FAMILIAR QUOTATIONS

Familiar Quotations

by
JOHN BARTLETT

A COLLECTION OF PASSAGES,
PHRASES AND PROVERBS
TRACED TO THEIR SOURCES
IN ANCIENT AND MODERN
LITERATURE

Thirteenth and
CENTENNIAL EDITION
Completely Revised

Little, Brown and Company · Boston · Toronto

LIBRARY OF CONGRESS CATALOG CARD NO. 55–10767

Thirteenth Edition Published November 1955

PRINTED IN THE UNITED STATES OF AMERICA

PREFACE TO THE THIRTEENTH AND CENTENNIAL EDITION

One hundred years ago there appeared the First Edition of FAMILIAR QUOTATIONS, a small, thin volume of 258 pages set in single column with an index which ran to a full 36 pages.

In his preface to the First Edition, John Bartlett wrote:

> The object of this work is to show, to some extent, the obligations our language owes to various authors for numerous phrases and familiar quotations which have become "household words."
>
> This Collection, originally made without any view of publication, has been considerably enlarged by additions from an English work on a similar plan, and is now sent forth with the hope that it may be found a convenient book of reference.
>
> Though perhaps imperfect in some respects, it is believed to possess the merit of accuracy, as the quotations have been taken from the original sources.
>
> Should this be favorably received, endeavors will be made to make it more worthy of the approbation of the public in a future edition.

Cambridge, May, 1855

The first nine editions of the book were under the editorship of John Bartlett, and the Ninth Edition, published in 1891, had grown to a volume of 1158 pages, 862 of text, 296 of index. In his preface to the Ninth Edition, Bartlett commented that it was the close of the volume's tentative life, a prophecy which was upset in 1914 with publication of the Tenth Edition under the editorship of Nathan Haskell Dole. Both the Eleventh Edition of 1937 and the Twelfth of 1948 continued to grow in size and stature under the joint editorship of Christopher Morley and Louella D. Everett.

The present Centennial Edition is, then, the thirteenth since the book first appeared. Our appreciation of the contributions of all those who have helped in the past is in no sense diminished by our belief that it is appropriate for this anniversary edition to be the responsibility of the firm's staff. We have borne in mind the original basis of selection which John Bartlett, a partner of Little, Brown, determined as "familiar or worthy of being familiar." We have learned to appreciate fully what John Bartlett said in his preface to the Fourth Edition: "It is not easy to determine in all cases the degree of familiarity that may belong to phrases and sentences which present themselves for admission; for what is familiar to one class of readers may be quite new to another."

In the laborious but stimulating task of revision the entire body of the text has been examined. Many quotations, because of the passage of time, seem to be no longer often repeated or likely to be remembered and have been dropped. Many well-known phrases which for one reason or another have never appeared in the book have been added.

The chronological sequence of authorship which has always made FAMILIAR QUOTATIONS of particular interest as a book to read as well as a book of reference has been preserved, and the debt of contemporary literature to that of other times and other tongues has been recognized by placing the ancient authors and those who wrote in foreign languages in chronological sequence. Only quotations from the Bible and those from unknown sources remain outside this pattern, which has been so useful in general reference and for showing the development of the language.

Because the body of our written and spoken expression has grown along so many avenues of knowledge, we have leaned heavily upon the advice and assistance of a large number of men and women of special scholarship and learning. Not only in this edition but through the years so many deep obligations to so many advisers have accrued that it is impossible here to make all the acknowledgments that should be made. It would be real negligence, however, not to mention the great contributions to the book made by Mr. Christopher Morley and Miss Louella D. Everett in preparation of the two preceding editions. In the Centennial Edition, which we hope will be as "favorably received" as was the First Edition, we must express our gratitude especially to Mrs. Emily Morison Beck, who has rendered highly competent and critical service in research and in processing the manuscript. Among other generous advisers, special thanks are due to Mr. Frank W. Cady, Professor Emeritus, of Middlebury College, Mr. Alston Hurd Chase of Phillips Academy at Andover, Mr. J. Frank

Dobie, Mr. Joseph Henry Jackson, Mr. W. Barton Leach of the Harvard Law School, Mr. David McCord and Mrs. Janet Payne Whitney. To the many unselfish individuals who write us almost daily with criticisms, suggestions and comments, we can only offer a blanket but appreciative word of thanks, for their interest does much toward perfecting BARTLETT.

Boston, Massachusetts
May 4, 1955

INDEX OF AUTHORS

Names preceded by the prepositional forms *d'*, *de*, *de la*, *du*, *van*, and *von* which are not British or American names are listed in the order of the name, and not the order of the prepositional form. Where custom warrants both listings, the name is so given (as with Jean de la Fontaine, who is listed under both Fontaine and La Fontaine).

The asterisk (*) preceding a name indicates that quotations from that author included as Notes are so numerous that the editors consider it impracticable to give the numbers of all the pages where they occur.

ix

ANONYMOUS AND COLLECTIVE WORKS

FAMILIAR QUOTATIONS

ANCIENT EGYPT

To resist him that is set in authority is evil.

The Instruction of Ptahhotep [1]
[Circa *2675* B. C.]

There it o'ertook me that I fell down for thirst, I was parched, my throat burned, and I said: "This is the taste of death."

The Story of Sinuke [1]
[Circa *2000* B. C.]

There is none that hath turned his shaft, there is none that hath bent his bow.

Ibid.

Then the ship perished, and of them that were in it not one survived. And I was cast on to an island by a wave of the sea.

*The Story of the Shipwrecked
Sailor* [1] [Circa *1700* B. C.?]

Everywhere he feels his Heart because its vessels run to all his limbs.

*The Beginning of the Secret
Book of the Physician* [2] [Circa
1550 B. C.]

Go not in and out in the court of justice, that thy name may not stink.

The Wisdom of Anii [1]
[Circa *900* B. C.]

HAMMURABI [3]
[*Floruit* 2100 B. C.]

I established law and justice in the land.

Prologue

If a man owe a debt and Adad [4] inundate his field and carry away the produce, or, through lack of water, grain have not grown in the field, in that year he shall not make any return of grain to the creditor, he shall alter his contract-tablet and he shall not pay the interest for that year.

Sect. 48

If a man destroy the eye of another man, they shall destroy his eye.

Sect. 196

HOMER [1]
[*Circa* 850 B. C.]

The wrath of Peleus' son, the direful spring
Of all the Grecian woes, O goddess, sing!

Iliad. [1] *Book I, Line 1*

The distant Trojans never injur'd me.

Ibid. Line 200

Words sweet as honey from his lips distill'd.

Ibid. Line 332

Shakes his ambrosial curls, and gives the nod, —
The stamp of fate, and sanction of the god.

Ibid. Line 684

And unextinguish'd laughter shakes the skies. [2]

Ibid. Line 771

The man who acts the least, upbraids the most.

Ibid. Book II, Line 311

Thick as autumnal leaves or driving sand.

Ibid. Line 970

The glorious gifts of the gods may not be cast aside.

Ibid. [3] *Book III, Line 65*

Chiefs, who no more in bloody fights engage,

---

[1] From ADOLF ERMAN [1854–1937]: *The Literature of the Ancient Egyptians,* translated [1927] by AYLWARD M. BLACKMAN.

[2] In *The Papyrus Ebers,* translated [1931] from the German version by CYRIL P. BRYAN.

[3] From ROBERT FRANCIS HARPER'S *The Code of Hammurabi King of Babylon,* about 2100 B.C., second edition.

[4] The storm god.

[1] The translation is that of ALEXANDER POPE [1715] unless otherwise noted.

[2] The same line occurs in the translation of the *Odyssey, Book VIII, L. 366.*

[3] Translated [1950] by CHASE AND PERRY.

But, wise through time, and narrative
with age,
In summer-days like grasshoppers rejoice,
A bloodless race, that send a feeble
voice.
> *Iliad. Book III, Line 199*

She moves a goddess, and she looks a
queen.
> *Ibid. Line 208*

But when he speaks, what elocution
flows!
Soft as the fleeces of descending snows
The copious accents fall, with easy art;
Melting they fall, and sink into the
heart.
> *Ibid. Line 283*

Ajax the great . . .
Himself a host.
> *Ibid. Line 293*

Wrapt in the cold embraces of the tomb.
> *Ibid. Line 312*

Plough the watery deep.
> *Ibid. Line 357*

And joyful nations join in leagues of
peace.
> *Ibid. Line 401*

The day shall come, the great avenging
day,
Which Troy's proud glories in the dust
shall lay,
When Priam's powers and Priam's self
shall fall,
And one prodigious ruin swallow all.
> *Ibid. Book IV, Line 196*

The first in banquets, but the last in
fight.
> *Ibid. Line 401*

Gods! How the son degenerates from
the sire!
> *Ibid. Line 451*

Not two strong men the enormous
weight could raise, —
Such men as live in these degenerate
days.[1]
> *Ibid. Book V, Line 371*

[1] A mass enormous! which in modern days
No two of earth's degenerate sons could
raise.
> *Book XX, L. 337*

Whose little body lodg'd a mighty
mind.
> *Iliad. Book V, Line 999*

He held his seat; a friend to human
race.
Fast by the road, his ever-open door
Obliged the wealthy, and reliev'd the
poor.[1]
> *Ibid. Book VI, Line 18*

Like leaves on trees the race of man is
found,
Now green in youth, now withering on
the ground:
Another race the following spring supplies:
They fall successive, and successive
rise.
> *Ibid. Line 181*

Inflaming wine, pernicious to mankind.
> *Ibid. Line 330*

If yet, not lost to all the sense of shame.
> *Ibid. Line 350*

He, from whose lips divine persuasion
flows.
> *Ibid. Book VII, Line 143*

Who dares think one thing, and another
tell,
My heart detests him as the gates of
Hell.[2]
> *Ibid. Book IX, Line 412*

Short is my date, but deathless my renown.
> *Ibid. Line 535*

Content to follow when we lead the
way.
> *Ibid. Book X, Line 141*

He serves me most, who serves his
country best.
> *Ibid. Line 201*

Praise from a friend, or censure from a
foe,
Are lost on hearers that our merits
know.
> *Ibid. Line 293*

The rest were vulgar deaths, unknown
to fame.
> *Ibid. Book XI, Line 394*

Without a sign, his sword the brave
man draws,

[1] See Sam Walter Foss, page 777b.
[2] See Pepys, page 284a.

4

And asks no omen but his country's cause.

Iliad. Book XII, Line 283

A day to fire the brave, and warm the cold,
To gain new glories, or augment the old.

Ibid. Line 321

And seem to walk on wings, and tread in air.

Ibid. Book XIII, Line 106

Not vain the weakest, if their force unite.

Ibid. Line 311

The best of things, beyond their measure, cloy.

Ibid. Line 795

Heroes as great have died, and yet shall fall.

Ibid. Book XV, Line 157

A noble mind disdains not to repent.

Ibid. Line 227

And for our country 'tis a bliss to die.[1]

Ibid. Line 583

Like strength is felt from hope, and from despair.

Ibid. Line 852

Two friends, two bodies with one soul inspir'd.[2]

Ibid. Book XVI, Line 267

Sleep and Death, two twins of winged race,
Of matchless swiftness, but of silent pace.

Ibid. Line 831

How vain, without the merit, is the name!

Ibid. Book XVII, Line 158

No season now for calm, familiar talk,
Like youths and maidens in an evening walk.

Ibid. Book XXII, Line 169

Achilles absent was Achilles still.

Ibid. Line 418

[1] See Horace, page 39a.
[2] A friend is one soul abiding in two bodies.
— DIOGENES LAERTIUS [*circa* A. D. 200]: *On Aristotle*
  Two souls with but a single thought,
  Two hearts that beat as one.
  VON MÜNCH BELLINGHAUSEN [1806–1871]: *Ingomar the Barbarian, Act II*

Forever honour'd, and forever mourn'd.

Iliad. Book XXII, Line 422

Unwept, unhonour'd, uninterr'd he lies! [1]

Ibid. Line 484

It is not strength, but art, obtains the prize,
And to be swift is less than to be wise.
'Tis more by art, than force of num'rous strokes.

Ibid. Book XXIII, Line 383

A green old age,[2] unconscious of decays.

Ibid. Line 929

Two urns by Jove's high throne have ever stood,
The source of evil one, and one of good.

Ibid. Book XXIV, Line 662

These things surely lie on the knees of the gods.

Odyssey.[3] *Book I, Line 267*

Soon as the early, rosy-fingered dawn appeared.

Ibid.[4] *Book II, Line 1*

Few sons are like their father, most are worse, few better than the father.

Ibid.[4] *Line 315*

A favorable wind clear-eyed Athene sent, a brisk west wind that sang along the wine-dark sea.

Ibid.[4] *Line 420*

An honest business never blush to tell.

Ibid.[5] *Book III, Line 20*

Urge him with truth to frame his fair replies;
And sure he will: for Wisdom never lies.

Ibid. Line 25

The lot of man; to suffer and to die.

Ibid. Line 117

[1] See Scott, page 414a.
Unknelled, uncoffined, and unknown. —
BYRON: *Childe Harold, Canto IV* [1818], St. 179
[2] See Dryden, page 276a.
[3] Translated [1879] by BUTCHER AND LANG.
[4] Translated [1884] by GEORGE H. PALMER.
[5] Translated [1725–1726] by ALEXANDER POPE. Pope engaged two friends, ELIJAH FENTON [1683–1730] and WILLIAM BROOME [1689–1745], to translate certain books of *The Odyssey* of Homer for him. The division of the work was: Pope — Books III, V, VII, IX, XIII, XIV, XVII, XXI, XXII, XXIV, and most of X and XV; Fenton — Books I, IV, XIX, and XX; Broome — Books II, VI, VIII, XI, XII, XVI, XVIII, XXIII.

A faultless body and a blameless mind.
Odyssey. Book III, Line 138
The long historian of my country's woes.
Ibid. Line 142
When now Aurora, daughter of the dawn,
With rosy lustre purpled o'er the lawn.
Ibid. Line 516
Wise to resolve, and patient to perform.
Ibid. Book IV (Fenton translation), Line 372
The leader, mingling with the vulgar host,
Is in the common mass of matter lost.
Ibid. Line 397
The people's parent, he protected all.
Ibid. Line 921
The big round tear stands trembling in her eye.
Ibid. Line 936
The windy satisfaction of the tongue.
Ibid. Line 1092
For a better and a higher gift than this there cannot be, when with accordant aims man and wife have a home. Great grief is it to foes and joy to friends; but they themselves best know its meaning.
Ibid.[1] *Book VI, Line 182*
No more was seen the human form divine.[2]
Ibid. Book X, Line 278
Ossa they strove to set upon Olympus, and upon Ossa leafy Pelion, that so the heavens might be scaled.
Ibid.[3] *Book XI, Line 426*

[1] Translated [1884] by GEORGE H. PALMER.
[2] See Milton, page 254b, and Blake, page 387b.
[3] Translated by GEORGE H. PALMER.
To pile Ossa on Pelion and roll leaf-crowned Olympus on Ossa. — VIRGIL [70–19 B.C.]: *Georgics, I, L. 28*
Then the omnipotent Father with his thunder made Olympus tremble, and from Ossa hurled Pelion. — OVID [43 B.C.–A.D. 17]: *Metamorphoses, I, L. 154*
Ossa they pressed down with Pelion's weight,
And on them both impos'd Olympus' hill.
FITZ-GEFFREY: *The Life and Death of Sir Francis Drake* [1596], *St. 99*
I would have you call to mind the strength

Oh woman, woman! when to ill thy mind
Is bent, all hell contains no fouler fiend.[1]
Odyssey. Book XI (Broome translation), Line 531
Rather I choose laboriously to bear
A weight of woes and breathe the vital air,
A slave to some poor hind that toils for bread,
Than reign the sceptred monarch of the dead.
Ibid. Line 597
And what so tedious as a twice-told tale.[2]
Ibid. Book XII (Broome translation), Line 538
He ceas'd; but left so pleasing on their ear
His voice, that list'ning still they seem'd to hear.
Ibid. Book XIII, Line 1
His native home deep imag'd in his soul.
Ibid. Line 38
The sex is ever to a soldier kind.
Ibid. Book XIV, Line 246
True friendship's laws are by this rule express'd,
Welcome the coming, speed the parting guest.[3]
Ibid. Book XV, Line 83
For too much rest itself becomes a pain.
Ibid. Line 429
Jove fix'd it certain that whatever day
Makes man a slave, takes half his worth away.
Ibid. Book XVII, Line 302
Unbless'd thy hand, if, in this low disguise,
Wander, perhaps, some inmate of the skies.[4]
Ibid. Line 576

of the ancient giants, that undertook to lay the high mountain Pelion on the top of Ossa, and set among those the shady Olympus. — RABELAIS: *Works, Book IV* [1548], *Chap. 38*
[1] See Otway, page 289b, and Congreve, page 298a.
[2] See Shakespeare, page 148a.
[3] See Pope, page 319b.
[4] See *Hebrews, XIII, 2,* on page 1063b.

Impatient straight to flesh his virgin sword.

> *Odyssey. Book XX (Fenton translation), Line 461*

So ends the bloody business of the day.

> *Ibid. Book XXII, Line 516*

HESIOD [1]
[Circa 720 B.C.?]

On the tongue of such an one they shed a honeyed dew,[2] and from his lips drop gentle words.

> *The Theogony. Line 82*

Night, having Sleep, the brother of Death.[3]

From whose eyelids also as they gazed dropped love.

> *Ibid. Line 910*

Both potter is jealous of potter and craftsman of craftsman; and poor man has a grudge against poor man, and poet against poet.[4]

> *Works and Days. Line 25*

Fools! they know not how much half exceeds the whole.[5]

> *Ibid. Line 40*

Oft hath even a whole city reaped the evil fruit of a bad man.[6]

> *Ibid. Line 240*

For himself doth a man work evil in working evils for another.

> *Ibid. Line 265*

Badness, look you, you may choose easily in a heap: level is the path, and

---

[1] Translated by J. BANKS, with a few alterations.

[2] He on honey-dew hath fed. — COLERIDGE [1772–1834]: *Kubla Khan*

[3] See Daniel, page 122a.
Death and his brother Sleep. — SHELLEY: *Queen Mab* [1813], *I*
Sleep, Death's twin-brother. — TENNYSON: *In Memoriam* [1850], *Part LXVIII*

[4] In ev'ry age and clime we see
Two of a trade can never agree.
GAY: *The Rat-catcher and Cats* [1727]
The potter envies the potter. — H. G. BOHN: *A Hand-Book of Proverbs* [1855]

[5] Pittacus said that half was more than the whole. — DIOGENES LAERTIUS [*circa* A.D. 200]: *Pittacus, II*

[6] One man's wickedness may easily become all men's curse. — PUBLILIUS SYRUS [*circa* 42 B.C.]: *Maxim 463*

---

right near it dwells. But before Virtue the immortal gods have put the sweat of man's brow; and long and steep is the way to it, and rugged at the first.

> *Works and Days. Line 287*

Let it please thee to keep in order a moderate-sized farm, that so thy garners may be full of fruits in their season.

> *Ibid. Line 304*

Invite the man that loves thee to a feast, but let alone thine enemy.

> *Ibid. Line 342*

A bad neighbour is as great a misfortune as a good one is a great blessing.

> *Ibid. Line 346*

Gain not base gains; base gains are the same as losses.

> *Ibid. Line 353*

If thou shouldst lay up even a little upon a little, and shouldst do this often, soon would even this become great.

> *Ibid. Line 360*

At the beginning of the cask and at the end take thy fill, but be saving in the middle; for at the bottom saving comes too late. Let the price fixed with a friend be sufficient, and even dealing with a brother call in witnesses, but laughingly.

> *Ibid. Line 366*

The morn, look you, furthers a man on his road, and furthers him too in his work.

> *Ibid. Line 579*

Observe moderation. In all, the fitting season is best.

> *Ibid. Line 694*

Neither make thy friend equal to a brother; but if thou shalt have made him so, be not the first to do him wrong.

> *Ibid. Line 707*

ARCHILOCHUS
[714?–676 B.C.]

The fox knows many things, but the hedgehog knows one big thing.[1]

> *Fragment 103*

---

[1] The fox has many tricks, and the hedgehog only one, but that is the best of all. — ERASMUS: *Adagia* [1500]

SOLON [1]
[638?–559 B. C.]

I grow old learning something new every day.
> VALERIUS MAXIMUS: *Book VIII, Chap. 7, Sect. 14*

MIMNERMUS
[*Floruit* 630–600 B. C.]

We are all clever enough at envying a famous man while he is yet alive, and at praising him when he is dead.
> *Fragment 1*

STESICHORUS [2]
[630–550 B. C.]

'Tis a vain and impotent thing to bewail the dead.
> STOBAEUS: *Anthology*

When a man dies, all his glory among men dies also.
> *Ibid.*

ALCAEUS [2]
[611–580 B. C.]

Not houses finely roofed or the stones of walls well-builded, nay nor canals and dockyards, make the city, but men able to use their opportunity.
> ARISTIDES: *Rhodian Oration*

Painting a lion from the claw.
> PLUTARCH: *On the Cessation of Oracles*

'Tis said that wrath is the last thing in a man to grow old.
> *Scholiast on Sophocles*

One that hath wine as a chain about his wits, such an one lives no life at all.
> DEMETRIUS: *On Poems* [3]

In fleeing the ashes he's fallen into the coals.
> APOSTOLIUS: *Proverbs*

[1] See also Diogenes Laertius' quotations from Solon, page 69b.
[2] Translated by J. M. EDMONDS.
[3] Papyrus of the first century B. C. found at Herculaneum.

SAPPHO OF LESBOS [1]
[*Circa* 610 B. C.]

Art thou the topmost apple
The gatherers could not reach,
Reddening on the bough?
> *To Atthis, paraphrase by* BLISS CARMAN

I loved thee, Atthis, once — long, long ago;
Long, long ago — the memory still is dear.
Stand face to face, friend, and unveil thine eyes,
Look deep in mine and keep the dead past clear
Of all regret.
> *To Atthis, paraphrase by* ANNE BUNNER

For to whomsoever I do good they harm me most.
> *Fragment 11* [2]

Evening, thou that bringest all, whatever the light-giving dawn scattered; thou bringest the sheep, thou bringest the goat, thou bringest the child to its mother.
> *Fragment 93* [2]

THEOGNIS
[570?–490? B. C.]

He who mistrusts most should be trusted least.
> *Sententiae. No. 223*

Be not too zealous; moderation is best in all things.
> *Ibid. No. 335*

Wine is wont to show the mind of man.[3]
> *Ibid. No. 500*

No one goes to Hades with all his immense wealth.[4]
> *Ibid. No. 725*

[1] Some say the Muses are nine but how carelessly! Look at the tenth, Sappho from Lesbos. — PLATO [427–347 B. C.] (Loeb Classical Library, *Greek Anthology, Vol. 3, P. 281*)
[2] Translated by MARY MILLS PATRICK.
[3] In wine there is truth. — PLINY [A. D. 23–79]: *Natural History, Book XIV, Sect. 141*
[4] For when he dieth he shall carry nothing away: his glory shall not descend after him. — *Psalm XLIX, 17*

ANACREON [1]
[563?–478 B.C.]

War spares not the brave but the cowardly.
The Greek Anthology. Book 7,
Epigram 160
Nor in those days did Persuasion shine all silver.
Scholiast on Pindar
Doorkeepers that fight are a mischief.
Etymologicum Magnum
Shining with desire and gleaming with unguents.
PLUTARCH: *Amatorius*

SIMONIDES OF CEOS
[556–469 B.C.]

In silence also there's a worth that brings no risk.
PLUTARCH: *Sayings of Emperors.*
Augustus Caesar
There's no joy even in beautiful Wisdom, unless one have holy Health.
SEXTUS EMPIRICUS: *Against the*
Mathematicians
Whereas gold is the kindest of all hosts when it shines in the sky, it comes an evil guest unto those that receive it in their hand.
PLUTARCH: *The Malignity of*
Herodotus
He that would live completely happy must before all things belong to a country that is of fair report.
AMMIANUS MARCELLINUS:
History
The city is the teacher of the man.
PLUTARCH: *Should Old Men*
Govern?
Go tell the Spartans, thou that passeth by,
That here, obedient to their laws, we lie.
Thermopylae [2]

[1] Translated by J. M. EDMONDS.
[2] Translated by WILLIAM LISLE BOWLES [1762–1850].
Ruskin said of this epitaph that it was the noblest group of words ever uttered by man. In Luderitzbucht Cemetery, South-West Africa, the lines, adapted to read:

AESOP
[*Floruit* 550 B.C.]

Any excuse will serve a tyrant.
The Wolf and the Lamb
Beware lest you lose the substance by grasping at the shadow.
The Dog and the Shadow
You may share the labours of the great, but you will not share the spoil.
The Lion's Share
You have put your head inside a wolf's mouth and taken it out again in safety. That ought to be reward enough for you.
The Wolf and the Crane
Better beans and bacon in peace than cakes and ale in fear.
The Town Mouse and the Country
Mouse
Only cowards insult dying majesty.
The Sick Lion
Little friends may prove great friends.
The Lion and the Mouse
Better no rule than cruel rule.
The Frogs Desiring a King
A huge gap appeared in the side of the mountains. At last a tiny mouse poked its little head out of the gap.[1]
The Mountains in Labour
Much outcry, little outcome.
Ibid.
There is always someone worse off than yourself.
The Hares and the Frogs
It is easy to be brave from a safe distance.
The Wolf and the Kid

Tell England, ye who pass this monument,
That we who rest here, die content,
mark the grave of Rex and Wilfred Wilmslow, who fell in the battle of Stetting [November, 1914]. In Southport, England, the War Memorial bears another adaptation of the epitaph:
Tell Britain, ye who mark this monument,
Faithful to her we fell, and rest content.
[1] See Horace, page 41b.
A mountain was in labour, sending forth dreadful groans, and there was in the region the highest expectation. After all, it brought forth a mouse. — PHAEDRUS [*circa* A.D. 8]: *Book IV, Fable 22, 1*

You will only injure yourself if you take notice of despicable enemies.[1]

The Bald Man and the Fly

Outside show is a poor substitute for inner worth.

The Fox and the Mask

Borrowed plumes.

The Jay and the Peacock

It is not only fine feathers that make fine birds.

Ibid.

Self-conceit may lead to self-destruction.

The Frog and the Ox

Gratitude is the sign of noble souls.

Androcles

We often despise what is most useful to us.

The Hart and the Hunter

They found that even the Belly, in its dull quiet way, was doing necessary work for the Body, and that all must work together or the Body will go to pieces.

The Belly and the Members

I am sure the grapes are sour.[2]

The Fox and the Grapes

It is easy to despise what you cannot get.

Ibid.

Be content with your lot; one cannot be first in everything.

The Peacock and Juno

Familiarity breeds contempt.[3]

The Fox and the Lion

We can easily represent things as we wish them to be.

The Lion and the Statue

Then the Grasshopper knew it is best to prepare for the days of necessity.

The Ant and the Grasshopper

The little Reed, bending to the force of the wind, soon stood upright again when the storm had passed over.

The Tree and the Reed

Obscurity often brings safety.

Ibid.

The Lamb that belonged to the Sheep, whose skin the Wolf was wearing, began to follow the Wolf in the Sheep's clothing.

The Wolf in Sheep's Clothing

Appearances are deceptive.

Ibid.

The Dog barked at the Ox and attempted to bite it when it approached the manger in the hope of getting at the straw.

The Dog in the Manger [1]

People often grudge others what they cannot enjoy themselves.

Ibid.

The boy called out "Wolf, Wolf!" and the villagers came out to help him. A few days afterward he tried the same trick, and again they came to his help. Shortly after this a Wolf actually came, but this time the villagers thought the boy was deceiving them again and nobody came to his help.

The Shepherd's Boy

A liar will not be believed, even when he speaks the truth.

Ibid.

Never soar aloft on an enemy's pinions.

The Tortoise and the Birds

Do but set the example yourself, and I will follow you. Example is the best precept.[2]

The Two Crabs

Never trust a friend who deserts you at a pinch.

The Two Fellows and the Bear

---

[1] A fly bit the bare pate of a bald man, who in endeavouring to crush it gave himself a hard slap. Then said the fly jeeringly, "You wanted to revenge the sting of a tiny insect with death; what will you do to yourself, who have added insult to injury?" — PHAE-DRUS [*circa* A.D. 8]: *Book V, Fable 3, 1*

[2] The fox, when he cannot reach the grapes, says they are not ripe. — GEORGE HERBERT: *Jacula Prudentum* [1640]

"They are too green," he said, "and only good for fools." — LA FONTAINE: *Book III* [1668], *Fable 11, The Fox and the Grapes*

[3] This is *Maxim 640* of Publilius Syrus.

See Shakespeare, page 180a.

I find my familiarity with thee has bred

contempt.—CERVANTES: *Don Quixote, Part I* [1605], *Book III, Chap. 6*

[1] See Robert Burton, page 222a.

[2] Example is always more efficacious than precept. — SAMUEL JOHNSON: *Rasselas* [1759], *Chap. XXX*

United we stand, divided we fall.[1]
> *The Four Oxen and the Lion*

A little thing in hand is worth more than a great thing in prospect.[2]
> *The Fisher and the Little Fish*

Little by little does the trick.
> *The Crow and the Pitcher*

I will have nought to do with a man who can blow hot and cold with the same breath.
> *The Man and the Satyr*

Thinking to get at once all the gold the Goose could give, he killed it and opened it only to find, — nothing.
> *The Goose with the Golden Eggs*

Put your shoulder to the wheel.
> *Hercules and the Waggoner*

The gods help them that help themselves.
> *Ibid.*

Please all, and you will please none.
> *The Man, the Boy, and the Donkey*

Who is to bell the Cat? It is easy to propose impossible remedies.
> *Belling the Cat*

When the Hare awoke from his nap, he saw the Tortoise just near the winning post. Plodding wins the race.
> *The Hare and the Tortoise*

We would often be sorry if our wishes were gratified.[3]
> *The Old Man and Death*

---

[1] See George Pope Morris, page 499a.

[2] He is a fool who lets slip a bird in the hand for a bird in the bush. — PLUTARCH [A. D. 46–120]: *Of Garrulity*

A bird in hand is worth two in the bush. — CERVANTES: *Don Quixote, Part I* [1605], *Book IV, Chap. 4*

Better one byrde in hande than ten in the wood. — JOHN HEYWOOD: *Proverbes* [1546], *Part I, Chap. XI*

A feather in hand is better than a bird in the air. — GEORGE HERBERT: *Jacula Prudentum* [1640]

[3] Granting our wish one of Fate's saddest jokes is! — J. R. LOWELL [1819–1891]: *Two Scenes from the Life of Blondel, Sc. II, St. 2*

Beware, my lord! Beware lest stern Heaven hate you enough to hear your prayers! — ANATOLE FRANCE: *The Crime of Sylvestre Bonnard* [1881], *Part II, Chap. 4*

When the gods wish to punish us they answer our prayers. — WILDE: *An Ideal Husband* [1895], *Act II*

Union gives strength.
> *The Bundle of Sticks*

While I see many hoof-marks going in, I see none coming out. It is easier to get into the enemy's toils than out again.
> *The Lion, the Fox, and the Beasts*

The haft of the arrow had been feathered with one of the eagle's own plumes. We often give our enemies the means of our own destruction.[1]
> *The Eagle and the Arrow*

Nature will out.
> *The Cat-Maiden*

Do not count your chickens before they are hatched.[2]
> *The Milkmaid and Her Pail*

Men often applaud an imitation, and hiss the real thing.
> *The Buffoon and the Countryman*

Never trust the advice of a man in difficulties.
> *The Fox and the Goat*

---

[1] So in the Libyan fable it is told
That once an eagle, stricken with a dart,
Said, when he saw the fashion of the shaft,
"With our own feathers, not by others' hands,
Are we now smitten."
> AESCHYLUS [‐25–456 B.C.]. *Fragment 135* (Plumptre's translation)

That eagle's fate and mine are one,
Which on the shaft that made him die
Espied a feather of his own,
Wherewith he wont to soar so high.
> EDMUND WALLER [1605–1687]: *To a Lady Singing a Song of his Composing*

Like a young eagle, who has lent his plume
To fledge the shaft by which he meets his doom,
See their own feathers pluck'd to wing the dart
Which rank corruption destines for their heart.
> THOMAS MOORE [1780–1852]: *Corruption*

See Byron, page 452a.

[2] Many count their chickens before they are hatched. — CERVANTES: *Don Quixote, Part II* [1615], *Chap. 55*

To swallow gudgeons ere they're catch'd,
And count their chickens ere they're hatch'd.
> SAMUEL BUTLER: *Hudibras, Part II* [1664], *Canto III, L. 923*

Reckon not on your chickens before they are hatched. — JEFFERYS TAYLOR [1792–1853]: *The Milkmaid*

IBYCUS [1]
[*Floruit circa* 550 B.C.]

You cannot find a medicine for life when once a man is dead.
> CHRYSIPPUS: *Negatives*

Every reef may be safely let out so long as the sail clears the top of the wave.
> *Scholiast on the Iliad*

Contests allow no excuses, no more do friendships.
> ZENOBIUS: *Proverbs*

The cranes of Ibycus.[2]

SIMPLICIUS
[*Floruit* 530 B.C.]

They [atoms] move in the void and catching each other up jostle together, and some recoil in any direction that may chance, and others become entangled with one another in various degrees according to the symmetry of their shapes and sizes and positions and order, and they remain together and thus the coming into being of composite things is effected.
> *De Caelo. 242, 15* [3]

HERACLITUS
[*Floruit* 513 B.C.]

Man's genius is a deity.
> PLUTARCH: *Platonic Questions*

Character is Destiny.
> MULLACH: *Fragments of Greek Philosophy*

There is nothing permanent except change.
> ROGERS: *Student's History of Philosophy*

---

[1] Translated by J. M. EDMONDS.

[2] According to legend, Ibycus was murdered at sea, and his murderers were discovered through cranes that followed the ship. Hence, the "cranes of Ibycus" became a proverb for the agency of the gods in revealing crime.

[3] Quoted by CYRIL BAILEY: *The Greek Atomists and Epicurus.*

AESCHYLUS
[525–456 B.C.]

I would far rather be ignorant than wise in the foreboding of evil.[1]
> *Suppliants. Line 453*

"Honour thy father and thy mother" stands written among the three laws of most revered righteousness.[2]
> *Ibid. Line 707*

Myriad laughter of the ocean waves.
> *Prometheus Bound. Line 89*

For somehow this is tyranny's disease, to trust no friends.
> *Ibid. Line 226*

Words are the physicians of a mind diseased.[3]
> *Ibid. Line 378*

Time as he grows old teaches many lessons.
> *Ibid. Line 981*

God's mouth knows not to utter falsehood, but he will perform each word.[4]
> *Ibid. Line 1032*

By suffering comes wisdom.
> *Agamemnon. Line 177*

Too lightly opened are a woman's ears;
Her fence downtrod by many trespassers.
> *Ibid. Line 486*

I think the slain
Care little if they sleep or rise again;
And we, the living, wherefore should we ache
With counting all our lost ones?
> *Ibid. Line 595*

Sweet is a grief well ended.
> *Ibid. Line 805*

---

[1] See Thomas Gray, page 347b.

[2] The reference is to three great laws ascribed to Triptolemus: namely, to honor parents; to worship the gods with the fruits of the earth; to hurt no living creature. The first two laws are also ascribed to the centaur Cheiron.
Honour thy father and thy mother. — *Exodus, XX, 12*

[3] Apt words have power to suage
The tumours of a troubl'd mind.
> MILTON: *Samson Agonistes* [1671], *L. 184*

[4] God is not a man that he should lie; . . . hath he said, and shall he not do it? — *Numbers, XXIII, 19*

For not many men, the proverb saith,
Can love a friend whom fortune pros-
  pereth
Unenvying.
                    Agamemnon. Line 832

I know how men in exile feed on
  dreams.
                    Ibid. Line 1668

Him who pitieth suffering men
Zeus pitieth, and his ways are sweet on
earth.
                    The Eumenides. Line 91

Fortune is a god and rules men's life.[1]
          The Choëphoroe. Line 59

Destiny
Waiteth alike for them that men call
  free,
And them by others mastered.
                    Ibid. Line 101

It is for the doer to suffer.
                    Ibid. Line 313

Pleasantest
Of all ties is the tie of host and guest.
                    Ibid. Line 699

For he wishes not to seem, but to be,
the best.[2]
          Seven Against Thebes. Line 592

God loves to help him who strives to
help himself.[3]
                    Fragment 223

O Death the Healer, scorn thou not, I
  pray,
To come to me: of cureless ills thou art

---

[1] Fortune commands men, and not men
fortune. — HERODOTUS [484–424 B. C.]: *Book
VII, Polymnia, Chap. 49*
[2] Meant, and taken by the audience, as a
reference to Aristides the Just.
[3] Heaven ne'er helps the men who will not
act. — SOPHOCLES [496–406 B. C.]: *Fragment
288* (Plumptre's translation)
  Try first thyself, and after call in God;
  For to the worker God himself lends aid.
          EURIPIDES [484–406 B. C.]: *Hippoly-
                    tus, Fragment 435*
  Help thyself, and God will help thee. —
GEORGE HERBERT: *Jacula Prudentum* [1640]
  Help thyself, Heaven will help thee. — LA
FONTAINE: *Book VI* [1678–1679], *Fable 18*
  God helps those who help themselves. —
ALGERNON SIDNEY: *Discourses on Govern-
ment* [1698], *Sect. XXIII.* FRANKLIN [1706–
1790]: *Poor Richard's Almanac*

The one physician. Pain lays not its
  touch
Upon a corpse.
                    Fragment 250 [1]

A prosperous fool is a grievous burden.
                    Fragment 383

Bronze is the mirror of the form;
wine, of the heart.
                    Fragment 384

It is not the oath that makes us believe the man, but the man the oath.
                    Fragment 385

PINDAR [2]
[522–442 B. C.]

The best of healers is good cheer.
                    Nemean Ode 4

Longer than deeds liveth the word.
                    Ibid.

It is the natal star that ruleth over
every deed.
                    Nemean Ode 5

For whatsoever one hath well said
goeth forth with a voice that never
dieth.
                    Isthmian Ode 4

Refrain from peering too far.
                    Olympian Ode 1

We are creatures of a day. What is
one, what is one not? Man is the dream
of a shadow.
                    Pythian Ode 8

The word that is overbearing is a
spur unto strife.
                    Fragment from Hymns

To foolish men belongeth a love for
things afar.
                    Paean 4

Every noble deed dieth, if suppressed in silence.
          *Eulogy on Alexander, Son of
                    Amyntas*

Whether the race of men on earth
mounteth a loftier tower by justice, or
by crooked wiles, my mind is divided
in telling clearly.

                    Fragment

---

[1] Translated by PLUMPTRE.
[2] Translated by SIR J. E. SANDYS.

SOPHOCLES
[496?–406 B. C.]

The ship of state — the gods once more,
After much rocking on a stormy surge,
Set her on even keel.
Antigone [1]

That pilot of the state
Who sets no hand to the best policy,
But remains tongue-tied through some terror, seems
Vilest of men.
Ibid.

None love the messenger who brings bad news.[2]
Ibid.

For money you would sell your soul.
Ibid.

A man of worth
In his own household will appear upright
In the state also.
Ibid.

There lives no greater fiend than Anarchy;
She ruins states, turns houses out of doors,
Breaks up in rout the embattled soldiery.
Ibid.

Do not persist, then, to retain at heart
One sole idea, that the thing is right
Which your mouth utters, and nought else beside.
Ibid.

Wonders are many, and none is more wonderful than man.[3]
Ibid.

Though a man be wise
It is no shame for him to live and learn.[4]
Ibid.

[1] Translated by SIR GEORGE YOUNG [1837–1930].
[2] See Shakespeare, page 152a.
[3] Translated by JEBB.
[4] It is good to live and learn. — CERVANTES: *Don Quixote, Part II* [1615], *Chap. 32*
Live and learn,
Not first learn and then live.
BROWNING: *Parleyings with Certain People, With Christopher Smart* [1887], *IX*

To err
From the right path is common to mankind.[1]
Antigone

A day can prostrate and upraise again
All that is human.
Ajax [2]

To behold harms of our own hands' doing,
Where none beside us wrought, causes sharp ruing.
Ibid.

A woman should be seen, not heard.
Ibid.

I would not take the fellow at a gift
Who warms himself with unsubstantial hopes;
But bravely to live on, or bravely end,[3]
Is due to gentle breeding.
Ibid.

In the ills of men
There is none sorer than Necessity.
Ibid.

Some mindfulness
A man should surely keep, of any thing
That pleased him once.
Ibid.

The happiest life consists in ignorance,
Before you learn to grieve and to rejoice.
Ibid.

Sleep, the universal vanquisher.
Ibid.

I for my own part, having learnt of late
Those hateful to us we are not to hate
As though they might not soon be friends again,
Intend to measure, now, the services
I render to my friend, as if not so
To abide for ever; for of mortals most
Find friendship an unstable anchorage.[4]
Ibid.

[1] That men may err was never yet denied.
— DRYDEN: *The Hind and the Panther* [1687], *L. 61*
See Pope, page 311b.
[2] Translated by SIR GEORGE YOUNG.
[3] Where life is more terrible than death, it is then the truest valour to dare to live. — SIR THOMAS BROWNE: *Religio Medici* [1642] (Everyman ed.), *P. 49*
[4] Love him so, as if you were one day to hate

'Tis a long road knows no turning.
Ajax

Men of perverse opinion do not know
The excellence of what is in their hands,
Till some one dash it from them.
Ibid.

Death is not the worst; rather, in vain
To wish for death, and not to compass
it.
Electra [1]

The flower
Of our young manhood.[2]
Oedipus Tyrannus [1]

Towers and ships are nothingness,
Void of our fellow men to inhabit them.
Ibid.

This dim-seen track-mark of an ancient
crime.
Ibid.

The Sphinx
With her enigma.
Ibid.

I benefit myself in aiding him.
Ibid.

Now am I hail-fellow-well-met with
all.
Ibid.

Pride, when puffed up, vainly, with
many things
Unseasonable, unfitting, mounts the
wall,
Only to hurry to that fatal fall.[3]
Ibid.

That kindred only should behold and
hear
The griefs of kin, fits best with decency.
Ibid.

---

him and hate him so, as you were one day to
love him. — Attributed to CHILO [*fl.* 556 B.C.]
in MONTAIGNE's essay, *Of Friendship*
   [1] Translated by SIR GEORGE YOUNG.
   [2] The very flower of youth. — TERENCE
[185–159 B.C.]: *Eunuchus, Act II, Sc. 3, L. 27*
   [3] See *Proverbs, XVI, 18*, on page 1039b.
   Pryde goeth before, and shame cometh behynde. — *Treatise of a Gallant* [*circa* 1510]
      Pryde will have a fall;
For pryde goeth before and shame cometh
after.
      JOHN HEYWOOD: *Proverbes* [1546],
                        Part I, Chap. X
Let pride go afore, shame will follow after.
—CHAPMAN, JONSON, AND MARSTON: *Eastward Ho* [1605], *Act IV, Sc. 1*

Of no mortal say
"That man is happy," till
Vexed by no grievous ill
He pass Life's goal.[1]
Oedipus Tyrannus. Closing lines

To know that all is well, even if late
We come to know it, is at least some
gain.
Trachiniae [2]

There is occasion for the vigilant
To fear for one who prospers, lest he
fall.
Ibid.

One must learn
By doing the thing; for though you
think you know it
You have no certainty, until you try.
Ibid.

If any
Count on two days, or any more, to
come,
He is a fool; for a man has no morrow,
Till with good luck he has got through
to-day.
Ibid.

War never slays a bad man in its course,
But the good always!
Philoctetes [2]

Winds are fair always, when you fly
from harm.
Ibid.

Who does not befriend himself
By doing good?
Oedipus Coloneus [2]

To the gods alone
Belongs it never to be old or die,
But all things else melt with all-power-
ful Time.
Ibid.

If a man to you
Refused a favour, when you begged
for it,

---

   [1] See Herodotus, page 18b.
   'Tis an old well-known proverb of mankind,
"You cannot tell men's fortunes till they die,
In any case, if they be good or bad."
                                    Trachiniae
   'Tis never seemly to felicitate
The fortunes of a man, as prosperous,
Before his life shall have been lived by him
Completely through.
         Tyndareus, Fragment 572
   [2] Translated by SIR GEORGE YOUNG.

And would give nothing, and then afterwards,
When you were satisfied of your desire,
And all the grace was graceless, proffered it,
Would not the pleasure so received be vain? [1]

Oedipus Coloneus

Never to have been born is much the best;
And the next best, by far,
To return thence, by the way speediest,
Where our beginnings are.

Ibid.

This is our portion at the close of life,
Strengthless — companionless.

Ibid.

It is the merit of a general
To impart good news, and to conceal the bad.

Ibid.

The very hair on my head
Stands up for dread.[2]

Ibid.

A remedy too strong for the disease.

Tereus. Fragment 514 [3]

Truly, to tell lies is not honourable;
But when the truth entails tremendous ruin,
To speak dishonourably is pardonable.

Creusa. Fragment 323

Sons are the anchors of a mother's life.

Phaedra. Fragment 612

To him who is in fear everything rustles.

Acrisius. Fragment 58

No falsehood lingers on into old age.

Ibid. Fragment 59

Lady, cheer up; most of our ills, blowing loudly
In dreams by night, grow milder when 'tis day.

Ibid. Fragment 63

No man loves life like him that's growing old.

Ibid. Fragment 64

War loves to prey upon the young.[1]

Scyrian Women. Fragment 498

Heaven ne'er helps the men who will not act.[2]

Unknown Dramas. Fragment 288

A wise gamester ought to take the dice
Even as they fall, and pay down quietly,
Rather than grumble at his luck.

Ibid. Fragment 686

Truth ever has most strength of what men say.

Ibid. Fragment 691

A woman's vows I write upon the wave.

Ibid. Fragment 694

The friends of the unlucky are far away.

Ibid. Fragment 773

If I am Sophocles, I am not mad;
and if I am mad, I am not Sophocles.

Vita Anonyma [3]

EURIPIDES
[484–406 B. C.]

Old men's prayers for death are lying prayers, in which they abuse old age and long extent of life. But when death draws near, not one is willing to die, and age no longer is a burden to them.

Alcestis.[4] *Line 669*

I care for riches, to make gifts
To friends, or lead a sick man back to health
With ease and plenty. Else small aid is wealth
For daily gladness; once a man be done
With hunger, rich and poor are all as one.

Electra.[5] *Line 539*

A hundred little things make likenesses
In brethren born, and show the father's blood.

Ibid. Line 642

[1] In peace, children inter their parents; war violates the order of nature, and causes parents to inter their children. — HERODOTUS [484–424 B. C.]: *Book I, Clio, Chap. 87*

[2] See Euripides, page 17a.
Help thyself, and God will help thee. — GEORGE HERBERT: *Jacula Prudentum* [1640]
See Franklin, page 330b.

[3] Translated by PLUMPTRE.
[4] Translated by MORRIS HICKEY MORGAN.
[5] Translated by SIR GILBERT MURRAY.

[1] See Samuel Johnson, page 339a.
[2] The hair of all stood up for fear. — Later in same drama
[3] The fragments are from the Everyman Edition of *The Dramas of Sophocles.*

Danger gleams
Like sunshine to a brave man's eyes.
　　Iphigenia in Tauris.[1] *Line 115*
How oft the darkest hour of ill
Breaks brightest into dawn.[2]
　　　　　　　Ibid. Line 723
I think that Fortune watcheth o'er our
　lives,
Surer than we. But well said: he who
　strives
Will find his gods strive for him
　equally.[3]
　　　　　　　Ibid. Line 910
　The night
Is the safe time for robbers, as the light
For just men.
　　　　　　　Ibid. Line 1024
Put not thy faith in any Greek.[4]
　　　　　　　Ibid. Line 1205
　The gifts of a bad man bring no good
with them.
　　　　　　　Medea.[5] *Line 618*
　Moderation, the noblest gift of
Heaven.
　　　　　　　Ibid. Line 636
I know, indeed, the evil of that I pur-
pose; but my inclination gets the better
of my judgment.[6]
　　　　　　　Ibid. Line 1078
To the fool, he who speaks wisdom
will sound foolish.
　　　　　　Bacchae. Line 480
　Slowly but surely withal moveth the
might of the gods.[7]
　　　　　　　Ibid. Line 882
　Slight not what's near through aim-
ing at what's far.
　　　　　　Rhesus.[5] *Line 482*

[1] Translated by SIR GILBERT MURRAY.
[2] The darkest hour is that before the dawn.
— HAZLITT: *English Proverbs*
[3] See Sophocles, page 16b.
[4] See Virgil, page 37a.
[5] Translated by MORRIS HICKEY MORGAN.
[6] See Ovid, page 42b, and *Romans, VII, 19,*
on page 1060a.
I find my growing judgment daily instruct
me how to be better, but my untamed affections and confirmed vitiosity makes me daily
do worse. — SIR THOMAS BROWNE: *Religio
Medici* [1642] (Everyman ed.), *P. 47*
We naturally know what is good, but naturally pursue what is evil. — *Ibid., P. 61*
[7] See George Herbert, page 234b.

Thou didst bring me forth for all
the Greeks in common, not for thyself
alone.
　　Iphigenia in Aulis.[1] *Line 1386*
The company of just and righteous
men is better than wealth and a rich
estate.
　　　　　Aegeus.[1] *Fragment 7*
A bad beginning makes a bad ending.
　　　　　Aeolus.[1] *Fragment 32*
Time will explain it all. He is a talker,
and needs no questioning before he
speaks.
　　　　　　Ibid. Fragment 38
Waste not fresh tears over old griefs.
　　　　　Alexander.[1] *Fragment 44*
The nobly born must nobly meet his
fate.[2]
　　　　　Alcymene.[1] *Fragment 100*
Woman is woman's natural ally.
　　　　　Alope.[1] *Fragment 109*
Man's best possession is a sympa-
thetic wife.
　　　　　Antigone.[1] *Fragment 164*
Second thoughts are ever wiser.[3]
　　　　　Hippolytus. Line 436
The tongue hath sworn, but the mind
is unsworn.[4]
　　　　　　　Ibid. Line 612
Toil, says the proverb, is the sire of
fame.
　　　　　Licymnius.[1] *Fragment 477*
Cowards do not count in battle; they
are there, but not in it.
　　　　　Meleager.[1] *Fragment 523*
A woman should be good for every-

[1] Translated by MORRIS HICKEY MORGAN.
[2] If there be any good in nobility, I trow it
to be only this, that it imposeth a necessity
upon those which are noble, that they should
not suffer their nobility to degenerate from
the virtues of their ancestors. — BOETHIUS
[A. D. 470–525]: *De Consolatione Philosophiae, III, 6, 25*
Noblesse oblige (Nobility has its obligation). — BOHN: *Foreign Proverbs*
[3] Second thoughts, they say, are best. —
DRYDEN: *The Spanish Friar* [1681], *Act II,
Sc. 2*
Is it so true that second thoughts are best?
— TENNYSON: *Sea Dreams* [1864]
[4] This line was always quoted as an example of Sophist casuistry.

thing at home, but abroad good for nothing.

Meleager.[1] *Fragment 525*
Silver and gold are not the only coin; virtue too passes current all over the world.

Oedipus.[1] *Fragment 546*
Where two discourse, if the one's anger rise,
The man who lets the contest fall is wise.

Protesilaus.[1] *Fragment 656*
When good men die their goodness does not perish,
But lives though they are gone. As for the bad,
All that was theirs dies and is buried with them.[2]

Temenidae.[1] *Fragment 734*
Every man is like the company he is wont to keep.

Phoenix.[1] *Fragment 809*
Who knows but life be that which men call death,
And death what men call life?[3]

Phrixus.[1] *Fragment 830*
Whoso neglects learning in his youth, loses the past and is dead for the future.

Ibid. Fragment 927
The gods visit the sins of the fathers upon the children.[4]

Ibid. Fragment 970
In a case of dissension, never dare to judge till you've heard the other side.

Heracleidae.[1] (*Quoted by* ARISTOPHANES *in The Wasps*)
Leave no stone unturned.[5]

Ibid. 1002

[1] Translated by MORRIS HICKEY MORGAN.
[2] See Shakespeare, page 168a.
[3] See Aristophanes, page 23a.
[4] See *Exodus, XX, 5,* on page 1024b.
The sins of the father are to be laid upon the children. — SHAKESPEARE: *Merchant of Venice* [1596-1597], *Act III, Sc. 5, L. 1*
[5] This may be traced to a response of the Delphic oracle given to Polycrates, as the best means of finding a treasure buried by Xerxes' general, Mardonius, on the field of Plataea. The oracle replied, "Turn every stone." — LEUTSCH AND SCHNEIDEWIN: *Corpus Paraemiographorum Graecorum, Vol. I, P. 146*
I commend the old proverb, "For we must look about under every stone, lest an orator

Those whom God wishes to destroy, he first deprives of their senses.[1]

Fragment, Greek Iambic
These men won eight victories over the Syracusans when the favor of the gods was equal for both sides.

Epitaph for the Athenians Slain in Sicily

HERODOTUS [2]
[484-424 B. C.]

A man trusts his ears less than his eyes.

Book I, Clio. Chap. 8
Call no man happy till you know the nature of his death; he is at best but fortunate.

Ibid. Chap. 32
They [the Persians] are accustomed to deliberate on matters of the highest moment when warm with wine; but whatever they in this situation may determine is again proposed to them on the morrow, in their cooler moments, by the person in whose house they had before assembled. If at this time also it meet their approbation, it is executed; otherwise it is rejected. Whatever also they discuss when sober, is always a second time examined after they have been drinking.[3]

Ibid. Chap. 133

bite us." — ARISTOPHANES [446-380 B.C.]: *The Trial of Euripides*
[1] Quos deus vult perdere, prius dementat.
In Boswell's *Life of Dr. Johnson* [1791] (Everyman ed.), *Vol. 2, Pp. 442-443,* this is quoted as a saying which everybody repeats, but nobody knows where to find.
Whom Fortune wishes to destroy she first makes mad. — PUBLILIUS SYRUS [*circa* 42 B.C.]: *Maxim 911*
When falls on man the anger of the gods, First from his mind they banish understanding.
      LYCURGUS [*fl.* 820 B.C.]
For those whom God to ruin has design'd, He fits for fate, and first destroys their mind.
      DRYDEN: *The Hind and the Panther* [1687], *Part III, L. 1093*
Whom the Gods would destroy they first make mad. — LONGFELLOW: *The Masque of Pandora* [1875], *VI*
[2] Translated by WILLIAM BELOE [1756-1817].
[3] The ancient Goths of Germany . . . had

They joined battle, and the Phocaeans won, yet it was but a Cadmean victory.[1]

Book I, Clio. Chap. 166

The art of medicine in Egypt is thus exercised: one physician is confined to the study and management of one disease; there are of course a great number who practice this art; some attend to the disorders of the eyes, others to those of the head, some take care of the teeth, others are conversant with all diseases of the bowels; whilst many attend to the cure of maladies which are less conspicuous.

Book II, Euterpe. Chap. 84

How much better it is to be envied than pitied.[2]

Book III, Thalia. Chap. 52

Envy is natural to man from the beginning.

Ibid. Chap. 80

They who mutually injure the state, mutually support each other.

Ibid. Chap. 82

You may have observed how the thunderbolt of Heaven chastises the insolence of the more enormous animals, whilst it passes over without injury the weak and insignificant: before these weapons of the gods you must have seen how the proudest palaces and the loftiest trees fall and perish.[3]

Book VII, Polymnia. Chap. 10

Every measure undertaken with temerity is liable to be perplexed with error, and punished by misfortune.

Book VII, Polymnia. Chap. 10

The Persian messengers travel with a velocity which nothing human can equal. . . . Neither snow, nor rain, nor heat, nor darkness, are permitted to obstruct their speed.[1]

Book VIII, Urania. Chap. 98

The king's arm is very long.

Ibid. Chap. 140

Nothing in human life is more to be lamented, than that a wise man should have so little influence.

Book IX, Calliope. Chap. 16

THUCYDIDES [2]
[471–401 B.C.]

Of the events of war, I have not ventured to speak from any chance information, nor according to any notion of my own; I have described nothing but what I saw myself, or learned from others of whom I made the most careful and particular inquiry. The task was a laborious one because eyewitnesses of the same occurrence gave different accounts of them as they remembered, or were interested in the actions of one side or the other. And very likely the strictly historical character of my narrative may be disappointing to the ear. But if he who desires to have before his eyes a true picture of the events which have happened, and of the like events which may be expected to happen hereafter in the order of human things, shall pronounce what I have written to be useful, then I shall be satisfied. My history is an everlasting possession, not

---

all of them a wise custom of debating everything of importance to their state, twice; that is, — once drunk, and once sober: — Drunk — that their councils might not want vigour; and sober — that they might not want discretion. —STERNE: *Tristram Shandy* [1760–1767], *Book V, Chap. 17*

Appeal from Philip drunk to Philip sober. — VALERIUS MAXIMUS [1st century A.D.]: *Book VI, Chap. 2*

[1] A Cadmean (or a Pyrrhic) victory was one in which the victors suffered as much as their enemies. "One more such victory," said Pyrrhus, "and I am lost."

See Plutarch, page 59a.

[2] Pindar expresses the same sentiment in *Pythian Ode, I, 164.*

[3] It is the lofty pine that by the storm
Is oftener tossed; towers fall with heavier crash

Which higher soar.

HORACE [65–8 B.C.]: *Odes, Book II, X, To Licinius, L. 9*

The bigger they come, the harder they fall. — ROBERT FITZSIMMONS [1862–1917], pugilist, before his fight with James J. Jeffries, a heavier man, in San Francisco [July 25, 1902]

[1] Neither snow, nor rain, nor heat, nor gloom of night stays these couriers from the swift completion of their appointed rounds. — *Inscription on the Main Post Office, New York City, adapted from Herodotus*

[2] Translated by JOWETT.

a prize composition which is heard and forgotten.

Peloponnesian War. Book I, 22

Mankind is tolerant of the praises of others so long as each hearer thinks he can do as well or nearly as well himself, but, when the speaker rises above him, jealousy is aroused and he begins to be incredulous.

Ibid. Book II, 35, Funeral Speech of Pericles

We are called a democracy, for the administration is in the hands of the many and not of the few. But while the law secures equal justice to all alike in their private disputes, the claim of excellence is also recognised; and when a citizen is in any way distinguished, he is preferred to the public service, not as a matter of privilege, but as the reward of merit. Neither is poverty a bar, but a man may benefit his country whatever be the obscurity of his condition. There is no exclusiveness in our public life, and in our private intercourse we are not suspicious of one another, nor angry with our neighbour if he does what he likes; we do not put on sour looks at him which, though harmless, are not pleasant. While we are thus unconstrained in our private intercourse, a spirit of reverence pervades our public acts; we are prevented from doing wrong by respect for authority and for the laws, having an especial regard to those which are ordained for the protection of the injured as well as to those unwritten laws which bring upon the transgressor of them the reprobation of the general sentiment.

Ibid. 37

We cultivate the mind. We are lovers of the beautiful, yet simple in our tastes, without loss of manliness.

Ibid. 40

Day by day fix your eyes upon the greatness of Athens, until you become filled with the love of her; and when you are impressed by the spectacle of her glory, reflect that this empire has

been acquired by men who knew their duty and had the courage to do it.

Peloponnesian War. Book II, 43, Funeral Speech of Pericles

The sacrifice which they collectively made was individually repaid to them; for they received again each one for himself a praise which grows not old, and the noblest of all sepulchres — I speak not of that in which their remains are laid, but of that in which their glory survives, and is proclaimed always and on every fitting occasion both in word and deed. For the whole earth is the sepulchre of famous men; not only are they commemorated by columns and inscriptions in their own country, but in foreign lands there dwells also an unwritten memorial of them, graven not on stone but in the hearts of men.

Ibid.

Men naturally despise those who court them, but respect those who do not give way to them.

Ibid. Book III, 39

SOCRATES [1]
[470–399 B. C.]

The life which is unexamined is not worth living.

Apology. 38

Either death is a state of nothingness and utter unconsciousness, or, as men say, there is a change and migration of the soul from this world to another.[2] . . . Now if death be of such a nature, I say that to die is to gain; for eternity is then only a single night.

Ibid. 40

No evil can happen to a good man, either in life or after death.

Ibid. 41

Man is a prisoner who has no right to open the door of his prison and run away. . . . A man should wait, and

[1] Translated by JOWETT.

[2] Either the soul is immortal and we shall not die, or it perishes with the flesh, and we shall not know that we are dead. Live, then, as if you were eternal. — ANDRÉ MAUROIS [1885–] (DURANT, *On the Meaning of Life, P. 53*)

not take his own life until God summons him.

Dialogues of PLATO. *Phaedo. 62*

Must not all things at the last be swallowed up in death?

Ibid. 72

Will you not allow that I have as much of the spirit of prophecy in me as the swans? For they, when they perceive that they must die, having sung all their life long, do then sing more lustily than ever, rejoicing in the thought that they are going to the god they serve.[1]

Ibid. 85

The partisan, when he is engaged in a dispute, cares nothing about the rights of the question, but is anxious only to convince his hearers of his own assertions.

Ibid. 91

False words are not only evil in themselves, but they infect the soul with evil.

Ibid.

The soul takes nothing with her to the other world but her education and culture; and these, it is said, are of the greatest service or of the greatest injury to the dead man, at the very beginning of his journey thither.

Ibid. 107

I think that I had better bathe before I drink the poison, and not give the women the trouble of washing my dead body.

Ibid. 115

I owe a cock to Asclepius; will you remember to pay the debt?

Ibid. 118 (The last words of Socrates)

---

[1] The jalous swan, ayens his deth that singeth. — CHAUCER: *The Parlement of Foules* [1372–1386], *L. 342*
    Makes a swan-like end,
    Fading in music.
        SHAKESPEARE: *The Merchant of Venice* [1596–1597], *Act III, Sc. 2, L. 44*
I will play the swan and die in music. — *Othello* [1604–1605], *Act V, Sc. 2, L. 245*
  See Shakespeare, page 148b.
  See Byron, page 458b.

HIPPOCRATES [1]
[460–377 B. C.]

I swear by Apollo Physician, by Asclepius, by Health, by Panacea, and by all the gods and goddesses, making them my witnesses, that I will carry out, according to my ability and judgment, this oath and this indenture. To hold my teacher in this art equal to my own parents; to make him partner in my livelihood; when he is in need of money to share mine with him; to consider his family as my own brothers, and to teach them this art, if they want to learn it, without fee or indenture. I will use treatment to help the sick according to my ability and judgment, but never with a view to injury and wrongdoing. I will keep pure and holy both my life and my art. In whatsoever houses I enter, I will enter to help the sick, and I will abstain from all intentional wrongdoing and harm. And whatsoever I shall see or hear in the course of my profession in my intercourse with men, if it be what should not be published abroad, I will never divulge, holding such things to be holy secrets. Now if I carry out this oath, and break it not, may I gain forever reputation among all men for my life and for my art; but if I transgress it and forswear myself, may the opposite befall me.

The Physician's Oath

Healing is a matter of time, but it is sometimes also a matter of opportunity.

Precepts. Chap. 1

Sometimes give your services for nothing, calling to mind a previous benefaction or present satisfaction. And if there be an opportunity of serving one who is a stranger in financial straits, give full assistance to all such. For where there is love of man, there is also love of the art. For some patients, though conscious that their condition is perilous, recover their health simply through their contentment with the

---

[1] Translated by WILLIAM HENRY RICH JONES [1817–1885].

goodness of the physician. And it is well to superintend the sick to make them well, to care for the healthy to keep them well, also to care for one's own self, so as to observe what is seemly.
Precepts. Chap. 6

In all abundance there is lack.
Ibid. Chap. 8

If for the sake of a crowded audience you do wish to hold a lecture, your ambition is no laudable one, and at least avoid all citations from the poets, for to quote them argues feeble industry.
Ibid. Chap. 12

Life is short and the art long.[1]
Aphorisms. Sect. I, 1

Extreme remedies are very appropriate for extreme diseases.[2]
Ibid. 6

ARISTOPHANES
[446–380 B. C.]

What heaps of things have bitten me to the heart!
A small few pleased me, very few, just four;
But those that vexed were sand-dune-hundredfold.
Acharnians [3]

If a word
Our orators let fall, save what pertains
To peace, I'll raise a storm of words, and rain
A very tempest of abuse upon them!
Ibid.[4]

He works and blows the coals

[1] Ars longa, vita brevis.
The lyf so short, the craft so long to lerne. — CHAUCER: *The Parlement of Foules* [1372–1386], *Proem, L. 1*
Art's long, though time is short. — BROWNING: *The Ring and the Book* [1868–1869], *IX, Juris Doctor Johannes-Baptista Bottinius*
See Longfellow, page 521a.
[2] See Shakespeare, page 177b.
For a desperate disease a desperate cure. — MONTAIGNE: *Essays* [1580–1595], *Book II, Chap. 3*
Desperate cures must be to desperate ills applied. — DRYDEN: *The Hind and the Panther* [1687], *Part III, L. 1111*
[3] Translated by B. B. ROGERS.
[4] Translated by JOHN HOOKHAM FRERE [1769–1846].

And has plenty of other irons in the fire.[1]
Acharnians

Master, shall I begin with the usual jokes
That the audience always laugh at?
Frogs [2]

Lodgings, — free from bugs and fleas, if possible,
If you know any such.
Ibid.

Brekeke-kesh, koash, koash.[3]
Ibid.

The men that stood for office, noted for acknowledged worth,
And for manly deeds of honour, and for honourable birth;
Train'd in exercise and art, in sacred dances and in song,
All are ousted and supplanted by a base ignoble throng.
Ibid.

He collected audiences about him,
And flourish'd, and exhibited, and harangued.
Ibid.

A vast expenditure of human voice.
Ibid.

Exalted ideas of fancy require
To be clothed in a suitable vesture of phrase.
Ibid.

I laugh'd till I cried.
Ibid.

If we withdraw the confidence we placed
In these our present statesmen, and transfer it
To those whom we mistrusted heretofore,
This seems I think our fairest chance for safety:
If with our present counsellors we fail,

[1]   It is always good
When a man has two irons in the fire.
FRANCIS BEAUMONT: *The Faithful Friends* [*circa* 1608], *Act I, Sc. 2*
[2] Translated by JOHN HOOKHAM FRERE [1769–1846].
[3] Adapted in college cheer: Brekeke-kex, koax, koax.

Then with their opposites we might succeed.

Frogs

Shame is the apprehension of a vision
Reflected from the surface of opinion —
The opinion of the public.

Ibid.

Perhaps death is life, and life is death,
And victuals and drink an illusion of
the senses;
For what is Death but an eternal sleep?
And does not Life consist in sleeping
and eating? [1]

Ibid.

Happy is the man possessing
The superior holy blessing
Of a judgment and a taste
Accurate, refined and chaste.

Ibid.

When shall I see those halcyon days? [2]

Clouds [3]

If you strike
Upon a thought that baffles you, break
off
From that entanglement and try another.
So shall your wits be fresh to start
again.

Ibid.

Old age is but a second childhood.

Ibid.

Throw fear to the wind.

Wasps [4]

Rais'd and swell'd with honours great
(such on bard yet never sate)
With meekness and modesty he bore
him;
And while his laurels grew, he kept ever
in his view
The heights yet unconquer'd before
him.

Ibid.

[1] See Euripides, page 18a.
[2] Expect Saint Martin's summer, halcyon days. — SHAKESPEARE: *King Henry VI, Part I* [1591], *Act I, Sc. 2, L. 131*
  The appellation of Halcyon-days, which was applied to a rare and bloodless week of repose. — GIBBON: *Decline and Fall of the Roman Empire* [1776–1788], *Chap. 48*
[3] Translated by THOMAS MITCHELL [1783–1845].
[4] Translated by RICHARD CUMBERLAND [1732–1811].

O the days that are gone by, O the days
that are no more,
When my eye was bold and fearless,
and my hand was on the oar.

Wasps

Bitt'rest stroke of all we feel it, that an
idle brood be fed
At our cost, who never handled oar or
jav'lin, never bled,
Nor so much as rais'd a blister in their
suff'ring country's stead.

Ibid.

The wise may learn many things from
their foes.

Birds

DIONYSIUS THE ELDER
[430–367 B.C.]

Let thy speech be better than silence,
or be silent.

Fragment 6

XENOPHON
[*Circa* 430–355 B.C.]

Apollo said that every one's true
worship was that which he found in
use in the place where he chanced to be.

Recollections of Socrates. I, 3, 1

The sea! The sea! [1]

Anabasis. IV, vii, 24

I knew my son was mortal.[2]

DIOGENES LAERTIUS: *Xenophon.*
Sect. 8

PLATO [3]
[427–347 B.C.]

He who is of a calm and happy nature
will hardly feel the pressure of age, but
to him who is of an opposite disposition
youth and age are equally a burden.

The Republic. Book I, 329–D

No physician, in so far as he is a
physician, considers his own good in
what he prescribes, but the good of his
patient; for the true physician is also

[1] Thalatta! Thalatta!
  Hail to thee, O Sea, ageless and eternal!
    HEINRICH HEINE [1797–1856]: *Tha-
    latta! Thalatta! St. 1*
[2] When his son was killed in battle.
[3] Translated by JOWETT.

a ruler having the human body as a subject, and is not a mere money-maker.

The Republic. Book I, 342–D

When there is an income-tax, the just man will pay more and the unjust less on the same amount of income.

Ibid. 343–D

Mankind censure injustice, fearing that they may be the victims of it and not because they shrink from committing it.

Ibid. 344–C

Necessity, who is the mother of invention.[1]

Ibid. Book II, 369–C

The beginning is the most important part of the work.

Ibid. 377–B

A fit of laughter which has been indulged to excess almost always produces a violent reaction.

Ibid. Book III, 388–E

Beauty of style and harmony and grace and good rhythm depend on simplicity.

Ibid. 400–D

Musical training is a more potent instrument than any other, because rhythm and harmony find their way into the inward places of the soul.

Ibid. 401–D

Gymnastic as well as music should begin in early years.

Ibid. 403–C

They do certainly give very strange and new-fangled names to diseases.

Ibid. 405–C

The judge should not be young; he should have learned to know evil, not from his own soul, but from late and long observation of the nature of evil

[1] Hunger is the teacher of the arts and the bestower of invention. — PERSIUS [A. D. 34–62]: *Prologue, L. 10*

Necessity, mother of invention. — WYCHERLEY: *Love in a Wood* [1671], *Act III, Sc. 3*

Art imitates Nature, and necessity is the mother of invention. — RICHARD FRANCK: *Northern Memoirs, edited by Scott* [written in 1658, published in 1694]

Sheer necessity, — the proper parent of an art so nearly allied to invention. — SHERIDAN: *The Critic* [1779], *Act I, Sc. 2*

in others: knowledge should be his guide, not personal experience.

The Republic. Book III, 409–B

Everything that deceives may be said to enchant.

Ibid. 413–C

Under the influence either of poverty or of wealth, workmen and their work are equally liable to degenerate.

Ibid. Book IV, 421–E

Wealth is the parent of luxury and indolence, and poverty of meanness and viciousness, and both of discontent.

Ibid. 422

The direction in which education starts a man will determine his future life.

Ibid. 425–B

What is the prime of life? May it not be defined as a period of about twenty years in a woman's life, and thirty in a man's?

Ibid. Book V, 460–E

Let there be one man who has a city obedient to his will, and he might bring into existence the ideal polity about which the world is so incredulous.

Ibid. 502–B

Behold! human beings living in an underground den . . . Like ourselves . . . they see only their own shadows, or the shadows of one another, which the fire throws on the opposite wall of the cave.

Ibid. Book VII, 515–B

Astronomy compels the soul to look upwards and leads us from this world to another.

Ibid. 529

I have hardly ever known a mathematician who was capable of reasoning.

Ibid. 531–E

Solon was under a delusion when he said that a man when he grows old may learn many things — for he can no more learn much than he can run much; youth is the time for any extraordinary toil.

Ibid. 536–D

Bodily exercise, when compulsory, does no harm to the body; but knowledge which is acquired under compulsion obtains no hold on the mind.

The Republic. Book VII, 536–E

Let early education be a sort of amusement; you will then be better able to find out the natural bent.

Ibid. 537

Oligarchy: A government resting on a valuation of property, in which the rich have power and the poor man is deprived of it.

Ibid. Book VIII, 550–C

Democracy, which is a charming form of government, full of variety and disorder, and dispensing a sort of equality to equals and unequals alike.[1]

Ibid. 558–C

The people have always some champion whom they set over them and nurse into greatness. . . . This and no other is the root from which a tyrant springs; when he first appears he is a protector.

Ibid. 565–C

In the early days of his power, he is full of smiles, and he salutes every one whom he meets.

Ibid. 566–D

When the tyrant has disposed of foreign enemies by conquest or treaty, and there is nothing to fear from them, then he is always stirring up some war or other, in order that the people may require a leader.

Ibid. 566–E

Has he not also another object which is that they may be impoverished by payment of taxes, and thus compelled to devote themselves to their daily wants and therefore less likely to conspire against him?

Ibid. 567

What a poor appearance the tales of poets make when stripped of the colours which music puts upon them, and recited in simple prose.

Ibid. Book X, 601–B

[1] See Aristotle, page 26b.

There are three arts which are concerned with all things: one which uses, another which makes, a third which imitates them.

The Republic. Book X, 601–D

No human thing is of serious importance.

Ibid.

The soul of man is immortal and imperishable.

Ibid. 608–D

These are the Fates, daughters of Necessity . . . Lachesis singing of the past, Clotho of the present, Atropos of the future.

Ibid. 617–C

Beloved Pan, and all ye other gods who haunt this place, give me beauty in the inward soul; and may the outward and inward man be at one. May I reckon the wise to be the wealthy, and may I have such a quantity of gold as none but the temperate can carry.

Phaedrus. 279

The greatest penalty of evil-doing — namely, to grow into the likeness of bad men.

Laws. 728

Of all the animals, the boy is the most unmanageable.

Ibid. 808

You are young, my son, and, as the years go by, time will change and even reverse many of your present opinions. Refrain therefore awhile from setting yourself up as a judge of the highest matters.

Ibid. 888

And this which you deem of no moment is the very highest of all: that is whether you have a right idea of the gods, whereby you may live your life well or ill.

Ibid.

Not one of them who took up in his youth with this opinion that there are no gods, ever continued until old age faithful to his conviction.

Ibid.

ZEUXIS
[*Circa* 400 B. C.]

Criticism comes easier than craftsmanship.

Quoted by PLINY *in Natural History*

AESCHINES
[389–314 B. C.]

The sinews of affairs are cut.[1]

Ctesiphon. Chap. 53

ARISTOTLE
[384–322 B. C.]

Poverty is the parent of revolution and crime.

Politics.[2] Book II

Even when laws have been written down, they ought not always to remain unaltered.

Ibid.

The law has no power to command obedience except that of habit, which can only be given by time, so that a readiness to change from old to new laws enfeebles the power of the law.

Ibid.

That judges of important causes should hold office for life is not a good thing, for the mind grows old as well as the body.

Ibid.

Man is by nature a political animal.[3]

Ibid. Book III

It is plain that the state is not determined merely by community of place and by the exchange of mutual protection from harm and of good offices. These things must, indeed, exist, if there is to be a city, yet the existence of all of them does not at once constitute a state; there must be, both in households and families, a sharing of the good life, in a form at once complete and self-sufficient.

Politics. Book III

If liberty and equality, as is thought by some, are chiefly to be found in democracy, they will be best attained when all persons alike share in the government to the utmost.[1]

Ibid. Book IV

The best political community is formed by citizens of the middle class. Those States are likely to be well administered in which the middle class is large, and larger if possible than both the other classes, or at any rate than either singly; for the addition of the middle class turns the scale and prevents either of the extremes from being dominant.

Ibid.

Inferiors revolt in order that they may be equal, and equals that they may be superior. Such is the state of mind which creates revolutions.

Ibid. Book V

Revolutions break out when opposite parties, the rich and the poor, are equally balanced, and there is little or nothing between them; for, if either party were manifestly superior, the other would not risk an attack upon them.

Ibid.

Democracies are most commonly corrupted by the insolence of demagogues.

Ibid.

One swallow does not make a spring.[2]

Nicomachean Ethics. I

---

[1] Ascribed to Demosthenes. DIOGENES LAERTIUS, in his *Life of Bion, Book IV, Chap. 7, Sect. 3*, represents Bion as saying, "Riches were the sinews of business," or, as the phrase may mean, "of the state." Referring perhaps to this maxim of the philosopher Bion, PLUTARCH says in his *Life of Cleomenes*, "He that first said that money was the sinews of affairs, seems especially in that saying to refer to war" (Modern Library Giant ed., *P. 986*). Accordingly we find money called expressly "the sinews of war" in LIBANIUS, *Oration 46*, and by the scholiast on PINDAR, *Olymp.*, *I, 4*, and in CICERO, *Philipp.*, *V, 2*, "nervos belli, infinitam pecuniam."

[2] Translated by JOWETT.

[3] This phrase is used elsewhere by Aristotle.

[1] See Plato, page 25a.

[2] One swallow maketh not summer. — JOHN HEYWOOD: *Proverbes* [1546], *Part II, Chap. 5*

One swallowe prouveth not that summer is neare. — NORTHBROOKE: *Treatise against Dancing* [1577]

One swallow never makes a summer. —

Of evils we must choose the least.[1]
Nicomachean Ethics. II

All admit that in a certain sense the several kinds of character are bestowed by nature. Justice, a tendency to Temperance, Courage, and the other types of character are exhibited from the moment of birth.
Ibid. VI

Mothers are fonder of their children. For they have a more painful share in their production and they are more certain that they are their own.
Ibid. IX

In practical matters the end is not mere speculative knowledge of what is to be done, but rather the doing of it. It is not enough to know about Virtue, then, but we must endeavour to possess it, and to use it, or to take any other steps that may make us good.
Ibid. X

The generality of men are naturally apt to be swayed by fear rather than by reverence, and to refrain from evil rather because of the punishment that it brings, than because of its own foulness.
Ibid.

What makes men good is held by some to be nature, by others habit or training, by others instruction. As for the goodness that comes by nature, this is plainly not within our control, but is bestowed by some divine agency on certain people who truly deserve to be called fortunate.
Ibid.

Misfortune unites men, when the same thing is harmful to both.
Rhetoric. I

No one loves him whom he fears.
Ibid. II

CERVANTES: *Don Quixote, Part I* [1605], *Book II, Chap. 4*
[1] Of two evils, the least should be chosen. — CICERO [106–43 B.C.]: *De Officiis, III, 1*
Of harmes two, the lesse is for to chese. — CHAUCER: *Troilus and Criseyde* [1372–1386], *Book II, L. 470*
Of two evils the less is always to be chosen. — THOMAS A KEMPIS [1380–1471]: *Imitation of Christ, Book III, Chap. 12*

God is mightiest in power, fairest in beauty, immortal in existence, supreme in virtue; therefore, being invisible to every mortal nature, he is seen through his works themselves.
De Mundo. Chap 6

DEMOSTHENES
[384–322 B.C.]

I do not purchase regret at such a price.
Reply to Laïs

Though a man escape every other danger, he can never wholly escape those who do not want such a person as he is to exist.
De Falsa Legatione.[1] 228

Every advantage in the past is judged in the light of the final issue.
First Olynthiac.[1] 11

Like the diet prescribed by doctors, which neither restores the strength of the patient nor allows him to succumb, so these doles that you are now distributing neither suffice to ensure your safety nor allow you to renounce them and try something else.
Third Olynthiac.[1] 33

To remind the man of the good turns you have done him is very much like a reproach.
De Corona.[1] 269

MENANDER [2]
[343–292 B.C.]

You knew not how to live in clover.
The Girl from Samos. Act 2, Sc. 4

The man who first invented the art of supporting beggars made many wretched.
The Fishermen. Fragment

We live, not as we wish to, but as we can.
The Lady of Andros. Fragment

In many ways the saying "Know thyself" is not well said. It were more practical to say "Know other people." [3]
Thrasyleon. Fragment

---

[1] Translated by C. A. AND J. H. VINCE.
[2] Translated by FRANCIS G. ALLINSON.
[3] See Plutarch, page 60a.

No one gets rich quickly if he is honest.[1]

The Flatterer. Fragment

Nor is it even possible for anyone to say while life lasts: "*That* is something that will not be my lot!"

The Drafting Officer. Fragment

I call a fig a fig, a spade a spade.[2]

Unidentified minor fragment

A woman is necessarily an evil, but he that gets the most tolerable one is lucky.

Ibid.

Marriage, if one will face the truth, is an evil, but a necessary evil.[3]

Ibid.

The land that gives poor nurture bears brave men.[4]

Ibid.

Manner, not gold, is woman's best adornment.

Fragment. Quoted in The Spectator, January 3, 1712

For our mind is God.

PLUTARCH: *Platonic Questions*

BIDPAI OR PILPAY [5]
[*Circa* 326 B.C.?]

We ought to do our neighbour all the good we can. If you do good, good will

be done to you; but if you do evil, the same will be measured back to you again.[1]

Chap. 1. Dabschelim and Pilpay

It has been the providence of Nature to give this creature [the cat] nine lives instead of one.[2]

Ibid. Fable 3, The Greedy and Ambitious Cat

There is no gathering the rose without being pricked by the thorns.[3]

Chap. 2. Fable 6, The Two Travellers

Wise men say that there are three sorts of persons who are wholly deprived of judgment, — they who are ambitious of preferments in the courts of princes; they who make use of poison to show their skill in curing it; and they who intrust women with their secrets.

Ibid.

Men are used as they use others.

Ibid. Fable 9, The King Who Became Just

What is bred in the bone will never come out of the flesh.[4]

Ibid. Fable 14, The Two Fishermen

Guilty consciences always make people cowards.[5]

Chap. 3. Fable 3, The Prince and His Minister

Whoever . . . prefers the service of princes before his duty to his Creator, will be sure, early or late, to repent in vain.

Ibid.

[1] No good man ever grew rich all at once. — PUBLILIUS SYRUS [*circa* 42 B.C.]: *Maxim 837*

[2] A similar saying is credited to Aristophanes by LUCIAN, *Quom. Hist. sit conscrib.*, 41

Brought up like a rude Macedon, and taught to call a spade a spade. — STEPHEN GOSSON: *Ephemerides of Phialo* [1579]

I think it good plain English, without fraud, To call a spade a spade, a bawd a bawd.

JOHN TAYLOR, the "Water Poet" [1580–1653]

[3] Marriage is an evil that most men welcome. — *Fragment, Monost. 102*. Motto of *The Spectator*, December 29, 1711.

[4] This and the preceding quotation are translated by A. H. CHASE.

[5] Theodor Benfey [1809–1881], German Orientalist, in tracing the name Pilpay or Bidpai, found that it was an appellative applied to the chief pandit or court scholar of an Indian prince. The *Fables of Pilpay*, or *Kalilah and Dimnah*, are the Arabic translation of the Pahlavi translation of the Sanskrit original of the *Panchatantra*. The first English translation appeared in 1570.

[1] And with what measure ye mete, it shall be measured to you again. — *Matthew, VII, 2*

[2] A woman hath nine lives like a cat. — JOHN HEYWOOD: *Proverbes* [1546], *Part II, Chap. 4*

[3] Ne'er the rose without the thorn. — HERRICK: *The Rose* [1648]

Flowers of all hue, and without thorn the rose. — MILTON: *Paradise Lost* [1667], *Book IV, L. 256*

[4] It will not out of the flesh that is bred in the bone. — JOHN HEYWOOD: *Proverbes* [1546], *Part II, Chap. 8*

[5] A guilty conscience never feels secure. — PUBLILIUS SYRUS [*circa* 42 B.C.]: *Maxim 617*

See Shakespeare, page 174b.

There are some who bear a grudge even to those that do them good.

> *Chap. 3. Fable 6, A Religious Doctor*

He that plants thorns must never expect to gather roses.[1]

> *Ibid. Fable 8, The Ignorant Physician*

Honest men esteem and value nothing so much in this world as a real friend. Such a one is as it were another self, to whom we impart our most secret thoughts, who partakes of our joy, and comforts us in our affliction; add to this, that his company is an everlasting pleasure to us.

> *Chap. 4. Choice of Friends*

That possession was the strongest tenure of the law.[2]

> *Chap. 5. Fable 4, The Cat and the Two Birds*

Wild elephants are caught by tame;
With money it is just the same.

> *The Panchatantra.*[3] *Book I*

EUCLID
[*Circa* 300 B. C.]

Pons asinorum (the bridge of asses).[4]

> *Elements. Book I, Proposition 5*

There is no royal road to geometry.[5]

> *Quoted by* PROCLUS: *Commentaria in Euclidem. Book 2, Chap. 4*

ARCHIMEDES
[287?–212 B. C.]

I have found it![6]

> VITRUVIUS POLLIO: *De Architectura. IX, 215*

---

[1] Whatsoever a man soweth, that shall he also reap. — *Galatians, VI, 7*
  See Samuel Butler, page 239a.
[2] Possession is eleven points in the law. — COLLEY CIBBER: *Woman's Wit* [1697], *Act I*
[3] Translation adapted from ARTHUR W. RYDER.
[4] Too difficult for asses, or stupid boys, to get over.
[5] Ptolemy I, King of Egypt, wished to study geometry, without going over the thirteen parts of Euclid's *Elements.* He said that a short cut would be agreeable, whereupon Euclid answered that there was no royal road to geometry. Often misquoted as "no royal road to learning."
[6] Eureka! Said when he found the principle of specific gravity.

Give me where to stand, and I will move the earth.[1]

> PAPPUS: *Collectio. Book VIII, Prop. 10, Sect. XI*

THEOCRITUS [2]
[THIRD CENTURY B. C.]

'Tis peace of mind, lad, we must find, and have a beldame nigh
To sit for us and spit for us and bid all ill go by.

> *The Harvest-Home. Line 126*

O cricket is to cricket dear, and ant for ant doth long,
The hawk's the darling of his fere, and o' me the Muse and her song.

> *The Third Country Singing-Match. Line 31*

O to be a frog, my lads, and live aloof from care.

> *The Reapers. Line 52*

Thou 'lt cut thy finger, niggard, a splitting caraway.

> *Ibid. Line 55*

A great love goes here with a little gift.

> *The Distaff. Line 24*

CALLIMACHUS
[*Floruit* 260 B. C.]

A big book is a big nuisance.

> *Fragmenta Incerta, No. 359*

This is the tomb of Callimachus that thou art passing.
He could sing well, and laugh well at the right time over the wine.

> *His Own Epitaph. Greek Anthology, Book VII, No. 415*

PLAUTUS [3]
[254–184 B. C.]

What is yours is mine, and all mine is yours.[4]

> *Trinummus. Act II, Sc. 2, Line 48*

Not by years but by disposition is wisdom acquired.

> *Ibid. Line 88*

---

[1] Said with reference to the lever.
[2] Translated by J. M. EDMONDS.
[3] Translated by HENRY THOMAS RILEY [1816–1878].
[4] What's mine is yours, and what is yours is mine. — SHAKESPEARE: *Measure for Measure* [1604–1605], *Act V, Sc. 1, L. 529*

He whom the gods favour dies in youth.[1]

    Bacchides. Act IV, Sc. 7, Line 18

You are seeking a knot in a bulrush.[2]

    Menaechmi. Act II, Sc. 1, Line 22

In the one hand he is carrying a stone, while he shows the bread in the other.[3]

    Aulularia. Act II, Sc. 2, Line 18

It was not for nothing that the raven was just now croaking on my left hand.[4]

    Ibid. Act. IV, Sc. 3, Line 1

There are occasions when it is undoubtedly better to incur loss than to make gain.

    Captivi. Act II, Sc. 2, Line 77

Patience is the best remedy for every trouble.[5]

    Rudens. Act II, Sc. 5, Line 71

Consider the little mouse, how sagacious an animal it is which never entrusts its life to one hole only.[6]

    Truculentus. Act. IV, Sc. 4, Line 15

---

[1] Those that God loves do not live long. — GEORGE HERBERT: *Jacula Prudentum* [2nd ed., 1651]

    See Wordsworth, page 410b.

    Heaven gives its favourites — early death. — BYRON: *Childe Harold, Canto IV* [1818], *St. 102*

    "Whom the gods love die young," was said of yore. — BYRON: *Don Juan* [1819–1824], *Canto IV, St. 12*

[2] A proverbial expression implying a desire to create doubts and difficulties where there really are none. It occurs in TERENCE: *Andria, Act V, Sc. 4, L. 38;* also in ENNIUS: *Saturae, 46.*

[3] What man is there of you, whom if his son ask bread, will he give him a stone? — *Matthew, VII, 9*

[4] That raven on yon left-hand oak
    (Curse on his ill-betiding croak!)
    Bodes me no good.
    JOHN GAY: *The Farmer's Wife and the Raven* [1727]

[5] Patience is a remedy for every sorrow. — PUBLILIUS SYRUS [*circa* 42 B.C.]: *Maxim 170*

[6] I holde a mouses herte nat worth a leek,
    That hath but oon hole for to sterte to,
    And if that faille, thanne is al y-do.
    CHAUCER: *The Canterbury Tales* [*circa* 1387], *The Wife of Bath's Prologue, L. 572*

    The mouse that hath but one hole is quickly taken. — GEORGE HERBERT: *Jacula Prudentum* [1640]

    The mouse that always trusts to one poor hole

Nothing is there more friendly to a man than a friend in need.[1]

    Epidicus. Act III, Sc. 3, Line 44

Things which you do not hope happen more frequently than things which you do hope.[2]

    Mostellaria. Act I, Sc. 3, Line 40

To blow and swallow at the same moment is not easy.

    Ibid. Act III, Sc. 2, Line 104

QUINTUS ENNIUS
[239–169 B.C.]

No sooner said than done — so acts your man of worth.

    Annals. Book 9 (Quoted by PRISCIANUS)

I never indulge in poetics
Unless I am down with rheumatics.

    Fragment of a Satire (Quoted by PRISCIANUS)

By delay he restored the state.[3]

    Quoted by CICERO *in De Senectute, IV*

Let no one pay me honor with tears, nor celebrate my funeral with mourning.[4]

    Quoted by CICERO, *Ibid. XX*

The ape, vilest of beasts, how like to us!

    Quoted by CICERO *in De Natura Deorum, Book I, Chap. 35*

No one regards what is before his feet; we all gaze at the stars.

    Iphigenia (Quoted by CICERO *in De Divinatione, Book II, Chap. 13)*

Can never be a mouse of any soul.
    POPE: *Paraphrase of the Prologue* [1714], *L. 298*

[1] A friend in need is a friend indeed. — HAZLITT: *English Proverbs*

[2] The unexpected always happens. — *A common saying*

[3] This refers to Quintus Fabius Maximus, "Cunctator." Hence the "Fabian policy" of waiting.

[4] No funeral gloom, my dears, when I am gone,
    Corpse-gazings, tears, black raiment, graveyard grimness.
    WILLIAM ALLINGHAM [1828–1889]: *Diary*

The idle mind knows not what it is it wants.

Iphigenia. Chorus

Whom they fear they hate.

Thyestes (Quoted by CICERO *in De Officiis, II, 7)*

When Fortune's fickle, the faithful friend is found.[1]

Quoted by CICERO *in De Amicitia, XVIII, 64*

MARCUS PORCIUS CATO
[234–149 B. C.]

Carthage must be destroyed.[2]

CAECILIUS STATIUS
[220–168 B. C.]

Let him draw out his old age to dotage drop by drop.

Hymnis (Quoted by FESTUS)

The facts will promptly blunt his ardor.

The Changeling (Quoted by CHARISIUS)

He plants trees to benefit another generation.

Synephebi (Quoted by CICERO *in De Senectute, VII)*

POLYBIUS
[SECOND CENTURY B. C.]

For peace, with justice and honor, is the fairest and most profitable of possessions, but with disgrace and shameful cowardice it is the most infamous and harmful of all.

Histories. IV, 31

Those who know how to win are much more numerous than those who know how to make proper use of their victories.

Ibid. X, 36

There is no witness so dreadful, no accuser so terrible as the conscience that dwells in the heart of every man.

Ibid. XVIII, 43

[1] In prosperity it is very easy to find a friend; but in adversity it is the most difficult of all things. — EPICTETUS [*circa* A. D. 60]: *Fragments, No. 127*

[2] Delenda est Carthago. Said to have been

TERENCE [1]
[185–159 B. C.]

Nothing in excess.[2]

Andria, Act. I, Sc. 1, Line 34

Of surpassing beauty and in the bloom of youth.

Ibid. Line 45

Hence these tears.

Ibid. Line 99

That is a true proverb which is wont to be commonly quoted, that "all had rather it were well for themselves than for another."

Ibid. Act II, Sc. 5, Line 15

The quarrels of lovers are the renewal of love.[3]

Ibid. Act III, Sc. 3, Line 23

Look you, I am the most concerned in my own interests.[4]

Ibid. Act IV, Sc. 1, Line 12

In fine, nothing is said now that has not been said before.[5]

Eunuchus. The Prologue, Line 41

Immortal gods! how much does one man excel another! What a difference there is between a wise person and a fool!

Ibid. Act II, Sc. 2, Line 1

I have everything, yet have nothing; and although I possess nothing, still of nothing am I in want.[6]

Ibid. Line 12

There are vicissitudes in all things.

Ibid. Line 45

the inevitable conclusion of all his speeches on any topic whatever.

[1] Translated by HENRY THOMAS RILEY [1816–1878].

[2] Ne quid nimis.

[3] The anger of lovers renews the strength of love. — PUBLILIUS SYRUS [*circa* 42 B.C.]: *Maxim 24*

The fallyng out of faithful frends renuyng is of love. — RICHARD EDWARDS: *The Paradise of Dainty Devices* [1576]

Let the falling out of friends be a renewing of affection. — LYLY: *Euphues* [1579]

The falling out of lovers is the renewing of love. — ROBERT BURTON: *Anatomy of Melancholy* [1621–1651], *Part III, Sect. 2*

[4] See Sir Thomas Browne, page 240b.

[5] See *Ecclesiastes, I, 10*, on page 1042a, and Robert Burton, page 221a.

[6] See *2 Corinthians, VI, 10*, on page 1062a, and Wotton, page 213a.

I did not care one straw.[1]

Eunuchus. Act III, Sc. 1, Line 21

Jupiter, now assuredly is the time when I could readily consent to be slain, lest life should sully this ecstasy with some disaster.[2]

Ibid. Sc. 5, Line 2

This and a great deal more like it I have had to put up with.

Ibid. Act IV, Sc. 6, Line 8

Take care and say this with presence of mind.[3]

Ibid. Line 31

It behooves a prudent person to make trial of everything before arms.

Ibid. Sc. 7, Line 19

I know the disposition of women: when you will, they won't; when you won't, they set their hearts upon you of their own inclination.

Ibid. Line 42

I took to my heels as fast as I could.

Ibid. Act V, Sc. 2, Line 5

Many a time, . . . from a bad beginning great friendships have sprung up.

Ibid. Line 34

I only wish I may see your head stroked down with a slipper.[4]

Ibid. Sc. 8, Line 1

I am a man, and nothing that concerns a man do I deem a matter of indifference to me.[5]

Heauton Timoroumenos. Act I, Sc. 1, Line 25

This is a wise maxim, "to take warning from others of what may be to your own advantage."

Ibid. Sc. 2, Line 36

That saying which I hear commonly repeated, — that time assuages sorrow.

Heauton Timoroumenos, Act III, Sc. 1, Line 12

Really, you have seen the old age of an eagle,[1] as the saying is.

Ibid. Sc. 2, Line 9

Many a time a man cannot be such as he would be, if circumstances do not admit of it.

Ibid. Act IV, Sc. 1, Line 53

Nothing is so difficult but that it may be found out by seeking.

Ibid. Sc. 2, Line 7

What now if the sky were to fall?[2]

Ibid. Line 41

Rigorous law is often rigorous injustice.[3]

Ibid. Sc. 4, Line 48

There is nothing so easy but that it becomes difficult when you do it with reluctance.

Ibid. Sc. 5, Line 1

Fortune helps the brave.[4]

Phormio. Act I, Sc. 4, Line 26

It is the duty of all persons, when affairs are the most prosperous, then in especial to reflect within themselves in what way they are to endure adversity.

Ibid. Act II, Sc. 1, Line 11

As many men, so many minds;[5] every one his own way.

Ibid. Sc. 4, Line 14

---

[1] Nor do they care a straw. — CERVANTES: *Don Quixote, Part I* [1605], *Book III, Chap. 9*

[2]
    If it were now to die,
    'Twere now to be most happy.

SHAKESPEARE: *Othello* [1604–1605], *Act II, Sc. 1, L. 192*

[3] Literally, "with a present mind" — equivalent to CAESAR's *praesentia animi* (*De Bello Gallico, V, 43, 4*).

[4] According to LUCIAN, there was a story that Omphale used to beat Hercules with her slipper or sandal.

[5] Quoted by CICERO in *De Officiis, I, 30.* In the Latin, Homo sum: humani nihil a me alienum puto.

[1] This was a proverbial expression, signifying a hale and vigorous old age.

[2] Some ambassadors from the Celtae, being asked by Alexander what in the world they dreaded most, answered, that they feared lest the sky should fall upon them. — ARRIANUS [*circa* A.D. 100–170]: *Book I, 4*

[3] Extreme law, extreme injustice, is now become a stale proverb in discourse. — CICERO [106–43 B.C.]: *De Officiis, I, 33*

Extreme justice is often injustice. — RACINE: *La Thébaïde* [1664], *Act IV, Sc. 3*

Mais l'extrême justice est une extrême injure. — VOLTAIRE: *Oedipe* [1718], *Act III, Sc. 3*

[4] PLINY THE YOUNGER says (*Book 6, Letter 16*) that PLINY THE ELDER said this during the eruption of Vesuvius: "Fortune favours the brave."

[5] Quot homines, tot sententiae.

So many heads so many wits. — JOHN

As the saying is, I have got a wolf by the ears.[1]

Phormio. *Act III, Sc. 2, Line 21*

I bid him look into the lives of men as though into a mirror, and from others to take an example for himself.

Adelphoe. *Act III, Sc. 3, Line 61*

According as the man is, so must you humour him.

Ibid. Line 77

It is a maxim of old that among themselves all things are common to friends.[2]

Ibid. Act V, Sc. 3, Line 18

It is the common vice of all, in old age, to be too intent upon our interests.[3]

Ibid. Sc. 8, Line 30

MARCUS TULLIUS CICERO
[106–43 B. C.]

If you aspire to the highest place it is no disgrace to stop at the second, or even the third.

De Oratore. *1*

The freer utterances of poetic license.[4]

Ibid. 38

For as lack of adornment is said to become some women, so this subtle oration, though without embellishment, gives delight.[5]

Ibid. 78

The mind of each man is the man himself.

De Republica. *VI, 26*

Thus in the beginning the world was so made that certain signs come before certain events.[6]

De Divinatione. *I, 118*

He was never less at leisure than when at leisure.[1]

De Officiis. *III, 1, quoting*
Scipio Africanus

What a time! What a civilization![2]

Catiline. *I, 1*

For how many things, which for our own sake we should never do, do we perform for the sake of our friends.

De Amicitia.[3] *XVI*

When Fortune is fickle, the faithful friend is found.[4]

Ibid. XVII

Nothing can be more disgraceful than to be at war with him with whom you have lived on terms of friendship.

Ibid. XXI

He removes the greatest ornament of friendship, who takes away from it respect.

Ibid. XXII

There is no greater bane to friendship than adulation, fawning, and flattery.

Ibid. XXV

Laws are dumb in the midst of arms.[5]

Pro Milone. *IV, 11*

Who stood to gain?[6]

Ibid. XII, 32

The good of the people is the chief law.[7]

De Legibus. *III, 3, 8*

I am a Roman citizen.[8]

In Verrem. *V, 57, 147*

Heywood: *Proverbes* [1546], *Part I, Chap. 2*

So many men so many mindes. — Gascoigne: *Glass of Government* [1575]

[1] A proverbial expression, which, according to Suetonius, was frequently in the mouth of Tiberius Caesar.

[2] All things are in common among friends. — Diogenes Laertius [*circa* A. D. 200]: *Diogenes, VI*

[3] Cicero quotes this in *Tusculan Disputations, Book 3*. The maxim was a favorite one with the Stoic philosophers.

[4] Poetarum licentiae liberiora.

[5] See Milton, page 256a.

[6] See Thomas Campbell, page 432b.

[1] I was never less alone than when by myself. — Edward Gibbon: *Memoirs* [1796]

Never less alone than when alone. — Samuel Rogers: *Human Life* [1819]

In solitude, where we are least alone. — Byron: *Childe Harold's Pilgrimage, Canto III* [1816], *St. 90*

[2] O tempora! O mores!

[3] Translated by Cyrus R. Edmonds.

[4] In prosperity it is very easy to find a friend; but in adversity it is the most difficult of all things. — Epictetus [*circa* A. D. 60]: *Fragments, No. 127*

See Ovid, page 43a.

[5] Silent enim leges inter arma.

The clatter of arms drowns the voice of the law. — Montaigne: *Essays* [1580–1595], *Book III, Chap. 1*

[6] Cui bono fuerit.

[7] Salus populi suprema est lex.

[8] Civis Romanus sum.

Let them hate, provided that they fear.[1]

　　Philippic. I, 14 (Quoted from the tragedian Accius)

Crimes are not to be measured by the issue of events, but from the bad intentions of men.

　　Paradox III

There is no place more delightful than home.

　　Epistolae. IV, 8

While the sick man has life there is hope.[2]

　　Ibid. IX, 10

I prefer to err with Plato.[3]

　　Tusculan Disputations. I, xvii, 39

For as I like a young man in whom there is something of the old, so I like an old man in whom there is something of the young; and he who follows this maxim, in body will possibly be an old man, but he will never be an old man in mind.

　　De Senectute.[4] XI

Old age is by nature rather talkative.

　　Ibid. XVI

Old age, especially an honored old age, has so great authority, that this is of more value than all the pleasures of youth.

　　Ibid. XVII

Intelligence, and reflection, and judgment, reside in old men, and if there had been none of them, no states could exist at all.

　　Ibid. XIX

The short period of life is long enough for living well and honourably.[5]

　　Ibid.

The harvest of old age is the recollection and abundance of blessings previously secured.

　　Ibid.

[1] Oderint, dum metuant.
[2] For the living there is hope, but for the dead there is none. — THEOCRITUS [THIRD CENTURY B. C.] *Idyl IV, 42*
See Gay, page 308a, and Goldsmith, page 353b.
[3] Errare malo cum Platone.
[4] Translated by CYRUS R. EDMONDS.
[5] Life is amply long for him who orders it properly. — SENECA [8 B. C.–A. D. 65]: *On the Shortness of Life, 1, 4*

Nor, in truth, would the honours of illustrious men continue after death, if their own spirits did not make us preserve a longer remembrance of them.

　　De Senectute. XXII

Old age is the consummation of life, just as of a play.

　　Ibid. XXIII

JULIUS CAESAR [1]
[102?–44 B. C.]

All Gaul is divided into three parts.[2]

　　De Bello Gallico, I, 1

LUCRETIUS
[95–55 B. C.]

To such evils could religion urge mankind.

　　De Rerum Natura. I, 101

Continual dropping wears away a stone.[3]

　　Ibid. 314

Pleasant it is, when winds disturb the surface of the vast sea, to watch from land another's mighty struggle.

　　Ibid. II, 1

The swift runners who hand over the lamp of life.

　　Ibid. 279

Why dost thou not withdraw from life like some sated banqueter and with calm spirit seek untroubled rest?

　　Ibid. III, 938

What is food to one man may be fierce poison to others.[4]

　　Ibid. IV, 637

[1] See also Plutarch, pages 56b and 59b.
[2] Gallia est omnis divisa in partes tres.
[3] For water continually dropping will wear hard rocks hollow. — PLUTARCH [A. D. 46–120]: *Of the Training of Children*
The soft droppes of rain perce the hard marble. — LYLY: *Euphues* [1579]
And drizling drops that often doe redound, The firmest flint doth in continuance weare.
　　EDMUND SPENSER: *Amoretti* [1595], *Sonnet 18*
[4] What's one man's poison, signor, Is another's meat or drink.
　　BEAUMONT AND FLETCHER: *Love's Cure* [1647], Act III, Sc. 2

In the midst of the fountain of wit there arises something bitter, which stings in the very flowers.[1]

　　　De Rerum Natura. IV, 1133

CATULLUS [2]
[87–54? B. C.]

Now he goes along the dark road, whence they say no one returns.

　　　Odes. III

Let us live and love, my Lesbia, and value at a penny all the talk of crabbed old men.

Suns may set and rise again. For us, when once our brief day has set, there's the sleep of one everlasting night.[3]

　　　Ibid. V

Over head and heels.[4]

　　　Ibid. XX

Everybody has his own delusion assigned to him: but we do not see that part of the bag which hangs on our back.[5]

　　　Ibid. XXII

Ah, what is more blessed than to put cares away, when the mind lays by its burden, and tired with labor of far travel we have come to our own home and rest on the couch we longed for? This it is which alone is worth all these toils.

　　　Ibid. XXXI

For there is nothing more silly than a silly laugh.

　　　Ibid. XXXIX

Oh, this age! how tasteless and ill-bred it is!

　　　Ibid. XLIII

---

[1] See Byron, page 452b.
[2] Translated by F. W. CORNISH.
[3] Translated by E. M. BECK.
[4] Per caputque pedesque.
[5] Whosoever shall call me madman, shall hear as much from me, and shall learn to look back upon the bag that hangs behind him. — HORACE [65–8 B. C.]: *Satires, Book II, III*
Jupiter has loaded us with a couple of wallets: the one, filled with our own vices, he has placed at our backs; the other, heavy with those of others, he has hung before. — PHAEDRUS [*circa* A. D. 8]: *Book IV, Fable 10*
Not a soul is there who seeks to search into himself — not one! But the wallet of the person in front is kept carefully in view. PERSIUS [A. D. 34–62]: *Satires, IV*

Now spring brings back balmy warmth.

　　　Odes. XLVI

Idleness ere now has ruined both kings and wealthy cities.

　　　Ibid. LI [*A Fragment*]

What is it, Catullus? why do you not make haste to die?

　　　Ibid. LII

Henceforth let no woman believe a man's oath, let none believe that a man's speeches can be trustworthy. They, while their mind desires something and longs eagerly to gain it, nothing fear to swear, nothing spare to promise; but as soon as the lust of their greedy mind is satisfied, they fear not then their words, they heed not their perjuries.[1]

　　　Ibid. LXIV

It is not fit that men should be compared with gods.

　　　Ibid. LXVIII

I hate and I love. Why I do so, perhaps you ask. I do not know, but I feel it and I am in torment.

　　　Ibid. LXXXV

For ever, brother, hail and farewell.[2]

　　　Ibid. CI

SALLUST
[86–34 B. C.]

The soul is the captain and ruler of the life of mortals.[3]

　　　Jugurtha. Chap. 1

Experience has shown that to be true which Appius [4] says in his verses, that every man is the architect of his own fortune;[5] and this proverb is especially

---

[1] What a woman says to her ardent lover should be written in wind and running water. — *Odes, LXX*
[2] In perpetuum, frater, ave atque vale.
[3] For man is man and master of his fate. — TENNYSON: *Idylls of the King, Geraint and Enid* [1859], *I, L. 355*
　　I am the master of my fate:
　　I am the captain of my soul.
　　　W. E. HENLEY [1849–1903]: *To R. T. Hamilton Bruce (Invictus)*
　Be the proud captain still of thine own fate. — J. B. KENYON [1858–1924]: *A Challenge*
[4] Appius Claudius Caecus, consul in 307 B. C.
[5] His own character is the arbiter of every

true of you, who have excelled others to such a degree that men are sooner wearied in singing the praises of your deeds than you in doing deeds worthy of praise.

Speech on the State, Addressed to Caesar in His Later Years. Chap. I, Sentence 2

CORNELIUS NEPOS
[*Floruit* 75 B.C.]

More brawn than brain.
Epaminondas. Chap. V, Line 21

VIRGIL
[70–19 B.C.]

Compare great things with small.[1]
Eclogues. I, Line 24

A great order of the ages is born anew. Now the virgin, now the reign of Saturn, comes again; now a new progeny descends from heaven.[2]
Ibid. IV, Line 5

We have now made you for a time out of marble.
Ibid. VII, Line 35

Age carries all things, even the mind, away.
Ibid. IX, Line 51

Love conquers all.[3]
Ibid. X, Line 69

Farthest Thule.[4]
Georgics. I, Line 30

Be favorable to bold beginnings.[1]
Georgics. I, Line 40

Practice, by taking thought, might little by little hammer out divers arts.
Ibid. Line 133

O but too happy the farmers, if they should know their own good fortune!
Ibid. Line 458

Let the fields and the gliding streams in the valleys delight me. Inglorious, let me court the rivers and forests.
Ibid. II, Line 485

Happy he who could learn the causes of things and who put beneath his feet all fears.[2]
Ibid. Line 490

Happy also he who knows the country gods — Pan and old Sylvanus and the sisterhood of the Nymphs.
Ibid. Line 493

Some trouble the dangerous seas with oars, others rush to arms.
Ibid. Line 503

Arms and the man I sing.[3]
Aeneid. Book I, Line 1

Fury ministers arms.[4]
Ibid. Line 150

God will give an end to these things too.
Ibid. Line 199

Perhaps some day it will be pleasant to remember these things.[5]
Ibid. Line 203

The leader in the deed a woman.[6]
Ibid. Line 364

She appeared a true goddess in her walk.
Ibid. Line 405

Happy they whose walls already rise.
Ibid. Line 437

---

one's fortune. — PUBLILIUS SYRUS [*circa* 42 B.C.]: *Maxim 283*
   Chiefly the mould of a man's fortune is in his own hands. — FRANCIS BACON: *Essays* [1597–1625], *Of Fortune*
   The brave man carves out his fortune, and every man is the son of his own works. — CERVANTES: *Don Quixote, Part I* [1605], *Chap. 4*

[1] To compare
Great things with small.
   MILTON: *Paradise Lost* [1667], *Book II, L. 921*

[2] Magnus ab integro saeculorum nascitur ordo.
Iam redit et Virgo, redeunt Saturnia regna;
Iam nova progenies caelo demittitur alto.
Interpreted by the Middle Ages as a prophecy of the birth of Christ. DANTE cites the lines in the *Purgatorio, Canto XXII, L. 70.*

[3] Omnia amor vincit.

[4] Ultima Thule.

[1] For the reverse side of the Great Seal of the United States (first used on the silver dollar certificates, series of 1935) this line of Virgil has been adapted, changed from the imperative mood, *Audacibus annue coeptis,* to the indicative mood, *Annuit coeptis,* He smiles on our beginnings.

[2] Virgil's tribute to Lucretius.

[3] Arma virumque cano.

[4] Furor arma ministrat.

[5] Forsan et haec olim meminisse iuvabit.

[6] Dux femina facti.

There are tears for misfortune.[1]

Aeneid. Book I, Line 462

A mind conscious of virtue may bring to thee suitable rewards.[2]

Ibid. Line 604

While rivers run into the sea, while on the mountains shadows move over the slopes, while heaven feeds the stars, ever shall thy honor, thy name, and thy praises endure.

Ibid. Line 607

Not unacquainted with sorrow, I have learned to aid the unfortunate.

Ibid. Line 630

I fear the Greeks, even when bringing gifts.[3]

Ibid. Book II, Line 49

I shudder at the word.[4]

Ibid. Line 204

The gods' thought was otherwise.[5]

Ibid. Line 428

O cursed lust for gold, to what dost thou not drive the hearts of men!

Ibid. Book III, Line 56

A fickle and changeful thing is woman ever.[6]

Ibid. Book IV, Line 569

Yield not to misfortunes but press forward the more boldly in their face.

Ibid. Book VI, Line 95

Easy is the descent to Hell; night and day the gates stand open; but to re-climb the slope, and escape to the outer air, this indeed is a task.

Ibid. Line 126

Faithful Achates.[7]

Ibid. Line 158 (and elsewhere)

---

[1] Sunt lacrimae rerum.

[2] The mind, conscious of rectitude, laughed to scorn the falsehood of report. — OVID [43 B.C.–A.D. 18]: *Fasti, Book IV, L. 311*

[3] Timeo Danaos et dona ferentes. See Euripides, page 17a.

[4] Horresco referens.

[5] Dis aliter visum.

[6] Varium et mutabile semper femina. Woman often changes; foolish the man who trusts her. — FRANCIS I OF FRANCE [1494–1547], written by him with his ring on a window of the château of Chambord (BRANTÔME: *Oeuvres, VII, 395*)

La donna è mobile. — PIAVE: *Libretto of* VERDI's *Rigoletto*, Duke's song

[7] Fidus Achates. Proverbial for a trusty

Fortunate isle, the abode of the blest.

Aeneid. Book VI, Line 639

Each of us suffers his own hell.

Ibid. Line 743

Others, I suppose, will more subtly mold the breathing bronze, draw forth the living features from the marble, plead causes better, mark with the rod the wanderings of the sky and foretell the rising stars: thou, Roman, be mindful to rule the peoples with imperial sway (these shall be thy arts) to impose the way of peace, to spare the conquered and put down the proud.

Ibid. Line 847

Implored the Genius of the place.

Ibid. Book VII, Line 136

Faith in the tale is old, but its fame is everlasting.

Ibid. Book IX, Line 79

It is enough to have perished once.

Ibid. Line 140

I could not bear a mother's tears.

Ibid. Line 289

Steep thyself in a bowl of summer-time.

Minor Poems. Copa: Syrisca, a Dancing Girl,[1] Line 29

Here's Death, twitching my ear: "Live," says he, "for I'm coming." [2]

Ibid. Line 38

These lines made I, another steals my honors;

So you for others, oxen, bear the yoke;

So you for others, bees, store up your honey;

So you for others, sheep, put on your fleece;

So you for others, birds, construct your nests.[3]

Epigram (From CAIUS TIBERIUS DONATUS: *Life of Virgil)*

---

comrade; Achates was the faithful companion of Aeneas.

[1] Attributed to Virgil by CHARISIUS, the Grammarian, and by SUETONIUS, though modern scholars question the authenticity of all the minor poems.

[2] Quoted by Justice Oliver Wendell Holmes in a radio address on his ninetieth birthday [March 8, 1931].

[3] Virgil wrote a distich praising Caesar, and

HORACE
[65–8 B.C.]

But if you give me a place among the bards of the lyre,
I shall lift my head till it strikes the stars.

Odes. Book I, i, Line 35

For mortal daring nothing is too high. In our blind folly we storm heaven itself.

Ibid. iii, Line 37

Pale Death, with impartial step, knocks at the poor man's cottage and at the palaces of kings.

Ibid. iv, Line 13

The brief span of life forbids us to cherish a long hope.

Ibid. Line 15

There's no cause for despair! [1]

Ibid. vii, Line 27

Tomorrow we again embark upon the boundless sea.

Ibid. Line 32

Melt me this cold, freely the firelogs throwing
On hearth, my Thaliarchus! And from crock
Two-eared, of Sabine make, unlock
Wine, with four years a-glowing! [2]

Ibid. ix, Line 5

What next morn's sun may bring, forebear to ask;
But count each day that comes by gift of chance
So much to the good.

Ibid. Line 13

Bathyllus claimed the lines. To expose him, Virgil wrote beneath the distich the following incomplete verses, and Caesar asked Bathyllus to finish the lines. He could not, and Virgil then supplied the missing words (italicized below):

Hos ego versiculos feci, tulit alter honores;
Sic vos non vobis, *fertis aratra boves;*
Sic vos non vobis, *mellificatis apes;*
Sic vos non vobis, *vellera fertis oves;*
Sic vos non vobis, *nidificatis aves.*

[1] Nil desperandum!
[2] Dissolve frigus, ligna super foco
Large reponens, atque benignius
Deprome quadrimum Sabina,
O Thaliarche, merum diota.

Inscription over the fireplace of the Harvard Club of Boston

Seize now and here the hour that is, nor trust some later day! [1]

Odes. Book I, xi, Last line

Thrice happy they, and more, whom an unbroken bond unites and whom love, unsevered by bitter quarrels, shall not release until the last day of all.

Ibid. xiii, Line 20

O fairer daughter of a fair mother.[2]

Ibid. xvi, Line 1

The pure in life and free from sin.[3]

Ibid. xxii, Line 1

What shame or measure can there be to our grief for one so dear?

Ibid. xxiv, Line 1

What cannot be removed, becomes lighter through patience.

Ibid. Line 19

One night waits all; Death's road we all must go.

Ibid. xxviii, Line 16

Grant that in age I may not drift Long years, my lyre forgot! [4]

Ibid. xxxi, Line 19

Now's the time for drinking! [5]

Ibid. xxxvii, Line 1

Cease your efforts to find where the last rose lingers.

Ibid. xxxviii, Line 3

Remember when life's path is steep to keep your mind even.

Ibid. Book II, iii, Line 1

Whoever cultivates the golden mean avoids both the poverty of a hovel and the envy of a palace.[6]

Ibid. x, Line 5

---

[1] Carpe diem, quam minimum credula postero.
[2] O matre pulchra filia pulchrior.
[3] Integer vitae, scelerisque purus.
[4] Not to be tuneless in old age! — DOBSON [1840–1921]: *Henry Wadsworth Longfellow*
[5] Nunc est bibendum!
[6] Keep the golden mean. — PUBLILIUS SYRUS [*circa* 42 B.C.]: *Maxim 1072*
He that holds fast the golden mean,
And lives contentedly between
The little and the great,
Feels not the wants that pinch the poor,
Nor plagues that haunt the rich man's door.
WILLIAM COWPER [1731–1800]: *Translation of Horace, Odes, Book II, x, St. 2*
The proper mean. — VOLTAIRE: *Letter to*

Spring's flowers, howe'er they bloom,
must fade again.
Odes. Book II, xi, Line 9

Alas, Postumus, the fleeting years
slip by.
Ibid. xiv, Line 1

Death's boatman takes no bribe, nor
brings
Ev'n skilled Prometheus back from
Hades' shore.
Ibid. xviii, Line 35

It is sweet and honourable to die for
one's country.[1]
Ibid. Book III, ii, Line 13

There is also a sure reward for faithful silence.
Ibid. Line 25

The man who is just and firm of
purpose can be shaken from his stern
resolve neither by the rage of the people
who urge him to crime nor by the
countenance of the threatening tyrant.
Ibid. iii, Line 1

Force without wisdom falls of its own
weight.
Ibid. iv, Line 65

Because you bear yourself as the
gods' inferior, you rule.
Ibid. vi, Line 5

Our sires' age was worse than our
grandsires'. We their sons are more
worthless than they: so in our turn we
shall give the world a progeny yet more
corrupt.[2]
Ibid. Line 46

Skilled in the works of both languages.
Ibid. viii, Line 5

With you I should love to live, with
you be ready to die.
Ibid. ix, Line 24

Gloriously false . . . a maid famous
to all time.
Ibid. xi, Line 35

I would not have borne this in my

flaming youth while Plancus was
consul.[1]
Odes. Book III, xiv, Line 27

As riches grow, care follows, and a
thirst
For more and more.
Ibid. xvi, Line 17

Learn calm to face what's pressing.
Ibid. xxix, Line 33

He will through life be master of
himself and a happy man who from day
to day can have said, "I have lived":
tomorrow the Father may fill the sky
with black clouds or with cloudless sunshine.[2]
Ibid. Line 41

I have built me a monument more
lasting than bronze.
Ibid. xxx, Line 1

I shall not wholly die. What's best of
me
Shall 'scape the tomb.[3]
Ibid. Line 6

Ev'n though the Golden Age upon the
earth
Once more may live.[4]
Ibid. Book IV, ii, Line 39

Summer treads
On heels of Spring.
Ibid. vii, Line 9

---

[1] In my hot youth, when George the Third
was king. — BYRON: *Don Juan* [1819–1824],
Canto 1, St. 212

[2] Tomorrow let my sun his beams display,
  Or in clouds hide them; I have lived my
  day.
    COWLEY: *Discourse XI, Of Myself*
      [1661], *St. 11*
Happy the man, and happy he alone,
  He who can call today his own;
  He who, secure within, can say,
  Tomorrow, do thy worst, for I have liv'd
  today.
    DRYDEN: *Imitation of Horace. Book
    III, Ode xxix* [1685], *L. 65*
Serenely full, the epicure would say,
Fate cannot harm me; I have dined today.
    SYDNEY SMITH [1771–1845]: *Recipe
      for Salad*

[3] I shall have more to say when I am dead.
    EDWIN ARLINGTON ROBINSON [1869–
      1935]: *John Brown, last line*

[4] The golden age, which a blind tradition
has hitherto placed in the past, is before us. —
C. H. SAINT-SIMON [1760–1825], quoted by
CARLYLE in *Sartor Resartus, Book 3, Chap. 5*

Count d'Argental [November 28, 1765]
[1] Dulce et decorum est pro patria mori.
See Homer, page 5a.
[2] See Homer, page 4a.

We are dust and a shadow.
>   *Odes. Book IV, vii, Line 16*

Brave men were living before Agamemnon; but all are overwhelmed in
unending night, unwept, unknown, because they lacked a sacred bard.[1]
>   *Ibid. ix, Line 25*

At the fit hour 'tis sweet to unbend.
>   *Ibid. xii, Line 28*

The laugh will then be mine.
>   *Epodes. xv, Line 24*

To bronze Jove changed Earth's golden
>   time;
With bronze, then iron, stamped the
>   age.
>   *Ibid. xvi, Line 64*

Another yet the same.
>   *Saecular Hymn.*[2] *Line 10*

Then, gods, to reverent youth grant
>   purity,
Grant, gods, to quiet age a peaceful
>   end.
>   *Ibid. Line 45*

No one lives content with his condition, whether reason gave it him, or
chance threw it in his way.
>   *Satires.*[3] *Book I, i, Line 1*

We rarely find a man who can say
he has lived happy, and content with
his life can retire from the world like
a satisfied guest.
>   *Ibid. Line 117*

It is grievous to be caught.
>   *Ibid. ii, Line 134*

This is a fault common to all singers,
that among their friends they never are
inclined to sing when they are asked,
unasked they never desist.
>   *Ibid. iii, Line 1*

The limbs of the mangled poet.
>   *Ibid. iv, Line 62*

There are many who recite their
writings in the middle of the forum;
and who do it while bathing: the close-

ness of the place gives melody to the
voice.
>   *Satires. Book I, iv, Line 74*

Ridicule often decides matters of importance more effectually, and in a better manner, than severity.
>   *Ibid. x, Line 14*

Carrying timber into a wood.[1]
>   *Ibid. Line 34*

You that intend to write what is
worthy to be read more than once, blot
frequently: and take no pains to make
the multitude admire you, content with
a few judicious readers.
>   *Ibid. Line 72*

Now learn what and how great benefits a temperate diet will bring along
with it. In the first place you will enjoy good health.
>   *Ibid. Book II, ii, Line 70*

In peace, as a wise man, he should
make suitable preparation for war.[2]
>   *Ibid. Line 110*

Live undaunted; and oppose gallant
breasts against the strokes of adversity.[3]
>   *Ibid. Line 135*

This was in my prayers.
>   *Ibid. vi, Line 1*

O nights and banquets of the gods!
>   *Ibid. Line 65*

At Rome, you long for the country;
when you are in the country, fickle, you
extol the absent city to the skies.
>   *Ibid. vii, Line 28*

Get place and wealth, if possible with
>   grace;

[1] "Carrying coals to Newcastle." — JAMES
MELVILLE: *Autobiography* [1583], I, L. 163
See Diogenes Laertius, page 71a.
[2] Who would desire peace should be pre-
pared for war. — VEGETIUS [*circa* 375 B.C.]:
De Rei Militari, Book III, Prologue
We should provide in peace what we need
in war. — PUBLILIUS SYRUS [*circa* 42 B.C.]:
Maxim 709
See Burton, page 223a, and Washington,
page 367a.
[3] The company is Spartan; see how all their
wounds are in front. — BASSUS: *The Greek
Anthology, Book 9, Epigram 279*

---

[1] How many, most famous while they lived,
are utterly forgotten for want of writers! —
BOETHIUS [A.D. 470?–525]: *De Consolatione
Philosophiae, II, 7*
[2] Translated by DR. JOHN MARSHALL.
[3] Translated by CHRISTOPHER SMART
[1722–1770].

If not, by any means get wealth and place.[1]

Epistles. Book I, i, Line 53

He has half the deed done, who has made a beginning.

Ibid. ii, Line 40

The covetous man is ever in want.

Ibid. Line 56

Sicilian tyrants never invented a greater torment than envy.

Ibid. Line 58

In the midst of hope and care, in the midst of fears and disquietudes, think every day that shines upon you is the last. Thus the hour, which shall not be expected, will come upon you an agreeable addition.

Ibid. iv, Line 12

When you have a mind to laugh, you shall see me, fat and sleek with good keeping, a hog of Epicurus' herd.

Ibid. Line 15

As soon as a man perceives how much the things he has discarded excel those which he pursues, let him return in time, and resume those which he relinquished.

Ibid. vii, Line 96

You may drive out nature with a fork, yet still she will return.

Ibid. x, Line 24

Whatever prosperous hour Providence bestows upon you, receive it with a thankful hand: and defer not the enjoyment of the comforts of life.

Ibid. xi, Line 22

They change their climate, not their disposition, who run beyond the sea.

Ibid. Line 27

That man is by no means poor, who has the use of everything he wants. If it is well with your belly, your back, and your feet, regal wealth can add nothing greater.

Ibid. xii, Line 4

Joys are not the property of the rich alone: nor has he lived ill, who at his

birth and at his death has passed unnoticed.

Epistles. Book I, xvii, Line 9

To have been acceptable to the great is not the last of praises. It is not every man's lot to gain Corinth.[1]

Ibid. Line 35

The man who makes the experiment deservedly claims the honour and the reward.

Ibid. Line 42

A word, once sent abroad, flies irrevocably.[2]

Ibid. xviii, Line 70

And seek for truth in the groves of Academe.

Ibid. Book II, ii, Line 45

I have to submit to much in order to pacify the touchy tribe of poets.

Ibid. Line 102

Poets desire either to teach or to give pleasure.

Ibid. iii, Line 333

Men ever had, and ever will have, leave
To coin new words well suited to the age.
Words are like leaves, some wither ev'ry year,
And ev'ry year a younger race succeeds.

Ars Poetica.[3] Line 73

For Nature forms, and softens us within,
And writes our fortune's changes in our face.

Ibid. Line 130

The lab'ring mountain scarce brings forth a mouse.[4]

Ibid. Line 168

Old men are only walking hospitals.

Ibid. Line 202

---

[1] Translated by ALEXANDER POPE.
  Get money; still get money, boy,
  No matter by what means.
  BEN JONSON: *Every Man in His Humour* [1598], *Act II, Sc. 3*

[1] 'Tis not every one who can afford to go to Corinth. — PLUTARCH [A. D. 46–120]: *Parallel Lives, Aristophanes*
  There is but one road that leads to Corinth. — WALTER PATER: *Marius the Epicurean* [1885], *Chap. 24*
  "There is but one way to Corinth," as of old. — ANDREW LANG: *Letters to Dead Authors* [1886], *To Lucian of Samosata*
[2] See *Ars Poetica, L. 438,* page 42a.
[3] Translated [1680] by the EARL OF ROSCOMMON.
[4] Parturient montes, nascetur ridiculus mus.

Five acts are the just measure of a play.
Ars Poetica. Line 226

And in one scene no more than three should speak.
Ibid. Line 229

Whatever you teach, be brief, that your readers' minds may readily comprehend and faithfully retain your words. Everything superfluous slips from the full heart.
Ibid. Line 335

He has carried every point who has mingled profit with pleasure.
Ibid. Line 343

A string may jar in the best master's hand,
And the most skilful archer miss his aim.
Ibid. Line 387

Homer himself hath been observ'd to nod.[1]
Ibid. Line 402

But words once spoke can never be recall'd.[2]
Ibid. Line 438

'Tis hard to find a man of great estate, That can distinguish flatterers from friends.
Ibid. Line 478

True friends appear less mov'd than counterfeit;
As men that truly grieve at funerals
Are not so loud, as those that cry for hire.
Ibid. Line 484

PROPERTIUS
[54 B.C.–A.D. 2]

Never change when love has found its home.
Book I. Elegy 1, Line 36

[1] Indignor quandoque bonus dormitat Homerus.
See Pope, page 310b.
[2] Thoughts unexpressed may sometimes fall back dead;
But God himself can't kill them when they're said.
WILL CARLETON [1845–1912]: *The First Settler's Story*
Four things come not back: the spoken word; the sped arrow; time past; the neg-

Let each man pass his days in that wherein his skill is greatest.
Book II. Elegy 1, Line 46

Scandal has ever been the doom of beauty.
Ibid. Elegy 32, Line 26

OVID
[43 B.C.–A.D. 18]

Every lover's a soldier and Cupid has his camps.
Amores. I, ix, Line 1

They come to see; they come that they themselves may be seen.[1]
The Art of Love. I, Line 99

It is expedient that there be gods, and, as it's expedient, let us believe there are.[2]
Ibid. Line 637

To be loved, be lovable.
Ibid. II, Line 107

Nothing is stronger than custom.
Ibid. Line 345

What you desire is not mortal.
Metamorphoses. II, Line 55

You will go most safely in the middle.
Ibid. Line 137

I see and approve better things, but follow worse.[3]
Ibid. VII, Line 20

Poetry comes fine spun from a mind at peace.
Tristia. Book I, Chap. 1, Line 39

lected opportunity. — OMAR IBN AL-HALIF: *Aphorism*
[1] Spectatum veniunt, veniunt spectentur ut ipsae.
And for to see, and eek for to be seye. — CHAUCER: *The Canterbury Tales* [circa 1387], *The Wife of Bath's Prologue, L.* 552
To see and to be seen. — BEN JONSON [1573?–1637]: *Epithalamion, St. III, L.* 4
To see, be seen, to tell, and gather tales. — POPE: *Paraphrases from Chaucer, The Wife of Bath* [1714], *L.* 282
[2] See Voltaire, page 325b.
[3] Video meliora, proboque; deteriora sequor.
I know and love the good, yet, ah! the worst pursue. — PETRARCH: *Sonnet CCXXV, Canzone XXI, To Laura in Life* [circa 1327]
The better I see and approve, the worse I follow. — SPINOZA'S translation in *Ethics* [1677], *Part IV*
See Euripides, page 17a, and *Romans, VII, 19*, on page 1060a.

While fortune smiles you'll have a host
of friends,
But they'll desert you when the storm
descends.[1]

> *Tristia. Book I, Chap. 9, Line 5*

It is annoying to be honest to no
purpose.

> *Epistolae ex Ponto. Book II,*
> *Chap. 3, Line 14*

Note too that a faithful study of the
liberal arts humanizes character and
permits it not to be cruel.

> *Ibid. Chap. 9, Line 47*

Grateful must we be that the heart
may go whithersoever it will.

> *Ibid. Book III, Chap. 5, Line 48*

How little you know about the age
you live in if you fancy that honey is
sweeter than cash in hand.

> *Fasti. Book I, Line 191*

Janus. I bar the doors in time of
peace, lest peace depart.

> *Ibid. Line 279*

PUBLILIUS SYRUS [2]
[*Circa* 42 B.C.]

As men, we are all equal in the presence of death.

> *Maxim 1*

To do two things at once is to do
neither.

> *Maxim 7*

We are interested in others when they
are interested in us.[3]

> *Maxim 16*

Every one excels in something in
which another fails.

> *Maxim 17*

A god could hardly love and be wise.[4]

> *Maxim 25*

The loss which is unknown is no loss
at all.[5]

> *Maxim 38*

He sleeps well who knows not that
he sleeps ill.

> *Maxim 77*

A good reputation is more valuable
than money.[1]

> *Maxim 108*

It is well to moor your bark with two
anchors.

> *Maxim 119*

Learn to see in another's calamity the
ills which you should avoid.[2]

> *Maxim 120*

An agreeable companion on a journey
is as good as a carriage.

> *Maxim 143*

Society in shipwreck is a comfort to
all.[3]

> *Maxim 144*

Many receive advice, few profit by it.

> *Maxim 149*

While we stop to think, we often
miss our opportunity.

> *Maxim 185*

Whatever you can lose, you should
reckon of no account.

> *Maxim 191*

Even a single hair casts its shadow.

> *Maxim 228*

It is sometimes expedient to forget
who we are.

> *Maxim 233*

We may with advantage at times forget what we know.

> *Maxim 234*

Crime is honest for a good cause.[4]

> *Maxim 244*

You should hammer your iron when
it is glowing hot.[5]

> *Maxim 262*

---

[1] See *Ecclesiastes, VII, 1*, on page 1042b, and
Bacon, page 120a.
A good name is better than riches. — CER-
VANTES: *Don Quixote, Part II* [1615], *Book
II, Chap. 33*
[2] The best plan is, as the common proverb
has it, to profit by the folly of others. —
PLINY [A.D. 23–79]: *Natural History, 18,
Sect. 31*
[3] See *Maxim 995*, page 46b.
[4] Honesta turpitudo est pro causa bona.
(The above is not Lyman's but a literal trans-
lation.)
[5] When the iron is hot, strike. — JOHN

[1] See Cicero, page 33b.
[2] Commonly called Publius, but spelled Publilius by PLINY in his *Natural History, 35,
Sect. 199.* Translated by DARIUS LYMAN. The
numbers are those of the translator.
[3] We always like those who admire us; we
do not always like those whom we admire. —
LA ROCHEFOUCAULD [1613–1680]: *Maxim 294*
[4] It is impossible to love and be wise. —
BACON: *Essays* [1597–1625], *Of Love*
[5] See Shakespeare, page 188b.

What is left when honour is lost?
Maxim 265

A fair exterior is a silent recommendation.
Maxim 267

Fortune is not satisfied with inflicting one calamity.
Maxim 274

When Fortune is on our side, popular favour bears her company.
Maxim 275

When Fortune flatters, she does it to betray.[1]
Maxim 277

Fortune is like glass, — the brighter the glitter, the more easily broken.
Maxim 280

It is more easy to get a favour from Fortune than to keep it.
Maxim 282

An overtaxed patience gives way to fury.[2]
Maxim 289

There are some remedies worse than the disease.[3]
Maxim 301

Powerful indeed is the empire of habit.[4]
Maxim 305

Amid a multitude of projects, no plan is devised.[5]
Maxim 319

It is easy for men to talk one thing and think another.
Maxim 322

When two do the same thing, it is not the same thing after all.
Maxim 338

A cock has great influence on his own dunghill.[1]
Maxim 357

Any one can hold the helm when the sea is calm.[2]
Maxim 358

No tears are shed when an enemy dies.
Maxim 376

The bow too tensely strung is easily broken.
Maxim 388

Treat your friend as if he might become an enemy.[3]
Maxim 402

No pleasure endures unseasoned by variety.[4]
Maxim 406

The judge is condemned when the criminal is absolved.[5]
Maxim 407

Practice is the best of all instructors.[6]
Maxim 439

He who is bent on doing evil can never want occasion.
Maxim 459

Never find your delight in another's misfortune.
Maxim 467

It is a bad plan that admits of no modification.
Maxim 469

It is better to have a little than nothing.
Maxim 484

Heywood: *Proverbes* [1546], *Part I, Chap. II*
Strike whilst the iron is hot. — Rabelais: *Book II* [1534], *Chap. 31*
Nothing like striking while the iron is hot. — Cervantes: *Don Quixote, Part II* [1615], *Book IV, Chap. 71*
[1] See Shakespeare, page 148a.
[2] See Dryden, page 277b.
[3] Marius said, "I see the cure is not worth the pain." — Plutarch [a.d. 46–120]: *Lives, Caius Marius*
The remedy is worse than the disease. — Bacon: *Essays* [1597–1625], *Of Seditions*
I find the medicine worse than the malady. — Beaumont and Fletcher: *Love's Cure* [1647], *Act III, Sc. 2*
[4] See Plutarch, page 60a.
[5] He that hath many irons in the fire, some of them will cool. — Hazlitt: *English Proverbs*

[1] Every cocke is proud on his owne dunghill. — John Heywood: *Proverbes* [1546], *Part I, Chap. XI*
[2] See Shakespeare, page 181a.
[3] Treat your friend as if he will one day be your enemy, and your enemy as if he will one day be your friend. — Laberius [105–43 b.c.]: *Fragment*
[4] See Cowper, page 364a.
[5] Judex damnatur cum nocens absolvitur — the motto adopted for the *Edinburgh Review.*
[6] Practice makes perfect. — *Proverb*
The saying, "Practice is everything," is Periander's. — Diogenes Laertius [*circa* 200 a.d.]: *Periander, 6*

It is an unhappy lot which finds no enemies.

Maxim 499

The fear of death is more to be dreaded than death itself.[1]

Maxim 511

A rolling stone gathers no moss.[2]

Maxim 524

Never promise more than you can perform.

Maxim 528

A wise man never refuses anything to necessity.[3]

Maxim 540

No one should be judge in his own cause.[4]

Maxim 545

Necessity knows no law except to conquer.[5]

Maxim 553

Nothing can be done at once hastily and prudently.[6]

Maxim 557

We desire nothing so much as what we ought not to have.

Maxim 559

It is only the ignorant who despise education.

Maxim 571

Do not turn back when you are just at the goal.[7]

Maxim 580

It is not every question that deserves an answer.

Maxim 581

No man is happy who does not think himself so.[1]

Maxim 584

Never thrust your own sickle into another's corn.[2]

Maxim 593

You cannot put the same shoe on every foot.

Maxim 596

He bids fair to grow wise who has discovered that he is not so.

Maxim 598

Every day should be passed as if it were to be our last.[3]

Maxim 633

Money alone sets all the world in motion.

Maxim 656

He who has plenty of pepper will pepper his cabbage.

Maxim 673

You should go to a pear-tree for pears, not to an elm.[4]

Maxim 674

It is a very hard undertaking to seek to please everybody.

Maxim 675

Look for a tough wedge for a tough log.

Maxim 723

How happy the life unembarrassed by the cares of business!

Maxim 725

---

[1] See Shakespeare, page 184b.
[2] The rolling stone never gathereth mosse. — JOHN HEYWOOD: *Proverbes* [1546], *Part I, Chap. XI*
The stone that is rolling can gather no moss. — TUSSER: *Five Hundred Points of Good Husbandry* [1557]
[3] Yet do I hold that mortal foolish who strives against the stress of necessity. — EURIPIDES [480–406 B.C.]: *Mad Heracles, L. 281*
[4] It is not permitted to the most equitable of men to be a judge in his own cause. — PASCAL [1623–1662]: *Pensées, Chap. 4, 1*
[5]   And with necessity,
The tyrant's plea, excus'd his devilish deeds.
MILTON: *Paradise Lost* [1667], *Book IV, L. 393*
Necessity is the argument of tyrants, it is the creed of slaves. — WILLIAM PITT: *Speech on the India Bill* [November, 1783]
[6] See Chaucer, page 82a, and Heywood, page 90b.
[7] When men are arrived at the goal, they should not turn back. — PLUTARCH [A.D. 46–120]: *Of the Training of Children*
[1] No man can enjoy happiness without thinking that he enjoys it. — SAMUEL JOHNSON [1709–1784]: *The Rambler*
[2] Did thrust as now in others' corn his sickle. — DU BARTAS: *Divine Weekes and Workes* [1578], *Part II, Second Weeke*
Not presuming to put my sickle in another man's corn. — NICHOLAS YONGE: *Musica Transalpina, Epistle Dedicatory* [1588]
[3] Thou wilt find rest from vain fancies if thou doest every act in life as though it were thy last. — MARCUS AURELIUS [A.D. 121–180]: *Meditations, II, 5*
[4] You may as well expect pears from an elm. — CERVANTES: *Don Quixote, Part II* [1615], *Book IV, Chap. 40*

Pardon one offence, and you encourage the commission of many.

Maxim 750

They who plough the sea do not carry the winds in their hands.[1]

Maxim 759

He gets through too late who goes too fast.

Maxim 767

In every enterprise consider where you would come out.[2]

Maxim 777

It takes a long time to bring excellence to maturity.

Maxim 780

The highest condition takes rise in the lowest.

Maxim 781

It matters not what you are thought to be, but what you are.

Maxim 785

No one knows what he can do till he tries.

Maxim 786

The next day is never so good as the day before.

Maxim 815

Good health and good sense are two of life's greatest blessings.

Maxim 827

It matters not how long you live, but how well.

Maxim 829

It is vain to look for a defence against lightning.

Maxim 835

Everything is worth what its purchaser will pay for it.[3]

Maxim 847

[1] The pilot cannot mitigate the billows or calm the winds. — PLUTARCH [A. D. 46–120]: *Of the Tranquillity of the Mind*

[2] In every affair, consider what precedes and what follows, and then undertake it. — EPICTETUS [*circa* A. D. 60]: *That Everything Is to be Undertaken with Circumspection, Chap. 15*

[3]   What is worth in anything
  But so much money as 'twill bring?
    BUTLER: *Hudibras, Part I* [1663],
       Canto I, L. 465

It is better to learn late than never.[1]

Maxim 864

Better be ignorant of a matter than half know it.[2]

Maxim 865

Better use medicines at the outset than at the last moment.[3]

Maxim 866

Prosperity makes friends, adversity tries them.

Maxim 872

Let a fool hold his tongue and he will pass for a sage.

Maxim 914

He knows not when to be silent who knows not when to speak.

Maxim 930

You need not hang up the ivy-branch over the wine that will sell.[4]

Maxim 968

It is a consolation to the wretched to have companions in misery.[5]

Maxim 995

Unless degree is preserved, the first place is safe for no one.[6]

Maxim 1042

Confession of our faults is the next thing to innocency.

Maxim 1060

I have often regretted my speech, never my silence.[7]

Maxim 1070

[1] See Shakespeare, page 145b.
[2] See Pope, page 310b.
[3] A stitch in time saves nine. — *Old Proverb*
[4] Good wine needs no bush. — SHAKESPEARE: *As You Like It* [1598–1600], *Epilogue, L. 4*
Good wine needs neither bush nor preface
To make it welcome.
    SIR WALTER SCOTT: *Peveril of the Peak* [1822], *Chap. 4*
[5] See *Maxim 144*, page 43b.
'Tis the only comfort of the miserable to have partners in their woes. — CERVANTES: *Don Quixote, Part I* [1605], *Book III, Chap. 10*
It is a comfort to the unhappy to have companions in misery. — SPINOZA: *Ethics* [1677], *Part 4, Proposition 57, Note*
[6] See Shakespeare, page 181a.
[7] Simonides said that "he never repented that he held his tongue, but often that he had spoken." — PLUTARCH [A. D. 46–120]: *Rules for the Preservation of Health*

Speech is a mirror of the soul: as a man speaks, so is he.

Maxim 1073

SENECA [1]
[8 B. C.–A. D. 65]

What fools these mortals be.[2]

Epistles. 1, 3

It is not the man who has too little, but the man who craves more, that is poor.

Ibid. 2, 2

Love of bustle is not industry.

Ibid. 3, 5

Live among men as if God beheld you; speak to God as if men were listening.

Ibid. 10, 5

The best ideas are common property.

Ibid. 12, 11

Men do not care how nobly they live, but only how long, although it is within the reach of every man to live nobly, but within no man's power to live long.

Ibid. 22, 17

A great pilot can sail even when his canvas is rent.

Ibid. 30, 3

Man is a reasoning animal.

Ibid. 41, 8

That most knowing of persons,— gossip.

Ibid. 43, 1

It is quality rather than quantity that matters.

Ibid. 45, 1

You can tell the character of every man when you see how he receives praise.

Ibid. 52, 12

Nothing is so certain as that the evils of idleness can be shaken off by hard work.

Ibid. 56, 9

Not lost, but gone before.[3]

Ibid. 63, 16

[1] Translated by W. H. D. ROUSE.
[2] Tanta stultitia mortalium est.
See Shakespeare, page 142a.
[3] Non amittuntur, sed praemittuntur.
Not dead, but gone before. — SAMUEL ROGERS: *Human Life* [1819]

All art is but imitation of nature.

Epistles. 65, 3

It is a rough road that leads to the heights of greatness.

Ibid. 84, 13

The pilot . . . who has been able to say, "Neptune, you shall never sink this ship except on an even keel," has fulfilled the requirements of his art.[1]

Ibid. 85, 33

I was shipwrecked before I got aboard.

Ibid. 87, 1

It is better, of course, to know useless things than to know nothing.

Ibid. 88, 45

Do not ask for what you will wish you had not got.

Ibid. 95, 1

We are mad, not only individually, but nationally. We check manslaughter and isolated murders; but what of war and the much vaunted crime of slaughtering whole peoples?

Ibid. 95, 30

A great step towards independence is a good-humored stomach.

Ibid. 123, 3

Fire is the test of gold; adversity, of strong men.[2]

Moral Essays. On Providence, 5, 9

Whom they have injured they also hate.[3]

Ibid. On Anger, 2, 33

I do not distinguish by the eye, but

[1] The mariner of old said thus to Neptune in a great tempest, "O God! thou mayest save me if thou wilt, and if thou wilt, thou mayest destroy me; but whether or no, I will steer my rudder true." — MONTAIGNE: *Essays* [1580–1595], *Book II, Chap. 16*
[2] See Beaumont and Fletcher, page 228a.
[3] It belongs to human nature to hate those you have injured. — TACITUS [A. D. 54–119]: *Agricola, 42, 15*
Chi fa ingiuria non perdona mai (He never pardons those he injures). — *Italian Proverb*
The offender never pardons. — GEORGE HERBERT: *Jacula Prudentum* [1640]
Forgiveness to the injured does belong;
But they ne'er pardon who have done the wrong.
　　DRYDEN: *The Conquest of Granada* [1670], *Part II, Act I, Sc. 2*

by the mind, which is the proper judge of the man.
> *Moral Essays. On the Happy Life, 2, 2*

There is no great genius without some touch of madness.[1]
> *Ibid. On Tranquillity of the Mind, 17, 10*

A great fortune is a great slavery.
> *Ibid. To Polybius on Consolation, 6, 5*

Wherever the Roman conquers, there he dwells.
> *Ibid. To Helvia on Consolation, 7, 7*

He who receives a benefit with gratitude, repays the first instalment on his debt.
> *On Benefits. Book 2, 22, 1*

You roll my log, and I will roll yours.
> *Apocolocyntosis. Chap. 9*

Do you seek Alcides' equal? None is, except himself.[2]
> *Hercules Furens. 1, 1, 84*

Successful and fortunate crime is called virtue.[3]
> *Ibid. 255*

A good mind possesses a kingdom.[4]
> *Thyestes. 380*

---

[1] An ancient commonplace, which Seneca says he quotes from ARISTOTLE: No excellent soul is exempt from a mixture of madness. *Problemata, 30, 1.* It is also in PLATO: *Phaedrus, 245 A.*
Good sense travels on the well-worn paths; genius, never. And that is why the crowd, not altogether without reason, is so ready to treat great men as lunatics. — CESARE LOMBROSO [1836–1909]: *The Man of Genius, Preface*
See Dryden, page 276b.
[2] None but himself can be his parallel. — LEWIS THEOBALD [1688–1744]: *The Double Falsehood*
And but herself admits no parallel. — MASSINGER [1583–1640]: *Duke of Milan, Act IV, Sc. 3*
[3] Treason doth never prosper; what's the reason?
Why, if it prosper, none dare call it treason.
> SIR JOHN HARINGTON [1561–1612]: *Epigrams, Of Treason*
[4] See Dyer, page 101b.

Light griefs are loquacious, but the great are dumb.[1]
> *Hippolytus. II, 3, 607*

PHAEDRUS [2]
[*Circa* A. D. 8]

Submit to the present evil, lest a greater one befall you.
> *Book I. Fable 2, 31*

He who covets what belongs to another deservedly loses his own.
> *Ibid. Fable 4, 1*

That it is unwise to be heedless ourselves while we are giving advice to others, I will show in a few lines.
> *Ibid. Fable 9, 1*

Whoever has even once become notorious by base fraud, even if he speaks the truth, gains no belief.
> *Ibid. Fable 10, 1*

By this story [The Fox and the Raven] it is shown how much ingenuity avails, and how wisdom is always an overmatch for strength.
> *Ibid. Fable 13, 13*

No one returns with good-will to the place which has done him a mischief.
> *Ibid. Fable 18, 1*

It has been related that dogs drink at the river Nile running along, that they may not be seized by the crocodiles.[3]
> *Ibid. Fable 25, 3*

Every one is bound to bear patiently the results of his own example.
> *Ibid. Fable 26, 12*

Come of it what may, as Sinon said.
> *Book III. The Prologue, 27*

Things are not always what they seem.[4]
> *Book IV. Fable 2, 5*

---

[1] See Montaigne, page 97b.
[2] Translated by HENRY THOMAS RILEY [1816–1878].
[3] PLINY, in his *Natural History, Book 8, Sect. 148,* and AELIAN, in his *Various Histories,* relate the same fact as to the dogs drinking from the Nile. "To treat a thing as the dogs do the Nile" was a common proverb with the ancients, signifying to do it superficially.
[4] Non semper ea sunt quae videntur.
See Longfellow, page 521a, and W. S. Gilbert, page 682b.

"I knew that before you were born." Let him who would instruct a wiser man consider this as said to himself.
Book V. Fable 9, 4

PLINY THE ELDER [1]
[A. D. 23–79]

In comparing various authors with one another, I have discovered that some of the gravest and latest writers have transcribed, word for word, from former works, without making acknowledgment.
Natural History. Book I,
Dedication, Sect. 22

It is ridiculous to suppose that the great head of things, whatever it be, pays any regard to human affairs.
Ibid. Book II, Sect. 20

Everything is soothed by oil, and this is the reason why divers send out small quantities of it from their mouths, because it smooths every part which is rough.[2]
Ibid. Sect. 234

It is far from easy to determine whether she [Nature] has proved to him a kind parent or a merciless stepmother.[3]
Ibid. Book VII, Sect. 1

[1] With some alterations, translated by JOHN BOSTOCK [1773–1846] and HENRY THOMAS RILEY [1816–1878].

[2] Why does pouring oil on the sea make it clear and calm? Is it for that the winds, slipping the smooth oil, have no force, nor cause any waves? — PLUTARCH [A. D. 46–120]: *Natural Questions, IX*

Bishop Adain [A. D. 651] gave to a company about to take a journey by sea "some holy oil, saying, 'I know that when you go abroad you will meet with a storm and contrary wind; but do you remember to cast this oil I give you into the sea, and the wind shall cease immediately.'" — BEDE [673–735]: *Ecclesiastical History, Book III, Chap. 14*

In JARED SPARKS'S edition of BENJAMIN FRANKLIN'S *Works, Vol. VI, P. 354,* there are letters between Franklin, Brownrigg, and Parish on the stilling of waves by means of oil.

[3] To man the earth seems altogether
No more a mother, but a step-dame rather.
DU BARTAS [1544–1590]: *Divine Weekes and Workes, First Weeke, Third Day*

Man alone at the very moment of his birth, cast naked upon the naked earth, does she abandon to cries and lamentations.[1]
Natural History. Book VII,
Sect. 2

To laugh, if but for an instant only, has never been granted to man before the fortieth day from his birth, and then it is looked upon as a miracle of precocity.[2]
Ibid.

Man is the only one that knows nothing, that can learn nothing without being taught. He can neither speak nor walk nor eat, and in short he can do nothing at the prompting of nature only, but weep.[3]
Ibid. Sect. 4

With man, most of his misfortunes are occasioned by man.[4]
Ibid. Sect. 5

Indeed, what is there that does not appear marvellous when it comes to our knowledge for the first time? [5] How many things, too, are looked upon as quite impossible until they have been actually effected?
Ibid. Sect. 6

The human features and countenance, although composed of but some ten parts or little more, are so fashioned that among so many thousands of men there are no two in existence who can-

[1] He is born naked, and falls a-whining at the first. — ROBERT BURTON: *Anatomy of Melancholy* [1621–1651], *Part I, Sect. 2, Memb. 3, Subsect. 10*

And when I was born, I drew in the common air, and fell upon the earth, which is of like nature; and the first voice which I uttered was crying, as all others do. — *The Wisdom of Solomon, VII, 3*

It was the custom among the ancients to place the newborn child upon the ground immediately after its birth.

[2] This term of forty days is mentioned by ARISTOTLE in his *Natural History.*

[3] See Tennyson, page 552a.

[4] See Burns, page 390a.

[5] Omne ignotum pro magnifico (Everything that is unknown is taken to be grand).
— TACITUS [A.D. 54–119]: *Agricola, 30*

not be distinguished from one another.[1]
Natural History. Book VII,
Sect. 8

All men possess in their bodies a poison which acts upon serpents; and the human saliva, it is said, makes them take to flight, as though they had been touched with boiling water. The same substance, it is said, destroys them the moment it enters their throat.[2]
Ibid. Sect. 15

It has been observed that the height of a man from the crown of the head to the sole of the foot is equal to the distance between the tips of the middle fingers of the two hands when extended in a straight line.
Ibid. Sect. 77

When a building is about to fall down, all the mice desert it.[3]
Ibid. Book VIII, Sect. 103

Bears when first born are shapeless masses of white flesh a little larger than mice, their claws alone being prominent. The mother then licks them gradually into proper shape.[4]
Ibid. Sect. 126

Cincinnatus was ploughing his four

jugera of land upon the Vaticanian Hill, — the same that are still known as the Quintian Meadows, — when the messenger brought him the dictatorship, finding him, the tradition says, stripped to the work.
Natural History. Book XVIII,
Sect. 20

The agricultural population, says Cato, produces the bravest men, the most valiant soldiers, and a class of citizens the least given of all to evil designs.
Ibid. Sect. 26

Why is it that we entertain the belief that for every purpose odd numbers are the most effectual?[1]
Ibid. Book XXVIII, Sect. 23

It was a custom with Apelles, to which he most tenaciously adhered, never to let any day pass, however busy he might be, without exercising himself by tracing some outline or other, — a practice which has now passed into a proverb.[2] It was also a practice with him, when he had completed a work, to exhibit it to the view of the passers-by in his studio, while he himself, concealed behind the picture, would listen to the criticisms. . . . Under these circumstances, they say that he was censured by a shoemaker for having represented the shoes with one latchet too few. The next day, the shoemaker, quite proud at seeing the former error corrected, thanks to his advice, began to

---

[1] It is the common wonder of all men, how among so many millions of faces there should be none alike. — SIR THOMAS BROWNE: *Religio Medici* [1642], *Part II, Sect. II*

Of a thousand shavers, two do not shave so much alike as not to be distinguished. — JOHNSON [1777]: *Boswell's Life, Vol. II, P. 120, Everyman ed.*

See Montaigne, page 99b.

[2] MADAME D'ABRANTES relates that when Bonaparte was in Cairo he sent for a serpent-detector (Psylli) to remove two serpents that had been seen in his house. He, having enticed one of them from his hiding place, caught it in one hand, just below the jawbone, in such a manner as to oblige the mouth to open, when, spitting into it, the effect was like magic: the reptile appeared struck with instant death. — *Memoirs, Vol. I, Chap. 59*

[3] This is alluded to by CICERO in his letters to Atticus, and is mentioned by AELIAN (*Animated Nature, Book VI, Chap. 41*). Compare the modern proverb, "Rats desert a sinking ship."

[4] Not unlike the bear which bringeth forth
   In the end of thirty dayes a shapeless
     birth;
   But after licking, it in shape she drawes,
   And by degrees she fashions out the pawes,

   The head, and neck, and finally doth bring
   To a perfect beast that first deformed
     thing.
      DU BARTAS: *Divine Weekes and*
      Workes [1578], *First Weeke, First*
      Day

I had not time to lick it into form, as a bear doth her young ones. — ROBERT BURTON: *Anatomy of Melancholy* [1621–1651], *Democritus to the Reader*

See Montaigne, page 99a.

[1] The god delights in an odd number. — VIRGIL [70–19 B.C.]: *Eclogues, 8, 75*

See Shakespeare, page 180b, and Samuel Lover, page 485b.

[2] Nulla dies abeat, quin linea ducta supersit. — ERASMUS [1465–1536]. Generally quoted, Nulla dies sine linea (No day without a line).

criticize the leg; upon which Apelles, full of indignation, popped his head out and reminded him that a shoemaker should give no opinion beyond the shoes,[1] — a piece of advice which has equally passed into a proverbial saying.
Natural History. Book XXXV,
Sect. 84

LUCAN [2]
[A. D. 39–65]

The conqueror's cause found favor with the gods, the conquered's with Cato.
The Civil War. Book I, Line 128
He stands the shadow of a mighty name.
Ibid. Line 135
Poverty, the mother of manhood.
Ibid. Line 165
Delay is ever fatal to those who are prepared.
Ibid. Line 281
When the whole world is nodding to its fall, happy the man who has been able to learn already the lowly place appointed for him.
Ibid. Book IV, Line 393
Boldness is a mask for fear, however great.
Ibid. Line 702
Yonder trouble concerns the sky and sea, but not our bark; for Caesar treads the deck.[3]
Ibid. Book V, Line 584

PETRONIUS [ARBITER]
[Died *circa* A. D. 66]

Beware of the dog.[4]
Satyricon. Sect. 29
Without why or wherefore.
Ibid. Sect. 37
A man who is always ready to believe what is told him will never do well.
Ibid. Sect. 43

[1] Ne supra crepidam sutor judicaret (Let not a shoemaker judge above his shoe), or, Let the cobbler stick to his last.
[2] Translated by J. D. Duff.
[3] See Plutarch, page 56b.
[4] Found with picture of a dog on a mosaic floor in Pompeii.

One good turn deserves another.
Satyricon. Sect. 45
A man must have his faults.
Ibid.
Not worth his salt.
Ibid. Sect. 57
My heart was in my mouth.
Ibid. Sect. 62
Beauty and wisdom are rarely conjoined.
Ibid. Sect. 94
The careful felicity of Horace.
Ibid. Sect. 118

DIO CHRYSOSTOM [1]
[A. D. 40–120]

Diogenes: The man I know not, for I am not acquainted with his mind.
Fourth Discourse on Kingship.
Chap. 17
Idleness and lack of occupation are the best things in the world to ruin the foolish.
Tenth Discourse, On Servants.
Chap. 7
Like men with sore eyes: they find the light painful, while the darkness, which permits them to see nothing, is restful and agreeable.
Eleventh, or Trojan, Discourse.
Chap. 2
Most men are so completely corrupted by opinion that they would rather be notorious for the greatest calamities than suffer no ill and be unknown.
Ibid. Chap. 6
Generally speaking, men are too cowardly to be willing to undergo severe suffering, since they fear death and pain, but they highly prize being mentioned as having suffered.
Ibid. Chap. 10

MARTIAL
[A. D. 40–102]

To yield to the stronger is valor's second prize.
On the Spectacles. Epigram 32

[1] Translated by J. W. Cohoon.

I write long epigrams, you yourself write nothing. Yours are shorter.[1]

Epigrams. Book I, 110

Nothing is more confident than a bad poet.[2]

Ibid. Book II, 63

He does not write at all whose poems no man reads.

Ibid. Book III, 9

The flaw which is hidden is deemed greater than it is.

Ibid. 52

The bee enclosed and through the amber shown
Seems buried in the juice which was his own.[3]

Ibid. Book IV, 32

They pass and are charged against us.[4]

Ibid. Book V, 20

What is the use of brevity if it constitute a book?

Ibid. Book VIII, 29

The good man prolongs his life; to be able to enjoy one's past life is to live twice.[5]

Ibid. Book X, 23

[1] An epigram of two lines has every merit, and if you exceed three lines it is rhapsody. — CYRILLUS: *The Greek Anthology, Book 9, Epigram 369*

[2] Quoted by MONTAIGNE in *Of Presumption.*

[3] Whence we see spiders, flies, or ants entombed and preserved forever in amber, a more than royal tomb. — FRANCIS BACON: *Historia Vitae et Mortis* [1623], *Sylva Sylvarum, Cent. I, Exper. 100*

I saw a flie within a beade
Of amber cleanly buried.

HERRICK [1591–1674]: *On a Fly Buried in Amber*

See Pope, page 318b.

[4] Of the days and hours.

[5] Thus would I double my life's fading space;
For he that runs it well, runs twice his race.

COWLEY [1618–1667]: *Discourse XI, Of Myself, St. XI*

For he lives twice who can at once employ
The present well, and ev'n the past enjoy.

POPE [1688–1744]: *Imitation of Martial*

Neither fear, nor wish for, your last day.[1]

Epigrams. Book X, 47

There is no glory in outstripping donkeys.

Ibid. Book XII, 36

I can't live with you or without you.

Ibid. 47

The country in town.[2]

Ibid. 57

QUINTILIAN
[A. D. 42–118]

We give to necessity the praise of virtue.[3]

*Institutiones Oratoriae.
Book I, 8, 14*

A liar should have a good memory.[4]

Ibid. Book IV, 2, 91

Vain hopes are often like the dreams of those who wake.

Ibid. Book VI, 2, 30

Those who wish to appear wise among fools, among the wise seem foolish.[5]

Ibid. Book X, 7, 21

[1] Nor love thy life, nor hate; but what thou liv'st
Live well; how long or short permit to Heaven.

MILTON: *Paradise Lost* [1667], *Book XI, L. 553*

[2] Rus in urbe.

[3] In the additions of Hadrianus Julius to the *Adages* of ERASMUS, he remarks, under the head of *Necessitatem edere*, that a very familiar proverb was current among his countrymen — "Necessitatem in virtutem commutare" (To make necessity a virtue).

Thus maketh vertue of necessitee. — CHAUCER: *Troilus and Criseyde* [1372–1386], *Book IV, L. 1586*

Others made a virtue of necessity. — RABELAIS: *Works, Book V* [1552], *Chap. 23*

Make a virtue of necessity. — ROBERT BURTON: *Anatomy of Melancholy* [1621–1651], *Part III, Sect. 3, Memb. 4, Subsect. I*

[4] He who has not a good memory should never take upon him the trade of lying. — MONTAIGNE: *Essays* [1580–1595], *Book I, Chap. IX, Of Liars*

Il faut bonne mémoire, après qu'on a menti. — CORNEILLE: *Le Menteur* [1642], *Act IV, Sc. 5*

Liars ought to have good memories. — ALGERNON SIDNEY: *Discourses on Government* [1698], *Chap. 2, Sect. XV*

[5] A wit with dunces, and a dunce with

PLUTARCH [1]
[A. D. 46–120]

As geographers, Sosius, crowd into the edges of their maps parts of the world which they do not know about, adding notes in the margin to the effect that beyond this lies nothing but sandy deserts full of wild beasts, and unapproachable bogs.[2]

Lives. Theseus, Page 3

From Theseus began the saying, "He is a second Hercules."

Ibid. Page 19

Caesar said he loved the treason, but hated the traitor.[3]

Ibid. Romulus, Page 36

The most perfect soul, says Heraclitus, is a dry light, which flies out of the body as lightning breaks from a cloud.

Ibid. Page 45

Anacharsis, coming to Athens, knocked at Solon's door, and told him that he, being a stranger, was come to be his guest, and contract a friendship with him; and Solon replying, "It is better to make friends at home," Ana-

charsis replied, "Then you that are at home make friendship with me."

Lives. Solon, Page 99

Themistocles said that he certainly could not make use of any stringed instrument; could only, were a small and obscure city put into his hands, make it great and glorious.

Ibid. Themistocles, Page 134

Themistocles said to Antiphates, . . . "Time, young man, has taught us both a lesson."

Ibid. Page 145

Laughing at his own son, who got his mother, and, by his mother's means, his father also, to indulge him, he told him that he had the most power of any one in Greece: "For the Athenians command the rest of Greece, I command the Athenians, your mother commands me, and you command your mother." [1]

Ibid.

Of two who made love to his daughter, he preferred the man of worth to the one who was rich, saying he desired a man without riches, rather than riches without a man.

Ibid.

Themistocles replied that a man's discourse was like to a rich Persian carpet, the beautiful figures and patterns of which can be shown only by spreading and extending it out; when it is contracted and folded up, they are obscure and lost.[2]

Ibid. Page 152

Moderation is best, and to avoid all extremes.

Ibid. Camillus, Page 159

Caesar once, seeing some wealthy strangers at Rome, carrying up and down with them in their arms and bosoms young puppy-dogs and monkeys, embracing and making much of them, took occasion not unnaturally to ask

---

wits. — POPE: *Dunciad* [1728], *Book IV, L. 90*
  A fool with judges, amongst fools a judge.
— COWPER: *Conversation* [1782], *L. 298*
  This man [Chesterfield], I thought, had been a lord among wits; but I find he is only a wit among lords. — SAMUEL JOHNSON: *Boswell's Life* [1791], *Vol. I, P. 159, Everyman ed.*
[1] Modern Library Giant edition.
[2] So geographers, in Afric maps,
  With savage pictures fill their gaps,
  And o'er unhabitable downs
  Place elephants for want of towns.
    SWIFT: *On Poetry, A Rhapsody* [1733]
[3] Princes in this case do hate the traitor, though they love the treason. — SAMUEL DANIEL: *Tragedy of Cleopatra* [1594], *Act IV, Sc. 1*
This principle is old, but true as fate,
Kings may love treason, but the traitor hate.
    DEKKER: *The Honest Whore* [1604], *Part 1, Act IV, Sc. 4*
  Though I love the treason, I hate the traitor.
— PEPYS: *Diary* [March 7, 1667]
T'abhor the makers, and their laws approve,
Is to hate traitors and the treason love.
    DRYDEN: *The Hind and the Panther* [1687], *Part III, L. 706*

[1] The same account appears in *Of the Training of Children* and in *Apophthegms of Kings and Great Commanders, Themistocles.*
[2] Also found in *Apophthegms of Kings and Great Commanders, Themistocles.*

whether the women in their country were not used to bear children.

Lives. Pericles, Page 182

He who busies himself in mean occupations produces, in the very pains he takes about things of little or no use, an evidence against himself of his negligence and indisposition to what is really good.

Ibid. Page 183

So very difficult a matter is it to trace and find out the truth of anything by history.

Ibid. Page 194

Be ruled by time, the wisest counsellor of all.

Ibid. Page 198

Old women should not seek to be perfumed.

Ibid. Page 203

Trees, when they are lopped and cut, grow up again in a short time,[1] but men, being once lost, cannot easily be recovered.

Ibid. Page 207

To be turned from one's course by men's opinions, by blame, and by misrepresentation, shows a man unfit to hold an office.

Ibid. Fabius, Page 216

You know, Hannibal, how to gain a victory, but not how to use it.

Ibid. Page 224

One colour, indeed, they say the chameleon cannot assume; it cannot itself appear white; but Alcibiades, whether with good men or bad, could adapt himself to his company.

Ibid. Alcibiades, Page 249

Menenius Agrippa concluded, at length, with the celebrated fable: "It once happened that all the other members of a man mutinied against the stomach, which they accused as the only idle, uncontributing part in the whole body, while the rest were put to hardships and the expense of much

labour to supply and minister to its appetites." [1]

Lives. Coriolanus, Page 266

Men are usually more stung and galled by reproachful words than hostile actions.

Ibid. Timoleon, Page 316

A Roman divorced from his wife, being highly blamed by his friends, who demanded, "Was she not chaste? Was she not fair? Was she not fruitful?" holding out his shoe, asked them whether it was not new and well made. "Yet," added he, "none of you can tell where it pinches me." [2]

Ibid. Aemilius Paulus, Page 322

Petty repeated annoyances, arising from unpleasantness or incongruity of character, have been the occasion of such estrangement as to make it impossible for man and wife to live together with any content.

Ibid.

A man without one scar to show on his skin, that is smooth and sleek with ease and home-keeping habits, will undertake to define the office and duties of a general.

Ibid. Page 340

The saying of old Antigonus, who when he was to fight at Andros, and one told him, "The enemy's ships are more than ours," replied, "For how many then wilt thou reckon me?"

Ibid. Pelopidas, Page 348

Archimedes had stated, that given the force, any given weight might be moved; and even boasted . . . that if there were another earth, by going into it he could remove this.

Ibid. Marcellus, Page 367

Asking him if Aristides had ever done him any injury, "None at all," said he, "neither know I the man; but I am tired

---

[1] The lopped tree in time may grow again,
Most naked plants renew both fruit and
flower.
ROBERT SOUTHWELL [1561–1595]:
Times Go by Turns

[1] See Aesop, page 10a.
[2] The wearer knows where the shoe wrings.
— GEORGE HERBERT: *Jacula Prudentum*
[1640]
I can tell where my own shoe pinches me.
— CERVANTES: *Don Quixote, Part I* [1605],
Book IV, Chap. 5

of hearing him everywhere called the Just."

Lives. Aristides, Page 396

Nor are we to use living creatures like old shoes or dishes and throw them away when they are worn out or broken with service.

Ibid. Marcus Cato, Page 415

It is a difficult task, O citizens, to make speeches to the belly, which has no ears.[1]

Ibid. Page 416

Cato used to assert that wise men profited more by fools, than fools by wise men; for that wise men avoided the faults of fools, but that fools would not imitate the good examples of wise men.

Ibid. Page 417

He said that in his whole life he most repented of three things: one was that he had trusted a secret to a woman; another, that he went by water when he might have gone by land; the third, that he had remained one whole day without doing any business of moment.

Ibid. Page 418

It was hard for him who had lived with one generation of men, to plead now before another.

Ibid. Page 422

Extraordinary rains pretty generally fall after great battles.

Ibid. Caius Marius, Page 507

Marius said that the law spoke too softly to be heard in such a noise of war.

Ibid. Page 511

Lycurgus . . . used to say that long hair made good-looking men more beautiful, and ill-looking men more terrible.

Ibid. Lysander, Page 525

Where the lion's skin will not reach, you must patch it out with the fox's.[2]

Ibid. Page 529

Moral habits, induced by public

practices, are far quicker in making their way into men's private lives, than the failings and faults of individuals are in infecting the city at large.

Lives. Lysander, Page 535

As it is in the proverb, played Cretan against Cretan.[1]

Ibid. Page 537

Did you not know, then, that to-day Lucullus dines with Lucullus?

Ibid. Lucullus, Page 622

Economy, which in things inanimate is but money-making, when exercised over men becomes policy.

Ibid. Crassus, Page 651

Whoever tries for great objects must suffer something.

Ibid. Page 669

It is no great wonder if in long process of time, while fortune takes her course hither and thither, numerous coincidences should spontaneously occur. If the number and variety of subjects to be wrought upon be infinite, it is all the more easy for fortune, with such an abundance of material, to effect this similarity of results.[2]

Ibid. Sertorius, Page 678

Perseverance is more prevailing than violence; and many things which cannot be overcome when they are together, yield themselves up when taken little by little.

Ibid. Page 688

Good fortune will elevate even petty minds, and give them the appearance of a certain greatness and stateliness, as from their high place they look down upon the world; but the truly noble and resolved spirit raises itself, and becomes

---

[1] The belly has no ears, nor is it to be filled with fair words. — RABELAIS: *Book IV* [1548], *Chap. 67*

[2] The prince must be a lion, but he must also know how to play the fox. — NICOLÒ MACHIAVELLI: *The Prince* [1532]

[1] Cheat against cheat. The Cretans were notorious as liars.

[2] History repeats itself. — *Proverb*
What is this day supported by precedents will hereafter become a precedent. — THUCYDIDES [471–401 B.C.]: *Annals, XI, 24*
'Tis one and the same Nature that rolls on her course, and whoever has sufficiently considered the present state of things might certainly conclude as to both the future and the past. — MONTAIGNE: *Essays* [1580–1595], *Book II, Chap. 12, Apology for Raimond Sebond*

more conspicuous in times of disaster and ill fortune.

Lives. Eumenes, Page 703

Agesilaus being invited once to hear a man who admirably imitated the nightingale, he declined, saying he had heard the nightingale itself.

Ibid. Agesilaus, Page 726

If all the world were just, there would be no need of valour.

Ibid. Page 727

It is circumstance and proper measure that give an action its character, and make it either good or bad.

Ibid. Page 736

No man ever asked a favour with less offence, or conferred one with a better grace. When he gave, it was without assumption; when he received, it was with dignity and honour.

Ibid. Pompey, Page 740

Pompey bade Sylla recollect that more worshipped the rising than the setting sun.[1]

Ibid. Page 749

A dead man cannot bite.

Ibid. Page 795

Whenever Alexander heard Philip had taken any town of importance, or won any signal victory, instead of rejoicing at it altogether, he would tell his companions that his father would anticipate everything, and leave him and them no opportunities of performing great and illustrious actions.[2]

Ibid. Alexander, Page 804

When Alexander asked Diogenes whether he wanted anything, "Yes," said he, "I would have you stand from between me and the sun."

Ibid. Page 810

[1] See David Garrick, page 347a.

He [Tiberius] upbraided Macro in no obscure and indirect terms "with forsaking the setting sun and turning to the rising." — TACITUS [A.D. 54–119]: *Annals, Book IV, Chap. 47, 20*

[2] While Alexander was a boy, Philip had great success in his affairs, at which he did not rejoice, but told the children that were brought up with him, "My father will leave me nothing to do." — *Apophthegms of Kings and Great Commanders, Alexander*

Alexander finding himself unable to untie the Gordian knot, the ends of which were secretly twisted round and folded up within it, cut it asunder with his sword.

Lives. Alexander, Page 813

When asked why he parted with his wife, Caesar replied, "I wished my wife to be not so much as suspected."[1]

Ibid. Caesar, Page 860

For my part, I had rather be the first man among these fellows, than the second man in Rome.[2]

Ibid. Page 861

He who reflects on another man's want of breeding, shows he wants it as much himself.

Ibid. Page 865

Using the proverb frequently in their mouths who enter upon dangerous and bold attempts, "The die is cast," he took the river.[3]

Ibid. Page 874

"And this," said Caesar, "you know, young man, is more disagreeable for me to say than to do."

Ibid. Page 876

Go on, my friend, and fear nothing; you carry Caesar and his fortune in your boat.[4]

Ibid. Page 877

[Cleopatra] was at a loss how to get in undiscovered, till she thought of putting herself into the coverlet of a bed and lying at length, whilst Apollodorus tied up the bedding and carried it on his back through the gates to Caesar's apartment.

Ibid. Page 883

Caesar's barber, a busy listening fellow.

Ibid.

Caesar said to the soothsayer, "The ides of March are come"; who answered

[1] Caesar's wife ought to be above suspicion. — *Roman Apophthegms, Caesar*

[2] I had rather be the first in this town than second in Rome. — *Ibid.*

[3] Iacta alea est. The river is the Rubicon.

[4] See Lucan, page 51a.

him calmly, "Yes, they are come, but they are not past." [1]

Lives. Caesar, Page 890

Phocion's oratory, like small coin of great value, was to be estimated, not by its bulk, but its intrinsic worth.

Ibid. Phocion, Page 898

Even a nod from a person who is esteemed is of more force than a thousand arguments or studied sentences from others.

Ibid.

Demosthenes told Phocion, "The Athenians will kill you some day when they once are in a rage." "And you," said he, "if they once are in their senses."

Ibid. Page 901

Men, steered by popular applause, though they bear the name of governors, are in reality the mere underlings of the multitude. The man who is completely wise and virtuous has no need at all of glory, except so far as it disposes and eases his way of action by the greater trust that it procures him.

Ibid. Agis, Page 960

Pytheas once, scoffing at Demosthenes, said that his arguments smelt of the lamp.

Ibid. Demosthenes, Page 1026

Demosthenes overcame and rendered more distinct his inarticulate and stammering pronunciation by speaking with pebbles in his mouth.

Ibid. Page 1028

In his house he had a large looking-glass, before which he would stand and go through his exercises.

Ibid.

Cicero called Aristotle a river of flowing gold, and said of Plato's Dialogues, that if Jupiter were to speak, it would be in language like theirs.

Ibid. Cicero, Page 1054

No beast is more savage than man when possessed with power answerable to his rage.

Ibid. Page 1068

Authority and place demonstrate and try the tempers of men, by moving

every passion and discovering every frailty.

Lives. Cicero, Page 1071

Medicine, to produce health, has to examine disease, and music, to create harmony, must investigate discord.

Ibid. Demetrius, Page 1073

Once Antigonus was told his son was ill, and went to see him. At the door he met some young beauty. Going in, he sat down by the bed and took his pulse. "The fever," said Demetrius, "has just left me." "Oh, yes," replied the father, "I met it going out at the door."

Ibid. Page 1083

"It is not," said Caesar, "these well-fed, long-haired men that I fear, but the pale and the hungry-looking"; meaning Brutus and Cassius, by whose conspiracy he afterwards fell.[1]

Ibid. Antony, Page 1111

There was no man of his time like Antony for addressing a multitude, or for carrying soldiers with him by the force of words.

Ibid. Page 1127

From PLUTARCH'S *Morals* [2]

It is a true proverb, that if you live with a lame man you will learn to halt.

Of the Training of Children

Eat not thy heart; which forbids to afflict our souls, and waste them with vexatious cares.

Ibid.

The very spring and root of honesty and virtue lie in the felicity of lighting on good education.

Ibid.

It is indeed a desirable thing to be well descended, but the glory belongs to our ancestors.

Ibid.

Nothing made the horse so fat as the king's eye.

Ibid.

Democritus said, words are but the shadow of actions.

Ibid.

---

[1] See Shakespeare, page 166a.

[1] See Shakespeare, page 166b.
[2] By various translators, revised by WILLIAM WATSON GOODWIN [1831–1912].

It is a point of wisdom to be silent when occasion requires, and better than to speak, though never so well.[1]

Of the Training of Children

Abstain from beans; that is, keep out of public offices, for anciently the choice of the officers of state was made by beans.

Ibid.

The whole life of man is but a point of time; let us enjoy it, therefore, while it lasts, and not spend it to no purpose.

Ibid.

An old doting fool, with one foot already in the grave.

Ibid.

Xenophanes said, "I confess myself the greatest coward in the world, for I dare not do an ill thing."

Of Bashfulness

One made the observation of the people of Asia that they were all slaves to one man, merely because they could not pronounce that syllable No.[2]

Ibid.

Euripides was wont to say, "Silence is an answer to a wise man."

Ibid.

Zeno first started that doctrine that knavery is the best defence against a knave.[3]

Ibid.

Alexander wept when he heard from Anaxarchus that there was an infinite number of worlds; and his friends asking him if any accident had befallen him, he returns this answer: "Do you not think it a matter worthy of lamentation that when there is such a vast multitude of them, we have not yet conquered one?"

On the Tranquillity of the Mind

Like the man who threw a stone at a bitch, but hit his step-mother, on which he exclaimed, "Not so bad!"

Ibid.

---

[1] Closed lips hurt no one, speaking may. — CATO THE CENSOR [234–149 B.C.]: *Book I, Distich 12*

[2] See Coleridge, page 424b.

[3] Set a thief to catch a thief. — BOHN: *Handbook of Proverbs*

Pittacus said, "Every one of you hath his particular plague, and my wife is mine; and he is very happy who hath this only."

On the Tranquillity of the Mind

He was a man, which, as Plato saith, is a very inconstant creature.[1]

Ibid.

All men whilst they are awake are in one common world; but each of them, when he is asleep, is in a world of his own.[2]

Of Superstition

I, for my own part, had much rather people should say of me that there neither is nor ever was such a man as Plutarch, than that they should say, "Plutarch is an unsteady, fickle, froward, vindictive, and touchy fellow."

Ibid.

Scilurus on his death-bed, being about to leave four-score sons surviving, offered a bundle of darts to each of them, and bade them break them. When all refused, drawing out one by one, he easily broke them, — thus teaching them that if they held together, they would continue strong; but if they fell out and were divided, they would become weak.[3]

Apophthegms of Kings and Great Commanders. Scilurus

Dionysius the Elder, being asked whether he was at leisure, he replied, "God forbid that it should ever befall me!"

Ibid. Dionysius

A prating barber asked Archelaus how he would be trimmed. He answered, "In silence."

Ibid. Archelaus

When Philip had news brought him of divers and eminent successes in one day, "O Fortune!" said he, "for all these so great kindnesses do me some small mischief."

Ibid. Philip

---

[1] See Montaigne, page 97b.

[2] A saying attributed to HERACLITUS.

[3] AESOP'S fable, *The Bundle of Sticks* has this theme.

See Franklin, page 331b.

Philip being arbitrator betwixt two wicked persons, he commanded one to fly out of Macedonia and the other to pursue him.

Apophthegms of Kings and
Great Commanders. Philip

Being about to pitch his camp in a likely place, and hearing there was no hay to be had for the cattle, "What a life," said he, "is ours, since we must live according to the convenience of asses!"

Ibid.

He made one of Antipater's recommendation a judge; and perceiving afterwards that his hair and beard were dyed, he removed him, saying, "I could not think one that was faithless in his hair could be trusty in his deeds."

Ibid.

Being nimble and light-footed, his father encouraged him to run in the Olympic race. "Yes," said he, "if there were any kings there to run with me."

Ibid. Alexander

Pyrrhus said, "If I should overcome the Romans in another fight, I were undone." [1]

Ibid. Pyrrhus

Themistocles being asked whether he would rather be Achilles or Homer, said, "Which would you rather be, — a conqueror in the Olympic games, or the crier that proclaims who are conquerors?"

Ibid. Themistocles

Alcibiades had a very handsome dog, that cost him seven thousand drachmas; and he cut off his tail, "that," said he, "the Athenians may have this story to tell of me, and may concern themselves no further with me."

Ibid. Alcibiades

To Harmodius, descended from the ancient Harmodius, when he reviled Iphicrates [a shoemaker's son] for his mean birth, "My nobility," said he, "begins with me, but yours ends in you." [2]

Ibid. Iphicrates

[1] See Herodotus, page 19a.
[2] Curtius Rufus seems to me to be descended from himself (a saying of Tiberius). — TACI-

Once when Phocion had delivered an opinion which pleased the people, . . . he turned to his friend and said, "Have I not unawares spoken some mischievous thing or other?" [1]

Apophthegms of Kings and
Great Commanders. Phocion

King Agis said, "The Lacedaemonians are not wont to ask how many, but where the enemy are."

Ibid. Agis

To one that promised to give him hardy cocks that would die fighting, "Prithee," said Cleomenes, "give me cocks that will kill fighting."

Ibid. Cleomenes

A soldier told Pelopidas, "We are fallen among the enemies." Said he, "How are we fallen among them more than they among us?"

Ibid. Pelopidas

Cato the Elder wondered how that city was preserved wherein a fish was sold for more than an ox.

Roman Apophthegms.
Cato the Elder

Cato requested old men not to add the disgrace of wickedness to old age, which was accompanied with many other evils.

Ibid.

He said they that were serious in ridiculous matters would be ridiculous in serious affairs.

Ibid.

Cicero said loud-bawling orators were driven by their weakness to noise, as lame men to take horse.

Ibid. Cicero

After he routed Pharnaces Ponticus at the first assault, he wrote thus to his friends: "I came, I saw, I conquered." [2]

Ibid. Caesar

As Caesar was at supper the discourse was of death, — which sort was the

TUS [A. D. 54–119]: *Annals, Book XI, Chap. 21, 16*

I am my own ancestor. — JUNOT, DUC D'ABRANTES [1771–1813], when asked about his ancestry

[1] See Diogenes Laertius, page 71b.
[2] Veni, vidi, vici.
See Shakespeare, page 153b.

best. "That," said he, "which is unexpected."

Roman Apophthegms.
Caesar

As Athenodorus was taking his leave of Caesar, "Remember," said he, "Caesar, whenever you are angry, to say or do nothing before you have repeated the four-and-twenty letters to yourself."

Ibid. Caesar Augustus

"Young men," said Caesar, "hear an old man to whom old men hearkened when he was young."

Ibid.

Custom is almost a second nature.[1]

Rules for the Preservation of Health. 18

Epaminondas is reported wittily to have said of a good man that died about the time of the battle of Leuctra, "How came he to have so much leisure as to die, when there was so much stirring?"

Ibid. 25

Socrates thought that if all our misfortunes were laid in one common heap, whence every one must take an equal portion, most persons would be contented to take their own and depart.[2]

Consolation to Apollonius

Diogenes the Cynic, when a little before his death he fell into a slumber, and his physician rousing him out of it asked him whether anything ailed him, wisely answered, "Nothing, sir; only one brother anticipates another, — Sleep before Death."

Ibid.

There are two sentences inscribed upon the Delphic oracle, hugely accommodated to the usages of man's life: "Know thyself,"[3] and "Nothing too

much"; and upon these all other precepts depend.

Consolation to Apollonius

Agesilaus was very fond of his children; and it is reported that once toying with them he got astride upon a reed as upon a horse, and rode about the room; and being seen by one of his friends, he desired him not to speak of it till he had children of his own.

Laconic Apophthegms. Of
Agesilaus the Great

Lysander, when Dionysius sent him two gowns, and bade him choose which he would carry to his daughter, said, "She can choose best," and so took both away with him.

Ibid. Of Lysander

And when the physician said, "Sir, you are an old man," "That happens," replied Pausanias, "because you never were my doctor."

Ibid. Of Pausanias

When one told Plistarchus that a notorious railer spoke well of him, "I'll lay my life," said he, "somebody hath told him I am dead, for he can speak well of no man living."

Ibid. Of Plistarchus

Said Periander, "Hesiod might as well have kept his breath to cool his pottage."[1]

The Banquet of the Seven
Wise Men. 14

Socrates said, "Bad men live that they may eat and drink, whereas good men eat and drink that they may live."[2]

How a Young Man Ought to
Hear Poems. 4

---

[1] Habit is a second nature. — MONTAIGNE: *Essays* [1580–1595], *Book III, Chap. 10*
See Shakespeare, page 132a.

[2] ADDISON's paper, *The Spectator, No. 558,* June 23, 1714, is on this theme.

[3] Plutarch ascribes this saying to Plato. It is also ascribed to Pythagoras, Chilo, Thales, Cleobulus, Bias, Solon, and Socrates; also to Phemonë, a mythical Greek poetess of the ante-Homeric period. JUVENAL (*Satire XI, 27*)

says that this precept descended from heaven.
Ful wys is he that can him-selven knowe.
— CHAUCER: *The Canterbury Tales* [*circa* 1387], *The Monk's Tale, Line 3329*
Make it thy business to know thyself, which is the most difficult lesson in the world. — CERVANTES: *Don Quixote, Part II* [1615], *Book IV, Chap. 42*
See Pope, page 316b.

[1] Spare your breath to cool your porridge. — RABELAIS: *Works, Book V* [1552], *Chap. 28*

[2] He used to say that other men lived to eat, but that he ate to live. — DIOGENES LAERTIUS [*circa* A.D. 200]: *Socrates, 14*
We should eat to live, not live to eat. —

That proverbial saying, "Ill news goes quick and far."

Of Inquisitiveness

Spintharus, speaking in commendation of Epaminondas, says he scarce ever met with any man who knew more and spoke less.

Of Hearing. 6

It is a thing of no great difficulty to raise objections against another man's oration, — nay, it is a very easy matter; but to produce a better in its place is a work extremely troublesome.

Ibid.

Antiphanes said merrily, that in a certain city the cold was so intense that words were congealed as soon as spoken, but that after some time they thawed and became audible; so that the words spoken in winter were articulated next summer.[1]

Of Man's Progress in Virtue

As those persons who despair of ever being rich make little account of small expenses, thinking that little added to a little will never make any great sum.

Ibid.

What is bigger than an elephant? But this also is become man's plaything, and a spectacle at public solemnities; and it learns to skip, dance, and kneel.

Of Fortune

No man ever wetted clay and then left it, as if there would be bricks by chance and fortune.

Ibid.

Alexander was wont to say, "Were I not Alexander, I would be Diogenes."

Of the Fortune or Virtue of Alexander the Great

When the candles are out all women are fair.[2]

Conjugal Precepts

MOLIÈRE: *L'Avare* [1668], *Act III, Sc. 5*
We must eat to live and live to eat. — FIELD-ING [1707–1754]: *The Miser, Act III, Sc. 3*
[1] Rabelais gives a somewhat similar account, referring to Antiphanes, in *Book IV, Chaps. 55* and *56*.
See Raspe (Baron Munchausen), page 369b.
[2] When all candles be out, all cats be gray. — JOHN HEYWOOD: *Proverbes* [1546], *Part I, Chap. 5*

Like watermen, who look astern while they row the boat ahead.[1]

Whether 'Twas Rightfully Said,
Live Concealed

Socrates said he was not an Athenian or a Greek, but a citizen of the world.[2]

Of Banishment

The great god Pan is dead.[3]

Why the Oracles Cease to
Give Answers

I am whatever was, or is, or will be; and my veil no mortal ever took up.[4]

Of Isis and Osiris

When Hermodotus in his poems described Antigonus as the son of Helios, "My valet-de-chambre," said he, "is not aware of this."[5]

Ibid.

---

[1] Like rowers, who advance backward. — MONTAIGNE: *Essays* [1580–1595], *Of Profit and Honour, Book III, Chap. I*
Like the watermen that row one way and look another. — ROBERT BURTON: *Anatomy of Melancholy* [1621–1651], *Democritus to the Reader*
[2] See Thomas Paine, page 371a, and William Lloyd Garrison, page 517a.
Diogenes, when asked from what country he came, replied, "I am a citizen of the world." — DIOGENES LAERTIUS [*circa* A.D. 200], *Diogenes, 6*
Citizen of the world, as I hold myself to be. — BOSWELL: *Life of Dr. Johnson* [1791], *Everyman Edition, Vol. I, P. 521*
[3] Great Pan is dead. — ELIZABETH BARRETT BROWNING [1806–1861]: *The Dead Pan, St. 26*
Plutarch relates (*Isis and Osiris*) that a ship well laden with passengers drove with the tide near the Isles of Paxi, when a loud voice was heard by most of the passengers calling unto one Thanus. The voice then said aloud to him, "When you are arrived at Palodes, take care to make it known that the great god Pan is dead."
[4] I am the things that are, and those that are to be, and those that have been. No one ever lifted my skirts; the fruit which I bore was the sun. — PROCLUS [A.D. 411?–485]: *On Plato's Timaeus* (Inscription in the temple of Neith at Sais, in Egypt)
[5] Few men have been admired by their domestics. — MONTAIGNE: *Essays* [1580–1595], *Book III, Chap. 2*
The phrase "No man is a hero to his valet" has often been attributed to Madame de Sévigné, but on the authority of MADAME AISSÉ (*Letters*, edited by Jules Ravenal, 1853) it belongs to Madame Cornuel [1614–1694].

We are more sensible of what is done against custom than against Nature.
Of Eating of Flesh. Tract 1

When Demosthenes was asked what was the first part of oratory, he answered, "Action"; and which was the second, he replied, "Action"; and which was the third, he still answered, "Action."
Lives of the Ten Orators

Xenophon says that there is no sound more pleasing than one's own praises.
Whether an Aged Man Ought to Meddle in State Affairs

Statesmen are not only liable to give an account of what they say or do in public, but there is a busy inquiry made into their very meals, beds, marriages, and every other sportive or serious action.
Political Precepts

Leo Byzantius said, "What would you do, if you saw my wife, who scarce reaches up to my knees? . . . Yet," went he on, "as little as we are, when we fall out with each other, the city of Byzantium is not big enough to hold us."
Ibid.

Cato said, "I had rather men should ask why my statue is not set up, than why it is."
Ibid.

It was the saying of Bion, that though the boys throw stones at frogs in sport, yet the frogs do not die in sport but in earnest.
Which Are the Most Crafty, Water or Land Animals? 7

For to err in opinion, though it be not the part of wise men, is at least human.[1]
Against Colotes

Simonides calls painting silent poetry, and poetry, speaking painting.
Whether the Athenians Were More Warlike or Learned. 3

Pythagoras, when he was asked what time was, answered that it was the soul of this world.
Platonic Questions

[1] See Pope, page 311b.

MANILIUS
[First Century a. d.]

As soon as we are born we begin to die, and the end depends upon the beginning.
Astronomica. IV, Line 16

JUVENAL
[a. d. 47–138]

Honesty is praised and starves.[1]
Satire I. Line 74

If nature refuses, indignation makes the verse.
Ibid. Line 79

Whatever men do — prayer, fear, anger, pleasure, joys, comings and goings — that is the stuff of which my little book is made.
Ibid. Line 85

He pardons the ravens and visits censure on the doves.
Satire II. Line 63

No man ever became extremely wicked all at once.[2]
Ibid. Line 83

Grammarian, orator, geometrician; painter, gymnastic teacher; fortune-teller, rope-dancer, physician, conjuror, — he knew everything.[3]
Satire III. Line 76

Unhappy poverty has no worse trait than that it makes men ridiculous.[4]
Ibid. Line 152

Not easily do they rise whose powers are hindered by straitened circumstances.
Ibid. Line 164

We all live in a state of ambitious poverty.
Ibid. Line 182

[1] A favorite quotation of Linnaeus, Swedish botanist and naturalist.
[2] Nemo repente fit turpissimus. See Beaumont and Fletcher, page 228b, and Racine, page 287b.
[3] See Dryden, page 277a.
[4] Nil habet infelix paupertas durius in se Quam quod ridiculos homines facit. See Samuel Johnson, page 335b.

A rare bird on earth and very like a black swan.[1]

Satire VI. Line 165

But who would guard the guards themselves?[2]

Ibid. Line 347

Nobility is the one only virtue.[3]

Satire VIII. Line 20

Hold it the greatest wrong to prefer life to honor and for life's sake to lose the reasons for living.

Ibid. Line 83

Two things only the people anxiously desire — bread and circuses.[4]

Satire X, Line 80

We should pray for a sane mind in a sound body.[5]

Ibid. Line 356

The greatest reverence is due a child! If you are contemplating a wicked act, despise not your child's tender years.

Satire XIV. Line 47

ONASANDER
[*Floruit* A. D. 49]

Vigor is found in the man who has not yet grown old, and discretion in the man who is not too young.

The General. Chap. 1, Sect. 10

Envy is a pain of mind that successful men cause their neighbours.

Ibid. Chap. 42, Paragraph 25

TACITUS
[A. D. 54–119]

The images of twenty of the most illustrious families — the Manlii, the Quinctii, and other names of equal splendour — were carried before it [the bier of Junia]. Those of Brutus and Cassius were not displayed; but for that very reason they shone with pre-eminent lustre.[6]

Annals. III, 76, 11

[1] Rara avis in terris nigroque simillima cygno.
[2] Sed quis custodiet ipsos custodes?
[3] See Chapman, page 117b.
[4] Duas tantum res anxius optat,
Panem et circenses.
[5] Orandum est ut sit mens sana in corpore sano.
[6] Lord John Russell, alluding to an expres-

He had talents equal to business, and aspired no higher.

Annals. VI, 39, 17

Some might consider him as too fond of fame; for the desire of glory clings even to the best men longer than any other passion.[1]

History. IV, 6, 36

Whatever is unknown is magnified.

Agricola. Sect. 30

To plunder, to slaughter, to steal, these things they misname empire; and where they make a desert, they call it peace.[2]

Ibid.

It is characteristic of human nature to hate the man whom you have wronged.

Ibid. Sect. 42

EPICTETUS [3]
[*Circa* A. D. 60]

To a reasonable creature, that alone is insupportable which is unreasonable; but everything reasonable may be supported.

Discourses. Chap. 2

When you have shut your doors, and darkened your room, remember never to say that you are alone, for you are not alone;[4] but God is within, and your genius is within, — and what need have they of light to see what you are doing?

Ibid. Chap. 14

sion used by him ("Conspicuous by his absence") in an address to the electors of the city of London, said, "It is not an original expression of mine, but is taken from one of the greatest historians of antiquity."
[1] Said of Helvidius Priscus.
See Milton, page 249a.
[2] Calgacus, addressing the Britons at the Battle of the Grampians, referring to the Romans.
Mark! where his carnage and his conquests cease!
He makes a solitude, and calls it — peace!
BYRON: *The Bride of Abydos* [1813], *Canto II, L. 428*
[3] Translated [1865] by THOMAS WENTWORTH HIGGINSON.
[4] Though in a wilderness, a man is never alone. — SIR THOMAS BROWNE: *Religio Medici* [1642] (Everyman ed.), *P. 82*

No great thing is created suddenly, any more than a bunch of grapes or a fig. If you tell me that you desire a fig, I answer you that there must be time. Let it first blossom, then bear fruit, then ripen.

Discourses. Chap. 15

Any one thing in the creation is sufficient to demonstrate a Providence to an humble and grateful mind.

Ibid. Chap. 16

Were I a nightingale, I would act the part of a nightingale; were I a swan, the part of a swan.

Ibid.

Since it is Reason which shapes and regulates all other things, it ought not itself to be left in disorder.

Ibid. Chap. 17

Practise yourself, for heaven's sake, in little things; and thence proceed to greater.

Ibid. Chap. 18

Why, then, do you walk as if you had swallowed a ramrod?

Ibid. Chap. 21

Difficulties are things that show what men are.

Ibid. Chap. 24

The good or ill of man lies within his own will.

Ibid Chap. 25

In theory there is nothing to hinder our following what we are taught; but in life there are many things to draw us aside.

Ibid. Chap. 26

Appearances to the mind are of four kinds. Things either are what they appear to be; or they neither are, nor appear to be; or they are, and do not appear to be; or they are not, and yet appear to be. Rightly to aim in all these cases is the wise man's task.

Ibid. Chap. 27

The appearance of things to the mind is the standard of every action to man.

That We Ought Not to Be Angry
with Mankind. 27

The materials of action are variable,

but the use we make of them should be constant.

How Nobleness of Mind May Be
Consistent with Prudence. 5

Shall I show you the muscular training of a philosopher? "What muscles are those?" — A will undisappointed; evils avoided; powers daily exercised; careful resolutions; unerring decisions.

Wherein Consists the Essence
of Good. 8

What is the first business of one who studies philosophy? To part with self-conceit. For it is impossible for any one to begin to learn what he thinks that he already knows.

How to Apply General Principles
to Particular Cases. 17

Every habit and faculty is preserved and increased by correspondent actions, — as the habit of walking, by walking; or running, by running.

How the Semblances of Things Are
to Be Combated. 18

Whatever you would make habitual, practise it; and if you would not make a thing habitual, do not practise it, but habituate yourself to something else.

Ibid.

Reckon the days in which you have not been angry. I used to be angry every day; now every other day; then every third and fourth day; and if you miss it so long as thirty days, offer a sacrifice of thanksgiving to God.

Ibid.

Be not hurried away by excitement, but say, "Semblance, wait for me a little. Let me see what you are and what you represent. Let me try you."

Ibid.

There are some things which men confess with ease, and others with difficulty.

Of Inconsistency. 21

Who is there whom bright and agreeable children do not attract to play and creep and prattle with them?

Concerning a Person Whom He
Treated with Disregard. 24

Two rules we should always have ready, — that there is nothing good or

evil save in the will; and that we are not to lead events, but to follow them.
In What Manner We Ought to Bear Sickness. Book III, 10

First say to yourself what you would be; and then do what you have to do.
Concerning Such as Read and Dispute Ostentatiously. 23

Let not another's disobedience to Nature become an ill to you; for you were not born to be depressed and unhappy with others, but to be happy with them. And if any is unhappy, remember that he is so for himself; for God made all men to enjoy felicity and peace.
That We Ought Not to Be Affected by Things Not in Our Own Power. 24

Remember that you ought to behave in life as you would at a banquet. As something is being passed around it comes to you; stretch out your hand, take a portion of it politely. It passes on; do not detain it. Or it has not come to you yet; do not project your desire to meet it, but wait until it comes in front of you. So act toward children, so toward a wife, so toward office, so toward wealth.
The Encheiridion. 15

Everything has two handles,—one by which it may be borne; another by which it cannot.[1]
Ibid. 43

PLINY THE YOUNGER [2]
[A. D. 61–105]

Modestus said of Regulus that he was "the biggest rascal that walks upon two legs."
Letters.[3] Book I, Letter 5, 14

There is nothing to write about, you say. Well, then, write and let me know just this,—that there *is* nothing to

[1] There is a right and wrong handle to everything. — RASPE: *Travels of Baron Munchausen* [1785], *Chap. 30*
[2] Translated [1746] by WILLIAM MELMOTH.
[3] Book VI, Letter 16, contains the description of the eruption of Vesuvius, A. D. 79, as witnessed by Pliny the Elder.

write about; or tell me in the good old style if you are well. That's right. I am quite well.[1]
Letters. Book I, Letter 11, 1

An object in possession seldom retains the same charm that it had in pursuit.[2]
Ibid. Book II, Letter 15, 1

He [Pliny the Elder] used to say that "no book was so bad but some good might be got out of it."[3]
Ibid. Book III, Letter 5, 10

This expression of ours, "Father of a family."[4]
Ibid. Book V, Letter 19, 2

That indolent but agreeable condition of doing nothing.[5]
Ibid. Book VIII, Letter 9, 3

Objects which are usually the motives of our travels by land and by sea are often overlooked and neglected if they lie under our eye. . . . We put off from time to time going and seeing what we know we have an opportunity of seeing when we please.
Ibid. Letter 20, 1

His only fault is that he has no fault.[6]
Ibid. Book IX, Letter 26, 1

EMPEROR HADRIAN
[A. D. 76–138]

Gentle little soul, hastening away, my body's guest and comrade, whither goest

[1] This comes to inform you that I am in a perfect state of health, hoping you are in the same. Ay, that's the old beginning. — GEORGE COLMAN THE YOUNGER: *The Heir at Law* [1797], *Act III, Sc. 2*
[2] It has been a thousand times observed, and I must observe it once more, that the hours we pass with happy prospects in view, are more pleasing than those crowned with fruition. — GOLDSMITH: *The Vicar of Wakefield* [1766], *Chap. 10*
[3] "There is no book so bad," said the bachelor, "but something good may be found in it." — CERVANTES: *Don Quixote, Part II* [1615], *Chap. 3*
[4] Paterfamilias.
[5] Dolce far niente (Sweet doing-nothing). — *Italian proverb*
[6] The greatest of faults, I should say, is to be conscious of none. — CARLYLE: *Heroes and Hero-Worship* [1841], *The Hero as Prophet*

thou now, pale, fearful, pensive, not jesting, as of old? [1]

Morientis, Ad Animam Suam
I've no mind to be a Florus,
Strolling round among the drink-shops,
Skulking round among the cook-shops,
Victim of fat-gorged mosquitoes.
Retort to Florus [2]

MARCUS AURELIUS ANTONINUS [3]
[A.D. 121–180]

This Being of mine, whatever it really is, consists of a little flesh, a little breath, and the part which governs.
Meditations. II, 2

The ways of the gods are full of providence.
Ibid. 3

Thou wilt find rest from vain fancies if thou doest every act in life as though it were thy last.[4]
Ibid. 5

No state sorrier than that of the man who keeps up a continual round, and pries into "the secrets of the nether world," as saith the poet, and is curious in conjecture of what is in his neighbour's heart.
Ibid. 13

Though thou be destined to live three thousand years and as many myriads besides, yet remember that no man loseth other life than that which he liveth, nor liveth other than that which he loseth.
Ibid. 14

For a man can lose neither the past

[1] Animula, vagula, blandula
Hospes comesque corporis,
Quae nunc abibis in loca,
Pallidula, frigida, nudula,
Nec, ut soles, dabis joca.
See Pope, page 312a.
[2] Florus, born in Africa [A.D. 74], Hadrian's friend, had addressed these lines to him (the third line has been lost):
I've no mind to be a Caesar,
Strolling round among the Britons

Victim of the Scythian hoar-frosts.
[3] Translated by Morris Hickey Morgan [1859–1910].
[4] See Publilius Syrus, *Maxim 633*, page 45b.

nor the future; for how can one take from him that which is not his? So remember these two points: first, that each thing is of like form from everlasting and comes round again in its cycle, and that it signifies not whether a man shall look upon the same things for a hundred years or two hundred, or for an infinity of time; second, that the longest lived and the shortest lived man, when they come to die, lose one and the same thing.
Meditations. II, 14

As for life, it is a battle and a sojourning in a strange land; but the fame that comes after is oblivion.
Ibid. 17

Waste not the remnant of thy life in those imaginations touching other folk, whereby thou contributest not to the common weal.
Ibid. III, 4

A man should *be* upright, not be *kept* upright.
Ibid. 5

Never esteem anything as of advantage to thee that shall make thee break thy word or lose thy self-respect.
Ibid. 7

By a tranquil mind I mean nothing else than a mind well ordered.
Ibid. IV, 3

Think on this doctrine, — that reasoning beings were created for one another's sake; that to be patient is a branch of justice, and that men sin without intending it.
Ibid.

The universe is change; our life is what our thoughts make it.
Ibid.

Nothing can come out of nothing,[1] any more than a thing can go back to nothing.
Ibid. 4

[1] De nihilo nihilum, in nihilum posse reverti. — Persius [A.D. 34–62]: *Satires*, 3, L. 84
Nothing can be produced out of nothing. — Diogenes Laertius [*circa* A.D. 200]: *Diogenes of Apollonia, 2*

Death, like birth, is a secret of Nature.

Meditations. IV, 5

That which makes the man no worse than he was makes his life no worse: it has no power to harm, without or within.

Ibid. 8

Whatever happens at all happens as it should; thou wilt find this true, if thou shouldst watch narrowly.

Ibid. 10

How much time he gains who does not look to see what his neighbour says or does or thinks, but only at what he does himself, to make it just and holy.

Ibid. 18

Whatever is in any way beautiful hath its source of beauty in itself, and is complete in itself; praise forms no part of it. So it is none the worse nor the better for being praised.

Ibid. 20

All that is harmony for thee, O Universe, is in harmony with me as well. Nothing that comes at the right time for thee is too early or too late for me. Everything is fruit to me that thy seasons bring, O Nature. All things come of thee, have their being in thee, and return to thee.

Ibid. 23

"Let thine occupations be few," saith the sage,[1] "if thou wouldst lead a tranquil life."

Ibid. 24

Love the little trade which thou hast learned, and be content therewith.

Ibid. 31

Remember this, — that there is a proper dignity and proportion to be observed in the performance of every act of life.

Ibid. 32

All is ephemeral, — fame and the famous as well.

Ibid. 35

Observe always that everything is the result of a change, and get used to

[1] DEMOCRITUS apud Senecam: *De Ira, III,* 6; *De Animi Tranquillitate,* 13

thinking that there is nothing Nature loves so well as to change existing forms and to make new ones like them.

Meditations. IV, 36

Search men's governing principles, and consider the wise, what they shun and what they cleave to.

Ibid. 38

Time is a sort of river of passing events, and strong is its current; no sooner is a thing brought to sight than it is swept by and another takes its place, and this too will be swept away.

Ibid. 43

All that happens is as usual and familiar as the rose in spring and the crop in summer.

Ibid. 44

Mark how fleeting and paltry is the estate of man, — yesterday in embryo, to-morrow a mummy or ashes. So for the hair's-breadth of time assigned to thee live rationally, and part with life cheerfully, as drops the ripe olive, extolling the season that bore it and the tree that matured it.

Ibid. 48

Deem not life a thing of consequence. For look at the yawning void of the future, and at that other limitless space, the past.

Ibid. 50

Always take the short cut; and that is the rational one. Therefore say and do everything according to soundest reason.

Ibid. 51

In the morning, when thou art sluggish at rousing thee, let this thought be present; "I am rising to a man's work."

Ibid. V, 1

A man makes no noise over a good deed, but passes on to another as a vine to bear grapes again in season.

Ibid. 6

Nothing happens to anybody which he is not fitted by nature to bear.

Ibid. 18

Live with the gods.

Ibid. 27

Look beneath the surface; let not the several quality of a thing nor its worth escape thee.

Meditations. VI, 3

The controlling Intelligence understands its own nature, and what it does, and whereon it works.

Ibid. 5

Do not think that what is hard for thee to master is impossible for man; but if a thing is possible and proper to man, deem it attainable by thee.

Ibid. 19

If any man can convince me and bring home to me that I do not think or act aright, gladly will I change; for I search after truth, by which man never yet was harmed.

Ibid. 21

What is not good for the swarm is not good for the bee.

Ibid. 54

How many, once lauded in song, are given over to the forgotten; and how many who sung their praises are clean gone long ago!

Ibid. VII, 6

One Universe made up of all that is; and one God in it all, and one principle of Being, and one Law, the Reason, shared by all thinking creatures, and one Truth.

Ibid. 9

The time is close when you shall forget all things and be by all forgotten.

Ibid. 21

It is man's peculiar duty to love even those who wrong him.

Ibid. 22

The art of living is more like wrestling than dancing, in so far as it stands ready against the accidental and the unforeseen, and is not apt to fall.

Ibid. 61

Remember this, — that very little is needed to make a happy life.

Ibid. 67

Remember that to change thy mind and to follow him that sets thee right, is to be none the less the free agent that thou wast before.

Ibid. VIII, 16

Look to the essence of a thing, whether it be a point of doctrine, of practice, or of interpretation.

Meditations. VIII, 22

Be not careless in deeds, nor confused in words, nor rambling in thought.

Ibid. 51

Think not disdainfully of death, but look on it with favour; for even death is one of the things that Nature wills.

Ibid. IX, 3

A wrong-doer is often a man that has left something undone, not always he that has done something.

Ibid. 5

Blot out vain pomp; check impulse; quench appetite; keep reason under its own control.

Ibid. 7

If you can, correct the evil by instruction; if not, remember that for this was patience given you. The gods, too, are patient with the like.

Ibid. 11

All things are the same, — familiar in enterprise, momentary in endurance, coarse in substance. All things now are as they were in the day of those whom we have buried.

Ibid. 14

Everything is in a state of metamorphosis. Thou thyself art in everlasting change and in corruption to correspond; so is the whole universe.

Ibid. 19

Forward, as occasion offers. Never look round to see whether any shall note it. . . . Be satisfied with success in even the smallest matter, and think that even such a result is no trifle.

Ibid. 29

Whatever may befall thee, it was preordained for thee from everlasting.

Ibid. X, 5

TERTULLIAN
[A. D. 160–240]

See how these Christians love one another.

Apologeticus. 39

Blood of the martyrs is the seed of the Church.
> *Apologeticus. 50*

It is certain because it is impossible.[1]
> *De Carne Christi. 5*

He who flees will fight again.[2]
> *De Fuga in Persecutione. 10*

ATHENAEUS [3]
[*Circa* A. D. 200]

It was a saying of Demetrius Phalereus, that "Men having often abandoned what was visible for the sake of what was uncertain, have not got what

[1] Certum est, quia impossibile est. This is usually misquoted, "Credo quia impossibile" (I believe it because it is impossible). Also attributed to St. Augustine in the form "Credo quia absurdum."

[2] A corresponding Greek passage is ascribed to Menander.
> That same man that runnith awaie
> Maie again fight an other daie.
>> ERASMUS: *Apothegms* [1542], translated by Udall

> Celuy qui fuit de bonne heure
> Peut combattre derechef.
> (He who flies in good time can fight again.)
>> *Satyre Menippée* [1594]

> Qui fuit peut revenir aussi;
> Qui meurt, il n'en est pas ainsi.
> (He who flies can also return; it is not so with him who dies.)
>> PAUL SCARRON [1610–1660]

> For those that fly may fight again,
> Which he can never do that's slain.
>> SAMUEL BUTLER: *Hudibras, Part III* [1678], *Canto III, L. 243*

> He that fights and runs away
> May turn and fight another day;
> But he that is in battle slain
> Will never rise to fight again.
>> JAMES RAY: *History of the Rebellion* [1752]

> For he who fights and runs away
> May live to fight another day;
> But he who is in battle slain
> Can never rise and fight again.
>> GOLDSMITH: *The Art of Poetry on a New Plan* [1761]

> But since the man that runs away
> Lives to die another day,
> And cowards' funerals, when they come,
> Are not wept so well at home,
> Therefore, though the best is bad,
> Stand and do the best, my lad.
>> A. E. HOUSMAN [1859–1936]: *The Day of Battle*

[3] Translated by CHARLES DUKE YONGE [1812–1891].

they expected, and have lost what they had, — being unfortunate by an enigmatical sort of calamity."
> *The Deipnosophists. VI, 23*

Every investigation which is guided by principles of Nature fixes its ultimate aim entirely on gratifying the stomach.[1]
> *Ibid. VII, 11*

Dorion, ridiculing the description of a tempest in the "Nautilus" of Timotheus, said that he had seen a more formidable storm in a boiling saucepan.[2]
> *Ibid. VIII, 19*

On one occasion some one put a very little wine into a wine-cooler, and said that it was sixteen years old. "It is very small for its age," said Gnathaena.
> *Ibid. XIII, 47*

DIOGENES LAERTIUS [3]
[*Circa* A. D. 200]

Writers differ with respect to the apophthegms of the Seven Sages, attributing the same one to various authors.
> *Thales. 14*

Solon used to say that speech was the image of actions; . . . that laws were like cobwebs, — for that if any trifling or powerless thing fell into them, they held it fast; while if it were something weightier, it broke through them and was off.
> *Solon. 10*

Solon gave the following advice: "Consider your honour, as a gentleman, of more weight than an oath."
> *Ibid. 12*

As some say, Solon was the author of the apophthegm, "Nothing in excess."
> *Ibid. 16*

[1] See Samuel Johnson, page 340a.
[2] A tempest in a teapot. — *Proverb*
[3] From *The Lives and Opinions of Eminent Philosophers,* translated by CHARLES DUKE YONGE [1812–1891].
There is scarce any Philosopher but dies twice or thrice in Laertius; nor almost any life without two or three deaths in Plutarch. — SIR THOMAS BROWNE: *Urn Burial* [1658], *Chap. 3*

o advised, "not to speak evil of
ad." [1]

Chilo. 2

raclitus says that Pittacus, when
he had got Alcaeus into his power, released him, saying, "Forgiveness is better than revenge." [2]

Pittacus. 3

One of his sayings was, "Even the
gods cannot strive against necessity." [3]

Ibid. 4

Another was, "Watch your opportunity." [4]

Ibid. 7

Bias used to say that men ought to
calculate life both as if they were fated
to live a long and a short time, and that
they ought to love one another as if at
a future time they would come to hate
one another; for that most men were
bad.

Bias. 5

Ignorance plays the chief part among
men, and the multitude of words. [5]

Cleobulus. 4

Anacharsis, on learning that the
sides of a ship were four fingers thick,
said that "the passengers were just that
distance from death." [6]

Anacharsis. 5

It was a common saying of Myson
that men ought not to investigate things
from words, but words from things; for
that things are not made for the sake
of words, but words for things.

Myson. 3

[1] De mortuis nil nisi bonum (Of the dead
nothing but good).

[2] Forgiveness is better than punishment;
for the one is proof of a gentle, the other of a
savage nature. — Quoted by EPICTETUS [*circa*
A.D. 60]: *Fragment 62*

[3] Necessity has no law. — RABELAIS: *Works,
Book V* [1564], *Chap. 15*
See Shakespeare, page 169a.

[4] Observe the opportunity. — *Apocrypha:
Ecclesiasticus, IV, 20*

[5] In the multitude of words there wanteth
not sin. — *Proverbs, X, 19*

[6] "How thick do you judge the planks of
our ship to be?" "Some two good inches and
upward," returned the pilot. "It seems, then,
we are within two fingers' breadth of damnation." — RABELAIS: *Works, Book IV* [1548],
Chap. 23

Epimenides was sent by his father
into the field to look for a sheep, turned
out of the road at mid-day and lay
down in a certain cave and fell asleep,
and slept there fifty-seven years; and
after that, when awake, he went on
looking for the sheep, thinking that he
had been taking a short nap. [1]

Epimenides. 2

Anaximander used to assert that the
primary cause of all things was the
Infinite, — not defining exactly whether
he meant air or water or anything else.

Anaximander. 2

Anaxagoras said to a man who was
grieving because he was dying in a
foreign land, "The descent to Hades is
the same from every place."

Anaxagoras. 6

Aristophanes turns Socrates into ridicule in his comedies, as making the
worse appear the better reason. [2]

Socrates. 5

Often when he was looking on at
auctions he would say, "How many
things there are which I do not need!"

Ibid. 10

Socrates said, "Those who want fewest things are nearest to the gods."

Ibid. 11

He said that there was one only good,
namely, knowledge; and one only evil,
namely, ignorance.

Ibid. 14

He declared that he knew nothing,
except the fact of his ignorance.

Ibid. 16

Being asked whether it was better to
marry or not, he replied, "Whichever
you do, you will repent it."

Ibid.

Aristippus being asked what were the
most necessary things for well-born
boys to learn, said, "Those things which
they will put in practice when they
become men."

Aristippus. 4

[1] The theme of IRVING's story of Rip Van
Winkle.
[2] See Milton, page 253b.

Like sending owls to Athens, as the proverb goes.[1]

Plato. 32

Time is the image of eternity.

Ibid. 41

There is a written and an unwritten law. The one by which we regulate our constitutions in our cities is the written law; that which arises from custom is the unwritten law.

Ibid. 51

Plato was continually saying to Xenocrates, "Sacrifice to the Graces."[2]

Xenocrates. 3

Of a rich man who was niggardly he said, "That man does not own his estate, but his estate owns him."

Bion. 3

Very late in life, when he was studying geometry, some one said to Lacydes, "Is it then a time for you to be learning now?" "If it is not," he replied, "when will it be?"

Lacydes. 5

The question was put to him, what hope is; and his answer was, "The dream of a waking man."

Aristotle. 11

He used to say that personal beauty was a better introduction than any letter; but others say that it was Diogenes who gave this description of it, while Aristotle called beauty "the gift of God"; that Socrates called it "a short-lived tyranny"; Theophrastus, "a silent deceit"; Theocritus, "an ivory mischief."

Ibid.

On one occasion Aristotle was asked how much educated men were superior to those uneducated: "As much," said he, "as the living are to the dead."[3]

Ibid.

It was a saying of his that education

[1] See Horace, page 40b.

[2] Let us sacrifice to the Muses. — PLUTARCH [A. D. 46–120]: *The Banquet of the Seven Wise Men* (A saying of Solon)

[3] This used to be quoted "with great warmth" by Dr. Johnson, according to Boswell in his *Life* of Dr. Johnson [1791].

was an ornament in prosperity and a refuge in adversity.

Aristotle. 11

Asked what he gained from philosophy, he answered, "To do without being commanded what others do from fear of the laws."

Ibid.

The question was once put to him, how we ought to behave to our friends; and the answer he gave was, "As we should wish our friends to behave to us."[1]

Ibid.

He used to define justice as "a virtue of the soul distributing that which each person deserved."

Ibid.

Another of his sayings was, that education was the best viaticum of old age.

Ibid.

It was a favourite expression of Theophrastus that time was the most valuable thing that a man could spend.[2]

Theophrastus. 10

Antisthenes used to say that envious people were devoured by their own disposition, just as iron is by rust.

Antisthenes. 4

When he was praised by some wicked men, he said, "I am sadly afraid that I must have done some wicked thing."[3]

Ibid.

When asked what learning was the most necessary, he said, "Not to unlearn what you have learned."

Ibid.

Diogenes would frequently praise those who were about to marry, and yet did not marry.

Diogenes. 4

"Bury me on my face," said Diogenes; and when he was asked why, he

[1] Therefore all things whatsoever ye would that men should do to you, do ye even so to them. — *Matthew, VII, 12*

[2] Nothing is so dear and precious as time. — RABELAIS: *Works, Book V* [1564], *Chap. 5*
Remember that time is money. — BENJAMIN FRANKLIN: *Advice to a Young Tradesman* [1748]

[3] See Plutarch, page 59b.

replied, "Because in a little while everything will be turned upside down."
Diogenes. 6

Plato having defined man to be a two-legged animal without feathers, Diogenes plucked a cock and brought it into the Academy, and said, "This is Plato's man." On which account this addition was made to the definition, — "With broad flat nails."
Ibid.

A man once asked Diogenes what was the proper time for supper, and he made answer, "If you are a rich man, whenever you please; and if you are a poor man, whenever you can." [1]
Ibid.

Diogenes lighted a candle in the daytime, and went round saying, "I am looking for a man." [2]
Ibid.

When asked what he would take to let a man give him a blow on the head, he said, "A helmet."
Ibid.

Once he saw a youth blushing, and addressed him, "Courage, my boy! that is the complexion of virtue." [3]
Ibid.

When asked what wine he liked to drink, he replied, "That which belongs to another."
Ibid.

When a man reproached him for going into unclean places, he said, "The sun too penetrates into privies, but is not polluted by them." [4]
Ibid.

[1] The rich when he is hungry, the poor when he has anything to eat. — RABELAIS: *Works, Book IV* [1548], *Chap. 64*

[2] Told also of Aesop.

[3] Blushing is the colour of virtue. — MATHEW HENRY [1662–1714]: *Commentaries, Jeremiah III*

[4] The spiritual virtue of a sacrament is like light: although it passes among the impure, it is not polluted. — ST. AUGUSTINE [A.D. 354–430]: *Tract on St. John, Chap. 5, 15*

The sun shineth upon the dunghill, and is not corrupted. — LYLY: *Euphues* [1579]

The sun, which passeth through pollutions and itself remains as pure as before. — BACON:

Diogenes said once to a person who was showing him a dial, "It is a very useful thing to save a man from being too late for supper."
Menedemus. 3

When Zeno was asked what a friend was, he replied, "Another I." [1]
Zeno. 19

They say that the first inclination which an animal has is to protect itself.
Ibid. 52

He calls drunkenness an expression identical with ruin. [2]
Pythagoras. 6

Among what he called his precepts were such as these: Do not stir the fire with a sword. Do not sit down on a bushel. Do not devour thy heart. [3]
Ibid. 17

In the time of Pythagoras that proverbial phrase "Ipse dixit" [4] was introduced into ordinary life.
Ibid. 25

It takes a wise man to discover a wise man.
Xenophanes. 3

Protagoras asserted that there were two sides to every question, exactly opposite to each other.
Protagoras. 3

Epicurus laid down the doctrine that pleasure was the chief good.
Epicurus. 6

LONGINUS
[*Circa* A.D. 210?–273]

Sublimity is the echo of a noble mind.
On the Sublime. Chap. IX

In the Odyssey one may liken Homer to the setting sun, of which the grandeur remains without the intensity.
Ibid.

Advancement of Learning [1605], *Book II*
Truth is as impossible to be soiled by any outward touch as the sunbeam. — MILTON: *The Doctrine and Discipline of Divorce* [1643]

[1] See Homer, page 5a.
[2] See Robert Hall, page 397b.
[3] See Plutarch, page 57b.
[4] He said it himself.

CONSTANTINE
[A. D. 288?–337]

In this sign shalt thou conquer.[1]
> EUSEBIUS: *Life of Constantine. I, 28*

ST. CHRYSOSTOM
[A. D. 327–407]

No one can harm the man who does himself no wrong.[2]
> *Letter to Olympia*

ST. JEROME [3]
[A. D. 345–420]

Avoid, as you would the plague, a clergyman who is also a man of business.
> *Letter 52, To Nepotian*

A fat paunch never breeds fine thoughts.
> *Ibid.*

The best almoner is he who keeps back nothing for himself.
> *Ibid.*

It is no fault of Christianity if a hypocrite falls into sin.
> *Letter 125, To Rusticus*

Preferring to store her money in the stomachs of the needy rather than hide it in a purse.
> *Letter 127, To Principia*

LONGUS
[FIFTH CENTURY]

There was never any yet that wholly could escape love, and never shall there be any, never so long as beauty shall be, never so long as eyes can see.
> *Daphnis and Chloe.*[4] *Proem, Chap. 2*

He is so poor that he could not keep a dog.
> *Ibid. Chap. 15*

---

[1] In hoc signo vinces. The words of Constantine's vision before his battle with Maxentius at Saxa Rubra, near Rome, A. D. 312.
[2] No one is injured save by himself. — ERASMUS [1465–1536]: *Adages*
[3] Translated by F. A. WRIGHT.
[4] The only known Greek prose romance (pastoral).

BOETHIUS
[A. D. 470?–525]

In every adversity of fortune, to have been happy is the most unhappy kind of misfortune.[1]
> *De Consolatione Philosophiae. Book II, 4, 4*

Who hath so entire happiness that he is not in some part offended with the condition of his estate?
> *Ibid. 41*

Nothing is miserable but what is thought so, and contrariwise, every estate is happy if he that bears it be content.
> *Ibid. 64*

From thee, great God, we spring, to thee we tend, —
Path, motive, guide, original and end.[2]
> *Ibid. Book III, 9, 27*

Who can give law to lovers? Love is a greater law to itself.
> *Ibid. 12, 47*

ST. BENEDICT [3]
[A. D. 480–543]

We are therefore about to establish a school of the Lord's service in which we hope to introduce nothing harsh or burdensome.
> *Rule of St. Benedict. Prologue*

ALI IBN-ABU-TALIB [4]
[602?–661]

He who has a thousand friends has not a friend to spare,

---

[1] See Dante, page 75b, and Chaucer, page 78b.
> This is truth the poet sings,
> That a sorrow's crown of sorrow is remembering happier things.
> TENNYSON: *Locksley Hall* [1842], *L. 75*
> There is no greater sorrow
> Than to be mindful of the happy time
> In misery.
> LONGFELLOW: *Inferno* [1867], *Canto V, L. 121*
[2] Translated by SAMUEL JOHNSON, and used as motto to *The Rambler, No. 7* [1750].
[3] Founder of Western monasticism.
[4] Ali ibn-abu-Talib, son-in-law of Mohammed, and fourth caliph, who was for his courage called "The Lion of God," was mur-

And he who has one enemy will meet him everywhere.[1]

CAEDMON
[*Floruit* 670]

Light was first
Through the Lord's word
Named day:
Beauteous, bright creation!
Creation.[2] The First Day

The fiend with all his comrades
Fell then from heaven above,
Through as long as three nights and days,
The angels from heaven into hell;
And them all the Lord transformed to devils,
Because they his deed and word
Would not revere.
Ibid. The Fall of the Rebel Angels

ALCUIN
[735–804]

The voice of the people is the voice of God.[3]
Letter to Charlemagne
[A. D. 800]

ABU MOHAMMED KASIM BEN ALI HARIRI
[1054–1122]

We praise Thee, O God,
For whatever perspicuity of language
Thou hast taught us
And whatever eloquence Thou hast inspired us with.
Makamat. Prayer

Guard us from error in narration,
And keep us from folly even in pleasantry,
So that we may be safe from the censure of sarcastic tongues.
Ibid.

---

dered A. D. 661. He was the author of *A Hundred Sayings*.
[1] Translated by EMERSON.
[2] From the text of BENJAMIN THORPE [1782–1870].
[3] Vox populi, vox Dei.

ARCHIPOETA
[TWELFTH CENTURY]

I have a rendezvous with death within a tavern.[1]

MOSES BEN MAIMON (MAIMONIDES)
[1135–1204]

Anticipate charity by preventing poverty; assist the reduced fellowman, either by a considerable gift, or a sum of money, or by teaching him a trade, or by putting him in the way of business, so that he may earn an honest livelihood, and not be forced to the dreadful alternative of holding out his hand for charity. This is the highest step and the summit of charity's golden ladder.
Charity's Eight Degrees

WALTER DE MAP
[1140–1210]

Die I must, but let me die drinking in an inn!
Hold the wine-cup to my lips sparkling from the bin!
So, when angels flutter down to take me from my sin,
"Ah, God have mercy on this sot," the cherubs will begin.
Quoted by J. R. GREEN, *in A Short History of the English People, Chap. 3, Sect. 1* [2]

THOMAS OF ERCILDOUN
[1220–1297]

Whate'er betide,
Haig shall be Haig of Bemersyde.
Quoted by SIR WALTER SCOTT: *Thomas the Rhymer, Part 2, Minstrelsy of the Scottish Border*

ALFONSO THE WISE
[1221–1284]

Had I been present at the creation,

---

[1] See Alan Seeger, page 947b.
[2] There is also a translation by LEIGH HUNT: "The Jovial Priest's Confession."

I would have given some useful hints for the better ordering of the universe.[1]

ST. THOMAS AQUINAS
[*Circa* 1225–1274]

Three things are necessary for the salvation of man: to know what he ought to believe; to know what he ought to desire; and to know what he ought to do.

Two Precepts of Charity [*1273*]

DANTE ALIGHIERI
[1265–1321]

In the middle of the journey of our life I came to myself in a dark wood where the straight way was lost.[2]

Divine Comedy [3] [Circa *1300*].
Inferno,[4] *Canto I, Line 1*

And as he, who with panting breath has escaped from the deep sea to the shore, turns to the dangerous water and gazes.

Ibid. Line 22

Thou art my master and my author; [5] thou alone art he from whom I took the good style that hath done me honour.

Ibid. Line 85

Leave all hope, ye that enter.[6]

Ibid. Canto III, Line 9

Here must all distrust be left; all cowardice must here be dead.

Ibid. Line 14

The wretched souls of those who lived without infamy and without praise maintain this miserable mode.[7]

Ibid. Line 34

[1] CARLYLE says, in his *History of Frederick the Great, Book II, Chap. 7*, that this saying of Alfonso about Ptolemy's astronomy, "that it seemed a crank machine; that it was pity the Creator had not taken advice," is still remembered by mankind — this and no other of his many sayings.
[2] Nel mezzo del cammin di nostra vita
　　Mi ritrovai per una selva oscura,
　　Che la diritta via era smarrita.
[3] Text from *The Temple Classics*, J. M. Dent & Sons [1900].
[4] Translated by JOHN AITKEN CARLYLE, *The Temple Classics*, unless otherwise noted.
[5] Virgil.
[6] Lasciate ogni speranza, voi ch'entrate!
[7] Translated by CHARLES ELIOT NORTON [1902].

Let us not speak of them; but look, and pass on.

Divine Comedy. Inferno,
Canto III, Line 51

These unfortunates, who never were alive.

Ibid. Line 64

Into the eternal darkness, into fire and into ice.

Ibid. Line 87

I came into a place void of all light, which bellows like the sea in tempest, when it is combated by warring winds.

Ibid. Canto V, Line 28

Love, which quickly lays hold on gentle heart, seized this one for the fair person that was taken from me, and the mode still hurts me.[1]

Ibid. Line 100

Love, which absolves no loved one from loving, seized me for the pleasing of him so strongly that, as thou seest, it does not even now abandon me.[1]

Ibid. Line 103

What sweet thoughts, what longing led them to the woeful pass.

Ibid. Line 113

There is no greater pain than to recall a happy time in wretchedness.[2]

Ibid. Line 121

That day we read in it no farther.[3]

Ibid. Line 138

Pride, Envy, and Avarice are the three sparks that have set the hearts of all on fire.

Ibid. Canto VI, Line 74

But when thou shalt be in the sweet world, I pray thee recall me to the memory of man.

Ibid. Line 88

O ye who have sound understandings, regard the doctrine that is hidden under the veil of the strange verses! [1]

Ibid. Canto IX, Line 61

Already I had fixed my look on his;

[1] Translated by CHARLES ELIOT NORTON [1902].
[2] 　　Nessun maggior dolore
　　Che ricordarsi del tempo felice
　　Nella miseria.
See Boethius, page 73b, and Chaucer, page 78b.
[3] Quel giorno più non vi leggemmo avante.

and he rose upright with breast and countenance, as if he entertained great scorn of Hell.
Divine Comedy. Inferno,
Canto X, Line 34
"If thou follow thy star, thou canst not fail of glorious haven."
Ibid. Canto XV, Line 55
So conscience chide me not, I am prepared for Fortune as she wills.
Ibid. Line 91
He listens well who notes it.
Ibid. Line 99
A fit request should be followed with the work in silence.
Ibid. Canto XXIV, Line 77
Consider your origin; ye were not formed to live like brutes, but to follow virtue and knowledge.
Ibid. Canto XXVI, Line 119
And thence we issued out, again to see the stars.[1]
Ibid. Canto XXXIV, Line 139
To run over better waters the little vessel of my genius now hoists her sails, as she leaves behind her a sea so cruel.
Ibid. Purgatorio,[2] Canto I, Line 1
He goes seeking liberty, which is so dear, as he knows who for it renounces life.
Ibid. Line 71
O conscience, upright and stainless, how bitter a sting to thee is a little fault!
Ibid. Canto III, Line 8
For to lose time is most displeasing to him who knows most.
Ibid. Line 78
The Infinite Goodness has such wide arms that it takes whatever turns to it.
Ibid. Line 121
Unless, before then, the prayer assist me which rises from a heart that lives in grace: what avails the other, which is not heard in heaven?
Ibid. Canto IV, Line 133
Stand like a firm tower that never

shakes its top for blowing of the winds.
Divine Comedy. Purgatorio,
Canto V, Line 14
[Beatrice] who shall be a light between truth and intellect.
Ibid. Canto VI, Line 45
It was now the hour that turns back desire in those that sail the sea, and softens their hearts, the day when they have said to their sweet friends farewell, and which pierces the new pilgrim with love, if he hear from afar a bell that seems to deplore the dying day.
Ibid. Canto VIII, Line 1
Give us this day the daily manna, without which, in this rough desert, he backward goes, who toils most to go on.
Ibid. Canto XI, Line 13
Worldly renown is naught but a breath of wind, which now comes this way and now comes that, and changes name because it changes quarter.
Ibid. Line 100
O human race, born to fly upward, wherefore at a little wind dost thou so fall.
Ibid. Canto XII, Line 95
To a greater force, and to a better nature, ye, free, are subject, and that creates the mind in you, which the heavens have not in their charge. Therefore if the present world go astray, the cause is in you, in you it is to be sought.
Ibid. Canto XVI, Line 79
Every one confusedly conceives of a good in which the mind may be at rest, and desires it; wherefore every one strives to attain to it.
Ibid. Canto XVII, Line 127
Love kindled by virtue always kindles another, provided that its flame appear outwardly.
Ibid. Canto XXII, Line 10
Less than a drop of blood remains in me that does not tremble; I recognize the signals of the ancient flame.[1]
Ibid. Canto XXX, Line 46
But so much the more malign and wild does the ground become with bad

---

[1] E quindi uscimmo a riveder le stelle.
[2] Translated by CHARLES ELIOT NORTON [1902].

[1]   Men che dramma
Di sangue m'è rimaso, che no tremi;
Conosco i segni dell' antica fiamma.

seed and untilled, as it has the more of good earthly vigor.
> *Divine Comedy. Purgatorio,*
> *Canto XXX, Line 118*

Pure and disposed to mount unto the stars.[1]
> *Ibid. Canto XXXIII, Line 145*

The glory of Him who moves everything penetrates through the universe, and is resplendent in one part more and in another less.
> *Ibid. Paradiso,*[2] *Canto I, Line 1*

Great flame follows a tiny spark.
> *Ibid. Line 34*

And his will is our peace.[3]
> *Ibid. Canto III, Line 85*

The greatest gift which God in His bounty bestowed in creating, and the most conformed to His own goodness, and that which He prizes the most, was the freedom of the will, with which the creatures that have intelligence, they all and they alone, were and are endowed.
> *Ibid. Canto V, Line 19*

Thou shalt make proof how the bread of others savors of salt, and how hard a path is the descending and the mounting of another's stairs.
> *Ibid. Canto XVII, Line 58*

Vanquishing me with the light of a smile, she said to me: "Turn thee, and listen, for not only in my eyes is Paradise."
> *Ibid. Canto XVIII, Line 19*

The night which hides things from us.
> *Ibid. Canto XXIII, Line 3*

The Love which moves the sun and the other stars.[4]
> *Ibid. Canto XXXIII, Line 145*

WILLIAM OF WYKEHAM
[1324–1404]

Manners makyth man.
> *Motto of his two foundations,*
> *Winchester College and New*
> *College, Oxford*

---

[1] Puro e disposto a salire alle stelle.
[2] Translated by CHARLES ELIOT NORTON [1902].
[3] E la sua volontate è nostra pace.
[4] L'amor che move il sole e l'altre stelle.

GEOFFREY CHAUCER [1]
[?1343–1400]

Hard is the herte that loveth nought
In May.
> *The Romaunt of the Rose*
> [Circa *1369*]. *Line 85*

The tyme, that may not sojourne,
But goth, and may never retourne,
As watir that doun renneth ay,
But never drope retourne may.
> *Ibid. Line 381*

As round as appil was his face.
> *Ibid. Line 819*

So that the more she yaf awey,
The more, ywis, she hadde alwey.
> *Ibid. Line 1159*

A ful gret fool is he, ywis,
That bothe riche and nygard is.
> *Ibid. Line 1171*

To rede, and drive the nyght away.
> *The Book of the Duchesse*
> [*1369*]. *Line 49*

Morpheus,
Thou knowest hym wel, the god of slep.
> *Ibid. Line 136*

I was waked
With smale foules a gret hepe,
That had affrayed me out of slepe.
> *Ibid. Line 294*

"Hyt is not al gold that glareth." [2]
> *The House of Fame* [*1374–*
> *1385*]. *Book I, Line 272*

---

[1] From the text of F. N. Robinson, *The Complete Works of Geoffrey Chaucer*, Houghton Mifflin Company [1933].

[2] Tyrwhitt says this is taken from the *Parabolae* of ALANUS DE INSULIS, who died in 1294: Non teneas aurum totum quod splendet ut aurum (Do not hold everything as gold which shines as gold).

But al thyng which that shineth as the gold Nis nat gold, as that I have herd it told.
> *The Canterbury Tales* [circa 1387],
> *The Canon's Yeoman's Tale, L. 962*

All is not golde that outward shewith bright. — LYDGATE [1370?–1451?]: *On the Mutability of Human Affairs*

Gold all is not that doth golden seem. — SPENSER: *Faerie Queene, Book II* [1590], *Canto VIII, St. 14*

All that glisters is not gold,
Often have you heard that told. —
SHAKESPEARE: *Merchant of Venice* [1596–1597], Act II, Sc. 7, L. 65

All is not gold that glisters. — CERVANTES:

Soun ys noght but eyr ybroken,
And every speche that ys spoken,
Lowd or pryvee, foul or fair,
In his substance ys but air.
> *The House of Fame. Book I,*
> *Line 765*

Venus clerk, Ovide,
That hath ysowen wonder wide
The grete god of Loves name.
> *Ibid. Book III, Line 1487*

The lyf so short, the craft so long to
lerne,[1]
Th'assay so hard, so sharp the con-
queryinge.
> *The Parliament of Fowls*
> *[1380–1386]. Line 1*

For out of olde feldes, as men seyth,
Cometh al this newe corn fro yer to
yere;
And out of olde bokes, in good feyth,
Cometh al this newe science that men
lere.
> *Ibid. Line 22*

Nature, the vicaire of the almyghty
lorde.
> *Ibid. Line 379*

"A fol can not be stille."
> *Ibid. Line 574*

Now welcome, somer, with thy sonne
softe,[2]
That hast this wintres weders overshake.
> *Ibid. Line 680*

A fool may ek a wys-man ofte gide.
> *Troilus and Criseyde* [Circa
> *1385]. Book I, Line 630*

Ek som tyme it is craft to seme fle
Fro thyng whych in effect men hunte
faste.
> *Ibid. Line 747*

Til crowes feet be growen under youre
yë.
> *Ibid. Book II, Line 403*

Don Quixote, Part II [1615], *Book III, Chap.*
33

All is not gold that glisteneth. — MIDDLE-
TON: *A Fair Quarrel* [1617], *Act V, Sc. 1*

All, as they say, that glitters is not gold. —
DRYDEN: *The Hind and the Panther* [1687],
L. 215

[1] See Hippocrates, page 22a.
[2] In a somer sesun, whan softe was the
sonne. — WILLIAM LANGLAND [1330?–1400?]:
The Vision of Piers Plowman, Prologue

Lord, this is an huge rayn!
This were a weder for to slepen inne!
> *Troilus and Criseyde. Book III,*
> *Line 656*

It is nought good a slepyng hound to
wake.[1]
> *Ibid. Line 764*

Right as an aspes leef she gan to quake.
> *Ibid. Line 1200*

For of fortunes sharpe adversitee
The worste kynde of infortune is this,
A man to han ben in prosperitee,
And it remembren, whan it passed is.[2]
> *Ibid. Line 1625*

Oon ere it herde, at tothir out it went.[3]
> *Ibid. Book IV, Line 434*

Ek wonder last but nyne nyght nevere
in towne.[4]
> *Ibid. Line 588*

But manly sette the world on six and
sevene;[5]
And if thow deye a martyr, go to
hevene!
> *Ibid. Line 622*

For tyme ylost may nought recovered
be.
> *Ibid. Line 1283*

I am right sory for youre hevynesse.
> *Ibid. Book V, Line 140*

For he that naught n'assaieth, naught
n'acheveth.
> *Ibid. Line 784*

Trewe as stiel.
> *Ibid. Line 831*

[1] See Dickens, page 579b.
[2] See Boethius, page 73b, and Dante, page
75b.
[3] Went in at the tone eare and out at
tother. — JOHN HEYWOOD: *Proverbes* [1546],
Part II, Chap. IX
[4] See Shakespeare, page 126b.
[5]   All is uneven,
And everything is left at six and seven.
    SHAKESPEARE: *Richard II* [1595–1596],
         Act II, Sc. 2, L. 120
Let things go at sixes and sevens. — CER-
VANTES: *Don Quixote, Part I* [1605], *Book
IV, Chap. 3*
Things going on at sixes and sevens. —
GOLDSMITH: *The Good-Natured Man* [1768],
Act I
    Say, why is everything
    Either at sixes or at sevens?
         W. S. GILBERT: *H.M.S. Pinafore*
         [1878], *Act II, Fair Moon*

This sodeyn Diomede.
> *Troilus and Criseyde. Book V,*
> *Line 1024*

Ye, fare wel al the snow of ferne yere! [1]
> *Ibid. Line 1176*

Ek gret effect men write in place lite;
Th' entente is al, and nat the lettres
space.
> *Ibid. Line 1629*

Go, litel bok, go, litel myn tragedye.
> *Ibid. Line 1786*

And for ther is so gret diversite
In Englissh and in writyng of oure
tonge,
So prey I God that non myswrite the,
Ne the mysmetre for defaute of tonge.
> *Ibid. Line 1793*

O moral Gower, this book I directe
To the.
> *Ibid. Line 1856*

Whan that the month of May
Is comen, and that I here the foules
synge,
And that the floures gynnen for to
spryngen,
Farewel my bok, and my devocioun!
> *The Legend of Good Women*
> [Circa *1386*]. *Line 36*

That, of al the floures in the mede,
Thanne love I most thise floures white
and rede,
Swiche as men callen daysyes in our
toun.
> *Ibid. Line 41*

Whan that Aprille with his shoures
soote
The droghte of March hath perced to
the roote.
> *The Canterbury Tales* [Circa
> *1387*]. *Prologue, Line 1*

And smale foweles maken melodye,
That slepen al the night with open yë,
(So priketh hem nature in hir corages);
Thanne longen folk to goon on pil-
grimages.
> *Ibid. Line 9*

He was a verray, parfit gentil knight.
> *Ibid. Line 72*

He was as fressh as is the month of
May.
> *Ibid. Line 92*

[1] See Villon, page 83b.

He koude songes make, and wel endyte.
> *The Canterbury Tales. Prologue,*
> *Line 95*

Ful wel she soong the service dyvyne,
Entuned in hir nose ful semely;
And Frenssh she spak ful faire and
fetisly,
After the scole of Stratford atte Bowe,
For Frenssh of Parys was to hir un-
knowe.
> *Ibid. Line 122*

His palfrey was as broun as is a berye.
> *Ibid. Line 207*

A Frere ther was, a wantowne and a
mery.
> *Ibid. Line 208*

Somwhat he lipsed, for his wantownesse,
To make his Englissh sweete upon his
tonge.
> *Ibid. Line 264*

A Clerk ther was of Oxenford also.
> *Ibid. Line 285*

For hym was levere have at his beddes
heed
Twenty bookes, clad in blak or reed,
Of Aristotle and his philosophie,
Than robes riche, or fithele, or gay
sautrie,
But al be that he was a philosophre,
Yet hadde he but litel gold in cofre.
> *Ibid. Line 293*

And gladly wolde he lerne, and gladly
teche.
> *Ibid. Line 308*

Nowher so bisy a man as he ther nas,
And yet he semed bisier than he was.
> *Ibid. Line 321*

For he was Epicurus owene sone.
> *Ibid. Line 336*

He was a good felawe.[1]
> *Ibid. Line 395*

His studie was but litel on the Bible.
> *Ibid. Line 438*

For gold in phisik is a cordial,
Therfore he lovede gold in special.
> *Ibid. Line 443*

[1] If he be not fellow with the best king,
thou shalt find him the best king of good
fellows. — SHAKESPEARE: *King Henry V*
[1598–1600], *Act V, Sc. 2, L. 259*

She was a worthy womman al hir lyve,
Housbondes at chirche dore she hadde
fyve.
> *The Canterbury Tales. Prologue,*
> *Line 459*

This noble ensample to his sheep he
yaf,
That first he wroghte, and afterward
he taughte.
> *Ibid. Line 496*

If gold ruste, what shal iren do?
> *Ibid. Line 500*

But Cristes loore, and his apostles
twelve,
He taughte, and first he folwed it hym-
selve.
> *Ibid. Line 527*

And yet he hadde a thombe of gold.[1]
> *Ibid. Line 563*

That hadde a fyr-reed cherubynnes
face.
> *Ibid. Line 624*

Wel loved he garleck, oynons, and eek
lekes,
And for to drynken strong wyn, reed as
blood.
> *Ibid. Line 634*

And whan that he wel dronken hadde
the wyn,
Than wolde he speke no word but
Latyn.
> *Ibid. Line 637*

Whoso shal telle a tale after a man,
He moot reherce as ny as evere he kan
Everich a word, if it be in his charge,
Al speke he never so rudeliche and
large,
Or ellis he moot telle his tale untrewe,
Or feyne thing, or finde wordes new.
> *Ibid. Line 731*

For May wol have no slogardye a-night.
The sesoun priketh every gentil herte,
And maketh him out of his sleep to
sterte.
> *Ibid. The Knight's Tale, Line 1042*

Ech man for hymself.
> *Ibid. Line 1182*

The bisy larke, messager of day.
> *Ibid. Line 1491*

[1] In allusion to the proverb, "Every honest
miller has a golden thumb."

May, with alle thy floures and thy
grene,
Welcome be thou, faire, fresshe May.
> *The Canterbury Tales. The*
> *Knight's Tale, Line 1510*

That "feeld hath eyen, and the wode
hath eres".[1]
> *Ibid. Line 1522*

Now up, now doun, as boket in a welle.
> *Ibid. Line 1533*

For pitee renneth soone in gentil herte.
> *Ibid. Line 1761*

Cupido,
Upon his shuldres wynges hadde he
two;
And blynd he was, as it is often seene;
A bowe he bar and arwes brighte and
kene.
> *Ibid. Line 1963*

Up roos the sonne, and up roose Emelye.
> *Ibid. Line 2273*

Myn be the travaille, and thyn be the
glorie!
> *Ibid. Line 2406*

And was al his chiere, as in his herte.
> *Ibid. Line 2683*

What is this world? what asketh men
to have?
Now with his love, now in his colde
grave
Allone, withouten any compaignye.
> *Ibid. Line 2777*

This world nys but a thurghfare ful of
wo,
And we been pilgrymes, passing to and
fro.
Deeth is an ende of every worldly soore.
> *Ibid. Line 2847*

Jhesu Crist, and seiynte Benedight,
Blesse this hous from every wikked
wight.
> *Ibid. The Miller's Tale, Line 3483*

[1] Fieldes have eies and woodes have eares.
— JOHN HEYWOOD: *Proverbes* [1546], *Part
II, Chap. V*
  Wode has erys, felde has sigt. — *King Ed-
ward and the Shepherd, MS.* [*circa* 1300]
  Walls have ears. — CERVANTES: *Don Quix-
ote, Part II* [1615], *Chap. 48*
  Woods have tongues
  As walls have ears.
TENNYSON: *Idylls of the King, Balin*
  and Balan [1885], *L. 522*

And broghte of myghty ale a large quart.

The Canterbury Tales. The Miller's Tale, Line 3497

Yet in our asshen olde is fyr yreke.[1]

Ibid. The Reeve's Prologue, Line 3882

The gretteste clerkes been noght the wisest men.[2]

Ibid. The Reeve's Tale, Line 4054

Thurgh thikke and thurgh thenne.[3]

Ibid. Line 4066

So was hir joly whistle wel ywet.

Ibid. Line 4155

At Cristemasse merie may ye daunce.

Ibid. The Man of Law's Prologue, Line 126

She is mirour of alle curteisye.[4]

Ibid. The Man of Law's Tale, Line 166

For in the sterres, clerer than is glas,
Is writen, God woot, whoso koude it rede,
The deeth of every man.

Ibid. Line 194

Sathan, that evere us waiteth to bigile.

Ibid. Line 582

In his owene grece I made hym frye.[5]

Ibid. The Wife of Bath's Prologue, Line 487

What thyng we may nat lightly have,
Therafter wol we crie alday and crave.

Ibid. Line 517

Greet prees at market maketh deere ware,

---

[1] E'en in our ashes live their wonted fires. — THOMAS GRAY: *Elegy in a Country Churchyard* [1750], *St. 23*

[2] The greatest Clerkes be not the wisest men. — JOHN HEYWOOD: *Proverbes* [1546], *Part II, Chap. V*

[3] Through thicke and thin. — DU BARTAS: *Divine Weeks and Works* [1578], *Second Week, Fourth Day*

[4] 　　Call him bounteous Buckingham, The mirror of all courtesy. SHAKESPEARE: *Henry VIII* [1613], *Act II, Sc. 1, L. 53*

[5] Frieth in her own grease. — JOHN HEYWOOD: *Proverbes* [1546], *Part I, Chap. XI*
The best way were to entertain him with hope, till the wicked fire of lust have melted him in his own grease. — SHAKESPEARE: *Merry Wives of Windsor* [1601], *Act II, Sc. 1, L. 60*

And to greet cheep is holde at litel prys.

The Canterbury Tales. The Wife of Bath's Prologue, Line 522

But yet I hadde alwey a coltes tooth.
Gat-toothed I was, and that bicam me weel.

Ibid. Line 601

"My lige lady, generally," quod he,
"Wommen desiren have sovereynetee
As well over hir housbond as hir love."

Ibid. The Wife of Bath's Tale, Line 1037

Looke who that is moost vertuous alway,
Pryvee and apert, and most entendeth ay
To do the gentil dedes that he kan;
Taak hym for the grettest gentil man.

Ibid. Line 1113

That he is gentil that dooth gentil dedis.[1]

Ibid. Line 1170

The lady of the hous ay stille sat.

Ibid. The Summoner's Tale, Line 2200

For though we slepe or wake, or rome, or ryde,
Ay fleeth the tyme, it nyl no man abyde.

Ibid. The Clerk's Tale, Line 118

Love is noght oold as whan that it is newe.

Ibid. Line 857

This flour of wyfly pacience.

Ibid. Line 919

No wedded man so hardy be t'assaille
His wyves pacience, in trust to fynde
Grisildis, for in certein he shal faille!

Ibid. Line 1180

It is no childes pley
To take a wyf withoute avysement.

Ibid. The Merchant's Tale, Line 1530

Love is blynd.[2]

Ibid. Line 1598

My wit is thynne.

Ibid. Line 1682

---

[1] Handsome is that handsome does. — GOLDSMITH: *The Vicar of Wakefield* [1766], *Chap. 1*

[2] See Shakespeare, page 144b.

Ther nys no werkman, whatsoevere he
be,
That may bothe werke wel and hast-
ily;[1]
This wol be doon at leyser parfitly.[2]
    The Canterbury Tales. The
       Merchant's Tale, Line 1832
The Pegasee,
The hors that hadde winges for to flee.
    Ibid. The Squire's Tale, Line 207
Therfore bihoveth hire a ful long spoon
That shal ete with a feend.[3]
       Ibid. Line 602
Men loven of propre kynde new fangel-
nesse.
       Ibid. Line 610
I am lorn with-outen remedye.
       Ibid. Line 629
Fy on possessioun
But-if a man be vertuous with-al.
       Ibid. Line 686
Pacience is an heigh vertu, certeyn.
    Ibid. The Franklin's Tale,
       Line 773
Servant in love, and lord in mariage.
       Ibid. Line 793
Taak this for fynal answere as of me.
       Ibid. Line 987
It is agayns the proces of nature.
       Ibid. Line 1345
Trouthe is the hyeste thyng that men
may kepe.
       Ibid. Line 1479
For dronkenesse is verray sepulture
Of mannes wit and his discrecioun.
    Ibid. The Pardoner's Tale,
       Line 558
Mordre wol out, certeyn, it wol nat
faille.[4]
    Ibid. The Prioress's Tale, Line 1776

[1] See John Heywood, page 90b, and Publilius Syrus, page 45a.
[2] Ease and speed in doing a thing do not
give the work lasting solidity or exactness of
beauty. — PLUTARCH [A.D. 46–120]: *Life of
Pericles*
[3] Hee must have a long spoon, shall eat
with the devill. — JOHN HEYWOOD: *Proverbs*
[1546], *Part II, Chap. V*
He must have a long spoon that must eat
with the devil. — SHAKESPEARE: *Comedy of
Errors* [1592–1593], *Act IV, Sc. 3, L. 64*
[4] Also in *The Nun's Priest's Tale, Lines
4242 and 4247.*

This may wel be rym dogerel.
    *The Canterbury Tales. Chaucer's
       Tale of Sir Thopas, Line 2115*
Ful wys is he that kan hymselven
knowe![1]
    Ibid. The Monk's Tale, Line 3329
He was of knyghthod and of fredom
flour.
       Ibid. Line 3832
For whan a man hath over-greet a wit,
Ful oft hym happeth to mysusen it.
    Ibid. The Canon Yeoman's Prologue,
       Line 648
The firste vertu, sone, if thou wolt leere,
Is to restreyne and kepe wel thy tonge.
    Ibid. The Manciple's Tale, Line 332
Thing that is seyd, is seyd; and forth
it gooth.
       Ibid. Line 355
For the proverbe seith that "manye
smale maken a greet."[2]
    Ibid. The Parson's Tale, Line 361
Reule wel thyself, that other folk canst
rede.
    Truth [Circa *1390*]. *Line 6*
And trouthe thee shal delivere, it is no
drede.
       Ibid. Line 7
The wrastling for this world axeth a fal.
       Ibid. Line 16

How easily murder is discovered! —
SHAKESPEARE: *Titus Andronicus* [1593–1594],
Act II, Sc. 3, L. 28
Truth will come to light; murder cannot be
hid long. — SHAKESPEARE: *Merchant of Venice*
[1596–1597], *Act II, Sc. 2, L. 86*
Murder, though it have no tongue, will speak
With most miraculous organ.
    SHAKESPEARE: *Hamlet* [1600–1601],
       Act II, Sc. 2, L. 630
Murder will out. — CERVANTES: *Don Quix-
ote, Part I* [1605], *Book III, Chap. 8*
Carcasses bleed at the sight of the mur-
derer. — ROBERT BURTON: *Anatomy of Mel-
ancholy* [1621–1651], *Part I, Sect. 1, Memb.
2, Subsect. 5*
Other sins only speak; murder shrieks out.
— JOHN WEBSTER: *Duchess of Malfi* [1623],
Act IV, Sc. 2
[1] See Plutarch, page 60a.
[2] Many small make a great. — JOHN HEY-
WOOD: *Proverbes* [1546], *Part I, Chap. XI*

JOHN WYCLIFFE
[? -1384]

I believe that in the end the truth will conquer.

To the Duke of Lancaster [1381]
(Quoted by J. R. GREEN: *A*
Short History of the English
People. Chap. 5)

THOMAS À KEMPIS
[1380–1471]

Be not angry that you cannot make others as you wish them to be, since you cannot make yourself as you wish to be.
Imitation of Christ [Circa 1420].
Book I, Chap. 16

Man proposes, but God disposes.[1]
Ibid. Chap. 19

What canst thou see elsewhere which thou canst not see here? Behold the heaven and the earth and all the elements; for of these are all things created.
Ibid. Chap. 20

It is easier not to speak a word at all than to speak more words than we should.
Ibid.

No man ruleth safely but he that is willingly ruled.
Ibid.

And when he is out of sight, quickly also is he out of mind.[2]
Ibid. Chap. 23

[1] This expression appears earlier in the *Chronicle of Battel Abbey*, P. 27 (Lower's translation), and in *The Vision of Piers Plowman*, L. 13994, ed. 1550.
Man appoints, and God disappoints. — CERVANTES: *Don Quixote, Part II* [1615], *Book IV, Chap. 55*
A man's heart deviseth his way; but the Lord directeth his steps. — *Proverbs, XVI, 9*
[2] Out of syght, out of mynd. — GOOGE: *Eglogs* [1563]
And out of mind as soon as out of sight. — FULKE GREVILLE [1554–1628]: *Sonnet LVI*
Fer from eze, fer from herte,
Quoth Hendyng.
HENDYNG: *Proverbs, MS.* [circa 1320]
I do perceive that the old proverbis be not alwaies trew, for I do finde that the absence of my Nath. doth breede in me the more continuall remembrance of him. — LADY ANN BACON, *Letter to Lady Jane Cornwallis* [1613]

Love is swift, sincere, pious, pleasant, gentle, strong, patient, faithful, prudent, long-suffering, manly and never seeking her own; for wheresoever a man seeketh his own, there he falleth from love.
Imitation of Christ. Book III,
Chap. 5

JOHN FORTESCUE
[*Circa* 1395–1476]

Moche Crye and no Wull.[1]
De Laudibus Legum Angliae
[1471]. Chap. 10

Comparisons are odious.[2]
Ibid. Chap. 19

HENRY VI
[1421–1471]

Kingdoms are but cares,
State is devoid of stay;
Riches are ready snares,
And hasten to decay.
From SIR JOHN HARINGTON'S
Nugae Antiquae [*Published*
1769]

FRANÇOIS VILLON
[1430–1484]

Where are the snows of yester-year?[3]
The Greater Testament.[4] *Ballad*
of Old-Time Ladies

All must come to the self-same bay;
Sons and servants, their days are told:
The wind carries their like away.
Ibid. Ballad of Old-Time Lords,
No. 2

[1] A great cry, but little wool. — CERVANTES: *Don Quixote, Part II* [1615], *Book III, Chap. 13*
All cry and no wool. — SAMUEL BUTLER: *Hudibras, Part I* [1663], *Canto I, L. 852*
[2] This was a well-known phrase in the 14th century, and has been repeated by many, including Lydgate, Shakespeare, and Swift.
[3] Où sont les neiges d'antan?
Alas for lovers! Pair by pair
The Wind has blown them all away;
The young and yare, the fond and fair;
Where are the Snows of Yesterday?
JUSTIN H. McCARTHY [1861–1936]:
A Ballad of Dead Ladies: After Villon, Envoy
[4] Translated by DANTE GABRIEL ROSSETTI [1828–1882].

Blonde or brunette, this rhyme applies,
Happy is he who knows them not.
> *The Greater Testament. Double*
> *Ballad to the Like Purport*

O Virgin clean,
To whom all sinners lift their hands on
　high,
Made whole in faith through Thee their
　go-between.
In this belief I will to live and die.
> *Ibid. Ballad of Homage to Our*
> *Lady*

There's no right speech out of Paris
town.
> *Ibid. Ballad of the Women of*
> *Paris*

If you have money, it doth not stay,
But this way and that it wastes amain:
What does it profit you, anyway?
Ill-gotten good is nobody's gain.
> *Ibid. Seemly Lesson to the Good-*
> *for-Noughts*

I know all save myself alone.
> *Ballad of Things Known and*
> *Unknown*

For he deserves not any fortune fair
Who would wish ill unto the realm of
　France.
> *Ballad Against Those Who Missay*
> *of France*

These traitorous thieves, accursèd and
　unfair,
The vintners that put water in our wine.
> *A Merry Ballad of Vintners*

In the amorous war
The wealthy gallant always gains the
　day.
> *Ballad of Ladies' Love, No. 1*

ALDUS (MANUTIUS)
[1450–1515]

Talk of nothing but business, and
despatch that business quickly.
> *Placard on the door of the Aldine*
> *Press, Venice, established about*
> *1490* [1]

[1] Quoted by Thomas Frognall Dibdin
[1776–1847] in *Introduction to the Knowledge of Rare and Valuable Editions of the
Greek and Latin Classics* [1802], *Vol. I, P. 436.*

LEONARDO DA VINCI
[1452–1519]

Whoever in discussion adduces authority uses not intellect but memory.
> *Note-Books* [1]

No counsel is more trustworthy than
that which is given upon ships that are
in peril.
> *Ibid.*

Intellectual passion drives out sensu-
ality.
> *Ibid.*

Let the street be as wide as the height
of the houses.
> *Ibid.*

No member needs so great a number
of muscles as the tongue; this exceeds
all the rest in the number of its movements.
> *Ibid.*

It is of no small benefit on finding
oneself in bed in the dark to go over
again in the imagination the main outlines of the forms previously studied, or
of other noteworthy things conceived
by ingenious speculation.
> *Ibid.*

As a well-spent day brings happy
sleep, so life well used brings happy
death.
> *Ibid.*

JOHN SKELTON
[Circa 1460–1529]

I saye, thou madde March hare.[2]
> *Replycation Against Certayne*
> *Yong Scolers*

There is nothynge that more dyspleaseth God,
Than from theyr children to spare the
　rod.[3]
> *Magnyfycence. Line 1954*
> *[Circa 1525]*

[1] Translated by Edward McCurdy.
[2] Mad as a March hare. — John Heywood:
Proverbes [1546], *Part II, Chap. V*
[3] He that spareth his rod hateth his son. —
Proverbs, XIII, 24
Spare the rod and spoil the child. — *English proverb, borrowed from the Latin and
traced to* circa a. d. 1000
They spare the rod and spoyl the child. —

He ruleth all the roste.[1]
Why Come Ye Not to Courte.
Line 198

By hoke ne by croke.[2]
Colyn Cloute [Circa *1519*].
Line 1240

The wolfe from the dore.
Ibid. Line 1531

Old proverbe says,
That byrd ys not honest
That fyleth hys owne nest.[3]
Poems against Garnesche

Maide, wydowe, or wyffe.
Philip Sparrow

DESIDERIUS ERASMUS
[1465–1536]

I know how busy you are in your library, which is your Paradise.[4]
Letter to Bishop Fisher [*1524*]

NICOLÒ MACHIAVELLI [5]
[1469–1527]

There is nothing more difficult to take in hand, more perilous to conduct, or more uncertain in its success, than to

---

RALPH VENNING: *Mysteries and Revelations* [1649]
[1] Rule the rost. — JOHN HEYWOOD: *Proverbes* [1546], *Part I, Chap. V*
Her that ruled the rost. — THOMAS HEYWOOD: *History of Women* [ed. 1624]
Rules the roast. — JONSON, CHAPMAN, MARSTON: *Eastward Ho* [1605], *Act II, Sc. 1*
[2] By hooke or crooke. — JOHN HEYWOOD: *Proverbes* [1546], *Part I, Chap. XI*
The phrase has been said to derive from the custom of some manors where tenants were authorized to take firebote *by hook or by crook;* that is, so much of the underwood as may be cut with a crook, and so much of the loose timber as may be collected from the boughs by means of a hook. One of the earliest citations of this proverb occurs in John Wycliffe's *Controversial Tracts* [*circa* 1370].
[3] It is a foule byrd that fyleth his owne nest. — JOHN HEYWOOD: *Proverbes* [1546], *Part II, Chap. V*
[4] Nec me fugit quam assiduus sis in bibliotheca, quae tibi Paradisi loco est. — P. S. ALLEN: *Selections from Erasmus, P. 128*
[5] Every Country hath its Machiavel. — SIR THOMAS BROWNE: *Religio Medici* [1642] (Everyman ed.), *P. 24*

take the lead in the introduction of a new order of things.
The Prince.[1] *Chap. 6*

The chief foundations of all states, new as well as old or composite, are good laws and good arms; and as there cannot be good laws where the state is not well armed, it follows that where they are well armed they have good laws.
Ibid. Chap. 12

A prince should therefore have no other aim or thought, nor take up any other thing for his study, but war and its organisation and discipline, for that is the only art that is necessary to one who commands.
Ibid. Chap. 14

Among other evils which being unarmed brings you, it causes you to be despised.
Ibid.

When neither their property nor their honour is touched, the majority of men live content.
Ibid. Chap. 19

There are three classes of intellects: one which comprehends by itself; another which appreciates what others comprehend; and a third which neither comprehends by itself nor by the showing of others; the first is the most excellent, the second is good, the third is useless.
Ibid. Chap. 22

Where the willingness is great, the difficulties cannot be great.
Ibid. Chap. 26

God is not willing to do everything, and thus take away our free will and that share of glory which belongs to us.
Ibid.

MICHELANGELO
[1474–1564]

The more the marble wastes, the more the statue grows.
Sonnet

If it be true that any beautiful thing

[1] Translated by W. K. MARRIOTT.

raises the pure and just desire of man from earth to God, the eternal fount of all, such I believe my love.

Sonnet

The power of one fair face makes my love sublime, for it has weaned my heart from low desires.

Sonnet

I live and love in God's peculiar light.

Ibid.

SIR THOMAS MORE [1]
[1478–1535]

They wonder much to hear that gold, which in itself is so useless a thing, should be everywhere so much esteemed, that even men for whom it was made, and by whom it has its value, should yet be thought of less value than it is.

Utopia [1516]. Of Jewels and Wealth

They have no lawyers among them, for they consider them as a sort of people whose profession it is to disguise matters.

Ibid. Of Law and Magistrates

Plato by a goodly similitude declareth, why wise men refrain to meddle in the commonwealth. For when they see the people swarm into the streets, and daily wet to the skin with rain, and yet can not persuade them to go out of the rain, they do keep themselves within their houses, seeing they cannot remedy the folly of the people.[2]

Ibid. Concerning the Best State of a Commonwealth

For men use, if they have an evil turn, to write it in marble: and whoso doth us a good turn we write it in dust.[3]

Richard III and his Miserable End [1543]

---

[1] Canonized by Pope Pius XI [1935].

[2] In the modern phrase, "not sense enough to come in out of the rain."

[3] Words writ in waters. — GEORGE CHAPMAN [1559?–1634?]: *Revenge for Honour, Act V, Sc. 2*

See Shakespeare, page 212a.

L'injure se grave en métal; et le bienfait

Assist me up, and in coming down I will shift for myself.

Said at the scaffold, on the way to execution

Wait till I put aside my beard, for that never committed treason.

To the headsman on the scaffold

MARTIN LUTHER
[1483–1546]

A mighty fortress is our God,
A bulwark never failing;
Our helper He amid the flood
Of mortal ills prevailing.[1]

Psalm, Ein' Feste Burg [2]

Tell your master that if there were as many devils at Worms as tiles on its roofs, I would enter.[3]

On approaching Worms

It is neither safe nor prudent to do aught against conscience. Here I stand —I cannot do otherwise. God help me. Amen.

Speech at the Diet of Worms

For where God built a church, there the Devil would also build a chapel.[4]

Table Talk. 67

---

s'escrit en l'onde. (An injury is engraved in metal, but a benefit is written in water.) — JEAN BERTAUT [*circa* 1611]

All your better deeds shall be in water writ, but this in marble. — BEAUMONT AND FLETCHER: *Philaster* [1620], *Act V, Sc. 3*

Here lies one whose name was writ in water. — *Keats's own Epitaph* [1821]

[1] Great God! there is no safety here below;
Thou art my fortress, thou that seem'st my foe.

FRANCIS QUARLES [1592–1644]:
Divine Poems

[2] Translated by FREDERIC H. HEDGE.

[3] On the 16th of April, 1521, Luther entered the imperial city [of Worms]. . . . On his approach . . . the Elector's chancellor entreated him, in the name of his master, not to enter a town where his death was decided. The answer which Luther returned was simply this. — BARON VON BUNSEN [1791–1860]: *Life of Luther*

[4] Where God hath a temple, the Devil will have a chapel. — ROBERT BURTON: *Anatomy of Melancholy* [1621–1651], *Part III, Sect. 4, Memb. 1, Subsect. 1*

No sooner is a temple built to God but the Devil builds a chapel hard by. — GEORGE HERBERT: *Jacula Prudentum* [1640]

A faithful and good servant is a real godsend; but truly 'tis a rare bird in the land.

Table Talk. 156

It makes a difference whose ox is gored.[1]

Works [1854 edition]. Vol. 62, Page 449

HUGH LATIMER
[1485–1555]

Play the man, Master Ridley; we shall this day light such a candle, by God's grace, in England, as I trust shall never be put out.[2]

Addressed to Nicholas Ridley [1500–1555] as they were being burned alive at Oxford, for heresy, October 16, 1555.[3] (Quoted by J. R. GREEN: A Short History of the English People, Chap. 7)

SIR DAVID LYNDSAY
[1490–1555]

They gave me first ane thing they call *citandum;*
Within aucht days I gat but *libellandum;*
Within ane month I gat *ad opponendum;*
In ane half year I gat *inter loquendum;*
An syne I gat — how call ye it? — *ad replicandum;*
But, I could never ane word yet understand him.

The Exactions and Delay of the Law

But or they came half gate to *concludendum,*

The fient a plack was left for to defend him.

The Exactions and Delay of the Law

Thus they postponed me twa year, with their train,
Syne, *hodie ad octo,* bade me come again.

Ibid.

Of *pronunciandum* they made me wonder fain;
But I gat ne'er my gude grey meir again.

Ibid.

ST. IGNATIUS LOYOLA [1]
[1491–1556]

Teach us, good Lord, to serve Thee as Thou deservest:
To give and not to count the cost;
To fight and not to heed the wounds;
To toil and not to seek for rest;
To labour and not ask for any reward
Save that of knowing that we do Thy will.

Prayer for Generosity [1548]

FRANCIS I OF FRANCE
[1494–1547]

All is lost save honour.[2]

Letter to his Mother [1525]

FRANÇOIS RABELAIS
[1495–1553]

I am going to seek a great perhaps.[3]

PETER ANTHONY MOTTEUX: *Life of Rabelais*

Let down the curtain: the farce is done.

Ibid.

---

[1] This is the moral of the fable of the lawyer, the farmer, and the farmer's ox, which was included in NOAH WEBSTER'S *American Spelling Book* [1802], entitled *The Partial Judge.*

[2] I shall light a candle of understanding in thine heart, which shall not be put out. — *2 Esdras, XIV, 25*

[3] See Latimer and Ridley in the might
Of Faith stand coupled for a common flight!
WORDSWORTH [1770–1850]: *Ecclesiastical Sonnets, Part II, XXXIV, Latimer and Ridley*

[1] Founder of the Society of Jesus.

[2] Tout est perdu fors l'honneur. The actual words written after his defeat at Pavia, 1525, were "De toutes choses ne m'est demeuré que l'honneur et la vie qui est saulvé." The letter is in DULAURE, *Histoire Civile, Physique et Morale de Paris* [1821–1825].

All gone but faith in God. — BISHOP JOHN McKIM [1852–1936]: Cabled message to the New York headquarters of the Episcopal Church after the destruction of the mission by the Japanese earthquake [1923].

[3] Je m'en vay chercher un grand Peut-estre. This and the next utterance are attributed to Rabelais on his deathbed.

He left a paper sealed up, wherein were found three articles as his last will: "I owe much; I have nothing; I give the rest to the poor."

PETER ANTHONY MOTTEUX: *Life of Rabelais*

One inch of joy surmounts of grief a span,
Because to laugh is proper to the man.
Works. To the Readers

To return to our wethers.[1]
Ibid. Book I [1532], Chap. 1

One falls to the ground in trying to sit on two stools.[2]
Ibid. Chap. 2

I drink no more than a sponge.
Ibid. Chap. 5

Appetite comes with eating, says Angeston.[3]
Ibid. Chap. 5

Thought the moon was made of green cheese.[4]
Ibid. Chap. 11

He always looked a given horse in the mouth.[5]
Ibid.

[1] Revenons à nos moutons. — A proverb taken from the farce *L'Avocat Pierre Patelin*, by BLANCHET [1459–1519]

[2] Between two stools one sits on the ground. — *Les Proverbes del Vilain*, MS. Bodleian [*circa* 1303]
While betweene two stooles my taile goe to the ground. — JOHN HEYWOOD: *Proverbes* [1546] *Part I, Chap. II*

[3] My appetite comes to me while eating. — MONTAIGNE: *Essays* [1580–1595], *Book III, Chap. 9, Of Vanity*

[4] The moone is made of a greene cheese. — JOHN HEYWOOD: *Proverbes* [1546], *Part II, Chap. VII*

[5] No man ought to looke a given horse in the mouth. — JOHN HEYWOOD: *Proverbes* [1546], *Part I, Chap. 5*
A gift-horse should not be looked in the mouth. — CERVANTES: *Don Quixote, Part II* [1615], *Book IV, Chap. 62*
He ne'er consider'd it, as loth
To look a gift-horse in the mouth.
SAMUEL BUTLER: *Hudibras, Part I,* [1663], *Canto I, L. 489*
This proverb occurs in *Vulgaria Stambrigi* [*circa* 1510]. Archbishop Trench says the proverb is certainly as old as Jerome of the fourth century, who, when some found fault with certain writings of his, replied that they were free-will offerings, and that it did not behove to look a gift horse in the mouth.

By robbing Peter he paid Paul,[1]
. . . and hoped to catch larks if ever the heavens should fall.[2]
Works. Book I, Chap. 11

You do not speak gospel.[3]
Ibid. Chap. 13

He laid him squat as a flounder.
Ibid. Chap. 27

Send them home as merry as crickets.
Ibid. Chap. 29

War begun without good provision of money beforehand for going through with it is but as a breathing of strength and blast that will quickly pass away. Coin is the sinews of war.[4]
Ibid. Chap. 46

How shall I be able to rule over others, that have not full power and command of myself?[5]
Ibid. Chap. 52

Subject to a kind of disease, which at that time they called lack of money.[6]
Ibid. Book II [1534], Chap. 16

He did not care a button for it.
Ibid.

How well I feathered my nest.[7]
Ibid. Chap. 17

[1] To robbe Peter and pay Poule. — JOHN HEYWOOD: *Proverbes* [1546], *Part I, Chap. XI*
Rob Peter, and pay Paul. — ROBERT BURTON: *Anatomy of Melancholy* [1621–1651], *Democritus to the Reader*
Give not Saint Peter so much, to leave Saint Paul nothing. — GEORGE HERBERT: *Jacula Prudentum* [1640]
To rob Peter and pay Paul is said to have had its origin when, in the reign of Edward VI, the lands of St. Peter at Westminster were appropriated to raise money for the repair of St. Paul's in London. Also found in Wycliffe's *Works, Vol. III, P. 174.*

[2] When the skie falth we shall have Larkes. — JOHN HEYWOOD: *Proverbes* [1546], *Part I, Chap. IV*

[3] All is not Gospell that thou doest speake. — JOHN HEYWOOD: *Proverbes* [1546], *Part II, Chap. II*

[4] See Aeschines, page 26a.

[5] See Thomas à Kempis, page 83a.

[6] See Shakespeare, page 152b.
Or that eternal want of pence,
Which vexes public men.
TENNYSON: *Will Waterproof's Lyrical Monologue* [1842], *St. 6*

[7] Mr. Coventry had already feathered his nest. — PEPYS: *Diary*, June 7, 1662

So much is a man worth as he esteems himself.

Works. Book II, Chap. 29

A good crier of green sauce.

Ibid. Chap. 31

Then I began to think that it is very true which is commonly said, that the one half of the world knoweth not how the other half liveth.

Ibid. Chap. 32

This flea which I have in mine ear.

Ibid. Book III [1545], Chap. 31

You have there hit the nail on the head.[1]

Ibid. Chap. 34

Above the pitch, out of tune, and off the hinges.

Ibid. Book IV [1548], Chap. 19

I'll go his halves.

Ibid. Chap. 23

The Devil was sick, — the Devil a monk would be;
The Devil was well, — the Devil a monk was he.

Ibid. Chap. 24

Do not believe what I tell you here any more than if it were some tale of a tub.[2]

Ibid. Chap. 38

Which was performed to a T.[3]

Ibid. Chap. 41

He that has patience may compass anything.

Ibid. Chap. 48

We will take the good will for the deed.[4]

Ibid. Chap. 49

[1] This hitteth the naile on the hed. — JOHN HEYWOOD: *Proverbes* [1546], *Part II, Chap. XI*

[2] The title of JONATHAN SWIFT's satire.

[3] We could manage this matter to a T. — STERNE: *Tristram Shandy, Book II* [1760], *Chap. 5*

You see they'd have fitted him to a T. — SAMUEL JOHNSON: *Boswell's Life* [1791]

You will find it shall echo my speech to a T. — THOMAS MOORE [1779–1852]: *Occasional Address for the Opening of the New Theatre of St. Stephen*

[4] The will for deed I doe accept. — DU BARTAS: *Divine Weeks and Works* [1578], *Second Week, Third Day, Part 2*

You must take the will for the deed. —

You are Christians of the best edition, all picked and culled.

Works. Book IV, Chap. 50

Would you damn your precious soul?

Ibid. Chap. 54

I perfectly feel even at my finger's end.

Ibid.

Let us fly and save our bacon.

Ibid. Chap. 55

Needs must when the Devil drives.[1]

Ibid. Chap. 57

Scampering as if the Devil drove them.

Ibid. Chap. 62

He freshly and cheerfully asked him how a man should kill time.

Ibid.

Whose cockloft is unfurnished.[2]

Ibid. Book V [1552], Author's Prologue

Speak the truth and shame the Devil.[3]

Ibid.

SWIFT: *Polite Conversation* [1738], *Dialogue II*

[1] He must needes goe whom the devill doth drive. — JOHN HEYWOOD: *Proverbes* [1546], *Part II, Chap. VII*

[2] Tall men are like houses of four stories, wherein commonly the uppermost room is worst furnished. — JAMES HOWELL (quoted): *Letter I, Book I, Sect. II* [1621]

Nature did never put her precious jewels into a garret four stories high, and therefore exceeding tall men had ever very empty heads. — FRANCIS BACON: *Apothegms* [1624], *No. 17*

Often the cockloft is empty in those whom Nature hath built many stories high. — THOMAS FULLER [1608–1661]: *Andronicus, Sect. VI, Par. 18, 1*

Such as take lodgings in a head
That's to be let unfurnished.
     SAMUEL BUTLER: *Hudibras, Part I* [1663], *Canto I, L. 161*

[3] While you live, tell truth and shame the devil! — SHAKESPEARE: *King Henry IV, Part I* [1597–1598], *Act III, Sc. 1, Line 58* —

I'd tell the truth, and shame the devil. — SAMUEL JOHNSON: *Boswell's Life* [1791] (Everyman Edition), *Vol. I, P. 460*

Truth being truth,
Tell it and shame the devil.
     BROWNING: *The Ring and the Book* [1868–1869], *III, The Other Half-Rome*

Plain as a nose in a man's face.[1]
Works. Book V, Author's Prologue
Like hearts of oak.[2]
Ibid.
You shall never want rope enough.
Ibid.
Looking as like . . . as one pea does like another.[3]
Ibid. Chap. 2
And thereby hangs a tale.
Ibid. Chap. 4
It is meat, drink, and cloth to us.
Ibid. Chap. 7
And so on to the end of the chapter.
Ibid. Chap. 10
What is got over the Devil's back is spent under the belly.[4]
Ibid. Chap. 11
We have here other fish to fry.[5]
Ibid. Chap. 12
What cannot be cured must be endured.
Ibid. Chap. 15
Thought I to myself, we shall never come off scot-free.
Ibid.
It is enough to fright you out of your seven senses.[6]
Ibid.

---

[1] See Shakespeare, page 132a.
As clear and as manifest as the nose in a man's face. — ROBERT BURTON: *Anatomy of Melancholy* [1621–1651], *Part III, Sect. 3, Memb. 4, Subsect. 1*
[2] See Garrick, page 347a.
[3] As lyke as one pease is to another. — LYLY: *Euphues* [1579]
　　　　They say we are
　　Almost as like as eggs.
　　　SHAKESPEARE: *The Winter's Tale* [1608–1611], *Act I, Sc. 2, L. 130*
As one egg is like another. — CERVANTES: *Don Quixote, Part II* [1615], *Book III, Chap. 14*
[4] Isocrates was in the right to insinuate that what is got over the Devil's back is spent under his belly. — LE SAGE: *Gil Blas* [1715–1735], *Book 8, Chap. 9*
[5] This is no time for me to mind niceties, and spelling of letters. I have other fish to fry. — CERVANTES: *Don Quixote, Part II* [1615], *Chap. 35*
[6] Huzza'd out of my seven senses. — ADDISON: *The Spectator*, November 5, 1714
Scared out of his seven senses. — SIR

Panurge had no sooner heard this, but he was upon the high-rope.
Works. Book V, Chap. 18
We saw a knot of others, about a baker's dozen.
Ibid. Chap. 23
I believe he would make three bites of a cherry.
Ibid.

JOHN HEYWOOD [1]
[1497–1580]

The loss of wealth is loss of dirt,
As sages in all times assert;
The happy man's without a shirt.[2]
Be Merry Friends

Let the world slide,[3] let the world go;
A fig for care, and a fig for woe!
If I can't pay, why I can owe,
And death makes equal the high and low.
Ibid.

Haste maketh waste.
Proverbes [1546]. Part I, Chap. II
Good to be merie and wise.
Ibid.

Beaten with his owne rod.
Ibid.

WALTER SCOTT: *Rob Roy* [1817], *Chap. 34*
[1] The *Proverbes* of JOHN HEYWOOD is the earliest collection of English colloquial sayings. It was first printed in 1546. The title of the edition of 1562 is *John Heywoodes Woorkes. A Dialogue conteyning the number in effect of all the proverbes in the English tounge, compact in a matter concernynge two maner of Maryages*, etc. The selection here given is from the edition of 1874 (a reprint of 1598), edited by JULIAN SHARMAN. See also the *Oxford Dictionary of English Proverbs* compiled by W. G. SMITH [1935].
[2] This line is the theme of many poems, e.g. SIR WALTER SCOTT: *The Search after Happiness; or, The Quest of Sultaun Solimaun*. JOHN HAY: *The Enchanted Shirt*. EDWIN MARKHAM: *The Shoes of Happiness*. EDGAR A. GUEST: *Envy*
[3] Let the world slide. — *Towneley Mysteries* [1420].
Let the world slip: we shall ne'er be younger. — SHAKESPEARE: *Taming of the Shrew* [1593–1594], *Induction, Sc. 2, L. 147*

Look ere ye leape.[1]
> *Proverbes. Part I, Chap. II*

He that will not when he may,
When he would he shall have nay.[2]
> *Ibid.*

The fat is in the fire.
> *Ibid.*

When the sunne shineth, make hay.
> *Ibid.*

The tide tarrieth no man.[3]
> *Ibid.*

Than catch and hold while I may,
fast binde, fast finde.[4]
> *Ibid.*

And while I at length debate and beate
the bush,
There shall steppe in other men and
catch the burdes.[5]
> *Ibid.*

Wedding is destiny,
And hanging likewise.[6]
> *Ibid.*

Happy man, happy dole.[7]
> *Ibid.*

[1] Thou shouldst have looked before thou
hadst leapt. — JONSON, CHAPMAN, MARSTON:
Eastward Ho [1605], *Act V, Sc. 1*
See Samuel Butler, page 239a.
[2] He that will not when he may,
When he will he shall have nay.
ROBERT BURTON: *Anatomy of Mel-
ancholy* [1621–1651], *Part III, Sect.
2, Memb. 5, Subsect. 5*
[3] See Chaucer, page 81b.
Time nor tide tarrieth no man. — ROBERT
GREENE: *Disputations* [1592]
Hoist up saile while gale doth last,
Tide and wind stay no man's pleasure.
ROBERT SOUTHWELL: *St. Peter's
Complaint* [1595]
Nae man can tether time or tide. — BURNS:
Tam O'Shanter [1787]
[4] Fast bind, fast find;
A proverb never stale in thrifty mind.
SHAKESPEARE: *Merchant of Venice*
[1596–1597], *Act II, Sc. 5, L. 54*
[5] It is this proverb which Henry V is re-
ported to have uttered at the siege of Orleans:
"Shall I beat the bush and another take the
bird?"
[6] Hanging and wiving go by destiny. —
The Schole-hous for Women [1541]
See Shakespeare, page 145a.
Marriage and hanging go by destiny;
matches are made in heaven. — ROBERT BUR-
TON: *Anatomy of Melancholy* [1621–1651],
Part III, Sect. 2, Memb. 5, Subsect. 5
[7] Happy man be his dole. — SHAKESPEARE:

God never sends th' mouth but he
sendeth meat.[1]
> *Proverbes. Part I, Chap. IV*

Like will to like.
> *Ibid.*

A hard beginning maketh a good
ending.
> *Ibid.*

More frayd then hurt.
> *Ibid.*

Feare may force a man to cast beyond the moone.[2]
> *Ibid.*

Nothing is impossible to a willing
hart.
> *Ibid.*

The wise man sayth, store is no sore.
> *Ibid. Chap. V*

Let the world wagge, and take mine
ease in myne Inne.[3]
> *Ibid.*

Hold their noses to grinstone.[4]
> *Ibid.*

Better to give then to take.[5]
> *Ibid.*

A sleveless errand.[6]
> *Ibid. Chap. VII*

Merry Wives [1600–1601], *Act III, Sc. 4,
L. 68; Winter's Tale* [1609–1611], *Act I,
Sc. 2, L. 163*
[1] God sendeth and giveth both mouth and
the meat. — THOMAS TUSSER: *Five Hundred
Points of Good Husbandry* [1557]
God sends meat, and the Devil sends cooks.
— JOHN TAYLOR: *Works* [1630], *Vol. II, P. 85*
The holy prophet Zoroaster said,
The Lord who made thy teeth shall give
thee bread.
> *Persian couplet*
[2] To "cast beyond the moon" is a phrase in
frequent use by the old writers. LYLY: *Euphues* [1579]. THOMAS HEYWOOD: *A Woman
Killed with Kindness* [1607].
[3] Shall I not take mine ease in mine inn? —
SHAKESPEARE: *Henry IV* [1597–1598], *Part I,
Act III, Sc. 3, L. 91*
[4] And hold one another's noses to the
grindstone hard. — ROBERT BURTON: *Anatomy of Melancholy* [1621–1651], *Part III,
Sect. 1, Memb. 3*
[5] It is more blessed to give than to receive.
— *Acts, XX, 35*
[6] Sending every one of her children upon
some sleeveless errand, as she terms it. —
JOSEPH ADDISON: *The Spectator, No. 47*
[April 24, 1711] (referring to April Fool errands)

Reckeners without their host must recken twice.[1]

> *Proverbes. Part I, Chap. VIII*

Cut my cote after my cloth.[2]

> *Ibid.*

The neer to the church, the further from God.[3]

> *Ibid. Chap. IX*

Now for good lucke, cast an old shooe after me.

> *Ibid.*

Better is to bow then breake.[4]

> *Ibid.*

It hurteth not the toung to give faire words.[5]

> *Ibid.*

Two heads are better then one.

> *Ibid.*

A short horse is soone currid.

> *Ibid. Chap. X*

To tell tales out of schoole.

> *Ibid.*

To hold with the hare and run with the hound.

> *Ibid.*

She is nether fish nor flesh, nor good red herring.[6]

> *Ibid.*

All is well that endes well.[1]

> *Proverbes. Part I, Chap. X*

Of a good beginning cometh a good end.[2]

> *Ibid.*

Better late than never.[3]

> *Ibid.*

When the steede is stolne, shut the stable durre.[4]

> *Ibid.*

She looketh as butter would not melt in her mouth.

> *Ibid.*

The still sowe eats up all the draffe.

> *Ibid.*

Ill weede growth fast.[5]

> *Ibid.*

It is a deere collop
That is cut out of th' owne flesh.[6]

> *Ibid.*

Beggars should be no choosers.

> *Ibid.*

A man may well bring a horse to the water,
But he cannot make him drinke without he will.[7]

> *Ibid.*

[1] He reckoneth without his Hostesse. Love knoweth no lawes. — LYLY: *Euphues* [1579]

[2] A relic of the Sumptuary Laws. One of the earliest instances occurs, 1530, in the interlude of *Godly Queene Hester*.

[3] Qui est près de l'église est souvent loin de Dieu (He who is near the Church is often far from God). — *Les Proverbes Communs* [circa 1500]

> To Kerke the narre, from God more farre,
> Has bene an old sayd sawe.
> And he that strives to touch the starre,
> Oft stombles at a strawe.
> SPENSER: *The Shepheardes Calender* [1579], July, L. 97

[4] Rather to bowe than breke is profitable; Humylite is a thing commendable.

> *The Morale Proverbs of Cristyne*, translated from the French [1390] by Earl Rivers, and printed by Caxton in 1478

[5] Fair words never hurt the tongue. — JONSON, CHAPMAN, MARSTON: *Eastward Ho* [1605], Act IV, Sc. 1

[6] Meat so dressed and sauced and seasoned that you didn't know whether it was beef or mutton — flesh, fowl, or good red herring. — GEORGE DU MAURIER: *Trilby* [1894]

[1] Si finis bonus est, totum bonum erit (If the end is good, all will be good). — *Gesta Romanorum* [1472], *Tale LXVII*

> SHAKESPEARE: *All's Well That Ends Well* [1601–1603]

[2] Who that well his warke beginneth,
The rather a good ende he winneth.

> GOWER: *Confessio Amantis* [circa 1386–1390]

[3] Potius sero quam nunquam. — LIVY [59 B.C.–A.D. 17]: *History, Book IV, Sect. 23*

[4] Quant le cheval est emblé dounke ferme fols l'estable (When the horse has been stolen, the fool shuts the stable). — *Les Proverbes del Vilain*

[5] Ewyl weed ys sone y-growe. — *MS. Harleian* [circa 1490]

> An ill weed grows apace. — GEORGE CHAPMAN: *An Humorous Day's Mirth* [1599]
> Great weeds do grow apace. — SHAKESPEARE: *Richard III* [1592–1593], Act II, Sc. 4, L. 13

[6] God knows thou art a collop of my flesh. — SHAKESPEARE: *Henry VI* [1591], Part I, Act V, Sc. 4, L. 18

[7] You may bring a horse to the river, but he will drink when and what he pleaseth. — GEORGE HERBERT: *Jacula Prudentum* [1640]

Men say, kinde will creepe where it may not goe.[1]

Proverbes. Part I, Chap. X

The cat would eate fish, and would not wet her feete.[2]

Ibid.

While the grasse groweth the horse starveth.[3]

Ibid.

Rome was not built in one day.

Ibid. Chap. XI

Yee have many strings to your bowe.[4]

Ibid.

Children learne to creepe ere they can learne to goe.

Ibid.

Better is halfe a lofe than no bread.

Ibid.

Nought venter nought have.[5]

Ibid.

Children and fooles cannot lye.[6]

Ibid.

All is fish that comth to net.[7]

Ibid.

Who is worse shod than the shoe-maker's wife?[8]

Ibid.

[1] You know that love
Will creep in service when it cannot go.
SHAKESPEARE: *Two Gentlemen of Verona* [1594–1595], *Act IV, Sc. 2, L. 19*
[2] Shakespeare alludes to this proverb in *Macbeth, Act I, Sc. 7, L. 44:*
Letting "I dare not" wait upon "I would,"
Like the poor cat i' the adage.
Cat lufat visch, ac he nele his feth wete. — MS. *Trinity College, Cambridge* [*circa* 1250]
[3] Whylst grass doth grow, oft sterves the seely steede. — WHETSTONE: *Promos and Cassandra* [1578]
While the grass grows —
The proverb is something musty.
SHAKESPEARE: *Hamlet* [1600–1601], *Act III, Sc. 2, L. 365*
[4] Two strings to his bow. — RICHARD HOOKER: *Laws of Ecclesiastical Polity, Book V* [1597], *Chap. LXXX*
[5] Nothing venture, nothing win. — W. S. GILBERT: *Iolanthe* [1882], *Act II*
[6] 'Tis an old saw, Children and fooles speake true. — LYLY: *Endymion* [1591]
[7] All's fish they get that cometh to net. — TUSSER: *Five Hundred Points of Good Husbandry* [1557], *February Abstract*
[8] Him that makes shoes go barefoot himself. — ROBERT BURTON: *Anatomy of Melancholy* [1621–1651], *Democritus to the Reader*

One good turne asketh another.

Proverbes. Part I, Chap. XI

Who waite for dead men shall goe long barefoote.

Ibid.

I pray thee let me and my fellow have A haire of the dog that bit us last night.[1]

Ibid.

But in deede,
A friend is never knowne till a man have neede.

Ibid.

New brome swepth cleene.

Ibid. Part II, Chap. I

All thing is the woorse for the wearing.

Ibid.

Burnt child fire dredth.[2]

Ibid. Chap. II

Love me litle, love me long.[3]

Ibid.

A fooles bolt is soone shot.[4]

Ibid. Chap. III

A woman hath nine lives like a cat[5]

Ibid. Chap. IV

A peny for your thought.

Ibid.

You stand in your owne light.

Ibid.

Though chaunge be no robbry.

Ibid.

Might have gone further and have fared worse.

Ibid.

The grey mare is the better horse.

Ibid.

Three may keepe counsayle, if two be away.[6]

Ibid. Chap. V

[1] In old receipt books we find it invariably advised that an inebriate should drink sparingly in the morning some of the same liquor which he had drunk to excess overnight.
[2] Brend child fur dredth,
Quoth Hendyng.
Proverbs of Hendyng, MS.
[*circa* 1320]
[3] Pray love me little, so you love me long. — HERRICK: *Love Me Little, Love Me Long* [1648]
[4] Sottes bolt is sone shote. — *Proverbs of Hendyng, MS.* [*circa* 1320]
[5] See Bidpai, page 28b.
[6] Two may keep counsel when the third's

Small pitchers have wyde eares.[1]
> *Proverbes. Part II, Chap. V*

Many hands make light worke.
> *Ibid.*

Out of Gods blessing into the warme Sunne.[2]
> *Ibid.*

There is no fire without some smoke.[3]
> *Ibid.*

A cat may looke on a King.
> *Ibid.*

Have yee him on the hip.[4]
> *Ibid.*

It had need to bee
A wylie mouse that should breed in the cats eare.[5]
> *Ibid.*

Leape out of the frying pan into the fyre.
> *Ibid.*

Time trieth troth in every doubt.[6]
> *Ibid.*

Much water goeth by the mill
That the miller knoweth not of.[7]
> *Ibid.*

---

away. — SHAKESPEARE: *Titus Andronicus* [1593–1594], *Act IV, Sc. 2, L. 145*
   Three can hold their peace if two be away. — GEORGE HERBERT: *Jacula Prudentum* [1640]
  [1] Pitchers have ears. — SHAKESPEARE: *The Taming of the Shrew* [1593–1594], *Act IV, Sc. 4, L. 52; Richard III* [1592–1593], *Act II, Sc. 4, L. 37*
   Little pitchers have wide ears. — GEORGE HERBERT: *Jacula Prudentum* [1640]
  [2] Thou shalt come out of a warme sunne into Gods blessing. — LYLY: *Euphues* [1579]
   Lest we leap out of the frying-pan into the fire; or, out of God's blessing into the warm sun. — CERVANTES: *Don Quixote, Part I* [1605], *Book III, Chap. 4*
   Thou out of Heaven's benediction comest
To the warm sun.
   SHAKESPEARE: *King Lear* [1605–1606], *Act II, Sc. 2, L. 168*
  [3] There can no great smoke arise, but there must be some fire. — LYLY: *Euphues* [1579]
  [4] See Shakespeare, page 144a.
  [5] A hardy mouse that is bold to breede
  In cattis eeris.
   Order of Foles [MS. *circa* 1450]
  [6] Time tries the troth in everything. — TUSSER: *Five Hundred Points of Good Husbandry* [1557], *Author's Epistle, Chap. I*
  [7]   More water glideth by the mill
   Than wots the miller of.
   SHAKESPEARE: *Titus Andronicus* [1593–1594], *Act II, Sc. 1, L. 85*

The moe the merrier.
> *Proverbes. Part II, Chap. VII*

To th' end of a shot and beginning of a fray.[1]
> *Ibid.*

It is better to be
An old man's derling than a yong man's werling.
> *Ibid.*

Be the day never so long,
Evermore at last they ring to evensong.[2]
> *Ibid.*

I know on which side my bread is buttred.
> *Ibid.*

Who is so deafe or so blinde as is hee
That wilfully will neither heare nor see?[3]
> *Ibid. Chap. IX*

The wrong sow by th' eare.
> *Ibid.*

Love me, love my dog.[4]
> *Ibid.*

An ill winde that bloweth no man to good.[5]
> *Ibid.*

For when I gave you an inch, you tooke an ell.[6]
> *Ibid.*

The miller sees not all the water that goes by his mill. — ROBERT BURTON: *Anatomy of Melancholy* [1621–1651], *Part III, Sect. 3, Memb. 4, Subsect. 1*
  [1] See Shakespeare, page 151b.
  [2] Be the day short or never so long,
  At length it ringeth to even song.
   Quoted at the stake by George Tankerfield [1555] (FOXE: *Book of Martyrs* [1563], *Chap. VII*)
  [3] See Mathew Henry, page 292b.
  [4] Qui me amat, amet et canem meum (Who loves me, let him love my dog also). — ST. BERNARD [*circa* 1150]: *Sermo Primus*
  [5] See Tusser, page 96a.
   Ill blows the wind that profits nobody. — SHAKESPEARE: *King Henry VI* [1591], *Part III, Act 2, Sc. 5, L. 55*
   Falstaff. What wind blew you hither, Pistol?
   Pistol. Not the ill wind which blows no man to good.
   SHAKESPEARE: *Henry IV* [1597–1598], *Part II, Act V, Sc. 3, L. 87*
  [6] Give an inch, he'll take an ell. — JOHN WEBSTER [1580–1625]: *Sir Thomas Wyatt*

Would yee both eat your cake and have your cake? [1]

Proverbes. Part II, Chap. IX

Every man for himselfe and God for us all. [2]

Ibid.

Though he love not to buy the pig in the poke. [3]

Ibid.

Enough is as good as a feast.

Ibid.

CHARLES V
[1500–1558]

To think that I attempted to force the reason and conscience of thousands of men into one mould and I cannot make two clocks agree! [4]

Quoted by HAVELOCK ELLIS: *The Task of Social Hygiene, Chap. 9*

Fortune hath somewhat the nature of a woman; if she be too much wooed, she is the farther off.

Quoted by FRANCIS BACON: *Advancement of Learning, Book II*

Myself and the lucky moment.

Quoted by PRESCOTT: *Philip II, Book I, Chap. 9*

Iron hand in a velvet glove.

Attributed to Charles V by CARLYLE: *Latter-Day Pamphlets, II*

[1] Wouldst thou both eat thy cake and have it? — GEORGE HERBERT: *The Size* [1633]

[2] Every man for himself, his own ends, the Devil for all. — ROBERT BURTON: *Anatomy of Melancholy* [1621–1651], *Part III, Sect. I, Memb. III*

[3] For buying or selling of pig in a poke. — TUSSER· *Five Hundred Points of Good Husbandry* [1557], *September Abstract*

[4] "When Charles V retired in weariness from the greatest throne in the world to the solitude of the monastery at Yuste, he occupied his leisure for some weeks in trying to regulate two clocks. It proved very difficult. One day, it is recorded, he turned to his assistant and said [the sentence quoted above]." — HAVELOCK ELLIS

JOHN KNOX
[1505–1572]

A man with God is always in the majority. [1]

Inscription on Reformation Monument, Geneva, Switzerland

JOHN BRADFORD
[1510–1555]

The familiar story, that, on seeing evil-doers taken to the place of execution, he was wont to exclaim: "But for the grace of God there goes John Bradford," is a universal tradition, which has overcome the lapse of time. [2]

Biographical Notice, Parker Society edition, The Writings of John Bradford [1853], *Page xliii*

SIR THOMAS VAUX
[1510–1556]

Companion none is like
Unto the mind alone;
For many have been harmed by speech,
Through thinking, few or none.

Of a Contented Mind [1557]

RICHARD GRAFTON
[?–1572]

Thirty dayes hath Nouember,
April, June, and September,
February hath xxviii alone,
And all the rest have xxxi. [3]

Chronicles of England [1562]

[1] Un homme avec Dieu est toujours dans la majorité.

[2] I never hear of such a case as this that I do not think of Baxter's words, and say, "There, but for the grace of God, goes Sherlock Holmes." — SIR ARTHUR CONAN DOYLE [1859–1930]: *The Boscombe Valley Mystery* (The reference is to RICHARD BAXTER [1615–1691], author of *The Saint's Everlasting Rest* and *The Call to the Unconverted*.)

[3] Junius, Aprilis, Septémq; Nouemq; tricenos,
Vnum plus reliqui, Februs tenet octo vicenos,
At si bissextus fuerit superadditur vnus.
WILLIAM HARRISON: *Description of Britain, prefixed to* HOLINSHED'S *Chronicle* [1577]
Thirty days hath September,
April, June, and November,

GEORGIUS FABRICIUS
[1516–1571]

He doth raise his country's fame with
    his own
And in the mouths of nations yet un-
    born
His praises shall be sung; Death comes
    to all
But great achievements raise a monu-
    ment
Which shall endure until the sun grows
    cold.

> *In Praise of Georgius Agricola*
> *[1494–1555]. Quoted by* HER-
> BERT CLARK HOOVER *and* LOU
> HENRY HOOVER *in their transla-*
> *tion of* AGRICOLA'S *De Re Metal-*
> *lica, Page xxiv*

THOMAS TUSSER
[1524–1580]

Except wind stands as never it stood,
It is an ill wind turns none to good.[1]

> *A Description of the Properties*
> *of Wind*

At Christmas play and make good
    cheer,
For Christmas comes but once a year.

> *The Farmer's Daily Diet*

February has twenty-eight alone,
All the rest have thirty-one;
Excepting leap year, — that's the time
When February's days are twenty-nine.

> *The Return from Parnassus* [1606]

Thirty days hath September,
April, June, and November;
All the rest have thirty-one,
Excepting February alone,
Which hath but twenty-eight, in fine,
Till leap year gives it twenty-nine.

> *Common in the New England states*

Fourth, eleventh, ninth, and sixth,
Thirty days to each affix;
Every other thirty-one
Except the second month alone.

> *Common in Chester County, Pennsyl-*
> *vania, among the Friends*

Compare the old Latin-class mnemonic:
In March, July, October, May,
The Ides are on the fifteenth day,
The Nones the seventh; all other months
    besides
Have two days less for Nones and Ides.

[1] See Heywood, page 94b.

Such mistress, such Nan,
Such master, such man.[1]

> *Five Hundred Points of Good Hus-*
> *bandry [1557]. April's Abstract*

Who goeth a borrowing
Goeth a sorrowing.

> *Ibid. June's Abstract*

'T is merry in hall
Where beards wag all.[2]

> *Ibid. August's Abstract*

Dry sun, dry wind;
Safe bind, safe find.[3]

> *Washing*

Hast thou a friend, as heart may wish at
    will?
Then use him so, to have his friendship
    still.
Wouldst have a friend, wouldst know
    what friend is best?
Have God thy friend, who passeth all
    the rest.

> *Posies for a Parlour*

To Death we must stoop, be we high,
    be we low,
But how, and how suddenly, few be
    that know;
What carry we then but a sheet to the
    grave,
To cover this carcass, of all that we
    have?

> *Tenants of God's Farmstead*

PIERRE DE RONSARD
[1524–1585]

When you are old, and in the candle
    light
Sit spinning by the fire at close of day,
You'll sing my songs in praise of you,
    and say:
"Thus Ronsard sang, whilst still my
    eyes were bright." [4]

> *Sonnet XLIII.*[5] *To Helen* [6]

[1] Tel maître, tel valet. Attributed to CHEVA-
LIER BAYARD by Cimber.

[2] Merry swithe it is in halle,
  When the beards waveth alle.
> *Life of Alexander* [1312]

[3] See Heywood, page 91a.

[4] "Ronsard me célébroit du temps que j'étois
belle."
Compare YEATS's adaptation: "When you
are old and gray and full of sleep," page 824a.

[5] Translated by WILLIAM A. DRAKE.

[6] Madame de Surgères.

WILLIAM STEVENSON
[1530?–1575]

I cannot eat but little meat,
My stomach is not good;
But sure I think that I can drink
With him that wears a hood.
Gammer Gurton's Needle [1575].
Drinking Song, Act II

Back and side go bare, go bare,
Both foot and hand go cold;
But, belly, God send thee good ale
enough,
Whether it be new or old.
Ibid. Refrain

GABRIEL MEURIER
[1530–1601]

He who excuses himself accuses himself.[1]

Trésor des Sentences

ELIZABETH, QUEEN OF ENGLAND
[1533–1603]

The use of the sea and air is common to all; neither can a title to the ocean belong to any people or private persons, forasmuch as neither nature nor public use and custom permit any possession thereof.
To the Spanish Ambassador [1580]

My care is like my shadow in the sun —
Follows me flying — flies when I pursue it.
On the Departure of Alençon
[1582]

I know I have the body of a weak and feeble woman, but I have the heart and stomach of a king, and of a king of England too; and think foul scorn that Parma or Spain, or any prince of Europe should dare to invade the borders of my realm.
Speech to the Troops at Tilbury on the Approach of the Armada, 1588

[1] Qui s'excuse, s'accuse.
See Shakespeare, page 148b.

Though God hath raised me high, yet this I count the glory of my crown: that I have reigned with your loves.
The Golden Speech, 1601

Semper eadem (Ever the same).
Motto

I am no lover of pompous title, but only desire that my name may be recorded in a line or two, which shall briefly express my name, my virginity, the years of my reign, the reformation of religion under it, and my preservation of peace.
To her ladies, discussing her epitaph

'Twas God the word that spake it,
He took the Bread and brake it;
And what the word did make it,
That I believe, and take it.[1]
S. CLARKE, *Marrow of Ecclesiastical History* [ed. 1675].
Part II, Life of Queen Elizabeth

MICHEL DE MONTAIGNE [2]
[1533–1592]

Man in sooth is a marvellous vain, fickle, and unstable subject.[3]
Essays.[4] *Book I* [1580], *Chap. 1, That Men by Various Ways Arrive at the Same End*

All passions that suffer themselves to be relished and digested are but moderate.[5]
Ibid. Chap. 2, Of Sorrow

The thing of which I have most fear is fear.[6]
Ibid. Chap. 17, Of Fear

He who should teach men to die

[1] Answer on being asked her opinion of Christ's presence in the Sacrament.
[2] Translated by CHARLES COTTON [1630–1687], revised by HAZLITT and WIGHT.
[3] See Plutarch, page 58b.
[4] This book of Montaigne the world has indorsed by translating it into all tongues. — EMERSON: *Representative Men* [1850], *Montaigne*
[5] See Seneca, page 48b, and Raleigh, page 111a.
[6] C'est de quoy j'ay le plus de peur que la peur.
See Thoreau, page 589a, and Roosevelt, page 918b.

97

would at the same time teach them to live.[1]

> *Essays. Book I, Chap. 19, That to Study Philosophy Is to Learn to Die*

The laws of conscience, which we pretend to be derived from nature, proceed from custom.

> *Ibid. Chap. 22, Of Custom*

Accustom him to everything, that he may not be a Sir Paris, a carpet-knight,[2] but a sinewy, hardy, and vigorous young man.

> *Ibid. Chap. 25, On the Education of Children*

It can be of no importance to me of what religion my physician or my lawyer is; this consideration has nothing in common with the offices of friendship which they owe me.

> *Ibid. Chap. 27, Of Friendship*

There are some defeats more triumphant than victories.[3]

> *Ibid. Chap. 30, Of Cannibals*

[1] I have taught you, my dear flock, for above thirty years how to live, and I will show you in a very short time how to die. — SIR EDWIN SANDYS [1561–1629]: *Anglorum Speculum*

There taught us how to live; and (oh, too high
The price for knowledge!) taught us how to die.
　　　THOMAS TICKELL: *On the Death of Mr. Addison* [1719], L. 81

Teach him how to live,
And, oh still harder lesson! how to die.
　　　BEILBY PORTEUS [1731–1808]: *Death, L. 316*

In teaching me the way to live
It taught me how to die.
　　　GEORGE POPE MORRIS [1802–1864]: *My Mother's Bible, St. 4*

[2] One of those carpet-knights that abandon themselves to sleep and lazy ease. — CERVANTES: *Don Quixote, Part I* [1605], Book III, Chap. 6

See Robert Burton, page 222a.

Carpet knights are men who are by the prince's grace and favour made knights at home. . . . They are called carpet knights because they receive their honours in the court and upon carpets. — GERVASE MARKHAM: *Booke of Honour* [1625]

[3] See Plutarch, page 59a.

Nothing is so firmly believed as what we least know.

> *Essays. Book I, Chap. 31, Of Divine Ordinances*

A wise man never loses anything if he have himself.

> *Ibid. Chap. 38, Of Solitude*

Even opinion is of force enough to make itself to be espoused at the expense of life.

> *Ibid. Chap. 40, Of Good and Evil*

To which we may add this other Aristotelian consideration, that he who confers a benefit on any one loves him better than he is beloved by him again.[1]

> *Ibid. Book II [1580], Chap. 8, Of the Affection of Fathers*

The middle sort of historians (of which the most part are) spoil all; they will chew our meat for us.

> *Ibid. Chap. 10, Of Books*

The only good histories are those that have been written by the persons themselves who commanded in the affairs whereof they write.

> *Ibid.*

She [virtue] requires a rough and stormy passage; she will have either outward difficulties to wrestle with, or internal difficulties.[2]

> *Ibid. Chap. 11, Of Cruelty*

There is, nevertheless, a certain respect, and a general duty of humanity, that ties us, not only to beasts that have life and sense, but even to trees and plants.

> *Ibid.*

Some impose upon the world that they believe that which they do not; others, more in number, make themselves believe that they believe, not being able to penetrate into what it is to believe.

> *Ibid. Chap. 12, Apology for Raimond Sebond[3]*

[1] Benefactors appear to love in a greater degree those whom they benefit than those who are benefited love their benefactors. — ARISTOTLE [384–322 B.C.]: *Nicomachean Ethics, Book IX, Chap. 1*

[2] See Milton, page 250b–251a.

[3] Raimond Sebond, Spaniard, died in 1436,

When I play with my cat, who knows whether I do not make her more sport than she makes me?

Essays. Book II, Chap. 12, Apology for Raimond Sebond

The souls of emperors and cobblers are cast in the same mould. . . . The same reason that makes us wrangle with a neighbour causes a war betwixt princes.

Ibid.

Man is certainly stark mad; he cannot make a worm, and yet he will be making gods by dozens.

Ibid.

Why may not a goose say thus: "All the parts of the universe I have an interest in: the earth serves me to walk upon, the sun to light me; [1] the stars have their influence upon me; I have such an advantage by the winds and such by the waters, there is nothing that yon heavenly roof looks upon so favourably as me. I am the darling of Nature! Is it not man that keeps, lodges, and serves me?"

Ibid.

Arts and sciences are not cast in a mould, but are formed and perfected by degrees, by often handling and polishing, as bears leisurely lick their cubs into form.

Ibid.

He that I am reading seems always to have the most force.

Ibid.

How many worthy men have we known to survive their own reputation! [2]

Ibid. Chap. 16, Of Glory

There is another sort of glory, which is the having too good an opinion of our own worth.

Ibid. Chap. 17, Of Presumption

One may be humble out of pride.

Ibid.

Nature has presented us with a large faculty of entertaining ourselves alone;

and often calls us to it, to teach us that we owe ourselves partly to society, but chiefly and mostly to ourselves.

Essays. Book II, Chap. 18, On Giving the Lie

I find that the best virtue I have has in it some tincture of vice.

Ibid. Chap. 20, That We Taste Nothing Pure

Saying is one thing, and doing is another.

Ibid. Chap. 31, Of Anger

Is it not a noble farce, wherein kings, republics, and emperors have for so many ages played their parts, and to which the whole vast universe serves for a theatre? [1]

Ibid. Chap. 36, Of the Most Excellent Men

Nature forms us for ourselves, not for others; to be, not to seem.

Ibid. Chap. 37, Of the Resemblance of Children to Their Brothers

There never was in the world two opinions alike, no more than two hairs or two grains; the most universal quality is diversity.[2]

Ibid. Of the Resemblance of Children to Their Fathers

The public weal requires that men should betray, and lie, and massacre.

Ibid. Book III [1595], Chap. 1, Of Profit and Honesty

I will follow the right side even to the fire, but excluding the fire if I can.

Ibid.

Does not he to whom you betray another, to whom you were as welcome as to himself, know that you will at another time do as much for him?

Ibid.

I speak truth, not so much as I would, but as much as I dare; and I dare a little the more, as I grow older.

Ibid. Chap. 2, Of Repentance

Few men have been admired by their own domestics.[3]

Ibid.

---

at Toulouse, where he had lived as professor of medicine and theology.

[1] See Pope, page 316a.
[2] See Bentley, page 292b.

[1] See Shakespeare, page 161a.
[2] See Pliny, page 49b.
[3] See Plutarch, page 61b.

It [marriage] happens as with cages: the birds without despair to get in, and those within despair of getting out.[1]

Essays. Book III, Chap. 5, Upon Some Verses of Virgil

And to bring in a new word by the head and shoulders, they leave out the old one.

Ibid.

All the world knows me in my book, and my book in me.

Ibid.

'Tis so much to be a king, that he only is so by being so. The strange lustre that surrounds him conceals and shrouds him from us; our sight is there broken and dissipated, being stopped and filled by the prevailing light.[2]

Ibid. Chap. 7, Of the Inconvenience of Greatness

We are born to inquire after truth; it belongs to a greater power to possess it. It is not, as Democritus said, hid in the bottom of the deeps, but rather elevated to an infinite height in the divine knowledge.

Ibid. Chap. 8, Of the Art of Conversation

I moreover affirm that our wisdom itself, and wisest consultations, for the most part commit themselves to the conduct of chance.[3]

Ibid.

[1] I myself have loved a lady and pursued her with a great deal of under-age protestation, whom some three or four gallants that have enjoyed would with all their hearts have been glad to have been rid of. 'Tis just like a summer bird-cage in a garden: the birds that are without despair to get in, and the birds that are within despair and are in a consumption for fear they shall never get out. — JOHN WEBSTER: *The White Devil* [1612], Act I, Sc. 2

Wedlock, indeed, hath oft compared been
To public feasts, where meet a public rout, —
Where they that are without would fain go in,
And they that are within would fain go out.

SIR JOHN DAVIES [1569–1626]: *Contention Betwixt a Wife, etc.*

[2] See Tennyson, page 554a.

[3] Although men flatter themselves with their great actions, they are not so often the

What if he has borrowed the matter and spoiled the form, as it oft falls out? [1]

Essays. Book III, Chap. 8, Of the Art of Conversation

The oldest and best known evil was ever more supportable than one that was new and untried.

Ibid. Chap. 9, Of Vanity

Not because Socrates said so,[2] but because it is in truth my own disposition — and perchance to some excess — I look upon all men as my compatriots, and embrace a Pole as a Frenchman, making less account of the national than of the universal and common bond.

Ibid.

There is no man so good, who, were he to submit all his thoughts and actions to the laws, would not deserve hanging ten times in his life.

Ibid.

Saturninus said, "Comrades, you have lost a good captain to make him an ill general."

Ibid.

A little folly is desirable in him that will not be guilty of stupidity.[3]

Ibid.

We seek and offer ourselves to be gulled.

Ibid. Chap. 11, Of Cripples

I have never seen a greater monster or miracle in the world than myself.

Ibid.

Men are most apt to believe what they least understand.

Ibid.

I have here only made a nosegay of culled flowers, and have brought noth-

result of great design as of chance. — LA ROCHEFOUCAULD [1613–1680]: *Maxim 57*

[1] Defacing first, then claiming for his own. CHARLES CHURCHILL [1731–1764]: *The Apology, L. 233*

[2] See Plutarch, page 61b.

[3] Mix a little folly with your wisdom; a little nonsense is pleasant now and then. — HORACE [65–8 B.C.]: *Odes, IV*
See Horace Walpole, page 350a.

ing of my own but the thread that ties them together.[1]

*Essays. Book III, Chap. 12,
Of Physiognomy*

I am further of opinion that it would be better for us to have [no laws] at all than to have them in so prodigious numbers as we have.

Ibid. Chap. 13, Of Experience

There is more ado to interpret interpretations than to interpret the things, and more books upon books than upon all other subjects; we do nothing but comment upon one another.

Ibid.

What can we do with those people who will not believe anything unless it is in print? . . . I would as soon quote one of my friends as I would Aulus Gellius or Macrobius.

Ibid.

For truth itself has not the privilege to be spoken at all times and in all sorts.

Ibid.

Sits he on never so high a throne, a man still sits on his bottom.

Ibid.

The diversity of physical arguments and opinions embraces all sorts of methods.

Ibid.

Let us a little permit Nature to take her own way; she better understands her own affairs than we.

Ibid.

I have ever loved to repose myself, whether sitting or lying, with my heels as high or higher than my head.

Ibid.

I, who have so much and so universally adored this "excellent mediocrity" of ancient times, and who have concluded the most moderate measure the most perfect, shall I pretend to an unreasonable and prodigious old age?

Ibid.

Que scais-je (What do I know)?

Motto on his seal

---

[1] I am but a gatherer and disposer of other men's stuff, at my best value. — SIR HENRY WOTTON: *Preface to the Elements of Architecture* [1624]

I do not understand; I pause; I examine.

Inscription for his library

EDWARD DYER
[*Circa* 1540–1607]

My mind to me a kingdom is;
Such present joys therein I find,
That it excels all other bliss
That earth affords or grows by kind:
Though much I want which most would
 have,
Yet still my mind forbids to crave.

Rawlinson Poetry MS. 85, P. 17 [1]

Some have too much, yet still do crave;
I little have, and seek no more:
They are but poor, though much they
 have,
And I am rich with little store:
They poor, I rich; they beg, I give;
They lack, I have; they pine, I live.

Ibid.

JAN ZAMOYSKI
[1541–1605]

The king reigns, but does not govern.[2]

*Speech in the Polish Parliament
[1605], referring to King Sigismund III*

MARY STUART, QUEEN OF SCOTS
[1542–1587]

In my end is my beginning.

Motto

---

[1] This poem became popular as a song, altered thus:
My mind to me a kingdom is;
Such perfect joy therein I find,
As far exceeds all earthly bliss
That God and Nature hath assigned.
Though much I want that most would have,
Yet still my mind forbids to crave.
BYRD: *Psalmes, Sonnets, etc.* [1588]
My mind to me an empire is,
While grace affordeth health.
ROBERT SOUTHWELL [1561–1595]:
Content and Rich
See Seneca, page 48a.

[2] Thiers adopted the epigram as the motto for his journal, the *Nationale*, which he established with Mignet and Carrel in 1830.

GUILLAUME DE SALLUSTE, SEIGNEUR DU BARTAS

[1544–1590]

The world's a stage,[1] where God's omnipotence,
His justice, knowledge, love, and providence
Do act the parts.

Divine Weekes and Workes[2]
[1578]. First Week, First Day

And reads, though running,[3] all these needful motions.

Ibid.

Mercy and justice, marching cheek by joule.

Ibid.

What is well done is done soon enough.

Ibid.

And swans seem whiter if swart crowes be by.

Ibid.

Night's black mantle covers all alike.[4]

Ibid.

Hot and cold, and moist and dry.[5]

Ibid. Second Day

Much like the French (or like ourselves, their apes),
Who with strange habit do disguise their shapes;
Who loving novels, full of affectation,
Receive the manners of each other nation.[6]

Ibid.

With tooth and nail.

Ibid.

From the foure corners of the worlde doe haste.[7]

Ibid.

---

[1] See Shakespeare, page 161a, and Du Bartas, page 103a.
[2] Translated [1606] by J. SYLVESTER [1563–1618].
[3] See *Habakkuk, II, 2*, on page 1049b, and Cowper, page 365b.
[4] Night . . . with thy black mantle. — SHAKESPEARE: *Romeo and Juliet* [1594–1595], *Act III, Sc. 2, L. 10 and 15*
[5] See Milton, page 254b.
[6] See Shakespeare, page 138b.
[7] See Shakespeare, page 149a and Donne, page 217b.

Oft seen in forehead of the frowning skies.[1]

Divine Weekes and Workes.
First Week, Second Day

Bright-flaming, heat-full fire,
The source of motion.

Ibid.

For where's the state beneath the firmament
That doth excel the bees for government?[2]

Ibid. Fifth Day, Part 1

These lovely lamps, these windows of the soul.[3]

Ibid. Sixth Day

Or almost like a spider, who, confin'd
In her web's centre, shakt with every winde,
Moves in an instant if the buzzing flie
Stir but a string of her lawn canapie.[4]

Ibid.

Which serves for cynosure
To all that sail upon the sea obscure.

Ibid. Seventh Day

Living from hand to mouth.

Ibid. Second Week, First Day, Part 4

---

[1] See Milton, page 249b.
[2] 　　So work the honey-bees,
Creatures that by a rule in Nature teach
The act of order to a peopled kingdom.
　　SHAKESPEARE: *King Henry V* [1598–1600], *Act I, Sc. 2, L. 187*
[3] The windows of mine eyes. — SHAKESPEARE: *King Richard III* [1592–1593], *Act V, Sc. 3, L. 117*
[4] Much like a subtle spider which doth sit
In middle of her web, which spreadeth wide;
If aught do touch the utmost thread of it
She feels it instantly on every side.
　　SIR JOHN DAVIES: *The Immortality of the Soul* [1599]
Our souls sit close and silently within,
And their own webs from their own entrails spin;
And when eyes meet far off, our sense is such
That, spider-like, we feel the tenderest touch.
　　DRYDEN: *Marriage à la Mode* [1673], *Act II, Sc. 1*
The spider's touch, how exquisitely fine!
Feels at each thread, and lives along the line.
　　POPE: *An Essay on Man* [1733–1734], *Epistle I, L. 217*

In the jaws of death.[1]

> *Divine Weekes and Workes. Second Week, First Day, Part 4*

Will change the pebbles of our puddly
    thought
To orient pearls.

> *Ibid. Third Day, Part 1*

Only that he may conform
To tyrant custom.

> *Ibid. Part 2*

Who breaks his faith, no faith is held
    with him.

> *Ibid. Fourth Day, Book 2*

Who well lives, long lives; for this age
    of ours
Should not be numbered by years, daies,
    and hours.

> *Ibid.*

My lovely living boy,
My hope, my hap, my love, my life, my
    joy.[2]

> *Ibid.*

Out of the book of Natur's learned
    brest.[3]

> *Ibid.*

Flesh of thy flesh, nor yet bone of thy
    bone.

> *Ibid.*

Weakened and wasted to skin and
    bone.

> *Ibid. Book 4*

I take the world to be but as a stage,
Where net-maskt men do play their
    personage.[4]

> *Dialogue Between Heraclitus and*
> *Democritus*

Made no more bones.

> *The Maiden Blush*

[1] Out of the jaws of death. — SHAKESPEARE: *Twelfth Night* [1598–1600], *Act III, Sc. 4, L. 396*
See Tennyson, page 553b.
[2] My fair son!
My life, my joy, my food, my all the world.
SHAKESPEARE: *King John* [1596–1597], *Act III, Sc. 4, L. 103*
[3] The book of Nature is that which the physician must read; and to do so he must walk over the leaves. — PARACELSUS [1493–1541]. Quoted in *Encyclopaedia Britannica* (11th ed.), *Vol. 20, P. 749*
[4] See Shakespeare, page 161a, and Du Bartas, page 102a.

MIGUEL DE CERVANTES
[1547–1616]

You are a King by your own Fireside, as much as any Monarch in his Throne.

> *Don Quixote*[1] [1605–1615]. *The*
> *Author's Preface, Page xix*

I was so free with him as not to mince
the matter.[2]

> *Ibid. Page xx*

They can expect nothing but their
labour for their pains.[3]

> *Ibid. Page xxiii*

Time out of mind.[4]

> *Ibid. Part I* [1605], *Book I,*
> *Chap. 1, Page 4*

Which I have earned with the sweat
of my brows.

> *Ibid. Chap. 4, Page 22*

By a small sample we may judge of
the whole piece.

> *Ibid. Page 25*

Put you in this pickle.

> *Ibid. Chap. 5, Page 30*

Can we ever have too much of a good
thing?

> *Ibid. Chap. 6, Page 37*

Fortune may have yet a better success in reserve for you, and they who
lose to-day may win to-morrow.

> *Ibid. Chap. 7, Page 39*

The charging of his enemy was but
the work of a moment.

> *Ibid. Chap. 8, Page 50*

I don't know that ever I saw one in
my born days.

> *Ibid. Book II, Chap. 2, Page 57*

Those two fatal words, Mine and
Thine.[5]

> *Ibid. Chap. 3, Page 63*

[1] Translated in 1700–1703 by PETER ANTHONY MOTTEUX [1660–1718]. The page numbers are those of the Modern Library Giant edition.
[2] See Shakespeare, page 187b.
You mince matters. — MOLIÈRE: *Tartuffe* [1667], *Act I, Sc. 1*
[3] See Shakespeare, page 181a.
[4] Time out o' mind. — SHAKESPEARE: *Romeo and Juliet* [1594–1595], *Act I, Sc. 4, L. 70*
[5] See Boileau, page 287a.

The eyes those silent tongues of Love.

> *Don Quixote. Part I, Book II,*
> *Chap. 3, Page 65*

As good-natured a soul as e'er trod on shoe of leather.

> *Ibid. Chap. 4, Page 69*

And had a face like a blessing.[1]

> *Ibid.*

He's a good man, I'll say that for him, and a true Christian every inch of him.

> *Ibid. Page 70*

There's not the least thing can be said or done, but people will talk and find fault.[2]

> *Ibid.*

Without a wink of sleep.[3]

> *Ibid. Page 72*

Everything disturbs an absent lover.

> *Ibid. Page 84*

It is a true saying, that a man must eat a peck of salt with his friend, before he knows him.

> *Ibid. Book III, Chap. 1, Page 92*

Fortune leaves always some door open to come at a remedy.

> *Ibid. Page 94*

Thank you for nothing.

> *Ibid.*

Fair and softly goes far.

> *Ibid. Chap. 2, Page 97*

May Old Nick [4] rock my cradle.

> *Ibid. Chap. 3, Page 103*

No limits but the sky.[5]

> *Ibid. Page 110*

---

[1] He had a face like a benediction. — JAR-VIS's translation

[2] See Samuel Dodge, page 557b.
Take wife, or cowl; ride you, or walk:
Doubt not but tongues will have their talk.
  LA FONTAINE: *The Miller, His Son,*
     and the Donkey [1694]
Do you think you could keep people from talking? — MOLIÈRE: *Tartuffe* [1667], *Act I, Sc. 1*

[3] I have not slept one wink. — SHAKE-SPEARE: *Cymbeline* [1609–1610], *Act III, Sc. 4, L. 103*

[4] Nick Machiavel had ne'er a trick,
  Though he gave his name to our Old Nick.
    BUTLER: *Hudibras, Part III* [1678],
            Canto 1, L. 1313

[5] Modern saying: The sky's the limit.

To give the devil his due.

> *Don Quixote. Part I, Book III,*
> *Chap. 3, Page 111*

A peck of troubles.

> *Ibid. Chap. 4, Page 112*

You're leaping over the hedge before you come to the stile.

> *Ibid. Page 117*

Paid him in his own coin.

> *Ibid. Page 119*

Bell, book, and candle.[1]

> *Ibid. Page 120*

Every tooth in a man's head is more valuable than a diamond.

> *Ibid. Page 121*

The famous Don Quixote de la Mancha, otherwise called The Knight of the Woeful Figure.[2]

> *Ibid. Chap. 5, Page 126*

Let the worst come to the worst.

> *Ibid. Page 127*

You are come off now with a whole skin.

> *Ibid.*

Fear is sharp-sighted, and can see things under ground, and much more in the skies.

> *Ibid. Chap. 6, Page 131*

A finger in every pie.[3]

> *Ibid. Page 133*

No better than she should be.

> *Ibid.*

Every dog has his day.

> *Ibid.*

That's the nature of women, . . . not to love when we love them, and to love when we love them not.[4]

> *Ibid.*

You may go whistle for the rest.

> *Ibid. Page 134*

Ill-luck, you know, seldom comes alone.[5]

> *Ibid. Page 135*

---

[1] See Shakespeare, page 148a.

[2] El Caballero de la Triste Figura. More accurately translated by Smollett as The Knight of the Sorrowful Countenance.

[3] No pie was baked at Castlewood but her little finger was in it. — THACKERAY: *The Virginians* [1857–1859], *Chap. 5*

[4] See Bernard Shaw, page 764b.

[5] See Shakespeare, page 178a.

Why do you lead me a wild-goose chase?

> *Don Quixote. Part I, Book III, Chap. 6, Page 136*

Experience, the universal Mother of Sciences.

> *Ibid. Chap. 7, Page 140*

I give up the ghost.

> *Ibid. Page 143*

Give me but that, and let the world rub, there I'll stick.

> *Ibid. Page 148*

Ne'er cringe nor creep, for what you by force may reap.

> *Ibid. Page 149*

'Tis an office of more trust to shave a man's beard than to saddle a horse.

> *Ibid. Page 151*

Sing away sorrow, cast away care.

> *Ibid. Chap. 8, Page 153*

After meat comes mustard; or, like money to a starving man at sea, when there are no victuals to be bought with it.

> *Ibid.*

Of good natural parts, and of a liberal education.

> *Ibid. Page 154*

A medley of kindred, that 'twould puzzle a convocation of casuists to resolve their degrees of consanguinity.

> *Ibid. Page 155*

Let every man mind his own business.

> *Ibid. Page 157*

Those who'll play with cats must expect to be scratched.

> *Ibid. Page 159*

Raise a hue and cry.

> *Ibid.*

Return to our flesh-pots of Egypt.

> *Ibid. Page 160*

'Tis the part of a wise man to keep himself to-day for to-morrow, and not venture all his eggs in one basket.

> *Ibid. Chap. 9, Page 162*

The ease of my burdens, the staff of my life.

> *Ibid. Page 163*

Within a stone's throw of it.

> *Ibid. Page 170*

The very remembrance of my former misfortune proves a new one to me.

> *Don Quixote. Part I, Book III, Chap. 10, Page 174*

Absence, that common cure of love.

> *Ibid. Page 177*

Lovers are commonly industrious to make themselves uneasy.

> *Ibid. Page 179*

From pro's and con's they fell to a warmer way of disputing.

> *Ibid. Page 181*

Naked came I into the world, and naked must I go out.

> *Ibid.*

Little said is soon amended.

> *Ibid. Page 184*

A close mouth catches no flies.

> *Ibid.*

She may guess what I should perform in the wet, if I do so much in the dry.[1]

> *Ibid. Chap. 11, Page 186*

Mere flim-flam stories, and nothing but shams and lies.

> *Ibid. Page 187*

Thou hast seen nothing yet.

> *Ibid. Page 190*

Between jest and earnest.

> *Ibid.*

Cutting the air as swift as a witch upon a broomstick.

> *Ibid. Page 191*

My love and hers have always been purely Platonic.

> *Ibid. Page 192*

There's no need to make an enquiry about a woman's pedigree, as there is of us men, when some badge of honour is bestowed on us.

> *Ibid. Page 194*

There are but two things that chiefly excite us to love a woman, an attractive beauty, and unspotted fame.

> *Ibid. Page 195*

'Tis ill talking of halters in the house of a man that was hanged.

> *Ibid.*

---

[1] An allusion to *Luke, XXIII, 31:* For if they do these things in a green tree, what shall be done in the dry?

My memory is so bad, that many times I forget my own name!

Don Quixote. Part I, Book III,
Chap. 11, Page 195

You're a devil at everything; and there's no kind of thing in the versal world but what you can turn your hand to.

Ibid. Page 196

'Twill grieve me so to the heart, that I shall cry my eyes out.

Ibid. Page 197

Ready to split his sides with laughing.

Ibid. Chap. 13, Page 208

As much a fool as he was, he loved money, and knew how to keep it when he had it, and was wise enough to keep his own counsel.

Ibid.

What man has assurance enough to pretend to know thoroughly the riddle of a woman's mind, and who could ever hope to fix her mutable nature? [1]

Ibid. Page 216

Demonstrations of love are never altogether displeasing to women, and the most disdainful, in spite of all their coyness, reserve a little complaisance in their hearts for their admirers.

Ibid. Book IV, Chap. 1, Page 226

My honour is dearer to me than my life.

Ibid. Page 228

On the word of a gentleman, and a Christian.

Ibid. Chap. 2, Page 236

Delay always breeds danger. [2]

Ibid. Page 240

Think before thou speakest.

Ibid. Chap. 3, Page 252

Let us forget and forgive injuries.

Ibid. Page 254

I must speak the truth, and nothing but the truth.

Ibid. Page 255

More knave than fool.

Ibid. Chap. 4, Page 261

A fig for your great captain.

Ibid. Chap. 5, Page 267

[1] See Virgil, page 37a.
[2] See Shakespeare, page 124b.

He that gives quickly gives twice. [1]

Don Quixote. Part I, Book IV,
Chap. 7, Page 291

Required in every good lover . . . the whole alphabet . . . Agreeable, Bountiful, Constant, Dutiful, Easy, Faithful, Gallant, Honourable, Ingenious, Kind, Loyal, Mild, Noble, Officious, Prudent, Quiet, Rich, Secret, True, Valiant, Wise . . . Young and Zealous.

Ibid. Page 292

Harp so on the same string.

Ibid. Chap. 8, Page 305

Virtue is the truest nobility.

Ibid. Chap. 9, Page 314

Here's the devil-and-all to pay.

Ibid. Chap. 10, Page 319

I begin to smell a rat.

Ibid.

I'll take my corporal oath on 't.

Ibid. Page 321

The proof of the pudding is in the eating.

Ibid. Page 322

Let none presume to tell me that the pen is preferable to the sword. [2]

Ibid. Page 325

It is past all controversy, that what costs dearest, is, and ought most to be valued.

Ibid. Chap. 11, Page 328

It seldom happens that any felicity comes so pure as not to be tempered and allayed by some mixture of sorrow.

Ibid. Chap. 14, Page 359

There's no striving against the stream; and the weakest still goes to the wall.

Ibid. Chap. 20, Page 404

The bow cannot always stand bent, nor can human frailty subsist without some lawful recreation.

Ibid. Chap. 21, Page 412

Faith without good works is dead.

Ibid. Chap. 23, Page 423

[1] Bis dat qui cito dat. — *Latin proverb*
[2] See Edward Bulwer Lytton, page 510b.
Scholars' pens carry farther, and give a louder report than thunder. — SIR THOMAS BROWNE: *Religio Medici* [1642] (Everyman ed.), *P. 70*

I would have nobody to control me, I would be absolute; and who but I? Now, he that is absolute can do what he likes; he that can do what he likes, can take his pleasure; he that can take his pleasure, can be content; and he that can be content, has no more to desire. So the matter's over; and come what will come, I am satisfied.

Don Quixote. Part I, Book IV,
Chap. 23, Page 423

Even a worm when trod upon, will turn again.

Ibid. Part II [1615], Book III,
Author's Preface, Page 440

It is not the hand, but the understanding of a man, that may be said to write.[1]

Ibid. Page 441

How blind must he be that can't see through a sieve.

Ibid. Chap. 1, Page 450

When the head aches, all the members partake of the pains.[2]

Ibid. Chap. 2, Page 455

Youngsters read it, grown men understand it, and old people applaud it.

Ibid. Chap. 3, Page 464

The most artful part in a play is the fool's.

Ibid. Page 465

There are men that will make you books, and turn 'em loose into the world, with as much dispatch as they would do a dish of fritters.

Ibid.

He that publishes a book runs a very great hazard, since nothing can be more impossible than to compose one that may secure the approbation of every reader.

Ibid. Page 466

[1] Cervantes's left hand was maimed for life by gunshot wounds in the battle of Lepanto.
[2] For let our finger ache, and it indues
   Our other healthful members even to that
   sense
   Of pain.
   SHAKESPEARE: *Othello* [1604–1605],
   Act III, Sc. 4, L. 145

Every man is as Heaven made him, and sometimes a great deal worse.

Don Quixote. Part II, Book III,
Chap. 4, Page 468

There's no sauce in the world like hunger.

Ibid. Chap. 5, Page 473

Birds of a feather flock together.

Ibid. Page 474

He casts a sheep's eye at the wench.

Ibid.

I ever loved to see everything upon the square.

Ibid. Page 475

Neither will I make myself anybody's laughing-stock.

Ibid.

Journey over all the universe in a map, without the expense and fatigue of travelling, without suffering the inconveniences of heat, cold, hunger, and thirst.

Ibid. Chap. 6, Page 479

Presume to put in her oar.

Ibid. Page 480

The fair sex.[1]

Ibid.

A little in one's own pocket is better than much in another man's purse. 'Tis good to keep a nest-egg. Every little makes a mickle.

Ibid. Chap. 7, Page 486

Remember the old saying, "Faint heart ne'er won fair lady."

Ibid. Chap. 10, Page 501

Fore-warned fore-armed.

Ibid. Page 502

As well look for a needle in a bottle of hay.

Ibid.

Are we to mark this day with a white or a black stone?

Ibid. Page 503

The very pink of courtesy.

Ibid. Chap. 13, Page 521

I'll turn over a new leaf.

Ibid. Page 524

[1] That sex which is therefore called fair. —
STEELE: *The Spectator, No. 302,* February 15, 1712

The pen is the tongue of the mind.
>*Don Quixote. Part II, Book III,*
>*Chap. 16, Page 543*

Modesty is a virtue not often found among poets, for almost every one of them thinks himself the greatest in the world.
>*Ibid. Chap. 18, Page 555*

Marriage is a noose.
>*Ibid. Chap. 19, Page 564*

There were but two families in the world, Have-much and Have-little.
>*Ibid. Chap. 20, Page 574*

He preaches well that lives well, quoth Sancho, that's all the divinity I understand.
>*Ibid. Page 575*

Love and War are the same thing, and stratagems and policy are as allowable in the one as in the other.
>*Ibid. Chap. 21, Page 580*

A private sin is not so prejudicial in this world as a public indecency.
>*Ibid. Chap. 22, Page 582*

There is no love lost, sir.[1]
>*Ibid.*

Come back sound, wind and limb.
>*Ibid. Page 587*

Patience, and shuffle the cards.[2]
>*Ibid. Chap. 23, Page 592*

Tell me thy company, and I'll tell thee what thou art.[3]
>*Ibid. Page 594*

---

[1] There is no hate lost between us. — MIDDLETON [1570–1627]: *The Witch, Act IV, Sc. 3*

[2] But patience, cousin, and shuffle the cards, till our hand is a stronger one. — SIR WALTER SCOTT: *Quentin Durward* [1823], *Chap. 8*

>Cut the fiercest quarrels short
>With "Patience, gentlemen, and shuffle."
>>W. M. PRAED [1802–1839]:
>>*Quince, St. 5*

Men disappoint me so, I disappoint myself so, yet courage, patience, shuffle the cards. — MARGARET FULLER OSSOLI [1810–1850]: *Letter to the Reverend W. H. Channing*

[3] Tell me what you eat, and I will tell you what you are. — ANTHELME BRILLAT-SAVARIN [1755–1826]: *Physiologie du Goût, Aphorism 4*

Show me your garden and I shall tell you

To-morrow will be a new day.
>*Don Quixote. Part II, Book III,*
>*Chap. 26, Page 618*

You can see farther into a millstone than he.
>*Ibid. Chap. 28, Page 628*

I can see with half an eye.
>*Ibid. Chap. 29, Page 632*

Scum of the world.[1]
>*Ibid. Page 635*

Old . . . that's an affront no woman can well bear.
>*Ibid. Chap. 31, Page 644*

One of the most considerable advantages the great have over their inferiors, is to have servants as good as themselves.
>*Ibid. Page 645*

Made 'em pay dear for their frolic.
>*Ibid. Chap. 32, Page 655*

Great persons are able to do great kindnesses.
>*Ibid. Page 662*

Honesty's the best policy.[2]
>*Ibid. Chap. 33, Page 666*

An honest man's word is as good as his bond.
>*Ibid. Book IV, Chap. 34, Page 674*

Heaven's help is better than early rising.
>*Ibid.*

He would not budge an inch.
>*Ibid. Page 677*

A blot in thy scutcheon to all futurity.
>*Ibid. Chap. 35, Page 681*

There's a time for some things, and a time for all things; a time for great things, and a time for small things.[3]
>*Ibid. Page 682*

With a grain of salt.
>*Ibid. Chap. 37, Page 690*

---

what you are. — ALFRED AUSTIN: *The Garden That I Love* [1905]

[1] See R. H. Schauffler, page 904b.

[2] I hold the maxim no less applicable to public than to private affairs, that honesty is always the best policy. — GEORGE WASHINGTON: *Farewell Address* [1796]

[3] See *Ecclesiastes, III, 1*, on page 1042b.

There's a time for all things. — SHAKESPEARE: *The Comedy of Errors* [1592–1593], *Act II, Sc. 2, L. 67*

They had best not stir the rice, though it sticks to the pot.
Don Quixote. Part II, Book IV, Chap. 37, Page 691

They cover a dunghill with a piece of tapestry when a procession goes by.
Ibid.

Good wits jump; [1] a word to the wise is enough.
Ibid. Page 692

My understanding has forsook me, and is gone a wool-gathering.[2]
Ibid. Chap. 38, Page 692

Diligence is the mother of good fortune.
Ibid. Page 724

What a man has, so much he's sure of.
Ibid. Page 725

When a man says, "Get out of my house! what would you have with my wife?" there's no answer to be made.
Ibid. Page 726

The pot calls the kettle black.
Ibid. Page 727

Mum's the word.[3]
Ibid. Chap. 44, Page 729

When thou art at Rome, do as they do at Rome.[4]
Ibid. Chap. 54, Page 806

He that proclaims the kindnesses he has received, shows his disposition to repay 'em if he could.
Ibid. Chap. 58, Page 835

He that errs in so considerable a passage, may well be suspected to have committed many gross errors through the whole history.
Ibid. Chap. 59, Page 843

[1] Great wits jump. — STERNE: *Tristram Shandy, Vol. III* [1761–1762], *Chap. 9*

[2] My thoughts ran a wool-gathering; and I did like the countryman, who looked for his ass while he was mounted on his back. — *Don Quixote, P. 827*
Have you summoned your wits from wool-gathering? — MIDDLETON: *The Family of Love* [1608], *Act V, Sc. 5*

[3] Cry "mum." — SHAKESPEARE: *The Merry Wives of Windsor* [1600–1601], *Act V, Sc. 2, L. 6*

[4] When they are at Rome, they do there as they see done. — ROBERT BURTON: *Anatomy of Melancholy* [1621–1651], *Memb. 2, Subsect. I*

I shall be as secret as the grave.
Don Quixote. Part II, Book IV, Chap. 62, Page 862

Now blessings light on him that first invented this same sleep! It covers a man all over, thoughts and all, like a cloak; 'tis meat for the hungry, drink for the thirsty, heat for the cold, and cold for the hot. 'Tis the current coin that purchases all the pleasures of the world cheap; and the balance that sets the king and the shepherd, the fool and the wise man even.
Ibid. Chap. 68, Page 898

The ass will carry his load, but not a double load; ride not a free horse to death.
Ibid. Chap. 71, Page 917

I thought it working for a dead horse, because I am paid beforehand.[1]
Ibid.

He . . . got the better of himself, and that's the best kind of victory one can wish for.
Ibid. Chap. 72, Page 924

Every man was not born with a silver spoon in his mouth.
Ibid. Chap. 73, Page 926

Die merely of the mulligrubs.
Ibid. Chap. 74, Page 932

Ne'er look for birds of this year in the nests of the last.[2]
Ibid. Page 933

There is a strange charm in the thoughts of a good legacy, or the hopes of an estate, which wondrously alleviates the sorrow that men would otherwise feel for the death of friends.
Ibid. Page 934

[1] It is a heart-rending delusion and a cruel snare to be paid for your work before you accomplish it. As soon as once your work is finished you ought to be promptly paid; but to receive your lucre one minute before it is due, is to tempt Providence to make a Micawber of you. — EDMUND GOSSE: *Gossip in a Library* [1891], *Beau Nash*

[2] For Time will teach thee soon the truth,
There are no birds in last year's nest!
LONGFELLOW [1807–1882]: *It Is Not Always May, St. 6*

For if he like a madman lived,
At least he like a wise one died.
> *Don Quixote. Part II, Book IV,*
> *Chap. 74, Page 935 (Don*
> *Quixote's Epitaph)*

Don't put too fine a point to your wit
for fear it should get blunted.
> *The Little Gypsy (La Gitanilla)*

My heart is wax moulded as she
pleases, but enduring as marble to retain.[1]
> *Ibid.*

GILES FLETCHER
[1549?–1611]

He is a path, if any be misled;
He is a robe, if any naked be;
If any chance to hunger, he is bread;
If any be a bondman, he is free;
If any be but weak, how strong is he!
To dead men life is he, to sick men,
  health;
To blind men, sight, and to the needy,
  wealth;
A pleasure without loss, a treasure with-
  out stealth.
> *Excellency of Christ*
> *[Circa 1593]*

A fool's paradise.[2]
> *The Sorcerer of Vain Delights*
> *[1593], Stanza 3*

SIR EDWARD COKE
[1552–1634]

The gladsome light of jurisprudence.
> *First Institute [1628]*

Reason is the life of the law; nay, the
common law itself is nothing else but

---

[1] Wax to receive, and marble to retain. —
BYRON: *Beppo* [1818], St. 34
[2] The earliest instance of this expression is
found in the *Paston Letters* [1462], No. 457.
The Paradise of Fools, to few unknown. —
MILTON: *Paradise Lost* [1667], Book III,
L. 496
Hence the fool's paradise. — ALEXANDER
POPE: *The Dunciad* [1728], Book III, L. 9
In this fool's paradise he drank delight. —
GEORGE DU MAURIER: *Peter Ibbetson* [1891]
XII, *Players*
What matter if it be a fool's paradise? Para-
dise is paradise, for whoever owns it! —
GEORGE DU MAURIER: *Peter Ibbetson* [1891]

reason. . . . The law, which is perfection of reason.[1]
> *First Institute*

For a man's house is his castle, *et
domus sua cuique tutissimum refu-
gium.*[2]
> *Third Institute [1644]*

The house of every one is to him as
his castle and fortress, as well for his
defence against injury and violence as
for his repose.
> *Semayne's Case. 5 Rep. 91*

They [corporations] cannot commit
treason, nor be outlawed nor excommu-
nicate, for they have no souls.
> *Case of Sutton's Hospital. 10 Rep. 32*

Magna Charta is such a fellow that
he will have no sovereign.
> *Debate in the Commons*
> *[May 17, 1628]*

Six hours in sleep, in law's grave study
  six,
Four spend in prayer, the rest on Nature fix.[3]
> *Translation of lines quoted by* COKE

SIR WALTER RALEIGH
[1552–1618]

If all the world and love were young,
And truth in every shepherd's tongue,
These pretty pleasures might me move
To live with thee, and be thy love.
> *The Nymph's Reply to the Pas-
> sionate Shepherd*[4] *(Printed in
> England's Helicon [1600]).
> Stanza 1*

---

[1] Let us consider the reason of the case. For
nothing is law that is not reason. — SIR JOHN
POWELL: *Coggs* vs. *Bernard, 2 Ld. Raym.
Rep. P. 911*
[2] One's home is the safest refuge to every-
one. — *Pandects* [6th Century A. D.], *Lib. II,
Tit. IV, De in Jus vocando*
I in mine own house am an emperor
  And will defend what's mine.
  MASSINGER: *The Roman Actor* [1629],
  Act I, Sc. 2
[3] Seven hours to law, to soothing slumber
  seven;
Ten to the world allot, and all to heaven.
  SIR WILLIAM JONES [1746–1794]
[4] An answer to MARLOWE's poem, *The Pas-
sionate Shepherd to His Love.* See page 123a.

Fain would I climb, yet fear I to fall.
Written on a Windowpane [1]

Fain would I, but I dare not; I dare,
and yet I may not;
I may, although I care not, for pleasure
when I play not.
Fain Would I

Passions are likened best to floods and
streams:
The shallow murmur, but the deep are
dumb.[2]
The Silent Lover. Prelude

Silence in love bewrays more woe
Than words, though ne'er so witty:
A beggar that is dumb, you know,
May challenge double pity.
Ibid. Stanza 7

Go, Soul, the body's guest,
Upon a thankless arrant:
Fear not to touch the best,
The truth shall be thy warrant:
Go, since I needs must die,
And give the world the lie.
The Lie. Stanza 1 [3] (*Printed in*
FRANCIS DAVISON'S *Poetical
Rhapsody* [*1608*]; *manuscript
copy traced to 1593*)

Give me my scallop-shell of quiet,
My staff of faith to walk upon,
My scrip of joy, immortal diet,
My bottle of salvation,
My gown of glory, hope's true gage,
And thus I'll take my pilgrimage.
His Pilgrimage [*1604*]

---

[1] Under this Queen Elizabeth wrote, "If
thy heart fails thee, climb not at all." —
THOMAS FULLER: *Worthies of England*
[*1662*]

[2] Altissima quaeque flumina minimo sono
labi (The deepest rivers flow with the least
sound). — QUINTUS CURTIUS [1st Century
A.D.], *VII, 4, 13*
Where the streame runneth smoothest, the
water is deepest. — LYLY: *Euphues and his
England* [*1580*]
Smooth runs the water where the brook is
deep. — SHAKESPEARE: *Henry VI* [*1591*],
Part II, Act III, Sc. 1, L. 53
Take heed of still waters, the quick pass
away. — GEORGE HERBERT: *Jacula Prudentum* [*1640*]

[3] This poem was probably written by
Raleigh during his imprisonment in 1592. It
has also been attributed to Sir John Davies,

Methought I saw the grave where
Laura lay.
Verses to Edmund Spenser

Shall I, like a hermit, dwell
On a rock or in a cell?
Poem

If she undervalue me,
What care I how fair she be? [1]
Ibid.

If she seem not chaste to me,
What care I how chaste she be?
Ibid.

[History] hath triumphed over time,
which besides it nothing but eternity
hath triumphed over.
Historie of the World [*1614*].
Preface

O eloquent, just, and mightie Death!
whom none could advise, thou hast per-
swaded; what none hath dared, thou
hast done; and whom all the world
hath flattered, thou only hast cast out
of the world and despised. Thou hast
drawne together all the farre stretched
greatnesse, all the pride, crueltie, and
ambition of man, and covered it all
over with these two narrow words, *Hic
jacet!*
*Ibid. Book V, Part I, Chap. 6,
Conclusion*

Cowards [may] fear to die; but courage stout,
Rather than live in snuff, will be put
out.
Remains [*ed. 1661*], *Page 258.
On the snuff of a candle the
night before he died*

Even such is time, that takes in trust
Our youth, our joys, our all we have,
And pays us but with age and dust;
Who in the dark and silent grave,
When we have wandered all our ways,
Shuts up the story of our days.
But from this earth, this grave, this
dust,

Joshua Sylvester, Lord Pembroke, and Rich-
ard Edwards.
[1] If she be not so to me,
What care I how fair she be?
GEORGE WITHER [*1588–1667*]:
The Shepherd's Resolution

My God shall raise me up, I trust!
Written the night before his death; found in his Bible in the Gate-house at Westminster

RICHARD HOOKER
[1553–1600]

Of Law there can be no less acknowledged than that her seat is the bosom of God, her voice the harmony of the world. All things in heaven and earth do her homage, — the very least as feeling her care, and the greatest as not exempted from her power.
Laws of Ecclesiastical Polity [*1594*]. *Book I*

That to live by one man's will became the cause of all men's misery.
Ibid.

GEORGE KEITH, FIFTH EARL MARISCHAL
[1553–1623]

Thai half said. Quhat say thai? Let thame say.[1]
Family motto, Mitchell Tower, Marischal College, Aberdeen, Scotland, founded in 1593

JOHN LYLY
[*Circa* 1553–1606]

Be valyaunt, but not too venturous. Let thy attyre bee comely, but not costly.[2]
Euphues [*1579*] (*Arber's reprint*). *Page 39*

The finest edge is made with the blunt whetstone.
Ibid. Page 47

It seems to me (said she) that you are in some brown study.[3]
Ibid. Page 80

---

[1] They say. What say they? Let them say. — *Motto over the fireplace in George Bernard Shaw's home*

[2] Costly thy habit as thy purse can buy,
But not express'd in fancy; rich, not gaudy.
SHAKESPEARE: *Hamlet* [1600–1601], *Act I, Sc. 3, L. 70*

[3] A brown study. — SWIFT: *Polite Conversation* [*circa* 1738]

Many strokes overthrow the tallest oaks.[1]
Euphues. Page 81

Lette me stande to the maine chance.
Ibid. Page 104

It is a world to see.
Ibid. Page 116

A clere conscience is a sure carde.
Ibid. Page 207

Goe to bed with the Lambe, and rise with the Larke.[2]
Euphues and his England [*1580*]. *Page 229*

A comely olde man as busie as a bee.
Ibid. Page 252

Maydens, be they never so foolyshe, yet beeing fayre they are commonly fortunate.
Ibid. Page 279

Your eyes are so sharpe that you cannot onely looke through a Milstone, but cleane through the minde.
Ibid. Page 289

I am glad that my Adonis hath a sweete tooth in his head.
Ibid. Page 308

A Rose is sweeter in the budde than full blowne.[3]
Ibid. Page 314

Cupid and my Campaspe play'd
At cards for kisses: Cupid paid.
Alexander and Campaspe [*1584*]. *Act III, Sc. 5*

How at heaven's gates she claps her wings,
The morne not waking til she sings.[4]
Ibid. Act V, Sc. 1

---

[1] Many strokes, though with a little axe,
Hew down and fell the hardest-timber'd oak.
SHAKESPEARE: *Henry VI* [1591], *Part III, Act II, Sc. 1, L. 54*

[2] To rise with the lark and go to bed with the lamb. — BRETON: *Court and Country* [1618]
Rise with the lark, and with the lark to bed. — JAMES HURDIS [1763–1801]: *The Village Curate*

[3] The rose is fairest when 'tis budding new. — SCOTT: *Lady of the Lake* [1810], *Canto III, St. 1*

[4] See Shakespeare, page 204a.

EDMUND SPENSER
[1553?–1599]

But of all burdens, that a man can
beare,
Moste is, a fooles talke to beare and to
heare.
> *The Shepheardes Calender
> [1579]. Maye, Line 140*

Fierce warres and faithfull loves shall
moralize my song.[1]
> *The Faerie Queene* [1590].
> *Introduction, Stanza 1*

A Gentle Knight was pricking on the
plaine.
> *Ibid. Book I, Canto 1, Stanza 1*

A bold bad man.
> *Ibid. Stanza 37*

Her angels face
As the great eye of heaven shyned
bright,
And made a sunshine in the shadie
place.
> *Ibid. Canto 3, Stanza 4*

Ay me, how many perils doe enfold
The righteous man, to make him daily
fall.[2]
> *Ibid. Canto 8, Stanza 1*

Is not short paine well borne, that
brings long ease,
And layes the soule to sleepe in quiet
grave?
Sleepe after toyle, port after stormie
seas,
Ease after warre, death after life does
greatly please.[3]
> *Ibid. Canto 9, Stanza 40*

All for love, and nothing for reward.
> *Ibid. Book II, Canto 8, Stanza 2*

Her berth was of the wombe of Morning dew,[4]

[1] And moralized his song. — POPE: *Epistle
to Dr. Arbuthnot* [1735], *L. 340*
[2] Ay me! what perils do environ
The man that meddles with cold iron!
SAMUEL BUTLER: *Hudibras, Part I*
[1663], *Canto III, L. 1*
[3] The last two lines are cut on Joseph Conrad's gravestone at Canterbury.
[4] The dew of thy birth is of the womb of
the morning. — *Book of Common Prayer,
Psalter, Psalm CX, 3*

And her conception of the joyous
Prime.
> *The Faerie Queene. Book III,
> Canto 6, Stanza 3*

Roses red and violets blew,
And all the sweetest flowres, that in the
forrest grew.
> *Ibid. Stanza 6*

All that in this delightfull Gardin
growes,
Should happie be, and have immortall
blis.
> *Ibid. Stanza 41*

That Squire of Dames.
> *Ibid. Canto 8, Stanza 44*

How over that same dore was likewise
writ,
Be bold, be bold, and every where *Be
bold.*[1]
> *Ibid. Canto 11, Stanza 54*

Another yron dore, on which was writ,
Be not too bold.
> *Ibid.*

Dan Chaucer, well of English unde-
tyled,
On Fames eternall beadroll worthie to
be fyled.
> *Ibid. Book IV* [1596],
> *Canto 2, Stanza 32*

For all that nature by her mother wit
Could frame in earth.
> *Ibid. Canto 10, Stanza 21*

Me seemes the world is runne quite out
of square,
From the first point of his appointed
sourse,
And being once amisse growes daily
wourse and wourse.
> *Ibid. Book V, Introduction,
> Stanza 1*

Ill can he rule the great, that cannot
reach the small.
> *Ibid. Canto 2, Stanza 43*

[1] De l'audace, encore de l'audace, et toujours de l'audace (Boldness, again boldness,
and always boldness). — DANTON: *Speech in
the Legislative Assembly* [1792]
Write on your doors the saying wise and
old,
"Be bold! be bold!" and everywhere — "Be
bold;
Be not too bold!"
LONGFELLOW: *Morituri Salutamus* [1875]

Who will not mercie unto others shew,
How can he mercy ever hope to have? [1]
> *The Faerie Queene. Book VI,*
> *Canto 1, Stanza 42*

The gentle minde by gentle deeds is
knowne.

For a man by nothing is so well be-
wrayed,
As by his manners.
> *Ibid. Canto 3, Stanza 1*

That here on earth is no sure happiness.
> *Ibid. Canto 11, Stanza 1*

    The ever-whirling wheele
Of *Change,* the which all mortall things
doth sway.
> *Ibid. Book VII, Canto 6, Stanza 1*

Warres and allarums unto Nations
wide.
> *Ibid. Stanza 3*

But Times do change and move continually.
> *Ibid. Stanza 47*

For deeds doe die, how ever noblie
donne,
And thoughts of men do as themselves
decay,
But wise wordes taught in numbers for
to runne,
Recorded by the Muses, live for ay.
> *The Ruines of Time* [*1591*].
> *Line 400*

Full little knowest thou that hast not
tride,
What hell it is, in suing long to bide:
To loose good dayes, that might be
better spent;
To wast long nights in pensive discontent;
To speed to-day, to be put back tomorrow;
To feed on hope, to pine with feare and
sorrow.
> *Mother Hubberds Tale* [*1591*].
> *Line 895*

To fret thy soule with crosses and with
cares;
To eate thy heart through comfortlesse
dispaires; [2]

[1] Blessed are the merciful, for they shall obtain mercy. — *Matthew, V, 7*
[2] See Plutarch, page 57b.

To fawne, to crowche, to waite, to ride,
to ronne,
To spend, to give, to want, to be un-
donne.

Unhappie wight, born to desastrous
end,
That doth his life in so long tendance
spend.
> *Mother Hubberds Tale. Line 903*

What more felicitie can fall to creature,
Than to enjoy delight with libertie.
> *Muiopotmos: or The Fate of the*
> *Butterflie* [*1591*]. *Line 209*

I hate the day, because it lendeth light
To see all things, and not my love to
see.
> *Daphnaida* [*1591*]. *Line 407*

Death slue not him, but he made death
his ladder to the skies.
> *An Epitaph upon Sir Philip Sidney*
> [*1591*]. *Line 20*

A sweet attractive kinde of grace,
A full assurance given by lookes,
Continuall comfort in a face,
The lineaments of Gospell bookes,
  I trowe that countenance cannot lie,
  Whose thoughts are legible in the eie.
> *An Elegie, or Friends Passion,*
> *for his Astrophill* (Sir Philip
> Sidney). *Line 103* [1]

Was never eie, did see that face,
Was never eare, did heare that tong,
Was never minde, did minde his grace,
That ever thought the travell long,
  But eies, and eares, and ev'ry
  thought,
  Were with his sweete perfections
  caught.
> *Ibid. Line 109*

Though last not least. [2]
> *Colin Clouts Come Home Again*
> [*1595*]. *Line 144*

Tell her the joyous time wil not be
staid

[1] This elegy was printed anonymously in a
miscellany, *The Phoenix' Nest* [1593]. It has
been erroneously ascribed to Mathew Roydon
[1580–1622].
[2] See Shakespeare, page 167b and page 190b.
The last, not least in honour or applause.
— Pope: *The Dunciad* [1728], *Book IV, L.*
577

Unlesse she doe him by the forelock take.[1]

Amoretti [*1595*]. *Sonnet 70*

The woods shall to me answer, and my Eccho ring.

Epithalamion [*1595*]. *Line 18*

Behold whiles she before the altar stands
Hearing the holy priest that to her speakes
And blesseth her with his two happy hands.

Ibid. Line 223

Ah! when will this long weary day have end,
And lende me leave to come unto my love?

Ibid. Line 278

For of the soule the bodie forme doth take:
For soule is forme, and doth the bodie make.

An Hymne in Honour of Beautie [*1596*]. *Line 132*

For all that faire is, is by nature good;[2]
That is a signe to know the gentle blood.

Ibid. Line 139

Sweete Themmes! runne softly, till I end my Song.[3]

Prothalamion [*1596*]. *Refrain*

I was promised on a time
To have reason for my rhyme;
From that time unto this season,
I received nor rhyme nor reason.

Lines on his Promised Pension (Quoted by THOMAS FULLER *in Worthies of England* [*1662*])

HENRY IV OF FRANCE
[1553–1610]

If God grants me the usual length of life, I hope to make France so pros-

---

[1] Take Time by the forelock. — THALES of Miletus [636–546 B.C.]
[2] See Shakespeare, page 185a.
[3] Sweet Thames, run softly till I end my song,
Sweet Thames, run softly, for I speak not loud or long.
T. S. ELIOT: *The Waste Land* [*1922*], *Part III*

perous that every peasant will have a chicken in his pot on Sunday [1]

Said when he was crowned king,
1589

Paris is well worth a mass.[2]

Caquets de l'Accouchée [*1622*]

SIR PHILIP SIDNEY
[1554–1586]

High-erected thoughts seated in the heart of courtesy.[3]

Arcadia [*1590*]. *Book I*

They are never alone that are accompanied with noble thoughts.[4]

Ibid.

Many-headed multitude.[5]

Ibid. Book II

My dear, my better half.

Ibid. Book III

"Fool!" said my muse to me, "look in thy heart, and write."[6]

Astrophel and Stella [*1591*]

With how sad steps, O Moon, thou climb'st the skies!

Ibid.

Have I caught my heav'nly jewel.[7]

Ibid. Second Song

My true-love hath my heart, and I have his,
By just exchange one for the other given:

---

[1] See Alexander Smith, page 650b.
[2] Paris vaut bien une messe. — *Attributed either to* HENRY IV *or to his minister* SULLY *in conversation with the king*
[3] Great thoughts come from the heart. — VAUVENARGUES [1715–1747]: *Maxim CXXVII*
[4] He never is alone that is accompanied with noble thoughts. — BEAUMONT AND FLETCHER: *Love's Cure* [1647], *Act III, Sc. 3*
[5] This many-headed monster, Multitude. — DANIEL: *History of the Civil Wars* [1595], *Book II, St. 13*
See Shakespeare, page 202a.
This many-headed monster. — MASSINGER: *The Roman Actor* [1629], *Act III, Sc. 2*
There still remains, to mortify a wit,
The many-headed monster of the pit.
ALEXANDER POPE: *Epistle I, Book II* [1734], *L. 304*
[6] Look, then, into thine heart and write. — LONGFELLOW: *Voices of the Night* [1839], *Prelude*
[7] Quoted by SHAKESPEARE in *Merry Wives of Windsor, Act III, Sc. 3, L. 45*

I hold his dear, and mine he cannot
    miss,
There never was a better bargain
    driven.
      The Bargain [*1591*]. *Stanza 1*

Sweet food of sweetly uttered knowledge.
      Defence of Poesy [*1595*]

He cometh unto you with a tale
which holdeth children from play, and
old men from the chimney-corner.
      Ibid.

I never heard the old song of Percy
and Douglas that I found not my heart
moved more than with a trumpet.
      Ibid.

THOMAS LODGE
[1558?–1625]

Love in my bosom like a bee
Doth suck his sweet.
      Rosalind [*1590*]

Her paps are centres of delight,
Her breasts are orbs of heavenly frame.
      Ibid.

GEORGE PEELE
[1558–1597]

His golden locks time hath to silver
    turned;
  O time too swift! O swiftness never
    ceasing!
His youth 'gainst time and age hath
    ever spurned,
  But spurned in vain; youth waneth
    by encreasing.
    Polyhymnia [*1590*]. *The Aged*
      Man-at-Arms, Stanza 1

His helmet now shall make a hive for
    bees,
  And lovers' songs be turned to holy
    psalms;
A man-at-arms must now serve on his
    knees,
  And feed on prayers, which are old
    age's alms.
      Ibid. Stanza 2

My merry, merry, merry roundelay
Concludes with Cupid's curse:

They that do change old love for new,
Pray gods, they change for worse!
      Cupid's Curse

GEORGE CHAPMAN
[1559–1634]

Promise is most given when the least
    is said.
      Hero and Leander [*1598*]

Black is a pearl in a woman's eye.[1]
    An Humorous Day's Mirth [*1599*]

Exceeding fair she was not; and yet fair
In that she never studied to be fairer
Than Nature made her.
      All Fools [*1605*]. *Act I, Sc. 1*

I tell thee Love is Nature's second sun,
Causing a spring of virtues where he
    shines.
      Ibid.

Cornelia. What flowers are these?
Gazetta. The pansy this.
Cornelia. Oh, that's for lovers'
    thoughts.[2]
      Ibid. Act. II, Sc. 1

Fortune, the great commandress of the
    world,
Hath divers ways to advance her fol-
    lowers:
To some she gives honour without de-
    serving,
To other some, deserving without hon-
    our.
      Ibid. Act V, Sc. 1

Young men think old men are fools;
but old men know young men are fools.
      Ibid.

Keep thy shop, and thy shop will
keep thee. Light gains make heavy
purses.[3]
    Eastward Ho [4] [*1605*]. *Act I, Sc. 1*

Make ducks and drakes with shillings.
      Ibid.

Only a few industrious Scots perhaps,
who indeed are dispersed over the face
of the whole earth. But as for them,

---

[1] Black men are pearls in beauteous ladies'
eyes. — SHAKESPEARE: *Two Gentlemen of Verona* [*1594–1595*], *Act V, Sc. 2, L. 12*
[2] See Shakespeare, page 178a.
[3] See Franklin, page 331a.
[4] By Chapman, Jonson, and Marston.

there are no greater friends to Englishmen and England, when they are out on't, in the world, than they are. And for my own part, I would a hundred thousand of them were there [Virginia]; for we are all one countrymen now, ye know, and we should find ten times more comfort of them there than we do here.[1]

Eastward Ho. Act III, Sc. 2

I will neither yield to the song of the siren nor the voice of the hyena, the tears of the crocodile [2] nor the howling of the wolf.

Ibid. Act. V, Sc. 1

For one heat, all know, doth drive out another,
One passion doth expel another still.[3]

Monsieur D'Olive [*1606*].
Act V, Sc. 1

To put a girdle round about the world.[4]

Bussy D'Ambois [*1607*].
Act I, Sc. 1

So our lives
In acts exemplary, not only win
Ourselves good names, but doth to others give
Matter for virtuous deeds, by which we live.

Ibid.

Who to himself is law no law doth need,
Offends no law, and is a king indeed.

Ibid. Act II, Sc. 1

Give me a spirit that on this life's rough sea
Loves t' have his sails fill'd with a lusty wind,
Even till his sail-yards tremble, his masts crack,

[1] This is the famous passage that gave offence to James I, and caused the imprisonment of the authors. The leaves containing it were cancelled and reprinted, and it only occurs in a few of the original copies. — RICHARD HERNE SHEPHERD

[2] These crocodile tears. — ROBERT BURTON: *Anatomy of Melancholy* [1621–1651], *Part III, Sect. 2, Memb. 2, Subsect. 4*
She's false, false as the tears of crocodiles. — SIR JOHN SUCKLING [1609–1642]: *The Sad One, Act IV, Sc. 5*

[3] See Shakespeare, page 134b.

[4] See Shakespeare, page 141b.

And his rapt ship run on her side so low
That she drinks water, and her keel plows air.

Conspiracy of Charles, Duke of Byron [*1608*]. *Act III, Sc. 1*

They're only truly great who are truly good.[1]

Revenge for Honour [*1654*].
Act V, Sc. 2

ROBERT GREENE
[1560–1592]

Sweet are the thoughts that savour of content;
The quiet mind is richer than a crown. . . .
A mind content both crown and kingdom is.

Farewell to Folly

SIR JOHN HARINGTON
[1561–1612]

Fortune, men say, doth give too much to many,
But yet she never gave enough to any.

Epigrams. Of Fortune

The readers and the hearers like my books,
But yet some writers cannot them digest;
But what care I? for when I make a feast
I would my guests should praise it, not the cooks.

Ibid. Of Writers Who Carp at Other Men's Books

ROBERT SOUTHWELL
[1561–1595]

What thought can think, another thought can mend.

Look Home

Let this suffice, by this conceive the rest,

[1] See Juvenal, page 63a.
'Tis only noble to be good. — TENNYSON: *Lady Clara Vere de Vere* [1833], St. 7

He should, he could, he would, he did
the best.
Look Home

Time goes by turns, and chances change
by course,
From foul to fair, from better hap to
worse.
Times Go by Turns

No joy so great but runneth to an end,
No hap so hard but may in time amend.
Ibid.

When sun is set the little stars will
shine.
Scorn Not the Least

He that high growth on cedars did bestow,
Gave also lowly mushrumps leave to
grow.
Ibid.

May never was the month of love,
For May is full of flowers;
But rather April, wet by kind,
For love is full of showers.
Love's Servile Lot

When Fortune smiles, I smile to think
How quickly she will frown.
I Envy Not Their Hap

As I in hoary winter night stood shivering in the snow,
Surprised was I with sudden heat which
made my heart to glow;
And lifting up a fearful eye to view
what fire was near
A pretty Babe all burning bright did
in the air appear.
*The Burning Babe. (A Christ-
mas poem praised by* BEN JON-
SON)

FRANCIS BACON
[1561–1626]

The monuments of wit survive the
monuments of power.
Essex's Device [*1595*]

Knowledge is power. — Nam et ipsa
scientia potestas est.[1]
Meditationes Sacrae [*1597*].
De Haeresibus

[1] A wise man is strong, yea, a man of knowledge increaseth strength. — *Proverbs, XXIV,
5.*

Knowledge is more than equivalent to

"Antiquitas saeculi juventus mundi."
These times are the ancient times, when
the world is ancient, and not those
which we account ancient *ordine retro-
grado,* by a computation backward
from ourselves.[1]
Advancement of Learning [*1605*].
Book I

For the glory of the Creator and the
relief of man's estate.
Ibid.

It [Poesy] was ever thought to have
some participation of divineness, because it doth raise and erect the mind
by submitting the shews of things to the
desires of the mind.
Ibid. Book II

Sacred and inspired divinity, the sa-
baoth and port of all men's labours and
peregrinations.
Ibid.

Cleanness of body was ever deemed
to proceed from a due reverence to
God.[2]
Ibid.

force. — SAMUEL JOHNSON: *Rasselas* [*1759*],
Chap. XIII

[1] As in the little, so in the great world, reason will tell you that old age or antiquity is
to be accounted by the farther distance from
the beginning and the nearer approach to the
end, — the times wherein we now live being
in propriety of speech the most ancient since
the world's creation. — GEORGE HAKEWILL:
*An Apologie or Declaration of the Power and
Providence of God in the Government of the
World* [*1627*]

For as old age is that period of life most
remote from infancy, who does not see that
old age in this universal man ought not to be
sought in the times nearest his birth, but in
those most remote from it? — PASCAL [*1623–
1662*]: *Preface to the Treatise on Vacuum*

It is worthy of remark that a thought which
is often quoted from Francis Bacon occurs in
[Giordano] Bruno's "Cena di Cenere," published in 1584: I mean the notion that the
later times are more aged than the earlier. —
WHEWELL: *Philosophy of the Inductive Sciences* [*1847*], *Vol. II, P. 198*

We are Ancients of the earth,
And in the morning of the times.
TENNYSON: *The Day Dream* [*1842*],
L'Envoi

[2] "Cleanliness is indeed next to godliness."
— JOHN WESLEY [*1703–1791*] (quoted): *Sermon XCII, On Dress*

According to Rabbi A. S. Bettelheim,

States as great engines move slowly.
Advancement of Learning.
Book II

I do plainly and ingenuously confess that I am guilty of corruption, and do renounce all defense. I beseech your Lordships to be merciful to a broken reed.[1]

On being charged by Parliament with corruption in the exercise of his office [*1621*]

Like the strawberry wives, that laid two or three great strawberries at the mouth of their pot, and all the rest were little ones.

Apothegms [*1624*]. *No. 54*

Sir Henry Wotton used to say that critics are like brushers of noblemen's clothes.

Ibid. No. 64

Sir Amice Pawlet, when he saw too much haste made in any matter, was wont to say, "Stay a while, that we may make an end the sooner."

Ibid. No. 76

Alonso of Aragon was wont to say in commendation of age, that age appears to be best in four things, — old wood best to burn, old wine to drink, old friends to trust, and old authors to read.[2]

Ibid. No. 97

this is found in the Hebrew fathers. He cites Phinehas ben Yair, as follows: "The doctrines of religion are resolved into carefulness; carefulness into vigorousness; vigorousness into guiltlessness; guiltlessness into abstemiousness; abstemiousness into cleanliness; cleanliness into godliness" — literally, next to godliness.

[1] Thou trustest in the staff of this broken reed. — *Isaiah, XXXVI, 6*

[2] Is not old wine wholesomest, old pippins toothsomest, old wood burns brightest, old linen wash whitest? Old soldiers, sweetheart, are surest, and old lovers are soundest. — JOHN WEBSTER: *Westward Hoe* [1607], Act II, Sc. 2

Old friends are best. King James used to call for his old shoes; they were easiest for his feet. — SELDEN: *Table Talk* [1689], *Friends*

I love everything that's old, — old friends, old times, old manners, old books, old wine .... and old friends are best! — GOLDSMITH: *She Stoops to Conquer* [1773], Act I

Old books, old wine, old Nankin blue. —

Cosmus, Duke of Florence, was wont to say of perfidious friends, that "We read that we ought to forgive our enemies; but we do not read that we ought to forgive our friends."

Apothegms. No. 206

Cato said the best way to keep good acts in memory was to refresh them with new.

Ibid. No. 247

Come home to men's business and bosoms.

Dedication to the Essays [*Edition 1625*]

No pleasure is comparable to the standing upon the vantage-ground of truth.

Of Truth

Men fear death as children fear to go in the dark; and as that natural fear in children is increased with tales, so is the other.

Of Death

Revenge is a kind of wild justice, which the more man's nature runs to, the more ought law to weed it out.

Of Revenge

It was a high speech of Seneca (after the manner of the Stoics), that "The good things which belong to prosperity are to be wished, but the good things that belong to adversity are to be admired."

Of Adversity

It is yet a higher speech of his than the other, "It is true greatness to have in one the frailty of a man and the security of a god."

Ibid.

Prosperity is the blessing of the Old Testament; adversity is the blessing of the New.

Ibid.

Prosperity is not without many fears and distastes; and adversity is not without comforts and hopes.

Ibid.

Virtue is like precious odours, —

AUSTIN DOBSON [1840–1921]: *Rondeau, To Richard Watson Gilder* most fragrant when they are incensed or crushed.[1]

Of Adversity

He that hath wife and children hath given hostages to fortune; for they are impediments to great enterprises, either of virtue or mischief.

Of Marriage and Single Life

Wives are young men's mistresses, companions for middle age, and old men's nurses.

Ibid.

A good name is like a precious ointment; it filleth all around about, and will not easily away; for the odors of ointments are more durable than those of flowers.[2]

Of Praise

Men in great place are thrice servants, — servants of the sovereign or state, servants of fame, and servants of business.

Of Great Place

Mahomet made the people believe that he would call a hill to him, and from the top of it offer up his prayers for the observers of his law. The people assembled. Mahomet called the hill to come to him, again and again; and when the hill stood still he was never a whit abashed, but said, "If the hill will not come to Mahomet, Mahomet will go to the hill."

Of Boldness

The desire of power in excess caused the angels to fall; the desire of knowledge in excess caused man to fall.[3]

Of Goodness

---

[1] As aromatic plants bestow
No spicy fragrance while they grow;
But crushed or trodden to the ground,
Diffuse their balmy sweets around.
GOLDSMITH: *The Captivity* [1764], *Act I*
The good are better made by ill,
As odours crushed are sweeter still.
SAMUEL ROGERS: *Jacqueline* [1814], *Stanza 3*
[2] See *Ecclesiastes, VII, 1,* on page 1042b, and Publilius Syrus, page 43b.
[3] Pride still is aiming at the blest abodes;
Men would be angels, angels would be gods.

I had rather believe all the fables in the legends and the Talmud and the Alcoran, than that this universal frame is without a mind.

Of Atheism

A little philosophy inclineth man's mind to atheism, but depth in philosophy bringeth men's minds about to religion.[1]

Ibid.

Travel, in the younger sort, is a part of education; in the elder, a part of experience. He that travelleth into a country before he hath some entrance into the language, goeth to school, and not to travel.

Of Travel

Princes are like to heavenly bodies, which cause good or evil times, and which have much veneration but no rest.[2]

Of Empire

Fortune is like the market, where many times, if you can stay a little, the price will fall.

Of Delays

In things that a man would not be seen in himself, it is a point of cunning to borrow the name of the world; as to say, "The world says," or "There is a speech abroad."

Of Cunning

There is a cunning which we in England call "the turning of the cat in the pan"; which is, when that which a man says to another, he lays it as if another had said it to him.

Ibid.

It is a good point of cunning for a man to shape the answer he would have in his own words and propositions, for it makes the other party stick the less.

Ibid.

Aspiring to be gods if angels fell,
Aspiring to be angels men rebel.
ALEXANDER POPE: *Essay on Man, Epistle I* [1733], *L. 125*
[1] A little skill in antiquity inclines a man to Popery; but depth in that study brings him about again to our religion. — THOMAS FULLER: *The Holy State* [1642], *The True Church Antiquary*
[2] See Shelley, page 467a.

It hath been an opinion that the French are wiser than they seem, and the Spaniards seem wiser than they are; but howsoever it be between nations, certainly it is so between man and man.
Of Seeming Wise

There is a wisdom in this beyond the rules of physic. A man's own observation, what he finds good of and what he finds hurt of, is the best physic to preserve health.
Of Regimen of Health

Discretion of speech is more than eloquence; and to speak agreeably to him with whom we deal is more than to speak in good words or in good order.
Of Discourse

If a man look sharply and attentively, he shall see Fortune; for though she is blind, she is not invisible.[1]
Of Fortune

Young men are fitter to invent than to judge, fitter for execution than for counsel, and fitter for new projects than for settled business.
Of Youth and Age

Virtue is like a rich stone, — best plain set.
Of Beauty

There is no excellent beauty that hath not some strangeness in the proportion.
Ibid.

God Almighty first planted a garden.[2]
Of Gardens

---

[1] Fortune is painted blind, with a muffler afore her eyes, to signify to you that Fortune is blind. — SHAKESPEARE: *Henry V* [1598–1600], *Act III, Sc. 6, L. 31*

[2] See *Genesis, II, 8,* on page 1021b.
Divina natura dedit agros, ars humana aedificavit urbes (Divine Nature gave the fields, human art built the cities). — VARRO [116–27 B.C.]: *De Re Rustica, III, 1*
Gardens were before gardeners, and but some hours after the earth. — SIR THOMAS BROWNE: *The Garden of Cyrus* [1658], *Chap. I*
God the first garden made, and the first city Cain. — COWLEY: *The Garden* [1664], *Essay V*
God made the country, and man made the town. — COWPER: *The Task* [1785], *Book I, L. 749*
See Shakespeare, page 178a.

And because the breath of flowers is far sweeter in the air (where it comes and goes, like the warbling of music) than in the hand, therefore nothing is more fit for that delight than to know what be the flowers and plants that do best perfume the air.
Of Gardens

It is generally better to deal by speech than by letter.
Of Negotiating

Some books are to be tasted, others to be swallowed, and some few to be chewed and digested.
Of Studies

Reading maketh a full man, conference a ready man, and writing an exact man.
Ibid.

Histories make men wise; poets, witty; the mathematics, subtile; natural philosophy, deep; moral, grave; logic and rhetoric, able to contend.
Ibid.

The greatest vicissitude of things amongst men is the vicissitude of sects and religions.
Of Vicissitude of Things

I bequeath my soul to God. . . . My body to be buried obscurely. For my name and memory, I leave it to men's charitable speeches, and to foreign nations, and the next age.
From his Will [*1626*]

The world's a bubble, and the life of man
Less than a span.[1]
The World [*1629*]

Who then to frail mortality shall trust
But limns on water, or but writes in dust.
Ibid.

What then remains but that we still should cry

---

[1] Whose life is a bubble, and in length a span. — WILLIAM BROWNE: *Britannia's Pastorals* [1613], *Book I, Song*
See Sir John Davies, page 213b, and *The New England Primer,* page 1000b.

For being born, and, being born, to
die? [1]
The World

I hold every man a debtor to his profession; from the which as men of
course do seek to receive countenance
and profit, so ought they of duty to endeavour themselves by way of amends
to be a help and ornament thereunto.
Maxims of the Law [1630].
Preface

Books must follow sciences, and not
sciences books.
Proposition touching Amend-
ment of Laws

SAMUEL DANIEL
[1562–1619]

Care-charmer Sleep, son of the sable
Night,
Brother to Death, in silent darkness
born.[2]
Sonnet: To Delia [1592]

Make me to say when all my griefs are
gone,
Happy the heart that sighed for such a
one!
Sonnet: I Must Not Grieve [1592]

And for the few that only lend their ear,
That few is all the world.
Musophilus [1599]. Stanza 97

This is the thing that I was born to do.
Ibid. Stanza 100

Unless above himself he can
Erect himself, how poor a thing is man!
To the Countess of Cumberland
[Circa 1600]. Stanza 12

---

[1] This line frequently occurs in almost exactly the same shape among the minor poems
of the time: "Not to be born, or, being born,
to die." — WILLIAM DRUMMOND: *Poems*
[1656]

[2] Care-charmer sleep, sweet ease in restless
misery,
The captive's liberty, and his freedom's
song,
Balm of the bruised heart, man's chief
felicity,
Brother of quiet death, when life is too,
too long!
BARTHOLOMEW GRIFFIN: *Fidessa*
More Chaste Than Kind [1596]
See Hesiod, page 7a.

Love is a sickness full of woes,
All remedies refusing.
Hymen's Triumph [1615]

MICHAEL DRAYTON
[1563–1631]

Fair stood the wind for France.
The Ballad of Agincourt [1605].
Stanza 1

O, when shall Englishmen
With such acts fill a pen,
Or England breed again
Such a King Harry?
Ibid. Stanza 15

Since there's no help, come let us kiss
and part.
Nay, I have done: you get no more of
me,
And I am glad, yea glad with all my
heart,
That thus so clearly, I myself can free.
Shake hands for ever, cancel all our
vows,
And when we meet at any time again,
Be it not seen in either of our brows,
That we one jot of former love retain;
Now at the last gasp of love's latest
breath,
When his pulse failing, passion speech-
less lies,
When faith is kneeling by his bed of
death,
And innocence is closing up his eyes,
Now if thou wouldst, when all have
given him over,
From death to life thou might'st him
yet recover.
Sonnet [1619]

The coast was clear.
Nymphidia [1627]

Had in him those brave translunary
things
That the first poets had.
(Said of MARLOWE) *To Henry*
Reynolds, of Poets and Poesy
[1627]

For that fine madness still he did retain
Which rightly should possess a poet's
brain.
Ibid.

CHRISTOPHER MARLOWE
[1564–1593]

My men, like satyrs grazing on the
    lawn,
Shall with their goat feet dance the
    antic hay.
> *Edward II* [*1594*]. *Act I, Sc. I*

I'm armed with more than complete
    steel, —
The justice of my quarrel.[1]
> *Lust's Dominion.*[2] *Act III, Sc. 4*

Who ever loved that loved not at first
    sight?[3]
> *Hero and Leander* [*1598*]

Come live with me, and be my love;
And we will all the pleasures prove
That hills and valleys, dales and fields,
Woods or steepy mountain yields.[4]
> *The Passionate Shepherd to*
> *his Love* [*1599*]

By shallow rivers, to whose falls
Melodious birds sing madrigals.[5]
> *Ibid.*

And I will make thee beds of roses
And a thousand fragrant posies.[5]
> *Ibid.*

Hell hath no limits, nor is circumscribed
In one self-place; for where we are is
    Hell,
And where Hell is, there must we ever
    be.
> *Doctor Faustus* [*1604*]. *Sc. 5*

When all the world dissolves,
And every creature shall be purified,
All places shall be hell that are not
    heaven.
> *Ibid.*

---

[1] See Shakespeare, page 125a.
[2] Attributed to Marlowe.
[3] Quoted in SHAKESPEARE's *As You Like It*,
Act III, Sc. 5, L. 82
  None ever loved but at first sight they
loved. — GEORGE CHAPMAN: *The Blind Beggar of Alexandria* [1598]
  I saw and loved. — GIBBON: *Memoirs*
[1796]
[4] See Donne, page 216a.
[5] To shallow rivers, to whose falls
  Melodious birds sing madrigals;
  There will we make our peds of roses,
  And a thousand fragrant posies.
> SHAKESPEARE: *Merry Wives of*
> *Windsor* [1600–1601], *Act III,*
> *Sc. 1, L. 17* (Sung by Evans)

Was this the face that launch'd a thou-
    sand ships,
And burnt the topless towers of Ilium?[1]
Sweet Helen, make me immortal with a
    kiss!
Her lips suck forth my soul:[2] see,
    where it flies!
> *Doctor Faustus. Sc. 14*

O, thou art fairer than the evening air
Clad in the beauty of a thousand stars.
> *Ibid.*

Now hast thou but one bare hour to
    live,
And then thou must be damned per-
    petually;
Stand still, you ever moving spheres of
    heaven,
That time may cease, and midnight
    never come.
> *Ibid. Sc. 16*

O lente, lente currite noctis equi:[3]
The stars move still, time runs, the
    clock will strike,
The devil will come, and Faustus must
    be damn'd.
O I'll leap up to my God: who pulls
    me down?
See see where Christ's blood streams in
    the firmament.
One drop would save my soul, half a
    drop, ah my Christ.
> *Ibid.*

Cut is the branch that might have
    grown full straight,
And burnèd is Apollo's laurel bough,[4]
That sometime grew within this learnèd
    man.
> *Ibid.*

I count religion but a childish toy,

---

[1] Was this fair face the cause, quoth she,
  Why the Grecians sacked Troy?
> SHAKESPEARE: *All's Well that Ends*
> *Well* [1601–1603], *Act I, Sc. 3, L. 75*
[2]   Once he drew
  With one long kiss my whole soul through
  My lips.
> TENNYSON: *Fatima* [1833] *St. 3*
[3] At si, quem malis, Cephalum complexa
  teneres,
  Clamares "lente currite noctis equi."
> OVID [43 B.C.–A.D. 18]: *Amores, i., 13*
[4] See Shakespeare, page 201b.

And hold there is no sin but ignorance.[1]
The Jew of Malta [Published
1633]. Act I
Infinite riches in a little room.
Ibid.
Excess of wealth is cause of covetousness.
Ibid.
Now will I show myself to have more of the serpent than the dove;[2] that is, more knave than fool.
Ibid. Act II

WILLIAM SHAKESPEARE [3]
[1564–1616]

Hung be the heavens with black, yield day to night!
King Henry VI [1591]. Part I,
Act I, Sc. 1, Line 1
Fight till the last gasp.
Ibid. Sc. 2, Line 127
Expect Saint Martin's summer, halcyon days.
Ibid. Line 131
Glory is like a circle in the water,
Which never ceaseth to enlarge itself,
Till by broad spreading it disperse to nought.
Ibid. Line 133
The sun with one eye vieweth all the world.
Ibid. Sc. 4, Line 84
Unbidden guests
Are often welcomest when they are gone.
Ibid. Act II, Sc. 2, Line 55
Between two hawks, which flies the higher pitch;
Between two dogs, which hath the deeper mouth;
Between two blades, which bears the better temper;

---

[1] There is no sin except stupidity. — OSCAR WILDE [1856–1900]: *The Critic as Artist, Part II*
[2] Be ye therefore wise as serpents, and harmless as doves. — *Matthew, X, 16*
[3] From the text of W. J. Craig, Oxford University Press. The dates and order, about which there is much conjecture, are those which Sir Edmund Chambers (*William Shakespeare* [1930]) thinks most probable.

Between two horses, which doth bear him best;
Between two girls, which hath the merriest eye;
I have, perhaps, some shallow spirit of judgment;
But in these nice sharp quillets of the law,
Good faith, I am no wiser than a daw.
King Henry VI. Part I, Act II,
Sc. 4, Line 12
I'll note you in my book of memory.
Ibid. Line 101
Just death, kind umpire of men's miseries.
Ibid. Sc. 5, Line 29
Fair be all thy hopes,
And prosperous be thy life in peace and war!
Ibid. Line 113
Chok'd with ambition of the meaner sort.
Ibid. Line 123
Friendly counsel cuts off many foes.
Ibid. Act III, Sc. 1, Line 184
Delays have dangerous ends.[1]
Ibid. Sc. 2, Line 33
Care is no cure, but rather corrosive,
For things that are not to be remedied.
Ibid. Sc. 3, Line 3
Of all base passions, fear is most accurs'd.
Ibid. Act V, Sc. 2, Line 18
She's beautiful and therefore to be wooed,
She is a woman, therefore to be won.[2]
Ibid. Sc. 3, Line 78
For what is wedlock forced, but a hell,
An age of discord and continual strife?
Whereas the contrary bringeth bliss,
And is a pattern of celestial peace.
Ibid. Sc. 5, Line 62
O Lord! that lends me life,
Lend me a heart replete with thankfulness!
Ibid. Part II, Act I, Sc. 1, Line 19

---

[1] See Cervantes, page 106a.
All delays are dangerous in war. — DRYDEN: *Tyrannic Love* [1669], *Act I, Sc. 1*
[2] See *Titus Andronicus*, page 129b.

Whose large style
Agrees not with the leanness of his
   purse.
      King Henry VI. Part II, Act I,
                Sc. 1, Line 112
'Tis not my speeches that you do mis-
   like,
But 'tis my presence that doth trouble
   ye.
Rancour will out.
                Ibid. Line 141
Could I come near your beauty with my
   nails
I'd set my ten commandments in your
   face.
         Ibid. Sc. 3, Line 144
Blessed are the peacemakers on earth.[1]
      Ibid. Act II, Sc. 1, Line 34
God be prais'd, that to believing souls
Gives light in darkness, comfort in de-
   spair! [2]
                Ibid. Line 66
God defend the right!
         Ibid. Sc. 3, Line 55
Sometimes hath the brightest day a
   cloud;
And after summer evermore succeeds
Barren winter, with his wrathful nip-
   ping cold:
So cares and joys abound, as seasons
   fleet.
          Ibid. Sc. 4, Line 1
Now 'tis the spring, and weeds are
   shallow-rooted;
Suffer them now and they'll o'ergrow
   the garden.
      Ibid. Act III, Sc. 1, Line 31
   In thy face I see
The map of honour, truth, and loyalty.
               Ibid. Line 202
What stronger breastplate than a heart
   untainted!
Thrice is he armed that hath his quar-
   rel just,

[1] Blessed are the peacemakers: for they
shall be called the children of God. — *Matthew, V, 9*
[2] Though hopeless love finds comfort in
   despair,
  It never can endure a rival's bliss!
    RICHARD BRINSLEY SHERIDAN: *The
      Critic* [1779], *Act III, Sc. 1*

And he but naked, though locked up in
   steel,
Whose conscience with injustice is cor-
   rupted.[1]
     King Henry VI. Part II, Act III,
               Sc. 2, Line 232
For wheresoe'er thou art in this world's
   globe,
I'll have an Iris that shall find thee out.
               Ibid. Line 406
He dies, and makes no sign.
          Ibid. Sc. 3, Line 29
Forbear to judge, for we are sinners all.[2]
Close up his eyes and draw the curtain
   close;
And let us all to meditation.
                Ibid. Line 31
The gaudy, blabbing, and remorseful
   day
Is crept into the bosom of the sea.
       Ibid. Act IV, Sc. 1, Line 1
Small things make base men proud.
               Ibid. Line 106
True nobility is exempt from fear.
               Ibid. Line 129
   I will make it felony to drink small
beer.[3]
           Ibid. Sc. 2, Line 75
   The first thing we do, let's kill all the
lawyers.
                Ibid. Line 86
   Is not this a lamentable thing, that
of the skin of an innocent lamb should
be made parchment? that parchment,
being scribbled o'er, should undo a
man?
                Ibid. Line 88
   Sir, he made a chimney in my father's
house, and the bricks are alive at this
day to testify it.
               Ibid. Line 160
   Thou hast most traitorously corrupted the youth of the realm in erect-

[1] See Marlowe, page 123a.
[2] Judge not, that ye be not judged. —
Matthew, VII, 1
[3] Doth it not show vilely in me to desire
small beer? — *King Henry IV* [1597–1598],
Part II, Act II, Sc. 2, L. 7
  See *Othello*, page 187a.
  That questionable superfluity — small beer.
— DOUGLAS JERROLD [1803–1857]: *The Trag-
edy of the Till*

ing a grammar-school; and whereas, before, our forefathers had no other books
but the score and the tally, thou hast
caused printing to be used; and, con-
trary to the king, his crown, and dig-
nity, thou hast built a paper-mill.
King Henry VI. Part II, Act IV,
Sc. 7, Line 35
Beggars mounted run their horse to
death.[1]
Ibid. Part III, Act I, Sc. 4, Line 127
O tiger's heart wrapp'd in a woman's
hide![2]
Ibid. Line 137
And many strokes, though with a little
axe,
Hew down and fell the hardest-timbered
oak.
Ibid. Act II, Sc. 1, Line 54
To weep is to make less the depth of
grief.
Ibid. Line 85
Didst thou never hear
That things ill got had ever bad suc-
cess?
And happy always was it for that son
Whose father for his hoarding went to
hell?
Ibid. Sc. 2, Line 45
Our hap is loss, our hope but sad
despair.[3]
Ibid. Sc. 3, Line 9
Thou setter up and plucker down of
kings.[4]
Ibid. Line 37
And what makes robbers bold but too
much lenity?
Ibid. Sc. 6, Line 22

[1] Set a beggar on horseback and he will
ride a gallop. — ROBERT BURTON: *Anatomy
of Melancholy* [1621–1651], *Part II, Sect. 2,
Memb. 2*
Set a beggar on horseback, and he'll outride
the Devil. — BOHN: *Foreign Proverbs, German* [1855]
[2] ROBERT GREENE in *A Groats-Worth of
Wit* [1592] burlesques this line: "Tyger's hart
wrapt in a Player's hide."
[3] Thus repuls'd, our final hope
Is flat despair.
MILTON: *Paradise Lost* [1667],
Book II, L. 142
[4] Proud setter up and puller down of kings.
— *Act III, Sc. 3, L. 156*

My crown is in my heart, not on my
head;
Not deck'd with diamonds and Indian
stones,
Nor to be seen: my crown is call'd con-
tent;
A crown it is that seldom kings enjoy.
King Henry VI. Part III,
Act III, Sc. 1, Line 62
'Tis a happy thing
To be the father unto many sons.
Ibid. Sc. 2, Line 104
Gloucester. That would be ten days'
wonder at the least.
Clarence. That's a day longer than a
wonder lasts.[1]
Ibid. Line 113
Like one that stands upon a promon-
tory,
And spies a far-off shore where he would
tread,
Wishing his foot were equal with his
eye.
Ibid. Line 135
Yield not thy neck
To fortune's yoke, but let thy dauntless
mind
Still ride in triumph over all mischance.
Ibid. Sc. 3, Line 16
For how can tyrants safely govern
home,
Unless abroad they purchase great al-
liance?
Ibid. Line 69
Having nothing, nothing can he lose.
Ibid. Line 152
Hasty marriage seldom proveth well.
Ibid. Act IV, Sc. 1, Line 18
Let us be back'd with God and with the
seas
Which he hath given for fence impreg-
nable,
And with their helps only defend our-
selves:
In them and in ourselves our safety lies.
Ibid. Line 43
What fates impose, that men must
needs abide;
It boots not to resist both wind and tide.
Ibid. Sc. 3, Line 57

[1] See Chaucer, page 78b.

Now join your hands, and with your
    hands your hearts.
     King Henry VI. Part III, Act IV,
               Sc. 6, Line 39

For many men that stumble at the
    threshold
Are well foretold that danger lurks
    within.
            Ibid. Sc. 7, Line 11

A little fire is quickly trodden out;
Which, being suffered, rivers cannot
    quench.
            Ibid. Sc. 8, Line 7

When the lion fawns upon the lamb,
The lamb will never cease to follow
    him.
              Ibid. Line 49

What is pomp, rule, reign, but earth and
    dust?
And, live we how we can, yet die we
    must.
       Ibid. Act V, Sc. 2, Line 27

Every cloud engenders not a storm.
            Ibid. Sc. 3, Line 13

We are advertis'd by our loving friends.
            Ibid. Sc. 3, Line 18

What though the mast be now blown
    over-board,
The cable broke, the holding anchor
    lost,
And half our sailors swallow'd in the
    flood?
Yet lives our pilot still.
            Ibid. Sc. 4, Line 3

So part we sadly in this troublous world
To meet with joy in sweet Jerusalem.
            Ibid. Sc. 5, Line 7

Men ne'er spend their fury on a child.
              Ibid. Line 57

He's sudden if a thing comes in his
    head.
              Ibid. Line 86

Suspicion always haunts the guilty
    mind;
The thief doth fear each bush an officer.
            Ibid. Sc. 6, Line 11

This word "love," which greybeards
    call divine.
              Ibid. Line 81

Now is the winter of our discontent

Made glorious summer by this sun of
    York.
     King Richard III [*1592–1593*].
           Act I, Sc. 1, Line 1

Grim-visaged war hath smoothed his
    wrinkled front.
              Ibid. Line 9

To leave this keen encounter of our
    wits.
         Ibid. Sc. 2, Line 116

His better doth not breathe upon the
    earth.
             Ibid. Line 141

Look, how my ring encompasseth thy
    finger,
Even so thy breast encloseth my poor
    heart;
Wear both of them, for both of them
    are thine.
             Ibid. Line 204

Was ever woman in this humour wooed?
Was ever woman in this humour won?
             Ibid. Line 229

Framed in the prodigality of nature.
             Ibid. Line 245

    The world is grown so bad,
That wrens make prey where eagles
    dare not perch.[1]
           Ibid. Sc. 3, Line 70

They that stand high have many blasts
    to shake them.
             Ibid. Line 259

And thus I clothe my naked villany
With odd old ends stol'n forth of holy
    writ,
And seem a saint when most I play the
    devil.
             Ibid. Line 336

Talkers are no good doers.
             Ibid. Line 351

O, I have passed a miserable night,
So full of ugly sights, of ghastly dreams,
That, as I am a Christian faithful man,
I would not spend another such a night,
Though 'twere to buy a world of happy
    days.
           Ibid. Sc. 4, Line 2

Lord, Lord! methought, what pain it
    was to drown:

---

[1] See Alexander Pope, page 312a.

What dreadful noise of waters in mine
    ears!
What ugly sights of death within mine
    eyes!
            King Richard III. Act I,
                    Sc. 4, Line 21
I pass'd, methought, the melancholy
    flood,
With that grim ferryman which poets
    write of,
Unto the kingdom of perpetual night.
            Ibid. Line 45
Sorrow breaks seasons and reposing
    hours,
Makes the night morning, and the noon-
    tide night.
            Ibid. Line 76
Thou art a widow; yet thou art a
    mother,
And hast the comfort of thy children
    left thee.
            Ibid. Act II, Sc. 2, Line 55
A parlous boy.
            Ibid. Sc. 4, Line 35
So wise so young, they say, do never
    live long.[1]
            Ibid. Act III, Sc. 1, Line 79
Off with his head!
            Ibid. Sc. 4, Line 75
Lives like a drunken sailor on a mast,
Ready with every nod to tumble down.
            Ibid. Line 98
Even in the afternoon of her best days.
            Ibid. Sc. 7, Line 185
Thou troublest me: I am not in the vein.
            Ibid. Act IV, Sc. 2, Line 117
The sons of Edward sleep in Abraham's
    bosom.[2]
            Ibid. Sc. 3, Line 38
A grievous burthen was thy birth to me;
Tetchy and wayward was thy infancy.
            Ibid. Sc. 4, Line 168
An honest tale speeds best being plainly
    told.
            Ibid. Line 359
Harp not on that string.
            Ibid. Line 365

[1] A little too wise, they say, do ne'er live
long. — MIDDLETON [1570–1627]: *The Phoenix, Act I, Sc. 1*
[2] The beggar died, and was carried by the
angels into Abraham's bosom. — *Luke, XVI,*
22

Thus far into the bowels of the land
Have we marched on without impedi-
    ment.
            King Richard III. Act V,
                    Sc. 2, Line 3
True hope is swift, and flies with swal-
    low's wings;
Kings it makes gods, and meaner crea-
    tures kings.
            Ibid. Line 23
The king's name is a tower of strength.
            Ibid. Sc. 3, Line 12
Give me another horse! bind up my
    wounds!
            Ibid. Line 178
O coward conscience, how dost thou
    afflict me!
            Ibid. Line 180
My conscience hath a thousand several
    tongues,
And every tongue brings in a several
    tale,
And every tale condemns me for a vil-
    lain.
            Ibid. Line 194
The early village cock
Hath twice done salutation to the morn.
            Ibid. Line 210
By the apostle Paul, shadows to-night
Have struck more terror to the soul of
    Richard
Than can the substance of ten thousand
    soldiers.
            Ibid. Line 217
Conscience is but a word that cowards
    use,
Devis'd at first to keep the strong in
    awe.
            Ibid. Line 310
A horse! a horse! my kingdom for a
    horse!
            Ibid. Sc. 4, Line 7
    I have set my life upon a cast,
And I will stand the hazard of the die:
I think there be six Richmonds in the
    field.
            Ibid. Line 9
The pleasing punishment that women
    bear.
            The Comedy of Errors [1592–
                    1593]. *Act I, Sc. 1, Line 46*

We may pity, though not pardon thee.
The Comedy of Errors.
Act I, Sc. 1, Line 97

To tell sad stories of my own mishaps.
Ibid. Line 120

Why, headstrong liberty is lash'd with
woe.
There's nothing situate under heaven's
eye
But hath his bound, in earth, in sea,
in sky.
Ibid. Act. II, Sc. 1, Line 15

A wretched soul, bruised with adversity.
Ibid. Line 34

Every why hath a wherefore.[1]
Ibid. Sc. 2, Line 45

There's no time for a man to recover
his hair that grows bald by nature.
Ibid. Line 74

What he hath scanted men in hair, he
hath given them in wit.
Ibid. Line 83

Time himself is bald, and therefore
to the world's end will have bald followers.
Ibid. Line 109

Small cheer and great welcome makes a
merry feast.
Ibid. Act III, Sc. 1, Line 26

There is something in the wind.
Ibid. Line 69

We'll pluck a crow together.
Ibid. Line 83

For slander lives upon succession,
For ever housed where it gets posses-
sion.
Ibid. Line 105

Be not thy tongue thy own shame's orator.
Ibid. Sc. 2, Line 10

Ill deeds are doubled with an evil word.
Ibid. Line 20

O! train me not, sweet mermaid, with
thy note,
To drown me in thy sister flood of
tears.
Ibid. Line 45

A back-friend, a shoulder-clapper.
*The Comedy of Errors. Act IV,
Sc. 2, Line 37*

Give me your hand and let me feel your
pulse.
Ibid. Sc. 4, Line 54

The venom clamours of a jealous
woman
Poison more deadly than a mad dog's
tooth.
Ibid. Act V, Sc. 1, Line 69

Unquiet meals make ill digestions.
Ibid. Line 74

One Pinch, a hungry lean-faced villain,
A mere anatomy.
Ibid. Line 238

A needy, hollow-eyed, sharp-looking
wretch,
A living-dead man.
Ibid. Line 241

I hope I shall have leisure to make good.
Ibid. Line 378

Sleep in peace, slain in your country's
wars!
*Titus Andronicus [1593–1594].
Act I, Sc. 1, Line 91*

Sweet mercy is nobility's true badge.
Ibid. Line 119

In peace and honour rest you here, my
sons;
Rome's readiest champions, repose you
here in rest,
Secure from worldly chances and mishaps!
Ibid. Line 150

These words are razors to my wounded
heart.
Ibid. Line 314

He lives in fame that died in virtue's
cause.
Ibid. Line 390

These dreary dumps.[1]
Ibid. Line 391

She is a woman, therefore may be
woo'd;
She is a woman, therefore may be won.[2]
Ibid. Act II, Sc. 1, Line 82

What you cannot as you would achieve,

---

[1] See *King Henry V*, page 156b.
For every why he had a wherefore. —
SAMUEL BUTLER: *Hudibras, Part I* [1663],
Canto I, L. 132

[1] And doleful dumps the mind oppress. —
Romeo and Juliet, Act IV, Sc. 5, L. 130
[2] See *King Henry VI*, page 124b.

You must perforce accomplish as you may.

Titus Andronicus. Act II, Sc. 1, Line 106

Poor harmless fly.

Ibid. Act. III, Sc. 2, Line 63

The eagle suffers little birds to sing.

Ibid. Act IV, Sc. 4, Line 82

And if the boy have not a woman's gift
To rain a shower of commanded tears,
An onion will do well for such a shift.

The Taming of the Shrew [*1593–1594*]. *Induction, Sc. 1, Line 124*

No profit grows where is no pleasure ta'en;
In brief, sir, study what you most affect.

Ibid. Act I, Sc. 1, Line 39

There's small choice in rotten apples.

Ibid. Line 137

Whom should I knock?

Ibid. Sc. 2, Line 6

To seek their fortunes further than at home,
Where small experience grows.

Ibid. Line 51

As curst and shrewd
As Socrates' Xanthippe.

Ibid. Line 70

Nothing comes amiss, so money comes withal.

Ibid. Line 82

Tush, tush! fear boys with bugs.

Ibid. Line 214

And do as adversaries do in law,
Strive mightily, but eat and drink as friends.

Ibid. Line 281

I must dance barefoot on her wedding day,
And, for your love to her, lead apes in hell.

Ibid. Act II, Sc. 1, Line 32

Old fashions please me best.

Ibid. Act III, Sc. 1, Line 81

Who wooed in haste and means to wed at leisure.[1]

Ibid. Sc. 2, Line 11

---

[1] Married in haste, we may repent at leisure. — CONGREVE: *The Old Bachelor* [1693], Act V, Sc. 1

A little pot and soon hot.[1]

The Taming of the Shrew. Act IV, Sc. 1, Line 6

It was the friar of orders grey,
As he forth walked on his way.[2]

Ibid. Line 148

Sits as one new-risen from a dream.

Ibid. Line 189

This is a way to kill a wife with kindness.

Ibid. Line 211

Kindness in women, not their beauteous looks,
Shall win my love.

Ibid. Sc. 2, Line 41

Our purses shall be proud, our garments poor:
For 'tis the mind that makes the body rich.

Ibid. Sc. 3, Line 173

And as the sun breaks through the darkest clouds,
So honour peereth in the meanest habit.

Ibid. Line 175

Forward, I pray, since we have come so far,
And be it moon, or sun, or what you please:
An if you please to call it a rush-candle,
Henceforth I vow it shall be so for me.

Ibid. Sc. 5, Line 12

So bedazzled with the sun
That everything I look on seemeth green.

Ibid. Line 46

My cake is dough.

Ibid. Act V, Sc. 1, Line 146

He that is giddy thinks the world turns round.

Ibid. Sc. 2, Line 20

A woman moved is like a fountain troubled,
Muddy, ill-seeming, thick, bereft of beauty.

Ibid. Line 143

---

[1] He is a little chimney, and heated hot in a moment. — LONGFELLOW: *The Courtship of Miles Standish* [1858]

[2] THOMAS PERCY [1728–1811] composed *The Friar of Orders Grey* of various fragments of ancient ballads found in Shakespeare's plays. See page 1011b.

Such duty as the subject owes the prince,
Even such a woman oweth to her husband.
> *The Taming of the Shrew.*
> *Act V, Sc. 2, Line 156*

Bid me discourse, I will enchant thine ear.
> *Venus and Adonis* [*1593*]. *Line 145*

Love is a spirit all compact of fire.
> *Ibid. Line 149*

A red morn, that ever yet betoken'd
Wrack to the seaman, tempest to the field.
> *Ibid. Line 453*

The owl, night's herald.
> *Ibid. Line 531*

The path is smooth that leadeth on to danger.
> *Ibid. Line 788*

Love comforteth like sunshine after rain.
> *Ibid. Line 799*

The text is old, the orator too green.
> *Ibid. Line 806*

Lo! here the gentle lark, weary of rest,
From his moist cabinet mounts up on high,
And wakes the morning.
> *Ibid. Line 853*

For he being dead, with him is beauty slain,
And, beauty dead, black chaos comes again.[1]
> *Ibid. Line 1019*

The grass stoops not, she treads on it so light.
> *Ibid. Line 1028*

Beauty itself doth of itself persuade
The eyes of men without an orator.
> *The Rape of Lucrece* [*1594*].
> *Line 29*

Those that much covet are with gain so fond,
For what they have not, that which they possess
They scatter and unloose it from their bond,
And so, by hoping more, they have but less.
> *Ibid. Line 134*

[1] See *Othello*, page 188a.

One for all, or all for one we gage.[1]
> *The Rape of Lucrece.*
> *Line 144*

Or sells eternity to get a toy.
> *Ibid. Line 214*

Time's glory is to calm contending kings,
To unmask falsehood, and bring truth to light.
> *Ibid. Line 939*

For greatest scandal waits on greatest state.
> *Ibid. Line 1006*

For men have marble, women waxen minds.
> *Ibid. Line 1240*

To see sad sights moves more than hear them told.
> *Ibid. Line 1324*

Cloud-kissing Ilion.
> *Ibid. Line 1370*

Lucrece swears he did her wrong.[2]
> *Ibid. Line 1462*

Home-keeping youth have ever homely wits.
> *The Two Gentlemen of Verona*
> [*1594–1595*]. *Act I, Sc. 1,*
> *Line 2*

I have no other but a woman's reason:
I think him so, because I think him so.
> *Ibid. Sc. 2, Line 23*

They do not love that do not show their love.
> *Ibid. Line 31*

O! they love least that let men know their love.
> *Ibid. Line 32*

Since maids, in modesty, say "No" to that
Which they would have the profferer construe "Ay."
> *Ibid. Line 53*

What is't that you took up so gingerly?
> *Ibid. Line 68*

O! how this spring of love resembleth
The uncertain glory of an April day!
> *Ibid. Sc. 3, Line 84*

[1] All for one, one for all, that is our device.
— ALEXANDRE DUMAS [1802–1870]: *The Three Musketeers, Chap. 9*
[2] Some villain hath done me wrong. — *King Lear* [1605–1606], *Act I, Sc. 2, L. 186*

O jest unseen, inscrutable, invisible,
As a nose on a man's face,[1] or a weath-
ercock on a steeple.
The Two Gentlemen of Verona.
Act II, Sc. 1, Line 145

He makes sweet music.
Ibid. Sc. 7, Line 28

That man that hath a tongue, I say, is
no man,
If with his tongue he cannot win a
woman.
Ibid. Act III, Sc. 1, Line 104

My thoughts do harbour with my
Sylvia nightly;
And slaves they are to me that send
them flying.
Ibid. Line 140

Who is Sylvia? what is she?
That all our swains commend her?
Holy, fair, and wise is she;
The heaven such grace did lend her.
Ibid. Act IV, Sc. 2, Line 40

Alas, how love can trifle with itself!
Ibid. Sc. 4, Line 185

How use doth breed a habit in a man![2]
Ibid. Act V, Sc. 4, Line 1

Make us heirs of all eternity.
Love's Labour's Lost [1594–
1595]. *Act I, Sc. 1, Line 7*

The huge army of the world's desires.
Ibid. Line 10

Or, having sworn too hard-a-keeping
oath,
Study to break it, and not break my
troth.
Ibid. Line 65

Why, all delights are vain; but that
most vain,
Which, with pain purchas'd, doth inherit pain.
Ibid. Line 72

Light seeking light doth light of light
beguile.
Ibid. Line 77

Study is like the heaven's glorious sun,
That will not be deep-search'd with
saucy looks;
Small have continual plodders ever
won,

[1] See Rabelais, page 90a.
[2] See Plutarch, page 60a.

Save base authority from others'
books.
These earthly godfathers of heaven's
lights
That give a name to every fixed star,
Have no more profit of their shining
nights
Than those that walk and wot not
what they are.
Love's Labour's Lost.
Act I, Sc. 1, Line 84

At Christmas I no more desire a rose
Than wish a snow in May's new-
fangled mirth;
But like of each thing that in season
grows.
Ibid. Line 105

A man in all the world's new fashion
planted,
That hath a mint of phrases in his brain.
Ibid. Line 163

And men sit down to that nourishment which is called supper.
Ibid. Line 237

That unlettered small-knowing soul.
Ibid. Line 251

A child of our grandmother Eve, a
female; or, for thy more sweet understanding, a woman.
Ibid. Line 263

Affliction may one day smile again;
and till then, sit thee down, sorrow!
Ibid. Line 312

Devise, wit; write, pen; for I am for
whole volumes in folio.
Ibid. Sc. 2, Line 194

Beauty is bought by judgment of the
eye,
Not utter'd by base sale of chapmen's
tongues.
Ibid. Act II, Sc. 1, Line 15

A man of sovereign parts he is esteem'd;
Well fitted in arts, glorious in arms:
Nothing becomes him ill that he would
well.
Ibid. Line 44

A merrier man,
Within the limit of becoming mirth,
I never spent an hour's talk withal.
Ibid. Line 66

Delivers in such apt and gracious words
That aged ears play truant at his tales,

And younger hearings are quite rav-
ished;
So sweet and voluble is his discourse.
Love's Labour's Lost.
Act II, Sc. 1, Line 73
Your wit's too hot, it speeds too fast,
'twill tire.
Ibid. Line 119
Warble, child; make passionate my
sense of hearing.
Ibid. Act III, Sc. 1, Line 1
Remuneration! O! that's the Latin
word for three farthings.
Ibid. Line 143
A very beadle to a humorous sigh.
Ibid. Line 185
This wimpled, whining, purblind, way-
ward boy,
This senior-junior, giant-dwarf, Dan
Cupid;
Regent of love-rhymes, lord of folded
arms,
The anointed sovereign of sighs and
groans,
Liege of all loiterers and malcontents.
Ibid. Line 189
He hath not fed of the dainties that
are bred in a book; he hath not eat pa-
per, as it were; he hath not drunk ink.
Ibid. Act IV, Sc. 2, Line 25
Many can brook the weather that love
not the wind.
Ibid. Line 34
You two are book-men.
Ibid. Line 35
These are begot in the ventricle of
memory, nourished in the womb of pia
mater, and delivered upon the mellow-
ing of occasion.
Ibid. Line 70
By heaven, I do love, and it hath
taught me to rhyme, and to be melan-
choly.
Ibid. Sc. 3, Line 13
The heavenly rhetoric of thine eye.
Ibid. Line 60
As upright as the cedar.
Ibid. Line 89
Sweet lords, sweet lovers, O! let us
embrace.
As true we are as flesh and blood can
be:

The sea will ebb and flow, heaven show
his face;
Young blood doth not obey an old
decree:
We cannot cross the cause why we
were born.
Love's Labour's Lost.
Act IV, Sc. 3, Line 214
For where is any author in the world
Teaches such beauty as a woman's eye?
Learning is but an adjunct to ourself.
Ibid. Line 312
But love, first learned in a lady's eyes,
Lives not alone immured in the brain.
Ibid. Line 327
It adds a precious seeing to the eye.
Ibid. Line 333
As sweet and musical
As bright Apollo's lute, strung with his
hair;
And when Love speaks, the voice of all
the gods
Makes heaven drowsy with the har-
mony.
Ibid. Line 342
From women's eyes this doctrine I de-
rive:
They sparkle still the right Promethean
fire;
They are the books, the arts, the aca-
demes,
That show, contain, and nourish all the
world.
Ibid. Line 350
He draweth out the thread of his ver-
bosity finer than the staple of his argu-
ment.
Ibid. Act V, Sc. 1, Line 18
Moth. They have been at a great
feast of languages, and stolen the
scraps.
Costard. O! they have lived long on
the alms-basket of words. I marvel thy
master hath not eaten thee for a word;
for thou art not so long by the head as
honorificabilitudinitatibus; thou art
easier swallowed than a flap-dragon.
Ibid. Line 39
In the posteriors of this day, which
the rude multitude call the afternoon.
Ibid. Line 96

Let me take you a button-hole lower.
Love's Labour's Lost.
Act V, Sc. 2, Line 705

The naked truth of it is, I have no shirt.
Ibid. Line 715

A jest's prosperity lies in the ear
Of him that hears it, never in the tongue
Of him that makes it.
Ibid. Line 869

When daisies pied and violets blue,
  And lady-smocks all silver-white,
And cuckoo-buds of yellow hue
  Do paint the meadows with delight,
The cuckoo then, on every tree,
Mocks married men; for thus sings he,
                    Cuckoo;
Cuckoo, cuckoo: O word of fear,
Unpleasing to a married ear.
Ibid. Line 902

When icicles hang by the wall,
  And Dick, the shepherd, blows his nail,
And Tom bears logs into the hall,
  And milk comes frozen home in pail,
When blood is nipp'd and ways be foul,
Then nightly sings the staring owl,
                    Tu-who;
Tu-whit, tu-who — a merry note,
While greasy Joan doth keel the pot.
When all aloud the wind doth blow,
And coughing drowns the parson's saw;
And birds sit brooding in the snow,
And Marion's nose looks red and raw,
When roasted crabs hiss in the bowl.
Ibid. Line 920

The words of Mercury are harsh after the songs of Apollo.
Ibid. Line 938

A pair of star-cross'd lovers.
Romeo and Juliet [*1594–1595*].
Act I, Prologue, Line 6

An hour before the worshipp'd sun
Peered forth the golden window of the east.
Ibid. Sc. 1, Line 124

As is the bud bit with an envious worm,
Ere he can spread his sweet leaves to the air,
Or dedicate his beauty to the sun.
Ibid. Line 156

Alas! that love, so gentle in his view,
Should be so tyrannous and rough in proof.
Romeo and Juliet. Act I,
Sc. 1, Line 174

Saint-seducing gold.
Ibid. Line 220

He that is strucken blind cannot forget
The precious treasure of his eyesight lost.
Ibid. Line 238

One fire burns out another's burning,[1]
One pain is lessen'd by another's anguish.
Ibid. Sc. 2, Line 47

I will make thee think thy swan a crow.
Ibid. Line 92

One fairer than my love! the all-seeing sun
Ne'er saw her match since first the world begun.
Ibid. Line 97

That book in many eyes doth share the glory
That in gold clasps locks in the golden story.
Ibid. Sc. 3, Line 91

For I am proverb'd with a grandsire phrase.
Ibid. Sc. 4, Line 37

We burn daylight.
Ibid. Line 43

Benvolio. O! then, I see Queen Mab
  hath been with you! . . .
Mercutio. She is the fairies' midwife,
  and she comes
In shape no bigger than an agate-stone
On the fore-finger of an alderman,
Drawn with a team of little atomies
Athwart men's noses as they lie asleep.
Ibid. Line 53

True, I talk of dreams,
Which are the children of an idle brain,
Begot of nothing but vain fantasy.
Ibid. Line 97

        Toes
Unplagu'd with corns.
Ibid. Sc. 5, Line 21

[1] See Chapman, page 117a.

For you and I are past our dancing days.[1]

> *Romeo and Juliet. Act I, Sc. 5, Line 35*

It seems she hangs upon the cheek of night
Like a rich jewel in an Ethiop's ear;
Beauty too rich for use, for earth too dear.

> *Ibid. Line 49*

My only love sprung from my only hate!
Too early seen unknown, and known too late!

> *Ibid. Line 142*

He jests at scars, that never felt a wound.
But, soft! what light through yonder window breaks?
It is the east, and Juliet is the sun.

> *Ibid. Act II, Sc. 2, Line 1*

She speaks, yet she says nothing.

> *Ibid. Line 12*

See, how she leans her cheek upon her hand.
O! that I were a glove upon that hand,
That I might touch that cheek.

> *Ibid. Line 23*

O Romeo, Romeo! wherefore art thou Romeo?[2]
Deny thy father, and refuse thy name;
Or, if thou wilt not, be but sworn my love,
And I'll no longer be a Capulet.

> *Ibid. Line 33*

What's in a name? That which we call a rose
By any other name would smell as sweet.

> *Ibid. Line 43*

For stony limits cannot hold love out.

> *Ibid. Line 67*

Alack! there lies more peril in thine eye
Than twenty of their swords.

> *Romeo and Juliet. Act II, Sc. 2, Line 71*

At lovers' perjuries,
They say, Jove laughs.[1]

> *Ibid. Line 92*

In truth, fair Montague, I am too fond.

> *Ibid. Line 98*

Romeo. Lady, by yonder blessed moon I swear,
That tips with silver all these fruit-tree tops, —
Juliet. O! swear not by the moon, the inconstant moon,
That monthly changes in her circled orb,
Lest that thy love prove likewise variable.

> *Ibid. Line 107*

Do not swear at all;
Or, if thou wilt, swear by thy gracious self,
Which is the god of my idolatry.

> *Ibid. Line 112*

Too like the lightning, which doth cease to be
Ere one can say it lightens.

> *Ibid. Line 119*

This bud of love, by summer's ripening breath,
May prove a beauteous flower when next we meet.

> *Ibid. Line 121*

A thousand times good-night!

> *Ibid. Line 154*

Love goes toward love, as schoolboys from their books;
But love from love, toward school with heavy looks.

> *Ibid. Line 156*

How silver-sweet sound lovers' tongues by night,
Like softest music to attending ears!

> *Ibid. Line 165*

---

[1] My dancing days are done. — BEAUMONT AND FLETCHER: *The Scornful Lady* [1616], *Act V, Sc. 3*

[2] HENRY FIELDING burlesqued this in *Life and Death of Tom Thumb the Great* [1730] as follows:

Huncamunca. O Tom Thumb! Tom Thumb! wherefore art thou Tom Thumb? — *Act II, Sc. 3*

[1] Perjuria ridet amantium Jupiter (Jupiter laughs at the perjuries of lovers.) — TIBULLUS [54?-18? B.C.]: *III, 6, 49*

And Jove but laughs at lovers' perjury. — DRYDEN: *Palamon and Arcite* [1680], *Book II, L. 758*

Dryden repeats this proverb in *Amphitryon* [1690], *Act I, Sc. 2.*

Good night, good night! parting is such
    sweet sorrow,
That I shall say good night till it be
    morrow.
      Romeo and Juliet. Act II,
            Sc. 2, Line 184

O! mickle is the powerful grace that lies
In herbs, plants, stones, and their true
    qualities:
For nought so vile that on the earth
    doth live
But to the earth some special good doth
    give,
Nor aught so good but strain'd from
    that fair use
Revolts from true birth, stumbling on
    abuse,
Virtue itself turns vice, being misap-
    plied;
And vice sometime's by action dignified.
        Ibid. Sc. 3, Line 15

Care keeps his watch in every old man's
    eye,
And where care lodges, sleep will never
    lie.
            Ibid. Line 35

Wisely and slow; they stumble that run
    fast.
            Ibid. Line 94

Stabbed with a white wench's black eye.
        Ibid. Sc. 4, Line 14

The courageous captain of compli-
    ments.
            Ibid. Line 21

One, two, and the third in your bosom.
            Ibid. Line 24

O flesh, flesh, how art thou fishified!
            Ibid. Line 41

If thy wits run the wild-goose chase,
I have done.
            Ibid. Line 77

A gentleman, nurse, that loves to
hear himself talk, and will speak more
in a minute than he will stand to in a
month.
           Ibid. Line 155

Love's heralds should be thoughts,
Which ten times faster glide than the
    sun's beams.
        Ibid. Sc. 5, Line 4

I would thou hadst my bones, and I
    thy news.
      Romeo and Juliet. Act II,
           Sc. 5, Line 27

The excuse that thou dost make in this
    delay
Is longer than the tale thou dost excuse.
            Ibid. Line 33

These violent delights have violent
    ends.
         Ibid. Sc. 6, Line 9

Therefore love moderately; long love
    doth so;
Too swift arrives as tardy as too slow.
            Ibid. Line 14

Here comes the lady: O! so light a foot
Will ne'er wear out the everlasting flint.
            Ibid. Line 16

Thy head is as full of quarrels as an
egg is full of meat.[1]
      Ibid. Act III, Sc. 1, Line 23

A word and a blow.[2]
            Ibid. Line 44

A plague o' both your houses!
            Ibid. Line 96

Romeo. Courage, man; the hurt cannot be much.
    Mercutio. No, 'tis not so deep as a
well, nor so wide as a church-door; but
'tis enough, 'twill serve.
           Ibid. Line 100

O! I am Fortune's fool.
            Ibid. Line 142

Gallop apace, you fiery-footed steeds,
Towards Phoebus' lodging.
        Ibid. Sc. 2, Line 1

When he shall die,
Take him and cut him out in little stars,
And he will make the face of heaven so
    fine
That all the world will be in love with
    night,
And pay no worship to the garish sun.
        Ibid. Sc. 2, Line 21

Was ever book containing such vile
    matter

---

[1] It's as full of good-nature as an egg's full
of meat. — RICHARD BRINSLEY SHERIDAN: *A
Trip to Scarborough* [1777], *Act III, Sc. 4*
[2] Word and a blow. — BUNYAN: *Pilgrim's
Progress* [1678], *Part I*

So fairly bound? O! that deceit should
dwell
In such a gorgeous palace.
*Romeo and Juliet. Act III,
Sc. 2, Line 83*
He was not born to shame:
Upon his brow shame is ashamed to sit.
Ibid. Line 91
Romeo, come forth; come forth, thou
fearful man:
Affliction is enamour'd of thy parts,
And thou art wedded to calamity.
Ibid. Sc. 3, Line 1
Adversity's sweet milk, philosophy.
Ibid. Line 54
Hang up philosophy!
Unless philosophy can make a Juliet.
Ibid. Line 56
The lark, the herald of the morn.
Ibid. Sc. 5, Line 6
Night's candles are burnt out, and joc-
und day
Stands tiptoe on the misty mountain-
tops.
Ibid. Line 9
I'll say yon grey is not the morning's
eye,
'Tis but the pale reflex of Cynthia's
brow;
Nor that is not the lark, whose notes
do beat
The vaulty heaven so high above our
heads:
I have more care to stay than will to go:
Come, death, and welcome: Juliet wills
it so.
How is't, my soul? let's talk; it is not
day.
Ibid. Line 19
Straining harsh discords and unpleasing
sharps.
Ibid. Line 28
All these woes shall serve
For sweet discourses in our time to
come.
Ibid. Line 52
Thank me no thankings, nor proud me
no prouds.
Ibid. Line 153
Is there no pity sitting in the clouds,
That sees into the bottom of my grief?
Ibid. Line 198

Past hope, past cure, past help!
*Romeo and Juliet. Act IV,
Sc. 1, Line 45*
Not stepping o'er the bounds of mod-
esty.
Ibid. Sc. 2, Line 28
My dismal scene I needs must act alone.
Ibid. Sc. 3, Line 19
My bosom's lord sits lightly in his
throne.
Ibid. Act V, Sc. 1, Line 3
Ah me! how sweet is love itself pos-
sess'd,
When but love's shadows are so rich in
joy.
Ibid. Line 10
Well, Juliet, I will lie with thee to-
night.
Ibid. Line 34
Meagre were his looks,
Sharp misery had worn him to the
bones.
Ibid. Line 40
A beggarly account of empty boxes.
Ibid. Line 45
Famine is in thy cheeks.
Ibid. Line 69
The world is not thy friend nor the
world's law.
Ibid. Line 72
Apothecary. My poverty, but not my
will, consents.
Romeo. I pay thy poverty, and not thy
will.
Ibid. Line 75
The strength
Of twenty men.
Ibid. Line 78
The time and my intents are savage-
wild,
More fierce and more inexorable far
Than empty tigers or the roaring sea.
Ibid. Sc. 3, Line 37
One writ with me in sour misfortune's
book.
Ibid. Line 82
Her beauty makes
This vault a feasting presence full of
light.
Ibid. Line 85

How oft when men are at the point of
death
Have they been merry!
*Romeo and Juliet. Act V,
Sc. 3, Line 88*
Beauty's ensign yet
Is crimson in thy lips and in thy cheeks,
And death's pale flag is not advanced
there.
Ibid. Line 94
Eyes, look your last!
Arms, take your last embrace!
Ibid. Line 112
O true apothecary!
Thy drugs are quick.
Ibid. Line 119
What's here? a cup, clos'd in my true
love's hand?
Ibid. Line 160
Pitiful sight! here lies the county slain,
And Juliet bleeding, warm, and newly
dead,
Who here hath lain these two days
buried.
Ibid. Line 174
The purest treasure mortal times afford
Is spotless reputation.
King Richard II [1595–1596].
Act I, Sc. 1, Line 177
Mine honour is my life; both grow in
one;
Take honour from me, and my life is
done.
Ibid. Line 182
The daintiest last, to make the end
most sweet.
Ibid. Sc. 3, Line 68
Truth hath a quiet breast.
Ibid. Line 96
How long a time lies in one little word!
Ibid. Line 213
Things sweet to taste prove in digestion
sour.
Ibid. Line 236
All places that the eye of heaven visits
Are to a wise man ports and happy
havens.
Ibid. Line 275
Suppose the singing birds musicians,
The grass whereon thou tread'st the
presence strew'd,

The flowers fair ladies, and thy steps
no more
Than a delightful measure or a dance;
For gnarling sorrow hath less power to
bite
The man that mocks at it and sets it
light.
*King Richard II. Act I,
Sc. 3, Line 288*
O, who can hold a fire in his hand
By thinking on the frosty Caucasus?
Or cloy the hungry edge of appetite
By bare imagination of a feast?
Or wallow naked in December snow
By thinking on fantastic summer's
heat?
O, no! the apprehension of the good
Gives but the greater feeling to the
worse.
Ibid. Line 294
Where'er I wander, boast of this I can,
Though banish'd, yet a true-born Eng-
lishman.[1]
Ibid. Line 308
The tongues of dying men
Enforce attention like deep harmony.
Ibid. Act II, Sc. 1, Line 5
The setting sun, and music at the close,
As the last taste of sweets, is sweetest
last,
Writ in remembrance, more than things
long past.
Ibid. Line 12
Report of fashions in proud Italy,
Whose manners still our tardy apish
nation
Limps after in base imitation.[2]
Ibid. Line 21
Small showers last long, but sudden
storms are short.
Ibid. Line 35
This royal throne of kings, this sceptred
isle,
This earth of majesty, this seat of Mars,
This other Eden, demi-paradise,
This fortress built by Nature for her-
self
Against infection and the hand of war,

---

[1] A stern, *a true-born Englishman.* — SAM-
UEL JOHNSON (BOSWELL: *Life* [1791])
[2] See Du Bartas, page 102a.

This happy breed of men, this little
　world,
This precious stone set in the silver sea,
Which serves it in the office of a wall
Or as a moat defensive to a house,
Against the envy of less happier lands,
This blessed plot, this earth, this realm,
　this England,
This nurse, this teeming womb of royal
　kings,
Fear'd by their breed and famous by
　their birth.
　　　　King Richard II. Act II,
　　　　　　　Sc. 1, Line 40
England, bound in with the triumphant
　sea,
Whose rocky shore beats back the en-
　vious siege
Of watery Neptune.
　　　　　　Ibid. Line 61
The ripest fruit first falls.
　　　　　　Ibid. Line 154
Your fair discourse hath been as sugar,
Making the hard way sweet and delec-
　table.
　　　　　Ibid. Sc. 3, Line 6
I count myself in nothing else so happy
As in a soul remembering my good
　friends.
　　　　　　Ibid. Line 46
Evermore thanks, the exchequer of the
　poor.
　　　　　　Ibid. Line 65
Grace me no grace, nor uncle me no
　uncle.
　　　　　　Ibid. Line 87
The caterpillars of the commonwealth,
Which I have sworn to weed and pluck
　away.
　　　　　　Ibid. Line 166
Things past redress are now with me
　past care.
　　　　　　Ibid. Line 171
I see thy glory like a shooting star
Fall to the base earth from the fir-
　mament.
　　　　　Ibid. Sc. 4, Line 19
Eating the bitter bread of banishment.
　　　　Ibid. Act III, Sc. 1, Line 21
Fires the proud tops of the eastern
　pines.
　　　　　Ibid. Sc. 2, Line 42

Not all the water in the rough rude sea
Can wash the balm off from an anointed
　king.
　　　　King Richard II. Act III,
　　　　　　　Sc. 2, Line 55
O, call back yesterday, bid time return!
　　　　　　Ibid. Line 69
The worst is death, and death will have
　his day.
　　　　　　Ibid. Line 103
Let's talk of graves, of worms, and
　epitaphs.
　　　　　　Ibid. Line 145
Let's choose executors and talk of wills.
　　　　　　Ibid. Line 148
And nothing can we call our own but
　death;
And that small model of the barren
　earth,
Which serves as paste and cover to our
　bones.
For God's sake, let us sit upon the
　ground,
And tell sad stories of the death of
　kings,
How some have been deposed, some
　slain in war,
Some haunted by the ghosts they have
　depos'd,
Some poison'd by their wives, some
　sleeping kill'd;
All murder'd: for within the hollow
　crown
That rounds the mortal temples of a
　king
Keeps Death his court.
　　　　　　Ibid. Line 152
Comes at the last, and with a little pin
Bores through his castle wall, and fare-
　well king!
　　　　　　Ibid. Line 169
Men judge by the complexion of the
　sky
The state and inclination of the day.
　　　　　　Ibid. Line 194
　　He is come to open
The purple testament of bleeding war.
　　　　　Ibid. Sc. 3, Line 93
　　O! that I were as great
As is my grief, or lesser than my name,

Or that I could forget what I have been,
Or not remember what I must be now.
                King Richard II. Act III, Sc. 3,
                                    Line 136
And my large kingdom for a little grave,
A little little grave, an obscure grave.
                        Ibid. Line 153
The noisome weeds, that without profit
        suck
The soil's fertility from wholesome
        flowers.
                    Ibid. Sc. 4, Line 38
Superfluous branches
We lop away that bearing boughs may
        live.
                    Ibid. Line 63
            Gave
His body to that pleasant country's
        earth,
And his pure soul unto his captain
        Christ,
Under whose colours he had fought so
        long.
                Ibid. Act IV, Sc. 1, Line 97
So Judas did to Christ: but he, in
        twelve,
Found truth in all but one; I, in twelve
        thousand, none.
                        Ibid. Line 170
Now is this golden crown like a deep
        well
That owes two buckets filling one an-
        other;
The emptier ever dancing in the air,
The other down, unseen and full of
        water:
That bucket down and full of tears
        am I,
Drinking my griefs, whilst you mount
        up on high.
                        Ibid. Line 184
You may my glories and my state de-
        pose,
But not my griefs; still am I king of
        those.
                        Ibid. Line 192
Some of you with Pilate wash your
        hands
Showing an outward pity.[1]
                        Ibid. Line 239

[1] Pilate . . . took water, and washed his
hands before the multitude, saying, I am in-

A mockery king of snow.
                    King Richard II. Act IV, Sc. 1,
                                    Line 260
As in a theatre, the eyes of men,
After a well-graced actor leaves the
        stage,
Are idly bent on him that enters next,
Thinking his prattle to be tedious.
                        Ibid. Act V, Sc. 2, Line 23
No word like "pardon."
                        Ibid. Sc. 3, Line 118
It is as hard to come as for a camel
To thread the postern of a small
        needle's eye.[1]
                        Ibid. Sc. 5, Line 16
How sour sweet music is
When time is broke and no proportion
        kept!
So is it in the music of men's lives.
                        Ibid. Line 42
I wasted time, and now doth time
        waste me;
For now hath time made me his num-
        bering clock;
My thoughts are minutes.
                        Ibid. Line 49
        The moon, like to a silver bow
New-bent in heaven.
        A Midsummer-Night's Dream
        [*1595–1596*]. *Act I, Sc. 1,*
        Line 9
To live a barren sister all your life,
Chanting faint hymns to the cold fruit-
        less moon.
                        Ibid. Line 72
But earthlier happy is the rose distill'd
Than that which withering on the virgin
        thorn [2]
Grows, lives, and dies in single blessed-
        ness.
                        Ibid. Line 76
        For aught that I could ever read,
Could ever hear by tale or history,

nocent of the blood of this just person. —
Matthew, XXVII, 24
[1] It is easier for a camel to go through the
eye of a needle, than for a rich man to enter
into the kingdom of God. — *Matthew, XIX,
24*
[2] Maidens withering on the stalk. — WORDS-
WORTH: *Personal Talk* [1806], *St. 1*

The course of true love never did run smooth.

A Midsummer-Night's Dream.
Act I, Sc. 1, Line 132

Swift as a shadow, short as any dream,
Brief as the lightning in the collied night,
That, in a spleen, unfolds both heaven and earth,
And ere a man hath power to say, "Behold!"
The jaws of darkness do devour it up:
So quick bright things come to confusion.

Ibid. Line 144

Love looks not with the eyes, but with the mind,
And therefore is wing'd Cupid painted blind.[1]

Ibid. Line 234

Masters, spread yourselves.

Ibid. Sc. 2, Line 16

This is Ercles' vein.

Ibid. Line 43

I'll speak in a monstrous little voice.

Ibid. Line 55

I am slow of study.

Ibid. Line 70

That would hang us, every mother's son.

Ibid. Line 81

I will roar you as gently as any sucking dove; I will roar you, as 'twere any nightingale.

Ibid. Line 85

A proper man, as one shall see in a summer's day.

Ibid. Line 89

I must go seek some dew-drops here,
And hang a pearl in every cowslip's ear.

Ibid. Act II, Sc. 1, Line 14

I am that merry wanderer of the night.
I jest to Oberon, and make him smile
When I a fat and bean-fed horse beguile,
Neighing in likeness of a filly foal:

[1] See Chaucer, page 81b.

> I have heard of reasons manifold
> Why Love must needs be blind,
> But this the best of all I hold, —
> His eyes are in his mind.
> COLERIDGE: *Reason for Love's*
> *Blindness* [1828]

And sometimes lurk I in a gossip's bowl,
In very likeness of a roasted crab.

A Midsummer-Night's Dream.
Act II, Sc. 1, Line 43

The human mortals.

Ibid. Line 101

The rude sea grew civil at her song,
And certain stars shot madly from their spheres
To hear the sea-maid's music.

Ibid. Line 152

And the imperial votaress passed on,
In maiden meditation, fancy-free.
Yet mark'd I where the bolt of Cupid fell:
It fell upon a little western flower,
Before milk-white, now purple with love's wound,
And maidens call it Love-in-idleness.

Ibid. Line 163

I'll put a girdle round about the earth
In forty minutes.[1]

Ibid. Line 175

It is not night when I do see your face.

Ibid. Line 221

For you in my respect are all the world:
Then how can it be said I am alone?

Ibid. Line 224

We cannot fight for love, as men may do;
We should be woo'd and were not made to woo.

Ibid. Line 241

I know a bank whereon the wild thyme blows,
Where oxlips and the nodding violet grows
Quite over-canopied with luscious woodbine,
With sweet musk-roses, and with eglantine.

Ibid. Line 249

Some to kill cankers in the musk-rose buds,
Some war with rere-mice for their leathern wings,
To make my small elves coats.

Ibid. Sc. 2, Line 3

The clamorous owl, that nightly hoots, and wonders

[1] See Chapman, page 117a.

At our quaint spirits.
A Midsummer-Night's Dream.
Act II, Sc. 2, Line 6
You spotted snakes with double tongue,
Thorny hedge-hogs, be not seen;
Newts, and blind-worms, do no wrong;
Come not near our fairy queen.
Ibid. Line 9
As a surfeit of the sweetest things
The deepest loathing to the stomach
brings.[1]
Ibid. Line 137
A lion among ladies is a most dread-
ful thing.
Ibid. Act III, Sc. 1, Line 32
A calendar, a calendar! look in the
almanack; find out moonshine.
Ibid. Line 55
Bless thee, Bottom! bless thee! thou
art translated.
Ibid. Line 124
Lord, what fools these mortals be! [2]
Ibid. Sc. 2, Line 115
So we grew together,
Like to a double cherry, seeming parted,
But yet an union in partition —
Two lovely berries moulded on one
stem.
Ibid. Line 208
Though she be but little, she is fierce.
Ibid. Line 325
I have a reasonable good ear in
music: let us have the tongs and the
bones.
Ibid. Act IV, Sc. 1, Line 32
Truly, a peck of provender; I could
munch your good dry oats. Methinks I
have a great desire to a bottle of hay:
good hay, sweet hay, hath no fellow.
Ibid. Line 36
I have an exposition of sleep come
upon me.
Ibid. Line 44
My Oberon! what visions have I seen!
Methought I was enamour'd of an ass.
Ibid. Line 82
I never heard
So musical a discord, such sweet
thunder.
Ibid. Line 118

I have had a dream, past the wit of
man to say what dream it was.
A Midsummer-Night's Dream.
Act IV, Sc. 1, Line 211
The eye of man hath not heard, the
ear of man hath not seen,[1] man's hand is
not able to taste, his tongue to conceive,
nor his heart to report, what my dream
was.
Ibid. Line 218
A paramour is, God bless us! a thing
of naught.
Ibid. Sc. 2, Line 14
Eat no onions nor garlic, for we are to
utter sweet breath.
Ibid. Line 44
The lunatic, the lover, and the poet
Are of imagination all compact:
One sees more devils than vast hell can
hold,
That is, the madman: the lover, all as
frantic,
Sees Helen's beauty in a brow of Egypt:
The poet's eye, in a fine frenzy rolling,
Doth glance from heaven to earth,
from earth to heaven;
And as imagination bodies forth
The forms of things unknown, the poet's
pen
Turns them to shapes, and gives to airy
nothing
A local habitation and a name.
Such tricks hath strong imagination,
That if it would but apprehend some
joy,
It comprehends some bringer of that
joy;
Or in the night, imagining some fear,
How easy is a bush supposed a bear!
Ibid. Act V, Sc. 1, Line 7
The true beginning of our end.[2]
Ibid. Line 111
The best in this kind are but shadows.
Ibid. Line 215
A very gentle beast, and of a good
conscience.
Ibid. Line 232

---

[1] Eye hath not seen, nor ear heard. — *1 Corinthians, II, 9*
[2] I see the beginning of my end. — MAS-SINGER: *The Virgin Martyr* [1622], *Act III, Sc. 3*

[1] See *King Henry IV*, page 151a.
[2] See Seneca, page 47a.

This passion, and the death of a dear friend, would go near to make a man look sad.

>   *A Midsummer-Night's Dream.*
>   *Act V, Sc. 1, Line 295*

With the help of a surgeon, he might yet recover and prove an ass.

>   *Ibid. Line 318*

The iron tongue of midnight hath told twelve.

>   *Ibid. Line 372*

My ventures are not in one bottom trusted,
Nor to one place.

>   *The Merchant of Venice [1596–*
>   *1597]. Act I, Sc. 1, Line 42*

Now, by two-headed Janus,
Nature hath framed strange fellows in her time.

>   *Ibid. Line 50*

You have too much respect upon the world:
They lose it that do buy it with much care.

>   *Ibid. Line 74*

I hold the world but as the world, Gratiano, —
A stage, where every man must play a part;
And mine a sad one.

>   *Ibid. Line 77*

Why should a man, whose blood is warm within,
Sit like his grandsire cut in alabaster?

>   *Ibid. Line 83*

There are a sort of men whose visages
Do cream and mantle like a standing pond.

>   *Ibid. Line 88*

I am Sir Oracle,
And when I ope my lips, let no dog bark!

>   *Ibid. Line 93*

I do know of these
That therefore only are reputed wise
For saying nothing.

>   *Ibid. Line 95*

Fish not, with this melancholy bait,
For this fool gudgeon, this opinion.

>   *Ibid. Line 101*

Gratiano speaks an infinite deal of nothing, more than any man in all Ven-

ice. His reasons are as two grains of wheat hid in two bushels of chaff: you shall seek all day ere you find them, and when you have them, they are not worth the search.

>   *The Merchant of Venice.*
>   *Act I, Sc. 1, Line 114*

In my school-days, when I had lost one shaft,
I shot his fellow of the selfsame flight
The selfsame way, with more advised watch,
To find the other forth; and by adventuring both,
I oft found both.

>   *Ibid. Line 141*

They are as sick that surfeit with too much, as they that starve with nothing.

>   *Ibid. Sc. 2, Line 5*

Superfluity comes sooner by white hairs, but competency lives longer.

>   *Ibid. Line 9*

If to do were as easy as to know what were good to do, chapels had been churches, and poor men's cottages princes' palaces.

>   *Ibid. Line 13*

The brain may devise laws for the blood, but a hot temper leaps o'er a cold decree.

>   *Ibid. Line 19*

He doth nothing but talk of his horse.

>   *Ibid. Line 43*

God made him, and therefore let him pass for a man.

>   *Ibid. Line 59*

When he is best, he is a little worse than a man; and when he is worst, he is little better than a beast.

>   *Ibid. Line 93*

I dote on his very absence.

>   *Ibid. Line 118*

My meaning in saying he is a good man, is to have you understand me that he is sufficient.

>   *Ibid. Sc. 3, Line 15*

Ships are but boards, sailors but men: there be land-rats and water-rats, water-thieves and land-thieves.

>   *Ibid. Line 22*

I will buy with you, sell with you, talk with you, walk with you, and so following; but I will not eat with you, drink with you, nor pray with you. What news on the Rialto?

The Merchant of Venice.
Act I, Sc. 3, Line 36

If I can catch him once upon the hip, I will feed fat the ancient grudge I bear him.

Ibid. Line 47

The devil can cite Scripture for his purpose.

Ibid. Line 99

A goodly apple rotten at the heart: O, what a goodly outside falsehood hath!

Ibid. Line 102

For sufferance is the badge of all our tribe.

Ibid. Line 110

You call me misbeliever, cut-throat dog, And spet upon my Jewish gaberdine.

Ibid. Line 111

Shall I bend low, and in a bondman's key, With bated breath and whispering humbleness, Say this?

Ibid. Line 124

O father Abram! what these Christians are, Whose own hard dealings teaches them suspect The thoughts of others!

Ibid. Line 161

I like not fair terms and a villain's mind.

Ibid. Line 180

Mislike me not for my complexion, The shadow'd livery of the burnish'd sun.

Ibid. Act II, Sc. 1, Line 1

An honest, exceeding poor man.

Ibid. Sc. 2, Line 54

The young gentleman, according to Fates and Destinies and such odd sayings, the Sisters Three and such branches of learning, is indeed deceased; or, as you would say in plain terms, gone to heaven.

Ibid. Line 66

The very staff of my age, my very prop.

The Merchant of Venice.
Act II, Sc. 2, Line 71

It is a wise father that knows his own child.

Ibid. Line 83

Go to; here's a simple line of life; here's a small trifle of wives; alas! fifteen wives is nothing: eleven widows and nine maids is a simple coming-in for one man; and then to 'scape drowning thrice, and to be in peril of my life with the edge of a feather-bed, — here are simple 'scapes. Well, if Fortune be a woman, she's a good wench for this gear.

Ibid. Line 158

And the vile squealing of the wry-necked fife.

Ibid. Sc. 5, Line 30

Who riseth from a feast With that keen appetite that he sits down?

Ibid. Sc. 6, Line 8

All things that are, Are with more spirit chased than enjoy'd.

Ibid. Line 12

But love is blind, and lovers cannot see The pretty follies that themselves commit.

Ibid. Line 36

Must I hold a candle to my shames?

Ibid. Line 41

A golden mind stoops not to show of dross.

Ibid. Sc. 7, Line 20

Young in limbs, in judgment old.

Ibid. Line 71

My daughter! O my ducats! O my daughter: Fled with a Christian! O my Christian ducats! Justice! the law! my ducats, and my daughter! A sealed bag, two sealed bags of ducats, Of double ducats, stol'n from me by my daughter!

Ibid. Sc. 8, Line 15

The fool multitude, that choose by show.

The Merchant of Venice.
Act II, Sc. 9, Line 26

Let none presume
To wear an undeserved dignity.
O! that estates, degrees, and offices
Were not deriv'd corruptly, and that clear honour
Were purchased by the merit of the wearer!

Ibid. Line 39

The ancient saying is no heresy:
"Hanging and wiving goes by destiny." [1]

Ibid. Line 83

Let him look to his bond.

Ibid. Act III, Sc. 1, Line 49

I am a Jew. Hath not a Jew eyes? Hath not a Jew hands, organs, dimensions, senses, affections, passions?

Ibid. Line 62

If you prick us, do we not bleed? if you tickle us, do we not laugh? if you poison us, do we not die? and if you wrong us, shall we not revenge?

Ibid. Line 65

The villany you teach me I will execute, and it shall go hard, but I will better the instruction.

Ibid. Line 76

I would not have given it for a wilderness of monkeys.

Ibid. Line 130

There's something tells me — but it is not love —
I would not lose you; and you know yourself,
Hate counsels not in such a quality.

Ibid. Sc. 2, Line 4

Makes a swan-like end,
Fading in music. [2]

Ibid. Line 44

Tell me where is fancy bred,
Or in the heart or in the head?
How begot, how nourished?
    Reply, reply.

Ibid. Line 63

In law, what plea so tainted and corrupt
But being season'd with a gracious voice,

[1] See Heywood, page 91a.
[2] See Socrates, page 21a.

Obscures the show of evil?

The Merchant of Venice.
Act III, Sc. 2, Line 75

There is no vice so simple but assumes
Some mark of virtue on his outward parts.

Ibid. Line 81

Thus ornament is but the guiled shore
To a most dangerous sea.

Ibid. Line 97

The seeming truth which cunning times put on
To entrap the wisest.

Ibid. Line 100

How all the other passions fleet to air,
As doubtful thoughts, and rash-embrac'd despair
And shuddering fear, and green-ey'd jealousy.
O love! be moderate; allay thy ecstasy;
In measure rain thy joy; scant this excess;
I feel too much thy blessing: make it less,
For fear I surfeit!

Ibid. Line 109

An unlesson'd girl, unschool'd, unpractis'd;
Happy in this, she is not yet so old
But she may learn.

Ibid. Line 160

Here are a few of the unpleasant'st words
That ever blotted paper!

Ibid. Line 252

Thus when I shun Scylla, your father, I fall into Charybdis, your mother. [1]

Ibid. Sc. 5, Line 17

A harmless necessary cat.

Ibid. Act IV, Sc. 1, Line 55

What! wouldst thou have a serpent sting thee twice?

Ibid. Line 69

The weakest kind of fruit
Drops earliest to the ground.

Ibid. Line 115

[1] Incidis in Scyllam cupiens vitare Charybdim (You fall into Scylla in seeking to avoid Charybdis). — PHILIPPE GUALTIER: *Alexandreis* [*circa* 1300], *Book V, L. 301*

To hold opinion with Pythagoras
That souls of animals infuse themselves
Into the trunks of men.[1]

   The Merchant of Venice.
   Act IV, Sc. 1, Line 131

I never knew so young a body with
so old a head.[2]

   Ibid. Line 163

The quality of mercy is not strain'd,
It droppeth as the gentle rain from
 heaven
Upon the place beneath. It is twice
 bless'd:
It blesseth him that gives and him that
 takes.
'Tis mightiest in the mightiest: it be-
 comes
The throned monarch better than his
 crown;
His sceptre shows the force of temporal
 power,
The attribute to awe and majesty,
Wherein doth sit the dread and fear of
 kings;
But mercy is above this sceptred sway,
It is enthroned in the hearts of kings,
It is an attribute to God himself;
And earthly power doth then show lik-
 est God's,
When mercy seasons justice. Therefore,
 Jew,
Though justice be thy plea, consider
 this,
That in the course of justice, none of us
Should see salvation: we do pray for
 mercy;
And that same prayer doth teach us all
 to render
The deeds of mercy.

   Ibid. Line 184

To do a great right, do a little wrong.

   Ibid. Line 216

---

[1] *Clown.* What is the opinion of Pythagoras
concerning wild fowl?
 Malvolio. That the soul of our grandam
might haply inhabit a bird.
  Twelfth-Night [1598–1600], *Act IV,
   Sc. 2, L. 55*
[2] He is young, but, take it from me, a very
staid head. — Thomas Wentworth, Earl of
Strafford [1593–1641]: Letter, commending
the Earl of Ormond to Charles I for appointment as Councillor

A Daniel come to judgment! yea, a
 Daniel!

   The Merchant of Venice.
   Act IV, Sc. 1, Line 223

How much more elder art thou than thy
 looks.

   Ibid. Line 251

Is it so nominated in the bond?

   Ibid. Line 260

'Tis not in the bond.

   Ibid. Line 263

For herein Fortune shows herself more
 kind
Than is her custom: it is still her use
To let the wretched man outlive his
 wealth,
To view with hollow eye and wrinkled
 brow
An age of poverty.

   Ibid. Line 268

Speak me fair in death.

   Ibid. Line 276

An upright judge, a learned judge!

   Ibid. Line 324

A Daniel, still say I, a second Daniel! —
I thank thee, Jew, for teaching me that
 word.

   Ibid. Line 341

You take my house, when you do take
 the prop
That doth sustain my house; you take
 my life,
When you do take the means whereby
 I live.

   Ibid. Line 376

He is well paid that is well satisfied.

   Ibid. Line 416

Lorenzo.   In such a night
Troilus methinks mounted the Troyan
 walls,
And sigh'd his soul toward the Grecian
 tents,
Where Cressid lay that night.
Jessica.   In such a night
Did Thisbe fearfully o'ertrip the dew,
And saw the lion's shadow ere himself,
And ran dismay'd away.
Lorenzo.   In such a night
Stood Dido with a willow in her hand

Upon the wild sea-banks, and waft her
    love
To come again to Carthage.
Jessica.   In such a night
Medea gather'd the enchanted herbs
That did renew old Aeson.
          The Merchant of Venice.
            Act V, Sc. 1, Line 3
How sweet the moonlight sleeps upon
    this bank!
Here we will sit and let the sounds of
    music
Creep in our ears: soft stillness and the
    night
Become the touches of sweet harmony.
Sit, Jessica. Look how the floor of
    heaven
Is thick inlaid with patines of bright
    gold:
There's not the smallest orb which
    thou behold'st
But in his motion like an angel sings,
Still quiring to the young-eyed cheru-
    bins.
Such harmony is in immortal souls;
But whilst this muddy vesture of decay
Doth grossly close it in, we cannot hear
    it.
                Ibid. Line 54
I am never merry when I hear sweet
    music.
                Ibid. Line 69
The man that hath no music in himself,
Nor is not mov'd with concord of sweet
    sounds,
Is fit for treasons, stratagems, and
    spoils;
The motions of his spirit are dull as
    night,
And his affections dark as Erebus.
Let no such man be trusted.
                Ibid. Line 83
How far that little candle throws his
    beams!
So shines a good deed in a naughty
    world.
                Ibid. Line 90
How many things by season season'd
    are
To their right praise and true perfec-
    tion!
                Ibid. Line 107

This night, methinks, is but the day-
    light sick.
          The Merchant of Venice.
            Act V, Sc. 1, Line 124
A light wife doth make a heavy hus-
    band.
                Ibid. Line 130
These blessed candles of the night.
                Ibid. Line 220
And if his name be George, I'll call him
    Peter;
For new-made honour doth forget men's
    names.
          King John [*1596–1597*]. *Act I*,
            Sc. 1, Line 186
Sweet, sweet, sweet poison for the age's
    tooth.
                Ibid. Line 213
Heaven lay not my transgression to my
    charge.
                Ibid. Line 256
A hazard of new fortunes.
          Ibid. Act II, Sc. 1, Line 71
For courage mounteth with occasion.
                Ibid. Line 82
Saint George, that swing'd the dragon,
    and e'er since
Sits on his horse back at mine hostess'
    door.
                Ibid. Line 288
He is the half part of a blessed man,
Left to be finished by such a she;
And she a fair divided excellence,
Whose fulness of perfection lies in him.
                Ibid. Line 437
Talks as familiarly of roaring lions
As maids of thirteen do of puppy-dogs!
                Ibid. Line 459
Zounds! I was never so bethump'd with
    words,
Since I first call'd my brother's father
    dad.[1]
                Ibid. Line 466
I will instruct my sorrows to be proud;
For grief is proud, and makes his owner
    stoop.
          Ibid. Act III, Sc. 1, Line 68
What hath this day deserv'd? what
    hath it done

[1] I was ne'er so thrummed since I was a
gentleman. — THOMAS DEKKER: *The Honest
Whore, Part I* [1604], *Act IV, Sc. 2*

That it in golden letters should be set
Among the high tides in the calendar?

King John. Act III, Sc. 1, Line 84

Thou wear a lion's hide! doff it for
shame,
And hang a calf's-skin on those recreant
limbs.

Ibid. Line 128

Bell, book and candle shall not drive
me back,
When gold and silver becks me to come
on.[1]

Ibid. Sc. 3, Line 12

I had a thing to say,
But I will fit it with some better time.

Ibid. Line 25

O, amiable lovely death![2]

Ibid. Sc. 4, Line 25

Grief fills the room up of my absent
child,
Lies in his bed, walks up and down with
me,
Puts on his pretty looks, repeats his
words,
Remembers me of all his gracious parts,
Stuffs out his vacant garments with his
form.

Ibid. Line 93

Life is as tedious as a twice-told tale,
Vexing the dull ear of a drowsy man.

Ibid. Line 108

When Fortune means to men most
good,
She looks upon them with a threatening eye.[3]

Ibid. Line 119

And he that stands upon a slippery
place
Makes nice of no vile hold to stay him
up.

Ibid. Line 137

To gild refined gold, to paint the lily,
To throw a perfume on the violet,
To smooth the ice, or add another hue
Unto the rainbow, or with taper-light
To seek the beauteous eye of heaven to
garnish,
Is wasteful and ridiculous excess.

Ibid. Act IV, Sc. 2, Line 11

And oftentimes excusing of a fault
Doth make the fault the worse by the
excuse.[1]

King John. Act IV, Sc. 2, Line 30

We cannot hold mortality's strong
hand.

Ibid. Line 82

There is no sure foundation set on
blood,
No certain life achiev'd by others'
death.

Ibid. Line 104

But if you be afeard to hear the worst,
Then let the worst unheard fall on your
head.

Ibid. Line 134

Make haste; the better foot before.[2]

Ibid. Line 170

Another lean unwash'd artificer.

Ibid. Line 201

How oft the sight of means to do ill
deeds
Makes ill deeds done!

Ibid. Line 219

Heaven take my soul, and England
keep my bones.

Ibid. Sc. 3, Line 10

I am amaz'd, methinks, and lose my
way
Among the thorns and dangers of this
world.

Ibid. Line 140

Mocking the air with colours idly
spread.

Ibid. Act V, Sc. 1, Line 72

The day shall not be up so soon as I,
To try the fair adventure of to-morrow.

Ibid. Sc. 5, Line 21

'Tis strange that death should sing.
I am the cygnet to this pale faint swan,
Who chants a doleful hymn to his own
death,[3]
And from the organ-pipe of frailty
sings
His soul and body to their lasting rest.

Ibid. Sc. 7, Line 20

Now my soul hath elbow-room.

Ibid. Line 28

---

[1] See Cervantes, page 104b.
[2] See Walt Whitman, page 609b.
[3] See Publilius Syrus, page 44a.

[1] See Meurier, page 97a.
[2] Put forward your best foot! — BROWN-
ING: *Respectability* [1855], *St. 3*
[3] See Socrates, page 21a.

This England never did, nor never shall,
Lie at the proud foot of a conqueror.
> *King John. Act V, Sc. 7, Line 112*

Come the three corners of the world in
arms,
And we shall shock them. Nought shall
make us rue,
If England to itself do rest but true.
> *Ibid. Line 116*

So shaken as we are, so wan with care.
> *King Henry IV [1597–1598].*
> *Part I, Act I, Sc. 1, Line 1*

In those holy fields
Over whose acres walk'd those blessed
feet
Which fourteen hundred years ago were
nail'd
For our advantage on the bitter cross.
> *Ibid. Line 24*

Here is a dear and true industrious
friend.
> *Ibid. Line 62*

The blessed sun himself a fair hot
wench in flame-colour'd taffeta, — I see
no reason why thou shouldst be so superfluous to demand the time of the
day.
> *Ibid. Sc. 2, Line 10*

Diana's foresters, gentlemen of the
shade, minions of the moon.
> *Ibid. Line 29*

So far as my coin would stretch; and
where it would not, I have used my
credit.
> *Ibid. Line 61*

Old father antic the law.
> *Ibid. Line 69*

I would to God thou and I knew
where a commodity of good names were
to be bought.
> *Ibid. Line 92*

Thou hast damnable iteration, and
art indeed able to corrupt a saint.
> *Ibid. Line 101*

'Tis my vocation, Hal; 'tis no sin
for a man to labour in his vocation.
> *Ibid. Line 116*

There's neither honesty, manhood,
nor good fellowship in thee.
> *Ibid. Line 154*

If all the year were playing holidays,
To sport would be as tedious as to work.
> *King Henry IV. Part I, Act I,*
> *Sc. 2, Line 226*

You tread upon my patience.
> *Ibid. Sc. 3, Line 4*

That title of respect
Which the proud soul ne'er pays but to
the proud.
> *Ibid. Line 8*

Fresh as a bridegroom; and his chin
new reap'd,
Showed like a stubble-land at harvest-
home;
He was perfumed like a milliner,
And 'twixt his finger and his thumb he
held
A pouncet-box, which ever and anon
He gave his nose and took 't away
again.
> *Ibid. Line 34*

And as the soldiers bore dead bodies
by,
He call'd them untaught knaves, un-
mannerly,
To bring a slovenly unhandsome corpse
Betwixt the wind and his nobility.
> *Ibid. Line 42*

So pester'd with a popinjay.
> *Ibid. Line 50*

God save the mark.
> *Ibid. Line 56*

And but for these vile guns,
He would himself have been a soldier.
> *Ibid. Line 63*

The blood more stirs
To rouse a lion than to start a hare!
> *Ibid. Line 197*

By heaven, methinks it were an easy
leap
To pluck bright honour from the pale-
faced moon,
Or dive into the bottom of the deep,
Where fathom-line could never touch
the ground,
And pluck up drowned honour by the
locks.
> *Ibid. Line 201*

Why, what a candy deal of courtesy
This fawning greyhound then did prof-
fer me!
> *Ibid. Line 251*

I know a trick worth two of that.
*King Henry IV. Part I, Act II,
Sc. 1, Line 40*

If the rascal have not given me medicines to make me love him, I'll be hanged.
Ibid. Sc. 2, Line 20

It would be argument for a week, laughter for a month, and a good jest for ever.
Ibid. Line 104

Falstaff sweats to death,
And lards the lean earth as he walks along.
Ibid. Line 119

Out of this nettle, danger, we pluck this flower, safety.
Ibid. Sc. 3, Line 11

I could brain him with his lady's fan.
Ibid. Line 26

Constant you are,
But yet a woman; and for secrecy,
No lady closer; for I well believe
Thou wilt not utter what thou dost not know;
And so far will I trust thee, gentle Kate.
Ibid. Line 113

A Corinthian, a lad of mettle, a good boy.
Ibid. Sc. 4, Line 13

A plague of all cowards, I say.
Ibid. Line 129

There live not three good men unhanged in England, and one of them is fat and grows old.
Ibid. Line 146

You care not who sees your back: call you that backing of your friends? A plague upon such backing!
Ibid. Line 168

I have peppered two of them. . . . I tell thee what, Hal, if I tell thee a lie, spit in my face; call me horse.
Ibid. Line 216

Give you a reason on compulsion! If reasons were as plentiful as blackberries, I would give no man a reason upon compulsion, I.
Ibid. Line 267

Mark now, how a plain tale shall put you down.
Ibid. Line 285

No more of that, Hal, an thou lovest me!
*King Henry IV. Part I, Act II,
Sc. 4, Line 316*

What doth gravity out of his bed at midnight?
Ibid. Line 328

A plague of sighing and grief! It blows a man up like a bladder.
Ibid. Line 370

You may buy land now as cheap as stinking mackerel.
Ibid. Line 399

That reverend vice, that grey iniquity, that father ruffian, that vanity in years.
Ibid. Line 505

If sack and sugar be a fault, God help the wicked! if to be old and merry be a sin, then many an old host that I know is damn'd: if to be fat be to be hated, then Pharaoh's lean kine are to be loved.
Ibid. Line 524

Banish plump Jack, and banish all the world.
Ibid. Line 534

Play out the play.
Ibid. Line 539

O, monstrous! but one half-pennyworth of bread to this intolerable deal of sack!
Ibid. Line 597

Diseased Nature oftentimes breaks forth
In strange eruptions.
Ibid. Act III, Sc. 1, Line 27

I am not in the roll of common men.
Ibid. Line 43

Glendower. I can call spirits from the vasty deep.

Hotspur. Why, so can I, or so can any man;
But will they come when you do call for them?
Ibid. Line 53

I had rather be a kitten and cry mew,
Than one of these same metre balladmongers.
Ibid. Line 128

But in the way of bargain, mark ye me,
I'll cavil on the ninth part of a hair.
> *King Henry IV. Part I, Act III,*
> *Sc. 1, Line 138*

A deal of skimble-skamble stuff.
> *Ibid. Line 153*

Those musicians that shall play to you
Hang in the air a thousand leagues from
hence.
> *Ibid. Line 226*

A good mouth-filling oath.
> *Ibid. Line 258*

A fellow of no mark nor likelihood.
> *Ibid. Sc. 2, Line 45*

And then I stole all courtesy from
heaven,
And drest myself in such humility
That I did pluck allegiance from men's
hearts.
> *Ibid. Line 52*

To loathe the taste of sweetness,
whereof a little
More than a little is by much too much.[1]
> *Ibid. Line 72*

The end of life cancels all bands.
> *Ibid. Line 157*

An I have not forgotten what the inside of a church is made of, I am a
pepper-corn.
> *Ibid. Sc. 3, Line 8*

Company, villanous company, hath
been the spoil of me.
> *Ibid. Line 10*

Rob me the exchequer.
> *Ibid. Line 204*

How has he the leisure to be sick
In such a justling time?
> *Ibid. Act IV, Sc. 1, Line 17*

This sickness doth infect
The very life-blood of our enterprise.
> *Ibid. Line 28*

That daffed the world aside,
And bid it pass.
> *Ibid. Line 96*

Baited like eagles having lately
bathed . . .
As full of spirit as the month of May,
And gorgeous as the sun at midsummer.
> *Ibid. Line 99*

[1] See *A Midsummer Night's Dream*, page
142a.

The cankers of a calm world and a long
peace.
> *King Henry IV. Part I, Act IV,*
> *Sc. 2, Line 32*

Food for powder, food for powder;
they'll fill a pit as well as better.
> *Ibid. Line 72*

To the latter end of a fray and the
beginning of a feast
Fits a dull fighter and a keen guest.[1]
> *Ibid. Line 86*

I could be well content
To entertain the lag-end of my life
With quiet hours.
> *Ibid. Act V, Sc. 1, Line 23*

I would 't were bedtime, Hal, and
all well.
> *Ibid. Line 126*

Honour pricks me on. Yea, but how
if honour prick me off when I come on,
— how then? Can honour set to a leg?
no: or an arm? no: or take away the
grief of a wound? no. Honour hath no
skill in surgery, then? no. What is honour? a word. What is in that word honour; what is that honour? air. A trim
reckoning! Who hath it? he that died o'
Wednesday. Doth he feel it? no. Doth
he hear it? no. It is insensible, then?
yea, to the dead. But will it not live
with the living? no. Why? detraction
will not suffer it. Therefore I'll none of
it. Honour is a mere scutcheon. And so
ends my catechism.
> *Ibid. Line 131*

Suspicion all our lives shall be stuck full
of eyes;
For treason is but trusted like the fox.
> *Ibid. Sc. 2, Line 8*

Let me tell the world.[2]
> *Ibid. Line 65*

The time of life is short;
To spend that shortness basely were too
long.
> *Ibid. Line 81*

[1] See John Heywood, page 94b.
[2] I'll tell the world. — SHAKESPEARE: *Measure for Measure* [1604–1605], Act II, Sc. 4,
L. 154
Ay, tell the world! — BROWNING: *Paracelsus* [1835], *Part II*

Two stars keep not their motion in one sphere.

King Henry IV. Part I, Act V,
Sc. 4, Line 65

This earth, that bears thee dead,
Bears not alive so stout a gentleman.

Ibid. Line 92

Thy ignominy sleep with thee in the grave,
But not remember'd in thy epitaph!

Ibid. Line 100

I could have better spared a better man.

Ibid. Line 104

The better part of valour is discretion.[1]

Ibid. Line 120

    Full bravely hast thou fleshed
Thy maiden sword.

Ibid. Line 132

Lord, Lord, how this world is given to lying! I grant you I was down and out of breath; and so was he. But we rose both at an instant, and fought a long hour by Shrewsbury clock.

Ibid. Line 148

I'll purge, and leave sack, and live cleanly.

Ibid. Line 168

    Rumour is a pipe
Blown by surmises, jealousies, conjectures,
And of so easy and so plain a stop
That the blunt monster with uncounted heads,
The still-discordant wavering multitude,[2]
Can play upon it.

Ibid. Part II, Induction, Line 15

Even such a man, so faint, so spiritless,
So dull, so dead in look, so woe-begone,
Drew Priam's curtain in the dead of night,
And would have told him half his Troy was burnt.

Ibid. Act I, Sc. 1, Line 70

Yet the first bringer of unwelcome news
Hath but a losing office, and his tongue
Sounds ever after as a sullen bell,

Remember'd knolling a departing friend.[1]

King Henry IV. Part II, Act I,
Sc. 1, Line 100

I am not only witty in myself, but the cause that wit is in other men.[2]

Ibid. Sc. 2, Line 10

A rascally yea-forsooth knave.

Ibid. Line 40

You lie in your throat if you say I am any other than an honest man.

Ibid. Line 97

Some smack of age in you, some relish of the saltness of time.

Ibid. Line 112

It is the disease of not listening, the malady of not marking, that I am troubled withal.

Ibid. Line 139

We that are in the vaward of our youth.

Ibid. Line 201

Have you not a moist eye, a dry hand, a yellow cheek, a white beard, a decreasing leg, an increasing belly?

Ibid. Line 206

Every part about you blasted with antiquity.

Ibid. Line 210

For my voice, I have lost it with hollaing and singing of anthems.

Ibid. Line 215

Pray that our armies join not in a hot day; for, by the Lord, I take but two shirts out with me, and I mean not to sweat extraordinarily.

Ibid. Line 237

It was always yet the trick of our English nation, if they have a good thing, to make it too common.

Ibid. Line 244

I were better to be eaten to death with rust than to be scoured to nothing with perpetual motion.

Ibid. Line 249

I can get no remedy against this consumption of the purse: borrowing only lingers and lingers it out, but the disease is incurable.

Ibid. Line 267

---

[1] It show'd discretion the best part of valour. — BEAUMONT AND FLETCHER: *A King and No King* [1619], *Act II, Sc. 3*
[2] See Sir Philip Sidney, page 115b.

[1] See Sophocles, page 14a.
[2] See Samuel Johnson, page 343a.

Who lined himself with hope,
Eating the air on promise of supply.
King Henry IV. Part II, Act I,
Sc. 3, Line 27
When we mean to build,
We first survey the plot, then draw the model;
And when we see the figure of the house,
Then must we rate the cost of the erection.[1]
Ibid. Line 41
A habitation giddy and unsure
Hath he that buildeth on the vulgar heart.
Ibid. Line 89
Past and to come seem best; things present worst.
Ibid. Line 108
A poor lone woman.
Ibid. Act II, Sc. 1, Line 37
I'll tickle your catastrophe.
Ibid. Line 68
He hath eaten me out of house and home.
Ibid. Line 82
Let the end try the man.
Ibid. Sc. 2, Line 52
Thus we play the fools with the time, and the spirits of the wise sit in the clouds and mock us.
Ibid. Line 155
He was indeed the glass
Wherein the noble youth did dress themselves.
Ibid. Sc. 3, Line 21
A good heart's worth gold.
Ibid. Sc. 4, Line 34
Aggravate your choler.
Ibid. Line 174
And let the welkin roar.
Ibid. Line 180
Is it not strange that desire should so many years outlive performance?
Ibid. Line 283
Now comes in the sweetest morsel of the night, and we must hence and leave it unpicked.
Ibid. Line 401

[1] Which of you, intending to build a tower, sitteth not down first, and counteth the cost, whether he have sufficient to finish it? — *Luke, XIV, 28*

O sleep, O gentle sleep,[1]
Nature's soft nurse! how have I frighted thee,
That thou no more wilt weigh my eyelids down
And steep my senses in forgetfulness?
King Henry IV. Part II, Act III,
Sc. 1, Line 5
With all appliances and means to boot.
Ibid. Line 29
Uneasy lies the head that wears a crown.
Ibid. Line 31
There is a history in all men's lives.
Ibid. Line 80
How many of mine old acquaintance are dead!
Ibid. Sc. 2, Line 37
Death, as the Psalmist saith, is certain to all; all shall die.
Ibid. Line 41
Accommodated; that is, when a man is, as they say, accommodated; or when a man is, being, whereby a' may be thought to be accommodated, — which is an excellent thing.
Ibid. Line 86
Most forcible Feeble.
Ibid. Line 181
We have heard the chimes at midnight.
Ibid. Line 231
A man can die but once: we owe God a death.
Ibid. Line 253
We ready are to try our fortunes
To the last man.
Ibid. Act IV, Sc. 2, Line 43
I may justly say, with the hook-nosed fellow of Rome, "I came, saw, and overcame."[2]
Ibid. Sc. 3, Line 44
If I had a thousand sons, the first human principle I would teach them should be, to forswear thin potations and to addict themselves to sack.
Ibid. Line 133
Will Fortune never come with both hands full

[1] Sleep, most gentle sleep. — Ovid [43 B.C.–A.D. 18]: *Metamorphoses, Book II, L. 624*
[2] See Plutarch, page 59b.

But write her fair words still in foulest letters?
> *King Henry IV. Part II, Act IV,*
> *Sc. 4, Line 103*

Golden care!
That keep'st the ports of slumber open wide
To many a watchful night!
> *Ibid. Sc. 5, Line 22*

Thy wish was father, Harry, to that thought.[1]
> *Ibid. Line 91*

Commit
The oldest sins the newest kind of ways.
> *Ibid. Line 124*

His cares are now all ended.
> *Ibid. Act. V, Sc. 2, Line 3*

I hope to see London once ere I die.
> *Ibid. Sc. 3, Line 61*

Falstaff. What! is the old king dead?
Pistol. As nail in door.[2]
> *Ibid. Line 123*

How ill white hairs become a fool and jester.
> *Ibid. Sc. 4, Line 53*

O! for a Muse of fire, that would ascend
The brightest heaven of invention!
> *King Henry V* [*1598–1600*].
> *Prologue, Line 1*

Consideration like an angel came,
And whipped the offending Adam out of him.
> *Ibid. Act I, Sc. 1, Line 28*

Hear him debate of commonwealth affairs,
You would say it hath been all in all his study.
> *Ibid. Line 41*

Turn him to any cause of policy,
The Gordian knot of it he will unloose,
Familiar as his garter: that when he speaks,
The air, a chartered libertine, is still.
> *Ibid. Line 45*

[1] Men's thoughts are much according to their inclination, their discourse and speeches according to their learning and infused opinions. — FRANCIS BACON: *Essays* [1597–1625], *Of Custom and Education*

[2] As dead as a door nail. — WILLIAM LANGLAND: *The Vision of Piers Plowman* [?1360–1399], *Part 2, L. 183*

Therefore doth heaven divide
The state of man in divers functions,
Setting endeavour in continual motion;
To which is fixed, as an aim or butt,
Obedience; for so work the honey-bees,
Creatures that by a rule in nature teach
The act of order to a peopled kingdom.
> *King Henry V. Act I,*
> *Sc. 2, Line 183*

The singing masons building roofs of gold.
> *Ibid. Line 198*

Many things, having full reference
To one consent, may work contrariously;
As many arrows, loosed several ways,
Fly to one mark;
As many several ways meet in one town;
As many fresh streams meet in one salt sea;
As many lines close in the dial's centre;
So may a thousand actions, once afoot,
End in one purpose, and be all well borne
Without defeat.
> *Ibid. Line 205*

'Tis ever common
That men are merriest when they are from home.
> *Ibid. Line 271*

Now all the youth of England are on fire,
And silken dalliance in the wardrobe lies.
> *Ibid. Act II, Prologue, Line 1*

O England! model to thy inward greatness,
Like little body with a mighty heart,
What mightst thou do, that honour would thee do,
Were all thy children kind and natural!
> *Ibid. Line 16*

A' made a finer end and went away an it had been any christom child; a' parted even just between twelve and one, even at the turning o' the tide: for after I saw him fumble with the sheets and play with flowers and smile upon his fingers' ends, I knew there was but one way; for his nose was as sharp

as a pen, and a' babbled of green fields.
King Henry V. Act II, Sc. 3,
Line 11

As cold as any stone.
Ibid. Line 26

Self-love, my liege, is not so vile a sin
As self-neglecting.
Ibid. Sc. 4, Line 74

Once more unto the breach, dear
friends, once more;
Or close the wall up with our English
dead!
In peace there's nothing so becomes a
man
As modest stillness and humility;
But when the blast of war blows in our
ears,
Then imitate the action of the tiger:
Stiffen the sinews, summon up the
blood,
Disguise fair nature with hard-favour'd
rage;
Then lend the eye a terrible aspect.
Ibid. Act III, Sc. 1, Line 1

And sheathed their swords for lack of
argument.
Ibid. Line 21

I see you stand like greyhounds in the
slips,
Straining upon the start. The game's
afoot:
Follow your spirit; and, upon this
charge
Cry "God for Harry! England and
Saint George!"
Ibid. Line 31

I would give all my fame for a pot
of ale and safety.
Ibid. Sc. 2, Line 14

Men of few words are the best men.
Ibid. Line 40

He will maintain his argument as well
as any military man in the world.
Ibid. Line 89

I know the disciplines of wars.
Ibid. Line 156

What is it then to me if impious war,
Array'd in flames like to the prince of
fiends,
Do, with his smirch'd complexion, all
fell feats

Enlink'd to waste and desolation?
King Henry V. Act III, Sc. 3,
Line 15

A man that I love and honour with
my soul, and my heart, and my duty,
and my life, and my living, and my
uttermost power.
Ibid. Sc. 6, Line 7

Giddy Fortune's furious fickle wheel,
That goddess blind,
That stands upon the rolling restless
stone.
Ibid. Line 28

I thought upon one pair of English legs
Did march three Frenchmen.
Ibid. Line 161

We are in God's hand.
Ibid. Line 181

That island of England breeds very
valiant creatures: their mastiffs are of
unmatchable courage.
Ibid. Sc. 7, Line 155

You may as well say that's a valiant
flea that dare eat his breakfast on the
lip of a lion.
Ibid. Line 160

The hum of either army stilly sounds,
That the fixed sentinels almost receive
The secret whispers of each other's
watch;
Fire answers fire, and through their
paly flames
Each battle sees the other's umbered
face;
Steed threatens steed, in high and boast-
ful neighs
Piercing the night's dull ear; and from
the tents
The armourers, accomplishing the
knights,
With busy hammers closing rivets up,
Give dreadful note of preparation.
Ibid. Act IV, Prologue, Line 5

There is some soul of goodness in things
evil,
Would men observingly distil it out.
Ibid. Act IV, Sc. 1, Line 4

When blood is their argument.
Ibid. Line 151

Every subject's duty is the king's;
but every subject's soul is his own.
Ibid. Line 189

What infinite heart's ease
Must kings neglect that private men
enjoy!
And what have kings that privates have
not too,
Save ceremony, save general ceremony?
And what art thou, thou idol ceremony?
What kind of god art thou, that suffer'st
more
Of mortal griefs than do thy worship-
pers?
What are thy rents? what are thy
comings-in?
O ceremony! show me but thy worth.

King Henry V. Act IV,
Sc. 1, Line 256

'Tis not the balm, the sceptre and the
ball,
The sword, the mace, the crown impe-
rial,
The intertissued robe of gold and pearl,
The farced title running 'fore the king,
The throne he sits on, nor the tide of
pomp
That beats upon the high shore of this
world,
No, not all these, thrice-gorgeous cere-
mony,
Not all these, laid in bed majestical,
Can sleep so soundly as the wretched
slave,
Who with a body filled and vacant mind
Gets him to rest, crammed with distress-
ful bread.

Ibid. Line 280

Winding up days with toil and nights
with sleep.

Ibid. Line 299

O God of battles, steel my soldiers'
hearts;
Possess them not with fear; take from
them now
The sense of reckoning, if the opposed
numbers
Pluck their hearts from them.

Ibid. Line 309

He is as full of valour as of kindness;
Princely in both.

Ibid. Sc. 3, Line 15

But if it be a sin to covet honour,
I am the most offending soul alive.

Ibid. Line 28

This day is called the feast of Crispian:
He that outlives this day, and comes
safe home,
Will stand a tip-toe when this day is
named.

King Henry V. Act IV, Sc. 3, Line 40

We few, we happy few, we band of
brothers.

Ibid. Line 60

Those that leave their valiant bones in
France,
Dying like men, though buried in your
dunghills,
They shall be fam'd; for there the sun
shall greet them,
And draw their honours reeking up to
heaven.

Ibid. Line 98

The saying is true, "The empty vessel makes the greatest sound."

Ibid. Sc. 4, Line 72

There is a river in Macedon, and
there is also moreover a river at Mon-
mouth; . . . and there is salmons in
both.

Ibid. Sc. 7, Line 28

There is occasions and causes why
and wherefore [1] in all things.

Ibid. Act V, Sc. 1, Line 3

By this leek, I will most horribly revenge. I eat and eat, I swear.

Ibid. Line 49

All hell shall stir for this.

Ibid. Line 72

A fellow of plain and uncoined constancy.

Ibid. Sc. 2, Line 160

My comfort is, that old age, that ill
layer-up of beauty, can do no more
spoil upon my face.

Ibid. Line 246

O Kate! nice customs curtsy to great
kings. Dear Kate, you and I cannot be
confined within the weak list of a country's fashion.

Ibid. Line 271

He hath indeed better bettered expectation.

Much Ado about Nothing [1598–
1600]. Act I, Sc. 1, Line 16

[1] See *The Comedy of Errors*, page 129a.

How much better is it to weep at joy than to joy at weeping.
Much Ado about Nothing.
Act I, Sc. 1, Line 28

A very valiant trencher-man.
Ibid. Line 52

There's a skirmish of wit between them.
Ibid. Line 64

He wears his faith but as the fashion of his hat.
Ibid. Line 76

The gentleman is not in your books.
Ibid. Line 79

What! my dear Lady Disdain! are you yet living?
Ibid. Line 123

I would my horse had the speed of your tongue, and so good a continuer.
Ibid. Line 151

Shall I never see a bachelor of three-score again?
Ibid. Line 209

Benedick the married man.
Ibid. Line 278

He is of a very melancholy disposition.
Ibid. Act II, Sc. 1, Line 6

I could not endure a husband with a beard on his face: I had rather lie in the woollen.
Ibid. Line 31

He that hath a beard is more than a youth, and he that hath no beard is less than a man.
Ibid. Line 38

As merry as the day is long.
Ibid. Line 52

Would it not grieve a woman to be over-mastered with a piece of valiant dust? to make an account of her life to a clod of wayward marl?
Ibid. Line 62

I have a good eye, uncle; I can see a church by daylight.
Ibid. Line 86

Speak low, if you speak love.
Ibid. Line 104

Friendship is constant in all other things
Save in the office and affairs of love:
Therefore, all hearts in love use their own tongues;

Let every eye negotiate for itself,
And trust no agent.
Much Ado about Nothing.
Act II, Sc. 1, Line 184

She speaks poniards, and every word stabs: if her breath were as terrible as her terminations, there were no living near her; she would infect to the north star.
Ibid. Line 257

Silence is the perfectest herald of joy: I were but little happy, if I could say how much.
Ibid. Line 319

It keeps on the windy side of care.[1]
Ibid. Line 328

There was a star danced, and under that was I born.
Ibid. Line 351

I will tell you my drift.[2]
Ibid. Line 406

He was wont to speak plain and to the purpose.
Ibid. Sc. 3, Line 19

Her hair shall be of what colour it please God.
Ibid. Line 36

Sigh no more, ladies, sigh no more,
　Men were deceivers ever;
One foot in sea and one on shore;
　To one thing constant never.
Ibid. Line 65

Sits the wind in that corner?
Ibid. Line 108

Bait the hook well: this fish will bite.
Ibid. Line 121

Happy are they that hear their detractions, and can put them to mending.
Ibid. Line 248

Shall quips and sentences and these paper bullets of the brain awe a man from the career of his humour? No; the world must be peopled. When I said I would die a bachelor, I did not think I should live till I were married.
Ibid. Line 260

The pleasant'st angling is to see the fish

---

[1] The windy side of the law. — *Twelfth-Night* [1598–1600], *Act III, Sc. 4, L. 183*
[2] We know your drift. — *Coriolanus* [1607–1608], *Act III, Sc. 3, L. 114*

Cut with her golden oars the silver stream,
And greedily devour the treacherous bait.

Much Ado about Nothing.
Act III, Sc. 1, Line 26

From the crown of his head to the sole of his foot, he is all mirth.

Ibid. Sc. 2, Line 9

He hath a heart as sound as a bell, and his tongue is the clapper; for what his heart thinks his tongue speaks.

Ibid. Line 12

Every one can master a grief but he that has it.

Ibid. Line 28

Are you good men and true?

Ibid. Sc. 3, Line 1

To be a well-favoured man is the gift of fortune; but to write and read comes by nature.

Ibid. Line 14

If they make you not then the better answer, you may say they are not the men you took them for.

Ibid. Line 49

They that touch pitch will be defiled.[1]

Ibid. Line 61

The fashion wears out more apparel than the man.

Ibid. Line 147

I thank God, I am as honest as any man living, that is an old man and no honester than I.

Ibid. Sc. 5, Line 15

A good old man, sir; he will be talking: as they say, When the age is in, the wit is out.

Ibid. Line 36

Well, God's a good man; an two men ride of a horse, one must ride behind.

Ibid. Line 39

O! what men dare do! what men may do! what men daily do, not knowing what they do!

Ibid. Act IV, Sc. 1, Line 19

[1] He that toucheth pitch shall be defiled therewith. — *Apocrypha: Ecclesiasticus, XIII, 1*

This pitch, as ancient writers do report, doth defile; so doth the company thou keepest. — *King Henry IV* [1597-1598], Part I, Act II, Sc. 4, L. 460

O! what authority and show of truth
Can cunning sin cover itself withal!

Much Ado about Nothing.
Act IV, Sc. 1, Line 35

I have mark'd
A thousand blushing apparitions
To start into her face; a thousand innocent shames
In angel whiteness beat away those blushes.

Ibid. Line 160

For it so falls out
That what we have we prize not to the worth
Whiles we enjoy it, but being lack'd and lost,
Why, then we rack the value; then we find
The virtue that possession would not show us
Whiles it was ours.

Ibid. Line 219

The idea of her life shall sweetly creep
Into his study of imagination,
And every lovely organ of her life
Shall come apparell'd in more precious habit,
More moving-delicate, and full of life
Into the eye and prospect of his soul.

Ibid. Line 226

Masters, it is proved already that you are little better than false knaves; and it will go near to be thought so shortly.

Ibid. Sc. 2, Line 23

Flat burglary as ever was committed.

Ibid. Line 54

Condemned into everlasting redemption.

Ibid. Line 60

O that he were here to write me down an ass!

Ibid. Line 80

A fellow that hath had losses, and one that hath two gowns, and every thing handsome about him.

Ibid. Line 90

Patch griefs with proverbs.

Ibid. Act V, Sc. 1, Line 17

Men
Can counsel and speak comfort to that grief

Which they themselves not feel.
>>> *Much Ado about Nothing.*
>>> *Act V, Sc. 1, Line 20*

Charm ache with air, and agony with
words.
>>> *Ibid. Line 26*

'Tis all men's office to speak patience
To those that wring under the load of
 sorrow;
But no man's virtue nor sufficiency
To be so moral when he shall endure
The like himself.
>>> *Ibid. Line 27*

For there was never yet philosopher
That could endure the toothache patiently.
>>> *Ibid. Line 35*

Some of us will smart for it.
>>> *Ibid. Line 108*

What though care killed a cat,[1] thou
hast mettle enough in thee to kill care.
>>> *Ibid. Line 135*

I was not born under a rhyming
planet.
>>> *Ibid. Sc. 2, Line 40*

Done to death by slanderous tongues.
>>> *Ibid. Sc. 3, Line 3*

Fleet the time carelessly, as they did
in the golden world.
>>> *As You Like It* [1598–1600].
>>> *Act I, Sc. 1, Line 126*

Always the dulness of the fool is the
whetstone of the wits.
>>> *Ibid. Sc. 2, Line 59*

The little foolery that wise men have
makes a great show.
>>> *Ibid. Line 97*

Well said: that was laid on with a
trowel.
>>> *Ibid. Line 113*

In the world I fill up a place, which
may be better supplied when I have
made it empty.
>>> *Ibid. Line 206*

Your heart's desires be with you!
>>> *Ibid. Line 214*

---

[1] Let care kill a cat,
 We'll laugh and grow fat.
>>> *Shirburn Ballads* [1585], *91*
Hang sorrow, care'll kill a cat. — JONSON:
Every Man in His Humour [1598], Act I,
Sc. 1

One out of suits with fortune.
>>> *As You Like It. Act I, Sc. 2,*
>>> *Line 263*

My pride fell with my fortunes.
>>> *Ibid. Line 269*

Hereafter, in a better world than this,
I shall desire more love and knowledge
 of you.
>>> *Ibid. Line 301*

Celia. Not a word?
Rosalind. Not one to throw at a
dog.
>>> *Ibid. Sc. 3, Line 2*

O, how full of briers is this working-
day world!
>>> *Ibid. Line 12*

Beauty provoketh thieves sooner than
 gold.
>>> *Ibid. Line 113*

We'll have a swashing and a martial
 outside,
As many other mannish cowards have.
>>> *Ibid. Line 123*

Hath not old custom made this life
 more sweet
Than that of painted pomp? Are not
 these woods
More free from peril than the envious
 court?
>>> *Ibid. Act II, Sc. 1, Line 2*

Sweet are the uses of adversity;
Which, like the toad, ugly and venom-
 ous,
Wears yet a precious jewel in his head;
And this our life, exempt from public
 haunt,
Finds tongues in trees, books in the run-
 ning brooks,
Sermons in stones, and good in every
 thing.
>>> *Ibid. Line 12*

The big round tears
Coursed one another down his innocent
 nose
In piteous chase.
>>> *Ibid. Line 38*

"Poor deer," quoth he, "thou mak'st a
 testament
As worldlings do, giving thy sum of
 more
To that which had too much."
>>> *Ibid. Line 47*

Sweep on, you fat and greasy citizens.
> *As You Like It. Act II, Sc. 1,*
> *Line 55*

And He that doth the ravens feed,
Yea, providently caters for the sparrow,
Be comfort to my age!
> *Ibid. Sc. 3, Line 43*

Though I look old, yet I am strong and
lusty;
For in my youth I never did apply
Hot and rebellious liquors in my blood.
> *Ibid. Line 47*

Therefore my age is as a lusty winter,
Frosty, but kindly.
> *Ibid. Line 52*

Thou art not for the fashion of these
times,
Where none will sweat but for promo-
tion.
> *Ibid. Line 59*

Ay, now am I in Arden: the more
fool I. When I was at home I was in a
better place; but travellers must be content.
> *Ibid. Sc. 4, Line 16*

If you remember'st not the slightest
folly
That ever love did make thee run into,
Thou hast not lov'd.
> *Ibid. Line 34*

We that are true lovers run into
strange capers.
> *Ibid. Line 53*

Thou speakest wiser than thou art
ware of.
> *Ibid. Line 57*

I shall ne'er be 'ware of mine own
wit, till I break my shins against it.
> *Ibid. Line 59*

Under the greenwood tree
Who loves to lie with me,
And turn his merry note
Unto the sweet bird's throat,
Come hither, come hither, come hither:
Here shall he see
No enemy
But winter and rough weather.
> *Ibid. Sc. 5, Line 1*

I can suck melancholy out of a song
as a weasel sucks eggs.
> *Ibid. Line 12*

Who doth ambition shun
And loves to live i' the sun,

Seeking the food he eats,
And pleas'd with what he gets.
> *As You Like It. Act II, Sc. 5,*
> *Line 38*

Amiens. What's that "ducdame"?
Jaques. 'Tis a Greek invocation to
call fools into a circle.[1]
> *Ibid. Line 58*

I met a fool i' the forest,
A motley fool.
> *Ibid. Sc. 7, Line 12*

And rail'd on Lady Fortune in good
terms,
In good set terms.
> *Ibid. Line 16*

And then he drew a dial from his poke,
And looking on it with lack-lustre eye,
Says, very wisely, "It is ten o'clock:
Thus we may see," quoth he, "how the
world wags." [2]
> *Ibid. Line 20*

And so from hour to hour we ripe and
ripe,
And then from hour to hour we rot and
rot;
And thereby hangs a tale.[3]
> *Ibid. Line 26*

My lungs began to crow like chanti-
cleer,
That fools should be so deep-contem-
plative;
And I did laugh sans intermission
An hour by his dial.
> *Ibid. Line 30*

Motley's the only wear.
> *Ibid. Line 34*

If ladies be but young and fair,
They have the gift to know it.
> *Ibid. Line 37*

I must have liberty
Withal, as large a charter as the wind,
To blow on whom I please.
> *Ibid. Line 47*

The "why" is plain as way to parish
church.
> *Ibid. Line 52*

[1] Your name, even in life, was, alas! a kind
of *ducdame* to bring people of no very great
sense into your circle. — ANDREW LANG: *Letters to Dead Authors* [1886], *To Percy
Bysshe Shelley*
[2] So wags the world. — SIR WALTER SCOTT:
Ivanhoe [1819], *Chap.* 37
[3] See Rabelais, page 90a.

Under the shade of melancholy boughs,
Lose and neglect the creeping hours of
time;
If ever you have look'd on better days,
If ever been where bells have knoll'd to
church,
If ever sat at any good man's feast.

>   *As You Like It. Act II,*
>   *Sc. 7, Line 111*

True is it that we have seen better
days.

>   *Ibid. Line 120*

And wiped our eyes
Of drops that sacred pity hath engender'd.

>   *Ibid. Line 122*

Oppress'd with two weak evils, age and
hunger.

>   *Ibid. Line 132*

The wide and universal theatre.

>   *Ibid. Line 137*

All the world 's a stage,
And all the men and women merely
players.[1]
They have their exits and their en-
trances;
And one man in his time plays many
parts,
His acts being seven ages. At first the
infant,
Mewling and puking in the nurse's
arms.
And then the whining school-boy, with
his satchel
And shining morning face, creeping like
snail
Unwillingly to school. And then the
lover,
Sighing like furnace, with a woful ballad
Made to his mistress' eyebrow. Then a
soldier,
Full of strange oaths, and bearded like
the pard;

---

[1] See Du Bartas, pages 102a and 103a, and
Montaigne, page 99b.
  The world's a theatre, the earth a stage,
  Which God and Nature do with actors fill.
    THOMAS HEYWOOD: *Apology for Actors*
                                [1612]
  The world's a stage on which all the parts
are played. — MIDDLETON: *A Game of Chess*
[1624], Act V, Sc. 1

Jealous in honour, sudden and quick in
quarrel,
Seeking the bubble reputation
Even in the cannon's mouth. And then
the justice,
In fair round belly with good capon
lined,
With eyes severe and beard of formal
cut,
Full of wise saws and modern in-
stances;
And so he plays his part. The sixth age
shifts
Into the lean and slipper'd pantaloon,
With spectacles on nose and pouch on
side;
His youthful hose, well saved, a world
too wide
For his shrunk shank; and his big
manly voice,
Turning again toward childish treble,
pipes
And whistles in his sound. Last scene of
all,
That ends this strange eventful history,
Is second childishness, and mere oblivion,
Sans teeth, sans eyes, sans taste, sans
everything.

>   *As You Like It. Act II,*
>   *Sc. 7, Line 139*

Blow, blow, thou winter wind!
Thou art not so unkind
  As man's ingratitude.

>   *Ibid. Line 174*

These trees shall be my books.

>   *Ibid. Act III, Sc. 2, Line 5*

The fair, the chaste, and unexpressive
she.

>   *Ibid. Line 10*

It goes much against my stomach.
Hast any philosophy in thee, shepherd?

>   *Ibid. Line 21*

He that wants money, means, and
content is without three good friends.

>   *Ibid. Line 25*

I am a true labourer: I earn that I
eat, get that I wear, owe no man hate,
envy no man's happiness, glad of other
men's good.

>   *Ibid. Line 78*

From the east to western Ind,
No jewel is like Rosalind.
As You Like It. Act III,
Sc. 2, Line 94
This is the very false gallop of verses.
Ibid. Line 120
Let us make an honourable retreat.
Ibid. Line 170
With bag and baggage.
Ibid. Line 171
O, wonderful, wonderful, and most
wonderful wonderful! and yet again
wonderful, and after that out of all
whooping.
Ibid. Line 202
Answer me in one word.
Ibid. Line 238
It is as easy to count atomies as to
resolve the propositions of a lover.
Ibid. Line 246
Do you not know I am a woman?
when I think, I must speak.
Ibid. Line 265
I do desire we may be better stran-
gers.
Ibid. Line 276
Jaques.   What stature is she of?
Orlando.   Just as high as my heart.
Ibid. Line 286
Time travels in divers paces with
divers persons. I'll tell you who Time
ambles withal, who Time trots withal,
who Time gallops withal, and who he
stands still withal.
Ibid. Line 328
Every one fault seeming monstrous
till his fellow fault came to match it.
Ibid. Line 377
Everything about you demonstrating
a careless desolation.
Ibid. Line 405
I would the gods had made thee poeti-
cal.
Ibid. Sc. 3, Line 16
The common executioner,
Whose heart the accustom'd sight of
death makes hard,
Falls not the axe upon the humbled
neck
But first begs pardon.
Ibid. Sc. 5, Line 3

The wounds invisible
That love's keen arrows make.
As You Like It. Act III,
Sc. 5, Line 30
Down on your knees,
And thank Heaven, fasting, for a good
man's love.
Ibid. Line 57
I am falser than vows made in wine.
Ibid. Line 73
It is a melancholy of mine own, com-
pounded of many simples, extracted
from many objects, and indeed the sun-
dry contemplation of my travels, which,
by often rumination, wraps me in a
most humorous sadness.
Ibid. Act IV, Sc. 1, Line 16
I had rather have a fool to make me
merry than experience to make me sad.
Ibid. Line 28
Farewell, Monsieur Traveller: look
you lisp and wear strange suits, disable
all the benefits of your own country, be
out of love with your nativity, and almost chide God for making you that
countenance you are, or I will scarce
think you have swam in a gondola.
Ibid. Line 35
I'll warrant him heart-whole.
Ibid. Line 51
Very good orators, when they are
out, they will spit; and for lovers, lack-
ing (God warn us!) matter, the clean-
liest shift is to kiss.
Ibid. Line 77
Men have died from time to time,
and worms have eaten them, but not
for love.
Ibid. Line 110
For ever and a day.
Ibid. Line 151
Men are April when they woo, De-
cember when they wed: maids are May
when they are maids, but the sky
changes when they are wives.
Ibid. Line 153
My affection hath an unknown bot-
tom, like the bay of Portugal.
Ibid. Line 219
The horn, the horn, the lusty horn
Is not a thing to laugh to scorn.
Ibid. Sc. 2, Line 17

Chewing the food of sweet and bitter fancy.

> *As You Like It. Act IV, Sc. 3, Line 103*

"So so" is good, very good, very excellent good; and yet it is not; it is but so so.

> *Ibid. Act V, Sc. 1, Line 30*

The fool doth think he is wise, but the wise man knows himself to be a fool.

> *Ibid. Line 35*

No sooner met but they looked; no sooner looked but they loved; no sooner loved but they sighed; no sooner sighed but they asked one another the reason; no sooner knew the reason but they sought the remedy.

> *Ibid. Sc. 2, Line 37*

How bitter a thing it is to look into happiness through another man's eyes!

> *Ibid. Line 48*

It was a lover and his lass,
With a hey, and a ho, and hey nonino,
That o'er the green cornfield did pass,
In the spring time, the only pretty ring time,
When birds do sing, hey ding a ding, ding;
Sweet lovers love the spring.

> *Ibid. Sc. 3, Line 18*

Here comes a pair of very strange beasts, which in all tongues are called fools.

> *Ibid. Sc. 4, Line 36*

An ill-favoured thing, sir, but mine own.[1]

> *Ibid. Line 60*

Rich honesty dwells like a miser, sir, in a poor house; as your pearl in your foul oyster.

> *Ibid. Line 62*

The Retort Courteous; . . . the Quip Modest; . . . the Reply Churlish; . . . the Reproof Valiant; . . . the Countercheck Quarrelsome; . . . the Lie Circumstantial; . . . the Lie Direct.

> *Ibid. Line 75*

[1] My glass is not large, but I drink out of my own. — ALFRED DE MUSSET [1810–1857]

Your "If" is the only peacemaker; much virtue in "If."

> *As You Like It. Act V, Sc. 4, Line 108*

What a case am I in.

> *Ibid. Epilogue, Line 7*

If music be the food of love,[1] play on;
Give me excess of it, that, surfeiting,
The appetite may sicken, and so die.
That strain again! it had a dying fall:
O! it came o'er my ear like the sweet sound
That breathes upon a bank of violets,
Stealing and giving odour!

> *Twelfth-Night* [1598–1600].
> *Act I, Sc. 1, Line 1*

O spirit of love! how quick and fresh art thou,
That notwithstanding thy capacity
Receiveth as the sea, nought enters there,
Of what validity and pitch soe'er,
But falls into abatement and low price,
Even in a minute: so full of shapes is fancy,
That it alone is high fantastical.

> *Ibid. Line 9*

When my tongue blabs, then let mine eyes not see.

> *Ibid. Sc. 2, Line 61*

I am sure care's an enemy to life.

> *Ibid. Sc. 3, Line 2*

Let them hang themselves in their own straps.

> *Ibid. Line 13*

I am a great eater of beef, and I believe that does harm to my wit.

> *Ibid. Line 92*

Wherefore are these things hid?

> *Ibid. Line 135*

Is it a world to hide virtues in?

> *Ibid. Line 142*

God give them wisdom that have it; and those that are fools, let them use their talents.

> *Ibid. Sc. 4, Line 14*

One draught above heat makes him a fool, the second mads him, and a third drowns him.

> *Ibid. Sc. 5, Line 139*

[1] Is not music the food of love? — RICHARD BRINSLEY SHERIDAN: *The Rivals* [1775], *Act II, Sc. 1*

We will draw the curtain and show you the picture.

> *Twelfth-Night. Act I, Sc. 5, Line 252*

'Tis beauty truly blent, whose red and white
Nature's own sweet and cunning hand laid on:
Lady, you are the cruell'st she alive
If you will lead these graces to the grave
And leave the world no copy.

> *Ibid. Line 259*

Make me a willow-cabin at your gate,
And call upon my soul within the house.

> *Ibid. Line 289*

Holla your name to the reverberate hills,
And make the babbling gossip of the air
Cry out.

> *Ibid. Line 293*

O mistress mine, where are you roaming?

> *Ibid. Act II, Sc. 3, Line 42*

Journeys end in lovers meeting,
Every wise man's son doth know.

> *Ibid. Line 46*

What is love? 'tis not hereafter;
Present mirth hath present laughter.

> *Ibid. Line 50*

Then come kiss me, sweet and twenty,
Youth's a stuff will not endure.

> *Ibid. Line 54*

He does it with a better grace, but I do it more natural.

> *Ibid. Line 91*

Is there no respect of place, persons, nor time in you?

> *Ibid. Line 100*

Sir Toby. Dost thou think, because thou art virtuous, there shall be no more cakes and ale?
Clown. Yes, by Saint Anne, and ginger shall be hot i' the mouth too.

> *Ibid. Line 124*

My purpose is, indeed, a horse of that colour.

> *Ibid. Line 184*

These most brisk and giddy-paced times.

> *Ibid. Sc. 4, Line 6*

If ever thou shalt love,
In the sweet pangs of it remember me;
For such as I am all true lovers are,
Unstaid and skittish in all motions else,
Save in the constant image of the creature
That is beloved.

> *Twelfth-Night. Act II, Sc. 4, Line 15*

Let still the woman take
An elder than herself: so wears she to him,
So sways she level in her husband's heart:
For, boy, however we do praise ourselves,
Our fancies are more giddy and unfirm,
More longing, wavering, sooner lost and worn,
Than women's are.

> *Ibid. Line 29*

Then let thy love be younger than thyself,
Or thy affection cannot hold the bent.
For women are as roses, whose fair flower
Being once display'd, doth fall that very hour.

> *Ibid. Line 36*

The spinsters and the knitters in the sun
And the free maids that weave their thread with bones,
Do use to chant it: it is silly sooth,
And dallies with the innocence of love,
Like the old age.

> *Ibid. Line 47*

Duke.　　　And what's her history?
Viola. A blank, my lord. She never told her love,
But let concealment, like a worm i' the bud,
Feed on her damask cheek: she pined in thought,
And with a green and yellow melancholy
She sat like patience on a monument,
Smiling at grief.

> *Ibid. Line 112*

I am all the daughters of my father's house,
And all the brothers too.

> *Ibid. Line 122*

Here comes the trout that must be caught with tickling.
Twelfth-Night. Act II, Sc. 5, Line 25
I know my place, as I would they should do theirs.
Ibid. Line 61
I may command where I adore.
Ibid. Line 116
Some are born great, some achieve greatness, and some have greatness thrust upon them.
Ibid. Line 159
He will come to her in yellow stockings, and 'tis a colour she abhors, and cross-garter'd, a fashion she detests.
Ibid. Line 220
Foolery, sir, does walk about the orb like the sun; it shines everywhere.
Ibid. Act III, Sc. 1, Line 44
This fellow's wise enough to play the fool,
And to do that well craves a kind of wit.
Ibid. Line 68
Music from the spheres.[1]
Ibid. Line 122
How apt the poor are to be proud.
Ibid. Line 141
Then westward-ho!
Ibid. Line 148
Oh, what a deal of scorn looks beautiful
In the contempt and anger of his lip!
Ibid. Line 159
Love sought is good, but given unsought, is better.
Ibid. Line 170
You will hang like an icicle on a Dutchman's beard.
Ibid. Sc. 2, Line 30
Let there be gall enough in thy ink.
Ibid. Line 54
Laugh yourselves into stitches.
Ibid. Line 75
I can no other answer make but thanks, And thanks, and ever thanks.
Ibid. Sc. 3, Line 14
Haply your eye shall light upon some toy

You have desire to purchase.
Twelfth-Night. Act III, Sc. 3, Line 44
This is very midsummer madness.
Ibid. Sc. 4, Line 62
Put thyself into the trick of singularity.
Ibid. Line 80
What, man! defy the Devil: consider, he's an enemy to mankind.
Ibid. Line 109
If this were played upon a stage now, I could condemn it as an improbable fiction.
Ibid. Line 142
More matter for a May morning.
Ibid. Line 158
Still you keep o' the windy side of the law.[1]
Ibid. Line 183
My remembrance is very free and clear from any image of offence done to any man.
Ibid. Line 251
Hob, nob, is his word: give 't or take 't.
Ibid. Line 265
I have heard of some kind of men that put quarrels purposely on others to taste their valour.
Ibid. Line 269
He's a very devil.
Ibid. Line 304
An I thought he had been valiant, and so cunning in fence, I'd have seen him damned ere I'd have challenged him.
Ibid. Line 314
Out of my lean and low ability I'll lend you something.
Ibid. Line 380
I hate ingratitude more in a man Than lying, vainness, babbling drunkenness,
Or any taint of vice whose strong corruption
Inhabits our frail blood.
Ibid. Line 390
As the old hermit of Prague, that

---

[1] The music of the spheres. — *Pericles* [1608–1609], Act V, Sc. 1, L. 231
See Sir Thomas Browne, page 240b.

[1] The windy side of care. — *Much Ado about Nothing* [1598–1600], Act II, Sc. 1, L. 328

never saw pen and ink, very wittily said
to a niece of King Gorboduc, "That
that is, is."

*Twelfth-Night. Act IV, Sc. 2,
Line 14*

Thus the whirligig of time brings in
his revenges.

Ibid. Act V, Sc. 1, Line 388

When that I was and a little tiny boy,
With hey, ho, the wind and the rain,
A foolish thing was but a toy,
For the rain it raineth every day.[1]

Ibid. Line 404

A surgeon to old shoes.

Julius Caesar [*1598–1600*].
Act I, Sc. 1, Line 26

As proper men as ever trod upon
neat's leather.

Ibid. Line 27

Have you not made a universal shout,
That Tiber trembled underneath her
banks,
To hear the replication of your sounds
Made in her concave shores?

Ibid. Line 48

Beware the ides of March.[2]

Ibid. Sc. 2, Line 18

Set honour in one eye and death i' the
other,
And I will look on both indifferently.

Ibid. Line 86

Well, honour is the subject of my story.
I cannot tell what you and other men
Think of this life; but, for my single
self,
I had as lief not be as live to be
In awe of such a thing as I myself.

Ibid. Line 92

Stemming it with hearts of controversy.

Ibid. Line 109

Why, man, he doth bestride the narrow
world
Like a Colossus; and we petty men
Walk under his huge legs, and peep
about
To find ourselves dishonourable graves.
Men at some time are masters of their
fates:

[1] Parodied by the Fool in *King Lear;* see
page 191b.
[2] See Plutarch, page 56b.

The fault, dear Brutus, is not in our
stars,
But in ourselves, that we are underlings.

*Julius Caesar. Act I, Sc. 2,
Line 134*

Upon what meat doth this our Caesar
feed,
That he is grown so great? Age, thou
art shamed!
Rome, thou hast lost the breed of noble
bloods!

Ibid. Line 148

There was a Brutus once that would
have brook'd
The eternal devil to keep his state in
Rome
As easily as a king.

Ibid. Line 158

Let me have men about me that are fat;
Sleek-headed men, and such as sleep o'
nights.
Yond Cassius has a lean and hungry
look;
He thinks too much: such men are dangerous.

Ibid. Line 191

He reads much;
He is a great observer, and he looks
Quite through the deeds of men.

Ibid. Line 200

Seldom he smiles, and smiles in such a
sort
As if he mock'd himself, and scorn'd his
spirit
That could be moved to smile at anything.

Ibid. Line 204

But, for my own part, it was Greek to
me.

Ibid. Line 288

Yesterday the bird of night did sit,
Even at noon-day, upon the market-
place,
Hooting and shrieking.

Ibid. Sc. 3, Line 26

O! he sits high in all the people's hearts:
And that which would appear offence
in us,
His countenance, like richest alchemy,
Will change to virtue and to worthiness.

Ibid. Line 157

[1] See Plutarch, page 57b.

'Tis a common proof,
That lowliness is young ambition's ladder,
Whereto the climber-upward turns his face;
But when he once attains the upmost round,
He then unto the ladder turns his back,
Looks in the clouds, scorning the base degrees
By which he did ascend.
Julius Caesar. Act II,
Sc. 1, Line 21

Therefore think him as a serpent's egg
Which, hatch'd, would, as his kind, grow mischievous,
And kill him in the shell.
Ibid. Line 32

Between the acting of a dreadful thing
And the first motion, all the interim is
Like a phantasma, or a hideous dream:
The Genius and the mortal instruments
Are then in council; and the state of man,
Like to a little kingdom, suffers then
The nature of an insurrection.
Ibid. Line 63

O conspiracy!
Sham'st thou to show thy dangerous brow by night,
When evils are most free?
Ibid. Line 77

Let's carve him as a dish fit for the gods.
Not hew him as a carcass fit for hounds.
Ibid. Line 173

But when I tell him he hates flatterers,
He says he does, being then most flattered.
Ibid. Line 207

Enjoy the honey-heavy dew of slumber.
Ibid. Line 230

You are my true and honourable wife,
As dear to me as are the ruddy drops
That visit my sad heart.[1]
Ibid. Line 288

Think you I am no stronger than my sex,

[1] Dear as the ruddy drops that warm my heart. — THOMAS GRAY: *The Bard* [1757], I, 3, L. 12

Being so father'd and so husbanded?
Julius Caesar. Act II, Sc. 1,
Line 296

When beggars die, there are no comets seen;
The heavens themselves blaze forth the death of princes.
Ibid. Sc. 2, Line 30

Cowards die many times before their deaths;
The valiant never taste of death but once.
Ibid. Line 32

Of all the wonders that I yet have heard,
It seems to me most strange that men should fear;
Seeing that death, a necessary end,
Will come when it will come.
Ibid. Line 32

See! Antony, that revels long o' nights,
Is notwithstanding up.
Ibid. Line 116

How hard it is for women to keep counsel.
Ibid. Sc. 4, Line 9

But I am constant as the northern star,
Of whose true-fix'd and resting quality
There is no fellow in the firmament.
Ibid. Act III, Sc. 1, Line 60

Et tu, Brute!
Ibid. Line 77

How many ages hence
Shall this our lofty scene be acted o'er,
In states unborn and accents yet unknown!
Ibid. Line 111

O mighty Caesar! dost thou lie so low?
Are all thy conquests, glories, triumphs, spoils,
Shrunk to this little measure?
Ibid. Line 148

The choice and master spirits of this age.
Ibid. Line 163

Though last, not least in love.[1]
Ibid. Line 189

O! pardon me, thou bleeding piece of earth,
That I am meek and gentle with these butchers!

[1] See Spenser, page 114b.

Thou art the ruins of the noblest man
That ever lived in the tide of times.
Julius Caesar. Act III,
Sc. 1, Line 254
Cry "Havoc!" and let slip the dogs of
war.
Ibid. Line 273
Romans, countrymen, and lovers!
hear me for my cause; and be silent,
that you may hear.
Ibid. Sc. 2, Line 13
Not that I loved Caesar less, but that
I loved Rome more.
Ibid. Line 22
As he was valiant I honour him: but,
as he was ambitious, I slew him.
Ibid. Line 27
If any, speak; for him have I of-
fended. I pause for a reply.
Ibid. Line 36
Friends, Romans, countrymen, lend me
your ears;
I come to bury Caesar, not to praise
him.
The evil that men do lives after them,
The good is oft interred with their
bones.[1]
Ibid. Line 79
For Brutus is an honourable man;
So are they all, all honourable men.
Ibid. Line 88
When that the poor have cried, Caesar
hath wept;
Ambition should be made of sterner
stuff.
Ibid. Line 97
O judgment! thou art fled to brutish
beasts,
And men have lost their reason.
Ibid. Line 110
But yesterday the word of Caesar might
Have stood against the world; now lies
he there,
And none so poor to do him reverence.
Ibid. Line 124
If you have tears, prepare to shed them
now.
Ibid. Line 174
See what a rent the envious Casca
made.
Ibid. Line 180

[1] See Euripides, page 18a.

This was the most unkindest cut of all.
Julius Caesar. Act III,
Sc. 2, Line 188
Great Caesar fell.
O! what a fall was there, my country-
men;
Then I, and you, and all of us fell down,
Whilst bloody treason flourish'd over
us.
Ibid. Line 194
What private griefs they have, alas! I
know not.
Ibid. Line 217
I come not, friends, to steal away your
hearts:
I am no orator, as Brutus is;
But, as you know me all, a plain blunt
man.
Ibid. Line 220
For I have neither wit, nor words, nor
worth,
Action, nor utterance, nor the power
of speech,
To stir men's blood: I only speak right
on.
Ibid. Line 225
Put a tongue
In every wound of Caesar, that should
move
The stones of Rome to rise and mutiny.
Ibid. Line 232
When love begins to sicken and decay,
It useth an enforced ceremony.
There are no tricks in plain and simple
faith.
Ibid. Act IV, Sc. 2, Line 20
You yourself
Are much condemn'd to have an itch-
ing palm.
Ibid. Sc. 3, Line 9
The foremost man of all this world.
Ibid. Line 22
I had rather be a dog, and bay the
moon,
Than such a Roman.
Ibid. Line 27
I'll use you for my mirth, yea, for my
laughter,
When you are waspish.
Ibid. Line 49
There is no terror, Cassius, in your
threats;

For I am arm'd so strong in honesty
That they pass by me as the idle wind,
Which I respect not.
> *Julius Caesar. Act IV,*
> *Sc. 3, Line 66*

A friend should bear his friend's infirmities,
But Brutus makes mine greater than they are.
> *Ibid. Line 85*

All his faults observed,
Set in a note-book, learn'd, and conn'd by rote.
> *Ibid. Line 96*

There is a tide in the affairs of men,
Which, taken at the flood, leads on to fortune;
Omitted, all the voyage of their life
Is bound in shallows and in miseries.
> *Ibid. Line 217*

We must take the current when it serves,
Or lose our ventures.
> *Ibid. Line 222*

The deep of night is crept upon our talk,
And nature must obey necessity.[1]
> *Ibid. Line 225*

But for your words, they rob the Hybla bees,
And leave them honeyless.
> *Ibid. Act V, Sc. 1, Line 34*

Forever, and forever, farewell, Cassius!
If we do meet again, why, we shall smile;
If not, why then, this parting was well made.
> *Ibid. Line 117*

O, that a man might know
The end of this day's business, ere it come.
> *Ibid. Line 123*

O Julius Caesar! thou art mighty yet!
Thy spirit walks abroad, and turns our swords
In our own proper entrails.
> *Ibid. Sc. 3, Line 94*

The last of all the Romans, fare thee well!
> *Ibid. Line 99*

[1] See Diogenes Laertius, page 70a.

This was the noblest Roman of them all.
> *Julius Caesar. Act V,*
> *Sc. 5, Line 68*

His life was gentle, and the elements
So mix'd in him that Nature might stand up
And say to all the world, "This was a man!"
> *Ibid. Line 73*

When my love swears that she is made of truth,
I do believe her, though I know she lies.
> *The Passionate Pilgrim* [*1599*].[1] *I*

Love's best habit is a soothing tongue.
> *Ibid.*

Bad in the best, though excellent in neither.
> *Ibid. VII*

Crabbed age and youth cannot live together.
Youth is full of pleasance, age is full of care.
> *Ibid. XII*

For this relief much thanks; 'tis bitter cold,
And I am sick at heart.
> *Hamlet* [*1600–1601*]. *Act I,*
> *Sc. 1, Line 8*

Not a mouse stirring.[2]
> *Ibid. Line 10*

But in the gross and scope of my opinion,
This bodes some strange eruption to our state.
> *Ibid. Line 68*

Whose sore task
Does not divide the Sunday from the week.
> *Ibid. Line 75*

This sweaty haste
Doth make the night joint-labourer with the day.
> *Ibid. Line 77*

In the most high and palmy state of Rome,
A little ere the mightiest Julius fell,
The graves stood tenantless and the sheeted dead

[1] The bulk of this volume is by others.
[2] See Clement Clarke Moore, page 437a.

Did squeak and gibber in the Roman streets.
> *Hamlet. Act I, Sc. 1, Line 113*

And then it started like a guilty thing
Upon a fearful summons.
> *Ibid. Line 148*

The cock, that is the trumpet of the morn.
> *Ibid. Line 150*

Whether in sea or fire, in earth or air,
The extravagant and erring spirit hies
To his confine.
> *Ibid. Line 153*

It faded on the crowing of the cock.
Some say that ever 'gainst that season comes
Wherein our Saviour's birth is celebrated,
The bird of dawning singeth all night long:
And then, they say, no spirit can walk abroad;
The nights are wholesome; then no planets strike,
No fairy takes, nor witch hath power to charm,
So hallow'd and so gracious is the time.
> *Ibid. Line 157*

So have I heard, and do in part believe it.
But, look, the morn in russet mantle clad,
Walks o'er the dew of yon high eastern hill.
> *Ibid. Line 165*

The memory be green.[1]
> *Ibid. Sc. 2, Line 2*

With one auspicious and one dropping eye,
With mirth in funeral and with dirge in marriage,
In equal scale weighing delight and dole.
> *Ibid. Line 11*

A little more than kin, and less than kind.
> *Ibid. Line 65*

Thou know'st 'tis common; all that live must die,

[1] See Thomas Moore, page 438a.

Passing through nature to eternity.
> *Hamlet. Act I, Sc. 2, Line 72*

Seems, madam! Nay, it is; I know not "seems."
'Tis not alone my inky cloak, good mother,
Nor customary suits of solemn black.
> *Ibid. Line 76*

But I have that within which passeth show;
These but the trappings and the suits of woe.
> *Ibid. Line 85*

O! that this too too solid flesh would melt,
Thaw and resolve itself into a dew;
Or that the Everlasting had not fix'd
His canon 'gainst self-slaughter! O God! O God!
How weary, stale, flat, and unprofitable
Seem to me all the uses of this world.
> *Ibid. Line 129*

Things rank and gross in nature
Possess it merely. That it should come to this!
> *Ibid. Line 136*

Hyperion to a satyr; so loving to my mother
That he might not beteem the winds of heaven
Visit her face too roughly.
> *Ibid. Line 140*

Why, she would hang on him,
As if increase of appetite had grown
By what it fed on.
> *Ibid. Line 143*

Frailty, thy name is woman!
> *Ibid. Line 146*

Like Niobe, all tears.
> *Ibid. Line 149*

A beast, that wants discourse of reason.
> *Ibid. Line 150*

It is not nor it cannot come to good.
> *Ibid. Line 158*

A truant disposition.
> *Ibid. Line 169*

Thrift, thrift, Horatio! the funeral baked meats
Did coldly furnish forth the marriage tables.

Would I had met my dearest foe [1] in heaven
Ere I had seen that day.
> *Hamlet. Act I, Sc. 2, Line 180*

In my mind's eye, Horatio.
> *Ibid. Line 185*

He was a man, take him for all in all,
I shall not look upon his like again.
> *Ibid. Line 187*

Season your admiration for a while.
> *Ibid. Line 192*

In the dead vast and middle of the night.
> *Ibid. Line 198*

Arm'd at points exactly, cap-a-pe.
> *Ibid. Line 200*

Distill'd
Almost to jelly with the act of fear.
> *Ibid. Line 204*

A countenance more in sorrow than in anger.
> *Ibid. Line 231*

While one with moderate haste might tell a hundred.
> *Ibid. Line 237*

Hamlet. His beard was grizzled, no?
Horatio. It was, as I have seen it in his life,
A sable silver'd.
> *Ibid. Line 239*

Give it an understanding, but no tongue.
> *Ibid. Line 249*

All is not well;
I doubt some foul play.
> *Ibid. Line 254*

Foul deeds will rise,
Though all the earth o'erwhelm them, to men's eyes.
> *Ibid. Line 256*

The chariest maid is prodigal enough
If she unmask her beauty to the moon:
Virtue itself 'scapes not calumnious strokes;
The canker galls the infants of the spring
Too oft before their buttons be disclosed,

[1] And dearest enemy. — THOMAS MIDDLETON [1570?–1627]: *Anything for a Quiet Life, Act V, Sc. 1*

And in the morn and liquid dew of youth
Contagious blastments are most imminent.
> *Hamlet. Act I, Sc. 3, Line 36*

Do not, as some ungracious pastors do,
Show me the steep and thorny way to heaven,
Whiles, like a puff'd and reckless libertine,
Himself the primrose path of dalliance treads,[1]
And recks not his own rede.[2]
> *Ibid. Line 47*

Give thy thoughts no tongue.
> *Ibid. Line 59*

Be thou familiar, but by no means vulgar;
Those friends thou hast, and their adoption tried,
Grapple them to thy soul with hoops of steel.
> *Ibid. Line 61*

Beware
Of entrance to a quarrel, but, being in,
Bear 't that the opposed may beware of thee.
Give every man thy ear, but few thy voice;
Take each man's censure, but reserve thy judgment.
Costly thy habit as thy purse can buy,
But not express'd in fancy; rich, not gaudy; [3]
For the apparel oft proclaims the man.
> *Ibid. Line 65*

Neither a borrower, nor a lender be;
For loan oft loses both itself and friend,
And borrowing dulls the edge of husbandry.
This above all: to thine own self be true,

[1] See *Macbeth*, page 196b.
[2] Wel oghte a preest ensample for to yive,
By his clennesse, how that his sheep shold live.
> CHAUCER: *Canterbury Tales* [circa 1387], *Prologue, L. 504*

And may you better reck the rede,
Than ever did the adviser.
> ROBERT BURNS [1759–1796]: *Epistle to a Young Friend*

[3] Neat, not gaudy. — CHARLES LAMB: *Letter to Wordsworth* [1806]

And it must follow, as the night the day,
Thou canst not then be false to any
man.

Hamlet. Act I, Sc. 3, Line 75

Springes to catch woodcocks.

Ibid. Line 115

When the blood burns, how prodigal the
soul
Lends the tongue vows.

Ibid. Line 116

Be somewhat scanter of your maiden
presence.

Ibid. Line 121

The air bites shrewdly.

Ibid. Sc. 4, Line 1

But to my mind, though I am native
here
And to the manner born, — it is a custom
More honoured in the breach than the
observance.

Ibid. Line 14

Angels and ministers of grace defend
us!

Ibid. Line 39

Be thy intents wicked or charitable,
Thou comest in such a questionable
shape
That I will speak to thee.

Ibid. Line 42

What may this mean,
That thou, dead corse, again in com-
plete steel
Revisit'st thus the glimpses of the
moon,
Making night hideous,[1] and we fools of
nature
So horridly to shake our disposition
With thoughts beyond the reaches of
our souls?

Ibid. Line 51

I do not set my life at a pin's fee.

Ibid. Line 65

My fate cries out,
And makes each petty artery in this
body
As hardy as the Nemean lion's nerve.

Ibid. Line 81

[1] And makes night hideous. — ALEXANDER
POPE: *The Dunciad, Book III* [1728], *L. 166*

Unhand me, gentlemen,
By heaven! I'll make a ghost of him
that lets me!

Hamlet. Act I, Sc. 4, Line 84

Something is rotten in the state of Denmark.

Ibid. Line 90

I could a tale unfold whose lightest
word
Would harrow up thy soul, freeze thy
young blood,
Make thy two eyes, like stars, start
from their spheres,
Thy knotted and combined locks to
part,
And each particular hair to stand an
end,
Like quills upon the fretful porpentine.

Ibid. Sc. 5, Line 15

And duller shouldst thou be than the fat
weed
That rots itself in ease on Lethe wharf.

Ibid. Line 32

O my prophetic soul!
My uncle!

Ibid. Line 40

O Hamlet, what a falling-off was there!

Ibid. Line 47

But, soft! methinks I scent the morning
air;
Brief let me be. Sleeping within my
orchard,
My custom always of the afternoon.

Ibid. Line 58

In the porches of mine ears.

Ibid. Line 63

Cut off even in the blossoms of my sin,
Unhousel'd, disappointed, unaneled,
No reckoning made, but sent to my ac-
count
With all my imperfections on my head.

Ibid. Line 76

Leave her to heaven
And to those thorns that in her bosom
lodge,
To prick and sting her.

Ibid. Line 86

The glow-worm shows the matin to be
near,
And 'gins to pale his uneffectual fire.

Ibid. Line 89

While memory holds a seat
In this distracted globe. Remember
thee!
Yea, from the table of my memory
I'll wipe away all trivial fond records.
Hamlet. Act I, Sc. 5, Line 96

Within the book and volume of my
brain.
Ibid. Line 103

O villain, villain, smiling, damned vil-
lain!
My tables, — meet it is I set it down,
That one may smile, and smile, and be
a villain;
At least I'm sure it may be so in Den-
mark.
Ibid. Line 106

There are more things in heaven and
earth, Horatio,
Than are dreamt of in your philosophy.
Ibid. Line 166

To put an antic disposition on.
Ibid. Line 172

Rest, rest, perturbed spirit!
Ibid. Line 182

The time is out of joint; O cursed spite,
That ever I was born to set it right!
Ibid. Line 188

Your bait of falsehood takes this carp
of truth:
And thus do we of wisdom and of reach,
With windlasses and with assays of
bias,
By indirections find directions out.
Ibid. Act II, Sc. 1, Line 63

Ungarter'd, and down-gyved to his
ankle.
Ibid. Line 80

This is the very ecstasy of love;
Whose violent property fordoes itself,
And leads the will to desperate under-
takings,
As oft as any passion under heaven
That does afflict our natures.
Ibid. Line 102

Brevity is the soul of wit.
Ibid. Sc. 2, Line 90

More matter, with less art.
Ibid. Line 95

That he is mad, 'tis true; 'tis true 'tis
pity;
And pity 'tis 'tis true.
Hamlet. Act II, Sc. 2, Line 97

Find out the cause of this effect,
Or rather say, the cause of this defect,
For this effect defective comes by cause.
Ibid. Line 101

Doubt thou the stars are fire;
Doubt that the sun doth move;
Doubt truth to be a liar;
But never doubt I love.
Ibid. Line 115

To be honest, as this world goes, is
to be one man picked out of ten thousand.
Ibid. Line 179

Still harping on my daughter.
Ibid. Line 190

Polonius. What do you read, my
lord?
Hamlet. Words, words, words.
Ibid. Line 195

They have a plentiful lack of wit.
Ibid. Line 204

Though this be madness, yet there is
method in 't.
Ibid. Line 211

These tedious old fools!
Ibid. Line 227

There is nothing either good or bad,
but thinking makes it so.
Ibid. Line 259

O God! I could be bounded in a nut-
shell, and count myself a king of infinite space, were it not that I have bad
dreams.
Ibid. Line 263

This goodly frame, the earth, seems
to me a sterile promontory; this most
excellent canopy, the air, look you, this
brave o'erhanging firmament, this majestical roof fretted with golden fire,
why, it appears no other thing to me
than a foul and pestilent congregation
of vapours. What a piece of work is a
man! how noble in reason! how infinite
in faculty! in form and moving how
express and admirable! in action how
like an angel! in apprehension how like
a god!
Ibid. Line 317

Man delights not me; no, nor woman neither.

    Hamlet. Act II, Sc. 2, Line 330

There is something in this more than natural, if philosophy could find it out.

    Ibid. Line 392

I am but mad north-north-west; when the wind is southerly, I know a hawk from a handsaw.

    Ibid. Line 405

They say an old man is twice a child.

    Ibid. Line 413

O Jephthah, judge of Israel, what a treasure hadst thou!

    Ibid. Line 431

One fair daughter and no more,
The which he loved passing well.

    Ibid. Line 435

Come, give us a taste of your quality.

    Ibid. Line 460

The play, I remember, pleased not the million; 'twas caviare to the general.

    Ibid. Line 465

They are the abstracts and brief chronicles of the time: after your death you were better have a bad epitaph than their ill report while you live.

    Ibid. Line 555

Use every man after his desert, and who should 'scape whipping?

    Ibid. Line 561

O, what a rogue and peasant slave am I!

    Ibid. Line 584

What's Hecuba to him or he to Hecuba,
That he should weep for her?

    Ibid. Line 593

But I am pigeon-livered, and lack gall
To make oppression bitter.

    Ibid. Line 613

    The play's the thing
Wherein I'll catch the conscience of the king.

    Ibid. Line 641

    With devotion's visage
And pious action we do sugar o'er
The devil himself.

    Ibid. Act III, Sc. 1, Line 47

To be, or not to be: that is the question:

Whether 'tis nobler in the mind to suffer
The slings and arrows of outrageous fortune,
Or to take arms against a sea of troubles,
And by opposing end them? To die: to sleep:
No more; and by a sleep to say we end
The heartache and the thousand natural shocks
That flesh is heir to, 'tis a consummation
Devoutly to be wish'd. To die, to sleep;
To sleep: perchance to dream: ay, there's the rub:
For in that sleep of death what dreams may come,
When we have shuffled off this mortal coil,
Must give us pause. There's the respect
That makes calamity of so long life;
For who would bear the whips and scorns of time,
The oppressor's wrong, the proud man's contumely,
The pangs of dispriz'd love, the law's delay,
The insolence of office and the spurns
That patient merit of the unworthy takes,
When he himself might his quietus make
With a bare bodkin? who would fardels bear,
To grunt and sweat under a weary life,
But that the dread of something after death,
The undiscover'd country from whose bourn
No traveller returns, puzzles the will
And makes us rather bear those ills we have
Than fly to others that we know not of?
Thus conscience does make cowards of us all; [1]
And thus the native hue of resolution
Is sicklied o'er with the pale cast of thought,

----

[1] See Bidpai, page 28b.

And enterprises of great pith and moment
With this regard their currents turn awry,
And lose the name of action.
Hamlet. Act III, Sc. 1, Line 56
Nymph, in thy orisons
Be all my sins remember'd.
Ibid. Line 89
For, to the noble mind
Rich gifts wax poor when givers prove unkind.
Ibid. Line 100
What should such fellows as I do crawling between earth and heaven? We are arrant knaves, all.
Ibid. Line 128
Be thou as chaste as ice, as pure as snow, thou shalt not escape calumny. Get thee to a nunnery, go.
Ibid. Line 142
I have heard of your paintings too, well enough; God has given you one face, and you make yourselves another.
Ibid. Line 150
O! what a noble mind is here o'erthrown:
The courtier's, soldier's, scholar's eye, tongue, sword.
Ibid. Line 159
The glass of fashion and the mould of form,
The observed of all observers!
Ibid. Line 162
Now see that noble and most sovereign reason,
Like sweet bells jangled, out of tune and harsh.
Ibid. Line 166
O, woe is me,
To have seen what I have seen, see what I see!
Ibid. Line 169
Speak the speech, I pray you, as I pronounced it to you, trippingly on the tongue; but if you mouth it, as many of your players do, I had as lief the town-crier spoke my lines. Nor do not saw the air too much with your hand, thus; but use all gently: for in the very torrent, tempest, and as I may say the whirlwind of passion, you must

acquire and beget a temperance, that may give it smoothness. Oh, it offends me to the soul to hear a robustious periwig-pated fellow tear a passion to tatters, to very rags, to split the ears of the groundlings, who for the most part are capable of nothing but inexplicable dumb-shows and noise. I would have such a fellow whipped for o'erdoing Termagant; it out-herods Herod.
Hamlet. Act III, Sc. 2, Line 1
Suit the action to the word, the word to the action; with this special observance, that you o'erstep not the modesty of nature.
Ibid. Line 20
To hold, as 'twere, the mirror up to nature; to show virtue her own feature, scorn her own image, and the very age and body of the time his form and pressure.
Ibid. Line 25
Though it make the unskilful laugh, cannot but make the judicious grieve
Ibid. Line 29
Not to speak it profanely.
Ibid. Line 35
I have thought some of Nature's journeymen had made men and not made them well, they imitated humanity so abominably.
Ibid. Line 38
No; let the candied tongue lick absurd pomp,
And crook the pregnant hinges of the knee
Where thrift may follow fawning.
Ibid. Line 65
A man that fortune's buffets and rewards
Hast ta'en with equal thanks.
Ibid. Line 72
They are not a pipe for fortune's finger
To sound what stop she please. Give me that man
That is not passion's slave, and I will wear him
In my heart's core, ay, in my heart of heart,
As I do thee. Something too much of this.
Ibid. Line 75

And my imaginations are as foul
As Vulcan's stithy.
                Hamlet. Act III, Sc. 2, Line 88
    Nay, then, let the devil wear black,
for I'll have a suit of sables.
                        Ibid. Line 138
    There's hope a great man's memory
may outlive his life half a year.
                        Ibid. Line 141
    This is miching mallecho; it means
mischief.
                        Ibid. Line 149
Where love is great, the littlest doubts
    are fear;
When little fears grow great, great love
    grows there.
                        Ibid. Line 183
What to ourselves in passion we pro-
    pose,
The passion ending, doth the purpose
    lose.
                        Ibid. Line 206
The lady doth protest too much, me-
    thinks.
                        Ibid. Line 242
    Let the galled jade wince, our withers
are unwrung.
                        Ibid. Line 256
Why, let the stricken deer go weep,[1]
    The hart ungalled play;
For some must watch, while some must
    sleep:
So runs the world away.
                        Ibid. Line 287
    You would pluck out the heart of my
mystery.
                        Ibid. Line 389
    Do you think I am easier to be played
on than a pipe?
                        Ibid. Line 393
    Hamlet. Do you see yonder cloud
that's almost in shape of a camel?
    Polonius. By the mass, and 'tis like
a camel, indeed.
    Hamlet. Methinks it is like a weasel.
    Polonius. It is backed like a weasel.
    Hamlet. Or like a whale?
    Polonius. Very like a whale.
                        Ibid. Line 400

[1] I was a stricken deer. — WILLIAM COW-
PER: *The Task* [1785], *Book III*

    They fool me to the top of my bent.
                Hamlet. Act III, Sc. 2, Line 408
By and by is easily said.
                        Ibid. Line 411
'Tis now the very witching time of
    night,
When churchyards yawn and hell itself
    breathes out
Contagion to this world.
                        Ibid. Line 413
I will speak daggers to her, but use
    none.
                        Ibid. Line 421
O! my offence is rank, it smells to
    heaven;
It hath the primal eldest curse upon 't,
A brother's murder.
                        Ibid. Sc. 3, Line 36
Now might I do it pat, now he is pray-
    ing;
And now I'll do't: — and so he goes to
    heaven;
And so I am revenged.
                        Ibid. Line 73
With all his crimes broad blown, as
    flush as May.
                        Ibid. Line 81
My words fly up, my thoughts remain
    below:
Words without thoughts never to
    heaven go.
                        Ibid. Line 97
Dead, for a ducat, dead!
                        Ibid. Sc. 4, Line 23
And let me wring your heart; for so I
    shall,
If it be made of penetrable stuff.
                        Ibid. Line 35
False as dicers' oaths.
                        Ibid. Line 45
A rhapsody of words.
                        Ibid. Line 48
See, what a grace was seated on this
    brow;
Hyperion's curls; the front of Jove him-
    self;
An eye like Mars, to threaten and com-
    mand,
A station like the herald Mercury
New-lighted on a heaven-kissing hill,
A combination and a form indeed,

Where every god did seem to set his
 seal,
To give the world assurance of a man.
Hamlet. Act III, Sc. 4, Line 55

At your age
The hey-day in the blood is tame, it's
 humble.
Ibid. Line 68

O shame! where is thy blush? Rebel-
lious hell,
If thou canst mutine in a matron's
 bones,
To flaming youth let virtue be as wax,
And melt in her own fire: proclaim no
 shame
When the compulsive ardour gives the
 charge,
Since frost itself as actively doth burn,
And reason panders will.
Ibid. Line 82

A king of shreds and patches.[1]
Ibid. Line 102

How is 't with you,
That you do bend your eye on vacancy?
Ibid. Line 115

Lay not that flattering unction to your
 soul.
Ibid. Line 145

Confess yourself to heaven;
Repent what's past; avoid what is to
 come.
Ibid. Line 149

For in the fatness of these pursy times
Virtue itself of vice must pardon beg.
Ibid. Line 153

Assume a virtue, if you have it not.
Ibid. Line 160

Refrain to-night,
And that shall lend a kind of easiness
To the next abstinence: the next more
 easy;
For use almost can change the stamp
 of nature.
Ibid. Line 165

I must be cruel, only to be kind.
Ibid. Line 178

[1] A wandering minstrel I —
 A thing of shreds and patches.
 W. S. GILBERT: *The Mikado*
 [1885], *Act I*

For 'tis the sport to have the enginer
Hoist with his own petar.
Hamlet. Act III, Sc. 4, Line 206

Diseases desperate grown
By desperate appliance are relieved,
Or not at all.[1]
Ibid. Act IV, Sc. 3, Line 9

A man may fish with the worm that
hath eat of a king, and eat of the fish
that hath fed of that worm.
Ibid. Line 29

We go to gain a little patch of ground,
That hath in it no profit but the name.
Ibid. Sc. 4, Line 18

How all occasions do inform against me,
And spur my dull revenge! What is a
 man,
If his chief good and market of his
 time
Be but to sleep and feed? a beast, no
 more.[2]
Sure, he that made us with such large
 discourse,
Looking before and after, gave us not
That capability and godlike reason
To fust in us unused.
Ibid. Line 32

Some craven scruple
Of thinking too precisely on th' event.
Ibid. Line 36

Rightly to be great
Is not to stir without great argument
But greatly to find quarrel in a straw
When honour's at the stake.
Ibid. Line 53

So full of artless jealousy is guilt,
It spills itself in fearing to be spilt.
Ibid. Sc. 5, Line 19

How should I your true love know
 From another one?
By his cockle hat and staff,
 And his sandal shoon.
Ibid. Line 23

He is dead and gone, lady,
 He is dead and gone;
At his head a grass-green turf,
 At his heels a stone.
Ibid. Line 29

[1] See Hippocrates, page 22a.
[2] The unmotived herd that only sleep and
feed. — JAMES RUSSELL LOWELL [1819–
1891]: *Under the Old Elm, Part VII, St. 3*

We know what we are, but know not what we may be.

Hamlet. Act IV, Sc. 5, Line 43

Come, my coach! Good night, sweet ladies; good night.

Ibid. Line 72

When sorrows come, they come not single spies,
But in battalions.

Ibid. Line 78

There's such divinity doth hedge a king,
That treason can but peep to what it would.

Ibid. Line 123

There's rosemary, that's for remembrance; . . . and there is pansies, that's for thoughts.[1]

Ibid. Line 174

You must wear your rue with a difference. There's a daisy; I would give you some violets, but they withered all when my father died.

Ibid. Line 181

A very riband in the cap of youth.

Ibid. Sc. 7, Line 77

One woe doth tread upon another's heel,
So fast they follow.[2]

Ibid. Line 164

Nature her custom holds,
Let shame say what it will.

Ibid. Line 188

There is no ancient gentlemen but gardeners, ditchers, and grave-makers; they hold up Adam's profession.[3]

Ibid. Act V, Sc. 1, Line 32

Cudgel thy brains no more about it.

Ibid. Line 61

[1] See Chapman, page 116b.
[2] Thus woe succeeds a woe, as wave a wave. — HERRICK: *Sorrows Succeed* [1648]
Woes cluster; rare are solitary woes;
They love a train, they tread each other's heel.
EDWARD YOUNG: *Night Thoughts* [1742–1745], *Night III, L. 63*
[3] See Francis Bacon, page 121a.
Oh, Adam was a gardener, and God who made him sees
That half a proper gardener's work is done upon his knees.
RUDYARD KIPLING [1865–1936]: *The Glory of the Garden, St. 8*

Has this fellow no feeling of his business, that he sings at grave-making?

Hamlet. Act V, Sc. 1, Line 71

Custom hath made it in him a property of easiness.

Ibid. Line 73

But age, with his stealing steps,
Hath claw'd me in his clutch.

Ibid. Line 77

A politician, . . . one that would circumvent God.

Ibid. Line 84

Why may not that be the skull of a lawyer? Where be his quiddities now, his quillets, his cases, his tenures, and his tricks?

Ibid. Line 104

One that was a woman, sir; but, rest her soul, she's dead.

Ibid. Line 145

How absolute the knave is! we must speak by the card, or equivocation will undo us.

Ibid. Line 147

The age is grown so picked that the toe of the peasant comes so near the heel of the courtier, he galls his kibe.

Ibid. Line 150

Alas, poor Yorick! I knew him, Horatio: a fellow of infinite jest, of most excellent fancy; he hath borne me on his back a thousand times; and now, how abhorred in my imagination it is! my gorge rises at it. Here hung those lips that I have kissed I know not how oft. Where be your gibes now? your gambols? your songs? your flashes of merriment, that were wont to set the table on a roar? Not one now, to mock your own grinning? quite chap-fallen? Now get you to my lady's chamber, and tell her, let her paint an inch thick, to this favour she must come; make her laugh at that.

Ibid. Line 201

To what base uses we may return, Horatio! Why may not imagination trace the noble dust of Alexander, till he find it stopping a bung-hole?

Ibid. Line 222

'Twere to consider too curiously, to consider so.

> *Hamlet. Act V, Sc. 1, Line 226*

Imperious Caesar, dead and turn'd to clay,
Might stop a hole to keep the wind away.

> *Ibid. Line 235*

Lay her i' the earth;
And from her fair and unpolluted flesh
May violets spring! [1]

> *Ibid. Line 260*

A ministering angel shall my sister be. [2]

> *Ibid. Line 263*

Sweets to the sweet: farewell!

> *Ibid. Line 265*

I thought thy bride-bed to have deck'd, sweet maid,
And not have strew'd thy grave.

> *Ibid. Line 267*

Though I am not splenetive and rash,
Yet have I in me something dangerous.

> *Ibid. Line 283*

Forty thousand brothers
Could not, with all their quantity of love,
Make up my sum.

> *Ibid. Line 291*

Nay, an thou'lt mouth,
I'll rant as well as thou.

> *Ibid. Line 305*

Let Hercules himself do what he may,
The cat will mew and dog will have his day.

> *Ibid. Line 313*

There's a divinity that shapes our ends,
Rough-hew them how we will.

> *Ibid. Sc. 2, Line 10*

I once did hold it, as our statists do,
A baseness to write fair.

> *Ibid. Line 33*

It did me yeoman's service.

> *Ibid. Line 36*

Popp'd in between the election and my hopes.

> *Ibid. Line 65*

---

[1] And from his ashes may be made
The violet of his native land.
  TENNYSON: *In Memoriam* [1850], XVIII
See *Rubaiyat*, page 531b.
[2] See Sir Walter Scott, page 414b.

The bravery of his grief did put me
Into a towering passion.

> *Hamlet. Act V, Sc. 2, Line 79*

'Tis the breathing time of day with me.

> *Ibid. Line 181*

The most fond and winnowed opinions.

> *Ibid. Line 201*

There's a special providence in the fall of a sparrow. [1] If it be now, 'tis not to come; if it be not to come, it will be now; if it be not now, yet it will come: the readiness is all. Since no man has aught of what he leaves, what is 't to leave betimes?

> *Ibid. Line 232*

A hit, a very palpable hit.

> *Ibid. Line 295*

This fell sergeant, death,
Is strict in his arrest.

> *Ibid. Line 350*

Report me and my cause aright.

> *Ibid. Line 353*

I am more an antique Roman than a Dane.

> *Ibid. Line 355*

Horatio, what a wounded name,
Things standing thus unknown, shall live behind me.
If thou didst ever hold me in thy heart,
Absent thee from felicity awhile,
And in this harsh world draw thy breath in pain,
To tell my story.

> *Ibid. Line 358*

The rest is silence.

> *Ibid. Line 372*

Now cracks a noble heart. Good-night, sweet prince,
And flights of angels sing thee to thy rest!

> *Ibid. Line 373*

O proud death! [2]
What feast is toward in thine eternal cell?

> *Ibid. Line 378*

---

[1] See Alexander Pope, page 316a.
[2] See Donne, page 217b.

I will make a Star-chamber matter of it.

The Merry Wives of Windsor [*1600–1601*]. *Act I, Sc. 1, Line 2*

All his successors gone before him have done 't; and all his ancestors that come after him may.

Ibid. Line 14

Seven hundred pounds and possibilities is goot gifts.

Ibid. Line 65

I had rather than forty shillings I had my Book of Songs and Sonnets here.

Ibid. Line 205

If there be no great love in the beginning, yet heaven may decrease it upon better acquaintance, when we are married and have more occasion to know one another: I hope, upon familiarity will grow more contempt.[1]

Ibid. Line 255

"Convey," the wise it call. "Steal!" foh! a fico for the phrase!

Ibid. Sc. 3, Line 30

I am almost out at heels.

Ibid. Line 32

Thou art the Mars of malcontents.

Ibid. Line 111

Here will be an old abusing of God's patience and the king's English.

Ibid. Sc. 4, Line 5

Dispense with trifles.

Ibid. Act II, Sc. 1, Line 47

There's the humour of it.

Ibid. Line 139

Faith, thou hast some crotchets in thy head now.

Ibid. Line 158

Why, then the world's mine oyster, Which I with sword will open.

Ibid. Sc. 2, Line 2

This is the short and the long of it.

Ibid. Line 62

Unless experience be a jewel.

Ibid. Line 216

Like a fair house built on another man's ground.

Ibid. Line 229

[1] See Aesop, page 10a.

Better three hours too soon than a minute too late.

The Merry Wives of Windsor. Act II, Sc. 2, Line 332

We have some salt of our youth in us; we are the sons of women.

Ibid. Sc. 3, Line 50

I cannot tell what the dickens his name is.

Ibid. Act III, Sc. 2, Line 20

He capers, he dances, he has eyes of youth, he writes verses, he speaks holiday, he smells April and May.

Ibid. Line 71

O, what a world of vile ill-favour'd faults Looks handsome in three hundred pounds a year!

Ibid. Sc. 4, Line 32

A woman would run through fire and water for such a kind heart.

Ibid. Line 106

If I be served such another trick, I'll have my brains ta'en out, and buttered, and give them to a dog for a new year's gift.

Ibid. Sc. 5, Line 7

I have a kind of alacrity in sinking.

Ibid. Line 13

As good luck would have it.[1]

Ibid. Line 86

The rankest compound of villanous smell that ever offended nostril.

Ibid. Line 95

A man of my kidney.

Ibid. Line 119

So curses all Eve's daughters, of what complexion soever.

Ibid. Act IV, Sc. 2, Line 24

Wives may be merry, and yet honest too.

Ibid. Line 110

This is the third time; I hope good luck lies in odd numbers. . . . There is divinity in odd numbers, either in nativity, chance, or death.[2]

Ibid. Act V, Sc. 1, Line 2

Life is a shuttle.

Ibid. Line 25

[1] As ill luck would have it. — CERVANTES: *Don Quixote, Part I* [1605], *Book I, Chap. II*
[2] See Pliny, page 50b.

Better a little chiding than a great deal of heartbreak.

The Merry Wives of Windsor.
Act V, Sc. 3, Line 10

I have had my labour for my travail.[1]
Troilus and Cressida [1601–1603].
Act I, Sc. 1, Line 73

Men prize the thing ungain'd more than it is.

Ibid. Sc. 2, Line 313

The sea being smooth
How many shallow bauble boats dare sail
Upon her patient breast.[2]

Ibid. Sc. 3, Line 34

The heavens themselves, the planets, and this centre,
Observe degree, priority, and place,
Insisture, course, proportion, season, form,
Office, and custom, in all line of order.

Ibid. Line 85

O! when degree is shak'd,
Which is the ladder to all high designs,
The enterprise is sick.[3]

Ibid. Line 101

Take but degree away, untune that string,
And, hark! what discord follows; each thing meets
In mere oppugnancy: the bounded waters
Should lift their bosoms higher than the shores
And make a sop of all this solid globe.

Ibid. Line 109

Then everything includes itself in power,
Power into will, will into appetite;
And appetite, an universal wolf,
So doubly seconded with will and power,
Must make perforce a universal prey,
And last eat up himself.

Ibid. Line 119

Like a strutting player, whose conceit
Lies in his hamstring, and doth think it rich
To hear the wooden dialogue and sound

'Twixt his stretch'd footing and the scaffoldage.

Troilus and Cressida. Act I, Sc. 3,
Line 153

And in such indexes, although small pricks
To their subsequent volumes, there is seen
The baby figure of the giant mass
Of things to come.

Ibid. Line 343

Mongrel beef-witted lord.

Ibid. Act II, Sc. 1, Line 14

Who wears his wit in his belly, and his guts in his head.

Ibid. Line 78

Modest doubt is call'd
The beacon of the wise, the tent that searches
To the bottom of the worst.

Ibid. Sc. 2, Line 15

'Tis mad idolatry
To make the service greater than the god.

Ibid. Line 56

The remainder viands
We do not throw in unrespective sink
Because we now are full.

Ibid. Line 70

The elephant hath joints, but none for courtesy: his legs are legs for necessity, not for flexure.

Ibid. Sc. 3, Line 114

He that is proud eats up himself; pride is his own glass, his own trumpet, his own chronicle.

Ibid. Line 165

Light boats sail swift, though greater hulks draw deep.

Ibid. Line 280

I am giddy, expectation whirls me round.
The imaginary relish is so sweet
That it enchants my sense.

Ibid. Act III, Sc. 2, Line 17

Words pay no debts.

Ibid. Line 56

To fear the worst oft cures the worse.

Ibid. Line 77

All lovers swear more performance than they are able, and yet reserve an ability that they never perform; vow-

---

[1] See Cervantes, page 103b.
[2] See Publilius Syrus, page 44b.
[3] See Publilius Syrus, page 46b.

ing more than the perfection of ten, and discharging less than the tenth part of one.

> *Troilus and Cressida. Act III, Sc. 2, Line 89*

For to be wise, and love,
Exceeds man's might; that dwells with gods above.

> *Ibid. Line 163*

Time hath, my lord, a wallet at his back,
Wherein he puts alms for oblivion.

> *Ibid. Sc. 3, Line 145*

Perseverance, dear my lord,
Keeps honour bright: to have done, is to hang
Quite out of fashion, like a rusty mail
In monumental mockery.

> *Ibid. Line 150*

For honour travels in a strait so narrow
Where one but goes abreast.

> *Ibid. Line 154*

Time is like a fashionable host
That slightly shakes his parting guest by the hand,
And with his arms outstretch'd, as he would fly
Grasps in the comer: welcome ever smiles,
And farewell goes out sighing.

> *Ibid. Line 168*

Beauty, wit,
High birth, vigour of bone, desert in service,
Love, friendship, charity, are subjects all
To envious and calumniating time.
One touch of nature makes the whole world kin.

> *Ibid. Line 171*

And give to dust that is a little gilt
More laud than gilt o'er-dusted.

> *Ibid. Line 178*

And, like a dew-drop from the lion's mane,
Be shook to air.

> *Ibid. Line 225*

My mind is troubled, like a fountain stirr'd;
And I myself see not the bottom of it.

> *Ibid. Line 314*

Be moderate, be moderate.

> *Troilus and Cressida. Act IV, Sc. 4, Line 1*

As many farewells as be stars in heaven.

> *Ibid. Line 44*

Sometimes we are devils to ourselves
When we will tempt the frailty of our powers,
Presuming on their changeful potency.

> *Ibid. Line 95*

The kiss you take is better than you give.

> *Ibid. Sc. 5, Line 38*

Fie, fie upon her!
There's language in her eye, her cheek, her lip,
Nay, her foot speaks; her wanton spirits look out
At every joint and motive of her body.

> *Ibid. Line 54*

Daughters of the game.

> *Ibid. Line 63*

What's past, and what's to come, is strew'd with husks
And formless ruin of oblivion.

> *Ibid. Line 165*

The end crowns all,
And that old common arbitrator, Time,
Will one day end it.

> *Ibid. Line 223*

He has not so much brain as ear-wax.

> *Ibid. Act V, Sc. 1, Line 58*

Words, words, mere words, no matter from the heart.

> *Ibid. Sc. 3, Line 109*

O world! world! world! thus is the poor agent despised.

> *Ibid. Sc. 10, Line 36*

Love all, trust a few,
Do wrong to none: be able for thine enemy
Rather in power than use, and keep thy friend
Under thine own life's key: be check'd for silence,
But never tax'd for speech.

> *All's Well that Ends Well [1601–1603]. Act I, Sc. 1, Line 74*

It were all one
That I should love a bright particular star

And think to wed it.
>   *All's Well that Ends Well.*
>   *Act I, Sc. 1, Line 97*

The hind that would be mated by the
lion
Must die for love.
>   *Ibid. Line 103*

Our remedies oft in ourselves do lie,
Which we ascribe to Heaven.
>   *Ibid. Line 235*

> Service is no heritage.
>   *Ibid. Sc. 3, Line 25*

My friends were poor, but honest.
>   *Ibid. Line 203*

>   Great floods have flown
From simple sources.
>   *Ibid. Act II, Sc. 1, Line 142*

Oft expectation fails, and most oft
there
Where most it promises.
>   *Ibid Line 145*

I will show myself highly fed and
lowly taught.
>   *Ibid. Sc. 2, Line 3*

They say miracles are past.
>   *Ibid. Sc. 3, Line 1*

From lowest place when virtuous things
proceed,
The place is dignified by the doer's
deed.
>   *Ibid. Line 132*

A young man married is a man that's
marr'd.
>   *Ibid. Line 315*

Make the coming hour o'erflow with
joy,
And pleasure drown the brim.
>   *Ibid. Sc. 4, Line 48*

No legacy is so rich as honesty.
>   *Ibid. Act III, Sc. 5, Line 13*

The web of our life is of a mingled
yarn, good and ill together.
>   *Ibid. Act IV, Sc. 3, Line 83*

I am a man whom Fortune hath
cruelly scratched.
>   *Ibid. Act V, Sc. 2, Line 28*

Whose words all ears took captive.
>   *Ibid. Sc. 3, Line 17*

>   Praising what is lost
Makes the remembrance dear.
>   *Ibid. Line 19*

The inaudible and noiseless foot of
Time.[1]
>   *All's Well that Ends Well.*
>   *Act V, Sc. 3, Line 41*

Love that comes too late,
Like a remorseful pardon slowly carried.
>   *Ibid. Line 57*

All impediments in fancy's course
Are motives of more fancy.
>   *Ibid. Line 216*

The bitter past, more welcome is the
sweet.
>   *Ibid. Line 339*

>   Spirits are not finely touch'd
But to fine issues.
>   *Measure for Measure* [1604–
>   1605]. *Act I, Sc. 1, Line 35*

He was ever precise in promise-keeping.
>   *Ibid. Sc. 2, Line 80*

Good counsellors lack no clients.
>   *Ibid. Line 115*

And liberty plucks justice by the nose.
>   *Ibid. Sc. 3, Line 29*

Who may, in the ambush of my name,
strike home.
>   *Ibid. Line 41*

I hold you as a thing ensky'd and
sainted.
>   *Ibid. Sc. 4, Line 34*

>   A man whose blood
Is very snow-broth; one who never feels
The wanton stings and motions of the
sense.
>   *Ibid. Line 57*

He arrests him on it;
And follows close the rigour of the
statute,
To make him an example.
>   *Ibid. Line 66*

Our doubts are traitors,
And make us lose the good we oft might
win
By fearing to attempt.
>   *Ibid. Line 78*

We must not make a scarecrow of the
law,
Setting it up to fear the birds of prey,

---

[1] How noiseless falls the foot of time !—
W. R. SPENCER [1769–1834]: *Lines to Lady
A. Hamilton*

And let it keep one shape, till custom
make it
Their perch, and not their terror.
Measure for Measure. Act II,
Sc. 1, Line 1

The jury, passing on the prisoner's life,
May in the sworn twelve have a thief
or two
Guiltier than him they try.
Ibid. Line 19

Some rise by sin, and some by virtue
fall.
Ibid. Line 38

Great with child, and longing for
stewed prunes.
Ibid. Line 94

They are not China dishes, but very
good dishes.
Ibid. Line 100

This will last out a night in Russia,
When nights are longest there.
Ibid. Line 144

His face is the worst thing about him.
Ibid. Line 167

Condemn the fault, and not the actor
of it?
Ibid. Sc. 2, Line 37

No ceremony that to great ones 'longs,
Not the king's crown, nor the deputed
sword,
The marshal's truncheon, nor the
judge's robe,
Become them with one half so good a
grace
As mercy does.[1]
Ibid. Line 59

Why, all the souls that were, were for-
feit once;
And He that might the vantage best
have took
Found out the remedy. How would you
be,
If He, which is the top of judgment,
should
But judge you as you are?
Ibid. Line 73

The law hath not been dead, though it
hath slept.
Ibid. Line 90

[1] See *Merchant of Venice*, page 146a.

O, it is excellent
To have a giant's strength; but it is
tyrannous
To use it like a giant.
Measure for Measure. Act II,
Sc. 2, Line 107

But man, proud man,
Drest in a little brief authority,
Most ignorant of what he's most as-
sured,
His glassy essence, like an angry ape,
Plays such fantastic tricks before high
heaven
As make the angels weep.
Ibid. Line 117

That in the captain's but a choleric
word
Which in the soldier is flat blasphemy.
Ibid. Line 130

It oft falls out,
To have what we would have, we speak
not what we mean.
Ibid. Sc. 4, Line 118

The miserable have no other medicine,
But only hope.
Ibid. Act III, Sc. 1, Line 2

A breath thou art,
Servile to all the skyey influences.
Ibid. Line 8

Thou hast nor youth nor age;
But, as it were, an after-dinner's sleep,
Dreaming on both; for all thy blessed
youth
Becomes as aged, and doth beg the alms
Of palsied eld; and when thou art old
and rich,
Thou hast neither heat, affection, limb,
nor beauty,
To make thy riches pleasant. What's
yet in this
That bears the name of life? Yet in this
life
Lie hid moe thousand deaths; yet
death we fear,
That makes these odds all even.
Ibid. Line 32

The sense of death is most in apprehension; [1]
And the poor beetle, that we tread upon,

[1] See Publilius Syrus, page 45a.

In corporal sufferance finds a pang as great
As when a giant dies.

    *Measure for Measure. Act III,
              Sc. 1, Line 76*

The cunning livery of hell.

              Ibid. Line 93

Ay, but to die, and go we know not where;
To lie in cold obstruction and to rot;
This sensible warm motion to become
A kneaded clod; and the delighted spirit
To bathe in fiery floods, or to reside
In thrilling region of thick-ribbed ice;
To be imprison'd in the viewless winds,
And blown with restless violence round about
The pendent world.

             Ibid. Line 116

The weariest and most loathed worldly life
That age, ache, penury, and imprisonment
Can lay on nature, is a paradise
To what we fear of death.

             Ibid. Line 127

I have no superfluous leisure.

             Ibid. Line 156

The hand that hath made you fair hath made you good.[1]

             Ibid. Line 182

Virtue is bold, and goodness never fearful.

             Ibid. Line 214

There, at the moated grange, resides this dejected Mariana.[2]

             Ibid. Line 279

Pygmalion's images, newly made woman.

             Ibid. Sc. 2, Line 48

This news is old enough, yet it is every day's news.

             Ibid. Line 249

He who the sword of heaven will bear
Should be as holy as severe.

             Ibid. Line 283

O, what may man within him hide,
Though angel on the outward side!

    *Measure for Measure. Act III,
             Sc. 2, Line 293*

Take, O take those lips away,
  That so sweetly were forsworn;
And those eyes, the break of day,
  Lights that do mislead the morn:
But my kisses bring again, bring again;
Seals of love, but sealed in vain, sealed in vain.[1]

       Ibid. Act IV, Sc. 1, Line 1

Every true man's apparel fits your thief.

             Ibid. Sc. 2, Line 46

Death's a great disguiser.

             Ibid. Line 185

We would, and we would not.

             Ibid. Sc. 4, Line 37

A forted residence 'gainst the tooth of time
And razure of oblivion.

         Ibid. Act V, Sc. 1, Line 12

Truth is truth
To the end of reckoning.

             Ibid. Line 45

Neither maid, widow, nor wife.

             Ibid. Line 173

They say best men are moulded out of faults,
And, for the most, become much more the better
For being a little bad.

             Ibid. Line 440

What's mine is yours, and what is yours is mine.[2]

             Ibid. Line 539

The bookish theoric.

    *Othello [1604–1605]. Act I,
             Sc. 1, Line 24*

We cannot all be masters.

             Ibid. Line 43

---

[1] See Spenser, page 115a.
[2] "Mariana in the moated grange." — The motto used by TENNYSON for the poem *Mariana* [1830].

[1] This song occurs in *Act V, Sc. 2* of FLETCHER's *Bloody Brother* [circa 1616], with the following additional stanza:
  Hide, O hide those hills of snow,
    Which thy frozen bosom bears,
  On whose tops the pinks that grow
    Are of those that April wears!
  But first set my poor heart free,
  Bound in those icy chains by thee.
[2] See Plautus, page 29b.

I will wear my heart upon my sleeve
For daws to peck at.
Othello. Act I, Sc. 1, Line 64
Trust not your daughters' minds
By what you see them act.
Ibid. Line 171
Keep up your bright swords, for the
dew will rust them.
Ibid. Sc. 2, Line 58
The wealthy curled darlings of our na-
tion.
Ibid. Line 68
Most potent, grave, and reverend
signiors,
My very noble and approv'd good
masters.
That I have ta'en away this old man's
daughter,
It is most true; true, I have married
her:
The very head and front of my offend-
ing
Hath this extent, no more. Rude am I
in my speech,
And little bless'd with the soft phrase
of peace.
Ibid. Sc. 3, Line 76
Little shall I grace my cause
In speaking for myself. Yet, by your
gracious patience,
I will a round unvarnish'd tale deliver
Of my whole course of love.
Ibid. Line 88
A maider never bold;
Of spirit so still and quiet, that her
motion
Blush'd at herself.
Ibid. Line 94
Still question'd me the story of my life
From year to year, the battles, sieges,
fortunes
That I have passed.
Ibid. Line 129
Wherein I spake of most disastrous
chances,
Of moving accidents by flood and field,
Of hair-breadth 'scapes i' the imminent
deadly breach.
Ibid. Line 134
Hills whose heads touch heaven.
Ibid. Line 141

And of the Cannibals that each other
eat,
The Anthropophagi, and men whose
heads
Do grow beneath their shoulders.
Othello. Act I, Sc. 3, Line 143
My story being done,
She gave me for my pains a world of
sighs:
She swore, in faith, 'twas strange, 'twas
passing strange,
'Twas pitiful, 'twas wondrous pitiful:
She wish'd she had not heard it, yet
she wish'd
That Heaven had made her such a man;
she thank'd me,
And bade me, if I had a friend that
loved her,
I should but teach him how to tell my
story,
And that would woo her. Upon this hint
I spake:
She loved me for the dangers I had
pass'd,
And I loved her that she did pity them.
This only is the witchcraft I have used.
Ibid. Line 158
I do perceive here a divided duty.
Ibid. Line 181
To mourn a mischief that is past and
gone
Is the next way to draw new mischief
on.
Ibid. Line 204
The robb'd that smiles, steals some-
thing from the thief.
Ibid. Line 208
But words are words; I never yet did
hear
That the bruis'd heart was pierced
through the ear.
Ibid. Line 218
Our bodies are our gardens, to the
which our wills are gardeners; . . .
either to have it sterile with idleness or
manured with industry.
Ibid. Line 324
Put money in thy purse.
Ibid. Line 345
The food that to him now is as lus-

cious as locusts, shall be to him shortly
as bitter as coloquintida.
> *Othello. Act I, Sc. 3, Line 354*

Framed to make women false.
> *Ibid. Line 404*

One that excels the quirks of blazoning
pens.
> *Ibid. Act II, Sc. 1, Line 63*

You are pictures out of doors,
Bells in your parlours, wild-cats in your
   kitchens,
Saints in your injuries, devils being
   offended,
Players in your housewifery, and housewives in your beds.
> *Ibid. Line 109*

For I am nothing if not critical.
> *Ibid. Line 119*

I am not merry; but I do beguile
The thing I am, by seeming otherwise.
> *Ibid. Line 122*

She that was ever fair and never proud,
Had tongue at will and yet was never
   loud.
> *Ibid. Line 148*

Iago. She that could think and ne'er
   disclose her mind,
See suitors following and not look behind,
She was a wight, if ever such wight
   were, —
Desdemona. To do what?
Iago. To suckle fools and chronicle
   small beer.[1]
Desdemona. O most lame and impotent
   conclusion!
> *Ibid. Line 158*

You may relish him more in the
soldier than in the scholar.
> *Ibid. Line 165*

If it were now to die,
'Twere now to be most happy.
> *Ibid. Line 192*

Base men being in love have then a
nobility in their natures more than is
native to them.
> *Ibid. Line 218*

Egregiously an ass.
> *Ibid. Line 321*

[1] See *King Henry VI*, page 125b.

I have very poor and unhappy brains
for drinking.
> *Othello. Act II, Sc. 3, Line 34*

Potations pottle-deep.
> *Ibid. Line 57*

King Stephen was a worthy peer,
   His breeches cost him but a crown;
He held them sixpence all too dear,
   With that he called the tailor lown.[1]
> *Ibid. Line 93*

'Tis pride that pulls the country down.
> *Ibid. Line 99*

Well, God's above all; and there be
souls must be saved, and there be souls
must not be saved.
> *Ibid. Line 106*

Silence that dreadful bell! it frights the
   isle
From her propriety.
> *Ibid. Line 177*

Your name is great
In mouths of wisest censure.
> *Ibid. Line 194*

But men are men; the best sometimes
   forget.
> *Ibid. Line 243*

Thy honesty and love doth mince this
   matter.[2]
> *Ibid. Line 249*

Reputation, reputation, reputation!
Oh! I have lost my reputation. I have
lost the immortal part of myself, and
what remains is bestial.
> *Ibid. Line 264*

Reputation is an idle and most false
imposition; oft got without merit, and
lost without deserving.
> *Ibid. Line 270*

O thou invisible spirit of wine! if
thou hast no name to be known by, let
us call thee devil!
> *Ibid. Line 285*

O God! that men should put an
enemy in their mouths to steal away
their brains; that we should with joy,

[1] These lines are from an old ballad, *Take
Thy Old Cloak About Thee.* See page 1011b.
[2] Mince the matter. — CERVANTES: *Don
Quixote* [1605], *Author's Preface*
   You mince matters. — MOLIÈRE: *Tartuffe*
[1664], *Act I, Sc. 1*

pleasance, revel, and applause, transform ourselves into beasts.

Othello. Act II, Sc. 3, Line 293

Good wine is a good familiar creature if it be well used.

Ibid. Line 315

How poor are they that have not patience!

Ibid. Line 379

Excellent wretch! Perdition catch my soul,
But I do love thee! and when I love thee not,
Chaos is come again.[1]

Ibid. Act III, Sc. 3, Line 90

Men should be what they seem.

Ibid. Line 126

Speak to me as to thy thinkings,
As thou dost ruminate, and give thy worst of thoughts
The worst of words.

Ibid. Line 131

Good name in man and woman, dear my lord,
Is the immediate jewel of their souls:
Who steals my purse steals trash; 'tis something, nothing;
'Twas mine, 'tis his, and has been slave to thousands;
But he that filches from me my good name
Robs me of that which not enriches him,
And makes me poor indeed.

Ibid. Line 155

O! beware, my lord, of jealousy;
It is the green-eyed monster which doth mock
The meat it feeds on: that cuckold lives in bliss
Who, certain of his fate, loves not his wronger;
But, O! what damned minutes tells he o'er
Who dotes, yet doubts; suspects, yet soundly loves!

Ibid. Line 165

Poor and content is rich, and rich enough.

Ibid. Line 172

[1] See *Venus and Adonis*, page 131a.

Think'st thou I'd make a life of jealousy,
To follow still the changes of the moon
With fresh suspicions? No; to be once in doubt
Is once to be resolved.

Othello. Act III, Sc. 3, Line 177

I humbly do beseech you of your pardon
For too much loving you.

Ibid. Line 212

If I do prove her haggard,
Though that her jesses were my dear heart-strings,
I'd whistle her off and let her down the wind,
To prey at fortune.

Ibid. Line 260

I am declined
Into the vale of years.

Ibid. Line 265

O curse of marriage!
That we can call these delicate creatures ours,
And not their appetites. I had rather be a toad,
And live upon the vapour of a dungeon,
Than keep a corner in the thing I love
For others' uses.

Ibid. Line 268

Trifles light as air
Are to the jealous confirmations strong
As proofs of holy writ.

Ibid. Line 323

Not poppy, nor mandragora,[1]
Nor all the drowsy syrups of the world,
Shall ever medicine thee to that sweet sleep
Which thou ow'dst yesterday.

Ibid. Line 331

I swear 'tis better to be much abused
Than but to know 't a little.

Ibid. Line 337

He that is robb'd, not wanting what is stolen,
Let him not know 't and he's not robb'd at all.[2]

Ibid. Line 343

O! now, for ever
Farewell the tranquil mind; farewell content!

[1] See *Antony and Cleopatra*, page 200a.
[2] See Publilius Syrus, page 43a.

Farewell the plumed troop and the big
wars
That make ambition virtue! O, fare-
well!
Farewell the neighing steed, and the
shrill trump,
The spirit-stirring drum, the ear-pierc-
ing fife,
The royal banner, and all quality,
Pride, pomp, and circumstance of glo-
rious war!
And, O you mortal engines, whose rude
throats
The immortal Jove's dread clamours
counterfeit,
Farewell! Othello's occupation's gone!
Othello. Act III, Sc. 3, Line 348
Be sure of it; give me the ocular proof.
Ibid. Line 361

No hinge nor loop
To hang a doubt on.
Ibid. Line 366
On horror's head horrors accumulate.
Ibid. Line 371
Take note, take note, O world!
To be direct and honest is not safe.
Ibid. Line 378
But this denoted a foregone conclusion.
Ibid. Line 429
Swell, bosom, with thy fraught,
For 'tis of aspics' tongues!
Ibid. Line 450
Like to the Pontick sea,
Whose icy current and compulsive
course
Ne'er feels retiring ebb, but keeps due
on
To the Propontic and the Hellespont,
Even so my bloody thoughts, with
violent pace,
Shall ne'er look back, ne'er ebb to hum-
ble love,
Till that a capable and wide revenge
Swallow them up.
Ibid. Line 454
Our new heraldry is hands, not hearts.
Ibid. Sc. 4, Line 48
'Tis the strumpet's plague
To beguile many, and be beguil'd by
one.
Ibid. Act IV, Sc. 1, Line 97

They laugh that win.
Othello. Act IV, Sc. 1, Line 123
My heart is turn'd to stone; I strike
it, and it hurts my hand. — O, the
world hath not a sweeter creature: she
might lie by an emperor's side, and
command him tasks.
Ibid. Line 190
O, she will sing the savageness out
of a bear!
Ibid. Line 198
But yet the pity of it, Iago! O! Iago,
the pity of it, Iago!
Ibid. Line 205
Is this the nature
Whom passion could not shake? whose
solid virtue
The shot of accident, nor dart of chance,
Could neither graze nor pierce?
Ibid. Line 277
I understand a fury in your words,
But not the words.
Ibid. Sc. 2, Line 31
Steep'd me in poverty to the very lips.
Ibid. Line 49
But, alas! to make me
A fixed figure for the time of scorn
To point his slow and moving finger at!
Ibid. Line 52
Patience, thou young and rose-lipp'd
cherubin.
Ibid. Line 62
O thou weed!
Who art so lovely fair and smell'st so
sweet
That the sense aches at thee, would
thou hadst ne'er been born.
Ibid. Line 66
O Heaven! that such companions
thou'dst unfold,
And put in every honest hand a whip
To lash the rascals naked through the
world.
Ibid. Line 141
Unkindness may do much:
And his unkindness may defeat my life,
But never taint my love.
Ibid. Line 159
The poor soul sat sighing by a sycamore
tree,
Sing all a green willow;

Her hand on her bosom, her head on her
knee
Sing willow, willow, willow.
> *Othello. Act IV, Sc. 3, Line 41*

It makes us, or it mars us.
> *Ibid. Act V, Sc. 1, Line 4*

Every way makes my gain.
> *Ibid. Line 14*

He hath a daily beauty in his life.
> *Ibid. Line 19*

This is the night
That either makes me or fordoes me
quite.
> *Ibid. Line 128*

And smooth as monumental alabaster.
> *Ibid. Sc. 2, Line 5*

Put out the light, and then put out the
light:
If I quench thee, thou flaming minister,
I can again thy former light restore
Should I repent me; but once put out
thy light,
Thou cunning'st pattern of excelling
nature,
I know not where is that Promethean
heat
That can thy light relume.
> *Ibid. Line 7*

It is the very error of the moon;
She comes more near the earth than she
was wont,
And makes men mad.
> *Ibid. Line 107*

Curse his better angel from his side,
And fall to reprobation.
> *Ibid. Line 206*

Here is my journey's end, here is my
butt,
And very sea-mark of my utmost sail.
> *Ibid. Line 268*

An honourable murderer, if you will;
For naught I did in hate, but all in
honour.
> *Ibid. Line 295*

I have done the state some service, and
they know 't;
No more of that. I pray you, in your
letters,
When you shall these unlucky deeds
relate,
Speak of me as I am; nothing extenuate,

Nor set down aught in malice: then,
must you speak
Of one that loved not wisely but too
well;
Of one not easily jealous, but, being
wrought,
Perplex'd in the extreme; of one whose
hand,
Like the base Indian, threw a pearl
away
Richer than all his tribe; of one whose
subdued eyes
Albeit unused to the melting mood,
Drop tears as fast as the Arabian trees
Their med'cinable gum.
> *Othello. Act V, Sc. 2, Line 338*

I took by the throat the circumcised
dog,
And smote him thus.
> *Ibid. Line 354*

My love's
More richer than my tongue.
> *King Lear [1605–1606]. Act I,*
> *Sc. 1, Line 79*

Now, our joy,
Although our last, not least.
> *Ibid. Line 84*

Nothing will come of nothing.
> *Ibid. Line 92*

Mend your speech a little,
Lest you may mar your fortunes.
> *Ibid. Line 96*

I want that glib and oily art,
To speak and purpose not.
> *Ibid. Line 227*

A still-soliciting eye, and such a tongue
That I am glad I have not.
> *Ibid. Line 234*

Who in the lusty stealth of nature take
More composition and fierce quality
Than doth, within a dull, stale, tired
bed,
Go to the creating a whole tribe of fops.
> *Ibid. Sc. 2, Line 11*

We have seen the best of our time:
machinations, hollowness, treachery,
and all ruinous disorders, follow us
disquietly to our graves.
> *Ibid. Line 125*

This is the excellent foppery of the
world, that, when we are sick in fortune, — often the surfeit of our own

behaviour, — we make guilty of our disasters the sun, the moon, and the stars: as if we were villains by necessity; fools by heavenly compulsion.
King Lear. Act I, Sc. 2, Line 129

That which ordinary men are fit for, I am qualified in; and the best of me is diligence.
Ibid. Sc. 4, Line 36

Truth's a dog must to kennel; he must be whipt out, when Lady the brach may stand by the fire and stink.
Ibid. Line 125

Have more than thou showest, Speak less than thou knowest, Lend less than thou owest.
Ibid. Line 133

Ingratitude, thou marble-hearted fiend! More hideous, when thou show'st thee in a child, Than the sea-monster.
Ibid. Line 283

How sharper than a serpent's tooth it is To have a thankless child!
Ibid. Line 312

Striving to better, oft we mar what's well.
Ibid. Line 371

The son and heir of a mongrel bitch.
Ibid. Act II, Sc. 2, Line 23

I have seen better faces in my time Than stands on any shoulder that I see Before me at this instant.
Ibid. Line 99

A good man's fortune may grow out at heels.
Ibid. Line 158

Fortune, good night, smile once more; turn thy wheel.
Ibid. Line 180

Hysterica passio! down, thou climbing sorrow! Thy element's below.
Ibid. Sc. 4, Line 57

That sir which serves and seeks for gain, And follows but for form, Will pack when it begins to rain, And leave thee in the storm.
Ibid. Line 79

Nature in you stands on the very verge Of her confine.
King Lear. Act II, Sc. 4, Line 149

Necessity's sharp pinch!
Ibid. Line 214

Our basest beggars Are in the poorest thing superfluous: Allow not nature more than nature needs, Man's life is cheap as beast's.
Ibid. Line 276

Let not women's weapons, waterdrops, Stain my man's cheeks!
Ibid. Line 280

I have full cause of weeping; but this heart Shall break into a hundred thousand flaws, Or e'er I'll weep. — O fool, I shall go mad!
Ibid. Line 287

Blow, winds, and crack your cheeks! rage! blow!
Ibid. Act III, Sc. 2, Line 1

I tax not you, you elements, with unkindness.
Ibid. Line 16

A poor, infirm, weak, and despised old man.
Ibid. Line 20

There was never yet fair woman but she made mouths in a glass.
Ibid. Line 35

I will be the pattern of all patience.
Ibid. Line 37

I am a man More sinn'd against than sinning.
Ibid. Line 59

The art of our necessities is strange, That can make vile things precious.
Ibid. Line 72

He that has and a little tiny wit, — With hey, ho, the wind and the rain, — Must make content with his fortunes fit, Though the rain it raineth every day.[1]
Ibid. Line 76

Oh! that way madness lies; let me shun that.
Ibid. Sc. 4, Line 21

[1] See *Twelfth-Night*, page 166a.

Poor naked wretches, wheresoe'er you
are,
That bide the pelting of this pitiless
storm,
How shall your houseless heads and un-
fed sides,
Your looped and windowed raggedness,
defend you
From seasons such as these?
King Lear. Act III, Sc. 4, Line 28
Take physic, pomp;
Expose thyself to feel what wretches
feel,
That thou mayst shake the superflux
to them,
And show the heavens more just.
Ibid. Line 33
Out-paramoured the Turk.
Ibid. Line 91
Is man no more than this? Consider
him well. Thou owest the worm no silk,
the beast no hide, the sheep no wool,
the cat no perfume. — Ha! here's
three on's are sophisticated! — Thou
art the thing itself: unaccommodated
man is no more but such a poor, bare
forkt animal as thou art. — Off, off, you
lendings!— Come, unbutton here.
Ibid. Line 105
'Tis a naughty night to swim in.
Ibid. Line 113
The green mantle of the standing
pool.
Ibid. Line 137
But mice and rats and such small deer
Have been Tom's food for seven long
year.
Ibid. Line 142
The prince of darkness is a gentleman.[1]
Ibid. Line 147
Poor Tom's a-cold.
Ibid. Line 151
Child Rowland to the dark tower came.[2]

[1] The Devil is a gentleman. — SHELLEY:
Peter Bell the Third [1819], *Part II, St. 2*
[2] Child Roland to the dark tower came. —
SIR WALTER SCOTT: *The Bridal of Triermain*
[1813]
Dauntless the slug-horn to my lips I set,
And blew. *"Childe Roland to the Dark
Tower came."*
BROWNING: *Childe Roland to the
Dark Tower Came* [1855], *St. 34*

His word was still, Fie, foh, and fum,
I smell the blood of a British man.
King Lear. Act III, Sc. 4, Line 185
He's mad that trusts in the tameness
of a wolf, a horse's health, a boy's love,
or a whore's oath.
Ibid. Sc. 6, Line 18
The little dogs and all,
Tray, Blanch, and Sweetheart, see, they
bark at me.
Ibid. Line 65
Is there any cause in nature that
makes these hard hearts?
Ibid. Line 80
I am tied to the stake, and I must stand
the course.
Ibid. Sc. 7, Line 54
Out, vile jelly!
Ibid. Line 83
The lowest and most dejected thing of
fortune.
Ibid. Act IV, Sc. 1, Line 3
The worst is not
So long as we can say, "This is the
worst."
Ibid. Line 27
As flies to wanton boys, are we to the
gods;
They kill us for their sport.
Ibid. Line 36
Sunshine and rain at once; her smiles
and tears.
Ibid. Sc. 3, Line 20
It is the stars,
The stars above us, govern our con-
ditions.
Ibid. Line 34
Our foster-nurse of nature is repose.
Ibid. Sc. 4, Line 12
In nothing am I chang'd
But in my garments.
Ibid. Sc. 6, Line 9
Come on, sir; here's the place: —
stand still. —
How fearful
And dizzy 'tis to cast one's eyes so low!
The crows and choughs that wing the
midway air
Show scarce so gross as beetles: half
way down
Hangs one that gathers samphire,
dreadful trade!

Methinks he seems no bigger than his
head:
The fishermen that walk upon the beach
Appear like mice.

King Lear. Act IV, Sc. 6, Line 11

Nature's above art in that respect.

Ibid. Line 87

Ay, every inch a king.

Ibid. Line 110

The wren goes to't, and the small gilded
fly
Does lecher in my sight.

Ibid. Line 115

Give me an ounce of civet, good
apothecary, to sweeten my imagination.

Ibid. Line 133

A man may see how this world goes
with no eyes. Look with thine ears: see
how yond justice rails upon yon simple
thief. Hark, in thine ear: change places;
and, handy-dandy, which is the justice,
which is the thief?

Ibid. Line 154

Through tatter'd clothes small vices do
appear;
Robes and furr'd gowns hide all. Plate
sin with gold,
And the strong lance of justice hurtless
breaks;
Arm it in rags, a pigmy's straw does
pierce it.

Ibid. Line 169

When we are born, we cry that we are
come
To this great stage of fools. — This' a
good block: —
It were a delicate stratagem to shoe
A troop of horse with felt: I'll put't in
proof;
And when I have stol'n upon these
sons-in-law,
Then, kill, kill, kill, kill, kill, kill!

Ibid. Line 187

Mine enemy's dog,
Though he had bit me, should have
stood that night
Against my fire.

Ibid. Sc. 7, Line 36

I am a very foolish, fond old man,
Fourscore and upward, not an hour
more or less;
And, to deal plainly,

I fear I am not in my perfect mind.

King Lear. Act IV, Sc. 7, Line 60

Pray you now, forget and forgive.

Ibid. Line 84

Men must endure
Their going hence, even as their com-
ing hither.
Ripeness is all.

Ibid. Act V, Sc. 2, Line 9

Come, let's away to prison;
We two alone will sing like birds i' the
cage:
When thou dost ask me blessing, I'll
kneel down,
And ask of thee forgiveness: and we'll
live,
And pray, and sing, and tell old tales
and laugh
At gilded butterflies, and hear poor
rogues
Talk of court news; and we'll talk with
them too,
Who loses, and who wins; who's in,
who's out;
And take upon's the mystery of things,
As if we were God's spies; and we'll
wear out,
In a wall'd prison, packs and sets of
great ones
That ebb and flow by the moon.

Ibid. Sc. 3, Line 8

Upon such sacrifices, my Cordelia,
The gods themselves throw incense.

Ibid. Line 20

The gods are just, and of our pleasant
vices
Make instruments to plague us.

Ibid. Line 172

The wheel is come full circle.

Ibid. Line 176

His flaw'd heart, —
Alack! too weak the conflict to support;
'Twixt two extremes of passion, joy and
grief,
Burst smilingly.

Ibid. Line 198

Her voice was ever soft,
Gentle, and low, an excellent thing in
woman.

Ibid. Line 274

And my poor fool is hang'd! No, no,
no life!

Why should a dog, a horse, a rat, have
life,
And thou no breath at all? Thou'lt come
no more,
Never, never, never, never, never!
Pray you, undo this button.
King Lear. Act V, Sc. 3, Line 307

Vex not his ghost: O! let him pass! he
hates him
That would upon the rack of this tough
world
Stretch him out longer.
Ibid. Line 315

The weight of this sad time we must
obey;
Speak what we feel, not what we ought
to say.
The oldest hath borne most: we that
are young
Shall never see so much, nor live so
long.
Ibid. Line 325

First Witch. When shall we three meet
again
In thunder, lightning, or in rain?
Second Witch. When the hurlyburly's
done,
When the battle's lost and won.
Macbeth [*1605–1606*]. *Act I,
Sc. 1, Line 1*

Fair is foul, and foul is fair:
Hover through the fog and filthy air.
Ibid. Line 12

Banners flout the sky.
Ibid. Sc. 2, Line 50

A sailor's wife had chestnuts in her lap,
And munch'd, and munch'd, and
munch'd: "Give me," quoth I:
"Aroint thee, witch!" the rump-fed
ronyon cries.
Ibid. Sc. 3, Line 4

Sleep shall neither night nor day
Hang upon his pent-house lid.
Ibid. Line 19

Dwindle, peak, and pine.
Ibid. Line 23

If you can look into the seeds of time,
And say which grain will grow and
which will not.
Ibid. Line 58

Stands not within the prospect of belief.
Macbeth. Act I, Sc. 3, Line 74

The earth hath bubbles, as the water
has,
And these are of them.
Ibid. Line 79

The insane root
That takes the reason prisoner.
Ibid. Line 84

And oftentimes, to win us to our harm,
The instruments of darkness tell us
truths,
Win us with honest trifles, to betray 's
In deepest consequence.
Ibid. Line 123

I am Thane of Cawdor:
If good, why do I yield to that sug-
gestion
Whose horrid image doth unfix my hair
And make my seated heart knock at my
ribs,
Against the use of nature? Present fears
Are less than horrible imaginings.
Ibid. Line 134

Come what come may,
Time and the hour runs through the
roughest day.
Ibid. Line 146

Nothing in his life
Became him like the leaving it; he died
As one that had been studied in his
death
To throw away the dearest thing he
owed,
As 'twere a careless trifle.
Ibid. Sc. 4, Line 7

There's no art
To find the mind's construction in the
face:
He was a gentleman on whom I built
An absolute trust.
Ibid. Line 11

More is thy due than more than all can
pay.
Ibid. Line 21

Glamis thou art, and Cawdor; and shalt
be
What thou art promis'd. Yet do I fear
thy nature;

It is too full o' the milk of human kindness [1]
To catch the nearest way.
> *Macbeth. Act I, Sc. 5, Line 16*

The raven himself is hoarse
That croaks the fatal entrance of Dun-
can
Under my battlements. Come, you
spirits
That tend on mortal thoughts! unsex
me here,
And fill me from the crown to the toe
top full
Of direst cruelty; make thick my blood,
Stop up the access and passage to re-
morse,
That no compunctious visitings of na-
ture
Shake my fell purpose.
> *Ibid. Line 38*

Nor heaven peep through the blanket
of the dark,
To cry "Hold, hold!"
> *Ibid. Line 53*

Your face, my thane, is as a book where
men
May read strange matters. To beguile
the time,
Look like the time; bear welcome in
your eye,
Your hand, your tongue: look like the
innocent flower,
But be the serpent under 't.
> *Ibid. Line 63*

Duncan. This castle hath a pleasant
seat; the air
Nimbly and sweetly recommends itself
Unto our gentle senses.
Banquo. This guest of summer,
The temple-haunting martlet, does ap-
prove
By his lov'd mansionry that the heav-
en's breath
Smells wooingly here: no jutty, frieze,
Buttress, nor coign of vantage, but this
bird
Hath made his pendent bed and procre-
ant cradle:

[1] The thunder of your words has soured
the milk of human kindness in my heart. —
RICHARD BRINSLEY SHERIDAN: *The Rivals*
[1775], *Act III, Sc. 4*

Where they most breed and haunt, I
have observed
The air is delicate.
> *Macbeth. Act I, Sc. 6, Line 1*

If it were done when 'tis done, then
'twere well
It were done quickly; if the assassina-
tion
Could trammel up the consequence,
and catch
With his surcease success; that but this
blow
Might be the be-all and the end-all here,
But here, upon this bank and shoal of
time,
We'd jump the life to come. But in
these cases
We still have judgment here; that we
but teach
Bloody instructions, which, being
taught, return
To plague the inventor; this even-
handed justice
Commends the ingredients of our poi-
son'd chalice
To our own lips.
> *Ibid. Sc. 7, Line 1*

Besides, this Duncan
Hath borne his faculties so meek, hath
been
So clear in his great office, that his vir-
tues
Will plead like angels, trumpet-tongued
against
The deep damnation of his taking-off;
And pity, like a naked new-born babe,
Striding the blast, or heaven's cheru-
bim, horsed
Upon the sightless couriers of the air,
Shall blow the horrid deed in every eye,
That tears shall drown the wind. I have
no spur
To prick the sides of my intent, but only
Vaulting ambition, which o'erleaps it-
self
And falls on the other.
> *Ibid. Line 16*

I have bought
Golden opinions from all sorts of people.
> *Ibid. Line 32*

Letting "I dare not" wait upon "I would,"
Like the poor cat i' the adage.[1]

Macbeth. Act I, Sc. 7, Line 44

I dare do all that may become a man;
Who dares do more is none.

Ibid. Line 46

　　Nor time nor place
Did then adhere.

Ibid. Line 51

Macbeth. If we should fail, —
Lady Macbeth.　　　　　We fail!
But screw your courage to the sticking-place,
And we'll not fail.

Ibid. Line 59

Memory, the warder of the brain.

Ibid. Line 65

　　There's husbandry in heaven;
Their candles are all out.

Ibid. Act II, Sc. 1, Line 4

　　Shut up
In measureless content.

Ibid. Line 16

Is this a dagger which I see before me,
The handle toward my hand? Come, let me clutch thee:
I have thee not, and yet I see thee still.
Art thou not, fatal vision, sensible
To feeling as to sight? or art thou but
A dagger of the mind, a false creation,
Proceeding from the heat-oppressed brain?

Ibid. Line 33

　　Now o'er the one half-world
Nature seems dead.

Ibid. Line 49

　　Thou sure and firm-set earth,
Hear not my steps, which way they walk, for fear
Thy very stones prate of my whereabout.

Ibid. Line 56

　　The bell invites me.
Hear it not, Duncan; for it is a knell
That summons thee to heaven or to hell.

Ibid. Line 62

It was the owl that shriek'd, the fatal bellman,
Which gives the stern'st good-night.

Ibid. Sc. 2, Line 4

[1] See John Heywood, page 93a.

　　The attempt and not the deed
Confounds us.

Macbeth. Act II, Sc. 2, Line 12

　　Had he not resembled
My father as he slept I had done 't.

Ibid. Line 14

I had most need of blessing, and "Amen"
Stuck in my throat.

Ibid. Line 33

Methought I heard a voice cry, "Sleep no more!
Macbeth does murder sleep!" the innocent sleep,
Sleep that knits up the ravell'd sleave of care,
The death of each day's life, sore labour's bath,
Balm of hurt minds, great nature's second course,
Chief nourisher in life's feast.

Ibid. Line 36

"Glamis hath murder'd sleep, and therefore Cawdor
Shall sleep no more, Macbeth shall sleep no more!"

Ibid. Line 43

　　Infirm of purpose!
Give me the daggers. The sleeping and the dead
Are but as pictures; 'tis the eye of childhood
That fears a painted devil.

Ibid. Line 52

Will all great Neptune's ocean wash this blood
Clean from my hand? No, this my hand will rather
The multitudinous seas incarnadine,
Making the green one red.

Ibid. Line 61

　　Go the primrose way to the everlasting bonfire.

Ibid. Sc. 3, Line 22

　It [drink] provokes the desire, but it takes away the performance.

Ibid. Line 34

The labour we delight in physics pain.

Ibid. Line 56

　　Tongue nor heart
Cannot conceive nor name thee!

Ibid. Line 70

Confusion now hath made his master-
piece!
Most sacrilegious murder hath broke
ope
The Lord's anointed temple, and stole
thence
The life o' the building!
> *Macbeth. Act II, Sc. 3, Line 72*
Downy sleep, death's counterfeit.
> *Ibid. Line 83*
Had I but died an hour before this
chance,
I had liv'd a blessed time; for, from
this instant,
There's nothing serious in mortality,
All is but toys; renown and grace is
dead.
The wine of life is drawn, and the mere
lees
Is left this vault to brag of.
> *Ibid. Line 98*
Who can be wise, amazed, temperate
and furious,
Loyal and neutral, in a moment?
> *Ibid. Line 115*
In the great hand of God I stand, and
thence
Against the undivulg'd pretence I fight
Of treasonous malice.
> *Ibid. Line 137*
To show an unfelt sorrow is an office
Which the false man does easy.
> *Ibid. Line 143*
A falcon, towering in her pride of place,
Was by a mousing owl hawk'd at and
kill'd.
> *Ibid. Sc. 4, Line 12*
I must become a borrower of the night
For a dark hour or twain.
> *Ibid. Act III, Sc. 1, Line 27*
Let every man be master of his time
Till seven at night.
> *Ibid. Line 41*
Murderer.   We are men, my liege.
Macbeth. Ay, in the catalogue ye go
for men.
> *Ibid. Line 91*
I am one, my liege,
Whom the vile blows and buffets of the
world
Have so incensed that I am reckless
what

I do to spite the world.
> *Macbeth. Act III, Sc. 1, Line 108*
So weary with disasters, tugg'd with for-
tune,
That I would set my life on any chance,
To mend it or be rid on 't.
> *Ibid. Line 112*
Things without all remedy
Should be without regard; what's done
is done.
> *Ibid. Sc. 2, Line 11*
We have scotch'd the snake, not kill'd
it.
> *Ibid. Line 13*
Duncan is in his grave;
After life's fitful fever he sleeps well;
Treason has done his worst: nor steel,
nor poison,
Malice domestic, foreign levy, nothing
Can touch him further.
> *Ibid. Line 22*
Come, seeling night,
Scarf up the tender eye of pitiful day,
And with thy bloody and invisible hand,
Cancel and tear to pieces that great
bond
Which keeps me pale! Light thickens,
and the crow
Makes wing to the rooky wood.
> *Ibid. Line 45*
Now spurs the lated traveller apace
To gain the timely inn.
> *Ibid. Sc. 3, Line 6*
But now I am cabin'd, cribb'd, confined,
bound in
To saucy doubts and fears.
> *Ibid. Sc. 4, Line 24*
Now, good digestion wait on appetite,
And health on both!
> *Ibid. Line 38*
Thou canst not say I did it; never shake
Thy gory locks at me.
> *Ibid. Line 50*
The air-drawn dagger.
> *Ibid. Line 62*
I drink to the general joy of the whole
table.
> *Ibid. Line 89*
Thou hast no speculation in those eyes
Which thou dost glare with!
> *Ibid. Line 95*

A thing of custom: 'tis no other;
Only it spoils the pleasure of the time.
      Macbeth. Act III, Sc. 4, Line 97
What man dare, I dare:
Approach thou like the rugged Russian
      bear,
The arm'd rhinoceros, or the Hyrcan
      tiger,
Take any shape but that, and my firm
      nerves
Shall never tremble.
      Ibid. Line 99
Hence, horrible shadow!
Unreal mockery, hence!
      Ibid. Line 106
Stand not upon the order of your going,
But go at once.
      Ibid. Line 119
Macbeth.   What is the night?
Lady Macbeth. Almost at odds with
      morning, which is which.
      Ibid. Line 126
I am in blood
Stepp'd in so far, that, should I wade
      no more,
Returning were as tedious as go o'er.
      Ibid. Line 136
My little spirit, see,
Sits in a foggy cloud, and stays for me.
      Ibid. Sc. 5, Line 35
Double, double toil and trouble;
Fire burn and cauldron bubble.
      Ibid. Act IV, Sc. 1, Line 10
Eye of newt, and toe of frog,
Wool of bat, and tongue of dog.
      Ibid. Line 14
Finger of birth-strangled babe,
Ditch-deliver'd by a drab.
      Ibid. Line 30
By the pricking of my thumbs,
Something wicked this way comes.
      Open, locks,
      Whoever knocks!
      Ibid. Line 44
How now, you secret, black, and mid-
      night hags!
      Ibid. Line 48
A deed without a name.
      Ibid. Line 49
Be bloody, bold, and resolute; laugh to
      scorn

The power of man, for none of woman
      born
Shall harm Macbeth.
      Macbeth. Act IV, Sc. 1, Line 79
I'll make assurance double sure,
And take a bond of fate.
      Ibid. Line 83
Macbeth shall never vanquish'd be un-
      til
Great Birnam wood to high Dunsinane
      hill
Shall come against him.[1]
      Ibid. Line 92
Show his eyes, and grieve his heart;
Come like shadows, so depart!
      Ibid. Line 110
What! will the line stretch out to the
      crack of doom?
      Ibid. Line 117
The weird sisters.
      Ibid. Line 136
When our actions do not,
Our fears do make us traitors.
      Ibid. Sc. 2, Line 3
Things at the worst will cease, or else
      climb upward
To what they were before.
      Ibid. Line 24
Angels are bright still, though the
      brightest fell.
      Ibid. Sc. 3, Line 22
Pour the sweet milk of concord into
      hell,
Uproar the universal peace, confound
All unity on earth.
      Ibid. Line 98
Give sorrow words; the grief that does
      not speak
Whispers the o'er-fraught heart and
      bids it break.
      Ibid. Line 209
What! all my pretty chickens and their
      dam
At one fell swoop?
      Ibid. Line 218
O! I could play the woman with mine
      eyes
And braggart with my tongue.
      Ibid. Line 229

[1] Till Birnam wood remove to Dunsinane,
I cannot taint with fear.
      Act V, Sc. 3, L. 2

Out, damned spot! out, I say!
Macbeth. Act V, Sc. 1, Line 38

Fie, my lord, fie! a soldier, and afeard?
Ibid. Line 40

Yet who would have thought the old man to have had so much blood in him?
Ibid. Line 42

The Thane of Fife had a wife: where is she now?
Ibid. Line 46

All the perfumes of Arabia will not sweeten this little hand.
Ibid. Line 56

Those he commands move only in command,
Nothing in love; now does he feel his title
Hang loose about him, like a giant's robe
Upon a dwarfish thief.
Ibid. Sc. 2, Line 19

The devil damn thee black, thou cream-faced loon!
Where gott'st thou that goose look?
Ibid. Sc. 3, Line 11

My way of life
Is fall'n into the sere, the yellow leaf;
And that which should accompany old age,
As honour, love, obedience, troops of friends,
I must not look to have; but in their stead,
Curses, not loud but deep; mouth-honour, breath,
Which the poor heart would fain deny, and dare not.
Ibid. Line 22

Doctor.   Not so sick, my lord,
As she is troubled with thick-coming fancies,
That keep her from her rest.
Macbeth.   Cure her of that:
Canst thou not minister to a mind diseas'd,
Pluck from the memory a rooted sorrow,
Raze out the written troubles of the brain,
And with some sweet oblivious antidote

Cleanse the stuff'd bosom of that perilous stuff
Which weighs upon the heart?
Doctor.   Therein the patient
Must minister to himself.
Macbeth. Throw physic to the dogs:
I'll none of it.
Macbeth. Act V, Sc. 3, Line 37

I would applaud thee to the very echo,
That should applaud again.
Ibid. Line 53

Hang out our banners on the outward walls;
The cry is still, "They come"; our castle's strength
Will laugh a siege to scorn.
Ibid. Sc. 5, Line 1

My fell of hair
Would at a dismal treatise rouse and stir
As life were in 't. I have supp'd full with horrors.
Ibid. Line 11

Tomorrow, and tomorrow, and tomorrow,
Creeps in this petty pace from day to day,
To the last syllable of recorded time;
And all our yesterdays have lighted fools
The way to dusty death. Out, out, brief candle!
Life's but a walking shadow, a poor player
That struts and frets his hour upon the stage
And then is heard no more: it is a tale
Told by an idiot, full of sound and fury,
Signifying nothing.
Ibid. Line 19

I 'gin to be aweary of the sun.
Ibid. Line 49

Blow, wind! come, wrack!
At least we'll die with harness on our back.
Ibid. Line 51

I bear a charmed life.
Ibid. Sc. 7, Line 41

And be these juggling fiends no more believ'd,
That palter with us in a double sense;

That keep the word of promise to our
ear
And break it to our hope.
> *Macbeth. Act V, Sc. 7, Line 48*

Live to be the show and gaze o' the time.
> *Ibid. Line 53*

Lay on, Macduff,
And damn'd be him that first cries,
"Hold, enough!"
> *Ibid. Line 62*

You shall see in him
The triple pillar of the world trans-
form'd
Into a strumpet's fool.
> *Antony and Cleopatra* [1606–
> 1607]. *Act I, Sc. 1, Line 12*

There's beggary in the love that can
be reckon'd.
> *Ibid. Line 15*

Let Rome in Tiber melt, and the wide
arch
Of the rang'd empire fall! Here is my
space.
> *Ibid. Line 33*

In nature's infinite book of secrecy
A little I can read.
> *Ibid. Sc. 2, Line 11*

On the sudden
A Roman thought hath struck him.
> *Ibid. Line 90*

Eternity was in our lips and eyes,
Bliss in our brows bent.
> *Ibid. Sc. 3, Line 35*

O! my oblivion is a very Antony,
And I am all forgotten.
> *Ibid. Line 90*

Give me to drink mandragora.[1] . . .
That I might sleep out this great gap
of time
My Antony is away.
> *Ibid. Sc. 5, Line 4*

The demi-Atlas of this earth, the arm
And burgonet of men.
> *Ibid. Line 23*

"Where's my serpent of old Nile?"
> *Ibid. Line 25*

A morsel for a monarch.
> *Ibid. Line 31*

My salad days,
When I was green in judgment.
> *Ibid. Line 73*

[1] See *Othello,* page 188b.

We, ignorant of ourselves,
Beg often our own harms, which the
wise powers
Deny us for our good; so find we profit
By losing of our prayers.
> *Antony and Cleopatra. Act II,
> Sc. 1, Line 5*

Epicurean cooks
Sharpen with cloyless sauce his appetite.
> *Ibid. Line 24*

You patch'd up your excuses.
> *Ibid. Sc. 2, Line 60*

The barge she sat in, like a burnish'd
throne,
Burn'd on the water; the poop was
beaten gold,
Purple the sails, and so perfumed that
The winds were love-sick with them;
the oars were silver,
Which to the tune of flutes kept stroke,
and made
The water which they beat to follow
faster,
As amorous of their strokes. For her
own person,
It beggar'd all description.
> *Ibid. Line 199*

Age cannot wither her, nor custom stale
Her infinite variety; other women cloy
The appetites they feed, but she makes
hungry
Where most she satisfies; for vilest
things
Become themselves in her, that the holy
priests
Bless her when she is riggish.
> *Ibid. Line 243*

I have not kept my square; but that to
come
Shall all be done by the rule.
> *Ibid. Sc. 3, Line 6*

'Twas merry when
You wager'd on your angling; when
your diver
Did hang a salt-fish on his hook, which
he
With fervency drew up.
> *Ibid. Sc. 5, Line 15*

Though it be honest, it is never good
To bring bad news.
> *Ibid. Line 85*

Come, thou monarch of the vine,
Plumpy Bacchus with pink eyne!
> *Antony and Cleopatra. Act II,*
> *Sc. 7, Line 120*

Who does i' the wars more than his
captain can
Becomes his captain's captain.
> *Ibid. Act III, Sc. 1, Line 21*

Celerity is never more admir'd
Than by the negligent.
> *Ibid. Sc. 7, Line 7*

We have kiss'd away
Kingdoms and provinces.
> *Ibid. Sc. 8, Line 7*

He wears the rose
Of youth upon him.
> *Ibid. Sc. 13, Line 20*

Men's judgments are
A parcel of their fortunes, and things
outward
Do draw the inward quality after them,
To suffer all alike.
> *Ibid. Line 31*

Let's have one other gaudy night.
> *Ibid. Line 182*

To business that we love we rise be-
time,
And go to 't with delight.
> *Ibid. Act IV, Sc. 4, Line 20*

This morning, like the spirit of a youth
That means to be of note, begins be-
• times.
> *Ibid. Line 26*

O infinite virtue! com'st thou smiling
from
The world's great snare uncaught?
> *Ibid. Sc. 8, Line 17*

The shirt of Nessus is upon me.
> *Ibid. Sc. 10, Line 56*

Sometimes we see a cloud that's drag-
onish;
A vapour sometime like a bear or lion,
A tower'd citadel, a pendant rock,
A forked mountain, or blue promontory
With trees upon 't.
> *Ibid. Sc. 12, Line 2*

That which is now a horse, even with
a thought
The rack dislimns, and makes it in-
distinct,
As water is in water.
> *Ibid. Line 9*

Unarm, Eros; the long day's task is
done,
And we must sleep.
> *Antony and Cleopatra. Act IV,*
> *Sc. 12, Line 35*

But I will be
A bridegroom in my death, and run
into 't
As to a lover's bed.
> *Ibid. Line 99*

I am dying, Egypt, dying; only
I here importune death awhile, until
Of many thousand kisses the poor last
I lay upon thy lips.
> *Ibid. Sc. 13, Line 18*

O! wither'd is the garland of the war,
The soldier's pole is fall'n; young boys
and girls
Are level now with men; the odds is
gone,
And there is nothing left remarkable
Beneath the visiting moon.
> *Ibid. Line 64*

Let's do it after the high Roman fashion.
> *Ibid. Line 87*

And it is great
To do that thing that ends all other
deeds,
Which shackles accidents, and bolts up
change.
> *Ibid. Act V, Sc. 2, Line 4*

For his bounty,
There was no winter in 't; an autumn
'twas
That grew the more by reaping.
> *Ibid. Line 86*

If there be, or ever were, one such,
It's past the size of dreaming.
> *Ibid. Line 96*

The bright day is done,
And we are for the dark.
> *Ibid. Line 192*

Mechanic slaves
With greasy aprons, rules, and hammers.
> *Ibid. Line 208*

A woman is a dish for the gods if the
devil dress her not.
> *Ibid. Line 274*

I have
Immortal longings in me.
　　　Antony and Cleopatra. Act V,
　　　　　　　Sc. 2, Line 282

If thou and nature can so gently part,
The stroke of death is as a lover's
　　pinch,
Which hurts, and is desir'd.
　　　　　　　Ibid. Line 296

Dost thou not see my baby at my
　　breast,
That sucks the nurse asleep?
　　　　　　　Ibid. Line 311

As she would catch another Antony
In her strong toil of grace.
　　　　　　　Ibid. Line 348

　　The gods sent not
Corn for the rich men only.
　　　Coriolanus [1607–1608]. *Act I,*
　　　　　　　Sc. 1, Line 213

Had I a dozen sons, each in my love
alike and none less dear than thine and
my good Marcius, I had rather eleven
die nobly for their country than one
voluptuously surfeit out of action.
　　　　　Ibid. Sc. 3, Line 24

　　All the yarn she spun in Ulysses' absence did but fill Ithaca full of moths.
　　　　　　　Ibid. Line 93

Nature teaches beasts to know their
friends.
　　　　Ibid. Act II, Sc. 1, Line 6

　　A cup of hot wine with not a drop of
allaying Tiber in't.[1]
　　　　　　　Ibid Line 52

　　Bid them wash their faces,
And keep their teeth clean.
　　　　　Ibid. Sc. 3, Line 65

I thank you for your voices: thank you,
Your most sweet voices.
　　　　　　　Ibid. Line 179

The mutable, rank-scented many.
　　　　Ibid. Act III, Sc. 1, Line 65

Hear you this Triton of the minnows?
　　Mark you
His absolute "shall"?
　　　　　　　Ibid. Line 88

---

[1] When flowing cups pass swiftly round
With no allaying Thames.
　　RICHARD LOVELACE: *To Althea from
　　　　　　Prison* [1649], *St. 2*

Enough, with over-measure.
　　　Coriolanus. Act III, Sc. 1, Line 139

What is the city but the people?
　　　　　　　Ibid. Line 198

His nature is too noble for the world:
He would not flatter Neptune for his
　　trident,
Or Jove for 's power to thunder. His
　　heart's his mouth:
What his breast forges, that his tongue
　　must vent;
And, being angry, does forget that ever
He heard the name of death.
　　　　　　　Ibid. Line 254

That it shall hold companionship in
　　peace
With honour, as in war.
　　　　　Ibid. Sc. 2, Line 49

　　I do love
My country's good with a respect more
　　tender,
More holy, more profound, than mine
　　own life.
　　　　　Ibid. Sc. 3, Line 109

　　Pride
Which out of daily fortune ever taints
The happy man.
　　　　Ibid. Act IV, Sc. 7, Line 37

So our virtues
Lie in the interpretation of the time.
　　　　　　　Ibid. Line 49

You know the very road into his kind-
　　ness,
And cannot lose your way.
　　　　Ibid. Act V, Sc. 1, Line 60

　　Chaste as the icicle
That's curdied by the frost from purest
　　snow
And hangs on Dian's temple.
　　　　　Ibid. Sc. 3, Line 65

　　Is't possible that so short a time can
alter the condition of a man?
　　　　　Ibid. Sc. 4, Line 10

They'll give him death by inches.
　　　　　　　Ibid. Line 43

Splitting the air with noise.
　　　　　Ibid. Sc. 5, Line 52

If you have writ your annals true, 'tis
　　there
That, like an eagle in a dove-cote, I

Flutter'd your Volscians in Corioli:
Alone I did it.
Coriolanus. Act V, Sc. 5, Line 114
Thou hast done a deed whereat valour
will weep.
Ibid. Line 135
He shall have a noble memory.
Ibid. Line 155
'Tis not enough to help the feeble up,
But to support him after.
Timon of Athens [*1607–1608*].
Act I, Sc. 1, Line 108
I call the gods to witness.
Ibid. Line 138
Satiety of commendations.
Ibid. Line 167
Ceremony was but devis'd at first
To set a gloss on faint deeds, hollow
welcomes,
Recanting goodness, sorry ere 'tis
shown;
But where there is true friendship, there
needs none.
Ibid. Sc. 2, Line 15
Here's that which is too weak to be a
sinner,
Honest water, which ne'er left man i'
the mire.[1]
Ibid. Line 60
Immortal gods, I crave no pelf;
I pray for no man but myself:
Grant I may never prove so fond,
To trust man on his oath or bond.
Ibid. Line 64
Men shut their doors against a setting
sun.
Ibid. Line 152
Every room
Hath blazed with lights and bray'd with
minstrelsy
Ibid. Act II, Sc. 2, Line 170
Every man has his fault, and honesty
is his.
Ibid. Act III, Sc. 1, Line 30
Policy sits above conscience.
Ibid. Sc. 2, Line 95
Nothing emboldens sin so much as
mercy.
Ibid. Sc. 5, Line 3

[1] Inscribed on the drinking fountain in the market-square of Stratford-on-Avon.

You fools of fortune, trencher-friends,
time's flies.
Timon of Athens. Act III, Sc. 6,
Line 107
We have seen better days.
Ibid. Act IV, Sc. 2, Line 27
O! the fierce wretchedness that glory
brings us.
Ibid. Line 30
I am Misanthropos, and hate mankind.
Ibid. Sc. 3, Line 53
I'll example you with thievery:
The sun's a thief, and with his great
attraction
Robs the vast sea; the moon's an ar-
rant thief,
And her pale fire she snatches from the
sun;
The sea's a thief, whose liquid surge re-
solves
The moon into salt tears; the earth's a
thief,
That feeds and breeds by a composture
stolen
From general excrement: each thing's
a thief.
Ibid. Line 441
Life's uncertain voyage.
Ibid. Act V, Sc. 1, Line 207
As an arrow shot
From a well-experienc'd archer hits the
mark
His eye doth level at.
Pericles [*1608–1609*]. *Act I, Sc. 1,*
Line 163
The sad companion, dull-eyed melan-
choly.
Ibid. Sc. 2, Line 2
Third Fisherman. Master, I marvel
how the fishes live in the sea.
First Fisherman. Why, as men do
aland; the great ones eat up the little
ones.[1]
Ibid. Act II, Sc. 1, Line 29
Lest the bargain should catch cold
and starve.
Cymbeline [*1609–1610*]. *Act I,*
Sc. 4, Line 186

[1] Men lived like fishes; the great ones devoured the small. — ALGERNON SIDNEY: *Dis-*
courses on Government [1698], *Chap. 2,*
Sect. XVIII

Hath his bellyful of fighting.
> *Cymbeline. Act II, Sc. 1, Line 24*

How bravely thou becomest thy bed!
> *Ibid. Sc. 2, Line 15*

The most patient man in loss, the most coldest that ever turned up ace.
> *Ibid. Sc. 3, Line 1*

Hark! hark! the lark at heaven's gate sings,
And Phoebus 'gins arise,[1]
His steeds to water at those springs
  On chaliced flowers that lies;
And winking Mary-buds begin
  To ope their golden eyes:
With everything that pretty is,
  My lady sweet, arise.
> *Ibid. Line 22*

As chaste as unsunn'd snow.
> *Ibid. Sc. 5, Line 13*

Some griefs are med'cinable.
> *Ibid. Act III, Sc. 2, Line 33*

Prouder than rustling in unpaid-for silk.
> *Ibid. Sc. 3, Line 24*

So slippery that
The fear's as bad as falling.
> *Ibid. Line 48*

The game is up.
> *Ibid. Line 107*

Slander,
Whose edge is sharper than the sword, whose tongue
Outvenoms all the worms of Nile, whose breath
Rides on the posting winds and doth belie
All corners of the world.
> *Ibid. Sc. 4, Line 35*

Against self-slaughter
There is a prohibition so divine
That cravens my weak hand.
> *Ibid. Line 78*

It is no act of common passage, but
A strain of rareness.
> *Ibid. Line 94*

Weariness
Can snore upon the flint when resty sloth
Finds the down pillow hard.
> *Ibid. Sc. 6, Line 33*

[1] See Lyly, page 112b.

An angel! or, if not,
An earthly paragon!
> *Cymbeline. Act III, Sc. 6, Line 42*

Society is no comfort
To one not sociable.
> *Ibid. Act IV, Sc. 2, Line 12*

I wear not
My dagger in my mouth.
> *Ibid. Line 78*

And put
My clouted brogues from off my feet.
> *Ibid. Line 213*

Fear no more the heat o' the sun,
  Nor the furious winter's rages;
Thou thy worldly task hast done,
  Home art gone, and ta'en thy wages.
Golden lads and girls all must,
As chimney-sweepers, come to dust.
> *Ibid. Line 258*

Fortune brings in some boats that are not steer'd.
> *Ibid. Sc. 3, Line 46*

By medicine life may be prolong'd, yet death
Will seize the doctor too.
> *Ibid. Act V, Sc. 5, Line 29*

To the onlie begetter.
> *Sonnets [Published 1609].*
> *Dedication*

When forty winters shall besiege my brow,
And dig deep trenches in thy beauty's field.
> *Sonnet 2*

Thou art thy mother's glass, and she in thee
Calls back the lovely April of her prime.
> *Sonnet 3*

Music to hear, why hear'st thou music sadly?
Sweets with sweet war not, joy delights in joy.
> *Sonnet 8*

Shall I compare thee to a summer's day?
Thou art more lovely and more temperate:
Rough winds do shake the darling buds of May,
And summer's lease hath all too short a date.
> *Sonnet 18*

But thy eternal summer shall not fade.
Sonnet 18

The painful warrior famoused for fight,
After a thousand victories, once foil'd,
Is from the books of honour razed quite,
And all the rest forgot for which he
toil'd.
Sonnet 25

When in disgrace with fortune and
men's eyes
I all alone beweep my outcast state.
And trouble deaf heaven with my boot-
less cries.
Sonnet 29

Desiring this man's art, and that man's
scope,
With what I most enjoy contented
least;
Yet in these thoughts myself almost
despising.
Ibid.

For thy sweet love remember'd such
wealth brings
That then I scorn to change my state
with kings.
Ibid.

When to the sessions of sweet silent
thought
I summon up remembrance of things
past,
I sigh the lack of many a thing I sought,
And with old woes new wail my dear
times' waste.
Sonnet 30

But if the while I think on thee, dear
friend,
All losses are restor'd and sorrows end.
Ibid.

Full many a glorious morning have I
seen.
Sonnet 33

Roses have thorns, and silver fountains
mud;
Clouds and eclipses stain both moon
and sun,
And loathsome canker lives in sweetest
bud.
All men make faults.
Sonnet 35

For nimble thought can jump both sea
and land.
Sonnet 44

Against that time when thou shalt
strangely pass,
And scarcely greet me with that sun,
thine eye,
When love, converted from the thing it
was,
Shall reasons find of settled gravity.
Sonnet 49

My grief lies onward, and my joy behind.
Sonnet 50

Like stones of worth they thinly placed
are,
Or captain jewels in the carcanet.
Sonnet 52

O! how much more doth beauty beauteous seem
By that sweet ornament which truth
doth give!
Sonnet 54

Not marble, nor the gilded monuments
Of princes, shall outlive this powerful
rhyme.
Sonnet 55

Like as the waves make towards the
pebbled shore,
So do our minutes hasten to their end.
Sonnet 60

Ruin hath taught me thus to ruminate, —
That Time will come and take my
love away.
Sonnet 64

Tir'd with all these, for restful death
I cry.
Sonnet 66

And art made tongue-tied by authority.
Ibid.

And simple truth miscall'd simplicity,
And captive good attending captain ill.
Ibid.

No longer mourn for me when I am
dead
Than you shall hear the surly sullen
bell
Give warning to the world that I am
fled
From this vile world, with vilest worms
to dwell.
Sonnet 71

That time of year thou may'st in me
behold

When yellow leaves, or none, or few, do hang
Upon those boughs which shake against the cold,
Bare ruin'd choirs, where late the sweet birds sang.
Sonnet 73

Clean starved for a look.
Sonnet 75

Your monument shall be my gentle verse,
Which eyes not yet created shall o'er-read;
And tongues to be your being shall rehearse,
When all the breathers of this world are dead;
You still shall live — such virtue hath my pen —
Where breath most breathes, — even in the mouths of men.
Sonnet 81

Who is it that says most? which can say more
Than this rich praise, — that you alone are you?
Sonnet 84

Farewell! thou art too dear for my possessing,
And like enough thou know'st thy estimate.
Sonnet 87

Do not, when my heart hath 'scap'd this sorrow,
Come in the rearward of a conquer'd woe;
Give not a windy night a rainy morrow,
To linger out a purpos'd overthrow.
Sonnet 90

The summer's flower is to the summer sweet,
Though to itself it only live and die.
Sonnet 94

Lilies that fester smell far worse than weeds.
Ibid.

The hardest knife ill-used doth lose his edge.
Sonnet 95

From you I have been absent in the spring,

When proud-pied April, dress'd in all his trim,
Hath put a spirit of youth in everything.
Sonnet 98

Sweets grown common lose their dear delight.
Sonnet 102

To me, fair friend, you never can be old,
For as you were when first your eye I ey'd
Such seems your beauty still.
Sonnet 104

Still constant is a wondrous excellence.
Sonnet 105

When in the chronicle of wasted time
I see descriptions of the fairest wights,
And beauty making beautiful old rime
In praise of ladies dead and lovely knights,
Then, in the blazon of sweet beauty's best,
Of hand, of foot, of lip, of eye, of brow,
I see their antique pen would have exprest
Even such a beauty as you master now.
Sonnet 106

Not mine own fears, nor the prophetic soul
Of the wide world dreaming on things to come
Can yet the lease of my true love control,
Suppos'd as forfeit to a confin'd doom.
The mortal moon hath her eclipse endur'd,
And the sad augurs mock their own presage.
Incertainties now crown themselves assured,
And peace proclaims olives of endless age.
Sonnet 107

That is my home of love; if I have ranged,
Like him that travels, I return again.
Sonnet 109

Alas, 'tis true I have gone here and there,
And made myself a motley to the view,
Gor'd mine own thoughts, sold cheap what is most dear,

Made old offences of affections new.
> *Sonnet 110*

My nature is subdu'd
To what it works in, like the dyer's
    hand.
> *Sonnet 111*

Let me not to the marriage of true
    minds
Admit impediments. Love is not love
Which alters when it alteration finds.
> *Sonnet 116*

O, no! it is an ever-fixed mark,
That looks on tempests and is never
    shaken;
It is the star to every wandering bark.
> *Ibid.*

If this be error, and upon me prov'd,
I never writ, nor no man ever lov'd.
> *Ibid.*

And ruin'd love, when it is built anew,
Grows fairer than at first, more strong,
    far greater.
> *Sonnet 119*

'Tis better to be vile than vile esteem'd,
When not to be receives reproach of be-
    ing;
And the just pleasure lost, which is so
    deem'd,
Not by our feeling, but by others' see-
    ing.
> *Sonnet 121*

No, I am that I am, and they that level
At my abuses reckon up their own.
> *Ibid.*

To kiss the tender inward of thy hand.
> *Sonnet 128*

The expense of spirit in a waste of
    shame
Is lust in action; and till action, lust
Is perjur'd, murd'rous, bloody, full of
    blame,
Savage, extreme, rude, cruel, not to
    trust.
Enjoyed no sooner but despised
    straight;
Past reason hunted; and no sooner had,
Past reason hated, as a swallow'd bait,
On purpose laid to make the taker mad:
Mad in pursuit, and in possession so;
Had, having, and in quest to have,
    extreme;

A bliss in proof, — and prov'd, a very
    woe;
Before, a joy propos'd; behind, a dream.
All this the world well knows; yet none
    knows well
To shun the heaven that leads men to
    this hell.
> *Sonnet 129*

My mistress' eyes are nothing like the
    sun;
Coral is far more red than her lips' red:
If snow be white, why then her breasts
    are dun;
If hairs be wires, black wires grow on
    her head.
> *Sonnet 130*

That full star that ushers in the even.
> *Sonnet 132*

When my love swears that she is made
    of truth,
I do believe her, though I know she lies.
> *Sonnet 138*

Two loves I have of comfort and de-
    spair,
Which like two spirits do suggest me
    still.
> *Sonnet 144*

For I have sworn thee fair, and thought
    thee bright,
Who art as black as hell, as dark as
    night.
> *Sonnet 147*

You pay a great deal too dear for
what's given freely.
> *The Winter's Tale* [1610–1611].
> *Act I, Sc. 1, Line 18*

We were as twinn'd lambs that did frisk
    i' the sun,
And bleat the one at the other: what
    we changed
Was innocence for innocence.
> *Ibid. Sc. 2, Line 67*

One good deed, dying tongueless,
Slaughters a thousand waiting upon
    that.
> *Ibid. Line 92*

Paddling palms and pinching fingers.
> *Ibid. Line 116*

Affection! thy intention stabs the
    centre:
Thou dost make possible things not so
    held,

Communicatest with dreams.
The Winter's Tale. Act I, Sc. 2,
Line 139
He makes a July's day short as December.
Ibid. Line 169
Black brows, they say,
Become some women best, so that there
be not
Too much hair there, but in a semicircle,
Or a half-moon made with a pen.
Ibid. Act II, Sc. 1, Line 8
A sad tale's best for winter.
Ibid. Line 24
There's some ill planet reigns:
I must be patient till the heavens look
With an aspect more favourable.
Ibid. Line 104
The silence often of pure innocence
Persuades when speaking fails.
Ibid. Sc. 2, Line 41
It is a heretic that makes the fire,
Not she which burns in 't.
Ibid. Sc. 3, Line 116
I am a feather for each wind that blows.
Ibid. Line 153
What's gone and what's past help
Should be past grief.
Ibid. Act III, Sc. 2, Line 223
This is fairy gold.
Ibid. Sc. 3, Line 127
Then comes in the sweet o' the year.
Ibid. Act IV, Sc. 2, Line 3
A snapper-up of unconsidered trifles.
Ibid. Line 26
A merry heart goes all the day,
Your sad tires in a mile-a.
Ibid. Line 135
There's rosemary and rue; these keep
Seeming and savour all the winter long.
Ibid. Sc. 3, Line 74
Daffodils,
That come before the swallow dares,
and take
The winds of March with beauty.
Ibid. Line 118
What you do
Still betters what is done.
Ibid. Line 135
When you do dance, I wish you

A wave o' the sea, that you might ever
do
Nothing but that.
The Winter's Tale. Act IV,
Sc. 3, Line 140
I love a ballad in print, a-life, for
then we are sure they are true.
Ibid. Line 262
The self-same sun that shines upon his
court
Hides not his visage from our cottage,
but
Looks on alike.
Ibid. Line 457
To unpathed waters, undreamed shores.
Ibid. Line 580
Prosperity's the very bond of love,
Whose fresh complexion and whose
heart together
Affliction alters.
Ibid. Line 586
Let me have no lying; it becomes
none but tradesmen.
Ibid. Line 747
To purge melancholy.
Ibid. Line 792
Stars, stars!
And all eyes else dead coals.
Ibid. Act V, Sc. 1, Line 67
I was no gentleman born.
Ibid. Sc. 2, Line 146
What fine chisel
Could ever yet cut breath?
Ibid. Sc. 3, Line 78
There's time enough for that.
Ibid. Line 128
He hath no drowning mark upon
him; his complexion is perfect gallows.
The Tempest [*1611–1612*].
Act I, Sc. 1, Line 33
Now would I give a thousand furlongs of sea for an acre of barren
ground.
Ibid. Line 70
I would fain die a dry death.
Ibid. Line 73
What seest thou else
In the dark backward and abysm of
time?
Ibid. Sc. 2, Line 49
I, thus neglecting worldly ends, all dedicated

To closeness and the bettering of my
  mind.
  The Tempest. Act I, Sc. 2, Line 89
    By telling of it,
Made such a sinner of his memory,
To credit his own lie.
                          Ibid. Line 99
    My library
Was dukedom large enough.
                          Ibid. Line 109
    The very rats
Instinctively have quit it.
                          Ibid. Line 147
Knowing I lov'd my books, he furnish'd
  me
From mine own library with volumes
  that   .
I prize above my dukedom.
                          Ibid. Line 166
From the still-vexed Bermoothes.
                          Ibid. Line 229
I will be correspondent to command,
And do my spiriting gently.
                          Ibid. Line 297
Come unto these yellow sands,
  And then take hands:
Curtsied when you have, and kiss'd
  The wild waves whist.
Foot it featly here and there.
                          Ibid. Line 375
This music crept by me upon the waters,
Allaying both their fury, and my pas-
  sion,
With its sweet air.
                          Ibid. Line 389
Full fathom five thy father lies;
  Of his bones are coral made;
Those are pearls that were his eyes:
  Nothing of him that doth fade
But doth suffer a sea-change
Into something rich and strange.[1]
                          Ibid. Line 394
The fringed curtains of thine eye ad-
  vance.
                          Ibid. Line 405
    Less too light winning
Make the prize light.
                          Ibid. Line 448
There's nothing ill can dwell in such a
  temple:

[1] The last three lines are inscribed on Shelley's gravestone.

If the ill spirit have so fair a house,
Good things will strive to dwell with 't.
  The Tempest. Act I, Sc. 2, Line 454
He receives comfort like cold por-
ridge.
                  Ibid. Act II, Sc. 1, Line 10
Gonzalo. Here is everything advanta-
geous to life.
Antonio. True; save means to live.
                          Ibid. Line 52
What is past is prologue.[1]
                          Ibid. Line 261
A very ancient and fish-like smell.
                  Ibid. Sc. 2, Line 27
Misery acquaints a man with strange
bedfellows.
                          Ibid. Line 42
I shall laugh myself to death.
                          Ibid. Line 167
'Ban, 'Ban, Ca-Caliban,
Has a new master — Get a new man.
                          Ibid. Line 197
Ferdinand.   Here's my hand.
Miranda. And mine, with my heart in't.
                  Ibid. Act III, Sc. 1, Line 89
Moon-calf.
                  Ibid. Sc. 2, Line 25
Keep a good tongue in your head.
                          Ibid. Line 41
He that dies pays all debts.
                          Ibid. Line 143
    The isle is full of noises,
Sounds and sweet airs, that give delight,
  and hurt not.
Sometimes a thousand twangling in-
  struments
Will hum about mine ears; and some-
  times voices,
That, if I then had wak'd after long
  sleep,
Will make me sleep again.
                          Ibid. Line 146
    A kind
Of excellent dumb discourse.
                  Ibid. Sc. 3, Line 38
    Do not give dalliance
Too much rein.
                  Ibid. Act IV, Sc. 1, Line 51

[1] Inscription on pedestal under "Female
Figure," East, National Archives Building,
Washington, D.C.

Our revels now are ended. These our
actors,
As I foretold you, were all spirits, and
Are melted into air, into thin air;
And, like the baseless fabric of this
vision,
The cloud-capp'd towers, the gorgeous
palaces,
The solemn temples, the great globe
itself,
Yea, all which it inherit, shall dissolve;
And, like this insubstantial pageant
faded,
Leave not a rack behind. We are such
stuff
As dreams are made on, and our little
life
Is rounded with a sleep.
The Tempest. Act IV, Sc. 1, Line 148

With foreheads villanous low.
Ibid. Line 252

I'll break my staff,
Bury it certain fathoms in the earth,
And, deeper than did ever plummet
sound
I'll drown my book.
Ibid. Act V, Sc. 1, Line 54

Where the bee sucks, there suck I;
In a cowslip's bell I lie.
There I couch when owls do cry.
On the bat's back I do fly
After summer merrily:
Merrily, merrily shall I live now,
Under the blossom that hangs on the
bough.
Ibid. Line 88

O brave new world,
That has such people in't!
Ibid. Line 183

Let us not burden our remembrances
With a heaviness that's gone.
Ibid. Line 199

My ending is despair.
Ibid. Epilogue, Line 15

Order gave each thing view.
King Henry VIII [1613]. Act I,
Sc. 1, Line 44

No man's pie is freed
From his ambitious finger.
Ibid. Line 52

The force of his own merit makes his
way.
King Henry VIII. Act I, Sc. 1,
Line 64

Anger is like
A full-hot horse, who being allow'd his
way,
Self-mettle tires him.
Ibid. Line 132

Heat not a furnace for your foe so hot
That it do singe yourself.
Ibid. Line 140

New customs,
Though they be never so ridiculous,
Nay, let 'em be unmanly, yet are fol-
low'd.
Ibid. Sc. 3, Line 2

The mirror of all courtesy.
Ibid. Act II, Sc. 1, Line 53

Go with me, like good angels, to my end:
And, as the long divorce of steel falls on
me,
Make of your prayers one sweet sacri-
fice,
And lift my soul to heaven.
Ibid. Line 75

This bold bad man.
Ibid. Sc. 2, Line 44

'Tis better to be lowly born,
And range with humble livers in con-
tent,
Than to be perked up in a glistering
grief
And wear a golden sorrow.
Ibid. Sc. 3, Line 19

I would not be a queen
For all the world.
Ibid. Line 45

Orpheus with his lute made trees,
And the mountain-tops that freeze,
Bow themselves when he did sing.
Ibid. Act III, Sc. 1, Line 3

Heaven is above all yet; there sits a
judge
That no king can corrupt.
Ibid. Line 99

'Tis well said again;
And 'tis a kind of good deed to say
well:
And yet words are no deeds.
Ibid. Sc. 2, Line 153

And then to breakfast with
What appetite you have.
> *King Henry VIII. Act III,*
> *Sc. 2, Line 203*

I have touched the highest point of all
my greatness;
And from that full meridian of my
glory,
I haste now to my setting: I shall fall
Like a bright exhalation in the evening,
And no man see me more.
> *Ibid. Line 224*

Press not a falling man too far!
> *Ibid. Line 334*

Farewell! a long farewell, to all my
greatness!
This is the state of man: to-day he puts
forth
The tender leaves of hopes; to-morrow
blossoms,
And bears his blushing honours thick
upon him;
The third day comes a frost, a killing
frost;
And, when he thinks, good easy man,
full surely
His greatness is a-ripening, nips his
root,
And then he falls, as I do. I have ventured,
Like little wanton boys that swim on
bladders,
This many summers in a sea of glory,
But far beyond my depth: my high-
blown pride
At length broke under me, and now has
left me,
Weary and old with service, to the
mercy
Of a rude stream, that must forever
hide me.
Vain pomp and glory of this world, I
hate ye:
I feel my heart new opened. O! how
wretched
Is that poor man that hangs on princes'
favours!
There is, betwixt that smile we would
aspire to,
That sweet aspect of princes, and their
ruin,

More pangs and fears than wars or
women have —
And when he falls, he falls like Lucifer,
Never to hope again.
> *King Henry VIII. Act III,*
> *Sc. 2, Line 352*

A peace above all earthly dignities,
A still and quiet conscience.
> *Ibid. Line 380*

A load would sink a navy.
> *Ibid. Line 384*

And sleep in dull cold marble.
> *Ibid. Line 434*

I charge thee, fling away ambition:
By that sin fell the angels.
> *Ibid. Line 441*

Love thyself last: cherish those hearts
that hate thee;
Corruption wins not more than honesty.
Still in thy right hand carry gentle
peace,
To silence envious tongues: be just, and
fear not:
Let all the ends thou aim'st at be thy
country's,
Thy God's, and truth's; then if thou
fall'st, O Cromwell,
Thou fall'st a blessed martyr!
> *Ibid. Line 444*

Had I but served my God with half the
zeal [1]
I served my king, he would not in mine
age
Have left me naked to mine enemies.
> *Ibid. Line 456*

An old man, broken with the storms of
state,
Is come to lay his weary bones among
ye;
Give him a little earth for charity!
> *Ibid. Act IV, Sc. 2, Line 21*

He gave his honours to the world again,
His blessed part to heaven, and slept in
peace.
> *Ibid. Line 29*

---

[1] Had I served God as well in every part
 As I did serve my king and master still,
 My scope had not this season been so
 short,
 Nor would have had the power to do
 me ill.
 THOMAS CHURCHYARD: *Death of*
 Morton [1593]

So may he rest; his faults lie gently on
him!
> *King Henry VIII. Act IV,*
> *Sc. 2, Line 31*

He was a man
Of an unbounded stomach.
> *Ibid. Line 33*

Men's evil manners live in brass; their
virtues
We write in water.[1]
> *Ibid. Line 45*

He was a scholar, and a ripe and good
one;
Exceeding wise, fair-spoken, and per-
suading;
Lofty and sour to them that loved him
not,
But to those men that sought him sweet
as summer.
> *Ibid. Line 51*

Yet in bestowing, madam,
He was most princely.
> *Ibid. Line 56*

After my death I wish no other herald,
No other speaker of my living actions,
To keep mine honour from corruption,
But such an honest chronicler as Grif-
fith.
> *Ibid. Line 69*

To dance attendance on their lordships'
pleasures.
> *Ibid. Act V, Sc. 2, Line 30*

'Tis a cruelty
To load a falling man.
> *Ibid. Sc. 3, Line 76*

You were ever good at sudden commendations.
> *Ibid. Line 122*

Those about her
From her shall read the perfect ways of
honour.
> *Ibid. Sc. 5, Line 37*

Nor shall this peace sleep with her;
but as when
The bird of wonder dies, the maiden
phoenix,
Her ashes new-create another heir
As great in admiration as herself.
> *Ibid. Line 40*

Wherever the bright sun of heaven shall
shine,

---

[1] See Sir Thomas More, page 86a.

His honour and the greatness of his
name
Shall be, and make new nations.
> *King Henry VIII. Act V, Sc. 5,*
> *Line 51*

A most unspotted lily shall she pass
To the ground, and all the world shall
mourn her.
> *Ibid. Line 62*

Some come to take their ease
And sleep an act or two.
> *Ibid. Epilogue, Line 2*

When as thine eye hath chose the
dame. . . .
Plainly say thou lov'st her well,
And set thy person forth to sell.
> *Sonnets to Sundry Notes of*
> *Music. IV*

The strongest castle, tower, and town,
The golden bullet beats it down.
> *Ibid.*

Have you not heard it said full oft,
A woman's nay doth stand for naught?
> *Ibid.*

Good friend, for Jesu's sake forbear
To dig the dust enclosed here.
Blest be the man that spares these
stones,
Cursed be he that moves my bones.
> *Shakespeare's Epitaph*

JOHN DAVIES
[1565?–1618]

Beauty's but skin deep.[1]
> *A Select Second Husband for*
> *Sir Thomas Overburie's Wife*
> *[1606]. VI*

THOMAS NASH
[1567–1601]

Spring, the sweet spring, is the year's
pleasant king;
Then blooms each thing, then maids
dance in a ring,

---

[1] All the beauty of the world, 'tis but skin
deep. — RALPH VENNING: *Orthodoxe Para-*
doxes [3d ed., 1650], *The Triumph of Assur-*
ance, P. 41
Many a dangerous temptation comes to us
in fine gay colours that are but skin-deep. —
MATHEW HENRY [1662–1714]: *Commen-*
taries, Genesis, III

Cold doth not sting, the pretty birds do
sing.
Cuckoo, jug-jug, pu-we, to-witta-woo!
Spring

Brightness falls from the air;
Queens have died young and fair;
Dust hath closed Helen's eye.
In Time of Pestilence

SIR HENRY WOTTON
[1568–1639]

Love lodged in a woman's breast
Is but a guest.
A Woman's Heart [1651]

How happy is he born and taught,
That serveth not another's will;
Whose armour is his honest thought,
And simple truth his utmost skill!
The Character of a Happy Life
[1651]. Stanza 1

Who God doth late and early pray
More of his grace than gifts to lend;
And entertains the harmless day
With a religious book or friend.
Ibid. Stanza 5

Lord of himself, though not of lands;
And having nothing, yet hath all.[1]
Ibid. Stanza 6

You meaner beauties of the night,
That poorly satisfy our eyes
More by your number than your light;
You common people of the skies, —
What are you when the moon[2] shall
rise?
On his Mistress, the Queen of
Bohemia.[3] Stanza 1

He first deceased; she for a little tried
To live without him, liked it not, and
died.
Upon the Death of Sir Albert
Morton's Wife [1651]

[1] As having nothing, and yet possessing all
things. — *2 Corinthians, VI, 10*
See Terence, page 31b.
[2] "Sun" in *Reliquiae Wottonianae* [eds.
1651, 1654, 1672, 1685]
[3] This was printed with music as early as
1624, in Est's "Sixth Set of Books," etc., and
is found in many MSS. — JOHN HANNAH:
The Courtly Poets [1870]

Hanging was the worst use a man
could be put to.
The Disparity Between Buck-
ingham and Essex [1651]

An ambassador is an honest man sent
to lie abroad for the commonwealth.[1]
Reliquiae Wottonianae [1651]

The itch of disputing will prove the
scab of churches.[2]
A Panegyric to King Charles [1651]

SIR JOHN DAVIES
[1569–1626]

What can we know? or what can we
discern,
When error chokes the windows of the
mind?
The Vanity of Human Learning
[1596]. Stanza 15

We that acquaint ourselves with ev'ry
zone,
And pass both tropics, and behold each
pole,
When we come home are to ourselves
unknown,
And unacquainted still with our own
soul.
Ibid. Stanza 25

I know my soul hath power to know all
things,
Yet is she blind and ignorant in all:
I know I'm one of Nature's little kings,
Yet to the least and vilest things am
thrall.
Ibid. Stanza 44

I know my life's a pain, and but a span;
I know my sense is mock'd in ev'ry
thing:
And to conclude, I know myself a man,

[1] In a letter to Velserus [1612] Wotton
says that this "merry definition of an ambas-
sador . . I had chanced to set down at my
friend's, Mr. Christopher Fleckamore, in his
Album."
[2] He directed the stone over his grave to be
inscribed:
Hic jacet hujus sententiae primus auctor:
DISPUTANDI PRURITUS ECCLESIARUM SCABIES.
Nomen alias quaere
(Here lies the author of this phrase: "The
itch for disputing is the sore of churches."
Seek his name elsewhere.) (IZAAK WALTON:
Life of Wotton [1651])

Which is a proud, and yet a wretched
   thing.
        The Vanity of Human Learning.
                Stanza 45

MARTYN PARKER
[?–1656]

Ye gentlemen of England
   That live at home at ease,
Ah! little do you think upon
   The dangers of the seas.
                 Song
When the stormy winds do blow.[1]
                 Ibid.

THOMAS MIDDLETON
[1570–1627]

Better the day, better the deed.[2]
      Michaelmas Term [1607].
               Act III, Sc. 1
As true as I live.
      The Family of Love [1608].
               Act V, Sc. 3
   That disease
Of which all old men sicken, — ava-
   rice.[3]
        The Roaring Girl [1611].
               Act I, Sc. 1
Beat all your feathers as flat down as
   pancakes.
                 Ibid.
As the case stands.
   The Old Law [1656]. *Act II, Sc. 1*
On his last legs.
        Ibid. Act V, Sc. 1
  As old Chaucer was wont to say, that
broad famous English poet.
   More Dissemblers besides Women
         [1657]. *Act I, Sc. 4*

[1] When the battle rages loud and long,
  And the stormy winds do blow.
       THOMAS CAMPBELL [1777–1844]:
          Ye Mariners of England
[2] The better the day, the worse deed. —
MATHEW HENRY [1662–1714]: *Commen-
taries, Genesis, III*
  The better the day the better the deed. —
DICKENS: *Edwin Drood* [1870], *Chap. 10*
[3] So for a good old-gentlemanly vice
  I think I must take up with avarice.
      BYRON: *Don Juan* [1819–1824],
           Canto I, St. 216

'Tis a stinger.[1]
   More Dissemblers besides Women.
              Act III, Sc. 2
How many honest words have suf-
fered corruption since Chaucer's days!
   No Wit, No Help, Like a Woman's
        [1657]. *Act II, Sc. 1*
Anything for a Quiet Life.
        Title of play [1662]
This was a good week's labour.
      Anything for a Quiet Life.
               Act V, Sc. 3
Black spirits and white, red spirits and
   gray,
Mingle, mingle, mingle, you that mingle
   may.[2]
      The Witch [*published 1778*].
               Act V, Sc. 2
Though I say it that should not say it.
   Wit at Several Weapons
   (*probably in collaboration
   with William Rowley* [1585?–
   1642?]). *Act II, Sc. 2*

THOMAS DEKKER
[1570?–1641]

The reason why fond women love to buy
Adulterate complexion: here 'tis
   read, —
False colours last after the true be dead.
   *A Description of a Lady by Her
                Lover*
This age thinks better of a gilded fool
Than of a threadbare saint in wisdom's
   school.
        Old Fortunatus [1600]
Honest labour bears a lovely face.
   Patient Grissell [1603]. *Act I, Sc. 1*
Cast away care, he that loves sorrow
Lengthens not a day, nor can buy to-
   morrow;
Money is trash, and he that will spend
   it,
Let him drink merrily, fortune will
   send it.
   The Sun's Darling [1624] (*Re-
       vised by John Ford*)

[1] He 'as had a stinger. — FLETCHER: *Wit
without Money* [1639], *Act IV, Sc. 1*
[2] These lines are introduced into *Macbeth,
Act IV, Sc. 1.* According to Steevens, "the
song was, in all probability, a traditional one."

The best of men
That e'er wore earth about him was a
   sufferer;
A soft, meek, patient, humble, tranquil
   spirit,
The first true gentleman that ever
   breathed.
   The Honest Whore. Part I [*1604*],
           Act I, Sc. 12

We are ne'er like angels till our passion
   dies.
   Ibid. Part II [*1630*], *Act I, Sc. 2*

JOHN DONNE [1]
[1573–1631]

I wonder by my troth, what thou, and I
Did, till we lov'd? were we not wean'd
   till then?
But suck'd on country pleasures, child-
   ishly?
Or snorted we in the seven sleepers'
   den?
      The Good Morrow. Stanza 1

And now good morrow to our waking
   souls,
Which watch not one another out of
   fear;
For love, all love of other sights controls,
And makes one little room, an everywhere.
Let sea-discoverers to new worlds have
   gone,
Let maps to other, worlds on worlds
   have shown,
Let us possess one world, each hath one,
   and is one.
           Ibid. Stanza 2

My face in thine eye, thine in mine
   appears,
And true plain hearts do in the faces
   rest,
Where can we find two better hemi-
   spheres

---

[1] Except where otherwise stated, these quotations are from the 1633 edition. The "Songs and Sonnets" were written by Donne before the turn of the century, according to Ben Jonson "ere he was twenty-five years old," but there is no evidence to show the exact date of their composition.

Without sharp North, without declining
   West?
      The Good Morrow. Stanza 3

Go, and catch a falling star,
   Get with child a mandrake root,
Tell me, where all past years are,
   Or who cleft the Devil's foot.
           Song. Stanza 1

And swear
   No where
Lives a woman true and fair.
           Ibid. Stanza 2

Though she were true, when you met
   her,
And last, till you write your letter,
      Yet she
      Will be
False, ere I come, to two, or three.
           Ibid. Stanza 3

I have done one braver thing
   Than all the Worthies did;
And yet a braver thence doth spring,
   Which is, to keep that hid.
      The Undertaking, Stanza 1

But he who loveliness within
   Hath found, all outward loathes,
For he who colour loves, and skin,
   Loves but their oldest clothes.
           Ibid. Stanza 4

And dare love that, and say so too,
And forget the He and She.
           Ibid. Stanza 5

Busy old fool, unruly Sun,
   Why dost thou thus,
Through windows, and through cur-
   tains call on us?
Must to thy motions lovers' seasons
   run?
      The Sun Rising. Stanza 1

She is all states, and all princes, I,
Nothing else is.
           Ibid. Stanza 3

For God sake hold your tongue, and
   let me love.
      The Canonization. Stanza 1

I am two fools, I know,
For loving, and for saying so
In whining poetry.
      The Triple Fool. Stanza 1

Who are a little wise, the best fools be.
           Ibid. Stanza 2

Sweetest love, I do not go,
　For weariness of thee,
Nor in hope the world can show
　A fitter love for me;
　　But since that I
Must die at last, 'tis best,
　To use my self in jest
Thus by feign'd deaths to die.
　　　　　　Song. Stanza 1

When I died last, and dear, I die
As often as from thee I go.
　　　　　　The Legacy. Stanza 1

Oh do not die, for I shall hate
All women so, when thou art gone.
　　　　　　The Fever. Stanza 1

Twice or thrice had I loved thee,
Before I knew thy face or name;
So in a voice, so in a shapeless flame,
Angels affect us oft, and worshipp'd be.
　　　　　Air and Angels. Stanza 1

Just such disparity
As is 'twixt air and Angels' purity,
'Twixt women's love, and men's will
　ever be.
　　　　　　Ibid. Stanza 2

All Kings, and all their favorites,
All glory of honours, beauties, wits,
The sun itself, which makes times, as
　they pass,
Is elder by a year, now, than it was
When thou and I first one another saw:
All other things, to their destruction
　draw,
　Only our love hath no decay;
This, no tomorrow hath, nor yesterday,
Running, it never runs from us away,
But truly keeps his first, last, everlast-
　ing day.
　　　　　　The Anniversary. Stanza 1

　At their best
Sweetness and wit, they are but
　mummy, possess'd.
　　　　　Love's Alchemy. Stanza 2

Come live with me, and be my love,
And we will some new pleasures prove
Of golden sands, and crystal brooks,
With silken lines, and silver hooks.
　　　　　　The Bait.[1] Stanza 1

Dull sublunary lovers' love
　(Whose soul is sense) cannot admit
Absence, because it doth remove
　Those things which elemented it.
　　*A Valediction Forbidding Mourn-
　　　　　　ing. Stanza 4*

Our two souls therefore, which are one,
　Though I must go, endure not yet
A breach, but an expansion,
　Like gold to airy thinness beat.
　　　　　　Ibid. Stanza 6

If they be two, they are two so
　As stiff twin compasses are two,
Thy soul the fixt foot, makes no show
　To move, but doth, if the other do.
　　　　　　Ibid. Stanza 7

Our eyes, upon one double string;
So to'entergraft our hands, as yet
Was all the means to make us one,
And pictures in our eyes to get
Was all our propagation.
　　　　　　The Extasy. Line 8

Love's mysteries in souls do grow,
But yet the body is his book.
　　　　　　Ibid. Line 71

I long to talk with some old lover's
　ghost,
Who died before the god of love was
　born.
　　　　　　Love's Deity. Stanza 1

A bracelet of bright hair about the bone.
　　　　　　The Relic. Stanza 1

So, so, break off this last lamenting kiss,
Which sucks two souls, and vapours
　both away.
　　　　　　The Expiration. Stanza 1

　Ah cannot we
As well as cocks and lions jocund be,
After such pleasures?
　　　　　　Farewell to Love [1635]

Love built on beauty, soon as beauty
　dies.
　　　　　Elegies. II, The Anagram

Nature's lay idiot, I taught thee to love.
　　　　　　Ibid. VII

She, and comparisons are odious.[1]
　　　　　Ibid. VIII, The Comparison

---

[1] Included by Izaak Walton in *The Compleat Angler* [1653], *Chap. 9*, as "made by
Dr. Donne, and made to shew the world that

he could make soft verses, when he thought
them fit and worth his labour."

See Marlowe, page 123a, and C. Day Lewis,
page 992b.

[1] See Fortescue, page 83b.

No spring, nor summer beauty hath
    such grace,
As I have seen in one autumnal face.
       Elegies. IX, The Autumnal
O my America! my new-found land.
      Ibid. XIX, To His Mistress
          Going to Bed [*1669*]
Sir, more than kisses, letters mingle
    souls;
For, thus friends absent speak.
    Verse Letter to Sir Henry Wotton.
                Line 1
Be thou thine own home, and in thy
    self dwell.
             Ibid. Line 47
And seeing the snail, which everywhere
    doth roam,
Carrying his own house still, still is at
    home,
Follow (for he is easy pac'd) this snail,
Be thine own palace, or the world's thy
    jail.
             Ibid. Line 49
And new Philosophy calls all in doubt,
The element of fire is quite put out;
The sun is lost, and the earth, and no
    man's wit
Can well direct him where to look for it.
And freely men confess that this world's
    spent,
When in the planets, and the firmament
They seek so many new; then see that
    this
Is crumbled out again to his atomies.
'Tis all in pieces, all coherence gone;
All just supply, and all relation:
Prince, subject, Father, Son, are things
    forgot.
    An Anatomie of the World. The
    First Anniversary of the Death of
    Mistress Elizabeth Drury [*1611*].
    Line 205

      Her pure, and eloquent blood
Spoke in her cheeks, and so distinctly
    wrought,
That one might almost say, her body
    thought.
    Of the Progress of the Soul. The
    Second Anniversary of the
    Death of Mistress Elizabeth
    Drury [*1612*]. *Line 244*

I am a little world made cunningly
Of elements, and an angelic sprite.
      Holy Sonnets. V [*1635*]
At the round earth's imagin'd corners,[1]
    blow
Your trumpets, angels, and arise, arise
From death, you numberless infinities
Of souls.
               Ibid. VII
All whom war, dearth, age, agues, tyr-
    annies,
Despair, law, chance, hath slain.
                 Ibid.
Death be not proud, though some have
    called thee
Mighty and dreadful, for thou art not
    so,
For those whom thou think'st thou dost
    overthrow,
Die not, poor death, nor yet canst thou
    kill me.
                Ibid. X
One short sleep past, we wake eternally,
And death shall be no more; death,
    thou shalt die.
                 Ibid.
Batter my heart, three-person'd God;
    for you
As yet but knock, breath, shine, and
    seek to mend.
              Ibid. XIV
Since I am coming to that holy room,
Where, with thy quire of saints for
    evermore,
I shall be made thy music; as I come
I tune the instrument here at the door,
And what I must do then, think here
    before.
      Hymn to God my God, in My
        Sickness [*1635*]. *Stanza 1*
Whilst my physicians by their love are
    grown
Cosmographers, and I their map, who
    lie
Flat on this bed.
            Ibid. Stanza 2
    I observe the physician with the same
diligence as he the disease.
       Devotions [*1624*]. *VI*

[1] See Du Bartas, page 102a.

The flea, though he kill none, he does all the harm he can.

Devotions. XII

No man is an island, entire of itself; every man is a piece of the continent, a part of the main; if a clod be washed away by the sea, Europe is the less, as well as if a promontory were, as well as if a manor of thy friends or of thine own were; any man's death diminishes me, because I am involved in mankind; and therefore never send to know for whom the bell tolls; it tolls for thee.

Ibid. XVII

I throw myself down in my chamber, and I call in and invite God and his angels thither, and when they are there, I neglect God and his angels, for the noise of a fly, for the rattling of a coach, for the whining of a door.

Sermon LXXX, At the Funeral of Sir William Cokayne [1626]

BEN JONSON [1]
[1573?–1637]

It was a mighty while ago.

Every Man in his Humour [1598]. Act I, Sc. 3

As he brews, so shall he drink.

Ibid. Act II, Sc. 1

It must be done like lightning.

Ibid. Act IV, Sc. 5

True happiness
Consists not in the multitude of friends,
But in the worth and choice.

Cynthia's Revels [1600]. Act III, Sc. 2

Queen and huntress, chaste and fair,
Now the sun is laid to sleep,
Seated in thy silver chair,
State in wonted manner keep:
  Hesperus entreats thy light,
  Goddess, excellently bright.

Ibid. Act V, Sc. 3

That old bald cheater, Time.

The Poetaster [1601]. Act I, Sc. 1

[1] O rare Ben Jonson! — SIR JOHN YOUNG: *Epitaph.* (Which was done at the charge of Jack Young, who, walking there when the grave was covering, gave the fellow 18 pence to cut it. — JOHN AUBREY [1626–1697]: *Brief Lives*)

The world knows only two, — that's Rome and I.

Sejanus [1603]. Act V, Sc. 1

Calumnies are answered best with silence.

Volpone [1607]. Act II, Sc. 2

Come my Celia, let us prove,
While we can, the sports of love;
Time will not be ours forever,
He at length our good will sever.
Spend not then his gifts in vain;
Suns that set may rise again,
But if once we lose this light,
'Tis with us perpetual night.[1]

Song, To Celia [1607]

Still to be neat, still to be drest,
As you were going to a feast.

Epicene; Or, The Silent Woman [1609]. Act I, Sc. 1

Give me a look, give me a face,
That makes simplicity a grace;
Robes loosely flowing, hair as free,
Such sweet neglect more taketh me
Than all the adulteries of art:
They strike mine eyes, but not my heart.[2]

Ibid.

The dignity of truth is lost with much protesting.

Catiline's Conspiracy [1611]. Act III, Sc. 2

Truth is the trial of itself
And needs no other touch,
And purer than the purest gold,
Refine it ne'er so much.

On Truth [1616]. Stanza 1

Follow a shadow, it still flies you;
Seem to fly it, it will pursue:
So court a mistress, she denies you;
Let her alone, she will court you.

Follow a Shadow [1616]. Stanza 1

Preserving the sweetness of proportion and expressing itself beyond expression.

The Masque of Hymen [1616]

Underneath this stone doth lie
As much beauty as could die;
Which in life did harbour give
To more virtue than doth live.

Epitaph on Elizabeth, L. H. [1616]

[1] See Catullus, page 35a.
[2] See Herrick, page 230b.

Whilst that for which all virtue now is
  sold,
And almost every vice, — almighty
  gold.[1]

*Epistle to Elizabeth, Countess of
    Rutland* [*1616*]

God wisheth none should wreck on a
  strange shelf:
To him man's dearer than to himself.

The Forest: To Sir Robert Wroth
[*1616*]

Drink to me only with thine eyes,
  And I will pledge with mine;
Or leave a kiss but in the cup
  And I'll not look for wine.[2]
The thirst that from the soul doth rise
  Doth ask a drink divine;
But might I of Jove's nectar sup,
  I would not change for thine.

Ibid. To Celia [*1616*]. *Stanza 1*

I sent thee late a rosy wreath,
  Not so much honouring thee
As giving it a hope that there
  It could not wither'd be.
But thou thereon didst only breathe,
  And sent'st it back to me;
Since when it grows and smells, I swear,
  Not of itself, but thee.

Ibid. Stanza 2

Reader, look,
Not at his picture, but his book.

*On the Portrait of Shakespeare
Prefixed to the First Folio* [*1623*]

Soul of the age!
The applause, delight, the wonder of
  our stage!
My Shakespeare, rise! I will not lodge
  thee by
Chaucer or Spenser, or bid Beaumont
  lie
A little further, to make thee a room:
Thou art a monument, without a tomb,
And art alive still, while thy book doth
  live,

---

[1] The flattering, mighty, nay, almighty
gold. — WOLCOT: *To Kien Long* [1782–1785],
Ode IV

See Irving, page 446b.

[2] Drink to me with your eyes alone. . . .
And if you will, take the cup to your lips
and fill it with kisses, and give it so to me. —
PHILOSTRATUS [*circa* A.D. 181–250]: *Letter
XXIV*

And we have wits to read, and praise to
  give.

To the Memory of Shakespeare
[*1623*]

Marlowe's mighty line.

Ibid.

Small Latin and less Greek.

Ibid.

He was not of an age but for all time.

Ibid.

Who casts to write a living line, must
  sweat.

Ibid.

For a good poet's made, as well as born.

Ibid.

Sweet Swan of Avon!

Ibid.

Let those that merely talk and never
  think,
That live in the wild anarchy of drink.[1]

Underwoods [*1640*]. *An Epistle,
  answering to One that asked to be
  sealed of the Tribe of Ben*

In small proportions we just beauties
  see,
And in short measures life may perfect
  be.

*Ibid. To the Immortal Memory
  of Sir Lucius Cary and Sir
  Henry Morison*

The players have often mentioned it
as an honor to Shakespeare, that in his
writing, whatsoever he penned, he never
blotted out line. My answer hath been,
"Would he had blotted a thousand."

*Timber, or Discoveries Made
  Upon Men and Matter* [*1640*]

I loved the man [Shakespeare] and
do honor his memory (on this side idolatry) as much as any.

Ibid.

Greatness of name in the father oft-
times overwhelms the son; they stand
too near one another. The shadow kills
the growth: so much, that we see the

---

[1] Who think too little, and who talk too
much. — DRYDEN: *Absalom and Achitophel*
[1680], *Part I, L. 534*

They never taste who always drink;
They always talk who never think.

MATTHEW PRIOR [1664–1721]: *Upon
    a Passage in the Scaligerana*

grandchild come more and oftener to be heir of the first.

Timber, or Discoveries Made Upon Men and Matter

Though the most be players, some must be spectators.

Ibid.

RICHARD BARNFIELD
[1574–1627]

The waters were his winding sheet, the sea was made for his tomb;
Yet for his fame the ocean sea, was not sufficient room.

Epitaph on Hawkins [*1595*]

As it fell upon a day
In the merry month of May,
Sitting in a pleasant shade
Which a grove of myrtles made.

Address to the Nightingale [1]

King Pandion he is dead,
All thy friends are lapp'd in lead.

Ibid.

Every one that flatters thee
Is no friend in misery.
Words are easy, like the wind;
Faithful friends are hard to find.
Every man will be thy friend
Whilst thou hast wherewith to spend:
But, if store of crowns be scant,
No man will supply thy want.

Ibid.

He that is thy friend indeed,
He will help thee in thy need.

Ibid.

JOSEPH HALL, BISHOP OF NORWICH
[1574–1656]

In bonds of love united, man and wife,
Long, yet too short, they spent a happy life.

Elegy on Sir Edward and Lady Lewkenor

So little in his purse, so much upon his back.

Portrait of a Poor Gallant

'Mongst all these stirs of discontented strife,
O, let me lead an academic life;
To know much, and to think for nothing, know
Nothing to have, yet think we have enow.

Discontent of Men with their Condition

Moderation is the silken string running through the pearl chain of all virtues.

Christian Moderation. Introduction

Death borders upon our birth, and our cradle stands in the grave.

Epistles. Decade III, Epistle 2

There is many a rich stone laid up in the bowels of the earth, many a fair pearl laid up in the bosom of the sea, that never was seen, nor never shall be.[1]

Contemplations. Book IV, The Veil of Moses

THOMAS CAMPION
[1575?–1620?]

Never love unless you can
Bear with all the faults of man:
Men will sometimes jealous be,
Though but little cause they see;
And hang the head, as discontent,
And speak what straight they will repent.

Never Love [*Circa 1617*].
Stanza 1

There is a garden in her face
  Where roses and white lilies blow;
A heav'nly paradise is that place,
  Wherein all pleasant fruits do grow;
There cherries grow that none may buy,
Till Cherry-ripe themselves do cry.

Cherry-Ripe [2] [*Circa 1617*].
Stanza 1

Those cherries fairly do enclose
  Of orient pearl a double row,
Which when her lovely laughter shows,

---

[1] This song, attributed to Shakespeare and included in his *Sonnets to Sundry Notes of Music,* is found in BARNFIELD's *Poems in Divers Humours,* published in 1598.

[1] See Thomas Gray, page 348b.
[2] "Cherry-ripe" was a familiar street cry of the time.
See Herrick, page 230a.

They look like rosebuds fill'd with snow.

> *Cherry-Ripe. Stanza 2*

The summer hath his joys,
And winter his delights;
Though love and all his pleasures are but toys,
They shorten tedious nights.

> *Winter Nights* [Circa *1617*].
> *Stanza 2*

ROBERT BURTON
[1577–1640]

Naught so sweet as melancholy.[1]

> *Anatomy of Melancholy*[2] [*1621–1651*]. *The Author's Abstract*

I would help others, out of a fellow-feeling.[3]

> *Ibid. Democritus to the Reader*

They lard their lean books with the fat of others' works.[4]

> *Ibid.*

We can say nothing but what hath been said.[5] Our poets steal from Homer.

---

[1] There's naught in this life sweet,
　If man were wise to see 't,
　But only melancholy;
　O sweetest Melancholy!
　　WILLIAM STRODE [1602–1645]:
　　A Song in Praise of Melancholy
JOHN FLETCHER introduced this song in his play, *The Nice Valour* [1647], *Act III, Sc. 3*; and it has also been attributed to him. See Fletcher, page 225b.
　There's not a string attuned to mirth
　But has its chord in melancholy.
　　HOOD [1799–1845]: *Ode to*
　　　Melancholy
[2] Burton's 'Anatomy of Melancholy,' he said, was the only book that ever took him out of bed two hours sooner than he wished to rise. — BOSWELL: *The Life of Dr. Johnson* [1791]
　If the reader has patience to go through his volumes, he will be more improved for literary conversation than by the perusal of any twenty other works with which I am acquainted. — BYRON [1807], in MOORE'S *Life*.
[3] A fellow-feeling makes one wondrous kind. — GARRICK: *Prologue on Quitting the Stage* [1776]
　See Virgil, page 37a.
[4] See Shakespeare, page 150a.
[5] See Terence, page 31b.

. . . Our story-dressers do as much; he that comes last is commonly best.

> *Anatomy of Melancholy.*
> *Democritus to the Reader*

I say with Didacus Stella, a dwarf standing on the shoulders of a giant may see farther than a giant himself.[1]

> *Ibid.*

It is most true, *stylus virum arguit,* — our style bewrays us.[2]

> *Ibid.*

As that great captain, Ziska, would have a drum made of his skin when he was dead, because he thought the very noise of it would put his enemies to flight.

> *Ibid.*

Smile with an intent to do mischief, or cozen him whom he salutes.

> *Ibid.*

Penny wise, pound foolish.

> *Ibid.*

Women wear the breeches.

> *Ibid.*

Like Aesop's fox, when he had lost his tail, would have all his fellow foxes cut off theirs.[3]

> *Ibid.*

Hannibal, as he had mighty virtues, so had he many vices; he had two distinct persons in him.

> *Ibid.*

Every man hath a good and a bad angel attending on him in particular, all his life long.

> *Ibid. Part I, Sect. 2, Memb. 1,*
> *Subsect. 2*

That which Pythagoras said to his scholars of old, may be for ever applied to melancholy men, *A fabis abstinete,* eat no beans.

> *Ibid. Memb. 2, Subsect. 1*

---

[1] Pigmaei gigantum humeris impositi plusquam ipsi gigantes vident. — DIDACUS STELLA, in LUCAN [A. D. 39–65]: *De Bello Civili, 10, II*
[2] Le style est l'homme même (The style is the man himself). — GEORGE LOUIS, COMTE DE BUFFON: *Discours sur le Style*, on admission to the French Academy [1753]
[3] AESOP [*floruit* 550 B. C.]: *Fables, Book V, Fable 5*

Cookery is become an art, a noble science; cooks are gentlemen.

Anatomy of Melancholy. Part I, Sect. 2, Memb. 2, Subsect. 2

As much valour is to be found in feasting as in fighting, and some of our city captains and carpet knights will make this good, and prove it.[1]

Ibid.

No rule is so general, which admits not some exception.

Ibid. Subsect. 3

Idleness is an appendix to nobility.

Ibid. Subsect. 6

Why doth one man's yawning make another yawn?

Ibid. Memb. 3, Subsect. 2

A nightingale dies for shame if another bird sings better.

Ibid. Subsect. 6

They do not live but linger.

Ibid. Subsect. 10

[Diseases] crucify the soul of man, attenuate our bodies, dry them, wither them, shrivel them up like old apples, make them so many anatomies.

Ibid.

[Desire] is a perpetual rack, or horsemill, according to Austin [St. Augustine], still going round as in a ring.

Ibid. Subsect. 11

[The rich] are indeed rather possessed by their money than possessors.

Ibid. Subsect. 12

Like a hog, or dog in the manger, he doth only keep it because it shall do nobody else good, hurting himself and others.[2]

Ibid.

Were it not that they are loath to lay out money on a rope, they would be hanged forthwith, and sometimes die to save charges.

Ibid.

A mere madness, to live like a wretch and die rich.

Ibid.

I may not here omit those two main plagues and common dotages of human

[1] See Montaigne, page 98a.
[2] See Aesop, page 10b.

kind, wine and women, which have infatuated and besotted myriads of people; they go commonly together.

Anatomy of Melancholy. Part I, Sect. 2, Memb. 3, Subsect. 13

All our geese are swans.[1]

Ibid. Subsect. 14

Though they [philosophers] write *contemptu gloriae*, yet as Hieron observes, they will put their names to their books.

Ibid.

They are proud in humility; proud in that they are not proud.[2]

Ibid.

We can make majors and officers every year, but not scholars.

Ibid. Subsect. 15

Hinc quam sic calamus saevior ense, patet. The pen worse than the sword.[3]

Ibid. Memb. 4, Subsect. 4

See one promontory (said Socrates of old), one mountain, one sea, one river, and see all.[4]

Ibid. Subsect. 7

Felix Plater notes of some young physicians, that study to cure diseases, catch them themselves, will be sick, and appropriate all symptoms they find related of others to their own persons.

Ibid. Sect. 3, Memb. 1, Subsect. 2

Aristotle said melancholy men of all others are most witty.

Ibid. Subsect. 3

[1] Every man thinks his own geese swans.
— DICKENS: *The Cricket on the Hearth* [1845], *Chirp the Second*
Let the long contention cease!
Geese are swans, and swans are geese.
MATTHEW ARNOLD: *The Last Word* [1867], *St. 2*
[2] See Coleridge, page 422b.
[3] See Bulwer Lytton, page 510b.
Pyrrhus was used to say that Cineas had taken more towns with his words than he with his arms. — PLUTARCH [A.D. 46–120]: *Pyrrhus*
[4] All places, all airs, make unto me one country; I am in England everywhere, and under any meridian. — SIR THOMAS BROWNE: *Religio Medici* [1642], *Part II, Sect. 1*
A blade of grass is always a blade of grass, whether in one country or another. — SAMUEL JOHNSON, in MRS. PIOZZI's *Anecdotes of Johnson* [1786]

Like him in Aesop, he whipped his horses withal, and put his shoulder to the wheel.[1]
Anatomy of Melancholy. Part II, Sect. 1, Memb. 2

Seneca thinks the gods are well pleased when they see great men contending with adversity.
Ibid. Sect. 2, Memb. 1, Subsect. 1

Machiavel says virtue and riches seldom settle on one man.
Ibid. Memb. 2

Almost in every kingdom the most ancient families have been at first princes' bastards; their worthiest captains, best wits, greatest scholars, bravest spirits in all our annals, have been base [born].
Ibid.

As he said in Machiavel, *omnes eodem patre nati*, Adam's sons, conceived all and born in sin, etc. "We are by nature all as one, all alike, if you see us naked; let us wear theirs and they our clothes, and what is the difference?"
Ibid.

Who cannot give good counsel? 'Tis cheap, it costs them nothing.
Ibid. Memb. 3

Many things happen between the cup and the lip.[2]
Ibid.

Everything, said Epictetus, hath two handles, — the one to be held by, the other not.
Ibid.

All places are distant from heaven alike.
Ibid. Memb. 4

The commonwealth of Venice in their armoury have this inscription: "Happy

---

[1] AESOP [*floruit* 550 B.C.]: *Hercules and the Waggoner*
[2] There is many a slip 'twixt the cup and the lip. — PALLADAS [*floruit* A.D. 400]: *Greek Anthology, Book X, Epigram 32.* A very ancient proverb, sometimes attributed to Homer.
Though men determine, the gods do dispose; and oft times many things fall out between the cup and the lip. — ROBERT GREENE: *Perimedes the Blacke-Smith* [1588]

is that city which in time of peace thinks of war." [1]
Anatomy of Melancholy. Part II, Sect. 2, Memb. 6

Every man, as the saying is, can tame a shrew but he that hath her.
Ibid.

Divers have been relieved [of melancholy] by exonerating themselves to a faithful friend.
Ibid.

Tobacco, divine, rare, superexcellent tobacco, which goes far beyond all the panaceas, potable gold and philosopher's stones, a sovereign remedy to all diseases.
Ibid. Sect. 4, Memb. 2, Subsect. 2

"Let me not live," said Aretine's Antonia, "if I had not rather hear thy discourse than see a play."
Ibid. Part III, Sect. 1, Memb. 1, Subsect. 1

Birds of a feather will gather together.[2]
Ibid. Subsect. 2

No cord nor cable can so forcibly draw, or hold so fast, as love can do with a twined thread.[3]
Ibid. Sect. 2, Memb. 1, Subsect. 2

To enlarge or illustrate this power and effect of love is to set a candle in the sun.
Ibid.

He is only fantastical that is not in fashion.
Ibid. Memb. 2, Subsect. 3

[Quoting Seneca] Cornelia kept her in talk till her children came from

---

[1] See Horace, page 40b, and George Washington, page 367a.
[2] Beast knows beast; birds of a feather flock together. — ARISTOTLE [384–322 B.C.]: *Rhetoric, Book I, Chap. 11, Sect. 25*
[3] One hair of a woman can draw more than a hundred pair of oxen. — JAMES HOWELL: *Letters* [1621], *Book II, IV*
She knows her man, and when you rant and swear,
Can draw you to her with a single hair.
　　DRYDEN: *Persius* [1693], *Satire V, L. 246*
Beauty draws us with a single hair. — POPE: *The Rape of the Lock* [1712], *Canto II, L. 27*

school, "and these," said she, "are my jewels."

> *Anatomy of Melancholy. Part III,*
> *Sect. 2, Memb. 2, Subsect. 3*

Diogenes struck the father when the son swore.

> *Ibid. Subsect. 5*

Though it rain daggers with their points downward.

> *Ibid. Memb. 3*

Going as if he trod upon eggs.

> *Ibid.*

I light my candle from their torches.

> *Ibid. Memb. 5, Subsect. 1*

England is a paradise for women and hell for horses; Italy a paradise for horses, hell for women, as the diverb goes.[1]

> *Ibid. Sect. 3, Memb. 1, Subsect. 2*

If the world will be gulled, let it be gulled.

> *Ibid. Sect. 4, Memb. 1, Subsect. 2*

For "ignorance is the mother of devotion," as all the world knows.

> *Ibid.*

The fear of some divine and supreme powers keeps men in obedience.[2]

> *Ibid.*

Out of too much learning become mad.[3]

> *Ibid.*

The Devil himself, which is the author of confusion and lies.

> *Ibid. Subsect. 3*

Isocrates adviseth Demonicus, when he came to a strange city, to worship by all means the gods of the place.

> *Ibid. Subsect. 5*

When they are at Rome, they do there as they see done.

> *Ibid. Memb. 2, Subsect. 1*

One religion is as true as another.

> *Ibid.*

[1] England is the paradise of women, purgatory of men, and the hell of horses. — JOHN FLORIO: *Second Frutes* [1591]

[2] The fear o' hell's a hangman's whip
To haud the wretch in order.
> ROBERT BURNS [1759–1796]: *Epistle*
> *to a Young Friend*

[3] Much learning doth make thee mad. — *Acts, XXVI, 24*

They have cheveril consciences that will stretch.

> *Anatomy of Melancholy. Part III,*
> *Sect. 4, Memb. 2, Subsect. 3*

THOMAS WARD
[1577–1639]

Where to elect there is but one,
'Tis Hobson's choice, — take that or none.[1]

> *England's Reformation* [1630].
> *Chapter IV*

JOHN FLETCHER
[1579–1625]

Man is his own star; and the soul that can
Render an honest and a perfect man
Commands all light, all influence, all fate.
Nothing to him falls early, or too late.
Our acts our angels are, or good or ill,
Our fatal shadows that walk by us still.

> *The Honest Man's Fortune*
> [1613]. (*In collaboration with*
> *three other authors*) *Epilogue*

Man is his own star; and that soul that can
Be honest is the only perfect man.[2]

> *Ibid.*

Weep no more, nor sigh, nor groan,
Sorrow calls no time that's gone;

[1] Thomas Hobson [1544–1631], of whom Steele wrote in *The Spectator, No. 509* [October 14, 1712]:

Mr. Tobias Hobson, from whom we have the expression, . . . was a carrier, . . . the first in this Island who let out hackney-horses. He lived in Cambridge, and observing that the scholars rid hard, his manner was to keep a large stable of horses, with boots, bridles, and whips. . . . When a man came for an horse, he was led into the stable, where there was great choice, but he obliged him to take the horse which stood next to the stable-door; so that every customer was alike well served according to his chance, and every horse ridden with the same justice. From whence it became a proverb, when what ought to be your election was forced upon you, to say Hobson's Choice.

[2] An honest man's the noblest work of God. — POPE: *Essay on Man, Epistle IV* [1734], L. 248

Violets plucked, the sweetest rain
Makes not fresh nor grow again.[1]
> *The Queen of Corinth* [*1617*].
> (*In collaboration with Mas-*
> *singer and a third author*)
> *Act III, Sc. 2*

Drink today, and drown all sorrow;
You shall perhaps not do't tomorrow.
> *The Bloody Brother* [*1616*].
> (*In collaboration with Jonson*
> *and others*) *Act II, Sc. 2*

And he that will to bed go sober
Falls with the leaf in October.[2]
> *Ibid.*

Three merry boys, and three merry
boys,
And three merry boys are we,[3]
As ever did sing in a hempen string
Under the gallows-tree.
> *Ibid. Act III, Sc. 3*

Of all the paths lead to a woman's love
Pity's the straightest.[4]
> *The Knight of Malta* [*1618-*
> *1619*]. (*In collaboration with*
> *Massinger*) *Act I, Sc. 1*

Go to grass.
> *The Little French Lawyer*
> [*Circa 1619*]. (*In collaboration*
> *with Massinger*) *Act IV, Sc. 7*

There is no jesting with edge tools.
> *Ibid.*

Let's meet, and either do or die.[5]
> *The Island Princess* [*1621*].
> *Act II, Sc. 4*

[1] See *The Friar of Orders Gray*, page 1011b.
[2] The following well-known catch, or glee,
is formed on this song:

He who goes to bed, and goes to bed sober,
Falls as the leaves do, and dies in October;
But he who goes to bed, and goes to bed mel-
low,
Lives as he ought to do, and dies an honest
fellow.

[3] Three merry men be we. — PEELE: *Old
Wives' Tale* [1595]
[4] Pity's akin to love. — THOMAS SOUTH-
ERNE: *Oroonoko* [1696], *Act II, Sc. 1*
For pity melts the mind to love. — DRY-
DEN: *Alexander's Feast* [1697], *L. 96*
Pity swells the tide of love. — EDWARD
YOUNG: *Night Thoughts* [1742-1745], *Night
III, L. 107*
[5] Let us do or die! — ROBERT BURNS [1759-
1796]: *Bannockburn*
This expression is a kind of common

Deeds, not words shall speak me.
> *The Lover's Progress* [*1623*].
> *Act III, Sc. 4*

Whistle, and she'll come to you.[1]
> *Wit Without Money* [*1639*].
> *Act IV, Sc. 4*

O woman, perfect woman! what distraction
Was meant to mankind when thou wast
made a devil!
> *Monsieur Thomas* [*1639*].
> *Act III, Sc. 1*

Hence, all you vain delights,
As short as are the nights
Wherein you spend your folly!
There's naught in this life sweet
But only melancholy.
> *Melancholy* [2] [*The Nice Valour,*
> *1647*]

JOHN WEBSTER
[1580-1625]

I saw him now going the way of all
flesh.[3]
> *Westward Hoe* [*1607*]. (*In col-*
> *laboration with Dekker*) *Act II,*
> *Sc. 2*

Call for the robin redbreast and the
wren,
Since o'er shady groves they hover,
And with leaves and flowers do cover
The friendless bodies of unburied men.
> *The White Devil* [*1612*].
> *Act V, Sc. 4*

But keep the wolf far thence, that's foe
to men,
For with his nails he'll dig them up
again.
> *Ibid.*

Prosperity doth bewitch men, seeming
clear;

property, being the motto, we believe, of a
Scottish family. — SIR WALTER SCOTT [1771-
1832]: *Review of* THOMAS CAMPBELL'S *Gertrude of Wyoming*
[1] Whistle, and I'll come to ye. — ROBERT
BURNS [1759-1796]: *Whistle, etc.*
[2] See Robert Burton, page 221b, and Milton,
page 245b.
[3] Title of the novel by Samuel Butler
[1903].

But seas do laugh, show white, when
    rocks are near.
       The White Devil. Act V, Sc. 6

Glories, like glow-worms, afar off shine
    bright,
But look'd too near have neither heat
    nor light.
       Duchess of Malfi [*1623*].
             Act IV, Sc. 2

I know death hath ten thousand sev-
    eral doors
For men to take their exit.[1]
                 Ibid.

Heaven-gates are not so highly arch'd
As princes' palaces; they that enter
    there
Must go upon their knees.
                 Ibid.

Ferdinand. Cover her face; mine eyes
    dazzle; she died young.
Bosola. I think not so; her infelicity
Seem'd to have years too many.
                 Ibid.

Vain the ambition of kings
Who seek by trophies and dead things
To leave a living name behind,
And weave but nets to catch the wind.
    The Devil's Law Case [*1623*].
                 Song

SIR THOMAS OVERBURY
[1581–1613]

Give me, next good, an understanding
    wife,
By nature wise, not learnèd much by
    art;
Some knowledge on her part will, all
    her life,
More scope of conversation impart.
           A Wife [*1614*]

In part to blame is she,
Which hath without consent been only
    tried:

---

[1] Death hath a thousand doors to let out
life. — MASSINGER: *A Very Woman* [1655],
Act V, Sc. 4
    Death hath so many doors to let out life.
— FLETCHER AND MASSINGER: *The Custom of
the Country* [1647], *Act II, Sc. 2*
    The thousand doors that lead to death. —
SIR THOMAS BROWNE: *Religio Medici* [1642],
Part I, Sect. XLIV

He comes too near that comes to be de-
    nied.
                A Wife

Books are a part of man's prerogative;
In formal ink they thoughts and voices
    hold,
That we to them our solitude may give,
And make time present travel that of
    old.
                 Ibid.

He disdains all things above his
reach, and preferreth all countries before his own.
    An Affectate Traveller [*1614*]

BISHOP RICHARD CORBET
[1582–1635]

Farewell rewards and fairies,[1]
Good housewives now may say.
    Farewell to the Fairies. Stanza 1

Nor too much wealth nor wit come to
    thee,
So much of either may undo thee.
    To His Son, Vincent Corbet

I wish thee all thy mother's graces,
Thy father's fortunes and his places.
                 Ibid.

PHILIP MASSINGER
[1583–1640]

Be wise;
Soar not too high to fall; but stoop to
    rise.
    Duke of Milan [*1623*]. *Act I, Sc. 2*

He that would govern others, first
    should be
Master of himself.
    The Bondman [*1624*]. *Act I, Sc. 3*

To be nobly born
Is now a crime.
    The Roman Actor [*1629*].
                 Act I, Sc. 1

Whose wealth
Arithmetic cannot number.
              Ibid. Sc. 3

Grim death.[2]
           Ibid. Act IV, Sc. 2

---

[1] *Rewards and Fairies*, title of a book by
Kipling [1910].
[2] See Milton, page 254b.

A New Way to Pay Old Debts.
Title of Play [*1632*]

THOMAS HEYWOOD
[*Died* 1650?]

Pack clouds away, and welcome day,
With night we banish sorrow.
Pack Clouds Away [*1630*].
Stanza 1

I hold he loves me best that calls me
Tom.
Hierarchie of the Blessed Angells
[*1635*]

Seven cities warred for Homer being
dead,
Who living had no roof to shroud his
head.[1]
Ibid.

JOHN SELDEN
[1584–1654]

Equity is a roguish thing. For Law
we have a measure, know what to trust
to; Equity is according to the conscience of him that is Chancellor, and
as that is larger or narrower, so is
Equity. 'Tis all one as if they should
make the standard for the measure we
call a "foot" a Chancellor's foot; what
an uncertain measure would this be!
One Chancellor has a long foot, another a short foot, a third an indifferent
foot. 'Tis the same thing in the Chancellor's conscience.
Table Talk [*1689*]. *Equity*

Humility is a virtue all preach, none
practise; and yet everybody is content
to hear.
Ibid. Humility

'Tis not the drinking that is to be
blamed, but the excess.
Ibid.

[1] Seven cities strive for the learned root of
Homer:
Smyrna, Chios, Colophon, Ithaca, Pylos,
Argos, Athens.
UNKNOWN (*Greek Anthology,
Book VI, Epigram 298*)
Seven wealthy towns contend for Homer
dead,
Through which the living Homer begged
his bread.
THOMAS SEWARD [*1708–
1790*]: *On Homer*

Commonly we say a judgment falls
upon a man for something in him we
cannot abide.
Table Talk. Judgments

Ignorance of the law excuses no
man; not that all men know the law,
but because 'tis an excuse every man
will plead, and no man can tell how to
refute him.
Ibid. Law

No man is the wiser for his learning.
Ibid. Learning

Wit and wisdom are born with a man.
Ibid.

Few men make themselves masters
of the things they write or speak.
Ibid.

Take a straw and throw it up into
the air, — you may see by that which
way the wind is.
Ibid. Libels

Philosophy is nothing but discretion.
Ibid. Philosophy

Marriage is a desperate thing.
Ibid. Marriage

Thou little thinkest what a little
foolery governs the world.[1]
Ibid. Pope

They that govern the most make the
least noise.
Ibid. Power

Syllables govern the world.
Ibid.

Never king dropped out of the
clouds.
Ibid.

Never tell your resolution beforehand.
Ibid. Wisdom

Wise men say nothing in dangerous
times.
Ibid.

Pleasure is nothing else but the intermission of pain.
Ibid. Pleasure

Preachers say, Do as I say, not as I
do.
Ibid. Preaching

[1] Behold, my son, with how little wisdom
the world is governed. — AXEL OXENSTIERN
[1583–1654]

A King is a thing men have made for their own sakes, for quietness' sake. Just as in a Family one man is appointed to buy the meat.
> *Table Talk. Of a King*

FRANCIS BEAUMONT
[1584–1616]

What things have we seen
Done at the Mermaid! heard words that
  have been
So nimble and so full of subtle flame
As if that everyone from whence they
  came
Had meant to put his whole wit in a
  jest,
And resolved to live a fool the rest
Of his dull life.
> *Letter to Ben Jonson* [*1640*]

BEAUMONT AND FLETCHER [1]

Francis Beaumont [1584–1616]
and John Fletcher
[1579–1625]

No better than you should be.[2]
> *The Coxcomb* [*1610*].
> *Act IV, Sc. 3*

The devil take the hindmost!
> *Philaster* [*1610*]. *Act V*

As cold as cucumbers.
> *Cupid's Revenge* [*1615*].
> *Act I, Sc. 1*

Calamity is man's true touchstone.[3]
> *Four Plays in One. The Triumph*
> *of Honour, Sc. 1*

Kiss till the cow comes home.
> *Scornful Lady* [*1616*].
> *Act III, Sc. 1*

Beggars must be no choosers.
> *Ibid. Act V, Sc. 3*

---

[1] Of whose partnership John Aubrey [1626–1697] said: "There was a wonderful consimility of fancy. They lived together not far from the playhouse, had one wench in the house between them, the same clothes and cloak, &c."
[2] She is no better than she should be. — Fielding: *The Temple Beau* [1730], *Act IV, Sc. 3*
[3] See Seneca, page 47b.

There is a method in man's wickedness, —
It grows up by degrees.[1]
> *A King and No King* [*1619*].
> *Act V, Sc. 4*

Upon my buried body lie lightly, gentle earth.
> *The Maid's Tragedy* [*1619*].
> *Act I, Sc. 2*

JOHN FORD
[1586–1639]

Diamond cut diamond.
> *The Lover's Melancholy* [*1629*].
> *Act I, Sc. 1*

'Tis Pity She's a Whore.
> *Title of Play* [*1633*]

THOMAS RAINBOROUGH
[? –1648]

The poorest he that is in England hath a life to live as the greatest he.
> *In the Army debates at Putney*
> [*October 29, 1647*]

THOMAS HOBBES
[1588–1679]

Words are wise men's counters, — they do but reckon by them; but they are the money of fools.
> *Leviathan. Part I* [*1651*],
> *Chap. IV*

The privilege of absurdity; to which no living creature is subject but man only.
> *Ibid. Chap. V*

Sudden glory is the passion which maketh those grimaces called laughter.
> *Ibid. Chap. VI*

The secret thoughts of a man run over all things, holy, profane, clean, obscene, grave, and light, without shame or blame.
> *Ibid. Chap. VIII*

During the time men live without a common power to keep them in awe, they are in that condition which is

---

[1] See Juvenal, page 62b, and Racine, page 287b.

called war; and such a war as is of every man against every man.

Leviathan. Part 1, Chap. XIII

As the nature of foul weather lieth not in a shower or two of rain but in an inclination thereto of many days together, so the nature of war consisteth not in actual fighting but in the known disposition thereto during all the time there is no assurance to the contrary. All other time is peace.

Ibid.

[In a state of nature] No arts, no letters, no society, and, which is worst of all, continual fear and danger of violent death, and the life of man solitary, poor, nasty, brutish, and short.

Ibid.

The praise of ancient authors proceeds not from the reverence of the dead, but from the competition and mutual envy of the living.

Ibid. Review and Conclusion

Such truth as opposeth no man's profit nor pleasure is to all men welcome.

Ibid.

GEORGE WITHER
[1588–1667]

Shall I, wasting in despair,
Die because a woman's fair?
Or make pale my cheeks with care,
'Cause another's rosy are?
Be she fairer than the day,
Or the flowery meads in May,
  If she be not so to me,
  What care I how fair she be?

Sonnet 4 [1619]. Stanza 1

If she love me, this believe,
I will die, ere she shall grieve,
If she slight me when I woo,
I can scorn and let her go;
  For if she be not for me,
  What care I for whom she be?

Ibid. Stanza 5

'Twas I that beat the bush,
The bird to others flew.

*A Love Sonnet [1622].
Stanza 11*

Though I am young, I scorn to flit
On the wings of borrowed wit.

The Shepherd's Hunting [1622]

WILLIAM BRADFORD
[1590–1657]

They knew they were pilgrims.[1]

Of Plymouth Plantation [1620–1647]. Chap. 7

So they committed themselves to the will of God and resolved to proceed.

Ibid. Chap. 9

Being thus arrived in a good harbor, and brought safe to land, they fell upon their knees and blessed the God of Heaven who had brought them over the vast and furious ocean, and delivered them from all the perils and miseries thereof, again to set their feet on the firm and stable earth, their proper element.

Ibid.

Our fathers were Englishmen which came over this great ocean, and were ready to perish in this wilderness.

Ibid.

The loss of . . . honest and industrious men's lives cannot be valued at any price.

Ibid. Chap. 12

But it pleased God to visit us then with death daily, and with so general a disease that the living were scarce able to bury the dead.

Ibid.

Cold comfort to fill their hungry bellies.

Ibid. Chap. 13

Behold, now, another providence of God. A ship comes into the harbor.

Ibid.

Thus out of small beginnings greater things have been produced by His hand that made all things of nothing, and gives being to all things that are; and, as one small candle may light a thousand, so the light here kindled hath

---

[1] It was owing to this passage, first printed in 1669, that the *Mayflower's* company came eventually to be called the Pilgrim Fathers.

shone unto many, yea in some sort to our whole nation.

Of Plymouth Plantation. Chap. 21

WILLIAM BROWNE
[1591–1643]

Underneath this sable hearse
Lies the subject of all verse:
Sidney's sister, Pembroke's mother.
Death, ere thou hast slain another
Fair and learn'd and good as she,
Time shall throw a dart at thee.

*Epitaph on the Countess of
Pembroke [1621]*

There is no season such delight can
   bring,
As summer, autumn, winter, and the
   spring.

Variety

ROBERT HERRICK
[1591–1674]

I sing of brooks, of blossoms, birds, and
   bowers:
Of April, May, of June, and July-
   flowers.
I sing of May-poles, Hock-carts, was-
   sails, wakes,
Of bride-grooms, brides, and of their
   bridal-cakes.

*Hesperides [1648]. Argument
of his Book*

What is a kiss? Why this, as some approve:
The sure, sweet cement, glue, and lime
   of love.

Ibid. A Kiss

Bid me to live, and I will live
   Thy Protestant to be,
Or bid me love, and I will give
   A loving heart to thee.

Ibid. To Anthea. Stanza 1

Cherry ripe, ripe, ripe, I cry,
Full and fair ones, — come and buy!
If so be you ask me where
They do grow, I answer, there,
Where my Julia's lips do smile, —
There's the land, or cherry-isle.

Ibid. Cherry Ripe [1]

[1] See Thomas Campion, page 220b.

Some asked how pearls did grow, and
   where?
Then spoke I to my girl
To part her lips, and showed them
   there
The quarelets of pearl.[1]

*Hesperides. The Rock of Rubies,
and the Quarrie of Pearls*

A sweet disorder in the dress
Kindles in clothes a wantonness.

Ibid. Delight in Disorder

A winning wave, deserving note,
In the tempestuous petticoat;
A careless shoe-string, in whose tie
I see a wild civility, —
Do more bewitch me than when art
Is too precise in every part.[2]

Ibid.

You say to me-wards your affection's
   strong;
Pray love me little, so you love me long.[3]

Ibid. Love me Little, Love me Long

Night makes no difference 'twixt the
   Priest and Clerk;
Joan as my Lady is as good i' the dark.

Ibid. No Difference i' th' Dark

Give me a kiss, and to that kiss a score;
Then to that twenty, add a hundred
   more:
A thousand to that hundred: so kiss on,
To make that thousand up a million.
Treble that million, and when that is
   done,
Let's kiss afresh, as when we first begun.

Ibid. To Anthea: Ah, My Anthea!

Gather ye rosebuds while ye may,
   Old Time is still a-flying,
And this same flower that smiles today
   Tomorrow will be dying.[4]

*Ibid. To the Virgins to make much
of Time*

Fair daffodils, we weep to see
You haste away so soon.

To Daffodils

[1] See Thomas Campion, page 220b.
[2] See Jonson, page 218b.
[3] See John Heywood, page 93b.
[4] Let us crown ourselves with rosebuds, before they be withered. — *Wisdom of Solomon, II, 8*
   Gather the rose of love, whilest yet is time.
— SPENSER: *The Faerie Queene, Book II* [1590], *Canto XII, St. 75*

Her pretty feet, like snails, did creep
  A little out, and then,[1]
As if they played at bo-peep,
  Did soon draw in again.
> *Hesperides. To Mistress
> Susanna Southwell*

Her eyes the glow-worm lend thee,
The shooting stars attend thee;
  And the elves also,
  Whose little eyes glow
Like the sparks of fire, befriend thee.
> *Ibid. The Night Piece to Julia*

Thus times do shift, — each thing his
  turn does hold;
New things succeed, as former things
  grow old.
> *Ibid. Ceremonies for
> Candlemas Eve*

Outdid the meat, outdid the frolic
  wine.
> *Ibid. Ode for Ben Jonson*

Attempt the end, and never stand to
  doubt;
Nothing's so hard but search will find
  it out.
> *Ibid. Seek and Find*

Here a little child I stand
Heaving up my either hand.
Cold as paddocks though they be,
Here I lift them up to Thee,
For a benison to fall
On our meat, and on us all.
> *Ibid. A Child's Grace*

Her legs were such Diana shows
When tuckt up she a-hunting goes
With buskins shortened to descry
The happy dawning of her thigh.
> *Ibid. The Vision*

Get up, sweet Slug-a-bed, and see
The dew bespangling herb and tree.
> *Ibid. Corinna's Going a-Maying*

Wash, dress, be brief in praying:
Few beads are best, when once we go
  a-Maying.
> *Ibid.*

Whenas in silks my Julia goes,
Then, then (methinks) how sweetly
  flows
That liquefaction of her clothes.
> *Ibid. Upon Julia's Clothes*

[1] See Suckling, page 261a.

HENRY KING, BISHOP
OF CHICHESTER
[1592–1669]

And that tame Lover who unlocks his
  heart
Unto his mistress, teaching her an art
To plague himself, shows her the secret
  way
How she may tyrannize another day!
> *The Steed that Comes to
> Understand* [1657]

Thou art the book, —
The library whereon I look.
> *Exequy on the Death of a
> Beloved Wife* [1657]

Then we shall rise
And view ourselves with clearer eyes
In that calm region where no night
Can hide us from each other's sight.
> *Ibid.*

Stay for me there; I will not fail
To meet thee in that hollow vale.
> *Ibid.*

FRANCIS QUARLES
[1592 1644]

Death aims with fouler spite
At fairer marks.[1]
> *Divine Fancies* [1632]

Sweet Phosphor, bring the day!
Light will repay
The wrongs of night.
> *Emblems* [1635]. *Book I,
> Emblem 14*

Be wisely worldly, be not worldly wise.
> *Ibid. Book II, Emblem 2*

This house is to be let for life or years;
Her rent is to sorrow, and her income
  tears.
Cupid, 't has long stood void; her bills
  make known,
She must be dearly let, or let alone.
> *Ibid. Emblem 10, Epigram*

The slender debt to Nature's quickly
  paid,[2]
Discharged, perchance, with greater
  ease than made.
> *Ibid. Emblem 13*

[1] See Edward Young, page 306a.
[2] To die is a debt we must all of us discharge. — EURIPIDES: *Alcestis, L. 418*

The next way home's the farthest way
about.[1]
> *Emblems. Book IV, Emblem 2,*
> *Epigram*

It is the lot of man but once to die.
> *Ibid. Book V, Emblem 7*

And what's a life? — a weary pilgrimage,
Whose glory in one day doth fill the
stage
With childhood, manhood, and decrepit
age.
> *What Is Life? Stanza 1*

Let all thy joys be as the month of
May,
And all thy days be as a marriage day:
Let sorrow, sickness, and a troubled
mind
Be stranger to thee, let them never find
Thy heart at home.
> *To a Bride*

The way to bliss lies not on beds of
down,
And he that has no cross deserves no
crown.
> *Esther*

THOMAS RAVENSCROFT
[1592?–1635]

Nose, nose, nose, nose!
And who gave thee that jolly red nose?
Sinament and Ginger, Nutmegs and
Cloves,
And that gave me my jolly red nose.
> *Deuteromelia* [*1609*]. *Song No. 7* [2]

GEORGE HERBERT
[1593–1633]

Sweet day, so cool, so calm, so bright,
The bridal of the earth and sky.
> *The Temple* [*1633*]. *Virtue,*
> *Stanza 1*

Sweet spring, full of sweet days and
roses,
A box where sweets compacted lie.
> *The Temple. Virtue, Stanza 3*

Only a sweet and virtuous soul,
Like seasoned timber, never gives.
> *Ibid. Stanza 4*

Love bade me welcome; yet my soul
drew back,
Guilty of dust and sin.
But quick-ey'd Love, observing me
grow slack
From my first entrance in,
Drew nearer to me, sweetly questioning
If I lack'd anything.
> *Ibid. Love, Stanza 1*

"You must sit down," says Love, "and
taste my meat."
So I did sit and eat.
> *Ibid. Stanza 3*

A verse may find him who a sermon
flies.[1]
And turn delight into a sacrifice.
> *Ibid. The Church Porch, Stanza 1*

Drink not the third glass, which thou
canst not tame,
When once it is within thee.
> *Ibid. Stanza 5*

Dare to be true: nothing can need a
lie;
A fault which needs it most, grows two
thereby.[2]
> *Ibid. Stanza 13*

By all means use sometimes to be alone.
> *Ibid. Stanza 25*

By no means run in debt: take thine
own measure.
Who cannot live on twenty pound a
year,
Cannot on forty.
> *Ibid. Stanza 30*

Wit's an unruly engine, wildly striking

---

[1] The longest way round is the shortest way
home. — BOHN: *Foreign Proverbs, Italian*

[2] Quoted by BEAUMONT AND FLETCHER, *The
Knight of the Burning Pestle* [1613], *Act I,
Sc. 3.* RAVENSCROFT's *Deuteromelia* was a supplement to his *Pammelia*, which was the earliest collection of rounds, catches, and canons
printed in England.

[1] That many people read a song
Who will not read a sermon.
> WINTHROP MACKWORTH PRAED [1802–
> 1839]:*The Chant of the Brazenhead,*
> *St. 1*

[2] And he that does one fault at first,
And lies to hide it, makes it two.
> ISAAC WATTS [1674–1748]:
> *Song XV*

Sometimes a friend, sometimes the engineer.

> *The Temple. The Church Porch,*
> *Stanza 41*

Be useful where thou livest.

> *Ibid. Stanza 55*

Sum up at night, what thou hast done by day.

> *Ibid. Stanza 76*

For thirty pence he did my death devise,[1]

Who at three hundred did the ointment prize.[2]

> *Ibid. The Sacrifice, Stanza 5*

Most things move th' under-jaw, the Crocodile not.[3]

Most things sleep lying, th' Elephant leans or stands.[4]

> *Ibid. Providence, Stanza 35*

Pulpits and Sundays, sorrow dogging sin,

Afflictions sorted, anguish of all sizes,

Fine nets and stratagems to catch us in,

Bibles laid open, millions of surprises.

> *Ibid. Sin, Stanza 2*

I struck the board, and cried, "No more;

    I will abroad."

What, shall I ever sigh and pine?

My lines and life are free; free as the road,

Loose as the wind, as large as store.

    Shall I be still in suit?

Have I no harvest but a thorn

To let me blood, and not restore

What I have lost with cordial fruit?

    Sure there was wine

Before my sighs did dry it; there was corn

Before my tears did drown it;

---

[1] See *King John and the Abbot of Canterbury,* page 1012a.

[2] Then saith one of his disciples, Judas Iscariot, Simon's son, which should betray him, Why was not this ointment sold for three hundred pence, and given to the poor? — *John, XII, 4–5*

[3] The crocodile does not move the lower jaw, but is the only animal that brings down its upper jaw to the under one. — HERODOTUS [484–424 B.C.], *Customs of the Egyptians*

[4] Leans the huge elephant. — JAMES THOMSON: *The Seasons, Summer* [1727], L. 725

Is the year only lost to me?

Have I no bays to crown it?

> *The Temple. The Collar*

But as I rav'd and grew more fierce and wild

    At every word,

Methought I heard one calling, "Child";

    And I replied, "My Lord."

> *Ibid.*

He would adore my gifts instead of Me,

And rest in Nature, not the God of Nature:

    So both should losers be.

> *Ibid. The Pulley, Stanza 3*

Let him be rich and weary, that at least,

If goodness lead him not, yet weariness

May toss him to my breast.

> *Ibid. Stanza 4*

Pleasing ware is half sold.

> *Jacula Prudentum* [1640]

Love, and a cough, cannot be hid.

> *Ibid.*

Deceive not thy physician, confessor, nor lawyer.

> *Ibid.*

Who would do ill ne'er wants occasion.

> *Ibid.*

A snow year, a rich year.

> *Ibid.*

Love your neighbour, yet pull not down your hedge.[1]

> *Ibid.*

The mill cannot grind with water that's past.

> *Ibid.*

Good words are worth much, and cost little.

> *Ibid.*

Hell is full of good meanings and wishings.[2]

> *Ibid.*

Whose house is of glass, must not throw stones at another.

> *Ibid.*

---

[1] See Robert Frost, page 879b.

[2] Sir, Hell is paved with good intentions. — SAMUEL JOHNSON [1775]: *Boswell's Life of Dr. Johnson, Everyman ed., Vol. I, P. 555* See William James, page 715a.

By suppers more have been killed than Galen ever cured.

Jacula Prudentum

The lion is not so fierce as they paint him.[1]

Ibid.

Go not for every grief to the physician, nor for every quarrel to the lawyer, nor for every thirst to the pot.

Ibid.

The best mirror is an old friend.

Ibid.

When you are an anvil, hold you still; when you are a hammer, strike your fill.[2]

Ibid.

He that lies with the dogs, riseth with fleas.

Ibid.

He that is not handsome at twenty, nor strong at thirty, nor rich at forty, nor wise at fifty, will never be handsome, strong, rich, or wise.

Ibid.

The buyer needs a hundred eyes, the seller not one.

Ibid.

My house, my house, though thou art small, thou art to me the Escurial.

Ibid.

Trust not one night's ice.

Ibid.

For want of a nail the shoe is lost, for want of a shoe the horse is lost, for want of a horse the rider is lost.[3]

Ibid.

Pension never enriched a young man.

Ibid.

One enemy is too much.[1]

Jacula Prudentum

Thursday come, and the week is gone.

Ibid.

Time is the rider that breaks youth.

Ibid.

Show me a liar, and I will show thee a thief.

Ibid.

One father is more than a hundred school-masters.

Ibid.

Reason lies between the spur and the bridle.

Ibid.

One sword keeps another in the sheath.

Ibid.

God's mill grinds slow, but sure.[2]

Ibid.

It is a poor sport that is not worth the candle.

Ibid.

He that lends, gives.

Ibid.

Poverty is no sin.

Ibid.

Words are women, deeds are men.[3]

Ibid.

To a close shorn sheep, God gives wind by measure.[4]

Ibid.

None knows the weight of another's burthen.

Ibid.

One hour's sleep before midnight is worth three after.

Ibid.

He hath no leisure who useth it not.

Ibid.

---

[1] The lion is not so fierce as painted. — THOMAS FULLER [1608-1661]: *Expecting Preferment*

[2] Stand like an anvil when it is beaten upon. — ST. IGNATIUS THEOPHORUS, Bishop of Antioch [A.D. 104]

When you are the anvil, bear —
When you are the hammer, strike.

EDWIN MARKHAM [1852–1940]: *Preparedness*

[3] A little neglect may breed mischief: for want of a nail, etc. — BENJAMIN FRANKLIN: *Maxim prefixed to Poor Richard's Almanac* [1757]

[1] See Ali Ibn-abu-Taleb, page 73b.

[2] See Euripides, page 17a.

Though the mills of God grind slowly, yet they grind exceeding small. — F. VON LOGAU [1604-1655]: *Retribution* (translated by LONGFELLOW)

[3] See Samuel Johnson, page 336b.

[4] Dieu mesure le froid à la brebis tondue (God proportions the wind to the shorn sheep). — HENRI ESTIENNE: *Prémices* [1594]

"God tempers the wind," said Maria, "to the shorn lamb." LAURENCE STERNE: *A Sentimental Journey* [1768]

Half the world knows not how the other half lives.

Jacula Prudentum

Life is half spent before we know what it is.

Ibid.

Every mile is two in winter.

Ibid.

The eye is bigger than the belly.

Ibid.

His bark is worse than his bite.

Ibid.

He that steals an egg will steal an ox.

Ibid. [*second edition, 1651*]

Of a pig's tail you can never make a good shaft.[1]

Ibid.

There is an hour wherein a man might be happy all his life could he find it.

Ibid.

Woe be to him who reads but one book.

Ibid.

IZAAK WALTON
[1593–1683]

But God, who is able to prevail, wrestled with him, as the angel did with Jacob, and marked him; marked him for his own.[2]

Life of Donne [*1640*]

Of which, if thou be a severe, sour-complexioned man, then I here disallow thee to be a competent judge.

The Compleat Angler [*1653–1655*]. *Author's Preface*

I have laid aside business, and gone a-fishing.

Ibid.

Angling may be said to be so like the

mathematics that it can never be fully learnt.

The Compleat Angler. Author's Preface

As no man is born an artist, so no man is born an angler.

Ibid.

I shall stay him no longer than to wish him a rainy evening to read this following discourse; and that if he be an honest angler, the east wind may never blow when he goes a fishing.

Ibid.

As the Italians say, Good company in a journey makes the way to seem the shorter.

Ibid. Part I, Chap. I

Doubt not but angling will prove to be so pleasant that it will prove to be, like virtue, a reward to itself.[1]

Ibid.

Sir Henry Wotton was a most dear lover and a frequent practiser of the Art of Angling; of which he would say, "'Twas an employment for his idle time, which was then not idly spent, a rest to his mind, a cheerer of his spirits, a diverter of sadness, a calmer of unquiet thoughts, a moderator of passions, a procurer of contentedness"; and "that it begat habits of peace and patience in those that professed and practised it."

Ibid.

You will find angling to be like the virtue of humility, which has a calmness of spirit and a world of other blessings attending upon it.[2]

Ibid.

---

[1] You can't make a silk purse out of a sow's ear. — JONATHAN SWIFT: *Polite Conversation* [?1738], *Dialogue II*

As certainly as you can make a velvet cap out of a sow's ear. — STERNE: *Tristram Shandy* [1761–1768], *Book IV*

The proverb says you can't make a silk purse out of a sow's ear. — DICKENS: *David Copperfield* [1849–1850], *Chap. 30*

[2] See Thomas Gray, page 349a.

[1] Ipsa quidem virtus sibimet pulcherrima merces (Virtue herself is her own fairest reward). — SILIUS ITALICUS [A.D. 25?–99]: *Punica, Lib. XIII, L. 663*

Virtue was sufficient of herself for happiness. — DIOGENES LAERTIUS [*circa* A.D. 200]: *Plato, XLII*

That virtue is her own reward, is but a cold principle. — SIR THOMAS BROWNE: *Religio Medici* [1642], *Part I, Sect. XLVII*

Virtue is its own reward. — PRIOR [1664–1721]: *Imitations of Horace, Book III, Ode 2*

[2] There is certainly something in angling . . . that tends to produce a gentleness of

I remember that a wise friend of mine did usually say, "That which is everybody's business is nobody's business."

> *The Compleat Angler.*
> *Part I, Chap. II*

An honest Ale-house where we shall find a cleanly room, Lavender in the Windows, and twenty Ballads stuck about the wall.

> *Ibid.*

Good company and good discourse are the very sinews of virtue.

> *Ibid.*

An excellent angler, and now with God.

> *Ibid. Chap. IV*

Old-fashioned poetry, but choicely good.

> *Ibid.*

I love such mirth as does not make friends ashamed to look upon one another next morning.

> *Ibid. Chap. V*

No man can lose what he never had.

> *Ibid.*

We may say of angling as Dr. Boteler[1] said of strawberries: "Doubtless God could have made a better berry, but doubtless God never did"; and so, if I might be judge, God never did make a more calm, quiet, innocent recreation than angling.

> *Ibid.*

I in these flowery meads would be;
These crystal springs should solace me,
To whose harmonious bubbling noise,
I with my angle would rejoice.

> *Ibid. The Angler's Wish. Stanza 1*

Thus use your frog: put your hook through his mouth and out at his gills, and then with a fine needle and silk sew the upper part of his leg with only one stitch to the arming wire of your hook, or tie the frog's leg above the upper joint to the armed wire; and in

spirit, and a pure serenity of mind. — WASHINGTON IRVING: *The Sketch-Book, The Angler*

[1] William Butler [1535–1618], styled by THOMAS FULLER in his *Worthies of England* the "Aesculapius of our age." This praise of the strawberry first appeared in the second edition of *The Angler*, 1655.

so doing use him as though you loved him.

> *The Compleat Angler. Part I,*
> *Chap. VIII*

This dish of meat is too good for any but anglers, or very honest men.

> *Ibid.*

Look to your health; and if you have it, praise God, and value it next to a good conscience; for health is the second blessing that we mortals are capable of, — a blessing that money cannot buy.

> *Ibid. Chap. XXI*

And upon all that are lovers of virtue, and dare trust in his Providence, and be quiet and go a-angling.

> *Ibid.*

The great secretary of Nature and all learning, Sir Francis Bacon.[1]

> *Life of Herbert* [*1670*]

THOMAS CAREW
[1595?–1639?]

Ask me no more where Jove bestows,
When June is past, the fading rose;
For in your beauty's orient deep
These flowers, as in their causes sleep.

> *To Celia* [*1640*]. *Stanza 1*

Ask me no more whither doth haste
The nightingale when May is past;
For in your sweet dividing throat
She winters and keeps warm her note.

> *Ibid. Stanza 3*

Ask me no more if East or West
The phoenix builds her spicy nest;
For unto you at last she flies,
And in your fragrant bosom dies.

> *Ibid. Stanza 5*

Give me more love or more disdain;
The torrid or the frozen zone:
Bring equal ease unto my pain;
The temperate affords me none.

> *Mediocrity in Love Rejected* [*1640*]

Thou shalt confess the vain pursuit
Of human glory yields no fruit
But an untimely grave.

> *On the Duke of Buckingham* [*1640*]

[1] Plato, Aristotle, and Socrates are secretaries of Nature. — JAMES HOWELL [1594–1666]: *Letters, Books II, Letter XI*

He that loves a rosy cheek,
 Or a coral lip admires,
Or from star-like eyes doth seek
 Fuel to maintain his fires; —
As old Time makes these decay,
So his flames must waste away.
            Disdain Returned [*1640*]. *Stanza 1*
The firstling of the infant year.
                        The Primrose [*1640*]
Then fly betimes, for only they
Conquer Love that run away.
            Conquest by Flight [*1640*]
The magic of a face.
      Epitaph on the Lady S—— [1640]

RENÉ DESCARTES
[1596–1650]

I think, therefore I am.[1]
      Le Discours de la Méthode [*1637*]
Good sense is of all things in the
world the most equally distributed, for
everybody thinks himself so abundantly
provided with it, that even those most
difficult to please in all other matters
do not commonly desire more of it than
they already possess.
                              Ibid.
The greatest minds are capable of
the greatest vices as well as of the greatest virtues.
                              Ibid.

JAMES SHIRLEY
[1596–1666]

How little room
Do we take up in death, that, living
      know
No bounds!
                  The Wedding [*1626*]
Only the actions of the just
Smell sweet and blossom in their dust.[2]
                              Ibid.
Death calls ye to the crowd of common
      men.
            Cupid and Death [*1653*]

[1] Cogito, ergo sum.
 Je pense donc je suis.
[2] The sweet remembrance of the just
 Shall flourish when he sleeps in dust.
 NAHUM TATE AND NICHOLAS BRADY:
      Psalm CXXXII [1696], 6

The glories of our blood and state
 Are shadows, not substantial things;
There is no armour against fate;
 Death lays his icy hand on kings.
      Contention of Ajax and Ulysses
                  [*1659*]. *Sc. 3*
The garlands wither on your brow;
Then boast no more your mighty deeds.
                              Ibid.

OLIVER CROMWELL
[1599–1658]

The State, in choosing men to serve
it, takes no notice of their opinions. If
they be willing faithfully to serve it,
that satisfies.
        *Before the Battle of Marston
            Moor* [*July 2, 1644*]
A few honest men are better than
numbers. If you choose godly, honest
men to be captains of horse, honest men
will follow them.
      Reorganization of the Army [*1645*]
I would have been glad to have lived
under my woodside, and to have kept
a flock of sheep, rather than to have
undertaken this government.
            To Parliament [*1658*]
Mr. Lely, I desire you would use all
your skill to paint my picture truly like
me, and not flatter me at all; but remark all these roughnesses, pimples,
warts, and everything as you see me,
otherwise I will never pay a farthing
for it.
      HORACE WALPOLE: *Anecdotes of
        Painting in England* [*1762–1771*]
I would be willing to live to be further serviceable to God and His people,
but my work is done! Yet God will be
with His people!
      [*September 1, 1658, two days
            before his death*]

SAMUEL BUTLER
[1600–1680]

When civil fury first grew high,
And men fell out they knew not why.
            Hudibras. Part I [*1663*],
                  Canto I, Line 1

And pulpit, drum ecclesiastic,[1]
Was beat with fist instead of a stick.
> *Hudibras. Part I, Canto I,*
> *Line 11*

We grant, although he had much wit,
He was very shy of using it.
> *Ibid. Line 45*

Beside, 'tis known he could speak
    Greek
As naturally as pigs squeak;[2]
That Latin was no more difficile
Than to a blackbird 'tis to whistle.
> *Ibid. Line 51*

He could distinguish and divide
A hair 'twixt south and southwest side,
On either which he would dispute,
Confute, change hands, and still con-
    fute.
> *Ibid. Line 67*

He'd run in debt by disputation,
And pay with ratiocination.
> *Ibid. Line 77*

For rhetoric, he could not ope
His mouth, but out there flew a trope.
> *Ibid. Line 81*

For all a rhetorician's rules
Teach nothing but to name his tools.
> *Ibid. Line 89*

A Babylonish dialect
Which learned pedants much affect.
> *Ibid. Line 93*

For he by geometric scale
Could take the size of pots of ale.
> *Ibid. Line 121*

And wisely tell what hour o' the day
The clock does strike, by algebra.
> *Ibid. Line 125*

Where entity and quiddity,
The ghosts of defunct bodies, fly.
> *Ibid. Line 145*

'Twas Presbyterian true blue.
> *Ibid. Line 189*

---

[1] This is the first we hear of the "drum ecclesiastic" beating up for recruits in worldly
warfare in our country. — WASHINGTON IRV-
ING: *Knickerbocker's History of New York*
[1809], *Book V, Chap. 7*

[2] He Greek and Latin speaks with greater
    ease
    Than hogs eat acorns, and tame pigeons
    peas.
    LIONEL CRANFIELD, EARL OF MIDDLE-
    SEX [1575–1645]: *Panegyric on Tom
    Coriate*

Such as do build their faith upon
The holy text of pike and gun.
> *Hudibras. Part I, Canto I,*
> *Line 193*

And prove their doctrine orthodox,
By apostolic blows and knocks.
> *Ibid. Line 199*

Compound for sins they are inclined to,
By damning those they have no mind
    to.
> *Ibid. Line 215*

The trenchant blade, Toledo trusty,
For want of fighting was grown rusty,
And ate into itself, for lack
Of somebody to hew and hack.
> *Ibid. Line 359*

For rhyme the rudder is of verses,
With which, like ships, they steer their
    courses.
> *Ibid. Line 463*

And force them, though it was in spite
Of Nature and their stars, to write.
> *Ibid. Line 647*

Great actions are not always true sons
Of great and mighty resolutions.
> *Ibid. Line 885*

I'll make the fur
Fly 'bout the ears of the old cur.
> *Ibid. Canto III, Line 277*

These reasons made his mouth to water.
> *Ibid. Line 379*

I am not now in fortune's power:
He that is down can fall no lower.[1]
> *Ibid. Line 871*

Cheer'd up himself with ends of verse
And sayings of philosophers.
> *Ibid. Line 1011*

Cleric before, and Lay behind;
A lawless linsey-woolsey brother,
Half of one order, half another.
> *Ibid. Line 1226*

But those that write in rhyme still
    make
The one verse for the other's sake;
For one for sense, and one for rhyme,
I think's sufficient at one time.
> *Ibid. Part II* [1664], *Canto I,*
> *Line 23*

Some have been beaten till they know
What wood a cudgel's of by th' blow;

---

[1] He that is down needs fear no fall. —
BUNYAN: *Pilgrim's Progress* [1678], *Part II*

Some kick'd until they can feel whether
A shoe be Spanish or neat's leather.
> *Hudibras. Part II, Canto I,*
> *Line 221*

Such great achievements cannot fail,
To cast salt on a woman's tail.
> *Ibid. Line 277*

Quoth she, I've heard old cunning stagers
Say fools for arguments use wagers.
> *Ibid. Line 297*

For what is worth in anything
But so much money as 'twill bring?
> *Ibid. Line 465*

She that with poetry is won
Is but a desk to write upon.
> *Ibid. Line 591*

Love is a boy by poets styl'd;
Then spare the rod and spoil the child.[1]
> *Ibid. Line 843*

The sun had long since in the lap
Of Thetis taken out his nap,
And, like a lobster boil'd the morn
From black to red began to turn.
> *Ibid. Canto II, Line 29*

Oaths are but words, and words but wind.
> *Ibid. Line 107*

For truth is precious and divine, —
Too rich a pearl for carnal swine.
> *Ibid. Line 257*

He that imposes an oath makes it,
Not he that for convenience takes it;
Then how can any man be said
To break an oath he never made?
> *Ibid. Line 377*

As the ancients
Say wisely, have a care o' th' main chance,[2]
And look before you ere you leap;[3]
For as you sow, ye are like to reap.[4]
> *Ibid. Line 501*

Doubtless the pleasure is as great
Of being cheated as to cheat.
> *Ibid. Canto III, Line 1*

[1] See Skelton, page 84b.
[2] See Lyly, page 112b.
[3] See Heywood, page 91a.
[4] Whatsoever a man soweth, that shall he also reap. — *Galatians, VI, 7*

He made an instrument to know
If the moon shine at full or no.
> *Hudibras. Part II, Canto III,*
> *Line 261*

But Hudibras gave him a twitch
As quick as lightning in the breech,
Just in the place where honour's lodg'd,
As wise philosophers have judg'd;
Because a kick in that part more
Hurts honour than deep wounds before.
> *Ibid. Line 1065*

As men of inward light are wont
To turn their optics in upon 't.
> *Ibid. Part III [1678], Canto I,*
> *Line 481*

What makes all doctrines plain and clear?
About two hundred pounds a year.
And that which was prov'd true before
Prove false again? Two hundred more.
> *Ibid. Line 1277*

Nick Machiavel had ne'er a trick,
Though he gave his name to our Old Nick.[1]
> *Ibid. Line 1313*

With crosses, relics, crucifixes,
Beads, pictures, rosaries, and pixes, —
The tools of working our salvation
By mere mechanic operation.
> *Ibid. Line 1495*

The saints engage in fierce contests
About their carnal interests.
> *Ibid. Canto II, Introduction*

True as the dial to the sun,[2]
Although it be not shin'd upon.
> *Ibid. Line 175*

He that complies against his will
Is of his own opinion still.
> *Ibid. Canto III, Line 547*

And poets by their sufferings grow,[3]
As if there were no more to do,

[1] Out of his surname they have coined an epithet for a knave, and out of his Christian name a synonym for the Devil. — MACAULAY: *Machiavelli* [1827]
[2] True as the needle to the pole,
Or as the dial to the sun.
> BARTON BOOTH [1681–1733]: *Song*
[3] Most wretched men
Are cradled into poetry by wrong;
They learn in suffering what they teach in song.
> SHELLEY: *Julian and Maddalo*
> [1818]

To make a poet excellent,
But only want and discontent.
Fragments

SIR KENELM DIGBY
[1603–1665]

The hot water is to remain upon it
[the tea] no longer than whiles you can
say the Miserere Psalm very leisurely.
The Closet Opened. Tea with Eggs

All Matter is indifferent to Form.
Of the Vegetation of Plants

SIR THOMAS BROWNE
[1605–1682]

I could never divide myself from
any man upon the difference of an opinion, or be angry with his judgment for
not agreeing with me in that from which
perhaps within a few days I should dissent myself.
Religio Medici [*1642*]. *Part I,*
Sect. VI

Many . . . have too rashly charged
the troops of error, and remain as
trophies unto the enemies of truth.
Ibid.

A man may be in as just possession of
truth as of a city, and yet be forced to
surrender.
Ibid.

I love to lose myself in a mystery, to
pursue my Reason to an *O altitudo!*
Ibid. Sect. IX

Rich with the spoils of Nature.[1]
Ibid. Sect. XIII

We carry with us the wonders, we
seek without us: there is all Africa and
her prodigies in us.
Ibid. Sect. XV

All things are artificial, for nature is
the art of God.[2]
Ibid. Sect. XVI

Obstinacy in a bad cause is but constancy in a good.
Ibid. Sect. XXV

[1] See Thomas Gray, page 348b.
[2] The course of Nature is the art of God. —
EDWARD YOUNG: *Night Thoughts* [*1742–
1745*], *Night IX, L. 1267*

Persecution is a bad and indirect way
to plant religion.
Religio Medici. Part I, Sect. XXV

This reasonable moderator, and equal
piece of justice, Death.
Ibid. Sect. XXXVIII

I am not so much afraid of death, as
ashamed thereof. 'Tis the very disgrace
and ignominy of our natures, that in a
moment can so disfigure us, that our
nearest friends, wife, and children,
stand afraid and start at us.
Ibid. Sect. XL

Whosoever enjoys not this life, I
count him but an apparition, though he
wear about him the sensible affections
of flesh. In these moral acceptions, the
way to be immortal is to die daily.
Ibid. Sect. XLV

How shall the dead arise, is no question of my Faith; to believe only possibilities, is not Faith, but mere philosophy.
Ibid. Sect. XLVIII

The heart of man is the place the
devils dwell in: I feel sometimes a hell
within myself.[1]
Ibid. Sect. LI

There is no road or ready way to
virtue.
Ibid. Sect. LV

They that endeavor to abolish vice,
destroy also virtue; for contraries,
though they destroy one another, are
yet the life of one another.
Ibid. Part II, Sect. IV

But how shall we expect charity towards others, when we are uncharitable
to our selves? *Charity begins at home,*
is the voice of the world; yet is every
man his greatest enemy, and, as it were,
his own executioner.
Ibid.

There is music even in the beauty,
and the silent note which Cupid strikes,
far sweeter than the sound of an instru-

[1] The mind is its own place, and in itself
Can make a heaven of hell, a hell of
heaven.
MILTON: *Paradise Lost* [*1667*],
Book I, L. 253
Which way I fly is Hell; myself am Hell.
— *Ibid., Book IV, L. 75*

ment; for there is a music wherever there is a harmony, order, or proportion; and thus far we may maintain the music of the spheres.
Religio Medici. Part II, Sect. IX

For the world, I count it not an inn, but an hospital; and a place not to live, but to die in.
Ibid. Sect. XI

There is surely a piece of divinity in us, something that was before the elements, and owes no homage unto the sun.
Ibid.

Ruat coelum, fiat voluntas tua.[1]
Ibid.

Sleep is a death; oh, make me try
By sleeping, what it is to die,
And as gently lay my head
On my grave, as now my bed!
Ibid. Sect. XII

When we desire to confine our words, we commonly say they are spoken under the rose.[2]
Vulgar Errors [1645]

An old and gray-headed error.
Ibid.

Times before you, when even living men were antiquities; when the living might exceed the dead, and to depart this world could not be properly said to go unto the greater number.[3]
Urn-Burial [1658]. Dedication

I look upon you as a gem of the old rock.[4]
Ibid.

[1] Though the sky fall, let Thy will be done. Fiat justitia et ruant coeli (Let justice be done though the heavens fall). — WILLIAM WATSON: *Ten Quodlibeticall Questions Concerning Religion and State* [1601]

[2] Sub rosa. This phrase, meaning secretly, is of unknown origin. With the ancients the rose was emblematic of secrecy, and when a host hung a rose above his tables, his guests understood that all words spoken under it were to remain secret. Later, roses were carved as decorations on the ceilings of council chambers and confessionals, with the same significance.

[3] 'Tis long since Death had the majority. — BLAIR: *The Grave* [1743], *Part II, L. 449*

[4] Adamas de rupe veteri praestantissimus

Quietly rested under the drums and tramplings of three conquests.
Urn-Burial. Chapter 5

Time which antiquates antiquities, and hath an art to make dust of all things.
Ibid.

What song the Sirens sang, or what name Achilles assumed when he hid himself among women.
Ibid.

The iniquity of oblivion blindly scattereth her poppy.
Ibid.

Herostratus lives that burnt the temple of Diana; he is almost lost that built it.[1]
Ibid.

Oblivion is not to be hired: the greater part must be content to be as though they had not been, to be found in the register of God, not in the record of man.
Ibid.

The night of time far surpasseth the day, and who knows when was the equinox?
Ibid.

Man is a noble animal, splendid in ashes and pompous in the grave, solemnizing nativities and deaths with equal lustre, nor omitting ceremonies of bravery in the infamy of his nature.
Ibid.

To keep our eyes open longer were but to act our antipodes. The huntsmen are up in America, and they are already past their first sleep in Persia. But who can be drowsy at that hour which freed us from everlasting sleep? or have slumbering thoughts at that time, when sleep itself must end, and, as some conjecture, all shall awake again?
The Garden of Cyrus [1658]

(A most excellent diamond from the old rock).

See Burke, page 360b.

[1] The aspiring youth that fired the Ephesian dome
Outlives in fame the pious fool that raised it.
CIBBER [1671–1757]: *Richard III, Act III, Sc. 1*

EDMUND WALLER
[1605–1687]

Illustrious acts high raptures do infuse,
And every conqueror creates a muse.
Panegyric on Cromwell

Under the tropic is our language spoke,
And part of Flanders hath receiv'd our
  yoke.
*Upon the Death of the
Lord Protector [1658]*

The yielding marble of her snowy
  breast.
*On a Lady Passing through a
Crowd of People [1664]*

To man, that was in th' evening made,
  Stars gave the first delight;
Admiring, in the gloomy shade,
  Those little drops of light.
*An Apology for Having Loved
Before [1664]*

That which her slender waist confin'd
Shall now my joyful temples bind;
No monarch but would give his crown
His arms might do what this has done.
On a Girdle [1664]. Stanza 1

My joy, my grief, my hope, my love,
Did all within this circle move!
Ibid. Stanza 2

A narrow compass! and yet there
Dwelt all that's good, and all that's
  fair;
Give me but what this riband bound,
Take all the rest the sun goes round!
Ibid. Stanza 3

  Go, lovely rose!
Tell her that wastes her time and me
  That now she knows,
When I resemble her to thee,
How sweet and fair she seems to be.
Go, Lovely Rose [1664]. Stanza 1

How small a part of time they share
That are so wondrous sweet and fair!
Ibid. Stanza 4

  For all we know
Of what the blessed do above
Is, that they sing, and that they love.
While I Listen to thy Voice

Poets that lasting marble seek
Must come in Latin or in Greek.
Of English Verse [1668]

And keeps the palace of the soul.[1]
Of Tea

Poets lose half the praise they should
  have got,
Could it be known what they discreetly
  blot.
*Upon Roscommon's Translation
of Horace, De Arte Poetica*

The soul's dark cottage, batter'd and
  decay'd,
Lets in new light through chinks that
  Time has made.[2]

Stronger by weakness, wiser men become
As they draw near to their eternal
  home:
Leaving the old, both worlds at once
  they view
That stand upon the threshold of the
  new.
On the Divine Poems [1686]

SIR WILLIAM DAVENANT
[1606–1668]

The lark now leaves his wat'ry nest
And, climbing, shakes his dewy wings.
Song [1637]. Stanza 1

For angling-rod he took a sturdy oak;
For line, a cable that in storm ne'er
  broke;
His hook was such as heads the end
  of pole
To pluck down house ere fire consumes
  it whole;
The hook was baited with a dragon's
  tail, —
And then on rock he stood to bob for
  whale.
Britannia Triumphans [1637]

The assembled souls of all that men
  held wise.
*Gondibert [1651]. Book II,
Canto V, Stanza 37*

I shall ask leave to desist, when I am

---

[1] The dome of thought, the palace of the
soul. — BYRON: *Childe Harold, Canto II*
[1812], *St. 6*
[2] To vanish in the chinks that Time has
made. — SAMUEL ROGERS: *Italy* [1822],
Paestum

interrupted by so great an experiment as dying.

His apology, in illness, for not having finished Gondibert

How much pleasure they lose (and even the pleasures of heroic poesy are not unprofitable) who take away the liberty of a poet, and fetter his feet in the shackles of a historian.

Prefatory Letter to Thomas Hobbes (Quoted in Biographia Literaria [1817] by S. T. COLE-RIDGE, Chapter 22

PIERRE CORNEILLE
[1606–1684]

Pierced to the depth of my heart by a blow unforeseen — and mortal.[1]

Le Cid [1636]. Act I, Sc. 6

He who cares naught for death cares naught for threats.

Ibid. Act II, Sc. 1

We triumph without glory when we conquer without danger.

Ibid. Sc. 2

Brave men are brave from the very first.

Ibid. Sc. 3

And the combat ceased for want of combatants.

Ibid. Act IV, Sc. 3

Do your duty, and leave the rest to heaven.

Horace [1639]. Act II, Sc. 8

All evils are equal when they are extreme.

Ibid. Act III, Sc. 4

Who is all-powerful should fear everything.

Cinna [1639]. Act IV, Sc. 2

By speaking of our misfortunes we often relieve them.

Polyeucte [1640]. Act I, Sc. 3

The manner of giving is worth more than the gift.

Le Menteur [1642]. Act I, Sc. 1

A liar is always lavish of oaths.

Ibid. Act III, Sc. 5

---

[1] Percé jusques au fond du coeur
D'une atteinte imprévue aussi bien que mortelle.

A good memory is needed after one has lied.[1]

Le Menteur. Act IV, Sc. 5

The fire which seems extinguished often slumbers beneath the ashes.

Rodogune [1644]. Act III, Sc. 4

He who allows himself to be insulted deserves to be.

Héraclius [1664]. Act I, Sc. 2

A service beyond all recompense Weighs so heavy that it almost gives offence.

Suréna [1674]. Act III, Sc. 1

THOMAS FULLER
[1608–1661]

Drawing near her death, she sent most pious thoughts as harbingers to heaven; and her soul saw a glimpse of happiness through the chinks of her sickness-broken body.

Life of Monica [1642]

He was one of a lean body and visage, as if his eager soul, biting for anger at the clog of his body, desired to fret a passage through it.[2]

Life of the Duke of Alva [1642]

She commandeth her husband, in any equal matter, by constant obeying him.

Holy and Profane State [1642]. The Good Wife

He knows little who will tell his wife all he knows.

Ibid. The Good Husband

One that will not plead that cause wherein his tongue must be confuted by his conscience.

Ibid. The Good Advocate

To smell to a turf of fresh earth is wholesome for the body; no less are thoughts of mortality cordial to the soul.

Ibid. The Virtuous Lady

Their heads sometimes so little that there is no room for wit; sometimes so

---

[1] Liars ought to have good memories. — ALGERNON SIDNEY: *Discourses on Government* [1698], *Chap. 2, Sect. XV*
[2] See Dryden, page 276b.

long that there is no wit for so much
room.
Holy and Profane State.
Of Natural Fools

Learning hath gained most by those
books by which the printers have lost.
Ibid. Of Books

Deceive not thy self by overexpecting happiness in the married estate.
Remember the nightingales which sing
only some months in the spring, but
commonly are silent when they have
hatched their eggs.
Ibid. Of Marriage

They that marry ancient people,
merely in expectation to bury them,
hang themselves in hope that one will
come and cut the halter.
Ibid.

Fame sometimes hath created something of nothing.
Ibid. Fame

Anger is one of the sinews of the soul;
he that wants it hath a maimed mind.
Ibid. Of Anger

Light, God's eldest daughter, is a
principal beauty in a building.
Ibid. Of Building

In Building, rather believe any man
than an Artificer for matter of charges.
Should they tell thee all the cost at the
first, it would blast a young Builder
in the budding.
Ibid.

JOHN MILTON
[1608–1674]

This is the month, and this the happy
morn,
Wherein the Son of Heav'n's eternal
King,
Of wedded maid and virgin mother
born,
Our great redemption from above did
bring;
For so the holy sages once did sing,
That He our deadly forfeit should re-
lease,

And with His Father work us a perpetual peace.
On the Morning of Christ's Na-
tivity [1629]. Stanza 1, Line 1

It was the winter wild
While the Heav'n-born child
All meanly wrapt in the rude manger
lies.
Ibid. Hymn, Stanza 1, Line 29

No war, or battle's sound
Was heard the world around.
The idle spear and shield were high up
hung.
Ibid. Stanza 4, Line 53

Time will run back and fetch the Age
of Gold.
Ibid. Stanza 14, Line 135

The Oracles are dumb;
No voice or hideous hum
Runs through the archèd roof in words
deceiving.
Ibid. Stanza 19, Line 173

From haunted spring and dale
Edg'd with poplar pale
The parting genius is with sighing sent.
Ibid. Stanza 20, Line 184

Peor and Baalim
Forsake their temples dim.
Ibid. Stanza 22, Line 197

What needs my Shakespeare for his
honour'd bones
The labour of an age in pilèd stones?
Or that his hallow'd relics should be
hid
Under a star-ypointing pyramid?
Dear son of memory, great heir of fame,
What need'st thou such weak witness
of thy name?
On Shakespeare [1630]

And so sepúlchred in such pomp dost
lie,
That kings for such a tomb would wish
to die.
Ibid.

How soon hath Time, the subtle thief of
youth,
Stol'n on his wing my three-and-twen-
tieth year.
On His Having Arrived at the Age
of Twenty-three [1631]

As ever in my great Taskmaster's eye.
Ibid.

Such sweet compulsion doth in music
lie.

> *Arcades* [*1630–1634*]. *Line 68*

Hence, loathèd Melancholy,
Of Cerberus and blackest Midnight
born,
In Stygian cave forlorn,
'Mongst horrid shapes, and shrieks, and
sights unholy.

> *L'Allegro* [*1632*]. *Line 1*

So buxom, blithe, and debonair.

> *Ibid. Line 24*

Haste thee, Nymph, and bring with
thee
Jest, and youthful Jollity,
Quips and Cranks and wanton Wiles,
Nods and Becks and wreathèd Smiles.

> *Ibid. Line 25*

Sport, that wrinkled Care derides,
And Laughter, holding both his sides.
Come, and trip it, as you go,
On the light fantastic toe.

> *Ibid. Line 31*

The mountain nymph, sweet Liberty.

> *Ibid. Line 36*

Mirth, admit me of thy crew,
To live with her, and live with thee,
In unreprovèd pleasures free.

> *Ibid. Line 38*

While the cock with lively din
Scatters the rear of darkness thin,
And to the stack, or the barn door,
Stoutly struts his dames before,
Oft list'ning how the hounds and horn
Cheerly rouse the slumb'ring morn.

> *Ibid. Line 49*

And every shepherd tells his tale
Under the hawthorn in the dale.

> *Ibid. Line 67*

Meadows trim, with daisies pied,
Shallow brooks, and rivers wide;
Towers and battlements it sees
Bosom'd high in tufted trees,
Where perhaps some beauty lies,
The cynosure of neighboring eyes.

> *Ibid. Line 75*

And the jocund rebecks sound
To many a youth, and many a maid,
Dancing in the chequered shade.

And young and old come forth to play
On a sunshine holiday.

> *L'Allegro. Line 94*

Then to the spicy nut-brown ale.

> *Ibid. Line 100*

Then lies him down the lubber fiend,
And stretch'd out all the chimney's
length,
Basks at the fire his hairy strength.

> *Ibid. Line 110*

Tower'd cities please us then,
And the busy hum of men.

> *Ibid. Line 117*

Ladies, whose bright eyes
Rain influence, and judge the prize.

> *Ibid. Line 121*

And pomp, and feast, and revelry,
With mask, and antique pageantry,
Such sights as youthful poets dream
On summer eves by haunted stream.
Then to the well-trod stage anon,
If Jonson's learned sock be on,
Or sweetest Shakespeare, Fancy's child,
Warble his native wood-notes wild.

> *Ibid. Line 127*

And ever, against eating cares,
Lap me in soft Lydian airs,
Married to immortal verse,[1]
Such as the meeting soul may pierce,
In notes with many a winding bout
Of linkèd sweetness long drawn out.

> *Ibid. Line 135*

Untwisting all the chains that tie
The hidden soul of harmony.

> *Ibid. Line 143*

Such strains as would have won the ear
Of Pluto, to have quite set free
His half-regain'd Eurydice.
These delights, if thou canst give,
Mirth, with thee, I mean to live.

> *Ibid. Line 148*

Hence vain deluding Joys,
The brood of Folly without father
bred!

> *Il Penseroso* [*1632*]. *Line 1*

The gay motes that people the sunbeams.

> *Ibid. Line 8*

---

[1] Wisdom married to immortal verse.—
WORDSWORTH: *The Excursion* [1814], *Book VII*

Come pensive Nun, devout and pure,
Sober, steadfast, and demure.
　　　　Il Penseroso. Line 31

And looks commercing with the skies,
Thy rapt soul sitting in thine eyes.
　　　　Ibid. Line 39

Forget thyself to marble.
　　　　Ibid. Line 42

And join with thee, calm Peace and Quiet,
Spare Fast, that oft with gods doth diet.
　　　　Ibid. Line 45

And add to these retired Leisure,
That in trim gardens takes his pleasure.
　　　　Ibid. Line 49

Sweet bird, that shunn'st the noise of folly,
Most musical, most melancholy!
　　　　Ibid. Line 61

　　I walk unseen
On the dry smooth-shaven green,
To behold the wandering moon,
Riding near her highest noon,
Like one that had been led astray
Through the heav'n's wide pathless way,
And oft, as if her head she bow'd,
Stooping through a fleecy cloud.
　　　　Ibid. Line 65

Oft, on a plat of rising ground,
I hear the far-off curfew sound
Over some wide-watered shore,
Swinging low with sullen roar.
　　　　Ibid. Line 73

Where glowing embers through the room
Teach light to counterfeit a gloom,
Far from all resort of mirth,
Save the cricket on the hearth.
　　　　Ibid. Line 79

Sometime let gorgeous Tragedy
In sceptred pall come sweeping by,
Presenting Thebes, or Pelops' line,
Or the tale of Troy divine.
　　　　Ibid. Line 97

Or bid the soul of Orpheus sing
Such notes as, warbled to the string,
Drew iron tears down Pluto's cheek.
　　　　Ibid. Line 105

Or call up him that left half told
The story of Cambuscan bold.
　　　　Il Penseroso. Line 109

Where more is meant than meets the ear.
　　　　Ibid. Line 120

When the gust hath blown his fill,
Ending on the rustling leaves,
With minute-drops from off the eaves.
　　　　Ibid. Line 128

Hide me from day's garish eye,
While the bee with honied thigh,
That at her flowery work doth sing,
And the waters murmuring
With such consort as they keep,
Entice the dewy-feather'd sleep.
　　　　Ibid. Line 141

And storied windows richly dight,
Casting a dim religious light.
There let the pealing organ blow,
To the full-voiced quire below,
In service high, and anthems clear
As may, with sweetness, through mine ear
Dissolve me into ecstasies,
And bring all Heaven before mine eyes.
　　　　Ibid. Line 159

Till old experience do attain
To something like prophetic strain.
　　　　Ibid. Line 173

Before the starry threshold of Jove's Court [1]
My mansion is.
　　　　Comus [1634]. Line 1

Above the smoke and stir of this dim spot
Which men call earth.
　　　　Ibid. Line 5

Yet some there be that by due steps aspire
To lay their just hands on that golden key
That opes the palace of Eternity.
　　　　Ibid. Line 12

An old, and haughty nation proud in arms.
　　　　Ibid. Line 33

What never yet was heard in tale or song,

[1] See William Blake, page 386b.

From old or modern bard, in hall or
bower.
Comus. Line 44

Bacchus, that first from out the purple
grape
Crush'd the sweet poison of misusèd
wine.
Ibid. Line 46

These my sky-robes, spun out of Iris'
woof.
Ibid. Line 83

The star that bids the shepherd fold.
Ibid. Line 93

And the gilded car of day,
His glowing axle doth allay
In the steep Atlantic stream.
Ibid. Line 95

Midnight shout and revelry,
Tipsy dance and jollity.
Ibid. Line 103

What hath night to do with sleep?
Ibid. Line 122

Ere the blabbing eastern scout,
The nice morn, on th' Indian steep,
From her cabin'd loop-hole peep.
Ibid. Line 138

When the gray-hooded Even,
Like a sad votarist in palmer's weed,
Rose from the hindmost wheels of
Phoebus' wain.
Ibid. Line 188

A thousand fantasies
Begin to throng into my memory,
Of calling shapes, and beck'ning shad-
ows dire,
And airy tongues that syllable men's
names
On sands and shores and desert wilder-
nesses.
Ibid. Line 205

Was I deceiv'd, or did a sable cloud
Turn forth her silver lining on the
night?
Ibid. Line 221

Sweet Echo, sweetest nymph, that liv'st
unseen
Within thy airy shell
By slow Meander's margent green,
And in the violet-embroidered
vale.
Ibid. Line 230

How sweetly did they float upon the
wings
Of silence, through the empty-vaulted
night,
At every fall smoothing the raven down
Of darkness till it smil'd!
Comus. Line 249

Such sober certainty of waking bliss.
Ibid. Line 263

With thy long levell'd rule of streaming light.
Ibid. Line 340

Virtue could see to do what Virtue
would
By her own radiant light, though sun
and moon
Were in the flat sea sunk. And Wis-
dom's self
Oft seeks to sweet retired solitude,
Where, with her best nurse Contem-
plation,
She plumes her feathers, and lets grow
her wings.
Ibid. Line 373

The unsunn'd heaps
Of miser's treasure.
Ibid. Line 398

'Tis Chastity, my brother, Chastity:
She that has that, is clad in complete
steel.
Ibid. Line 420

Some say no evil thing that walks by
night,
In fog or fire, by lake or moorish fen,
Blue meagre hag, or stubborn unlaid
ghost,
That breaks his magic chains at curfew
time,
No goblin, or swart faery of the mine,
Hath hurtful power o'er true virginity.
Ibid. Line 432

How charming is divine philosophy!
Not harsh and crabbed, as dull fools
suppose,
But musical as is Apollo's lute,[1]
And a perpetual feast of nectar'd sweets
Where no crude surfeit reigns.
Ibid. Line 476

---

[1]   As sweet and musical
As bright Apollo's lute.
SHAKESPEARE: *Love's Labour's Lost*
[1594–1595], *Act IV, Sc. 3, L. 342*

Fill'd the air with barbarous dissonance.

Comus. Line 550

I was all ear,
And took in strains that might create a soul
Under the ribs of Death.

Ibid. Line 560

That power
Which erring men call Chance.

Ibid. Line 587

Praising the lean and sallow abstinence.

Ibid. Line 709

Beauty is Nature's coin, must not be hoarded,
But must be current, and the good thereof
Consists in mutual and partaken bliss.

Ibid. Line 739

Beauty is Nature's brag, and must be shown
In courts, at feasts, and high solemnities,
Where most may wonder at the workmanship;
It is for homely features to keep home, —
They had their name thence; coarse complexions
And cheeks of sorry grain will serve to ply
The sampler, and to tease the huswife's wool.
What need a vermeil-tinctur'd lip for that,
Love-darting eyes, or tresses like the morn?

Ibid. Line 745

Enjoy your dear wit, and gay rhetoric,
That hath so well been taught her dazzling fence.

Ibid. Line 790

Sabrina fair,
Listen where thou art sitting
Under the glassy, cool, translucent wave,
In twisted braids of lilies knitting
The loose train of thy amber-dropping hair;
Listen for dear honour's sake,

Goddess of the silver lake,
Listen and save.

Comus. Line 859

But now my task is smoothly done:
I can fly, or I can run.

Ibid. Line 1012

Love Virtue, she alone is free,
She can teach ye how to climb
Higher than the sphery chime;
Or, if Virtue feeble were,
Heav'n itself would stoop to her.

Ibid. Line 1019

I come to pluck your berries harsh and crude,
And with forc'd fingers rude
Shatter your leaves before the mellowing year.

Lycidas [1637]. Line 3

He knew
Himself to sing, and build the lofty rhyme.

Ibid. Line 10

Without the meed of some melodious tear.

Ibid. Line 14

Hence with denial vain, and coy excuse.

Ibid. Line 18

Under the opening eyelids of the morn,
We drove afield; and both together heard
What time the gray-fly winds her sultry horn,
Batt'ning our flocks with the fresh dews of night.

Ibid. Line 26

But oh the heavy change, now thou art gone,
Now thou art gone and never must return!

Ibid. Line 37

The gadding vine.

Ibid. Line 40

As killing as the canker to the rose.

Ibid. Line 45

Alas! what boots it with incessant care
To tend the homely slighted shepherd's trade,
And strictly meditate the thankless Muse?
Were it not better done as others use,

To sport with Amaryllis in the shade,
Or with the tangles of Neaera's hair?
                    Lycidas. Line 64
Fame is the spur that the clear spirit
    doth raise [1]
(That last infirmity of noble mind) [2]
To scorn delights, and live laborious
    days;
But the fair guerdon when we hope to
    find,
And think to burst out into sudden
    blaze,
Comes the blind Fury with th' abhorred
    shears
And slits the thin-spun life.
                    Ibid. Line 70
Fame is no plant that grows on mortal
    soil.
                    Ibid. Line 78
The strain I heard was of a higher mood.
                    Ibid. Line 87
It was that fatal and perfidious bark
Built in th' eclipse, and rigg'd with
    curses dark,
That sunk so low that sacred head of
    thine.
                    Ibid. Line 100
The Pilot of the Galilean lake;
Two massy keys he bore of metals
    twain
(The golden opes, the iron shuts
    amain).
                    Ibid. Line 109
        Such as for their bellies' sake,
Creep and intrude, and climb into the
    fold.
                    Ibid. Line 114
The hungry sheep look up, and are not
    fed,
But, swoln with wind and the rank mist
    they draw,
Rot inwardly and foul contagion
    spread;
Besides what the grim wolf with privy
    paw

[1] See Tacitus, page 63b.
[2] That thirst (for applause), if the last infirmity of noble minds, is also the first infirmity of weak ones; and, on the whole, the
strongest impulsive influence of average
humanity. — RUSKIN: *Sesame and Lilies*
[1865], *Of Kings' Treasuries, 3*

Daily devours apace, and nothing said.
                    Lycidas. Line 123
But that two-handed engine at the door
Stands ready to smite once, and smite
    no more.
                    Ibid. Line 130
Throw hither all your quaint enamell'd
    eyes,
That on the green turf suck the honied
    showers,
And purple all the ground with vernal
    flowers.
                    Ibid. Line 139
Whether beyond the stormy Hebrides,
Where thou perhaps under the whelm-
    ing tide
Visit'st the bottom of the monstrous
    world.
                    Ibid. Line 156
Look homeward, Angel, now, and melt
    with ruth.
                    Ibid. Line 163
For Lycidas your sorrow is not dead,
Sunk though he be beneath the watery
    floor;
So sinks the day-star in the ocean bed,
And yet anon repairs his drooping head,
And tricks his beams, and with new-
    spangled ore
Flames in the forehead of the morning
    sky.
                    Ibid. Line 166
He touch'd the tender stops of various
    quills,
With eager thought warbling his Doric
    lay.
                    Ibid. Line 188
At last he rose, and twitch'd his mantle
    blue:
Tomorrow to fresh woods and pastures
    new.
                    Ibid. Line 192
    The lazy leaden-stepping Hours,
Whose speed is but the heavy plum-
    met's pace.
                    On Time [Circa *1637*]
    All this earthy grossness quit,
Attired with stars we shall for ever sit,
Triumphing over Death, and Chance,
    and thee, O Time.
                    Ibid.

Thy liquid notes that close the eye of
day.
> *Sonnet: To the Nightingale*
> [Circa *1637*]

Where the bright seraphim in burning
row
Their loud up-lifted angel trumpets
blow.
> *At a Solemn Music* [Circa *1637*]

A poet soaring in the high reason of
his fancies, with his garland and singing robes about him.
> *The Reason of Church Gov-
> ernment* [*1641*]. *Book II,
> Introduction*

By labour and intent study (which
I take to be my portion in this life),
joined with the strong propensity of
nature, I might perhaps leave something so written to after times as they
should not willingly let it die.
> *Ibid.*

Beholding the bright countenance of
truth in the quiet and still air of delightful studies.
> *Ibid.*

He who would not be frustrate of his
hope to write well hereafter in laudable
things ought himself to be a true poem.
> *Apology for Smectymnuus* [*1642*]

His words, like so many nimble and
airy servitors, trip about him at command.
> *Ibid.*

Litigious terms, fat contentions, and
flowing fees.
> *Tractate of Education* [*1644*]

Enflamed with the study of learning
and the admiration of virtue; stirred up
with high hopes of living to be brave
men and worthy patriots, dear to God,
and famous to all ages.
> *Ibid.*

Ornate rhetorick taught out of the
rule of Plato. . . . To which poetry
would be made subsequent, or indeed
rather precedent, as being less subtle
and fine, but more simple, sensuous,
and passionate.
> *Ibid.*

In those vernal seasons of the year,
when the air is calm and pleasant, it
were an injury and sullenness against
Nature not to go out and see her riches,
and partake in her rejoicing with heaven
and earth.
> *Tractate of Education*

Books are not absolutely dead things,
but do contain a potency of life in them
to be as active as that soul was whose
progeny they are; nay they do preserve
as in a vial the purest efficacy and extraction of that living intellect that
bred them.
> *Areopagitica* [*1644*]

As good almost kill a man as kill a
good book: who kills a man kills a
reasonable creature, God's image; but
he who destroys a good book kills
reason itself.
> *Ibid.*

A good book is the precious life-blood
of a master-spirit, embalmed and treasured up on purpose to a life beyond
life.
> *Ibid.*

I cannot praise a fugitive and clois-
tered virtue, unexercised and un-
breathed, that never sallies out and
sees her adversary, but slinks out of the
race where that immortal garland is to
be run for, not without dust and heat.
> *Ibid.*

Who shall silence all the airs and
madrigals that whisper softness in
chambers?
> *Ibid.*

Where there is much desire to learn,
there of necessity will be much arguing,
much writing, many opinions; for opinion in good men is but knowledge in the
making.
> *Ibid.*

Methinks I see in my mind a noble
and puissant nation rousing herself like
a strong man after sleep, and shaking
her invincible locks: methinks I see her
as an eagle mewing her mighty youth,
and kindling her undazzled eyes at the
full midday beam.
> *Ibid.*

Though all the winds of doctrine [1]

[1] *Winds of Doctrine,* used as title of a
book by GEORGE SANTAYANA [1913].

were let loose to play upon the earth, so Truth be in the field, we do ingloriously, by licensing and prohibiting, to misdoubt her strength. Let her and Falsehood grapple: who ever knew Truth put to the worse in a free and open encounter?[1]

Areopagitica

Men of most renowned virtue have sometimes by transgressing most truly kept the law.

Tetrachordon [*1644–1645*]

That old man eloquent.

To the Lady Margaret Ley [*1644?*]

That would have made Quintilian stare and gasp.

On the Detraction which followed upon my writing certain Treatises [*1645*]

License they mean when they cry Liberty;
For who loves that must first be wise and good.

Ibid. II

In mirth that after no repenting draws.

Sonnet XI. To Cyriack Skinner [*1646–1647?*]

For other things mild Heav'n a time ordains,
And disapproves that care, though wise in show,
That with superfluous burden loads the day,
And, when God sends a cheerful hour, refrains.

Ibid.

For such kind of borrowing as this, if it be not bettered by the borrower, among good authors is accounted Plagiarè.

Iconoclastes [*1649*]. *XXIII*

Peace hath her victories
No less renown'd than war.

To the Lord General Cromwell [*1652*]

When I consider how my light is spent,

[1] See Montaigne, page 98b.

Error of opinion may be tolerated where reason is left free to combat it. — JEFFERSON: *Inaugural Address* [March 4, 1801]

Ere half my days, in this dark world and wide,
And that one talent which is death to hide
Lodg'd with me useless.

Sonnet XV. On His Blindness [*1652*]

"Doth God exact day-labour, light denied?"

Ibid.

Who best
Bear his mild yoke, they serve him best; his state
Is kingly; thousands at his bidding speed,
And post o'er land and ocean without rest;
They also serve who only stand and wait.

Ibid.

Avenge, O Lord, thy slaughter'd saints, whose bones
Lie scatter'd on the Alpine mountains cold;
Ev'n them who kept thy truth so pure of old
When all our fathers worshipt stocks and stones.

On the Late Massacre in Piedmont [*1655*]

Yet I argue not
Against Heav'n's hand or will, nor bate one jot
Of heart or hope; but still bear up and steer
Right onward.

Sonnet XVII. To Cyriack Skinner, Upon his Blindness [*1655?*]

Methought I saw my late espoused saint,[1]
Brought to me like Alcestis from the grave.

On his Deceased Wife [*1658?*]

But oh! as to embrace me she inclin'd,
I wak'd, she fled, and day brought back my night.

Ibid.

Of Man's first disobedience, and the fruit
Of that forbidden tree whose mortal taste

[1] See Sir Walter Raleigh, page 111b.

Brought death into the world, and all
our woe.
> *Paradise Lost* [*1667*]. *Book I,*
> *Line 1*

Things unattempted yet in prose or
rhyme.
> *Ibid. Line 16*

What in me is dark
Illumine, what is low raise and support;
That to the height of this great argu-
ment
I may assert eternal Providence,
And justify the ways of God to men.[1]
> *Ibid. Line 22*

The infernal serpent; he it was, whose
guile,
Stirr'd up with envy and revenge, deceived
The mother of mankind.
> *Ibid. Line 34*

Him the Almighty Power
Hurled headlong flaming from th' eter-
nal sky
With hideous ruin and combustion
down
To bottomless perdition, there to dwell
In adamantine chains and penal fire
Who durst defy th' Omnipotent to
arms.
> *Ibid. Line 44*

As far as angels' ken.
> *Ibid. Line 59*

Where peace
And rest can never dwell, hope never
comes
That comes to all.
> *Ibid. Line 65*

What though the field be lost?
All is not lost — th' unconquerable
will,
And study of revenge, immortal hate,
And courage never to submit or yield.
> *Ibid. Line 105*

Vaunting aloud, but racked with deep
despair.
> *Ibid. Line 126*

[1] See *Samson Agonistes*, page 260a.
But vindicate the ways of God to man. —
POPE: *Essay on Man* [1733–1734], *Epistle I,*
L. 16

To be weak is miserable,
Doing or suffering.
> *Paradise Lost. Book I, Line 157*

And out of good still to find means of
evil.
> *Ibid. Line 165*

The seat of desolation, void of light.
> *Ibid. Line 181*

A mind not to be chang'd by place or
time.
The mind is its own place, and in itself
Can make a heaven of hell, a hell of
heaven.[1]
> *Ibid. Line 253*

Better to reign in hell than serve in
heaven.
> *Ibid. Line 263*

His spear, to equal which the tallest
pine
Hewn on Norwegian hills to be the mast
Of some great ammiral, were but a
wand
He walk'd with, to support uneasy steps
Over the burning marle.
> *Ibid. Line 292*

Thick as autumnal leaves that strow
the brooks
In Vallombrosa.
> *Ibid. Line 302*

Awake, arise, or be forever fallen!
> *Ibid. Line 330*

Spirits, when they please,
Can either sex assume, or both.
> *Ibid. Line 423*

When night
Darkens the streets, then wander forth
the sons
Of Belial, flown with insolence and
wine.
> *Ibid. Line 500*

Th' imperial ensign, which, full high
advanc'd,
Shone like a meteor, streaming to the
wind.[2]
> *Ibid. Line 536*

Sonorous metal blowing martial sounds:
At which the universal host up sent

[1] See Sir Thomas Browne, page 240b, and
Book IV, L. 73, page 255a.
[2] Stream'd like a meteor to the troubled
air. — THOMAS GRAY: *The Bard* [1757], *I, 2,*
L. 6

A shout that tore hell's concave, and beyond
Frighted the reign of Chaos and old Night.
> *Paradise Lost. Book I, Line 540*

Anon they move
In perfect phalanx, to the Dorian mood
Of flutes and soft recorders.
> *Ibid. Line 549*

His form had yet not lost
All her original brightness, nor appear'd
Less than archangel ruin'd, and th' excess
Of glory obscur'd.
> *Ibid. Line 591*

The sun . . . .
In dim eclipse, disastrous twilight sheds
On half the nations, and with fear of change
Perplexes monarchs.
> *Ibid. Line 594*

Thrice he assay'd, and thrice, in spite of scorn,
Tears, such as angels weep, burst forth.
> *Ibid. Line 619*

Who overcomes
By force hath overcome but half his foe.
> *Ibid. Line 648*

Mammon, the least erected spirit that fell
From heaven; for ev'n in heaven his looks and thoughts
Were always downward bent, admiring more
The riches of heaven's pavement, trodden gold,
Than aught divine or holy else enjoy'd
In vision beatific.
> *Ibid. Line 679*

Let none admire
That riches grow in hell: that soil may best
Deserve the precious bane.
> *Ibid. Line 690*

From morn
To noon he fell, from noon to dewy eve,
A summer's day; and with the setting sun

Dropp'd from the Zenith, like a falling star.
> *Paradise Lost. Book I, Line 742*

High on a throne of royal state, which far
Outshone the wealth of Ormus and of Ind,
Or where the gorgeous East with richest hand
Showers on her kings barbaric pearl and gold,
Satan exalted sat, by merit rais'd
To that bad eminence.
> *Ibid. Book II, Line 1*

The strongest and the fiercest spirit
That fought in heaven, now fiercer by despair.
> *Ibid. Line 44*

Rather than be less,
Car'd not to be at all.
> *Ibid. Line 47*

My sentence is for open war.
> *Ibid. Line 51*

Which, if not victory, is yet revenge.
> *Ibid. Line 105*

But all was false and hollow; though his tongue
Dropp'd manna, and could make the worse appear
The better reason,[1] to perplex and dash
Maturest counsels.
> *Ibid. Line 112*

For who would lose,
Though full of pain, this intellectual being,
Those thoughts that wander through eternity,
To perish rather, swallow'd up and lost
In the wide womb of uncreated night,
Devoid of sense and motion?
> *Ibid. Line 146*

His red right hand.[2]
> *Ibid. Line 174*

Unrespited, unpitied, unrepriev'd.
> *Ibid. Line 185*

The never-ending flight
Of future days.
> *Ibid. Line 221*

[1] See Diogenes Laertius, page 70b.
[2] *Rubente dextera.* — HORACE [65–8 B. C.]: *Ode I, 2, 2, To Caesar Augustus*

Thus Belial with words clothed in reason's garb
Counselled ignoble ease, and peaceful sloth,
Not peace.
Paradise Lost. Book II, Line 226
With grave
Aspect he rose, and in his rising seem'd
A pillar of state; deep on his front engraven
Deliberation sat, and public care;
And princely counsel in his face yet shone,
Majestic though in ruin.
Ibid. Line 300
The palpable obscure.
Ibid. Line 406
Long is the way
And hard, that out of hell leads up to light.
Ibid. Line 432
Their rising all at once was as the sound
Of thunder heard remote.
Ibid. Line 476
Others apart sat on a hill retir'd,
In thoughts more elevate, and reason'd high
Of providence, foreknowledge, will, and fate,
Fix'd fate, free-will, foreknowledge absolute;
And found no end, in wand'ring mazes lost.
Ibid. Line 557
Arm th' obdur'd breast
With stubborn patience as with triple steel.
Ibid. Line 568
Far off from these a slow and silent stream,
Lethe the River of Oblivion.
Ibid. Line 582
At certain revolutions all the damn'd
Are brought: and feel by turns the bitter change
Of fierce extremes, — extremes by change more fierce;
From beds of raging fire to starve in ice
Their soft ethereal warmth, and there to pine

Immovable, infix'd, and frozen round,
Periods of time; thence hurried back to fire.
Paradise Lost. Book II, Line 596
Whence and what art thou, execrable shape?
Ibid. Line 681
Before mine eyes in opposition sits
Grim Death, my son and foe.
Ibid. Line 803
Hot, cold, moist, and dry, four champions fierce,
Strive here for mast'ry.
Ibid. Line 898
With ruin upon ruin, rout on rout,
Confusion worse confounded.
Ibid. Line 995
And fast by, hanging in a golden chain,
This pendent world, in bigness as a star
Of smallest magnitude close by the moon.
Ibid. Line 1051
Hail, holy light! offspring of heav'n first-born.
Ibid. Book III, Line 1
Thus with the year
Seasons return; but not to me returns
Day, or the sweet approach of even or morn,
Or sight of vernal bloom or summer's rose,
Or flocks, or herds, or human face divine;
But cloud instead, and ever-during dark
Surrounds me; from the cheerful ways of men
Cut off, and for the book of knowledge fair
Presented with a universal blank
Of Nature's works, to me expung'd and raz'd,
And wisdom at one entrance quite shut out.
Ibid. Line 40
See golden days, fruitful of golden deeds,
With joy and love triumphing.
Ibid. Line 337
Dark with excessive bright.
Ibid. Line 380

The hell within him.
>   *Paradise Lost. Book IV, Line 20*

Now conscience wakes despair
That slumber'd, — wakes the bitter
>   memory
Of what he was, what is, and what must
>   be
Worse.
>   *Ibid. Line 23*

At whose sight all the stars
Hide their diminish'd heads.[1]
>   *Ibid. Line 34*

A grateful mind
By owing owes not, but still pays, at
>   once
Indebted and discharg'd.
>   *Ibid. Line 55*

Which way shall I fly
Infinite wrath and infinite despair?
Which way I fly is hell; myself am
>   hell; [2]
And in the lowest deep a lower deep,
Still threat'ning to devour me, opens
>   wide,
To which the hell I suffer seems a
>   heaven.
>   *Ibid. Line 73*

So farewell hope, and, with hope, fare-
>   well fear,
Farewell remorse; all good to me is lost.
Evil, be thou my good.
>   *Ibid. Line 108*

And on the Tree of Life,
The middle tree and highest there that
>   grew,
Sat like a cormorant.
>   *Ibid. Line 194*

A heaven on earth.
>   *Ibid. Line 208*

Flowers of all hue, and without thorn
>   the rose.[3]
>   *Ibid. Line 256*

For contemplation he and valour
>   form'd,
For softness she and sweet attractive
>   grace;

[1] Ye little stars! hide your diminished rays.
— POPE: *Moral Essays* [1731–1735], *Epistle III, L. 282*

[2] See Sir Thomas Browne, page 240b, and
Book I, L. 253, page 252b.

[3] See Bidpai, page 28b.

He for God only, she for God in him.
>   *Paradise Lost. Book IV, Line 297*

Implied
Subjection, but requir'd with gentle
>   sway,
And by her yielded, by him best re-
>   ceiv'd, —
Yielded with coy submission, modest
>   pride,
And sweet, reluctant, amorous delay.
>   *Ibid. Line 307*

Adam the goodliest man of men since
>   born
His sons, the fairest of her daughters
>   Eve.
>   *Ibid. Line 323*

And with necessity,
The tyrant's plea,[1] excus'd his devilish
>   deeds.
>   *Ibid. Line 393*

Imparadis'd in one another's arms.
>   *Ibid. Line 506*

Live while ye may,
Yet happy pair.
>   *Ibid. Line 533*

Now came still evening on, and twilight
>   gray
Had in her sober livery all things clad.
>   *Ibid. Line 598*

The wakeful nightingale,
She all night long her amorous descant
>   sung;
Silence was pleas'd: now glow'd the
>   firmament
With living sapphires; Hesperus, that
>   led
The starry host, rode brightest, till the
>   moon,
Rising in clouded majesty, at length
Apparent queen, unveil'd her peerless
>   light,
And o'er the dark her silver mantle
>   threw.
>   *Ibid. Line 602*

The timely dew of sleep.
>   *Ibid. Line 614*

With thee conversing I forget all time,
All seasons, and their change; all please
>   alike.

[1] Necessity is the argument of tyrants, it is
the creed of slaves. — WILLIAM PITT: *Speech
on the India Bill* [November, 1783]

Sweet is the breath of morn, her rising
 sweet,
With charm of earliest birds; pleasant
 the sun
When first on this delightful land he
 spreads
His orient beams on herb, tree, fruit,
 and flower,
Glist'ring with dew; fragrant the fertile
 earth
After soft showers; and sweet the coming on
Of grateful ev'ning mild, then silent
 night
With this her solemn bird, and this fair
 moon,
And these the gems of heaven, her
 starry train.
    Paradise Lost. Book IV, Line 639

Millions of spiritual creatures walk the
 earth
Unseen, both when we wake, and when
 we sleep.
        Ibid. Line 677

    In naked beauty more adorn'd,
More lovely, than Pandora.[1]
        Ibid. Line 713

    Eas'd the putting off
These troublesome disguises which we
 wear.
        Ibid. Line 739

Hail, wedded love, mysterious law, true
 source
Of human offspring.
        Ibid. Line 750

Squat like a toad, close at the ear of
 Eve.
        Ibid. Line 800

    Abash'd the devil stood,
And felt how awful goodness is, and
 saw
Virtue in her shape how lovely.
        Ibid. Line 846

All hell broke loose.
        Ibid. Line 918

Like Teneriff or Atlas unremoved.
        Ibid. Line 987

[1] See Cicero, page 33a.
    When unadorned, adorned the most. —
THOMSON: *Autumn* [1730], *L. 204*

    The starry cope
Of heaven.
    Paradise Lost. Book IV, Line 992
    His sleep
Was aery light, from pure digestion
 bred.
        Ibid. Book V, Line 3

    My latest found,
Heaven's last, best gift, my ever-new
 delight!
        Ibid. Line 18

    Good, the more
Communicated, more abundant grows.
        Ibid. Line 71

These are thy glorious works, Parent
 of good!
        Ibid. Line 153

A wilderness of sweets.
        Ibid. Line 294

So saying, with despatchful looks in
 haste
She turns, on hospitable thoughts intent.
        Ibid. Line 331

    Nor jealousy
Was understood, the injur'd lover's hell.
        Ibid. Line 449

The bright consummate flower.
        Ibid. Line 481

    Midnight brought on the dusky hour
Friendliest to sleep and silence.
        Ibid. Line 667

Innumerable as the stars of night,
Or stars of morning, dewdrops which
 the sun
Impearls on every leaf and every
 flower.
        Ibid. Line 745

Among the faithless, faithful only he.
        Ibid. Line 897

    Morn,
Wak'd by the circling hours, with rosy
 hand
Unbarr'd the gates of light.
        Ibid. Book VI, Line 2

Servant of God, well done! Well hast
 thou fought
The better fight, who single hast maintained
Against revolted multitudes the cause

Of truth, in word mightier than they in
arms.
Paradise Lost. Book VI, Line 29
He onward came; far off his coming
shone.
Ibid. Line 768
Let it profit thee to have heard,
By terrible example, the reward
Of disobedience.
Ibid. Line 909
More safe I sing with mortal voice, un-
chang'd
To hoarse or mute, though fall'n on
evil days,
On evil days though fall'n, and evil
tongues,
In darkness, and with dangers com-
pass'd round,
And solitude.
Ibid. Book VII, Line 24
Still govern thou my song,
Urania, and fit audience find, though
few.
Ibid. Line 30
Out of one man a race
Of men innumerable.
Ibid. Line 155
Heaven open'd wide
Her ever-during gates, harmonious
sound,
On golden hinges moving.
Ibid. Line 205
God saw the Light was good;
And light from darkness by the hemi-
sphere
Divided: Light the Day, and Darkness
Night,
He named. Thus was the first Day even
and morn.
Ibid. Line 249
There Leviathan
Hugest of living creatures, on the deep
Stretch'd like a promontory sleeps or
swims,
And seems a moving land, and at his
gills
Draws in, and at his trunk spouts out a
sea.
Ibid. Line 412
Endued
With sanctity of reason.
Ibid. Line 507

The Planets in their stations list'ning
stood,
While the bright Pomp ascended jubi-
lant.
Open, ye everlasting gates, they sung,
Open, ye heavens, your living doors;
let in
The great Creator from his work re-
turn'd
Magnificent, his six days' work, a world.
Paradise Lost. Book VII, Line 563
A broad and ample road, whose dust
is gold,
And pavement stars, as stars to thee ap-
pear
Seen in the galaxy, that milky way
Which nightly as a circling zone thou
seest
Powder'd with stars.
Ibid. Line 577
The Angel ended, and in Adam's ear
So charming left his voice that he awhile
Thought him still speaking, still stood
fix'd to hear.
Ibid. Book VIII, Line 1
To know
That which before us lies in daily life
Is the prime wisdom.
Ibid. Line 192
Liquid lapse of murmuring streams.
Ibid. Line 263
And feel that I am happier than I know.
Ibid. Line 282
Among unequals what society
Can sort, what harmony or true de-
light?
Ibid. Line 383
Her virtue, and the conscience of her
worth,
That would be woo'd, and not unsought
be won.
Ibid. Line 502
The sum of earthly bliss.
Ibid. Line 522
Accuse not Nature! she hath done her
part;
Do thou but thine!
Ibid. Line 561
Oft times nothing profits more
Than self-esteem, grounded on just and
right

Well-manag'd.
Paradise Lost. Book VIII, Line 571
My unpremeditated verse.
Ibid. Book IX, Line 24
Pleas'd me, long choosing and beginning late.
Ibid. Line 26
    Unless an age too late, or cold
Climate, or years, damp my intended wing.
Ibid. Line 44
Revenge, at first though sweet,[1]
Bitter ere long back on itself recoils.
Ibid. Line 171
For solitude sometimes is best society,
And short retirement urges sweet return.
Ibid. Line 249
At shut of evening flowers.
Ibid. Line 278
As one who long in populous city pent,[2]
Where houses thick and sewers annoy the air.
Ibid. Line 445
God so commanded, and left that command
Sole daughter of his voice;[3] the rest, we live
Law to ourselves, our reason is our law.
Ibid. Line 652
    His words, replete with guile,
Into her heart too easy entrance won.
Ibid. Line 733
    Her rash hand in evil hour
Forth reaching to the fruit, she pluck'd, she eat:
Earth felt the wound, and Nature from her seat,
Sighing through all her works, gave signs of woe
That all was lost.
Ibid. Line 780
So dear I love him that with him all deaths
I could endure, without him live no life.
Ibid. Line 832

---

[1] Sweet is revenge — especially to women. — BYRON: *Don Juan* [1819–1824], *Canto 1, St. 124*
[2] See Keats, page 477a.
[3] See Wordsworth, page 409b.

    In her face excuse
Came prologue, and apology too prompt.
Paradise Lost. Book IX, Line 853
O fairest of Creation, last and best
Of all God's works, creature in whom excelled
Whatever can to sight or thought be formed,
Holy, divine, good, amiable, or sweet!
How art thou lost, how on a sudden lost,
Defac'd, deflower'd, and now to Death devote?
Ibid. Line 896
    Yet I shall temper so
Justice with mercy, as may illustrate most
Them fully satisfy'd, and thee appease.
Ibid. Book X, Line 77
She gave me of the tree, and I did eat.
Ibid. Line 143
Pandemonium, city and proud seat
Of Lucifer.
Ibid. Line 424
A dismal universal hiss, the sound
Of public scorn.
Ibid. Line 508
Death . . . on his pale horse.
Ibid. Line 588
    How gladly would I meet
Mortality, my sentence, and be earth
Insensible! how glad would lay me down
As in my mother's lap!
Ibid. Line 775
Demoniac frenzy, moping melancholy,
And moon-struck madness.
Ibid. Book XI, Line 485
And over them triumphant Death his dart
Shook, but delay'd to strike, though oft invok'd.
Ibid. Line 491
So may'st thou live, till, like ripe fruit, thou drop
Into thy mother's lap, or be with ease
Gathered, not harshly plucked, for death mature:
This is old age.
Ibid. Line 535
Nor love thy life, nor hate; but what thou liv'st

Live well; how long or short permit to
Heaven.[1]
>*Paradise Lost. Book XI, Line 553*

A bevy of fair women.
>*Ibid. Line 582*

The evening star,
Love's harbinger.
>*Ibid. Line 588*

The brazen throat of war.
>*Ibid. Line 713*

An olive-leaf he brings, pacific sign.
>*Ibid. Line 860*

In me is no delay; with thee to go,
Is to stay here; without thee here to
stay,
Is to go hence unwilling; thou to me
Art all things under Heaven, all places
thou,
Who for my willful crime art banished
hence.
>*Ibid. Book XII, Line 615*

The world was all before them, where
to choose
Their place of rest, and Providence
their guide.
They hand in hand, with wand'ring
steps and slow,
Through Eden took their solitary way.
>*Ibid. Line 646*

Most men admire
Virtue who follow not her lore.
>*Paradise Regained* [*1671*].
>*Book I, Line 482*

Skill'd to retire, and in retiring draw
Hearts after them tangled in amorous
nets.
>*Ibid. Book II, Line 161*

Beauty stands
In the admiration only of weak minds
Led captive.
>*Ibid. Line 220*

Rocks whereon greatest men have oftest wreck'd.
>*Ibid. Line 228*

Of whom to be disprais'd were no small
praise.
>*Ibid. Book III, Line 56*

Elephants indorsed with towers.
>*Ibid. Line 329*

----

[1] See Martial, page 52b.

Dusk faces with white silken turbans
wreath'd.
>*Paradise Regained. Book IV,*
>*Line 76*

What honour that,
But tedious waste of time, to sit and
hear
So many hollow compliments and lies,
Outlandish flatteries?
>*Ibid. Line 122*

The childhood shows the man,
As morning shows the day.[1]
>*Ibid. Line 220*

Athens, the eye of Greece, mother of
arts
And eloquence.
>*Ibid. Line 240*

The olive grove of Academe,
Plato's retirement, where the Attic bird
Trills her thick-warbled notes the sum-
mer long.
>*Ibid. Line 244*

Socrates . . .
Whom, well inspir'd, the oracle pro-
nounc'd
Wisest of men.
>*Ibid. Line 274*

The first and wisest of them all professed
To know this only, that he nothing
knew.[2]
>*Ibid. Line 293*

Deep vers'd in books, and shallow in
himself.
>*Ibid. Line 327*

Till morning fair
Came forth with pilgrim steps, in amice
gray.
>*Ibid. Line 426*

Eyeless in Gaza, at the mill with slaves.
>*Samson Agonistes* [*1671*]. *Line 41*

O loss of sight, of thee I most complain!
>*Ibid. Line 68*

O dark, dark, dark, amid the blaze of
noon,
Irrecoverably dark, total eclipse
Without all hope of day!
>*Ibid. Line 80*

----

[1] See Wordsworth, page 406b.
[2] See Diogenes Laertius, page 70b.

The sun to me is dark
And silent as the moon,
When she deserts the night,
Hid in her vacant interlunar cave.
Samson Agonistes. Line 86
To live a life half dead, a living death
Ibid. Line 100
Ran on embattled armies clad in iron,
And, weaponless himself,
Made arms ridiculous.
Ibid. Line 129
Just are the ways of God,
And justifiable to men; [1]
Unless there be who think not God at all.
Ibid. Line 293
A grain of manhood.
Ibid. Line 408
What boots it at one gate to make defence,
And at another to let in the foe?
Ibid. Line 560
God of our fathers, what is man!
That thou towards him with hand so various,
(Or might I say contrarious?)
Temper'st thy providence through his short course.
Ibid. Line 667
But who is this, what thing of sea or land, —
Female of sex it seems —
That so bedeck'd, ornate, and gay,
Comes this way sailing
Like a stately ship
Of Tarsus, bound for th' isles
Of Javan or Gadire,
With all her bravery on, and tackle trim,
Sails fill'd, and streamers waving,
Courted by all the winds that hold them play,
An amber scent of odorous perfume
Her harbinger?
Ibid. Line 710
Dalila. In argument with men a woman ever
Goes by the worse, whatever be her cause.

[1] See *Paradise Lost, Book I, L. 22*, page 252a.

Samson. For want of words, no doubt, or lack of breath!
Samson Agonistes. Line 903
Fame, if not double-faced, is double-mouthed,
And with contrary blast proclaims most deeds;
On both his wings, one black, the other white,
Bears greatest names in his wild aery flight.
Ibid. Line 971
Yet beauty, though injurious, hath strange power,
After offence returning, to regain
Love once possess'd.
Ibid. Line 1003
Love-quarrels oft in pleasing concord end;
Not wedlock-treachery.
Ibid. Line 1008
Boast not of what thou would'st have done, but do
What then thou would'st.
Ibid. Line 1104
He's gone, and who knows how he may report
Thy words by adding fuel to the flame?
Ibid. Line 1350
For evil news rides post, while good news baits.
Ibid. Line 1538
Suspense in news is torture.
Ibid. Line 1569
Nothing is here for tears, nothing to wail
Or knock the breast; no weakness, no contempt,
Dispraise, or blame; nothing but well and fair,
And what may quiet us in a death so noble.
Ibid. Line 1721
All is best, though we oft doubt
What the unsearchable dispose
Of Highest Wisdom brings about.
Ibid. Line 1745
Calm of mind, all passion spent.
Ibid. Line 1758
Such bickerings to recount, met often in these our writers, what more worth is it than to chronicle the wars of kites

or crows flocking and fighting in the air?

> *The History of England*
> *[1670]. Book IV*

SIR JOHN SUCKLING
[1609–1642]

Why so pale and wan, fond lover?
Prithee, why so pale?
Will, when looking well can't move her,
Looking ill prevail?

> *Song [1638]. Stanza 1*

Quit, quit, for shame, this will not move,
This cannot take her.
If of herself she will not love,
Nothing can make her.
The devil take her!

> *Ibid. Stanza 3*

Death's no punishment: it is the sense,
The pains and fears afore, that makes
a death.

> *Aglaura [1638]. Act V, Sc. 1*

But as when an authentic watch is
shown,
Each man winds up and rectifies his
own,
So in our very judgments.[1]

> *Ibid. Epilogue*

High characters (cries one), and he
would see
Things that ne'er were, nor are, nor
ne'er will be.[2]

> *The Goblins [1639]. Epilogue*

Her feet beneath her petticoat
Like little mice, stole in and out,[3]
As if they feared the light;

[1] 'Tis with our judgments as our watches,
none
Go just alike, yet each believes his own.
  POPE: *An Essay on Criticism*
  [1711], Part I, L. 9
[2] Whoever thinks a faultless piece to see,
Thinks what ne'er was, nor is, nor e'er
shall be.
  POPE: *An Essay on Criticism*
  [1711], Part II, L. 53
There's no such thing in Nature, and
you'll draw
A faultless monster which the world ne'er
saw.
  JOHN SHEFFIELD, DUKE OF BUCK-
  INGHAMSHIRE [1648–1721]: *Essay
  on Poetry*
[3] See Herrick, page 231a.

But oh, she dances such a way!
No sun upon an Easter-day
Is half so fine a sight.

> *A Ballad upon a Wedding [1641].*
> *Stanza 8*

Her lips were red, and one was thin,
Compared with that was next her chin,
Some bee had stung it newly.

> *Ibid. Stanza 11*

I prithee send me back my heart,
Since I cannot have thine;
For if from yours you will not part,
Why then shouldst thou have mine?

> *Fragmenta Aurea [1646].*
> *Song, Stanza 1*

'Tis not the meat, but 'tis the appetite
Makes eating a delight.

> *Ibid. Of Thee, Kind Boy,*
> *Stanza 3*

Spare diet is the cause love lasts,
For surfeits sooner kill than fasts.

> *Ibid. Against Absence*

Out upon it, I have loved
Three whole days together;
And am like to love three more,
If it prove fair weather.

> *Ibid. A Poem with the Answer,*
> *Stanza 1*

'Tis expectation makes a blessing dear,
Heaven were not heaven, if we knew
what it were.

> *Ibid. Against Fruition, Stanza 4*

Women are the baggage of life: they
are
Troublesome, and hinder us in the great
march,
And yet we cannot be without 'em.

> *The Tragedy of Brennoralt [1646].*
> *Act I, Sc. 1*

Success is a rare paint, hides all the
ugliness.

> *Ibid.*

Sleep is as nice as woman,
The more I court it, the more it flies me.

> *Ibid. Act II, Sc. 1*

She is pretty to walk with,
And witty to talk with,
And pleasant, too, to think on.

> *Ibid.*

Her face is like the milky way i' the
sky, —

A meeting of gentle lights without name.

> *The Tragedy of Brennoralt.*
> *Act III, Sc. 1*

SIR MATTHEW HALE [1]
[1609–1676]

Be not too rigid in matters purely conscientious, where all the harm is diversity of judgment.

> *Things Necessary to be Continually Had in Remembrance*

Be not biassed with compassion to the poor, or favour to the rich, in point of justice.

> *Ibid.*

Not to be solicitous what men will say or think.

> *Ibid.*

To abhor all private solicitations in matters depending.

> *Ibid.*

To be short, and sparing, at meals, that I may be the fitter for business.

> *Ibid.*

WILLIAM CARTWRIGHT
[1611–1643]

St. Francis and St. Benedight,
Bless this house from wicked wight,
From the nightmare and the Goblin
That is hight Good Fellow Robin.
Keep it from all evil spirits,
Fairies, weasels, bats, and ferrets
From curfew time to the next prime.

> *A House Blessing* [1651] [2]

Love makes those young whom age doth chill,
And whom he finds young, keeps young still.

> *To Chloe* [1651]

Tell me no more of minds embracing minds,
And hearts exchanged for hearts;
That spirits spirits meet, as winds do winds,
And mix their subtlest parts;

[1] Lord Chief Justice of England.
[2] Matthew, Mark, Luke, and John,
The bed be blest that I lye on.
THOMAS ADY: *A Candle in the Dark* [1656]

That two unbodied essences may kiss,
And then like angels, twist and feel one bliss.

> *No Platonic Love* [1651]. *Stanza 1*

I was that silly thing that once was wrought
To practise this thin love;
I climbed from sex to soul, from soul to thought;
But thinking there to move,
Headlong I rolled from thought to soul, and then
From soul I lighted at the sex again.

> *Ibid. Stanza 2*

JAMES GRAHAM,
FIRST MARQUESS OF
MONTROSE
[1612–1650]

He either fears his fate too much,
Or his deserts are small,
That dares not put it to the touch
To gain or lose it all. [1]

> *My Dear and Only Love. Stanza 2*

I'll make thee glorious by my pen,
And famous by my sword. [2]

> *Ibid. Stanza 5*

THOMAS JORDAN
[1612–1685]

Let us drink and be merry, dance, joke, and rejoice,
With claret and sherry, theorbo and voice!

> *Coronemus Nos Rosis Antequam Marcescant.* [3] *Stanza 1*

Fish dinners will make a man spring like a flea.

> *Ibid. Stanza 2*

Though now she be pleasant and sweet to the sense,

[1] That puts it not unto the touch
To win or lose it all.
MARK NAPIER [1798–1879]: *Montrose and the Covenanters*
[2] I'll make thee famous by my pen,
And glorious by my sword.
SCOTT: *Legend of Montrose* [1819], *Chap. XV*
[3] One of the songs of Sir Henry Morgan's buccaneers was an adaptation of this poem.

Will be damnable mouldy a hundred
years hence.

Coronemus Nos Rosis Antequam
Marcescant. Stanza 3

For health, wealth and beauty, wit,
learning, and sense,

Must all come to nothing a hundred
years hence.

Ibid. Stanza 4

ISAAC DE BENSERADE
[1612–1691]

In bed we laugh, in bed we cry;
And, born in bed, in bed we die.
The near approach a bed may show
Of human bliss to human woe.

A Son Lit (Translated by DR.
SAMUEL JOHNSON)

RICHARD CRASHAW
[1613–1649]

The conscious water saw its God and
blushed.[1]

Epigrammata Sacra [1634].
Aquae in Vinum Versae

Two went to pray? Oh, rather say
One went to brag, the other to pray;
One stands up close and treads on high
Where the other dares not send his eye;
One nearer to God's altar trod,
The other to the altar's God.

Two Went Up to the Temple
to Pray [1648]

Whoe'er she be,
That not impossible she,
That shall command my heart and me.

Wishes to His Supposed
Mistress [1648]

Where'er she lie,

[1] Nympha pudica Deum vidit et erubuit. —
Quoted by SAMUEL JOHNSON [1778], *Bos-*
well's Life of Dr. Johnson, Vol. II, P. 218,
Everyman ed. A footnote states that this line
has frequently been attributed to Dryden, but
appeared in Crashaw's *Epigrammata Sacra*
[1634].
  The bashful stream hath seen its God and
blushed. — AARON HILL [1685–1750]
  The water hears thy faintest word,
  And blushes into wine.
    JOHN SAMUEL BEWLEY MONSELL
    [1811–1875]: *Mysterious is Thy*
    Presence, Lord, St. 1

Locked up from mortal eye,
In shady leaves of destiny.

Wishes to His Supposed Mistress

Days that need borrow
No part of their good morrow
From a fore-spent night of sorrow.

Ibid.

Life that dares send
A challenge to his end,
And when it comes, say, Welcome,
friend!

Ibid.

Sydnaeian showers
Of sweet discourse, whose powers
Can crown old Winter's head with
flowers.

Ibid.

I would be married, but I'd have no
wife,
I would be married to a single life.

On Marriage [1648]

All is Caesar's; and what odds
So long as Caesar's self is God's?

Mark XII [1648]

All those fair and flagrant things.

The Flaming Heart Upon the
Book of Saint Teresa [1652].
Line 34

Love's passives are his activ'st part.
The wounded is the wounding heart.

Ibid. Line 71

O thou undaunted daughter of desires!

Ibid. Line 93

By all the eagle in thee, all the dove.

Ibid. Line 95

Poor world, said I, what wilt thou do
To entertain this starry stranger?
Is the best thou canst bestow,
A cold and not too cleanly manger?
Contend, ye powers of heav'n and earth,
To fit a bed for this huge birth.

Hymn of the Nativity [1652].
Stanza 6

Proud world, said I, cease your contest,
And let the mighty babe alone —
The phoenix builds the phoenix' nest,
Love's architecture is his own;
The babe whose birth embraves this
morn,
Made his own bed ere he was born.

Ibid. Stanza 7

Welcome, all wonders in one sight!
Eternity shut in a span.
Hymn of the Nativity. Full Chorus
A happy soul, that all the way
To heaven hath a summer's day.
*In Praise of Lessius's Rule of
Health*
The modest front of this small floor,
Believe me, reader, can say more
Than many a braver marble can, —
"Here lies a truly honest man!"
Epitaph upon Mr. Ashton

JEREMY TAYLOR
[1613–1667]

When Abraham sat at his tent-door,
according to his custom, waiting to entertain strangers, he espied an old man
stooping and leaning on his staff, weary
with age and travel, coming toward
him, who was an hundred years of age;
he received him kindly, washed his feet,
provided supper, caused him to sit
down; but observing that the old man
ate and prayed not, nor begged for a
blessing on his meat, asked him why he
did not worship the God of heaven. The
old man told him that he worshiped the
fire only, and acknowledged no other
God: at which answer Abraham grew
so zealously angry, that he thrust the
old man out of his tent, and exposed
him to all the evils of the night and an
unguarded condition. When the old
man was gone, God called to him and
asked him where the stranger was; he
replied, "I thrust him away because he
did not worship thee"; God answered
him, "I have suffered him these hundred years, although he dishonored me,
and couldst thou not endure him one
night, when he gave thee no trouble?"
Upon this, saith the story, Abraham
fetched him back again, and gave him
hospitable entertainment and wise instruction. Go thou and do likewise, and
thy charity will be rewarded by the
God of Abraham.
The Liberty of Prophesying [1646]
Every man hath in his own life sins
enough, in his own mind trouble

enough: so that curiosity after the affairs of others cannot be without envy
and an evil mind. What is it to me if
my neighbour's grandfather were a
Syrian, or his grandmother illegitimate,
or that another is indebted five thousand pounds, or whether his wife be
expensive?
Holy Living [1650–1651]
He that is most knowing hath a capacity to become happy, which a less
knowing prince or a rich person hath
not.
XXVIII Sermons [1651]
No man ever repented that he arose
from the table sober, healthful, and
with his wits about him.
XXV Sermons [1653]

FRANÇOIS, DUC DE LA ROCHEFOUCAULD
[1613–1680]

Our virtues are most frequently but
vices disguised.[1]
*Reflections, or Sentences and
Moral Maxims* [2]
We all have strength enough to en-
dure the misfortunes of others.
Maxim 19
Philosophy triumphs easily over past
evils and future evils; but present evils
triumph over it.[3]
Maxim 22
We need greater virtues to sustain
good fortune than bad.
Maxim 25
Neither the sun nor death can be
looked at steadily.
Maxim 26
If we had no faults, we would not
take so much pleasure in noticing them
in others.
Maxim 31

[1] This epigraph, which is the key to the
system of La Rochefoucauld, is found in another form as No. 179 of the Maxims of the
first edition, 1665; it is omitted from the second and third, and reappears for the first
time in the fourth edition at the head of the
Reflections. — AIMÉ MARTIN
[2] The fifth edition [1678] is the standard
one.
[3] See Goldsmith, page 355a.

Jealousy feeds upon suspicion, and it turns into fury or it ends as soon as we pass from suspicion to certainty.

Maxim 32

Self-interest speaks all sorts of tongues, and plays all sorts of roles, even that of disinterestedness.

Maxim 39

We are never so happy nor so unhappy as we imagine.

Maxim 49

To succeed in the world, we do everything we can to appear successful.

Maxim 56

There is no disguise which can for long conceal love where it exists or simulate it where it does not.

Maxim 70

There are very few people who are not ashamed of having been in love when they no longer love each other.

Maxim 71

True love is like ghosts, which everybody talks about and few have seen.

Maxim 76

The love of justice is simply, in the majority of men, the fear of suffering injustice.

Maxim 78

Silence is the best tactic for him who distrusts himself.

Maxim 79

What men call friendship is only a reciprocal conciliation of interests, an exchange of good offices; it is in short simply a form of barter from which self-love always expects to gain something.

Maxim 83

It is more ignominious to mistrust our friends than to be deceived by them.

Maxim 84

Everyone complains of his memory, and no one complains of his judgment.

Maxim 89

Old people like to give good advice, as solace for no longer being able to provide bad examples.

Maxim 93

A man who is ungrateful is sometimes less to blame for it than his benefactor.

Maxim 96

The understanding is always the dupe of the heart.

Maxim 102

Nothing is given so profusely as advice.

Maxim 110

The true way to be deceived is to think oneself more clever than others.

Maxim 127

We would rather speak ill of ourselves than not talk about ourselves at all.

Maxim 138

Usually we praise only to be praised.

Maxim 146

Our repentance is not so much regret for the ill we have done as fear of the ill that may happen to us in consequence.

Maxim 180

Most people judge men only by their success or their good fortune.

Maxim 212

Hypocrisy is the homage that vice pays to virtue.

Maxim 218

Too great haste in paying off an obligation is a kind of ingratitude.

Maxim 226

There is great skill in knowing how to conceal one's skill.

Maxim 245

The pleasure of love is in loving. We are happier in the passion we feel than in that we arouse.[1]

Maxim 259

We always like those who admire us; we do not always like those whom we admire.

Maxim 294

The gratitude of most men is merely a secret desire to receive greater benefits.[2]

Maxim 298

[1] See Shelley, page 465b.
[2] Sir Robert Walpole's [1676–1745] definition of the gratitude of place-expectants, "That it is a lively sense of *future* favours." — WILLIAM HAZLITT: *English Comic Writers* [1819], *Wit and Humour*

Lovers never get tired of each other, because they are always talking about themselves.
Maxim 312

We pardon to the extent that we love.
Maxim 330

We rarely find that people have good sense unless they agree with us.[1]
Maxim 347

Jealousy is always born together with love, but it does not always die when love dies.
Maxim 361

Mediocre minds usually dismiss anything which reaches beyond their own understanding.
Maxim 375

The greatest fault of a penetrating wit is to go beyond the mark.
Maxim 377

We may give advice, but we do not inspire conduct.
Maxim 378

The veracity which increases with old age is not far from folly.
Maxim 416

Nothing prevents our being natural so much as the desire to appear so.
Maxim 431

In their first passion women love their lovers, in the others they love love.[2]
Maxim 471

Quarrels would not last long if the fault were only on one side.
Maxim 496

In the misfortune of our best friends we find something that is not exactly displeasing.[3]
Maxim 583

---

[1] "That was excellently observed," say I when I read a passage in another where his opinion agrees with mine. When we differ, then I pronounce him to be mistaken.—SWIFT [1667–1745]: *Thoughts on Various Subjects*

[2] See Byron, page 458a.

[3] In all distresses of our friends
We first consult our private ends;
While Nature, kindly bent to ease us,
Points out some circumstance to please us.
SWIFT [1667–1745]: *A Paraphrase of Rochefoucauld's Maxim*
Maxim 583 is one of the "Maximes sup-

To win that wonder of the world,
A smile from her bright eyes,
I fought my King, and would have hurled
The gods out of their skies.
To Madame de Longueville

RICHARD BAXTER
[1615–1691]

I preached as never sure to preach again,
And as a dying man to dying men.
Love Breathing Thanks and Praise

SIR JOHN DENHAM
[1615–1669]

Oh, could I flow like thee,[1] and make thy stream
My great example, as it is my theme!
Though deep, yet clear, though gentle yet not dull;
Strong without rage, without o'erflowing full.
Cooper's Hill [1642]. *Line 189*

I can no more believe old Homer blind,
Than those who say the sun hath never shined:
The age wherein he lived was dark, but he
Could not want sight who taught the world to see.
Progress of Learning [1668]

But whither am I strayed? I need not raise
Trophies to thee from other men's dispraise;
Nor is thy fame on lesser ruins built;
Nor needs thy juster title the foul guilt
Of Eastern kings, who, to secure their reign,
Must have their brothers, sons, and kindred slain.[2]
On Mr. John Fletcher's Works [1668]

---

primées" discarded before the 1678 edition.

[1] The River Thames.

[2] Poets are sultans, if they had their will;
For every author would his brother kill.
ROGER BOYLE, FIRST EARL OF ORRERY [1621–1679]

See Pope, page 318b.

SIR ROGER L'ESTRANGE
[1616–1704]

Though this may be play to you,
'Tis death to us.
Fables from Several Authors.
Fable 398

ABRAHAM COWLEY
[1618–1667]

What shall I do to be forever known,
And make the age to come my own?
The Motto

This only grant me, that my means may
lie
Too low for envy, for contempt too
high.
The Vote [1636]

Well then! I now do plainly see
This busy world and I shall ne'er agree;
The very honey of all earthly joy
Does of all meats the soonest cloy,
    And they, methinks, deserve my pity,
Who for it can endure the stings,
The crowd, and buzz and murmurings,
    Of this great hive, the city.
The Wish [1647]

Ah yet, ere I descend to the grave
May I a small house and large garden
    have;
And a few friends, and many books,
    both true,
Both wise, and both delightful too!
Ibid.

A mistress moderately fair.
Ibid.

The world's a scene of changes, and to
    be
Constant, in Nature were inconstancy.
Inconstancy [1647]

Th' adorning thee with so much art
    Is but a barb'rous skill;
'Tis like the pois'ning of a dart,
    Too apt before to kill.
The Waiting Maid [1647]

The thirsty earth soaks up the rain,
And drinks, and gapes for drink again.
The plants suck in the earth, and are
With constant drinking fresh and fair.
From Anacreon [1656].
II, Drinking

Fill all the glasses there, for why
Should every creature drink but I?
Why, man of morals, tell me why?
From Anacreon. II, Drinking

A mighty pain to love it is,
And 'tis a pain that pain to miss;
But of all pains, the greatest pain
It is to love, but love in vain.
Ibid. VII, Gold

His time is forever, everywhere his
    place.
Friendship in Absence

Nothing is there to come, and nothing
    past,
But an eternal now does always last.[1]
Davideis [1656]. Book I,
Line 25

Ye fields of Cambridge, our dear Cam-
    bridge, say,
Have ye not seen us walking every day?
Was there not a tree about which did
    not know
    The love betwixt us two?
On the Death of Mr. William
Harvey

Life is an incurable disease.
To Dr. Scarborough [1656]

Let but thy wicked men from out thee
    go,
And all the fools that crowd thee so,
Even thou, who dost thy millions boast,
A village less than Islington wilt grow,
A solitude almost.
Of Solitude. VII

The fairest garden in her looks,
And in her mind the wisest books.
The Garden. I

Hence, ye profane! I hate ye all,
Both the great vulgar and the small.[2]
Horace. Book III, Ode 1

Charm'd with the foolish whistling of a
    name.[3]
Virgil, Georgics. Book II, Line 72

[1] One of our poets (which is it?) speaks of
an everlasting now. — ROBERT SOUTHEY: *The
Doctor* [1834–1847], *Chap. XXV*
[2] Odi profanum vulgus.
[3] Ravish'd with the whistling of a name. —
POPE: *Essay on Man* [1732–1734], *Epistle IV,*
L. 283

Words that weep and tears that speak.[1]
The Prophet
Poet and Saint! to thee alone are given
The two most sacred names of earth
  and Heaven.
On the Death of Mr. Crashaw
[1668]
His *faith*, perhaps, in some nice tenets
  might
Be wrong; his *life*, I'm sure, was in the
  right.[2]
Ibid.

RICHARD LOVELACE
[1618–1658]

Oh, could you view the melody
  Of every grace
  And music of her face,[3]
You'd drop a tear;
  Seeing more harmony
  In her bright eye
Than now you hear.
Orpheus to Beasts [1649]
Tell me not, sweet, I am unkind,
  That from the nunnery
Of thy chaste breast and quiet mind,
  To war and arms I fly.
To Lucasta: Going to the Wars
[1649]. Stanza 1
I could not love thee, dear, so much,
Lov'd I not honour more.
Ibid. Stanza 3
When I lie tangled in her hair,
  And fettered to her eye,
The gods that wanton in the air
  Know no such liberty.
To Althea: From Prison
[1649]. Stanza 1
Fishes that tipple in the deep,
Know no such liberty.
Ibid. Stanza 2
Stone walls do not a prison make,[4]
  Nor iron bars a cage;

Minds innocent and quiet take
  That for an hermitage;
If I have freedom in my love,
  And in my soul am free,
Angels alone that soar above
  Enjoy such liberty.[1]
To Althea: From Prison. Stanza 4
If to be absent were to be
  Away from thee;
Or that when I am gone,
  You and I were alone;
Then, my Lucasta, might I crave
Pity from blust'ring wind, or swallow-
  ing wave.
To Lucasta: Going Beyond the
Seas [1649]. Stanza 1

ANDREW MARVELL
[1620–1678]

The inglorious arts of peace.
Upon Cromwell's return from
Ireland [1650]
He [2] nothing common did, or mean,
Upon that memorable scene,
But with his keener eye
The axe's edge did try.
Ibid.
But bowed his comely head
Down as upon a bed.
Ibid.
So much one man can do,
That does both act and know.
Ibid.
Had we but world enough, and time,
This coyness, lady, were no crime.
To His Coy Mistress
[1650–1652]
  I would
Love you ten years before the Flood:
And you should, if you please, refuse
Till the conversion of the Jews.
My vegetable love should grow
Vaster than empires, and more slow.
Ibid.

---

[1] Thoughts that breathe, and words that
burn. — THOMAS GRAY: *Progress of Poesy*
[1754], *III, 3, 4*
[2] See Pope, page 317b.
[3] The mind, the music breathing from her
face. — BYRON: *Bride of Abydos* [1813],
Canto I, St. 6
[4] Stone walls a prisoner make, but not a
slave. — WORDSWORTH [1770–1850]: *Humanity*

[1] But though my wing is closely bound,
  My heart's at liberty;
  My prison walls cannot control
  The flight, the freedom of the soul.
    JEANNE GUYON [1648–1717]:
    A Prisoner's Song, Castle of
    Vincennes, France, St. 4
[2] King Charles I.

But at my back I always hear
Time's wingèd chariot hurrying near;
And yonder all before us lie
Deserts of vast eternity.
                To His Coy Mistress
    Then worms shall try
That long preserved virginity,
And your quaint honour turn to dust,
And into ashes all my lust.
The grave's a fine and private place,
But none, I think, do there embrace.
                        Ibid.
        Though we cannot make our sun
Stand still, yet we will make him run.
                        Ibid.
Annihilating all that's made
To a green thought in a green shade.
                The Garden [*1650–1652*]
Casting the body's vest aside,
My soul into the boughs does glide.
                        Ibid.
The world in all doth but two nations
    bear, —
The good, the bad; and these mixed
    everywhere.
                The Loyal Scot [*1650–1652*]
My love is of a birth as rare
As 'tis for object strange and high;
It was begotten by despair
Upon impossibility.
                The Definition of Love [*1650–
                1652*]. *Stanza 1*
As lines, so loves oblique, may well
Themselves in every angle greet;
But ours, so truly parallel,
Though infinite, can never meet.
                        Ibid. Stanza 7
Where the remote Bermudas ride,
In th' ocean's bosom unespied.
                        Bermudas [*1657*]
    Orange bright,
Like golden lamps in a green light.
                        Ibid.
And all the way, to guide their chime,
With falling oars they kept the time.[1]
                        Ibid.

---

[1] Faintly as tolls the evening chime
    Our voices keep tune and our oars keep
    time.
        THOMAS MOORE [1780–1852]:
        A Canadian Boat Song, St. 1

JEAN DE LA FONTAINE
[1621–1695]
We believe no evil till the evil's done.
        Fables. Book I [*1668*], *Fable 8*
We heed no instincts but our own.
                        Ibid.
The opinion of the strongest is al-
ways the best.
                Ibid. Fable 10
By the work one knows the workman.
                Ibid. Fable 21
It is a double pleasure to deceive the
deceiver.
        Ibid. Book II [*1668*], *Fable 15*
It is impossible to please all the world
and one's father.
        Ibid. Book III [*1668*], *Fable 1*
In everything one must consider the
end.[1]
                Ibid. Fable 5
    Beware, as long as you live, of
judging people by appearances.
        Ibid. Book VI [*1668*], *Fable 5*
The sign brings customers.
        Ibid. Book VII [*1678–1679*],
                        Fable 15
Let ignorance talk as it will, learning
has its value.
        Ibid. Book VIII [*1678–1679*],
                        Fable 19
People who make no noise are dan-
gerous.
                Ibid. Fable 23
He knows the universe, and himself
he does not know.
                Ibid. Fable 26
No path of flowers leads to glory.
        Ibid. Book X [*1678–1679*],
                        Fable 14

JEAN BAPTISTE MOLIÈRE
[1622–1673]
I always make the first verse well,
but I have trouble making the others.
        Les Précieuses Ridicules
                [*1659*]. *Sc. 11*

---

[1] Whatsoever thou takest in hand, remember the end, and thou shalt never do amiss. —
Apocrypha, Ecclesiasticus, III, 36

The world, dear Agnes, is a strange affair.

L'École des Femmes [*1662*].
Act II, Sc. 6

There are fagots and fagots.

Le Médecin Malgré Lui
[*1666*]. *Act I, Sc. 6*

We have changed all that.

Ibid. Act II, Sc. 6

He's a wonderful talker, who has the art of telling you nothing in a great harangue.

Le Misanthrope [*1666*].
Act II, Sc. 5

He makes his cook his merit, and the world visits his dinners and not him.

Ibid.

You see him laboring to produce *bons mots.*

Ibid.

The more we love our friends, the less we flatter them; it is by excusing nothing that pure love shows itself.

Ibid.

Doubts are more cruel than the worst of truths.

Ibid. Act III, Sc. 7

Anyone may be an honourable man, and yet write verse badly.

Ibid. Act IV, Sc. 1

If everyone were clothed with integrity, if every heart were just, frank, kindly, the other virtues would be well-nigh useless, since their chief purpose is to make us bear with patience the injustice of our fellows.

Ibid. Act V, Sc. 1

It is a wonderful seasoning of all enjoyments to think of those we love.

Ibid. Sc. 4

There is no rampart that will hold out against malice.

Tartuffe [*1667*]. *Act I, Sc. 1*

Those whose conduct gives room for talk are always the first to attack their neighbours.

Ibid.

She is laughing up her sleeve at you.

Ibid. Sc. 6

A woman always has her revenge ready.

Ibid. Act II, Sc. 2

A heart that forgets us puts us on our mettle to forget just as quickly, and, if we don't succeed, at least we make believe we have succeeded.

Tartuffe. Act II, Sc. 4

Although I am a pious man, I am not the less a man.

Ibid. Act III, Sc. 3

I prefer an accommodating vice to an obstinate virtue.

Amphitryon [*1668*]. *Act I, Sc. 4*

One must eat to live, and not live to eat.

Ibid. Act III, Sc. 1

The true Amphitryon is the Amphitryon who gives dinners.[1]

Ibid. Sc. 5

You wanted it so, Georges Dandin, you wanted it so![2] This suits you very nicely, and you are served right; you have precisely what you deserve.

Georges Dandin [*1668*].
Act I, Sc. 9

The beautiful eyes of my money-box! He speaks of it as a lover of his mistress!

L'Avare [*1668*]. *Act V, Sc. 3*

You are speaking before a man to whom all Naples is known.

Ibid. Sc. 5

Good Heavens! For more than forty years I have been speaking prose without knowing it.

Le Bourgeois Gentilhomme
[*1670*]. *Act II, Sc. 4*

All that is not prose is verse; and all that is not verse is prose.

Ibid.

My fair one, let us swear an eternal friendship.[3]

Ibid. Act IV, Sc. 1

[1] Le véritable Amphitryon est l'Amphitryon où l'on dine.
[2] Vous l'avez voulu, Georges Dandin, vous l'avez voulu.
[3] A sudden thought strikes me — let us swear an eternal friendship. — FRERE: *The Rovers* [1798]
Madam, I have been looking for a person who disliked gravy all my life; let us swear eternal friendship. — SYDNEY SMITH [1771–1845]: *Lady Holland's Memoir, Vol. I, Chap. 9*

I will maintain it before the whole world.
Le Bourgeois Gentilhomme.
Act IV, Sc. 5

What the devil was he doing in that galley? [1]
Les Fourberies de Scapin
[1671]. Act II, Sc. 11

Grammar, which knows how to control even kings. [2]
Les Femmes Savantes [1672].
Act II, Sc. 6

It is seasoned throughout with Attic salt.
Ibid. Act III, Sc. 2

Ah, there are no longer any children!
Le Malade Imaginaire [1673].
Act II, Sc. 11

Nearly all men die of their remedies, and not of their illnesses.
Ibid. Act III, Sc. 3

RICHARD RUMBOLD
[1622–1685]

I never could believe that Providence had sent a few men into the world, ready booted and spurred to ride, and millions ready saddled and bridled to be ridden.
On the scaffold [1685] (MA-CAULAY's *History of England,*
Chap. 1)

[1] Que diable allait-il faire dans cette galère? What the deuce did he want on board a Turk's galley? — CYRANO DE BERGERAC: *Le Pédant Joué* [1654], *Act II, Sc. 4*
The saying of Molière came into his head: "But what the devil was he doing in that galley?" and he laughed at himself. — TOLSTOI: *War and Peace* [1865–1872], *Part IV, Chap. 6*
Often misquoted, "in that gallery," as in DICKENS's *A Tale of Two Cities* [1859], *Book I, Chap. 5:* "What the devil do you do in that gallery there!"
[2] Sigismund [1361–1437], Emperor of the Holy Roman Empire, at the Council of Constance [1414], said to a prelate who had objected to his Majesty's grammar: "Ego sum rex Romanus, et supra grammaticam" (I am the Roman king, and am above grammar).

ALGERNON SIDNEY
[1622–1683]

This hand, unfriendly to tyrants,
Seeks with the sword placid repose under liberty. [1]
Life and Memoirs of Algernon
Sidney

It is not necessary to light a candle in the sun. [2]
Discourses on Government
[1698]. Sect. XXIII

HENRY VAUGHAN
[1622–1695]

Dear Night! this world's defeat;
The stop to busy fools; care's check and curb;
The day of spirits; my soul's calm retreat
Which none disturb!
Christ's progress, and His prayer-time;
The hours to which high Heaven doth chime.
Silex Scintillans [1655].
The Night, Line 25

My soul, there is a country
Far beyond the stars
Where stands a wingèd sentry
All skilful in the wars:
There, above noise and danger,
Sweet Peace is crown'd with smiles,
And One born in a manger
Commands the beauteous files.
Ibid. Peace, Stanza 1

I saw Eternity the other night
Like a great ring of pure and endless light.
All calm, as it was bright;
And round beneath it, Time in hours, days, years,

[1]   Manus haec, inimica tyrannis,
Ense petit placidam sub libertate quietem.
The second line is the motto of the Commonwealth of Massachusetts.
[2] Like his that lights a candle to the sun. — ANDREW FLETCHER [1655–1716]: *Letter to Sir Walter Aston*
And hold their farthing candle to the sun. — EDWARD YOUNG: *Satire VII* [1725–1728], *L. 56*
And hold their glimmering tapers to the sun. — GEORGE CRABBE: *The Parish Register* [1807], *Part I, Introduction*

Driv'n by the spheres
Like a vast shadow mov'd; in which the
world
And all her train were hurled.
Silex Scintillans. The World

Happy those early days, when I
Shin'd in my angel-infancy.
Before I understood this place
Appointed for my second race.
Ibid. The Retreat

But felt through all this fleshly dress
Bright shoots of everlastingness.
Ibid.

They are all gone into the world of
light,
And I alone sit lingering here;
Their very memory is fair and bright,
And my sad thoughts doth clear.
Ibid. They Are All Gone,
Stanza 1

I see them walking in an air of glory
Whose light doth trample on my
days, —
My days, which are at best but dull
and hoary,
Mere glimmering and decays.
Ibid. Stanza 3

Dear, beauteous death, the jewel of the
just!
Shining nowhere but in the dark;
What mysteries do lie beyond thy dust,
Could man outlook that mark!
Ibid. Stanza 5

BLAISE PASCAL
[1623–1662]

Things are always at their best in
their beginning.
Lettres Provinciales [1656–
1657]. No. 4

Too much and too little education
hinder the mind.
Pensées [1670]. Sect. II, No. 72

I lay it down as a fact that, if all men
knew what others say of them, there
would not be four friends in the world.
Ibid. No. 101

The state of man: inconstancy,
boredom, anxiety.[1]
Pensées. Sect. II, No. 127

Cleopatra's nose, had it been shorter,
the whole aspect of the world would
have been changed.
Ibid. No. 162

The eternal silence of these infinite
spaces terrifies me.
Ibid. Sect. III, No. 206

We shall die alone.[2]
Ibid. No. 211

Between us and hell or heaven there
is nothing but life, which of all things
is the frailest.
Ibid. No. 213

The heart has its reasons which reason knows nothing of.[3]
Ibid. Sect. IV, No. 277

We know the truth, not only by the
reason, but by the heart.
Ibid. No. 282

Man is but a reed, the weakest in
nature, but he is a thinking reed.[4]
Ibid. Sect. VI, No. 347

Man is neither angel nor brute; and
the misfortune is that he who would
act the angel acts the brute.[5]
Ibid. No. 358

Evil is easy, and has infinite forms.
Ibid. No. 408

To ridicule philosophy is really to
philosophize.[6]
Ibid. Sect. VII, No. 430

What a chimera then is man! What a
novelty! What a monster, what a chaos,
what a contradiction, what a prodigy!
Judge of all things, feeble worm of the
earth, depository of truth, a sink of

[1] Condition de l'homme: inconstance, ennui, inquiétude.
[2] On mourra seul.
[3] Le coeur a ses raisons que la raison ne
connaît point.
[4] L'homme n'est qu'un roseau, le plus faible
de la nature, mais c'est un roseau pensant.
[5] L'homme n'est ni ange, ni bête; et le malheur veut que qui veut faire l'ange fait la
bête.
[6] Se moquer de la philosophie, c'est vrai-
ment philosopher.

uncertainty and error, the glory and the shame of the universe.[1]

> *Pensées. Sect. VII, No. 434*

Self is hateful.[2]

> *Ibid. No. 455*

Men never do evil so completely and cheerfully as when they do it from religious conviction.

> *Ibid. Sect. XIV, No. 894*

WILLIAM WALKER
[1623–1684]

Learn to read slow: all other graces
Will follow in their proper places.[3]

> *The Art of Reading*

GEORGE FOX [4]
[1624–1691]

The Lord showed me, so that I did see clearly, that he did not dwell in these temples which men had commanded and set up, but in people's hearts . . . his people were his temple, and he dwelt in them.

> *Journal* [*1694*]

I used in my dealings the word *verily*, and it was a common saying among people that knew me, if George says *verily* there is no altering him.

> *Ibid.*

The Lord opened unto me that being bred at Oxford or Cambridge was not enough to fit and qualify men to be ministers of Christ.

> *Ibid.*

My relations were much troubled at me that I would not go with them to hear the priest; for I would get into the orchard or the fields with my Bible by myself.

> *Ibid.*

I was glad that I was commanded to turn people to that inward light, spirit

---

[1] See Pope, pages 316b–317a.
[2] Le moi est haïssable.
[3] Take time enough; all other graces
  Will soon fill up their proper places.
    JOHN BYROM [1692–1763]: *Advice
      to Preach Slow*
[4] The founder of the Society of Friends (Quakers).

and grace, by which all might know their salvation, and their way to God.

> *Journal*

When the Lord sent me forth into the world, He forbade me to put off my hat to any, high or low.

> *Ibid.*

Justice Bennet of Derby, was the first that called us Quakers, because I bid them tremble at the word of the Lord. This was in the year 1650.

> *Ibid.*

He [Oliver Cromwell] said: "I see there is a people risen, that I cannot win either with gifts, honours, offices or places; but all other sects and people I can."

> *Ibid.*

JOHN AUBREY
[1626–1697]

He [Hobbes] had read much, but his contemplation was much more than his reading. He was wont to say that if he had read as much as other men, he should have known no more than other men.

> *Brief Lives* [*Edition 1898*]. *I, 349*

[William Oughtred, mathematician] His wife was a penurious woman, and would not allow him to burne candle after supper, by which means many a good notion is lost.

> *Ibid. II, 110*

Mr. William Shakespear was borne at Stratford upon Avon in the county of Warwick. His father was a butcher, and I have been told heretofore by some of the neighbours, that when he was a boy he exercised his father's trade, but when he killed a calfe he would doe it in a high style and make a speech. Ben Johnson and he did gather humours of men dayly where ever they came.

> *Ibid. II, 225*

JOHN BUNYAN
[1628–1688]

And so I penned
It down, until at last it came to be,

For length and breadth, the bigness which you see.

Pilgrim's Progress [*1678*].
Apology for His Book

Some said, "John, print it"; others said, "Not so."

Some said, "It might do good"; others said, "No."

Ibid.

As I walk'd through the wilderness of this world.

Ibid. Part I

The name of the slough was Despond.
Ibid.

Every fat [vat] must stand upon his bottom.[1]

Ibid.

The name of the one was Obstinate and the name of the other was Pliable.
Ibid.

The gentleman's name was Mr. Worldly-Wise-Man.

Ibid.

He came to the house of the Interpreter.

Ibid.

The palace Beautiful.
Ibid.

The valley of Humiliation.
Ibid.

A foul Fiend coming over the field to meet him; his name is Apollyon.
Ibid.

The pilgrim they laid in a large upper chamber, whose window opened toward the sun-rising; the name of the chamber was Peace.

Ibid.

I will talk of things heavenly, or things earthly; things moral, or things evangelical; things sacred, or things profane; things past, or things to come; things foreign, or things at home; things more essential, or things circumstantial.

Ibid.

It beareth the name of Vanity Fair,

[1] Every tub must stand upon its bottom. — CHARLES MACKLIN: *The Man of the World* [1781], *Act I, Sc. 2*

because the town where 'tis kept is lighter than vanity.

Pilgrim's Progress. Part I

Hanging is too good for him, said Mr. Cruelty.

Ibid.

A castle called Doubting Castle, the owner whereof was Giant Despair.
Ibid.

They came to the Delectable Mountains.

Ibid.

A great horror and darkness fell upon Christian.

Ibid.

So I awoke, and behold it was a dream.

Ibid.

Some things are of that nature as to make

One's fancy chuckle, while his heart doth ache.

Ibid. The Author's Way of Sending Forth His Second Part of the Pilgrim

A man that could look no way but downwards with a muckrake in his hand.

Ibid. Part II

The first string that the musician usually touches is the bass, when he intends to put all in tune. God also plays upon this string first, when he sets the soul in tune for himself.

Ibid.

My sword I give to him that shall succeed me in my pilgrimage, and my courage and skill to him that can get it. My marks and scars I carry with me, to be a witness for me, that I have fought his battles who now will be my rewarder.

Ibid.

So he passed over, and all the trumpets sounded for him on the other side.
Ibid.

The captain of all these men of death that came against him to take him away, was the Consumption, for it was that that brought him down to the grave.

> *The Life and Death of Mr. Badman*

SIR WILLIAM TEMPLE
[1628–1699]

Books, like proverbs, receive their chief value from the stamp and esteem of ages through which they have passed.

> *Miscellanea, Part II* [*1690*].
> *Ancient and Modern Learning*

When all is done, human life is, at the greatest and the best, but like a froward child, that must be played with and humoured a little to keep it quiet till it falls asleep, and then the care is over.

> *Ibid. Of Poetry*

No clap of thunder in a fair frosty day could more astonish the world than our declaration of war against Holland in 1672.

> *Memoirs* [*1692*]. *Vol. II*

JOHN TILLOTSON
[1630–1694]

If God were not a necessary Being of Himself, He might almost seem to be made for the use and benefit of men.[1]

> *Sermon*

They who are in highest places, and have the most power, have the least liberty, because they are most observed.

> *Reflections*

WALTER POPE
[1630?–1714]

May I govern my passions with absolute sway,
And grow wiser and better, as strength wears away,
Without gout or stone, by a gentle decay.

> *The Old Man's Wish* [*1685*]

---

[1] If God did not exist, it would be necessary to invent him. — VOLTAIRE [1694–1778]: *A l'Auteur du Livre des trois Imposteurs, Épitre CXL*

JOHN DRYDEN
[1631–1700]

And threat'ning France, plac'd like a painted Jove,
Kept idle thunder in his lifted hand.

> *Annus Mirabilis* [*1667*].
> *Stanza 39*

I am resolved to grow fat, and look young till forty.[1]

> *Secret Love, or The Maiden Queen* [*1667*]. *Act III, Sc. 1*

He [Shakespeare] was the man who of all modern, and perhaps ancient poets, had the largest and most comprehensive soul.

> *Essay of Dramatic Poesy* [*1668*]

He was naturally learn'd; he needed not the spectacles of books to read Nature; he looked inwards, and found her there.

> *Ibid.*

Pains of love be sweeter far
Than all other pleasures are.

> *Tyrannic Love* [*1669*].
> *Act IV, Sc. 1*

I am as free as Nature first made man,
Ere the base laws of servitude began,
When wild in woods the noble savage ran.

> *The Conquest of Granada* [*1669–1670*]. *Part I, Act I, Sc. 1*

Fame then was cheap, and the first comer sped;
And they have kept it since by being dead.

> *Ibid. Epilogue*

But Shakespeare's magic could not copied be;
Within that circle none durst walk but he.

> *The Tempest* [*1670*]. *Prologue*

Death in itself is nothing; but we fear
To be we know not what, we know not where.

> *Aureng-Zebe* [*1676*].
> *Act IV, Sc. 1*

When I consider life, 'tis all a cheat.
Yet fool'd with hope, men favour the deceit;

---

[1] See Sir Walter Scott, page 417b.

Trust on, and think tomorrow will repay.
Tomorrow's falser than the former
day;
Lies worse, and while it says we shall be
blest
With some new joys, cuts off what we
possest.
Strange cozenage! None would live past
years again,
Yet all hope pleasure in what yet re-
main;
And from the dregs of life think to re-
ceive
What the first sprightly running could
not give.
        Aureng-Zebe. Act IV, Sc. 1
'Tis not for nothing that we life pur-
sue;
It pays our hopes with something still
that's new.
                        Ibid.
Errors, like straws, upon the surface
flow;
He who would search for pearls must
dive below.
        All for Love [*1678*]. *Prologue*
Men are but children of a larger growth.
        Ibid. Act IV, Sc. 1
With how much ease believe we what
we wish! [1]
Whatever is, is in its causes just.[2]
        Oedipus [*1679*] (*With* NA-
        THANIEL LEE). *Act III, Sc. 1*
His hair just grizzled,
As in a green old age.[3]
                        Ibid.
Of no distemper, of no blast he died,
But fell like autumn fruit that mellow'd
long, —
Even wonder'd at, because he dropp'd
no sooner.
Fate seem'd to wind him up for four-
score years,
Yet freshly ran he on ten winters more;
Till like a clock worn out with eating
time,

[1] Men freely believe that which they desire.
— CAESAR [102?-44 B.C.]: *De Bello Gallico,
Book III, Sect. 18*
   [2] See Pope, page 316b.
   [3] See Homer, page 5b.

The wheels of weary life at last stood
still.
        Oedipus (*With* NATHANIEL LEE).
                        Act IV, Sc. 1
Whate'er he did was done with so much
ease,
In him alone, 'twas natural to please.
        Absalom and Achitophel.
        Part I [*1680*], *Line 27*
Of these the false Achitophel was first,
A name to all succeeding ages curst.
For close designs and crooked counsels
fit,
Sagacious, bold, and turbulent of wit,
Restless, unfixed in principles and
place,
In power unpleas'd, impatient of dis-
grace;
A fiery soul, which, working out its
way,
Fretted the pygmy-body to decay:
And o'er-inform'd the tenement of
clay.[1]
A daring pilot in extremity;
Pleas'd with the danger, when the
waves went high
He sought the storms; but for a calm
unfit,
Would steer too nigh the sands to boast
his wit.
Great wits are sure to madness near
allied,
And thin partitions do their bounds
divide.[2]
                        Ibid. Line 150
Bankrupt of life, yet prodigal of ease.
                        Ibid. Line 168
And all to leave what with his toil he
won
To that unfeather'd two-legg'd thing,
a son.
                        Ibid. Line 169
In friendship false, implacable in hate,
Resolv'd to ruin or to rule the state.
                        Ibid. Line 173

[1] See Thomas Fuller, page 243b.
[2] Remembrance and reflection how allied!
   What thin partitions sense from thought
   divide!
        POPE: *Essay on Man* [*1733-1734*],
                        Epistle I, L. 225
See Seneca, page 48a.

And heaven had wanted one immortal
song.
> *Absalom and Achitophel.*
> *Part I, Line 197*

The people's prayer, the glad diviner's
theme,
The young men's vision, and the old
men's dream! [1]
> *Ibid. Line 238*

Behold him setting in his western skies,
The shadows lengthening as the vapours rise.
> *Ibid. Line 268*

Than a successive title long and dark,
Drawn from the mouldy rolls of Noah's
ark.
> *Ibid. Line 301*

His courage foes, his friends his truth
proclaim.
> *Ibid. Line 357*

Let him give on till he can give no more.
> *Ibid. Line 389*

All empire is no more than power in
trust.
> *Ibid. Line 411*

Better one suffer, than a nation grieve.
> *Ibid. Line 416*

Who think too little, and who talk too
much.[2]
> *Ibid. Line 534*

A man so various, that he seem'd to be
Not one, but all mankind's epitome;
Stiff in opinions, always in the wrong,
Was everything by starts, and nothing
long;
But, in the course of one revolving
moon
Was chymist, fiddler, statesman, and
buffoon.[3]
> *Ibid. Line 545*

So over violent, or over civil,
That every man with him was God or
Devil.
> *Ibid. Line 557*

His tribe were God Almighty's gentlemen.
> *Ibid. Line 645*

[1] Your old men shall dream dreams, your
young men shall see visions. — *Joel, II, 28*
[2] See Jonson, page 219b.
[3] See Juvenal, page 62b.

Large was his wealth, but larger was
his heart.
> *Absalom and Achitophel.*
> *Part I, Line 826*

Him of the western dome, whose
weighty sense
Flows in fit words and heavenly eloquence.
> *Ibid. Line 868*

Of ancient race by birth, but nobler yet
In his own worth.
> *Ibid. Line 900*

Beware the fury of a patient man.[1]
> *Ibid. Line 1005*

Made still a blund'ring kind of melody;
Spurr'd boldly on, and dashed through
thick and thin,
Through sense and nonsense, never out
nor in.
> *Ibid. Part II* [*1682*], *Line 413*

For every inch that is not fool is rogue.
> *Ibid. Line 463*

There is a pleasure sure
In being mad which none but madmen
know.[2]
> *The Spanish Friar* [*1681*].
> *Act II, Sc. 1*

And, dying, bless the hand that gave
the blow.[3]
> *Ibid.*

He's a sure card.
> *Ibid.*

They say everything in the world is
good for something.
> *Ibid. Act III, Sc. 2*

Or break the eternal Sabbath of his rest.
> *Ibid. Act V, Sc. 2*

All human things are subject to decay,
And, when fate summons, monarchs
must obey.
> *Mac Flecknoe* [*1682*]. *Line 1*

The rest to some faint meaning make
pretence,
But Shadwell never deviates into sense.
Some beams of wit on other souls may
fall,

[1] See Publilius Syrus, page 44a.
[2] There is a pleasure in poetic pains
Which only poets know.
> COWPER [1731–1800]: *The*
> *Timepiece, L. 285*
[3] Adore the hand that gives the blow. —
POMFRET [1667–1702]: *Verses to His Friend*

Strike through and make a lucid interval;
But Shadwell's genuine night admits no ray,
His rising fogs prevail upon the day.
Mac Flecknoe. Line 19

And torture one poor word ten thousand ways.
Ibid. Line 208

Wit will shine
Through the harsh cadence of a rugged line.
To the Memory of Mr. Oldham
[1684]. Line 15

Happy the man, and happy he alone,
He who can call today his own;
He who, secure within, can say,
Tomorrow, do thy worst, for I have liv'd today.[1]
Imitation of Horace. Book III,
Ode 29 [1685], Line 65

Not heaven itself upon the past has power;
But what has been, has been, and I have had my hour.
Ibid. Line 71

I can enjoy her [2] while she's kind;
But when she dances in the wind,
And shakes the wings and will not stay,
I puff the prostitute away.
Ibid. Line 81

And virtue, though in rags, will keep me warm.
Ibid. Line 87

Ill news is wing'd with fate, and flies apace.
Threnodia Augustalis [1685].
Line 49

Men met each other with erected look,
The steps were higher that they took;
Friends to congratulate their friends made haste,
And long inveterate foes saluted as they pass'd.
Ibid. Line 124

Since heaven's eternal year is thine.
To the Pious Memory of Mrs.
Anne Killegrew [1686]. Line 15

[1] See Horace, page 39b.
[2] Fortune.

O gracious God! how far have we
Profan'd thy heavenly gift of poesy!
To the Pious Memory of Mrs.
Anne Killegrew. Line 56

Her wit was more than man, her innocence a child.[1]
Ibid. Line 70

Art she had none, yet wanted none,
For nature did that want supply:
So rich in treasures of her own,
She might our boasted stores defy.
Ibid. Line 71

From harmony, from heavenly harmony,
This universal frame began:
From harmony to harmony
Through all the compass of the notes it ran,
The diapason closing full in Man.
A Song for St. Cecilia's Day
[1687]. Stanza 1

What passion cannot Music raise and quell?
Ibid. Stanza 2

The trumpet's loud clangour
Excites us to arms,
With shrill notes of anger,
And mortal alarms.
The double double double beat
Of the thundering drum
Cries Hark! the foes come.
Ibid. Stanza 3

The soft complaining flute,
In dying notes, discovers
The woes of hopeless lovers.
Ibid. Stanza 4

The trumpet shall be heard on high
The dead shall live, the living die,
And Music shall untune the sky!
Ibid. Grand Chorus

She fear'd no danger, for she knew no sin.
The Hind and the Panther
[1687]. Part I, Line 4

And doom'd to death, though fated not to die.
Ibid. Line 8

For truth has such a face and such a mien,

[1] Of manners gentle, of affections mild,
In wit a man; simplicity a child.
POPE: *Epitaph on Gay* [1730]

As to be lov'd needs only to be seen.[1]
> *The Hind and the Panther.*
> *Part I, Line 33*

Of all the tyrannies on human kind
The worst is that which persecutes
the mind.
> *Ibid. Line 239*

And kind as kings upon their coronation
day.
> *Ibid. Line 271*

Too black for heaven, and yet too white
for hell.
> *Ibid. Line 343*

And leaves the private conscience for
the guide.
> *Ibid. Line 478*

Eternal house, not built with mortal
hands!
> *Ibid. Line 494*

Who can believe what varies every day,
Nor ever was, nor will be at a stay?
> *Ibid. Part II, Line 36*

All have not the gift of martyrdom.
> *Ibid. Line 59*

When the cause goes hard, the guilty
man
Excepts, and thins his jury all he can.
> *Ibid. Line 242*

Reason to rule, mercy to forgive:
The first is law, the last prerogative.
> *Ibid. Line 261*

War seldom enters but where wealth
allures.
> *Ibid. Line 706*

Much malice mingled with a little wit.
> *Ibid. Part III, Line 1*

Jealousy, the jaundice of the soul.
> *Ibid. Line 73*

For present joys are more to flesh and
blood
Than a dull prospect of a distant good.
> *Ibid. Line 364*

T'abhor the makers, and their laws approve,
Is to hate traitors and the treason love.[2]
> *Ibid. Line 706*

Secret guilt by silence is betrayed.
> *Ibid. Line 763*

[1] See Pope, page 317a.
[2] He loved treachery but hated a traitor. —
PLUTARCH [A. D. 46–120]: *Lives, Romulus,*
Chap. 17, Sect. 3

Possess your soul with patience.[1]
> *The Hind and the Panther.*
> *Part III, Line 839*

Our vows are heard betimes! and
Heaven takes care
To grant, before we can conclude the
prayer:
Preventing angels met it half the way,
And sent us back to praise, who came
to pray.[2]
> *Britannia Rediviva* [*1688*]. *Line 1*

Three poets, in three distant ages born,
Greece, Italy, and England did adorn.
The first in loftiness of thought sur-
pass'd;
The next, in majesty; in both the last.
The force of Nature could no further
go.
To make a third, she join'd the former
two.
> *Under Mr. Milton's Picture*
> [*1688*]

This is the porcelain clay of humankind.[3]
> *Don Sebastian* [*1690*]. *Act I, Sc. 1*

I have a soul that like an ample shield
Can take in all, and verge enough for
more.[4]
> *Ibid.*

A knock-down argument: 'tis but a
word and a blow.
> *Amphitryon* [*1690*]. *Act I, Sc. 1*

Whistling to keep myself from being
afraid.[5]
> *Ibid. Act III, Sc. 1*

So softly death succeeded life in her,
She did but dream of heaven, and she
was there.
> *Eleonora* [*1692*]. *Line 315*

Theirs was the giant race, before the
flood
> *Epistle to Congreve* [*1693*]. *Line 5*

[1] In your patience possess ye your souls. —
Luke, XXI, 19
[2] See Goldsmith, page 356a.
[3] The precious porcelain of human clay. —
BYRON: *Don Juan* [1819–1824], *Canto IV,*
St. 11
[4] Give ample room and verge enough. —
THOMAS GRAY: *The Bard* [1757], *II, 1*
[5] Whistling aloud to bear his courage up. —
BLAIR: *The Grave* [1743], *L. 58*

Genius must be born, and never can be taught.
> *Epistle to Congreve. Line 60*

Be kind to my remains; and oh defend,
Against your judgment, your departed friend!
> *Ibid. Line 72*

Look round the habitable world: how few
Know their own good, or knowing it, pursue.
> *Juvenal. Satire X* [*1693*]

None but the brave deserves the fair.
> *Alexander's Feast* [*1697*]. *Line 15*

With ravish'd ears
The monarch hears;
Assumes the god,
Affects to nod,
And seems to shake the spheres.
> *Ibid. Line 37*

Bacchus, ever fair and ever young.
> *Ibid. Line 54*

Rich the treasure,
Sweet the pleasure, —
Sweet is pleasure after pain.
> *Ibid. Line 58*

Sooth'd with the sound, the king grew vain;
Fought all his battles o'er again;
And thrice he routed all his foes, and thrice he slew the slain.
> *Ibid. Line 66*

Fallen from his high estate,
And welt'ring in his blood;
Deserted, at his utmost need,
By those his former bounty fed,
On the bare earth expos'd he lies,
With not a friend to close his eyes.
> *Ibid. Line 78*

Softly sweet, in Lydian measures,
Soon he sooth'd his soul to pleasures.
War, he sung, is toil and trouble;
Honour but an empty bubble;
Never ending, still beginning,
Fighting still, and still destroying.
If all the world be worth thy winning,
Think, oh think it worth enjoying:
Lovely Thais sits beside thee,
Take the good the gods provide thee.
> *Ibid. Line 97*

Sigh'd and look'd, and sigh'd again.
> *Ibid. Line 120*

And, like another Helen, fir'd another Troy.
> *Alexander's Feast. Line 154*

Could swell the soul to rage, or kindle soft desire.
> *Ibid. Line 160*

He rais'd a mortal to the skies,
She drew an angel down.
> *Ibid. Line 169*

Words, once my stock, are wanting to commend
So great a poet and so good a friend.
> *Epistle to Peter Antony Motteux* [*1698*]. *Line 54*

Better to hunt in fields, for health unbought,
Than fee the doctor for a nauseous draught.
The wise, for cure, on exercise depend;
God never made his work for man to mend.
> *Epistle to John Dryden of Chesterton* [*1700*]. *Line 92*

A very merry, dancing, drinking,
Laughing, quaffing, and unthinking time.
> *The Secular Masque* [*1700*]. *Line 38*

The sword within the scabbard keep,
And let mankind agree.
> *Ibid. Line 61*

All, all of a piece throughout:
Thy chase had a beast in view;
Thy wars brought nothing about;
Thy lovers were all untrue.
'Tis well an old age is out,
And time to begin a new.
> *Ibid. Line 86*

And new-laid eggs, which Baucis' busy care
Turn'd by a gentle fire and roasted rare.
> *Ovid, Metamorphoses* [*1700*]. *Book VIII, Baucis and Philemon, Line 97*

Ill habits gather by unseen degrees, —
As brooks make rivers, rivers run to seas.
> *Ibid. Book XV, The Worship of Aesculapius, Line 155*

Here is God's plenty. [Of Chaucer's
Canterbury Tales]
Fables [*1700*]. *Preface*

For Art may err, but Nature cannot
miss.
Ibid. The Cock and the Fox.
Line 452

Old as I am, for ladies' love unfit,
The power of beauty I remember yet.
Ibid. Cymon and Iphigenia. Line 1

He trudg'd along unknowing what he
sought,
And whistled as he went, for want of
thought.
Ibid. Line 84

Love taught him shame; and shame,
with love at strife,
Soon taught the sweet civilities of life.
Ibid. Line 133

She hugg'd the offender, and forgave
the offence:
Sex to the last.[1]
Ibid. Line 367

And raw in fields the rude militia
swarms,
Mouths without hands; maintain'd at
vast expense,
In peace a charge, in war a weak defence.
Ibid. Line 400

Of seeming arms to make a short essay,
Then hasten to be drunk, — the busi-
ness of the day.
Ibid. Line 407

He was exhal'd; his great Creator drew
His spirit, as the sun the morning dew.[2]
On the Death of a Very Young
Gentleman [*1704*]

[1] And love the offender, yet detest the offence. — POPE: *Eloisa to Abelard* [*1717*],
L. 192
[2] Early, bright, transient, chaste as morning
dew,

She sparkl'd, was exhal'd, and went to
heaven.
EDWARD YOUNG: *Night Thoughts*
[*1742–1745*], *Night V, L. 600*

WILLIAM STOUGHTON
[1631–1701]

God sifted a whole nation that he
might send choice grain over into this
wilderness.[1]
Election Sermon at Boston
[*April 29, 1669*]

BENEDICT (BARUCH)
SPINOZA [2]
[1632–1677]

Nature abhors a vacuum.
Ethics [*1677*].[3] *Part I, Prop. XV,*
Note

God and all the attributes of God are
eternal.
Ibid. Prop. XIX

Nothing exists from whose nature
some effect does not follow.
Ibid. Prop. XXXVI

He who would distinguish the true
from the false must have an adequate
idea of what is true and false.
Ibid. Part II, Prop. XLII, Proof

Will and Intellect are one and the
same thing.
Ibid. Prop. XLIX, Corollary

He that can carp in the most eloquent or acute manner at the weakness
of the human mind is held by his fellows as almost divine.
Ibid. Part III, Preface

Surely human affairs would be far
happier if the power in men to be silent
were the same as that to speak. But ex-

[1] God had sifted three kingdoms to find
the wheat for this planting. — LONGFELLOW:
Courtship of Miles Standish [*1858*], *IV*
[2] Ein Gottbetrunkener Mensch (A God-
intoxicated man). — NOVALIS (FRIEDRICH VON
HARDENBERG) [*1772–1801*]
The Lord blot out his name under heaven.
The Lord set him apart for destruction from
all the tribes of Israel, with all the curses of
the firmament which are written in the Book
of the Law. . . . There shall no man speak
to him, no man write to him, no man show
him any kindness, no man stay under the
same roof with him, no man come nigh him.
— Amsterdam Synagogue's curse on Spinoza
[*1656*]
[3] Everyman edition, translated by ANDREW
BOYLE.

perience more than sufficiently teaches that men govern nothing with more difficulty than their tongues.

Ethics. Part III, Prop. II, Note

Pride is therefore pleasure arising from a man's thinking too highly of himself.

Ibid. Prop. XXVI, Note

It may easily come to pass that a vain man may become proud and imagine himself pleasing to all when he is in reality a universal nuisance.

Ibid. Prop. XXX, Note

Sadness diminishes or hinders a man's power of action.

Ibid. Prop. XXXVII, Proof

Self-complacency is pleasure accompanied by the idea of oneself as cause.

Ibid. Prop. LI, Note

It therefore comes to pass that every one is fond of relating his own exploits and displaying the strength both of his body and his mind, and that men are on this account a nuisance one to the other.

Ibid. Prop. LIV, Note

I refer those actions which work out the good of the agent to courage, and those which work out the good of others to nobility. Therefore temperance, sobriety, and presence of mind in danger, etc., are species of courage; but modesty, clemency, etc., are species of nobility.

Ibid. Prop. LIX, Note

Fear cannot be without hope nor hope without fear.

Ibid. Definition XIII, Explanation

So long as a man imagines that he cannot do this or that, so long is he determined not to do it: and consequently, so long it is impossible to him that he should do it.

Ibid. Definition XXVIII, Explanation

Those who are believed to be most abject and humble are usually most ambitious and envious.

Ibid. Definition XXIX, Explanation

One and the same thing can at the same time be good, bad, and indifferent, e.g., music is good to the melancholy,

bad to those who mourn, and neither good nor bad to the deaf.

Ethics. Part IV, Preface

Man is a social animal.

Ibid. Prop. XXXV, Note

Men will find that they can prepare with mutual aid far more easily what they need, and avoid far more easily the perils which beset them on all sides, by united forces.

Ibid.

Avarice, ambition, lust, etc., are nothing but species of madness, although not enumerated among diseases.[1]

Ibid. Prop. XLIV, Note

It is the part of a wise man to feed himself with moderate pleasant food and drink, and to take pleasure with perfumes, with the beauty of growing plants, dress, music, sports, and theatres, and others places of this kind which man may use without any hurt to his fellows.

Ibid. Prop. XLV, Note 2

He whose honour depends on the opinion of the mob must day by day strive with the greatest anxiety, act and scheme in order to retain his reputation. For the mob is varied and inconstant, and therefore if a reputation is not carefully preserved it dies quickly.

Ibid. Prop. LVIII, Note

In refusing benefits caution must be used lest we seem to despise or to refuse them for fear of having to repay them in kind.

Ibid. Prop. LXX, Note

To give aid to every poor man is far beyond the reach and power of every man. . . . Care of the poor is incumbent on society as a whole.

Ibid. Appendix, XVII

None are more taken in by flattery than the proud, who wish to be the first and are not.

Ibid. XXI

---

[1] To me, avarice seems not so much a vice, as a deplorable piece of madness. — SIR THOMAS BROWNE: *Religio Medici* [1642]

Those are most desirous of honour and glory who cry out the loudest of its abuse and the vanity of the world.
Ethics. Part V, Prop. X, Note

We feel and know that we are eternal.
Ibid. Prop. XXIII, Note

All excellent things are as difficult as they are rare.
Ibid. Prop. XLII, Note

The things which . . . are esteemed as the greatest good of all, . . . can be reduced to these three headings: to wit, Riches, Fame, and Pleasure. With these three the mind is so engrossed that it cannot scarcely think of any other good.
Tractatus de Intellectus Emendatione [*1677*]. *I, 3*

Fame has also this great drawback, that if we pursue it we must direct our lives in such a way as to please the fancy of men, avoiding what they dislike and seeking what is pleasing to them.
Ibid. 5

The more intelligible a thing is, the more easily it is retained in the memory, and contrariwise, the less intelligible it is, the more easily we forget it.
Ibid. XI, 81

JOHN LOCKE
[*1632–1704*]

New opinions are always suspected, and usually opposed, without any other reason but because they are not already common.
Essay on Human Understanding [*1690*]. *Dedicatory Epistle*

No man's knowledge here can go beyond his experience.
Ibid. Book II, Chap. 1, Sect. 19

It is one thing to show a man that he is in error, and another to put him in possession of truth.
Ibid. Book IV, Chap. 7, Sect. 11

All men are liable to error; and most men are, in many points, by passion or interest, under temptation to it.
Ibid. Chap. 20, Sect. 17

A sound mind in a sound body,[1] is a short but full description of a happy state in this world.
Some Thoughts on Education [*1693*]. *Sect. 1*

Virtue is harder to be got than knowledge of the world; and, if lost in a young man, is seldom recovered.
Ibid. Sect. 64

He that will have his son have a respect for him and his orders, must himself have a great reverence for his son.
Ibid. Sect. 65

The only fence against the world is a thorough knowledge of it.
Ibid. Sect. 88

BISHOP RICHARD CUMBERLAND
[*1632–1718*]

It is better to wear out than to rust out.
Quoted by BISHOP GEORGE HORNE [*1730–1792*]: *Sermon on the Duty of Contending for the Truth*

WENTWORTH DILLON, EARL OF ROSCOMMON
[*1633–1685*]

Remember Milo's end,
Wedged in that timber which he strove to rend.
Essay on Translated Verse [*1684*]. *Line 87*

And choose an author as you choose a friend.
Ibid. Line 96

Immodest words admit of no defence,
For want of decency is want of sense.
Ibid. Line 113

The multitude is always in the wrong.
Ibid. Line 184

My God, my Father, and my Friend,
Do not forsake me in my end.
Translation of Dies Irae

[1] Mens sana in corpore sano. — JUVENAL [A. D. 40–125]: *Satire X, L. 356*

SAMUEL PEPYS
[1633–1703]

I pray God to keep me from being proud.

Diary. March 22, 1660

This morning came home my fine camlet cloak, with gold buttons, and a silk suit, which cost me much money, and I pray God to make me able to pay for it.

Ibid. July 1, 1660

And so to bed.

Ibid. July 22, 1660; December 7, 1660; May 19, 1662; etc.

I am unwilling to mix my fortune with him that is going down the wind.

Ibid. September 6, 1660

I did give ten shillings and no more, though I believe most of the rest did give more, and did believe that I did so too.

Ibid. November 5, 1660

One, by his own confession to me, that can put on two several faces, and look his enemies in the face with as much love as his friends. But, good God! what an age is this, and what a world is this! that a man cannot live without playing the knave and dissimulation.

Ibid. September 1, 1661

Though he be a fool, yet he keeps much company, and will tell all he sees or hears, so a man may understand what the common talk of the town is.

Ibid. September 2, 1661

Besides us and my uncle Fenner's family, there was none of any quality, but poor and rascally people.

Ibid. September 15, 1661

My wife, poor wretch.

Ibid. September 18, 1661; December 19, 1662; etc.

Thanks be to God, since my leaving drinking of wine, I do find myself much better, and do mind my business better, and do spend less money, and less time lost in idle company.

Ibid. January 26, 1662

As happy a man as any in the world, for the whole world seems to smile upon me.

Diary. October 31, 1662

Great talk among people how some of the Fanatiques do say that the end of the world is at hand, and that next Tuesday is to be the day. Against which, whenever it shall be, good God fit us all!

Ibid. November 25, 1662

Bought Hudibras again, it being certainly some ill humour to be so against that which all the world cries up to be the example of wit; for which I am resolved once more to read him, and see whether I can find it or no.[1]

Ibid. February 6, 1663

Got my father, brother Tom, and myself together, and I advised my father to good husbandry, and to be living within the compass of £50 a year, and all in such kind words, as not only made both them but myself to weep.

Ibid. May 1, 1663

Troubled to see my wife forced to sit in the back of the coach, though pleased to see her company none but women and one parson.

Ibid. June 15, 1663

Find myself £43 worse than I was the last month . . . chiefly arisen from my layings-out in clothes for myself and wife; viz., for her about £12, and for myself £55.

Ibid. October 31, 1663

Home, and dined, where I found an excellent mastiffe — his name Towser — sent me by a surgeon.

Ibid. February 17, 1664

To the Trinity House, where a very good dinner among the old soakers.

Ibid. February 15, 1665

I am at a loss to know whether it be my hare's foot which is my preservative, or my taking of a pill of turpentine every morning.

Ibid. March 26, 1665

[1] Pepys had bought *Hudibras,* December 26, 1662, but thought it "so silly an abuse of the Presbyter Knight going to the wars" that he sold it the same day.

Thus I ended this month with the greatest joy that ever I did any in my life, because I have spent the greatest part of it with abundance of joy, and honour, and pleasant journeys, and brave entertainments, and without cost of money.

Diary. July 31, 1665

But Lord! how everybody's looks, and discourse in the street, is of death, and nothing else; and few people going up and down, that the town is like a place distressed and forsaken.[1]

Ibid. August 30, 1665

Saw a wedding in the church; and strange to see what delight we married people have to see these poor fools de-coyed into our condition.

Ibid. December 25, 1665

Musick and women I cannot but give way to, whatever my business is.

Ibid. March 9, 1666

The truth is, I do indulge myself a little the more in pleasure, knowing that this is the proper age of my life to do it; and, out of my observation that most men that do thrive in the world do forget to take pleasure during the time that they are getting their estate, but reserve that till they have got one, and then it is too late for them to enjoy it.

Ibid. March 10, 1666

Home, and, being washing-day, dined upon cold meat.

Ibid. April 4, 1666

Anon comes home my wife from Brampton, not looked for till Saturday, which will hinder me of a little pleasure, but I am glad of her coming.

Ibid. April 19, 1666

Musick is the thing of the world that I love most.

Ibid. July 30, 1666

Thus ends this year of publick won-der and mischief to this nation, and, therefore, generally wished by all peo-ple to have an end.

Ibid. December 31, 1666

Busy till night, pleasing myself mightily to see what a deal of business

[1] The time of the Great Plague.

goes off a man's hands when he stays by it.

Diary. January 14, 1667

Did satisfy myself mighty fair in the truth of the saying that the world do not grow old at all, but is in as good condition in all respects as ever it was.

Ibid. February 3, 1667

This day I am, by the blessing of God, 34 years old, in very good health and mind's content, and in condition of estate much beyond whatever my friends could expect of a child of their's, this day 34 years. The Lord's name be praised! and may I be thankful for it.

Ibid. February 23, 1667

To church; and with my mourning, very handsome, and new periwigg, make a great show.

Ibid. March 31, 1667

But to think of the clatter they make with his coach, and their own fine cloathes, and yet how meanly they live within doors, and nastily, and borrow-ing everything of neighbours.

Ibid. April 1, 1667

I have had it much in my thoughts lately that it is not too much for me now, in degree or cost, to keep a coach, but contrarily, that I am almost ashamed to be seen in a hackney.

Ibid. April 21, 1667

Whose red nose makes me ashamed to be seen with him.

Ibid. May 3, 1667

I staid talking below, while my wife dressed herself, which vexed me that she was so long about it.[1]

Ibid. July 14, 1667

Gives me some kind of content to re-member how painful it is sometimes to keep money, as well as to get it.

Ibid. October 11, 1667

And there all my Fellow-Officers, and all the world that was within hearing, did congratulate me, and cry my speech as the best thing they ever heard.

Ibid. March 5, 1668

[1] In fairness to Mrs. Pepys, it should be added that they were rising at 4 A. M. that warm morning, for a picnic in the country.

Not to make any more speech, which, while my fame is good, I will avoid, for fear of losing it.

Diary. March 13, 1668

I find my wife hath something in her gizzard, that only waits an opportunity of being provoked to bring up; but I will not, for my content-sake, give it.

Ibid. June 17, 1668

I by little words find that she hath heard of my going to plays, and carrying people abroad every day, in her absence; and that I cannot but help the storm will break out in a little time.

Ibid. June 18, 1668

In appearance, at least, he being on all occasions glad to be at friendship with me, though we hate one another, and know it on both sides.

Ibid. September 22, 1668

I do hate to be unquiet at home.

Ibid. January 22, 1669

And so I betake myself to that course, which is almost as much as to see myself go into my grave; for which, and all the discomforts that will accompany my being blind, the good God prepare me!

Ibid. May 31, 1669 (final entry)

GEORGE SAVILE,
MARQUESS OF HALIFAX
[1633–1695]

Children and fools want everything, because they want wit to distinguish; there is no stronger evidence of a crazy understanding than the making too large a catalogue of things necessary.

Advice to a Daughter [1688]

Popularity is a crime from the moment it is sought; it is only a virtue where men have it whether they will or no.

Moral Thoughts and Reflections [1750]

Misspending a man's time is a kind of self-homicide.

Ibid.

ROBERT SOUTH
[1634–1716]

Speech was given to the ordinary sort of men whereby to communicate their mind; but to wise men, whereby to conceal it.[1]

Sermon [1676]

NICHOLAS BOILEAU-
DESPRÉAUX
[1636–1711]

Happy who in his verse can gently steer
From grave to light, from pleasant to severe.[2]

The Art of Poetry [1674].[3]
Canto I, Line 75

Whate'er is well-conceived is clearly said,
And the words to say it flow with ease.

Ibid. Line 153

Every age has its pleasures, its style of wit, and its own ways.

Ibid. Canto III, Line 374

The wisest man is he who does not fancy that he is so at all.

Satire 1. Line 46

He [Molière] pleases all the world, but cannot please himself.

Ibid. Line 94

In spite of every sage whom Greece can show,
Unerring wisdom never dwelt below;

[1] Speech was made to open man to man, and not to hide him; to promote commerce, and not betray it. — DAVID LLOYD [1635–1692]: *The Statesmen and Favourites of England since the Reformation* [1665, edited by Whitworth], *Vol. I, P. 503*
Men talk only to conceal the mind. — EDWARD YOUNG: *Love of Fame* [1725–1728], *Satire II, L. 208*
The true use of speech is not so much to express our wants as to conceal them. — GOLDSMITH: *The Bee, No. 3* [October 20, 1759]
Ils ne se servent de la pensée que pour autoriser leurs injustices, et n'emploient les paroles que pour déguiser leurs pensées (Men use thought only to justify their wrongdoings, and employ speech only to conceal their thoughts). — VOLTAIRE: *Dialogue XIV, Le Chapon et la Poularde* [1766]

[2] See Pope, page 318a.

[3] Translated by DRYDEN.

Folly in all of every age we see,
The only difference lies in the degree.
Satire 4. Line 37

Greatest fools are oft most satisfied.
Ibid. Line 128

If your descent is from heroic sires,
Show in your life a remnant of their fires.
Satire 5. Line 43

Of all the creatures that creep, swim, or fly,
Peopling the earth, the waters, and the sky,
From Rome to Iceland, Paris to Japan,
I really think the greatest fool is man.
Satire 8. Line 1

Follows his wife like fringe upon her gown.
Ibid. Line 47

A hero may be dragged in a romance
Through ten long volumes by the laws of France.
Hence every year our books in torrents run,
And Paris counts an author in each son.
Satire 9. Line 103

But satire, ever moral, ever new,
Delights the reader and instructs him, too.
She, if good sense refine her sterling page,
Oft shakes some rooted folly of the age.
Ibid. Line 257

Honor is like an island, rugged and without a beach; once we have left it, we can never return.
Satire 10. Line 167

Now two punctilious envoys, Thine and Mine,
Embroil the earth about a fancied line;
And, dwelling much on right and much on wrong,
Prove how the right is chiefly with the strong.
Satire 11. Line 141

All Europe by conflicting Faiths was rent,
And e'en the Orthodox on carnage bent;
The blind avengers of Religion's cause

Forgot each precept of her peaceful laws.
Satire 12. Line 169

The terrible burden of having nothing to do.
Epistle XI

BISHOP THOMAS KEN
[1637–1711]

Teach me to live, that I may dread
The grave as little as my bed.
Morning and Evening Hymn.
Stanza 3

Praise God, from whom all blessings flow!
Praise Him, all creatures here below!
Praise Him above, ye heavenly host!
Praise Father, Son, and Holy Ghost!
Ibid. Stanza 10

JEAN RACINE
[1639–1699]

It is no longer a passion hidden in my veins: it is the goddess Venus herself fastened on her prey.[1]
Phèdre [1677]. Act I, Sc. 3

Innocence has nothing to dread.
Ibid. Act III, Sc. 6

Crime like virtue has its degrees; and timid innocence was never known to blossom suddenly into extreme license.[2]
Ibid. Act IV, Sc. 2

According to ancient, sacred custom.
Athalie [1691]. Act I, Sc. 1

To repair the irreparable ravages of time.
Ibid. Act II, Sc. 5

SIR CHARLES SEDLEY
[1639?–1701]

When change itself can give no more,
'Tis easy to be true.
Reasons for Constancy. Stanza 4

Phyllis is my only joy,
Faithless as the winds or seas;

[1] Ce n'est plus une ardeur dans mes veines cachée:
C'est Vénus toute entière à sa proie attachée.
[2] See Juvenal, page 62b.

287

Sometimes coming, sometimes coy,
Yet she never fails to please.
Song [*1702*]. *Stanza 1*

SIR ISAAC NEWTON
[1642–1727]

I do not know what I may appear to the world; but to myself I seem to have been only like a boy playing on the seashore, and diverting myself in now and then finding a smoother pebble or a prettier shell than ordinary, whilst the great ocean of truth lay all undiscovered before me.
BREWSTER's *Memoirs of Newton* [*1855*]. *Vol. II, Chap. XXVII*

O Diamond! Diamond! thou little knowest the mischief done!
Said to a pet dog who knocked over a candle and set fire to his papers

WILLIAM PENN
[1644–1718]

The receipts of cookery are swelled to a volume; but a good stomach excels them all.
Fruits of Solitude [1] [*1693*]

Truth often suffers more by the heat of its defenders, than from the arguments of its opposers.
Ibid.

Men are generally more careful of the breed of their horses and dogs than of their children.
Ibid.

It were endless to dispute upon everything that is disputable.
Ibid.

Have a care where there is more sail than ballast.
Ibid.

Passion is a sort of fever in the mind,

[1] A copy of this little book, wrote ROBERT LOUIS STEVENSON, "I carried in my pocket all about the San Francisco streets, read in street-cars and ferry-boats when I was sick unto death, and found in all times and places a peaceful and sweet companion."

which ever leaves us weaker than it found us.
Fruits of Solitude

The public must and will be served.
Ibid.

Much reading is an oppression of the mind, and extinguishes the natural candle, which is the reason of so many senseless scholars in the world.
Advice to His Children [*1699*]

JEAN DE LA BRUYÈRE
[1645–1696]

Liberality consists less in giving a great deal than in gifts well timed.
Les Caractères [*1688–1697*].
Du Coeur

To laugh at men of sense is the privilege of fools.
Ibid. De la Société

Most men make use of the first part of their life to render the other part wretched.
Ibid. De l'Homme

If women were by nature what they makes themselves by artifice, if their faces suddenly became as bright or as leaden as they make them with paint and powder, they would be inconsolable.
Ibid. Des Femmes

HENRY ALDRICH
[1647–1710]

If all be true that I do think,
There are five reasons we should drink:
Good wine — a friend — or being dry —
Or lest we should be by and by —
Or any other reason why.
Five Reasons for Drinking

JOHN WILMOT, EARL OF ROCHESTER
[1647–1680]

Here lies our sovereign lord the king,
Whose word no man relies on;

He never says a foolish thing,
  Nor ever does a wise one.
    *Written on the Bedchamber Door
      of Charles II* [1]

For pointed satire I would Buckhurst
  choose,
The best good man with the worst-
  natured muse.[2]
    *An Allusion to Horace. Satire X,
      Book I*

A merry monarch, scandalous and poor.
    A Satire on King Charles II

The world appears like a great family,
Whose lord, oppressed with pride and
  poverty,
(That to the few great bounty he may
  show)
Is fain to starve the numerous train
  below.
    Like a Great Family

There's not a thing on earth that I can
  name,
So foolish, and so false, as common
  fame.
    Did E'er This Sauay World

Reason, which fifty times to one does
  err,
Reason, an *ignis fatuus* of the mind.
    A Satire Against Mankind [1675].
      Line 11

Books bear him up a while, and make
  him try
To swim with bladders of philosophy.
    Ibid. Line 20

Then Old Age and Experience, hand in
  hand,
Lead him to death, and make him understand,
After a search so painful and so long,
That all his life he has been in the
  wrong.
    Ibid. Line 25

Dead, we become the lumber of the
  world.
    After Death

[1] Charles II's reply to Lord Rochester's
epigram was: "That is very true: for my
words are my own, and my actions are my
ministers'."
[2] Thou best-humour'd man with the worst-
humour'd muse! — GOLDSMITH: *Retaliation*
[1774], *Postscript*

JOHN SHEFFIELD, DUKE OF BUCKINGHAMSHIRE
[1648–1721]

Of all those arts in which the wise excel,
Nature's chief masterpiece is writing
  well.
    Essay on Poetry [1682]

Read Homer once, and you can read
  no more;
For all books else appear so mean, so
  poor,
Verse will seem prose; but still persist
  to read,
And Homer will be all the books you
  need.
    Ibid.

And when I feigned an angry look,
Alas! I loved you best.
    The Reconcilement [1701]

WILLIAM III, PRINCE OF ORANGE
[1650–1702]

There is one certain means by which
I can be sure never to see my country's
ruin: I will die in the last ditch.
    HUME: *History of England*
    [1754–1757]. *Chap. 65*

THOMAS OTWAY
[1651–1685]

What mighty ills have not been done by
  woman!
Who was 't betrayed the Capitol? — A
  woman!
Who lost Mark Antony the world? —
  A woman!
Who was the cause of a long ten years'
  war,
And laid at last old Troy in ashes? —
  Woman!
Destructive, damnable, deceitful
  woman!
    The Orphan [1680]. *Act III, Sc. 1*

Let us embrace, and from this very
moment vow an eternal misery together.
    Ibid. Act IV, Sc. 2

O woman! lovely woman! Nature
made thee

To temper man: we had been brutes
without you.
Venice Preserved [*1682*].
Act I, Sc. 1

FRANÇOIS DE SALIGNAC DE LA MOTHE FÉNELON
[1651–1715]

That weary listlessness, which renders life unsupportable to the voluptuous and the indolent, is unknown to those who can employ themselves by reading.
Télémaque [*1699*]. *Book II*
There were some who said that a man at the point of death was more free than all others, because death breaks every bond, and over the dead the united world has no power.
Ibid. Book V
Love is conquered only by flight. Against such an enemy, true courage consists in fear and retreat, in retreat without deliberation, and without looking back.
Ibid. Book VI
By labor Wisdom gives poignancy to pleasure, and by pleasure she restores vigor to labor.
Ibid. Book VII
Do not men die fast enough without being destroyed by each other? Can any man be insensible of the brevity of life? and can he who knows it, think life too long!
Ibid.
They that defy the tempest to gratify avarice and luxury, deserve shipwreck.
Ibid.
Courage is a virtue only in proportion as it is directed by prudence.
Ibid. Book X
No distinction so little excites envy as that which is derived from ancestors by a long descent.
Ibid.
To be always ready for war, said Mentor, is the surest way to avoid it.[1]
Ibid.

[1] See Horace, page 40b, and Washington, page 367a.

Some of the most dreadful mischiefs that afflict mankind proceed from wine; it is the cause of disease, quarrels, sedition, idleness, aversion to labour, and every species of domestic disorder.
Télémaque. Book X
The blood of a nation ought never to be shed except for its own preservation in the utmost extremity.
Ibid. Book XIII
Mankind, by the perverse depravity of their nature, esteem that which they have most desired as of no value the moment it is possessed, and torment themselves with fruitless wishes for that which is beyond their reach.
Ibid. Book XVIII

NAHUM TATE
[1652–1715]
AND
NICHOLAS BRADY
[1659–1726]

And though he promise to his loss,
He makes his promise good.
Psalms [*1696*]. *XV, 5*
The sweet remembrance of the just
Shall flourish when he sleeps in dust.
Ibid. CXII, 6
Permit the transports of a British Muse,
And pardon raptures that yourselves infuse.
Tate, *as Poet Laureate, to the Parliament* [*1701*]

THOMAS D'URFEY
[1653–1723]

O'er the hills and far away.[1]
Pills to Purge Melancholy

ANDREW FLETCHER OF SALTOUN
[1655–1716]

Give me the making of the songs of a nation, and I care not who makes its laws.
Conversation Concerning a Right Regulation of Government for the Common Good of Mankind [*1703*]

[1] See Gay, page 308b.

NATHANIEL LEE
[1655–1692]

Then he will talk — good gods! how he will talk!
> *The Rival Queens, or, The Death of Alexander the Great* [*1677*]. *Act I, Sc. 3*

Vows with so much passion, swears with so much grace,
That 'tis a kind of heaven to be deluded by him.
> *Ibid.*

When Greeks joined Greeks, then was the tug of war.
> *Ibid. Act IV, Sc. 2*

'Tis beauty calls, and glory shows the way.[1]
> *Ibid.*

Man, false man, smiling, destructive man!
> *Theodosius* [*1680*]. *Act III, Sc. 2*

JOHN DENNIS
[1657–1734]

A man who could make so vile a pun would not scruple to pick a pocket.
> *The Gentleman's Magazine. Vol. LI* [*1781*], *Page 324*

They will not let my play run; and yet they steal my thunder.[2]

[1] "Leads the way" in the stage editions, which contain various interpolations, among them

  See the conquering hero comes!
  Sound the trumpet, beat the drums!

which was first used by Handel in *Joshua*, and afterwards transferred to *Judas Maccabaeus*. The text of both oratorios was written by Dr. Thomas Morell [1703–1784], a clergyman.

[2] For his play *Appius and Virginia* [1709], Dennis had invented a new species of thunder. "The tragedy however was coldly received, notwithstanding such assistance, and was acted but a short time. Some nights after, Mr. Dennis, being in the pit at the representation of *Macbeth*, heard his own thunder made use of; upon which he rose in a violent passion, and exclaimed, with an oath, that it was his thunder. 'See,' said he, 'how the rascals use me! They will not let my play run, and yet they steal my thunder!'" — *Biographia Britannica, Vol. V, P. 103*

JOHN NORRIS
[1657–1711]

How fading are the joys we dote upon!
Like apparitions seen and gone.
But those which soonest take their flight
Are the most exquisite and strong, —
Like angels' visits, short and bright;[1]
Mortality's too weak to bear them long.
> *The Parting*

When after some delays, some dying strife,
The soul stands shivering on the ridge of life;
With what a dreadful curiosity
Does she launch out into the sea of vast eternity.
> *The Meditation*

DANIEL DEFOE
[1661–1731]

Wherever God erects a house of prayer,
The Devil always builds a chapel there;[2]
And 'twill be found, upon examination,
The latter has the largest congregation.
> *The True-Born Englishman* [*1701*]. *Part I, Line 1*

From this amphibious ill-born mob began
That vain, ill-natur'd thing, an Englishman.
> *Ibid. Line 132*

Great families of yesterday we show,
And Lords whose parents were the Lord knows who.
> *Ibid. Line 372*

In their religion they are so uneven,
That each man goes his own By-way to heaven.
> *Ibid. Part II, Line 104*

And of all plagues with which mankind are curst,
Ecclesiastic tyranny's the worst.
> *Ibid. Line 299*

[1] Like those of angels, short and far between. — Robert Blair: *The Grave* [1743], *L. 588*

Like angel visits, few and far between. — Thomas Campbell: *Pleasures of Hope* [1799], *Part II, L. 378*

[2] See Luther, page 86b.

When kings the sword of justice first
    lay down,
They are no kings, though they possess
    the crown.
Titles are shadows, crowns are empty
    things,
The good of subjects is the end of
    kings.
       The True-Born Englishman.
          Part II, Line 313

He bade me observe it, and I should
always find, that the calamities of life
were shared among the upper and lower
part of mankind; but that the middle
station had the fewest disasters.
          Robinson Crusoe [*1719*]

One day, about noon, going towards
my boat, I was exceedingly surprised
with the print of a man's naked foot on
the shore, which was very plain to be
seen on the sand.
                 Ibid.

I let him know his name should be
Friday, which was the day I saved his
life.
                 Ibid.

I took my man Friday with me.
                 Ibid.

SIR SAMUEL GARTH
[1661–1719]

A barren superfluity of words.
        The Dispensary[1] [*1699*].
           Canto II, Line 95
To die is landing on some silent shore
Where billows never break, nor tem-
    pests roar;
Ere well we feel the friendly stroke, 'tis
    o'er.
        Ibid. Canto III, Line 225
Hard was their lodging, homely was
    their food;
For all their luxury was doing good.[2]
         Claremont. Line 148

[1] Thou hast no faults, or I no faults can
    spy;
Thou art all beauty, or all blindness I.
    CHRISTOPHER CODRINGTON [1668–
    1710]: *Lines Addressed to Garth
    on His Dispensary*
[2] And learn the luxury of doing good. —
GOLDSMITH: *The Traveller* [1764], *L. 22*

RICHARD BENTLEY
[1662–1742]

It is a maxim with me that no man
was ever written out of reputation but
by himself.[1]
        MONK'S *Life of Bentley*
The fortuitous or casual concourse of
atoms.
      Works [*1692*]. *Vol. III, Sermon
            VII, Page 147*

MATHEW HENRY
[1662–1714]

He rolls it under his tongue as a
sweet morsel.
      Commentaries [*1708–1710*].
           Psalm XXXVI
Our creature comforts.
          Ibid. Psalm XXXVII
They that die by famine die by
inches.
          Ibid. Psalm LIX
To fish in troubled waters.
          Ibid. Psalm LX
Here is bread, which strengthens
man's heart, and therefore called the
staff of life.[2]
          Ibid. Psalm CIV
Hearkners, we say, seldom hear good
of themselves.
        Ibid. Ecclesiastes, VII
It was a common saying among the
Puritans, "Brown bread and the Gospel
is good fare."
          Ibid. Isaiah, XXX
None so blind as those that will not
see.[3]
         Ibid. Jeremiah, XX

[1] See Montaigne, page 99a.
[2] For, behold, the Lord, the Lord of hosts,
doth take away from Jerusalem and from
Judah the stay and the staff, the whole stay
of bread, and the whole stay of water. —
Isaiah, III, 1
Bread is the staff of life. — SWIFT: *Tale of
a Tub* [1704]
Corn, which is the staff of life. — EDWARD
WINSLOW: *Good News from New England*
[1624]
[3] O foolish people, and without understanding; which have eyes and see not; which have
ears, and hear not. — *Jeremiah, V, 21*

Judas had given them the slip.
Commentaries. Matthew, XXII
After a storm comes a calm.
Ibid. Acts, IX
It is good news, worthy of all accep-
tation! and yet not too good to be true.
Ibid. Timothy, I
It is not fit the public trusts should
be lodged in the hands of any, till they
are first proved and found fit for the
business they are to be entrusted with.[1]
Ibid. Timothy, III

THOMAS (TOM) BROWN
[1663–1704]

I do not love thee, Doctor Fell.
The reason why I cannot tell;
But this alone I know full well,
I do not love thee, Doctor Fell.[2]
*Written while a student at
Christ Church, Oxford*
To treat a poor wretch with a bottle
of Burgundy, and fill his snuff-box, is
like giving a pair of laced ruffles to a
man that has never a shirt on his back.[3]
Laconics [1707]

WILLIAM WALSH
[1663–1708]

Of all the plagues a lover bears,
Sure rivals are the worst.
Song. Stanza 1
I can endure my own despair,
But not another's hope.
Ibid. Stanza 2

[1] See Burke, page 361b, Thomas Jefferson,
page 375a, Clay, page 433b, Calhoun, page
442a, and Cleveland, page 689a.
The phrase, "public office is a public trust,"
has of late become common property. —
CHARLES SUMNER [1872]
[2] Non amo te, Sabidi, nec possum dicere
    quare;
Hoc tantum possum dicere, non amo te.
(I do not love thee, Sabidius, nor can I say
why; but this much I can say, I do not love
thee). — MARTIAL [A.D. 40–102]: *Epigram I,
33*
    Je ne vous aime pas, Hylas;
    Je n'en saurois dire la cause,
    Je sais seulement une chose;
    C'est que je ne vous aime pas.
      COMTE DE BUSSY-RABUTIN
          [1618–1693]
[3] See Goldsmith, page 358a.

MATTHEW PRIOR
[1664–1721]

All jargon of the schools.[1]
I Am That I Am, An Ode [1688]
Our hopes, like towering falcons, aim
At objects in an airy height;
The little pleasure of the game
Is from afar to view the flight.
To the Hon. Charles Montague
Odds life! must one swear to the truth
of a song?
A Better Answer
Be to her virtues very kind;
Be to her faults a little blind.
Let all her ways be unconfin'd;
And clap your padlock — on her mind!
An English Padlock [1707]
That if weak women went astray,
Their stars were more in fault than
they.
Hans Carvel
The end must justify the means.
Ibid.
And thought the nation ne'er would
thrive
Till all the whores were burnt alive.
Paulo Purganti
And often took leave, but was loth to
depart.[2]
The Thief and the Cordelier
Nobles and heralds, by your leave,
  Here lies what once was Matthew
  Prior;
The son of Adam and of Eve:
  Can Bourbon or Nassau claim
  higher?[3]
Epitaph. Extempore

[1] Noisy jargon of the schools. — POMFRET
[1667–1702]: *Reason*
The sounding jargon of the schools. —
COWPER: *Truth* [1782], *L. 367*
[2] As men that be lothe to departe do often
take their leff [JOHN CLERK TO WOLSEY]. —
HENRY ELLIS [1777–1869]: *Letters, Third Series, Vol. I, P. 262*
"A loth to depart" was the common term
for a song, or a tune played, on taking leave
of friends.
[3] The following epitaph was written long
before the time of Prior:
    Johnnie Carnegie lais heer.
      Descendit of Adam and Eve.
    Gif ony con gang hieher,
      Ise willing give him leve.

Lays the rough paths of peevish Nature
   even,
And opens in each heart a little heaven.
                                    Charity

His noble negligences teach
What others' toils despair to reach.
                        Alma. Canto II, Line 7

Till their own dreams at length deceive
   'em,
And oft repeating, they believe 'em.
                    Ibid. Canto III, Line 13

Abra was ready ere I called her name;
And though I called another, Abra
   came.
   *Solomon on the Vanity of the
      World* [*1718*]. *Book II, Line 364*

Who breathes must suffer, and who
   thinks must mourn;
And he alone is bless'd who ne'er was
   born.
            Ibid. Book III, Line 240

To John I ow'd great obligation;
But John, unhappily, thought fit
To publish it to all the nation:
Sure John and I are more than quit.
                        Epigram [*1718*]

In public employments industrious and
   grave,
And alone with his friends, Lord! how
   merry was he!
                    For My Own Monument

SIR JOHN VANBRUGH
[1664–1726]

No man worth having is true to his
wife, or can be true to his wife, or ever
was, or ever will be so.
                        The Relapse [*1697*].
                                Act III, Sc. 2

Belinda. Ay, but you know we must
return good for evil.
Lady Brute. That may be a mistake
in the translation.
                    The Provoked Wife [*1698*].
                                    Act I, Sc. 1

Much of a muchness.
            The Provoked Husband [*1728*].
            Act I, Sc. 1 (*Completed by
            Cibber*).

JOHN POMFRET
[1667–1702]

Heaven is not always angry when he
   strikes,
But most chastises those whom most
   he likes.[1]
            *Verses to His Friend under
                        Affliction*

JONATHAN SWIFT
[1667–1745]

Seamen have a custom, when they
meet a whale, to fling him out an empty
tub by way of amusement, to divert him
from laying violent hands upon the
ship.
            Tale of a Tub [*1704*]. *Preface*

Books, the children of the brain.
                            Ibid. Sect. I

As boys do sparrows, with flinging
salt upon their tails.
                        Ibid. Sect. VII

When a man's fancy gets astride on
his reason; when imagination is at cuffs
with the senses; and common understanding, as well as common sense, is
kicked out of doors; the first proselyte
he makes is himself.
                        Ibid. Sect. IX

This is the sublime and refined point
of felicity, called the possession of being
well-deceived: the serene, peaceful
state of being a fool among knaves.
                                    Ibid.

Satire is a sort of glass, wherein beholders do generally discover everybody's face but their own.
        Battle of the Books [*1704*]. *Preface*

The two noblest things, which are
sweetness and light.[2]
                                    Ibid.

Laws are like cobwebs, which may
catch small flies, but let wasps and
hornets break through.
        *A Tritical Essay upon the Facul-
                    ties of the Mind* [*1707*]

[1] Whom the Lord loveth he chasteneth. —
Hebrews, XII, 6
[2] See Matthew Arnold, page 623a.

There is nothing in this world constant, but inconstancy.

> *A Tritical Essay upon the Faculties of the Mind*

'Tis very warm weather when one's in bed.

> *Journal to Stella. November 8, 1710*

With my own fair hands.

> *Ibid. January 4, 1711*

We are so fond of one another, because our ailments are the same.

> *Ibid. February 1, 1711*

I love good creditable acquaintance; I love to be the worst of the company.

> *Ibid. May 17, 1711*

We were to do more business after dinner; but after dinner is after dinner —an old saying and a true, "much drinking, little thinking."

> *Ibid. February 26, 1712*

We have just enough religion to make us hate, but not enough to make us love one another.

> *Thoughts on Various Subjects* [1711]

Censure is the tax a man pays to the public for being eminent.

> *Ibid.*

Every man desires to live long, but no man would be old.

> *Ibid.*

'Tis an old maxim in the schools,
That flattery's the food of fools;
Yet now and then your men of wit
Will condescend to take a bit.

> *Cadenus and Vanessa* [1] [1713]

If Heaven had looked upon riches to be a valuable thing, it would not have given them to such a scoundrel.

> *Letter to Miss Vanhomrigh* [August 12, 1720]

He [the Emperor] is taller by almost the breadth of my nail, than any of his court, which alone is enough to strike an awe into the beholders.

> *Gulliver's Travels* [1727]. *Part I, Chap. II, Voyage to Lilliput*

Big-endians and small-endians.[1]

> *Ibid. Chap. IV*

It is computed, that eleven thousand persons have, at several times, suffered death, rather than submit to break their eggs at the smaller end.

> *Ibid.*

I cannot but conclude the bulk of your natives to be the most pernicious race of little vermin that nature ever suffered to crawl upon the surface of the earth.

> *Ibid. Part II, Chap. VII, Voyage to Brobdingnag*

And he gave it for his opinion, that whoever could make two ears of corn, or two blades of grass, to grow upon a spot of ground where only one grew before, would deserve better of mankind, and do more essential service to his country, than the whole race of politicians put together.[2]

> *Ibid.*

He had been eight years upon a project for extracting sunbeams out of cucumbers, which were to be put in phials hermetically sealed, and let out to warm the air in raw inclement summers.

> *Ibid. Part III, Chap. V, Voyage to Laputa*

A set of phrases learn't by rote;
A passion for a scarlet coat;
When at a play to laugh, or cry,
Yet cannot tell the reason why:
Never to hold her tongue a minute;
While all she prates has nothing in it.

> *The Furniture of a Woman's Mind* [1727]

---

[1] When the poem of "Cadenus and Vanessa" was the general topic of conversation, some one said, "Surely that Vanessa must be an extraordinary woman that could inspire the Dean to write so finely upon her." Mrs. Johnson smiled, and answered that "she thought that point not quite so clear; for it was well known the Dean could write finely upon a broomstick." — SAMUEL JOHNSON: *Lives of the Poets* [1779–1781], *Life of Swift*

[1] As the political parties of Whig and Tory are pointed out by the high and low heels of the Lilliputians (Framecksan and Hamecksan), those of Papist and Protestant are designated under the Big-endians and Small-endians.

[2] He who makes two blades of grass grow in place of one renders a service to the State. — VOLTAIRE: *Letter to M. Moreau* [1765]

For conversation well endu'd;
She calls it witty to be rude;
And, placing raillery in railing,
Will tell aloud your greatest failing.
*The Furniture of a Woman's
Mind*

In party, furious to her pow'r;
A bitter Whig, or Tory sour;
Her arguments directly tend
Against the side she would defend.
Ibid.

Not die here in a rage, like a poisoned
rat in a hole.
*Letter to Bolingbroke
[March 21, 1729]*

Yet malice never was his aim;
He lash'd the vice but spar'd the name.
No individual could resent,
Where thousands equally were meant.
His satire points at no defect
But what all mortals may correct;
For he abhorr'd that senseless tribe
Who call it humor when they gibe.
*Verses on the Death of Dean
Swift [1731]. Line 459*

Hobbes clearly proves that every crea-
ture
Lives in a state of war by nature.[1]
On Poetry, A Rhapsody [1733].

So, naturalists observe, a flea
Hath smaller fleas that on him prey;
And these have smaller still to bite
'em;
And so proceed *ad infinitum.*
Thus every poet, in his kind,
Is bit by him that comes behind.
Ibid.

Conversation is but carving!
Give no more to every guest
Than he's able to digest.
Give him always of the prime,
And but little at a time.
Carve to all but just enough,
Let them neither starve nor stuff,
And that you may have your due,
Let your neighbour carve for you.
Conversation

Under this window in stormy weather
I marry this man and woman together;

[1] See Hobbes, pages 228b–229a.

Let none but Him who rules the thun-
der
Put this man and woman asunder.
*Marriage Service from His
Chamber Window*

The sight of you is good for sore
eyes.[1]
*Polite Conversation [1738?].
Dialogue I*

'Tis as cheap sitting as standing.
Ibid.

I hate nobody: I am in charity with
the world.
Ibid.

I won't quarrel with my bread and
butter.
Ibid.

She's no chicken; she's on the wrong
side of thirty, if she be a day.
Ibid.

She wears her clothes as if they were
thrown on with a pitchfork.
Ibid.

He was a bold man that first eat an
oyster.
Ibid. Dialogue II

That is as well said as if I had said it
myself.
Ibid.

Fingers were made before forks, and
hands before knives.
Ibid.

She has more goodness in her little
finger than he has in his whole body.
Ibid.

Lord! I wonder what fool it was that
first invented kissing.
Ibid.

The best doctors in the world are
Doctor Diet, Doctor Quiet, and Doc-
tor Merryman.[2]
Ibid.

[1] What a sight for sore eyes that would be!
—WILLIAM HAZLITT [1778–1830]: *Of Per-
sons One Would Have Seen*
[2] Use three physicians
First, Dr. Quiet;
Next, Dr. Merryman,
And Dr. Dyet.
Regimen Sanitatis Salernitanum
[1607]

I'll give you leave to call me anything, if you don't call me "spade."
Polite Conversation. Dialogue II

May you live all the days of your life.
Ibid.

I always like to begin a journey on Sundays, because I shall have the prayers of the Church to preserve all that travel by land or by water.
Ibid.

I know Sir John will go, though he was sure it would rain cats and dogs.
Ibid.

I thought you and he were hand-in-glove.
Ibid.

She watches him as a cat would watch a mouse.
Ibid. Dialogue III

There was all the world and his wife.
Ibid.

Hail, fellow, well met,
All dirty and wet:
Find out if you can,
Who's master, who's man.
My Lady's Lamentation [*1765*].
Line 171

I shall be like that tree, — I shall die at the top.
Sir Walter Scott's *Life of Swift* [*1814*]

Ubi saeva indignatio ulterius cor lacerare nequit.[1]
Epitaph: Inscribed on Swift's grave, St. Patrick's, Dublin

SUSANNAH CENTLIVRE
[*1667?–1723*]

The real Simon Pure.
A Bold Stroke for a Wife [*1718*].
Act V, Sc. 1

ALAIN RENÉ LE SAGE
[*1668–1747*]

It may be said that his wit shines at the expense of his memory.[2]
Gil Blas [*1715–1735*].
Book III, Chap. 11

A flatterer can risk everything with great personages.
Gil Blas. Book IV, Chap. 7

Pride and conceit were the original sin of man.
Ibid. Book VII, Chap. 3

I wish you all sorts of prosperity with a little more taste.
Ibid. Chap. 4

The pleasure of talking is the inextinguishable passion of a woman, coeval with the act of breathing.
Ibid. Chap. 7

Glory is the true and honorable recompense of gallant actions.
Ibid. Chap. 12

Facts are stubborn things.[1]
Ibid. Book X, Chap. 1

Plain as a pike-staff.
Ibid. Book XII, Chap. 8

WILLIAM CONGREVE
[*1670–1729*]

Eternity was in that moment.
The Old Bachelor [*1693*].
Act IV, Sc. 7

It is the business of a comic poet to paint the vices and follies of human kind.
The Double Dealer [*1694*].
Epistle Dedicatory

Retired to their tea and scandal, according to their ancient custom.
Ibid. Act I, Sc. 1

Tho' marriage makes man and wife one flesh, it leaves 'em still two fools.
Ibid. Act II, Sc. 3

No mask like open truth to cover lies,
As to go naked is the best disguise.
Ibid. Act V, Sc. 4

Thou liar of the first magnitude.
Love for Love [*1695*].
Act II, Sc. 2

I warrant you, if he danced till doomsday, he thought I was to pay the piper.
Ibid.

---

[1] Where savage indignation can no longer tear the heart.

[2] See Sheridan, page 382b.

[1] Facts are contrary 'z mules. — James Russell Lowell: *Biglow Papers, Series II* [1862], *No. 4*

Women are like tricks by sleight of
hand,
Which, to admire, we should not understand.
> *Love for Love. Act IV, Sc. 3*

Music hath charms to soothe the savage
breast,[1]
To soften rocks, or bend a knotted oak.
> *The Mourning Bride [1697].*
> *Act I, Sc. 1*

By magic numbers and persuasive
sound.
> *Ibid.*

Heaven has no rage like love to hatred
turned,
Nor hell a fury like a woman scorned.[2]
> *Ibid. Act III, Sc. 8*

Love's but a frailty of the mind,
When 'tis not with ambition joined:
A sickly flame, which, if not fed, ex-
pires,
And feeding, wastes in self-consuming
fires.
> *The Way of the World [1700].*
> *Act III, Sc. 12*

Thou art a retailer of phrases, and
dost deal in remnants of remnants.
> *Ibid. Act IV, Sc. 9*

If there's delight in love, 'tis when I
see
That heart which others bleed for, bleed
for me.
> *Ibid.*

Defer not till tomorrow to be wise,
Tomorrow's sun to thee may never
rise.[3]
> *Letter to Cobham*

RICHARD LEVERIDGE
[1670–1758]

When mighty roast beef was the Englishman's food,

It ennobled our hearts, and enriched
our blood,
Our soldiers were brave and our courtiers were good.
Oh! the roast beef of old England![1]
> *The Roast Beef of Old England.*
> *Stanza 1*

COLLEY CIBBER
[1671–1757]

As good be out of the world as out of
the fashion.
> *Love's Last Shift [1696]. Act II*

Words are but empty thanks.
> *Woman's Wit [1697]. Act V*

Perish that thought!
> *Richard III (altered) [1700].*
> *Act V, Sc. 5*

This business will never hold water.
> *She Wou'd and She Wou'd Not*
> *[1703]. Act IV*

Old houses mended,
Cost little less than new before they're
ended.
> *The Double Gallant [1707].*
> *Prologue*

Oh, how many torments lie in the
small circle of a wedding-ring!
> *Ibid. Act I, Sc. 2*

Stolen sweets are best.
> *The Rival Fools [1709]. Act I*

JOSEPH ADDISON
[1672–1719]

For wheresoe'er I turn my ravish'd
eyes,
Gay gilded scenes and shining prospects
rise,
Poetic fields encompass me around,
And still I seem to tread on classic
ground.
> *A Letter from Italy [1703]*

And, pleased the Almighty's orders to
perform,

---

[1] Music hath charms, we all may find,
Ingratiate deeply with the mind.
— MATTHEW GREEN [1696–1737]:
The Spleen, L. 141
[2] We shall find no fiend in hell can match
the fury of a disappointed woman. — COLLEY
CIBBER: *Love's Last Shift* [1696], *Act IV*
[3] Be wise today; 'tis madness to defer. —
EDWARD YOUNG: *Night Thoughts* [1742–
1745], *Night I, L. 390*

[1] Oh, the roast beef of England,
And old England's roast beef!
FIELDING [1707–1754]: *The Grub
Street Opera, Act III, Sc. 2*

Rides in the whirlwind and directs the
storm.[1]
   The Campaign [*1704*]. *Line 91*

Reading is to the mind what exercise
is to the body.
   The Tatler [*1709–1711*].
     No. 147

The spacious firmament on high,
With all the blue ethereal sky,
And spangled heavens, a shining frame,
Their great Original proclaim.
  Ode [*in The Spectator, No. 465,*
    August 23, 1712]

Soon as the evening shades prevail,
The moon takes up the wondrous tale,
And nightly to the listening earth
Repeats the story of her birth;
While all the stars that round her burn,
And all the planets in their turn,
Confirm the tidings as they roll,
And spread the truth from pole to pole.
     Ibid.

For ever singing as they shine,
"The hand that made us is divine."
     Ibid

Should the whole frame of Nature
 round him break,
In ruin and confusion hurled,
He, unconcerned, would hear the
 mighty crack,
And stand secure amidst a falling
 world.
  Horace. Ode III, Book III

Thy steady temper, Portius,
Can look on guilt, rebellion, fraud, and
 Caesar,
In the calm lights of mild philosophy.
   Cato [2] [*1713*]. *Act I, Sc. 1*

'Tis not in mortals to command success,
But we'll do more, Sempronius, — we'll
 deserve it.
     Ibid. Sc. 2

Blesses his stars and thinks it luxury.
     Ibid. Sc. 4

'Tis pride, rank pride, and haughtiness
 of soul;
I think the Romans call it stoicism.
    Cato. Act I, Sc. 4

Were you with these, my prince, you'd
 soon forget
The pale, unripened beauties of the
 north.
     Ibid.

Beauty soon grows familiar to the lover,
Fades in his eye, and palls upon the
 sense.

The virtuous Marcia towers above her
 sex.
     Ibid.

  My voice is still for war.
Gods! can a Roman senate long debate
Which of the two to choose, slavery or
 death?
    Ibid. Act II, Sc. 1

The woman that deliberates is lost.
    Ibid. Act IV, Sc. 1

Curse on his virtues! they've undone
 his country.
     Ibid. Sc. 4

  What pity is it
That we can die but once to save our
 country![1]
     Ibid.

When vice prevails, and impious men
 bear sway,
The post of honour is a private station.[2]
     Ibid.

It must be so, — Plato, thou reasonest
 well!
Else whence this pleasing hope, this
 fond desire,
This longing after immortality?
Or whence this secret dread, and inward horror
Of falling into naught? Why shrinks
 the soul

---

[1] This line is frequently ascribed to Pope,
as it is repeated in his *Dunciad, Book III*
[*1728*], *L. 264.*

[2] The *Massachusetts Spy* used the following
lines from *Cato* as its motto from November
22, 1771 to April 6, 1775:

Do thou Great Liberty inspire our Souls —
And make our Lives in thy Possession happy —
Or, our Deaths glorious in thy just Defence.

[1] I only regret that I have but one life to
lose for my country. — NATHAN HALE [before
his execution, September 22, 1776]

[2] Give me, kind Heaven, a private station,
A mind serene for contemplation!
Title and profit I resign;
The post of honour shall be mine.
  GAY: *Fables, Part II* [*1738*], *The*
  Vulture, The Sparrow, and Other
  Birds

Back on herself, and startles at destruction?
'Tis the divinity that stirs within us;
'Tis Heaven itself that points out an hereafter,
And intimates eternity to man.
Eternity! thou pleasing, dreadful thought!

Cato. Act V, Sc. 1

Sweet are the slumbers of the virtuous man.

Ibid. Sc. 4

From hence, let fierce contending nations know
What dire effects from civil discord flow.

Ibid.

Round-heads and wooden-shoes are standing jokes.

The Drummer. Prologue, Line 8

If I can any way contribute to the diversion or improvement of the country in which I live, I shall leave it, when I am summoned out of it, with the secret satisfaction of thinking that I have not lived in vain.[1]

The Spectator. No. 1,
March 1, 1711

I shall endeavour to enliven morality with wit, and to temper wit with morality.

Ibid. No. 10, March 11, 1711

True happiness is of a retired nature, and an enemy to pomp and noise; it arises, in the first place, from the enjoyment of one's self; and, in the next, from the friendship and conversation of a few select companions.

Ibid. No. 15, March 17, 1711

In all thy humours, whether grave or mellow,
Thou'rt such a touchy, testy, pleasant fellow;
Hast so much wit, and mirth, and spleen about thee,

There is no living with thee, nor without thee.[1]

The Spectator. No. 68,
May 18, 1711

There is not a more unhappy being than a superannuated idol.

Ibid. No. 73, May 24, 1711

A man that has a taste of music, painting, or architecture, is like one that has another sense, when compared with such as have no relish of those arts.

Ibid. No. 93, June 16, 1711

There is not so variable thing in nature as a lady's head-dress.

Ibid. No. 98, June 21, 1711

There is no defence against reproach but obscurity.

Ibid. No. 101, June 26, 1711

Much may be said on both sides.

Ibid. No. 122, July 20, 1711

Authors have established it as a kind of rule, that a man ought to be dull sometimes; as the most severe reader makes allowances for many rests and nodding-places in a voluminous writer.

Ibid. No. 124, July 23, 1711

Books are the legacies that a great genius leaves to mankind, which are delivered down from generation to generation, as presents to the posterity of those who are yet unborn.

Ibid. No. 166, September 10, 1711

Good-nature is more agreeable in conversation than wit, and gives a certain air to the countenance which is more amiable than beauty.

Ibid. No. 169, September 13, 1711

Were I to prescribe a rule for drinking, it should be formed upon a saying quoted by Sir William Temple: the first glass for myself, the second for my friends, the third for good humour, and the fourth for mine enemies.

Ibid. No. 195, October 13, 1711

A true critic ought to dwell rather upon excellencies than imperfections, to discover the concealed beauties of a writer, and communicate to the world

---

[1] I shall pass through this world but once. If, therefore, there be any kindness I can show, or any good thing I can do, let me do it now; let me not defer it or neglect it, for I shall not pass this way again.— *Attributed to* ETIENNE DE GRELLET [1773–1855]

[1] A translation of MARTIAL [A. D. 40–102], *XII, 47,* who imitated OVID [43 B. C.–A. D. 18], *Amores, III, 11, 39.*

such things as are worth their observation.

> *The Spectator. No. 291,*
> *February 2, 1712*

Death only closes a man's reputation, and determines it as good or bad.

> *Ibid. No. 349, April 10, 1712*

Mirth is like a flash of lightning, that breaks through a gloom of clouds, and glitters for a moment; cheerfulness keeps up a kind of daylight in the mind, and fills it with a steady and perpetual serenity.

> *Ibid. No. 381, May 17, 1712*

Sir Roger made several reflections on the greatness of the British Nation; as, that one Englishman could beat three Frenchmen; that we could never be in danger of Popery so long as we took care of our fleet; that the Thames was the noblest river in Europe . . . with many other honest prejudices which naturally cleave to the heart of a true Englishman.

> *Ibid. No. 383, May 20, 1712*

The fraternity of the henpecked.[1]

> *Ibid. No. 482, September 12, 1712*

A man should always consider how much he has more than he wants, and how much more unhappy he might be than he really is.

> *Ibid. No. 574, July 30, 1714*

We are always doing something for Posterity, but I would fain see Posterity do something for us.

> *Ibid. No. 587, August 20, 1714*

See in what peace a Christian can die.

> *Dying words [1719], in* YOUNG,
> *Conjectures on Original Composition* [1759]

SIR RICHARD STEELE

[1672–1729]

I am come to a tavern alone to eat a steak, after which I shall return to the office.

> *Letters to His Wife.*
> *October 28, 1707*

I have partly succeeded in my business today, and enclose two guineas.

[1] See Byron, page 457a.

Dear Prue, I can't come home to dinner.

> *Letters to His Wife.*
> *January 3, 1708*

I was going home two hours ago, but was met by Mr. Griffith, who has kept me ever since. I will come within a pint of wine.

> *Ibid. Eleven at Night,*
> *January 5, 1708*

A little in drink, but at all times your faithful husband.

> *Ibid. September 27, 1708*

If you do not hear of me before three tomorrow afternoon, believe I am too fuddled to take care to observe your orders.

> *Ibid. October 25, 1708*

The finest woman in nature should not detain me an hour from you; but you must sometimes suffer the rivalship of the wisest men.

> *Ibid. September 17, 1712*

Though her mien carries much more invitation than command, to behold her is an immediate check to loose behaviour; to love her was a liberal education.[1]

> *Tatler [1709]. No. 49*

When you fall into a man's conversation, the first thing you should consider is, whether he has a greater inclination to hear you, or that you should hear him.

> *The Spectator. No. 49,*
> *April 26, 1711*

Of all the affections which attend human life, the love of glory is the most ardent.

> *Ibid. No. 139, August 9, 1711*

An old gentleman t'other day in discourse with a friend of his, (reflecting upon some adventures they had in youth together) cry'd out, Oh Jack, those were happy days!

> *Ibid. No. 153, August 25, 1711*

Age in a virtuous person, of either sex, carries in it an authority which makes it preferable to all the pleasures of youth.

> *Ibid. No. 153, August 25, 1711*

[1] Lady Elizabeth Hastings [1682–1739].

Among all the diseases of the mind there is not one more epidemical or more pernicious than the love of flattery.

The Spectator. No. 238,
December 3, 1711

Will Honeycomb calls these over-offended ladies the outrageously virtuous.

Ibid. No. 266, January 4, 1712

A favour well bestowed is almost as great an honour to him who confers it as to him who receives it.

Ibid. No. 497, September 30, 1712

BENJAMIN SCHMOLKE
[1672–1737]

If wind and sky were always fair
The sailor would not watch the star,
And David's Psalms had ne'er been
  sung
If grief his heart had never wrung.

Bearing the Burden. Stanza 4

EDMOND HOYLE [1]
[1672–1769]

When in doubt, win the trick.

Twenty-four Rules for Learners.
Rule 12

NICHOLAS ROWE
[1673–1718]

As if Misfortune made the throne her
  seat,
And none could be unhappy but the
  great.[2]

The Fair Penitent [1703].
Prologue

At length the morn and cold indifference came.

Ibid. Act I, Sc. 1

Is this that haughty gallant, gay Lothario?

Ibid. Act V, Sc. 1

---

[1] Hoyle published [1742] a *Short Treatise on Whist,* which in subsequent editions added rules for playing piquet, backgammon, chess, and other games. His *Laws* [1760] ruled whist playing until 1864, hence the saying, "according to Hoyle."

[2] None think the great unhappy, but the great. — EDWARD YOUNG: *The Love of Fame* [1725–1728], *Satire 1, L. 238*

ISAAC WATTS
[1674–1748]

Were I so tall to reach the pole,
  Or grasp the ocean with my span,
I must be measured by my soul:
  The mind's the standard of the man.

Horae Lyricae [1706]. Book II,
False Greatness

Let dogs delight to bark and bite,
  For God hath made them so;
Let bears and lions growl and fight,
  For 'tis their nature too.

Divine Songs [1715]. XVI

But, children, you should never let
  Such angry passions rise;
Your little hands were never made
  To tear each other's eyes.

Ibid.

Birds in their little nests agree;
  And 'tis a shameful sight
When children of one family
  Fall out, and chide, and fight.

Ibid. XVII

How doth the little busy bee
  Improve each shining hour,[1]
And gather honey all the day
  From every opening flower!

Ibid. XX

For Satan finds some mischief still
  For idle hands to do.

Ibid.

Hush, my dear, lie still and slumber!
  Holy angels guard thy bed!
Heavenly blessings without number
  Gently falling on thy head.

A Cradle Hymn

'Tis the voice of the sluggard; I heard
  him complain,
"You have wak'd me too soon, I must
  slumber again." [2]

The Sluggard. Stanza 1

Let me be dress'd fine as I will,
Flies, worms, and flowers, exceed me
  still.

Against Pride in Clothes. Stanza 4

Lord, in the morning thou shalt hear
My voice ascending high.

Psalm V [1719]

---

[1] See Lewis Carroll, page 656a.
[2] See Lewis Carroll, page 657b.

O God, our help in ages past,
Our hope for years to come,
Our shelter from the stormy blast,
And our eternal home.
> *Psalm XC* [*1719*]. *Stanza 1*

A thousand ages in Thy sight
Are like an evening gone;
Short as the watch that ends the night
Before the rising sun.
> *Ibid. Stanza 4*

Time, like an ever-rolling stream,
Bears all its sons away;
They fly forgotten, as a dream
Dies at the opening day.
> *Ibid. Stanza 5*

Joy to the world! the Lord is come;
Let earth receive her King.
Let ev'ry heart prepare Him room,
And heav'n and nature sing.
> *Psalm XCVIII* [*1719*]. *Stanza 1*

And while the lamp holds out to burn,
The vilest sinner may return.
> *Hymns and Spiritual Songs.*
> *Book I, Hymn 88*

Strange that a harp of thousand strings
Should keep in tune so long!
> *Ibid. Book II, Hymn 19*

Hark! from the tombs a doleful sound.
> *Ibid. Hymn 63*

The tall, the wise, the reverend head
Must lie as low as ours.
> *Ibid.*

When I can read my title clear
To mansions in the skies,
I'll bid farewell to every fear,
And wipe my weeping eyes.
> *Ibid. Hymn 65*

There is a land of pure delight,
Where saints immortal reign;
Infinite day excludes the night,
And pleasures banish pain.
> *Ibid. Hymn 66*

WILLIAM SOMERVILLE [1]
[1675–1742]

How humble, and how complaisant
Is the proud man reduced to want!

[1] Of whom DR. JOHNSON, in his *Lives of the Poets*, made the famous remark, "He writes very well for a gentleman."

With what a silly, hanging face
He bears his unforeseen disgrace!
> *Ready Money* [*1727*]

Let all the learned say what they can,
'Tis ready money makes the man.
> *Ibid.*

There is something in a face,
An air, and a peculiar grace,
Which boldest painters cannot trace.
> *The Lucky Hit* [*1727*]

So in each action 'tis success
That gives it all its comeliness.
> *Ibid.*

For what is virtue, courage, wit,
In all men, but a lucky hit?
> *Ibid.*

So, safe on shore the pensioned sailor
    lies,
And all the malice of the storm defies;
With ease of body blest and peace of
    mind
Pities the restless crew he left behind;
Whilst, in his cell, he meditates alone
On his great voyage to the world un-
    known.
> *The Author, an Old Man, to*
> *His Arm-chair* [*1750*]

SIR ROBERT WALPOLE
[1676–1745]

The balance of power.
> *Speech* [*1741*]

Flowery oratory he despised. He ascribed to the interested views of themselves or their relatives the declara-
tions of pretended patriots, of whom he
said, "All those men have their price."
> WILLIAM COXE: *Memoirs of Wal-*
> *pole* [*1798*], *Vol. IV, P. 369*

Anything but history, for history
must be false.
> *Walpoliana. No. 141*

HENRY ST. JOHN,
VISCOUNT BOLINGBROKE
[1678–1751]

Truth lies within a little and certain
compass, but error is immense.
> *Reflections Upon Exile* [*1716*]

I have read somewhere or other, —
in Dionysius of Halicarnassus, I think,

— that history is philosophy teaching by examples.[1]
> *On the Study and Use of History*
> *[1752]. Letter 2*

Nations, like men, have their infancy.
> *Ibid. Letter 4*

They [Thucydides and Xenophon] maintained the dignity of history.
> *Ibid. Letter 5*

It is the modest, not the presumptuous, inquirer who makes a real and safe progress in the discovery of divine truths. One follows Nature and Nature's God; that is, he follows God in his works and in his word.[2]
> *Letter to Mr. Pope*

GEORGE FARQUHAR
[1678–1707]

Like hungry guests, a sitting audience looks.
> *The Inconstant* [*1702*].
> *Prologue*

The prologue is the grace,
Each act, a course, each scene, a different dish.
> *Ibid.*

Cos. Pray now, what may be that same bed of honour?
Kite. Oh, a mighty large bed! bigger by half than the great bed at Ware: ten thousand people may lie in it together, and never feel one another.
> *The Recruiting Officer* [*1706*].
> *Act I, Sc. 1*

I believe they talked of me, for they laughed consumedly.
> *The Beaux' Stratagem* [*1707*].
> *Act III, Sc. 1*

---

[1] The contact with manners then is education; and this Thucydides appears to assert when he says history is philosophy learned from examples. — Dionysius of Halicarnassus [54?–7? b.c.]: *Ars Rhet. XI, 2*
[2] Slave to no sect, who takes no private road,
But looks through Nature up to Nature's God.
> Pope: *Essay on Man* [*1732–1734*], *Epistle IV, L. 331*

'Twas for the good of my country that I should be abroad.[1]
> *The Beaux' Stratagem.*
> *Act III, Sc. 2*

THOMAS PARNELL
[1679–1718]

My days have been so wondrous free
The little birds that fly
With careless ease from tree to tree,
Were but as bless'd as I.
> *Song*[2] [*1714*]. *Stanza 1*

Still an angel appear to each lover beside,
But still be a woman to you.
> *When Thy Beauty Appears*
> [*1722*]. *Stanza 3*

We call it only pretty Fanny's way.
> *An Elegy to an Old Beauty*
> [*1722*]. *Stanza 4*

Let those love now who never loved before;
Let those who always loved, now love the more.
> *Translation of the Pervigilium*
> *Veneris*[3]

EDWARD YOUNG
[1683–1765]

The love of praise, howe'er conceal'd by art,

---

[1] Leaving his country for his country's sake.
— Charles Fitz-Geffrey: *The Life and Death of Sir Francis Drake* [1596], *St. 213*
True patriots all; for, be it understood,
We left our country for our country's good.
> George Barrington: *Prologue Written for the Opening of the Playhouse at New South Wales, January 16, 1796*
(According to the *Oxford Companion to English Literature*, "Barrington" was the adopted name of a notorious pickpocket who was transported to the penal settlement at Botany Bay.)
[2] Set to music by Francis Hopkinson; one of the earliest American songs.
[3] Written *circa* a.d. 350:
Cras amet qui nunquam amavit, quique amavit cras amet.
(Let him love tomorrow who never loved before; and he who has loved, let him love tomorrow.)

Reigns more or less, and glows in ev'ry
heart.
>   *Love of Fame* [*1725–1728*].
>   *Satire I, Line 51*

Some for renown, on scraps of learning
dote,
And think they grow immortal as they
quote.
>   *Ibid. Line 89*

They that on glorious ancestors enlarge,
Produce their debt instead of their discharge.
>   *Ibid. Line 147*

Be wise with speed;
A fool at forty is a fool indeed.
>   *Ibid. Satire II, Line 282*

For her own breakfast she'll project a
scheme,
Nor take her tea without a stratagem.
>   *Ibid. Satire VI, Line 190*

Think naught a trifle, though it small
appear;
Small sands the mountain, moments
make the year.
>   *Ibid. Line 208*

One to destroy is murder by the law,
And gibbets keep the lifted hand in
awe;
To murder thousands takes a specious
name,
War's glorious art, and gives immortal
fame.[1]
>   *Ibid. Satire VII, Line 55*

The man that makes a character makes
foes.
>   *To Mr. Pope. Epistle I, Line 28*

Their feet through faithless leather met
the dirt,
And oftener chang'd their principles
than shirt.
>   *Ibid. Line 277*

In records that defy the tooth of time.
>   *The Statesman's Creed*

Tired nature's sweet restorer, balmy
sleep!
>   *Night Thoughts* [*1742–1745*].
>   *Night I, Line 1*

Night, sable goddess! from her ebon
throne,

[1] See Porteus, page 366a–366b.

In rayless majesty, now stretches forth
Her leaden sceptre o'er a slumbering
world.
>   *Night Thoughts. Night I, Line 18*

Creation sleeps! 'Tis as the general
pulse
Of life stood still, and Nature made a
pause, —
An awful pause! prophetic of her end.
>   *Ibid. Line 23*

Procrastination is the thief of time.
>   *Ibid. Line 393*

At thirty, man suspects himself a fool;
Knows it at forty, and reforms his plan;
At fifty chides his infamous delay,
Pushes his prudent purpose to resolve;
In all the magnanimity of thought
Resolves, and re-resolves; then dies the
same.
>   *Ibid. Line 417*

All men think all men mortal but themselves.
>   *Ibid. Line 424*

Thy purpose firm is equal to the deed:
Who does the best his circumstance allows
Does well, acts nobly; angels could no
more.
>   *Ibid. Night II, Line 90*

"I've lost a day!" — the prince who
nobly cried,
Had been an emperor without his
crown.[1]
>   *Ibid. Line 99*

Ah, how unjust to Nature and himself
Is thoughtless, thankless, inconsistent
man!
>   *Ibid. Line 112*

Whose yesterdays look backwards with
a smile.
>   *Ibid. Line 334*

[1] Once at supper, reflecting that he [Em-
peror Titus] had done nothing for any that
day, he broke out into that memorable and
justly admired saying, "My friends, I have
lost a day!" — SUETONIUS [A. D. 70?–140?]:
Lives of the Twelve Caesars
Think that day lost whose descending sun
Views from thy hand no noble action done.
>   J. BOBART: *Virtus sui Gloria* [1697]

Thoughts shut up want air,
And spoil, like bales unopen'd to the
sun.
Night Thoughts. Night II,
Line 466
How blessings brighten as they take
their flight!
Ibid. Line 602
Man wants but little, nor that little
long.[1]
Ibid. Night IV, Line 118
A Christian is the highest style of man.
Ibid. Line 788
By night an atheist half believes a God.[2]
Ibid. Night V, Line 177
We see time's furrows on another's
brow,
And death intrench'd, preparing his as-
sault;
How few themselves in that just mirror
see!
Ibid. Line 627
Like our shadows,
Our wishes lengthen as our sun de-
clines.
Ibid. Line 661
Death loves a shining mark, a signal
blow.[3]
Ibid. Line 1011
The man that blushes is not quite a
brute.
Ibid. Night VII, Line 496
Too low they build, who build beneath
the stars.[4]
Ibid. Night VIII, Line 215
Final Ruin fiercely drives
Her ploughshare o'er creation.[5]
Ibid. Night IX, Line 167
An undevout astronomer is mad.
Ibid. Line 771

SIR WILLIAM PULTENEY [6]
[1684–1764]

For twelve honest men have decided
the cause,

[1] See Goldsmith, page 354b.
[2] See W. T. Cummings, page 991b.
[3] See Quarles, page 231b.
[4] Inscription on a wall of the Library of
Congress, Washington, D.C.
[5] See Burns, page 391a.
[6] One of "the three grand allies," the others

Who are judges alike of the facts and
the laws.
The Honest Jury

GEORGE BERKELEY, BISHOP OF CLOYNE
[1685–1753]

[Tar water] is of a nature so mild
and benign and proportioned to the
human constitution, as to warm with-
out heating, to cheer but not inebriate.[1]
Siris [1744]. Paragraph 217
He who says there is no such thing
as an honest man, you may be sure is
himself a knave.
Maxims Concerning Patriotism
Ferments of the worst kind succeed
to perfect inaction.
Ibid.
Westward the course of empire takes
its way; [2]
The four first acts already past,
A fifth shall close the drama with the
day:
Time's noblest offspring is the last.
On the Prospect of Planting
Arts and Learning in Amer-
ica [1752]. Stanza 6
Our youth we can have but today,
We may always find time to grow old.
Can Love Be Controlled by
Advice? [3]

JANE BRERETON
[1685–1740]

The picture placed the busts between
Adds to the thought much strength;
Wisdom and Wit are little seen,
But Folly's at full length.
On Beau Nash's Picture at Full
Length between the Busts of Sir
Isaac Newton and Mr. Pope [4]

being Stanhope and Walpole. Walpole said
that he feared Pulteney's tongue more than
another man's sword.
[1] See Cowper, page 364b.
[2] Westward the star of empire takes its way.
— JOHN QUINCY ADAMS: *Oration at Plym-*
outh [1802]
[3] In AIKEN: *Vocal Poetry* [1810]
[4] In ALEXANDER DYCE [1798–1869]: *Speci-*
mens of British Poetesses (This epigram is
generally ascribed to Chesterfield.)

AARON HILL
[1685–1750]

First, then, a woman will or won't, depend on 't;
If she will do 't she will; and there's
   an end on 't.
But if she won't, since safe and sound
   your trust is,
Fear is affront, and jealousy injustice.
                 Zara. Epilogue

Tender-handed stroke a nettle,
   And it stings you for your pains;
Grasp it like a man of mettle,
   And it soft as silk remains.[1]

'Tis the same with common natures:
   Use 'em kindly, they rebel;
But be rough as nutmeg-graters,
   And the rogues obey you well.
    Verses Written on a Window
                 in Scotland

SAMUEL MADDEN
[1686–1765]

In an orchard there should be enough
to eat, enough to lay up, enough to be
stolen, and enough to rot upon the
ground.
   Quoted by SAMUEL JOHNSON
   [1783] (BOSWELL's *Life, Vol.*
   II, Page 457, Everyman edition)

ALLAN RAMSAY
[1686–1758]

Farewell to Lochaber, farewell to my
   Jean,
Where heartsome wi' thee I hae mony
   days been;
For Lochaber no more, Lochaber no
   more,
We'll maybe return to Lochaber no
   more.
      Lochaber No More [1724].
                  Stanza 1

My Peggy is a young thing,
Just entered in her teens.
               Peggy [1734?]

[1] The world's a nettle; disturb it, it stings:
   Grasp it firmly, it stings not.
   E. R. BULWER-LYTTON: *Lucile* [1860],
         Part 1, Canto 3, II

THOMAS TICKELL
[1686–1740]

Just men, by whom impartial laws were
   given;
And saints who taught and led the way
   to heaven.
    On the Death of Mr. Addison
             [1719]. Line 41

The sweetest garland to the sweetest
   maid.
    To a Lady with a Present of
              Flowers [1729]

HENRY CAREY
[1687?–1743]

Namby Pamby's little rhymes,
Little jingle, little chimes.
             Namby Pamby [1]

Aldiborontiphoscophornio!
Where left you Chrononhotonthologos?
   Chrononhotonthologos. Act I, Sc. 1

His cogitative faculties immersed
In cogibundity of cogitation.
                    Ibid.

Of all the girls that are so smart,
   There's none like pretty Sally.
She is the darling of my heart,
   And she lives in our alley.
    Sally in Our Alley [1729]. Stanza 1

Of all the days that's in the week
   I dearly love but one day,
And that's the day that comes betwixt
   A Saturday and Monday.
            Ibid. Stanza 4

God save our gracious king!
Long live our noble king!
   God save the king!
       God Save the King [1740?]

JOHN GAY
[1688–1732]

'Twas when the sea was roaring
With hollow blasts of wind,

[1] Ambrose Phillips . . . who had the honour of bringing into fashion a species of composition which has been called, after his name,
Namby Pamby. — MACAULAY: *Review of
Aikin's Life of Addison* [1843]

A damsel lay deploring,
All on a rock reclin'd.
>   *The What d'ye Call It* [*1715*].
>   *Act II, Sc. 8*

All in the Downs the fleet was moor'd.
>   *Sweet William's Farewell to*
>   *Black-eyed Susan* [*1720*]

Adieu, she cried, and waved her lily
hand.
>   *Ibid.*

My lodging is on the cold ground,
    And hard, very hard, is my fare,
But that which grieves me more
    Is the coldness of my dear.
>   *My Lodging is on the Cold*
>   *Ground* [*1720*]. *Stanza 1*

Remote from cities liv'd a swain,
Unvex'd with all the cares of gain;
His head was silver'd o'er with age,
And long experience made him sage.
>   *Fables, Part I* [*1727*]. *The*
>   *Shepherd and the Philosopher*

Whence is thy learning? Hath thy toil
O'er books consum'd the midnight oil?
>   *Ibid.*

Where yet was ever found a mother
Who'd give her booby for another?
>   *Ibid. The Mother, the Nurse,*
>   *and the Fairy*

When we risk no contradiction,
It prompts the tongue to deal in fiction.
>   *Ibid. The Elephant and the*
>   *Bookseller*

Lest men suspect your tale untrue,
Keep probability in view.
>   *Ibid. The Painter who Pleased*
>   *Nobody and Everybody*

Is there no hope? the sick man said;
The silent doctor shook his head.
>   *Ibid. The Sick Man and the Angel*

While there is life there's hope, he
cried.[1]
>   *Ibid.*

Those who in quarrels interpose
Must often wipe a bloody nose.
>   *Ibid. The Mastiffs*

I hate the man who builds his name
On ruins of another's fame.
>   *Ibid. The Poet and the Rose*

[1] See Cicero, page 34a.

The child whom many fathers share
Hath seldom known a father's care.
>   *Fables, Part I. The Hare*
>   *and Many Friends*

And when a lady's in the case,
You know all other things give place.
>   *Ibid.*

From wine what sudden friendship
springs!
>   *Ibid. Part II* [*1738*]. *The*
>   *Squire and His Cur*

O Polly, you might have toy'd and
kiss'd,
By keeping men off, you keep them on.
>   *The Beggar's Opera* [*1728*].
>   *Act I, Sc. 4, Air IX*

If with me you'd fondly stray.
Over the hills and far away.[1]
>   *Ibid. Sc. 13, Air XVI*

Fill ev'ry glass, for wine inspires us,
    And fires us
With courage, love and joy.
Women and wine should life employ.
Is there ought else on earth desirous?
>   *Ibid. Act II, Sc. 1, Air XIX*

If the heart of a man is depress'd with
cares,
The mist is dispell'd when a woman appears.
>   *Ibid. Sc. 3, Air XXI*

Youth's the season made for joys,
Love is then our duty.
>   *Ibid. Sc. 4, Air XXII*

Man may escape from rope and gun;
Nay, some have outliv'd the doctor's
pill:
Who takes a woman must be undone,
That basilisk is sure to kill.
The fly that sips treacle is lost in the
sweets,
So he that tastes woman, woman,
woman,
He that tastes woman, ruin meets.
>   *Ibid. Sc. 8, Air XXVI*

How happy could I be with either,
Were t'other dear charmer away!
>   *Ibid. Sc. 13, Air XXXV*

The charge is prepar'd; the lawyers are
met;

[1] See D'Urfey, page 290b.

The judges all ranged, — a terrible show!

The Beggar's Opera. Act III, Sc. 11, Air LVII

Life is a jest, and all things show it;
I thought so once, but now I know it.[1]

My Own Epitaph

ALEXANDER POPE [2]
[1688–1744]

Happy the man whose wish and care
A few paternal acres bound,
Content to breathe his native air
  In his own ground.

Ode on Solitude [Circa *1700*].
Stanza 1

Thus let me live, unseen, unknown,
Thus unlamented let me die;
Steal from the world, and not a stone
  Tell where I lie.

Ibid. Stanza 5

Not chaos-like together crush'd and
  bruis'd,
But, as the world, harmoniously con-
  fus'd:
Where order in variety we see,
And where, though all things differ, all
  agree.

Windsor Forest [*1704*]. *Line 13*

Oft, as in airy rings they skim the
  heath,
The clam'rous lapwings feel the leaden
  death;
Oft, as the mounting larks their notes
  prepare,
They fall, and leave their little lives
  in air.

Ibid. Line 131

To dear-bought wisdom give the credit
  due,

And think for once a woman tells you
  true.

*Paraphrases from Chaucer. The
Wife of Bath, Her Prologue*
[Circa *1709*], *Line 3*

Curtain lectures made a restless night.

Ibid. Line 165

Let all mankind this certain maxim
  hold;
Marry who will, our sex is to be sold.

With empty hands no tassels you can
  lure,
But fulsome love for gain we can endure;
For gold we love the impotent and old,
And heave, and pant, and kiss, and
  cling, for gold.

Yet with embraces curses oft I mixt,
Then kiss'd again, and chid, and rail'd
  betwixt.

Ibid. Line 170

How quaint an appetite in women
  reigns!
Free gifts we scorn, and love what
  costs us pains.
Let men avoid us, and on them we leap;
A glutted market makes provision
  cheap.

Ibid. Line 259

The wasting moth ne'er spoil'd my best
  array;
The cause was this, I wore it every day.

Ibid. Line 288

  Whoe'er it be
That tells my faults, I hate him mortally!

Ibid. Line 351

Love seldom haunts the breast where
  learning lies,
And Venus sets ere Mercury can rise.

Ibid. Line 369

How vain that second life in others'
  breath,[1]
Th' estate which wits inherit after
  death!
Ease, health, and life for this they must
  resign,
(Unsure the tenure, but how vast the
  fine!)

---

[1] Life is an empty dream. — BROWNING:
Paracelsus, II [1835]
  Life seems a jest of Fate's contriving. —
J. R. LOWELL: *Harvard Commemoration Ode*
[1865], *IV*

[2] A thousand years may elapse before there
shall appear another man with a power of
versification equal to that of Pope. — DR.
JOHNSON [1781]: BOSWELL'S *Life of Dr.
Johnson*

[1] See *Essay on Man*, page 317b.

The great man's curse, without the
gains, endure,
Be envied, wretched; and be flatter'd,
poor;
All luckless wits their enemies profest,
And all successful, jealous friends at
best.
Nor Fame I slight, nor for her favours
call;
She comes unlook'd for, if she comes at
all.
The Temple of Fame [*1711*].
Line 505
Unblemish'd let me live or die un-
known;
Oh, grant an honest fame, or grant me
none!
Ibid. Line 523
How vast a memory has Love!
Sappho to Phaon [*1712*]. *Line 52*
'Tis with our judgments as our watches,
none
Go just alike, yet each believes his
own.[1]
Essay on Criticism [*1711*].
Part I, Line 9
Let such teach others who themselves
excel,
And censure freely who have written
well.
Ibid. Line 15
Some are bewilder'd in the maze of
schools,
And some made coxcombs Nature
meant but fools.
Ibid. Line 26
One science only will one genius fit;
So vast is art, so narrow human wit.
Ibid. Line 60
First follow Nature, and your judgment
frame
By her just standard, which is still the
same;
Unerring Nature, still divinely bright,
One clear, unchanged, and universal
light,
Life, force, and beauty must to all im-
part,
At once the source, and end, and test of
Art.
Ibid. Line 68

[1] See Suckling, page 261a.

Music resembles poetry; in each
Are nameless graces which no methods
teach,
And which a master-hand alone can
reach.
Essay on Criticism. Part I,
Line 143
Those oft are stratagems which errors
seem,
Nor is it Homer nods, but we that
dream.[1]
Ibid. Line 177
O may some spark of your celestial fire
The last, the meanest of your sons in-
spire,
(That on weak wings, from far, pursues
your flights,
Glows while he reads, but trembles as
he writes)
To teach vain Wits a science little
known,
T'admire superior sense, and doubt
their own.
Ibid. Line 195
Of all the causes which conspire to
blind
Man's erring judgment, and misguide
the mind,
What the weak head with strongest
bias rules,
Is pride, the never-failing vice of fools.
Ibid. Part II, Line 1
A little learning is a dangerous thing;
Drink deep, or taste not the Pierian
spring:
There shallow draughts intoxicate the
brain,
And drinking largely sobers us again.
Ibid. Line 15
Hills peep o'er hills, and Alps on Alps
arise!
Ibid. Line 32
'T is not a lip or eye we beauty call,
But the joint force and full result of all.
Ibid. Line 45
Whoever thinks a faultless piece to see,
Thinks what ne'er was, nor is, nor e'er
shall be.[2]
Ibid. Line 53
True wit is Nature to advantage
dress'd,

[1] See Horace, page 42a.
[2] See Suckling, page 261a.

What oft was thought, but ne'er so well express'd.

Essay on Criticism. Part II, Line 97

Words are like leaves; and where they most abound,
Much fruit of sense beneath is rarely found.

Ibid. Line 109

Such labour'd nothings, in so strange a style,
Amaze th' unlearn'd, and make the learned smile.

Ibid. Line 126

In words, as fashions, the same rule will hold,
Alike fantastic if too new or old:
Be not the first by whom the new are tried,
Nor yet the last to lay the old aside.

Ibid. Line 133

Some to church repair,
Not for the doctrine, but the music there.
These equal syllables alone require,
Though oft the ear the open vowels tire;
While expletives their feeble aid do join,
And ten low words oft creep in one dull line.

Ibid. Line 142

A needless Alexandrine ends the song,
That, like a wounded snake, drags its slow length along.

Ibid. Line 156

True ease in writing comes from art, not chance,
As those move easiest who have learn'd to dance.[1]
'Tis not enough no harshness gives offence;
The sound must seem an echo to the sense.

Ibid. Line 162

At ev'ry trifle scorn to take offence.

Ibid. Line 186

Yet let not each gay turn thy rapture move;

[1] Also in *Epistle II, Book II of Horace* [1737], *L. 178.*

For fools admire, but men of sense approve.

Essay on Criticism. Part II, Line 190

Some judge of authors' names, not works, and then
Nor praise nor blame the writings, but the men.

Ibid. Line 212

What woeful stuff this madrigal would be
In some starv'd hackney sonneteer or me!
But let a lord once own the happy lines,
How the wit brightens! how the style refines!

Ibid. Line 218

Some praise at morning what they blame at night,
But always think the last opinion right.

Ibid. Line 230

Envy will merit as its shade pursue,
But like a shadow proves the substance true.

Ibid. Line 266

To err is human, to forgive divine.[1]

Ibid. Line 325

All seems infected that th' infected spy,
As all looks yellow to the jaundic'd eye.

Ibid. Line 358

Be silent always when you doubt your sense.

Ibid. Part III, Line 6

Men must be taught as if you taught them not,
And things unknown proposed as things forgot.

Ibid. Line 15

The bookful blockhead ignorantly read,
With loads of learned lumber in his head,
With his own tongue still edifies his ears,
And always list'ning to himself appears.

[1] See Sophocles, page 14b.
Then gently scan your brother man,
  Still gentler sister woman;
Though they may gang a kennin' wrang,
  To step aside is human.
      ROBERT BURNS: *Address to the Unco Guid* [1787]

All books he reads, and all he reads assails.
                    *Essay on Criticism. Part III,
                    Line 53*

For fools rush in where angels fear to tread.
                    Ibid. Line 66

But where's the man who counsel can bestow,
Still pleas'd to teach, and yet not proud to know?[1]
                    Ibid. Line 72

Careless of censure, nor too fond of fame,
Still pleas'd to praise, yet not afraid to blame,
Averse alike to flatter or offend,
Not free from faults, nor yet too vain to mend.
                    Ibid. Line 182

Vital spark of heav'nly flame,
Quit, oh quit, this mortal frame!
Trembling, hoping, ling'ring, flying,
Oh, the pain, the bliss of dying![2]
Cease, fond Nature, cease thy strife,
And let me languish into life!
        *The Dying Christian to His Soul
                    [1712]. Stanza 1*

What dire offence from amorous causes springs!
What mighty contests rise from trivial things!
        *The Rape of the Lock [1712].
                    Canto I, Line 1*

On her white breast a sparkling cross she wore,
Which Jews might kiss, and infidels adore.
                    Ibid. Canto II, Line 7

If to her share some female errors fall,
Look on her face, and you'll forget 'em all.
                    Ibid. Line 17

Fair tresses man's imperial race ensnare,
And beauty draws us with a single hair.[3]
                    Ibid. Line 27

[1] See Chaucer, page 79b.
[2] See Hadrian, page 65b.
[3] See Robert Burton, page 223b.

Here thou, great Anna! whom three realms obey,
Dost sometimes counsel take — and sometimes tea.
                    *The Rape of the Lock.
                    Canto III, Line 7*

At every word a reputation dies.
                    Ibid. Line 16

The hungry judges soon the sentence sign,
And wretches hang that jurymen may dine.
                    Ibid. Line 21

Coffee, which makes the politician wise.
                    Ibid. Line 117

But when to mischief mortals bend their will,
How soon they find fit instruments of ill!
                    Ibid. Line 125

The meeting points the sacred hair dissever
From the fair head, forever, and forever!
Then flash'd the living lightning from her eyes,
And screams of horror rend th' affrighted skies.
                    Ibid. Line 153

Steel could the labour of the gods destroy,
And strike to dust th' imperial towers of Troy;
Steel could the works of mortal pride confound
And hew triumphal arches to the ground.
                    Ibid. Line 173

Charms strike the sight, but merit wins the soul.
                    Ibid. Canto V, Line 34

To wake the soul by tender strokes of art,
To raise the genius, and to mend the heart;
To make mankind, in conscious virtue bold,
Live o'er each scene, and be what they behold:

For this the Tragic Muse first trod the stage.
> *Prologue to Mr. Addison's Cato [1713]. Line 1*

A brave man struggling in the storms of fate,
And greatly falling with a falling state.
> *Ibid. Line 21*

Ignobly vain, and impotently great.
> *Ibid. Line 29*

Dear, damn'd, distracting town, farewell!
Thy fools no more I'll tease:
This year in peace, ye critics, dwell,
Ye harlots, sleep at ease!
> *A Farewell to London [1715]. Stanza 1*

Luxurious lobster-nights, farewell,
For sober, studious days!
> *Ibid. Stanza 12*

Oh name for ever sad! for ever dear!
Still breath'd in sighs, still usher'd with a tear.
> *Eloisa to Abelard [1717]. Line 31*

Now warm in love, now with'ring in my bloom,
Lost in a convent's solitary gloom!
> *Ibid. Line 37*

Speed the soft intercourse from soul to soul,
And waft a sigh from Indus to the Pole.
> *Ibid. Line 57*

Curse on all laws but those which love has made!
Love, free as air at sight of human ties,
Spreads his light wings, and in a moment flies.
> *Ibid. Line 74*

No, make me mistress to the man I love;
If there be yet another name more free,
More fond than mistress, make me that to thee!
> *Ibid. Line 88*

And if I lose thy love, I lose my all.
> *Ibid. Line 118*

How happy is the blameless vestal's lot!
The world forgetting, by the world forgot.
> *Ibid. Line 207*

One thought of thee puts all the pomp to flight,
Priests, tapers, temples, swim before my sight.[1]
> *Eloisa to Abelard. Line 273*

He best can paint them who shall feel them most.
> *Ibid. Line 366*

What beck'ning ghost along the moonlight shade
Invites my steps, and points to yonder glade?
> *Elegy to the Memory of an Unfortunate Lady [1717]. Line 1*

Is it, in Heav'n, a crime to love too well?
To bear too tender or too firm a heart,
To act a lover's or a Roman's part?
Is there no bright reversion in the sky
For those who greatly think, or bravely die?
> *Ibid. Line 6*

Ambition first sprung from your blest abodes,
The glorious fault of Angels and of Gods.
> *Ibid. Line 13*

By foreign hands thy dying eyes were clos'd,
By foreign hands thy decent limbs compos'd,
By foreign hands thy humble grave adorn'd,
By strangers honour'd, and by strangers mourn'd!
> *Ibid. Line 51*

How lov'd, how honour'd once, avails thee not,
To whom related, or by whom begot;
A heap of dust alone remains of thee:
'Tis all thou art, and all the proud shall be!
> *Ibid. Line 71*

It is certain no literal translation can be just to an excellent original in a superior language: but it is a great mistake to imagine (as many have done)

---

[1] Priests, altars, victims, swam before my sight. — EDMUND SMITH: *Phaedra and Hippolytus, adapted from Racine* [1707], *Act I, Sc. 1*

paraphrase can make amends
eneral defect: which is no less
to lose the spirit of an ancient,
by deviating into the modern manners
of expression. If there be sometimes
a darkness, there is often a light in antiquity, which nothing better preserves
than a version almost literal.

Preface to the Iliad [*1717*]

Simplicity is the mean between ostentation and rusticity.

Ibid.

The fate of all extremes is such:
Men may be read, as well as books, too
  much.

Moral Essays [*1720–1735*].
Epistle I [*1733*], *Line 9*

To observations which ourselves we
  make,
We grow more partial for th' observer's
  sake.

Ibid. Line 11

Like following life through creatures
  you dissect,
You lose it in the moment you detect.

Ibid. Line 29

Not always actions show the man; we
  find
Who does a kindness is not therefore
  kind.

Ibid. Line 109

Who combats bravely is not therefore
  brave,
He dreads a death-bed like the meanest
  slave.
Who reasons wisely is not therefore
  wise;
His pride in reasoning, not in acting,
  lies.

Ibid. Line 115

'Tis education forms the common
  mind:
Just as the twig is bent the tree's inclined.

Ibid. Line 149

Manners with fortunes, humours turn
  with climes,
Tenets with books, and principles with
  times.

Ibid. Line 172

Give this cheek a little red.

Ibid. Line 251

And you, brave Cobham! to the latest
  breath
Shall feel your ruling passion strong in
  death.

Moral Essays. Epistle I, Line 262

Most women have no characters at all.

Ibid. Epistle II [*1735*], *Line 2*

Whether the charmer sinner it or saint
  it,
If folly grow romantic, I must paint it.

Ibid. Line 15

Choose a firm cloud before it fall, and
  in it
Catch, ere she change, the Cynthia of
  this minute.

Ibid. Line 19

Fine by defect, and delicately weak.

Ibid. Line 43

Chaste to her husband, frank to all
  beside,
A teeming mistress, but a barren bride.

Ibid. Line 71

Wise wretch! with pleasures too refin'd
  to please;
With too much spirit to be e'er at ease;
With too much quickness ever to be
  taught;
With too much thinking to have common thought.

Ibid. Line 95

"With ev'ry pleasing, ev'ry prudent
  part,
Say, what can Chloe want?" — She
  wants a heart,
She speaks, behaves, and acts just as
  she ought,
But never, never reach'd one gen'rous
  thought.

Ibid. Line 159

In men, we various ruling passions find;
In women, two almost divide the kind;
Those, only fixed, they first or last
  obey,
The love of pleasure, and the love of
  sway.

Ibid. Line 207

Men, some to business, some to pleasure
  take;
But every woman is at heart a rake.

Ibid. Line 215

She who ne'er answers till a husband
  cools,

Or if she rules him, never shows she
rules;
Charms by accepting, by submitting,
sways,
Yet has her humour most, when she
obeys.
Moral Essays. Epistle II, Line 261

And mistress of herself though china
fall.
Ibid. Line 268

Woman's at best a contradiction still.
Ibid. Line 270

Who shall decide when doctors disagree? [1]
Ibid. Epistle III [1732], Line 1

Blest paper-credit! last and best supply!
That lends corruption lighter wings to
fly!
Ibid. Line 39

But thousands die without or this or
that,
Die, and endow a college or a cat.
Ibid. Line 95

The ruling passion, be it what it will,
The ruling passion conquers reason
still.
Ibid. Line 153

Who builds a church to God, and not
to fame,
Will never mark the marble with his
name.
Ibid. Line 285

Satan now is wiser than of yore,
And tempts by making rich, not mak-
ing poor.
Ibid. Line 351

Good sense, which only is the gift of
Heaven,
And though no science, fairly worth the
seven.
Ibid. Epistle IV [1731], Line 43

Statesman, yet friend to truth; of soul
sincere,
In action faithful, and in honour clear;
Who broke no promise, serv'd no private end,

[1] When doctors differ who decides amid
the milliard-headed throng? — SIR RICHARD
FRANCIS BURTON [1821–1890]: *The Kasidah
of Haji Abdu El-Yazdi, VIII, 29*

Who gain'd no title, and who lost no
friend;
Ennobled by himself, by all approv'd
And prais'd, unenvied by the Muse he
lov'd.
*Moral Essays. Epistle V [1720],
Line 67*

Blessed is he who expects nothing,
for he shall never be disappointed. [1]
Letter to Gay [October 6, 1727]

You beat your pate, and fancy wit will
come:
Knock as you please, there's nobody
at home. [2]
Epigram: An Empty House [1727]

Ye Gods! annihilate but space and
time,
And make two lovers happy.
*Martinus Scriblerus on the Art of
Sinking in Poetry [1728]. Chap. XI*

Of manners gentle, of affections mild;
In wit a man, simplicity a child.
Epitaph on Gay [1732]

Awake, my St. John! leave all meaner
things
To low ambition and the pride of kings.
Let us, since life can little more supply
Than just to look about us, and to die,
Expatiate free o'er all this scene of
man;
A mighty maze! but not without a
plan.
*Essay on Man [1733–1734].
Epistle I, Line 1*

Eye Nature's walks, shoot folly as it
flies,
And catch the manners living as they
rise;
Laugh where we must, be candid where
we can,
But vindicate the ways of God to man. [3]
Ibid. Line 13

[1] Pope calls this the eighth beatitude (Ros-
coe's edition of Pope, *Vol. X, P. 184*).
Blessed are those that nought expect,
For they shall not be disappointed.
JOHN WOLCOT ("Peter Pindar")
[1738–1819]: *Ode to Pitt*

[2] His wit invites you by his looks to come,
But when you knock, it never is at home.
COWPER: *Conversation* [1782],
L. 303

[3] See Milton, page 252a.

Say first, of God above or man below,
What can we reason but from what we
 know?
> *Essay on Man. Epistle I, Line 17*

Pleased to the last, he crops the flowery
 food,
And licks the hand just raised to shed
 his blood.
> *Ibid. Line 83*

Who sees with equal eye, as God of all,
A hero perish or a sparrow fall,
Atoms or systems into ruin hurl'd,
And now a bubble burst, and now a
 world.
> *Ibid. Line 87*

Hope springs eternal in the human
 breast:
Man never is, but always to be, blest.
> *Ibid. Line 95*

Lo, the poor Indian! whose untutor'd
 mind
Sees God in clouds, or hears him in the
 wind;
His soul proud Science never taught to
 stray
Far as the solar walk or milky way;
Yet simple nature to his hope has giv'n,
Behind the cloud-topped hill, an
 humbler heav'n.
> *Ibid. Line 99*

But thinks, admitted to that equal sky,
His faithful dog shall bear him company.
> *Ibid. Line 111*

In pride, in reas'ning pride, our error
 lies;
All quit their sphere, and rush into the
 skies!
Pride still is aiming at the bless'd
 abodes,
Men would be Angels, Angels would be
 Gods.
Aspiring to be Gods if Angels fell,
Aspiring to be Angels men rebel.
> *Ibid. Line 123*

Seas roll to waft me, suns to light me
 rise;
My footstool earth, my canopy the
 skies.[1]
> *Ibid. Line 139*

[1] See Montaigne, page 99a.

All are but parts of one stupendous
 whole,
Whose body Nature is, and God the
 soul.
> *Essay on Man. Epistle I, Line 267*

As full, as perfect, in vile man that
 mourns
As the rapt seraph that adores and
 burns.
To Him no high, no low, no great, no
 small;[1]
He fills, he bounds, connects, and equals
 all!
> *Ibid. Line 277*

All nature is but art, unknown to thee;
All chance, direction, which thou canst
 not see;
All discord, harmony not understood;
All partial evil, universal good;
And spite of pride, in erring reason's
 spite,
One truth is clear, Whatever is, is
 right.[2]
> *Ibid. Line 289*

Know then thyself, presume not God
 to scan;
The proper study of mankind is man.[3]
Placed on this isthmus of a middle state,
A being darkly wise and rudely great:
With too much knowledge for the Scep-
 tic side,
With too much weakness for the Stoic's
 pride,
He hangs between, in doubt to act or
 rest;
In doubt to deem himself a God or
 Beast;
In doubt his mind or body to prefer;
Born but to die, and reas'ning but to
 err;

[1] There is no great and no small
 To the Soul that maketh all.
 EMERSON [1803–1882]: *Epigraph
 to History*

[2] See Dryden, page 276a.

[3] See Plutarch, page 60a.
 La vraie science et la vraie étude de
l'homme, c'est l'homme (The true science and
the true study of man is man). — PIERRE
CHARRON: *Traité de la Sagesse* [1601], *Book
I, Preface*
 Trees and fields tell me nothing: men are
my teachers. — PLATO [427–347 B.C.]: *Phaedrus*

Alike in ignorance, his reason such,
Whether he thinks too little or too
   much;
Chaos of thought and passion, all con-
   fused;
Still by himself abused or disabused;
Created half to rise, and half to fall;
Great lord of all things, yet a prey to
   all;
Sole judge of truth, in endless error
   hurled;
The glory, jest, and riddle of the world.
   Essay on Man. Epistle II, Line 1
Fix'd like a plant on his peculiar spot,
To draw nutrition, propagate, and rot.
   Ibid. Line 63
On life's vast ocean diversely we sail,
Reason the card, but passion is the gale.
   Ibid. Line 107
And hence one master-passion in the
   breast,
Like Aaron's serpent, swallows up the
   rest.[1]
   Ibid. Line 131
The young disease, that must subdue
   at length,
Grows with his growth, and strength-
   ens with his strength.
   Ibid. Line 135
Vice is a monster of so frightful mien,
As to be hated needs but to be seen;
Yet seen too oft, familiar with her face,
We first endure, then pity, then em-
   brace.
   Ibid. Line 217
The learn'd is happy Nature to explore,
The fool is happy that he knows no
   more;
The rich is happy in the plenty giv'n,
The poor contents him with the care of
   Heav'n.
   Ibid. Line 263
Behold the child, by Nature's kindly
   law,
Pleased with a rattle, tickled with a
   straw:
Some livelier plaything gives his youth
   delight,

[1] For they cast down every man his rod,
and they became serpents: but Aaron's rod
swallowed up their rods. — *Exodus, VII, 12*

A little louder, but as empty quite:
Scarfs, garters, gold, amuse his riper
   stage,
And beads and prayer-books are the
   toys of age.
Pleased with this bauble still, as that
   before,
Till tired he sleeps, and life's poor play
   is o'er.
   Essay on Man. Epistle II, Line 274
Learn of the little nautilus to sail,
Spread the thin oar, and catch the
   driving gale.
   Ibid. Epistle III, Line 177
For forms of government let fools con-
   test;
Whate'er is best administer'd is best:
For modes of faith let graceless zealots
   fight;
His can't be wrong whose life is in the
   right.[1]
In faith and hope the world will dis-
   agree,
But all mankind's concern is charity.
   Ibid. Line 303
O happiness! our being's end and aim!
Good, pleasure, ease, content! whate'er
   thy name:
That something still which prompts the
   eternal sigh,
For which we bear to live, or dare to
   die.
   Ibid. Epistle IV, Line 1
Reason's whole pleasure, all the joys of
   sense,
Lie in three words — health, peace, and
   competence.
   Ibid. Line 79
Worth makes the man, and want of it
   the fellow;
The rest is all but leather or prunella.
   Ibid. Line 203
What's Fame? a fancy'd life in others'
   breath,
A thing beyond us, ev'n before our
   death.
   Ibid. Line 237
A wit's a feather, and a chief a rod;

[1] See Cowley, page 268a.

An honest man's the noblest work of
God.[1]

Essay on Man. Epistle IV, Line 247
One self-approving hour whole years
outweighs
Of stupid starers and of loud huzzas:
And more true joy Marcellus exil'd feels
Than Caesar with a senate at his heels.

Ibid. Line 255
If parts allure thee, think how Bacon
shin'd,
The wisest, brightest, meanest of mankind!
Or ravish'd with the whistling of a
name,[2]
See Cromwell, damn'd to everlasting
fame!

Ibid. Line 281
Slave to no sect, who takes no private
road,
But looks through Nature up to Nature's God.[3]

Ibid. Line 331
Form'd by thy converse, happily to
steer
From grave to gay, from lively to
severe.[4]

Ibid. Line 379
Say, shall my little bark attendant sail,
Pursue the triumph and partake the
gale?

Ibid. Line 385
Thou wert my guide, philosopher, and
friend.[5]

Ibid. Line 390
"Shut, shut the door, good John!"
fatigued, I said;
"Tie up the knocker! say I'm sick, I'm
dead."

Epistle to Dr. Arbuthnot [*1735*].
Prologue to the Satires, Line 1
Fire in each eye, and papers in each
hand,
They rave, recite, and madden round
the land.

Ibid. Line 5

[1] See Burns, page 390b.
[2] See Cowley, page 267b.
[3] See Bolingbroke, page 304a.
[4] See Boileau, page 286b.
[5] Is this my guide, philosopher, and friend?
— *Epistle I, Book I of Horace* [1733–1738],
L. 177

Is there a parson much bemused in
beer,
A maudlin poetess, a rhyming peer,
A clerk foredoom'd his father's soul to
cross,
Who pens a stanza when he should
engross?

*Epistle to Dr. Arbuthnot. Prologue
to the Satires, Line 15*
Fired that the house[1] reject him,
" 'Sdeath, I'll print it,
And shame the fools."

Ibid. Line 61
No creature smarts so little as a fool.

Ibid. Line 84
Destroy his fib, or sophistry — in vain!
The creature's at his dirty work again.

Ibid. Line 91
As yet a child, nor yet a fool to fame,
I lisp'd in numbers, for the numbers
came.

Ibid. Line 127
This long disease, my life.

Ibid. Line 132
Pretty! in amber to observe the forms
Of hairs, or straws, or dirt, or grubs, or
worms.[2]
The things, we know, are neither rich
nor rare,
But wonder how the devil they got
there.

Ibid. Line 169
Means not, but blunders round about
a meaning;
And he whose fustian's so sublimely
bad,
It is not poetry, but prose run mad.

Ibid. Line 186
Were there one whose fires
True Genius kindles, and fair Fame
inspires,
Bless'd with each talent and each art to
please,
And born to write, converse, and live
with ease;
Should such a man, too fond to rule
alone,
Bear, like the Turk, no brother near the
throne;[3]

[1] The theater.
[2] See Martial, page 52a.
[3] See Denham, page 266b.

View him with scornful, yet with jealous eyes,
And hate for arts that caus'd himself to rise;
Damn with faint praise, assent with civil leer,
And without sneering teach the rest to sneer; [1]
Willing to wound, and yet afraid to strike,
Just hint a fault, and hesitate dislike;
Alike reserv'd to blame or to commend,
A tim'rous foe, and a suspicious friend;
Dreading ev'n fools; by flatterers besieged,
And so obliging that he ne'er obliged;
Like Cato, give his little Senate laws, [2]
And sit attentive to his own applause.

Epistle to Dr. Arbuthnot. Prologue to the Satires, Line 193

Oh let me live my own, and die so too
(To live and die is all I have to do)!
Maintain a poet's dignity and ease,
And see what friends, and read what books I please.

Ibid. Line 261

Curst be the verse, how well soe'er it flow,
That tends to make one worthy man my foe.

Ibid. Line 283

Let Sporus tremble — What? that thing of silk,
Sporus, that mere white curd of ass's milk?
Satire or sense, alas! can Sporus feel?
Who breaks a butterfly upon a wheel?

Ibid. Line 305

Yet let me flap this bug with gilded wings,
This painted child of dirt, that stinks and stings;

---

[1] When needs he must, yet faintly then he praises;
Somewhat the deed, much more the means he raises:
So marreth what he makes, and praising most, dispraises.
PHINEAS FLETCHER: *The Purple Island* [1633], *Canto VII*
[2] While Cato gives his little senate laws. —
Prologue to Mr. Addison's Cato [1713], *L. 23*

Whose buzz the witty and the fair annoys,
Yet wit ne'er tastes, and beauty ne'er enjoys.

Epistle to Dr. Arbuthnot. Prologue to the Satires, Line 309

Eternal smiles his emptiness betray,
As shallow streams run dimpling all the way.

Ibid. Line 315

Wit that can creep, and pride that licks the dust.

Ibid. Line 333

Unlearn'd, he knew no schoolman's subtle art,
No language but the language of the heart.

Ibid. Line 398

Me, let the tender office long engage
To rock the cradle of reposing age;
With lenient arts extend a mother's breath,
Make languor smile, and smooth the bed of death;
Explore the thought, explain the asking eye,
And keep awhile one parent from the sky.

Ibid. Line 408

I cannot sleep a wink.

Satires, Epistles, and Odes of Horace [1733–1738]. *Satire I, Book II, Line 12*

Satire's my weapon, but I'm too discreet
To run amuck, and tilt at all I meet.

Ibid. Line 69

But touch me, and no minister so sore.

Ibid. Line 76

There St. John mingles with my friendly bowl,
The feast of reason and the flow of soul.

Ibid. Line 127

For I, who hold sage Homer's rule the best,
Welcome the coming, speed the going guest. [1]

Ibid. Satire II, Book II, Line 159

---

[1] This line is repeated in the translation of the *Odyssey, Book XV, L. 83*, with "parting" instead of "going." See Homer, page 6b.

I've often wish'd that I had clear,
For life, six hundred pounds a year;
A handsome house to lodge a friend,
A river at my garden's end,
A terrace walk, and half a rood
Of land set out to plant a wood.
> *Satires, Epistles, and Odes of Horace. Satire VI, Book II, Line 1*

Give me again my hollow tree,
A crust of bread, and liberty.
> *Ibid. Line 220*

A patriot is a fool in ev'ry age.
> *Epilogue to the Satires. Dialogue I, Line 41*

Laugh then at any but at fools or foes;
These you but anger, and you mend not those.
Laugh at your friends, and if your friends are sore,
So much the better, you may laugh the more.
> *Ibid. Line 53*

Let humble Allen, with an awkward shame,
Do good by stealth, and blush to find it fame.
Virtue may choose the high or low degree.
> *Ibid. Line 135*

Never gallop Pegasus to death.
> *Epistle I. Book I, Line 14*

When the brisk minor pants for twenty-one.
> *Ibid. Line 38*

Not to go back is somewhat to advance,
And men must walk, at least, before they dance.
> *Ibid. Line 53*

He's armed without that's innocent within.
> *Ibid. Line 94*

Get place and wealth, if possible with grace;
If not, by any means get wealth and place.
> *Ibid. Line 103*

Above all Greek, above all Roman fame.
> *Ibid. Book II, Line 26*

The mob of gentlemen who wrote with ease.
> *Epistle I. Book II, Line 108*

One simile that solitary shines
In the dry desert of a thousand lines.
> *Ibid. Line 111*

Then marble, soften'd into life, grew warm,
And yielding metal flow'd to human form.[1]
> *Ibid. Line 147*

Who says in verse what others say in prose.
> *Ibid. Line 202*

What will a child learn sooner than a song?
> *Ibid. Line 205*

Ev'n copious Dryden wanted, or forgot,
The last and greatest art — the art to blot.
> *Ibid. Line 280*

There still remains, to mortify a wit,
The many-headed monster of the pit.[2]
> *Ibid. Line 304*

We poets are (upon a poet's word)
Of all mankind the creatures most absurd:
The season when to come, and when to go,
To sing, or cease to sing, we never know.
> *Ibid. Line 358*

Call, if you will, bad rhyming a disease,
It gives men happiness, or leaves them ease.
> *Epistle II. Book II, Line 182*

The worst of madmen is a saint run mad.
> *Epistle VI. Book I, Line 27*

Vain was the chief's, the sage's pride!
They had no poet, and they died.
> *Odes. Book IV, Ode 9, Stanza 4*

Father of all! in every age,
In every clime adored,

---

[1] The canvas glow'd beyond ev'n Nature warm;
The pregnant quarry teem'd with human form.
GOLDSMITH: *The Traveller* [1764], *L. 137*

[2] See Sir Philip Sidney, page 115b.

By saint, by savage, and by sage,
Jehovah, Jove, or Lord!
> *The Universal Prayer* [*1738*].
> *Stanza 1*

And binding Nature fast in fate,
Left free the human will.
> *Ibid. Stanza 3*

And deal damnation round the land.
> *Ibid. Stanza 7*

Teach me to feel another's woe,
  To hide the fault I see;
That mercy I to others show,
  That mercy show to me.[1]
> *Ibid. Stanza 10*

I am his Highness'[2] dog at Kew;
Pray tell me, sir, whose dog are you?
> *On the Collar of a Dog*

Nature and Nature's laws lay hid in
  night:
God said, Let Newton be! and all was
  light.
> *Epitaph Intended for Sir
> Isaac Newton*

Who dare to love their country, and
  be poor.
> *On His Grotto at Twickenham*
> [*1740*]

Party is the madness of many for the
gain of a few.
> *Thoughts on Various Subjects*
> [*1741*]

I never knew any man in my life
who could not bear another's misfortunes perfectly like a Christian.[3]
> *Ibid.*

A man should never be ashamed to
own he has been in the wrong, which is
but saying, in other words, that he is
wiser today than he was yesterday.
> *Ibid.*

It is with narrow-souled people as
with narrow-necked bottles; the less
they have in them the more noise they
make in pouring out.
> *Ibid.*

When men grow virtuous in their old

age, they only make a sacrifice to God
of the devil's leavings.[1]
> *Thoughts on Various Subjects*

True disputants are like true sports-
men, their whole delight is in the pursuit.
> *Ibid.*

There, take (says Justice), take ye each
  a shell:
We thrive at Westminster on fools like
  you;
'Twas a fat oyster — live in peace, —
  adieu.[2]
> *Verbatim from Boileau*

Whether thou choose Cervantes' serious air,
Or laugh and shake in Rabelais' easy
  chair.
> *The Dunciad* [*1743*].
> *Book I, Line 21*

Poetic Justice, with her lifted scale,
Where, in nice balance, truth with gold
  she weighs,
And solid pudding against empty
  praise.
> *Ibid. Line 52*

While pensive poets painful vigils keep,
Sleepless themselves to give their readers sleep.
> *Ibid. Line 93*

Next o'er his books his eyes begin to
  roll,
In pleasing memory of all he stole.
> *Ibid. Line 127*

Or where the pictures for the page
  atone,
And Quarles is sav'd by beauties not his
  own.
> *Ibid. Line 139*

How index-learning turns no student
  pale,
Yet holds the eel of science by the tail.
> *Ibid. Line 279*

---

[1] See Spenser, page 114a.
[2] Frederick, Prince of Wales.
[3] See La Rochefoucauld, page 264b.

[1] See La Rochefoucauld, page 265a.
[2] "Tenez voilà," dit-elle, "à chacun une
    écaille,
Des sottises d'autrui nous vivons au
    Palais;
Messieurs, l'huître étoit bonne. Adieu. Vi-
    vez en paix."
    BOILEAU [1636–1711]: *Epître II
    (à M. l'Abbé des Roches)*

And gentle Dullness ever loves a joke.
The Dunciad. Book II, Line 34
A brain of feathers, and a heart of lead.
Ibid. Line 44
Peel'd, patch'd, and piebald, linsey-
woolsey brothers,
Grave mummers! sleeveless some and
shirtless others.
That once was Britain.
Ibid. Book III, Line 115
And proud his mistress' order to per-
form,
Rides in the whirlwind and directs the
storm.[1]
Ibid. Line 263
A wit with dunces, and a dunce with
wits.[2]
Ibid. Book IV, Line 90
"The right divine of kings to govern
wrong."
Ibid. Line 188
Stuff the head
With all such reading as was never read:
For thee explain a thing till all men
doubt it,
And write about it, Goddess, and about
it.
Ibid. Line 249
To happy convents, bosom'd deep in
vines,
Where slumber abbots purple as their
wines.
Ibid. Line 301
Led by my hand, he saunter'd Europe
round,
And gather'd every vice on Christian
ground.
Ibid. Line 311
Ev'n Palinurus nodded at the helm.
Ibid. Line 614
Religion, blushing, veils her sacred fires,
And unawares Morality expires.
Nor public flame nor private dares to
shine;
Nor human spark is left, nor glimpse
divine!
Lo! thy dread empire Chaos! is re-
stor'd,
Light dies before thy uncreating word:

[1] See Addison, pages 298b–299a.
[2] See Quintilian, page 52b.

Thy hand, great Anarch! lets the cur-
tain fall,
And universal darkness buries all.
The Dunciad. Book IV, Line 649

LADY MARY WORTLEY MONTAGU
[1689–1762]

And we meet with champagne and a
chicken, at last.
The Lover [1748]
Be plain in dress, and sober in your
diet;
In short, my deary, kiss me, and be
quiet.
*A Summary of Lord Lyttelton's
Advice*
Satire should, like a polished razor
keen,
Wound with a touch that's scarcely
felt or seen.
*To the Imitator of the First Satire
of Horace. Book II*
This world consists of men, women,
and Herveys.[1]
Letters [1763]. Vol. I
But the fruit that can fall without shak-
ing
Indeed is too mellow for me.
*Letters and Works [1837].
The Answer*

JOHN BYROM
[1692–1763]

God bless the King, — I mean the
faith's defender!
God bless — no harm in blessing — the
Pretender!
But who pretender is, or who is king, —
God bless us all! — that's quite another
thing.[2]
*Miscellaneous Poems [1773].
To an Officer of the Army, ex-
tempore*

[1] As the French say, there are three sexes,
— men, women, and clergymen. — SYDNEY
SMITH [1771–1845]: *Lady Holland's Memoir,
Vol. I, Chap. 9*
[2] Quoted by SIR WALTER SCOTT in *Red-
gauntlet, Vol. II, Chap. 1,* Edinburgh edition
[1832].

Some say, compar'd to Bononcini,
That Mynheer Handel's but a ninny;
Others aver that he to Handel
Is scarcely fit to hold a candle.
Strange all this difference should be
'Twixt Tweedledum and Tweedledee.
Miscellaneous Poems. On the Feuds between Handel and Bononcini
As clear as a whistle.
Epistle to Lloyd

PHILIP DORMER STANHOPE, EARL OF CHESTERFIELD
[1694–1773]

Measures not men.[1]
Letters. March 6, 1742
Whatever is worth doing at all, is worth doing well.
Ibid. March 10, 1746
The knowledge of the world is only to be acquired in the world, not in a closet.
Ibid. October 4, 1746
An injury is much sooner forgotten than an insult.
Ibid. October 9, 1746
Do as you would be done by, is the surest method of pleasing.
Ibid. October 9, 1747
Take the tone of the company that you are in.
Ibid.
I knew once a very covetous, sordid fellow,[2] who used to say, "Take care of the pence, for the pounds will take care of themselves."
Ibid. November 6, 1747
Advice is seldom welcome; and those who want it most always like it least.
Ibid. January 29, 1748
Speak of the moderns without contempt, and of the ancients without idolatry.
Ibid. February 22, 1748
Wear your learning, like your watch, in a private pocket: and do not pull it

[1] See Goldsmith, page 355b, and Burke, page 359a.
[2] William Lowndes [1652–1724], Secretary of the Treasury in the reigns of William III, Queen Anne, and George I.

out and strike it, merely to show that you have one.
Letters. February 22, 1748
Manners must adorn knowledge, and smooth its way through the world. Like a great rough diamond, it may do very well in a closet by way of curiosity, and also for its intrinsic value.
Ibid. July 1, 1748
Women, then, are only children of a larger growth.
Ibid. September 5, 1748
Women who are either indisputably beautiful, or indisputably ugly, are best flattered upon the score of their understandings; but those who are in a state of mediocrity, are best flattered upon their beauty, or at least their graces; for every woman who is not absolutely ugly thinks herself handsome.
Ibid.
Without some dissimulation no business can be carried on at all.
Ibid. May 22, 1749
Idleness is only the refuge of weak minds.
Ibid. July 20, 1749
Style is the dress of thoughts.
Ibid. November 24, 1749
Religion must still be allowed to be a collateral security, at least, to Virtue.
Ibid. January 8, 1750
Despatch is the soul of business.
Ibid. February 5, 1750
Knowledge may give weight, but accomplishments give lustre, and many more people see than weigh.
Ibid. May 8, 1750
Let blockheads read what blockheads write.
Ibid. November 1, 1750
Is it possible to love such a man?[1] No. The utmost I can do for him is to consider him as a respectable Hottentot.
Ibid. February 28, 1751
It is commonly said, and more particularly by Lord Shaftesbury,[2] that ridicule is the best test of truth.
Ibid. February 6, 1752

[1] Lord Lyttelton.
[2] Truth, 'tis supposed, may bear all lights; and one of those principal lights or natural

Every woman is infallibly to be gained by every sort of flattery, and every man by one sort or other.
Letters. March 16, 1752

Chapter of accidents.[1]
Ibid. February 16, 1753

Women, and young men, are very apt to tell what secrets they know, from the vanity of having been trusted.
Letters to His Son

I assisted at the birth of that most significant word "flirtation," which dropped from the most beautiful mouth in the world.
The World. No. 101

Unlike my subject now shall be my song;
It shall be witty, and it sha'n't be long.
Impromptu Lines

The dews of the evening most carefully shun, —
Those tears of the sky for the loss of the sun.
Advice to a Lady in Autumn

The nation looked upon him as a deserter, and he shrunk into insignificancy and an earldom.
Character of Pulteney

He adorned whatever subject he either spoke or wrote upon, by the most splendid eloquence.[2]
Character of Bolingbroke

FRANCIS HUTCHESON
[1694–1746]

That action is best which procures

the greatest happiness for the greatest numbers.[1]
Inquiry Concerning Moral Good and Evil [1720]. Sect. 3

VOLTAIRE
(FRANÇOIS MARIE AROUET)
[1694–1778]

Virtue debases itself in justifying itself.
Oedipe [1718]. Act I, Sc. 4

Crime has its heroes, error has its martyrs:
Of true zeal and false, what vain judges we are!
Henriade [1728]. Chant V, Line 200

He who is merely just is severe.
Letter to the King of Prussia [1740]

The first who was king was a fortunate soldier:
Who serves his country well has no need of ancestors.[2]
Mérope [1743]. Act I, Sc. 3

It is better to risk saving a guilty person than to condemn an innocent one.
Zadig [1747]. Chap. 6

The king [Frederick the Great] has sent me some of his dirty linen to wash; I will wash yours another time.[3]
Reply to General Manstein [1752]

This agglomeration which was called and which still calls itself the Holy Roman Empire is neither holy, nor Roman, nor an Empire.
Essai sur les Moeurs [1756]

All is for the best in the best of possible worlds.[4]
Candide [1759]. Chap. 1

---

mediums by which things are to be viewed in order to a thorough recognition is ridicule itself. — ANTHONY ASHLEY COOPER, LORD SHAFTESBURY: *Essay on the Freedom of Wit and Humour* [1709], *Part I, Sect. 1*

[1] The Chapter of Accidents is the longest chapter in the book. — Attributed to JOHN WILKES by SOUTHEY in *The Doctor* [1837], *Chap. 118*

[2] See Johnson, page 337b.

Il embellit tout ce qu'il touche (He adorns whatever he touches). — FÉNELON [1651–1715]: *Lettre sur les Occupations de l'Académie Française, Sect. IV*

[1] Priestley was the first (unless it was Beccaria) who taught my lips to pronounce this sacred truth, — that the greatest happiness of the greatest number is the foundation of morals and legislation. — JEREMY BENTHAM [1748–1832]: *Works, Vol. X, P. 142*

[2] What can they see in the longest kingly line in Europe, save that it runs back to a successful soldier? — SIR WALTER SCOTT: *Woodstock* [1826], *Chap. 37*

[3] See Napoleon, page 399b.

[4] Referring to the philosophy of Leibnitz and his followers.

If this is the best of possible worlds, what then are the others?
Candide. Chap. 6

Optimism, said Candide, is a mania for maintaining that all is well when things are going badly.
Ibid. Chap. 19

For what end, then, has this world been formed? . . . To plague us to death.
Ibid. Chap. 21

In this country [England] it is found good, from time to time, to kill one admiral to encourage the others.
Ibid. Chap. 23

This is the happiest of mortals, for he is above everything he possesses.
Ibid. Chap. 26

Labour preserves us from three great evils — weariness, vice, and want.
Ibid. Chap. 30

Let us work without disputing; it is the only way to render life tolerable.
Ibid.

We must cultivate our garden.[1]
Ibid.

In the case of news, we should always wait for the sacrament of confirmation.
Letter to Count d'Argental
[August 28, 1760]

The first among languages is that which possesses the largest number of excellent works.
Letter to Deodati de Tovazzi
[January 24, 1761]

There are truths which are not for all men, nor for all times.
Letter to Cardinal de Bernis
[April 23, 1761]

Whatever you do, crush the infamous thing [superstition], and love those who love you.[2]
Letter to d'Alembert
[November 28, 1762]

Common sense is not so common.
Dictionnaire Philosophique
[1764]. Self-love

In general, the art of government consists in taking as much money as

possible from one class of citizens to give to the other.
Dictionnaire Philosophique. Money

The best is the enemy of the good.[1]
Ibid. Dramatic Art

Very learned women are to be found, in the same manner as female warriors; but they are seldom or never inventors.
Ibid. Women

The proper mean.[2]
Letter to Count d'Argental
[November 28, 1765]

Men use thought only to justify their wrongdoings, and speech only to conceal their thoughts.[3]
Dialogue 14. Le Chapon et la
Poularde [1766]

I have never made but one prayer to God, a very short one: "O Lord, make my enemies ridiculous." And God granted it.
Letter to M. Damiliville
[May 16, 1767]

History is little else than a picture of human crimes and misfortunes.[4]
L'Ingénu [1767]. Chap. 10

It is said that God is always for the big battalions.[5]
Letter to M. le Riche
[February 6, 1770]

Thought depends absolutely on the stomach, but in spite of that, those who have the best stomachs are not the best thinkers.
Letter to d'Alembert
[August 20, 1770]

If God did not exist, it would be necessary to invent him.[6]
Épître à l'Auteur du Livre des
Trois Imposteurs
[November 10, 1770]

Change everything, except your loves.
Sur l'Usage de la Vie

---

1 Le mieux est l'ennemi du bien.
2 Le juste milieu. See Horace, page 38b.
3 See Robert South, page 286b.
4 See Gibbon, page 369a.
5 See Gibbon, page 369b.
Providence is always on the side of the last reserve. — *Attributed to* NAPOLEON
6 See Ovid, page 42b, and Tillotson, page 275a.

1 Il faut cultiver notre jardin.
2 Quoi que vous fassiez, écrasez l'infâme, et aimez qui vous aime.

I am very fond of truth, but not at all of martyrdom.
> *Letter to d'Alembert*
> [*February, 1776*]

The secret of being a bore is to tell everything.
> *L'Enfant Prodigue. Preface*

The embarrassment of riches.
> *Le Droit du Seigneur.*
> *Act II, Sc. 6*

He who thinks himself wise, O heavens! is a great fool.
> *Ibid. Act IV, Sc. 1*

He who has not the spirit of his age,
Of his age has all the misery.[1]
> *Letter to Cideville*

The superfluous, a very necessary thing.
> *Le Mondain. Line 21*

Love truth, but pardon error.
> *Discours sur l'Homme. Discours 3*

It seems clear to me that God designed us to live in society — just as He has given the bees the honey; and as our social system could not subsist without the sense of justice and injustice, He has given us the power to acquire that sense.
> *Letter to Frederick the Great* [2]

I advise you to go on living solely to enrage those who are paying your annuities. It is the only pleasure I have left.
> *Letter to Madame du Deffand* [2]

Liberty of thought is the life of the soul.
> *Essay on Epic Poetry*
> (*written in English*)

Whoe'er thou art, behold thy master,
He is, or was, or is to be.[3]
> *On a Statuette of Cupid in the*
> *Cirey Gardens*

I disapprove of what you say, but I will defend to the death your right to say it.
> *Attributed to Voltaire* [4]

[1] Qui n'a pas l'esprit de son âge,
De son âge a tout le malheur.
[2] S. G. TALLENTYRE: *Voltaire in His Letters* [1919]
[3] Qui que tu sois, voici ton maître;
Il l'est — le fut — ou le doit être.
[4] This sentence is not Voltaire's, but was

FRANÇOIS QUESNAY
[1694–1774]

Laissez faire, laissez passer.[1]
> *Attributed to Quesnay*

MATTHEW GREEN
[1696–1737]

Fling but a stone, the giant dies.
> *The Spleen* [1737]. *Line 93*

Laugh and be well.
> *Ibid. Line 94*

Happy the man, who, innocent,
Grieves not at ills he can't prevent;
His skiff does with the current glide,
Not puffing pulled against the tide.
> *Ibid. Line 365*

By happy alchemy of mind
They turn to pleasure all they find.
> *Ibid. Line 610*

Though pleased to see the dolphins play,
I mind my compass and my way.
> *Ibid. Line 826*

WILLIAM OLDYS
[1696–1761]

Busy, curious, thirsty fly,
Drink with me, and drink as I.
> *On a Fly Drinking out of a Cup*
> *of Ale. Stanza 1*

Three-score summers, when they're gone,
Will appear as short as one.
> *Ibid. Stanza 2*

first used in quoting a letter from Voltaire to Helvétius in *The Friends of Voltaire* [1906] by S. G. TALLENTYRE (E. Beatrice Hall). She claims it was a paraphrase of Voltaire's words in the *Essay on Tolerance,* "Think for yourselves and let others enjoy the privilege to do so too."
[1] Let it be, let it pass. The phrase is not readily translatable, and also appears as "Laissez faire, laissez aller." It has been attributed to PIERRE LE PESANT BOISGUILBERT [1676–1714] and JEAN CLAUDE GOURNAY [1712–1759], as well as to Quesnay. It was widely used by the Physiocrats in urging freedom from government interference, and was adopted by ADAM SMITH [1723–1790].

MADAME DU DEFFAND
[1697–1784]

He [Voltaire] has invented history.
FOURNIER: *L'Esprit dans l'Histoire*
The distance is nothing; it is only
the first step which counts.[1]
Letter to d'Alembert
[July 7, 1763]

CHARLES MACKLIN
[?–1797]

The law is a sort of hocus-pocus
science.[2]
Love à la Mode [1759]. *Act II, Sc. 1*

RICHARD SAVAGE
[1698–1743]

He lives to build, not boast, a generous
race;
No tenth transmitter of a foolish face.
The Bastard [1728]. *Line 7*
May see thee now, though late, redeem
thy name,
And glorify what else is damn'd to
fame.
Character of Foster

WILLIAM WARBURTON,
BISHOP OF GLOUCESTER
[1698–1779]

Orthodoxy is my doxy — heterodoxy
is another man's doxy.[3]
Quoted by JOSEPH PRIESTLEY
[1733–1804]: Memoirs, Vol. I,
Page 572

---

[1] This remark refers to the legend that St.
Denis, carrying his head in his hands, walked
two leagues.
Voltaire wrote to Madame du Deffand
[January, 1764] that one of her bon mots
was quoted in the notes of *La Pucelle, Canto
1*: "Il n'y a que le premier pas qui coûte."
[2] Hocus was an old cunning attorney. — DR.
JOHN ARBUTHNOT: *Law is a Bottomless Pit:
or, History of John Bull* [1712], *Chap. 5*
The words of consecration, "*Hoc est corpus,*" were travestied into a nickname for jugglery, as "Hocus-pocus." — JOHN RICHARD
GREEN: *A Short History of the English People* [1874], *Chap. VII, Sect. 1*
[3] Priestley relates that, in a debate on the
Test Laws, Lord Sandwich said: "I have
heard frequent use of the words 'orthodoxy'

JOHN DYER
[1699–1758]

A little rule, a little sway,
A sunbeam in a winter's day,
Is all the proud and mighty have
Between the cradle and the grave.
Grongar Hill [1726]. *Line 89*

JAMES THOMSON
[1700–1748]

See, Winter comes to rule the varied
year,[1]
Sullen and sad.
The Seasons. Winter [1726], *Line 1*
Welcome, kindred gloom!
Congenial horrors, hail!
Ibid. Line 5
Cruel as death, and hungry as the
grave.
Ibid. Line 393
There studious let me sit,
And hold high converse with the mighty
dead.
Ibid. Line 431
The kiss, snatch'd hasty from the side-
long maid.
Ibid. Line 625
The meek-ey'd Morn appears, mother
of dews.
Ibid. Summer [1727], *Line 47*
Ships dim-discover'd dropping from the
clouds.
Ibid. Line 946
Sigh'd and look'd unutterable things.
Ibid. Line 1188
Who stemm'd the torrent of a down-
ward age.
Ibid. Line 1505
Come, gentle Spring! ethereal Mild-
ness! come.
Ibid. Spring [1728], *Line 1*
But who can paint
Like Nature? Can imagination boast,
Amid its gay creation, hues like hers?
Ibid. Line 465

---

and 'heterodoxy' but I confess myself at a loss
to know precisely what they mean." Bishop
Warburton whispered his definition to him.
[1] O Winter, ruler of the inverted year. —
COWPER: *The Task* [1784], *Book IV, Winter
Evening, L. 34*

Delightful task! to rear the tender thought,
To teach the young idea how to shoot.
    The Seasons. Spring, Line 1149
An elegant sufficiency, content,
Retirement, rural quiet, friendship, books.
    Ibid. Line 1158
Crown'd with the sickle, and the wheaten sheaf,
While Autumn, nodding o'er the yellow plain,
Comes jovial on.
    Ibid. Autumn [*1730*], *Line 1*
For loveliness
Needs not the foreign aid of ornament,
But is when unadorn'd adorn'd the most.[1]
    Ibid. Line 208
He saw her charming, but he saw not half
The charms her downcast modesty conceal'd.
    Ibid. Line 233
For still the world prevail'd, and its dread laugh,
Which scarce the firm philosopher can scorn.
    Ibid. Line 237
Or where the Northern ocean, in vast whirls,
Boils round the naked melancholy isles
Of farthest Thulè, and th' Atlantic surge
Pours in among the stormy Hebrides.
    Ibid. Line 871
Shade, unperceiv'd, so softening into shade.
    Hymn [*1730*]. *Line 25*
From seeming evil still educing good.
    Ibid. Line 114
Come then, expressive silence, muse His praise.
    Ibid. Line 118
O Sophonisba! Sophonisba, O!
    Sophonisba [*1729*]. *Act III, Sc. 2*
As those we love decay, we die in part,
String after string is severed from the heart;
Till loosen'd life, at last but breathing clay,
[1] See Milton, page 256a.

Without one pang is glad to fall away.
    On the Death of Mr. Aikman [1]
Forever, Fortune, wilt thou prove
An unrelenting foe to love;
And when we meet a mutual heart,
Come in between and bid us part?
    To Fortune
When Britain first, at Heaven's command,
    Arose from out the azure main,
This was the charter of the land,
    And guardian angels sung this strain:
Rule, Britannia! Britannia, rule the waves!
Britons never will be slaves.
    Alfred [*1740*]. *Act II, Sc. 5*
A pleasing land of drowsy head it was,
Of dreams that wave before the half-shut eye;
And of gay castles in the clouds that pass,
Forever flushing round a summer sky:
There eke the soft delights that witchingly
Instill a wanton sweetness through the breast,
And the calm pleasures always hover'd nigh;
But whate'er smack'd of noyance or unrest
Was far, far off expell'd from this delicious nest.
    The Castle of Indolence [*1748*].
    Canto I, Stanza 6
O fair undress, best dress! it checks no vein,
But every flowing limb in pleasure drowns,
And heightens ease with grace.
    Ibid. Stanza 26
Plac'd far amid the melancholy main.
    Ibid. Stanza 30
"A penny saved is a penny got" —
Firm to this scoundrel maxim keepeth he.
    Ibid. Stanza 50
A bard here dwelt, more fat than bard beseems,
Who, void of envy, guile, and lust of gain,
[1] William Aikman [1682–1731], portrait painter.

a

On virtue still, and nature's pleasing
   themes,
Pour'd forth his unpremeditated strain.
     The Castle of Indolence. Canto I,
                   Stanza 68
A little round, fat, oily man of God.
               Ibid. Stanza 69
I care not, Fortune, what you me deny:
You cannot rob me of free Nature's
   grace,
You cannot shut the windows of the
   sky
Through which Aurora shows her
   brightening face.
       Ibid. Canto II, Stanza 3
Health is the vital principle of bliss,
And exercise, of health.
            Ibid. Stanza 55

PHILIP DODDRIDGE
[1702–1751]

Live while you live, the epicure would
   say,
And seize the pleasures of the present
   day;
Live while you live, the sacred preacher
   cries,
And give to God each moment as it flies.
Lord, in my views, let both united be:
I live in pleasure when I live to thee.
     Epigram on His Family Arms [1]
Awake, my soul! stretch every nerve,
   And press with vigour on;
A heavenly race demands thy zeal,
   And an immortal crown.
   Hymns [1755]. *Zeal and Vigour*
   in the Christian Race, Stanza 1

ROBERT DODSLEY
[1703–1764]

One kind kiss before we part,
   Drop a tear and bid adieu;
Though we sever, my fond heart
   Till we meet shall pant for you. [2]
      The Parting Kiss [1745]
No state of life but must to patience
   bow:

[1] The Latin proverb: Dum vivimus, viva-
mus (Let us live while we live).
[2] See Burns, page 392a.

b

The tradesman must have patience
   for his bill;
He must have patience who to law will
   go;
And should he lose his right, more
   patience still;
Yea, to prevent or heal full many a
   strife,
How oft, how long must man have
   patience with his wife.
        To Patience [1745]

JONATHAN EDWARDS
[1703–1758]

Resolved, never to do anything which
I should be afraid to do if it were the
last hour of my life.
       Seventy Resolutions
Intend to live in continual mortifica-
tion, and never to expect or desire any
worldly ease or pleasure.
          Diary. 1723
A little, wretched, despicable creature; a worm, a mere nothing, and less
than nothing; a vile insect that has
risen up in contempt against the majesty of Heaven and earth.
   The Justice of God in the Damna-
       tion of Sinners [1734]
I assert that nothing ever comes to
pass without a cause.
     The Freedom of the Will [1754]
This dictate of common sense.
                Ibid.

JOHN WESLEY
[1703–1791]

I look upon the world as my parish.
     Journal. June 11, 1739
That execrable sum of all villanies,
commonly called the Slave Trade.
     Ibid. February 12, 1772
Though I am always in haste, I am
never in a hurry.
     Letters. December 10, 1777
Do all the good you can,
By all the means you can,
In all the ways you can,
In all the places you can,
At all the times you can,

To all the people you can,
As long as ever you can.
John Wesley's Rule

SOAME JENYNS
[1704–1787]

Let each fair maid, who fears to be
disgraced,
Ever be sure to tie her garters fast,
Lest the loosed string, amidst the public
hall,
A wished-for prize to some proud fop
should fall.
The Art of Dancing [1752]

NATHANIEL COTTON
[1705–1788]

If solid happiness we prize,
Within our breasts this jewel lies,
  And they are fools who roam.
The world has nothing to bestow;
From our own selves our joys must
  flow,
  And that dear hut, our home.
The Fireside. Stanza 3
To be resign'd when ills betide,
Patient when favours are deni'd,
  And pleas'd with favours given, —
Dear Chloe, this is wisdom's part;
This is that incense of the heart [1]
Whose fragrance smells to heaven.
Ibid. Stanza 11
Yet still we hug the dear deceit.
Content. Vision IV
Hold the fleet angel fast until he bless
thee.[2]

Tomorrow

BENJAMIN FRANKLIN [3]
[1706–1790]

We are a kind of posterity in respect
to them.
Letter to William Strahan [1745]

---

[1] The incense of the heart may rise. — JOHN
PIERPONT [1785–1866]: *Every Place a Temple*
[2] I will not let thee go, except thou bless
me. — *Genesis, XXXII, 26*
    Like the patriarch's angel hold it fast
    Till it gives its blessing.
        WHITTIER [1807–1892]: *My Soul
            and I, St. 34*
[3] Eripuit coelo fulmen sceptrumque tyran-

8th and lastly. They are so grateful!!
*Reasons for Preferring an Elderly
Mistress* [1745]
Remember that time is money.[1]
Advice to a Young Tradesman
[1748]
God helps them that help themselves.[2]
*Maxims prefixed to Poor Richard's
Almanac* [1757]
Dost thou love life? Then do not
squander time, for that is the stuff life
is made of.
Ibid.
Early to bed and early to rise,
Makes a man healthy, wealthy, and
wise.[3]
Ibid.
Plough deep while sluggards sleep.
Ibid.
Never leave that till tomorrow which
you can do today.
Ibid.
Three removes are as bad as a fire.
Ibid.
Little strokes fell great oaks.
Ibid.
A little neglect may breed mischief:
for want of a nail the shoe was lost; for
want of a shoe the horse was lost; and
for want of a horse the rider was lost.[4]
Ibid.
He that goes a borrowing goes a
sorrowing.
Ibid.
Vessels large may venture more,
But little boats should keep near shore.
Ibid.

---

nis (He snatched the lightning from heaven,
and the scepter from tyrants) — a line attributed to Turgot, and inscribed on Houdon's
bust of Franklin. Frederick von der Trenck
[1726–1794] asserted at his trial [1794] that
he was the author of this line.
[1] We reckon hours and minutes to be dollars and cents. — T. C. HALIBURTON [1796–
1865]: *The Clockmaster*
[2] See Sophocles, page 16b.
[3] JOHN CLARKE: *Paraemiolgia* [1639]
My hour is eight o'clock, though it is an
infallible rule, "Sanat, sanctificat, et ditat,
surgere mane" (That he may be healthy,
happy, and wise, let him rise early). — *A
Health to the Gentle Profession of Serving-
men* [1598]
[4] See Herbert, page 234a.

It is hard for an empty sack to stand upright.

> *Maxims prefixed to Poor Richard's Almanac*

Experience keeps a dear school, but fools will learn in no other.

> *Ibid.*

A word to the wise is enough, and many words won't fill a bushel.

> *Preface to Poor Richard Improved [1758]*

The used key is always bright.

> *Ibid.*

Lost time is never found again.

> *Ibid.*

He that riseth late, must trot all day.

> *Ibid.*

Keep thy shop, and thy shop will keep thee.[1]

> *Ibid.*

They that can give up essential liberty to obtain a little temporary safety deserve neither liberty nor safety.

> *Historical Review of Pennsylvania [1759]*

Idleness and pride tax with a heavier hand than kings and parliaments. If we can get rid of the former, we may easily bear the latter.

> *Letter on the Stamp Act [July 11, 1765]*

The grand leap of the whale up the Fall of Niagara is esteemed, by all who have seen it, as one of the finest spectacles in nature.

> *To the editor of a London newspaper [1765], intended to chaff the English for their ignorance of America*

Here Skugg lies snug
As a bug in a rug.

> *Letter to Miss Georgiana Shipley [September, 1772]*

There never was a good war or a bad peace.[2]

> *Letter to Josiah Quincy [September 11, 1773]*

1 See Chapman, page 116b.

2 I cease not to advocate peace; even though unjust it is better than the most just war. — CICERO [106–43 B. C.]: *Epistolae ad Atticum, Book VII, Epistle 14*

It hath been said that an unjust peace is

You and I were long friends: you are now my enemy, and I am

> Yours,
> B. Franklin
> *Letter to William Strahan [July 5, 1775]*

We must all hang together, or assuredly we shall all hang separately.

> *At the signing of the Declaration of Independence [July 4, 1776]*

He has paid dear, very dear, for his whistle.

> *The Whistle [1779]*

Here you would know and enjoy what posterity will say of Washington. For a thousand leagues have nearly the same effect with a thousand years.

> *Letter to Washington [March 5, 1780]*

George Washington, Commander of the American armies, who, like Joshua of old, commanded the sun and the moon to stand still, and they obeyed him.

> *A Toast at a Dinner in Versailles*[1]

I wish the bald eagle had not been chosen as the representative of our country; he is a bird of bad moral character; like those among men who live by sharping and robbing, he is generally poor, and often very lousy.

The turkey is a much more respectable bird, and withal a true original native of America.

> *Letter to Sarah Bache [January 26, 1784]*

He [the sun] gives light as soon as he rises.

> *An Economical Project*[2] *[1784]*

Our Constitution is in actual operation; everything appears to promise

to be preferred before a just war. — SAMUEL BUTLER: *Butler's Remains [1759], Speeches in the Rump Parliament*

1 The British Minister had proposed a toast to George III, in which he likened him to the sun, and the French Minister had toasted Louis XVI, comparing him with the moon.

2 A letter to the *Journal de Paris* advocating daylight saving.

that it will last; but in this world nothing is certain but death and taxes.
Letter to M. Leroy [*1789*]

The next thing most like living one's life over again seems to be a recollection of that life, and to make that recollection as durable as possible by putting it down in writing.
Autobiography [*1793–1868*].
Chap. I

Often I sat up in my room reading the greatest part of the night, when the book was borrowed in the evening and to be returned early in the morning, lest it should be missed or wanted.
Ibid.

Persons of good sense, I have since observed, seldom fall into disputation, except lawyers, university men, and men of all sorts that have been bred at Edinburgh.
Ibid.

Eat not to dullness; drink not to elevation.
Ibid. Chap. VI

An advantage itinerant preachers have over those who are stationary, the latter cannot well improve their delivery of a sermon by so many rehearsals.
Ibid. Chap. VII

I shall never ask, never refuse, nor ever resign an office.
Ibid. Chap. VIII

Human felicity is produced not so much by great pieces of good fortune that seldom happen, as by little advantages that occur every day.
Ibid. Chap. IX

When men are employed, they are best contented; for on the days they worked they were good-natured and cheerful, and, with the consciousness of having done a good day's work, they spent the evening jollily; but on our idle days they were mutinous and quarrelsome.
Ibid. Chap. X

HENRY FIELDING
[1707–1754]

All Nature wears one universal grin.
Tom Thumb the Great [*1730*].
Act I, Sc. 1

Today it is our pleasure to be drunk;
And this our queen shall be as drunk as we.
Ibid. Sc. 2

When I'm not thank'd at all, I'm thank'd enough;
I've done my duty, and I've done no more.
Ibid. Sc. 3

Lo, when two dogs are fighting in the streets,
With a third dog one of the two dogs meets;
With angry teeth he bites him to the bone,
And this dog smarts for what that dog has done.[1]
Ibid. Sc. 6

I am as sober as a judge.
Don Quixote in England [*1734*].
Act III, Sc. 14

This story will never go down.
Tumble-down Dick

The dusky night rides down the sky,
And ushers in the morn;
The hounds all join in glorious cry,
The huntsman winds his horn,
And a-hunting we will go.[2]
A-Hunting We Will Go [*1734*].
Stanza 1

[1] Thus when a barber and a collier fight,
The barber beats the luckless collier — white;
The dusty collier heaves his ponderous sack,
And big with vengeance beats the barber — black.
In comes the brick-dust man, with grime o'erspread,
And beats the collier and the barber — red:
Black, red, and white in various clouds are tost,
And in the dust they raise the combatants are lost.
CHRISTOPHER SMART [1722–1770]:
The Trip to Cambridge
[2] It's of three jovial huntsmen, and a-hunting they did go;

To whom nothing is given, of him can nothing be required.
Joseph Andrews [*1742*].
Book II, Chap. 8

I describe not men, but manners; not an individual, but a species.
Ibid. Book III, Chap. 1

They are the affectation of affectation.
Ibid. Chap. 3

Public schools are the nurseries of all vice and immorality.
Ibid. Chap. 5

Some folks rail against other folks, because other folks have what some folks would be glad of.
Ibid. Book IV, Chap. 6

Can any man have a higher notion of the rule of right and the eternal fitness of things?
The History of Tom Jones [*1749*].
Book IV, Chap. 4

Wisdom, whose lessons have been represented as so hard to learn by those who never were at her school, only teaches us to extend a simple maxim universally known. And this is, not to buy at too dear a price.
Ibid. Book VI, Chap. 3

Distinction without a difference.
Ibid. Chap. 13

The too inordinate fondness of a father . . . must be allowed the name of an amiable weakness.[1]
Ibid. Book X, Chap. 8

Nothing more aggravates ill success than the near approach to good.
Ibid. Book XIII, Chap. 2

Hairbreadth missings of happiness look like the insults of Fortune.
Ibid.

The republic of letters.
Ibid. Book XIV, Chap. 1

And they hunted, and they hollo'd, and they blew their horns also; Look ye there!
The Three Jovial Huntsmen (old English ballad), *St. 1*

[1] Amiable weaknesses of human nature. — GIBBON: *Decline and Fall of the Roman Empire* [1776–1788], *Chap. XIV*
It was an amiable weakness. — SHERIDAN: *The School for Scandal* [1777]

It hath been often said, that it is not death, but dying which is terrible.
Amelia [*1751*]. *Book III, Chap. 4*

These are called the pious frauds of friendship.
Ibid. Book VI, Chap. 6

When widows exclaim loudly against second marriages, I would always lay a wager that the man, if not the wedding-day, is absolutely fixed on.
Ibid. Chap. 8

There is not in the universe a more ridiculous, nor a more contemptible animal, than a proud clergyman.
Ibid. Chap. 10

One of my illustrious predecessors.[1]
Covent Garden Journal
[*January 11, 1752*]

Perhaps there is more of ostentation than of real utility in ships of this vast and unwieldy burthen.
Journal of a Voyage to Lisbon
[*1755*]

CARL LINNAEUS
[*1707–1778*]

To live by medicine is to live horribly.
Diaeta Naturalis. Introduction

Nature does not proceed by leaps.[2]
Philosophia Botanica. Sect. 77

Mingle your joys sometimes with your earnest occupation.
Quoted in biography of Linnaeus by BENJAMIN DAYDON JONES, *Chap. 9*

A professor can never better distinguish himself in his work than by encouraging a clever pupil, for the true discoverers are among them, as comets amongst the stars.
Ibid.

---

[1] Illustrious predecessor. — BURKE: *The Present Discontents* [1770]
I tread in the footsteps of illustrious men. . . . In receiving from the people the sacred trust twice confided to my illustrious predecessor [Andrew Jackson]. — MARTIN VAN BUREN: *Inaugural Address* [March 4, 1837]
[2] Natura non facit saltus.

Live innocently; God is here.
Quoted in biography of Linnaeus. Chap. 15 (Inscribed over the door of Linnaeus's bedchamber)

If a tree dies, plant another in its place.

Ibid.

GEORGES LOUIS LECLERC DE BUFFON
[1707–1788]

The style is the man himself.[1]
Discourse [On his admission to the French Academy, 1753]

Genius is nothing but a great aptitude for patience.
Attributed [2]

CHARLES WESLEY
[1707–1788]

"Christ, the Lord, is risen today,"
Sons of men and angels say,
Raise your joys and triumphs high,
Sing, ye heavens, and earth reply.
Hymns and Sacred Poems [1739].
Christ, the Lord, is Risen Today

Jesus, lover of my soul,
Let me to Thy bosom fly,
While the waters nearer roll,
While the tempest still is high;
Hide me, O my Saviour, hide,
Till the storm of life is past;
Safe into the haven glide,
O receive my soul at last.
Ibid. [1740]. Jesus, Lover of My Soul

Gentle Jesus, meek and mild,
Look upon a little child;

[1] Le style est l'homme même.
[2] Le génie n'est autre chose qu'une grande aptitude à la patience.

This is quoted by MATTHEW ARNOLD in his *Essays in Criticism, A French Coleridge* [1865]. There is also a popular proverb: "Genius is patience." DISRAELI, *The Young Duke* [1831]: "Patience is a necessary ingredient of genius." LESLIE STEPHEN [1832–1904]: "Genius is a capacity for taking trouble." JAN WALAEUS also says: "Genius is an intuitive talent for labor." LORD SYDENHAM [1799–1841] defined genius as a consummate sense of proportion.

See Carlyle, page 476a.

Pity my simplicity,
Suffer me to come to thee.
Hymns and Sacred Poems [1742].
Gentle Jesus, Meek and Mild

Soldiers of Christ, arise,
And put your armour on.
Ibid. [1749] Soldiers of Christ, Arise

Hark! the herald angels sing
Glory to the new-born King;
Peace on earth, and mercy mild,
God and sinners reconciled!
Joyful all ye nations rise,
Join the triumph of the skies;
With th' angelic host proclaim
Christ is born in Bethlehem.[1]
Ibid. [1753]. Christmas Hymn: Hark! the Herald Angels Sing

WILLIAM PITT, EARL OF CHATHAM
[1708–1778]

The atrocious crime of being a young man, which the honorable gentleman [Walpole] has with such spirit and decency charged upon me, I shall neither attempt to palliate nor deny; but content myself with wishing that I may be one of those whose follies may cease with their youth, and not of that number who are ignorant in spite of experience.
Speech in the House of Commons [2]
[March 6, 1741]

I rejoice that America has resisted. Three millions of people, so dead to all the feelings of liberty, as voluntarily to submit to be slaves, would have been fit instruments to make slaves of the rest.
Ibid. [January 14, 1766]

[1] George Whitefield altered lines 1 and 2, 7 and 8 from Wesley's original:
Hark, how all the welkin rings,
"Glory to the King of kings."

Universal nature say,
"Christ the Lord is born today."
[2] This is the composition of Johnson, founded on some note or statement of the actual speech. Johnson said, "That speech I wrote in a garret, in Exeter Street." — BOSWELL: *Life of Dr. Johnson [1791]*

Confidence is a plant of slow growth in an aged bosom; youth is the season of credulity.

> *Speech in the House of Commons*
> *[January 14, 1766]*

Unlimited power is apt to corrupt the minds of those who possess it.[1]

> *Case of Wilkes. Speech*
> *[January 9, 1770]*

Where law ends, tyranny begins.

> *Ibid.*

A long train of these practices has at length unwillingly convinced me that there is something behind the throne greater than the King himself.

> *Chatham Correspondence. Speech*
> *[March 2, 1770]*

Reparation for our rights at home, and security against the like future violations.[2]

> *Letter to the Earl of Shelburne*
> *[September 29, 1770]*

You cannot conquer America.

> *Speech [November 18, 1777]*

If I were an American, as I am an Englishman, while a foreign troop was landed in my country I never would lay down my arms, — never! never! never!

> *Ibid.*

I invoke the genius of the Constitution.

> *Ibid.*

The poorest man may in his cottage bid defiance to all the force of the Crown. It may be frail; its roof may shake; the wind may blow through it; the storms may enter, the rain may enter, — but the King of England cannot enter; all his forces dare not cross the threshold of the ruined tenement!

> *Speech on the Excise Bill*

[1] Power tends to corrupt; absolute power corrupts absolutely. — LORD ACTON: *Letter to Bishop Mandell Creighton* [1887]

[2] Indemnity for the past and security for the future. — LORD JOHN RUSSELL: *Life and Times of Charles James Fox* [1859–1860], *Vol. III, P. 345, Letter to the Hon. T. Maitland*

SAMUEL JOHNSON
[1709–1784]

Of all the griefs that harass the distrest,
Sure the most bitter is a scornful jest.[1]

> *London [1738]. Line 166*

This mournful truth is ev'rywhere confess'd, —
Slow rises worth, by poverty depress'd.[2]

> *Ibid. Line 176*

When learning's triumph o'er her barb'rous foes
First rear'd the stage, immortal Shakespeare rose;
Each change of many-colour'd life he drew,
Exhausted worlds, and then imagin'd new:
Existence saw him spurn her bounded reign,
And panting Time toil'd after him in vain.

> *Prologue at the Opening of Drury*
> *Lane Theatre [1747]*

Cold approbation gave the ling'ring bays,
For those who durst not censure, scarce could praise.

> *Ibid.*

Declamation roar'd, while Passion slept.

> *Ibid.*

The wild vicissitudes of taste.

> *Ibid.*

For we that live to please must please to live.

> *Ibid.*

Studious to please, yet not ashamed to fail.

> *Prologue to the Tragedy of Irene*
> *[1749]*

Let observation with extensive view
Survey mankind, from China to Peru.[3]

> *Vanity of Human Wishes [1749].*
> *Line 1*

[1] See Juvenal, page 62b.

[2] Three years later Johnson wrote, "Mere unassisted merit advances slowly, if — what is not very common — it advances at all."

[3] DE QUINCEY quotes with approval, but without naming him, the criticism of a writer who contends that this couplet amounts in effect to this: "Let observation with extensive

Deign on the passing world to turn
thine eyes,
And pause a while from learning to be
wise.
There mark what ills the scholar's life
assail, —
Toil, envy, want, the patron, and the
jail.
Vanity of Human Wishes. Line 157

A frame of adamant, a soul of fire,
No dangers fright him, and no labours
tire.
Ibid. Line 191

He left the name at which the world
grew pale,
To point a moral, or adorn a tale.
Ibid. Line 221

Enlarge my life with multitude of days,
In health, in sickness, thus the sup-
pliant prays;
Hides from himself his state, and shuns
to know
That life protracted is protracted woe.
Ibid. Line 255

Superfluous lags the veteran on the
stage.
Ibid. Line 308

Must helpless man, in ignorance sedate,
Roll darkling down the torrent of his
fate?
Ibid. Line 345

Secure, whate'er he gives, he gives the
best.
Ibid. Line 356

With these celestial Wisdom calms the
mind,
And makes the happiness she does not
find.
Ibid. Line 367

From thee, great God, we spring, to
thee we tend, —
Path, motive, guide, original and end.[1]
*Motto to The Rambler, No. 7
[1750]*

Curiosity is one of the permanent
and certain characteristics of a vigorous
mind.
The Rambler [March 12, 1751]

No place affords a more striking conviction of the vanity of human hopes,
than a public library.
The Rambler [March 23, 1751]

Parnassus has its flowers of transient
fragrance, as well as its oaks of towering height, and its laurels of eternal
verdure.
Ibid.

Life is surely given us for higher
purposes than to gather what our ancestors have wisely thrown away.
Ibid. [May 14, 1751]

It is one of the maxims of the civil
law, that definitions are hazardous.
Ibid. [May 28, 1751]

Praise like gold and diamonds owes
its value only to its scarcity.
Ibid. [June 6, 1751]

Almost all absurdity of conduct
arises from the imitation of those whom
we can not resemble.
Ibid. [July 2, 1751]

I am not so lost in lexicography as
to forget that *words are the daughters
of earth, and that things are the sons
of heaven.*[1]
Preface to His Dictionary [1755]

I dismiss it with frigid tranquillity,
having little to fear or hope from censure or from praise.
Ibid.

CLUB — An assembly of good fellows, meeting under certain conditions.
Definition in the Dictionary

ESSAY — A loose sally of the mind;
an irregular indigested piece; not a
regular and orderly composition.
Ibid.

EXCISE — A hateful tax levied upon
commodities, and adjudged not by
the common judges of property, but
wretches hired by those to whom excise
is paid.
Ibid.

GRUBSTREET — The name of a street
near Moorsfield, London, much inhabited by writers of small histories, dictionaries, and temporary poems.
Ibid.

observation observe mankind extensively." —
Rhetoric [1828]
[1] A translation of Boethius's *De Consolatione Philosophiae, III, 9, 27.*

[1] See Herbert, page 234b.

OATS — A grain which in England is generally given to horses, but in Scotland supports the people.[1]

Definition in the Dictionary

He is no wise man that will quit a certainty for an uncertainty.

The Idler [1758–1760]. No. 57

What is read twice is commonly better remembered than what is transcribed.

Ibid. No. 74

Ye who listen with credulity to the whispers of fancy, and pursue with eagerness the phantoms of hope; who expect that age will perform the promises of youth, and that the deficiencies of the present day will be supplied by the morrow, — attend to the history of Rasselas, Prince of Abyssinia.

Rasselas [1759]. Chap. I

"I fly from pleasure," said the prince, "because pleasure has ceased to please; I am lonely because I am miserable, and am unwilling to cloud with my presence the happiness of others."

Ibid. Chap. III

A man used to vicissitudes is not easily dejected.

Ibid. Chap. XII

Few things are impossible to diligence and skill.

Ibid.

I live in the crowd of jollity, not so much to enjoy company as to shun myself.

Ibid. Chap. XVI

Many things difficult to design prove easy to performance.

Ibid.

The first years of man must make provision for the last.

Ibid. Chap. XVII

The endearing elegance of female friendship.

Ibid. Chap. XLVI

How small of all that human hearts endure,
That part which laws or kings can cause or cure!
Still to ourselves in every place consigned,
Our own felicity we make or find.

Lines Added to GOLDSMITH's Traveller [1763–1764]

That man is little to be envied whose patriotism would not gain force upon the plain of Marathon, or whose piety would not grow warmer among the ruins of Iona.

Journey to the Western Islands [1775]. Inch Kenneth

"To Oliver Goldsmith, Poet, Naturalist, Historian, who left scarcely any style of writing untouched, and touched nothing that he did not adorn."[1]

Epitaph on Goldsmith [June 22, 1776]

Whoever wishes to attain an English style, familiar but not coarse, and elegant but not ostentatious, must give his days and nights to the volumes of Addison.

Lives of the Poets [1779–1781]. Life of Addison

To be of no church is dangerous. Religion, of which the rewards are distant, and which is animated only by faith and hope, will glide by degrees out of the mind unless it be invigorated and reimpressed by external ordinances, by stated calls to worship, and the salutary influence of example.

Ibid. Life of Milton

His [Garrick's] death eclipsed the gayety of nations, and impoverished the public stock of harmless pleasure.[2]

Ibid. Life of Edmund Smith

Officious, innocent, sincere,
Of every friendless name the friend.

Verses on the Death of Mr. Robert Levet [1783]. Stanza 2

---

[1] It was pleasant to me to find, that "oats," the "food of horses," were so much used as the food of the people in Dr. Johnson's own town. — BOSWELL: *Life of Dr. Johnson* [1791], *Everyman ed., Vol. I, P. 628*

I own that by my definition of *oats* I meant to vex them [the Scotch]. — *Ibid., Vol. II, P. 434*

[1] Olivarii Goldsmith, Poetae, Physici, Historici, Qui nullum fere scribendi genus non tetigit, Nullum quod tetigit non ornavit.

[2] Quoted by BOSWELL, *Life of Dr. Johnson, Everyman ed., Vol. I, P. 39,* and *Vol. II, P. 275.*

In misery's darkest cavern known,
His useful care was ever nigh.
Where hopeless anguish pour'd his
groan,
And lonely want retir'd to die.
*Verses on the Death of Mr.
Robert Levet. Stanza 5*
His virtues walk'd their narrow round,
Nor made a pause, nor left a void.
Ibid. Stanza 7
Then, with no throbs of fiery pain,[1]
No cold gradations of decay,
Death broke at once the vital chain,
And freed his soul the nearest way.
Ibid. Stanza 9
Tomorrow I purpose to regulate my
room.
*Prayers and Meditations [Pub-
lished 1785]. 1764*
Preserve me from unseasonable and
immoderate sleep.
Ibid. 1767
Every man naturally persuades him-
self that he can keep his resolutions,
nor is he convinced of his imbecility but
by length of time and frequency of ex-
periment.
Ibid. 1770
This world, where much is to be done
and little to be known.
*Ibid. Against Inquisitive and
Perplexing Thoughts*
Gratitude is a fruit of great cultiva-
tion; you do not find it among gross
people.
*Boswell's Tour to the Hebrides
[Published 1785]. [September
20, 1773]*
A fellow that makes no figure in com-
pany, and has a mind as narrow as the
neck of a vinegar-cruet.
Ibid. [September 30, 1773]
Here closed in death th' attentive eyes
That saw the manners in the face.
Epitaph on Hogarth [1786]
The hoary Sage replied,
Come, my lad, and drink some beer.
*Mrs. Piozzi: Anecdotes of Samuel
Johnson [1786]*
If the man who turnips cries

[1] Variant: Then with no throbbing fiery
pain.

Cry not when his father dies,
'Tis a proof that he had rather
Have a turnip than his father.[1]
*Mrs. Piozzi: Anecdotes of
Samuel Johnson*
He was a very good hater.
Ibid.
The law is the last result of human
wisdom acting upon human experience
for the benefit of the public.
Ibid.
The use of travelling is to regulate
imagination by reality, and instead of
thinking how things may be, to see them
as they are.
Ibid.
Dictionaries are like watches; the
worst is better than none, and the best
cannot be expected to go quite true.
Ibid.
Books that you may carry to the fire
and hold readily in your hand, are the
most useful after all.
*Apophthegms from Hawkins's
Life of Johnson [1787]*
Round numbers are always false.
Ibid.
As with my hat [2] upon my head
I walk'd along the Strand,
I there did meet another man
With his hat in his hand.[3]
*Ibid. Anecdotes of Johnson by
George Steevens*
Abstinence is as easy to me as tem-
perance would be difficult.
*Anecdotes of Johnson by
Hannah More*
Boswell. That, Sir, was great forti-
tude of mind.
Johnson. No, Sir; stark insensibility.
*Boswell's Life of Dr. Johnson [4]
[1791]. Vol. I, Page 28*

[1] Burlesque of Lope de Vega's lines,
"Se acquier los leones vence," etc.
[2] Elsewhere found, "I put my hat."
[3] A parody on the ballad, *The Hermit of
Warkworth.*
[4] Everyman edition, 2 volumes.
The Life of Johnson is assuredly a great, a
very great work. Homer is not more decidedly
the first of heroic poets, Shakespeare is not
more decidedly the first of dramatists, Demosthenes is not more decidedly the first of
orators, than Boswell is the first of biogra-

On clean-shirt-day he went abroad, and paid visits.

BOSWELL's *Life of Dr. Johnson.*
Vol. I, Page 56

Tom Birch is as brisk as a bee in conversation; but no sooner does he take a pen in his hand, than it becomes a torpedo to him, and benumbs all his faculties.

Ibid. Page 92

I'll come no more behind your scenes, David; for the silk stockings and white bosoms of your actresses excite my amorous propensities.[1]

Ibid. Page 117

Wretched un-idea'd girls.

Ibid. Page 148

Is not a patron, my lord, one who looks with unconcern on a man struggling for life in the water, and when he has reached ground encumbers him with help? The notice which you have been pleased to take of my labours, had it been early, had been kind; but it has been delayed till I am indifferent, and cannot enjoy it; till I am solitary, and cannot impart it; till I am known, and do not want it.[2]

Ibid. Page 156

Sir, he [Bolingbroke] was a scoundrel and a coward; a scoundrel for charging a blunderbuss against religion and morality; a coward, because he had not resolution to fire it off himself, but left half a crown to a beggarly Scotchman to draw the trigger at his death.

Ibid. Page 160

If a man does not make new acquaintances as he advances through life, he will soon find himself left alone. A man,

sir, should keep his friendship in a constant repair.

BOSWELL's *Life of Dr. Johnson.*
Vol. I, Page 182

Towering in the confidence of twenty-one.[1]

Ibid. Page 197

Being in a ship is being in a jail, with the chance of being drowned.

Ibid. Page 215

Nothing is little to him that feels it with great sensibility.[2]

Ibid. Page 230

Bounty always receives part of its value from the manner in which it is bestowed.[3]

Ibid. Page 233

Every man's affairs, however little, are important to himself.[4]

Ibid. Page 235

A man of genius has been seldom ruined but by himself.[5]

Ibid. Page 236

Sir, I think all Christians, whether Papists or Protestants, agree in the essential articles, and that their differences are trivial, and rather political than religious.[6]

Ibid. Page 251

The noblest prospect which a Scotchman ever sees, is the high-road that leads him to England.

Ibid. Page 264

A man ought to read just as inclina-

[1] Letter to Bennet Langton [January 9, 1758].
[2] Letter to Joseph Baretti [July 20, 1762].
[3] Letter to the Earl of Bute [July 20, 1762].
[4] To the same [November 3, 1762].
[5] Letter to Joseph Baretti [December 21, 1762].
[6] All denominations of Christians have really little difference in point of doctrine, though they may differ widely in external forms. — *Vol. I, P. 411* [1772]

I do not find that the age or country makes the least difference; no, nor the language the actor spoke, nor the religion which they professed, — whether Arab in the desert, or Frenchman in the Academy. I see that sensible men and conscientious men all over the world were of one religion of well-doing and daring. — EMERSON: *Lectures and Biographical Sketches* [1884], *The Preacher*

See Disraeli, page 513b.

phers. He has no second. — MACAULAY: *Samuel Johnson* [1831]

[1] To David Garrick [1749].
[2] Letter to Lord Chesterfield [February 7, 1755].

What is a Patron? Johnson knew,
And well that lifelike portrait drew.
He is a Patron who looks down
With careless eye on men who drown;
But if they chance to reach the land,
Encumbers them with helping hand.
AUSTIN DOBSON [1840–1921]: *The Noble Patron*

See Sophocles, pages 15b–16a.

tion leads him; for what he reads as a task will do him little good.[1] A young man should read five hours in a day, and so may acquire a great deal of knowledge.

BOSWELL's *Life of Dr. Johnson.*
Vol. I, Page 266

If he does really think that there is no distinction between virtue and vice, why, sir, when he leaves our houses let us count our spoons.

Ibid. Page 268

If I accustom a servant to tell a lie for *me*, have I not reason to apprehend that he will tell many lies for *himself?*
Ibid. Page 270

Sir, your levellers wish to level *down* as far as themselves; but they cannot bear levelling *up* to themselves.

Ibid. Page 277

Sherry[2] is dull, naturally dull; but it must have taken him a great deal of pains to become what we now see him. Such an excess of stupidity, sir, is not in Nature.

Ibid. Page 280

Sir, a woman preaching is like a dog's walking on his hind legs. It is not done well; but you are surprised to find it done at all.

Ibid. Page 287

I look upon it, that he who does not mind his belly will hardly mind anything else.[3]

Ibid. Page 290

This was a good dinner enough, to be sure, but it was not a dinner to *ask* a man to.

Ibid. Page 291

The gloomy calm of idle vacancy.[4]
Ibid. Page 294

---

[1] The book which you read from a sense of duty, or because for any reason you must, does not commonly make friends with you. — WILLIAM DEAN HOWELLS: *My Literary Passions* [1895], *Chap. 7*

[2] Thomas Sheridan [1719–1788], actor, lecturer, and author.

[3] See Athenaeus, page 69b.

[4] Letter to Boswell [December 8, 1763]. See Cowper, page 365a.

[Of Sir John Hawkins] A very unclubable man.

BOSWELL's *Life of Dr. Johnson.*
Vol. I, Page 298

He[1] is one of the many who have made themselves *public*, without making themselves *known*.

Ibid. Page 310

I cannot see that lectures can do so much good as reading the books from which the lectures are taken.

Ibid. Page 315

Were he not to marry again, it might be concluded that his first wife had given him a disgust to marriage; but by taking a second wife he pays the highest compliment to the first, by showing that she made him so happy as a married man, that he wishes to be so a second time.

Ibid. Page 360

It matters not how a man dies, but how he lives.

Ibid. Page 378

That fellow seems to me to possess but one idea, and that is a wrong one.[2]
Ibid. Page 393

A gentleman who had been very unhappy in marriage, married immediately after his wife died: Johnson said, it was the triumph of hope over experience.

Ibid. Page 394

A decent provision for the poor is the true test of civilization.

Ibid. Page 396

Whatever philosophy may determine of material nature, it is certainly true of intellectual nature, that it abhors a vacuum.

Ibid. Page 403

Nobody can write the life of a man, but those who have eat and drunk and lived in social intercourse with him.[3]
Ibid. Page 422

---

[1] William Kenrick [1725–1779], a writer who attacked Goldsmith, Garrick, Fielding, Johnson, and Colman.

[2] See Disraeli, page 512a.

[3] They only who live with a man can write his life with any genuine exactness and discrimination; and few people who have lived

The way to make sure of power and influence is by lending money confidentially to your neighbours at a small interest, or perhaps no interest at all, and having their bonds in your possession.

BOSWELL's *Life of Dr. Johnson.*
Vol. I, Page 422

I am a great friend to public amusements; for they keep people from vice.
Ibid. Page 424

A cow is a very good animal in the field; but we turn her out of a garden.
Ibid. Page 436

Much may be made of a Scotchman if he be caught young.
Ibid. Page 440

The way to spread a work is to sell it at a low price. No man will send to buy a thing that costs even sixpence, without an intention to read it.
Ibid. Page 465

An old tutor of a college said to one of his pupils: Read over your composition, and wherever you meet with a passage which you think is particularly fine, strike it out.[1]
Ibid. Page 470

You are the most unscottified of your countrymen.
Ibid. Page 473

Was ever poet so trusted before? [2]
Ibid. Page 502

Attack is the reaction. I never think I have hit hard unless it rebounds.
Ibid. Page 540

A man will turn over half a library to make one book.
Ibid. Page 545

Patriotism is the last refuge of a scoundrel.
Ibid. Page 547

Knowledge is of two kinds: we know a subject ourselves, or we know where we can find information upon it.
Ibid. Page 558

In lapidary inscriptions a man is not upon oath.

BOSWELL's *Life of Dr. Johnson.*
Vol. I, Page 589

There is now less flogging in our great schools than formerly, but then less is learned there; so that what the boys get at one end they lose at the other.
Ibid.

There is nothing which has yet been contrived by man by which so much happiness is produced as by a good tavern or inn.[1]
Ibid. Page 620

A man is very apt to complain of the ingratitude of those who have risen far above him.
Ibid. Vol. II, Page 5

If a man could say nothing against a character but what he can prove, history could not be written.
Ibid. Page 13

No man but a blockhead ever wrote except for money.
Ibid. Page 16

While grief is fresh, every attempt to divert only irritates.
Ibid. Page 21

Life is a progress from want to want, not from enjoyment to enjoyment.
Ibid. Page 36

Life admits not of delays; when pleasure can be had, it is fit to catch it. Every hour takes away part of the things that please us, and perhaps part of our disposition to be pleased.[2]
Ibid. Page 98

In every volume of poems something good may be found.
Ibid. Page 117

---

with a man know what to remark about him. — *Vol. I, P. 617*

[1] See Sydney Smith, page 419b.

[2] Of Oliver Goldsmith, in a letter to Boswell [July 4, 1774].

[1] Whoe'er has travell'd life's dull round,
   Where'er his stages may have been,
May sigh to think he still has found
   His warmest welcome at an inn.
   WILLIAM SHENSTONE [1714–1763]:
   Written on a Window of an Inn at Henley
ROBERT LEIGHTON [1611–1684], Archbishop of Glasgow, often said that if he were to choose a place to die in, it should be an inn. — *Works, Vol. I, P. 76*

[2] Letter to Boswell [September 1, 1777].

When a man is tired of London, he is tired of life; for there is in London all that life can afford.
Boswell's Life of Dr. Johnson.
Vol. II, Page 131

Everything that enlarges the sphere of human powers, that shows man he can do what he thought he could not do, is valuable.
Ibid. Page 168

It is a man's own fault, it is from want of use, if his mind grows torpid in old age.
Ibid. Page 183

Johnson had said that he could repeat a complete chapter of "The Natural History of Iceland," from the Danish of Horrebow, the whole of which was exactly (Ch. LXXII. *Concerning snakes*) thus: "There are no snakes to be met with throughout the whole island." [1]
Ibid. Page 201

As the Spanish proverb says, "He, who would bring home the wealth of the Indies, must carry the wealth of the Indies with him," so it is in travelling, a man must carry knowledge with him if he would bring home knowledge.
Ibid. Page 216

It is better to live rich, than to die rich.
Ibid. Page 218

I would rather be attacked than unnoticed. For the worst thing you can do to an author is to be silent as to his works.
Ibid. Page 257

I remember a passage in Goldsmith's "Vicar of Wakefield," which he was afterwards fool enough to expunge: "I do not love a man who is zealous for nothing."
Ibid. Page 267

Claret is the liquor for boys, port for men; but he who aspires to be a hero must drink brandy.
Ibid. Page 271

[1] Chapter XLII is still shorter: "There are no owls of any kind in the whole island."

Worth seeing? yes; but not worth going to see.
Boswell's Life of Dr. Johnson.
Vol. II, Page 291

A Frenchman must be always talking, whether he knows anything of the matter or not; an Englishman is content to say nothing, when he has nothing to say.
Ibid. Page 326

Of Dr. Goldsmith he said, "No man was more foolish when he had not a pen in his hand, or more wise when he had."
Ibid. Page 336

The applause of a single human being is of great consequence.
Ibid. Page 338

Come to me, my dear Bozzy, and let us be as happy as we can.[1]
Ibid. Page 366

The potentiality of growing rich beyond the dreams of avarice.[2]
Ibid. Page 376

Classical quotation is the *parole* of literary men all over the world.
Ibid. Page 386

My friend was of opinion that when a man of rank appeared in that character [as an author], he deserved to have his merits handsomely allowed.[3]
Ibid. Page 393

A jest breaks no bones.
Ibid. Page 405

To let friendship die away by negligence and silence, is certainly not wise. It is voluntarily to throw away one of the greatest comforts of this weary pilgrimage.
Ibid. Page 417

Whatever you have, spend less.[4]
Ibid. Page 427

[1] Letter to Boswell [March 14, 1781].
[2] I am rich beyond the dreams of avarice. —Edward Moore: *The Gamester* [1753], Act II, Sc. 2
[3] Usually quoted as "When a nobleman writes a book, he ought to be encouraged."
[4] Letter to Boswell [December 7, 1782].

I never have sought the world; the world was not to seek me.[1]

BOSWELL's *Life of Dr. Johnson. Vol. II, Page 436*

He is not only dull himself, but the cause of dullness in others.[2]

Ibid. Page 441

Clear your mind of cant.

Ibid. Page 469

Who drives fat oxen should himself be fat.[3]

Ibid. Page 535

I have found you an argument; I am not obliged to find you an understanding.

Ibid. Page 536

Blown about with every wind of criticism.[4]

Ibid. Page 539

Don't *attitudenize*.

Ibid. Page 541

I look upon every day to be lost, in which I do not make a new acquaintance.

Ibid. Page 579

Life is very short, and very uncertain; let us spend it as well as we can.

Ibid. Page 583

God bless you, my dear.

Ibid. Page 609 (His last words)

GEORGE, LORD LYTTELTON
[1709-1773]

Women, like princes, find few real friends.

Advice to a Lady

What is your sex's earliest, latest care, Your heart's supreme ambition? To be fair.

Ibid.

The lover in the husband may be lost.

Ibid.

[1] I have not loved the world, nor the world me. — BYRON: *Childe Harold, Canto III* [1816], *St. 113*

See Emerson, pages 502b–503a.

[2] See Shakespeare, page 152b.

[3] A parody on "Who rules o'er freemen should himself be free," from BROOKE's *Gustavus Vasa* [1739].

[4] Carried about with every wind of doctrine. — *Ephesians, IV, 14*

Where none admire, 'tis useless to excel; Where none are beaux, 'tis vain to be a belle.

Soliloquy on a Beauty in the Country

ALICIA [1] RUTHERFORD COCKBURN
[1712-1794]

I've seen the smiling Of Fortune beguiling, I've felt all her favours and found her decay; Sweet was her blessing, Kind her caressing: But now they are fled, are fled far away.

The Flowers of the Forest. Stanza 1

GEORGE GRENVILLE
[1712-1770]

A wise government knows how to enforce with temper or to conciliate with dignity.

Speech against the Expulsion of John Wilkes, House of Parliament [1769]

EDWARD MOORE
[1712-1757]

Can't I another's face commend, And to her virtues be a friend, But instantly your forehead lowers, As if *her* merit lessen'd *yours?*

The Farmer, the Spaniel, and the Cat [1756]

The maid who modestly conceals Her beauties, while she hides, reveals; Give but a glimpse, and fancy draws Whate'er the Grecian Venus was.

The Spider and the Bee [1756]

Time still, as he flies, brings increase to her truth, And gives to her mind what he steals from her youth.

The Happy Marriage [1756]

[1] Sometimes given as Alison.

JEAN JACQUES ROUSSEAU
[1712–1778]

Never exceed your rights, and they will soon become unlimited.
A Discourse on Political Economy
[*1758*]

Money is the seed of money, and the first guinea is sometimes more difficult to acquire than the second million.
Ibid.

Man is born free, and everywhere he is in chains.[1]
Contrat Social [*1762*]. *Book I, Chap. 1*

The strongest is never strong enough to be always the master, unless he transforms strength into right, and obedience into duty.
Ibid. Chap. 3

The right of conquest has no foundation other than the right of the strongest.
Ibid. Chap. 4

The body politic, like the human body, begins to die from its birth, and bears in itself the causes of its destruction.
Ibid. Book III, Chap. 11

As soon as public service ceases to be the chief business of the citizens, and they would rather serve with their money than with their persons, the State is not far from its fall.
Ibid. Chap. 15

Good laws lead to the making of better ones; bad ones bring about worse. As soon as any man says of the affairs of the State, "What does it matter to me?" the State may be given up for lost.
Ibid.

God makes all things good; man meddles with them and they become evil.
Émile, ou De l'Éducation [*1762*].
Book I

I shall always maintain that whoso says in his heart, "There is no God,"

while he takes the name of God upon his lips, is either a liar or a madman.
Émile, ou De l'Éducation. Book I

People who know little are usually great talkers, while men who know much say little.
Ibid.

What wisdom can you find that is greater than kindness?
Ibid. Book II

The happiest is he who suffers least; the most miserable is he who enjoys least. Ever more sorrow than joy, — this is the lot of all of us.
Ibid.

Nature never deceives us; it is always we who deceive ourselves.
Ibid. Book III

There exists one book, which, to my taste, furnishes the happiest treatise of natural education. What then is this marvelous book? Is it Aristotle? Is it Pliny, is it Buffon? No, — it is *Robinson Crusoe*.
Ibid.

Self-love makes more libertines than love.
Ibid. Book IV

Provided a man is not mad, he can be cured of every folly but vanity.
Ibid.

A man says what he knows, a woman says what will please.
Ibid. Book V

Where is the man who owes nothing to the land in which he lives? Whatever that land may be, he owes to it the most precious thing possessed by man, the morality of his actions and the love of virtue.
Ibid.

I have entered on a performance which is without precedent, and will have no imitator. I propose to show my fellow-mortals a man in all the integrity of nature; and this man shall be myself.
Confessions [*1782*]. *Book I*

Remorse goes to sleep during a prosperous period and wakes up in adversity.
Ibid.

---

[1] L'homme est né libre, et partout il est dans les fers.

It is too difficult to think nobly when one only thinks to get a living.
Confessions. Book II

Hatred, as well as love, renders its votaries credulous.
Ibid. Book V

At length I recollected the thoughtless saying of a great princess, who, on being informed that the country people had no bread, replied, "Let them eat cake."[1]
Ibid. Book VI

The thirst after happiness is never extinguished in the heart of man.
Ibid. Book IX

He thinks like a philosopher, and acts like a king.
Ibid. Book XII

JOSIAH TUCKER, DEAN OF GLOUCESTER
[1712–1799]

What is true of a shopkeeper is true of a shopkeeping nation.[2]
Tract Against Going to War for the Sake of Trade [1763]

LAURENCE STERNE
[1713–1768]

Only the brave know how to forgive. . . . A coward never forgave; it is not in his nature.
Sermons. Vol. I [1760], *No. 12*

"Pray, my dear," quoth my mother, "have you not forgot to wind up the clock?" — "Good G—!" cried my father, making an exclamation, but taking care to moderate his voice at the

[1] "Qu'ils mangent de la brioche."
This remark is usually attributed to Marie Antoinette, after her arrival in France in 1770, but the sixth book of the *Confessions* was written two or three years before that date.

[2] See Adam Smith, page 352b.
Let Pitt then boast of his victory to his nation of shopkeepers. — BERTRAND BARÈRE: *Speech* [June 11, 1794]
But it may be said as a rule, that every Englishman in the Duke of Wellington's army paid his way. The remembrance of such a fact surely becomes a nation of shopkeepers. — THACKERAY: *Vanity Fair* [1847–1848], *Vol. I, Chap. 28*

same time, — "Did ever woman, since the creation of the world, interrupt a man with such a silly question?"[1]
Tristram Shandy. Book I [1760], *Chap. 1*

So long as a man rides his hobby-horse peaceably and quietly along the King's highway, and neither compels you or me to get up behind him, — pray, Sir, what have either you or I to do with it?
Ibid. Chap. 7

For every ten jokes, thou hast got an hundred enemies.
Ibid. Chap. 12

He was within a few hours of giving his enemies the slip for ever.
Ibid.

Whistled up to London, upon a Tom Fool's errand.
Ibid. Chap. 16

'Tis known by the name of perseverance in a good cause, — and of obstinacy in a bad one.
Ibid. Chap. 17

Persuasion hung upon his lips.
Ibid. Chap. 19

Digressions, incontestably, are the sunshine; — they are the life, the soul of reading; — take them out of this book for instance, — you might as well take the book along with them.
Ibid. Chap. 22

The history of a soldier's wound beguiles the pain of it.
Ibid. Chap. 25

The desire of knowledge, like the thirst of riches, increases ever with the acquisition of it.
Ibid. Book II [1760], *Chap. 3*

Writing, when properly managed (as you may be sure I think mine is) is but a different name for conversation.
Ibid. Chap. 11

Go, poor devil, get thee gone! Why should I hurt thee? This world surely

[1] I wish either my father or my mother, or indeed both of them, as they were in duty both equally bound to it, had minded what they were about when they begot me. — *Ibid.*

is wide enough to hold both thee and me.[1]

> *Tristram Shandy. Book II,*
> *Chap. 12*

That's another story,[2] replied my father.

> *Ibid. Chap. 17*

Trust that man in nothing who has not a Conscience in everything.

> *Ibid. Chap. 17*

Good — bad — indifferent.

> *Ibid. Book III* [*1761–1762*],
> *Chap. 2*

"Our armies swore terribly in Flanders," cried my uncle Toby, — "but nothing to this."

> *Ibid. Chap. 11*

Of all the cants which are canted in this canting world, though the cant of hypocrites may be the worst, the cant of criticism is the most tormenting!

> *Ibid. Chap. 12*

When Ernulphus[3] cursed — no part escaped him.

> *Ibid.*

'Twould be as much as my life was worth.

> *Ibid. Chap. 20*

Before an affliction is digested, consolation ever comes too soon; and after it is digested, it comes too late.

> *Ibid. Chap. 29*

The sweat of a man's brows, and the exudations of a man's brains, are as much a man's own property as the breeches upon his backside.

> *Ibid. Chap. 34*

One of the two horns of my dilemma.

> *Ibid. Book IV* [*1761–1762*],
> *Chap. 26*

The feather put into his cap of having been abroad.

> *Ibid. Chap. 31*

Now or never was the time.

> *Tristram Shandy. Book IV,*
> *Chap. 31*

Sciences may be learned by rote, but wisdom not.

> *Ibid. Book V* [*1761–1762*],
> *Chap. 32*

O blessed health! . . . thou art above all gold and treasure . . . . He that has thee, has little more to wish for; — and he that is so wretched as to want thee, — wants everything with thee.

> *Ibid. Chap. 33*

The Accusing Spirit, which flew up to heaven's chancery with the oath, blushed as he gave it in; and the Recording Angel, as he wrote it down, dropped a tear upon the word and blotted it out forever.[1]

> *Ibid. Book VI* [*1761–1762*],
> *Chap. 8*

A man should know something of his own country, too, before he goes abroad.

> *Ibid. Book VII* [*1765*], *Chap. 2*

I am sick as a horse.

> *Ibid.*

Ho! 'tis the time of salads.

> *Ibid. Chap. 17*

"They order," said I, "this matter better in France."

> *A Sentimental Journey* [*1768*].
> *Line 1*

I pity the man who can travel from Dan to Beersheba and cry, " 'Tis all barren!"

> *Ibid. In the Street, Calais*

Tant pis and *tant mieux,* being two of the great hinges in French conversation, a stranger would do well to set himself right in the use of them before he gets to Paris.

> *Ibid. Montreuil*

Hail, ye small, sweet courtesies of life! for smooth do ye make the road of it.

> *Ibid. The Pulse, Paris*

---

[1] Uncle Toby to the fly.
[2] But that is another story. — KIPLING: *Plain Tales from the Hills* [1888], *Three and — an Extra*
[3] Ernulph or Arnulph [1040–1124], French Benedictine and Bishop of Rochester.

[1] But sad as angels for the good man's sin, Weep to record, and blush to give it in. CAMPBELL: *Pleasures of Hope* [1799], *Part II, L. 357*

"Disguise thyself as thou wilt, still, Slavery," said I, "still thou art a bitter draught."

A Sentimental Journey. The Passport, The Hotel at Paris

"God tempers the wind," said Maria, "to the shorn lamb." [1]

Ibid. Maria

WILLIAM SHENSTONE
[1714–1763]

Her cap, far whiter than the driven snow,
Emblems right meet of decency does yield.

*The Schoolmistress [1737].
Stanza 6*

WILLIAM WHITEHEAD
[1715–1785]

With indignation I survey
Such skill and judgment thrown away;
The time profusely squandered there
On vulgar arts beneath thy care,
If well employed at less expense
Had taught thee honour, virtue, sense.

*The Youth and the Philosopher
[1774]*

DAVID GARRICK
[1716–1779]

Let others hail the rising sun:
I bow to that whose course is run.

On the Death of Mr. Pelham

Heart of oak are our ships,
Heart of oak are our men,
We always are ready,
Steady, boys, steady,
We'll fight, and we'll conquer again and again.

Heart of Oak [Circa *1770*]

Here lies Nolly Goldsmith, for shortness called Noll,
Who wrote like an angel, and talk'd like poor Poll.

Impromptu Epitaph on Goldsmith

[1] See Herbert, page 234b.

THOMAS GRAY
[1716–1771]

Ye distant spires, ye antique towers,
That crown the wat'ry glade.

*On a Distant Prospect of Eton
College [1742]. Stanza 1*

Still as they run they look behind,
They hear a voice in every wind,
And snatch a fearful joy.

Ibid. Stanza 4

Alas! regardless of their doom,
The little victims play;
No sense have they of ills to come,
Nor care beyond today.

Ibid. Stanza 6

Grim-visag'd comfortless Despair.

Ibid. Stanza 7

To each his suff'rings; all are men,
Condemn'd alike to groan, —
The tender for another's pain,
Th' unfeeling for his own.
Yet ah! why should they know their fate,
Since sorrow never comes too late,
And happiness too swiftly flies?
Thought would destroy their paradise.
No more; where ignorance is bliss,
'Tis folly to be wise. [1]

Ibid. Stanza 10

Daughter of Jove, relentless power,
Thou tamer of the human breast,
Whose iron scourge and torturing hour
The bad affright, afflict the best!

*Hymn to Adversity [1742].
Stanza 1*

What sorrow was, thou bad'st her know,
And from her own she learn'd to melt at others' woe.

Ibid. Stanza 2

What female heart can gold despise?
What cat's averse to fish?

*On the Death of a Favourite Cat
[1747]. Stanza 4*

A fav'rite has no friend!

Ibid. Stanza 6

As sickly plants betray a niggard earth,

[1] He that increaseth knowledge increaseth sorrow. — *Ecclesiastes, I, 18*

Whose barren bosom starves her gen'rous birth.

> *The Alliance of Education and Government* [Circa *1748*]

The social smile, the sympathetic tear.

> *Ibid.*

When love could teach a monarch to be wise,
And gospel-light first dawn'd from Bullen's eyes.[1]

> *Ibid.*

The curfew tolls the knell of parting day,
The lowing herd wind slowly o'er the lea,
The ploughman homeward plods his weary way,
And leaves the world to darkness and to me.

> *Elegy in a Country Churchyard* [*1750*]. *Stanza 1*

Now fades the glimmering landscape on the sight,
And all the air a solemn stillness holds,
Save where the beetle wheels his droning flight,
And drowsy tinklings lull the distant folds.

> *Ibid. Stanza 2*

Save that from yonder ivy-mantled tow'r
The moping owl does to the moon complain.

> *Ibid. Stanza 3*

Each in his narrow cell forever laid,
The rude forefathers of the hamlet sleep.

> *Ibid. Stanza 4*

Nor grandeur hear with a disdainful smile
The short and simple annals of the poor.

> *Ibid. Stanza 8*

The boast of heraldry, the pomp of pow'r,
And all that beauty, all that wealth e'er gave,
Await alike the inevitable hour:

The paths of glory lead but to the grave.

> *Elegy in a Country Churchyard.*
> *Stanza 9*

Where thro' the long-drawn aisle and fretted vault
The pealing anthem swells the note of praise.

> *Ibid. Stanza 10*

Can storied urn, or animated bust
Back to its mansion call the fleeting breath?
Can honour's voice provoke the silent dust,
Or flatt'ry soothe the dull cold ear of death?

> *Ibid. Stanza 11*

Hands, that the rod of empire might have sway'd,
Or waked to ecstasy the living lyre.

> *Ibid. Stanza 12*

But Knowledge to their eyes her ample page
Rich with the spoils of time did ne'er unroll; [1]
Chill penury repress'd their noble rage,
And froze the genial current of the soul.

> *Ibid. Stanza 13*

Full many a gem of purest ray serene.[2]
The dark unfathom'd caves of ocean bear:
Full many a flower is born to blush unseen,
And waste its sweetness on the desert air.

> *Ibid. Stanza 14*

Some village Hampden, that with dauntless breast
The little tyrant of his fields withstood,
Some mute inglorious Milton here may rest,
Some Cromwell guiltless of his country's blood.

> *Ibid. Stanza 15*

[1] The monarch is Henry VIII; Anne Boleyn's name is here spelled (as it is in Shakespeare's *Henry VIII*) as it is pronounced.

[1] See Sir Thomas Browne, page 240a.

[2] Every single phrase is a string of perfect gems, of purest ray serene, strung together on a loose golden thread. — GEORGE DU MAURIER: *Trilby, Part VI* [1894]

Forbade to wade through slaughter to
   a throne,
And shut the gates of mercy on man-
   kind.
    Elegy in a Country Churchyard.
                 Stanza 17
Far from the madding crowd's ignoble
   strife
Their sober wishes never learn'd to
   stray;
Along the cool sequester'd vale of life
They kept the noiseless tenor of their
   way.[1]
               Ibid. Stanza 19
Implores the passing tribute of a sigh.
               Ibid. Stanza 20
For who, to dumb forgetfulness a prey,
This pleasing anxious being e'er re-
   sign'd,
Left the warm precincts of the cheer-
   ful day,
Nor cast one longing ling'ring look
   behind?
               Ibid. Stanza 22
E'en from the tomb the voice of nature
   cries,
E'en in our ashes live their wonted
   fires.[2]
               Ibid. Stanza 23
Mindful of th' unhonour'd dead.
               Ibid. Stanza 24
Here rests his head upon the lap of
   earth,
A youth to fortune and to fame un-
   known.
Fair Science frown'd not on his hum-
   ble birth,
And Melancholy mark'd him for her
   own.[3]
    Ibid. The Epitaph, Stanza 1
Large was his bounty, and his soul sin-
   cere,
Heaven did a recompense as largely
   send:
He gave to mis'ry (all he had) a tear,

---

[1]   In sober state,
  Through the sequestered vale of rural life,
  The venerable patriarch guileless held
  The tenor of his way.
    PORTEUS [1731–1808]: *Death, L. 108*
[2] See Chaucer, page 81a.
[3] See Walton, page 235a.

He gained from Heav'n ('twas all he
   wish'd) a friend.
    Elegy in a Country Churchyard.
         The Epitaph, Stanza 2
No farther seek his merits to disclose,
Or draw his frailties from their dread
   abode,
(There they alike in trembling hope
   repose),
The bosom of his Father and his God.
                Ibid. Stanza 3
The meanest floweret of the vale,
The simplest note that swells the gale,
The common sun, the air, the skies,
To him are opening paradise.
    *Ode on the Pleasure Arising from
      Vicissitude* [*1754*]. *Line 53*
O'er her warm cheek and rising bosom
   move
The bloom of young Desire and purple
   light of Love.
      The Progress of Poesy [*1754*].
              I, 3, Line 16
Far from the sun and summer-gale,
In thy green lap was Nature's Darling [1]
   laid.
          Ibid. III, 1, Line 1
Or ope the sacred source of sympa-
   thetic tears.
         Ibid. III, 1, Line 12
He [2] pass'd the flaming bounds of
   place and time:
The living throne, the sapphire-blaze,
Where angels tremble while they gaze,
He saw; but, blasted with excess of
   light,
Closed his eyes in endless night.
              Ibid. 2, Line 4
Ruin seize thee, ruthless king,
Confusion on thy banners wait;
Though fann'd by Conquest's crimson
   wing,
They mock the air with idle state.
      The Bard [*1759*]. *I, 1, Line 1*
Weave the warp, and weave the woof,
The winding-sheet of Edward's race.
Give ample room and verge enough,
The characters of hell to trace.
           Ibid. II, 1, Line 1

---

[1] Shakespeare.
[2] Milton.

Fair laughs the morn, and soft the
zephyr blows,
While proudly riding o'er the azure
realm,
In gallant trim the gilded vessel goes,
Youth on the prow, and Pleasure at
the helm;
Regardless of the sweeping whirlwind's
sway,
That, hush'd in grim repose, expects
his evening prey.
The Bard. II, 2, Line 9

Visions of glory, spare my aching
sight;
Ye unborn ages, crowd not on my soul!
Ibid. III, 1, Line 11

And truth severe, by fairy fiction drest.
Ibid. 3, Line 3

Now my weary lips I close;
Leave me, leave me to repose!
Descent of Odin [*1761*]. *Line 71*

Iron sleet of arrowy shower
Hurtles in the darken'd air.
The Fatal Sisters [*1761*]

Too poor for a bribe, and too proud to
importune;
He had not the method of making a
fortune.
On His Own Character [*1761*]

Sweet is the breath of vernal shower,
The bee's collected treasures sweet,
Sweet music's melting fall, but sweeter
yet
The still small voice of gratitude.
Ode for Music [*1769*]

HORACE WALPOLE
[1717–1797]

Harry Vane, Pulteney's toad-eater.
Letter to Sir Horace Mann [*1742*]
The world is a comedy to those that
think, a tragedy to those that feel.
Ibid. [*1769*]
A careless song, with a little non-
sense in it now and then, does not mis-
become a monarch.[1]
Ibid. [*1774*]

[1] A little nonsense now and then
Is relished by the wisest men.
ANONYMOUS

The whole [Scotch] nation hitherto
has been void of wit and humour, and
even incapable of relishing it.
Letter to Sir Horace Mann [*1778*]
Prognostics do not always prove
prophecies, — at least the wisest prophets make sure of the event first.
Letter to Thomas Walpole [*1785*]

SAMUEL FOOTE
[1720–1777]

Born in a cellar, and living in a garret.[1]
The Author. Act II

Matt Minikin won't set fire to the
Thames though he lives near the
Bridge.
Trip to Calais [*1776*]

So she went into the garden to cut
a cabbage leaf to make an apple pie;
and at the same time a great she-bear,
coming up the street, pops its head into
the shop. "What! no soap?" So he died,
and she very imprudently married the
barber; and there were present the
Picninnies, and the Joblillies, and the
Garyulies, and the Grand Panjandrum
himself, with the little round button at
top, and they all fell to playing the
game of catch as catch can, till the
gunpowder ran out at the heels of their
boots.
*Nonsense written to test the
boasted memory of Charles
Macklin, The Quarterly Review* [*1854*], *Credited to Foote
by* MARIA EDGEWORTH *in Harry
and Lucy, Concluded, Volume
II*

THOMAS GIBBONS
[1720–1785]

That man may last, but never lives,
Who much receives, but nothing gives;
Whom none can love, whom none can
thank, —
Creation's blot, creation's blank.
When Jesus Dwelt

[1] Born in the garret, in the kitchen bred. —
BYRON: *A Sketch* [1816]

DENNIS O'KELLY
[1720–1787]

It will be Eclipse first, the rest nowhere.

Declaration at Epsom [May 3, 1769] when the great race horse, Eclipse, was to run his first race. Annals of Sporting, Volume II, Page 271

JOHN WOOLMAN
[1720–1772]

Though the change from day to night is by a motion so gradual as scarcely to be perceived, yet when night is come we behold it very different from the day; and thus as people become wise in their own eyes, and prudent in their own sight, customs rise up from the spirit of this world, and spread by little, and little, till a departure from the simplicity that there is in Christ becomes as distinguishable as light from darkness, to such who are crucified to the world.

Considerations on the True Harmony of Mankind

GILBERT WHITE
[1720–1793]

The tortoise, like other reptiles, has an arbitrary stomach as well as lungs; and can refrain from eating as well as breathing for a great part of the year.
Natural History of Selborne. April 12, 1772

WILLIAM COLLINS
[1721–1759]

Well may your hearts believe the truths I tell:
'Tis virtue makes the bliss, where'er we dwell.
Persian Eclogues [1742]. I, Selim, or The Shepherd's Moral, Line 5

Curst be the gold and silver which persuade

Weak men to follow far-fatiguing trade.
Persian Eclogues. II, Hassan, or The Camel Driver, Line 31

How sleep the brave, who sink to rest
By all their country's wishes bless'd!
Ode Written in the Year 1746. Stanza 1

By fairy hands their knell is rung;
By forms unseen their dirge is sung.
There Honour comes, a pilgrim grey,
To bless the turf that wraps their clay,
And Freedom shall awhile repair,
To dwell a weeping hermit there!
Ibid. Stanza 2

In numbers warmly pure and sweetly strong.
Ode to Simplicity [1747]. Stanza 1

Now air is hush'd, save where the weak-eyed bat,
With short shrill shriek, flits by on leathern wing,
Or where the beetle winds
His small but sullen horn.
Ode to Evening [1747]. Stanza 3

'Twas sad by fits, by starts 'twas wild.
The Passions [1747]. Line 28

With eyes up-rais'd, as one inspir'd,
Pale Melancholy sate retir'd;
And, from her wild, sequester'd seat,
In notes by distance made more sweet,
Pour'd thro' the mellow horn her pensive soul.
Ibid. Line 57

In hollow murmurs died away.
Ibid. Line 68

O Music, sphere-descended maid,
Friend of Pleasure, Wisdom's aid!
Ibid. Line 95

JEANNE, MARQUISE DE POMPADOUR
[1721–1764]

After us the deluge.[1]
Reputed reply to Louis XV [November 5, 1757] after the defeat of the French and Austrian armies by Frederick the Great in the battle of Rossbach

[1] Après nous le déluge.
The attribution to Mme. de Pompadour is

TOBIAS SMOLLETT
[1721–1771]

He was formed for the ruin of our sex.
    Roderick Random [*1748*]. *Chap. 22*
Thy fatal shafts unerring move,
I bow before thine altar, Love!
    Ibid. Chap. 40

CHRISTOPHER SMART
[1722–1770]

O servant of God's holiest charge,
The minister of praise at large.
    A Song to David. Stanza 3

SIR WILLIAM BLACKSTONE
[1723–1780]

The royal navy of England hath ever been its greatest defence and ornament; it is its ancient and natural strength, — the floating bulwark of our island.
    Commentaries [*1765–1769*].
    Vol. I, Book I, Chap. XIII
Time whereof the memory of man runneth not to the contrary.[1]
    Ibid. Chap. XVIII

ADAM SMITH
[1723–1790]

The real price of everything, what everything really costs to the man who wants to acquire it, is the toil and trouble of acquiring it.
    Wealth of Nations [*1776*]
To found a great empire for the sole purpose of raising up a people of customers may at first sight appear a project fit only for a nation of shopkeepers. It is, however, a project altogether unfit for a nation of shopkeepers; but extremely fit for a nation whose

made by DESPRÉS in *Mémoires de Madame de Hausset,* also by SAINTE-BEUVE and LA TOUR, but LAROUSSE in *Fleurs Historiques* attributes the saying to the King. It was original with neither, for it is an old French proverb.
[1] The favorite phrase of their law is "a custom whereof the memory of man runneth not back to the contrary." — EMERSON: *English Traits* [*1856*]

Government is influenced by shopkeepers.[1]
    Wealth of Nations

JOHN HOME
[1724–1808]

In the first days
Of my distracting grief, I found myself
As women wish to be who love their lords.
    Douglas [*1756*]. *Act I, Sc. 1*
I'll woo her as the lion woos his brides.
    Ibid.
My name is Norval; on the Grampian hills
My father feeds his flocks; a frugal swain,
Whose constant cares were to increase his store,
And keep his only son, myself, at home.
    Ibid. Act III, Sc. 1
Like Douglas conquer, or like Douglas die.
    Ibid. Act V, Sc. 1

RICHARD GIFFORD
[1725–1807]

Verse sweetens toil, however rude the sound;
    She feels no biting pang the while she sings;
Nor, as she turns the giddy wheel around,
    Revolves the sad vicissitudes of things.[2]
    Contemplation

LOGAN, MINGO CHIEF
[1725–1780]

I appeal to any white man to say if he ever entered Logan's cabin hungry and he gave him not meat; if ever he came cold and naked and he clothed him not?
    Message to Lord Dunmore, Governor of Virginia [*November 11, 1774*], *in Notes on Virginia, by* THOMAS JEFFERSON

[1] See Josiah Tucker, page 345a.
[2] See Bacon, page 121b.

JAMES OTIS
[1725–1783]

An act against the constitution is void.
Argument Against the Writs of Assistance [1] [1761]

Taxation without representation is tyranny.[2]
Attributed [1763]

WILLIAM PRESCOTT
[1726–1795]

Don't fire until you see the whites of their eyes.[3]
At Bunker Hill, June 17, 1775

OLIVER GOLDSMITH
[1728–1774]

One writer, for instance, excels at a plan or a title-page, another works away the body of the book, and a third is a dab at an index.
The Bee. No. 1, October 6, 1759

What cities, as great as this, have . . . promised themselves immortality! Posterity can hardly trace the situation of some. The sorrowful traveller wanders over the awful ruins of others. . . . Here stood their citadel, but now grown over with weeds; there their senate-house, but now the haunt of every noxious reptile; temples and theatres stood here, now only an undistinguished heap of ruins.
Ibid. No. 4, October 27, 1759

Good people all, with one accord,
  Lament for Madam Blaize,

Who never wanted a good word —
  From those who spoke her praise.
Elegy on Mrs. Mary Blaize [1759]. *Stanza 1*

A night-cap deck'd his brows instead of bay,
A cap by night, a stocking all the day.
Description of an Author's Bed-chamber [1760]

That strain once more; it bids remembrance rise.
The Captivity, An Oratorio [1764]. *Act I*

O Memory! thou fond deceiver.
Ibid.

To the last moment of his breath,
  On hope the wretch relies;
And even the pang preceding death
  Bids expectation rise.[1]
Ibid. Act II

Hope, like the gleaming taper's light,
  Adorns and cheers our way;
And still, as darker grows the night,
  Emits a brighter ray.
Ibid.

Remote, unfriended, melancholy, slow,
Or by the lazy Scheldt, or wandering Po.
The Traveller [1764]. *Line 1*

Where'er I roam, whatever realms to see,
My heart untravell'd fondly turns to thee;
Still to my brother turns, with ceaseless pain,
And drags at each remove a lengthening chain.
Ibid. Line 7

Such is the patriot's boast, where'er we roam,
His first, best country ever is, at home.
Ibid. Line 73

Where wealth and freedom reign contentment fails,
And honour sinks where commerce long prevails.
Ibid. Line 91

Man seems the only growth that dwindles here.[2]
Ibid. Line 126

---

[1] In John Adams, *Works* [1850–1856], Vol. II, P. 522.
[2] This maxim was the guide and watchword of all the friends of liberty. Otis actually said: "No parts of His Majesty's dominions can be taxed without their consent." *Rights of the Colonies* [1764], *P. 64.*
[3] Silent till you see the whites of their eyes. — PRINCE CHARLES OF PRUSSIA, at Jagerndorf, May 23, 1745
By push of bayonets; no firing till you see the whites of their eyes. — FREDERICK THE GREAT, at Prague, May 6, 1757

[1] See Cicero, page 34a.
[2] Italy.

By sports like these are all their cares
beguil'd,
The sports of children satisfy the child.
The Traveller. Line 153

But winter ling'ring chills the lap of
May.
Ibid. Line 172

Cheerful at morn, he [1] wakes from short
repose,
Breasts the keen air, and carols as he
goes.
Ibid. Line 185

So the loud torrent, and the whirlwind's roar,
But bind him to his native mountains
more.
Ibid. Line 217

They please, are pleas'd, they give to
get esteem,
Till, seeming blest, they grow to what
they seem.[2]
Ibid. Line 266

To men of other minds my fancy flies,
Embosom'd in the deep where Holland
lies.
Methinks her patient sons before me
stand,
Where the broad ocean leans against
the land.
Ibid. Line 281

Pride in their port, defiance in their
eye,
I see the lords of humankind [3] pass by.
Ibid. Line 327

The land of scholars, and the nurse of
arms.[4]
Ibid. Line 356

For just experience tells, in every soil,
That those that think must govern
those that toil.
Ibid. Line 372

Laws grind the poor, and rich men rule
the law.
Ibid. Line 386

Vain, very vain, my weary search to
find

[1] The Swiss peasant.
[2] The character of the French.
[3] The British.
[4] England.

That bliss which only centres in the
mind.
The Traveller. Line 423

I . . . chose my wife, as she did her
wedding-gown, not for a fine glossy
surface, but such qualities as would
wear well.
The Vicar of Wakefield [1766].
Chap. 1

We sometimes had those little rubs
which Providence sends to enhance the
value of its favours.
Ibid.

Handsome is that handsome does.[1]
Ibid.

That virtue which requires to be
ever guarded is scarce worth the sen-
tinel.
Ibid. Chap. 5

I find you want me to furnish you
with argument and intellects too.
Ibid. Chap. 7

Man wants but little here below,
Nor wants that little long.[2]
*Ibid. Chap. 8, The Hermit (Edwin
and Angelina), Stanza 8*

She was all of a muck of sweat.
Ibid. Chap. 9

They would talk of nothing but high
life, and high-lived company, with
other fashionable topics, such as pictures, taste, Shakespeare, and the musical glasses.[3]
Ibid.

Conscience is a coward, and those
faults it has not strength enough to prevent it seldom has justice enough to
accuse.
Ibid. Chap. 13

A kind and gentle heart he had,
To comfort friends and foes;
The naked every day he clad
When he put on his clothes.
*Ibid. Chap. 17, An Elegy on the
Death of a Mad Dog, Stanza 3*

[1] See Chaucer, page 81b.
[2] See Edward Young, page 306a, and
Oliver Wendell Holmes, page 536a.
[3] "Shall we talk about Shakespeare?" he
asked sarcastically. "Or the musical glasses?"
— ALDOUS HUXLEY: *Point Counter Point*
[1928], *Chap. 21*

And in that town a dog was found,
As many dogs there be,
Both mongrel, puppy, whelp, and
hound,
And curs of low degree.

*The Vicar of Wakefield. Chap.
17, An Elegy on the Death of a
Mad Dog, Stanza 4*

The dog, to gain some private ends,
Went mad, and bit the man.

Ibid. Stanza 5

The man recovered of the bite —
The dog it was that died.

Ibid. Stanza 8

When lovely woman stoops to folly,
And finds too late that men betray,
What charm can soothe her melan-
choly?
What art can wash her guilt away? [1]

Ibid. Chap. 24, Song, Stanza 1

The only art her guilt to cover,
To hide her shame from every eye,
To give repentance to her lover,
And wring his bosom, is — to die.

Ibid. Stanza 2

To what a fortuitous concurrence do
we not owe every pleasure and convenience of our lives.

Ibid. Chap. 31

This same philosophy is a good horse
in the stable, but an arrant jade on a
journey.[2]

The Good-Natur'd Man [1768].
Act I

He calls his extravagance, generosity; and his trusting everybody, universal benevolence.

Ibid.

All his faults are such that one loves
him still the better for them.

Ibid.

Friendship is a disinterested commerce between equals; love, an abject
intercourse between tyrants and slaves.

Ibid.

Silence gives consent.

Ibid. Act II

Measures, not men, have always been
my mark.[1]

The Good-Natur'd Man. Act II

Sweet Auburn! loveliest village of the
plain.

The Deserted Village [1770].
Line 1

The hawthorn bush, with seats beneath
the shade,
For talking age and whispering lovers
made.

Ibid. Line 13

The bashful virgin's sidelong looks of
love.

Ibid. Line 29

Ill fares the land, to hastening ills a
prey,
Where wealth accumulates, and men
decay;
Princes and lords may flourish or may
fade;
A breath can make them, as a breath
has made;
But a bold peasantry, their country's
pride,
When once destroy'd, can never be supplied.

Ibid. Line 51

His best companions, innocence and
health;
And his best riches, ignorance of
wealth.

Ibid. Line 61

How happy he who crowns in shades
like these,
A youth of labour with an age of ease!

Ibid. Line 99

Bends to the grave with unperceived
decay,
While resignation gently slopes the
way,
And all his prospects brightening to
the last,
His heaven commences ere the world
be past.

Ibid. Line 109

The watch-dog's voice that bay'd the
whispering wind,

---

[1] See T. S. Eliot, page 944a.
[2] See La Rochefoucauld, page 264b.

[1] See Chesterfield, page 323a, and Burke,
page 359a.

And the loud laugh that spoke the vacant mind.[1]

The Deserted Village. Line 121

A man he was to all the country dear,
And passing rich with forty pounds a year.

Ibid. Line 141

Careless their merits or their faults to scan,
His pity gave ere charity began.
Thus to relieve the wretched was his pride,
And even his failings lean'd to Virtue's side.

Ibid. Line 161

And, as a bird each fond endearment tries
To tempt its new-fledg'd offspring to the skies,
He tried each art, reprov'd each dull delay,
Allur'd to brighter worlds, and led the way.

Ibid. Line 167

Truth from his lips prevail'd with double sway,
And fools, who came to scoff, remain'd to pray.[2]

Ibid. Line 179

Even children follow'd with endearing wile,
And pluck'd his gown, to share the good man's smile.

Ibid. Line 183

A man severe he was, and stern to view;
I knew him well, and every truant knew;
Well had the boding tremblers learn'd to trace
The day's disasters in his morning face;
Full well they laugh'd, with counterfeited glee,
At all his jokes, for many a joke had he;

Full well the busy whisper, circling round,
Convey'd the dismal tidings when he frown'd.
Yet was he kind; or if severe in aught,
The love he bore to learning was in fault;
The village all declar'd how much he knew;
'Twas certain he could write, and cipher too.

The Deserted Village. Line 197

In arguing too, the parson own'd his skill,
For e'en though vanquished, he could argue still;
While words of learned length and thundering sound
Amaz'd the gazing rustics rang'd around,
And still they gaz'd, and still the wonder grew,
That one small head could carry all he knew.

Ibid. Line 209

Where village statesmen talk'd with looks profound,
And news much older than their ale went round.

Ibid. Line 223

The whitewash'd wall, the nicely sanded floor,
The varnish'd clock that click'd behind the door;
The chest contriv'd a double debt to pay, —
A bed by night, a chest of drawers by day.[1]

Ibid. Line 227

The twelve good rules, the royal game of goose.[2]

Ibid. Line 232

---

[1] Frequent and loud laughter is the characteristic of folly and ill manners: it is the manner in which the mob express their silly joy at silly things, and they call it being merry. In my mind there is nothing so illiberal and so ill-bred as audible laughter. — LORD CHESTERFIELD: *Letters* [March 9, 1748]

[2] See Dryden, page 279b.

[1] A cap by night, a stocking all the day. — *Description of an Author's Bed-chamber.* See page 353b.

[2] The twelve good rules were ascribed to Charles I: (1) urge no healths; (2) profane no divine ordinances; (3) touch no state matters; (4) reveal no secrets; (5) pick no quarrels; (6) make no comparisons; (7) maintain no ill opinions; (8) keep no bad company; (9) encourage no vice; (10) make no long

To me more dear, congenial to my
  heart,
One native charm, than all the gloss
  of art.
          The Deserted Village. Line 253
And, ev'n while fashion's brightest arts
  decoy,
The heart distrusting asks, if this be
  joy.
          Ibid. Line 263
Her modest looks the cottage might
  adorn,
Sweet as the primrose peeps beneath
  the thorn.
          Ibid. Line 329
In all the silent manliness of grief.
          Ibid. Line 384
O Luxury! thou curst by Heaven's de-
  cree!
          Ibid. Line 385
Thou source of all my bliss and all my
  woe,
That found'st me poor at first, and
  keep'st me so.
          Ibid. Line 413
The very pink of perfection.
    She Stoops to Conquer [1773].
          Act I
Let schoolmasters puzzle their brain,
  With grammar, and nonsense, and
  learning;
Good liquor, I stoutly maintain,
  Gives genius a better discerning.
          Ibid.
The genteel thing is the genteel thing
at any time. If so be that a gentleman
bees in a concatenation accordingly.
          Ibid.
I'll be with you in the squeezing of a
lemon.
          Ibid.
A modest woman, dressed out in all
her finery, is the most tremendous ob-
ject of the whole creation.
          Ibid. Act II

This is Liberty Hall.
          She Stoops to Conquer. Act II
They liked the book the better the
more it made them cry.
          Ibid.
Ask me no questions, and I'll tell you
no fibs.[1]
          Ibid. Act III
The very pink of courtesy and cir-
cumspection.
          Ibid. Act IV
Our Garrick's a salad; for in him we
see
Oil, vinegar, sugar, and saltness agree!
          Retaliation [1774]. *Line 11*
Here lies our good Edmund,[2] whose
  genius was such,
We scarcely can praise it, or blame it
  too much;
Who, born for the universe, narrow'd
  his mind,
And to party gave up what was meant
  for mankind . . .
Who, too deep for his hearers, still went
  on refining,
And thought of convincing, while they
  thought of dining:
Though equal to all things, for all
  things unfit;
Too nice for a statesman, too proud for
  a wit.
          Ibid. Line 29
His conduct still right, with his argument wrong.
          Ibid. Line 46
A flattering painter,[3] who made it his
  care
To draw men as they ought to be, not
  as they are.
          Ibid. Line 63
Here lies David Garrick, describe me,
  who can,
An abridgment of all that was pleasant
  in man.
          Ibid. Line 93

---

meals; (11) repeat no grievances; (12) lay
no wagers.
  Goose: A game played with counters on a
board divided into compartments, in some of
which a goose was depicted. — *Oxford English Dictionary*

[1] Them that asks no questions isn't told a
lie. — KIPLING [1865–1936]: *A Smuggler's
Song*, St. 6
[2] Edmund Burke.
[3] Richard Cumberland [1732–1811], author of such sentimental comedies as *The
West Indian* and *The Brothers.*

As a wit, if not first, in the very first
line.
> *Retaliation. Line 96*

On the stage he was natural, simple,
affecting;
'Twas only that when he was off he was
acting.
> *Ibid. Line 101*

He cast off his friends, as a huntsman
his pack,
For he knew when he pleas'd he could
whistle them back.
> *Ibid. Line 107*

Who pepper'd the highest was surest
to please.
> *Ibid. Line 112*

When they talk'd of their Raphaels,
Correggios, and stuff,
He shifted his trumpet and only took
snuff.[1]
> *Ibid. Line 145*

Such dainties to them, their health it
might hurt;
It's like sending them ruffles, when
wanting a shirt.[2]
> *The Haunch of Venison* [*1776*]

[To Dr. Johnson] If you were to
make little fishes talk, they would talk
like whales.
> BOSWELL's *Life of Dr. Johnson*
> [*1791*]. *Vol. I, Page 466, Every-*
> *man Edition*

I consider an author's literary reputation to be alive only while his name
will insure a good price for his copy
from the bookseller's.
> *Ibid. Page 468*

There is no arguing with Johnson:
for if his pistol misses fire, he knocks
you down with the butt end of it.
> *Ibid. Vol. II, Page 509*

THOMAS WARTON
[1728–1790]

All-powerful Ale! whose sorrow-sooth-
ing sweets

---

[1] Sir Joshua Reynolds, who was exceedingly
deaf.
[2] See Tom Brown, page 293a.

Oft I repeat in vacant afternoon.
> *A Panegyric on Oxford Ale* [1]

With British ale improving British
worth.
> *Ibid.*

Thus too, the matchless bard, whose
lay resounds
The Splendid Shilling's praise, in
nightly gloom
Of lonesome garret, pined for cheerful
ale.[2]
> *Ibid.*

Nor rough, nor barren, are the winding ways
Of hoar antiquity, but strewn with
flowers.
> *Written on a Blank Leaf of*
> DUGDALE's *Monasticon* [*1777*]

JOHN STARK
[1728–1822]

There, my boys, are your enemies,
redcoats and Tories. You must beat
them — or Molly Stark is a widow tonight.
> *At the Battle of Bennington,*
> *August 16, 1777*

JOHN PARKER
[1729–1775]

Stand your ground. Don't fire unless
fired upon; but if they mean to have a
war, let it begin here!
> *To his Minute Men at Lexington,*
> *April 19, 1775*

EDMUND BURKE
[1729–1797]

The writers against religion, whilst
they oppose every system, are wisely

---

[1] From *The Oxford Sausage* [*1764*], a famous miscellany of Oxford rhymes and satires, reprinted in several subsequent editions.
[2] Happy the man, who, void of care and
strife,
In silken or in leathern purse retains
A splendid shilling. He nor hears with pain
New oysters cried, nor sighs for cheerful
ale.
> JOHN PHILIPS: *The Splendid*
> *Shilling* [*1701*]

careful never to set up any of their own.

A Vindication of Natural Society [*1756*]

I am convinced that we have a degree of delight, and that no small one, in the real misfortunes and pains of others.[1]

On the Sublime and Beautiful [*1756*]. *Sect. XIV*

Custom reconciles us to everything.

Ibid. Sect. XVIII

There is, however, a limit at which forbearance ceases to be a virtue.

Observations on a Late Publication on the Present State of the Nation [*1769*]

The wisdom of our ancestors.[2]

Ibid.

When bad men combine, the good must associate; else they will fall one by one, an unpitied sacrifice in a contemptible struggle.

Thoughts on the Cause of the Present Discontents [*April 23, 1770*]

Of this stamp is the cant of, Not men, but measures;[3] a sort of charm by which many people get loose from every honourable engagement.

Ibid.

So to be patriots as not to forget we are gentlemen.

Ibid.

Public life is a situation of power and energy; he trespasses against his duty who sleeps upon his watch, as well as he that goes over to the enemy.

Ibid.

Reflect how you are to govern a people who think they ought to be free, and think they are not. Your scheme yields no revenue; it yields nothing but discontent, disorder, disobedience; and such is the state of America, that after wading up to your eyes in blood, you could only end just where you begun; that is, to tax where no revenue is to be

[1] See La Rochefoucauld, page 266a.
[2] Also in the *Discussion on the Traitorous Correspondence Bill* [1793].
[3] See Goldsmith, page 355b.

found, to — my voice fails me; my inclination indeed carries me no farther — all is confusion beyond it.

First Speech on Conciliation with America. American Taxation [*April 19, 1774*]

It ought to be the happiness and glory of a representative to live in the strictest union, the closest correspondence, and the most unreserved communication with his constituents. Their wishes ought to have great weight with him; their opinion high respect; their business unremitted attention. It is his duty to sacrifice his repose, his pleasures, his satisfaction, to theirs; and above all, ever, and in all cases, to prefer their interests to his own.

Speech to the Electors of Bristol [*November 3, 1774*]

Your representative owes you, not his industry only, but his judgment; and he betrays instead of serving you if he sacrifices it to your opinion.

Ibid.

The concessions of the weak are the concessions of fear.

Second Speech on Conciliation with America. The Thirteen Resolutions [*March 22, 1775*]

There is America, which at this day serves for little more than to amuse you with stories of savage men and uncouth manners, yet shall, before you taste of death, show itself equal to the whole of that commerce which now attracts the envy of the world.

Ibid.

When we speak of the commerce with our colonies, fiction lags after truth, invention is unfruitful, and imagination cold and barren.

Ibid.

A people who are still, as it were, but in the gristle, and not yet hardened into the bone of manhood.

Ibid.

Through a wise and salutary neglect [of the colonies], a generous nature has been suffered to take her own way to perfection; when I reflect upon these effects, when I see how profitable they have been to us, I feel all the pride of power sink and all presumption in the wisdom of human contrivances melt and die away within me. My rigour relents. I pardon something to the spirit of liberty.

Second Speech on Conciliation with America. The Thirteen Resolutions

The use of force alone is but *temporary*. It may subdue for a moment; but it does not remove the necessity of subduing again: and a nation is not governed, which is perpetually to be conquered.

Ibid.

Abstract liberty, like other mere abstractions, is not to be found.

Ibid.

The religion most prevalent in our northern colonies is a refinement on the principles of resistance: it is the dissidence of dissent, and the protestantism of the Protestant religion.

Ibid.

In no country [America] perhaps in the world is law so general a study. . . . This study renders men acute, inquisitive, dexterous, prompt in attack, ready in defence, full of resources. . . . They augur misgovernment at a distance, and snuff the approach of tyranny in every tainted breeze.

Ibid.

I do not know the method of drawing up an indictment against an whole people.

Ibid.

It is not, what a lawyer tells me I *may* do; but what humanity, reason, and justice, tell me I ought to do.

Ibid.

The march of the human mind is slow.

Ibid.

Freedom and not servitude is the cure of anarchy; as religion, and not atheism, is the true remedy for superstition.

Ibid.

All government — indeed, every human benefit and enjoyment, every virtue and every prudent act — is founded on compromise and barter.

Second Speech on Conciliation with America. The Thirteen Resolutions

Instead of a standing revenue, you will have therefore a perpetual quarrel.

Ibid.

Slavery they can have anywhere. It is a weed that grows in every soil.

Ibid.

Deny them this participation of freedom, and you break that sole bond, which originally made, and must still preserve the unity of the empire.

Ibid.

It is the love of the British people; it is their attachment to their government, from the sense of the deep stake they have in such a glorious institution, which gives you both your army and your navy, and infuses into both that liberal obedience, without which your army would be a base rabble, and your navy nothing but rotten timber.

Ibid.

Magnanimity in politics is not seldom the truest wisdom; and a great empire and little minds go ill together.

Ibid.

By adverting to the dignity of this high calling, our ancestors have turned a savage wilderness into a glorious empire: and have made the most extensive, and the only honourable conquests, not by destroying, but by promoting the wealth, the number, the happiness of the human race.

Ibid.

He was not merely a chip of the old block, but the old block itself.

On Pitt's First Speech [February 26, 1781]. From WRAXALL'S *Memoirs, First Series, Vol. I, Page 342*

The people never give up their liberties but under some delusion.

Speech at County Meeting of Buckinghamshire [1784]

There never was a bad man that had ability for good service.

Speech in Opening the Impeachment of Warren Hastings [*1788*]

They made and recorded a sort of institute and digest of anarchy, called the Rights of Man.

On the Army Estimates [*1790*]

People will not look forward to posterity who never look backward to their ancestors.[1]

Reflections on the Revolution in France [*1790*]

You had that action and counter-action which, in the natural and in the political world, from the reciprocal struggle of discordant powers draws out the harmony of the universe.

Ibid.

The unbought grace of life, the cheap defence of nations, the nurse of manly sentiment and heroic enterprise is gone.

Ibid.

That chastity of honour which felt a stain like a wound.

Ibid.

Vice itself lost half its evil by losing all its grossness.

Ibid.

Kings will be tyrants from policy, when subjects are rebels from principle.

Ibid.

Learning will be cast into the mire and trodden down under the hoofs of a swinish multitude.

Ibid.

Because half-a-dozen grasshoppers under a fern make the field ring with their importunate chink, whilst thousands of great cattle, reposed beneath the shadow of the British oak, chew the cud and are silent, pray do not imagine that those who make the noise are the only inhabitants of the field; that of course they are many in number; or that, after all, they are other than the little shrivelled, meagre, hopping, though loud and

troublesome insects of the hour.

Reflections on the Revolution in France

In their nomination to office they will not appoint to the exercise of authority as to a pitiful job, but as to a holy function.

Ibid.

He that wrestles with us strengthens our nerves and sharpens our skill. Our antagonist is our helper.

Ibid.

To execute laws is a royal office; to execute orders is not to be a king. However, a political executive magistracy, though merely such, is a great trust.[1]

Ibid.

You can never plan the future by the past.[2]

Letter to a Member of the National Assembly [*1791*]

The cold neutrality of an impartial judge.

Preface to Brissot's Address [*1794*]

All men that are ruined, are ruined on the side of their natural propensities.

On a Regicide Peace [*1796*]

Example is the school of mankind, and they will learn at no other.

Ibid.

Mere parsimony is not economy. . . . Expense, and great expense, may be an essential part of true economy.

Letter to a Noble Lord [*1796*]

Economy is a distributive virtue, and consists not in saving but in selection. Parsimony requires no providence, no sagacity, no powers of combination, no comparison, no judgment.

Ibid.

I would rather sleep in the southern corner of a little country churchyard than in the tomb of the Capulets.

Letter to Matthew Smith

And having looked to Government

---

[1] The Democratic Party is like a mule — without pride of ancestry or hope of posterity. — IGNATIUS DONNELLY [1831–1901]: *Speech in the Minnesota Legislature*

[1] See Mathew Henry, page 293a, Jefferson, page 375a, Clay, page 433b, and Calhoun, page 442a.

[2] See Patrick Henry, page 368b.

for bread, on the very first scarcity they will turn and bite the hand that fed them.
Thoughts and Details on Scarcity [1800]

JOHN SCOTT
[1730–1783]

I hate that drum's discordant sound,
Parading round, and round, and round:
To me it talks of ravaged plains,
And burning towns, and ruined swains,
And mangled limbs, and dying groans,
And widows' tears, and orphans' moans;
And all that Misery's hand bestows
To fill the catalogue of human woes.
I Hate That Drum's Discordant Sound. Stanza 2

JOSIAH WEDGWOOD
[1730–1795]

Am I not a man and brother?
On a Medallion [1] *[1787]*

CHARLES CHURCHILL
[1731–1764]

He mouths a sentence as curs mouth a bone.
The Rosciad [1761]. Line 322
But, spite of all the criticising elves,
Those who would make us feel — must feel themselves.[2]
Ibid. Line 961
Apt alliteration's artful aid.
The Prophecy of Famine [1763]. Line 86
There webs were spread of more than common size,
And half-starved spiders prey'd on half-starved flies.
Ibid. Line 327

[1] Representing a Negro in chains, with one knee on the ground and both hands lifted up to heaven. This was adopted as a seal by the Anti-Slavery Society of London.
[2] *Si vis me flere, dolendum est Primum ipsi tibi*
(If you wish me to weep, you yourself must first feel grief).
HORACE [65–8 B.C.]: *Ars Poetica, L. 102*

With curious art the brain, too finely wrought,
Preys on herself, and is destroyed by thought.
Epistle to William Hogarth [1763]. Line 645
Men the most infamous are fond of fame,
And those who fear not guilt yet start at shame.
The Author [1763]. Line 233
Be England what she will,
With all her faults she is my country still.[1]
The Farewell. Line 27

WILLIAM COWPER
[1731–1800]

What peaceful hours I once enjoy'd!
How sweet their memory still!
But they have left an aching void
The world can never fill.
Olney Hymns [1779]. Walking with God
God moves in a mysterious way
His wonders to perform;
He plants his footsteps in the sea
And rides upon the storm.
Ibid. Light Shining out of Darkness
Behind a frowning providence
He hides a shining face.
Ibid.
Happiness depends, as Nature shows,
Less on exterior things than most suppose.
Table Talk [1782]. Line 246
Freedom has a thousand charms to show,

[1] England, with all thy faults I love thee still,
My country!
COWPER: *The Task [1784], Book II, The Timepiece, L. 206*
Our country! In her intercourse with foreign nations may she always be in the right; but our country, right or wrong. — STEPHEN DECATUR: *Toast given at Norfolk [April, 1816]*
I hope to find my country in the right: however, I will stand by her, right or wrong. — JOHN JORDAN CRITTENDEN [1787–1863]: *On the Mexican War*

That slaves, howe'er contented, never know.

> *Table Talk. Line 260*

Manner is all in all, whate'er is writ,
The substitute for genius, sense, and wit.

> *Ibid. Line 542*

Low ambition and the thirst of praise.[1]

> *Ibid. Line 591*

Made poetry a mere mechanic art.

> *Ibid. Line 654*

Lights of the world, and stars of human race.

> *The Progress of Error [1782].*
> *Line 97*

How much a dunce that has been sent to roam
Excels a dunce that has been kept at home!

> *Ibid. Line 415*

A fool must now and then be right by chance.

> *Conversation [1782]. Line 96*

He would not, with a peremptory tone,
Assert the nose upon his face his own.

> *Ibid. Line 121*

A moral, sensible, and well-bred man
Will not affront me, — and no other can.

> *Ibid. Line 193*

Pernicious weed![2] whose scent the fair annoys,
Unfriendly to society's chief joys:
Thy worst effect is banishing for hours
The sex whose presence civilizes ours.

> *Ibid. Line 251*

I cannot talk with civet in the room,
A fine puss-gentleman that's all perfume.

> *Ibid. Line 283*

Our wasted oil unprofitably burns,
Like hidden lamps in old sepulchral urns.

> *Ibid. Line 357*

A business with an income at its heels
Furnishes always oil for its own wheels.

> *Retirement [1782]. Line 615*

Absence of occupation is not rest,[3]

A mind quite vacant is a mind distress'd.

> *Retirement. Line 623*

An idler is a watch that wants both hands,
As useless if it goes as if it stands.

> *Ibid. Line 681*

Built God a church, and laugh'd His word to scorn.[1]

> *Ibid. Line 688*

Philologists, who chase
A panting syllable through time and space,
Start it at home, and hunt it in the dark
To Gaul, to Greece, and into Noah's ark.

> *Ibid. Line 691*

I praise the Frenchman,[2] his remark was shrewd, —
How sweet, how passing sweet, is solitude!
But grant me still a friend in my retreat,
Whom I may whisper, Solitude is sweet.

> *Ibid. Line 739*

I am monarch of all I survey,
My right there is none to dispute.

> *Verses Supposed to be Written*
> *by Alexander Selkirk [1782].*
> *Stanza 1*

O Solitude! where are the charms
That sages have seen in thy face?

> *Ibid.*

How fleet is a glance of the mind!
Compared with the speed of its flight
The tempest itself lags behind,
And the swift-winged arrows of light.

> *Ibid. Stanza 6*

There goes the parson, O illustrious spark!
And there, scarce less illustrious, goes the clerk.

> *On Observing Some Names of*
> *Little Note [1782]*

That though on pleasure she was bent,
She had a frugal mind.

> *History of John Gilpin [1785].*
> *Stanza 8*

---

[1] See Pope, page 315b.
[2] Tobacco.
[3] See John Sullivan Dwight, page 583a.

[1] Voltaire, who built a church at Ferney [1760–1761], with the inscription "Deo erexit Voltaire."
[2] La Bruyère.

A hat not much the worse for wear.
History of John Gilpin. Stanza 46

Now let us sing, Long live the king,
And Gilpin, Long live he;
And when he next doth ride abroad,
May I be there to see!
Ibid. Stanza 63

God made the country, and man made the town.[1]
The Task [1785]. *Book I,*
The Sofa, Line 749

Oh for a lodge in some vast wilderness,[2]
Some boundless contiguity of shade,
Where rumour of oppression and deceit,
Of unsuccessful or successful war,
Might never reach me more.
Ibid. Book II, The Timepiece,
Line 1

Mountains interposed
Make enemies of nations, who had else
Like kindred drops been mingled into one.
Ibid. Line 17

Slaves cannot breathe in England; if their lungs
Receive our air, that moment they are free!
They touch our country, and their shackles fall.
Ibid. Line 40

Presume to lay their hand upon the ark[3]
Of her magnificent and awful cause.
Ibid. Line 231

Transforms old print
To zigzag manuscript, and cheats the eyes
Of gallery critics by a thousand arts.
Ibid. Line 363

Variety's the very spice of life.[4]
Ibid. Line 606

[1] See Bacon, page 121a.
[2] Oh that I had in the wilderness a lodging-place of wayfaring men! — *Jeremiah, IX, 2*
See Byron, page 454b.
[3] Uzzah put forth his hand to the ark of God, and took hold of it . . . and the anger of the Lord was kindled against Uzzah. — *2 Samuel, VI, 6–7*
[4] See Publilius Syrus, page 44b.

His head,
Not yet by time completely silver'd o'er,
Bespoke him past the bounds of freakish youth,
But strong for service still, and unimpair'd.
The Task. Book II, The
Timepiece, Line 702

Guilty splendour.
Ibid. Book III, The Garden,
Line 70

I was a stricken deer[1] that left the herd
Long since.
Ibid. Line 108

Great contest follows, and much learned dust.
Ibid. Line 161

From reveries so airy, from the toil
Of dropping buckets into empty wells,
And growing old in drawing nothing up.[2]
Ibid. Line 188

Riches have wings,[3] and grandeur is a dream.
Ibid. Line 265

Who loves a garden loves a greenhouse too.
Ibid. Line 566

Now stir the fire, and close the shutters fast,
Let fall the curtains, wheel the sofa round,
And while the bubbling and loud-hissing urn
Throws up a steamy column, and the cups
That cheer but not inebriate wait on each,
So let us welcome peaceful evening in.
Ibid. Book IV, The Winter
Evening, Line 36

'Tis pleasant, through the loopholes of retreat,
To peep at such a world, to see the stir
Of the great Babel; and not feel the crowd.
Ibid. Line 88

[1] See Shakespeare, page 176a.
[2] See Sydney Smith, page 419a.
[3] Riches certainly make themselves wings. — *Proverbs, XXIII, 5*

O Winter, ruler of the inverted year! [1]
> *The Task. Book IV, The Winter*
> *Evening, Line 120*

With spots quadrangular of diamond form,
Ensanguined hearts, clubs typical of strife,
And spades, the emblems of untimely graves.
> *Ibid. Line 217*

In indolent vacuity of thought.[2]
> *Ibid. Line 297*

It seems the part of wisdom.
> *Ibid. Line 336*

All learned, and all drunk!
> *Ibid. Line 478*

Gloriously drunk, obey the important call.
> *Ibid. Line 510*

Silently as a dream the fabric rose;
No sound of hammer or of saw was there.[3]
> *Ibid. Book V, The Winter*
> *Morning Walk, Line 144*

But war's a game, which, were their subjects wise,
Kings would not play at.
> *Ibid. Line 187*

There is in souls a sympathy with sounds;
And as the mind is pitch'd the ear is pleased
With melting airs or martial, brisk or grave;
Some chord in unison with what we hear
Is touch'd within us, and the heart replies.
How soft the music of those village bells

Falling at intervals upon the ear
In cadence sweet!
> *The Task. Book VI, Winter Walk*
> *at Noon, Line 1*

Here the heart
May give a useful lesson to the head,
And Learning wiser grow without his books.
> *Ibid. Line 85*

Knowledge is proud that he has learn'd so much;
Wisdom is humble that he knows no more.
> *Ibid. Line 96*

An honest man, close-button'd to the chin,
Broadcloth without, and a warm heart within.
> *Epistle to Joseph Hill [1785]*

Shine by the side of every path we tread
With such a lustre, he that runs may read.[1]
> *Tirocinium [1785]. Line 79*

Toll for the brave!
 The brave that are no more,
All sunk beneath the wave,
 Fast by their native shore!
> *On the Loss of the Royal George [2]*
> *[1791]. Stanza 1*

And still to love, though prest with ill,
In wintry age to feel no chill,
With me is to be lovely still,
 My Mary!
> *To Mary [1791]. Stanza 11*

Beware of desp'rate steps! The darkest day
(Live till tomorrow) will have pass'd away.
> *The Needless Alarm [1794].*
> *Moral*

---

[1] See Thomson, page 327b.
[2] See Samuel Johnson, page 340a.
[3] So that there was neither hammer nor axe, nor any tool of iron heard in the house while it was in building. — *1 Kings, VI, 7*

No hammers fell, no ponderous axes rung,
Like some tall palm the mystic fabric sprung,
Majestic silence!
>   REGINALD HEBER [1783–1826]:
>   *Palestine*

[1] Write the vision, and make it plain, upon tables, that he may run that readeth it. — *Habakkuk, II, 2*
[2] The *Royal George* was an English man-of-war of 108 guns, which suddenly heeled over, under the strain caused by the shifting of her guns, while being refitted at Spithead, August 29, 1782. The commander, Admiral Kempenfeldt, and eight hundred of the sailors, marines, and visitors on board, were drowned.

I shall not ask Jean Jacques Rousseau
If birds confabulate or no.
> *Pairing Time Anticipated*
> [*Circa 1794*]

Misses! the tale that I relate
This lesson seems to carry, —
Choose not alone a proper mate,
But proper time to marry.
> *Ibid. Moral*

Oh that those lips had language! Life
has pass'd
With me but roughly since I heard thee
last.
> *On the Receipt of My Mother's*
> *Picture* [*1798*]

ERASMUS DARWIN
[*1731–1802*]

No radiant pearl which crested For-
tune wears,
No gem that twinkling hangs from
Beauty's ears,
Not the bright stars which Night's
blue arch adorn,
Nor rising suns that gild the vernal
morn,
Shine with such lustre as the tear that
flows
Down Virtue's manly cheek for others'
woes.
> *The Botanic Garden. Part II*
> [*1789*], *Canto III, Line 459*

CHARLES LEE
[*1731–1782*]

Beware that your Northern laurels
do not change to Southern willows.[1]
> *To General Horatio Gates after*
> *surrender of Burgoyne at Sara-*
> *toga* [*October 17, 1777*]

BEILBY PORTEUS
[*1731–1808*]

One murder made a villain,
Millions, a hero. Princes were privileged

[1] Gates was later defeated by Cornwallis at
Camden, South Carolina [August 16, 1780],
and was relieved of his command.

To kill, and numbers sanctified the
crime.[1]
> *Death. Line 154*

War its thousands slays, Peace, its ten
thousands.
> *Ibid. Line 178*

Love is something so divine,
Description would but make it less;
'Tis what I feel, but can't define,
'Tis what I know, but can't express.
> *On Love*

GEORGE WASHINGTON
[*1732–1799*]

Labour to keep alive in your breast
that little spark of celestial fire, —
conscience.
> *Rule from the copybook of*
> *Washington when a schoolboy.*
> JARED SPARKS'S *Life of Wash-*
> *ington* [*1839*], *Vol. II, Page*
> *109*

When is the time for brave men to
exert themselves in the cause of liberty
and their country, if this is not? Should
any difficulties that they may have to
encounter at this important crisis, deter
them? God knows, there is not a difficulty, that you both [Schuyler and
General Montgomery] very justly complain of, which I have not in an eminent
degree experienced, that I am not every
day experiencing; but we must bear up
against them, and make the best of
mankind as they are, since we cannot
have them as we wish.
> *To Major General Philip Schuyler*
> [*December 24, 1775*]

It follows then as certain as that
night succeeds the day, that without a
decisive Naval force we can do nothing
definitive. And with it, every thing
honourable and glorious.
> *To Lafayette* [*November 15,*
> *1781*]

If men are to be precluded from offering their sentiments on a matter,
which may involve the most serious and
alarming consequences that can invite
the consideration of mankind, reason is

[1] See Young, page 305a.

of no use to us; the freedom of speech may be taken away, and dumb and silent we may be led, like sheep to the slaughter.

Address to Officers of the Army [March 15, 1783]

Almighty God, we make our earnest prayer that Thou wilt keep the United States in Thy holy protection; that Thou wilt incline the hearts of the citizens to cultivate a spirit of subordination and obedience to government; to entertain a brotherly affection and love for one another and for their fellow-citizens of the United States at large.

Prayer after Inauguration [1789]

To be prepared for war is one of the most effectual means of preserving peace.[1]

First Annual Address, to both Houses of Congress [January 8, 1790]

The basis of our political system is the right of the people to make and to alter their constitutions of government.

Farewell Address [September 17, 1796]

Let me now . . . warn you in the most solemn manner against the baneful effects of the spirit of party.

Ibid.

Observe good faith and justice toward all nations. Cultivate peace and harmony with all. . . . The nation which indulges toward another an habitual hatred or an habitual fondness is in some degree a slave. It is a slave to its animosity or to its affection, either of which is sufficient to lead it astray from its duty and its interest.

Ibid.

It is our true policy to steer clear of permanent alliances with any portion of the foreign world.

Ibid.

There can be no greater error than to expect or calculate upon real favors from nation to nation.

Ibid.

[1] See Horace, page 40b, and Burton, page 223a.

PIERRE DE BEAUMARCHAIS
[1732–1799]

I quickly laugh at everything, for fear of having to cry.[1]

Le Barbier de Séville [1775]. Act I, Sc. 2

If you assure me that your intentions are honourable.

Ibid. Act IV, Sc. 6

JOHN ADAMS
[1735–1826]

All great changes are irksome to the human mind, especially those which are attended with great dangers and uncertain effects.

Letter to James Warren [April 22, 1776]

Yesterday the greatest question was decided which ever was debated in America; and a greater perhaps never was, nor will be, decided among men. A resolution was passed without one dissenting colony, that these United Colonies are, and of right ought to be, free and independent States.

Letter to Abigail Adams [July 3, 1776]

The second day of July, 1776,[2] will be the most memorable epocha in the history of America. I am apt to believe that it will be celebrated by succeeding generations as the great anniversary festival. It ought to be commemorated as the day of deliverance, by solemn acts of devotion to God Almighty. It ought to be solemnized with pomp and parade, with shows, games, sports, guns, bells, bonfires, and illuminations, from one end of this continent to the other, from this time forward for evermore.

Ibid.

[1] Je me presse de rire de tout, de peur d'être obligé d'en pleurer.

See Byron, page 458b, and Lincoln, page 540a.

[2] On July 2, 1776, the resolution for independence, drafted by Richard Henry Lee of Virginia, was adopted by a committee including John Adams. On July 4 the Declaration of Independence was agreed to, en-

The happiness of society is the end of government.
> *Thoughts on Government* [*1776*]

Fear is the foundation of most governments.
> *Ibid.*

Where annual elections end, there slavery begins.
> *Ibid.*

The judicial power ought to be distinct from both the legislative and executive, and independent upon both, that so it may be a check upon both.
> *Ibid.*

A government of laws, and not of men.
> *Original Draft of Massachusetts Constitution* [*1779*]

JAMES BEATTIE
[1735–1803]

He thought as a sage, though he felt as a man.
> *The Hermit*

ISAAC BICKERSTAFF
[1735–1812?]

There was a jolly miller once lived on the River Dee;
He worked and sang from morn till night; no lark more blithe than he.
> *Love in a Village* [*1762*].
> *Act I, Sc. 2*

And this the burthen of his song, for ever used to be,
"I care for nobody, not I, if no one cares for me." [1]
> *Ibid.*

JOHN LANGHORNE
[1735–1779]

The child of misery, baptized in tears.
> *The Country Justice. Part I*

---

grossed, signed by John Hancock, and sent to the legislatures of the States.

[1] Naebody cares for me,
I care for naebody.
> ROBERT BURNS [1759–1796]: *I Hae a Wife o' My Ain*, St. 4

I envy none, no, no, not I,
And no one envies me.
> CHARLES MACKAY [1814–1889]: *The King and the Miller*

WILLIAM JULIUS MICKLE
[1735–1788]

The dews of summer nights did fall,
The moon (sweet regent of the sky) [1]
Silvered the walls of Cumnor Hall
And many an oak that grew thereby.
> *Cumnor Hall* [*1784*]. *Stanza 1*

For there's nae luck about the house,
There's nae luck at a';
There's little pleasure in the house
When our gudeman's awa.
> *The Mariner's Wife. Stanza 1*

CHARLES JOSEPH, PRINCE DE LIGNE
[1735–1814]

The Congress doesn't run — it waltzes. [2]
> *Comment to La Garde–Chambonacs* [*1814*]

PATRICK HENRY
[1736–1799]

Caesar had his Brutus; Charles the First his Cromwell; and George the Third ["Treason!" cried the Speaker] — *may profit by their example*. If *this* be treason, make the most of it.
> *Speech on the Stamp Act, House of Burgesses, Williamsburg, Virginia* [*May 29, 1765*]

I am not a Virginian, but an American.
> *Speech in First Continental Congress, Philadelphia* [*October 14, 1774*]

I have but one lamp by which my feet are guided, and that is the lamp of experience. I know no way of judging of the future but by the past. [3]
> *Speech in Virginia Convention, St. John's Episcopal Church, Richmond, Virginia* [*March 23, 1775*]

We are not weak if we make a proper

[1] Now Cynthia, named fair regent of the night. — GAY: *Trivia* [1716], *Book III*
[2] Le Congrès ne marche pas, il danse. Said of the Congress of Vienna.
[3] See Burke, page 361b.

use of those means which the God of Nature has placed in our power. . . . The battle, sir, is not to the strong alone; [1] it is to the vigilant, the active, the brave.

> *Speech in Virginia Convention, St. John's Episcopal Church, Richmond, Virginia*

Is life so dear, or peace so sweet, as to be purchased at the price of chains and slavery? Forbid it, Almighty God! I know not what course others may take, but as for me, give me liberty, or give me death!

> *Ibid.*

EDWARD GIBBON
[1737–1794]

The various modes of worship, which prevailed in the Roman world, were all considered by the people as equally true; by the philosopher, as equally false; and by the magistrate, as equally useful.

> *Decline and Fall of the Roman Empire [1776–1788]. Chap. 2*

The reign of Antoninus is marked by the rare advantage of furnishing very few materials for history; which is indeed little more than the register of the crimes, follies, and misfortunes of mankind.[2]

> *Ibid. Chap. 3*

It has been calculated by the ablest politicians that no State, without being soon exhausted, can maintain above the hundredth part of its members in arms and idleness.

> *Ibid. Chap. 5*

In every deed of mischief he [Adronicus] had a heart to resolve, a head to contrive, and a hand to execute.[3]

> *Ibid. Chap. 48*

[1] The race is not to the swift, nor the battle to the strong. — *Ecclesiastes, IX, 11*
[2] See Voltaire, page 325b.
[3] He [Hampden] had a head to contrive, a tongue to persuade, and a hand to execute any mischief. — EDWARD HYDE, EARL OF CLARENDON [1608–1674]: *History of the Rebellion* [1702–1704], *Vol. III, Book 7, Sect. 84*
See Junius, page 1002a.

Our sympathy is cold to the relation of distant misery.

> *Decline and Fall of the Roman Empire. Chap. 49*

The winds and waves are always on the side of the ablest navigators.[1]

> *Ibid. Chap. 68*

Vicissitudes of fortune, which spares neither man nor the proudest of his works, which buries empires and cities in a common grave.

> *Ibid. Chap. 71*

All that is human must retrograde if it do not advance.

> *Ibid.*

I saw and loved.

> *Memoirs*

On the approach of spring I withdrew without reluctance from the noisy and extensive scene of crowds without company, and dissipation without pleasure.

> *Ibid.*

RUDOLF ERICH RASPE
[1737–1794]

What in the dark I had taken to be a stump of a little tree appearing above the snow, to which I had tied my horse, proved to have been the weathercock of the church steeple.

> *Travels of Baron Munchausen [1785]. Chap. 2*

We all did our duty, which, in the patriot's, soldier's, and gentleman's language, is a very comprehensive word, of great honour, meaning, and import.

> *Ibid. Chap. 5*

The sprigs took root in my horse's body, grew up, and formed a bower over me.

> *Ibid.*

His tunes were frozen up in the horn, and came out now by thawing.[2]

> *Ibid. Chap. 6*

If any of the company entertain a doubt of my veracity, I shall only say to such, I pity their want of faith.

> *Ibid.*

[1] See Voltaire, page 325b.
[2] See Plutarch, page 61a.

I had the very sling in my pocket which assisted David in slaying Goliath.
Travels of Baron Munchausen.
Chap. 10

Upon this island of cheese grows great plenty of corn, the ears of which produce loaves of bread, ready made.
Ibid. Chap. 20

I have ever confined myself to facts.
Ibid.

A traveller has a right to relate and embellish his adventures as he pleases, and it is very unpolite to refuse that deference and applause they deserve.
Ibid. Chap. 21

There is a right and wrong handle to everything.[1]
Ibid. Chap. 30

THOMAS PAINE
[1737–1809]

From the east to the west blow the
trumpet to arms!
Through the land let the sound of it
flee;
Let the far and the near all unite, with
a cheer,
In defence of our Liberty Tree.
The Liberty Tree [*July, 1775*].
Stanza 4

Society in every state is a blessing, but government, even in its best state, is but a necessary evil; in its worst state, an intolerable one.
Common Sense [*1776*]

Suspicion is the companion of mean souls, and the bane of all good society.
Ibid.

When we are planning for posterity, we ought to remember that virtue is not hereditary.
Ibid.

These are the times that try men's souls. The summer soldier and the sunshine patriot will, in this crisis, shrink from the service of his country; but he that stands it *now*, deserves the love and thanks of man and woman. Tyranny, like hell, is not easily conquered; yet we have this consolation with us,

[1] See Epictetus, page 65a.

that the harder the conflict, the more glorious the triumph. What we obtain too cheap, we esteem too lightly; 'tis dearness only that gives everything its value. Heaven knows how to put a proper price upon its goods; and it would be strange indeed, if so celestial an article as *Freedom* should not be highly rated.
The American Crisis. No. I
[*December 23, 1776*]

Panics, in some cases, have their uses; they produce as much good as hurt. Their duration is always short; the mind soon grows through them and acquires a firmer habit than before. But their peculiar advantage is, that they are the touchstone of sincerity and hypocrisy, and bring things and men to light, which might otherwise have lain forever undiscovered.
Ibid.

Not a place upon earth might be so happy as America. Her situation is remote from all the wrangling world, and she has nothing to do but to trade with them.
Ibid.

A bad cause will ever be supported by bad means and bad men.
Ibid. No. II [*January 13, 1777*]

Those who expect to reap the blessings of freedom must, like men, undergo the fatigue of supporting it.
Ibid. No. IV [*September 12, 1777*]

It is not a field of a few acres of ground, but a cause, that we are defending, and whether we defeat the enemy in one battle, or by degrees, the consequences will be the same.
Ibid.

We fight not to enslave, but to set a country free, and to make room upon the earth for honest men to live in.
Ibid.

It is the object only of war that makes it honourable. And if there was ever a *just* war since the world began, it is this in which America is now engaged.
Ibid. No. V [*March 21, 1778*]

Character is much easier kept than recovered.
The American Crisis. No. XIII
[April 19, 1783]

War involves in its progress such a train of unforeseen and unsupposed circumstances that no human wisdom can calculate the end. It has but one thing certain, and that is to increase taxes.
Prospects on the Rubicon [1787]

[Burke] is not affected by the reality of distress touching his heart, but by the showy resemblance of it striking his imagination. He pities the plumage, but forgets the dying bird.
Rights of Man. Part I [1791]

My country is the world, and my religion is to do good.[1]
Ibid. Part II [1792], Chap. 5

And the final event to himself [Burke] has been, that, as he rose like a rocket, he fell like a stick.
Letter to the Addressers

I believe in one God and no more, and I hope for happiness beyond this life. I believe in the equality of man; and I believe that religious duties consist in doing justice, loving mercy, and endeavoring to make our fellow-creatures happy.
The Age of Reason [1793]. Part I

It is with a pious fraud as with a bad action; it begets a calamitous necessity of going on.
Ibid.

When authors and critics talk of the sublime, they see not how nearly it borders on the ridiculous.[2]
Ibid. Part II, Note

JACQUES DELILLE
[1738-1813]

Fate makes our relatives, choice makes our friends.
La Pitié [1803]. Canto I

[1] See W. L. Garrison, page 517a.
[2] See Napoleon, page 399b.

JOHN WOLCOT
("PETER PINDAR")
[1738-1819]

What rage for fame attends both great and small!
Better be damned than mentioned not at all.
To the Royal Academicians

Care to our coffin adds a nail, no doubt,
And every grin so merry draws one out.
Expostulatory Odes. XV

HESTER LYNCH THRALE
(PIOZZI)
[1739-1821]

The tree of deepest root is found
Least willing still to quit the ground:
'Twas therefore said by ancient sages,
That love of life increased with years
So much, that in our latter stages,
When pain grows sharp and sickness rages,
The greatest love of life appears.
Three Warnings

Johnson's conversation was by much too strong for a person accustomed to obsequiousness and flattery; it was mustard in a young child's mouth.
Quoted in BOSWELL's Life of Dr. Johnson [1791], Vol. II, Page 396, Everyman Edition

DANIEL BLISS
[1740-1806]

God wills us free, man wills us slaves,
I will as God wills, God's will be done.
Epitaph on gravestone of John Jack, "A Native of Africa, who died March 1773, aged about 60 years. Tho' born in a land of slavery he was born free."

JAMES BOSWELL
[1740-1795]

See also under SAMUEL JOHNSON

That favourite subject, Myself.
Letter to Temple [July 26, 1763]

We cannot tell the precise moment when friendship is formed. As in filling a vessel drop by drop, there is at last a drop which makes it run over; so in a series of kindnesses there is at last one which makes the heart run over.

> *Life of Dr. Johnson* [*1791*],
> *Everyman Edition, Vol. II,*
> *Page 122*

I think no innocent species of wit or pleasantry should be suppressed; and that a good pun may be admitted among the smaller excellencies of lively conversation.

> *Ibid. Page 537*

AUGUSTUS MONTAGUE TOPLADY
[1740–1778]

Rock of Ages, cleft for me,
Let me hide myself in thee.
> *Rock of Ages* [*1775*]. *Stanza 1*

LOUIS SÉBASTIEN MERCIER
[1740–1814]

Extremes meet.
> *Tableaux de Paris* [*1782*].
> *Vol. IV, Chap. 348, Title*

SÉBASTIEN R. N. CHAMFORT
[1741–1794]

The most wasted day of all is that on which we have not laughed.
> *Maxims and Thoughts. 1*

Chance is a nickname for Providence.
> *Ibid. 62*

JOHANN KASPAR LAVATER
[1741–1801]

Say not you know another entirely, till you have divided an inheritance with him.
> *Aphorisms on Man* [1] [Circa
> *1788*]. *No. 157*

He who, when called upon to speak a disagreeable truth, tells it boldly and has done is both bolder and milder than

[1] These Aphorisms were much admired and privately annotated by WILLIAM BLAKE. See the one-volume edition of BLAKE'S *Poetry and Prose*, edited by GEOFFREY KEYNES.

he who nibbles in a low voice and never ceases nibbling.[1]
> *Aphorisms on Man. No. 302*

Trust not him with your secrets, who, when left alone in your room, turns over your papers.
> *Ibid. No. 449*

The public seldom forgive twice.
> *Ibid. No. 606*

Venerate four characters: the sanguine, who has checked volatility and the rage for pleasure; the choleric who has subdued passion and pride; the phlegmatic emerged from indolence; and the melancholy who has dismissed avarice, suspicion and asperity.
> *Ibid. No. 609*

If you mean to know yourself, interline such of these aphorisms as affect you agreeably in reading, and set a mark to such as left a sense of uneasiness with you; and then shew your copy to whom you please.
> *Ibid. No. 643*

WILLIAM PALEY
[1743–1805]

Who can refute a sneer?
> *Moral Philosophy* [*1785*]. *Vol. II,*
> *Book V, Chap. 9*

ANNA LETITIA (AIKIN) BARBAULD
[1743–1825]

Life! we've been long together
Through pleasant and through cloudy
    weather;
'Tis hard to part when friends are
    dear,—
Perhaps 'twill cost a sigh, a tear;
Then steal away, give little warning,
    Choose thine own time;
Say not "Good night," but in some
    brighter clime
Bid me "Good morning."
> *Life. Stanza 3*

This dead of midnight is the noon of
    thought.
> *A Summer's Evening Meditation*

[1] Blake's marginal comment on this was "Damn such!"

THOMAS JEFFERSON
[1743–1826]

A lively and lasting sense of filial duty is more effectually impressed on the mind of a son or daughter by reading King Lear, than by all the dry volumes of ethics, and divinity, that ever were written.

Letter to Robert Skipwith
[August 3, 1771]

The God who gave us life, gave us liberty at the same time.

Summary View of the Rights of
British America [1774]

When, in the course of human events, it becomes necessary for one people to dissolve the political bands which have connected them with another, and to assume among the powers of the earth the separate and equal station to which the laws of nature and of nature's God [1] entitle them, a decent respect to the opinions of mankind requires that they should declare the causes which impel them to the separation. We hold these truths to be self-evident; that all men are created equal; that they are endowed by their creator with certain unalienable rights; [2] that among these are life, liberty, and the pursuit of happiness; that to secure these rights, governments are instituted among men, deriving their just powers from the consent of the governed; that whenever any form of government becomes destructive to these ends, it is the right of the people to alter or to abolish it, and to institute new government, laying its foundation on such principles, and organizing its powers in such form, as to them shall seem most likely to effect their safety and happiness.

Declaration of Independence
[July 4, 1776]

[1] See Bolingbroke, page 304a.
[2] The phrase is frequently misquoted "inalienable."
All men are born free and equal, and have certain natural, essential and unalienable rights. — *Constitution of Massachusetts* [1778]

We must therefore . . . hold them [the British] as we hold the rest of mankind, enemies in war, in peace friends.

Declaration of Independence

And for the support of this declaration, with a firm reliance on the protection of divine providence, we mutually pledge to each other our lives, our fortunes, and our sacred honor.

Ibid.

Ignorance is preferable to error; and he is less remote from the truth who believes nothing, than he who believes what is wrong.

Notes on the State of Virginia
[1781–1785]. Query VI

A single zealot may commence persecutor, and better men be his victims.

Ibid. Query XVII

Indeed, I tremble for my country when I reflect that God is just.

Ibid. Query XVIII

Those who labor in the earth are the chosen people of God, if ever he had a chosen people, whose breasts He has made His peculiar deposit for substantial and genuine virtue.

Ibid. Query XIX

He who permits himself to tell a lie once, finds it much easier to do it a second and third time, till at length it becomes habitual; he tells lies without attending to it, and truths without the world's believing him. This falsehood of the tongue leads to that of the heart, and in time depraves all its good dispositions.

Letter to Peter Carr [August 19, 1785]

The basis of our government being the opinion of the people, the very first object should be to keep that right; and were it left to me to decide whether we should have a government without newspapers, or newspapers without a government, I should not hesitate a moment to prefer the latter.

Letter to Colonel Edward Carrington [January 16, 1787]

Experience declares that man is the only animal which devours his own kind; for I can apply no milder term to the governments of Europe, and to the general prey of the rich on the poor.

Letter to Colonel Edward Carrington [January 16, 1787]

I hold it, that a little rebellion, now and then, is a good thing, and as necessary in the political world as storms in the physical.

Letter to James Madison [January 30, 1787]

What country before ever existed a century and a half without a rebellion? . . . The tree of liberty must be refreshed from time to time with the blood of patriots and tyrants. It is its natural manure.

Letter to William Stevens Smith [November 13, 1787]

The republican is the only form of government which is not eternally at open or secret war with the rights of mankind.

Letter to William Hunter [March 11, 1790]

We are not to expect to be translated from despotism to liberty in a featherbed.

Letter to Lafayette [April 2, 1790]

Let what will be said or done, preserve your *sang froid* immovably, and to every obstacle, oppose patience, perseverance, and soothing language.

Letter to William Short [March 18, 1792]

Delay is preferable to error.

Letter to George Washington [May 16, 1792]

Offices are as acceptable here as elsewhere, and whenever a man has cast a longing eye on them, a rottenness begins in his conduct.

Letter to Tench Coxe [May 21, 1799]

I have sworn upon the altar of God, eternal hostility against every form of tyranny over the mind of man.

Letter to Dr. Benjamin Rush [September 23, 1800]

If there be any among us who would wish to dissolve this Union or to change its republican form, let them stand undisturbed as monuments of the safety with which error of opinion may be tolerated where reason is left free to combat it.

First Inaugural Address [March 4, 1801]

But would the honest patriot, in the full tide of successful experiment, abandon a government which has so far kept us free and firm, on the theoretic and visionary fear that this government, the world's best hope, may by possibility want energy to preserve itself?

Ibid.

Sometimes it is said that man cannot be trusted with the government of himself. Can he, then, be trusted with the government of others? Or have we found angels in the forms of kings to govern him? Let history answer this question.

Ibid.

Still one thing more, fellow citizens — a wise and frugal government, which shall restrain men from injuring one another, which shall leave them otherwise free to regulate their own pursuits of industry and improvement, and shall not take from the mouth of labor the bread it has earned. This is the sum of good government, and this is necessary to close the circle of our felicities.

Ibid.

Equal and exact justice to all men, of whatever state or persuasion, religious or political; peace, commerce, and honest friendship with all nations — entangling alliances with none; . . . freedom of religion; freedom of the press; freedom of person under the protection of the *habeas corpus;* and trial by juries impartially selected — these principles form the bright constellation which has gone before us, and guided our steps through an age of revolution and reformation. The wisdom of our sages and the blood of our heroes have been devoted to their attainment. They should be the creed of our political faith

— the text of civil instruction — the touchstone by which to try the services of those we trust; and should we wander from them in moments of error or alarm, let us hasten to retrace our steps and to regain the road which alone leads to peace, liberty, and safety.

First Inaugural Address

Of the various executive abilities, no one excited more anxious concern than that of placing the interests of our fellow-citizens in the hands of honest men, with understanding sufficient for their stations.

Letter to Elias Shipman and Others of New Haven [*July 12, 1801*]

If a due participation of office is a matter of right, how are vacancies to be obtained? Those by death are few; by resignation, none.

Ibid.

Whensoever hostile aggressions . . . require a resort to war, we must meet our duty and convince the world that we are just friends and brave enemies.

Letter to Andrew Jackson [*December 3, 1806*]

When a man assumes a public trust, he should consider himself as public property.[1]

Remark to Baron von Humboldt [*1807*]

If, in my retirement to the humble station of a private citizen, I am accompanied with the esteem and approbation of my fellow citizens, trophies obtained by the blood-stained steel, or the tattered flags of the tented field, will never be envied. The care of human life and happiness, and not their destruction, is the first and only legitimate object of good government.

To the Republican Citizens of Washington County, Maryland [*March 31, 1809*]

Politics, like religion, hold up the torches of martyrdom to the reformers of error.

Letter to James Ogilvie [*August 4, 1811*]

[1] See Mathew Henry, page 293a, Burke, page 361b, and Calhoun, page 442a.

The earth belongs to the living, not to the dead.

Letter to John W. Eppes [*June 24, 1813*]

I agree with you that there is a natural aristocracy among men. The grounds of this are virtue and talents.

Letter to John Adams [*October 28, 1813*]

Merchants have no country. The mere spot they stand on does not constitute so strong an attachment as that from which they draw their gains.

Letter to Horatio G. Spafford [*March 17, 1814*]

If a nation expects to be ignorant and free, in a state of civilization, it expects what never was and never will be.

Letter to Colonel Charles Yancey [*January 6, 1816*]

Enlighten the people generally, and tyranny and oppressions of body and mind will vanish like evil spirits at the dawn of day.

Letter to Du Pont de Nemours [*April 24, 1816*]

I have the consolation to reflect that during the period of my administration not a drop of the blood of a single fellow citizen was shed by the sword of war or of the law.

Letter to Count Dugnani, Papal Nuncio [*February 14, 1818*]

I know no safe depository of the ultimate powers of the society but the people themselves; and if we think them not enlightened enough to exercise their control with a wholesome discretion, the remedy is not to take it from them, but to inform their discretion.

Letter to William Charles Jarvis [*September 28, 1820*]

Amplification is the vice of modern oratory. It is an insult to an assembly of reasonable men, disgusting and revolting instead of persuading. Speeches measured by the hour, die by the hour.

Letter to David Harding, President of the Jefferson Debating Society of Hingham [*April 20, 1824*]

Men by their constitutions are naturally divided into two parties: 1. Those who fear and distrust the people, and wish to draw all powers from them into the hands of the higher classes. 2. Those who identify themselves with the people, have confidence in them, cherish and consider them as the most honest and safe, although not the most wise depository of the public interests. In every country these two parties exist; and in every one where they are free to think, speak, and write, they will declare themselves.

Letter to Henry Lee
[August 10, 1824]

Never buy what you do not want, because it is cheap; it will be dear to you.

A Decalogue of Canons for Observation in Practical Life [February 21, 1825]

When angry, count ten before you speak; if very angry, an hundred.
Ibid.

The good old Dominion, the blessed mother of us all.
Thoughts on Lotteries [1826]

CONSTITUTION OF THE UNITED STATES
[1787]

We the People of the United States, in Order to form a more perfect Union, establish Justice, insure domestic tranquillity, provide for the common welfare, and secure the blessings of liberty to ourselves and our posterity, do ordain and establish this Constitution for the United States of America.
Preamble

Treason against the United States, shall consist only in levying War against them, or in adhering to their Enemies, giving them aid and comfort. No person shall be convicted of Treason unless on the Testimony of two witnesses to the same overt act, or on confession in open court.
Article III, Section 3

Congress shall make no law respecting an establishment of religion, or prohibiting the free exercise thereof; or abridging the freedom of speech, or of the press; or the right of the people peaceably to assemble, and to petition the government for a redress of grievances.
First Amendment [1791]

JOSIAH QUINCY
[1744–1775]

Blandishments will not fascinate us, nor will threats of a "halter" intimidate. For, under God, we are determined that wheresoever, whensoever, or howsoever we shall be called to make our exit, we will die free men.
Observations on the Boston Port Bill [1774]

ROWLAND HILL
[1744–1833]

Why should the Devil have all the good tunes?
Sermons. Quoted in BROOME,
Life, Page 93

HANNAH MORE
[1745–1833]

Since trifles make the sum of human things,
And half our misery from our foibles springs.
Sensibility

In men this blunder still you find, —
All think their little set mankind.
Florio and His Friend

Small habits well pursued betimes
May reach the dignity of crimes.
Ibid.

Some phrase that with the public took
Was all he read of any book.
Ibid.

WILLIAM SCOTT, LORD STOWELL
[1745–1836]

A dinner lubricates business.
> *Quoted in* BOSWELL'S *Life of Dr. Johnson, London edition [1835], Vol. VIII, Page 67*

The elegant simplicity of the three per cents.[1]
> *Quoted in* CAMPBELL'S *Lives of the Lord Chancellors [1857], Vol. X, Chap. 212*

CHARLES DIBDIN
[1745–1814]

Did you ever hear of Captain Wattle?
He was all for love, and a little for the bottle.
> *Captain Wattle and Miss Roe*

Here, a sheer hulk, lies poor Tom Bowling,
The darling of our crew;
No more he'll hear the tempest howling,
For death has broach'd him to.
> *Tom Bowling*

Faithful below he did his duty,
But now he's gone aloft.
> *Ibid.*

Spanking Jack was so comely, so pleasant, so jolly,
Though winds blew great guns, still he'd whistle and sing;
Jack loved his friend, and was true to his Molly,
And if honour gives greatness, was great as a king.
> *The Sailor's Consolation*

WILLIAM PITT
[? –1840]

One night came on a hurricane,
The sea was mountains rolling,
When Barney Buntline turned his quid,
And said to Billy Bowling:
"A strong nor-wester's blowing, Bill;
Hark! don't ye hear it roar, now?
Lord help 'em, how I pities all
Unhappy folks on shore now!"
> *The Sailor's Consolation. Stanza 1*

[1] The sweet simplicity of the three per cents. — DISRAELI: *Endymion* [1880], *Chap. 96*

JAMES HOOK
[1746–1827]

A little farm well tilled,
A little barn well filled,
A little wife well willed,
Give me, give me.
> *The Soldier's Return. Stanza 1*

I like the farm well tilled,
And I like the house well filled,
But no wife at all
Give me, give me.
> *Ibid. Stanza 3*

SIR WILLIAM JONES
[1746–1794]

On parent knees, a naked new-born child,
Weeping thou sat'st while all around thee smiled;
So live, that sinking in thy last long sleep,
Calm thou mayst smile, while all around thee weep.
> *From the Persian [1786]*

CHARLES COTESWORTH PINCKNEY
[1746–1825]

Millions for defence, but not one cent for tribute.[1]
> *When Minister to the French Republic [1797]*

JOHN PAUL JONES
[1747–1792]

I have not yet begun to fight.
> *Aboard the Bonhomme Richard,[2] September 23, 1779*

JOHN O'KEEFFE
[1747–1833]

A glass is good, and a lass is good,
And a pipe to smoke in cold weather;

[1] Inscribed on the cenotaph in his memory in St. Michael's Church, Charleston, South Carolina. What Pinckney really said was more forcible — "not *a damned penny* for tribute."
[2] Engaged with the British frigate *Serapis*, off Flamborough Head, England.

The world is good, and the people are
good,
And we're all good fellows together.
Sprigs of Laurel. Act II, Sc. 1
And why I'm so plump the reason I
tell, —
Who leads a good life is sure to live
well.
*Merry Sherwood. A Friar of
Orders Gray, Stanza 1*

SAMUEL PARR [1]
[1747–1825]

Now that the old lion is dead, every
ass thinks he may kick at him.
*While dining with Sir Joshua
Reynolds, after the death of Dr.
Johnson. Quoted in* BOSWELL'S
*Life of Dr. Johnson [1791],
Vol. II, Page 612, Everyman
Edition*

JOHN LOGAN
[1748–1788]

Thou hast no sorrow in thy song,
No winter in thy year.
To the Cuckoo
Oh could I fly, I'd fly with thee!
We'd make with joyful wing
Our annual visit o'er the globe,
Companions of the spring.
Ibid.

JOHN EDWIN
[1749–1790]

A man's ingress into the world is naked
and bare,
His progress through the world is
trouble and care;
And lastly, his egress out of the world,
is nobody knows where.
If we do well here, we shall do well
there:
I can tell you no more if I preach a
whole year.
*The Eccentricities of John Ed-
win [second edition, London,
1791], Vol. I, Page 74*

[1] Dr. Parr composed the Latin epitaph for
the monument to Dr. Johnson, placed in St.
Paul's Cathedral, London, February, 1790.

JOHANN WOLFGANG
VON GOETHE
[1749–1832]

If you inquire what the people are
like here, I must answer, "The same as
everywhere!"
*The Sorrows of Werther
[1774–1787]. May 17th*

The history of science is science itself; the history of the individual, the
individual.
Mineralogy and Geology

Who never ate his bread in sorrow,
Who never spent the darksome hours
Weeping, and watching for the mor-
row, —
He knows you not, ye heavenly
Powers.
*Wilhelm Meister's Apprenticeship
[1786–1830]. Book II, Chap. 13*

Who longs in solitude to live,
Ah! soon his wish will gain:
Men hope and love, men get and give,
And leave him to his pain.
Ibid. Book III, Chap. 1

Know'st thou the land where the lemon-
trees bloom,
Where the gold orange glows in the deep
thicket's gloom,
Where a wind ever soft from the blue
heaven blows,
And the groves are of laurel and myrtle
and rose? [1]
Ibid.

One ought, every day at least, to hear
a little song, read a good poem, see a
fine picture, and, if it were possible, to
speak a few reasonable words. [2]
Ibid. Book V, Chap. 1

To know of some one here and there
whom we accord with, who is living on
with us, even in silence, — this makes
our earthly ball a peopled garden.
Ibid. Book VII, Chap. 5

Art is long, life short; [3] judgment
difficult, opportunity transient.
Ibid. Chap. 9

[1] See Byron, page 455b.
[2] See Charles Eliot Norton, page 637b.
[3] See Hippocrates, page 22a.

Three things are to be looked to in a building: that it stand on the right spot; that it be securely founded; that it be successfully executed.

Elective Affinities [1] [*1808*].
Book I, Chap. 9

The sum which two married people owe to one another defies calculation. It is an infinite debt, which can only be discharged through all eternity.
Ibid.

A pretty foot is a great gift of nature.
Ibid. Chap. 11

One is never satisfied with a portrait of a person that one knows.
Ibid. Book II, Chap. 2

The fate of the architect is the strangest of all. How often he expends his whole soul, his whole heart and passion, to produce buildings into which he himself may never enter.
Ibid. Chap. 3

Let us live in as small a circle as we will, we are either debtors or creditors before we have had time to look round.
Ibid. Chap. 4

Mediocrity has no greater consolation than in the thought that genius is not immortal.
Ibid. Chap. 5

A teacher who can arouse a feeling for one single good action, for one single good poem, accomplishes more than he who fills our memory with rows on rows of natural objects, classified with name and form.
Ibid. Chap. 7

No one feels himself easy in a garden which does not look like the open country.
Ibid. Chap. 8

We lay aside letters never to read them again, and at last we destroy them out of discretion, and so disappears the most beautiful, the most immediate breath of life, irrecoverably for ourselves and for others.
Ibid. Chap. 9

[1] Translated by JAMES ANTHONY FROUDE [1818–1894].

Know'st thou yesterday, its aim and reason?
Work'st thou well today for worthier things?
Then calmly wait the morrow's hidden season,
And fear thou not what hap soe'er it brings.

Zahme Xenien. Book IV
[*1821*]

If I work incessantly to the last, nature owes me another form of existence when the present one collapses.
Letter to Eckermann
[*February 4, 1829*]

The artist may be well advised to keep his work to himself till it is completed, because no one can readily help him or advise him with it . . . but the scientist is wiser not to withhold a single finding or a single conjecture from publicity.

Essay on Experimentation

Man errs, while his struggle lasts.[1]
Faust [*1808–1832*], Part I
[*1808*]. *Prologue in Heaven*

Two souls dwell, alas! in my breast.[2]
Ibid. Before the Gate

I am the spirit that always denies.[3]
Ibid. Study

My peace is gone,
My heart is heavy.[4]
Ibid. Gretchen at the Spinning Wheel

Who strives always to the utmost, him can we save.[5]
Ibid. Part II [*1832*]

He only earns his freedom and existence who daily conquers them anew.[6]
Ibid.

[1] Es irrt der Mensch, so lang er strebt.
[2] Zwei Seelen wohnen, ach! in meiner Brust.
[3] Ich bin der Geist der stets verneint.
[4] Meine Ruh' ist hin,
Mein Herz ist schwer.
[5] Wer immer strebens sich bemüht,
Den können wir erlösen.
[6] Nur der verdient sich Freiheit wie das Leben
Der täglich sie erobern muss.

I was fair, too, and that was my undoing! [1]
> *Faust. Part II*

The Eternal Feminine draws us on.[2]
> *Ibid. Last line*

Without haste, but without rest.[3]
> *Motto*

More light! [4]
> *Last words*

EDWARD JENNER
[1749–1823]

The hollow winds begin to blow;
The clouds look black, the glass is low;
The soot falls down, the spaniels sleep,
And spiders from their cobwebs peep.
'Twill surely rain; I see with sorrow
Our jaunt must be put off tomorrow.
> *Forty Signs of Rain*

LADY ANNE BARNARD
[1750–1825]

When the sheep are in the fauld, and
the kye's come hame,
And a' the weary warld to rest are gone,
The waes o' my heart fall in showers
frae my ee,
Unkenn'd by my gudeman, who sleeps
sound by me.
> *Auld Robin Gray* [*1771*]. *Stanza 1*

So I will do my best a gude wife to be,
For Auld Robin Gray he is kind to me.
> *Ibid. Stanza 9*

JOHN PHILPOT CURRAN
[1750–1817]

It is the common fate of the indolent
to see their rights become a prey to the
active. The condition upon which God
hath given liberty to man is eternal
vigilance; [5] which condition if he break,

servitude is at once the consequence of
his crime and the punishment of his
guilt.
> *Speech upon the Right of*
> *Election* [*1790*]

JOHN TRUMBULL
[1750–1831]

But optics sharp it needs, I ween,
To see what is not to be seen.
> *McFingal* [*1782*]. *Canto I, Line 67*

But as some muskets so contrive it
As oft to miss the mark they drive at,
And though well aimed at duck or
plover,
Bear wide, and kick their owners over.
> *Ibid. Line 93*

As though there were a tie
And obligation to posterity.
We get them, bear them, breed, and
nurse:
What has posterity done for us?
> *Ibid. Canto II, Line 121*

No man e'er felt the halter draw,
With good opinion of the law.
> *Ibid. Canto III, Line 489*

RICHARD BRINSLEY
SHERIDAN
[1751–1816]

Mrs. Malaprop. Illiterate him, I say,
quite from your memory.
> *The Rivals* [*1775*]. *Act I, Sc. 2*

'Tis safest in matrimony to begin
with a little aversion.
> *Ibid.*

A circulating library in a town is as
an evergreen tree of diabolical knowledge.
> *Ibid.*

A progeny of learning.
> *Ibid.*

Don't let your simplicity be imposed
on.
> *Ibid.*

Never say more than is necessary.
> *Ibid. Act II, Sc. 1*

---

[1] Schön war ich auch, und das war mein
Verderben.
[2] Das Ewig-Weibliche zieht uns hinan.
[3] Ohne Hast, aber ohne Rast.
[4] Mehr Licht!
[5] Commonly quoted: Eternal vigilance is
the price of liberty.
There is one safeguard known generally to
the wise, which is an advantage and security

to all, but especially to democracies as against
despots. What is it? Distrust. — DEMOSTHE-
NES [*circa* 385–322 B.C.]: *Philippic 2, Sect. 24*

I know you are laughing in your sleeve.

The Rivals. Act II, Sc. 1

He is the very pine-apple of politeness!

Ibid. Act III, Sc. 3

If I reprehend anything in this world, it is the use of my oracular tongue, and a nice derangement of epitaphs!

Ibid.

As headstrong as an allegory on the banks of the Nile.

Ibid.

Too civil by half.

Ibid. Sc. 4

Our ancestors are very good kind of folks; but they are the last people I should choose to have a visiting acquaintance with.

Ibid. Act IV, Sc. 1

No caparisons, miss, if you please. Caparisons don't become a young woman.

Ibid. Sc. 2

We will not anticipate the past; so mind, young people, — our retrospection will be all to the future.

Ibid.

You are not like Cerberus, three gentlemen at once, are you?

Ibid.

The quarrel is a very pretty quarrel as it stands; we should only spoil it by trying to explain it.

Ibid. Sc. 3

You're our envoy; lead the way, and we'll precede.

Ibid. Act V, Sc. 1

There's nothing like being used to a thing.

Ibid. Sc. 3

My valour is certainly going! it is sneaking off! I feel it oozing out, as it were, at the palm of my hands!

Ibid.

I own the soft impeachment.

Ibid.

Thro' all the drama — whether damned or not —
Love gilds the scene, and women guide the plot.

Ibid. Epilogue

An apothecary should never be out of spirits.

St. Patrick's Day [1775].
Act I, Sc. 1

A fluent tongue is the only thing a mother don't like her daughter to resemble her in.

Ibid. Sc. 2

Death's a debt; his mandamus binds all alike — no bail, no demurrer.

Ibid. Act II, Sc. 4

I had rather follow you to your grave than see you owe your life to any but a regular-bred physician.

Ibid.

I ne'er could any lustre see
In eyes that would not look on me;
I ne'er saw nectar on a lip
But where my own did hope to sip.

The Duenna [1775]. Act I, Sc. 2

I loved him for himself alone.

Ibid. Sc. 3

I was struck all of a heap.

Ibid. Act II, Sc. 2

A bumper of good liquor
Will end a contest quicker
Than justice, judge, or vicar.[1]

Ibid. Sc. 3

Conscience has no more to do with gallantry than it has with politics.

Ibid. Sc. 4

Tale-bearers are as bad as the tale-makers.

The School for Scandal [1777].
Act I, Sc. 1

You shall see them on a beautiful quarto page, where a neat rivulet of text shall meander through a meadow of margin.

Ibid.

You had no taste when you married me.

Ibid. Sc. 2

Here's to the maiden of bashful fifteen;
Here's to the widow of fifty;
Here's to the flaunting, extravagant quean,

[1] The government of a nation is often decided over a cup of coffee, or the fate of empires changed by an extra bottle of Johannisberg. — G. P. R. JAMES: *Richelieu* [1829], *Chap. 16*

And here's to the housewife that's
thrifty!
  Let the toast pass;
  Drink to the lass;
I'll warrant she'll prove an excuse for
the glass.
The School for Scandal.
Act III, Sc. 3

An unforgiving eye, and a damned
disinheriting countenance.
Ibid. Act IV, Sc. 1

Be just before you're generous.
Ibid.

There is not a passion so strongly
rooted in the human heart as envy.
The Critic [1779]. Act I, Sc. 1

The newspapers! Sir, they are the
most villainous, licentious, abominable,
infernal — Not that I ever read them!
No, I make it a rule never to look into
a newspaper.
Ibid.

Egad, I think the interpreter is the
hardest to be understood of the two!
Ibid. Sc. 2

A practitioner in panegyric, or, to
speak more plainly, a professor of the
art of puffing.
Ibid.

The number of those who undergo
the fatigue of judging for themselves
is very small indeed.[1]
Ibid.

Certainly nothing is unnatural that
is not physically impossible.
Ibid. Act II, Sc. 1

Though hopeless love finds comfort in
despair,
It never can endure a rival's bliss! [2]
Ibid. Act III, Sc. 1

An oyster may be crossed in love.[2]
Ibid.

---

[1] See J. R. Lowell, page 603b, and Bryce,
page 698a.
  We must view with profound respect the
infinite capacity of the human mind to resist the introduction of useful knowledge. —
THOMAS RAYNESFORD LOUNSBURY [1838–
1915]: Quoted in *The Freshman and His
College* [1913], by FRANCIS CUMMINS LOCK-
WOOD, *P. 44*
[2] From the interpolated tragedy, *The Spanish Armada.*

The Right Honorable gentleman is
indebted to his memory for his jests,
and to his imagination for his facts.
Sheridaniana. Speech in Reply to
Mr. Dundas

You write with ease to show your
breeding,
But easy writing's curst hard reading.
Clio's Protest. In THOMAS
MOORE'S *Life of Sheridan*
[1825], Vol. I, Page 155

JAMES MADISON
[1751–1836]

To secure the public good, and private rights, against the danger of . . .
faction, and at the same time to preserve
the spirit and form of popular government, is then the great object to which
our inquiries are directed.
The Federalist [1787–1788].
No. 10

I believe there are more instances of
the abridgment of the freedom of the
people by gradual and silent encroachments of those in power than by violent
and sudden usurpations.
Speech in the Virginia Convention
[June 16, 1788]

JOHANN HEINRICH VOSS
[1751–1826]

Who does not love wine, women, and
song
Remains a fool his whole life long.[1]
Couplet

PHILIP FRENEAU
[1752–1832]

From Susquehanna's utmost springs
Where savage tribes pursue their
game,
His blanket tied with yellow strings,
A shepherd of the forest came.
The Indian Student. Stanza 1

---

[1] Wer nicht liebt Wein, Weib und Gesang,
  Der bleibt ein Narr sein Leben lang.
  The couplet has also been attributed to
Luther, apparently on no better authority
than an eighteenth-century jingle in which
"Luther" is needed to rhyme with "Futter."
It is REDLICH who ascribes it to Voss.

In spite of all the learned have said,
  I still my old opinion keep;
The posture that we give the dead
  Points out the soul's eternal sleep.
    The Indian Burying-Ground.
                        Stanza 1

Then rushed to meet the insulting foe;
They took the spear, but left the
  shield.[1]
    To the Memory of the Ameri-
    cans who Fell at Eutaw [Sep-
    tember 8, 1781]

LEONARD McNALLY
[1752-1820]

On Richmond Hill there lived a lass
  More bright than May-day morn;
Whose smiles all other maids' surpass,
  A rose without a thorn.
    The Lass of Richmond Hill.
                        Stanza 1

ROBERT HAWKER
[1753-1827]

Lord, dismiss us with thy blessing,
  Hope, and comfort from above;
Let us each, thy peace possessing,
  Triumph in redeeming love.
                        Benediction

MADAME ROLAND
[1754-1793]

O Liberty! Liberty! what crimes are
committed in thy name!
    LAMARTINE: *Histoire des*
                Girondins [1847]

JOEL BARLOW
[1754-1813]

The laws of husking every wight can
  tell —
And sure no laws he ever keeps so
  well:
For each red ear a general kiss he gains.
                        Hasty-Pudding

[1] When Prussia hurried to the field,
  And snatched the spear, but left the shield.
    SCOTT: *Marmion* [1808], *Introduction*
                        to Canto III

WILLIAM DRENNAN
[1754-1820]

Nor one feeling of vengeance presume
  to defile
The cause, or the men, of the Emerald
  Isle.[1]
    Erin [1795]. Stanza 3

GEORGE CRABBE
[1754-1832]

Books cannot always please, however
  good;
Minds are not ever craving for their
  food.
    The Borough [1810]. Letter
                XXIV, Schools
In idle wishes fools supinely stay;
Be there a will, and wisdom finds a way.
    The Birth of Flattery
Cut and come again.
    Tales [1812]. VII, The Widow's
                        Tale
But 'twas a maxim he had often tried,
That right was right, and there he
  would abide.
    Ibid. XV, The Squire and
                the Priest
And took for truth the test of ridicule.[2]
    Tales of the Hall [1819].
    Book VIII, The Sisters
Time has touched me gently in his race,
And left no odious furrows in my face.
    Ibid. Book XVII, The Widow

[1] The first known use of this appellation
for Ireland.
[2] How comes it to pass, then, that we appear such cowards in reasoning, and are so
afraid to stand the test of ridicule? — AN-
THONY COOPER, EARL OF SHAFTESBURY [1671–
1713]: *Characteristics, A Letter Concerning
Enthusiasm, Sect. 2*
Truth, 'tis supposed, may bear all lights;
and one of those principal lights or natural
mediums by which things are to be viewed in
order to a thorough recognition is ridicule
itself. — SHAFTESBURY: *Essay on the Freedom
of Wit and Humour, Sect. 1*
'Twas the saying of an ancient sage (Gor-
gias Leontinus, *apud* Aristotle's "Rhetoric,"
lib. iii. c. 18), that humour was the only test
of gravity, and gravity of humour. For a subject which would not bear raillery was suspicious; and a jest which would not bear a
serious examination was certainly false wit. —
Ibid., Sect. 5

The ring, so worn as you behold,
So thin, so pale, is yet of gold.
A Marriage Ring

CHARLES MAURICE DE TALLEYRAND-PÉRIGORD
[1754–1838]

Black as the devil,
Hot as hell,
Pure as an angel,
Sweet as love.[1]
Recipe for Coffee

They have learned nothing, and forgotten nothing.[2]
Attributed to Talleyrand by the Chevalier de Panat in a letter to Mallet du Pan [January, 1796]

It is the beginning of the end.[3]
Quoted in EDOUARD FOURNIER: *L'Esprit dans l'Histoire [1857]*

BERTRAND BARÈRE
[1755–1841]

The tree of liberty only grows when watered by the blood of tyrants.
Speech in the National Convention [1792]

It is only the dead who do not return.
Speech [1794]

HENRY LEE
[1756–1818]

To the memory of the Man, first in war, first in peace, and first in the hearts of his countrymen.
Resolutions Presented to the House of Representatives on the Death of Washington [December, 1799]

[1] Noir comme le diable,
Chaud comme l'enfer,
Pur comme un ange,
Doux comme l'amour.
This appears as an inscription on many old coffeepots.

[2] Ils n'ont rien appris, ni rien oublié. Said of the Bourbons.

[3] "C'est le commencement de la fin." Reported to have been Talleyrand's comment on receiving the news of the battle of Borodino in 1812.

JAMES GILLRAY
[1757–1815]

The Old Lady of Threadneedle Street.[1]
Title of cartoon [1797]

WILLIAM BLAKE
[1757–1827]

How sweet I roam'd from field to field,
And tasted all the summer's pride,
Till I the prince of love beheld
Who in the sunny beams did glide.
Poetical Sketches [1783].
Song, Stanza 1

He loves to sit and hear me sing,
Then, laughing, sports and plays
with me;
Then stretches out my golden wing,
And mocks my loss of liberty.
Ibid. Stanza 4

My silks and fine array,
My smiles and languish'd air,
By love are driv'n away;
And mournful lean despair
Brings me yew to deck my grave:
Such end true lovers have.
Ibid. Song, Stanza 1

Like a fiend in a cloud,
With howling woe,
After night I do crowd,
And with night will go;
I turn my back to the east,
From whence comforts have increas'd;
For light doth seize my brain
With frantic pain.
Ibid. Mad Song, Stanza 3

How have you left the ancient love
That bards of old enjoy'd in you!
The languid strings do scarcely move!
The sound is forc'd, the notes are
few!
Ibid. To the Muses, Stanza 4

Does the eagle know what is in the pit?
Or wilt thou go ask the mole?
Can Wisdom be put in a silver rod?
Or Love in a golden bowl?
The Book of Thel [1789].
Thel's Motto

[1] The Bank of England.

Piping down the valleys wild,
Piping songs of pleasant glee,
On a cloud I saw a child.
　　　　Songs of Innocence [*1789*].
　　　　　　Introduction, Stanza 1

And I made a rural pen,
And I stain'd the water clear,
And I wrote my happy songs
Every child may joy to hear.
　　　　　　　Ibid. Stanza 5

Little Lamb, who made thee?
Dost thou know who made thee?
Gave thee life, and bid thee feed
By the stream and o'er the mead;
Gave thee clothing of delight,
Softest clothing, woolly, bright.
　　　　Ibid. The Lamb, Stanza 1

My mother bore me in the southern
　　wild,
And I am black, but O! my soul is
　　white;
White as an angel is the English child,
But I am black, as if bereav'd of light.
　　　　Ibid. The Little Black Boy,
　　　　　　　　Stanza 1

"And we are put on earth a little space,
That we may learn to bear the beams
　　of love;
And these black bodies and this sun-
　　burnt face
Is but a cloud, and like a shady grove."
　　　　　　　Ibid. Stanza 4

I'll shade him from the heat, till he can
　　bear
To lean in joy upon our father's knee;
And then I'll stand and stroke his silver
　　hair,
And be like him, and he will then love
　　me.
　　　　　　　Ibid. Stanza 7

When my mother died I was very
　　young,
And my father sold me while yet my
　　tongue
Could scarcely cry " 'weep! 'weep!
　　'weep!"
So your chimneys I sweep, and in soot
　　I sleep.
　　　　Ibid. The Chimney Sweeper,
　　　　　　　　Stanza 1

To Mercy, Pity, Peace, and Love
All pray in their distress;
And to these virtues of delight
Return their thankfulness.
　　　　Songs of Innocence. The Divine
　　　　　　　Image, Stanza 1

The moon like a flower
In heaven's high bower,
With silent delight
Sits and smiles on the night.
　　　　Ibid. Night, Stanza 1

And there the lion's ruddy eyes
Shall flow with tears of gold,
And pitying the tender cries,
And walking round the fold,
Saying "Wrath, by his meekness,
And by his health, sickness,
Is driven away
From our immortal day."
　　　　　　Ibid. Stanza 5

"For, wash'd in life's river,
My bright mane for ever
Shall shine like the gold
As I guard o'er the fold."
　　　　　　Ibid. Stanza 6

When the voices of children are heard
　　on the green
And laughing is heard on the hill,
My heart is at rest within my breast
　　And everything else is still.
　　　　Ibid. Nurse's Song, Stanza 1

Can I see another's woe,
And not be in sorrow too?
Can I see another's grief,
And not seek for kind relief?
　　　　Ibid. On Another's Sorrow,
　　　　　　　　Stanza 1

Rintrah roars and shakes his fires in
　　the burden'd air;
Hungry clouds swag on the deep.
　　　　The Marriage of Heaven and
　　　　Hell [Circa *1793*]. *The Argu-*
　　　　ment

The busy bee has no time for sorrow.
　　　　Ibid. Proverbs of Hell

No bird soars too high, if he soars
with his own wings.
　　　　　　　　Ibid.

The pride of the peacock is the glory
of God.

The lust of the goat is the bounty of
God.

The wrath of the lion is the wisdom of God.

The nakedness of woman is the work of God.

> *The Marriage of Heaven and Hell.*
> *Proverbs of Hell*

Think in the morning. Act in the noon. Eat in the evening. Sleep in the night.

> *Ibid.*

The weak in courage is strong in cunning.

> *Ibid.*

Improvement makes straight roads; but the crooked roads without improvement are roads of genius.

> *Ibid.*

Never seek to tell thy love
Love that never told can be;
For the gentle wind does move
Silently, invisibly.

I told my love, I told my love,
I told her all my heart,
Trembling, cold, in ghastly fears —
Ah, she doth depart.

Soon as she was gone from me
A traveller came by
Silently, invisibly —
O, was no deny.

> *Poems from MSS.* [Circa *1793*].
> *Untitled Poem*

I asked a thief to steal me a peach:
He turned up his eyes.
I ask'd a lithe lady to lie her down:
Holy and meek she cries.

As soon as I went an angel came:
He wink'd at the thief
And smil'd at the dame,
And without one word spoke
Had a peach from the tree,
And 'twixt earnest and joke
Enjoy'd the Lady.

> *Ibid. Untitled Poem*

Sleep, Sleep, beauty bright
Dreaming o'er the joys of night.
Sleep, Sleep: in thy sleep
Little sorrows sit and weep.

> *Ibid. A Cradle Song, Stanza 1*

Love to faults is always blind,
Always is to joy inclin'd,
Lawless, wing'd, and unconfin'd,
And breaks all chains from every mind.

> *Poems from MSS. Untitled Poem*

The sword sung on the barren heath,
The sickle in the fruitful field:
The sword he sung a song of death,
But could not make the sickle yield.

> *Ibid. Untitled Poem*

Abstinence sows sand all over
The ruddy limbs and flaming hair,
But desire gratified
Plants fruits of life and beauty there.

> *Ibid. Untitled Poem*

If you trap the moment before it's ripe,
The tears of repentance you'll certainly wipe;
But if once you let the ripe moment go
You can never wipe off the tears of woe.

> *Ibid. Untitled Poem*

He who binds to himself a joy
Does the winged life destroy;
But he who kisses the joy as it flies
Lives in eternity's sun rise.

> *Ibid. Eternity*

What is it men in women do require?
The lineaments of Gratified Desire.
What is it women do in men require?
The lineaments of Gratified Desire.

> *Ibid. The Question Answer'd*

The look of love alarms
Because 'tis fill'd with fire;
But the look of soft deceit
Shall win the lover's hire.

> *Ibid. Untitled Poem*

Hear the voice of the Bard!
Who Present, Past, and Future, sees;
Whose ears have heard
The Holy Word
That walk'd among the ancient trees.

> *Songs of Experience* [*1794*].
> *Introduction, Stanza 1*

"Turn away no more;
Why wilt thou turn away?
The starry floor,
The wat'ry shore,
Is giv'n thee till the break of day." [1]

> *Ibid. Stanza 4*

"Love seeketh not itself to please,
Nor for itself hath any care,

[1] See Milton, page 246b.

But for another gives its ease,
And builds a Heaven in Hell's despair."
    *Songs of Experience. The Clod
    and the Pebble, Stanza 1*

"Love seeketh only self to please,
To bind another to its delight,
Joys in another's loss of ease,
And builds a Hell in Heaven's despite."
    Ibid. Stanza 3

O Rose, thou art sick!
The invisible worm
That flied in the night,
In the howling storm,

Has found out thy bed
Of crimson joy,
And his dark secret love
Does thy life destroy.
    Ibid. The Sick Rose.

Little Fly,
Thy summer's play
My thoughtless hand
Has brush'd away.
    Ibid. The Fly, Stanza 1

Am not I
A fly like thee?
Or art not thou
A man like me?
    Ibid. Stanza 2

For I dance,
And drink, and sing,
Till some blind hand
Shall brush my wing.
    Ibid. Stanza 3

Tiger! Tiger! burning bright
In the forests of the night,
What immortal hand or eye
Could frame thy fearful symmetry?
    Ibid. The Tiger, Stanza 1

In what distant deeps or skies
Burnt the fire of thine eyes?
On what wings dare he aspire?
What the hand dare seize the fire?
    Ibid. Stanza 2

What the hammer? what the chain?
In what furnace was thy brain?
What the anvil? what dread grasp
Dare its deadly terrors clasp?
    Ibid. Stanza 4

When the stars threw down their spears,
And water'd heaven with their tears,
Did he smile his work to see?
Did he who made the Lamb make thee?
    *Songs of Experience. The
    Tiger, Stanza 5*

In every cry of every man,
In every infant's cry of fear,
In every voice, in every ban,
The mind-forg'd manacles I hear.
    Ibid. London, Stanza 2

But most thro' midnight streets I hear
How the youthful harlot's curse
Blasts the new born infant's tear,
And blights with plagues the marriage
    hearse.
    Ibid. Stanza 4

My mother groan'd! my father wept.
Into the dangerous world I leapt:
Helpless, naked, piping loud:
Like a fiend hid in a cloud.
    Ibid. Infant Sorrow, Stanza 1

I was angry with my friend:
I told my wrath, my wrath did end.
I was angry with my foe:
I told it not, my wrath did grow.
    Ibid. A Poison Tree, Stanza 1

Cruelty has a human heart,
And jealousy a human face;
Terror the human form divine,
And secrecy the human dress.
    Ibid. A Divine Image, Stanza 1

My spectre around me night and day
Like a wild beast guards my way.
My emanation far within
Weeps incessantly for my sin.
    Poems From MSS. [Circa
    1800–1803]. *Untitled Poem,
    Stanza 1*

And throughout all eternity
I forgive you, you forgive me.
    Ibid. Stanza 14

Mock on, mock on, Voltaire, Rousseau;
Mock on, mock on: 'tis all in vain!
You throw the sand against the wind,
And the wind blows it back again.
    Ibid. Untitled Poem, Stanza 1

Terror in the house does roar,
But Pity stands before the door.
    Ibid. Fragment

There is a smile of love,
And there is a smile of deceit,

And there is a smile of smiles
In which these two smiles meet.
> *Poems* [Circa *1803*]. *The Smile,*
> *Stanza 1*

And there is a frown of hate,
And there is a frown of disdain,
And there is a frown of frowns
Which you strive to forget in vain.
> *Ibid. Stanza 2*

For it sticks in the heart's deep core
And it sticks in the deep back bone;
And no smile that ever was smil'd,
But only one smile alone.
> *Ibid. Stanza 3*

To see a world in a grain of sand
And a heaven in a wild flower,
Hold infinity in the palm of your hand
And eternity in an hour.
> *Ibid. Auguries of Innocence,*
> *Line 1*

A robin redbreast in a cage
Puts all Heaven in a rage.
> *Ibid. Line 5*

A dog starv'd at his master's gate
Predicts the ruin of the state.
> *Ibid. Line 9*

He who shall hurt the little wren
Shall never be belov'd by men.
> *Ibid. Line 29*

A truth that's told with bad intent
Beats all the lies you can invent.
> *Ibid. Line 53*

Every tear from every eye
Becomes a babe in eternity.
> *Ibid. Line 67*

He who shall teach the child to doubt
The rotting grave shall ne'er get out.
> *Ibid. Line 77*

He who doubts from what he sees
Will ne'er believe, do what you please.
If the sun and moon should doubt,
They'd immediately go out.
> *Ibid. Line 97*

The harlot's cry from street to street
Shall weave old England's winding
sheet.
> *Ibid. Line 105*

Every night and every morn
Some to misery are born.
Every morn and every night
Some are born to sweet delight.
> *Ibid. Line 109*

And did those feet in ancient time
Walk upon England's mountains green?
And was the holy Lamb of God
On England's pleasant pastures seen?
> *Milton* [*1804–1808*]. *Stanza 1*

And did the countenance divine
Shine forth upon our clouded hills?
And was Jerusalem builded here
Among those dark Satanic mills?
> *Ibid. Stanza 2*

Bring me my bow of burning gold:
Bring me my arrows of desire:
Bring me my spear: O clouds unfold!
Bring me my chariot of fire.
> *Ibid. Stanza 3*

I will not cease from mental fight,
Nor shall my sword sleep in my hand
Till we have built Jerusalem
In England's green and pleasant land.
> *Ibid. Stanza 4*

The Angel that presided at my birth
Said: "Little creature, formed of joy
and mirth,
Go, love without the help of any thing
on earth."
> *Fragment* [Circa *1810*]

The vision of Christ that thou dost see
Is my vision's greatest enemy:
Thine has a great hook nose like thine,
Mine has a snub nose like to mine.
> *The Everlasting Gospel*
> [Circa *1818*]

Both read the Bible day and night,
But thou read'st black where I read
white.
> *Ibid.*

This life's dim windows of the soul
Distorts the heavens from pole to pole
And leads you to believe a lie
When you see with, not thro', the eye
That was born in a night to perish in a
night.
> *Ibid.*

Poetry fettered fetters the human
race. Nations are destroyed or flourish
in proportion as their poetry, painting,
and music are destroyed or flourish.
> *Jerusalem* [*1804–1820*].
> *Chap. I, Preface*

For a tear is an intellectual thing,
And a sigh is the sword of an angel king,

And the bitter groan of a martyr's woe
Is an arrow from the Almighty's bow.
Jerusalem. Chap. II, Sect. 52
England! awake! awake! awake!
Jerusalem thy sister calls!
Why wilt thou sleep the sleep of death
And close her from thy ancient walls?
Ibid. Chap. III, Sect. 77,
Stanza 1
And now the time returns again:
Our souls exult, and London's towers
Receive the Lamb of God to dwell
In England's green and pleasant
bowers.
Ibid. Stanza 3

JOHN PHILIP KEMBLE
[1757–1823]

Perhaps it was right to dissemble your
love,
But — why did you kick me down
stairs?
The Panel. Act I, Sc. 1

ROYALL TYLER [1]
[1757–1826]

Why should our thoughts to distant
countries roam,
When each refinement may be found
at home?
The Contrast [1787]. Prologue
This outlandish lingo.
Ibid. Act II, Sc. 2
By the living jingo, you look so top-
ping, I took you for one of the agents
to Congress.
Ibid.
Since General Shays has sneaked off
and given us the bag to hold.
Ibid.
I am at the end of my tether.
Ibid. Act III, Sc. 1

[1] Tyler was born in Boston, was graduated
from Harvard, practiced law, and helped to
suppress Shays's Rebellion. Three weeks after
seeing *The School for Scandal* in New York,
he wrote *The Contrast,* the second play to
be written by an American. He also wrote a
novel, *The Algerine Captive* [1797], and was
Chief Justice of the State Supreme Court in
Vermont from 1807 to 1813.

JAMES MONROE
[1758–1831]

National honor is national property
of the highest value.
First Inaugural Address
[March 4, 1817]
The American continents . . . are
henceforth not to be considered as subjects for future colonization by any European powers.
Annual Message to Congress
[December, 1823] (The Mon-
roe Doctrine)
We owe it, therefore, to candor, and
to the amicable relations existing between the United States and those powers to declare that we should consider
any attempt on their part to extend
their system to any portion of this
hemisphere as dangerous to our peace
and safety. With the existing colonies
or dependencies of any European power
we . . . shall not interfere. But with
the governments . . . whose independence we have . . . acknowledged, we
could not view any interposition for
the purpose of oppressing them, or controlling, in any other manner, their
destiny, by any European power, in any
other light than as a manifestation of
an unfriendly disposition towards the
United States.
Ibid.

HORATIO NELSON
[1758–1805]

In the battle off Cape St. Vincent,
Nelson gave orders for boarding the
San Josef, exclaiming "Westminster
Abbey, or victory!"
Southey's *Life of Nelson*
[1813]. Vol. I
England expects every man will do
his duty.[1]
Ibid. Vol. II [Battle of
Trafalgar]

[1] This famous sentence is thus first reported: "Say to the fleet, England confides
that every man will do his duty." Captain
Pasco, Nelson's flag lieutenant, suggested sub-
stituting "expects" for "confides," which was

Kiss me, Hardy.
SOUTHEY's *Life of Nelson. Vol. II*
[*Battle of Trafalgar*]
May the great God, whom I worship, grant to my country and for the benefit of Europe in general, a great and glorious victory, and may no misconduct in anyone tarnish it, and may humanity after the victory be the predominant feature in the British fleet.
Prayer written in his diary
[*October 21, 1805*]

ROBERT BURNS
[1759–1796]

Wee, sleekit, cowrin, tim'rous beastie,
O, what a panic's in thy breastie!
Thou need na start awa sae hasty
Wi' bickering brattle!
To a Mouse [*1785*]. *Stanza 1*
I'm truly sorry man's dominion
Has broken Nature's social union.
Ibid. Stanza 2
The best laid schemes o' mice and men
Gang aft a-gley;
An' lea'e us nought but grief and pain,
For promis'd joy.
Ibid. Stanza 7
When chill November's surly blast
Made fields and forests bare.
Man Was Made to Mourn
[*1786*]. *Stanza 1*
Man's inhumanity to man
Makes countless thousands mourn.
Ibid. Stanza 7
Beneath the milk-white thorn that scents the evening gale.
The Cotter's Saturday Night
[*1786*]. *Stanza 9*
He wales a portion with judicious care;
And "Let us worship God," he says, with solemn air.
Ibid. Stanza 12
From scenes like these, old Scotia's grandeur springs,
That makes her loved at home, revered abroad:

---

adopted. Captain Blackwood, who commanded the *Euryalus*, says that the correction suggested was from "Nelson expects" to "England expects."

Princes and lords are but the breath of kings,[1]
"An honest man's the noblest work of God." [2]
The Cotter's Saturday Night.
Stanza 19
Gie me ae spark o' Nature's fire,
That's a' the learning I desire.
First Epistle to J. Lapraik
[*1786*]. *Stanza 13*
Gif ye want ae friend that's true,
I'm on your list.
Ibid. Stanza 15
I winna blaw about mysel,
As ill I like my fauts to tell.
Ibid. Stanza 16
My worthy friend, ne'er grudge an' carp,
Tho' Fortune use you hard an' sharp.
Second Epistle to J. Lapraik
[*1786*]. *Stanza 8*
The social, friendly, honest man,
Whate'er he be,
'Tis he fulfills great Nature's plan,
And none but he.
Ibid. Stanza 15
Morality, thou deadly bane,
Thy tens o' thousands thou hast slain!
A Dedication to Gavin Hamilton
[*1786*]
It's hardly in a body's pow'r,
To keep, at times, frae being sour.
Epistle to Davie [*1786*].
Stanza 2
O Life! how pleasant, in thy morning,
Young Fancy's rays the hills adorning!
Cold-pausing Caution's lesson scorning,
We frisk away,
Like schoolboys, at th' expected warning,
To joy an' play.
Epistle to James Smith
[*1786*]. *Stanza 15*
Misled by fancy's meteor ray,
By passion driven;
But yet the light that led astray
Was light from heaven.
The Vision [*1786*]. *II, Stanza 18*

[1] See Goldsmith, page 355b.
[2] See Pope, pages 317b–318a.

And, like a passing thought, she fled
   In light away.
       The Vision. II, Stanza 24
His lockèd, lettered, braw brass collar
Showed him the gentleman an' scholar.
       The Twa Dogs [*1786*]. *Stanza 3*
An' there began a lang digression
About the lords o' the creation.
       Ibid. Stanza 6
Oh wad some power the giftie gie us
To see oursels as others see us!
It wad frae monie a blunder free us,
   An' foolish notion.
       To a Louse [*1786*]. *Stanza 8*
Wee, modest, crimson-tippèd flow'r,
Thou's met me in an evil hour;
For I maun crush amang the stoure
   Thy slender stem:
To spare thee now is past my pow'r,
   Thou bonie gem.
       To a Mountain Daisy
       [*1786*]. *Stanza 1*
Stern Ruin's ploughshare drives elate,
   Full on thy bloom.[1]
       Ibid. Stanza 9
O life! thou art a galling load,
Along a rough, a weary road,
   To wretches such as I!
   Despondency [*1786*]. *Stanza 1*
Perhaps it may turn out a sang,
Perhaps turn out a sermon.
       Epistle to a Young Friend
       [*1786*]. *Stanza 1*
A man may tak a neebor's part,
Yet hae nae cash to spare him.
       Ibid. Stanza 4
I waive the quantum o' the sin,
The hazard of concealing;
But, och! it hardens a' within,
And petrifies the feeling!
       Ibid. Stanza 6
To catch Dame Fortune's golden smile,
Assiduous wait upon her;
And gather gear by ev'ry wile
That's justified by honor:
Not for to hide it in a hedge,
Nor for a train-attendant;
But for the glorious privilege
Of being independent.
       Ibid. Stanza 7

[1] See Edward Young, page 306a.

An atheist's laugh's a poor exchange
For Deity offended!
     Epistle to a Young Friend. Stanza 9
There's nought but care on ev'ry han',
In every hour that passes, O:
What signifies the life o' man,
An' 't were nae for the lasses, O.
       Green Grow the Rashes, O
       [*1787*]. *Stanza 1*
Auld Nature swears, the lovely dears
Her noblest work she classes, O:
Her prentice han' she try'd on man,
An' then she made the lasses, O.
       Ibid. Stanza 5
Green grow the rashes, O;
Green grow the rashes, O;
The sweetest hours that e'er I spend,
Are spent among the lasses, O.
       Ibid. Chorus
Some books are lies frae end to end.
      Death and Dr. Hornbook
       [*1787*]. *Stanza 1*
John Barleycorn got up again,
And sore surpris'd them all.
     John Barleycorn [*1787*]. *Stanza 3*
Affliction's sons are brothers in distress;
A brother to relieve, — how exquisite
   the bliss!
     A Winter Night [*1787*]. *Stanza 8*
A dear-lov'd lad, convenience snug,
A treach'rous inclination —
But, let me whisper i' your lug,
Ye're aiblins nae temptation.
     Address to the Unco Guid
       [*1787*]. *Stanza 6*
Then gently scan your brother man,
Still gentler sister woman;
Tho' they may gang a kennin wrang,
To step aside is human:
One point must still be greatly dark,
The moving *why* they do it;
And just as lamely can ye mark
How far perhaps they rue it.
       Ibid. Stanza 7
O, my luve is like a red, red rose,
That's newly sprung in June.
O, my luve is like the melodie,
That's sweetly play'd in tune.
     Johnson's Musical Museum
     [*1787–1796*]. *A Red, Red*
     Rose, Stanza 1

Contented wi' little, and cantie wi' mair.
Johnson's Musical Museum. Contented wi' Little, Stanza 1

Ye banks and braes o' bonie Doon,
How can ye bloom sae fresh and fair?
How can ye chant, ye little birds,
And I sae weary fu' o' care!
Thou'll break my heart, thou warbling bird,
That wantons thro' the flowering thorn!
Thou minds me o' departed joys,
Departed never to return.
*Ibid. The Banks o' Doon,
Stanza 1*

Chords that vibrate sweetest pleasure
Thrill the deepest notes of woe.
*Ibid. Sensibility How Charming,
Stanza 4*

Ae fond kiss, and then we sever!
Ae farewell, and then forever!
Ibid. Ae Fond Kiss, Stanza 1

But to see her was to love her,
Love but her, and love for ever.[1]
Had we never lov'd sae kindly,
Had we never lov'd sae blindly,
Never met — or never parted —
We had ne'er been broken-hearted.
Ibid. Stanza 2

It was a' for our rightfu' King
We left fair Scotland's strand.
*Ibid. It Was A' For Our Rightfu'
King, Stanza 1*

Now a' is done that men can do,
And a' is done in vain.
Ibid. Stanza 2

He turn'd him right and round about
Upon the Irish shore,
And gae his bridle reins a shake,
With adieu for evermore,
My dear —
And adieu for evermore!
Ibid. Stanza 3

John Anderson my jo, John,
When we were first acquent,
Your locks were like the raven,
Your bonie brow was brent;
But now your brow is beld, John,
Your locks are like the snaw,

[1] See Samuel Rogers, page 396b, and Halleck, page 462b.

But blessings on your frosty pow,
John Anderson my jo!
*Johnson's Musical Museum. John
Anderson My Jo, Stanza 1*

John Anderson my jo, John,
We clamb the hill thegither,
And monie a cantie day, John,
We've had wi' ane anither;
Now we maun totter down, John,
And hand in hand we'll go,
And sleep thegither at the foot,
John Anderson my jo!
Ibid. Stanza 2

Farewell to the Highlands, farewell to the North,
The birthplace of valour, the country of worth!
Wherever I wander, wherever I rove,
The hills of the Highlands for ever I love.
*Ibid. My Heart's in the
Highlands, Stanza 1*

My heart's in the Highlands, my heart is not here,
My heart's in the Highlands a-chasing the deer.
Ibid. Chorus

Should auld acquaintance be forgot,
And never brought to mind?
Should auld acquaintance be forgot,
And auld lang syne!
Auld Lang Syne [*1788*].
Stanza 1

For auld lang syne, my dear,
For auld lang syne,
We'll tak a cup o' kindness yet
For auld lang syne!
Ibid. Chorus

Flow gently, sweet Afton, among thy green braes!
Flow gently, I'll sing thee a song in thy praise!
My Mary's asleep by thy murmuring stream —
Flow gently, sweet Afton, disturb not her dream!
Sweet Afton [*1789*]. *Stanza 1*

Thou stock dove whose echo resounds thro' the glen,
Ye wild whistling blackbirds in yon thorny den,

Thou green-crested lapwing, thy
screaming forbear —
I charge you, disturb not my slumbering fair!
Sweet Afton. Stanza 2

To make a happy fireside clime
To weans and wife,
That's the true pathos and sublime
Of human life.
Epistle to Dr. Blacklock
[1789]. Stanza 9

This day Time winds th' exhausted
chain,
To run the twelvemonth's length again.
New Year's Day, 1791. Stanza 1

The voice of Nature loudly cries,
And many a message from the skies,
That something in us never dies.
Ibid. Stanza 3

When Nature her great masterpiece
design'd,
And fram'd her last, best work, the hu-
man mind,
Her eye intent on all the wondrous
plan,
She form'd of various stuff the various
Man.
To Robert Graham [1791].
Stanza 1

She is a winsome wee thing,
She is a handsome wee thing,
She is a lo'esome wee thing,
This sweet wee wife o' mine.
My Wife's a Winsome Wee Thing
[1792]. Chorus

The golden hours on angel wings
Flew o'er me and my dearie;
For dear to me as light and life
Was my sweet Highland Mary.
Highland Mary [1792]. Stanza 2

But, oh! fell death's untimely frost,
That nipt my flower sae early.
Ibid. Stanza 3

If there's a hole in a' your coats,
I rede you tent it;
A chiel's amang you takin' notes,
And faith he'll prent it.
On the Late Captain Grose's
Peregrinations thro' Scotland
[1793]. Stanza 1

Some hae meat and canna eat,
And some wad eat that want it;
But we hae meat, and we can eat,
And sae the Lord be thankit.
The Selkirk Grace [1793]

O Mary, at thy window be!
It is the wish'd, the trysted hour.
Mary Morison [1793]. Stanza 1

The lovely Mary Morison!
Ibid.

Whare sits our sulky, sullen dame,
Gathering her brows like gathering
storm,
Nursing her wrath to keep it warm.
Tam o' Shanter [1793]. Stanza 1

Ah, gentle dames! it gars me greet
To think how monie counsels sweet,
How monie lengthened, sage advices,
The husband frae the wife despises.
Ibid. Stanza 4

His ancient, trusty, drouthy cronie;
Tam lo'ed him like a vera brither, —
They had been fou for weeks thegither.
Ibid. Stanza 5

The landlady and Tam grew gracious
Wi' secret favours, sweet and precious.
Ibid.

The landlord's laugh was ready chorus.
Ibid.

Kings may be blest, but Tam was
glorious,
O'er a' the ills o' life victorious.
Ibid. Stanza 6

But pleasures are like poppies spread,
You seize the flower, its bloom is shed;
Or like the snow falls in the river,
A moment white, then melts forever.
Ibid. Stanza 7

That hour, o' night's black arch the
keystane.
Ibid.

Inspiring bold John Barleycorn,
What dangers thou canst make us
scorn!
Ibid. Stanza 11

As Tammie glow'red, amazed, and curious,
The mirth and fun grew fast and furious.
Ibid. Stanza 13

Her cutty sark,[1] o' Paisley harn,
That while a lassie she had worn,
In longitude tho' sorely scanty,
It was her best, and she was vauntie.
Tam o' Shanter. Stanza 16

Life is but a day at most,
Sprung from night, — in darkness lost:
Hope not sunshine ev'ry hour,
Fear not clouds will always lour.
Written in Friars Carse Hermitage [*1793*]. *Stanza 2*

Scots, wha hae wi' Wallace bled,
Scots, wham Bruce has aften led,
Welcome to your gory bed
Or to victorie!
Scots, Wha Hae [*1794*].
Stanza 1

Now's the day, and now's the hour:
See the front o' battle lour,
See approach proud Edward's power —
Chains and slaverie!
Ibid. Stanza 2

Lay the proud usurpers low!
Tyrants fall in every foe!
Liberty's in every blow!
Let us do, or die!
Ibid. Stanza 6

The rank is but the guinea's stamp,
The man's the gowd for a' that.
Is There for Honest Poverty
[*1795*]. *Stanza 1*

A prince can mak a belted knight,
A marquis, duke, and a' that;
But an honest man's aboon his might,
Guid faith, he mauna fa' that.
Ibid. Stanza 4

For a' that, and a' that,
An' twice as muckle 's a' that,
I've lost but ane, I've twa behin',
I've wife eneugh for a' that.
Posthumous Pieces. The Jolly Beggars, Chorus

God knows, I'm no the thing I should be,
Nor am I even the thing I could be.
Ibid. To the Reverend John M'Math, Stanza 8

If there's another world, he lives in bliss;
If there is none, he made the best of this.
Posthumous Pieces. Epitaph on William Muir

In durance vile here must I wake and weep,
And all my frowsy couch in sorrow steep.
Ibid. Epistle from Esopus to Maria

It's guid to be merry and wise,
It's guid to be honest and true,
It's guid to support Caledonia's cause
And bide by the buff and the blue.
Ibid. Here's a Health to Them That's Awa', Stanza 1

JOHANN CHRISTOPH FRIEDRICH VON SCHILLER
[*1759–1805*]

There are three lessons I would write,
Three words as with a burning pen,
In tracings of eternal light,
Upon the hearts of men.
Hope, Faith, and Love. Stanza 1

Thus grave these lessons on thy soul, —
Hope, faith, and love; and thou shalt find
Strength when life's surges rudest roll,
Light when thou else wert blind!
Ibid. Stanza 5

The richest monarch in the Christian world;
The sun in my own dominions never sets.[1]
Don Carlos [*1787*]. *Act I, Sc. 6*

When the wine goes in, strange things come out.
The Piccolomini [*1799*].
Act II, Sc. 12

Against stupidity the very gods
Themselves contend in vain.[2]
The Maid of Orleans [*1801*].
Act III, Sc. 6

---

[1] The famous tea clipper, *Cutty Sark*, designed by Hercules Linton and built in 1869, had the story of Tam o' Shanter carved upon her bow and counter. Nannie with flying locks and scanty shift was the figurehead.

[1] See Scott, page 417b, and Daniel Webster, page 444a.
[2] Against boredom even the gods themselves struggle in vain. — NIETZSCHE [1844–1900]: *The Antichrist, 48*

This feat of Tell, the archer, will be told
While yonder mountains stand upon
  their base.
By Heaven! the apple's cleft right
  through the core.
  William Tell [1804]. Act III, Sc. 3

MASON LOCKE WEEMS
[1759–1825]

"George," said his father, "do you
know who killed that beautiful little
cherry tree yonder in the garden?" . . .
Looking at his father with the sweet
face of youth brightened with the
inexpressible charm of all-conquering
truth, he bravely cried out, "I can't tell
a lie. I did cut it with my hatchet."
  *The Life of George Washing-
  ton: With Curious Anecdotes,
  Equally Honorable to Himself
  and Exemplary to His Young
  Countrymen [1800]*

JOSEPH ROUGET DE LISLE
[1760–1836]

Ye sons of France, awake to glory!
Hark! hark! what myriads bid you rise!

To arms! to arms! ye brave!
The avenging sword unsheathe!
March on! march on! all hearts re-
  solved
On victory or death!
  The Marseillaise [1] *[1792]*

AUGUST FRIEDRICH
FERDINAND VON KOTZEBUE
[1761–1819]

There is another and a better world.
  The Stranger [1798]. Act I, Sc. 1

[1] Allons, enfants de la patrie,
  Le jour de gloire est arrivé!

  Aux armes, citoyens!
  Formez vos bataillons!
  Marchons! Marchons! Qu'un sang impur
  Abreuve nos sillons!
Composed in the garrison at Strasbourg
and originally called *Chant de guerre de l'ar-
mée du Rhin,* the *Marseillaise* took its name
from the patriots of Marseilles who first made

JOANNA BAILLIE
[1762–1851]

Oh, swiftly glides the bonnie boat,
Just parted from the shore,
And to the fisher's chorus-note
Soft moves the dipping oar.[1]
  *Oh, Swiftly Glides the Bonnie
  Boat*
The wild-fire dances on the fen,
The red star sheds its ray;
Uprouse ye then, my merry men!
It is our op'ning day.
  The Outlaw's Song. Stanza 1
Oh, who shall lightly say that fame
Is nothing but an empty name,
When but for those, our mighty dead,
All ages past a blank would be.
  The Worth of Fame. Stanza 2
Good-morrow to thy sable beak
And glossy plumage dark and sleek,
Thy crimson moon and azure eye,
Cock of the heath, so wildly shy.
  The Heath-Cock. Stanza 1

ANDREW CHERRY
[1762–1812]

Loud roared the dreadful thunder,
The rain a deluge showers.
  The Bay of Biscay
As she lay, on that day,
In the bay of Biscay, O!
  Ibid.

GEORGE COLMAN, THE
YOUNGER
[1762–1836]

Tell 'em Queen Anne's dead.[2]
  The Heir-at-Law [1797]
On their own merits modest men are
  dumb.
  Ibid. Epilogue
And what's impossible can't be,
And never, never comes to pass.
  The Maid of the Moor

it known in Paris. The English version in the
text is that usually found in the songbooks.
  [1] See Marvell, page 269a.
  [2] The phrase became proverbial for telling
what everybody knows.

But when ill indeed,
E'en dismissing the doctor don't always
　succeed.
Lodgings for Single Gentlemen
When taken,
To be well shaken.
The Newcastle Apothecary
O Miss Bailey!
Unfortunate Miss Bailey!
Love Laughs at Locksmiths.
Act II, Song
'Tis a very fine thing to be father-in-
　law
To a very magnificent three-tailed Ba-
　shaw!
Blue Beard. Act II, Sc. 5
I had a soul above buttons.
Sylvester Daggerwood, or New
Hay at the Old Market. Sc. 1
Mynheer Vandunck, though he never
　was drunk,
Sipped brandy and water gayly.
Mynheer Vandunck

JOSEPH FOUCHÉ
[1763–1820]

"It is more than a crime; it is a
blunder," [1] — words which I record,
because they have been repeated and
attributed to others.
Memoirs

Death is an eternal sleep.
Inscription placed by his orders
on the gates of the cemeteries
[*1794*]

SAMUEL ROGERS
[1763–1855]

Sweet Memory! wafted by thy gentle
　gale,
Oft up the stream of Time I turn my
　sail.
The Pleasures of Memory
[*1792*]. *Part II, 1*

She was good as she was fair,
None — none on earth above her!
As pure in thought as angels are:
To know her was to love her. [1]
Jacqueline [2] [*1814*]. *Stanza 1*
A guardian angel o'er his life presiding,
Doubling his pleasures, and his cares
　dividing.
Human Life
To fireside happiness, to hours of ease
Blest with that charm, the certainty to
　please.
Ibid.
The soul of music slumbers in the shell
Till waked and kindled by the master's
　spell;
And feeling hearts, touch them but
　rightly, pour
A thousand melodies unheard before!
Ibid.
Mine be a cot beside the hill;
A beehive's hum shall soothe my ear;
A willowy brook that turns a mill,
With many a fall shall linger near. [3]
A Wish. Stanza 1
That very law which moulds a tear
And bids it trickle from its source, —
That law preserves the earth a sphere,
And guides the planets in their course.
On a Tear. Stanza 6
Go! you may call it madness, folly;
You shall not chase my gloom away!
There's such a charm in melancholy
I would not if I could be gay.
To ——. Stanza 1
Ward has no heart, they say, but I
　deny it:
He has a heart, and gets his speeches
　by it.
Epigram

ROBERT HALL
[1764–1831]

His [Burke's] imperial fancy has
laid all Nature under tribute, and has

---

[1] "C'est plus qu'un crime, c'est une faute,"
reputedly Fouché's comment on the murder of
the Duc d'Enghien [1804]. Fouché's family
denied the authenticity of the *Memoirs,* and
the remark has also been commonly attributed
to Talleyrand. Sainte-Beuve ascribes it to
Boulay de la Meurthe.

[1] See Burns, page 392a, and Halleck, page
462b.
[2] First published in the same volume with
Byron's *Lara,* neither author appending his
name to his work.
[3] See Yeats, page 824b.

collected riches from every scene of the creation and every walk of art.
Apology for the Freedom of the Press

Call things by their right names. . . . Glass of brandy and water! That is the current but not the appropriate name: ask for a glass of liquid fire and distilled damnation.
GREGORY's *Life of Hall*

THOMAS MORTON
[1764–1838]

Push on, — keep moving.
A Cure for the Heartache [*1797*]. *Act II, Sc. 1*

Approbation from Sir Hubert Stanley is praise indeed.
Ibid. Act V, Sc. 2

What will Mrs. Grundy say? What will Mrs. Grundy think?[1]
Speed the Plough [*1798*]. *Act I, Sc. 1*

ANN RADCLIFFE
[1764–1823]

Fate sits on these dark battlements and frowns,
And as the portal opens to receive me,
A voice in hollow murmurs through the courts
Tells of a nameless deed.[2]
Motto of her novel The Mysteries of Udolpho [*1794*]

HELEN D'ARCY CRANSTOUN (MRS. DUGALD STEWART)
[1765–1838]

I weep not for the silent dead,
Their pains are past, their sorrows o'er.[3]
The Song of Genius

CATHERINE MARIA FANSHAWE
[1765–1834]

'Twas whisper'd in heaven, 'twas mutter'd in hell,
And echo caught faintly the sound as it fell;
On the confines of earth 'twas permitted to rest,
And the depths of the ocean its presence confess'd.
Enigma: The Letter H

MARY LAMB
[1765–1847]

Thou straggler into loving arms,
Young climber-up of knees.
A Child. Stanza 3

SIR JAMES MACKINTOSH
[1765–1832]

Diffused knowledge immortalizes itself.
Vindiciae Gallicae [*1791*]

The Commons, faithful to their system, remained in a wise and masterly inactivity.
Ibid.

The frivolous work of polished idleness.
Dissertation on Ethical Philosophy [*1830*]. *Remarks on Thomas Brown*

Disciplined inaction.
History of the Revolution in England in 1688 [*1834*]. *Chap. VII*

MADAME DE STAËL
[1766–1817]

The sight of such a monument is like a continuous and stationary music.[1]
Corinne [*1807*]. *Book IV, Chap. 3*

[1] Since it [architecture] is music in space, as it were a frozen music. . . . If architecture in general is frozen music. — FRIEDRICH VON SCHELLING [1775–1854]: *Philosophie der Kunst, Pp. 576, 593*

[1] See Herbert Spencer, page 614b.
[2] See Shakespeare, page 198a.
[3] Quoted by SIR WALTER SCOTT in *The Talisman* [*1825*], *Chap. 26*.

To understand all makes us very indulgent.[1]

> *Corinne. Book XVIII, Chap. 5*

ERNST F. MÜNSTER [2]
[1766–1839]

Absolutism tempered by assassination.

> *Description of the Russian*
> *Constitution*

ISAAC D'ISRAELI
[1766–1848]

Whatever is felicitously expressed risks being worse expressed: it is a wretched taste to be gratified with mediocrity when the excellent lies before us.

> *Curiosities of Literature* [*1834*].
> *On Quotation*

They [the early writers] looked with alarm upon the halo of immortality that encircled the printing-press.

> *Amenities of Literature* [*1841*].
> *Vol. II, Page 278*

CAROLINA OLIPHANT,
LADY NAIRNE
[1766–1845]

Sweet's the laverock's note and lang,
  Lilting wildly up the glen;
But aye to me he sings ae sang,
  Will ye no come back again?

> *Will Ye No Come Back Again?*
> [*1846*]. *Stanza 5*

Would you be young again?
  So would not I —
One tear to memory given,
  Onward I'd hie.

> *Would You Be Young Again?*
> [*Looking Backward*]. *Stanza 1*

---

[1] To all the gossip that I hear
I'll give no faith; to what I see
But only half, for it is clear
All that led up is dark to me.
Learn we the larger life to live,
To comprehend is to forgive.
HENRIETTA A. HUXLEY [1825–1914]:
"*Tout Comprendre, C'est Tout Pardonner*"
[2] Hanoverian envoy at St. Petersburg.

Gude nicht, and joy be wi' you a'.

> *Gude Nicht* [*1846*]

A penniless lass wi' a lang pedigree.

> *The Laird o' Cockpen* [*1846*].
> *Stanza 2*

NANCY DENNIS SPROAT
[1766–1826]

How pleasant is Saturday night,
When I've tried all the week to be
  good,
And not spoke a word that was bad,
And obliged every one that I could.

> *Lullabies for Children* [*1818*].
> *Saturday Night, Stanza 1*

HENRI BENJAMIN
CONSTANT
[1767–1830]

I am not the rose, but I have lived with her.[1]

> *Attributed*

JOHN QUINCY ADAMS
[1767–1848]

Think of your forefathers! Think of your posterity![2]

> *Speech at Plymouth*
> [*December 22, 1802*]

In charity to all mankind, bearing no malice or ill-will to any human being, and even compassionating those who hold in bondage their fellow-men, not knowing what they do.[3]

> *Letter to A. Bronson*
> [*July 30, 1838*]

My wants are many, and, if told,
  Would muster many a score;
And were each wish a mint of gold,
  I still should long for more.

> *The Wants of Man* [*1841*].
> *Stanza 1*

This is the last of earth! I am content.

> *Last Words* [*February 21, 1848*]

---

[1] Je ne suis pas la rose, mais j'ai vécu avec elle. — Attributed to CONSTANT by ABRAHAM HAYWARD in his introduction to the *Autobiography and Letters* [1861] of Mrs. PIOZZI
[2] Et majores vestros et posteros cogitate. — TACITUS [*circa* A.D. 55–117]: *Agricola, 32, 26*
[3] See Abraham Lincoln, page 542a.

ANDREW JACKSON
[1767–1845]

Our Federal Union: it must be preserved.

Toast given on the Jefferson Birthday Celebration [1830]

It is to be regretted that the rich and powerful too often bend the acts of government to their selfish purposes. . . . Every man is equally entitled to protection by law; but when the laws undertake to add . . . artificial distinctions, to grant titles, gratuities, and exclusive privileges, to make the rich richer and the potent more powerful, the humble members of society — the farmers, mechanics, and laborers — who have neither the time nor the means of securing like favors to themselves, have a right to complain of the injustice of their government.

Message Vetoing the Bank Bill [July 10, 1832]

There are no necessary evils in government. Its evils exist only in its abuses. If it would confine itself to equal protection, and, as Heaven does its rains, shower its favors alike on the high and the low, the rich and the poor, it would be an unqualified blessing.

Ibid.

You are uneasy; you never sailed with *me* before, I see.[1]

PARTON'S *Life of Jackson. Vol. III, Page 493*

NAPOLEON BONAPARTE
[1769–1821]

Soldiers, from the summit of yonder pyramids forty centuries look down upon you.

In Egypt [July 21, 1798]

Go, sir, gallop, and don't forget that the world was made in six days. You can ask me for anything you like, except time.

To one of his aides [1803]. Quoted in R. M. JOHNSTON, The Corsican

From the sublime to the ridiculous is but a step.[1]

To the Abbé du Pradt, on the return from Russia [1812], referring to the retreat from Moscow

What is the throne? — a bit of wood gilded and covered with velvet. I am the state [2] — I alone am here the representative of the people. Even if I had done wrong you should not have reproached me in public — people wash their dirty linen at home. France has more need of me than I of France.

To the Senate [1814]

France is invaded; I go to put myself at the head of my troops, and, with God's help and their valour, I hope soon to drive the enemy beyond the frontier.

At Paris [January 23, 1814]

The bullet that will kill me is not yet cast.

At Montereau [February 17, 1814]

The Allied Powers having proclaimed that the Emperor Napoleon is the sole obstacle to the re-establishment of peace in Europe, he, faithful to his oath, declares that he is ready to descend from the throne, to quit France, and even to relinquish life, for the good of his country.

Act of Abdication [April 4, 1814]

Unite for the public safety, if you would remain an independent nation.

Proclamation to the French People [June 22, 1815]

[1] Du sublime au ridicule il n'y a qu'un pas. The saying has been attributed also to Talleyrand.

See Paine, page 371a.

[2] The expression "L'état c'est moi" ("I am the state"), commonly attributed to Louis XIV, was apparently first ascribed to him by DULAURE in his *Histoire de Paris* [1863], and can claim no historical authenticity. Even if a pure fabrication of Dulaure's, however, it has a usefulness of its own in providing a concise symbol of the attitude of Louis XIV toward absolute monarchy.

[1] A remark made to an elderly gentleman who was sailing with Jackson down Chesapeake Bay in an old steamboat.

Wherever wood can swim, there I am sure to find this flag of England.
At Rochefort [*July, 1815*]

Whatever shall we do in that remote spot? Well, we will write our Memoirs. Work is the scythe of time.
On board H. M. S. Bellerophon [*August, 1815*]

I generally had to give in [speaking of his relations with the Empress Josephine].
On St. Helena [*May 19, 1816*]

My maxim was, *la carrière est ouverte aux talents*, without distinction of birth or fortune.
On St. Helena [*March 3, 1817*]

Our hour is marked, and no one can claim a moment of life beyond what fate has predestined.
To Dr. Arnott [*April, 1821*]

I am neither an atheist nor a rationalist; I believe in God, and am of the religion of my father. I was born a Catholic, and will fulfill all the duties of that church, and receive the assistance which she administers.
On St. Helena [*April 18, 1821*]

I could not unbend the bow; and France has been deprived of the liberal institutions I intended to give her.
BOURRIENNE: *Memoirs, Vol. X, Page 425* [*May 3, 1821*]

All was not lost until the moment when all had succeeded.
Ibid. On anniversary of Battle of Waterloo, Page 39

Madame Montholon having inquired what troops he considered the best, "Those which are victorious, Madame," replied the Emperor.
Ibid. Page 399

Tête d'armée (Head of the army).
Last words [*May 5, 1821*]

Two o'clock in the morning courage.
Quoted in LAS CASES, *Napoleon at St. Helena* [*1823*]

An army marches on its stomach.
Attributed to Napoleon

Every French soldier carries a marshal's baton in his knapsack.[1]
Attributed to Napoleon

JOHN HOOKHAM FRERE
[1769–1846]

And don't confound the language of the nation
With long-tailed words in *osity* and *ation*.
The Monks and the Giants. Canto I, Line 6

Despair in vain sits brooding over the putrid eggs of hope.
The Rovers. Act I, Sc. 2

ARTHUR WELLESLEY,
DUKE OF WELLINGTON
[1769–1852]

Nothing except a battle lost can be half so melancholy as a battle won.
Dispatch [*1815*]

There is no mistake; there has been no mistake; and there shall be no mistake.
Letter to Mr. Huskisson

I care not one twopenny damn.[2]
Quoted in GEORGE OTTO TREVELYAN: *Life and Letters of Lord Macaulay* [*1876*], *Vol. II, Page 221*

It is very true that I have said that I considered Napoleon's presence in the field equal to forty thousand men in the balance. This is a very loose way of talking; but the idea is a very different one from that of his presence at a battle being equal to a reinforcement of forty thousand men.
STANHOPE, *Conversations with Wellington* [*1888*], *Page 81*

The battle of Waterloo was won on the playing fields of Eton.
Quoted in FRASER, *Words on Wellington* [*1889*]

---

[1] Tout soldat français porte dans sa giberne le bâton de maréchal de France.
[2] Quoted, as the Duke's oath, in a letter from MACAULAY to T. F. Ellis, March 6, 1849.

DAVID EVERETT
[1770–1813]

You'd scarce expect one of my age
To speak in public on the stage;
And if I chance to fall below
Demosthenes or Cicero,
Don't view me with a critic's eye,
But pass my imperfections by.
Large streams from little fountains flow,
Tall oaks from little acorns grow.[1]
*Lines written for a school dec-
lamation for Ephraim H. Far-
rar, aged seven, New Ipswich,
New Hampshire* [*1791*]

These thoughts inspire my youthful mind
To be the greatest of mankind;
Great, not like Caesar, stained with blood,
But only great as I am good.
*Lines written for a school dec-
lamation* [*1791*]

GEORGE CANNING
[1770–1827]

When our perils are past, shall our gratitude sleep?
No, — here's to the pilot that weathered the storm.
*Song for the Inauguration of the
Pitt Club* [*May 25, 1802*]

I give thee sixpence! I will see thee damned first.
*The Friend of Humanity and the
Knife-Grinder. Stanza 9*

A steady patriot of the world alone,
The friend of every country but his own.[2]
New Morality. Line 113

And finds, with keen, discriminating sight,
Black's not so black, — nor white so *very* white.
Ibid. Line 199

[1] The lofty oak from a small acorn grows. — LEWIS DUNCOMBE [1711–1730]: *De Minimis Maxima* (translation)
Parvis e glandibus quercus. — *Latin motto*
[2] This refers to the Jacobin.
See Overbury, page 226b.

Give me the avowed, the erect, the manly foe,
Bold I can meet, — perhaps may turn his blow!
But of all plagues, good Heaven, thy wrath can send,
Save, save, oh save me from the *candid friend!* [1]
New Morality. Line 207

I think of those companions true
Who studied with me at the U-
-niversity of Göttingen.
*Song sung by Rogero in the bur-
lesque play, The Rovers. Stanza 1*

Here rests, and let no saucy knave
Presume to sneer and laugh,
To learn that mouldering in the grave
Is laid a British Calf.
*Epitaph on the Tombstone
Erected over the Marquis of
Anglesea's Leg, Lost at the
Battle of Waterloo. Stanza 1*

She saw two legs were lost on him
Who never meant to run.
Ibid. Stanza 9

In matters of commerce the fault of the Dutch
Is offering too little and asking too much.
*Dispatch to Sir Charles Bagot,
British Minister at The Hague*
[*January 31, 1826*]

I called the New World into existence to redress the balance of the Old.
The King's Message [*December
12, 1826*]

GEORG WILHELM
FRIEDRICH HEGEL
[1770–1831]

Peoples and governments never have learned anything from history, or acted on principles deduced from it.
Philosophy of History [*1832*].[2]
Introduction

[1] Defend me from my friends; I can defend myself from my enemies. — *Remark attributed to Maréchal Villars when taking
leave of Louis XIV*
[2] Translated by J. SIBREE.

Amid the pressure of great events, a general principle gives no help.

Philosophy of History.
Introduction

To him who looks upon the world rationally, the world in its turn presents a rational aspect. The relation is mutual.

Ibid.

The history of the world is none other than the progress of the consciousness of freedom.

Ibid.

We may affirm absolutely that nothing great in the world has been accomplished without passion.

Ibid.

It is easier to discover a deficiency in individuals, in states, and in Providence, than to see their real import and value.

Ibid.

Life has a value only when it has something valuable as its object.

Ibid.

Serious occupation is labor that has reference to some want.

Ibid. Part I, Sect. 2, Chap. 1

It is a matter of perfect indifference where a thing originated; the only question is: "Is it true in and for itself?"

Ibid. Part III, Sect. 3, Chap. 2

When liberty is mentioned, we must always be careful to observe whether it is not really the assertion of private interests which is thereby designated.

Ibid. Part IV, Sect. 3, Chap. 2

The Few assume to be the *deputies,* but they are often only the *despoilers* of the Many.

Ibid. Chap. 3

JAMES HOGG [1]
[1770–1835]

She left this world of sorrow and pain,
And returned to the Land of Thought again.

Kilmeny

[1] The "Ettrick Shepherd."

Charlie is my darling,
The young Chevalier.
　　Charlie Is My Darling. Refrain
Love is like a dizziness,
It winna let a poor body
Gang about his bizziness.
　　Love Is Like a Dizziness. Stanza 1

PIERRE JACQUES ÉTIENNE, COUNT CAMBRONNE
[1770–1842]

The Guard dies, but never surrenders.[1]

Inscribed upon the monument
erected to him at Nantes

JOSEPH HOPKINSON
[1770–1842]

Hail, Columbia! happy land!
Hail, ye heroes! heaven-born band!
Who fought and bled in Freedom's cause,
Who fought and bled in Freedom's cause,
And when the storm of war was gone,
Enjoyed the peace your valor won.
Let independence be our boast,
Ever mindful what it cost;
Ever grateful for the prize,
Let its altar reach the skies!
　　Hail, Columbia.[2] Stanza 1

WILLIAM ROBERT SPENCER
[1770–1834]

When the black-lettered list to the gods was presented,

[1] This phrase, attributed to Cambronne, who was made prisoner at Waterloo, was vehemently denied by him. It was invented by Rougemont, a prolific author of *mots,* two days after the battle, in the "Indépendant." — FOURNIER: *L'Esprit dans l'Histoire*

[2] The musical setting of *Hail, Columbia,* generally attributed to Philip Phile, was originally *The President's March,* written in 1789 as an inaugural march for George Washington. In 1798, Joseph Hopkinson was asked by Mr. Fox, a young actor-singer, to write verses to the music of the march, to introduce at a benefit performance. The song was repeated eight times, and when sung the ninth time, the audience stood and joined in the chorus.

(The list of what Fate for each mortal intends,)
At the long string of ills a kind goddess relented,
And slipped in three blessings — wife, children, and friends.
Wife, Children, and Friends.
Stanza 1

Oh! where does faithful Gêlert roam,
The flow'r of all his race?
So true, so brave; a lamb at home,
A lion in the chase!
Beth-Gêlert. Stanza 4

JOHN TOBIN
[1770–1804]

The man that lays his hand upon a woman,
Save in the way of kindness, is a wretch
Whom 'twere gross flattery to name a coward.
The Honeymoon [1805]. Act II, Sc. 1

She's adorned
Amply that in her husband's eye looks lovely, —
The truest mirror that an honest wife
Can see her beauty in.
Ibid. Act III, Sc. 4

WILLIAM WORDSWORTH [1]
[1770–1850]

And homeless near a thousand homes I stood,
And near a thousand tables pined and wanted food.
Guilt and Sorrow [Written 1791–1794]. Part II, Stanza 41

A simple child,
That lightly draws its breath,
And feels its life in every limb,
What should it know of death?
We Are Seven [1798]. Stanza 1

O Reader! had you in your mind
Such stores as silent thought can bring,

---

[1] Coleridge said to Wordsworth, "Since Milton, I know of no poet with so many *felicities* and unforgettable lines and stanzas as you." — HENRY NELSON COLERIDGE: *Memoir* [1847]

O gentle Reader! you would find
A tale in everything.
Simon Lee [1798]. Stanza 9

In that sweet mood when pleasant thoughts
Bring sad thoughts to the mind.
Lines Written in Early Spring [1798]. Stanza 1

And 'tis my faith, that every flower
Enjoys the air it breathes.
Ibid. Stanza 3

Nor less I deem that there are Powers
Which of themselves our minds impress;
That we can feed this mind of ours
In a wise passiveness.
Expostulation and Reply [1798].
Stanza 6

Up! up! my friend, and quit your books;
Or surely you'll grow double:
Up! up! my friend, and clear your looks;
Why all this toil and trouble?
The Tables Turned [1798].
Stanza 1

Come forth into the light of things,
Let Nature be your teacher.
Ibid. Stanza 4

One impulse from a vernal wood
May teach you more of man,
Of moral evil and of good,
Than all the sages can.
Ibid. Stanza 6

Sensations sweet,
Felt in the blood, and felt along the heart.
Lines Composed a Few Miles Above Tintern Abbey [1798]

That best portion of a good man's life, —
His little, nameless, unremembered, acts
Of kindness and of love.
Ibid.

That blessed mood,
In which the burthen of the mystery,
In which the heavy and the weary weight
Of all this unintelligible world,
Is lightened.
Ibid.

The sounding cataract
Haunted me like a passion; the tall rock,
The mountain, and the deep and gloomy wood,
Their colours and their forms, were then to me
An appetite; a feeling and a love,
That had no need of a remoter charm,
By thoughts supplied, nor any interest
Unborrowed from the eye.
Lines Composed a Few Miles
Above Tintern Abbey
But hearing oftentimes
The still, sad music of humanity.
Ibid.
A sense sublime
Of something far more deeply interfused,
Whose dwelling is the light of setting suns,
And the round ocean and the living air,
And the blue sky, and in the mind of man;
A motion and a spirit, that impels
All thinking things, all objects of all thought,
And rolls through all things.
Ibid.
Knowing that Nature never did betray
The heart that loved her.
Ibid.
Men who can hear the Decalogue and feel
No self-reproach.
The Old Cumberland Beggar
[Written 1798]
As in the eye of Nature he has lived,
So in the eye of Nature let him die!
Ibid.
Full twenty times was Peter feared,
For once that Peter was respected.
Peter Bell [Written 1798].
Part I, Stanza 3
A primrose by a river's brim
A yellow primrose was to him,
And it was nothing more.
Ibid. Stanza 12
The soft blue sky did never melt
Into his heart; he never felt
The witchery of the soft blue sky!
Ibid. Stanza 15

On a fair prospect some have looked,
And felt, as I have heard them say,
As if the moving time had been
A thing as steadfast as the scene
On which they gazed themselves away.
Peter Bell. Part I, Stanza 16
As if the man had fixed his face,
In many a solitary place,
Against the wind and open sky!
Ibid. Stanza 26 [1]
Many are our joys
In youth, but oh! what happiness to live
When every hour brings palpable access
Of knowledge, when all knowledge is delight,
And sorrow is not there!
The Prelude [Written 1799–
1805]. Book II
Where the statue stood
Of Newton with his prism and silent face,
The marble index of a mind forever
Voyaging through strange seas of thought, alone.
Ibid. Book III
There's not a man
That lives who hath not known his god-like hours.
Ibid.
When from our better selves we have too long
Been parted by the hurrying world, and droop,
Sick of its business, of its pleasures tired,
How gracious, how benign, is Solitude.
Ibid. Book IV
'Tis told by one whom stormy waters threw,
With fellow-sufferers by the shipwreck spared,

[1] The original edition [1819] had the following as the fourth stanza from the end of Part I, which was omitted in all subsequent editions:
Is it a party in a parlour?
Crammed just as they on earth were crammed, —
Some sipping punch, some sipping tea,
But, as you by their faces see,
All silent and all damned.

Upon a desert coast, that having
  brought
To land a single volume, saved by
  chance,
A treatise on Geometry.
  The Prelude. Book VI
  Multitudes of hours
Pilfered away, by what the Bard who
  sang
Of the Enchanter Indolence [1] hath
  called
"Good-natured lounging," and behold
  a map
Of my collegiate life.
  Ibid.
  How men lived
Even next-door neighbours, as we say,
  yet still
Strangers, not knowing each the other's
  name.
  Ibid. Book VII
Bliss was it in that dawn to be alive,
But to be young was very heaven!
  Ibid. Book XI
One of those heavenly days that can-
  not die.
  Nutting [*1799*]
What fond and wayward thoughts will
  slide
  Into a lover's head!
"O mercy!" to myself I cried,
  "If Lucy should be dead!"
  Strange Fits of Passion Have I
  Known [*1799*]. *Stanza 7*
She dwelt among the untrodden ways
  Beside the springs of Dove,
A maid whom there were none to praise
  And very few to love.[2]
  Lucy: She Dwelt Among the Un-
  trodden Ways [*1799*]. *Stanza 1*
A violet by a mossy stone
  Half hidden from the eye! —

[1] THOMSON's *Castle of Indolence* [1748].
[2] He lived amidst th' untrodden ways
    To Rydal Lake that lead;
  A bard whom there were none to praise,
    And very few to read.
  Unread his works — his "Milk White Doe"
    With dust is dark and dim;
  It's still in Longmans' shop, and oh!
    The difference to him!
    — *Parody by* HARTLEY COLERIDGE
    [1796–1849]

Fair as a star, when only one
  Is shining in the sky.
  Lucy: She Dwelt Among the Un-
  trodden Ways. Stanza 2
She lived unknown, and few could
  know
  When Lucy ceased to be;
But she is in her grave, and, oh,
  The difference to me!
  Ibid. Stanza 3
Three years she grew in sun and shower,
Then Nature said, "A lovelier flower
On earth was never sown;
This Child I to myself will take;
She shall be mine, and I will make
A Lady of my own."
  Lucy: Three Years She Grew in
  Sun and Shower [*1799*]. *Stanza 1*
"The stars of midnight shall be dear
To her; and she shall lean her ear
In many a secret place
Where rivulets dance their wayward
  round,
And beauty born of murmuring sound
Shall pass into her face."
  Ibid. Stanza 5
A slumber did my spirit seal;
  I had no human fears:
She seemed a thing that could not feel
  The touch of earthly years.

No motion has she now, no force;
  She neither hears nor sees;
Rolled round in earth's diurnal course,
  With rocks, and stones, and trees.
  A Slumber Did My Spirit Seal
  [*1799*]
One that would peep and botanize
Upon his mother's grave.
  A Poet's Epitaph [*1799*]. *Stanza 5*
And you must love him, ere to you
He will seem worthy of your love.
  Ibid. Stanza 11
The harvest of a quiet eye.
  Ibid. Stanza 13
Yet sometimes, when the secret cup
Of still and serious thought went
  round,
It seemed as if he drank it up —
He felt with spirit so profound.
  Matthew [*1799*]. *Stanza 7*

The sweetest thing that ever grew
Beside a human door.
> *Lucy Gray* [*1799*]. *Stanza 2*

A youth to whom was given
So much of earth — so much of heaven.
> *Ruth* [*1799*]. *Stanza 21*

Poetry is the breath and finer spirit of all knowledge; it is the impassioned expression which is in the countenance of all Science.
> *Lyrical Ballads, Second Edition*
> [*1800*]. *Preface*

In spite of difference of soil and climate, of language and manners, of laws and customs, — in spite of things silently gone out of mind, and things violently destroyed, the Poet binds together by passion and knowledge the vast empire of human society, as it is spread over the whole earth, and over all time.
> *Ibid.*

I have said that poetry is the spontaneous overflow of powerful feelings: it takes its origin from emotion recollected in tranquillity.
> *Ibid.*

All men feel an habitual gratitude, and something of an honourable bigotry, for the objects which have long continued to please them.
> *Ibid.*

Something between a hindrance and a help.
> *Michael* [*1800*]

Drink, pretty creature, drink!
> *The Pet Lamb* [*1800*]

May no rude hand deface it,
And its forlorn *hic jacet!*
> *Ellen Irwin* [*1800*]. *Stanza 7*

She gave me eyes, she gave me ears;
And humble cares, and delicate fears;
A heart, the fountain of sweet tears;
And love, and thought, and joy.
> *The Sparrows' Nest* [*1801*].
> *Stanza 2*

My heart leaps up when I behold
A rainbow in the sky:
So was it when my life began;
So is it now I am a man.
> *My Heart Leaps Up When I*
> *Behold* [*1802*]

The Child is father of the Man; [1]
And I could wish my days to be
Bound each to each by natural piety.
> *My Heart Leaps Up When I Behold*

Sweet childish days, that were as long
As twenty days are now.
> *To a Butterfly* [*1802*]. *Part II,*
> *I've Watched You Now a Full*
> *Half-hour, Stanza 2*

Often have I sighed to measure
By myself a lonely pleasure,
Sighed to think, I read a book
Only read, perhaps, by me.
> *To the Small Celandine* [*1802*].
> *Part II, Stanza 4*

I thought of Chatterton, the marvellous boy,
The sleepless soul that perished in his pride;
Of him who walked in glory and in joy
Following his plough, along the mountain-side:
By our own spirits are we deified:
We Poets in our youth begin in gladness;
But thereof come in the end despondency and madness.
> *Resolution and Independence*
> [*1802*]. *Stanza 7*

That heareth not the loud winds when they call,
And moveth all together, if it moves at all.
> *Ibid. Stanza 11*

Choice word and measured phrase, above the reach
Of ordinary men.
> *Ibid. Stanza 14*

And mighty poets in their misery dead.
> *Ibid. Stanza 17*

Earth has not anything to show more fair:
Dull would he be of soul who could pass by
A sight so touching in its majesty.
> *Composed Upon Westminster*
> *Bridge* [*September 3, 1802*]

Ne'er saw I, never felt, a calm so deep!
The river glideth at his own sweet will;

[1] See Milton, page 259b.

Dear God! the very houses seem asleep;
And all that mighty heart is lying still!
Composed Upon Westminster Bridge

It is a beauteous evening, calm and free,
The holy time is quiet as a nun
Breathless with adoration.
It Is a Beauteous Evening [*1802*]

Thou liest in Abraham's bosom all the year;
And worship'st at the Temple's inner shrine,
God being with thee when we know it not.
Ibid.

Once did She hold the gorgeous east in fee:
And was the safeguard of the west.
On the Extinction of the Venetian Republic [*1802*]

Men are we, and must grieve when even the shado
Of that which once was great, is passed away.
Ibid.

And, when she took unto herself a Mate,
She must espouse the everlasting Sea.
Ibid.

Thou hast left behind
Powers that will work for thee; air, earth, and skies;
There's not a breathing of the common wind
That will forget thee; thou hast great allies;
Thy friends are exultations, agonies,
And love, and man's unconquerable mind.
To Toussaint L'Ouverture

Plain living and high thinking are no more:
The homely beauty of the good old cause
Is gone; our peace, our fearful innocence,
And pure religion breathing household laws.
O Friend! I Know Not Which Way I Must Look [*1802*]

Milton! thou should'st be living at this hour:
England hath need of thee; she is a fen
Of stagnant waters.
London, 1802

Thy soul was like a star, and dwelt apart:
Thou hadst a voice whose sound was like the sea:
Pure as the naked heavens, majestic, free,
So didst thou travel on life's common way,
In cheerful godliness.
Ibid.

We must be free or die, who speak the tongue
That Shakespeare spake; the faith and morals hold
Which Milton held.
It Is Not To Be Thought Of [*1802*]

We meet thee, like a pleasant thought,
When such are wanted.
To the Daisy [*1802*]. *Stanza 3*

The poet's darling.
Ibid. Stanza 4

Thou unassuming commonplace
Of Nature.
To the Same Flower [*1802*].
Stanza 1

Oft on the dappled turf at ease
I sit, and play with similes,
Loose type of things through all degrees.
Ibid. Stanza 2

And stepping westward seemed to be
A kind of heavenly destiny.
Stepping Westward [*1803*].
Stanza 2

For old, unhappy, far-off things,
And battles long ago.
The Solitary Reaper [*1803*].
Stanza 3

Some natural sorrow, loss, or pain,
That has been, and may be again.
Ibid.

The music in my heart I bore
Long after it was heard no more.
Ibid. Stanza 4

Because the good old rule
Sufficeth them, the simple plan,

That they should take, who have the power,
And they should keep who can.
Rob Roy's Grave [*1803*]. *Stanza 9*

Yon foaming flood seems motionless as ice;
Its dizzy turbulence eludes the eye,
Frozen by distance.
Address to Kilchurn Castle [*1803*]

A brotherhood of venerable trees.
Sonnet Composed at —— Castle [*1803*]

A remnant of uneasy light.
The Matron of Jedborough [*1803*]

Oh for a single hour of that Dundee
Who on that day the word of onset gave!
Sonnet, in the Pass of Killicranky [*1803*]

There was a time when meadow, grove, and stream,
The earth, and every common sight,
To me did seem
Apparelled in celestial light,
The glory and the freshness of a dream.
It is not now as it hath been of yore; —
Turn wheresoe'er I may,
By night or day,
The things which I have seen I now can see no more.
Ode. Intimations of Immortality [1]
[*1803–1806*]. *Stanza 1*

The Rainbow comes and goes,
And lovely is the Rose.
Ibid. Stanza 2

The sunshine is a glorious birth;
But yet I know, where'er I go,
That there hath passed away a glory from the earth.
Ibid.

Where is it now, the glory and the dream?
Ibid. Stanza 4

Our birth is but a sleep and a forgetting:
The soul that rises with us, our life's star,
Hath had elsewhere its setting,

[1] The Ode on Immortality is the high water mark which the intellect has reached in this age. — EMERSON: *English Traits* [1856]

And cometh from afar:
Not in entire forgetfulness,
And not in utter nakedness,
But trailing clouds of glory do we come
From God, who is our home:
Heaven lies about us in our infancy! [1]
Shades of the prison-house begin to close
Upon the growing boy.
Ode. Intimations of Immortality. *Stanza 5*

At length the man perceives it die away,
And fade into the light of common day.
Ibid.

As if his whole vocation
Were endless imitation.
Ibid. Stanza 7

High instincts before which our mortal nature
Did tremble like a guilty thing surprised.
Ibid. Stanza 9

Truths that wake,
To perish never.
Ibid.

Though inland far we be,
Our souls have sight of that immortal sea
Which brought us hither.
Ibid.

Though nothing can bring back the hour
Of splendour in the grass, of glory in the flower.
Ibid. Stanza 10

In years that bring the philosophic mind.
Ibid.

The clouds that gather round the setting sun
Do take a sober colouring from an eye
That hath kept watch o'er man's mortality.
Ibid. Stanza 11

[1] Not only around our infancy
Doth heaven with all its splendors lie;
Daily, with souls that cringe and plot,
We Sinais climb and know it not.
    JAMES RUSSELL LOWELL: *The Vision of Sir Launfal* [1848], *Part I, Prelude, St. 2*

To me the meanest flower that blows can give
Thoughts that do often lie too deep for tears.
> *Ode. Intimations of Immortality.*
> *Stanza 11*

O blithe New-comer! I have heard,
I hear thee and rejoice.
O Cuckoo! shall I call thee bird,
Or but a wandering voice?
> *To the Cuckoo [1804]. Stanza 1*

She was a phantom of delight
When first she gleamed upon my sight;
A lovely apparition, sent
To be a moment's ornament;
Her eyes as stars of twilight fair,
Like twilight's, too, her dusky hair,
But all things else about her drawn
From May-time and the cheerful dawn.
> *She Was a Phantom of Delight*
> *[1804]. Stanza 1*

A creature not too bright or good
For human nature's daily food;
For transient sorrows, simple wiles,
Praise, blame, love, kisses, tears, and smiles.
> *Ibid. Stanza 2*

And now I see with eye serene
The very pulse of the machine.
> *Ibid. Stanza 3*

The reason firm, the temperate will,
Endurance, foresight, strength, and skill;
A perfect woman, nobly planned,
To warn, to comfort, and command.
> *Ibid.*

I wandered lonely as a cloud
That floats on high o'er vales and hills,
When all at once I saw a crowd,
A host, of golden daffodils;
Beside the lake, beneath the trees,
Fluttering and dancing in the breeze.
> *I Wandered Lonely as a Cloud*
> *[1804]. Stanza 1*

Ten thousand saw I at a glance,
Tossing their heads in sprightly dance.
> *Ibid. Stanza 2*

A poet could not but be gay,
In such a jocund company:
I gazed — and gazed — but little thought

What wealth to me the show had brought.
> *I Wandered Lonely as a Cloud.*
> *Stanza 3*

That inward eye
Which is the bliss of solitude.
> *Ibid. Stanza 4*

Stern Daughter of the Voice of God! [1]
> *Ode to Duty [1805]. Stanza 1*

A light to guide, a rod
To check the erring, and reprove.
> *Ibid.*

Thou dost preserve the stars from wrong;
And the most ancient heavens, through Thee, are fresh and strong.
> *Ibid. Stanza 6*

The light that never was, on sea or land;
The consecration, and the Poet's dream.
> *Suggested by a Picture of Peele*
> *Castle in a Storm [1805]. Stanza 4*

Shalt show us how divine a thing
A woman may be made.
> *To a Young Lady [1805]. Dear*
> *Child of Nature, Stanza 2*

But an old age serene and bright,
And lovely as a Lapland night,
   Shall lead thee to thy grave.
> *Ibid. Stanza 3*

Who is the happy Warrior? Who is he
That every man in arms would wish to be?
> *Character of the Happy Warrior*
> *[1806]*

But who, if he be called upon to face
Some awful moment to which Heaven has joined
Great issues, good or bad for humankind,
Is happy as a lover.
> *Ibid.*

And, through the heat of conflict, keeps the law
In calmness made, and sees what he foresaw.
> *Ibid.*

Whom neither shape of danger can dismay,

[1] See Milton, page 258a.

Nor thought of tender happiness be-
tray.
   Character of the Happy Warrior
Like, — but oh how different!
   Yes, It Was the Mountain Echo
      [1806]
The world is too much with us; late
and soon,
Getting and spending, we lay waste our
powers:
Little we see in Nature that is ours.
   *The World Is Too Much With
      Us [1806]*
Great God! I'd rather be
A Pagan suckled in a creed outworn; [1]
So might I, standing on this pleasant
lea,
Have glimpses that would make me
less forlorn;
Have sight of Proteus rising from the
sea;
Or hear old Triton blow his wreathed
horn.
   Ibid.
Where lies the land to which yon Ship
must go? [2]
Fresh as a lark mounting at break of
day,
Festively she puts forth in trim array.
   Where Lies the Land [1806]
Blessed barrier between day and day.
   *To Sleep [1806]. II, A Flock
      of Sheep*
Maidens withering on the stalk. [3]
   *Personal Talk [1806].
      Sonnet 1*
Dreams, books, are each a world; and
books, we know,
Are a substantial world, both pure and
good.

Round these, with tendrils strong as
flesh and blood,
Our pastime and our happiness will
grow.
   Personal Talk. Sonnet 3
A power is passing from the earth.
   *Lines on the Expected Dissolution
      of Mr. Fox [1806]. Stanza 5*
Two voices are there: one is of the
sea,[1]
One of the mountains; each a mighty
voice.
   *Thought of a Briton on the Sub-
      jugation of Switzerland [1807]*
The silence that is in the starry sky,
The sleep that is among the lonely
hills.
   *Song at the Feast of Brougham
      Castle [1807]*
A few strong instincts, and a few plain
rules.
   *Alas! What Boots the Long
      Laborious Quest? [1809]*
Strongest minds
Are often those of whom the noisy
world
Hears least.
   The Excursion [2] *[Published
      1814]. Book I*
The imperfect offices of prayer and
praise.
   Ibid.
The good die first,[3]
And they whose hearts are dry as sum-
mer dust
Burn to the socket.
   Ibid.
Wrongs unredressed, or insults un-
avenged.
   Ibid. Book III
Society became my glittering bride.
   Ibid.

---

[1]   Good Lord! I'd rather be
Quite unacquainted with the A.B.C.
Than write such hopeless rubbish as thy
  worst.
    JAMES KENNETH STEPHEN: *Sonnet,
      Wordsworth* [1891]
[2] Where lies the land to which the ship
  would go?
Far, far ahead, is all her seamen know.
    ARTHUR HUGH CLOUGH [1819–1861]:
      Songs of Absence
[3] Withering on the virgin thorn. — SHAKE-
SPEARE: *A Midsummer-Night's Dream* [1595–
1596], *Act I, Sc. 1, L. 77*

[1] Two voices are there: one is of the deep.
And one is of an old half-witted sheep
Which bleats articulate monotony,
And indicates that two and one are three.
    JAMES KENNETH STEPHEN: *Sonnet,
      Wordsworth* [1891]
[2] This will never do. — FRANCIS JEFFREY:
Opening sentence, review of WORDSWORTH'S
Excursion, Edinburgh Review [1814]
[3] See Plautus, page 30a.

There is a luxury in self-dispraise;
And inward self-disparagement affords
To meditative spleen a grateful feast.
The Excursion. Book IV

I have seen
A curious child, who dwelt upon a
tract
Of inland ground, applying to his ear
The convolutions of a smooth-lipped
shell,
To which, in silence hushed, his very
soul
Listened intensely; and his counte-
nance soon
Brightened with joy, for from within
were heard
Murmurings, whereby the monitor ex-
pressed
Mysterious union with its native sea.[1]
Ibid.

One in whom persuasion and belief
Had ripened into faith, and faith be-
come
A passionate intuition.
Ibid.

Spires whose "silent finger points to
heaven."[2]
Ibid. Book VI

Wisdom married to immortal verse.
Ibid. Book VII

A man he seems of cheerful yesterdays
And confident tomorrows.
Ibid.

---

[1] But I have sinuous shells of pearly hue ...
Shake one, and it awakens; then apply
Its polisht lips to your attentive ear,
And it remembers its august abodes,
And murmurs as the ocean murmurs there.
WALTER SAVAGE LANDOR: *Gebir,
Book I* [1798]
Upon a mountain height, far from the sea,
I found a shell,
And to my listening ear the lonely thing
Ever a song of ocean seemed to sing,
Ever a tale of ocean seemed to tell.
EUGENE FIELD [1850–1895]:
The Wanderer, St. 1

[2] An instinctive taste teaches men to build
their churches in flat countries with spire
steeples, which, as they cannot be referred to
any other object, point as with silent finger to
the sky and stars. — COLERIDGE: *The Friend*
[1809], *No. 14*

Her bosom heaves and spreads, her
stature grows;
And she expects the issue in repose.
Laodamia [*1814*]. *Stanza 2*

The gods approve
The depth, and not the tumult, of the
soul.
Ibid. Stanza 13

An ampler ether, a diviner air.
Ibid. Stanza 18

But thou that didst appear so fair
To fond imagination,
Dost rival in the light of day
Her delicate creation.
Yarrow Visited [*1814*]. *Stanza 6*

And beauty, for confiding youth,
Those shocks of passion can prepare
That kill the bloom before its time;
And blanch, without the owner's crime,
The most resplendent hair.
Lament of Mary Queen of Scots
[*1817*]. *Stanza 6*

Enough if something from our hands
have power
To live, and act, and serve the future
hour.
*The River Duddon, Sonnet:
Afterthought* [*1820*]

We feel that we are greater than we
know.
Ibid.

The feather, whence the pen
Was shaped that traced the lives of
these good men,
Dropped from an angel's wing.[1]
*Ecclesiastical Sonnets. Part III, V,
Walton's Book of Lives* [*1821*]

Give all thou canst; high Heaven re-
jects the lore
Of nicely-calculated less or more.
*Ibid. XLIII, Inside of King's Col-
lege Chapel, Cambridge* [*1821*]

But hushed be every thought that
springs
From out the bitterness of things.
*Elegiac Stanzas, Addressed to
Sir G. H. B.* [*1824*]. *Stanza 7*

---

[1] The pen wherewith thou dost so heavenly
sing
Made of a quill from an angel's wing.
HENRY CONSTABLE [1562–
1613]: *Sonnet*

Ethereal minstrel! pilgrim of the sky!
To a Skylark [*1825*]. *Stanza 1*

Type of the wise who soar, but never roam,
True to the kindred points of heaven and home.
Ibid. Stanza 2

Scorn not the sonnet. Critic, you have frowned,
Mindless of its just honours; with this key
Shakespeare unlocked his heart.[1]
Scorn Not the Sonnet [*1827*]

Look for the stars, you'll say that there are none;
Look up a second time, and, one by one,
You mark them twinkling out with silvery light,
And wonder how they could elude the sight!
Calm Is the Fragrant Air [*1832*]

Small service is true service while it lasts.
Of humblest friends, bright creature! scorn not one:
The daisy, by the shadow that it casts,
Protects the lingering dewdrop from the sun.
To a Child, Written in her Album [*1834*]

How does the meadow-flower its bloom unfold?
Because the lovely little flower is free
Down to its root, and, in that freedom, bold.
A Poet! He Hath Put His Heart to School [*1842*]

Minds that have nothing to confer
Find little to perceive.
Yes, Thou art Fair [*1845*]. *Stanza 2*

[1]   "With this same key
Shakespeare unlocked his heart" once more!
Did Shakespeare? If so, the less Shakespeare he!
ROBERT BROWNING: *House* [1876], *St. 10*

THOMAS DIBDIN
[1771–1841]

Oh, it's a snug little island!
A right little, tight little island.
The Snug Little Island

JAMES MONTGOMERY
[1771–1854]

Tomorrow — oh, 'twill never be,
If we should live a thousand years!
Our time is all today, today.
Today

Give me the hand that is honest and hearty,
Free as the breeze and unshackled by party.
Give Me Thy Hand. Stanza 2

The rose has but a summer reign,
The daisy never dies.
The Daisy. Stanza 10

"The Press! — What is the Press?" I cried;
When thus a wondrous voice replied:
"In me all human knowledge dwells;
The oracle of oracles,
Past, present, future, I reveal,
Or in oblivion's silence seal;
What I preserve can perish never,
What I forego is lost forever."
The Press. Stanza 1

All that philosophers have sought,
Science discovered, genius wrought;
All that reflective memory stores,
Or rich imagination pours,
All that the wit of man conceives,
All that he wishes, hopes, believes;
All that he loves, or fears, or hates,
All that to heaven and earth relates,
— These are the lessons that I teach
In speaking silence, silent speech.
Ibid. Stanza 4

Counts his sure gains, and hurries back for more.
The West Indies. Part III

Hope against hope, and ask till ye receive.
The World before the Flood.
Canto V, Stanza 10

Joys too exquisite to last,
And yet *more* exquisite when past.
The Little Cloud. Stanza 9

Bliss in possession will not last;
Remembered joys are never past;
At once the fountain, stream, and sea,
They were, they are, they yet shall be.
The Little Cloud. Stanza 10

Friend after friend departs;
  Who hath not lost a friend?
There is no union here of hearts
  That finds not here an end.
Friends. Stanza 1

'Tis not the whole of life to live,
Nor all of death to die.
*The Issues of Life and Death.
Stanza 2*

Who, that hath ever been,
  Could bear to be no more?
Yet who would tread again the scene
  He trod through life before?
The Falling Leaf. Stanza 7

Here in the body pent,
  Absent from Him I roam,
Yet nightly pitch my moving tent
  A day's march nearer home.
At Home in Heaven

Prayer is the soul's sincere desire,
  Uttered or unexpressed;
The motion of a hidden fire
  That trembles in the breast.
What is Prayer? Stanza 1

Prayer is the burden of a sigh,
  The falling of a tear;
The upward glancing of an eye,
  When none but God is near.
Ibid. Stanza 2

SIR WALTER SCOTT
[1771–1832]

The way was long, the wind was cold,
The Minstrel was infirm and old;
His withered cheek, and tresses gray,
Seem'd to have known a better day.
*The Lay of the Last Minstrel
[1805]. Introduction*

Such is the custom of Branksome Hall.
Ibid. Canto I, Stanza 7

What shall be the maiden's fate?
Who shall be the maiden's mate?
Ibid. Stanza 16

If thou would'st view fair Melrose
  aright,

Go visit it by the pale moonlight.
*The Lay of the Last Minstrel.
Canto II, Stanza 1*

I cannot tell how the truth may be;
I say the tale as 'twas said to me.
Ibid. Stanza 22

In peace, Love tunes the shepherd's
  reed;
In war, he mounts the warrior's steed;
In halls, in gay attire is seen;
In hamlets, dances on the green.
Love rules the court, the camp, the
  grove,
And men below, and saints above;
For love is heaven, and heaven is love.
Ibid. Canto III, Stanza 2

Her blue eyes sought the west afar,
For lovers love the western star.
Ibid. Stanza 24

Ne'er
Was flattery lost on poet's ear;
A simple race! they waste their toil
For the vain tribute of a smile.
*Ibid. Canto IV, Interlude
after Stanza 35*

Call it not vain: they do not err
Who say, that when the poet dies,
Mute Nature mourns her worshipper,
And celebrates his obsequies.
Ibid. Canto V, Stanza 1

True love's the gift which God has
  given
To man alone beneath the heaven:
It is not fantasy's hot fire,
  Whose wishes, soon as granted, fly;
It liveth not in fierce desire,
  With dead desire it doth not die;
It is the secret sympathy,
The silver link, the silken tie,
Which heart to heart and mind to mind
In body and in soul can bind.
Ibid. Stanza 13

Breathes there the man, with soul so
  dead,
Who never to himself hath said,
  This is my own, my native land!
Whose heart hath ne'er within him
  burn'd [1]
As home his footsteps he hath turn'd,

[1] Did not our heart burn within us while
he talked with us by the way? — *Luke,
XXIV, 32*

From wandering on a foreign strand?
If such there breathe, go, mark him
    well;
For him no minstrel raptures swell;
High though his titles, proud his name,
Boundless his wealth as wish can
    claim, —
Despite those titles, power, and pelf,
The wretch, concentred all in self,
Living, shall forfeit fair renown,
And, doubly dying, shall go down
To the vile dust, from whence he
    sprung,
Unwept, unhonour'd, and unsung.[1]
        The Lay of the Last Minstrel.
            Canto VI, Stanza 1

O Caledonia! stern and wild,
Meet nurse for a poetic child!
Land of brown heath and shaggy wood;
Land of the mountain and the flood!
            Ibid. Stanza 2

November's sky is chill and drear,
November's leaf is red and sear.
        Marmion [1808]. *Introduction
            to Canto I, Stanza 1*

Stood for his country's glory fast,
And nail'd her colors to the mast!
            Ibid. Stanza 10

Just at the age 'twixt boy and youth,
When thought is speech, and speech is
    truth.
        *Ibid. Introduction to Canto II,
            Stanza 4*

When, musing on companions gone,
We doubly feel ourselves alone.
            Ibid. Stanza 5

To bring my tribute to his grave: —
'Tis little — but 'tis all I have.
        *Ibid. Introduction to Canto IV,
            Stanza 5*

Where's the coward that would not
    dare
To fight for such a land?
        Ibid. Canto IV, Stanza 30

Lightly from fair to fair he flew,
And loved to plead, lament, and sue;
Suit lightly won, and short-lived pain,
For monarchs seldom sigh in vain.
        Ibid. Canto V, Stanza 9

[1] See Homer, page 5b.

Oh, young Lochinvar is come out of the
    West,
Through all the wide Border his steed
    was the best.
        Marmion. Canto V, Stanza 12
            [*Lochinvar, Stanza 1*]

So faithful in love, and so dauntless in
    war,
There never was knight like the young
    Lochinvar.
            Ibid.

For a laggard in love, and a dastard in
    war,
Was to wed the fair Ellen of brave
    Lochinvar.
        Ibid. [*Lochinvar, Stanza 2*]

With a smile on her lips, and a tear in
    her eye.
        Ibid. [*Lochinvar, Stanza 5*]

Heap on more wood! — the wind is
    chill;
But let it whistle as it will,
We'll keep our Christmas merry still.
        *Ibid. Introduction to Canto VI,
            Stanza 1*

England was merry England, when
Old Christmas brought his sports again.
'Twas Christmas broach'd the mightiest
    ale;
'Twas Christmas told the merriest tale;
A Christmas gambol oft could cheer
The poor man's heart through half the
    year.
Still linger, in our northern clime,
Some remnants of the good old time.
            Ibid. Stanza 4

And dar'st thou, then,
To beard the lion in his den,
The Douglas in his hall?
            Ibid. Canto VI, Stanza 14

Oh, what a tangled web we weave,
When first we practise to deceive!
            Ibid. Stanza 17

O woman! in our hours of ease,
Uncertain, coy, and hard to please,
And variable as the shade
By the light quivering aspen made;
When pain and anguish wring the
    brow,
A ministering angel thou! [1]
            Ibid. Stanza 30

[1] See Shakespeare, page 179a.

"Charge, Chester, charge! on, Stanley,
   on!"
Were the last words of Marmion.
Marmion. Canto VI,
Stanza 32
To all, to each, a fair good-night,
And pleasing dreams, and slumbers
   light.
Ibid. L'Envoy, To the Reader
The stag at eve had drunk his fill,
Where danced the moon on Monan's
   rill,
And deep his midnight lair had made
In lone Glenartney's hazel shade.
The Lady of the Lake [*1810*].
Canto I, Stanza 1
In listening mood she seemed to stand,
The guardian Naiad of the strand.
Ibid. Stanza 17
And ne'er did Grecian chisel trace
A Nymph, a Naiad, or a Grace
Of finer form, or lovelier face.
Ibid. Stanza 18
A foot more light, a step more true,
Ne'er from the heath-flower dash'd the
   dew.
Ibid.
On his bold visage middle age
Had slightly press'd its signet sage,
Yet had not quench'd the open truth
And fiery vehemence of youth:
Forward and frolic glee was there,
The will to do, the soul to dare.
Ibid. Stanza 21
Soldier, rest! thy warfare o'er,
Sleep the sleep that knows not break-
   ing,
Dream of battled fields no more,
Days of danger, nights of waking.
Ibid. Stanza 31
Hail to the Chief who in triumph ad-
   vances! [1]
Ibid. Canto II, Stanza 19
Some feelings are to mortals given,
With less of earth in them than heaven.
Ibid. Stanza 22
Like the dew on the mountain,
  Like the foam on the river,

---

[1] These verses were set to music by JAMES
SANDERSON [1769–1841?], and this march has
become traditionally attached to the President
of the United States.

Like the bubble on the fountain,
  Thou art gone, and forever!
The Lady of the Lake. Canto III,
Stanza 16 [*Coronach, Stanza 3*]
Come one, come all! this rock shall fly
From its firm base as soon as I.
Ibid. Canto V, Stanza 10
And the stern joy which warriors feel
In foemen worthy of their steel.
Ibid.
Who o'er the herd would wish to reign,
Fantastic, fickle, fierce, and vain!
Vain as the leaf upon the stream,
And fickle as a changeful dream;
Fantastic as a woman's mood,
And fierce as Frenzy's fever'd blood.
Thou many-headed monster [1] thing,
Oh who would wish to be thy king!
Stanza 30
Where, where was Roderick then!
One blast upon his bugle horn
Were worth a thousand men!
Ibid. Canto VI, Stanza 18
Where lives the man that has not tried
How mirth can into folly glide,
   And folly into sin!
The Bridal of Triermain [*1813*].
Canto I, Stanza 21
Long loved, long woo'd, and lately won,
My life's best hope, and now mine own.
Ibid. Introduction to Canto II,
Stanza 1
Two sisters by the goal are set,
Cold Disappointment and Regret;
One disenchants the winner's eyes,
And strips of all its worth the prize,
While one augments its gaudy show,
More to enhance the loser's woe.
Rokeby [*1813*]. *Canto I,*
Stanza 31
Still are the thoughts to memory dear.
Ibid. Stanza 33
A mother's pride, a father's joy.
Ibid. Canto III, Stanza 15
Oh, Brignall banks are wild and fair,
  And Greta woods are green,
And you may gather garlands there
  Would grace a summer's queen.
Ibid. Stanza 16
The tear down childhood's cheek that
  flows

---

[1] See Sir Philip Sidney, page 115b.

Is like the dewdrop on the rose;
When next the summer breeze comes by,
And waves the bush, the flower is dry.
   Rokeby. Canto IV, Stanza 1

Thus aged men, full loth and slow,
The vanities of life forego,
And count their youthful follies o'er,
Till Memory lends her light no more.
   Ibid. Canto V, Stanza 1

Oh, many a shaft at random sent
Finds mark the archer little meant!
And many a word, at random spoken,
May soothe or wound a heart that's
 broken!
   The Lord of the Isles [*1815*].
     Canto V, Stanza 18

Randolph, thy wreath has lost a rose.[1]
   Ibid. Canto VI, Stanza 18

There was — and O! how many sor-
 rows crowd
Into these two brief words!
   Ibid. Conclusion

Then strip, lads, and to it, though
 sharp be the weather,
And if, by mischance, you should
 happen to fall,
There are worse things in life than a
 tumble on heather,
And life is itself but a game at football.
   Song [2] [*1815*]. *Stanza 5*

 A lawyer without history or literature is a mechanic, a mere working
mason; if he possesses some knowledge
of these, he may venture to call himself
an architect.
   Guy Mannering [*1815*]. *Chap. 37*

Bluid is thicker than water.[3]
   Ibid. Chap. 38

 It's no fish ye're buying, it's men's
lives.[4]
   The Antiquary [*1816*]. *Chap. 11*

----

[1] Robert Bruce's censure of Randolph for
permitting a body of English cavalry to pass
his flank on the day before the battle of Bannockburn [June 24, 1314].
 A rose hath fallen from thy chaplet. —
Halidon Hall [*1822*], *Act II, Sc. 2*
 [2] On the lifting of the banner of the House
of Buccleuch at a great football match on
Carterhaugh.
 [3] This proverb is found as early as the
seventeenth century.
 [4] See Thomas Hood, page 489a.

Come as the winds come, when
 Forests are rended;
Come as the waves come, when
 Navies are stranded.
   Pibroch of Donald Dhu [*1816*].
     Stanza 4

Sound, sound the clarion, fill the fife!
 To all the sensual world proclaim,
One crowded hour of glorious life
 Is worth an age without a name.[1]
   Old Mortality [*1816*]. *Chap. 34*

Time will rust the sharpest sword,
Time will consume the strongest cord;
That which moulders hemp and steel,
Mortal arm and nerve must feel.
   Harold the Dauntless [*1817*].
     Canto I, Stanza 4

 Cursed war and racking tax
Have left us scarcely raiment to our
 backs.
   The Search after Happiness [2]
     [*1817*]. *Stanza 16*

Paddy had not — a shirt to his back!
   Ibid. Stanza 22

 Sea of upturned faces.
   Rob Roy [*1817*]. *Chap. 20*

 Lochow and the adjacent districts
formed the original seat of the Campbells. The expression of "a far cry to
Lochow" was proverbial.
   Ibid. Chap. 29, Note

 There's a gude time coming.
   Ibid. Chap. 32

 My foot is on my native heath, and
my name is MacGregor.
   Ibid. Chap. 34

 Jock, when ye hae naething else to
do, ye may be aye sticking in a tree; it
will be growing, Jock, when ye're sleeping.[3]
   The Heart of Midlothian
     [*1818*]. *Chap. 8*

Vacant heart, and hand, and eye,
Easy live and quiet die.
   The Bride of Lammermoor
   [*1819*]. *Chap. 3, Lucy Ashton's*
   Song

----

[1] See *Count Robert of Paris*, page 418a.
[2] See John Heywood, page 90b.
[3] The dying words of a Highland laird to
his son.

The happy combination of fortuitous circumstances.[1]

> *The Monastery* [*1820*]. *Answer of the Author of Waverley to the Letter of Captain Clutterbuck*

Within that awful volume [2] lies
The mystery of mysteries!

> *Ibid. Chap. 12*

And better had they ne'er been born,
Who read to doubt, or read to scorn.

> *Ibid.*

When we are handfasted, as we term it, we are man and wife for a year and day; that space gone by, each may choose another mate, or, at their pleasure, may call the priest to marry them for life; and this we call handfasting.[3]

> *Ibid. Chap. 25*

Spur not an unbroken horse; put not your ploughshare too deep into new land.

> *Ibid.*

Meat eaten without either mirth or music is ill of digestion.

> *Ibid.*

When I hae a saxpence under my
  thumb,
Then I get credit in ilka town;
But when I am poor, they bid me gae
  by,
O, poverty parts good company.

> *The Abbot* [*1820*]. *Chap. 7*

The jolly old landlord said, "nothing's to pay."

> *The Pirate* [*1821*]. *Chap. 23*

Ah, County Guy, the hour is nigh,
  The sun has left the lea.
The orange flower perfumes the bower,
  The breeze is on the sea.

> *Quentin Durward* [*1823*]. *Chap. 4*

Fat, fair, and forty.[1]

> *St. Ronan's Well* [*1823*]. *Chap. 7*

Tell that to the marines — the sailors won't believe it.[2]

> *Redgauntlet* [*1824*]. *Vol. II, Chap. 7*

Too much rest is rust.[3]

> *The Betrothed* [*1825*]. *Chap. 13*

The playbill, which is said to have announced the tragedy of Hamlet, the character of the Prince of Denmark being left out.

> *The Talisman* [*1825*]. *Introduction*

Rouse the lion from his lair.

> *Ibid. Heading, Chap. 6*

Recollect that the Almighty, who gave the dog to be companion of our pleasures and our toils, hath invested him with a nature noble and incapable of deceit.

> *Ibid. Chap. 24*

If you keep a thing seven years, you are sure to find a use for it.

> *Woodstock* [*1826*]. *Chap. 28*

The sun never sets on the immense empire of Charles V.[4]

> *Life of Napoleon* [*1827*]

Come fill up my cup, come fill up my can,
Come saddle your horses, and call up your men;

---

[1] See Dryden, page 275b.
Lord —— is going to marry Lady ——, a fat, fair, and fifty card-playing resident of the Crescent. — Mrs. MELESINA TRENCH [1768–1827], in a letter [February 18, 1816]
[2] "Right," quoth Ben, "that will do for the marines." — BYRON: *The Island* [1823], *Canto II, last line*
"That will do for the marines, but the sailors won't believe it" is an old saying.
[3] German proverb: Rast ich, so rost ich (When I rest, I rust).
[4] See Daniel Webster, page 444a.
Why should the brave Spanish soldier brag the sun never sets in the Spanish dominions, but ever shineth on one part or other we have conquered for our king? — CAPTAIN JOHN SMITH: *Advertisements for the Unexperienced, &c.* [1631]
It may be said of them [the Hollanders] as of the Spaniards, that the sun never sets on their dominions. — GAGE: *New Survey of the West Indies* [1648], *Epistle Dedicatory*

---

[1] See Daniel Webster, page 444a.
Fortuitous combination of circumstances. — DICKENS: *Our Mutual Friend* [1864–1865], *Vol. II, Chap. 7.*
[2] The Bible.
[3] This custom of handfasting actually prevailed in the upland days. It arose partly from the want of priests. While the convents subsisted, monks were detached on regular circuits through the wilder districts, to marry those who had lived in this species of connexion. — ANDREW LANG: *Note in his edition of The Monastery.*

Come open the West Port, and let me
gang free,
And it's room for the bonnets of Bonny
Dundee!
    The Doom of Devorgoil [*1830*].
    Bonny Dundee, Chorus

One hour of life, crowded to the full
with glorious action, and filled with
noble risks, is worth whole years of
those mean observances of paltry decorum.[1]
    Count Robert of Paris [*1832*].
    Chap. 25

Heaven knows its time; the bullet
has its billet.
    Ibid.

SYDNEY SMITH
[1771–1845]

The schoolboy whips his taxed top;
the beardless youth manages his taxed
horse with a taxed bridle on a taxed
road; and the dying Englishman, pouring his medicine, which has paid seven
per cent, into a spoon that has paid
fifteen per cent, flings himself back
upon his chintz bed which has paid
twenty-two per cent, and expires in the
arms of an apothecary who has paid a
license of a hundred pounds for the
privilege of putting him to death.
    Review of Seybert's *Annals of*
    the United States [*1820*]

In the four quarters of the globe,
who reads an American book, or goes
to an American play, or looks at an
American picture or statue?
    Ibid.

Correspondences are like small-
clothes before the invention of suspenders; it is impossible to keep them up.
    Letter to Mrs. Crowe
    [*January 31, 1841*]

If you choose to represent the various parts in life by holes upon a table,
of different shapes, — some circular,
some triangular, some square, some oblong, — and the persons acting these
parts by bits of wood of similar shapes,
we shall generally find that the trian-

[1] See *Old Mortality*, page 416b.

gular person has got into the square
hole, the oblong into the triangular,
and a square person has squeezed himself into the round hole. The officer
and the office, the doer and the thing
done, seldom fit so exactly that we can
say they were almost made for each
other.[1]
    Sketches of Moral Philosophy
    [*1850*]

That knuckle-end of England, —
that land of Calvin, oat-cakes, and
sulphur.
    Lady Holland's *Memoir*
    [*1855*]. *Vol. I, Chap. 2*

No one minds what Jeffrey says:
. . . it is not more than a week ago
that I heard him speak disrespectfully
of the equator.
    Ibid.

Preaching has become a by-word for
long and dull conversation of any
kind; and whoever wishes to imply, in
any piece of writing, the absence of
everything agreeable and inviting,
calls it a sermon.
    Ibid. Chap. 3

It is always right that a man should
be able to render a reason for the faith
that is within him.
    Ibid.

Avoid shame, but do not seek glory,
— nothing so expensive as glory.
    Ibid. Chap. 4

It is no part of the duty of a clergyman to preach upon subjects purely
political, but it is not therefore his
duty to avoid religious subjects which
have been distorted into political subjects.
    Ibid.

Take short views, hope for the best,
and trust in God.
    Ibid. Chap. 6

Hope is the belief, more or less
strong, that joy will come; desire is
the wish it may come. There is no
word to designate the remembrance of
joys past.
    Ibid.

[1] Generally accepted as the origin of the
phrase "A square peg in a round hole."

Looked as if she had walked straight out of the ark.

Lady Holland's Memoir.
Vol. I, Chap. 7

Great men hallow a whole people, and lift up all who live in their time.

Ibid.

Not body enough to cover his mind decently with; his intellect is improperly exposed.

Ibid. Chap. 9

He has spent all his life in letting down empty buckets into empty wells; and he is frittering away his age in trying to draw them up again.[1]

Ibid.

Ah, you flavour everything; you are the vanilla of society.

Ibid.

My living in Yorkshire was so far out of the way, that it was actually twelve miles from a lemon.

Ibid.

As the French say, there are three sexes, — men, women, and clergymen.[2]

Ibid.

Daniel Webster struck me much like a steam-engine in trousers.

Ibid.

"Heat, ma'am!" I said; "it was so dreadful here, that I found there was nothing left for it but to take off my flesh and sit in my bones."

Ibid.

I have gout, asthma, and seven other maladies, but am otherwise very well.

Ibid. Chap. 10

When you rise in the morning, form a resolution to make the day a happy one to a fellow-creature.

Ibid.

Live always in the best company when you read.

Ibid.

Never give way to melancholy; resist it steadily, for the habit will encroach.

Ibid.

He was a one-book man. Some men

[1] See Cowper, page 364b.
[2] See Lady Mary Wortley Montagu, page 322b.

have only one book in them; others, a library.

Lady Holland's Memoir.
Vol. I, Chap. 11

Marriage resembles a pair of shears, so joined that they can not be separated; often moving in opposite directions, yet always punishing anyone who comes between them.[1]

Ibid.

Macaulay is like a book in breeches. . . . He has occasional flashes of silence, that make his conversation perfectly delightful.

Ibid.

Let onion atoms lurk within the bowl And, half suspected, animate the whole.

Ibid. Recipe for Salad

Don't tell me of facts, I never believe facts; you know Canning said nothing was so fallacious as facts, except figures.

Ibid.

What you don't know would make a great book.

Ibid.

In composing, as a general rule, run your pen through every other word you have written; you have no idea what vigor it will give your style.[2]

Ibid.

Thank God for tea! What would the world do without tea? — how did it exist? I am glad I was not born before tea.

Ibid.

That sign of old age, extolling the past at the expense of the present.

Ibid.

We know nothing of tomorrow; our business is to be good and happy today.

Ibid. Chap. 12

WILLIAM BARNES RHODES
[1772–1826]

Bombastes. So have I heard on Afric's burning shore

[1] We are the two halves of a pair of scissors, when apart, Pecksniff, but together we are something. — DICKENS: *Martin Chuzzlewit* [1843–1844], *Chap. 11*
[2] See Samuel Johnson, page 341a.

A hungry lion give a grievous roar;
The grievous roar echoed along the
    shore.
Artaxaminous. So have I heard on
    Afric's burning shore
Another lion give a grievous roar;
And the first lion thought the last a
    bore.
      Bombastes Furioso [*1810*].
          Act I, Sc. 4

FRANÇOIS HORACE BASTIEN SÉBASTIANI
[1772–1851]

Order reigns in Warsaw.[1]
    Announcement of the fall of
               Warsaw

JOSIAH QUINCY, JR.
[1772–1864]

If this bill [for the admission of Orleans Territory as a State] passes, I am
compelled to declare it as my deliberate
opinion that the bonds of this Union
are virtually dissolved; that the States
which compose it are free from their
moral obligations; and that, as it will
be the right of all, so it will be the duty
of some, to prepare definitely for a
separation — amicably if they can;
violently if they must.[2]
    Speech in the U. S. House of
    Representatives, January 14,
    1811

SAMUEL TAYLOR COLERIDGE
[1772–1834]

Poor little Foal of an oppressed race!
I love the languid patience of thy face.
      To a Young Ass [*1794*]

---

[1] Des lettres que je reçois de Pologne m'an-
noncent que la tranquillité règne à Varsovie.
—DUMAS [1802–1870]: *Mémoires, Second
Series, Vol. IV, Chap. 3*

[2] The gentleman [Quincy] cannot have forgotten his own sentiment, uttered even on the
floor of this House, "Peaceably if we can,
forcibly if we must." — HENRY CLAY: *Speech*
[January 8, 1813]

Ere sin could blight or sorrow fade,
    Death came with friendly care;
The opening bud to heaven conveyed,
    And bade it blossom there.
      Epitaph on an Infant [*1794*]

Blest hour! it was a luxury — to be
    left!
    Reflections on Having Left a
      Place of Retirement [*1795*]

This Lime-tree Bower My Prison.
        Title of Poem [*1797*]

In Xanadu did Kubla Khan
A stately pleasure-dome decree:
Where Alph, the sacred river, ran
Through caverns measureless to man
Down to a sunless sea.
So twice five miles of fertile ground
With walls and towers were girdled
    round.
      Kubla Khan [*1797*]

A savage place! as holy and enchanted
As e'er beneath a waning moon was
    haunted
By woman wailing for her demon-lover.
               Ibid.

Ancestral voices prophesying war!
               Ibid.

A damsel with a dulcimer
In a vision once I saw:
It was an Abyssinian maid,
And on her dulcimer she played,
Singing of Mount Abora.
               Ibid.

That sunny dome! those caves of ice!
And all who heard should see them
    there,
And all should cry, Beware! Beware!
His flashing eyes, his floating hair!
Weave a circle round him thrice,
And close your eyes with holy dread,
For he on honey-dew hath fed,[1]
And drunk the milk of Paradise.
               Ibid.

And the spring comes slowly up this
    way.
      Christabel. Part I [*1797*]

Her gentle limbs did she undress,
And lay down in her loveliness.
               Ibid.

A sight to dream of, not to tell!
               Ibid.

---

[1] See Hesiod, page 7a.

And constancy lives in realms above;
And life is thorny; and youth is vain;
And to be wroth with one we love
Doth work like madness in the brain.
Christabel. Part II [1800]
It is an ancient Mariner,
And he stoppeth one of three.
"By thy long grey beard and glittering
eye,
Now wherefore stopp'st thou me?"
The Ancient Mariner [1798–
1834]. Part I, Stanza 1
The guests are met, the feast is set:
May'st hear the merry din.
Ibid. Stanza 2
He holds him with his glittering eye —
The Wedding-Guest stood still,
And listens like a three years' child:
The Mariner hath his will.
Ibid. Stanza 4
The ship was cheered, the harbour
cleared,
Merrily did we drop
Below the kirk, below the hill,
Below the lighthouse top.
Ibid. Stanza 6
The Wedding-Guest here beat his
breast,
For he heard the loud bassoon.
Ibid. Stanza 8
The bride hath paced into the hall,
Red as a rose is she.
Ibid. Stanza 9
And now there came both mist and
snow,
And it grew wondrous cold:
And ice, mast-high, came floating by,
As green as emerald.
Ibid. Stanza 13
The ice was here, the ice was there,
The ice was all around:
It cracked and growled, and roared and
howled,
Like noises in a swound!
Ibid. Stanza 15
"God save thee, ancient Mariner!
From fiends, that plague thee thus! —
Why look'st thou so?" — "With my
cross-bow
I shot the Albatross."
Ibid. Stanza 20

The fair breeze blew, the white foam
flew,
The furrows followed free;
We were the first that ever burst
Into that silent sea.
The Ancient Mariner.
Part II, Stanza 5
As idle as a painted ship
Upon a painted ocean.
Ibid. Stanza 8
Water, water, every where,
Nor any drop to drink.
Ibid. Stanza 9
The very deep did rot: O Christ!
That ever this should be!
Yea, slimy things did crawl with legs
Upon the slimy sea.
Ibid. Stanza 10
About, about, in reel and rout
The death-fires danced at night.
Ibid. Stanza 11
I bit my arm, I sucked the blood,
And cried, A sail! a sail!
Ibid. Part III, Stanza 4
Without a breeze, without a tide,
She steadies with upright keel!
Ibid. Stanza 6
Her lips were red, her looks were free,
Her locks were yellow as gold:
Her skin was white as leprosy,
The nightmare Life-in-Death was she,
Who thicks man's blood with cold.
Ibid. Stanza 11
The sun's rim dips, the stars rush out:
At one stride comes the dark;
With far-heard whisper o'er the sea
Off shot the spectre-bark.
Ibid. Stanza 13
We listened and looked sideways up!
Fear at my heart, as at a cup,
My life-blood seemed to sip.
Ibid. Stanza 14
The hornèd Moon, with one bright star
Within the nether tip.
Ibid.
Each turned his face with a ghastly
pang,
And cursed me with his eye.
Ibid. Stanza 15

And thou art long, and lank, and
   brown,
As is the ribbed sea-sand.[1]
The Ancient Mariner.
Part IV, Stanza 1

Alone, alone, all, all alone;
Alone on a wide, wide sea.
Ibid. Stanza 3

The moving moon went up the sky,
And nowhere did abide;
Softly she was going up,
And a star or two beside.
Ibid. Stanza 10

Her beams bemocked the sultry main,
Like April hoar-frost spread;
But where the ship's huge shadow lay,
The charmèd water burnt alway
A still and awful red.
Ibid. Stanza 11

A spring of love gushed from my heart,
And I blessed them unaware.
Ibid. Stanza 14

Oh sleep! it is a gentle thing,
Beloved from pole to pole.
Ibid. Part V, Stanza 1

A noise like of a hidden brook
In the leafy month of June,
That to the sleeping woods all night
Singeth a quiet tune.
Ibid. Stanza 17

"The man hath penance done,
And penance more will do."
Ibid. Stanza 25

Like one that on a lonesome road
Doth walk in fear and dread,
And having once turned round, walks
   on,
And turns no more his head;
Because he knows a frightful fiend
Doth close behind him tread.
Ibid. Part VI, Stanza 10

Is this the hill? is this the kirk?
Is this mine own countree?
Ibid. Stanza 14

O Wedding-Guest! This soul hath been
Alone on a wide wide sea:
So lonely 'twas, that God himself
Scarce seemèd there to be.
Ibid. Part VII, Stanza 19

[1] A note by Coleridge in *Sibylline Leaves*
[1817] says: "For [these] lines I am indebted
to Mr. Wordsworth."

He prayeth well who loveth well
Both man and bird and beast.
The Ancient Mariner.
Part VII, Stanza 22

He prayeth best who loveth best
All things both great and small;
For the dear God who loveth us,
He made and loveth all.
Ibid. Stanza 23

A sadder and a wiser man
He rose the morrow morn.
Ibid. Stanza 25

Yes, while I stood and gazed, my tem-
   ples bare,
And shot my being through earth, sea,
   and air,
Possessing all things with intensest
   love,
O Liberty! my spirit felt thee there.
France: An Ode [1798]. V

Forth from his dark and lonely hiding-
   place
(Portentous sight!) the owlet Atheism,
Sailing on obscene wings athwart the
   noon,
Drops his blue-fringèd lids, and holds
   them close,
And hooting at the glorious sun in
   heaven
Cries out, "Where is it?"
Fears in Solitude [1798]

And the Devil did grin, for his darling
   sin
Is pride that apes humility.[1]
The Devil's Thoughts [2] [1799].
Stanza 6

Strongly it bears us along in swelling
   and limitless billows;
Nothing before and nothing behind but
   the sky and the ocean.
The Homeric Hexameter (trans-
lated from Schiller) [1799?]

In the hexameter rises the fountain's
   silvery column,
In the pentameter aye falling in melody
   back.
The Ovidian Elegiac Metre
(from Schiller) [1799]

[1] See Robert Burton, page 222b.
[2] This poem was written in collaboration

All thoughts, all passions, all delights,
Whatever stirs this mortal frame,
All are but ministers of Love,
And feed his sacred flame.
Love [*1799*]. *Stanza 1*

Saved from outrage worse than death.
Ibid. Stanza 14

Tranquillity! thou better name
Than all the family of Fame.
Ode to Tranquillity [*1801*].
Stanza 1

Aloof with hermit-eye I scan
The present work of present man —
A wild and dream-like trade of blood
and guile,
Too foolish for a tear, too wicked for a
smile.
Ibid. Stanza 4

Hast thou a charm to stay the morning
star
In his steep course?
Hymn in the Vale of Chamouni
[*1802*]

Risest from forth thy silent sea of
pines.
Ibid.

Motionless torrents! silent cataracts!
Ibid.

Ye living flowers that skirt the eternal
frost.
Ibid.

Earth, with her thousand voices, praises
God.
Ibid.

What is an Epigram? A dwarfish
whole,
Its body brevity, and wit its soul.[1]
An Epigram [*1802*]

I see, not feel, how beautiful they are.
Dejection: An Ode [*1802*].
Stanza 2

O Lady! we receive but what we give
And in our life alone does Nature live.
Ibid. Stanza 4

Joy is the sweet voice, Joy the luminous
cloud —
We in ourselves rejoice!

---

with Southey, who also imitated it in *The
Devil's Walk*, quoted on page 427a.

[1] See Shakespeare, page 173a.

And thence flows all that charms or ear
or sight,
All melodies the echoes of that voice,
All colours a suffusion of that light.
Dejection: An Ode. Stanza 5

How seldom, friend! a good great man
inherits
Honor or wealth, with all his worth and
pains!
It sounds like stories from the land of
spirits
If any man obtains that which he merits,
Or any merit that which he obtains.

Greatness and goodness are not means,
but ends!
Hath he not always treasures, always
friends,
The good great man? Three treasures,
— love, and light,
And calm thoughts, regular as infant's
breath; —
And three firm friends, more sure than
day and night, —
Himself, his Maker, and the Angel
Death.
The Good Great Man [*1802*]

Trochee trips from long to short;
From long to long in solemn sort
Slow Spondee stalks.
Metrical Feet [*1806*]

What outward form and feature are
He guesseth but in part;
But what within is good and fair
He seeth with the heart.
Reason For Love's Blindness
[*1811?*]

Poetry is not the proper antithesis to
prose, but to science. Poetry is opposed
to science, and prose to metre. The
proper and immediate object of science
is the acquirement, or communication,
of truth; the proper and immediate object of poetry is the communication of
immediate pleasure.
Definitions of Poetry [*1811*]

Reviewers are usually people who
would have been poets, historians, biographers, if they could; they have tried

their talents at one or the other, and have failed; therefore they turn critics.[1]

Lectures on Shakespeare and
Milton [1811–1812]

Iago's soliloquy, the motive-hunting of a motiveless malignity — how awful it is!

Ibid.

I wish our clever young poets would remember my homely definitions of prose and poetry; that is, prose, — words in their best order; poetry, — the best words in their best order.

Ibid.

That passage is what I call the sublime dashed to pieces by cutting too close with the fiery four-in-hand round the corner of nonsense.

Ibid.

Not the poem which we have read, but that to which we return, with the greatest pleasure, possesses the genuine power, and claims the name of essential poetry.

Biographia Literaria [1817].
Chap. 1

Every reform, however necessary, will by weak minds be carried to an excess, that itself will need reforming.

Ibid.

Experience informs us that the first defence of weak minds is to recriminate.

Ibid. Chap. 2

Through all the works of Chaucer, there reigns a cheerfulness, a manly hilarity, which makes it almost impossible to doubt a correspondent habit of feeling in the author himself.

Ibid.

Men whose dearest wishes are fixed on objects wholly out of their own power, become in all cases more or less impatient and prone to anger.

Ibid.

[1] Reviewers, with some rare exceptions, are a most stupid and malignant race. As a bankrupt thief turns thief-taker in despair, so an unsuccessful author turns critic. — SHELLEY: *Fragments of Adonais* [1821]
See Disraeli, page 513a.

Veracity does not consist in *saying*, but in the intention of *communicating* truth.

Biographia Literaria. Chap. 9

The lamentable difficulty I have always experienced in saying "No."

Ibid. Chap. 10

To have lived in vain must be a painful thought to any man, and especially so to him who has made literature his profession.

Ibid.

Never pursue literature as a trade.

Ibid. Chap. 11

The first range of hills that encircles the scanty vale of human life is the horizon for the majority of its inhabitants. On *its* ridges the common sun is born and departs. From *them* the stars rise, and touching *them*, they vanish.

Ibid. Chap. 12

It was agreed that my endeavors [in the plan of the *Lyrical Ballads*] should be directed to persons and characters supernatural, or at least romantic; yet so as to transfer from our inward nature a human interest and a semblance of truth sufficient to procure for these shadows of imagination that willing suspension of disbelief for the moment, which constitutes poetic faith.

Ibid. Chap. 14

Good sense is the body of poetic genius, fancy its drapery, motion its life, and imagination the soul.

Ibid.

Our myriad-minded Shakespeare.[1]

Ibid. Chap. 15

The sense of musical delight, with the power of producing it, is a gift of imagination; and this together with the power of reducing multitude into unity of effect, and modifying a series of thoughts by some one predominant thought or feeling, may be cultivated and improved, but can never be learned. It is in these that *poeta nascitur non fit.*

Ibid.

[1] "A phrase," says Coleridge, "which I have borrowed from a Greek monk, who applies it to a patriarch of Constantinople."

Polysyllabic (or what the common people call, *dictionary*) words.
Biographia Literaria. Chap. 20

The infallible test of a blameless style: namely, its untranslatableness in words of the same language, without injury to the meaning.
Ibid. Chap. 22

A poem is not necessarily obscure, because it does not aim to be popular. It is enough if a work be perspicuous to those for whom it is written.
Ibid.

Talk of the devil, and his horns appear, says the proverb.
Ibid. Chap. 23

The knight's bones are dust,
And his good sword rust;
His soul is with the saints, I trust.
The Knight's Tomb [*1817?*]

The Eighth Commandment was not made for bards.
The Reproof and Reply [*1823*]

Nought cared this body for wind or weather,
When youth and I lived in 't together.
Youth and Age [*1823–1832*].
Stanza 1

Flowers are lovely; love is flower-like;
Friendship is a sheltering tree;
Oh the joys that came down shower-like,
Of friendship, love, and liberty,
Ere I was old!
Ibid. Stanza 2

In many ways doth the full heart reveal
The presence of the love it would conceal.
Motto to Poems Written in Later Life [*1826*]

I counted two-and-seventy stenches,
All well defined, and several stinks.
Cologne [*1828*]

The river Rhine, it is well known,
Doth wash your city of Cologne;
But tell me, nymphs! what power divine
Shall henceforth wash the river Rhine?
Ibid.

The happiness of life is made up of minute fractions — the little soon forgotten charities of a kiss or smile, a kind look, a heartfelt compliment, and the countless infinitesimals of pleasurable and genial feeling.
The Friend. The Improvisatore
[*1828*]

Beneath this sod
A poet lies, or that which once seemed he —
Oh, lift a thought in prayer for S.T.C.!
That he, who many a year, with toil of breath,
Found death in life, may here find life in death.
Epitaph written for himself
[*1833*]

JOHN RANDOLPH
[1773–1833]

The surest way to prevent war is not to fear it.
Speech, U. S. House of Representatives [*March 5, 1806*]

He is a man of splendid abilities, but utterly corrupt. He shines and stinks like rotten mackerel by moonlight.[1]
Of Edward Livingston

WILLIAM HENRY HARRISON
[1773–1841]

We admit of no government by divine right . . . the only legitimate right to govern is an express grant of power from the governed.
Inaugural Address [*March 4, 1841*]

Never with my consent shall an officer of the people, compensated for his services out of their pockets, become the pliant instrument of the Executive will.
Ibid.

[1] Quoted in W. CABELL BRUCE: *John Randolph of Roanoke* [1923], *Vol. II, P. 197.*
'Tis vain for present fame to wish.
Our persons first must be forgotten;
For poets are like stinking fish,
They never shine until they're rotten.
MACDONALD CLARKE [1798–1842]: *Epigram*

A decent and manly examination of the acts of Government should be not only tolerated, but encouraged.
Inaugural Address

ROBERT SOUTHEY
[1774–1843]

"You are old, Father William," the young man cried,
"The few locks which are left you are gray;
You are hale, Father William, a hearty old man, —
Now tell me the reason I pray."
The Old Man's Comforts, and How He Gained Them.[1] *Stanza 1*

"In the days of my youth," Father William replied,
"I remembered that youth could not last;
I thought of the future, whatever I did,
That I never might grieve for the past."
Ibid. Stanza 4

Bishop Hatto fearfully hastened away,
And he crossed the Rhine without delay,
And reached his tower, and barred with care
All the windows, and doors, and loopholes there.
God's Judgment on a Wicked Bishop.[2] *Stanza 12*

[1] Of several parodies of this poem, the one by Lewis Carroll is probably better known than the original. See page 656a.
"You are old, Father William, and though one would think
All the veins in your body were dry,
Yet the end of your nose is red as a pink;
I beg your indulgence, but why?"
LEE O. HARRIS AND JAMES WHITCOMB RILEY: *Father William, St. 1*

[2] Hatto, in the time of the great famine of 914, when he saw the poor exceedingly oppressed by famine, assembled a great company of them together into a barn at Kaub and burnt them . . . because he thought the famine would sooner cease if those poor folks were despatched out of the world. . . . But God . . . sent against him a plague of mice . . . and the prelate retreated to a tower in the Rhine . . . . but the mice chased him con-

It was a summer's evening;
Old Kaspar's work was done,
And he before his cottage door
Was sitting in the sun;
And by him sported on the green
His little grandchild Wilhelmine.
The Battle of Blenheim [*1798*].
Stanza 1

He came to ask what he had found,
That was so large, and smooth, and round.
Ibid. Stanza 2

" 'Tis some poor fellow's skull," said he,
"Who fell in the great victory."
Ibid. Stanza 3

But what they fought each other for,
I could not well make out.
Ibid. Stanza 6

"And every body praised the Duke,
Who this great fight did win."
Ibid. Stanza 6

"But what good came of it at last?"
Quoth little Peterkin.
"Why, that I cannot tell," said he;
"But 'twas a famous victory."
Ibid. Stanza 11

One dreadful sound could the Rover hear,
A sound as if with the Inchcape Bell
The Devil below was ringing his knell.
The Inchcape Rock.[1] *Stanza 17*

Where Washington hath left
His awful memory
A light for after times!
Ode Written during the War with America [*1814*]

My days among the dead are past;
Around me I behold,
Where'er these casual eyes are cast,
The mighty minds of old;
My never-failing friends are they,
With whom I converse night and day.
My Days Among the Dead Are Past [*1818*]. *Stanza 1*

tinually . . . and at last he was most miserably devoured. — THOMAS CORYAT: *Crudities* [*1611*]
[1] A rock in the North Sea, off the Firth of Tay, Scotland, dangerous to navigators because it is covered with every tide. There is a tradition that a warning bell was fixed on the rock by the Abbot of Aberbrothok, which was stolen by a sea pirate, who perished on the rock a year later. Southey's ballad deals with this tradition.

Yet leaving here a name, I trust,
That will not perish in the dust.
> *My Days Among the Dead*
> *Are Past. Stanza 4*

The laws are with us, and God on our side.
> *On the Rise and Progress of*
> *Popular Disaffection* [*1817*]

Agreed to differ.
> *Life of Wesley* [*1820*]

The Satanic school.
> *Vision of Judgment* [*1821*].
> *Original Preface*

So I told them in rhyme,
For of rhymes I had store.
> *The Cataract of Lodore*

And so never ending, but always descending.
> *Ibid.*

"And wherefore do the poor complain?"
The rich man asked of me —
"Come walk abroad with me," I said,
"And I will answer thee."
> *The Complaints of the Poor.*
> *Stanza 1*

From his brimstone bed, at break of day,
A-walking the Devil is gone,
To look at his little snug farm of the World,
And see how his stock went on.
> *The Devil's Walk. Stanza 1*

How then was the Devil dressed?
O, he was in his Sunday's best;
His coat was red, and his breeches were blue,
And there was a hole where his tail came through.
> *Ibid. Stanza 3*

He passed a cottage with a double coach-house, —
A cottage of gentility;
And he owned with a grin,
That his favourite sin
Is pride that apes humility.[1]
> *Ibid. Stanza 8*

He was always found
Among your ten and twenty pound subscribers,

[1] See Coleridge, page 422b.

Your benefactors in the newspapers.
His alms were money put to interest
In the other world.
> *The Alderman's Funeral*

As frozen as charity.[1]
> *The Soldier's Wife. Stanza 4*

Blue, darkly, deeply, beautifully blue.[2]
> *Madoc in Wales. Part I, 5*

What will not woman, gentle woman dare,
When strong affection stirs her spirit up?
> *Ibid. Part II, 2*

And last of all an Admiral came,
A terrible man with a terrible name, —
A name which you all know by sight very well,
But which no one can speak, and no one can spell.
> *The March to Moscow. Stanza 8*

They sin who tell us love can die;
With life all other passions fly,
All others are but vanity. . . .
Love is indestructible,
Its holy flame forever burneth;
From heaven it came, to heaven returneth. . . .
It soweth here with toil and care,
But the harvest-time of love is there.
> *The Curse of Kehama. Canto X,*
> *Stanza 10*

Thou hast been called, O sleep! the friend of woe;
But 'tis the happy that have called thee so.
> *Ibid. Canto XV, Stanza 11*

JANE AUSTEN
[1775–1817]

What dreadful hot weather we have!
It keeps me in a continual state of inelegance.
> *Letter to her sister Cassandra.*
> *September 18, 1796*

[1] See Hood, page 489b, and O'Reilly, page 729b.

[2] "Darkly, deeply, beautifully blue,"
As some one somewhere sings about the sky.
> BYRON: *Don Juan* [*1819–1824*],
> *Canto IV, St. 110*

Miss Blachford is agreeable enough. I do not want people to be very agreeable, as it saves me the trouble of liking them a great deal.

> *Letter to her sister Cassandra.*
> *December 24, 1798*

She was highly rouged, and looked rather quietly and contentedly silly than anything else.

> *Ibid. May 12, 1801*

It is a truth universally acknowledged, that a single man in possession of a good fortune, must be in want of a wife.

However little known the feelings or views of such a man may be on his first entering a neighbourhood, this truth is so well fixed in the minds of the surrounding families, that he is considered as the rightful property of some one or other of their daughters.

> *Pride and Prejudice* [*1813*].
> *Chap. 1*

Mr. Collins had only to change from Jane to Elizabeth — and it was soon done — done while Mrs. Bennet was stirring the fire.

> *Ibid. Chap. 15*

My dear, I have two small favours to request. First, that you will allow me the free use of my understanding on the present occasion; and secondly, of my room. I shall be glad to have the library to myself as soon as may be.

> *Ibid. Chap. 20*

Those who do not complain are never pitied.

> *Ibid.*

Mrs. Bennet was restored to her usual querulous serenity.

> *Ibid. Chap. 42*

You ought certainly to forgive them, as a Christian, but never to admit them in your sight, or allow their names to be mentioned in your hearing.

> *Ibid. Chap. 57*

For what do we live, but to make sport for our neighbours, and laugh at them in our turn?

> *Ibid.*

I have been a selfish being all my life, in practice, though not in principle.

> *Pride and Prejudice. Chap. 58*

The little bit (two inches wide) of ivory on which I work with so fine a brush as produces little effect after much labour.[1]

> *Letter to J. Edward Austen.*
> *December 16, 1816*

"Only a novel" . . . in short, only some work in which the greatest powers of the mind are displayed, in which the most thorough knowledge of human nature, the happiest delineation of its varieties, the liveliest effusions of wit and humour are conveyed to the world in the best chosen language.

> *Northanger Abbey* [*1818*].
> *Chap. 5*

You [men] have difficulties, and privations, and dangers enough to struggle with. You are always labouring and toiling, exposed to every risk and hardship. Your home, country, friends, all quitted. Neither time, nor health, nor life, to be called your own. It would be too hard, indeed . . . if woman's feelings were to be added to all this.

> *Persuasion* [*1818*]. *Chap. 23*

CHARLES LAMB
[1775–1834]

I have had playmates, I have had companions,
In my days of childhood, in my joyful school-days.
All, all are gone, the old familiar faces.

> *Old Familiar Faces* [*1796*]

I have something more to do than feel.

> *Letter to Coleridge after the*
> *death of Lamb's mother* [*1796*]

---

[1] [Miss Austen] had a talent for describing the involvements and feelings and characters of ordinary life which is to me the most wonderful I ever met with. The Big Bow-Wow strain I can do myself like any now going; but the exquisite touch, which renders ordinary commonplace things and characters interesting, from the truth of the description and the sentiment, is denied to me. — SCOTT: *Journal* [March 14, 1826]

The not unpeaceful evening of a day
Made black by morning storms.
> *Poem-letter to Coleridge* [*1797*]

For God's sake (I never was more
serious) don't make me ridiculous any
more by terming me gentle-hearted
in print [1] . . . substitute drunken dog,
ragged head, seld-shaven, odd-eyed,
stuttering, or any other epithet which
truly and properly belongs to the gentleman in question.
> *Letter to Coleridge* [*August, 1800*]

Separate from the pleasure of your
company, I don't much care if I never
see a mountain in my life. I have passed
all my days in London, until I have
formed as many and intense local attachments, as any of you mountaineers
can have done with dead nature. The
lighted shops of the Strand and Fleet
Street, the innumerable trades, tradesmen and customers, coaches, waggons,
playhouses, all the bustle and wickedness round about Covent Garden, the
very women of the town, the watch-
men, drunken scenes, rattles. . . . I
often shed tears in the motley Strand
from fullness of joy at so much life.
> *Letter to Wordsworth* [*1801*]

I have confessed to you my utter in-
ability to remember in any comprehensive way what I read. I can vehemently applaud, or perversely stickle,
at *parts;* but I cannot grasp at a whole.
> *Letter to Godwin* [*1803*]

Gone before
To that unknown and silent shore.
> *Hester* [*1803*]. *Stanza 7*

A good-natured woman, which is as
much as you can expect from a friend's
wife, whom you got acquainted with a
bachelor.
> *Letter to Hazlitt* [*1805*]

Neat, not gaudy.
> *Letter to Wordsworth* [*1806*]

This very night I am going to leave
off tobacco! Surely there must be some

---

[1] For thee, my gentle-hearted Charles, to
whom
No sound is dissonant which tells of life.
> COLERIDGE: *This Lime-tree Bower
My Prison* [1797]

other world in which this unconquerable purpose shall be realized.
> *Letter to Thomas Manning* [*1815*]

Anything awful makes me laugh. I
misbehaved once at a funeral.
> *Letter to Southey* [*1815*]

An archangel a little damaged.
> *Lamb's Description of Coleridge.*
> *Letter to Wordsworth* [*1816*]

Fanny Kelly's divine plain face.
> *Letter to Mrs. Wordsworth*
> [*1818*]

The red-letter days, now become, to
all intents and purposes, dead-letter
days.
> *Essays of Elia* [*1823*]. *Oxford*
> *in the Vacation* [1]

The human species, according to the
best theory I can form of it, is composed of two distinct races, the men
who borrow, and the men who lend.
> *Ibid. The Two Races of Men*

Borrowers of books — those mutila-
tors of collections, spoilers of the symmetry of shelves, and creators of odd
volumes.
> *Ibid.*

Of all sound of all bells — (bells,
the music nighest bordering upon
heaven) — most solemn and touching
is the peal which rings out the Old
Year.
> *Ibid. New Year's Eve*

A clear fire, a clean hearth, and the
rigour of the game.
> *Ibid. Mrs. Battle's Opinions on*
> *Whist*

Sentimentally I am disposed to harmony; but organically I am incapable
of a tune.
> *Ibid. A Chapter on Ears*

Credulity is the man's weakness, but
the child's strength.
> *Ibid. Witches, and Other Night*
> *Fears*

Parents do not know what they do
when they leave tender babes alone to
go to sleep in the dark.
> *Ibid.*

---

[1] Which, it has been pointed out, was actually written at Cambridge. See E. V. LUCAS:
Lamb and the Universities.

Not many sounds in life, and I include all urban and all rural sounds, exceed in interest a knock at the door.[1]
Essays of Elia. Valentine's Day

A God-send, as our familiarly pious ancestors termed a benefit received where the benefactor was unknown.
Ibid.

The custom of saying grace at meals had, probably, its origin in the early times of the world, and the hunter-state of man, when dinners were precarious things, and a full meal was something more than a common blessing.
Ibid. Grace Before Meat

A fair sepulchre in the grateful stomach of the judicious epicure.
Ibid. A Dissertation upon Roast Pig

Presents, I often say, endear absents.
Ibid.

It argues an insensibility.
Ibid.

Nothing is to me more distasteful than that entire complacency and satisfaction which beam in the countenances of a new-married couple.
Ibid. The Behaviour of Married People

I came home for ever!
Letter to Bernard Barton [1825], on leaving his "33 years' desk" at the East India House

Who first invented work, and bound the free
And holiday-rejoicing spirit down . . . .
To that dry drudgery at the desk's dead wood?
Work

The economy of Heaven is dark
And wisest clerks have missed the mark.
On an Infant Dying as Soon as Born [1827]

[1] Doorbells are like a magic game,
Or the grab-bag at a fair —
You never know when you hear one ring
Who may be waiting there.
RACHEL FIELD [1894–1942]: *Doorbells*

Martin, if dirt was trumps, what hands you would hold!
Lamb's Suppers, in LEIGH HUNT: *Lord Byron and His Contemporaries [1828]*

Some cry up Haydn, some Mozart,
Just as the whim bites. For my part,
I do not care a farthing candle
For either of them, nor for Handel.
Letter to Mrs. William Hazlitt [1830]

A bird appears a thoughtless thing . . .
No doubt he has his little cares,
And very hard he often fares,
The which so patiently he bears.
Crumbs to the Birds

Reputation said: "If once we sever,
Our chance of future meeting is but vain:
Who parts from me, must look to part for ever,
For Reputation lost comes not again."
Love, Death, and Reputation. Stanza 4

For thy sake, tobacco, I
Would do anything but die.
A Farewell to Tobacco

He has left off reading altogether, to the great improvement of his originality.
Last Essays of Elia [1833]. Detached Thoughts on Books and Reading

Books think for me.
Ibid.

Books which are no books.
Ibid.

To be strong-backed and neat-bound is the desideratum of a volume. Magnificence comes after.
Ibid.

Newspapers always excite curiosity. No one ever lays one down without a feeling of disappointment.
Ibid.

If there be a regal solitude, it is a sick bed.
Ibid. The Convalescent

How sickness enlarges the dimensions of a man's self to himself.
Ibid.

Let me caution persons grown old in active business, not lightly, nor without weighing their own resources, to forego their customary employment all at once, for there may be danger in it.
Last Essays of Elia. The Superannuated Man

Your absence of mind we have borne, till your presence of body came to be called in question by it.
Ibid. Amicus Redivivus

A pun is a pistol let off at the ear; not a feather to tickle the intellect.
Ibid. Popular Fallacies: IX, That the Worst Puns are the Best

A presentation copy . . . is a copy of a book which does not sell, sent you by the author, with his foolish autograph at the beginning of it; for which, if a stranger, he only demands your friendship; if a brother author, he expects from you a book of yours, which does not sell, in return.
Ibid. XI, That We Must Not Look a Gift-Horse in the Mouth

The growing infirmities of age manifest themselves in nothing more strongly, than in an inveterate dislike of interruption.
Ibid. XII, That Home is Home Though it is Never so Homely

The good things of life are not to be had singly, but come to us with a mixture.
Ibid. XIII, That You Must Love Me and Love My Dog

It has happened not seldom that one work of some author has so transcendently surpassed in execution the rest of his compositions, that the world has agreed to pass a sentence of dismissal upon the latter, and to consign them to total neglect and oblivion.
Eliana. Estimate of Defoe's Secondary Novels

Cannot the heart in the midst of crowds feel frightfully alone?
Ibid.

The greatest pleasure I know is to do a good action by stealth, and to have it found out by accident.
Table Talk. In the Athenaeum [*1834*]

WALTER SAVAGE LANDOR
[1775–1864]

Rose Aylmer, whom these wakeful eyes
　May weep, but never see,
A night of memories and of sighs
　I consecrate to thee.
Rose Aylmer [*1806*]

There are no fields of amaranth on this side of the grave; there are no voices, O Rhodopè, that are not soon mute, however tuneful; there is no name, with whatever emphasis of passionate love repeated, of which the echo is not faint at last.
Imaginary Conversations [*1824–1829*]. *Aesop and Rhodopè, I*

Elegance in prose composition is mainly this: a just admission of topics and of words; neither too many nor too few of either; enough of sweetness in the sound to induce us to enter and sit still; enough of illustration and reflection to change the posture of our minds when they would tire; and enough of sound matter in the complex to repay us for our attendance.
Ibid. Chesterfield and Chatham

Of all failures, to fail in a witticism is the worst, and the mishap is the more calamitous in a drawn out and detailed one.
Ibid.

'Tis verse that gives
Immortal youth to mortal maids.
Verse

Around the child bend all the three
Sweet Graces — Faith, Hope, Charity.
Around the man bend other faces —
Pride, Envy, Malice, are his Graces.
Around the Child

Children are what the mothers are.
No fondest father's fondest care
Can fashion so the infant heart.
Children

When we play the fool, how wide
The theatre expands! beside,
How long the audience sits before us!
How many prompters! what a chorus!
Plays [1846]. Stanza 2

There is delight in singing, tho' none
  hear
Beside the singer.
To Robert Browning [1846]

I strove with none, for none was worth
  my strife;
Nature I loved; and next to Nature,
  Art.
I warm'd both hands before the fire of
  life;
It sinks, and I am ready to depart.
Dying Speech of an Old
Philosopher [1853]

THOMAS CAMPBELL
[1777–1844]

'Tis distance lends enchantment to the
  view,
And robes the mountain in its azure
  hue.[1]
Pleasures of Hope [1799].
Part I, Line 7

Hope, for a season, bade the world farewell,
And Freedom shriek'd as Kosciusko
  fell!
Ibid. Line 381

Who hath not own'd, with rapture-
  smitten frame,
The power of grace, the magic of a
  name?
Ibid. Part II, Line 5

And muse on Nature with a poet's eye.
Ibid. Line 98

That gems the starry girdle of the year.
Ibid. Line 194

Cease, every joy, to glimmer on my
  mind,
But leave, oh leave the light of Hope
  behind!

[1] The mountains too, at a distance, appear
airy masses and smooth, but seen near at hand
they are rough. — DIOGENES LAERTIUS [*circa*
A. D. 200]: *Pyrrho, IX*

What though my wingèd hours of bliss
  have been
Like angel visits, few and far between.[1]
Pleasures of Hope. Part II, Line 375

On the green banks of Shannon, when
  Sheelah was nigh,
No blithe Irish lad was so happy as I;
No harp like my own could so cheerily
  play,
And wherever I went was my poor dog
  Tray.
The Harper [1799]. Stanza 1

Ye mariners of England,
That guard our native seas;
Whose flag has braved, a thousand
  years,
The battle and the breeze!
Ye Mariners of England [1800].
Stanza 1

Britannia needs no bulwarks,
No towers along the steep;
Her march is o'er the mountain waves,
Her home is on the deep.
Ibid. Stanza 3

The meteor flag of England
Shall yet terrific burn,
Till danger's troubled night depart,
And the star of peace return.
Ibid. Stanza 4

Oh! once the harp of Innisfail
Was strung full high to notes of glad-
  ness;
But yet it often told a tale
Of more prevailing sadness.
O'Connor's Child. Stanza 1

'Tis the sunset of life gives me mystical
  lore,
And coming events cast their shadows
  before.[2]
Lochiel's Warning [1802]

The combat deepens. On, ye brave,
Who rush to glory or the grave!

[1] See John Norris, page 291b.
[2] See Cicero, page 33a.
Often do the spirits
Of great events stride on before the events,
And in today already walks tomorrow.
COLERIDGE: *Wallenstein* [1799–
1800], *Part II, Act V, Sc. 1*
Poets are the hierophants of an unappre-
hended inspiration; the mirrors of the gigantic
shadows which futurity casts upon the present.
— SHELLEY: *A Defence of Poetry* [1821]

Wave, Munich! all thy banners wave,
And charge with all thy chivalry!
> *Hohenlinden* [*1802*]. *Stanza 7*

Few, few shall part where many meet!
The snow shall be their winding-sheet
And every turf beneath their feet
Shall be a soldier's sepulchre.
> *Ibid. Stanza 8*

There was silence deep as death,
And the boldest held his breath,
For a time.
> *Battle of the Baltic* [*1805*].
> *Stanza 2*

For his country he sigh'd, when at twilight repairing
To wander alone by the wind-beaten
hill.
> *The Exile of Erin. Stanza 1*

Star that bringest home the bee,
And sett'st the weary labourer free!
> *Song to the Evening Star. Stanza 1*

Oh, how hard it is to find
The one just suited to our mind!
> *Song. Stanza 1*

To live in hearts we leave behind
Is not to die.[1]
> *Hallowed Ground. Stanza 6*

Oh leave this barren spot to me!
Spare, woodman, spare the beechen
tree! [2]
> *The Beech-Tree's Petition. Stanza 1*

Drink ye to her that each loves best!
And if you nurse a flame
That's told but to her mutual breast,
We will not ask her name.
> *Drink Ye to Her. Stanza 1*

A stoic of the woods, — a man without
a tear.
> *Gertrude of Wyoming* [*1809*].
> *Part I, Stanza 23*

Triumphal arch, that fill'st the sky
When storms prepare to part,
I ask not proud Philosophy
To teach me what thou art.
> *To the Rainbow* [*1819*].
> *Stanza 1*

[1] They are not dead who live
In hearts they leave behind.
HUGH ROBERT ORR [1887–   ]:
They Softly Walk, St. 1
[2] See George Pope Morris, page 498b.

HENRY CLAY
[1777–1852]

If you wish to avoid foreign collision,
you had better abandon the ocean.
> *Speech, U. S. House of Repre-*
> *sentatives* [*January 22, 1812*]

It would not be thought very just or
wise to arraign the honorable professions of law and physic because the one
produces the pettifogger and the other
the quack.
> *Speech, U. S. House of Repre-*
> *sentatives* [*April 26, 1820*]

Government is a trust, and the officers of the government are trustees; and
both the trust and the trustees are created for the benefit of the people.[1]
> *Speech at Ashland, Kentucky*
> [*March, 1829*]

The arts of power and its minions
are the same in all countries and in all
ages. It marks its victim; denounces it;
and excites the public odium and the
public hatred, to conceal its own abuses
and encroachments.
> *Speech, U. S. Senate* [*March 14,*
> *1834*]

Precedents deliberately established
by wise men are entitled to great
weight. They are evidence of truth, but
only evidence. . . . But a solitary
precedent . . . which has never been
re-examined, can not be conclusive.
> *Speech, U. S. Senate* [*February*
> *18, 1835*]

I have heard something said about
allegiance to the South. I know no
South, no North, no East, no West, to
which I owe any allegiance.
> *Speech* [*1848*]

Sir, I would rather be right than be
President.
> *Speech* [*1850*]

General Alexander Smyth, a tedious
speaker in Congress, observed: "You,
sir, speak for the present generation;
but I speak for posterity."

"Yes," said Mr. Clay, "and you seem

[1] See Burke, page 361b, Jefferson, page
375a, and Calhoun, page 442a.

resolved to speak until the arrival of your audience."

Quoted by EPES SARGENT *in*
Life of Henry Clay

COLONEL VALENTINE BLACKER
[1778–1823]

Put your trust in God, my boys, and keep your powder dry!

Oliver Cromwell's Advice [*1834*]

WILLIAM HAZLITT
[1778–1830]

One of the pleasantest things in the world is going a journey; but I like to go by myself.

On Going a Journey

The soul of a journey is liberty, perfect liberty, to think, feel, do just as one pleases.

Ibid.

Oh! it is great to shake off the trammels of the world and of public opinion — to lose our importunate, tormenting, everlasting personal identity and become the creature of the moment, clear of all ties . . . to be known by no other title than *the Gentleman in the parlour!*

Ibid.

What I mean by living to one's self is living in the world, as in it, not of it. . . . It is to be a silent spectator of the mighty scene of things; . . . to take a thoughtful, anxious interest or curiosity in what is passing in the world, but not to feel the slightest inclination to make or meddle with it.

On Living to One's Self

Even in the common affairs of life, in love, friendship, and marriage, how little security have we when we trust our happiness in the hands of others!

Ibid.

There is not a more mean, stupid, dastardly, pitiful, selfish, spiteful, envious, ungrateful animal than the Public.

It is the greatest of cowards, for it is afraid of itself.

On Living to One's Self

When a man is dead, they put money in his coffin, erect monuments to his memory, and celebrate the anniversary of his birthday in set speeches. Would they take any notice of him if he were living? No!

Ibid.

Horas non numero nisi serenas [1] — is the motto of a sun-dial near Venice. There is a softness and a harmony in the words and in the thought unparalleled.

On a Sun-Dial

If our hours were all serene, we might probably take almost as little note of them, as the dial does of those that are clouded.

Ibid.

No young man believes he shall ever die.

The Feeling of Immortality in Youth

There is a feeling of Eternity in youth, which makes us amends for everything. To be young is to be as one of the Immortal Gods.

Ibid.

The young are prodigal of life from a superabundance of it; the old are tenacious on the same score, because they have little left, and cannot enjoy even what remains of it.

Ibid.

As we advance in life, we acquire a keener sense of the value of time. Nothing else, indeed, seems of any consequence; and we become misers in this respect.

Ibid.

The only true retirement is that of the heart; the only true leisure is the repose of the passions. To such persons it makes little difference whether they are young or old; and they die as they have lived, with graceful resignation.

Ibid.

If I have not read a book before, it

[1] I count only the sunny hours.

is, to all intents and purposes, new to me, whether it was printed yesterday or three hundred years ago.
On Reading New Books

When I take up a work that I have read before (the oftener the better) I know what I have to expect. The satisfaction is not lessened by being anticipated.
On Reading Old Books

Persons without education certainly do not want either acuteness or strength of mind in what concerns themselves, or in things immediately within their observation; but they have no power of abstraction, no general standard of taste, or scale of opinion. They see their objects always near, and never in the horizon. Hence arises that egotism which has been remarked as the characteristic of self-taught men.
The Round Table. I, 26

It is better to be able neither to read nor write than to be able to do nothing else.
On the Ignorance of the Learned

Men of genius do not excel in any profession because they labour in it, but they labour in it, because they excel.
Characteristics

We are not hypocrites in our sleep.
On Dreams

"The English," says Froissart, "amused themselves sadly after the fashion of their country." They have indeed a way of their own. Their mirth is a relaxation from gravity, a challenge to dull care to be gone; and one is not always clear at first, whether the appeal is successful.
Merry England

When a person dies who does any one thing better than any one else in the world, it leaves a gap in society.
Table Talk [1821–1822] (On the death of John Cavanagh, famous player of fives, a kind of handball)

HENRY PETER, LORD BROUGHAM
[1778–1868]

Let the soldier be abroad if he will, he can do nothing in this age. There is another personage, — a personage less imposing in the eyes of some, perhaps insignificant. The schoolmaster is abroad,[1] and I trust to him, armed with his primer, against the soldier in full military array.
Speech, Opening of Parliament [January 29, 1828]

In my mind, he was guilty of no error, he was chargeable with no exaggeration, he was betrayed by his fancy into no metaphor, who once said that all we see about us, kings, lords, and Commons, the whole machinery of the State, all the apparatus of the system, and its varied workings, end in simply bringing twelve good men into a box.
Present State of the Law [February 7, 1828]

Pursuit of Knowledge under Difficulties.
Title of Book [1830]

Death was now armed with a new terror.
Attributed to Brougham[2]

JOHN GALT
[1779–1839]

From the lone sheiling of the misty island

[1] At the first meeting of the London Mechanics' Institution, 1825, John Reynolds, head of a school in Clerkenwell, acted as secretary of the meeting. Lord Brougham, who spoke at this meeting, said in the course of his remarks, "Look out, gentlemen, the schoolmaster is abroad." The phrase attracted little attention at that time, but when used in a speech three years later, it at once became popular.
[2] Brougham delivered a very warm panegyric upon the ex-Chancellor, and expressed a hope that he would make a good end, although to an expiring Chancellor death was now armed with a new terror. — LORD JOHN CAMPBELL: *Lives of the Chancellors* [1849], Vol. VII, P. 163
Lord St. Leonards attributes this phrase to

Mountains divide us, and the waste of
    seas —
Yet still the blood is strong, the heart is
    Highland,
And we in dreams behold the Hebrides.[1]
      Canadian Boat Song. Stanza 2

FRANCIS SCOTT KEY
[1779–1843]

Oh, say can you see by the dawn's early
    light,
What so proudly we hailed at the twi-
    light's last gleaming?
Whose broad stripes and bright stars,
    thro' the perilous fight,
O'er the ramparts we watched were so
    gallantly streaming?
And the rockets' red glare, the bombs
    bursting in air,
Gave proof thro' the night that our
    flag was still there.
Oh, say does that star-spangled banner
    yet wave
O'er the land of the free and the home
    of the brave?
      The Star-Spangled Banner [Sep-
      tember 14, 1814]. Stanza 1

Then conquer we must, for our cause
    it is just, —
And this be our motto, — "In God is
    our trust!"
      Ibid. Stanza 4

JOSEPH STORY
[1779–1845]

Whene'er you speak, remember every
    cause

Sir Charles Wetherell, who used it on the occasion referred to by Lord Campbell.

[1] This poem appeared in *Noctes Ambrosi-
anae*, No. 46, in *Blackwood's Magazine*, September, 1829. It is generally credited to John
Galt, but JOHN WILSON ("Christopher
North") has also been suggested as the author.
JOHN GIBSON LOCKHART noted, on a copy of
the poem in his own handwriting, that the
song had been sent to him by a friend in
Upper Canada. Galt, author of *Annals of the
Parish*, was in Canada in 1824 and 1826. The
poem was likewise found in the handwriting
of Hugh Montgomerie, twelfth Earl of Eglin-
ton [1739–1819], ascribed to a Gaelic origin.

Stands not on eloquence, but stands on
    laws;
Pregnant in matter, in expression brief,
Let every sentence stand with bold re-
    lief;
On trifling points not time nor talents
    waste,
A sad offence to learning and to taste;
Nor deal with pompous phrase, nor e'er
    suppose
Poetic flights belong to reasoning prose.
      Advice to Young Lawyers.
                   Stanza 1

Here shall the Press the People's right
    maintain,
Unaw'd by influence and unbrib'd by
    gain;
Here patriot Truth her glorious precepts
    draw,
Pledg'd to Religion, Liberty, and Law.
      Motto of the Salem Register
      (In W. W. STORY, *Life and Let-*
      ters of Joseph Story [1851])

HORACE SMITH
[1779–1849]

Thinking is but an idle waste of
    thought,
And nought is everything, and every-
    thing is nought.
      Rejected Addresses. Cui Bono?
                   Stanza 8

In the name of the Prophet — figs.
      Johnson's Ghost

Although corruption may our frame
    consume,
The immortal spirit in the skies may
    bloom.
      Address to the Mummy at Bel-
      zoni's Exhibition. Stanza 13

WILLIAM LAMB,
VISCOUNT MELBOURNE
[1779–1848]

I wish I was as cocksure of anything
as Tom Macaulay is of everything.
      In COWPER, *Melbourne's Papers*
      [1889]. Preface

THOMAS, LORD DENMAN
[1779–1854]

A delusion, a mockery, and a snare.
*O'Connell v. The Queen (in 11
Clark and Finnelly Reports)*

The mere repetition of the *Cantilena*
of lawyers cannot make it law, unless
it can be traced to some competent authority; and if it be irreconcilable, to
some clear legal principle.

Ibid.

CLEMENT CLARKE MOORE
[1779–1863]

'Twas the night before Christmas, when
  all through the house
Not a creature was stirring, — not even
  a mouse; [1]
The stockings were hung by the chimney with care,
In hopes that St. Nicholas soon would
  be there.

*A Visit from St. Nicholas
[December, 1823]*

"Happy Christmas to all, and to all a
  good-night!"

Ibid.

CHARLES CALEB COLTON
[1780–1832]

Imitation is the sincerest of flattery.
The Lacon

WILLIAM ELLERY CHANNING
[1780–1842]

I call that mind free which jealously
guards its intellectual rights and
powers, which calls no man master,
which does not content itself with a
passive or hereditary faith, which opens
itself to light whencesoever it may
come, which receives new truth as
an angel from Heaven.

Spiritual Freedom

[1] See Shakespeare, page 169b.

The office of government is not to
confer happiness, but to give men opportunity to work out happiness for
themselves.

*The Life and Character of
Napoleon Bonaparte*

CHARLES MINER
[1780–1865]

When I see a merchant over-polite
to his customers, begging them to taste
a little brandy and throwing half his
goods on the counter, — thinks I, that
man has an axe to grind.

Who'll Turn Grindstones [1]

THOMAS MOORE
[1780–1852]

Weep on! and, as thy sorrows flow,
I'll taste the luxury of woe.

*Juvenile Poems. Anacreontic,
Press the Grape, Stanza 2*

How shall we rank thee upon glory's
  page?
Thou more than soldier and just less
  than sage!

*Poems Relating to America. To
Thomas Hume, Stanza 6*

I knew by the smoke, that so gracefully
  curl'd
Above the green elms, that a cottage
  was near;
And I said, "If there's peace to be found
  in the world,
A heart that was humble might hope
  for it here!"

Ibid. Ballad Stanzas, 1

They made her a grave, too cold and
  damp
For a soul so warm and true;
And she's gone to the Lake of the Dis-
  mal Swamp,
Where, all night long, by a firefly lamp,
She paddles her white canoe.

*Ibid. The Lake of the Dismal
Swamp, Stanza 1*

[1] From *Essays from the Desk of Poor
Robert the Scribe* [1815].

437

Faintly as tolls the evening chime,
Our voices keep tune and our oars keep
　time.[1]
　　　*Poems Relating to America. A
　　　Canadian Boat-Song, Stanza 1*
Row, brothers, row, the stream runs
　fast,
The rapids are near, and the daylight's
　past.
　　　　　　　　　　　　　　Ibid.
Go where glory waits thee!
But while fame elates thee,
　Oh, still remember me!
　　　*Irish Melodies [1807–1834].
　　　Go Where Glory Waits Thee,
　　　Stanza 1*
Oh, breathe not his name! let it sleep
　in the shade,
Where cold and unhonour'd his relics
　are laid.
　　　*Ibid. Oh Breathe Not His Name,
　　　　　　　　　　　Stanza 1*
And the tear that we shed, though in
　secret it rolls,
Shall long keep his memory green in our
　souls.[2]
　　　　　　　　　　Ibid. Stanza 2
The harp that once through Tara's halls
　The soul of music shed,
Now hangs as mute on Tara's walls
　As if that soul were fled.
So sleeps the pride of former days,
　So glory's thrill is o'er;
And hearts that once beat high for
　praise
Now feel that pulse no more.
　　　*Ibid. The Harp That Once
　　　Through Tara's Halls, Stanza 1*
And the heart that is soonest awake to
　the flowers
Is always the first to be touch'd by the
　thorns.
　　　*Ibid. Oh, Think Not My Spirits
　　　Are Always as Light, Stanza 1*
Rich and rare were the gems she wore,
And a bright gold ring on her wand
　she bore.
　　　*Ibid. Rich and Rare Were the
　　　Gems She Wore, Stanza 1*

[1] See Marvell, page 269a.
[2] See Shakespeare, page 170a.

There is not in the wide world a valley
　so sweet
As that vale in whose bosom the bright
　waters meet.[1]
　　　*Irish Melodies. The Meeting of
　　　　　　the Waters, Stanza 1*
Come, send round the wine, and leave
　points of belief
To simpleton sages, and reasoning fools.
　　　*Ibid. Come, Send Round the
　　　　　　Wine, Stanza 1*
Shall I ask the brave soldier, who fights
　by my side
In the cause of mankind, if our creeds
　agree?
Shall I give up the friend I have valued
　and tried,
If he kneel not before the same altar
　with me?[2]
　　　　　　　　　　Ibid. Stanza 2
Ah! little they think who delight in her
　strains,
How the heart of the Minstrel is break-
　ing.
　　　*Ibid. She is Far from the Land,
　　　　　　　　　　　Stanza 2*
Believe me, if all those endearing young
　charms
Which I gaze on so fondly today,
Were to change by tomorrow and fleet
　in my arms,
Like fairy gifts fading away,
Thou would'st still be adored as this
　moment thou art,
Let thy loveliness fade as it will,
And around the dear ruin each wish of
　my heart
Would entwine itself verdantly still.
　　　*Ibid. Believe Me, If All Those
　　　Endearing Young Charms,
　　　Stanza 1*

[1] The vale of Avoca, County Wicklow, Ire-
land, where the Avonmore and Avonbeg meet
to form the river Avoca.
[2] I do not question school nor creed
　Of Christian, Protestant, or Priest;
　I only know that creeds to me
　Are but new names for mystery,
　That good is good from east to east,
　And more I do not know nor need
　To know, to love my neighbor well.
　　　JOAQUIN MILLER [1841–1913]: *The
　　　　　Tale of the Tall Alcalde*

No, the heart that has truly lov'd never
    forgets,
But as truly loves on to the close;
As the sunflower turns on her god, when
    he sets,
The same look which she turn'd when
    he rose.
    Irish Melodies. Believe Me, If
      All Those Endearing Young
      Charms, Stanza 2
And when once the young heart of a
    maiden is stolen,
The maiden herself will steal after it
    soon.
    Ibid. Ill Omens, Stanza 1
'Tis sweet to think, that, where'er we
    rove,
  We are sure to find something bliss-
    ful and dear;
And that when we're far from the lips
    we love,
  We've but to make love to the lips
    we are near.
    Ibid. 'Tis Sweet to Think,
      Stanza 1
But there's nothing half so sweet in life
As love's young dream.
    Ibid. Love's Young Dream,
      Stanza 1
To live with them is far less sweet,
Than to remember thee.
    Ibid. I Saw Thy Form, Stanza 3
Eyes of unholy blue.
    Ibid. By That Lake Whose
      Gloomy Shore, Stanza 2
'Tis the last rose of summer,
  Left blooming alone;
All her lovely companions
  Are faded and gone;
No flower of her kindred,
  No rosebud is nigh,
To reflect back her blushes,
  Or give sigh for sigh.
    Ibid. The Last Rose of Summer,
      Stanza 1
When true hearts lie wither'd
  And fond ones are flown,
Oh, who would inhabit
  This bleak world alone?
    Ibid. Stanza 3
And the best of all ways
  To lengthen our days

Is to steal a few hours from the night,
  my dear.
    Irish Melodies. The Young May
      Moon, Stanza 1
You may break, you may shatter the
  vase if you will,
But the scent of the roses will hang
  round it still.
    Ibid. Farewell! But Whenever
No eye to watch, and no tongue to
  wound us,
All earth forgot, and all heaven around
  us.
    Ibid. Come O'er the Sea,
      Stanza 2
The light that lies [1]
In woman's eyes.
    Ibid. The Time I've Lost in
      Wooing, Stanza 1
  My only books
  Were woman's looks,
And folly's all they've taught me.
    Ibid.
I know not, I ask not, if guilt's in that
  heart,
I but know that I love thee, whatever
  thou art.
    Ibid. Come, Rest in This Bosom,
      Stanza 2
A Persian's heaven is easily made:
'Tis but black eyes and lemonade.
    Intercepted Letters, or The Two-
      Penny Post Bag [1813]. VI
Oft in the stilly night,
  Ere slumber's chain has bound me,
Fond memory brings the light
  Of other days around me;
    The smiles, the tears,
    Of boyhood's years,
The words of love then spoken;
    The eyes that shone
    Now dimmed and gone,
The cheerful hearts now broken.
    National Airs [1815]. Oft in the
      Stilly Night, Stanza 1

---

[1]   O dreamy eyes,
    They tell sweet lies of Paradise;
    And in those eyes the love-light lies
    And lies — and lies — and lies!
      ANITA OWEN: *Dreamy Eyes*
        [circa 1894]

I feel like one,
Who treads alone
Some banquet-hall deserted,
Whose lights are fled,
Whose garlands dead,
And all but he departed.
> *National Airs. Oft in the Stilly*
> *Night, Stanza 2*

Came but for Friendship and took away
Love.
> *Ibid. A Temple to Friendship,*
> *Stanza 2*

As half in shade and half in sun
This world along its path advances,
May that side the sun's upon
Be all that e'er shall meet thy glances!
> *Ibid. Peace Be Around Thee,*
> *Stanza 2*

If I speak to thee in friendship's name,
Thou think'st I speak too coldly;
If I mention love's devoted flame,
Thou say'st I speak too boldly.
> *Ibid. How Shall I Woo? Stanza 1*

A friendship that like love is warm;
A love like friendship steady.
> *Ibid. Stanza 3*

Young Love may go,
For aught I care,
To Jericho!
> *Ibid. When Love Is Kind, Stanza 6*

So Life's year begins and closes;
Days though shortening still can
shine;
What though youth gave love and roses,
Age still leaves us friends and wine.
> *Ibid. Spring and Autumn,*
> *Stanza 1*

Give smiles to those who love you less,
But keep your tears for me.
> *When Midst the Gay I Meet.*
> *Stanza 1*

This world is all a fleeting show,
For man's illusion given;
The smiles of joy, the tears of woe,
Deceitful shine, deceitful flow, —
There's nothing true but Heaven.
> *Sacred Songs. This World is All*
> *a Fleeting Show, Stanza 1*

Sound the loud timbrel o'er Egypt's
dark sea!

Jehovah has triumph'd, — his people
are free.
> *Sacred Songs. Sound the*
> *Loud Timbrel*

As down in the sunless retreats of the
ocean
Sweet flowers are springing no mortal
can see,
So, deep in my soul the still prayer of
devotion,
Unheard by the world, rises silent to
Thee.
> *Ibid. As Down in the Sunless*
> *Retreats, Stanza 1*

Ask a woman's advice, and, whate'er
she advise,
Do the very reverse and you're sure to
be wise.
> *Satirical and Humorous Poems.*
> *How to Make a Good Politician,*
> *Stanza 1*

There was a little man, and he had a
little soul;
And he said, Little Soul, let us try, try,
try!
> *Ibid. Little Man and Little Soul,*
> *Stanza 1*

Oh, call it by some better name,
For friendship sounds too cold.
> *Ballads and Songs. Oh, Call It*
> *by Some Better Name, Stanza 1*

To sigh, yet feel no pain;
To weep, yet scarce know why;
To sport an hour with Beauty's chain,
Then throw it idly by.
> *Miscellaneous Poems. The Blue*
> *Stocking, VI*

And from the lips of Truth one mighty
breath
Shall like a whirlwind scatter in its
breeze
The whole dark pile of human mockeries: —
Then shall the reign of mind commence
on earth,
And starting fresh as from a second
birth,
Man in the sunshine of the world's new
spring

Shall walk transparent like some holy
thing!
> *Lalla Rookh* [*1817*]. *Part I, The*
> *Veiled Prophet of Khorassan*

The heaven of each is but what each
desires.
> *Ibid.*

There's a bower of roses by Bendemeer's stream,
And the nightingale sings round it all
the day long.[1]
> *Ibid. Part II*

But Faith, fanatic Faith, once wedded
fast
To some dear falsehood, hugs it to the
last.
> *Ibid. Part III*

One morn a Peri at the gate
Of Eden stood disconsolate.
> *Ibid. Part IV, Paradise and the Peri*

Take all the pleasures of all the spheres
And multiply each through endless
years, —
One minute of heaven is worth them
all.
> *Ibid.*

But the trail of the serpent is over them
all.
> *Ibid.*

Oh! ever thus, from childhood's hour,
I've seen my fondest hope decay;
I never loved a tree or flower,
But 'twas the first to fade away.
I never nurs'd a dear gazelle
To glad me with its soft black eye,
But when it came to know me well
And love me it was sure to die.[2]
> *Ibid. Part V, The Fire-Worshippers*

Paradise itself were dim
And joyless, if not shared with him!
> *Ibid. Part VI*

---

[1] As I recall them the roses bloom again,
and the nightingales sing by the calm Bendemeer. — THACKERAY: *The Newcomes* [*1853-
1855*], *Chap. 1*
[2] I never had a piece of toast
Particularly long and wide
But fell upon the sanded floor,
And always on the buttered side.
> JAMES PAYN: *Poem* [*1884*]

Alas! how light a cause may move
Dissension between hearts that love!
> *Lalla Rookh. Part VIII, The*
> *Light of the Haram*

Like that celestial bird whose nest
Is found beneath far Eastern skies,
Whose wings though radiant when at
rest
Lose all their glory when he flies.
> *Ibid.*

Fly to the desert, fly with me,
Our Arab tents are rude for thee.
> *Ibid.*

Humility, that low, sweet root
From which all heavenly virtues shoot.
> *The Loves of the Angels* [*1823*].
> *Third Angel's Story*

COMMANDER JAMES LAWRENCE, U.S.N.
[1781–1813]

Tell the men to fire faster and not to
give up the ship; fight her till she sinks.
> *On Board the Chesapeake*
> [*June 1, 1813*]

EBENEZER ELLIOTT
[1781–1849]

When wilt Thou save the people?
O God of mercy, when?
Not kings and lords, but nations!
Not thrones and crowns, but men!
Flowers of Thy heart, O God, are they;
Let them not pass, like weeds, away —
God save the people!
> *Corn Law Rhymes* [*1828*]. *When*
> *Wilt Thou Save the People?*
> *Stanza 1*

What is a communist? One who hath
yearnings
For equal division of unequal earnings.
> *Poetical Works* [*1846*]. *Epigram*

THOMAS HART BENTON
[1782–1858]

This new page opened in the book of
our public expenditures, and this new
departure taken, which leads into the

bottomless gulf of civil pensions and family gratuities.

Speech, U. S. Senate, Against a Grant to President Harrison's Widow [April, 1841]

JOHN C. CALHOUN
[1782–1850]

Protection and patriotism are reciprocal.

Speech, U. S. House of Representatives [December 12, 1811]

The very essence of a free government consists in considering offices as public trusts,[1] bestowed for the good of the country, and not for the benefit of an individual or a party.

Speech [February 13, 1835]

A power has risen up in the government greater than the people themselves, consisting of many and various and powerful interests, combined into one mass, and held together by the cohesive power of the vast surplus in the banks.[2]

Speech [May 27, 1836]

The surrender of life is nothing to sinking down into acknowledgment of inferiority.

Speech, U. S. Senate [February 19, 1847]

ANN TAYLOR
[1782–1866]
JANE TAYLOR
[1783–1824]

Who ran to help me when I fell,
And would some pretty story tell,
Or kiss the place to make it well?
  My mother.

Original Poems for Infant Minds [1804]. My Mother [By ANN TAYLOR], Stanza 6

One honest John Tompkins, a hedger and ditcher,
Although he was poor, did not want to be richer;

[1] See Burke, page 361b, Jefferson, page 375a, and Clay, page 433b.
[2] From this speech comes the phrase, "Cohesive power of public plunder."

For all such vain wishes in him were prevented
By a fortunate habit of being contented.

Original Poems for Infant Minds. Contented John [By JANE TAYLOR], Stanza 1

Twinkle, twinkle, little star,
How I wonder what you are,
Up above the world so high,
Like a diamond in the sky.[1]

Rhymes for the Nursery [1806]. The Star, Stanza 1

I thank the goodness and the grace
  Which on my birth have smiled,
And made me, in these Christian days,
  A happy Christian child.

Hymns for Infant Minds [1810]. A Child's Hymn of Praise, Stanza 1

Oh, that it were my chief delight
  To do the things I ought!
Then let me try with all my might
  To mind what I am taught.

Ibid. For a Very Little Child

There's hardly anything so small,
  So trifling or so mean,
That we may never want at all,
  For service unforeseen;
And wilful waste, depend upon 't,
Brings, almost always, woeful want!

Ibid. The Pin [By ANN TAYLOR], Stanza 6

'Twas fancied by some, who but slightly had seen them,
There was not a pin to be chosen between them.

Ibid. Jane and Eliza [By ANN TAYLOR], Stanza 2

DANIEL WEBSTER
[1782–1852]

Whatever makes men good Christians, makes them good citizens.

Speech at Plymouth, Massachusetts [2] [December 22, 1820]

[1] Twinkle, twinkle, little bat!
How I wonder what you're at!
Up above the world you fly,
Like a tea-tray in the sky.
LEWIS CARROLL: *Alice's Adventures in Wonderland* [1865]
[2] This oration will be read five hundred

Labor in this country is independent and proud. It has not to ask the patronage of capital, but capital solicits the aid of labor.[1]

Speech [April 2, 1824]

We wish that this column, rising towards heaven among the pointed spires of so many temples dedicated to God, may contribute also to produce in all minds a pious feeling of dependence and gratitude. We wish, finally, that the last object to the sight of him who leaves his native shore, and the first to gladden his who revisits it, may be something which shall remind him of the liberty and the glory of his country.

Address on Laying the Corner-Stone of the Bunker Hill Monument [June 17, 1825]

Mind is the great lever of all things; human thought is the process by which human ends are ultimately answered.

Ibid.

Knowledge, in truth, is the great sun in the firmament. Life and power are scattered with all its beams.

Ibid.

Let our object be our country, our whole country, and nothing but our country.

Ibid.

Sink or swim, live or die, survive or perish, I give my hand and my heart to this vote.[2]

Discourse in Commemoration of Adams and Jefferson, Faneuil Hall, Boston [August 2, 1826]

It is my living sentiment, and by the blessing of God it shall be my dying sentiment, — Independence now and Independence forever.[1]

Discourse in Commemoration of Adams and Jefferson, Faneuil Hall, Boston

Washington is in the clear upper sky.

Ibid.

The gentleman has not seen how to reply to this, otherwise than by supposing me to have advanced the doctrine that a national debt is a national blessing.[2]

Second Speech on Foote's Resolution [January 26, 1830]

I shall enter on no encomium upon Massachusetts; she needs none. There she is.[3] Behold her, and judge for yourselves. There is her history; the world knows it by heart. The past, at least, is secure. There is Boston and Concord and Lexington and Bunker Hill; and there they will remain forever.

Ibid.

The people's government, made for the people, made by the people, and answerable to the people.[4]

Ibid.

When my eyes shall be turned to behold for the last time the sun in heaven, may I not see him shining on the broken and dishonored fragments of a once glorious Union; on States dissevered, discordant, belligerent; on a land rent with civil feuds, or drenched, it may be, in fraternal blood.

Ibid.

---

years hence with as much rapture as it was heard. It ought to be read at the end of every century, and indeed at the end of every year, forever and ever. — JOHN ADAMS: *Letter to Webster* [December 23, 1821]

[1] See Lincoln, page 539b.

[2] Mr. Adams, describing a conversation with Jonathan Sewall in 1774, says: "I answered that the die was now cast; I had passed the Rubicon. Swim or sink, live or die, survive or perish with my country was my unalterable determination." — JOHN ADAMS: *Works* [1850–1856], *Vol. IV, P. 8*

Live or die, sink or swim. — GEORGE PEELE: *Edward I* [1584?]

Both Adams and Jefferson died on July 4, 1826.

[1] Mr. Webster says of Mr. Adams: "On the day of his death, hearing the noise of bells and cannon, he asked the occasion. On being reminded that it was 'Independent Day,' he replied, 'Independence forever.' " — *Webster's Works* [1903], *Vol. I, P. 150*

[2] A national debt, if it is not excessive, will be to us a national blessing. — ALEXANDER HAMILTON: *Letter to Robert Morris* [April 30, 1781]

[3] This is generally misquoted as "Massachusetts, there she stands."

[4] Our sovereign, the people. — CHARLES JAMES FOX: Toast [1798], for which his name was erased from the Privy Council.

See Lincoln, page 541a, and Theodore Parker, page 560a.

Liberty and Union, now and forever, one and inseparable.

Second Speech on Foote's Resolution

There is no refuge from confession but suicide; and suicide is confession.

Argument on the Murder of Captain White [April 6, 1830]

There is nothing so powerful as truth, — and often nothing so strange.[1]

Ibid.

Fearful concatenation of circumstances.[2]

Ibid.

A sense of duty pursues us ever. It is omnipresent, like the Deity. If we take to ourselves the wings of the morning, and dwell in the uttermost parts of the sea, duty performed or duty violated is still with us, for our happiness or our misery. If we say the darkness shall cover us, in the darkness as in the light our obligations are yet with us.

Ibid.

He smote the rock of the national resources, and abundant streams of revenue gushed forth. He touched the dead corpse of Public Credit, and it sprung upon its feet.[3]

Speech on Hamilton [March 10, 1831]

God grants liberty only to those who love it, and are always ready to guard and defend it.

Speech [June 3, 1834]

On this question of principle, while actual suffering was yet afar off, they [the Colonies] raised their flag against a power to which, for purposes of foreign conquest and subjugation, Rome in the height of her glory is not to be compared, — a power which has dotted over the surface of the whole globe with her possessions and military posts,

whose morning drum-beat, following the sun,[1] and keeping company with the hours, circles the earth with one continuous and unbroken strain of the martial airs of England.

Speech [May 7, 1834]

One country, one constitution, one destiny.

Speech [March 15, 1837]

There are persons who constantly clamor. They complain of oppression, speculation, and pernicious influence of wealth. They cry out loudly against all banks and corporations, and a means by which small capitalists become united in order to produce important and beneficial results. They carry on mad hostility against all established institutions. They would choke the fountain of industry and dry all streams.

Speech, U. S. Senate [March 12, 1838]

When tillage begins, other arts follow. The farmers therefore are the founders of human civilization.

Remarks on Agriculture [January 13, 1840]

America has furnished to the world the character of Washington. And if our American institutions had done nothing else, that alone would have entitled them to the respect of mankind.

Completion of Bunker Hill Monument [June 17, 1843]

Thank God! I — I also — am an American!

Ibid.

Justice, sir, is the great interest of man on earth.

On Mr. Justice Story [September 12, 1845]

Inconsistencies of opinion, arising from changes of circumstances, are often justifiable.[2]

Speech [July 25 and 27, 1846]

---

[1] See Byron, page 460a.
[2] See Scott, page 417a.
[3] He it was that first gave to the law the air of a science. He found it a skeleton, and clothed it with life, colour, and complexion; he embraced the cold statue, and by his touch it grew into youth, health, and beauty. — BARRY YELVERTON, LORD AVONMORE [1736–1805]: *On Blackstone*

[1] See Scott, page 417b.
[2] L'homme absurde est celui qui ne change jamais (The absurd man is he who never changes). — AUGUSTE MARSEILLE BARTHÉLEMY: *Ma Justification* [1832]

Liberty exists in proportion to wholesome restraint.

Speech at the Charleston Bar Dinner [May 10, 1847]

The law: It has honored us; may we honor it.

Ibid.

I have read their platform, and though I think there are some unsound places in it, I can stand upon it pretty well. But I see nothing in it both new and valuable. "What is valuable is not new, and what is new is not valuable."

Speech at Marshfield, Massachusetts [September 1, 1848]

I was born an American; I will live an American; I shall die an American.[1]

Speech [July 17, 1850]

Faneuil Hall, the cradle of American liberty.

Letter [April, 1851]

Men hang out their signs indicative of their respective trades: shoemakers hang out a gigantic shoe; jewelers, a monster watch; and the dentist hangs out a gold tooth; but up in the mountains of New Hampshire, God Almighty has hung out a sign to show that there He makes men.

The Old Man of the Mountain [2]

I still live.

Last words [October 24, 1852]

REGINALD HEBER
[1783–1826]

Failed the bright promise of your early day.

Palestine

Brightest and best of the sons of the morning,
Dawn on our darkness, and lend us thine aid.

Hymns. Epiphany, Stanza 1

By cool Siloam's shady rill
How sweet the lily grows!

Ibid. First Sunday after Epiphany, No. II

[1] See Patrick Henry, page 368b.
[2] A natural rock formation in the shape of a human profile, in the Presidential Range of the White Mountains. It gave Hawthorne the theme of his story *The Great Stone Face.*

The Son of God goes forth to war,
A kingly crown to gain;
His blood-red banner streams afar;
Who follows in His train?

Hymns. The Son of God Goes Forth to War, Stanza 1

From Greenland's icy mountains,
From India's coral strand,
Where Afric's sunny fountains
Roll down their golden sand.

Ibid. Missionary Hymn, Stanza 1

Though every prospect pleases,
And only man is vile:
In vain with lavish kindness
The gifts of God are strown;
The heathen in his blindness
Bows down to wood and stone.

Ibid. Stanza 2

Holy, Holy, Holy! Lord God Almighty!
Early in the morning our song shall rise to Thee:
Holy, Holy, Holy! Merciful and Mighty!
God in Three Persons, Blessed Trinity.

Ibid. Holy, Holy, Holy!

Holy, Holy, Holy! all the Saints adore Thee,
Casting down their golden crowns around the glassy sea.

Ibid.

WASHINGTON IRVING
[1783–1859]

How convenient it would be to many of our great men and great families of doubtful origin, could they have the privilege of the heroes of yore, who, whenever their origin was involved in obscurity, modestly announced themselves descended from a god.

Knickerbocker's History of New York [1809]. Book II, Chap. 3

Who ever hears of fat men heading a riot, or herding together in turbulent mobs? — no — no, 'tis your lean, hungry men who are continually worrying society, and setting the whole community by the ears.[1]

Ibid. Book III, Chap. 2

[1] See Shakespeare, page 166b.

Your true dull minds are generally preferred for public employ, and especially promoted to city honors; your keen intellects, like razors, being considered too sharp for common service.

Knickerbocker's History of New York. Book III, Chap. 2

His wife "ruled the roast," and in governing the governor, governed the province, which might thus be said to be under petticoat government.

Ibid. Book IV, Chap. 4

The most glorious hero that ever desolated nations might have mouldered into oblivion among the rubbish of his own monument, did not some historian take him into favor, and benevolently transmit his name to posterity.

Ibid. Book V, Chap. 1

There is in every true woman's heart a spark of heavenly fire, which lies dormant in the broad daylight of prosperity; but which kindles up, and beams and blazes in the dark hour of adversity.

The Sketch-Book [1819–1820].
The Wife

Those men are most apt to be obsequious and conciliating abroad, who are under the discipline of shrews at home.

Ibid. Rip Van Winkle

A curtain lecture is worth all the sermons in the world for teaching the virtues of patience and long-suffering.

Ibid.

A sharp tongue is the only edge tool that grows keener with constant use.

Ibid.

That happy age when a man can be idle with impunity.

Ibid.

A woman's whole life is a history of the affections.

Ibid. The Broken Heart

Language gradually varies, and with it fade away the writings of authors who have flourished their allotted time.

Ibid. The Mutabilities of Literature

There rise authors now and then, who seem proof against the mutability of language, because they have rooted themselves in the unchanging principles of human nature.

The Sketch-Book. The Mutabilities of Literature

His [the author's] renown has been purchased, not by deeds of violence and blood, but by the diligent dispensation of pleasure.

Ibid. Westminster Abbey [The Poets' Corner]

The sorrow for the dead is the only sorrow from which we refuse to be divorced. Every other wound we seek to heal, every other affliction to forget; but this wound we consider it a duty to keep open; this affliction we cherish and brood over in solitude.

Ibid. Rural Funerals

Whenever a man's friends begin to compliment him about looking young, he may be sure that they think he is growing old.

Bracebridge Hall [1822].
Bachelors

The land of literature is a fairy land to those who view it at a distance, but, like all other landscapes, the charm fades on a nearer approach, and the thorns and briars become visible. The republic of letters is the most factious and discordant of all republics, ancient or modern.

Tales of a Traveller [1824].
Notoriety

The almighty dollar,[1] that great object of universal devotion throughout our land, seems to have no genuine devotees in these peculiar villages.

Wolfert's Roost [1855]. The Creole Village

Those calm, sunny seasons in the commercial world, which are known by the name of "times of unexampled prosperity."

Ibid. "A Time of Unexampled Prosperity"

[Captain Delaplace[2]] gazed at [Ethan] Allen in bewildered astonish-

---

[1] See Jonson, page 219a.
[2] Commandant at Fort Ticonderoga, New York, May 10, 1775.

ment. "By whose authority do you act?" exclaimed he. "In the name of the great Jehovah, and the Continental Congress!" replied Allen.

> *Life of Washington* [*1855–1859*].
> *Vol. I, Chap. 38*

HENRI BEYLE (STENDHAL)
[1783–1842]

One can acquire everything in solitude — except character.

> *Fragments. I*

Prudery is a kind of avarice, the worst of all.

> *Ibid. V*

In matters of sentiment, the public has very crude ideas; and the most shocking fault of women is that they make the public the supreme judge of their lives.

> *Ibid. IX*

A wise woman never yields by appointment. It should always be an unforeseen happiness.

> *De l'Amour* [*1822*]. *Chap. 60*

The Baron could not produce epigrams; he required at least four sentences of six lines each to be brilliant.

> *The Red and the Black* [*1831*].
> *Chap. 34*

I see but one rule: *to be clear*. If I am not clear, all *my world* crumbles to nothing.

> *Reply to Balzac. October 30,*
> *1840* [1]

Wit lasts no more than two centuries.

> *Ibid.*

It is the nobility of their style which will make our writers of 1840 unreadable forty years from now.

> *Manuscript Note* [*1840*]

ALLAN CUNNINGHAM
[1784–1842]

A wet sheet and a flowing sea,
A wind that follows fast,

[1] In reference to *The Charterhouse of Parma* [1839].

And fills the white and rustling sail,
And bends the gallant mast.

> *The Songs of Scotland* [*1825*].
> *A Wet Sheet and a Flowing Sea,*
> *Stanza 1*

While the hollow oak our palace is,
Our heritage the sea.

> *Ibid. Stanza 3*

When looks were fond and words were few.

> *Ibid. Poet's Bridal-day Song,*
> *Stanza 2*

John Grumlie swore by the light o' the moon,
And the green leaves on the tree,
That he could do more work in a day
Than his wife could do in three.

> *Ibid. John Grumlie,* [1] *Stanza 1*

But henceforth I maun mind the plow,
And ye maun bide at hame.

> *Ibid. Stanza 6*

It's hame and it's hame, hame fain wad I be,
O, hame, hame, hame to my ain countree!

> *Ibid. It's Hame and It's Hame*

LEIGH HUNT
[1784–1859]

This Adonis in loveliness was a corpulent man of fifty. [2]

> *The Examiner* [*March 22, 1812*]

Where the light woods go seaward from the town.

> *The Story of Rimini* [*1816*].
> *Canto I, Line 18*

But most he loved a happy human face.

> *Ibid. Canto III, Line 110*

[1] Adapted from the old ballad *The Wife of Auchtermuchty*. Another adaptation is *Darby and Joan*, by St. John Honeywood [1763–1798]:

> When Darby saw the setting sun,
> He swung his scythe and home he run,
> Sat down, drank off his quart, and said:
> "My work is done, I'll go to bed."

[2] For this reference to the Prince Regent, Hunt was imprisoned. But he was allowed to redecorate the walls of his prison with a trellis of roses, had his family with him, and visitors were freely admitted — Byron, indeed, gave a dinner party in his honor at the jail.

With spots of sunny openings, and with
  nooks
To lie and read in, sloping into brooks.
The Story of Rimini. Canto III,
Line 418

The world was all forgot, the struggle
  o'er,
Desperate the joy. — That day they
  read no more.[1]
Ibid. Line 607

Green little vaulter in the sunny grass.
To the Grasshopper and the
Cricket [1817]

Abou Ben Adhem (may his tribe increase!)
Awoke one night from a deep dream
  of peace.
Abou Ben Adhem [1838]

An angel writing in a book of gold.
Ibid.

Write me as one who loves his fellow-
  men.
Ibid.

And show'd the names whom love of
  God had bless'd,
And lo! Ben Adhem's name led all the
  rest.
Ibid.

Jenny kissed me when we met,
Jumping from the chair she sat in;
Time, you thief, who love to get
Sweets into your list, put that in:
Say I'm weary, say I'm sad,
Say that health and wealth have
  missed me,
Say I'm growing old, but add,
Jenny kissed me.[2]
Rondeau [1838]

Stolen sweets are always sweeter,
Stolen kisses much completer,
Stolen looks are nice in chapels,
Stolen, stolen, be your apples.
Song of Fairies Robbing an
Orchard

Oh for a seat in some poetic nook,

Just hid with trees and sparkling with
  a brook!
Politics and Poetics. Line 72

"No love," quoth he, "but vanity, sets
  love a task like that."
The Glove and the Lions.[1]
Stanza 4

Learn the right
Of coining words in the quick mint of
  joy.
A Rustic Walk and Dinner.
Line 33

Some people say it is a very easy
thing to get up of a cold morning. You
have only, they tell you, to take the
resolution; and the thing is done.
Getting Up on Cold Mornings

She thinks the young women of the
present day too forward, and the men
not respectful enough; but hopes her
grandchildren will be better; though
she differs with her daughter in several
points respecting their management.
The Old Lady

Those who have lost an infant are
never, as it were, without an infant
child. They are the only persons who,
in one sense, retain it always.
Deaths of Little Children

A fireside is a great opiate.
A Few Thoughts on Sleep

It has been said of ladies when they
write letters, that they put their minds
in their postscripts — let out the real
objects of their writing, as if it were
a second thought, or a thing comparatively indifferent.
Anacreon

The only place a new hat can be carried into with safety is a church, for
there is plenty of room there.
A Chapter on Hats

The maid-servant, the sailor, and
the schoolboy, are the three beings that
enjoy a holiday beyond all the rest of
the world.
The Maid-Servant

---

[1] See Dante, page 75b.
[2] The "Jenny" was Jane Welsh Carlyle, who
kissed Hunt when he brought Carlyle good
news.

[1] SCHILLER wrote a poem on the same
theme, and BROWNING's *The Glove* [1845] is
a later version of the familiar legend.

JAMES SHERIDAN KNOWLES
[1784–1862]

A sound so fine, there's nothing lives
'Twixt it and silence.
Virginius [1820]. Act V, Sc. 2

LADY CAROLINE LAMB
[1785–1828]

Mad, bad, and dangerous to know.
Of Byron, in her Journal

THOMAS DE QUINCEY
[1785–1859]

It is notorious that the memory strengthens as you lay burdens upon it, and becomes trustworthy as you trust it.
Confessions of an English Opium-Eater[1] *[1822–1856]. Page 30*

Call for the grandest of all earthly spectacles, what is that? It is the sun going to his rest. Call for the grandest of all human sentiments, what is that? It is that man should forget his anger before he lies down to sleep.[2]
Ibid. Page 86

The reception one meets with from the women of a family generally determines the tenor of one's whole entertainment.
Ibid. Page 132

Mails from the North — the East — the West — the South — whence, according to some curious etymologists, comes the magical word NEWS.
Ibid. Page 145

Oxford Street, stony-hearted stepmother, thou that listenest to the sighs of orphans, and drinkest the tears of children.
Ibid. Page 174

Dyspepsy is the ruin of most things: empires, expeditions, and everything else.
Letter to Hessey [1823]

If once a man indulges himself in murder, very soon he comes to think little of robbing; and from robbing he

next comes to drinking and Sabbath-breaking, and from that to incivility and procrastination.
Murder Considered as One of the Fine Arts [1827]

Worlds of fine thinking lie buried in that vast abyss [newspapers], never to be disentombed or restored to human admiration.
Reminiscences of the English Lake Poets. Coleridge

THOMAS LOVE PEACOCK
[1785–1866]

How troublesome is day!
It calls us from our sleep away;
It bids us from our pleasant dreams
    awake,
And sends us forth to keep or break
Our promises to pay.
How Troublesome Is Day

None better knew the feast to sway,
    Or keep mirth's boat in better trim;
For Nature had but little clay
    Like that of which she moulded him.
*Headlong Hall [1816]. Chap. 5,
In His Last Binn Sir Peter Lies,
Stanza 2*

A heeltap! a heeltap! I never could
    bear it!
So fill me a bumper, a bumper of
    claret!
Ibid. Song.

Not drunk is he who from the floor
Can rise alone and still drink more;
But drunk is he, who prostrate lies,
Without the power to drink or rise.
*The Misfortunes of Elphin
[1829]. Heading, Chap. 3,
translated from the Welsh*

The mountain sheep are sweeter,
But the valley sheep are fatter;
We therefore deemed it meeter
To carry off the latter.
Ibid. Chap. 11

Ancient sculpture is the true school of modesty. But where the Greeks had modesty, we have cant; where they had poetry, we have cant; where they had patriotism, we have cant; where they had anything that exalts, delights, or

---

[1] Everyman edition.
[2] See *Ephesians, IV, 26*, at page 1062b.

adorns humanity, we have nothing but cant, cant, cant.
> *Crotchet Castle* [*1831*]. *Chap. 7*

He remembered too late, on his thorny green bed,
Much that well may be thought cannot wisely be said.
> *Ibid. The Priest and the Mulberry Tree, Stanza 5*

OLIVER HAZARD PERRY
[1785–1820]

We have met the enemy, and they are ours.
> *Letter to General Harrison* [*dated "United States Brig Niagara. Off the Western Sisters. Sept. 10, 1813, 4 P. M."*]

JOHN PIERPONT
[1785–1866]

The Yankee boy, before he's sent to school,
Well knows the mystery of that magic tool,
The pocket-knife.
> *Whittling, A Yankee Portrait. Stanza 1*

SAMUEL WOODWORTH
[1785–1842]

How dear to this heart are the scenes of my childhood,
When fond recollection presents them to view.
> *The Old Oaken Bucket*

Then soon with the emblem of truth overflowing,
And dripping with coolness, it rose from the well.
> *Ibid.*

The old oaken bucket, the iron-bound bucket,
The moss-covered bucket, which hung in the well.
> *Ibid.*

Pickaxe, shovel, spade, crowbar, hoe, and barrow,

Better not invade, Yankees have the marrow.
> *The Patriotic Diggers* [*1814*]. *Stanza 1*

We'll show him that Kentucky boys
Are Alligator-horses.
> *The Hunters of Kentucky.*[1] *Stanza 2*

So Pakenham he made his brags
If he in fight was lucky,
He'd have their gals and cotton bags,
In spite of old Kentucky.
> *Ibid. Stanza 4*

DAVID CROCKETT
[1786–1836]

I leave this rule for others when I'm dead,
Be always sure you're right — then go ahead.[2]
> *Autobiography* [*1834*]

Don't shoot, colonel, I'll come down:
I know I'm a gone coon.[3]
> *Story told by Crockett of a treed raccoon*

WILLIAM LEARNED MARCY
[1786–1857]

They see nothing wrong in the rule that to the victors belong the spoils of the enemy.
> *Speech, U. S. Senate* [*January, 1832*]

WINFIELD SCOTT
[1786–1866]

Say to the seceded States, "Wayward sisters, depart in peace."
> *Letter to W. H. Seward* [*March 3, 1861*]

[1] This ballad, having the subtitle *Half Horse and Half Alligator*, celebrates the participation of the Kentuckians, under the command of General John Coffee, in the Battle of New Orleans, January 8, 1815. It was published as a broadside in Boston, and, in 1826, collected in a volume, *Melodies, Duets, Trios, Songs, and Ballads*, by JAMES M. CAMPBELL.
[2] Crockett's motto in the War of 1812.
[3] The expression "gone coon" was current during the Revolutionary War, originating in the plea of a spy, dressed in raccoon skins, to his discoverer, an English rifleman. — *Century Cyclopedia of Names*

RICHARD HENRY DANA
[1787–1879]

A voice within us speaks the startling word,
"Man, thou shalt never die!"
Immortality

BRYAN WALLER PROCTER ("BARRY CORNWALL")
[1787–1874]

The sea! the sea! the open sea!
The blue, the fresh, the ever free!
The Sea. Stanza 1

Touch us gently, Time! [1]
Let us glide adown thy stream
Gently, — as we sometimes glide
Through a quiet dream.
A Petition to Time. Stanza 1

Humble voyagers are we,
O'er life's dim, unsounded sea.
Ibid. Stanza 2

EMMA WILLARD
[1787–1870]

Rocked in the cradle of the deep,
I lay me down in peace to sleep.
The Cradle of the Deep [1831]

RICHARD HARRIS BARHAM
[1788–1845]

The Lady Jane was tall and slim,
The Lady Jane was fair.
Ingoldsby Legends [1840]. *The Knight and the Lady*

The Devil must be in that little Jackdaw!
Ibid. The Jackdaw of Rheims

The Cardinal rose with a dignified look,
He call'd for his candle, his bell, and his book!
In holy anger, and pious grief,
He solemnly cursed that rascally thief!
He cursed him at board, he cursed him in bed;
From the sole of his foot to the crown of his head;
He cursed him in sleeping, that every night

[1] See Crabbe, page 383b.

He should dream of the devil, and wake in a fright;
He cursed him in living, he cursed him in drinking,
He cursed him in coughing, in sneezing, in winking;
He cursed him in sitting, in standing, in lying;
He cursed him in walking, in riding, in flying,
He cursed him living, he cursed him dying! —
Never was heard such a terrible curse!
But what gave rise to no little surprise,
Nobody seem'd one penny the worse!
Ingoldsby Legends. The Jackdaw of Rheims

Heedless of grammar, they all cried,
That's him!
Ibid.

GEORGE NOEL GORDON, LORD BYRON
[1788–1824]

Friendship is Love without his wings.
L'Amitié est l'Amour sans Ailes [1806]

I only know we loved in vain;
I only feel — farewell! farewell!
Farewell! If Ever Fondest Prayer [1808]. *Stanza 2*

When we two parted
In silence and tears,
Half broken-hearted,
To sever for years.
When We Two Parted [1808].
Stanza 1

Near this spot are deposited the remains of one who possessed Beauty without Vanity, Strength without Insolence, Courage without Ferocity, and all the Virtues of Man, without his Vices. This Praise, which would be unmeaning Flattery if inscribed over human ashes, is but a just tribute to the Memory of Boatswain, a Dog.
Inscription on the Monument of a Newfoundland Dog [1808]

The poor dog, in life the firmest friend,

The first to welcome, foremost to defend.

Inscription on the Monument of a Newfoundland Dog

I'll publish right or wrong:
Fools are my theme, let satire be my song.

English Bards and Scotch Reviewers [1809]. Line 5

'Tis pleasant, sure, to see one's name in print;
A book's a book, although there's nothing in 't.

Ibid. Line 51

A man must serve his time to every trade
Save censure — critics are all ready made.

Ibid. Line 63

With just enough of learning to misquote.

Ibid. Line 66

As soon
Seek roses in December, ice in June;
Hope constancy in wind, or corn in chaff;
Believe a woman or an epitaph,
Or any other thing that's false, before
You trust in critics.

Ibid. Line 75

Better to err with Pope, than shine with Pye.

Ibid. Line 102

'Twas thine own genius gave the final blow,
And help'd to plant the wound that laid thee low:
So the struck eagle, stretch'd upon the plain,
No more through rolling clouds to soar again,
View'd his own feather on the fatal dart,
And wing'd the shaft that quiver'd in his heart.[1]

Ibid. Line 826

Though Nature's sternest painter, yet the best.[2]

Ibid. Line 839

[1] See Aesop, page 11b.
[2] Crabbe.

Maid of Athens, ere we part,
Give, oh give me back my heart!

Maid of Athens [1810]. Stanza 1

Vex'd with mirth the drowsy ear of night.

Childe Harold's Pilgrimage. Canto I [1812], Stanza 2

Had sigh'd to many, though he loved but one.

Ibid. Stanza 5

Maidens, like moths, are ever caught by glare,
And Mammon wins his way where seraphs might despair.

Ibid. Stanza 9

Might shake the saintship of an anchorite.

Ibid. Stanza 11

Adieu! adieu! my native shore
Fades o'er the waters blue.

Ibid. Stanza 13

My native land, good night!

Ibid.

Still from the fount of joy's delicious springs
Some bitter o'er the flowers its bubbling venom flings.[1]

Ibid. Stanza 82

War, war is still the cry, — "war even to the knife!"[2]

Ibid. Stanza 86

The dome of thought, the palace of the soul.[3]

Ibid. Canto II [1812], Stanza 6

Once more upon the waters, yet once more!
And the waves bound beneath me as a steed
That knows his rider!

Ibid. Canto III [1816], Stanza 2

There was a sound of revelry by night,
And Belgium's capital had gather'd then
Her beauty and her chivalry, and bright
The lamps shone o'er fair women and brave men.

[1] See Lucretius, page 35a.
[2] "War even to the knife" was the reply of Palafox, the governor of Saragossa, when summoned to surrender by the French, who besieged that city in 1808.
[3] See Waller, page 242b.

A thousand hearts beat happily; and
　when
Music arose with its voluptuous swell,
Soft eyes look'd love to eyes which
　spake again,
And all went merry as a marriage bell.
But hush! hark! a deep sound strikes
　like a rising knell!
　　　　Childe Harold's Pilgrimage.
　　　　　Canto III, Stanza 21

Did ye not hear it? — No! 'twas but
　the wind,
Or the car rattling o'er the stony street.
On with the dance! let joy be uncon-
　fined;
No sleep till morn, when Youth and
　Pleasure meet
To chase the glowing hours with flying
　feet.
　　　　　　　Ibid. Stanza 22

And there was mounting in hot haste.
　　　　　　　Ibid. Stanza 25

Or whispering, with white lips, "The
　foe! They come! they come!"
　　　　　　　　　Ibid.

Like to the apples on the Dead Sea's
　shore,
All ashes to the taste.
　　　　　　　Ibid. Stanza 34

He who ascends to mountain-tops, shall
　find
The loftiest peaks most wrapt in clouds
　and snow;
He who surpasses or subdues mankind
Must look down on the hate of those
　below.
　　　　　　　Ibid. Stanza 45

All tenantless, save to the crannying
　wind.
　　　　　　　Ibid. Stanza 47

History's purchased page to call them
　great.
　　　　　　　Ibid. Stanza 48

The castled crag of Drachenfels
Frowns o'er the wide and winding
　Rhine.
　　　　　　　Ibid. Stanza 55

To fly from, need not be to hate, man-
　kind.
　　　　　　　Ibid. Stanza 69

By the blue rushing of the arrowy
　Rhone.
　　　　Childe Harold's Pilgrimage.
　　　　　Canto III, Stanza 71

I live not in myself, but I become
Portion of that around me: [1] and to me
High mountains are a feeling, but the
　hum
Of human cities torture.
　　　　　　　Ibid. Stanza 72

The sky is changed, — and such a
　change! O night
And storm, and darkness! ye are
　wondrous strong,
Yet lovely in your strength, as is the
　light
Of a dark eye in woman!
　　　　　　　Ibid. Stanza 92

Exhausting thought,
And hiving wisdom with each studious
　year.
　　　　　　　Ibid. Stanza 107

Sapping a solemn creed with solemn
　sneer.
　　　　　　　　　Ibid.

Fame is the thirst of youth.
　　　　　　　Ibid. Stanza 112

I have not loved the world, nor the
　world me; [2]
I have not flatter'd its rank breath,
　nor bow'd
To its idolatries a patient knee.
　　　　　　　Ibid. Stanza 113

I stood
Among them, but not of them; in a
　shroud
Of thoughts which were not their
　thoughts.
　　　　　　　　　Ibid.

I stood in Venice on the Bridge of
　Sighs,
A palace and a prison on each hand.
　　　Ibid. Canto IV [1818], Stanza 1

Where Venice sate in state, throned on
　her hundred isles.
　　　　　　　　　Ibid.

The thorns which I have reap'd are of
　the tree

[1] I am a part of all that I have met. —
TENNYSON: *Ulysses* [1842]
[2] See Johnson, page 343a, and Emerson,
pages 502b–503a.

I planted; they have torn me, and I
    bleed.
I should have known what fruit would
    spring from such a seed.
            Childe Harold's Pilgrimage.
                Canto IV, Stanza 10
Parting day
Dies like the dolphin, whom each pang
    imbues
With a new colour as it gasps away,
The last still loveliest, till — 'tis gone,
    and all is gray.
            Ibid. Stanza 29
Italia! O Italia! thou who hast
The fatal gift of beauty.[1]
            Ibid. Stanza 42
Let these describe the undescribable.
            Ibid. Stanza 53
The starry Galileo, with his woes.
            Ibid. Stanza 54
Ungrateful Florence! Dante sleeps
    afar,
Like Scipio, buried by the upbraiding
    shore.
            Ibid. Stanza 57
The poetry of speech.
            Ibid. Stanza 58
Then farewell Horace, whom I hated
    so,
Not for thy faults, but mine.
            Ibid. Stanza 77
O Rome! my country! city of the soul!
            Ibid. Stanza 78
The Niobe of nations! there she stands,
Childless and crownless, in her voiceless
    woe.
            Ibid. Stanza 79
I speak not of men's creeds — they
    rest between
Man and his Maker.
            Ibid. Stanza 95
Yet, Freedom! yet thy banner, torn,
    but flying,
Streams like the thunder-storm against
    the wind.
            Ibid. Stanza 98
'Tis but the same rehearsal of the
    past . . .

[1] Based on the famous sonnet of VINCENZO
DA FILICAJA [1642–1707]:
    Italia, Italia! O tu cui feo la sorte.

And History, with all her volumes vast,
Hath but one page.
            Childe Harold's Pilgrimage.
                Canto IV, Stanza 108
Egeria! sweet creation of some heart
Which found no mortal resting-place
    so fair
As thine ideal breast.
            Ibid. Stanza 115
Death, the sable smoke where vanishes
    the flame.
            Ibid. Stanza 124
Butcher'd to make a Roman holiday!
            Ibid. Stanza 141
"While stands the Coliseum, Rome
    shall stand;
When falls the Coliseum, Rome shall
    fall;
And when Rome falls — the world." [1]
            Ibid. Stanza 145
Oh! that the desert were my dwelling-
    place,[2]
With one fair spirit for my minister,
That I might all forget the human
    race,
And, hating no one, love but only her!
            Ibid. Stanza 177
There is a pleasure in the pathless
    woods,
There is a rapture on the lonely shore,
There is society, where none intrudes,
By the deep sea, and music in its roar:
I love not man the less, but Nature
    more.
            Ibid. Stanza 178
Roll on, thou deep and dark blue ocean,
    roll!
Ten thousand fleets sweep over thee in
    vain;
Man marks the earth with ruin, — his
    control
Stops with the shore.
            Ibid. Stanza 179
Time writes no wrinkle on thine azure
    brow —

[1] The saying of the ancient pilgrims, quoted
from BEDE by GIBBON, *The Decline and Fall
of the Roman Empire* [1781], *Chap. LXXI.*
[2] Oh that I had in the wilderness a lodging-
place of wayfaring men! — *Jeremiah, IX, 2*
See Cowper, page 364a.

Such as creation's dawn beheld, thou
rollest now.[1]
Childe Harold's Pilgrimage.
Canto IV, Stanza 182

Thou glorious mirror, where the Almighty's form
Glasses itself in tempests.
Ibid. Stanza 183

And I have loved thee, Ocean! and my
joy
Of youthful sports was on thy breast
to be
Borne, like thy bubbles, onward; from
a boy
I wantoned with thy breakers, . . .
And trusted to thy billows far and near,
And laid my hand upon thy mane,[2] —
as I do here.
Ibid. Stanza 184

I awoke one morning and found myself famous.
Entry in Memoranda after publication of first two cantos of Childe Harold's Pilgrimage. Quoted by THOMAS MOORE, *Life of Byron* [*1830*], *Chap. 14*

Such is the aspect of this shore;
'Tis Greece, but living Greece no more!
So coldly sweet, so deadly fair,
We start, for soul is wanting there.
The Giaour [*1813*]. *Line 90*

Shrine of the mighty! can it be
That this is all remains of thee?
Ibid. Line 106

And lovelier things have mercy shown
To every failing but their own;
And every woe a tear can claim,
Except an erring sister's shame.
Ibid. Line 418

The keenest pangs the wretched find
Are rapture to the dreary void,
The leafless desert of the mind,
The waste of feelings unemployed.
Ibid. Line 957

---

[1] And thou vast ocean, on whose awful face
Time's iron feet can print no ruin-trace.
ROBERT MONTGOMERY: *The Omnipresence of the Deity* [1830]

[2] He laid his hand upon "the Ocean's mane,"
And played familiar with his hoary locks.
ROBERT POLLOK [1798–1827]: *The Course of Time, Book IV, L. 689*

Better to sink beneath the shock
Than moulder piecemeal on the rock.
The Giaour. Line 969

The cold in clime are cold in blood,
Their love can scarce deserve the name.
Ibid. Line 1099

I die, — but first I have possess'd,
And come what may, I *have been*
bless'd.
Ibid. Line 1114

She was a form of life and light
That, seen, became a part of sight,
And rose, where'er I turn'd mine eye,
The morning-star of memory!
Ibid. Line 1127

Know ye the land where the cypress
and myrtle
Are emblems of deeds that are done
in their clime;
Where the rage of the vulture, the love
of the turtle,
Now melt into sorrow, now madden
to crime? [1]
The Bride of Abydos [*1813*].
Canto I, Stanza 1

Where the virgins are soft as the roses
they twine,
And all save the spirit of man is divine?
Ibid.

The fatal facility of the octosyllabic
verse.
The Corsair [*1814*]. *Dedication*

He left a corsair's name to other times,
Link'd with one virtue, and a thousand
crimes.
Ibid. Canto III, Stanza 24

The Cincinnatus of the West,
Whom envy dared not hate,
Bequeathed the name of Washington
To make man blush there was but
one! [2]
Ode to Napoleon Bonaparte
[*1814*]. *II*

Lord of himself, — that heritage of
woe!
Lara [*1814*]. *Canto I,*
Stanza 2

---

[1] See Goethe, page 378b.

[2] See *Don Juan*, page 459a, and *The Age of Bronze*, page 460b.

The hand that kindles cannot quench
    the flame.
                Lara. Canto II, Stanza 11

She walks in beauty, like the night
    Of cloudless climes and starry skies;
And all that's best of dark and bright
    Meet in her aspect and her eyes;
Thus mellow'd to that tender light
    Which Heaven to gaudy day denies.
            *Hebrew Melodies [1815]. She
            Walks in Beauty, Stanza 1*

The Assyrian came down like the wolf
    on the fold,
And his cohorts were gleaming in pur-
    ple and gold;
And the sheen of their spears was like
    stars on the sea,
When the blue wave rolls nightly on
    deep Galilee.
        *Ibid. The Destruction of Sen-
            nacherib,*[1] *Stanza 1*

For the Angel of Death spread his wings
    on the blast.
                Ibid. Stanza 3

And the might of the Gentile, unsmote
    by the sword,
Hath melted like snow in the glance
    of the Lord!
                Ibid. Stanza 6

Fare thee well! and if forever,
Still forever, fare thee well.
        Fare Thee Well [1816]. Stanza 1

Sighing that Nature form'd but one
    such man,
And broke the die, in moulding Sheri-
    dan.[2]
        *Monody on the Death of Sheridan
            [1816]. Line 117*

My hair is gray, but not with years,
    Nor grew it white
        In a single night,

[1] And it came to pass that night, that the angel of the Lord went out, and smote in the camp of the Assyrians an hundred fourscore and five thousand: and when they arose early in the morning, behold, they were all dead corpses. — *2 Kings, XIX, 35*

[2] Natura il fece, e poi ruppe la stampa (Nature made him, and then broke the mould). — ARIOSTO: *Orlando Furioso* [1532], Canto X, St. 84

As men's have grown from sudden fears.
        *The Prisoner of Chillon [1816].
                            Stanza 1*

O God! it is a fearful thing
To see the human soul take wing
In any shape, in any mood.
                Ibid. Stanza 8

A light broke in upon my brain, —
    It was the carol of a bird;
It ceased, and then it came again,
    The sweetest song ear ever heard.
                Ibid. Stanza 10

I had a dream which was not all a
    dream.
                Darkness [1816]

Though the day of my destiny's over,
And the star of my fate hath declined.
        *Stanzas to Augusta [1816].
                            Stanza 1*

My boat is on the shore,
    And my bark is on the sea;
But, before I go, Tom Moore,
    Here's a double health to thee!
        *To Thomas Moore [1817].
                            Stanza 1*

Here's a sigh to those who love me,
    And a smile to those who hate;
And, whatever sky's above me,
    Here's a heart for every fate.[1]
                Ibid. Stanza 2

So we'll go no more a-roving
So late into the night.
            *Letter to Thomas Moore
                [February 26, 1817]*

Mont Blanc is the monarch of moun-
    tains;
    They crowned him long ago
On a throne of rocks, in a robe of
    clouds,
    With a diadem of snow.
            Manfred [1817]. Act I, Sc. 1

She was not old, nor young, nor at the
    years
Which certain people call a "certain
    age,"
Which yet the most uncertain age ap-
    pears.
            Beppo [1818]. Stanza 22

For most men (till by losing rendered
    sager)

[1] See Longfellow, page 521a.

Will back their own opinions by a wager.

    Beppo. Stanza 27

Besides, they always smell of bread and butter.

    Ibid. Stanza 39

  That soft bastard Latin,
Which melts like kisses from a female mouth.

    Ibid. Stanza 44

One hates an author that's all author.

    Ibid. Stanza 75

O Mirth and Innocence! O milk and water!
Ye happy mixtures of more happy days.

    Ibid. Stanza 80

And if we do but watch the hour,
There never yet was human power
Which could evade, if unforgiven,
The patient search and vigil long
Of him who treasures up a wrong.

    Mazeppa [1819]. Stanza 10

In virtues nothing earthly could surpass her,
Save thine "incomparable oil," Macassar!

   Don Juan. Canto I [1819],
      Stanza 17

But, oh! ye lords of ladies intellectual,
Inform us truly, — have they not henpeck'd you all? [1]

    Ibid. Stanza 22

The languages, especially the dead,
The sciences, and most of all the abstruse,
The arts, at least all such as could be said
To be the most remote from common use.

    Ibid. Stanza 40

Her maids were old, and if she took a new one,
You might be sure she was a perfect fright.

    Ibid. Stanza 48

Her stature tall, — I hate a dumpy woman.

    Ibid. Stanza 61

[1] See Addison, page 301a.

What men call gallantry, and gods adultery,
Is much more common where the climate's sultry.

   Don Juan. Canto I, Stanza 63

Christians have burnt each other, quite persuaded
That all the Apostles would have done as they did.

    Ibid. Stanza 83

A little still she strove, and much repented,
And whispering, "I will ne'er consent," — consented.

    Ibid. Stanza 117

'Tis sweet to hear the watch-dog's honest bark
Bay deep-mouth'd welcome as we draw near home;
'Tis sweet to know there is an eye will mark
Our coming, and look brighter when we come.

    Ibid. Stanza 123

Sweet is revenge — especially to women.[1]

    Ibid. Stanza 124

Man's love is of man's life a thing apart;
'Tis woman's whole existence.

    Ibid. Stanza 194

There's nought, no doubt, so much the spirit calms
As rum and true religion.

   Ibid. Canto II [1819],
      Stanza 34

A solitary shriek, the bubbling cry
Of some strong swimmer in his agony.

    Ibid. Stanza 53

'Tis very certain the desire of life
Prolongs it.

    Ibid. Stanza 64

'Tis said that persons living on annuities
Are longer lived than others.

    Ibid. Stanza 65

  All who joy would win
Must share it, — happiness was born a twin.

    Ibid. Stanza 172

[1] See Milton, page 258a.

Let us have wine and women, mirth and laughter,
Sermons and soda-water the day after.[1]
    Don Juan. Canto II, Stanza 178

In her first passion woman loves her lover,
In all the others, all she loves is love.[2]
    Ibid. Canto III [1821], Stanza 3

Think you, if Laura had been Petrarch's wife,
He would have written sonnets all his life?
    Ibid. Stanza 7

All tragedies are finished by a death,
All comedies are ended by a marriage.
    Ibid. Stanza 9

He was the mildest manner'd man
That ever scuttled ship or cut a throat.
    Ibid. Stanza 41

Even good men like to make the public stare.
    Ibid. Stanza 81

The isles of Greece, the isles of Greece!
Where burning Sappho loved and sung. . . .
Eternal summer gilds them yet,
But all, except their sun, is set.
    Ibid. Stanza 86, 1

The mountains look on Marathon,
And Marathon looks on the sea;
And musing there an hour alone,
I dreamed that Greece might still be free.
    Ibid. 3

And where are they? and where art thou,
My country? On thy voiceless shore
The heroic lay is tuneless now —
The heroic bosom beats no more!
And must thy lyre, so long divine,
Degenerate into hands like mine?
    Ibid. 5

Earth! render back from out thy breast
A remnant of our Spartan dead!
Of the three hundred grant but three,
To make a new Thermopylae.
    Ibid. 7

You have the Pyrrhic dance as yet,
Where is the Pyrrhic phalanx gone?

[1] See Dickens, page 577a, and George Ade, page 829a.
[2] See La Rochefoucauld, page 266a.

Of two such lessons, why forget
The nobler and the manlier one?
You have the letters Cadmus gave —
Think ye he meant them for a slave?
    Don Juan. Canto III, Stanza 86, 10

Fill high the bowl with Samian wine!
    Ibid. 11

Place me on Sunium's marble steep,
Where nothing save the waves and I
May hear our mutual murmurs sweep;
There, swan-like, let me sing and die.[1]
A land of slaves shall ne'er be mine —
Dash down yon cup of Samian wine!
    Ibid. 16

But words are things, and a small drop of ink,
Falling like dew upon a thought, produces
That which makes thousands, perhaps millions, think.
    Ibid. Stanza 88

And glory long has made the sages smile,
'Tis something, nothing, words, illusion, wind —
Depending more upon the historian's style
Than on the name a person leaves behind.
    Ibid. Stanza 90

Ah, surely nothing dies but something mourns.
    Ibid. Stanza 108

And if I laugh at any mortal thing,
'Tis that I may not weep.[2]
    Ibid. Canto IV [1821], Stanza 4

And her face so fair
Stirr'd with her dream, as rose-leaves with the air.[3]
    Ibid. Stanza 29

These two hated with a hate
Found only on the stage.
    Ibid. Stanza 93

[1] See Socrates, page 21a.
[2] See Beaumarchais, page 367b, and Lincoln, page 540a.
[3] All her innocent thoughts
Like rose-leaves scatter'd.
    JOHN WILSON ("CHRISTOPHER NORTH"): *On the Death of a Child* [1812]

"Arcades ambo," — *id est*, blackguards both.

> *Don Juan. Canto IV, Stanza 93*

I've stood upon Achilles' tomb,
And heard Troy doubted: time will doubt of Rome.

> *Ibid. Stanza 101*

There's not a sea the passenger e'er pukes in,
Turns up more dangerous breakers than the Euxine.

> *Ibid. Canto V [1821], Stanza 5*

And put himself upon his good behaviour.

> *Ibid. Stanza 47*

That all-softening, overpowering knell,
The tocsin of the soul — the dinner bell.

> *Ibid. Stanza 49*

The women pardon'd all except her face.

> *Ibid. Stanza 113*

Polygamy may well be held in dread,
Not only as a sin, but as a bore.

> *Ibid. Canto VI [1823], Stanza 12*

The drying up a single tear has more
Of honest fame than shedding seas of gore.

> *Ibid. Canto VIII [1823], Stanza 3*

Not so Leonidas and Washington,
Whose every battle-field is holy ground,
Which breathes of nations saved, not worlds undone.[1]

> *Ibid. Stanza 5*

Half-pay for life makes mankind worth destroying.

> *Ibid. Stanza 14*

George Washington had thanks and nought beside,
Except the all-cloudless glory (which few men's is)
To free his country.[1]

> *Ibid. Canto IX [1823], Stanza 8*

"Gentlemen farmers" — a race worn out quite.

> *Ibid. Stanza 32*

[1] See *Ode to Napoleon*, page 455b, and *The Age of Bronze*, page 460b.

When Bishop Berkeley said "there was no matter,"
And proved it, — 'twas no matter what he said.

> *Don Juan. Canto XI [1823], Stanza 1*

And, after all, what is a lie? 'Tis but
The truth in masquerade; and I defy
Historians, heroes, lawyers, priests, to put
A fact without some leaven of a lie.

> *Ibid. Stanza 37*

'Tis strange the mind, that very fiery particle,
Should let itself be snuff'd out by an article.

> *Ibid. Stanza 60*

Ready money is Aladdin's lamp.

> *Ibid. Canto XII [1823], Stanza 12*

Cervantes smil'd Spain's chivalry away.

> *Ibid. Canto XIII [1823], Stanza 11*

Society is now one polish'd horde,
Formed of two mighty tribes, the *Bores* and *Bored*.

> *Ibid. Stanza 95*

All human history attests
That happiness for man, — the hungry sinner! —
Since Eve ate apples, much depends on dinner.[1]

> *Ibid. Stanza 99*

Death, so called, is a thing which makes men weep,
And yet a third of life is passed in sleep.

> *Ibid. Canto XIV [1823], Stanza 3*

Of all the horrid, hideous notes of woe,
Sadder than owl-songs or the midnight blast,
Is that portentous phrase, "I told you so."

> *Ibid. Stanza 50*

[1] For a man seldom thinks with more earnestness of anything than he does of his dinner. — PIOZZI: *Anecdotes of Samuel Johnson* [1786]

'Tis strange, but true; for truth is always strange, —
Stranger than fiction.[1]
> *Don Juan. Canto XIV,*
> *Stanza 101*

The Devil hath not, in all his quiver's choice,
An arrow for the heart like a sweet voice.
> *Ibid. Canto XV [1824],*
> *Stanza 13*

A lovely being, scarcely formed or moulded,
A rose with all its sweetest leaves yet folded.
> *Ibid. Stanza 43*

The antique Persians taught three useful things, —
To draw the bow, to ride, and speak the truth.
> *Ibid. Canto XVI [1824],*
> *Stanza 1*

All farewells should be sudden.
> *Sardanapalus [1821]. Act V*

The best of prophets of the future is the past.
> *Journal [January 28, 1821]*

The world is a bundle of hay,
  Mankind are the asses that pull,
Each tugs in a different way, —
And the greatest of all is John Bull!
> *Letter to Thomas Moore*
> *[June 22, 1821]*

He seems
To have seen better days, as who has not
Who has seen yesterday?
> *Werner [1822]. Act I, Sc. 1*

The "good old times" — all times when old are good.
> *The Age of Bronze [1823].*
> *Stanza 1*

Whose [2] game was empires and whose stakes were thrones,

---

[1] Le vrai peut quelquefois n'être pas vraisemblable (Truth may sometimes be improbable). — BOILEAU [1636–1711]: *L'Art Poétique, III, L. 48*
  See Daniel Webster, page 444a.
  Truth is stranger than fiction, but not so popular. — AUTHOR UNKNOWN
[2] Napoleon.

Whose table earth, whose dice were human bones.
> *The Age of Bronze. Stanza 3*

While Franklin's quiet memory climbs to heaven,
Calming the lightning which he thence had riven,
Or drawing from the no less kindled earth
Freedom and peace to that which boasts his birth;
While Washington's a watchword, such as ne'er
Shall sink while there's an echo left to air.[1]
> *Ibid. Stanza 5*

How often we forget all time, when lone,
Admiring Nature's universal throne,
Her woods, her wilds, her waters, the intense
Reply of hers to our intelligence.
> *The Island [1823]. Canto II,*
> *Stanza 16*

Sublime tobacco! which from east to west
Cheers the tar's labour or the Turkman's rest.[2]
> *Ibid. Stanza 19*

Divine in hookas, glorious in a pipe
When tipp'd with amber, mellow, rich, and ripe;
Like other charmers, wooing the caress
More dazzlingly when daring in full dress;
Yet thy true lovers more admire by far
Thy naked beauties — give me a cigar!
> *Ibid.*

What's drinking?
A mere pause from thinking!
> *The Deformed Transformed*
> *[1824]. Act III, Sc. 1*

My days are in the yellow leaf; [3]

---

[1] See *Ode to Napoleon*, page 455b, and *Don Juan*, page 459a.
[2] Whatever Aristotle, and his worthy cabal, may say of it,
  Tobacco is divine, there is nothing to equal it.
  PIERRE CORNEILLE: *Le Festin de Pierre [1673], Act I, Sc. 1*
[3] See Shakespeare, pages 199a and 205b–206a.

The flowers and fruits of love are
  gone;
The worm, the canker, and the grief
Are mine alone!
    On My Thirty-sixth Year [*1824*].
                              Stanza 2
Seek out — less often sought than
  found —
A soldier's grave, for thee the best;
Then look around, and choose thy
  ground,
And take thy rest.
              Ibid. Stanza 10

ARTHUR SCHOPENHAUER
[1788–1860]

Hatred comes from the heart; contempt from the head; and neither feeling is quite within our control.
        Studies in Pessimism.[1]
        Psychological Observations
If a man sets out to hate all the miserable creatures he meets, he will not
have much energy left for anything
else; whereas he can despise them, one
and all, with the greatest ease.
                              Ibid.
Every man takes the limits of his own
field of vision for the limits of the
world.
                              Ibid.
Not to go to the theatre is like making one's toilet without a mirror.
                              Ibid.
Every parting gives a foretaste of
death; [2] every coming together again a
foretaste of the resurrection.
                              Ibid.
There is no absurdity so palpable but
that it may be firmly planted in the human head if you only begin to inculcate
it before the age of five, by constantly
repeating it with an air of great solem-
nity.
                              Ibid.
It is a curious fact that in bad days
we can very vividly recall the good time

that is now no more; but that in good
days we have only a very cold and imperfect memory of the bad.
    Studies in Pessimism. Psycho-
              logical Observations
The fundamental fault of the female
character is that it has no sense of justice.
                    Ibid. On Women
Dissimulation is innate in woman,
and almost as much a quality of the
stupid as of the clever.
                              Ibid.
Noise is the most impertinent of all
forms of interruption. It is not only an
interruption, but also a disruption of
thought.
                      Ibid. On Noise
The most general survey shows us
that the two foes of human happiness
are pain and boredom.
    Essays. Personality, or What a
                              Man Is
A man who has no mental needs, because his intellect is of the narrow and
normal amount, is, in the strict sense of
the word, what is called a *philistine*.[1]
                              Ibid.
Pride is an established conviction of
one's own paramount worth in some
particular respect; while vanity is the
desire of rousing such a conviction in
others. Pride works from within; it is
the direct appreciation of oneself. Vanity is the desire to arrive at this appreciation indirectly, from without.
                        Ibid. Pride
Ignorance is degrading only when
found in company with riches.
        Ibid. On Books and Reading
Intellect is invisible to the man who
has none.[2]
        Ibid. Our Relation to Others,
                            Sect. 23
There is no more mistaken path to
happiness than worldliness, revelry,
high life.
        Ibid. Our Relation to Ourselves,
                            Sect. 24
To be alone is the fate of all great

---

[1] Translated by T. BAILEY SAUNDERS, Modern Library edition.
[2] Partir c'est mourir un peu. — *French
proverb*

[1] See Matthew Arnold, page 621b.
[2] See La Rochefoucauld, page 266a.

minds — a fate deplored at times, but still always chosen as the less grievous of two evils.

Essays. Our Relation to
Ourselves, Sect. 24

Do not shorten the morning by getting up late; look upon it as the quintessence of life, as to a certain extent sacred.

Counsels and Maxims. Chap. 2

Speak without emphasizing your words. Leave other people to discover what it is that you have said; and as their minds are slow, you can make your escape in time.

Ibid. Chap. 3

HANNAH FLAGG GOULD
[1789–1865]

Alone I walked the ocean strand;
A pearly shell was in my hand;
I stooped and wrote upon the sand
    My name — the year — the day.

A Name on the Sand. Stanza 1

A wave came rolling high and fast,
And washed my lines away.

Ibid.

WILLIAM KNOX
[1789–1825]

Oh why should the spirit of mortal be proud?
Like a fast-flitting meteor, a fast-flying cloud,
A flash of the lightning, a break of the wave,
He passes from life to his rest in the grave.

Songs of Israel [1824]. Mortality,[1]
Stanza 1

'Tis the wink of an eye, 'tis the draught of a breath,
From the blossom of health to the paleness of death.

Ibid. Stanza 14

CHARLES PHILLIPS
[1789–1859]

Grand, gloomy, and peculiar, he sat upon the throne a sceptred hermit,

[1] This poem was a favorite of Abraham Lincoln.

wrapped in the solitude of his own originality.

The Character of Napoleon

SARAH JOSEPHA HALE
[1790–1879]

Mary had a little lamb,
    Its fleece was white as snow,
And everywhere that Mary went
    The lamb was sure to go;
He followed her to school one day,
    That was against the rule;
It made the children laugh and play
    To see a lamb in school.

Mary's Lamb. In the Juvenile
Miscellany [September, 1830]

FITZ-GREENE HALLECK
[1790–1867]

Strike — till the last armed foe expires;
Strike — for your altars and your fires;
Strike — for the green graves of your sires;
    God — and your native land!

Marco Bozzaris.[1] Stanza 3

But to the hero, when his sword
    Has won the battle for the free,
Thy voice sounds like a prophet's word,
    And in its hollow tones are heard
The thanks of millions yet to be.

Ibid. Stanza 6

One of the few, the immortal names
That were not born to die.

Ibid. Stanza 7

Green be the turf above thee,
    Friend of my better days!
None knew thee but to love thee,[2]
    Nor named thee but to praise.

On the Death of Joseph Rodman
Drake

They love their land because it is their own,
And scorn to give aught other reason why;
Would shake hands with a king upon his throne,

[1] A Greek patriot, born about 1788, killed in a night attack against the Turks, near Missolonghi, Greece, August 20, 1823.
[2] See Burns, page 392a, and Rogers, page 396b.

And think it kindness to his Majesty.
Connecticut
This bank-note world.
Alnwick Castle. Stanza 7

ALPHONSE DE LAMARTINE
[1790–1869]

"O time, arrest your flight! and you, propitious hours, arrest your course! Let us savor the fleeting delights of our most beautiful days!" [1]
The Lake [1820]. Stanza 6

I say to this night: "Pass more slowly"; and the dawn will come to dispel the night. [2]
Ibid. Stanza 8

Limited in his nature, infinite in his desires, man is a fallen god who remembers the heavens.
Méditations Poétiques [1820]. Sermon 2

What is our life but a succession of preludes to that unknown song whose first solemn note is sounded by Death? [3]
Ibid. Second Series, Sermon 15

Man, it seems, is not able to bear the languid rest on Nature's bosom, and when the trumpet sounds the signal of danger, he hastens to join his comrades, no matter what the cause that calls him to arms. He rushes into the thickest of the fight and amid the uproar of the battle regains confidence in himself and his powers.
Ibid.

Experience is the only prophecy of wise men.
Speech, at Mâcon [1847]

To love for the sake of being loved is human, but to love for the sake of loving is angelic.
Graziella [1849]. Part IV, Chap. 5

[1] "O temps, suspends ton vol! et vous, heures propices,
   Suspendez votre cours!
Laissez-nous savourer les rapides délices
   Des plus beaux de nos jours!"
[2] Je dis à cette nuit: "Sois plus lente"; et l'aurore
   Va dissiper la nuit.
[3] This passage was used by Liszt as a heading for his tone poem *Les Préludes*.

The more I see of the representatives of the people, the more I admire my dogs.
From COUNT D'ORSAY: Letter to John Forster [1850]

SAMUEL GILMAN
[1791–1858]

Fair Harvard! Thy sons to thy Jubilee throng,
   And with blessings surrender thee o'er,
By these festival rites, from the age that is past,
   To the age that is waiting before.
Ode, Bicentennial, Harvard University [September 8, 1836]. Stanza 1

First flower of their wilderness, star of their night,
Calm rising through change and through storm.
Ibid.

HENRY HART MILMAN
[1791–1868]

And the cold marble leapt to life a god.
The Belvedere Apollo

Too fair to worship, too divine to love.
Ibid.

LYDIA HUNTLEY SIGOURNEY
[1791–1865]

Ye say that all have passed away —
   That noble race and brave —
But their name is on your waters [1] —
   Ye may not wash it out.
Indian Names. Stanza 1

Your mountains build their monument,
Though ye destroy their dust.
Ibid. Stanza 5

Through the open window's space
Behold, a camel thrust his face.

[1] We will give the names of our fearless race
   To each bright river whose course we trace.
FELICIA D. HEMANS [1793–1835]: *Song of Emigration*

"My nose is cold," he meekly cried,
"Oh, let me warm it by thy side."
The Camel's Nose. Stanza 1

To evil habit's earliest wile
Lend neither ear, nor glance, nor
smile —
Choke the dark fountain ere it flows,
Nor e'en admit the camel's nose.
Ibid. Stanza 4

CHARLES SPRAGUE
[1791–1875]

Here lived and loved another race
of beings. Beneath the same sun that
rolls over your heads the Indian hunter
pursued the panting deer. . . . The
Indian of falcon glance and lion bearing, the theme of the touching ballad,
the hero of the pathetic tale, is gone.
The American Indian

CHARLES WOLFE
[1791–1823]

Not a drum was heard, not a funeral
note,
As his corse to the rampart we hurried.
*The Burial of Sir John Moore
at Corunna [1817]. Stanza 1*

But he lay like a warrior taking his
rest
With his martial cloak around him.
Ibid. Stanza 3

We carved not a line, and we raised
not a stone,
But we left him alone with his glory.
Ibid. Stanza 8

JOHN KEBLE
[1792–1866]

The trivial round, the common task,
Would furnish all we ought to ask.
*The Christian Year [1827].
Morning, Stanza 10*

Abide with me from morn till eve,
For without Thee I cannot live;
Abide with me when night is nigh,
For without Thee I dare not die.
Ibid. Evening, Stanza 4

JOHN HOWARD PAYNE
[1792–1852]

'Mid pleasures and palaces though we
may roam,
Be it ever so humble, there's no place
like home; [1]
A charm from the skies seems to hal-
low us there,
Which sought through the world is
ne'er met with elsewhere.
*Home, Sweet Home (From the opera
Clari, the Maid of Milan [1823])*

PERCY BYSSHE SHELLEY
[1792–1822]

Once, early in the morning,
Beelzebub arose,
With care his sweet person adorning,
He put on his Sunday clothes. [2]
*The Devil's Walk, A Ballad
[1812]. Stanza 1*

How wonderful is Death,
Death and his brother Sleep. [3]
Queen Mab [1813]. I

Power, like a desolating pestilence,
Pollutes whate'er it touches; and obe-
dience,
Bane of all genius, virtue, freedom,
truth,
Makes slaves of men, and, of the hu-
man frame,
A mechanized automaton.
Ibid. III

Heaven's ebon vault,
Studded with stars unutterably bright,
Through which the moon's unclouded
grandeur rolls,
Seems like a canopy which love had
spread
To curtain her sleeping world.
Ibid. IV

The awful shadow of some unseen
Power
Floats though unseen among us,
— visiting

[1] Home is home, be it never so homely. —
English Proverb [circa 1300]
[2] See Southey, page 427a.
[3] See Hesiod, page 7a, and Daniel, page
122a.

This various world with as inconstant wing
As summer winds that creep from flower to flower.
> *Hymn to Intellectual Beauty [1816]. Stanza 1*

Spirit of Beauty, that dost consecrate
With thine own hues all thou dost shine upon
Of human thought or form.
> *Ibid. Stanza 2*

Some say that gleams of a remoter world
Visit the soul in sleep, — that death is slumber,
And that its shapes the busy thoughts outnumber
Of those who wake and live.
> *Mont Blanc [1816]. Stanza 3*

I met a traveller from an antique land
Who said: "Two vast and trunkless legs of stone
Stand in the desert. Near them, on the sand,
Half sunk, a shattered visage lies, whose frown,
And wrinkled lip, and sneer of cold command,
Tell that its sculptor well those passions read."
> *Ozymandias [1817]*

"My name is Ozymandias, king of kings:
Look on my works, ye Mighty, and despair!"
Nothing beside remains. Round the decay
Of that colossal wreck, boundless and bare
The lone and level sands stretch far away.
> *Ibid.*

With hue like that when some great painter dips
His pencil in the gloom of earthquake and eclipse.
> *The Revolt of Islam [1817]. Canto V, Stanza 23*

I could lie down like a tired child,
And weep away the life of care

Which I have borne and yet must bear.
> *Stanzas Written in Dejection near Naples [1818]. Stanza 4*

Forms more real than living man,
Nurslings of immortality!
> *Prometheus Unbound [1818–1819]. Act I*

Like stars half quencht in mists of silver dew.
> *Ibid. Act II, Sc. 1*

All love is sweet,
Given or returned. Common as light is love,
And its familiar voice wearies not ever. . . .
They who inspire it most are fortunate,
As I am now; but those who feel it most
Are happier still.[1]
> *Ibid. Sc. 5*

Death is the veil which those who live call life;
They sleep, and it is lifted.
> *Ibid. Act III, Sc. 3*

Good, great and joyous, beautiful and free;
This is alone Life, Joy, Empire, and Victory.
> *Ibid. Act IV, closing lines*

I love all waste
And solitary places; where we taste
The pleasure of believing what we see
Is boundless, as we wish our souls to be.
> *Julian and Maddalo [1819]. Line 14*

Thou Paradise of exiles, Italy!
> *Ibid. Line 57*

It is our will
That thus enchains us to permitted ill —
We might be otherwise — we might be all
We dream of happy, high, majestical.
Where is the love, beauty and truth we seek,
But in our mind?
> *Ibid. Line 170*

Me — who am as a nerve o'er which do creep

[1] See La Rochefoucauld, page 265b.

The else unfelt oppressions of this earth.
> *Julian and Maddalo.* Line *449*

Most wretched men
Are cradled into poetry by wrong;
They learn in suffering what they teach in song.[1]
> *Ibid.* Line *543*

Chameleons feed on light and air:
Poets' food is love and fame.
> *An Exhortation* [*1819*]. *Stanza 1*

O wild West Wind, thou breath of Autumn's being,
Thou, from whose unseen presence the leaves dead
Are driven, like ghosts from an enchanter fleeing,
Yellow, and black, and pale, and hectic red,
Pestilence-stricken multitudes.
> *Ode to the West Wind* [*1819*].
> *Stanza 1*

Wild Spirit, which art moving everywhere;
Destroyer and preserver; hear, oh, hear!
> *Ibid.*

Make me thy lyre, even as the forest is:
What if my leaves are falling like its own!
The tumult of thy mighty harmonies
Will take from both a deep, autumnal tone,
Sweet though in sadness. Be thou, Spirit fierce,
My spirit! Be thou me, impetuous one!
> *Ibid. Stanza 5*

O Wind,
If Winter comes, can Spring be far behind?
> *Ibid.*

The seed ye sow, another reaps;
The wealth ye find, another keeps;
The robes ye weave, another wears;
The arms ye forge, another bears.
> *Song to the Men of England*
> [*1819*]. *Stanza 5*

Nothing in the world is single,
All things by a law divine

[1] See Butler, page 239b.

In one spirit meet and mingle.
> *Love's Philosophy* [*1819*].
> *Stanza 1*

I arise from dreams of thee
In the first sweet sleep of night,
When the winds are breathing low,
And the stars are shining bright.
> *The Indian Serenade* [*1819*].
> *Stanza 1*

The Champak odours fail,
Like sweet thoughts in a dream.
> *Ibid. Stanza 2*

Hell is a city much like London —
A populous and smoky city.
> *Peter Bell the Third* [*1819*].
> *Part III, Stanza 1*

Teas,
Where small talk dies in agonies.
> *Ibid. Stanza 12*

He had as much imagination
As a pint-pot.
> *Ibid. Part IV, Stanza 8*

A lovely lady, garmented in light
From her own beauty.
> *The Witch of Atlas* [*1820*].
> *Stanza 5*

A Sensitive Plant in a garden grew,
And the young winds fed it with silver dew.
> *The Sensitive Plant* [*1820*].
> *I, Stanza 1*

For love and beauty and delight,
There is no death nor change.
> *Ibid. Conclusion, Stanza 6*

I bring fresh showers for the thirsting flowers,
From the seas and the streams.
> *The Cloud* [*1820*].
> *Stanza 1*

That orbèd maiden with white fire laden,
Whom mortals call the moon.
> *Ibid. Stanza 4*

I am the daughter of Earth and Water,
And the nursling of the Sky;
I pass through the pores of the ocean and shores,
I change, but I cannot die.
> *Ibid. Stanza 6*

Hail to thee, blithe spirit!
Bird thou never wert.

That from Heaven, or near it,
  Pourest thy full heart
In profuse strains of unpremeditated
  art.
      To a Skylark [*1821*]. *Stanza 1*
And singing still dost soar, and soar-
  ing ever singest.
          Ibid. Stanza 2
Thou art unseen, — but yet I hear thy
  shrill delight.
          Ibid. Stanza 4
We look before and after,
  And pine for what is not;
Our sincerest laughter
  With some pain is fraught;
Our sweetest songs are those that tell
  of saddest thought.
          Ibid. Stanza 18
Teach me half the gladness
  That thy brain must know,
Such harmonious madness
  From my lips would flow,
The world should listen then, as I am
  listening now.
          Ibid. Stanza 21
Kings are like stars — they rise and
  set, they have
The worship of the world, but no re-
  pose.[1]
        Hellas [*1821*]. *Line 195*
The world's great age begins anew,
  The golden years return,
The earth doth like a snake renew
  Her winter weeds outworn.
          Ibid. Line 1060
The world is weary of the past,
Oh, might it die or rest at last!
        Ibid. Final Chorus
What! alive, and so bold, O earth?
  Written on Hearing the News of
  the Death of Napoleon [*1821*].
  Stanza 1
I weep for Adonais — he is dead!
Oh, weep for Adonais! though our tears
Thaw not the frost which binds so dear
  a head!
        Adonais [*1821*]. *I*
Till the Future dares
Forget the Past, his fate and fame shall
  be

[1] See Bacon, page 120b.

An echo and a light unto eternity!
          Adonais. I
Most musical of mourners, weep again!
          Ibid. IV
But now, thy youngest, dearest one has
  perished,
The nursling of thy widowhood.
          Ibid. VI
To that high Capital, where kingly
  Death
Keeps his pale court in beauty and
  decay,
He came.
          Ibid. VII
Lost Angel of a ruined Paradise!
She knew not 't was her own; as with
  no stain
She faded, like a cloud which had out-
  wept the rain.
          Ibid. X
Desires and Adorations,
Winged Persuasions and veiled Desti-
  nies,
Splendours, and Glooms, and glimmer-
  ing Incarnations
Of hopes and fears, and twilight Fan-
  tasies;
And Sorrow, with her family of Sighs,
And Pleasure, blind with tears, led by
  the gleam
Of her own dying smile instead of eyes,
Came in slow pomp.
          Ibid. XIII
Ah woe is me! Winter is come and gone,
But grief returns with the revolving
  year.
          Ibid. XVIII
Alas! that all we loved of him should
  be,
But for our grief, as if it had not been,
And grief itself be mortal!
          Ibid. XXI
As long as skies are blue, and fields
  are green,
Evening must usher night, night urge
  the morrow,
Month follow month with woe, and
  year wake year to sorrow.
          Ibid.
Why didst thou leave the trodden paths
  of men

Too soon, and with weak hands though
  mighty heart
Dare the unpastured dragon in his den?
Defenceless as thou wert, oh, where was
  then
Wisdom the mirrored shield, or scorn
  the spear?
  Adonais. XXVII

The Pilgrim of Eternity,[1] whose fame
Over his living head like heaven is
  bent,
An early but enduring monument,
Came, veiling all the lightnings of his
  song
In sorrow.
  Ibid. XXX

A pard-like spirit, beautiful and swift.
  Ibid. XXXII

In mockery of monumental stone.
  Ibid. XXXV

Peace, peace! he is not dead, he doth
  not sleep —
He hath awakened from the dream of
  life.
  Ibid. XXXIX

He has outsoared the shadow of our
  night;
Envy and calumny and hate and pain,
And that unrest which men miscall
  delight
Can touch him not and torture not
  again;
From the contagion of the world's
  slow stain
He is secure, and now can never mourn
A heart grown cold, a head grown gray
  in vain.
  Ibid. XL

He lives, he wakes — 'tis Death is dead,
  not he.
  Ibid. XLI

He is made one with Nature: there is
  heard
His voice in all her music, from the
  moan
Of thunder to the song of night's sweet
  bird.
  Ibid. XLII

He is a portion of the loveliness
Which once he made more lovely.
  Ibid. XLIII

[1] Byron.

And many more, whose names on
  Earth are dark,
But whose transmitted effluence can
  not die
So long as fire outlives the parent
  spark,
Rose, robed in dazzling immortality.
  Adonais. XLVI

The One remains, the many change and
  pass;
Heaven's light forever shines, Earth's
  shadows fly;
Life, like a dome of many-coloured
  glass,
Stains the white radiance of Eternity,
Until Death tramples it to fragments.
  Ibid. LII

The soul of Adonais, like a star,
Beacons from the abode where the
  Eternal are.
  Ibid. LV

Music, when soft voices die,
Vibrates in the memory;
Odours, when sweet violets sicken,
Live within the sense they quicken.

Rose leaves, when the rose is dead,
Are heaped for the beloved's bed;
And so thy thoughts, when thou art
  gone,
Love itself shall slumber on.
  *To —— : Music, When Soft Voices
  Die* [*1821*]

The desire of the moth for the star,
  Of the night for the morrow,
The devotion to something afar
  From the sphere of our sorrow.
  *To —— : One Word Is Too Often
  Profaned* [*1821*]. *Stanza 2*

Rarely, rarely, comest thou,
Spirit of Delight!
  *Song: Rarely, Rarely, Comest
  Thou* [*1821*]. *Stanza 1*

I love tranquil solitude
And such society
As is quiet, wise, and good.
  Ibid. Stanza 7

Poets are the hierophants of an unapprehended inspiration; the mirrors

of the gigantic shadows which futurity casts upon the present.[1]

A Defence of Poetry [1821]

Poetry is the record of the best and happiest moments of the happiest and best minds.

Ibid.

Poets are the unacknowledged legislators of the world.

Ibid.

We rest. A dream has power to poison sleep;
We rise. One wandering thought pollutes the day.

Mutability [1821]. I, Stanza 3

Man's yesterday may ne'er be like his morrow;
Naught may endure but Mutability.

Ibid. Stanza 4

The flower that smiles today
Tomorrow dies;
All that we wish to stay
Tempts and then flies.
What is this world's delight?
Lightning that mocks the night,
Brief even as bright.

Ibid. II, Stanza 1

There is no sport in hate when all the rage
Is on one side.

Lines to a Reviewer [1821]

When the lamp is shattered
The light in the dust lies dead: —
When the cloud is scattered
The rainbow's glory is shed.

*When the Lamp is Shattered [1822].
Stanza 1*

Best and brightest, come away!
Fairer far than this fair day.

To Jane. An Invitation [1822]

Sing again, with your dear voice revealing
A tone
Of some world far from ours,
Where music and moonlight and feeling
Are one.

*To Jane: The Keen Stars Were
Twinkling [1822]. Stanza 4*

[1] See Campbell, page 432b.

FREDERICK MARRYAT
[1792–1848]

I haven't the gift of the gab, my sons —
because I'm bred to the sea.

The Old Navy. Stanza 1

JOHN CLARE
[1793–1864]

I am! yet what I am who cares, or knows?
My friends forsake me like a memory lost.

*Written in Northampton
County Asylum*

The world was on thy page
Of victories but a comma.

To Napoleon

The wind and clouds, now here, now there,
Hold no such strange dominion
As woman's cold, perverted will,
And soon estranged opinion.

When Lovers Part

If life had a second edition, how I would correct the proofs.[1]

*In a letter to a friend.
Quoted in Foreword to
J. W. AND ANNE TIBBLE'S
John Clare: A Life [1932]*

FELICIA DOROTHEA
HEMANS
[1793–1835]

The stately homes of England!
How beautiful they stand,
Amidst their tall ancestral trees,
O'er all the pleasant land! [2]

The Homes of England. Stanza 1

[1] Compare the epitaph written for himself (at the age of twenty-two) by BENJAMIN FRANKLIN: "Benjamin Franklin, Printer . . . Will Appear Once More, In a New and More Elegant Edition, Revised and Corrected by the Author."

[2] Those comfortably padded lunatic asylums, which are known, euphemistically, as the stately homes of England. — VIRGINIA

The breaking waves dashed high
  On a stern and rock-bound coast,
And the woods, against a stormy sky,
  Their giant branches tossed.
            The Landing of the Pilgrim
                  Fathers. Stanza 1

A band of exiles moored their bark
On a wild New England shore.
            Ibid. Stanza 2

Ay, call it holy ground,
  The soil where first they trod!
They have left unstained what there
  they found —
  Freedom to worship God.
            Ibid. Stanza 10

The boy [1] stood on the burning deck,
  Whence all but he had fled;
The flame that lit the battle's wreck
  Shone round him o'er the dead.
            Casabianca. Stanza 1

There came a burst of thunder sound;
The boy, — oh! where was he?
            Ibid. Stanza 9

In the busy haunts of men.
            Tale of the Secret Tribunal.
                  Part I

Oh, call my brother back to me!
  I cannot play alone:
The summer comes with flower and
  bee, —
  Where is my brother gone?
            The Child's First Grief. Stanza 1

Wave may not foam nor wild wind
  sweep
Where rest not England's Dead.
            England's Dead

Woolf [1882–1941]: *The Common Reader:*
Lady Dorothy Nevill
      The stately homes of England,
        How beautiful they stood
      Before their recent owners
        Relinquished them for good.
            E. V. Knox [1881–   ]: *The*
                  Stately Homes
  [1] Giacomo Casabianca, whose father, Louis,
at the battle of the Nile, 1798, commanded
the flagship *Orient*. It took fire and blew up,
the commander was mortally wounded, and
when most of the crew fled, Giacomo remained aboard, in an effort to help his gallant
father.

WILLIAM CULLEN BRYANT
[1794–1878]

To him who in the love of Nature holds
Communion with her visible forms,
  she speaks
A various language.
            Thanatopsis [1817–1821]

Go forth, under the open sky, and list
To Nature's teachings.
            Ibid.

The hills,
Rock-ribbed, and ancient as the sun.
            Ibid.

Old ocean's gray and melancholy
  waste.
            Ibid.

      All that tread
The globe are but a handful to the
  tribes
That slumber in its bosom.
            Ibid.

So live, that when thy summons comes
  to join
The innumerable caravan which
  moves
To that mysterious realm, where each
  shall take
His chamber in the silent halls of
  death,
Thou go not, like the quarry-slave at
  night,
Scourged to his dungeon, but, sustained
  and soothed
By an unfaltering trust, approach thy
  grave,
Like one that wraps the drapery of his
  couch
About him, and lies down to pleasant
  dreams.
            Ibid.

He who, from zone to zone,
Guides through the boundless sky thy
  certain flight,
In the long way that I must tread alone,
Will lead my steps aright.
            To a Waterfowl [1818]. *Stanza 8*

Here the free spirit of mankind, at
  length,
Throws its last fetters off; and who
  shall place

A limit to the giant's unchained
   strength,
Or curb his swiftness in the forward
   race?
      The Ages [*1821*]. *Stanza 33*
The stormy March has come at last,
With wind, and cloud, and changing
   skies;
I hear the rushing of the blast,
That through the snowy valley flies.
      March. Stanza 1
The groves were God's first temples.
      A Forest Hymn
Rogue's Island once — but when the
   rogues were dead,
Rhode Island was the name it took
   instead.
   A Meditation on Rhode Island
      Coal. Stanza 1
The melancholy days are come, the
   saddest of the year,
Of wailing winds, and naked woods,
   and meadows brown and sere.
   The Death of the Flowers [*1832*].
      Stanza 1
Chained in the market-place he stood,
   A man of giant frame,
Amid the gathering multitude
   That shrunk to hear his name.
      The African Chief. Stanza 1
Loveliest of lovely things are they,
On earth, that soonest pass away.
The rose that lives its little hour
Is prized beyond the sculptured flower.
   A Scene on the Banks of the
      Hudson. Stanza 3
Thou blossom bright with autumn dew,
And colored with the heaven's own
   blue,
That openest when the quiet light
Succeeds the keen and frosty night.
   To the Fringed Gentian [*1832*].
      Stanza 1
These are the gardens of the Desert,
   these
The unshorn fields, boundless and
   beautiful,
For which the speech of England has
   no name —
The Prairies.
      The Prairies

The praise of those who sleep in earth,
The pleasant memory of their worth,
The hope to meet when life is past,
Shall heal the tortured mind at last.
      The Living Lost. Stanza 3
Truth, crushed to earth, shall rise
   again;
   The eternal years of God are hers;
But Error, wounded, writhes in pain,
   And dies among his worshippers.
      The Battle-Field. Stanza 9
The fiercest agonies have shortest reign.
      Mutation
Oh mother of a mighty race,
Yet lovely in thy youthful grace!
   Oh Mother of a Mighty Race.
      Stanza 1
Man foretells afar
The courses of the stars; the very hour
He knows when they shall darken or
   grow bright;
Yet doth the eclipse of Sorrow and of
   Death
Come unforewarned.
      An Evening Revery
Oh, slow to smite and swift to spare,
   Gentle and merciful and just!
Who, in the fear of God, didst bear
   The sword of power, a nation's
     trust!
   The Death of Lincoln. Stanza 1

EDWARD EVERETT
[1794–1865]

As a work of art, I know few things
more pleasing to the eye, or more capable of affording scope and gratifica-
tion to a taste for the beautiful, than
a well-situated, well-cultivated farm.
   Address at Buffalo, New York
      [*October 9, 1857*]
I am no aristocrat. I do not own a
quadruped larger than a cat, and she
an indifferent mouser; nor any kind of
vehicle, with the exception, possibly, of
a wheelbarrow.
      Mount Vernon Papers. No. 7
The days of palmy prosperity are
not those most favorable to the display
of public virtue or the influence of wise
and good men. In hard, doubtful, un-

prosperous, and dangerous times, the disinterested and patriotic find their way, by a species of public instinct, unopposed, joyfully welcomed, to the control of affairs.

> *Mount Vernon Papers. No. 14*

When I contemplate the extent to which the moral sentiments, the intelligence, the affections of so many millions of people, — sealed up by a sacred charm within the cover of a letter, — daily circulate through a country, I am compelled to regard the Post-office, next to Christianity, as the right arm of our modern civilization.

> *Ibid. No. 27*

WILLIAM WHEWELL
[1794–1866]

And so no force, however great, can stretch a cord, however fine, into a horizontal line which shall be absolutely straight.[1]

> *Elementary Treatise on Mechanics [1819]. The Equilibrium of Forces on a Point*

JOHN GARDINER CALKINS BRAINARD
[1795–1828]

Death has shaken out the sands of thy glass.

> *Lament for Long Tom*

NARCISSE ACHILLE, COMTE DE SALVANDY
[1795–1856]

We are dancing on a volcano.

> *At a fête given by the Duc d'Orléans to the King of Naples [1830]*

JOHN WOODCOCK GRAVES
[1795–1886]

D' ye ken John Peel with his coat so gay?
D' ye ken John Peel at the break of day?

[1] Reputed to be an example of unconscious but perfect rhyme.

D' ye ken John Peel when he's far far away
With his hounds and his horn in the morning?
'Twas the sound of his horn brought me from my bed,
And the cry of his hounds, which he oft-times led,
For Peel's view-hallo would waken the dead,
Or the fox from his lair in the morning.

> *John Peel [1832]*

THOMAS CARLYLE
[1795–1881]

He who would write heroic poems should make his whole life a heroic poem.

> *Life of Schiller [1823–1824]*

The only thing connected with him [Richter], we think, that has reached this country is his saying, — imported by Madame de Staël, and thankfully pocketed by most newspaper critics, — "Providence has given to the French the empire of the land; to the English that of the sea; to the Germans that of — the air!"

> *Richter [1827]*

True humour springs not more from the head than from the heart; it is not contempt, its essence is love; it issues not in laughter, but in still smiles, which lie far deeper.

> *Ibid.*

The great law of culture is: Let each become all that he was created capable of being.

> *Ibid.*

Literary men are . . . . a perpetual priesthood.

> *State of German Literature [1827]. Fichte*

In every man's writings, the character of the writer must lie recorded.

> *Goethe [1828]*

We are firm believers in the maxim that, for all right judgment of any man or thing, it is useful, nay essential, to see his good qualities before pronouncing on his bad.

Goethe

How does the poet speak to men, with power, but by being still more a man than they?

Burns [*1828*]

A poet without love were a physical and metaphysical impossibility.

Ibid.

Aesop's Fly, sitting on the axle of the chariot, has been much laughed at for exclaiming: What a dust I do raise!

On Boswell's Life of Johnson [*1832*]

Whoso belongs only to his own age, and reverences only its gilt Popinjays or soot-smeared Mumbojumbos, must needs die with it.

Ibid.

The stupendous Fourth Estate, whose wide world-embracing influences what eye can take in? [1]

Ibid.

Of all outward evils Obscurity is perhaps in itself the least.

Ibid.

Loud clamor is always more or less insane.

Ibid.

All work is as seed sown; it grows and spreads, and sows itself anew.

Ibid.

Love is ever the beginning of Knowledge, as fire is of light.

Essays. Death of Goethe [*1832*]

Music is well said to be the speech of angels.

Ibid. The Opera

[1] The gallery in which the reporters sit has become a fourth estate of the realm. — MACAULAY: *On Hallam's Constitutional History* [1828]

Burke said there were Three Estates in Parliament; but, in the Reporters' Gallery yonder, there sat a Fourth Estate more important far than they all. It is not a figure of speech, or witty saying; it is a literal fact, — very momentous to us in these times. — *Heroes and Hero-Worship* [1841], *The Hero as Man of Letters*

A mystic bond of brotherhood makes all men one.

Essays. Goethe's Works [*1832*]

Everywhere the human soul stands between a hemisphere of light and another of darkness on the confines of two everlasting hostile empires, — Necessity and Free Will.

Ibid.

Man makes the circumstances, and spiritually as well as economically is the artificer of his own fortune. . . . Man's circumstances are the element he is appointed to live and work in; . . . so that in another no less genuine sense, it can be said circumstances make the man.[1]

Diderot [*1833*]

No man who has once heartily and wholly laughed can be altogether irreclaimably bad.

Sartor Resartus [*1833–1834*]. *Book I, Chap. 4*

The man who cannot laugh is not only fit for treasons, stratagems and spoils; but his whole life is already a treason and a stratagem.

Ibid.

He who first shortened the labor of Copyists by device of *Movable Types* was disbanding hired Armies, and cashiering most Kings and Senates, and creating a whole new Democratic world: he had invented the Art of printing.

Ibid. Chap. 5

Be not the slave of Words.

Ibid. Chap. 8

Wonder is the basis of Worship.

Ibid. Chap. 10

Biography is by nature the most universally profitable, universally pleasant of all things: especially biography of distinguished individuals.

Ibid. Chap. 11

What you see, yet can not see over, is as good as infinite.

Ibid. Book II, Chap. 1

Sarcasm I now see to be, in general, the language of the Devil; for which

[1] See Disraeli, page 511a.

reason I have, long since, as good as renounced it.

 Sartor Resartus. Book II, Chap. 4

To consume your own choler, as some chimneys consume their own smoke;[1] to keep a whole Satanic School spouting, if it must spout, inaudibly, is a negative yet no slight virtue, nor one of the commonest in these times.

   Ibid. Chap. 6

Alas! the fearful Unbelief is unbelief in yourself.

   Ibid. Chap. 7

Produce! Were it but the pitifulest infinitesimal fraction of a product, produce it in God's name.

   Ibid. Chap. 9

As the Swiss inscription says: *Sprechen ist silbern, Schweigen ist golden,* — "Speech is silvern, Silence is golden"; or, as I might rather express it, Speech is of Time, Silence is of Eternity.[2]

  Ibid. Book III, Chap. 3

Wouldst thou plant for Eternity, then plant into the deep infinite faculties of man.

     Ibid.

Two men I honour, and no third. First, the toilworn craftsman that with earth-made implement laboriously conquers the earth, and makes her man's. . . . A second man I honour, and still more highly: Him who is seen toiling for the spiritually indispensable; not daily bread, but the bread of life.

   Ibid. Chap. 4

That there should one man die ignorant who had capacity for knowledge, this I call a tragedy.

     Ibid.

[1] See *Heroes and Hero-Worship*, page 475b.
Consume your own smoke. — BROWNING: *Pacchiarotto* [1876], *XXV*
Would that he consumed his own smoke. — MELVILLE: *Moby Dick* [1851], *Chap. XCVI*
See Osler, page 743b.
[2] Silence is deep as Eternity; speech is shallow as Time. — CARLYLE: *Sir Walter Scott* [1838]

Trust not the heart of that man for whom old clothes are not venerable.

 Sartor Resartus. Book III, Chap. 6

The Public is an old woman. Let her maunder and mumble.

    Journal [*1835*]

It is now almost my sole rule of life to clear myself of cants and formulas, as of poisonous Nessus shirts.

  Letter to His Wife [*1835*]

No lie you can speak or act but it will come, after longer or shorter circulation, like a bill drawn on Nature's Reality, and be presented there for payment, — with the answer, No effects.

 The French Revolution [*1837*].
  Vol. I, Book III, Chap. 1

To a shower of gold most things are penetrable.

   Ibid. Chap. 7

"The people may eat grass":[1] hasty words, which fly abroad irrevocable, — and will send back tidings.

   Ibid. Chap. 9

O poor mortals, how ye make this earth bitter for each other.

  Ibid. Book V, Chap. 5

Battles, in these ages, are transacted by mechanism; with the slightest possible development of human individuality or spontaneity; men now even die, and kill one another, in an artificial manner.

  Ibid. Book VII, Chap. 4

There were certain runaways whom Fritz the Great bullied back into the battle with a: "*R* — , *wollt ihr ewig leben,* Unprintable Offscouring of Scoundrels, would ye live forever!"[2]

  Ibid. Vol. II, Book I, Chap. 4

There is no heroic poem in the world but is at bottom a biography, the life of a man; also, it may be said, there is no life of a man, faithfully recorded,

[1] The remark of Foullon, when his finance scheme raised the question: What will the people do?
[2] A similar phrase was current during both World Wars. See Sandburg, page 898b.

but is a heroic poem of its sort, rhymed or unrhymed.

Sir Walter Scott [1838]

There is a great discovery still to be made in Literature, that of paying literary men by the quantity they do not write.

Ibid.

No man lives without jostling and being jostled; in all ways he has to elbow himself through the world, giving and receiving offence.

Ibid.

All greatness is unconscious, or it is little and naught.

Ibid.

The uttered part of a man's life, let us always repeat, bears to the un-uttered, unconscious part a small unknown proportion. He himself never knows it, much less do others.

Ibid.

It can be said of him, when he departed he took a Man's life along with him. No sounder piece of British manhood was put together in that eighteenth century of Time.

Ibid.

The Christian religion of late ages has been continually dissipating itself into Metaphysics; and threatens now to disappear, as some rivers do, in deserts of barren sand.

Ibid.

Nothing that was worthy in the past departs; no truth or goodness realized by man ever dies, or can die.

Ibid.

The barrenest of all mortals is the sentimentalist.

Ibid.

Democracy is, by the nature of it, a self-cancelling business; and gives in the long run a net result of zero.

Chartism [1839]. Chap. 6,
Laissez-Faire

No sadder proof can be given by a man of his own littleness than disbelief in great men.

Heroes and Hero-Worship [1841].
The Hero as Divinity

The history of the world is but the biography of great men.[1]

Heroes and Hero-Worship. The
Hero as Divinity

We must get rid of Fear.

Ibid.

A vein of poetry exists in the hearts of all men.

Ibid. The Hero as Poet

The Age of Miracles is forever here!

Ibid. The Hero as Priest

In books lies the soul of the whole Past Time: the articulate audible voice of the Past, when the body and material substance of it has altogether vanished like a dream.

Ibid. The Hero as Man of Letters

All that mankind has done, thought, gained or been: it is lying as in magic preservation in the pages of books.

Ibid.

The true University of these days is a Collection of Books.

Ibid.

The suffering man ought really to consume his own smoke; there is no good in emitting smoke till you have made it into fire.[2]

Ibid.

Adversity is sometimes hard upon a man; but for one man who can stand prosperity, there are a hundred that will stand adversity.

Ibid.

"A fair day's-wages for a fair day's-work": it is as just a demand as governed men ever made of governing. It is the everlasting right of man.

Past and Present [1843].
Book I, Chap. 3

Fire is the best of servants; but what a master![3]

Ibid. Book II, Chap. 9

All work, even cotton-spinning, is noble; work is alone noble. . . . A

---

[1] History is the essence of innumerable biographies. — *On History* [1830]
See Emerson, page 501b.

[2] See *Sartor Resartus*, page 474a.

[3] Mammon is like fire: the usefulest of all servants, if the frightfulest of all masters! — *Book IV, Chap.* 7

life of ease is not for any man, nor for any god.

> *Past and Present. Book III,*
> *Chap. 4*

Every noble crown is, and on earth will forever be, a crown of thorns.

> *Ibid. Chap. 7*

Even in the meanest sorts of Labor, the whole soul of a man is composed into a kind of real harmony the instant he sets himself to work.

> *Ibid. Chap. 11*

Blessed is he who has found his work; let him ask no other blessedness.

> *Ibid.*

There is endless merit in a man's knowing when to have done.

> *Francia [1845]*

He that works and *does* some Poem, not he that merely *says* one, is worthy of the name of Poet.

> *Introduction to Cromwell's*
> *Letters and Speeches [1845]*

Respectable Professors of the Dismal Science.[1]

> *Latter Day Pamphlets. No. 1 [1850]*

A Parliament speaking through reporters to Buncombe and the twenty-seven millions, mostly fools.

> *Ibid. No. 6*

The fine arts once divorcing themselves from *truth* are quite certain to fall mad, if they do not die.

> *Ibid. No. 8*

A healthy hatred of scoundrels.

> *Ibid. No. 12*

Genius . . . which is the transcendent capacity for taking trouble first of all.[2]

> *Life of Frederick the Great [1858–*
> *1865]. Book IV, Chap. III*

[1] Referring to political economy and social science, Carlyle also in his *Occasional Discourse on the Negro Question* [1849] speaks of "What we might call, by way of Eminence, the Dismal Science."

[2] The more widely current version is "an infinite capacity for taking pains." See Buffon, page 334a.

Happy the people whose annals are blank in history-books.[1]

> *Life of Frederick the Great.*
> *Book XVI, Chap. 1*

So here hath been dawning
  Another blue day:
Think, wilt thou let it
  Slip useless away?

> *Today*

What is Man? A foolish baby,
  Vainly strives, and fights, and frets.
Demanding all, deserving nothing,
  One small grave is what he gets.

> *Cui Bono. Stanza 3*

My whinstone house my castle is;
I have my own four walls.

> *My Own Four Walls*

Lord Bacon could as easily have created the planets as he could have written Hamlet.

> *Remark in discussion*

JOSEPH RODMAN DRAKE
[1795–1820]

When Freedom from her mountain-height
  Unfurled her standard to the air,
She tore the azure robe of night,
  And set the stars of glory there.
She mingled with its gorgeous dyes
The milky baldric of the skies,
And striped its pure, celestial white
With streakings of the morning light.

> *The American Flag [1819]. Stanza 1*

Forever float that standard sheet!
  Where breathes the foe but falls before us,
With Freedom's soil beneath our feet,
  And Freedom's banner streaming o'er us?

> *Ibid. Stanza 5*

JOHN KEATS
[1795–1821]

I stood tip-toe upon a little hill,
The air was cooling, and so very still.

> *Poems [1817]. I Stood Tip-toe,*
> *Line 1*

[1] Carlyle identifies this as "Montesquieu's aphorism."

And then there crept
A little noiseless noise among the leaves,
Born of the very sigh that silence
heaves.
> *Poems. I Stood Tip-toe, Line 10*

Open afresh your round of starry folds,
Ye ardent marigolds!
> *Ibid. Line 47*

Where swarms of minnows show their
little heads,
Staying their wavy bodies 'gainst the
streams.
> *Ibid. Line 72*

Sometimes goldfinches one by one will
drop
From low hung branches; little space
they stop;
But sip, and twitter, and their feathers
sleek;
Then off at once, as in a wanton freak:
Or perhaps, to show their black, and
golden wings,
Pausing upon their yellow flutterings.
> *Ibid. Line 87*

Woman! when I behold thee flippant,
vain,
Inconstant, childish, proud, and full of
fancies.
> *Ibid. Woman! When I Behold Thee Flippant, Vain*

To one who has been long in city pent,
'Tis very sweet to look into the fair
And open face of heaven.
> *Ibid. Sonnet, To One Who Has Been Long in City Pent*

E'en like the passage of an angel's tear
That falls through the clear ether silently.
> *Ibid.*

Much have I travell'd in the realms of
gold,
And many goodly states and kingdoms
seen;
Round many western islands have I
been
Which bards in fealty to Apollo hold.
> *Ibid. Sonnet, On First Looking into Chapman's Homer*

Then felt I like some watcher of the
skies
When a new planet swims into his ken;

Or like stout Cortez when with eagle
eyes
He star'd at the Pacific — and all his
men
Look'd at each other with a wild surmise —
Silent, upon a peak in Darien.
> *Poems. Sonnet, On First Looking into Chapman's Homer*

Hear ye not the hum
Of mighty workings? —
Listen awhile ye nations, and be dumb.
> *Ibid. Sonnet, Addressed to Haydon*

The poetry of earth is never dead.
> *Ibid. On the Grasshopper and the Cricket*

Life is but a day;
A fragile dew-drop on its perilous way
From a tree's summit.
> *Ibid. Sleep and Poetry, Line 85*

O for ten years, that I may overwhelm
Myself in poesy.
> *Ibid. Line 96*

A drainless shower
Of light is poesy; 'tis the supreme of
power;
'Tis might half slumb'ring on its own
right arm.
> *Ibid. Line 235*

But strength alone though of the Muses
born
Is like a fallen angel: trees uptorn,
Darkness, and worms, and shrouds, and
sepulchres
Delight it; for it feeds upon the burrs,
And thorns of life; forgetting the great
end
Of poesy, that it should be a friend
To soothe the cares, and lift the
thoughts of man.
> *Ibid. Line 241*

My spirit is too weak — mortality
Weighs heavily on me like unwilling
sleep,
And each imagin'd pinnacle and steep
Of godlike hardship, tells me I must die
Like a sick Eagle looking at the sky.
> *Sonnet, On Seeing the Elgin Marbles [Written 1817]*

It keeps eternal whisperings around
Desolate shores, and with its mighty
  swell
Gluts twice ten thousand Caverns.
      Sonnet, On the Sea [Written
                          1817]
In a drear-nighted December
  Too happy, happy tree
Thy branches ne'er remember
  Their green felicity.
            Stanzas [Written 1817]
  I am certain of nothing but the holiness of the heart's affections and the truth of imagination — what the imagination seizes as beauty must be truth — whether it existed before or not.
        Letter to Benjamin Bailey
              [November 22, 1817]
  O for a life of Sensations rather than of Thoughts!
                            Ibid.
  At once it struck me what quality went to form a Man of Achievement, especially in Literature, and which Shakespeare possessed so enormously — I mean *Negative Capability*, that is, when a man is capable of being in uncertainties, mysteries, doubts, without any irritable reaching after fact and reason.
      Letter to George and Thomas
        Keats [December 22, 1817]
  We hate poetry that has a palpable design upon us — and if we do not agree, seems to put its hand in its breeches pocket. Poetry should be great and unobtrusive, a thing which enters into one's soul, and does not startle or amaze with itself, but with its subject.
  Letter to John Hamilton Reynolds
              [February 3, 1818]
  Poetry should surprise by a fine excess, and not by singularity. It should strike the reader as a wording of his own highest thoughts, and appear almost as a remembrance.
      Letter to John Taylor [February
                          27, 1818]
  If poetry comes not as naturally as leaves to a tree it had better not come at all.
                            Ibid.

  Axioms in philosophy are not axioms until they are proved upon our pulses: we read fine things but never feel them to the full until we have gone the same steps as the author.[1]
    Letter to John Hamilton Reynolds
              [May 3, 1818]
Shed no tear — O shed no tear!
The flower will bloom another year.
Weep no more — O weep no more!
Young buds sleep in the root's white
  core.
        Faery Songs. I [Written 1818]
Blue! Gentle cousin of the forest-green,
Married to green in all the sweetest
      flowers, —
Forget-me-not, — the blue bell, —
      and, that Queen
Of secrecy, the violet.
            Sonnet, Blue [Written 1818]
  There is not a fiercer hell than the failure in a great object.
        Endymion [1818]. Preface
  The imagination of a boy is healthy, and the mature imagination of a man is healthy; but there is a space of life between, in which the soul is in a ferment, the character undecided, the way of life uncertain, the ambition thick-sighted: thence proceeds mawkishness, and the thousand bitters which those men I speak of must necessarily taste in going over the following pages.
                            Ibid.
A thing of beauty is a joy for ever:
Its loveliness increases; it will never
Pass into nothingness; but still will
  keep
A bower quiet for us, and a sleep
Full of sweet dreams, and health, and
  quiet breathing.
          Ibid. Book 1, Line 1
  The grandeur of the dooms
We have imagined for the mighty dead.
                  Ibid. Line 20
O magic sleep! O comfortable bird,

[1] Nothing ever becomes real till it is experienced — even a proverb is no proverb to you till your life has illustrated it. — *Letter to George and Georgiana Keats* [February 14– May 3, 1819]

That broodest o'er the troubled sea of
the mind
Till it is hush'd and smooth!
Endymion. Book I, Line 453

Time, that aged nurse,
Rock'd me to patience.
Ibid. Line 705

Wherein lies happiness? In that which
becks
Our ready minds to fellowship divine,
A fellowship with essence; till we
shine,
Full alchemiz'd, and free of space. Be-
hold
The clear religion of heaven!
Ibid. Line 777

The crown of these
Is made of love and friendship, and sits
high
Upon the forehead of humanity.
Ibid. Line 800

A hope beyond the shadow of a dream.
Ibid. Line 857

Pleasure is oft a visitant; but pain
Clings cruelly to us.
Ibid. Line 906

'Tis the pest
Of love, that fairest joys give most un-
rest.
Ibid. Book II, Line 365

To sorrow,
I bade good-morrow,
And thought to leave her far away
behind;
But cheerly, cheerly,
She loves me dearly;
She is so constant to me, and so kind.
Ibid. Book IV, Line 173

There is an awful warmth about my
heart like a load of immortality.
Letter to John Hamilton Reynolds
[September 22, 1818]

I begin to get a little acquainted
with my own strength and weakness.
Praise or blame has but a momentary
effect on the man whose love of beauty
in the abstract makes him a severe
critic on his own works.
Letter to James Hessey
[October 9, 1818]

In *Endymion,* I leaped headlong into
the sea, and thereby have become better acquainted with the soundings, the
quicksands, and the rocks, than if I
had stayed upon the green shore, and
piped a silly pipe, and took tea and
comfortable advice.
Letter to James Hessey
[October 9, 1818]

I would sooner fail than not be
among the greatest.
Ibid.

When I have fears that I may cease to
be
Before my pen has glean'd my teeming
brain.
Sonnet, When I Have Fears
[Written 1818]

When I behold, upon the night's starr'd
face,
Huge cloudy symbols of a high romance.
Ibid.

Then on the shore
Of the wide world I stand alone, and
think
Till love and fame to nothingness do
sink.
Ibid.

Bright star, would I were stedfast as
thou art —
Not in lone splendour hung aloft the
night
And watching, with eternal lids apart,
Like nature's patient, sleepless Eremite,
The moving waters at their priestlike
task
Of pure ablution round earth's human
shores.
Sonnet, Bright Star [Written
1819]

Pillow'd upon my fair love's ripening
breast,
To feel for ever its soft fall and swell,
Awake for ever in a sweet unrest,
Still, still to hear her tender-taken
breath,
And so live ever — or else swoon to
death.
Ibid.

The day is gone, and all its sweets are
gone!

Sweet voice, sweet lips, soft hand, and
softer breast.
Sonnet, The Day Is Gone
[*Written 1819*]

O what can ail thee, knight at arms,
Alone and palely loitering?
The sedge has withered from the lake,
And no birds sing!
La Belle Dame Sans Merci
[*Written 1819*]. *Stanza 1*

I met a lady in the meads
Full beautiful, a faery's child;
Her hair was long, her foot was light,
And her eyes were wild.
Ibid. Stanza 4

She looked at me as she did love,
And made sweet moan.
Ibid. Stanza 5

"La belle dame sans merci
Thee hath in thrall!"
Ibid. Stanza 10

A man's life of any worth is a continual Allegory — and very few eyes
can see the mystery of his life — a life
like the Scriptures, figurative. . . .
Lord Byron cuts a figure, but he is not
figurative. Shakespeare led a life of
allegory: his works are the comments
on it.
*Letter to George and Georgiana
Keats* [*February 14–May 3,
1819*]

This living hand, now warm and ca-
pable
Of earnest grasping, would, if it were
cold
And in the icy silence of the tomb,
So haunt thy days and chill thy dream-
ing nights
That thou would wish thine own heart
dry of blood
So in my veins red life might stream
again,
And thou be conscience-calm'd — see
here it is —
I hold it towards you.
*Lines Supposed to Have Been
Addressed to Fanny Brawne*
[*Written 1819*]

Love in a hut, with water and a crust,
Is — Love, forgive us! — cinders,
ashes, dust.
Poems [*1820*]. *Lamia, Part II,
Line 1*

There was an awful rainbow once in
heaven:
We know her woof, her texture; she is
given
In the dull catalogue of common
things.
Philosophy will clip an angel's wings.
Ibid. Line 231

Too many tears for lovers have been
shed,
Too many sighs give we to them in fee,
Too much of pity after they are dead,
Too many doleful stories do we see,
Whose matter in bright gold were best
be read.
Ibid. Isabella (*The Pot of
Basil*), *Stanza 12*

St. Agnes' Eve — Ah, bitter chill it
was!
The owl, for all his feathers, was a-cold.
The hare limp'd trembling through the
frozen grass,
And silent was the flock in woolly fold.
Ibid. The Eve of St. Agnes, Stanza 1

The silver, snarling trumpets 'gan to
chide.
Ibid. Stanza 4

She sigh'd for Agnes' dreams, the sweetest of the year.
Ibid. Stanza 7

Asleep in lap of legends old.
Ibid. Stanza 15

Sudden a thought came like a full-
blown rose,
Flushing his brow, and in his pained
heart
Made purple riot.
Ibid. Stanza 16

A poor, weak, palsy-stricken, churchyard thing.
Ibid. Stanza 18

As though a tongueless nightingale
should swell
Her throat in vain, and die, heart-
stifled in her dell.
Ibid. Stanza 23

Full on this casement shone the wintry moon,
And threw warm gules on Madeline's fair breast.
>> *Poems. The Eve of St. Agnes,
Stanza 25*

Unclasps her warmed jewels one by one;
Loosens her fragrant bodice; by degrees
Her rich attire creeps rustling to her knees.
>> *Ibid. Stanza 26*

And still she slept an azure-lidded sleep.
>> *Ibid. Stanza 30*

And the long carpets rose along the gusty floor.
>> *Ibid. Stanza 40*

And they are gone: aye, ages long ago
These lovers fled away into the storm.
>> *Ibid. Stanza 42*

My heart aches, and a drowsy numbness pains
My sense, as though of hemlock I had drunk,
Or emptied some dull opiate to the drains
One minute past, and Lethe-wards had sunk.
>> *Ibid. Ode to a Nightingale,
Stanza 1*

Thou, light-winged Dryad of the trees,
In some melodious plot
Of beechen green, and shadows numberless,
Singest of summer in full-throated ease.
>> *Ibid.*

O, for a draught of vintage! that hath been
Cool'd a long age in the deep-delved earth,
Tasting of Flora and the country green,
Dance, and Provençal song, and sunburnt mirth!
O, for a beaker full of the warm South,
Full of the true, the blushful Hippocrene,

With beaded bubbles winking at the brim,
And purple-stained mouth.
>> *Poems. Ode to a Nightingale,
Stanza 2*

Fade far away, dissolve, and quite forget
What thou among the leaves hast never known,
The weariness, the fever, and the fret
Here, where men sit and hear each other groan.
>> *Ibid. Stanza 3*

Where youth grows pale, and spectre-thin, and dies;
Where but to think is to be full of sorrow
And leaden-eyed despairs.
>> *Ibid.*

Already with thee! tender is the night.
>> *Ibid. Stanza 4*

I cannot see what flowers are at my feet,
Nor what soft incense hangs upon the boughs,
But, in embalmed darkness, guess each sweet.
>> *Ibid. Stanza 5*

The murmurous haunt of flies on summer eves.
>> *Ibid.*

Darkling I listen; and, for many a time
I have been half in love with easeful Death,
Call'd him soft names in many a mused rhyme,
To take into the air my quiet breath;
Now more than ever seems it rich to die,
To cease upon the midnight with no pain,
While thou art pouring forth thy soul abroad
In such an ecstasy!
Still wouldst thou sing, and I have ears in vain —
To thy high requiem become a sod.
>> *Ibid. Stanza 6*

Thou wast not born for death, immortal Bird!
No hungry generations tread thee down;
The voice I hear this passing night was heard

In ancient days by emperor and
  clown:
Perhaps the self-same song that found
  a path
    Through the sad heart of Ruth,
  when, sick for home,
  She stood in tears amid the alien
  corn;
      The same that oft-times hath
Charm'd magic casements, opening on
  the foam
Of perilous seas, in faery lands for-
  lorn.
    Poems. Ode to a Nightingale,
                Stanza 7
Forlorn! the very word is like a bell
To toll me back from thee to my sole
  self!
           Ibid. Stanza 8
Was it a vision, or a waking dream?
Fled is that music: — Do I wake or
  sleep?
                Ibid.
Thou still unravish'd bride of quiet-
  ness,
  Thou foster-child of silence and slow
  time,
Sylvan historian, who canst thus ex-
  press
  A flowery tale more sweetly than our
  rhyme:
What leaf-fring'd legend haunts about
  thy shape?
    Ibid. Ode on a Grecian Urn,
                Stanza 1
What men or gods are these? What
  maidens loth?
What mad pursuit? What struggle to
  escape?
  What pipes and timbrels? What
  wild ecstasy?
                Ibid.
Heard melodies are sweet, but those
  unheard
Are sweeter.
           Ibid. Stanza 2
For ever wilt thou love, and she be
  fair!
                Ibid.
Who are these coming to the sacrifice?
  To what green altar, O mysterious
  priest,

Lead'st thou that heifer lowing at the
  skies,
And all her silken flanks with gar-
  lands drest?
    Poems. Ode on a Grecian Urn,
                Stanza 4
O Attic shape! Fair attitude!
           Ibid. Stanza 5
"Beauty is truth, truth beauty," —
  that is all
Ye know on earth, and all ye need to
  know.
                Ibid.
    To make delicious moan
Upon the midnight hours.
    Ibid. Ode to Psyche, Stanza 3
A bright torch, and a casement ope at
  night,
To let the warm Love in!
           Ibid. Stanza 5
Ever let the fancy roam,
Pleasure never is at home.
         Ibid. Fancy, Line 1
Bards of Passion and of Mirth,
Ye have left your souls on earth!
Have ye souls in heaven too?
    Ibid. Ode Written on the Blank
    Page before Beaumont and
    Fletcher's Fair Maid of the Inn
Souls of Poets dead and gone,
What Elysium have ye known,
Happy field or mossy cavern,
Choicer than the Mermaid Tavern?
Have ye tippled drink more fine
Than mine host's Canary wine?
    Ibid. Lines on the Mermaid
                Tavern
Season of mists and mellow fruitfulness,
Close bosom-friend of the maturing sun.
    Ibid. To Autumn, Stanza 1
Who hath not seen thee oft amid thy
  store?
Sometimes whoever seeks abroad may
  find
Thee sitting careless on a granary floor,
  Thy hair soft-lifted by the winnow-
  ing wind;
Or on a half-reap'd furrow sound
  asleep,
  Drows'd with the fume of poppies,
  while thy hook

Spares the next swath and all its twined flowers.
> *Poems. To Autumn, Stanza 2*

Then in a wailful choir the small gnats mourn
Among the river sallows.
> *Ibid. Stanza 3*

No, no, go not to Lethe, neither twist
Wolf's-bane, tight-rooted, for its poisonous wine.
> *Ibid. Ode on Melancholy, Stanza 1*

Nor let the beetle, nor the death-moth be
Your mournful Psyche.
> *Ibid.*

Then glut thy sorrow on a morning rose.
> *Ibid. Stanza 2*

She dwells with Beauty — Beauty that must die.
> *Ibid. Stanza 3*

His soul shall taste the sadness of her might,
And be among her cloudy trophies hung.
> *Ibid.*

Deep in the shady sadness of a vale
Far sunken from the healthy breath of morn,
Far from the fiery noon, and eve's one star,
Sat gray-hair'd Saturn, quiet as a stone.
> *Ibid. Hyperion, Book I, Line 1*

That large utterance of the early Gods!
> *Ibid. Line 51*

For to bear all naked truths,
And to envisage circumstance, all calm,
That is the top of sovereignty.
> *Ibid. Book II, Line 203*

Here lies one whose name was writ in water.[1]
> *Epitaph for himself* [*1821*]

---

[1] Among the many things he has requested of me to-night, this is the principal, — that on his gravestone shall be this inscription. — *Letter from Severn, in* RICHARD MONCKTON MILNES: *Life, Letters, and Literary Remains of John Keats* [1848]
See Sir Thomas More, page 86a.

SIR THOMAS NOON TALFOURD
[1795–1854]

'Tis a little thing
To give a cup of water; yet its draught
Of cool refreshment, drained by fevered lips,
May give a shock of pleasure to the frame
More exquisite than when nectarean juice
Renews the life of joy in happiest hours.
> *Ion* [*1835*]. *Act I, Sc. 2*

ALFRED BUNN
[1796–1860]

I dreamt that I dwelt in marble halls,
With vassals and serfs at my side.
> *The Bohemian Girl* [*1843*].
> *Act II, Song*

But — I also dreamt, which pleas'd me most,
That you loved me still the same.
> *Ibid.*

HARTLEY COLERIDGE
[1796–1849]

The soul of man is larger than the sky,
Deeper than ocean, or the abysmal dark
Of the unfathomed center.
> *To Shakespeare*

She is not fair to outward view
  As many maidens be;
Her loveliness I never knew
  Until she smiled on me:
Oh! then I saw her eye was bright,
A well of love, a spring of light.
> *Song, She Is Not Fair*

Her very frowns are fairer far
Than smiles of other maidens are.
> *Ibid.*

THOMAS CHANDLER HALIBURTON ("SAM SLICK")
[1796–1865]

I want you to see Peel, Stanley, Graham, Shiel, Russell, Macauley, Old Joe, and so on. These men are all upper-crust here.[1]

Sam Slick in England.[2] Chap. XXIV

Circumstances alter cases.

The Old Judge. Chap. XV

We can do without any article of luxury we have never had; but when once obtained, it is not in human natur' to surrender it voluntarily.

The Clockmaker

HORACE MANN
[1796–1859]

Lost, yesterday, somewhere between sunrise and sunset, two golden hours, each set with sixty diamond minutes. No reward is offered, for they are gone forever.

Aphorism

Be ashamed to die until you have won some victory for humanity.

Commencement Address, Antioch College [1859]

JAMES ROBINSON PLANCHÉ
[1796–1880]

Gentle Zitella, whither away?
Love's ritornella list, while I play.

The Brigand. Love's Ritornella

WILLIAM HICKLING PRESCOTT
[1796–1859]

The surest test of the civilization of a people — at least, as sure as any — afforded by mechanical art is to be found in their architecture, which presents so noble a field for the display of the grand and the beautiful, and which, at the same time, is so intimately connected with the essential comforts of life.

The Conquest of Peru [1847].
Book I, Chap. 5

Where there is no free agency, there can be no morality. Where there is no

temptation, there can be little claim to virtue.[1] Where the routine is rigorously proscribed by law, the law, and not the man, must have the credit of the conduct.

The Conquest of Peru. Book I, Chap. 5

Drawing his sword he [Pizarro] traced a line with it on the sand from East to West. Then, turning towards the South, "Friends and comrades!" he said, "on that side are toil, hunger, nakedness, the drenching storm, desertion, and death; on this side ease and pleasure. There lies Peru with its riches; here, Panama and its poverty. Choose, each man, what best becomes a brave Castilian. For my part, I go to the South." So saying, he stepped across the line.

Ibid. Book II, Chap. 4

RICHARD RYAN
[1796–1849]

O, saw ye the lass wi' the bonnie blue een?
Her smile is the sweetest that ever was seen,
Her cheek like the rose is, but fresher, I ween,
She's the loveliest lassie that trips on the green.

O, Saw Ye the Lass

JOSEPH AUGUSTINE WADE
[1796–1845]

Meet Me by Moonlight Alone.

Title of Poem

THOMAS HAYNES BAYLY
[1797–1839]

Those who have wealth must be watchful and wary,
Power, alas! naught but misery brings!

I'd Be a Butterfly. Stanza 2

---

[1] Those families, you know, are our upper-crust, — not upper ten thousand. — JAMES FENIMORE COOPER: *The Ways of the Hour* [1850], *Chap. VI*

[2] The "Sam Slick" papers first appeared in a weekly paper in Nova Scotia in 1836.

[1] There's many a life of sweet content
Whose virtue is environment.
WALTER LEARNED [1847–1915]: *On the Fly-Leaf of Manon Lescaut*

Oh no! we never mention her, —
Her name is never heard;
My lips are now forbid to speak
That once familiar word.
Oh No! We Never Mention Her

Why don't the men propose, Mamma?
Why don't the men propose?
Why Don't the Men Propose?

She wore a wreath of roses
The first night that we met.
She Wore a Wreath

Friends depart, and memory takes them
To her caverns, pure and deep.
Teach Me to Forget

Tell me the tales that to me were so
dear,
Long, long ago, long, long ago.
Long, Long Ago [1]

Oh pilot, 'tis a fearful night!
There's danger on the deep.
The Pilot

Absence makes the heart grow fonder: [2]
Isle of Beauty, fare thee well!
Isle of Beauty

My fond affection thou hast seen,
Then judge of my regret
To think more happy thou hadst been
If we had never met.
To My Wife

I'm saddest when I sing.
You Think I Have a Merry Heart

SAMUEL LOVER
[1797–1868]

Reproof on her lip, but a smile in her
eye.
Rory O'More [1836]. *Stanza 1*

For dhrames always go by contrairies,
my dear.
Ibid. Stanza 2

[1] A popular temperance song, *Where Are
the Friends That to Me Were So Dear?* was
set to the tune of *Long, Long Ago.*
[2] I find that absence still increases love. —
CHARLES HOPKINS: *To C. C.* [1694]
Distance sometimes endears friendship, and
absence sweeteneth it. — JAMES HOWELL: *Familiar Letters* [1650], *Book I, Sect. 1, No. 6*

"That's eight times today that you've
kissed me before."
"Then here goes another," says he, "to
make sure,
For there's luck in odd numbers," says
Rory O'More. [1]
Rory O'More. Stanza 3

As she sat in the low-backed car
The man at the turn-pike bar
Never asked for the toll
But just rubbed his old poll
And looked after the low-backed car.
The Low-Backed Car. Stanza 1

And with my advice, faith I wish you'd
take me.
Widow Machree [1839]

Sure the shovel and tongs
To each other belongs.
Ibid.

HEINRICH HEINE [2]
[1797–1856]

"Oh, 'tis Love that makes us grateful,
Oh, 'tis Love that makes us rich!"
So sings man, and every fateful
Echo bears his amorous speech.
O, die Liebe macht uns selig.
Stanza 1

Toward France there journeyed two
grenadiers
Who had been captured in Russia;
And they hung their heads and their
eyes had tears
As they came to the border of Prus-
sia.
*Nach Frankreich zogen zwei
Grenadier'. Stanza 1*

A pine tree stands so lonely
In the North where the high winds
blow,
He sleeps; and the whitest blanket
Wraps him in ice and snow.
Ein Fichtenbaum steht einsam.
Stanza 1

[1] See Pliny, page 50b.
[2] Translated by LOUIS UNTERMEYER.
Therefore a secret unrest
Tortured thee, brilliant and bold.
MATTHEW ARNOLD: *Heine's Grave*
[1867]

From grief too great to banish
Come songs, my lyric minions.[1]
    Aus meinen grossen Schmerzen.
            Stanza 1

When two who love are parted,
  They talk, as friend to friend,
Clasp hands and weep a little,
  And sigh without an end.
    Wenn zwei von einander scheiden.
            Stanza 1

I do not know why this confronts me,
  This sadness, this echo of pain;
A curious legend still haunts me,
  Still haunts and obsesses my brain.[2]
    Ich weiss nicht, was soll es be-
    deuten (The Lorelei). *Stanza 1*

The years keep coming and going,
  Men will arise and depart;
Only one thing is immortal:
  The love that is in my heart.
    Die Jahre kommen und gehen.
            Stanza 1

Child, you are like a flower,
So sweet and pure and fair.[3]
  Du bist wie eine Blume. Stanza 1

He who, for the first time, loves,
Even vainly, is a God.
But the man who loves again,
And still vainly, is a fool.
    Wer zum erstenmale liebt.
            Stanza 1

Oh what lies there are in kisses!
    In den Küssen, welche Lüge.
            Stanza 1

The sea has its pearls,
The heaven its stars, —
But my heart, my heart,
My heart has its love.
    Das Meer hat seine Perlen.
            Stanza 1

The deep, blue eyes of Springtime
  Peer from the grass beneath;

---

[1] Out of my own great woe
  I make my little songs.
    Translated by ELIZABETH BARRETT
               BROWNING
See Butler, page 239b.
[2] Ich weiss nicht, was soll es bedeuten,
  Dass ich so traurig bin;
  Ein Märchen aus alten Zeiten,
  Das kommt mir nicht aus dem Sinn.
[3] Du bist wie eine Blume,
  So hold und schön und rein.

They are the tender violets
  That I will twine in a wreath.
    Die blauen Frühlingsaugen.
            Stanza 1

Your eyes' blue depths are lifted,
  With love and friendship stirred.
They smile; and, lost in dreaming,
  I cannot speak a word.[1]
    Mit deinen blauen Augen.
            Stanza 1

Good-Fortune is a giddy maid,
  Fickle and restless as a fawn;
She smooths your hair; and then the
    jade
Kisses you quickly, and is gone.[2]
    Das Glück ist eine leichte Dirne.
            Stanza 1

But Madam Sorrow scorns all this,
  She shows no eagerness for flitting;
But with a long and fervent kiss
  Sits by your bed — and brings her
    knitting.
            Ibid. Stanza 2

This is America!
This is the new world!
Not the present European
Wasted and withering sphere.
    Vitzliputzli. Prelude, Dieses ist
            Amerika! Stanza 1

For Sleep is good, but Death is better
  still —
The best is never to be born at all.[3]
    Gross ist die Ähnlichkeit der
         beiden schönen

If one has no heart, one cannot write
for the masses.
    Letter to Julius Campe
       [*March 18, 1840*]

---

[1] Mit deinen blauen Augen
  Siehst du mich lieblich an,
  Da wird mir so träumend zu Sinne,
  Dass ich nicht sprechen kann.
[2] See Dryden, page 278a.
Good Luck is the gayest of all gay girls,
Long in one place she will not stay,
Back from your brow she strokes the curls,
  Kisses you quick and flies away.
But Madame Bad Luck soberly comes . . .
  And sits by your bed, and brings her knit-
    ting.
    JOHN HAY [1838–1905]: *Good and*
         Bad Luck (After Heine)
[3] See Sophocles, page 16a.

Ordinarily he is insane, but he has lucid moments when he is only stupid.

Of Savoye, appointed ambassador to Frankfurt by Lamartine [*1848*]

To publish even one line of an author which he himself has not intended for the public at large — especially letters which are addressed to private persons — is to commit a despicable act of felony.

Quoted by SWINBURNE *as heading for In Sepulcretis*

WILLIAM MOTHERWELL
[1797–1835]

I've wandered east, I've wandered west,
  Through mony a weary way;
But never, never can forget
  The luve o' life's young day!
        Jeannie Morrison. Stanza 1

MARY WOLLSTONECRAFT SHELLEY
[1797–1851]

I beheld the wretch — the miserable monster whom I had created.

      Frankenstein [*1818*]. *Chap. 5*

MACDONALD CLARKE
[1798–1842]

Whilst twilight's curtain spreading far,
Was pinned with a single star.
      Death in Disguise. Line 227
Ha! see where the wild-blazing Grog-shop appears,
As the red waves of wretchedness swell;
How it burns on the edge of tempestuous years —
The horrible Light-house of Hell!
        The Rum-hole

JOHN ADAMS DIX
[1798–1879]

If any one attempts to haul down the American flag, shoot him on the spot.

Official Dispatch to Treasury Officer in New Orleans [*January 29, 1861*]

ROBERT GILFILLAN
[1798–1850]

There's a hope for every woe,
  And a balm for every pain,
But the first joys of our heart
  Come never back again!
      The Exile's Song. Stanza 4

THOMAS HOOD
[1798–1845]

Ben Battle was a soldier bold,
  And used to war's alarms;
But a cannon-ball took off his legs,
  So he laid down his arms!
      Faithless Nellie Gray [*1826*].
            Stanza 1

His death, which happened in his berth,
  At forty-odd befell:
They went and told the sexton, and
  The sexton tolled the bell.
      Faithless Sally Brown [*1826*].
           Stanza 17

There is a silence where hath been no sound,
There is a silence where no sound may be,
In the cold grave — under the deep, deep sea,
Or in wide desert where no life is found.
      Sonnet, Silence [*1827*]

We watched her breathing through the night,
  Her breathing soft and low,
As in her breast the wave of life
  Kept heaving to and fro.
      The Death-Bed [*1827*]. *Stanza 1*
Our very hopes belied our fears,
  Our fears our hopes belied; —
We thought her dying when she slept,
  And sleeping when she died.
        Ibid. Stanza 3
I remember, I remember
The house where I was born,
The little window where the sun
Came peeping in at morn;
He never came a wink too soon
Nor brought too long a day.
      I Remember, I Remember
          [*1827*]. *Stanza 1*

I remember, I remember
The fir-trees dark and high;
I used to think their slender tops
Were close against the sky:
It was a childish ignorance,
But now 'tis little joy
To know I'm farther off from heaven
Than when I was a boy.

> *I Remember, I Remember. Stanza 4*

She stood breast-high amid the corn,[1]
Clasped by the golden light of morn,
Like the sweetheart of the sun,
Who many a glowing kiss had won.

> *Ruth* [*1827*]. *Stanza 1*

Thus she stood amid the stooks,
Praising God with sweetest looks.

> *Ibid. Stanza 4*

And there is even a happiness
That makes the heart afraid.

> *Ode to Melancholy* [*1827*]

There's not a string attuned to mirth
But has its chord in melancholy.

> *Ibid.*

But evil is wrought by want of thought,
As well as want of heart.

> *The Lady's Dream* [*1827*].
> *Stanza 16*

I saw old Autumn in the misty morn
Stand shadowless like silence, listening
To silence.

> *Ode, Autumn* [*1827*]. *Stanza 1*

Peace and rest at length have come,
All the day's long toil is past,
And each heart is whispering, "Home,
Home at last."

> *Home at Last* [*1827*]

Straight down the Crooked Lane,
And all round the Square.

> *A Plain Direction. Stanza 1*

Two stern-faced men set out from Lynn
Through the cold and heavy mist,
And Eugene Aram walked between,
With gyves upon his wrist.

> *The Dream of Eugene Aram*
> [*1829*]. *Stanza 36*

Never go to France
Unless you know the lingo,
If you do, like me,
You will repent, by jingo.

> *French and English* [*1839*].
> *Stanza 1*

[1] See Keats, page 482a.

No warmth, no cheerfulness, no healthful ease,
No comfortable feel in any member —
No shade, no shine, no butterflies, no
bees,
No fruits, no flowers, no leaves, no
birds,
     November!

> *No*

Seem'd washing his hands with invisible soap
In imperceptible water.

> *Miss Kilmansegg and Her Pre-*
> *cious Leg* [*1841–1843*]. *Her*
> *Christening, Stanza 10*

O bed! O bed! delicious bed!
That heaven upon earth to the weary
head!

> *Ibid. Her Dream, Stanza 7*

He lies like a hedgehog rolled up the
wrong way,
Tormenting himself with his prickles.

> *Ibid. Stanza 14*

There's a double beauty whenever a
swan
Swims on a lake, with her double
thereon.[1]

> *Ibid. Her Honeymoon, Stanza 9*

Home-made dishes that drive one from
home.

> *Ibid. Her Misery, Stanza 1*

Gold! Gold! Gold! Gold!
Bright and yellow, hard and cold.

> *Ibid. Her Moral*

Spurned by the young, but hugged by
the old
To the very verge of the churchyard
mould.

> *Ibid.*

How widely its agencies vary, —
To save — to ruin — to curse — to
bless, —
As even its minted coins express,
Now stamped with the image of Good
Queen Bess,
And now of a Bloody Mary.

> *Ibid.*

[1] The swan on still St. Mary's lake
Float double, swan and shadow!
> WORDSWORTH: *Yarrow Unvisited*
> [1803], *St. 6*

Another tumble! — that's his precious
  nose!
    Parental Ode to My Infant Son.
                     Stanza 3

Boughs are daily rifled
  By the gusty thieves,
And the book of Nature
  Getteth short of leaves.
        The Season. Stanza 2

With fingers weary and worn,
  With eyelids heavy and red,
A woman sat in unwomanly rags
  Plying her needle and thread —
    Stitch! stitch! stitch!
    The Song of the Shirt [*1843*].
                 Stanza 1

O men, with sisters dear!
  O men, with mothers and wives!
It is not linen you're wearing out,
  But human creatures' lives! [1]
        Ibid. Stanza 4

Sewing at once with a double thread,
A shroud as well as a shirt.
                     Ibid.

O God! that bread should be so dear,
And flesh and blood so cheap!
        Ibid. Stanza 5

No blessed leisure for love or hope,
But only time for grief.
        Ibid. Stanza 10

My tears must stop, for every drop
Hinders needle and thread.
                    Ibid.

A wife who preaches in her gown,
And lectures in her night-dress.
    The Surplice Question. Stanza 2

One more unfortunate,
  Weary of breath,
Rashly importunate,
  Gone to her death!
    The Bridge of Sighs [*1844*].
                 Stanza 1

Take her up tenderly,
  Lift her with care;
Fashioned so slenderly,
  Young, and so fair!
        Ibid. Stanza 2

[1] See Scott, page 416a.

Alas for the rarity
Of Christian charity
  Under the sun! [1]
    The Bridge of Sighs. Stanza 9

O'er the earth there comes a bloom;
Sunny light for sullen gloom;
Warm perfume for vapour cold —
I smell the rose above the mould!
    Farewell, Life [*1845*]. *Stanza 2*

GEORGE LINLEY
[1798–1865]

Among our ancient mountains,
And from our lovely vales,
Oh, let the prayer re-echo:
"God bless the Prince of Wales!"
    God Bless the Prince of Wales.
                 Stanza 1

Tho' lost to sight, to memory dear
  Thou ever wilt remain;
One only hope my heart can cheer, —
  The hope to meet again.
                  Song [2]

ROBERT POLLOK
[1798–1827]

Sorrows remembered sweeten present
  joy.
  The Course of Time. Book I, Line 464

HENRY SCOTT RIDDELL
[1798–1870]

Then Scotland's dales and Scotland's
  vales,
  And Scotland's hills for me;
I'll drink a cup to Scotland yet,
  Wi' a' the honours three.
      Scotland Yet. Stanza 2

[1] See Southey, page 427b, and O'Reilly,
page 729b.
[2] This song was written and composed,
probably about 1830, by Linley for the well-
known tenor Augustus Braham, and sung by
him.
  Absent or dead, still let a friend be dear. —
ALEXANDER POPE: *Epistle to Robert, Earl of
Oxford and Mortimer* [1721]

AMOS BRONSON ALCOTT
[1799–1888]

Greater is he who is above temptation than he who being tempted overcomes.
> *Orphic Sayings* [1840]. *No. 12*

The true teacher defends his pupils against his own personal influence. He inspires self-distrust. He guides their eyes from himself to the spirit that quickens him. He will have no disciple.
> *Ibid. The Teacher*

Who loves a garden still his Eden keeps,
Perennial pleasures plants, and wholesome harvests reaps.
> *Tablets* [1868]

Nature is thought immersed in matter.
> *Ibid.*

I press thee to my heart as Duty's faithful child.
> *Sonnet to Louisa May Alcott* [1882]

RUFUS CHOATE
[1799–1859]

The courage of New England was the "courage of Conscience." It did not rise to that insane and awful passion, the love of war for itself.
> *Address at Ipswich Centennial* [1834]

The final end of Government is not to exert restraint but to do good.
> *Speech, U. S. Senate* [July 2, 1841]

There was a state without king or nobles; there was a church without a bishop;[1] there was a people governed by grave magistrates which it had selected, and by equal laws which it had framed.
> *Speech before the New England Society* [December 22, 1843]

We join ourselves to no party that does not carry the flag and keep step to the music of the Union.
> *Letter to the Whig Convention, Worcester* [October 1, 1855]

Its constitution the glittering and sounding generalities[1] of natural right which make up the Declaration of Independence.
> *Letter to the Maine Whig Committee* [1856]

HONORÉ DE BALZAC
[1799–1850]

I believe in the incomprehensibility of God.
> *Letter to Madame de Hanska* [1837]

Those sweetly smiling angels with pensive looks, innocent faces, and cash-boxes for hearts.
> *Cousin Bette* [1846]. *Chap. 15*

Love and hate are emotions that feed on themselves; but of the two hate is the more enduring. Love is limited by our limited strength — it draws its power from living and giving; but hate is like death and avarice — it is a sort of active abstraction, apart from people and things.
> *Ibid. Chap. 16*

MARY HOWITT
[1799–1888]

Old England is our home, and Englishmen are we;

---

[1] See Junius, page 1002a.

It [Calvinism] established a religion without a prelate, a government without a king. — GEORGE BANCROFT: *History of the United States* [1834–1876], *Vol. III, Chap. VI*

Compare the anonymous poem, *The Puritans' Mistake*, published by Oliver Ditson in 1844:
Oh, we are weary pilgrims; to this wilderness we bring
A Church without a bishop, a State without a King.

---

[1] Six years earlier, Choate gave a lecture in Providence, a review of which, by FRANKLIN J. DICKMAN, appeared in the *Journal* of December 14, 1849. Dickman wrote: "We fear that the glittering generalities of the speaker have left an impression more delightful than permanent." It would seem that Dickman must have the credit of inventing the phrase "glittering generalities," unless his report was merely echoing words used by Choate in the lecture.

Our tongue is known in every clime,
our flag in every sea.
Old England Is Our Home

"Will you walk into my parlour?" said
the spider to the fly;
" 'Tis the prettiest little parlour that
ever you did spy."
The Spider and the Fly

Buttercups and daisies,
Oh, the pretty flowers;
Coming ere the Springtime,
To tell of sunny hours.
Buttercups and Daisies

GEORGE PAYNE
RAINSFORD JAMES
[1799–1860]

Thou'rt an ass, Robin, thou'rt an ass,
To think that great men be
More gay than I that lie on the grass
Under the greenwood tree.
I tell thee no, I tell thee no,
The Great are slaves to their gilded
show.
Richelieu [*1829*]. *Chap. 3,
Robber's Song, Stanza 1*

Turning over a page or two in the
book of Nature, I found that the most
brilliant actions and the greatest events
were generally brought about from the
meanest motives and most petty
causes.
Ibid. Chap. 5

A single word has sometimes lost or
won an empire — even less than a
single word, if we may believe the history of Darius's horse, who proclaimed
his master emperor without speaking.[1]
Ibid. Chap. 6

Age is the most terrible misfortune
that can happen to any man; other
evils will mend, this is every day getting worse.
Ibid. Chap. 14

[1] The seven candidates for the throne of
Persia agreed that he should be king whose
horse neighed first. The horse of Darius was
the first.

THOMAS NOEL
[1799–1861]

Rattle his bones over the stones!
He's only a pauper, whom nobody
owns!
The Pauper's Drive. Stanza 1

Let him push at the door, — in the
chimney roar,
And rattle the window-pane;
Let him in at us spy with his icicle eye,
But he shall not entrance gain.
Old Winter. Stanza 5

JULIA CRAWFORD
[1800–1885]

Kathleen mavourneen! the grey dawn
is breaking,
The horn of the hunter is heard on the
hill.
Kathleen Mavourneen [*1835*].
Stanza 1

Hast thou forgotten how soon we must
sever?
Oh! hast thou forgotten this day we
must part?
It may be for years, and it may be
forever;
Then why art thou silent, thou voice
of my heart?
Ibid.

THOMAS BABINGTON,
LORD MACAULAY
[1800–1859]

That is the best government which
desires to make the people happy, and
knows how to make them happy.
*On Mitford's History of
Greece* [*1824*]

Free trade, one of the greatest blessings which a government can confer on
a people, is in almost every country unpopular.
Ibid.

Press where ye see my white plume
shine, amidst the ranks of war,
And be your oriflamme today the helmet of Navarre.
Ivry [*1824*]. *Line 29*

Nobles by the right of an earlier creation, and priests by the imposition of a mightier hand.

On Milton [*1825*]

The dust and silence of the upper shelf.

Ibid.

Perhaps no person can be a poet, or even can enjoy poetry, without a certain unsoundness of mind.

Ibid.

Nothing is so useless as a general maxim.

On Niccolo de Machiavelli [*1827*]

The English Bible, — a book which if everything else in our language should perish, would alone suffice to show the whole extent of its beauty and power.

On John Dryden [*1828*]

His imagination resembled the wings of an ostrich. It enabled him to run, though not to soar.

Ibid.

Ye diners-out from whom we guard our spoons.[1]

Political Georgics

Men are never so likely to settle a question rightly as when they discuss it freely.

Southey's Colloquies [*1830*]

Nothing is so galling to a people, not broken in from the birth, as a paternal or, in other words, a meddling government, a government which tells them what to read and say and eat and drink and wear.

Ibid.

He had a head which statuaries loved to copy, and a foot the deformity of which the beggars in the streets mimicked.

On Moore's Life of Lord Byron [*1831*]

We know no spectacle so ridiculous as the British public in one of its periodical fits of morality.

Ibid.

From the poetry of Lord Byron they drew a system of ethics compounded of misanthropy and voluptuousness, — a system in which the two great commandments were to hate your neighbour and to love your neighbour's wife.

On Moore's Life of Lord Byron

What a singular destiny has been that of this remarkable man! — To be regarded in his own age as a classic, and in ours as a companion! To receive from his contemporaries that full homage which men of genius have in general received only from posterity; to be more intimately known to posterity than other men are known to their contemporaries!

On Boswell's Life of Johnson [*1831*]

That wonderful book, while it obtains admiration from the most fastidious critics, is loved by those who are too simple to admire it.

On Bunyan's Pilgrim's Progress [*1831*]

The conformation of his mind was such that whatever was little seemed to him great, and whatever was great seemed to him little.

On Horace Walpole [*1833*]

Such night in England ne'er had been, nor ne'er again shall be.

The Armada [*1833*]. *Line 34*

An acre in Middlesex is better than a principality in Utopia.[1]

On Lord Bacon [*1837*]

Every schoolboy knows who imprisoned Montezuma, and who strangled Atahualpa.

On Lord Clive [*1840*]

She [the Roman Catholic Church] may still exist in undiminished vigour when some traveller from New Zealand shall, in the midst of a vast solitude, take his stand on a broken arch of London Bridge to sketch the ruins of St. Paul's.[2]

On Ranke's History of the Popes [*1840*]

---

[1] The louder he talked of his honor, the faster we counted our spoons. — EMERSON: *Conduct of Life* [1860], *Worship*

[1] See Tennyson, page 549a.
[2] Macaulay used a similar image in 1824 in the concluding paragraph of a review of MIT-

She [the Catholic Church] thoroughly understands what no other Church has ever understood, how to deal with enthusiasts.

On Ranke's History of the Popes

The Chief Justice was rich, quiet, and infamous.

On Warren Hastings [1841]

I shall not be satisfied unless I produce something which shall for a few days supersede the last fashionable novel on the tables of young ladies.

Letter to Macvey Napier
[November 5, 1841]

In order that he might rob a neighbour whom he had promised to defend, black men fought on the coast of Coromandel and red men scalped each other by the great lakes of North America.

On Frederic the Great [1842]

We hardly know an instance of the strength and weakness of human nature

---

FORD'S *Greece* and in his review of MILL'S *Essay on Government* in 1829.

Who knows but that hereafter some traveller like myself will sit down upon the banks of the Seine, the Thames, or the Zuyder Zee, where now, in the tumult of enjoyment, the heart and the eyes are too slow to take in the multitude of sensations? Who knows but he will sit down solitary amid silent ruins, and weep a people inurned and their greatness changed into an empty name? — CONSTANTIN DE VOLNEY [1757–1820]: *Ruins, Chap. II*

The next Augustan age will dawn on the other side of the Atlantic. There will, perhaps, be a Thucydides at Boston, a Xenophon at New York, in time a Virgil at Mexico, and a Newton at Peru. At last some curious traveller from Lima will visit England, and give a description of the ruins of St. Paul's, like the editions of Balbec and Palmyra. — HORACE WALPOLE: *Letter to Sir Horace Mann* [November 24, 1774]

In the firm expectation that when London shall be a habitation of bitterns, when St. Paul and Westminster Abbey shall stand shapeless and nameless ruins in the midst of an unpeopled marsh, when the piers of Waterloo Bridge shall become the nuclei of islets of reeds and osiers, and cast the jagged shadows of their broken arches on the solitary stream, some Transatlantic commentator will be weighing in the scales of some new and now unimagined system of criticism the respective merits of the Bells and the Fudges and their historians. — SHELLEY: *Dedication to Peter Bell the Third* [1819]

so striking and so grotesque as the character of this haughty, vigilant, resolute, sagacious blue-stocking, half Mithridates and half Trissotin, bearing up against a world in arms, with an ounce of poison in one pocket and a quire of bad verses in the other.

On Frederic the Great

Lars Porsena of Clusium
  By the Nine Gods he swore
That the great house of Tarquin
  Should suffer wrong no more.
By the Nine Gods he swore it,
  And named a trysting day,
And bade his messengers ride forth
East and west and south and north,
  To summon his array.

Lays of Ancient Rome [1842].
Horatius, Stanza 1

To every man upon this earth
  Death cometh soon or late;
And how can man die better
  Than facing fearful odds
For the ashes of his fathers,
  And the temples of his gods?

Ibid. Stanza 27

Those behind cried "Forward!"
And those before cried "Back!"

Ibid. Stanza 50

Oh, Tiber! father Tiber!
  To whom the Romans pray,
A Roman's life, a Roman's arms,
  Take thou in charge this day.

Ibid. Stanza 59

A man who has never looked on Niagara has but a faint idea of a cataract; and he who has not read Barère's Memoirs may be said not to know what it is to lie.

Mémoires de Bertrand Barère
[1843]

The highest proof of virtue is to possess boundless power without abusing it.

Review of Aikin's Life of
Addison [1843]

There you sit,[1] doing penance for the disingenuousness of years.

Speech, House of Commons
[April 14, 1845]

[1] Sir Robert Peel.

Forget all feuds, and shed one English
tear
O'er English dust. A broken heart lies
here.
> *Epitaph on a Jacobite* [*1845*]

Those who compare the age in which
their lot has fallen with a golden age
which exists only in imagination, may
talk of degeneracy and decay; but no
man who is correctly informed as to the
past, will be disposed to take a morose
or desponding view of the present.
> *History of England* [*1849–1861*].
> *Vol. I, Chap. 1*

I shall cheerfully bear the reproach
of having descended below the dignity
of history if I can succeed in placing
before the English of the nineteenth
century a true picture of the life of
their ancestors.
> *Ibid.*

The Puritan hated bear-baiting, not
because it gave pain to the bear, but
because it gave pleasure to the spectators.[1]
> *Ibid. Chap. 2*

There were gentlemen and there
were seamen in the navy of Charles II.
But the seamen were not gentlemen, and
the gentlemen were not seamen.
> *Ibid. Chap. 3*

The ambassador [of Russia] and
the grandees who accompanied him
were so gorgeous that all London
crowded to stare at them, and so filthy
that nobody dared to touch them. They
came to the court balls dropping pearls
and vermin.
> *Ibid. Vol. V, Chap. 23*

Your Constitution is all sail and no
anchor.
> *Letter to H. S. Randall, author*
> *of a Life of Thomas Jefferson*
> [*May 23, 1857*]

I met Sir Bulwer Lytton, or Lytton
Bulwer. He is anxious about some
scheme for some association of literary
men. I detest all such associations. I

[1] Even bear-baiting was esteemed heathen-
ish and unchristian: the sport of it, not the
inhumanity, gave offence. — HUME: *History
of England* [1754–1757], *Vol. I, Chap. LXII*

hate the notion of gregarious authors.
The less we have to do with each other,
the better.
> *Quoted in* GEORGE OTTO TRE-
> VELYAN: *Life and Letters of*
> *Lord Macaulay* [*1877*]. *Vol. II,*
> *Page 245*

Soon fades the spell, soon comes the
night;
Say will it not be then the same,
Whether we played the black or white,
Whether we lost or won the game?
> *Sermon in a Churchyard. Stanza 8*

Who never forgot that the end of
Government is the happiness of the
governed.
> *Inscription for the Statue of*
> *Lord William Bentinck*

SIR HENRY TAYLOR
[1800–1886]

His food
Was glory, which was poison to his
mind
And peril to his body.
> *Philip Van Artevelde* [*1834*].
> *Part I, Act I, Sc. 5*

The world knows nothing of its greatest men.
> *Ibid.*

He that lacks time to mourn, lacks
time to mend.
Eternity mourns that.
> *Ibid.*

We figure to ourselves
The thing we like; and then we build
it up,
As chance will have it, on the rock or
sand, —
For thought is tired of wandering o'er
the world,
And homebound Fancy runs her bark
ashore.
> *Ibid.*

Such souls,
Whose sudden visitations daze the
world,
Vanish like lightning, but they leave
behind
A voice that in the distance far away
Wakens the slumbering ages.
> *Ibid.*

RICHARD BETHELL, LORD WESTBURY
[1800–1873]

Take a note of that; his Lordship says he will turn it over in what he is pleased to call his mind.[1]

NASH: *Life of Lord Westbury*
[*1888*]. *Vol. I, Page 158*

JANE WELSH CARLYLE
[1801–1866]

Medical men all over the world having merely entered into a tacit agreement to call all sorts of maladies people are liable to, in cold weather, by one name; so that one sort of treatment may serve for all, and their practice be thereby greatly simplified.

Letter to John Welsh
[*March 4, 1837*]

Some new neighbours, that came a month or two ago, brought with them an accumulation of all the things to be guarded against in a London neighbourhood, viz., a pianoforte, a lap-dog, and a parrot.

Letter to Mrs. Carlyle
[*May 6, 1839*]

Never does one feel oneself so utterly helpless as in trying to speak comfort for great bereavement. I will not try it. Time is the only comforter for the loss of a mother.

Letter to Thomas Carlyle
[*December 27, 1853*]

If peace and quietness be not in one's own power, one can always give oneself at least bodily fatigue — no such bad succedaneum after all.

Journal. October 23, 1855

When one has been threatened with a great injustice, one accepts a smaller as a favour.

Ibid. November 21, 1855

[1] Reported to have been spoken in an audible whisper, from the barristers' table, in reference to a presiding judge. According to Nash, Lord Westbury always disclaimed invention of the mot.

DAVID GLASGOW FARRAGUT
[1801–1870]

Damn the torpedoes! Captain Drayton, go ahead! Jouett, full speed!

At Mobile Bay [*August 5, 1864*]

JOHN HENRY, CARDINAL NEWMAN
[1801–1890]

Time hath a taming hand.

Persecution [*1832*]. *Stanza 3*

Lead, kindly Light, amid the encircling gloom;
Lead thou me on!
The night is dark, and I am far from home;
Lead thou me on!
Keep thou my feet: I do not ask to see
The distant scene; one step enough for me.

The Pillar of the Cloud [*1833*].
Stanza 1

And with the morn, those angel faces smile
Which I have loved long since, and lost awhile.

Ibid. Stanza 3

Growth is the only evidence of life.

Apologia pro Vita Sua [*1864*]

It is thy very energy of thought
Which keeps thee from thy God.

Dream of Gerontius [*1866*].
Part III

Who lets his feelings run
In soft luxurious flow,
Shrinks when hard service must be done,
And faints at every woe.

Flowers Without Fruit [*1868*]

Living Nature, not dull Art
Shall plan my ways and rule my heart.

Nature and Art [*1868*]. *Stanza 12*

Weep not for me:
Be blithe as wont, nor tinge with gloom
The stream of love that circles home,
Light hearts and free!

Joy in the gifts Heaven's bounty lends,
Nor miss my face, dear friends!
I still am near.
A Voice from Afar [Knowledge]
[1868]. Stanza 1

It is almost a definition of a gentleman to say he is one who never inflicts pain.
Idea of a University [1873]. The
Man of the World

If he be an unbeliever, he will be too profound and large-minded to ridicule religion or to act against it; he is too wise to be a dogmatist or fanatic in his infidelity. He respects piety and devotion; he even supports institutions as venerable, beautiful, or useful, to which he does not assent; he honours the ministers of religion, and it contents him to decline its mysteries without assailing or denouncing them.
Ibid.

A great memory does not make a philosopher, any more than a dictionary can be called a grammar.
Ibid. Knowledge in Relation to
Learning

Ex Umbris et Imaginibus in Veritatem! (From shadows and symbols into the truth.)
Epitaph at Edgbaston, composed
by himself

BRIGHAM YOUNG
[1801–1877]

This is the place!
On first seeing the valley of the
Great Salt Lake, July 24, 1847 [1]

ALLEN C. SPOONER
[*Floruit* 1846]

I mused upon the Pilgrim flock
Whose luck it was to land

[1] Brigham Young and 142 men, three women and two children were the vanguard of Mormon pioneers who explored westward from Nebraska to find a new home for their Church. Mahonri M. Young, noted sculptor and grandson of Brigham Young, designed the "This is The Place Monument," which was dedicated on the spot on the centennial, July 24, 1947.

Upon almost the only rock
Among the Plymouth sand.
Old Times and New. Stanza 2
(Written for the New England
Society Festival, New York,
December 22, 1846)

ALEXANDRE DUMAS
THE ELDER
[1802–1870]

There are virtues which become crimes by exaggeration.
The Count of Monte Cristo
[1841–1845]. Chap. 90

Great is truth. Fire cannot burn, nor water drown it.
Ibid. Chap. 113

All human wisdom is summed up in two words, — wait and hope.
Ibid. Chap. 117

All for one, one for all, that is our device.[1]
The Three Musketeers [1844].
Chap. 9

Nothing succeeds like success.[2]
Ange Pitou [1854]. Vol. I, Page 72

Let us look for the woman.[3]
The Mohicans of Paris
[1854–1855]. Vol. III,
Chaps. 10 and 11

VICTOR HUGO
[1802–1885]

Let us, while waiting for new monuments, preserve the ancient monuments.
Note added to the Definitive
Edition of Notre Dame de Paris
[1832]

Popularity? It is glory's small change.
Ruy Blas [1838]. Act III, Sc. 5

The three problems of the age — the degradation of man by poverty, the ruin of woman by starvation, and the

[1] See Shakespeare, page 131b.
[2] Rien ne réussit comme le succès. — *French proverb*
[3] Cherchons la femme. "Cherchez la femme" is attributed to Joseph Fouché [1759–1820].

dwarfing of childhood by physical and spiritual night.
Les Misérables [1] [*1862*].
Preface

The supreme happiness of life is the conviction that we are loved.
Ibid. Fantine, Book V, Chap. 4

For prying into any human affairs, none are equal to those whom it does not concern.
Ibid. Chap. 8

The malicious have a dark happiness.
Ibid. Chap. 9

Great grief is a divine and terrible radiance which transfigures the wretched.
Ibid. Chap. 13

Napoleon . . . mighty somnambulist of a vanished dream.
Ibid. Cosette, Book I, Chap. 13

Thank heaven, nations are great aside from the dismal chances of the sword.
Ibid. Chap. 16

Waterloo is a battle of the first rank won by a captain of the second.
Ibid.

Would you realize what Revolution is, call it Progress; and would you realize what Progress is, call it Tomorrow.
Ibid. Chap. 17

What is that to the Infinite?
Ibid. Chap. 18

Great blunders are often made, like large ropes, of a multitude of fibres.
Ibid. Book V, Chap. 10

Upon the first goblet he read this inscription: Monkey wine; upon the second: lion wine; upon the third: sheep wine; upon the fourth: swine wine. These four inscriptions expressed the four descending degrees of drunkenness: the first, that which enlivens; the second, that which irritates; the third, that which stupefies; finally the last, that which brutalizes.
Ibid. Book VI, Chap. 9

[1] Translated by CHARLES E. WILBOUR, Modern Library Giant.

A man is not idle because he is absorbed in thought. There is a visible labour and there is an invisible labour.
Les Misérables. Cosette, Book VII, Chap. 8

To be buried in Père Lachaise is like having mahogany furniture.
Ibid. Book VIII, Chap. 5

No one ever keeps a secret so well as a child.
Ibid. Chap. 8

The peculiarity of prudery is to multiply sentinels, in proportion as the fortress is less threatened.[1]
Ibid. Marius, Book II, Chap. 8

Nothing will mix and amalgamate more easily than an old priest and an old soldier. In reality, they are the same kind of man. One has devoted himself to his country upon earth, the other to his country in heaven; there is no other difference.
Ibid. Book III, Chap. 2

He had the appearance of a caryatid in vacation; he was supporting nothing but his reverie.
Ibid. Book IV, Chap. 2

Life, misfortunes, isolation, abandonment, poverty, are battlefields which have their heroes; obscure heroes, sometimes greater than the illustrious heroes.
Ibid. Book V, Chap. 1

A creditor is worse than a master; for a master owns only your person, a creditor owns your dignity, and can belabour that.
Ibid. Chap. 2

Social prosperity means man happy, the citizen free, the nation great.
Ibid. Saint Denis, Book I, Chap. 4

Nothing is more dangerous than discontinued labour; it is habit lost. A habit easy to abandon, difficult to resume.
Ibid. Book II, Chap. 1

[1] That is the refuge of all old coquettes; it is hard for them to be deserted by the gallants, and from such a desertion, in their spite, they take refuge in the trade of a prude. — MOLIÈRE: *Tartuffe* [1667], *Act I, Sc. 1*

Thought is the labour of the intellect,
reverie is its pleasure.
Les Misérables. Saint Denis,
Book II, Chap. 1

Where the telescope ends, the microscope begins. Which of the two has the
grander view?
Ibid. Book III, Chap. 3

A compliment is something like a kiss
through a veil.
Ibid. Book VIII, Chap. 1

Great perils have this beauty, that
they bring to light the fraternity of
strangers.
Ibid. Book XII, Chap. 4

Philosophy is the microscope of
thought.
Ibid. Jean Valjean, Book II,
Chap. 2

When grace is joined with wrinkles,
it is adorable. There is an unspeakable
dawn in happy old age.
Ibid. Book V, Chap. 2

Nothing is more gentle than smoke,
nothing more frightful. . . . Smoke
rising through the trees may signify the
most charming thing in the world, the
hearth; or the most terrible, a con-
flagration.
Ninety-Three [1879]. Part I,
Book IV, Chap. 7

The sublimest song to be heard on
earth is the lisping of the human soul
on the lips of children.
Ibid. Part III, Book III, Chap. 1

Nothing is so like a soul as a bee. It
goes from flower to flower as a soul
from star to star, and it gathers honey
as a soul gathers light.
Ibid. Chap. 3

To rise at six, to dine at ten,
To sup at six, to sleep at ten,
Makes a man live for ten times ten.
Inscription over the door
of Hugo's study

I represent a party which does not
yet exist: the party of revolution, civilization.
This party will make the twentieth
century.
There will issue from it first the
United States of Europe, then the
United States of the World.
Prophecy in autograph on the
wall of the room in which Hugo
died, Place des Vosges, Paris

LYDIA MARIA CHILD
[1802–1880]

Genius hath electric power
Which earth can never tame,
Bright suns may scorch and dark
clouds lower,
Its flash is still the same.
Marius Amid the Ruins of Carthage

Over the river and through the wood,
To grandfather's house we'll go;
The horse knows the way
To carry the sleigh,
Through the white and drifted snow.
Thanksgiving Day. Stanza 1

ALBERT GORTON GREENE
[1802–1868]

Old Grimes is dead, that good old man
We never shall see more;
He used to wear a long black coat
All buttoned down before.
Old Grimes. Stanza 1

He had no malice in his mind,
No ruffles on his shirt.
Ibid. Stanza 8

His knowledge hid from public gaze,
He did not bring to view,
Nor made a noise town-meeting days,
As many people do.
Ibid. Stanza 10

LETITIA ELIZABETH
LANDON
[1802–1838]

Few, save the poor, feel for the poor.
The Poor

Were it not better to forget
Than but remember and regret?
Despondency

GEORGE POPE MORRIS
[1802–1864]

Woodman, spare that tree!
Touch not a single bough! [1]

[1] See Campbell, page 433a.

In youth it sheltered me,
And I'll protect it now.
Woodman, Spare That Tree
[1830]. Stanza 1
The iron-armed soldier, the true-
hearted soldier,
The gallant old soldier of Tippecanoe.[1]
Campaign Song for William
Henry Harrison [1840]
A song for our banner! The watchword
recall
Which gave the Republic her station:
"United we stand, divided we fall!"[2]
It made and preserves us a nation![3]
The Flag of Our Union.
'Tis ever thus, when in life's storm
Hope's star to man grows dim,
An angel kneels, in woman's form,
And breathes a prayer for him.
Pocahontas. Stanza 3

EDWARD COOTE PINKNEY
[1802–1828]

I fill this cup to one made up
Of loveliness alone,
A woman, of her gentle sex
The seeming paragon;
To whom the better elements
And kindly stars have given
A form so fair, that, like the air,
'Tis less of earth than heaven.
A Health [1825]. Stanza 1
Her every tone is music's own,
Like those of morning birds,
And something more than melody
Dwells ever in her words.
Ibid. Stanza 2

[1] Morris's words, sung to the tune of "The
Old Oaken Bucket," were immensely popular.
For the first time in our land the power of
song was invoked to aid a Presidential candidate. — BEN PERLEY POORE: *Reminiscences*
[1886]
[2] See Aesop, page 11a.
Then join hand in hand, brave Americans all!
By uniting we stand, by dividing we fall.
JOHN DICKINSON: *The Liberty Song*
[1768]
[3] Bless'd with victory and peace,
may our Heaven-rescued land
Praise the Power that hath made
and preserved us a nation.
FRANCIS SCOTT KEY: *The Star-Spangled*
Banner [1814], St. 4

Look out upon the stars, my love,
And shame them with thine eyes.
A Serenade [1825]

WINTHROP MACKWORTH
PRAED
[1802–1839]

And oh! I shall find how, day by day,
All thoughts and things look older;
How the laugh of pleasure grows less
gay,
And the heart of friendship colder.
Twenty-eight and Twenty-nine
She was our queen, our rose, our star;
And then she danced — O Heaven, her
dancing!
The Belle of the Ball
His talk was like a stream which runs
With rapid change from rocks to roses,
It slipped from politics to puns;
It passed from Mahomet to Moses.
The Vicar. Stanza 5
Events are writ by History's pen:
Though causes are too much to care
for:—
Fame talks about the where and when,
While folly asks the why and where-
fore.
Epitaph on the Late King of
the Sandwich Islands. Stanza 4
Dame Fortune is a fickle gipsy,
And always blind, and often tipsy;
Sometimes for years and years together,
She'll bless you with the sunniest
weather,
Bestowing honour, pudding, pence,
You can't imagine why or whence; —
Then in a moment — Presto, pass! —
Your joys are withered like the grass.
The Haunted Tree

DAVID CHRISTY
[1802– ?]

Cotton is King; or, The Economical
Relations of Slavery.
Title of Book [1855] [1]

[1] Take away *time is money*, and what is
left of England? take away *cotton is king*,
and what is left of America? — VICTOR HUGO:
Les Misérables [1862], *Marius, Book IV,*
Chap. 4

THOMAS LOVELL BEDDOES
[1803–1849]

The anchor heaves, the ship swings free,
The sails swell full. To sea, to sea!
Sailor's Song. Stanza 2

If there were dreams to sell,
  What would you buy?
Some cost a passing-bell;
  Some a light sigh.
Dream-Pedlary

That divinest hope, which none can know of
Who have not laid their dearest in the grave.
Death's Jest Book [1850]

If thou wilt ease thine heart
Of love and all its smart,
Then sleep, dear, sleep.

But wilt thou cure thy heart
Of love and all its smart,
Then die, dear, die.
Ibid.

WILLIAM ALLEN
[1803–1879]

Fifty-four forty, or fight! [1]
Speech, U. S. Senate [1844]

GEORGE BORROW
[1803–1881]

O England! long, long may it be ere the sun of thy glory sink beneath the wave of darkness! Though gloomy and portentous clouds are now gathering rapidly around thee, still, still may it please the Almighty to disperse them, and to grant thee a futurity longer in duration and still brighter in renown than thy past! Or, if thy doom be at hand, may that doom be a noble one,

and worthy of her who has been styled the Old Queen of the waters!
The Bible in Spain [1842]

O ye gifted ones, follow your calling, for, however various your talents may be, ye can have but one calling capable of leading ye to eminence and renown; follow resolutely the one straight path before you, it is that of your good angel, let neither obstacles nor temptations induce ye to leave it; bound along if you can; if not, on hands and knees follow in it, perish in it, if needful; but ye need not fear that; no one ever yet died in the true path of his calling before he had attained the pinnacle.
Lavengro [1851]. Chap. 21

Trust not a man's words if you please, or you may come to very erroneous conclusions; but at all times place implicit confidence in a man's countenance in which there is no deceit; and of necessity there can be none. If people would but look each other more in the face, we should have less cause to complain of the deception of the world; [1] nothing so easy as physiognomy nor so useful.
Ibid. Chap. 22

Translation is at best an echo.
Ibid. Chap. 25

There's night and day, brother, both sweet things; sun, moon, and stars, brother, all sweet things; there's likewise a wind on the heath. Life is very sweet, brother; who would wish to die?
Ibid.

I learnt . . . to fear God, and to take my own part.
Ibid. Chap. 86

Youth is the only season for enjoyment, and the first twenty-five years of one's life are worth all the rest of the longest life of man, even though those five-and-twenty be spent in penury and contempt, and the rest in the possession of wealth, honours, respectability.
The Romany Rye [1857]. Chap. 30

---

[1] This phrase was adopted as the slogan of the war party, in the presidential election of 1844. At the time, war with England regarding the Oregon question seemed imminent. The Democratic convention of 1844 had demanded the reoccupation of the whole of Oregon up to 54° 40', but the new president, James K. Polk, compromised with Great Britain on the forty-ninth parallel.

[1] See Dickens, page 580a.

WILLIAM DRIVER
[1803–1886]

I name thee Old Glory.
> *Words on Hoisting the Flag* [1]

RALPH WALDO EMERSON
[1803–1882]

Four snakes gliding up and down a hollow for no purpose that I could see — not to eat, not for love, but only gliding.
> *Journal. April 11, 1834*

Give me health and a day, and I will make the pomp of emperors ridiculous.
> *Nature* [1836]. *Chap. 3, Beauty*

He who has mastered any law in his private thoughts, is master to that extent of all men whose language he speaks, and of all into whose language his own can be translated.
> *The American Scholar* [1837]

Wherever Macdonald sits, there is the head of the table.[2]
> *Ibid.*

If the single man plant himself indomitably on his instincts, and there abide, the huge world will come round to him.[3]
> *Ibid.*

Men grind and grind in the mill of a truism, and nothing comes out but what was put in. But the moment they desert the tradition for a spontaneous thought, then poetry, wit, hope, virtue, learning, anecdote, all flock to their aid.
> *Literary Ethics* [1838]

[1] On August 10, 1831, a large American flag was presented to Captain William Driver of the brig *Charles Doggett* by a band of women, in recognition of his humane service in bringing back the British mutineers of the ship *Bounty* from Tahiti to their former home, Pitcairn Island. As the flag was hoisted to the masthead, Captain Driver proclaimed, "I name thee Old Glory." The flag is now in the Smithsonian Institution, Washington, D. C.

[2] Emerson's sentence is usually quoted with the substitution of "Macgregor" for "Macdonald."

[3] See Disraeli, page 512a.
All things come round to him who will but wait. — LONGFELLOW: *Tales of a Wayside Inn, The Student's Tale* [1863]

I wish to write such rhymes as shall not suggest a restraint, but contrariwise the wildest freedom.
> *Journal. June 27, 1839*

Time dissipates to shining ether the solid angularity of facts.
> *Essays: First Series* [1841]. *History*

There is properly no History; only Biography.[1]
> *Ibid.*

Nature is a mutable cloud, which is always and never the same.
> *Ibid.*

A man is a bundle of relations, a knot of roots, whose flower and fruitage is the world.
> *Ibid.*

The virtue in most request is conformity. Self-reliance is its aversion. It loves not realities and creators, but names and customs.
> *Ibid. Self-Reliance*

Whoso would be a man must be a non-conformist.
> *Ibid.*

A foolish consistency is the hobgoblin of little minds, adored by little statesmen and philosophers and divines.
> *Ibid.*

To be great is to be misunderstood.
> *Ibid.*

An institution is the lengthened shadow of one man.
> *Ibid.*

Nothing can bring you peace but yourself.
> *Ibid.*

Every sweet has its sour; every evil its good.
> *Ibid. Compensation*

For every thing you have missed, you have gained something else; and for every thing you gain, you lose something.
> *Ibid.*

Everything in Nature contains all the powers of Nature. Everything is made of one hidden stuff.
> *Ibid.*

[1] See Carlyle, page 475b.

It is as impossible for a man to be cheated by any one but himself, as for a thing to be, and not to be, at the same time.

Essays: First Series. Compensation

There is no luck in literary reputation. They who make up the final verdict upon every book are not the partial and noisy readers of the hour when it appears; but a court as of angels, a public not to be bribed, not to be entreated, and not to be overawed, decides upon every man's title to fame.

Ibid. Spiritual Laws

All mankind love a lover.

Ibid. Love

No man ever forgot the visitations of that power to his heart and brain, which created all things new; which was the dawn in him of music, poetry, and art.

Ibid.

Thou art to me a delicious torment.

Ibid. Friendship

Happy is the house that shelters a friend.

Ibid.

A friend is a person with whom I may be sincere. Before him, I may think aloud.

Ibid.

A friend may well be reckoned the masterpiece of Nature.

Ibid.

Two may talk and one may hear, but three cannot take part in a conversation of the most sincere and searching sort.

Ibid.

The only reward of virtue is virtue; the only way to have a friend is to be one.

Ibid.

I do then with my friends as I do with my books. I would have them where I can find them, but I seldom use them.

Ibid.

Do what we can, summer will have its flies. If we walk in the woods, we must feed mosquitoes.

Ibid. Prudence

In skating over thin ice our safety is in our speed.

Essays: First Series. Prudence

Heroism feels and never reasons and therefore is always right.

Ibid. Heroism

Nothing great was ever achieved without enthusiasm.

Ibid. Circles

Nothing astonishes men so much as common sense and plain dealing.

Ibid. Art

There is always a certain meanness in the argument of conservatism, joined with a certain superiority in its fact.

The Conservative [*1842*]

Nature and Books belong to the eyes that see them.

Essays: Second Series [*1844*]. *Experience*

No house, though it were the Tuileries, or the Escurial, is good for anything without a master.

Ibid. Manners

The only gift is a portion of thyself.[1]

Ibid. Gifts

The less government we have, the better — the fewer laws, and the less confided power.

Ibid. Politics

Money, which represents the prose of life, and which is hardly spoken of in parlors without an apology, is, in its effects and laws, as beautiful as roses.

Ibid. Nominalist and Realist

Every man is wanted, and no man is wanted much.

Ibid.

And with Caesar to take in his hand the army, the empire, and Cleopatra, and say, "All these will I relinquish if you will show me the fountains of the Nile."

Ibid. New England Reformers

The reward of a thing well done, is to have done it.

Ibid.

Good-bye, proud world! I'm going home;

[1] See J. R. LOWELL, page 600a, and Whitman, page 608a–608b.

Thou art not my friend and I'm not
   thine.[1]
    Poems [*1847*]. *Good-bye, Stanza 1*
Oh, when I am safe in my sylvan home,
I tread on the pride of Greece and
   Rome;
And when I am stretched beneath the
   pines
Where the evening star so holy shines,
I laugh at the lore and the pride of
   man,
At the sophist schools, and the learned
   clan;
For what are they all in their high con-
   ceit,
When man in the bush with God may
   meet?
      Ibid. Stanza 4
Nor knowest thou what argument
Thy life to thy neighbor's creed has
   lent.
All are needed by each one;
Nothing is fair or good alone.
    Ibid. Each and All, Stanza 1
I wiped away the weeds and foam,
I fetched my sea-born treasures home;
But the poor, unsightly, noisome things
Had left their beauty on the shore,
With the sun and the sand and the wild
   uproar.
      Ibid. Stanza 3
I like a church; I like a cowl;
I love a prophet of the soul;
And on my heart monastic aisles
Fall like sweet strains or pensive
   smiles;
Yet not for all his faith can see
Would I that cowlèd churchman be.
    Ibid. The Problem, Stanza 1
Not from a vain or shallow thought
His awful Jove young Phidias brought.
      Ibid. Stanza 2
The hand that rounded Peter's dome,
And groined the aisles of Christian
   Rome,
Wrought in a sad sincerity;
Himself from God he could not free;
He builded better than he knew; —
The conscious stone to beauty grew.
      Ibid.

[1] See Johnson, page 343a.

Earth proudly wears the Parthenon
As the best gem upon her zone.
    Poems. The Problem, Stanza 3
The passive Master lent his hand
To the vast soul that o'er him planned.[1]
      Ibid.
Enclosed
In a tumultuous privacy of storm.
    Ibid. The Snow-Storm
To mimic in slow structures, stone by
   stone,
Built in an age, the mad wind's night-
   work,
The frolic architecture of the snow.
      Ibid.
Life is too short to waste
In critic peep or cynic bark,
Quarrel or reprimand:
'Twill soon be dark;
Up! mind thine own aim, and
God speed the mark!
    Ibid. To J. W.
There's no rood has not a star above it.
    Ibid. Musketaquid
   All sorts of things and weather
Must be taken in together,
To make up a year
And a Sphere.
   Ibid. Fable, The Mountain and
          the Squirrel
   If eyes were made for seeing,
Then Beauty is its own excuse for be-
   ing.[2]
    Ibid. The Rhodora
Things are in the saddle,
And ride mankind.
    Ibid. Ode Inscribed to
      W. H. Channing
There are two laws discrete,
Not reconciled, —
Law for man, and law for thing.
      Ibid.
Olympian bards who sung
  Divine ideas below,
Which always find us young,
  And always keep us so.
    Ibid. Ode to Beauty

[1] This couplet is inscribed on the boulder
marking Emerson's grave in Sleepy Hollow
Cemetery, Concord, Massachusetts.
[2] See Elizabeth Barrett Browning, page
519b, and Whittier, page 526b.

Heartily know,
When half-gods go,
The gods arrive.
> *Poems. Give All to Love, Stanza 4*

Love not the flower they pluck, and
    know it not,
And all their botany is Latin names.
> *Ibid. Blight*

By the rude bridge that arched the
    flood,
Their flag to April's breeze unfurled,
Here once the embattled farmers stood,
And fired the shot heard round the
    world.
> *Ibid. Hymn Sung at the Com-
> pletion of the Battle Monu-
> ment, Concord [July 4, 1837],
> Stanza 1*

Hast thou named all the birds without
a gun? [1]
Loved the wood-rose, and left it on its
    stalk?
> *Ibid. Forbearance*

I hate quotations. Tell me what you
know.
> *Journal. May, 1849*

He is great who is what he is from
Nature, and who never reminds us of
others.
> *Representative Men [1850].
> Uses of Great Men*

When nature removes a great man,
people explore the horizon for a successor; but none comes, and none will.
His class is extinguished with him. In
some other and quite different field, the
next man will appear.
> *Ibid.*

Every hero becomes a bore at last.
> *Ibid.*

Great geniuses have the shortest biographies.
> *Ibid. Plato, or, The Philosopher*

Keep cool: it will be all one a hundred years hence. [2]
> *Ibid. Montaigne, or, The Skeptic*

[1] See S. W. Foss, page 777b.
[2] What matters what anybody thinks? "It
will be all the same a hundred years hence."

Is not marriage an open question,
when it is alleged, from the beginning
of the world, that such as are in the institution wish to get out, and such as
are out wish to get in? [1]
> *Representative Men. Montaigne,
> or, The Skeptic*

Thought is the property of him who
can entertain it, and of him who can
adequately place it.
> *Ibid. Shakespeare, or, The Poet*

"There shall be no Alps," he said.
> *Ibid. Napoleon, or, The Man of
> the World*

[Napoleon] directed Bourrienne to
leave all his letters unopened for three
weeks, and then observed with satisfaction how large a part of the correspondence had thus disposed of itself,
and no longer required an answer.
> *Ibid.*

The word *liberty* in the mouth of Mr.
Webster sounds like the word *love* in
the mouth of a courtezan.
> *Journal. February 12 (?), 1851*

I trust a good deal to common fame,
as we all must. If a man has good corn,
or wood, or boards, or pigs, to sell, or
can make better chairs or knives, cru-
cibles or church organs, than anybody
else, you will find a broad hard-beaten
road to his house, though it be in the
woods. [2]
> *Ibid. February, 1855*

That is the most sensible proverb ever invented. — GEORGE DU MAURIER: *Peter Ibbetson* [1891]

[1] See Montaigne, page 100a.
[2] The editors, E. W. EMERSON and W. E.
FORBES, appended a footnote: "There has
been much inquiry in the newspapers recently
as to whether Mr. Emerson wrote a sentence
very like the above which has been attributed
to him in print. The Editors do not find the
latter in his works, but there can be little
doubt that it was a memory quotation by
some hearer, or, quite probably, correctly
reported from one of his lectures, the same
image in differing words."
If a man can write a better book, preach a
better sermon, or make a better mouse-trap
than his neighbor, though he builds his
house in the woods the world will make a
beaten path to his door. — SARAH S. B. YULE
AND MARY S. KEENE: *Borrowings* [1889], *re-*

Classics which at home are drowsily read have a strange charm in a country inn, or in the transom of a merchant brig.

English Traits [*1856*]

I find the Englishman to be him of all men who stands firmest in his shoes.

Ibid. Manners

A creative economy is the fuel of magnificence.

Ibid. Aristocracy

Coal is a portable climate.

Conduct of Life [*1860*]. *Wealth*

The world is his, who has money to go over it.

Ibid.

The farmer is covetous of his dollar, and with reason. . . . He knows how many strokes of labor it represents. His bones ache with the day's work that earned it.

Ibid.

Art is a jealous mistress,[1] and, if a man have a genius for painting, poetry, music, architecture, or philosophy, he makes a bad husband, and an ill-provider.

Ibid.

One of the benefits of a college education is to show the boy its little avail.

Ibid. Culture

All educated Americans, first or last, go to Europe.

Ibid.

Solitude, the safeguard of mediocrity, is to genius the stern friend.

Ibid.

A man known to us only as a celebrity in politics or in trade, gains largely in our esteem if we discover that he has some intellectual taste or skill.

Ibid.

There is always a best way of doing everything, if it be to boil an egg. Manners are the happy ways of doing things.

Ibid. Behavior

Your manners are always under examination, and by committees little sus-

pected, — a police in citizens' clothes, — but are awarding or denying you very high prizes when you least think of it.

Ibid.

Conduct of Life. Behavior

The alleged power to charm down insanity, or ferocity in beasts, is a power behind the eye.

Ibid.

Fine manners need the support of fine manners in others.

Ibid.

The highest compact we can make with our fellow is, — "Let there be truth between us two forevermore."

Ibid.

It is sublime to feel and say of another, I need never meet, or speak, or write to him: we need not reinforce ourselves, or send tokens of remembrance: I rely on him as on myself: if he did thus or thus, I know it was right.

Ibid.

There is no beautifier of complexion, or form, or behavior, like the wish to scatter joy and not pain around us.

Ibid.

We must be as courteous to a man as we are to a picture, which we are willing to give the advantage of a good light.

Ibid.

There is one topic peremptorily forbidden to all well-bred, to all rational mortals, namely, their distempers. If you have not slept, or if you have slept, or if you have headache, or sciatica, or leprosy, or thunder-stroke, I beseech you, by all angels, to hold your peace.

Ibid.

Shallow men believe in luck.[1]

Ibid. Worship

'Tis a Dutch proverb, that "paint costs nothing," such are its preserving qualities in damp climates.

Ibid. Considerations by the Way

Our chief want in life is somebody who shall make us do what we can.

Ibid.

---

ported by Mrs. Yule as having been used by Emerson in an address

[1] See Sharswood, page 560b.

[1] Luck is infatuated with the efficient. —*Persian proverb*

Make yourself necessary to somebody.
Conduct of Life. Considerations by the Way

Beauty without grace is the hook without the bait.
Ibid. Beauty

Never read any book that is not a year old.
Ibid. In Praise of Books

I should as soon think of swimming across Charles River, when I wish to go to Boston, as of reading all my books in originals, when I have them rendered for me in my mother tongue.
Ibid.

Great men are they who see that spiritual is stronger than any material force; that thoughts rule the world.
Progress of Culture, Phi Beta Kappa Address [July 18, 1867]

And striving to be man, the worm
Mounts through all the spires of form.
May-Day and Other Pieces [1867].
May-Day

God said, I am tired of kings,
I suffer them no more.
Ibid. Boston Hymn [Read January 1, 1863], Stanza 2

Oh, tenderly the haughty day
Fills his blue urn with fire.
Ibid. Ode [Sung July 4, 1857], Stanza 1

Go put your creed into your deed,
Nor speak with double tongue.
Ibid. Stanza 5

I think no virtue goes with size.
Ibid. The Titmouse

For well the soul, if stout within,
Can arm impregnably the skin.
Ibid.

So nigh is grandeur to our dust,
So near is God to man,
When Duty whispers low, *Thou must*,
The youth replies, *I can.*
Ibid. Voluntaries, III

Nor sequent centuries could hit
Orbit and sum of Shakespeare's wit.
Ibid. Solution

Born for success he seemed,
With grace to win, with heart to hold,

With shining gifts that took all eyes.
May-Day and Other Pieces.
In Memoriam E. B. E.

Nor mourn the unalterable Days
That Genius goes and Folly stays.
Ibid.

Fear not, then, thou child infirm,
There's no god dare wrong a worm.
Ibid. Compensation, I

He thought it happier to be dead,
To die for Beauty, than live for bread.
Ibid. Beauty

Wilt thou seal up the avenues of ill?
Pay every debt, as if God wrote the bill.
Ibid. "Suum Cuique"

Too busied with the crowded hour to
fear to live or die.
Ibid. Nature

Damsels of Time, the hypocritic Days,
Muffled and dumb like barefoot dervishes,
And marching single in an endless file,
Bring diadems and fagots in their hands.
Ibid. Days

I, too late,
Under her solemn fillet saw the scorn.
Ibid.

It is time to be old,
To take in sail.
Ibid. Terminus

Obey the voice at eve obeyed at prime.
Ibid.

Though love repine, and reason chafe,
There came a voice without reply, —
" 'Tis man's perdition to be safe,
When for the truth he ought to die."
Ibid. Sacrifice

For what avail the plough or sail,
Or land or life, if freedom fail?
Ibid. Boston, Stanza 5

What care though rival cities soar
Along the stormy coast,
Penn's town, New York, and Baltimore,
If Boston knew the most!
Ibid. Stanza 9

If the red slayer think he slays,
Or if the slain think he is slain,
They know not well the subtle ways
I keep, and pass, and turn again.
Ibid. Brahma

They reckon ill who leave me out;
  When me they fly, I am the wings;
I am the doubter and the doubt,
  And I the hymn the Brahmin sings.
      May-Day and Other Pieces.
          Brahma
Draw, if thou canst, the mystic line,
Severing rightly his from thine,
Which is human, which divine.
      Ibid. Worship
That book is good
Which puts me in a working mood.
Unless to Thought is added Will,
Apollo is an imbecile.
  Ibid. Fragments on the Poetic Gift
In the vaunted works of Art
The master-stroke is Nature's part.[1]
      Ibid. Art
I am the owner of the sphere,
Of the seven stars and the solar year,
Of Caesar's hand, and Plato's brain,
Of Lord Christ's heart, and Shake-
  speare's strain.
      Ibid. History
Ever from one who comes tomorrow
Men wait their good and truth to bor-
  row.
      Ibid. Merlin's Song
The music that can deepest reach,
And cure all ill, is cordial speech.
      Ibid.
A day for toil, an hour for sport,
But for a friend is life too short.
      Ibid.
Some of your hurts you have cured,
And the sharpest you still have sur-
  vived,
But what torments of grief you en-
  dured
From evils which never arrived![2]
  Ibid. Borrowing [From the French]
A ruddy drop of manly blood
  The surging sea outweighs,

---

[1] Nature paints the best part of a picture,
carves the best part of the statue, builds the
best part of the house, and speaks the best
part of the oration. — *Society and Solitude*
[1870], *Art*
[2] Let us be of good cheer, however, remembering that the misfortunes hardest to
bear are those which never come. — JAMES
RUSSELL LOWELL: *Democracy and Addresses*
[1884]

The world uncertain comes and goes,
  The lover rooted stays.
      May-Day and Other Pieces.
          Friendship
Me too thy nobleness has taught
  To master my despair;
The fountains of my hidden life
  Are through thy friendship fair.
      Ibid.
God may forgive sins, he said, but
awkwardness has no forgiveness in
heaven or earth.
      Society and Solitude [1870]
The most advanced nations are al-
ways those who navigate the most.
      Ibid. Civilization
Hitch your wagon to a star.
      Ibid.
The true test of civilization is, not
the census, nor the size of cities, nor
the crops — no, but the kind of man
the country turns out.
      Ibid.
Raphael paints wisdom; Handel sings
it, Phidias carves it, Shakespeare writes
it, Wren builds it, Columbus sails it,
Luther preaches it, Washington arms
it, Watt mechanizes it.
      Ibid. Art
Every genuine work of art has as
much reason for being as the earth and
the sun.
      Ibid.
We boil at different degrees.
      Ibid. Eloquence
The ornament of a house is the
friends who frequent it.
      Ibid. Domestic Life
We have the newspaper, which does
its best to make every square acre of
land and sea give an account of itself
at your breakfast-table.
      Ibid. Works and Days
Can anybody remember when the
times were not hard and money not
scarce?
      Ibid.
A man builds a fine house; and now
he has a master, and a task for life; he
is to furnish, watch, show it, and keep
it in repair the rest of his days.
      Ibid.

'Tis the good reader that makes the good book.
Society and Solitude. Success

We do not count a man's years until he has nothing else to count.
Ibid. Old Age

Poetry teaches the enormous force of a few words, and, in proportion to the inspiration, checks loquacity.
Parnassus [1874]. Preface

There are two classes of poets,— the poets by education and practice, these we respect; and poets by nature, these we love.
Ibid.

No lover of poetry can spare Chaucer, or should grudge the short study required to command the archaisms of his English, and the skill to read the melody of his verse.
Ibid.

Life is not so short but that there is always time enough for courtesy.
Letters and Social Aims [1876].
Social Aims

I have heard with admiring submission the experience of the lady who declared that the sense of being perfectly well-dressed gives a feeling of inward tranquillity which religion is powerless to bestow.
Ibid.

Do not say things. What you are stands over you the while, and thunders so that I cannot hear what you say to the contrary.
Ibid.

Abraham Lincoln . . . who was at home and welcome with the humblest, and with a spirit and a practical vein in the times of terror that commanded the admiration of the wisest. His heart was as great as the world, but there was no room in it to hold the memory of a wrong.
Ibid. Greatness

Next to the originator of a good sentence is the first quoter of it.[1]
Ibid. Quotation and Originality

[1] There is not less wit nor less invention in applying rightly a thought one finds in a book, than in being the first author of that

When Shakespeare is charged with debts to his authors, Landor replies, "Yet he was more original than his originals. He breathed upon dead bodies and brought them into life."
Letters and Social Aims. Quotation
and Originality

In fact, it is as difficult to appropriate the thoughts of others as it is to invent.
Ibid.

By necessity, by proclivity, and by delight, we all quote.
Ibid.

Every good poem that I know I recall by its rhythm also. Rhyme is a pretty good measure of the latitude and opulence of a writer. If unskilled, he is at once detected by the poverty of his chimes.
Ibid. Poetry and Imagination

Wit makes its own welcome, and levels all distinctions.
Ibid. The Comic

The perception of the comic is a tie of sympathy with other men.
Ibid.

What is a weed? A plant whose virtues have not yet been discovered.[1]
Fortune of the Republic [1878]

All thoughts of a turtle are turtles, and of a rabbit, rabbits.
The Natural History of
Intellect [1893]

When you strike at a king, you must kill him.
Recollected by OLIVER WENDELL
HOLMES, JR. *Quoted in* MAX
LERNER: *The Mind and Faith of*
Justice Holmes [1943]

thought. — BAYLE: *Dictionnaire Historique et Critique* [1697–1702]
 Though old the thought and oft exprest,
 'Tis his at last who says it best.
JAMES RUSSELL LOWELL: *For an*
Autograph [1868]
 [1] A weed is no more than a flower in disguise. — JAMES RUSSELL LOWELL: *A Fable for Critics* [1848]
 A weed is but an unloved flower! — ELLA WHEELER WILCOX [1850–1919]: *The Weed,*
St. 1

ROBERT STEPHEN HAWKER
[1803-1875]

And shall Trelawny die?
Here's twenty thousand Cornish men
Will know the reason why.
The Song of the Western Men.[1]
Stanza 1

RICHARD HENRY HENGIST HORNE
[1803-1884]

'Tis always morning somewhere in the world.
Orion [1843]. Book III,
Canto II
A sweet content
Passing all wisdom or its fairest flower.
Ibid.
The wisdom of mankind creeps slowly on,
Subject to every doubt that can retard
Or fling it back upon an earlier time.
Ibid.

DOUGLAS JERROLD
[1803-1857]

He is one of those wise philanthropists who in a time of famine would vote for nothing but a supply of toothpicks.
Wit and Opinions of Douglas
Jerrold [1859]
Dogmatism is puppyism come to its full growth.
Ibid.
The surest way to hit a woman's heart is to take aim kneeling.
Ibid.
That fellow would vulgarize the day of judgment.
Ibid. A Comic Author

[1] This ballad commemorates the commitment to the Tower of London of Sir Jonathan Trelawny [1650-1721], with six other prelates, in 1688, for refusing to recognize the Declaration of Indulgence issued by James II. "And shall Trelawny die?" has been a popular phrase throughout Cornwall since the imprisonment of the seven bishops. Hawker wrote the ballad in 1825.

The best thing I know between France and England is the sea.
Wit and Opinions of Douglas Jer-
rold. The Anglo-French Alliance
Some people are so fond of ill-luck that they run half-way to meet it.
Ibid. Meeting Troubles Half-Way
Earth is here [Australia] so kind, that just tickle her with a hoe and she laughs with a harvest.
Ibid. A Land of Plenty
The ugliest of trades have their moments of pleasure. Now, if I were a grave-digger, or even a hangman, there are some people I could work for with a great deal of enjoyment.
Ibid. Ugly Trades
He was so good he would pour rose-water on a toad.
Ibid. A Charitable Man
As for the brandy, "nothing extenuate"; and the water, put nought in in malice.
Ibid. Shakespeare Grog
Talk to him of Jacob's ladder, and he would ask the number of the steps.
Ibid. A Matter-of-fact Man

CHARLES SWAIN
[1803-1874]

Let tomorrow take care of tomorrow, —
Leave things of the future to fate;
What's the use to anticipate sorrow? —
Life's troubles come never too late!
Imaginary Evils. Stanza 1

SARAH HELEN POWER WHITMAN
[1803-1878]

Star of resplendent front! Thy glorious eye
Shines on me still from out yon clouded sky.
Arcturus (To Edgar Allan Poe)
The summer skies are darkly blue,
The days are still and bright,
And Evening trails her robes of gold
Through the dim halls of Night.[1]
Summer's Call

[1] See Longfellow, page 520b.

ROBERT SMITH SURTEES
[1803–1864]

Full o' beans and benevolence.
Handley Cross [*1843*]. *Chap. 27*
Three things I never lends — my
'oss, my wife, and my name.
Hillingdon Hall [*1845*]. *Chap. 33*
More people are flattered into virtue
than bullied out of vice.
The Analysis of the Hunting Field
[*1846*]. *Chap. 1*
Better be killed than frightened to
death.
Mr. Facey Romford's Hounds
[*1865*]. *Chap. 32*

EDWARD BULWER LYTTON
[1803–1873]

A good heart is better than all the
heads in the world.
The Disowned [*1828*]. *Chap. 33*
The easiest person to deceive is one's
own self.
Ibid. Chap. 42
The magic of the tongue is the most
dangerous of all spells.
Eugene Aram [*1832*]. *Book I,*
Chap. 7
When stars are in the quiet skies,
Then most I pine for thee;
Bend on me then thy tender eyes,
As stars look on the sea.
Ernest Maltravers [*1837*].
Book III, Chap. 1
Rank is a great beautifier.
The Lady of Lyons [*1838*].
Act II, Sc. 1
Love, like Death,
Levels all ranks, and lays the shep-
herd's crook
Beside the sceptre.
Ibid. Act III, Sc. 2
You speak
As one who fed on poetry.
Richelieu [*1839*]. *Act I, Sc. 1*
The mate for beauty
Should be a man, and not a money-
chest.
Ibid. Sc. 2

Great men gain doubly when they
make foes their friends.
Richelieu. Act I, Sc. 2
Beneath the rule of men entirely great,
The pen is mightier than the sword.[1]
Ibid. Act II, Sc. 2
In the lexicon of youth, which fate re-
serves
For a bright manhood, there is no such
word
As "fail."
Ibid.
To what a reed
We bind our destinies, when man we
love.[2]
The Duchess de la Vallière.
Act III, Sc. 3
What's affection, but the power we
give another to torment us?
Darnley. Act II, Sc. 1
A good cigar is as great a comfort to
a man as a good cry to a woman.
Ibid. Act III, Sc. 2
He who has little silver in his pouch
must have the more silk on his tongue.
The Last of the Barons [*1843*].
Book I, Chap. 3
Out-babying Wordsworth and out-
glittering Keats.[3]
The New Timon [*1846*]. *Part I*
Alone! — that worn-out word,
So idly spoken, and so coldly heard;
Yet all that poets sing and grief hath
known
Of hopes laid waste, knells in that word
ALONE!
Ibid. Part II
That should be a warning to you
never again to fall into the error of
the would-be scholar — namely, quote
second-hand.
My Novel [*1853*]. *Chap. 19*
The worst part of an eminent man's
conversation is, nine times out of ten,

1 See Burton, page 222b.
Eloquence a hundred times has turned the
scale of war and peace at will. — EMERSON:
Progress of Culture [1867]
2 See Pascal, page 272b.
3 Tennyson.

to be found in that part which he means to be clever.

Caxtonia. Differences Between the Urban and Rural Temperament

In science, read, by preference, the newest works; in literature, the oldest. The classic literature is always modern.

Ibid. Hints on Mental Culture

In science, address the few, in literature the many. In science, the few must dictate opinion to the many; in literature, the many, sooner or later, force their judgment on the few.

Ibid. Readers and Writers

BENJAMIN DISRAELI, EARL OF BEACONSFIELD
[1804–1881]

The microcosm of a public school.

Vivian Grey [1826]. Book I, Chap. II

I hate definitions.

Ibid. Book II, Chap. VI

Experience is the child of Thought, and Thought is the child of Action. We can not learn men from books.

Ibid. Book V, Chap I

Variety is the mother of Enjoyment.

Ibid. Chap. IV

There is moderation even in excess.

Ibid. Book VI, Chap. I

I repeat . . . that all power is a trust; that we are accountable for its exercise; that from the people and for the people all springs, and all must exist.[1]

Ibid. Chap. VII

Man is not the creature of circumstances. Circumstances are the creatures of men.[2]

Ibid.

The disappointment of manhood succeeds to the delusion of youth: let us hope that the heritage of old age is not despair.

Ibid. Book VIII, Chap. IV

A dark horse which had never been thought of, and which the careless St.

James had never even observed in the list, rushed past the grand stand in sweeping triumph.

The Young Duke [1831]. Book I, Chap. V

Yes, I am a Jew, and when the ancestors of the right honourable gentleman were brutal savages in an unknown island, mine were priests in the temple of Solomon.[1]

Reply to a taunt by Daniel O'Connell [2]

What we anticipate seldom occurs; [3] what we least expected generally happens.

Henrietta Temple [1837]. Book II, Chap. IV

Nature has given us two ears but only one mouth.

Ibid. Book VI, Chap. XXIV

Though I sit down now, the time will come when you will hear me.[4]

Maiden Speech in the House of Commons [1837]

---

[1] In his *Reminiscences of Sixty Years in the National Metropolis* [1886], BEN PERLEY POORE quotes this reply of Senator Judah P. Benjamin [1811–1884] to a Senator of German extraction who taunted him with being a Jew: "The gentleman will please remember that when his half-civilized ancestors were hunting the wild boar in the forests of Silesia, mine were the Princes of the earth."

[2] Disraeli's name shows he is by descent a Jew. His father became a convert. He is the better for that in this world, and I hope he will be the better for it in the next. I have the happiness of being acquainted with some Jewish families in London, and among them more accomplished ladies, or more humane, cordial, high-minded, or better-educated gentlemen I have never met. It will not be supposed, therefore, that when I speak of Disraeli as the descendant of a Jew, that I mean to tarnish him on that account. They were once the chosen people of God. There were miscreants among them, however, also, and it must certainly have been from one of these that Disraeli descended. He possesses just the qualities of the impenitent thief who died upon the Cross, whose name, I verily believe, must have been Disraeli. — DANIEL O'CONNELL: *Speech,* at trades union meeting in Dublin [1835]

[3] See Emerson, page 507a.

[4] See William Lloyd Garrison, page 517a.

[1] See Webster, page 443b, Lincoln, page 541a, and Parker, page 560a.

[2] See Carlyle, page 473b.

Free trade is not a principle, it is an expedient.[1]

On Import Duties [April 25, 1843]

The noble lord [2] is the Rupert of debate.

Speech [April, 1844]

Youth is a blunder; manhood a struggle; old age a regret.

Coningsby [1844]. Book III, Chap. I

Property has its duties as well as its rights.[3]

Sybil [1845]. Book II, Chap. XI

Little things affect little minds.

Ibid. Book III, Chap. II

We all of us live too much in a circle.[4]

Ibid. Chap. VII

Mr. Kremlin was distinguished for ignorance; for he had only one idea, and that was wrong.[5]

Ibid. Book IV, Chap. V

The right honorable gentleman [6] caught the Whigs bathing and walked away with their clothes.

Speech, House of Commons [February 28, 1845]

A conservative government is an organized hypocrisy.

Speech on Agricultural Interests [March 17, 1845]

He was fresh and full of faith that "something would turn up." [7]

Tancred [1847]. Book III, Chap. VI

Everything comes if a man will only wait.[8]

Ibid. Book IV, Chap. VIII

[1] It is a condition which confronts us, not a theory. — Grover Cleveland: *Annual Message* [1887], referring to the tariff
[2] Lord Stanley.
[3] Property has its duties as well as its rights. — Captain Thomas Drummond (inventor of the Drummond light): *Letter to the Landlords of Tipperary* [May 22, 1838]
[4] The life of man is a self-evolving circle. — Emerson: *Essays, First Series* [1841], *Circles*
[5] See Johnson, page 340b.
[6] Sir Robert Peel.
[7] See Dickens, page 579a.
[8] See Emerson, page 501a.

A precedent embalms a principle.

Speech on the Expenditures of the Country [February 22, 1848]

Justice is truth in action.

Speech [February 11, 1851]

This shows how much easier it is to be critical than to be correct.

Speech [January 24, 1860]

Posterity is a most limited assembly. Those gentlemen who reach posterity are not much more numerous than the planets.

Speech [June 3, 1862]

The characteristic of the present age is craving credulity.

Speech at Oxford Diocesan Conference [November 25, 1864]

Is man an ape or an angel? [1] I, my lord, I am on the side of the angels. I repudiate with indignation and abhorrence those new fangled theories.

Ibid.

In the character of the victim [Lincoln], and even in the accessories of his last moments, there is something so homely and innocent that it takes the question, as it were, out of all the pomp of history and the ceremonial of diplomacy — it touches the heart of nations and appeals to the domestic sentiment of mankind.

Address, House of Commons [May 1, 1865]

Ignorance never settles a question.

Ibid. [May 14, 1866]

Individualities may form communities, but it is institutions alone that can create a nation.

Speech at Manchester [1866]

However gradual may be the growth of confidence, that of credit requires still more time to arrive at maturity.

Speech [November 9, 1867]

The secret of success is constancy to purpose.

Speech [June 24, 1870]

When a man fell into his anecdotage, it was a sign for him to retire.

Lothair [1870]. Chap. XXVIII

[1] See Charles Darwin, page 530b.

Every woman should marry — and no man.
Lothair. Chap. XXX

You know who the critics are? The men who have failed in literature and art.[1]
Ibid. Chap. XXXV

"My idea of an agreeable person," said Hugo Bohun, "is a person who agrees with me."
Ibid.

Increased means and increased leisure are the two civilizers of man.
Speech to the Conservatives of Manchester [April 3, 1872]

A university should be a place of light, of liberty, and of learning.
Speech, House of Commons [March 11, 1873]

The author who speaks about his own books is almost as bad as a mother who talks about her own children.
Speech [November 19, 1873]

The health of the people is really the foundation upon which all their happiness and all their powers as a State depend.
Speech [July 24, 1877]

A sophistical rhetorician [Gladstone], inebriated with the exuberance of his own verbosity, and gifted with an egotistical imagination that can at all times command an interminable and inconsistent series of arguments to malign an opponent and to glorify himself.
Speech at Riding School, London [July 27, 1878]

A series of congratulatory regrets.
Lord Hartington's Resolution on the Berlin Treaty [July 27, 1878]

The hare-brained chatter of irresponsible frivolity.
Speech, Guildhall, London [November 9, 1878]

His Christianity was muscular.
Endymion [1880]. Chap. XIV

The Athanasian Creed is the most splendid ecclesiastical lyric ever poured forth by the genius of man.
Ibid. Chap. LII

[1] See Coleridge, page 423b.

The world is a wheel, and it will all come round right.
Endymion. Chap. LXX

"As for that," said Waldershare, "sensible men are all of the same religion." "And pray, what is that?" inquired the prince. "Sensible men never tell."
Ibid. Chap. LXXXI

NATHANIEL HAWTHORNE
[1804–1864]

Sleeping or waking, we hear not the airy footsteps of the strange things that almost happen.
Twice-Told Tales [1837]. David Swan

The sky, now gloomy as an author's prospects.
Ibid. Sights from a Steeple

Our Creator would never have made such lovely days, and have given us the deep hearts to enjoy them, above and beyond all thought, unless we were meant to be immortal.
Mosses from an Old Manse [1846]. The Old Manse

That lack of energy that distinguishes the occupants of almshouses, and all other human beings who depend for subsistence on charity, on monopolized labor, or anything else, but their own independent exertions.
The Scarlet Letter [1850]. The Custom-House

Human nature will not flourish, any more than a potato, if it be planted and replanted, for too long a series of generations, in the same worn-out soil.
Ibid.

Neither the front nor the back entrance of the Custom-House opens on the road to Paradise.
Ibid.

It is a good lesson — though it may often be a hard one — for a man who has dreamed of literary fame . . . to step aside out of the narrow circle in which his claims are recognized, and to find how utterly devoid of significance,

beyond that circle, is all that he achieves, and all he aims at.
The Scarlet Letter. The Custom-House

The black flower of civilized society, a prison.
Ibid. Chap. 1

On the breast of her gown, in red cloth, surrounded with an elaborate embroidery and fantastic flourishes of gold-thread, appeared the letter A.
Ibid. Chap. 2

It is to the credit of human nature, that, except where its selfishness is brought into play, it loves more readily than it hates.
Ibid. Chap. 13

Let men tremble to win the hand of woman, unless they win along with it the utmost passion of her heart.
Ibid. Chap. 15

No man, for any considerable period, can wear one face to himself, and another to the multitude, without finally getting bewildered as to which may be the true.
Ibid. Chap. 20

Life is made up of marble and mud.
The House of the Seven Gables [1851]. Chap. 2

Providence seldom vouchsafes to mortals any more than just that degree of encouragement which suffices to keep them at a reasonably full exertion of their powers.
Ibid. Chap. 3

A stale article, if you dip it in a good, warm, sunny smile, will go off better than a fresh one that you've scowled upon.
Ibid. Chap. 4

Life, within doors, has few pleasanter prospects than a neatly arranged and well-provisioned breakfast-table.
Ibid. Chap. 7

What other dungeon is so dark as one's own heart! What jailer so inexorable as one's self!
Ibid. Chap. 11

There is no greater bugbear than a strong-willed relative, in the circle of his own connections.
The House of the Seven Gables. Chap. 11

Once in every half-century, at longest, a family should be merged into the great, obscure mass of humanity, and forget all about its ancestors.
Ibid. Chap. 12

The world owes all its onward impulses to men ill at ease. The happy man inevitably confines himself within ancient limits.
Ibid. Chap. 20

Of all the events which constitute a person's biography, there is scarcely one . . . . to which the world so easily reconciles itself as to his death.
Ibid. Chap. 21

A revolution, or anything that interrupts social order, may afford opportunities for the individual display of eminent virtues; but its effects are pernicious to general morality.
The Snow Image [1851]. Old News, Chap. 3

It is a token of healthy and gentle characteristics, when women of high thoughts and accomplishments love to sew; especially as they are never more at home with their own hearts than while so occupied.
The Marble Faun [1860]. Chap. 5

Every young sculptor seems to think that he must give the world some specimen of indecorous womanhood, and call it Eve, Venus, a Nymph, or any name that may apologize for a lack of decent clothing.
Ibid. Chap. 14

This greatest mortal consolation, which we derive from the transitoriness of all things — from the right of saying, in every conjuncture, — "This, too, will pass away." [1]
Ibid. Chap. 16

At no time are people so sedulously careful to keep their trifling appoint-

[1] See Lincoln, page 538b.

ments, attend to their ordinary occupations, and thus put a commonplace aspect on life, as when conscious of some secret that if suspected would make them look monstrous in the general eye.
The Marble Faun. Chap. 20

Nobody, I think, ought to read poetry, or look at pictures or statues, who cannot find a great deal more in them than the poet or artist has actually expressed.[1]
Ibid. Chap. 41

Caskets! — a vile modern phrase, which compels a person of sense and good taste to shrink more disgustfully than ever before from the idea of being buried at all.
Our Old Home [*1863*].
About Warwick

That odd state of mind wherein we fitfully and teasingly remember some previous scene or incident, of which the one now passing appears to be but the echo and reduplication.
Ibid. Near Oxford

Old soldiers, I know not why, seem to be more accostable than old sailors.
Ibid. Up the Thames

It is not the statesman, the warrior, or the monarch that survives, but the despised poet, whom they may have fed with their crumbs, and to whom they owe all that they now are or have — a name.
Ibid.

Mountains are earth's undecaying monuments.
Sketches from Memory [*1868*]. *The Notch of the White Mountains*

THOMAS KIBBLE HERVEY
[1804–1859]

Like ships, that sailed for sunny isles,
But never came to shore.
The Devil's Progress

[1] Every book is written with a constant secret reference to the few intelligent persons whom the writer believes to exist in the million. . . . The artist has always the masters in his eye. — EMERSON: *Progress of Culture* [1867]

SARAH FLOWER ADAMS
[1805–1848]

Though like the wanderer,
  The sun gone down,
Darkness be over me,
  My rest a stone;
Yet in my dreams I'd be
Nearer, my God, to Thee,
  Nearer to Thee.
Nearer, My God, to Thee. Stanza 2

He sendeth sun, he sendeth shower,
Alike they're needful to the flower;
And joys and tears alike are sent
To give the soul fit nourishment.
As comes to me or cloud or sun,
Father! thy will, not mine, be done.
He Sendeth Sun, He Sendeth Shower

Once have a priest for enemy, good bye
To peace.
Vivia Perpetua. Act III, Sc. 2

WILLIAM HARRISON AINSWORTH
[1805–1884]

She must be seen to be appreciated.
Old Saint Paul's [*1841*].
Book I, Chap. 3

ALEXIS DE TOCQUEVILLE
[1805–1859]

I know of no country, indeed, where the love of money has taken stronger hold on the affections of men and where a profounder contempt is expressed for the theory of the permanent equality of property.
Democracy in America.[1] *Part I* [*1835*], *Chap. 3*

Within these limits the power vested in the American courts of justice of pronouncing a statute to be unconstitutional forms one of the most powerful barriers that have ever been devised against the tyranny of political assemblies.
Ibid. Chap. 6

I have never been more struck by the

[1] The Henry Reeve text, as revised by Francis Bowen, corrected and edited by Phillips Bradley [1945].

good sense and the practical judgment of the Americans than in the manner in which they elude the numberless difficulties resulting from their Federal Constitution.

Democracy in America. Part I,
Chap. 8

In this question, therefore, there is no medium between servitude and license; in order to enjoy the inestimable benefits that the liberty of the press ensures, it is necessary to submit to the inevitable evils that it creates.

Ibid. Chap. 9

An American cannot converse, but he can discuss, and his talk falls into a dissertation. He speaks to you as if he was addressing a meeting; and if he should chance to become warm in the discussion, he will say "Gentlemen" to the person with whom he is conversing.

Ibid. Chap. 14

I cannot believe that a republic could hope to exist at the present time if the influence of lawyers in public business did not increase in proportion to the power of the people.

Ibid. Chap. 16

They [the Americans] have all a lively faith in the perfectibility of man, they judge that the diffusion of knowledge must necessarily be advantageous, and the consequences of ignorance fatal; they all consider society as a body in a state of improvement, humanity as a changing scene, in which nothing is, or ought to be, permanent; and they admit that what appears to them today to be good, may be superseded by something better tomorrow.

Ibid. Chap. 18

America is a land of wonders, in which everything is in constant motion and every change seems an improvement. The idea of novelty is there indissolubly connected with the idea of amelioration. No natural boundary seems to be set to the efforts of man; and in his eyes what is not yet done is only what he has not yet attempted to do.

Ibid.

Democratic nations care but little for what has been, but they are haunted by visions of what will be; in this direction their unbounded imagination grows and dilates beyond all measure. . . . Democracy, which shuts the past against the poet, opens the future before him.

Democracy in America. Part II
[1840], First Book, Chap. 17

Thus not only does democracy make every man forget his ancestors, but it hides his descendants and separates his contemporaries from him; it throws him back forever upon himself alone and threatens in the end to confine him entirely within the solitude of his own heart.

Ibid. Second Book, Chap. 2

It is strange to see with what feverish ardor the Americans pursue their own welfare, and to watch the vague dread that constantly torments them lest they should not have chosen the shortest path which may lead to it.

Ibid. Chap. 13

If I were asked . . . to what the singular prosperity and growing strength of that people [the Americans] ought mainly to be attributed, I should reply: To the superiority of their women.

Ibid. Third Book, Chap. 12

The love of wealth is therefore to be traced, as either a principal or accessory motive, at the bottom of all that the Americans do; this gives to all their passions a sort of family likeness. . . . It may be said that it is the vehemence of their desires that makes the Americans so methodical; it perturbs their minds, but it disciplines their lives.

Ibid. Chap. 17

SAMUEL WILBERFORCE [1]
[1805–1873]

If I were a cassowary
On the plains of Timbuctoo,

[1] Bishop of Oxford, and later of Winchester — nicknamed "Soapy Sam."

I would eat a missionary,
  Coat and bands and hymn-book, too.[1]
                              Impromptu

WILLIAM LLOYD GARRISON
[1805–1879]

My country is the world; my countrymen are mankind.[2]
  Prospectus of The Public Liberator
                              [1830]
I am in earnest. I will not equivocate; I will not excuse; I will not retreat a single inch; and I will be heard! [3]
  Salutatory of The Liberator
                  [January 1, 1831]
I will be as harsh as truth and as uncompromising as justice.
  The Liberator. Vol. I, No. 1
                              [1831]
The compact which exists between the North and the South is a covenant with death and an agreement with hell.[4]
  Resolution adopted by the Anti-Slavery Society [January 27, 1843]
With reasonable men, I will reason; with humane men I will plead; but to tyrants I will give no quarter, nor waste arguments where they will certainly be lost.
  W. P. AND F. J. T. GARRISON:
  William Lloyd Garrison [1885–1889]. Vol. I, Page 188
Since the creation of the world there has been no tyrant like Intemperance, and no slaves so cruelly treated as his.
                  Ibid. Page 268
We may be personally defeated, but our principles never.
                  Ibid. Page 402
Wherever there is a human being, I see God-given rights inherent in that being, whatever may be the sex or complexion.
                  Ibid. Vol. III, Page 390

[1] Variant: Skin and bones and hymn-book, too.
[2] See Plutarch, page 61b, and Paine, page 371a.
[3] See Disraeli, page 511b.
[4] We have made a covenant with death, and with hell are we at agreement. — *Isaiah, XXVIII, 15*

The success of any great moral enterprise does not depend upon numbers.
  W. P. AND F. J. T. GARRISON: *William Lloyd Garrison. Vol. III, Page 473*
You can not possibly have a broader basis for any government than that which includes all the people, with all their rights in their hands, and with an equal power to maintain their rights.[1]
  Ibid. Vol. IV, Page 224

WILLIAM PITT PALMER
[1805–1884]

I couldn't stand it, sir, at all,
But up and kissed her on the spot!
I know — boo-hoo — I ought to not,
But, somehow, from her looks — boo-hoo —
I thought she kind o' wished me to!
                  The Smack in School

COLONEL SIDNEY SHERMAN
[1805–1873]

Remember the Alamo!
  Battle Cry, San Jacinto [April 21, 1836]

JOHN STUART MILL
[1806–1873]

The sole end for which mankind are warranted, individually or collectively, in interfering with the liberty of action of any of their number is self-protection.
  Liberty [1859]. Introduction
If all mankind minus one, were of one opinion, and only one person were of the contrary opinion, mankind would be no more justified in silencing that one person, than he, if he had the power, would be justified in silencing mankind.
                  Ibid. Chap. 2
We can never be sure that the opinion we are endeavoring to stifle is a false opinion; and if we were sure, stifling it would be an evil still.
                              Ibid.

[1] See Webster, page 443b, Lincoln, page 541a, and Parker, page 560a.

To question all things; — never to turn away from any difficulty; to accept no doctrine either from ourselves or from other people without a rigid scrutiny by negative criticism; letting no fallacy, or incoherence, or confusion of thought, step by unperceived; above all, to insist upon having the meaning of a word clearly understood before using it, and the meaning of a proposition before assenting to it; — these are the lessons we learn from ancient dialecticians.

> *Inaugural Address as Rector,*
> *University of St. Andrews*
> *[February 1, 1867]*

ELIZABETH BARRETT BROWNING
[1806–1861]

Of all the thoughts of God that are
Borne inward into souls afar,
Along the Psalmist's music deep,
Now tell me if that any is,
For gift or grace, surpassing this:
"He giveth his beloved — sleep." [1]

> *The Sleep* [*1838*]. *Stanza 1*

Thou large-brained woman and large-hearted man.

> *To George Sand, A Desire* [*1844*]

Or from Browning some "Pomegranate," which, if cut deep down the middle,
Shows a heart within blood-tinctured of a veined humanity.

> *Lady Geraldine's Courtship*
> [*1844*]. *Stanza 41*

Poets ever fail in reading their own verses to their worth.

> *Ibid. Stanza 42*

There Shakespeare, on whose forehead climb
The crowns o' the world; O eyes sublime
With tears and laughters for all time!

> *A Vision of Poets* [*1844*].
> *Line 298*

[1] *Psalm CXXVII, 2*

Life treads on life, and heart on heart;
We press too close in church and mart
To keep a dream or grave apart.

> *A Vision of Poets. Conclusion,*
> *Line 820*

Knowledge by suffering entereth,
And life is perfected by death.

> *Ibid. Line 929*

And I smiled to think God's greatness flowed around our incompleteness, —
Round our restlessness, His rest.

> *Rhyme of the Duchess May*
> [*1844*]. *Conclusion, Stanza 11*

Do ye hear the children weeping, O my brothers,
Ere the sorrow comes with years?

> *The Cry of the Children*
> [*1844*]. *Stanza 1*

The child's sob in the silence curses deeper
Than the strong man in his wrath.

> *Ibid. Stanza 13*

I tell you hopeless grief is passionless.

> *Grief* [*1844*]

Therefore to this dog will I,
Tenderly not scornfully,
Render praise and favor:
With my hand upon his head,
Is my benediction said
Therefore and for ever.

> *To Flush, My Dog* [*1844*].
> *Stanza 14*

And lips say "God be pitiful,"
Who ne'er said "God be praised."

> *The Cry of the Human* [*1844*].
> *Stanza 1*

But since he had
The genius to be loved, why let him have
The justice to be honoured in his grave.

> *Crowned and Buried* [*1844*].
> *Stanza 27*

"Yes," I answered you last night;
"No," this morning, sir, I say:
Colors seen by candle-light
Will not look the same by day. [1]

> *The Lady's "Yes"* [*1844*].
> *Stanza 1*

[1] To say why gals acts so or so,
Or don't, 'ould be presumin';

By thunders of white silence, over-
thrown.
Hiram Powers's Greek Slave
[1850]

Unless you can muse in a crowd all day
On the absent face that fixed you;
Unless you can love, as the angels may,
With the breadth of heaven betwixt
you;
Unless you can dream that his faith is
fast,
Through behoving and unbehoving;
Unless you can die when the dream is
past —
Oh, never call it loving!
A Woman's Shortcomings
[1850]. Stanza 5

"Guess now who holds thee?" —
"Death," I said. But there
The silver answer rang, — "Not Death,
but Love."
Sonnets from the Portuguese
[1850]. I

Go from me. Yet I feel that I shall stand
Henceforward in thy shadow.
Ibid. VI

The widest land
Doom takes to part us, leaves thy hand
in mine
With pulses that beat double. What I do
And what I dream include thee, as the
wine
Must taste of its own grapes.
Ibid.

If thou must love me, let it be for
nought
Except for love's sake only.
Ibid. XIV

Mebby to mean *yes* an' say *no*
Comes nateral to women.
JAMES RUSSELL LOWELL: *The Biglow
Papers, Series II* [1867], *St. 18*

You gave me the key to your heart, my
love;
Then why do you make me knock?
"Oh, that was yesterday; Saints above,
Last night I changed the lock!"
JOHN BOYLE O'REILLY [1844–
1890]: *Constancy*

And if I loved you Wednesday,
Well, what is that to you?
I do not love you Thursday —
So much is true.
EDNA ST. VINCENT MILLAY [1892–
1950]: *Thursday*

When our two souls stand up erect and
strong,
Face to face, silent, drawing nigh and
nigher.
Sonnets from the Portuguese. XXII

To drop some golden orb of perfect song
Into our deep, dear silence.
Ibid.

God only, who made us rich, can make
us poor.
Ibid. XXIV

How do I love thee? Let me count the
ways.
Ibid. XLIII

I shall but love thee better after death.
Ibid.

Women know
The way to rear up children (to be
just),
They know a simple, merry, tender
knack
Of tying sashes, fitting baby-shoes,
And stringing pretty words that make
no sense.
Aurora Leigh [1] *[1857]. Book I,
Line 47*

Life, struck sharp on death,
Makes awful lightning.
Ibid. Line 210

The beautiful seems right
By force of Beauty, and the feeble
wrong
Because of weakness.
Ibid. Line 753

As sings the lark when sucked up out
of sight
In vortices of glory and blue air.
Ibid. Line 1055

Men do not think
Of sons and daughters, when they fall
in love.
Ibid. Book II, Line 608

I should not dare to call my soul my
own.
Ibid. Line 786

God answers sharp and sudden on some
prayers,
And thrusts the thing we have prayed
for in our face,
A gauntlet with a gift in 't.
Ibid. Line 952

[1] See Edward Fitzgerald, page 533b.

Every wish
Is like a prayer, with God.[1]
> *Aurora Leigh. Book II, Line 954*

Is the blue in eyes
As awful as in stockings?
> *Ibid. Book III, Line 379*

How many desolate creatures on the earth
Have learnt the simple dues of fellowship
And social comfort, in a hospital.
> *Ibid. Line 1122*

A little sunburnt by the glare of life.
> *Ibid. Book IV, Line 1140*

Let no one till his death
Be called unhappy. Measure not the work
Until the day's out and the labor done.
> *Ibid. Book V, Line 76*

Men get opinions as boys learn to spell,
By reiteration chiefly.
> *Ibid. Book VI, Line 6*

Since when was genius found respectable?
> *Ibid. Line 275*

Earth's crammed with heaven,
And every common bush afire with God;
But only he who sees takes off his shoes —
The rest sit round it and pluck blackberries.
> *Ibid. Book VII, Line 820*

We walked too straight for fortune's end,
We loved too true to keep a friend;
At last we're tired, my heart and I.
> *My Heart and I [1862]. Stanza 2*

Grief may be joy misunderstood;
Only the Good discerns the good.
> *De Profundis [1862]. Stanza 21*

CHARLES FENNO HOFFMAN
[1806–1884]

We were not many — we who stood
Before the iron sleet that day;
Yet many a gallant spirit would

[1] See James Montgomery, page 413a.

Give half his years, if he but could
Have been with us at Monterey.
> *Monterey. Stanza 1*

NATHANIEL PARKER WILLIS
[1806–1867]

The shadows lay along Broadway,
'Twas near the twilight tide.
> *Unseen Spirits. Stanza 1*

The sin forgiven by Christ in Heaven
By man is cursed alway.
> *Ibid. Stanza 5*

CHARLES FRANCIS ADAMS
[1807–1886]

It would be superfluous in me to point
out to your Lordship that this is war.
> *Dispatch to Earl Russell*
> *[September 5, 1863]*

CHARLES JEFFERYS
[1807–1865]

Oh! if I were Queen of France, or still
    better, Pope of Rome,
I'd have no fighting men abroad, no
    weeping maids at home;
All should be at peace; or, if kings must
    show their might,
Why, let them who make the quarrel be
    the only men to fight.
> *Jeannette and Jeannot. Stanza 4*

Were only kings themselves to fight,
    there'd be an end of war.
> *Jeannot's Answer. Stanza 4*

HENRY WADSWORTH LONGFELLOW
[1807–1882]

Music is the universal language of
mankind, — poetry their universal
pastime and delight.
> *Outre-Mer [1833–1834]*

I heard the trailing garments of the
    Night [1]
Sweep through her marble halls.
> *Hymn to Night [1839]. Stanza 1*

Tell me not, in mournful numbers,
    Life is but an empty dream!

[1] See Sarah Whitman, page 509b.

For the soul is dead that slumbers,
  And things are not what they seem.[1]
      A Psalm of Life [*1839*]. *Stanza 1*
Life is real! Life is earnest!
  And the grave is not its goal;
Dust thou art, to dust returnest,
  Was not spoken of the soul.
      Ibid. Stanza 2
Art is long, and Time is fleeting,[2]
  And our hearts, though stout and
    brave,
Still, like muffled drums, are beating
  Funeral marches to the grave.[3]
      Ibid. Stanza 4
Trust no Future, howe'er pleasant!
  Let the dead Past bury its dead!
Act, act in the living present!
  Heart within, and God o'erhead!
      Ibid. Stanza 6
Lives of great men all remind us
  We can make our lives sublime,
And, departing, leave behind us
  Footprints on the sands of time.
      Ibid. Stanza 7
Let us, then, be up and doing,
  With a heart for any fate; [4]
Still achieving, still pursuing,
  Learn to labour and to wait.
      Ibid. Stanza 9
There is a Reaper whose name is
    Death,
  And, with his sickle keen,
He reaps the bearded grain at a breath,
  And the flowers that grow between.
    The Reaper and the Flowers
      [*1839*]. *Stanza 1*
The hooded clouds, like friars,
Tell their beads in drops of rain.
    Midnight Mass for the Dying
      Year [*1839*]. *Stanza 4*
Who ne'er his bread in sorrow ate,
Who ne'er the mournful midnight hours
Weeping upon his bed has sate,
He knows you not, ye Heavenly
  Powers.[5]
    Hyperion [*1839*]. *Book I, Motto*

[1] See Phaedrus, page 48b.
[2] See Hippocrates, page 22a.
[3] Our lives are but our marches to the
grave. — BEAUMONT AND FLETCHER: *The Humorous Lieutenant* [1619], *Act III, Sc. 5*
[4] See Byron, page 456b.
[5] Wer nie sein Brod mit Thränen ass,

Look not mournfully into the Past.
It comes not back again. Wisely improve the Present. It is thine. Go forth
to meet the shadowy Future, without
fear, and with a manly heart.[1]
    Hyperion. Book IV, Chap. 8
It was the schooner Hesperus,
  That sailed the wintry sea;
And the skipper had taken his little
    daughter,
  To bear him company.
    The Wreck of the Hesperus
      [*1842*]. *Stanza 1*
Blue were her eyes as the fairy-flax.
      Ibid. Stanza 2
Christ save us all from a death like this,
On the reef of Norman's Woe!
      Ibid. Stanza 22
Under the spreading chestnut-tree
  The village smithy stands;
The smith a mighty man is he
  With large and sinewy hands.
    The Village Blacksmith [*1842*].
      Stanza 1
His brow is wet with honest sweat,
  He earns whate'er he can,
And looks the whole world in the face,
  For he owes not any man.
      Ibid. Stanza 2
Something attempted, something done,
Has earned a night's repose.
      Ibid. Stanza 7
No one is so accursed by fate,
No one so utterly desolate,
But some heart, though unknown,
Responds unto his own.
    Endymion [*1842*]. *Stanza 8*

Wer nicht die kummervollen Nächte
Auf seinem Bette weinend sass,
Der kennt euch nicht, ihr himmlischen
  Mächte.
    GOETHE: *Wilhelm Meister's Apprenticeship* [1786–1830], *Book
    II, Chap. 13*
[1] Blicke nicht trauernd in die Vergangenheit,
  Sie kommt nicht wieder, nutze weise die
    Gegenwart,
  Sie ist dein, der düsteren Zukunft geh
    ohne
  Furcht mit männliche Sinne entgegen.
    *Inscription on Chapel of St. Gilgen,
      near Salzburg*

Into each life some rain must fall,
Some days must be dark and dreary.
    The Rainy Day [*1842*]. *Stanza 3*
I like that ancient Saxon phrase, which
  calls
The burial-ground God's-Acre!
      God's-Acre [*1842*]. *Stanza 1*
Standing with reluctant feet,
Where the brook and river meet,
Womanhood and childhood fleet!
    Maidenhood [*1842*]. *Stanza 3*
A banner with the strange device,
  Excelsior!
    Excelsior [*1842*]. *Stanza 1*
Stars of the summer night!
  Far in yon azure deeps,
Hide, hide your golden light!
  She sleeps.
    The Spanish Student [*1842*].
      Act I, Sc. 3, Serenade
She floats upon the river of his thoughts.
      Ibid. Act II, Sc. 3
Were half the power, that fills the world
  with terror,
Were half the wealth, bestowed on
  camps and courts,
Given to redeem the human mind from
  error,
There were no need of arsenals or
  forts.
    The Arsenal at Springfield
      [*1845*]. *Stanza 9*
The day is done, and the darkness
  Falls from the wings of Night,
As a feather is wafted downward
  From an eagle in his flight.
    The Day Is Done [*1845*].
      Stanza 1
A feeling of sadness and longing
  That is not akin to pain,
And resembles sorrow only
  As the mist resembles the rain.
    Ibid. Stanza 3
Some simple and heartfelt lay.
    Ibid. Stanza 4
  The bards sublime,
Whose distant footsteps echo
  Through the corridors of Time.
    Ibid. Stanza 5
And the night shall be filled with music,
  And the cares, that infest the day,

Shall fold their tents, like the Arabs,
  And as silently steal away.
    The Day Is Done. Stanza 11
The horologe of Eternity
Sayeth this incessantly, —
  "Forever — never!
  Never — forever!"
    The Old Clock on the Stairs
      [*1845*]. *Stanza 9*
I shot an arrow into the air,
It fell to earth, I knew not where.
    The Arrow and the Song
      [*1845*]. *Stanza 1*
Though the mills of God grind slowly,
  yet they grind exceeding small; [1]
Though with patience He stands wait-
  ing, with exactness grinds He all.
    Retribution
This is the forest primeval. The mur-
  muring pines and the hemlocks.
    Evangeline [*1847*]. *Prelude*
  Alike were they free from
Fear, that reigns with the tyrant, and
  envy, the vice of republics.
    Ibid. Part I, 1
When she had passed, it seemed like
  the ceasing of exquisite music.
    Ibid.
Silently one by one, in the infinite
  meadows of heaven
Blossomed the lovely stars, the forget-
  me-nots of the angels.
    Ibid. 3
Talk not of wasted affection! affection
  never was wasted;
If it enrich not the heart of another, its
  waters, returning
Back to their springs, like the rain, shall
  fill them full of refreshment:
That which the fountain sends forth
  returns again to the fountain.
    Ibid. Part II, 1
  Give what you have. To some one,
it may be better than you dare to think.
    Kavanagh [*1849*]
  Sail on, O Ship of State!
Sail on, O Union, strong and great!
Humanity with all its fears,
With all the hopes of future years,
Is hanging breathless on thy fate!
    The Building of the Ship [*1849*]
  [1] See George Herbert, page 234b.

Our hearts, our hopes, are all with thee,
Our hearts, our hopes, our prayers, our
   tears,
Our faith triumphant o'er our fears,
Are all with thee, — are all with thee!
The Building of the Ship
There is no flock, however watched and
   tended,
   But one dead lamb is there!
There is no fireside, howsoe'er de-
   fended,
   But has one vacant chair!
Resignation [*1849*]. *Stanza 1*
There is no Death! What seems so is
   transition;
   This life of mortal breath
Is but a suburb of the life elysian,
   Whose portal we call Death.
Ibid. Stanza 5
Nothing useless is, or low;
   Each thing in its place is best;
And what seems but idle show
   Strengthens and supports the rest.
The Builders [*1849*]. *Stanza 2*
God sent his Singers upon earth
With songs of sadness and of mirth.
The Singers [*1849*]. *Stanza 1*
But the great Master said, "I see
No best in kind, but in degree;
I gave a various gift to each,
To charm, to strengthen, and to teach."
Ibid. Stanza 6
All your strength is in your union.
All your danger is in discord;
Therefore be at peace henceforward,
And as brothers live together.
The Song of Hiawatha
[*1855*]. *Part I*
By the shore of Gitche Gumee,
By the shining Big-Sea-Water,
Stood the wigwam of Nokomis,
Daughter of the Moon, Nokomis.
Ibid. Part III
From the waterfall he named her,
Minnehaha, Laughing Water.
Ibid. Part IV
As unto the bow the cord is,
So unto the man is woman,
Though she bends him, she obeys him,
Though she draws him, yet she follows,
Useless each without the other!
Ibid. Part X

If we could read the secret history
of our enemies, we should find in each
man's life sorrow and suffering enough
to disarm all hostility.
Driftwood [*1857*]
If I am not worth the wooing, I
surely am not worth the winning.
The Courtship of Miles Standish
[*1858*]. *Part III*
"Why don't you speak for yourself,
John?"
Ibid.
God had sifted three kingdoms to find
the wheat for this planting.
Ibid. Part IV
Saint Augustine! well hast thou said,
That of our vices we can frame
A ladder, if we will but tread
Beneath our feet each deed of shame.[1]
The Ladder of Saint Augustine
[*1858*]. *Stanza 1*
The heights by great men reached and
   kept
Were not attained by sudden flight,
But they, while their companions slept,
Were toiling upward in the night.
Ibid. Stanza 10
All houses wherein men have lived and
   died
Are haunted houses.
Haunted Houses [*1858*]. *Stanza 1*
The long mysterious Exodus of death.
The Jewish Cemetery at Newport
[*1858*]. *Stanza 1*
Pride and humiliation hand in hand
Walked with them through the world
   where'er they went;
Trampled and beaten were they as the
   sand,
And yet unshaken as the continent.
Ibid. Stanza 12
A boy's will is the wind's will,
And the thoughts of youth are long,
   long thoughts.
My Lost Youth [*1858*]. *Stanza 1*
Spanish sailors with bearded lips,
And the beauty and mystery of the
   ships,
And the magic of the sea.
Ibid. Stanza 3

[1] See Tennyson, page 551b.

A Lady with a Lamp [1] shall stand
In the great history of the land,
A noble type of good,
Heroic womanhood.
　　　Santa Filomena [*1858*]. *Stanza 10*
Ye are better than all the ballads
　That ever were sung or said;
For ye are living poems,
　And all the rest are dead.
　　　　　　Children [*1858*]. *Stanza 9*
Between the dark and the daylight,
　When the night is beginning to lower,
Comes a pause in the day's occupations,
　That is known as the Children's
　　Hour.
　　　The Children's Hour [*1860*].
　　　　　　　　　　Stanza 1
I hear in the chamber above me
The patter of little feet.
　　　　　　　Ibid. Stanza 2
Grave Alice, and laughing Allegra,
And Edith with golden hair.
　　　　　　　Ibid. Stanza 3
Listen, my children, and you shall hear,
Of the midnight ride of Paul Revere,
On the eighteenth of April, in Seventy-
　five;
Hardly a man is now alive
Who remembers that famous day and
　year.
　　　Tales of a Wayside Inn [*1863–*
　　　1874]. *Paul Revere's Ride,*
　　　Stanza 1
One if by land, and two if by sea;
And I on the opposite shore will be,
Ready to ride and spread the alarm
Through every Middlesex village and
　farm.
　　　　　　　Ibid. Stanza 2
The fate of a nation was riding that
　night.
　　　　　　　Ibid. Stanza 8
A voice in the darkness, a knock at the
　door,
And a word that shall echo forever-
　more!
　　　　　　　Ibid. Stanza 14
A town that boasts inhabitants like me
Can have no lack of good society.
　　Ibid. The Birds of Killingworth,
　　　　　　　　　　Stanza 6

[1] Florence Nightingale [1820–1910].

His form was ponderous, and his step
　was slow;
There never was so wise a man before;
He seemed the incarnate "Well, I told
　you so!"
　　Tales of a Wayside Inn. The Birds
　　　　of Killingworth, Stanza 9
How can I tell the signals and the signs
By which one heart another heart di-
　vines?
How can I tell the many thousand ways
By which it keeps the secret it betrays?
　　Ibid. Emma and Eginhard, Stanza 8
Ships that pass in the night, and speak
　each other in passing,
Only a signal shown and a distant voice
　in the darkness;
So on the ocean of life we pass and
　speak one another, [1]
Only a look and a voice; then darkness
　again and a silence.
　　　　　　Ibid. Elizabeth, IV
Time has laid his hand
Upon my heart, gently, not smiting it,
But as a harper lays his open palm
Upon his harp to deaden its vibrations.
　　　The Golden Legend [*1872*].
　　　　　IV, The Cloisters
The grave itself is but a covered bridge
Leading from light to light, through a
　brief darkness. [2]
　　　Ibid. V, A Covered Bridge at
　　　　　　　　　　Lucerne
Don't cross the bridge till you come
　to it,
Is a proverb old, and of excellent wit.
　　　Ibid. VI, The School of Salerno

[1] And soon, too soon, we part with pain,
　To sail o'er silent seas again.
　　THOMAS MOORE [1779–1852]: *Meet-*
　　　ing of the Ships
Two lives that once part are as ships that
divide. — EDWARD BULWER LYTTON [1805–
1873]: *A Lament*
　As vessels starting from ports thousands of
miles apart pass close to each other in the
naked breadths of the ocean, nay, sometimes
even touch in the dark. — HOLMES: *Professor
at the Breakfast Table* [1860]
[2] Death seems but a covered way
　Which opens into light.
　　WHITTIER [1807–1892]: *My
　　　Psalm, St. 14*

"O Caesar, we who are about to die
Salute you!" was the gladiators' cry
In the arena, standing face to face
With death and with the Roman popu-
lace.
  Morituri Salutamus [*1875*].
                            Stanza 1

Let him not boast who puts his armor on
As he who puts it off, the battle done.
                    Ibid. Stanza 9

Better like Hector in the field to die,
Than like a perfumed Paris turn and
  fly.
                    Ibid. Stanza 10

Ye, against whose familiar names not
  yet
The fatal asterisk of death is set.
                    Ibid. Stanza 11

The love of learning, the sequestered
  nooks,
And all the sweet serenity of books.
                    Ibid. Stanza 21

        Ah, nothing is too late,
Till the tired heart shall cease to palpi-
  tate.
Cato learned Greek at eighty; Sophocles
Wrote his grand Oedipus, and Simonides
Bore off the prize of verse from his
  compeers,
When each had numbered more than
  fourscore years.
                    Ibid. Stanza 22

For age is opportunity no less
Than youth itself, though in another
  dress,
And as the evening twilight fades away
The sky is filled with stars, invisible
  by day.
                    Ibid. Stanza 24

So when a great man dies,
For years beyond our ken,
The light he leaves behind him lies
Upon the paths of men.
    From Collections [*1875–1882*].
        Charles Sumner, Stanza 9

Sweet the memory is to me
Of a land beyond the sea,
Where the waves and mountains meet,

Where, amid her mulberry-trees
Sits Amalfi in the heat.
    From Collections. Amalfi, Stanza 1

The birds, God's poor who cannot wait.
    Ibid. The Sermon of St. Francis,
                            Stanza 3

She knew the life-long martyrdom,
  The weariness, the endless pain
Of waiting for some one to come
  Who nevermore would come again.
    Ibid. Vittoria Colonna, Stanza 6

Stay, stay at home, my heart, and rest;
Home-keeping hearts are happiest.
            Ibid. Song, Stanza 1

So Nature deals with us, and takes
  away
Our playthings one by one, and by the
  hand
Leads us to rest.
                    Ibid. Nature

Not in the clamor of the crowded street,
Not in the shouts and plaudits of the
  throng,
But in ourselves, are triumph and defeat.
                Ibid. The Poets

Nothing that is can pause or stay;
The moon will wax, the moon will wane,
The mist and cloud will turn to rain,
The rain to mist and cloud again,
  Tomorrow be today.
                Kéramos [*1878*]

Turn, turn, my wheel! 'Tis nature's
  plan
The child should grow into the man.
                            Ibid.

The willow pattern, that we knew
In childhood, with its bridge of blue.
                            Ibid.

Three Silences there are: the first of
  speech,
The second of desire, the third of
  thought;
This is the lore a Spanish monk, dis-
  traught
With dreams and visions, was the first
  to teach.
    The Three Silences of Molinos [1]

[1] Miguel Molinos [1640–1696], Spanish
mystic, one of the early Quietists.

In the long, sleepless watches of the
　night.
　　　　The Cross of Snow [*1879*]
The holiest of all holidays are those
Kept by ourselves in silence and apart;
The secret anniversaries of the heart.
　　　　　　　　　　　Holidays
Your silent tents of green [1]
　We deck with fragrant flowers;
Yours has the suffering been,
　The memory shall be ours.
　　　　　Decoration Day. Stanza 6
Great is the art of beginning, but greater
　the art is of ending;
Many a poem is marred by a super-
　fluous verse.
　　　　　Elegiac Verse. Stanza 14
Out of the shadows of night
The world rolls into light;
It is daybreak everywhere.
　　　The Bells of San Blas.[2] *Stanza 11*
There was a little girl
Who had a little curl
Right in the middle of her forehead;
　And when she was good
　She was very, very good,
But when she was bad she was horrid.
　　　　　There Was a Little Girl [3]

ROBERT MONTGOMERY
[1807–1855]

The soul aspiring pants its source to
　mount,
As streams meander level with their
　fount.[4]
　　　The Omnipresence of the Deity
　　　　　　　　　[*1828*]. *Part I*

[1]　　The low green tent
Whose curtain never outward swings.
　　　　WHITTIER: *Snow-Bound* [1866]
[2] The last poem written by Longfellow,
dated March 15, 1882. He died March 24.
[3] BLANCHE ROOSEVELT TUCKER, in *The
Home Life of Henry W. Longfellow* [1882],
states that these lines were written by the poet
for his children on a day when Edith did not
want to have her hair curled.
[4] We take this to be, on the whole, the
worst similitude in the world. In the first
place, no stream meanders or can possibly
meander level with the fount. In the next
place, if streams did meander level with their
founts, no two motions can be less like each
other than that of meandering level and that

RICHARD CHENEVIX
TRENCH
[1807–1886]

True servant's title he may wear,
　He only who has not
For his lord's gifts, how rich soe'er,
　His lord himself forgot.
　　　　　The Spilt Pearls. Stanza 8
Lord, what a change within us one
　short hour
Spent in Thy presence will prevail to
　make!
　　　　　　　　　　　Prayer
We kneel, how weak! we rise, how full
　of power!
　　　　　　　　　　　Ibid.
Make channels for the stream of love
Where they may broadly run,
And love has overflowing streams
To fill them every one.
　　　　　　The Law of Love

JOHN GREENLEAF
WHITTIER
[1807–1892]

The Present, the Present is all thou hast
　For thy sure possessing;
Like the patriarch's angel hold it fast
　Till it gives its blessing.[1]
　　　　My Soul and I. Stanza 34
The Night is mother of the Day,
　The Winter of the Spring,
And ever upon old Decay
　The greenest mosses cling.
　　　A Dream of Summer. Stanza 4
Art's perfect forms no moral need,
　And beauty is its own excuse;[2]
But for the dull and flowerless weed
Some healing virtue still must plead.
　　　　　Songs of Labor [*1850*].
　　　　　Dedication, Stanza 5
Heap high the farmer's wintry hoard!
Heap high the golden corn!

of mounting upwards. — MACAULAY: *Review
of Montgomery's Poems* [1830]
　These lines were omitted in the subsequent
edition of the poem.
[1] See Cotton, page 330a.
[2] In a footnote, Whittier acknowledges his
indebtedness for this line to EMERSON'S *The
Rhodora.* See Emerson, page 503b.

No richer gift has Autumn poured
From out her lavish horn!
The Corn-Song. Stanza 1

What calls back the past, like the rich
pumpkin pie?
The Pumpkin. Stanza 3

The tissue of the Life to be
  We weave with colors all our own,
And in the field of Destiny
  We reap as we have sown.
Raphael. Stanza 16

So fallen! so lost! the light withdrawn
  Which once he wore!
The glory from his gray hairs gone
  Forevermore!
Ichabod [1] *[1850]. Stanza 1*

From those great eyes
  The soul has fled:
When faith is lost, when honor dies,
  The man is dead!
Ibid. Stanza 8

Yet sometimes glimpses on my sight,
Through present wrong the eternal
  right;
And, step by step, since time began,
I see the steady gain of man.
The Chapel of the Hermits
[1853]. Stanza 11

Search thine own heart. What paineth
  thee
In others in thyself may be.
Ibid. Stanza 85

Blessings on thee, little man,
Barefoot boy, with cheek of tan!
The Barefoot Boy [1856].
Stanza 1

Health that mocks the doctor's rules,
Knowledge never learned of schools.
Ibid. Stanza 2

The age is dull and mean. Men creep,
Not walk.
Lines Inscribed to Friends under
Arrest for Treason Against the
Slave Power [1856]. Stanza 1

[1] This poem was the outcome of the surprise and grief and forecast of evil consequences which I felt on reading the seventh of March speech of Daniel Webster in support of the "compromise," and the Fugitive Slave Law. — WHITTIER'S *Note*

God's ways seem dark, but, soon or
  late,
They touch the shining hills of day.
Lines Inscribed to Friends under
Arrest for Treason Against the
Slave Power. Stanza 5

Nature speaks in symbols and in signs.
To Charles Sumner

Tradition wears a snowy beard, romance is always young.
Mary Garvin. Stanza 4

Better heresy of doctrine, than heresy
  of heart.
Ibid. Stanza 22

For of all sad words of tongue or pen,
The saddest are these: "It might have
  been!"
Maud Muller [1856]. Stanza 53

Old Floyd Ireson, for his hard heart,
Tarred and feathered and carried in a
  cart
By the women of Marblehead.
Skipper Ireson's Ride
[1860]. Stanza 1

Round the silver domes of Lucknow,
  Moslem mosque and Pagan shrine,
Breathed the air to Britons dearest,
  The air of Auld Lang Syne.[1]
The Pipes at Lucknow. Stanza 9

The windows of my soul I throw
Wide open to the sun.
My Psalm. Stanza 2

No longer forward nor behind
  I look in hope or fear;
But, grateful, take the good I find,
  The best of now and here.
Ibid. Stanza 3

Perish with him the folly that seeks
  through evil good.
Brown of Ossawatomie. Stanza 6

"Shoot, if you must, this old gray head,
But spare your country's flag," she said.
Barbara Frietchie [1864].
Stanza 18

A shade of sadness, a blush of shame,
Over the face of the leader came.
Ibid. Stanza 19

[1] It was the pipes of the Highlanders,
And now they played "Auld Lang Syne."
ROBERT TRAILL SPENCE LOWELL
[1816-1891]: *The Relief of Lucknow, September 25, 1857*

"Who touches a hair of yon gray head
Dies like a dog! March on!" he said.
　　　Barbara Frietchie. Stanza 21
Shut in from all the world without,
We sat the clean-winged hearth about.
　　　　Snow-Bound [*1866*]
Melt not in an acid sect
The Christian pearl of charity.
　　　　　　　　Ibid.
Angel of the backward look.
　　　　　　　　Ibid.
Life is ever lord of Death
And Love can never lose its own.
　　　　　　　　Ibid.
To eat the lotus of the Nile
And drink the poppies of Cathay.
　　　The Tent on the Beach
　　　　　[*1867*]. *Stanza 4*
And so beside the Silent Sea
I wait the muffled oar.
　　　The Eternal Goodness
　　　　[*1867*]. *Stanza 19*
I know not where His islands lift
　Their fronded palms in air;
I only know I cannot drift
　Beyond His love and care.
　　　　Ibid. Stanza 20
Flowers spring to blossom where she
　walks
The careful ways of duty;
Our hard, stiff lines of life with her
Are flowing curves of beauty.[1]
　　　Among the Hills [*1869*].
　　　　　　　Stanza 52
If woman lost us Eden, such
As she alone restore it.
　　　　Ibid. Stanza 60
Sweeter than any sung
My songs that found no tongue;
Nobler than any fact
My wish that failed of act.
　　　My Triumph. Stanza 9
Others shall sing the song,
Others shall right the wrong, —
Finish what I begin,
And all I fail of win.
　　　　Ibid. Stanza 10

[1] Straight is the line of Duty,
　Curved is the line of Beauty,
　Follow the straight line, thou shalt see
　The curved line ever follow thee.
　　WILLIAM MACCALL [1812–1888]: *Duty*

Dear Lord and Father of mankind,
　Forgive our foolish ways!
Reclothe us in our rightful mind,
In purer lives Thy service find,
　In deeper reverence, praise.
　　The Brewing of Soma [*1872*]
God is and all is well.[1]
　　　　My Birthday. Stanza 2
He brings cool dew in his little bill,
　And lets it fall on the souls of sin:
You can see the mark on his red breast
　still
　Of fires that scorch as he drops it in.[2]
　　　　The Robin. Stanza 4

SALMON PORTLAND CHASE
[1808–1873]

The Constitution, in all its provisions, looks to an indestructible Union composed of indestructible States.
　　　Decision in Texas v. *White,*
　　　　7 Wallace 725 [*1868*]

The only way to resumption is to resume.
　　　Letter to Horace Greeley
　　　　　[*March 17, 1866*]

[1] See Browning, page 567a.
[2] Far, far away, is a land of woe and darkness, spirits of evil and fire. Day after day a little bird flies there, bearing in his bill a drop of water to quench the flame. So near the burning stream does he fly that his feathers are scorched by it, and hence he is named "Bron-rhuddyn" — breast-burned. — *Carmarthenshire Legend of the Robin*
　Sweet Robin, I have heard them say
　That thou wert there upon the day
　That Christ was crowned in cruel scorn,
　And bore away one bleeding thorn;
　That so the blush upon thy breast
　In shameful sorrow was imprest,
　And thence thy genial sympathy
　With our redeemed humanity.
　　WILLIAM CROSWELL DOANE [1832–1913]: *Robin Redbreast*
　When Christ was taken from the rood,
　　One thorn upon the ground,
　Still moistened with the Precious Blood,
　　An early robin found,
　And wove it crosswise in his nest,
　Where, lo, it reddened all his breast!
　　JOHN BANISTER TABB [1845–1909]:
　　　　　Robin Redbreast

FRANCES DANA GAGE
[1808–1884]

The home we first knew on this beautiful earth,
The friends of our childhood, the place of our birth,
In the heart's inner chamber sung always will be,
As the shell ever sings of its home in the sea! [1]

Home

MAURICE DE MACMAHON
[1808–1893]

Here I am, and here I stay. [2]
At Sevastopol [September, 1855]

ANDREW JOHNSON
[1808–1875]

We are swinging round the circle.
On the Presidential Reconstruction Tour [August, 1866]

THOMAS MILLER
[1808–1874]

What though upon his hoary head
Have fallen many a winter's snow?
His wreath is still as green and red
As 'twas a thousand years ago.
For what has he to do with care!
His wassail-bowl and old arm-chair
Are ever standing ready there,
For Christmas comes but once a year.

Christmas Comes but Once a Year

---

[1] As a sea-shell of the sea
Ever shall I sing of thee.
GEORGE MEREDITH [1828–1909]:
Love Within the Lover's Breast
Gather a shell from the strown beach
And listen at its lips: they sigh
The same desire and mystery,
The echo of the whole sea's speech.
DANTE GABRIEL ROSSETTI [1828–1882]: *The Sea Limits*, St. 4
See Wordsworth, page 411a.

[2] J'y suis, j'y reste. Reply to the Commander-in-Chief, from the trenches before Malakoff, in the siege of Sevastopol, when warned to beware of an explosion which might follow the retreat of the Russians.

CAROLINE ELIZABETH SHERIDAN NORTON, LADY MAXWELL
[1808–1877]

Love not! love not! ye hapless sons of clay;
Hope's gayest wreaths are made of earthly flowers —
Things that are made to fade and fall away,
Ere they have blossomed for a few short hours.

Love Not

A soldier of the Legion lay dying in Algiers;
There was lack of woman's nursing, there was dearth of woman's tears.

Bingen on the Rhine. Stanza 1

GEORGE WASHINGTON PATTEN
[1808–1882]

Keep honor, like your sabre, bright,
Shame coward fear — and then,
If we must perish in the fight,
Oh! let us die like men.

Oh! Let Us Die Like Men. Stanza 4

Joys that we've tasted
May sometimes return,
But the torch when once wasted,
Ah! how can it burn?

Joys That We've Tasted. Stanza 1

SAMUEL FRANCIS SMITH
[1808–1895]

My country, 'tis of thee,
Sweet land of liberty,
Of thee I sing:
Land where my fathers died,
Land of the pilgrims' pride,
From every mountain-side
Let freedom ring.

America [1831]

Our fathers' God, to thee,
Author of liberty,
To thee I sing;
Long may our land be bright
With freedom's holy light;

Protect us by thy might,
Great God, our King!
America

CHARLES ROBERT DARWIN
[1809–1882]

I have called this principle, by which each slight variation, if useful, is preserved, by the term Natural Selection.
The Origin of Species
[1859]. Chap. 3
The expression often used by Mr. Herbert Spencer, of the Survival of the Fittest, is more accurate, and is sometimes equally convenient.[1]
Ibid.
We will now discuss in a little more detail the Struggle for Existence.[2]
Ibid.
Even when we are quite alone, how often do we think with pleasure or pain of what others think of us — of their imagined approbation or disapprobation.
The Descent of Man
[1871]. Chap. 4
The highest possible stage in moral culture is when we recognize that we ought to control our thoughts.
Ibid.
The presence of a body of well-instructed men, who have not to labor for their daily bread, is important to a degree which cannot be overestimated; as all high intellectual work is carried on by them, and on such work material progress of all kinds mainly depends, not to mention other and higher advantages.
Ibid. Chap. 5
Progress has been much more general than retrogression.
Ibid.

[1] This survival of the fittest which I have here sought to express in mechanical terms, is that which Mr. Darwin has called "natural selection, or the preservation of favoured races in the struggle for life." — HERBERT SPENCER: *Principles of Biology* [1864–1867], *Indirect Equilibration*
[2] The perpetual struggle for room and food. — MALTHUS: *On Population* [1798], *Chap. III*

The Simiadae then branched off into two great stems, the New World and Old World monkeys; and from the latter at a remote period, Man, the wonder and the glory of the universe, proceeded.[1]
The Descent of Man. Chap. 6
False facts are highly injurious to the progress of science, for they often endure long; but false views, if supported by some evidence, do little harm, for every one takes a salutary pleasure in proving their falseness.
Ibid. Chap. 21
Physiological experiment on animals is justifiable for real investigation, but not for mere damnable and detestable curiosity.[2]
Letter to E. Ray Lankester
I love fools' experiments. I am always making them.
Remark cited in Life of Darwin
As for a future life, every man must judge for himself between conflicting vague probabilities.
Life and Letters, Edited by
FRANCIS DARWIN [1887]
Believing as I do that man in the distant future will be a far more perfect creature than he now is, it is an intolerable thought that he and all other sentient beings are doomed to

[1] I confess freely to you, I could never look long upon a monkey, without very mortifying reflections. — CONGREVE: *Letter to Dennis* [1695]
Pouter, tumbler and fantail are from the same source;
The racer and hack may be traced to one horse;
So men were developed from monkeys, of course,
Which nobody can deny.
LORD CHARLES NEAVES [1800–1876]: *The Origin of Species*
See Benjamin Disraeli, page 512b.
[2] The main cause of this unparalleled progress in physiology, pathology, medicine and surgery has been the fruitful application of the experimental method of research, just the same method which has been the great lever of all scientific advance in modern times. — DR. WILLIAM H. WELCH [1850–1934]: *Argument against Antivivisection Bill* (Senate No. 34), Fifty-sixth Congress, First Session [February 21, 1900]

complete annihilation after such long-continued slow progress. To those who fully admit the immortality of the human soul, the destruction of our world will not appear so dreadful.

Life and Letters, Edited by
FRANCIS DARWIN

EDWARD FITZGERALD
[1809–1883]

Wake! For the Sun who scatter'd into flight
The Stars before him from the Field of night,
  Drives Night along with them from Heav'n and strikes
The Sultan's Turret with a Shaft of Light.

The Rubáiyát of Omar Khayyám.[1] Stanza 1

Awake! for Morning in the Bowl of Night
Has flung the Stone that puts the Stars to flight:
  And Lo! the Hunter of the East has caught
The Sultan's Turret in a Noose of Light.

Ibid. Stanza 1, First Edition

Now the New Year reviving old Desires,
The thoughtful Soul to Solitude retires.

Ibid. Stanza 4

Iram indeed is gone with all his Rose.

Ibid. Stanza 5

Come, fill the Cup, and in the fire of Spring
Your Winter-garment of Repentance fling:
  The Bird of Time has but a little way
To flutter — and the Bird is on the Wing.

Ibid. Stanza 7

The Leaves of Life keep falling one by one.

Ibid. Stanza 8

Each Morn a thousand Roses brings, you say:

[1] Translated in four editions, 1859, 1868, 1872, and 1879. The fourth edition is used here, unless otherwise stated.

Yes, but where leaves the Rose of Yesterday?

The Rubáiyát of Omar Khayyám.
Stanza 9

A Book of Verses underneath the Bough,
A Jug of Wine, a Loaf of Bread — and Thou
  Beside me singing in the Wilderness —
Oh, Wilderness were Paradise enow!

Ibid. Stanza 12

Ah, take the Cash, and let the Credit go,
Nor heed the rumble of a distant Drum!

Ibid. Stanza 13

The Worldly Hope men set their Hearts upon
Turns Ashes — or it prospers; and anon,
  Like Snow upon the Desert's dusty Face,
Lighting a little hour or two — is gone.

Ibid. Stanza 16

Think, in this batter'd Caravanserai
Whose Portals are alternate Night and Day,
  How Sultan after Sultan with his Pomp
Abode his destin'd Hour, and went his way.

Ibid. Stanza 17

They say the Lion and the Lizard keep
The Courts where Jamshyd gloried and drank deep:
  And Bahram, that great Hunter — the Wild Ass
Stamps o'er his Head, but cannot break his sleep.

Ibid. Stanza 18

I sometimes think that never blows so red
The Rose as where some buried Caesar bled;
  That every Hyacinth the Garden wears
Dropt in her Lap from some once lovely Head.[1]

Ibid. Stanza 19

Ah, my Belovèd, fill the Cup that clears

[1] See Shakespeare, page 179a, and Tennyson, page 551b.

TODAY of past Regrets and future
Fears:
Tomorrow! — Why, Tomorrow I
may be
Myself with Yesterday's Sev'n thou-
sand Years.
The Rubáiyát of Omar Khayyám.
Stanza 21

For some we loved, the loveliest and the
best
That from his Vintage rolling Time
hath prest.
Ibid. Stanza 22

Ah, make the most of what we yet may
spend,
Before we too into the Dust descend;
Dust into Dust, and under Dust, to
lie,
Sans Wine, sans Song, sans Singer, and
— sans End!
Ibid. Stanza 24

Myself when young did eagerly fre-
quent
Doctor and Saint, and heard great argu-
ment
About it and about: but evermore
Came out by the same door where in I
went.
Ibid. Stanza 27

And this was all the Harvest that I
reap'd —
"I came like Water, and like Wind I
go."
Ibid. Stanza 28

There was the Door to which I found no
Key;
There was the Veil through which I
might not see.
Some little talk awhile of ME and
THEE
There was — and then no more of
THEE and ME.
Ibid. Stanza 32

"While you live,
Drink! — for, once dead, you never
shall return."
Ibid. Stanza 35

Tomorrow's tangle to the winds resign.
Ibid. Stanza 41

So when that Angel of the darker Drink
At last shall find you by the river-brink,

And, offering his Cup, invite your
Soul
Forth to your Lips to quaff — you shall
not shrink.
The Rubáiyát of Omar Khayyám.
Stanza 43

And fear not lest Existence closing your
Account, and mine, should know the
like no more;
The Eternal Sákí from that Bowl
has pour'd
Millions of Bubbles like us, and will
pour.[1]
Ibid. Stanza 46

A Hair perhaps divides the False and
True.
Ibid. Stanza 49

Waste not your Hour, nor in the vain
pursuit
Of This and That endeavour and dispute.
Ibid. Stanza 54

Striking from the Calendar
Unborn Tomorrow and dead Yester-
day.
Ibid. Stanza 57

The Grape that can with Logic absolute
The Two-and-Seventy jarring Sects
confute.
Ibid. Stanza 59

The Flower that once has blown for
ever dies.
Ibid. Stanza 63

Strange, is it not? that of the myriads
who
Before us pass'd the door of Darkness
through,
Not one returns to tell us of the Road,
Which to discover we must travel too.
Ibid. Stanza 64

I sent my Soul through the Invisible,
Some letter of that After-life to spell:
And by and by my Soul return'd to
me,
And answer'd "I Myself am Heav'n and
Hell."[2]
Ibid. Stanza 66

[1] See Tennyson, page 546b.
[2] See Milton, page 252b.

Heav'n but the Vision of fulfill'd Desire,
And Hell the Shadow from a Soul on
fire.
The Rubáiyát of Omar Khayyám.
Stanza 67

We are no other than a moving row
Of Magic Shadow-shapes that come
and go.
Ibid. Stanza 68

This Chequer-board of Nights and
Days.
Ibid. Stanza 69

The Moving Finger writes; and, having
writ,
Moves on: nor all your Piety nor Wit
Shall lure it back to cancel half a
Line,
Nor all your Tears wash out a Word
of it.
Ibid. Stanza 71

That inverted Bowl they call the Sky,
Whereunder crawling coop'd we live
and die.
Ibid. Stanza 72

And this I know: whether the one True
Light
Kindle to Love, or Wrath-consume me
quite,
One Flash of It within the Tavern
caught
Better than in the Temple lost outright.
Ibid. Stanza 77

"And He that with his hand the Vessel
made
Will surely not in after Wrath destroy."
Ibid. Stanza 85

Indeed the Idols I have loved so long
Have done my credit in this World
much wrong:
Have drown'd my Glory in a shallow
Cup,
And sold my Reputation for a Song.
Ibid. Stanza 93

I wonder often what the Vintners buy
One half so precious as the stuff they
sell.
Ibid. Stanza 95

Yet Ah, that Spring should vanish with
the Rose!

That Youth's sweet-scented manuscript
should close!
The Rubáiyát of Omar Khayyám.
Stanza 96

Ah Love! could you and I with Him
conspire
To grasp this Sorry Scheme of Things
entire,
Would not we shatter it to bits —
and then
Remould it nearer to the Heart's Desire!
Ibid. Stanza 99

Yon rising Moon that looks for us
again —
How oft hereafter will she wax and
wane;
How oft hereafter rising look for us
Through this same Garden — and for
one in vain!
Ibid. Stanza 100

And when like her, O Sákí, you shall
pass
Among the Guests Star-scatter'd on the
Grass,
And in your joyous errand reach the
spot
Where I made One — turn down an
empty Glass!
Ibid. Stanza 101

The King in a carriage may ride,
And the Beggar may crawl at his side;
But in the general race,
They are traveling all the same pace.
Chronomoros

Mrs. Browning's death was rather a
relief to me, I must say; no more Aurora Leighs, thank God!
Letter [July 15, 1861] [1]

Taste is the feminine of genius.
Letter to James Russell Lowell
[October, 1877]

[1] Aye, dead! and were yourself alive, good
Fitz,
How to return your thanks would pass
my wits.
Kicking you seems the common lot of
curs,
While more appropriate greeting lends you
grace.
Surely to spit there glorifies your face,
Spitting with lips once sanctified by hers.
ROBERT BROWNING in *The Athe-
naeum* [July 13, 1889]

WILLIAM EWART GLADSTONE
[1809–1898]

To be engaged in opposing wrong affords, under the conditions of our mental constitution, but a slender guarantee for being right.
> *Time and Place of Homer* [*1858*]. *Introduction*

Decision by majorities is as much an expedient as lighting by gas.
> *Speech, House of Commons* [*1858*]

The disease of an evil conscience is beyond the practice of all the physicians of all the countries in the world.
> *Speech, Plumstead* [*1878*]

National injustice is the surest road to national downfall.
> *Ibid.*

All the world over, I will back the masses against the classes.
> *Speech, Liverpool* [*June 28, 1886*]

I have always regarded that Constitution as the most remarkable work known to me in modern times to have been produced by the human intellect, at a single stroke (so to speak), in its application to political affairs.[1]
> *Letter to the committee in charge of the celebration of the Centennial Anniversary of the American Constitution* [*July 20, 1887*]

Selfishness is the greatest curse of the human race.
> *Speech, Hawarden* [*May 28, 1890*]

OLIVER WENDELL HOLMES [2]
[1809–1894]

Ay, tear her tattered ensign down!
Long has it waved on high,

And many an eye has danced to see
That banner in the sky.
> *Old Ironsides* [*1830*]. *Stanza 1*

Nail to the mast her holy flag,
Set every threadbare sail,
And give her to the god of storms,
The lightning and the gale!
> *Ibid. Stanza 3*

Thou say'st an undisputed thing
In such a solemn way.
> *To an Insect. Stanza 7*

One sad, ungathered rose
On my ancestral tree.
> *My Aunt. Stanza 6*

You think they are crusaders, sent
From some infernal clime,
To pluck the eyes of Sentiment
And dock the tail of Rhyme,
To crack the voice of Melody
And break the legs of Time.
> *The Music Grinders. Stanza 9*

And silence, like a poultice, comes
To heal the blows of sound.
> *Ibid. Stanza 10*

And since, I never dare to write
As funny as I can.
> *The Height of the Ridiculous. Stanza 8*

When the last reader reads no more.
> *The Last Reader*

Age, like distance, lends a double charm.[1]
> *A Rhymed Lesson. Urania*

And when you stick on conversation's burs,
Don't strew your pathway with those dreadful *urs*.
> *Ibid.*

Be sure your tailor is a man of sense.
> *Ibid.*

Wear seemly gloves; not black, nor yet too light,
And least of all the pair that once was white.
> *Ibid.*

Have a good hat; the secret of your looks

---

[1] As the British Constitution is the most subtle organism which has proceeded from progressive history, so the American Constitution is the most wonderful work ever struck off at a given time by the brain and purpose of man. — *Kin Beyond the Sea* [*North American Review*, September, 1878]

[2] The most successful combination the world has ever seen, of physician and man of

letters. — Sir William Osler, quoted in Harvey Cushing: *Life of Sir William Osler* [1925], *Vol. I, Chap. 15*

[1] See Campbell, page 432a.

Lives with the beaver in Canadian
brooks;
Virtue may flourish in an old cravat,
But man and nature scorn the shock-
ing hat.[1]
A Rhymed Lesson. Urania
Learn the sweet magic of a cheerful
face;
Not always smiling, but at least serene.
The Morning Visit
Wake in our breast the living fires,
The holy faith that warmed our sires;
Thy hand hath made our Nation free;
To die for her is serving Thee.
Army Hymn. Stanza 2
The lusty days of long ago,
When you were Bill and I was Joe.
Bill and Joe. Stanza 1
Where are the Marys, and Anns, and
Elizas,
Loving and lovely of yore?
Questions and Answers. Stanza 3
Oh for one hour of youthful joy!
Give back my twentieth spring!
The Old Man Dreams. Stanza 1
Old Time is a liar! We're twenty to-
night!
The Boys. Stanza 1
Where the snow-flakes fall thickest
there's nothing can freeze!
Ibid. Stanza 2
One flag, one land, one heart, one hand,
One Nation, evermore!
Voyage of the Good Ship Union.
Stanza 12
Good to the heels the well-worn slipper
feels
When the tired player shuffles off the
buskin;
A page of Hood may do a fellow good
After a scolding from Carlyle or
Ruskin.
How Not to Settle It. Stanza 3
When lawyers take what they would
give
And doctors give what they would take.
Latter-day Warnings. Stanza 4
Learn to give
Money to colleges while you live.
Don't be silly and think you'll try

[1] See *The Autocrat of the Breakfast-Table*,
page 536a.

To bother the colleges, when you die,
With codicil this, and codicil that,
That Knowledge may starve while Law
grows fat;
For there never was pitcher that
wouldn't spill,
And there's always a flaw in a donkey's
will.
Parson Turell's Legacy
Where we love is home,
Home that our feet may leave, but not
our hearts.
Homesick in Heaven. Stanza 5
There is no time like the old time, when
you and I were young.[1]
No Time Like the Old Time.
Stanza 1
'Tis like stirring living embers when,
at eighty, one remembers
All the achings and the quakings of "the
times that tried men's souls." [2]
Grandmother's Story of Bunker
Hill Battle. Stanza 1
The style's the man, so books avow;
The style's the woman, anyhow.
How the Old Horse Won the Bet.
Stanza 2
I read it in the story-book, that, for to
kiss his dear,
Leander swam the Hellespont, — and
I will swim this here.
The Ballad of the Oysterman.
Stanza 3
Lean, hungry, savage, anti-everythings.
A Modest Request. The Speech.
This body in which we journey
across the isthmus between the two
oceans is not a private carriage, but an
omnibus.
The Guardian Angel. Chap. 3
A thought is often original, though
you have uttered it a hundred times.
The Autocrat of the Break-
fast-Table [1858]. I

[1] The good old times, the grand old times,
the great old times! — DICKENS: *The Chimes*
[1844], *First Quarter*
There are no days like the good old days,
The days when we were youthful!
EUGENE FIELD [1850–1895]: *Old*
Times, Old Friends, Old Love
[2] See Thomas Paine, page 370a.

Everybody likes and respects self-made men. It is a great deal better to be made in that way than not to be made at all.
The Autocrat of the Breakfast-Table. I

Insanity is often the logic of an accurate mind overtaxed.
Ibid.

Put not your trust in money, but put your money in trust.
Ibid. II

Sin has many tools, but a lie is the handle which fits them all.
Ibid. VI

There is that glorious epicurean paradox uttered by my friend the historian,[1] in one of his flashing moments: "Give us the luxuries of life, and we will dispense with its necessaries."[2]
Ibid.

Boston State-house is the hub of the solar system. You couldn't pry that out of a Boston man, if you had the tire of all creation straightened out for a crowbar.
Ibid.

The axis of the earth sticks out visibly through the centre of each and every town or city.
Ibid.

The world's great men have not commonly been great scholars, nor its great scholars great men.
Ibid.

Knowledge and timber shouldn't be much used till they are seasoned.
Ibid.

The hat is the *ultimum moriens* of respectability.[3]
Ibid. XIII

Little I ask; my wants are few,
I only wish a hut of stone,

[1] John Lothrop Motley [1814–1877].
[2] Said Scopas of Thessaly, "We rich men count our felicity and happiness to lie in these superfluities, and not in those necessary things." — PLUTARCH [A. D. 46–120]: *On the Love of Wealth*
[3] See *A Rhymed Lesson*, pages 534b–535a.

(A *very plain* brown stone will do,)
That I may call my own.[1]
Contentment [*1858*]. *Stanza 1*

Build thee more stately mansions, O my soul,
As the swift seasons roll!
Leave thy low-vaulted past!
Let each new temple, nobler than the last,
Shut thee from heaven with a dome more vast,
Till thou at length art free,
Leaving thine outgrown shell by life's unresting sea!
The Chambered Nautilus [*1858*]. *Stanza 5*

Have you heard of the wonderful one-hoss shay,
That was built in such a logical way
It ran a hundred years to a day?
The Deacon's Masterpiece [*1858*]. *Stanza 1*

A general flavor of mild decay.
Ibid. Stanza 10

It went to pieces all at once, —
All at once, and nothing first,
Just as bubbles do when they burst.
Ibid. Stanza 11

I firmly believe that if the whole *materia medica* as now used could be sunk to the bottom of the sea, it would be all the better for mankind — and all the worse for the fishes.[2]
Address, Massachusetts Medical Society [*May 30, 1860*]

He comes of the Brahmin caste of New England. This is the harmless, inoffensive, untitled aristocracy.
The Brahmin Caste of New England [*1860*]

It makes men imperious to sit a horse.
Elsie Venner [*1861*]

[1] See Goldsmith, page 354b.
[2] Stir the mixture well
Lest it prove inferior,
Then put half a drop
Into Lake Superior.
Every other day
Take a drop in water,
You'll be better soon
Or at least you oughter.
BISHOP WILLIAM CROSWELL DOANE [1832–1913]: *Lines on Homoeopathy*

To be seventy years young is sometimes far more cheerful and hopeful than to be forty years old.

> *On the Seventieth Birthday of Julia Ward Howe* [*May 27, 1889*]

ABRAHAM LINCOLN
[1809–1865]

If the good people, in their wisdom, shall see fit to keep me in the background, I have been too familiar with disappointments to be very much chagrined.

> *Address, New Salem, Illinois* [*March 9, 1832*]

I go for all sharing the privileges of the government who assist in bearing its burdens.

> *Letter to Editor of the Sangamon Journal, New Salem, Illinois* [*June 13, 1836*]

If destruction be our lot we must ourselves be its author and finisher. As a nation of freemen we must live through all time, or die by suicide.

> *Address, Young Men's Lyceum, Springfield, Illinois* [*January 27, 1838*]

There is no grievance that is a fit object of redress by mob law.

> *Ibid.*

Towering genius disdains a beaten path. It seeks regions hitherto unexplored.

> *Ibid.*

I am not a Know-Nothing; that is certain. How could I be? How can any one who abhors the oppression of Negroes be in favor of degrading classes of white people? Our progress in degeneracy appears to me to be pretty rapid. As a nation we began by declaring that "all men are created equal." We now practically read it "all men are created equal, except Negroes." When the Know-Nothings get control, it will read "all men are created equal, except Negroes and foreigners and Catholics." When it comes to this, I shall prefer emigrating to some country where they make no pretense of loving liberty — to

Russia, for instance, where despotism can be taken pure, and without the base alloy of hypocrisy.

> *Letter to Joshua F. Speed* [*August 24, 1855*]

"A house divided against itself cannot stand."[1] I believe this government cannot endure permanently half slave and half free. I do not expect the Union to be dissolved — I do not expect the house to fall — but I do expect it will cease to be divided. It will become all one thing, or all the other. Either the opponents of slavery will arrest the further spread of it, and place it where the public mind shall rest in the belief that it is in the course of ultimate extinction; or its advocates will push it forward till it shall become alike lawful in all the States, old as well as new, North as well as South.

> *Speech, Republican State Convention, Springfield, Illinois* [*June 16, 1858*]

Nobody has ever expected me to be President. In my poor, lean, lank face nobody has ever seen that any cabbages were sprouting out.

> *Second Campaign Speech against Douglas,[2] Springfield, Illinois* [*July 17, 1858*]

As I would not be a *slave*, so I would not be a *master*. This expresses my idea of democracy. Whatever differs from this, to the extent of the difference, is no democracy.[3]

> *Fragment* [*August 1, 1858?*], *in* ROY P. BASLER: *The Collected Works of Abraham Lincoln* [*1953*]. *Vol. II, Page 532*

When . . . you have succeeded in dehumanizing the Negro; when you

[1] If a house be divided against itself, that house cannot stand. — *Mark, III, 25*

[2] They have seen in his [Douglas's] round, jolly, fruitful face, post-offices, land-offices, marshalships and cabinet appointments, chargéships and foreign missions, bursting and sprouting out in wonderful exuberance, ready to be laid hold of by their greedy hands. — *Ibid.*

[3] See *Address to Indiana Regiment*, page 542a–542b.

have put him down and made it impossible for him to be but as the beasts of the field; when you have extinguished his soul in this world and placed him where the ray of hope is blown out as in the darkness of the damned, are you quite sure that the demon you have roused will not turn and rend you? What constitutes the bulwark of our own liberty and independence? It is not our frowning battlements, our bristling sea coasts, our army and our navy. These are not our reliance against tyranny. All of those may be turned against us without making us weaker for the struggle. Our reliance is in the love of liberty which God has planted in us. Our defence is in the spirit which prized liberty as the heritage of all men, in all lands everywhere. Destroy this spirit and you have planted the seeds of despotism at your own doors. Familiarize yourselves with the chains of bondage and you prepare your own limbs to wear them. Accustomed to trample on the rights of others, you have lost the genius of your own independence and become the fit subjects of the first cunning tyrant who rises among you.

Speech, Edwardsville, Illinois
[September 11, 1858]

That is the issue that will continue in this country when these poor tongues of Judge Douglas and myself shall be silent. It is the eternal struggle between these two principles — right and wrong — throughout the world. They are the two principles that have stood face to face from the beginning of time; and will ever continue to struggle. The one is the common right of humanity, and the other the divine right of kings. It is the same principle in whatever shape it develops itself. It is the same spirit that says, "You toil and work and earn bread, and I'll eat it." No matter in what shape it comes, whether from the mouth of a king who seeks to bestride the people of his own nation and live by the fruit of their labor, or from one race of men as an apology for enslaving another race, it is the same tyrannical principle.

Reply, Seventh and Last Joint Debate, Alton, Illinois [October 15, 1858]

This is a world of compensation; and he who would be no slave must consent to have no slave. Those who deny freedom to others deserve it not for themselves, and, under a just God, cannot long retain it.

Letter to H. L. Pierce and Others [April 6, 1859]

It is said an Eastern monarch once charged his wise men to invent him a sentence to be ever in view, and which should be true and appropriate in all times and situations. They presented him the words: "And this, too, shall pass away." [1] How much it expresses! How chastening in the hour of pride! How consoling in the depths of affliction! . . . And yet, let us hope, it is not quite true. Let us hope, rather, that by the best cultivation of the physical world beneath and around us, and the best intellectual and moral world within us, we shall secure an individual, social, and political prosperity and happiness, whose course shall be onward and upward, and which, while the earth endures, shall not pass away.

Address, Wisconsin State Agricultural Society, Milwaukee [September 30, 1859]

Let us have faith that right makes might, and in that faith let us to the end dare to do our duty as we understand it.

Address, Cooper Union, New York [February 27, 1860]

No one, not in my situation, can appreciate my feeling of sadness at this parting. To this place, and the kindness of these people, I owe everything. Here I have lived a quarter of a century, and have passed from a young to an old man. Here my children have been born, and one is buried. I now leave, not knowing when or whether ever I may return, with a task before

1 See Hawthorne, page 514b.

me greater than that which rested upon Washington. Without the assistance of that Divine Being who ever attended him, I cannot succeed. With that assistance I cannot fail. Trusting in Him who can go with me, and remain with you, and be everywhere for good, let us confidently hope that all will yet be well.

Farewell Address, Springfield, Illinois [February 11, 1861]

If we do not make common cause to save the good old ship of the Union on this voyage, nobody will have a chance to pilot her on another voyage.

Address, Cleveland, Ohio [February 15, 1861]

I have never had a feeling, politically, that did not spring from the sentiments embodied in the Declaration of Independence. . . . I have often inquired of myself what great principle or idea it was that kept this Confederacy so long together. . . . It was that which gave promise that in due time the weights would be lifted from the shoulders of all men, and that all should have an equal chance.

Speech in Independence Hall, Philadelphia [February 22, 1861]

It is safe to assert that no government proper ever had a provision in its organic law for its own termination.

First Inaugural Address [March 4, 1861]

This country, with its institutions, belongs to the people who inhabit it. Whenever they shall grow weary of the existing government, they can exercise their constitutional right of amending it, or their revolutionary right to dismember or overthrow it.

Ibid.

Why should there not be a patient confidence in the ultimate justice of the people? Is there any better or equal hope in the world?

Ibid.

While the people retain their virtue and vigilance, no administration, by any extreme of wickedness or folly, can very seriously injure the government in the short space of four years.

First Inaugural Address

We are not enemies, but friends. We must not be enemies. Though passion may have strained, it must not break our bonds of affection. The mystic chords of memory, stretching from every battlefield and patriot grave to every living heart and hearth-stone all over this broad land, will yet swell the chorus of the Union when again touched, as surely they will be, by the better angels of our nature.

Ibid.

I think the necessity of being *ready* increases. — Look to it.

Letter (this is the whole message) to Governor Andrew G. Curtin of Pennsylvania [April 8, 1861]

Labor is prior to, and independent of, capital. Capital is only the fruit of labor, and could never have existed if labor had not first existed. Labor is the superior of capital, and deserves much the higher consideration. Capital has its rights, which are as worthy of protection as any other rights.

First Annual Message to Congress [December 3, 1861]

It is difficult to make a man miserable while he feels he is worthy of himself and claims kindred to the great God who made him.

Address on Colonization to a Negro Deputation at Washington [August 14, 1862]

My paramount object in this struggle is to save the Union, and is not either to save or to destroy slavery. If I could save the Union without freeing any slave, I would do it; and if I could do it by freeing all the slaves, I would do it; and if I could save it by freeing some and leaving others alone, I would also do that.

Letter to Horace Greeley [August 22, 1862]

I shall try to correct errors when shown to be errors, and I shall adopt new views so fast as they shall appear to be true views. . . . and I intend no modification of my oft-expressed personal wish that all men everywhere could be free.

Letter to Horace Greeley
[August 22, 1862]

The President takes the result of the New York elections philosophically, and will, doubtless, profit by the lesson. When Colonel Forney inquired of him how he felt about New York, he replied: "Somewhat like the boy in Kentucky, who stubbed his toe while running to see his sweetheart. The boy said he was too big to cry, and far too badly hurt to laugh." [1]

Frank Leslie's Illustrated Weekly
[November 22, 1862]

A nation may be said to consist of its territory, its people, and its laws. The territory is the only part which is of certain durability.

Second Annual Message to Congress
[December 1, 1862]

If there ever could be a proper time for mere catch arguments, that time surely is not now. In times like the present, men should utter nothing for which they would not willingly be responsible through time and in eternity.

Ibid.

Fellow-citizens, we cannot escape history. We of this Congress and this administration will be remembered in spite of ourselves. No personal significance or insignificance can spare one or another of us. The fiery trial through which we pass will light us down, in honor or dishonor, to the last generation. We say we are for the Union. The world will not forget that we say this. We know how to save the Union. The world knows we do

[1] The election referred to resulted in a victory for Horatio Seymour, Democratic candidate for governor of New York. Moreover, throughout the North the Democrats picked up a number of congressional seats and won a number of state elections.

Adlai E. Stevenson, Democratic candidate for the presidency in 1952, quoted this remark of Lincoln's in a television speech after losing the election.

know how to save it. We — even we here — hold the power and bear the responsibility. In giving freedom to the slave, we assure freedom to the free — honorable alike in what we give and what we preserve. We shall nobly save or meanly lose the last, best hope of earth. Other means may succeed; this could not fail. The way is plain, peaceful, generous, just — a way which, if followed, the world will forever applaud, and God must forever bless.

Second Annual Message
to Congress

Beware of rashness, but with energy and sleepless vigilance go forward and give us victories.

Letter to Major-General Joseph
Hooker [January 26, 1863]

The Father of Waters [1] again goes unvexed to the sea.

Letter to James C. Conkling
[August 26, 1863]

Among freemen there can be no successful appeal from the ballot to the bullet, and . . . they who take such appeal are sure to lose their case and pay the cost.

Ibid.

I have endured a great deal of ridicule without much malice; and have received a great deal of kindness, not quite free from ridicule. I am used to it.

Letter to James H. Hackett
[November 2, 1863]

Fourscore and seven years ago our fathers brought forth on this continent a new nation, conceived in liberty, and dedicated to the proposition that all men are created equal.

Now we are engaged in a great civil war, testing whether that nation, or any nation so conceived and so dedicated, can long endure. We are met on a great battlefield of that war. We have come to dedicate a portion of that field as a final resting-place for those who here gave their lives that that nation might live. It is altogether fitting and proper that we should do this.

But, in a larger sense, we cannot

[1] See Stephen Vincent Benét, page 979b.

dedicate — we cannot consecrate — we cannot hallow — this ground. The brave men, living and dead, who struggled here, have consecrated it far above our poor power to add or detract. The world will little note nor long remember what we say here, but it can never forget what they did here. It is for us, the living, rather to be dedicated here to the unfinished work which they who fought here have thus far so nobly advanced. It is rather for us to be here dedicated to the great task remaining before us — that from these honored dead we take increased devotion to that cause for which they gave the last full measure of devotion; that we here highly resolve that these dead shall not have died in vain; that this nation, under God, shall have a new birth of freedom; and that government of the people, by the people, for the people, shall not perish from the earth.[1]

Address at Gettysburg
[November 19, 1863]

I claim not to have controlled events, but confess plainly that events have controlled me.

Letter to A. G. Hodges
[April 4, 1864]

The world has never had a good definition of the word liberty, and the American people, just now, are much in want of one.

Address, Sanitary Fair, Baltimore
[April 18, 1864]

It is no fault in others that the Methodist Church sends more soldiers to the field, more nurses to the hospital, and more prayers to heaven than any. God bless the Methodist Church. Bless all the churches, and blessed be God, who, in this our great trial, giveth us the churches.

To a Methodist Delegation
[May 14, 1864]

I do not allow myself to suppose that either the convention or the League have concluded to decide that I am either the greatest or best man in Amer-

ica, but rather they have concluded that it is not best to swap horses while crossing the river, and have further concluded that I am not so poor a horse that they might not make a botch of it in trying to swap.

Reply to the National Union
League [June 9, 1864]

Truth is generally the best vindication against slander.

Letter to Secretary Stanton, refusing to dismiss Postmaster-General Montgomery Blair
[July 18, 1864]

It has long been a grave question whether any government, not too strong for the liberties of its people, can be strong enough to maintain its existence in great emergencies.

Response to a Serenade
[November 10, 1864]

Human nature will not change. In any future great national trial, compared with the men of this, we shall have as weak and as strong, as silly and as wise, as bad and as good.

Ibid.

DEAR MADAM: I have been shown in the files of the War Department a statement of the Adjutant-General of Massachusetts that you are the mother of five sons who have died gloriously on the field of battle. I feel how weak and fruitless must be any words of mine which should attempt to beguile you from the grief of a loss so overwhelming. But I cannot refrain from tendering to you the consolation that may be found in the thanks of the Republic they died to save. I pray that our heavenly Father may assuage the anguish of your bereavement, and leave you only the cherished memory of the loved and lost, and the solemn pride that must be yours to have laid so costly a sacrifice upon the altar of freedom.

Letter to Mrs. Bixby, whose five sons were reported killed in battle [1] *[November 21, 1864]*

---

[1] See Webster, page 443b, Garrison, page 517b, and Theodore Parker, page 560a.

[1] In reality, only two of Mrs. Bixby's sons had died in action, but Lincoln was unaware of this when he wrote the letter.

It may seem strange that any men should dare to ask a just God's assistance in wringing their bread from the sweat of other men's faces; but let us judge not, that we be not judged.
Second Inaugural Address
[March 4, 1865]
The Almighty has His own purposes.
Ibid.

Fondly do we hope — fervently do we pray — that this mighty scourge of war may speedily pass away. Yet, if God wills that it continue until all the wealth piled by the bondsman's two hundred and fifty years of unrequited toil shall be sunk, and until every drop of blood drawn with the lash shall be paid by another drawn with the sword, as was said three thousand years ago, so still it must be said, "The judgments of the Lord are true and righteous altogether."
Ibid.

With malice toward none; with charity for all; with firmness in the right, as God gives us to see the right,[1] let us strive on to finish the work we are in; to bind up the nation's wounds; to care for him who shall have borne the battle, and for his widow, and his orphan — to do all which may achieve and cherish a just and lasting peace among ourselves, and with all nations.
Ibid.

Men are not flattered by being shown that there has been a difference of purpose between the Almighty and them. To deny it, however, in this case, is to deny that there is a God governing the world. It is a truth which I thought needed to be told, and, as whatever of humiliation there is in it falls most directly on myself, I thought others might afford for me to tell it.
Letter to Thurlow Weed
[March 15, 1865]

I have always thought that all men should be free; but if any should be slaves, it should be first those who desire it for themselves, and secondly

¹ See John Quincy Adams, page 398b.

those who desire it for others. Whenever I hear any one arguing for slavery, I feel a strong impulse to see it tried on him personally.[1]
Address to an Indiana Regiment
[March 17, 1865]
Important principles may and must be flexible.
Last public address, Washington
[April 11, 1865]

If you once forfeit the confidence of your fellow citizens, you can never regain their respect and esteem. It is true that you may fool all the people some of the time; you can even fool some of the people all the time; but you can't fool all of the people all the time.
To a caller at the White House.
In ALEXANDER K. McCLURE:
Lincoln's Yarns and Stories
[1904], Page 124

One night he dreamed that he was in a crowd, when someone recognized him as the President, and exclaimed in surprise, "He is a very common-looking man." Whereupon he answered, "Friend, the Lord prefers common-looking people. That is the reason he makes so many of them."
JAMES MORGAN: *Our Presidents*
[1924], Chap. 6

If I were to try to read, much less answer, all the attacks made on me, this shop might as well be closed for any other business. I do the very best I know how — the very best I can; and I mean to keep doing so until the end. If the end brings me out all right, what is said against me won't amount to anything. If the end brings me out wrong, ten angels swearing I was right would make no difference.
Conversation at the White House, reported by FRANCIS B. CARPENTER: *Six Months at the White House with Abraham Lincoln* *[1866]*

If you call a tail a leg, how many legs has a dog? Five? No, calling a tail a leg don't *make* it a leg.
Traditionally attributed to Lincoln

¹ See *Fragment*, page 537b.

RICHARD MONCKTON MILNES (BARON HOUGHTON)
[1809–1885]

I wandered by the brookside,
  I wandered by the mill;
I could not hear the brook flow,
  The noisy wheel was still.
The Brookside. Stanza 1

The beating of my own heart
Was all the sound I heard.
Ibid.

The hills of manhood wear a noble face
  When seen from far;
The mist of light from which they take
    their grace
  Hides what they are.
Carpe Diem

Mohammed's truth lay in a holy Book,
Christ's in a sacred Life.
Mohammedanism

A fair little girl sat under a tree,
Sewing as long as her eyes could see;
Then smoothed her work, and folded it
    right,
And said, "Dear work, good-night,
    good-night."
Good-Night and Good-Morning.
Stanza 1

They who have steeped their souls in
    prayer
Can every anguish calmly bear.
The Sayings of Rabia. IV

Lady Moon, Lady Moon, where are
    you roving?
  Over the sea.
Lady Moon, Lady Moon, whom are
    you loving?
  All that love me!
A Child's Song

The sense of humour is the just balance of all the faculties of man, the best security against the pride of knowledge and the conceits of the imagination, the strongest inducement to submit with a wise and pious patience to the vicissitudes of human existence.
Memoir of Thomas Hood

EDGAR ALLAN POE
[1809–1849]

O, human love! thou spirit given,
On Earth, of all we hope in Heaven!
Which fall'st into the soul like rain
Upon the Siroc-wither'd plain.
Tamerlane [1827]

All that we see or seem
Is but a dream within a dream.
A Dream Within a Dream [1827]

Sound loves to revel in a summer night.
Al Aaraaf [1829]. Part II

It is with literature as with law or empire—an established name is an estate in tenure, or a throne in possession.
Poems [1831]. Preface, Letter to Mr. B——

Helen, thy beauty is to me
  Like those Nicean barks of yore,
That gently, o'er a perfumed sea,
  The weary, wayworn wanderer bore
  To his own native shore.
To Helen [1831]. Stanza 1

On desperate seas long wont to roam,
  Thy hyacinth hair, thy classic face,
Thy Naiad airs have brought me home
  To the glory that was Greece,
And the grandeur that was Rome.
Ibid. Stanza 2

In Heaven a spirit doth dwell
  "Whose heart-strings are a lute"; [1]
None sing so wildly well
As the angel Israfel.
Israfel [1831]. Stanza 1

If I could dwell
Where Israfel
  Hath dwelt, and he where I,
He might not sing so wildly well
  A mortal melody,
While a bolder note than this might
    swell
From my lyre within the sky.
Ibid. Stanza 8

Whose wreathed friezes intertwine
The viol, the violet, and the vine.
The City in the Sea [1831].
Stanza 2

[1] And the angel Israfel, whose heart-strings are a lute, and who has the sweetest voice of all God's creatures. — *The Koran*

While from a proud tower in the town
Death looks gigantically down.
>> *The City in the Sea. Stanza 3*

Ah, broken is the golden bowl! [1] — the
spirit flown forever!
Let the bell toll! — a saintly soul floats
on the Stygian river;
And, Guy De Vere, hast *thou* no tear?
— weep now or never more!
>> *Lenore* [*1831*]. *Stanza 1*

A dirge for her the doubly dead in that
she died so young.
>> *Ibid.*

Vastness! and Age! and Memories of
Eld!
Silence! and Desolation! and dim
Night!
>> *The Coliseum* [*1833*]. *Stanza 1*

Thou wast that all to me, love,
For which my soul did pine —
A green isle in the sea, love,
A fountain and a shrine,
All wreathed with fairy fruits and
flowers,
And all the flowers were mine.
>> *To One in Paradise* [*1834*].
>> *Stanza 1*

And all my days are trances,
And all my nightly dreams
Are where thy grey eye glances,
And where thy footstep gleams —
In what ethereal dances,
By what eternal streams.
>> *Ibid. Stanza 4*

Those who dream by day are cog-
nizant of many things which escape
those who dream only by night.
>> *Eleonora* [*1841*]

There are chords in the hearts of the
most reckless which can not be touched
without emotion. Even with the utterly lost, to whom life and death are
equally jests, there are matters of which
no jest can be made.
>> *The Masque of the Red*
>> *Death* [*1842*]

And much of Madness, and more of Sin,
And Horror the soul of the plot.
>> *The Conqueror Worm* [*1843*].
>> *Stanza 3*

[1] See *Ecclesiastes, XII, 6,* on page 1043b.

While the angels, all pallid and wan,
Uprising, unveiling, affirm
That the play is the tragedy, "Man,"
And its hero, the Conqueror Worm.
>> *The Conqueror Worm. Stanza 5*

There is something in the unselfish
and self-sacrificing love of a brute,
which goes directly to the heart of him
who has had frequent occasion to test
the paltry friendship and gossamer
fidelity of mere Man.
>> *The Black Cat* [*1843*]

Perverseness is one of the primitive
impulses of the human heart.
>> *Ibid.*

The boundaries which divide Life
from Death are at best shadowy and
vague. Who shall say where the one
ends, and where the other begins?
>> *The Premature Burial* [*1844*]

With me poetry has been not a purpose, but a passion; and the passions
should be held in reverence: they must
not — they cannot at will be excited,
with an eye to the paltry compensations, or the more paltry commendations, of mankind.
>> *The Raven and Other Poems*
>> [*1845*]. *Preface*

Once upon a midnight dreary, while I
pondered, weak and weary,
Over many a quaint and curious volume
of forgotten lore —
While I nodded, nearly napping, suddenly there came a tapping,
As of some one gently rapping, rapping
at my chamber door.
>> *The Raven* [*1845*].
>> *Stanza 1*

Ah, distinctly I remember it was in the
bleak December;
And each separate dying ember wrought
its ghost upon the floor.
Eagerly I wished the morrow; — vainly
I had sought to borrow
From my books surcease of sorrow —
sorrow for the lost Lenore —
For the rare and radiant maiden whom
the angels name Lenore —
Nameless *here* for evermore.
>> *Ibid. Stanza 2*

And the silken sad uncertain rustling of
each purple curtain
Thrilled me — filled me with fantastic
terrors never felt before.
The Raven. Stanza 3

Deep into that darkness peering, long
I stood there, wondering, fearing,
Doubting, dreaming dreams no mortal
ever dared to dream before.
Ibid. Stanza 5

Perched upon a bust of Pallas just
above my chamber door —
Perched, and sat, and nothing more.
Ibid. Stanza 7

"Ghastly grim and ancient Raven wan-
dering from the Nightly shore —
Tell me what thy lordly name is on the
Night's Plutonian shore!"
Quoth the Raven, "Nevermore."
Ibid. Stanza 8

Whom unmerciful Disaster
Followed fast and followed faster.
Ibid. Stanza 11

"Prophet!" said I, "thing of evil! —
prophet still, if bird or devil!
By that Heaven that bends above us —
by that God we both adore —
Tell this soul with sorrow laden."
Ibid. Stanza 16

"Take thy beak from out my heart, and
take thy form from off my door!"
Quoth the Raven, "Nevermore."
Ibid. Stanza 17

And the Raven, never flitting, still is
sitting, *still* is sitting
On the pallid bust of Pallas just above
my chamber door;
And his eyes have all the seeming of a
demon's that is dreaming,
And the lamp-light o'er him streaming
throws his shadow on the floor;
And my soul from out that shadow that
lies floating on the floor
Shall be lifted — nevermore!
Ibid. Stanza 18

The Imp of the Perverse.
Title of Story [1845]

The object Truth, or the satisfaction
of the intellect, and the object Passion,
or the excitement of the heart, are, although attainable, to a certain extent,
in poetry, far more readily attainable
in prose.
The Philosophy of Composition
[1846]

The skies they were ashen and sober;
The leaves they were crispèd and
sere —
The leaves they were withering and
sere;
It was night in the lonesome October
Of my most immemorial year.
Ulalume [1847]. Stanza 1

It was down by the dank tarn of
Auber,
In the ghoul-haunted woodland of
Weir.
Ibid.

Here once, through an alley Titanic,
Of cypress, I roamed with my soul —
Of cypress, with Psyche, my soul.
Ibid. Stanza 2

And now, as the night was senescent
And star-dials pointed to morn —
As the star-dials hinted of morn —
At the end of our path a liquescent
And nebulous lustre was born.
Ibid. Stanza 4

Thus I pacified Psyche and kissed her,
And tempted her out of her gloom.
Ibid. Stanza 8

Can it be fancied that Deity ever vin-
dictively
Made in his image a mannikin merely
to madden it? [1]
The Rationale of Verse [1848]

A Quixotic sense of the honorable —
of the chivalrous.
Letter to Mrs. Whitman
[October 18, 1848]

And o'er his heart a shadow
Fell as he found
No spot of ground
That looked like Eldorado.
Eldorado [1849]

And the fever called "Living"
Is conquered at last.
For Annie [1849]

---

[1] What! out of senseless Nothing to provoke
A conscious Something to resent the yoke.
FITZGERALD: *The Rubáiyát of Omar
Khayyám* [1859–1879], St. 78

And this maiden she lived with no
   other thought
Than to love and be loved by me.
      Annabel Lee [*1849*]. *Stanza 1*

She was a child and *I* was a child,
   In this kingdom by the sea,
But we loved with a love that was more
   than love —
I and my Annabel Lee —
With a love that the wingèd seraphs
   of Heaven
Coveted her and me.
      Ibid. Stanza 2

And neither the angels in Heaven above
   Nor the demons down under the sea,
Can ever dissever my soul from the
   soul
Of the beautiful Annabel Lee.
      Ibid. Stanza 5

In her sepulchre there by the sea —
In her tomb by the side of the sea.
      Ibid. Stanza 6

Keeping time, time, time,
   In a sort of Runic rhyme,
To the tintinnabulation that so musi-
   cally wells
From the bells, bells, bells, bells,
   Bells, bells, bells.
      The Bells [*1849*]. *Stanza 1*

Hear the loud alarum bells —
   Brazen bells!
What a tale of terror, now, their
   turbulency tells!
      Ibid. Stanza 3

I would define, in brief, the Poetry
of words as the Rhythmical Creation of
Beauty. Its sole arbiter is Taste.
      The Poetic Principle [*1850*]

ALFRED, LORD TENNYSON
[1809–1892]

Dowered with the hate of hate, the
   scorn of scorn,
The love of love.
      The Poet [*1830*]. *Stanza 1*

For it was in the golden prime
Of good Haroun Alraschid.
      *Recollections of the Arabian
      Nights* [*1830*]. *Stanza 2*

She said, "I am aweary, aweary,
I would that I were dead!"
      Mariana [*1830*]. *Refrain*

A still small voice spake unto me,
"Thou art so full of misery,
Were it not better not to be?"
      The Two Voices [*1833*]. *Stanza 1*

This truth within thy mind rehearse,
That in a boundless universe
Is boundless better, boundless worse.
      Ibid. Stanza 9

Tho' thou wert scattered to the wind,
Yet is there plenty of the kind.[1]
      Ibid. Stanza 11

I know that age to age succeeds,
Blowing a noise of tongues and deeds,
A dust of systems and of creeds.
      Ibid. Stanza 69

Like glimpses of forgotten dreams.
      Ibid. Stanza 127

No life that breathes with human
   breath
Has ever truly longed for death.
      Ibid. Stanza 132

   In after-dinner talk,
Across the walnuts and the wine.
      The Miller's Daughter [*1833*].
      Stanza 4

O mother Ida, many-fountained Ida,
Dear mother Ida, hearken ere I die.
      Oenone [*1833*]. *Line 22*

Self-reverence, self-knowledge, self-
   control,
These three alone lead life to sovereign
   power.
      Ibid. Line 142

I built my soul a lordly pleasure-house,
Wherein at ease for aye to dwell.
      The Palace of Art [*1833*].
      Stanza 1

At me you smiled, but unbeguiled
I saw the snare, and I retired:
The daughter of a hundred Earls,
You are not one to be desired.
      Lady Clara Vere de Vere [*1833*].
      Stanza 1

A simple maiden in her flower
Is worth a hundred coats-of-arms.
      Ibid. Stanza 2

[1] See Fitzgerald, page 532b.

The lion on your old stone gates
Is not more cold to you than I.
> *Lady Clara Vere de Vere. Stanza 3*

Her manners had not that repose
Which stamps the caste of Vere de
Vere.
> *Ibid. Stanza 5*

From yon blue heavens above us bent,
The gardener Adam and his wife
Smile at the claims of long descent.
> *Ibid. Stanza 7*

Kind hearts are more than coronets,
And simple faith than Norman blood.
> *Ibid.*

If time be heavy on your hands,
Are there no beggars at your gate,
Nor any poor about your lands?
Oh! teach the orphan-boy to read,
Or teach the orphan-girl to sew.
> *Ibid. Stanza 9*

You must wake and call me early, call
me early, mother dear;
Tomorrow 'ill be the happiest time of
all the glad New Year, —
Of all the glad New Year, mother, the
maddest, merriest day;
For I'm to be Queen o' the May, mother,
I'm to be Queen o' the May.
> *The May Queen* [*1833*].
> *Stanza 1*

There is sweet music here that softer
falls
Than petals from blown roses on the
grass.
> *The Lotos-Eaters* [*1833*]. *Choric*
> *Song, Stanza 1*

Music that gentlier on the spirit lies,
Than tir'd eyelids upon tir'd eyes;
Music that brings sweet sleep down
from the blissful skies.
> *Ibid.*

Ah, why
Should life all labour be?
> *Ibid. Stanza 4*

Let us alone. Time driveth onward fast,
And in a little while our lips are dumb.
Let us alone. What is it that will last?
All things are taken from us, and be-
come
Portions and parcels of the dreadful
Past.
> *Ibid.*

Give us long rest or death, dark death
or dreamful ease.
> *The Lotos-Eaters. Choric Song.*
> *Stanza 4*

A daughter of the gods, divinely tall,
And most divinely fair.
> *A Dream of Fair Women* [*1833*].
> *Stanza 22*

God gives us love. Something to love
He lends us; but when love is grown
To ripeness, that on which it throve
Falls off, and love is left alone.
> *To J. S.* [*1833*]. *Stanza 4*

Sleep sweetly, tender heart, in peace;
Sleep, holy spirit, blessed soul,
While the stars burn, the moons in-
crease,
And the great ages onward roll.
> *Ibid. Stanza 18*

Willows whiten, aspens quiver,
Little breezes dusk and shiver.
> *The Lady of Shalott* [*1833*].
> *Part I, Stanza 1*

But who hath seen her wave her hand?
Or at the casement seen her stand?
Or is she known in all the land,
The Lady of Shalott?
> *Ibid. Stanza 3*

All in the blue unclouded weather.
> *Ibid. Part III, Stanza 3*

"Tirra lirra," by the river
Sang Sir Lancelot.
> *Ibid. Stanza 4*

She left the web, she left the loom,
She made three paces thro' the room,
She saw the water-lily bloom,
She saw the helmet and the plume,
She looked down to Camelot.
> *Ibid. Stanza 5*

But Lancelot mused a little space;
He said, "She has a lovely face;
God in his mercy lend her grace,
The Lady of Shalott."
> *Ibid. Part IV, Stanza 6*

The old order changeth, yielding place
to new;
And God fulfills himself in many ways,
Lest one good custom should corrupt
the world.
> *Morte d'Arthur* [*1842*].
> *Line 408*

More things are wrought by prayer Than this world dreams of. Wherefore, let thy voice Rise like a fountain for me night and day.

> *Morte d'Arthur. Line 415*

More black than ashbuds in the front of March.

> *The Gardener's Daughter* [*1842*]

The long mechanic pacings to and fro, The set gray life, and apathetic end.

> *Love and Duty* [*1842*]

Ah! when shall all men's good Be each man's rule, and universal peace Lie like a shaft of light across the land?

> *The Golden Year* [*1842*]. *Line 47*

Thro' all the circle of the golden year.

> *Ibid. Line 50*

It little profits that an idle king, By this still hearth, among these barren crags, Match'd with an aged wife, I mete and dole Unequal laws unto a savage race.

> *Ulysses* [*1842*]. *Line 1*

Much have I seen and known; cities of men And manners, climates, councils, governments, Myself not least, but honour'd of them all; And drunk delight of battle with my peers, Far on the ringing plains of windy Troy.

> *Ibid. Line 13*

How dull it is to pause, to make an end, To rust unburnished, not to shine in use, As tho' to breathe were life!

> *Ibid. Line 22*

This gray spirit yearning in desire To follow knowledge like a sinking star, Beyond the utmost bound of human thought.

> *Ibid. Line 30*

This is my son, mine own Telemachus.

> *Ibid. Line 33*

The deep Moans round with many voices. Come, my friends,

'Tis not too late to seek a newer world.

> *Ulysses. Line 55*

It may be we shall touch the Happy Isles, And see the great Achilles, whom we knew.

> *Ibid. Line 63*

To strive, to seek, to find, and not to yield.[1]

> *Ibid. Line 70*

Comrades, leave me here a little, while as yet 'tis early morn: Leave me here, and when you want me, sound upon your bugle horn.

> *Locksley Hall* [*1842*]. *Line 1*

In the spring a livelier iris changes on the burnished dove; In the spring a young man's fancy lightly turns to thoughts of love.

> *Ibid. Line 19*

He will hold thee, when his passion shall have spent its novel force, Something better than his dog, a little dearer than his horse.

> *Ibid. Line 49*

The many-winter'd crow that leads the clanging rookery home.

> *Ibid. Line 68*

Like a dog, he hunts in dreams.

> *Ibid. Line 79*

With a little hoard of maxims preaching down a daughter's heart.

> *Ibid. Line 94*

But the jingling of the guinea helps the hurt that Honour feels.

> *Ibid. Line 105*

For I dipt into the future, far as human eye could see, Saw the Vision of the world, and all the wonder that would be; Saw the heavens fill with commerce, argosies of magic sails, Pilots of the purple twilight, dropping down with costly bales; Heard the heavens fill with shouting, and there rain'd a ghastly dew

[1] Inscribed on the memorial cross erected to the memory of Captain Robert Falcon Scott and his men at Hut Point in the Antarctic.

From the nations' airy navies grappling
in the central blue.

> *Locksley Hall. Line 119*

Till the war drum throbbed no longer
and the battle flags were furled
In the Parliament of Man, the Federation of the world.

> *Ibid. Line 127*

Yet I doubt not through the ages one
increasing purpose runs,
And the thoughts of men are widened
with the process of the suns.

> *Ibid. Line 137*

Knowledge comes, but wisdom lingers.

> *Ibid. Line 141*

Woman is the lesser man, and all thy
passions, match'd with mine,
Are as moonlight unto sunlight, and as
water unto wine.

> *Ibid. Line 151*

I will take some savage woman, she
shall rear my dusky race.

> *Ibid. Line 168*

I the heir of all the ages, in the foremost files of time.

> *Ibid. Line 178*

Let the great world spin forever down
the ringing grooves of change.

> *Ibid. Line 182*

Better fifty years of Europe than a
cycle of Cathay.

> *Ibid. Line 184*

And on her lover's arm she leant,
And round her waist she felt it fold,
And far across the hills they went
In that new world which is the old.

> *The Day-Dream [1842]. The
> Departure, Stanza 1*

And o'er the hills, and far away
Beyond their utmost purple rim,
Beyond the night, across the day,
Thro' all the world she followed him.

> *Ibid. Stanza 4*

My strength is as the strength of ten,
Because my heart is pure.

> *Sir Galahad [1842]. Stanza 1*

Others' follies teach us not,
Nor much their wisdom teaches;
And most, of sterling worth, is what
Our own experience preaches.

> *Will Waterproof's Lyrical Monologue [1842]. Stanza 22*

And wheresoe'r thou move, good luck
Shall fling her old shoe after.

> *Will Waterproof's Lyrical Monologue. Stanza 27*

As she fled fast through sun and shade
The happy winds upon her played,
Blowing the ringlet from the braid.

> *Sir Launcelot and Queen Guinevere [1842]. Stanza 5*

Cophetua sware a royal oath;
"This beggar maid shall be my
queen!"[1]

> *The Beggar Maid [1842].
> Stanza 2*

For now the poet can not die,
Nor leave his music as of old,
But round him ere he scarce be cold
Begins the scandal and the cry.

> *To ——, after Reading a Life and
> Letters [1842]. Stanza 1*

He gave the people of his best:
His worst he kept, his best he gave.

> *Ibid. Stanza 7*

Break, break, break,
On thy cold gray stones, O Sea!
And I would that my tongue could utter
The thoughts that arise in me.

> *Break, Break, Break [1842].
> Stanza 1*

O well for the fisherman's boy,
That he shouts with his sister at
play!
O well for the sailor lad,
That he sings in his boat on the bay!

> *Ibid. Stanza 2*

And the stately ships go on
To their haven under the hill;
But O for the touch of a vanish'd hand,
And the sound of a voice that is still!

> *Ibid. Stanza 3*

But the tender grace of a day that is
dead
Will never come back to me.

> *Ibid. Stanza 4*

Veneer'd with sanctimonious theory.

> *The Princess [1847]. Prologue,
> Line 117*

With prudes for proctors, dowagers for
deans,

---

[1] See *Ballads*, page 1011b.

And sweet girl-graduates in their golden hair.

The Princess. Prologue, Line 141

A rosebud set with little willful thorns,
And sweet as English air could make her, she.

Ibid. Line 153

A little street half garden and half house.

Ibid. Part I, Line 211

When we fall out with those we love
And kiss again with tears!

Ibid. Part II, Song

And quoted odes, and jewels five-words-long
That on the stretched forefinger of all Time
Sparkle forever.

Ibid. Line 355

Sweet and low, sweet and low,
  Wind of the western sea,
Low, low, breathe and blow,
  Wind of the western sea!
Over the rolling waters go,
Come from the dying moon, and blow,
  Blow him again to me;
While my little one, while my pretty one, sleeps.

Ibid. Part III, Song

The splendour falls on castle walls
And snowy summits old in story.
The long light shakes across the lakes,
And the wild cataract leaps in glory.
Blow, bugle, blow, set the wild echoes flying,
Blow, bugle; answer, echoes, dying, dying, dying.

Ibid. Part IV, Song, Stanza 1

The horns of Elfland faintly blowing.

Ibid. Stanza 2

O Love, they die in yon rich sky,
  They faint on hill or field or river:
Our echoes roll from soul to soul,
  And grow forever and forever.

Ibid. Stanza 3

There sinks the nebulous star we call the sun.

Ibid. Line 1

Tears, idle tears, I know not what they mean,
Tears from the depth of some divine despair

Rise in the heart, and gather to the eyes,
In looking on the happy autumn-fields,
And thinking of the days that are no more.

The Princess. Part IV, Song, Stanza 1

Dear as remembered kisses after death,
And sweet as those by hopeless fancy feign'd
On lips that are for others; deep as love,
Deep as first love, and wild with all regret;
O Death in Life, the days that are no more.

Ibid. Stanza 4

O Swallow, Swallow, flying, flying South,
Fly to her, and fall upon her gilded eaves,
And tell her, tell her, what I tell to thee.

Ibid. Song, Stanza 1

Man is the hunter; woman is his game.

Ibid. Part V, Line 147

Man for the field and woman for the hearth:
Man for the sword and for the needle she:
Man with the head and woman with the heart:
Man to command and woman to obey;
All else confusion.

Ibid. Line 427

Home they brought her warrior dead.
She nor swoon'd, nor utter'd cry:
All her maidens, watching, said,
"She must weep or she will die."

Ibid. Part VI, Song, Stanza 1

The woman is so hard
Upon the woman.

Ibid. Line 205

Ask me no more: thy fate and mine are seal'd:
I strove against the stream and all in vain:
Let the great river take me to the main:
No more, dear love, for at a touch I yield;
  Ask me no more.

Ibid. Part VII, Song, Stanza 3

Now sleeps the crimson petal, now the white;
Nor waves the cypress in the palace walk;
Nor winks the gold fin in the porphyry font:
The fire-fly wakens: waken thou with me.

The Princess. Part VII, Song, Stanza 1

Now lies the Earth all Danaë to the stars,
And all thy heart lies open unto me.

Ibid. Stanza 3

Sweet is every sound,
Sweeter thy voice, but every sound is sweet;
Myriads of rivulets hurrying thro' the lawn,
The moan of doves in immemorial elms,
And murmuring of innumerable bees.

Ibid. Line 203

Happy he
With such a mother! faith in woman-kind
Beats with his blood, and trust in all things high
Comes easy to him; and tho' he trip and fall,
He shall not blind his soul with clay.

Ibid. Line 308

Some sense of duty, something of a faith,
Some reverence for the laws ourselves have made,
Some patient force to change them when we will,
Some civic manhood firm against the crowd.

Ibid. Conclusion, Line 54

Strong Son of God, immortal Love,
Whom we, that have not seen thy face,
By faith, and faith alone, embrace,
Believing where we cannot prove.

In Memoriam [1850]. Prologue, Stanza 1

Our little systems have their day.

Ibid. Stanza 5

Let knowledge grow from more to more,
But more of reverence in us dwell;

That mind and soul, according well,
May make one music as before.

In Memoriam. Prologue, Stanza 7

I held it truth, with him who sings
To one clear harp in divers tones,
That men may rise on stepping-stones
Of their dead selves to higher things.

Ibid. Part I, Stanza 1

I sometimes hold it half a sin
To put in words the grief I feel;
For words, like Nature, half reveal
And half conceal the Soul within.

Ibid. Part V, Stanza 1

But, for the unquiet heart and brain
A use in measured language lies;
The sad mechanic exercise,
Like dull narcotics numbing pain.

Ibid. Stanza 2

Never morning wore
To evening, but some heart did break.

Ibid. Part VI, Stanza 2

And topples round the dreary west
A looming bastion fringed with fire.

Ibid. Part XV, Stanza 5

And from his ashes may be made
The violet of his native land.[1]

Ibid. Part XVIII, Stanza 1

I do but sing because I must,
And pipe but as the linnets sing.[2]

Ibid. Part XXI, Stanza 6

The shadow cloaked from head to foot.

Ibid. Part XXIII, Stanza 1

Who keeps the keys of all the creeds.

Ibid. Stanza 2

And Thought leapt out to wed with Thought
Ere Thought could wed itself with Speech.

Ibid. Stanza 4

And round us all the thicket rang
To many a flute of Arcady.

Ibid. Stanza 6

'Tis better to have loved and lost
Than never to have loved at all.[3]

Ibid. Part XXVII, Stanza 4

[1] See Shakespeare, page 179a, and Fitzgerald, page 531b.
[2] Ich singe, wie der Vogel singt
Der in den Zweigen wohnet.
GOETHE: *Wilhelm Meister's Apprenticeship* [1786–1830], *Book II, Chap. 11*
[3] Say what you will, 'tis better to be left

Her eyes are homes of silent prayer.
In Memoriam. Part XXXII,
Stanza 1

Thrice blest whose lives are faithful
prayers,
Whose loves in higher love endure;
What souls possess themselves so
pure,
Or is there blessedness like theirs?
Ibid. Stanza 4

Whose faith has centre everywhere,
Nor cares to fix itself to form.
Ibid. Part XXXIII, Stanza 1

How fares it with the happy dead?
Ibid. Part XLIV, Stanza 1

Short swallow-flights of song, that dip
Their wings in tears, and skim away.
Ibid. Part XLVIII, Stanza 4

Be near me when my light is low.
Ibid. Part L, Stanza 1

And Time, a maniac scattering dust,
And Life, a Fury slinging flame.
Ibid. Stanza 2

Do we indeed desire the dead
Should still be near us at our side?
Ibid. Part LI, Stanza 1

Hold thou the good; define it well;
For fear divine Philosophy
Should push beyond her mark, and
be
Procuress to the Lords of Hell.
Ibid. Part LIII, Stanza 4

Oh yet we trust that somehow good
Will be the final goal of ill.
Ibid. Part LIV, Stanza 1

But what am I?
An infant crying in the night:
An infant crying for the light:
And with no language but a cry.[1]
Ibid. Stanza 5

---

than never to have been loved. — CONGREVE:
The Way of the World [1700], *Act II, Sc. 6*
Better to love amiss than nothing to have
loved. — CRABBE: *Tales* [1812], *XIV, The*
Struggles of Conscience
What voice did on my spirit fall,
Peschiera, when thy bridge I crost?
'Tis better to have fought and lost
Than never to have fought at all.
ARTHUR HUGH CLOUGH [1819–1861]:
Peschiera

[1] See Pliny, page 49b.

So careful of the type she seems,
So careless of the single life.
In Memoriam. Part LV,
Stanza 2

The great world's altar-stairs,
That slope through darkness up to God.
Ibid. Stanza 4

And faintly trust the larger hope.
Ibid. Stanza 5

Nature, red in tooth and claw.
Ibid. Part LVI, Stanza 4

Who battled for the True, the Just.
Ibid. Stanza 5

The sweetest soul
That ever look'd with human eyes.
Ibid. Part LVII, Stanza 3

Who breaks his birth's invidious bar,
And grasps the skirts of happy chance,
And breasts the blows of circumstance.
Ibid. Part LXIV, Stanza 2

And lives to clutch the golden keys,
To mould a mighty state's decrees,
And shape the whisper of the throne.
Ibid. Stanza 3

So many worlds, so much to do,
So little done, such things to be.[1]
Ibid. Part LXXIII, Stanza 1

O last regret, regret can die!
Ibid. Part LXXVIII, Stanza 5

The little speedwell's darling blue.
Ibid. Part LXXXIII, Stanza 2

God's finger touch'd him, and he slept.
Ibid. Part LXXXV, Stanza 5

There lives more faith in honest doubt,[2]
Believe me, than in half the creeds.
Ibid. Part XCVI, Stanza 3

He seems so near, and yet so far.
Ibid. Part XCVII, Stanza 6

Ring out, wild bells, to the wild sky!
Ibid. Part CVI, Stanza 1

Ring out the old, ring in the new,
Ring, happy bells, across the snow!
Ibid. Stanza 2

---

[1] How little I have gained,
How vast the unattained.
WHITTIER [1807–1892]: *My Triumph,*
St. 7

[2] Who never doubted never half believed.
Where doubt there truth is — 'tis her
shadow.
P. J. BAILEY [1816–1902]: *Festus:*
A Country Town

Ring in the nobler modes of life
With sweeter manners, purer laws.
In Memoriam. Part CVI,
Stanza 4

Ring out old shapes of foul disease,
Ring out the narrowing lust of gold;
Ring out the thousand wars of old,
Ring in the thousand years of peace!
Ibid. Stanza 7

Ring in the valiant man and free,
The larger heart, the kindlier hand!
Ring out the darkness of the land,
Ring in the Christ that is to be!
Ibid. Stanza 8

The blind hysterics of the Celt.
Ibid. Part CIX, Stanza 4

And thus he bore without abuse
The grand old name of gentleman,
Defamed by every charlatan,
And soiled with all ignoble use.
Ibid. Part CXI, Stanza 6

Wearing all that weight
Of learning lightly like a flower.
Ibid. Conclusion, Stanza 10

One God, one law, one element,
And one far-off divine event,
To which the whole creation moves.
Ibid. Stanza 36

He clasps the crag with crooked hands;
Close to the sun in lonely lands,
Ring'd with the azure world he stands.

The wrinkled sea beneath him crawls;
He watches from his mountain walls,
And like a thunderbolt he falls.
The Eagle [1851]

This laurel greener from the brows
Of him that utter'd nothing base.[1]
To the Queen [1851]. Stanza 2

Broad-based upon her people's will,
And compass'd by the inviolate sea.
Ibid. Stanza 9

Rich in saving common-sense,
And, as the greatest only are,
In his simplicity sublime.
Oh good gray head which all men knew!
Ode on the Death of the Duke of
Wellington [1852]. Stanza 4

O iron nerve to true occasion true,
O fall'n at length, that tower of
strength
Which stood four-square to all the
winds that blew.
Ode on the Death of the Duke
of Wellington. Stanza 4

Not once or twice in our rough island
story
The path of duty was the way to glory.[1]
Ibid. Stanza 8

We are not cotton-spinners all.
The Third of February, 1852.
Stanza 8

Half a league, half a league,
Half a league onward,
All in the valley of death
Rode the six hundred.
The Charge of the Light Brigade
[1854]. Stanza 1

Some one had blundered:
Theirs not to make reply,
Theirs not to reason why,
Theirs but to do and die.
Ibid. Stanza 2

Cannon to right of them,
Cannon to left of them,
Cannon in front of them
Volley'd and thunder'd. . . .
Into the jaws of death,
Into the mouth of hell
Rode the six hundred.
Ibid. Stanza 3

For men may come and men may go,
But I go on forever.
Song from The Brook [1855].
Stanza 6

Faultily faultless, icily regular, splendidly null.
Maud [1855]. Part I, II

That jewelled mass of millinery,
That oiled and curled Assyrian Bull.
Ibid. VI, Stanza 6

One still strong man in a blatant land.
Ibid. X, Stanza 5

Gorgonized me from head to foot,
With a stony British stare.
Ibid. XIII, Stanza 2

Come into the garden, Maud,
For the black bat, night, has flown,

[1] Wordsworth, Tennyson's predecessor as poet laureate.

[1] See Thomas Gray, page 348a–348b.

Come into the garden, Maud,
  I am here at the gate alone.
        Maud. Part I, XXII, Stanza 1
All night have the roses heard
  The flute, violin, bassoon;
All night has the casement jessamine
    stirr'd
  To the dancers dancing in tune;
Till a silence fell with the waking bird,
  And a hush with the setting moon.
          Ibid. Stanza 3
Queen rose of the rosebud garden of
    girls.
          Ibid. Stanza 9
She is coming, my own, my sweet;
  Were it ever so airy a tread,
My heart would hear her and beat,
  Were it earth in an earthy bed;
My dust would hear her and beat,
  Had I lain for a century dead;
Would start and tremble under her feet,
  And blossom in purple and red.
          Ibid. Stanza 11
Ah Christ, that it were possible
  For one short hour to see
The souls we loved, that they might
    tell us
What and where they be.
      Ibid. Part II, IV, Stanza 3
And after many a summer dies the
    swan.
          Tithonus [1860]. Line 4
Here at the quiet limit of the world.
            Ibid. Line 7
Wearing the white flower of a blame-
    less life,
Before a thousand peering littlenesses,
In that fierce light which beats upon a
    throne,
And blackens every blot.
    Idylls of the King [1859–1885].
                Dedication, Line 24
Man's word is God in man.
      Ibid. The Coming of Arthur,
                    Line 132
Large divine and comfortable words.[1]
            Ibid. Line 267
Live pure, speak true, right wrong, fol-
    low the King —

[1] Hear what comfortable words our Saviour
Christ saith unto all who truly turn to him. —
Book of Common Prayer, Holy Communion

Else, wherefore born?
    Idylls of the King. Gareth and
                Lynette, Line 117
A damsel of high lineage, and a brow
May-blossom, and a cheek of apple-
    blossom,
Hawk-eyes; and lightly was her slen-
    der nose
Tip-tilted like the petal of a flower.
          Ibid. Line 574
Our hoard is little, but our hearts are
    great.
      Ibid. The Marriage of Geraint,
                    Line 352
For man is man and master of his fate.[1]
            Ibid. Line 355
The useful trouble of the rain.
    Ibid. Geraint and Enid, Line 770
The world will not believe a man re-
    pents;
And this wise world of ours is mainly
    right.
          Ibid. Line 899
The whole wood-world is one full peal
    of praise.
      Ibid. Balin and Balan, Line 444
Mere white truth in simple nakedness.
            Ibid. Line 509
As love, if love be perfect, casts out
    fear,
So hate, if hate be perfect, casts out
    fear.
      Ibid. Merlin and Vivien, Line 41
Faith and unfaith can ne'er be equal
    powers:
Unfaith in aught is want of faith in all.
            Ibid. Line 384
It is the little rift within the lute,
That by and by will make the music
    mute,
And ever widening slowly silence all.
            Ibid. Line 386
Blind and naked Ignorance
Delivers brawling judgments, un-
    ashamed,
On all things all day long.
            Ibid. Line 662
For men at most differ as heaven and
    earth,

[1] See Sallust, page 35b.

But women, worst and best, as heaven
and hell.
>   *Idylls of the King. Merlin and*
>   *Vivien, Line 812*

Elaine the fair, Elaine the loveable,
Elaine, the lily maid of Astolat.
>   *Ibid. Lancelot and Elaine. Line 1*

But, friend, to me
He is all fault who hath no fault at all.
For who loves me must have a touch
of earth.
>   *Ibid. Line 131*

In me there dwells
No greatness, save it be some far-off
touch
Of greatness to know well I am not
great.
>   *Ibid. Line 447*

The shackles of an old love straitened
him,
His honour rooted in dishonour stood,
And faith unfaithful kept him falsely
true.
>   *Ibid. Line 870*

Sweet is true love tho' given in vain,
in vain;
And sweet is death who puts an end
to pain.
>   *Ibid. Line 1000*

He makes no friend who never made
a foe.
>   *Ibid. Line 1082*

Figs out of thistles.
>   *Ibid. The Last Tournament,*
>   *Line 356*

The greater man the greater courtesy.
>   *Ibid. Line 628*

The vow that binds too strictly snaps
itself.
>   *Ibid. Line 652*

For courtesy wins woman all as well
As valor may.
>   *Ibid. Line 702*

For manners are not idle, but the fruit
Of loyal nature and of noble mind.
>   *Ibid. Guinevere, Line 333*

To love one maiden only, cleave to her,
And worship her by years of golden
deeds.
>   *Ibid. Line 472*

No more subtle master under heaven
Than is the maiden passion for a maid,

Not only to keep down the base in man,
But teach high thought, and amiable
words
And courtliness, and the desire of fame,
And love of truth, and all that makes
a man.
>   *Idylls of the King. Guinevere,*
>   *Line 475*

To where beyond these voices there is
peace.
>   *Ibid. Line 692*

I found Him in the shining of the stars,
I mark'd Him in the flowering of His
fields,
But in His ways with men I find Him
not.
>   *Ibid. The Passing of Arthur,*
>   *Line 9*

For why is all around us here
As if some lesser god had made the
world,
But had not force to shape it as he
would?
>   *Ibid. Line 13*

Clothed in white samite, mystic, wonderful.
>   *Ibid. Line 199*

Cast all your cares on God; that anchor holds.
>   *Enoch Arden* [1864]

Insipid as the queen upon a card.
>   *Aylmer's Field* [1864]

Marriages are made in Heaven.[1]
>   *Ibid.*

He that wrongs his friend
Wrongs himself more, and ever bears
about
A silent court of justice in his breast,
Himself the judge and jury, and him-
self
The prisoner at the bar, ever con-
demn'd.
>   *Ibid.*

The worst is yet to come.[2]
>   *Ibid.*

---

[1] Marriage is Destiny, made in heaven.
—LYLY: *Mother Bombie* [1594]
      If marriages
Are made in Heaven, they should be happier.
   SOUTHERNE: *The Fatal Marriage* [1694]
   See Heywood, page 91a.
[2] See Browning, page 572a, and Philander
Johnson, page 830a.

That a lie which is half a truth is ever
the blackest of lies,
That a lie which is all a lie may be met
and fought with outright,
But a lie which is part a truth is a
harder matter to fight.
The Grandmother [*1864*].
Stanza 8

Doänt thou marry for munny, but goä
wheer munny is!
Northern Farmer: New Style
[*1869*]. *Stanza 5*

Speak to Him thou for He hears, and
Spirit with Spirit can meet —
Closer is He than breathing, and nearer
than hands and feet.
The Higher Pantheism [*1869*].
Stanza 6

Flower in the crannied wall,
I pluck you out of the crannies,
I hold you here, root and all, in my
hand,
Little flower — but *if* I could under-
stand
What you are, root and all, and all in
all,
I should know what God and man is.
Flower in the Crannied Wall
[*1869*]

At Flores in the Azores Sir Richard
Grenville lay,
And a pinnace, like a flutter'd bird,
came flying from far away;
"Spanish ships of war at sea! we have
sighted fifty-three!"
The Revenge [*1878*]. *Stanza 1*

Then sware Lord Thomas Howard:
" 'Fore God I am no coward."
Ibid.

"I should count myself the coward if I
left them, my Lord Howard,
To these Inquisition dogs and the devildoms of Spain."
Ibid. Stanza 2

All the charm of all the Muses often
flowering in a lonely word.
To Virgil [*1882*]

Old men must die, or the world would
grow mouldy, would only breed
the past again.
Becket [*1884*]. *Prologue*

Cleave ever to the sunnier side of
doubt,
And cling to Faith beyond the forms
of Faith.
The Ancient Sage [*1885*]

The shell must break before the bird
can fly.
Ibid.

Slav, Teuton, Kelt, I count them all
My friends and brother souls,
With all the peoples, great and small,
That wheel between the poles.
*The Charge of the Heavy
Brigade. Epilogue* [*1885*]

The song that nerves a nation's heart
Is in itself a deed.
Ibid.

That man's the best Cosmopolite
Who loves his native country best.
Hands All Round [*1885*]

Love your enemy, bless your haters,
said the Greatest of the great;
Christian love among the Churches
looked the twin of heathen hate.
*Locksley Hall Sixty Years
After* [*1886*]. *Line 85*

Charm us, orator, till the lion look no
larger than the cat.
Ibid. Line 112

Authors — essayist, atheist, novelist,
realist, rhymester, play your part,
Paint the mortal shame of nature with
the living hues of art.
Ibid. Line 139

Not of the sunlight,
Not of the moonlight,
Not of the starlight!
O young Mariner,
Down to the haven,
Call your companions,
Launch your vessel
And crowd your canvas,
And, ere it vanishes
Over the margin,
After it, follow it,
Follow the Gleam.[1]
Merlin and the Gleam [*1889*].
Stanza 10

[1] The Gleam . . . signifies in my poem
the higher poetic imagination. — *In* HALLAM
TENNYSON: *Alfred, Lord Tennyson, A
Memoir* [1897], *Vol. II, P. 366*

Sunset and evening star,
  And one clear call for me!
And may there be no moaning of the
    bar,
  When I put out to sea.
        Crossing the Bar [*1889*].
                Stanza 1
But such a tide as moving seems asleep,
  Too full for sound and foam,
When that which drew from out the
    boundless deep
  Turns again home.
        Ibid. Stanza 2
Twilight and evening bell,
  And after that the dark.
        Ibid. Stanza 3
I hope to see my Pilot face to face
When I have crossed the bar.
        Ibid. Stanza 4

ROBERT CHARLES WINTHROP
[1809–1894]

Our Country, — whether bounded
by the St. John's and the Sabine, or
however otherwise bounded[1] or described, and be the measurements more
or less, — still our Country, to be
cherished in all our hearts, to be defended by all our hands.
        Toast at Faneuil Hall [*Fourth
            of July, 1845*]
  A star for every State, and a State
for every star.
        Address on Boston Common [*1862*]
  Slavery is but half abolished, eman-
cipation is but half completed, while
millions of freemen with votes in their
hands are left without education. Justice to them, the welfare of the States
in which they live, the safety of the
whole Republic, the dignity of the elective franchise, — all alike demand that
the still remaining bonds of ignorance
shall be unloosed and broken, and the

[1] The United States — bounded on the
north by the Aurora Borealis, on the south by
the precession of the equinoxes, on the east
by the primeval chaos, and on the west by the
Day of Judgment. — JOHN FISKE [1842–
1901]: *Bounding the United States*

minds as well as the bodies of the eman-
cipated go free.
        Yorktown Oration [*1881*]

SAMUEL DODGE
[*Floruit* 1868]

You may go through this world, but
    'twill be very slow
If you listen to all that is said as you
    go;
You'll be worried and fretted and kept
    in a stew,
For meddlesome tongues must have
    something to do,
For people will talk, you know.
        People Will Talk. Stanza 1

PHINEAS TAYLOR BARNUM
[1810–1891]

There's a sucker born every minute.
        Attributed

WILLIAM HENRY CHANNING
[1810–1884]

To live content with small means; to
seek elegance rather than luxury, and
refinement rather than fashion; to be
worthy, not respectable, and wealthy,
not rich; to study hard, think quietly,
talk gently, act frankly; to listen to
stars and birds, to babes and sages,
with open heart; to bear all cheerfully,
do all bravely, await occasions, hurry
never. In a word, to let the spiritual,
unbidden and unconscious, grow up
through the common. This is to be my
symphony.
        My Symphony

DANIEL CLEMENT COLESWORTHY
[1810–1893]

A little word in kindness spoken,
  A motion or a tear,

Has often healed the heart that's broken,
And made a friend sincere.
A Little Word. Stanza 1

Then deem it not an idle thing
A pleasant word to speak;
The face you wear — the thoughts you bring —
The heart may heal or break.
Ibid. Stanza 3

SIR FRANCIS HASTINGS DOYLE
[1810–1888]

Last night, among his fellow roughs,
He jested, quaffed, and swore;
A drunken private of the Buffs,
Who never looked before.
Today, beneath the foeman's frown,
He stands in Elgin's place,
Ambassador from Britain's crown,
And type of all her race.
The Private of the Buffs. Stanza 1

ELIZABETH CLEGHORN GASKELL
[1810–1865]

A man is *so* in the way in the house.
Cranford [1851–1853]. Chap. 1

Correspondence, which bears much the same relation to personal intercourse that the books of dried plants I sometimes see ("Hortus Siccus," I think they call the thing) do to the living and fresh flowers in the lanes and meadows.
Ibid. Chap. 3

One gives people in grief their own way.
Ibid. Chap. 6

A little credulity helps one on through life very smoothly.
Ibid. Chap. 11

I'll not listen to reason. . . . Reason always means what some one else has got to say.
Ibid. Chap. 14

GENERAL PIERRE BOSQUET
[1810–1861]

It is magnificent, but it is not war.[1]
Said of the charge of the Light Brigade at the battle of Balaklava [October 25, 1854]

ALFRED DE MUSSET
[1810–1857]

How glorious it is — and also how painful — to be an exception.
Le Merle Blanc. I

Things they don't understand always cause a sensation among the English.
Ibid. VIII

Never were there so many sleepless nights as in the time of this man [Napoleon]. Never did one see so many anguished mothers gaze from the ramparts of the towns. Never was there such silence when one spoke of death. And yet there was never so much joy, life, warlike music, in all hearts. There was never such pure sunshine as that which dried all this blood. People said that God made it for this man; they called it Austerlitz weather. But he made it himself with his incessant gunfire, and the only clouds were on the morrow of his battles.
Confession d'un Enfant du Siècle [1836]. Chap. 2

POPE LEO XIII (GIACCHINO PECCI)
[1810–1903]

Every man has by nature the right to possess property as his own.
Encyclical Letter on the Condition of Labor [May 15, 1891]

It is impossible to reduce human society to one level.
Ibid.

It is one thing to have a right to the possession of money, and another to have a right to use money as one pleases.
Ibid.

[1] C'est magnifique, mais ce n'est pas la guerre.
See Tennyson, page 553b.

When a society is perishing, the true advice to give to those who would restore it is to recall it to the principles from which it sprung.

*Encyclical Letter on the
Condition of Labor*

Among the purposes of a society should be to try to arrange for a continuous supply of work at all times and seasons.

Ibid.

JAMES SLOANE GIBBONS
[1810–1892]

We are coming, Father Abraham, three
hundred thousand more,
From Mississippi's winding stream and
from New England's shore;
We leave our ploughs and workshops,
our wives and children dear,
With hearts too full for utterance, with
but a silent tear.

Three Hundred Thousand More.[1]
Stanza 1

WILLIAM MILLER
[1810–1872]

Wee Willie Winkie rins through the
toun,
Upstairs and dounstairs, in his nicht-
goun,
Tirlin' at the window, cryin' at the
lock,
"Are the weans in their bed? for it's
nou ten o'clock."

Willie Winkie

MARGARET FULLER
(OSSOLI)
[1810–1850]

I myself am more divine than any I
see.

*Letter to Emerson
[March 1, 1838]*

The golden-rod is one of the fairy, magical flowers; it grows not up to seek human love amid the light of day, but

[1] First printed in the *New York Evening Post,* July 16, 1862.

to mark to the discerning what wealth lies hid in the secret caves of earth.

Journal [September, 1840]

Beware of over-great pleasure in being popular or even beloved. As far as an amiable disposition and powers of entertainment make you so, it is happiness, but if there is one grain of plausibility, it is a poison.

*Letter to her brother Arthur
[December 20, 1840]*

What I mean by the Muse is that unimpeded clearness of the intuitive powers, which a perfectly truthful adherence to every admonition of the higher instincts would bring to a finely organized human being. . . . Should these faculties have free play, I believe they will open new, deeper and purer sources of joyous inspiration than have yet refreshed the earth.

*Woman in the Nineteenth
Century [1845]*

It does not follow because many books are written by persons born in America that there exists an American literature. Books which imitate or represent the thoughts and life of Europe do not constitute an American literature. Before such can exist, an original idea must animate this nation and fresh currents of life must call into life fresh thoughts along its shores.

In the New York Tribune [1846]

Truth is the nursing mother of genius. No man can be absolutely true to himself, eschewing cant, compromise, servile imitation, and complaisance, without becoming original for there is in every creature a fountain of life which, if not choked back by stones and other dead rubbish, will create a fresh atmosphere, and bring to life fresh beauty.

Ibid.

When an immortal poet was secure only of a few copyists to circulate his works, there were princes and nobles to patronize literature and the arts. Here is only the public, and the public must learn how to cherish the nobler and rarer plants, and to plant the aloe, able to wait a hundred years for its bloom, or its garden will contain, presently, nothing but potatoes and pot-herbs.

In the New York Tribune

This was one of the rye-bread days, all dull and damp without.

Diary. Quoted by THOMAS WENTWORTH HIGGINSON: *Life of Margaret Fuller Ossoli [1884], Chap. 7*

For precocity some great price is always demanded sooner or later in life.

Ibid. Chap. 18

Genius will live and thrive without training, but it does not the less reward the watering-pot and pruning-knife.

Ibid.

I accept the universe.[1]

Attributed

THEODORE PARKER
[1810–1860]

Truth never yet fell dead in the streets; it has such affinity with the soul of man, the seed however broadcast will catch somewhere and produce its hundredfold.

A Discourse of Matters Pertaining to Religion [1842]

Truth stood on one side and Ease on the other; it has often been so.

Ibid.

Man never falls so low that he can see nothing higher than himself.

Essay, A Lesson for the Day

All men desire to be immortal.

A Sermon on the Immortal Life [September 20, 1846]

A democracy, — that is a government of all the people, by all the people, for all the people;[2] of course, a government of the principles of eternal justice, the unchanging law of God; for shortness' sake I will call it the idea of Freedom.

The American Idea[1] *[1850]*

We look to Thee; Thy truth is still the Light
Which guides the nations, groping on their way,
Stumbling and falling in disastrous night,
Yet hoping ever for the perfect day.

The Way, the Truth, and the Life.
Stanza 2

EDMUND HAMILTON SEARS
[1810–1876]

Calm on the listening ear of night
Come Heaven's melodious strains,
Where wild Judea stretches far
Her silver-mantled plains.

Christmas Song [1834]

It came upon the midnight clear,
That glorious song of old,
From Angels bending near the earth
To touch their harps of gold;
"Peace on the earth, good will to men
From Heaven's all gracious King."
The world in solemn stillness lay
To hear the angels sing.

The Angels' Song [1850]

When Peace shall over all the earth
Its ancient splendors fling
And the whole world send back the song
Which now the angels sing.

Ibid.

GEORGE SHARSWOOD
[1810–1883]

It is not uncommon to hear the expression, "The law is a jealous mistress." It is true that this profession, like all others, demands of those who

---

[1] By God! she'd better. — CARLYLE's *reported comment*

[2] See Daniel Webster, page 443b, William Lloyd Garrison, page 517b, and Lincoln, page 541a.
Parker used the same phrase in a speech delivered in Boston [May 31, 1854] and in a sermon in Music Hall, Boston [July 4, 1858]. WILLIAM H. HERNDON visited Boston and on his return to Springfield, Illinois, took with him some of Parker's sermons and addresses. In his *Abraham Lincoln, Vol. II, P. 65,* Herndon says that Lincoln marked with pencil the portion of the Music Hall address, "Democracy is direct self-government, over all the people, by all the people, for all the people."

[1] Speech at the New England Anti-Slavery Convention, Boston [May 29, 1850].

would succeed in it an earnest and entire devotion.[1]

Memoir of William Blackstone,
Blackstone's Commentaries
[1860]

MARTIN FARQUHAR TUPPER
[1810–1889]

A babe in a house is a well-spring of pleasure.

Proverbial Philosophy [*1838–*
1842]. *Of Education*

Analogy is milk for babes, but abstract truths are strong meat.

Ibid.

God, from a beautiful necessity, is Love.

Ibid. Of Immortality

Error is a hardy plant: it flourisheth in every soil.

Ibid. Of Truth in Things False

Wait, thou child of hope, for Time shall teach thee all things.

Ibid. Of Good in Things Evil

Clamorous pauperism feasteth While honest Labor, pining, hideth his sharp ribs.

Ibid. Of Discretion

Well-timed silence hath more eloquence than speech.

Ibid.

It is well to lie fallow for a while.

Ibid. Of Recreation

A good book is the best of friends, the same today and for ever.

Ibid. Of Reading

Who can wrestle against Sleep? —
Yet is that giant very gentleness.

Ibid. Of Beauty

Nature's own Nobleman, friendly and frank,
Is a man with his heart in his hand!

Nature's Nobleman [*1844*].
Stanza 1

[1] I will not say with Lord Hale, that "The Law will admit of no rival," . . . but I will say that it is a jealous mistress, and requires a long and constant courtship. It is not to be won by trifling favors, but by lavish homage. — JOSEPH STORY: *The Value and Importance of Legal Studies* [1829]

See Emerson, page 505a.

Hope and be happy that all's for the best!

All's for the Best [*1844*].
Stanza 3

Never go gloomily, man with a mind!
Hope is a better companion than fear.

Cheer Up [*1844*]. *Stanza 1*

JOHN BRIGHT
[1811–1889]

And even if I were alone, if mine were a solitary voice, raised amid the din of arms and the clamours of a venal press, I should have the consolation I have tonight — and which I trust will be mine to the last moment of my existence — the priceless consolation that no word of mine has tended to the squandering of my country's treasure or the spilling of one single drop of my country's blood.[1]

Speech on the Crimean War,
House of Commons [*December*
22, 1854]

The Angel of Death has been abroad throughout the land; you may almost hear the beating of his wings.

Speech, House of Commons
[*February 23, 1855*]

Force is no remedy.

On the Irish Troubles [*1880*]

My opinion is that the Northern States will manage somehow to muddle through.

Said during the American Civil
War. Quoted in JUSTIN MC-
CARTHY: *Reminiscences* [*1899*]

THÉOPHILE GAUTIER
[1811–1872]

Everything passes. Robust art alone is eternal. The bust outlasts the citadel.[2]

L'Art

[1] See Jefferson, page 375b.
[2] Tout passe. L'art robuste
Seul a l'éternité;
Le buste
Survit à la cité.

HORACE GREELEY
[1811–1872]

A widow of doubtful age will marry almost any sort of a white man.
> *Letter to Dr. Rufus Wilmot Griswold*

If, on a full and final review, my life and practice shall be found unworthy of my principles, let due infamy be heaped on my memory; but let none be thereby led to distrust the principles to which I proved recreant, nor yet the ability of some to adorn them by a suitable life and conversation. To unerring time be all this committed.
> *Statement* [*1846*], *quoted in* JAMES PARTON: *Life of Horace Greeley* [*1855*]

The best business you can go into you will find on your father's farm or in his workshop. If you have no family or friends to aid you, and no prospect opened to you there, turn your face to the great West,[1] and there build up a home and fortune.
> *To Aspiring Young Men. Ibid. Page 414*

The illusion that times that were are better than those that are, has probably pervaded all ages.
> *The American Conflict* [*1864–1866*]

Wisdom is never dear, provided the article be genuine.
> *Address on Agriculture, Houston, Texas* [*May 23, 1871*]

FRANCES SARGENT OSGOOD
[1811–1850]

Work — for some good, be it ever so slowly;
Cherish some flower, be it ever so lowly;
Labor! — all labor is noble and holy!
Let thy great deeds be thy prayer to thy God!
> *Laborare est Orare.*[2] *Stanza 6*

[1] See J. B. L. Soule, page 585a.
[2] To labor is to pray. — Motto of BENEDICT [480–543], *founder of the Benedictine Order*

WENDELL PHILLIPS
[1811–1884]

Take the whole range of imaginative literature, and we are all wholesale borrowers. In every matter that relates to invention, to use, or beauty or form, we are borrowers.
> *Lecture, The Lost Arts* [*1838*]

We live under a government of men — and morning newspapers.
> *Speech* [*January 28, 1852*]

Revolutions are not made; they come. A revolution is as natural a growth as an oak. It comes out of the past. Its foundations are laid far back.
> *Ibid.*

The best use of laws is to teach men to trample bad laws under their feet.
> *Speech* [*April 12, 1852*]

What the Puritans gave the world was not thought, but action.
> *Speech* [*December 21, 1855*]

One on God's side is a majority.
> *Speech* [*November 1, 1859*]

Every man meets his Waterloo at last.
> *Ibid.*

Truth is one forever absolute, but opinion is truth filtered through the moods, the blood, the disposition of the spectator.
> *Idols* [*October 4, 1859*]

Difference of religion breeds more quarrels than difference of politics.
> *Speech* [*November 7, 1860*]

Governments exist to protect the rights of minorities. The loved and the rich need no protection, — they have many friends and few enemies.
> *Speech* [*December 21, 1860*]

Revolutions never go backward.[1]
> *Speech* [*February 17, 1861*]

Some doubt the courage of the Negro. Go to Haiti and stand on those fifty thousand graves of the best sol-

[1] I know, and all the world knows, that revolutions never go backward. — WILLIAM HENRY SEWARD: *Speech at Rochester on the Irrepressible Conflict* [October, 1858]

diers France ever had, and ask them what they think of the Negro's sword.

Address on Toussaint L'Ouverture [*1861*]

Aristocracy is always cruel.

Ibid.

HARRIET BEECHER STOWE [1]
[1811–1896]

Eliza made her desperate retreat across the river just in the dusk of twilight. The grey mist of evening, rising slowly from the river, enveloped her as she disappeared up the bank, and the swollen current and floundering masses of ice presented a hopeless barrier between her and her pursuer.

Uncle Tom's Cabin [*1852*].
Chap. 8

I 'spect I growed. Don't think nobody never made me.

Ibid. Chap. 20

I's wicked — I is. I's mighty wicked, anyhow. I can't help it.

Ibid.

Whipping and abuse are like laudanum: you have to double the dose as the sensibilities decline.

Ibid.

It lies around us like a cloud,
  A world we do not see;
Yet the sweet closing of an eye
  May bring us there to be.

The Other World [*1867*].
Stanza 1

CHARLES SUMNER
[1811–1874]

There is the National flag. He must be cold, indeed, who can look upon its folds rippling in the breeze without pride of country. If in a foreign land,

the flag is companionship, and country itself, with all its endearments.

Are We a Nation? [*November 19, 1867*]

White is for purity; red, for valor; blue for justice. And altogether, bunting, stripes, stars, and colors, blazing in the sky, make the flag of our country, to be cherished by all our hearts, to be upheld by all our hands.

Ibid.

WILLIAM MAKEPEACE THACKERAY
[1811–1863]

Although I enter not,
Yet round about the spot
  Ofttimes I hover;
And near the sacred gate,
With longing eyes I wait,
  Expectant of her.

At the Church Gate [1]

The play is done; the curtain drops,
  Slow falling to the prompter's bell:
A moment yet the actor stops,
  And looks around, to say farewell.
It is an irksome word and task;
  And when he's laughed and said his say,
He shows, as he removes the mask,
  A face that's anything but gay.

Doctor Birch and His Young Friends. Epilogue, The End of the Play, Stanza 1

Christmas is here:
Winds whistle shrill,
Icy and chill,
Little care we;
Little we fear
Weather without,
Sheltered about
The Mahogany Tree.

The Mahogany Tree. Stanza 1

Though more than half the world was his,

He [2] died without a rood his own;

---

[1] We have seen an American woman write a novel of which a million copies were sold in all languages, and which had one merit, of speaking to the universal heart, and was read with equal interest to three audiences, namely, in the parlor, in the kitchen, and in the nursery of every house. — EMERSON: *Society and Solitude* [1870], *Success*

[1] In *Pendennis* [1848–1850], *Vol. I, Chap. 31,* the third and fourth lines read:
  Sometimes I hover,
  And at the sacred gate.

[2] Napoleon Bonaparte; the ballad was written in Paris at the time of the second funeral of Napoleon [1840].

And borrow'd from his enemies
Six foot of ground to lie upon.
The Chronicle of the Drum. Part II

Werther had a love for Charlotte
Such as words could never utter;
Would you know how first he met her?
She was cutting bread and butter.[1]
Sorrows of Werther. Stanza 1

Charlotte was a married lady,
And a moral man was Werther,
And for all the wealth of Indies,
Would do nothing for to hurt her.
Ibid. Stanza 2

So he sighed and pined and ogled,
And his passion boiled and bubbled,
Till he blew his silly brains out
And no more was by it troubled.
Ibid. Stanza 3

Charlotte, having seen his body
Borne before her on a shutter,
Like a well-conducted person,
Went on cutting bread and butter.
Ibid. Stanza 4

Away from the world and its toils and
its cares,
I've a snug little kingdom up four pairs
of stairs.
The Cane-Bottom'd Chair. Stanza 1

A man — I let the truth out —
Who's had almost every tooth out,
Cannot sing as once he sung,
When he was young as you are young,
When he was young and lutes were
strung,
And love-lamps in the casement hung.
Mrs. Katherine's Lantern. Stanza 6

The rose upon my balcony the morning
air perfuming,
Was leafless all the winter time and
pining for the spring.
The Rose Upon My Balcony.
Stanza 1

There lived a sage in days of yore,
And he a handsome pigtail wore;

[1] Charlotte held a brown loaf in her hand, and was cutting slices for the little ones all round in proportion to their age and appetite. — GOETHE: *The Sorrows of Werther* [1774]

But wondered much and sorrowed more
Because it hung behind him.
A Tragic Story (from von
Chamisso). Stanza 1

In the brave days when I was twenty-
one.
The Garret. Refrain

There were three sailors of Bristol City
Who took a boat and went to sea.
But first with beef and captain's bis-
cuits
And pickled pork they loaded she.
There was gorging Jack and guzzling
Jimmy,
And the youngest he was little Billee.
Now when they got as far as the
Equator
They'd nothing left but one split pea.
Little Billee

Says gorging Jim to guzzling Jacky,
We have no wittles, so we must eat *we*.
Ibid.

There's little Bill as is young and
tender,
We're old and tough — so let's eat *he*.
Ibid.

This I set down as a positive truth.
A woman with fair opportunities, and
without a positive hump, may marry
whom she likes.[1]
Vanity Fair [1847–1848].
Vol. I, Chap. 4

Them's my sentiments.
Ibid. Chap. 21

Everybody in Vanity Fair must have
remarked how well those live who are
comfortably and thoroughly in debt;
how they deny themselves nothing;
how jolly and easy they are in their
minds.
Ibid. Chap. 22

When we say of a gentleman that he
lives elegantly on nothing a year, we
use the word "nothing" to signify some-

[1] I should like to see any kind of a man, distinguishable from a gorilla, that some good and even pretty woman could not shape a husband out of. — OLIVER WENDELL HOLMES: *The Professor at the Breakfast-Table* [1860]
The whole world is strewn with snares, gins and pitfalls for the capture of men by women. — BERNARD SHAW: *Man and Superman* [1903], *Epistle Dedicatory*

thing unknown; meaning, simply, that we don't know how the gentleman in question defrays the expenses of his establishment.

Vanity Fair. Vol. I, Chap. 35

How to Live Well on Nothing a Year.

Ibid. Title of Chap. 36

Mother is the name for God in the lips and hearts of little children.[1]

Ibid. Chap. 37

I think I could be a good woman if I had five thousand a year.[2]

Ibid. Vol. II, Chap. 1

A comfortable career of prosperity, if it does not make people honest, at least keeps them so.

Ibid.

By economy and good management, — by a sparing use of ready money and by paying scarcely anybody, — people can manage, for a time at least, to make a great show with very little means.

Ibid. Chap. 11

Ah! *Vanitas Vanitatum!* Which of us is happy in this world? Which of us has his desire? or, having it, is satisfied? — Come, children, let us shut up the box and the puppets, for our play is played out.

Ibid. Chap. 27

He who meanly admires mean things is a Snob.

The Book of Snobs [1848].
Chap. 2

Rake's Progress.[3]

Pendennis [1848–1850]. Title of Chap. 19

Yes, I am a fatal man, Madame Fribsbi. To inspire hopeless passion is my destiny.

Ibid. Chap. 23

Remember, it's as easy to marry a rich woman as a poor woman.

Pendennis. Chap. 28

Of the Corporation of the Goose-quill — of the Press, ... of the fourth estate.[1] . . . There she is — the great engine — she never sleeps. She has her ambassadors in every quarter of the world — her courtiers upon every road. Her officers march along with armies, and her envoys walk into statesmen's cabinets. They are ubiquitous.

Ibid. Chap. 30

The best way is to make your letters safe. I never wrote a letter in all my life that would commit me, and demmy, sir, I have had some experience of women.

Ibid. Chap. 64

How hard it is to make an Englishman acknowledge that he is happy!

Ibid. Chap. 69

This Bouillabaisse a noble dish is —
A sort of soup, or broth, or brew.

The Ballad of Bouillabaisse [1849].
Stanza 2

Ho, pretty page, with the dimpled chin,
That never has known the barber's shear,
All your wish is woman to win,
This is the way that boys begin, —
Wait till you come to Forty Year.

Rebecca and Rowena [1850]. The Age of Wisdom, Stanza 1

'Tis not the dying for a faith that's so hard, Master Harry — every man of every nation has done that — 'tis the living up to it that's difficult.[2]

Henry Esmond [1852]. Book I, Chap. 6

'Tis strange what a man may do, and a woman yet think him an angel.

Ibid. Chap. 7

Fiction carries a greater amount of truth in solution than the volume which purports to be all true.

The English Humorists [1853]. Steele

Harlequin without his mask is known to present a very sober countenance,

---

[1] The mother's face and voice are the first conscious objects as the infant soul unfolds, and she soon comes to stand in the very place of God to her child. — GRANVILLE STANLEY HALL: *Article in Pedagogical Seminary* [June, 1891]

[2] See Huxley, page 633b.

[3] *The Rake's Progress* is the title of one of the famous series of paintings and engravings by William Hogarth [1697–1764].

[1] See Carlyle, page 473a.

[2] See Adlai E. Stevenson, page 986b.

and was himself, the story goes, the melancholy patient whom the Doctor advised to go and see Harlequin.[1]

The English Humorists. Swift

The true pleasure of life is to live with your inferiors.

The Newcomes [*1853–1855*].
Chap. 9

The wicked are wicked, no doubt, and they go astray and they fall, and they come by their deserts; but who can tell the mischief which the very virtuous do?

Ibid. Chap. 20

Just as the last bell struck, a peculiar sweet smile shone over his face, and he lifted up his head a little, and quickly said "Adsum!" and fell back. It was the word we used at school, when names were called; and lo, he, whose heart was as that of a little child, had answered to his name, and stood in the presence of The Master.

Ibid. Chap. 80

A pedigree reaching as far back as the Deluge.

The Rose and the Ring [*1855*].
Chap. 2

The book of female logic is blotted all over with tears, and Justice in their courts is forever in a passion.

The Virginians [*1857–1859*].
Chap. 4

Heaven does not choose its elect from among the great and wealthy.

Ibid. Chap. 5

Women like not only to conquer, but to be conquered.

Ibid.

Next to the very young, I suppose the very old are the most selfish.

Ibid. Chap. 61

'Tis hard with respect to Beauty, that its possessor should not have even

---

[1] A patient one day presented himself to Abernethy; after careful examination the celebrated practitioner said, "You need amusement; go and hear Grimaldi; he will make you laugh, and that will be better for you than any drugs." "My God," exclaimed the invalid, "but I *am* Grimaldi!" — CESARE LOMBROSO [1836–1909]: *The Man of Genius, Part I, Chap. 2*

a life-enjoyment of it, but be compelled to resign it after, at the most, some forty years' lease.

The Virginians. Chap. 73

For a steady self-esteem and indomitable confidence in our own courage, greatness, magnanimity, who can compare with Britons, except their children across the Atlantic?

Ibid. Chap. 89

Through all the doubt and darkness, the danger and long tempest of the war, I think it was only the American leader's[1] indomitable soul that remained entirely steady.

Ibid. Chap. 90

To endure is greater than to dare; to tire out hostile fortune; to be daunted by no difficulty; to keep heart when all have lost it; to go through intrigue spotless; to forego even ambition when the end is gained — who can say this is not greatness?

Ibid. Chap. 92

Bravery never goes out of fashion.

The Four Georges [*1860*].
George II

As we go on the downhill journey, the milestones are gravestones, and on each more and more names are written; unless haply you live beyond man's common age, when friends have dropped off, and, tottering, and feeble, and unpitied, you reach the terminus alone.

The Roundabout Papers [*1861–1862*]. *On Letts' Diary*

ROBERT BROWNING
[1812–1889]

Sun-treader,[2] life and light be thine forever!

Pauline [*1833*]

I go to prove my soul!

I see my way as birds their trackless way.

I shall arrive! what time, what circuit first,

I ask not; but unless God send his hail

---

[1] George Washington.
[2] Shelley.

Or blinding fire-balls, sleet or stifling
    snow,
In some time, his good time, I shall
    arrive:
He guides me and the bird. In his good
    time!
                    Paracelsus [1835]. Part I
Measure your mind's height by the
    shade it casts!
                    Ibid. Part III
        Every joy is gain
And gain is gain, however small.
                    Ibid. Part IV
Over the sea our galleys went.
                    Ibid.
The sad rhyme of the men who proudly
    clung
To their first fault, and withered in
    their pride.
                    Ibid.
I give the fight up: let there be an end,
A privacy, an obscure nook for me.
I want to be forgotten even by God.
                    Ibid. Part V
Would you have your songs endure?
Build on the human heart.
                    Sordello [1840]. II
        Thoughts may be
Over-poetical for poetry.
                    Ibid. III
'Twere too absurd to slight
For the hereafter the today's delight!
                    Ibid. VI
        Any nose
May ravage with impunity a rose.
                    Ibid.
Day!
Faster and more fast,
O'er night's brim, day boils at last.
    Pippa Passes [1841]. Introduction
The year's at the spring
And day's at the morn;
Morning's at seven;
The hillside's dew-pearled;
The lark's on the wing;
The snail's on the thorn:
God's in his heaven —
All's right with the world.[1]
                    Ibid. Part I

[1] See Voltaire, page 324b, and Whittier,
page 528b.

One may do whate'er one likes
In Art: the only thing is, to make sure
That one does like it.
                    Pippa Passes. Part II
Some unsuspected isle in far-off seas.
                    Ibid.
In the morning of the world,
When earth was nigher heaven than
    now.
                    Ibid. Part III
All service ranks the same with God:
With God, whose puppets, best and
    worst,
Are we; there is no last nor first.
                    Ibid. Part IV
Marching along, fifty-score strong,
Great-hearted gentlemen, singing this
    song.
            Bells and Pomegranates [1841–
            1846]. Cavalier Tunes, I,
            Marching Along
Boot, saddle, to horse, and away!
            Ibid. III, Boot and Saddle
Just for a handful of silver he left us,
Just for a riband to stick in his coat.
            Ibid. The Lost Leader [1]
We that had loved him so, followed
    him, honoured him,
    Lived in his mild and magnificent
    eye,
Learned his great language, caught his
    clear accents,
    Made him our pattern to live and to
    die!
                    Ibid.
Shakespeare was of us, Milton was for
    us,
Burns, Shelley, were with us — they
    watch from their graves!
                    Ibid.
One more devils'-triumph and sorrow
    for angels,
One more wrong to man, one more insult
    to God!
                    Ibid.
We shall march prospering, — not thro'
    his presence;
    Songs may inspirit us, — not from
    his lyre;
Deeds will be done, — while he boasts
    his quiescence,

[1] Often taken as reference to Wordsworth.

Still bidding crouch whom the rest
bade aspire.
            Bells and Pomegranates.
                     The Lost Leader
Never glad confident morning again!
                              Ibid.
I sprang to the stirrup, and Joris, and
    he;
I galloped, Dirck galloped, we galloped
    all three.
        *Ibid. How They Brought the
        Good News from Ghent to Aix,
        Stanza 1*
And into the midnight we galloped
    abreast.
                              Ibid.
Round the cape of a sudden came the
    sea,
And the sun looked over the moun-
    tain's rim:
And straight was a path of gold for
    him,
And the need of a world of men for
    me.
        Ibid. Parting at Morning
Let's contend no more, Love,
    Strive nor weep:
All be as before, Love,
    — Only sleep!
        *Ibid. A Woman's Last Word,
                     Stanza 1*
Where the apple reddens
    Never pry —
Lest we lose our Edens,
    Eve and I.
                     Ibid. Stanza 5
Teach me, only teach, Love!
    As I ought
I will speak thy speech, Love,
    Think thy thought.
                     Ibid. Stanza 7
That shall be tomorrow
    Not tonight:
I must bury sorrow
    Out of sight.
                     Ibid. Stanza 9
Beautiful Evelyn Hope is dead!
        Ibid. Evelyn Hope, Stanza 1
You will wake, and remember, and
    understand.
                     Ibid. Stanza 7

Where the quiet-coloured end of eve-
    ning smiles.
        *Bells and Pomegranates. Love
                Among the Ruins, Stanza 1*
Earth's returns
For whole centuries of folly, noise and
    sin!
                     Ibid. Stanza 7
This world, and the wrong it does.
        *Ibid. Old Pictures in Florence,
                              Stanza 7*
What a man's work comes to! So he
    plans it,
Performs it, perfects it, makes amends
For the toiling and moiling, and then,
    sic transit!
                     Ibid. Stanza 10
What's come to perfection perishes.
Things learned on earth, we shall prac-
    tise in heaven:
    Works done least rapidly, Art most
        cherishes.
                     Ibid. Stanza 17
Your ghost will walk, you lover of trees,
    (If our loves remain)
In an English lane.
                Ibid. De Gustibus
Italy! my Italy!
Queen Mary's saying serves for me —
    (When fortune's malice
    Lost her — Calais):
Open my heart, and you will see
Graved inside of it, "Italy."
                              Ibid.
Oh, to be in England,
    Now that April's there,
And whoever wakes in England
    Sees, some morning, unaware,
That the lowest boughs and the brush-
    wood sheaf
    Round the elm-tree bole are in tiny
        leaf,
While the chaffinch sings on the orchard
    bough
    In England — now!
        *Ibid. Home-Thoughts, from
                     Abroad, Stanza 1*
That's the wise thrush; he sings each
    song twice over,

Lest you should think he never could recapture
The first fine careless rapture!
> *Bells and Pomegranates. Home-Thoughts, from Abroad, Stanza 2*

Nobly, nobly Cape St. Vincent to the North-west died away;
Sunset ran, one glorious blood-red, reeking into Cadiz Bay.
> *Ibid. Home-thoughts, from the Sea*

How well I know what I mean to do
When the long dark autumn evenings come.
> *Ibid. By the Fireside, Stanza 1*

O woman-country! [1] wooed not wed.
> *Ibid. Stanza 6*

Oh, the little more, and how much it is!
And the little less, and what worlds away!
> *Ibid. Stanza 39*

If two lives join, there is oft a scar.
They are one and one, with a shadowy third;
One near one is too far.
> *Ibid. Stanza 46*

Only I discern
Infinite passion, and the pain
Of finite hearts that yearn.
> *Ibid. Two in the Campagna, Stanza 12*

This is a spray the Bird clung to,
Making it blossom with pleasure.
> *Ibid. Misconceptions, Stanza 1*

Room after room,
I hunt the house through
We inhabit together.
> *Ibid. Love in a Life, Stanza 1*

Escape me?
Never —
Beloved!
While I am I, and you are you.
> *Ibid. Life in a Love, Stanza 1*

To dry one's eyes and laugh at a fall,
And baffled, get up and begin again.
> *Ibid. Stanza 2*

Ah, did you once see Shelley plain,
And did he stop and speak to you,
And did you speak to him again?
How strange it seems and new! [2]
> *Ibid. Memorabilia, I*

[1] Italy.
[2] And did you once find Browning plain?

There's a woman like a dewdrop, she's so purer than the purest.
> *Bells and Pomegranates. A Blot in the 'Scutcheon, Act I, Sc. 3*

When is man strong until he feels alone? [1]
> *Ibid. Colombe's Birthday, Act III*

You know, we French stormed Ratisbon.
> *Ibid. Incident of the French Camp, Stanza 1*

"You're wounded!" "Nay," the soldier's pride
Touched to the quick, he said:
"I'm killed, Sire!" And his chief beside,
Smiling the boy fell dead.
> *Ibid. Stanza 5*

That's my last Duchess painted on the wall.
> *Ibid. My Last Duchess*

She had
A heart — how shall I say? — too soon made glad.
> *Ibid.*

The lie was dead,
And damned, and truth stood up instead.
> *Ibid. Count Gismond, Stanza 13*

Morning, evening, noon and night,
"Praise God!" sang Theocrite.
> *Ibid. The Boy and the Angel*

Just my vengeance complete,
The man sprang to his feet,
Stood erect, caught at God's skirts, and prayed!
—So, *I* was afraid!
> *Ibid. Instans Tyrannus, Stanza 7*

When a man's busy, why, leisure
Strikes him as wonderful pleasure:
'Faith, and at leisure once is he?
Straightway he wants to be busy.
> *Ibid. The Glove, Stanza 1*

And did he really seem quite clear?
And did you read the book again?
How strange it seems and queer.
CHARLES WILLIAM STUBBS [1845–1912]:
Parody
[1] The strongest man on earth is he who stands most alone. — IBSEN: *An Enemy of the People* [1882], *Act V*

Who knows but the world may end tonight?
Bells and Pomegranates. The Last Ride Together, Stanza 2

Fail I alone, in words and deeds?
Why, all men strive, and who succeeds?
Ibid. Stanza 5

All labor, yet no less
Bear up beneath their unsuccess.
Look at the end of the work, contrast
The petty done, the undone vast,
This present of theirs with the hopeful past!
Ibid.

What hand and brain went ever paired?
What heart alike conceived and dared?
What act proved all its thought had been?
Ibid. Stanza 6

Sing, riding's a joy! For me I ride.
Ibid. Stanza 7

Earth being so good, would heaven seem best?
Ibid. Stanza 9

Hamelin Town's in Brunswick,
By famous Hanover city.
Ibid. The Pied Piper of Hamelin, Stanza 1

Rats!
They fought the dogs and killed the cats,
And bit the babies in the cradles,
And ate the cheeses out of the vats,
And licked the soup from the cooks' own ladles.
Ibid. Stanza 2

With shrieking and squeaking
In fifty different sharps and flats.
Ibid.

When the liquor's out, why clink the cannikin?
Ibid. The Flight of the Duchess, XVI

It's a long lane that knows no turnings.
Ibid. XVII

That low man seeks a little thing to do,
Sees it and does it;
This high man, with a great thing to pursue,
Dies ere he knows it.

That low man goes on adding one to one,
His hundred's soon hit;
This high man, aiming at a million,
Misses an unit.
That has the world here — should he need the next,
Let the world mind him!
This throws himself on God, and unperplexed
Seeking shall find Him.
Bells and Pomegranates. A Grammarian's Funeral

And inasmuch as feeling, the East's gift,
Is quick and transient, — comes, and lo, is gone —
While Northern thought is slow and durable.
Ibid. Luria, Act V

Ah, but a man's reach should exceed his grasp,
Or what's a heaven for?
Men and Women [1855]. Andrea del Sarto [1]

How I shall lie through centuries,
And hear the blessed mutter of the mass,
And see God made and eaten all day long,
And feel the steady candle-flame, and taste
Good strong thick stupefying incense smoke!
Ibid. The Bishop Orders His Tomb at Saint Praxed's Church

Truth that peeps
Over the glass's edge when dinner's done,
And body gets its sop and holds its noise
And leaves soul free a little.
Ibid. Bishop Blougram's Apology

The common problem, yours, mine, every one's,
Is — not to fancy what were fair in life
Provided it could be, — but, finding first

[1] The poem is based on the account of the artist given in VASARI'S *Lives of the Painters*.

What may be, then find how to make it
fair
Up to our means.
*Men and Women. Bishop
Blougram's Apology*

Just when we are safest, there's a sun-
set-touch,
A fancy from a flower-bell, some one's
death,
A chorus-ending from Euripides.
Ibid.

One wise man's verdict outweighs all
the fools'.
Ibid.

Our interest's on the dangerous edge of
things.
The honest thief, the tender murderer,
The superstitious atheist, demirep
That loves and saves her soul in new
French books.
Ibid.

You call for faith:
I show you doubt, to prove that faith
exists.
The more of doubt, the stronger faith,
I say,
If faith o'ercomes doubt.
Ibid.

When the fight begins within himself,
A man's worth something.
Ibid.

Dear dead women, with such hair, too
— what's become of all the gold
Used to hang and brush their bosoms?
I feel chilly and grown old.
*Ibid. A Toccata of Galuppi's,
Stanza 15*

The sin I impute to each frustrate ghost
Is — the unlit lamp and the ungirt loin.
*Ibid. The Statue and the Bust,
Stanza 83*

God made all the creatures, and gave
them our love and our fear,
To give sign, we and they are his children, one family here.
Ibid. Saul, VI

How good is man's life, the mere living! how fit to employ
All the heart and the soul and the senses
forever in joy!
Ibid. IX

I have lived, seen God's hand through
a lifetime, and all was for best.
Men and Women. Saul, IX

God is seen God
In the star, in the stone, in the flesh,
in the soul and the clod.
Ibid. XVII

'Tis not what man Does which exalts
him, but what man Would do!
Ibid. XVIII

The sprinkled isles,
Lily on lily, that o'erlace the sea.
Ibid. Cleon

And I have written three books on the
soul,
Proving absurd all written hitherto,
And putting us to ignorance again.
Ibid.

Rafael made a century of sonnets.
Ibid. One Word More, II

Does he paint? he fain would write a
poem, —
Does he write? he fain would paint a
picture.
Ibid. VIII

Where my heart lies, let my brain lie
also.
Ibid. XIV

God be thanked, the meanest of his
creatures
Boasts two soul-sides, one to face the
world with,
One to show a woman when he loves
her!
Ibid. XVII

Oh, their Rafael of the dear Madonnas,
Oh, their Dante of the dread Inferno,
Wrote one song — and in my brain I
sing it,
Drew one angel — borne, see, on my
bosom!
Ibid. XIX

Was there naught better than to enjoy?
No feat which, done, would make
time break,
And let us pent-up creatures through
Into eternity, our due?
No forcing earth teach heaven's em-
ploy?
*Dramatis Personae [1864]. Dis
Aliter Visum, Stanza 24*

That out of three sounds he frame, not
  a fourth sound, but a star.
> *Dramatis Personae. Abt Vogler,*[1]
> *Stanza 7*

What was good shall be good, with for
  evil so much good more;
On the earth the broken arcs; in the
  heaven, a perfect round.
> *Ibid. Stanza 9*

The high that proved too high, the
  heroic for earth too hard,
The passion that left the ground to lose
  itself in the sky.
> *Ibid. Stanza 10*

Sorrow is hard to bear, and doubt is
  slow to clear,
Each sufferer says his say, his scheme
  of the weal and woe:
But God has a few of us whom he
  whispers in the ear;
The rest may reason and welcome:
  'tis we musicians know.
> *Ibid. Stanza 12*

Grow old along with me!
The best is yet to be,
The last of life, for which the first was
  made.
Our times are in his hand.
> *Ibid. Rabbi Ben Ezra, Stanza 1*

Irks care the crop-full bird? Frets
  doubt the maw-crammed beast?
> *Ibid. Stanza 4*

Then welcome each rebuff
That turns earth's smoothness rough,
Each sting that bids nor sit nor stand,
  but go!
Be our joys three-parts pain!
  Strive, and hold cheap the strain;
Learn, nor account the pang; dare,
  never grudge the throe!
> *Ibid. Stanza 6*

What I aspired to be,
And was not, comforts me.
> *Ibid. Stanza 7*

Therefore I summon age
To grant youth's heritage.
> *Ibid. Stanza 13*

Thou waitedst age: wait death nor be
  afraid!
> *Ibid. Stanza 19*

[1] The Abt or Abbé George Joseph Vogler

Look not thou down but up!
> *Dramatis Personae. Rabbi*
> *Ben Ezra, Stanza 30*

Stung by the splendour of a sudden
  thought.
> *Ibid. A Death in the Desert*

Progress, man's distinctive mark alone,
Not God's, and not the beasts': God is,
  they are;
Man partly is, and wholly hopes to be.
> *Ibid.*

Letting the rank tongue blossom into
  speech.
> *Ibid. Caliban upon Setebos*

How sad and bad and mad it was —[1]
But then, how it was sweet!
> *Ibid. Confessions, Stanza 9*

Fear death? — to feel the fog in my
  throat,
The mist in my face.
> *Ibid. Prospice*

No! let me taste the whole of it, fare
  like my peers,
  The heroes of old,
Bear the brunt, in a minute pay glad
  life's arrears
  Of pain, darkness, and cold.
> *Ibid.*

Hold me but safe again within the bond
Of one immortal look.
> *Ibid. Eurydice to Orpheus*

This could but have happened once, —
And we missed it, lost it forever.
> *Ibid. Youth and Art, Stanza 17*

All that I own is a print,
An etching, a mezzotint.
> *Ibid. A Likeness*

He never saw, never before today,
What was able to take his breath away.
A face to lose youth for, to occupy age
With the dream of, meet death with.[2]
> *Ibid.*

We find great things are made of little
  things,
And little things go lessening till at last

[1749–1824] was a composer, professor,
Kapellmeister, and writer on music.
[1] See Swinburne, page 695a.
[2] A face that a man might die for. — SIR
ARTHUR CONAN DOYLE: *The Adventures of
Sherlock Holmes: A Scandal in Bohemia*
[1892]

Comes God behind them.
> *Dramatis Personae. Mr. Sludge,*
> *"The Medium"*

I'm — now the President, now Jenny
Lind,
Now Emerson, now the Benicia Boy.[1]
> *Ibid.*

Boston's a hole, the herring-pond is
wide,
V-notes are something, liberty still
more.
Beside, is he the only fool in the world?
> *Ibid.*

It's wiser being good than bad;
It's safer being meek than fierce;
It's fitter being sane than mad.
My own hope is, a sun will pierce
The thickest cloud earth ever stretched;
That, after Last, returns the First,
Though a wide compass round be
fetched;
That what began best can't end
worst,
Nor what God blessed once, prove
accurst.
> *Ibid. Apparent Failure, Stanza 7*

O Lyric Love, half angel and half bird,
And all a wonder and a wild desire.
> *The Ring and the Book*
> *[1868–1869]. I*

Call in law when a neighbor breaks
your fence,
Cribs from your field, tampers with
rent or lease,
Touches the purse or pocket, — but
woos your wife?
No: take the old way trod when men
were men!
> *Ibid. II, Half-Rome*

There is but one way to browbeat this
world,
Dumb-founder doubt, and repay scorn
in kind, —
To go on trusting, namely, till faith
move
Mountains.
> *Ibid. III, The Other Half-Rome*

"The serpent tempted me and I did
eat."
So much of paradisal nature, Eve's!

[1] The Benicia Boy was John C. Heenan, a
prizefighter of Benicia, California.

Her daughters ever since prefer to urge
"Adam so starved me I was fain accept
The apple any serpent pushed my
way."
> *The Ring and the Book. IV,*
> *Tertium Quid*

The truth was felt by instinct here,
— Process which serves a world of
trouble and time.
> *Ibid.*

'Twas a thief said the last kind word
to Christ:
Christ took the kindness and forgave
the theft.
> *Ibid. VI, Giuseppe Caponsacchi*

All poetry is difficult to read,
— The sense of it is, anyhow.
> *Ibid. VII, Pompilia*

No work begun shall ever pause for
death!
> *Ibid.*

So, let him wait God's instant men call
years;
Meantime hold hard by truth and his
great soul,
Do out the duty! Through such souls
alone
God stooping shows sufficient of his
light
For us i' the dark to rise by.
> *Ibid.*

Faultless to a fault.
> *Ibid. IX, Juris Doctor Johannes-*
> *Baptista Bottinius*

The curious crime, the fine
Felicity and flower of wickedness.
> *Ibid. X, The Pope*

What I call God,
And fools call Nature.[1]
> *Ibid.*

Why comes temptation, but for man to
meet
And master and make crouch beneath
his foot,
And so be pedestaled in triumph?
> *Ibid.*

[1] Some call it Evolution,
And others call it God.

Some of us call it Autumn,
And others call it God.
> W. H. CARRUTH [1859–1924]: *Each in*
> *His Own Tongue*

White shall not neutralize the black,
nor good
Compensate bad in man, absolve him
so:
Life's business being just the terrible
choice.
The Ring and the Book. X,
The Pope

You never know what life means till
you die:
Even throughout life, 'tis death that
makes life live,
Gives it whatever the significance.
Ibid. XI, Guido

Save the squadron, honor France, love
thy wife the Belle Aurore!
Hervé Riel [1871]. Stanza 11

A man in armor is his armor's slave.
Herakles [1871]

Life's a little thing!
Such as it is, then, pass life pleasantly
From day to night, nor once grieve all
the while.
Ibid.

In God's good time,
Which does not always fall on Satur-
day
When the world looks for wages.[1]
Ibid.

The great mind knows the power of
gentleness,
Only tries force, because persuasion
fails.
Ibid.

'Twas not for every Gawain to gaze
upon the Grail!
Fifine at the Fair [1872]. IV

No creature's made so mean
But that, some way, it boasts, could we
investigate,
Its supreme worth.
Ibid. XXIX

So absolutely good is truth, truth never
hurts
The teller.
Ibid. XXXII

Death reads the title clear —
What each soul for itself conquered
from out things here.
Fifine at the Fair. LV

Clash forth life's common chord,
whence, list how there ascend
Harmonics far and faint, till our perception end.
Ibid. LXII

That far land we dream about,
Where every man is his own architect.
Red Cotton Night-Cap
Country [1873]. II

A secret's safe
'Twixt you, me, and the gate-post!
The Inn Album [1875]. II

Ignorance is not innocence but sin.
Ibid. V

No ear! or if ear, so tough-gristled —
He thought that he sung while he
whistled.
Pacchiarotto [1876]. XXVI

Have you found your life distasteful?
My life did and does smack sweet.
Was your youth of pleasure wasteful?
Mine I saved and hold complete.
Do your joys with age diminish?
When mine fail me, I'll complain.
Must in death your daylight finish?
My sun sets to rise again.
At the "Mermaid" [1876]. Stanza 10

I find earth not gray but rosy,
Heaven not grim but fair of hue.
Do I stoop? I pluck a posy.
Do I stand and stare?[1] All's blue.
Ibid. Stanza 12

"With this same key
Shakespeare unlocked his heart"[2] once
more!
Did Shakespeare? If so, the less Shake-
speare he!
House [1876]. Stanza 10

Because a man has shop to mind
In time and place, since flesh must
live,
Needs spirit lack all life behind,

---

[1] The old Tuscan proverb, *"Iddio non paga sabato"; "*God does not pay Saturdays." — *Life in Letters of William Dean Howells, Vol. II, P. 169, Letter to Mrs. James T. Fields* [February 23, 1903]

[1] What is this life if, full of care,
We have no time to stand and stare?
WILLIAM HENRY DAVIES [1871–1940]:
Leisure
[2] See Wordsworth, page 412a.

All stray thoughts, fancies fugitive,
All loves except what trade can give?
　　　　　Shop [*1876*]. *Stanza 20*
Good, to forgive;
　Best, to forget!
　Living, we fret;
Dying, we live.
　　　La Saisiaz [*1877*]. *Introduction,*
　　　　　　　　　　　　Stanza 1
Can we love but on condition that the
　thing we love must die?
　　　　　　　　　　　　　Ibid.
Such a starved bank of moss
　Till, that May-morn,
Blue ran the flash across:
　Violets were born!
　The Two Poets of Croisic [*1878*].
　　　　　Introduction, Stanza 1
Sky — what a scowl of cloud
　Till, near and far,
Ray on ray split the shroud:
　Splendid, a star!
　　　　　　　Ibid. Stanza 2
　As if true pride
Were not also humble!
　Lines Written in an Album [*1882*]
Wanting is — what?
　Summer redundant,
　Blueness abundant,
　— Where is the blot?
　　Wanting is — What? [1] [*1883*]
Out of the wreck I rise.
　　　　　　　Ixion [*1883*]
　Climb the rounds
Of life's long ladder, one by slippery
　one.
　Jochanan Hakkadosh [*1883*].
　　　　　　　　　　Stanza 27
What Youth deemed crystal, Age finds
　out was dew
Morn set a-sparkle, but which noon
　quick dried.
　　　　　　　Ibid. Stanza 101
Never the time and the place
And the loved one all together!
　　　*Never the Time and the
　　　　　　　　Place* [*1883*]

[1] Browning is — what?
　Riddle redundant,
　Baldness abundant,
　Sense, who can spot?
ANONYMOUS, in *Punch* [April 21, 1883]

Help me with knowledge — for Life's
　Old — Death's New!
　　*Epitaph on Levi Lincoln
　　　　　Thaxter, 1824–1884*
What if the rose-streak of morning
Pale and depart in a passion of tears?
Once to have hoped is no matter for
　scorning!
Love once — e'en love's disappoint-
　ment endears!
A minute's success pays the failure of
　years.
　　Apollo and the Fates [*1886*].
　　　　　　　　　　Stanza 42
Oh, fancies that might be, oh, facts
　that are!
　　　　Asolando [*1889*].
　　　　　　Inapprehensiveness
Songs, Spring thought perfection,
　Summer criticizes:
What in May escaped detection,
　August, past surprises,
Notes, and names each blunder.
　　*Ibid. Flute-Music, with an
　　Accompaniment, Stanza 11*
One who never turned his back but
　marched breast forward,
Never doubted clouds would break,
Never dreamed, though right were
　worsted, wrong would triumph,
Held we fall to rise, are baffled to fight
　better,
Sleep to wake.
　　　　Ibid. Epilogue, Stanza 3
No, at noonday in the bustle of man's
　work-time
Greet the unseen with a cheer!
　　　　　　Ibid. Stanza 4

SAMUEL DICKINSON
BURCHARD
[1812–1891]

We are Republicans, and don't propose to leave our party and identify
ourselves with the party whose ante-
cedents have been Rum, Romanism,
and Rebellion.
　　*Speaking for a deputation of
　　clergymen calling upon James
　　G. Blaine, the Republican
　　Presidential candidate, New
　　York* [*October 29, 1884*]

CHARLES DICKENS
[1812–1870]

I hold my inventive faculty on the stern condition that it must master my whole life, often have complete possession of me, make its own demands upon me, and sometimes for months together put everything else away from me.

Letters [*1833–1870*] (*Edited by* MAMIE DICKENS AND GEORGINA HOGARTH

He had used the word in its Pickwickian sense.

Pickwick Papers [*1836–1837*]. *Chap. 1*

Did it ever strike you on such a morning as this that drowning would be happiness and peace?

Ibid. Chap. 5

"It wasn't the wine," murmured Mr. Snodgrass, in a broken voice. "It was the salmon."

Ibid. Chap. 8

I wants to make your flesh creep.

Ibid.

"Can I unmoved see thee dying
On a log
Expiring frog!"

Ibid. Chap. 15

Tongue; well that's a wery good thing when it an't a woman's.

Ibid. Chap. 19

Be wery careful o' vidders all your life.

Ibid. Chap. 20

The wictim o' connubiality, as Blue Beard's domestic chaplain said, with a tear of pity, ven he buried him.

Ibid.

Despair seldom comes with the first severe shock of misfortune. A man has confidence in untried friends, he remembers the many offers of service so freely made by his boon companions when he wanted them not; he has hope — the hope of happy inexperience.

Ibid. Chap. 21

I have heerd how many ord'nary women one vidder's equal to, in pint o' comin' over you. I think it's five-and-twenty, but I don't rightly know vether it a'n't more.

Pickwick Papers. Chap. 23

Bold Turpin vunce, on Hounslow Heath,
His bold mare Bess bestrode.

Ibid. Chap. 43, Romance

Please, sir, I want some more.

Oliver Twist [*1837–1838*]. *Chap. 2*

There are books of which the backs and covers are by far the best parts.

Ibid. Chap. 14

I'll eat my head.

Ibid.

I only know two sorts of boys. Mealy boys, and beef-faced boys.

Ibid.

There is something about a roused woman, especially if she add to all her other strong passions, the fierce impulses of recklessness and despair, which few men like to provoke.

Ibid. Chap. 16

There's light enough for wot I've got to do.

Ibid. Chap. 47

"If the law supposes that," said Mr. Bumble, . . . "the law is a ass, a idiot."

Ibid. Chap. 51

He had but one eye, and the popular prejudice runs in favour of two.

Nicholas Nickleby [*1838–1839*]. *Chap. 4*

Subdue your appetites, my dears, and you've conquered human natur.

Ibid. Chap. 5

There are only two styles of portrait painting; the serious and the smirk.

Ibid. Chap. 10

Oh! they're too beautiful to live, much too beautiful!

Ibid. Chap. 14

I pity his ignorance and despise him.

Ibid. Chap. 15

The two countesses had no outlines at all, and the dowager's was a demd outline.

Ibid. Chap. 34

A demd, damp, moist, unpleasant body!

Ibid.

Bring in the bottled lightning, a clean tumbler, and a corkscrew.

Nicholas Nickleby. Chap. 49

All is gas and gaiters.

Ibid.

My life is one demd horrid grind.

Ibid. Chap. 64

He has gone to the demnition bow-wows.

Ibid.

What is the odds so long as the fire of soul is kindled at the taper of conwiviality, and the wing of friendship never moults a feather . . . and the present moment is the least happiest of our existence.

The Old Curiosity Shop [1841].
Chap. 2

She's the ornament of her sex.

Ibid. Chap. 5

In love of home, the love of country has its rise.

Ibid. Chap. 38

That vague kind of penitence which holidays awaken next morning.

Ibid. Chap. 40

The memory of those who lie below passes away so soon. At first they tend them, morning, noon, and night; they soon begin to come less frequently; from once a day, to once a week; from once a week to once a month; then at long and uncertain intervals; then, not at all.

Ibid. Chap. 54

"Did you ever taste beer?" "I had a sip of it once," said the small servant. "Here's a state of things!" cried Mr. Swiveller. . . . "She *never* tasted it — it can't be tasted in a sip!"

Ibid. Chap. 57

It was a maxim with Foxey — our revered father, gentlemen — "Always suspect everybody."

Ibid. Chap. 66

When Death strikes down the innocent and young, for every fragile form from which he lets the panting spirit free, a hundred virtues rise, in shapes of mercy, charity, and love, to walk the world, and bless it.

Ibid. Chap. 72

Oh gracious, why wasn't I born old and ugly?

Barnaby Rudge [1841]. *Chap. 70*

Any man may be in good spirits and good temper when he's well dressed. There an't much credit in that.

Martin Chuzzlewit [1843–1844].
Chap. 5

With affection beaming in one eye, and calculation shining out of the other.

Ibid. Chap. 8

Regrets are the natural property of gray hairs.

Ibid. Chap. 10

Keep up appearances whatever you do.

Ibid. Chap. 11

"Do other men for they would do you." That's the true business precept.

Ibid.

Buy an annuity cheap, and make your life interesting to yourself and everybody else that watches the speculation.

Ibid. Chap. 18

Leave the bottle on the chimley-piece, and don't ask me to take none, but let me put my lips to it when I am so disposed.

Ibid. Chap. 19

"She's the sort of woman now," said Mould, . . . "one would almost feel disposed to bury for nothing: and do it neatly, too!"

Ibid. Chap. 25

He'd make a lovely corpse.

Ibid.

What we've got to do, is to keep up our spirits, and be neighbourly. We shall come all right in the end, never fear.

Ibid. Chap. 33

A man ain't got no right to be a public man, unless he meets the public views.

Ibid. Chap. 34

Here are all kinds of employers wanting all sorts of servants, and all sorts of servants wanting all kinds of employers, and they never seem to come together.

Martin Chuzzlewit. Chap. 36

Oh Sairey, Sairey, little do we know wot lays afore us!

Ibid. Chap. 40

I don't believe there's no sich a person!

Ibid. Chap. 49

Old Marley was as dead as a doornail. . . . The wisdom of our ancestors is in the simile.

A Christmas Carol [1843].
Stave One

Secret, and self-contained, and solitary as an oyster.

Ibid.

I wear the chain I forged in life.

Ibid.

In came a fiddler — and tuned like fifty stomach-aches. In came Mrs. Fezziwig, one vast substantial smile.

Ibid. Stave Two

Let's have the shutters up . . . before a man can say Jack Robinson.[1]

Ibid.

As good as gold.

Ibid. Stave Three

"God bless us every one!" said Tiny Tim, the last of all.

Ibid.

It *was* a turkey! He could never have stood upon his legs, that bird! He would have snapped 'em off short in a minute, like sticks of sealing-wax.

Ibid. Stave Five

It was always said of him, that he knew how to keep Christmas well if any man alive possessed the knowledge.

Ibid. Stave Five

Facts and Figures! Put 'em down!

The Chimes [1844]. First Quarter

The New Year, like an Infant Heir to the whole world, was waited for, with welcomes, presents, and rejoicings.

Ibid. Second Quarter

O let us love our occupations,
Bless the squire and his relations,
Live upon our daily rations,
And always know our proper stations.

The Chimes. Second Quarter

Oh the nerves, the nerves; the mysteries of this machine called Man! Oh the little that unhinges it: poor creatures that we are!

Ibid. Third Quarter

Give us, in mercy, better homes when we're a-lying in our cradles; give us better food when we're a-working for our lives; give us kinder laws to bring us back when we're a-going wrong; and don't set Jail, Jail, Jail afore us, everywhere we turn.

Ibid.

He's tough, ma'am, tough, is J. B. Tough and devilish sly.

Dombey and Son [1848]. Chap. 7

I want to know what it says. . . . The sea, Floy, what it is that it keeps on saying.[1]

Ibid. Chap. 8

"Wal'r, my boy," replied the Captain, "in the Proverbs of Solomon you will find the following words, 'May we never want a friend in need, nor a bottle to give him!' When found, make a note of."

Ibid. Chap. 15

Cows are my passion.

Ibid. Chap. 21

A mind equal to any undertaking that he puts it alongside of.

Ibid. Chap. 23

The bearings of this observation lays in the application on it.

Ibid.

You'll find us rough, Sir, but you'll find us ready.

David Copperfield [1849–1850].
Chap. 3

I am a lone lorn creetur . . . and everythink goes contrairy with me.

Ibid.

I'd better go into the house, and die and be a riddance!

Ibid.

---

[1] I'd do it as soon as say Jack Robinson. — FANNY BURNEY: *Evelina* [1778], *Letter 82*
I'd get her off before you could say Jack Robinson. — MARIA EDGEWORTH: *The Absentee* [1812], *Chap. 2*

[1] See Joseph Edwards Carpenter, page 582b.

Barkis is willin'.
David Copperfield. Chap. 5
That he may be ready — in case of anything turning up.[1]
Ibid. Chap. 12
I never will desert Mr. Micawber.
Ibid.

Annual income twenty pounds, annual expenditure nineteen nineteen six, result happiness. Annual income twenty pounds, annual expenditure twenty pounds ought and six, result misery.
Ibid.
It's a mad world. Mad as Bedlam.
Ibid. Chap. 14
I'm a very umble person.[2]
Ibid. Chap. 16
The winds you are going to tempt, have wafted thousands upon thousands to fortune, and brought thousands upon thousands happily back.
Ibid.
The mistake was made of putting some of the trouble out of King Charles's head into my head.[3]
Ibid. Chap. 17
I only ask for information.
Ibid. Chap. 20
It was as true . . . as turnips is. It was as true . . . as taxes is. And nothing's truer than them.
Ibid. Chap. 21
What a world of gammon and spinnach it is, though, ain't it!
Ibid. Chap. 22
Nobody's enemy but his own.
Ibid. Chap. 25
Accidents will occur in the best-regulated families.
Ibid. Chap. 28
Ride on! Rough-shod if need be, smooth-shod if that will do, but ride

on! Ride on over all obstacles, and win the race!
David Copperfield. Chap. 28
A long pull, and a strong pull, and a pull all together.
Ibid. Chap. 30
People can't die, along the coast . . . except when the tide's pretty nigh out. They can't be born, unless it's pretty nigh in — not properly born, till flood. He's a going out with the tide.[1]
Ibid.
There wasn't room to swing a cat there.
Ibid. Chap. 35
I ate umble pie with an appetite.
Ibid. Chap. 39
Let sleeping dogs lie — who wants to rouse 'em?
Ibid.
Skewered through and through with office-pens, and bound hand and foot with red tape.
Ibid. Chap. 43
It's only my child-wife.
Ibid. Chap. 44
A man must take the fat with the lean.
Ibid. Chap. 51
Trifles make the sum of life.
Ibid. Chap. 53
The seamen said it blew great guns.
Ibid. Chap. 55
This is a London particular. . . . A fog, miss.
Bleak House [1852–1853]. Chap. 3
Not to put too fine a point upon it.
Ibid. Chap. 32
One always begins to forgive a place as soon as it's left behind.
Little Dorrit [1857–1858].
Book I, Chap. 2
Whatever was required to be done, the Circumlocution Office was beforehand with all the public departments in the art of perceiving — HOW NOT TO DO IT.
Ibid. Chap. 10

---

[1] See Disraeli, page 512a.
[2] Not only humble but umble, which I look upon to be the comparative, or, indeed, superlative degree. — ANTHONY TROLLOPE: *Doctor Thorne* [1858], *Chap. 4*
[3] "King Charles's Head" has passed into common use in the English language as a phrase meaning some whimsical obsession. — G. B. STERN [1890–   ]: *Monogram*

[1] See Sir James Frazer, page 759a.

A person who can't pay, gets another person who can't pay, to guarantee that he can pay.
Little Dorrit. Book I, Chap. 23

Papa, potatoes, poultry, prunes, and prism, are all very good words for the lips: especially prunes and prism.
Ibid. Book II, Chap. 5

It is at least as difficult to stay a moral infection as a physical one.
Ibid. Chap. 13

It was the best of times, it was the worst of times, it was the age of wisdom, it was the age of foolishness, it was the epoch of belief, it was the epoch of incredulity, it was the season of Light, it was the season of Darkness, it was the spring of hope, it was the winter of despair.
A Tale of Two Cities [1859].
Book I, Chap. 1

A wonderful fact to reflect upon, that every human creature is constituted to be that profound secret and mystery to every other.
Ibid. Chap. 3

The calm that must follow all storms — emblem to humanity of the rest and silence into which the storm called Life must hush at last.
Ibid. Chap. 6

Detestation of the high is the involuntary homage of the low.
Ibid. Book II, Chap. 9

It is a far, far better thing that I do, than I have ever done; it is a far, far better rest that I go to, than I have ever known.
Ibid. Book III, Chap. 15

I have known a vast quantity of nonsense talked about bad men not looking you in the face. Don't trust that conventional idea. Dishonesty will stare honesty out of countenance, any day in the week, if there is anything to be got by it.
Hunted Down [1859]. Chap. 2

In the little world in which children have their existence, whosoever brings them up, there is nothing so finely perceived and so finely felt, as injustice.
Great Expectations [1860–1861].
Chap. 9

Probably every new and eagerly expected garment ever put on since clothes came in, fell a trifle short of the wearer's expectation.
Ibid. Chap. 19

Throughout life, our worst weaknesses and meannesses are usually committed for the sake of the people whom we most despise.
Ibid. Chap. 27

My best of wishes for your merry Christmases and your happy New Years, your long lives and your true prosperities. Worth twenty pound good if they are delivered as I send them. Remember? Here's a final prescription added, "To be taken for life."
Doctor Marigold's Prescriptions
[1865]. Chap. 1

EDWARD LEAR
[1812–1888]

There was an Old Man with a beard,
Who said: "It is just as I feared!
 Two Owls and a Hen,
 Four Larks and a Wren,
Have all built their nests in my beard."
 Book of Nonsense [1846]. Limerick

How pleasant to know Mr. Lear!
 Who has written such volumes of
 stuff!
Some think him ill-tempered and queer,
 But a few think him pleasant enough.
 Nonsense Songs [1871].
 Preface, Stanza 1

His body is perfectly spherical,
He weareth a runcible hat.
 Ibid. Stanza 5

The Owl and the Pussy-cat went to sea
 In a beautiful pea-green boat,
They took some honey, and plenty of
 money,
 Wrapped up in a five-pound note.
The Owl looked up to the stars above,
 And sang to a small guitar,
"O lovely Pussy! O Pussy, my love,

What a beautiful Pussy you are,
  You are,
  You are!
What a beautiful Pussy you are!"
   *Nonsense Songs. The Owl and
     the Pussy-cat, Stanza 1*
Pussy said to the Owl, "You elegant
  fowl!
How charmingly sweet you sing!
O let us be married! too long we have
  tarried:
But what shall we do for a ring?"
They sailed away, for a year and a day,
  To the land where the Bong-tree
  grows
And there in a wood a Piggy-wig stood
With a ring at the end of his nose.
        Ibid. Stanza 2
"Dear Pig, are you willing to sell for
  one shilling
Your ring?" Said the Piggy, "I will."
        Ibid. Stanza 3
They dined on mince, and slices of
  quince,
  Which they ate with a runcible
  spoon;
And hand in hand, on the edge of the
  sand,
  They danced by the light of the
  moon.
        Ibid.
They went to sea in a Sieve, they did,
  In a Sieve they went to sea:
In spite of all their friends could say.
   Ibid. The Jumblies, Stanza 1
But we don't care a button! we don't
  care a fig!
In a Sieve we'll go to sea!
Far and few, far and few,
  Are the lands where the Jumblies
  live;
Their heads are green, and their hands
  are blue,
And they went to sea in a Sieve.
        Ibid.
Calico Pie,
  The little Birds fly
Down to the calico tree,
  Their wings were blue,
  And they sang "Tilly-loo!"
Till away they flew, —
And they never came back to me!

They never came back!
They never came back!
They never came back to me!
   *Nonsense Songs. Calico Pie,
          Stanza 1*
Calico Jam,
  The little Fish swam,
Over the syllabub sea.
        Ibid. Stanza 2
Who, or why, or which, or what,
Is the Akond of Swat?
   The Akond of Swat [1] *[1873]*
She sate upon her Dobie,
  To watch the Evening Star,
And all the Punkahs as they passed,
  Cried, "My! how fair you are!"
    *The Cummerbund [1874].
          Stanza 1*
On the top of the Crumpetty Tree
  The Quangle Wangle sat,
But his face you could not see,
  On account of his Beaver Hat.
   *Nonsense Songs [1877]. The
   Quangle Wangle's Hat, Stanza 1*
On the coast of Coromandel
  Where the early pumpkins blow,
   In the middle of the woods
  Lived the Yonghy-Bonghy-Bò.
Two old chairs, and half a candle,
One old jug without a handle, —
  These were all his worldly goods.
   *Ibid. The Courtship of the
   Yonghy-Bonghy-Bò, Stanza 1*

---

[1] What, what, what,
  What's the news from Swat?
    Sad news,
    Bad news,
Comes by cable led
Through the Indian Ocean's bed,
Through the Persian Gulf, the Red
Sea and the Med-
Iterranean — he's dead;
The Ahkoond is dead!
   GEORGE THOMAS LANIGAN: *A
        Threnody* [1878], *St. 1*
Now the Ahkoond of Swat is a vague sort of
  man
Who lives in a country far over the sea;
Pray tell me, good reader, if tell me you can,
What's the Ahkoond of Swat to you folks
  or to me?
   EUGENE FIELD: *The Ahkoond of Swat*
                     [1884]

There he heard a Lady talking,
To some milk-white Hens of Dork-
ing, —
'Tis the Lady Jingly Jones!
  Nonsense Songs. The Courtship of
  the Yonghy-Bonghy-Bò, Stanza 2
"I would be your wife most gladly!"
(Here she twirled her fingers madly,)
"But in England I've a mate!"
  Ibid. Stanza 5
When awful darkness and silence reign
Over the great Gromboolian plain,
  Through the long, long wintry nights.
  Ibid. The Dong with the
  Luminous Nose, Stanza 1
The Pobble who has no toes
Had once as many as we;
When they said, "Some day you may
  lose them all;" —
He replied, — "Fish fiddle de-dee!"
  Ibid. The Pobble Who Has No
  Toes, Stanza 1
Ploffskin, Pluffskin, Pelican jee!
We think no Birds so happy as we!
Plumpskin, Ploshkin, Pelican jill!
We think so then, and we thought so
  still.
  Ibid. The Pelican Chorus

WILLIAM JAMES LINTON
[1812–1898]

He boasts nor wealth nor high descent,
  yet he may claim to be
A gentleman to match the best of any
  pedigree:
His blood hath run in peasant veins
  through many a noteless year;
Yet, search in every prince's court,
  you'll rarely find his peer.
For he's one of Nature's Gentlemen,
  the best of every time.
  Nature's Gentleman.[1] *Stanza 1*

NORMAN MACLEOD
[1812–1872]

Courage, brother! do not stumble,
  Though thy path be dark as night;
There's a star to guide the humble,
  Trust in God and do the Right.
  Trust in God [1857]. *Stanza 1*

[1] See Eliza Cook, page 591a.

WILLIAM EDMONDSTOUNE AYTOUN
[1813–1865]

News of battle! — news of battle!
  Hark! 'tis ringing down the street;
And the archways and the pavement
  Bear the clang of hurrying feet.
  Edinburgh after Flodden
  [1849]. *Stanza 1*
Nowhere beats the heart so kindly
As beneath the tartan plaid!
  Charles Edward at Versailles
  on the Anniversary of Culloden
  [1849]. *Line 219*
They bore within their breasts the grief
That fame can never heal —
The deep, unutterable woe
Which none save exiles feel.
  The Island of the Scots
  [1849]. *Stanza 12*

HENRY WARD BEECHER
[1813–1887]

A thoughtful mind, when it sees a
Nation's flag, sees not the flag only,
but the Nation itself; and whatever
may be its symbols, its insignia, he
reads chiefly in the flag the Government, the principles, the truths, the
history which belongs to the Nation
that sets it forth.
  The American Flag
Where is human nature so weak as
in the book-store!
  Star Papers. Subtleties of Book
  Buyers
You cannot forget if you would,
those golden kisses all over the cheeks
of the meadow, queerly called dandelions.
  Ibid. A Discourse on Flowers

JOSEPH EDWARDS CARPENTER
[1813–1885]

What are the wild waves saying,[1]
  Sister, the whole day long,

[1] See Dickens, page 578b.

That ever amid our playing
I hear but their low, lone song?
> *What Are the Wild Waves
> Saying? Stanza 1*

Yes! but there's something greater
That speaks to the heart alone:
'Tis the voice of the great Creator
Dwells in that mighty tone.
> *Ibid. Refrain*

CHRISTOPHER PEARSE CRANCH
[1813–1892]

Thought is deeper than all speech,
Feeling deeper than all thought;
Souls to souls can never teach
What unto themselves was taught.
> *Thought [Gnosis]. Stanza 1*

We are spirits clad in veils;
Man by man was never seen;
All our deep communing fails
To remove the shadowy screen.
> *Ibid. Stanza 2*

O Light divine! we need no fuller test
That all is ordered well;
We know enough to trust that all is best
Where Love and Wisdom dwell.
> *Oh, Love Supreme*

JOHN SULLIVAN DWIGHT
[1813–1893]

Is not true leisure
One with true toil? [1]
> *Rest. Stanza 1*

Rest is not quitting
The busy career,
Rest is the fitting
Of self to its sphere.
> *Ibid. Stanza 4*

'Tis the brook's motion,
Clear without strife,
Fleeing to ocean
After its life.
> *Ibid. Stanza 5*

Work, and thou wilt bless the day
Ere the toil be done;
They that work not, can not pray,
Can not feel the sun.
God is living, working still,

[1] See Cowper, page 363a.

All things work and move;
Work, or lose the power to will,
Lose the power to love.
> *Working*

JOSEPH HOOKER
[1813–1879]

Well, General, we have not had many dead cavalrymen lying about lately.
> *Remark to General William
> Woods Averell, of the Cavalry
> [November, 1862]*

ELIJAH KELLOGG
[1813–1901]

If ye are men, follow me! Strike down your guard, gain the mountain passes, and then do bloody work, as did your sires at old Thermopylae! Is Sparta dead? Is the old Grecian spirit frozen in your brains, that you do cower like a belabored hound beneath his master's lash? O comrades, warriors, Thracians! If we must fight, let us fight for ourselves. If we must slaughter, let it be under the clear sky, by the bright waters, in noble, honorable battle!
> *Spartacus to the Gladiators
> [1846]*

EPES SARGENT
[1813–1880]

A life on the ocean wave,
A home on the rolling deep;
Where the scattered waters rave,
And the winds their revels keep!
Like an eagle caged I pine
On this dull, unchanging shore:
Oh, give me the flashing brine,
The spray and the tempest's roar!
> *A Life on the Ocean Wave
> [1847]. Stanza 1*

HENRY STEVENSON WASHBURN
[1813–1903]

We shall meet, but we shall miss him,
There will be one vacant chair;

We shall linger to caress him
When we breathe our evening prayer.[1]
The Vacant Chair. Stanza 1

THOMAS OSBORNE DAVIS
[1814–1845]

Come in the evening, or come in the
morning,
Come when you're looked for, or come
without warning.
The Welcome. Stanza 1

FREDERICK WILLIAM
FABER
[1814–1863]

The sea, unmated creature, tired and
lone,
Makes on its desolate sands eternal
moan.
The Sorrowful World

Hark! Hark! my soul, angelic songs
are swelling
O'er earth's green fields, and ocean's
wave-beat shore;
How sweet the truth those blessed
strains are telling
Of that new life when sin shall be no
more!
Pilgrims of the Night

O Paradise! O Paradise!
Who doth not crave for rest?
Who would not seek the happy land
Where they that love are blest?
Paradise

CHARLES MACKAY
[1814–1889]

But the sunshine aye shall light the
sky,
As round and round we run;
And the truth shall ever come upper-
most,
And justice shall be done.
Eternal Justice. Stanza 4

Cannon-balls may aid the truth,
But thought's a weapon stronger;
We'll win our battles by its aid; —
Wait a little longer.
The Good Time Coming. Stanza 1

[1] See Longfellow, page 523a.

The smallest effort is not lost,
Each wavelet on the ocean tost
Aids in the ebb-tide or the flow;
Each rain-drop makes some floweret
blow;
Each struggle lessens human woe.
The Old and the New

There is no such thing as death.
In Nature nothing dies.
From each sad remnant of decay
Some forms of life arise.
There Is No Such Thing as Death

Old Tubal Cain was a man of might,
In the days when earth was young.
Tubal Cain. Stanza 1

Not alone for the blade was the bright
steel made,
And he fashioned the first plowshare.[1]
Ibid. Stanza 4

To the West! to the West! to the land
of the free,
Where the mighty Missouri rolls down
to the sea.
To the West. Stanza 1

Where the prairies, like seas where the
billows have rolled,
Are broad as the kingdoms and empires of old.
Ibid. Stanza 2

Make my coffee strong!
The Quarrel

If happy I and wretched he,
Perhaps the king would change with
me.
Differences

MICHAEL WENTWORTH
BECK
[1815–1843]

This world is not so bad a world
As some would like to make it;
Though whether good, or whether bad,
Depends on how we take it.
The World As It Is. Stanza 1

[1] Tubal fashioned the hand-flung spears
And showed his neighbours peace.
KIPLING [1865–1936]: *Jubal and Tubal
Cain, St. 3*

RICHARD HENRY DANA
[1815–1882]

Six days shalt thou labor and do all
thou art able,
And on the seventh — holystone the
decks and scrape the cable.
*Two Years Before the Mast
[1840]. Chap. 3, Philadelphia
Catechism*

Like a true ship, committed to her
element once for all at her Launching,
she perished at sea.
*Ibid. Twenty-Four Years After
[1869]*

DANIEL DECATUR EMMETT
[1815–1904]

I wish I was in de land ob cotton,
Old times dar am not forgotten.
Look away, look away,
Look away, Dixie Land.
Dixie [1859]

In Dixie's land, we'll took our stand,
To lib an' die in Dixie!
Away, away,
Away down South in Dixie.
Ibid.

JOHN BABSONE LANE SOULE
[1815–1891]

Go west, young man.[1]
*Article in the Terre Haute,
Indiana, Express [1851]*

ANTHONY TROLLOPE
[1815–1882]

He argued that the principal duty
which a parent owed to a child was to
make him happy.
Doctor Thorne [1858]. Chap. 3

[1] Horace Greeley [1811–1872] used the
expression in an editorial in *The New York
Tribune* (see Greeley, page 562a). As the
saying, "Go west, young man, and grow up
with the country," gained popularity, Greeley
printed Soule's article, to show the source of
his inspiration.
Many men have stated that the advice was
given to them by Greeley, among them William S. Verity [1837–1930], who said Greeley
had given it to him in 1859.

In these days a man is nobody unless his biography is kept so far posted
up that it may be ready for the national
breakfast-table on the morning after
his demise.
Doctor Thorne. Chap. 25

How I do hate those words, "an excellent marriage." In them is contained
more of wicked worldliness than any
other words one ever hears spoken.
*The Small House at Allington
[1864]. Chap. 39*

Those who offend us are generally
punished for the offence they give; but
we so frequently miss the satisfaction
of knowing that we are avenged!
Ibid. Chap. 50

She understood how much louder a
cock can crow in its own farmyard than
elsewhere.
*The Last Chronicle of Barset
[1867]. Vol. I, Chap. 17*

Always remember that when you go
into an attorney's office door, you will
have to pay for it, first or last.
Ibid. Chap. 20

It is a comfortable feeling to know
that you stand on your own ground.
Land is about the only thing that can't
fly away.
Ibid. Vol. II, Chap. 58

It's dogged as does it.
Ibid. Chap. 61

Nothing reopens the springs of love
so fully as absence, and no absence so
thoroughly as that which must needs
be endless.
Ibid. Chap. 67

PHILIP JAMES BAILEY
[1816–1902]

Let each man think himself an act of
God,
His mind a thought, his life a breath of
God;
And let each try, by great thoughts and
good deeds,
To show the most of Heaven he hath
in him.
Festus [1839]. Proem

Evil and good are God's right hand
and left.
> *Festus. Proem*

Art is man's nature; nature is God's
art.
> *Ibid.*

It matters not how long we live, but
how.
> *Ibid. Wood and Water*

The world must have great minds, even
as great spheres
Or suns, to govern lesser restless minds.
> *Ibid. Water and Wood*

Men might be better if we better
deemed
Of them. The worst way to improve the
world
Is to condemn it.[1]
> *Ibid. A Mountain, Sunrise*

It is much less what we do
Than what we think, which fits us for
the future.
> *Ibid. Alcove and Garden*

The first and worst of all frauds is to
cheat
Oneself.
> *Ibid. Anywhere*

We live in deeds, not years; in
thoughts, not breaths;
In feelings, not in figures on a dial.
We should count time by heart-throbs.
He most lives
Who thinks most — feels the noblest
— acts the best.
> *Ibid. A Country Town*

Envy's a coal comes hissing hot from
hell.
> *Ibid.*

The sole equality on earth is death.
> *Ibid.*

America, thou, half-brother of the
world;
With something good and bad of every
land.
> *Ibid. The Surface*

Who can mistake great thoughts?
They seize upon the mind — arrest,
and search,

[1] The surest plan to make a Man
Is, think him so.
JAMES RUSSELL LOWELL: *The Biglow
Papers* [1848], *Jonathan to John, St. 9*

And shake it.
> *Festus. A Village Feast*

The worst men often give the best advice.
> *Ibid.*

Man is a military animal,
Glories in gunpowder, and loves parade.
> *Ibid. A Metropolis*

There is no disappointment we endure
One half so great as that we are to ourselves.[1]
> *Ibid. The Sun*

CHARLOTTE BRONTË
[1816–1855]

Life, believe, is not a dream
So dark as sages say;
Oft a little morning rain
Foretells a pleasant day.
> *Life* [*1846*]. *Stanza 1*

The human heart has hidden treasures,
In secret kept, in silence sealed; —
The thoughts, the hopes, the dreams,
the pleasures,
Whose charms were broken if re-
vealed.
> *Evening Solace* [*1846*]. *Stanza 1*

Reader, I married him.
> *Jane Eyre* [*1847*]. *Chap. 38*

An abundant shower of curates has
fallen upon the north of England.
> *Shirley* [*1849*]. *Chap. 1*

FRANCES BROWN
[1816–1864]

Oh! those blessed times of old! with
their chivalry and state;
I love to read their chronicles, which
such brave deeds relate;
I love to sing their ancient rhymes, to
hear their legends told —
But, Heaven be thanked! I live not in
those blessed times of old!
> *Oh! the Pleasant Days of Old.*
> *Stanza 7*

[1] Every really able man, if you talk sincerely with him, considers his work, however
much admired, as far short of what it should
be. — EMERSON: *Immortality* [1875]

JAMES THOMAS FIELDS
[1816–1881]

How sweet and gracious, even in com-
　mon speech,
Is that fine sense which men call Cour-
　tesy!
Courtesy

It transmutes aliens into trusting
　friends,
And gives its owner passport round the
　globe.
Ibid.

Just then, with a wink and a sly normal
　lurch,
The owl, very gravely, got down from
　his perch,
Walked round, and regarded his fault-
　finding critic
(Who thought he was stuffed) with a
　glance analytic.
The Owl-Critic

"I'm an owl; you're another. Sir Critic,
　good day!"
And the barber kept on shaving.
Ibid.

The skipper stormed, and tore his hair,
　Hauled on his boots and roared to
　　Marden,
"Nantucket's sunk, and here we are
　Right over old Marm Hackett's gar-
　　den!"
The Nantucket Skipper. Stanza 10

'Tis a fearful thing in winter
　To be shattered in the blast,
And to hear the rattling trumpet
　Thunder, "Cut away the mast!"
Ballad of the Tempest. Stanza 2

Is not God upon the ocean,
Just the same as on the land?[1]
Ibid. Stanza 5

[1] Sir Humphrey Gilbert [1539?–1583], on
embarking on his ill-fated voyage homeward,
— "We are as near to Heaven by sea as by
land." — J. R. Green: *A Short History of
the English People* [1874], *Chap. 8*
　　"Do not fear! Heaven is as near,"
　He said, "by water as by land!"
　　Longfellow: *Sir Humphrey Gilbert*
　　　　　[1849], *St. 6*

ELLEN STURGIS HOOPER
[1816–1841]

I slept and dreamed that life was
　beauty.
I woke — and found that life was
　duty;
Was my dream, then, a shadowy lie?
Toil on, sad heart, courageously,
And thou shalt find thy dream shall be
A noonday light and truth to thee.
Beauty and Duty

JOHN GODFREY SAXE
[1816–1887]

There's a castle in Spain, very charm-
　ing to see,
　Though built without money or toil;
Of this handsome estate I am owner in
　fee,
　And paramount lord of the soil.
My Castle in Spain. Stanza 1

Though we may think we are specially
　blest,
We are certain to pay for the favors we
　get!
The Gifts of the Gods. Stanza 1

I wish that practising was not
So different from preaching.
Wishing. Stanza 4

I'm growing fonder of my staff;
　I'm growing dimmer in the eyes;
I'm growing fainter in my laugh;
　I'm growing deeper in my sighs;
I'm growing careless of my dress;
　I'm growing frugal of my gold;
I'm growing wise; I'm growing —
　yes, —
I'm growing old!
I'm Growing Old. Stanza 3

He takes the strangest liberties, —
But never takes his leave!
My Familiar. Stanza 2

A frown is no extinguisher —
It does not put him out!
Ibid. Stanza 6

In battle or business, whatever the
　game,
In law or in love, it is ever the same;
In the struggle for power, or the scram-
　ble for pelf,

Let this be your motto, — Rely on
    yourself!
For, whether the prize be a ribbon or
    throne,
The victor is he who can go it alone! [1]
      The Game of Life. Stanza 7

It was six men of Indostan
    To learning much inclined,
Who went to see the Elephant
    (Though all of them were blind),
That each by observation
    Might satisfy his mind.
    The Blind Men and the Elephant.
          Stanza 1

'Tis wise to learn; 'tis God-like to
    create.
          The Library

I asked of Echo, 't other day
(Whose words are few and often
    funny),
What to a novice she could say
Of courtship, love, and matrimony?
    Quoth Echo, plainly: — "Matter-o'-
    money."
          Echo. Stanza 1

MICHAEL JOSEPH BARRY
[1817–1889]

But whether on the scaffold high
    Or in the battle's van,
The fittest place where man can die
Is where he dies for man!
    The Place Where Men Should Die.[2]
          Stanza 5

JOHN BARTHOLOMEW
GOUGH
[1817–1886]

What is a minority? The chosen heroes of this earth have been in a minority. There is not a social, political, or
religious privilege that you enjoy today that was not bought for you by the
blood and tears and patient suffering
of the minority. It is the minority that
have stood in the van of every moral

conflict, and achieved all that is noble
in the history of the world.
          What Is a Minority?

TOM TAYLOR
[1817–1880]

You lay a wreath on murdered Lin-
    coln's bier,
You, who, with mocking pencil, wont
    to trace,
Broad for the self-complacent British
    sneer,
His length of shambling limb, his fur-
    rowed face.
     *Abraham Lincoln Foully
     Assassinated.*[1] *Stanza 1*

HENRY DAVID THOREAU
[1817–1862]

I am a parcel of vain strivings tied
By a chance bond together.
        Sic Vita [1841]. Stanza 1

Great God, I ask thee for no meaner
    pelf
Than that I may not disappoint myself,
That in my action I may soar as high
As I can now discern with this clear
    eye.
        A Prayer [1842]. Stanza 1

Any man more right than his neighbors constitutes a majority of one.
      Civil Disobedience [1849]

My life is like a stroll upon the beach,
As near the ocean's edge as I can go.
    *My Life Is Like a Stroll upon
     the Beach [1849]. Stanza 1*

It takes two to speak the truth, —
one to speak, and another to hear.
    *A Week on the Concord and
    Merrimack Rivers [1849].
    Wednesday*

I saw a delicate flower had grown up
two feet high between the horses' feet
and the wheel track. An inch more to
right or left had sealed its fate, or an
inch higher. Yet it lived to flourish, and

---

[1] He travels the fastest who travels alone.
— KIPLING [1865–1936]: *The Winners*
[2] Printed in *The Dublin Nation*, September
28, 1844.

[1] Printed in *Punch*, London, May 6, 1865.
(Taylor became editor of *Punch* in 1874.) It
was at a performance of Taylor's play, *Our
American Cousin,* that Lincoln was shot.

never knew the danger it incurred. It did not borrow trouble, nor invite an evil fate by apprehending it.

Journal. September, 1850

Nothing is so much to be feared as fear.[1]

Ibid. September 7, 1851

The blue-bird carries the sky on his back.

Ibid. April 3, 1852

The perception of beauty is a moral test.

Ibid. June 21, 1852

The youth gets together his materials to build a bridge to the moon, or, perchance, a palace or temple on the earth, and, at length, the middle-aged man concludes to build a woodshed with them.[2]

Ibid. July 14, 1852

Fire is the most tolerable third party.

Ibid. January 2, 1853

Some circumstantial evidence is very strong, as when you find a trout in the milk.

Ibid. November 11, 1854

That man is the richest whose pleasures are the cheapest.

Ibid. March 11, 1856

When the playful breeze drops in the pool, it springs to right and left, quick as a kitten playing with dead leaves.

Ibid. April 9, 1859

The savage in man is never quite eradicated.

Ibid. September 26, 1859

The fate of the country . . . does not depend on what kind of paper you drop into the ballot-box once a year, but on what kind of man you drop from your chamber into the street every morning.

Slavery in Massachusetts [1854]

I have travelled a good deal in Concord.

Walden [1854]. I, Economy

---

[1] See F. D. Roosevelt, page 918b.

[2] At noon he bounded out for food, and nothing less than roast lion would content him. But by suppertime milk toast would do. — Quoted without provenance in *We Accept With Pleasure*, by BERNARD DE VOTO [1897–   ]

Public opinion is a weak tyrant compared with our own private opinion. What a man thinks of himself, that it is which determines, or rather indicates, his fate.

Walden. I, Economy

The mass of men lead lives of quiet desperation.

Ibid.

It is a characteristic of wisdom not to do desperate things.

Ibid.

As if you could kill time without injuring eternity.

Ibid.

Most of the luxuries, and many of the so-called comforts, of life are not only not indispensable, but positive hindrances to the elevation of mankind.

Ibid.

It is true, I never assisted the sun materially in his rising; but, doubt not, it was of the last importance only to be present at it.

Ibid.

For many years I was self-appointed inspector of snow-storms and rain-storms, and did my duty faithfully.

Ibid.

Beware of all enterprises that require new clothes.

Ibid.

The swiftest traveller is he that goes afoot.

Ibid.

It is not necessary that a man should earn his living by the sweat of his brow, unless he sweats easier than I do.

Ibid.

The man who goes alone can start today; but he who travels with another must wait till that other is ready.

Ibid.

There is no odor so bad as that which arises from goodness tainted.

Ibid.

There are a thousand hacking at the branches of evil to one who is striking at the root.

Ibid.

Philanthropy is almost the only virtue which is sufficiently appreciated by mankind.

Walden. I, Economy

To him whose elastic and vigorous thought keeps pace with the sun, the day is a perpetual morning.

Ibid. II, Where I Lived, and What I Lived For

To be awake is to be alive.

Ibid.

I went to the woods because I wished to live deliberately, to front only the essential facts of life, and see if I could not learn what it had to teach, and not, when I came to die, discover that I had not lived.

Ibid.

Our life is frittered away by detail. . . . Simplify, simplify.

Ibid.

Time is but the stream I go a-fishing in.

Ibid.

Books must be read as deliberately and reservedly as they were written.

Ibid. III, Reading

What is called eloquence in the forum is commonly found to be rhetoric in the study.

Ibid.

The works of the great poets have never yet been read by mankind, for only great poets can read them.

Ibid.

How many a man has dated a new era in his life from the reading of a book.

Ibid.

I love a broad margin to my life.

Ibid. IV, Sounds

Our horizon is never quite at our elbows.

Ibid. V, Solitude

I never found the companion that was so companionable as solitude. We are for the most part more lonely when we go abroad among men than when we stay in our chambers. A man thinking or working is always alone, let him be where he will.

Ibid.

I had three chairs in my house: one for solitude, two for friendship, three for society.

Walden. VI, Visitors

Ministers who spoke of God as if they enjoyed a monopoly of the subject.

Ibid.

I was determined to know beans.

Ibid. VII, The Beanfield

There is never an instant's truce between virtue and vice. Goodness is the only investment that never fails.

Ibid. XI, Higher Laws

While men believe in the infinite, some ponds will be thought to be bottomless.

Ibid. XVI, The Pond in Winter

Through our own recovered innocence we discern the innocence of our neighbors.

Ibid. XVII, Spring

If one advances confidently in the direction of his dreams, and endeavors to live the life which he has imagined, he will meet with a success unexpected in common hours.

Ibid. XVIII, Conclusion

If a man does not keep pace with his companions, perhaps it is because he hears a different drummer. Let him step to the music which he hears, however measured or far away.

Ibid.

Love your life, poor as it is. You may perhaps have some pleasant, thrilling, glorious hours, even in a poorhouse. The setting sun is reflected from the windows of the almshouse as brightly as from the rich man's abode.

Ibid. Conclusion

It is life near the bone where it is sweetest.

Ibid.

Rather than love, than money, than fame, give me truth.

Ibid.

Men will lie on their backs, talking about the fall of man, and never make an effort to get up.

Life Without Principle [*1863*]

Whate'er we leave to God, God does
And blesses us.
Inspiration [_1894_]. _Proem_
I hear beyond the range of sound,
I see beyond the range of sight,
New earths and skies and seas around,
And in my day the sun doth pale his
light.
Ibid. Stanza 7
She with one breath attunes the spheres,
And also my poor human heart.
Ibid. Stanza 15

ELIZA COOK
[1818–1889]

Whom do we dub as Gentlemen? The
knave, the fool, the brute —
If they but own full tithe of gold, and
wear a courtly suit.
Nature's Gentleman. Stanza 1
They hold the rank no king can give,
no station can disgrace;
Nature puts forth her Gentleman, and
monarchs must give place.[1]
Ibid. Stanza 6
I love it, I love it; and who shall dare
To chide me for loving that old arm-
chair?
The Old Arm-Chair
How cruelly sweet are the echoes that
start
When memory plays an old tune on the
heart!
Old Dobbin. Stanza 16
Better build schoolrooms for "the boy"
Than cells and gibbets for "the man." [2]
A Song for the Ragged Schools.
Stanza 12
How busy we are on Tom Tiddler's
ground
Looking for gold and silver.[3]
Tom Tiddler's Ground. Stanza 1
Whenever you find your heart despair
Of doing some goodly thing,

[1] See Linton, page 582a.
[2] Give them a chance — if you stint them
now, tomorrow you'll have to pay
A larger bill for a darker ill.
DENIS A. McCARTHY [1870–1931]:
Give Them a Place to Play, St. 4
[3] Here we are on Tom Tiddler's ground,
picking up gold and silver. — _A children's
game_

Con over this strain, try bravely again,
And remember the Spider and King.[1]
Try Again. Stanza 16

CECIL FRANCES
ALEXANDER
[1818–1895]

All things bright and beautiful,
All creatures great and small,
All things wise and wonderful,
The Lord God made them all.
All Things Bright and Beautiful
[_1848_]. _Stanza 1_
The rich man in his castle,
The poor man at his gate,
God made them, high or lowly,
And ordered their estate.
Ibid. Stanza 3
There is a green hill far away,
Without a city wall,
Where the dear Lord was crucified,
Who died to save us all.
There Is a Green Hill [_1848_].
Stanza 1
Once in royal David's city
Stood a lowly cattle shed,
Where a Mother laid her Baby
In a manger for his bed:
Mary was that Mother mild,
Jesus Christ her little Child.
Once in Royal David's City
[_1848_]. _Stanza 1_

EMILY BRONTË
[1818–1848]

Sleep not, dream not; this bright day
Will not, cannot last for aye;
Bliss like thine is bought by years
Dark with torment and with tears.
Sleep Not [_1846_]. _Stanza 1_
The Bluebell is the sweetest flower
That waves in summer air:
Its blossoms have the mightiest power
To soothe my spirit's care.
The Bluebell [_1846_]. _Stanza 1_
Love is like the wild rose-briar;
Friendship like the holly-tree.

[1] Robert Bruce, liberator and king [1306–
1329] of Scotland.

The holly is dark when the rose-briar blooms,
But which will bloom most constantly?
Love and Friendship [*1846*].
Stanza 1

I'll walk where my own nature would be leading —
It vexes me to choose another guide —
Where the grey flocks in ferny gléns are feeding,
Where the wild wind blows on the mountain-side.
Often Rebuked [*1846*]. *Stanza 4*

Cold in the earth — and fifteen wild Decembers
From those brown hills have melted into spring:
Faithful, indeed, is the spirit that remembers
After such years of change and suffering!
Remembrance [*1846*]

No coward soul is mine,
No trembler in the world's storm-troubled sphere:
I see Heaven's glories shine,
And faith shines equal, arming me from fear.
Last Lines [*1846*]. *Stanza 1*

There is not room for Death.[1]
Ibid. Stanza 7

I lingered round them, under that benign sky: watched the moths fluttering among the heath and hare-bells; listened to the soft wind breathing through the grass; and wondered how any one could ever imagine unquiet slumbers for the sleepers in that quiet earth.
Wuthering Heights [*1847*].
Last Words

WILLIAM ELLERY CHANNING
[1818–1901]

Habitant of castle gray,
Creeping thing in sober way,

[1] See Dylan Thomas, page 996b.

Visible sage mechanician,
Skillfulest arithmetician.
The Spider

Most joyful let the Poet be;
It is through him that all men see.
The Poet of the Old and New Times

A wail in the wind is all I hear;
A voice of woe for a lover's loss.
Lament for Thoreau

The hills are reared, the seas are scooped in vain
If learning's altar vanish from the plain.
Inscription for the Alcott House [1]

GEORGE DUFFIELD
[1818–1888]

Stand up! — stand up for Jesus!
Hymn

WILLIAM MAXWELL EVARTS
[1818–1901]

The pious ones of Plymouth, who, reaching the Rock, first fell upon their own knees and then upon the aborigines.[2]
Quoted by HENRY WATTERSON
in The Louisville Courier-Journal [*July 4, 1913*]

JOHN JAMES ROBERT MANNERS, DUKE OF RUTLAND
[1818–1906]

Let wealth and commerce, laws and learning die,
But leave us still our old nobility.
England's Trust. Part III, Line 231

JOHN MASON NEALE
[1818–1866]

Good King Wenceslas look'd out,
On the Feast of Stephen;

[1] This couplet is painted over the mantel in Alcott House, Concord, Massachusetts.
[2] This pun has also been attributed to Oliver Wendell Holmes, Bill Nye, and George Frisbie Hoar.

When the snow lay round about,
　Deep and crisp and even.
　　　　Good King Wenceslas. Stanza 1
"Bring me flesh and bring me wine,
Bring me pine-logs hither."
　　　　　　　　Ibid. Stanza 3
Page and monarch, forth they went,
　Forth they went together,
Through the rude winds' wild lament
And the bitter weather.
　　　　　　　　　　Ibid.

In his master's steps he trod,
　Where the snow lay dinted;
Heat was in the very sod
　Which the Saint had printed.
Wherefore, Christian men, be sure,
　Wealth or rank possessing,
Ye who now do bless the poor
　Shall yourselves find blessing.
　　　　　　　　Ibid. Stanza 5
O come, O come, Emmanuel,
And ransom captive Israel.
　　　　O Come, O Come, Emmanuel
　　　　(translated from the Latin,
　　　　Veni, Veni, Emmanuel)
Jerusalem the golden, with milk and
　honey blest,
Beneath thy contemplation sink heart
　and voice oppressed.
　　　　Hymn (translated from the
　　　　Latin, Urbs Syon Aurea)
Brief life is here our portion.
　　　　　　　　　　Hymn

KARL MARX
[1818–1883]

Religion . . . is the opium of the
people.
　　　　Critique of the Hegelian Phi-
　　　　losophy of Right [1844]. In-
　　　　troduction
The history of all hitherto existing
society is the history of class struggles.
　　　　Manifesto of the Communist
　　　　Party [1] *[1848]. I*
Of all the classes that stand face to
face with the bourgeoisie today the
proletariat alone is a really revolutionary class. The other classes decay and

[1] Written in collaboration with FRIEDRICH
ENGELS. Translated by SAMUEL MOORE.

finally disappear in the race of modern
industry; the proletariat is its special
and essential product.[1]
　　　　Manifesto of the Communist
　　　　　　　　　　Party. I
Pauperism develops more rapidly
than population and wealth.
　　　　　　　　　　Ibid.
In proportion as the antagonism be-
tween classes within the nation van-
ishes, the hostility of one nation to another will come to an end.
　　　　　　　　　　Ibid. II
The ruling ideas of each age have
ever been the ideas of its ruling class.
　　　　　　　　　　Ibid.
Christian Socialism is but the holy
water with which the priest consecrates
the heartburnings of the aristocrat.
　　　　　　　　　　Ibid. III
The proletarians have nothing to lose
but their chains. They have a world to
win. Workers of the world, unite!
　　　　　　　　　　Ibid. IV
Nothing can have value without being an object of utility. If it be useless, the labor contained in it is useless,
cannot be reckoned as labor, and cannot therefore create value.
　　　　Capital [2] *[1867–1883]. Part II,*
　　　　　　　　Chap. 3, Page 33
The capitalist himself is a practical
man, who, it is true, does not always
reflect on what he says outside his office,
but who always knows what he does
inside the latter.
　　　　　　Ibid. Chap. 5, Page 43
Constant labor of one uniform kind
destroys the intensity and flow of a
man's animal spirits, which find recrea-

[1] By bourgeoisie is meant the class of modern capitalists, owners of the means of social
production and employers of wage-labor. By
proletariat, the class of modern wage-laborers
who, having no means of production of their
own, are reduced to selling their labor-power
in order to live. — FRIEDRICH ENGELS [1820–
1895]: *Footnote to Manifesto of the Communist Party*
[2] Abridged edition prepared by JULIAN
BORCHARDT, translated by STEPHEN L. TRASK,
Modern Library edition.

tion and delight in mere change of activity.

Capital. Part II, Chap. 9,
Page 74

The intellectual desolation, artificially produced by converting immature human beings into mere machines.

Ibid. Chap. 10, Page 102

The battle of competition is fought by cheapening of commodities.

Ibid. Chap. 13, Page 168

The only part of the so-called national wealth that actually enters into the collective possessions of modern peoples is their national debt.

Ibid. Chap. 14, Page 199

Capitalist production begets, with the inexorability of a law of nature, its own negation.

Ibid. Chap. 15, Page 204

When commercial capital occupies a position of unquestioned ascendancy, it everywhere constitutes a system of plunder.

Ibid. Chap. 21, Page 262

From each according to his abilities, to each according to his needs.

Critique of the Gotha Program [1]
[1875]

IVAN SERGEYEVICH TURGENIEV
[1818–1883]

That air of superiority to the rest of the world which usually disappears when once the twenties have been passed.

Fathers and Sons [2] *[1862].*
Chap. 4

That awkwardness which overtakes a young man when, just ceased to be a boy, he returns to the spot where hitherto he has ranked as a mere child.

Ibid.

That dim, murky period when regrets come to resemble hopes, and hopes are beginning to resemble regrets.

Ibid. Chap. 7

[1] Modern Library edition.
[2] Translated by C. J. HOGARTH.

I agree with no man's opinions. I have some of my own.

Fathers and Sons. Chap. 13

The temerity to believe in nothing.

Ibid. Chap. 14

A picture may instantly present what a book could set forth only in a hundred pages.

Ibid. Chap. 16

The sensuous joy of magnanimity.

Ibid. Chap. 17

Whatever a man prays for, he prays for a miracle. Every prayer reduces itself to this: "Great God, grant that twice two be not four."

Prayer

Don't forget me, but do not call me to mind either, in the midst of daily cares, pleasures and needs. . . . I do not want to disturb your life, I do not want to impede its quiet course.

Literary Remains [published in 1930]. When I Shall Be No More

HENRY WHEELER SHAW ("JOSH BILLINGS")
[1818–1885]

A sekret ceases tew be a sekret if it iz once confided — it iz like a dollar bill, once broken, it iz never a dollar agin.

Affurisms [1] *[1865]*

Love iz like the meazles; we kant have it bad but onst, and the later in life we have it the tuffer it goes with us.

Ibid.

Put an Englishman into the garden of Eden, and he would find fault with the whole blarsted consarn; — put a Yankee in, and he would see where he could alter it to advantage; — put an Irishman in, and he would want tew boss the thing; — put a Dutchman in, and he would proceed tew plant it.

Ibid.

Better make a weak man your enemy than your friend.

Ibid.

[1] From *Josh Billings: His Sayings.*

I never knu a man trubbled with melankolly, who had plenty to dew, and did it.

Afurisms

Poverty iz the step-mother ov genius.

Ibid.

Manifest destiny iz the science ov going tew bust, or enny other place before yu git thare.

Manifest Destiny

Thare iz such a thing az manifest destiny, but when it occurs it iz like the number ov rings on the rakoon's tale, ov no great consequense only for ornament.

Ibid.

The wheel that squeaks the loudest Is the one that gets the grease.

The Kicker

It is better to know nothing than to know what ain't so.[1]

Proverb [1874]

MAX SCHNECKENBURGER
[1819–1849]

So long as blood shall warm our veins, While for the sword one hand remains, One arm to bear a gun, — no more Shall foot of foeman tread thy shore! Dear Fatherland, no fear be thine, Firm stands thy guard along the Rhine.

The Watch on the Rhine.[2]
Stanza 4

ARTHUR HUGH CLOUGH
[1819–1861]

Grace is given of God, but knowledge is bought in the market.

The Bothie of Tober-na-Vuolich
[1848]. Part IV

A world where nothing is had for nothing.

Ibid. Part VIII

As ships, becalmed at eve, that lay With canvas drooping, side by side, Two towers of sail, at dawn of day

Are scarce long leagues apart descried.

Qua Cursum Ventus [1849].
Stanza 1

It fortifies my soul to know That, though I perish, Truth is so: That, howsoe'er I stray and range, Whate'er I do, Thou dost not change. I steadier step when I recall That, if I slip, Thou dost not fall.

"With Whom Is No Variableness"[1]
[1862]

Because we can't do all we would, Does it follow, to do nothing's good?

Dipsychus [1862]. Part I, Sc. 4

And almost every one when age, Disease, or sorrows strike him, Inclines to think there is a God, Or something very like Him.

Ibid. Sc. 5

This world is very odd we see, We do not comprehend it; But in one fact we all agree, God won't, and we can't, mend it.

Ibid. Part II, Sc. 2

How pleasant it is to have money!

Ibid.

Haunt not the fringy edges of the fight But the pell-mell of men.

Ibid. Sc. 4

That out of sight is out of mind[2] Is true of most we leave behind; It is not sure, nor can be true, My own and only love, of you.

Songs of Absence [1862]

Say not, the struggle naught availeth, The labour and the wounds are vain, The enemy faints not, nor faileth, And as things have been they remain.

Say Not the Struggle Naught
Availeth [1862]. Stanza 1

For while the tired waves, vainly breaking, Seem here no painful inch to gain, Far back, through creeks and inlets making, Comes silent, flooding in, the main.

Ibid. Stanza 3

---

[1] Better know nothing than half-know many things. — NIETZSCHE: *Thus Spake Zarathustra* [1883–1891], *Part IV, 64*

[2] Translated by JOHN R. THOMPSON [1823–1873].

[1] *James, I, 17.*

[2] See Thomas à Kempis, page 83a.

And not by eastern windows only,
When daylight comes, comes in the light;
In front, the sun climbs slow, how slowly,
But westward, look, the land is bright.

> *Say Not the Struggle Naught*
> *Availeth. Stanza 4*

GEORGE ELIOT
(MARIAN EVANS CROSS)
[1819–1880]

'Tis God gives skill,
But not without men's hands: He could not make
Antonio Stradivari's violins
Without Antonio.

> *Stradivarius*

O may I join the choir invisible
Of those immortal dead who live again
In minds made better by their presence.

> *O May I Join the Choir Invisible*

May I reach
That purest heaven, be to other souls
The cup of strength in some great agony.

> *Ibid.*

Life is too precious to be spent in this weaving and unweaving of false impressions, and it is better to live quietly under some degree of misrepresentation than to attempt to remove it by the uncertain process of letter-writing.

> *Letter to Mrs. Peter Taylor*
> *[June 8, 1856]*

Boots and shoes are the greatest trouble of my life. Everything else one can turn and turn about, and make old look like new; but there's no coaxing boots and shoes to look better than they are.

> *Amos Barton* [*1857*]. *Chap. 2*

It's no trifle at her time of life to part with a doctor who knows her constitution.

> *Janet's Repentance* [*1857*].
> *Chap. 3*

Any coward can fight a battle when he's sure of winning; but give me the man who has pluck to fight when he's sure of losing. That's my way, sir; and there are many victories worse than a defeat.

> *Janet's Repentance. Chap. 6*

Opposition may become sweet to a man when he has christened it persecution.

> *Ibid. Chap. 8*

It's but little good you'll do a-watering the last year's crops.

> *Adam Bede* [*1859*]. *Chap. 18*

He was like a cock who thought the sun had risen to hear him crow.

> *Ibid. Chap. 33*

I've never any pity for conceited people, because I think they carry their comfort about with them.[1]

> *The Mill on the Floss* [*1860*].
> *Book V, Chap. 4*

Below their names it was written: "In their death they were not divided."[2]

> *Ibid. Last line of book*

The years seem to rush by now, and I think of death as a fast approaching end of a journey — double and treble reason for loving as well as working while it is day.

> *Letter to Miss Sara Hennell*
> *[November 22, 1861]*

It seems to me much better to read a man's own writing than to read what others say about him, especially when the man is first-rate and the "others" are third-rate.

> *Letter to Miss Hennell*
> *[October 28, 1865]*

I have the conviction that excessive literary production is a social offence.

> *Letter to Alexander Main*
> *[September 11, 1871]*

I like not only to be loved, but also to be told that I am loved. I am not sure that you are of the same kind. But the realm of silence is large enough beyond the grave. This is the world of

---

[1] There is not enough of love and goodness in the world to throw any of it away on conceited people. — NIETZSCHE [1844–1900]: *Human, All Too Human, 129*

[2] 2 Samuel, I, 23

light and speech, and I shall take leave to tell you that you are very dear.

Letter to Mrs. Burne-Jones
[May 11, 1875]

All biography diminishes in interest when the subject has won celebrity — or some reputation that hardly comes up to a celebrity. But autobiography at least saves a man or woman that the world is curious about from the publication of a string of mistakes called "Memoirs."

Letter to Miss Sara Hennell
[November 22, 1876]

Blessed is the man who, having nothing to say, abstains from giving in words evidence of the fact.

Impressions of Theophrastus
Such [1879]

THOMAS DUNN ENGLISH
[1819–1902]

Oh! don't you remember sweet Alice, Ben Bolt?
Sweet Alice, whose hair was so brown,
Who wept with delight when you gave her a smile,
And trembled with fear at your frown?

Ben Bolt [1]

Though little dangers they may fear,
When greater dangers men environ
Then women show a front of iron;
And, gentle in their manner, they
Do bold things in a quiet way.

Betty Zane. [2] *Stanza 1*

JOSIAH GILBERT HOLLAND
[1819–1881]

Heaven is not reached at a single bound;

[1] First published in *The New York Mirror,* September 2, 1843. It was set to music, an adaptation of an old German melody, by NELSON KNEASS, and sung in the play *The Battle of Buena Vista.* In 1894 GEORGE DU MAURIER used the song in his novel *Trilby* and it at once became popular.
[2] Fort Henry (now Wheeling, West Virginia) was attacked by Simon Girty and a band of Wyandot Indians, September 27–28, 1777. Betty Zane ran from the blockhouse to the log hut on the hill, and returned with a cask of gunpowder wrapped in her apron.

But we build the ladder by which we rise
From the lowly earth to the vaulted skies,
And we mount to its summit round by round. [1]

Gradatim. Stanza 1

He could see naught but vanity in beauty,
And naught but weakness in a fond caress,
And pitied men whose views of Christian duty
Allowed indulgence in such foolishness.

Daniel Gray. Stanza 9

God give us men! A time like this demands
Strong minds, great hearts, true faith, and ready hands;
Men whom the lust of office does not kill;
Men whom the spoils of office cannot buy;
Men who possess opinions and a will;
Men who have honor; men who will not lie.

The Day's Demand

JULIA WARD HOWE
[1819–1910]

Mine eyes have seen the glory of the coming of the Lord;
He is trampling out the vintage where the grapes of wrath are stored;
He hath loosed the fateful lightning of His terrible, swift sword;
His truth is marching on.

Battle Hymn of the Republic
[1862]. Stanza 1

In the beauty of the lilies Christ was born across the sea,
With a glory in His bosom that transfigures you and me;
As He died to make men holy, let us die to make men free.

Ibid. Stanza 5

Weave no more silks, ye Lyons looms,
To deck our girls for gay delights!

[1] Step after step the ladder is ascended. — GEORGE HERBERT: *Jacula Prudentum* [1640]

The crimson flower of battle blooms,
And solemn marches fill the nights.
Our Orders

CHARLES KINGSLEY
[1819–1875]

Oh! that we two were Maying.
The Saint's Tragedy [*1848*].
Act II, Sc. 9

"O Mary, go and call the cattle home,
And call the cattle home,
And call the cattle home,
Across the sands of Dee;"
The western wind was wild and dank
with foam,
And all alone went she.
The Sands of Dee. Stanza 1

The cruel crawling foam.
Ibid. Stanza 4

For men must work, and women must
weep,
And there's little to earn and many to
keep,
Though the harbor bar be moaning.
The Three Fishers. Stanza 1

For men must work, and women must
weep,
And the sooner it's over, the sooner to
sleep;
And good-bye to the bar and its
moaning.
Ibid. Stanza 3

Be good, sweet maid, and let who will
be clever;
Do noble things, not dream them, all
day long;
And so make Life, Death, and that vast
Forever
One grand sweet song.
A Farewell. Stanza 3

The world goes up and the world goes
down,
And the sunshine follows the rain;
And yesterday's sneer and yesterday's
frown
Can never come over again.
Dolcino to Margaret

Oh England is a pleasant place for
them that's rich and high,

But England is a cruel place for such
poor folks as I.
The Last Buccaneer. Stanza 1

In the light of fuller day,
Of purer science, holier laws.[1]
On the Death of a Certain Journal [2]
[*1848–1849*]. *Stanza 5*

A lone man's companion, a bachelor's
friend, a hungry man's food, a sad man's
cordial, a wakeful man's sleep, and a
chilly man's fire . . . there's no herb
like unto it [tobacco] under the canopy
of heaven.
Westward Ho [*1855*]. *Chap. 7*

More ways of killing a cat than chok-
ing her with cream.
Ibid. Chap. 20

Thank God every morning when you
get up that you have something to do
that day which must be done, whether
you like it or not. Being forced to work,
and forced to do your best, will breed
in you temperance and self-control,
diligence and strength of will, cheerfulness and content, and a hundred virtues which the idle never know.
Town and Country Sermons [*1861*]

Clear and cool, clear and cool,
By laughing shallow, and dreaming
pool;
Cool and clear, cool and clear,
By shining shingle, and foaming wear;
Under the crag where the ouzel sings,
And the ivied wall where the church-bell
rings;
Undefiled, for the undefiled;
Play by me, bathe in me, mother and
child.
Water Babies [*1863*]. *Song I,*
Stanza 1

When all the world is young, lad,
And all the trees are green;
And every goose a swan, lad,
And every lass a queen;
Then hey for boot and horse, lad,
And round the world away:
Young blood must have its course, lad,
And every dog his day.[3]
Ibid. Song II, Stanza 1

[1] See Tennyson, page 553a.
[2] *The Christian Socialist.*
[3] See Shakespeare, page 179a.

When all the world is old, lad,
And all the trees are brown;
And all the sport is stale, lad,
And all the wheels run down.
　　　Water Babies. Song II, Stanza 2
God grant you find one face there
You loved when all was young!
　　　　　　　　　　　　Ibid.
I once had a sweet little doll, dears,
The prettiest doll in the world;
Her cheeks were so red and so white,
　　dears,
And her hair was so charmingly curled.
　　　Ibid. Song IV, Stanza 1
　We were crawling slowly along, looking out for Virgin Garda; the first of those numberless isles which Columbus, so goes the tale, discovered on St. Ursula's day, and named them after the saint and her eleven thousand mythical virgins. Unfortunately, English buccaneers have since given to most of them less poetic names. The Dutchman's Cap, Broken Jerusalem, The Dead Man's Chest,[1] Rum Island, and so forth, mark a time and race more prosaic.
　　　　At Last [*1870*]. *Chap. 1*
　To be discontented with the divine discontent, and to be ashamed with the noble shame, is the very germ and first upgrowth of all virtue.
　　　Health and Education [*1874*].
　　　　　The Science of Health
　Some say that the age of chivalry is past, that the spirit of romance is dead. The age of chivalry is never past, so long as there is a wrong left unredressed on earth.
　　　Life [*1879*]. *Vol. II, Chap. 28*

JAMES RUSSELL LOWELL
[1819–1891]

She doeth little kindnesses
Which most leave undone, or despise.
　　　　My Love [*1840*]. *Stanza 4*
Be noble! and the nobleness that lies
In other men, sleeping, but never dead,
Will rise in majesty to meet thine own.
　　　　　Sonnet IV [*1840*]

[1] See R. L. Stevenson, pages 749b–750a.

Great Truths are portions of the soul
　of man;
Great souls are portions of Eternity.
　　　　　　　Sonnet VI [*1841*]
His words were simple words enough,
　And yet he used them so,
That what in other mouths was rough
　In his seemed musical and low.
　　　The Shepherd of King Admetus
　　　　　　[*1842*]. *Stanza 5*
All thoughts that mould the age begin
Deep down within the primitive soul.
　　　An Incident in a Railroad Car
　　　　　　[*1842*]. *Stanza 13*
Who speaks the truth stabs Falsehood
　to the heart.
　　　　　　　L'Envoi [*1843*]
No man is born into the world whose
　work
Is not born with him; there is always
　work,
And tools to work withal, for those who
　will;
And blessèd are the horny hands of toil.
　　　A Glance Behind the Curtain
　　　　　　　　[*1843*]
They are slaves who fear to speak
For the fallen and the weak. . . .
They are slaves who dare not be
In the right with two or three.
　　　Stanzas on Freedom [*1843*]. *IV*
The nurse of full-grown souls is solitude.
　　　　　　Columbus [*1844*]
Once to every man and nation comes
　the moment to decide,
In the strife of Truth with Falsehood,
　for the good or evil side.
　　　　The Present Crisis [*1844*].
　　　　　　　　Stanza 5
Truth forever on the scaffold, Wrong
　forever on the throne.[1]
　　　　　　Ibid. Stanza 8
Then it is the brave man chooses, while
　the coward stands aside,

[1] Worth on foot, and rascals in the coach.
—DRYDEN: *Art of Poetry* [*1685*], L. *376*
Wrong rules the land, and waiting Justice sleeps. — J. G. HOLLAND [1819–1881]: *The Day's Demand*

Doubting in his abject spirit, till his
Lord is crucified.
The Present Crisis. Stanza 11

They must upward still, and onward,
who would keep abreast of Truth.
Ibid. Stanza 18

Dear common flower, that grow'st be-
side the way,
Fringing the dusty road with harmless
gold.
To the Dandelion [1845].
Stanza 1

The birch, most shy and ladylike of
trees.
An Indian-Summer Reverie [1846].
Stanza 8

Not only around our infancy
Doth heaven with all its splendors lie;
Daily, with souls that cringe and plot,
We Sinais climb and know it not.
The Vision of Sir Launfal [1848].
Part I, Prelude, Stanza 2

'Tis heaven alone that is given away;
'Tis only God may be had for the ask-
ing.
Ibid. Stanza 4

And what is so rare as a day in June?
Then, if ever, come perfect days;
Then Heaven tries the earth if it be in
tune,
And over it softly her warm ear lays.
Ibid. Stanza 5

He gives only the worthless gold
Who gives from a sense of duty.
Ibid. Part I, Stanza 6

The gift without the giver is bare; [1]
Who gives himself with his alms feeds
three, —
Himself, his hungering neighbor, and
me.
Ibid. Part II, Stanza 8

Got the ill name of augurs, because
they were bores.
A Fable for Critics [1848]

There comes Emerson first, whose rich
words, every one,
Are like gold nails in temples to hang
trophies on;
Whose prose is grand verse, while his
verse, the Lord knows,

[1] See Emerson, page 502b.

Is some of it pr— No, 'tis not even
prose.[1]
A Fable for Critics

And I honor the man who is willing to
sink
Half his present repute for the freedom
to think,
And, when he has thought, be his cause
strong or weak,
Will risk t' other half for the freedom
to speak.
Ibid.

There comes Poe, with his raven, like
Barnaby Rudge,
Three fifths of him genius and two
fifths sheer fudge.
Ibid.

Nature fits all her children with something to do,
He who would write and can't write,
can surely review.[2]
Ibid.

Ez fer war, I call it murder, —
There you hev it plain an' flat;
I don't want to go no furder
Than my Testyment fer that. . . .
An' you've gut to git up airly
Ef you want to take in God.
The Biglow Papers. Series I
[1848], No. 1, Stanza 5

Laborin' man an' laborin' woman
Hev one glory an' one shame;
Ev'y thin' thet's done inhuman
Injers all on 'em the same.
Ibid. Stanza 10

This goin' ware glory waits ye haint
one agreeable feetur.
Ibid. No. 2, Stanza 6

But John P.
Robinson, he
Sez they didn't know everythin' down
in Judee.
Ibid. No. 3, Stanza 8

A marciful Providunce fashioned us
holler
O' purpose thet we might our principles
swaller.
Ibid. No. 4, Stanza 2

[1] Meredith is a prose Browning, and so
is Browning — OSCAR WILDE [1854–1900]:
The Critic as Artist
[2] See Disraeli, page 513a.

I should like to shoot
The holl gang, by the gret horn spoon!
The Biglow Papers. Series I,
No. 5, Stanza 2
I du believe with all my soul
In the gret Press's freedom,
To pint the people to the goal
An' in the traces lead 'em.
Ibid. No. 6, Stanza 7
I *don't* believe in princerple,
But oh I *du* in interest.
Ibid. Stanza 9
It ain't by princerples nor men
My preudunt course is steadied, —
I scent wich pays the best, an' then
Go into it baldheaded.
Ibid. Stanza 10
Of my merit
On thet pint you yourself may jedge;
All is, I never drink no sperit,
Nor I haint never signed no pledge.
Ibid. No. 7, Stanza 9
Ez to my princerples, I glory
In hevin' nothin' o' the sort.
Ibid. Stanza 10
God makes sech nights, all white an'
still,
Fur'z you can look or listen.
Ibid. Series II [1866], The
Courtin', Stanza 1
His heart kep' goin' pity-pat,
But hern went pity-Zekle.
Ibid. Stanza 15
All kin' o' smily round the lips,
An' teary round the lashes.
Ibid. Stanza 21
My gran'ther's rule was safer 'n 'tis
to crow:
Don't never prophesy — onless ye
know.
Ibid. No. 2
It's 'most enough to make a deacon
swear.
Ibid.
Folks never understand the folks they
hate.
Ibid.
Ef you want peace, the thing you've
gut tu du
Is jes' to show you're up to fightin', tu.[1]
Ibid.

[1] See Washington, page 367a.

Bad work follers ye ez long's ye live.
The Biglow Papers. Series II,
No. 2
Our papers don't purtend to print on'y
wut Guv'ment choose,
An' thet insures us all to git the very
best o' noose.
Ibid. No. 3
No, never say nothin' without you're
compelled tu,
An' then don't say nothin' thet you can
be held tu.
Ibid. No. 5
Wut's words to them whose faith an'
truth
On War's red techstone rang true
metal,
Who ventered life an' love an' youth
For the gret prize o' death in battle?
Ibid. No. 10, Stanza 17
They came three thousand miles, and
died,
To keep the Past upon its throne;
Unheard, beyond the ocean tide,
Their English mother made her moan.[1]
Graves of Two English Sol-
diers on Concord Battle-
ground [1849]. Stanza 3
Slowly the Bible of the race is writ,
And not on paper leaves nor leaves of
stone;
Each age, each kindred, adds a verse
to it,
Texts of despair or hope, of joy or
moan.
Bibliolatres [1849]. Stanza 6
There is nothing so desperately mo-
notonous as the sea, and I no longer
wonder at the cruelty of pirates.
Fireside Travels [1864]. At Sea
It is by presence of mind in untried
emergencies that the native metal of a
man is tested.
Abraham Lincoln [1864]
What men call treasure and the Gods
call dross.
Ode Recited at the Harvard
Commemoration [1865]. IV

[1] Inscribed on the memorial to the two
British soldiers, Concord, Massachusetts.

Each year to ancient friendships adds
    a ring,
As to an oak.
       Under the Willows [*1868*]
The shell disdained a soul had gained,
The lyre had been discovered.
      The Finding of the Lyre [*1868*].
                Stanza 4
Not failure, but low aim, is crime.
    For an Autograph [*1868*]. *Stanza 5*
When I was a beggarly boy,
    And lived in a cellar damp,
I had not a friend nor a toy,
    But I had Aladdin's lamp.
         Aladdin [*1868*]. *Stanza 1*
Safe in the hallowed quiets of the past.
    The Cathedral [1] [*1869*]. *Stanza 9*
The one thing finished in this hasty
    world.
                    Ibid.
The wisest man could ask no more of
    Fate
Than to be simple, modest, manly, true,
Safe from the Many, honored by the
    Few;
To count as naught in World, or
    Church, or State;
But inwardly in secret to be great.
    Sonnet, Jeffries Wyman [*1874*]
For me Fate gave, whate'er she else
    denied,
A nature sloping to the southern side;
I thank her for it, though when clouds
    arise
Such Natures double-darken gloomy
    skies.
    Epistle to George William Curtis
            [*1874*]. *Postscript*
Like him who, in the desert's awful
    frame,
Notches his cockney initials on the
    Sphinx.
    Sonnet on Being Asked for an
      Autograph in Venice [*1875*]
The Maple puts her corals on in May.
            The Maple [*1875*]
In vain we call old notions fudge,
And bend our conscience to our deal-
    ing;

[1] Chartres.

The Ten Commandments will not
    budge,
And stealing will continue stealing.[1]
    International Copyright
        [*November 20, 1885*]
These pearls of thought in Persian gulfs
    were bred,
Each softly lucent as a rounded moon;
The diver Omar plucked them from
    their bed,
Fitzgerald strung them on an English
    thread.
    In a Copy of Omar Khayyám
          [*1888*]. *Stanza 1*
  As brief
As a dragon-fly's repose.
    Scherzo [*1888*]. *Stanza 3*
In life's small things be resolute and
    great
To keep thy muscle trained: know'st
    thou when Fate
Thy measure takes, or when she'll say
    to thee,
"I find thee worthy; do this deed for
    me"?
          Sayings [*1888*]. *1*
As life runs on, the road grows strange
With faces new, and near the end
The milestones into headstones change,
    'Neath every one a friend.
    Sixty-Eighth Birthday [*1889*]
  Solitude is as needful to the imagi-
nation as society is wholesome for the
character.
                  Dryden
  A wise scepticism is the first attribute
of a good critic.
      Shakespeare Once More
  Truly there is a tide in the affairs of
men, but there is no gulf-stream setting forever in one direction.
    New England Two Centuries Ago
  There is no better ballast for keeping
the mind steady on its keel, and saving
it from all risk of crankiness, than business.
                    Ibid.
  Puritanism, believing itself quick
with the seed of religious liberty, laid,

[1] Motto of the American Copyright League.

without knowing it, the egg of democracy.

New England Two Centuries Ago

It was in making education not only common to all, but in some sense compulsory on all, that the destiny of the free republics of America was practically settled.

Ibid.

Talent is that which is in a man's power; genius is that in whose power a man is.

Rousseau and the Sentimentalists

Every man feels instinctively that all the beautiful sentiments in the world weigh less than a single lovely action.

Ibid.

It is singular how impatient men are with over-praise of others, how patient with over-praise of themselves; and yet the one does them no injury, while the other may be their ruin.

Literary Remains of the Reverend Homer Wilbur

Things always seem fairer when we look back at them, and it is out of that inaccessible tower of the past that Longing leans and beckons.

A Few Bits of Roman Mosaic

An umbrella is of no avail against a Scotch Mist.

On a Certain Condescension in Foreigners

The soil out of which such men as he are made is good to be born on, good to live on, good to die for and to be buried in.

Garfield

Mishaps are like knives, that either serve us or cut us, as we grasp them by the blade or the handle.

Cambridge Thirty Years Ago

No man, I suspect, ever lived long in the country without being bitten by these meteorological ambitions. He likes to be hotter and colder, to have been more deeply snowed up, to have more trees and larger blown down than his neighbors.

My Garden Acquaintance

As if old age were never kindly as well as frosty; as if it had no reverend

graces of its own as good in their way as the noisy impertinence of childhood, the elbowing self-conceit of youth, or the pompous mediocrity of middle life!

A Good Word for Winter

What a sense of security in an old book which Time has criticised for us!

A Library of Old Authors

There is no good in arguing with the inevitable. The only argument available with an east wind is to put on your overcoat.

Democracy and Addresses

It is curious how tyrannical the habit of reading is, and what shifts we make to escape thinking.[1] There is no bore we dread being left alone with so much as our own minds.

A Moosehead Journal

There are few brains that would not be better for living on their own fat a little while.

Ibid.

HERMAN MELVILLE
[1819–1891]

Sailor or landsman, there is some sort of Cape Horn for all. Boys! beware of it; prepare for it in time. Greybeards! thank God it is passed.

White-Jacket [1850]. Chap. 26

Call me Ishmael.

Moby Dick [1851]. Chap. 1

But oh! shipmates! on the starboard hand of every woe, there is a sure delight; and higher the top of that delight, than the bottom of the woe is deep. Is not the main-truck higher than the kelson is low? Delight is to him — a far, far upward, and inward delight — who against the proud gods and commodores of this earth, ever stands forth his own inexorable self.

Ibid. Chap. 9

And eternal delight and deliciousness will be his, who coming to lay him down, can say with his final breath — O Father! — chiefly known to me by Thy rod — mortal or immortal, here I

[1] See Sheridan, page 382a, and Bryce, page 698a.

die. I have striven to be Thine, more than to be this world's, or mine own. Yet this is nothing; I leave eternity to Thee; for what is man that he should live out the lifetime of his God?

Moby Dick. Chap. 9

The Nantucketer, out of sight of land, furls his sails and lays him to his rest, while under his very pillow rush herds of walruses and whales.

Ibid. Chap. 14

A whale ship was my Yale College and my Harvard.

Ibid. Chap. 24

Thou great democratic God! who didst not refuse to the swart convict, Bunyan, the pale poetic pearl; Thou who didst clothe with doubly hammered leaves of finest gold, the stumped and paupered arm of old Cervantes; Thou who didst pick up Andrew Jackson from the pebbles; who didst hurl him upon a warhorse; who didst thunder him higher than a throne!

Ibid. Chap. 26

The starred and stately nights seemed haughty dames in jewelled velvets, nursing at home in lonely pride the memory of their absent conquering Earls, the golden helmeted suns!

Ibid. Chap. 29

This it is, that for ever keeps God's true princes of the Empire from the world's hustings; and leaves the highest honors that this air can give, to those men who become famous more through their infinite inferiority to the choice hidden handful of the Divine Inert, than through their undoubted superiority over the dead level of the mass.

Ibid. Chap. 33

For as this appalling ocean surrounds the verdant land, so in the soul of man there lies one insular Tahiti, full of peace and joy, but encompassed by all the horrors of the half known life.

Ibid. Chap. 58

Give me a condor's quill! Give me Vesuvius' crater for an inkstand! . . . To produce a mighty book, you must choose a mighty theme.

Ibid. Chap. 104

And meet it is, that over these sea-pastures, wide-rolling watery prairies and Potters' Fields of all four continents, the waves should rise and fall, and ebb and flow unceasingly; for here, millions of mixed shades and shadows, drowned dreams, somnambulisms, reveries; all that we call lives and souls, lie dreaming, dreaming, still; tossing like slumberers in their beds; the ever-rolling waves but made so by their restlessness.

Moby Dick. Chap. 111

Where lies the final harbor, whence we unmoor no more?

Ibid. Chap. 114

But if the great sun move not of himself; but is as an errand-boy in heaven; nor one single star can revolve, but by some invisible power; how then can this one small heart beat; this one small brain think thoughts; unless God does that beating, does that thinking, does that living, and not I. By heaven, man, we are turned round and round in this world, like yonder windlass, and Fate is the handspike.

Ibid. Chap. 132

Thinking is, or ought to be, a coolness and a calmness; and our poor hearts throb, and our poor brains beat too much for that.

Ibid. Chap. 135

An old, old sight, and yet somehow so young; aye, and not changed a wink since I first saw it, a boy, from the sandhills of Nantucket! The same! — the same! — the same to Noah as to me. There's a soft shower to leeward. Such lovely leewardings! They must lead somewhere — to something else than common land, more palmy than the palms.

Ibid.

Now small fowls flew screaming over the yet yawning gulf; a sullen white surf beat against its steep sides; then all collapsed, and the great shroud of the sea rolled on as it rolled five thousand years ago.

Ibid.

There is no faith, and no stoicism, and no philosophy, that a mortal man can possibly evoke, which will stand the final test in a real impassioned onset of Life and Passion upon him. Faith and philosophy are air, but events are brass.

Pierre [*1852*]

All dies! and not alone
The aspiring trees and men and grass;
The poets' forms of beauty pass,
And noblest deeds they are undone,
Even truth itself decays, and lo,
From truth's sad ashes pain and false-
    hood grow.

The Lake

THOMAS WILLIAM PARSONS
[1819–1892]

Sorrow and the scarlet leaf,
    Sad thoughts and sunny weather:
Ah me, this glory and this grief
    Agree not well together!

A Song for September

JOHN RUSKIN
[1819–1900]

He is the greatest artist who has embodied, in the sum of his works, the greatest number of the greatest ideas.

Modern Painters. Vol. I [*1843*],
Part I, Chap. 2, Sect. 9

The greatest thing a human soul ever does in this world is to *see* something, and tell what it *saw* in a plain way. Hundreds of people can talk for one who can think, but thousands can think for one who can see. To see clearly is poetry, prophecy, and religion, all in one.

Ibid. Vol. III [*1856*], *Part IV,
Chap. 16, Sect. 28*

In order that people may be happy in their work, these three things are needed: They must be fit for it: They must not do too much of it: And they must have a sense of success in it.

Pre-Raphaelitism [*1851*]

Remember that the most beautiful things in the world are the most useless; peacocks and lilies for instance.

The Stones of Venice [*1851–1853*].
Vol. I, Chap. 2

It is chiefly by private, not by public, effort that your city must be adorned.

*Lectures on Architecture and
Painting* [*1853*]. *I*

Blue colour is everlastingly appointed by the Deity to be a source of delight.

Ibid.

There is no Wealth but Life.

Unto This Last [*1862*]. *Sect. 77*

That country is the richest which nourishes the greatest number of noble and happy human beings; that man is richest who, having perfected the functions of his own life to the utmost, has also the widest helpful influence, both personal, and by means of his possessions, over the lives of others.

Ibid.

Life being very short, and the quiet hours of it few, we ought to waste none of them in reading valueless books.[1]

Sesame and Lilies [*1865*]. *Preface*

The greatest efforts of the race have always been traceable to the love of praise, as its greatest catastrophes to the love of pleasure.

Ibid. Of Kings' Treasuries, Sect. 3

All books are divisible into two classes: the books of the hour, and the books of all time.

Ibid. Sect. 8

There are masked words abroad, I say, which nobody understands, but which everybody uses, and most people will also fight for, live for, or even die for, fancying they mean this, or that, or the other, of things dear to them.

Ibid. Sect. 16

The very cheapness of literature is making even wise people forget that if a book is worth reading, it is worth buying. No book is worth anything which is not worth *much;* nor is it

[1] Life is too short for reading inferior books. — JAMES BRYCE: *Address at Rutgers College* [November 10, 1911]

serviceable, until it has been read, and re-read, and loved, and loved again; and marked, so that you can refer to the passages you want in it.
Sesame and Lilies. Of Kings' Treasuries, Sect. 32

When men are rightly occupied, their amusement grows out of their work, as the colour-petals out of a fruitful flower.
Ibid. Sect. 39

He only is advancing in life, whose heart is getting softer, whose blood warmer, whose brain quicker, whose spirit is entering into living peace. And the men who have this life in them are the true lords or kings of the earth — they, and they only.
Ibid. Sect. 42

This is the true nature of home — it is the place of Peace; the shelter, not only from all injury, but from all terror, doubt, and division.
Ibid. Of Queens' Gardens, Sect. 68

Borrowers are nearly always ill-spenders, and it is with lent money that all evil is mainly done, and all unjust war protracted.
The Crown of Wild Olive [1866]. Work, Sect. 34

Give a little love to a child, and you get a great deal back.
Ibid. Sect. 49

There's no music in a "rest," Katie, that I know of: but there's the making of music in it. And people are always missing that part of the life-melody.
Ethics of the Dust [1866]. Lecture 4, The Crystal Orders

Life without industry is guilt, industry without art is brutality.
Lectures on Art [1870]. III, The Relation of Art to Morals

Engraving, then, is, in brief terms, the Art of Scratch.
Ariadne Florentina [1873–1876]. Lecture I

Trust thou thy Love: if she be proud, is she not sweet?

Trust thou thy Love: if she be mute, is she not pure?
Lay thou thy soul full in her hands, low at her feet;
Fail, Sun and Breath! — yet, for thy peace, she shall endure.
Trust Thou Thy Love

WILLIAM WETMORE STORY
[1819–1895]

Give me the old enthusiasms back,
Give me the ardent longings that I lack, —
The glorious dreams that fooled me in my youth,
The sweet mirage that lured me on its track, —
And take away the bitter, barren truth.
Ah, yes! Success, I fear, has come too late!
Girolamo, Detto Il Fiorentino

Mosquito critics with a poisonous sting.
Ibid.

Of every noble work the silent part is best,
Of all expression that which can not be expressed.
The Unexpressed

We live as much in all that we have lost
As what we own.
Sonnet, After Long Days of Dull Perpetual Rain

QUEEN VICTORIA
[1819–1901]

We are not amused.
Comment, upon seeing an imitation of herself by the Honorable Alexander Grantham Yorke, Groom-in-Waiting to the Queen

WILLIAM ROSS WALLACE
[1819–1881]

The hand that rocks the cradle is the hand that rules the world.
The Hand That Rules the World. Stanza I

WALT WHITMAN
[1819–1892]

The United States themselves are essentially the greatest poem. . . . Here at last is something in the doings of man that corresponds with the broadcast doings of the day and night.
Preface to Leaves of Grass [1855],
First Edition

The proof of a poet is that his country absorbs him as affectionately as he has absorbed it.
Ibid.

Once fully enslaved, no nation, state, city of this earth, ever afterward resumes its liberty.
Leaves of Grass [1855–1892].[1]
To the States

I hear America singing, the varied carols I hear.
Ibid. I Hear America Singing

Shut not your doors to me proud libraries.
Ibid. Shut Not Your Doors

I will write the evangel-poem of comrades and of love.
Ibid. Starting from Paumanok, 6

I say the whole earth and all the stars in the sky are for religion's sake.
Ibid. 7

None has begun to think how divine he himself is, and how certain the future is.
Ibid.

I say the real and permanent grandeur of these States must be their religion.
Ibid.

[1] The first edition of *Leaves of Grass* consisted of 94 quarto pages and included the preface which set forth Whitman's faith and his poetic theory. Enlarged and revised editions followed. The tenth edition (from which the text used here is taken) was the last edition supervised by Whitman himself, literally from his deathbed, and hence it is sometimes called the "Deathbed Edition." Whitman wrote of it, "as there are now several editions of *Leaves of Grass,* different texts and dates, I wish to say that I prefer and recommend this present one."

Nothing can happen more beautiful than death.[1]
Leaves of Grass. Starting from
Paumanok, 12

I celebrate myself and sing myself, And what I assume you shall assume.
Ibid. Song of Myself, 1

I loafe and invite my soul.
Ibid.

Creeds and schools in abeyance.
Ibid.

Urge and urge and urge, Always the procreant urge of the world.
Ibid. 3

I have no mockings or arguments; I witness and wait.
Ibid. 4

A kelson of the creation is love.
Ibid. 5

A child said *What is grass?* fetching it to one with full hands.
Ibid. 6

Or I guess it is the handkerchief of the Lord.
Ibid.

And now it seems to me the beautiful uncut hair of graves.
Ibid.

All goes onward and outward, nothing collapses, And to die is different from what any one supposed, and luckier.
Ibid.

I find no sweeter fat than sticks to my own bones.
Ibid. 20

Whether I come to my own [2] today or in ten thousand or ten million years,

[1] Why fear death? Death is only a beautiful adventure. — CHARLES FROHMAN [1860–1915]: Last words to a group of friends as the *Lusitania* was sinking [May 7, 1915]
Why should I fear Death's call? Can there e'er be
In life more beautiful adventure than
To re-embark upon that unknown sea?
JAMES TERRY WHITE [1845–1920]:
Why Fear? St. 1

[2] Nor time, nor space, nor deep, nor high, Can keep my own away from me.
JOHN BURROUGHS [1837–1931]:
Waiting, St. 6

I can cheerfully take it now, or with
equal cheerfulness I can wait.
*Leaves of Grass. Song of
Myself, 20*

I am he that walks with the tender and
growing night,
I call to the earth and sea half-held by
the night.
Press close bare-bosom'd night — press
close magnetic nourishing night!
Night of south winds — night of the
large few stars!
Still nodding night — mad naked summer night.
Ibid. 21

I dote on myself, there is that lot of
me and all so luscious.
Ibid. 24

I hear the violoncello, ('tis the young
man's heart's complaint).
Ibid. 26

I believe a leaf of grass is no less than
the journey-work of the stars.
Ibid. 31

And the tree-toad is a chef-d'oeuvre
for the highest. . . .
And a mouse is miracle enough to stagger sextillions of infidels.
Ibid.

I think I could turn and live with
animals, they are so placid and
self-contain'd,
I stand and look at them long and long.
They do not sweat and whine about
their condition,
They do not lie awake in the dark and
weep for their sins,
They do not make me sick discussing
their duty to God,
Not one is dissatisfied, not one is de-
mented with the mania of owning
things,
Not one kneels to another, nor to his
kind that lived thousands of years
ago,
Not one is respectable or unhappy over
the whole earth.
Ibid. 32

Behold, I do not give lectures or a little
charity,

When I give I give myself.[1]
*Leaves of Grass. Song of
Myself, 40*

And when you rise in the morning you
will find what I tell you is so.
Ibid.

I have said that the soul is not more
than the body,
And I have said that the body is not
more than the soul,
And nothing, not God, is greater to one
than one's self is.
Ibid. 48

In the faces of men and women I see
God.
Ibid.

Do I contradict myself?
Very well then I contradict myself,
(I am large, I contain multitudes.)
Ibid. 51

I sound my barbaric yawp over the
roofs of the world.
Ibid. 52

If any thing is sacred the human body
is sacred.
*Ibid. Children of Adam, I Sing
the Body Electric, 8*

I hear it was charged against me that
I sought to destroy institutions,
But really I am neither for nor against
institutions.
*Ibid. I Hear It Was Charged
Against Me*

When I peruse the conquer'd fame of
heroes and the victories of mighty
generals, I do not envy the generals.
*Ibid. When I Peruse the
Conquer'd Fame*

Afoot and light-hearted I take to
the open road,
Healthy, free, the world before me,
The long brown path before me lead-
ing wherever I choose.
Ibid. Song of the Open Road, 1

Henceforth I ask not good-fortune, I
myself am good-fortune,
Henceforth I whimper no more, post-
pone no more, need nothing,
Done with indoor complaints, libraries,
querulous criticisms,

[1] See Emerson, page 502b.

Strong and content I travel the open road.

Leaves of Grass. Song of the Open Road, 1

The earth, that is sufficient,
I do not want the constellations any nearer,
I know they are very well where they are,
I know they suffice for those who belong to them.

Ibid.

A great city is that which has the greatest men and women.

Ibid. Song of the Broad-Axe, 4

In this broad earth of ours,
Amid the measureless grossness and the slag,
Enclosed and safe within its central heart,
Nestles the seed perfection.

Ibid. Song of the Universal, 1

Through the battle, through defeat, moving yet and never stopping,
Pioneers! O pioneers!

Ibid. Pioneers! O Pioneers! 13

Youth, large, lusty, loving — Youth, full of grace, force, fascination,
Do you know that Old Age may come after you, with equal grace, force, fascination?

Ibid. Youth, Day, Old Age and Night, 1

Out of the cradle endlessly rocking,
Out of the mocking-bird's throat, the musical shuttle.

Ibid. Out of the Cradle Endlessly Rocking

Soothe! soothe! soothe!
Close on its wave soothes the wave behind,
And again another behind embracing and lapping every one close,
But my love soothes not me, not me.

Ibid.

O darkness! O in vain!
O I am very sick and sorrowful.

Ibid.

Whereto answering, the sea,
Delaying not, hurrying not,
Whisper'd me through the night, and very plainly before daybreak,

Lisp'd to me the low and delicious word death.

Leaves of Grass. Out of the Cradle Endlessly Rocking

Roaming in thought over the Universe,
I saw the little that is Good steadily hastening towards immortality,
And the vast that is Evil I saw hastening to merge itself and become lost and dead.[1]

Ibid. Roaming in Thought After Reading Hegel

Over all the sky — the sky! far, far out of reach, studded, breaking out, the eternal stars.

Ibid. Bivouac on a Mountain Side

Give me the splendid silent sun, with all his beams full-dazzling!

Ibid. Give Me the Splendid Silent Sun, 1

Beautiful that war and all its deeds of carnage must in time be utterly lost,
That the hands of the sisters Death and Night incessantly softly wash again and ever again, this soiled world;
For my enemy is dead, a man divine as myself is dead.

Ibid. Reconciliation

When lilacs last in the door-yard bloom'd,
And the great star early droop'd in the western sky in the night,
I mourn'd, and yet shall mourn with ever-returning spring.

Ibid. When Lilacs Last in the Door-yard Bloom'd, 1

O sane and sacred death.

Ibid. 7

Come lovely and soothing death,[2]
Undulate round the world, serenely arriving, arriving,
In the day, in the night, to all, to each,
Sooner or later, delicate death.

Ibid. 14

Prais'd be the fathomless universe,

[1] Evil perpetually tends to disappear. — HERBERT SPENCER [1820–1903]: *The Evanescence of Evil*
[2] See Shakespeare, page 148a.

For life and joy, and for objects and
   knowledge curious,
And for love, sweet love — But praise!
   praise! praise!
For the sure-enwinding arms of cool-
   enfolding Death.
   Leaves of Grass. When Lilacs Last
   in the Door-yard Bloom'd, 14
O Captain! my Captain! our fearful
   trip is done!
The ship has weather'd every rack,
   the prize we sought is won,
The port is near, the bells I hear, the
   people all exulting.
   Ibid. O Captain! My Captain! 1
The ship is anchor'd safe and sound, its
   voyage closed and done,
From fearful trip the victor ship comes
   in with object won.
   Ibid. 3
Exult O shores, and ring O bells!
But I with mournful tread,
Walk the deck my Captain lies,
Fallen cold and dead.
   Ibid.
This dust was once the man,
Gentle, plain, just and resolute, under
   whose cautious hand,
Against the foulest crime in history
   known in any land or age,
Was saved the Union of these States.
   Ibid. This Dust Was Once the Man
The whole theory of the universe is
   directed unerringly to one single
   individual — namely to You.
   Ibid. By Blue Ontario's Shore, 15
Not till the sun excludes you do I ex-
   clude you.
   Ibid. To a Common Prostitute
Liberty is to be subserved whatever
   occurs.
   Ibid. To a Foil'd European
   Revolutionaire, 1
O we can wait no longer,
We too take ship O soul,
Joyous we too launch out on trackless
   seas,
Fearless for unknown shores.
   Ibid. Passage to India, 8
What do you suppose will satisfy the

soul, except to walk free and own
   no superior?
   Leaves of Grass. Laws for
   Creations, 3
To me every hour of the light and dark
   is a miracle,
Every cubic inch of space is a miracle.
   Ibid. Miracles, 2
Sail, sail thy best, ship of Democracy.
Of value is thy freight, 'tis not the
   Present only,
The Past is also stored in thee.
   Ibid. Thou Mother with Thy
   Equal Brood, 4
Society waits unform'd, and is for a
   while between things ended and
   things begun.
   Ibid. Thoughts, 1
Our life is closed, our life begins,
The long, long anchorage we leave,
The ship is clear at last, she leaps!
She swiftly courses from the shore,
Joy, shipmate, joy.
   Ibid. Joy, Shipmate, Joy!
Camerado, this is no book,
Who touches this touches a man.
   Ibid. So Long!
The world, the race, the soul — in
   space and time the universes,
All bound as is befitting each — all
   surely going somewhere.
   Ibid. Going Somewhere
I am the Poem of Earth, said the voice
   of the rain,
Eternal I rise impalpable out of the
   land and the bottomless sea.
   Ibid. The Voice of the Rain
Soon to be lost for aye in the darkness
   — loth, O so loth to depart!
Garrulous to the very last.
   Ibid. After the Supper and Talk
None of the artists or pictures has
   caught the deep, though subtle and in-
   direct expression of this man's face.
There is something else there. One of
   the great portrait painters of two or
   three centuries ago is needed.
   Specimen Days. Of Lincoln,
   August 12, 1863
I never see that man [Lincoln] with-
   out feeling that he is one to become personally attach'd to, for his combination

of purest, heartiest tenderness, and native western form of manliness.
Specimen Days. The Inauguration, March 4, 1865

He leaves for America's history and biography, so far, not only its most dramatic reminiscence — he leaves, in my opinion, the greatest, best, most characteristic, artistic, moral personality.
Ibid. Death of President Lincoln, April 16, 1865

The real war will never get in the books.
Ibid. The Real War, etc.

Tone your wants and tastes down low enough, and make much of negatives, and of mere daylight and the skies.
Ibid. An Interregnum Paragraph

After you have exhausted what there is in business, politics, conviviality, and so on — have found that none of these finally satisfy, or permanently wear — what remains? Nature remains.
Ibid. New Themes Entered Upon

In the civilization of to-day it is undeniable that, over all the arts, literature dominates, serves beyond all.
Democratic Vistas [1871]

The main social, political spine-character of the States will probably run along the Ohio, Missouri and Mississippi rivers, and west and north of them, including Canada.
Ibid.

Political democracy, as it exists and practically works in America, with all its threatening evils, supplies a training-school for making first-class men. It is life's gymnasium, not of good only, but of all.
Ibid.

It is native personality, and that alone, that endows a man to stand before presidents or generals, or in any distinguish'd collection, with *aplomb* — and *not* culture, or any knowledge or intellect whatever.
Ibid.

To have great poets, there must be great audiences, too.
Notes Left Over. Ventures, on an Old Theme

Hast Thou, pellucid, in Thy azure depths, medicine for case like mine?
Specimen Days. The Sky, October 20, 1876

One is never entirely without the instinct of looking around.
Ibid. One of the Human Kinks

You must not know too much, or be too precise or scientific about birds and trees and flowers and water-craft; a certain free margin, and even vagueness — perhaps ignorance, credulity — helps your enjoyment of these things.
Ibid. Birds, May 14, 1881

No really great song can ever attain full purport till long after the death of its singer — till it has accrued and incorporated the many passions, many joys and sorrows, it has itself aroused.
November Boughs [1888]. The Bible as Poetry

No one will ever get at my verses who insists upon viewing them as a literary performance.
Goodbye, My Fancy [1891]. A Backward Glance O'er Travel'd Roads

There is no week nor day nor hour, when tyranny may not enter upon this country, if the people lose their roughness and spirit of defiance — Tyranny may always enter — there is no charm, no bar against it — the only bar against it is a large resolute breed of men.
Notes for Lecturers on Democracy and "Adhesiveness." C. J. FURNESS: *Walt Whitman's Workshop [1928]*

URANIA LOCKE STOUGHTON BAILEY ("JULIA GILL") [1820–1882]

I want to be an angel,
    And with the angels stand,
A crown upon my forehead,
    A harp within my hand.
I Want to Be an Angel. Stanza 1

WILLIAM COX BENNETT
[1820–1895]

"God wills but ill," the doubter said,
  "Lo, time doth evil only bear;
Give me a sign His love to prove,
  His vaunted goodness to declare!"
The poet pointed where a flower,
  A simple daisy, starred the sod,
And answered, "Proof of love and
    power
Behold, behold a smile of God!"
            A Thought

Oh! come you from the Indies, and,
  soldier, can you tell
Aught of the gallant Ninetieth, and
  who are safe and well?
O soldier, say my son is safe — for
  nothing else I care,
And you shall have a mother's thanks
  — shall have a widow's prayer.
         From India. Stanza 1

HENRY HOWARD BROWNELL
[1820–1872]

As vonce I valked by a dismal svamp,
There sot an Old Cove in the dark and
  damp,
And at everybody as passed that road
A stick or a stone this Old Cove
  throwed.
And venever he flung his stick or his
  stone,
He'd set up a song of "Let me alone."[1]
         Let Us Alone

ALICE CARY
[1820–1871]

Work, and your house shall be duly fed:
Work, and rest shall be won;
I hold that a man had better be dead
Than alive when his work is done.
            Work

Kiss me, though you make believe;
Kiss me, though I almost know
You are kissing to deceive.
         Make Believe

[1] All we ask is to be let alone. — JEFFERSON DAVIS: *First Message to the Confederate Congress* [March, 1861]

Three little bugs in a basket,
And hardly room for two.
         Three Bugs

JEAN INGELOW
[1820–1897]

But two are walking apart forever,
And wave their hands for a mute
  farewell.
         Divided. VI, 5

A sweeter woman ne'er drew breath
Than my sonne's wife, Elizabeth.
  *High Tide on the Coast of
    Lincolnshire, 1571. Stanza 11*

Man dwells apart, though not alone,
  He walks among his peers unread;
The best of thoughts which he hath
    known
For lack of listeners are not said.
    Afterthought. Stanza 1

It is a comely fashion to be glad, —
Joy is the grace we say to God.
         Dominion

Like coral insects multitudinous
The minutes are whereof our life is
  made.
            Work

  Blondel, when his lay
Pierced the strong tower, and Richard
  answered it.[1]
         Wishing

I marked my love by candle-light
Sewing her long white seam.
  The Long White Seam. Stanza 1

A land where all the men are stones,
Or all the stones are men.
      *A Land That Living
        Warmth Disowns*

THEODORE O'HARA
[1820–1867]

On Fame's eternal camping-ground
  Their silent tents are spread,

[1] There is a tradition that Blondel, a French troubadour, attendant and friend of Richard Coeur de Lion, discovered Richard, imprisoned in the castle of Dürrenstein, by singing beneath the tower window a song which they had composed and to which the king responded.

And Glory guards, with solemn round,
The bivouac of the dead.
The Bivouac of the Dead.[1]
Stanza 1
Sons of the Dark and Bloody ground,[2]
Ye must not slumber there,
Where stranger steps and tongues resound
Along the heedless air.
Ibid. Stanza 9

GEORGE FREDERICK ROOT
[1820–1895]

Tramp! Tramp! Tramp! the boys are marching,
Cheer up, comrades, they will come,
And beneath the starry flag
We shall breathe the air again
Of the free land in our own beloved home.
Tramp! Tramp! Tramp! [1862]
Yes, we'll rally round the flag, boys,
we'll rally once again,
Shouting the battle-cry of Freedom,
We will rally from the hill-side, we'll
gather from the plain,
Shouting the battle-cry of Freedom.
The Battle-Cry of Freedom [1863]

SIR WILLIAM HOWARD RUSSELL
[1820–1907]

The Russians dashed on towards that thin red-line streak tipped with a line of steel.[3]
Correspondence to the London Times from the Crimea, describing the British infantry at Balaklava [*October 25, 1854*]

[1] Written in August, 1847, to commemorate the Americans slain in the battle of Buena Vista, February 22–23, 1847.
[2] Translation of the Indian name Kentucky.
[3] Soon the men of the column began to see that though the scarlet line was slender, it was very rigid and exact. — A. W. KINGLAKE [1809–1891]: *Invasion of the Crimea, Vol. III, P. 455*
It's "Thin red line of 'eroes" when the drums begin to roll. — KIPLING [1865–1936]: *Tommy, St. 3*

WILLIAM TECUMSEH SHERMAN
[1820–1891]

War is cruel and you cannot refine it.
Reply to the protest of the Atlanta, Georgia, city government on invasion [*1864*]
Hold the fort! I am coming!
Signaled to General Corse in Allatoona from the top of Kenesaw [*October 5, 1864*]
I am tired and sick of war. Its glory is all moonshine. It is only those who have neither fired a shot nor heard the shrieks and groans of the wounded who cry aloud for blood, more vengeance, more desolation. War is hell.
Attributed to an address before the graduating class, Michigan Military Academy [*June 19, 1879*], *in a letter published in The National Tribune, Washington, D. C., November 26, 1914*

JOHN TYNDALL
[1820–1893]

Heat Considered as a Mode of Motion.
Title of Treatise [*1863*]
It is not my habit of mind to think otherwise than solemnly of the feeling which prompts prayer. It is a power which I should like to see guided, not extinguished — devoted to practicable objects instead of wasted upon air.
Fragments of Science. Vol. II, Prayer as a Form of Physical Energy
Life is a wave, which in no two consecutive moments of its existence is composed of the same particles.
Ibid. Vitality
We are truly heirs of all the ages; but as honest men it behooves us to learn the extent of our inheritance, and as brave ones not to whimper if it should prove less than we had supposed.
Ibid. Matter and Force
The mind of man may be compared to a musical instrument with a certain

range of notes, beyond which in both directions we have an infinitude of silence.

> *Fragments of Science. Vol. II,*
> *Matter and Force*

The brightest flashes in the world of thought are incomplete until they have been proved to have their counterparts in the world of fact.

> *Ibid. Scientific Materialism*

Believing, as I do, in the continuity of nature, I cannot stop abruptly where our microscopes cease to be of use. Here the vision of the mind authoritatively supplements the vision of the eye. By a necessity engendered and justified by science I cross the boundary of the experimental evidence, and discern in that Matter which we, in our ignorance of its latent powers, and notwithstanding our professed reverence for its Creator, have hitherto covered with opprobrium, the promise and potency of all terrestrial Life.

> *Ibid. Address at Belfast*
> *[August 19, 1874]*

It is as fatal as it is cowardly to blink facts because they are not to our taste.

> *Ibid. Science and Man*

Charles Darwin, the Abraham of scientific men — a searcher as obedient to the command of truth as was the patriarch to the command of God.

> *Ibid.*

Superstition may be defined as constructive religion which has grown incongruous with intelligence.

> *Ibid.*

Religious feeling is as much a verity as any other part of human consciousness; and against it, on the subjective side, the waves of science beat in vain.

> *Ibid. Professor Virchow and*
> *Evolution*

HERBERT SPENCER
[1820–1903]

Progress, therefore, is not an accident, but a necessity. . . . It is a part of nature.

> *Social Statics [1851]. Part I,*
> *Chap. 2*

Education has for its object the formation of character.

> *Social Statics. Part II, Chap. 17*

Opinion is ultimately determined by the feelings, and not by the intellect.

> *Ibid. Part IV, Chap. 30*

Morality knows nothing of geographical boundaries or distinctions of race.

> *Ibid.*

No one can be perfectly free till all are free; no one can be perfectly moral till all are moral; no one can be perfectly happy till all are happy.

> *Ibid.*

Architecture, sculpture, painting, music, and poetry, may truly be called the efflorescence of civilized life.

> *Essays on Education [1861].*
> *Education: What Knowledge Is*
> *of Most Worth?*

Every cause produces more than one effect.

> *Ibid. On Progress: Its Law*
> *and Cause*

The tyranny of Mrs. Grundy [1] is worse than any other tyranny we suffer under.

> *Ibid. On Manners and Fashion*

Old forms of government finally grow so oppressive that they must be thrown off even at the risk of reigns of terror.

> *Ibid.*

Music must take rank as the highest of the fine arts — as the one which, more than any other, ministers to human welfare.

> *Ibid. On the Origin and Function*
> *of Music*

We too often forget that not only is there "a soul of goodness in things evil," [2] but very generally a soul of truth in things erroneous.

> *First Principles [1861]*

The fact disclosed by a survey of the past that majorities have been wrong must not blind us to the complemen-

---

[1] See Thomas Morton, page 397a.
[2] There is some soul of goodness in things evil
Would men observingly distill it out.
SHAKESPEARE: *King Henry V* [1598–1600], *Act IV, Sc. 1, L. 4*

tary fact that majorities have usually not been entirely wrong.
First Principles

Volumes might be written upon the impiety of the pious.
Ibid.

We have unmistakable proof that throughout all past time, there has been a ceaseless devouring of the weak by the strong.
Ibid.

This survival of the fittest.
Principles of Biology [*1864–1867*].
Part III, Chap. 12

The Republican form of government is the highest form of government: but because of this it requires the highest type of human nature — a type nowhere at present existing.
Essays [*1891*]. *The Americans*

The ultimate result of shielding men from the effects of folly is to fill the world with fools.
Ibid State Tamperings with Money Banks

GUSTAVE NADAUD
[1820–1893]

I'm growing old, I've sixty years;
  I've labored all my life in vain.
In all that time of hopes and fears,
  I've failed my dearest wish to gain.
I see full well that here below
  Bliss unalloyed there is for none,
My prayer would else fulfillment
  know —
Never have I seen Carcassonne! [1]
Carcassonne.[2] *Stanza 1*

They tell me every day is there
  Not more nor less than Sunday gay;
In shining robes and garments fair
  The people walk upon their way.
Ibid. Stanza 3

[1] I can scarce believe the tale
  Borne to me on every gale!
  You have been to Carcassonne?
  Looked its stately towers upon?
  JULIA CAROLINE RIPLEY DORR [1825–1913]: *To One Who Went to Carcassonne, St. 1*
[2] Translated by JOHN R. THOMPSON [1823–1873].

SIR RICHARD FRANCIS BURTON
[1821–1890]

Why meet we on the bridge of Time to
  'change one greeting and to part?
The Kasidah of Haji Abdu El-Yazdi. I, 11

Why must we meet, why must we part,
  why must we bear this yoke of MUST,
Without our leave or asked or given,
  by tyrant Fate on victim thrust?
Ibid. 13

Hardly we learn to wield the blade before the wrist grows stiff and old;
Hardly we learn to ply the pen ere Thought and Fancy faint with cold.
Ibid. III, 32

Life, atom of that Infinite Space that stretcheth, 'twixt the Here and There.
Ibid. 36

Indeed he knows not how to know who knows not also how to un-know.
Ibid. VI, 18

Mankind a future life must have to balance life's unequal lot.
Ibid. VIII, 9

Do what thy manhood bids thee do, from none but self expect applause;
He noblest lives and noblest dies who makes and keeps his self-made laws.
Ibid. 37

JOSEPH WARREN FABENS
[1821–1875]

I've seen the land of all I love
  Fade in the distance dim;
I've watched above the blighted heart,
  Where once proud hope had been;
But I've never known a sorrow
  That could with that compare,
When off the blue Canaries
  I smoked my last cigar.
My Last Cigar. Stanza 4

FREDERICK LOCKER-LAMPSON
[1821–1895]

"Vanitas vanitatum" has rung in the ears
Of gentle and simple for thousands of years;
The wail still is heard, yet its notes never scare
Either simple or gentle from Vanity Fair.
Vanity Fair

What an arm — what a waist
For an arm!
To My Grandmother

The world's as ugly, ay, as Sin, —
And almost as delightful.
The Jester's Plea

And many are afraid of God —
And more of Mrs. Grundy.[1]
Ibid.

WILLIAM H. VANDERBILT
[1821–1885]

The public be damned.[2]
Reply to a newspaper reporter
[circa 1883]

GEORGE JOHN WHYTE-MELVILLE
[1821–1878]

When you sleep in your cloak there's no lodging to pay.
Boots and Saddles

For everything created
In the bounds of earth and sky
Has such longing to be mated,
It must couple or must die.
Like to Like

In the choice of a horse and a wife, a man must please himself, ignoring the opinion and advice of friends.
Riding Recollections [1878]

Education should be as gradual as the moonrise, perceptible not in progress but in result.
Ibid.

[1] See Thomas Morton, page 397a.
[2] There are various versions of the occasion of this remark. See letters in *New York Times,* August 25, 1918, and *New York Herald,* October 1, 1918.

Pluck takes us into a difficulty, nerve brings us out of it. Both are comprised in the noble quality we call valor.
Riding Recollections

MARY BAKER EDDY
[1821–1910]

The prayer that reforms the sinner and heals the sick is an absolute faith that all things are possible to God, — a spiritual understanding of Him, an unselfed love.
Science and Health with Key to the Scriptures [1875]. *Page 1*

In the year 1866, I discovered the Christ Science or divine laws of Life, Truth, and Love, and named my discovery Christian Science.[1]
Ibid. Page 107

Jesus of Nazareth was the most scientific man that ever trod the globe. He plunged beneath the material surface of things, and found the spiritual cause.
Ibid. Page 313

The basis of all health, sinlessness, and immortality is the great fact that God is the only Mind; and this Mind must be not merely believed, but it must be understood.
Ibid. Page 339

Spirit is the real and eternal; matter is the unreal and temporal.
Ibid. Page 468

Sickness, sin and death, being inharmonious, do not originate with God, nor belong to His government.
Ibid. Page 472

Being is holiness, harmony, immortality. It is already proved that a knowledge of this, even in small degree, will uplift the physical and moral standard of mortals, will increase longevity, will purify and elevate character. Thus

[1] The words "Christian Science" were not original with Mary Baker Eddy, but she was the first to give them wide circulation. In 1840, Abraham Coles used the words in verse, as also did Sara Josepha Hale, in 1848. In 1850, William Adams published a series of addresses on Moral Philosophy and called his work *Christian Science.* — NORMAN BEASLEY: *The Cross and the Crown* [1952], *P. 13n*

progress will finally destroy all error, and bring immortality to light.
Science and Health with Key to the Scriptures. Page 492
Divine Love always has met and always will meet every human need.
Ibid. Page 494
How would you define Christian Science?

As the law of God, the law of good, interpreting and demonstrating the divine Principle and rule of universal harmony.
Rudimental Divine Science [1891]. Page 1
To live and let live, without clamor for distinction or recognition; to wait on divine Love; to write truth first on the tablet of one's own heart, — this is the sanity and perfection of living, and my human ideal.
Message to the Mother Church for 1902. Page 2
To live so as to keep human consciousness in constant relation with the divine, the spiritual, and the eternal, is to individualize infinite power; and this is Christian Science.
The First Church of Christ, Scientist, and Miscellany [1906]. Page 160
It matters not what be thy lot,
So Love doth guide;
For storm or shine, pure peace is thine,
Whate'er betide.
Satisfied. Stanza 1
Blest Christmas morn, though murky clouds
Pursue thy way,
Thy light was born where storm enshrouds
Nor dawn nor day!
Christmas Morn. Stanza 1
O'er waiting harp-strings of the mind
There sweeps a strain,
Low, sad, and sweet, whose measures bind
The pow'r of pain.
O'er Waiting Harp-strings of the Mind. Stanza 1
My prayer, some daily good to do
To Thine, for Thee —

An off'ring pure of Love, whereto
God leadeth me.
O'er Waiting Harp-strings of the Mind. Stanza 7

HENRI-FRÉDÉRIC AMIEL
[1821–1881]

Truth is the secret of eloquence and of virtue, the basis of moral authority; it is the highest summit of art and of life.
Journal [1883]
Doing easily what others find difficult is talent; doing what is impossible for talent is genius.
Ibid.

A man without passion is only a latent force, only a possibility, like a stone waiting for the blow from the iron to give forth sparks.
Ibid.

If ignorance and passion are the foes of popular morality, it must be confessed that moral indifference is the malady of the cultivated classes.
Ibid.

Pure truth cannot be assimilated by the crowd; it must be communicated by contagion.
Ibid.

FYODOR DOSTOYEVSKY
[1821–1881]

Man is a pliable animal, a being who gets accustomed to everything!
The House of the Dead (Prison Life in Siberia) [1] *[1861–1862]. Part I, Chap. 2*
With ready-made opinions one cannot judge of crime. Its philosophy is a little more complicated than people think. It is acknowledged that neither convict prisons, nor the hulks, nor any system of hard labour ever cured a criminal.
Ibid.
Humane treatment may raise up one in whom the divine image has long been

[1] Everyman edition.

obscured. It is with the unfortunate, above all, that humane conduct is necessary.

> *The House of the Dead (Prison Life in Siberia). Part I, Chap. 9*

Tyranny is a habit capable of being developed, and at last becomes a disease. . . . . The man and the citizen disappear for ever in the tyrant.

> *Ibid. Part II, Chap. 3*

Even those who have renounced Christianity and attack it, in their inmost being still follow the Christian ideal, for hitherto neither their subtlety nor the ardour of their hearts has been able to create a higher ideal of man and of virtue than the ideal given by Christ of old. When it has been attempted, the result has been only grotesque.

> *The Brothers Karamazov* [1] [*1880*]. *Part II, Book IV, Chap. 1*

Until you have become really, in actual fact, a brother to every one, brotherhood will not come to pass. No sort of scientific teaching, no kind of common interest, will ever teach men to share property and privileges with equal consideration for all. Every one will think his share too small and they will be always envying, complaining and attacking one another.

> *Ibid. Book VI, Chap. 2*

The true security is to be found in social solidarity rather than in isolated individual effort.

> *Ibid.*

Be not forgetful of prayer. Every time you pray, if your prayer is sincere, there will be new feeling and new meaning in it, which will give you fresh courage, and you will understand that prayer is an education.

> *Ibid. Chap. 3*

Love all God's creation, the whole and every grain of sand in it. Love every leaf, every ray of God's light. Love the animals, love the plants, love

everything. If you love everything, you will perceive the divine mystery in things. Once you perceive it, you will begin to comprehend it better every day. And you will come at last to love the whole world with an all-embracing love.

> *The Brothers Karamazov. Part II, Book VI, Chap. 3*

Men reject their prophets and slay them, but they love their martyrs and honour those whom they have slain.

> *Ibid.*

CHARLES BAUDELAIRE
[1821–1867]

The poet is like the prince of the clouds who haunts the tempest and laughs at the man with the bow; exiled on the ground amid the hue and cry, his giant's wings prevent him from walking.[1]

> *Fleurs du Mal* [*1861*]. *L'Albatros, Stanza 4*

Mother of memories, mistress of mistresses.[2]

> *Ibid. Le Balcon, Stanza 1*

My child, my sister, think of the sweetness of going away there to live together![3]

> *Ibid. L'Invitation au Voyage, Stanza 1*

There, all is order and beauty, luxury, calm, and voluptuousness.[4]

> *Ibid. Refrain*

I have more memories than if I were a thousand years old.[5]

> *Ibid. Spleen, Line 1*

---

[1] Le Poète est semblable au prince des nuées
Qui hante la tempête et se rit de l'archer;
Exilé sur le sol au milieu des huées,
Ses ailes de géant l'empêchent de marcher.
[2] Mère des souvenirs, maîtresse des maîtresses.
[3]   Mon enfant, ma soeur,
    Songe à la douceur
D'aller là-bas vivre ensemble!
[4] Là, tout n'est qu'ordre et beauté,
Luxe, calme et volupté.
[5] J'ai plus de souvenirs que si j'avais mille ans.

---

[1] Translated by CONSTANCE GARNETT. Modern Library edition.

To the best, to the most beautiful
who is my joy and my well-being.[1]

> *Les Epaves* [*1866*]. *Hymne,*
> *Stanza 5*

What do I care that you are good?
Be beautiful! and be sad! [2]

> *Nouvelles Fleurs du Mal* [*1866–*
> *1868*]. *Madrigal Triste, Stanza 1*

There can be no progress (real, that
is, moral) except in the individual and
by the individual himself.

> *Mon Coeur Mis à Nu* [*1887*]. *XV*

There are in every man, at every
hour, two simultaneous postulations,
one towards God, the other towards
Satan.

> *Ibid. XIX*

There exist only three beings worthy
of respect: the priest, the soldier, the
poet. To know, to kill, to create.

> *Ibid. XXII*

To be a great man and a saint for
oneself, that is the one important thing.

> *Ibid. LII*

MATTHEW ARNOLD
[1822–1888]

One lesson, Nature, let me learn of thee.

> *Sonnet 1, Quiet Work* [*1849*]

Be his
My special thanks, whose even-
balanced soul,
From first youth tested up to extreme
old age,
Business could not make dull, nor pas-
sion wild:
Who saw life steadily and saw it whole.[3]

> *Sonnet 2, To a Friend* [*1849*]

Others abide our question. Thou art
free.
We ask and ask: Thou smilest and art
still,
Out-topping knowledge.

> *Sonnet 3, Shakespeare* [*1849*]

The will is free:
Strong is the Soul, and wise, and beautiful:

---

[1] A la très-bonne, à la très-belle
   Qui fait ma joie et ma santé.
[2] Que m'importe que tu sois sage?
   Sois belle! et sois triste!
[3] Sophocles.

The seeds of godlike power are in us
still:
Gods are we, Bards, Saints, Heroes, if
we will.

> *Sonnet 4, Written in Emerson's*
> *Essays* [*1849*]

France, famed in all great arts, in none
supreme.

> *Sonnet 10, To a Republican*
> *Friend, 1848* [*1849*]

To its own impulse every creature stirs:
Live by thy light, and Earth will live by
hers.

> *Sonnet 11, Religious Isolation*
> [*1849*]

Come, dear children, let us away;
Down and away below.
Now my brothers call from the bay;
Now the great winds shorewards blow;
Now the salt tides seawards flow;
Now the wild white horses play,
Champ and chafe and toss in the spray.

> *The Forsaken Merman*
> [*1849*], *Stanza 1*

One last look at the white-wall'd town,
And the little grey church on the windy
shore.

> *Ibid. Stanza 3*

Sand-strewn caverns, cool and deep,
Where the winds are all asleep;
Where the spent lights quiver and
gleam;
Where the salt weed sways in the
stream;
Where the sea-beasts rang'd all round
Feed in the ooze of their pasture-
ground.

> *Ibid. Stanza 4*

Children dear, were we long alone?
The sea grows stormy, the little ones
moan.

> *Ibid. Stanza 6*

She will start from her slumber
When gusts shake the door;
She will hear the winds howling,
Will hear the waves roar.

> *Ibid. Stanza 8*

Here came a mortal,
But faithless was she.
And alone dwell for ever
The kings of the sea.

> *Ibid.*

From grief that is but passion;
From mirth that is but feigning;
From tears that bring no healing;
From wild and weak complaining;
  Thine old strength revealing;
    Save, oh, save.
                Stagirius [1849]
Fate gave, what Chance shall not control,
His sad lucidity of soul.
            Resignation [1849]
Yet they, believe me, who await
No gifts from Chance, have conquered
  Fate.
                        Ibid.
Resolve to be thyself: and know, that
  he
Who finds himself, loses his misery.
        *Self-Dependence [1852].
                    Stanza 8*
We cannot kindle when we will
The fire that in the heart resides.
    Morality [1852]. Stanza 1
But tasks in hours of insight will'd
Can be through hours of gloom fulfill'd.
                        Ibid.
With aching hands and bleeding feet
  We dig and heap, lay stone on stone;
We bear the burden and the heat
  Of the long day, and wish 'twere
    done.
Not till the hours of light return
All we have built do we discern.
                Ibid. Stanza 2
Calm Soul of all things! make it mine
  To feel, amid the city's jar,
That there abides a peace of thine,
  Man did not make, and can not mar.
    *Lines Written in Kensington
    Gardens [1852]. Stanza 10*
Physician of the Iron Age,
Goethe has done his pilgrimage.
He took the suffering human race,
He read each wound, each weakness
  clear —
And struck his finger on the place
And said — Thou ailest here, and here.
        *Memorial Verses [1852].
                    Stanza 3*
Time may restore us in his course
Goethe's sage mind and Byron's force;

But where will Europe's latter hour
Again find Wordsworth's healing
  power?
        Memorial Verses. Stanza 5
Children of men! not that your age
  excel
  In pride of life the ages of your sires;
But that ye think clear, feel deep, bear
  fruit well,
  The Friend of man desires.
                Progress [1852]
Still bent to make some port he knows
  not where,
Still standing for some false impossible
  shore.
        A Summer Night [1852]
Be neither saint nor sophist-led, but be
  a man.
        *Empedocles on Etna [1852].
            Act I, Sc. 2, Line 136*
We do not what we ought;
  What we ought not, we do;
And lean upon the thought
  That Chance will bring us through.
                Ibid. Line 237
Nature, with equal mind,
Sees all her sons at play,
Sees man control the wind,
The wind sweep man away.
                Ibid. Line 257
Is it so small a thing
To have enjoyed the sun,
To have lived light in the spring,
To have loved, to have thought, to have
  done;
To have advanced true friends, and
  beat down baffling foes?
            Ibid. Act II, Line 397
The day in its hotness,
The strife with the palm;
The night in its silence,
The stars in their calm.
                Ibid. Line 465
The same heart beats in every human
  breast.
        The Buried Life [1852]. Stanza 2
But often in the world's most crowded
  streets,
But often, in the din of strife,
There rises an unspeakable desire
After the knowledge of our buried life.
                Ibid. Stanza 6

A man becomes aware of his life's flow.
The Buried Life. Stanza 7

And then he thinks he knows
The Hills where his life rose,
And the Sea where it goes.
Ibid. Stanza 8

Go, for they call you, Shepherd, from the hill.
The Scholar Gypsy [1853].
Stanza 1

Crossing the stripling Thames at Bab-lock-hithe,
Trailing in the cool stream thy fingers wet,
As the slow punt swings round.
Ibid. Stanza 8

Thou waitest for the spark from heaven! and we,
Light half-believers in our casual creeds . . .
Who hesitate and falter life away,
And lose tomorrow the ground won today.
Ibid. Stanza 18

This strange disease of modern life.
Ibid. Stanza 21

Still nursing the unconquerable hope,
Still clutching the inviolable shade.
Ibid. Stanza 22

Strew on her roses, roses,
And never a spray of yew!
In quiet she reposes;
Ah, would that I did too!
Requiescat [1853]. Stanza 1

Her cabin'd, ample spirit,
It flutter'd and fail'd for breath.
Tonight it doth inherit
The vasty hall of death.
Ibid. Stanza 4

Hark! ah, the nightingale —
The tawny-throated!
Hark, from that moonlit cedar what a burst!
What triumph! hark! — what pain!
Philomela [1853]. Stanza 1

Eternal passion!
Eternal pain!
Ibid. Stanza 3

What shelter to grow ripe is ours?
What leisure to grow wise?
Stanzas in Memory of the Author of "Obermann" [1] *[1853].*
Stanza 18

We, in some unknown Power's employ,
Move on a rigorous line;
Can neither, when we will, enjoy;
Nor, when we will, resign.
Ibid. Stanza 34

Truth sits upon the lips of dying men.
Sohrab and Rustum [1853].
Line 656

Wandering between two worlds, one dead,
The other powerless to be born.
Stanzas from the Grande Char-treuse [1855]. Stanza 15

Peace, peace is what I seek, and public calm;
Endless extinction of unhappy hates.
Merope [1858]

With women the heart argues, not the mind.
Ibid.

Whispering from her towers the last enchantments of the Middle Age [Ox-ford]. . . . Home of lost causes, and forsaken beliefs, and unpopular names, and impossible loyalties!
Essays in Criticism, First Series
[1865]. Preface

I am bound by my own definition of criticism: a disinterested endeavor to learn and propagate the best that is known and thought in the world.
Ibid. Functions of Criticism at
the Present Time

Poetry is simply the most beautiful, impressive and widely effective mode of saying things, and hence its importance.
Ibid. Heinrich Heine

Philistine must have originally meant, in the mind of those who invented the nickname, a strong, dogged, unenlightened opponent of the children of the light.
Ibid.

[1] Étienne Pivert de Sénancour [1770–1846], French author. His most notable work, *Ober-mann*, was published in 1804.

On the breast of that huge Mississippi of falsehood called history, a foam-bell more or less is of no consequence.[1]

*Essays in Criticism, First Series.
Literary Influence of Academies*

The great apostle of the Philistines, Lord Macaulay.

Ibid. Joubert

The sea is calm tonight,
The tide is full, the moon lies fair
Upon the Straits.

Dover Beach [*1867*]. *Stanza 1*

Begin, and cease, and then again begin,
With tremulous cadence slow, and bring
The eternal note of sadness in.

Ibid.

The sea of faith
Was once, too, at the full, and round earth's shore
Lay like the folds of a bright girdle furl'd;
But now I only hear
Its melancholy, long, withdrawing roar,
Retreating to the breath
Of the night-wind down the vast edges drear
And naked shingles of the world.

Ibid. Stanza 3

Ah, love, let us be true
To one another! for the world, which seems
To lie before us like a land of dreams,
So various, so beautiful, so new,
Hath really neither joy, nor love, nor light,
Nor certitude, nor peace, nor help for pain;
And we are here as on a darkling plain

[1] History never embraces more than a small part of reality. — LA ROCHEFOUCAULD [1613–1680]: *Paul Sabatier*
How oft we sigh
When histories charm to think that histories lie!
THOMAS MOORE [1780–1852]:
The Skeptic
History is nothing more than the belief in the senses, the belief in falsehood. — NIETZSCHE [1844–1900]: *The Twilight of the Idols, "Reason" in Philosophy, 1*
History is bunk. — HENRY FORD [1863–1947]

Swept with confused alarms of struggle and flight,
Where ignorant armies clash by night.

Dover Beach. Stanza 4

It is — last stage of all —
When we are frozen up within, and quite
The phantom of ourselves,
To hear the world applaud the hollow ghost
Which blamed the living man.

Growing Old [*1867*]. *Stanza 7*

Hear it, O Thyrsis, still our Tree is there!
Ah, vain! These English fields, this upland dim,
These brambles pale with mist engarlanded,
That lone, sky-pointing tree, are not for him.
To a boon southern country he is fled,
And now in happier air,
Wandering with the great Mother's train divine . . .
Within a folding of the Apennine.

Thyrsis [*1867*]. *Stanza 18*

Creep into thy narrow bed,
Creep, and let no more be said!
Vain thy onset! all stands fast;
Thou thyself must break at last.

The Last Word [*1867*]. *Stanza 1*

Let the long contention cease!
Geese are swans, and swans are geese.[1]

Ibid. Stanza 2

Charge once more, then, and be dumb!
Let the victors, when they come,
When the forts of folly fall,
Find thy body by the wall.

Ibid. Stanza 4

Was Christ a man like us? — Ah! let us try
If we then, too, can be such men as he!

The Better Part [*1867*]

Spare me the whispering, crowded room,
The friends who come and gape and go,
The ceremonious air of gloom —
All, which makes death a hideous show.

A Wish [*1867*]. *Stanza 4*

[1] See Burton, page 222b.

Cruel, but composed and bland,
Dumb, inscrutable and grand,
So Tiberius might have sat,
Had Tiberius been a cat.
                Poor Matthias [*1867*]
Coldly, sadly descends
The autumn evening. The Field
Strewn with its dank yellow drifts
Of withered leaves, and the elms,
Fade into dimness apace.
            Rugby Chapel [*1867*]. *Stanza 1*
Most men eddy about
Here and there — eat and drink,
Chatter and love and hate,
Gather and squander, are raised
Aloft, are hurl'd in the dust,
Striving blindly, achieving
Nothing; and then they die.
                Ibid. Stanza 6
Friends who set forth at our side
Falter, are lost in the storm!
We, we only, are left!
                Ibid. Stanza 8
Then, in such hour of need
Of your fainting, dispirited race,
Ye, like angels, appear,
Beacons of Hope ye appear!
Languor is not in your heart,
Weakness is not in your word,
Weariness not on your brow.
                Ibid. Stanza 13
  Our society distributes itself into
Barbarians, Philistines, and Populace;
and America is just ourselves, with the
Barbarians quite left out, and the
Populace nearly.
            Culture and Anarchy [*1869*].
                        Preface
  The pursuit of perfection, then, is the
pursuit of sweetness and light.[1] . . .
He who works for sweetness and light
united, works to make reason and the
will of God prevail.
                        Ibid.
  One has often wondered whether
upon the whole earth there is anything
so unintelligent, so unapt to perceive
how the world is really going, as an
ordinary young Englishman of our
upper class.
                        Ibid.

[1] See Swift, page 294b.

Below the surface stream, shallow and
    light,
Of what we say and feel — below the
    stream,
As light, of what we think we feel, there
    flows
With noiseless current, strong, obscure
    and deep,
The central stream of what we feel in-
    deed.
        St. Paul and Protestantism [1]
                        [*1870*]
  Culture, the acquainting ourselves
with the best that has been known and
said in the world.
        Literature and Dogma [*1873*].
                        Preface
  Conduct is three-fourths of our life
and its largest concern.
                Ibid. Chap. 1
  A beautiful and ineffectual angel,
beating in the void his luminous wings
in vain.
        *Essays in Criticism, Second
            Series* [*1888*]. *Shelley*

ULYSSES S. GRANT
[1822–1885]

  No terms except an unconditional
and immediate surrender can be accepted. I propose to move immediately
upon your works.
        *To General S. B. Buckner, Fort
            Donelson* [*February 16, 1862*]
  I propose to fight it out on this line,
if it takes all summer.
        *Dispatch to Washington, Be-
            fore Spottsylvania Court House*
            [*May 11, 1864*]
  Let us have peace.
        *Accepting a Nomination for the
            Presidency* [*May 29, 1868*]
  I know no method to secure the repeal of bad or obnoxious laws so effective as their stringent execution.
                Inaugural Address
                [*March 4, 1869*]
  Let no guilty man escape, if it can
be avoided. No personal considerations

[1] For an acknowledgment of Arnold's authorship of this interpolated verse, see his
Letters, Vol. II, P. 32, February 21, 1870.

should stand in the way of performing a public duty.

> *Indorsement of a Letter relating to the Whiskey Ring [July 29, 1875]*

Leave the matter of religion to the family altar, the church, and the private school, supported entirely by private contributions. Keep the church and the State for ever separate.

> *Speech at Des Moines, Iowa [1875]*

Labor disgraces no man; unfortunately you occasionally find men disgrace labor.

> *Speech at Midland International Arbitration Union, Birmingham, England [1877]*

They [the Pilgrim Fathers] fell upon an ungenial climate, where there were nine months of winter and three months of cold weather and that called out the best energies of the men, and of the women too, to get a mere subsistence out of the soil, with such a climate. In their efforts to do that they cultivated industry and frugality at the same time — which is the real foundation of the greatness of the Pilgrims.

> *Speech at New England Society Dinner [December 22, 1880]*

EDWARD EVERETT HALE
[1822–1909]

I am only one,
But still I am one.
I cannot do everything,
But still I can do something;
And because I cannot do everything
I will not refuse to do the something
   that I can do.

> *For the Lend-a-Hand Society*

Its pink and white are everywhere,
A ray of sun — and all the slope
Laughs with its white and red.
"It is the Mayflower of our hope;
The spring is come."

> *The Finding of the First Mayflower. Stanza 3*

Behind all these men you have to do with, behind officers, and government, and people even, there is the Country Herself, your Country, and . . . you belong to Her as you belong to your own mother. Stand by Her, boy, as you would stand by your mother.

> *The Man Without a Country [1865]*

He loved his country as no other man has loved her, but no man deserved less at her hands.

> *Ibid. Epitaph of Philip Nolan*

I taught him four speeches. . . .
1. "Very well, thank you. And you?" This for an answer to casual salutations.
2. "I am very glad you liked it."
3. "There has been so much said, and, on the whole, so well said, that I will not occupy the time."
4. "I agree, in general, with my friend the other side of the room."

> *My Double and How He Undid Me [1868]*

It is not necessary to finish your sentences in a crowd, but by a sort of mumble, omitting sibilants and dentals. This, indeed, if your words fail you, answers even in public extempore speech, but better where other talking is going on.

> *Ibid.*

To look up and not down,
To look forward and not back,
To look out and not in, and
To lend a hand.[1]

> *Ten Times One Is Ten [1870]*

Let the scroll
Fill as it may as years unroll;
But when again she calls her youth
To serve her in the ranks of Truth,
May she find all one heart, one soul —
At home or on some distant shore —
"All present, or accounted for!"

> *Alma Mater's Roll [For a Harvard dinner, 1875]*

[1] Rule of the Harry Wadsworth Club.

THOMAS HUGHES
[1822–1896]

Life isn't all beer and skittles;[1] but beer and skittles, or something better of the same sort, must form a good part of every Englishman's education.
Tom Brown's School-days
[1857]. Part I, Chap. 2

He never wants anything but what's right and fair; only when you come to settle what's right and fair, it's everything that he wants and nothing that you want. And that's his idea of a compromise. Give me the Brown compromise when I'm on his side.
Ibid. Part II, Chap. 2

GEORGE LIPPARD
[1822–1854]

There was tumult in the city,
In the quaint old Quaker town,
And the streets were rife with people
Pacing restless up and down.
Independence Bell. Stanza 1

When a nation's life's at hazard,
We've no time to think of men!
Ibid. Stanza 3

"IK. MARVEL" (DONALD GRANT MITCHELL)
[1822–1908]

Ashes follow blaze inevitably as death follows life. Misery treads on the heels of joy; anguish rides swift after pleasure.
Reveries of a Bachelor [1850].
First Reverie, Part III

Blessed be letters — they are the monitors, they are also the comforters, and they are the only true heart-talkers.
Ibid. Second Reverie

JOHN TYLER PETTEE
[1822–1907]

Pray for peace and grace and spiritual food,

For wisdom and guidance, for all these are good,
But don't forget the potatoes.
Prayer and Potatoes

EDWARD JOHN PHELPS
[1822–1900]

Waiting for that delusive train
That, always coming, never comes,
Till weary and worn, cold and forlorn,
And paralyzed in every function,
I hope in hell
Their souls may dwell
Who first invented Essex Junction.
Essex Junction. Stanza 1

THOMAS BUCHANAN READ
[1822–1872]

The old, old sea, as one in tears,
Comes murmuring with its foamy lips,
And knocking at the vacant piers,
Calls for its long-lost multitude of ships.
Come, Gentle Trembler. Stanza 5

I stood by the open casement
And looked upon the night,
And saw the westward-going stars
Pass slowly out of sight.
The Celestial Army. Stanza 1

Boone, the pioneer,
Whose statue, in the eternal niche of fame,
Leans on his gleaming rifle; and whose name
Is carved so deep in the Kentuckian rocks,
It may not be effaced.
The New Pastoral. Book XXVII

The terrible grumble, and rumble, and roar,
Telling the battle was on once more,
And Sheridan twenty miles away.
Sheridan's Ride. Stanza 1

I hate the sin, but I love the sinner.
What a Word May Do. Stanza 1

---

[1] It's a regular holiday to them — all porter and skittles. . . . Down-hearted fellers as can't svig away at the beer, nor play at skittles neither. — DICKENS: *Pickwick Papers* [1836–1837], *Chap. 41*

BERNARD ELLIOTT BEE
[1823–1861]

See, there is Jackson, standing like a stone-wall.
> *Of General T. J. Jackson, at the Battle of Bull Run* [1] *[July 21, 1861]*

GEORGE HENRY BOKER
[1823–1890]

"Freedom!" their battle-cry, —
"Freedom! or leave to die!"
> *The Black Regiment. Stanza 5*

Lay him low, lay him low,
In the clover or the snow!
What cares he? he cannot know.
> *Dirge for a Soldier.* [2] *Stanza 1*

"Give me but two brigades," said Hooker, frowning at fortified Lookout.
> *Battle of Lookout Mountain.* [3] *Stanza 1*

All through the long, long polar day,
The vessels westward sped;
And wherever the sail of Sir John was blown,
The ice gave way and fled.
> *The Ballad of Sir John Franklin.* [4] *Stanza 7*

And there, while thread shall hang to thread,
Oh, let that ensign fly!
The noblest constellation set
Against the Northern sky.
> *The Cumberland.* [5] *Stanza 37*

I am that blessing which men fly from
— Death.
> *Countess Laura. Stanza 13*

Love is that orbit of the restless soul
Whose circle grazes the confines of space,

---

[1] Bee was killed in this battle.
[2] General Philip Kearny, killed near Chantilly, Virginia, September 1, 1862.
[3] Chattanooga, Tennessee, November 24, 1863.
[4] Arctic explorer [1786–1847].
[5] Sunk by the *Merrimac*, off Hampton Roads, Virginia [March 8, 1862]. Commanded by Lieutenant George U. Morris, she went down with all on board and colors flying. Most of the crew were lost.

Bounding within the limits of its race
Utmost extremes.
> *Sonnet, Love*

WILLIAM BRIGHTY RANDS ("MATTHEW BROWNE")
[1823–1882]

Never do today what you can
Put off till tomorrow.[1]
> *Lilliput Levee*

Great wide, beautiful, wonderful world,
With the wonderful waters round you curled,
And the wonderful grass upon your breast,
World, you are beautifully drest.
> *The Child's World. Stanza 1*

You are more than the earth, though you are such a dot;
You can love and think, and the earth cannot!
> *Ibid. Stanza 5*

JULIA A. FLETCHER CARNEY
[1823–1908]

Little drops of water, little grains of sand,
Make the mighty ocean and the pleasant land.
So the little moments, humble though they be,
Make the mighty ages of eternity.
> *Little Things [1845]*

Little deeds of kindness, little words of love,
Help to make earth happy like the heaven above.
> *Ibid.*

WILLIAM JOHNSON CORY
[1823–1892]

All beauteous things for which we live
By laws of time and space decay.

---

[1] No idleness, no laziness, no procrastination; never put off till tomorrow what you can do today. — LORD CHESTERFIELD: *Letters*, December 26, 1749

But oh, the very reason why
I clasp them, is because they die.
Mimnermus in Church. Stanza 4
Somewhere beneath the sun,
These quivering heart-strings prove it,
Somewhere there must be one
Made for this soul, to move it.
Amaturus
For waste of scheme and toil we grieve,
For snowflakes on the wave we sigh,
For writings on the sand that leave
Naught for tomorrow's passer-by.
On Livermead Sands. Stanza 1
They told me, Heraclitus, they told me
you were dead;
They brought me bitter news to hear
and bitter tears to shed.
I wept, as I remembered, how often you
and I
Had tired the sun with talking and sent
him down the sky.
And now that thou art lying, my dear
old Carian guest,
A handful of grey ashes, long long ago
at rest,
Still are thy pleasant voices, thy
Nightingales,[1] awake,
For Death, he taketh all away, but
them he cannot take.
Heraclitus,[2] Paraphrase from
Callimachus [3]

BARTHOLOMEW DOWLING
[1823–1863]

We meet 'neath the sounding rafter,
And the walls around are bare;

[1] *The Nightingales* was the title of the poems left by HERACLITUS [*floruit* 500 B.C.].
[2] They tell me, Heraclitus, thou art dead,
And many are the tears for thee I shed,
With memories of those summer nights opprest
When we together talked the sun to rest.
Alas! my guest, my friend! no more art thou;
Long, long ago wert ashes, and yet now
Thy Nightingales live on, I hear them sing,
E'en death spares them, who spares not anything.
LILLA CABOT PERRY [1848–1933]: translated from CALLIMACHUS, *Greek Anthology, Book VII, Epigram 80*
[3] *Floruit* 260 B.C.

As they shout back our peals of laughter
It seems that the dead are there.
Then stand to your glasses steady!
We drink in our comrades' eyes:
One cup to the dead already —
Hurrah for the next that dies!
The Revel.[1] Stanza 1

THOMAS WENTWORTH HIGGINSON
[1823–1911]

The test of an author is not to be found merely in the number of his phrases that pass current in the corner of newspapers . . . but in the number of passages that have really taken root in younger minds.
Margaret Fuller Ossoli [1884].
Chap. 18
When a thought takes one's breath away, a lesson on grammar seems an impertinence.
Preface to EMILY DICKINSON'S
Poems, First Series [1890]
An easy thing, O Power Divine,
To thank Thee for these gifts of Thine,
For summer's sunshine, winter's snow,
For hearts that kindle, thoughts that glow;
But when shall I attain to this —
To thank Thee for the things I miss?
The Things I Miss
Age, I make light of it,
Fear not the sight of it,
Time's but our playmate, whose toys are divine.
Sixty and Six: A Fountain
of Youth

JOHN KELLS INGRAM
[1823–1907]

Who fears to speak of Ninety-eight?
Who blushes at the name?
When cowards mock the patriot's fate,
Who hangs his head for shame?
The Memory of the Dead.[2]
Stanza 1

[1] Commemorating those who died in a great cholera epidemic in India.
[2] First published anonymously in *The Dublin Nation*, April 1, 1843.

GEORGE MARTIN LANE
[1823–1897]

The waiter he to him doth call,
And gently whispers — "One Fishball."
The waiter roars it through the hall,
The guests they start at "One Fish-
  ball!"
The guest then says, quite ill at ease,
"A piece of bread, sir, if you please."
The waiter roars it through the hall:
"We don't give bread with one Fish-
  ball!"

> One Fish-ball,[1] Couplets 7–10
> [*Harper's Monthly, July, 1855*]

FRANCIS PARKMAN
[1823–1893]

The growth of New England was a result of the aggregate efforts of a busy multitude, each in his narrow circle toiling for himself, to gather competence or wealth. The expansion of New France was the achievement of a gigantic ambition striving to grasp a continent. It was a vain attempt.

> *Pioneers of France in the New World* [*1865*]. *Introduction*

A boundless vision grows upon us; an untamed continent; vast wastes of forest verdure; mountains silent in primeval sleep; river, lake, and glimmering pool; wilderness oceans mingling with the sky. Such was the domain which France conquered for Civilization. Plumed helmets gleamed in the shade of its forests, priestly vestments in its dens and fastnesses of ancient barbarism. Men steeped in antique learning, pale with the close breath of the cloister, here spent the noon and evening of their lives, ruled savage hordes with a mild, parental sway, and stood serene before the direst shapes of death. Men of courtly nurture, heirs to the polish of a far-reaching ancestry, here, with their

---

[1] The author was Professor of Latin at Harvard; PROFESSOR MORGAN's memoir of him says that the embarrassment of the "lone fish-ball" was an actual experience.

dauntless hardihood, put to shame the boldest sons of toil.

> *Pioneers of France in the New World. Introduction*

Faithfulness to the truth of history involves far more than a research, however patient and scrupulous, into special facts. Such facts may be detailed with the most minute exactness, and yet the narrative, taken as a whole, may be unmeaning or untrue. The narrator must seek to imbue himself with the life and spirit of the time. He must study events in their bearings near and remote; in the character, habits, and manners of those who took part in them. He must himself be, as it were, a sharer or a spectator of the action he describes.

> *Ibid.*

If any pale student, glued to his desk, here seek an apology for a way of life whose natural fruit is that pallid and emasculate scholarship of which New England has had too many examples, it will be far better that this sketch had not been written. For the student there is, in its season, no better place than the saddle, and no better companion than the rifle or the oar.

> *Autobiography* [*1868*] (*Proceedings of the Massachusetts Historical Society, Vol. VIII, Page 353*)

The most momentous and far-reaching question ever brought to issue on this continent was: Shall France remain here or shall she not?

> *Montcalm and Wolfe* [*1884*]. *Introduction*

The French Revolution began at the top — in the world of fashion, birth, and intellect — and propagated itself downwards.

> *Ibid.*

Versailles was a gulf into which the labor of France poured its earnings, and it was never full.

> *Ibid. Page 11*

France built its best colony on a prin-

ciple of exclusion, and failed: England reversed the system, and succeeded.
Montcalm and Wolfe. Page 22

JAMES MATTHEWS LEGARÉ
[1823–1859]

Go bow thy head in gentle spite,
Thou lily white,
For she who spies thee waving here,
With thee in beauty can compare
As day with night.
To a Lily

Thou in thy lake dost see
Thyself: so she
Beholds her image in her eyes
Reflected. Thus did Venus rise
From out the sea.
Ibid.

CAROLINE ATHERTON BRIGGS MASON
[1823–1890]

Do they miss me at home — do they miss me?
'Twould be an assurance most dear,
To know that this moment some loved one
Were saying, "I wish he were here."
Do They Miss Me at Home?
Stanza 1

His grave a nation's heart shall be,
His monument a people free!
President Lincoln's Grave

EDWARD HAZEN PARKER
[1823–1896]

Life's race well run,
Life's work well done,
Life's victory won,
    Now cometh rest.
Funeral Ode on James A. Garfield.
Stanza 1

COVENTRY PATMORE
[1823–1896]

Life is not life at all without delight.
Victory in Defeat
None thrives for long upon the happiest dream.
Tired Memory

Grant me the power of saying things
Too simple and too sweet for words!
The Angel in the House [1854–1856]. Book I, Canto 1, Prelude 1, The Impossibility

Love, sole mortal thing
Of worth immortal.
Ibid. Prelude 2, Love's Reality

Ah, wasteful woman! she who may
On her sweet self set her own price,
Knowing man cannot choose but pay,
How has she cheapened Paradise!
How given for nought her priceless gift,
How spoiled the bread and spilled the wine,
Which, spent with due respective thrift,
Had made brutes men and men divine!
Ibid. Canto 3, Prelude 3, Unthrift

Love wakes men, once a lifetime each;
They lift their heavy lids, and look;
And, lo, what one sweet page can teach
They read with joy, then shut the book.
Ibid. Canto 8, Prelude 2,
The Revelation

Why, having won her, do I woo?
Because her spirit's vestal grace
Provokes me always to pursue,
But, spirit-like, eludes embrace.
Ibid. Book II, Canto 12, Prelude 1,
The Married Lover

For want of me the world's course will not fail:
When all its work is done, the lie shall rot;
The truth is great, and shall prevail,
When none cares whether it prevail or not.
The Unknown Eros [1877]. Book I,
Canto 12, Magna est Veritas

If I were dead, you'd sometimes say,
"Poor Child!"
Ibid. Canto 14, If I Were Dead

A Woman is a foreign land,
Of which, though there he settle young,
A man will ne'er quite understand
The customs, politics, and tongue.
Woman

Some who do not consider that Christianity has proved a failure, do, nevertheless, hold that it is open to question whether the race, as a race,

has been much affected by it, and whether the external and visible evil and good which have come of it do not pretty nearly balance one another.
Christianity and Progress

Atheism in art, as well as in life, has only to be pressed to its last consequences in order to become ridiculous.
Emotional Art

The poet, as a rule, should avoid religion altogether as a direct subject.
Bad Morality Is Bad Art

It is a great consolation to reflect that, among all the bewildering changes to which the world is subject, the character of woman cannot be altered.
Ibid.

EDWARD POLLOCK
[1823–1858]

There's something in the parting hour
Will chill the warmest heart,
Yet kindred, comrades, lovers, friends,
Are fated all to part.
The Parting Hour
The one who goes is happier
Than those he leaves behind.
Ibid.

THEODORE DE BANVILLE
[1823–1891]

We'll to the woods no more, the laurel-trees are cut.[1]
Nous n'irons plus aux bois

PHOEBE CARY
[1824–1874]

I think true love is never blind,
But rather brings an added light,
An inner vision quick to find
The beauties hid from common sight.
True Love. Stanza 1
Give plenty of what is given to you,
And listen to pity's call;
Don't think the little you give is great
And the much you get is small.
A Legend of the Northland. I,
Stanza 8

[1] Nous n'irons plus aux bois, les lauriers sont coupés. (From an old nursery rhyme.)

Sometimes, I think, the things we see
Are shadows of the things to be;
That what we plan we build;
That every hope that hath been crossed,
And every dream we thought was lost,
In heaven shall be fulfilled.
Dreams and Realities. Stanza 7
And though hard be the task,
"Keep a stiff upper lip."
Keep a Stiff Upper Lip
One sweetly solemn thought
Comes to me o'er and o'er;
I am nearer home today
Than I ever have been before.
Nearer Home. Stanza 1
For of all the hard things to bear and grin,
The hardest is being taken in.
Kate Ketcham (Parody on WHITTIER'S *Maud Muller)*

LUCY LARCOM
[1824–1893]

Oh, her heart's adrift, with one
On an endless voyage gone!
Night and morning
Hannah's at the window binding shoes.
Hannah Binding Shoes. Stanza 2
I do not own an inch of land,
But all I see is mine.
A Strip of Blue
If the world seems cold to you,
Kindle fires to warm it!
Three Old Saws
If the world's a wilderness,
Go, build houses in it!
Ibid.
If the world's a vale of tears,
Smile, till rainbows span it!
Ibid.
There is light in shadow and shadow in light,
And black in the blue of the sky.
Black in Blue Sky. Stanza 2

GEORGE WILLIAM CURTIS
[1824–1892]

While we read history we make history.
The Call of Freedom

Every great crisis of human history is a pass of Thermopylae, and there is always a Leonidas and his three hundred to die in it, if they can not conquer.
The Call of Freedom

Imagination is as good as many voyages — and how much cheaper.
Prue and I [*1856*]. *Preface*

Happiness is speechless.
Ibid. Chap. 4

The pride of ancestry increases in the ratio of distance.
Ibid. Chap. 6

It is a great pity that men and women forget that they have been children. Parents are apt to be foreigners to their sons and daughters. Maturity is the gate of Paradise which shuts behind us; and our memories are gradually weaned from the glories in which our nativity was cradled.
Ibid. Chap. 7

Love is the coldest of critics.
Ibid.

Gentlemen, this is the convention of free speech, and I have been given the floor. I have only a few words to say to you, but I shall say them if I stand here until tomorrow morning.
At the Republican National Convention [*1860*]

CHARLES GODFREY LELAND
[1824–1903]

Hans Breitmann gife a barty —
Where ish dat barty now?
Hans Breitmann's Barty [*1857*]

If all the world must see the world
  As the world the world hath seen,
Then it were better for the world
  That the world had never been.
The World and the World

"A New Year's gift to the world," said the Frost,
"Rich lace curtains which nothing cost."
Frost Pictures. Stanza 4

They saw a Dream of Loveliness descending from the train.
The Masher

The brave deserve the lovely — every woman may be won.
The Masher

ALEXANDRE DUMAS
THE YOUNGER
[1824–1895]

Business? It's quite simple. It's other people's money.
La Question d'Argent [*1857*].
Act II, Sc. 7

GEORGE MACDONALD
[1824–1905]

Alas! how easily things go wrong!
A sigh too much or a kiss too long,
And there follows a mist and a weeping rain,
And life is never the same again.
Phantastes. Song

Where did you come from, baby dear?
Out of the everywhere into the here.
At the Back of the North Wind.
Baby, Stanza 1

Where did you get those eyes so blue?
Out of the sky as I came through.
Ibid. Stanza 2

They were all looking for a king
  To slay their foes and lift them high;
Thou cam'st, a little baby thing
  That made a woman cry.
That Holy Thing. Stanza 1

Said the Wind to the Moon, "I will blow you out!"
The Wind and the Moon.
Stanza 1

WALTER CHALMERS SMITH
[1824–1908]

And all through life I see a cross —
  Where sons of God yield up their breath;
There is no gain except by loss;
  There is no life except by death;
  There is no vision but by faith.
Olrig Grange. Book 6

JOHN WHITTAKER WATSON
[1824–1890]

O the snow, the beautiful snow,
Filling the sky and the earth below.
Over the house-tops, over the street,
Over the heads of the people you meet,
    Dancing,
      Flirting,
        Skimming along,
Beautiful snow, it can do nothing
    wrong.
      Beautiful Snow [*1869*]. *Stanza 1*

HENRY DE LAFAYETTE WEBSTER
[1824–1896]

The years creep slowly by, Lorena,
The snow is on the grass again.
      Lorena.[1] *Stanza 1*

ADELINE DUTTON TRAIN WHITNEY
[1824–1906]

The sun of life has crossed the line;
The summer-shine of lengthened light
Faded and failed — till, where I stand,
'Tis equal day and equal night.
      Equinoctial. Stanza 1
I bow me to the threatening gale:
I know when that is overpast,
Among the peaceful harvest days
An Indian Summer comes at last.
      Ibid. Stanza 6

EDWARD HENRY BICKERSTETH, BISHOP OF EXETER
[1825–1906]

    Give us men!
Men from every rank,
Fresh and free and frank;
Men of thought and reading,
Men of light and leading,
Men of loyal breeding,
The nation's welfare speeding.
      Give Us Men. Stanza 1

[1] One of the most popular songs of the Civil
War period.

RICHARD DODDRIDGE BLACKMORE
[1825–1900]

Women, who are, beyond all doubt,
the mothers of all mischief, also nurse
that babe to sleep when he is too noisy.
      Lorna Doone [*1869*]. *Chap. 57*

WILLIAM ALLEN BUTLER
[1825–1902]

Dresses for breakfasts, and dinners,
    and balls;
Dresses to sit in, and stand in, and
    walk in;
Dresses to dance in, and flirt in, and
    talk in;
Dresses in which to do nothing at all;
Dresses for Winter, Spring, Summer,
    and Fall.
      Nothing to Wear [1]
This same Miss McFlimsey of Madison
    Square,
The last time we met was in utter de-
    spair,
Because she had nothing whatever to
    wear!
      Ibid.

JULIA CAROLINE RIPLEY DORR
[1825–1913]

Under thy hooded mantle I can see
Thy wavelets of soft hair, like those
    that lie
On a girl's forehead; and thy unlined
    brow,
Pregnant with thought inbreathed, be-
    trayeth not
One of thy secrets saving this alone, —
That thou hast loved and suffered.[2]
      In Rock Creek Cemetery

[1] *Harper's Weekly,* February 7, 1857.
[2] The sculpture by Augustus Saint-Gaudens
for the grave of Mrs. Henry Adams, Rock
Creek Cemetery, Washington, D. C.
  This is not death, nor sorrow, nor sad Hope;
  Nor rest that follows strife, but oh, more
    dread!
'Tis Life, for all its agony, serene,
Immortal, and unmournful and content.
  RICHARD WATSON GILDER [1844–1909]:
    The Saint-Gaudens Memorial

HENRIETTA A. HEATHORN
(MRS. THOMAS H. HUXLEY)
[1825–1914]

Be not afraid, ye waiting hearts that
weep,
For God still giveth His belovèd sleep,[1]
And if an endless sleep He wills — so
best.[2]
> *Browning's Funeral, December 31,*
> *1889*

To all the gossip that I hear
I'll give no faith; to what I see
But only half, for it is clear
All that led up is dark to me.
    Learn we the larger life to live,
    To comprehend is to forgive.
        "Tout Comprendre, C'est Tout
        Pardonner"

THOMAS HENRY HUXLEY
[1825–1895]

I cannot but think that he who finds
a certain proportion of pain and evil
inseparably woven up in the life of the
very worms, will bear his own share
with more courage and submission.
> *On the Educational Value of*
> *the Natural History Sciences*
> *[1854]*

To a person uninstructed in natural
history, his country or seaside stroll is
a walk through a gallery filled with
wonderful works of art, nine-tenths of
which have their faces turned to the
wall.
> *Ibid.*

Education is the instruction of the
intellect in the laws of Nature, under
which name I include not merely things
and their forces, but men and their
ways; and the fashioning of the affections and of the will into an earnest and
loving desire to move in harmony with
those laws.
> *A Liberal Education [1868]*

For every man the world is as fresh
as it was at the first day, and as full of

[1] He giveth his beloved sleep. — *Psalm
CXXVII, 2*
[2] These lines were carved on Huxley's tomb
by his own request.

untold novelties for hi...
eyes to see them.
> *A Lib...*

The chess-board is the ...
pieces are the phenomena of th...
verse, the rules of the game are wh...
we call the laws of Nature. The player
on the other side is hidden from us.
We know that his play is always fair,
just, and patient. But also we know, to
our cost, that he never overlooks a mistake, or makes the smallest allowance
for ignorance.
> *Ibid.*

If some great Power would agree to
make me always think what is true
and do what is right, on condition of
being turned into a sort of clock and
wound up every morning before I got
out of bed, I should instantly close with
the offer.
> *On Descartes' Discourse on Method*
> *[1870]. Method and Results*

There is the greatest practical benefit
in making a few failures early in life.
> *On Medical Education [1870]*

That mysterious independent variable of political calculation, Public
Opinion.
> *Universities, Actual and Ideal*
> *[1874]*

Veracity is the heart of morality.
> *Ibid.*

Becky Sharp's acute remark that it
is not difficult to be virtuous on ten
thousand a year [1] has its application to
nations; and it is futile to expect a
hungry and squalid population to be
anything but violent and gross.
> *Joseph Priestley [1874]*

Logical consequences are the scarecrows of fools and the beacons of wise
men.
> *Animal Automatism [1874]*

Size is not grandeur, and territory
does not make a nation.
> *On University Education [1876]*

Perhaps the most valuable result of
all education is the ability to make
yourself do the thing you have to do,

[1] See Thackeray, page 565a.

when it ought to be done, whether you like it or not; it is the first lesson that ought to be learned; and however early a man's training begins, it is probably the last lesson that he learns thoroughly.
Technical Education [*1877*]

The great end of life is not knowledge but action.
Ibid.

If a little knowledge is dangerous, where is the man who has so much as to be out of danger?
On Elemental Instruction in Physiology [*1877*]

Irrationally held truths may be more harmful than reasoned errors.
The Coming of Age of "The Origin of Species" [*1880*]

It is the customary fate of new truths to begin as heresies and to end as superstitions.
Ibid.

FRANCIS TURNER PALGRAVE
[1825–1897]

Time's corrosive dewdrop eats
The giant warrior to a crust
Of earth in earth and rust in rust.
A Danish Barrow

ADELAIDE ANNE PROCTER
[1825–1864]

One by one the sands are flowing,
One by one the moments fall;
Some are coming, some are going;
Do not strive to grasp them all.
One by One. Stanza 1

Seated one day at the organ,
I was weary and ill at ease,
And my fingers wandered idly
Over the noisy keys.
A Lost Chord. Stanza 1

But I struck one chord of music
Like the sound of a great Amen.
Ibid. Stanza 2

It seemed the harmonious echo
From our discordant life.
Ibid. Stanza 4

RICHARD HENRY STODDARD
[1825–1903]

Pale in her fading bowers the Summer stands,
Like a new Niobe with claspèd hands,
Silent above the flowers, her children lost,
Slain by the arrows of the early Frost.
Ode

Joy may be a miser,
But Sorrow's purse is free.
Persian Song

BAYARD TAYLOR
[1825–1878]

Till the sun grows cold,
And the stars are old,
And the leaves of the Judgment Book unfold.
Bedouin Song

They sang of love, and not of fame;
Forgot was Britain's glory;
Each heart recalled a different name,
But all sang "Annie Laurie."
The Song of the Camp. Stanza 5

The bravest are the tenderest, —
The loving are the daring.
Ibid. Stanza 11

The violet loves a sunny bank,
The cowslip loves the lea;
The scarlet creeper loves the elm,
But I love — thee.
Proposal. Stanza 1

Learn to live, and live to learn,
Ignorance like a fire doth burn,
Little tasks make large return.
To My Daughter. Stanza 1

WILLIAM WHITING
[1825–1878]

Eternal Father! strong to save,
Whose arm hath bound the restless wave,
Who bidd'st the mighty ocean deep
Its own appointed limits keep:
O, hear us when we cry to Thee
For those in peril on the sea!
Eternal Father, Strong to Save.
Stanza 1

G. W. HUNT
[*Floruit* 1878]

We don't want to fight, but, by jingo,
  if we do,
We've got the ships, we've got the men,
  we've got the money, too.
We've fought the Bear before, and
  while Britons shall be true,
The Russians shall not have Constantinople.
                    Song [1] [*1878*]

FREDERICK TEMPLE HAMILTON BLACKWOOD, LORD DUFFERIN
[1826–1902]

In the market-place lay a dead dog.
Of the group gathered around it, one
said: "This carcass is disgusting." Another said, "The sight of it is torment."
Every man spoke in this strain. But
Jesus drew near and said, "Pearls are
not equal in whiteness to his teeth.
Look not on the failures of others and
the merits of thyself; cast thine eye on
thine own fault."
        *Installation Address as Lord
        Rector of St. Andrew's Univer-
        sity* [*1891*]

GEORGE W. BUNGAY
[1826–1892]

In rituals and faith excel!
Chimed out the Episcopalian bell.
        The Creeds of the Bells. Stanza 2
All is well! is well! is well!
Pealed out the good old Dutch church
  bell.
                    Ibid. Stanza 3
O swell! ye rising waters, swell!
Pealed out the clear-toned Baptist bell.
                    Ibid. Stanza 4
        Do well!
Rang out the Unitarian bell.
                    Ibid. Stanza 5

[1] Sung by Gilbert Hastings Macdermott
(Farrell) [1845–1901], "the great Macdermott." The song gave the terms "jingo" and
"jingoism" to the political vocabulary, though
the phrase "by jingo" had been used earlier
by Goldsmith and Thomas Hood.

Salvation's free, we tell! we tell!
Shouted the Methodistic bell.
        The Creeds of the Bells. Stanza 6
        No hell!
Rang out the Universalist bell.
                    Ibid. Stanza 7
All hail, ye saints, the chorus swell!
Chimed in the Roman Catholic bell.
                    Ibid. Stanza 10
Drink from the well!
In rapture rang the Temperance bell.
                    Ibid. Stanza 11

DINAH MARIA MULOCK CRAIK
[1826–1887]

Two hands upon the breast,
  And labour's done; [1]
Two pale feet crossed in rest,
  The race is won.
                    Now and Afterwards
Love that asketh love again
Finds the barter nought but pain;
Love that giveth in full store
Aye receives as much, and more.
        Love that Asketh Love Again
God rest ye, merry gentlemen! let
  nothing you dismay,
For Jesus Christ, our Saviour, was
  born on Christmas day.
        A Christmas Carol. Stanza 1
Douglas, Douglas, tender and true!
        Douglas, Tender and True. [2]
                    Stanza 1
Oh, my son's my son till he gets him a
  wife,
But my daughter's my daughter all her
  life.
                    Young and Old

STEPHEN COLLINS FOSTER
[1826–1864]

The day goes by like a shadow o'er the
  heart,
With sorrow where all was delight;

[1] Two hands upon the breast, and labor is
past. — *Russian proverb*
[2] O Douglas, O Douglas!
Tendir and trewe.
    SIR RICHARD HOLLAND: *The Buke of
    the Howlat* [*circa* 1450], *St. 31*

The time has come when the darkies
  have to part:
Then my old Kentucky Home, good
  night!
  My Old Kentucky Home.
  Stanza 2

Weep no more, my lady,
Oh! weep no more today!
We will sing one song for the old Ken-
  tucky Home,
For the old Kentucky Home far away.
  Ibid. Chorus

Way down upon the Swanee River,
  Far, far away,
There's where my heart is turning ever;
  There's where the old folks stay.
All up and down the whole creation,
  Sadly I roam,
Still longing for the old plantation,
  And for the old folks at home.
  The Old Folks at Home. Stanza 1

All the world is sad and dreary
  Ev'rywhere I roam,
Oh! darkies, how my heart grows
  weary,
Far from the old folks at home.
  Ibid. Chorus

I'm coming, I'm coming, for my head is
  bending low;
I hear those gentle voices calling, "Old
  Black Joe."
  Old Black Joe. Stanza 3

O, Susanna! O, don't you cry for me,
I've come from Alabama, wid my banjo
  on my knee.
  O, Susanna. Chorus

I come down dah wid my hat caved in,
  Doodah! doodah!
I go back home wid a pocket full of tin,
  Oh! doodah day!
Gwine to run all night!
Gwine to run all day!
I'll bet my money on de bobtail nag —
Somebody bet on de bay.
  Camptown Races

I dream of Jeanie with the light brown
  hair,
Borne like a vapor on the summer air;
I see her tripping where the bright
  streams play,

Happy as the daisies that dance on her
  way.
  Jeanie with the Light Brown
  Hair. Stanza 1

Beautiful dreamer, wake unto me,
Starlight and dewdrop are waiting for
  thee;
Sounds of the rude world heard in the
  day,
Lulled by the moonlight have all
  passed away.
  Beautiful Dreamer. Stanza 1

COATES KINNEY
[1826–1904]

What a bliss to press the pillow
  Of a cottage-chamber bed
And to listen to the patter
  Of the soft rain overhead!
  Rain on the Roof. Stanza 1

That subdued, subduing strain
Which is played upon the shingles
By the patter of the rain.
  Ibid. Stanza 6

ETHEL LYNN BEERS
[1827–1879]

All quiet along the Potomac tonight,
  No sound save the rush of the river,
While soft falls the dew on the face of
  the dead, —
  The picket's off duty forever.
  The Picket Guard [1861].
  Stanza 6

EDWARD STUYVESANT
BRAGG
[1827–1912]

They love him most for the enemies
he has made.[1]
  Speech seconding the nomina-
  tion of Grover Cleveland for
  the Presidency, Democratic
  National Convention, Chicago
  [July 9, 1884]

[1] An adaptation of Governor Bragg's expression became a Cleveland campaign slogan:
"We love him for the enemies he has made."

MORTIMER COLLINS
[1827–1876]

There was an Ape in the days that were
    earlier;
Centuries passed, and his hair became
    curlier;
Centuries more gave a thumb to his
    wrist —
Then he was Man — and a Positivist.
                The Positivists
A man is as old as he's feeling,
A woman as old as she looks.
              How Old Are You?

ROSE TERRY COOKE
[1827–1892]

Yet courage, soul! nor hold thy
    strength in vain,
In hope o'ercome the steeps God set
    for thee;
For past the Alpine summits of great
    pain,
Lieth thine Italy.[1]
              Beyond. Stanza 4

CHARLES B. FAIRBANKS
("AGUECHEEK")
[1827–1859]

Cleanliness is a great virtue; but
when it is carried to such an extent that
you cannot find your books and papers
which you left carefully arranged on
your table — when it gets to be a mon-
omania with man or woman — it becomes a bore.
    My Unknown Chum. Antwerp
             and Brussels
Slander, like Death, loves a shining
mark.[2]
    Ibid. Napoleon the Third
Foreign travel ought to soften prejudices, religious or political, and liberal-
ize a man's mind; but how many there
are who seem to have travelled for the
purpose of getting up their rancour

[1] Hannibal, encouraging his men: Quarum
alterum latus Italiae sit. — LIVY [59 B.C.–
A.D. 17]: *Ab Urbe Condita Libri, XXI, 30, 5*
[2] See Edward Young, page 306a.

against all that is opposed to their notions.
    My Unknown Chum. The Philos-
      ophy of Foreign Travel

FRANCIS MILES FINCH
[1827–1907]

These in the robings of glory,
    Those in the gloom of defeat,
All with the battle-blood gory,
    In the dusk of eternity meet:
Under the sod and the dew,
    Waiting the judgment-day;
Under the laurel, the Blue,
    Under the willow, the Gray.
    The Blue and the Gray. Stanza 2

CHARLES ELIOT NORTON
[1827–1908]

I think that a knowledge of Greek
thought and life, and of the arts in
which the Greeks expressed their
thought and sentiment, essential to
high culture. A man may know everything else, but without this knowledge
he remains ignorant of the best intellectual and moral achievements of his
own race.
    Letter to F. A. Tupper [1885]
Whatever your occupation may be
and however crowded your hours with
affairs, do not fail to secure at least a
few minutes every day for refreshment
of your inner life with a bit of poetry.
    Used by a Boston newspaper as
    a heading for a column of re-
    printed poems

JOHN TOWNSEND
TROWBRIDGE
[1827–1916]

Men are polished, through act and
    speech,
    Each by each,
As pebbles are smoothed on the rolling
    beach.
              A Home Idyl

With years a richer life begins,
  The spirit mellows:
Ripe age gives tone to violins,
  Wine, and good fellows.
                    Three Worlds

WILLIAM ALLINGHAM
[1828–1889]

Up the airy mountain,
  Down the rushy glen,
We daren't go a-hunting
  For fear of little men.
            The Fairies. Stanza 1

ROBERT BARNABAS BROUGH
[1828–1860]

My Lord Tomnoddy is thirty-four;
The Earl can last but a few years more.
My Lord in the Peers will take his
  place:
Her Majesty's councils his words will
  grace.
Office he'll hold and patronage sway;
Fortunes and lives he will vote away;
And what are his qualifications? —
  ONE!
He's the Earl of Fitzdotterel's eldest
  son.
                My Lord Tomnoddy

ELIZABETH RUNDLE CHARLES
[1828–1896]

To know how to say what other people only think, is what makes men poets and sages; and to dare to say what others only dare to think, makes men martyrs or reformers.
        *Chronicles of the Schönberg-
            Cotta Family, XIV*

GERALD MASSEY
[1828–1907]

Where our vanguard camps Today
Our rear shall march Tomorrow.
                Today and Tomorrow

GEORGE MEREDITH
[1828–1913]

I expect that Woman will be the last thing civilized by Man.
    *The Ordeal of Richard Feverel
        [1859]. Chap. 1*
Who rises from prayer a better man, his prayer is answered.
            Ibid. Chap. 12
The sun is coming down to earth, and the fields and the waters shout to him golden shouts.
            Ibid. Chap. 19
Kissing don't last: cookery do!
            Ibid. Chap. 28
See ye not, Courtesy
Is the true Alchemy,
Turning to gold all it touches and tries?
    The Song of Courtesy [1859]. IV
The old hound wags his shaggy tail,
  And I know what he would say:
It's over the hills we'll bound, old
    hound,
  Over the hills, and away.
            Over the Hills [1859]
I've studied men from my topsy-turvy
  Close, and, I reckon, rather true.
Some are fine fellows: some, right
    scurvy:
  Most, a dash between the two.
        Juggling Jerry [1859]. VII
Two of a trade, lass, never agree.
                Ibid. IX
Life is but the pebble sunk;
Deeds, the circle growing!
        *The Head of Bran the Blest
            [1860]. IV, Stanza 4*
Not till the fire is dying in the grate,
Look we for any kinship with the stars.
Oh, wisdom never comes when it is gold,
And the great price we pay for it full
    worth;
We have it only when we are half earth.
            Modern Love [1862]. IV
And if I drink oblivion of a day,
So shorten I the stature of my soul.
                Ibid. XII
The actors are, it seems, the usual
    three:
Husband, and wife, and lover.
                Ibid. XXV

That rarest gift
To Beauty, Common Sense.
 Modern Love. XXXII

How many a thing which we cast to
 the ground,
When others pick it up becomes a
 gem!
  Ibid. XLI

In tragic life, God wot,
No villain need be! Passions spin the
 plot:
We are betrayed by what is false
 within.
  Ibid. XLIII

Their sense is with their senses all
 mixed in,
Destroyed by subtleties these women
 are!
  Ibid. XLVIII

Ah, what a dusty answer gets the soul
When hot for certainties in this our
 life!
  Ibid. L

Into the breast that gives the rose
Shall I with shuddering fall?
 The Spirit of Earth in Autumn
  [*1862*]. *Stanza 1*

Earth knows no desolation.
She smells regeneration
In the moist breath of decay.
  Ibid. Stanza 14

Cynicism is intellectual dandyism.
 The Egoist [*1879*]. *Chap. 7*

In . . . the book of Egoism, it is
written, Possession without obligation
to the object possessed approaches
felicity.
  Ibid. Chap. 14

On a starred night Prince Lucifer up-
 rose.
Tired of his dark dominion swung the
 fiend . . .
He reached a middle height, and at the
 stars,
Which are the brain of heaven, he
 looked, and sank.
Around the ancient track marched, rank
 on rank,
The army of unalterable law.
 Lucifer in Starlight [*1883*]

Enter these enchanted woods,
 You who dare.
 The Woods of Westermain
  [*1883*]. *Stanza 1*

She whom I love is hard to catch and
 conquer,
Hard, but O the glory of the winning
 were she won!
 Love in the Valley [*1883*].
  Stanza 2

Darker grows the valley, more and
 more forgetting:
So were it with me if forgetting could
 be willed.

Tell the grassy hollow that holds the
 bubbling well-spring,
Tell it to forget the source that keeps
 it filled.
  Ibid. Stanza 5

Love that so desires would fain keep
 her changeless;
Fain would fling the net, and fain have
 her free.
  Ibid. Stanza 6

 Thence had he the laugh . . .
Broad as ten thousand beeves
At pasture.
 The Spirit of Shakespeare [*1883*]

Civil limitation daunts
His utterance never; the nymphs blush,
 not he.
 An Orson of the Muse [*Walt
  Whitman*] [*1883*]

A witty woman is a treasure; a witty
beauty is a power.
 Diana of the Crossways
  [*1885*]. *Chap. 1*

The well of true wit is truth itself.
  Ibid.

Ireland gives England her soldiers,
her generals too.
  Ibid. Chap. 2

With patient inattention hear him
 prate.
 Bellerophon [*1887*]. *Stanza 4*

Full lasting is the song, though he,
The singer, passes.
 The Thrush in February
  [*1888*]. *Stanza 17*

Cannon his name,
Cannon his voice, he came.
 Napoleon [*1891*]. *I*

For Order's cause he laboured, as in-
    clined
A soldier's training and his Euclid
    mind. . . .
That creature, woman, was the sofa
    soft,
When warriors their dusty armour
    doffed,
And read their manuals for the mak-
    ing truce
With rosy frailties framed to repro-
    duce.
                    Napoleon. IX
Evermore shall tyrant Force
Beget the greater for its overthrow.
                    Ibid. XIII
For iron Winter held her firm;
Across her sky he laid his hand;
And bird he starved, he stiffened worm;
A sightless heaven, a shaven land.
                    Tardy Spring [1891]
Now the North wind ceases,
The warm South-west awakes,
The heavens are out in fleeces,
And earth's green banner shakes.
                            Ibid.
Sword of Common Sense! . . .
Bright, nimble of the marrow-nerve
To wield thy double edge, retort
Or hold the deadlier reserve.
            Ode to the Comic Spirit [1892]

FITZ-JAMES O'BRIEN
[1828–1862]

The enchanted circle of the Upper
Ten.[1]
            The Diamond Lens [1858].
                            Chap. 2
It was of a famous vintage, that of
1848, a year when war and wine throve
together.
                    Ibid. Chap. 4

DANTE GABRIEL ROSSETTI
[1828–1882]

The blessed damozel leaned out
    From the gold bar of Heaven:
Her eyes were deeper than the depth
    Of waters stilled at even;

[1] See Haliburton, page 483b.

She had three lilies in her hand,
And the stars in her hair were seven.
            The Blessed Damozel [1850].
                            Stanza 1
And the souls mounting up to God
Went by her like thin flames.
                    Ibid. Stanza 7
I have been here before,
    But when or how I can not tell;
I know the grass beyond the door,
    The sweet keen smell,
The sighing sound, the lights around
    the shore.
            Sudden Light [1881]. Stanza 1
Still we say as we go, —
    "Strange to think by the way,
Whatever there is to know,
    That shall we know one day."
            The Cloud Confines [1881].
                            Stanza 1
Was it a friend or foe that spread these
    lies?
Nay, who but infants question in such
    wise,
'Twas one of my most intimate en-
    emies.
                    Fragment [1881]
A Sonnet is a moment's monument, —
Memorial from the Soul's eternity
To one dead deathless hour.
            The House of Life [1881].
                            Proem
And though thy soul sail leagues and
    leagues beyond, —
Still, leagues beyond those leagues,
    there is more sea.
            Ibid. 73, The Choice, III
Look in my face: my name is Might-
    have-been;
I am also called No-more, Too-late,
    Farewell.
            Ibid. 97, A Superscription

GEORGE WALTER
THORNBURY
[1828–1876]

The fool that eats till he is sick must
    fast till he is well,
The wooer who can flatter most will
    bear away the belle.
                    The Jester's Sermon

HENRIK IBSEN
[1828–1906]

A lie, turned topsy-turvy, can be prinked and tinseled out, decked in plumage new and fine, till none knows its lean old carcass.

Peer Gynt [*1867*]. *Act I*

For fortune such as I've enjoyed I have to thank America. My amply furnished library I owe to Germany's later schools. From France, again, I get my waistcoats, my manners, and my spice of wit — from England an industrious hand, and keen sense for my own advantage. The Jew has taught me how to wait. Some taste for *dolce far niente* I have received from Italy — and one time, in a perilous pass, to eke the measure of my days, I had recourse to Swedish steel.

Ibid. Act IV

Marriage is a thing you've got to give your whole mind to.

The League of Youth [*1869*]. *Act IV*

These heroes of finance are like beads on a string — when one slips off, all the rest follow.

Ibid.

He has the luck to be unhampered by either character, or conviction, or social position; so that Liberalism is the easiest thing in the world for him.

Ibid. Act V

Look into any man's heart you please, and you will always find, in every one, at least one black spot which he has to keep concealed.

Pillars of Society [*1877*]. *Act III*

The spirit of truth and the spirit of freedom — they are the pillars of society.

Ibid. Act IV

There can be no freedom or beauty about a home life that depends on borrowing and debt.

A Doll's House [*1879*]. *Act I*

A barrister's profession is such an uncertain thing, especially if he won't undertake unsavory cases.

A Doll's House. Act I

There are some people one loves best, and others whom one would almost always rather have as companions.

Ibid. Act II

To crave for happiness in this world is simply to be possessed by a spirit of revolt. What right have we to happiness?

Ghosts [*1881*]. *Act I*

It is not only what we have inherited from our fathers that exists again in us, but all sorts of old dead ideas and all kinds of old dead beliefs and things of that kind. They are not actually alive in us; but there they are dormant, all the same, and we can never be rid of them. Whenever I take up a newspaper and read it, I fancy I see ghosts creeping between the lines. There must be ghosts all over the world.

Ibid. Act II

I hold that man is in the right who is most closely in league with the future.

Letter to Georg Brandes [*January 3, 1882*]

A community is like a ship; every one ought to be prepared to take the helm.

An Enemy of the People [*1882*]. *Act I*

The most crying need in the humbler ranks of life is that they should be allowed some part in the direction of public affairs. That is what will develop their faculties and intelligence and self-respect.

Ibid. Act II

The public doesn't require any new ideas. The public is best served by the good, old-fashioned ideas it already has.

Ibid.

An editor cannot always act as he would prefer. He is often obliged to bow to the wishes of the public in unimportant matters. Politics are the most important thing in life — for a newspaper.

Ibid. Act III

The most dangerous enemy to truth

641

and freedom among us is the compact majority.

> *An Enemy of the People. Act. IV*

You should never wear your best trousers when you go out to fight for freedom and truth.

> *Ibid. Act V*

Rob the average man of his life-illusion, and you rob him of his happiness at the same stroke.

> *The Wild Duck* [*1884*]. *Act V*

Vine-leaves in his hair.

> *Hedda Gabler* [*1890*]. *Act II*

COUNT LYOF NIKOLAYE-VITCH TOLSTOI
[1828–1910]

The Frenchman is conceited from supposing himself mentally and physically to be inordinately fascinating both to men and to women. An Englishman is conceited on the ground of being a citizen of the best-constituted state in the world, and also because he as an Englishman always knows what is the correct thing to do, and knows that everything that he, as an Englishman, does do is indisputably the correct thing. An Italian is conceited from being excitable and easily forgetting himself and other people. A Russian is conceited precisely because he knows nothing and cares to know nothing, since he does not believe it possible to know anything fully. A conceited German is the worst of them all, and the most hardened of all, and the most repulsive of all; for he imagines that he possesses the truth in a science of his own invention, which is to him absolute truth.

> *War and Peace* [*1865–1872*].[1]
> *Part IX, Chap. 10*

The subject of history is the life of peoples and of humanity. To catch and pin down in words — that is, to describe directly the life, not only of humanity, but even of a single people, appears to be impossible.[2]

> *Ibid. Epilogue, Part II, Chap. 1*

[1] Translated by CONSTANCE GARNETT. Modern Library Giant.
[2] See Francis Parkman, page 628b.

If the will of every man were free, that is, if every man could act as he chose, the whole of history would be a tissue of disconnected accidents.

> *War and Peace. Epilogue, Part II,*
> *Chap. 8*

The most powerful weapon of ignorance — the diffusion of printed matter.

> *Ibid.*

Time is infinite movement without one moment of rest.

> *Ibid. Chap. 10*

All happy families resemble one another; every unhappy family is unhappy in its own fashion.

> *Anna Karenina* [*1875–1876*].[1]
> *Part I, Chap. 1*

War on the one hand is such a terrible, such an atrocious, thing, that no man, especially no Christian man, has the right to assume the responsibility of beginning it.

> *Ibid. Part VIII, Chap. 15*

Error is the force that welds men together; truth is communicated to men only by deeds of truth.

> *My Religion* [*1884*]. *Chap. 12*

The happiness of men consists in life. And life is in labor.

> *What Shall We Do Then?*
> [*1886*]. *Chap. 38*

The vocation of every man and woman is to serve other people.

> *Ibid. Chap. 40, Note*

The whole trade in the luxuries of life is brought into existence and supported by the requirements of women.

> *The Kreutzer Sonata* [*1890*].
> *Chap. 9*

His face was of that insipidly pleasing kind which women call "not bad-looking."

> *Ibid. Chap. 19*

The more is given the less the people will work for themselves, and the less

[1] Translated by NATHAN HASKELL DOLE [1852–1935].

they work the more their poverty will increase.[1]

Help for the Starving. Part III [January, 1892]

The only significance of life consists in helping to establish the kingdom of God; and this can be done only by means of the acknowledgment and profession of the truth by each one of us.

The Kingdom of God [1893]. Chap. 12

Art is a human activity having for its purpose the transmission to others of the highest and best feelings to which men have risen.

What Is Art? [1898]. Chap. 8

GEORGE WILLIAM CHILDS
[1829–1894]

Do not keep the alabaster boxes of your love and tenderness sealed up until your friends are dead. Fill their lives with sweetness. Speak approving, cheering words while their ears can hear them, and while their hearts can be thrilled and made happier by them.

A Creed

ROSCOE CONKLING
[1829–1888]

He will hew to the line of right, let the chips fall where they may.

Speech nominating General Grant for a third term, National Republican Convention, Chicago [June 5, 1880]

CHARLES GRAHAM HALPINE
("MILES O'REILLY")
[1829–1868]

And if asked what state he hails from,
    This our sole reply shall be,
"From near Appomattox Court-house,
    With its famous apple-tree." [2]

A Bumper to Grant. Stanza 8

[1] If you stop supporting that crowd, it will support itself. — SENECA [8 B.C.–A. D. 65]: *Epistle 20, 7*

[2] Quoted by Roscoe Conkling in his speech nominating Grant for the Presidency, Republican Convention [June, 1880].

There's never a bond, old friend, like this, —
We have drunk from the same canteen!

The Canteen. Stanza 1

The constellation of O'Ryan, ignorantly and falsely spelled Orion.

Subtitle of poem, Irish Astronomy

JOSEPH JEFFERSON
[1829–1905]

God bless the little church around the corner.[1]

In GEORGE MACADAM: *The Little Church Around the Corner [1925]*

SILAS WEIR MITCHELL
[1829–1914]

Death's but one more tomorrow.

Of One Who Seemed to Have Failed

Show me his friends and I the man shall know;
This wiser turn a larger wisdom lends:
Show me the books he loves and I shall know
The man far better than through mortal friends.

Books and the Man. Stanza 1

The first thing to be done by a biographer in estimating character is to examine the stubs of the victim's cheque-books.

Quoted in CUSHING: *Life of Sir William Osler [1925]. Vol. I, Chap. 21, Page 583*

JOSHUA DAVENPORT ROBINSON
[1829–1866]

I shall see his toys and his empty chair,
    And the horse he used to ride,

[1] Said after the death of George Holland, a well-loved old actor, in December, 1870. A certain New York rector declined to hold the funeral in his church and recommended Jefferson to "a little church around the corner." This was the Church of the Transfiguration, East 29th Street, popularly known ever since by that term of affection.

And they will speak with a silent speech
Of the little boy that died.
The Little Boy That Died.
Stanza 3

CARL SCHURZ
[1829–1906]

Ideals are like stars; you will not succeed in touching them with your hands. But like the seafaring man on the desert of waters, you choose them as your guides, and following them you will reach your destiny.[1]
Address, Faneuil Hall, Boston
[April 18, 1859]

You are underrating the President [Lincoln]. I grant that he lacks higher education and his manners are not in accord with European conceptions of the dignity of a chief magistrate. He is a well-developed child of nature and is not skilled in polite phrases and poses. But he is a man of profound feeling, correct and firm principles and incorruptible honesty. His motives are unquestionable, and he possesses to a remarkable degree the characteristic, God-given trait of this people, sound common sense.
Letter to Theodore Petrasch
[October, 1864]

Our country, right or wrong.[2] When right, to be kept right; when wrong, to be put right.
Address, Anti-Imperialistic Conference, Chicago [October 17, 1899]

HENRY TIMROD
[1829–1867]

Spring, with that nameless pathos in
the air
Which dwells with all things fair,
Spring, with her golden suns and silver
rain,
Is with us once again.
Spring. Stanza 1

[1] See Emerson, page 507b.
[2] See Charles Churchill, page 362b.

There is no holier spot of ground
Than where defeated valor lies,
By mourning beauty crowned!
Ode, Decorating the Graves of the Confederate Dead, Magnolia Cemetery, Charleston, South Carolina [1867]. Stanza 5

CHARLES DUDLEY WARNER
[1829–1900]

To own a bit of ground, to scratch it with a hoe, to plant seeds, and watch the renewal of life, — this is the commonest delight of the race, the most satisfactory thing a man can do.
My Summer in a Garden [1870].
Preliminary

Broad acres are a patent of nobility; and no man but feels more of a man in the world if he have a bit of ground that he can call his own. However small it is on the surface, it is four thousand miles deep; and that is a very handsome property.
Ibid.

What a man needs in gardening is a cast-iron back, with a hinge in it.
Ibid. Third Week

If you wish to save men from any particular vice, set up a tremendous cry of warning about some other, and they will all give their special efforts to the one to which attention is called.[1]
Ibid. Tenth Week

If you do things by the job, you are perpetually driven: the hours are scourges. If you work by the hour, you gently sail on the stream of Time, which is always bearing you on to the haven of Pay, whether you make any effort, or not.
Ibid. Eleventh Week

The toad, without which no garden would be complete.
Ibid. Thirteenth Week

[1] When classes are exasperated against each other, the peace of the world is always kept by striking a new note. Instantly the units part, and form in a new order, and those who were opposed are now side by side. — EMERSON: *Progress of Culture* [1883]

True it is that politics makes strange bedfellows.

> *My Summer in a Garden.*
> *Fifteenth Week*

What small potatoes we all are, compared with what we might be!

> *Ibid.*

Public opinion is stronger than the legislature, and nearly as strong as the ten commandments.

> *Ibid. Sixteenth Week*

The thing generally raised on city land is taxes.

> *Ibid.*

CHARLES HAMILTON AÏDÉ
[1830–1906]

I sit beside my lonely fire
And pray for wisdom yet:
For calmness to remember
Or courage to forget.

> *Remember or Forget*

CHARLOTTE ALINGTON BARNARD ("CLARIBEL")
[1830–1869]

I cannot sing the old songs I sang long
years ago,
For heart and voice would fail me, and
foolish tears would flow.

> *I Cannot Sing the Old Songs* [1]

Take back the heart that thou gavest,
What is my anguish to thee?
Take back the freedom thou cravest,
Leaving the fetters to me.

> *Take Back the Heart*

NOAH BROOKS
[1830–1903]

Conductor, when you receive a fare,
Punch in the presence of the passenjare.
A blue trip slip for an eight cent fare,
A buff trip slip for a six cent fare,
A pink trip slip for a five cent fare,
Punch in the presence of the passenjare.

[1] I can not sing the old songs now!
  It is not that I deem them low;
  'Tis that I can't remember how
    They go.
  C. S. CALVERLEY [1831–1884]: *Changed*

Punch, brothers, punch with care,
Punch in the presence of the passenjare.

> *Inspired by a notice to conductors, posted in New York horsecars* [1]

THOMAS EDWARD BROWN
[1830–1897]

A Garden is a lovesome thing, God wot!
  Rose plot,
  Fringed pool,
  Ferned grot —
  The veriest school
  Of Peace; and yet the fool
Contends that God is not —
Not God! in Gardens! when the eve is
  cool?
Nay, but I have a sign:
'Tis very sure God walks in mine.

> *My Garden*

EMILY DICKINSON [2]
[1830–1886]

This is my letter to the world,
That never wrote to me, —
The simple news that Nature told,
With simple majesty.

> *Part I, Life. Fly-leaf, Stanza 1*

Success is counted sweetest
By those who ne'er succeed.

> *Ibid. I, Stanza 1*

Our share of night to bear,
Our share of morning.

> *Ibid. II, Stanza 1*

Here a star, and there a star,
Some lose their way.
Here a mist, and there a mist,
Afterwards — day!

> *Ibid. Stanza 2*

If I can stop one heart from breaking,
I shall not live in vain;
If I can ease one life the aching,
Or cool one pain,
Or help one fainting robin

[1] The jingle attained celebrity following its publication in MARK TWAIN's *Literary Nightmare* (*Punch, Brothers, Punch*) [1876]. An account of its origin is given in A. B. PAINE's *Mark Twain* [1912], Vol. I, P. 555.
[2] *The Poems of Emily Dickinson*, edited by BIANCHI AND HAMPSON [1937].

Unto his nest again,
I shall not live in vain.
　　　　　　　　Part I, Life. VI

Much madness is divinest sense
To a discerning eye;
Much sense the starkest madness.
'Tis the majority
In this, as all, prevails.
Assent, and you are sane;
Demur, — you're straightway danger-
　　ous,
And handled with a chain.
　　　　　　　　Ibid. XI

The soul selects her own society,
Then shuts the door.
　　　　　　　　Ibid. XIII, Stanza 1

To fight aloud is very brave,
But gallanter, I know,
Who charge within the bosom,
The cavalry of woe.
　　　　　　　　Ibid. XVI, Stanza 1

I taste a liquor never brewed,
From tankards scooped in pearl.
　　　　　　　　Ibid. XX, Stanza 1

Inebriate of air am I,
And debauchee of dew,
Reeling, through endless summer days,
From inns of molten blue.
　　　　　　　　Ibid. Stanza 2

Till seraphs swing their snowy hats,
And saints to windows run,
To see the little tippler
Leaning against the sun!
　　　　　　　　Ibid. Stanza 4

He ate and drank the precious words,
His spirit grew robust;
He knew no more that he was poor,
Nor that his frame was dust.
He danced along the dingy days,
And this bequest of wings
Was but a book. What liberty
A loosened spirit brings.
　　　　　　　　Ibid. XXI

I'm nobody! Who are you?
Are you nobody, too?
Then there's a pair of us — don't tell!
They'd banish us, you know.
　　　　　　　　Ibid. XXVII, Stanza 1

How dreary to be somebody!
How public, like a frog

To tell your name the livelong day
To an admiring bog!
　　　　　　　　Part I, Life. XXVII, Stanza 2

Hope is the thing with feathers
That perches in the soul,
And sings the tune without the words,
And never stops at all.
　　　　　　　　Ibid. XXXII, Stanza 1

For each ecstatic instant
We must an anguish pay
In keen and quivering ratio
To the ecstasy.
　　　　　　　　Ibid. XXXVII, Stanza 1

The thought beneath so slight a film
Is more distinctly seen, —
As laces just reveal the surge,
Or mists the Apennine.
　　　　　　　　Ibid. XL

The soul unto itself
Is an imperial friend, —
Or the most agonizing spy
An enemy could send.
　　　　　　　　Ibid. XLI, Stanza 1

God gave a loaf to every bird,
But just a crumb to me.
　　　　　　　　Ibid. LIII, Stanza 1

Just lost when I was saved!
Just felt the world go by!
Just girt me for the onset with eternity,
When breath blew back,
And on the other side
I heard recede the disappointed tide!
　　　　　　　　Ibid. LXXXIII, Stanza 1

A word is dead
When it is said,
　Some say.
I say it just
Begins to live
　That day.
　　　　　　　　Ibid. LXXXIX

My life closed twice before its close;
It yet remains to see
If Immortality unveil
A third event to me.

So huge, so hopeless to conceive,
As these that twice befell.
Parting is all we know of heaven,
And all we need of hell.
　　　　　　　　Ibid. XCVI

We never know how high we are
Till we are called to rise;
And then, if we are true to plan,
Our statures touch the skies.
Part I, Life. XCVII, Stanza 1

There is no frigate like a book
To take us lands away,
Nor any coursers like a page
Of prancing poetry.

This traverse may the poorest take
Without oppress of toll;
How frugal is the chariot
That bears a human soul!
Ibid. XCIX

A bird came down the walk:
He did not know I saw;
He bit an angle-worm in halves
And ate the fellow, raw.
Part II, Nature. XXIII, Stanza 1

God made a little gentian;
It tried to be a rose
And failed, and all the summer laughed.
Ibid. XLVIII

Besides the autumn poets sing,
A few prosaic days
A little this side of the snow
And that side of the haze.
Ibid. XLIX, Stanza 1

The pedigree of honey
Does not concern the bee;
A clover, any time, to him
Is aristocracy.
Ibid. LVI

Some keep the Sabbath going to church;
I keep it staying at home,
With a bobolink for a chorister,
And an orchard for a dome.
Ibid. LVII, Stanza 1

I'll tell you how the sun rose, —
A ribbon at a time.
The steeples swam in amethyst,
The news like squirrels ran.
Ibid. LXXIII, Stanza 1

These are the days when birds come
back,
A very few, a bird or two,
To take a backward look.
Ibid. LXXVIII, Stanza 1

These are the days when skies put on
The old, old sophistries of June, —
A blue and gold mistake.
Part II, Nature. LXXVIII,
Stanza 2

The morns are meeker than they were,
The nuts are getting brown;
The berry's cheek is plumper,
The rose is out of town.
Ibid. LXXIX, Stanza 1

The sky is low, the clouds are mean,
A travelling flake of snow
Across a barn or through a rut
Debates if it will go.

A narrow wind complains all day
How some one treated him;
Nature, like us, is sometimes caught
Without her diadem.
Ibid. LXXX

There's a certain slant of light,
On winter afternoons,
That oppresses, like the weight
Of cathedral tunes.
Ibid. LXXXII, Stanza 1

Alter? When the hills do.
Falter? When the sun
Question if his glory
Be the perfect one.
Part III, Love. III, Stanza 1

Elysium is as far as to
The very nearest room,
If in that room a friend await
Felicity or doom.
Ibid. IV, Stanza 1

"Going to him! Happy letter! Tell
him —
Tell him the page I didn't write;
Tell him I only said the syntax,
And left the verb and pronoun out."
Ibid. XXIII, Stanza 1

Love is anterior to life,
Posterior to death,
Initial of creation, and
The exponent of breath.
Ibid. XXXVII

Heart, we will forget him!
You and I, to-night!
You may forget the warmth he gave,
I will forget the light.
XLVII, Stanza 1

That short, potential stir
That each can make but once,
That bustle so illustrious
'Tis almost consequence,

Is the *éclat* of death.
Oh, thou unknown renown
That not a beggar would accept,
Had he the power to spurn!
Part IV, Time and Eternity. XIII

I never saw a moor,
I never saw the sea;
Yet know I how the heather looks,
And what a wave must be.

I never spoke with God,
Nor visited in heaven;
Yet certain am I of the spot
As if the chart were given.
Ibid. XVII

The sweeping up the heart,
And putting love away
We shall not want to use again
Until eternity.
Ibid. XXII, Stanza 2

Afraid? Of whom am I afraid?
Not death; for who is he?
The porter of my father's lodge
As much abasheth me.
Ibid. XXIV, Stanza 1

Because I could not stop for Death,
He kindly stopped for me;
The carriage held but just ourselves
And Immortality.
Ibid. XXVII, Stanza 1

If I shouldn't be alive
When the robins come,
Give the one in red cravat
A memorial crumb.
Ibid. XXXVII, Stanza 1

Adventure most unto itself
The Soul condemned to be;
Attended by a Single Hound —
Its own Identity.
Part V, The Single Hound. I

Glory is that bright tragic thing,
That for an instant
Means Dominion,
Warms some poor name
That never felt the sun,

Gently replacing
In oblivion.
Part V, The Single Hound. XX

This quiet Dust was Gentlemen and
    Ladies,
  And Lads and Girls;
Was laughter and ability and sighing,
  And frocks and curls.
Ibid. LXXIV

Eden is that old-fashioned House
We dwell in every day,
Without suspecting our abode
Until we drive away.
Ibid. CVIII

Of course I prayed —
And did God care?
He cared as much
As on the air
A bird had stamped her foot
And cried "Give me!"
Part VI, Further Poems. 2,
XXXVIII, Stanza 1

A bayonet's contrition
Is nothing to the Dead!
Part VII, Additional Poems. 1, I,
Stanza 4

I thought that nature was enough
Till human nature came,
But that the other did absorb
As firmament a flame.
New Poems.[1] 149, Stanza 1

I tasted careless then.
I did not know the wine
Came once a world, did you?
Oh, had you told me so,
This thirst would blister easier now!
Ibid. 292, Stanza 3

The dying is a trifle, past,
But living — this include
The dying multifold without
The respite to be dead.
Ibid. 305, Stanza 2

But blossom were I,
I would rather be
Thy moment
Than a bee's eternity.
Ibid. 311, Stanza 2

The poets light but lamps,
Themselves go out;

[1] *Bolts of Melody* [1945] edited by Mabel
Loomis Todd and Millicent Todd Bingham.

The wicks they stimulate,
If vital light

Inhere as do the suns,
Each age a lens
Disseminating their
Circumference.
> *New Poems. 432*

If I read a book and it makes my whole body so cold no fire can ever warm me, I know that is poetry. If I feel physically as if the top of my head were taken off, I know that is poetry. These are the only ways I know it. Is there any other way?
> *Quoted in Life and Letters of Emily Dickinson* [*1924*], *by* MARTHA GILBERT DICKINSON BIANCHI

PAUL HAMILTON HAYNE
[1830–1886]

I see the cloud-born squadrons of the gale,
Their lines of rain like glittering spears deprest.
> *A Storm in the Distance. Stanza 1*

JAMES PROCTOR KNOTT
[1830–1911]

Duluth! The word fell upon my ear with a peculiar and indescribable charm, like the gentle murmur of a low fountain stealing forth in the midst of roses, or the soft sweet accent of an angel's whisper in the bright, joyous dream of sleeping innocence. 'Twas the name for which my soul had panted for years, as the hart panteth for the water-brooks.[1]
> *Speech on the St. Croix & Bayfield Railroad Bill, U. S. House of Representatives* [*January 27, 1871*]

[1] Congressman Knott's ironic eulogy of Duluth — then a mere wilderness village — helped to defeat the railroad bill and, paradoxically, furnished Duluth its title of "zenith city of the unsalted seas."

CHRISTINA GEORGINA ROSSETTI
[1830–1894]

Hope is like a harebell trembling from its birth,
Love is like a rose the joy of all the earth,
Faith is like a lily lifted high and white,
Love is like a lovely rose the world's delight.
Harebells and sweet lilies show a thornless growth,
But the rose with all its thorns excels them both.
> *Hope Is Like a Harebell*

Does the road wind up-hill all the way?
Yes, to the very end.
> *Up-Hill* [*1861*]. *Stanza 1*

My heart is like a singing bird.
> *A Birthday* [*1861*]. *Stanza 1*

When I am dead, my dearest,
　Sing no sad songs for me;
Plant thou no roses at my head,
　Nor shady cypress tree.
> *Song* [*1862*]. *Stanza 1*

I shall not see the shadows,
I shall not feel the rain.
> *Ibid. Stanza 2*

Remember me when I am gone away,
Gone far away into the silent land.
> *Remember* [*1862*]

Better by far you should forget and smile
Than that you should remember and be sad.
> *Ibid.*

All earth's full rivers can not fill
The sea, that drinking thirsteth still.
> *By the Sea*

One day in the country
Is worth a month in town.
> *Summer*

O Earth, lie heavily upon her eyes;
Seal her sweet eyes weary of watching, Earth.
> *Rest* [*1862*]

Silence more musical than any song.
> *Ibid.*

In the bleak mid-winter
　Frosty wind made moan,
Earth stood hard as iron,

Water like a stone;
Snow had fallen, snow on snow,
Snow on snow,
In the bleak mid-winter,
Long ago.
Mid-Winter

ALEXANDER SMITH
[1830–1867]

Some books are drenchèd sands
On which a great soul's wealth lies all
in heaps,
Like a wrecked argosy.
A Life Drama [1853]. *Sc. 2*

Like a pale martyr in his shirt of fire.
Ibid.

In winter, when the dismal rain
Came down in slanting lines,
And Wind, that grand old harper, smote
His thunder-harp of pines.
Ibid.

A poem round and perfect as a star.
Ibid.

The saddest thing that can befall a soul
Is when it loses faith in God and
woman.
Ibid. Sc. 12

The soul of man is like the rolling
world,
One half in day, the other dipt in night;
The one has music and the flying cloud,
The other, silence and the wakeful
stars.
Horton

Each time we love,
We turn a nearer and a broader mark
To that keen archer, Sorrow, and he
strikes.
A Boy's Dream

Time has fallen asleep in the afternoon sunshine.
Dreamthorp [1863]. *First Essay*

It is not of so much consequence
what you say, as how you say it. Memorable sentences are memorable on account of some single irradiating word.
Ibid. On the Writing of Essays

The world is not so much in need
of new thoughts as that when thought
grows old and worn with usage it
should, like current coin, be called in,
and, from the mint of genius, reissued
fresh and new.
*Dreamthorp. On the
Writing of Essays*

Death is the ugly fact which Nature
has to hide, and she hides it well.
*Ibid. Of Death and the
Fear of Dying*

Everything is sweetened by risk.
Ibid.

In life there is nothing more unexpected and surprising than the arrivals
and departures of pleasure. If we find
it in one place today, it is vain to seek
it there tomorrow. You can not lay a
trap for it.
Ibid.

A man's real possession is his memory. In nothing else is he rich, in nothing else is he poor.
Ibid.

Scotland had invaded England more
than once, but the blue bonnets never
went over the border [1] so triumphantly
as when they did so in the shape of
songs and ballads.
Ibid. William Dunbar

Just consider what a world this would
be if ruled by the best thoughts of men
of letters! Ignorance would die at once,
war would cease, taxation would be
lightened, not only every Frenchman,
but every man in the world, would have
his hen in the pot.[2]
Ibid. Men of Letters

To be occasionally quoted is the only
fame I care for.
Ibid.

A man gazing on the stars is proverbially at the mercy of the puddles
on the road.
Ibid.

Trifles make up the happiness or the
misery of mortal life. The majority of
men slip into their graves without having encountered on their way thither

[1] When the Blue Bonnets came over the
Border. — SCOTT: *The Monastery* [1820],
Chap. 25, Border Ballad
[2] See Henry IV, page 115a–115b.
A chicken in every pot. — *Republican cam-
paign slogan* [1932]

any signal catastrophe or exaltation of fortune or feeling.

Dreamthorp. Men of Letters

The skin of the man of letters is peculiarly sensitive to the bite of the critical mosquito; and he lives in a climate in which such mosquitoes swarm. He is seldom stabbed to the heart — he is often killed by pin-pricks.

Ibid.

Every man's road in life is marked by the graves of his personal likings.

Ibid. On the Importance of a Man to Himself

In the wide arena of the world, failure and success are not accidents as we so frequently suppose, but the strictest justice. If you do your fair day's work, you are certain to get your fair day's wage — in praise or pudding, whichever happens to suit your taste.

Ibid.

The great man is the man who does a thing for the first time.

Ibid.

How deeply seated in the human heart is the liking for gardens and gardening.[1]

Ibid. Books and Gardens

A man does not plant a tree for himself, he plants it for posterity.

Ibid.

A good portrait is a kind of biography, and neither painter nor biographer can carry out his task satisfactorily unless he be admitted behind the scenes.

Ibid. On Vagabonds

CHARLES STUART CALVERLEY
[1831–1884]

I have a liking old
For thee, though manifold
Stories, I know, are told,
Not to thy credit!

Ode to Tobacco. Stanza 2

I sit alone at present, dreaming darkly of a Dun.

In the Gloaming

[1] See Charles Dudley Warner, page 644b.

The farmer's daughter hath soft brown hair

(*Butter and eggs and a pound of cheese*)

And I met with a ballad, I can't say where,

That wholly consisted of lines like these.

Ballad, after William Morris [The Auld Wife]. Part I, Stanza 6

And this song is considered a perfect gem,

And as to the meaning, it's what you please.

Ibid. Part II, Stanza 4

Mine was a joke for the ages;
  Full of intricate meaning and pith;
A feast for your scholars and sages —
  How it would have rejoiced Sydney Smith!
'Tis such thoughts that ennoble a mortal;
  And, singling him out from the herd,
Fling wide immortality's portal —
  — But what was the word?

Flight. Stanza 9

As the flight of a bird in the air
Is the flight of a joke.

Ibid. Stanza 10

Forever; 'tis a single word!
  Our rude forefathers deemed it two:
Can you imagine so absurd
  A view?

Forever

When the forest-nymphs are beading
  Fern and flower with silvery dew
My infallible proceeding
  Is to wake, and think of you.

The 14th of February

MARY MAPES DODGE
[1831–1905]

Whimpy, little Whimpy,
  Cried so much one day,
His grandma couldn't stand it,
  And his mother ran away.

Little Whimpy. Stanza 1

Whenever a snowflake leaves the sky,
It turns and turns to say "Good-by!
Good-by, dear clouds, so cool and gray!"

Then lightly travels on its way.
Snowflakes
Life is a mystery as deep as ever death
can be;
Yet oh, how sweet it is to us, this life
we live and see!
The Two Mysteries. Stanza 3
But I believe that God is overhead;
And as life is to the living, so death is to
the dead.
Ibid. Stanza 5

JAMES ABRAM GARFIELD
[1831–1881]

Fellow-citizens! God reigns, and the
Government at Washington still lives!
*Speech on Assassination of
Lincoln, New York [April 15,
1865]*
For mere vengeance I would do nothing. This nation is too great to look for
mere revenge. But for the security of
the future I would do everything.
Ibid.
I am not willing that this discussion
should close without mention of the
value of a true teacher. Give me a log
hut, with only a simple bench, Mark
Hopkins [1] on one end and I on the
other, and you may have all the buildings, apparatus and libraries without
him.
*Address to Williams College
Alumni, New York [December
28, 1871] [2]*

HELEN HUNT JACKSON
[1831–1885]

O suns and skies and clouds of June,
And flowers of June together,

[1] Mark Hopkins [1802–1887], president of
Williams College [1836–1872], and president
of the American Board of Commissioners for
Foreign Missions [1857–1881].
For Education is, Making Men;
So is it now, so was it when
Mark Hopkins sat on one end of a log
And James Garfield sat on the other.
ARTHUR GUITERMAN [1871–1943]:
Education
[2] In BURKE A. HINSDALE: *President Gar-
field and Education* [1882], P. 43.

Ye cannot rival for one hour
October's bright blue weather.
*October's Bright Blue Weather.
Stanza 1*
Find me the men on earth who care
Enough for faith or creed today
To seek a barren wilderness
For simple liberty to pray.
The Pilgrim Forefathers. Stanza 5
On the king's gate the moss grew gray;
The king came not. They called him
dead
And made his eldest son one day
Slave in his father's stead.
Coronation. Stanza 10
Oh, write of me, not "Died in bitter
pains,"
But "Emigrated to another star!"
Emigravit
Father, I scarcely dare to pray,
So clear I see, now it is done,
How I have wasted half my day,
And left my work but just begun.
A Last Prayer. Stanza 1
My body, eh. Friend Death, how now?
Why all this tedious pomp of writ?
Thou hast reclaimed it sure and slow
For half a century, bit by bit.
Habeas Corpus.[1] Stanza 1
There is nothing so skilful in its own
defence as imperious pride.
Ramona [1884]. Chap. 13
Wounded vanity knows when it is
mortally hurt; and limps off the field,
piteous, all disguises thrown away. But
pride carries its banner to the last.
Ibid.
There cannot be found in the animal
kingdom a bat, or any other creature, so
blind in its own range of circumstance
and connection, as the greater majority
of human beings are in the bosoms of
their families.
Ibid.
That indescribable expression peculiar to people who hope they have not
been asleep, but know they have.
Ibid. Chap. 14

[1] Her last poem, left unfinished.

EDWARD ROBERT BULWER LYTTON, EARL OF LYTTON ("OWEN MEREDITH") [1]
[1831–1891]

Love thou the rose, yet leave it on its stem.[2]
> *The Wanderer* [*1857*]. *Prologue,*
> *Part I, 19*

But I am sick of all the din
That's made in praising Verdi,
Who only know a violin
Is not a hurdy-gurdy.
> *The Wanderer in France.*
> *"Prensus in Aegaeo"*

My life is a torn book. But at the end
A little page, quite fair, is saved, my friend,
Where thou didst write thy name.
> *The Wanderer in Holland.*
> *Jacqueline*

The heart of a man's like that delicate weed
Which requires to be trampled on, boldly indeed,
Ere it gives forth the fragrance you wish to extract.
> *Lucile* [*1860*]. *Part I, Canto 1, IV*

Whene'er I hear French spoken as I approve,
I feel myself quietly falling in love.
> *Ibid. Canto 2, XII*

We may live without poetry, music and art;
We may live without conscience and live without heart;
We may live without friends; we may live without books;
But civilized man can not live without cooks.
> *Ibid. XIX*

He may live without books, — what is knowledge but grieving?
He may live without hope, — what is hope but deceiving?
He may live without love, — what is passion but pining?

But where is the man that can live without dining?
> *Lucile. Part I, Canto 2, XXIV*

The face the most fair to our vision allowed
Is the face we encounter and lose in the crowd.
The thought that most thrills our existence is one
Which, before we can frame it in language, is gone.
> *Ibid. Canto 5, I*

Ay, there are some good things in life, that fall not away with the rest.
And, of all best things upon earth, I hold that a faithful friend is the best.
> *Last Words of a Sensitive*
> *Second-Rate Poet*

Talk not of genius baffled. Genius is master of man.
Genius does what it must, and talent does what it can.
> *Ibid.*

PHILIP HENRY SHERIDAN
[1831–1888]

The only good Indians I ever saw were dead.[1]
> *Remark at Fort Cobb, Indian*
> *Territory* [*January, 1869*]

ROWLAND HOWARD
[*Floruit* 1876]

Waste not, want not, is a maxim I would teach.
Let your watchword be dispatch, and practise what you preach;
Do not let your chances like sunbeams pass you by,
For you never miss the water till the well runs dry.
> *You Never Miss the Water* [2]

---

[1] Lord Lytton, the Viceroy, who still lives in the literary hall of fame as the author of Lucile — a vast, stale Victorian piece of poetry. — WILLIAM E. WOODWARD: *Meet General Grant* [1928], *Part 4, Chap. 30*

[2] See Emerson, page 504a.

[1] Edward Sylvester Ellis [1840–1916] reported that after Custer's fight with Black Kettle's band of Cheyenne Indians, the Comanche Chief Toch-a-way (Turtle Dove) was presented to General Sheridan. The Indian said: "Me Toch-a-way, me good Indian." The General's reply, as reported by Ellis, is given in the text; the phrase is more often heard in the version "The only good Indian is a dead Indian."

[2] In *Peterson's Magazine,* 1876.

LOUISA MAY ALCOTT
[1832–1888]

Christmas won't be Christmas without any presents.
> *Little Women* [*1868*]. *Chap. 1*

A little kingdom I possess,
Where thoughts and feelings dwell;
And very hard the task I find
  Of governing it well.
> Quoted in EDNAH D. CHENEY:
> *Louisa May Alcott, Her Life,
> Letters, and Journals* [*1889*].
> *Chap. 3, My Kingdom,*[1] *Stanza 1*

I do not ask for any crown
  But that which all may win;
Nor try to conquer any world
  Except the one within.
> *Ibid. Stanza 4*

I had a pleasant time with my mind, for it was happy.
> *Ibid.*

Resolved to take Fate by the throat and shake a living out of her.
> *Ibid.*

For such as he there is no death; —
His life the eternal life commands;
Above man's aims his nature rose.
The wisdom of a just content
Made one small spot a continent,
And tuned to poetry Life's prose.[2]
> *Ibid. Chap. 7, Thoreau's Flute,*[3]
> *Stanza 2*

My definition [of a philosopher] is of a man up in a balloon, with his family and friends holding the ropes which confine him to earth and trying to haul him down.
> *Ibid. Chap. 10*

Now I am beginning to live a little, and feel less like a sick oyster at low tide.
> *Ibid. Chap. 11*

Philosophers sit in their sylvan hall
And talk of the duties of man,
Of Chaos and Cosmos, Hegel and Kant,
With the Oversoul well in the van;
All on their hobbies they amble away

And a terrible dust they make;
Disciples devout both gaze and adore,
As daily they listen and bake.
> *Philosophers* [1]

ELIZABETH AKERS ALLEN
[1832–1911]

Backward, turn backward, O Time, in
  your flight,
Make me a child again just for tonight!
> *Rock Me to Sleep* [*1860*].
> *Stanza 1*

Behold, we live through all things —
  famine, thirst,
Bereavement, pain; all grief and
  misery,
All woe and sorrow; life inflicts its
  worst
On soul and body — but we can not die,
Though we be sick, and tired, and faint,
  and worn, —
Lo, all things can be borne!
> *Endurance. Stanza 5*

  Unremembered and afar
I watched you as I watched a star,
Through darkness struggling into view,
And loved you better than you knew.
> *Left Behind. Stanza 5*

Let all unselfish spirits heed
The story of Johnny Appleseed.
He had another and prouder name
In far New England, whence he came,
But by this title, and this alone,
Was the kindly wanderer loved and
  known.
> *Johnny Appleseed.*[2] *Stanza 1*

Carve not upon a stone when I am dead
The praises which remorseful mourners
  give

---

[1] Written at the age of thirteen.
[2] The word "tuned" is frequently misprinted as "turned."
[3] In *The Atlantic Monthly*, September, 1863.

[1] Quoted in FLORENCE WHITING BROWN: *Alcott and the Concord School of Philosophy* [1926], *P. 46.*
[2] John Chapman [1774–1847].
Remember Johnny Appleseed,
All ye who love the apple;
He served his kind by Word and Deed,
In God's grand greenwood chapel.
  WILLIAM HENRY VENABLE [1836–1918]:
> *Johnny Appleseed, St. 25*

See Vachel Lindsay, page 903b.

To women's graves — a tardy recompense —
But speak them while I live.[1]
           Till Death. Stanza 6

SIR EDWIN ARNOLD
[1832–1904]

Shall any gazer see with mortal eyes,
Or any searcher know by mortal mind?
Veil after veil will lift — but there must
   be
Veil upon veil behind.
        The Light of Asia [1879].
                Book VIII

Weep awhile, if ye are fain, —
Sunshine still must follow rain;
Only not at death, for death,
Now I know, is that first breath
Which our souls draw when we enter
Life, which is of all life centre.
        After Death In Arabia

Nor ever once ashamed
So we be named
Press-men; Slaves of the Lamp; Serv-
   ants of Light.
      The Tenth Muse. Stanza 18

Not an eye, however dull,
But seems — somewhere — beautiful.
      Facies Non Omnibus Una

We are they who will not take
   From palace, priest, or code,
A meaner Law than "Brotherhood" —
   A lower Lord than God.
     *Armageddon: A War Song of
       the Future. Stanza 4*

[1] I fancy when I go to rest some one will
   bring to light
Some kindly word or goodly act long buried
   out of sight;
But, if it's all the same to you, just give to
   me, instead,
The bouquets while I'm living and the knocking when I'm dead.
     Louis Edwin Thayer [1878–   ]:
       Of Post-Mortem Praises, St. 1
If with pleasure you are viewing any work a
   man is doing,
If you like him or you love him, tell him now.
.   .   .   .
Do not wait till life is over and he's underneath the clover,
For he cannot read his tombstone when he's
   dead!
     Berton Braley [1882–   ]: *Do It
          Now, St. 1 and 2*

Somewhere there waiteth in this world
   of ours
For one lone soul, another lonely soul —
Each chasing each through all the
   weary hours,
And meeting strangely at one sudden
   goal;
Then blend they — like green leaves
   with golden flowers,
Into one beautiful and perfect whole —
And life's long night is ended, and the
   way
Lies open onward to eternal day.[1]
                Destiny

We are the voices of the wandering
   wind,
Which moan for rest and rest can never
   find;
Lo! as the wind is, so is mortal life,
A moan, a sigh, a sob, a storm, a strife.
           The Deva's Song

WILLIAM CROSWELL DOANE
[1832–1913]

Their Lent is over, and their Easter
   won.
                Death

I am quite sure he thinks that I am
   God —
Since he is God on whom each one de-
   pends
For life and all things that His bounty
   sends —
My dear old dog, most constant of all
   friends.
                Cluny

LEWIS CARROLL
(CHARLES LUTWIDGE
DODGSON)
[1832–1898]

All in the golden afternoon
   Full leisurely we glide
For both our oars, with little skill
   By little arms are plied

[1] A sublime hope cheers ever the faithful
heart, that elsewhere, in other regions of the
universal powers, souls are now acting, enduring and daring, which can love us, and which
we can love. — Emerson: *Friendship* [1841]

While little hands make vain pretence
Our wanderings to guide.
> *Alice's Adventures in Wonderland* [*1865*].   *Introduction, Stanza 1*

"What is the use of a book," thought Alice, "without pictures or conversations?"
> *Ibid. Chap. 1*

Do cats eat bats? . . . Do bats eat cats?
> *Ibid.*

Curiouser and curiouser!
> *Ibid. Chap. 2*

How doth the little crocodile
Improve his shining tail,
And pour the waters of the Nile
On every golden scale! [1]

How cheerfully he seems to grin,
How neatly spreads his claws,
And welcomes little fishes in
With gently smiling jaws!
> *Ibid.*

"I'll be judge, I'll be jury," said cunning old Fury; "I'll try the whole cause, and condemn you to death."
> *Ibid. Chap. 3*

Oh my fur and whiskers!
> *Ibid. Chap. 4*

"I can't explain *myself*, I'm afraid, sir," said Alice, "because I'm not myself, you see."

"I don't see," said the Caterpillar.
> *Ibid. Chap. 5*

"You are old, Father William," the young man said,
"And your hair has become very white;
And yet you incessantly stand on your head —
Do you think, at your age, it is right?" [2]
> *Ibid. Stanza 1*

"In my youth," said his father, "I took to the law,
And argued each case with my wife;
And the muscular strength, which it gave to my jaw,
Has lasted the rest of my life."
> *Ibid. Stanza 6*

"I have answered three questions, and that is enough,"

[1] See Isaac Watts, page 302b.
[2] See Southey, page 426a.

Said his father. "Don't give yourself airs!
Do you think I can listen all day to such stuff?
Be off, or I'll kick you down-stairs!"
> *Alice's Adventures in Wonderland.*
> *Chap. 5, Stanza 8*

"I shall sit here," he said, "on and off, for days and days."
> *Ibid. Chap. 6*

"If everybody minded their own business," said the Duchess in a hoarse growl, "the world would go round a deal faster than it does."
> *Ibid.*

"Talking of axes," said the Duchess, "chop off her head!"
> *Ibid.*

Speak roughly to your little boy,
And beat him when he sneezes:
He only does it to annoy,
Because he knows it teases.
> *Ibid.*

"All right," said the Cat; and this time it vanished quite slowly, beginning with the end of the tail, and ending with the grin, which remained some time after the rest of it had gone.
> *Ibid.*

"Then you should say what you mean," the March Hare went on.

"I do," Alice hastily replied; "at least — at least I mean what I say — that's the same thing, you know."

"Not the same thing a bit!" said the Hatter. "Why, you might just as well say that 'I see what I eat' is the same thing as 'I eat what I see'!"
> *Ibid. Chap. 7*

"It was the *best* butter," the March Hare meekly replied.
> *Ibid.*

Twinkle, twinkle, little bat!
How I wonder what you're at!
Up above the world you fly,
Like a tea-tray in the sky.
> *Ibid.*

"Take some more tea," the March Hare said to Alice, very earnestly.

"I've had nothing yet," Alice replied in an offended tone: "so I can't take more."

"You mean you can't take *less*," said the Hatter: "it's very easy to take *more* than nothing."

Alice's Adventures in Wonderland.
Chap. 7

They drew all manner of things — everything that begins with an M . . . , such as mouse-traps, and the moon, and memory, and muchness — you know you say things are "much of a muchness."

Ibid.

The Queen turned crimson with fury, and after glaring at her for a moment like a wild beast, began screaming, "Off with her head! Off with —"

Ibid. Chap. 8

"Tut, tut, child," said the Duchess. "Everything's got a moral if only you can find it."

Ibid. Chap. 9

And the moral of that is — "Oh, 'tis love, 'tis love, that makes the world go round!"

Ibid.

Take care of the sense and the sounds will take care of themselves.

Ibid.

"We called him Tortoise because he taught us," said the Mock Turtle angrily. "Really you are very dull!"

Ibid.

"Reeling and Writhing, of course, to begin with," the Mock Turtle replied, "and the different branches of Arithmetic — Ambition, Distraction, Uglification, and Derision."

Ibid.

"Will you walk a little faster?" said a whiting to a snail,
"There's a porpoise close behind us, and he's treading on my tail."

Ibid. Chap. 10

"Will you, won't you, will you, won't you, will you join the dance?"

Ibid.

"The further off from England the nearer is to France —
Then turn not pale, beloved snail, but come and join the dance."

Ibid. Stanza 3

'Tis the voice of the Lobster: I heard him declare
"You have baked me too brown, I must sugar my hair." [1]

Alice's Adventures in Wonderland.
Chap. 10, Stanza 3

Soup of the evening, beautiful soup!

Ibid.

Sentence first — verdict afterwards.

Ibid. Chap. 12

Child of the pure, unclouded brow
And dreaming eyes of wonder!
Though time be fleet and I and thou
Are half a life asunder,
Thy loving smile will surely hail
The love-gift of a fairy-tale.

Alice Through the Looking-Glass [*1872*]. *Introduction, Stanza 1*

"The horror of that moment," the King went on, "I shall never, *never* forget!"

"You will, though," the Queen said, "if you don't make a memorandum of it."

Ibid. Chap. 1

'Twas brillig, and the slithy toves
Did gyre and gimble in the wabe;
All mimsy were the borogoves,
And the mome raths outgrabe.

Ibid. Jabberwocky, Stanza 1

"Beware the Jabberwock, my son!
The jaws that bite, the claws that catch!
Beware the Jubjub bird, and shun
The frumious Bandersnatch!"

Ibid. Stanza 2

And, as in uffish thought he stood,
The Jabberwock, with eyes of flame,
Came whiffling through the tulgey wood,
And burbled as it came!

Ibid. Stanza 4

One, two! One, two! And through and through
The vorpal blade went snicker-snack!
He left it dead, and with its head
He went galumphing back.

Ibid. Stanza 5

"And hast thou slain the Jabberwock?
Come to my arms, my beamish boy!

[1] See Isaac Watts, page 302b.

O frabjous day! Callooh! Callay!"
  He chortled in his joy.
        Alice Through the Looking-Glass.
          Chap. 1, Jabberwocky, Stanza 6

Curtsey while you're thinking what
to say. It saves time.
                Ibid. Chap. 2

"Now! Now!" cried the Queen.
"Faster! Faster!"
                        Ibid.

"A slow sort of country!" said the
Queen. "Now, *here,* you see, it takes all
the running you can do, to keep in the
same place. If you want to get somewhere else, you must run at least twice
as fast as that!"
                        Ibid.

Speak in French when you can't
think of the English for a thing — turn
out your toes when you walk — and remember who you are!
                        Ibid.

"If you think we're wax-works," he
said, "you ought to pay, you know.
Wax-works weren't made to be looked
at for nothing. Nohow!"
                Ibid. Chap. 4

"Contrariwise," continued Tweedledee, "if it was so, it might be; and if it
were so, it would be; but as it isn't, it
ain't. That's logic."
                        Ibid.

The sun was shining on the sea,
  Shining with all his might:
He did his very best to make
  The billows smooth and bright —
And this was odd, because it was
  The middle of the night.
        Ibid. The Walrus and the
          Carpenter, Stanza 1

The Walrus and the Carpenter
  Were walking close at hand:
They wept like anything to see
  Such quantities of sand:
"If this were only cleared away,"
  They said, "it would be grand!"
                Ibid. Stanza 4

"If seven maids with seven mops
  Swept it for half a year,
Do you suppose," the Walrus said,
  "That they could get it clear?"

"I doubt it," said the Carpenter,
  And shed a bitter tear.
        Alice Through the Looking-
          Glass. Chap. 4, The Walrus and
          the Carpenter, Stanza 5

"O Oysters, come and walk with us!"
  The Walrus did beseech.
"A pleasant walk, a pleasant talk,
  Along the briny beach."
                Ibid. Stanza 6

And thick and fast they came at last,
  And more, and more, and more —
All hopping through the frothy waves,
  And scrambling to the shore.
                Ibid. Stanza 9

"The time has come," the Walrus said,
  "To talk of many things:
Of shoes — and ships — and sealing-
  wax —
Of cabbages — and kings —
And why the sea is boiling hot —
  And whether pigs have wings."
                Ibid. Stanza 11

"But wait a bit," the Oysters cried,
  "Before we have our chat;
For some of us are out of breath,
  And all of us are fat!"
                Ibid. Stanza 12

The Carpenter said nothing but
  "The butter's spread too thick!"
                Ibid. Stanza 16

"I weep for you," the Walrus said:
  "I deeply sympathize."
With sobs and tears he sorted out
  Those of the largest size,
Holding his pocket-handkerchief
  Before his streaming eyes.
                Ibid. Stanza 17

But answer came there none —
And this was scarcely odd, because
  They'd eaten every one.
                Ibid. Stanza 18

Twopence a week, and jam every
other day.
                Ibid. Chap. 5

"The rule is, jam to-morrow, and
jam yesterday — but never jam today."

"It must come sometimes to 'jam today,'" Alice objected.

"No, it can't," said the Queen. "It's

jam every other day: to-day isn't any other day, you know."

Alice Through the Looking-Glass.
Chap. 5

"It's a poor sort of memory that only works backwards," the Queen remarked.

Ibid.

Consider anything, only don't cry!

Ibid.

"There's no use trying," she said: "one *can't* believe impossible things."

"I daresay you haven't had much practice," said the Queen. "When I was your age, I always did it for half-an-hour a day. Why, sometimes I've believed as many as six impossible things before breakfast."

Ibid.

They gave it me — for an un-birthday present.

Ibid. Chap. 6

"But 'glory' doesn't mean 'a nice knock-down argument,' " Alice objected.

"When *I* use a word," Humpty Dumpty said, in rather a scornful tone, "it means just what I choose it to mean — neither more nor less."

"The question is," said Alice, "whether you *can* make words mean so many different things."

"The question is," said Humpty Dumpty, "which is to be master — that's all."

Ibid.

It's as large as life and twice as natural.

Ibid. Chap. 7

His answer trickled through my head, Like water through a sieve.

Ibid. Chap. 8

What's the French for fiddle-de-dee?

Ibid. Chap. 9

It isn't etiquette to cut any one you've been introduced to. Remove the joint!

Ibid.

He would answer to "Hi!" or to any loud cry
Such as "Fry me!" or "Fritter my wig!"
To "What-you-may-call-um!" or

"What-was-his-name!"
But especially "Thing-um-a-jig!"

The Hunting of the Snark [1876].
Fit I, Stanza 9

"What's the good of Mercator's North Poles and Equators,
Tropics, Zones and Meridian Lines?"
So the Bellman would cry: and the crew would reply
"They are merely conventional signs!"

Ibid. Fit II, Stanza 3

It frequently breakfasts at five-o'clock tea,
And dines on the following day.

Ibid. Stanza 17

There was silence supreme! Not a shriek, not a scream,
Scarcely even a howl or a groan,
As the man they called "Ho!" told his story of woe
In an antediluvian tone.

Ibid. Fit III, Stanza 3

It is this, it is this that oppresses my soul.

Ibid. Stanza 11

And my heart is like nothing so much as a bowl
Brimming over with quivering curds.

Ibid.

You may charge me with murder — or want of sense —
(We are all of us weak at times):
But the slightest approach to a false pretence
Was never among my crimes!

Ibid. Fit IV, Stanza 4

They sought it with thimbles, they sought it with care;
They pursued it with forks and hope;
They threatened its life with a railway-share;
They charmed it with smiles and soap.

Ibid. Fit V, Stanza 1

For the Snark *was* a Boojum, you see.

Ibid. Fit VIII, Stanza 9

He thought he saw an Elephant,
   That practised on a fife:
He looked again, and found it was
   A letter from his wife.
"At length I realize," he said,
   "The bitterness of Life!"

Sylvie and Bruno [1889]. Chap. 5

He thought he saw a Buffalo
  Upon the chimney-piece:
He looked again, and found it was
  His sister's husband's niece.
      Sylvie and Bruno. Chap. 6
He thought he saw an Albatross
  That fluttered round the lamp:
He looked again, and found it was
  A penny-postage-stamp.
"You'd best be getting home," he said,
  "The nights are very damp."
      Ibid. Chap. 12

BENJAMIN H. HILL
[1832–1882]

He was a foe without hate, a friend without treachery, a soldier without cruelty, and a victim without murmuring. He was a public officer without vices, a private citizen without wrong, a neighbor without reproach, a Christian without hypocrisy, and a man without guilt. He was Caesar without his ambition, Frederick without his tyranny, Napoleon without his selfishness, and Washington without his reward.
    Tribute to Robert E. Lee [1]

NORA PERRY
[1832–1896]

Tying her bonnet under her chin,
She tied her raven ringlets in;
But not alone in the silken snare
Did she catch her lovely floating hair,
For, tying her bonnet under her chin,
She tied a young man's heart within.
      The Love-Knot. Stanza 1
What silences we keep, year after year,
With those who are most near to us, and dear!
      Too Late. Stanza 1
Some day of days, threading the street
  With idle, heedless pace,
  Unlooking for such grace,
  I shall behold your face!
      Some Day of Days. Stanza 1
Who knows the thoughts of a child?
      Who Knows? Stanza 1

[1] Quoted in *Robert E. Lee* [1911], by THOMAS NELSON PAGE.

They sat and combed their beautiful hair,
Their long, bright tresses, one by one,
As they laughed and talked in the chamber there,
After the revel was done.
      After the Ball. Stanza 1

HENRY CLAY WORK
[1832–1884]

Father, dear father, come home with me now,
  The clock in the belfry strikes one;
You said you were coming right home from the shop
  As soon as your day's work was done.
    Come Home, Father [1864].
           Stanza 1
Bring the good old bugle, boys, we'll sing another song;
Sing it with a spirit that will start the world along,
Sing it as we used to sing it — fifty thousand strong,
  As we were marching through Georgia.
    Marching Through Georgia
      [1865]. Stanza 1
"Hurrah! hurrah! we bring the Jubilee!
Hurrah! Hurrah! the flag that makes you free!"
So we sang the chorus from Atlanta to the sea,
  As we were marching through Georgia.
      Ibid. Chorus

WILHELM BUSCH [1]
[1832–1908]

Youth should heed the older-witted
  When they say, don't go too far —
Now their sins are all committed,
  Lord, how virtuous they are!
    Pious Helen (Die fromme
           Helene)

[1] Famous artist and cartoonist, author of the German classic for children, *Max and Moritz* [1865].

ISAAC HILL BROMLEY
[1833–1898]

Listen! John A. Logan is the Head Center, the Hub, the King Pin, the Main Spring, Mogul and Mugwump [1] of the final plot by which partisanship was installed in the Commission.

Editorial in New York Tribune
[February 16, 1877]

Bring me honey of Hymettus, bring me
stores of Attic salt;
I am weary of the commonplace, to dulness call a halt!
These dinner speeches tire me, they are
tedious, flat, and stale:
From a hundred thousand banquet tables comes a melancholy wail,
As a hundred thousand banqueters sit
up in evening dress
And salute each mouldy chestnut with
a signal of distress.

Our Chauncey.[2] *Stanza 2*

MARY ABIGAIL DODGE
("GAIL HAMILTON")
[1833–1896]

Whatever an author puts between the two covers of his book is public property; whatever of himself he does not put there is his private property, as much as if he had never written a word.

Country Living and Country
Thinking [1862]. Preface

The moment an audacious head is lifted one inch above the general level, pop! goes the unerring rifle of some biographical sharpshooter, and it is all over with the unhappy owner.

Skirmishes and Sketches. The
New School of Biography

What's virtue in man can't be vice in a cat.

Both Sides

[1] A mugwump is a person educated beyond his intellect. — HORACE PORTER [1837–1921] in the Cleveland-Blaine campaign [1884]
[2] In praise of Chauncey M. Depew, read at the annual dinner of the New York Yale Alumni Association [January 23, 1891].

ADAM LINDSAY GORDON
[1833–1870]

Question not, but live and labour
Till yon goal be won,
Helping every feeble neighbour,
Seeking help from none;
Life is mostly froth and bubble,[1]
Two things stand like stone —
Kindness in another's trouble,
Courage in our own.

Ye Wearie Wayfarer. Finis
Exoptatus, Stanza 8

For good undone and gifts misspent
and resolutions vain,
'Tis somewhat late to trouble. This I
know —
I should live the same life over, if I had
to live again;
And the chances are I go where most
men go.

The Sick Stockrider

A little season of love and laughter,
Of light and life, and pleasure and pain,
And a horror of outer darkness after,
And dust returneth to dust again.

The Swimmer

In a thousand years we shall all forget
The things that trouble us now.

After the Quarrel

On earth there's little worth a sigh,
And nothing worth a tear!

To My Sister. Stanza 8

Lay me low, my work is done,
I am weary. Lay me low.

Valedictory

JOHN JAMES INGALLS
[1833–1900]

Every man is the center of a circle, whose fatal circumference he can not pass.

Eulogy on Benjamin Hill, U. S.
Senate [January 23, 1882]

The purification of politics is an iri-descent dream.

Article in New York World
[1890]

Next in profusion to the divine pro-fusion of water, light and air, those three physical facts which render exist-

[1] See Gay, page 309a.

ence possible, may be reckoned the universal beneficence of grass.
Blue Grass

I knock unbidden once at every gate!
If sleeping, wake; if feasting, rise before
I turn away. It is the hour of fate.
Opportunity [1891]

ROBERT GREEN INGERSOLL
[1833–1899]

Like an armed warrior, like a plumed knight, James G. Blaine marched down the halls of the American Congress and threw his shining lance full and fair against the brazen forehead of every traitor to his country and every maligner of his fair reputation.
Speech, nominating Blaine for President, at the National Republican Convention, Cincinnati [June 15, 1876]

Though Scotland boasts a thousand names,
Of patriot, king and peer,
The noblest, grandest of them all
Was loved and cradled here.
The Birthplace of Burns, Ayr [1] *[August 19, 1878]*

These heroes are dead. They died for liberty — they died for us. They are at rest. They sleep in the land they made free, under the flag they rendered stainless, under the solemn pines, the sad hemlocks, the tearful willows, the embracing vines. They sleep beneath the shadows of the clouds, careless alike of sunshine or storm, each in the windowless palace of rest. Earth may run red with other wars — they are at peace. In the midst of battles, in the roar of conflict, they found the serenity of death.
Vision of War [Speech at Indianapolis, September 21, 1876]

I am the inferior of any man whose rights I trample under foot. Men are not superior by reason of the accidents

[1] This poem hangs in Burns's birthplace, Ayr.

of race or color. They are superior who have the best heart — the best brain.
Liberty

The superior man is the providence of the inferior. He is eyes for the blind, strength for the weak, and a shield for the defenseless. He stands erect by bending above the fallen. He rises by lifting others.
Ibid.

Every cradle asks us, "Whence?" and every coffin, "Whither?" The poor barbarian, weeping above his dead, can answer these questions as intelligently as the robed priest of the most authentic creed.
Address at a Little Boy's Grave

We, too, have our religion, and it is this: Help for the living, hope for the dead.
Ibid.

Few rich men own their own property. The property owns them.
Address to the McKinley League, New York [October 29, 1896]

An honest God is the noblest work of man.
The Gods

In nature there are neither rewards nor punishments — there are consequences.
Some Reasons Why

Justice is the only worship.
Love is the only priest.
Ignorance is the only slavery.
Happiness is the only good.
The time to be happy is now,
The place to be happy is here,
The way to be happy is to make others so.
Creed

DAVID ROSS LOCKE
("PETROLEUM V. NASBY")
[1833–1888]

The contract 'twixt Hannah, God and me,
Was not for one or twenty years, but for eternity.
Hannah Jane [1871]. Stanza 29

SIR LEWIS MORRIS
[1833–1907]

The wind that sighs before the dawn
  Chases the gloom of night,
The curtains of the East are drawn,
  And suddenly — 'tis light.
          Le Vent de l'Esprit. Stanza 1

Call no faith false which e'er hath
    brought
  Relief to any laden life,
Cessation from the pain of thought,
  Refreshment 'mid the dust of strife.
            Tolerance. Stanza 1

EDMUND CLARENCE STEDMAN
[1833–1908]

Prison-mate and dock-yard fellow,
  Blades to Meg and Molly dear,
Off to capture Porto Bello
  Sailed with Morgan the Buccaneer!
            Morgan.[1] *Stanza 1*

Crops failed; wealth took a flight;
    house, treasure, land,
Slipped from my hold — thus plenty
    comes and goes.
One friend I had, but he too loosed his
    hand
(Or was it I?) the year I met with Rose.
        The World Well Lost. Stanza 2

"Oh, anywhere! Forward! 'Tis all the
    same, Colonel:
You'll find lovely fighting along the
    whole line!"
        Kearny[2] *at Seven Pines. Stanza 3*

Look on this cast, and know the hand
That bore a nation in its hold:
From this mute witness understand
What Lincoln was, — how large of
    mould.
            The Hand of Lincoln. Stanza 1

Give us a man of God's own mould,
  Born to marshal his fellow-men;
One whose fame is not bought and sold
  At the stroke of a politician's pen.
            Wanted — A Man. Stanza 2

[1] The old bold mate of Henry Morgan. —
JOHN MASEFIELD [1878–   ]: *Captain Stratton's Fancy*

[2] General Philip Kearny [1815–1862].

Not thou, not thou — 'tis we
Are deaf, are dumb, are blind!
            Helen Keller. Stanza 4

JULIA LOUISE MATILDA WOODRUFF
[1833–1909]

Out of the strain of the Doing,
Into the peace of the Done.
            Harvest Home [*1910*]

JOHN EMERICH EDWARD DALBERG, LORD ACTON
[1834–1902]

Power tends to corrupt; absolute
power corrupts absolutely.
        *Letter to Bishop Mandell
            Creighton, 1887*

HORATIO ALGER
[1834–1899]

'Twas on Lake Erie's broad expanse,
  One bright midsummer day,
The gallant steamer Ocean Queen
  Swept proudly on her way.
            John Maynard.[1] *Stanza 1*

Three hundred grateful voices rise
  In praise to God that He
Hath saved them from the fearful fire,
  And from the engulfing sea.
            Ibid. Stanza 11

GEORGE ARNOLD
[1834–1865]

"Learn while you're young," he often
    said,
"There is much to enjoy down here be-
    low;
Life for the living, and rest for the
    dead!"
Said the jolly old pedagogue, long ago.
        The Jolly Old Pedagogue. Stanza 2

[1] John Maynard was a pilot on a steamboat
plying between Detroit and Buffalo. The
steamer did not carry boats, and one summer
afternoon, when proceeding with large quantities of resin and tar on board, it caught fire,
seven miles from Buffalo. Passengers and crew
crowded the forward part of the ship. John
Maynard stayed at the helm and beached the

"The living need charity more than the dead."

The Jolly Old Pedagogue. Stanza 3

I,
Being dry,
Sit, idly sipping here
My Beer.

Beer

SIR JOHN LUBBOCK, LORD AVEBURY
[1834–1913]

The world would be better and brighter if our teachers would dwell on the Duty of Happiness as well as on the Happiness of Duty, for we ought to be as cheerful as we can, if only because to be happy ourselves is a most effectual contribution to the happiness of others.

*The Pleasures of Life
[1887–1889]*

The idle man does not know what it is to enjoy rest. Hard work, moreover, not only tends to give us rest for the body, but, what is even more important, peace to the mind.

Ibid.

SABINE BARING-GOULD
[1834–1924]

Onward, Christian soldiers,
Marching as to war,
With the Cross of Jesus
Going on before.

Onward, Christian Soldiers

Through the night of doubt and sorrow
Onward goes the pilgrim band,
Singing songs of expectation,
Marching to the Promised Land.

*Through the Night of Doubt
and Sorrow: Translated from
the Danish of B. S. INGEMANN*

Now the day is over,
Night is drawing nigh;
Shadows of the evening
Steal across the sky.

Now the Day Is Over. Stanza 1

Comfort every sufferer
Watching late in pain;
Those who plan some evil,
From their sin restrain.

Now the Day Is Over. Stanza 5

CHARLES FARRAR BROWNE ("ARTEMUS WARD")
[1834–1867]

The Puritans nobly fled from a land of despotism to a land of freedim, where they could not only enjoy their own religion, but could prevent everybody else from enjoyin *his*.

The London Punch Letters.[1]
No. V [1866]

My pollertics, like my religion, being of an exceedin' accommodatin' character.

The Crisis

The fack can't be no longer disgised that a Krysis is onto us.

Ibid.

I am not a politician, and my other habits are good.

Fourth of July Oration

The prevailin' weakness of most public men is to Slop over. G. Washington never slopt over.

Ibid.

I can't sing. As a singist I am not a success. I am saddest when I sing. So are those who hear me. They are sadder even than I am.

Artemus Ward's Lecture

N. B. This is rote Sarcastikul.

A Visit to Brigham Young

Did you ever have the measels, and if so, how many?

The Census

I have alreddy given Two cousins to the war, & I stand reddy to sacrifiss my wife's brother ruther 'n not see the rebelyin krusht. And if wuss comes to wuss, I'll shed ev'ry drop of blud my able-bodid relations has got.

To the Prince of Wales

---

ship, all lives being saved except his own. — JOHN B. GOUGH [1817–1886]: *Sermon*

[1] The Puritan's idea of Hell is a place where everybody has to mind his own business. — *Attributed to* WENDELL PHILLIPS [1811–1884]

Why is this thus? What is the reason of this thusness?

Moses, the Sassy

He is dreadfully married. "He's the most married man I ever saw in my life."

Ibid.

Let us all be happy and live within our means, even if we have to borrow the money to do it with.

Natural History

The sun has a right to "set" where it wants to, and so, I may add, has a hen.

A Morman Romance. IV

They cherish his mem'ry, and them as sell pictures of his birth-place, etc., make it prof'tible cherishin' it.

At the Tomb of Shakespeare

GEORGE LOUIS PALMELLA BUSSON DU MAURIER
[1834–1896]

That aristocratic flavor, so grateful and comforting to scholar and ignoramus alike, which the costly British public-school system (and the British accent) alone can impart to a dead language.

Peter Ibbetson [*1891*]. *Page 49*

The wretcheder one is, the more one smokes; and the more one smokes, the wretcheder one gets — a vicious circle!

Ibid. Page 135

Songs without words are best.

Ibid. Page 162

Happiness is like time and space — we make and measure it ourselves; it is a fancy — as big, as little, as you please; just a thing of contrasts and comparisons.

Ibid. Page 399

All will be well for us all, and of such a kind that all who do not sigh for the moon will be well content.

Ibid. Page 415

He had never heard such music as this, never dreamt such music was possible. He was conscious, while it lasted, that he saw deeper into the beauty, the sadness of things, the very heart of them, and their pathetic evanescence, as with a new inner eye — even into eternity itself, beyond the veil.

Trilby.[1] Part I

Lovely female shapes are terrible complicators of the difficulties and dangers of this earthly life, especially for their owner.

Ibid.

A wave of religious emotion rolled over Little Billee and submerged him; swept him off his little legs, swept him out of his little self, drowned him in a great seething surge of love — love of his kind, love of love, love of life, love of death, love of all that is and ever was and ever will be.

Ibid. Part III

That is the worst of those dear people who have charm; they are so terrible to do without, when once you have got accustomed to them and all their ways.

Ibid. Part V

She was one of those rarely gifted beings who cannot look or speak or even stir without waking up (and satisfying) some vague longing that lies dormant in the hearts of most of us.

Ibid. Part VII

There can be prayers without words just as well as songs, I suppose.

Ibid. Part VIII

Grief tires more than anything, and brings a deeper slumber.

Ibid.

A little work, a little play,
To keep us going — and so, good-day!

A little warmth, a little light,
Of love's bestowing — and so, good-night! [2]

[1] *Trilby* was published serially in *Harper's Monthly,* beginning with the January, 1894, issue.

[2] La vie est vaine:
  Un peu d'amour,
  Un peu de haine . . .
  Et puis — Bonjour!

  La vie est brève:
  Un peu d'espoir,
  Un peu de rêve

A little fun, to match the sorrow
Of each day's growing — and so, good-
　　morrow!

A little trust that when we die
We reap our sowing! and so — good-
　　by!
Trilby. Part VIII

CHARLES WILLIAM ELIOT
[1834–1926]

In the modern world the intelligence of public opinion is the one indispensable condition of social progress.
Inaugural Address [1869]
Enter to grow in wisdom.
Inscription on the Outside of the 1890 Gate to Harvard Yard
Depart better to serve thy country and mankind.
Inscription on the Inside of the 1890 Gate to Harvard Yard
To the Fifty-fourth Regiment of Massachusetts Infantry:
　The white officers, taking life and honor in their hands, cast in their lot with men of a despised race unproved in war, and risked death as inciters of servile insurrection if taken prisoners, besides encountering all the common perils of camp march and battle.
　The black rank and file volunteered when disaster clouded the Union cause, served without pay for eighteen months till given that of white troops, faced threatened enslavement if captured, were brave in action, patient under heavy and dangerous labors, and cheerful amid hardships and privations.
　Together they gave to the nation and the world undying proof that Americans of African descent possess the pride, courage, and devotion of the patriot soldier. One hundred and eighty thousand such Americans enlisted under the Union flag in 1863–1865.
Inscription on Robert Gould Shaw Monument, Boston Common [1897]

Et puis — Bon soir!
LEON MONTENAEKEN [1859–?]:
Peu de Chose

Carrier of news and knowledge
Instrument of trade and commerce
Promoter of mutal acquaintance
Among men and nations and hence
Of peace and good will.

Carrier of love and sympathy
Messenger of friendship
Consoler of the lonely
Servant of the scattered family
Enlarger of the public life.
Inscriptions for the East and West Pavilions, Post Office, Washington, D. C.[1]

WALTER KITTREDGE
[1834–1905]

We're tenting tonight on the old camp-
　　ground,
　Give us a song to cheer
Our weary hearts, a song of home
　And friends we love so dear.
Tenting on the Old Camp-ground. Stanza 1

WILLIAM MORRIS
[1834–1896]

I know a little garden-close,
Set thick with lily and red rose,
Where I would wander if I might
From dewy morn to dewy night.
The Life and Death of Jason [1867]. A Garden by the Sea, Stanza 1
The idle singer of an empty day.
The Earthly Paradise [1868–1870]. An Apology, Stanza 1
Dreamer of dreams, born out of my
　　due time,

[1] These inscriptions were edited by WOODROW WILSON, to read:
　Carrier of news and knowledge
　Instrument of trade and
　Promoter of mutual acquaintance
　Of peace and good will
　Among men and nations.

　Messenger of sympathy and love
　Servant of parted friends
　Consoler of the lonely
　Bond of the scattered family
　Enlarger of the common life.

Why should I strive to set the crooked
　straight?
>　　　　*The Earthly Paradise. An*
>　　　　　　*Apology, Stanza 4*

Forget six counties overhung with
　smoke,
Forget the snorting steam and piston
　stroke,
Forget the spreading of the hideous
　town;
Think rather of the pack-horse on the
　down,
And dream of London, small, and white,
　and clean.
>　　　　　　*Ibid. Prologue*

Love is enough, though the world be
　a-waning.
>　　　　　*Love Is Enough*

RODEN BERKELEY
WRIOTHESLEY NOEL
[1834–1894]

After battle sleep is best,
After noise, tranquillity.
>　　　　　　*The Old*

The bass eternal of the sea.
>　　　　　　*Beatrice*

RICHARD REALF
[1834–1878]

Back of the canvas that throbs, the
　painter is hinted and hidden;
Into the statue that breathes, the soul
　of the sculptor is bidden.
>　　　*Indirection. Stanza 3*

Back of the sound broods the silence,
　back of the gift stands the giving;
Back of the hand that receives thrill
　the sensitive nerves of receiving.
>　　　　　*Ibid. Stanza 4*

ABRAM JOSEPH RYAN
[1834–1886]

But far on the deep there are billows
That never shall break on the beach;
And I have heard songs in the Silence
That never shall float into speech.
>　　*Song of the Mystic. Stanza 9*

Hearts that are great are always lone,
They never will manifest their best;
Their greatest greatness is unknown —
Earth knows a little — God, the rest.
>　　　　*A Thought. Stanza 3*

A land without ruins is a land without memories — a land without memories is a land without history.
>　　　*A Land Without Ruins.*
>　　　　　　*Foreword*

Crowns of roses fade — crowns of
thorns endure. Calvaries and crucifix-
ions take deepest hold of humanity —
the triumphs of might are transient —
they pass and are forgotten — the sufferings of right are graven deepest on
the chronicle of nations.
>　　　　　　*Ibid.*

FRANK RICHARD STOCKTON
[1834–1902]

He could open either door he pleased.
. . . If he opened the one, there came
out of it a hungry tiger, the fiercest and
most cruel that could be procured,
which immediately sprang upon him,
and tore him to pieces, as a punishment
for his guilt. . . . But if the accused
person opened the other door, there
came forth from it a lady, the most
suitable to his years and station that
his Majesty could select among his fair
subjects. . . . So I leave it with all of
you: Which came out of the opened
door — the lady or the tiger?
>　　*The Lady or the Tiger? [1884]*

JAMES THOMSON
[1834–1882]

Give a man a horse he can ride,
　Give a man a boat he can sail;
And his rank and wealth, his strength
　and health
　On sea nor shore shall fail.
>　　*Sunday Up the River [1869].*
>　　　　　*XV, Stanza 1*

Give a man a pipe he can smoke,
　Give a man a book he can read:
And his home is bright with a calm de-
　light,

Though the room be poor indeed.
> *Sunday Up the River. XV,*
> *Stanza 2*

The City is of Night; perchance of
Death,
But certainly of Night.
> *The City of Dreadful Night*
> *[1874]. Proem*

Dateless oblivion and divine repose.
> *Ibid. XIII*

The wine of Love is music,
And the feast of Love is song:
And when Love sits down to the ban-
quet,
Love sits long.
> *The Vine. Stanza 1*

CHARLES HENRY WEBB
("JOHN PAUL")
[1834–1905]

Turn out more ale, turn up the light;
I will not go to bed tonight.
Of all the foes that man should dread
The first and worst one is a bed.
> *Dum Vivimus Vigilamus.*
> *Stanza 1*

Friends I have had both old and young,
And ale we drank and songs we sung:
Enough you know when this is said,
That, one and all, — they died in bed.
In bed they died and I'll not go
Where all my friends have perished so.
> *Ibid.*

That 'tis well to be off with the old love
Before one is on with the new
Has somehow passed into a proverb,[1]
But who follows its teaching may rue.
> *Proverbum Sap. Stanza 1*

Were the proverb not wiser if mended,
And the fickle and wavering told
To be sure that they're on with the new
love
Before being off with the old?
> *Ibid. Stanza 3*

[1] It's gude to be merry and wise,
It's gude to be honest and true;
It's gude to be off with the old love,
Before you are on with the new.
Anonymous [1816]: Quoted by An-
thony Trollope in *Barchester Tow-
ers* [1857], *Chap. 46.*
See Bernard Shaw, page 764a.

Of Christian souls more have been
wrecked on shore
Than ever were lost at sea.
> *With a Nantucket Shell. Stanza 3*

JAMES McNEILL WHISTLER
[1834–1903]

Two and two continue to make four,
in spite of the whine of the amateur for
three, or the cry of the critic for five.
> *Whistler v. Ruskin* [1] *[1878]*

Nature sings her exquisite song to the
artist alone, her son and her master —
her son in that he loves her, her master
in that he knows her.
> *Ten O'Clock [1888]*

The rare Few, who, early in Life,
have rid Themselves of the Friendship
of the Many.
> *The Gentle Art of Making Enemies*
> *[1890]. Dedication*

To say of a picture, as is often said
in its praise, that it shows great and
earnest labour, is to say that it is incomplete and unfit for view.
> *Ibid. Propositions, 2*

Industry in Art is a necessity — not
a virtue — and any evidence of the
same, in the production, is a blemish,
not a quality; a proof, not of achievement, but of absolutely insufficient
work, for work alone will efface the
footsteps of work.[2]
> *Ibid.*

The masterpiece should appear as
the flower to the painter — perfect in
its bud as in its bloom — with no reason
to explain its presence — no mission to
fulfill — a joy to the artist, a delusion
to the philanthropist — a puzzle to the
botanist — an accident of sentiment
and alliteration to the literary man.
> *Ibid.*

[1] In Whistler's lawsuit for libel. Ruskin had
written of Whistler's *Nocturne in Black and
Gold,* "I have seen, and heard, much of
Cockney impudence before now; but never
expected to hear a coxcomb ask two hundred
guineas for flinging a pot of paint in the
public's face." — *Fors Clavigera, Letter 79*
[1877]
[2] Ars est celare artem (Art lies in concealing
art). — *Latin proverb*

Art should be independent of all clap-trap — should stand alone, and appeal to the artistic sense of eye and ear, without confounding this with emotions entirely foreign to it, as devotion, pity, love, patriotism, and the like. All these have no kind of concern with it.

The Gentle Art of Making Enemies.
Propositions, 2

The imitator is a poor kind of creature. If the man who paints only the tree, or flower, or other surface he sees before him were an artist, the king of artists would be the photographer. It is for the artist to do something beyond this: in portrait painting to put on canvas something more than the face the model wears for that one day; to paint the man, in short, as well as his features.

Ibid.

One cannot continually disappoint a Continent.[1]

Ibid.

Wilde. I wish I'd said that.
Whistler. You will, Oscar, you will.

Quoted in L. C. INGLEBY: *Oscar*
Wilde [*1907*]

I am not arguing with you — I am telling you.

Quoted by JOSEPH AND ELIZABETH ROBINS PENNELL *in Life*
of Whistler [*1908*]

"I only know of two painters in the world," said a newly introduced feminine enthusiast to Whistler, "yourself and Velasquez." "Why," answered Whistler in dulcet tones, "why drag in Velasquez?"

D. C. SEITZ: *Whistler Stories*
[*1913*]

ALFRED AUSTIN
[1835–1913]

So long as Faith with Freedom reigns,
  And loyal Hope survives,
And gracious Charity remains
  To leaven lowly lives;

[1] Referring to a contemplated visit to the United States.

While there is one untrodden tract
  For intellect or will,
And men are free to think and act,
  Life is worth living still.
        Is Life Worth Living? [1]

Why should we lodge in marble or in bronze
Spirits more vast than earth, or sea, or sky?
Wiser the silent worshiper who cons
Their page for Wisdom that will never die.
    On the Proposal to Erect a Statue
        to Shakespeare in London

Gods for themselves are monuments enough.
        Ibid.

An earl by right, by courtesy a man.
        The Season

THOMAS BRIGHAM BISHOP
[1835–1905]

John Brown's body lies a-mouldering in the grave,
His soul goes marching on.
        John Brown's Body

Shoo, fly! don't bodder me! I belong to Company G,
I feel like a morning star.
        Shoo, Fly. Refrain

PHILLIPS BROOKS
[1835–1893]

O little town of Bethlehem!
  How still we see thee lie;
Above thy deep and dreamless sleep
  The silent stars go by;
Yet in thy dark streets shineth
  The everlasting Light;
The hopes and fears of all the years
  Are met in thee tonight.
    O Little Town of Bethlehem.
        Stanza 1

While mortals sleep, the angels keep
  Their watch of wond'ring love.
O morning stars together

[1] See William James, page 715b.

Proclaim the holy birth,
And praises sing to God the King
And peace to men on earth.
O Little Town of Bethlehem.
Stanza 2

Life comes before literature, as the material always comes before the work. The hills are full of marble before the world blooms with statues.
Literature and Life

Do not pray for easy lives. Pray to be stronger men! Do not pray for tasks equal to your powers. Pray for powers equal to your tasks.
Sermons. Going up to Jerusalem

Greatness, after all, in spite of its name, appears to be not so much a certain size as a certain quality in human lives. It may be present in lives whose range is very small.
Ibid. Purpose and Use of Comfort

May I try to tell you again where your only comfort lies? It is not in forgetting the happy past. People bring us well-meant but miserable consolation when they tell what time will do to help our grief. We do not want to lose our grief, because our grief is bound up with our love and we could not cease to mourn without being robbed of our affections.
Letter to a friend on the death of his mother [*November 19, 1891*]

SAMUEL BUTLER
[1835–1902]

The man who lets himself be bored is even more contemptible than the bore.
The Fair Haven [*1873*]. *Memoir, Chap. 3*

Stowed away in a Montreal lumber room
The Discobolus standeth and turneth his face to the wall;
Dusty, cobweb-covered, maimed and set at naught,

Beauty crieth in an attic and no man regardeth.
O God! O Montreal!
A Psalm of Montreal.[1] *Stanza 1*
The Discobolus is put here because he is vulgar —
He has neither vest nor pants with which to cover his limbs;
I, Sir, am a person of most respectable connections. —
My brother-in-law is haberdasher to Mr. Spurgeon.
O God! O Montreal!
Ibid. Stanza 5

A hen is only an egg's way of making another egg.
Life and Habit [*1877*]. *Chap. 8*

It is far safer to know too little than too much. People will condemn the one, though they will resent being called upon to exert themselves to follow the other.
The Way of All Flesh[2] [*1903*]. *Chap. 5*

Adversity, if a man is set down to it by degrees, is more supportable with equanimity by most people than any great prosperity arrived at in a single lifetime.[3]
Ibid.

It is our less conscious thoughts and our less conscious actions which mainly mould our lives and the lives of those who spring from us.
Ibid.

To me it seems that youth is like spring, an over-praised season — delightful if it happen to be a favoured one, but in practice very rarely favoured and more remarkable, as a general rule, for biting east winds than genial breezes.
Ibid. Chap. 6

In old age we live under the shadow of Death, which, like a sword of Dam-

[1] This satirical presentation of the conflict between Greek art and modern gospels was evoked by the discovery of a plaster cast of the Discobolus in a Montreal storeroom. The poem was written in Canada in 1875, and published in 1884.
[2] See John Webster, page 225b.
[3] See Carlyle, page 475b.

ocles, may descend at any moment, but we have so long found life to be an affair of being rather frightened than hurt that we have become like the people who live under Vesuvius, and chance it without much misgiving.

The Way of All Flesh. Chap. 6

A pair of lovers are like sunset and sunrise: there are such things every day but we very seldom see them.

Ibid. Chap. 11

Taking numbers into account, I should think more mental suffering had been undergone in the streets leading from St. George's, Hanover Square, than in the condemned cells of Newgate.

Ibid. Chap. 13

Every man's work, whether it be literature or music or pictures or architecture or anything else, is always a portrait of himself, and the more he tries to conceal himself the more clearly will his character appear in spite of him.

Ibid. Chap. 14

A virtue, to be serviceable, must, like gold, be alloyed with some commoner but more durable metal.

Ibid. Chap. 19

One great reason why clergymen's households are generally unhappy is because the clergyman is so much at home and close about the house.

Ibid. Chap. 24

The advantage of doing one's praising for oneself is that one can lay it on so thick and exactly in the right places.

Ibid. Chap. 34

The best liar is he who makes the smallest amount of lying go the longest way — who husbands it too carefully to waste it where it can be dispensed with.

Ibid. Chap. 39

If people would dare to speak to one another unreservedly, there would be a good deal less sorrow in the world a hundred years hence.

Ibid. Chap. 44

Everyone has a mass of bad work in him which he will have to work off and get rid of before he can do better — and indeed, the more lasting a man's ultimate good work, the more sure he is to pass through a time, and perhaps a very long one, in which there seems very little hope for him at all. We must all sow our spiritual wild oats.

The Way of All Flesh. Chap. 51

It is in the uncompromisingness with which dogma is held and not in the dogma or want of dogma that the danger lies.

Ibid. Chap. 68

When people get it into their heads that they are being specially favoured by the Almighty, they had better as a general rule mind their p's and q's.

Ibid. Chap. 71

An empty house is like a stray dog or a body from which life has departed.[1]

Ibid. Chap. 72

A man's friendships are, like his will, invalidated by marriage — but they are also no less invalidated by the marriage of his friends.

Ibid. Chap. 75

I reckon being ill as one of the great pleasures of life, provided one is not too ill and is not obliged to work till one is better.

Ibid. Chap. 80

Life is the art of drawing sufficient conclusions from insufficient premises.

Note-Books [*1912*]. *Lord, What Is Man?*

All progress is based upon a universal innate desire on the part of every organism to live beyond its income.

Ibid.

Though analogy is often misleading, it is the least misleading thing we have.

Ibid. Music, Pictures, and Books

I have gone in for posthumous fame. . . . Posterity will give a man a fair

---

[1] I suppose I've passed it a hundred times,
   but I always stop for a minute
And look at the house, the tragic house,
   the house with nobody in it.
    JOYCE KILMER [1886–1918]: *The House With Nobody In It*

hearing; his own times will not do so if he is attacking vested interests, and I have attacked two powerful sets of vested interests at once — the Church and Science.

Note-Books. Homo Unius Libri

Ideas and opinions, like living organisms, have a normal rate of growth which cannot be either checked or forced beyond a certain point. The more unpopular an opinion is, the more necessary is it that the holder should be somewhat punctilious in his observance of conventionalities generally.

Ibid. The Art of Propagating Opinion

I do not think America is a good place in which to be a genius. A genius can never expect to have a good time anywhere, but America is about the last place in which life will be endurable at all for an inspired writer.

Ibid. Cash and Credit

Genius . . . has been defined as a supreme capacity for taking trouble. . . . It might be more fitly described as a supreme capacity for getting its possessors into trouble of all kinds and keeping them therein so long as the genius remains.

Ibid. Genius

An apology for the Devil: It must be remembered that we have only heard one side of the case. God has written all the books.

Ibid. Higgledy-Piggledy: An Apology for the Devil

God is Love, I dare say. But what a mischievous devil Love is.

Ibid. God Is Love

To live is like love, all reason is against it, and all healthy instinct for it.

Ibid. Life and Love

The Ancient Mariner would not have taken so well if it had been called *The Old Sailor*.

Ibid. Titles and Subjects

The public buys its opinions as it buys its meat, or takes in its milk, on the principle that it is cheaper to do this than to keep a cow. So it is, but the milk is more likely to be watered.

Note-Books. Sequel to "Alps and Sanctuaries"

I do not mind lying, but I hate inaccuracy.

Ibid. Truth and Convenience: Falsehood

How holy people look when they are sea-sick!

Ibid. The Channel Passage

O Critics, Cultured Critics!
Who will praise me after I am dead,
Who will see in me both more and less
    than I intended,
But who will swear that whatever it was
    it was all perfectly right;
You will think you are better than the
    people who, when I was alive,
    swore that whatever I did was
    wrong,
And damned my books for me as fast as
    I could write them;
But you will not be better, you will be
    just the same, neither better nor
    worse,
And you will go for some future Butler
    as your fathers have gone for me;
Oh, how I should have hated you!

To Critics and Others

RICHARD GARNETT
[1835–1906]

Man and Woman may only enter Paradise hand in hand. Together, the myth tells us, they left it and together must they return.

De Flagello Myrteo [1905]. Preface, XII

Evergreens are said to be associated with Death as emblems of immortality, and this is true. But there is another and perhaps a deeper symbol: that all seasons are alike to him, as to them.

Ibid. Preface, XXXI

The three eldest children of Necessity: God, the World, and Love.

Ibid. I

Love is God's essence; Power but

his attribute; therefore is his love greater than his power.
De Flagello Myrteo. IV

To become Love, Friendship needs what Morality needs to become Religion — the fire of emotion.
Ibid. LV

Perfect Love casts out Prudery together with Fear.
Ibid. LIX

Joy to forgive and joy to be forgiven
Hang level in the balances of Love.
Ibid. LXII

When Silence speaks for Love she has much to say.
Ibid. XCIX

Is life worth living? This if thou inquire,
'Tis probable that thou hast never lived,
And palpable that thou hast never loved.[1]
Ibid. CCVII

Sweet are the words of Love, sweeter his thoughts:
Sweetest of all what Love nor says nor thinks.
Ibid. CCL

Ascend above the restrictions and conventions of the World, but not so high as to lose sight of them.
Ibid. CCCXXXIII

"Let the man that woos to win
Woo with an unhairy chin."
Thus she said, and as she bid
Each devoted Vizier did.
The Fair Circassian. Stanza 3

SIR ALFRED COMYN LYALL
[1835–1911]

"I think till I'm weary of thinking,"
Said the sad-eyed Hindu King,
"And I see but shadows around me,
Illusion in everything."
The Hindu King's Reply to the Missionary

[1] See Alfred Austin, page 669a–669b, and William James, page 715b.

JOHN LUCKEY McCREERY
[1835–1906]

There is no death! The stars go down
To rise upon some other shore,
And bright in heaven's jeweled crown
They shine for evermore.
There Is No Death [*1863*].
Stanza 1

ADAH ISAACS MENKEN
[1835–1868]

Where is the promise of my years,
Once written on my brow?
Ere errors, agonies, and fears
Brought with them all that speaks in tears,
Ere I had sunk beneath my peers; —
Where sleeps that promise now?
El Suspiro (Infelix) [*1868*]

I stand a wreck on Error's shore,
A spectre not within the door,
A houseless shadow evermore,
An exile lingering here.
Ibid.

LOUISE CHANDLER MOULTON
[1835–1908]

Bend low, O dusky Night,
And give my spirit rest,
Hold me to your deep breast,
And put old cares to flight.
Give back the lost delight
That once my soul possest,
When Love was loveliest.
Tonight

I hied me off to Arcady —
The month it was the month of May,
And all along the pleasant way,
The morning birds were mad with glee,
And all the flowers sprang up to see,
As I went on to Arcady.
The Secret of Arcady

BISHOP HENRY CODMAN POTTER
[1835–1908]

We have exchanged the Washingtonian dignity for the Jeffersonian simplicity, which was in truth only another name for the Jacksonian vulgarity.

Address at the Washington Centennial Service in St. Paul's Chapel, New York [April 30, 1889]

HARRIET PRESCOTT SPOFFORD
[1835–1921]

The awful phantom of the hungry poor.
Sonnet, A Winter's Night

CELIA LAIGHTON THAXTER
[1835–1894]

Sad soul, take comfort, nor forget
That sunrise never failed us yet.
The Sunrise Never Failed Us Yet. Stanza 4

Across the narrow beach we flit,
One little sand-piper and I;
And fast I gather, bit by bit,
The scattered drift-wood, bleached and dry.
The wild waves reach their hands for it,
The wild wind raves, the tide runs high,
As up and down the beach we flit,
One little sand-piper and I.
The Sand-Piper

MARK TWAIN [1]
(SAMUEL LANGHORNE CLEMENS)
[1835–1910]

I'll resk forty dollars that he can outjump any frog in Calaveras county.
The Celebrated Jumping Frog [1865]

[1] I was a fresh, new journalist, and needed a *nom de guerre;* so I confiscated the ancient mariner's discarded one ["Mark Twain"], and have done my best to make it remain what it was in his hands — a sign and symbol and warrant that whatever is found in its company may be gambled on as being the petrified truth. — *Life on the Mississippi* [1883], *Chap. 50* (The earlier use of the pen name was by Captain Isaiah Sellers, in *The New Orleans Picayune.*)
The phrase "mark twain," meaning "two

I don't see no p'ints about that frog that's any better'n any other frog.
The Celebrated Jumping Frog

Soap and education are not as sudden as a massacre, but they are more deadly in the long run.
The Facts Concerning the Recent Resignation [1867]

Tomorrow night I appear for the first time before a Boston audience — 4000 critics.
Letter to Pamela Clemens Moffet [November 9, 1869]

They spell it Vinci and pronounce it Vinchy; foreigners always spell better than they pronounce.
The Innocents Abroad [1869]. Chap. 19

I do not want Michael Angelo for breakfast — for luncheon — for dinner — for tea — for supper — for between meals.
Ibid. Chap. 27

Lump the whole thing! say that the Creator made Italy from designs by Michael Angelo!
Ibid.

Guides cannot master the subtleties of the American joke.
Ibid.

There's millions in it!
The Gilded Age [1] [1873]

Barring that natural expression of villainy which we all have, the man looked honest enough.
A Mysterious Visit [1875]

This poor little one-horse town.
The Undertaker's Chat [1875]

Tom appeared on the sidewalk with a bucket of whitewash and a long-handled brush. He surveyed the fence, and all gladness left him and a deep

fathoms deep," was employed in making soundings on the Mississippi river boats.
By American literature in the proper sense we ought to mean literature written in an American way, with an American turn of language and an American cast of thought. The test is that it couldn't have been written anywhere else. — STEPHEN LEACOCK [1869–1944]: *Mark Twain as a National Asset*
[1] Written in collaboration with CHARLES DUDLEY WARNER.

melancholy settled down upon his spirit.
Thirty yards of board fence nine feet
high. Life to him seemed hollow, and
existence but a burden.

The Adventures of Tom Sawyer
[1876]. Chap. 2

Work consists of whatever a body is
obliged to do . . . Play consists of
whatever a body is not obliged to do.

Ibid.

The minister gave out his text and
droned along monotonously through an
argument that was so prosy that many
a head by and by began to nod — and
yet it was an argument that dealt in
limitless fire and brimstone and thinned
the predestined elect down to a company so small as to be hardly worth the
saving.

Ibid. Chap. 5

There was no getting around the
stubborn fact that taking sweetmeats
was only "hooking," while taking bacon
and hams and such valuables was plain
simple *stealing* — and there was a command against that in the Bible. So they
inwardly resolved that so long as they
remained in the business, their piracies
should not again be sullied with the
crime of stealing.

Ibid. Chap. 13

To promise not to do a thing is the
surest way in the world to make a body
want to go and do that very thing.

Ibid. Chap. 22

She makes me wash, they comb me
all to thunder . . . The widder eats
by a bell; she goes to bed by a bell; she
gits up by a bell — everything's so
awful reg'lar a body can't stand it.

Ibid. Chap. 35

A baby is an inestimable blessing and
bother.

Letter to Annie Webster
[September 1, 1876]

There is a sumptuous variety about
the New England weather that compels
the stranger's admiration — and regret.
The weather is always doing something
there; always attending strictly to business; always getting up new designs
and trying them on people to see how

they will go. But it gets through more
business in Spring than in any other
season. In the Spring I have counted
one hundred and thirty-six different
kinds of weather inside of twenty-four
hours.

New England Weather, Speech
at dinner of New England So-
ciety, New York [December 22,
1876]

Probable nor'-east to sou'-west
winds, varying to the southard and
westard and eastard and points between; high and low barometer, sweeping round from place to place; probable areas of rain, snow, hail, and
drought, succeeded or preceded by
earthquakes with thunder and lightning.

Ibid.

We haven't all had the good fortune
to be ladies; we haven't all been generals, or poets, or statesmen; but when
the toast works down to the babies, we
stand on common ground.

Answering a Toast to the Babies,
Banquet in Honor of General
U. S. Grant, Palmer House, Chi-
cago [November 14, 1879]

Among the three or four million
cradles now rocking in the land are
some which this nation would preserve
for ages as sacred things, if we could
know which ones they are.

Ibid.

It is the longest river in the world —
four thousand three hundred miles.
. . . It is also the crookedest river in
the world, since in one part of its journey it uses up one thousand three hundred miles to cover the same ground
that the crow would fly over in six
hundred and seventy-five.

Life on the Mississippi [1883].
Chap. 1

The world and the books are so accustomed to use, and over-use, the word
"new" in connection with our country,
that we early get and permanently retain the impression that there is nothing
old about it.

Ibid.

Sired by a hurricane, dam'd by an earthquake.

Life on the Mississippi. Chap. 3

When I'm playful I use the meridians of longitude and parallels of latitude for a seine, and drag the Atlantic Ocean for whales. I scratch my head with the lightning and purr myself to sleep with the thunder.

Ibid.

The Child of Calamity.

Ibid.

I was gratified to be able to answer promptly, and I did. I said I didn't know.

Ibid. Chap. 6

Your true pilot cares nothing about anything on earth but the river, and his pride in his occupation surpasses the pride of kings.

Ibid. Chap. 7

By the Shadow of Death, but he's a lightning pilot!

Ibid.

A limb of Satan.[1]

Ibid. Chap. 8

I'll learn him or kill him.

Ibid.

Give an Irishman lager for a month, and he's a dead man. An Irishman is lined with copper, and the beer corrodes it. But whiskey polishes the copper and is the saving of him.

Ibid. Chap. 23

Spread open on the rack, where the plaintive singer had left it, *Ro*-holl on, silver *moo*-hoon, guide the *trav*-el-lerr his *way*.

Ibid. Chap. 38

All the modern inconveniences.

Ibid. Chap. 43

The educated Southerner has no use for an *r*, except at the beginning of a word.

Ibid. Chap. 44

The Northern word "guess" — imported from England, where it used to be common, and now regarded by satirical Englishmen as a Yankee original —

[1] Also in *The Prince and the Pauper, Chap. 13.*

is but little used among Southerners. They say "reckon."

Life on the Mississippi. Chap. 44

In the South the war is what A. D. is elsewhere; they date from it.

Ibid. Chap. 45

War talk by men who have been in a war is always interesting; whereas moon talk by a poet who has not been in the moon is likely to be dull.

Ibid.

Sir Walter [Scott] had so large a hand in making Southern character as it existed before the war that he is in great measure responsible for the war.

Ibid. Chap. 46

It was without a compeer among swindles. It was perfect, it was rounded, symmetrical, complete, colossal.

Ibid. Chap. 52

When I retired from the rebel army in '61 I retired upon Louisiana in good order; at least in good enough order for a person who had not yet learned how to retreat according to the rules of war, and had to trust to native genius.

Ibid. Chap. 53

Persons attempting to find a motive in this narrative will be prosecuted; persons attempting to find a moral in it will be banished; persons attempting to find a plot in it will be shot.

By Order of the Author.

Adventures of Huckleberry Finn [1884]. Notice

You don't know about me without you have read a book by the name of *The Adventures of Tom Sawyer;* but that ain't no matter. That book was made by Mr. Mark Twain, and he told the truth, mainly. There was things which he stretched, but mainly he told the truth.

Ibid. Chap. 1

Jim was most ruined for a servant, because he got stuck up on account of having seen the devil and been rode by witches.

Ibid. Chap. 2

We catched fish and talked, and we took a swim now and then to keep off sleepiness. It was kind of solemn, drift-

ing down the big, still river, laying on our backs looking up at the stars, and we didn't ever feel like talking loud, and it warn't often that we laughed — only a little kind of a low chuckle. We had mighty good weather as a general thing, and nothing ever happened to us at all.
*Adventures of Huckleberry Finn.
Chap. 12*

It most froze me to hear such talk. . . . Thinks I, this is what comes of my not thinking. Here was this nigger, which I had as good as helped to run away, coming right out flat-footed and saying he would steal his children — children that belonged to a man I didn't even know, a man that hadn't ever done me no harm.
Ibid. Chap. 16

Pilgrim's Progress, about a man that left his family, it didn't say why. I read considerable in it now and then. The statements was interesting but tough.
Ibid. Chap. 17

There warn't anybody at the church, except maybe a hog or two, for there warn't any lock on the door, and hogs likes a puncheon floor in summer-time because it's cool. If you notice, most folks don't go to church only when they've got to; but a hog is different.
Ibid. Chap. 18

We said there warn't no home like a raft, after all. Other places do seem so cramped up and smothery, but a raft don't. You feel mighty free and easy and comfortable on a raft.
Ibid.

A monstrous big river.
Ibid. Chap. 19

I was trying to make my mouth say I would do the right thing and the clean thing, and go and write to that nigger's owner and tell where he was; but deep down in me I knowed it was a lie, and He knowed it. You can't pray a lie — I found that out.
Ibid. Chap. 21

I was a-trembling because I'd got to decide forever betwixt two things, and I knowed it. I studied for a minute, sort

of holding my breath, and then says to myself, "All right, then, I'll *go* to hell."
*Adventures of Huckleberry Finn.
Chap. 21*

Hain't we got all the fools in town on our side? And ain't that a big enough majority in any town? [1]
Ibid. Chap. 26

An experienced, industrious, ambitious, and often quite picturesque liar.
The Private History of a Campaign That Failed [1885]

He is now fast rising from affluence to poverty.
Henry Ward Beecher's Farm
[1885]

He [George Washington Cable] has taught me to abhor and detest the Sabbath-day and hunt up new and troublesome ways to dishonor it.
Letter to William Dean Howells
[*February 27, 1885*]

Whenever the literary German dives into a sentence, that is the last you are going to see of him till he emerges on the other side of his Atlantic with his verb in his mouth.
A Connecticut Yankee at King Arthur's Court [1889]. *Chap. 22*

Weather is a literary speciality, and no untrained hand can turn out a good article on it.
The American Claimant [1892].
Foreword

Tell the truth or trump — but get the trick.
Pudd'nhead Wilson [1894].
Pudd'nhead Wilson's Calendar, Chap. 1

Adam was but human — this explains it all. He did not want the apple for the apple's sake, he wanted it only because it was forbidden.
Ibid. Chap. 2

Whoever has lived long enough to find out what life is, knows how deep a debt of gratitude we owe to Adam, the

[1] See *Pudd'nhead Wilson's New Calendar,* page 679a.

first great benefactor of our race. He brought death into the world.

> *Pudd'nhead Wilson. Pudd'nhead Wilson's Calendar, Chap. 3*

Training is everything. The peach was once a bitter almond; cauliflower is nothing but cabbage with a college education.

> *Ibid. Chap. 5*

Habit is habit, and not to be flung out of the window by any man, but coaxed down-stairs a step at a time.

> *Ibid. Chap. 6*

One of the most striking differences between a cat and a lie is that a cat has only nine lives.

> *Ibid. Chap. 7*

The holy passion of Friendship is of so sweet and steady and loyal and enduring a nature that it will last through a whole lifetime, if not asked to lend money.

> *Ibid. Chap. 8*

Why is it that we rejoice at a birth and grieve at a funeral? It is because we are not the person involved.

> *Ibid. Chap. 9*

All say, "How hard it is that we have to die" — a strange complaint to come from the mouths of people who have had to live.

> *Ibid. Chap. 10*

When angry, count four; when very angry, swear.[1]

> *Ibid.*

Courage is resistance to fear, mastery of fear — not absence of fear.

> *Ibid. Chap. 12*

Nothing so needs reforming as other people's habits.

> *Ibid. Chap. 15*

Put all your eggs in the one basket and — WATCH THAT BASKET.

> *Ibid.*

If you pick up a starving dog and make him prosperous, he will not bite you. This is the principal difference between a dog and a man.

> *Ibid. Chap. 16*

[1] See Jefferson, page 376a.

Few things are harder to put up with than the annoyance of a good example.

> *Pudd'nhead Wilson. Pudd'nhead Wilson's Calendar, Chap. 19*

It were not best that we should all think alike; it is difference of opinion that makes horse-races.

> *Ibid.*

Be good and you will be lonesome.

> *Following the Equator [1897]. Caption for Author's Photograph on Shipboard, Frontispiece of First Edition*

When in doubt tell the truth.

> *Ibid. Vol. I, Pudd'nhead Wilson's New Calendar, Chap. 2*

Truth is the most valuable thing we have. Let us economize it.

> *Ibid. Chap. 7*

It could probably be shown by facts and figures that there is no distinctly native American criminal class except Congress.

> *Ibid. Chap. 8*

Everything human is pathetic. The secret source of Humor itself is not joy but sorrow. There is no humor in heaven.

> *Ibid. Chap. 10*

We should be careful to get out of an experience only the wisdom that is in it — and stop there; lest we be like the cat that sits down on a hot stove-lid. She will never sit down on a hot stove-lid again — and that is well; but also she will never sit down on a cold one anymore.

> *Ibid. Chap. 11*

We can secure other people's approval, if we do right and try hard; but our own is worth a hundred of it, and no way has been found out of securing that.

> *Ibid. Chap. 14*

It is easier to stay out than get out.

> *Ibid. Chap. 18*

Pity is for the living, envy is for the dead.

> *Ibid. Chap. 19*

It is by the goodness of God that in our country we have those three unspeakably precious things: freedom of speech, freedom of conscience, and the prudence never to practise either of them.

> *Following the Equator. Vol. I, Pudd'nhead Wilson's New Calendar, Chap. 20*

"*Classic.*" A book which people praise and don't read.

> *Ibid. Chap. 25*

Man is the Only Animal that blushes. Or needs to.

> *Ibid. Chap. 27*

Let us be thankful for the fools. But for them the rest of us could not succeed.[1]

> *Ibid. Chap. 28*

There are several good protections against temptations, but the surest is cowardice.

> *Ibid. Chap. 36*

There is an old time toast which is golden for its beauty. "When you ascend the hill of prosperity may you not meet a friend."

> *Ibid. Vol. II, Chap. 5*

Each person is born to one possession which outvalues all his others — his last breath.

> *Ibid. Chap. 6*

It takes your enemy and your friend, working together, to hurt you to the heart; the one to slander you and the other to get the news to you.

> *Ibid. Chap. 9*

Grief can take care of itself, but to get the full value of a joy you must have somebody to divide it with.

> *Ibid. Chap. 12*

In statesmanship get the formalities right, never mind about the moralities.

> *Ibid. Chap. 29*

Everyone is a moon, and has a dark side which he never shows to anybody.

> *Ibid. Chap. 30*

The reports of my death are greatly exaggerated.

> *Cable from London to the Associated Press* [*1897*]

A round man cannot be expected to

[1] See *Huckleberry Finn*, page 677b.

fit in a square hole right away. He must have time to modify his shape.

> *More Tramps Abroad* [*1897*]

In Boston they ask, How much does he know? In New York, How much is he worth? In Philadelphia, Who were his parents?

> *What Paul Bourget Thinks of Us* [*1899*]

The silent colossal National Lie that is the support and confederate of all the tyrannies and shams and inequalities and unfairnesses that afflict the peoples — that is the one to throw bricks and sermons at.

> *My First Lie, and How I Got Out of It* [*1900*]

Always do right. This will gratify some people, and astonish the rest.[1]

> *To the Young People's Society, Greenpoint Presbyterian Church, Brooklyn* [*February 16, 1901*]

A powerful agent is the right word. Whenever we come upon one of those intensely right words in a book or a newspaper the resulting effect is physical as well as spiritual, and electrically prompt.

> *Essay on William Dean Howells* [*1906*]

It may be called the Master Passion, the hunger for self-approval.

> *What Is Man?* [*1906*]*. Chap. 6*

The fact that man knows right from wrong proves his *intellectual* superiority to the other creatures; but the fact that he can *do* wrong proves his *moral* inferiority to any creature that *cannot*.

> *Ibid.*

Thunder is good, thunder is impressive; but it is lightning that does the work.

> *Letter to an Unidentified Person* [*1908*]

As out of place as a Presbyterian in Hell.

> *Quoted in* ALBERT BIGELOW PAINE: *Mark Twain* [*1912*]

[1] President Truman kept this saying on his desk in the White House.

"You tell me whar a man gits his corn pone, en I'll tell you what his 'pinions is."

*Europe and Elsewhere [1925].
Corn Pone Opinions*

Its name is Public Opinion. It is held in reverence. It settles everything. Some think it is the voice of God.

Ibid.

Biographies are but the clothes and buttons of the man — the biography of the man himself cannot be written.

*Autobiography [1924]. Vol. I,
Page 2*

Of all the creatures that were made he [man] is the most detestable. Of the entire brood he is the only one — the solitary one — that possesses malice. That is the basest of all instincts, passions, vices — the most hateful. . . . He is the only creature that inflicts pain for sport, knowing it to *be* pain. . . . Also — in all the list he is the only creature that has a nasty mind.

Ibid. Vol. II, Page 7

The trade of critic, in literature, music, and the drama, is the most degraded of all trades.

Ibid. Page 69

I believe that our Heavenly Father invented man because he was disappointed in the monkey.

Quoted in BERNARD DE VOTO: *Mark
Twain in Eruption [1940]*

Familiarity breeds contempt — and children.

Notebooks

Good breeding consists in concealing how much we think of ourselves and how little we think of the other person.

Ibid.

Death, the only immortal who treats us all alike, whose pity and whose peace and whose refuge are for all — the soiled and the pure, the rich and the poor, the loved and the unloved.

*Ibid. Memorandum written on
his deathbed*

Loyalty to petrified opinion never yet broke a chain or freed a human soul.

*Inscription beneath his bust in
the Hall of Fame*

The calm confidence of a Christian with four aces.

Attributed

THOMAS BAILEY ALDRICH
[1836–1907]

Somewhere — in desolate wind-swept space —
In Twilight-land — in No-man's land —
Two hurrying Shapes met face to face,
And bade each other stand.

Identity. Stanza 1

So precious life is! Even to the old
The hours are as a miser's coins!

Broken Music. Stanza 4

A man should live in a garret aloof,
And have few friends, and go poorly clad,
With an old hat stopping a chink in the roof,
To keep the Goddess constant and glad.

*The Flight of the Goddess.
Stanza 1*

We knew it would rain, for the poplars showed
The white of their leaves.

Before the Rain. Stanza 3

You do poets and their song
A grievous wrong,
If your own soul does not bring
To their high imagining
As much beauty as they sing.

Appreciation. Stanza 2

It has become almost an honor
Not to be crowned.

Popularity

Some weep because they part,
And languish broken-hearted,
And others — O my heart! —
Because they never parted.

The Difference

Sweet courtesy has done its most
If you have made each guest forget
That he himself is not the host.

Hospitality

My mind lets go a thousand things,
Like dates of wars and deaths of kings.

Memory

I vex me not with brooding on the years

That were ere I drew breath: why
should I then
Distrust the darkness that may fall
again
When life is done?
I Vex Me Not

What is more cheerful, now, in the
fall of the year, than an open-wood-
fire? Do you hear those little chirps
and twitters coming out of that piece
of apple-wood? Those are the ghosts of
the robins and blue-birds that sang
upon the bough when it was in blossom last Spring. In Summer whole
flocks of them come fluttering about
the fruit-trees under the window: so I
have singing birds all the year round.
Miss Mehitabel's Son

It was very pleasant to me to get a
letter from you the other day. Perhaps
I should have found it pleasanter if I
had been able to decipher it. I don't
think that I mastered anything beyond
the date (which I knew) and the signature (which I guessed at). There's
a singular and a perpetual charm in a
letter of yours; it never grows old, it
never loses its novelty. . . . Other
letters are read and thrown away and
forgotten, but yours are kept forever
— unread. One of them will last a
reasonable man a lifetime.
*Letter to Professor Edward
Sylvester Morse*

EDWARD ERNEST BOWEN
[1836–1901]

Forty years on, when afar and asunder
Parted are those who are singing today.
*Forty Years On, Harrow Foot-
ball Song [1872]*

JOSEPH CHAMBERLAIN
[1836–1914]

I never like being hit without striking
back.
*Speech on Tariff Reform,
Greenock, Scotland [October 7,
1903]*

Provided that the City of London remains as it is at present, the clearing-
house of the world.
*Speech, Guildhall, London
[January 19, 1904]*

The day of small nations has long
passed away. The day of Empires has
come.
*Speech, Birmingham
[May 12, 1904]*

JOHN CLIFFORD
[1836–1923]

And so, I thought, the anvil of God's
Word
For ages skeptic blows have beat upon;
Yet, though the noise of falling blows
was heard,
The anvil is unharmed — the hammers
gone.
Hammer and Anvil. Stanza 3

WILLIAM SCHWENCK
GILBERT [1]
[1836–1911]

Of all the ships upon the blue,
No ship contain'd a better crew
Than that of worthy Captain Reece,
Commanding of The Mantelpiece.
*The "Bab" Ballads [1866–
1871]. Captain Reece, Stanza 1*
The Times and Saturday Review
Beguiled the leisure of the crew.
Ibid. Stanza 7
I write the pretty mottoes which you
find inside the crackers.
Ibid. Ferdinando and Elvira
And down in fathoms many went the
captain and the crew;
Down went the owners — greedy men
whom hope of gain allured:
Oh, dry the starting tear, for they were
heavily insured.
Ibid. Etiquette, Stanza 1
Oh, I am a cook and a captain bold
And the mate of the *Nancy* brig,

[1] His foe was folly and his weapon wit. —
ANTHONY HOPE HAWKINS, *Inscription on Gilbert Memorial, Victoria Embankment, London*

And a bo'sun tight, and a midshipmite,
And the crew of the captain's gig.
*The "Bab" Ballads. The Yarn of
the "Nancy Bell," Stanza 3*

As innocent as a new-laid egg.
Engaged [*1877*]. *Act I*

I'm called Little Buttercup — dear
little Buttercup,
Though I could never tell why.
H. M. S. Pinafore [*1878*]. *Act I*

I am the Captain of the *Pinafore*;
And a right good captain too!
Ibid.

And I'm never, never sick at sea!
What, never?
No, never!
What, *never*?
Hardly ever!
He's hardly ever sick at sea!
Then give three cheers, and one cheer
more
For the hardy Captain of the *Pinafore!*
Ibid.

Bad language or abuse,
I never, never use,
Whatever the emergency;
Though "Bother it" I may
Occasionally say,
I never never use a big, big D.
Ibid.

And so do his sisters, and his cousins,
and his aunts!
His sisters and his cousins,
Whom he reckons up by dozens,
And his aunts!
Ibid.

When I was a lad I served a term
As office boy to an Attorney's firm.
I cleaned the windows and I swept the
floor
And I polished up the handle of the big
front door.
I polished up that handle so care-
fullee
That now I am the Ruler of the
Queen's Navee!
Ibid.

Now landsmen all, whoever you may be,
If you want to rise to the top of the tree
If your soul isn't fettered to an office
stool,

Be careful to be guided by this golden
rule —
Stick close to your desks and *never go
to sea,*
And you all may be Rulers of the
Queen's Navee!
H. M. S. Pinafore. Act I

Things are seldom what they seem,
Skim milk masquerades as cream.[1]
Ibid. Act II

He is an Englishman!
For he himself has said it,
And it's greatly to his credit,
That he is an Englishman!
Ibid.

For he might have been a Roosian,
A French or Turk or Proosian,
Or perhaps Itali-an.
But in spite of all temptations
To belong to other nations,
He remains an Englishman.
Ibid.

It is, it is a glorious thing
To be a Pirate King.
Pirates of Penzance [*1879*].
Act I

I am the very model of a modern
Major-General.
Ibid.

I know the Kings of England, and I
quote the fights historical,
From Marathon to Waterloo, in order
categorical.
Ibid.

When the foeman bares his steel,
Tarantara, tarantara!
We uncomfortable feel,
Tarantara.
Ibid. Act II

When constabulary duty's to be done,
The policeman's lot is not a happy one!
Ibid.

Come, friends, who plough the sea,
Truce to navigation,
Take another station;
Let's vary piracee
With a little burglaree.[2]
Ibid.

---

[1] See Phaedrus, page 48b, and Longfellow,
page 521a.
[2] The roistering chorus "Hail, hail, the

Twenty love-sick maidens we,
Love-sick all against our will.
Patience [*1881*]. *Act I*

You must lie upon the daisies and discourse in novel phrases of your
complicated state of mind,
The meaning doesn't matter if it's only
idle chatter of a transcendental
kind.
 And everyone will say,
 As you walk your mystic way,
"If this young man expresses himself in
terms too deep for *me*,
Why, what a very singularly deep
young man this deep young man
must be!"
Ibid.

Then a sentimental passion of a vegetable fashion must excite your
languid spleen,
An attachment à la Plato for a bashful
young potato, or a not too French
French bean!
Though the Philistines may jostle, you
will rank as an apostle in the high
aesthetic band,
If you walk down Piccadilly with a
poppy or a lily in your medieval
hand.
 And everyone will say,
 As you walk your flowery way,
"If he's content with a vegetable love
which would certainly not suit *me*,
Why, what a most particularly pure
young man this pure young man
must be!"
Ibid.

Prithee, pretty maiden, will you marry
me?
(Hey, but I'm hopeful, willow, willow,
waly!)
Ibid.

While this magnetic,
Peripatetic
Lover, he lived to learn,
By no endeavor,
Can magnet ever
Attract a Silver Churn!
Ibid. Act II

gang's all here" is sung to Sir Arthur Sullivan's music for these lines.

Sing "Hey to you — good day to
 you" —
Sing "Bah to you — ha! ha! to you" —
Sing "Booh to you — pooh, pooh, to
 you."
Patience. Act II

"High diddle diddle"
Will rank as an idyll,
If I pronounce it chaste!
Ibid.

Francesca di Rimini, miminy, piminy,
Je-ne-sais-quoi young man!
Ibid.

A greenery-yallery, Grosvenor Gallery,
Foot-in-the-grave young man!
Ibid.

I see no objection to stoutness, in
 moderation.
Iolanthe [*1882*]. *Act I*

None shall part us from each other,
 One in life and death are we:
All in all to one another —
 I to thee and thou to me!
Thou the tree and I the flower —
 Thou the idol; I the throng —
Thou the day and I the hour —
 Thou the singer; I the song!
Ibid.

Bow, bow, ye lower middle classes!
Bow, bow, ye tradesmen, bow, ye
 masses.
Ibid.

The Law is the true embodiment
Of everything that's excellent.
It has no kind of fault or flaw,
And I, my Lords, embody the Law.
Ibid.

Pretty young wards in Chancery.
Ibid.

A pleasant occupation for
A rather susceptible Chancellor!
Ibid.

For I'm not so old, and not so plain,
And I'm quite prepared to marry again.
Ibid.

Spurn not the nobly-born
With love affected,
Nor treat with virtuous scorn
The well-connected.
Ibid.

Hearts just as pure and fair
May beat in Belgrave Square

683

As in the lowly air
Of Seven Dials.
Iolanthe. Act I

Here's a pretty kettle of fish!
Ibid. Act II

When I went to the Bar as a very young
man,
(Said I to myself, said I).
Ibid.

I am an intellectual chap,
And think of things that would astonish
you.

I often think it's comical
How nature always does contrive
That every boy and every gal,
That's born into the world alive,
Is either a little Liberal,
Or else a little Conservative!
Ibid.

The House of Peers, throughout the
war,
Did nothing in particular,
And did it very well.
Ibid.

Oh, Captain Shaw!
Type of true love kept under!
Could thy Brigade
With cold cascade
Quench my great love, I wonder!
Ibid.

When you're lying awake with a dismal
headache, and repose is taboo'd by
anxiety,
I conceive you may use any language
you choose to indulge in, without
impropriety.
Ibid.

For you dream you are crossing the
Channel, and tossing about in a
steamer from Harwich —
Which is something between a large
bathing machine and a very small
second class carriage.
Ibid.

Faint heart never won fair lady!
Nothing venture, nothing win —
Blood is thick, but water's thin —
In for a penny, in for a pound —
It's Love that makes the world go
round!
Ibid.

Politics we bar,
They are not our bent:
On the whole we are
Not intelligent.
Princess Ida [*1884*]. *Act I*

I love my fellow-creatures — I do all
the good I can —
Yet everybody says I'm such a disagree-
able man!
And I can't think why!
Ibid.

Darwinian Man, though well-behaved,
At best is only a monkey shaved!
Ibid. Act II

A wandering minstrel I —
A thing of shreds and patches,
Of ballads, songs and snatches,
And dreamy lullaby!
The Mikado [*1885*]. *Act I*

I can't help it. I was born sneering.
Ibid.

As some day it may happen that a victim must be found,
I've got a little list — I've got a little
list.
Of society offenders who might well be
under ground,
And who never would be missed —
who never would be missed.
Ibid.

The idiot who praises, with enthusiastic
tone,
All centuries but this, and every country but his own.[1]
Ibid.

Three little maids from school are we,
Pert as a schoolgirl well can be,
Filled to the brim with girlish glee.
Ibid.

Ah, pray make no mistake,
We are not shy;
We're very wide awake,
The moon and I!
Ibid.

Here's a pretty state of things!
Here's a pretty how-de-do.
Ibid.

[1] See Overbury, page 226b, and Canning,
page 401a.

My object all sublime
I shall achieve in time —
To make the punishment fit the crime.
The Mikado. Act II

A source of innocent merriment!
Of innocent merriment.
Ibid.

On a cloth untrue
With a twisted cue
And elliptical billiard balls.
Ibid.

I drew my snickersnee!
Ibid.

The flowers that bloom in the spring,
Tra la,
Have nothing to do with the case.
Ibid.

On a tree by a river a little tom-tit
Sang "Willow, titwillow, titwillow!"
And I said to him, "Dicky-bird, why do
you sit
Singing 'Willow, titwillow, titwillow!' "
Ibid.

"Is it weakness of intellect, birdie?" I
cried,
"Or a rather tough worm in your little
inside?"
With a shake of his poor little head he
replied,
"Oh, Willow, titwillow, titwillow!"
Ibid.

There's a fascination frantic
In a ruin that's romantic;
Do you think you are sufficiently de-
cayed?
Ibid.

Hail the Bridegroom — hail the Bride!
When the nuptial knot is tied.
Ruddigore [1887]. Act I

I have a song to sing O!
Sing me your song, O!
*The Yeomen of the Guard
[1888]. Act I*

It's a song of a merryman, moping
mum,
Whose soul was sad, and whose glance
was glum,
Who sipped no sup, and who craved no
crumb,
As he sighed for the love of a ladye.
Ibid.

He led his regiment from behind —
He found it less exciting.
The Gondoliers [1889]. Act I

That celebrated,
Cultivated,
Underrated
Nobleman,
The Duke of Plaza Toro!
Ibid.

No soldier in that gallant band
Hid half as well as he did.
He lay concealed throughout the war,
And this preserved his gore, O!
Ibid.

Of that there is no manner of doubt —
No probable, possible shadow of
doubt —
No possible doubt whatever.
Ibid.

Life's a pudding full of plums;
Care's a canker that benumbs,
Wherefore waste our elocution
On impossible solution?
Life's a pleasant institution,
Let us take it as it comes!
Ibid.

Life's perhaps the only riddle
That we shrink from giving up.
Ibid.

The gratifying feeling that our duty has
been done.
Ibid.

Take a pair of sparkling eyes.
Ibid.

The world has joked incessantly for
over fifty centuries,
And every joke that's possible has long
ago been made.
*His Excellency: The Played-
Out Humorist [1894]*

Humour is a drug which it's the fashion
to abuse.
Ibid.

WASHINGTON GLADDEN
[1836–1918]

In the darkest night of the year,
When the stars have all gone out,
That courage is better than fear,
That faith is truer than doubt.
Ultima Veritas. Stanza 4

BRET HARTE (FRANCIS BRETT HARTE)
[1836–1902]

The patient stars
Lean from their lattices, content to wait.
All is illusion till the morning bars
Slip from the levels of the Eastern gate.
Night is too young, O friend! day is too
    near;
Wait for the day that maketh all things
    clear.
    Not yet, O friend, not yet!
        Cadet Grey. Song, Not Yet

All is not true,
All is not ever as it seemeth now.
                  Ibid.
What lieth dark, O love, bright day will
    fill;
Wait for thy morning, be it good or ill.
                  Ibid.

Fades the light,
    And afar
Goeth day, cometh night;
    And a star
Leadeth all,
Speedeth all
    To their rest.[1]
        Ibid. Bugle Song

Love, good-night!
    Must thou go
    When the day
And the light
    Need thee so?
                  Ibid.

Until points of gravest import yielded
    slowly one by one,
And by Love was consummated what
    Diplomacy begun.
        Concepcion de Arguello
Never a tear bedims the eye
That time and patience will not dry;
Never a lip is curved with pain
That can't be kissed into smiles again.
        The Lost Galleon [1867]

---

[1] Fading light
    Dims the sight,
      And the stars gem the sky,
    Gleaming bright,
      From afar drawing nigh,
    Falls the night.
    JOSEPH BERG ESENWEIN [1867–1946]:
                  Taps, St. 1

Which I wish to remark,
    And my language is plain,
That for ways that are dark
    And for tricks that are vain,
The heathen Chinee is peculiar.
    Plain Language from Truthful
        James [1870]. Stanza 1
Ah Sin was his name.
              Ibid. Stanza 2
With the smile that was childlike and
    bland.
              Ibid. Stanza 4
We are ruined by Chinese cheap labor.
              Ibid. Stanza 7
And ever since then, when the clock
    strikes two,
She walks unbidden from room to
    room,
And the air is filled that she passes
    through
With a subtle, sad perfume.
        A Newport Romance. Stanza 6
And on that grave where English oak
    and holly
    And laurel wreaths entwine,
Deem it not all a too presumptuous
    folly,
This spray of Western pine!
        Dickens in Camp. Stanza 10
These things are managed so well in
    France.[1]
            The Tale of a Pony
Brief words, when actions wait, are
    well:
The prompter's hand is on his bell;
The coming heroes, lovers, kings,
Are idly lounging in the wings;
Behind the curtain's mystic fold
The glowing future lies unrolled.
    Address at opening of the Cali-
    fornia Theatre, San Francisco
        [January 19, 1870]
What was it the Engines said,
Pilots touching, — head to head
Facing on the single track,
Half a world behind each back?
    What the Engines Said (Open-
    ing of the Pacific Railroad) [2]

---

[1] See Sterne, page 346b.
[2] Drill, ye tarriers, drill,
    And it's work all day
    Without sugar in your tay,

I reside at Table Mountain, and my
name is Truthful James;
I am not up to small deceit, or any sinful games.
The Society upon the Stanislaus

He smiled a kind of sickly smile, and
curled up on the floor,
And the subsequent proceedings interested him no more.
Ibid.

For there be women, fair as she,
Whose verbs and nouns do more agree.
Mrs. Judge Jenkins

Oh, yer's yer good old whiskey,
Drink it down.
Two Men of Sandy Bar [1876].
Act IV

One big vice in a man is apt to keep
out a great many smaller ones.
Ibid.

Give me a man that is capable of a
devotion to anything, rather than a
cold, calculating average of all the virtues!
Ibid.

I'm acquainted with affliction,
Chiefly in the form of fiction,
As 'tis offered up by strangers
At the consul's open door.
At the Consul's Open Door [1]

I think I know all fancy
Styles of active mendicancy.
Ibid.

I know the worthy tourist,
Who by accident the purest,
Lost his letters, watch and wallet,
From the cold deck coming o'er.
Ibid.

When you're working for the U.P. Railway.
Laborers' song during the construc-
tion of the Union Pacific Railway
[1] Written while Harte was United States
consul at Glasgow [1880–1885], after receiving a note of warning from Bristol, England, that an impostor pretending to be a
destitute American had been procuring money
from United States consuls.

FRANCES RIDLEY
HAVERGAL
[1836–1879]

Silence is no certain token
That no secret grief is there;
Sorrow which is never spoken
Is the heaviest load to bear.
Misunderstood. Stanza 15

FITZHUGH LUDLOW
[1836–1870]

While we wait for the napkin, the soup
gets cold,
While the bonnet is trimming, the face
grows old,
When we've matched our buttons, the
pattern is sold,
And everything comes too late — too
late.
Too Late. Stanza 2

SARAH MORGAN BRYANT
PIATT
[1836–1919]

Other suns will shine as golden,
Other skies be just as blue;
Other south winds blow as softly,
Gently drinking up the dew.
Today. Stanza 1

WILLIAM JEFFREY PROWSE
[1836–1870]

Though the latitude's rather uncertain,
And the longitude likewise is vague,
Still the people I pity who know not the
City,
The beautiful City of Prague.
The City of Prague. Stanza 5

MARY ASHLEY TOWNSEND
[1836–1901]

I believe if I should die
And you should kiss my eyelids when I
lie
Cold, dead, and dumb to all the world
contains,

The folded orbs would open at thy
    breath,
And, from its exile in the isles of death,
Life would come gladly back along my
    veins.

Creed. Stanza 1

WILLIAM WINTER
[1836–1917]

Who cares for nothing alone is free, —
Sit down, good fellow, and drink with
    me!

Orgia

His love was like the liberal air, —
    Embracing all, to cheer and bless;
And every grief that mortals share
    Found pity in his tenderness.

I. H. Bromley

Fierce for the right, he bore his part
    In strife with many a valiant foe;
But Laughter winged his polished dart,
    And kindness tempered every blow.

Ibid.

Cold the stars are, cold the earth is,
    Everything is grim and cold!
Strange and drear the sound of mirth is
    — Life and I are old.

Age

CESARE LOMBROSO
[1836–1909]

Klopstock was questioned regarding
the meaning of a passage in his poem.
He replied, "God and I both knew what
it meant once; now God alone knows." [1]

*The Man of Genius. Part I,
    Chap. 2*

The appearance of a single great
genius is more than equivalent to the
birth of a hundred mediocrities.

Ibid. Part II, Chap. 2

"Lawsuit mania" . . . a continual
craving to go to law against others,
while considering themselves the injured party.

Ibid. Part III, Chap. 3

The ignorant man always adores
what he cannot understand.

Ibid.

[1] Also attributed to Browning, apropos of
his *Sordello.*

Men in general, but more particularly the insane, love to speak of themselves, and on this theme they even
become eloquent.

*The Man of Genius.
    Part IV, Chap. 1*

MARY GARDINER
BRAINARD
[1837–1905]

I see not a step before me as I tread on
    another year;
But I've left the Past in God's keeping,
    — the Future His mercy shall
    clear;
And what looks dark in the distance,
    may brighten as I draw near.

Not Knowing. Stanza 2

JOHN BURROUGHS
[1837–1921]

In sorrow he learned this truth —
One may return to the place of his
    birth,
He cannot go back to his youth.

The Return. Stanza 3

Serene, I fold my hands and wait,
    Nor care for wind, nor tide, nor sea;
I rave no more 'gainst time or fate,
    For lo! my own shall come to me.

Waiting. Stanza 1

I was born with a chronic anxiety
about the weather.

Is It Going to Rain?

Literature is an investment of genius
which pays dividends to all subsequent
times.

Literary Fame

It is always easier to believe than to
deny. Our minds are naturally affirmative.

*The Light of Day. The Modern
    Skeptic*

Time does not become sacred to us
until we have lived it.

The Spell of the Past

Nature teaches more than she
preaches. There are no sermons in

stones. It is easier to get a spark out of a stone than a moral.
>   *Time and Change. The Gospel of Nature*

I go to books and to nature as a bee goes to the flower, for a nectar that I can make into my own honey.
>   *The Summit of the Years*

Life is a struggle, but not a warfare.
>   *Ibid.*

GROVER CLEVELAND
[1837–1908]

Public officers are the servants and agents of the people, to execute the laws which the people have made.
>   *Letter accepting the nomination for Governor of New York* [*October, 1882*]

Your every voter, as surely as your chief magistrate, exercises a public trust.[1]
>   *Inaugural Address* [*March 4, 1885*]

However plenty silver dollars may become, they will not be distributed as gifts among the people.
>   *First Annual Message* [*December 8, 1885*]

The so-called debtor class . . . are not dishonest because they are in debt.
>   *Ibid.*

After an existence of nearly twenty years of almost innocuous desuetude these laws are brought forth.
>   *Message* [*March 1, 1886*]

When more of the people's sustenance is exacted through the form of taxation than is necessary to meet the just obligations of Government and expenses of its economical administration, such exaction becomes ruthless extor-

[1] The familiar saying "Public office is a public trust" seems to have been paraphrased from various campaign speeches by Cleveland in 1884.
See Mathew Henry, page 293a, Burke, page 361b, Jefferson, page 375a, Clay, page 433b, and Calhoun, page 442a.

tion and a violation of the fundamental principles of a free Government.
>   *Second Annual Message* [*December, 1886*]

It is a condition which confronts us — not a theory.[1]
>   *Third Annual Message* [*December 6, 1887*]

The lessons of paternalism ought to be unlearned and the better lesson taught that while the people should patriotically and cheerfully support their Government, its functions do not include the support of the people.
>   *Inaugural Address* [*March 4, 1893*]

I have tried so hard to do the right.
>   *Last Words*

ADMIRAL GEORGE DEWEY
[1837–1917]

You may fire when you are ready, Gridley.
>   *Addressed to the Captain of Dewey's Flagship, at the Battle of Manila Bay, May 1, 1898*

WILLIAM DEAN HOWELLS
[1837–1920]

We live, but a world has passed away
With the years that perished to make us men.
>   *The Mulberries*

Lord, for the erring thought
Not into evil wrought:
Lord, for the wicked will
Betrayed and baffled still;
For the heart from itself kept,
Our thanksgiving accept.
>   *Thanksgiving*

Though I move with leaden feet,
Light itself is not so fleet;
And before you know me gone
Eternity and I are one.
>   *Time*

I know his name, I know his note,
That so with rapture takes my soul;
Like flame the gold beneath his throat,
His glossy cope is black as coal.
>   *The Song the Oriole Sings*

[1] See Disraeli, page 512a.

He who sleeps in continual noise is
wakened by silence.
Pordenone. IV
See how today's achievement is only
tomorrow's confusion;
See how possession always cheapens the
thing that was precious.
Ibid.
Yes, death is at the bottom of the cup,
And every one that lives must drink it
up;
And yet between the sparkle at the top
And the black lees where lurks that bit-
ter drop,
There swims enough good liquor,
Heaven knows,
To ease our hearts of all their other
woes.
If
The first night, when at night I went
about
Locking the doors and windows every-
where,
After she died, I seemed to lock her out
In the starred silence and the homeless
air.
Experience
Tossing his mane of snows in wildest
eddies and tangles,
Lion-like March cometh in, hoarse,
with tempestuous breath.
Earliest Spring. Stanza 1
They were Americans, and they knew
how to worship a woman.
The Lady of the Aroostook
[1879]
The Bostonian who leaves Boston
ought to be condemned to perpetual
exile.
The Rise of Silas Lapham [1885].
Chap. 5
The man of letters must make up his
mind that in the United States the fate
of a book is in the hands of the women.
Literature and Life [1902]
Does it afflict you to find your books
wearing out? I mean literally. . . .
The mortality of all inanimate things is
terrible to me, but that of books most
of all.
Letter to Charles Eliot Norton
[April 6, 1903]

I am not sorry for having wrought in
common, crude material so much; that
is the right American stuff; and perhaps hereafter, when my din is done,
if any one is curious to know what that
noise was, it will be found to have proceeded from a small insect which was
scraping about on the surface of our
life and trying to get into its meaning
for the sake of the other insects larger
or smaller. That is, such has been my
unconscious work; consciously, I was
always, as I still am, trying to fashion
a piece of literature out of the life next
at hand.
Letter to Charles Eliot Norton
[April 26, 1903]

Last night, after I got back from my
Balfour tailor, I expressed my surprise
that B. should go to such a simple shop.
"Well, I don't think, sir, Mr. Balfour
cares much for his clothes, sir. Them
distinguished men can't, sir. Their
thoughts soars to 'igher things, sir."
Letter to Mrs. Howells [April
12, 1904], quoting his London
landlord

Spain, where most of my boyhood
was passed while I was working at case
in my father's printing-office in Northern Ohio.
Letter to Brander Matthews
[July 22, 1911], referring to his
love for Don Quixote

HENRY SAMBROOKE LEIGH
[1837–1883]

In form and feature, face and limb,
I grew so like my brother,
That folks got taking me for him
And each for one another.
The Twins. Stanza 1

And when I died the neighbors came
And buried brother John.
Ibid. Stanza 5

My love she is a kitten,
And my heart's a ball of string.
My Love and My Heart. Stanza 1

JOHN L. PARKER
[1837–1917]

The little brown button,
The sacred bronze button,
The Grand Army button
He wears on his coat.
The Little Bronze Button

INNES RANDOLPH
[1837–1887]

I am a good old rebel —
   Yes; that's just what I am —
And for this land of freedom
   I do not give a dam'.
I'm glad I fit agin 'em,
   And I only wish we'd won;
And I don't ax no pardon
   For anything I've done.
      A Good Old Rebel (Unrecon-
      structed). Stanza 1

ALGERNON CHARLES SWINBURNE
[1837–1909]

Maiden and mistress of the months and
   stars
Now folded in the flowerless fields of
   heaven.
      Atalanta in Calydon [*1865*].
      Line 1

When the hounds of spring are on
   winter's traces,
The mother of months in meadow or
   plain
Fills the shadows and windy places
With lisp of leaves and ripple of rain;
And the brown bright nightingale
   amorous
Is half assuaged for Itylus,
For the Thracian ships and the foreign
   faces,
The tongueless vigil, and all the pain.
      Ibid. Chorus, Stanza 1

Come with bows bent and with empty-
   ing of quivers,
Maiden most perfect, lady of light,
With a noise of winds and many rivers,
With a clamour of waters, and with
   might;
Bind on thy sandals, O thou most fleet,

Over the splendour and speed of thy
   feet,
For the faint east quickens, the wan
   west shivers,
Round the feet of the day and the feet
   of the night.
      Atalanta in Calydon. Chorus,
      Stanza 2

For winter's rains and ruins are over,
And all the season of snows and sins;
The days dividing lover and lover,
The light that loses, the night that wins;
And time remembered is grief forgotten.
And frosts are slain and flowers begotten,
And in green underwood and cover
Blossom by blossom the spring begins.
      Ibid. Stanza 4

Before the beginning of years
There came to the making of man
Time, with a gift of tears;
Grief, with a glass that ran;
Pleasure, with pain for leaven;
Summer, with flowers that fell;
Remembrance fallen from heaven,
And madness risen from hell;
Strength without hands to smite;
Love that endures for a breath;
Night, the shadow of light,
And life, the shadow of death.
      Ibid. Chorus, Stanza 1

Eyesight and speech they wrought
For the veils of the soul therein,
A time for labour and thought,
A time to serve and to sin; [1]
They gave him light in his ways,
And love, and a space for delight,
And beauty and length of days,
And night, and sleep in the night.
His speech is a burning fire;
With his lips he travaileth;
In his heart is a blind desire,
In his eyes foreknowledge of death;
He weaves, and is clothed with derision;
Sows, and he shall not reap;
His life is a watch or a vision
Between a sleep and a sleep.
      Ibid. Stanza 3

We have seen thee, O Love, thou art
   fair; thou art goodly, O Love.
      Ibid. Chorus

[1] See *Ecclesiastes, III, 2*, on page 1042b.

For words divide and rend;
But silence is most noble till the end.
Atalanta in Calydon. Chorus

O wise among women, and wisest,
Our Lady of Pain.
Dolores [1866]. Stanza 5

Change in a trice
The lilies and languors of virtue
For the raptures and roses of vice.
Ibid. Stanza 9

O splendid and sterile Dolores,
Our Lady of Pain.
Ibid.

Ah beautiful passionate body
That never has ached with a heart!
Ibid. Stanza 11

The delight that consumes the desire,
The desire that outruns the delight.
Ibid. Stanza 14

Despair the twin-born of devotion.
Ibid.

I have passed from the outermost portal
To the shrine where a sin is a prayer.
Ibid. Stanza 17

For the crown of our life as it closes
Is darkness, the fruit thereof dust;
No thorns go as deep as a rose's,
And love is more cruel than lust.
Time turns the old days to derision,
Our loves into corpses or wives;
And marriage and death and division
Make barren our lives.
Ibid. Stanza 20

What ailed us, O gods, to desert you
For creeds that refuse and restrain?
Come down and redeem us from virtue,
Our Lady of Pain.
Ibid. Stanza 35

Then love was the pearl of his oyster,
And Venus rose red out of wine.
Ibid. Stanza 39

Lo, this is she that was the world's delight.
Laus Veneris [1866]. Stanza 3

Ah yet would God this flesh of mine might be
Where air might wash and long leaves cover me,
Where tides of grass break into foam of flowers,

Or where the wind's feet shine along the sea.
Laus Veneris. Stanza 14

O sad kissed mouth, how sorrowful it is!
Ibid. Stanza 79

To have known love, how bitter a thing it is.
Ibid. Stanza 103

There will no man do for your sake, I think,
What I would have done for the least word said.
I had wrung life dry for your lips to drink,
Broken it up for your daily bread.
*The Triumph of Time [1866].
Stanza 12*

I wish we were dead together today,
Lost sight of, hidden away out of sight,
Clasped and clothed in the cloven clay,
Out of the world's way, out of the light.
Ibid. Stanza 15

At the door of life, by the gate of breath,
There are worse things waiting for men than death.
Ibid. Stanza 20

I will go back to the great sweet mother,
Mother and lover of men, the sea.
Ibid. Stanza 33

There lived a singer in France of old,
By the tideless dolorous midland sea.
In a land of sand and ruin and gold
There shone one woman, and none but she.
Ibid. Stanza 41

O brother, the gods were good to you.
Sleep, and be glad while the world endures.
Be well content as the years wear through;
Give thanks for life, and the loves and lures.
Ibid. Stanza 43

I shall never be friends again with roses;
I shall loathe sweet tunes.
Ibid. Stanza 45

Marvellous mercies and infinite love.
*Les Noyades [1866].
Stanza 1*

I am sick of singing; the bays burn deep
  and chafe: I am fain
To rest a little from praise and grievous
  pleasure and pain.
    Hymn to Proserpine: After the
    Proclamation in Rome of the
    Christian Faith [*1866*]
Thou hast conquered, O pale Galilean;
  the world has grown grey from thy
  breath;
We have drunken of things Lethean,
  and fed on the fullness of death.
Laurel is green for a season, and love is
  sweet for a day;
But love grows bitter with treason, and
  laurel outlives not May.
Sleep, shall we sleep after all? for the
  world is not sweet in the end;
For the old faiths loosen and fall, the
  new years ruin and rend.
            Ibid.
I shall die as my fathers died, and sleep
  as they sleep; even so.
For the glass of the years is brittle
  wherein we gaze for a span.
            Ibid.
For there is no God found stronger than
  death; and death is a sleep.
            Ibid.
If you loved me ever so little,
  I could bear the bonds that gall,
I could dream the bonds were brittle;
  You do not love me at all.
  Satia Te Sanguine [*1866*]. *Stanza 1*
While he lives let a man be glad,
For none hath joy of his death.
    A Lamentation [*1866*]. *I, 4*
If love were what the rose is,
  And I were like the leaf,
Our lives would grow together
In sad or singing weather.
    A Match [*1866*]. *Stanza 1*
If you were April's lady,
  And I were lord in May.
        Ibid. Stanza 5
If you were queen of pleasure,
  And I were king of pain,
We'd hunt down love together,
Pluck out his flying feather,
And teach his feet a measure,
  And find his mouth a rein.
        Ibid. Stanza 6

For in the time we know not of
    Did fate begin
Weaving the web of days that wove
    Your doom, Faustine.
    Faustine [*1866*]. *Stanza 24*
  A love machine
With clockwork joints of supple gold —
  No more, Faustine.
        Ibid. Stanza 36
Take hand and part with laughter;
  Touch lips and part with tears;
Once more and no more after,
  Whatever comes with years.
    Rococo [*1866*]. *Stanza 1*
Forget that I remember,
And dream that I forget.
        Ibid. Stanza 2
The burden of long living. Thou shalt
  fear
Waking, and sleeping mourn upon thy
  bed;
And say at night "Would God the day
  were here,"
And say at dawn "Would God the day
  were dead."[1]
    A Ballad of Burdens [*1866*].
            Stanza 4
For life is sweet, but after life is death.
This is the end of every man's desire.
       Ibid. L'Envoy
O love, O lover, loose or hold me fast,
I had thee first, whoever have thee last.
      Erotion [*1866*]
I shall remember while the light lives
  yet
And in the night-time I shall not forget.
Though (as thou wilt) thou leave me
  ere life leave,
I will not, for thy love I will not, grieve.
            Ibid.
Here, where the world is quiet;
  Here, where all trouble seems
Dead winds' and spent waves' riot
  In doubtful dreams of dreams.
    The Garden of Proserpine [*1866*].
            Stanza 1

[1] In the morning thou shalt say, Would God
it were even! and at even thou shalt say,
Would God it were morning! for the fear of
thine heart wherewith thou shalt fear, and for
the sight of thine eyes which thou shalt see. —
Deuteronomy, XXVIII, 67

I am tired of tears and laughter,
　And men that laugh and weep;
Of what may come hereafter
　For men that sow and reap:
I am weary of days and hours,
Blown buds of barren flowers,
Desires and dreams and powers
　And everything but sleep.
　　　The Garden of Proserpine.
　　　　　Stanza 2

We are not sure of sorrow,
　And joy was never sure.
Today will die tomorrow;
　Time stoops to no man's lure;
And love, grown faint and fretful,
With lips but half regretful
Sighs, and with eyes forgetful
　Weeps that no loves endure.
　　　　Ibid. Stanza 10

From too much love of living,
　From hope and fear set free,
We thank with brief thanksgiving
　Whatever gods may be
That no life lives forever;
That dead men rise up never;
That even the weariest river
　Winds somewhere safe to sea.[1]
　　　　Ibid. Stanza 11

Ah that such sweet things should be fleet,
Such fleet things sweet!
　　　Félise [1866]. Stanza 22

Those eyes the greenest of things blue,
The bluest of things grey.
　　　　Ibid. Stanza 24

Eyes colored like a water-flower,
And deeper than the green sea's glass;
Eyes that remember one sweet hour —
In vain we swore it should not pass.
　　　　Ibid. Stanza 36

Live and let live, as I will do,
Love and let love, and so will I.
But, sweet, for me no more with you:
Not while I live, not though I die.
　　　Good-night, good-bye.
　　　　Ibid. Stanza 59

I remember the way we parted,
　The day and the way we met;
You hoped we were both broken-
　hearted

[1] No matter how long the river, the river
will reach the sea. — EUGENE FITCH WARE
("IRONQUILL") [1841–1911]: *The Blizzard*

And knew we should both forget.
　　　An Interlude [1866]. Stanza 11

And the best and the worst of this is
　That neither is most to blame,
If you have forgotten my kisses
　And I have forgotten your name.
　　　　Ibid. Stanza 14

And through the trumpet of a child of
　Rome
Rang the pure music of the flutes of
　Greece.
　　　*Song for the Centenary of
　　　Walter Savage Landor [1866].
　　　　Stanza 17*

I am that which began;
　Out of me the years roll;
Out of me God and man;
　I am equal and whole;
God changes, and man, and the form of
　them bodily; I am the soul.
　　　　Hertha [1871]. Stanza 1

Before ever land was,
　Before ever the sea,
Or soft hair of the grass,
　Or fair limbs of the tree,
Or the flesh-coloured fruit of my
　branches,
I was, and thy soul was in me.
　　　　Ibid. Stanza 2

A creed is a rod,
　And a crown is of night;
But this thing is God,
　To be man with thy might,
To grow straight in the strength of thy
　spirit, and to live out thy life as the
　light.
　　　　Ibid. Stanza 15

In the grey beginning of years, in the
　twilight of things that began,
The word of the earth in the ears of
　the world, was it God? was it man?
　　　　Hymn of Man [1871]

Ask nothing more of me, sweet,
All I can give you I give;
Heart of my heart, were it more,
More would be laid at your feet:
Love that should help you to live,
Song that should spur you to soar.
　　　The Oblation [1871]. Stanza 1

It is long since Mr. Carlyle expressed
his opinion that if any poet or other
literary creature could really be "killed

off by one critique" or many, the sooner he was so despatched the better; a sentiment in which I for one humbly but heartily concur.
> *Under the Microscope* [*1872*]

A blatant Bassarid of Boston, a rampant Maenad of Massachusetts.[1]
> *Ibid.*

To wipe off the froth of falsehood from the foaming lips of inebriated virtue, when fresh from the sexless orgies of morality and reeling from the delirious riot of religion, may doubtless be a charitable office.
> *Ibid.*

The more congenial page of some tenth-rate poeticule worn out with failure after failure and now squat in his hole like the tailless fox, he is curled up to snarl and whimper beneath the inaccessible vine of song.
> *Ibid.*

The tadpole poet will never grow into anything bigger than a frog; not though in that stage of development he should puff and blow himself till he bursts with windy adulation at the heels of the laureled ox.
> *Ibid.*

Many loves of many a mood and many a kind
Fill the life of man, and mould the secret mind.
> *Erechtheus* [*1876*]

Poor splendid wings so frayed and soiled and torn!
> *A Ballad of François Villon* [*1878*]. *Stanza 3*

Villon, our sad bad glad mad brother's name.[2]
> *Ibid. Refrain*

In a coign of the cliff between lowland and highland,
At the sea-down's edge between windward and lee,

[1] The reference is to Harriet Beecher Stowe, whose accusations against Byron in her article, "The True Story of Lady Byron's Life" [*Atlantic Monthly*, September, 1869], and in her book, *Lady Byron Vindicated* [1870], aroused strong protests in England.
[2] See Browning, page 572b.

Walled round with rocks as an inland island,
The ghost of a garden fronts the sea.[1]
> *A Forsaken Garden* [*1878*]. *Stanza 1*

There is no help for these things; none to mend,
And none to mar; not all our songs, O friend,
Will make death clear or make life durable.
> *Ave atque Vale: In Memory of Charles Baudelaire* [*1878*]. *Stanza 16*

Sleep; and if life was bitter to thee, pardon,
If sweet, give thanks; thou hast no more to live;
And to give thanks is good, and to forgive.
> *Ibid. Stanza 17*

Body and spirit are twins: God only knows which is which.
> *The Higher Pantheism in a Nutshell* [*1880*]. *Stanza 7*

God, whom we see not, is: and God, who is not, we see:
Fiddle, we know, is diddle: and diddle, we take it, is dee.
> *Ibid. Stanza 12*

A little soul scarce fledged for earth
Takes wing with heaven again for goal
Even while we hailed as fresh from birth
A little soul.
> *A Baby's Death* [*1883*]. *I, 1*

Who knows but on their sleep may rise
Such light as never heaven let through
To lighten earth from Paradise?
> *Ibid. IV, 2*

All our past acclaims our future: Shakespeare's voice and Nelson's hand,
Milton's faith and Wordsworth's trust in this our chosen and chainless land,

[1] On the grass of the cliff, at the edge of the steep,
God planted a garden, a garden of sleep.
CLEMENT W. SCOTT [1841–1904]: *The Garden of Sleep*

Bear as witness: come the world against
her, England yet shall stand.
England, An Ode [*1884*]. *II, 5*

Faith in faith established evermore
Stands a sea-mark in the tides of time.
A Sea-Mark [*1884*]. *Stanza 5*

Not with dreams, but with blood and
with iron,[1]
Shall a nation be moulded to last.
A Word for the Country [*1884*].
Stanza 13

Is not Precedent indeed a King of men?
A Word from the Psalmist [*1884*].
Stanza 4

HENRY BROOKS ADAMS
[1838–1918]

Accident counts for much in companionship as in marriage.
The Education of Henry Adams
[*1907*]. *Chap. 4*

Women have, commonly, a very positive moral sense; that which they will,
is right; that which they reject, is
wrong; and their will, in most cases,
ends by settling the moral.
Ibid. Chap. 6

All experience is an arch, to build
upon.[2]
Ibid.

Only on the edge of the grave can
man conclude anything.
Ibid.

Although the Senate is much given to
admiring in its members a superiority
less obvious or quite invisible to out-
siders, one Senator seldom proclaims
his own inferiority to another, and still
more seldom likes to be told of it.
Ibid. Chap. 7

Friends are born, not made.
Ibid.

[1] Not by speechifying and counting majorities are the great questions of the time to be
solved . . . but by iron and blood [Eisen
und Blut]. — BISMARCK: *Speech, Prussian
Diet* [September 30, 1862]
[2] Yet all experience is an arch wherethrough
Gleams that untraveled world.
TENNYSON: *Ulysses* [1842]

A friend in power is a friend lost.[1]
The Education of Henry Adams.
Chap. 7

The effect of power and publicity on
all men is the aggravation of self, a
sort of tumor that ends by killing the
victim's sympathies.
Ibid. Chap. 10

Young men have a passion for regarding their elders as senile.
Ibid. Chap. 11

Knowledge of human nature is the
beginning and end of political education.
Ibid. Chap. 12

These questions of taste, of feeling,
of inheritance, need no settlement.
Everyone carries his own inch-rule of
taste, and amuses himself by applying
it, triumphantly, wherever he travels.
Ibid.

Intimates are predestined.
Ibid. Chap. 13

His first struggle with a sleeping-car
made him doubt the value — to him —
of a Pullman civilization.
Ibid. Chap. 16

Chaos often breeds life, when order
breeds habit.
Ibid.

At best, the renewal of broken relations is a nervous matter.
Ibid.

Sumner's[2] mind had reached the
calm of water which receives and reflects images without absorbing them;
it contained nothing but itself.
Ibid.

The difference is slight, to the influence of an author, whether he is read
by five hundred readers, or by five hundred thousand; if he can select the five
hundred, he reaches the five hundred
thousand.
Ibid. Chap. 17

The newspaper-man is, more than
most men, a double personality; and his
person feels best satisfied in its double

[1] See *Chap. 28*, page 697b.
[2] Charles Sumner [1811–1874].

instincts when writing in one sense and thinking in another.

*The Education of Henry Adams.
Chap. 17*

A teacher affects eternity; he can never tell where his influence stops.

Ibid. Chap. 20

One friend in a lifetime is much; two are many; three are hardly possible. Friendship needs a certain parallelism of life, a community of thought, a rivalry of aim.

Ibid.

What one knows is, in youth, of little moment; they know enough who know how to learn.

Ibid. Chap. 21

He had often noticed that six months' oblivion amounts to newspaper-death, and that resurrection is rare. Nothing is easier, if a man wants it, than rest, profound as the grave.

Ibid. Chap. 22

Morality is a private and costly luxury.

Ibid.

Nothing is more tiresome than a superannuated pedagogue.

Ibid. Chap. 23

The study of history is useful to the historian by teaching him his ignorance of women. . . . The woman who is known only through a man is known wrong.

Ibid.

He too serves a certain purpose who only stands and cheers.[1]

Ibid. Chap. 24

Practical politics consists in ignoring facts.

Ibid.

Nothing in education is so astonishing as the amount of ignorance it accumulates in the form of inert facts.

Ibid. Chap. 25

[1] And if I should lose, let me stand by the road
And cheer as the winners go by!
BERTON BRALEY [1882–   ]: *Prayer of a Sportsman*

Power when wielded by abnormal energy is the most serious of facts.

*The Education of Henry Adams.
Chap. 28*

Those who seek education in the paths of duty are always deceived by the illusion that power in the hands of friends is an advantage to them.[1]

Ibid.

Power is poison. Its effect on Presidents had been always tragic, chiefly as an almost insane excitement at first, and a worse reaction afterwards; but also because no mind is so well balanced as to bear the strain of seizing unlimited force without habit or knowledge of it; and finding it disputed with him by hungry packs of wolves and hounds whose lives depend on snatching the carrion.

Ibid.

A certain chronic irritability — a sort of Bostonitis — which, in its primitive Puritan forms, seemed due to knowing too much of his neighbors and thinking too much of himself.

Ibid.

Modern politics is, at bottom, a struggle not of men but of forces.

Ibid.

We combat obstacles in order to get repose, and, when got, the repose is insupportable.

Ibid. Chap. 29

Simplicity is the most deceitful mistress that ever betrayed man.

Ibid. Chap. 30

No one means all he says, and yet very few say all they mean, for words are slippery and thought is viscous.

Ibid. Chap. 31

The movement from unity into multiplicity, between 1200 and 1900, was unbroken in sequence, and rapid in acceleration. Prolonged one generation longer, it would require a new social mind.

Ibid. Chap. 34

Even in America, the Indian Summer of life should be a little sunny and a little sad, like the season, and infinite

[1] See *Chap. 7*, page 696b.

in wealth and depth of tone — but never hustled.

> *The Education of Henry Adams.*
> *Chap. 35*

Perhaps some day — say 1938, their centenary — they [1] might be allowed to return together for a holiday, to see the mistakes of their own lives made clear in the light of the mistakes of their successors; and perhaps then, for the first time since man began his education among the carnivores, they would find a world that sensitive and timid natures could regard without a shudder.

> *Ibid. Closing words*

JAMES BRYCE [2]
[1838–1922]

Law will never be strong or respected unless it has the sentiment of the people behind it. If the people of a State make bad laws, they will suffer for it. They will be the first to suffer. Suffering, and nothing else, will implant that sentiment of responsibility which is the first step to reform.

> *The American Commonwealth*
> *[1888]. Vol. I, Page 352*

To the vast majority of mankind nothing is more agreeable than to escape the need for mental exertion. . . . To most people nothing is more troublesome than the effort of thinking. [3]

> *Studies in History and Jurisprudence [1901]. Obedience*

The greatest liberty that man has taken with Nature. [4]

> *South America [1912]*

What you want [in Washington] is to have a city which every one who comes from Maine, Texas, Florida, Arkansas, or Oregon can admire as being something finer and more beautiful than he had ever dreamed of before;

something which makes him even more proud to be an American.

> *The Nation's Capital* [1]

You have never sufficiently foreseen how enormously rich and populous a nation you are going to be.

> *Ibid.*

Medicine, the only profession that labours incessantly to destroy the reason for its own existence.

> *Address at dinner for General W. C. Gorgas [March 23, 1914]*

GEORGE COOPER
[1838–1927]

Sweet Genevieve,
The days may come, the days may go,
But still the hands of mem'ry weave
The blissful dreams of long ago.

> *Sweet Genevieve [Circa 1877]*

JOHN HAY
[1838–1905]

A keerless man in his talk was Jim,
  And an awkward hand in a row,
He never flunked, and he never lied, —
  I reckon he never knowed how.

> *Jim Bludso*

"I'll hold her nozzle agin the bank
Till the last galoot's ashore."

> *Ibid.*

And they all had trust in his cussedness,
And knowed he would keep his word.

> *Ibid.*

He weren't no saint — but at jedgment
  I'd run my chance with Jim,
'Longside of some pious gentlemen
  That wouldn't shook hands with him.
He seen his duty, a dead-sure thing, —
  And went for it thar and then;
And Christ ain't a-going to be too hard
  On a man that died for men.

> *Ibid.*

I don't go much on religion,
  I never ain't had no show;
But I've got a middlin' tight grip, sir,
  On the handful o' things I know.
I don't pan out on the prophets

---

[1] Adams and his two friends John Hay [1838–1905] and Clarence King [1842–1901].

[2] Ambassador from Great Britain to the United States, 1906–1913.

[3] See R. B. Sheridan, page 382a.

[4] The Panama Canal.

[1] In *The National Geographic Magazine*, 1913.

And free-will, and that sort of
  thing, —
But I b'lieve in God and the angels
Ever sence one night last spring.
Little Breeches

And I think that saving a little child,
  And fotching him to his own,
Is a derned sight better business
  Than loafing around The Throne.
Ibid.

The night comes down, the lights burn
  blue;
And at my door the Pale Horse stands,[1]
To bear me forth to unknown lands.
The Stirrup Cup

Bring me tonight a lotus tied
With thread from a house where none
  has died.[2]
The Law of Death

There are three species of creatures who
  when they seem coming are going,
When they seem going they come:
  Diplomats, women, and crabs.
Distichs. II

When you break up housekeeping, you
  learn the extent of your treasures.
Ibid. IX

Who would succeed in the world should
  be wise in the use of his pronouns.
Utter the You twenty times, where you
  once utter the I.
Ibid. XIII

True luck consists not in holding the
  best of the cards at the table:
Luckiest he who knows just when to
  rise and go home.
Ibid. XV

Try not to beat back the current, yet be
  not drowned in its waters;
Speak with the speech of the world,
  think with the thoughts of the few.
Ibid. XVII

[1] A pale horse: and his name that sat on him
was Death. — *Revelation, VI, 8*
[2] "A grain of mustard-seed," the sage replied,
"Found where none old or young has ever
  died,
Will cure the pain you carry in your
  side."
JOHN WHITE CHADWICK [1840–1904]:
  Buddha's Lesson

GEORGE WASHINGTON JOHNSON
[1838–1917]

I wandered today to the hill, Maggie,
  To watch the scene below,
The creek and the old rusty mill,
  Maggie,
As we used to, long ago.
When You and I Were Young,
Maggie [*1866*]. *Stanza 1*

To me you're as fair as you were, Mag-
  gie,
When you and I were young.
Ibid. Stanza 3

And now we are aged and gray, Maggie,
  The trials of life nearly done,
Let us sing of the days that are gone,
  Maggie,
When you and I were young.
Refrain

WILLIAM EDWARD HARTPOLE LECKY
[1838–1903]

Offspring of an idle hour,
Whence has come thy lasting power?
On an Old Song

The stately ship is seen no more,
The fragile skiff attains the shore;
And while the great and wise decay,
And all their trophies pass away,
Some sudden thought, some careless
  rhyme,
Still floats above the wrecks of Time.
Ibid.

JOHN, VISCOUNT MORLEY
[1838–1923]

No man can climb out beyond the
limitations of his own character.
Critical Miscellanies [*1871*].
Robespierre

A great interpreter of life ought not
himself to need interpretation.
Emerson

The most frightful idea that has
ever corroded human nature — the
idea of eternal punishment.
Vauvenargues

Where it is a duty to worship the sun it is pretty sure to be a crime to examine the laws of heat.

Voltaire [1872]

A man will already be in no mean Paradise if at the hour of sunset a ray of good hope may fall upon him like harmonies of music.

Ibid.

Those who would treat politics and morality apart will never understand the one or the other.

Rousseau [1873]

You can not demonstrate an emotion or prove an aspiration.

Ibid.

Evolution is not a force but a process; not a cause but a law.

On Compromise [1874]

It is not enough to do good; one must do it the right way.

Ibid.

You have not converted a man because you have silenced him.

Ibid.

Literature — the most seductive, the most deceiving, the most dangerous of professions.

Burke [1879]

Great economic and social forces flow with a tidal sweep over communities that are only half conscious of that which is befalling them. Wise statesmen are those who foresee what time is thus bringing, and endeavor to shape institutions and to mold men's thought and purpose in accordance with the change that is silently surrounding them.

Life of Richard Cobden [1881]

The great business of life is to be, to do, to do without, and to depart.

Address on Aphorisms [1887]

The gravity and concision of Thucydides are of specially wholesome example in these days of over-coloured and over-voluminous narrative.

Ibid.

Simplicity of character is no hindrance to subtlety of intellect.

Life of Gladstone [1903]

Every man of us has all the centuries in him.

Ibid.

There are some books which cannot be adequately reviewed for twenty or thirty years after they come out.

Recollections [1917]. Vol. I, Book 2, Chap. 8

The proper memory for a politician is one that knows what to remember and what to forget.

Ibid. Vol. II, Book 4, Chap. 2

In my creed, waste of public money is like the sin against the Holy Ghost.

Ibid. Book 5, Chap. 3

Success depends on three things: who says it, what he says, how he says it; and of these three things, what he says is the least important.

Ibid. Chap. 4

Excess of severity is not the path to order. On the contrary, it is the path to the bomb.

Ibid.

MARGARET ELIZABETH SANGSTER
[1838–1912]

I know — yet my arms are empty,
  That fondly folded seven,
And the mother heart within me
  Is almost starved for heaven.

Are the Children at Home?

Never yet was a springtime,
  Late though lingered the snow,
That the sap stirred not at the whisper
  Of the southwind, sweet and low;
Never yet was a springtime
  When the buds forgot to blow.

Awakening

GEORGE LEYBOURNE
[? –1884]

He flies through the air with the greatest of ease,
This daring young man on the flying trapeze;

His figure is handsome, all girls he can
　please,
And my love he purloined her away!
　　The Man on the Flying Trapeze
　　　　　　　　　　　　　[*1860*]

JOSEPH MALINES [1]
[*Floruit* 1895]

Better put a strong fence 'round the
　top of the cliff,
Than an ambulance down in the valley.
　　　　A Fence or an Ambulance.
　　　　　　　　　　　Stanza 7

HEZEKIAH BUTTERWORTH
[1839–1905]

The bird with the broken pinion
Never soared as high again.
　　The Bird with a Broken Wing
One taper lights a thousand,
　Yet shines as it has shone;
And the humblest light may kindle
　A brighter than its own.
　　　The Taper. Stanza 10

FRANCIS PHARCELLUS
CHURCH
[1839–1906]

Virginia, your little friends are wrong.
They have been affected by the skepticism of a skeptical age. They do not believe except they see. They think that
nothing can be which is not compre-
hensible by their little minds. All minds,
Virginia, whether they be men's or children's, are little. In this great universe
of ours man is a mere insect, an ant,
in his intellect, as compared with the
boundless world about him, as measured by the intelligence capable of
grasping the whole of truth and knowledge.
　　　Editorial: Is There a Santa
　　　　　　　　　　　Claus? [2]
Not believe in Santa Claus? You
might as well not believe in fairies.
. . . No Santa Claus! Thank God, he

[1] Editor of *The Reciter,* an English publication.
[2] First published in *The New York Sun,*
September 21, 1897, in reply to an inquiry
from Virginia O'Hanlon.

lives, and he lives forever. A thousand
years from now, Virginia, nay, ten
times ten thousand years from now, he
will continue to make glad the heart of
childhood.
　　Editorial: Is There a Santa Claus?

WALTER PATER
[1839–1894]

Every intellectual product must be
judged from the point of view of the
age and the people in which it was produced.
　　　The Renaissance [*1873*].
　　　　　　　　　　Mirandola
　Its generous belief that nothing which
had ever interested the human mind
could wholly lose its vitality.
　　　　　　　　　　　　Ibid.
That sweet look of devotion which
men have never been able altogether to
love, and which still makes the born
saint an object almost of suspicion to
his earthly brethren.
　　　　　　　Ibid. Botticelli
The sunless pleasures of weary people, whose care for external things is
slackening.
　　　　　　　Ibid. Michelangelo
Hers is the head upon which all "the
ends of the world are come," and the
eyelids are a little weary. It is a beauty
wrought out from within upon the flesh,
the deposit, little cell by cell, of strange
thoughts and fantastic reveries and exquisite passions. Set it for a moment
beside one of those white Greek goddesses or beautiful women of antiquity,
and how would they be troubled by this
beauty, into which the soul with all its
maladies has passed?
　　　Ibid. Leonardo da Vinci
　　　　　　　　　　[*Mona Lisa*]
She is older than the rocks among
which she sits; like the vampire, she
has been dead many times, and learned
the secrets of the grave; and has been
a diver in deep seas, and keeps their
fallen day about her; and trafficked for
strange webs with Eastern merchants:
and as Leda, was the mother of Helen

of Troy, and, as Saint Anne, the mother
of Mary; and all this has been to her
but as the sound of lyres and flutes, and
lives only in the delicacy with which
it has moulded the changing lineaments,
and tinged the eyelids and the hands.

*The Renaissance. Leonardo
da Vinci [Mona Lisa]*

All art constantly aspires towards the
condition of music.

Ibid. The School of Giorgione

They [1] form a circle which in an age
of great troubles, losses, anxieties, can
amuse itself with art, poetry, intrigue.

Ibid. Du Bellay

Religions, as they grow by natural
laws out of man's life, are modified by
whatever modifies his life.

Ibid. Winckelmann

Let us understand by poetry all literary production which attains the power
of giving pleasure by its form, as distinct from its matter.

Ibid.

To burn always with this hard, gem-
like flame, to maintain this ecstasy, is
success in life.

Ibid. Conclusion

What we have to do is to be for ever
curiously testing new opinions and
courting new impressions.

Ibid.

Art comes to you proposing frankly
to give nothing but the highest quality
to your moments as they pass.

Ibid.

A book, like a person, has its fortunes
with one; is lucky or unlucky in the
precise moment of its falling in our
way, and often by some happy accident
counts with us for something more than
its independent value.

*Marius the Epicurean
[1885]. Chap. 6*

To know when one's self is interested, is the first condition of interesting other people.

Ibid.

Given the hardest terms, supposing
our days are indeed but a shadow, even

[1] The poets of the *Pléiade.*

so, we may well adorn and beautify, in
scrupulous self-respect, our souls, and
whatever our souls touch upon.

Marius the Epicurean. Chap. 8

By the attainment of a true philosophy to attain happiness; or, having
missed both, to perish, as one of the
vulgar herd.

Ibid. Chap. 24

I hardly know wherein philosophy
and wine are alike unless it be in
this, that the philosophers exchange
their ware for money, like the wine-
merchants; some of them with a mixture of water or worse, or giving short
measure.

Ibid.

We need some imaginative stimulus,
some not impossible ideal such as may
shape vague hope, and transform it into
effective desire, to carry us year after
year, without disgust, through the
routine-work which is so large a part of
life.

Ibid. Chap. 25

The aim of a true philosophy must
lie, not in futile efforts towards the complete accommodation of man to the
circumstances in which he chances to
find himself, but in the maintenance of
a kind of candid discontent, in the face
of the very highest achievement.

Ibid.

Through the survival of their children, happy parents are able to think
calmly, and with a very practical affection, of a world in which they are to
have no direct share.

Ibid.

JAMES RYDER RANDALL
[1839–1908]

Hark to an exiled son's appeal,
    Maryland, my Maryland!
My Mother State, to thee I kneel.

*Maryland, My Maryland [1861].
Stanza 2*

From hill to hill, from creek to creek,
Potomac calls to Chesapeake,
    Maryland, my Maryland.

Ibid. Stanza 7

SAMUEL JOHN STONE
[1839–1900]

Where did I come from, then? Ah,
   where indeed?
This is a riddle monstrous hard to read.
I have it! Why, of course,
All things are moulded by some plastic
   force
Out of some atoms somewhere up in
   space,
Fortuitously concurrent anyhow —
There, now!
That's plain as is the beak upon my
   face.
     *Soliloquy of a Rationalistic
           Chicken* [1]

What I can't see, I never will believe in!
               Ibid.

WILFRID SCAWEN BLUNT
[1840–1922]

He who has once been happy is for aye
Out of destruction's reach.
       Sonnet, With Esther
Nor has the world a better thing,
   Though one should search it round,
Than thus to live one's own sole king,
   Upon one's own sole ground.
       The Old Squire. Stanza 14
Ay, this is the famed rock, which Her-
   cules
And Goth and Moor bequeathed us. At
   this door
England stands sentry.
       Sonnet, Gibraltar

HENRY BURTON
[1840–1930]

Have you had a kindness shown?
   Pass it on.
       Pass It On. [2] *Stanza 1*
Hold thy lighted lamp on high,
Be a star in someone's sky.
       Ibid. Stanza 4

[1] In *Harper's Monthly*, September, 1875.
[2] Official poem of the International Sunshine Society.

TIMOTHY J. CAMPBELL
[1840–1904]

What's the Constitution between
friends? [1]
     Attributed [Circa *1885*]

JOHN WHITE CHADWICK
[1840–1904]

If good men were only better,
Would the wicked be so bad?
     A Timely Question. Stanza 1
It singeth low in every heart,
   We hear it each and all, —
A song of those who answer not,
   However we may call.
     Auld Lang Syne. Stanza 1

HENRY AUSTIN DOBSON
[1840–1921]

Once at the Angelus
   (Ere I was dead),
Angels all glorious
   Came to my bed.
      "Good-Night, Babette!"
Time goes, you say? Ah no!
Alas, Time stays, *we* go.
     The Paradox of Time. Stanza 1
The ladies of St. James's!
   They're painted to the eyes;
Their white it stays for ever,
   Their red it never dies:
But Phyllida, my Phyllida!
   Her color comes and goes;
It trembles to a lily, —
   It wavers to a rose.
     The Ladies of St. James's. Stanza 4
Far better, in some nook unknown,
   To sleep for once — and soundly —
Than still survive in wistful stone,
   Forgotten more profoundly.
     *To an Unknown Bust in the
       British Museum. Stanza 6*
Yet would today when Courtesy grows
   chill,
And life's fine loyalties are turned to
   jest,

[1] Campbell's reported comment to President Cleveland, who refused to support a
bill urged by Campbell on the grounds that
it was unconstitutional. Campbell was a Tam-
many representative from New York.

Some fire of thine might burn within us
  still!
Ah, would but one might lay his lance
  in rest,
And charge in earnest — were it but
  a mill!
> *Don Quixote*

Form is the Cage and Sense the Bird.
The Poet twirls them in his Mind,
And wins the Trick with both combined.
> *The Toyman*

He praised the Thing he understood;
'Twere well if every Critic would.
> *The 'Squire at Vauxhall. Moral 2*

I intended an Ode,
And it turned to a Sonnet.
It began *à la mode*,
I intended an Ode;
But Rose crossed the road
In her latest new bonnet;
I intended an Ode;
And it turned to a Sonnet.
> *Urceus Exit*

Love comes back to his vacant dwelling, —
The old, old Love that we knew of
  yore!
> *The Wanderer. Stanza 1*

In the work-a-day world, — for its
  needs and woes,
There is place and enough for the pains
  of prose;
But whenever the May-bells clash and
  chime,
Then hey! — for the ripple of laughing
  rhyme!
> *The Ballad of Prose and Rhyme.*
> *Envoy*

Fame is a food that dead men eat, —
I have no stomach for such meat.
> *Fame Is a Food that Dead Men*
> *Eat. Stanza 1*

The Press is too much with us: small
  and great;
We are undone of chatter and *on dit*,
Report, retort, rejoinder, repartee,
Mole-hill and mare's nest, fiction up-to-
date.
> *A Pleasant Invective Against*
> *Printing*

WILLIAM CHANNING GANNETT

[1840–1923]

The poem hangs on the berry bush
  When comes the poet's eye;
The street begins to masquerade
  When Shakespeare passes by.
The Christ sees white in Judas's heart
  And loves His traitor well;
The God, to angel His new heaven,
  Explores His lowest hell.
> *We See as We Are*

THOMAS HARDY

[1840–1928]

When I set out for Lyonnesse,
  A hundred miles away,
  The rime was on the spray,
And starlight lit my lonesomeness.
> *When I Set Out for Lyonnesse*
> [1870]

Good, but not religious-good.
> *Under the Greenwood Tree*
> [1872]. *Chap. 2*

The kingly brilliance of Sirius pierced
the eye with a steely glitter, the star
called Capella was yellow, Aldebaran
and Betelgueux shone with a fiery red.
To persons standing alone on a hill
during a clear midnight such as this, the
roll of the world eastward is almost a
palpable movement.
> *Far From the Madding Crowd*
> [1874]. *Chap. 2*

In fact, precisely at this transitional
point of its nightly roll into darkness
the great and particular glory of the
Egdon waste began, and nobody could
be said to understand the heath who
had not been there at such a time. It
could best be felt when it could not
clearly be seen.
> *The Return of the Native* [1878].
> *Chap. 1*

The place became full of a watchful
intentness now; for when other things
sank brooding to sleep the heath appeared slowly to awake and listen.
> *Ibid.*

The great inviolate place had an ancient permanence which the sea cannot

claim. Who can say of a particular sea that it is old? Distilled by the sun, kneaded by the moon, it is renewed in a year, in a day, or in an hour. The sea changed, the fields changed, the rivers, the villages, and the people changed, yet Egdon remained.

The Return of the Native. Chap. 1

Like the British Constitution, she owes her success in practice to her inconsistencies in principle.

The Hand of Ethelberta [1876]

A lover without indiscretion is no lover at all.

Ibid.

That cold accretion called the world, which, so terrible in the mass, is so unformidable, even pitiable, in its units.

*Tess of the D'Urbervilles [1891].
Chap. 13*

That shabby corner of God's allotment where He lets the nettles grow, and where all unbaptized infants, notorious drunkards, suicides, and others of the conjecturally damned are laid.

Ibid. Chap. 14

The chronic melancholy which is taking hold of the civilized races with the decline of belief in a beneficent power.

Ibid. Chap. 18

The debatable land between predilection and love.

Ibid. Chap. 20

Patience, that blending of moral courage with physical timidity.

Ibid. Chap. 43

"Justice" was done, and the President of the Immortals (in Aeschylean phrase) had ended his sport with Tess.

Ibid. Chap. 59

William Dewy, Tranter Reuben,
  Farmer Ledlow late at plough,
Robert's kin, and John's and Ned's,
And the Squire, and Lady Susan, lie in
  Mellstock churchyard now!

Friends Beyond [1898]. Stanza 1

We have triumphed: this achievement
  turns the bane to antidote,
Unsuccesses to success,

Many thought-worn eves and morrows
  to a morrow free of thought.

Friends Beyond. Stanza 4

No more need we corn and clothing,
  feel of old terrestrial stress;
Chill detraction stirs no sigh;
Fear of death has even bygone us:
  death gave all that we possess.

Ibid. Stanza 5

That faiths by which my comrades
  stand
Seem fantasies to me,
And mirage-mists their Shining Land,
  Is a strange destiny.

*The Impercipient [1898].
Stanza 1*

He who breathes All's-Well to these
Breathes no All's-Well to me.

Ibid. Stanza 3

I leant upon a coppice gate
When Frost was spectre-gray,
And Winter's dregs made desolate
The weakening eye of day.

*The Darkling Thrush [1900].
Stanza 1*

An aged thrush, frail, gaunt, and small,
In blast-beruffled plume.

Ibid. Stanza 3

So little cause for carollings
Of such ecstatic sound
Was written on terrestrial things
Afar or nigh around,
That I could think there trembled
  through
His happy good-night air
Some blessed Hope, whereof he knew
And I was unaware.

Ibid. Stanza 4

What of the Immanent Will and its designs?
The Will has woven with an absent heed
Since life first was; and ever so will
  weave.

*The Dynasts [1904–1908].
Part I, Fore-Scene*

A local cult called Christianity.

Ibid. Spirit of the Years, Sc. 6

Aggressive Fancy working spells
Upon a mind o'erwrought.

Ibid. Sc. 6, Napoleon

Ere systemed suns were globed and lit
The slaughters of the race were writ.
> *The Dynasts. Part II, Sc. 5,*
> *Semi-chorus*

My argument is that War makes rattling good history; but Peace is poor reading.
> *Ibid. Spirit Sinister*

To see stand weeping by
A woman once embraced, will try
The tension of a man the most austere.
> *The Contretemps. Stanza 6*

One pairing is as good as another
Where all is venture!
> *Ibid. Stanza 10*

You have not known
Men's lives, deaths, toils, and teens;
You are but a heap of stick and stone:
A new house has no sense of the have-
beens.[1]
> *The Two Houses. Stanza 5*

"Yes; quaint and curious war is!
You shoot a fellow down
You'd treat if met where any bar is,
Or help to half-a-crown."
> *The Man He Killed. Stanza 5*

We have lost somewhat, afar and near,
Gentlemen,
The thinning of our ranks each year
Affords a hint we are nigh undone,
That we shall not be ever again
The marked of many, loved of one.
> *An Ancient to Ancients. Stanza 3*

Much is there waits you we have
missed;
Much lore we leave you worth the
knowing;
Much, much has lain outside our ken.
Nay, rush not: time serves; we are
going.
> *Ibid. Stanza 10*

A star looks down at me,
And says: "Here I and you

---

[1] There's nothing mournful about it; it cannot be sad and lone
For the lack of something within it that
it has never known.
JOYCE KILMER [1886–1918]: *The House
with Nobody in It, St. 5*

Stand, each in our degree:
What do you mean to do?"
> *Waiting Both. Stanza 1*

We two kept house, the Past and I,
The Past and I;
I tended while it hovered nigh,
Leaving me never alone.
> *The Ghost of the Past. Stanza 1*

Woman much missed, how you call to
me, call to me,
Saying that now you are not as you were
When you had changed from the one
who was all to me,
But as at first, when our day was fair.
> *The Voice [1912]*

What of the faith and fire within us
Men who march away
Ere the barn-cocks say
Night is growing gray?
> *Men Who March Away [1914]*

Only a man harrowing clods
In a slow silent walk
With an old horse that stumbles and
nods
Half asleep as they stalk.

Only thin smoke without flame
From the heaps of couch grass;
Yet this will go onward the same
Though Dynasties pass.

Yonder a maid and her wight
Come whispering by;
War's annals will cloud into night
Ere their story die.
> *In Time of "The Breaking of*
> *Nations" [1915]*

Yes, yes; I am old. In me appears
The history of a hundred years.
Empires', kings', captives' births and
deaths;
Strange faiths and fleeting shibboleths;
Tragedy, comedy, through my pages
Beyond all mummed on any stages;
Cold hearts beat hot, hot hearts beat
cold,
And I beat on.
> *The Newspaper Soliloquizes:*
> *London Observer, March 14,*
> *1926*

ROSSITER JOHNSON
[1840–1931]

O for a lodge in a garden of cucumbers! [1]
O for an iceberg or two at control!
O for a vale which at mid-day the dew cumbers!
O for a pleasure trip up to the Pole!
Ninety-nine in the Shade. Stanza 1

WILLIAM HENRY HARRISON ("ADIRONDACK") MURRAY
[1840–1904]

Ah, friends, dear friends, as years go on and heads get gray, how fast the guests do go!
Touch hands, touch hands, with those that stay.
Strong hands to weak, old hands to young, around the Christmas board, touch hands.
The false forget, the foe forgive, for every guest will go and every fire burn low and cabin empty stand.
Forget, forgive, for who may say that Christmas day may ever come to host or guest again.
Touch hands!
John Norton's Vagabond

ROSSITER WORTHINGTON RAYMOND
[1840–1918]

Life is eternal; and love is immortal; and death is only a horizon; and a horizon is nothing save the limit of our sight.
A Commendatory Prayer

WILLIAM GRAHAM SUMNER
[1840–1910]

The Forgotten Man [2] . . . delving away in patient industry, supporting his family, paying his taxes, casting his vote, supporting the church and the school . . . but he is the only one for whom there is no provision in the great

[1] As a lodge in a garden of cucumbers. — *Isaiah*, I, 8
[2] See Franklin D. Roosevelt, page 918b.

scramble and the big divide. Such is the Forgotten Man. He works, he votes, generally he prays — but his chief business in life is to pay. . . . Who and where is the Forgotten Man in this case, who will have to pay for it all?
Speech, The Forgotten Man [1883]

JOHN ADDINGTON SYMONDS
[1840–1893]

No seed shall perish which the soul hath sown.
Sonnet: Versöhnung, A Belief

Gods fade; but God abides and in man's heart
Speaks with the clear unconquerable cry
Of energies and hopes that can not die.
Sonnet, On the Sacro Monte

She smiled, and the shadows departed;
She shone, and the snows were rain;
And he who was frozen-hearted
Bloomed up into love again.
Eyebright

These things shall be, — a loftier race
Than e'er the world hath known shall rise
With flame of freedom in their souls,
And light of knowledge in their eyes.
The Days That Are to Be

KATHARINE KENT CHILD WALKER
[1840–1916]

However divinity schools may refuse to "skip" in unison, and may butt and butter each other about the doctrine and origin of human depravity, all will join devoutly in the credo, I believe in the total depravity of inanimate things.
The Total Depravity of Inanimate Things [1864]

The elusiveness of soap, the knottiness of strings, the transitory nature of buttons, the inclination of suspenders to twist and of hooks to forsake their

lawful eyes, and cleave only unto the hairs of their hapless owner's head.
The Total Depravity of Inanimate Things

HENRY WATTERSON
[1840–1921]

Things have come to a helluva pass
When a man can't cudgel his own jackass.
Reply when rebuked for criticizing the Governor of Kentucky

ELIZABETH WORDSWORTH
[1840–1932]

If all the good people were clever,
  And all clever people were good,
The world would be nicer than ever
  We thought that it possibly could.

But somehow, 'tis seldom or never
  The two hit it off as they should;
The good are so harsh to the clever,
  The clever so rude to the good!
The Clever and the Good [*1890*]

ÉMILE ZOLA
[1840–1902]

Truth is on the march and nothing can stop it.
J'Accuse [*1898*]

JOHN WILSON [1]
[? –1889]

Oh for a book and a shady nook,
  either in door or out;
With the green leaves whisp'ring overhead, or the street cries all about.
Where I may read all at my ease,
  both of the new and old;
For a jolly good book whereon to
  look is better to me than gold.
For a Catalogue of Secondhand Books

ROBERT BUCHANAN
[1841–1901]

The Fleshly School of Poetry.
Title of Article [*1871*]

[1] A London bookseller, friend of Austin Dobson.

The sweet post-prandial cigar.
De Berny
Alone at nights,
I read my Bible more and Euclid less.
An Old Dominie's Story
Beauty and Truth, tho' never found, are worthy to be sought.
To David in Heaven

I saw the starry Tree
Eternity
Put forth the blossom Time.
Proteus

Full of a sweet indifference.
Charmian

I say, the world is lovely,
And that loveliness is enough.
Artist and Model

A race that binds
Its body in chains and calls them Liberty,
And calls each fresh link Progress.
Political Mystics. Titan and Avatar

JUSTICE OLIVER WENDELL HOLMES, JR.
[1841–1935]

The life of the law has not been logic: it has been experience.
The Common Law [*1881*]

I think that, as life is action and passion, it is required of a man that he should share the passion and action of his time at peril of being judged not to have lived.
Memorial Day Address [*1884*]

Through our great good fortune, in our youth our hearts were touched with fire.
Ibid.

The Law, wherein, as in a magic mirror, we see reflected not only our own lives, but the lives of all men that have been! When I think on this majestic theme, my eyes dazzle.[1]
To the Suffolk Bar Association [*1885*]

[1] See John Webster, page 226a.

I say to you in all sadness of conviction, that to think great thoughts you must be heroes as well as idealists.

The Profession of the Law [*1886*]

Thus only can you gain the secret isolated joy of the thinker, who knows that, a hundred years after he is dead and forgotten, men who never heard of him will be moving to the measure of his thought, — the subtile rapture of a postponed power, which the world knows not because it has no external trappings, but which to his prophetic vision is more real than that which commands an army.

Ibid.

The prophecies of what the courts will do in fact, and nothing more pretentious, are what I mean by the law.

The Path of the Law [*1897*]

Certainty generally is illusion, and repose is not the destiny of man.

Ibid.

The remoter and more general aspects of the law are those which give it universal interest. It is through them that you not only become a great master in your calling, but connect your subject with the universe and catch an echo of the infinite, a glimpse of its unfathomable process, a hint of the universal law.

Ibid.

The rule of joy and the law of duty seem to me all one.

Speech at Bar Association Dinner, Boston [*1900*]

Life is an end in itself, and the only question as to whether it is worth living is whether you have enough of it.

Ibid.

A great man represents a great ganglion in the nerves of society, or, to vary the figure, a strategic point in the campaign of history, and part of his greatness consists in his being *there.*

John Marshall [*1901*]

Taxes are what we pay for civilized society.

Compañia de Tabacos v. *Collector, 275 U. S. 87, 100* [*1904*]

Great cases like hard cases make bad law.

Northern Securities Co. v. *United States, 193 U. S. 197, 400* [*1904*]

The Fourteenth Amendment does not enact Mr. Herbert Spencer's *Social Statics.*

Lochner v. *New York, 198 U. S. 45, 75* [*1905*]

General propositions do not decide concrete cases. The decision will depend on a judgment or intuition more subtle than any articulate major premise.

Ibid. Page 78

Life is painting a picture, not doing a sum.

The Class of '61 [*Speeches, 1913*]

I learned in the regiment and in the class the conclusion, at least, of what I think the best service that we can do for our country and for ourselves: To see so far as one may, and to feel the great forces that are behind every detail . . . ; to hammer out as compact and solid a piece of work as one can, to try to make it first rate, and to leave it unadvertised.

Ibid.

The only prize much cared for by the powerful is power. The prize of the general is not a bigger tent, but command.

Law and the Court [*1913*]

Judges are apt to be naif, simpleminded men, and they need something of Mephistopheles. We too need education in the obvious — to learn to transcend our own convictions and to leave room for much that we hold dear to be done away with short of revolution by the orderly change of law.

Ibid.

I recognize without hesitation that judges do and must legislate, but they can do so only interstitially; they are confined from molar to molecular motions.

Southern Pacific Co. v. *Jensen, 244 U. S. 205, 221* [*1917*]

The common law is not a brooding omnipresence in the sky but the articulate voice of some sovereign or quasi-sovereign that can be identified.

Southern Pacific Co. v. *Jensen, 244 U. S. 205, 221. Page 222*

Certitude is not the test of certainty.

Natural Law [*1918*]

When men have realized that time has upset many fighting faiths, they may come to believe even more than they believe the very foundations of their own conduct that the ultimate good desired is better reached by free trade in ideas — that the best test of truth is the power of the thought to get itself accepted in the competition of the market, and that truth is the only ground upon which their wishes safely can be carried out. That at any rate is the theory of our Constitution. It is an experiment, as all life is an experiment.

Abrams v. *United States, 250 U. S. 616, 630* [*1919*]

Upon this point a page of history is worth a volume of logic.

New York Trust Co. v. *Eisner, 256 U. S. 345, 349* [*1921*]

It is said that this manifesto is more than a theory, that it was an incitement. Every idea is an incitement.

Gitlow v. *New York, 268 U. S. 652, 673* [*1925*]

Three generations of imbeciles are enough.

Buck v. *Bell, 274 U. S. 200, 207* [*1927*]

For my part I think it a less evil that some criminals should escape than that the government should play an ignoble part. . . . If the existing code does not permit district attorneys to have a hand in such dirty business, it does not permit the judge to allow such iniquities to succeed.

Olmstead v. *United States, 277 U. S. 438, 470* [*1928*]

If there is any principle of the Constitution that more imperatively calls for attachment than any other it is the principle of free thought — not free thought for those who agree with us but freedom for the thought that we hate.

United States v. Schwimmer, 279 U. S. 644, 653 [*1928*]

The riders in a race do not stop short when they reach the goal. There is a little finishing canter before coming to a standstill. There is time to hear the kind voice of friends and to say to one's self: "The work is done." But just as one says that, the answer comes: "The race is over, but the work never is done while the power to work remains." The canter that brings you to a standstill need not be only coming to rest. It cannot be, while you still live. For to live is to function. That is all there is in living.

Radio address on his ninetieth birthday [*March 8, 1931*]

Life seems to me like a Japanese picture which our imagination does not allow to end with the margin. We aim at the infinite and when our arrow falls to earth it is in flames.

Message to the Federal Bar Association [*February 29, 1932*]

WILLIAM HENRY HUDSON
[1841–1922]

When I meet with a falsehood, I care not who the great persons who proclaim it may be, I do not try to like it or believe it or mimic the fashionable prattle of the world about it.

The Purple Land [*1885*]. *Chap. 28*

You cannot fly like an eagle with the wings of a wren.

Afoot in England [*1909*]. *Chap. 6*

When I hear people say they have not found the world and life so agreeable or interesting as to be in love with it, or that they look with equanimity to its end, I am apt to think they have never been properly alive nor seen with clear vision the world they think so meanly of, or anything in it — not a blade of grass. Only I know that mine is an exceptional case, that the visible world is to me more beautiful and interesting than to most persons, that the delight I experienced in my communings with Nature did not pass away, leaving nothing but a recollection of vanished happiness to intensify a present pain. The happiness was never lost, . . . so that in my worst times, when I was compelled to exist shut out from Nature in London for long periods, sick and poor and friendless, I could yet always feel that it was infinitely better to be than not to be.

Far Away and Long Ago [*1918*].
Chap. 24

SIR RICHARD CLAVER-HOUSE JEBB
[1841–1905]

At the middle point of the [Greek] stage, some steps — known as "Charon's staircase," because the ghost sometimes comes up by them — lead down into what we should call the pit.

Greek Literature [*1877*]

MARY ARTEMISIA LATHBURY [1]
[1841–1913]

Day is dying in the west;
Heaven is touching earth with rest.
Day Is Dying in the West
[*1877*]. *Stanza 1*

Children of yesterday,
Heirs of tomorrow,
What are you weaving?
Labor and sorrow?
Look to your looms again,
Faster and faster
Fly the great shuttles
Prepared by the Master.
Life's in the loom,
Room for it — room!
Song of Hope. Stanza 1

[1] Miss Lathbury was known as the Chautauqua Laureate.

JOAQUIN [1] MILLER (CINCINNATUS HEINE MILLER)
[1841?–1913]

That man who lives for self alone
Lives for the meanest mortal known.
Walker in Nicaragua. Chant I,
Stanza 1

In men whom men condemn as ill
I find so much of goodness still,[2]
In men whom men pronounce divine
I find so much of sin and blot,
I do not dare to draw a line
Between the two, where God has not.[3]
Byron

The bravest battle that ever was fought;
Shall I tell you where and when?
On the maps of the world you will find it not;
It was fought by the mothers of men.
The Bravest Battle. Stanza 1

The soul that feeds on books alone —
I count that soul exceeding small
That lives alone by book and creed, —
A soul that has not learned to read.
The Larger College. Stanza 10

Honor and glory forever more
To this good man gone to rest;
Peace on the dim Plutonian shore;[4]
Rest in the land of the blest.
Peter Cooper, April, 1883.
Stanza 1

[1] In a paper, *How I Came to be a Writer of Books* [*Lippincott's Magazine*, 1886], quoted in STUART P. SHERMAN's introduction to *The Poetical Works of Joaquin Miller* [1923], Miller explains the origin of his pen name. His first writing was a public letter in defense of Joaquin Murietta, the outlaw. A Sacramento newspaper banteringly identified him with the outlaw, and friends continued the banter. The name "Joaquin" clung to him, so Miller accepted it and used it in the title of his first book and thereafter.

[2] See Shakespeare, page 155b.

[3] There is so much good in the worst of us,
And so much bad in the best of us,
That it hardly behooves any of us
To talk about the rest of us.
First printed in *The Marion* (Kansas) *Record*, owned by Governor Edward Wallis Hoch [1849–1925], and assumed to have been written by him

[4] See Poe, page 545a.

The biggest dog has been a pup.
>*William Brown of Oregon.*
>*Stanza 5*

Behind him lay the gray Azores,
Behind the Gates of Hercules;
Before him not the ghost of shores,
Before him only shoreless seas.
>*Columbus. Stanza 1*

He gained a world; he gave that world
Its grandest lesson: "On! sail on!"
>*Ibid. Stanza 5*

The Lightning reached a fiery rod,
And on Death's fearful forehead wrote
The autograph of God.
>*With Love to You and Yours.*
>*Part I, Canto III*

PIERRE AUGUSTE RENOIR
[1841–1919]

I have a predilection for painting
that lends joyousness to a wall.
>AMBROISE VOLLARD: *Renoir*
>*[1919]*

MINOT JUDSON SAVAGE
[1841–1918]

There comes an hour of sadness
With the setting of the sun,
Not for the sins committed,
But the things I have not done.
>*Things Not Done*

A man's truest monument must be a
man.
>*The Song of a Man (Phillips*
>*Brooks). Stanza 8*

CLEMENT WILLIAM SCOTT
[1841–1904]

Oh, promise me that some day you and I
Will take our love together to some sky
Where we can be alone and faith renew,
And find the hollows where those flowers
grew.
>*Oh, Promise Me [1888]*

EDWARD ROWLAND SILL
[1841–1887]

At the punch-bowl's brink
Let the thirsty think
What they say in Japan:

"First the man takes a drink,
Then the drink takes a drink,
Then the drink takes the man!"
>*An Adage from the Orient*

No pity, Lord, could change the heart
From red with wrong to white as wool;
The rod must heal the sin: but Lord,
Be merciful to me, a fool!
>*The Fool's Prayer*

'Tis by our follies that so long
We hold the earth from heaven away.
>*Ibid.*

The ill-timed truth we might have
kept —
Who knows how sharp it pierced and
stung?
The word we had not sense to say —
Who knows how grandly it had rung?
>*Ibid.*

Earth bears no balsam for mistakes;
Men crown the knave, and scourge the
tool
That did his will.[1]
>*Ibid.*

What may we take into the vast For-
ever?
That marble door
Admits no fruit of all our long endeavor,
No fame-wreathed crown we wore,
No garnered lore.
>*The Future*

SIR HENRY MORTON
STANLEY
[1841–1904]

Doctor Livingstone, I presume?
>*On meeting Livingstone in Ujiji,*
>*Central Africa [November 10,*
>*1871]*

EUGENE FITCH WARE
("IRONQUILL")
[1841–1911]

Human hopes and human creeds
Have their root in human needs.
>*The Rhymes of Ironquill.*
>*Preface*

---

[1] The law locks up both man and woman
Who steals the goose from off the common,

Man builds no structure which outlives a book.

The Book

O Dewey was the morning
Upon the first of May,
And Dewey was the Admiral
Down in Manila Bay;
And Dewey were the Regent's eyes,
"Them" orbs of royal blue!
And Dewey feel discouraged?
I Dew not think we Dew.

In the Topeka (Kansas) Daily Capital, May 3, 1898

Work brings its own relief;
He who most idle is
Has most of grief.

Today

No evil deed live oN.

The Palindrome

I'm ignorant of music, but still, in spite of that,
I always drop a quarter in an organ-grinder's hat.

The Organ-Grinder

The ballads of the people are the bulwarks of the State.

Ibid.

The highest of renown
Are the surest stricken down;
But the stupid and the clown
They remain.

Paresis

The Turks,
Becoming somewhat sad,
Surrendered every
Consonant they had.

The Siege of Djklxprwbz

Oft the statesman and the saint
Think they're doing good, but ain't.

Aesop's Fables. No. 17

The days of long-haired poets now are o'er;
The short-haired poet seems to have the floor.

The Short-Haired Poet. Stanza 3

But lets the greater felon loose
Who steals the common from the goose.
ANONYMOUS. *Quoted by* EDWARD POTTS CHEYNEY: *Social and Industrial History of England* [1901], *Introduction*

The farmer works the soil,
The agriculturist works the farmer.

The Kansas Bandit

CHARLES FOLLEN ADAMS
[1842–1918]

I haf von funny leedle poy
Vot gomes schust to mine knee;
Der queerest schap, der createst rogue,
As efer you dit see.
He runs, und schumps, und schmashes dings
In all barts off der house:
But vot off dot? He vas mine son,
Mine leedle Yawcob Strauss.

Yawcob Strauss. Stanza 1

I vants to gondradict dot shap
Dot made dis leedle shoke:
"A voman vas der glinging vine,
Und man der shturdy oak."

Der Oak und der Vine. Stanza 1

AMBROSE BIERCE
[1842–1914 ?]

Mark how my fame rings out from zone to zone:
A thousand critics shouting: "He's unknown!"

Couplet

Cynic, perforce, from study of mankind
In the false volume of his single mind,
He damned his fellows for his own unworth,
And, bad himself, thought nothing good on earth.
He yearned to squander what he lived to save
And did not, for he could not, cheat the grave.

An Epitaph

To men a man is but a mind. Who cares
What face he carries or what form he wears?
But woman's body is the woman. O
Stay thou, my sweetheart, and do never go.

The Devil's Dictionary [1] *[1906]*

---

[1] First published as *The Cynic's Word Book*, retitled in 1911.

Advice: the smallest current coin.
The Devil's Dictionary

Bore: a person who talks when you wish him to listen.
Ibid.

Edible: good to eat, and wholesome to digest, as a worm to a toad, a snake to a pig, a pig to a man, and a man to a worm.
Ibid.

Garter: an elastic band intended to keep a woman from coming out of her stockings and desolating the country.
Ibid.

Labor: one of the processes by which A acquires property for B.
Ibid.

Marriage: a community consisting of a master, a mistress, and two slaves, making in all, two.
Ibid.

Piracy: commerce without its folly-swaddles, just as God made it.
Ibid.

Prejudice: a vagrant opinion without visible means of support.
Ibid.

Saint: a dead sinner revised and edited.
Ibid.

Woman would be more charming if one could fall into her arms without falling into her hands.
Epigrams

You are not permitted to kill a woman who has injured you, but nothing forbids you to reflect that she is growing older every minute. You are avenged 1440 times a day.
Ibid.

Self-denial is indulgence of a propensity to forego.
Ibid.

CHARLES EDWARD CARRYL
[1842–1920]

The night was thick and hazy
When the *Piccadilly Daisy*

Carried down the crew and Captain in the sea;
And I think the water drowned 'em,
For they never, never found 'em,
And I know they didn't come ashore with me.
Robinson Crusoe. Stanza 1

I had that fellow Friday
Just to keep the tavern tidy.
Ibid. Stanza 3

Canary birds feed on sugar and seed,
Parrots have crackers to crunch;
And as for the poodles, they tell me the noodles
Have chicken and cream for their lunch.
But there's never a question
About my digestion —
Anything does for me!
The Plaint of the Camel.
Stanza 1

A capital ship for an ocean trip
Was the "Walloping Window-blind."
No gale that blew dismayed her crew
Or troubled the Captain's mind.
The man at the wheel was taught to feel
Contempt for the wildest blow,
And it often appeared, when the weather had cleared,
That he'd been in his bunk below.
Davy and the Goblin, A Nautical
Ballad. Stanza 1

INA DONNA COOLBRITH
[1842–1928]

He walks with God upon the hills!
And sees, each morn, the world arise
New-bathed in light of paradise.
The Poet

CHARLES MONROE DICKINSON
[1842–1924]

When the lessons and tasks are all ended,
And the school for the day is dismissed,
And the little ones gather around me
To bid me "good-night" and be kissed.
The Children. Stanza 1

WILLIAM JAMES
[1842–1910]

Habit is thus the enormous fly-wheel of society, its most precious conservative agent. It alone is what keeps us all within the bounds of ordinance.

The Principles of Psychology [1890]. Chap. 10

It is well for the world that in most of us, by the age of thirty, the character has set like plaster, and will never soften again.

Ibid.

There is no more miserable human being than one in whom nothing is habitual but indecision.

Ibid.

No matter how full a reservoir of *maxims* one may possess, and no matter how good one's *sentiments* may be, if one have not taken advantage of every concrete opportunity to *act*, one's character may remain entirely unaffected for the better. With mere good intentions, hell is proverbially paved.[1]

Ibid.

Keep the faculty of effort alive in you by a little gratuitous exercise every day. That is, be systematically ascetic or heroic in little unnecessary points, do every day or two something for no other reason than that you would rather not do it, so that when the hour of dire need draws nigh, it may find you not unnerved and untrained to stand the test.

Ibid.

The hell to be endured hereafter, of which theology tells, is no worse than the hell we make for ourselves in this world by habitually fashioning our characters in the wrong way.

Ibid.

No state [of mind] once gone can recur and be identical with what it was before.

Ibid. Chap. 11

[1] Hell is paved with good intentions. — JOHN RAY: *English Proverbs* [1670]
See George Herbert, page 233b.
Hell is paved with good intentions, not with bad ones. — BERNARD SHAW [1856–1950]: *Maxims for Revolutionists*

We are not only gregarious animals, liking to be in sight of our fellows, but we have an innate propensity to get ourselves noticed, and noticed favorably, by our kind. No more fiendish punishment could be devised, were such a thing physically possible, than that one should be turned loose in society and remain absolutely unnoticed by all the members thereof.

The Principles of Psychology. Chap. 12

In the practical as in the theoretic life, the man whose acquisitions *stick* is the man who is always achieving and advancing, whilst his neighbors, spending most of their time in relearning what they once knew but have forgotten, simply hold their own.

Ibid. Chap. 18

Genius, in truth, means little more than the faculty of perceiving in an unhabitual way.

Ibid. Chap. 20

The great source of terror to infancy is solitude.

Ibid. Chap. 25

A thing is important if any one *think* it important.

Ibid. Chap. 28

If this life be not a real fight, in which something is eternally gained for the universe by success, it is no better than a game of private theatricals from which one may withdraw at will. But it *feels* like a real fight.

The Will to Believe [1897]

The deepest thing in our nature is . . . this dumb region of the heart in which we dwell alone with our willingnesses and unwillingnesses, our faiths and fears.

Ibid.

Be not afraid of life. Believe that life *is* worth living, and your belief will help create the fact.[1]

Ibid.

The whole drift of my education goes to persuade me that the world of our present consciousness is only one out of

[1] See Alfred Austin, page 669a–669b.

many worlds of consciousness that exist.
> *The Varieties of Religious Experience* [*1902*]. *Lecture XX*

Man, biologically considered, and whatever else he may be in the bargain, is simply the most formidable of all the beasts of prey, and, indeed, the only one that preys systematically on its own species.
> *Remarks at the Peace Banquet* [*October 7, 1904*]

Man lives *by* habits, indeed, but what he lives *for* is thrills and excitements.
> *Ibid.*

JOHN ALEXANDER JOYCE
[1842–1915]

You must leave your many millions
  And the gay and festive crowd;
Though you roll in royal billions,
  There's no pocket in a shroud.[1]
> *There's No Pocket in a Shroud.* *Stanza 1*

I shall love you in December
With the love I gave in May! [2]
> *Question and Answer. Stanza 8*

SIDNEY LANIER
[1842–1881]

The sun is a-wait at the ponderous gate of the West.
> *The Marshes of Glynn* [*1877*]. *IV, 3*

Ye marshes, how candid and simple and
    nothing-withholding and free
Ye publish yourselves to the sky and
    offer yourselves to the sea!
Tolerant plains, that suffer the sea and
    the rains and the sun,
Ye spread and span like the catholic
    man who hath mightily won
God out of knowledge and good out of
    infinite pain

[1] You Can't Take It With You. — *Title of Comedy by* Moss Hart and George Kaufman [1937]

[2] Will you love me in December as you do in May? — James J. Walker, *set to music by* Ernest R. Ball [1905]

And sight out of blindness and purity
    out of a stain.
> *The Marshes of Glynn. IV, 6*

As the marsh-hen secretly builds on the
    watery sod,
Behold I will build me a nest on the
    greatness of God:
I will fly in the greatness of God as the
    marsh-hen flies
In the freedom that fills all the space
    'twixt the marsh and the skies:
By so many roots as the marsh-grass
    sends in the sod
I will heartily lay me a-hold on the
    greatness of God:
Oh, like to the greatness of God is the
    greatness within
The range of the marshes, the liberal
    marshes of Glynn.
> *Ibid. 7*

Out of the hills of Habersham,
Down the valleys of Hall.
> *Song of the Chattahoochee* [*1877*]. *Stanza 1*

Downward the voices of Duty call —
Downward, to toil and be mixed with
    the main,
The dry fields burn, and the mills are to
    turn.
> *Ibid. Stanza 5*

The incalculable Up-and-Down of
    Time.
> *Clover* [*1877*]

Life! thou sea-fugue, writ from east to
    west,
  Love, Love alone can pore
  On thy dissolving score
Of harsh half-phrasings,
  Blotted ere writ,
And double erasings
  Of chords most fit.
> *The Symphony* [*1877*]

Music is Love in search of a word.
> *Ibid.*

Into the woods my Master went,
Clean forspent, forspent.
Into the woods my Master came,
Forspent with love and shame.
> *A Ballad of Trees and the Master* [*1877*]. *Stanza 1*

'Twas on a tree they slew Him — last
When out of the woods He came.
A Ballad of Trees and the Master.
Stanza 2

Now in the sea's red vintage melts the
sun,
As Egypt's pearl dissolved in rosy
wine,
And Cleopatra night drinks all.
Evening Song. Stanza 2

My soul is sailing through the sea,
But the Past is heavy and hindereth me.
Barnacles [1877]. Stanza 1

DAVID LAW PROUDFIT
("PELEG ARKWRIGHT")
[1842–1897]

A man sat on a rock and sought
Refreshment from his thumb;
A dinotherium wandered by
And scared him some.
His name was Smith. The kind of rock
He sat upon was shale.
One feature quite distinguished him —
He had a tail.
Prehistoric Smith

Nature abhors imperfect work
And on it lays her ban;
And all creation must despise
A tailless man.
Ibid.

MAY RILEY SMITH
[1842–1927]

Strange we never prize the music
Till the sweet-voiced bird has flown,
Strange that we should slight the violets
Till the lovely flowers are gone.
If We Knew [1867]

HUGH ANTOINE D'ARCY
[1843–1925]

"Say, boys! if you give me just another
whiskey I'll be glad,
And I'll draw right here a picture of the
face that drove me mad.
Give me that piece of chalk with which
you mark the baseball score,

You shall see the lovely Madeleine
upon the bar-room floor."
The Face upon the Floor [1887] [1]

With chalk in hand the vagabond began
To sketch a face that well might buy
the soul of any man.
Then as he placed another lock upon
the shapely head,
With a fearful shriek he leaped and fell
across the picture — dead!
Ibid.

SARAH DOUDNEY
[1843–1926]

Oh, the wasted hours of life
That have drifted by!
Oh, the good that might have been,
Lost without a sigh!
The Lesson of the Water-Mill
[1864]

ANNA E. HAMILTON
[1843–1876]

This learned I from the shadow of a
tree,
That to and fro did sway against a wall,
Our shadow selves, our influence, may
fall
Where we ourselves can never be.
Influence

HENRY JAMES
[1843–1916]

The face of nature and civilization
in this our country is to a certain point a
very sufficient literary field. But it will
yield its secrets only to a really *grasping*
imagination. . . . To write well and
worthily of American things one need
even more than elsewhere to be a
master.
Letter to Charles Eliot Norton
[January 16, 1871]

It's a complex fate, being an American, and one of the responsibilities it

[1] Often given as "The Face on the Barroom
Floor."

entails is fighting against a superstitious valuation of Europe.

> *Letter [1872]. Quoted in* PERCY
> LUBBOCK, *Letters of Henry*
> *James [1920], Vol. I, Page 13*

If the picturesque were banished
from the face of the earth, I think the
idea would survive in some typical
American breast.

> *Transatlantic Sketches [1875]*

It takes a great deal of history to
produce a little literature.

> *Hawthorne [1879]. Chap. 1*

Whatever question there may be of
his [Thoreau's] talent, there can be
none, I think, of his genius. It was a
slim and crooked one, but it was eminently personal. He was unperfect, unfinished, inartistic; he was worse than
provincial — he was parochial.

> *Ibid. Chap. 4*

Cats and monkeys, monkeys and cats
— all human life is there.

> *The Madonna of the Future*
> *[1879]*

There are few hours in life more
agreeable than the hour dedicated to
the ceremony known as afternoon tea.

> *The Portrait of a Lady [1881]*

At moments she discovered she was
grotesquely wrong, and then she treated
herself to a week of passionate humility.

> *Ibid.*

The real offence, as she ultimately
perceived, was her having a mind of her
own at all. Her mind was to be his —
attached to his own like a small garden-
plot to a deer-park.

> *Ibid.*

The only reason for the existence of a
novel is that it does attempt to represent life.

> *The Art of Fiction [1888]*

The only obligation to which in advance we may hold a novel, without
incurring the accusation of being arbitrary, is that it be interesting.

> *Ibid.*

The advantage, the luxury, as well as
the torment and responsibility of the
novelist, is that there is no limit to

what he may attempt as an executant —
no limit to his possible experiments, efforts, discoveries, successes.

> *The Art of Fiction*

The power to guess the unseen from
the seen, to trace the implications of
things, to judge the whole piece by the
pattern, the condition of feeling life in
general so completely that you are well
on your way to knowing any particular
corner of it — this cluster of gifts may
almost be said to constitute experience.
. . . If experience consists of impressions, it may be said that impressions
are experience. . . . Therefore, if I
should certainly say to a novice, "Write
from experience and experience only,"
I should feel that this was rather a
tantalizing monition if I were not careful immediately to add, "Try to be one
of the people on whom nothing is lost."

> *Ibid.*

We must grant the artist his subject,
his idea, his *donnée:* our criticism is applied only to what he makes of it. . . .
If we pretend to respect the artist at all,
we must allow him his freedom of
choice, in the face, in particular cases,
of innumerable presumptions that the
choice will not fructify. Art derives a
considerable part of its beneficial exercise from flying in the face of presumptions.

> *Ibid.*

There are few things more exciting to
me . . . than a psychological reason.

> *Ibid.*

The practice of "reviewing" . . . in
general has nothing in common with
the art of criticism.

> *Criticism [1893]*

The critical sense is so far from frequent that it is absolutely rare, and the
possession of the cluster of qualities that
minister to it is one of the highest distinctions. . . . In this light one sees
the critic as the real helper of the artist, a torch-bearing outrider, the interpreter, the brother. . . . Just in proportion as he is sentient and restless,
just in proportion as he reacts and

reciprocates and penetrates, is the critic a valuable instrument.

Criticism

However incumbent it may be on most of us to do our duty, there is, in spite of a thousand narrow dogmatisms, nothing in the world that any one is under the least obligation to *like* — not even (one braces one's self to risk the declaration) a particular kind of writing.

Flaubert [*1893*]

The time-honored bread-sauce of the happy ending.

Theatricals: Second Series [*1895*]

"Live all you can; it's a mistake not to. It doesn't so much matter what you do in particular, so long as you have had your life. If you haven't had that what *have* you had? . . . What one loses one loses; make no mistake about that. . . . The right time is *any* time that one is still so lucky as to have. . . . Live!"

The Ambassadors [*1903*]. *Book Fifth, Chap. 2*

Really, universally, relations stop nowhere, and the exquisite problem of the artist is eternally but to draw, by a geometry of his own, the circle within which they shall happily *appear* to do so.

Prefaces [*1907–1909*]. *Roderick Hudson*

There is, I think, no more nutritive or suggestive truth . . . than that of the perfect dependence of the "moral" sense of a work of art on the amount of felt life concerned in producing it. The question comes back thus, obviously, to the kind and the degree of the artist's prime sensibility, which is the soil out of which his subject springs.

Ibid. The Portrait of a Lady

To see deep difficulty braved is at any time, for the really addicted artist, to feel almost even as a pang the beautiful incentive, and to feel it verily in such sort as to wish the danger intensified. The difficulty most worth tackling

can only be for him, in these conditions, the greatest the case permits of.

Prefaces. The Portrait of a Lady

Life being all inclusion and confusion, and art being all discrimination and selection, the latter, in search of the hard latent *value* with which it alone is concerned, sniffs round the mass as instinctively and unerringly as a dog suspicious of some buried bone.

Ibid. The Spoils of Poynton

The fatal futility of Fact.

Ibid.

No themes are so human as those that reflect for us, out of the confusion of life, the close connexion of bliss and bale, of the things that help with the things that hurt, so dangling before us for ever that bright hard medal, of so strange an alloy, one face of which is somebody's right and ease and the other somebody's pain and wrong.

Ibid. What Maisie Knew

The effort really to see and really to represent is no idle business in face of the *constant* force that makes for muddlement. The great thing is indeed that the muddled state too is one of the very sharpest of the realities, that it also has colour and form and character, has often in fact a broad and rich comicality.

Ibid.

To criticise is to appreciate, to appropriate, to take intellectual possession, to establish in fine a relation with the criticised thing and to make it one's own.

Ibid.

The historian, essentially, wants more documents than he can really use; the dramatist only wants more liberties than he can really take.

Ibid. The Aspern Papers

The ever-importunate murmur, "Dramatise it, dramatise it!"

Ibid. The Altar of the Dead

In art economy is always beauty.

Ibid.

The terrible *fluidity* of self-revelation.

Ibid. The Ambassadors

The anomalous fact is that the theatre, so called, can flourish in barbarism, but that any *drama* worth speaking of can develop but in the air of civilization.
*Letter to C. E. Wheeler
[April 9, 1911]*

I'm glad you like adverbs — I adore them; they are the only qualifications I really much respect.
Letter to Miss M. Betham Edwards [January 5, 1912]

We must know, as much as possible, in our beautiful art, . . . what we are talking about — and the only way to know is to have lived and loved and cursed and floundered and enjoyed and suffered. I think I don't regret a single "excess" of my responsive youth — I only regret, in my chilled age, certain occasions and possibilities I didn't embrace.
*Letter to Hugh Walpole
[August 21, 1913]*

I still, in presence of life . . . have reactions — as many as possible. . . . It's, I suppose, because I am that queer monster, the artist, an obstinate finality, an inexhaustible sensibility. Hence the reactions — appearances, memories, many things, go on playing upon it with consequences that I note and "enjoy" (grim word!) noting. It all takes doing — and I *do*. I believe I shall do yet again — it is still an act of life.
*Letter to Henry Adams
[March 21, 1914]*

The effect, if not the prime office, of criticism is to make our absorption and our enjoyment of the things that feed the mind as aware of itself as possible, since that awareness quickens the mental demand, which thus in turn wanders further and further for pasture. This action on the part of the mind practically amounts to a reaching out for the reasons of its interest, as only by its ascertaining them can the interest grow more various. This is the very education of our imaginative life.
The New Novel [1914]

It is art that *makes* life, makes interest, makes importance, for our consideration and application of these things, and I know of no substitute whatever for the force and beauty of its process.
*Letter to H. G. Wells
[July 10, 1915]*

The full, the monstrous demonstration that Tennyson was not Tennysonian.
*The Middle Years [1917].
Chap. 6*

To take what there *is*, and use it, without waiting forever in vain for the preconceived — to dig deep into the actual and get something out of *that* — this doubtless is the right way to live.
Notebooks [1948]

FREDERIC WILLIAM HENRY MYERS
[1843–1901]

Look when the clouds are blowing
And all the winds are free:
In fury of their going
They fall upon the sea.
But though the blast is frantic,
And though the tempest raves,
The deep immense Atlantic
Is still beneath the waves.
Wind, Moon, and Tides

Coldly sublime, intolerably just.
Saint Paul

In no single act or passion can salvation stand; far hence, beyond Orion and Andromeda, the cosmic process works and shall work forever through unbegotten souls.
Human Personality. Chap. X

JOSEPHINE POLLARD
[1843–1892]

Though he has Eden to live in,
Man cannot be happy alone.
*We Cannot Be Happy Alone.
Stanza 5*

GEORGE BIRDSEYE
[1844–1919]

The longest day is in June, they say;
　The shortest in December.
They did not come to me that way:
　The shortest I remember
You came a day with me to stay,
　And filled my heart with laughter;
The longest day — you were away —
　The very next day after.
　　　　Shortest and Longest [*1889*]

ROBERT BRIDGES [1]
[1844–1930]

Beneath the crisp and wintry carpet hid
A million buds but stay their blossoming;
And trustful birds have built their nests
　amid
The shuddering boughs, and only wait
　to sing
Till one soft shower from the south shall
　bid,
And hither tempt the pilgrim steps of
　Spring.
　　　The Growth of Love [*1876*].
　　　　　　　　Sonnet 6

Beauty being the best of all we know
Sums up the unsearchable and secret
　aims
Of nature.
　　　　　Ibid. Sonnet 8

I live on hope and that I think do all
Who come into this world.
　　　　　Ibid. Sonnet 63

Behind the western bars
The shrouded day retreats,
And unperceived the stars
Steal to their sovran seats.
　　　The Clouds Have Left the Sky.
　　　　　　　　Stanza 3

And whiter grows the foam,
The small moon lightens more;
And as I turn me home,
My shadow walks before.
　　　　　Ibid. Stanza 4

Whither, O splendid ship, thy white
　sails crowding,

[1] Poet laureate from 1913 until his death.
He was succeeded by John Masefield.

Leaning across the bosom of the urgent
　West,
That fearest nor sea rising, nor sky
　clouding,
Whither away, fair rover, and what thy
　quest?
　　　　　A Passer-By. Stanza 1

I have loved flowers that fade,
　Within whose magic tents
Rich hues have marriage made
　With sweet unmemoried scents.
　　　I Have Loved Flowers That Fade.
　　　　　　　　Stanza 1

Ah! little at best can all our hopes avail
　us
To lift this sorrow, or cheer us, when in
　the dark,
　Unwilling, alone we embark,
And the things we have seen and have
　known and have heard of, fail us.
　　　　　On a Dead Child. Stanza 7

Gird on thy sword, O man, thy strength
　endue,
In fair desire thine earth-born joy re-
　new.
Live thou thy life beneath the making
　sun
Till Beauty, Truth, and Love in thee
　are one.
　　　A Hymn of Nature. VII, Stanza 1

When first we met we did not guess
That Love would prove so hard a mas-
　ter.
Of more than common friendliness
When first we met we did not guess.
　　　　　　　　Triolet

So sweet love seemed that April morn,
When first we kissed beside the thorn,
So strangely sweet, it was not strange
We thought that love could never
　change.
　　　　Shorter Poems. Book V, 5

My delight and thy delight
Walking, like two angels white,
In the gardens of the night.
　　　　　New Poems. Number 9

Love, from whom the world begun,
Hath the secret of the sun.
Love can tell, and love alone,
Whence the million stars were strewn,
Why each atom knows its own.
　　　　　　　　Ibid.

Wisdom will repudiate thee, if thou
  think to enquire
WHY things are as they are or whence
  they came: thy task
is first to learn WHAT IS, and in pur-
  suant knowledge
pure intellect will find pure pleasure
  and the only ground
for a philosophy conformable to truth.
  The Testament of Beauty
  [*1929*]
Our hope is ever livelier than despair,
  our joy
livelier and more abiding than our sorrows are.
  Ibid.
For what were pleasure if never contemplation gave
a spiritual significance to objects of
  sense,
nor in thought's atmosphere poet vision
  arose?
  Ibid.
Man, in the unsearchable darkness,
  knoweth one thing
that as he is, so was he made: and if
  the Essence
and characteristic faculty of humanity
is our conscient Reason and our desire
  of knowledge,
that was Nature's Purpose in the making of man.
  Ibid.

ROBERT JONES BURDETTE
[1844–1914]

I love the man who knows it all,
From east to west, from north to south,
Who knows all things, both great and
  small,
And tells it with his tiresome mouth.
  He Knows It All. Stanza 1

There are two days in the week about
which and upon which I never worry.
Two carefree days, kept sacredly free
from fear and apprehension. One of
these days is Yesterday. . . . And the
other day I do not worry about is Tomorrow.
  The Golden Day

It isn't the experience of today that
drives men mad. It is the remorse for
something that happened yesterday,
and the dread of what tomorrow may
disclose.
  The Golden Day

GEORGE WASHINGTON
CABLE
[1844–1925]

There came to port last Sunday night
  The queerest little craft,
Without an inch of rigging on;
  I looked and looked — and laughed!
  The New Arrival. Stanza 1
She has no manifest but this,
  No flag floats o'er the water;
She's too new for the British Lloyd's —
  My daughter! O my daughter!
  Ibid. Stanza 2

EDWARD CARPENTER
[1844–1929]

There is nothing that is evil except
because a man has not mastery over it;
and there is no good thing that is not
evil if it have a mastery over a man.
  Towards Democracy. The Secret
  of Time and Satan
Every new movement or manifestation of human activity, when unfamil-
iar to people's minds, is sure to be misrepresented and misunderstood.
  The Drama of Love and Death.
  Chap. 8, Note
The first condition of social happiness and prosperity must be the sense
of the Common Life.
  Pagan and Christian Creeds.
  Chap. 17

EDWARD A. CHURCH
[1844–1929]

Of all the words the Evangelists record,
To comfort souls perplexèd and dis-
  tressed,
This ever seems to me divinest, best —
The thought that Peter spoke — "Thou
  knowest, Lord."
  Sonnet, Thou Knowest

MARY AINGE DE VERE
("MADELINE BRIDGES")
[1844–1920]

There are loyal hearts, there are spirits
  brave,
There are souls that are pure and true;
Then give to the world the best you
  have,
And the best will come back to you.
Life's Mirror. Stanza 1

ANATOLE FRANCE
[1844–1924]

I do not know any reading more
easy, more fascinating, more delightful
than a catalogue.
*The Crime of Sylvestre Bon-
nard* [1] *[1881]. The Log, December 24, 1849*
All the historical books which contain no lies are extremely tedious.
Ibid.
Lovers who love truly do not write
down their happiness.
Ibid. November 30, 1859
To know is nothing at all; to imagine
is everything.
Ibid. Part II, Chap. 2
He flattered himself on being a man
without any prejudices; and this pretension itself is a very great prejudice.
Ibid. Chap. 4
Those who have given themselves the
most concern about the happiness of
peoples have made their neighbours
very miserable.
Ibid.
Man is so made that he can only find
relaxation from one kind of labor by
taking up another.[2]
Ibid.
People who have no weaknesses are
terrible; there is no way of taking advantage of them.
Ibid.
The whole art of teaching is only the
art of awakening the natural curiosity

[1] Translated by LAFCADIO HEARN. Modern
Library edition.
[2] See Karl Marx, pages 593b–594a.

of young minds for the purpose of satis-
fying it afterwards.
*The Crime of Sylvestre Bonnard.
Part II, Chap. 4*
The faculty of doubting is rare
among men. A few choice spirits carry
the germ of it in them, but these do not
develop without training.
*Penguin Island [1908].
Book VI, Chap. 2*
A tale without love is like beef with-
out mustard: an insipid dish.
*The Revolt of the Angels
[1914]. Chap. 8*
We have medicines to make women
speak; we have none to make them keep
silence.
*The Man Who Married a Dumb
Wife.*[1] *Act II, Sc. 4*
The good critic is he who narrates the
adventures of his soul among master-
pieces.
La Vie Littéraire. Preface
We reproach people for talking about
themselves; but it is the subject they
treat best.
Ibid. Journal des Goncourt

RICHARD WATSON GILDER
[1844–1909]

Through love to light! Oh wonderful
  the way
That leads from darkness to the per-
  fect day!
After-song
How to the singer comes the song?
How to the summer fields
Come flowers? How yields
Darkness to happy morn? How doth
  the night
Bring stars?
*How to the Singer Comes the
Song? Stanza 4*
What is a sonnet? 'Tis a pearly shell
That murmurs of the far-off murmur-
  ing sea;
A precious jewel carved most curi-
  ously;
It is a little picture painted well.
The Sonnet

[1] Translated by CURTIS HIDDEN PAGE.

I count my time by times that I meet
  thee;
These are my yesterdays, my morrows,
  noons
And nights; these my old moons and
  my new moons.
              The New Day. Book IV, 6

GERARD MANLEY
HOPKINS [1]
[1844–1889]

The world is charged with the grandeur
  of God. . . .
There lives the dearest freshness deep
  down things.
              God's Grandeur [2]

Glory be to God for dappled things —
For skies of couple-colour as a brindled
  cow;
For rose-moles all in stipple upon trout
  that swim.
              Pied Beauty

All things counter, original, spare,
  strange;
Whatever is fickle, freckled (who
  knows how?)
With swift, slow; sweet, sour; adazzle,
  dim;
He fathers-forth whose beauty is past
  change:
      Praise him.
              Ibid.

I caught this morning morning's minion,
  kingdom of daylight's dauphin,
  dapple-dawn-drawn Falcon, in his
  riding
Of the rolling level underneath him
  steady air, and striding
High there, how he rung upon the rein
  of a wimpling wing
In his ecstasy!
              The Windhover

[1] He has left us only 90 poems — but so
essential that they will colour and convert the
development of English poetry for many decades to come. — HERBERT READ [1893–   ]
in *The Criterion*, April, 1931

[2] Hopkins's poems were published posthumously, first in a small selection by Robert
Bridges, then in a nearly complete edition in
1918, reissued with some additions in 1930.

Brute beauty and valour and act, oh,
  air, pride, plume, here
Buckle!
              The Windhover

As kingfishers catch fire, dragonflies
  draw flame.
              Sonnet

Each mortal thing does one thing and
  the same:
Deals out that being indoors each one
  dwells.
              Ibid.

Nor worst, there is none. Pitched past
  pitch of grief.
              Sonnet

O the mind, mind has mountains;
  cliffs of fall
Frightful, sheer, no-man-fathomed.
              Sonnet

Elected Silence, sing to me
And beat upon my whorlèd ear,
Pipe me to pastures still and be
The music that I care to hear.
              The Habit of Perfection

I say that we are wound
With mercy round and round
As if with air.
              Mary Mother of Divine Grace
World-mothering air, air wild,
Wound with thee, in thee isled,
Fold home, fast fold thy child.
              Ibid.

Summer ends now; now, barbarous in
  beauty, the stooks rise
Around; up above, what wind-walks!
  what lovely behaviour
Of silk-sack clouds! Has wilder, willful-wavier
Meal-drift moulded ever and melted
  across skies?
              Hurrahing in Harvest

I have asked to be
  Where no storms come,
Where the green swell is in the havens
  dumb
  And out of the swing of the sea.
              Heaven-Haven

I kiss my hand
To the stars, lovely-asunder
Starlight, wafting him out of it; and
Glow, glory in thunder. . . .

Since tho' he is under the world's
 splendour and wonder,
His mystery must be instressed,
 stressed;
For I greet him the days I meet him,
 and bless when I understand.
>> *The Wreck of the Deutschland.*
>> *Stanza 5*

That night, that year
Of now done darkness I wretch lay
 wrestling with (my God!) my God.
>> *Carrion Comfort*

To lift up the hands in prayer gives
God glory, but a man with a dungfork
in his hand, a woman with a slop-pail,
give him glory too. He is so great that
all things give him glory if you mean
they should. So then, my brethren, live.
>> *An Address on St. Ignatius*

ANDREW LANG
[1844–1912]

You can cover a great deal of country
in books.
>> *To the Gentle Reader. Stanza 5*

Here stand my books, line upon line
They reach the roof, and row by row,
They speak of faded tastes of mine,
And things I did, but do not, know.
>> *Ballade of His Books. Stanza 1*

Why, why are rhymes so rare to *love?*
>> *Ballade of Difficult Rhymes*

There's a joy without canker or cark,
There's a pleasure eternally new,
'Tis to gloat on the glaze and the mark
Of china that's ancient and blue.
>> *Ballade of Blue China. Stanza 1*

Here's a pot with a cot in a park,
In a park where the peach-blossoms
 blew;
Where the lovers eloped in the dark,
Lived, died, and were changed into two
Bright birds that eternally flew
Through the boughs of the may, as they
 sang;
'Tis a tale was undoubtedly true
In the reign of the Emperor Hwang.
>> *Ibid. Stanza 3*

So gladly, from the songs of modern
 speech

Men turn, and see the stars, and feel the
 free
Shrill wind beyond the close of heavy
 flowers;
And, through the music of the languid
 hours,
They hear like ocean on a western
 beach
The surge and thunder of the Odyssey.
>> *Sonnet, The Odyssey*

Why ladies read what they *do* read
Is a thing that no man may explain.
>> *A Remonstrance with the Fair.*
>> *Stanza 1*

Who wins his love shall lose her,
Who loses her shall gain.
>> *Lost Love. Stanza 1*

In dreams she grows not older
 The lands of dream among;
Though all the world wax colder,
 Though all the songs be sung,
In dreams doth he behold her
 Still fair and kind and young.
>> *Ibid. Stanza 4*

And, if one Rag of Character they
 spare,
Comes the Biographer, and strips it
 bare!
>> *Letters to Dead Authors* [*1886*].
>> *Epistle to Mr. Alexander Pope*

Contemporary spites do not harm
true genius.
>> *Ibid. To M. Chapelain*

The dusty and stony ways of contemporary criticism.
>> *Ibid. To Edgar Allan Poe*

The eye of each man sees but what
it has the power of seeing.
>> *Ibid. To Homer*

My mind is gay but my soul is melancholy.
>> *Quoted by* Mrs. Lang *in Pref-*
>> *ace, The Poetical Works of*
>> *Andrew Lang* [*1923*]

JAMES HILARY MULLIGAN
[1844–1916]

The moonlight is the softest, in Kentucky,

Summer days come oftest, in Kentucky,
Friendship is the strongest,
Love's fires glow the longest,
Yet a wrong is always wrongest,
In Kentucky.
In Kentucky. Stanza 1

Songbirds are sweetest, in Kentucky,
Thoroughbreds the fleetest, in Kentucky;
The mountains tower proudest,
Thunder peals the loudest,
The landscape is the grandest,
And politics the damnedest,
In Kentucky.
Ibid. Stanza 7

FRIEDRICH WILHELM NIETZSCHE
[1844–1900]

Our destiny exercises its influence over us even when, as yet, we have not learned its nature: it is our future that lays down the law of our today.
Human, All Too Human [1] *[1878]. 7*

One must have a good memory to be able to keep the promises one makes.
Ibid. 59

One will rarely err if extreme actions be ascribed to vanity, ordinary actions to habit, and mean actions to fear.
Ibid. 74

How poor the human mind would be without vanity! It resembles a well stocked and ever renewed ware-emporium that attracts buyers of every class: they can find almost everything, have almost everything, provided they bring with them the right kind of money — admiration.
Ibid.

Every tradition grows ever more venerable — the more remote is its origin, the more confused that origin is. The reverence due to it increases from generation to generation. The tradition finally becomes holy and inspires awe.
Ibid. 96

[1] Translated by ALEXANDER HARVEY.

I teach you the Superman. Man is something that is to be surpassed.
Thus Spake Zarathustra [1] *[1883–1891]. Prologue, Chap. 3*

Man is a rope stretched between the animal and the Superman — a rope over an abyss.
Ibid. Chap. 4

I want to teach men the sense of their existence, which is the Superman, the lightning out of the dark cloud man.
Ibid. Chap. 7

No small art is it to sleep: it is necessary for that purpose to keep awake all day.
Ibid. Part I, Chap. 2

This is the hardest of all: to close the open hand out of love, and keep modest as a giver.
Ibid. Part II, Chap. 23

Beggars, however, one should entirely do away with! Verily, it annoyeth one to give unto them, and it annoyeth one not to give unto them.[2]
Ibid. Chap. 25

Distrust all in whom the impulse to punish is powerful.
Ibid. Chap. 29

Thoughts that come with doves' footsteps guide the world.
Ibid. Chap. 44

We ought to learn from the kine one thing: ruminating.
Ibid. Part IV, Chap. 68

Then learnedst thou how much harder it is to give properly than to take properly, and that bestowing well is an art — the last, subtlest master-art of kindness.
Ibid.

If ye would go up high, then use your own legs! Do not get yourselves *carried* aloft; do not seat yourselves on other people's backs and heads!
Ibid. Chap. 73

[1] Translated by THOMAS COMMON.
[2] There is surely a Physiognomy, which those experienced and Master Mendicants observe, whereby they instantly discover a merciful aspect, and will single out a face wherein they spy the signatures and marks of Mercy. — SIR THOMAS BROWNE: *Religio Medici* [1642] (Everyman ed.), *P. 66*

From people who merely pray we must become people who bless.
Notes on Thus Spake Zarathustra. 82

It is certainly not the least charm of a theory that it is refutable.
Beyond Good and Evil [1] *[1885–1886]. I, 18*

No one is such a liar as the indignant man.
Ibid. II, 26

It is not the strength but the duration of great sentiments that makes great men.
Ibid. IV, 72

Woman learns how to hate in proportion as she forgets how to charm.
Ibid. 84

Where there is neither love nor hatred in the game, woman's play is mediocre.
Ibid. 115

In revenge and in love woman is more barbarous than man.
Ibid. 139

The thought of suicide is a great consolation: [2] by means of it one gets successfully through many a bad night.
Ibid. 157

There are few pains so grievous as to have seen, divined, or experienced how an exceptional man has missed his way and deteriorated.
Ibid. V, 203

Blessed are the forgetful: for they get the better even of their blunders.
Ibid. VII, 217

Is not life a hundred times too short for us to bore ourselves?
Ibid. 227

One does not know — cannot know — the best that is in one.
Ibid. VIII, 249

The melancholia of everything completed!
Ibid. IX, 277

The "masters" have been done away with; the morality of the vulgar man has triumphed.
Genealogy of Morals [1] *[1887].*
First Essay, Aphorism 9

The broad effects which can be obtained by punishment in man and beast, are the increase of fear, the sharpening of the sense of cunning, the mastery of the desires; so it is that punishment tames man, but does not make him "better."
Ibid. Second Essay, Aphorism 15

A married philosopher belongs to comedy.
Ibid. Third Essay, Aphorism 7

Every tiny step forward in the world was formerly made at the cost of mental and physical torture.
Ibid. Aphorism 9

The sick are the greatest danger for the healthy; it is not from the strongest that harm comes to the strong, but from the weakest.
Ibid. Aphorism 14

A strong and well-constituted man digests his experiences (deeds and misdeeds all included) just as he digests his meats, even when he has some tough morsels to swallow.
Ibid. Aphorism 16

Nothing ever succeeds which exuberant spirits have not helped to produce.
The Twilight of the Idols [2] *[1888].*
Preface

Contentment preserves one even from catching cold. Has a woman who knew that she was well dressed ever caught cold? — No, not even when she had scarcely a rag to her back.
Ibid. Maxims and Missiles, 25

Without music life would be a mistake.
Ibid. 33

He who laughs best today, will also laugh last. [3]
Ibid. 43

---

[1] Translated by HELEN ZIMMERN.
[2] We are in the power of no calamity while death is in our own. — SIR THOMAS BROWNE: *Religio Medici* [1642] (Everyman ed.), P. 50

[1] Translated by HORACE B. SAMUEL.
[2] Translated by ANTHONY M. LUDOVICI.
[3] Better the last smile than the first laughter. — JOHN RAY: *English Proverbs* [1670]. This is a variant of the familiar saying, "He laughs

That which needs to be proved cannot be worth much.

The Twilight of the Idols. The Problem of Socrates, 5

Unconscious gratitude for a good digestion (sometimes called "brotherly love").

Ibid. Morality as the Enemy of Nature, 3

Two great European narcotics, alcohol and Christianity.

Ibid. Things the Germans Lack, 2

Dancing in all its forms cannot be excluded from the curriculum of all noble education: dancing with the feet, with ideas, with words, and, need I add that one must also be able to dance with the pen?

Ibid. 7

In the architectural structure, man's pride, man's triumph over gravitation, man's will to power, assume a visible form. Architecture is a sort of oratory of power by means of forms.

Ibid. Skirmishes in a War with the Age, 11

If a man have a strong faith he can indulge in the luxury of scepticism.

Ibid. 12

The sick man is a parasite of society. In certain cases it is indecent to go on living. To continue to vegetate in a state of cowardly dependence upon doctors and special treatments, once the meaning of life, the right to life, has been lost, ought to be regarded with the greatest contempt by society.

Ibid. 36

Liberal institutions straightway cease from being liberal the moment they are soundly established: once this is attained no more grievous and more thorough enemies of freedom exist than liberal institutions.

Ibid. 38

It is my ambition to say in ten sentences what everyone else says in a whole book, — what everyone else does *not* say in a whole book.

Ibid. 51

Love is the state in which man sees things most widely different from what they are. The force of illusion reaches its zenith here, as likewise the sweetening and transfiguring power. When a man is in love he endures more than at other times; he submits to everything.

The Antichrist [1] [*1888*]. *Aphorism 23*

Our statesmen — a body of men who are otherwise so unembarrassed, and such thorough anti-Christians in deed — still declare themselves Christians and still flock to communion.[2]

Ibid. Aphorism 39

God created woman. And boredom did indeed cease from that moment — but many other things ceased as well! Woman was God's *second* mistake.

Ibid. Aphorism 48

Life always gets harder toward the summit — the cold increases, responsibility increases.

Ibid. Aphorism 57

I call Christianity the one great curse, the one enormous and innermost perversion, the one great instinct of revenge, for which no means are too venomous, too underhand, too underground and too petty, — I call it the one immortal blemish of mankind.

Ibid. Aphorism 62

My doctrine is: Live that thou mayest desire to live again, — that is thy duty, — for in any case thou wilt live again!

Eternal Recurrence. [1] *27*

Even a thought, even a possibility, can shatter us and transform us.

Ibid. 30

Nothing on earth consumes a man more quickly than the passion of resentment.

Ecce Homo [1] [*1888*]

I believe only in French culture, and regard everything else in Europe which calls itself "culture" as a misunderstanding. I do not even take the German kind into consideration.

Ibid.

best who laughs last," known in many languages.

[1] Translated by ANTHONY M. LUDOVICI.
[2] The reference is probably to Bismarck.

Wherever Germany extends her sway, she ruins culture.

Ecce Homo

As an artist, a man has no home in Europe save in Paris.

Ibid.

Simply by being compelled to keep constantly on his guard, a man may grow so weak as to be unable any longer to defend himself.

Ibid.

My time has not yet come either; some are born posthumously.

Ibid.

No one can draw more out of things, books included, than he already knows. A man has no ears for that to which experience has given him no access.

Ibid.

The Germans are like women, you can scarcely ever fathom their depths — they haven't any.[1]

Ibid.

After coming in contact with a religious man, I always feel that I must wash my hands.

Ibid.

All prejudices may be traced back to the intestines. A sedentary life is the real sin against the Holy Ghost.[2]

Ibid.

One must separate from anything that forces one to repeat No again and again.

Ibid.

JOHN BOYLE O'REILLY
[1844–1890]

They who see the Flying Dutchman never, never reach the shore.

The Flying Dutchman

Doubt is brother-devil to Despair.

Prometheus

The world is large when weary leagues
  two loving hearts divide

[1] Man thinks woman profound — why? Because he can never fathom her depths. Woman is not even shallow. — *The Twilight of the Idols, Maxims and Missiles,* 27

[2] Translated by CLIFTON P. FADIMAN. Modern Library edition.

But the world is small when your enemy
  is loose on the other side.

Distance

The red rose whispers of passion
  And the white rose breathes of love;
O, the red rose is a falcon,
  And the white rose is a dove.

A White Rose. Stanza 1

You may grind their souls in the self-
  same mill,
You may bind them, heart and brow;
But the poet will follow the rainbow
  still,
And his brother will follow the plow.

The Rainbow's Treasure.
Stanza 5

The wealth of mankind is the wisdom
  they leave.

Rules of the Road

Be silent and safe — silence never betrays you.

Ibid.

"I had" is a heartache, "I have" is a
  fountain,
You're worth what you saved, not the
  million you made.

Ibid.

This truth keep in sight, — every man
  on the planet
Has just as much right as yourself to
  the road.

Ibid.

The organized charity, scrimped and
  iced,
In the name of a cautious, statistical
  Christ.[1]

In Bohemia. Stanza 5

Oh, I long for the glow of a kindly
  heart and the grasp of a friendly
  hand!
And I'd rather live in Bohemia than in
  any other land.

Ibid. Stanza 6

Well blest is he who has a dear one
  dead;
A friend he has whose face will never
  change —

[1] See Southey, page 427b, and Hood, page 489b.

A dear communion that will not grow
   strange;
The anchor of a love is death.
         Forever. Stanza 3

ARTHUR WILLIAM EDGAR O'SHAUGHNESSY
[1844–1881]

We are the music-makers,
   And we are the dreamers of dreams,
Wandering by lone sea-breakers,
   And sitting by desolate streams;
World-losers and world-forsakers,
   On whom the pale moon gleams:
Yet we are the movers and shakers
   Of the world for ever, it seems.
         Ode. Stanza 1
One man with a dream, at pleasure,
   Shall go forth and conquer a crown;
And three with a new song's measure
   Can trample an empire down.
         Ibid. Stanza 2
For each age is a dream that is dying,
Or one that is coming to birth.
         Ibid. Stanza 3

WILLIAM ARCHIBALD SPOONER [1]
[1844–1930]

Kinquering Congs their titles take.
   Announcing the hymn in college
            chapel
You have deliberately tasted two
worms and you can leave Oxford by the
town drain.
      Dismissing a student
This audience of beery wenches.
      At a woman's college
I remember your name perfectly, but
I just can't think of your face.
         A greeting

MAURICE THOMPSON
[1844–1901]

A soft Kentucky strain was in his voice,
And the Ohio's deeper boom was there,

---

[1] Canon Spooner, for many years warden
of New College, Oxford, was famous for un-
intentional transpositions of word and
thought. This form of metathesis became
known as a "spoonerism."

With some wild accents of old Wabash
   days,
   And winds of Illinois;
And when he spoke he took us unaware,
   With his high courage and unselfish
   ways.
         At Lincoln's Grave

MRS. EDWARD CRASTER

The centipede was happy quite
   Until a toad in fun
Said, "Pray, which leg goes after
   which?"
That worked her mind to such a pitch,
She lay distracted in a ditch,
   Considering how to run.
    Credited, in Cassell's Weekly,
     to Pinafore Poems [1871]

DR. BREWSTER HIGLEY

Oh, give me a home where the buffalo
   roam,
Where the deer and the antelope play,
Where seldom is heard a discouraging
   word
And the skies are not cloudy all day.
     Home on the Range [1873]

JARRETT AND PALMER
[Floruerunt 1866]

Legs are staple articles and will never
go out of fashion while the world lasts.
   Of the original production
   [1866] of their Grand Magical
   Spectacular Drama, The Black
   Crook, by Charles M. Barras
   [1826–1873]

R. L. SHARPE
[Floruit 1890]

Each is given a bag of tools,
A shapeless mass,
A book of rules;
And each must make,
Ere life is flown,
A stumbling-block
Or a stepping-stone.
   Stumbling-Block or Stepping-
       Stone. Stanza 2

JOHN B. BOGART [1]
[1845-1921]

When a dog bites a man, that is not news, because it happens so often. But if a man bites a dog, that is news.
Quoted by FRANK M. O'BRIEN
in The Story of The Sun [1918]

JOHN HENRY BONER
[1845-1903]

Ah, we fondly cherish
  Faded things
That had better perish.
  Memory clings
To each leaf it saves.
      Gather Leaves and Grasses
Here lived the soul enchanted
  By melody of song;
Here dwelt the spirit haunted
  By a demoniac throng.
      Poe's Cottage at Fordham

WILL CARLETON
[1845-1912]

Worm or beetle — drought or tempest
  — on a farmer's land may fall,
Each is loaded full o' ruin, but a mort-
  gage beats 'em all.
      The Tramp's Story
I've watched my duty, straight an'
  true,
  An' tried to do it well;
Part of the time kept heaven in view,
  An' part steered clear of hell.
      The New Church Doctrine.
      Stanza 2
Not a log in this buildin' but its mem-
  ories has got,
And not a nail in this old floor but
  touches a tender spot.
      Out of the Old House, Nancy.
      Stanza 17
He has seen old views and patients dis-
  appearing, one by one,
He has learned that Death is master
  both of Science and of Art.
      The Country Doctor. Stanza 3

[1] City editor of *The Sun*, New York, 1873-1890.

Things at home are crossways, and Betsey and I are out.
      Betsey and I Are Out. Stanza 1
I have talked with Betsey, and Betsey
  has talked with me,
And so we've agreed together that we
  can't never agree.
      Ibid. Stanza 3
Betsey, like all good women, had a
  temper of her own.
      Ibid. Stanza 4
The more we arg'ed the question the
  more we didn't agree.
      Ibid. Stanza 5
You see, when we came to division,
  there was things that wouldn't
  divide.
      Betsey Destroys the Paper.
      Stanza 6
I'm going away today with a handsomer man than you.
      Gone with a Handsomer Man.
      Stanza 4
To appreciate heaven well
'Tis good for a man to have some fifteen minutes of hell.
      Ibid. Stanza 20
Over the hill to the poor-house I'm
  trudgin' my weary way.
      Over the Hill to the Poor-House.
      Stanza 1
She had an edication, an' that was good
  for her;
But when she twitted me on mine,
  'twas carryin' things too fur.
      Ibid. Stanza 14

WILLIAM ULICK O'CONNOR CUFFE (LORD DESART)
[1845-1898]

Mother Hubbard, you see, was old: there being no mention of others, we may presume she was alone; a widow — a friendless, old, solitary widow. Yet did she despair? Did she sit down and weep, or read a novel, or wring her hands? No! She went to the cupboard.
      Mock Sermon: Old Mother
      Hubbard [1877]

CHARLES FLETCHER DOLE
[1845–1927]

Good Will is the mightiest practical force in the universe.
Cleveland Address

The Golden Rule works like gravitation.
Ibid.

Democracy is on trial in the world, on a more colossal scale than ever before.
The Spirit of Democracy

EDWARD HARRIGAN
[1845–1911]

The drums and fifes, how sweetly they did play,
As we march'd, march'd, march'd in the Mulligan Guard.
The Mulligan Guard [*1873*]

DANIEL WEBSTER HOYT
[1845–1936]

If you have a friend worth loving,
Love him. Yes, and let him know
That you love him, ere life's evening
Tinge his brow with sunset glow.
Why should good words ne'er be said
Of a friend till he is dead? [1]
A Sermon in Rhyme [*1878*].
Stanza 1

If you hear a song that thrills you,
Sung by any child of song,
Praise it. Do not let the singer
Wait deservèd praises long.
Why should one who thrills your heart
Lack the joy you may impart?
Ibid. Stanza 2

MARGARET THOMSON JANVIER ("MARGARET VANDEGRIFT")
[1845–1913]

You needn't be trying to comfort me —
I tell you my dolly is dead!
There's no use in saying she isn't, with a crack like that in her head.
The Dead Doll. Stanza 1

[1] See Elizabeth Akers Allen, pages 654b–655a.

GEORGE KENNAN
[1845–1924]

Heroism, the Caucasian mountaineers say, is endurance for one moment more.
Letter to Henry Munroe Rogers
[*July 25, 1921*]

EUGENE LEE-HAMILTON
[1845–1907]

Things bygone are the only things that last:
The present is mere grass, quick-mown away;
The past is stone, and stands for ever fast.
Roman Baths

HAMILTON WRIGHT MABIE
[1845–1916]

The peculiarity of the New England hermit has not been his desire to get near to God, but his anxiety to get away from man.
Backgrounds of Literature.
Emerson and Concord

GEORGE SAINTSBURY
[1845–1933]

It must be remembered that the point of honour which decrees that a man must not under any circumstances accept money from a woman with whom he is on certain terms, is of very modern growth, and is still tempered by the proviso that he may take as much as he likes or can get from his wife.
Preface to FIELDING's *Tom Jones*

One of the commonest but most uncritical faults of criticism — the refusal to consider what it is that the author intended to give us.
Ibid.

Men will try to persuade themselves, or at least others, that they read poetry because it is a criticism of life, because it expresses the doubts and fears and thoughts and hopes of the time, because it is a substitution for religion, because it is a relief from serious work, because and because and because. As a matter of fact, they (that is to say, those of them who like it generally) read it because they like it, because it communicates an experience of half-sensual, half-intellectual pleasure to them.

Corrected Impressions [1895].
Tennyson

Criticism is the endeavor to find, to know, to love, to recommend, not only the best, but all the good, that has been known and thought and written in the world.

A History of Criticism [1900–1904]

It is the first duty of the novelist to let himself be read — anything else that he gives you is a bonus, a trimming, a dessert.

History of the English Novel
[1913]

I have never tried to be in the fashion for the sake of being in it, and seldom, I think, to be out of it for the sake of being out of it. Logic and history have been the only external guides I have accepted in temporal things, except where pure taste has reigned alone.

Notes on a Cellar Book [1920].
Preface

When they [wines] were good they pleased my sense, cheered my spirits, improved my moral and intellectual powers, besides enabling me to confer the same benefits on other people.

Ibid.

ARABELLA EUGENIA SMITH
[1845–1916]

If I should die tonight,
My friends would look upon my quiet face,
Before they laid it in its resting place,
And deem that death had left it almost fair.

If I Should Die Tonight.[1]
Stanza 1

[1] The parody by BEN KING [1857–1894] has become better known than the original:
If I should die tonight
And you should come in deepest grief and woe —

CHARLES WILLIAM STUBBS
[1845–1912]

I sat alone with my conscience
In a place where time had ceased,
And we talked of my former living
In the land where the years increased.

Conscience and Future
Judgment [1876]

To sit alone with my conscience
Will be judgment enough for me.[1]

Ibid.

JOHN BANISTER TABB
[1845–1909]

The ghost am I
Of winds that die
Alike on land or sea.

The Fog. Stanza 1

How many an acorn falls to die
For one that makes a tree!
How many a heart must pass me by
For one that cleaves to me!

Compensation. Stanza 1

Out of the dusk a shadow,
Then a spark;
Out of the cloud a silence,
Then a lark;
Out of the heart a rapture,
Then a pain;
Out of the dead, cold ashes,
Life again.

Evolution

Back to the primal gloom
Where life began.

Going Blind

And in the School of Darkness learn
What mean
"The things unseen."

Ibid.

JAMES TERRY WHITE
[1845–1920]

If thou of fortune be bereft
And in thy store there be but left

And say: "Here's that ten dollars that I owe,"
I might arise in my large white cravat
And say, "What's that?"

[1] There's just ae thing I cannae bear,
An' that's my conscience.
R. L. STEVENSON [1850–1894]: *In Scots,*
XIV, My Conscience

Two loaves, sell one and with the dole
Buy hyacinths to feed thy soul.
*Not by Bread Alone: After
Hippocrates* [*1907*]

SARAH CHAUNCEY WOOLSEY ("SUSAN COOLIDGE")
[1845–1905]

Men die, but sorrow never dies.
The "Cradle Tomb" at Westminster
These are weighty secrets, and we must
whisper them.
Secrets

"A commonplace life," we say, and we
sigh;
But why should we sigh as we say?
The commonplace sun in the common-
place sky
Makes up the commonplace day.
Commonplace

And God, who studies each commonplace soul,
Out of commonplace things makes His
beautiful whole.
Commonplace

CHARLES DUPEE BLAKE
[1846–1903]

Rock-a-bye-baby on the tree top,
When the wind blows the cradle will
rock,
When the bough breaks the cradle will
fall,
And down will come baby, cradle and
all.
Attributed

"MICHAEL FIELD" (KATHARINE BRADLEY)
[1846–1914]
(EDITH COOPER)
[1862–1913]

The enchanting miracles of change.
Renewal
Come, mete out my loneliness, O wind,
For I would know
How far the living who must stay be-
hind
Are from the dead who go.
Mete Out My Loneliness

Among the hills I trace the path that I
must wend;
I watch, not bidding him farewell, the
sun descend.
Sweet and of their nature vacant are
the days I spend —
Quiet as a plough laid by at the furrow's end.
Old Age

JOSEPH IGNATIUS CONSTANTINE CLARKE
[1846–1925]

"Wherever there's Kellys there's trou-
ble," said Burke.
"Wherever fighting's the game,
Or a spice of danger in grown man's
work,"
Said Kelly, "you'll find my name."
The Fighting Race. Stanza 2
"Oh, the fighting races don't die out,
If they seldom die in bed."
Ibid. Stanza 5

RICHARD LEWIS NETTLESHIP
[1846–1892]

The only strength for me is to be
found in the sense of a personal presence everywhere, it scarcely matters
whether it be called human or divine; a
presence which only makes itself felt at
first in this and that particular form
and feature.
Lectures and Memories. I, 72

ALEXANDER MacGREGOR ROSE
[1846–1898]

Der Kaiser auf der Vaterland
Und Gott on high, all dings gommand,
Ve two, ach, don'd you understandt?
Meinself — und Gott.
*Hoch! Der Kaiser (Kaiser &
Co.)* [1] [*1897*]. *Stanza 1*

[1] These verses created a stir when recited
by Captain (later Rear Admiral) Joseph Bul-
lock Coghlan [1844–1908] at a dinner given
in his honor at the Union League Club, New
York, April 21, 1899.

Gott pulls mit me, und I mit him.
Hoch! Der Kaiser (Kaiser & Co.).
Stanza 16

HENRYK SIENKIEWICZ
[1846–1916]

The greater philosopher a man is, the more difficult it is for him to answer the foolish questions of common people.
Quo Vadis.[1] *Chap. 19*

EDWARD NOYES WESTCOTT
[1846–1898]

Yes, an' no, an' mebbe, an' mebbe not.
David Harum [1898]. Chap. 1
Do unto the other feller the way he'd like to do unto you an' do it fust.
Ibid. Chap. 20
They say a reasonable number of fleas is good fer a dog — keeps him from broodin' over bein' a dog.
Ibid. Chap. 32
The' ain't nothin' truer in the Bible 'n that sayin' thet them that has gits.
Ibid Chap. 35
I've often had to notice that a man'll sometimes do the foolishest thing or meanest thing in his hull life after he's dead.
Ibid.

JOHN PETER ALTGELD [2]
[1847–1902]

In writing "Progress and Poverty," he dipped his pen into the tears of the human race, and with celestial clearness wrote down what he conceived to be eternal truths.
Memorial Address on Henry George [1897]
When he died, there was nowhere a soul that cried out: "There is one iron hand less to grind us, one wolf less to

tear our flesh," but everywhere a feeling that a friend of the race had gone.
Memorial Address on Henry George

HENRY AUGUSTIN BEERS
[1847–1926]

He sang one song and died — no more but that;
A single song and carelessly complete.
The Singer of One Song [1]
So through the poets' orchestra, which weaves
One music from a thousand stops and strings,
Pierces the note of that immortal song:
"High over all the lonely bugle grieves." [2]
Ibid.

ALEXANDER GRAHAM BELL
[1847–1922]

Mr. Watson, come here, I want you.
To his assistant [March 10, 1876]; the first intelligible words transmitted by telephone

THOMAS ALVA EDISON
[1847–1931]

There is no substitute for hard work.
Life [1932]. Chap. 24
Genius is one per cent inspiration and ninety-nine per cent perspiration.
Ibid.

EDGAR FAWCETT
[1847–1904]

She remembers so many graves
That no one else will remember.
The Grass. Stanza 3
In some blithe moment, was it Nature's choice
To dower a scrap of sunset with a voice?
To an Oriole

---

[1] Translated by JEREMIAH CURTIN [1838–1906].
[2] VACHEL LINDSAY's poem on Altgeld, *The Eagle That Is Forgotten,* is cited on page 902b.

[1] Grenville Mellen [1799–1841].
[2] And high above the fight the lonely bugle grieves! — GRENVILLE MELLEN: *Ode on the Celebration of the Battle of Bunker Hill, June 17, 1825*

WALTER LEARNED
[1847–1915]

A lure more strong, a wish more faint,
Makes one a monster, one a saint.
On the Flyleaf of "Manon Lescaut"

O carping world! If there's an age
Where youth and manhood keep
An equal poise, alas! I must
Have passed it in my sleep.
To Critics. Stanza 3

Her lips were so near
That — what else could I do?
An Explanation

This world is a difficult world, indeed,
And people are hard to suit,
And the man who plays on the violin
Is a bore to the man with the flute.
Consolation. Stanza 4

JOHN LOCKE
[1847–1889]

O Ireland, isn't it grand you look —
Like a bride in her rich adornin'?
And with all the pent-up love of my
heart
I bid you the top o' the mornin'!
*The Exile's Return (Dawn on
the Irish Coast). Stanza 1*

ALICE MEYNELL
[1847–1922]

My heart shall be thy garden. Come,
my own,
Into thy garden; thine be happy hours
Among my fairest thoughts, my tallest
flowers,
From root to crowning petal thine alone.
Sonnet, The Garden

She walks — the lady of my delight —
A shepherdess of sheep.
Her flocks are thoughts. She keeps them
white;
She guards them from the steep.
The Shepherdess. Stanza 1

She holds her little thoughts in sight,
Though gay they run and leap.
She is so circumspect and right;
She has her soul to keep.
Ibid. Stanza 2

I must not think of thee; and, tired yet
strong,
I shun the thought that lurks in all
delight —
The thought of thee — and in the blue
heaven's height
And in the sweetest passage of a song.
Sonnet, Renouncement

With the first dream that comes with
the first sleep
I run, I run, I am gathered to thy
heart.
Ibid.

O heavenly colour, London town
Has blurred it from her skies;
And, hooded in an earthly brown,
Unheaven'd the city lies.
November Blue. Stanza 1

It is principally for the sake of the
leg that a change in the dress of man is
so much to be desired. . . . The leg is
the best part of the figure . . . and the
best leg is the man's. Man should no
longer disguise the long lines, the strong
forms, in those lengths of piping or tubing that are of all garments the most
stupid.
Essays. Unstable Equilibrium

LLOYD MIFFLIN
[1847–1921]

Inscrutable, colossal, and alone.
Sesostris

JULIA A. MOORE [1]
[1847–1920]

Dear Friends, I write for money,
With a kind heart and hand,
I wish to make no Enemies
Throughout my native land.
Kind friends, now I close my rhyme,
And lay my pen aside,
Between me and my critics
I leave you to decide.
*To My Friends and Critics.
Stanza 6*

[1] "The Sweet Singer of Michigan," of whom
Mark Twain wrote: "The one and unfaiiing
great quality which distinguishes her poetry
from Shakespeare's and makes it precious to
us is its stern and simple irrelevancy." — *Following the Equator* [1897], *Vol. II, Chap. 8*

Leave off the agony, leave off style,
Unless you've got money by you all the
  while.
If you look about you you'll often have
  to smile
To see so many poor people putting on
  style.
          Leave Off the Agony in Style

MILTON NOBLES
[1847–1924]

The villain still pursued her.
          The Phoenix [1875]. Act I, Sc. 3

WILLIAM EDWARD NORRIS
[1847–1925]

If your lips would keep from slips,
  Five things observe with care:
To whom you speak; of whom you
  speak;
And how, and when, and where.
          Nursery Rhyme, Quoted in
          Thirlby Hall

JAMES JEFFREY ROCHE
[1847–1908]

  A brave endeavor
To do thy duty, whate'er its worth,
Is better than life with love forever,
And love is the sweetest thing on earth.
          Sir Hugo's Choice

What gain is it to the people that a God
  laid down His life,
If twenty centuries after, His world be
  a world of strife?
          For the People. Stanza 4

Yea, the gateway shall be free
Unto all, from sea to sea;
And no fratricidal slaughter
Shall defile its sacred water;
But — the hand that ope'd the gate
  shall forever hold the key!
          Panama

I'd rather be handsome than homely;
  I'd rather be youthful than old;
If I can't have a bushel of silver
  I'll do with a barrel of gold.
          Contentment

All loved Art in a seemly way
With an earnest soul and a capital A.
          The V-A-S-E

ARCHIBALD PHILIP PRIMROSE, EARL OF ROSEBERY
[1847–1929]

Few speeches which have produced
an electrical effect on an audience can
bear the colourless photography of a
printed record.
          Life of Pitt [1891]

It is beginning to be hinted that we
are a nation of amateurs.
          Rectorial Address, Glasgow
          [November 16, 1900]

GEORGE ROBERT SIMS
[1847–1922]

Lor', but women's rum cattle to deal
  with, the first man found that to
  his cost,
And I reckon it's just through a woman
  the last man on earth'll be lost.
          Moll Jarvis o' Morley

O gleaming lamps of London,
That gem of the city's crown,
What fortunes be within you,
O Lights of London Town?
          The Lights of London Town.
          Stanza 1

You come here to see how paupers the
  season of Christmas spend;
You come here to watch us feeding, as
  they watch the captured beast.
          Christmas Day in the
          Workhouse. Stanza 8

ARTHUR JAMES BALFOUR
[1848–1930]

  The energies of our system will decay, the glory of the sun will be dimmed,
and the earth, tideless and inert, will no
longer tolerate the race which has for a
moment disturbed its solitude. Man will
go down into the pit, and all his
thoughts will perish.
          The Foundations of Belief [1895]

Biography should be written by an acute enemy.

> *Quoted by* S. K. RATCLIFFE *in The London Observer, January 30, 1927*

JOHN VANCE CHENEY
[1848–1922]

Who drives the horses of the sun
  Shall lord it but a day;
Better the lowly deed were done,
  And kept the humble way.
> *The Happiest Heart. Stanza 1*

The happiest heart that ever beat
  Was in some quiet breast
That found the common daylight sweet,
  And left to Heaven the rest.
> *Ibid. Stanza 3*

JOHN CHURTON COLLINS
[1848–1908]

Truth is the object of philosophy, but not always of philosophers.
> *Aphorisms quoted by* LOGAN PEARSALL SMITH: *A Treasury of English Aphorisms*

Mistrust a subordinate who never finds fault with his superior.
> *Ibid.*

The secret of success in life is known only to those who have not succeeded.
> *Ibid.*

If men were as unselfish as women, women would very soon become more selfish than men.
> *Ibid.*

DIGBY MACKWORTH DOLBEN
[1848–1867]

The world is young today:
  Forget the gods are old,
  Forget the years of gold
When all the months were May.
> *A Song*

SAMUEL MILLER HAGEMAN
[1848–1905]

Every sound shall end in silence, but
  the silence never dies.
> *Silence [1876]. Stanza 10*

Earth is but the frozen echo of the silent voice of God.
> *Silence. Stanza 19*

JOEL CHANDLER HARRIS
[1848–1908]

How many po' sinners'll be kotched out late
En fin' no latch ter de golden gate?
No use fer ter wait twell ter-morrer,
De sun mus'n't set on yo' sorrer, —
Sin's ez sharp ez a bamboo-brier, —
O Lord! fetch de mo'ners up higher!
> *Uncle Remus: His Songs and His Sayings [1881]*

Hit look lak sparrer-grass, hit feel lak sparrer-grass, hit tas'e lak sparrer-grass, en I bless ef 'taint sparrer-grass.
> *Nights with Uncle Remus [1883]. Chap. 27*

No 'pollygy aint gwine ter make h'ar come back whar de b'iling water hit.
> *Ibid. Chap. 45*

Tar-baby ain't sayin' nuthin', en Brer Fox, he lay low.
> *Uncle Remus: Legends of the Old Plantation*

Ez soshubble ez a baskit er kittens.
> *Ibid.*

Bred en bawn in a brier-patch, Brer Fox.
> *Ibid.*

You do de pullin', Sis Cow, en I'll do de gruntin'.
> *Ibid.*

He diggy, diggy, diggy, but no meat dar!
> *Ibid.*

W'en ole man Rabbit say "scoot," dey scooted, en w'en old Miss Rabbit say "scat," dey scatted.
> *Ibid.*

Lazy fokes' stummucks don't git tired.
> *Uncle Remus: Plantation Proverbs*

Jay-bird don't rob his own nes'.
> *Ibid.*

Licker talks mighty loud w'en it gits loose fum de jug.
> *Ibid.*

Hongry rooster don't cackle w'en he fine a wum.
Uncle Remus: Plantation Proverbs

Youk'n hide de fier, but w'at you gwine do wid de smoke?
Ibid.

Dogs don't bite at de front gate.
Ibid.

Watch out w'en youer gittin' all you want. Fattenin' hogs ain't in luck.
Ibid.

Hop light, ladies,
  Oh, Miss Loo!
Oh, swing dat yaller gal!
  Do, boys, do!
Plantation Play Song

When you've got a thing to say,
Say it! Don't take half a day.
When your tale's got little in it,
Crowd the whole thing in a minute!
Life is short — a fleeting vapor —
Don't you fill the whole blamed paper
With a tale which, at a pinch,
Could be cornered in an inch!
Boil her down until she simmers,
Polish her until she glimmers.
Advice to Writers for the
Daily Press

JORIS KARL HUYSMANS
[1848–1907]

The pleasure of travel, which only exists as a matter of fact in retrospect and seldom in the present, at the instant when it is being experienced.
Against the Grain [1] [*1884*].
Chap. 3

One could revel, for instance, in long explorations while near one's own fireside, stimulating the restive or sluggish mind, if need be, by reading some narrative of travel in distant lands.
Ibid.

Is there a woman, whose form is more dazzling, more splendid than the two locomotives that pass over the Northern Railroad lines?
Ibid.

[1] Translated by JOHN HOWARD.

The diamond has become notoriously common since every tradesman has taken to wearing it on his little finger.
Against the Grain. Chap. 5

The loveliest tune imaginable becomes vulgar and insupportable as soon as the public begins to hum it and the hurdy-gurdies make it their own.
Ibid. Chap. 9

Perfumes, in fact, rarely come from the flowers whose names they bear . . . with the exception of the inimitable jasmine, which it is impossible to counterfeit.
Ibid. Chap. 10

Art is the only clean thing on earth, except holiness.
Les Foules de Lourdes [*1906*]

RICHARD JEFFERIES
[1848–1887]

Give me fullness of life like to the sea and the sun; give me fullness of physical life, mind equal and beyond their fullness; give me a greatness and perfection of soul higher than all things; give me my inexpressible desire.
The Story of My Heart [*1883*].
Chap. VI

No thought which I have ever had has satisfied my soul.
Ibid.

The most extraordinary spectacle is the vast expenditure of labor and time wasted in obtaining mere subsistence.
Ibid. Chap. X

The world works only for today, as the world worked twelve thousand years ago, and our children's children will still have to toil and slave for the bare necessities of life.
Ibid.

I hope succeeding generations will be able to be idle. I hope that nine-tenths of their time will be leisure time; that they may enjoy their days, and the earth, and the beauty of this beautiful world; that they may rest by the sea and dream; that they may dance and sing, and eat and drink.
Ibid. Chap. XI

Let me exhort everyone to do their utmost to think outside and beyond our present circle of ideas. For every idea gained is a hundred years of slavery remitted.

The Story of My Heart. Chap. XI

VILFREDO PARETO
[1848–1923]

Give me a fruitful error any time, full of seeds, bursting with its own corrections. You can keep your sterile truth for yourself.

Comment on Kepler

CHARLOTTE AUGUSTA ("CARLOTTA") PERRY
[1848–1914]

The sails we see on the ocean
　Are as white as white can be;
But never one in the harbor
　As white as the sails at sea.
*Distance, the Enchantress.
Stanza 1*

It was only a glad "Good morning,"
　As she passed along the way,
But it spread the morning's glory
　Over the livelong day.
Good Morning

EBEN EUGENE REXFORD
[1848–1916]

Darling, I am growing old,
Silver threads among the gold
Shine upon my brow today;
Life is fading fast away.
*Silver Threads Among
the Gold [1873]*

BARONESS BERTHA VON SUTTNER
[1848–1914]

After the verb "To Love," "To Help" is the most beautiful verb in the world!
Epigram

WILL HENRY THOMPSON
[1848–1918]

Then at the brief command of Lee
Moved out that matchless infantry,

With Pickett leading grandly down,
To rush against the roaring crown
Of those dread heights of destiny.[1]
*The High Tide at Gettysburg
[1888]. Stanza 2*

The voice that rang through Shiloh's
　woods
And Chickamauga's solitudes,
The fierce South cheering on her sons!
Ibid. Stanza 3

FREDERIC EDWARD WEATHERLY
[1848–1929]

Playing all my heart remembers,
　Old, old songs from far away;
Golden Junes and bleak Decembers
　Rise around me as I play.
Fiddle and I. Stanza 2

Always the same, Darby, my own,
Always the same to your old wife Joan.
Darby and Joan. Stanza 1

The sailor's wife the sailor's star shall
be.
Nancy Lee

ROLLIN JOHN WELLS
[1848–1923]

A little more tired at close of day,
A little less anxious to have our way;
A little less ready to scold and blame,
A little more care of a brother's name;
And so we are nearing our journey's
　end,
Where time and eternity meet and
　blend.
Growing Old. Stanza 1

JAMES LANE ALLEN
[1849–1925]

The birds are moulting. If man could only moult also — his mind once a year its errors, his heart once a year its useless passions.
A Kentucky Cardinal [1894]

By degrees the comforting light of what you may actually do and be in an imperfect world will shine close to you and all around you, more and more. It

[1] See Cone, page 781b.

is this that will lead you never to perfection, but always toward it.
The Choir Invisible [*1897*].
Chap. 20

JOSEPH GREEN FRANCIS
[1849–1930]

A Tam o' Shanter Dog
And a plaintive piping Frog,
With a Cat whose one extravagance
    was clothes,
Went to see a Bounding Bug
Dance a jig upon a rug,
While a Beetle balanced bottles on his
    nose.
The Book of Cheerful Cats

EDMUND GOSSE
[1849–1928]

The girls nowadays display a shocking freedom; but they were partly led into it by the relative laxity of their mothers, who, in their turn, gave great anxiety to a still earlier generation.
The Whole Duty of Woman
There never, we suppose, from the beginning of the world, was a man-preacher who did not warn the women of his congregation against the vanity of fair raiment.
Ibid.
The wizard silence of the hours of dew.
The White Throat
The Past is like a funeral gone by,
The Future comes like an unwelcome
    guest.
May-Day
I do not hunger for a well-stored mind,
I only wish to live my life, and find
My heart in unison with all mankind.
Lying in the Grass

WILLIAM ERNEST HENLEY
[1849–1903]

The Hospital, grey, quiet, old,
Where Life and Death like friendly
    chafferers meet.
In Hospital [*1888*]. *Enter Patient*
Far in the stillness a cat
Languishes loudly.
Ibid. Vigil

A well-bred silence always at command.
In Hospital. Lady-Probationer
From the winter's grey despair,
From the summer's golden languor,
Death, the lover of Life,
Frees us for ever.
Ibid. Ave, Caesar
Bland as a Jesuit, sober as a hymn.
Ibid. House-Surgeon
Valiant in velvet, light in ragged luck,
Most vain, most generous, sternly critical,
Buffoon and poet, lover and sensualist:
A deal of Ariel, just a streak of Puck,
Much Antony, of Hamlet most of all,
And something of the Shorter-Catechist.
Ibid. Apparition [*Robert Louis Stevenson*]
As dust that drives, as straws that blow,
Into the night go one and all.
Ballade of Dead Actors
The ways of Death are soothing and
    serene,
And all the words of Death are grave
    and sweet.
In Memoriam R. G. C. B. [*1888*]
What is to come we know not. But we
    know
That what has been was good.
What Is to Come [*1888*]
Out of the night that covers me,
Black as the Pit from pole to pole,
I thank whatever gods may be
For my unconquerable soul.
Echoes. IV [*1888*], *In Memoriam R. T. Hamilton Bruce* [*"Invictus"*], *Stanza 1*
In the fell clutch of circumstance,
I have not winced nor cried aloud:
Under the bludgeonings of chance
My head is bloody, but unbowed.
Ibid. Stanza 2
It matters not how strait the gate,
How charged with punishments the
    scroll,
I am the master of my fate;
I am the captain of my soul.[1]
Ibid. Stanza 4
The nightingale has a lyre of gold,
    The lark's is a clarion call,

[1] See Sallust, page 35b.

And the blackbird plays but a boxwood
    flute,
  But I love him best of all.
            Echoes. XVIII [*1888*],
                    To A. D.

A late lark twitters from the quiet skies.
    Ibid. XXXV [*1888*], *In Memoriam*
                Margaritae Sorori

Night with her train of stars
And her great gift of sleep.
                            Ibid.

So be my passing!
My task accomplished and the long day
    done,
My wages taken, and in my heart
Some late lark singing.
                            Ibid.

Or ever the knightly years were gone
  With the old world to the grave,
I was a King in Babylon
  And you were a Christian Slave.
    Ibid. XXXVII [*1888*], *To W. A.*

The Spirit of Wine
Sang in my glass, and I listened
With love to his odorous music,
His flushed and magnificent song.
            Ibid. XLI, To R. A. M. S.

    These poor Might-Have-Beens,
These fatuous, ineffectual Yesterdays!
    To James McNeill Whistler

For Death and Time bring on the prime
Of God's own chosen weather,
And we lie in the peace of the Great
    Release
As once in the grass together.
            In Memoriam R. L. S.

What have I done for you,
England, my England?
        Rhymes and Rhythms. XXV

In the street of By-and-By
Stands the hostelry of Never,
Dream from deed he must dissever
Who his fortune here would try.
        In the Street of By-and-By

SARAH ORNE JEWETT
[1849–1909]

A harbor, even if it is a little harbor,
is a good thing, since adventurers come

into it as well as go out, and the life in
it grows strong, because it takes something from the world and has something
to give in return.
        Country By-Ways. River
                    Driftwood

We were standing where there was a
fine view of the harbor and its long
stretches of shore all covered by the
great army of the pointed firs, darkly
cloaked and standing as if they waited
to embark. As we looked far seaward
among the outer islands, the trees
seemed to march seaward still, going
steadily over the heights and down to
the water's edge.
    The Country of the Pointed Firs
                        [*1896*]

God bless them all who die at sea!
If they must sleep in restless waves,
God make them dream they are ashore,
With grass above their graves.
    The Gloucester Mother [*1908*].
                    Stanza 3

The thing that teases the mind over
and over for years, and at last gets
itself put down rightly on paper —
whether little or great, it belongs to
Literature.
        Letter to Willa Cather. Quoted
        in Preface to The Country of
        the Pointed Firs and Other
        Stories [*1925*]

EMMA LAZARUS
[1849–1887]

Give me your tired, your poor,
Your huddled masses yearning to
    breathe free,
The wretched refuse of your teeming
    shore,
Send these, the homeless, tempest-
    tossed, to me:
I lift my lamp beside the golden door.
    The New Colossus: Inscription
    for the Statue of Liberty, New
    York Harbor

SIR WILLIAM OSLER
[1849–1919]

The greater the ignorance the greater the dogmatism.

*In Montreal Medical Journal
[1902]*

The philosophies of one age have become the absurdities of the next, and the foolishness of yesterday has become the wisdom of tomorrow.

Ibid.

The natural man has only two primal passions, to get and to beget.

*Science and Immortality [1904].
Chap. 2*

We forget that the measure of the value of a nation to the world is neither the bushel nor the barrel, but mind; and that wheat and pork, though useful and necessary, are but dross in comparison with those intellectual products which alone are imperishable.

*Aequanimitas and Other Addresses
[1904]. Teacher and Student*

When schemes are laid in advance, it is surprising how often the circumstances fit in with them.

*Ibid. Internal Medicine as a
Vocation*

A well trained sensible family doctor is one of the most valuable assets in a community, worth today, as in Homer's time, many another man. . . . Few men live lives of more devoted self-sacrifice.

Ibid. Chauvinism in Medicine

Amid an eternal heritage of sorrow and suffering our work is laid.

Ibid. The Student Life

Tact is the saving virtue without which no woman can be a success.

*Commencement Address to
Nurses, Johns Hopkins University [May 7, 1913]*

Speck in cornea, 50¢.

*Entry in his account-book, first
fee as a practicing physician.
From Life of Sir William Osler
by* HARVEY CUSHING *[1925],
Vol. I, Chap. 6*

After all, there is no such literature as a Dictionary.

*Life of Sir William Osler.
Vol. I, Chap. 11*

The desire to take medicine is perhaps the greatest feature which distinguishes man from animals.

Ibid. Chap. 14

This is yet the childhood of the world, and a supine credulity is still the most charming characteristic of man.

Ibid.

We are here to add what we can *to*, not to get what we can *from*, Life.[1]

Ibid.

Humanity has but three great enemies; fever, famine and war; of these by far the greatest, by far the most terrible, is fever.

Ibid.

Though a little one, the master-word [Work] looms large in meaning. It is the open sesame to every portal, the great equalizer in the world, the true philosopher's stone which transmutes all the base metal of humanity into gold.[2]

Ibid. Chap. 22

Things cannot always go your way. Learn to accept in silence the minor aggravations, cultivate the gift of taciturnity and consume your own smoke [3] with an extra draught of hard work, so that those about you may not be annoyed with the dust and soot of your complaints.

Ibid.

Take the sum of human achievement in action, in science, in art, in literature — subtract the work of the men above forty, and while we should miss great treasures, even priceless treasures, we would practically be where we are

[1] Also in *Doctor and Nurse,* in *Aequanimitas and Other Addresses* [1904].
[2] Lecture, *The Master-Word in Medicine,* Toronto, October 1, 1903, also in *Aequanimitas.*
[3] See Carlyle, page 474a.

to-day. . . . The effective, moving, vitalizing work of the world is done between the ages of twenty-five and forty.[1]

Life of Sir William Osler. Vol. I, Chap. 24 (The Fixed Period)

My second fixed idea is the uselessness of men above sixty years of age, and the incalculable benefit it would be in commercial, political, and in professional life, if as a matter of course, men stopped work at this age.[2]

Ibid.

In that charming novel, "The Fixed Period," [by] Anthony Trollope, . . . the plot hinges upon the admirable scheme of a college into which at sixty men retired for a year of contemplation before a peaceful departure by chloroform. That incalculable benefits might follow such a scheme is apparent to anyone who, like myself, is nearing the limit, and who has made a careful study of the calamities which may befall men during the seventh and eighth decades.[2]

Ibid.

Nothing will sustain you more potently than the power to recognize in your humdrum routine, as perhaps it may be thought, the true poetry of life — the poetry of the commonplace, of the ordinary man, of the plain, toil-worn woman, with their loves and their joys, their sorrows and their griefs.

Ibid. (The Student Life)

Lift up one hand to heaven and thank your stars if they have given you the proper sense to enable you to appreciate the inconceivably droll situations in which we catch our fellow creatures.

Ibid.

[1] Address at Johns Hopkins University, Baltimore, February 22, 1905.
[2] This valedictory address caused much discussion and misquotation. It was headlined in the press "OSLER RECOMMENDS CHLOROFORM AT SIXTY," and occasioned many columns of letters, caustic cartoons, and the like, until to "Oslerize" became a byword.

I have three personal ideals. One, to do the day's work well and not to bother about to-morrow. . . . The second ideal has been to act the Golden Rule, as far as in me lay, toward my professional brethren and toward the patients committed to my care. And the third has been to cultivate such a measure of equanimity as would enable me to bear success with humility, the affection of my friends without pride, and to be ready when the day of sorrow and grief came to meet it with the courage befitting a man.

Life of Sir William Osler. Vol. I, Chap. 24 (Farewell Dinner [May 2, 1905])

Throw all the beer and spirits into the Irish Channel, the English Channel, and the North Sea for a year, and people in England would be infinitely better. It would certainly solve all the problems with which the philanthropists, the physicians, and the politicians have to deal.[1]

Ibid. Vol. II, Chap. 26

No man is really happy or safe without a hobby, and it makes precious little difference what the outside interest may be — botany, beetles or butterflies, roses, tulips or irises; fishing, mountaineering or antiquities — anything will do so long as he straddles a hobby and rides it hard.[2]

Ibid. Chap. 29

Nothing in life is more wonderful than faith — the one great moving force which we can neither weigh in the balance nor test in the crucible.

Ibid. Chap. 30

In the life of a young man the most essential thing for happiness is the gift of friendship.

Ibid. Chap. 31

[1] Address at Working Men's College, Camden Town, November 17, 1906.
[2] Address, Medical Library Association, Belfast, July 28, 1909.

No bubble is so iridescent or floats longer than that blown by the successful teacher.

> *Life of Sir William Osler.*
> *Vol. II, Chap. 31*

The nation's Valhalla [Westminster Abbey].

> *Ibid. Chap. 32*

It is one of the greatest blessings that so many women are so full of tact. The calamity happens when a woman who has all the other riches of life just lacks that one thing.[1]

> *Ibid. Chap. 33*

The quest for righteousness is Oriental, the quest for knowledge, Occidental.[2]

> *Ibid. Chap. 34*

In science the credit goes to the man who convinces the world, not to the man to whom the idea first occurs.[3]

> *Ibid. Chap. 38*

JAMES WHITCOMB RILEY
[1849–1916]

O'er folded blooms
  On swirls of musk,
The beetle booms adown the glooms
And bumps along the dusk.

> *The Beetle. Stanza 7*

The ripest peach is highest on the tree.

> *The Ripest Peach. Stanza 1*

An' the Gobble-uns'll git you
Ef you don't watch out.

> *Little Orphant Annie. Stanza 1*

His Mammy heered him holler, an' his
  Daddy heered him bawl,
An' when they turn't the kivvers down,
  he wasn't there at all!

> *Ibid. Stanza 2*

It hain't no use to grumble and complain,
  It's jest as easy to rejoice;

[1] Commencement Address, Johns Hopkins Hospital School of Nursing, May 7, 1913.
[2] Address, Jewish Historical Society of England, April 27, 1914.
[3] Address, Royal Society of Medicine, Historical Section, May 15, 1918.

When God sorts out the weather and
  sends rain,
Why rain's my choice.

> *Wet-Weather Talk*

Heaven holds all for which you sigh —
There! little girl; don't cry!

> *A Life-Lesson. Stanza 3*

I can see the pink sunbonnet and the
  little checkered dress
She wore when first I kissed her and she
  answered the caress
With the written declaration that, "as
  surely as the vine
Grew 'round the stump," she loved me
  — that old sweetheart of mine.

> *An Old Sweetheart of Mine.*
> *Stanza 12*

When over the fair fame of friend or foe
The shadow of disgrace shall fall,
  instead
Of words of blame, or proof of thus and
  so,
Let something good be said.

> *Let Something Good Be Said.*
> *Stanza 1*

Fer the world is full of roses, and the
  roses full of dew,
And the dew is full of heavenly love
  that drips fer me and you.

> *Thoughts fer the Discuraged*
> *Farmer. Stanza 5*

Tell you what I like the best —
'Long about knee-deep in June,
Bout the time strawberries melts
On the vine, — some afternoon
Like to jes' git out and rest,
And not work at nothin' else.

> *Knee-deep in June. Stanza 1*

Oh! the old swimmin'-hole! When I
  last saw the place,
The scene was all changed, like the
  change in my face.

> *The Old Swimmin'-Hole. Stanza 5*

Work is the least o' my idees
When the green, you know, gits back in
  the trees!

> *When the Green Gits Back in*
> *the Trees. Stanza 1*

O, the Raggedy Man he works fer Pa,
An' he's the goodest man ever you saw!

> *The Raggedy Man. Stanza 1*

There's a boil on his ear and a corn on
his chin, —
He calls it a dimple — but dimples
stick in.
The Man in the Moon. Stanza 3

A pictur' that no painter has the col-
orin' to mock —
When the frost is on the punkin and the
fodder's in the shock.
When the Frost Is on the Punkin.
Stanza 2

Le's go a-visitin' back to Griggsby's
Station —
Back where we ust to be so happy and
so pore!
Griggsby's Station. Stanza 1

EDWARD BELLAMY [1]
[1850–1898]

If we could have devised an arrangement for providing everybody with
music in their homes, perfect in quality,
unlimited in quantity, suited to every
mood, and beginning and ceasing at
will, we should have considered the
limit of human felicity already attained.
Looking Backward [1887]

Your system was liable to periodical
convulsions, overwhelming alike the
wise and unwise, the successful cut-
throat as well as his victim. I refer to
the business crises at intervals of five to
ten years, which wrecked the industries
of the nation.
Ibid.

AUGUSTINE BIRRELL
[1850–1933]

Libraries are not made; they grow.
Obiter Dicta. Book-Buying

Good as it is to inherit a library, it is
better to collect one.
Ibid.

[1] There is at least a fair chance that another fifty years will confirm Edward Bellamy's position as one of the most authentic
prophets of our age. — HEYWOOD BROUN
[1931]

FLORENCE EARLE COATES
[1850–1927]

The messenger of sure and swift relief,
Welcomed with wailings and reproach-
ful grief;
The friend of those that have no friend
but me,
I break all chains, and set all captives
free.
Death. Stanza 2

There is always room for beauty: mem-
ory
A myriad lovely blossoms may enclose,
But, whatsoe'er hath been, there still
must be
Room for another rose.
The Poetry of Earth. Stanza 1

EUGENE FIELD
[1850–1895]

I feel a sort of yearnin' 'nd a chokin' in
my throat
When I think of Red Hoss Mountain
'nd of Casey's tabble dote!
Casey's Table d'Hôte. Stanza 1

He could whip his weight in wildcats.
Modjesky as Cameel. Stanza 10

Let my temptation be a book,
Which I shall purchase, hold, and keep.
The Bibliomaniac's Prayer.
Stanza 2

No matter what conditions
Dyspeptic come to feaze,
The best of all physicians
Is Apple-pie and cheese!
Apple-Pie and Cheese. Stanza 5

I like the Anglo-Saxon speech
With its direct revealings;
It takes a hold, and seems to reach
'Way down into your feelings.
"Good-by — God Bless You!"
Stanza 1

I'm sure no human heart goes wrong
That's told "Good-by — God bless
you!"
Ibid. Stanza 2

I never lost a little fish — yes, I am free
to say
It always was the biggest fish I caught
that got away.
Our Biggest Fish. Stanza 2

How gracious those dews of solace that
over my senses fall
At the clink of the ice in the pitcher the
boy brings up the hall!
The Clink of the Ice. Stanza 1

When one's all right, he's prone to spite
The doctor's peaceful mission;
But when he's sick, it's loud and quick
He bawls for a physician.[1]
Doctors. Stanza 2

When I demanded of my friend what
viands he preferred,
He quoth: "A large cold bottle, and a
small hot bird!"
The Bottle and the Bird. Stanza 1

Have you ever heard of the Sugar-Plum
Tree?
'Tis a marvel of great renown!
It blooms on the shore of the Lollipop
sea
In the garden of Shut-Eye Town.
The Sugar-Plum Tree. Stanza 1

Wynken, Blynken, and Nod one night
Sailed off in a wooden shoe —
Sailed on a river of crystal light
Into a sea of dew.
Wynken, Blynken, and Nod.
Stanza 1

The little toy dog is covered with dust,
But sturdy and stanch he stands;
And the little toy soldier is red with
rust,
And his musket moulds in his hands;
Time was when the little toy dog was
new,
And the soldier was passing fair;
And that was the time when our Little
Boy Blue
Kissed them and put them there.
Little Boy Blue. Stanza 1

The Rock-a-By Lady from Hushaby
street
Comes stealing; comes creeping.
The Rock-a-By Lady. Stanza 1

Have you ever heard the wind go
"Yooooo"?

[1] Three faces wears the doctor: when first
sought
An Angel's; and a god's the cure half-
wrought;

'Tis a pitiful sound to hear!
It seems to chill you through and
through
With a strange and speechless fear.
The Night Wind. Stanza 1

The Dinkey-Bird goes singing
In the amfalula tree!
The Dinkey-Bird. Stanza 1

The gingham dog went "Bow-wow-
wow!"
And the calico cat replied "Mee-ow!"
The air was littered, an hour or so,
With bits of gingham and calico.
The Duel. Stanza 2

Father calls me William, sister calls me
Will,
Mother calls me Willie, but the fellers
call me Bill!
Jest 'Fore Christmas. Stanza 1

'Most all the time, the whole year
round, there ain't no flies on me,
But jest 'fore Christmas I'm as good
as I kin be!
Ibid.

Shuffle-Shoon and Amber-Locks
Sit together, building blocks;
Shuffle-Shoon is old and gray,
Amber-Locks a little child,
But together at their play
Age and Youth are reconciled.
Shuffle-Shoon and Amber-Locks.
Stanza 1

Mother tells me "Happy dreams!" and
takes away the light,
An' leaves me lyin' all alone an' seein'
things at night.
Seein' Things. Stanza 1

Strive not to hew your path through
life — it really doesn't pay;
Be sure the salve of flattery soaps all
you do and say;
Herein the only royal road to fame and
fortune lies:
Put not your trust in vinegar — molasses catches flies!
Uncle Eph. Stanza 4

But when, the cure complete, he seeks his
fee,
The Devil looks less terrible than he.
ANONYMOUS

FRED GILBERT
[1850–1903]

The Man Who Broke the Bank at Monte Carlo.
Title of song [1892]

JOHN CHEEVER GOODWIN
[1850–1912]

For that elephant ate all night,
  And that elephant ate all day;
Do what he could to furnish him food,
  The cry was still *more hay.*
Wang: The Man with an Elephant on His Hands [1891]

LAFCADIO HEARN
[1850–1904]

My friends are much more dangerous than my enemies. . . . These latter help me so much by their unconscious aid that I almost love them. They help me to maintain the isolation indispensable to quiet regularity of work.
Letter to Ernest Fenollosa, 1899. Quoted by VERA MCWILLIAMS: *Lafcadio Hearn [1946]*

HENRY CABOT LODGE
[1850–1924]

New England has a harsh climate, a barren soil, a rough and stormy coast, and yet we love it, even with a love passing that of dwellers in more favored regions.
Address, New England Society of New York [December 22, 1884]

Of "Americanism" of the right sort we cannot have too much. Mere vaporing and boasting become a nation as little as a man. But honest, outspoken pride and faith in our country are infinitely better and more to be respected than the cultivated reserve which sets it down as ill-bred and in bad taste ever to refer to our country except by way of deprecation, criticism, or general negation.
Ibid.

Let every man honor and love the land of his birth and the race from which he springs and keep their memory green. It is a pious and honorable duty. But let us have done with British-Americans and Irish-Americans and German-Americans, and so on, and all be Americans. . . . If a man is going to be an American at all let him be so without any qualifying adjectives; and if he is going to be something else, let him drop the word American from his personal description.[1]
The Day We Celebrate (Forefathers' Day), Address, New England Society of Brooklyn [December 21, 1888]

It is the flag just as much of the man who was naturalized yesterday, as of the man whose people have been here many generations.
Address [1915]

He was a great patriot, a great man; above all, a great American. His country was the ruling, mastering passion of his life from the beginning even unto the end.
Theodore Roosevelt: Address Before Congress [February 9, 1919]

PHILIP BOURKE MARSTON
[1850–1887]

A little time for laughter,
A little time to sing,
A little time to kiss and cling,
And no more kissing after.[2]
After. Stanza 1

LAURA ELIZABETH RICHARDS
[1850–1943]

Sure, honor's name will aye be richer
For the bright name of Molly Pitcher.
Molly Pitcher

Great is truth and shall prevail,[3]
Therefore must we weep and wail.
The Mameluke and the Hospodar

[1] See Theodore Roosevelt, page 780a.
[2] See Du Maurier, pages 665b–666a.
[3] See *1 Esdras*, IV, 41, on page 1065a. For (magna est veritas & praevalebit) great

748

Every little wave had its nightcap on.
A Song for Hal
Ponsonby Perks,
He fought with Turks,
Performing many wonderful works.
Nonsense Verses. Stanza 2

ROBERT RICHARDSON
[1850–1901]

Warm summer sun, shine friendly here;
Warm western wind, blow kindly here;
Green sod above, rest light, rest light —
Good-night, Annette! Sweetheart, good-night.[1]
To Annette

ROBERT LOUIS STEVENSON
[1850–1894]

Mankind was never so happily inspired as when it made a cathedral.
An Inland Voyage [*1878*]. *Noyon*

Every man is his own doctor of divinity, in the last resort.
Ibid.

For my part, I travel not to go anywhere, but to go. I travel for travel's sake. The great affair is to move.
Travels with a Donkey [*1878*]

Marriage is like life in this — that it is a field of battle, and not a bed of roses.
Virginibus Puerisque [*1881*].
I, Chap. 1

Times are changed with him who marries; there are no more by-path meadows, where you may innocently linger, but the road lies long and straight and dusty to the grave.
Ibid. Chap. 2

---

is truth, & shall prevail. — Thomas Brooks:
The Crown and Glory of Christianity [*1662*]
[1] Mark Twain adapted this verse, by the Australian poet Richardson, for the stone marking the grave of his daughter, Olivia Susan Clemens, who died August 18, 1896, aged twenty-four:
Warm summer sun, shine kindly here;
Warm southern wind, blow softly here;
Green sod above, lie light, lie light —
Good-night, dear heart, good-night, good-night.

Man is a creature who lives not upon bread alone but principally by catch-words.
Virginibus Puerisque. I, Chap. 2

The cruellest lies are often told in silence.
Ibid. Chap. 4, Truth of Intercourse

Old and young, we are all on our last cruise.
Ibid. II, Crabbed Age and Youth

It is better to be a fool than to be dead.
Ibid.

Give me the young man who has brains enough to make a fool of himself.
Ibid.

Books are good enough in their own way, but they are a mighty bloodless substitute for life.
Ibid. III, An Apology for Idlers

Perpetual devotion to what a man calls his business, is only to be sustained by perpetual neglect of many other things.
Ibid.

There is no duty we so much underrate as the duty of being happy.
Ibid.

To travel hopefully is a better thing than to arrive.
Ibid. VI, El Dorado

To be what we are, and to become what we are capable of becoming, is the only end of life.
Familiar Studies of Men and Books [*1882*]

I am in the habit of looking not so much to the nature of a gift as to the spirit in which it is offered.
New Arabian Nights [*1882*].
The Suicide Club

Fifteen men on the Dead Man's Chest —[1]
Yo-ho-ho, and a bottle of rum!

---

[1] Treasure Island came out of Kingsley's "At Last," where I got the Dead Man's Chest — and that was the seed. — R. L. Stevenson, *Letter to Sidney Colvin*
See Charles Kingsley, page 599a.

Drink and the devil had done for the
　　rest —
Yo-ho-ho, and a bottle of rum!
　　　　　　Treasure Island [*1883*]

Doctors is all swabs.
　　　　Ibid. Chap. 3 [*Billy Bones*]

Many's the long night I've dreamed
of cheese — toasted, mostly.
　　　　Ibid. Chap. 15 [*Ben Gunn*]

There's no music like a little river's.
It plays the same tune (and that's the
favourite) over and over again, and yet
does not weary of it like men fiddlers.
It takes the mind out of doors; and
though we should be grateful for good
houses, there is, after all, no house like
God's out-of-doors.
　　　　Prince Otto [*1885*]. *Chap. 2*

For all the story-books you read:
For all the pains you comforted:
For all you pitied, all you bore,
In sad and happy days of yore . . .
Take, nurse, the little book you hold!
　　　A Child's Garden of Verses
　　　[*1885*]. *To Alison Cunningham*
　　　from Her Boy

In winter I get up at night
And dress by yellow candle-light.
In summer, quite the other way,
I have to go to bed by day.
　　　Ibid. Bed in Summer, Stanza 1

I have to go to bed and see
The birds still hopping on the tree,
Or hear the grown-up people's feet
Still going past me on the street.
　　　　　　Ibid. Stanza 2

A child should always say what's true
And speak when he is spoken to,
And behave mannerly at table;
At least as far as he is able.
　　　Ibid. Whole Duty of Children

Whenever the moon and stars are set,
Whenever the wind is high,
All night long in the dark and wet,
A man goes riding by.
Late in the night when the fires are out,
Why does he gallop and gallop about?
　　　Ibid. Windy Nights, Stanza 1

Dark brown is the river,
　　Golden is the sand,

It flows along for ever,
　　With trees on either hand.
　　　A Child's Garden of Verses. Where
　　　　　Go the Boats, Stanza 1

The pleasant land of counterpane.
　　　Ibid. The Land of Counterpane,
　　　　　　　　　　Stanza 4

I have a little shadow that goes in and
　　out with me,
And what can be the use of him is more
　　than I can see.
He is very, very like me from the heels
　　up to the head;
And I see him jump before me, when I
　　jump into my bed.
　　　Ibid. My Shadow, Stanza 1

The friendly cow all red and white,
　　I love with all my heart:
She gives me cream with all her might,
　　To eat with apple-tart.
　　　　Ibid. The Cow, Stanza 1

The world is so full of a number of
　　things,
I'm sure we should all be as happy as
　　kings.
　　　　　Ibid. Happy Thought

The eternal dawn, beyond a doubt,
　　Shall break on hill and plain,
And put all stars and candles out
　　Ere we be young again.
　　　　　　　To Minnie

Little Indian, Sioux or Crow,
Little frosty Eskimo,
Little Turk or Japanee,
O! don't you wish that you were me?
　　　　Ibid. Foreign Children

I feel very strongly about putting
questions; it partakes too much of the
style of the day of judgment. You start
a question, and it's like starting a stone.
You sit quietly on the top of a hill; and
away the stone goes, starting others.
　　　The Strange Case of Dr. Jekyll and
　　　　　　　Mr. Hyde [*1886*]

Am I no a bonny fighter?
　　　Kidnapped [*1886*]. *Chap. 10*
　　　　　　　　　[Alan Breck]

Of all my verse, like not a single line;
But like my title, for it is not mine.
That title from a better man [1] I stole:

　[1] Ben Jonson.

Ah, how much better, had I stol'n the whole!

Underwoods [*1887*]. *Foreword*

There are men and classes of men that stand above the common herd: the soldier, the sailor, and the shepherd not unfrequently; the artist rarely; rarelier still, the clergyman; the physician almost as a rule. He is the flower (such as it is) of our civilization.

Ibid. Dedication

Generosity he has, such as is possible to those who practise an art, never to those who drive a trade; discretion, tested by a hundred secrets; tact, tried in a thousand embarrassments; and what are more important, Heraclean cheerfulness and courage.

Ibid.

Gratitude is but a lame sentiment; thanks, when they are expressed, are often more embarrassing than welcome.

Ibid.

Go, little book, and wish to all
Flowers in the garden, meat in the hall,
A bin of wine, a spice of wit,
A house with lawns enclosing it,
A living river by the door,
A nightingale in the sycamore!

Ibid. Envoy

Youth now flees on feathered foot.

Ibid. To Will H. Low [1]

Life is over, life was gay:
We have come the primrose way.

Ibid.

Dear Andrew, with the brindled hair.[2]

Ibid. To Andrew Lang

Under the wide and starry sky,
Dig the grave and let me lie.
Glad did I live and gladly die,
And I laid me down with a will.

Ibid. Requiem, Stanza 1

[1] American painter [1853–1932], whose wife translated Stevenson's *Strange Case of Dr. Jekyll and Mr. Hyde* into French.

[2] Dear Louis of the awful cheek!
Who told you it was right to speak,
Where all the world might hear and stare,
Of other fellows' "brindled hair"?
ANDREW LANG [1844–1912]: *To R. L. S.*

This be the verse you grave for me:
Here he lies where he longed to be;
Home is the sailor, home from sea,
  And the hunter home from the hill.

Underwoods. Requiem, Stanza 2

If I have faltered more or less
In my great task of happiness.

Ibid. The Celestial Surgeon

If beams from happy human eyes
Have moved me not; if morning skies,
Books, and my food, and summer rain
Knocked on my sullen heart in vain: —
Lord, thy most pointed pleasure take
And stab my spirit broad awake.

Ibid.

Yet, O stricken heart, remember, O remember
How of human days he lived the better part.
April came to bloom and never dim December
Breathed its killing chills upon the head or heart.

Ibid. In Memoriam F. A.
Stilwell [1] [*1881*]

Let first the onion flourish there,
Rose among roots, the maiden-fair
Wine-scented and poetic soul
Of the capacious salad bowl.

Ibid. To a Gardener

My body, which my dungeon is,
And yet my parks and palaces.

Ibid. XXXVII

There are kind hearts still, for friends to fill
And fools to take and break them;
But the nearest friends are the auldest friends
And the grave's the place to seek them.

Ibid. In Scots, XVI, Stanza 3

I have thus played the sedulous ape to Hazlitt, to Lamb, to Wordsworth, to Sir Thomas Browne, to Defoe, to Hawthorne, to Montaigne, to Baudelaire and to Obermann.

Memories and Portraits [*1887*].
A College Magazine

[1] Lady Colvin's son by her first marriage; he died at the age of eighteen.

"A Penny Plain and Twopence Coloured."

Memories and Portraits. Essay about Skelt's Juvenile Drama

Wealth I ask not, hope nor love,
  Nor a friend to know me;
All I ask, the heaven above
  And the road below me.

Songs of Travel. The Vagabond, Stanza 4

I will make you brooches and toys for
  your delight
Of bird-song at morning and star-shine
  at night.

Ibid. Romance, Stanza 1

And this shall be for music when no
  one else is near,
The fine song for singing, the rare song
  to hear!

Ibid. Stanza 3

God, if this were enough,
That I see things bare to the buff.

Ibid. If This Were Faith

Bright is the ring of words
When the right man rings them.

Ibid. XIV

In the highlands, in the country places,
Where the old plain men have rosy
  faces,
And the young fair maidens
  Quiet eyes.

Ibid. XV

I have trod the upward and the downward slope;
I have endured and done in days before;
I have longed for all, and bid farewell
  to hope;
And I have lived and loved and closed
  the door.

Ibid. XXII

Trusty, dusky, vivid, true,
With eyes of gold and bramble-dew,
Steel-true and blade-straight
The great artificer
Made my mate.

Ibid. XXV, To My Wife, Stanza 1

Be it granted me to behold you again
  in dying,
Hills of home!

Ibid. XLIII, To S. R. Crockett

Let any man speak long enough, he
will get believers.

*The Master of Ballantrae [1889].
Summary of Events*

Not every man is so great a coward
as he thinks he is — nor yet so good a
Christian.

Ibid. Mr. Mackellar's Journey

Do you know what the Governor of
South Carolina said to the Governor
of North Carolina? It's a long time
between drinks, observed that powerful
thinker.[1]

*The Wrong Box [1889].
Chap. 8*

If I have at all learned the trade of
using words to convey truth and to
arouse emotion, you have at last furnished me with a subject.

*An Open Letter on Father
Damien*

Still obscurely fighting the lost fight
of virtue, still clinging, in the brothel
or on the scaffold, to some rag of honour, the poor jewel of their souls!

*Across the Plains [1892].
Pulvis et Umbra*

So long as we love we serve; so long
as we are loved by others, I would almost say that we are indispensable; and
no man is useless while he has a friend.

Ibid. Lay Morals

To be honest, to be kind — to earn
a little and spend a little less, to make
upon the whole a family happier for his
presence, to renounce when that shall
be necessary and not to be embittered,
to keep a few friends, but these without
capitulation — above all, on the same
grim condition, to keep friends with

[1] Of the several traditions relating to the
origin of this remark, the most reasonable one
traces it to John Motley Morehead [1796–
1866], who was Governor of North Carolina
1841–1845. He was visited by James H. Hammond [1807–1864], who was Governor of
South Carolina 1842–1844. They engaged in
discussion and argument, and when the latter
waxed hot, Governor Morehead was reported
by a servant to have exclaimed: "It's a long
time between drinks." — Personal letter from
John Motley Morehead, November 21, 1934

himself — here is a task for all that a man has of fortitude and delicacy.
A Christmas Sermon

If your morals make you dreary, depend upon it, they are wrong. I do not say give them up, for they may be all you have, but conceal them like a vice lest they should spoil the lives of better and simpler people.
Ibid.

Here lies one who meant well, tried a little, failed much: — surely that may be his epitaph of which he need not be ashamed.
Ibid.

Chiefs! Our road is not built to last a thousand years, yet in a sense it is. When a road is once built, it is a strange thing how it collects traffic, how every year as it goes on, more and more people are found to walk thereon, and others are raised up to repair and perpetuate it, and keep it alive.[1]
Vailima Letters [1895]. Address to the Chiefs on the Opening of the Road of Gratitude, October, 1894

You cannot run away from a weakness; you must some time fight it out or perish; and if that be so, why not now, and where you stand?
The Amateur Emigrant [1896]

To be a gentleman is to be one all the world over, and in every relation and grade of society.
Ibid.

Culture is not measured by the greatness of the field which is covered by our knowledge, but by the nicety with which we can perceive relations in that field, whether great or small.
Ibid.

[1] Robert Louis Stevenson was a roadmender. . . . Ay, and with more than his pen. . . . I wonder was he ever so truly great, so entirely the man we know and love, as when he inspired the chiefs to make a highway in the wilderness. Surely no more fitting monument could exist to his memory than the Road of Gratitude, cut, laid, and kept by the pureblood tribe kings of Samoa. — MICHAEL FAIRLESS (MARGARET FAIRLESS BARBER) [1869–1901]: *The Roadmender, Chap. 5*

Ice and iron cannot be welded.
Weir of Hermiston [1896]

Give us grace and strength to forbear and to persevere. Give us courage and gaiety and the quiet mind, spare to us our friends, soften to us our enemies.
Prayer [1]

Youth is wholly experimental.
Letter to a Young Gentleman

ROSE HARTWICK THORPE
[1850–1939]

She breathed the husky whisper:—
"Curfew must not ring tonight."
Curfew Must Not Ring Tonight. Stanza 2

Long, long years I've rung the curfew from that gloomy, shadowed tower;
Every evening, just at sunset, it has told the twilight hour;
I have done my duty ever, tried to do it just and right,
Now I'm old I will not falter, — Curfew it must ring tonight.
Ibid. Stanza 3

Out she swung — far out; the city seemed a speck of light below,
There 'twixt heaven and earth suspended as the bell swung to and fro.
Ibid. Stanza 7

ELLA WHEELER WILCOX
[1850–1919]

Talk happiness. The world is sad enough
Without your woe. No path is wholly rough.
Speech. Stanza 1

Talk faith. The world is better off without
Your uttered ignorance and morbid doubt.
Ibid. Stanza 2

Talk health. The dreary, never-ending tale
Of mortal maladies is more than stale;

[1] On the bronze memorial to Stevenson in St. Giles Cathedral, Edinburgh, Scotland.

You cannot charm or interest or please
By harping on that minor chord, dis-
ease.
Say you are well, or all is well with you,
And God shall hear your words and
make them true.
Speech. Stanza 3

The two kinds of people on earth that
I mean
Are the people who lift and the people
who lean.
To Lift or to Lean

It ever has been since time began,
And ever will be, till time lose breath,
That love is a mood — no more — to
man,
And love to woman is life or death.
Blind. Stanza 1

Laugh, and the world laughs with you;
Weep, and you weep alone;
For the sad old earth must borrow its
mirth,
But has trouble enough of its own.
Solitude. Stanza 1

Feast, and your halls are crowded;
Fast, and the world goes by.
Ibid. Stanza 3

So many gods, so many creeds,
So many paths that wind and wind,
When just the art of being kind
Is all this sad world needs.
The World's Need

No question is ever settled
Until it is settled right.
Settle the Question Right

We flatter those we scarcely know,
We please the fleeting guest,
And deal full many a thoughtless blow
To those who love us best.
Life's Scars. Stanza 3

ROSE HENNIKER HEATON

She answered by return of post
The invitation of her host.
She caught the train she said she would,
And changed at junctions as she should.
She brought a light and smallish box
And keys belonging to the locks.
The Perfect Guest

She left no little things behind
Excepting loving thoughts and kind.
Ibid.

SAMUEL VALENTINE COLE
[1851–1925]

"Hammer away, ye hostile hands,
Your hammers break, God's anvil
stands."
The Unthwarted Plan

Where'er men go, in heaven, or earth,
or hell,
They find themselves, and that is all
they find.
The Difference

The man who knows and knows he
knows,[1]
To him your homage bring;
He wields the power that waits and
wins,
And he is rightful king.
An Old Saw Reset. Stanza 1

FERDINAND FOCH
[1851–1929]

A guest at a dinner given in honor of
Marshal Foch in Denver, Colorado,
said that there was nothing but wind
in French politeness. Marshal Foch re-
torted: "Neither is there anything but
wind in a pneumatic tire, yet it eases
wonderfully the jolts along life's highway."
Attributed

My center is giving way, my right is
pushed back, situation excellent, I am
attacking.[2]
*Said at the Second Battle of
the Marne, 1918*

EDWARD SMITH UFFORD
[1851–1929]

Throw out the life-line across the dark
wave,

[1] He who knows not, and knows not that
he knows not, is a fool. Shun him.
He who knows not, and knows that he
knows not, is simple. Teach him.
He who knows, and knows not that he
knows, is asleep. Waken him.
He who knows, and knows that he knows,
is wise. Follow him.
Arabic apothegm

[2] Mon centre cède, ma droite recule, situation excellente, j'attaque. — *Quoted by* B. H.
LIDDELL HART, *Reputations Ten Years After*
[1928]

There is a brother whom someone
should save,
Throw out the life-line, throw out the
life-line,
Someone is sinking today.
Throw Out the Life-line
(revivalist hymn) [*1884*]

FRANCIS WILLIAM BOURDILLON
[1852–1921]

The night has a thousand eyes,
And the day but one;
Yet the light of the bright world dies,
With the dying sun.
Light. Stanza 1

The mind has a thousand eyes,
And the heart but one;
Yet the light of a whole life dies,
When love is done.
Ibid. Stanza 2

Upon the valley's lap
The dewy morning throws
A thousand pearly drops
To wash a single rose.
So, often in the course
Of life's few fleeting years,
A single pleasure costs
The soul a thousand tears.
Upon the Valley's Lap

ROBERT BONTINE CUNNINGHAME-GRAHAM
[1852–1936]

Success, which touches nothing that
it does not vulgarize, should be its own
reward . . . the odium of success is
hard enough to bear, without the added
ignominy of popular applause.
Success [*1902*]

The ancient seat of pedantry [Ox-
ford], where they manufacture prigs as
fast as butchers in Chicago handle
hogs.
With the North-West Wind

God forbid that I should go to any
heaven in which there are no horses.
Letter to Theodore Roosevelt
[*1917*]

Handsomely, as he who lay in it
might well have said, they lowered the
coffin down. The priest had left his
Latin and said a prayer or two in English, and I was glad of it, for English
surely was the speech the Master Mariner most loved, and honoured in the
loving with new graces of his own.
Harboured [*The burial of*
Joseph Conrad, 1924]

NATHAN HASKELL DOLE [1]
[1852–1935]

What other State compares with Maine
In glorious coasts, where ocean tides
Have for long ages beat in vain
To storm the coves where safety
hides;
Where pillared cliffs like sentries stand
To guard the entries to the land,
From Kittery to Calais!
The State of Maine. Stanza 1

EDWIN MARKHAM
[1852–1940]

Why build these cities glorious
If man unbuilded goes?
In vain we build the world, unless
The builder also grows.
Man-Making

Bowed by the weight of centuries he
leans
Upon his hoe and gazes on the ground,
The emptiness of ages in his face,
And on his back the burden of the
world.
The Man with the Hoe [2] [*1899*].
Stanza 1

O masters, lords and rulers in all lands,
Is this the handiwork you give to God?
Ibid. Stanza 3

Here was a man to hold against the
world,
A man to match the mountains [3] and
the sea.
Lincoln, the Man of the People
[*1901*]. *Stanza 1*

[1] Editor of the tenth edition of *Bartlett's*
Familiar Quotations [1914].
[2] Millet's painting.
[3] A man to match his mountains, not to
creep

The color of the ground was in him, the red earth,
The smack and tang of elemental things.
Lincoln, the Man of the People.
Stanza 2
So came the Captain with the mighty heart;
And when the judgment thunders split the house,
Wrenching the rafters from their ancient rest,
He held the ridgepole up, and spiked again
The rafters of the Home.
Ibid. Stanza 4
And when he fell in whirlwind, he went down
As when a lordly cedar, green with boughs,
Goes down with a great shout upon the hills,
And leaves a lonesome place against the sky.
Ibid.
Three times I came to your friendly door;
Three times my shadow was on your floor.
I was the beggar with bruisèd feet;
I was the woman you gave to eat;
I was the child on the homeless street.
How the Great Guest Came
He drew a circle that shut me out —
Heretic, rebel, a thing to flout.
But Love and I had the wit to win:
We drew a circle that took him in.
Outwitted

GEORGE MOORE
[1852–1933]

After all there is but one race — humanity.
The Bending of the Bough. Act III
The difficulty in life is the choice.
Act IV

Dwarfed and abased below them.
WHITTIER: *Among the Hills* [1869],
Prelude
Bring me men to match my mountains. —
SAM WALTER FOSS [1858–1911]: *The Coming American*

The wrong way always seems the more reasonable.
The Bending of the Bough. Act IV
A quotation, a chance word heard in an unexpected quarter, puts me on the trail of the book destined to achieve some intellectual advancement in me.
Confessions of a Young Man
[1888]. *XII*
English, Scotchmen, Jews, do well in Ireland — Irishmen never; even the patriot has to leave Ireland to get a hearing.
Ave [1911]. *Overture*
My one claim to originality among Irishmen is that I have never made a speech.
Ibid. Chap. 4
As the moon is more interested in the earth than in any other thing, there is always some woman more interested in a man's mind than in anything else, who is willing to follow it sentence by sentence.
Ibid. Chap. 10
A man travels the world over in search of what he needs and returns home to find it.
The Brook Kerith [1916].
Chap. 11
My definition of pure poetry, something that the poet creates outside of his own personality.
Anthology of Pure Poetry.
Introduction

HENRY VAN DYKE
[1852–1933]

If all the skies were sunshine,
Our faces would be fain
To feel once more upon them
The cooling plash of rain.
If All the Skies. Stanza 1
Men have dulled their eyes with sin,
And dimmed the light of heaven with doubt,
And built their temple-walls to shut thee in,
And framed their iron creeds to shut thee out.
God of the Open Air. Stanza 3

"Raise the stone, and thou shalt find me; cleave the wood and there am I." [1]
The Toiling of Felix. Part I,
Prelude

This is the gospel of labour, ring it, ye bells of the kirk!
The Lord of Love came down from above, to live with the men who work;
This is the rose that He planted, here in the thorn-curst soil:
Heaven is blest with perfect rest, but the blessing of Earth is toil.
Ibid. Envoy, Stanza 5

So it's home again, and home again, America for me.
My heart is turning home again, and there I long to be.
"America for Me." Stanza 2

Oh, London is a man's town, there's power in the air;
And Paris is a woman's town, with flowers in her hair.
Ibid. Stanza 3

I want a ship that's westward bound to plough the rolling sea,
To the blessèd Land of Room Enough beyond the ocean bars,
Where the air is full of sunlight and the flag is full of stars.
Ibid. Stanza 6

This is my work; my blessing, not my doom;
Of all who live, I am the one by whom
This work can best be done in the right way.
The Three Best Things. I, Work

Not to the swift, the race:
Not to the strong, the fight: [2]
Not to the righteous, perfect grace:
Not to the wise, the light.
Reliance. Stanza 1

---

[1] *Oxyrhynchus Logia Agrapha, The Unwritten Sayings of Jesus, Fifth Logion.*
[2] See *Ecclesiastes, IX, 11,* on page 1043a.
In anguish we uplift
A new unhallowed song:
The race is to the swift;
The battle to the strong.
JOHN DAVIDSON [1857–1909]:
War-Song, St. 1

Oh, was I born too soon, my dear, or were you born too late,
That I am going out the door while you come in the gate?
Rencontre. Stanza 1

The lintel low enough to keep out pomp and pride:
The threshold high enough to turn deceit aside.
For the Friends at Hurstmont.
The Door

Self is the only prison that can ever bind the soul.
The Prison and the Angel

Individuality is the salt of common life. You may have to live in a crowd, but you do not have to live like it, nor subsist on its food.
The School of Life

It is with rivers as it is with people: the greatest are not always the most agreeable nor the best to live with.
Little Rivers. Chap. 2

The first day of spring is one thing, and the first spring day is another. The difference between them is sometimes as great as a month.
Fisherman's Luck. Chap. 5

YOUNG EWING ALLISON
[1853–1932]

The very texture of every enduring work of art must imbed the glowing life of its own times and the embers of the past. If it does not cover space as history it must plumb the depths of emotion in an individual to reach the universal perception.
"My Old Kentucky Home"

HALL CAINE
[1853–1931]

I reject the monstrous theory that while a man may redeem the past a woman never can.
The Eternal City. Part VI,
Chap. 18

A great outrage on the spirit of Justice breaks down all barriers of race and nationality.
Ibid. Part VII, Chap. 5

EDGAR WATSON HOWE
[1853–1937]

A really busy person never knows how much he weighs.
Country Town Sayings [*1911*]

What people say behind your back is your standing in the community.
Ibid.

There is nothing so well known as that we should not expect something for nothing — but we all do and call it Hope.
Ibid.

ROBERT UNDERWOOD JOHNSON
[1853–1937]

For lover or nightingale who can wait?
Whenever he cometh he cometh late.
Spring at the Villa Conti

Song's but solace for a day;
Wine's a traitor not to trust;
Love's a kiss and then away;
Time's a peddler deals in dust.
Hearth-Song. Stanza 2

CECIL JOHN RHODES
[1853–1902]

I desire to encourage and foster an appreciation of the advantages which will result from the union of the English-speaking peoples throughout the world, and to encourage in the students from the United States of America an attachment to the country from which they have sprung without I hope withdrawing them or their sympathies from the land of their adoption or birth.
Will, establishing the Rhodes Scholarships

Educational relations make the strongest tie.
Ibid.

So little done — so much to do.
Last words

IRWIN RUSSELL [1]
[1853–1879]

De man what keeps pullin' de grape-vine shakes down a few bunches at leas'.
Precepts at Parting [*1888*].
Stanza 3

You mus' reason with a mule.
Nebuchadnezzar [*1888*].
Stanza 3

You bless us, please sah, eben ef we's
doin' wrong tonight,
Kase den we'll need de blessin' more'n
ef we's doin' right;
An' let de blessin' stay wid us untel we
comes to die
An' goes to keep our Christmas wid
dem sheriffs in de sky.
Christmas Night in the Quarters
[*1917*]. *Blessing the Dance*

JAMES A. BLAND
[1854–1911]

Carry me back to old Virginny,
There's where the cotton and the corn
and taters grow;
There's where the birds warble sweet
in the springtime,
There's where this old darky's heart am
long'd to go.
Carry Me Back to Old Virginny
[*1875*]

WILLIAM HENRY DRUMMOND
[1854–1907]

De win' can blow lak hurricane
An' s'pose she blow some more,
You can't get drown on Lac St. Pierre
So long you stay on shore.
The Wreck of the "Julie Plante."
Stanza 6

Do w'at you lak wit' your old gran-
'pere

[1] Among the first — if not the very first — of Southern writers to appreciate the literary possibilities of the Negro character. — JOEL CHANDLER HARRIS [1848–1908]

For w'en you're beeg feller he won't be
   dere —
  Leetle Bateese!
           Little Bateese. Stanza 7
To the hut of the peasant, or lordly
  hall,
To the heart of the king, or humblest
  thrall,
Sooner or late, love comes to all.
         The Grand Seigneur. Stanza 1

SIR JAMES GEORGE FRAZER
[1854–1941]

Dwellers by the sea cannot fail to be
impressed by the sight of its ceaseless
ebb and flow, and are apt, on the principles of that rude philosophy of sympathy and resemblance . . . . to trace a
subtle relation, a secret harmony, between its tides and the life of man. . . . .
The belief that most deaths happen at
ebb tide is said to be held along the
east coast of England from Northum-
berland to Kent.[1]
       The Golden Bough.[2] *Chap. 3*
  The heaviest calamity in English
history, the breach with America,
might never have occurred if George
the Third had not been an honest dullard.
                   Ibid.
  By religion, then, I understand a
propitiation or conciliation of powers
superior to man which are believed to
direct and control the course of nature
and of human life.
            Ibid. Chap. 4
  It is a common rule with primitive
people not to waken a sleeper, because
his soul is away and might not have
time to get back.
           Ibid. Chap. 18
  The awe and dread with which the
untutored savage contemplates his

[1] Just between twelve and one, even at the
turning o' the tide. — SHAKESPEARE: *King
Henry V* [1598–1600], *Act II, Sc. 3* (Falstaff's
death)
  See Dickens, page 579b.
[2] Abridged one-volume edition [1922]. The
original appeared in twelve volumes from
1890 to 1915.

mother-in-law are amongst the most
familiar facts of anthropology.
       The Golden Bough. Chap. 18
  The world cannot live at the level of
its great men.
             Ibid. Chap. 37

THOMAS RILEY MARSHALL
[1854–1925]

What this country needs is a good
five-cent cigar.[1]
     Remark to John Crockett, Chief
    Clerk of the United States Senate

CHARLES LEONARD MOORE
[1854–1923]

Thine the great grave where dark De
  Soto sleeps —
A new Columbus of the forest deeps.
         To America [*1896*]
And now for what comes next
Thou waitest in thine invulnerable
  West,
Blazoning more large thy living-lettered
  text,
"Chance and the tools to those who use
  them best."
                   Ibid.

EVA MARCH TAPPAN
[1854–1930]

We drove the Indians out of the land,
But a dire revenge these redmen
  planned,
For they fastened a name to every
  nook,
And every boy with a spelling-book
Will have to toil till his hair turns gray
Before he can spell them the proper
  way.[2]
        On the Cape. Stanza 1

EDITH MATILDA THOMAS
[1854–1925]

The god of music dwelleth out of doors.
                  Music

[1] What this country needs is a good five-
cent nickel. — FRANKLIN P. ADAMS [1932]
[2] See Lydia Sigourney, page 463b.

The love of my life came not
As love unto others is cast;
For mine was a secret wound —
But the wound grew a pearl, at last.
The Deep-Sea Pearl. Stanza 1

WILLARD DUNCAN VANDIVER
[1854–1932]

I come from a State that raises corn
and cotton and cockleburs and Democrats, and frothy eloquence neither
convinces nor satisfies me. I am from
Missouri. You have got to show me.
*Speech at a naval banquet in
Philadelphia, while a Representative in Congress from Missouri, and a member of the
House Committee on Naval Affairs [1899]*

MARY DOW BRINE
[*Floruit* 1878]

She's somebody's mother, boys, you
know,
For all she's aged and poor and slow.
Somebody's Mother [1878]

GERALD BRENNAN
[*Floruit* 1899]

Th' mem'ry comes like a banshee me-
self an' me wealth between,
An' I long for a mornin's mornin' in
Shanahan's ould shebeen.
*Shanahan's Ould Shebeen
[1899]. Stanza 4*
If you couldn't afford good whiskey,
he'd take you on trust for beer.
Ibid. Stanza 5

WILLIAM COWPER BRANN [1]
[1855–1898]

Boston runs to brains as well as to
beans and brown bread. But she is
cursed with an army of cranks whom

[1] Known as "The Iconoclast," from the
name of his paper, first published in Austin,
Texas, and later in Waco.

nothing short of a strait-jacket or a
swamp-elm club will ever control.
*From The Iconoclast. Beans
and Blood*
No man can be a patriot on an empty
stomach.
Ibid. Old Glory [July 4, 1893]
It has the subtle flavor of an old
pair of sox.
Ibid. Godey's Magazine
The Lydian notes of Andrew Carnegie as he warbles a riant roundelay in
praise of poverty, or laments in pathetic
spondees the woes of the man with
spondulix.
Ibid. Our American Czars
Every few years our industrial system gets the jim-jams. Capital flies to
cover, factories close and labor goes
tramping across the country seeking
honest employment and receiving a
warm welcome — from militia companies with shotted guns. . . . We are
slowly emerging from the crash of '93,
and the cuckoos are cock-sure that a
country fairly bursting with wealth was
saved from the demnition bowwows by
the blessed expedient of going into debt.
*Speech, Slave or Sovereign
[August 10, 1895]*

HENRY CUYLER BUNNER
[1855–1896]

Love must kiss that mortal's eyes
Who hopes to see fair Arcady.
The Way to Arcady
That pitcher of mignonette
Is a garden in heaven set
To the little sick child in the basement.
A Pitcher of Mignonette
Off with your hat as the flag goes by!
And let the heart have its say;
You're man enough for a tear in your
eye
That you will not wipe away.
The Old Flag. Stanza 1
It was an old, old, old, old lady,
And a boy that was half-past three;
And the way that they played together
Was beautiful to see.
"One, Two, Three." Stanza 1

I have a bookcase, which is what
Many much better men have not.
There are no books inside, for books,
I am afraid, might spoil its looks.
But I've three busts, all second-hand,
Upon the top. You understand
I could not put them underneath —
Shake, Mulleary and Go-ethe.
Shake, Mulleary and Go-ethe.
Stanza 1

EUGENE VICTOR DEBS
[1855–1926]

While there is a lower class I am in
it, while there is a criminal element I
am of it; while there is a soul in prison,
I am not free.
Labor and Freedom

FRANK FRANKFORT MOORE
[1855–1931]

He knew that to offer a man friendship when love is in his heart is like
giving a loaf of bread to one who is
dying of thirst.
The Jessamy Bride. Chap. 9

To strike at a serpent that hisses may
only cause it to spring.
Ibid. Chap. 19

Destiny has more resources than the
most imaginative composer of fiction.
Ibid. Chap. 22

WALTER HINES PAGE
[1855–1918]

Every letter of declination ought to
be written by a skilful man — a diplo-
matist who can write an unpleasant
truth without offence.
A Publisher's Confession [*1905*]

There is one thing better than good
government, and that is government in
which all the people have a part.
Life and Letters [*1922–1925*].
Vol. III, Page 31

SIR ARTHUR WING PINERO
[1855–1934]

You may dive into many waters, but
there is *one* social Dead Sea.
The Second Mrs. Tanqueray
[*1893*]. *Act I*

From forty till fifty a man is at heart
either a stoic or a satyr.
Ibid.

There are two sorts of affection —
the love for a woman you respect, and
the love for the woman you — love.
Ibid. Act II

It is only one step from toleration to
forgiveness.
Ibid.

I believe the future is only the past
again, entered through another gate.
Ibid. Act IV

How many "coming men" has one
known! Where on earth do they all
go to?
The Notorious Mrs. Ebbsmith
[*1895*]. *Act I*

There's only one hour in a woman's
life. . . . One supreme hour. Her poor
life is like the arch of a crescent; so
many years lead up to that hour, so
many weary years decline from it.
Ibid. Act III

Vanity is the cause of a great deal of
virtue in men; the vainest are those who
like to be thought respectable.
Ibid. Act IV

OLIVE SCHREINER
("RALPH IRON")
[1855–1920]

It came to pass that after a time the
artist was forgotten, but the work lived.
Dreams. The Artist's Secret

If you are an artist, may no love of
wealth or fame or admiration and no
fear of blame or misunderstanding
make you ever paint, with pen or brush,
an ideal or a picture of external life
otherwise than as you see it.
Ibid. Chap. 7

WILLIAM SHARP
("FIONA MACLEOD")
[1855–1905]

My heart is a lonely hunter that hunts
on a lonely hill.
The Lonely Hunter. Stanza 6

I hear the little children of the wind
Crying solitary in lonely places.
Little Children of the Wind

CY WARMAN
[1855–1914]

Every daisy in the dell knows my se-
cret, knows it well,
And yet I dare not tell, sweet Marie.
Sweet Marie [1893]. Stanza 1

GEORGE EDWARD
WOODBERRY
[1855–1930]

O, inexpressible as sweet,
Love takes my voice away;
I cannot tell thee when we meet
What most I long to say.
Song

Where are the friends that I knew in my
Maying,
In the days of my youth, in the first of
my roaming?
We were dear; we were leal; oh, far we
went straying,
Now never a heart to my heart comes
homing!
Comrades. Stanza 1

JOSEPH TABRAR
[*Floruit* 1892]

Daddy wouldn't buy me a bow-wow!
bow-wow!
Daddy wouldn't buy me a bow-wow!
bow-wow!
I've got a little cat,
And I'm very fond of that,
But I'd rather have a bow-wow, wow.
Daddy Wouldn't Buy Me a
Bow-Wow [1892]

SUSAN HART DYER
[*Floruit* 1912]

Zamboanga! Zamboanga! [1]
With the starlight on the sea,
And the blue hills of Basilan
Looming off mysteriously.
Zamboanga [1912]. Stanza 2

FRANCIS BELLAMY
[1856–1931]

I pledge allegiance to the flag of the
United States and to the republic for
which it stands, one nation, indivisible,
with liberty and justice for all.[2]
The Pledge of Allegiance to the
Flag [1892]

KENYON COX
[1856–1919]

Work thou for pleasure — paint, or
sing, or carve
The thing thou lovest, though the body
starve —
Who works for glory misses oft the
goal;
Who works for money coins his very
soul.
Work for the work's sake, then, and it
may be
That these things shall be added unto
thee.
Work [1895]

[1] Oh, the monkeys have no tails in Zam-
boanga,
They were chewed off by the whales. . . .
Zamboanga, Mindanao.
From the transport you look damn well,
But before I'd serve again in Zambo-
anga,
I'd rather serve a hitch in hell.
U. S. Infantry song of the Philippines
[2] In 1888 James B. Upham [1845–1905]
wrote a rough draft of the pledge which
Bellamy, as chairman of a committee for a
national school program to celebrate the four-
hundredth anniversary of the discovery of
America, helped to put into its final form.
The pledge was officially emended to read
"one nation under God" by a joint resolution
of Congress approved by the President,
June 14, 1954.

ELBERT HUBBARD
[1856–1915]

It is not book learning young men need, nor instruction about this and that, but a stiffening of the vertebrae which will cause them to be loyal to a trust, to act promptly, concentrate their energies, do a thing — "carry a message to Garcia."[1]

A Message to Garcia [*1900*]

The man who is anybody and who does anything is surely going to be criticized, vilified, and misunderstood. This is a part of the penalty for greatness, and every great man understands it; and understands, too, that it is no proof of greatness. The final proof of greatness lies in being able to endure contumely without resentment.

Get Out or Get in Line

If you work for a man, in heaven's name work for him! If he pays you wages that supply you your bread and butter, work for him — speak well of him, think well of him, stand by him and stand by the institution he represents.

Ibid.

ABBOTT LAWRENCE LOWELL
[1856–1943]

While a bright future beckoned, they freely gave their lives and fondest hopes for us and our allies, that we might learn from them courage in peace to spend our lives making a better world for others.

Inscription, Memorial Church, Harvard College, above the names of Harvard men who died in the First World War

[1] After the declaration of the Spanish-American War, Andrew Summers Rowan, then Lieutenant, United States Bureau of Military Intelligence, was sent to communicate with General Calixto Garcia. He landed in an open boat near Turquino Peak, April 24, 1898, executed the mission, and brought back information regarding the insurgent army.

EDWARD SANDFORD MARTIN
[1856–1939]

A Little Brother of the Rich.

Title of poem

Succor the Poor, my sisters, I,
While heaven shall still vouchsafe me health,
Will strive to share and mollify
The trials of abounding wealth.

A Little Brother of the Rich.
Stanza 5

Within my earthly temple there's a crowd.
There's one of us that's humble; one that's proud.
There's one that's broken-hearted for his sins,
And one who, unrepentant, sits and grins.
There's one who loves his neighbor as himself,
And one who cares for naught but fame and pelf.
From much corroding care would I be free
If once I could determine which is Me.

Mixed

ROBERT EDWIN PEARY
[1856–1920]

We returned from the Pole to Cape Columbia in only sixteen days . . . the exhilaration of success lent wings to our sorely battered feet. But Ootah, the Eskimo, had his own explanation. Said he: "The devil is asleep or having trouble with his wife, or we should never have come back so easily."

The North Pole [*1910*]

HENRI PHILIPPE PÉTAIN
[1856–1951]

They shall not pass.[1]

Verdun, February 26, 1916

[1] Ils ne passeront pas. The inscription on the Verdun medal is: "On ne passe pas."

LIZETTE WOODWORTH REESE
[1856–1935]

When I consider Life and its few
   years —
A wisp of fog betwixt us and the sun;
A call to battle, and the battle done
Ere the last echo dies within our ears.
                Tears

The burst of music down an unlistening
   street.
                Ibid.

How each hath back what once he
   stayed to weep;
Homer his sight, David his little lad!
                Ibid.

Creeds grow so thick along the way,
Their boughs hide God.
                Doubt

Glad that I live am I;
That the sky is blue;
Glad for the country lanes,
And the fall of dew.
    A Little Song of Life. Stanza 1

GEORGE BERNARD SHAW
[1856–1950]

My method is to take the utmost
trouble to find the right thing to say,
and then to say it with the utmost lev-
ity.
      Answers to Nine Questions

A prosperous man of business, who
probably never read anything but a
newspaper since he left school.
    Cashel Byron's Profession
        [1886]. Chap. 5

All this struggling and striving to
make the world better is a great mistake; not because it isn't a good thing
to improve the world if you know how
to do it, but because striving and struggling is the worst way you could set
about doing anything.
         Ibid. Chap. 6

It's well to be off with the Old
Woman before you're on with the
New.[1]
    The Philanderer [1893]. Act II

[1] See C. H. Webb, page 668a.

The fickleness of the women I love is
only equalled by the infernal constancy
of the women who love me.
       The Philanderer. Act II

The test of a man or woman's breeding is how they behave in a quarrel.
           Ibid. Act IV

People are always blaming their circumstances for what they are. I don't
believe in circumstances. The people
who get on in this world are the people
who get up and look for the circumstances they want, and, if they can't
find them, make them.
    Mrs. Warren's Profession
        [1893]. Act II

There are no secrets better kept than
the secrets that everybody guesses.
          Ibid. Act III

A great devotee of the Gospel of Getting On.
          Ibid. Act IV

We have no more right to consume
happiness without producing it than to
consume wealth without producing it.
     Candida [1898]. Act I

I'm only a beer teetotaller, not a
champagne teetotaller.
          Ibid. Act III

We don't bother much about dress
and manners in England, because, as a
nation we don't dress well and we've no
manners.
      You Never Can Tell
        [1898]. Act I

A family enjoying the unspeakable
peace and freedom of being orphans.
         Ibid. Act II

The great advantage of a hotel is that
it's a refuge from home life.
           Ibid.

There is only one religion, though
there are a hundred versions of it.
   Plays Pleasant and Unpleasant
    [1898]. Vol. II, Preface

You're not a man, you're a machine.
    Arms and the Man [1898].
           Act III

The worst sin towards our fellow
creatures is not to hate them, but to be

indifferent to them: that's the essence of inhumanity.

> *The Devil's Disciple* [*1901*].
> Act II

This is the true joy in life, the being used for a purpose recognized by yourself as a mighty one; the being thoroughly worn out before you are thrown on the scrap heap; the being a force of Nature instead of a feverish selfish little clod of ailments and grievances complaining that the world will not devote itself to making you happy.

> *Man and Superman* [*1903*].
> Epistle Dedicatory

A lifetime of happiness! No man alive could bear it: it would be hell on earth.

> *Ibid. Act I*

The more things a man is ashamed of, the more respectable he is.

> *Ibid.*

You think that you are Ann's suitor; that you are the pursuer and she the pursued; that it is your part to woo, to persuade, to prevail, to overcome. Fool: it is you who are the pursued, the marked-down quarry, the destined prey.

> *Ibid. Act II*

Marry Ann; and at the end of a week you'll find no more inspiration in her than in a plate of muffins.

> *Ibid.*

An Englishman thinks he is moral when he is only uncomfortable.

> *Ibid. Act III*

He who can, does. He who cannot, teaches.

> *Ibid. Maxims for Revolutionists,*
> Page 230

Marriage is popular because it combines the maximum of temptation with the maximum of opportunity.

> *Ibid. Page 231*

If you strike a child, take care that you strike it in anger, even at the risk of maiming it for life. A blow in cold blood neither can nor should be forgiven.

> *Ibid. Page 234*

The greatest of evils and the worst of crimes is poverty.

> *Major Barbara* [*1907*]. *Preface*

I can't talk religion to a man with bodily hunger in his eyes.

> *Ibid. Act II*

Home life as we understand it is no more natural to us than a cage is natural to a cockatoo.

> *Getting Married* [*1911*].
> Preface

In the extreme instances of reaction against convention, female murderers get sheaves of offers of marriage.

> *Ibid.*

When two people are under the influence of the most violent, most insane, most delusive, and most transient of passions, they are required to swear that they will remain in that excited, abnormal, and exhausting condition continuously until death do them part.

> *Ibid.*

A man is like a phonograph with half-a-dozen records. You soon get tired of them all; and yet you have to sit at table whilst he reels them off to every new visitor.

> *Ibid. (The Play)*

In England we always let an institution strain itself until it breaks.

> *Ibid.*

The whole strength of England lies in the fact that the enormous majority of the English people are snobs.

> *Ibid.*

You don't learn to hold your own in the world by standing on guard, but by attacking, and getting well hammered yourself.

> *Ibid.*

Religion is a great force — the only real motive force in the world; but what you fellows don't understand is that you must get at a man through his own religion and not through yours.

> *Ibid.*

The modest cough of a minor poet.

> *The Dark Lady of the Sonnets*
> [*1914*]

This writing of plays is a great matter, forming as it does the minds and

affections of men in such sort that whatsoever they see done in show on the stage, they will presently be doing in earnest in the world, which is but a larger stage.
The Dark Lady of the Sonnets

I like a bit of a mongrel myself, whether it's a man or a dog; they're the best for every day.
Misalliance [*1914*]. *Episode I*

If parents would only realize how they bore their children!
Ibid.

He's a gentleman: look at his boots.
Pygmalion [*1916*]. *Act I*

Women upset everything. When you let them into your life, you find that the woman is driving at one thing and you're driving at another.
Ibid. Act II

I have to live for others and not for myself; that's middle class morality.
Ibid. Act V

The great secret, Eliza, is not having bad manners or good manners or any other particular sort of manners, but having the same manner for all human souls: in short, behaving as if you were in Heaven, where there are no third-class carriages, and one soul is as good as another.
Ibid.

Independence? That's middle class blasphemy. We are all dependent on one another, every soul of us on earth.
Ibid.

All great truths begin as blasphemies.
Annajanska. [*1919*]

The nauseous sham goodfellowship our democratic public men get up for shop use.
Back to Methuselah [*1921*]. *Gospel of the Brothers Barnabas*

Life is a disease; and the only difference between one man and another is the stage of the disease at which he lives.
Ibid.

I enjoy convalescence. It is the part that makes the illness worth while.
Back to Methuselah. Gospel of the Brothers Barnabas

A nap, my friend, is a brief period of sleep which overtakes superannuated persons when they endeavor to entertain unwelcome visitors or to listen to scientific lectures.
Ibid. Tragedy of an Elderly Gentleman

Everything happens to everybody sooner or later if there is time enough.
Ibid. As Far As Thought Can Reach

Silence is the most perfect expression of scorn.
Ibid.

The worst cliques are those which consist of one man.
Ibid.

Assassination is the extreme form of censorship.
The Rejected Statement. Part 1

The Jews generally give value. They make you pay; but they deliver the goods. In my experience the men who want something for nothing are invariably Christians.
Saint Joan [*1924*]. *Scene IV*

One man that has a mind and knows it, can always beat ten men who haven't and don't.
The Apple Cart [*1930*]. *Act I*

Every person who owes his life to civilized society and who has enjoyed since his childhood its very costly protections and advantages should appear at reasonable intervals before a properly qualified jury to justify his existence, which should be summarily and painlessly terminated if he fails to justify it and it develops that he is a positive nuisance and more trouble than he is worth. Nothing less will really make people responsible citizens.
Radio address from London to America [*October 11, 1931*]

You put up in New York Harbor a

monstrous idol which you called "Liberty." [1]

Speech, Metropolitan Opera House, [2] *New York* [*April 11, 1933*]

You in America should trust to that volcanic political instinct which I have divined in you.

Ibid.

BOOKER TALIAFERRO WASHINGTON
[1856–1915]

No race can prosper till it learns that there is as much dignity in tilling a field as in writing a poem.

Up From Slavery [*1901*]

KATE DOUGLAS WIGGIN
[1856–1923]

My heart is open wide tonight
For stranger, kith or kin.
I would not bar a single door
Where Love might enter in.

The Romance of a Christmas Card

OSCAR FINGAL O'FLAHERTIE WILLS WILDE
[1856–1900]

Tread lightly, she is near
Under the snow,
Speak gently, she can hear
The daisies grow.

Requiescat. Stanza 1

Think of all
The suns that go to make one speedwell blue!

Quia Multum Amavi. Stanza 4

These are the letters which Endymion wrote
To one he loved in secret, and apart.

[1] "I see," said he, speaking to some American friends, "that you too put up monuments to your great dead!" — Story of a distinguished Frenchman on a visit to the United States during Prohibition, in RALPH NEVILL: *Paris of Today* [1924]

[2] A radio broadcast, made before the Academy of Political Science.

And now the brawlers of the auction mart
Bargain and bid for each poor blotted note.

On the Sale by Auction of Keats's Love Letters

And yet, and yet,
These Christs that die upon the barricades,
God knows it I am with them, in some ways.

Sonnet to Liberty: Not That I Love Thy Children

Down the long and silent street,
The dawn, with silver-sandaled feet,
Crept like a frightened girl.

The Harlot's House

A poet can survive everything but a misprint.

The Children of the Poets

As for borrowing Mr. Whistler's ideas about art, the only thoroughly original ideas I have ever heard him express have had reference to his own superiority as a painter over painters greater than himself.

Reply to an attack by James McNeill Whistler, Truth [*January 9, 1890*]

Meredith is a prose Browning, and so is Browning. He used poetry as a medium for writing in prose.

The Critic as Artist [*1891*]. *Part I*

An age that has no criticism is either an age in which art is immobile, hieratic, and confined to the reproduction of formal types, or an age that possesses no art at all.

Ibid.

It is through Art, and through Art only, that we can realize our perfection; through Art and Art only that we can shield ourselves from the sordid perils of actual existence.

Ibid. Part II

As long as war is regarded as wicked, it will always have its fascination. When it is looked upon as vulgar, it will cease to be popular.

Ibid.

There is no sin except stupidity.[1]
The Critic as Artist. Part II
There is no such thing as a moral or
an immoral book. Books are well writ-
ten, or badly written. That is all.
The Picture of Dorian Gray
[1891]. Preface
All art is quite useless.
Ibid.

There is only one thing in the world
worse than being talked about, and that
is not being talked about.
Ibid. Chap. 1
Conscience and cowardice are really
the same things.
Ibid.

Laughter is not at all a bad beginning
for a friendship, and it is far the best
ending for one.
Ibid.
The only way to get rid of a tempta-
tion is to yield to it.
Ibid. Chap. 2
He knew the precise psychological
moment [2] when to say nothing.
Ibid.
The only difference between a ca-
price and a lifelong passion is that the
caprice lasts a little longer.
Ibid.
Children begin by loving their par-
ents; as they grow older they judge
them; sometimes they forgive them.
Ibid. Chap. 5
Conscience makes egotists of us all.
Ibid. Chap. 8
When a woman marries again it is
because she detested her first husband.
When a man marries again, it is because

---

[1] See Marlowe, page 124a.
[2] In all considerations the psychological momentum or factor must be allowed to play a
prominent part, for without its co-operation
there is little to be hoped from the work of the
artillery. — *Neue Preussische Kreuzzeitung,*
December 16, 1870, commenting upon the
siege of Paris.
An error in translation gave us "psychological moment" (i.e. the critical moment). The
Parisians ridiculed the phrase as an example
of German pedantry, but it speedily became
universal.

he adored his first wife.[1] Women try
their luck; men risk theirs.
The Picture of Dorian Gray.
Chap. 15
Over the piano was printed a notice:
Please do not shoot the pianist. He is
doing his best.
Impressions of America. Leadville
Now-a-days we are all of us so hard
up, that the only pleasant things to pay
are compliments. They're the only
things we *can* pay.
Lady Windermere's Fan
[1892]. Act I
I can resist everything except temp-
tation.
Ibid.
We are all in the gutter, but some of
us are looking at the stars.
Ibid. Act III
In this world there are only two trag-
edies. One is not getting what one
wants, and the other is getting it.
Ibid.
What is a cynic? A man who knows
the price of everything, and the value
of nothing.
Ibid.
Experience is the name everyone
gives to their mistakes.
Ibid.
I have never admitted that I am more
than twenty-nine, or thirty at the most.
Twenty-nine when there are pink
shades, thirty when there are not.[2]
Ibid. Act IV
Mrs. Allonby. They say, Lady Hun-
stanton, that when good Americans die
they go to Paris.[3]
Lady Hunstanton. Indeed? And
when bad Americans die, where do
they go to?

---

[1] See Samuel Johnson, page 340b.
[2] When you come to write my epitaph,
Charles, let it be in these delicious words,
"She had a long twenty-nine."—JAMES M.
BARRIE [1860–1937]: *Rosalind*
[3] Good Americans, when they die, go to
Paris. — THOMAS GOLD APPLETON [1812–
1884], *quoted by* OLIVER WENDELL HOLMES
in *Autocrat of the Breakfast Table* [1858]

Lord Illingworth. Oh, they go to America.

> *A Woman of No Importance*
> [*1893*]. *Act I*

The youth of America is their oldest tradition. It has been going on now for three hundred years.

> *Ibid.*

Nothing spoils a romance so much as a sense of humour in the woman.

> *Ibid.*

Men always want to be a woman's first love. That is their clumsy vanity. We women have a more subtle instinct about things. What we like is to be a man's last romance.

> *Ibid. Act II*

I suppose society is wonderfully delightful. To be in it is merely a bore. But to be out of it simply a tragedy.

> *Ibid. Act III*

Talk to every woman as if you loved her, and to every man as if he bored you, and at the end of your first season you will have the reputation of possessing the most perfect social tact.

> *Ibid.*

I delight in men over seventy. They always offer one the devotion of a lifetime.

> *Ibid. Act IV*

Really, if the lower orders don't set us a good example, what on earth is the use of them?

> *The Importance of Being*
> *Earnest* [*1895*]. *Act I*

I have invented an invaluable permanent invalid called Bunbury, in order that I may be able to go down into the country whenever I choose.

> *Ibid.*

Memory is the diary that we all carry about with us.

> *Ibid. Act II*

I never travel without my diary. One should always have something sensational to read in the train.

> *Ibid.*

No woman should ever be quite accurate about her age. It looks so calculating.

> *Ibid. Act III*

An acquaintance that begins with a compliment is sure to develop into a real friendship.

> *An Ideal Husband* [*1895*]. *Act I*

Nothing produces such an effect as a good platitude.

> *Ibid.*

Private information is practically the source of every large modern fortune.

> *Ibid. Act II*

To love oneself is the beginning of a lifelong romance.

> *Ibid. Act III*

I never saw a man who looked
With such a wistful eye
Upon that little tent of blue
Which prisoners call the sky,
And at every wandering cloud that trailed
Its ravelled fleeces by.

> *The Ballad of Reading Gaol*
> [*1898*]. *Part I, Stanza 3*

When a voice behind me whispered low,
"That fellow's got to swing."

> *Ibid. Stanza 4*

Yet each man kills the thing he loves,
By each let this be heard,
Some do it with a bitter look,
Some with a flattering word.
The coward does it with a kiss,
The brave man with a sword!

> *Ibid. Stanza 7*

It is sweet to dance to violins
When Love and Life are fair:
To dance to flutes, to dance to lutes
Is delicate and rare:
But it is not sweet with nimble feet
To dance upon the air!

> *Ibid. Part II, Stanza 9*

Like two doomed ships that pass in storm
We had crossed each other's way:
But we made no sign, we said no word,
We had no word to say.

> *Ibid. Stanza 12*

Something was dead in each of us,
And what was dead was Hope.

> *Ibid. Stanza 31*

And the wild regrets, and the bloody sweats,
None knew so well as I:

For he who lives more lives than one
More deaths than one must die.
> *The Ballad of Reading Gaol.*
> *Part II, Stanza 37*

I know not whether Laws be right,
Or whether Laws be wrong;
All that we know who lie in gaol
Is that the wall is strong;
And that each day is like a year,
A year whose days are long.
> *Ibid. Part V, Stanza 1*

The vilest deeds like poison-weeds
Bloom well in prison-air:
It is only what is good in Man
That wastes and withers there:
Pale Anguish keeps the heavy gate
And the Warder is Despair.
> *Ibid. Stanza 5*

How else but through a broken heart
May Lord Christ enter in?
> *Ibid. Stanza 14*

Where there is sorrow there is holy
ground.
> *De Profundis* [*1905*]

WOODROW WILSON
[1856–1924]

The United States must be neutral in
fact as well as in name. . . . We must
be impartial in thought as well as in
action.
> *Message to the U. S. Senate*
> [*August 19, 1914*]

You deal in the raw material of
opinion, and, if my convictions have
any validity, opinion ultimately governs
the world.
> *Address to the Associated Press*
> [*April 20, 1915*]

There is such a thing as a man being
too proud to fight.
> *Address to Foreign-Born Citizens*
> [*May 10, 1915*]

The things that the flag stands for
were created by the experiences of a
great people. Everything that it stands
for was written by their lives. The flag
is the embodiment, not of sentiment,
but of history. It represents the experiences made by men and women, the ex-

periences of those who do and live under that flag.
> *Address* [*June 14, 1915*]

We have stood apart, studiously
neutral.
> *Message to Congress*
> [*December 7, 1915*]

There must be, not a balance of
power, but a community of power; not
organized rivalries, but an organized
common peace.
> *Address to the U. S. Senate*
> [*January 22, 1917*]

It must be a peace without victory.
. . . Victory would mean peace forced
upon the loser, a victor's terms imposed
upon the vanquished. It would be accepted in humiliation, under duress, at
an intolerable sacrifice, and would leave
a sting, a resentment, a bitter memory
upon which terms of peace would rest,
not permanently, but only as upon
quicksand. Only a peace between equals
can last.
> *Ibid.*

I am seeking only to face realities and
to face them without soft concealments.
> *Ibid.*

A little group of willful men reflecting no opinion but their own have rendered the great Government of the
United States helpless and contemptible.
> *Statement made in reference to*
> *certain members of the Senate* [1]
> [*March 4, 1917*]

Armed neutrality is ineffectual
enough at best.
> *Address to Congress, asking for*
> *a declaration of war* [*April 2,*
> *1917*]

The world must be made safe for
democracy.
> *Ibid.*

It is a fearful thing to lead this great
peaceful people into war . . . we shall
fight for the things which we have al-

[1] Eleven Senators had conducted a filibuster
against a bill authorizing the arming of American merchant vessels.

ways carried nearest our hearts, — for democracy, for the right of those who submit to authority to have a voice in their own Governments, for the rights and liberties of small nations, for a universal dominion of right by such a concert of free peoples as shall bring peace and safety to all nations and make the world itself at last free. To such a task we can dedicate our lives and our fortunes, everything that we are and everything that we have, with the pride of those who know that the day has come when America is privileged to spend her blood and her might for the principles that gave her birth and happiness and the peace which she has treasured. God helping her, she can do no other.

> *Address to Congress, asking for a declaration of war [April 2, 1917]*

1. Open covenants of peace, openly arrived at.

2. Absolute freedom of navigation upon the seas.

5. A free, open-minded, and absolutely impartial adjustment of all colonial claims.

8. The wrong done to France by Prussia in 1871 in the matter of Alsace-Lorraine . . . should be righted.

10. The peoples of Austria-Hungary . . . should be accorded the freest opportunity of autonomous development.

13. An independent Polish state should be erected . . . which should be assured a free and secure access to the sea.

14. A general association of nations must be formed . . . for the purpose of affording mutual guarantees of political independence and territorial integrity to great and small states alike.

> *Address to Congress (The Fourteen Points) [January 8, 1918]*

Sometimes people call me an idealist. Well, that is the way I know I am an American. America is the only idealistic nation in the world.

> *Address at Sioux Falls [September 8, 1919]*

The highest and best form of efficiency is the spontaneous cooperation of a free people.

> *Quoted by* BERNARD BARUCH, *in American Industry at War: A Report of the War Industries Board [March, 1921]*

I cannot refrain from saying it: I am not one of those who have the least anxiety about the triumph of the principles I have stood for. I have seen fools resist Providence before and I have seen their destruction, as will come upon these again — utter destruction and contempt. That we shall prevail is as sure as that God reigns.

> *Last public words, to a group of people gathered outside his house on Armistice Day, 1923*

GERTRUDE FRANKLIN ATHERTON
[1857–1948]

Women love the lie that saves their pride, but never an unflattering truth.

> *The Conqueror [1902]. Book III, Chap. 6*

To put a tempting face aside when duty demands every faculty . . . is a lesson which takes most men longest to learn.

> *Ibid.*

The perfect friendship of two men is the deepest and highest sentiment of which the finite mind is capable; women miss the best in life.

> *Ibid. Chap. 12*

No matter how hard a man may labor, some woman is always in the background of his mind. She is the one reward of virtue.

> *Ibid. Book IV, Chap. 3*

ALICE BROWN
[1857–1948]

Praise not the critic, lest he think
You crave the shelter of his ink;
But pray his halo, when he dies,
May tip the steelyards of the skies.

> *The Critic*

Yet thou, O banqueter on worms,
Who wilt not let corruption pass! —
Dost search out mildew, mould and
  stain,
Beneath a magnifying-glass.
The Slanderer

JOSEPH CONRAD
[1857–1924]

A work that aspires, however humbly, to the condition of art should carry its justification in every line.
The Nigger of the Narcissus
[1898]. Preface

But the artist appeals to that part of our being which is not dependent on wisdom; to that in us which is a gift and not an acquisition — and, therefore, more permanently enduring. He speaks to our capacity for delight and wonder, to the sense of mystery surrounding our lives: to our sense of pity, and beauty, and pain.
Ibid.

The ship, a fragment detached from the earth, went on lonely and swift like a small planet.
Ibid. Chap. 2

Goodbye, brothers! You were a good crowd. As good a crowd as ever fisted with wild cries the beating canvas of a heavy foresail; or tossing aloft, invisible in the night, gave back yell for yell to a westerly gale.
Ibid. Chap. 5

I am a great foe of favouritism in public life, in private life, and even in the delicate relationship of an author to his works.
Lord Jim [1900]. Author's Note

There is a weird power in a spoken word. . . . And a word carries far — very far — deals destruction through time as the bullets go flying through space.
Ibid. Chap. 15

That faculty of beholding at a hint the face of his desire and the shape of his dream, without which the earth would know no lover and no adventurer.
Ibid. Chap. 16

Felicity, felicity — how shall I say it? — is quaffed out of a golden cup in every latitude: the flavour is with you — with you alone, and you can make it as intoxicating as you please.
Lord Jim. Chap. 16

It is when we try to grapple with another man's intimate need that we perceive how incomprehensible, wavering, and misty are the beings that share with us the sight of the stars and the warmth of the sun.
Ibid.

You shall judge of a man by his foes as well as by his friends.
Ibid. Chap. 34

Vanity plays lurid tricks with our memory.
Ibid. Chap. 41

Some great men owe most of their greatness to the ability of detecting in those they destine for their tools the exact quality of strength that matters for their work.
Ibid. Chap. 42

Only a moment; a moment of strength, of romance, of glamour — of youth! . . . A flick of sunshine upon a strange shore, the time to remember, the time for a sigh, and — goodbye! — Night — Goodbye . . . !
Youth [1902]

She strode like a grenadier, was strong and upright like an obelisk, had a beautiful face, a candid brow, pure eyes, and not a thought of her own in her head.
Tales of Unrest [1902].
The Return

What greatness had not floated on the ebb of that river [the Thames] into the mystery of an unknown earth! . . . The dreams of men, the seed of commonwealths, the germs of empires.
Heart of Darkness [1902]

Running all over the sea trying to get behind the weather.
Typhoon [1902]. Chap. 2

The sea never changes and its works, for all the talk of men, are wrapped in mystery.
Ibid.

I have known the sea too long to believe in its respect for decency.
Typhoon. Chap. 2

An elemental force is ruthlessly frank.
Ibid.

The air of the New World seems favorable to the art of declamation.
Nostromo [*1904*]. *Chap. 6*

Efficiency of a practically flawless kind may be reached naturally in the struggle for bread. But there is something beyond — a higher point, a subtle and unmistakable touch of love and pride beyond mere skill; almost an inspiration which gives to all work that finish which is almost art — which *is* art.
The Mirror of the Sea [*1906*].
The Fine Art

The East Wind, an interloper in the dominions of Westerly Weather, is an impassive-faced tyrant with a sharp poniard held behind his back for a treacherous stab.
Ibid. Rulers of East and West

The autocratic sway of the West Wind, whether forty north or forty south of the equator, is characterized by an open, generous, frank, barbarous recklessness. For he is a great autocrat, and to be a great autocrat you must be a great barbarian.
Ibid.

What all men are really after is some form, or perhaps only some formula, of peace.
Under Western Eyes [*1911*].
Part I

A man's real life is that accorded to him in the thoughts of other men by reason of respect or natural love.
Ibid. 1

Let a fool be made serviceable according to his folly.
Ibid. 3

The belief in a supernatural source of evil is not necessary; men alone are quite capable of every wickedness.
Ibid. Part II, 4

Why should a man certain of immortality think of his life at all?
Under Western Eyes. Part II, 4

No woman is an absolute fool. . . .
No woman is ever completely deceived.
Ibid. 5

That strange impulse of indiscretion, common to men who lead secret lives, and accounting for the invariable existence of "compromising documents" in all the plots and conspiracies of history.
Ibid. Part III, 1

You can't ignore the importance of a good digestion. The joy of life . . . depends on a sound stomach, whereas a bad digestion inclines one to skepticism, incredulity, breeds black fancies and thoughts of death.
Ibid. 3

All ambitions are lawful except those which climb upward on the miseries or credulities of mankind.
A Personal Record [*1912*].
Preface

The sight of human affairs deserves admiration and pity. And he is not insensible who pays them the undemonstrative tribute of a sigh which is not a sob, and of a smile which is not a grin.
Ibid.

Only in men's imagination does every truth find an effective and undeniable existence. Imagination, not invention, is the supreme master of art as of life.
Ibid. Chap. 1

For Englishmen especially, of all the races of the earth, a task, any task, undertaken in an adventurous spirit acquires the merit of romance.
Ibid. Chap. 5

There are on earth no actors too humble and obscure not to have a gallery; that gallery which envenoms the play by stealthy jeers, counsels of anger, amused comments, or words of perfidious compassion.
Chance [*1914*]. *Part II, Chap. 4*

There is no rest for a messenger till the message is delivered.
The Rescue [*1920*]. *Part VI, 8*

In plucking the fruit of memory one runs the risk of spoiling its bloom.
> *The Arrow of Gold* [*1919*].
> *Author's Note*

Historian of fine consciences.
> *Notes on Life and Letters* [*1921*]. *Henry James, An Appreciation*

Most of us, if you will pardon me for betraying the universal secret, have, at some time or other, discovered in ourselves a readiness to stray far, ever so far, on the wrong road.
> *Ibid. A Happy Wanderer*

What humanity needs is not the promise of scientific immortality, but compassionate pity in this life and infinite mercy on the Day of Judgment.
> *Ibid. The Life Beyond*

JOHN DAVIDSON
[1857–1909]

My feet are heavy now but on I go,
My head erect beneath the tragic years.
> *I Felt the World A-spinning*

Fame is the breath of power:
What valid work was ever for itself
Wrought solely, be it war, art, statesmanship?
> *Smith*

Dance and sing, we are eternal;
Let us still be mad with drinking:
'Tis a madness less infernal
Than the madness caused by thinking.
> *Song of Bacchantes and Satyrs.*
> *Stanza 1*

The lowliest men would sooner face
A thousand dreadful deaths, than come
Before their loved ones in disgrace.
> *A Ballad of a Coward. Stanza 12*

Some diplomat no doubt
Will launch a heedless word,
And lurking war leap out.
> *War-Song*

And blood in torrents pour
In vain — always in vain,
For war breeds war again.
> *Ibid.*

Do I believe in Heaven and Hell? I do;
We have them here; the world is nothing else.
> *Dedication to the Generation Knocking at the Door*

Men should no longer degrade themselves under such appellations as Christian, Mohammedan, Agnostic, Monist, etc. Men are the Universe become conscious: the simplest man should consider himself too great to be called after any name.
> *Fleet Street and Other Poems* [*1909*]. *Foreword*

HENRY BLAKE FULLER
[1857–1929]

The martyrdom involved in a fortnight's entertainment of anybody whomsoever.[1]
> *The Chevalier of Pensieri-Vani.*
> *Chap. 10*

GEORGE GISSING
[1857–1903]

In the days to come, as through all time that is past, man will lord it over his fellow, and earth will be stained red from veins of young and old. That sweet and sounding name of *patria* becomes an illusion and a curse.
> *By the Ionian Sea* [*1901*]. *XVIII*

It is because nations tend to stupidity and baseness that mankind moves so slowly; it is because individuals have a capacity for better things that it moves at all.
> *The Private Papers of Henry Ryecroft* [*1903*]. *I, 16*

The mind which renounces, once and for ever, a futile hope, has its compensation in ever-growing calm.
> *Ibid. 20*

Education is a thing of which only the few are capable; teach as you will

---

[1] No one can be so welcome a guest that he will not annoy his host after three days. —
PLAUTUS: *Miles Gloriosus* [205 B.C.]
Fish and guests in three days are stale. —
JOHN LYLY: *Euphues* [1579]

only a small percentage will profit by your most zealous energy.

The Private Papers of Henry Ryecroft. I, 22

For the man sound in body and serene of mind there is no such thing as bad weather; every sky has its beauty, and storms which whip the blood do but make it pulse more vigorously.

Ibid. IV, 1

BENJAMIN FRANKLIN KING, JR.
[1857–1894]

Old friends are most too home-like now.
They know your age, and when
You got expelled from school, and lots
Of other things.

Like the New Friends Best

Nothing to do but work,
Nothing to eat but food,
Nothing to wear but clothes
To keep one from going nude.

The Pessimist (The Sum of Life).
Stanza 1

Nothing to breathe but air,
Quick as a flash 'tis gone;
Nowhere to fall but off,
Nowhere to stand but on.

Ibid. Stanza 2

Nowhere to go but out,
Nowhere to come but back.

Ibid. Stanza 4

Her folks an' hiz'n
An' hiz'n an' her'n
Never speak to each other
From what I can learn.

Her Folks an' Hiz'n

SIR RONALD ROSS [1]
[1857–1932]

I know this little thing
A myriad men will save.
O Death, where is thy sting?
Thy victory, O grave?

Referring to the discovery that malaria is carried by mosquitoes

---

[1] Ross received a Nobel prize in 1902 for his researches in malaria control.

EDGAR SMITH
[1857–1938]

You may tempt the upper classes
With your villainous demi-tasses,
But Heaven will protect the Working Girl.

Heaven Will Protect the Working Girl [1]

FRANK LEBBY STANTON
[1857–1927]

Jest a-wearyin' fer you —
All the time a-feelin' blue;
Wishin' fer you — wonderin' when
You'll be comin' home again.

Wearyin' for You. Stanza 1

Sweetes' li'l' feller —
Everybody knows;
Dunno what ter call 'im,
But he's mighty lak' a rose!

Mighty Lak' a Rose. Stanza 1

THORSTEIN VEBLEN
[1857–1929]

Conspicuous consumption of valuable goods is a means of reputability to the gentleman of leisure.

The Theory of the Leisure Class [1899]. Chap. 4

With the exception of the instinct of self-preservation, the propensity for emulation is probably the strongest and most alert and persistent of the economic motives proper.

Ibid. Chap. 5

The requirement of conspicuous wastefulness is not commonly present, consciously, in our canons of taste, but it is none the less present as a constraining norm selectively shaping and sustaining our sense of what is beautiful, and guiding our discrimination with respect to what may legitimately be approved as beautiful and what may not.

Ibid. Chap. 6

The dog . . . commends himself to our favour by affording play to our pro-

---

[1] Sung by Marie Dressler [1873–1934] in *Tillie's Nightmare.*

pensity for mastery, and as he is also an item of expense, and commonly serves no industrial purpose, he holds a well-assured place in men's regard as a thing of good repute.

The Theory of the Leisure Class.
Chap. 6

The visible imperfections of the hand-wrought goods, being honorific, are accounted marks of superiority in point of beauty, or serviceability, or both. Hence has arisen that exaltation of the defective, of which John Ruskin and William Morris were such eager spokesmen in their time. . . . The Kelmscott Press reduced the matter to an absurdity by issuing books for modern use, edited with the obsolete spelling, printed in black-letter, and bound in limp vellum fitted with thongs.

Ibid.

Priestly vestments show, in accentuated form, all the features that have been shown to be evidence of a servile status and a vicarious life.

Ibid. Chap. 7

The walking-stick serves the purpose of an advertisement that the bearer's hands are employed otherwise than in useful effort, and it therefore has utility as an evidence of leisure.

Ibid. Chap. 10

The sporting man's sense of luck and chance is an inarticulate or inchoate animism . . . it implies the possibility of propitiating, or of deceiving and cajoling, or otherwise disturbing the unfolding of propensities resident in the objects which constitute the apparatus and accessories of any game of skill or chance. There are few sporting men who are not in the habit of wearing charms or talismans.

Ibid. Chap. 11

The adoption of the cap and gown is one of the striking atavistic features of modern college life.

Ibid. Chap. 14

The classics have scarcely lost in absolute value as a voucher of scholastic respectability, since for this purpose it is only necessary that the scholar should be able to put in evidence some learning which is conventionally recognized as evidence of wasted time.

The Theory of the Leisure Class.
Chap. 14

As felicitous an instance of futile classicism as can well be found is the conventional spelling of the English language. English orthography satisfies all the requirements of the canons of reputability under the law of conspicuous waste. It is archaic, cumbrous, and ineffective; its acquisition consumes much time and effort; failure to acquire it is easy of detection.

Ibid.

HENRY WILLARD AUSTIN
[1858–1912]

Genius, that power which dazzles mortal eyes,
Is oft but perseverance in disguise.

Perseverance Conquers All

JOHN BURNS
[1858–1943]

The St. Lawrence is water, and the Mississippi is muddy water; but that, sir, is liquid history.

Said on the terrace of the House of Commons, to transatlantic visitors who belittled the size of the Thames

WILLISTON FISH
[1858–1939]

I, Charles Lounsbury, being of sound and disposing mind and memory [he lingered on the word memory], do now make and publish this my last will and testament, in order, as justly as I may, to distribute my interests in the world among succeeding men.

A Last Will [1]

I leave to children exclusively, but only for the life of their childhood, all and every the dandelions of the fields

[1] In *Harper's Weekly,* September 3, 1898, reprinted by request of many readers in the issue of December 12, 1908.

and the daisies thereof, with the right to play among them freely.
A Last Will

And I devise to children the yellow shores of creeks and the golden sands beneath the waters thereof, with the dragon-flies that skim the surface of said waters.
Ibid.

To lovers I devise their imaginary world, with whatever they may need, as the stars of the sky, the red, red roses by the wall, the snow of the hawthorn, the sweet strains of music, or aught else they may desire to figure to each other the lastingness and beauty of their love.
Ibid.

To those who are no longer children, or youths, or lovers, I leave, too, the knowledge of what a rare, rare world it is.
Ibid.

SAM WALTER FOSS
[1858–1911]

The plain man is the basic clod
From which we grow the demigod;
And in the average man is curled
The hero stuff that rules the world.
In Memoriam. Stanza 2

Seek not for fresher founts afar,
Just drop your bucket where you are.
Opportunity

No financial throe volcanic
Ever yet was known to scare it;
Never yet was any panic
Scared the firm of Grin and Barrett.
The Firm of Grin and Barrett. Stanza 1

A hundred thousand men were led
By one calf near three centuries dead.
They followed still his crooked way,
And lost one hundred years a day;
For thus such reverence is lent
To well-established precedent.
The Calf-Path

A rodless Walton of the brooks,
A bloodless sportsman, I. [1]
The Bloodless Sportsman

The woods are made for the hunters of dreams,
The brooks for the fishers of song;
To the hunters who hunt for the gunless game
The streams and the woods belong.
Ibid.

Let me live in my house by the side of the road
    Where the race of men go by;
They are good, they are bad, they are weak, they are strong,
    Wise, foolish — so am I.
Then why should I sit in the scorner's seat,
    Or hurl the cynic's ban?
Let me live in my house by the side of the road
    And be a friend of man.
The House by the Side of the Road. [2] *Stanza 5*

On the thirty-second day of the thirteenth month of the eighth day of the week,
On the twenty-fifth hour and the sixty-first minute, we'll find all things that we seek.
The Eighth Day of the Week

I say the very things that make the greatest Stir
An' the most interestin' things, are things that didn't occur. [3]
Things That Didn't Occur

He had a startling genius, but somehow it didn't emerge;
Always on the evolution of things that wouldn't evolve;
Always verging toward some climax, but he never reached the verge;

[1] See Emerson, page 504a.
[2] See Homer, page 4b.
    And greatly was he loved, for courteously
    He welcomed to his house beside the way
    All comers.
        HOMER [*circa* 850 B.C.]: *Iliad, Book VI,* translated by WILLIAM CULLEN BRYANT
[3] See Emerson, page 507a, and James Russell Lowell, page 507a, footnote 2.

Always nearing the solution of some
theme he could not solve.
The Inventor [1]

REMY DE GOURMONT
[1858–1915]

Aesthetic emotion puts man in a
state favorable to the reception of
erotic emotion. Art is the accomplice of
love. Take love away and there is no
longer art.
Decadence [2]

I do not believe it useful to generalize
opinions, to teach admirations. It is for
each man to procure himself the emotion he needs, and the morality which
suits him.
Ibid.

It is because peoples do not know
each other that they hate each other so
little.
Ibid.

There are too few obscure writers in
French. We accustom ourselves like
cowards to love only writing that is
easy and that will soon be elementary.
Ibid.

JOHN TROTWOOD MOORE
[1858–1929]

Only the game fish swims up stream.[3]
The Unafraid

EDITH NESBIT
[1858–1924]

The chestnut's proud, and the lilac's
pretty,
The poplar's gentle and tall,

But the plane tree's kind to the poor
dull city —
I love him best of all!
Child's Song in Spring

ADOLPH S. OCHS
[1858–1935]

All the news that's fit to print.
Motto of The New York Times [1]

AGNES REPPLIER
[1858–1950]

That little band of authors who, unknown to the wide careless world, remain from generation to generation the
friends of a few fortunate readers.
Preface to James Howell

THEODORE ROOSEVELT
[1858–1919]

I wish to preach, not the doctrine
of ignoble ease,[2] but the doctrine of
the strenuous life.
Speech before the Hamilton Club,
Chicago [April 10, 1899]

Far better it is to dare mighty things,
to win glorious triumphs, even though
checkered by failure, than to take rank
with those poor spirits who neither enjoy much nor suffer much, because they
live in the gray twilight that knows not
victory nor defeat.
Ibid.

We must remember not to judge any
public servant by any one act, and especially should we beware of attacking
the men who are merely the occasions
and not the causes of disaster.
Ibid.

---

[1] Ef you want to be sick of your life,
Jest come and change places with me a
spell — for I'm an inventor's wife.
MRS. E. T. CORBETT: *The Inventor's
Wife* [1883]

[2] Translated by W. A. BRADLEY.

[3] Quoted by GRANTLAND RICE [1880–1954]
in *The Ballade of the Gamefish* and *Expanding
the Theme.*
Only the gamefish swims upstream,
But the sensible fish swims down.
OGDEN NASH [1902–   ]: *When You
Say That, Smile*

[1] When Adolph Ochs bought *The New York
Times* in 1896 he adopted this motto, which
has been printed in every issue since.
"It is hard to think of any group of seven
words that have aroused more newspaper
controversy." — GERALD W. JOHNSON: *An
Honorable Titan* (biography of Ochs) [1946]

[2]   Me . . . dulcis alebat
Parthenope, studiis florentem ignobilis
otii (Sweet Parthenope [Naples] nourished
me flourishing in studies of ignoble ease).
VIRGIL [70–19 B.C.]: *Georgics, Book 4, L. 563*

Death is always and under all circumstances a tragedy, for if it is not, then it means that life itself has become one.
Letter to Cecil Spring-Rice
[March 12, 1900]

I am as strong as a bull moose and you can use me to the limit.
Letter to Mark Hanna
[June 27, 1900]

No man is justified in doing evil on the ground of expediency.
The Strenuous Life *[1900]*

If we seek merely swollen, slothful ease and ignoble peace, if we shrink from the hard contests where men must win at the hazard of their lives and at the risk of all they hold dear, then bolder and stronger peoples will pass us by, and will win for themselves the domination of the world.
Ibid.

The first requisite of a good citizen in this Republic of ours is that he shall be able and willing to pull his weight.
Speech, New York *[November 11, 1902]*

There is a homely adage which runs, "Speak softly and carry a big stick; you will go far." If the American nation will speak softly and yet build and keep at a pitch of the highest training a thoroughly efficient navy, the Monroe Doctrine will go far.
Speech at Minnesota State Fair
[September 2, 1901]

A man who is good enough to shed his blood for his country is good enough to be given a square deal afterwards. More than that no man is entitled to, and less than that no man shall have.
Speech at Springfield, Illinois
[July 4, 1903]

Chronic wrongdoing, or an impotence which results in a general loosening of the ties of civilized society, may in America . . . ultimately require intervention by some civilized nation, and in the Western Hemisphere the adherence of the United States to the Monroe Doctrine may force the United States, however reluctantly, in flagrant cases of such wrongdoing or impotence, to the exercise of an international police power.
Annual Message to Congress
(Corollary to the Monroe Doctrine) *[December 6, 1904]*

Men with the muck-rake are often indispensable to the well-being of society, but only if they know when to stop raking the muck.
Address, Laying of the Cornerstone, Office Building of House of Representatives, Washington
[April 14, 1906]

Malefactors of great wealth.
Speech at Provincetown, Massachusetts *[August 20, 1907]*

Nature-faker.
Everybody's Magazine
[September, 1907]

To waste, to destroy, our natural resources, to skin and exhaust the land instead of using it so as to increase its usefulness, will result in undermining in the days of our children the very prosperity which we ought by right to hand down to them amplified and developed.
Message to Congress *[December 3, 1907]*

The object of government is the welfare of the people. The material progress and prosperity of a nation are desirable chiefly so far as they lead to the moral and material welfare of all good citizens.
The New Nationalism *[1910]*

Every man holds his property subject to the general right of the community to regulate its use to whatever degree the public welfare may require it.
Speech, Osawatomie
[August 31, 1910]

The lunatic fringe in all reform movements.
Autobiography *[1913]*

We demand that big business give the people a square deal; in return we must insist that when any one engaged in big business honestly endeavors to do right he shall himself be given a square deal.
Ibid.

We stand equally against government by a plutocracy and government by a mob. There is something to be said for government by a great aristocracy which has furnished leaders to the nation in peace and war for generations; even a democrat like myself must admit this. But there is absolutely nothing to be said for government by a plutocracy, for government by men very powerful in certain lines and gifted with "the money touch," but with ideals which in their essence are merely those of so many glorified pawn-brokers.

Letter to Sir Edward Grey
[November 15, 1913]

There is no room in this country for hyphenated Americanism. . . . The one absolutely certain way of bringing this nation to ruin, of preventing all possibility of its continuing to be a nation at all, would be to permit it to become a tangle of squabbling nationalities.

Speech before the Knights of Columbus, New York [October 12, 1915]

We have room for but one language here, and that is the English language, for we intend to see that the crucible turns our people out as Americans, and not as dwellers in a polyglot boarding house.[1]

Letter read at the All-American Festival, New York [January 5, 1919]

LANGDON SMITH
[1858–1908]

When you were a tadpole and I was a fish,
In the Paleozoic time.
Evolution [1895]. Stanza 1

CLARENCE URMY
[1858–1923]

Old songs are best — how sweet to hear
The strains to home and memory dear!

[1] See Henry Cabot Lodge, page 748b.

Old books are best — how tale and rhyme
Float with us down the stream of time!
Old Songs Are Best

Not what we have, but what we use;
Not what we see, but what we choose —
These are the things that mar or bless
The sum of human happiness.
The Things that Count. Stanza 1

SIR WILLIAM WATSON
[1858–1935]

April, April,
Laugh thy girlish laughter;
Then, the moment after,
Weep thy girlish tears.
Song

What is so sweet and dear
As a prosperous morn in May,
The confident prime of the day,
And the dauntless youth of the year,
When nothing that asks for bliss,
Asking aright, is denied,
And half of the world a bridegroom is,
And half of the world a bride.
Ode in May. Stanza 2

The Poet gathers fruit from every tree,
Yea, grapes from thorns, and figs from thistles, he.
Epigram

Say what thou wilt, the young are happy never.
Give me bless'd Age, beyond the fire and fever, —
Past the delight that shatters, hope that stings,
And eager flutt'ring of life's ignorant wings.
Epigram

Strange the world about me lies,
Never yet familiar grown —
Still disturbs me with surprise,
Haunts me like a face half known.
World-Strangeness. Stanza 1

Five-and-thirty black slaves,
Half-a-hundred white,
All their duty but to sing
For their Queen's delight.
The Key-board. Stanza 1

For still the ancient riddles mar
Our joy in man, in leaf, in star.

The Whence and Whither give no rest,
The Wherefore is a hopeless quest.
> *An Epistle to N. A. Stanza 4*

To dress, to call, to dine, to break
  No canon of the social code,
The little laws that lacqueys make,
  The futile decalogue of Mode, —
How many a soul for these things lives,
  With pious passion, grave intent!
While Nature careless-handed gives
  The things that are more excellent.
> *The Things That Are More*
> *Excellent. Stanza 6*

The sense of greatness keeps a nation
great.
> *Our Eastern Treasure*

Lo, with the ancient
Roots of man's nature,
Twines the eternal
  Passion of song.
> *England My Mother. Part II,*
> *Stanza 1*

Ever Love fans it,
Ever Life feeds it,
Time cannot age it,
  Death cannot slay.
> *Ibid. Stanza 2*

Trees in their blooming,
Tides in their flowing,
Stars in their circling,
  Tremble with song.
> *Ibid. Stanza 5*

She is not old, she is not young,
The woman with the serpent's tongue.
> *The Woman With the Serpent's*
> *Tongue* [1]

Who half makes love to you today,
Tomorrow gives her guest away.
> *Ibid.*

KATHARINE LEE BATES
[1859–1929]

O beautiful for spacious skies,
  For amber waves of grain,
For purple mountain majesties
  Above the fruited plain!
America! America!

[1] Was he a "guest" — who dares to wrong
  His hostess in so foul a song?
O poet with the coward's tongue!
  Richard Le Gallienne [1866–1947]:
    The Poet with a Coward's Tongue

God shed his grace on thee
And crown thy good with brotherhood
  From sea to shining sea!
> *America the Beautiful* [*1893*].
> *Stanza 1*

O beautiful for patriot dream
  That sees beyond the years
Thine alabaster cities gleam
  Undimmed by human tears!
> *Ibid. Stanza 4*

HAROLD EDWIN BOULTON
[1859–1935]

Speed, bonnie boat, like a bird on the
  wing;
  Onward, the sailors cry:
Carry the lad that's born to be King
  Over the sea to Skye.
> *Skye Boat Song. Stanza 1*

HELEN GRAY CONE
[1859–1934]

Pickett's Virginians were passing
  through;
Supple as steel and brown as leather,
Rusty and dusty of hat and shoe,
Wonted to hunger and war and
  weather;
Peerless, fearless, an army's flower!
Sterner soldiers the world saw never,
Marching lightly, that summer hour,
To death and failure and fame forever.[1]
> *Greencastle Jenny. Stanza 4*

SIR ARTHUR CONAN DOYLE
[1859–1930]

  London, that great cesspool into
which all the loungers of the Empire are
irresistibly drained.
> *A Study in Scarlet* [*1887*]

  When you have eliminated the impossible, whatever remains, however improbable, must be the truth.
> *The Sign of Four* [*1890*]. *Chap. 6*

  It is my belief, Watson, founded
upon my experience, that the lowest
and vilest alleys of London do not
present a more dreadful record of sin

[1] See Will Henry Thompson, page 740a–740b.

than does the smiling and beautiful countryside.
> *The Adventures of Sherlock Holmes*
> *[1891]. Copper Beeches*

To Sherlock Holmes she is always *the* woman.
> *Ibid. A Scandal in Bohemia*

You know my methods, Watson.
> *The Memoirs of Sherlock Holmes*
> *[1894]. The Crooked Man*

"Excellent!" I [Watson] cried. "Elementary," said he [Holmes].
> *Ibid.*

Art in the blood is liable to take the strangest forms.
> *Ibid. The Greek Interpreter*

They were the footprints of a gigantic hound!
> *The Hound of the Baskervilles*
> *[1902]. Chap. 2*

Come, Watson, come! The game is afoot.
> *The Return of Sherlock Holmes*
> *[1904]. The Adventure of the*
> *Abbey Grange*

The fair sex is your department.
> *Ibid. (To Dr. Watson) The*
> *Second Stain*

It is a great thing to start life with a small number of really good books which are your very own.
> *Through the Magic Door [1908]*

No British autobiography has ever been frank, and consequently no British autobiography has ever been good. Of all forms of literature it is the one least adapted to the national genius. You could not imagine a British Rousseau, still less a British Benvenuto Cellini.
> *Ibid.*

Several incidents in my life have convinced me of spiritual interposition — of the promptings of some beneficent force outside ourselves, which tries to help us where it can.
> *Ibid.*

The bow was made in England,
Of true wood, of yew wood,
The wood of English bows.
> *The Song of the Bow. Stanza 1*

One favor we entreat,
We were called a little early, and our toilet's not complete.
We've no quarrel with the shirt,
But the breeches wouldn't hurt,
For the evening air is chilly in Cremona.[1]
> *Cremona. Stanza 20*

ARTHUR WENTWORTH HAMILTON EATON
[1859–1937]

O give me a place in the garden of song,
I would linger and labor there all summer long,
There are corners to care for, stray beds to make bloom,
I ask not for wages, I only seek room
In the garden of song.
> *The Garden of Song. Stanza 1*

HAVELOCK ELLIS
[1859–1939]

To be a leader of men one must turn one's back on men.
> *Introduction to* HUYSMANS'
> *Against the Grain*

The text of the Bible is but a feeble symbol of the Revelation held in the text of Men and Women.
> *Impressions and Comments*

God is an Unutterable Sigh in the Human Heart, said the old German mystic.
> *Ibid.*

Without an element of the obscene there can be no true and deep aesthetic or moral conception of life. . . . It is only the great men who are truly obscene. If they had not dared to be obscene they could never have dared to be great.
> *Ibid.*

The omnipresent process of sex, as it is woven into the whole texture of

---

[1] In the surprise attack on Cremona, February 1, 1702, the Irish Brigade rushed out to resist the invaders, without waiting to dress.

our man's or woman's body, is the pattern of all the process of our life.

The New Spirit

If men and women are to understand each other, to enter into each other's nature with mutual sympathy, and to become capable of genuine comradeship, the foundation must be laid in youth.

The Task of Social Hygiene.
Chap. 1

The larger our great cities grow, the more irresistible becomes the attraction which they exert on the children of the country, who are fascinated by them, as the birds are fascinated by the lighthouse or the moths by the candle.

Ibid. Chap. 5

There are few among us who have not suffered from too early familiarity with the Bible and the conceptions of religion.

Ibid. Chap. 7

The German feels nothing of that sensitive jealousy with which the French seek to guard private life and the rights of the individual.

Ibid. Chap. 9

The Englishman's reverence for the individual's rights goes beyond the Frenchman's, for in France there is a tendency to subordinate the individual to the family, and in England the interests of the individual predominate.

Ibid.

So far as business and money are concerned, a country gains nothing by a successful war, even though that war involves the acquisition of immense new provinces.

Ibid. Chap. 10

Conquest brings self-conceit and intolerance, the reckless inflation and dissipation of energies. Defeat brings prudence and concentration; it ennobles and fortifies.

Ibid.

There has never been any country at every moment so virtuous and so wise

that it has not sometimes needed to be saved from itself.

The Task of Social Hygiene.
Chap. 10

Those persons who are burning to display heroism may rest assured that the course of social evolution will offer them every opportunity.

Ibid.

The family only represents one aspect, however important an aspect, of a human being's functions and activities. . . . A life is beautiful and ideal, or the reverse, only when we have taken into our consideration the social as well as the family relationship.

Little Essays of Love and Virtue.
Chap. 1

One can know nothing of giving aught that is worthy to give unless one also knows how to take.

Ibid.

That indeed were a world fit to perish, wherein the moralist had set up the ignoble maxim: Safety first.

Ibid. Chap. 2

The by-product is sometimes more valuable than the product.

Ibid. Chap. 3

All civilization has from time to time become a thin crust over a volcano of revolution.

Ibid. Chap. 7

The greatest task before civilization at present is to make machines what they ought to be, the slaves, instead of the masters of men.

Ibid.

The art of dancing stands at the source of all the arts that express themselves first in the human person. The art of building, or architecture, is the beginning of all the arts that lie outside the person; and in the end they unite.

The Dance of Life. Chap. 2

Dancing is the loftiest, the most moving, the most beautiful of the arts, because it is no mere translation or abstraction from life; it is life itself.

Ibid.

The place where optimism most flourishes is the lunatic asylum.
The Dance of Life. Chap. 3

Thinking in its lower grades is comparable to paper money, and in its higher forms it is a kind of poetry.
Ibid.

In philosophy, it is not the attainment of the goal that matters, it is the things that are met with by the way.
Ibid.

Every man of genius sees the world at a different angle from his fellows, and there is his tragedy.
Ibid.

The mathematician has reached the highest rung on the ladder of human thought.
Ibid.

A man must not swallow more beliefs than he can digest.
Ibid. Chap. 5

The Promised Land always lies on the other side of a wilderness.
Ibid.

What we call "morals" is simply blind obedience to words of command.
Ibid. Chap. 6

The world's greatest thinkers have often been amateurs; for high thinking is the outcome of fine and independent living, and for that a professional chair offers no special opportunities.
Ibid.

For the artist life is always a discipline, and no discipline can be without pain. That is so even of dancing, which of all the arts is most associated in the popular mind with pleasure. To learn to dance is the most austere of disciplines.
Ibid.

The prevalence of suicide, without doubt, is a test of height in civilization; it means that the population is winding up its nervous and intellectual system to the utmost point of tension and that sometimes it snaps.[1]
Ibid. Chap. 7

The sun and the moon and the stars would have disappeared long ago — as

[1] See Nietzsche, page 727a.

even their infinitely more numerous analogues on the earth beneath are likely to disappear — had they happened to be within the reach of predatory human hands.
The Dance of Life. Chap. 7

Had there been a Lunatic Asylum in the suburbs of Jerusalem, Jesus Christ would infallibly have been shut up in it at the outset of his public career. That interview with Satan on a pinnacle of the Temple would alone have damned him, and everything that happened after could but have confirmed the diagnosis.
Impressions and Comments. Series III

H. W. FOWLER
[1859–1933]
AND
F. G. FOWLER
[1871–1918]

Prefer geniality to grammar.
The King's English [1906]. Chap. 2

The obvious is better than obvious avoidance of it.
Modern English Usage[1] *[1926]*

KENNETH GRAHAME
[1859–1932]

As a rule, indeed, grown-up people are fairly correct on matters of fact; it is in the higher gift of imagination that they are so sadly to seek.
The Golden Age [1895]. The Finding of the Princess

A man can stand very much in the cause of love: poverty, aunts, rivals, barriers of every sort, — all these only serve to fan the flame. But personal ridicule is a shaft that reaches the very vitals.
Ibid. "Young Adam Cupid"

The year was in its yellowing time, and the face of Nature a study in old gold.
Ibid. A Harvesting

[1] Written by H. W. Fowler.

Those who painfully and with bleeding feet have scaled the crags of mastery over musical instruments have yet their loss in this, — that the wild joy of strumming has become a vanished sense.
The Golden Age. A Harvesting

I began to like this man. He answered your questions briefly and to the point, and never tried to be funny. I felt I could be confidential with him.
Ibid. The Roman Road

Monkeys, who very sensibly refrain from speech, lest they should be set to earn their livings.
Ibid. "Lusisti Satis"

Grown-up people really ought to be more careful. Among themselves it may seem but a small thing to give their word and take back their word.
The Magic Ring

There is nothing — absolutely nothing — half so much worth doing as simply messing about in boats . . . or with boats. . . . In or out of 'em, it doesn't matter.
The Wind in the Willows [1908].
Chap. 1

ALFRED EDWARD HOUSMAN [1]
[1859–1936]

Loveliest of trees, the cherry now
Is hung with bloom along the bough.
A Shropshire Lad [1896]. II

[1] I was brought up in the Church of England and in the High Church party, which is much the best religion I have ever come across. But Lemprière's "Classical Dictionary," read when I was eight, made me prefer paganism to Christianity; I abandoned Christianity at thirteen, and became an atheist at twenty-one. . . .

I am not a pessimist but a pejorist (as George Eliot said she was not an optimist but a meliorist); and that philosophy is founded on my observation of the world, not on anything so trivial and irrelevant as personal history. Secondly, I did not begin to write poetry in earnest until the really emotional part of my life was over; and my poetry, so far as I could make out, sprang chiefly from physical causes, such as a relaxed

Now, of my threescore years and ten,
Twenty will not come again,
And take from seventy springs a score,
It only leaves me fifty more.
A Shropshire Lad. II

And since to look at things in bloom
Fifty springs are little room,
About the woodlands I will go
To see the cherry hung with snow.
Ibid.

Clay lies still, but blood's a rover;
Breath's a ware that will not keep.
Up, lad: when the journey's over
There'll be time enough to sleep.
Ibid. IV, Reveille

If the heats of hate and lust
In the house of flesh are strong,
Let me mind the house of dust
Where my sojourn shall be long.
Ibid. XII

When I was one-and-twenty
I heard a wise man say,
"Give crowns and pounds and guineas
But not your heart away;
Give pearls away and rubies
But keep your fancy free."
But I was one-and-twenty,
No use to talk to me.
Ibid. XIII

"The heart out of the bosom
Was never given in vain;
'Tis paid with sighs a-plenty
And sold for endless rue."
And I am two-and-twenty,
And Oh, 'tis true, 'tis true.
Ibid.

His folly has not fellow
Beneath the blue of day
That gives to man or woman
His heart and soul away.
Ibid. XIV

Oh, when I was in love with you,
Then I was clean and brave,
And miles around the wonder grew
How well I did behave.
Ibid. XVIII

And now the fancy passes by,
And nothing will remain,

sore throat during my most prolific period, the first five months of 1895.
Autobiographical note written for a
French translation of his poems

And miles around they'll say that I
  Am quite myself again.
                    A Shropshire Lad. XVIII

Today, the roads all runners come,
Shoulder-high, we bring you home,
And set you at your threshold down,
Townsman of a stiller town.
              *Ibid. XIX, To an Athlete
                            Dying Young*

And silence sounds no worse than
    cheers
After earth has stopped the ears.
                                    Ibid.

In summertime on Bredon
  The bells they sound so clear;
Round both the shires they ring them
  In steeples far and near,
  A happy noise to hear.
                          Ibid. XXI

Here of a Sunday morning
  My love and I would lie,
And see the colored counties,
  And hear the larks so high
  About us in the sky.
                              Ibid.

They tolled the one bell only,
  Groom there was none to see,
The mourners followed after,
  And so to church went she,
  And would not wait for me.
                              Ibid.

The bells they sound on Bredon,
  And still the steeples hum.
"Come all to church, good people," —
  Oh, noisy bells, be dumb;
  I hear you, I will come.
                              Ibid.

That is the land of lost content,
  I see it shining plain,
The happy highways where I went
  And cannot come again.
                          Ibid. XL

Oh, 'tis jesting, dancing, drinking
  Spins the heavy world around.
If young hearts were not so clever,
Oh, they would be young for ever:
Think no more; 'tis only thinking
  Lays lads underground.
                          Ibid. XLIX

With rue my heart is laden
  For golden friends I had,

For many a rose-lipt maiden
  And many a lightfoot lad.
                    A Shropshire Lad. LIV

By brooks too broad for leaping
  The lightfoot boys are laid.
                                    Ibid.

And cowards' funerals, when they
    come,
Are not wept so well at home,
Therefore, though the best is bad,
Stand and do the best, my lad.
              Ibid. LVI, The Day of Battle

Why, if 'tis dancing you would be,
There's brisker pipes than poetry.
                          Ibid. LXII

Oh many a peer of England brews
Livelier liquor than the Muse,
And malt does more than Milton can
To justify God's ways to man.[1]
Ale, man, ale's the stuff to drink
For fellows whom it hurts to think.
                                    Ibid.

Oh, I have been to Ludlow fair
And left my necktie God knows where,
And carried half way home, or near,
Pints and quarts of Ludlow beer.
                                    Ibid.

Luck's a chance, but trouble's sure,
I'd face it as a wise man would,
And train for ill and not for good.
                                    Ibid.

Mithridates, he died old.[2]
                                    Ibid.

We'll to the woods no more,
The laurels all are cut,[3]
The bowers are bare of bay
That once the Muses wore.
              Last Poems [1922]. Foreword

The troubles of our proud and angry
    dust
Are from eternity, and shall not fail.
Bear them we can, and if we can we
    must.

---

[1] See Milton, page 252a.
[2] Housman's passage is based on the belief
of the ancients that Mithridates the Great
[*circa* 135–63 B. C.] had so saturated his body
with poisons that none could injure him.
When captured by the Romans he tried in
vain to poison himself, then ordered a Gallic
mercenary to kill him.
[3] See Théodore de Banville, page 630a.

Shoulder the sky, my lad, and drink
  your ale.
> *Last Poems. IX*

Pass me the can, lad; there's an end of
  May.
> *Ibid.*

Could man be drunk for ever
  With liquor, love, or fights,
Lief should I rouse at morning
  And lief lie down of nights.
> *Ibid. X*

But men at whiles are sober
  And think by fits and starts.
And if they think, they fasten
  Their hands upon their hearts.
> *Ibid.*

The laws of God, the laws of man,
He may keep that will and can;
Not I: let God and man decree
Laws for themselves and not for me.
> *Ibid. XII*

And how am I to face the odds
Of man's bedevilment and God's?
I, a stranger and afraid
In a world I never made.
> *Ibid.*

These, in the day when heaven was
  falling,
The hour when earth's foundations fled,
Followed their mercenary calling
And took their wages and are dead.
> *Ibid. XXXVII, Epitaph on an*
> *Army of Mercenaries* [1]

They say my verse is sad: no wonder;
  Its narrow measure spans
Tears of eternity, and sorrow,
  Not mine, but man's.
> *More Poems* [*1936*]

The thoughts of others
  Were light and fleeting,
Of lovers' meeting
  Or luck or fame;
Mine were of trouble
  And mine were steady,
So I was ready
  When trouble came.
> *Ibid. VI*

The rainy Pleiads wester,
  Orion plunges prone,

And midnight strikes and hastens,
  And I lie down alone.
> *More Poems. XI*

Oh, the pearl seas are yonder,
  The gold and amber shore;
Shires where the girls are fonder,
  Towns where the pots hold more.
> *Ibid. XXXIII*

Silent hills indenting
The orange band of eve.
> *Ibid.*

We now to peace and darkness
  And earth and thee restore
Thy creature that thou madest
  And wilt cast forth no more.
> *Ibid. XLVII, For My Funeral*

Good night. Ensured release,
Imperishable peace,
  Have these for yours.[1]
While sky and sea and land
And earth's foundations stand
  And heaven endures.
> *Ibid. XLVIII, Alta Quies*

Good literature continually read for
pleasure must, let us hope, do some
good to the reader: must quicken his
perception though dull, and sharpen
his discrimination though blunt, and
mellow the rawness of his personal opinions.
> *The Name and Nature of Poetry* [2]

Poems very seldom consist of poetry
and nothing else; and pleasure can be
derived also from their other ingredients.
> *Ibid.*

Good religious poetry, whether in
Keble or Dante or Job, is likely to be
most justly appreciated and most dis-
criminatingly relished by the undevout.
> *Ibid.*

Even when poetry has a meaning, as
it usually has, it may be inadvisable to
draw it out. . . . Perfect understanding will sometimes almost extinguish
pleasure.
> *Ibid.*

[1] These three lines are on the tablet over
Housman's grave in the parish church at
Ludlow, Shropshire.

[2] The Leslie Stephen Lecture, delivered at
Cambridge University, May 9, 1933.

[1] The British regulars who made the retreat
from Mons, beginning August 24, 1914.

Experience has taught me, when I am shaving of a morning, to keep watch over my thoughts, because, if a line of poetry strays into my memory, my skin bristles so that the razor ceases to act. . . . The seat of this sensation is the pit of the stomach.

The Name and Nature of Poetry

I have seldom written poetry unless I was rather out of health, and the experience, though pleasurable, was generally agitating and exhausting.

Ibid.

JEROME KLAPKA JEROME
[1859–1927]

Let your boat of life be light, packed with only what you need — a homely home and simple pleasures, one or two friends, worth the name, some one to love and some one to love you,[1] a cat, a dog, and a pipe or two, enough to eat and enough to wear, and a little more than enough to drink; for thirst is a dangerous thing.

Three Men in a Boat [1889]. *Chap. 3*

Fox-terriers are born with about four times as much original sin in them as other dogs.

Ibid. Chap. 13

They [bagpipes] appear to be a trying instrument to perform upon. You have to get enough breath for the whole tune before you start.

Ibid. Chap. 14

It is in the circumstantial detail, the embellishing touches of probability, the general air of scrupulous — almost of pedantic — veracity, that the experienced angler is seen.

Ibid. Chap. 17

"Nothing, so it seems to me," said the stranger, "is more beautiful than the love that has weathered the storms of life. . . . The love of the young for the young, that is the beginning of life.

[1] Find someone to love . . . and, oh, someone to love you. — SACHA GUITRY: *Deburau* [1918]

But the love of the old for the old, that is the beginning of — of things longer."

The Passing of the Third Floor Back [1908]

There is a certain satisfaction in feeling you are bearing with heroic resignation the irritating folly of others.

Ibid.

Leave-takings are but wasted sadness. Let me pass out quietly.

Ibid.

WILLIAM JAMES LAMPTON
[1859–1917]

Same old slippers,
  Same old rice,
Same old glimpse of
  Paradise.

June Weddings. Stanza 10

Where the corn is full of kernels
And the colonels full of corn.

Kentucky

CHARLES FLETCHER LUMMIS
[1859–1928]

I am bigger than anything that can happen to me. All these things, sorrow, misfortune, and suffering, are outside my door. I am in the house and I have the key.

Epigram

NORA ARCHIBALD SMITH
[1859–1934]

They'd knock on a tree and would timidly say
To the Spirit who might be within there that day:
"Fairy fair, Fairy fair, wish thou me well;
'Gainst evil witcheries weave me a spell!"

Knocking on Wood. Stanza 3

SIR CECIL ARTHUR SPRING-RICE
[1859–1918]

I vow to thee, my country — all earthly things above —

Entire and whole and perfect, the service of my love,
The love that asks no questions: the
  love that stands the test,
That lays upon the altar the dearest
  and the best:
The love that never falters, the love
  that pays the price,
The love that makes undaunted the
  final sacrifice.
          I Vow to Thee, My Country [1]

CHARLES E. STANTON [2]
[1859–1933]

Lafayette, we are here. [3]
  Address at the Tomb of Lafayette,
  Picpus Cemetery, Paris [*July 4,*
  1917]

JAMES KENNETH STEPHEN
⌈1859–1892]

When the Rudyards cease from kipling
And the Haggards ride no more.
          Lapsus Calami. To R. K.
If all the harm that women have done
Were put in a bundle and rolled into
  one,
Earth would not hold it,
The sky could not enfold it,
It could not be lighted nor warmed by
  the sun.
          Ibid. A Thought, Stanza 1

[1] Written January 12, 1918, on his last
night as British Ambassador in Washington.
[2] Nephew of Edwin M. Stanton, Secretary
of War in Lincoln's Cabinet. He was chief
disbursing officer of the American Expeditionary Forces in France, and was deputed by
General Pershing to speak on behalf of the
A. E. F. on this occasion.
[3] The remark has also been attributed to
General Pershing, who in *My Experiences in
the World War* [1931] says he cannot remember having said "anything so splendid." However, one of the uniformed American corre-
spondents present upon the July 4, 1917, occasion, Naboth Hedin, states that he heard
Pershing pronounce the phrase three weeks
earlier on June 14, his second day in Paris.
"Pershing stepped up to it [Lafayette's grave]
and saluted in his best manner and then said
in a loud voice, 'Lafayette, we are here.' I
was about twenty feet away." (*Letter from
Naboth Hedin to Samuel Eliot Morison* [June

Of sentences that stir my bile,
  Of phrases I detest,
There's one beyond all others vile:
  "He did it for the best."
          Lapsus Calami. The Malefactor's
                    Plea, Stanza 1
Once there was a famous nation
  With a long and glorious past:
Very splendid was its station,
  And its territory vast.
          A Political Allegory
To the nation now occurred an
  Opportunity of saying
What they thought about the burden
  Which the government was laying
On their shoulders: and they said it
  In uncompromising terms.
                              Ibid.
But the nation — mark the moral,
  For its value is untold —
During each successive quarrel
  Grew and prospered as of old.
                              Ibid.

FRANCIS THOMPSON
[1859–1907]

The fairest things have fleetest end,
  Their scent survives their close:
But the rose's scent is bitterness
  To him that loved the rose.
          Daisy. Stanza 10
She went her unremembering way,
  She went and left in me
The pang of all the partings gone,
  And partings yet to be.
          Ibid. Stanza 12
Nothing begins, and nothing ends,
  That is not paid with moan;
For we are born in other's pain,
  And perish in our own.
          Ibid. Stanza 15
Look for me in the nurseries of Heaven. [1]
          To My Godchild
The innocent moon, which nothing does
  but shine,
Moves all the labouring surges of the
  world.
          Sister Songs. Part II
____
21, 1954].) Stanton used the phrase again on
July 14.
[1] This line is inscribed on Thompson's
tombstone in Kensal Green.

I fear to love thee, Sweet, because
Love's the ambassador of loss.
To Olivia

I fled Him, down the nights and down
the days;
I fled Him, down the arches of the
years;
I fled Him, down the labyrinthine ways
Of my own mind; and in the mist
of tears
I hid from Him, and under running
laughter.
The Hound of Heaven [1893].
Stanza 1

Across the margent of the world I fled,
And troubled the gold gateways of
the stars.
Ibid. Stanza 2

Still with unhurrying chase,
And unperturbèd pace,
Deliberate speed, majestic instancy,
Came on the following Feet,
And a Voice above their beat —
"Naught shelters thee, who wilt not
shelter Me."
Ibid.

I stand amid the dust o' the mounded
years —
My mangled youth lies dead beneath
the heap.
My days have crackled and gone up in
smoke.
Ibid. Stanza 4

Ever and anon a trumpet sounds
From the hid battlements of Eternity.
Ibid.

All which I took from thee I did but
take,
Not for thy harms,
But just that thou might'st seek it
in My arms.
All which thy child's mistake
Fancies as lost, I have stored for thee
at home.
Ibid. Stanza 5

There is no expeditious road
To pack and label men for God,
And save them by the barrel-load.
A Judgment in Heaven. Epilogue

Thou canst not stir a flower
Without troubling of a star.
The Mistress of Vision

From stones and poets you may know,
Nothing so active is, as that which least
seems so.
Contemplation

Happiness is the shadow of things past,
Which fools still take for that which is
to be!
From the Night of Forebeing

O world invisible, we view thee,
O world intangible, we touch thee,
O world unknowable, we know thee.
*The Kingdom of God ("In No
Strange Land"). Stanza 1*

The drift of pinions, would we hearken,
Beats at our own clay-shuttered doors.
Ibid. Stanza 3

The angels keep their ancient places; —
Turn but a stone, and start a wing!
'Tis ye, 'tis your estrangèd faces,
That miss the many-splendoured thing.
Ibid. Stanza 4

Upon thy so sore loss
Shall shine the traffic of Jacob's ladder
Pitched betwixt Heaven and Charing
Cross.
Ibid. Stanza 5

Short arm needs man to reach to
Heaven
So ready is Heaven to stoop to him.
Grace of the Way. Stanza 6

Know you what it is to be a child?
It is to be something very different
from the man of to-day. It is to have
a spirit yet streaming from the waters
of baptism; it is to believe in love, to
believe in loveliness, to believe in belief; it is to be so little that the elves
can reach to whisper in your ear; it is to
turn pumpkins into coaches, and mice
into horses, lowness into loftiness, and
nothing into everything, for each child
has its fairy godmother in its soul.
Shelley [1]

Children's griefs are little, certainly;
but so is the child, so is its endurance,
so is its field of vision, while its nervous
impressionability is keener than ours.
Grief is a matter of relativity; the sorrow should be estimated by its propor-

[1] In *The Dublin Review*, July, 1908.

tion to the sorrower; a gash is as painful to one as an amputation to another.
Shelley

Few poets were so mated before, and no poet was so mated afterwards, until Browning stooped and picked up a faircoined soul that lay rusting in a pool of tears.
Ibid.

The designs of his bright imagination were never etched by the sharp fumes of necessity.
Ibid.

A poet must to some extent be a chameleon, and feed on air. But it need not be the musty breath of the multitude.
Ibid.

NIXON WATERMAN
[1859–1944]

We shall do so much in the years to
  come,
But what have we done today?
We shall give our gold in a princely
  sum,
But what did we give today?
  What Have We Done Today?

No man can feel himself alone
The while he bravely stands
Between the best friends ever known —
His two good, honest hands.
Interludes

SIDNEY WEBB
(BARON PASSFIELD)
[1859–1947]
AND
BEATRICE WEBB
[1858–1943]

The inevitability of gradualness.
Presidential address, British Labour Party Congress [1923]

JANE ADDAMS
[1860–1935]

Private beneficence is totally inadequate to deal with the vast numbers of the city's disinherited.
Twenty Years at Hull House [1910]

The common stock of intellectual enjoyment should not be difficult of access because of the economic position of him who would approach it.
Twenty Years at Hull House

JAMES MATTHEW BARRIE
[1860–1937]

The humourist's like a man firin' at a target — he doesna ken whether he hits or no till them at the target tells 'im.
A Window in Thrums [1889].
Chap. 5

Those who bring sunshine to the lives of others cannot keep it from themselves.
Ibid. Chap. 18

The life of every man is a diary in which he means to write one story, and writes another; and his humblest hour is when he compares the volume as it is with what he vowed to make it.
The Little Minister [1891].
Chap. 1

The most gladsome thing in the world is that few of us fall very low; the saddest that, with such capabilities, we seldom rise high.
Ibid. Chap. 3

It's a weary warld, and nobody bides in't.
Ibid. Chap. 4

Has it ever struck you that the trouts bite best on the Sabbath? God's critters tempting decent men.
Ibid. Chap. 8

You canna expect to be baith grand and comfortable.
Ibid. Chap. 10

A house is never still in darkness to those who listen intently; there is a whispering in distant chambers, an unearthly hand presses the snib of the window, the latch rises. Ghosts were created when the first man woke in the night.
Ibid. Chap. 22

Let no one who loves be called altogether unhappy. Even love unreturned has its rainbow.

The Little Minister. Chap. 24

Them that has china plates themsels is the maist careful no to break the china plates of others.

Ibid. Chap. 26

Though it was really one laugh with a tear in the middle I counted it as two.

Margaret Ogilvy [1896]. Chap. 1

We never understand how little we need in this world until we know the loss of it.

Ibid. Chap. 8

In dinner talk it is perhaps allowable to fling on any faggot rather than let the fire go out.

Tommy and Grizel [1900].
Chap. 3

Shall we make a new rule of life from tonight: always to try to be a little kinder than is necessary?

The Little White Bird [1902].
Chap. 4

Poets are people who despise money except what you need for today.

Ibid. Chap. 15

When the first baby laughed for the first time, the laugh broke into a thousand pieces and they all went skipping about, and that was the beginning of fairies.

Peter Pan [1904]. Act I

Every time a child says "I don't believe in fairies" there is a little fairy somewhere that falls down dead.

Ibid.

Do you believe in fairies? . . . If you believe, clap your hands!

Ibid. Act IV

Alick. What *is* charm, exactly, Maggie?

Maggie. Oh, it's — it's a sort of bloom on a woman. If you have it, you don't need to have anything else; and if you don't have it, it doesn't much matter what else you have. Some women, the few, have charm for all;

and most have charm for one. But some have charm for none.[1]

What Every Woman Knows [1908].
Act I

The tragedy of a man who has found himself out.

Ibid. Act IV

Every man who is high up loves to think that he has done it all himself; and the wife smiles, and lets it go at that.

Ibid.

One's religion is whatever he is most interested in, and yours is Success.

The Twelve-Pound Look [1910]

The greatest glory that has ever come to me was to be swallowed up in London, not knowing a soul, with no means of subsistence, and the fun of working till the stars went out. To have known any one would have spoilt it. I did not even quite know the language.

Courage: Rectorial Address at St.
Andrew's [May 3, 1922]

Mighty are the Universities of Scotland, and they will prevail. But even in your highest exultations never forget that they are not four, but five. The greatest of them is the poor, proud homes you come out of, which said so long ago: "There shall be education in this land."

Ibid.

For several days after my first book was published I carried it about in my pocket, and took surreptitious peeps at

[1] What is charm? It is what the violet has and the camellia has not. — Marion Crawford [1854-1909]: *Children of the King, Chap. 5*

"Charm" — which means the power to effect work without employing brute force — is indispensable to women. Charm is a woman's strength just as strength is a man's charm. — Havelock Ellis [1859-1939]: *The Task of Social Hygiene, Chap. 3*

Charm is the measure of attraction's power
To chain the fleeting fancy of the hour,
And rival all the spell of Beauty's dower.
    Louisa Carroll Thomas [1865-]: *What Is Charm? St. 1*

it to make sure that the ink had not faded.
> *Speech at the Critics' Circle, London [1922]*

JOHN COLLINS BOSSIDY
[1860–1928]

And this is good old Boston,
The home of the bean and the cod,
Where the Lowells talk to the Cabots
And the Cabots talk only to God.[1]
> *Toast, Midwinter Dinner, Holy Cross Alumni [1910]*

WILLIAM JENNINGS BRYAN
[1860–1925]

The humblest citizen of all the land, when clad in the armor of a righteous cause, is stronger than all the hosts of Error.
> *Speech at the National Democratic Convention, Chicago [1896]*

You shall not press down upon the brow of labor this crown of thorns. You shall not crucify mankind upon a cross of gold.
> *Ibid.*

If the Father deigns to touch with divine power the cold and pulseless heart of the buried acorn and to make it burst forth from its prison walls, will He leave neglected in the earth the soul of man made in the image of his Creator?
> *The Prince of Peace*

If matter mute and inanimate, though changed by the forces of Nature into a multitude of forms, can never die, will the spirit of man suffer annihilation when it has paid a brief visit, like a royal guest, to this tenement of clay?
> *Ibid.*

[1] Patterned on the toast given at the twenty-fifth anniversary dinner of the Harvard Class of 1880, by a Westerner.
Here's to old Massachusetts,
  The home of the sacred cod,
Where the Adamses vote for Douglas,
  And the Cabots walk with God.

CHARLES TOWNSEND COPELAND
[1860–1952]

For the common man, the best memorial is some beneficent thing or function that shall bear his name.
> *Tribute to Nathaniel Southgate Shaler [1906]. Copeland Reader*

A man is always better than a book.
> *Ibid.*

To blame him were absurd; to pity were profane.
> *Not "Poor Charles Lamb." Copeland Reader Introduction*

Whenever we encounter the typical essayist, he is found to be a tatler, a spectator, a rambler, a lounger, and, in the best sense, a citizen of the world.
> *Ibid.*

HARRY MICAJAH DAUGHERTY
[1860–1941]

In a smoke-filled room in some hotel.[1]
> *Republican National Convention, Chicago, June, 1920*

HAMLIN GARLAND
[1860–1940]

Do you fear the force of the wind,
  The slash of the rain?
Go face them and fight them,
  Be savage again.
> *Do You Fear the Wind?*

The palms of your hands will thicken,
  The skin of your cheek will tan,
You'll go ragged and weary and swarthy,
  But you'll walk like a man!
> *Ibid.*

[1] Daugherty, manager for Senator Warren G. Harding, predicted that the convention would be deadlocked and would be decided by a group of men who "will sit down about two o'clock in the morning around a table in a smoke-filled room." The room was in the suite occupied by George Harvey, rooms 804–805 in the Blackstone Hotel.

CHARLOTTE PERKINS STETSON GILMAN
[1860–1935]

Cried all, "Before such things can come,
You idiotic child,
You must alter Human Nature!"
And they all sat back and smiled.
            Similar Cases

Said I, in scorn all burning hot,
   In rage and anger high,
"You ignominious idiot!
   Those wings are made to fly!"
         A Conservative. Stanza 5

"I do not want to be a fly!
I want to be a worm!"
            Ibid. Stanza 6

I ran against a Prejudice
That quite cut off the view.
        An Obstacle. Stanza 1

There's a whining at the threshold —
There's a scratching at the floor —
To work! To work! In Heaven's name!
The wolf is at the door!
     The Wolf at the Door. Stanza 6

The people people have for friends
   Your common sense appal,
But the people people marry
   Are the queerest folk of all.
            Queer People

Human life consists in mutual service. No grief, pain, misfortune, or "broken heart," is excuse for cutting off one's life while any power of service remains. But when all usefulness is over, when one is assured of an unavoidable and imminent death, it is the simplest of human rights to choose a quick and easy death in place of a slow and horrible one.
   Note written before her suicide
         [August 17, 1935]

WILLIAM RALPH INGE
[1860–1954]

Literature flourishes best when it is half a trade and half an art.
      The Victorian Age [1922]

JUSTIN HUNTLY M'CARTHY
[1860–1936]

On level lines of woodwork stand
My books obedient to my hand.
            My Books

The playwrights mouth, the preachers jangle,
The critics challenge and defend,
And Fiction turns the Muses' mangle —
Of making books there is no end.[1]
     A Ballade of Book-Making.
            Stanza 2

JAMES BALL NAYLOR
[1860–1945]

King David and King Solomon
   Led merry, merry lives,
With many, many lady friends
   And many, many wives;
But when old age crept over them —
   With many, many qualms,
King Solomon wrote the Proverbs
   And King David wrote the Psalms.
         Ancient Authors

BLISS PERRY
[1860–1953]

The fact is, we are not a book-reading people. The vast majority of our ninety-odd millions of population have no literary appetites which cannot be supplied by the newspapers, the magazines, and an occasional "best-seller" novel.
   The Praise of Folly. Criticism in
         American Periodicals

FRANK DEMPSTER SHERMAN
[1860–1916]

Of all the threads of rhyme
   Which I have spun,
I shall be glad if Time
   Save only one.
            His Desire

Out of the scabbard of the night,
   By God's hand drawn,

[1] See *Ecclesiastes, XII, 12,* on page 1044a.

Flashes his shining sword of light,
And lo, — the dawn!

Dawn

Hark to the noisy caravans of brown,
Intrepid Sparrows, — Arabs of the air!

City Sparrows

OWEN WISTER
[1860–1938]

When you call me that, *smile!*

The Virginian [*1902*]. *Chap. 2*

RICHARD BURTON
[1861–1940]

From their folded mates they wander
far,
Their ways seem harsh and wild;
They follow the beck of a baleful star,
Their paths are dream-beguiled.

Black Sheep

BLISS CARMAN
[1861–1929]

An open hand, an easy shoe,
And a hope to make the day go through.

The Joys of the Road

No fidget and no reformer, just
A calm observer of ought and must.

Ibid.

Make me over, mother April,
When the sap begins to stir!

Spring Song. Stanza 1

Make me over in the morning
From the rag-bag of the world!
Scraps of dream and duds of daring,
Home-brought stuff from far sea-faring.

Ibid. Stanza 12

The scarlet of the maples can shake me
like a cry
Of bugles going by.

A Vagabond Song. Stanza 2

There is something in October sets the
gypsy blood astir.

Ibid. Stanza 3

Here we came when love was young.
Now that love is old,

Shall we leave the floor unswept
And the hearth acold?

The Homestead. Stanza 1

I took a day to search for God,
And found Him not. But as I trod
By rocky ledge, through woods un-
tamed,
Just where one scarlet lily flamed,
I saw His footprint in the sod.

Vestigia. Stanza 1

I often wish that I could rid the
world of the tyranny of facts. What
are facts but compromises? A fact
merely marks the point where we have
agreed to let investigation cease.

In The Atlantic Monthly,
May, 1906

LOUISE IMOGEN GUINEY
[1861–1920]

He has done with roofs and men,
Open, Time, and let him pass.

Ballad of Kenelm

A short life in the saddle, Lord!
Not long life by the fire.

The Knight Errant. Stanza 2

Cowley said it engagingly: *Bene qui
latuit, bene vixit:* he lives well, that has
lain well hidden. The pleasantest condition of life is in incognito.

Patrins. On the Delights of an
Incognito

A passing salute to this world and her
pitiful beauty.

The Wild Ride. Stanza 5

A certain sesquipedalianism is natural to Americans: witness our press
editorials, our Fourth of July orations,
and the public messages of all our Presidents since Lincoln.

In Scribner's Magazine,
January, 1911

Quotations (such as have point and
lack triteness) from the great old authors are an act of filial reverence on
the part of the quoter, and a blessing
to a public grown superficial and external.

Ibid.

JOHN LUTHER LONG
[1861–1927]

To die with honour when one can no longer live with honour.[1]
Madame Butterfly [*1897*] (*inscription on Samurai blade*)

EDWARD MacDOWELL
[1861–1908]

A house of Dreams untold
That looks out over the whispering
    tree-tops
And faces the setting sun.
House of Dreams [2]

BYRON RUFUS NEWTON
[1861–1938]

Vulgar of manner, overfed,
Overdressed and underbred;
Heartless, Godless, hell's delight,
Rude by day and lewd by night.
Owed to New York [*1906*]
Purple-robed and pauper-clad,
Raving, rotting, money-mad;
A squirming herd in Mammon's mesh,
A wilderness of human flesh;
Crazed with avarice, lust, and rum,
New York, thy name's Delirium.
Ibid.

"JOHN OXENHAM" (WILLIAM ARTHUR DUNKERLEY)
[1861–1941]

Art thou lonely, O my brother?
Share thy little with another!
Stretch a hand to one unfriended,
And thy loneliness is ended.
Lonely Brother
But see how high!—
It reaches up
To God's blue sky!
The Philosopher's Garden

[1] One should die proudly when it is no longer possible to live proudly. — NIETZSCHE [1844–1900]: *The Twilight of the Idols, Skirmishes in a War with the Age, 36*
[2] Preface to his composition, *From a Log Cabin*, and inscribed on the memorial tablet near his grave.

Kneel always when you light a fire!
The Sacrament of Fire
Thank God for sleep!
And, when you cannot sleep,
Still thank Him that you live
To lie awake.
The Sacrament of Sleep
To every man there openeth
A Way, and Ways, and a Way,
The High Soul climbs the High Way,
The Low Soul gropes the Low,
And in between, on the misty flats,
The rest drift to and fro.
The Ways
And every man decideth
The Way his soul shall go.
Ibid.
Only through Me can come the great
    awakening;
Wrong cannot right the wrongs that
    Wrong hath done;
Only through Me, all other gods for-
    saking,
Can ye attain the heights that must
    be won.
Dies Irae — Dies Pacis

SIR WALTER RALEIGH [1]
[1861–1922]

I wish I loved the Human Race;
I wish I loved its silly face;
I wish I liked the way it walks;
I wish I liked the way it talks;
And when I'm introduced to one
I wish I thought *What Jolly Fun!*
Wishes of an Elderly Man (*Wished at a Garden-Party, June, 1914*)

WENDELL PHILLIPS STAFFORD
[1861–   ]

My heart is where the hills fling up
    Green garlands to the day.
'Tis where the blue lake brims her cup,
    The sparkling rivers play.
My heart is on the mountain still,
    Where'er my steps may be,

[1] Professor of English literature at Oxford from 1904, and author of critical works on Milton, Wordsworth, Shakespeare, and others.

Vermont, O maiden of the hills,
My heart is there with thee!
Vermont: A Song. Stanza 1

RABINDRANATH TAGORE
[1861–1941]

When one knows thee, then alien there is none, then no door is shut. Oh, grant me my prayer that I may never lose the touch of the one in the play of the many.
Gitanjali [1913]

Come out of thyself,
Stand in the open;
Within thy heart wilt thou hear
The response of all the world.
Sheaves. The Invitation

When I bring you coloured toys, my child, I understand why there is such a play of colours on clouds, on water, and why flowers are painted in tints.
The Crescent Moon [1913].
When and Why

I do not love him because he is good, but because he is my little child.
Ibid. The Judge

I alone have a right to blame and punish, for he only may chastise who loves.[1]
Ibid.

Years mature into fruit
So that some small seeds of moments
May outlive them.
On Visiting Yale University
[1932]

ALFRED NORTH WHITEHEAD
[1861–1947]

The human body is an instrument for the production of art in the life of the human soul.
Adventures of Ideas [1933].
Chap. 18

A general definition of civilization: a civilized society is exhibiting the five qualities of Truth, Beauty, Adventure, Art, Peace.
Ibid. Chap. 19

[1] See Pomfret, page 294b.

The deliberate aim at Peace very easily passes into its bastard substitute, Anaesthesia.
Adventures of Ideas. Chap. 20

Youth is life as yet untouched by tragedy. . . . When youth has once grasped where Beauty dwells — with a real knowledge and not as a mere matter of literary phraseology — its self-surrender is absolute.
Ibid.

There are no whole truths; all truths are half-truths. It is trying to treat them as whole truths that plays the devil.
Dialogues of Alfred North Whitehead [1953].[1] *Page 16*

The vitality of thought is in adventure. *Ideas won't keep.* Something must be done about them. When the idea is new, its custodians have fervour, live for it, and, if need be, die for it.
Ibid. Page 100

Intelligence is quickness to apprehend as distinct from ability, which is capacity to act wisely on the thing apprehended.
Ibid. Page 135

Our minds are finite, and yet even in these circumstances of finitude we are surrounded by possibilities that are infinite, and the purpose of human life is to grasp as much as we can out of that infinitude.
Ibid. Page 163

A culture is in its finest flower before it begins to analyze itself.
Ibid. Page 169

The ideas of Freud were popularized by people who only imperfectly understood them, who were incapable of the great effort required to grasp them in their relationship to larger truths, and who therefore assigned to them a prominence out of all proportion to their true importance.
Ibid. Page 211

Art is the imposing of a pattern on experience, and our esthetic enjoyment in recognition of the pattern.
Ibid. Page 228

[1] As recorded by Lucien Price.

A philosopher of imposing stature doesn't think in a vacuum. Even his most abstract ideas are, to some extent, conditioned by what is or is not known in the time when he lives.

Dialogues of Alfred North Whitehead. Page 229

With the sense of sight, the idea communicates the emotion, whereas, with sound, the emotion communicates the idea, which is more direct and therefore more powerful.

Ibid. Page 231

Intellect is to emotion as our clothes are to our bodies: we could not very well have civilized life without clothes, but we would be in a poor way if we had only clothes without bodies.

Ibid. Page 232

No period of history has ever been great or ever can be that does not act on some sort of high, idealistic motives, and idealism in our time has been shoved aside, and we are paying the penalty for it.

Ibid. Page 276

The English never abolish anything. They put it in cold storage.

Ibid. Page 309

Shakespeare wrote better poetry for not knowing too much; Milton, I think, knew too much finally for the good of his poetry.

Ibid. Page 369

JOHN KENDRICK BANGS
[1862–1922]

Shakespeare was not accounted great
When good Queen Bess ruled England's
    state,
So why should I today repine
Because the laurel is not mine?

Consolation. Stanza 1

I think mankind by thee would be less
    bored
If only thou wert not thine own reward.

A Hint to Virtue

To dig and delve in nice clean dirt
Can do a mortal little hurt.

Gardening

"I'm just as big for me," said he,
"As you are big for you!"

The Little Elfman. Stanza 2

ARTHUR CHRISTOPHER BENSON
[1862–1925]

Land of Hope and Glory, Mother of
    the Free,
How shall we extol thee, who are born
    of thee?
Wider still and wider shall thy bounds
    be set;
God, who made thee mighty, make thee
    mightier yet.

Land of Hope and Glory. Chorus

Edward Fitzgerald said that he wished we had more lives of obscure persons; one wants to know what other people are thinking and feeling about it all. . . . If the dullest person in the world would only put down sincerely what he or she thought about his or her life, about work and love, religion and emotion, it would be a fascinating document.

From a College Window

ALBERT JEREMIAH BEVERIDGE
[1862–1927]

This party comes from the grass roots. It has grown from the soil of the people's hard necessities.

Address as Temporary Chairman of the Bull Moose Convention, Chicago [August 5, 1912]

JAMES W. BLAKE
[1862–1935]

East Side, West Side, all around the
    town,
The tots sang "Ring-a-rosie," "London
    Bridge is falling down";
Boys and girls together, me and Mamie
    O'Rourke,

Tripped the light fantastic on the sidewalks of New York.
> *The Sidewalks of New York* [1]
> [*1894*]

CARRIE JACOBS BOND
[*1862–1946*]

When you come to the end of a perfect day.
> *A Perfect Day. Stanza 1*

For mem'ry has painted this perfect day
With colors that never fade,
And we find at the end of a perfect day
The soul of a friend we've made.
> *Ibid. Stanza 2*

NICHOLAS MURRAY BUTLER
[*1862–1947*]

An expert is one who knows more and more about less and less.
> *Commencement Address,*
> *Columbia University*

GOLDSWORTHY LOWES DICKINSON
[*1862–1932*]

A fundamental, and as many believe, the most essential part of Christianity, is its doctrine of reward and punishment in the world beyond; and a religion which had nothing at all to say about this great enigma we should hardly feel to be a religion at all.
> *The Greek View of Life* [*1898*].
> *Chap. 1, Sect. 11*

Dissatisfaction with the world in which we live and determination to realize one that shall be better, are the prevailing characteristics of the modern spirit.
> *Ibid. Chap. 5*

Chinese poetry is of all poetry I know the most human and the least symbolic or romantic. It contemplates life just as it presents itself, without any veil of ideas, any rhetoric or sentiment; it simply clears away the obstruction

[1] The music of the song was composed by Charles B. Lawlor [*1852–1925*].

which habit has built up between us and the beauty of things.
> *An Essay on the Civilizations of*
> *India, China, and Japan* [*1914*].
> *Page 47*

The United States of America — the greatest potential force, material, moral, and spiritual, in the world.
> *The Choice Before Us* [*1917*].
> *Chap. 1*

To the man who has the religion of peace, the supreme value is love. To the man who has the religion of war, the supreme value is strife.
> *Ibid. Chap. 3*

Government is everywhere to a great extent controlled by powerful minorities, with an interest distinct from that of the mass of the people.
> *Ibid. Chap. 4*

The true way for one civilization to "conquer" another is for it to be so obviously superior in this or that point that others desire to imitate it.
> *Ibid. Chap. 5*

War is not "inevitable," but proceeds from definite and removable causes.
> *Ibid. Chap. 9*

Nations are quite capable of starving every other side of life — education, sanitation, housing, public health, everything that contributes to life, physical, intellectual, moral, and spiritual, in order to maintain their armaments.
> *Ibid. Chap. 11*

ANNIE JOHNSON FLINT
[*1862–1932*]

The thrones are rocking to their fall —
It is the twilight of the Kings!
> *The Twilight of the Kings*

Have you come to the Red Sea place in your life,
Where, in spite of all you can do,
There is no way out, there is no way back,
There is no other way but through?
> *At the Place of the Sea. Stanza 1*

NORMAN GALE
[1862–1942]

Here in the country's heart
Where the grass is green,
Life is the same sweet life
As it e'er hath been.
The Country Faith. Stanza 1

Write: — He had made a finer man
And left increased renown behind,
If he had only shut his books
To read the chapters of mankind!
Last Words. Stanza 10

EDWARD, VISCOUNT GREY OF FALLODON
[1862–1933]

The lamps are going out all over Europe; we shall not see them lit again in our lifetime.
Comment, August 4, 1914, standing at the windows of his room in the Foreign Office, London, as the lamplighters were turning off the lights in St. James's Park

O. HENRY (WILLIAM SYDNEY PORTER)
[1862–1910]

No calamity so touches the common heart of humanity as does the straying of a little child. Their feet are so uncertain and feeble; the ways are so steep and strange.
*The Four Million [1906].
Between Rounds*

If men knew how women pass the time when they are alone, they'd never marry.
Ibid. Memoirs of a Yellow Dog

What a woman wants is what you're out of. She wants more of a thing when it's scarce.
*Heart of the West [1907].
Cupid à la Carte*

Love and business and family and religion and art and patriotism are nothing but shadows of words when a man's starving.
Ibid.

Esau, that swapped his copyright for a partridge.
*Heart of the West.
Cupid à la Carte*

There is one day that is ours. There is one day when all we Americans who are not self-made go back to the old home to eat saleratus biscuits and marvel how much nearer to the porch the old pump looks than it used to. . . . Thanksgiving Day . . . is the one day that is purely American.
*The Trimmed Lamp [1907].
Two Thanksgiving Day Gentlemen*

One day the christeners of apartment houses and the cognominators of sleeping-cars will meet, and there will be some jealous and sanguinary knifing.
Ibid. The Country of Elusion

Perhaps there is no happiness in life so perfect as the martyr's.
Ibid.

Bohemia is nothing more than the little country in which you do not live.
Ibid.

Lost, your Excellency. Lost associations and societies. Lost right reverends and wrong reverends of every order. Lost reformers and lawmakers, born with heavenly compassion in your hearts, but with the reverence of money in your souls. And lost thus around us every day.[1]
Ibid. Elsie in New York

When a poor man finds a long-hidden quarter-dollar that has slipped through a rip in his vest lining, he sounds the pleasure of life with a deeper plummet than any millionaire can hope to cast.
*The Voice of the City [1908].
The Complete Life of John Hopkins*

You're the goods.
Ibid. From Each According to His Ability

It was beautiful and simple as all truly great swindles are.
*The Gentle Grafter [1908].
The Octopus Marooned*

[1] A paraphrase of the closing lines of Chapter 47 of Dickens's *Bleak House*.

There are two times when you can never tell what is going to happen. One is when a man takes his first drink; and the other is when a woman takes her latest.

The Gentle Grafter. The Octopus Marooned

He was outwardly decent and managed to preserve his aquarium, but inside he was impromptu and full of unexpectedness.

Ibid.

It brings up happy old days when I was only a farmer and not an agriculturist.

Ibid. Modern Rural Sports

Living as high as prize fighters out of training.

Ibid. A Tempered Wind

Busy as a one-armed man with the nettle-rash pasting on wall-paper.

Ibid. The Ethics of Pig

Bagdad-on-the-Subway.[1]

Roads of Destiny [*1909*]. *The Discounters of Money*

History is bright and fiction dull with homely men who have charmed women.

Ibid. "Next to Reading Matter"

You can't appreciate home till you've left it, money till it's spent, your wife till she's joined a woman's club, nor Old Glory till you see it hanging on a broomstick on the shanty of a consul in a foreign town.

Ibid. The Fourth in Salvador

Men to whom life had appeared as a reversible coat — seamy on both sides.

Options [*1909*]. *The Hiding of Black Bill*

A man asleep is certainly a sight to make angels weep. Now, a woman asleep you regard as different. No matter how she looks, you know it's better for all hands for her to be that way.

Ibid.

The big city is like a mother's knee to many who have strayed far and found the roads rough beneath their uncertain feet. At dusk they come home and sit upon the door-step.

Options. Supply and Demand

Better fifty years of Europe than a cyclone in the bay.[1]

Ibid. He Also Serves

She would have made a splendid wife, for crying only made her eyes more bright.

Ibid. No Story

A kind of mixture of fools and angels — they rush in and fear to tread at the same time.[2]

Ibid. The Moment of Victory

A story with a moral appended is like the bill of a mosquito. It bores you, and then injects a stinging drop to irritate your conscience.

Strictly Business [*1910*]. *The Gold That Glittered*

Except in street cars one should never be unnecessarily rude to a lady.

Ibid

She plucked from my lapel the invisible strand of lint (the universal act of woman to proclaim ownership).

Ibid. A Ramble in Aphasia

Californians are a race of people; they are not merely inhabitants of a State.

Ibid. A Municipal Report

Take of London fog 30 parts; malaria 10 parts; gas leaks 20 parts; dewdrops gathered in a brick-yard at sunrise 25 parts; odor of honeysuckle 15 parts. Mix. The mixture will give you an approximate conception of a Nashville drizzle.

Ibid.

Most wonderful of all are words, and how they make friends one with another, being oft associated, until not even obituary notices them do part.

Whirligigs [*1910*]. *Calloway's Code*

It couldn't have happened anywhere but in little old New York.[3]

Ibid. A Little Local Color

---

[1] Also in *A Madison Square Arabian Night,* *A Night in New Arabia,* and *"What You Want."*

[1] See Tennyson, page 549a.
[2] See Pope, page 312a.
[3] Also in *A Midsummer Knight's Dream,*

There was too much scenery and fresh air. What I need is a steam-heated flat with no ventilation or exercise.
Letter [April 15, 1910]

I was made by a Dago and presented to the American people on behalf of the French Government for the purpose of welcomin' Irish immigrants into the Dutch city of New York.
Sixes and Sevens [1911]. The Lady Higher Up [1]

May his liver turn to water, and the bones of him crack in the cold of his heart. May dog fennel grow upon his ancestors' graves, and the grandsons of his children be born without eyes. May whiskey turn to clabber in his mouth, and every time he sneezes may he blister the soles of his feet. And the smoke of his pipe — may it make his eyes water, and the drops fall on the grass that his cows eat and poison the butter that he spreads on his bread.[2]
Ibid. Transformation of Martin Burney

A straw vote only shows which way the hot air blows.
Rolling Stones [1913]. A Ruler of Men

We may achieve climate, but weather is thrust upon us.
Ibid. A Fog in Santone

Take it from me — he's got the goods.
The Unprofitable Servant

"You can tell your paper," the great man said,
"I refused an interview.
I have nothing to say on the question, sir;
Nothing to say to you."
And then he talked till the sun went down
And the chickens went to roost.
Poems. Nothing to Say

Turn up the lights; I don't want to go home in the dark.
Last words (quoted in the biography by C. ALPHONSO SMITH)

ELLA HIGGINSON
[1862–1940]

Oh, every year hath its winter,
And every year hath its rain —
But a day is always coming
When the birds go north again.
When the Birds Go North Again. Stanza 1

One leaf is for hope, and one is for faith,
And one is for love, you know,
And God put another in for luck.
Four-Leaf Clover. Stanza 2

Forgive you? — Oh, of course, dear,
A dozen times a week!
We women were created
Forgiveness but to speak.
Wearing Out Love. Stanza 1

MAURICE MAETERLINCK
[1862–1949]

The future is a world limited by ourselves; in it we discover only what concerns us and, sometimes, by chance, what interests those whom we love the most.
Joyzelle. Act I

Men's weaknesses are often necessary to the purposes of life.
Ibid. Act II

I have never for one instant seen clearly within myself; how then would you have me judge the deeds of others? [1]
Pelleas and Melisande [1892]. Act I, Sc. 3

Each young and beautiful being shapes around it events that are themselves young, beautiful, and happy.
Ibid. Act IV, Sc. 2

Past One at Rooney's, and *The Rubber Plant's Story.*
[1] The Statue of Liberty.
[2] See Synge, pages 856b–857a.

[1] No man can justly censure or condemn another, because indeed no man truly knows another. . . . Further, no man can judge another, because no man knows himself. — SIR THOMAS BROWNE: *Religio Medici* [1642]

Old men have need to touch sometimes with their lips the brow of a woman or the cheek of a child, that they may believe again in the freshness of life.
Pelleas and Melisande.
Act IV, Sc. 2

There are no dead.
The Blue Bird [*1909*].
Act IV, Sc. 2

WALT MASON
[1862–1939]

The little green tents where the soldiers sleep and the sunbeams play and the women weep, are covered with flowers today.
The Little Green Tents

The statesman throws his shoulders back, and straightens out his tie,
And says, "My friends, unless it rains, the weather will be dry."
And when this thought into our brains has percolated through,
We common people nod our heads and loudly cry, "How true!"
The Statesman

There's a man in the world who is never turned down, wherever he chances to stray; he gets the glad hand in the populous town, out where the farmers make hay; he's greeted with pleasure on deserts of sand, and deep in the aisles of the woods; wherever he goes there's the welcoming hand — he's the Man Who Delivers the Goods.
The Man Who Delivers the Goods

Little drops of water poured into the milk, give the milkman's daughter lovely gowns of silk. Little grains of sugar mingled with the sand, make the grocer's assets swell to beat the band.
Little Things

SIR HENRY NEWBOLT
[1862–1938]

To set the cause above renown,
To love the game beyond the prize,
To honor, while you strike him down,
The foe that comes with fearless eyes;

To count the life of battle good
And dear the land that gave you birth,
And dearer yet the brotherhood
That binds the brave of all the earth.
The Island Race. Clifton Chapel,
Stanza 2

Qui procul hinc, the legend's writ, —
The frontier-grave is far away —
Qui ante diem periit:
Sed miles, sed pro patria.[1]
Ibid. Stanza 4

Drake he was a Devon man, an' ruled the Devon seas.
Ibid. Drake's Drum, Stanza 2

"Take my drum to England, hang et by the shore,
Strike et when your powder's runnin' low;
If the Dons sight Devon, I'll quit the port o' Heaven,
An' drum them up the Channel as we drummed them long ago."
Ibid.

When the strong command
Obedience is best.
A Ballad of John Nicholson

And now he saw with lifted eyes
The East like a great chancel rise,
And deep through all his senses drawn,
Received the sacred wine of dawn.
The Last Word

Now the sunset breezes shiver,
And she's fading down the river,
But in England's song for ever
She's the Fighting Téméraire.
The Fighting Téméraire

"Play up! play up! and play the game!"
Vitai Lampada

England! where the sacred flame
Burns before the inmost shrine,
Where the lips that love thy name
Consecrate their hopes and thine,
Where the banners of thy dead
Weave their shadows overhead,
Watch beside thine arms tonight,
Pray that God defend the Right.
The Vigil. Stanza 1

[1] Who died far away, before his time: but as a soldier, for his country.

EDEN PHILLPOTTS
[1862–   ]

A sudden wakin', a sudden weepin',
A li'l suckin', a li'l sleepin';
A cheel's full joys an' a cheel's short
    sorrows,
Wi' a power o' faith in gert to-morrows.
        Man's Days. Stanza 1

His father's sister had bats in the
belfry and was put away.
        Peacock House

ROBERT CAMERON ROGERS
[1862–1912]

The hours I spent with thee, dear heart,
    Are as a string of pearls to me;
I count them over, every one apart,
    My rosary, my rosary.
        My Rosary

Visions I no longer see,
And smoke is only smoke to me,
    Now I am old.
        The Old Smoker

EDITH WHARTON
[1862–1937]

There are two ways of spreading light:
    to be
The candle or the mirror that reflects
    it.
        Vesalius in Zante

Mrs. Ballinger is one of the ladies
who pursue Culture in bands, as though
it were dangerous to meet it alone.
        Xingu [*1916*]

I was never allowed to read the popular American children's books of my
day because, as my mother said, the
children spoke bad English *without the
author's knowing it.*
        A Backward Glance [*1934*].
            Chap. 3

To [Henry] James's intimates, however, these elaborate hesitancies, far
from being an obstacle, were like a cobweb bridge flung from his mind to
theirs, an invisible passage over which
one knew that silver-footed ironies,
veiled jokes, tiptoe malices, were steal-

ing to explode a huge laugh at one's
feet.
        A Backward Glance. Chap. 8
"Summer afternoon — summer afternoon; to me those have always been the
two most beautiful words in the English
language."
        (*Said by* HENRY JAMES *to* MRS.
        WHARTON) *Ibid. Chap. 10*

THE REVEREND E. J. HARDY
[*Floruit* 1910]

How To Be Happy Though Married.
        Title of book [*1910*]

HENRY HOLCOMB BENNETT
[1863–1924]

Hats off!
Along the street there comes
A blare of bugles, a ruffle of drums,
A flash of color beneath the sky:
    Hats off!
The flag is passing by.
        The Flag Goes By. Stanza 1

GAMALIEL BRADFORD
[1863–1932]

I sometimes wish that God were back
    In this dark world and wide;
For though some virtues he might lack,
    He had his pleasant side.
        Exit God

That odd, fantastic ass, Rousseau,
    Declared himself unique.
How men persist in doing so,
    Puzzles me more than Greek.
        Rousseau

The sins that tarnish whore and thief
    Beset me every day.
My most ethereal belief
    Inhabits common clay.
        Ibid.

OLIVER HERFORD
[1863–1935]

God made Man
    Frail as a bubble;
God made Love,
    Love made Trouble.

God made the Vine,
　Was it a sin
That Man made Wine
　To drown Trouble in?
A Plea

The Gargoyle often makes his perch
On a cathedral or a church,
Where, mid ecclesiastic style,
He smiles an early-Gothic smile.
The Gargoyle

Children, behold the Chimpanzee:
He sits on the ancestral tree
From which we sprang in ages gone.
The Chimpanzee

Ermined and minked and Persian-
　lambed,
Be-puffed (be-painted, too, alas!)
Be-decked, be-diamonded —
　be-damned!
The women of the better class.
The Women of the Better Class.
Stanza 4

RUFUS M. JONES
[1863–1948]

A little five-year-old boy, who had
been bombed out of his home and
evacuated to the country, said: "Now
I am nobody's nothing."
American Friends Service
Committee, Annual Report
[1943]. Foreword

JAMES MICHAEL KIERAN [1]
[1863–1936]

The Brain Trust.
Description of the professorial
advisers chosen by Franklin D.
Roosevelt in his first Presiden-
tial campaign [1932]

JOSEPH P. MacCARTHY
[1863–1934]

You must select the Puritans for
your ancestors. You must have a sheltered youth and be a graduate of Harvard. . . . Eat beans on Saturday
night and fish-balls on Sunday morn-

[1] Dr. Kieran was president of Hunter College, New York City.

ing. . . . You must be a D.A.R., a
Colonial Dame, an S.A.R. or belong
to the Mayflower Society. . . . You
must read the Atlantic Monthly. . . .
You must make sure in advance that
your obituary appears in the Boston
Transcript. There is nothing else.
To be Happy in New England,
Letter to the Editor of The
Christian Register

ARTHUR MACHEN
[1863–1947]

It was better, he thought, to fail in
attempting exquisite things than to
succeed in the department of the utterly contemptible.
The Hill of Dreams [1907].
Chap. 5

A. EDWARD NEWTON
[1863–1940]

Young man, get a hobby; preferably
get two, one for indoors and one for
out; get a pair of hobby-horses that
can safely be ridden in opposite directions.
Amenities of Book-Collecting
[1918]. Chap. 1

Possession is the grave of bliss. No
sooner do we own some great book than
we want another.
Ibid. Chap. 3

Only when a man is safely ensconced
under six feet of earth, with several
tons of enlauding granite upon his
chest, is he in a position to give advice
with any certainty, and then he is silent.
Ibid. Chap. 4

From contemplation one may become wise, but knowledge comes only
from study.
A Magnificent Farce [1921].
Chap. 8

I wish that some one would give a
course in how to live. It can't be taught
in the colleges: that's perfectly obvi-

ous, for college professors don't know any better than the rest of us.
> *This Book-Collecting Game* [*1928*]. *Chap. 10*

Gilbert White discovered the formula for complete happiness, but he died before making the announcement, leaving it for me to do so. It is to be very busy with the unimportant.
> *Ibid.*

CLARENCE OUSLEY
[1863–1948]

When the mint is in the liquor and its fragrance on the glass,
It breathes a recollection that can never, never pass.
> *When the Mint Is in the Liquor.* *Stanza 1*

SIR ARTHUR THOMAS QUILLER-COUCH
[1863–1944]

Literature is not an abstract science, to which exact definitions can be applied. It is an art, the success of which depends on personal persuasiveness, on the author's skill to give as on ours to receive.
> *Inaugural Lecture at Cambridge University* [*1913*]

JAMES HARVEY ROBINSON
[1863–1935]

Political campaigns are designedly made into emotional orgies which endeavor to distract attention from the real issues involved, and they actually paralyze what slight powers of cerebration man can normally muster.
> *The Human Comedy* [*1937*]. *Chap. 9*

With supreme irony, the war to "make the world safe for democracy" [1] ended by leaving democracy more unsafe in the world than at any time since the collapse of the revolutions of 1848.
> *Ibid.*

[1] See Woodrow Wilson, page 770b.

GEORGE SANTAYANA
[1863–1952]

O World, thou choosest not the better part!
It is not wisdom to be only wise,
And on the inward vision close the eyes,
But it is wisdom to believe the heart.
> *O World, Thou Choosest Not* [*1894*]

Columbus found a world, and had no chart,
Save one that faith deciphered in the skies;
To trust the soul's invincible surmise
Was all his science and his only art.
> *Ibid.*

Heaven is to be at peace with things;
Come chaos now, and in a whirlwind's rings
Engulf the planets. I have seen the best.
> *Sonnet 49* [*1894*]

Beauty is pleasure regarded as the quality of a thing.
> *The Sense of Beauty* [*1896*]. *The Nature of Beauty*

The infinity which moves us is the sense of multiplicity in uniformity. Accordingly, things which have enough multiplicity, as the lights of a city seen across water, have an effect similar to that of the stars, if less intense; whereas a star, if alone, because the multiplicity is lacking, makes a wholly different impression.
> *Ibid. Form*

Beauty as we feel it is something indescribable: what it is or what it means can never be said.
> *Ibid. Expression*

Beauty is a pledge of the possible conformity between the soul and nature, and consequently a ground of faith in the supremacy of the good.
> *Ibid.*

Fanaticism consists in redoubling your efforts when you have forgotten your aim.
> *The Life of Reason* [*1905–1906*]. *Vol. I*

The human race, in its intellectual life, is organized like the bees: the masculine soul is a worker, sexually atrophied, and essentially dedicated to impersonal and universal arts; the feminine is a queen, infinitely fertile, omnipresent in its brooding industry, but passive and abounding in intuitions without method and passions without justice.

The Life of Reason. Vol. II

Let a man once overcome his selfish terror at his own finitude, and his finitude is, in one sense, overcome.

Introduction to The Ethics of Spinoza [1910]

Perhaps the only true dignity of man is his capacity to despise himself.

Ibid.

Miracles are propitious accidents, the natural causes of which are too complicated to be readily understood.

Ibid.

The Bible is literature, not dogma.

Ibid.

American life is a powerful solvent. It seems to neutralise every intellectual element, however tough and alien it may be, and to fuse it in the native good-will, complacency, thoughtlessness, and optimism.

Character and Opinion in the United States [1920]

All his life he [the American] jumps into the train after it has started and jumps out before it has stopped; and he never once gets left behind, or breaks a leg.

Ibid.

He carries his English weather in his heart wherever he goes, and it becomes a cool spot in the desert, and a steady and sane oracle amongst all the delirium of mankind.

Soliloquies in England [1922]. The British Character

England is the paradise of individuality, eccentricity, heresy, anomalies, hobbies, and humours.

Ibid.

The world is a perpetual caricature of itself; at every moment it is the mockery and the contradiction of what it is pretending to be.

Ibid. Dickens

There is no cure for birth and death save to enjoy the interval.

Soliloquies in England. War Shrines

I like to walk about amidst the beautiful things that adorn the world; but private wealth I should decline, or any sort of personal possessions, because they would take away my liberty.

Ibid. The Irony of Liberalism

My atheism, like that of Spinoza, is true piety towards the universe and denies only gods fashioned by men in their own image, to be servants of their human interests.

Ibid. On My Friendly Critics

The young man who has not wept is a savage, and the old man who will not laugh is a fool.

Dialogues in Limbo [1925]. III

There is nothing impossible in the existence of the supernatural: its existence seems to me decidedly probable.

The Genteel Tradition at Bay [1931]

ERNEST LAWRENCE THAYER

[1863–1940]

The outlook wasn't brilliant for the Mudville nine that day.

Casey at the Bat.[1] Stanza 1

There was ease in Casey's manner as he stepped into his place,
There was pride in Casey's bearing, and a smile on Casey's face,
And when, responding to the cheers, he lightly doffed his hat,
No stranger in the crowd could doubt 'twas Casey at the bat.

Ibid. Stanza 6

"Strike one," the umpire said.

Ibid. Stanza 8

[1] First printed in *The San Francisco Examiner*, June 3, 1888.

Yet I'd take my chance with fame,
Calmly let it go at that,
With the right to sign my name
Under "Casey at the Bat."

GRANTLAND RICE [1880–1954]: *The Masterpiece*

From the benches black with people
    there went up a muffled roar,
Like the beating of the storm-waves on
    a stern and distant shore.
          Casey at the Bat. Stanza 9
With a smile of Christian charity great
    Casey's visage shone;
He stilled the rising tumult; he bade
    the game go on.
              Ibid. Stanza 10
Oh! somewhere in this favored land the
    sun is shining bright;
The band is playing somewhere, and
    somewhere hearts are light;
And somewhere men are laughing and
    somewhere children shout,
But there is no joy in Mudville —
    mighty Casey has struck out.
              Ibid. Stanza 13

HARRY BRAISTED
[*Floruit* 1896]

You're Not the Only Pebble on the
Beach.
           Title of song [*1896*]

JOSEPH HAYDEN
[*Floruit* 1896]

There'll be a hot time in the old town
tonight.
    A Hot Time in the Old Town [1]
                  [*1896*]

OSCAR W. FIRKINS
[1864–1932]

I should have enjoyed the country
[Switzerland] more thoroughly if the
poets and romancers had not corrupted
my mind with their pestiferous superlatives.
        Letter [*August 3, 1913*] [2]

[1] Theodore August Metz [1848–1936]
composed a march, *A Hot Time in the Old
Town Tonight,* in 1886 for the McIntyre
and Heath minstrel show. In 1896 Joseph
Hayden wrote words for the music, and the
song was published. It became the favorite
rallying song of Theodore Roosevelt's Rough
Riders in Cuba, and later was Roosevelt's
campaign song.
[2] These quotations are from *Memoirs and
Letters of O. W. Firkins,* 1934.

My state is contentment *within* despair.
      Letter [*December 29, 1922*]
The great art includes much that the
small art excludes: humor, pain, and
evil. Much that is repulsive when alone
becomes beautiful in its relation. To
find the ennobling relation is the task
of life and of art.
                Lecture Notes
A classic is produced by the cooperation of the public with the author. A
classic is a work which is fit to enter
into permanent relations with a large
section of mankind.[1]
                     Ibid.

RICHARD HOVEY
[1864–1900]

Whose furthest footstep never strayed
Beyond the village of his birth
Is but a lodger for the night
In this old wayside inn of earth.
    More Songs from Vagabondia
        [*1896*]. *Envoy, Stanza 1*
For it's always fair weather
When good fellows get together
With a stein on the table and a good
    song ringing clear.
    A Stein Song [*1898*]. *Stanza 1*
I do not know beneath what sky
    Nor on what seas shall be thy fate:
I only know it shall be high,
    I only know it shall be great.
    Unmanifest Destiny [*1898*].
                  Stanza 7
There are worser ills to face
    Than foeman in the fray;
And many a man has fought because —
    He feared to run away.
    The Marriage of Guenevere.
             Act IV, Sc. 3
I have need of the sky,
I have business with the grass.
      I Have Need of the Sky
Eleazar Wheelock was a very pious
    man;
He went into the wilderness to teach
    the Indian,

[1] See Mark Twain, page 679a.

With a *Gradus ad Parnassum,* a Bible,
and a drum,
And five hundred gallons of New England rum. . . .
Eleazar was the faculty, and the whole
curriculum
Was five hundred gallons of New England rum.
Dartmouth College song

MARK ANTONY DE WOLFE HOWE
[1864–   ]

The village sleeps, a name unknown, till
men
With life-blood stain its soil, and pay
the due
That lifts it to eternal fame, — for then
'Tis grown a Gettysburg or Waterloo.
Distinction

Not for the star-crowned heroes, the
men that conquer and slay,
But a song for those that bore them, the
mothers braver than they!
With never a blare of trumpets, with
never a surge of cheers,
They march to the unseen hazard —
pale, patient volunteers.
The Valiant

Now, thieving Time, take what you
must —
Quickness to hear, to move, to see;
When dust is drawing near to dust
Such diminutions needs must be.
Yet leave, O leave exempt from plunder
My curiosity, my wonder!
*Thieving Time (Aged eighty-
seven)*

ROBERT LOVEMAN
[1864–1923]

It is not raining rain to me,
It's raining daffodils;
In every dimpled drop I see
Wild flowers on the hills.
April Rain [1901]. Stanza 1

A health unto the happy!
A fig for him who frets! —
It is not raining rain to me,
It's raining violets.
Ibid. Stanza 4

PAUL ELMER MORE [1]
[1864–1937]

As our private memory is not a
merely passive retention of sensations,
so in literature the critical spirit is at
work as a conscious energy of selection. The function of criticism is far
removed from the surrender to luxurious revery.
*Shelburne Essays [1904–1935].
Criticism*

Great music is a psychical storm,
agitating to fathomless depths the mystery of the past within us. Or we might
say that it is a prodigious incantation.
There are tones that call up all ghosts
of youth and joy and tenderness; —
there are tones that evoke all phantom
pains of perished passion; — there are
tones that revive all dead sensations of
majesty and might and glory, — all ex-
pired exultations, — all forgotten mag-
nanimities. Well may the influence of
music seem inexplicable to the man
who idly dreams that his life began
less than a hundred years ago! He who
has been initiated into the truth knows
that to every ripple of melody, to every billow of harmony, there answers
within him, out of the Sea of Death
and Birth, some eddying immeasurable
of ancient pleasure and pain.
Ibid. Lafcadio Hearn

ANDREW BARTON ("BANJO") PATERSON
[1864–1941]

Once a jolly swagman camped by a
billy-bong,
Under the shade of a kulibar tree,
And he sang as he sat and waited for
his billy-boil,

[1] To read him is to enter an austere and
elevated realm of ideas and to know a man
who, in the guise of a critic, is authentically
concerned with the first and last things of
human experience. — WALTER LIPPMANN, in
The Saturday Review of Literature, March
15, 1930

"You'll come a-waltzing, Matilda, with me." [1]
> *Waltzing Matilda. Australian Soldiers' Marching Song*

STEPHEN PHILLIPS
[1864–1915]

Thy face remembered is from other worlds,
It has been died for, though I know not when,
It has been sung of, though I know not where.
> *Marpessa*

The half of music, I have heard men say,
Is to have grieved.
> *Ibid.*

Out of our sadness have we made this world
So beautiful.
> *Ibid.*

The constable with lifted hand
Conducting the orchestral Strand.
> *The Wife*

JOSEPH BERT SMILEY
[1864–1903]

Thirty years with that tongue so sharp?
Ho! Angel Gabriel! Give him a Harp!
> *St. Peter at the Gate (Thirty Years with a Shrew). Stanza 13*

See that on finest ambrosia he feeds,
He's had about all the Hades he needs;
It isn't just hardly the thing to do
To roast him on earth and the future, too.
> *Ibid. Stanza 14*

ISRAEL ZANGWILL
[1864–1926]

Scratch the Christian and you find the pagan — spoiled.
> *Children of the Ghetto [1892]*

America is God's Crucible, the great Melting-Pot where all the races of Europe are melting and re-forming!
> *The Melting Pot [1908]. Act I*

[1] Swagman = highwayman; billy-bong = brook; kulibar = gum tree; billy-boil = coffee.

In how many lives does Love really play a dominant part? The average taxpayer is no more capable of a "grand passion" than of a grand opera.
> *Romeo and Juliet and Other Love Stories*

JOHN BENNETT
[1865–   ]

If Life's a lie, and Love's a cheat,
As I have heard men say,
Then here's a health to fond deceit —
God bless you, dear, today!
> *God Bless You, Dear, Today. Stanza 3*

A hundred years from now, dear heart,
We shall not care at all.
It will not matter then a whit,
The honey or the gall.
> *In a Rose Garden [1895]. Stanza 1*

We are all but fellow-travellers
Along Life's weary way;
If any man can play the pipes,
In God's name, let him play.
> *Year Book, Poetry Society of South Carolina [1921]*

MADISON JULIUS CAWEIN
[1865–1914]

Some reckon time by stars,
And some by hours;
Some measure days by dreams,
And some by flowers;
My heart alone records
My days and hours.
> *Some Reckon Time by Stars. Stanza 1*

Here is the place where Loveliness keeps house,
Between the river and the wooded hills.
> *Here Is the Place*

An old Spanish saying is that "a kiss without a moustache is like an egg without salt."
> *Nature-Notes*

ROBERT WILLIAM CHAMBERS
[1865–1933]

Sez Corporal Madden to Private Mc-Fadden:

"Yer figger wants padd'n —
Sure, man, ye've no shape!
Behind ye yer shoulders
Stick out like two bowlders;
Yer shins are as thin
As a pair of pen-holders!"
The Recruit. Stanza 3

FRANK MOORE COLBY
[1865–1925]

True satire is not the sneering substance that we know, but satire that includes the satirist.
The Colby Essays [*1926*]. *Vol. I*

Men will confess to treason, murder, arson, false teeth, or a wig. How many of them will own up to a lack of humor?
Ibid.

Nobody can describe a fool to the life, without much patient self-inspection.
Ibid.

Every man ought to be inquisitive through every hour of his great adventure down to the day when he shall no longer cast a shadow in the sun. For if he dies without a question in his heart, what excuse is there for his continuance? [1]
Ibid.

In spite of the large population of this planet, men and women remain to-day the most inaccessible things on it.
Ibid. Vol. II

A new movement is not a stampede to some new object, but a stampede away from some old person.
Ibid.

The attempt to turn a complex problem of the head into a simple moral question for the heart to answer, is of course a necessary part of all political discussions.
Ibid.

I have found some of the best reasons I ever had for remaining at the bottom simply by looking at the men at the top.
Ibid.

[1] See M. A. De Wolfe Howe, page 809a.

A "new thinker," when studied closely, is merely a man who does not know what other people have thought.
The Margin of Hesitation

Were it not for the presence of the unwashed and the half-educated, the formless, queer and incomplete, the unreasonable and absurd, the infinite shapes of the delightful human tadpole, the horizon would not wear so wide a grin.
Imaginary Obligations

In public we say the race is to the strongest; in private we know that a lopsided man runs the fastest along the little side-hills of success.
Constrained Attitudes

Journalists have always been our most old-fashioned class, being too busy with the news of the day to lay aside the mental habits of fifty years before.
Ibid.

HOLMAN FRANCIS DAY
[1865–1935]

He pasted a sheet of postage stamps
  from snout clear down to tail,
Put on a quick delivery stamp, and
  sent the cod by mail.
Cure for Homesickness

The purest affection the heart can hold
Is the honest love of a nine-year-old.
That May-basket for Mabel Fry

If ye only knew the backaches in an
  old stun' wall!
An Old Stun' Wall

H. A. L. FISHER [1]
[1865–1940]

All political decisions are taken under great pressure, and if a treaty serves its turn for ten or twenty years, the

[1] Fisher was Warden of New College, Oxford, and one of the eminent historians of Trevelyan's era. He wrote a life of Napoleon and *The History of the Napoleonic Tradition*.

wisdom of its framers is sufficiently confirmed.[1]

Political Prophecies [1918]

It is easier for eight or nine elderly men to feel their way towards unanimity, if they are not compelled to conduct their converging manoeuvres under the microscopes and telescopes of the Press, but are permitted to shuffle about a little in slippers.

An International Experiment [2]
[1921]

Purity of race does not exist. Europe is a continent of energetic mongrels.

A History of Europe [1934].
Chap. 1

Politics is the art of human happiness.

Ibid. Chap. 31

Taine pointed out that history was made by men, that men had bodies, that bodies were now healthy, now disordered, and that the state of the body inevitably affected the action of the mind. The study of the human body was part of the historian's duty. The accidents of health had more to do with the march of great events than was ordinarily suspected.

Paris at High Noon [1941]

KING GEORGE V
[1865–1936]

If I may be regarded as in some true sense the head of this great and widespread family, sharing its life and sustained by its affection, this will be a full reward for the long and sometimes anxious labours of my reign.

Radio greeting to the British Empire [Christmas Day, 1934]

FREDERIC WILLIAM GOUDY
[1865–1947]

I am the voice of today, the herald of tomorrow. . . . I coin for you the

[1] Thirty years is the life of most great treaties. — R. B. MOWAT: *A History of Great Britain* [1922]
[2] The League of Nations.

enchanting tale, the philosopher's moralizing, and the poet's visions. . . . I am the leaden army that conquers the world — I am TYPE.

The Type Speaks

"LAURENCE HOPE" (ADELA FLORENCE CORY NICOLSON)
[1865–1904]

Less than the dust, beneath thy chariot
  wheel,
Less than the weed, that grows beside
  thy door,
Less than the rust, that never stained
  thy sword,
Less than the need thou hast in life of
  me,
  Even less am I.

Less Than the Dust. Stanza 1

For this is Wisdom; to love, to live,
To take what Fate, or the Gods, may
  give.

The Teak Forest

To have, — to hold, — and, — in time,
  — let go!

Ibid.

Pale hands I loved beside the Shalimar,
Where are you now? Who lies beneath
  your spell?
Whom do you lead on Rapture's roadway, far,
Before you agonize them in farewell?

Kashmiri Song. Stanza 1

Yet I, this little while ere I go hence,
Love very lightly now, in self-defence.

Verse by Taj Mahomed

Men should be judged, not by their tint
  of skin,
The Gods they serve, the Vintage that
  they drink,
Nor by the way they fight, or love, or
  sin,
But by the quality of thought they
  think.

Men Should Be Judged

Often devotion to virtue arises from
  sated desire.

I Arise and Go Down to
the River. Stanza 6

LAURENCE HOUSMAN
[1865–]

Minority is no disproof:
Wisdom is not so strong and fleet
As never to have known defeat.
Advocatus Diaboli

RUDYARD KIPLING
[1865–1936]

I have eaten your bread and salt.
I have drunk your water and wine.
The deaths ye died I have watched
beside
And the lives ye led were mine.
Departmental Ditties [*1886*].
Prelude, Stanza 1

Little Tin Gods on Wheels.
Public Waste. Stanza 4

Trust me, Today's Most Indispensables,
Five hundred men can take your place
or mine.
The Last Department. Stanza 8

The blush that flies at seventeen
Is fixed at forty-nine.
My Rival. Stanza 2

The toad beneath the harrow knows
Exactly where each tooth-point goes;
The butterfly upon the road
Preaches contentment to that toad.
Pagett, M. P.

Cross that rules the Southern Sky!
Stars that sweep, and turn, and fly,
Hear the Lovers' Litany: —
"Love like ours can never die!"
The Lovers' Litany. Stanza 2

And a woman is only a woman, but a
good cigar is a Smoke.
The Betrothed. Stanza 25

The temper of chums, the love of your
wife,[1] and a new piano's tune —
Which of the three will you trust at the
end of an Indian June?
Certain Maxims of Hafiz. IV

[1] It is as foolish to make experiments upon
the constancy of a friend, as upon the chastity
of a wife. — SAMUEL JOHNSON: *Letter to
James Boswell* [September 9, 1779]

You'll never plumb the Oriental mind,
And if you did, it isn't worth the toil.
One Viceroy Resigns

It takes a great deal of Christianity
to wipe out uncivilized Eastern instincts, such as falling in love at first
sight.
Plain Tales from the Hills [*1888*].
Lispeth

Ride with an idle whip, ride with an
unused heel,
But, once in a way, there will come a
day
When the colt must be taught to feel
The lash that falls, and the curb that
galls, and the sting of the rowelled steel.
*Ibid. The Conversion of
Aurelian McGoggin*

Never praise a sister to a sister, in
the hope of your compliments reaching
the proper ears.
Ibid. False Dawn

If you hit a pony over the nose at
the outset of your acquaintance, he may
not love you, but he will take a deep
interest in your movements ever afterwards.
Ibid.

Meddling with another man's folly is
always thankless work.
Ibid. The Rescue of Pluffles

Many religious people are deeply
suspicious. They seem — for purely religious purposes, of course — to know
more about iniquity than the Unregenerate.
Ibid. Watches of the Night

She was as immutable as the Hills.
But not quite so green.
Ibid. Venus Annodomini

Youth had been a habit of hers for
so long, that she could not part with it.
Ibid.

Every one is more or less mad on one
point.[1]
*Ibid. On the Strength of a
Likeness*

[1] Semel insanivimus omnes (We have all
once been mad). — JOHANNES BAPTISTA
MANTUANUS [1448–1516]: *Eclogues, No. I*

After marriage arrives a reaction, sometimes a big, sometimes a little, one; but it comes sooner or later, and must be tided over by both parties if they desire the rest of their lives to go with the current.

> *Plain Tales from the Hills.*
> *Three and — an Extra*

This is worth remembering. Speaking to, or crying over, a husband never did any good yet.

> *Ibid.*

A woman's guess is much more accurate than a man's certainty.

> *Ibid.*

The silliest woman can manage a clever man; but it needs a very clever woman to manage a fool!

> *Ibid.*

Lo, I have wrought in common clay
Rude figures of a rough-hewn race.

> *Soldiers Three* [*1888*]. *Dedication, Stanza 2*

Oh, East is East, and West is West, and
    never the twain shall meet,
Till Earth and Sky stand presently at
    God's great Judgment Seat.
But there is neither East nor West, Bor-
    der, nor Breed, nor Birth,
When two strong men stand face to
    face, though they come from the
    ends of the earth!

> *The Ballad of East and West*
> [*1889*]

The first proof a man gives of his interest in a woman is by talking to her about his own sweet self. If the woman listens without yawning, he begins to like her. If she flatters the animal's vanity, he ends by adoring her.

> *Under the Deodars* [*1889*].
> *The Education of Otis Veere*

More men are killed by overwork than the importance of the world justifies.

> *The Phantom 'Rickshaw* [*1889*]

There aren't twelve hundred people in the world who understand pictures. The others pretend and don't care.

> *The Light That Failed* [*1890*].
> *Chap. 7*

Overloaded, undermanned, meant to
    founder, we
Euchred God Almighty's storm, bluffed
    the Eternal Sea!

> *The Ballad of the "Bolivar"*
> [*1890*]. *Stanza 12*

Man that is born of woman is small potatoes and few in a hill.

> *Life's Handicap* [*1891*]. *The*
> *Head of the District*

The end of the fight is a tombstone
    white with the name of the late
    deceased,
And the epitaph drear: "A Fool lies
    here who tried to hustle the East."

> *The Naulahka* [*1892*]. *Chap. 5*

When Earth's last picture is painted,
    and the tubes are twisted and
    dried,
When the oldest colours have faded,
    and the youngest critic has died,
We shall rest, and, faith, we shall need
    it — lie down for an aeon or two,
Till the Master of All Good Workmen
    shall put us to work anew.

> *When Earth's Last Picture Is*
> *Painted* [*1892*]. *Stanza 1*

I am sick of endless sunshine, sick of
    blossom-burdened bough.
Give me back the leafless woodlands
    where the winds of Springtime
    range —
Give me back one day in England, for
    it's Spring in England now! [1]

> *In Springtime. Stanza 1*

They rise to their feet as He passes by,
    gentlemen unafraid.

> *Barrack Room Ballads* [*1892*].
> *Dedication, Stanza 5*

The Liner she's a lady, and if a war
    should come,
The Man-o'-War's 'er 'usband, and 'e'd
    bid 'er stay at home;
But, oh, the little cargo-boats that fill
    with every tide!
'E'd 'ave to up an' fight for them for
    they are England's pride.

> *The Liner She's a Lady. Stanza 5*

And what should they know of England
    who only England know?

> *The English Flag*

[1] See Browning, page 568b.

There be triple ways to take, of the
    eagle or the snake,
Or the way of a man with a maid; [1]
But the sweetest way to me is a ship's
    upon the sea
    In the heel of the North-East Trade.
        The Long Trail. Stanza 4

We have fed our sea for a thousand
    years
  And she calls us, still unfed,
Though there's never a wave of all her
    waves
  But marks our English dead.
    *A Song of the English [1893]. The
    Song of the Dead, II, Stanza 1*

If blood be the price of admiralty,
Lord God, we ha' paid in full!
             Ibid.

Deeper than speech our love, stronger
    than life our tether,
But we do not fall on the neck or kiss
    when we come together.
    Ibid. England's Answer

Go to your work and be strong, halting
    not in your ways,
Baulking the end half-won for an in-
    stant dole of praise.
Stand to your work and be wise — cer-
    tain of sword and pen,
Who are neither children nor Gods, but
    men in a world of men!
             Ibid.

  He wrapped himself in quotations [2]
— as a beggar would enfold himself in
the purple of Emperors.
    *Many Inventions [1893]. The
    Finest Story in the World*

Ever the wide world over, lass,
  Ever the trail held true,
Over the world and under the world,
  And back at the last to you.
    The Gipsy Trail. Stanza 2

The wild hawk to the wind-swept sky,
  The deer to the wholesome wold

---

[1] See *Proverbs, XXX, 19,* on page 1041b.
[2] In literature quotation is good only when
the writer whom I follow goes my way, and,
being better mounted than I, gives me a cast.
— EMERSON: *Quotation and Originality*
[1876]

And the heart of a man to the heart of
    a maid,
  As it was in the days of old.
        The Gipsy Trail. Stanza 11

They change their skies above them,
  But not their hearts that roam.
        The Native-born. Stanza 2

There's a Legion that never was 'listed,
That carries no colours or crest.
        The Lost Legion. Stanza 1

To go and find out and be damned
  (Dear boys!).
             Ibid.

I can rip your very heartstrings out
  with those.
    *The Song of the Banjo [1894].
             Stanza 6*

"Something hidden. Go and find it. Go
  and look behind the Ranges —
Something lost behind the Ranges.
  Lost and waiting for you. Go!" [1]
        The Explorer. Stanza 2

Who hath desired the Sea? — the sight
  of salt water unbounded —
The heave and the halt and the hurl
  and the crash of the comber wind-
  hounded?
    The Sea and the Hills. Stanza 1

So and no otherwise — hillmen desire
  their Hills!
             Ibid.

Absolute, unvarying rigidity, rigidity!
    The Ship that Found Herself

They copied all they could follow, but
  they couldn't copy my mind.
    The "Mary Gloster" [1894]

When Pack meets with Pack in the
  Jungle, and neither will go from
  the trail,
Lie down till the leaders have spoken
  — it may be fair words shall prevail.
    *The Second Jungle Book [1895].
    The Law of the Jungle, Stanza 6*

Now these are the Laws of the Jungle,
  and many and mighty are they;
But the head and the hoof of the Law

---

[1] "Because it is there." — *Said by* GEORGE
LEIGH MALLORY [1886–1924] *when asked
why he wanted to climb Mt. Everest*

and the haunch and the hump is
— Obey!
*The Second Jungle Book. The Law
of the Jungle, Refrain*

He who rebukes the world is rebuked
by the world.
Ibid. The Undertakers

He had been, as the old law recommends, twenty years a youth, twenty
years a fighter, though he had never
carried a weapon in his life, and twenty
years head of a household.
Ibid. Miracle of Purun Bhagat

Cock the gun that is not loaded, cook
the frozen dynamite —
But oh, beware my Country, when my
Country grows polite!
*Et Dona Ferentes [1896].
Stanza 11*

Daughter am I in my mother's house;
But mistress in my own.
Our Lady of the Snows [1] *[1897].
Stanza 1*

God of our fathers, known of old,
Lord of our far-flung battle-line,
Beneath whose awful Hand we hold
Dominion over palm and pine —
Lord God of Hosts, be with us yet,
Lest we forget — lest we forget!
Recessional [1897]. Stanza 1

The tumult and the shouting dies;
The Captains and the Kings depart:
Still stands Thine ancient sacrifice,
An humble and a contrite heart.
Ibid. Stanza 2

Lo, all our pomp of yesterday
Is one with Nineveh and Tyre!
Ibid. Stanza 3

If, drunk with sight of power, we loose
Wild tongues that have not Thee in
awe,
Such boastings as the Gentiles use,
Or lesser breeds without the Law.
Ibid. Stanza 4

And he wrote for them wonderful verses
that swept the land like flame,
Till the fatted souls of the English were
scourged with the thing called
Shame.
*The Last of the Light Brigade.
Stanza 8*

[1] The Dominion of Canada.

God gives all men all earth to love,
But since man's heart is small,
Ordains for each one spot shall prove
Belovèd over all.
Sussex. Stanza 12

A fool there was and he made his prayer
(Even as you and I!)
To a rag and a bone and a hank of hair
(We called her the woman who did not
care)
But the fool he called her his lady
fair —
(Even as you and I!)
The Vampire [1897]. Stanza 1

Oh, the years we waste and the tears
we waste
And the work of our head and hand
Belong to the woman who did not
know . . .
And did not understand.
Ibid. Stanza 2

Make ye no truce with Adam-zad —
the Bear that walks like a Man! [1]
The Truce of the Bear. Stanza 2

The Goth and the shameless Hun!
The Rowers. Stanza 11

All we have of freedom, all we use or
know —
This our fathers bought for us long and
long ago.
The Old Issue. Stanza 5

Ancient Right unnoticed as the breath
we draw —
Leave to live by no man's leave, underneath the law.
Ibid. Stanza 6

Little Friend of All the World.
Kim [1901]. Chap. 1

We have had a jolly good lesson, and it
serves us jolly well right!
The Lesson [1902]. Stanza 2

We have forty million reasons for failure, but not a single excuse.
Ibid. Stanza 8

With the flannelled fools at the wicket
or the muddied oafs at the goals.
The Islanders [1902]

No doubt but ye are the People — absolute, strong, and wise;
Whatever your heart has desired ye
have not withheld from your eyes.

[1] Russia.

On your own heads, in your own hands,
the sin and the saving lies!
The Islanders

Creation's cry goes up on high
From age to cheated age:
"Send us the men who do the work
For which they draw the wage!"
The Wage-Slaves. Stanza 3

This is our lot if we live so long and
labour unto the end —
That we outlive the impatient years
and the much too patient friend:
And because we know we have breath
in our mouth and think we have
thoughts in our head,
We shall assume that we are alive,
whereas we are really dead.
The Old Men. Stanza 1

Take up the White Man's burden.
The White Man's Burden.
Stanza 1

Your new-caught, sullen peoples,
Half-devil and half-child.
Ibid.

But, spite all modern notions, I've
found her first and best —
The only certain packet for the Islands
of the Blest.
The Three-Decker. Stanza 1

The Devil whispered behind the leaves,
"It's pretty, but is it Art?"
The Conundrum of the Workshops

Ah! what avails the classic bent
And what the cultured word,
Against the undoctored incident
That actually occurred?
The Benefactors. Stanza 1

It is not learning, grace nor gear,
Nor easy meat and drink,
But bitter pinch of pain and fear
That makes creation think.
Ibid. Stanza 3

There are nine and sixty ways of con-
structing tribal lays,
And—every—single—one—of—them—is—
right.
In the Neolithic Age. Stanza 5

You must hack through much deposit
Ere you know for sure who was it
Came to burial with such honour in the
Files

(Only seven seasons back beneath the
Files).
"Very great our loss and grievous —
So our best and brightest leave us,
And it ends the Age of Giants," say
the Files.
The Files

When your Imp of Blind Desire
Bids you set the Thames afire,
You'll remember men have done so —
in the Files.
Ibid.

And the naked soul of Tomlinson grew
white as a rain-washed bone.
Tomlinson

The sin they do by two and two they
must pay for one by one.
Ibid.

Those who have passed to the further
shore
May be hailed — at a price — on the
road to En-dor.[1]
En-Dor. Stanza 2

The female of the species is more
deadly than the male.
The Female of the Species.
Stanza 1

"Confound Romance!". . . And all
unseen
Romance brought up the nine-fifteen.
The King

My son was killed while laughing at
some jest. I would I knew
What it was, and it might serve me in
a time when jests are few.
Epitaphs of the War. A Son

"What are the bugles blowin' for?" said
Files-on-Parade.
To turn you out, to turn you out," the
Colour-Sergeant said.
Danny Deever. Stanza 1

They've taken of his buttons off an' cut
his stripes away,
An' they're hangin' Danny Deever in
the mornin'.
Ibid.

We aren't no thin red 'eroes.[2]
Tommy. Stanza 4

[1] Behold there is a woman that hath
a familiar spirit at En-dor. — *1 Samuel,*
XXVIII, 7
[2] See Sir W. H. Russell, page 613a.

Single men in barricks don't grow into
  plaster saints.
                    Tommy. Stanza 4
It's Tommy this, an' Tommy that, an'
  "Chuck 'im out, the brute!"
But it's "Saviour of 'is country," when
  the guns begin to shoot.
                    Ibid. Stanza 5
So 'ere's *to* you, Fuzzy-Wuzzy, at your
  'ome in the Soudan;
You're a pore benighted 'eathen but a
  first-class fightin' man.
                    "Fuzzy-Wuzzy." Stanza 1
'E's all 'ot sand an' ginger when alive,
An' 'e's generally shammin' when 'e's
  dead.
                    Ibid. Stanza 4
The uniform 'e wore
Was nothin' much before,
An' rather less than 'arf o' that be'ind.
                    Gunga Din. Stanza 2
An' for all 'is dirty 'ide
'E was white, clear white, inside
When 'e went to tend the wounded
  under fire!
                    Ibid. Stanza 3
Though I've belted you an' flayed you,
By the livin' Gawd that made you,
You're a better man than I am, Gunga
  Din!
                    Ibid. Stanza 5
'Ave you 'eard o' the Widow at Wind-
  sor
With a hairy gold crown on 'er 'ead?
         The Widow at Windsor. Stanza 1
Walk wide o' the Widow at Windsor,
  For 'alf o' Creation she owns:
We 'ave bought 'er the same with the
  sword an' the flame,
  An' we've salted it down with our
    bones!
                    Ibid. Stanza 2
By the old Moulmein Pagoda, lookin'
  lazy at the sea,
There's a Burma girl a-settin', and I
  know she thinks o' me;
For the wind is in the palm-trees, and
  the temple-bells they say:
"Come you back, you British soldier;
  come you back to Mandalay!"
  Come you back to Mandalay,
  Where the old Flotilla lay;

Can't you 'ear their paddles chunkin'
  from Rangoon to Mandalay?
On the road to Mandalay,
  Where the flyin'-fishes play,
An' the dawn comes up like thunder
  outer China 'crost the Bay!
                    Mandalay. Stanza 1
I've a neater, sweeter maiden in a
  cleaner, greener land.
                    Ibid. Stanza 5
Ship me somewheres east of Suez,
  where the best is like the worst,
Where there aren't no Ten Command-
  ments an' a man can raise a thirst.
                    Ibid. Stanza 6
Back to the Army again, sergeant,
  Back to the Army again.
Out o' the cold an' the rain.
           "Back to the Army Again."
                                Refrain
For there isn't a job on the top of the
  earth the beggar don't know, nor
  do.
           "Soldier an' Sailor Too." Stanza 2
'E's a sort of a bloomin' cosmopolouse
  — soldier an' sailor too.
                                Ibid.
To stand an' be still to the *Birken'ead*
  drill [1] is a damn' tough bullet to
  chew.
                    Ibid. Stanza 5
I've taken my fun where I've found it.
                    The Ladies. Stanza 1
An' I learned about women from 'er.
                    Ibid. Refrain
For the Colonel's Lady an' Judy
  O'Grady
Are sisters under their skins!
                    Ibid. Stanza 8
We met upon the level an' we parted
  on the Square,
An' I was Junior Deacon in my Mother-
  Lodge out there.
                    The Mother-Lodge. Refrain
To the legion of the lost ones, to the
  cohort of the damned.
                Gentlemen-Rankers. Stanza 1
We're poor little lambs who've lost our
  way,
  Baa! Baa! Baa!

See Anonymous, page 1003b.

We're little black sheep who've gone
    astray,
    Baa-aa-aa!
Gentlemen-rankers out on the spree,
Damned from here to Eternity,
God ha' mercy on such as we,
    Baa! Yah! Baa!
        Gentlemen-Rankers. Refrain

We have done with Hope and Honour,
    we are lost to Love and Truth,
We are dropping down the ladder rung
    by rung;
And the measure of our torment is the
    measure of our youth.
God help us, for we knew the worst too
    young!
        Ibid. Stanza 4

The backbone of the Army is the Non-
    commissioned Man!
        The 'Eathen. Stanza 18

For to admire an' for to see,
For to be'old this world so wide —
It never done no good to me
But I can't drop it if I tried!
        "For to Admire." Refrain

He's an absent-minded beggar, but he
    heard his country's call,
And his reg'ment didn't need to send
    to find him!
        The Absent-minded Beggar.
                Stanza 3

Boots — boots — boots — boots —
    movin' up and down again!
There's no discharge in the war! [1]
        Boots. Stanza 1

The bachelor may risk 'is 'ide
    To 'elp you when you're downed;
But the married man will wait beside
    Till the ambulance comes round.
        The Married Man. Stanza 5

The married man must sink or swim
An' — 'e can't afford to sink!
        Ibid. Stanza 7

If England was what England seems,
An' not the England of our dreams,
But only putty, brass, an' paint,
'Ow quick we'd drop 'er! But she ain't.
        The Return. Refrain

One man in a thousand, Solomon says,
Will stick more close than a brother.[1]
        The Thousandth Man. Stanza 1

But the Thousandth Man will stand by
    your side
To the gallows-foot — and after!
        Ibid. Stanza 4

Down to Gehenna or up to the Throne,
He travels the fastest who travels
    alone.[2]
        The Winners. Stanza 1

When the body that lived at your single
    will,
With its whimper of welcome, is stilled
    (how still!)
When the spirit that answered your
    every mood
Is gone — wherever it goes — for good,
You will discover how much you care,
And will give your heart to a dog to
    tear.
        The Power of the Dog. Stanza 4

The arrows of our anguish
Fly farther than we guess.
        The Rabbi's Song. Stanza 3

I keep six honest serving-men
    (They taught me all I knew);
Their names are What and Why and
    When
And How and Where and Who.
        Just-So Stories [*1902*]. *The*
                Elephant's Child

The great grey-green, greasy Lim-
    popo River, all set about with fever-
    trees.
        Ibid.

Yes, weekly from Southampton,
Great steamers, white and gold,
Go rolling down to Rio
(Roll down — roll down to Rio!).
And I'd like to roll to Rio
Some day before I'm old!
        Ibid. The Beginning of the
            Armadilloes, Stanza 4

When the ship goes *wop* (with a wiggle
    between)
And the steward falls into the soup-
    tureen . . . .

---

[1] There is no discharge in that war. — *Ecclesiastes, VIII, 8*

[1] See *Ecclesiastes, VII, 28*, on page 1043a.
[2] He may well win the race that runs by
himself. — BENJAMIN FRANKLIN: *Poor Richard's Almanac* [1757]

Why, then you will know (if you haven't guessed)
You're "Fifty North and Forty West!"
Just-So Stories. How the Whale Got His Throat

The Camel's hump is an ugly lump
Which well you may see at the Zoo;
But uglier yet is the Hump we get
From having too little to do.
Ibid. How the Camel Got His Hump

We get the Hump—
Cameelious Hump—
The Hump that is black and blue!
Ibid.

The cure for this ill is not to sit still,
Or frowst with a book by the fire;
But to take a large hoe and a shovel also,
And dig till you gently perspire.
Ibid.

The Cat. He walked by himself, and all places were alike to him.
Ibid. The Cat That Walked By Himself

He went through the Wet Wild Woods, waving his wild tail, and walking by his wild lone. But he never told anybody.
Ibid.

We must go back with Policeman Day—
Back from the City of Sleep!
The City of Sleep. Stanza 1

If I were damned of body and soul,
I know whose prayers would make me whole,
Mother o' mine, O mother o' mine.
Mother o' Mine

'Tisn't beauty, so to speak, nor good talk necessarily. It's just It. Some women'll stay in a man's memory if they once walked down a street.
Traffics and Discoveries [1904]. Mrs. Bathurst

Anything green that grew out of the mould
Was an excellent herb to our fathers of Old.
"Our Fathers of Old." Stanza 1

Wonderful little our fathers knew,
Half their remedies cured you dead —
Most of their teaching was quite untrue.
"Our Fathers of Old." Stanza 3

Of all the trees that grow so fair,
  Old England to adorn,
Greater are none beneath the Sun,
  Than Oak, and Ash, and Thorn.[1]
*Puck of Pook's Hill [1906].
A Tree Song, Stanza 1*

Land of our Birth, we pledge to thee
Our love and toil in the years to be.
Ibid. The Children's Song, Stanza 1

Teach us Delight in simple things,
And Mirth that has no bitter springs.
Ibid. Stanza 7

Take of English earth as much
As either hand may rightly clutch.
In the taking of it breathe
Prayer for all who lie beneath.
*Rewards and Fairies [1910].
A Charm, Stanza 1*

If you can meet with Triumph and Disaster
And treat those two impostors just the same.
Ibid. If, Stanza 2

If you can talk with crowds and keep your virtue,
Or walk with Kings — nor lose the common touch.
Ibid. Stanza 4

Yours is the Earth and everything that's in it,
And — which is more — you'll be a Man, my son!
Ibid.

And thrones on Shrieking Circumstance
The Sacredly Absurd.
The Necessitarian. Stanza 3

If once you have paid him the Danegeld
You never get rid of the Dane.
Danegeld. Stanza 4

Say "we," "us" and "ours" when you're talking instead of "you fellows" and "I."
Norman and Saxon. Stanza 6

[1] See *Glasgerion*, page 1012a.

At Runnymede, at Runnymede,
What say the reeds at Runnymede?
The Reeds of Runnymede.
Stanza 1
When Crew and Captain understand
each other to the core,
It takes a gale and more than a gale to
put their ship ashore.
Together. Stanza 2
The snow lies thick on Valley Forge,
The ice on the Delaware,
But the poor dead soldiers of King
George
They neither know nor care.
The American Rebellion. II,
After, Stanza 1
When 'Omer smote 'is bloomin' lyre,
He'd 'eard men sing by land an' sea;
An' what he thought 'e might require,
'E went an' took — the same as me!
When 'Omer Smote 'is Bloomin'
Lyre. Stanza 1
Our England is a garden, and such gar-
dens are not made
By singing: — "Oh, how beautiful!"
and sitting in the shade.
The Glory of the Garden.
Stanza 5
As I pass through my incarnations in
every age and race,
I make my proper prostrations to the
gods of the Market Place;
Peering through reverent fingers, I
watch them flourish and fall,
And the Gods of the Copybook Max-
ims, I notice, outlast them all.
The Gods of the Copybook
Maxims. Stanza 1
For all we take we must pay, but the
price is cruel high.
The Courting of Dinah Shadd.
Chap. 1
Never show a woman that ye care
the snap av a finger for her, an' begad
she'll come bleatin' to your boot heels.
Ibid. Chap. 2
As the day wears and the impetus of
the morning dies away, there will come
upon you an overwhelming sense of the
uselessness of your toil. This must be
striven against.
The Judgment of Dungara

Hot and bothered.
Independence [1]
If you have not your own rations you
must feed out of your Tribe's hands —
with all that that implies.
Ibid.
A man may be festooned with the
whole haberdashery of success, and go
to his grave a castaway.
Ibid.
Enough work to do, and strength
enough to do the work.
A Doctor's Work [2]
That packet of assorted miseries
which we call a Ship.
The First Sailor
Never again will I spend another
winter in this accursed bucket-shop of
a refrigerator called England.
Letter to Sidney Colvin [3]
For all we have and are,
For all our children's fate,
Stand up and take the war.
The Hun is at the gate!
"For All We Have and Are"
[1914]. Stanza 1
There is but one task for all —
One life for each to give.
What stands if Freedom fall?
Who dies if England live?
Ibid. Stanza 4
He became an officer *and* a gentle-
man, which is an enviable thing.
Only a Subaltern
Tea fights. [4]
Ibid.
An imperfectly denatured animal in-
termittently subject to the unpredicta-
ble reactions of an unlocated spiritual
area.
Surgeons and the Soul [1923]
(Definition of man)
I taught Turkey all he ever knew of
French, and he tried to make Stalky

[1] Rectorial Address, St. Andrew's, October
10, 1923.
[2] Address, October, 1908, at Middlesex Hospital (where Kipling died in 1936).
[3] Quoted by E. V. LUCAS: *The Colvins and
Their Friends* [1928], P. 294.
[4] Giggle, gabble, gobble, git. — OLIVER
WENDELL HOLMES [1809–1894], *description
of a tea party*

and me comprehend a little Latin.
There is much to be said for this system,
if you want a boy to learn anything,
because he will remember what he gets
from an equal where his master's words
are forgotten.
> *Something of Myself for My*
> *Friends Known and Unknown*
> [*1937*]. *Chap. 2.*

When your Daemon is in charge, do
not try to think consciously. Drift,
wait, and obey.
> *Ibid. Chap. 8*

If I have given you delight
By aught that I have done,
Let me lie quiet in that night
Which shall be yours anon.
> *The Appeal.*[1] *Stanza 1*

ERICH FRIEDRICH WILHELM LUDENDORFF
[1865–1937]

I decline Christianity because it
is Jewish, because it is international
and because, in cowardly fashion, it
preaches Peace on Earth.
> *Deutsche Gottesglaube*

MORGAN SHEPARD ("JOHN MARTIN")
[1865–1947]

Perhaps I ain't relijus,
But when I say a prayer,
I sort er feel inside er me
That God is always there.
> *Relijus. Stanza 1*

LOGAN PEARSALL SMITH [2]
[1865–1946]

What a bore it is, waking up in the
morning always the same person. I wish

---

[1] Final poem in the Definitive Edition of
Rudyard Kipling's Verse [1940].
[2] Two weeks before his death, a friend asked
him half jokingly if he had discovered any
meaning in life. "Yes," he replied, "there is
a meaning; at least, for me, there is one thing
that matters — to set a chime of words tinkling in the minds of a few fastidious people."
— CYRIL CONNOLLY [1903–   ]: *A Tribute
to Logan Pearsall Smith,* in *The New Statesman and Nation*

I were unflinching and emphatic, and
had big, bushy eyebrows and a Message for the Age. I wish I were a deep
Thinker, or a great Ventriloquist.
> *Trivia [1902]. Green Ivory*

But when in modern books, reviews,
and thoughtful magazines I read about
the Needs of the Age, its Complex
Questions, its Dismays, Doubts, and
Spiritual Agonies, I feel an impulse to
go out and comfort that bewildered
Epoch, to wipe away its tears, still its
cries, and speak edifying words of Consolation to it.
> *Ibid. My Mission*

The minds of all of us are haunted
by thoughts which have not yet found
expression, and it is often the happy
fortune of the aphorist to drag from
its obscurity some such dim intuition,
or confused bit of experience; to clothe
it in words and bring it into daylight
for our delighted recognition.
> *A Treasury of English Aphorisms*
> [*1928*]. *Introduction*

There are two things to aim at in life:
first, to get what you want; and, after
that, to enjoy it. Only the wisest of
mankind achieve the second.
> *Afterthoughts [1931]*

Happiness is a wine of the rarest
vintage, and seems insipid to a vulgar
taste.
> *Ibid.*

How awful to reflect that what people say of us is true!
> *Ibid.*

Solvency is entirely a matter of temperament and not of income.
> *Ibid.*

That we should practise what we
preach is generally admitted; but anyone who preaches what he and his hearers practise must incur the gravest
moral disapprobation.
> *Ibid.*

It is almost always worth while to
be cheated; people's little frauds have
an interest which more than repays
what they cost us.
> *Ibid.*

Why are happy people not afraid of Death, while the insatiable and the unhappy so abhor that grim feature?

Afterthoughts

When they come downstairs from their Ivory Towers, Idealists are apt to walk straight into the gutter.

Ibid.

The indefatigable pursuit of an unattainable Perfection, even though it consist in nothing more than in the pounding of an old piano, is what alone gives a meaning to our life on this unavailing star.

Ibid.

Eat with the Rich, but go to the play with the Poor, who are capable of Joy.

Ibid.

We need new friends; some of us are cannibals who have eaten their old friends up: others must have everrenewed audiences before whom to reenact an ideal version of their lives.

Ibid.

A best-seller is the gilded tomb of a mediocre talent.

Ibid.

What I like in a good author is not what he says, but what he whispers.

Ibid.

People say that life is the thing, but I prefer reading.

Ibid.

Most of all I envy the octogenarian poet [1] who joined three words —
"Go, lovely Rose" —
so happily together, that he left his name to float down through Time on the wings of a phrase and a flower.

Ibid.

Thank heavens, the sun has gone in, and I don't have to go out and enjoy it.

Ibid.

What with its crude awakenings can youth know of the rich returns of awareness to elderly people from their afternoon naps; of their ironic thoughts and long retrospections, and the sweetness they taste of not being dead?

Ibid.

[1] Edmund Waller [1606–1687]. See page 242a.

How I should like to distil my disesteem of my contemporaries into prose so perfect that all of them would have to read it!

Afterthoughts

ARTHUR SYMONS
[1865–1945]

And I would have, now love is over,
An end to all, an end:
I cannot, having been your lover,
Stoop to become your friend!

After Love. Stanza 3

Life is a dream in the night, a fear among fears,
A naked runner lost in a storm of spears.

In the Wood of Finvara. Stanza 1

I broider the world upon a loom,
I broider with dreams my tapestry;
Here in a little lonely room
I am master of earth and sea,
And the planets come to me.

The Loom of Dreams. Stanza 1

He knew that the whole mystery of beauty can never be comprehended by the crowd, and that while clearness is a virtue of style, perfect explicitness is not a necessary virtue.

The Symbolist Movement in Literature [1899]. Gérard de Nerval

Without charm there can be no fine literature, as there can be no perfect flower without fragrance.

Ibid. Stéphane Mallarmé

The mystic too full of God to speak intelligibly to the world.

Ibid. Arthur Rimbaud

Many excellent writers, very many painters, and most musicians are so tedious on any subject but their own.

Ibid.

Criticism is properly the rod of divination: a hazel-switch for the discovery of buried treasure, not a birch-twig for the castigation of offenders.

An Introduction to the Study of Browning [1906]. Preface

The great things in poetry are song at the core, but externally mere speech.
Dramatis Personae [*1923*].
Sir William Watson

HERBERT TRENCH
[1865–1923]

A circumnavigator of the soul.
Shakespeare. Stanza 4

WILLIAM BUTLER YEATS
[1865–1939]

Down by the salley gardens my love and I did meet;
She passed the salley gardens with little snow-white feet.
She bid me take love easy, as the leaves grow on the tree;
But I, being young and foolish, with her would not agree.
Down by the Salley Gardens [*1889*]
She bid me take life easy, as the grass grows on the weirs;
But I was young and foolish, and now am full of tears.
Ibid.
The years like great black oxen tread the world
And God, the herdsman, goads them on behind.
The Countess Cathleen [*1892*]
Red Rose, proud Rose, sad Rose of all my days!
Come near me, while I sing the ancient ways.
To the Rose Upon the Rood of Time [*1893*]. *Stanza 1*
I find under the boughs of love and hate,
In all poor foolish things that live a day,
Eternal beauty wandering on her way.
Ibid.
When you are old and grey and full of sleep,
And nodding by the fire, take down this book.[1]
When You Are Old [*1893*]
How many loved your moments of glad grace,

[1] See Ronsard, page 96b.

And loved your beauty, with love false or true,
But one man loved the pilgrim soul in you,
And loved the sorrows of your changing face.
When You Are Old
I will arise and go now, and go to Innisfree,
And a small cabin build there, of clay and wattles made:
Nine bean-rows will I have there, a hive for the honeybee,
And live alone in the bee-loud glade.
The Lake Isle of Innisfree [1] [*1893*].
Stanza 1
And I shall have some peace there, for peace comes dropping slow,
Dropping from the veils of the morning to where the cricket sings;
There midnight's all a glimmer, and noon a purple glow,
And evening full of the linnet's wings.
Ibid. Stanza 2
I hear it in the deep heart's core.
Ibid. Stanza 3
A pity beyond all telling
Is hid in the heart of love.
The Pity of Love [*1893*]
The brawling of a sparrow in the eaves,
The brilliant moon and all the milky sky,
And all that famous harmony of leaves,
Had blotted out man's image and his cry.

A girl arose that had red mournful lips
And seemed the greatness of the world in tears,
Doomed like Odysseus and the labouring ships
And proud as Priam murdered with his peers;

[1] I had still the ambition, formed in Sligo in my teens, of living in imitation of Thoreau on Innisfree, a little island in Lough Gill, and when walking through Fleet Street very homesick I heard a little tinkle of water and saw a fountain in a shop-window which balanced a little ball upon its jet, and began to remember lake water. From the sudden remembrance came my poem Innisfree. — *The Trembling of the Veil* (autobiography) [*1926*]
See Samuel Rogers, page 396b.

Arose, and on the instant clamorous
  eaves,
A climbing moon upon an empty sky,
And all that lamentation of the leaves,
Could but compose man's image and
  his cry.
  The Sorrow of Love [*1893*]
The land of faery,
Where nobody gets old and godly and
  grave,
Where nobody gets old and crafty and
  wise,
Where nobody gets old and bitter of
  tongue.
  The Land of Heart's Desire [*1894*]
When we are young
We long to tread a way none trod be-
  fore,
But find the excellent old way through
  love
And through the care of children to the
  hour
For bidding Fate and Time and Change
  good-bye.
                              Ibid.
I would mould a world of fire and dew
With no one bitter, grave, or over wise,
And nothing marred or old to do you
  wrong.
                              Ibid.
  Land of Heart's Desire,
Where beauty has no ebb, decay no
  flood,
But joy is wisdom, Time an endless
  song.
                              Ibid.
Though I am old with wandering
Through hollow lands and hilly lands,
I will find out where she has gone,
And kiss her lips and take her hands;
And walk among long dappled grass,
And pluck till time and times are done
The silver apples of the moon,
The golden apples of the sun.
  The Song of Wandering Aengus
                [*1899*]. *Stanza 3*
All things uncomely and broken, all
  things worn out and old,
The cry of a child by the roadway, the
  creak of a lumbering cart,
The heavy steps of the ploughman,
  splashing the wintry mould,

Are wronging your image that blossoms
  a rose in the deeps of my heart.
  *The Lover Tells of the Rose in
    His Heart* [*1899*]. *Stanza 1*
The wrong of unshapely things is a
  wrong too great to be told.
                    Ibid. Stanza 2
Had I the heavens' embroidered cloths,
Enwrought with gold and silver light.
  *He Wishes for the Cloths of
              Heaven* [*1899*]
But I, being poor, have only my
  dreams;
I have spread my dreams under your
  feet;
Tread softly because you tread on my
  dreams.
                              Ibid.
When I play on my fiddle in Dooney,
Folk dance like a wave of the sea.
  The Fiddler of Dooney [*1899*].
                             Stanza 1
For the good are always the merry,
Save by an evil chance,
And the merry love the fiddle,
And the merry love to dance.
                    Ibid. Stanza 4
O heart! O heart! if she'd but turn her
  head,
You'd know the folly of being com-
  forted.
  The Folly of Being Comforted
                            [*1904*]
Never give all the heart, for love
Will hardly seem worth thinking of
To passionate women if it seem
Certain, and they never dream
That it fades out from kiss to kiss.
  Never Give All the Heart [*1904*]
I heard the old, old men say,
"All that's beautiful drifts away
Like the waters."
  *The Old Men Admiring Them-
    selves in the Water* [*1904*]
Why, what could she have done, being
  what she is?
Was there another Troy for her to
  burn?
        No Second Troy [*1910*]
The fascination of what's difficult
Has dried the sap out of my veins, and
  rent

Spontaneous joy and natural content
Out of my heart.
> *The Fascination of What's*
> *Difficult* [*1910*]

Wine comes in at the mouth
And love comes in at the eye;
That's all we shall know for truth
Before we grow old and die.
> *A Drinking Song* [*1910*]

Though leaves are many, the root is
one;
Through all the lying days of my youth
I swayed my leaves and flowers in the
sun;
Now I may wither into the truth.
> *The Coming of Wisdom with Time*
> [*1910*]

Be secret and exult,
Because of all things known
That is most difficult.
> *To a Friend Whose Work Has*
> *Come to Nothing* [*1914*]

I made my song a coat
Covered with embroideries
Out of old mythologies
From heel to throat;
But the fools caught it,
Wore it in the world's eyes
As though they'd wrought it.
Song, let them take it,
For there's more enterprise
In walking naked.
> *A Coat* [*1914*]

I know that I shall meet my fate
Somewhere among the clouds above;
Those that I fight I do not hate,
Those that I guard I do not love;
My country is Kiltartan Cross,
My countrymen Kiltartan's poor.
> *An Irish Airman Foresees His*
> *Death* [*1919*]

Nor law, nor duty bade me fight,
Nor public men, nor cheering crowds,
A lonely impulse of delight
Drove to this tumult in the clouds;
I balanced all, brought all to mind,
The years to come seemed waste of
breath,
A waste of breath the years behind
In balance with this life, this death.
> *Ibid.*

All the wild witches, those most noble
ladies,
For all their broom-sticks and their
tears,
Their angry tears, are gone.
> *Lines Written in Dejection* [*1919*]

I mourn for that most lonely thing; and
yet God's will be done:
I knew a phoenix in my youth, so let
them have their day.
> *His Phoenix* [*1919*]. *Stanza 4*

We have lit upon the gentle, sensitive
mind
And lost the old nonchalance of the
hand;
Whether we have chosen chisel, pen or
brush,
We are but critics, or but half create.
> *Ego Dominus Tuus* [*1919*]

All changed, changed utterly:
A terrible beauty is born.
> *Easter 1916* [*1921*]

Nothing that we love over-much
Is ponderable to our touch.
> *Towards Break of Day* [*1921*].
> *Stanza 3*

The blood-dimmed tide is loosed, and
everywhere
The ceremony of innocence is drowned;
The best lack all conviction, while the
worst
Are full of passionate intensity.
> *The Second Coming* [*1921*]

And what rough beast, its hour come
round at last,
Slouches towards Bethlehem to be
born?
> *Ibid.*

For such,
Being made beautiful overmuch,
Consider beauty a sufficient end,
Lose natural kindness and maybe
The heart-revealing intimacy
That chooses right, and never find a
friend.
> *A Prayer for My Daughter*
> [*1921*]. *Stanza 3*

If there's no hatred in a mind
Assault and battery of the wind
Can never tear the linnet from the leaf.
> *Ibid. Stanza 7*

An intellectual hatred is the worst,
So let her think opinions are accursed.
A Prayer for My Daughter. Stanza 8

A musician who would give me pleasure should not repeat a line, or put more than one note to a syllable. I am a poet not a musician, and dislike to have my words distorted or their animation destroyed, even though the musician claims to have expressed their meaning in a different medium.
A Note on the Setting of These Poems to Music [1922]

An aged man is but a paltry thing,
A tattered coat upon a stick, unless
Soul clap its hands and sing.
Sailing to Byzantium [1928]. Stanza 2

Consume my heart away; sick with desire
And fastened to a dying animal
It knows not what it is; and gather me
Into the artifice of eternity.
Ibid. Stanza 3

Once out of nature I shall never take
My bodily form from any natural thing,
But such a form as Grecian goldsmiths make
Of hammered gold and gold enamelling
To keep a drowsy Emperor awake;
Or set upon a golden bough to sing
To lords and ladies of Byzantium
Of what is past, or passing, or to come.[1]
Ibid. Stanza 4

Does the imagination dwell the most
Upon a woman won or a woman lost?
The Tower [1928]. II, Stanza 13

Much did I rage when young,
Being by the world oppressed,
But now with flattering tongue
It speeds the parting guest.
Youth and Age [1928]

Everything that man esteems
Endures a moment or a day.
Love's pleasure drives his love away,

----

[1] I have read somewhere that in the Emperor's palace at Byzantium was a tree made of gold and silver, and artificial birds that sang. — YEATS's *Note*

The painter's brush consumes his dreams.
Two Songs From a Play [1928]. II, Stanza 2

But what is Whiggery?
A levelling, rancorous, rational sort of mind
That never looked out of the eye of a saint
Or out of a drunkard's eye.
The Seven Sages [1933]

No man has ever lived that had enough
Of children's gratitude or woman's love.
Vacillation [1933]. Stanza 3

What were all the world's alarms
To mighty Paris when he found
Sleep upon a golden bed
That first dawn in Helen's arms?
Words for Music Perhaps [1933]. Lullaby, Stanza 1

Speech after long silence; it is right,
All other lovers being estranged or dead,

.   .   .   .   .

That we descant and yet again descant
Upon the supreme theme of Art and Song:
Bodily decrepitude is wisdom; young
We loved each other and were ignorant.
Ibid. After Long Silence

I carry the sun in a golden cup,
The moon in a silver bag.
Ibid. Those Dancing Days Are Gone, Refrain

I gave what other women gave
That stepped out of their clothes,
But when this soul, its body off,
Naked to naked goes,
He it has found shall find therein
What none other knows.
A Woman Young and Old [1933]. A Last Confession, Stanza 3

He that sings a lasting song
Thinks in a marrow-bone.
A Prayer for Old Age [1935]. Stanza 1

I pray — for fashion's word is out
And prayer comes round again —
That I may seem, though I die old,
A foolish, passionate man.
Ibid. Stanza 3

Irish poets, learn your trade,
Sing whatever is well made.
Last Poems [1936–1939].
Under Ben Bulben, V
On limestone quarried near the spot
By his command these words are cut:
Cast a cold eye
On life, on death.
Horseman, pass by! [1]
Ibid. VI

HARRY DACRE
[*Floruit* 1892]

Daisy, Daisy, give me your answer, do!
I'm half crazy, all for the love of you!
It won't be a stylish marriage,
I can't afford a carriage,
But you'll look sweet upon the seat
Of a bicycle built for two!
Daisy Bell [1892]

HENRY J. SAYERS
[? –1932]

Ta-ra-ra-boom-de-ay!
Title of minstrel show number
[1891], made famous by Lottie
Collins in 1892 [2]
A sweet Tuxedo girl you see,
Queen of swell society,
Fond of fun as fond can be
When it's on the strict Q. T.
I'm not too young, I'm not too old,
Not too timid, not too bold,
Just the kind you'd like to hold —
Just the kind for sport I'm told —
Ta-ra-ra-boom-de-ay.
Ibid. Stanza 1 of original version

GEORGE W. YOUNG
[*Floruit* 1900]

The word must be spoken that bids you
depart —
Though the effort to speak it should
shatter my heart —

[1] These lines are now inscribed on Yeats's
grave.
[2] Douglas Gilbert, in *Lost Chords* [1942],
quotes the *New York Herald*: "London has
gone stark mad over the refrain" [February
28, 1892].

Though in silence, with blighted affec-
tion, I pine,
Yet the lips that touch liquor must
never touch mine!
The Lips That Touch Liquor.
Stanza 5

GEORGE ADE [1]
[1866–1944]

A good folly is worth what you pay
for it.
Fables in Slang [1899]. A Lot
for Three Dollars

In uplifting, get underneath.
Ibid. The Good Fairy

He had been kicked in the Head by
a Mule when young and believed everything he read in the Sunday Papers.
Ibid. The Slim Girl

Only the more rugged mortals should
attempt to keep up with current literature.
Ibid. Didn't Care for Story-books

Never put off until Tomorrow what
should have been Done early in the
Seventies.
Forty Modern Fables [1901].
The Third and Last Call

To insure Peace of Mind ignore the
Rules and Regulations.
Ibid. The Crustacean

If it were not for the Presents, an
Elopement would be Preferable.
Ibid. The General Manager of
the Love Affair

Stay with the Procession or you will
Never Catch up.
Ibid. The Old-Time Pedagogue

The Time to enjoy a European trip
is about Three Weeks after Unpacking.
Ibid. The Hungry Man

Draw your Salary before Spending it.
Ibid. The People's Choice

[1] Somehow I always like to think
Of *Georgeade* as a Summer Drink,
Sparkling and cool, with just a Tang
Of Pleasant Effervescent Slang.
OLIVER HERFORD [1863–1935]:
Celebrities I Have Never Met

The Man was a Pinhead in a good
many Respects, but he was Wise as a
Serpent.
> *Forty Modern Fables. The*
> *Wise Piker*

For Parlor Use the Vague Generality
is a Life-Saver.
> *Ibid.*

Last night at twelve I felt immense,
But now I feel like thirty cents.
> *The Sultan of Sulu* [*1902*]. *Remorse*

But, R – e – m – o – r – s – e!
The water-wagon is the place for me;
It is no time for mirth and laughter,
The cold, gray dawn of the morning
after! [1]
> *Ibid.*

MARTIIA GILBERT
DICKINSON BIANCHI [2]
[1866–1943]

Deeper than chords that search the
soul and die,
Mocking to ashes color's hot array, —
Closer than touch, — within our hearts
they lie
The words we do not say.
> *The Words We Do Not Say*

HENRY BLOSSOM
[1866–1919]

I Want What I Want When I Want
It.
> *Mlle. Modiste* [*1905*]. *Title of song*

GELETT BURGESS
[1866–1951]

I'd rather have Fingers than Toes,
I'd rather have Eyes than a Nose;
  And as for my Hair
  I'm glad it's all there,
I'll be awfully sad when it goes.
> *Nonsense Verses*

Leave the lady, Willy, let the racket rip,
She is going to fool you, you have lost
  your grip,

[1] See Byron, page 458a, and Dickens, page
577a.
[2] Niece of Emily Dickinson.

Your brain is in a muddle, and your
  heart is in a whirl,
Come along with me, Willy, never mind
  the girl!
> *Willy and the Lady. Stanza 1*

I never saw a Purple Cow,
  I never hope to see one;
But I can tell you, anyhow,
  I'd rather see than be one.
> *The Purple Cow* [*1895*]

Ah, yes, I wrote the "Purple Cow" —
  I'm sorry, now, I wrote it!
But I can tell you, anyhow,
  I'll kill you if you quote it.
> *Cinq Ans Après*

Not the quarry, but the chase,
Not the laurel, but the race,
Not the hazard, but the play,
Make me, Lord, enjoy alway.
> *A Prayer*

EDMUND VANCE COOKE
[1866–1932]

The Woman tempted me — and tempts
  me still!
Lord God, I pray You that she ever
  will!
> *Adam*

'Tis not the weight of jewel or plate,
  Or the fondle of silk and fur;
'Tis the spirit in which the gift is rich,
  As the gifts of the wise ones were;
And we are not told whose gift was gold
Or whose was the gift of myrrh.
> *The Spirit of the Gift*

Oh, a trouble's a ton, or a trouble's an
  ounce,
  Or a trouble is what you make it,
And it isn't the fact that you're hurt
  that counts,
But only how did you take it.
> *How Did You Die? Stanza 1*

My pa held me up to the moo-cow-moo,
  So clost I could almost touch,
En' I fed him a couple of times or two,
En' I wasn't a fraid-cat — much.
> *The Moo-Cow-Moo. Stanza 1*

PHILANDER JOHNSON
[1866–1939]

Sometimes the new friends
  Leave the heart aglow,
But it's when they're like the men
  We cherished long ago.
                    Old Friends. Stanza 2

Cheer up, the worst is yet to come.[1]
                    Shooting Stars

RICHARD LE GALLIENNE
[1866–1947]

There's too much beauty upon this
    earth
For lonely men to bear.
        A Ballad of Too Much Beauty.
                    Stanza 1

One asked of Regret,
  And I made reply:
To have held the bird,
  And let it fly.
                    Regret

Shadow and sun — so too our lives are
    made —
Here learn how great the sun, how
    small the shade!
                    For Sundials

May is building her house. With apple
    blooms
She is roofing over the glimmering
    rooms.
        May Is Building Her House.
                    Stanza 1

Behind the times I know I am,
But what is a tired man to do?
I light my pipe, and read Charles Lamb.
        Ballade of the Noisiness of the
                    Times. Stanza 1

Ah London! London! our delight,
Great flower that opens but at night.
                    A Ballad of London

Yet all the while my Lord I meet
In every London lane and street.
                    The Second Crucifixion

"Name your favorite writer" should
be one of the first questions in the Engagement Catechism.
        The Quest of the Golden Girl
                    [1896]. Book II, Chap. 6

———
[1] See Tennyson, page 555b.

Wild oats will get sown some time,
and one of the arts of life is to sow them
at the right time.
        The Quest of the Golden Girl.
                    Book III, Chap. 9

WALTER MALONE
[1866–1915]

They do me wrong who say I come no
    more
When once I knock and fail to find you
    in;
For every day I stand outside your
    door,
And bid you wake, and rise to fight and
    win.
                    Opportunity. Stanza 1

And if a lowly singer dries one tear,
Or soothes one humble human heart
    in pain,
Be sure his homely verse to God is dear,
And not one stanza has been sung in
    vain.
                    The Humbler Poets. Stanza 3

THOMAS L. MASSON
[1866–1934]

Obey That Impulse.
        Subscription slogan for "Life," of
        which he was editor, 1893–1922

A Safe and Sane Fourth.
                    Slogan

GEORGE BARR McCUTCHEON
[1866–1928]

"You brute!" hissed the Countess.
        Graustark [1901]. Chap. 16

GILBERT MURRAY
[1866–   ]

Romantic plays with happy endings
are almost of necessity inferior in artistic value to true tragedies. Not, one
would hope, simply because they end
happily; happiness in itself is certainly
not less beautiful than grief; but because a tragedy in its great moments
can generally afford to be sincere, while

romantic plays live in an atmosphere of ingenuity and make-believe.

> *Preface to the Iphigenia in Tauris of Euripides*

The life and liberty and property and happiness of the common man throughout the world are at the absolute mercy of a few persons whom he has never seen, involved in complicated quarrels that he has never heard of.

> *The League of Nations and the Democratic Idea [1921]*

JOHN JEROME ROONEY
[1866–1934]

The steel decks rock with the lightning shock, and shake with the great recoil,
And the sea grows red with the blood of the dead and reaches for his spoil —
But not till the foe has gone below or turns his prow and runs,
Shall the voice of peace bring sweet release to the men behind the guns!

> *The Men Behind the Guns. Stanza 4*

LINCOLN STEFFENS
[1866–1936]

"So you've been over into Russia?" said Bernard Baruch, and I answered very literally, "I have been over into the future, and it works."[1]

> *Autobiography [1931]. Chap. 18*

BERT LESTON TAYLOR
[1866–1921]

When quacks with pills political would dope us,
When politics absorbs the livelong day,
I like to think about the star Canopus,
So far, so far away!

> *Canopus. Stanza 1*

These scoffers, these obstructionists,
These fossils — who are they?

[1] On Steffens's return from the Bullitt mission, 1919.

The glad young, mad young futurists
Who prance around today.

> *So Shall It Be. Stanza 6*

Everywhere I look I see —
Fact or fiction, life or play,
Still the little game of Three:
B and C in love with A.

> *Old Stuff. Stanza 3*

And when the fragrant day is done,
Night — and a shoal of stars.

> *The Road to Anywhere. Stanza 5*

HERBERT GEORGE WELLS
[1866–1946]

The past is but the beginning of a beginning, and all that is and has been is but the twilight of the dawn. . . . A day will come when beings who are now latent in our thoughts and hidden in our loins shall stand upon this earth as one stands upon a footstool, and shall laugh and reach out their hands amid the stars.

> *The Discovery of the Future [1901]*

Nothing could have been more obvious to the people of the early twentieth century than the rapidity with which war was becoming impossible. And as certainly they did not see it. They did not see it until the atomic bombs burst in their fumbling hands.

> *The World Set Free [1914]*

The catastrophe of the atomic bombs which shook men out of cities and businesses and economic relations, shook them also out of their old-established habits of thought, and out of the lightly held beliefs and prejudices that came down to them from the past.

> *Ibid.*

Human history becomes more and more a race between education and catastrophe.

> *The Outline of History [1920]. Chap. 15*

The professional military mind is by necessity an inferior and unimaginative mind; no man of high intellectual quality would willingly imprison his gifts in such a calling.

The Outline of History. Chap. 40
The Great War and the Petty Peace.
Ibid.

Human history is in essence a history of ideas.
Ibid.

Every one of these hundreds of millions of human beings is in some form seeking happiness. . . . Not one is altogether noble nor altogether trustworthy nor altogether consistent; and not one is altogether vile. Not a single one but has at some time wept.
Ibid.

A federation of all humanity, together with a sufficient measure of social justice to ensure health, education, and a rough equality of opportunity, would mean such a release and increase of human energy as to open a new phase in human history.
Ibid. Chap. 41
Our true nationality is mankind.
Ibid.

An artist who theorizes about his work is no longer artist but critic.
The Temptation of Harringay
While the poor little affairs of obscure, industrious men of letters are made the subject of intensive research, the far more romantic, thrilling and illuminating documents about the seekers and makers of great fortunes, are neither gathered nor cherished.
The Work, Wealth and Happiness of Mankind [*1931*]. *Chap. 10*
In England we have come to rely upon a comfortable time-lag of fifty years or a century intervening between the perception that something ought to be done and a serious attempt to do it.
Ibid. Chap. 11
The Shape of Things to Come.[1]
Title of Book [*1933*]
The crazy combative patriotism that plainly threatens to destroy civilization

[1] The baby figure of the giant mass
Of things to come.
SHAKESPEARE: *Troilus and Cressida*
[1601–1603], *Act I, Sc. 3, L. 345*

is very largely begotten by the schoolmaster and the schoolmistress in their history lessons. They take the growing mind at a naturally barbaric phase and they inflame and fix its barbarism.
The Informative Content of Education [*1937*]

STANLEY BALDWIN
[1867–1947]

When you think about the defence of England you no longer think of the chalk cliffs of Dover. You think of the Rhine. That is where our frontier lies today.
Speech in the House of Commons
[*July 30, 1934*]

ENOCH ARNOLD BENNETT
[1867–1931]

The Old Wives' Tale.[1]
Title of novel [*1908*]
Being a husband is a whole-time job.
The Title [*1918*]. *Act I*
Pessimism, when you get used to it, is just as agreeable as optimism.
Things That Have Interested Me
[*1918*]
The price of justice is eternal publicity.
Ibid. Second Series [*1923*]

ROSCOE CONKLING ENSIGN BROWN
[1867–1946]

With equal care weigh well the record of the wisdom and the folly of mankind.
Inscription for the wall of the Central Library, Brooklyn
Farther than the arrow, higher than wings, fly poet's song and prophet's word.
Inscription for a door of the Library

[1] A fool he is to believe the tales of an old wife. — ALEXANDER BARCLAY: *The Ship of Fools* [1508]
Old wives' foolish tales of Robin Hood. — NICHOLAS UDALL [1542]

WILLIAM CECIL DAMPIER-WHETHAM
[1867–1952]

Beyond the bright searchlights of science,
Out of sight of the windows of sense,
Old riddles still bid us defiance,
Old questions of Why and of Whence.
The Recent Development of
Physical Science [1904]

ERNEST DOWSON
[1867–1900]

They are not long, the weeping and
the laughter,
Love and desire and hate:
I think they have no portion in us
after
We pass the gate.
Vitae Summa Brevis [1896].
Stanza 1

I have been faithful to thee, Cynara!
in my fashion.
Non Sum Qualis Eram Bonae Sub
Regno Cynarae [1] [1896]. *Refrain*

I have forgot much, Cynara! gone with
the wind,
Flung roses, roses, riotously with the
throng.
Ibid. Stanza 3

I cried for madder music and for
stronger wine.
Ibid. Stanza 4

You would have understood me, had
you waited;
I could have loved you, dear! as well
as he:
Had we not been impatient, dear! and
fated
Always to disagree.
You Would Have Understood
Me [1896]. *Stanza 1*

What is the use of speech? Silence were
fitter:
Lest we should still be wishing things
unsaid.
Ibid. Stanza 2

[1] I am not the man I was under the reign
of the good Cynara. — HORACE [65–8 B. C.]
Book IV, Ode 1, Ad Venerem

From troublous sights and sounds set
free;
In such a twilight hour of breath,
Shall one retrace his life, or see,
Through shadows, the true face of
death?
Extreme Unction. Stanza 3

FINLEY PETER DUNNE
("MR. DOOLEY")
[1867–1936]

An Anglo-Saxon, Hinnissy, is a German that's forgot who was his parents.
. . . I'm wan iv th' hottest Anglo-
Saxons that iver come out iv Anglo-
Saxony.
Mr. Dooley in Peace and in War
[1898]. On the Anglo-Saxon

Life'd not be worth livin' if we didn't
keep our inimies.
Ibid. On New Year's Resolutions

Whin th' case is all over, the jury'll
pitch th' tistimony out iv the window,
an' consider three questions: "Did Loot-
gert look as though he'd kill his wife?
Did his wife look as though she ought
to be kilt? Isn't it time we wint to supper?"
Ibid. On Expert Testimony

Th' dead ar-re always pop'lar. I
knowed a society wanst to vote a mon-
yment to a man an' refuse to help his
fam'ly, all in wan night.
Ibid. On Charity

"Th' American nation in th' Sixth
Ward is a fine people," he says. "They
love th' eagle," he says, "on th' back
iv a dollar."
Ibid. On Oratory in Politics

'Tis . . . "Hands acrost th' sea an'
into some wan's pocket," an' "Take up
th' white man's burden an' hand it to
th' coons," an' "An open back dure an'
a closed fr-ront dure."
Mr. Dooley in the Hearts of His
Countrymen [1899]. The De-
cline of National Feeling

"I think," said Mr. Dooley, "that if
th' Christyan Scientists had some
science an' th' doctors more Christianity, it wudden't make anny diff'rence

which ye called in — if ye had a good nurse."

Mr. Dooley's Opinions [*1900*].
Christian Science

No matther whether th' constitution follows th' flag or not, th' supreme coort follows th' iliction returns.

Ibid. The Supreme Court's Decisions

In me younger days 't was not considhered rayspictable f'r to be an athlete. An athlete was always a man that was not sthrong enough f'r wurruk. Fractions dhruv him fr'm school an' th' vagrancy laws dhruv him to baseball.

Ibid. On Athletics

I think a lie with a purpose is wan iv th' worst kind an' th' mos' profitable.

Ibid. On Lying

Th' dimmycratic party ain't on speakin' terms with itsilf.

Ibid. Mr. Dooley Discusses Party Politics

Th' raypublican party broke ye, but now that ye're down we'll not turn a cold shoulder to ye. Come in an' we'll keep ye — broke.

Ibid.

Hogan's r-right whin he says: "Justice is blind." Blind she is, an' deef an' dumb an' has a wooden leg.

Ibid. Cross-Examinations

No wan cares to hear what Hogan calls: "Th' short an' simple scandals iv th' poor."

Ibid.

'Twas founded be th' Puritans to give thanks f'r bein' presarved fr'm th' Indyans, an' . . . we keep it to give thanks we are presarved fr'm th' Puritans.

Ibid. Thanksgiving

Vice . . . is a creature of such heejous mien . . . that th' more ye see it th' betther ye like it.

Ibid. The Crusade Against Vice

Glory be, whin business gets above sellin' tinpinny nails in a brown paper cornucopy, 't is hard to tell it fr'm murther.

Ibid. On Wall Street

Degrees is good things because they livils all ranks.

Mr. Dooley's Opinions.
Colleges and Degrees

"D' ye think th' colledges has much to do with th' progress iv th' wurruld?" asked Mr. Hennessy.

"D'ye think," said Mr. Dooley, " 'tis th' mill that makes th' wather run?"

Ibid.

'Tis "Th' Biography iv a Hero be Wan who Knows." [1] 'Tis "Th' Darin' Exploits iv a Brave Man be an Actual Eye Witness." 'Tis "Th' Account iv th' Desthruction iv Spanish Power in th' Ant Hills," as it fell fr'm th' lips iv Tiddy Rosenfelt an' was took down be his own hands. . . . But if I was him I'd call th' book "Alone in Cubia."

Mr. Dooley's Philosophy [*1900*].
A Book Review

A war expert . . . is a man ye niver heerd iv befure. If ye can think iv annywan whose face is onfamilyar to ye an' ye don't raymimber his name, an' he's got a job on a pa-aper ye didn't know was published, he's a war expert.

Ibid. The War Expert

Th' enthusyasm iv this counthry, Hinnissy, always makes me think iv a bonfire on an ice-floe. It burns bright so long as ye feed it, an' it looks good, but it don't take hold, somehow, on th' ice.

Ibid. The Boer Mission

" 'Twill civilize th' Chinnymen," said Mr. Hennessy.

" 'Twill civilize thim stiff," said Mr. Dooley.

Ibid. The Future of China (*On German intervention in China*)

"Me dear boy, what special branch iv larnin' wud ye like to have studied f'r ye be our compitint profissors?"

Ibid. The Education of the Young (*A college president to a prospective student*)

If ye live enough befure thirty ye won't care to live at all afther fifty.

Ibid. Casual Observations

[1] Theodore Roosevelt's *The Rough Riders* [1899].

Among men, Hinnissy, wet eye manes dhry heart.

Mr. Dooley's Philosophy.
Casual Observations

A fanatic is a man that does what he thinks th' Lord wud do if He knew th' facts iv th' case.

Ibid.

A vote on th' tallysheet is worth two in the box.

Ibid.

I care not who makes th' laws iv a nation if I can get out an injunction.

Ibid.

'Tis as hard f'r a rich man to enther th' kingdom iv Hiven as it is f'r a poor man to get out iv Purgatory.

Ibid.

Thrust ivrybody — but cut th' ca-ards.

Ibid.

A man that'd expict to thrain lobsters to fly in a year is called a loonytic; but a man that thinks men can be tu-rrned into angels be an iliction is called a rayformer an' remains at large.

Ibid.

Miracles are laughed at be a nation that r-reads thirty millyon newspapers a day an' supports Wall sthreet.

Ibid.

Th' higher up a coort is, the less [the judges] see iv each other. Their office hours are fr'm a quarther to wan leap years. Ye take a lively lawyer that's wurruked twinty hours a day suin' sthreet railrood comp'nies an' boost him onto a high coort an' he can't think out iv a hammock. Th' more exalted . . . th' joodicyal station, th' more it's like a dormitory.

Observations by Mr. Dooley
[1902]. The Law's Delays

Unforchunitly diplomacy on'y goes as far as the dure. It is onable to give protection to th' customer, so whin he laves th' shop th' sthrong arm men iv th' Sinit knocks him down an' takes fr'm him ivrything he got inside an' more too. Di-plomacy has become a philanthropic pursoot like shop-keepin',

but politics, me lords, is still th' same ol' spoort iv highway robb'ry.

Observations by Mr. Dooley.
International Amenities

Ye see, a prince is a gr-reat man in th' ol' counthry, but he niver is as gr-reat over there as he is here. Whin he's at home he's something th' people can't help an' they don't mind him. He's like an iron lamp post, station'ry, ornymintal, an' useful to let people know where they are. But whin he comes to this home iv raypublican simplicity, he's all that th' wurrud prince wud imply, an' it implies more to us thin to annywan else.

Ibid. Prince Henry's Reception

Spain was our frind till th' war was over. Thin she rounded on us an' sold us th' Ph'lippines.

Ibid. European Intervention

Th' flag [1] floats free an' well guarded over th' govermint offices, an' th' cheery people go an' come on their errands — go out alone an' come back with th' throops. Iverywhere happiness, contint, love iv th' shtep-mother counthry, excipt in places where there ar-re people.

Ibid. The Philippine Peace

A rayformer thinks he was ilicted because he was a rayformer, whin th' thruth iv th' matther is he was ilicted because no wan knew him. Ye can always ilict a man in this counthry on that platform. If I was runnin' f'r office, I'd change me name, an' have printed on me cards: "Give him a chanst; he can't be worse."

Ibid. Reform Administration

A reg'lar pollytician can't give away an' alley without blushin', but a business man who is in pollytics jus' to see that th' civil sarvice law gets thurly enfoorced, will give Lincoln Park an' th' public libr'y to th' beef thrust, charge an admission price to th' lake front an' make it a felony f'r annywan to buy stove polish outside iv his store, an' have it all put down to public im-

---

[1] The American flag in the Philippines.

provemints with a pitcher iv him in th' corner stone.
Observations by Mr. Dooley.
Reform Administration

"I don't like a rayformer," said Mr. Hennessy.

"Or anny other raypublican," said Mr. Dooley.
Ibid.

If a man is wise, he gets rich an' if he gets rich, he gets foolish, or his wife does. That's what keeps the money movin' around.
Ibid. Newport

"Oh, well," said Mr. Hennessy, "we are as th' Lord made us."

"No," said Mr. Dooley, "lave us be fair. Lave us take some iv th' blame oursilves."
Ibid.

"What d'ye think iv th' man down in Pinnsylvanya [1] who says th' Lord an' him is partners in a coal mine?" asked Mr. Hennessy. . . .

"Has he divided th' profits?" asked Mr. Dooley.
Ibid. Machinery

But th' best thing about a little judicyous swearin' is that it keeps th' temper. 'Twas intinded as a compromise between runnin' away an' fightin'. Befure it was invinted they was on'y th' two ways out iv an argymint.
Ibid. Swearing

It must be a good thing to be good or ivrybody wudden't be pretendin' he was. But I don't think they'se anny such thing as hypocrisy in th' wurruld. They can't be. If ye'd turn on th' gas in th' darkest heart ye'd find it had a good raison for th' worst things it done, a good varchous raison, like needin' th' money or punishin' th' wicked or tachin' people a lesson to be more careful, or protectin' th' liberties iv mankind, or needin' th' money.
Ibid. Hypocrisy

I don't think we injye other people's sufferin', Hinnissy. It isn't acshally injyement. But we feel betther f'r it.
Ibid. Enjoyment

[1] George Baer.

Whin a woman discovers she has a soul, Hinnissy, 'tis time she was sint to a rest-cure. It niver comes till late in life, an' ye can't tell what she'll do about it.
Dissertations by Mr. Dooley
[1906]. Royal Doings

Why shud a woman want to be thin onless she is thin? Th' idee iv female beauty that all gr-reat men, fr'm Julius Caesar to mesilf, has held, is much more like a bar'l thin a clothespole.
Ibid. Banting

"Ye know a lot about [raising children]," said Mr. Hennessy.

"I do," said Mr. Dooley. "Not bein' an author, I'm a gr-reat critic."
Ibid. The Bringing Up of Children

Th' old story iv th' ant an' th' grasshopper — th' ant that ye can step on an' th' grasshopper ye can't catch.
Ibid. The Labor Troubles

It's too bad that th' goolden days has passed, Hinnissy. Capital still pats labor on th' back, but on'y with an axe. Labor rayfuses to be threated as a frind. It wants to be threated as an inimy. It thinks it gets more that way. They ar-re still a happy fam'ly, but it's more like an English fam'ly. They don't speak.
Ibid.

"Annyhow, I bet no wan iver took Binjamin Franklin f'r a waiter."

"I wondher why?" asked Mr. Hennessy.

"I don't know," said Mr. Dooley, "onless it was that even in th' prisince iv a king Binjamin Franklin niver felt like a waiter."
Ibid. Diplomatic Uniforms

"If ye had a boy wud ye sind him to colledge?" asked Mr. Hennessy.

"Well," said Mr. Dooley, "at th' age whin a boy is fit to be in colledge I wudden't have him around th' house."
Ibid. The Intellectual Life

Th' prisidincy is th' highest office in th' gift iv th' people. Th' vice-prisidincy is th' next highest an' th' lowest. It isn't a crime exactly. Ye can't be sint to jail f'r it, but it's a kind iv a disgrace. It's like writin' anonymous letters.

> *Dissertations by Mr. Dooley.*
> *The Vice-President*

Some vice-prisidints have been so anxious f'r th' prisidint's safety that they've had to be warned off th' White House grounds.

> *Ibid.*

It is his jooty to rigorously enforce th' rules iv th' Sinit. There ar-re none. Th' Sinit is ruled be courtesy, like th' longshoreman's union.

> *Ibid.*

Prisidint Eliot . . . has communicated th' sad fact to th' clargy. Nawthin' th' clargy likes so much as a sad fact.

> *Ibid. The American Family*

Libries niver encouraged lithrachoor anny more thin tombstones encourage livin'. No wan iver wrote annythin' because he was tol' that a hundherd years fr'm now his books might be taken down fr'm a shelf in a granite sepulcher an' some wan wud write "Good" or "This man is crazy" in th' margin. What lithrachoor needs is fillin' food.

> *Ibid. The Carnegie Libraries*

Slug-ye'er-spouse is an internaytional spoort that has niver become pop'lar on our side iv th' wather. An American lady is not th' person that anny man but a thrained athlete wud care to raise his hand again' save be way iv smoothin' her hair.

> *Ibid. Corporal Punishment*

Won't [public flogging] be fine? Th' govermint gives us too little amusemint nowadays. Th' fav'rite pastime iv civilized man is croolty to other civilized man.

> *Ibid.*

"Spare th' rod an' spile th' child," said Mr. Hennessy.

"Yes," said Mr. Dooley, "but don't spare th' rod an' ye spile th' rod, th' child, an' th' child's father."

> *Ibid.*

This home iv opporchunity where

ivry man is th' equal iv ivry other man befure th' law if he isn't careful.

> *Dissertations by Mr. Dooley.*
> *The Food We Eat*

"Ye ra-aly do think dhrink is a nicissry evil?" said Mr. Hennessy.

"Well," said Mr. Dooley, "if it's an evil to a man, it's not nicissry, an' if it's nicissry it's an evil."

> *Ibid. The Bar*

"He made [money]," said Mr. Dooley, "because he honestly loved it with an innocint affiction. He was thrue to it. Th' reason ye have no money is because ye don't love it f'r itsilf alone. Money won't iver surrinder to such a flirt."

> *Mr. Dooley on Making a Will*
> *and Other Evil Necessities*
> *[1919]. On Making a Will*

"Is th' President[1] a good goluf player, d'ye know, at all?" asked Mr. Hennessy . . .

"As a goluf player he cud give Lincoln a sthroke a hole," said Mr. Dooley.

> *Ibid. On Golf*

JOHN GALSWORTHY
[1867–1933]

Justice is a machine that, when some one has once given it the starting push, rolls on of itself.

> *Justice [1910]. Act II*

Public opinion's always in advance of the Law.

> *Windows [1922]. Act I*

The value of a sentiment is the amount of sacrifice you are prepared to make for it.

> *Ibid. Act II*

By the cigars they smoke, and the composers they love, ye shall know the texture of men's souls.

> *Indian Summer of a Forsyte*
> *[1920]. Chap. 1*

He ordered himself a dozen oysters; but, suddenly remembering that the

---

[1] President Wilson.

month contained no "r," changed them to a fried sole.[1]

The White Monkey [*1924*].
Part III, Chap. 7

It has often been remarked that the breakfast-tables of people who avow themselves indifferent to what the Press may say of them are garnished by all the newspapers on the morning when there is anything to say.

The Silver Spoon [*1926*].
Part II, Chap. 2

If you do not think about the future, you cannot have one.

Swan Song [*1928*].
Part II, Chap. 6

A man of action, forced into a state of thought, is unhappy until he can get out of it.

Maid in Waiting [*1931*].
Chap. 3

Politicians are marvels of energy and principle when they're out of office, but when they get in, they simply run behind the machine.

Ibid. Chap. 5

There's just one rule for politicians all over the world: Don't say in Power what you say in Opposition; if you do, you only have to carry out what the other fellows have found impossible.

Ibid. Chap. 7

One's eyes are what one is, one's mouth what one becomes.

Flowering Wilderness [*1932*].
Chap. 2

The beginnings and endings of all human undertakings are untidy, the building of a house, the writing of a novel, the demolition of a bridge, and, eminently, the finish of a voyage.

Over the River [*1933*]. *Chap. 1*

How to save the old that's worth sav-

---

[1] It is unseasonable and unwholesome in all months that have not an *R* in their name to eat an oyster. — WILLIAM BUTLER: *Dyet's Dry Dinner* [1599]

Let's sing a song of glory to Themistocles O'Shea,
Who ate a dozen oysters on the second day of May.

STODDARD KING [1889–1933]: *The Man Who Dared*

ing, whether in landscape, houses, manners, institutions, or human types, is one of our greatest problems, and the one that we bother least about.

Over the River. Chap. 39

LLOYD McKIM GARRISON
[1867–1900]

Like misers, our usurious memories bring
Their coins each day of greedy reckoning —
Grieved, if they miss one as they count their store,
Or find one brass, long loved as gold before.

Souvenirs

"JOHN OLIVER HOBBES"
(MRS. P. M. T. CRAIGIE)
[1867–1906]

A false success made by the good humor of outside influences is always peaceful; a real success made by the qualities of the thing itself is always a declaration of war.

The Dream and the Business
[*1906*]

LIONEL JOHNSON
[1867–1902]

The splendid silence clings
Around me: and around
The saddest of all kings
Crown'd, and again discrown'd.

By the Statue of King Charles
at Charing Cross. Stanza 2

Vanquished in life, his death
By beauty made amends.

Ibid. Stanza 8

I know you: solitary griefs,
Desolate passions, aching hours!
I know you: tremulous beliefs,
Agonized hopes, and ashen flowers!

The Precept of Silence. Stanza 1

Some players upon plaintive strings
Publish their wistfulness abroad;
I have not spoken of these things,
Save to one man, and unto God.

Ibid. Stanza 3

ERNEST FENWICK JOHNSTONE
[1867–1938]

I dreamed that I went to the City of Gold,
To Heaven resplendent and fair,
And after I entered that beautiful fold
By one in authority there I was told
That not a Vermonter was there.
No Vermonters in Heaven.
Stanza 1

We give them the best the Kingdom provides;
They have everything here that they want,
But not a Vermonter in Heaven abides;
A very brief period here he resides,
Then hikes his way back to Vermont.
Ibid. Stanza 6

CHARLES EDWARD MONTAGUE
[1867–1928]

A gifted small girl has explained that pins are a great means of saving life, "by not swallowing them."
Dramatic Values [*1911*]

"The freedom of Europe," "The war to end war," "The overthrow of militarism," "The cause of civilization" — most people believe so little now in anything or anyone that they would find it hard to understand the simplicity and intensity of faith with which these phrases were once taken among our troops, or the certitude felt by hundreds of thousands of men who are now dead that if they were killed their monument would be a new Europe not soured or soiled with the hates and greeds of the old.
Disenchantment [*1922*]. *Chap. 13*

A lie will easily get you out of a scrape, and yet, strangely and beautifully, rapture possesses you when you have taken the scrape and left out the lie.
Ibid. Chap. 15

War hath no fury like a non-combatant.
Ibid.

"I was born below par to th' extent of two whiskies."
Fiery Particles [*1923*]

Burgundy was the winiest wine, the central, essential, and typical wine, the soul and greatest common measure of all the kindly wines of the earth.
Judith

GEORGE W. RUSSELL ("AE")
[1867–1935]

Our hearts were drunk with a beauty
Our eyes could never see.
The Unknown God

Twilight, a timid fawn, went glimmering by,
And Night, the dark-blue hunter, followed fast.
Refuge

With these heaven-assailing spires
All that was in clay or stone
Fabled of rich Babylon
By these children is outdone.
New York. Stanza 1

HENRY LEWIS STIMSON [1]
[1867–1950]

The only way to make a man trustworthy is to trust him; and the surest way to make him untrustworthy is to distrust him and show your distrust.
The Bomb and the Opportunity [*Harper's Magazine, March, 1946*]

The only deadly sin I know is cynicism.
On Active Service in Peace and War [*1948*]. *Introduction*

HARRY LEON WILSON
[1867–1939]

I can be pushed just so far.
Ruggles of Red Gap [*1915*]

MARY HUNTER AUSTIN
[1868–1934]

Whisper of the wind along the sage,
Only wait till I can get the word —

[1] Secretary of War, 1911–1913 and 1940–1945; Secretary of State, 1929–1933.

Never was it printed in a page,
Never was it spoken, never heard.
Whisper of the Wind
What need has he of clocks who knows
When highest peaks are gilt and rose
Day has begun?
Clocks and Calendars. Stanza 1

THOMAS WILLIAM
HODGSON CROSLAND
[1868–1924]

The Unspeakable Scot.
Title of satiric essay

NORMAN DOUGLAS
[1868–   ]

You can tell the ideals of a nation by
its advertisements.
South Wind [1917]. Chap. 7
Men have lost sight of distant hori-
zons. Nobody writes for humanity, for
civilization; they write for their country, their sect; to amuse their friends
or annoy their enemies.
Ibid. Chap. 8
No one can expect a majority to be
stirred by motives other than ignoble.
Ibid. Chap. 10
A love-match is generally a failure
and a money-match is always a mistake. The heroes, the saints and sages
— they are those who face the world
alone.
Ibid. Chap. 11
No great man is ever born too soon or
too late. When we say that the time is
not ripe for this or that celebrity, we
confess by implication that this very
man, and no other, is required.
Ibid. Chap. 13
For three consecutive months they
could barely afford the most unnecessary luxuries of life.
Ibid. Chap. 20
Many a man who thinks to found a
home discovers that he has merely
opened a tavern for his friends.
Ibid. Chap. 24

WILLIAM EDWARD
BURGHARDT DuBOIS
[1868–   ]

Herein lies the tragedy of the age:
not that men are poor — all men know
something of poverty; not that men are
wicked — who is good? Not that men
are ignorant — what is truth? Nay, but
that men know so little of men.
The Souls of Black Folk [1903]

MAXIM GORKY
[1868–1936]

It is quiet here and restful and the air
is delicious. There are gardens everywhere, nightingales sing in the gardens
and police spies lie in the bushes. There
are nightingales in every garden, but
police spies only in mine, I think. They
sit under my windows in the darkness
of the night and try to get a glimpse of
how I spread sedition in Russia.
Letter to Chekhov
Lies — there you have the religion of
slaves and taskmasters.[1]
The Lower Depths [1903]
The double-headed eagle of the autocracy was not merely the coat of arms
of the Empire, but an exceedingly live
and actively pernicious bird.
Talks on Craftsmanship

RONALD ARTHUR HOPWOOD
[1868–1949]

The strength of the ship is the Service,
And the strength of the Service, the
ship.
The Laws of the Navy. Stanza 2
On the strength of one link in the cable
Dependeth the might of the chain:
Who knows when thou mayest be
tested?
So live that thou bearest the strain.
Ibid. Stanza 5
They prosper who burn in the morning
The letters they wrote over night.
Ibid. Stanza 17

[1] The censor forbade this line to be spoken
on the stage.

FRANK McKINNEY ("KIN") HUBBARD ("ABE MARTIN")
[1868–1930]

Miss Fawn Lippincut says she wouldn' marry th' best man on earth, but we supposed she wuz much younger.
Abe Martin's Sayings and Sketches [*1915*]

Miss Tawney Apple is confined t' her home by a swollen dresser drawer.
Ibid.

Mr. and Mrs. Lettie Plum, married in June, couldn' git ther car out o' garage last evenin', so they had to go to bed hungry.
Ibid.

It's no disgrace t' be poor, but it might as well be.
Ibid.

He was a power politically fer years, but he never got prominent enough t' have his speeches garbled.
Ibid.

When a fellow says it hain't the money but the principle o' the thing, it's th' money.
Hoss Sense and Nonsense [*1926*]

Nobuddy ever fergits where he buried a hatchet.
Abe Martin's Broadcast [*1930*]

GRENVILLE KLEISER
[1868–1953]

She gleans how long you wish to stay;
She lets you go without delay.
The Ideal Hostess
She is not difficult to please;
She can be silent as the trees.
She shuns all ostentatious show;
She knows exactly when to go.[1]
The Ideal Guest

HERMAN W. KNICKERBOCKER
[1868–1934]

If I had the power today by the simple turning of my hand to endow myself

[1] See Rose Henniker Heaton, page 754a.

with personal immortality, in my infinite ignorance I would refuse to turn my hand. God knows best.
Eulogy at the funeral of Riley Grannan, Rawhide, Nevada [*April 3, 1908*]

AGNES LEE
[1868–1939]

Bed is the boon for me!
It's well to bake and sweep,
But hear the word of old Lizette:
It's better than all to sleep.
Old Lizette on Sleep. Stanza 1
There's nothing, nothing, nothing, I say,
That's worth the lying awake!
Ibid. Stanza 3

EDWARD VERRALL LUCAS
[1868–1938]

The French never allow a distinguished son of France to lack a statue.
Wanderings and Diversions [*1926*].
Zigzags in France
Americans are people who prefer the Continent to their own country, but refuse to learn its languages.
Ibid. The Continental Dictionary
Ticket Collector. — The man who never wants to see your ticket unless you are asleep.
Ibid.
He says one of the two things that men who have lasted for a hundred years always say — either that they have drunk whisky and smoked all their lives, or that neither tobacco nor spirits ever made the faintest appeal to them.
Ibid. Secrets
People in hotels strike no roots. The French phrase for chronic hotel guests even says so: they are called dwellers *sur la branche.*
Ibid. To Be Let or Sold
A genius is a man who does unique things of which nobody would expect him to be capable.
Reading, Writing and Remembering [*1932*]

There can be no defence like elaborate courtesy.
Reading, Writing and
Remembering

Has any reader ever found perfect accuracy in the newspaper account of any event of which he himself had inside knowledge?
Of Accuracy

The art of life is to keep down acquaintances. One's friends one can manage, but one's acquaintances can be the devil.
Over Bremerton's

WILLIAM TYLER PAGE
[1868–1942]

I believe in the United States of America as a Government of the people, by the people, for the people; whose just powers are derived from the consent of the governed; a democracy in a republic, a sovereign Nation of many sovereign States; a perfect Union one and inseparable; established upon those principles of freedom, equality, justice and humanity for which American patriots sacrificed their lives and fortunes. I therefore believe it is my duty to my country to love it, to support its Constitution, to obey its laws, to respect its flag, and to defend it against all enemies.
The American's Creed[1]

EDMOND ROSTAND
[1868–1918]

A great nose indicates a great man —
Genial, courteous, intellectual,
Virile, courageous.
Cyrano de Bergerac[2] *[1897].*
Act I

Free fighters, free lovers, free spenders —
The Cadets of Gascoyne — the defenders
Of old homes, old names, and old splendors.
Ibid. Act II

[1] Adopted by the House of Representatives, April 3, 1918.
[2] Translated by BRIAN HOOKER.

A Bear. How do you know I am a diplomat?
Chinese Woman. Why, by the skilful way you hide your claws.
L'Aiglon[1] *[1900]. Act IV*
(A Masquerade)

I fall back dazzled at beholding myself all rosy red,
At having, I myself, caused the sun to rise.
Chantecler [1907]. Act II, Sc. 3

And sounding in advance its victory,
My song jets forth so clear, so proud, so peremptory,
That the horizon, seized with a rosy trembling,
Obeys me.
Ibid.

ROBERT FALCON SCOTT
[1868–1912]

Make the boy interested in natural history if you can; it is better than games; they encourage it at some schools.
Last Message to His Wife

He [Oates][2] said: "I am just going outside, and may be some time." He went out into the blizzard, and we have not seen him since. . . . We knew that poor Oates was walking to his death, but though we tried to dissuade him, we knew that it was the act of a brave man and an English gentleman. We all hope to meet the end with a similar spirit, and assuredly the end is not far.
Diary. March 16, 1912

Had we lived, I should have had a tale to tell of the hardihood, endurance, and courage of my companions which would have stirred the heart of every Englishman. These rough notes and our dead bodies must tell the tale.
Journal. Message to the Public[3]

[1] Translated by LOUIS N. PARKER.
[2] Lawrence Edward Grace Oates [1880–1912], of the Inniskilling Dragoons, a member of Scott's last Antarctic expedition.
[3] Inscribed on the memorial to Captain Scott and his companions, Waterloo Place, London.

WILLIAM ALLEN WHITE
[1868–1944]

And thus the King of Boyville first set his light little foot upon the soil of an unknown country.
> *The King of Boyville [1896]*

What's the Matter with Kansas?
> *Editorial in Emporia Gazette.*
> *August 15, 1896*

Tin horn politicians.
> *Emporia Gazette. October 25, 1901*

"Company" merges into the family when clean towels are not kept in the bathroom every morning. A man is no longer company when they change sheets on his bed only once in two weeks. . . . When sons-in-law come home to visit for years at a time, the question will be seen to have considerable importance.
> *Ibid. June 4, 1906*

The fresh-water college is doing a great work.
> *Ibid. June 10, 1907*

All dressed up, with nowhere to go.
> *Of the Progressive Party in 1916, after Theodore Roosevelt retired from Presidential competition*

Put fear out of your heart. This Nation will survive, this State will prosper, the orderly business of life will go forward if only men can speak in whatever way given them to utter what their hearts hold — by voice, by posted card, by letter or by press. Reason never has failed men. Only force and oppression have made the wrecks in the world.
> *Emporia Gazette. 1922*

Consistency is a paste jewel that only cheap men cherish.[1]
> *Ibid. November 17, 1923*

The talent of a meat packer, the morals of a money changer and the manners of an undertaker.
> *Obituary of Frank A. Munsey.*
> *December, 1925*

[1] Commenting on an item in the Topeka *Capital:* "The Emporia Gazette is the best loved paper in Kansas because its editor never looks in yesterday's files to see if what he proposes to write today is consistent."

LAURENCE BINYON
[1869–1943]

For Mercy, Courage, Kindness, Mirth,
There is no measure upon earth.
Nay, they wither, root and stem,
If an end be set to them.
> *A Song*

They shall grow not old, as we that are
> left grow old:
Age shall not weary them, nor the years
> condemn.
At the going down of the sun and in the
> morning
We will remember them.
> *For the Fallen. Stanza 4*

ELLIS PARKER BUTLER
[1869–1937]

Pigs is Pigs.
> *Title of story [1906]*

It is other folks' dogs and children that make most of the bad feelin's between neighbors.
> *The Confessions of a Daddy*
> *[1907]. Chap. 1*

NEVILLE CHAMBERLAIN
[1869–1940]

For the second time in our history, a British Prime Minister has returned from Germany bringing peace with honor. I believe it is peace for our time. . . . Go home and get a nice quiet sleep.[1]
> *Address from 10 Downing Street,*
> *September 30, 1938, upon return*
> *to London after the Munich conference with Hitler, Daladier,*
> *and Mussolini*

[1] As reported in the *New York Times,* October 1, 1938.
While we endeavor to maintain peace, I certainly should be the last to forget that, if peace cannot be maintained with honour, it is no longer peace. — Lord John Russell: *Speech at Greenock, Scotland* [September 19, 1853]
Lord Salisbury and myself have brought you back peace — but a peace, I hope, with honour, which may satisfy our sovereign, and tend to the welfare of the country. — Benjamin Disraeli: *Report on the Berlin Congress* [July 16, 1878]

Hitler has missed the bus.
Speech in the House of Commons,
April 4, 1940

"MICHAEL FAIRLESS"
(MARGARET FAIRLESS
BARBER)
[1869–1901]

The people who make no roads are ruled out from intelligent participation in the world's brotherhood.
The Roadmender. I, 5
Necessity can set me helpless on my back, but she cannot keep me there; nor can four walls limit my vision.
Ibid. II, 6
Revelation is always measured by capacity.
Ibid. III, 3

ANDRÉ GIDE
[1869–1951]

What another would have done as well as you, do not do it. What another would have said as well as you, do not say it; written as well, do not write it. Be faithful to that which exists nowhere but in yourself — and thus make yourself indispensable.
Les Nourritures Terrestres. Envoi
A unanimous chorus of praise is not an assurance of survival; authors who please everyone at once are quickly exhausted. I would prefer to think that a hundred years hence people will say we did not properly understand him [Anatole France].
Pretexts

STRICKLAND GILLILAN
[1869–1954]

Make 'em brief, Finnigin!
Finnigin to Flannigan. Stanza 3
Bilin' down 's repoort, wuz Finnigin!
An' he writed this here: "*Musther Flannigan* —
Off agin, on agin,
Gone agin. — FINNIGIN."
Ibid. Stanza 6

Just stand aside and watch yourself go by;
Think of yourself as "he" instead of "I."
Watch Yourself Go By. Stanza 1

FREDERIC LAWRENCE
KNOWLES
[1869–1905]

Each little lyrical
Grave or satirical
Musical miracle!
On a Flyleaf of Burns's Songs
Helen's lips are drifting dust; [1]
Ilion is consumed with rust.
Love Triumphant
This body is my house — it is not I:
Triumphant in this faith I live and die.
The Tenant
Joy is a partnership,
Grief weeps alone;
Many guests had Cana,
Gethsemane had one.
Grief and Joy

STEPHEN LEACOCK
[1869–1944]

If I were founding a university I would found first a smoking room; then when I had a little more money in hand I would found a dormitory; then after that, or more probably with it, a decent reading room and a library. After that, if I still had more money that I couldn't use, I would hire a professor and get some textbooks.
Oxford As I See It
He flung himself from the room, flung himself upon his horse and rode madly off in all directions.
Gertrude the Governess
Golf may be played on Sunday, not being a game within the view of the law, but being a form of moral effort.
Other Fancies [1923]. Why
I Refuse to Play Golf
The average man goes to church six times a year and has attended Sunday

[1] See Thomas Nash, page 213a.

School for two afternoons and can sing half a hymn.
> *Winnowed Wisdom* [*1926*].
> *Preface*

The general idea, of course, in any first class laundry, is to see that no shirt or collar ever comes back twice.
> *Ibid. Chap. 6*

EDGAR LEE MASTERS
[1869–1950]

All, all, are sleeping on the hill.
> *Spoon River Anthology* [*1915*].
> *The Hill, Refrain*

Out of me unworthy and unknown
The vibrations of deathless music;
"With malice toward none, with charity for all."
> *Ibid. Anne Rutledge*

I am Anne Rutledge who sleep beneath these weeds,
Beloved in life of Abraham Lincoln,
Wedded to him, not through union,
But through separation.
> *Ibid.*

To this generation I would say:
Memorize some bit of verse of truth or beauty.
> *Ibid. Mrs. George Reece*

Hats may make divorces.
> *Ibid. Mrs. Williams*

And there is the silence of age,
Too full of wisdom for the tongue to utter it
In words intelligible to those who have not lived
The great range of life.
> *Silence*

WILLIAM VAUGHN MOODY
[1869–1910]

Jill-o'er-the-ground is purple blue,
Blue is the quaker-maid,
The wild geranium holds its dew
Long in the boulder's shade.
> *Gloucester Moors* [*1901*]. *Stanza 2*

This earth is not the steadfast place
We landsmen build upon;
From deep to deep she varies pace,
And while she comes is gone.
> *Ibid. Stanza 4*

But on, but on does the old earth steer
As if her port she knew.
> *Gloucester Moors. Stanza 5*

Then not to kneel, almost
Seemed like a vulgar boast.
> *Good Friday* [*1901*]. *Stanza 9*

Gigantic, wilful, young,
Chicago sitteth at the northwest gates,
With restless violent hands and casual tongue
Moulding her mighty fates.
> *An Ode in Time of Hesitation*
> [*1901*]. *Stanza 3*

Our fluent men of place and consequence
Fumble and fill their mouths with hollow phrase,
Or for the end-all of deep arguments
Intone their dull commercial liturgies.
> *Ibid. Stanza 7*

Blindness we may forgive, but baseness we will smite.
> *Ibid. Stanza 9*

Shrill and high, newsboys cry
The worst of the city's infamy.
> *In New York* [*1901*]. *Stanza 4*

The roaring street is hung for miles
With fierce electric fire.
> *Ibid. Stanza 9*

JESSIE BELLE RITTENHOUSE
[1869–1948]

My debt to you, Belovèd,
Is one I cannot pay
In any coin of any realm
On any reckoning day.
> *Debt*

I worked for a menial's hire,
Only to learn, dismayed,
That any wage I had asked of Life,
Life would have paid.
> *My Wage*

EDWIN ARLINGTON
ROBINSON
[1869–1935]

We cannot know how much we learn
From those who never will return,
Until a flash of unforeseen
Remembrance falls on what has been.
> *Flammonde*

To shake the tree
Of life itself and bring down fruit un-
heard-of.
Ben Jonson Entertains a Man
from Stratford

I would have rid the earth of him
Once, in my pride. . . .
I never knew the worth of him
Until he died.
An Old Story

Life is the game that must be played:
This truth at least, good friends, we
know;
So live and laugh, nor be dismayed
As one by one the phantoms go.
Ballade by the Fire. Envoy

The songs of one who strove to play
The broken flutes of Arcady.
Ballade of Broken Flutes

There be two men of all mankind
That I'm forever thinking on:
They chase me everywhere I go, —
Melchizedek, Ucalegon.
Two Men

Like dead, remembered footsteps on old
floors.
The Pity of the Leaves

And thus we die,
Still searching, like poor old astrono-
mers
Who totter off to bed and go to sleep
To dream of untriangulated stars.
Octaves. XI

The saddest among kings of earth,
Bowed with a galling crown, this man
Met rancor with a cryptic mirth,
Laconic — and Olympian.
The Master: Lincoln

Wearing upon his forehead, with no
fear,
The laurel of approved iniquity.
Uncle Ananias

Miniver Cheevy, child of scorn,
Grew lean while he assailed the
seasons;
He wept that he was ever born,
And he had reasons.
Miniver Cheevy [1910]. Stanza 1

Miniver loved the Medici,
Albeit he had never seen one;

He would have sinned incessantly
Could he have been one.
Miniver Cheevy. Stanza 5

Miniver Cheevy, born too late,
Scratched his head and kept on
thinking;
Miniver coughed and called it fate,
And kept on drinking.
Ibid. Stanza 8

Who of us, being what he is,
May scoff at others' ecstasies?
However we may shine today,
More-shining ones are on the way.
Atherton's Gambit

I shall have more to say when I am
dead.
John Brown

Like a physician who can do no good,
But knows how soon another would
have his fee
Were he to tell the truth.
Avon's Harvest

Art's long hazard, where no man may
choose
Whether he play to win, or toil to lose.
Caput Mortuum

Love that's wise
Will not say all it means.
Tristram [1927]. Part VII

For when a woman is left too much
alone,
Sooner or later she begins to think;
And no man knows what then she may
discover.
Ibid.

There is a little watchman in my heart
Who is always telling me what time
it is.
Ibid. Part VIII

Love must have wings to fly away from
love,
And to fly back again.
Ibid.

I like rivers
Better than oceans, for we see both
sides.
An ocean is forever asking questions
And writing them aloud along the
shore.
Roman Bartholow. Part III

Once in a life, they tell us, and once
only,
So great a thing as a great love may
come —
To crown us, or to mark us with a scar
No craft or custom shall obliterate.
Roman Bartholow. Part IV

Of all small things
That have the most infernal power to
grow,
Few may be larger than a few small
words
That may not say themselves and be
forgotten.
Genevieve and Alexandra

Here where the wind is always north-
north-east
And children learn to walk on frozen
toes.
New England

GEORGE STERLING
[1869–1926]

Thou art the star for which all evening
waits.
Aldebaran at Dusk

BOOTH TARKINGTON
[1869–1946]

Penrod was doing something very un-
usual and rare, something almost never
accomplished except by colored people or by a boy in school on a spring
day: he was doing really nothing at all.
He was merely a state of being.
Penrod [1914]. Chap. 8

There are two things that will be believed of any man whatsoever, and one
of them is that he has taken to drink.
Ibid. Chap. 10

They were upon their great theme:
"When I get to be a man!" Being human, though boys, they considered
their present estate too commonplace to
be dwelt upon. So, when the old men
gather, they say: "When I was a boy!"
It really is the land of nowadays that
we never discover.
Ibid. Chap. 26

CAROLYN WELLS
[1869–1942]

Youth is a silly, vapid state;
Old age with fears and ills is rife;
This simple boon I beg of Fate —
A thousand years of Middle Life!
My Boon

"A noble theme!" the tyro cried,
And straightway scribbled off a sonnet.
"A noble theme," the poet sighed,
"I am not fit to write upon it."
Humility

I love the Christmas-tide, and yet,
I notice this, each year I live;
I always like the gifts I get,
But how I love the gifts I give!
A Thought

The books we think we ought to read
are poky, dull and dry;
The books that we would like to read
we are ashamed to buy;
The books that people talk about we
never can recall;
And the books that people give us, Oh,
they're the worst of all.
On Books

The Smile That Won't Come Off.
Winning slogan in a contest

FRANK LLOYD WRIGHT
[1869–   ]

No house should ever be *on* any hill
or on anything. It should be *of* the
hill, belonging to it, so hill and house
could live together each the happier for
the other.
An Autobiography [1932]

BERNARD MANNES BARUCH
[1870–   ]

America has never forgotten — and
will never forget — the nobler things
that brought her into being and that
light her path — the path that was entered upon only one hundred and fifty
years ago. . . . . How young she is! It
will be centuries before she will adopt
that maturity of custom — the cloth-

ing of the grave — that some people believe she is already fitted for.

> *Address on accepting The Churchman Award, New York* [*May 23, 1944*]

Oh, oh — someone's taken the office.

> *On finding the park bench, where he usually held conference, occupied by others* [TIME, *April 22, 1946*]

HILAIRE BELLOC
[1870–1953]

Child! do not throw this book about;
Refrain from the unholy pleasure
Of cutting all the pictures out!
Preserve it as your chiefest treasure.

> *A Bad Child's Book of Beasts.*
> *Dedication*

When people call this beast to mind,
They marvel more and more
At such a little tail behind,
So large a trunk before.

> *Ibid. The Elephant*

I shoot the Hippopotamus
With bullets made of platinum,
Because if I use leaden ones
His hide is sure to flatten 'em.

> *Ibid. The Hippopotamus*

The Whale that wanders round the Pole
Is not a table fish.
You cannot bake or boil him whole
Nor serve him in a dish.

> *Ibid. The Whale*

Balliol made me, Balliol fed me,
Whatever I had she gave me again:
And the best of Balliol loved and led me.
God be with you, Balliol men.

> *To the Balliol Men Still in Africa*
> [*1900*]

Here richly, with ridiculous display,
The Politician's corpse was laid away.
While all of his acquaintance sneered and slanged,
I wept; for I had longed to see him hanged.

> *Epitaph on the Politician Himself*

Oh, he didn't believe in Adam and Eve —
He put no faith therein;

His doubts began with the fall of man,
And he laughed at original sin.

> *Song of the Pelagian Heresy*

The Tipple's aboard and the night is young,
The door's ajar and the Barrel is sprung,
I am singing the best song ever was sung
And it has a rousing chorus.

> *West Sussex Drinking Song.*
> *Chorus*

How slow the Shadow creeps: but when 'tis past
How fast the Shadows fall. How fast! How fast!

> *For a Sundial*

Loss and Possession, Death and Life are one,
There falls no shadow where there shines no sun.

> *Ibid.*

The moon on the one hand, the dawn on the other:
The moon is my sister, the dawn is my brother.
The moon on my left and the dawn on my right.
My brother, good morning: my sister, good night.

> *The Early Morning*

The great hills of the South Country
They stand along the sea;
And it's there walking in the high woods
That I could wish to be,
And the men that were boys when I was a boy
Walking along with me.

> *The South Country. Stanza 2*

If I ever become a rich man,
Or if ever I grow to be old,
I will build a house with deep thatch
To shelter me from the cold,
And there shall the Sussex songs be sung
And the story of Sussex told.

> *Ibid. Stanza 9*

And the men that were boys when I was a boy
Shall sit and drink with me.

> *Ibid. Stanza 10*

From quiet homes and first beginning,
  Out to the undiscovered ends,
There's nothing worth the wear of win-
  ning
  But laughter and the love of friends.
                    Dedicatory Ode
Of Courtesy, it is much less
Than Courage of Heart or Holiness,
Yet in my walks it seems to me
That the Grace of God is in Courtesy.
                    Courtesy
Do you remember an Inn,
Miranda?
Do you remember an Inn?
And the tedding and the spreading
Of the straw for a bedding,
And the fleas that tease in the High
  Pyrenees,
And the wine that tasted of the tar?
                    Tarantella
I said to Heart, "How goes it?" Heart
  replied:
"Right as a Ribstone Pippin!" But it
  lied.
                    The False Heart
Now just imagine how it feels
When first your toes and then your
  heels,
And then by gradual degrees,
Your shins and ankles, calves and
  knees,
Are slowly eaten, bit by bit.
No wonder Jim detested it!
                    Cautionary Tales. Jim
The Chief Defect of Henry King
Was chewing little bits of String.
                    Ibid. Henry King
Physicians of the Utmost Fame
Were called at once; but when they
  came
They answered, as they took their Fees,
"There is no Cure for this Disease."
                    Ibid.
"Oh, my Friends, be warned by me,
That Breakfast, Dinner, Lunch and
  Tea
Are all the Human Frame re-
  quires . . ."
With that the Wretched Child expires.
                    Ibid.
Matilda told such Dreadful Lies,

It made one Gasp and Stretch one's
  Eyes;
Her Aunt, who, from her Earliest
  Youth,
Had kept a Strict Regard for Truth,
Attempted to Believe Matilda:
The effort very nearly killed her.
                  Cautionary Tales. Matilda
It happened that a few Weeks later
Her Aunt was off to the Theatre
To see that Interesting Play
The Second Mrs. Tanqueray.
                    Ibid.
For every time She shouted "Fire!"
They only answered "Little Liar!"
And therefore when her Aunt returned,
Matilda, and the House, were burned.
                    Ibid.
The nicest child I ever knew
Was Charles Augustus Fortescue.
        Ibid. Charles Augustus Fortescue
When I am dead, I hope it may be said:
"His sins were scarlet, but his books
  were read."
                    On His Books

BENJAMIN NATHAN CARDOZO
[1870–1938]

A trustee is held to something stricter
than the morals of the market place.
Not honesty alone, but the punctilio
of an honor the most sensitive, is then
the standard of behavior.
          *Meinhard v. Salmon, 249 N.Y.
                    458, 464 [1928]*

JOHN IRVING DILLON
[1870–1938]

I lift my glass in a grateful toast
To those glorious days of the used-to-
  be —
Days that live on in memory,
Bathed in a shimmering golden haze —
Our still-remembered "olden days"!
          Those Olden Days. Stanza 11

LORD ALFRED DOUGLAS
[1870–1945]

I have been profligate of happiness
And reckless of the world's hostility,

The blessèd part has not been given to
  me
Gladly to suffer fools.[1]
To Olive

MRS. J. BORDEN HARRIMAN
[1870–   ]

Next to entertaining or impressive
talk, a thoroughgoing silence manages
to intrigue most people.
From Pinafores to Politics [*1923*].
Chap. 4

ARTHUR J. LAMB
[1870–1928]

Her beauty was sold for an old man's
  gold,
She's a bird in a gilded cage.
A Bird in a Gilded Cage [*1900*]
"He don't know Nellie like I do,"
Said the saucy little bird on Nellie's hat.
The Bird on Nellie's Hat [*1906*]

SIR HARRY LAUDER
[1870–1950]

Oh, it's nice to get up in the mornin',
But it's nicer to lie in bed.
Song

Just a wee doch-an'-dorris
Before we gang awa' . . .
If y' can say
It's a braw brecht moonlecht necht,
Yer a' recht, that's a'.
Song

Roamin' in the gloamin'
By the bonny banks of Clyde.
Song

I Love a Lassie.
Title of Song

NIKOLAI LENIN
[1870–1924]

Political institutions are a superstructure resting on an economic foundation.
*The Three Sources and Three
Constituent Parts of Marxism* [2]
[*1913*]

[1] For ye suffer fools gladly, seeing ye yourselves are wise. — *2 Corinthians, XI, 19*
[2] Translated by MAX EASTMAN.

Capital, created by the labour of the
worker, oppresses the worker by undermining the small proprietor and creating an army of the unemployed.
*The Three Sources and Three
Constituent Parts of Marxism*

Capital has conquered throughout
the world, but its victory is only an
earnest of the victory of labour over
capital.
Ibid.

People always have been and they
always will be stupid victims of deceit
and self-deception in politics, until they
learn behind every kind of moral, religious, political, social phrase, declaration and promise to seek out the interests of this or that class or classes.
Ibid.

Uneven economic and political development is an absolute law of capitalism. Hence, the victory of socialism is
possible, first in a few or even one single
capitalist country taken separately.
*Collected Works. Vol. XVIII,
Page 272*

International imperialism disposing
of the might of capital cannot coexist
with the Soviet Republic. Conflict is
unavoidable, and here is the greatest
difficulty of the Russian Revolution,
its greatest historical task, that of pro-
voking the International Revolution.
Ibid. Vol. XXII, Page 37

It is true that liberty is precious —
so precious that it must be rationed.
Attributed. Quoted by SIDNEY
AND BEATRICE WEBB *in Soviet
Communism: A New Civiliza-
tion?* [*1936*]. *Page 1036*

The most important thing in illness
is never to lose heart.
To his mother. Quoted by HEW-
LETT JOHNSON *in The Secret
of Soviet Strength* [*1943*]

DENIS ALOYSIUS McCARTHY
[1870–1931]

This is the land where hate should die,
  No feuds of faith, no spleen of race,

No darkly-brooding fear should try
Beneath our flag to find a place.
> *This Is the Land Where Hate*
> *Should Die. Stanza 1*

HECTOR HUGH MUNRO ("SAKI")
[1870–1916]

She took to telling the truth about her age; she said she was forty-two and five months. . . . It may have been pleasing to the angels, but her elder sister was not gratified.
> *Reginald* [*1904*]. *Reginald on*
> *Besetting Sins*

The cook was a good cook, as cooks go; and as cooks go she went.
> *Ibid.*

Women and elephants never forget an injury.
> *Ibid.*

I might have been a gold-fish in a glass bowl for all the privacy I got.
> *Ibid. The Innocence of Reginald*

The Western custom of one wife and hardly any mistresses.
> *Reginald in Russia* [*1910*]. *A*
> *Young Turkish Catastrophe*

Hating anything in the way of ill-natured gossip ourselves, we are always grateful to those who do it for us and do it well.
> *Ibid. The Soul of Laploshka*

Poverty keeps together more homes than it breaks up.
> *The Chronicles of Clovis* [*1911*].
> *Esmé*

His socks compelled one's attention without losing one's respect.
> *Ibid. "Ministers of Grace"*

"It was their Silver Wedding; such lots of silver presents, quite a show."
"We must not grudge them their show of presents after twenty-five years of married life; it is the silver lining to their cloud."
> *The Unbearable Bassington* [*1912*]

Sherard Blaw, the dramatist who had discovered himself, and who had given so ungrudgingly of his discovery to the world.
> *Ibid.*

The sacrifices of friendship were beautiful in her eyes as long as she was not asked to make them.
> *Beasts and Super-Beasts* [*1914*].
> *Fur*

"The man is a common murderer."
"A common murderer, possibly, but a very uncommon cook."
> *Ibid. The Blind Spot*

Waldo is one of those people who would be enormously improved by death.
> *Ibid. The Feast of Nemesis*

Children with Hyacinth's temperament don't know better as they grow older; they merely know more.
> *The Toys of Peace* [*1919*].
> *Hyacinth*

In baiting a mouse-trap with cheese, always leave room for the mouse.
> *The Square Egg* [*1924*]. *The*
> *Infernal Parliament*

Confront a child, a puppy, and a kitten with a sudden danger; the child will turn instinctively for assistance, the puppy will grovel in abject submission, the kitten will brace its tiny body for a frantic resistance.
> *Ibid. The Achievement of the Cat*

A little inaccuracy sometimes saves tons of explanation.
> *Ibid. The Comments of Moung Ka*

FRANK NORRIS
[1870–1902]

He's the kind of man that gets up a reputation for being clever and artistic by running down the very one particular thing that every one likes, and cracking up some book or picture or play that no one has ever heard of.
> *The Pit* [*1903*]. *Chap. 2*

ROSCOE POUND
[1870–   ]

The law must be stable, but it must not stand still.
> *Introduction to the Philosophy*
> *of Law* [*1922*]

EDDIE NEWTON AND T. LAURENCE SEIBERG
[*Floruerunt* 1900]

Casey Jones! Orders in his hand.
Casey Jones! Mounted to the cabin,
Took his farewell journey to that promised land.
> *Casey Jones* [*1900*] (*Adapted from verses and melody by* WALLACE SAUNDERS) [1]

HAROLD BEGBIE
[1871–1929]

"The Christian ideal," it is said, "has not been tried and found wanting; it has been found difficult, and left untried."
> *Life of William Booth*

JOHN JOY BELL
[1871–1934]

I've never traveled for more 'n a day,
 I never was one to roam,
But I likes to sit on the busy quay,
 Watchin' the ships that says to me —
"Always somebody goin' away,
Somebody gettin' home."
> *On the Quay. Stanza 1*

RALPH BERGENGREN
[1871–1947]

Christmas itself may be called into question
If carried so far it creates indigestion.[2]
> *The Unwise Christmas*

[1] Of the many versions of this traditional ballad, the most familiar is printed in CARL SANDBURG'S *The American Songbag* [1927]. It begins:
 Come all you rounders, for I want you to hear
 The story of a brave engineer.
 Casey Jones was the rounder's name.
 On a big eight-wheeler of a mighty fame.
[2] Ye Tables groan before ye Feaste,
 Ye Feasters groan thereafter.
 ARTHUR GUITERMAN [1871–1943]:
 A True Bill Agaynst Christmasse

STEPHEN CRANE
[1871–1900]

He had fought like a pagan who defends his religion.
> *The Red Badge of Courage* [*1895*].
> *Chap. 17*

Within him, as he hurled himself forward, was born a love, a despairing fondness for this flag which was near him. It was a creation of beauty and invulnerability.
> *Ibid. Chap. 19*

None of them knew the color of the sky.
> *The Open Boat* [*1898*]

A man said to the universe:
"Sir, I exist!"
"However," replied the universe,
"The fact has not created in me
A sense of obligation."
> *War Is Kind* [*1899*]. *Fragment*

THOMAS AUGUSTINE DALY
[1871–1948]

I gotta love for Angela,
 I love Carlotta, too.
I no can marry both o' dem,
 So w'at I gona do?
> *Between Two Loves. Stanza 1*

Da spreeng ees com'; but oh, da joy
 Eet ees too late!
He was so cold, my leetla boy,
 He no could wait.
> *Da Leetla Boy. Stanza 1*

Flo was fond of Ebenezer —
 "Eb," for short, she called her beau.
Talk of tides of love, great Caesar!
 You should see them — Eb and Flo.
> *The Tides of Love*

Sing clear, O! throstle,
 Thou golden-tongued apostle
And little brown-frocked brother
 Of the loved Assisian!
> *To a Thrush*

W'at good eesa wife eef she don'ta be fat?
> *Da Styleesha Wife*

"Eat hearty, and give the old ship a good name!"
> *Grace for the Ship*

The Man, the One and Only One —
First Gentleman on Earth —
Said: "How about a little fun?
Come! let us have some mirth!"
          The First New Year's Eve.
                    Stanza 1

"Fifteen-two and a pair" —
Look at them! Granny and Gramp',
Playing so peacefully there —
And what of the wild young scamp [1]
Who fashioned this quiet game
For numberless Darbies and Joans?
Gone with the wind like a flame;
Peace to his mouldering bones!
          The Game of Cribbage

WILLIAM HENRY DAVIES
[1871–1940]

What glorious sunsets have their birth
In Cities fouled by smoke!
This tree — whose roots are in a
    drain —
Becomes the greenest Oak!
          Love's Rivals

Fools have their second childhood, but
    the Great
Still keep their first, and have no second
    state.
          Men That Think

I am as certain of my song,
When first it warms the brain,
As woman of her unborn child,
Or wind that carries rain.
          The Birth of Song

I had Ambition, by which sin
The angels fell;
I climbed and, step by step, O Lord,
Ascended into Hell.
          Ambition

I'll make my Joy a secret thing,
My face shall wear a mask of care;
And those who hunt a Joy to death,
Shall never know what sport is there!
          Hunting Joy. Stanza 3

[1] Cribbage was invented by Sir John
Suckling [1609–1642], according to the account in the *Brief Lives* of JOHN AUBREY
[1626–1697].

LADY PAMELA WYNDHAM GLENCONNER
[1871–1928]

Bitter are the tears of a child:
    Sweeten them.
Deep are the thoughts of a child:
    Quiet them.
Sharp is the grief of a child:
    Take it from him.
Soft is the heart of a child:
    Do not harden it.
          A Child

Giving presents is a talent; to know
what a person wants, to know when and
how to get it, to give it lovingly, and
well. Unless a character possesses this
talent there is no moment more annihilating to ease than that in which a present is received and given.
          Edward Wyndham Tennant:
                    A Memoir. Chap. 5

ARTHUR GUITERMAN
[1871–1943]

The Antiseptic Baby and the Prophy-
    lactic Pup
Were playing in the garden when the
    Bunny gamboled up;
They looked upon the Creature with a
    loathing undisguised; —
It wasn't Disinfected and it wasn't
    Sterilized.
          Strictly Germ-Proof. Stanza 1

The Cat on your hearthstone to this
    day presages,
By solemnly sneezing, the coming of
    rain! [1]
          The First Cat. Stanza 7

Oh, the saddest of sights in a world of
    sin
Is a little lost pup with his tail tucked
    in!
          Little Lost Pup. Stanza 1

[1] While rain depends, the pensive cat gives
    o'er
    Her frolics, and pursues her tail no more.
    JONATHAN SWIFT: *Description of a
          City Shower* [1710]

The finest thing in London is the
Bobby; [1]
Benignant information is his hobby.
The Lyric Baedeker. London

Amoebas at the start
  Were not complex;
They tore themselves apart
  And started Sex.
Sex. Stanza 1

The three-toed tree-toad
Sings his sweet ode
  To the moon.
Nocturne

Of all cold words of tongue or pen
The worst are these: "I knew him
when —" [2]
Prophets in Their Own Country

Oh, the Brown Missouri Mule has a
  copper-plated throat
And the welkin splits apart when he
  hits an upper note.
Mule Song. Stanza 1

BURTON J. HENDRICK
[1871–1949]

The dissenting opinions of one generation become the prevailing interpretation of the next.
Bulwark of the Republic [1937]

RALPH HODGSON
[1871–   ]

'Twould ring the bells of Heaven
The wildest peal for years,
If Parson lost his senses
And people came to theirs,
And he and they together
Knelt down with angry prayers
For tamed and shabby tigers
And dancing dogs and bears,
And wretched, blind pit ponies,
And little hunted hares.
The Bells of Heaven

But oh, the den of wild things in
The darkness of her eyes!
The Gypsy Girl

[1] The constable with lifted hand
Conducting the orchestral Strand.
STEPHEN PHILLIPS [1864–1915]:
The Wife
[2] See Whittier, page 527b.

God loves an idle rainbow
No less than labouring seas.
A Wood Song

Time, you old gypsy man,
  Will you not stay,
Put up your caravan
  Just for one day?
*Time, You Old Gypsy Man.
Stanza 1*

Pity him, this dupe of dream,
Leader of the herd again
Only in his daft old brain,
Once again the bull supreme.
The Bull

Oh, had our simple Eve
Seen through the make-believe!
Eve. Stanza 5

I climbed the hill as light fell short,
And rooks came home in scramble sort.
The Song of Honor

I stared into the sky,
As wondering men have always done
Since beauty and the stars were one,
Though none so hard as I.
Ibid.

Reason has moons, but moons not hers
  Lie mirrored on her sea,
Confounding her astronomers,
  But O! delighting me.
Reason

JAMES WELDON JOHNSON
[1871–1938]

O black and unknown bards of long
  ago,
How came your lips to touch the sacred
  fire?
How, in your darkness, did you come to
  know
The power and beauty of the minstrel's
  lyre?
*O Black and Unknown Bards.
Stanza 1*

And God stepped out on space,
And He looked around and said,
*"I'm lonely —
I'll make me a world."*
*The Creation: A Negro Sermon.
Stanza 1*

CHARLES RANN KENNEDY
[1871–1950]

A peculiar kind of fear they call courage.
The Terrible Meek [*1912*]

The meek, the terrible meek, the fierce agonizing meek, are about to enter into their inheritance.
Ibid.

WILBUR DICK NESBIT
[1871–1927]

Who waits upon the when and how
Remains forever in the rear.
A Plea for the Friendless Present.
Stanza 4

Each page of them Quotations that this
  Bartlett man got out
Is sure to have old Ibid's prose or
  poems strung about.
"Old Ibid." Stanza 2

I'm gettin' so, when I read things particularly fine,
I know that Ibid's name will be below
  the endin' line.
Ibid.

HERBERT GEORGE PONTING
[1871–1935]

On the outside grows the furside, on the
  inside grows the skinside;
So the furside is the outside, and the
  skinside is the inside.
The Sleeping Bag [1]

MARCEL PROUST
[1871–1922]

When from a long-distant past nothing subsists, after the people are dead, after the things are broken and scattered, still, alone, more fragile, but with more vitality, more unsubstantial, more persistent, more faithful, the smell and taste of things remain poised a long

time, like souls, ready to remind us, waiting and hoping for their moment, amid the ruins of all the rest; and bear unfaltering, in the tiny and almost impalpable drop of their essence, the vast structure of recollection.
Remembrance of Things Past [1]
[1913–1926]. Swann's Way

In his younger days a man dreams of possessing the heart of the woman whom he loves; later, the feeling that he possesses the heart of a woman may be enough to make him fall in love with her.
Ibid.

What artists call posterity is the posterity of the work of art.
Ibid. Within a Budding Grove,
Part I

The time which we have at our disposal every day is elastic; the passions that we feel expand it, those that we inspire contract it; and habit fills up what remains.
Ibid.

Untruthfulness and dishonesty were with me, as with most people, called into being in so immediate, so contingent a fashion, and in self-defence, by some particular interest, that my mind, fixed on some lofty ideal, allowed my character, in the darkness below, to set about those urgent, sordid tasks, and did not look down to observe them.
Ibid. The Guermantes Way, Part I

Like everybody who is not in love, he imagined that one chose the person whom one loved after endless deliberations and on the strength of various qualities and advantages.
Ibid. Cities of the Plain, Part I

We passionately long that there may be another life in which we shall be similar to what we are here below. But we do not pause to reflect that, even without waiting for that other life, in this life, after a few years we are un-

---

[1] For *The South Polar Times*, Midwinter Day, June 22, 1911, prepared by the men of Captain Robert Falcon Scott's last Antarctic expedition. Ponting was the photographer for the Scott expedition.

[1] *A la Recherche du Temps Perdu*, translated by C. K. SCOTT MONCRIEFF, except the last section, *The Past Recaptured*, which was translated by FREDERICK A. BLOSSOM.

faithful to what we have been, to what we wished to remain immortally.

Remembrance of Things Past.
Cities of the Plain, Part II

It is often simply from want of the creative spirit that we do not go to the full extent of suffering. And the most terrible reality brings us, with our suffering, the joy of a great discovery, because it merely gives a new and clear form to what we have long been ruminating without suspecting it.

Ibid.

The bonds that unite another person to ourself exist only in our mind. Memory as it grows fainter relaxes them, and notwithstanding the illusion by which we would fain be cheated and with which, out of love, friendship, politeness, deference, duty, we cheat other people, we exist alone. Man is the creature that cannot emerge from himself, that knows his fellows only in himself; when he asserts the contrary, he is lying.

Ibid. The Sweet Cheat Gone

We do not succeed in changing things according to our desire, but gradually our desire changes. The situation that we hoped to change because it was intolerable becomes unimportant. We have not managed to surmount the obstacle, as we were absolutely determined to do, but life has taken us round it, led us past it, and then if we turn round to gaze at the remote past, we can barely catch sight of it, so imperceptible has it become.

Ibid.

There is not a woman in the world the possession of whom is as precious as that of the truths which she reveals to us by causing us to suffer.

Ibid.

We are healed of a suffering only by experiencing it to the full.

Ibid.

Happiness is beneficial for the body but it is grief that develops the powers of the mind.

Ibid. The Past Recaptured

As for happiness, it has hardly more than one useful quality, namely to make unhappiness possible. In our happiness, we should form very sweet bonds, full of confidence and attachment, in order that the sundering of them may cause us that priceless rending of the heart which is called unhappiness.

Remembrance of Things Past.
The Past Recaptured

JOHN MILLINGTON SYNGE
[1871–1909]

It's in a lonesome place you do have to be talking with someone, and looking for someone, in the evening of the day.

In the Shadow of the Glen [*1903*]

What is the price of a thousand horses against a son where there is one son only?

Riders to the Sea [*1904*]

Bartley will have a fine coffin out of the white boards, and a deep grave surely. What more can we want than that? No man at all can be living for ever, and we must be satisfied.

Ibid.

When I was writing "The Shadow of the Glen" I got more aid than any learning could have given me from a chink in the floor of the old Wicklow house where I was staying, that let me hear what was being said by the servant girls in the kitchen.

The Playboy of the Western World [*1907*]. *Preface*

Drink a health to the wonders of the western world, the pirates, preachers, poteen-makers, with the jobbing jockies; parching peelers, and the juries fill their stomachs selling judgments of the English law.

Ibid. Act II

May I meet him with one tooth and it aching, and one eye to be seeing seven and seventy divils in the twists of the road, and one old timber leg on him to limp into the scalding grave. There he is now crossing the strands, and that the

Lord God would send a high wave to wash him from the world.[1]

> *The Playboy of the Western World. Act II*

Aid me for to win her, and I'll be asking God to stretch a hand to you in the hour of death, and lead you short cuts through the Meadows of Ease, and up the floor of Heaven to the Footstool of the Virgin's Son.

> *Ibid.*

A man who is not afraid of the sea will soon be drowned, he said, for he will be going out on a day he shouldn't. But we do be afraid of the sea, and we do only be drownded now and again.

> *The Aran Islands [1907]*

There is no language like the Irish for soothing and quieting.

> *Ibid.*

A translation is no translation, he said, unless it will give you the music of a poem along with the words of it.

> *Ibid.*

PAUL VALÉRY
[1871–1945]

The folly of mistaking a paradox for a discovery, a metaphor for a proof, a torrent of verbiage for a spring of capital truths, and oneself for an oracle, is inborn in us.

> *Introduction to the Method of Leonardo da Vinci* [2]

Collect all the facts that can be collected about the life of Racine and you will never learn from them the art of his verse. All criticism is dominated by the outworn theory that the man is the cause of the work as in the eyes of the law the criminal is the cause of the

[1] May the grass grow at your door and the fox build his nest on your hearthstone. May the light fade from your eyes, so you never see what you love. May your own blood rise against you, and the sweetest drink take be the bitterest cup of sorrow. May you die without benefit of clergy; may there be none to shed a tear at your grave, and may the hearthstone of hell be your best bed forever. — *Traditional Wexford curse*

See O. Henry, page 802a.

[2] Translated by THOMAS McGREEVY.

crime. Far rather are they both the effects.

> *Introduction to the Method of Leonardo da Vinci*

ALBERT EDWARD WIGGAM
[1871–]

Intelligence appears to be the thing that enables a man to get along without education. Education appears to be the thing that enables a man to get along without the use of his intelligence.

> *The New Decalogue of Science* [1923]

Statesmanship should quickly learn the lesson of biology, as stated by Conklin, that "Wooden legs are not inherited, but wooden heads are."

> *Ibid.*

EVERARD JACK APPLETON
[1872–1931]

Somewhere she waits to make you win,
Your soul in her firm white hands;
Somewhere the gods have made for you
The woman who understands.

> *The Woman Who Understands*

SIR MAX BEERBOHM
[1872–]

Most women are not so young as they are painted.

> *A Defence of Cosmetics*

Zuleika, on a desert island, would have spent most of her time in looking for a man's foot-print.

> *Zuleika Dobson [1911]. Chap. 2*

She was hardly more affable than a cameo.

> *Ibid. Chap. 3*

The dullard's envy of brilliant men is always assuaged by the suspicion that they will come to a bad end.

> *Ibid. Chap. 4*

Ordinary saints grow faint to posterity; whilst quite ordinary sinners pass vividly down the ages.

> *Ibid. Chap. 6*

She was one of the people who say "I don't know anything about music really, but I know what I like." [1]
Zuleika Dobson. Chap. 9

The Oxford spirit — that gentlest spirit, so lingering and searching, so dear to them who as youths were brought into ken of it, so exasperating to them who were not.
Ibid. Chap. 12

Of all the objects of hatred, a woman once loved is the most hateful.
Ibid. Chap. 13

I have known no man of genius who had not to pay, in some affliction or defect either physical or spiritual, for what the gods had given him.
No. 2, The Pines

It seems to be a law of nature that no man ever is loth to sit for his portrait. A man may be old, he may be ugly, he may be burdened with grave responsibilities to the nation, and that nation be at a crisis of its history; but none of these considerations, nor all of them together, will deter him from sitting for his portrait.
Quia Imperfectum

To say that a man is vain means merely that he is pleased with the effect he produces on other people. A conceited man is satisfied with the effect he produces on himself.
Ibid.

Strange, when you come to think of it, that of all the countless folk who have lived before our time on this planet not one is known in history or in legend as having died of laughter.
Laughter

LÉON BLUM
[1872–1950]

Life does not give itself to one who tries to keep all its advantages at once.

I have often thought morality may perhaps consist solely in the courage of making a choice.
Quoted in The Practical Cogitator. [1]
Page 97

No government can remain stable in an unstable society and an unstable world.
A l'Échelle Humaine [1945].
Page 54

JAMES BONE
[1872–   ]

"London!" It has the sound of distant thunder.
The London Perambulator [1925]

The mighty fleet of Wren, with their topgallants and mainsails of stone.
Ibid.

It was in London that Whistler discovered the nocturne.
Ibid.

The City of Dreadful Height.
Description of New York [2]

To make a cliché is to make a classic. [3]
Farewell speech on Fleet Street,
December 29, 1945

He made righteousness readable.
Of C. P. Scott [1846–1932], editor
of the Manchester Guardian

PATRICK REGINALD CHALMERS
[1872–1942]

Oh, bright as a berry,
  They're red and they're rare,
The setters from Kerry,
  And Cork and Kildare!
The Red Dogs

"I find," said 'e, "things very much as 'ow I've always found,

---

[1] Bromide No. 1. — GELETT BURGESS: *Are You a Bromide?* [1906]
  In art I pull no high-brow stuff,
  I know what I like, and that's enough.
  WILLIAM W. WOOLLCOTT [1877–1949]: *I Am a One Hundred Percent American, St. 3*

[1] Selected and arranged by CHARLES P. CURTIS, JR., and FERRIS GREENSLET [1945].
[2] In *The Manchester Guardian.*
[3] Apropos the phrase "ocean greyhound," first said by his father, David Drummond Bone, Glasgow journalist, referring to the *Alaska* [1881], first ship to cross the Atlantic in less than a week.

For mostly they goes up and down or
    else goes round and round."
                Roundabouts and Swings.
                            Stanza 2
What's lost upon the roundabouts we
    pulls up on the swings!
                                Ibid.
A little dog
Walked out that day with These,
Round eyes agog
    For butterflies and bees,
Wet nose for smells that please.
                A Chosen Saint.[1] Stanza 3

CALVIN COOLIDGE
[1872–1933]

There is no right to strike against the
public safety by anybody, anywhere,
any time.
    *Telegram to Samuel Gompers,
    President of the American Fed-
    eration of Labor, on the occa-
    sion of the Boston police strike
    [September 14, 1919]*
Inflation is repudiation.
    Speech, Chicago [January 11, 1922]
The business of America is business.
    *Speech before the Society of
    American Newspaper Editors
    [January 17, 1925]*
They hired the money, didn't they?
    *Referring to the European war
    debts [1925]*
I do not choose to run for President
in 1928.
    *Statement to reporters, Rapid
    City, South Dakota [August 2,
    1927]*
I love Vermont because of her hills
and valleys, her scenery and invigor-
ating climate, but most of all because
of her indomitable people.
    *Address from train platform,
    Bennington, Vermont [Septem-
    ber 21, 1928]*

[1] Go thou with this man, and God, which
dwelleth in heaven, prosper your journey,
and the angel of God keep you company. So
they went forth both, and the young man's
dog with them. — *The Apocrypha: Tobit,
V, 16*

JAMES B. DOLLARD
[1872–   ]

I'm sick o' New York City an' the
    roarin' o' the thrains
That rowl above the blessèd roofs an'
    undernaith the dhrains;
Wid dust an' smoke an' divilmint I'm
    moidhered head an' brains,
    An' I'm thinkin' o' the skies of ould
Kilkinny!
                Ould Kilkinny!

PAUL LAURENCE DUNBAR
[1872–1906]

Folks ain't got no right to censuah otha
    folks about dey habits;
Him dat giv' de squir'ls de bushtails
    made de bobtails fu' de rabbits.
                        Accountability
You cain't sta't no notes a-flyin'
    Lak de ones dat rants and rings
From de kitchen to de big woods
    When Malindy sings.
                    When Malindy Sings
There is a heaven, for ever, day by day,
The upward longing of my soul doth
    tell me so.
There is a hell, I'm quite as sure; for
    pray,
If there were not, where would my
    neighbors go?
                            Theology
Speak up, Ike, an' 'spress yo'se'f.
                        Encouragement
Sweetah den de music of a lovesick
    mockin'-bird,
Comin' f'om de gal you loves better den
    yo' kin,
"Howdy, honey, howdy, won't you step
    right in?"
                "Howdy, Honey, Howdy!"
Heish yo' mouf, I's only tu'nin' of de
    chillun in de bed.
                *The Turning of the Babies
                            in the Bed*
It's easy 'nough to titter w'en de stew
    is smokin' hot,
But hit's mighty ha'd to giggle w'en
    dey's nuffin' in de pot.
                            Philosophy

Poor was the loan at best —
God! but the interest!
The Debt. Stanza 3

LEARNED HAND
[1872–   ]

Justice, I think, is the tolerable accommodation of the conflicting interests of society, and I don't believe there is any royal road to attain such accommodations concretely.
Quoted by PHILIP HAMBURGER: *The Great Judge* [LIFE, *November 4, 1946*]

I had rather take my chance that some traitors will escape detection than spread abroad a spirit of general suspicion and distrust, which accepts rumor and gossip in place of undismayed and unintimidated inquiry.
Speech, Convocation of the Board of Regents, University of the State of New York [*October 24, 1952*]

That community is already in the process of dissolution where each man begins to eye his neighbor as a possible enemy, where nonconformity with the accepted creed, political as well as religious, is a mark of disaffection; where denunciation, without specification or backing, takes the place of evidence; where orthodoxy chokes freedom of dissent; where faith in the eventual supremacy of reason has become so timid that we dare not enter our convictions in the open lists, to win or lose.
Ibid.

The mutual confidence on which all else depends can be maintained only by an open mind and a brave reliance upon free discussion.
Ibid.

MILDRED HOWELLS
[1872–   ]

And so it criticized each flower,
This supercilious seed;
Until it woke one summer hour,
And found itself a weed.
The Difficult Seed. Stanza 5

Oh, tell me how my garden grows,
Where I no more may take delight,
And if some dream of me it knows,
Who dream of it by day and night.
Oh, Tell Me How My Garden Grows. Stanza 5

RUPERT HUGHES
[1872–1948]

Dear little child, this little book
Is less a primer than a key
To sunder gates where wonder waits
Your "Open Sesame!"
With a First Reader

JOHN McCRAE
[1872–1918]

In Flanders fields the poppies blow
Between the crosses, row on row.
In Flanders Fields.[1] *Stanza 1*
Take up our quarrel with the foe:
To you from failing hands we throw
The torch; be yours to hold it high.
If ye break faith with us who die
We shall not sleep, though poppies grow
In Flanders fields.
Ibid. Stanza 3

PATRICK F. O'KEEFE
[1872–1934]

Say It with Flowers.[2]
Slogan for the Society of American Florists [*1917*]

CALE YOUNG RICE
[1872–1943]

Spring has come up from the South again,
With soft mists in her hair,
And a warm wind in her mouth again,
And budding everywhere.
The Immortal. Stanza 1
You who are old,
And have fought the fight,
And have won or lost or left the fight,

[1] In *Punch*, December 8, 1915.
[2] Say It with Music. — *Title of song by* IRVING BERLIN [1921]

Weight us not down
With fears of the world, as we run!
The Young to the Old

BERTRAND RUSSELL
[1872–   ]

It is preoccupation with possession, more than anything else, that prevents men from living freely and nobly.
*Principles of Social Recon-
struction* [*1916*]

Mathematics possesses not only truth, but supreme beauty — a beauty cold and austere, like that of sculpture, without appeal to any part of our weaker nature, sublimely pure, and capable of a stern perfection such as only the greatest art can show.
The Study of Mathematics

Mathematics takes us into the region of absolute necessity, to which not only the actual world, but every possible world, must conform.
Ibid.

The psychology of adultery has been falsified by conventional morals, which assume, in monogamous countries, that attraction to one person cannot coexist with a serious affection for another. Everybody knows that this is untrue.
Marriage and Morals [*1929*]. *XVI*

A good society is a means to a good life for those who compose it; not something having a kind of excellence on its own account.
Authority and the Individual
[*1949*]

ELLERY SEDGWICK
[1872–   ]

Autobiographies ought to begin with Chapter Two.
The Happy Profession [*1946*].
Chap. 1

Maternal testimony notwithstanding, babies are like as biscuits in a pan.
Ibid.

In America, getting on in the world means getting out of the world we have known before.
Ibid.

Democracy's real test lies in its respect for minority opinion.
The Happy Profession. Chap. 5

Against the misuse of words every editorial prejudice should be fixed in concrete.
Ibid. Chap. 18

ALBERT PAYSON TERHUNE
[1872–1942]

Win without boasting. Lose without excuse.
More About Dog Shows

ERNEST VINCENT WRIGHT
[1872–1939]

Then all of us prepare to rise
And hold our bibs before our eyes,
And be prepared for some surprise
When father carves the duck.
When Father Carves the Duck
[*1891*]. *Stanza 1*

CARL LOTUS BECKER
[1873–1945]

Economic distress will teach men, if anything can, that realities are less dangerous than fancies, that fact-finding is more effective than fault-finding.
Progress and Power [*1935*]

The significance of man is that he is that part of the universe that asks the question, What is the significance of Man? He alone can stand apart imaginatively and, regarding himself and the universe in their eternal aspects, pronounce a judgment: The significance of man is that he is insignificant and is aware of it.
Ibid.

Those of us who think that we are a nation of starry-eyed idealists [1] who have been twice tricked by the British into a European war in order to pull their chestnuts out of the fire have read the history of this country to little purpose. . . . The truth is rather that the existence and friendliness of the British

[1] See Henry Agard Wallace, page 948b.

861

Empire and the power of the British Fleet have for more than a century enabled us to roast our own chestnuts at leisure and eat them in security.
Progress and Power

HENRY NOEL BRAILSFORD
[1873–   ]

Music is neither secular nor religious. It can at best suggest the beating of the pulse, the rhythm of the blood that accompanies a given order of ideas.
On Handel's Largo

The musician who tries to rival the painter by describing external things, is a magician who has thrown aside his wand to wield a quarter-staff.
The Sea in Music

GUY WETMORE CARRYL
[1873–1904]

You call it a waste of time, this taste
  For popular tunes, and yet
Good-bye to care when you whistle the
  air
Of the song that you can't forget.
The Organ Man. Stanza 3

And in his dim, uncertain sight
Whatever wasn't must be right,
From which it follows he had strong
Convictions that what was, was wrong.
*The Iconoclastic Rustic and the
Apropos Acorn. Stanza 2*

In every new and smart disease,
From housemaid's knee to heart disease,
She recognized the symptoms as her own!
*How Jack Found That Beans May
Go Back on a Chap. Stanza 2*

The people wait at the haven's gate to greet the men who win!
Thank God for peace! Thank God for peace, when the great gray ships come in!
*When the Great Gray Ships
Come In. Stanza 4*

ARTHUR CHAPMAN
[1873–1935]

Out where the handclasp's a little
  stronger,
Out where the smile dwells a little
  longer,
That's where the West begins.
*Out Where the West Begins.
Stanza 1*

Out where the skies are a trifle bluer,
Out where friendship's a little truer.
Ibid. Stanza 2

Where there's more of singing and less
  of sighing,
Where there's more of giving and less of
  buying,
And a man makes friends without half
  trying.
Ibid. Stanza 3

WALTER DE LA MARE
[1873–   ]

Slowly, silently, now the moon
Walks the night in her silver shoon.
Silver

"World of divine delight," heart whispereth,
Though all its all lie but 'twixt birth and death.
Divine Delight

Here lies a most beautiful lady,
Light of step and heart was she.
An Epitaph

"Is there anybody there?" said the
  Traveller,
  Knocking on the moonlit door;
And his horse in the silence champed
  the grasses
  Of the forest's ferny floor.
The Listeners

"Tell them that I came, and no one
  answered,
That I kept my word," he said.
Ibid.

If I were Lord of Tartary,
  Myself and me alone,
My bed should be of ivory,
  Of beaten gold my throne.
Tartary. Stanza 1

'Tis the immortal thought
  Whose passion still
Makes of the unchanging
  The unchangeable.
When the Rose Is Faded.
Stanza 3

No lovelier hills than thine have laid
  My tired thoughts to rest:
No peace of lovelier valleys made
  Like peace within my breast.
England. Stanza 1

Hi! handsome hunting man,
Fire your little gun.
Bang! Now the animal
Is dead and dumb and done.
Nevermore to peep again, creep again,
  leap again,
Eat or sleep or drink again, oh, what
  fun!
Hi!

Memory — that strange deceiver!
Who can trust her? How believe her —
While she hoards with equal care
The poor and trivial, rich and rare;
Yet flings away, as wantonly,
Grave fact and loveliest fantasy?
Memory

Poor Jim Jay
Got stuck fast
In Yesterday.
Jim Jay

It's a very odd thing —
As odd as can be —
That whatever Miss T. eats
Turns into Miss T.
Miss T.

Three jolly gentlemen,
In coats of red,
Rode their horses
Up to bed.
The Huntsmen

Not the briefest moment — yours or
  mine —
Can ever come again.
Not One. Stanza 2

Be not too wildly amorous of the far,
Nor lure thy fantasy to its utmost scope.
The Imagination's Pride

I met at eve the Prince of Sleep,
  His was a still and lovely face,

He wandered through a valley steep,
  Lovely in a lonely place.
I Met at Eve

MARK FENDERSON
[1873–1944]

What's the use? Yesterday an egg,
tomorrow a feather duster.
Caption of Cartoon, The
Dejected Rooster

FORD MADOX (HUEFFER)
FORD
[1873–1939]

Sometimes wind and sometimes rain,
Then the sun comes back again;
Sometimes rain and sometimes snow,
Goodness, how we'd like to know
Why the weather alters so.
Children's Song. Stanza 1

Only two classes of books are of universal appeal: the very best and the
very worst.
Joseph Conrad [*1924*]

PERCY HAMMOND
[1873–1936]

The female knee is a joint and not an
entertainment.
Dramatic Review

DANIEL GREGORY MASON
[1873–   ]

The ideal of Independence requires
resistance to the herd spirit now so
widespread, to our worship of quantity and indifference to quality, to our
unthinking devotion to organization,
standardization, propaganda, and ad-
vertising.
Artistic Ideals [*1927*]

Art of any profundity can be appreciated only slowly, gradually, in leisurely contemplation.
Ibid.

JAMES JACKSON MONTAGUE
[1873–1941]

My beagle bit a Kleagle
Of the Ku Klux Klan.
Doomed. Stanza 1

But no one ever is allowed in Sleepy-
town, unless
He goes to bed in time to take the
Sleepytown Express!
The Sleepytown Express. Stanza 1

ELIZABETH CUTTER
(MRS. DWIGHT WHITNEY)
MORROW
[1873–1955]

My friend and I have built a wall
Between us thick and wide:
The stones of it are laid in scorn
And plastered high with pride.
Wall. Stanza 1

There is no lover like an island shore
For lingering embrace;
No tryst so faithful as the turning tide
At its accustomed place.
Islands. Stanza 1

ALBERT JAY NOCK
[1873–1945]

All Souls College, Oxford, planned
better than it knew when it limited the
number of its undergraduates to four;
four is exactly the right number for any
college which is really intent on getting
results.
*Memoirs of a Superfluous Man
[1943]. III, Chap. 3*

Money does not pay for anything,
never has, never will. It is an economic
axiom as old as the hills that goods and
services can be paid for only with goods
and services.
Ibid. Chap. 13

As sheer casual reading-matter, I still
find the English dictionary the most
interesting book in our language.
Ibid. IV, Chap. 1

SIME SILVERMAN [1]
[1873–1933]

Wall Street Lays An Egg.
*Headline announcing the stock
market crash of October, 1929*

Sticks Nix Hicks Pix.
*Headline, meaning that the
rural audiences do not care for
moving pictures dealing with
country themes*

ALFRED EMANUEL SMITH [2]
[1873–1944]

The kiss of death.
*Alluding to Hearst's support of
Ogden Mills, Smith's unsuccess-
ful opponent in the 1926 cam-
paign for Governor of New
York State*

Let's look at the record.
Campaign Speeches [1928]

The Governor of New York State
does not have to be an acrobat.
*Speech in behalf of Franklin
D. Roosevelt [1928]*

Nobody shoots at Santa Claus.
Campaign Speeches [1936]

No matter how thin you slice it, it's
still boloney.
Ibid.

H. M. TOMLINSON
[1873–   ]

The sea is at its best at London, near
midnight, when you are within the
arms of a capacious chair, before a
glowing fire, selecting phases of the
voyages you will never make.
The Sea and the Jungle [1912]

[1] Silverman, who founded and edited the
famous theatrical trade paper *Variety* [1905],
had perhaps more influence on American
slang than any man of his time.

[2] He is the Happy Warrior of the political
battlefield. — FRANKLIN D. ROOSEVELT: *Nominating Speech, Democratic National Convention* [June 26, 1924] (See Wordsworth,
pages 409b–410a.)

Al Smith knew as much as any living man
of the art of democratic government. — EL-
LERY SEDGWICK: *The Happy Profession*
[1946], *Chap. 17*

How many grave speeches, which have surprised, shocked, and directed the nation, have been made by Great Men too soon after a noble dinner, words winged by the Press without an accompanying and explanatory wine list.

Waiting for Daylight [*1922*]

The reader who is illuminated is, in a real sense, the poem.

Between the Lines [*1930*]

Bad and indifferent criticism of books is just as serious as a city's careless drainage.

Ibid.

What was created in Concord, though in so airy a fashion, may be standing to America's credit when her vast engine shops are homes for spiders.

The Road to Concord [*1931*]

LENA GUILBERT FORD
[*Floruit* 1915]

Keep the home fires burning,
While your hearts are yearning,
Though your lads are far away
They dream of home.
There's a silver lining
Through the dark cloud shining,
Turn the dark cloud inside out,
Till the boys come home.

Keep the Home Fires Burning
[*1915*]

SIR NORMAN ANGELL
[1874–   ]

The Great Illusion.

Title of book [*1910*] *on the
futility of war*

The power of words is such that they have prevented our learning some of the most important events in the world's history.

Let the People Know [*1943*].
*Chap. 7: Words That Are
Assassins*

MAURICE BARING
[1874–1945]

All theories of what a good play is, or how a good play should be written, are futile. A good play is a play which when acted upon the boards makes an audience interested and pleased. A play that fails in this is a bad play.

Have You Anything to Declare?

CHARLES AUSTIN BEARD
[1874–1948]
AND
MARY RITTER BEARD
[1876–   ]

At no time, at no place, in solemn convention assembled, through no chosen agents, had the American people officially proclaimed the United States to be a democracy. The Constitution did not contain the word or any word lending countenance to it, except possibly the mention of "We, the people," in the preamble . . . when the Constitution was framed no respectable person called himself or herself a democrat.

America in Midpassage [*1939*].
Chap. 17

SIR DAVID WILLIAM BONE
[1874–   ]

We sailors are jealous for our vessels. Abuse us if you will, but have a care for what you may say of our ships. We alone are entitled to call them bitches, wet brutes, stubborn craft, but we will stand for no such liberties from the beach.

Merchantmen-at-Arms

GORDON BOTTOMLEY
[1874–1948]

Many deaths have place in men
  Before they come to die;
Joys must be used and spent, and then
  Abandoned and passed by.

New Year's Eve, 1913

When you destroy a blade of grass
You poison England at her roots.

To Ironfounders and Others

Your worship is your furnaces,
Which, like old idols, lost obscenes,
Have molten bowels; your vision is
Machines for making more machines.
To Ironfounders and Others

ANNA HEMPSTEAD BRANCH
[1874-1937]

Order is a lovely thing;
On disarray it lays its wing,
Teaching simplicity to sing.
The Monk in the Kitchen
His screaming stallions maned with
    whistling wind.
Nimrod Wars with the Angels
God wove a web of loveliness,
Of clouds and stars and birds,
But made not anything at all
So beautiful as words.
*Songs for My Mother: Her
Words. Stanza 5*
Oh, grieve not, ladies, if at night
Ye wake to feel your beauty going.
It was a web of frail delight,
Inconstant as an April snowing.
Grieve Not, Ladies. Stanza 1

ARTHUR HENRY REGINALD BULLER
[1874-1944]

There was a young lady named Bright,
Whose speed was far faster than light;
    She set out one day
    In a relative way,
And returned home the previous night.
Limerick [1]

GILBERT KEITH CHESTERTON
[1874-1936]

Nothing sublimely artistic has ever
arisen out of mere art, any more than
anything essentially reasonable has
ever arisen out of the pure reason.
There must always be a rich moral soil
for any great aesthetic growth.
A Defence of Nonsense

[1] *Punch,* December 19, 1923.

Every great literature has always
been allegorical — allegorical of some
view of the whole universe.
A Defence of Nonsense
The whole difference between construction and creation is exactly this:
that a thing constructed can only be
loved after it is constructed; but a
thing created is loved before it exists.
Preface to DICKENS'S
Pickwick Papers
A man knows what style of book he
wants to write when he knows nothing
else about it.
Ibid.
A good joke is the one ultimate and
sacred thing which cannot be criticized.
Our relations with a good joke are di-
rect and even divine relations.
Ibid.
The world will never starve for won-
ders; but only for want of wonder.
*Inscription on General Motors
Building, Century of Progress
Exposition, Chicago*
But they that fought for England,
Following a fallen star,
Alas, alas for England
They have their graves afar.
Elegy in a Country Churchyard
Thieves respect property. They
merely wish the property to become
their property that they may more per-
fectly respect it.
Ibid.
Mr. Max Beerbohm attempted to
analyze the jokes at which the mob
laughs. He divided them into three sec-
tions: jokes about bodily humiliation,
jokes about things alien, such as foreigners, and jokes about bad cheese.
Cockneys and Their Jokes
Art is limitation; the essence of
every picture is the frame.
Orthodoxy. Chap. 3
You can free things from alien or accidental laws, but not from the laws of
their own nature. . . . Do not go
about as a demagogue, encouraging tri-
angles to break out of the prison of
their three sides. If a triangle breaks

out of its three sides, its life comes to a lamentable end.

Orthodoxy. Chap. 3

Heights were made to be looked at, not to be looked from.

The Innocence of Father Brown
(The Hammer of God)

The English poor, broken in every revolt, bullied by every fashion, long despoiled of property, and now being despoiled of liberty, entered history with a noise of trumpets, and turned themselves in two years into one of the iron armies of the world.

A Short History of England [*1917*]

The cold queen of England is looking in the glass;
The shadow of the Valois is yawning at the Mass.

Lepanto

Don John of Austria is going to the war.

Ibid.

The hidden room in man's house where God sits all the year,
The secret window whence the world looks small and very dear.

Ibid.

Cervantes on his galley sets the sword back in the sheath
(Don John of Austria rides homeward with a wreath).

And he sees across a weary land a straggling road in Spain,
Up which a lean and foolish knight forever rides in vain.

Ibid.

To an open house in the evening
Home shall men come,
To an older place than Eden
And a taller town than Rome.

The House of Christmas

Burn from my brain and from my breast
Sloth, and the cowardice that clings,
And stiffness and the soul's arrest:
And feed my brain with better things.

A Ballade of a Book-Reviewer

The strangest whim has seized me . . . After all
I think I will not hang myself today.

A Ballade of Suicide

St. George he was for England,
And before he killed the dragon
He drank a pint of English ale
Out of an English flagon.

The Englishman

Step softly, under snow or rain,
To find the place where men can pray;
The way is all so very plain
That we may lose the way.

The Wise Men

And Noah he often said to his wife when he sat down to dine,
"I don't care where the water goes if it doesn't get into the wine."

Wine and Water

Before the Roman came to Rye or out to Severn strode,
The rolling English drunkard made the rolling English road.

The Rolling English Road

Tea is like the East he grows in,
A great yellow Mandarin
With urbanity of manner
And unconsciousness of sin.

The Song of Right and Wrong

Cocoa is a cad and coward.

Ibid.

For the great Gaels of Ireland
Are the men that God made mad,
For all their wars are merry,
And all their songs are sad.[1]

The Ballad of the White Horse.
Book II

And if ever ye ride in Ireland,
The jest may yet be said,
There is the land of broken hearts,
And the land of broken heads.

Ibid. Book V

I also had my hour;
One far fierce hour and sweet:
There was a shout about my ears,
And palms before my feet.

The Donkey

The Yankee is a dab at electricity and crime,
He tells you how he hustles and it takes him quite a time,

[1] For the Young Gaels of Ireland
Are the lads that drive me mad;
For half their words need footnotes,
And half their rhymes are bad.
ARTHUR GUITERMAN [1871–1943]:
The Young Celtic Poets, St. 2

I like his hospitality that's cordial and
frank,
I do not mind his money but I do not
like his swank.
                    A Song of Self-Esteem

The face of Father Brown . . .
could shine with ignorance as well as
with knowledge.[1]
            The Wisdom of Father Brown

SIR WINSTON SPENCER
CHURCHILL [2]
[1874–   ]

I pass with relief from the tossing
sea of Cause and Theory to the firm
ground of Result and Fact.
        The Malakand Field Force [*1898*]

It is better to be making the news
than taking it; to be an actor rather
than a critic.
                            Ibid.

Nothing in life is so exhilarating as
to be shot at without result.
                            Ibid.

There are men in the world who derive as stern an exaltation from the
proximity of disaster and ruin, as others
from success.
                            Ibid.

Terminological inexactitude.
        Speech, House of Commons,
                February 22, 1906

The maxim of the British people is
"Business as usual."
    Speech, Guildhall, November 9,
                            1914

By being so long in the lowest form
[at Harrow] I gained an immense advantage over the cleverer boys. . . .
I got into my bones the essential structure of the ordinary British sentence —
which is a noble thing. Naturally I am

---

[1] My father, a good man, told me "Never
lose your ignorance; you cannot replace it."
— ERICH MARIA REMARQUE, interviewed in
The New York Times, January 27, 1946
[2] See also Roosevelt and Churchill, page
922a.

biassed in favor of boys learning English; and then I would let the clever
ones learn Latin as an honor, and Greek
as a treat.
        Roving Commission: My Early
                    Life [*1930*]

Decided only to be undecided, resolved to be irresolute, adamant for
drift, solid for fluidity, all-powerful to
be impotent.[1]
            While England Slept [*1936*]

Dictators ride to and fro upon tigers
which they dare not dismount. And the
tigers are getting hungry.
                            Ibid.

I have watched this famous island
descending incontinently, fecklessly,
the stairway which leads to a dark gulf.
It is a fine broad stairway at the beginning, but after a bit the carpet ends.
A little farther on there are only flag-
stones, and a little farther on still these
break beneath your feet.
                            Ibid.

The German dictator, instead of
snatching the victuals from the table,
has been content to have them served
to him course by course.
        *Speech on the Munich Agree-
        ment, House of Commons,
        October 5, 1938*

That long [Canadian] frontier from
the Atlantic to the Pacific Oceans,
guarded only by neighborly respect
and honorable obligations, is an example to every country and a pattern
for the future of the world.
        *Speech in honor of R. B.
        Bennett, Canada Club, London,
        April 20, 1939*

I cannot forecast to you the action
of Russia. It is a riddle wrapped in a
mystery inside an enigma.
        Broadcast, October 1, 1939

For each and for all, as for the
Royal Navy, the watchword should be,
"Carry on, and dread nought."
        *Speech on Traffic at Sea, House
        of Commons, December 6, 1939*

---

[1] Of Stanley Baldwin's policies.

I have nothing to offer but blood, toil, tears and sweat.[1]

First Statement as Prime Minister, House of Commons, May 13, 1940

Victory at all costs, victory in spite of all terror, victory however long and hard the road may be; for without victory there is no survival.

Ibid.

We shall not flag or fail. We shall fight in France, we shall fight on the seas and oceans, we shall fight with growing confidence and growing strength in the air, we shall defend our island, whatever the cost may be, we shall fight on the beaches, we shall fight on the landing grounds, we shall fight in the fields and in the streets, we shall fight in the hills; we shall never surrender.

Speech on Dunkirk, House of Commons, June 4, 1940

If we open a quarrel between the past and the present, we shall find that we have lost the future.

Speech, House of Commons (later broadcast), June 18, 1940

Let us therefore brace ourselves to our duties, and so bear ourselves that, if the British Empire and its Common-

---

[1] Mollifie it with thy teares, or sweat, or blood. — JOHN DONNE: *An Anatomy of the World* [1611], *I, 430–431*

Year after year they voted cent per cent,
Blood, sweat, and tear-wrung millions —
why? for rent!
BYRON: *The Age of Bronze* [1823], *XIV*
A similar phrase was also used by GIUSEPPE GARIBALDI [1807–1882] in his *Address to the Thousand.*
It [poetry] is forged slowly and patiently, link by link, with sweat and blood and tears. — LORD ALFRED DOUGLAS: *Collected Poems* [1919]
Their sweat, their tears, their blood bedewed the endless plain. — WINSTON S. CHURCHILL: *The Unknown War* [1931], referring to the armies of the Czar before the Russian Revolution
Churchill referred to his promise of blood, toil, tears and sweat in subsequent speeches on October 8, 1940, May 7 and December 2, 1941, and January 27 and November 10, 1942.

---

wealth last for a thousand years, men will still say: "This was their finest hour."

Speech, House of Commons, June 18, 1940

We shall defend every village, every town and every city. The vast mass of London itself, fought street by street, could easily devour an entire hostile army; and we would rather see London laid in ruins and ashes than that it should be tamely and abjectly enslaved.

Radio Broadcast, July 14, 1940

Never in the field of human conflict was so much owed by so many to so few.

Tribute to the Royal Air Force, House of Commons, August 20, 1940

The British Empire and the United States will have to be somewhat mixed up together in some of their affairs for mutual and general advantage. For my own part, looking out upon the future, I do not view the process with any misgivings. I could not stop it if I wished; no one can stop it. Like the Mississippi, it just keeps rolling along.[1] Let it roll. Let it roll on full flood, inexorable, irresistible, benignant, to broader lands and better days.

Ibid.

This wicked man Hitler, the repository and embodiment of many forms of soul-destroying hatred, this monstrous product of former wrongs and shame.

Radio Broadcast, September 11, 1940

Death and sorrow will be the companions of our journey; hardship our garment; constancy and valor our only shield. We must be united, we must be undaunted, we must be inflexible.

Report on the War Situation, House of Commons, October 8, 1940

---

[1] Ol' Man River [Mississippi] . . . he keeps on rollin' along. — OSCAR HAMMERSTEIN 2ND [1927], *music by* JEROME KERN

We are waiting for the long-promised invasion. So are the fishes.

Radio Broadcast to the French People, October 21, 1940

The only guide to a man is his conscience; the only shield to his memory is the rectitude and sincerity of his actions.

Tribute to Neville Chamberlain, House of Commons, November 12, 1940

To die at the height of a man's career, the highest moment of his effort here in this world, universally honored and admired, to die while great issues are still commanding the whole of his interest, to be taken from us at a moment when he could already see ultimate success in view — is not the most unenviable of fates.[1]

Report on the War Situation, House of Commons, December 19, 1940

I do not resent criticism, even when, for the sake of emphasis, it parts for the time with reality.

Speech, House of Commons, January 22, 1941

Here is the answer which I will give to President Roosevelt. . . . Give us the tools, and we will finish the job.

Radio Broadcast, February 9, 1941

This is one of those cases in which the imagination is baffled by the facts.

Remark in the House of Commons, May 13, 1941 [following the parachute descent in Scotland by Rudolf Hess]

The British nation is unique in this respect. They are the only people who like to be told how bad things are, who like to be told the worst.

Report on the War Situation, House of Commons, June 10, 1941

A vile race of quislings[2] — to use

the new word which will carry the scorn of mankind down the centuries.

Speech at St. James's Palace, London, June 12, 1941

The destiny of mankind is not decided by material computation. When great causes are on the move in the world . . . we learn that we are spirits, not animals, and that something is going on in space and time, and beyond space and time, which, whether we like it or not, spells duty.

Radio Broadcast to America on receiving the Honorary Degree of Doctor of Laws from the University of Rochester, New York, June 16, 1941

We will have no truce or parley with you [Hitler], or the grisly gang who work your wicked will. You do your worst — and we will do our best.

Speech, London County Council, July 14, 1941

The V sign is the symbol of the unconquerable will of the occupied territories, and a portent of the fate awaiting the Nazi tyranny.

A Message to the People of Europe on the Launching of the "V for Victory" Propaganda Campaign, July 20, 1941

Nothing is more dangerous in wartime than to live in the temperamental atmosphere of a Gallup Poll,[1] always feeling one's pulse and taking one's temperature.

Report on the War Situation, House of Commons, September 30, 1941

Do not let us speak of darker days; let us speak rather of sterner days. These are not dark days: these are great days — the greatest days our country has ever lived; and we must all thank God that we have been allowed, each of us according to our stations, to

[1] Lord Lothian, British Ambassador to the United States, died in Washington, December 12, 1940.

[2] Vidkun Quisling, head of the Nasjonal Samling party in Norway, who co-operated and collaborated with the Nazis when Ger-

many invaded Norway, April 9, 1940. Quisling was executed October 23, 1945.

[1] Dr. George H. Gallup founded the British Institute of Public Opinion in 1936.

play a part in making these days memorable in the history of our race.

Address to the Boys of Harrow School, October 29, 1941

In the past we have had a light which flickered, in the present we have a light which flames, and in the future there will be a light which shines over all the land and sea.

Speech on War with Japan, House of Commons, December 8, 1941, and later broadcast

What kind of people do they [the Japanese] think we are?

Speech to United States Congress, December 24, 1941

We have not journeyed all this way across the centuries, across the oceans, across the mountains, across the prairies, because we are made of sugar candy.

Speech to the Canadian Senate and House of Commons, Ottawa, broadcast, December 30, 1941

When I warned [the French] that Britain would fight on alone whatever they did, their generals told their Prime Minister and his divided Cabinet, "In three weeks England will have her neck wrung like a chicken." Some chicken; some neck.

Ibid.

The late M. Venizelos [1] observed that in all her wars England — he should have said Britain, of course — always wins one battle — the last.

Speech at the Lord Mayor's Day Luncheon, London, November 10, 1942

Now this is not the end. It is not even the beginning of the end.[2] But it is, perhaps, the end of the beginning.

Ibid.

I have not become the King's First Minister in order to preside over the liquidation of the British Empire.

Ibid.

[1] Eleutherios Venizelos [1864–1936], Greek statesman.

[2] See Talleyrand, page 384a.

The soft under-belly of the Axis.

Report on the War Situation, House of Commons, November 11, 1942

There is no finer investment for any community than putting milk into babies.

Radio Broadcast: A Four Years' Plan, March 21, 1943

The proud German Army has once again proved the truth of the saying, "The Hun is always either at your throat or at your feet."

Speech to United States Congress, May 19, 1943

I quote the words of your great general, Nathan Bedford Forrest, the eminently successful Confederate leader. Asked the secret of his victories, Forrest said, "I git thar fustest with the mostest men." [1]

A Talk to the American Press in Washington, May 25, 1943

The House of Commons thrives on criticism, it is perfectly impervious to newspaper abuse or taunts from any quarter, and it is capable of digesting almost anything or almost any body of gentlemen, whatever be the views with which they arrive.

Speech on Rebuilding the House of Commons, October 28, 1943

There was a man who sold a hyena skin while the beast still lived and who was killed in hunting it.

Speech on Allied War Gains, House of Commons, August 2, 1944

"Not in vain" may be the pride of those who survived and the epitaph of those who fell.[2]

Speech, House of Commons, September 28, 1944

[1] General Nathan Bedford Forrest [1821–1877], Confederate cavalry leader. Historians deny that the General said it in such rustic terms, but the saying has become classic in this version.

[2] The eight thousand paratroopers of the First British Airborne Division who landed in Arnhem, Holland, behind the German lines, in September, 1944, and held the area for nine days and nights, with a loss of six thou-

The United States is a land of free speech. Nowhere is speech freer — not even here where we sedulously cultivate it even in its most repulsive form.
Speech, House of Commons, September 28, 1944

He died in harness, and we may well say in battle harness, like his soldiers, sailors and airmen who died side by side with ours and carrying out their tasks to the end all over the world. What an enviable death was his.
Tribute to President Franklin D. Roosevelt in the House of Commons, April 17, 1945

In Franklin Roosevelt there died the greatest American friend we have ever known — and the greatest champion of freedom who has ever brought help and comfort from the new world to the old.
Ibid.

I think "No comment" is a splendid expression. I am using it again and again. I got it from Sumner Welles.
To reporters at Washington airport, after conferring with President Truman at the White House, February 12, 1946

An iron curtain [1] has descended across the Continent.
Address at Westminster College, Fulton, Missouri, March 5, 1946

This address to which I have given the title, "The Sinews of Peace."
Ibid.

In War: Resolution. In Defeat: Defiance. In Victory: Magnanimity. In Peace: Good Will.
The Second World War: Moral of the Work. Vol. I, The Gathering Storm [1948]

No one can guarantee success in war, but only deserve it.
The Second World War: Moral of the Work. Vol. II, Their Finest Hour [1949]

When you have to kill a man it costs nothing to be polite.
Ibid. Vol. III, The Grand Alliance [1950]

This is the sort of impertinence up with which I will not put.[1]
Attributed

ISABEL FISKE CONANT
[1874–   ]

He who loves an old house
Never loves in vain,
How can an old house
Used to sun and rain,
To lilac and larkspur,
And an elm above,
Ever fail to answer
The heart that gives it love?
Old House. Stanza 1

CLARENCE DAY
[1874–1935]

When eras die, their legacies
Are left to strange police.
Professors in New England guard
The glory that was Greece.
Thoughts Without Words

The parting injunctions
Of mothers and wives
Are one of those functions
That poison their lives.
Scenes from the Mesozoic

It is possible that our race may be an accident, in a meaningless universe, living its brief life uncared-for, on this dark, cooling star: but even so — and all the more — what marvelous creatures we are! What fairy story, what tale from the Arabian Nights of the jinns, is a hundredth part as wonderful

---

sand men. Major General R. E. Urquhart, the Division commander, sent the radio message to Field Marshal Montgomery: "All will be ordered to break out rather than surrender."

[1] According to the London *Times*, the expression "iron curtain" was coined by Ludwig Schwerin von Krosigk, Hitler's Minister of Finance, and was used by Goebbels in his propaganda material for some years before Churchill adopted it.

[1] Reportedly a press worker had "corrected," on the printer's proof of Churchill's memoirs, a sentence which had ended idiomatically with a preposition; Churchill restored the original order, with the marginal comment quoted above.

as this true fairy story of simians! It is so much more heartening, too, than the tales we invent. A universe capable of giving birth to many such accidents is — blind or not — a good world to live in, a promising universe.
This Simian World [*1920*]. *XIX*

Father declared he was going to buy a new plot in the cemetery, a plot all for himself. "And I'll buy one on a corner," he added triumphantly, "where I can get out!"

Mother looked at him, startled but admiring, and whispered to me, "I almost believe he could do it."
Life with Father [*1935*]

THEODOSIA GARRISON
[1874–1944]

I never crossed your threshold with a grief
But that I went without it.
The Closed Door. Stanza 1

The kindliest thing God ever made,
His hand of very healing laid
Upon a fevered world, is shade.
Shade. Stanza 1

ELLEN GLASGOW
[1874–1945]

I have observed with wonder so many intellectual and literary fashions that I have come at last to rely positively upon one conviction alone. No idea is so antiquated that it was not once modern. No idea is so modern that it will not some day be antiquated. . . . To seize the flying thought before it escapes us is our only touch with reality.
Address to the Modern Language Association [*1936*]

Preserve, within a wild sanctuary, an inaccessible valley of reveries.
A Certain Measure [*1943*]

Tilling the fertile soil of man's vanity.
Ibid.

HARRY GRAHAM
[1874–1936]

Billy, in one of his nice new sashes,
Fell in the fire and was burnt to ashes;
Now, although the room grows chilly,
I haven't the heart to poke poor Billy.
Ruthless Rhymes for Heartless Homes [*1899*]. *Tender-Heartedness*

Auntie, did you feel no pain
Falling from that apple tree?
Would you do it, please, again?
'Cos my friend here didn't see.
Ibid. Appreciation

HERBERT CLARK HOOVER
[1874–   ]

A great social and economic experiment [Prohibition], noble in motive and far-reaching in purpose.
Letter to Senator William E. Borah, February 28, 1928

The American system of rugged individualism.
Campaign speech, New York [*October 22, 1928*]

While I can make no claim for having introduced the term "rugged individualism," I should be proud to have invented it. It has been used by American leaders for over a half-century in eulogy of those God-fearing men and women of honesty whose stamina and character and fearless assertion of rights led them to make their own way in life.
The Challenge to Liberty [*1934*]. *Chap. 5*

A good many things go around in the dark besides Santa Claus.
Address, John Marshall Republican Club, St. Louis, Missouri [*December 16, 1935*]

Older men declare war. But it is youth that must fight and die. And it is youth who must inherit the tribula-

tion, the sorrow, and the triumphs that are the aftermath of war.[1]
Speech, Republican National Convention, Chicago, June 27, 1944

HAROLD L. ICKES
[1874–1952]

I am against government by crony.
On resigning as Secretary of the Interior, February, 1946

ALVIN SAUNDERS JOHNSON
[1874–]

As in the bosom of the earth vestiges of all earlier life may still be found, so in the bosom of public opinion are to be found vestiges of the early dinosaurs of thought.
On German Pacification [1944]

HEWLETT JOHNSON [2]
[1874–]

Not so easily does a people liberate itself from its social past. Many ideas, customs, intolerances, and tolerances, too, cling on unperceived by those who think that they live in days where all things are new.
The Soviet Power: The Socialist Sixth of the World [1940]. Book II, 2

Nothing is better calculated to drive men to desperation than when, in attempting to carry out beneficial reform, they find the whole world aligned against them. The more especially so if amongst those so aligned they discover men who had preached the same ideal, but now dreaded its concrete realization.
Ibid. 3

W. L. MACKENZIE KING
[1874–1950]

Labor can do nothing without capital, capital nothing without labor, and neither labor or capital can do anything without the guiding genius of management; and management, however wise its genius may be, can do nothing without the privileges which the community affords.
Canadian Club Speech, Montreal [March 17, 1919]

Government, in the last analysis, is organized opinion. Where there is little or no public opinion, there is likely to be bad government, which sooner or later becomes autocratic government.
Message of the Carillon [1927]. Page 139

HENRY HERBERT KNIBBS
[1874–1945]

When he is hidden from the sun,
And grasses grow where he is laid,
Men mark the good a man has done,
And glorify the name he made.
The Journey

Adventure was his coronal,
And all his wealth was wandering.
Ibid.

After the coffee things ain't so bad.
That Inside Song

You haven't whipped religion; just a man.
The Fighting Parson

AMY LOWELL
[1874–1925]

Hung all over with mouse-traps of metres, and cages
Of bright-plumaged rhythms, with pages and pages
Of colors slit up into streaming confetti.
A Critical Fable [1922] (passage describing herself)

I walk down the garden paths,
And all the daffodils
Are blowing, and the bright blue squills.
Patterns

A pattern called a war.
Christ! What are patterns for?
Ibid.

[1] See Grantland Rice, page 910a.
[2] Dean of Canterbury.

All about us peal the loud, sweet Te
    Deums of the Canterbury bells.
      Madonna of the Evening Flowers
Heart-leaves of lilac all over New Eng-
    land,[1]
Roots of lilac under all the soil of New
    England,
Lilac in me because I am New England.
                         Lilacs
The sight of a white church above thin
    trees in a city square
Amazes my eyes as though it were the
    Parthenon.
            Meeting-House Hill

WILLIAM SOMERSET MAUGHAM
[1874–   ]

There are two good things in life,
freedom of thought and freedom of
action.
      Of Human Bondage [*1915*].
                    Chap. 23
Like all weak men he laid an exaggerated stress on not changing one's
mind.
                 Ibid. Chap. 39
People ask you for criticism, but
they only want praise.
                 Ibid. Chap. 50
There is nothing so degrading as the
constant anxiety about one's means of
livelihood. . . . Money is like a sixth
sense without which you cannot make
a complete use of the other five.
                 Ibid. Chap. 51
The mystic sees the ineffable, and
the psycho-pathologist the unspeakable.
      The Moon and Sixpence [*1919*].
                     Chap. 1
I forget who it was that recommended men for their soul's good to do
each day two things they disliked: [2]
. . . it is a precept that I have fol-

---

[1] Stands the lilac-bush tall-growing with
heart-shaped leaves of rich green. — WALT
WHITMAN: *When Lilacs Last in the Door-
yard Bloom'd* [1865–1866]

[2] See William James, page 715a, and T. H.
Huxley, pages 633b–634a.

lowed scrupulously; for every day I
have got up and I have gone to bed.
      The Moon and Sixpence. Chap. 2
Impropriety is the soul of wit.[1]
                 Ibid. Chap. 4
Conscience is the guardian in the individual of the rules which the community has evolved for its own preservation.
                 Ibid. Chap. 14
It is not true that suffering ennobles
the character; happiness does that
sometimes, but suffering, for the most
part, makes men petty and vindictive.
                 Ibid. Chap. 17
A woman can forgive a man for the
harm he does her, but she can never
forgive him for the sacrifices he makes
on her account.
                 Ibid. Chap. 41
He made one laugh sometimes by
speaking the truth, but this is a form of
humour which gains its force only by
it unusualness.
                 Ibid. Chap. 44
Do you know that conversation is
one of the greatest pleasures in life?
But it wants leisure.
      The Trembling of a Leaf
             [*1921*]. *Chap. 3*
The tragedy of love is indifference.
                 Ibid. Chap. 4
I would sooner read a time-table or
a catalogue than nothing at all. They
are much more entertaining than half
the novels that are written.
        The Summing Up [*1938*]
Life is too short to do anything for
oneself that one can pay others to do
for one.
                        Ibid.
You must not pursue a success, but
fly from it.
                        Ibid.
If a nation values anything more
than freedom, it will lose its freedom;
and the irony of it is that if it is comfort or money that it values more, it
will lose that too.
      Strictly Personal [*1941*].
                    Chap. 31

---

[1] See Shakespeare, page 173a.

As deserted as a playwright after the first night of an unsuccessful play.
                    The Razor's Edge [*1944*].
                              Chap. 3
As mean as cat's meat.
        Quoted in THOMAS F. BRADY:
        *The Eighty Years of Mr.
        Maugham, New York Times
        Magazine* [*January 24, 1954*]
I am an agnostic with sympathies.
                              Ibid.

ALICE DUER MILLER
[1874–1942]

When a woman like that whom I've
    seen so much
All of a sudden drops out of touch,
Is always busy and never can
Spare you a moment, it means a Man.
        Forsaking All Others [*1931*]
I have loved England, dearly and
    deeply,
Since that first morning, shining and
    pure,
The white cliffs of Dover, I saw rising
    steeply
Out of the sea that once made her se-
    cure.
        The White Cliffs [*1940*]
I am American bred,
I have seen much to hate here — much
    to forgive,
But in a world where England is fin-
    ished and dead,
I do not wish to live.
                              Ibid.

ROSELLE MERCIER
MONTGOMERY
[1874–1933]

Companioned years have made them
    comprehend
The comradeship that lies beyond a
    kiss.
The young ask much of life — they ask
    but this,
To fare the road together to its end.
        For a Wedding Anniversary
Oh, there are many things that women
    know,

That no one tells them, no one needs
    to tell;
And that they know, their dearest never
    guess! [1]
        Ulysses Returns: Penelope Speaks
Never a ship sails out of the bay
But carries my heart as a stowaway.
                    The Stowaway

PAUL RICHARD
[1874–   ]

The vagabond, when rich, is called a
tourist.
                The Scourge of Christ
                    [*1929*]. *Page 40*
When the rich assemble to concern
themselves with the business of the
poor it is called charity. When the poor
assemble to concern themselves with
the business of the rich it is called
anarchy.
                        Ibid. Page 63
Hunting — the   least   honourable
form of war on the weak.
                        Ibid. Page 142

EDWARD HERSEY
RICHARDS
[1874–   ]

A wise old owl sat on an oak,
The more he saw the less he spoke;
The less he spoke the more he heard;
Why aren't we like that wise old bird?
                        A Wise Old Owl

JOHN DAVISON
ROCKEFELLER, JR.
[1874–   ]

I believe that every right implies a
responsibility; every opportunity, an
obligation; every possession, a duty.
        *Ten Principles: Address in be-
        half of United Service Organiza-
        tions, New York* [*July 8, 1941*]

[1] Never believe her love is blind,
    All his faults are locked securely
    In a closet of her mind.
    SARA TEASDALE [1884–1933]: *Appraisal*

ROBERT WILLIAM SERVICE
[1874–]

This is the Law of the Yukon, that only
　the Strong shall thrive;
That surely the Weak shall perish, and
　only the Fit survive.[1]
Dissolute, damned and despairful, crip-
　pled and palsied and slain,
This is the Will of the Yukon, — Lo,
　how she makes it plain!
The Law of the Yukon

Master, I've done Thy bidding, and the
　light is low in the west,
And the long, long shift is over . . .
Master, I've earned it — Rest.
The Song of the Wage-Slave

Back of the bar, in a solo game, sat
　Dangerous Dan McGrew,
And watching his luck was his light-o'-
　love, the lady that's known as
　Lou.
The Shooting of Dan McGrew.
Stanza 1

The Northern Lights have seen queer
　sights,
But the queerest they ever did see
Was that night on the marge of Lake
　Lebarge
I cremated Sam McGee.
The Cremation of Sam McGee.
Stanza 1

A promise made is a debt unpaid.
Ibid. Stanza 8

There's a race of men that don't fit in,
A race that can't stay still;
So they break the hearts of kith and
　kin,
And they roam the world at will.
The Men That Don't Fit In.
Stanza 1

Fate has written a tragedy; its name is
　"The Human Heart."
The Theatre is the House of Life,
　Woman the mummer's part;

[1] Now this is the Law of the Jungle — as
　old and as true as the sky;
And the Wolf that shall keep it may
　prosper, but the Wolf that shall
　break it must die.
KIPLING: *The Law of the Jungle* [1895]

The Devil enters the prompter's box
and the play is ready to start.
The Harpy. Stanza 12

God made a heart of gold, of gold,
　Shining and sweet and true;
Gave it a home of fairest mould,
　Blest it, and called it — You.
Sunshine. VI

I just think that dreams are best,
　Just to sit and fancy things;
Give your gold no acid test,
　Try not how your silver rings.
Dreams Are Best. Stanza 1

The man who can fight to Heaven's
　own height
Is the man who can fight when he's
　losing.
Carry On

Ah! the clock is always slow;
It is later than you think.
It Is Later than You Think

That classic that the world has lost,
The Little Book I Never Wrote.
My Masterpiece. Stanza 2

When we, the Workers, all demand:
　"What are we fighting for?" . . .
Then, then we'll end that stupid crime,
　that devil's madness — War.
Michael

GERTRUDE STEIN
[1874–1946]

Rose is a rose is a rose is a rose.
Sacred Emily

The Autobiography of Alice B.
Toklas.
Title of book [*1933*]

Pigeons in the grass alas.
Four Saints in Three Acts [*1934*]

Before the Flowers of Friendship
Faded Friendship Faded.
Title

In the United States there is more
space where nobody is than where anybody is.

This is what makes America what
it is.
The Geographical History
of America [*1936*]

ARTHUR STRINGER
[1874–1950]

Beauty is not immortal. In a day
Blossom and June and rapture pass
away.
A Fragile Thing Is Beauty.
Stanza 2

Our bitterest wine is always drained
from crushed ideals.
The Devastator

HARRY WILLIAMS
[1874–1924]
AND JACK JUDGE
[1878–1938]

It's a long way to Tipperary, it's a long
way to go;
It's a long way to Tipperary, to the
sweetest girl I know!
Good-bye, Piccadilly, farewell, Leices-
ter Square,
It's a long, long way to Tipperary, but
my heart's right there!
Tipperary [*1908*]

In the Shade of the Old Apple Tree.
Title of Song

WILLIAM E. WOODWARD
[1874–1950]

The turning points of lives are not
the great moments. The real crises are
often concealed in occurrences so trivial
in appearance that they pass unob-
served.
George Washington [*1926*].
Chap. 3, Part 2

Vanity as an impulse has without
doubt been of far more benefit to civilization than modesty has ever been.
Ibid. Chap. 5, Part 1

Here is another bead on the string of
confusions.
Meet General Grant [*1929*].
Chap. 27, Part 5

EDMUND CLERIHEW
BENTLEY
[1875–]

Sir Christopher Wren
Said "I am going to dine with some
men.
If anybody calls
Say I am designing St. Paul's."
Biography for Beginners

John Stuart Mill
By a mighty effort of will
Overcame his natural bonhomie
And wrote "Principles of Political
Economy."
Ibid.

George the Third
Ought never to have occurred.
One can only wonder
At so grotesque a blunder.[1]
Ibid.

ABBIE FARWELL BROWN
[1875–1927]

They named their rocky farmlands,
Their hamlets by the sea,
For the mother-towns that bred them
In racial loyalty.
Names. Stanza 7

No matter what my birth may be,
No matter where my lot is cast,
I am the heir in equity
Of all the precious Past.
The Heritage. Stanza 1

JOHN BUCHAN,
LORD TWEEDSMUIR
[1875–1940]

We can only pay our debt to the past
by putting the future in debt to ourselves.
*Address to the People of Can-
ada, on the Coronation of
George VI, May 12, 1937*

[1] George the First was always reckoned
Vile, but viler George the Second;
And what mortal ever heard
Any good of George the Third?
When from earth the Fourth descended
God be praised, the Georges ended!
WALTER SAVAGE LANDOR: *Epigram,
after hearing* THACKERAY'S *lectures
on the Four Georges* [*1855*]

LOUISE DRISCOLL
[1875–   ]

There you will find what
Every man needs,
Wild religion
Without any creeds.
Spring Market. Stanza 5

Villon among the birds is he,
A bold, bright rover, bad and free;
Yet not without such loveliness
As makes the curse upon him less.
The Blue Jay. Stanza 1

GILBERT EMERY
[1875–1945]

They're a poor lot, the men, all of
'em, and dirty, too — but the thing is,
darlin', to get one that cleans easy.
Tarnish [1923]. Act III

ELLEN THORNEYCROFT FOWLER
[1875–1929]

The inner half of every cloud
Is bright and shining;
I therefore turn my clouds about,
And always wear them inside out
To show the lining.
The Wisdom of Folly. Stanza 3

ROBERT FROST
[1875–   ]

I'm going out to clean the pasture
spring;
I'll only stop to rake the leaves away
(And wait to watch the water clear, I
may):
I shan't be gone long. — You come too.
The Pasture

Ah, when to the heart of man
Was it ever less than a treason
To go with the drift of things,
To yield with a grace to reason,
And bow and accept the end
Of a love or a season?
Reluctance [1913]. Stanza 4

Something there is that doesn't love a
wall.
Mending Wall [1914]

My apple trees will never get across
And eat the cones under his pines, I
tell him.
He only says, "Good fences make good
neighbors."
Mending Wall

The nearest friends can go
With anyone to death, comes so far
short
They might as well not try to go at all.
Home Burial [1914]

Nothing to look backward to with
pride,
And nothing to look forward to with
hope.
*The Death of the Hired Man
[1914]*

"Home is the place where, when you
have to go there,
They have to take you in." "I should
have called it
Something you somehow haven't to deserve."
Ibid.

As a child misses the unsaid Good-
night,
And falls asleep with heartache.
The Black Cottage [1914]

Most of the change we think we see in
life
Is due to truths being in and out of
favor.
Ibid.

The blue's but a mist from the breath
of the wind,
A tarnish that goes at a touch of the
hand.
Blueberries [1914]

The best way out is always through.
A Servant to Servants [1914]

Pressed into service means pressed out
of shape.
The Self-Seeker [1914]

Two roads diverged in a wood, and I —
I took the one less traveled by,
And that has made all the difference.
The Road Not Taken [1916]

I'd like to get away from earth awhile
And then come back to it and begin
over.
May no fate willfully misunderstand
me

And half grant what I wish and snatch
me away
Not to return. Earth's the right place
for love:
I don't know where it's likely to go
better.
Birches [*1916*]

I wonder about the trees:
Why do we wish to bear
Forever the noise of these
More than another noise
So close to our dwelling place?
The Sound of the Trees [*1916*]

The Hyla breed
That shouted in the mist a month ago,
Like ghost of sleigh-bells in a ghost of
snow.
Hyla Brook [*1916*]

I met a Californian who would
Talk California — a state so blessed,
He said, in climate, none had ever died
there
A natural death.
New Hampshire [*1923*].
Stanza 3

Do you know,
Considering the market, there are more
Poems produced than any other thing?
No wonder poets sometimes have to
seem
So much more business-like than busi-
ness men.
Their wares are so much harder to get
rid of.
Ibid. Stanza 17

She's one of the two best states in the
Union.
Vermont's the other.
Ibid. Stanza 18

Anything I can say about New Hampshire
Will serve almost as well about Vermont,
Excepting that they differ in their
mountains.
The Vermont mountains stretch extended straight;
New Hampshire mountains curl up in a
coil.
Ibid. Stanza 19

Why make so much of fragmentary
blue

In here and there a bird, or butterfly,
Or flower, or wearing-stone, or open
eye,
When heaven presents in sheets the
solid hue?
Fragmentary Blue [*1923*].
Stanza 1

Keep cold, young orchard. Good-bye
and keep cold.
Dread fifty above more than fifty below.
Good-bye and Keep Cold [*1923*]

Whose woods these are I think I know.
His house is in the village though;
He will not see me stopping here
To watch his woods fill up with snow.
*Stopping by Woods on a Snowy
Evening* [*1923*]. *Stanza 1*

My little horse must think it queer
To stop without a farmhouse near.
Ibid. Stanza 2

He gives his harness bells a shake
To ask if there is some mistake.
Ibid. Stanza 3

The woods are lovely, dark and deep.
But I have promises to keep,
And miles to go before I sleep.
Ibid. Stanza 4

Some say the world will end in fire,
Some say in ice.
From what I've tasted of desire
I hold with those who favor fire.
But if it had to perish twice,
I think I know enough of hate
To say that for destruction ice
Is also great
And would suffice.
Fire and Ice [*1923*]

We heard the miniature thunder where
he fled.
The Runaway [*1923*]

Love at the lips was touch
As sweet as I could bear;
And once that seemed too much;
I lived on air.
To Earthward [*1923*]. *Stanza 1*

Now no joy but lacks salt
That is not dashed with pain
And weariness and fault;
I crave the stain

Of tears, the aftermark
Of almost too much love,
The sweet of bitter bark
And burning clove.
Ibid. Stanzas 5 and 6
Tree at my window, window tree,
My sash is lowered when night comes
on;
But let there never be curtain drawn
Between you and me.
Tree at My Window [1928].
Stanza 1
That day she put our heads together,
Fate had her imagination about her,
Your head so much concerned with
outer,
Mine with inner, weather.
Ibid. Stanza 4
I have been one acquainted with the
night.
Acquainted with the Night
[1928]
If, as they say, some dust thrown in my
eyes
Will keep my talk from getting over-
wise,
I'm not the one for putting off the
proof.
Let it be overwhelming.
Dust in the Eyes [1928]
Don't join too many gangs. Join few if
any.
Join the United States and join the
family —
But not much in between unless a col-
lege.
Build Soil [1932]
Never ask of money spent
Where the spender thinks it went.
Nobody was ever meant
To remember or invent
What he did with every cent.
The Hardship of Accounting
[1936]
I never dared be radical when young
For fear it would make me conservative
when old.
Precaution [1936]
And were an epitaph to be my story
I'd have a short one ready for my own.
I would have written of me on my
stone:

I had a lover's quarrel with the world.
The Lesson for Today [1942]
Happiness Makes Up in Height for
What It Lacks in Length.
Title of poem [1942]
Any eye is an evil eye
That looks in on to a mood apart.
A Mood Apart [1947]

ZANE GREY
[1875–1939]

We'll use a signal I have tried and
found far-reaching and easy to yell.
Waa-hoo!
The Last of the Plainsmen.
Chap. 4

MINNIE LOUISE HASKINS
[1875–   ]

And I said to the man who stood at
the gate of the year: "Give me a light
that I may tread safely into the unknown." And he replied: "Go out into
the darkness and put your hand into
the hand of God. That shall be to you
better than light and safer than a
known way." [1] So I went forth, and
finding the Hand of God, trod gladly
into the night. And He led me towards
the hills and the breaking of day in
the lone East.
God Knows [1908]. Proem

FREDERICK PALMER
LATIMER
[1875–1940]

I wish I were a little rock,
  A-sitting on a hill,
A-doing nothing, all day long,
  But just a-sitting still;
I wouldn't eat, I wouldn't sleep,
  I wouldn't even wash —
I'd sit and sit a thousand years,
  And rest myself, b'Gosh!
The Weary Wisher

[1] Quoted by George VI in a radio broadcast to the Empire, December 25, 1939.

PERCY MACKAYE
[1875–   ]

Because he [1] never wore his sentient
  heart
For crows and jays to peck, ofttimes to
  such
He seemed a silent fellow, who o'er-
  much
Held from the general gossip-ground
  apart,
Or tersely-spoke, and tart.

Uriel. Stanza 11

Inward, not outward, throbs the eternal
  war
Where each is his own Norman Conqueror.

Sonnet, Norman Conquest
[1944]

THOMAS MANN
[1875–   ]

We are most likely to get angry and
excited in our opposition to some idea
when we ourselves are not quite certain
of our own position, and are inwardly
tempted to take the other side.

Buddenbrooks [1903]. *Part*
VIII, Chap. 2

Grandfather used to say about a
dish that had no particular taste or
consistency: it tastes as if you were
hanging your tongue out of the window!

Ibid. Part X, Chap. 1

Beauty can pierce one like a pain.

Ibid. Part XI, Chap. 2

Space, like time, engenders forgetfulness; but it does so by setting us bodily
free from our surroundings and giving
us back our primitive, unattached state.
. . . Time, we say, is Lethe; but
change of air is a similar draught, and,
if it works less thoroughly, does so more
quickly.

The Magic Mountain [1924].[2]
Chap. 1

A man lives not only his personal
life, as an individual, but also, con-

sciously or unconsciously, the life of
his epoch and his contemporaries.

The Magic Mountain. Chap. 2

The solemn, discreet, almost overawed bearing which the young German's respect for authority leads him
to assume in the presence of pens, ink,
and paper, or anything else which bears
to his mind an official stamp.

Ibid. Chap. 4

I have the feeling that once I am at
home again I shall need to sleep three
weeks on end to get rested from the
rest I've had!

Ibid.

The only religious way to think of
death is as part and parcel of life; to
regard it, with the understanding and
the emotions, as the inviolable condition of life.

Ibid. Chap. 5

Time has no divisions to mark its
passage, there is never a thunder-storm
or blare of trumpets to announce the
beginning of a new month or year.
Even when a new century begins it is
only we mortals who ring bells and fire
off pistols.

Ibid.

Order and simplification are the first
steps toward the mastery of a subject
— the actual enemy is the unknown.

Ibid.

The proud embarrassment of the
artist, tasting the enjoyment of looking
on his own works with the eyes of
strangers.

Ibid.

Human reason needs only to will
more strongly than fate, and she *is*
fate.

Ibid. Chap. 6

Opinions cannot survive if one has
no chance to fight for them.

Ibid.

Chop-fallen funeral processions, with
their dignity curtailed by present-day
traffic conditions.

Ibid.

One quickly gets readiness in an art
where strong desire comes in play.

Ibid.

---

[1] William Vaughn Moody.
[2] Translated by H. T. Lowe-Porter.

All interest in disease and death is only another expression of interest in life.

The Magic Mountain. Chap. 6

What perplexes the world is the disparity between the swiftness of the spirit, and the immense unwieldiness, sluggishness, inertia, permanence of matter.

Ibid.

The invention of printing and the Reformation are and remain the two outstanding services of central Europe to the cause of humanity.

Ibid.

Speech is civilization itself. The word, even the most contradictory word, preserves contact — it is silence which isolates.

Ibid.

A man's dying is more the survivors' affair than his own.

Ibid.

What we call mourning for our dead is perhaps not so much grief at not being able to call them back as it is grief at not being able to want to do so.

Ibid. Chap. 7

Time cools, time clarifies; no mood can be maintained quite unaltered through the course of hours.

Ibid.

Seven is a good handy figure in its way, picturesque, with a savour of the mythical; one might say that it is more filling to the spirit than a dull academic half-dozen.

Ibid.

In the Word is involved the unity of humanity, the wholeness of the human problem, which permits nobody to separate the intellectual and artistic from the political and social, and to isolate himself within the ivory tower of the "cultural" proper.

An Exchange of Letters [1]
[January, 1937]

[1] Reply, written from Zurich, to the Dean of the Philosophical Faculty at Bonn University. The latter had written to Thomas Mann, who had left Germany in 1933, that his name had been struck off the list of Honorary Doctors.

God help our darkened and desecrated country and teach it to make its peace with the world and with itself.

An Exchange of Letters

Hold fast the time! Guard it, watch over it, every hour, every minute! Unregarded it slips away, like a lizard, smooth, slippery, faithless, a pixy-wife. Hold every moment sacred. Give each clarity and meaning, each the weight of thine awareness, each its true and due fulfilment.

The Beloved Returns [*1939*]

HUGHES MEARNS
[1875–   ]

As I was going up the stair
I met a man who wasn't there.
He wasn't there again today.
I wish, I wish he'd stay away.

The Psychoed

FRANK WARD O'MALLEY
[1875–1932]

Life is just one damned thing after another.[1]

Quoted in The Literary Digest,
November 5, 1932

VILDA SAUVAGE OWENS
[1875–1950]

If I ever have time for things that matter,
If ever I have the smallest chance,
I'm going to live in
Little Broom Gardens,
Moat-by-the-Castle,
Nettlecombe, Hants.

If I Ever Have Time for the
Things That Matter. Stanza 1

[1] Also attributed to Elbert Hubbard; the phrase probably precedes them both.
ODTAA, title of book by John Masefield [1926]; and Tom Treanor, war correspondent, entitled his book *One Damn Thing After Another* [1944].

RAINER MARIA RILKE
[1875–1926]

Her smile was not meant to be seen by anyone and served its whole purpose in being smiled.
The Journal of My Other Self [1]

He was a poet and hated the approximate.
Ibid.

Love consists in this, that two solitudes protect and touch and greet each other.
Letters to a Young Poet [2]

The future enters into us, in order to transform itself in us, long before it happens.
Ibid.

We're never single-minded, unperplexed, like migratory birds.
The Duino Elegies. Fourth Elegy

The most visible joy can only reveal itself to us when we've transformed it, within.
Ibid. Seventh Elegy

Death is the side of life which is turned away from us.
Letter to his Polish Translator, W. von Hulewicz

A good marriage is that in which each appoints the other guardian of his solitude.
Letters [3]

Once the realization is accepted that even between the *closest* human beings infinite distances continue to exist, a wonderful living side by side can grow up, if they succeed in loving the distance between them which makes it possible for each to see the other whole against the sky.
Ibid.

In the difficult are the friendly forces, the hands that work on us.
Ibid.

Works of art are indeed always products of having-been-in-danger, of

[1] Translated by JOHN LINTON [1930].
[2] Translated by M. D. HERTER NORTON [1934].
[3] Translated by JANE BARNARD GREENE and M. D. HERTER NORTON.

having-gone-to-the-very-end in an experience, to where man can go no further.
Letters

RAFAEL SABATINI
[1875–1950]

Born with the gift of laughter and the sense that the world was mad,[1] and that was his only patrimony.
Scaramouche. Chap. 1

RIDGELY TORRENCE
[1875–1950]

God gave them Youth, God gave them Love, and even God can give no more.
The House of a Hundred Lights. The Young Lovers

Of all the languages of earth in which the human kind confer
The Master Speaker is the Tear: it is the Great Interpreter.
Ibid. The Conclusion of the Whole Matter

I was weak as a rained-on bee.
Eye-Witness. The Tramp Sings

EVELYN UNDERHILL
[1875–1941]

I saw the race fulfil
The spiral of its steep ascent, predestined of the Will.
Yet not unled, but shepherded by one they may not see —
The one who walked with starry feet the western road by me!
Uxbridge Road. Stanza 5

[1] Inscribed over a door in the Hall of Graduate Studies, Yale University. The architect, John Donald Tuttle, explained in a letter in *The New Yorker* [December 8, 1934] his recoiling from collegiate Gothic, "a type of architecture that had been designed expressly . . . to enable yeomen to pour molten lead through slots on their enemies below. As a propitiatory gift to my gods . . . and to make them forget by appealing to their senses of humor, I carved the inscription over the door."

THOMAS WALSH
[1875–1928]

A little world — we truly say
While days are young and careless-
hearted;
From clime to clime we speed today,
Earth's paths are cleared and ocean's
charted;
But ah, how large a world we stray
When thou and I are parted!
Zither Song

MOIRA O'NEILL
[*Floruit* 1900]

Youth's for an hour,
Beauty's a flower,
But love is the jewel that wins the
world.
Songs of the Glens of Antrim
[*1900*]. *Beauty's a Flower*
"If she was tall?" Like a king's own
daughter.
"If she was fair?" Like a mornin' o'
May.
A Broken Song. Stanza 2
The memory's fairly spoilt on me
Wid mindin' to forget.
Forgettin'. Stanza 5

SHERWOOD ANDERSON
[1876–1941]

Everyone in the world is Christ and
they are all crucified.
Winesburg, Ohio [*1919*]. *The
Philosopher*
I am a lover and have not found my
thing to love.
Ibid. Tandy

WILLA SIBERT CATHER
[1876–1947]

Oh, this is the joy of the rose:
That it blows,
And goes.
In Rose-Time
Where are the loves that we have loved
before
When once we are alone, and shut the
door?
L'Envoi

Fireflies gleam in the damp and
mould, —
All that is left of the Caesars' gold.
The Palatine. Stanza 3
No one can build his security upon
the nobleness of another person.
Alexander's Bridge [*1912*].
Chap. 8
There are only two or three human
stories, and they go on repeating them-
selves as fiercely as if they had never
happened before.
O Pioneers! [*1913*]. *Part II,
Chap. 4*
I like trees because they seem more
resigned to the way they have to live
than other things do.
Ibid. Chap. 8
We all like people who do things,
even if we only see their faces on a
cigar-box lid.
The Song of the Lark [*1915*].
Part I, Chap. 18
Artistic growth is, more than it is
anything else, a refining of the sense
of truthfulness. The stupid believe
that to be truthful is easy; only the
artist, the great artist, knows how
difficult it is.
Ibid. Part VI, Chap. 11
Winter lies too long in country
towns; hangs on until it is stale and
shabby, old and sullen.
My Ántonia [*1918*]. *Book II,
Chap. 7*
Old men are like that, you know. It
makes them feel important to think
they're in love with somebody.
Ibid. Book III, Chap. 4
Art, it seems to me, should simplify.
That, indeed, is very nearly the whole
of the higher artistic process; finding
what conventions of form and what detail one can do without and yet preserve the spirit of the whole — so that
all that one has suppressed and cut
away is there to the reader's consciousness as much as if it were in type
on the page.
On the Art of Fiction [*1920*]

That irregular and intimate quality of things made entirely by the human hand.
Death Comes for the Archbishop [*1927*]. *Book I, Chap. 3*

The Miracles of the Church seem to me to rest not so much upon faces or voices or healing power coming suddenly near to us from afar off, but upon our perceptions being made finer, so that for a moment our eyes can see and our ears can hear what is there about us always.
Ibid. Chap. 4

The universal human yearning for something permanent, enduring, without shadow of change.
Ibid. Book III, Chap. 3

Only solitary men know the full joys of friendship. Others have their family; but to a solitary and an exile his friends are everything.
Shadows on the Rock [*1931*].
Book III, Chap. 5

There are all those early memories; one cannot get another set; one has only those.
Ibid. Book IV, Chap. 2

These coppers, big and little, these brooms and clouts and brushes, were tools; and with them one made, not shoes or cabinet-work, but life itself. One made a climate within a climate; one made the days, — the complexion, the special flavor, the special happiness of each day as it passed; one made life.
Ibid. Chap. 3

Sometimes a neighbor whom we have disliked a lifetime for his arrogance and conceit lets fall a single commonplace remark that shows us another side, another man, really; a man uncertain, and puzzled, and in the dark like ourselves.
Ibid. Epilogue

SARAH NORCLIFFE CLEGHORN
[1876–   ]

The golf links lie so near the mill
That almost every day

The laboring children can look out
And watch the men at play.
Quatrain [*1915*]

IRVIN SHREWSBURY COBB
[1876–1944]

It smells like gangrene starting in a mildewed silo, it tastes like the wrath to come, and when you absorb a deep swig of it you have all the sensations of having swallowed a lighted kerosene lamp. A sudden, violent jolt of it has been known to stop the victim's watch, snap his suspenders and crack his glass eye right across.
Definition of "Corn Licker" given to the Distillers' Code Authority, N. R. A.

Echoes, stealing upward, from those beneath the sod;
"No creed or dogma has produced a satisfying God."
Schedule for Plan for Going Elsewhere

I charge my family . . . that they shall put on none of the bogus habiliments of so-called mourning. Folds of black crepe never ministered to the memory of the departed.
Letter of Instructions to be opened after his death

Lay my ashes at the roots of a dogwood tree in Paducah at the proper planting season. Should the tree live, that will be monument enough for me.
Ibid.

CLARENCE JAMES DENNIS
[1876–1938]

Me name is Mud.
The Sentimental Bloke [*1916*].
A Spring Song, Stanza 2

A suddin notion stops me wiv a jar —
Wot if Doreen, I thinks, should grow to be
A fat ole weepin' willer like 'er Mar!
Ibid. Mar, Stanza 24

RICHARD BUTLER GLAENZER
[1876–1937]

Indian only in this:
Your sudden way
Of stealing on us — but to kiss
With peace, not slay!
Indian Summer. Stanza 1

WALLACE IRWIN
[1876–   ]

It's happy goes as lucky goes
To Romany in June.
From Romany to Rome. Stanza 1

Of all the fish that swim or swish
In ocean's deep autocracy,
There's none possess such haughtiness
As the codfish aristocracy.
Codfish Aristocracy. Stanza 1

I ask to know.
Letters of a Japanese Schoolboy

"Sayin' nothin'," says the goldsmith,
"is a woman's rarest skill."
"Birds should sing," remarked the Doctor, "but a woman should be still."
The Chamber of Tranquillity.
Stanza 10

CHARLES FRANCIS KETTERING
[1876–   ]

A man must have a certain amount of intelligent ignorance to get anywhere.
On his seventieth birthday,
August 29, 1946

We should all be concerned about the future because we will have to spend the rest of our lives there.
Seed for Thought [1949]

MAXIM MAXIMOVICH LITVINOV
[1876–1951]

To strengthen the League of Nations is to abide by the principle of collective security . . . to abide by the principle that peace is indivisible.[1]
Speech at League of Nations, Geneva, condemning Italian aggression in Ethiopia [July 1, 1936]

GRACE FALLOW NORTON
[1876–   ]

I have loved many, the more and the few —
I have loved many, that I might love you.
Song of the Sum of All

POPE PIUS XII (EUGENIO PACELLI)
[1876–   ]

Whoever dared raise a hand against Rome would be guilty of matricide in the eyes of the civilized world and in the eternal judgments of God.
Address to the College of Cardinals, Rome [June 2, 1944]

Private property is a natural fruit of labor, a product of intense activity of man, acquired through his energetic determination to ensure and develop with his own strength his own existence and that of his family, and to create for himself and his own an existence of just freedom, not only economic, but also political, cultural and religious.
Radio broadcast [September 1, 1944]

If a worker is deprived of hope to acquire some personal property, what other natural stimulus can be offered him that will inspire him to hard work, labor, saving and sobriety today, when so many nations and men have lost everything and all they have left is their capacity for work?
Ibid.

[1] In an earlier speech at the League, on September 5, 1935, during the Italian preparations for the invasion, Litvinov used a similar phrase: "The thesis of the indivisibility of peace. . . . It has now become clear to the whole world that each war is the creation of a preceding war and the generator of new present or future wars."

The church contradicts and condemns State Absolutism based on the false principle that the authority of the state is unlimited and controls the entire field of public and private life, invading even the realm of ideas, beliefs and conscience.
Wisdom — Not Weapons of War [1]
The American people have a genius for splendid and unselfish action, and into the hands of America God has placed the destinies of afflicted humanity.
Ibid.

A. S. W. ROSENBACH
[1876–1952]

After love, book collecting is the most exhilarating sport of all.
A Book Hunter's Holiday [*1936*]
Brooklyn has the proud distinction of having had more distinguished bibliophiles than any other city of its size in the world.
Ibid.

GEORGE MACAULAY TREVELYAN
[1876–   ]

A man and what he loves and builds have but a day and then disappear; nature cares not — and renews the annual round untired. It is the old law, sad but not bitter. Only when man destroys the life and beauty of nature, there is the outrage.
Grey of Fallodon [*1937*].
Book I, Chap. 3
Serbia . . . that little land of ferocious heroes.
Ibid. Book II, Chap. 8
Disinterested intellectual curiosity is the life blood of real civilisation.
English Social History [*1942*].
Preface
Education . . . has produced a vast population able to read but unable to distinguish what is worth reading.
Ibid. Chap. 18

[1] In *Collier's*, January 5, 1946.

BERTHA ADAMS BACKUS
[*Floruit* 1911]

Build for yourself a strong-box,
Fashion each part with care;
When it's strong as your hand can make it,
Put all your troubles there.
Then Laugh [*1911*]. *Stanza 1*

TED OLSON
[*Floruit* 1912]

Honor and truth and manhood —
These are the things that stand,
Though the sneer and jibe of the cynic tribe
Are loud through the width of the land.
Things That Endure. Stanza 1
But a lie, whatever the guise it wears,
Is a lie as it was of yore,
And a truth that has lasted a million years
Is good for a million more.
Ibid. Stanza 3

THOMAS CURTIS CLARK
[1877–   ]

Let us no more be true to boasted race or clan,
But to our highest dream, the brotherhood of man.
The New Loyalty

GRACE NOLL (MRS. NORMAN H.) CROWELL
[1877–   ]

God wrote His loveliest poem on the day
He made the first tall silver poplar tree,
And set it high upon a pale-gold hill
For all the new enchanted earth to see.
Silver Poplars. Stanza 1

ANTHONY EUWER
[1877–   ]

As a beauty I'm not a great star.
Others are handsomer far;

But my face — I don't mind it
Because I'm behind it;
It's the folks out in front that I jar.
Limerick [1]

WILHELM FRICK
[1877–1946]

Right is for National Socialists that
which serves the German people.
Address to Lawyers,
October 3, 1933

ROSE FYLEMAN
[1877–   ]

The Fairies have never a penny to
spend,
They haven't a thing put by,
But theirs is the dower of bird and of
flower,
And theirs are the earth and the sky.
The Fairies Have Never a Penny
to Spend. Stanza 1
There are fairies at the bottom of our
garden!
The Fairies. Stanza 1
The Queen — now can you guess who
that could be
(She's a little girl by day, but at night
she steals away)?
Well — it's me!
Ibid. Stanza 3

SIR JAMES HOPWOOD JEANS
[1877–1946]

Taking a very gloomy view of the
future of the human race, let us suppose that it can only expect to survive
for two thousand million years longer,
a period about equal to the past age of
the earth. Then, regarded as a being
destined to live for threescore years and
ten, humanity, although it has been
born in a house seventy years old, is
itself only three days old.
The Wider Aspects of
Cosmogony [1928]

[1] Often quoted by Woodrow Wilson.

RICHARD R. KIRK
[1877–   ]

Thrice blessed are our friends: they
come, they stay,
And presently they go away.
Thrice Blessed
A book's an Inn whose patrons' praise
Depends on seasons and on days,
On dispositions, and — in fine —
Not wholly on the landlord's wine.
A Book's an Inn

DOUGLAS MALLOCH
[1877–1938]

Here's the secret of the riddle for suc-
cesses everywhere —
There's some little second fiddle that
is carrying the air.
The Plain Member. Stanza 3
The river belongs to the Nation,
The levee, they say, to the State;
The Government runs navigation,
The Commonwealth, though, pays the
freight.
Now, here is the problem that's
heavy —
Please, which is the right or the
wrong —
When the water runs over the levee,
To whom does the river belong?
Uncle Sam's River. Stanza 1
If it's your Mississippi in dry time,
If it's yours, Uncle Sam, when it's wet,
If it's your Mississippi in fly time,
In flood time it's your Mississippi yet.
Ibid. Stanza 6
Courage is to feel
The daily daggers of relentless steel
And keep on living.
Courage. Stanza 2
You have to believe in happiness,
Or happiness never comes. . . .
Ah, that's the reason a bird can sing —
On his darkest day he believes in
Spring.
You Have to Believe
He who makes a garden
Works hand-in-hand with God.
Who Makes a Garden

ANGELO PATRI
[1877–   ]

In one sense there is no death. The life of a soul on earth lasts beyond his departure. You will always feel that life touching yours, that voice speaking to you, that spirit looking out of other eyes, talking to you in the familiar things he touched, worked with, loved as familiar friends. He lives on in your life and in the lives of all others that knew him.[1]
Keep Children from Funerals
[November 30, 1938]

LEONARD H. ROBBINS
[1877–1947]

Be true while there yet is time.
For this is the cry of a thousand souls
that down to the Pit have trod —
Who keeps the Truth from the people
stands in the way of God!
The Truth and John Billington.
Stanza 8

THEODORE GOODRIDGE ROBERTS
[1877–1953]

The wide seas and the mountains called
to him
And gray dawn saw his campfires in
the rain.
A Vagrant's Epitaph. Stanza 1

LAURA SIMMONS
[1877–1949]

What though you hide it in your
trunk —
Ere sailing hour has set?
Jammed down beneath your old blue
serge?
Don't think you can forget!

[1] Even the death of friends will inspire us as much as their lives. . . . Their memories will be incrusted over with sublime and pleasing thoughts, as their monuments are overgrown with moss. — THOREAU: *A Week on the Concord and Merrimack Rivers* [1849], *Concord River*

The face within that passport book
Will rise to haunt you yet.
Your Passport Picture

CHARLES HANSON TOWNE
[1877–1949]

Youth, there are countless stories
spread
By gentlemen whose hair is gray.
Believe them not, but me instead —
The Nineties were not really gay.
Ballade of Gentle Denial

I need not shout my faith. Thrice eloquent
Are quiet trees and the green listening
sod.
Hushed are the stars, whose power is
never spent;
The hills are mute — yet how they
speak of God!
Silence

How softly runs the afternoon
Beneath the billowy clouds of June!
How Softly Runs the Afternoon

ARTHUR UPSON
[1877–1908]

My days are phantom days, each one
The shadow of a hope;
My real life never was begun
Nor any of my real deeds done.
Phantom Life

Wine that was spilt in haste
Arising in fumes more precious;
Garlands that fell forgot
Rooting to wondrous bloom.
After a Dolmetsch Concert.
Stanza 2

WILLIAM W. WOOLLCOTT
[1877–1949]

I am a One Hundred Percent Ameri-
can;
I am a super patriot.
I Am a One Hundred Percent
American. Stanza 1

I am an anti-Darwin intellectual.
The man that says that any nice young
boy or gal

Is a descendant of the ape
Shall never from Hell's fire escape.
I Am a One Hundred Percent
American. Stanza 2

McLANDBURGH WILSON
[*Floruit* 1915]

Our hero is a man of peace,
Preparedness he implores;
His sword within its scabbard sleeps,
But mercy, how it snores!
Theodore Roosevelt
'Twixt the optimist and pessimist
The difference is droll:
The optimist sees the doughnut
But the pessimist sees the hole.
Optimist and Pessimist

LOUIS KAUFMAN
ANSPACHER
[1878–1947]

Marriage is that relation between
man and woman in which the independence is equal, the dependence mutual,
and the obligation reciprocal.
Address, Boston [*December 30,*
1934]

KARLE WILSON
(MRS. THOMAS ELLIS)
BAKER
[1878–]

Brother, the creed would stifle me
That shelters you.[1]
Creeds. Stanza 2
Let me grow lovely, growing old —
So many fine things do:
Laces, and ivory, and gold,
And silks need not be new.
Old Lace: Let Me Grow Lovely
Today I have grown taller from walk-
ing with the trees.
Good Company

[1] My creed may have no lift of hope for
you,
And yours might drive me down the
slopes of hell.
LEWIS WORTHINGTON SMITH
[1866–]: *Creeds*

I love the friendly faces of old sorrows;
I have no secrets that they do not
know.
I Love the Friendly Faces.
Stanza 1

AMELIA JOSEPHINE BURR
[1878–]

As one who looks on a face through a
window, through life I have looked
on God.
Because I have loved life, I shall have
no sorrow to die.
A Song of Living. Stanza 3

HENRY SEIDEL CANBY
[1878–]

We can put our children on wheels to
see the world, but we cannot give them
the kind of home that any town provided in the nineties, not at any price.
The Age of Confidence. Chap. 14
Arrogance, pedantry, and dogmatism
are the occupational diseases of those
who spend their lives directing the intellects of the young.
Alma Mater
[Walt Whitman] remembered things
impossible for us, impossible but intelligible, and which will become unintelligible at our peril.
Classic Americans. Walt Whitman
Skunk cabbages! a thousand sonnets
died in that misnomer.
Meditations in the Woods

PIERRE CARTIER
[1878–]

While in France we consider it takes
three generations to go from shirtsleeves to wealth,[1] here, in America,
where accelerated speed is an important
element of success, it takes but one generation to complete the same process.
Address, French Chamber of
Commerce of the United States,
New York, September 27, 1940

[1] There's no' but three generations atween
clog and clog. — *Lancashire Proverb*
Three generations from shirtsleeves to
shirtsleeves. — *Attributed to* ANDREW CAR-
NEGIE [1835–1919]

GEORGE MICHAEL COHAN
[1878–1942]

No matter what may happen, whatever
  may befall,
I only know I'm mighty glad I'm living,
  that is all.
I'm Mighty Glad I'm Living

You won't do any business, if you
  haven't got a band:
The folks expect a street parade and
  uniforms so grand.
You Won't Do Any Business

Always Leave Them Laughing When
You Say Good-bye.
Title of song

Give my regards to Broadway,
  Remember me to Herald Square,
Tell all the gang at Forty-second Street
  That I will soon be there.
Give My Regards to Broadway
[*1904*]

Hurried and worried until we're buried,
  and there's no curtain call,
Life's a very funny proposition, after
  all.
Life's a Funny Proposition [*1907*]

The Yanks are coming,
The drums rum-tumming everywhere.
Over There [*1917*]

And we won't come back till it's over
  over there.
Ibid.

What's all the shootin' for?
The Tavern [*1920*]

GRACE HAZARD CONKLING
[1878–   ]

I have an understanding with the hills
At evening when the slanted radiance
  fills
Their hollows, and the great winds let
  them be,
And they are quiet and look down at
  me.
After Sunset

Invisible beauty has a word so brief
A flower can say it or a shaken leaf,
But few may ever snare it in a song.
Ibid.

To build the trout a crystal stair.
The Whole Duty of
Berkshire Brooks

He who gives a passion-flower
Always asks it back.
Tampico

ALFRED EDGAR COPPARD
[1878–   ]

Truth is truth and love is love,
Give us grace to taste thereof;
But if truth offend my sweet,
Then I will have none of it.
Mendacity. Stanza 1

Ere this trick of truth undo me,
Little love, my love, come to me.
Ibid. Stanza 3

ADELAIDE CRAPSEY
[1878–1914]

These be
Three silent things:
The falling snow . . . the hour
Before the dawn . . . the mouth of
  one
Just dead.
Cinquain: Triad

EDWARD JOHN MORETON
DRAX PLUNKETT,
LORD DUNSANY
[1878–   ]

A new thing came and they could not
  see,
A new wind blew and they would not
  feel it.
In His Own Country. Stanza 1

May you go safe, my friend, across that
  dizzy way
No wider than a hair, by which your
  people go
From Earth to Paradise; may you go
  safe today
With stars and space above, and time
  and stars below.
May You Go Safe: On the
Death of a Muhammedan
Friend. Stanza 1

When we break up under the heavy years and go down into eternity our thoughts like small lost rafts float on awhile upon Oblivion's sea. They will not carry much over those tides, our names and a phrase or two and little else.
Fifty-One Tales. The Raft Builders

HARRY EMERSON FOSDICK
[1878–   ]

The Sea of Galilee and the Dead Sea are made of the same water. It flows down, clear and cool, from the heights of Hermon and the roots of the cedars of Lebanon. The Sea of Galilee makes beauty of it, for the Sea of Galilee has an outlet. It gets to give. It gathers in its riches that it may pour them out again to fertilize the Jordan plain. But the Dead Sea with the same water makes horror. For the Dead Sea has no outlet. It gets to keep.
The Meaning of Service [*1920*]

WILFRID WILSON GIBSON
[1878–   ]

One song leads on to another,
One friend to another friend,
So I'll travel along
With a friend and a song.
The Empty Purse. Stanza 1

All life moving to one measure —
Daily bread.
All Life Moving to One Measure

Just what it meant to smile and smile
And let my son go cheerily —
My son . . . and wondering all the while
What stranger would come back to me.
The Return. Stanza 2

OLIVER ST. JOHN GOGARTY
[1878–   ]

Only the Lion and the Cock,
As Galen says, withstand Love's shock.
So, Dearest, do not think me rude
If I yield now to lassitude,

But sympathize with me. I know
You would not have me roar, or crow.
After Galen

I give more praise to Troy's redoubt
For Love kept in, than War kept out.
On Troy

And up the back-garden
The sound comes to me
Of the lapsing, unsoilable,
Whispering sea.
Ringsend

What should we know,
For better or worse,
Of the Long Ago,
Were it not for Verse?
Verse

A vitalized symbol
Of earth and of storm,
Of Chaos contracted
To intricate form.
The Crab Tree

If but the will be firmly bent,
No stuff resists the mind's intent.
The Image-Maker

DONALD ROBERT PERRY MARQUIS
[1878–1937]

The saddest ones are those that wear
The jester's motley garb.
The Tavern of Despair

The world hath just one tale to tell, and
  it is very old;
A little tale — a simple tale — a tale
  that's easy told:
"There was a youth in Babylon who
  greatly loved a maid!"
News from Babylon

No doubt the cherubs earn their wage
Who wind each ticking star.
The Rebel

Noah an' Jonah an' Cap'n John Smith,
Mariners, travelers, magazines of myth,
Settin' up in Heaven, chewin' and a-
  chawin'
Eatin' their terbaccy, talkin' and a-
  jawin'.
*Noah an' Jonah an' Cap'n
John Smith* [*1921*]

For I want to hire out as the Skipper
(Who dodges life's stress and its
  strains)
Of the Trolley, the Toonerville Trolley,
The Trolley that Meets all the Trains.
The Toonerville Trolley:
To Fontaine Fox

A dollar a line,
The Uplifting stuff brings a dollar a
  line!
Yes, Song Is Coming into Its
Own Again

And similar goddamned phrases.
Ballade of Goddamned Phrases [1]

I pray Thee make my column read,
And give me thus my daily bread.
Endow me, if Thou grant me wit,
Likewise with sense to mellow it.
Prayer

Comet, shake out your locks and let
  them flare
Across the startled heaven of my soul!
Pluck out the hairpins, Sue, and let her
  roll!
Don't be so stingy with your blooming
  hair.
Sonnets to a Red-Haired Lady
[1922]. I

I love you as New Englanders love pie!
Ibid. XII

One boob may die, but deathless is
  The royal race of hicks —
When Ahab went to Ascalon
  They sold him gilded bricks.
Boob Ballad

Oh, what the hell, it's Spring!
And just for the sake of argyment, I'll
  show 'em who is king.
David and Bathsheba (As Inter-
preted by the Old Soak)

There will be no beans in the Almost
Perfect State. [2]
The Almost Perfect State [1927]

For a territory the size of the United
States five millions of people would be
about right. . . . The human population of the entire world should be kept

well under a hundred millions. . . . If
the world were not so full of people,
and most of them did not have to work
so hard, there would be more time for
them to get out and lie on the grass,
and there would be more grass for
them to lie on.
The Almost Perfect State

Of middle age the best that can be
said is that a middle-aged person has
likely learned how to have a little fun
in spite of his troubles.
Ibid.

oh i should worry and fret
death and i will coquette
there s a dance in the old dame yet
toujours gai toujours gai
archy [1] *and mehitabel [1927].*
the song of mehitabel

procrastination is the
art of keeping
up with yesterday
ibid. certain maxims of archy

an optimist is a guy that has never
  had much experience
ibid.

what in hell
have i done to deserve all these kittens
ibid. mehitabel and her kittens

dance mehitabel dance
caper and shake a leg
what little blood is left
will fizz like wine in a keg
ibid. mehitabel dances with boreas

i have noticed that when chickens
quit quarreling over their food they
often find that there is enough for all
of them i wonder if it might not be the
same way with the human race
archy's life of mehitabel [1933].
random thoughts by archy

so unlucky
that he runs into accidents
which started out to happen
to somebody else
ibid. archy says

theres life in the old dame yet
ibid. the retreat from hollywood

---

[1] Inspired by a protest from General Ian
Hamilton, Commander of the Mediterranean
Expeditionary Force [1915], against turning
his cables into hackneyed phrases.
[2] See Robert Burton, page 221b.

[1] archy, a cockroach, is unable to use the
shift key on the typewriter and therefore
cannot print capital letters.

Dreadful things are just as apt to happen when stupid people control a situation as when definitely ill-natured people are in charge.

Chapters for the Orthodox [*1934*].
Chap. 8

All religion, all life, all art, all expression come down to this: to the effort of the human soul to break through its barrier of loneliness, of intolerable loneliness, and make some contact with another seeking soul, or with what all souls seek, which is (by any name) God.

Ibid. Chap. 11

it is a cheering thought to think
that god is on the side of the best digestion [1]

archy does his part [*1935*].
the big bad wolf

there is bound to be a certain amount of
trouble running any country
if you are president the trouble happens to you
but if you are a tyrant you can arrange things so
that most of the trouble happens to other people

ibid. archy's newest deal

there is always
a comforting thought
in time of trouble when
it is not our trouble

ibid. comforting thoughts

too many creatures
both insects and humans
estimate their own value
by the amount of minor irritation
they are able to cause
to greater personalities than themselves

ibid. pride

the females of all species are most dangerous when they appear to retreat

ibid. a farewell

To stroke a platitude until it purrs like an epigram.

The Sun Dial

---

[1] Give me a good digestion, Lord,
And also something to digest.
ANONYMOUS: *A Pilgrim's Grace, St. 1*

Publishing a volume of verse is like dropping a rose-petal down the Grand Canyon and waiting for the echo.

The Sun Dial

Poetry is what Milton saw when he went blind.

Ibid.

If you make people think they're thinking, they'll love you. If you really make them think they'll hate you.

Ibid.

An Idea isn't responsible for the people who believe in it.

Ibid.

A man has jest naturally got to have something to cuss around and boss, so's to keep himself from finding out he don't amount to nothing.

Danny's Own Story

JOHN MASEFIELD [1]
[1878–　]

Theirs be the music, the colour, the glory, the gold;
Mine be a handful of ashes, a mouthful of mould.
Of the maimed, of the halt and the blind in the rain and the cold —
Of these shall my songs be fashioned, my tales be told.

A Consecration. Stanza 7

I must down to the seas again, to the lonely sea and the sky,
And all I ask is a tall ship and a star to steer her by,
And the wheel's kick and the wind's song and the white sail's shaking,
And a grey mist on the sea's face and a grey dawn breaking.

Sea-Fever [*1902*]. *Stanza 1*

I must down to the seas again, for the call of the running tide
Is a wild call and a clear call that may not be denied.

Ibid. Stanza 2

I must down to the seas again, to the vagrant gypsy life,
To the gull's way and the whale's way where the wind's like a whetted knife;

---

[1] Appointed Poet Laureate, 1930.

And all I ask is a merry yarn from a
laughing fellow-rover,
And quiet sleep and a sweet dream
when the long trick's over.
Sea-Fever. Stanza 3

Dunno about Life — it's jest a tramp
alone
From wakin'-time to doss.
Dunno about Death — it's jest a quiet
stone
All over-grey wi' moss.
Vagabond

It's a warm wind, the west wind, full of
birds' cries.
The West Wind

One road leads to London,
One road runs to Wales,
My road leads me seawards
To the white dipping sails.
Roadways

My road calls me, lures me
West, east, south, and north;
Most roads lead men homewards,
My road leads me forth.
Ibid.

In quest of that one beauty
God put me here to find.
Ibid.

The schooners and the merry crews are
laid away to rest,
A little south the sunset in the Islands
of the Blest.
A Ballad of John Silver

Commonplace people dislike tragedy,
because they dare not suffer and cannot
exult. The truth and rapture of man are
holy things, not lightly to be scorned.
A carelessness of life and beauty marks
the glutton, the idler, and the fool in
their deadly path across history.
The Tragedy of Nan [*1909*].
Preface

And he who gives a child a treat
Makes joy-bells ring in Heaven's street,
And he who gives a child a home
Builds palaces in Kingdom come.
The Everlasting Mercy [*1911*]

To get the whole world out of bed
And washed, and dressed, and warmed,
and fed,

To work, and back to bed again,
Believe me, Saul, costs worlds of pain.
The Everlasting Mercy

O Christ who holds the open gate,
O Christ who drives the furrow
straight,
O Christ, the plough, O Christ, the
laughter
Of holy white birds flying after.
Ibid.

The rain that makes things new,
The earth that hides things old.
Ibid.

The days that make us happy make us
wise.
Biography

In the dark womb where I began
My mother's life made me a man.
Through all the months of human birth
Her beauty fed my common earth.
I cannot see, nor breathe, nor stir,
But through the death of some of her.
C. L. M. Stanza 1

Quinquireme of Nineveh from distant
Ophir,
Rowing home to haven in sunny Pales-
tine,
With a cargo of ivory,
And apes and peacocks,[1]
Sandalwood, cedarwood, and sweet
white wine.
Cargoes. Stanza 1

Dirty British coaster with a salt-caked
smoke stack,
Butting through the Channel in the
mad March days,
With a cargo of Tyne coal,
Road-rail, pig-lead,
Firewood, iron-ware, and cheap tin
trays.
Ibid. Stanza 3

So I'm for drinking honestly, and dying
in my boots.
Captain Stratton's Fancy. Stanza 7

Oh London Town's a fine town, and
London sights are rare,

---

[1] Once in three years came the navy of
Tharshish, bringing gold, and silver, ivory,
and apes, and peacocks. — *1 Kings, X, 22*

And London ale is right ale, and brisk's
    the London air.
                    London Town. Stanza 1
All the great things of life are swiftly
    done,
Creation, death, and love the double
    gate.
However much we dawdle in the sun
We have to hurry at the touch of Fate;
When Life knocks at the door no one
    can wait,
When Death makes his arrest we have
    to go.
                    The Widow in the Bye Street
                    [1912]. Part 2
Love is a flame to burn out human
    wills,
Love is a flame to set the will on fire,
Love is a flame to cheat men into mire.
One of the three, we make Love what
    we choose.
                    Ibid.
What good can painting do to anyone?
I don't say never do it; far from
    that —
No harm in sometimes painting just
    for fun.
Keep it for fun, and stick to what
    you're at.
                    Dauber [1913]. Part 2
Spit brown, my son, and get a hairy
    breast.
                    Ibid.
What am I, Life? A thing of watery
    salt
Held in cohesion by unresting cells,
Which work they know not why, which
    never halt,
Myself unwitting where their Master
    dwells?
                    Sonnets. 14
O beautiful is love and to be free
Is beautiful, and beautiful are friends.
Love, freedom, comrades, surely make
    amends
For all these thorns through which we
    walk to death.
                    Enslaved
Bitter it is, indeed, in human Fate
When Life's supreme temptation comes
    too late.
                    The Woman Speaks

Go forth to seek: the quarry never
    found
Is still a fever to the questing hound,
The skyline is a promise, not a bound.
                    The Wanderer of Liverpool
I touch my country's mind, I come to
    grips
With half her purpose, thinking of
    these ships,
That art untouched by softness, all
    that line
Drawn ringing hard to stand the test
    of brine.
                    Ships
Then the black-bright, smooth-running,
    clicking clean
Brushed, oiled and dainty typewriting
    machine,
With tins of ribbons waiting for the
    blows
Which soon will hammer them to verse
    and prose.
                    Shopping in Oxford
Man consists of body, mind, and imagination. His body is faulty, his mind
untrustworthy, but his imagination
has made him remarkable. In some
centuries, his imagination has made life
on this planet an intense practice of all
the lovelier energies.
                    Shakespeare and Spiritual Life
                    [1924]
There is another way to truth: by
the minute examination of facts. That
is the way of the scientist: a hard and
noble and thankless way. It is not the
way of the great poet, the rare unreasonable who comes once in ten generations. He apprehends truth by power:
the truth which he apprehends cannot
be defined, save by greater power, and
there is no greater power.
                    Ibid.
One ought to see everything that one
has a chance of seeing; because in life
not many have one chance and none
has two.
                    Sard Harker [1924]
When Custom presses on the souls
    apart,
Who seek a God not worshipped by the
    herd,

Forth, to the wilderness, the chosen
　start
Content with ruin, having but the
　Word.
　　　Lines on the Tercentenary of
　　　　Harvard College [*1936*]

CARL SANDBURG
[1878–　]

I am the people — the mob — the
　crowd — the mass.
Do you know that all the great work
　of the world is done through me?
　　　I Am the People, the Mob
　　　　　　　　　　　　[*1916*]

I know a Jew fish crier down on Max-
　well Street with a voice like a
　north wind blowing over corn
　stubble in January. . . .
His face is that of a man terribly glad
　to be selling fish.
　　　　　　　　Fish Crier [*1916*]

Hog Butcher for the World,
Tool Maker, Stacker of Wheat,
Player with Railroads and the Nation's
　Freight Handler;
Stormy, husky, brawling,
City of the Big Shoulders.
　　　　　　　　Chicago [*1916*]

I won't take my religion from any man
　who never works except with his
　mouth and never cherishes any
　memory except the face of the
　woman on the American silver dol-
　lar.
　　　To a Contemporary Bunk-
　　　　shooter [*1916*]

The fog comes on little cat feet.
　　　　　　　　　Fog [*1916*]

Pile the bodies high at Austerlitz and
　Waterloo.
Shovel them under and let me work —
　I am the grass; I cover all.
　　　　　　　　Grass [*1918*]
And pile them high at Gettysburg
And pile them high at Ypres and Ver-
　dun.
Shovel them under and let me work.
Two years, ten years, and passengers
　ask the conductor:

What place is this?
Where are we now?
　　　　　　　　　　　Grass
O prairie mother, I am one of your
　boys.
I have loved the prairie as a man with
　a heart shot full of pain over love.
　　　　　　　　　　　Prairie
I tell you the past is a bucket of ashes.
　　　　　　　　　　　Ibid.

The peace of great churches be for you,
Where the players of lofty pipe organs
Practice old lovely fragments, alone.
　　　　　　　　　　　For You
The peace of great books be for you,
Stains of pressed clover leaves on pages,
Bleach of the light of years held in
　leather.
　　　　　　　　　　　Ibid.
For the gladness here where the sun is
　shining at evening on the weeds of
　the river,
Our prayer of thanks.
　　　　Our Prayer of Thanks
For the laughter of children who tum-
　ble barefooted and bareheaded in
　the summer grass.
　　　　　　　　　　　Ibid.
The republic is a dream.
Nothing happens unless first a dream.
　　　Washington Monument by Night
When Abraham Lincoln was shoveled
　into the tombs, he forgot the cop-
　perheads and the assassin . . . in
　the dust, in the cool tombs.
　　　　　　Cool Tombs [*1918*]
That sergeant at Belleau Woods,
Walking into the drumfires, calling his
　men,
"Come on, you . . . Do you want to
　live forever?" [1]
　　　　　　　　Losers [*1921*]
Always he kept on asking: "Where did
　that blood come from?"
　　　　　　Ossawatomie [*1921*]
The French who found the Ohio River
　named it
La Belle Rivière, meaning a woman
　easy to look at.
　　　Whiffs of the Ohio River at
　　　　　　　　　　Cincinnati

[1] See Thomas Carlyle, page 474b.

The marvelous rebellion of man at all signs reading "Keep Off." [1]

Who Am I?

Take any streetful of people buying clothes and groceries, cheering a hero or throwing confetti and blowing tin horns . . . tell me if the lovers are losers . . . tell me if any get more than the lovers . . . in the dust . . . in the cool tombs.

Ibid.

Lay me on an anvil, O God.
Beat me and hammer me into a crowbar.
Let me pry loose old walls.
Let me lift and loosen old foundations.

Prayers of Steel

Look out how you use proud words.
When you let proud words go, it is not easy to call them back.
They wear long boots, hard boots.

Primer Lesson

Time is a sandpile we run our fingers in.

Hotel Girl

Man is a long time coming.
Man will yet win.
Brother may yet line up with brother:
This old anvil laughs at many broken hammers.
There are men who can't be bought.

The People Will Live On [*1936*]

Time is a great teacher.
Who can live without hope?
In the darkness with a great bundle of grief the people march.

Ibid.

LOUIS EDWIN THAYER
[1878–   ]

Here is a toast that I want to give
 To a fellow I'll never know;
To the fellow who's going to take my place

[1] It was marked, in large black letters, "Office of the Manager — Keep Out." So Jurgen opened this door. — JAMES BRANCH CABELL: *Jurgen* [1919], *Chap. 44*

When it's time for me to go.

To My Successor [*1909*].
Stanza 1

EDWARD THOMAS
[1878–1917]

Out of the night, two cocks together crow,
Cleaving the darkness with a silver blow.

Cock-Crow

HANS ZINSSER
[1878–1940]

Now death is merciful. He calls me hence
Gently, with friendly soothing of my fears
Of ugly age and feeble impotence
And cruel disintegration of slow years.

Sonnets

How sweet the Summer! And the Autumn shone
Like warmth within our hearts as in the sky,
Ripening rich harvests that our love had sown.
How good that ere the Winter comes, I die!
Then, ageless in your heart, I'll come to rest
Serene and proud, as when you loved me best.

Ibid.

ETHEL BARRYMORE
[1879–   ]

That's all there is: there isn't any more.

Added, with permission of the author [Thomas Raceward], as the curtain line of "Sunday" [*1904*]

SIR WILLIAM BEVERIDGE
[1879–   ]

Simple effluxion of time.[1]

Social Insurance [*1942*]

[1] The *Oxford English Dictionary* traces the phrase "effluxion of time" back to JOHN MOLLE: *The Living Librarie* [1621].

The object of government in peace and in war is not the glory of rulers or of races, but the happiness of the common man.

Social Insurance

JAMES BRANCH CABELL
[1879–   ]

Why is the King of Hearts the only one that hasn't a moustache?

The Rivet in Grandfather's Neck [1915]

Divers queens who die with Antony But live a great while first with Julius.

Retractions. V

"Men's hands are by ordinary soiled in climbing," quoth the Centaur.

Jurgen [1919]. Chap. 5

Now I am wiser: for I know there is not any memory with less satisfaction in it than the memory of some temptation we resisted.

Ibid. Chap. 7

I am willing to taste any drink once.

Ibid. Chap. 16

I shall marry in haste, and repeat at leisure.

Ibid. Chap. 38

There is no faith stronger than that of a bad-tempered woman in her own infallibility.

Ibid. Chap. 39

Poetry is man's rebellion against being what he is.

Ibid. Chap. 44

The optimist proclaims that we live in the best of all possible worlds; and the pessimist fears this is true.

The Silver Stallion [1926]. Chap. 26

LEE WILSON DODD
[1879–1933]

Much that I sought, I could not find;
Much that I found, I could not bind;
Much that I bound, I could not free;
Much that I freed returned to me.

Ronde Macabre

ALBERT EINSTEIN
[1879–1955]

The most beautiful thing we can experience is the mysterious. It is the source of all true art and science.

"What I Believe," Forum [October, 1930]

As long as there are sovereign nations possessing great power, war is inevitable.

Einstein on the Atomic Bomb. Atlantic Monthly, November, 1945

I do not believe that civilization will be wiped out in a war fought with the atomic bomb. Perhaps two thirds of the people of the earth might be killed, but enough men capable of thinking, and enough books, would be left to start again, and civilization could be restored.

Ibid.

Since I do not foresee that atomic energy is to be a great boon for a long time, I have to say that for the present it is a menace. Perhaps it is well that it should be. It may intimidate the human race into bringing order into its international affairs, which, without the pressure of fear, it would not do.

Ibid.

Every intellectual who is called before one of the committees ought to refuse to testify, i. e., he must be prepared . . . for the sacrifice of his personal welfare in the interest of the cultural welfare of his country. . . . This kind of inquisition violates the spirit of the Constitution.

If enough people are ready to take this grave step they will be successful. If not, then the intellectuals of this country deserve nothing better than the slavery which is intended for them.

Letter to William Frauenglass,[1] May 16, 1953

[1] Einstein's letter was published in the *New York Times,* June 12, 1953; Mr. Frauenglass had been subpoenaed to testify before the Senate Internal Security Subcommittee, then under the chairmanship of Senator Jenner of Indiana.

JOHN ERSKINE
[1879–1951]

The Moral Obligation to Be Intelligent.

Title of book [1915]

The body travels more easily than the mind, and until we have limbered up our imagination we continue to think as though we had stayed home. We have not really budged a step until we take up residence in someone else's point of view.

The Complete Life [1943].
Chap. 8, Foreigners

W. C. FIELDS
[1879–1946]

It ain't a fit night out for man or beast.

The Fatal Glass of Beer

DOROTHY CANFIELD FISHER
[1879–   ]

A mother is not a person to lean on but a person to make leaning unnecessary.

Her Son's Wife [1926]

The skull of life suddenly showed through its smile.

Bonfire [1933]

EDWARD MORGAN FORSTER
[1879–   ]

Railway termini . . . are our gates to the glorious and the unknown. Through them we pass out into adventure and sunshine, to them, alas! we return. In Paddington all Cornwall is latent and the remoter west; down the inclines of Liverpool Street lie fenlands and the illimitable Broads; Scotland is through the pylons of Euston; Wessex behind the poised chaos of Waterloo.

Howards End [1910]. Chap. 2

It will be generally admitted that Beethoven's Fifth Symphony is the most sublime noise that has ever penetrated into the ear of man.

Howards End. Chap. 5

It is thus, if there is any rule, that we ought to die — neither as victim nor as fanatic, but as the seafarer who can greet with an equal eye the deep that he is entering, and the shore that he must leave.

Ibid. Chap. 12

Only connect! That was the whole of her sermon. Only connect the prose and the passion, and both will be exalted, and human love will be seen at its height. Live in fragments no longer. Only connect, and the beast and the monk, robbed of the isolation that is life to either, will die.

Ibid. Chap. 22

The historian must have some conception of how men who are not historians behave.

Abinger Harvest [1936].
Captain Edward Gibbon

It is not that the Englishman can't feel — it is that he is afraid to feel. He has been taught at his public school that feeling is bad form. He must not express great joy or sorrow, or even open his mouth too wide when he talks — his pipe might fall out if he did.

Ibid. Notes on English Character

English literature is a flying fish. It is a sample of the life that goes on day after day beneath the surface; it is a proof that beauty and emotion exist in the salt, inhospitable sea.

Ibid.

How rare, how precious is frivolity! How few writers can prostitute all their powers! They are always implying "I am capable of higher things."

Ibid. Ronald Firbank

EDMUND L. GRUBER
[1879–1941]

Over hill, over dale, we have hit the dusty trail
And those caissons go rolling along.
Countermarch! Right about! hear those wagon soldiers shout

While those caissons go rolling along.
Oh, it's hi-hi-yee! for the field artil-
leree,
Shout out your numbers loud and
strong,
And where'er we go, you will always
know
That those caissons are rolling along.
The Caisson Song [1]

JOHN HAYNES HOLMES
[1879–   ]

If Christians were Christians, there
would be no anti-Semitism. Jesus was
a Jew. There is nothing that the ordinary Christian so dislikes to remember as this awkward historical fact. But
it happens, none the less, to be true.
*The Sensible Man's View of
Religion* [1933]

Priests are no more necessary to religion than politicians to patriotism.
Ibid.

The universe is not hostile, nor yet
is it friendly. It is simply indifferent.
Ibid.

The life of humanity upon this
planet may yet come to an end, and a
very terrible end. But I would have
you notice that this end is threatened
in our time not by anything that the
universe may do to us, but only by
what man may do to himself.
Ibid.

VACHEL LINDSAY
[1879–1931]

Record it for the grandson of your
son —
A city is not builded in a day:

Our little town cannot complete her
soul
Till countless generations pass away.
On the Building of Springfield
[*1912*]. *Stanza 2*

Booth died blind and still by faith he
trod,
Eyes still dazzled by the ways of God.
*General William Booth Enters
into Heaven* [*1913*]

Sleep softly . . . eagle forgotten . . .
under the stone,
Time has its way with you there and
the clay has its own.
Sleep on, O brave-hearted, O wise man,
that kindled the flame —
To live in mankind is far more than to
live in a name.
The Eagle That Is Forgotten [1]
[*1913*]. *Stanza 5*

Factory windows are always broken.
Somebody's always throwing bricks,
Somebody's always heaving cinders,
Playing ugly Yahoo tricks.
Factory Windows. Stanza 1

See how the generations pass
Like sand through Heaven's blue hour-
glass.
Shantung

I want live things in their pride to re-
main.
I will not kill one grasshopper vain
Though he eats a hole in my shirt like
a door.
I let him out, give him one chance
more.
Perhaps, while he gnaws my hat in his
whim,
Grasshopper lyrics occur to him.
The Santa Fé Trail [*1914*]

Fat black bucks in a wine-barrel room,
Barrel-house kings; with feet unstable,
Sagged and reeled and pounded on the
table,
Pounded on the table,

---

[1] Major Gruber wrote this song when he
was a lieutenant in the 5th Field Artillery in
the Philippines. In April, 1908, the 1st Battalion came from the United States to relieve
the 2nd Battalion, and Lieutenant Gruber
was asked to write a song that would sym-
bolize the spirit of the reunited regiment.
There are many variant wordings.

[1] John Peter Altgeld [1847–1902], Governor of Illinois, 1893–1897, widely criticized
for pardoning, in June, 1893, the anarchists
who had been serving life terms in prison
since the Haymarket riot in Chicago, May 4,
1886. Altgeld, in pardoning them, declared
that "the judge conducted the trial with
malicious ferocity."

Beat an empty barrel with the handle
 of a broom.
> *The Congo* [*1914*]. *Part I*

Then I saw the Congo, creeping
 through the black,
Cutting through the forest with a
 golden track.
> *Ibid.*

Be careful what you do,
Or Mumbo-Jumbo, God of the Congo,
And all of the other
Gods of the Congo,
Mumbo-Jumbo will hoo-doo you.
> *Ibid.*

A bronzed, lank man! His suit of ancient black,
A famous high top-hat and plain worn
 shawl
Make him the quaint great figure that
 men love,
The prairie-lawyer, master of us all.
> *Abraham Lincoln Walks at*
> *Midnight* [*1914*]. *Stanza 3*

They spoke, I think, of perils past.
They spoke, I think, of peace at last.
One thing I remember:
Spring came on forever,
Spring came on forever,
Said the Chinese nightingale.
> *The Chinese Nightingale* [*1917*]

Then you died on the prairie, and
 scorned all disgraces,
O broncho that would not be broken of
 dancing.
> *The Broncho That Would Not*
> *Be Broken* [*1917*]. *Stanza 5*

Highly establish
In the name of God,
The United States of Europe, Asia, and
 the World.
> *Sew the Flags Together* [*1918*]

The flower-fed buffaloes of the spring
In the days of long ago,
Ranged where the locomotives sing
And the prairie flowers lie low.
> *The Flower-Fed Buffaloes*

God make our blunders wise.
> *Litany of the Heroes, Stanza 16*

Come let us forget our ivory-towers,[1]
 brothers,
Come let us be bold with our songs.
> *Every Soul Is a Circus. Part IV,*
> *The Pontoon Bridge Miracle*

Planting the trees that would march
 and train
On, in his name to the great Pacific,
Like Birnam Wood to Dunsinane,[2]
Johnny Appleseed swept on.[3]
> *In Praise of Johnny Appleseed*

I find strange thoughts in me, on war
and peace. . . . This is not the last
chance good men all over the world
will have to fight.
> *Letter to Eleanor Dougherty,*
> *October 12, 1918* [4]

The more probable chance for me
will come in some little row where
strikers are being shot down. . . .
I would be with the fool strikers, right
or wrong.
> *Ibid.*

[1] Charles-Augustin Sainte-Beuve [1804–1869] is the first writer known to have likened a poet's retreat to an ivory tower. In his *Pensées d'Août, To M. Villemain, St. 3*, dated October, 1837, he wrote:

> Hugo, dur partisan
> . . . combattit sous l'armure,
> Et tint haut sa bannière au milieu du mur-
> mure:
> Il la maintient encore; et Vigny, plus secret,
> Comme en sa tour d'ivoire, avant midi, ren-
> trait

> (Hugo, stern partisan
> . . . fought under armor,
> And held his banner high in the midst of the
> tumult:
> He holds it still; and Vigny, more secret,
> As if in his tower of ivory, retired before
> noon).

The poet, retired in his Tower of Ivory, isolated, according to his desire, from the world of man, resembles, whether he so wishes or not, another solitary figure, the watcher enclosed for months at a time in a lighthouse at the head of a cliff. — JULES DE GAULTIER [1858–?]: *La Guerre et les Destinées de l'Art*

The Ivory Tower is the title of an unfinished novel [1917] by Henry James.

[2] See Shakespeare, page 198b.

[3] See E. A. Allen, page 654b.

[4] Published by his sister, Olive Lindsay Wakefield, in the *Saturday Review of Literature,* October 20, 1945.

ST. JOHN LUCAS
[1879–1934]

The curate thinks you have no soul;
I know that he has none.[1]

My Dog

GEORGE WASHINGTON LYON
[1879–   ]

Worry, the interest paid by those who borrow trouble.

Epigram, in Judge,
March 1, 1924

DIXON LANIER MERRITT
[1879–   ]

A wonderful bird is the pelican,
His bill will hold more than his belican.
He can take in his beak
Food enough for a week,
But I'm damned if I see how the helican.

The Pelican [1910]

HAROLD MONRO
[1879–1932]

How lonely we shall be!
What shall we do,
You without me,
I without you?

Midnight Lamentation

FELIX RIESENBERG
[1879–1939]

The sea has always been a seducer, a careless lying fellow, not feminine, as many writers imagine, but strongly masculine in its allurement. The king of the sea, with his whiskers of weed and his trident and dolphins, truly represents the main and gives it character. The sea, like a great sultan, supports thousands of ships, his lawful wives. These he caresses and chastises as the case may be. This explains the feminine gender of all proper vessels.

Vignettes of the Sea

---

[1] There are things that even the youngest curate cannot explain. — LEONARD MERRICK: *One Man's View* [1897]

WILL ROGERS
[1879–1935]

All I know is just what I read in the papers.

Prefatory remark

I tell you Folks, all Politics is Apple Sauce.

The Illiterate Digest [1924].
Page 30

Everything is funny as long as it is happening to somebody else.

Ibid. Page 131

More men have been elected between Sundown and Sunup, than ever were elected between Sunup and Sundown.

Ibid. Page 152

I never met a man I didn't like.

Address, Boston [June, 1930]

A comedian can only last till he either takes himself serious or his audience takes him serious.

Syndicated newspaper article,
June 28, 1931

I not only "don't choose to run"[1] [for President] but I don't even want to leave a loophole in case I am drafted, so I won't "choose." I will say "won't run" no matter how bad the country will need a comedian by that time.

Ibid.

Politics has got so expensive that it takes lots of money to even get beat with.

Ibid.

ROBERT HAVEN SCHAUFFLER
[1879–   ]

At the gate of the West I stand,
On the isle where the nations throng,
We call them "scum o' the earth."[2]

Scum o' the Earth

JOSEPH STALIN
[1879–1953]

The Soviet regime possesses all the requisites for the upbuilding of a fully

---

[1] See Calvin Coolidge, page 859a.
[2] See Cervantes, page 108b.

socialized society, provided it can overcome its internal difficulties. We are witnessing a temporary stabilization of capitalism and the stabilization of the Soviet regime. A temporary equilibrium has been established between the two stabilizations. This compromise is the basic feature of the present situation.[1]
Speech to Party Officials,
May 9, 1925

In the U.S.S.R. work is the duty of every able-bodied citizen, according to the principle: "He who does not work, neither shall he eat."

In the U.S.S.R. the principle of socialism is realised: "From each according to his ability, to each according to his work." [2]
Constitution of the Union
of Soviet Socialist Republics
[1936]. Article 12

Citizens of the U.S.S.R. have the right to work.
Ibid. Article 118

Citizens of the U.S.S.R. have the right to rest.
Ibid. Article 119

Citizens of the U.S.S.R. have the right to maintenance in old age.
Ibid. Article 120

Citizens of the U.S.S.R. have the right to education
Ibid. Article 121

The victory of socialism in Russia is not complete because the danger of intervention from capitalist countries continues. The problem can be solved only by uniting the serious efforts of the international proletariat with the still more serious efforts of the entire Soviet people.
Letter to Comrade Ivanov,
February 14, 1938

Socialism can succeed only on the basis of a high productivity of labor, higher than under capitalism, on the basis of an abundance of products and

[1] This statement was popularized as "socialism in one country" and used in arguing against the position of Leon Trotsky.
[2] See Karl Marx, page 594a.

of articles of consumption of all kinds, on the basis of a prosperous and cultured life for all members of society.
Quoted by HEWLETT JOHNSON *in The Soviet Power: The Socialist Sixth of the World [1940], Book III, 8*

History shows that there are no invincible armies.
Address broadcast, Declaration of War, July 3, 1941 (Germany invaded Russia June 22, 1941)

In case of a forced retreat of Red Army units, all rolling stock must be evacuated; to the enemy must not be left a single engine, a single railway car, not a single pound of grain or a gallon of fuel. . . . In occupied regions conditions must be made unbearable for the enemy and all his accomplices. They must be hounded and annihilated at every step and all their measures frustrated.
Ibid. [The "scorched earth" edict]

All working people must be roused to defend our freedom, our honor, our country. . . . All the forces of the people for the demolition of the enemy.
Ibid.

The Hitlerite blackguards have covered Europe with gallows and concentration camps. . . . They have turned Europe into a prison of nations, and this they call the new order in Europe.
Address to the Moscow Soviet,
November 6, 1942

BESSIE ANDERSON (MRS. ARTHUR J.) STANLEY [1879–   ]

He has achieved success who has lived well, laughed often and loved much.
Success (prize-winning definition in a contest conducted by the Brown Book Magazine, 1904)

WALLACE STEVENS
[1879–]

Complacencies of the peignoir, and late
Coffee and oranges in a sunny chair.
Sunday Morning [*1923*]. *Stanza 1*

In the isolation of the sky,
At evening, casual flocks of pigeons
make
Ambiguous undulations as they sink,
Downward to darkness, on extended
wings.
Ibid. Stanza 8

Just as my fingers on these keys
Make music, so the self-same sounds
On my spirit make a music, too.
Peter Quince at the Clavier [*1923*].
Stanza 1

Beauty is momentary in the mind —
The fitful tracing of a portal;
But in the flesh it is immortal.
The body dies; the body's beauty lives.
Ibid. Stanza 4

The essential gaudiness of poetry.
*Stevens's note to The Emperor
of Ice-Cream*

The essential thing in form is to be
free in whatever form is used. A free
form does not assure freedom. As a
form, it is just one more form. So that
it comes to this, I suppose, that I believe in freedom regardless of form.
A Note on Poetry [*1937*]

ROSE PASTOR STOKES
[1879–1933]

Some pray to marry the man they love,
My prayer will somewhat vary:
I humbly pray to Heaven above
That I love the man I marry.
My Prayer

SIMEON STRUNSKY
[1879–1948]

Statistics are the heart of democracy.
*Topics of the Times,
November 30, 1944*

No colonization without misrepresentation.
No Mean City [1] [*1944*]. *Chap. 1*

People who want to understand
democracy should spend less time in
the library with Aristotle and more
time on the buses and in the subway.
Ibid. Chap. 2

To renew ties with the past need not
always be daydreaming; it may be tapping old sources of strength for new
tasks.
Ibid. Chap. 20

Nearly a century ago the foreigners
were saying that the national American
motto was "Hurry up!" They were the
first words which the immigrant heard
at Castle Garden, probably from his
own kinsmen who had preceded him to
America by a few years and were now
hustling him home from the dock.
Ibid. Chap. 30

Famous remarks are very seldom
quoted correctly.
Ibid. Chap. 38

GEORGE ASAF
(GEORGE H. POWELL)
[1880–1951]

What's the use of worrying?
It never was worth while,
So, pack up your troubles in your old
kit-bag,
And smile, smile, smile.
*Pack Up Your Troubles in
Your Old Kit-Bag* [*1915*]

HENRY HOWARTH
BASHFORD
[1880–]

As I came down the Highgate Hill
I met the sun's bravado,
And saw below me, fold on fold,
Grey to pearl and pearl to gold,
This London like a land of old,
The land of Eldorado.
Romances. Stanza 1

[1] A citizen of no mean city. — *Acts, XXI,
39*

JOSEPH CLARK GREW
[1880–]

This [sartorial convention] is a real problem with which I shall have to wrestle during the next few days, for of such stuff is diplomacy made.[1]
Ten Years in Japan [*1944*].
July 20, 1932

We have a phrase in English "straight from the horse's mouth." I never knew why the particular animal chosen was a horse, especially as most horses are generally not very communicative. But the meaning is clear enough. What I shall say in Japan in the ensuing months comes "straight from the horse's mouth."[2]
Ibid. October 19, 1939

ROBERT BROWNING HAMILTON
[1880–]

I walked a mile with Pleasure.
She chattered all the way,
But left me none the wiser
For all she had to say.
Along the Road. Stanza 1

I walked a mile with Sorrow,
And ne'er a word said she;
But, oh, the things I learned from her
When Sorrow walked with me!
Ibid. Stanza 2

BRIAN HOOKER
[1880–1946]

O youth foregone, foregoing!
O dream unseen, unsought!
God give you joy of knowing
What life your death has bought.[3]
A. D. 1919. Stanza 5

[1] In a diplomat's soul you may find iron ore, but it is usually oil — and in a whale of a diplomat you'll find the whole equipment — the blubber of charity, the whalebone of flexibility, the oil of commodity. A great diplomat is a regular Moby Dick. — FRANCIS HACKETT: *Review of* ROGER B. MERRIMAN, *Suleiman the Magnificent, The New York Times* [January 4, 1945]
[2] Address before the America-Japan Society.
[3] Inscription on a tablet at Yale University

HELEN KELLER
[1880–]

Literature is my Utopia. Here I am not disfranchised. No barrier of the senses shuts me out from the sweet, gracious discourse of my book-friends. They talk to me without embarrassment or awkwardness.
The Story of My Life [*1902*]

DOUGLAS MacARTHUR
[1880–]

I shall return.
Message on leaving Corregidor for Australia, March 11, 1942

The President of the United States has ordered me to break through the Japanese lines and proceed from Corregidor to Australia for the purpose, as I understand it, of organizing the American offensive against Japan. A primary purpose of this is relief of the Philippines. I came through and I shall return.
Statement on arrival from Philippines in Adelaide, Australia[1]
[*March 20, 1942*]

This is the Voice of Freedom, General MacArthur speaking. People of the Philippines: I have returned.
Upon landing at Leyte Island [*October 20, 1944*]

I see that the old flagpole still stands. Have your troops hoist the colors to its peak, and let no enemy ever haul them down.
To Colonel George M. Jones and 503rd Regimental Combat Team, who recaptured Corregidor [*March 2, 1945*]

It is fatal to enter any war without the will to win it.
Speech, Republican National Convention [*July 7, 1952*]

commemorating the Yale men who died in the First World War.
[1] On assuming Supreme Command in the Southwest Pacific.

907

GEORGE
CATLETT MARSHALL
[1880–   ]

The refusal of the British and Russian peoples to accept what appeared to be inevitable defeat was the great factor in the salvage of our civilization.

Biennial Report of the Chief of Staff of the U. S. Army, September 1, 1945

If man does find the solution for world peace it will be the most revolutionary reversal of his record we have ever known.

Ibid.

HENRY LOUIS MENCKEN
[1880–   ]

The virulence of the national appetite for bogus revelation.

A Book of Prefaces [*1917*].
Chap. 1, Sect. 2

To the man with an ear for verbal delicacies — the man who searches painfully for the perfect word, and puts the way of saying a thing above the thing said — there is in writing the constant joy of sudden discovery, of happy accident.

Ibid. Chap. 2, Sect. 2

Poverty is a soft pedal upon all branches of human activity, not excepting the spiritual.

Ibid. Chap. 4, Sect. 3

Formalism is the hall-mark of the national culture.

Ibid. Sect. 6

Time is a great legalizer, even in the field of morals.

Ibid.

The prophesying business is like writing fugues; it is fatal to every one save the man of absolute genius.

Prejudices, First Series [*1919*].
Chap. 2

The public . . . demands certainties; it must be told definitely and a bit raucously that this is true and that is false. But there *are* no certainties.

Ibid. Chap. 3

All successful newspapers are ceaselessly querulous and bellicose. They never defend anyone or anything if they can help it; if the job is forced upon them, they tackle it by denouncing someone or something else.

Prejudices, First Series. Chap. 13

The great artists of the world are never Puritans, and seldom even ordinarily respectable.

Ibid. Chap. 16

To be in love is merely to be in a state of perceptual anaesthesia — to mistake an ordinary young man for a Greek god or an ordinary young woman for a goddess.

Ibid.

All the more pretentious American authors try to write chastely and elegantly; the typical literary product of the country is still a refined essay in the *Atlantic Monthly*, perhaps gently jocose but never rough — by Emerson, so to speak, out of Charles Lamb.

The American Language [*1919*]

Philadelphia is the most pecksniffian of American cities, and thus probably leads the world.

Ibid.

It is the dull man who is always sure, and the sure man who is always dull.

Prejudices, Second Series [*1920*].
Chap. 1

There are no mute, inglorious Miltons,[1] save in the hallucinations of poets. The one sound test of a Milton is that he functions as a Milton.

Ibid. Third Series [*1922*], *Chap. 3*

Nine times out of ten, in the arts as in life, there is actually no truth to be discovered; there is only error to be exposed.

Ibid.

Injustice is relatively easy to bear; what stings is justice.

Ibid.

Poetry is a comforting piece of fiction set to more or less lascivious music.

Ibid. Chap. 7

---

[1] See Gray, page 348b.

Faith may be defined briefly as an illogical belief in the occurrence of the improbable.

Prejudices, Third Series. Chap. 14

To be happy one must be (*a*) well fed, unhounded by sordid cares, at ease in Zion, (*b*) full of a comfortable feeling of superiority to the masses of one's fellow men, and (*c*) delicately and unceasingly amused according to one's taste. It is my contention that, if this definition be accepted, there is no country in the world wherein a man constituted as I am — a man of my peculiar weakness, vanities, appetites, and aversions — can be so happy as he can be in the United States. Going further, I lay down the doctrine that it is a sheer physical impossibility for such a man to live in the United States and *not* be happy.

On Being an American [*1922*]

The difference between a moral man and a man of honor is that the latter regrets a discreditable act, even when it has worked and he has not been caught.

Prejudices, Fourth Series [*1924*].
Chap. 11

Nothing can come out of an artist that is not in the man.

Ibid. Fifth Series [*1926*].
Chap. 5

Christian endeavor is notoriously hard on female pulchritude.

The Aesthetic Recoil

The learned are seldom pretty fellows, and in many cases their appearance tends to discourage a love of study in the young.

The New Webster International Dictionary [*1934*]

The Gaseous Vertebrata who own, operate and afflict the universe have treated me with excessive politeness.

Happy Days [*1940*]. *Preface*

When A annoys or injures B on the pretense of improving B, A is a scoundrel.

Newspaper Days: 1899–1906
[*1941*]

I've made it a rule never to drink by daylight and never to refuse a drink after dark.

Quoted in New York Post,
September 18, 1945

ALFRED NOYES
[1880–]

There's a magic in the distance, where the sea-line meets the sky.

Forty Singing Seamen. Stanza 9

Go down to Kew in lilac-time (it isn't far from London!)
And you shall wander hand in hand with love in summer's wonderland.

Barrel-Organ. Stanza 5

The wind was a torrent of darkness among the gusty trees,
The moon was a ghostly galleon tossed upon cloudy seas,
The road was a ribbon of moonlight over the purple moor,
And the highwayman came riding —
Riding — riding —
The highwayman came riding, up to the old inn-door.

The Highwayman

The landlord's black-eyed daughter,
Bess, the landlord's daughter,
Plaiting a dark red love-knot into her long black hair.

Ibid.

I'll come to thee by moonlight, though hell should bar the way.

Ibid.

Calling as he used to call, faint and far away,
In Sherwood, in Sherwood, about the break of day.

Sherwood

The cymbals crash,
And the dancers walk,
With long silk stockings
And arms of chalk.

A Victory Dance.[1] *Stanza 1*

God how the dead men
Grin by the wall,

[1] The symphonic poem *Victory Ball*, composed by Ernest Schelling [1876–1939], was inspired by this poem.

Watching the fun
Of the Victory Ball.
A Victory Dance. Stanza 9

EDMUND LESTER PEARSON
[1880–1937]

No agreement about books can make us look upon another man with so friendly an eye as the discovery that he belonged to our period, and shared our special enthusiasms about reading, in the years that stretched between the sixth birthday and the sixteenth.
Books in Black or Red [1923]

GRANTLAND RICE
[1880–1954]

Where the puddle is shallow, the weakfish stay
To drift along with the current's flow;
To take the tide as it moves each day
With the idle ripples that come and go.
Ballade of the Gamefish
When the One Great Scorer comes to write against your name —
He marks — not that you won or lost
— but how you played the game.[1]
Alumnus Football
All wars are planned by old men
In council rooms apart,
Who plan for greater armament
And map the battle chart.[2]
Two Sides of War. Stanza 1
I've noticed nearly all the dead
Were hardly more than boys.
Ibid. Stanza 4

LYTTON STRACHEY
[1880–1932]

Bertie[3] seemed to display a deep-seated repugnance to every form of mental exertion.
Queen Victoria [1921]. Chap. 6
In women's hearts he[4] had always

[1] But just this line ye grave for me:
"He played the game."
ROBERT WILLIAM SERVICE [1874–   ]:
The Lost Master
[2] See Herbert Hoover, pages 873b–874a.
[3] Edward VII as a child.
[4] Disraeli.

read as in an open book. . . . He realised everything — the interacting complexities of circumstance and character, the pride of place mingled so inextricably with personal arrogance, the super-abundant emotionalism, the ingenuousness of outlook, the solid, the laborious respectability, shot through so incongruously by temperamental cravings for the coloured and the strange, the singular intellectual limitations, and the mysteriously essential female elements impregnating every particle of the whole. A smile hovered over his impassive features, and he dubbed Victoria "the Faery."
Queen Victoria. Chap. 8
Perhaps of all the creations of man language is the most astonishing.
Words and Poetry

RICHARD HENRY TAWNEY
[1880–   ]

The burden of our civilization is . . . that industry itself has come to hold a position of exclusive predominance among human interests, which no single interest, and least of all the provision of the material means of existence, is fit to occupy.
The Acquisitive Society
Industrialized communities neglect the very objects for which it is worth while to acquire riches in their feverish preoccupation with the means by which riches can be acquired.
Ibid.

NANCY BYRD TURNER
[1880–   ]

When I go up to London
'Twill be in April weather.
I'll have a riband on my rein
And flaunt a scarlet feather.
Going Up to London
Death is only an old door
Set in a garden wall.
Death a Quiet Door

MARGARET WIDDEMER
[1880–   ]

I have shut my little sister in from life
    and light
(For a rose, for a ribbon, for a wreath
    across my hair),
I have made her restless feet still until
    the night,
Locked from sweets of summer and
    from wild spring air.
                The Factories. Stanza 1

The old road to Paradise
Easy it is missed!
            The Old Road to Paradise.
                        Stanza 2

Carnations and my first love! And he
    was seventeen,
And I was only twelve years — a
    stately gulf between.
                Carnations. Stanza 1

Well, if the thing is over, better it is
    for me,
The lad was ever a rover, loving and
    laughing and free.
            Mary, Helper of Heartbreak.
                        Stanza 1

Mary, helper of heartbreak, send him
    to me tonight!
                Ibid. Stanza 3

THOMAS RUSSELL YBARRA
[1880–   ]

A Christian is a man who feels
    Repentance on a Sunday
For what he did on Saturday
    And is going to do on Monday.
                The Christian

ALBERT JAY COOK
[*Floruit* 1917]

It's Heaven, Hell or Hoboken [1] before
    next Christmas Day.
            Heaven, Hell or Hoboken [2]

[1] Hoboken was a port of embarkation and
return for the American Expeditionary Forces
during the First World War.
[2] Published in *The Stars and Stripes.*

LASCELLES ABERCROMBIE
[1881–1938]

Crumble, crumble,
Voiceless things;
No faith can last
That never sings.
            The Stream's Song. Stanza 6
For the last hour
To joy belongs;
The steadfast perish,
But not the songs.
                Ibid. Stanza 7

FRANKLIN PIERCE ADAMS
("F.P.A.")
[1881–   ]

Christmas is over and Business is
Business.
                For the Other 364 Days
"Up, to the office, . . . and so to bed."
            A Ballade of Mr. Samuel Pepys.
                        Refrain

If vigilance yet above you
Hover, count the times I love you;
And if slumber still repel you,
Count the times I do not tell you.
                        Lullaby
Ruthlessly pricking our gonfalon bub-
    ble,
Making a Giant hit into a double,
Words that are weighty with nothing
    but trouble:
"Tinker to Evers to Chance."
                Baseball's Sad Lexicon
The rich man has his motor car,
    His country and his town estate.
He smokes a fifty-cent cigar
    And jeers at Fate.
                The Rich Man. Stanza 1
Yet though my lamp burn low and dim,
    Though I must slave for liveli-
    hood —
Think you that I would change with
    him?
You bet I would!
                Ibid. Stanza 3
The best you get is an even break.
            Ballade of Schopenhauer's
                        Philosophy

I shot a poem into the air,
It was reprinted everywhere
From Bangor to the Rocky Range
And always credited to
— Exchange.
Frequently

O bards of rhyme and metre free,
My gratitude goes out to ye
For all your deathless lines — ahem!
Let's see now . . . What *is* one of
them?
To a Vers Librist

Of making many books there is no
end —
So Sancho Panza said, and so say I.
Thou wert my guide, philosopher and
friend
When only one is shining in the sky.
Lines on and from "Bartlett's Familiar Quotations"

Go, lovely Rose that lives its little
hour!
Go, little booke! and let who will be
clever!
Roll on! From yonder ivy-mantled
tower
The moon and I could keep this up
forever.
Ibid.

Prints, approaches the well-known
date;
Time to wallop and stigmatize;
Time for the wearisome old debate;
Why did it win the Pulitzer Prize?
*Ballade of the Annual Query.
L'Envoi*

MARY ANTIN
[1881–1949]

So at last I was going to America!
Really, really going, at last! The
boundaries burst. The arch of heaven
soared. A million suns shone out for
every star. The winds rushed in from
outer space, roaring in my ears, "America! America!"
The Promised Land [1912]

WITTER BYNNER
[1881–]

Name me no names for my disease,
With uninforming breath;
I tell you I am none of these,
But homesick unto death.
*The Patient to the Doctors.
Stanza 1*

Give her such beauty of body and mind
As the leaves of an aspen tree
When they vary from silver to green in
the wind,
And who shall be lovely as she?
A Prayer for Beauty

You must keep your goal in sight,
Labor toward it day and night,
Then at last arriving there —
You shall be too old to care.
Wisdom

What's the use of a new-born
child? [1] . . .
To raise the dead heart? — to set wild
The fettered hope?
Poor Richard

A leader is best
When people barely know that he
exists.
*The Way of Life According to
Laotzu*

The biggest problem in the world
Could have been solved when it was
small.
Ibid.

JOSEPH CAMPBELL
[1881–1944]

As a white candle
In a holy place,
So is the beauty
Of an aged face.
The Old Woman. Stanza 1

Her thoughts as still
As the waters
Under a ruined mill.
Ibid. Stanza 3

[1] "What is the use of this new invention?"
some one asked Franklin. "What is the use
of a new-born child?" was his reply.—
JAMES PARTON: *The Life and Times of
Benjamin Franklin* [1864], *Vol. II, P. 514.*
(A footnote states that the anecdote is taken
from the memoirs of Baron de Grimm.)

FRANCIS CARLIN (J. F. C. MacDONNELL)
[1881–1945]

That which is in disorder
  Has neither rule nor rhyme,
Like the stars at Heaven's border
  And the troubled laughter of Time.
    The Raveled Edge. Stanza 3

ROBERT WILLIAM CHAPMAN
[1881–   ]

A house is infinitely communicative, and tells many things besides the figure of its master's income. There are houses that confess intellectual penury, and houses that reek of enlightenment.
    The Portrait of a Scholar
    [1920]
A quotation, like a pun, should come unsought, and then be welcomed only for some propriety or felicity justifying the intrusion.
    Ibid. The Art of Quotation
A collector should not be too careful to be sure of what he buys, or the sporting spirit will atrophy; and he who collects that he may have the best collection, or a better than his friend's, is little more than a miser.
    Ibid. Silver Spoons

PADRAIC COLUM
[1881–   ]

Oh, to have a little house!
To own the hearth and stool and all!
    An Old Woman of the Roads.
    Stanza 1
And I am praying God on high,
  And I am praying Him night and day,
For a little house — a house of my own —
  Out of the wind's and the rain's way.
    Ibid. Stanza 6

JOHN FREEMAN
[1881–1929]

Who may regret what was, since it has made

Himself himself? All that I was I am,
And the old childish joy now lives in me
At sight of a green field or a green tree.
    All That I Was I Am

EDGAR ALBERT GUEST
[1881–   ]

Somebody said that it couldn't be done,
  But he with a chuckle replied
That "maybe it couldn't," but he would be one
Who wouldn't say so till he'd tried.
    It Couldn't Be Done [1]

The things that haven't been done before,
  Those are the things to try;
Columbus dreamed of an unknown shore
  At the rim of the far-flung sky.
    The Things That Haven't Been
    Done Before

It takes a heap o' livin' in a house
  t' make it home,
A heap o' sun an' shadder, an' ye sometimes have t' roam
Afore ye really 'preciate the things ye
  lef' behind,
An' hunger fer 'em somehow, with 'em
  allus on yer mind.
    Home

Let me be a little kinder,
Let me be a little blinder
To the faults of those around me,
Let me praise a little more.
    A Creed

I'd rather see a sermon than hear one
  any day;
I'd rather one should walk with me
  than merely tell the way.
    Sermons We See

In this bright little package, now isn't it odd?
You've a dime's worth of something known only to God!
    The Package of Seeds

[1] The world would sleep if things were run
By men who say, "It can't be done!"
    PHILANDER JOHNSON [1866–1939]:
    "It Can't Be Done"

Here is one of God's miracles soon to
unfold,
Thus for ten cents an ounce is Divinity
sold!
The Package of Seeds

JOHN EDWARD HAZZARD
[1881–1935]

It worries me to beat the band
To hear folks say our lives is grand;
Wish they'd try some one-night stand.
Ain't it awful, Mabel!
Ain't It Awful, Mabel!

WILLIAM McFEE
[1881–   ]

A trouble is a trouble, and the gen-
eral idea, in the country, is to treat it
as such.
Casuals of the Sea [1916].
Book I, 4
The world belongs to the enthusiast
who keeps cool.
Ibid. 14
The nobility of soul which is libel-
lously miscalled "proper pride."
Ibid. 17
If fate means you to lose, give him
a good fight anyhow.
Ibid. Book II, 2
Doing what's right is no guarantee
against misfortune.
Ibid. 6
It's the people who're comfortable
who have time to worry over little
trivial things.
Ibid.
Responsibility's like a string we can
only see the middle of. Both ends are
out of sight.
Ibid.
The alluring yet ineluctable problem
of human folly.
Aliens [1917]. Preface
A certain incomprehensible reticence
of soul which is peculiar to the English.
Command [1922]. Chap. 6
The bourgeois artist who retains his
integrity is the only really happy man
in the modern world. He is unable to

envy anybody because nobody has anything he can use which is not his already.
More Harbours of Memory
[1934]. Introduction

JOHN GNEISENAU
NEIHARDT
[1881–   ]

Give me high noon — and let it then
be night!
Let Me Live Out My Years
And grant me, when I face the grisly
Thing,
One haughty cry to pierce the gray
Perhaps!
O let me be a tune-swept fiddlestring
That feels the Master Melody — *and
snaps!*
Ibid.

STUART PRATT SHERMAN
[1881–1926]

The delectable form which intelligence takes in its moments of surplus
power — the form of wit.
*Introduction [1923] to Ameri-
can Prose Masters by* W. C.
BROWNELL

WILLIAM TEMPLE
(ARCHBISHOP OF CANTER-
BURY)
[1881–1944]

There is no structural organization
of society which can bring about the
coming of the Kingdom of God on
earth, since all systems can be perverted by the selfishness of man.
The Malvern Manifesto [1]
Human status ought not to depend
upon the changing demands of the economic process.
Ibid.
The existing industrial order tends
to recklessness and sacrilege in the

[1] Drawn up by a Conference of the Province of York, January 10, 1941; signed for
the Conference by Temple, then Archbishop
of York.

treatment of natural resources . . . it is largely responsible for the problem of the "mass man" who easily develops the herd psychology.
The Malvern Manifesto

MARY WEBB
[1881–1927]

The past is only the present become invisible and mute; and because it is invisible and mute, its memoried glances and its murmurs are infinitely precious. We are tomorrow's past.
Precious Bane [*1924*].[1]
Foreword

It made me gladsome to be getting some education, it being like a big window opening.
Ibid. Book I, Chap. 5

Saddle your dreams afore you ride 'em.
Ibid. Chap. 6

If you stop to be kind, you must swerve often from your path.
Ibid. Book II, Chap. 3

It's the folk that depend on us for this and for the other that we most do miss. So the mother is more let and hindered lacking the little creatures clinging to her skirt than she is when they be there, for she has no heart for her work.
Ibid. Book IV, Chap. 4

PELHAM GRENVILLE WODEHOUSE
[1881–   ]

He spoke with a certain what-is-it in his voice, and I could see that, if not actually disgruntled, he was far from being gruntled.
The Code of the Woosters

[1]   That soil may best
Deserve the precious bane.
MILTON: *Paradise Lost* [*1667*],
Book I, L. 689

BERTON BRALEY
[1882–   ]

The grammar has a rule absurd
  Which I would call an outworn myth:
"A preposition is a word
  You mustn't end a sentence with!"[1]
No Rule to Be Afraid Of.
Stanza 1

And so they sailed away, these three,
  Mencken,
  Nathan
  And God.[2]
Three Minus One. Stanza 1

With doubt and dismay you are smitten,
You think there's no chance for you, son?
Why, the best books haven't been written,
The best race hasn't been run.
Opportunity. Stanza 1

Back of the beating hammer
  By which the steel is wrought,
Back of the workshop's clamor
  The seeker may find the Thought.
The Thinker. Stanza 1

Back of the Job — the Dreamer
Who's making the dream come true!
Ibid. Stanza 4

JOHN DRINKWATER
[1882–1937]

This be my pilgrimage and goal,
  Daily to march and find
The secret phrases of the soul,
  The evangels of the mind.
Vocation

And not a girl goes walking
  Along the Cotswold lanes
But knows men's eyes in April
  Are quicker than their brains.
Cotswold Love

Grant us the will to fashion as we feel,
Grant us the strength to labor as we know,

[1] See Churchill, page 872b.
[2] See Eugene Field, page 747a.

Grant us the purpose, ribbed and edged
with steel,
To strike the blow.
> *A Prayer. Stanza 9*

SIR ARTHUR STANLEY EDDINGTON
[1882–1944]

It is one thing for the human mind to extract from the phenomena of nature the laws which it has itself put into them; it may be a far harder thing to extract laws over which it has no control. It is even possible that laws which have not their origin in the mind may be irrational, and we can never succeed in formulating them.
> *Space, Time, and Gravitation*
> *[1920]*

SAMUEL GOLDWYN
[1882–   ]

For years I have been known for saying "include me out," but today I am giving it up forever. From now on let me say: "Oxford and Balliol, include me in."
> *Address to the Students of Balliol*
> *College, Oxford [March 1, 1945]*

In two words: im-possible.
> *Quoted by* ALVA JOHNSON:
> *The Great Goldwyn*

HERMANN HAGEDORN
[1882–   ]

Down the fair-chambered corridor of
years,
The quiet shutting, one by one, of
doors.
> *Doors*

WILLIAM FREDERICK HALSEY, JR.
[1882–   ]

Strike repeat Strike.
> *Reply to division commanders*
> *in South Pacific, when asked for*
> *his instructions, October 24,*
> *1942*

Hit hard, hit fast, hit often.
> *Formula for waging war*

Send them our latitude and longitude.
> *Retort to the enemy's question,*
> *"Where is the American Fleet?"*
> *October, 1944*

Our ships have been salvaged and are retiring at high speed toward the Japanese fleet.
> *Radio message, October, 1944,*
> *after Japanese claims that most*
> *of the U. S. Third Fleet had*
> *either been sunk or had retired*

HUGH S. JOHNSON
[1882–1942]

There was never a war at arms that was not merely the extension of a preceding war of commerce grown fiercer until the weapons of commerce seemed no longer sufficiently deadly.[1]
> *Radio broadcast for "World*
> *Peaceways" [1935]*

JAMES JOYCE
[1882–1941]

When thou hast heard his name upon
The bugles of the cherubim,
Begin thou softly to unzone
Thy girlish bosom unto him
And softly to undo the snood
That is the sign of maidenhood.
> *Chamber Music [1907].*
> *XI, Stanza 2*

Pity is the feeling which arrests the mind in the presence of whatsoever is grave and constant in human sufferings and unites it with the human sufferer.
> *A Portrait of the Artist as a*
> *Young Man [1916]. Chap. 5*

Welcome, O life! I go to encounter for the millionth time the reality of experience and to forge in the smithy of my soul the uncreated conscience of my

[1] War is not merely a political act, but also a political instrument, a continuation of political relations, a carrying out of the same by other means. — KARL VON CLAUSEWITZ: *On War* [1832]

race. Old father, old artificer, stand me now and ever in good stead.

A Portrait of the Artist as a Young Man. Concluding words of Stephen Dedalus

A man of genius makes no mistakes. His errors are volitional and are the portals of discovery.

Ulysses [1] *[1922]. II*

Around us fear, descending
Darkness of fear above
And in my heart how deep unending
Ache of love!

Pomes Penyeach [1927]. On the Beach at Fontana

Why, why, why! Weh, O weh!
I'se so silly to be flowing but I no canna stay!

Finnegans Wake [1939]. Song of The River

FIORELLO H. LaGUARDIA
[1882–1948]

Ticker tape ain't spaghetti.

Speech to the United Nations Relief and Rehabilitation Administration, March 29, 1946

WINIFRED MARY LETTS
[1882–]

I saw the spires of Oxford
As I was passing by,
The gray spires of Oxford
Against a pearl-gray sky.

The Spires of Oxford. Stanza 1

That God once loved a garden
We learn in Holy writ.
And seeing gardens in the Spring
I well can credit it.

Stephen's Green. Stanza 1

---

[1] In respect of the recurrent emergence of the theme of sex in the minds of his characters, it must always be remembered that his locale was Celtic and his season Spring . . . whilst in many places the effect of "Ulysses" on the reader undoubtedly is somewhat emetic, nowhere does it tend to be an aphrodisiac. "Ulysses" may, therefore, be admitted into the United States. — JUDGE JOHN M. WOOLSEY: *Decision of U. S. District Court* [December 6, 1933]

PHILIP HENRY KERR, MARQUESS OF LOTHIAN [1]
[1882–1940]

A limitation of armaments by political appeasement.[2]

Letter to The Times (London), May, 1934

JACQUES MARITAIN
[1882–]

In the modern social order, the *person* is sacrificed to the *individual*. The individual is given universal suffrage, equality of rights, freedom of opinion; while the person, isolated, naked, with no social armor to sustain and protect him, is left to the mercy of all the devouring forces which threaten the life of the soul, exposed to relentless actions and reactions of conflicting interests and appetites. . . . It is a homicidal civilization.

Three Reformers [1925]

ALAN ALEXANDER MILNE
[1882–]

Hush! Hush! Whisper who dares!
Christopher Robin is saying his prayers.

When We Were Very Young. Vespers

They're changing guard at Buckingham Palace —
Christopher Robin went down with Alice.

Ibid. Buckingham Palace

The King asked
The Queen, and
The Queen asked
The Dairymaid:
"Could we have some butter for
The Royal slice of bread?"

Ibid. The King's Breakfast

"Nobody, my darling,
Could call me
A fussy man —
BUT

---

[1] See Winston Churchill, page 870a.
[2] One of the most portentous slogans of the period was coined here. — KONRAD HEIDEN: *Der Führer* [1944], P. 714

I do like a little bit of butter to my
  bread!"
        When We Were Very Young.
          The King's Breakfast

It isn't really
Anywhere!
It's somewhere else
Instead!
    Ibid. Halfway Down, Stanza 2

What shall I call my dear little dor-
  mouse?
His eyes are small, but his tail is e-nor-
  mouse.
        Ibid. The Christening

Christopher Robin goes
Hoppity, hoppity,
Hoppity, hoppity, hop.
Whenever I tell him
Politely to stop it, he
Says he can't possibly stop.
        Ibid. Hoppity

  James James
  Morrison Morrison
  Weatherby George Dupree
  Took great
  Care of his Mother
  Though he was only three.
  James James
  Said to his Mother,
  "Mother," he said, said he:
"You must never go down to the end of
    the town, if you don't go down
    with me."
        Ibid. Disobedience

Christopher Robin
Had wheezles
And sneezles.
        Now We Are Six. Sneezles

If I were a bear,
  And a big bear, too,
I shouldn't much care
  If it froze or snew.
        Ibid. Furry Bear

I am a Bear of Very Little Brain,
and long words Bother me.
        Winnie-the-Pooh. Chap. 4

Time for a little something.
        Ibid. Chap. 6

FRANKLIN DELANO
ROOSEVELT
[1882–1945]

There is nothing I love as much as a
good fight.
        Interview, New York Times
          [January 22, 1911]

These unhappy times call for the
building of plans . . . that build from
the bottom up and not from the top
down, that put their faith once more in
the forgotten man [1] at the bottom of
the economic pyramid.
        Radio address [April 7, 1932]

The country needs and, unless I mistake its temper, the country demands
bold, persistent experimentation. It is
common sense to take a method and
try it: If it fails, admit it frankly and
try another. But above all, try something.
        Address at Oglethorpe University
          [May 22, 1932]

I pledge you, I pledge myself,
to a new deal for the American people.
        Speech accepting the nomina-
          tion for the Presidency, Demo-
          cratic National Convention,
          Chicago [July 2, 1932]

This campaign marks the beginning
of a new deal in American politics, and
in the conduct of the American government.
        Campaign speech at Indianapolis
          [October 20, 1932]

There is no indispensable man.
        Campaign speech at New York
          [November 3, 1932]

The only thing we have to fear is
fear itself.[2]
        First Inaugural Address
          [March 4, 1933]

[1] See William Graham Summer, page 707a–
707b.
All honor to the one that in this hour
Cries to the world as from a lighted tower —
Cries for the Man Forgotten.
  EDWIN MARKHAM [1852–1940]: *The*
                        Forgotten Man
[2] See Thoreau, page 589a.

The money changers have fled from their high seats in the temple of our civilization.
First Inaugural Address

In the field of world policy I would dedicate this nation to the policy of the good neighbor.[1]
Ibid.

If I were asked to state the great objective which Church and State are both demanding for the sake of every man and woman and child in this country, I would say that that great objective is "a more abundant life."
Address before Federal Council of Churches of Christ [December 6, 1933]

I am not for a return to that definition of liberty under which for many years a free people were being gradually regimented into the service of the privileged few. I prefer and I am sure you prefer that broader definition of liberty under which we are moving forward to greater freedom, to greater security for the average man than he has ever known before in the history of America.
Fireside Chat [September 30, 1934]

We have earned the hatred of entrenched greed.
Message to Congress [January 3, 1936]

The truth is found when men are free to pursue it.
Address at Temple University [February 22, 1936]

Out of this modern civilization economic royalists carved new dynasties. . . . The royalists of the economic order have conceded that political freedom was the business of the Government, but they have maintained that economic slavery was nobody's business.
Speech accepting renomination [June 27, 1936]

[1] I am as desirous of being a good neighbor as I am of being a bad subject. — THOREAU: *Civil Disobedience* [1849]

This generation of Americans has a rendezvous with destiny.
Speech accepting renomination

I have seen war. . . . I hate war.
Address at Chautauqua [August 14, 1936]

I have not sought, I do not seek, I repudiate the support of any advocate of Communism or of any other alien "ism" which would by fair means or foul change our American democracy.
Address at Syracuse [September 29, 1936]

I should like to have it said of my first Administration that in it the forces of selfishness and of lust for power met their match. I should like to have it said of my second Administration that in it these forces met their master.
Speech, Madison Square Garden [October 31, 1936]

Men with a passion for anonymity.
Report of President's Committee on Administrative Management [January 12, 1937]

We have always known that heedless self-interest was bad morals; we know now that it is bad economics.
Second Inaugural Address [January 20, 1937]

I see one-third of a nation ill-housed, ill-clad, ill-nourished.
Ibid.

The test of our progress is not whether we add more to the abundance of those who have much; it is whether we provide enough for those who have too little.
Ibid.

The epidemic of world lawlessness is spreading. When an epidemic of physical disease starts to spread, the community approves and joins in a quarantine of the patients in order to protect the health of the community against the spread of the disease. . . . The will for peace on the part of peace-loving nations must express itself to the end that nations that may be tempted to violate their agreements and the rights of others will desist from such a course. There must be positive endeavors to preserve peace.

> *Speech at Chicago* [1] *[October 5, 1937]*

War is a contagion.

> *Ibid.*

History proves that dictatorships do not grow out of strong and successful governments, but out of weak and helpless ones. If by democratic methods people get a government strong enough to protect them from fear and starvation, their democracy succeeds; but if they do not, they grow impatient. Therefore, the only sure bulwark of continuing liberty is a government strong enough to protect the interests of the people, and a people strong enough and well enough informed to maintain its sovereign control over its government.

> *Fireside Chat [April 14, 1938]*

Remember, remember always that all of us, and you and I especially, are descended from immigrants and revolutionists.[2]

> *Address to Daughters of the American Revolution [April 21, 1938]*

A program whose basic thesis is not that the system of free private enterprise for profit has failed in this generation, but that it has not yet been tried.

> *Message on Concentration of Economic Power [April 29, 1938]*

The Democratic Party will live and continue to receive the support of the majority of Americans just so long as it remains a liberal party.

> *Address, Denton, Maryland [September 5, 1938]*

The Soviet Union, as everybody who has the courage to face the fact knows, is run by a dictatorship as absolute as any other dictatorship in the world.

> *Address to American Youth Congress [February 10, 1940]*

On this tenth day of June, 1940, the

---

[1] The "Quarantine the Aggressors" speech.
[2] See *Campaign Speech, Boston,* page 921b.

---

hand that held the dagger has struck it into the back of its neighbor.[1]

> *Address to the Graduating Class, University of Virginia, Charlottesville [June 10, 1940]*

Eternal truths will be neither true nor eternal unless they have fresh meaning for every new social situation.

> *Address, University of Pennsylvania [September 20, 1940]*

And while I am talking to you mothers and fathers, I give you one more assurance. I have said this before, but I shall say it again and again and again: Your boys are not going to be sent into any foreign wars.

> *Campaign speech in Boston [October 30, 1940]*

That great historic trio . . . Martin, Barton and Fish.[2]

> *Ibid.*

It is an unfortunate human failing that a full pocketbook often groans more loudly than an empty stomach.

> *Speech in Brooklyn [November 1, 1940]*

We must be the great arsenal of democracy.

> *Fireside Chat [December 29, 1940]*

In the future days, which we seek to make secure, we look forward to a world founded upon four essential human freedoms. The first is freedom of speech and expression — everywhere in the world. The second is freedom of every person to worship God in his own way — everywhere in the world. The third is freedom from want . . . everywhere in the world. The fourth is freedom from fear . . . anywhere in the world.

> *Message to Congress [January 6, 1941]*

One great difference which has characterized this division [between liberal

---

[1] A few hours before President Roosevelt's address, Count Ciano, Italy's Foreign Minister, had notified the French Ambassador that Italy considered herself at war with France beginning June 11.
[2] Joseph Martin, Bruce Barton, and Hamilton Fish.

and conservative parties] has been that the liberal party — no matter what its particular name was at the time — believed in the wisdom and efficacy of the will of the great majority of the people, as distinguished from the judgment of a small minority. . . . The other great difference between the two parties has been this: The liberal party is a party which believes that, as new conditions and problems arise beyond the power of men and women to meet as individuals, it becomes the duty of the Government itself to find new remedies with which to meet them. The liberal party insists that the Government has the definite duty to use all its power and resources to meet new social problems with new social controls — to insure to the average person the right to his own economic and political life, liberty, and the pursuit of happiness.
Introduction to Public Papers and Addresses, 1938 Volume [*1941*]

We, too, born to freedom, and believing in freedom, are willing to fight to maintain freedom. We, and all others who believe as deeply as we do, would rather die on our feet than live on our knees.[1]
Response on receiving the degree of Doctor of Civil Law conferred by Oxford University, at a special convocation, Harvard University [2] [*June 19, 1941*]

When you see a rattlesnake poised to strike, you do not wait until he has struck before you crush him.
Fireside Chat [*September 11, 1941*]

Yesterday, December 7, 1941 — a date which will live in infamy — the United States of America was suddenly and deliberately attacked by naval and air forces of the Empire of Japan.
War Message to Congress [*December 8, 1941*]

[1] The phrase was a watchword with the Republican forces in the Spanish Civil War, 1936–1939, and is usually attributed to the celebrated woman leader, La Pasionaria.
[2] Read by Major General Edwin M. Watson, serving as proxy for President Roosevelt.

Never before have we had so little time in which to do so much.[1]
Fireside Chat [*February 23, 1942*]

We all know that books burn — yet we have the greater knowledge that books cannot be killed by fire. People die, but books never die. No man and no force can abolish memory. . . . In this war, we know, books are weapons.
Message to the American Booksellers Association [*April 23, 1942*]

It is not a tax bill but a tax relief bill providing relief not for the needy but for the greedy.
Message to the House vetoing the tax bill [*February 22, 1944*]

These Republican leaders have not been content with attacks on me, or my wife, or on my sons. No, not content with that, they now include my little dog, Fala. Well, of course, I don't resent attacks, . . . but Fala *does* resent them. . . . I think I have a right to resent, to object to libelous statements about my dog.[2]
Speech, Teamsters' Dinner, Washington [*September 23, 1944*]

All of our people all over the country — except the pure-blooded Indians — are immigrants or descendants of immigrants, including even those who came over here on the Mayflower.[3]
Campaign Speech, Boston [*November 4, 1944*]

The American people are quite competent to judge a political party that works both sides of a street.
Ibid.

[1] See Churchill, page 869b.
[2] This was Roosevelt's rejoinder to the charge that the President, at a cost of several million dollars to the taxpayers, had sent a destroyer back to the Aleutian Islands to fetch his Scottie, Fala, allegedly stranded there. When Fala heard these baseless stories of government extravagance on his account, "his Scotch soul was furious. He has not been the same dog since."
[3] See *Address to D. A. R.*, page 920a.

Perfectionism, no less than isolationism or imperialism or power politics, may obstruct the paths to international peace.

State of the Union Message
[January 6, 1945]

We have learned that we cannot live alone, at peace; that our own well-being is dependent on the well-being of other nations, far away. We have learned that we must live as men, and not as ostriches, nor as dogs in the manger. We have learned to be citizens of the world, members of the human community.

Fourth Term Inaugural Address
[January 20, 1945]

More than an end to war, we want an end to the beginnings of all wars.

Address written for Jefferson Day Dinners broadcast, April 13, 1945 [1]

The only limit to our realization of tomorrow will be our doubts of today. Let us move forward with strong and active faith.

Ibid.

FRANKLIN D. ROOSEVELT
AND
WINSTON CHURCHILL

FIRST, their countries seek no aggrandizement, territorial or other.

SECOND, they desire to see no territorial changes that do not accord with the freely expressed wishes of the peoples concerned. . . .

The Atlantic Charter, drawn up aboard U.S.S. Augusta, off the coast of Maine, issued August 14, 1941

SIXTH, after the final destruction of the Nazi tyranny, they hope to see established a peace which will afford to all nations the means of dwelling in safety within their own boundaries, and which will afford assurance that all

[1] President Roosevelt died April 12, at Warm Springs, Georgia.

the men in all the lands may live out their lives in freedom from fear and want. . . .

The Atlantic Charter

EIGHTH, they believe that all of the nations of the world, for realistic as well as spiritual reasons, must come to the abandonment of the use of force. Since no future peace can be maintained if land, sea or air armaments continue to be employed by nations which threaten, or may threaten, aggression outside of their frontiers, they believe, pending the establishment of a wider and permanent system of general security, that the disarmament of such nations is essential.

Ibid.

JAMES STEPHENS
[1882–1950]

I hear a sudden cry of pain!
There is a rabbit in a snare.

The Snare

Forgive us all our trespasses,
Little creatures, everywhere!

Little Things. Stanza 5

In cloud and clod to sing
Of everything and anything.

The Pit of Bliss

I heard a bird at dawn
Singing sweetly on a tree,
That the dew was on the lawn,
And the wind was on the lea;
But I didn't listen to him,
For he didn't sing to me.

The Rivals. Stanza 1

I was singing all the time,
Just as prettily as he.

Ibid. Stanza 3

Women are wiser than men because they know less and understand more.

The Crock of Gold [1930].
Chap. 2

Virtue is the performance of pleasant actions.

Ibid. Chap. 10

Women and birds are able to see without turning their heads, and that is indeed a necessary provision, for they are both surrounded by enemies.

The Demi-Gods. Chap. 2

If a person desires to be a humorist it is necessary that the people around him shall be at least as wise as he is, otherwise his humor will not be comprehended.

Ibid. Chap. 27

Something depressing comes on the mind when it has been too extensively occupied with the female sex.

In the Land of Youth. Chap. 28

The Bad poet is super-abundant in all anthologies of verse.

Preface to A Trophy of Arms [1936], by RUTH PITTER

VIRGINIA WOOLF [1]
[1882–1941]

Those comfortably padded lunatic asylums which are known, euphemistically, as the stately homes of England.[2]

The Common Reader [1925].
Lady Dorothy Nevill

Trivial personalities decomposing in the eternity of print.

Ibid. The Modern Essay

There is no room for the impurities of literature in an essay.

Ibid.

That complete statement which is literature.

Ibid. How It Strikes a Contemporary

The word-coining genius, as if thought plunged into a sea of words and came up dripping.

Ibid. An Elizabethan Play

[1] Virginia Woolf is the best living example of that sort of mind which had its innings in letters in the eighteenth century — a mind partly critical, partly philosophical, highly imaginative, incapable of the vaster emotions but so subtle in its emotionalized intellectuality, so polished, that it makes most other contemporary writers appear to be parvenus of the intellect. — MARY M. COLUM in *The New York Herald-Tribune*, May 8, 1927

The talent of this generation which is most certain of survival. — REBECCA WEST: *Ending in Earnest* [1931]

[2] See Felicia D. Hemans, page 469b.

The beauty of the world has two edges, one of laughter, one of anguish, cutting the heart asunder.

A Room of One's Own [1929]

Women have served all these centuries as looking-glasses possessing the magic and delicious power of reflecting the figure of man at twice its natural size.

Ibid.

Surely it was time someone invented a new plot, or that the author came out from the bushes.

Between the Acts [1941]

SIR ANDREW BROWNE CUNNINGHAM
[1883–   ]

We are so outnumbered there's only one thing to do. We must attack.[1]

Before attacking the Italian fleet at Taranto, November, 1940

MAX EASTMAN
[1883–   ]

I don't know why it is we are in such a hurry to get up when we fall down. You might think we would lie there and rest a while.

The Enjoyment of Laughter [1936]. Part III, Chap. 4

Modernity is a poor thing to feel priggish about; it only makes you a more obvious mark for the prigs of a new modernity to sneer back at. No man can keep up with the times for more than seventy years, and after that his frantic efforts to do so look silly forever.

Ibid. Part V, Chap. 4

ARTHUR DAVISON FICKE
[1883–1945]

No man of elder years than fifty Should be empowered with lands and gold.

[1] Quoted in *British Commanders*, published by British Information Services [1945].

It turns them shrewd and over-thrifty,
It makes them cruel and blind and cold.
Youth and Age. Stanza 1

Old men in impotence can beget
New wars to kill the lusty young.
Young men can sing: old men forget
That any song was ever sung.
Ibid. Stanza 3

KAHLIL GIBRAN
[1883–1931]

Let there be spaces in your together-
ness.[1]
The Prophet [1923]. On Marriage

You may give them your love but
not your thoughts,
For they have their own thoughts.
You may house their bodies but not
their souls,
For their souls dwell in the house of
tomorrow, which you cannot visit, not
even in your dreams.
You may strive to be like them, but
seek not to make them like you.
For life goes not backward nor tar-
ries with yesterday.
You are the bows from which your
children as living arrows are sent forth.
Ibid. On Children

You give but little when you give of
your possessions. It is when you give
of yourself that you truly give.[2]
Ibid. On Giving

Work is love made visible. And if
you cannot work with love but only
with distaste, it is better that you
should leave your work and sit at the
gate of the temple and take alms of
those who work with joy.
Ibid. On Work

The lust for comfort, that stealthy
thing that enters the house a guest, and
then becomes a host, and then a master.
Ibid. On Houses

When one of you falls down he falls
for those behind him, a caution against
the stumbling stone. Ay, and he falls
for those ahead of him, who though

[1] See Rilke, page 884a.
[2] See James Russell Lowell, page 600a.

faster and surer of foot, yet removed
not the stumbling stone.
*The Prophet. On Crime and
Punishment*

You pray in your distress and in
your need; would that you might pray
also in the fullness of your joy and in
your days of abundance.
Ibid. On Prayer

He who wears his morality but as his
best garment were better naked.
Ibid. On Religion

I have learned silence from the talkative, toleration from the intolerant, and
kindness from the unkind; yet strange,
I am ungrateful to those teachers.
Sand and Foam [1926]

We shall never understand one another until we reduce the language to
seven words.
Ibid.

JOHN CEREDIGION JONES
[1883–1947]

All's well, for over there among his
peers
A happy warrior sleeps.[1]
The Returning Man. Stanza 4

HARRY KEMP
[1883–　　]

I pitied him in his blindness;
But can I boast, "I see"?
Perhaps there walks a spirit
Close by, who pities me.
Blind. Stanza 2

JOHN MAYNARD KEYNES
(LORD KEYNES)
[1883–1946]

He [Clemenceau] had one illusion
— France; and one disillusion — man-
kind, including Frenchmen.
*Economic Consequences of the
Peace [1919]. Chap. 3*

Watching the company, with six or

[1] These lines are inscribed over the arch-
way of the Memorial Chamber in the Peace
Tower, Parliament Buildings, Ottawa.
See Wordsworth, pages 409b–410a.

seven senses not available to ordinary men, judging character, motive, and subconscious impulse, perceiving what each was thinking and even what each was going to say next, and compounding with telepathic instinct the argument or appeal best suited to the vanity, weakness, or self interest of his immediate auditor.[1]

Economic Consequences of the Peace. Chap. 3

He [Woodrow Wilson] could write Notes from Sinai or Olympus; he could remain unapproachable in the White House or even in the Council of Ten and be safe. But if he once stepped down to the intimate quality of the Four, the game was evidently up.

Ibid.

To make the defeated Central Empires into good neighbors.

Ibid. Chap. 6

We have been moved already beyond endurance, and need rest.

Ibid. Chap. 7

Marxian Socialism must always remain a portent to the historians of Opinion — how a doctrine so illogical and so dull can have exercised so powerful and enduring an influence over the minds of men, and, through them, the events of history.

The End of Laissez-Faire [*1925*].
Chap. 3

Thrift may be the handmaid and nurse of Enterprise. But equally she may not. . . . For the engine which drives Enterprise is not Thrift, but Profit.

A Treatise on Money [*1930*]

The love of money as a possession — as distinguished from the love of money as a means to the enjoyments and realities of life — will be recognised for what it is, a somewhat disgusting morbidity, one of those semi-criminal, semi-pathological propensities which one hands over with a shudder to the specialists in mental disease.

Essays in Persuasion
[*1931*]. *Part V*

[1] Lloyd George.

In the United States, it is almost inconceivable what rubbish a public man has to utter today if he is to keep respectable.

In the Atlantic Monthly
[*May, 1932*]

Words ought to be a little wild for they are the assault of thoughts on the unthinking.

In the New Statesman and Nation
[*July 15, 1933*]

His [Newton's] peculiar gift was the power of holding continuously in his mind a purely mental problem until he had seen through it. . . . Anyone who has ever attempted a pure scientific or philosophical thought knows how one can hold a problem momentarily in one's mind and apply all one's power of concentration to piercing through it, and how it will dissolve and escape and you find that what you are surveying is a blank.

Essays in Biography [*1933*]

There is no harm in being sometimes wrong — especially if one is promptly found out.

Ibid.

Practical men, who believe themselves to be quite exempt from any intellectual influences, are usually the slaves of some defunct economist. . . . It is ideas, not vested interests, which are dangerous for good or evil.

The General Theory of Employment, Interest and Money [*1936*]

BENITO MUSSOLINI
[1883–1945]

War alone brings up to its highest tension all human energy and puts the stamp of nobility upon the peoples who have the courage to face it.

Written for The Italian Encyclopedia [1]

Fortunately the Italian people is not yet accustomed to eating several times per day.

Speech [*December, 1930*] [1]

[1] Quoted in George Seldes: *Sawdust Caesar* [1935].

We have buried the putrid corpse of liberty.

Speech [1]

The Italian race is a race of sheep. Eighteen years are not enough to change them. It takes a hundred and eighty, and maybe a hundred and eighty centuries.

Quoted in The Ciano Diaries
[January 29, 1940]

It is humiliating to remain with our hands folded while others write history. It matters little who wins. To make a people great it is necessary to send them to battle even if you have to kick them in the pants. This is what I shall do.

Ibid. [April 11, 1940]

GEOFFREY ANKETELL STUDDERT-KENNEDY ("WOODBINE WILLIE" [2])
[1883–1929]

When Jesus came to Birmingham, they
   simply passed Him by,
They never hurt a hair of Him, they
   only let Him die.

Indifference

HOWARD ARNOLD WALTER
[1883–1918]

I would be true, for there are those who
   trust me;
I would be pure, for there are those
   who care;
I would be strong, for there is much to
   suffer;
I would be brave, for there is much to
   dare.

My Creed

ANGELA MORGAN
[Floruit 1920]

Work!
Thank God for the swing of it,

[1] Quoted in MAURICE PARMELEE: *Bolshevism, Fascism and the Liberal-Democratic State* [1934].

[2] The affectionate nickname given him by the soldiers to whom, while chaplain, he distributed cigarettes in the trenches.

For the clamoring, hammering ring
   of it,
Passion of labor daily hurled
On the mighty anvils of the world.

Work: A Song of Triumph

LAURA BENÉT
[1884–   ]

Lost in the spiral of his conscience, he
Detachedly takes rest.

The Snail

ERNEST BEVIN
[1884–1951]

There has never been a war yet which, if the facts had been put calmly before the ordinary folk, could not have been prevented. The common man is the greatest protection against war.

Speech, House of Commons
[November, 1945]

WILL CUPPY
[1884–1949]

The Dodo never had a chance. He seems to have been invented for the sole purpose of becoming extinct and that was all he was good for.

How to Become Extinct [1941]

EDOUARD DALADIER
[1884–   ]

If French and German blood is now to be spilled, as it was twenty-five years ago . . . then each of the two peoples will fight confident of its own victory. But surely Destruction and Barbarism will be the real victors.

Letter to Adolf Hitler,
August 26, 1939

The weakness of democracies is that once a general has been built up in public opinion it becomes impossible to remove him.

Quoted by PERTINAX [1] in Grave Diggers of France [1944]. Page 87

[1] André Géraud.

A phrase has spread from civilians to soldiers and back again: "This is a phony war."[1]
> Quoted by PERTINAX *in Grave Diggers of France. Page 139 [Speech to the Deputies, December 22, 1939]*

JAMES ELROY FLECKER
[1884–1915]

Oh shall I never be home again?
Meadows of England shining in the rain
Spread wide your daisied lawns.
> *Brumana*

I am Don Juan, curst from age to age
By priestly tract and sentimental stage:
Branded a villain or believed a fool,
Battered by hatred, seared by ridicule.
> *Don Juan Declaims*

My brother and good friend, the Sun.
> *A Western Voyage*

West of these out to seas colder than the Hebrides
  I must go
Where the fleet of stars is anchored and the young
  Star-captains glow.
> *The Dying Patriot*

We who with songs beguile your pilgrimage
And swear that Beauty lives though lilies die,
We Poets of the proud old lineage
Who sing to find your hearts, we know not why.
> *The Golden Journey to Samarkand [1913]. Prologue*

When even lovers find their peace at last,
And Earth is but a star, that once had shone.
> *Ibid.*

What would ye, ladies? It was ever thus;
Men are unwise and curiously planned.
> *Ibid. Epilogue*

I have seen old ships sail like swans asleep.
> *The Old Ships [1915]*

[1] The French was "une drôle de guerre."

A ship, an isle, a sickle moon —
With few but with how splendid stars.[1]
> *A Ship, An Isle, A Sickle Moon*

TEXAS GUINAN
[1884–1933]

Hello, sucker!
> *Greeting to night club patrons*

A big butter-and-egg man.[2]
> *Describing a lavish spender or theatrical "angel"*

FRANZ KAFKA
[1884–1924]

The true way goes over a rope which is not stretched at any great height but just above the ground. It seems more designed to make people stumble than to be walked upon.
> *The Great Wall of China. Reflections*

You do not need to leave your room. Remain sitting at your table and listen. Do not even listen, simply wait. Do not even wait, be quite still and solitary. The world will freely offer itself to you to be unmasked, it has no choice, it will roll in ecstasy at your feet.
> *Ibid.*

Only our concept of Time makes it possible for us to speak of the Day of Judgment by that name; in reality it is a summary court in perpetual session.
> *Letters[3]*

All human error is impatience, a premature renunciation of method, a delusive pinning down of a delusion.
> *Ibid.*

There are two cardinal sins from which all the others spring; impatience and laziness.
> *Ibid.*

FANNY HEASLIP LEA
[1884–1955]

It's odd to think we might have been
Sun, moon and stars unto each other —

[1] See Whitman, page 608a.
[2] Title of play by George S. Kaufman, 1925.
[3] Quoted in *Franz Kafka* by MAX BROD.

Only, I turned down one little street
As you went up another.
Fate. Stanza 5

SEAN O'CASEY
[1884–   ]

The whole world is in a state of chassis.
Juno and the Paycock

CHARLES LEO O'DONNELL
[1884–1934]

I have never been able to school my eyes
Against young April's blue surprise.
Wonder

KEITH PRESTON
[1884–1927]

Imperial Caesar dead and turned to clay
Estopped a hole to keep the wind away;
The great god Ra whose shrine once covered acres
Is filler now for cross-word puzzle makers.
The Destiny That Shapes Our Ends

Love, lay thy phobias to rest,
Inhibit thy taboo!
We twain shall share, forever blest,
A complex built for two.
Love Song, Freudian

Among our literary scenes,
Saddest this sight to me,
The graves of little magazines
That died to make verse free.
The Liberators

He must not laugh at his own wheeze:
A snuff box has no right to sneeze.
The Humorist

I am the captain of my soul;[1]
I rule it with stern joy;
And yet I think I had more fun
When I was a cabin boy.
An Awful Responsibility

[1] See W. E. Henley, page 741b.

ODELL SHEPARD
[1884–   ]

October in New England,
And I not there to see
The glamour of the goldenrod,
The flame of the maple tree!
Home Thoughts. Stanza 1

SARA TEASDALE
[1884–1933]

When I am dead and over me bright April
Shakes out her rain-drenched hair,
Though you should lean above me broken-hearted,
I shall not care.
I Shall Not Care. Stanza 1

When I can look Life in the eyes,
Grown calm and very coldly wise,
Life will have given me the Truth,
And taken in exchange — my youth.
Wisdom

How many million Aprils came
Before I ever knew
How white a cherry bough could be,
A bed of squills, how blue!
Blue Squills. Stanza 1

Strephon's kiss was lost in jest,
Robin's lost in play,
But the kiss in Colin's eyes
Haunts me night and day.
The Look. Stanza 2

Let it be forgotten, as a flower is forgotten,
Forgotten as a fire that once was singing gold,
Let it be forgotten for ever and ever,
Time is a kind friend, he will make us old.
Let It Be Forgotten. Stanza 1

I make the most of all that comes,
And the least of all that goes.
The Philosopher. Stanza 4

For better than the minting
Of a gold crowned king
Is the safe memory
Of a lovely thing.
The Coin

Spend all you have for loveliness,
Buy it, and never count the cost;

For one white singing hour of peace
Count many a year of strife well lost.
                              Barter
Forget me for a month, a year,
  But, oh, beloved, think of me
When unexpected beauty burns
  Like sudden sunlight on the sea.
        Vignettes Overseas: Off Algiers

HARRY S. TRUMAN
[1884–   ]

When they told me yesterday what
had happened, I felt like the moon, the
stars and all the planets had fallen on
me.
        Statement to reporters, April 13,
        1945, the day after his accession
        to the Presidency
The responsibility of the great states
is to serve and not to dominate the
world.
        First Message to Congress,
                    April 16, 1945
When Kansas and Colorado have a
quarrel over the water in the Arkansas
River they don't call out the National
Guard in each State and go to war over
it. They bring a suit in the Supreme
Court of the United States and abide
by the decision. There isn't a reason in
the world why we cannot do that inter-
nationally.
        Speech in Kansas City, April, 1945
Sixteen hours ago an American airplane dropped one bomb on Hiroshima.
. . . It is a harnessing of the basic
power of the universe. The force from
which the sun draws its power has been
loosed against those who brought war
to the Far East.
        First announcement of the
        atomic bomb, August 6, 1945
The release of atomic energy constitutes a new force too revolutionary to
consider in the framework of old ideas.[1]
        Message to Congress on atomic
                    energy, October 3, 1945

[1] At Magny's dinner. They said that Berthe-
lot had predicted that in a hundred years
of physical and chemical science man would
learn to know the atom, and that with this
knowledge he would be able, at his will, to

Means of destruction hitherto unknown, against which there can be no
adequate military defense, and in the
employment of which no single nation
can in fact have a monopoly.
        Declaration on Atomic Energy
        by President Truman and Prime
        Ministers Clement Attlee and
        W. L. Mackenzie King at the
        White House, Washington, No-
        vember 15, 1945
Effective, reciprocal, and enforceable
safeguards acceptable to all nations.
                              Ibid.
We must embark on a bold new program for making the benefits of our
scientific advances and industrial progress available for the improvement and
growth of under-developed areas. More
than half the people of the world are living in conditions approaching misery.
Their food is inadequate. They are the
victims of disease. Their economic life is
primitive and stagnant. Their poverty
is a handicap and a threat both to them
and to more prosperous areas.
        Inaugural Address (Point Four
        Program) [January 20, 1949]

SOPHIE TUCKER
[1884–   ]

From birth to age eighteen, a girl
needs good parents. From eighteen
to thirty-five, she needs good looks.
From thirty-five to fifty-five, she needs

dim, extinguish or relight the sun like a
Carcel lamp. Claude Bernard, for his part, is
said to have announced that with a hundred
years more of physiological knowledge we
would be able to make the organic law ourselves — to manufacture human life, in competition with the Creator.
  For our part we did not raise any objection
to all this talk, but we do believe that at that
particular stage of scientific development, the
good Lord, with a flowing white beard, will
arrive on Earth with his chain of keys and
will say to humanity, just as they do at
the Art Gallery at five o'clock, "Gentlemen,
it's closing time." (*"Messieurs, on ferme."*)
— EDMOND DE GONCOURT AND JULES DE GON-
COURT: *Journals*, April 7, 1869

a good personality. From fifty-five on, she needs good cash.

Said at sixty-nine

HUGH WALPOLE
[1884–1941]

We are so largely the playthings of Fate in our fears. To one, fear of the dark, to another of physical pain, to a third of public ridicule, to a fourth of poverty, to a fifth of loneliness — for all of us our own particular creature lurks in ambush. Nor is it our choice of place or creature.

The Old Ladies [*1924*]

ANNA WICKHAM
(MRS. PATRICK HEPBURN)
[1884–]

The true male never yet walked
Who liked to listen when his mate talked.

The Affinity

Because of the body's hunger are we born,
And by contriving hunger are we fed;
Because of hunger is our work well done,
And so our songs well sung, and things well said.

Sehnsucht

ARTHUR WALLACE CALHOUN
[1885–]

Gentlemen of the old régime in the South would say, "A woman's name should appear in print but twice — when she marries and when she dies."

Social History of the American Family [*1918*], *Vol. II, Page 326, citing* MYRTA LOCKETT AVARY: *Dixie After the War* [*1906*], *Page 23*

ISAK DINESEN
[1885–]

What is man, when you come to think upon him, but a minutely set, ingenious machine for turning, with in-

finite artfulness, the red wine of Shiraz into urine?

Seven Gothic Tales

WILL DURANT
[1885–]

A statesman cannot afford to be a moralist.

What Is Civilization?

The finger that turns the dial rules the air.

Ibid.

Civilization exists by geological consent, subject to change without notice.

Ibid.

The health of nations is more important than the wealth of nations.

Ibid.

Conscience is the deposit of a Mississippi of prohibitions.

Ibid.

DuBOSE HEYWARD
[1885–1940]

It is cruel for a woman with her man gone,
An' the younguns allus hungry, an' winter comin' on.

Black Christmas

Here lies a spendthrift who believed
That only those who spend may keep;
Who scattered seeds, yet never grieved
Because a stranger came to reap.

Epitaph for a Poet

KAREN HORNEY, M.D.
[1885–]

Fortunately [psycho-]analysis is not the only way to resolve inner conflicts. Life itself still remains a very effective therapist.

Our Inner Conflicts [*1945*]

RING LARDNER
[1885–1933]

A good many young writers make the mistake of enclosing a stamped, self-addressed envelope, big enough for the manuscript to come back in. This is too much of a temptation to the editor.

How to Write Short Stories [*1924*]

Mother set facing the front of the train, as it makes her giddy to ride backwards. I set facing her, which does not affect me.

The Golden Honeymoon [*1924*]

D. H. LAWRENCE
[1885-1930]

I never saw a wild thing
Sorry for itself.

Self-Pity

When I wish I was rich, then I know I
   am ill.

Riches

When I read Shakespeare I am struck
   with wonder
That such trivial people should muse
   and thunder
In such lovely language.

When I Read Shakespeare.
Stanza 1

And Hamlet, how boring, how boring to
   live with,
So mean and self-conscious, blowing
   and snoring
His wonderful speeches, full of other
   folks' whoring!

Ibid. Stanza 3

My mother was a superior soul
   A superior soul was she,
Cut out to play a superior role
   In the god-damn bourgeoisie.

Red-Herring. Stanza 2

One realm we have never conquered
— the pure present. One great mystery of time is terra incognita to us — the instant. The most superb mystery we have hardly recognized — the immediate, instant self. The quick of all time is the instant. The quick of all the universe, of all creation, is the incarnate, carnal self.

New Poems [*1918*]. *Preface*

Men are free when they are in a living homeland, not when they are straying and breaking away. . . . The most unfree souls go west, and shout of free-

dom. Men are freest when they are most unconscious of freedom. The shout is a rattling of chains.

Studies in Classic American
Literature [*1923*]. *Chap. 1*

Necessary, for ever necessary, to burn out false shames and smelt the heaviest ore of the body into purity.

Lady Chatterley's Lover [*1928*]

SINCLAIR LEWIS
[1885-1951]

Not only Gopher Prairie, but ten thousand towns from Albany to San Diego . . . not a dozen buildings which suggested that, in the fifty years of Gopher Prairie's existence, the citizens had realized that it was either desirable or possible to make this, their common home, amusing or attractive.

Main Street [*1920*]. *Chap. 4*

His name was George F. Babbitt, and . . . he was nimble in the calling of selling houses for more than people could afford to pay.

Babbitt [*1922*]. *Chap. 1*

A sensational event was changing from the brown suit to the gray the contents of his pockets. He was earnest about these objects. They were of eternal importance, like baseball or the Republican Party.

Ibid.

Pastoral visiting:
  No partiality.
  Don't neglect hired girls, be cordial.
  Guard conversation, pleasing manner and laugh and maybe one funny story but no scandal or crit. of others.
  Stay only 15–30 minutes.
  Ask if like to pray with, not insist.
  Rem gt opportunities during sickness, sorrow, marriage.
  Ask jokingly why husband not oftener to church.

Elmer Gantry [*1927*]. *Chap. 8,*
notes on Practical Theology
lectures

Every compulsion is put upon writers to become safe, polite, obedient, and sterile. In protest, I declined election to the National Institute of Arts and Letters some years ago, and now I must decline the Pulitzer Prize.[1]

> *Letter declining the Pulitzer Prize for his novel, Arrowsmith [1926]*

To a true-blue professor of literature in an American university, literature is not something that a plain human being, living today, painfully sits down to produce. No; it is something dead.

> *The American Fear of Literature, address given at Stockholm, on receiving the Nobel Prize for Literature [December 12, 1930]*

Our American professors like their literature clear and cold and pure and very dead.

> *Ibid.*

It Can't Happen Here.

> *Title of Book [1935]*

A "lady" is a woman so incompetent as to have to take refuge in a secluded class, like kings and idiots, who have to be treated with special kindness because they can't take it.

> *Debate with Lewis Browne: Has the Modern Woman Made Good? Town Hall, New York [November 19, 1941]*

ANDRÉ MAUROIS
[1885–   ]

The minds of different generations are as impenetrable one by the other as are the monads of Leibniz.

> *Ariel* [2] *[1924]. Chap. 12*

If in the eyes of an Irishman there is any one being more ridiculous than an Englishman, it is an Englishman who loves Ireland.

> *Ibid. Chap. 13*

Learning is nothing without cultivated manners, but when the two are combined in a woman you have one of the most exquisite products of civilization.

> *Ibid. Chap. 16*

[1] Lewis became a member of the National Institute in 1935.
[2] Translated by ELLA D'ARCY.

Modesty and unselfishness — these are virtues which men praise — and pass by.

> *Ariel. Chap. 24*

That mixture of Christian sorrow and mundane relish which the virtuous employ in talking of the vicious.

> *Ibid. Chap. 26*

There are certain persons for whom pure Truth is a poison.

> *Ibid. Chap. 29*

Housekeeping in common is for women the acid test.

> *Ibid. Chap. 35*

CHESTER WILLIAM NIMITZ
[1885–   ]

A ship is always referred to as "she" because it costs so much to keep one in paint and powder.

> *Talk before the Society of Sponsors of the United States Navy [February 13, 1940]*

WILLIAM ALEXANDER PERCY
[1885–1942]

I heard a bird at break of day
Sing from the autumn trees
A song so mystical and calm,
So full of certainties.

> *Overtones*

EZRA POUND
[1885–   ]

Sing we for love and idleness,
Naught else is worth the having.

> *An Immortality*

And I would rather have my sweet,
Though rose-leaves die of grieving,
Than do high deeds in Hungary
To pass all men's believing.

> *Ibid.*

The apparition of these faces in the crowd;
Petals on a wet, black bough.

> *In a Station of the Metro [1916]*

That age is gone;
Pierre de Maensac is gone.

I have walked over these roads;
I have thought of them living.
> *Provincia Deserta* [*1916*]

Some other mouth
May be as fair as hers,
Might, in new ages, gain her wor-
shippers,
When our two dusts with Waller's shall
be laid,
Siftings on siftings in oblivion,
Till change hath broken down
All things save Beauty alone.
> *Hugh Selwyn Mauberley*
> [*1920*]. *Envoi*

I was
And I no more exist;
Here drifted
An hedonist.
> *Ibid. The Age Demanded*

They will come no more,
The old men with beautiful manners.
> *I Vecchii*

Poetry ought to be as well written as
prose.
> *Quoted by T. S. Eliot: The Use
> of Poetry* [*1933*], *Chap. 4*

Real education must ultimately be
limited to men who insist on knowing, the rest is mere sheep-herding.
> *A, B, C of Reading* [*1934*].
> *Page 70*

It is only after long experience that
most men are able to define a thing
in terms of its own genus, painting as
painting, writing as writing. You can
spot the bad critic when he starts by
discussing the poet and not the poem.
> *Ibid. Page 71*

There is no reason why the same
man should like the same book at 18
and at 48.
> *Ibid. Page 72*

Any one who is too lazy to master the
comparatively small glossary necessary to understand Chaucer deserves to
be shut out from the reading of good
books forever.
> *Ibid. Page 87*

Men do not understand books until
they have had a certain amount of life,
or at any rate no man understands a
deep book, until he has seen and lived
at least part of its contents.
> *A, B, C of Reading. Page 88*

KENNETH ROBERTS
[1885–]

On every side of us are men who
hunt perpetually for their personal
Northwest Passage, too often sacri-
ficing health, strength, and life itself to the search; and who shall say
they are not happier in their vain but
hopeful quest than wiser, duller folks
who sit at home, venturing nothing
and, with sour laughs, deriding the
seekers for that fabled thoroughfare?
> *Northwest Passage* [*1937*].
> *Foreword*

GEOFFREY SCOTT
[1885–1929]

In my garden goes a fiend
Dark and wild, whose name is Wind.
> *Wind*

LOUIS UNTERMEYER
[1885–]

And though these shattering walls are
thin,
May they be strong to keep hate out
And hold love in.
> *Prayer for a New House.*
> *Stanza 4*

God, if You wish for our love,
Fling us a handful of stars!
> *Caliban in the Coal Mines.*
> *Stanza 4*

God, though this life is but a wraith,
Although we know not what we use,
Although we grope with little faith,
Give me the heart to fight — and lose.
> *Prayer. Stanza 1*

From compromise and things half
done,
Keep me with stern and stubborn
pride;
And when at last the fight is won,
God, keep me still unsatisfied.
> *Ibid. Stanza 5*

CARL VAN DOREN
[1885–1950]

The first writers are first and the rest, in the long run, nowhere but in anthologies.

What Is American Literature?

I give him back, in his grand dimensions, to his nation and the world.

Benjamin Franklin [1938]

HAROLD TUCKER WEBSTER
[1885–1952]

Caspar Milquetoast: The Timid Soul.

Character in Series of Cartoons

The Thrill that Comes Once in a Lifetime.

Title of Series of Cartoons

HUMBERT WOLFE
[1885–1940]

Who thought of the lilac?
"I," dew said,
"I made up the lilac
out of my head."

The Lilac. Stanza 1

Like a small grey
coffee-pot
sits the squirrel.

The Grey Squirrel. Stanza 1

Listen! the wind is rising,
and the air is wild with leaves,
We have had our summer evenings,
now for October eves!

Autumn (Resignation). Stanza 2

ELINOR HOYT WYLIE
[1885–1928]

We shall walk in velvet shoes:
Wherever we go
Silence will fall like dews
On white silence below.

Velvet Shoes [1921]. Stanza 4

Avoid the reeking herd,
Shun the polluted flock,
Live like that stoic bird
The eagle of the rock.

The Eagle and the Mole [1921].
Stanza 1

If you would keep your soul
From spotted sight or sound,
Live like the velvet mole;
Go burrow underground.

The Eagle and the Mole. Stanza 5

Say not of Beauty she is good,
Or aught but beautiful.

Beauty [1921]

Enshrine her and she dies, who had
The hard heart of a child.

Ibid.

Down to the Puritan marrow of my bones
There's something in this richness that I hate.
I love the look, austere, immaculate,
Of landscapes drawn in pearly monotones.

Wild Peaches [1921]. Stanza 4

I was, being human, born alone;
I am, being woman, hard beset;
I live by squeezing from a stone
The little nourishment I get.

Let No Charitable Hope [1923].
Stanza 2

My soul, be not disturbed
By planetary war;
Remain securely orbed
In this contracted star.

Address to My Soul [1928].
Stanza 1

A subtle spirit has my path attended,
In likeness not a lion but a pard;
And when the arrows flew like hail, and hard,
He licked my wounds, and all my wounds were mended.

One Person [1928]. Sonnet IX

My lord, adjudge my strength, and set me where
I bear a little more than I can bear.

Ibid. Sonnet XVI

My late discovered earth and early sky.

Ibid. Sonnet XVII

If any have a stone to throw
It is not I, ever or now.

The Pebble

Pity the prickly star that frightens
The Christ Child with its shattered spear;

Pity the midnight when it lightens;
Pity me, my dear.
Pity Me. Stanza 3
The worst and best are both inclined
To snap like vixens at the truth;
But, O, beware the middle mind
That purrs and never shows a tooth!
Nonsense Rhyme. Stanza 2
Honied words like bees,
Gilded and sticky, with a little sting.
Pretty Words
Hail, element of earth, receive thy
own,
And cherish, at thy charitable breast,
This man, this mongrel beast:
He plows the sand, and, at his hardest
need,
He sows himself for seed.
Hymn to Earth [1929]. Stanza 6
Receive him as thy lover for an hour
Who will not weary, by a longer stay,
The kind embrace of clay.
Ibid. Stanza 7

ZOË AKINS
[1886–]

The Greeks Had a Word For It.
Title of play [1930]
So much do I love wandering,
So much I love the sea and sky,
That it will be a piteous thing
In one small grave to lie.
The Wanderer. Stanza 2

WILLIAM ROSE BENÉT
[1886–1950]

I flung my soul to the air like a falcon
flying. . . .
I shall start a heron soon
In the marsh beneath the moon —
A strange white heron rising with silver
on its wings.
*The Falconer of God [1914].
Stanza 1*
I beat forever
The fens and the sedges.
The pledge is still the same — for all
disastrous pledges,
All hopes resigned!

My soul still flies above me for the
quarry it shall find.
The Falconer of God. Stanza 4
Rain, with a silver flail;
Sun, with a golden ball;
Ocean, wherein the whale
Swims minnow-small.
Whale. Stanza 1
Monarch is night
Of all eldest things,
Pain and affright,
Rapturous wings.
Night. Stanza 3
O Love, a thousand, thousand voices,
From night to dawn, from dawn to
night,
Have cried the passion of their choices
To orb your name and keep it bright.
The Name of Love. Stanza 1
In vast infant sagacity brooding.
Mad Blake
Jesse James was a two-gun man
(*Roll on, Missouri!*)
Jesse James: American Myth
In seven states he cut up dadoes.
He's gone with the buffler an' the des-
peradoes.
Ibid.
What did your body say to mine
deep in velvet night's delight?
*On heaven's wall a golden vine clambers
bright.*
*The Dust Which Is God [1941].
That Rin Sae Deep*

VAN WYCK BROOKS
[1886–]

His wife not only edited his works
but edited him.
*The Ordeal of Mark Twain [1920].
Chap. 5*
Even the Concord ice had bubbles
in it. As wood and grass were its only
staples, Emerson advised his fellow
townsmen to manufacture schoolteachers and make them the best in the
world.
*The Flowering of New England
[1936]. Chap. 13*

FRANCES CORNFORD
[1886–   ]

O why do you walk through the fields
    in gloves,
    Missing so much and so much?
O fat white woman whom nobody loves,
Why do you walk through the fields in
    gloves
When the grass is as soft as the breast
    of doves
    And shivering-sweet to the touch?
    To a Fat Lady Seen from the Train

ROY HELTON
[1886–   ]

Oaks are the true conservatives;
They hold old leaves till summer gives
A green exchange
    Come Back to Earth. XLIX
What is a common man?
    Where is a common tree?
I'll pick one common buttercup
    But challenge two or three,
For every one bears instant proof
    Of its identity.
    Ibid. LIII, Stanza 1

AL JOLSON
[1886–1950]

You ain't heard nothin' yet, folks.
    Ad lib remark introduced in the
    first talking motion picture,
    "The Jazz Singer," July, 1927

JOYCE KILMER
[1886–1918]

Because the road was steep and long
    And through a dark and lonely land,
God set upon my lips a song
    And put a lantern in my hand.
    Love's Lantern
They say that life is a highway and its
    milestones are the years.
    Roofs
I think that I shall never see
A poem lovely as a tree.
A tree whose hungry mouth is prest

Against the earth's sweet flowing
    breast.
    Trees [1]
Poems are made by fools like me,
But only God can make a tree.
    Ibid.
The pleasantest sort of poet
Is the poet who's old and wise.
    Old Poets
Her lips' remark was: "Oh, you kid!"
Her soul spoke thus (I know it did):
"O king of realms of endless joy,
My own, my golden grocer's boy."
    Servant Girl and Grocer's Boy
A house that has echoed a baby's laugh
    and held up his stumbling feet,
Is the saddest sight, when it's left alone,
    that ever your eyes could meet.
    The House with Nobody in It
In a wood they call the Rouge Bouquet
There is a new-made grave today,
Built by never a spade nor pick
Yet covered with earth ten metres
    thick.
    Rouge Bouquet

ARTHUR KROCK
[1886–   ]

The President [Franklin D. Roosevelt] told the chairman to "clear everything with Sidney" (Hillman),[2] which gave to the C. I. O. organization that dominated the proceedings the veto power it later exercised.
    New York Times, July 25, 1944
The words ["clear everything with Sidney"] applied only to the Vice Presidential nomination of the Democrats at Chicago.
    Ibid. October 24, 1944

DAVID MORTON
[1886–   ]

Who walks with Beauty has no need of
    fear;

[1] First published in *Poetry: A Magazine of Verse*, Chicago, August, 1913.
See Heywood Broun, page B-952, and Ogden Nash, page B-121.
[2] Sidney Hillman [1887–1946], Chairman of the Political Action Committee of the C. I. O., and president of the Amalgamated Clothing Workers.

The sun and moon and stars keep pace
  with him;
Invisible hands restore the ruined year,
And time, itself, grows beautifully dim.
                    Who Walks with Beauty

My faith is all a doubtful thing,
  Wove on a doubtful loom, —
Until there comes, each showery spring,
  A cherry-tree in bloom.
                    Symbol

SHAEMAS O'SHEEL
[1886–1954]

They went forth to battle, but they
  always fell; [1]
Their eyes were fixed above the sullen
  shields;
Nobly they fought and bravely, but not
  well,
And sank heart-wounded by a subtle
  spell.
            They Went Forth to Battle.
                    Stanza 1

He whom a dream hath possessed
  knoweth no more of doubting.
            He Whom a Dream Hath
            Possessed. Stanza 1

SIEGFRIED SASSOON
[1886–   ]

Soldiers are citizens of death's grey
  land.
                    Dreamers

Soldiers are dreamers; when the guns
  begin
They think of firelit homes, clean beds,
  and wives.
                    Ibid.

And when the war is done and youth
  stone dead
I'd toddle safely home and die — in
  bed.
                    Base Details

Who will remember, passing through
  this Gate,
The unheroic Dead who fed the guns?

[1] They came forth to battle, but they
always fell. — JAMES MACPHERSON [1736–
1796]: *Poems of Ossian, Cath-Loda, Duan
Second*

Who shall absolve the foulness of their
  fate, —
Those doomed, conscripted, unvictorious ones?
            On Passing the New Menin Gate

VINCENT STARRETT
[1886–   ]

The day before yesterday always has
been a glamor day. The present is sordid and prosaic. Time colors history as
it does a meerschaum pipe.
            Buried Caesars. Robert Neilson
            Stephens and The Costume
            Novel

CARROLL A. WILSON
[1886–1947]

"Familiar quotations" . . . are more
than familiar; they are something part
of us. . . . These echoes from the past
have two marked characteristics — a
simple idea, and an accurate rhythmic
beat.
            Preface to First Appearance in
            Print of Some 400 Familiar
            Quotations [1935]

ED WYNN
[1886–   ]

Every radish I ever pulled up seemed
to have a mortgage attached to it.
            Explaining Why He Sold His Farm

LEONARD BACON
[1887–1954]

Technique! The very word is like the
  shriek
Of outraged Art. It is the idiot name
Given to effort by those who are too
  weak,
Too weary, or too dull to play the
  game.
The mighty have no theory of technique.
            Ph.D's. Sophia Trenton

Those who dwell upon ivory towers [1]
Have heads of the same material.
                    Tower of Ivory

[1] See Vachel Lindsay, page 903b.

BRUCE BAIRNSFATHER
[1887–   ]

Well, if you knows of a better 'ole,
go to it.
Fragments from France [1915].
Caption of cartoon

RUPERT BROOKE
[1887–1915]

Somewhere, behind Space and Time.
Is wetter water, slimier slime!
Heaven

And in that Heaven of all their wish,
There shall be no more land, say fish.
Ibid.

The hawthorn hedge puts forth its
buds,
And my heart puts forth its pain.
All Suddenly the Spring Comes Soft

Unkempt about those hedges blows
An English unofficial rose.
The Old Vicarage, Grantchester

Curates, long dust, will come and go
On lissom, clerical, printless toe.
Ibid.

England's the one land, I know,
Where men with Splendid Hearts may
go;
And Cambridgeshire, of all England,
The shire for Men who Understand.
Ibid.

For Cambridge people rarely smile,
Being urban, squat, and packed with
guile.
Ibid.

Stands the Church clock at ten to three?
And is there honey still for tea?
Ibid.

Breathless, we flung us on the windy
hill,
Laughed in the sun, and kissed the
lovely grass.
The Hill

And then you suddenly cried, and
turned away.
Ibid.

For what they'd never told me of,
And what I never knew,

It was that all the time, my love,
Love would be merely you.
Song

But there's wisdom in women, of more
than they have known,
And thoughts go blowing through them,
are wiser than their own.
There's Wisdom in Women

These I have loved:
White plates and cups, clean-gleam-
ing . . .
The cool kindliness of sheets, that soon
Smooth away trouble; and the rough
male kiss
Of blankets; grainy wood; live hair
that is
Shining and free; blue-massing clouds;
the keen
Unpassioned beauty of a great ma-
chine;
The benison of hot water; furs to touch,
The good smell of old clothes.
The Great Lover

If I should die, think only this of me:
That there's some corner of a foreign
field
That is for ever England.
The Soldier

This heart, all evil shed away,
A pulse in the eternal mind, no less
Gives somewhere back the thoughts by
England given.
Ibid.

Now, God be thanked, Who has
matched us with His hour,
And caught our youth, and wakened us
from sleeping.
Peace

The worst friend and enemy is but
Death.
Ibid.

Blow out, you bugles, over the rich
dead!
There's none of these so lonely and
poor of old,
But, dying, has made us rarer gifts
than gold.
The Dead. I

Honour has come back, as a king, to
earth,
And paid his subjects with a royal
wage;

And Nobleness walks in our ways
  again;
And we have come into our heritage.
                          The Dead. I

ISAAC GOLDBERG
[1887–1938]

Diplomacy is to do and say
The nastiest thing in the nicest way.
                          The Reflex

JAMES NORMAN HALL
[1887–1951]

The thing that numbs the heart is this:
  That men cannot devise
Some scheme of life to banish fear
  That lurks in most men's eyes.
                          Fear

SIDNEY HILLMAN [1]
[1887–1946]

Politics is the science of how who
gets what, when and why.
    Political Primer for All Americans
                                 [1944]

EARNEST A. HOOTON
[1887–1954]

Up from the Ape.
                Title of Book [1931]
Why Men Behave Like Apes, and
Vice Versa.
                Title of Book [1940]

ROBINSON JEFFERS
[1887–   ]

The gulls, the cloud-calligraphers of
  windy spirals before a storm.
                          The Cycle
While this America settles in the mould
  of its vulgarity, heavily thicken-
  ing to empire,
And protest, only a bubble in the
  molten mass, pops and sighs out,
  and the mass hardens.
          Shine, Perishing Republic
                      [1924]. Stanza 1

[1] See Arthur Krock, page 936b.

All these tidal gatherings, growth and
  decay,
Shining and darkening, are forever
Renewed; and the whole cycle impeni-
  tently
Revolves, and all the past is fu-
  ture.
                      Practical People
All the arts lose virtue
Against the essential reality
Of creatures going about their business
  among the equally
Earnest elements of nature.
                  Boats in a Fog [1924]
Lend me the stone strength of the past
  and I will lend you
The wings of the future, for I have
  them.
          *To the Rock That Will Be a
                          Cornerstone*
Divinely superfluous beauty
Rules the games, presides over des-
  tinies, makes trees grow
And hills tower, waves fall.
The incredible beauty of joy.
          Divinely Superfluous Beauty
The beauty of things was born before
  eyes and sufficient to itself; the
  heart-breaking beauty
Will remain when there is no heart to
  break for it.
                          Credo
          The deep dark-shining
Pacific leans on the land,
Feeling his cold strength
To the outmost margins.
                      Night [1925]
Humanity is the mold to break away
  from, the crust to break through,
  the coal to break into fire,
The atom to be split.
                Roan Stallion [1925]

SIR BERNARD
MONTGOMERY
(VISCOUNT MONTGOMERY
OF ALAMEIN)
[1887–   ]

To us is given the honor of striking
a blow for freedom which will live in
history, and in the better days that lie

ahead men will speak with pride of our doings.

> *Message to his troops, June 5, 1944, on the eve of the Allied invasion of Europe*

I am not a bit anxious about my battles. If I am anxious I don't fight them. I wait until I am ready.

> *Quoted in "British Commanders," published [1945] by British Information Services*

MARIANNE MOORE
[1887–   ]

The monkeys
winked too much and were afraid of
    snakes. The zebras, supreme in
their abnormality; the elephants, with
    their fog-colored skin
and strictly practical appendages
    were there.
> *The Monkeys [1921]*

Denunciations do not affect
    the culprit; nor blows, but it
is torture to him to not be spoken to.
> *Spenser's Ireland [1941]. Stanza 1*

The Irish say your trouble is their
    trouble and your
joy their joy? I wish
I could believe it;
I am troubled, I'm dissat-
    isfied, I'm Irish.
> *Ibid. Stanza 6*

They're fighting that I
may yet recover from the disease, *my
self;* some have it lightly, some will
die.[1]
> *In Distrust of Merits [1944].
> Stanza 3*

There never was a war that was
    not inward; I must
fight till I have conquered in myself
    what
causes war, but I would not believe it.
I inwardly did nothing.
    O Iscariotlike crime!
Beauty is everlasting
    And dust is for a time.
> *Ibid. Stanza 8*

[1] See Pascal, page 273a.

SAMUEL ELIOT MORISON
[1887–   ]

A tough but nervous, tenacious but restless race [the Yankees]; materially ambitious, yet prone to introspection, and subject to waves of religious emotion. . . . A race whose typical member is eternally torn between a passion for righteousness and a desire to get on in the world.

> *Maritime History of Massachusetts [1921]. Chap. 2*

Never, in these United States, has the brain of man conceived, or the hand of man fashioned, so perfect a thing as the clipper ship. . . . The *Flying Cloud* was our Rheims, the *Sovereign of the Seas* our Parthenon, the *Lightning* our Amiens; but they were monuments carved from snow. For a brief moment of time they flashed their splendor around the world, then disappeared with the sudden completeness of the wild pigeon.

> *Ibid. Chap. 23*

He [Columbus] enjoyed long stretches of pure delight such as only a seaman may know, and moments of high, proud exultation that only a discoverer can experience.

> *Admiral of the Ocean Sea [1942].
> Chap. 49*

FAIRFIELD OSBORN
[1887–   ]

We do not live to extenuate the miseries of the past nor to accept as incurable those of the present.

> *The Limits of the Earth.
> Chap. 10*

H. I. PHILLIPS
[1887–   ]

Horse-sense in an atmosphere of
Pomp and glory,
Self-effacement in a generation
Of self-salesmanship,
A Vermont Yankee in
King Ballyhoo's Court!
> *Calvin Coolidge*

EDITH SITWELL
[1887–   ]

Every hundred years or so it becomes necessary for a change to take place in the body of poetry . . . a fresh movement appears and produces a few great men, and once more the force and vigour die from the results of age; the movement is carried on by weak and worthless imitators, and a change becomes necessary again.
Poetry and Criticism [*1926*]

Still falls the Rain —
Dark as the world of man, black as our
    loss —
Blind as the nineteen hundred and
    forty nails
Upon the Cross.
Still Falls the Rain [*1940*]

ALEXANDER WOOLLCOTT
[1887–1943]

The two oldest professions in the world — ruined by amateurs.[1]
The Knock at the Stage-Door
[*The Actor and the Street-*
walker]

"Ladies, just a little more virginity, if you don't mind."
Capsule Criticism [*Beerbohm*
Tree to the Extras]

There is less in this than meets the eye.
A companion's comment at a
Maeterlinck play [*attributed to*
Tallulah Bankhead]

I must get out of these wet clothes and into a dry Martini.
Quoted in Reader's Digest

Babies in silk hats playing with dynamite.
Of diplomats. Quoted by SAM-
UEL HOPKINS ADAMS: *A. Wooll-*
cott [*1945*]

[1] The most ancient profession in the world. — KIPLING: *Soldiers Three* [1888], *On the City Wall*

Germany was the cause of Hitler just as much as Chicago is responsible for the Chicago *Tribune*.
Last words before the micro-
phone [*January 23, 1943*],
"People's Platform" program

ROLAND YOUNG
[1887–1953]

And here's the happy bounding flea —
You cannot tell the he from she.
The sexes look alike, you see;
But she can tell, and so can he.
The Flea

OWEN HALL
(JAMES DAVIS)
[? –1907]

O tell me, pretty maiden, are there any more at home like you?
Floradora [*1900*]. *Act II*

IRVING BERLIN
[1888–   ]

Come on and hear, come on and hear,
Alexander's Ragtime Band.
Alexander's Ragtime Band [*1911*]

You've got to get up, you've got to get
    up,
You've got to get up this morning!
Oh! How I Hate to Get Up in
the Morning [*1917*]

God bless America,
Land that I love;
Stand beside her and guide her
Through the night with a light from
    above.
God Bless America [1]

HENRY BESTON
[1888–   ]

The neon glow of the age of comfort and violence.
Review of John Burroughs's
America, in The Freeman
[*February 11, 1952*]

[1] The song was written in 1917, and first sung by Kate Smith, Armistice Day, 1938. (Copyright, 1939.)

HEYWOOD BROUN
[1888–1939]

In the march up to the heights of fame there comes a spot close to the summit in which man reads "nothing but detective stories."

G.K.C. [*1922*]

"Trees" (if I have the name right) is one of the most annoying pieces of verse within my knowledge. The other one is Kipling's "If," with third place reserved for Henley's "Invictus."

"Trees" maddens me, because it contains the most insincere line ever written by mortal man. Surely the Kilmer tongue must have been not far from the Kilmer cheek when he wrote, "Poems are made by fools like me."

It Seems to Me [*1935*]. *"Trees," "If," and "Invictus"*

Life is a copycat and can be bullied into following the master artist who bids it come to heel.

Ibid. Nature the Copycat

I have known people to stop and buy an apple on the corner and then walk away as if they had solved the whole unemployment problem.

Ibid. Chummy Charlie

The Irish are the cry-babies of the Western world. Even the mildest quip will set them off into resolutions and protests.

Ibid. The Piece That Got Me Fired

The swaggering underemphasis of New England.

Heywood Broun: Collected Edition [*1941*]

DANA BURNET
[1888–   ]

I'd rather have an inch of dog than miles of pedigree.

The Road to Vagabondia, Stanza 3

DALE CARNEGIE
[1888–   ]

How to Win Friends and Influence People.

Title of book [*1938*]

J. FRANK DOBIE
[1888–   ]

The average Ph.D. thesis is nothing but a transference of bones from one graveyard to another.

A Texan in England [*1945*]. *Chap. 1*

Conform and be dull.

The Voice of the Coyote [*1949*]. *Introduction*

Putting on the spectacles of science in expectation of finding the answer to everything looked at signifies inner blindness.

Ibid.

Reading great books whets but never slacks the thirst for greatness.

Tom Lea: A Portfolio of Six Paintings [*1953*]. *Introduction*

THOMAS STEARNS ELIOT
[1888–   ]

Let us go then, you and I,
When the evening is spread out against the sky
Like a patient etherised upon a table.

The Love Song of J. Alfred Prufrock [*1917*]

In the room the women come and go
Talking of Michelangelo.

Ibid.

I have measured out my life with coffee spoons.

Ibid.

I should have been a pair of ragged claws
Scuttling across the floors of silent seas.

Ibid.

Should I, after tea and cakes and ices,
Have the strength to force the moment
to its crisis?
*The Love Song of J. Alfred
Prufrock*

I have seen the moment of my greatness
flicker,
And I have seen the eternal Footman
hold my coat, and snicker,
And in short, I was afraid.
Ibid.

I grow old . . . I grow old . . .
I shall wear the bottoms of my trousers
rolled.
Ibid.

Do I dare to eat a peach?
I shall wear white flannel trousers, and
walk upon the beach.
I have heard the mermaids singing,
each to each.
I do not think that they will sing to me.
Ibid.

The readers of the *Boston Evening
Transcript*
Sway in the wind like a field of ripe
corn.
The Boston Evening Transcript
[*1917*]

Upon the glazen shelves kept watch
Matthew and Waldo, guardians of the
faith,
The army of unalterable law.[1]
Cousin Nancy

We have been, let us say, to hear the
latest Pole
Transmit the Preludes, through his hair
and finger-tips.
Portrait of a Lady [*1917*]. *I*

My smile falls heavily among the bric-
à-brac.
Ibid. III

I am aware of the damp souls of house-
maids
Sprouting despondently at area gates.
Morning at the Window [*1917*]

Stand on the highest pavement of the
stair —
Lean on a garden urn —
Weave, weave the sunlight in your hair.
La Figlia Che Piange [*1917*]

[1] See Meredith, page 639a.

Simple and faithless as a smile and
shake of the hand.
La Figlia Che Piange

It [tradition] cannot be inherited,
and if you want it you must obtain it
by great labour.
*Tradition and the Individual
Talent* [*1919*]

There is a great deal, in the writing
of poetry, which must be conscious and
deliberate. In fact, the bad poet is usually unconscious where he ought to be
conscious, and conscious where he
ought to be unconscious.
Ibid.

Poetry is not a turning loose of emotion, but an escape from emotion; it is
not the expression of personality, but
an escape from personality. But, of
course, only those who have personality and emotions know what it means
to want to escape from these things.
Ibid.

The broad-backed hippopotamus
Rests on his belly in the mud;
Although he seems so firm to us
He is merely flesh and blood.
The Hippopotamus [*1920*]

Webster was much possessed by death
And saw the skull beneath the skin.
Whispers of Immortality [*1920*]

Uncorseted, her friendly bust
Gives promise of pneumatic bliss.
Ibid.

Reorganized upon the floor
She yawns and draws a stocking up.
Sweeney Among the Nightingales
[*1920*]

After such knowledge, what forgive-
ness? Think now
History has many cunning passages,
contrived corridors
And issues, deceives with whispering
ambitions,
Guides us by vanities.
Gerontion [*1920*]

April is the cruellest month, breeding
Lilacs out of the dead land, mixing
Memory and desire, stirring
Dull roots with spring rain.
The Waste Land [*1922*]. *I, The
Burial of the Dead*

And I will show you something different
from either
Your shadow at morning striding be-
hind you
Or your shadow at evening rising to
meet you;
I will show you fear in a handful of
dust.
*The Waste Land. I, The
Burial of the Dead*

Hurry up please its time.
Ibid. II, A Game of Chess

But at my back from time to time I
hear
The sound of horns and motors, which
shall bring
Sweeney to Mrs. Porter in the spring.
O the moon shone bright on Mrs. Porter
And on her daughter
They wash their feet in soda water.
Ibid. III, The Fire Sermon

When lovely woman stoops to folly and
Paces about her room again, alone,
She smoothes her hair with automatic
hand,
And puts a record on the gramophone.
Ibid.

Between the idea
And the reality
Between the motion
And the act
Falls the Shadow.
The Hollow Men [1925]. V

This is the way the world ends
Not with a bang but a whimper.
Ibid.

Humility is the most difficult of all
virtues to achieve; nothing dies harder
than the desire to think well of oneself.
*Shakespeare and the Stoicism of
Seneca [1927]*

We know too much, and are convinced of too little. Our literature is a
substitute for religion, and so is our
religion.
*A Dialogue on Dramatic Poetry
[1928]*

Because I do not hope to turn again
Because I do not hope
Because I do not hope to turn.
Ash-Wednesday [1930]. I

Lady, three white leopards sat under
a juniper-tree.
Ash-Wednesday. II

Blown hair is sweet, brown hair over
the mouth blown.
Ibid.

The white sails still fly seaward, sea-
ward flying
Unbroken wings.
Ibid. VI

And the lost heart stiffens and rejoices
In the lost lilac and the lost sea voices
And the weak spirit quickens to rebel
For the bent golden-rod and the lost
sea smell.
Ibid.

Teach us to care and not to care
Teach us to sit still
Even among these rocks,
Our peace in His will.[1]
Ibid.

What seas what shores what grey rocks
and what islands
What water lapping the bow
And scent of pine and the woodthrush
singing through the fog
What images return
O my daughter.
Marina [1930]

Yet we have gone on living,
Living and partly living.
*Murder in the Cathedral [1935].
Part I*

The last temptation is the greatest
treason:
To do the right deed for the wrong
reason.
Ibid.

Human kind cannot bear very much
reality.
Ibid. Part II

Footfalls echo in the memory
Down the passage which we did not
take
Towards the door we never opened
Into the rose-garden.
*Four Quartets [1943].
Burnt Norton*

Garlic and sapphires in the mud
Clot the bedded axle-tree.
Ibid.

[1] See Dante, page 77a.

In my beginning is my end.
> *Four Quartets. East Coker*

Each venture
Is a new beginning, a raid on the inarticulate
With shabby equipment always deteri-
orating
In the general mess of imprecision of
feeling.
> *Ibid.*

In my end is my beginning.[1]
> *Ibid.*

I do not know much about gods; but
I think that the river
Is a strong brown god — sullen, un-
tamed and intractable.
> *Ibid. The Dry Salvages*

The backward look behind the assurance
Of recorded history, the backward half-
look
Over the shoulder, towards the primitive terror.
> *Ibid.*

Music heard so deeply
That it is not heard at all, but you
are the music
While the music lasts.
> *Ibid.*

Only undefeated
Because we have gone on trying;
We, content at the last
If our temporal reversion nourish
(Not too far from the yew-tree)
The life of significant soil.
> *Ibid.*

What the dead had no speech for, when
living,
They can tell you, being dead: the
communication
Of the dead is tongued with fire beyond the language of the living.
> *Ibid. Little Gidding*

ALINE (MRS. JOYCE) KILMER
[1888–1941]

I shall not be afraid any more,
  Either by night or day;

[1] See Mary, Queen of Scots, page 101b.

What would it profit me to be afraid
  With you away?
> *I Shall Not Be Afraid. Stanza 1*

I'm sorry you are wiser,
  I'm sorry you are taller;
I liked you better foolish,
  And I liked you better smaller.
> *For the Birthday of a Middle-*
> *Aged Child. Stanza 1*

Things have a terrible permanence
When people die.
> *Things. Stanza 6*

WILLIAM L. LAURENCE
[1888–   ]

The Atomic Age began at exactly
5:30 Mountain War Time on the morning of July 16, 1945, on a stretch of
semi-desert land about fifty airline
miles from Alamogordo, New Mexico.

At that great moment in history,
ranking with the moment in the long
ago when man first put fire to work for
him and started on his march to civilization, the vast energy locked within
the hearts of the atoms of matter was
released for the first time in a burst of
flame such as had never before been
seen on this planet.[1]
> *In the New York Times,*
> *September 26, 1945*

A great ball of fire about a mile in
diameter, changing colors as it kept
shooting upward, from deep purple to
orange, expanding, growing bigger, rising as it was expanding, an elemental
force freed from its bonds after being
chained for billions of years.
> *Ibid.*

At first it was a giant column that
soon took the shape of a supramun-
dane mushroom. For a fleeting instant
it took the form of the Statue of Liberty magnified many times.
> *Ibid.*

[1] As if the earth, water, gases, lightning and
caloric had not a million energies, the discovery of any one of which could change the art
of war again, and put an end to war by the
exterminating forces man can apply. —
EMERSON: *The Fortune of the Republic*
[1878]

T. E. LAWRENCE [1]
[1888–1935]

I loved you, so I drew these tides of men into my hands and wrote my will across the sky in stars.
Seven Pillars of Wisdom [*1926*].
Dedication

Arabs could be swung on an idea as on a cord; for the unpledged allegiance of their minds made them obedient servants. None of them would escape the bond till success had come, and with it responsibility and duty and engagements. Then the idea was gone and the work ended — in ruins.
Ibid. Chap. 3

There could be no honour in a sure success, but much might be wrested from a sure defeat.
Revolt in the Desert [*1927*].
Chap. 19

It came upon me freshly how the secret of uniform was to make a crowd solid, dignified, impersonal: to give it the singleness and tautness of an upstanding man. This death's livery which walled its bearers from ordinary life, was sign that they had sold their wills and bodies to the State: and contracted themselves into a service not the less abject for that its beginning was voluntary.
Ibid. Chap. 35

EUGENE O'NEILL
[1888–1953]

Dat ole davil, sea.
Anna Christie [*1922*]. *Act I*

We's all poor nuts and things happen, and we yust get mixed in wrong, that's all.
Ibid. Act IV

[1] Changed his name to T. E. Shaw, 1927. Appearing first in the war news from Arabia as a personage rather more incredible than Prester John, and presently emerging into clear definition as the author of one of the great histories of the world, recording his own conquests at an age at which young company officers are hardly allowed to speak at the mess table. — BERNARD SHAW, in *The New York Evening Post*, April 16, 1927

For de little stealin' dey gits you in jail soon or late. For de big stealin' dey makes you emperor and puts you in de Hall o' Fame when you croaks. If dey's one thing I learns in ten years on de Pullman cars listenin' to de white quality talk, it's dat same fact.
The Emperor Jones [*1920*]. *Sc. 1*

Yank. Sure! Lock me up! Put me in a cage! Dat's de on'y answer yuh know. G'wan, lock me up!
Policeman. What you been doin'?
Yank. Enough to gimme life for! I was born, see? Sure, dat's de charge. Write it in de blotter. I was born, get me!
The Hairy Ape [*1922*]

He couldn't design a cathedral without it looking like the First Supernatural Bank!
The Great God Brown [*1926*]

Our lives are merely strange dark interludes in the electrical display of God the Father!
Strange Interlude [*1928*]

JOHN CROWE RANSOM
[1888–   ]

Two evils, monstrous either one apart,
Possessed me, and were long and loath at going:
A cry of Absence, Absence, in the heart,
And in the wood the furious winter blowing.
Winter Remembered

Hands hold much of heat in little storage.
They Hail the Sunrise

The lazy geese, like a snow cloud
Dripping their snow on the green grass,
Tricking and stopping, sleepy and proud,
Who cried in goose, Alas.
Bells for John Whiteside's Daughter

Here lies a lady of beauty and high degree.
Of chills and fever she died, of fever and chills,
The delight of her husband, her aunts, an infant of three,

And of medicos marvelling sweetly on
her ills.
Here Lies a Lady

Long, long before men die I sometimes
read
Their stoic backs as plain as graveyard
stones.
The Resurrection

And kept their blue eyes blue to any
weather.
Men

Mouth he remembered: the quaint ori-
fice
From which came heat that flamed
upon the kiss.
The Equilibrists

In Heaven you have heard no marriage
is,
No white flesh tinder to your lecheries,
Your male and female tissue sweetly
shaped
Sublimed away, and furious blood
escaped.
Ibid.

Equilibrists lie here; stranger, tread
light;
Close, but untouching in each other's
sight;
Mouldered the lips and ashy the tall
skull,
Let them lie perilous and beautiful.
Ibid.

He rose and was himself again.
Simply another morning, and simply
Jane.
Morning

God have mercy on the sinner
Who must write with no dinner,
No gravy and no grub,
No pewter and no pub,
No belly and no bowels,
Only consonants and vowels.
Survey of Literature

Athens, a fragile kingdom by the foam,
Assumed the stranger's yoke; but then
behold how meek
Those unbred Caesars grew, who spent
their fruits of Rome
Forever after, trying to be Greek.
Triumph

ROBERT EMMONS ROGERS
[1888–1941]

Marry the boss's daughter.
*Advice to the Class of 1929, Mas-
sachusetts Institute of Technology*

LEW SARETT
[1888–   ]

God, let me flower as I will!
For I am weary of the chill
Companionship of waxen vines
And hothouse-nurtured columbines.
Let Me Flower as I Will

In yonder room he lies
With pennies on his eyes.
Requiem for a Croesus

ALAN SEEGER
[1888–1916]

Whether I am on the winning or losing side is not the point with me: it is
being on the side where my sympathies
lie that matters, and I am ready to see
it through to the end. Success in life
means doing that thing than which
nothing else conceivable seems more
noble or satisfying or remunerative,
and this enviable state I can truly say
that I enjoy, for had I the choice I
would be nowhere else in the world
than where I am.[1]
Letter to his mother [*July 3, 1915*]

I have a rendezvous with Death [2]
At some disputed barricade,
When Spring comes back with rustling
shade
And apple-blossoms fill the air.
I Have a Rendezvous with Death

When Spring trips north again this
year,

---

[1] I think he would not wish himself any
where but where he is. — SHAKESPEARE: *King
Henry V* [1598–1600], *Act IV, Sc. 1, L. 125*
[2] See Archipoeta, page 74b.
I have a rendezvous with Life,
When Spring's first heralds hum.
COUNTEE CULLEN [1903–1946]: *I Have
a Rendezvous with Life*

And I to my pledged word am true,
I shall not fail that rendezvous.
> *I Have a Rendezvous with Death*

SAMUEL SHELLABARGER
[1888–1954]

Frequent indifference to external fact, though regrettable, is still relatively unimportant, for portraiture is not photography.
> *The Chevalier Bayard* [*1928*].
> *Chap. 1*

A man, a nation, a millennium, grows and is strong, or declines and perishes, in proportion to the spiritual content of each. But when nothing spiritual remains, what is left to man but the worship of vanity? Lord Vanity rules our present world.
> *Lord Vanity* [*1953*]. *Chap. 14*

When it has leveled everything, fire burns itself out, and so does a lie.
> *Ibid.*

BARTOLOMEO VANZETTI
[1888–1927]

I found myself compelled to fight back from my eyes the tears, and quanch my heart trobling to my throat to not weep before him. But Sacco's name will live in the hearts of the people when your name, your laws, institutions and your false god are but a dim rememoring of a cursed past in which man was wolf to the man.
> *Last Speech to the Court* [1]

HENRY AGARD WALLACE
[1888–   ]

The object of this war is to make sure that everybody in the world has the privilege of drinking a quart of milk a day.[2]
> *Address: The Price of Free*
> *World Victory* [*May 8, 1942*]

[1] Vanzetti and Nicolo Sacco, Italian anarchists, were executed August 23, 1927, by the Commonwealth of Massachusetts on charges, never conclusively proved, of murder and robbery.

[2] This statement became twisted into the

The century on which we are entering can be and must be the century of the common man.
> *Address: The Price of Free*
> *World Victory*

The hair goes with the hide.
> *Answer when questioned by reporters why he had not mentioned the Democratic Vice-Presidential candidate, Harry S. Truman, in his campaign speech in Madison Square Garden, New York, September 21, 1944*

The people who are fighting against me know that they are not fighting a starry-eyed liberal or mystic. If they really thought that, they wouldn't be worried.[1]
> *Speech at Testimonial Dinner,*
> *New York, January 29, 1945*

CONRAD AIKEN
[1889–   ]

Music I heard with you was more than music,
And bread I broke with you was more than bread.
> *Music I Heard with You* [*1914*]

Stars in the purple dusk above the rooftops
Pale in a saffron mist and seem to die,
And I myself on a swiftly tilting planet
Stand before a glass and tie my tie.
> *Senlin. Morning Song*

One by one in the moonlight there,
Neighing far off on the haunted air,
The unicorns come down to the sea.
> *Ibid. Evening Song*

Rock meeting rock can know love better
Than eyes that stare or lips that touch.
All that we know in love is bitter,
And it is not much.
> *Annihilation. Stanza 8*

All lovely things will have an ending,
All lovely things will fade and die,

purported slogan "Milk for Hottentots," which was disclaimed by Mr. Wallace.
[1] See C. L. Becker, page 861b.

And youth, that's now so bravely
    spending,
Will beg a penny by and by.
            *All Lovely Things Will Have an
                        Ending*
O Altitudo in the bloodstream swims.[1]
    And in the Human Heart [*1940*].
                    Sonnet VI
Ice is the silent language of the peak;
and fire the silent language of the star.
                Ibid. Sonnet X
Shadow to you, the subtle — light to
    me,
the nimble — and the twilight soul
    between,
in which, embracing, we may learn to
    be,
and having learned to be, may learn to
    mean.
                Ibid. Sonnet X
For brief as water falling will be death,
and brief as flower falling, or a leaf,
brief as the taking, and the giving,
    breath;
thus natural, thus brief, my love, is
    grief.
                Ibid. Sonnet XVIII
Shape has no shape, nor will your think-
    ing shape it;
space has no confines; and no borders
    time.
And yet, to think the abyss is to escape
    it.
                Ibid. Sonnet XXVI
Nor will that morning come which is
    not strange,
who have, each day, such wonders to
    exchange.
                Ibid. Sonnet XXXVIII

HERVEY ALLEN
[1889–1949]

Mornings, the flower-women hawk their
    wares —
Bronze caryatids of a genial race,
Bearing the bloom-heaped baskets on
    their heads.
                    Palmetto Town
Grow up as soon as you can. It pays.
The only time you really live fully is

[1] See Sir Thomas Browne, page 240a.

from thirty to sixty. . . . The young
are slaves to dreams; the old servants
of regrets. Only the middle-aged have
all their five senses in the keeping of
their wits.
    Anthony Adverse [*1933*]. *Chap. 31*
What is even a wise book but a blast
from the lungs made visible to the
eyes?
                        Ibid.
Practise what I call a decent mam-
malian philosophy.
                        Ibid.

ROBERT CHARLES
BENCHLEY
[1889–1945]

I haven't been abroad in so long that
I almost speak English without an accent.
            The Old Sea Rover Speaks
Can anyone help me out by furnishing the last three words to the following stanza which I learned in school
and of which I have forgotten the last
three words, thereby driving myself
crazy! —
"I'm sorry that I spelt the word,
    I hate to go above you,
Because — the brown eyes lower fell,
    Because, you see, — —— ——."
                Inside Benchley [*1921*]
An Austrian scientist has come out
with the announcement that there is no
such thing as a hundred per cent male
or a hundred per cent female. If this is
true, it is really a big step forward.
        *Ibid. A Talk to Young Men:
        Graduation Address on "The
        Decline of Sex"*

CHRISTOPHER DAWSON
[1889–   ]

As soon as men decide that all means
are permitted to fight an evil, then their
good becomes indistinguishable from
the evil that they set out to destroy.
        *The Judgment of the Nations
                        [1942]*
Religion has withdrawn into isolated
strongholds, where it remains on the

defensive, surveying the land through the narrow loopholes in the fortifications.

The Judgment of the Nations

CHARLES DIVINE
[1889–1950]

Where hearts were high and fortunes low, and onions in the stew.
At the Lavender Lantern. Stanza 3
A crooked street goes past my door, entwining love of every land;
It wanders, singing, round the world, to Askelon and Samarkand.
*The Crooked Street of Dreams.
Stanza 1*

PHILIP GUEDALLA
[1889–1944]

Biography, like big game hunting, is one of the recognized forms of sport, and it is as unfair as only sport can be.
Supers and Supermen [1920]
No picture of life in Calais was too ludicrous to be believed in Dover; that is one of the advantages of being an Island Race.[1]
Ibid.
There is no Gibbon but Gibbon, and Gibbon is his prophet.[2] The solemn march of his cadences, the majestic impropriety of his innuendo are without rivals in the respective annals of British eloquence and British indelicacy.
Ibid.
The work of Henry James has always seemed divisible by a simple dynastic arrangement into three reigns: James I, James II, and the Old Pretender.
Ibid.
An Englishman is a man who lives on an island in the North Sea governed by Scotsmen.
Ibid.

[1] There are several versions of a supposed London newspaper headline, the best known perhaps being "THICK FOG OVER CHANNEL: CONTINENT ISOLATED."
[2] There is no God but God, and Mohammed is his prophet. — *Moslem creed* (the first phrase is from *The Koran, Chap. 3*)

The cheerful clatter of Sir James Barrie's cans as he went round with the milk of human kindness.
Some Critics
Strange that pre-eminence in Germany has more than once been indicated by an eccentric pattern in the hair upon the upper lip.
The Hundred Years [1936]
The true history of the United States is the history of transportation . . . in which the names of railroad presidents are more significant than those of Presidents of the United States.
Ibid.
There is no plant in the whole world of more cautious growth than Anglo-American negotiation.
Mr. Churchill [1942] (apropos the wedding of Mr. Churchill's parents)
The little ships, the unforgotten un-Homeric catalogue of *Mary Jane* and *Peggy IV,* of *Folkestone Belle, Boy Billy,* and *Ethel Maud,* of *Lady Haig* and *Skylark* . . . the little ships of England brought the army home.
Ibid. (Evacuation of Dunkirk)

ADOLF HITLER
[1889–1945]

During the next thousand years no revolution will take place in Germany.
*Address at Party Rally,
September, 1934*
The Sudetenland is the last territorial claim I have to make in Europe.
*Address at Sports Palast,
September 26, 1938*
I know that one is able to win people far more by the spoken than by the written word, and that every great movement on this globe owes its rise to the great speakers and not to the great writers.
Mein Kampf.[1] Preface
The one means that wins the easiest victory over reason: terror and force.
Ibid. Vol. I, Chap. 2, Page 53

[1] Complete and Unabridged Edition [1940].

A majority can never replace the man. . . . . Just as a hundred fools do not make one wise man, an heroic decision is not likely to come from a hundred cowards.

Mein Kampf. Vol. I, Chap. 3, Page 105

There is only one real "statesman" once in a blue moon in one nation, and not a hundred or more at a time.

Ibid. Page 113

For if a man is not ready or able to fight for his existence, righteous Providence has already decreed his doom. The world is not intended for cowardly nations.

Ibid. Page 123

Every movement with great aims has anxiously to watch that it does not lose connection with the great masses.

Ibid. Page 137

I consider the foundation or the destruction of a religion essentially more important than the foundation or destruction of a State, let alone a party.

Ibid. Page 148

The efficiency of the truly national leader consists primarily in preventing the division of the attention of a people, and always in concentrating it on a single enemy.

Ibid. Page 152

Mankind has grown strong in eternal struggles and it will only perish through eternal peace.

Ibid. Chap. 4, Page 175

The greater the amount of room a people has at its disposal, the greater is also its natural protection; because military victories over nations crowded in small territories have always been reached more quickly and more easily.

Ibid. Page 177

Strength lies not in defense but in attack.

Ibid. Page 191

All propaganda has to be popular and has to adapt its spiritual level to the perception of the least intelligent of those towards whom it intends to direct itself.

Ibid. Chap. 6, Page 232

As soon as by one's own propaganda even a glimpse of right on the other side is admitted, the cause for doubting one's own right is laid.

Mein Kampf. Vol. I, Chap. 6, Page 237

In the size of the lie there is always contained a certain factor of credibility, since the great masses of the people . . . will more easily fall victims to a great lie than to a small one.

Ibid. Chap. 10, Page 313

If an idea is right in itself, and if thus armed it embarks on the struggle in this world, it is invincible and every persecution will lead to its inner strengthening.

Ibid. Chap. 12, Page 487

Germany will be either a world power or will not be at all.

Ibid. Vol. II, Chap. 14, Page 950

Never tolerate the establishment of two continental powers in Europe.

Ibid. Page 963

An intelligent victor will, whenever possible, present his demands to the vanquished in installments.

Ibid. Chap. 15, Page 968

The more extortions thus cheerfully accepted, the more unjustified does it seem to people finally to set about defending themselves.

Ibid.

After fifteen years of work I have achieved, as a common German soldier and merely with my fanatical will power, the unity of the German nation, and have freed it from the death sentence of Versailles.[1]

Proclamation to the Troops on taking over the leadership of the German armed forces [December 21, 1941]

[1] The Allied and Associated Governments affirm and Germany accepts the responsibility of Germany and her Allies for causing all the loss and damage to which the Allied and Associated Governments and their nationals have been subjected as a consequence of the war imposed upon them by the aggression of Germany and her Allies. — *Treaty of Versailles, Article 231 (the "War Guilt Clause")* [June 28, 1919]

This war no longer bears the characteristics of former inter-European conflicts. It is one of those elemental conflicts which usher in a new millennium and which shake the world once in a thousand years.

Speech before the Reichstag
[April 26, 1942]

Whomsoever England allies herself with, she will see her allies stronger than she is herself at the end of this war.

Ibid.

If the German people despair, they will deserve no better than they get. If they despair, I will not be sorry for them if God lets them down.

Speech at Munich on the Twentieth Anniversary of the Munich Beer Hall Putsch, broadcast November 8, 1943

EDWIN POWELL HUBBLE
[1889–   ]

On the grand scale, the Observable Region [of space] is very much the same everywhere and in all directions — in other words, it is homogeneous.

The Exploration of Space [1945]

STODDARD KING
[1889–1933]

A writer owned an Asterisk,
And kept it in his den,
Where he wrote tales (which had large sales)
Of frail and erring men;
And always, when he reached the point
Where carping censors lurk,
He called upon the Asterisk
To do his dirty work.

The Writer and the Asterisk.
Stanza 1

There's a long, long trail a-winding
Into the land of my dreams,
Where the nightingales are singing
And a white moon beams:
There's a long, long night of waiting
Until my dreams all come true,

Till the day when I'll be going down
That long, long trail with you.

The Long, Long Trail [1913]

WALTER LIPPMANN
[1889–   ]

Copeland of Harvard once remarked when he was asked whether he had enjoyed a tea party, "if I had not been there I should have been very much bored." [1]

William Bolitho — A Memoir

In foreign relations, as in all other relations, a policy has been formed only when commitments and power have been brought into balance.

U. S. Foreign Policy [1943]

The final test of a leader is that he leaves behind him in other men the conviction and the will to carry on. . . . The genius of a good leader is to leave behind him a situation which common sense, without the grace of genius, can deal with successfully.

Roosevelt Has Gone
[April 14, 1945]

KATHERINE MANSFIELD
[1889–1923]

Whenever I prepare for a journey I prepare as though for death. Should I never return, all is in order. This is what life has taught me.

Journal, 1922

I want, by understanding myself, to understand others. I want to be all that I am capable of becoming. . . . This all sounds very strenuous and serious. But now that I have wrestled with it, it's no longer so. I feel happy — deep down. *All is well.*

Ibid. (end of her journal)

---

[1] I quite agree with Alexandre Dumas who, when asked how he had enjoyed a fearfully dull party, said, "I should not have enjoyed it if *I* had not been there." How delightful one is to oneself. — LAURA TENNANT: *Letter to Sidney Colvin,* December, 1884 (*Quoted in* E. V. LUCAS: *The Colvins and Their Friends, P. 188*)

FRANCIS JOSEPH, CARDINAL SPELLMAN
[1889–   ]

Somewhere — the place it matters not
  — somewhere
I saw a child, hungry and thin of
  face —
Eyes in whose pools life's joys no
  longer stirred,
Lips that were dead to laughter's eager
  kiss,
Yet parted fiercely to a crust of bread.
     Prayer for Children [*1944*]

W. J. TURNER
[1889–1946]

If love means affection, I
  Love old trees, hats, coats and
  things,[1]
Anything that's been with me
In my daily sufferings.
     Epithalamium. Stanza 3
How often does a man need to see a
  woman?
Once!
Once is enough, but a second time will
  confirm it.
     The Word Made Flesh?

ELMER FRANK ANDREWS
[1890–   ]

If a man has an office with a desk on
which there is a buzzer, and if he can
press that buzzer and have somebody
come dashing in response — then he's
an executive.
     *Address before the Trade Asso-
     ciation Executives' Forum of
     Chicago* [*December 9, 1938*]

WILLIAM BOLITHO
[1890–1930]

The adventurer is within us, and he
contests for our favour with the social
man we are obliged to be. These two
sorts of life are incompatibles; one we
hanker after, the other we are obliged

[1] See Bacon, page 119a.

to. There is no other conflict so deep
and bitter as this.
     Twelve Against the Gods [*1929*].
     Introduction

We, like the eagles, were born to be
free. Yet we are obliged, in order to live
at all, to make a cage of laws for ourselves and to stand on the perch. We
are born as wasteful and unremorseful
as tigers; we are obliged to be thrifty,
or starve, or freeze. We are born to
wander, and cursed to stay and dig.
     Ibid.

His real glory is that of all adventurers: to have been the tremendous
outsider.
     Ibid. Christopher Columbus

The world will never learn to beware
of these stately gentlemen with the
fixed calm look straight in your eyes,
who never joke, and never waver, profuse in cautious hints and allusions,
but practised in rightly placed silences
— which is why the confidence trick is
still running.
     Ibid.

The most dangerous enterprise in
the world, the foundation of a religion.
     Ibid. Mahomet

That great bourn of all common
sense: compromise.
     Ibid.

You need more tact in the dangerous
art of giving presents than in any other
social action.[1]
     Ibid. Lola Montez

Contrary to male sentimentality and
psychology, the confrontation of a hostile crowd, to a woman, is like a tonic.
     Ibid.

An adventure differs from a mere
feat in that it is tied to the eternally
unattainable. Only one end of the rope
is in the hand, the other is not visible,
and neither prayers, nor daring, nor
reason can shake it free.
     Ibid. Napoleon III

Freeing oppressed nationalities is
perhaps the most dangerous of all
philanthropic enterprises.
     Ibid.

[1] See Lady Glenconner, page 853b.

The voice of the people needs a whole art of harmonic transcription to be understood.
Twelve Against the Gods.
Woodrow Wilson

VANNEVAR BUSH
[1890–]

The scene changes but the aspirations of men of good will persist.
Modern Arms and Free Men [*1949*]. *Foreword*
If democracy loses its touch, then no great war will be needed to overwhelm it. If it keeps and enhances its strength, no great war need come again.
Ibid. Page 263
Fear can not be banished, but it can be calm and without panic; and it can be mitigated by reason and evaluation.
Ibid.

KAREL ČAPEK
[1890–1938]

Rossum's Universal Robots.[1]
R. U. R. [*1920*]
O Lord, grant that in some way it may rain every day, say from about midnight until three o'clock in the morning . . . gentle and warm so that it can soak in . . . that there may be plenty of dew and little wind, enough worms, no plant-lice and snails, no mildew, and that once a week thin liquid manure and guano may fall from heaven.
The Gardener's Year [*1931*].
The Gardener's Prayer

MARCUS COOK CONNELLY
[1890–]

Gangway for de Lawd God Jehovah!
The Green Pastures [2]
God. I'll jest r'ar back an' pass a miracle.
Ibid.

[1] The term "robot" came into English through Čapek's play.
[2] First produced in 1930. Suggested by Roark Bradford's stories, *Ol' Man Adam an' His Chillun.*

Gabriel. How about cleanin' up de whole mess of 'em and sta'tin all over ag'in wid some new kind of animal?
God. An' admit I'm licked?
The Green Pastures
Even bein' Gawd ain't a bed of roses.
Ibid.

ELMER DAVIS
[1890–]

Atomic warfare is bad enough; biological warfare would be worse; but there is something that is worse than either. The French can tell you what it is; or the Czechs, or the Greeks, or the Norwegians, or the Filipinos; it is subjection to an alien oppressor.
No World, If Necessary [1]
One world or none, say the atomic scientists. Has it occurred to them that if their one world turned out to be totalitarian and obscurantist, we might better have no world at all?
Ibid.

CHARLES ANDRÉ JOSEPH MARIE DE GAULLE
[1890–]

France has lost a battle. But France has not lost the war.
Broadcast from London to the French people after the fall of France, June 18, 1940

DWIGHT DAVID EISENHOWER
[1890–]

Humility must always be the portion of any man who receives acclaim earned in the blood of his followers and the sacrifices of his friends.
Address at Guildhall on receiving the Freedom of the City of London, July 12, 1945
Since this century's beginning a time of tempest has seemed to come upon the continents of the earth.
Inaugural Address [*January 20, 1953*]

[1] In the *Saturday Review of Literature*, March 30, 1946.

In the final choice a soldier's pack is not so heavy a burden as a prisoner's chains.

Inaugural Address

As it is an ancient truth that freedom cannot be legislated into existence, so it is no less obvious that freedom cannot be censored into existence.

President's Letter to American Library Association Convention [June, 1953]

SIR ALAN PATRICK HERBERT
[1890–   ]

When laughing Ann trips down the street
The sun comes out as well,
The town is at her twinkling feet,
The crier rings his bell,
The young men leap like little fish,
Policemen stand and purr,
While husbands look behind and wish
That they had married her.

Laughing Ann. Stanza 1

I'm not a jealous woman, but I *can't* see what he sees in her,
I can't see *what* he sees in her, I can't see what he *sees* in her!

I Can't Think What He Sees in Her

Holy Deadlock.

Title of novel [1934] satirizing the paradoxes of British divorce law [1]

The Common Law of England has been laboriously built upon a mythical figure — the figure of "The Reasonable Man."

Uncommon Law [1935]. Page 1

The critical period in matrimony is breakfast-time.

Ibid. Page 98

An Act of God was defined as *something which no reasonable man could have expected.*

Ibid. Page 316

[1] Herbert's book and his campaign in the House of Commons were of major importance in bringing about the reform embodied in the Matrimonial Causes Bill of 1937.

I regard the pub as a valuable institution.

Letter to the Electors of Oxford University [1935] [1]

They tell us that capitalism is doomed: Karl Marx, I believe, made the same announcement 80 years ago. He may still be right: but the old clock ticks on.

Ibid.

We shall not produce equality by turning everything upside-down.

Ibid.

SAMUEL HOFFENSTEIN
[1890–1947]

I play with the bulls and the bears;
I'm the Bartlett of market quotations.

Songs for an Old-Fashioned Lute. VI

The stars, like measles, fade at last.

The Mimic Muse. V

Babies haven't any hair;
Old men's heads are just as bare; —
Between the cradle and the grave
Lies a haircut and a shave.

Songs of Faith in the Year after Next. VIII

Little by little we subtract
Faith and Fallacy from Fact,
The Illusory from the True,
And starve upon the residue.

Rag-Bag, II. Observation, Stanza 1

The heart's dead
Are never buried.

Summer Day

GERALD WHITE JOHNSON
[1890–   ]

A man who has tried to play Mozart, and failed, through that vain effort comes into position better to understand the man who tried to paint the Sistine Madonna, and did.

A Little Night-Music [1937]

England has proved that the heroes are not all dead. England has shown

[1] Herbert was elected to the House of Commons, November, 1935, as one of the two representatives of Oxford University.

that there are also brave men after Agamemnon.[1] England has taught us that even our generation can produce glory and honor and undying fame. England restores our belief that faith and loyalty are still able to lift common men to greatness.

Editorial, In Praise of England.
The Baltimore Sun [September, 1940]

Nothing changes more constantly than the past; for the past that influences our lives does not consist of what actually happened, but of what men believe happened.

American Heroes and Hero-Worship [1943]. Chap. 1

Heroes are created by popular demand, sometimes out of the scantiest materials . . . such as the apple that William Tell never shot, the ride that Paul Revere never finished, the flag that Barbara Frietchie never waved.

Ibid.

ROBERT LEY
[1890–1945]

Strength through Joy.[2]
Instruction for the German Labor Front, December 2, 1933

CHRISTOPHER MORLEY
[1890–   ]

And of all man's felicities
  The very subtlest one, say I,
Is when for the first time he sees
  His hearthfire smoke against the sky.
A Hallowe'en Memory. Stanza 5

Heaven is not built of country seats,
But little queer suburban streets.
To the Little House. Stanza 4

The man who never in his life
Has washed the dishes with his wife
Or polished up the silver plate —
He still is largely celibate.
Washing the Dishes. Stanza 4

Now fades the glossy, cherished anthracite;

[1] See Horace, page 40a.
[2] Kraft durch Freude.

The radiators lose their temperature:
How ill avail, on such a frosty night,
The short and simple flannels of the poor.[1]
Elegy Written in a Country Coal-Bin

Unhappy lovers always should be Frenchmen,
So sweet a tongue for any kind of pain!
Toulemonde. III

  Women all
Raiment themselves most brightly for the dark
Which is, on information and belief,
  Their true dominion.
Ibid. VI

I bid you, mock not Eros;
  He knows not doubt or shame,
And, unaware of proverbs,
  The burnt child craves the flame.
Of a Child That Had Fever

When you sell a man a book you don't sell him just twelve ounces of paper and ink and glue — you sell him a whole new life.
Parnassus on Wheels [1917]. Chap. 4

"Dear me," cried Mrs. Spaniel, "what will the neighbors think?"

"They won't," said Gissing, "I don't doubt they'll talk, but they won't think. Thinking is very rare."
Where the Blue Begins [1922]

He is too experienced a parent ever to make positive promises.
Thunder on the Left [1925]. Chap. 5

If you have to keep reminding yourself of a thing, perhaps it isn't so.
Ibid. Chap. 9

April prepares her green traffic light and the world thinks Go.
John Mistletoe [1931]. 8

[1] Daily she came from Bromley to the City,
  Pink underclothes of crêpe de Chine she wore,
  So that in each backyard she viewed with pity
  The short and simple flannels of the poor.
  OLIVER HERFORD(?), *quoted by*
  A. EDWARD NEWTON, *Derby Day*

A human being: an ingenious assembly of portable plumbing.
> *Human Being* [*1932*]. *Chap. 11*

How great a bonfire the savages of New York kindle for their evening meal!
> *Ibid. Chap. 33*

That faint but sensitive enteric expectancy which suggests the desirability of a cocktail. . . . A drink has been arranged and will shortly take place.
> *Swiss Family Manhattan* [*1932*]. *Chap. 9*

The enemies of the Future are always the very nicest people.
> *Kitty Foyle* [*1939*]. *Chap. 5*

Dancing is wonderful training for girls, it's the first way you learn to guess what a man is going to do before he does it.
> *Ibid. Chap. 11*

The evening papers print what they do and get away with it because by afternoon the human mind is ruined anyhow.
> *Ibid. Chap. 25*

New York, the nation's thyroid gland.
> *Shore Leave* [*1939*]

Town that made thinking feel, and feeling think;
She has a motto to recall when needed:
I may make heavy weather, but not sink.
> *"Fluctuat nec Mergitur"* [1] [*1940*]

There was so much handwriting on the wall
That even the wall fell down.
> *Around the Clock* [*1943*]

Since men learned print, no night is wholly black.
> *The Watchman's Sonnet*

All joys I bless, but I confess
There is one greatest thrill:
What the dentist does when he stops the buzz
And puts away the drill.
> *Song in a Dentist's Chair. Stanza 1*

Man must learn, or his name is mud,
To relish the ebb as well as the flood.
> *Toulemonde: Intermezzo* [*1944*]

[1] The motto of Paris.

Global citizens began it
When Men-about-town became Men-about-planet.
> *Toulemonde: Intermezzo*

When ego, fantailed like a peacock
Can find the needle in the haycock
And hold the needle's eye and thread it —
Is that millennium? You said it!
> *Ibid.*

Chattering voltage like a broken wire
The wild cicada cried, Six weeks to frost!
> *End of August*

Why do they put the Gideon Bibles only in the bedrooms, where it's usually too late, and not in the barroom downstairs?
> *Contribution to a Contribution*

ALLAN NEVINS
[1890–　]

The former allies had blundered in the past by offering Germany too little, and offering even that too late,[1] until finally Nazi Germany had become a menace to all mankind.
> *Germany Disturbs the Peace,*
> *in Current History, May, 1935*

GEORGE SELDES
[1890–　]

Sawdust Caesar.[2]
> *Title of book* [*1932*]

FRED M. VINSON
[1890–1953]

Wars are not "acts of God." They are caused by man, by man-made insti-

[1] It is the old trouble — too late. Too late with Czechoslovakia, too late with Poland, certainly too late with Finland. It is always too late, or too little, or both. — DAVID LLOYD GEORGE: *Speech, House of Commons,* March 13, 1940, *the day after the fall of Finland*
"Too Late," caption of famous cartoon by SIR JOHN TENNIEL in *Punch* [February, 1885], when the relief expedition to Khartoum reached there two days after the death of Gordon.
[2] Mussolini.

tutions, by the way in which man has organized his society. What man has made, man can change.

Speech at Arlington National Cemetery, Memorial Day, 1945

AGATHA CHRISTIE

It is completely unimportant. That is why it is so interesting.

The Murder of Roger Ackroyd [*1926*]

"RED" ROWLEY
[*Floruit* 1915]

Mademoiselle from Armenteers,
Hasn't been kissed in forty years,
Hinky dinky, parley-voo.

Mademoiselle from Armentières [1]
Mademoiselle from St. Nazaire,
She never heard of underwear.

Ibid.

ELY CULBERTSON [2]
[1891–]

The bizarre world of cards . . . a world of pure power politics where rewards and punishments were meted out immediately. A deck of cards was built like the purest of hierarchies, with every card a master to those below it, a lackey to those above it. And there were "masses" — long suits — which always asserted themselves in the end, triumphing over the kings and aces.

Total Peace [*1943*]. *Chap. 1*

Power politics is the diplomatic name for the law of the jungle.

Must We Fight Russia? [*1946*]. *Chap. 2*

We must conquer war, or war will conquer us.

Ibid.

[1] Soldier song of World War I, with innumerable versions. The tune and verse structure were based on a song long known in the British Army, composed by Alfred James Walden ("Harry Wincott") [1867–1947].
[2] I became a kind of one-man Peace Foundation, endowed not by Carnegie or Rockefeller but by the bridge players. — ELY CULBERTSON, in *The Commonweal*

God and the politicians willing, the United States can declare peace upon the world, and win it.

Must We Fight Russia? Chap. 5

DAVID LOW
[1891–]

I have never met anybody who wasn't against War. Even Hitler and Mussolini were, according to themselves.

*In the New York Times,
February 10, 1946*

ELLIOT PAUL
[1891–]

She had a complete ignorance of everything a woman does not need to know.

The Life and Death of a Spanish Town [*1942*]. *Chap. 1*

Patience makes women beautiful in middle age.

Ibid. Chap. 2

There was Madrid, and I carry it like a photograph in the inside-pocket of my mind and each day it wears, is soiled, gets thinner, cracks, wrinkles — still it is Madrid.

Ibid. Chap. 7

Government forms which had been printed in such a way that there was never enough space in which to provide answers to ambiguous questions.

The Last Time I Saw Paris [1]
[*1942*]. *Part I, 3*

The last time I see Paris will be on the day I die. The city was inexhaustible, and so is its memory.

Ibid. Part II, 23

[1] The last time I saw Paris, her heart was warm and gay,
I heard the laughter of her heart in every street café.
OSCAR HAMMERSTEIN 2ND [1895–]:
The Last Time I Saw Paris

HAROLD WILLIAM THOMPSON
[1891–]

Body, Boots and Britches.[1]
Title of a volume of New York folklore [*1940*]

HERBERT V. WILEY
[1891–1954]

Stand by to crash.
Last command to the crew of the falling U. S. Navy dirigible Akron [*April 4, 1933*]

STELLA BENSON
[1892–1933]

Call no man foe, but never love a stranger.
Build up no plan, nor any star pursue.
Go forth with crowds; in loneliness is danger.
To the Unborn. Stanza 3
Family jokes, though rightly cursed by strangers, are the bond that keeps most families alive.
Pipers and a Dancer. Chap. 9

JOHN PEALE BISHOP
[1892–1944]

Things I have hated: A certain shade of brown
Which elder ladies love; wet roofs that drip
Their huge drops on your neck; short sheets that slip
And leave your ankles freezing; fires that smoke;
Carved, heavy furniture of varnished oak.
The Great Hater

PEARL S. BUCK
[1892–]

Be born anywhere, little embryo novelist, but do not be born under the shadow of a great creed, not under the burden of original sin, not under the

[1] A New York State phrase to express completeness, as "lock, stock and barrel."

doom of salvation. Go out and be born among gypsies or thieves or among happy workaday people who live in the sun and do not think about their souls.
Advice to Unborn Novelists

RAYMOND CLAPPER
[1892–1945]

It's a wise crack that knows its own father.
Quoted in Washington Tapestry by OLIVE EWING CLAPPER [*1946*]

ROBERT PETER TRISTRAM COFFIN
[1892–1955]

If men could still be holy anywhere,
It would be in towers such as these
That line the coasts with lamps and warn the ships —
The holy towers of the silences.
Towers of Silence
A man should choose with careful eye
The things to be remembered by.
The Weather Vane
Life and death upon one tether
And running beautiful together.
Crystal Moment

J. B. S. HALDANE
[1892–]

Science is vastly more stimulating to the imagination than are the classics.
Daedalus

ROBERT H. JACKSON
[1892–1954]

The first trial in history for crimes against the peace of the world imposes a grave responsibility. The wrongs which we seek to condemn and punish have been so calculated, so malignant and so devastating that civilization cannot tolerate their being ignored because it cannot survive their being repeated.
Opening Address before the International Military Tribunal [*1945*]

The day that this country ceases to be free for irreligion, it will cease to be free for religion.

> *Dissenting opinion, Zorach* v. *Clausor, 343 U.S. 306, 325* [*1952*]

HOWARD MUMFORD JONES
[1892–]

They say the forties are the dangerous ages.

> *The Forties* [*1937*]

Therefore we are leaders, we who are dull
But eminent. Our shining names are told,
Our notable acts, our virtues are enrolled
In Who's Who in America for you to cull.

> *Ibid. V*

A few unrepentant old sinners wonder if Marx
Also explains the unsocialized pairs in the parks.

> *Ibid. XXXII*

Persecution is the first law of society because it is always easier to suppress criticism than to meet it.

> *Primer of Intellectual Freedom* [*1949*]. *Introduction*

JOHN KIERAN
[1892–]

Who harbors in memory a wealth of valued verse has laid up unto himself treasures that moths will not corrupt nor thieves break in and steal. This is the conviction of one who . . . as a soldier in World War I, trudged the desolate sector of the Somme and the ruined region of Arras with little limp volumes of Shakespeare in his pockets and miniature collections of Burns, Browning, Swinburne, and Tennyson wedged in his pack between the top of the blanket roll and the strapped-down flap that held his mess kit.

> *Poems I Remember* [*1942*]. *Foreword*

ARCHIBALD MacLEISH
[1892–]

Sometimes within the brain's old ghostly house,
I hear, far off, at some forgotten door,
A music and an eerie faint carouse,
And stir of echoes down the creaking floor.

> *Chambers of Imagery. Stanza 1*

Beauty is that Medusa's head
Which men go armed to seek and sever.
It is most deadly when most dead,
And dead will stare and sting forever.

> *Beauty*

The trumpet of
Time in our ears and the brazen and
Breaking shout of our days!

> *Panic: Chorus*

A poem should not mean
But be.

> *Ars Poetica* [*1926*]

There with vast wings across the canceled skies,
There in the sudden blackness the black pall
Of nothing, nothing, nothing — nothing at all.

> *The End of the World* [*1926*]

The world was always yours: you would not take it.

> *Speech to a Crowd*

And here face downward in the sun
To feel how swift how secretly
The shadow of the night comes on . . .

> *You, Andrew Marvell* [*1930*]

Christ but this earth goes over to the squall of time!
Hi but she heels to it — rail down: ribs down: rolling
Dakotas under her hull! And the night climbing
Sucking the green from the ferns by these Berkshire boulders!

> *The Sunset Piece*

She lies on her left side her flank golden:
Her hair is burned black with the strong sun:
The scent of her hair is of rain in the dust on her shoulders:

She has brown breasts and the mouth
of no other country.
> *Frescoes for Mr. Rockefeller's
> City [1933]. Landscape as a
> Nude*

The one man who should never attempt an explanation of a poem is its author. If the poem can be improved by its author's explanations it never should have been published, and if the poem cannot be improved by its author's explanations the explanations are scarcely worth reading.
> *Poems [1938]. Author's Note*

America was promises . . .
It was Man who had been promised.
> *America Was Promises [1939]*

The perversion of the mind is only possible when those who should be heard in its defense are silent.
> *The Irresponsibles [1940]*

The scholar digs his ivory cellar in the ruins of the past and lets the present sicken as it will.
> *Ibid.*

Races didn't bother the Americans. They were something a lot better than any race. They were a People. They were the first self-constituted, self-declared, self-created People in the history of the world. And their manners were their own business. And so were their politics. And so, but ten times so, were their souls.
> *A Time to Act [1943]*

EARL MARLATT
[1892–   ]

Fancy the rapture
Of being there
When the world was made!
> *May Morning.[1] Stanza 1*

EDWARD POWYS MATHERS
[1892–   ]

A love-sick heart dies when the heart is
whole,

[1] It must have been May Morning when the world was made. — *Old Provençal chanson*

For all the heart's health is to be sick
with love.
> *Fard. Translation from the
> Hindustani of Miyan Jagnu,
> Eighteenth Century*

Before you love,
Learn to run through snow
Leaving no footprint.
> *Translation of a Turkish Proverb*

EDNA ST. VINCENT MILLAY
[1892–1950]

And what are you that, missing you,
  I should be kept awake
As many nights as there are days
  With weeping for your sake?
> *The Philosopher*

Death devours all lovely things:
  Lesbia with her sparrow
Shares the darkness, — presently
  Every bed is narrow.
> *Passer Mortuus Est. Stanza 1*

All I could see from where I stood
Was three long mountains and a wood.
> *Renascence [1917]*

I would I were alive again
To kiss the fingers of the rain,
To drink into my eyes the shine
Of every slanting silver line,
To catch the freshened, fragrant breeze
From drenched and dripping apple-
  trees.
> *Ibid.*

I know not how such things can be,
I only know there came to me
A fragrance such as never clings
To aught save happy living things.
> *Ibid.*

The world stands out on either side
No wider than the heart is wide;
Above the world is stretched the sky, —
No higher than the soul is high.[1]
The heart can push the sea and land
Farther away on either hand;
The soul can split the sky in two,
And let the face of God shine through.
> *Ibid.*

[1] See Hartley Coleridge, page 483b.

The fabric of my faithful love
No power shall dim or ravel
Whilst I stay here, — but oh, my dear,
If I should ever travel!
To the Not Impossible Him.
Stanza 3

I know I am but summer to your heart,
And not the full four seasons of the
year.
Two Seasons. Sonnet 1

I drank at every vine.
The last was like the first.
I came upon no wine
So wonderful as thirst.
Feast. Stanza 1

I only know that summer sang in me
A little while, that in me sings no more.
What Lips My Lips Have Kissed

Euclid alone
Has looked on Beauty bare.[1] Fortunate
they
Who, though once only and then but
far away,
Have heard her massive sandal set on
stone.
The Harp-Weaver [1923].
Sonnet 22

Pity me that the heart is slow to learn
What the swift mind beholds at every
turn.
Sonnet: Pity Me Not Because
the Light of Day

My candle burns at both ends;
It will not last the night;
But, ah, my foes, and, oh, my friends —
It gives a lovely light.[2]
Figs from Thistles. First Fig

Oh, come again to Astolat!
I will not ask you to be kind;

[1] Mathematics possesses not only truth, but supreme beauty — a beauty cold and austere, like that of sculpture, without appeal to any part of our weaker nature, yet sublimely pure, and capable of a stern perfection such as only the greatest art can show. — BERTRAND RUSSELL: *The Principles of Mathematics* [1903]

[2] I burned my candle at both ends,
And now have neither foes nor friends.
SAMUEL HOFFENSTEIN [1890–1947]:
Songs of Fairly Utter Despair, VIII

And you may go when you will go,
And I will stay behind.
Elaine. Stanza 1

Music my rampart, and my only one.
On Hearing a Symphony of
Beethoven

Read me, do not let me die!
Search the fading letters, finding
Steadfast in the broken binding
All that once was I!
The Poet and His Book. Stanza 6

Who builds her a house with love for
timber,
Builds her a house of foam;
And I'd rather be bride to a lad gone
down
Than widow to one safe home.
Keen. Stanza 5

If ever I said, in grief or pride,
I tired of honest things, I lied.
The Goose Girl

I will be the gladdest thing under the
sun!
I will touch a hundred flowers and not
pick one.
Afternoon on a Hill

Life goes on forever like the gnawing of
a mouse.
Ashes of Life. Stanza 3

Thanks be to God, the world is wide,
And I am going far from home!
And I forgot in Camelot
The man I loved in Rome.
Fugitive. Stanza 1

My heart is warm with the friends I
make,
And better friends I'll not be knowing;
Yet there isn't a train I wouldn't take,
No matter where it's going.
Travel. Stanza 3

I am not resigned to the shutting away
of loving hearts in the hard
ground.
So it is, and so it will be, for so it has
been, time out of mind:
Into the darkness they go, the wise and
the lovely. Crowned
With lilies and with laurel they go;
but I am not resigned.
Dirge Without Music. Stanza 1

I had a little Sorrow,
Born of a little Sin.
> *The Penitent. Stanza 1*

Whether or not we find what we are
seeking
Is idle, biologically speaking.
> *Sonnet: I Shall Forget You*
> *Presently*

Love is not all: it is not meat nor
drink
Nor slumber nor a roof against the
rain;
Nor yet a floating spar to men that
sink.
> *Fatal Interview. XXX*

See how these masses mill and swarm
And troop and muster and assail:
God! we could keep this planet warm
By friction, if the sun should fail.
> *Three Sonnets in Tetrameter*
> *[1938]. I*

This little life, from here to there —
Who lives it safely anywhere? . . .
(The tidal wave devours the shore:
There *are* no islands any more.)
> *There Are No Islands, Any More* [1]
> *[June 14, 1940]*

HENRY VOLLAM MORTON
[1892–   ]

One drink of wine, and you act like
a monkey; two drinks, and you strut
like a peacock; three drinks, and you
roar like a lion; and four drinks — you
behave like a pig.[2]
> *In the Steps of St. Paul* [1936].
> *Chap. 1*

The perfect place for a writer is in
the hideous roar of a city, with men
making a new road under his window
in competition with a barrel organ, and
on the mat a man waiting for the rent.
> *Ibid. Chap. 4*

---

[1] Great Britain no longer is an island. The
strategic implication will be clear very soon
England is an island in so far as she is lonely,
cut off from the world. Hunger is staring her
in the face. — HITLER: *Radio speech*, July 1,
1940.
We cannot be an island. — FRANKLIN D.
ROOSEVELT: *Radio address*, March 8, 1941
[2] Moral of an Arabian story about Adam
and the fruit of a vine.

St. Nicholas, in addition to protect-
ing sailors, children, travellers, and
merchants, is also the patron saint of
pawnbrokers. The story goes that a
nobleman of the saint's native town,
Parara in Asia Minor, had lost all his
money, and did not know how he could
endow his three beautiful daughters. St.
Nicholas, hearing of his trouble, went
by night and flung through the window
three bags of gold with which the nobleman was able to provide handsome
dowries. These three bags are shown in
all early ikons as three gold apples, and
the gold apples of St. Nicholas are the
origin of the pawnbroker's sign.[1]
> *In the Steps of St. Paul. Chap. 7*

REINHOLD NIEBUHR
[1892–   ]

Goodness, armed with power, is corrupted; and pure love without power is
destroyed.
> *Beyond Tragedy* [1938]

Man's capacity for justice makes
democracy possible, but man's inclination to injustice makes democracy necessary.
> *The Children of Light and the*
> *Children of Darkness* [1944]

BASIL O'CONNOR
[1892–   ]

The world cannot continue to wage
war like physical giants and to seek
peace like intellectual pygmies.
> *Address at National Conference of*
> *Christians and Jews* [1945]

LEVERETT SALTONSTALL
[1892–   ]

The real New England Yankee is a
person who takes the midnight train
home from New York.
> *Press conference* [*May 4, 1939*]

---

[1] *Webster's New International Dictionary*
says that the pawnbroker's three gilt balls
are "from the coat of arms of Lombardy.
The first moneylenders in London were
Lombards."

SIR OSBERT SITWELL
[1892–   ]

Nothing exists which the British bour-
geoisie
Does not understand;
Therefore there is no death
— And, of course, no life.
> *At the House of Mrs. Kinfoot*

WENDELL LEWIS WILLKIE
[1892–1944]

There are no distant points in the
world any longer. . . . Our thinking
in the future must be world-wide
> *Radio Address [October 26, 1942]*
> *and One World [1943]. Chap. 1*

I believe the moral losses of expediency always far outweigh the temporary
gains. And I believe that every drop of
blood saved through expediency will
be paid for by twenty drawn by the
sword.[1]
> *One World. Chap. 4*

There exists in the world today a
gigantic reservoir of good will toward
us, the American people.
> *Ibid. Chap. 10*

Freedom is an indivisible word.[2] If
we want to enjoy it, and fight for it, we
must be prepared to extend it to everyone, whether they are rich or poor,
whether they agree with us or not, no
matter what their race or the color of
their skin.
> *Ibid. Chap. 13*

From the battlefields of Italy to the
gold-star homes here in America, Negroes have learned that there is nothing
more democratic than a bullet or a
splinter of steel.
> *An American Program [1944].*
> *Chap. 2*

The Constitution does not provide
for first and second class citizens.
> *Ibid.*

Our sovereignty is not something to
be hoarded, but something to be used.
> *Ibid. Chap. 7*

[1] See Lincoln, page 542a.
[2] See Litvinov, page 887a–887b.

FAITH BALDWIN
[1893–   ]

I think that Life has spared those mor-
tals much —
And cheated them of more — who have
not kept
A breathless vigil by the little bed
Of some beloved child.
> *Vigil*

MORRIS BISHOP
[1893–   ]

After the day is over
  And the passers-by are rare
The lights burn low in the barber-shop
  And the shades are drawn with care
To hide the haughty barbers
  Cutting each other's hair.
> *The Tales the Barbers Tell*

There I stood, and humbly scanned
  The miracle that sense appals,
And I watched the tourists stand
  Spitting in Niagara Falls.
> *Public Aid for Niagara Falls.*
> *Stanza 4*

OMAR BRADLEY
[1893–   ]

But it [Pearl Harbor], and the subsequent lessons we learned, day by day,
until September 1945, should have
taught all military men that our military forces are one team — in the game
to win regardless of who carries the
ball. This is no time for "fancy dans"
who won't hit the line with all they
have on every play, unless they can
call the signals. Each player on this
team — whether he shines in the spot-
light of the backfield or eats dirt in
the line — must be an all-American.
> *Testimony, Hearings Before the*
> *Committee on Armed Services,*
> *House of Representatives [Oc-*
> *tober 19, 1949]*

Red China is not the powerful nation
seeking to dominate the world. Frankly,
in the opinion of the Joint Chiefs of
Staff, this strategy would involve us in
the wrong war, at the wrong place, at

the wrong time, and with the wrong enemy.

> *Testimony, Hearings Before the Committee on Armed Services and the Committee on Foreign Affairs, U. S. Senate [May 15, 1951]*

ELIZABETH COATSWORTH
[1893–   ]

To a life that seizes
  Upon content,
Locality seems
  But accident.
> *To Daughters, Growing Up.
> Stanza 7*

JAMES BRYANT CONANT
[1893–   ]

Behavior which appears superficially correct but is intrinsically corrupt always irritates those who see below the surface.
> *Baccalaureate Address, Harvard College [June 17, 1934]*

Slogans are both exciting and comforting, but they are also powerful opiates for the conscience. . . . Some of mankind's most terrible misdeeds have been committed under the spell of certain magic words or phrases.
> *Ibid.*

He who enters a university walks on hallowed ground.
> *Notes on the Harvard Tercentenary [1936]*

Each honest calling, each walk of life, has its own elite, its own aristocracy based on excellence of performance.
> *Our Fighting Faith. "In This Country There Are No Classes"* [1]

Liberty like charity must begin at home.
> *Ibid. Our Unique Heritage* [2]

[1] Baccalaureate Sermon, June 16, 1940. The title is taken from a statement in an address by JAMES A. GARFIELD [1831–1881]: *The Future of the Republic: Its Dangers and its Hopes* [1873].

[2] Address, opening of the first wartime

The primary concern of American education today is not the development of the appreciation of the "good life" in young gentlemen born to the purple. . . . Our purpose is to cultivate in the largest possible number of our future citizens an appreciation of both the responsibilities and the benefits which come to them because they are Americans and are free.
> *Annual Report to the Board of Overseers, Harvard University* [1]
> *[January 11, 1943]*

HANS FALLADA
(RUDOLF DITZEN)
[1893–1947]

Little Man, What Now?
> *Title of novel [1932]*

HERMANN GOERING
[1893–1946]

Shoot first and inquire afterwards, and if you make mistakes, I will protect you.
> *Instruction for the Prussian Police, 1933*

HAROLD JOSEPH LASKI
[1893–1950]

It would be madness to let the purposes or the methods of private enterprise set the habits of the age of atomic energy.
> *Plan or Perish [1945]*

ANITA LOOS
[1893–   ]

Gentlemen always seem to remember blondes.
> *Gentlemen Prefer Blondes [1925].
> Chap. 1*

summer term, Harvard College, June 30, 1942.

[1] Describing his purpose, as President of Harvard University, in appointing a University Committee on the Objectives of a General Education in a Free Society. The committee's report was published [1945] under the title *General Education in a Free Society*.

She always believed in the old adage, "Leave them while you're looking good."
Gentlemen Prefer Blondes. Chap. 1

A girl never really looks as well as she does on board a steamship, or even a yacht.
Ibid.

JOHN PHILLIPS MARQUAND
[1893–]

It is worth while for anyone to have behind him a few generations of honest, hard-working ancestry.
The Late George Apley [*1937*]. *Chap. 3*

His father watched him across the gulf of years and pathos which always must divide a father from his son.
Ibid. Chap. 10

Marriage . . . is a damnably serious business, particularly around Boston.
Ibid. Chap. 11

There is a certain phase in the life of the aged when the warmth of the heart seems to increase in direct proportion with the years. This is a time of life when a solicitous family does well to watch affectionately over the vagaries of its unattached relatives, particularly of those who are comfortably off.
Ibid. Chap. 23

WILFRED OWEN
[1893–1918]

What passing-bells for these who died as cattle?
Only the monstrous anger of the guns.
Only the stuttering rifles' rapid rattle
Can patter out their hasty orisons.
The Anthem for Doomed Youth

DOROTHY PARKER
[1893–]

Where's the man could ease a heart
Like a satin gown?
The Satin Dress. Stanza 1

Yet this the need of woman, this her curse:
To range her little gifts, and give, and give,
Because the throb of giving's sweet to bear.
I Know I Have Been Happiest

Four be the things I am wiser to know:
Idleness, sorrow, a friend, and a foe.
Inventory

Four be the things I'd been better without:
Love, curiosity, freckles, and doubt.
Ibid.

And this is the sum of a lasting lore:
Scratch a lover, and find a foe.
Ballade of a Great Weariness. Stanza 1

Men seldom make passes
At girls who wear glasses.
News Item

Accursed from their birth they be
Who seek to find monogamy,
Pursuing it from bed to bed —
I think they would be better dead.
Reuben's Children

You are brief and frail and blue —
Little sisters, I am, too.
You are heaven's masterpieces —
Little loves, the likeness ceases.
Sweet Violets

Guns aren't lawful;
Nooses give;
Gas smells awful;
You might as well live.
Résumé

Why is it no one ever sent me yet
One perfect limousine, do you suppose?
Ah no, it's always just my luck to get
One perfect rose.
One Perfect Rose. Stanza 3

Then if my friendships break and bend,
There's little need to cry
The while I know that every foe
Is faithful till I die.
The Leal. Stanza 2

He lies below, correct in cypress wood,
And entertains the most exclusive worms.
Epitaph for a Very Rich Man

The man she had was kind and clean
And well enough for every day,

But, oh, dear friends, you should have
seen
The one that got away!
> *The Fisherwoman*

There was nothing more fun than a
man!
> *The Little Old Lady in
> Lavender Silk*

The affair between Margot Asquith
and Margot Asquith will live as one of
the prettiest love stories in all literature.
> *Review in the New Yorker of
> the Autobiography of Margot
> Asquith*

SIR HERBERT READ
[1893–   ]

The only literature which is at the
same time vital and popular is the literature of the music-hall.
> *Phases of English Poetry [1928]*

Poetry can never again become a
popular art until the poet gives himself
wholly to "the cadence of consenting
feet." [1]
> *Ibid.*

The no-man's-years between the
wars. [1919–1939]
> *Annals of Innocence and
> Experience [1940]*

JOACHIM VON
RIBBENTROP
[1893–1945]

The Führer is always right.
> *Königsberg address,
> August 24, 1939*

ROBERT LEROY RIPLEY
[1893–1949]

Believe It or Not.
> *Title of syndicated
> newspaper feature*

[1] The quotation is from FRANCIS BARTON
GUMMERE: *The Beginnings of Poetry* [1901].

DOROTHY LEIGH SAYERS
[1893–   ]

Death seems to provide the minds of
the Anglo-Saxon race with a greater
fund of innocent amusement than any
other single subject . . . the tale must
be about dead bodies or very wicked
people, preferably both, before the
Tired Business Man can feel really
happy.
> *The Third Omnibus of Crime
> [1935]. Introduction*

Do you promise that your Detectives
shall well and truly detect the Crimes
presented to them, using those Wits
which it shall please you to bestow
upon them and not placing reliance
upon, nor making use of, Divine Revelation, Feminine Intuition, Mumbo-
Jumbo, Jiggery-Pokery, Coincidence or
the Act of God?
> *The Mind of the Maker [1941].
> Chap. XI (Membership oath of
> the Detection Club, London,
> quoted by Miss Sayers)*

HAROLD CLAYTON UREY [1]
[1893–   ]

We need first of all to be thoroughly
frightened.
> *Speech on the Atomic Bomb,
> December 3, 1945*

The most dangerous situation that
humanity has ever faced in all history.
> *One World or None [1946].
> Chap. 2*

JOHN VAN ALSTYN WEAVER
[1893–1938]

Don't you ever try to go there —
It's to dream of, not to find.
Lovely things like that is always
Mostly in your mind.
> *Legend. Stanza 7*

Sure enough, the towers and castles
Went like lightnin' out of sight —
Nothin' there but filthy Jersey
On a drizzly night.
> *Ibid. Stanza 9*

[1] Winner of Nobel Prize for Physics, 1934.

WINIFRED WELLES
[1893–1939]

My squirrel with his tail curved up
Like half a silver lyre.
Silver for Midas. Stanza 4
Oh all you safe and smooth of heart
Listen to song from me,
Whose wooden throat was once a part
Of the north side of a tree! [1]
The Violin. Stanza 4

MAE WEST
[1893–   ]

Come up and see me sometime.
Diamond Lil [2] *[1932]*
Beulah, peel me a grape.
She Done Him Wrong [1933]

DON BLANDING
[1894–   ]

It's more than just an easy word for
casual good-bye;
It's gayer than a greeting, and it's sad-
der than a sigh.
Aloha Oe: Its Meaning
It's said a hundred different ways, in
sadness and in joy,
Aloha means "I love you." So I say
"Aloha Oe."
Ibid.

EDWARD ESTLIN
CUMMINGS [3]
[1894–   ]

All in green went my love riding
on a great horse of gold
into the silver dawn.
*All in green went my love riding
[1923]*

[1] Arbor viva, tacui; mortua, cano. (When
I was part of a living tree, I was silent; now
dead, I sing.) — *Inscription found on an old
violin*
[2] The play was later made into a movie,
She Done Him Wrong.
[3] The terror of typesetters, an enigma to
book reviewers, and the special target of all
the world's literary philistines. — *Publisher's
note, Modern Library edition of The Enormous Room*

Softer be they than slippered sleep
the lean lithe deer
the fleet flown deer.
All in green went my love riding
four lean hounds crouched low and
smiling
my heart fell dead before.
Ibid.
turning from the tremendous lie of
sleep
i watch the roses of the day grow deep.
*it is at moments after i have
dreamed [1923]*
Humanity i love you because
when you're hard up you pawn your
intelligence to buy a drink.
Humanity i love you [1925]
this is the garden: colours come and go,
frail azures fluttering from night's outer
wing
strong silent greens serenely lingering,
absolute lights like baths of golden
snow.
this is the garden [1925]
among
the slow deep trees perpetual of sleep
some silver-fingered fountain steals the
world.
Ibid
for life's not a paragraph
And death i think is no parenthesis.
Since feeling is first [1926]
along the brittle treacherous bright
streets
of memory comes my heart, singing like
an idiot, whispering like a drunken man

who(at a certain corner, suddenly)
meets
the tall policeman of my mind.
*along the brittle treacherous
bright streets [1926]*
nobody, not even the rain, has such
small hands
*somewhere i have never
travelled [1931]*
Always the beautiful answer who
asks a more beautiful question.
*Collected Poems [1938].
Introduction*
lady through whose profound and fragile lips

the sweet small clumsy feet of April
came
into the ragged meadow of my soul.
Collected Poems. 189
King Christ, this world is all aleak;
and lifepreservers there are none:
and waves which only He may walk
Who dares to call Himself a man.
Ibid. 258
open your thighs to fate and (if you can
withholding nothing) World, conceive
a man.
Ibid. 293
he sang his didn't he danced his did.
50 Poems. 29

RACHEL FIELD
[1894–1942]

You won't know why, and you can't
say now
Such a change upon you came,
But — once you have slept on an
island
You'll never be quite the same!
*If Once You Have Slept On An
Island* [*1926*]

ESTHER FORBES
[1894 ? –]

Women have almost a genius for
anti-climaxes.
O Genteel Lady! [*1926*]
Most American heroes of the Revolutionary period are by now two men,
the actual man and the romantic image.
Some are even three men — the actual
man, the image, and the debunked remains.
Paul Revere [*1942*]

AGNES KENDRICK GRAY
[1894–]

Sure, 'tis God's ways is very quare,
An' far beyont my ken,
How o' the selfsame clay he makes
Poets an' useful men.
The Shepherd to the Poet. Stanza 4

ALDOUS LEONARD HUXLEY
[1894–]

It is far easier to write ten passably
effective Sonnets, good enough to take
in the not too inquiring critic, than one
effective advertisement that will take in
a few thousand of the uncritical buying
public.
On the Margin [*1923*]
There are not enough *bon mots* in
existence to provide any industrious
conversationalist with a new stock for
every social occasion.
Point Counter Point [*1928*].
Chap. 7
A bad book is as much of a labour to
write as a good one; it comes as sin-
cerely from the author's soul.
Ibid. Chap. 13
There is no substitute for talent. In-
dustry and all the virtues are of no
avail.
Ibid.
Parodies and caricatures are the most
penetrating of criticisms.
Ibid. Chap. 28
There's only one corner of the uni-
verse you can be certain of improving,
and that's your own self.
Time Must Have a Stop [*1944*]
Blood of the world, time stanchless
flows;
The wound is mortal and is mine.
Seasons
Over her the swan shook slowly free
The folded glory of his wings, and made
A white-walled tent of soft and lumi-
nous shade.
Leda
A poor degenerate from the ape,
Whose hands are four, whose tail's a
limb,
I contemplate my flaccid shape
And know I may not rival him
Save with my mind.
First Philosopher's Song
But when the wearied Band
Swoons to a waltz, I take her hand,
And there we sit in peaceful calm
Quietly sweating palm to palm.
Frascati's

JOSEPH HENRY JACKSON
[1894–   ]

Did you ever hear anyone say "That work had better be banned because I might read it and it might be very damaging to me"?

In the San Francisco Chronicle
[*1953*]

CHARLES LANGBRIDGE MORGAN
[1894–   ]

The art of living does not consist in preserving and clinging to a particular mood of happiness, but in allowing happiness to change its form without being disappointed by the change; for happiness, like a child, must be allowed to grow up.

An English Retrospect [1]

Freedom from interruption may be counted by artists as not the least of the five freedoms.

A Fifth Freedom [2]

ROBERT NATHAN
[1894–   ]

Because my grief seems quiet and apart,
Think not for such a reason it is less.
True sorrow makes a silence in the heart,
Joy has its friends, but grief its loneliness.

A Cedar Box [*1929*]. *Sonnet VII*

Toward men and toward God, she maintained a respectful attitude, lightened by the belief that in a crisis she could deal adequately with either of them.

The Road of Ages [*1935*].
Chap. 2

Bells in the country,
They sing the heart to rest
When night is on the high road
And day is in the west.

Bells in the Country

[1] *Menander's Mirror, Times Literary Supplement,* London, May 20, 1944.
[2] *Menander's Mirror,* April 28, 1945.

It is but just that there should rise,
At peace beneath our Western skies,
From out the hearts of free-born men,
This little town again.[1]

Lidice. Stanza 2

WESTBROOK PEGLER
[1894–   ]

The Era of Wonderful Nonsense.[2]

Mr. Gump Himself

For the fifth year in succession I have pored over the catalogue of dogs in the show at Madison Square Garden without finding a dog named Rover, Towser, Sport, Spot or Fido.

Who is the man who can call from his back door at night: "Here, Champion Alexander of Clane o' Wind-Holme! Here, Champion Alexander of Clane o' Wind-Holme"?

Here, Rover!

I am a member of the rabble in good standing.

The Lynching Story

After a quiet study of the rules and tools of civilized table warfare your correspondent has decided that the French combine the greatest simplicity with the best results.

France in One Easy Lesson

PHELPS PUTNAM
[1894–1948]

We have insulted you as Lady Luck.

Hymn to Chance

Hard-boiled, unbroken egg, what can you care
For the enfolded passion of the Rose?

Hasbrouck and the Rose

[1] On July 12, 1942, a group of Americans, predominantly of Czech origin, renamed their town of Stern Park Garden, Illinois, in memory of Lidice, the village destroyed by Hitler. The inscription on a granite shaft reads: "In memory of the people of Lidice, Czechoslovakia, destroyed by barbarism but living forever in the hearts of all those who love freedom, this monument is erected by the free people of America at Lidice, Illinois."
[2] The period of spending and speculation during the "Coolidge Prosperity."

KENNETH CLAIBORNE ROYALL [1]
[1894–   ]

A "brass hat" is an officer of at least one rank higher than you whom you don't like and who doesn't like you.[2]
Speech, Chamber of Commerce, Wilson, North Carolina, February 15, 1946

BEARDSLEY RUML
[1894–   ]

It takes only a period of about a dozen years to implant a basic culture in the mind of man — the period between the age of two and the age of fourteen. In a psycho-biological sense, history, tradition and custom are only about twelve years old.
World Trade and Peace: Address, National Foreign Trade Convention, November 14, 1945

MARGARET E. SANGSTER
[1894–   ]

Oh, cakes and friends we should choose with care;
Not always the fanciest cake that's there
Is the best to eat! And the plainest friend
Is sometimes the finest one in the end!
French Pastry. Stanza 3

GENEVIEVE TAGGARD
[1894–1948]

Try tropic for your balm,
Try storm,
And after storm, calm.
Try snow of heaven, heavy, soft, and slow,
Brilliant and warm.
Nothing will help, and nothing do much harm.
Of the Properties of Nature for Healing an Illness. Stanza 1

[1] Brigadier-General in World War II.
[2] Some big brass hat from the War Office. —JAMES HILTON: *Good-bye, Mr. Chips* [1934], *Chap. 14*

Terror touches me when I
Dream I am touching a butterfly.
The Enamel Girl

Defiant even now, it tugs and moans
To be untangled from these mother's bones.
With Child. Stanza 3

JAMES THURBER
[1894–   ]

Well, if I called the wrong number, why did you answer the 'phone?
Caption for cartoon

The War Between Men and Women.
Series of cartoons

Humor is emotional chaos remembered in tranquillity.[1]
Quoted by MAX EASTMAN *in The Enjoyment of Laughter* [1936]

Is Sex Necessary?
Title of Book [1929] *written with* E. B. WHITE

Let Your Mind Alone.
Title of Book [1937]

Early to rise and early to bed makes a male healthy and wealthy and dead.
Fables for Our Time [1940]. *The Shrike and the Chipmunks*

You might as well fall flat on your face as lean over too far backward.
Ibid. The Bear Who Let It Alone

MARK VAN DOREN
[1894–   ]

Wit is the only wall
Between us and the dark.
Wit. Stanza 1

He talked, and as he talked
Wallpaper came alive;
Suddenly ghosts walked
And four doors were five.
The Story Teller. Stanza 1

Grass nibbling inward
Like green fire.
Former Barn Lot. Stanza 3

The sun
Drew semicircles smooth and high.

[1] See Wordsworth, page 406a.

A week was seven domes across a
  desert,
And any afternoon took long to die.
The Difference. Stanza 1

DUKE OF WINDSOR
(KING EDWARD VIII)
[1894–   ]

I have found it impossible to carry
the heavy burden of responsibility and
to discharge my duties as King as I
would wish to do without the help and
support of the woman I love.
Farewell broadcast after abdica-
tion [December 11, 1936]

RICHARD BUCKMINSTER
FULLER
[1895–   ]

We must think of our whole eco-
nomics in terms of a preventive pathol-
ogy instead of a curative pathology.
Don't oppose forces; use them.
God is a verb,
Not a noun.
No More Secondhand God

KING GEORGE VI
[1895–1952]

The highest of distinctions is service
to others.
Broadcast greeting to the em-
pire after his coronation, May
12, 1937
We shall prevail.
Broadcast on declaration of war,
September 3, 1939

ROBERT GRAVES
[1895–   ]

As you are woman, so be lovely:
As you are lovely, so be various,
Merciful as constant, constant as vari-
  ous,
So be mine, as I yours for ever.
Pygmalion to Galatea

With a fork drive Nature out,
She will ever yet return.[1]
Marigolds
Hate is a fear, and fear is rot
That cankers root and fruit alike:
Fight cleanly then, hate not, fear not,
Strike with no madness when you
  strike.
Hate Not, Fear Not
"How is your trade, Aquarius,
This frosty night?"
"Complaints is many and various,
And my feet are cold," says Aquarius.
Star Talk. Stanza 5
I do not love the Sabbath,
  The soapsuds and the starch,
The troops of solemn people
  Who to Salvation march.
The Boy Out of Church
Resolved that church and Sabbath
Were never made for man.[2]
Ibid.
A well-chosen anthology is a com-
plete dispensary of medicine for the
more common mental disorders, and
may be used as much for prevention
as cure.
On English Poetry. XXIX
"Blonde or dark, sir?" says enough
Whether of women, drink, or snuff.
Blonde or Dark?
Truth-loving Persians do not dwell
  upon
The trivial skirmish fought near Mara-
  thon.
The Persian Version

ROBERT HILLYER
[1895–   ]

Men lied to them, and so they went to
  die.
Thermopylae and Golgotha [1919]
We whom life changes with its every
  whim
Remember now his steadfastness. In
  him
Was a perfection, an unconscious grace,

---

[1] Naturam expelles furca, tamen usque re-
curret. — HORACE [65–8 B.C.]: *Epistles, I,*
10, 24
[2] See *Mark, II, 27,* on page 1055b.

Life could not mar, and death can not efface.

A Parting in April. In Memoriam: Le Baron Russell Briggs [1934]

Each finger nail a crimson petal, seen
Through a pale garnishing of nicotine.

A Letter to the Editor [1936]

Silence! the Columnist is on the sill! . . .
She enters with triumphant condescension
Exuding promises of Sunday mention.
Impishly coy, grandiloquent with power,
She bids await the inevitable hour
When printer's ink shall scatter her largesse
On writers who have won their own success.

Ibid.

ROBERT KEITH LEAVITT
[1895–   ]

People don't ask for facts in making up their minds. They would rather have one good, soul-satisfying emotion than a dozen facts.

Voyages and Discoveries [1939]

You do not have to shout. But if you whisper . . . the whisper had better be good.

Ibid. [1940]

LEWIS MUMFORD
[1895–   ]

People have hesitated to call Whitman's poems poetry; it is useless to deny that they belong to sacred literature.

The Golden Day [1926]. V

The jolly and comfortable bourgeois tradition of the Victorian age, a state of mind composed of felt slippers and warm bellywash.

Ibid. VIII

In Whitman and Melville letters

again became as racy as the jabber of a waterside saloon.

The Golden Day. VIII

EDWARD E. PARAMORE, JR.
[1895–   ]

Oh, the North Countree is a hard countree
That mothers a bloody brood;
And its icy arms hold hidden charms
For the greedy, the sinful and lewd.
And strong men rust, from the gold and the lust
That sears the Northland soul.

The Ballad of Yukon Jake [1921]

Oh, tough as a steak was Yukon Jake —
Hard-boiled as a picnic egg.

Ibid.

FULTON JOHN SHEEN
[1895–   ]

Baloney is flattery so thick it cannot be true, and blarney is flattery so thin we like it.

Address before the Ancient Order of Hibernians, Boston [December 3, 1938]

PIERRE VAN PAASSEN
[1895–   ]

That detached and baronial air of superiority the Briton habitually affects when circumstances beyond his control bring him into the presence of creatures of a lesser breed.

That Day Alone [1941]. Sect. I

Recklessness — that appearance of courage, which is not true courage.

Ibid. Sect. IV, 8

Half of our misery and weakness derives from the fact that we have broken with the soil and that we have allowed the roots that bound us to the earth to rot. We have become detached from the earth, we have abandoned her. And a man who abandons nature has begun to abandon himself.

Ibid. Sect. VI

LEON SAMSON
[*Floruit* 1930]

Money is the power of impotence.
The New Humanism [*1930*].
Page 206
The Diplomat sits in silence, watching the world with his ears.
Ibid. Page 291
Property is the pivot of civilization.
Ibid. Page 316
War is a transfer of property from nation to nation.
Ibid.
Revolution is a transfer of property from class to class.
Ibid.

JOHN RODERIGO DOS PASSOS
[1896–   ]

The chilly December day
two shivering bicycle mechanics from Dayton, Ohio,[1]
first felt their homemade contraption
whittled out of hickory sticks,
gummed together with Arnstein's bicycle cement,
stretched with muslin they'd sewn on their sister's sewingmachine in their own backyard on Hawthorn Street in Dayton, Ohio,
soar into the air
above the dunes and the wide beach at Kitty Hawk.[2]
The Big Money [*1936*]. (*The Campers at Kitty Hawk*)

IRA C. EAKER,[3]
[1896–   ]

I do not intend to do any talking until we have done more fighting, but this I can say now. I hope when we have gone you will all be glad we came.
Speech before Mayor, the Town Council and servicemen welcoming the American Eighth Air Force at High Wycombe, England, July, 1942

[1] The Wright brothers, Wilbur and Orville.
[2] December 17, 1903.
[3] Lieutenant General, United States Air Force.

IRWIN EDMAN
[1896–1954]

Whene'er with wild elation
Tremblingly I smite the lyre,
Comes the swift and kind damnation:
"He's a clever versifier."
The Curse of Faint Praise
The gift of gaiety may itself be the greatest good fortune, and the most serious step toward maturity.
In The Bookman [*May, 1926*]

F. SCOTT FITZGERALD
[1896–1940]

The victor belongs to the spoils.
The Beautiful and Damned [*1921*]
The test of a first-rate intelligence is the ability to hold two opposed ideas in the mind at the same time, and still retain the ability to function.
The Crack-up [*1936*]
In a real dark night of the soul it is always three o'clock in the morning.[1]
Ibid.
It was about then [1920] that I wrote a line which certain people will not let me forget: "She was a faded but still lovely woman of twenty-seven."
Early Success [*1937*]
Egyptian Proverb: The worst things:
To be in bed and sleep not,
To want for one who comes not,
To try to please and please not.
Note-Books[2]
The rhythm of the weekend, with its birth, its planned gaieties, and its announced end, followed the rhythm of life and was a substitute for it.
Ibid.
Show me a hero and I will write you a tragedy.
Ibid.
Fitzgerald. The rich are different from us.

[1] See Napoleon, page 400a.
[2] In *The Crack-up*, edited by Edmund Wilson [1945].

Hemingway. Yes, they have more money.

Note-Books [1]

It grows harder to write, because there is much less weather than when I was a boy and practically no men and women at all.

Ibid.

"I had to sink my yacht to make the guests go home."

Ibid.

Draw your chair up close to the edge of the precipice and I'll tell you a story.

Ibid.

It is in the thirties that we want friends. In the forties we know they won't save us any more than love did.

Ibid.

The easiest way to get a reputation is to go outside the fold, shout around for a few years as a violent atheist or a dangerous radical, and then crawl back to the shelter.

Ibid.

The hangover became a part of the day as well allowed-for as the Spanish siesta.

My Lost City [2]

HAROLD N. GILBERT
[1896–   ]

Keep 'em flying.
Slogan of the Air Forces, poster caption, World War II

LOUIS GINSBERG
[1896–   ]

Love that is hoarded moulds at last
Until we know some day
The only thing we ever have
Is what we give away.

Song. Stanza 1

GRAHAM LEE HEMMINGER
[1896–1949]

Tobacco is a dirty weed. I like it.
It satisfies no normal need. I like it.

[1] Quoted in a footnote by Edmund Wilson.
[2] In *The Crack-up*, edited by Edmund Wilson [1945].

It makes you thin, it makes you lean,
It takes the hair right off your bean.
It's the worst darn stuff I've ever seen.
I like it. [1]

Tobacco

JOE JACOBS
[1896–1940]

We was robbed!
After the fight between Max Schmeling and Jack Sharkey, June 21, 1932, when Sharkey had been awarded the decision and the heavyweight title, Jacobs, Schmeling's manager, shouted into the radio microphone this protest which was heard from coast to coast

I should of stood in bed.
Jacobs left a sick-bed to go to Detroit in October, 1935, to attend the World's Series. He bet on Chicago, which lost to Detroit. When he returned to New York he made this comment to the sports writers who came to interview him.

ERIC A. JOHNSTON
[1896–   ]

America and defeat cannot be made to rhyme.

America Unlimited [1944]

DODIE SMITH
[1896–   ]

I have found that sitting in a place where you have never sat before can be inspiring.

I Capture the Castle

DIXIE WILLSON
[1896–   ]

He may look just the same to you,
And he may be just as fine,
But the next-door dog is the next-door dog,
And mine — is — mine!

Next-Door Dog

[1] First published in *Penn State Froth*, November, 1915.

LUTHER W. YOUNGDAHL
[1896–   ]

When public excitement runs high as to alien ideologies, is the time when we must be particularly alert not to impair the ancient landmarks set up in the Bill of Rights.

United States v. *Lattimore, 112 F. Supp. 507, 518, May 2, 1953*

JOSEPH AUSLANDER
[1897–   ]

Spring had come
Like the silver needle-note of a fife,
Like a white plume and a green lance and a glittering knife
And a jubilant drum.

Steel

ELIZABETH ASQUITH BIBESCO
[1897–1945]

I have made a great discovery. What I love belongs to me. Not the chairs and tables in my house, but the masterpieces of the world.
It is only a question of loving them enough.

Balloons [*1923*]

Being in a hurry is one of the tributes he pays to life.

Ibid.

It is sometimes the man who opens the door who is the last to enter the room.

The Fir and the Palm [*1924*]. *Chap. 13*

You are such a wonderful Baedeker to life. All the stars are in the right places.

Ibid.

It is never any good dwelling on good-byes. It is not the being together that it prolongs, it is the parting.

Ibid. Chap. 15

BERNARD DE VOTO
[1897–   ]

New England is a finished place. Its destiny is that of Florence or Venice, not Milan, while the American empire careens onward toward its unpredicted end. . . . It is the first American section to be finished, to achieve stability in the conditions of its life. It is the first old civilization, the first permanent civilization in America.

New England: There She Stands. Harper's Magazine, March, 1932

The West begins where the average annual rainfall drops below twenty inches. When you reach the line which marks that drop — for convenience, the one hundredth meridian — you have reached the West.

The Plundered Province. Harper's Magazine, August, 1934

Pessimism is only the name that men of weak nerves give to wisdom.

Mark Twain: The Ink of History. Address, University of Missouri, December, 1935

Art is the terms of an armistice signed with fate.

Mark Twain at Work [*1942*]

The achieved West had given the United States something that no people had ever had before, an internal, domestic empire.

The Year of Decision [*1943*]

Between the amateur and the professional, . . . there is a difference not only in degree but in kind. The skillful man is, within the function of his skill, a different integration, a different nervous and muscular and psychological organization. . . . A tennis player or a watchmaker or an airplane pilot is an automatism but he is also criticism and wisdom.

Across the Wide Missouri [*1947*]

Novelists, whatever else they may be besides, are also children talking to children — in the dark.

The World of Fiction [*1950*]

You can no more keep a martini in the refrigerator than you can keep a kiss there. The proper union of gin and vermouth is a great and sudden glory; it is one of the happiest marriages on earth and one of the shortest-lived.

The Hour [*1951*]

The water of life was given to us to

make us see for a while that we are more nearly men and women, more nearly kind and gentle and generous, pleasanter and stronger, than without its vision there is any evidence we are.
The Hour [*1951*]

One of the facts which define the United States is that its national and its imperial boundaries are the same. Another is that it is a political unit which occupies a remarkably coherent geographical unit of continental extent.
The Course of Empire [*1952*]

History abhors determinism but cannot tolerate chance.
Ibid.

The dawn of knowledge is usually the false dawn.
Ibid.

SIR ANTHONY EDEN
[1897–   ]

Every succeeding scientific discovery makes greater nonsense of old-time conceptions of sovereignty.
Speech, House of Commons, November 22, 1945

WILLIAM FAULKNER
[1897–   ]

He [the writer] must teach himself that the basest of all things is to be afraid; and, teaching himself that, forget it forever, leaving no room in his workshop for anything but the old verities and truths of the heart, the old universal truths lacking which any story is ephemeral and doomed — love and honor and pity and pride and compassion and sacrifice.
Speech upon receiving the Nobel Prize, Stockholm, December 10, 1950

I decline to accept the end of man.
Ibid.

I believe that man will not merely endure: he will prevail.
Ibid.

PAUL JOSEPH GOEBBELS
[1897–1945]

We can do without butter, but, despite all our love of peace, not without arms. One cannot shoot with butter but with guns.[1]
Address in Berlin, January 17, 1936

DAVID McCORD
[1897–   ]

A handful of sand is an anthology of the universe.
Once and for All [*1929*].
Introduction

Call home the child, whose credulous
first hours
Burn at the heart of living, and surprise
The better reason with unbidden truth.
A Bucket of Bees [*1934*]

March is outside the door
Flaming some old desire
As man turns uneasily from his fire.
The Crows [*1934*]

The cricket's gone, we only hear machines;
In erg and atom they exact their pay.
And life is largely lived on silver screens,
And chemistry anneals the common clay.
Ballade of Time and Space [*1935*]

By and by
God caught his eye.
Epitaphs: The Waiter

Still for us where Cottons mather
In the spring the Willas cather
    As of yore.
And What's More: On Stopping at a New Hampshire Inn [*1941*]

I recommend for plain dis-ease
A good post-operative sneeze;
You might as well be on the rack
When every stitch takes up its slack.
Ibid. Convalescence: The Sneeze

[1] Probably the origin of the slogan, "Guns or butter," popularly attributed to Hermann Goering, who in a radio broadcast later in the year said: "Guns will make us powerful; butter will only make us fat."

The sun lies supple on the bricks;
I walk the fluent street.
> *Yellow Chartreuse* [*1941*]

I want to know not his earning power
but his yearning power.[1]
> *Epigram*

RUTH PITTER
[1897–   ]

Though our world burn, the small dim
    words
Stand here in steadfast grace,
And sing, like the indifferent birds
    About a ruined place.
> *On an Old Poem. Stanza 2*

I go about, but cannot find
The blood-relations of the mind.
> *The Lost Tribe. Stanza 1*

ERICH MARIA REMARQUE
[1897–   ]

The army report confined itself to
the single sentence: All quiet on the
Western Front.
> *All Quiet on the Western
Front* [2] [*1929*]

ANDERSON M. SCRUGGS
[1897–   ]

Yet after brick and steel and stone are
    gone,
And flesh and blood are dust, the dream
    lives on.
> *Sonnet. Only the Dream is Real*

THORNTON NIVEN WILDER
[1897–   ]

The whole purport of literature,
which is the notation of the heart. Style
is but the faintly contemptible vessel
in which the bitter liquid is recommended to the world.
> *The Bridge of San Luis Rey*
> [*1927*]. *II*

[1] There are three ingredients in the good
life: learning, earning, and yearning. —
CHRISTOPHER MORLEY: *Parnassus on Wheels*
[1917], *Chap. 10*
[2] Im Westen Nichts Neues.

For what human ill does not dawn
seem to be an alleviation?
> *The Bridge of San Luis Rey. III*

We come from a world where we
have known incredible standards of excellence, and we dimly remember beauties which we have not seized again.
> *Ibid. IV*

A man looks pretty small at a wedding, George. All those good women
standing shoulder to shoulder, making
sure that the knot's tied in a mighty
public way.
> *Our Town* [*1938*]

The dead don't stay interested in us
living people for very long. Gradually,
gradually, they let go hold of the earth
. . . and the ambitions they had . . .
and the pleasures they had . . . and
the things they suffered . . . and the
people they loved. They get weaned
away from earth — that's the way I
put it, weaned away.
> *Ibid.*

That's what it was to be alive. To
move about in a cloud of ignorance; to
go up and down trampling on the feelings of those about you. To spend and
waste time as though you had a million years. To be always at the mercy
of one self-centered passion, or another. Now you know — that's the
happy existence you wanted to go back
to.
> *Ibid.*

STEPHEN VINCENT BENÉT
[1898–1943]

I died in my boots like a pioneer
With the whole wide sky above me.
> *The Ballad of William Sycamore*

He could fiddle all the bugs off a sweet-
    potato-vine.
> *The Mountain Whippoorwill*
> [*1923*]. *Stanza 22*

Oh, Georgia booze is mighty fine booze,
The best yuh ever poured yuh,
But it eats the soles right offen yore
    shoes,
For Hell's broke loose in Georgia.
> *Ibid. Stanza 48*

He cleansed and anointed, took fresh
    apparel,
And worshiped the Lord in a tuneful
    carol.
      King David [*1923*]. *Part VI,*
                Stanza 5

Down where the taproots of New Eng-
    land trees
Suck bare existence from the broken
    stones.
      The Golden Corpse [*1925*].
                Sonnet 4

The years have hardier tasks
Than listening to a whisper or a sigh.
They creep among us with a bag of
    masks
And fit them to our brows obsequiously.
              Ibid. Sonnet 5

I have fallen in love with American
    names,
The sharp names that never get fat,
The snakeskin-titles of mining-claims,
The plumed war-bonnet of Medicine
    Hat,
Tucson and Deadwood and Lost Mule
    Flat.
      American Names [*1927*]. *Stanza 1*

American Muse, whose strong and
    diverse heart
So many men have tried to understand
But only made it smaller with their
    art,
Because you are as various as your
    land.
      John Brown's Body [*1928*].
                Invocation

Thames and all the rivers of the kings
Ran into Mississippi and were drowned.
                    Ibid.

Honesty rare as a man without self-
    pity,
Kindness as large and plain as a prairie
    wind.
                    Ibid.

The small, dim noises, thousand-fold,
That all old houses and forests hold.
                Ibid. Book 2

Make war on the men — the ladies
    have too-long memories.
               Ibid. Book 4

Broad-streeted Richmond . . .
The trees in the streets are old trees
    used to living with people,
Family-trees that remember your
    grandfather's name.
      John Brown's Body. Book 4

Stonewall Jackson, wrapped in his
    beard and his silence.
                    Ibid.

Such horses are
The jewels of the horseman's hands
    and thighs,
They go by the word and hardly need
    the rein.
                    Ibid.

A great victor, in defeat as great,
No more, no less, always himself in
    both.
                    Ibid.

The ant finds kingdoms in a foot of
    ground.
                    Ibid.

But all of them are sure they know
    God's will.
I am the only man who does not know
    it.
                Ibid. Book 5

"Let us cross the river," he said, "and
    rest under the shade of the trees." [1]
                Ibid. Book 6

Sherman's buzzin' along to de sea,
Like Moses ridin' on a bumblebee.
                Ibid. Book 8

Rolling, rolling from Arkansas, Kansas,
    Iowa,
Rolling from Ohio, Wisconsin, Illinois,
Rolling and shouting:
Till, at last, it is Mississippi,
The Father of Waters. [2]
      Ode to Walt Whitman [*1935*]. *I*

This is the man they ate at the green
    table
Pulling their gloves on ere they touched
    the meat.
This is the fruit of war, the fruit of
    peace,

---

[1] Stonewall Jackson's last words actually
were, "Let us cross the river and rest in the
shade." [May 10, 1863]
[2] See Lincoln, page 540b.

The ripeness of invention, the new lamb.
> *Litany for Dictatorships* [*1936*]

We thought we were done with these things but we were wrong.
We thought, because we had power, we had wisdom.
> *Ibid.*

Our fathers and ourselves sowed dragon's teeth.
Our children know and suffer the armed men.
> *Ibid.*

If two New Hampshiremen aren't a match for the devil, we might as well give the country back to the Indians.
> *The Devil and Daniel Webster* [*1936*]

Even the damned may salute the eloquence of Mr. Webster.
> *Ibid.*

The fall with his sachem colors, the summer wind by the shore,
The spring like an Indian runner, beautiful, stripped, and swift,
They knew these things in their season
— and yet there was something more
And they thought not only of harvest, when they thanked their God for His gift.
> *Ode for the Tercentenary of the Founding of New Haven, Connecticut, June 6, 1938*

Our earth is but a small star in the great universe. Yet of it we can make, if we choose, a planet unvexed by war, untroubled by hunger or fear, undivided by senseless distinctions of race, color or theory.
> *Prayer, written for and read by President Franklin D. Roosevelt to the United Nations on Flag Day, June 14, 1942*

They were half of the first families in Virginia.
Well, where do you start, when you start counting F.F.V.s?
> *Western Star* [*1943*]. *Book I, Page 81*

That queer sense of relief and shame
Which comes to those who make sensible decisions.
> *Western Star. Book I, Page 128*

There were human beings aboard the Mayflower,
Not merely ancestors.
> *Ibid. Page 133*

Remember that when you say
"I will have none of this exile and this stranger
For his face is not like my face and his speech is strange,"
You have denied America with that word.
> *Ibid. Page 180*

HORACE GREGORY
[1898–   ]

My boyhood saw
Greek islands floating over Harvard Square.[1]
> *Chorus for Survival. XIV*

CECILY R. HALLACK
[1898–1938]

Lord of the pots and pipkins, since I have no time to be
A saint by doing lovely things and vigilling with Thee,
By watching in the twilight dawn, and storming Heaven's gates,
Make me a saint by getting meals and washing up the plates!
> *The Divine Office of the Kitchen. Stanza 1*

CLIVE STAPLES LEWIS
[1898–   ]

The safest road to Hell is the gradual one — the gentle slope, soft underfoot, without sudden turnings, without milestones, without signposts.
> *The Screwtape Letters* [*1941*]. *XII*

The Future is something which everyone reaches at the rate of sixty minutes an hour, whatever he does, whoever he is.
> *Ibid. XXV*

[1] The speaker in the poem is Emerson.

The long, dull, monotonous years of middle-aged prosperity or middle-aged adversity are excellent campaigning weather [for the Devil].

The Screwtape Letters. XXVIII

ANTHONY CLEMENT McAULIFFE
[1898–　　]

Nuts!

Reply [December 23, 1944] to German major and captain who brought an ultimatum from their commander, demanding the surrender of the men of the 101st Airborne Division who had been trapped for seven days at Bastogne

DONALD CULROSS PEATTIE
[1898　　　]

It is natural that women should like the birds whose domestic affairs can be observed under the eaves; they love the sweetest singers, the brightest plumage, the species not too shy to be seen at close range. For them the waders and swimmers, the awkward of leg, the harsh of cry, the wild of soul, have seldom the same appeal. But that which flees from men, that will men have. Women of all people ought to understand this, but they do not, quite.

An Almanac for Moderns [1935].
November 9

In Thomas Henry Huxley Darwinism had a champion in invincible armor. For sheer glitter his mind has seldom had an equal in any land or age and he laid waste about him with the weapon of truth. "The cradle of every science," he chuckled, "is surrounded by dead theologians as that of Hercules was with strangled serpents."

Ibid. February 13

The beauty of a butterfly's wing, the beauty of all things, is not a slave to purpose, a drudge sold to futurity. It is excrescence, superabundance, random ebullience, and sheer delightful waste to be enjoyed in its own high right.

An Almanac for Moderns.
March 13

The time to hear bird music is between four and six in the morning. Seven o'clock is not too late, but by eight the fine rapture is over, due, I suspect, to the contentment of the inner man that comes with breakfast; a poet should always be hungry or have a lost love.

Ibid. April 22

AMELIA EARHART PUTNAM
[1898–1937]

Courage is the price that life exacts for
　granting peace.
The soul that knows it not, knows no
　release
From little things.

Courage

DOROTHY E. REID

A goosegirl ermined is a goosegirl still
And geese will gabble everywhere she
　goes.

Not in Andersen

LOUIS ADAMIC
[1899–1951]

There is a certain blend of courage, integrity, character and principle which has no satisfactory dictionary name but has been called different things at different times in different countries. Our American name for it is "guts."

A Study in Courage [1] *[1944]*

NOEL COWARD
[1899–　　]

Mad dogs and Englishmen go out in
　the mid-day sun;
The Japanese don't care to, the Chinese
　wouldn't dare to;
Hindus and Argentines sleep firmly
　from twelve to one,
But Englishmen detest a siesta.

Mad Dogs and Englishmen

[1] An essay on Marshal Tito of Yugoslavia.

In Rangoon the heat of noon is just
    what the natives shun . . .
In Bangkok at twelve o'clock they foam
    at the mouth and run . . .
In Bengal to move at all is seldom if
    ever done.
        Mad Dogs and Englishmen

HART CRANE
[1899–1932]

Adagios of islands, O my Prodigal.
        Voyages [*1926*]. *II*
Damp tonnage and alluvial march of
    days . . .
Tortured with history, its one will —
    flow.
    The Bridge [*1930*]. *The River*
                (Mississippi)
Bunched in mutual glee
The bearings glint, — O murmurless
    and shined
In oilrinsed circles of blind ecstasy!
        Ibid. The Power House
O, early following thee, I searched the
    hill
Blue-writ and odor-firm with violets.
        To Walt Whitman
Why do I often meet your visage here,[1]
Your eyes like agate lanterns — on and
    on
Below the toothpaste and the dandruff
    ads?
    The Tunnel (*New York Subway*)

ERNEST HAYCOX
[1899–1950]

No sensible man watches his feet
hit ground. He looks ahead to see what
kind of ground they'll hit next.
    Pioneer Loves. Call This
                Land Home

ERNEST HEMINGWAY [2]
[1899–   ]

The real thing, the sequence of motion and fact which made the emotion
and which would be as valid in a year

---

[1] Edgar Allan Poe.
[2] Awarded the Nobel Prize in 1954 for
The Old Man and the Sea [1952].

or in ten years or, with luck and if you
stated it purely enough, always, was
beyond me and I was working very
hard to try to get it.
    Death in the Afternoon [*1932*].
                Chap. 1

So far, about morals, I know only
that what is moral is what you feel
good after and what is immoral is what
you feel bad after.
        Ibid.

All our words from loose using have
lost their edge.
        Ibid. Chap. 7

Bullfighting is the only art in which
the artist is in danger of death and in
which the degree of brilliance in the
performance is left to the fighter's
honor.
        Ibid. Chap. 9

When writing a novel a writer should
create living people; people not characters. A *character* is a caricature.
        Ibid. Chap. 16

Prose is architecture, not interior
decoration, and the Baroque is over.
        Ibid.

There are some things which cannot
be learned quickly, and time, which is
all we have, must be paid heavily for
their acquiring. They are the very simplest things and because it takes a
man's life to know them the little new
that each man gets from life is very
costly and the only heritage he has to
leave.
        Ibid.

Every novel which is truly written
contributes to the total of knowledge
which is there at the disposal of the
next writer who comes, but the next
writer must pay, always, a certain
nominal percentage in experience to
be able to understand and assimilate
what is available as his birthright and
what he must, in turn, take his departure from.
        Ibid.

A serious writer is not to be confused with a solemn writer. A serious

writer may be a hawk or a buzzard or even a popinjay, but a solemn writer is always a bloody owl.
Death in the Afternoon. Chap. 16

A growing ecstasy of ordered, formal, passionate, increasing disregard for death. . . . It is impossible to believe the emotional and spiritual intensity and pure, classic beauty that can be produced by a man, an animal and a piece of scarlet serge draped over a stick.
Ibid. Chap. 18

All modern American literature comes from one book by Mark Twain called *Huckleberry Finn.* If you read it you must stop where the Nigger Jim is stolen from the boys. That is the real end. The rest is just cheating. But it's the best book we've had. All American writing comes from that. There was nothing before. There has been nothing as good since.
The Green Hills of Africa [*1935*]. *Chap. 1*

Not this August, nor this September; you have this year to do in what you like. Not next August, nor next September; that is still too soon; they are still too prosperous from the way things pick up when armament factories start at near capacity; they never fight as long as money can still be made without. . . . But the year after that or the year after that they fight.
Notes on the Next War [1]

The Fifth Column. [2]
Title of play [*1938*]

The world is a fine place and worth fighting for.
For Whom the Bell Tolls [*1940*]

And he felt the earth move out and away from under them.
Ibid.

[1] In *Esquire,* September, 1935.
[2] The phrase originated in a radio address by one of Franco's generals, Emilio Mola, during the Spanish Civil War [1936–1939]. He was leading four columns of troops against Madrid, and boasted that he had a "fifth column" of sympathizers within Madrid who would support him.

Cowardice, as distinguished from panic, is almost always simply a lack of ability to suspend the functioning of the imagination. Learning to suspend your imagination and live completely in the very second of the present with no before and no after is the greatest gift a soldier can acquire.
Men at War [*1942*]. *Introduction*

Easy writing makes hard reading.
Quoted in SAMUEL PUTNAM, *Paris Was Our Mistress* [*1947*]

The first and most important thing of all, at least for writers today, is to strip language clean, to lay it bare down to the bone.
Ibid.

All good books are alike in that they are truer than if they had really happened and after you are finished reading one you will feel that all that happened to you and afterwards it all belongs to you; the good and the bad, the ecstasy, the remorse and sorrow, the people and the places and how the weather was. If you can get so that you can give that to people, then you are a writer.
Quoted in CARLOS BAKER, *Hemingway: The Writer as Artist* [*1952*], *Chap. 3*

ROBERT MAYNARD HUTCHINS
[1899–　]

The most distressing aspect of the world into which you are going is its indifference to the basic issues, which now, as always, are moral issues.
Convocation Address, University of Chicago, June, 1945

We call Japanese soldiers fanatics when they die rather than surrender, whereas American soldiers who do the same thing are heroes.
Ibid.

A world community means common understanding, a common tradition, common ideas, and common ideals.

. . . The task is overwhelming, and the chance of success is slight. We must take the chance or die.

The Atomic Bomb versus Civilization, December, 1945

We do not know what education could do for us, because we have never tried it.

Ibid.

The policy of repression of ideas cannot work and never has worked.

Testimony before the Boyles Committee [*1949*]

ERIC LINKLATER
[1899–   ]

Scratch my back with a garden rake.

The Pirates in the Deep Green Sea [*1949*]. *Chap. 2*

ALAN PORTER
[1899–1942]

Every countenance
That warms and lights the heart of the beholder
Shews, clear and true, the signature of pain.

The Signature of Pain

Let him that beds a princess fear
To show himself too free,
And ceremoniously draw near:
There should between true lovers be
An excellent immodesty.

A Plea That Shame Be Forgotten

I am not one that would be thinned
Into an immaterial wind:
I have no longing to be seen
A part of April's fledge of green,
Or burn where summer suns have been.

Death. Stanza 2

Were death forgotten, days were white
Circles of unimpaired delight.

Ibid. Stanza 4

LELAND STOWE
[1899–   ]

An American will tinker with anything he can put his hands on. But how

rarely can he be persuaded to tinker with an abstract idea.

They Shall Not Sleep [*1944*]

E. B. WHITE
[1899–   ]

The critic leaves at curtain fall
To find, in starting to review it,
He scarcely saw the play at all
For watching his reaction to it.

Critic

All poets who, when reading from their own works, experience a choked feeling, are major. For that matter, all poets who read from their own works are major, whether they choke or not.

How to Tell a Major Poet from a Minor Poet

"It's broccoli, dear."
"I say it's spinach, and I say the hell with it."

Caption for cartoon by Carl Rose in The New Yorker

Commuter — one who spends his life
In riding to and from his wife;
A man who shaves and takes a train
And then rides back to shave again.

Commuter

It is easier for a man to be loyal to his club than to his planet; the by-laws are shorter, and he is personally acquainted with the other members.

One Man's Meat

Democracy is the recurrent suspicion that more than half of the people are right more than half of the time.

World Government and Peace [1]

His words leap across rivers and mountains, but his thoughts are still only six inches long.

Ibid.

Everybody likes to hear about a man laying down his life for his country, but nobody wants to hear about a country giving her shirt for her planet.

Ibid.

[1] Reprinted from *The New Yorker*, 1943–1945.

OSCAR WILLIAMS
[1900–   ]

The prodigious exuberance of the miniature human beings
Tests the chutes of gravitation, seventeen trees from the zoo.
                The Children's Playground
Get up and out, my man, the day is
bursting with moments . . .
Rise, my good man, from your bed of
straws in the wind.
                            The Answer

DENIS WILLIAM BROGAN
[1900–   ]

The Englishman is interested in contemporary America. It evokes no response to tell him that Boston is like
an English town. He has seen quite
enough English towns and would rather
hear about New York or Chicago,
which are not like English towns.
                The English People [1943]
American social fences have to be
continually repaired; in England they
are like wild hedges; they grow if left
alone.
                            Ibid.
A people that has licked a more
formidable enemy than Germany or
Japan, primitive North America . . .
a country whose national motto has
been "root, hog, or die."
            The American Character [1944]
Any well-established village in New
England or the northern Middle West
could afford a town drunkard, a town
atheist, and a few Democrats.
                            Ibid.

JOHN MASON BROWN
[1900–   ]

Brutus seemed no more than a re-
sounding set of vocal cords wrapped up
in a toga.
                Two on the Aisle [1938]
To many people dramatic criticism
must seem like an attempt to tattoo
soap bubbles.
                Broadway in Review [1940]

Death re-creates an individual out of
someone who has fallen singly from the
ranks. In his loneliness by a foreign
roadside, this man or that ceases to be
Government Issue, a mass commodity
produced by a mass response out of
a mass need and hope. He once again
becomes man's issue, and woman's, too.
                Many a Watchful Night [1944]

ELIZABETH, QUEEN MOTHER OF ENGLAND
[1900–   ]

The children will not leave unless I
do. I shall not leave unless their father
does, and the King will not leave the
country in any circumstances whatever.
                Reported answer to press query
                regarding the Princesses' leaving
                England after the bombing of
                Buckingham Palace in 1940

JAMES HILTON
[1900–1954]

Anno domini — that's the most fatal
complaint of all in the end.
                Good-bye, Mr. Chips [1934].
                            Chap. 1
The austere serenity of Shangri-La.
Its forsaken courts and pale pavilions
shimmered in repose from which all the
fret of existence had ebbed away, leaving a hush as if moments hardly dared
to pass.
                Lost Horizon [1933]. *Chap. 5*
When the High Lama asked him
whether Shangri-La was not unique in
his experience, and if the Western
world could offer anything in the least
like it, he answered with a smile: "Well,
yes — to be quite frank it reminds me
very slightly of Oxford."
                            Ibid. Chap. 9
Perhaps the exhaustion of the passions is the beginning of wisdom, if you
care to alter the proverb. That also, my
son, is the doctrine of Shangri-La.
                            Ibid. Chap. 10
Memory put a red star in the corner
like pictures in a gallery that get sold.
                Time and Time Again [1953]

If you forgive people enough you belong to them, and they to you, whether either person likes it or not — squatter's rights of the heart.

Time and Time Again

RICHARD HUGHES
[1900–]

Puddings should be
Full of currants, for me:
Boiled in a pail,
Tied in the tail
Of an old bleached shirt:
So hot that they hurt.

Poets, Painters, Puddings

MARTHA OSTENSO
[1900–]

Pity the Unicorn,
Pity the Hippogriff,
Souls that were never born
Out of the land of If!

*The Unicorn and the Hippogriff.
Stanza 1*

ERNIE PYLE
[1900–1945]

I write from the worm's-eye point of view.

Here Is Your War [*1943*]

If you go long enough without a bath even the fleas will let you alone.

Ibid.

Then darkness enveloped the whole American armada. Not a pinpoint of light showed from those hundreds of ships as they surged on through the night toward their destiny, carrying across the ageless and indifferent sea tens of thousands of young men, fighting for . . . for . . . well, at least for each other.[1]

Brave Men [*1944*]

ADLAI STEVENSON
[1900–]

More important than winning the election, is governing the nation. That

[1] Description of the Normandy beachhead, June, 1944.

is the test of a political party — the acid, final test.

*Speech accepting nomination,
Democratic National Convention, Chicago, July 26, 1952*

Let's talk sense to the American people. Let's tell them the truth, that there are no gains without pains.

Ibid.

What do we mean by patriotism in the context of our times? . . . A patriotism that puts country ahead of self; a patriotism which is not short, frenzied outbursts of emotion, but the tranquil and steady dedication of a lifetime. There are words that are easy to utter, but this is a mighty assignment. For it is often easier to fight for principles than to live up to them.[1]

*Speech, New York City,
August 27, 1952*

When an American says that he loves his country, he means not only that he loves the New England hills, the prairies glistening in the sun, the wide and rising plains, the great mountains, and the sea. He means that he loves an inner air, an inner light in which freedom lives and in which a man can draw the breath of self-respect.

Ibid.

This is the first time I have ever heard of a party going into battle under the slogan, "Throw the rascals in."

*Speech, Phoenix, Arizona,
September 12, 1952*

A hungry man is not a free man.

*Speech, Kasson, Minnesota,
September 6, 1952*

A wise man does not try to hurry history.

*Speech, San Francisco,
September 9, 1952*

The time to stop a revolution is at the beginning, not the end.

Ibid.

Your public servants serve you right.

*Speech, Los Angeles,
September 11, 1952*

[1] See Thackeray, page 565b.

Those who corrupt the public mind are just as evil as those who steal from the public purse.

Speech, Albuquerque, New Mexico, September 12, 1952

Nature is neutral. Man has wrested from nature the power to make the world a desert or to make the deserts bloom. There is no evil in the atom; only in men's souls.[1]

Speech, Hartford, Connecticut, September 18, 1952

Government [in a democracy] cannot be stronger or more tough-minded than its people. It cannot be more inflexibly committed to the task than they. It cannot be wiser than the people.

Speech, Chicago, September 29, 1952

As citizens of this democracy, you are the rulers and the ruled, the lawgivers and the law-abiding, the beginning and the end.

Ibid.

VIOLET ALLEYN STOREY
[1900–   ]

I have a small-town soul.
It makes me want to know
Wee, unimportant things
About the folks that go
Past on swift journeyings.

Ironical

WILLIAM LINDSAY WHITE
[1900–   ]

They Were Expendable.

Title of book [1942]

THOMAS WOLFE
[1900–1938]

Which of us has known his brother? Which of us has looked into his father's heart? Which of us has not remained forever prison-pent? Which of us is not forever a stranger and alone?

Look Homeward, Angel! [2] [*1929*]. *Foreword*

[1] See J. Robert Oppenheimer, page 992b.
[2] See Milton, page 249b.

Most of the time we think we're sick, it's all in the mind.

Look Homeward, Angel! Part I, 1

Making the world safe for hypocrisy.

Ibid. Part III, 36

It is Europeans, for the most part, who have constructed these great ships, but without America they have no meaning. These ships are alive with the supreme ecstasy of the modern world, which is the voyage to America.

Of Time and the River [*1935*]. *Book VIII*

The young men of this land are not, as they are often called, a "lost" race — they are a race that never yet has been discovered. And the whole secret, power, and knowledge of their own discovery is locked within them — they know it, feel it, have the whole thing in them — and they cannot utter it.

The Web and the Rock [*1939*]. *Chap. 13*

There is no spectacle on earth more appealing than that of a beautiful woman in the act of cooking dinner for someone she loves.

Ibid. Chap. 28

If a man has a talent and cannot use it, he has failed. If he has a talent and uses only half of it, he has partly failed. If he has a talent and learns somehow to use the whole of it, he has gloriously succeeded, and won a satisfaction and a triumph few men ever know.

Ibid. Chap. 30

EMPEROR HIROHITO OF JAPAN
[1901–   ]

The ties between us and our people have always stood upon mutual trust and affection. They do not depend upon mere legends and myths. They are not predicated on the false conception that the Emperor is divine and that the Japanese people are superior to other races and fated to rule the world.

New Year Rescript [*1946*]

CORNELIA OTIS SKINNER
[1901–]

Woman's virtue is man's greatest invention.

Paris '90

CORNELIA OTIS SKINNER
[1901–]
AND
EMILY KIMBROUGH
[1899–]

We were young enough still to harbor the glad illusion that organized forms of get-together were commendable.

Our Hearts Were Young and Gay

JAN STRUTHER
[1901–1952]

She saw every personal relationship as a pair of intersecting circles. . . . Probably perfection is reached when the area of the two outer crescents, added together, is exactly equal to that of the leaf-shaped piece in the middle. On paper there must be some neat mathematical formula for arriving at this; in life, none.

Mrs. Miniver [*1940*]

It took me forty years on earth
To reach this sure conclusion:
There is no Heaven but clarity,
No Hell except confusion.

All Clear

CHARLES A. WAGNER
[1901–]

When I loved you and you loved me,
You were the sky, the sea, the tree.
Now skies are skies, and seas are seas,
And trees are brown and they are trees.

When I Loved You

ROY CAMPBELL
[1902–]

You praise the firm restraint with
which they write —
I'm with you there, of course:

They use the snaffle and the curb all
right,
But where's the bloody horse?

On Some South African Novelists

We had no time for make-believe
So early each began
To wear his liver on his sleeve,
To snarl, and be an angry man.

Poets in Africa. Stanza 2

I love to see, when leaves depart,
The clear anatomy arrive,
Winter, the paragon of art,
That kills all forms of life and feeling
Save what is pure and will survive.

Autumn. Stanza 1

THOMAS EDMUND DEWEY
[1902–]

That's why it's time for a change.[1]

*Campaign speech, San Francisco,
September 21, 1944*

DANIEL WHITEHEAD HICKY
[1902–]

No friend like music when the last
word's spoken
And every pleading is a plea in vain;
No friend like music when the heart is
broken,
To mend its wings and give it flight
again.

No Friend Like Music

LANGSTON HUGHES
[1902–]

De railroad bridge's
A sad song in de air.
Ever' time de trains pass
I wants to go somewhere.

Homesick Blues. Stanza 1

I swear to the Lord
I still can't see
Why Democracy means
Everybody but me.

The Black Man Speaks

[1] The phrase was used extensively in the campaigns of 1944, 1948, and 1952.

CHARLES AUGUSTUS LINDBERGH
[1902–   ]

We (that's my ship and I) took off rather suddenly. We had a report somewhere around 4 o'clock in the afternoon before that the weather would be fine, so we thought we would try it.
Lindbergh's Own Story, in The New York Times, May 23, 1927

I saw a fleet of fishing boats. . . . I flew down almost touching the craft and yelled at them, asking if I was on the right road to Ireland.
They just stared. Maybe they didn't hear me. Maybe I didn't hear them. Or maybe they thought I was just a crazy fool. An hour later I saw land.
Ibid.

OGDEN NASH
[1902–   ]

O money, money, money, I'm not necessarily one of those who think thee holy,
But I often stop to wonder how thou canst go out so fast when thou comest in so slowly.
Hymn to the Thing That Makes the Wolf Go [1]

There are two kinds of people who blow through life like a breeze,
And one kind is gossipers, and the other kind is gossipees.
I'm a Stranger Here Myself. I Have It on Good Authority

Another good thing about gossip is that it is within everybody's reach,
And it is much more interesting than any other form of speech.
Ibid.

Bankers Are Just Like Anybody Else, Except Richer
Ibid. Verse title

[1] From the *New York American*, January, 1934.

Dogs display reluctance and wrath
If you try to give them a bath.
They bury bones in hideaways
And half the time they trot sideaways.
I'm a Stranger Here Myself. An Introduction to Dogs, Stanza 4

City people always want the most faucets
And the comfortablest caucets.
Ibid. The City, Stanza 4

Barmaids Are Diviner Than Mermaids
Ibid. Verse title

There was a young belle of old Natchez
Whose garments were always in patchez.
When comment arose
On the state of her clothes,
She drawled, When Ah itchez, Ah scratchez!
Ibid. Requiem

There is only one way to achieve happiness on this terrestrial ball,
And that is to have either a clear conscience, or none at all.
Ibid. Inter-Office Memorandum

Sleep is perverse as human nature,
Sleep is perverse as a legislature,
Sleep is as forward as hives or goiters,
And where it is least desired, it loiters.
The Face Is Familiar. Read This Vibrant Exposé

Home is heaven and orgies are vile,
But I like an orgy, once in a while.
Ibid. Home, 99 44/100% Sweet Home

Women would rather be right than reasonable.
Good Intentions. Frailty, Thy Name Is a Misnomer

Candy
Is dandy
But liquor
Is quicker.
Many Long Years Ago. Reflections on Ice-Breaking

I think that I shall never see
A billboard lovely as a tree.
Indeed, unless the billboards fall
I'll never see a tree at all.
Ibid. Song of the Open Road

One would be in less danger
From the wiles of the stranger
If one's own kin and kith
Were more fun to be with.
Many Long Years Ago.
Family Court

The turtle lives 'twixt plated decks
Which practically conceal its sex.
I think it clever of the turtle
In such a fix to be so fertile.
Ibid. The Turtle

They have such refined and delicate
palates
That they can discover no one worthy
of their ballots,
And then when someone terrible gets
elected
They say, There, that's just what I expected!
Ibid. Election Day Is a Holiday

A bit of talcum
Is always walcum.
Ibid. Reflection on Babies

The old men know when an old man
dies.
Ibid. Old Men

There is something about a Martini,
A tingle remarkably pleasant;
A yellow, a mellow Martini;
I wish that I had one at present.
There is something about a Martini,
Ere the dining and dancing begin,
And to tell you the truth,
It is not the vermouth —
I think that perhaps it's the gin.
Ibid. A Drink with Something in It

They take a paper and they read the
headlines,
So they've heard of unemployment and
they've heard of breadlines,
And they philanthropically cure them
all
By getting up a costume charity ball.
Ibid. Pride Goeth Before a Raise

There are some people who are very re-
sourceful
At being remorseful,
And who apparently feel that the best
way to make friends
Is to do something terrible and then
make amends.
Ibid. Hearts of Gold

Women are ethereal beings, subsisting
entirely on chocolate marshmallow
nut sundaes and cantaloupe,
But they open up a package of cigarettes like a lioness opening up an
antelope.
Versus. Thoughts Thought
After a Bridge Party

Middle age is when you've met so many
people that every new person you
meet reminds you of someone else.
Ibid. Let's Not Climb the Wash-
ington Monument Tonight

A commuter is one who never knows
how a show comes out because he
has to leave early to catch a train
to get him back to the country in
time to catch a train to bring him
back to the city.
Ibid. The Banker's Special

I believe a little incompatibility is the
spice of life, particularly if he has
income and she is pattable.
Ibid. I Do, I Will, I Have

My garden will never make me famous,
I'm a horticultural ignoramus,
I can't tell a stringbean from a soybean,
Or even a girl bean from a boy bean.
Ibid. He Digs, He Dug, He Has Dug

When I remember bygone days
I think how evening follows morn;
So many I loved were not yet dead,
So many I love were not yet born.
Ibid. The Middle

He tells you when you've got on too
much lipstick,
And helps you with your girdle when
your hips stick.
Ibid. The Perfect Husband

A door is what a dog is perpetually on
the wrong side of.
The Private Dining Room. A
Dog's Best Friend Is His Il-
literacy

They are a higher form of life,
My dog, my daughter, and my wife,
Inhabitants of a fourth dimension
Too mystic for my comprehension.
Ibid. Father-in-Law of the Groom

THEODORE SPENCER
[1902–1949]

Eunuchs, abortive Platonists and priests
Speak always very wisely about love.
An Act of Life [1944]

JOHN ERNST STEINBECK
[1902–   ]

Man, unlike any other thing organic or inorganic in the universe, grows beyond his work, walks up the stairs of his concepts, emerges ahead of his accomplishments.
The Grapes of Wrath [1939].
Chap. 14
"Okie use' ta mean you was from Oklahoma. Now it means you're scum. Don't mean nothing itself, it's the way they say it."
Ibid. Chap. 18
They had hoped to find a home, and they found only hatred. Okies — the owners hated them because the owners knew they were soft and the Okies strong, that they were fed and the Okies hungry.
Ibid. Chap. 19

ERSKINE CALDWELL
[1903–   ]

Tobacco Road.
Title of novel [1] [1932]

CYRIL CONNOLLY
[1903–   ]

Spring is a call to action, hence to disillusion, therefore April is called "the cruellest month." [2]
The Unquiet Grave [1945]
There is no fury like a woman searching for a new lover.
Ibid.
Obesity is a mental state, a disease brought on by boredom and disappointment.
Ibid.

[1] The play [1933], adapted by JACK KIRKLAND, had one of the longest runs in American stage history.
[2] See T. S. Eliot, page 943b.

Melancholy and remorse form the deep leaden keel which enables us to sail into the wind of reality; we run aground sooner than the flat-bottomed pleasure-lovers, but we venture out in weather that would sink them.
The Unquiet Grave

COUNTEE CULLEN
[1903–1946]

She thinks that even up in heaven
Her class lies late and snores,
While poor black cherubs rise at seven
To do celestial chores.
Epitaph: A Lady I Know
Though wet nor blow nor space I fear,
Yet fear I deeply, too,
Lest Death should meet and claim me ere
I keep Life's rendezvous.
I Have a Rendezvous with Life [1]

WILLIAM THOMAS CUMMINGS [2]
[1903–1944]

There are no atheists in the foxholes. [3]
Field Sermon on Bataan [1942]

MERRILL MOORE
[1903–   ]

Water has sunk more grievances than wine
And will continue to.
Hymn for Water. Stanza 2
The noise that Time makes.
M: 1000 Sonnets [1938]

GEORGE ORWELL
[1903–1950]

All animals are equal, but some animals are more equal than others.
Animal Farm [1945]. Chap. 10

[1] See Alan Seeger, page 947b.
[2] Father Cummings, of Maryknoll Mission, was a member of the Chaplains Corps. He was aboard an unmarked Japanese ship that was transporting prisoners from the Philippines to Japan when sunk by an American submarine, December 15, 1944.
[3] Quoted by CARLOS P. ROMULO, *I Saw the Fall of the Philippines* [1942], *P. 263.*

WILLIAM PLOMER
[1903–]

That was the Africa we knew,
Where, wandering alone,
We saw, heraldic in the heat,
A scorpion on a stone.
The Scorpion

PETER ARNO
[1904–]

I consider your conduct unethical
and lousy.
Caption for cartoon

CLIFTON FADIMAN
[1904–]

Ennui, felt on the proper occasions,
is a sign of intelligence.
Reading I've Liked [*1941*]

Man's painful desire to communicate
without coalescing.
Ibid.

MARGARET FISHBACK
[1904–]

The same old charitable lie
Repeated as the years scoot by
Perpetually makes a hit —
"You really haven't changed a bit!"
The Lie of the Land

CECIL DAY LEWIS
[1904–]

Tempt me no more; for I
Have known the lightning's hour,
The poet's inward pride,
The certainty of power.
Tempt Me No More. Stanza 1

And if our blood alone
Will melt this iron earth,
Take it. It is well spent
Easing a savior's birth.
Ibid. Stanza 7

I've heard them lilting at loom and
belting,
Lasses lilting before dawn of day:
But now they are silent, not gamesome
and gallant —

The flowers of the town are rotting
away.[1]
A Time to Dance

Come, live with me and be my love,
And we will all the pleasures prove [2]
Of peace and plenty, bed and board,
That chance employment may afford.
Ibid.

Rest from loving and be living.
Fallen is fallen past retrieving.
Rest from Loving

Slow drip the seconds, time is stalactite.
*As One Who Wanders into
Old Workings*

Make us a wind to shake the world!
The Magnetic Mountain. 31

Spring through death's iron guard
Her million blades shall thrust;
Love that was sleeping, not extinct,
Throw off the nightmare crust.
Ibid. 35

Sleep-walking on that silver wall, the
furious
Sick shapes and pregnant fancies of
your world.
Newsreel [*1941*]. *Stanza 3*

J. ROBERT OPPENHEIMER
[1904–]

In some sort of crude sense which no
vulgarity, no humor, no over-statement
can quite extinguish, the physicists have
known sin; and this is a knowledge
which they cannot lose.
*Physics in the Contemporary
World, lecture at Massachusetts
Institute of Technology, November 25, 1947*

EMERY REVES
[1904–]

The Golden Calf to which the most
devoted and mystic adoration of the
masses goes in our days is: Sovereignty.
No symbol carrying the pretension of a

---

[1] I've heard them lilting at our ewe-milking,
Lasses a-lilting before dawn o' day;
But now they are moaning on ilka green
loaning:
"The Flowers of the Forest are a' wede
away."
JANE ELLIOTT [*1727–1805*]:
A Lament for Flodden

[2] See Marlowe, page 123a.

deity caused so much misery, hatred, starvation and mass execution as the notion "Sovereignty of the Nation."
A Democratic Manifesto [*1942*].
Chap. 6

GRETA GARBO
[1905–   ]

I want to be alone.[1]
Attributed

PHYLLIS McGINLEY
[1905–   ]

We never sit down to our pottage,
We never go calm to our rest,
But lo! at the door of our cottage,
The knock of the Guest.
Elegy from a Country Dooryard.
Stanza 3

Meek-eyed parents hasten down the ramps
To greet their offspring, terrible from camps.
Ode to the End of Summer

HERBERT J. MULLER
[1905–   ]

Few have heard of Fra Luca Parioli, the inventor of double-entry bookkeeping; but he has probably had much more influence on human life than has Dante or Michelangelo.
The Uses of the Past [*1952*].
Chap. 8

ROBERT PENN WARREN
[1905–   ]

The annual sacrament of sea and sun,
Which browns the face and heals the heart . . .
But the mail lurks in the box at the house where you live.
End of Season. Stanzas 5 and 6

ALFRED BARRETT, S.J.
[1906–   ]

See how in God's design,
Layette to mound,

[1] Garbo maintains that her most famous remark has always been misquoted. . . . "I only said, 'I want to be *let* alone!'" — JOHN BAINBRIDGE, in *Life* [January 24, 1955]

A lifetime of linen
Laps us round.
Linen

WYSTAN HUGH AUDEN
[1907–   ]

Cathedrals,
Luxury liners laden with souls,
Holding to the east their hulls of stone.
On This Island. XVII

Underneath the abject willow,
Lover, sulk no more;
Act from thought should quickly follow:
What is thinking for?
Ibid. XXII

Come to our bracing desert
Where eternity is eventful,
For the weather-glass
Is set at Alas,
The thermometer at Resentful.
For the Time Being. The Flight into Egypt

Come to our well-run desert
Where anguish arrives by cable,
And the deadly sins
May be bought in tins
With instructions on the label.
Ibid.

In the nightmare of the dark
All the dogs of Europe bark,
And the living nations wait,
Each sequestered in its hate.
In Memory of W. B. Yeats [*1939*]

Intellectual disgrace
Stares from every human face,
And the seas of pity lie
Locked and frozen in each eye.
Ibid.

O stern proconsul of intractable provinces,
O poet of the difficult, dear addicted artist.
At the Grave of Henry James.
Stanza 5

Sob, heavy world
Sob as you spin,
Mantled in mist, remote from the happy.
The Age of Anxiety

CHRISTOPHER FRY
[1907–   ]

But life has such
Diversity, I sometimes remarkably lose
Eternity in the passing moment.
The Lady's Not for Burning
[*1950*]. *Act I*

Something compels us into
The terrible fallacy that man is desirable
And there's no escaping into truth.
Ibid. Act II

Campaigning
Love still pitches his tent of light among
The suns and moons.
Ibid.

The best
Thing we can do is to make wherever we're lost in
Look as much like home as we can.
Ibid. Act III

ANNE MORROW LINDBERGH
[1907–   ]

Rivers perhaps are the only physical features of the world that are at their best from the air. . . . Rivers stretch out serenely ahead as far as the eye can reach.
North to the Orient [*1935*].
Chap. 17

What did they call it in New England when they felt this same thing?
. . . "Journey-proud."
"Listen! the Wind" [1] [*1938*].
Chap. 18

One can never pay in gratitude; one can only pay "in kind" somewhere else in life.
Ibid. Chap. 19

The wave of the future is coming and there is no fighting it.
The Wave of the Future [*1940*]

Lost time was like a run in a stocking. It always got worse.
The Steep Ascent [*1944*]. *Chap. 3*

[1] See Humbert Wolfe, page 934a.

LOUIS MACNEICE
[1907–   ]

Holidays should be like this,
Free from over-emphasis,
Time for soul to stretch and spit
Before the world comes back on it.
Epilogue, for W. H. Auden [*1936*]

I have no liking to defer
To capitalist or bureaucrat;
As for your Social Register
You know what you can do with that!
Ballade in a Bad Temper [*1940*]

PAUL ENGLE
[1908–   ]

Wytham, Water Eaton, Wolvercote,
Old names worn water-smooth under the tongue.
Corn [*1939*]

I came to that dark water-wandered town,
Where, before proud stone was piled on stone
To mark the frantic limits of the mind,
Oxen forded the mild, midland river.
Ibid. (Oxford)

The tense American nerve relaxed, I lived
With a gray quietness that let the mind
Grow inward like a root.
Ibid.

I heard, down the long valley of my bones,
The cry of home run like a calling hound . . .
Belly and brain, I lived America.
Ibid.

HOWELL M. FORGY
[1908–   ]

Praise the Lord and pass the ammunition.[1]
Said at Pearl Harbor,
December 7, 1941

[1] Lieutenant Commander Forgy was serving as chaplain on a cruiser at the time of the Japanese attack, when he said these words to a chain of men handling ammunition. (Also title of a popular song by Frank Loesser [September, 1942].)

WILLIAM SAROYAN
[1908–   ]

The Time of Your Life.
Title of play [1] *[1939]*

What they do, boys, is creep up on you,
And I don't mean Indians.
I mean Americans, over the radio.
The Propagandists [1940]

If you listen to them, you will be lis-
    tened to,
Saying what they said, and no longer
    the man you were.
Ibid.

If you give to a thief he cannot steal
from you, and he is then no longer a
thief.
The Human Comedy [1943].
Chap. 4

"How much does it cost to send a
telegram to New Jersey?"
"Not nearly as much as it's worth."
Ibid. Chap. 17

STEPHEN SPENDER
[1909–   ]

I think continually of those who were
    truly great —
The names of those who in their lives
    fought for life,
Who wore at their hearts the fire's cen-
    ter.
I Think Continually of Those

Born of the sun they traveled a short
    while towards the sun,
And left the vivid air signed with their
    honour.
Ibid.

GEORGE CASPAR HOMANS
[1910–   ]

Liberty is a beloved discipline.
The Human Group [1950].
Chap. 12

W. R. RODGERS

Laugh at the skinny notice of your
    birth,
Or roar at your obese obituary.
Words

[1] Awarded the 1940 Pulitzer Prize, which
Saroyan refused.

Your doubts are the private detectives
Employed by your dislike, to make a
    case
Against change or choice.
Words

GEORGE BARKER
[1913–   ]

What is all but a Woolworth welter
    of things?
Seven Munich Elegies. 5

Life is torpedoed and like a Titanic
    goes under
Threshing her ensigns
Against the dreadnought seas of blood
    and thunder
That flood our visions.
Ibid. 6

The chaos is come of the organized dis-
    order,
The consistently inappropriate and the
    simple wrong.
First American Ode

NATHALIA CRANE
[1913–   ]

Oh, I'm in love with the janitor's boy,
    And the janitor's boy loves me;
He's going to hunt for a desert isle
    In our geography.
The Janitor's Boy [1924]. Stanza 1

I linger on the flathouse roof, the moon-
    light is divine.
But my heart is all a-flutter like the
    washing on the line.
The Flathouse Roof. Stanza 1

Once a pallid vestal
    Doubted truth in blue;
Listed red as ruin,
    Harried every hue.
The Vestal. Stanza 1

Every gaudy color
Is a bit of truth.
Ibid. Stanza 5

In the darkness, who would answer for
    the color of a rose,
Or the vestments of the May moth and
    the pilgrimage it goes?
The Blind Girl. Stanza 1

When the moon comes over Brooklyn

On time with the borough clock,
'Tis the same that saw Palmyra
And the walls of Antioch.
The Moon of Brooklyn. Stanza 1
There is a glory
In a great mistake.
Imperfection

DONALD FRANCIS MASON
[1913–   ]

Sighted sub, sank same.
*Radio message to U. S. Navy
Base, January 8, 1942*

MURIEL RUKEYSER
[1913–   ]

Women and poets see the truth arrive,
Then it is acted out,
The lives are lost, and all the newsboys
shout.
Beast in View [1944]. *Letter to
the Front*
The world of man's selection
May widen more and more.
Women in drudgery knew
They must be one of four:
Whores, artists, saints, and wives.
Ibid. Wreath of Women

KARL JAY SHAPIRO
[1913–   ]

He cast his vote,
Distrusting all the elected but not the
law.
Elegy for a Dead Soldier
[1944]. *VII*
Above all else he loathed the homily,
The slogan and the ad. He paid his bill
But not for Congressmen at Bunker
Hill.
Ideals were few and those there were
not made
For conversation. He belonged to
church
But never spoke of God. The Christmas
tree,
The Easter egg, baptism, he observed,
Never denied the preacher on his perch,
And would not sign Resolved That or
Whereas.
Ibid. VIII

IRWIN SHAW
[1913–   ]

There are too many books I haven't
read, too many places I haven't seen,
too many memories I haven't kept long
enough.
Bury the Dead [1936]
I got a religion that wants to take
heaven out of the clouds and plant it
right here on the earth where most of us
can get a slice of it.
Ibid.

ROSS PARKER
[1914–   ]
AND
HUGHIE CHARLES
[1907–   ]

There'll always be an England
While there's a busy street,
Wherever there's a turning wheel,
A million marching feet.
*There'll Always Be an
England* [1939]

DELMORE SCHWARTZ
[1914–   ]

In Dreams Begin Responsibilities.
Title of book of poems [1938]
Save postage stamps or photographs,
But save your soul! Only the past is
immortal.
The Repetitive Heart

DYLAN THOMAS [1]
[1914–1953]

Light breaks where no sun shines;
Where no sea runs, the waters of the
heart
Push in their tides.
Light breaks where no sun shines
And death shall have no dominion.[2]
Title and refrain of poem

[1] All these selections are from *Collected
Poems* [1953].
[2] See *Romans, VI, 9,* on page 1059b, and
Emily Brontë, page 592a.

After the first death there is no other.
A Refusal to Mourn the Death, by
*　　Fire, of a Child in London*
Forgotten mornings when he walked
　　with his mother
　Through the parables
　　Of sun light
And the legend of the green chapels.
*　　　　　Poem in October*
Do not go gentle into that good night,
Old age should burn and rave at close
　of day;
Rage, rage against the dying of the
　light.
*　　　　Do not go gentle into*
*　　　　　that good night*
Now as I was young and easy under
　the apple boughs
About the lilting house and happy as
　the grass was green.
*　　　Fern Hill. Stanza 1*
　And the sabbath rang slowly
In the pebbles of the holy stream.
*　　　　Ibid. Stanza 2*
In the sun that is young once only,
　Time let me play and be
Golden in the mercy of his means.
*　　　　　　　Ibid.*
And honoured among foxes and pheas-
　ants by the gay house
Under the new made clouds and happy
　as the heart was long,
　In the sun born over and over,
　　I ran my heedless ways.
*　　　　Ibid. Stanza 5*
　Time held me green and dying
Though I sang in my chains like the
　sea.
*　　　　Ibid. Stanza 6*

HAROLD ADAMSON

Comin' in on a Wing and a Prayer.
Title of popular song of World
*　　　　　War II [1943]*

FLORENCE FRENCH
DUNBAR
[1916–　　]

The Spring comes truly when, between
　the rains,

The stiff new wasps ascend the window
　panes.
*　　　　　　　Wasp Time*

JOHN WALLER
[1917–　　]

Guns are left to do what words
Might have done earlier, properly used.
*　　　　　　　In Beirut*
How frequently the last time
Comes and we do not know.
*　　　　The Meaning of War*

WILLIAM H. ("BILL")
MAULDIN
[1921–　　]

I feel like a fugitive from th' law of
averages.
*　　　Up Front [1944]. Caption*
*　　　　　　　for cartoon*
　Look at an infantryman's eyes and
you can tell how much war he has seen.
*　　　　　　　Ibid.*
"He's right, Joe, when we ain't
fightin' we should ack like sojers."
*　　　　　　　Ibid.*

QUEEN ELIZABETH II
OF ENGLAND
[1926–　　]

My whole life, whether it be long or
short, shall be devoted to your service
and the service of our great imperial
family to which we all belong, but I
shall not have strength to carry out this
resolution alone unless you join in it
with me.
*　　Radio broadcast from Capetown,*
*　　South Africa, to the British Com-*
*　　monwealth on her twenty-first*
*　　birthday [April 21, 1947]*

CHARTER OF THE UNITED
NATIONS

We, the peoples of the United Nations, determined to save succeeding
generations from the scourge of war,
which twice in our lifetime has brought
untold sorrow to mankind, and to re-
affirm faith in fundamental human

rights, in the dignity and worth of the human person, in the equal right of men and women and of nations large and small . . .

And for these ends to practice tolerance and live together in peace with one another as good neighbors . . .

Have resolved to combine our efforts to accomplish these aims.

Preamble [1] [*June, 1945*]

[1] The preamble was based on the draft written by JAN CHRISTIAN SMUTS [1870–1950].

ANONYMOUS

Sumer is icumen in,
  Lhude sing cuccu!
Groweth sed, and bloweth med,
And springth the wude nu —
    Sing cuccu!
        Cuckoo Song [*Circa 1250*]

Castles in Spain.[1]
    Phrase from the French
         [*13th century*]

When Adam delved and Eve span
Who was then a gentleman?
    Text used by JOHN BALL *for
his speech at Blackheath to the
men in Wat Tyler's Rebellion*
  [*1381*]

Forgive and forget.
    *Saying current since the
         14th century*

I sing of a maiden
  That is makeless;
King of all kings
  To her son she ches.
    Carol. I Sing of a Maiden
       [*15th century*]

Western wind, when wilt thou blow?
The small rain down can rain, —
Christ, if my love were in my arms
And I in my bed again!
    Western Wind [*Circa 1530*]

Multiplication is vexation,
Division is as bad;
The rule of three doth puzzle me,
And practice drives me mad.
    Elizabethan MS. [*1570*]

There is a lady sweet and kind,
Was never face so pleased my mind;
I did but see her passing by,
And yet I love her till I die.
        Song [*1570*]

Greensleeves was all my joy,
  Greensleeves was my delight,

Greensleeves was my heart of gold,
  And who but my Lady Greensleeves?
    A Handful of Pleasant Delites
      [*1584*]. *Greensleeves*

Alas, my love, you do me wrong
  To cast me off discourteously,
When I have loved you so long,
  Delighting in your company.
           Ibid.

Shall I bid her go? What, and if I do?
Shall I bid her go, and spare not?
O no, no, no, I dare not.[1]
    Corydon's Farewell to Phillis.
         Stanza 2

Where griping griefs the heart would
  wound
And doleful dumps the mind oppress,
There music with her silver sound
With speed is wont to send redress.[2]
    A Song to the Lute in Musicke.
         Stanza 1

A fool and his money are soon parted.
    *Saying current since the
         16th century*

Turn again Whittington,
Lord Mayor of London.[3]
    *Refrain of Bow Bells heard by
    Dick Whittington* [*Circa 1605*]

Love not me for comely grace,
For my pleasing eye or face,
Nor for any outward part,
No, nor for a constant heart.
    In JOHN WILBYE, *Second Set of
        Madrigals* [*1608*]

If wishes were horses, beggars might
ride.
    From JOHN RAY'S *English
        Proverbs* [*1670*]

---

[1] Paraphrased by Shakespeare in *Twelfth-Night* [*1598–1600*], Act II, Sc. 3.

[2] Another version is used by Shakespeare in *Romeo and Juliet* [*1594–1595*], Act IV, Sc. 5.

[3] Richard Whittington, son of a London mercer, rose to be mayor of London three times before his death in 1423.

[1] Thou shalt make castels than in Spayne,
  And dreme of joye, al but in vayne.
    JEAN DE MEUN: *Romaunt of the Rose,
    Fragment B, L. 2573* [*circa 1277*]

Begone, dull Care! I prithee begone
from me!
Begone, dull Care! thou and I shall
never agree.
In JOHN PLAYFORD, *Musical
Companion* [*1687*]

Though little, I'll work as hard as a
Turk,
If you'll give me employ,
To plow and sow, and reap and mow,
And be a farmer's boy.
The Farmer's Boy [*before 1689*].
Stanza 2

Carriages without horses shall go,
And accidents fill the world with woe.
*Prophecy Attributed to Mother
Shipton* [1] [*17th century*]

Around the world thoughts shall fly
In the twinkling of an eye.
Ibid.

Under water men shall walk,
Shall ride, shall sleep, and talk;
In the air men shall be seen
In white, in black, and in green.
Ibid.

Iron in the water shall float
As easy as a wooden boat.
Ibid.

A swarm of bees in May
Is worth a load of hay;
A swarm of bees in June
Is worth a silver spoon;
A swarm of bees in July
Is not worth a fly.
Old English saying

When poverty comes in at the door,
love flies out the window.
*Saying current since the 17th
century*

Please to remember the Fifth of November,
Gunpowder Treason and Plot.
*Guy Fawkes's Rhyme, tradi-
tional in England since the
17th century*

[1] Most of the prophecies attributed to
Mother Shipton — a witch and prophetess,
according to tradition, who lived in Yorkshire
in Tudor times — are fabrications of the seventeenth century and later.

THE NEW ENGLAND
PRIMER [1]

In Adam's fall
We sinned all.

My Book and Heart
Must never part.

Young Obadias,
David, Josias, —
All were pious.

Peter denied
His Lord, and cryed.

Young Timothy
Learnt sin to fly.

Xerxes did die,
And so must I.

Zaccheus he
Did climb the tree
Our Lord to see.

Our days begin with trouble here,
    Our life is but a span,[2]
And cruel death is always near,
    So frail a thing is man.

Now I lay me down to take my sleep,[3]
I pray the Lord my soul to keep;
If I should die before I wake,
I pray the Lord my soul to take.

Sabina has a thousand charms
    To captivate my heart;
Her lovely eyes are Cupid's arms,
    And every look a dart:
But when the beauteous idiot speaks,
    She cures me of my pain;
Her tongue the servile fetters breaks
    And frees her slave again.
From Amphion Anglicus [*1700*]

[1] As early as 1691, Benjamin Harris of
Boston advertised the forthcoming second
impression of the the *New England Primer*.
The oldest known copy extant is dated 1737.
[2] See Bacon, page 121b.
[3] The first record of this prayer is found
in the *Enchiridion Leonis* [A. D. 1160]. The
early editions of the *Primer* give the prayer
as above. In the edition of 1784 the first line
is altered to read, "Now I lay me down to
sleep." In the edition of 1814 the second line
reads, "I pray thee, Lord, my soul to keep."

The Campbells are comin', oho, oho.
　　　　　　Song [*Circa 1715*]
The Girl I Left Behind Me.
　　　　　　Title of song [*1759*]
The United Voice of all His Majesty's free and loyal Subjects in America — Liberty and Property, and no Stamps.
　　　　Motto of various American colonial newspapers [*1765–1766*]
Yankee Doodle came to town
Upon a little pony,
He stuck a feather in his hat
And called it macaroni.
　　　　　　Yankee Doodle [1]
Yankee Doodle, keep it up,
　Yankee Doodle dandy,
Mind the music and the step,
And with the girls be handy.
　　　　　　Ibid. Chorus
It's all in the day's work.
　　　Saying current since the 18th century
Man may work from sun to sun,
But woman's work is never done.
　　　　　　Old saying

JUNIUS [2]

One precedent creates another. They soon accumulate and constitute law.

[1] This version was sufficiently popular in America in 1767 to be used in the ballad opera *The Disappointment, or, The Force of Credulity* [1767], by ANDREW BARTON.
　Father and I went up to camp,
　　Along with Captain Goodwin;
　And there we saw the men and boys,
　　As thick as hasty-pudding.
　　　Yankee doodle do.
　　Version used in The Contrast [1790], *by* ROYALL TYLER
The origin of *Yankee Doodle* remains as mysterious as ever, unless it be deemed a positive result to have eliminated definitely every theory thus far advanced. — OSCAR GEORGE THEODORE SONNECK: *Report on The Star-Spangled Banner, Hail Columbia, America, Yankee Doodle* [1909]
[2] Pseudonym of the author of a series of letters that appeared in the *Public Advertiser* from 1769 to 1771, published in book form in 1772; they have been attributed, among others, to Sir Philip Francis, Lord Shelburne, Lord George Sackville, and Lord Temple.

What yesterday was fact, today is doctrine.
　　The Letters of Junius [*1769–1771*]. *Dedication to the English Nation*

The liberty of the press is the Palladium of all the civil, political, and religious rights of an Englishman.
　　　　　　Ibid.

These are the gloomy companions of a disturbed imagination; the melancholy madness of poetry, without the inspiration.
　　Ibid. VII, To Sir William Draper [*March 3, 1769*]

There are some hereditary strokes of character by which a family may be as clearly distinguished as by the blackest features of the human face.
　　Ibid. XII, To the Duke of Grafton [*May 30, 1769*]

I believe there is yet a spirit of resistance in this country, which will not submit to be oppressed; but I am sure there is a fund of good sense in this country, which cannot be deceived.
　　Ibid. XVI, To the Printer of the Public Advertiser (H. S. Woodfall) [*July 19, 1769*]

We owe it to our ancestors to preserve entire those rights, which they have delivered to our care: we owe it to our posterity, not to suffer their dearest inheritance to be destroyed.
　　Ibid. XX, To the Printer of the Public Advertiser [*August 8, 1769*]

When the constitution is openly invaded, when the first original right of the people, from which all laws derive their authority, is directly attacked, inferior grievances naturally lose their force, and are suffered to pass by without punishment or observation.
　　Ibid. XXX, To the Printer of the Public Advertiser [*October 17, 1769*]

There is a moment of difficulty and danger at which flattery and falsehood can no longer deceive, and simplicity it-self can no longer be misled.

> *The Letters of Junius. XXXV,*[1]
> *To the Printer of the Public Ad-vertiser* [*December 19, 1769*]

They [the Americans] equally detest the pageantry of a King, and the super-cilious hypocrisy of a bishop.[2]

> *Ibid.*

There is a holy mistaken zeal in politics as well as in religion. By per-suading others, we convince ourselves.

> *Ibid.*

The least considerable man among us has an interest equal to the proudest nobleman, in the laws and constitution of his country, and is equally called upon to make a generous contribution in support of them; — whether it be the heart to conceive, the understand-ing to direct, or the hand to execute.[3]

> *Ibid. XXXVII, To the Printer of the Public Advertiser* [*March 19, 1770*]

We lament the mistakes of a good man, and do not begin to detest him until he affects to renounce his prin-ciples.

> *Ibid. XLI, To Lord Mansfield* [*November 14, 1770*]

The injustice done to an individual is sometimes of service to the public. Facts are apt to alarm us more than the most dangerous principles.

> *Ibid.*

An honest man, like the true religion, appeals to the understanding, or mod-estly confides in the internal evidence of his conscience. The impostor em-ploys force instead of argument, im-poses silence where he cannot convince, and propagates his character by the sword.

> *Ibid.*

[1] This letter is of great significance in the history of the freedom of the press. The pub-lisher was prosecuted for seditious libel, and the jury brought in a verdict of "guilty of printing and publishing only." After a second trial, Woodfall was freed on payment of costs.
[2] See Rufus Choate, page 490a.
[3] See Gibbon, page 369a.

If individuals have no virtues, their vices may be of use to us.

> *The Letters of Junius. LIX, To the Printer of the Public Ad-vertiser* [*October 5, 1771*]

The temple of fame is the shortest passage to riches and preferment.

> *Ibid.*

Rebellion to tyrants is obedience to God.[1]

> *Motto on Thomas Jefferson's Seal* [*Circa 1776*]

Lost is our old simplicity of times,
The world abounds with laws, and teems with crimes.

> *On the Proceedings Against America.*[2] *Stanza 1*

Our cargoes of meat, drink, and cloaths beat the Dutch.

> *Siege of Boston* [*1775*]

There is nothing new except what is forgotten.

> *Attributed to Mademoiselle Bertin, milliner to Marie An-toinette* [*Circa 1785*]

O Paddy dear, an' did ye hear the news that's goin' round?
The shamrock is by law forbid to grow on Irish ground!
No more St. Patrick's Day we'll keep, his colour can't be seen,
For there's a cruel law agin the wearin' o' the Green!

> *The Shan-von-Voght. Irish Song quoted in* TRENCH: *Realities of Irish Life*

For they're hangin' men an' women there for wearin' o' the Green.

> *Ibid.*

Christmas is coming, the geese are get-ting fat,
Please to put a penny in the old man's hat;
If you haven't got a penny, a ha'penny will do,

[1] The motto of one, I believe, of the regi-cides of Charles I. — *Letter from Jefferson to Edward Everett* [February 24, 1823]
Jefferson's reference probably is to John Bradshaw [1602–1659].
[2] In *The Pennsylvania Gazette,* February 8, 1775, "from a late London Magazine."

If you haven't got a ha'penny, God
   bless you!
                     Beggar's rhyme

From ghoulies and ghosties and long-
   leggety beasties
And things that go bump in the night,
Good Lord, deliver us!
                     Scottish prayer

The woods are full of them.
   Quoted by ALEXANDER WIL-
   SON: *American Ornithology*
   [*1808*]. *Preface*

The cunning seldom gain their ends;
The wise are never without friends.
   The Fox and the Hen, Moral [1]

A fox went out in a hungry plight
And he begged of the moon to give him
   light,
For he'd many miles to go that night
Before he could reach his den-O.
   The Gray Goose. Stanza 1

One night when the wind it blew cold,
Blew bitter across the wild moor,
Young Mary she came with her child,
Wandering home to her own father's
   door.
   Mary of the Wild Moor. [2]
                     Stanza 1

Oh, the praties they are small —
   Over here, over here.
Oh, the praties they are small
When we dig 'em in the fall,
And we eat 'em, coats and all,
   Full of fear, full of fear.
   Irish Famine Song [*1846–1847*]

Oh, ye'll tak' the high road an' I'll tak'
   the low road,
An' I'll be in Scotland bafore ye;
But I and my true love will never meet
   again,
On the bonnie, bonnie banks o' Loch
   Lomond.
   Scottish Song, Loch Lomond.
                     Refrain

So I said, "Old man, for whom digg'st
   thou this grave

[1] In JOHN PIERPONT'S *Young Reader*
[*1843*].
[2] Set to music by C. H. Keith and arranged for piano by Joseph W. Turner
[*1846*].

In the heart of London town?"
And the deep-toned voice of the digger
   replied —
"We're laying a gas-pipe down!"
   From the Sublime to the
                 Ridiculous. [1] *Stanza 3*

Went out to milk and I didn't know
   how,
I milked the goat instead of the cow;
A monkey sittin' on a pile of straw
A-winkin' at his mother-in-law.
Turkey in the straw, turkey in the hay,
Roll 'em up and twist 'em up a high
   tuckahaw,
And hit 'em up a tune called Turkey in
   the Straw.
   Turkey in the Straw. [2]
           Stanza 1 and refrain

Sugar in the gourd and honey in the
   horn,
I never was so happy since the hour I
   was born.
   Ibid. Stanza 6

You pays your money, and you takes
your choice.
   Caption to cartoon by JOHN
   LEECH *in Punch, January 3,*
   1846

It's the 'ammer, 'ammer, 'ammer
along the 'ard 'igh road.
   Ibid. May 31, 1856 (A vet-
   erinary and a horseman discuss-
   ing a horse's legs)

Women and children first.
   The Birkenhead Drill [3] [*Febru-*
                   ary 26, 1852]

Frankie and Johnny were lovers, my
   gawd, how they could love,
Swore to be true to each other, true as
   the stars above;

[1] Included in *Course of Composition and
Rhetoric* by GEORGE PAYN QUACKENBOS
[*1826–1881*]
[2] The classical American rural tune . . .
steps around like an apple-faced farmhand
. . . as American as Andrew Jackson, Johnny
Appleseed, and Corn on the Cob. — CARL
SANDBURG: *The American Songbag* [*1927*]
[3] The women and children were the first to
be removed from the sinking ship *Birkenhead*.
See Kipling, page 818b.

He was her man, but he done her wrong.
> *Frankie and Johnny.*[1] *Stanza 1*

Och, Johnny, I hardly knew ye!
With drums and guns, and guns and drums
The enemy nearly slew ye.
My darling dear, you look so queer,
Och, Johnny, I hardly knew ye.
> *Irish Folk Song. Stanza 1*

Where are the legs with which you run,
When you went to carry a gun?
Indeed your dancing days are done —
Och, Johnny, I hardly knew ye.
> *Ibid. Stanza 3*

Up and down the City Road,
In and out the Eagle,
That's the way the money goes —
Pop goes the weasel!
> *Popular song in London*[2]
> *[Circa 1853]*

All I want of you is a little see-vility, and that of the commonest goddamned-est kind.[3]
> *"The New Bedford Classic," as reported in* ZEPHANIAH W. PEASE, *The History of New Bedford* [1918]. *Supposed to be said by the mate of a whaler to his ill-humored captain*

You-all means a race or section,
Family, party, tribe, or clan;
You-all means the whole connection
Of the individual man.
> *You-All (From The Richmond Times-Dispatch)*

Some talk of Alexander, and some of Hercules;
Of Hector, and Lysander, and such great names as these;
But of all the world's brave heroes, there's none that can compare

With a tow, row, row, row, row, row for the British Grenadier.
> *The British Grenadiers*

The holly and the ivy,
When they are both full grown,
Of all the trees that are in the wood,
The holly bears the crown:
The rising of the sun
And the running of the deer,
The playing of the merry organ,
Sweet singing in the choir.
> *Carol. The Holly and the Ivy*

From the halls of Montezuma,
  To the shores of Tripoli,
We fight our country's battles
  On the land as on the sea.
> *U. S. Marines' Song. Stanza 1*

If the Army and the Navy
  Ever look on Heaven's scenes,
They will find the streets are guarded by
  The United States Marines.
> *Ibid. Stanza 4*

There is a tavern in the town,
And there my true love sits him down,
And drinks his wine with laughter and with glee,
And never, never thinks of me.
> *There Is a Tavern in the Town.*
> *Stanza 1*

Fare thee well for I must leave thee,
Do not let this parting grieve thee,
But remember that the best of friends must part.
> *Ibid. Refrain*

Adieu, adieu, kind friends, adieu, adieu, adieu,
I can no longer stay with you.
I'll hang my harp on a weeping willow-tree,[1]
And may the world go well with thee.
> *Ibid. Stanza 2*

Mr. Finney had a turnip,
  And it grew behind the barn,
And it grew, and it grew,
  And the turnip did no harm.
> *Mr. Finney's Turnip.*[2] *Stanza 1*

---

[1] Traditional ballad; there are innumerable versions and verses.
[2] The weasel was a hatter's tool, and "pop" was a term meaning to pawn or "hock." The Eagle was a music hall in the City Road. The song is attributed to W. R. MANDALE.
[3] Another traditional version, repudiated by New Bedford authority, is that the skipper said: "All I want out of you is silence, and damn little of that."

[1] See *Psalm CXXXVII, 2*, on page 1038a.
[2] Often attributed to Longfellow, who denied the authorship in a letter to George Anderson, July 11, 1881.

Of all the funny things that live, in
woodland, marsh, or bog,
That creep the ground or fly the air,
the funniest thing's a frog.
> *The Scientific Frog [Circa*
> *1865]. Stanza 1*

I belong to that highly respectable
tribe
Which is known as the Shabby Genteel . . .
Too proud to beg, too honest to steal.
> *The Shabby Genteel (Sung by*
> *Sol Smith Russell [1848–1901]*
> *in A Poor Relation)*

If any lift of mine may ease
The burden of another,
God give me love and care and strength
To help my ailing brother.
> *If Any Little Word of Mine*
> *[1880]. Stanza 2*

The sons of the prophet are brave men
and bold,
And quite unaccustomed to fear,
But the bravest by far in the ranks of
the Shah
Was Abdul the Bulbul Amir.
> *Abdul the Bulbul Amir. Stanza 1*

Now the heroes were plenty and well
known to fame
In the troops that were led by the
Czar,
And the bravest of these was a man by
the name
Of Ivan Petruski Skavar.
> *Ibid. Stanza 3*

I'm Terence O'Reilly, I'm a man of renown . . .
If they'd let me be, I'd have Ireland
free,
On the railroads you'd not pay any
fare,
I'd have the United States under my
thumb,
And I'd sleep in the President's chair.
> *Is That Mr. Reilly?* [1] *[1882].*
> *Stanza 1*

Is that Mr. Reilly, can anyone tell?
Is that Mr. Reilly that owns the hotel?

[1] Assumed to be the origin of the phrase
"leading the life of Riley," meaning to have
an easy time.

Well, if that's Mr. Reilly, they speak of
so highly,
Upon me soul, Reilly, you're doin' quite
well.
> *Is That Mr. Reilly? Chorus*

Sow a Thought, and you reap an Act;
Sow an Act, and you reap a Habit;
Sow a Habit, and you reap a Character;
Sow a Character, and you reap a Des-
tiny.
> *Quoted by* SAMUEL SMILES
> *[1812–1904], in Life and La-*
> *bour [1887]*

Now is the time for all good men to
come to the aid of the party.
> *Practice sentence used in type-*
> *writing* [1]

As Maine goes, so goes the nation.[2]
> *American political maxim*
> *[Circa 1888]*

Sister Anne, do you see any one coming?
> *The anxious cry of Fatima, one*
> *of the wives of Bluebeard*

Slide, Kelly, Slide.
> *Title of song by* J. W. KELLY
> *[1889]*

Oh, Shenandoah, I long to hear you.
Away, you rolling river,
Oh Shenandoah, I long to hear you.
Away, I'm bound to go
'Cross the wide Missouri.
> *Song*

In the first person, simply *shall* foretells,
In *will* a threat or else a promise
dwells;
Shall in the second and third does
threat,

[1] Charles Weller, a court reporter, originated this expression in . . . 1867 to test the
efficiency of the first practical typewriter
which his friend Christopher Sholes had constructed. — *Life*, April 11, 1955
[2] As Maine goes, so goes Vermont. —
JAMES FARLEY: *Statement to press* [Novem-
ber 4, 1936] *after predicting that Roosevelt
would carry 46 states in the presidential election*

Will then simply foretells a future feat.
> *Grammar, Irish National Schools*

Try what you will, there's nothing like leather.
> *Nothing Like Leather*

The sweetest lives are those to duty wed,
Whose deeds, both great and small,
Are close-knit strands of an unbroken thread,
Where love ennobles all.
The world may sound no trumpet, ring no bells;
The book of life the shining record tells.
> *Attributed to Elizabeth Barrett Browning, but not found in her writings*

Ladling the butter from adjacent tubs,
Stubbs butters Freeman, Freeman butters Stubbs.
> *Variously quoted [Circa 1890], alluding to the mutual praise of two famous Oxford historians*

Lizzie Borden took an axe
And gave her mother forty whacks;
When she saw what she had done
She gave her father forty-one!
> *Rhyme popular after the murder trial of Lizzie Borden at Fall River, Massachusetts [June, 1893]*

The little cares that fretted me,
  I lost them yesterday,
Among the fields above the sea,
  Among the winds at play.
> *Out in the Fields, in St. Paul's Magazine, August 20, 1898*

Out in the fields with God!
> *Ibid.*

Remember the Maine! [1]
> *Slogan, Spanish-American War [1898]*

The halls of fame are open wide
  And they are always full;
Some go in by the door called "push,"
  And some by the door called "pull."
> *Quoted by Stanley Baldwin [1867–1947] in a speech in the House of Commons*

[1] On February 15, 1898, the American battleship *Maine* was blown up in Havana harbor, Cuba.

He who whispers down a well
About the goods he has to sell,
Will never reap the golden dollars
Like him who shows them round and hollers.
> *Quoted by the then Prince of Wales [1894–   ] (Duke of Windsor); thought to be of American origin*

The codfish lays ten thousand eggs,
  The homely hen lays one.
The codfish never cackles
  To tell you what she's done.
And so we scorn the codfish,
  While the humble hen we prize,
Which only goes to show you
  That it pays to advertise.
> *It Pays to Advertise*

Two ears and but a single tongue
By nature's laws to man belong;
The lesson she would teach is clear:
Repeat but half of what you hear.
> *Old jingle*

One white foot — try him,
Two white feet — buy him,
Three white feet — look well about him;
Four white feet — go without him.[1]
> *Rhyme for a horse-buyer*

An apple a day keeps the doctor away.
> *Current since the 19th century*

The great unwashed.
> *19th century expression*

The way to a man's heart is through his stomach.
> *Current since the 19th century*

All the world is queer save me and thee; and sometimes I think thee is a little queer.
> *Attributed to an unidentified Quaker, speaking to his wife*

Man is the only animal that eats when he is not hungry, drinks when he

[1] Three white feet and a white nose,
  Rip off his skin and throw him to the crows.
  New Hampshire version of last two lines

is not thirsty, and makes love at all seasons.

Source unknown

You can always tell a Harvard man, but you can't tell him much.

Attributed to JAMES BARNES
[*1866–1936*]

Keeping up with the Joneses.

Popular saying

Paying through the nose.[1]

Popular phrase for excessive payment

Rest and be thankful.

Inscription on stone seat in the Scottish Highlands, and title of one of Wordsworth's poems

Wisdom of many and the wit of one.

Definition of a proverb [2]

Doesn't amount to Hannah Cook.[3]

Saying common in Maine and on Cape Cod

Drive a coach and six through an Act of Parliament.

Credited to Sir Stephen Rice [1637–1715], Chief Baron of the Exchequer, by MACAULAY *in History of England [1849–1861], Chap. 12*

Free soil, free men, free speech, Frémont.

Rallying cry of the Republican Party in 1856, when John Charles Frémont [1813–1890] was the party's candidate for the presidency

---

[1] Grimm says that Odin had a poll-tax which was called in Sweden a nose-tax; it was a penny per nose, or poll. — *Deutsche Rechts Alterthümer*

[2] Probably based on the definition of a proverb which Lord John Russell gave one morning at breakfast at Mardock's: "One man's wit, and all men's wisdom." — *Memoirs of Sir James Mackintosh* [*1765–1832*], Vol. I, Page 473

[3] Variously explained as a character who once lived on Campobello Island; a corruption of a phrase in Indian dialect; and a comparison with the worthlessness (for navigation) of a cook on board ship.

Dirty work at the crossroads.

Attributed [1] *to* WALTER MELVILLE'S *melodrama The Girl Who Took the Wrong Turning, or, No Wedding Bells for Him*

The goose hangs high.[2]

Common saying for a favorable situation

Hit's a lot worse to be soul-hungry than to be body-hungry.

A Kentucky mountain woman asking for her granddaughter to be admitted to Berea College high school [Circa 1900]. Quoted by CARL R. WOODWARD.[3]

The Great White Way.

Title of novel [1901] by ALBERT BIGELOW PAINE [*1861–1937*]

There ain't no such animal.

Comment of a New Jersey farmer looking at a dromedary at a circus: cartoon in Life, November 7, 1907, credited to Everybody's Magazine

How old is Ann?

Popular saying in the early 20th century [4]

The Pyramids first, which in Egypt were laid;
Next Babylon's Garden, for Amytis made;
Then Mausolos' Tomb of affection and guilt;
Fourth, the Temple of Dian in Ephesus built;
The Colossus of Rhodes, cast in brass, to the Sun;
Sixth, Jupiter's Statue, by Phidias done;

---

[1] In *Notes and Queries* (London).

[2] Originally, perhaps, "the goose *honks* high" — it cries and flies high. Wild geese fly higher when the weather is fine or promises to be fine. Hence, the prospects are bright; everything is favourable. — *Century Dictionary*

[3] In *The Wonderful World of Books*, edited by ALFRED STEFFERUD [*1953*].

[4] This question became well known when *The New York Press*, October 16, 1903, printed the problem: "Mary is 24 years old. She is twice as old as Ann was when Mary was as old as Ann is now. How old is Ann?" The answer is that Ann is 18.

The Pharos of Egypt comes last, we are
  told,
Or the Palace of Cyrus, cemented with
  gold.
                        Seven Wonders of the
                        Ancient World
Use it up, wear it out;
Make it do, or do without.
                        New England maxim
  Earned a precarious living by tak-
ing in one another's washing.
                        Origin unknown
Something old, something new,
Something borrowed, something blue,
And a lucky sixpence in her shoe.[1]
                        Wedding rhyme
  God looks after fools, drunkards, and
the United States.
                        Epigram
Oh, why don't you work
Like other men do?
How the hell can I work
When there's no work to do?
                        Hallelujah, I'm a Bum
                        [Circa 1907]
Every time I come to town
The boys keep kicking my dawg
  around;
Makes no difference if he is a hound,
They've got to quit kicking my dawg
  around.
                        Champ Clark campaign song
                        [1912]
Old soldiers never die;
They only fade away!
                        War song, British Army
                        [1914–1918]
She was poor but she was honest,
And her parents were the same,
Till she met a city feller,
And she lost her honest name.
                        War song [1914–1918]
  Fifty million Frenchmen can't be
wrong.[2]
                        Saying popular with American
                        soldiers during World War I
                        [1917–1918]

My aunt's charwoman's sister's son
Heard a policeman on his beat
Say to a nursemaid down our street
That he knew a man who had a friend
And he could tell when the war would
  end.
                        Jingle popular in 1917–1918
Don't sell America short.[1]
                        Popular American saying
                        [1925–1929]
Lord, through this hour
  Be Thou our Guide,
So by Thy power
  No foot shall slide.
                        Westminster Chimes
Climb high
Climb far
Your goal the sky
Your aim the star.
                        Inscription on Hopkins Memo-
                        rial Steps, Williams College,
                        Williamstown, Massachusetts
Mother, may I go out to swim?
Yes, my darling daughter:
Hang your clothes on a hickory limb
And don't go near the water.
                        Origin dubious
Lives of great men all remind us
  As their pages o'er we turn,
That we're apt to leave behind us
  Letters that we ought to burn.
                        Quoted by DR. A. S. W. ROSEN-
                        BACH *in A Book Hunter's Holi-*
                        day [1936]
See the happy moron,
  He doesn't give a damn.
I wish I were a moron —
  My God, perhaps I am!
                        Incorrectly attributed to
                        Dorothy Parker
You will eat, bye and bye,
In that glorious land above the sky;

---

[1] There are variants for the less familiar
last line, such as "And a silver sixpence in
each shoe."
[2] Sometimes "forty" or "thirty" is heard
instead of "fifty." When Texas Guinan and

her troupe were refused entry into France in
1931, she was quoted as saying: "It goes to
show that fifty million Frenchmen *can* be
wrong." She promptly renamed her show *Too
Hot for Paris*, and toured the United States
with it.
[1] The phrase may have stemmed from
"Never be a bear on the United States," attributed variously to JUNIUS S. MORGAN
[1813–1890] and J. P. MORGAN [1837–1913].

Work and pray, live on hay,
You'll get pie in the sky when you die.
The Preacher and the Slave [1]
The difficult we do immediately. The
impossible takes a little longer.
*Slogan of United States Army
Air Forces*
G. I. Joe.
*World War II term for
infantryman* [2]
Stay with me, God. The night is dark,
The night is cold: my little spark
Of courage dies. The night is long;
Be with me, God, and make me strong.
A Soldier — His Prayer. [3] *Stanza 1*
We sure liberated the hell out of this
place.
*American soldier in the ruins of
a French village, 1944; quoted
by* MAX MILLER *in The Far
Shore* [1945]
Spartan simplicity must be observed.
Nothing will be done merely because it
contributes to beauty, convenience,
comfort, or prestige.
*From the Office of the Chief
Signal Officer, U. S. Army,
May 29, 1945*
Soldiers who wish to be a hero
Are practically zero,
But those who wish to be civilians,
Jesus, they run into the millions.
*Army latrine inscription quoted
by* NORMAN ROSTEN *in The Big
Road* [1945]
Since wars begin in the minds of
men, it is in the minds of men that the
defences of peace must be constructed.
*Constitution of the United Na-
tions Educational, Scientific and
Cultural Organization* [1946]

[1] Attributed to Joe Hill in the 1927 edition
of *I.W.W. Songs.*
[2] This name, chosen for the soldier in
Lieutenant DAVE BREGER's comic strip for
Yank, the Army weekly, first appeared in
the issue of June 17, 1942. Writing in *Time*
[February 26, 1945], Lieutenant Breger said:
"I decided on 'G. I. Joe,' the 'G. I.' [Govern-
ment Issue] because of its prevalence in Army
talk, and the 'Joe' for the alliterative effect."
[3] This poem, found on a scrap of paper
in a slit trench in Tunisia during the battle
of El Agheila, was printed in *Poems from the*

We are not dealing simply with a
military or scientific problem but with
a problem in statecraft and the ways
of the human spirit.
*Report on the International
Control of Atomic Energy, published March 16, 1946* [1]
Relief from the terrible fear which
can do so much to engender the very
thing feared.
Ibid.
Anything constructive in relation to
atomic energy must inevitably be novel
and immensely difficult.
Ibid.

FOREIGN PROVERBS
AND SAYINGS

LATIN

Actus non facit reum, nisi mens sit
rea.
The act is not criminal unless the
intent is criminal.
Legal maxim
Ad majorem Dei gloriam.
To the greater glory of God.
Motto of the Society of Jesus
Adeste, fideles,
Laeti triumphantes;
Venite, venite in Bethlehem.

O come, all ye faithful,
Joyful and triumphant,
O come ye, O come ye to Bethlehem.
Hymn, 18th Century
Ave Caesar, morituri te salutamus.
Hail Caesar, we who are about to
die salute you.
*Salutation of the Roman glad-
iators upon entering the arena*
Caveat emptor.
Let the buyer beware.
Proverb

Desert, by members of the British Eighth
Army [1944].
[1] Prepared for the Department of State by
a Board of Consultants: Chester I. Barnard,
J. Robert Oppenheimer, Charles A. Thomas,
Harry A. Winne, and David E. Lilienthal,
Chairman.

Cucullus non facit monachum.[1]
The cowl does not make a monk.
Medieval Latin proverb

De gustibus non disputandum.
There is no arguing about tastes.
Proverb

De minimis non curat lex.
The law is not concerned with trifles.
Legal maxim

Deus vult.
God wills it.
Motto of the Crusades [*1095*]

Divide et impera.
Divide and rule.
Ancient political maxim cited by
MACHIAVELLI

E Pluribus Unum.
One out of many.
*Motto on title page of the
Gentleman's Journal* [*January,
1692*], *adopted as motto for
seal of the United States, June
20, 1782*

Et in Arcadia ego.
I too have lived in Arcadia.[2]
*Inscription on a tomb in a
painting by Guercino* [*Circa
1623*]

Festina lente.
Make haste slowly.
Borrowed from the Greek

Mea culpa.
The fault is mine.
*Latin phrase derived from the
Mass*

Non conscire sibi.
Conscious of no fault.
Latin saying

Omnis festinatio est a diabolo.
All haste is from the devil.
Medieval Latin proverb

[1] It takes more than a hood and sad eyes
to make a monk. — *Albanian Proverb*
[2] This translation is now usually considered
erroneous. The accepted translation is: I too
am in Arcadia — that is, Even in Arcadia there
am I [Death].
Also in a painting by Poussin [*circa* 1630].
E. PANOFSKY discusses the phrase in *Philosophy and History: Essays Presented to E. Cas-
sirer* [1936].

Post hoc, ergo propter hoc.
After this, therefore because of this.
Definition of fallacy in logic

Pro bono publico.
For the public good.
Saying

Semper fidelis.
Ever faithful.
Motto of the U. S. Marine Corps

Si monumentum requiris, circum-
spice.
If you seek a monument, look about
you.
*Inscription on Sir Christopher
Wren's tomb in St. Paul's
Cathedral, London*

Sic semper tyrannis.[1]
Thus ever to tyrants.
Motto of State of Virginia
[*Adopted 1779*]

Sic transit gloria mundi.
Thus passes away the glory of this
world.
Saying

FRENCH

Il ne faut pas être plus royaliste que
le roi.
One must not be more royalist than
the king.
*Saying which originated under
Louis XVI*

Liberté! Egalité! Fraternité!
Liberty! Equality! Fraternity!
*Phrase dating from before the
French Revolution, officially
adopted in 1793*

Rien ne réussit comme le succès.
Nothing succeeds like success.
Proverb

Tout passe, tout casse, tout lasse.
Everything passes, everything per-
ishes, everything palls.
Proverb

[1] The words of John Wilkes Booth as he
shot Lincoln at Ford's Theater [April 14,
1865].

Ah, les bons vieux temps où nous étions si malheureux!

Oh, the good old times when we were so unhappy!

Saying

MISCELLANEOUS

Whatever kind of word thou speakest the like shalt thou hear.

Greek Anthology. Book IX, Epigram 382

When I am dead let fire destroy the world; it matters not to me, for I am safe.

Ibid. Fragment 430

Envy slays itself by its own arrows.

Ibid. Book X, Epigram 111

Give me today, and take tomorrow.

Quoted and condemned by St. Chrysostom

One picture is worth more than ten thousand words.

Chinese proverb

On the day of victory no one is tired.

Arab proverb

I came to the place of my birth, and cried, "The friends of my youth, where are they?" And echo answered, "Where are they?"

Arab saying

BALLADS

For in my mind, of all mankind
I love but you alone.

The Nut-Brown Maid [15th century]. Refrain

For I must to the green-wood go,
Alone, a banished man.

Ibid.

No burial this pretty pair
  Of any man receives,
Till Robin Red-breast piously
  Did cover them with leaves.

The Children in the Wood. Stanza 16

The king sits in Dunfermline town
Drinking the blude-red wine.

Sir Patrick Spens. Stanza 1

"To Noroway, to Noroway,
To Noroway o'er the faem;
The king's daughter o' Noroway,
'Tis thou must bring her hame."

Sir Patrick Spens. Stanza 4

The first word that Sir Patrick read
So loud, loud laughed he;
The neist word that Sir Patrick read
The tear blinded his e'e.

Ibid. Stanza 5

"I saw the new moon late yestreen
Wi' the auld moon in her arm;
And if we gang to sea, master,
I fear we'll come to harm."

Ibid. Stanza 10

Half-owre, half-owre to Aberdour,
'Tis fifty fathoms deep;
And there lies gude Sir Patrick Spens,
Wi' the Scots lords at his feet!

Ibid. Stanza 19

The blinded boy that shoots so trim,[1]
From heaven down did hie.

King Cophetua and the Beggar-maid. Stanza 2

It was a friar of orders gray[2]
Walked forth to tell his beads.

The Friar of Orders Gray.[3] Stanza 1

Our joys as wingèd dreams do fly;
  Why then should sorrow last?
Since grief but aggravates thy loss,
  Grieve not for what is past.

Ibid. Stanza 13

King Stephen was a worthy peer,
His breeches cost him but a crown.

Take Thy Old Cloak About Thee.[4] Stanza 7

It's pride that puts this country down;
Man, take thine old cloak about thee.

Ibid.

[1] Young Adam Cupid, he that shot so trim,
  When King Cophetua loved the beggar-maid!
    SHAKESPEARE: *Romeo and Juliet* [1594–1595], *Act II, Sc. 1, L. 13*
[2] See Shakespeare, page 130b.
[3] THOMAS PERCY [1728–1811] composed this ballad from various fragments of ancient ballads found in Shakespeare's plays. It appeared in his *Reliques of Ancient English Poetry* [1765].
[4] See Shakespeare, page 187b.

Fight on, my merry men all;
For why, my life is at an end.[1]
> *Chevy Chase*

A fairer lady there never was seen
Than the blind beggar's daughter of
Bethnall Green.
> *The Beggar's Daughter of*
> *Bethnall Green.[2] Stanza 33*

When captains courageous,[3] whom
death could not daunt,
Did march to the siege of the city of
Gaunt,
They mustered their soldiers by two
and by three,
And the foremost in battle was Mary
Ambree.
> *Mary Ambree.[4] Stanza 1*

Then let Jane Shore with sorrow sing,
That was belovèd of a king.
> *Jane Shore. Stanza 1*

"I'll rest," said he, "but thou shalt
walk";
So doth this wandering Jew
From place to place, but cannot rest
For seeing countries new.
> *The Wandering Jew. Stanza 9*

For thirty pence our Saviour was sold
Among the false Jews, as I have been
told;
And twenty-nine is the worth of thee,
For I think thou art one penny worser
than he.
> *King John and the Abbot of*
> *Canterbury. Stanza 21*

Glasgerion swore a full great oath,
By oak, and ash and thorn.[5]
> *Glasgerion. Stanza 19*

[1] Says Johnnie, "Fight on, my merry men all,
I'm a little wounded, but I am not slain;
I will lay me down for to bleed a while,
Then I'll rise and fight with you again."
Johnnie Armstrong's Last Good-night,
St. 18 (DRYDEN's *Miscellanies* [1702])
[2] This very house was built by the blind
beggar of Bednall Green, so much talked of
and sung in ballads. — SAMUEL PEPYS: *Diary*
[June 26, 1663]
[3] Source of the title of RUDYARD KIPLING's
Captains Courageous.
[4] BEN JONSON calls any virago Mary Am-
bree, and JOHN FLETCHER alludes to Mary
Ambree in *The Scornful Lady* [1616].
[5] See Kipling, page 820b.

In Scarlet town, where I was born,
There was a fair maid dwellin',
Made every youth cry Well-a-way!
Her name was Barbara Allen.
> *Barbara Allen's Cruelty.*
> *Stanza 1*

All in the merry month of May,
When green buds they were swellin',
Young Jemmy Grove on his death-bed
lay,
For love of Barbara Allen.
> *Ibid. Stanza 2*

So slowly, slowly rase she up,
And slowly she came nigh him,
And when she drew the curtain by —
"Young man, I think you're dyin'."
> *Ibid. Stanza 4*

True Thomas lay on Huntlie Bank;
A ferlie he spied wi' his e'e;
And there he saw a lady bright
Come riding down by the Eildon Tree.
> *Thomas the Rhymer. Stanza 1*

"A bed, a bed," Clerk Saunders said,
"A bed for you and me!"
"Fye na, fye na," said may Margaret,
"Till anes we married be!"
> *Clerk Saunders. Stanza 2*

There were twa sisters sat in a bour;
Binnorie, O Binnorie!
There came a knight to be their wooer,
By the bonnie milldams o' Binnorie.
> *Binnorie. Stanza 1*

There were three ravens sat on a tree,
They were as black as they might be.
> *The Three Ravens. Stanza 1*

The one of them said to his make,
"Where shall we our breakfast take?"
> *Ibid. Stanza 2*

Down there came a fallow doe
As great with young as she might go.
> *Ibid. Stanza 6*

She buried him before the prime,
She was dead herself ere evensong
time.
> *Ibid. Stanza 9*

God send every gentleman
Such hounds, such hawks, and such a
leman.
> *Ibid. Stanza 10*

Ye Highlands and ye Lawlands,
O where hae ye been?

They hae slain the Earl of Murray,
And hae laid him on the green.
The Bonny Earl of Murray.
Stanza 1

O waly, waly, up the bank,
And waly, waly, doun the brae,
And waly, waly, yon burn-side,
Where I and my Love wont to gae!
Waly, Waly. Stanza 1

O waly, waly, gin love be bonnie,
A little time while it is new!
But when 'tis auld it waxeth cauld,
And fades awa' like morning dew.
Ibid. Stanza 2

But had I wist, before I kist,
That love had been sae ill to win,
I had lock'd my heart in a case o' gowd,
And pinn'd it wi' a siller pin.
Ibid. Stanza 5

"What gat ye to your dinner, Lord
  Randal, my Son?
What gat ye to your dinner, my hand-
  some young man?"
"I gat eels boil'd in broo'; mother,
  make my bed soon,
For I'm weary wi' hunting, and fain
  wald lie down."
Lord Randal

A ship I have got in the North Country
And she goes by the name of the
  Golden Vanity,
O, I fear she will be taken by a Spanish
  Gal-la-lee,
As she sails by the Low-lands low.
The Golden Vanity. Stanza 1

And when with envy Time, trans-
  ported,
Shall think to rob us of our joys,
You'll in your girls again be courted,
And I'll go wooing in my boys.
Winifreda.¹ Stanza 8

But in vain she did conjure him
To depart her presence so;
Having a thousand tongues to allure
  him,
And but one to bid him go.
Dulcina.² Stanza 2

¹ *Winifreda* appeared in LEWIS's *Collection*
[1726].
² This song is mentioned by IZAAK WALTON
in *The Compleat Angler* [1653]. It has been
ascribed to Raleigh, on very doubtful authority.

Over the mountains,
And over the waves,
Under the fountains
And under the graves;
Under floods that are deepest,
Which Neptune obey,
Over rocks that are steepest,
Love will find out the way.
Love Will Find Out the Way.
Stanza 1

O what a plague is love
How shall I bear it?
She will inconstant prove,
I greatly fear it.
Phillida Flouts Me. Stanza 1

And let all women strive to be
As constant as Penelope.
Constant Penelope. Stanza 18

For without money, George,
  A man is but a beast:
But bringing money, thou shalt be
  Always my welcome guest.
George Barnwell.¹ Part II,
Stanza 25

EPITAPHS

A zealous Lock-Smith dyed of late,
And did arrive at heaven gate,
He stood without and would not
  knocke,
Because he meant to picke the locke.
Epitaph upon a Puritanicall
Lock-Smith; quoted by WIL-
LIAM CAMDEN *in Remaines*
Concerning Britaine [1637]

All the brothers were valiant, and
all the sisters virtuous.
From the inscription on the
tomb of the Duchess of New-
castle in Westminster Abbey
[1673]

A house she hath, 'tis made of such
  good fashion,
The tenant ne'er shall pay for reparation,
Nor will the landlord ever raise her rent
Or turn her out of doors for non-pay-
  ment;

¹ Inspired by GEORGE LILLO's play, *The
London Merchant, or, The History of George
Barnwell,* first acted in 1731.

From chimney-tax this cell is free,
To such a house who would not tenant
    be?
    For Rebecca Bogess, Folkestone,
                    August 22, 1688
It is so soon that I am done for,
I wonder what I was begun for.
        For a child aged three weeks,
                Cheltenham Churchyard
She tasted of life's bitter cup,
Refused to drink the potion up;
She turned her little head aside,
Disgusted with the task and died.
        For a child aged six months
Here lies John Knott:
His father was Knott before him,
He lived Knott, died Knott,
Yet underneath this stone doth lie
Knott christened, Knott begot,
And here he lies and still is Knott.
            Perthshire Churchyard
Here lie I, Martin Elginbrodde:
Ha'e mercy o' my soul, Lord God,
As I wad do, were I Lord God
And ye were Martin Elginbrodde.
        Aberdeen Churchyard (Quoted
        by GEORGE MACDONALD *in his*
        novel, David Elginbrod [1862],
        Chap. 13)
Beneath this stone, a lump of clay,
    Lies Arabella Young,
Who on the 24th of May
    Began to hold her tongue.
            British Museum Collection
Beneath this stone a lump of clay
    Lies Uncle Peter Daniels
Who too early in the month of May
    Took off his winter flannels.
        Medway, Massachusetts, 1746
Here sleeps in peace a Hampshire Gren-
    adier,
Who caught his death by drinking cold
    small beer;
Soldiers, take heed from his untimely
    fall,
And when you're hot, drink strong, or
    not at all.
            Winchester Churchyard, 1764
A dying preacher I have been,
To dying hearers such as you.
Though dead, a preacher still I am
To such as come my grave to view.

Let this to you a warning be
That quickly you must follow me.
        Elder Samuel Waldo, South
        Dover (Wingdale) Cemetery,
        Dutchess County, New York,
        September 10, 1798
Immaturus obi: sed tu felicior annos
Vive meos, Bona Respublica! Vive
    tuos.
(I died young; but thou, O Good Re-
    public,
Live out my years for me with better
    fortune.)
        Inscription, perhaps chosen by
        Thomas Jefferson, on the tomb
        of Meriwether Lewis [1774–
        1809], explorer of the Lewis
        and Clark expedition
    Here lies Sir Jenkin Grout, who loved
his friend, and persuaded his enemy:
what his mouth ate, his hand paid for:
what his servants robbed, he restored:
if a woman gave him pleasure, he supported her in pain: he never forgot his
children: and whoso touched his finger,
drew after it his whole body.
        Quoted by RALPH WALDO EM-
        ERSON *in his essay, Manners*
        [1856]
This is the grave of Mike O'Day
Who died maintaining his right of way.
His right was clear, his will was strong,
But he's just as dead as if he'd been
    wrong.
                    20th century

NURSERY RHYMES

Old Mother Goose,
When she wanted to wander,
Would ride through the air
On a very fine gander
            Old Mother Goose
Cock a doodle doo!
My dame has lost her shoe;
My master's lost his fiddling-stick,
And knows not what to do.
            Cock a Doodle Doo
Three blind mice, see how they run!
They all ran after the farmer's wife,
She cut off their tails with a carving-
    knife,

Did you ever see such a sight in your
    life,
      As three blind mice?
             Three Blind Mice

A frog he would a-wooing go.
    "Heigh-ho!" says Rowley.
      A Frog He Would A-wooing Go

With a rowley powley gammon and
    spinach,
Heigh-ho! says Anthony Rowley.
            Ibid. Chorus

Old King Cole
Was a merry old soul,
And a merry old soul was he,
He called for his pipe,
And he called for his bowl,
And he called for his fiddlers three.
            Old King Cole

The King of France went up the hill,
With forty thousand men;
The King of France came down the hill,
And ne'er went up again.
        The King of France

Jack Sprat could eat no fat,
His wife could eat no lean;
And so between them both, you see,
They licked the platter clean.
              Jack Sprat

Rain, rain, go away,
Come again another day.
              Rain, Rain

Pat-a-cake, pat-a-cake, baker's man,
Bake me a cake as fast as you can;
Pat it and prick it, and mark it with B,
Put it in the oven for baby and me.
             Pat-a-cake

The lion and the unicorn
Were fighting for the crown;
The lion beat the unicorn
All round the town.
Some gave them white bread,
And some gave them brown;
Some gave them plum cake,
And sent them out of town.
    The Lion and the Unicorn

Little Jack Horner sat in the corner,
Eating a Christmas pie:
He put in his thumb, and pulled out a
    plum,
And said, "What a good boy am I!"
          Little Jack Horner

London Bridge is falling down,
My fair lady.
            London Bridge

As I was going to St. Ives,
I met a man with seven wives,
Each wife had seven sacks,
Each sack had seven cats,
Each cat had seven kits:
Kits, cats, sacks, and wives,
How many were there going to St.
    Ives?
      As I Was Going to St. Ives

The man in the wilderness asked of me
How many strawberries grew in the
    sea.
I answered him as I thought good,
"As many as red herrings grow in the
    wood."
    The Man in the Wilderness

Lady-bug, lady-bug, fly away home,
Your house is on fire, and your children
    will burn.
        Lady-bug, Lady-bug

Hickory, dickory dock,
The mouse ran up the clock,
The clock struck one,
The mouse ran down;
Hickory, dickory dock.
       Hickory, Dickory Dock

Baa, baa, black sheep,
Have you any wool?
Yes, sir, yes, sir,
Three bags full:
One for my master,
And one for my dame,
And one for the little boy
Who lives down the lane.
      Baa, Baa, Black Sheep

Mary, Mary, quite contrary,
How does your garden grow?
With silver bells, and cockle shells,
And pretty maids all in a row.
    Mary, Mary, Quite Contrary

Oranges and lemons,
Say the bells of St. Clement's.
When will you pay me?
Say the bells of Old Bailey.
When I grow rich,
Say the bells of Shoreditch.
      Oranges and Lemons

Here comes a candle to light you to
    bed,

Here comes a chopper to chop off your
   head.

Oranges and Lemons

"Who killed Cock Robin?"
"I," said the sparrow,
"With my bow and arrow,
I killed Cock Robin." [1]

Who Killed Cock Robin?

"Who saw him die?"
"I," said the Fly,
"With my little eye,
I saw him die."

Ibid.

This little pig went to market;
This little pig stayed home;
This little pig had roast beef;
This little pig had none;
And this little pig cried, Wee, wee, wee!
All the way home.

This Little Pig

Little boy blue, come blow your horn,
The sheep's in the meadow, the cow's
   in the corn;
But where is the boy who looks after
   the sheep?
He's under the haystack fast asleep.
Will you wake him? No, not I,
For if I do, he'll be sure to cry.

Little Boy Blue

Simple Simon met a pieman
   Going to the fair:
Says Simple Simon to the pieman,
   "Let me taste your ware."

Simple Simon

Ding, dong, bell,
Pussy's in the well.
Who put her in?
Little Johnny Green.
Who pulled her out?
Big Jack Stout.

Ding, Dong, Bell

Little Tommy Tucker
Sings for his supper;
What shall we give him?
White bread and butter.

Little Tommy Tucker

[1] "Who killed John Keats?"
   "I," said the Quarterly,
   So savage and tartarly,
   " 'Twas one of my feats."

BYRON: *Letter to John Murray*
[July 30, 1821]

How shall he cut it
Without any knife?
How will he marry
Without any wife?

Little Tommy Tucker

Cross-patch,
Draw the latch,
Sit by the fire and spin:
Take a cup
And drink it up,
Then call your neighbors in.

Cross-patch

Hey diddle diddle
The cat and the fiddle,
The cow jumped over the moon;
The little dog laughed
To see such sport,
And the dish ran away with the spoon.

Hey Diddle Diddle

Three wise men of Gotham
Went to sea in a bowl:
If the bowl had been stronger,
My song would have been longer.

Three Wise Men of Gotham

Jack and Jill went up the hill
To fetch a pail of water;
Jack fell down and broke his crown,
And Jill came tumbling after.

Jack and Jill

See-saw, Margery Daw,
Jacky shall have a new master;
Jacky must have but a penny a day,
Because he can't work any faster.

See-saw, Margery Daw

Taffy was a Welshman, Taffy was a
   thief;
Taffy came to my house and stole a
   piece of beef.

Taffy Was a Welshman

The Queen of Hearts
She made some tarts,
   All on a summer's day;
The Knave of Hearts
He stole the tarts,
   And took them clean away.

The Queen of Hearts

Bye, baby bunting,
Daddy's gone a-hunting,
Gone to get a rabbit skin
To wrap the baby bunting in.

Bye, Baby Bunting

Come, let's to bed,
Says Sleepy-head;
Tarry a while, says Slow;
Put on the pot,
Says Greedy-gut,
We'll sup before we go.

Let's to Bed

Four and twenty tailors went to kill a
  snail,
The best man among them durst not
  touch her tail.
She put out her horns like a little
  Kyloe cow,
Run, tailors, run, or she'll kill you all
  e'en now.

Four and Twenty Tailors

Goosey goosey gander,
Whither shall I wander?
Upstairs and downstairs,
And in my lady's chamber;
There I met an old man who wouldn't
  say his prayers;
I took him by the left leg,
And threw him down the stairs.

Goosey Goosey Gander

Sing a song of sixpence,
  A pocket full of rye,
Four and twenty blackbirds,
  Baked in a pie;
When the pie was opened,
  The birds began to sing;
Wasn't that a dainty dish
  To set before a king?

Sing a Song of Sixpence

The king was in his counting-house
  Counting out his money;
The queen was in the parlor
  Eating bread and honey;
The maid was in the garden
  Hanging out the clothes,
Along came a blackbird,
  And snipped off her nose.

Ibid.

There was an old woman who lived in
  a shoe,
She had so many children she didn't
  know what to do;
She gave them some broth without any
  bread,
She whipped them all soundly and put
  them to bed.

There Was an Old Woman

Ride a cock-horse to Banbury Cross,
To see a fine lady upon a white horse;
Rings on her fingers and bells on her
  toes,
She shall have music wherever she goes.

Ride a Cock-Horse

Tom, Tom, the piper's son,
Stole a pig, and away he run;
The pig was eat, and Tom was beat,
And Tom went howling down the
  street.

Tom, Tom, the Piper's Son

Tom, Tom, the piper's son,
He learned to play when he was young.
But all the tune that he could play,
Was "Over the hills and far away." [1]

Ibid.

"Where are you going to, my pretty
  maid?"
"I'm going a-milking, sir," she said.

*Where Are You Going To, My
Pretty Maid?*

"My face is my fortune, sir," she said.

Ibid.

"Nobody asked you, sir," she said.

Ibid.

One a penny, two a penny, hot cross-
  buns;
If you have no daughters, give them
  to your sons.

Hot Cross-Buns

Pease-porridge hot, pease-porridge cold,
Pease-porridge in the pot, nine days
  old.

Pease-porridge Hot

Curly-locks, Curly-locks,
Wilt thou be mine?
Thou shalt not wash dishes
Nor yet feed the swine.
But sit on a cushion
And sew a fine seam,
And feed upon strawberries,
Sugar and cream.

Curly-Locks

I had a little nut tree, nothing would it
  bear
But a silver nutmeg and a golden pear;
The king of Spain's daughter came to
  visit me,

[1] See D'Urfey, page 290b and Gay, page
308b.

And all for the sake of my little nut
   tree.
         I Had a Little Nut Tree
Humpty Dumpty sat on a wall,
Humpty Dumpty had a great fall;
All the king's horses
And all the king's men
Couldn't put Humpty Dumpty together
   again.
         Humpty Dumpty
Little Bo-Peep has lost her sheep,
   And can't tell where to find them;
Leave them alone, and they'll come
   home,
   Wagging their tails behind them.
         Little Bo-Peep
Little Polly Flinders
Sat among the cinders,
Warming her pretty little toes.
Her mother came and caught her,
And whipped her little daughter
For spoiling her nice new clothes.
         Little Polly Flinders
The north wind doth blow,
And we shall have snow,
And what will poor robin do then,
   Poor thing?
He'll sit in a barn,
To keep himself warm,
And hide his head under his wing,
   Poor thing!
       The North Wind Doth Blow
Old Mother Hubbard
Went to the cupboard,
To fetch her poor dog a bone;
But when she got there
The cupboard was bare,
And so the poor dog had none.
         Old Mother Hubbard
Pussy cat, pussy cat, where have you
   been?
I've been to London to look at the
   queen.
Pussy cat, pussy cat, what did you
   there?
I frightened a little mouse under the
   chair.
         Pussy-Cat
Peter Piper picked a peck of pickled
   peppers;
A peck of pickled peppers Peter Piper
   picked.

If Peter Piper picked a peck of pickled
   peppers,
Where's the peck of pickled peppers
   Peter Piper picked?
         Peter Piper
Monday's child is fair of face,
Tuesday's child is full of grace,
Wednesday's child is full of woe,
Thursday's child has far to go,
Friday's child is loving and giving,
Saturday's child has to work for its
   living,
But a child that's born on the Sabbath
   day
Is fair and wise and good and gay.
         Rhyme
Solomon Grundy,
Born on a Monday,
Christened on Tuesday,
Married on Wednesday,
Took ill on Thursday,
Worse on Friday,
Died on Saturday,
Buried on Sunday:
This is the end
Of Solomon Grundy.
         Solomon Grundy
What are little boys made of?
Snips and snails, and puppy-dogs' tails;
That's what little boys are made of.
      What Are Little Boys Made Of?
What are little girls made of?
Sugar and spice, and everything nice;
That's what little girls are made of.
         Ibid.
Hickety, pickety, my black hen,
She lays eggs for gentlemen;
Gentlemen come every day
To see what my black hen doth lay.
         Hickety, Pickety
Little Miss Muffet
Sat on a tuffet,
Eating some curds and whey.
Along came a spider,
And sat down beside her,
And frightened Miss Muffet away.
         Little Miss Muffet
Peter, Peter Pumpkin-eater,
Had a wife and couldn't keep her;
He put her in a pumpkin shell,
And there he kept her very well.
      Peter, Peter Pumpkin-Eater

Jack, be nimble,
Jack, be quick,
Jack, jump over the candle-stick.
            Jack Be Nimble
There was a crooked man, and he went
    a crooked mile,
He found a crooked sixpence against a
    crooked stile;
He bought a crooked cat, which caught
    a crooked mouse,
And they all lived together in a little
    crooked house.
       There Was a Crooked Man
Diddle, diddle, dumpling, my son John,
He went to bed with his stockings on;
One shoe off, one shoe on;
Diddle, diddle, dumpling, my son John.
      Diddle, Diddle, Dumpling
Rub-a-dub-dub,
Three men in a tub,
And who do you think they be?
The butcher, the baker,
The candlestick-maker;
Turn 'em out, knaves all three!
          Rub-a-Dub-Dub
I saw three ships come sailing by,
Come sailing by, come sailing by,
I saw three ships come sailing by,
On New Year's Day in the morning.
         I Saw Three Ships
In fir tar is,
In oak none is.
In mud eel is,
In clay none is.
Goats eat ivy.
Mares eat oats.
               Rhyme
Lucy Locket lost her pocket,
Kitty Fisher found it;
There was not a penny in it,
But a ribbon round it.
           Lucy Locket
There were three jolly huntsmen,
As I have heard them say,
And they would go a-hunting
Upon St. David's Day.
   There Were Three Jolly Huntsmen
All day they hunted,
And nothing did they find,
But a ship a-sailing,
A-sailing with the wind.
               Ibid.

O do you know the muffin man,
The muffin man, the muffin man,
O do you know the muffin man,
That lives in Drury Lane?
          The Muffin Man
To market, to market to buy a fat pig,
Home again, home again, jiggety-jig.
       To Market, To Market
Doctor Foster went to Gloucester
In a shower of rain;
He stepped in a puddle, up to his
    middle,
And never went there again.
           Doctor Foster
There was an old woman
Lived under a hill;
And if she's not gone,
She lives there still.
     There Was an Old Woman
There was a little man, and he had a
    little gun,
And his bullets were made of lead, lead,
    lead;
He went to the brook, and saw a little
    duck,
And shot it through the head, head,
    head.
      There Was a Little Man
Lavender's blue, dilly, dilly, lavender's
    green;
When I am king, dilly, dilly, you shall
    be queen.
           Lavender's Blue
A dillar, a dollar,
A ten o'clock scholar,
What makes you come so soon?
You used to come at ten o'clock,
And now you come at noon.
         A Dillar, a Dollar
I had a little pony,
His name was Dapple-Gray;
I lent him to a lady
To ride a mile away.
She whipped him, she slashed him,
She rode him through the mire;
I would not lend my pony now
For all the lady's hire.
         I Had a Little Pony
Polly, put the kettle on,
Polly, put the kettle on,
Polly, put the kettle on,
We'll all have tea.

Sukey, take it off again,
Sukey, take it off again,
Sukey, take it off again,
They've all gone away.
Polly, Put the Kettle On

Little Tommy Tittlemouse
Lived in a little house;
He caught fishes
In other men's ditches.
Little Tommy Tittlemouse

The farmer in the dell, the farmer in
the dell,
Heigho! the derry oh, the farmer in the
dell.
The Farmer in the Dell

Hark! Hark! The dogs do bark,
The beggars are coming to town;
Some in rags, some in tags,
And some in velvet gowns.
Hark! Hark!

Ten little Indians standing in a line —
One went home, and then there were
nine.
Ten Little Indians

When good King Arthur ruled this
land,
He was a goodly king,
He bought three pecks of barley meal,
To make a bag pudding.
Good King Arthur

One misty, moisty morning,
When cloudy was the weather,
I chanced to meet an old man
Clothed all in leather;
He began to compliment,
And I began to grin —
"How do you do?" and "How do you
do?"
And "How do you do?" again!
One Misty, Moisty Morning

Bobby Shaftoe's gone to sea,
Silver buckles on his knee;

He'll come back and marry me,
Pretty Bobby Shaftoe.
Bobby Shaftoe

Bobby Shaftoe's fat and fair,
Combing down his yellow hair;
He's my love forevermore,
Pretty Bobby Shaftoe.
Ibid.

Fe, Fi, Fo, Fum!
I smell the blood of an Englishman;
Be he alive or be he dead,
I'll grind his bones to make my bread.
Fe, Fi, Fo, Fum

There was a man in our town,
And he was wondrous wise;
He jumped into a bramble bush
And scratched out both his eyes.
There Was a Man in Our Town

There were two blackbirds,
Sitting on a hill,
The one named Jack,
    The other named Jill;
Fly away, Jack! Fly Away, Jill!
Come again, Jack! Come again, Jill!
Two Blackbirds

This is the farmer sowing the corn,
That kept the cock that crowed in the
morn,
That waked the priest all shaven and
shorn,
That married the man all tattered and
torn,
That kissed the maiden all forlorn,
That milked the cow with the crumpled
horn,
That tossed the dog
That worried the cat
That killed the rat
That ate the malt
That lay in the house that Jack built.
The House that Jack Built

THE HOLY BIBLE

WYCLIFFE TRANSLATION
[1384]

This Bible is for the Government of the People, by the People, and for the People.

General Prologue

THE KING JAMES VERSION [1]
[1611]

OLD TESTAMENT

In the beginning God created the heaven and the earth.

Genesis. I, 1

And the earth was without form, and void; and darkness was upon the face of the deep. And the Spirit of God moved upon the face of the waters.

Ibid. 2

And God said, Let there be light; and there was light.

Ibid. 3

And the evening and the morning were the first day.

Ibid. 5

And God saw that it was good.

Ibid. 10

And God said, Let us make man in our image, after our likeness.

Ibid. 26

Male and female created he them.

Ibid. 27

Be fruitful, and multiply, and replenish the earth, and subdue it: and have dominion over the fish of the sea, and over the fowl of the air, and over

every living thing that moveth upon the earth.

Genesis. I, 28

And the Lord God formed man of the dust of the ground, and breathed into his nostrils the breath of life; and man became a living soul.

Ibid. II, 7

And the Lord God planted a garden eastward in Eden.

Ibid. 8

The tree of life also in the midst of the garden.

Ibid. 9

But of the tree of the knowledge of good and evil, thou shalt not eat of it: for in the day that thou eatest thereof thou shalt surely die.

Ibid. 17

It is not good that the man should be alone; I will make him an help meet for him.

Ibid. 18

And the Lord God caused a deep sleep to fall upon Adam, and he slept; and he took one of his ribs, and closed up the flesh instead thereof.

Ibid. 21

And the rib, which the Lord God had taken from man, made he a woman.

Ibid. 22

Bone of my bones, and flesh of my flesh.

Ibid. 23

Therefore shall a man leave his father and his mother, and shall cleave unto his wife: and they shall be one flesh.

Ibid. 24

Now the serpent was more subtile than any beast of the field.

Ibid. III, 1

Your eyes shall be opened, and ye shall be as gods, knowing good and evil.

Ibid. 5

[1] Among all our joys, there was no one that more filled our hearts, than the blessed continuance of the preaching of God's sacred Word among us; which is that inestimable treasure, which excelleth all the riches of the earth; because the fruit thereof extendeth itself, not only to the time spent in this transitory world, but directeth and disposeth men unto that eternal happiness which is above in heaven. — *The Translators' Dedication to James I*

And they sewed fig leaves together, and made themselves aprons.

Genesis. III, 7

And they heard the voice of the Lord God walking in the garden in the cool of the day.

Ibid. 8

The woman whom thou gavest to be with me, she gave me of the tree, and I did eat.

Ibid. 12

What is this that thou hast done? And the woman said, The serpent beguiled me, and I did eat.

Ibid. 13

In sorrow thou shalt bring forth children.

Ibid. 16

In the sweat of thy face shalt thou eat bread, till thou return unto the ground; for out of it wast thou taken: for dust thou art, and unto dust shalt thou return.

Ibid. 19

And Adam called his wife's name Eve; because she was the mother of all living.

Ibid. 20

So he drove out the man: and he placed at the east of the garden of Eden cherubims, and a flaming sword which turned every way, to keep the way of the tree of life.

Ibid. 24

And Abel was a keeper of sheep, but Cain was a tiller of the ground.

Ibid. IV, 2

Am I my brother's keeper?

Ibid. 9

The voice of thy brother's blood crieth unto me from the ground.

Ibid. 10

A fugitive and a vagabond shalt thou be in the earth.

Ibid. 12

My punishment is greater than I can bear.

Ibid. 13

And the Lord set a mark upon Cain.

Ibid. 15

And Cain went out from the presence of the Lord, and dwelt in the land of Nod.

Genesis. IV, 16

The father of such as dwell in tents.

Ibid. 20

Jubal: he was the father of all such as handle the harp and organ.

Ibid. 21

And Enoch walked with God.

Ibid. V, 24

And all the days of Methuselah were nine hundred sixty and nine years.

Ibid. 27

And Noah begat Shem, Ham, and Japheth.

Ibid. 32

There were giants in the earth in those days.

Ibid. VI, 4

Mighty men which were of old, men of renown.

Ibid.

Make thee an ark of gopher wood.

Ibid. 14

And of every living thing of all flesh, two of every sort shalt thou bring into the ark.

Ibid. 19

And the rain was upon the earth forty days and forty nights.

Ibid. VII, 12

But the dove found no rest for the sole of her foot.

Ibid. VIII, 9

And lo, in her mouth was an olive leaf plucked off.

Ibid. 11

For the imagination of man's heart is evil from his youth.

Ibid. 21

While the earth remaineth, seedtime and harvest, and cold and heat, and summer and winter, and day and night shall not cease.

Ibid. 22

I do set my bow in the cloud, and it shall be for a token of a covenant between me and the earth.

Ibid. IX, 13

Even as Nimrod the mighty hunter before the Lord.
Genesis. X, 9
Babel; because the Lord did there confound the language of all the earth.
Ibid. XI, 9
Let there be no strife, I pray thee, between me and thee . . . for we be brethren.
Ibid. XIII, 8
In a good old age.
Ibid. XV, 15
His [Ishmael's] hand will be against every man, and every man's hand against him.
Ibid. XVI, 12
Thy name shall be Abraham; for a father of many nations have I made thee.
Ibid. XVII, 5
My Lord, if now I have found favour in thy sight, pass not away, I pray thee, from thy servant.
Ibid. XVIII, 3
But his [Lot's] wife looked back from behind him, and she became a pillar of salt.
Ibid. XIX, 26
My son, God will provide himself a lamb for a burnt offering.
Ibid. XXII, 8
And he [Esau] sold his birthright unto Jacob.
Ibid. XXV, 33
The voice is Jacob's voice, but the hands are the hands of Esau.
Ibid. XXVII, 22
Thy brother came with subtilty, and hath taken away thy blessing.
Ibid. 35
He [Jacob] dreamed, and behold a ladder set up on the earth, and the top of it reached to heaven: and behold the angels of God ascending and descending on it.
Ibid. XXVIII, 12
Surely the Lord is in this place; and I knew it not.
Ibid. 16
This is none other but the house of God, and this is the gate of heaven.
Ibid. 17

Jacob served seven years for Rachel; and they seemed unto him but a few days, for the love he had to her.
Genesis. XXIX, 20
Mizpah; for he said, The Lord watch between me and thee, when we are absent one from another.
Ibid. XXXI, 49
I will not let thee go, except thou bless me.
Ibid. XXXII, 26
For I have seen God face to face, and my life is preserved.
Ibid. 30
Behold, this dreamer cometh.
Ibid. XXXVII, 19
They stript Joseph out of his coat, his coat of many colours.
Ibid. 23
And the lean and the ill-favoured kine did eat up the first seven fat kine.
Ibid. XLI, 20
There come seven years of great plenty throughout all the land of Egypt: And there shall arise after them seven years of famine.
Ibid. 29, 30
Ye shall bring down my gray hairs with sorrow to the grave.
Ibid. XLIV, 29
And ye shall eat the fat of the land.
Ibid. XLV, 18
Unstable as water, thou shalt not excel.
Ibid. XLIX, 4
Unto the utmost bound of the everlasting hills.
Ibid. 26
She took for him an ark of bulrushes, and daubed it with slime and with pitch.
Exodus. II, 3
I have been a stranger in a strange land.
Ibid. 22
Behold, the bush burned with fire, and the bush was not consumed.
Ibid. III, 2
Put off thy shoes from off thy feet, for the place whereon thou standest is holy ground.
Ibid. 5

A land flowing with milk and honey.[1]

Exodus. III, 8

And God said unto Moses, I AM THAT I AM.

Ibid. 14

I am slow of speech, and of a slow tongue.

Ibid. IV, 10

Ye shall no more give the people straw to make brick.

Ibid. V, 7

And he hardened Pharaoh's heart.

Ibid. VII, 13.

Let my people go.

Ibid. 16

Darkness which may be felt.

Ibid. X, 21

Your lamb shall be without blemish.

Ibid. XII, 5

And thus shall ye eat it; with your loins girded, your shoes on your feet, and your staff in your hand; and ye shall eat it in haste: it is the Lord's passover.

Ibid. 11

For I will pass through the land of Egypt this night, and will smite all the firstborn in the land of Egypt, both man and beast; and against all the gods of Egypt I will execute judgment: I am the Lord.

Ibid. 12

This day [Passover] shall be unto you for a memorial; and ye shall keep it a feast to the Lord throughout your generations.

Ibid. 14

Seven days shall ye eat unleavened bread.

Ibid. 15

There was a great cry in Egypt: for there was not a house where there was not one dead.

Ibid. 30

Remember this day, in which ye came out from Egypt, out of the house of bondage.

Ibid. XIII, 3

And the Lord went before them by day in a pillar of a cloud, to lead them

[1] Also in *XXXIII, 3, and Jeremiah, XI, 5.*

the way; and by night in a pillar of fire.

Exodus. XIII, 21

And Moses stretched out his hand over the sea; and the Lord caused the sea to go back by a strong east wind all that night, and made the sea dry land, and the waters were divided.

Ibid. XIV, 21

I will sing unto the Lord, for he hath triumphed gloriously: the horse and his rider hath he thrown into the sea.

Ibid. XV, 1

The Lord is my strength and song, and he is become my salvation.

Ibid. 2

The Lord is a man of war.

Ibid. 3

Thou sentest forth thy wrath, which consumed them as stubble.

Ibid. 7

Would to God we had died by the hand of the Lord in the land of Egypt, when we sat by the fleshpots, and when we did eat bread to the full.

Ibid. XVI, 3

It is manna.

Ibid. 15

Thou shalt have no other gods before me.

Ibid. XX, 2

Thou shalt not make unto thee any graven image.

Ibid. 4

For I the Lord thy God am a jealous God, visiting the iniquity of the fathers upon the children unto the third and fourth generation of them that hate me.

Ibid. 5

Thou shalt not take the name of the Lord thy God in vain.

Ibid. 7

Remember the sabbath day, to keep it holy.

Ibid. 8

Six days shalt thou labour, and do all thy work;
But the seventh day . . . thou shalt not do any work.

Ibid. 9, 10

Honour thy father and thy mother: that thy days may be long upon the land which the Lord thy God giveth thee.
Exodus. XX, 12

Thou shalt not kill

Thou shalt not commit adultery.

Thou shalt not steal.

Thou shalt not bear false witness against thy neighbour.

Thou shalt not covet thy neighbour's house, thou shalt not covet thy neighbour's wife, nor his manservant, nor his maidservant, nor his ox, nor his ass, nor any thing that is thy neighbour's.
Ibid. 13–17

But let not God speak with us, lest we die.
Ibid. 19

He that smiteth a man, so that he die, shall be surely put to death.
XXI. 12

Eye for eye, tooth for tooth,[1] hand for hand, foot for foot.
Ibid. 24

Behold, I send an Angel before thee, to keep thee in the way.
Ibid. XXIII, 20

Thou art a stiffnecked people.
Ibid. XXXIII, 3

Thou canst not see my face: for there shall no man see me, and live.
Ibid. 20

And he [Moses] was there with the Lord forty days and forty nights; he did neither eat bread, nor drink water. And he wrote upon the tables the words of the covenant, the ten commandments.
Ibid. XXXIV, 28

The swine . . . is unclean to you. Of their flesh shall ye not eat.
Leviticus. XI, 7, 8

Let him go for a scapegoat into the wilderness.
Ibid. XVI, 10

Thou shalt not go up and down as a talebearer among thy people.
Ibid. XIX, 16

Thou shalt love thy neighbour as thyself.[1]
Leviticus. XIX, 18

The Lord bless thee, and keep thee: The Lord make his face shine upon thee, and be gracious unto thee: The Lord lift up his countenance upon thee, and give thee peace.
Numbers. VI, 24, 25, 26

Sent to spy out the land.
Ibid. XIII, 16

And your children shall wander in the wilderness forty years.
Ibid. XIV, 33

The Lord opened the mouth of the ass, and she said unto Balaam, What have I done unto thee?
Ibid. XXII, 28

Let me die the death of the righteous, and let my last end be like his!
Ibid. XXIII, 10

God is not a man, that he should lie.
Ibid. 19

How goodly are thy tents, O Jacob, and thy tabernacles, O Israel!
Ibid. XXIV, 5

Be sure your sin will find you out.
Ibid. XXXII, 23

Thou shalt love the Lord thy God with all thine heart, and with all thy soul, and with all thy might.
Deuteronomy. VI, 5

The Lord thy God hath chosen thee to be a special people unto himself.
Ibid. VII, 6

Man doth not live by bread only,[2] but by every word that proceedeth out of the mouth of the Lord doth man live.
Ibid. VIII, 3

A dreamer of dreams.
Ibid. XIII, 1

The wife of thy bosom.
Ibid. 6

The poor shall never cease out of the land.
Ibid. XV, 11

---

[1] Also in *Matthew, V, 38.*

[1] Also in *Matthew, XIX, 19; XXII, 39; Mark, XII, 31, 33; Romans, XIII, 9; Galatians, V, 14; James, II, 8.*

[2] Also in *Matthew, IV, 4.*

And thou shalt become an astonishment, a proverb, and a byword, among all nations.

Deuteronomy. XXVIII, 37

In the morning thou shalt say, Would God it were even! and at even thou shalt say, Would God it were morning!

Ibid. 67

The secret things belong unto the Lord our God.

Ibid. XXIX, 29

He kept him as the apple of his eye.

Ibid. XXXII, 10

Jeshurun waxed fat, and kicked.

Ibid. 15

As thy days, so shall thy strength be.

Ibid. XXXIII, 25

The eternal God is thy refuge, and underneath are the everlasting arms.

Ibid. 27

No man knoweth of his [Moses's] sepulchre unto this day.

Ibid. XXXIV, 6

As I was with Moses, so I will be with thee: I will not fail thee, nor forsake thee.

Joshua. I, 5

Be strong and of a good courage;[1] be not afraid, neither be thou dismayed: for the Lord thy God is with thee whithersoever thou goest.

Ibid. 9

Mighty men of valour.

Ibid. VI, 2

And it came to pass, when the people heard the sound of the trumpet, and the people shouted with a great shout, that the wall fell down flat, so that the people went up into the city.

Ibid. 20

His fame was noised throughout all the country.

Ibid. 27

Hewers of wood and drawers of water.

Ibid. IX, 21

The sun stood still, and the moon stayed.

Ibid. X, 13

[1] Also in *Deuteronomy, XXI, 6, 7, 23.*

Old and stricken in years.

Joshua. XIII, 1

I am going the way of all the earth.

Ibid. XXIII, 14

They shall be as thorns in your sides.

Judges. II, 3

I arose a mother in Israel.

Ibid. V, 7

The stars in their courses fought against Sisera.

Ibid. 20

She brought forth butter in a lordly dish.

Ibid. 25

She [Jael] put her hand to the nail, and her right hand to the workmen's hammer; and with the hammer she smote Sisera, she smote off his head.

Ibid. 26

At her feet he bowed, he fell, he lay down: at her feet he bowed, he fell: where he bowed, there he fell down dead.

Ibid. 27

Why tarry the wheels of his chariots?

Ibid. 28

Is not the gleaning of the grapes of Ephraim better than the vintage of Abiezer?

Ibid. VIII, 2

Say now Shibboleth: and he said Sibboleth: for he could not frame to pronounce it right.

Ibid. XII, 6

There was a swarm of bees and honey in the carcase of the lion.

Ibid. XIV, 8

Out of the eater came forth meat, and out of the strong came forth sweetness.

Ibid. 14

If ye had not plowed with my heifer, ye had not found out my riddle.

Ibid. 18

He smote them hip and thigh.

Ibid. XV, 8

With the jawbone of an ass . . . have I slain a thousand men.

Ibid. 16

The Philistines be upon thee, Samson.

Ibid. XVI, 9

So the dead which he slew at his death were more than they which he slew in his life.

Judges. XVI, 30

From Dan even to Beer-sheba.

Ibid. XX, 1

All the people arose as one man.

Ibid. 8

In those days there was no king in Israel: every man did that which was right in his own eyes.

Ibid. XXI, 25

Whither thou goest, I will go; and where thou lodgest, I will lodge: thy people shall be my people, and thy God my God.

Ruth. I, 16

Let me glean and gather after the reapers among the sheaves.

Ibid. II, 7

Go not empty unto thy mother in law.

Ibid. III, 17

In the flower of their age.

1 Samuel. II, 33

The Lord called Samuel; and he answered, Here am I.

Ibid. III, 4

Speak, Lord; for thy servant heareth.

Ibid. 9

Be strong, and quit yourselves like men.

Ibid. IV, 9

The glory is departed from Israel: for the ark of God is taken.

Ibid. 22

Is Saul also among the prophets?

Ibid. X, 11

And all the people shouted, and said, God save the king.

Ibid. 24

A man after his own heart.

Ibid. XIII, 14

Every man's sword was against his fellow.

Ibid. XIV, 20

To obey is better than sacrifice, and to hearken than the fat of rams.

Ibid. XV, 22

For rebellion is as the sin of witchcraft, and stubbornness is as iniquity and idolatry.

1 Samuel. XV, 23

For the Lord seeth not as man seeth; for man looketh on the outward appearance, but the Lord looketh on the heart.

Ibid. XVI, 7

Let no man's heart fail because of him [Goliath].

Ibid. XVII, 32

And he [David] . . . chose him five smooth stones out of the brook.

Ibid. 40

So David prevailed over the Philistine with a sling and with a stone.

Ibid. 50

Saul hath slain his thousands, and David his ten thousands.

Ibid. XVIII, 7

And Jonathan . . . loved him [David] as he loved his own soul.

Ibid. XX, 17

I have played the fool.

Ibid. XXVI, 21

Tell it not in Gath, publish it not in the streets of Askelon.

2 Samuel. I, 20

Saul and Jonathan were lovely and pleasant in their lives, and in their death they were not divided: they were swifter than eagles, they were stronger than lions.

Ibid. 23

How are the mighty fallen in the midst of the battle!

Ibid. 25

Thy love to me was wonderful, passing the love of women.

Ibid. 26

How are the mighty fallen, and the weapons of war perished!

Ibid. 27

Abner . . . smote him under the fifth rib.

Ibid. II, 23

Know ye not that there is a prince and a great man fallen this day in Israel?

Ibid. III, 38

And David and all the house of Israel played before the Lord on all manner of instruments made of fir wood, even on harps, and on psalteries, and on timbrels, and on cornets, and on cymbals.

2 Samuel. VI, 5

And David danced before the Lord.

Ibid. 14

Tarry at Jericho until your beards be grown.[1]

Ibid. X, 5

Set ye Uriah in the forefront of the hottest battle.

Ibid. XI, 15

The poor man had nothing, save one little ewe lamb.

Ibid. XII, 3

Thou art the man.

Ibid. 7

Now he is dead, wherefore should I fast? Can I bring him back again? I shall go to him, but he shall not return to me.

Ibid. 23

For we must needs die, and are as water spilt on the ground, which cannot be gathered up again.

Ibid. XIV, 14

Would God I had died for thee, O Absalom, my son, my son!

Ibid. XVIII, 33

The Lord is my rock, and my fortress, and my deliverer.

Ibid. XXII, 2

David the son of Jesse . . . the sweet psalmist of Israel.

Ibid. XXIII, 1

A wise and an understanding heart.

1 Kings. III, 12

And the king said, Divide the living child in two, and give half to the one, and half to the other.

Ibid. 25

Then spake the woman whose the living child was unto the king, for her bowels yearned upon her son, and she said, O my lord, give her the living child, and in no wise slay it.

Ibid. 26

[1] Also in *1 Chronicles, XIX, 5.*

Then the king answered and said, Give her the living child.

1 Kings. III, 27

Many, as the sand which is by the sea in multitude.

Ibid. IV, 20

He [Solomon] spake three thousand proverbs: and his songs were a thousand and five.

Ibid. 32

So that there was neither hammer nor axe nor any tool of iron heard in the house, while it was in building.

Ibid. VI, 7

When the queen of Sheba heard of the fame of Solomon . . . she came to prove him with hard questions.

Ibid. X, 1

The half was not told me.

Ibid. 7

Once in three years came the navy of Tharshish, bringing gold, and silver, ivory, and apes, and peacocks.

Ibid. 22

King Solomon loved many strange women.

Ibid. XI, 1

And he had seven hundred wives, princesses, and three hundred concubines: and his wives turned away his heart.

Ibid. 3

My father hath chastised you with whips, but I will chastise you with scorpions.

Ibid. XII, 11

To your tents, O Israel.

Ibid. 16

He went and dwelt by the brook Cherith, that is before Jordan.

Ibid. XVII, 5

And the ravens brought him bread and flesh in the morning, and bread and flesh in the evening; and he drank of the brook.

Ibid. 6

I have commanded a widow woman there to sustain thee.

Ibid. 9

An handful of meal in a barrel, and a little oil in a cruse.

Ibid. 12

And the barrel of meal wasted not, neither did the cruse of oil fail.
1 Kings. XVII, 16

How long halt ye between two opinions?
Ibid. XVIII, 21

There ariseth a little cloud out of the sea, like a man's hand.
Ibid. 44

And he girded up his loins, and ran before Ahab.
Ibid. 46

But the Lord was not in the wind: and after the wind an earthquake; but the Lord was not in the earthquake:

And after the earthquake a fire; but the Lord was not in the fire: and after the fire a still small voice.
Ibid. XIX, 11, 12

Let not him that girdeth on his harness boast himself as he that putteth it off.
Ibid. XX, 11

Hast thou found me, O mine enemy?
Ibid. XXI, 20

The dogs shall eat Jezebel by the wall of Jezreel.
Ibid. 23

There appeared a chariot of fire, and horses of fire . . . and Elijah went up by a whirlwind into heaven.
2 Kings. II, 11

There is death in the pot.
Ibid. IV, 40

Are not Abana and Pharpar, rivers of Damascus, better than all the waters of Israel?
Ibid. V, 12

Is not the sound of his master's feet behind him?
Ibid. VI, 32

Is thy servant a dog, that he should do this great thing?
Ibid. VIII, 13

What hast thou to do with peace? turn thee behind me.
Ibid. IX, 18

The driving is like the driving of Jehu, the son of Nimshi; for he driveth furiously.
Ibid. 20

Jezebel heard of it; and she painted her face, and tired her head, and looked out at a window.
2 Kings. IX, 30

A land of corn and wine.
Ibid. XVIII, 32

Set thine house in order.
Ibid. XX, 1

I will wipe Jerusalem as a man wipeth a dish, wiping it, and turning it upside down.
Ibid. XXI, 13

His mercy endureth for ever.
1 Chronicles. XVI, 41

The Lord searcheth all hearts, and understandeth all the imaginations of the thoughts.
Ibid. XXVIII, 9

Our days on the earth are as a shadow.
Ibid. XXIX, 15

He [David] died in a good old age, full of days, riches, and honour.
Ibid. 28

The man whom the king delighteth to honour.
Esther. VI, 6

One that feared God, and eschewed evil.
Job. I, 1

Satan came also.
Ibid. 6

And the Lord said unto Satan, Whence comest thou? Then Satan answered the Lord, and said, From going to and fro in the earth, and from walking up and down in it.
Ibid. 7

Doth Job fear God for nought?
Ibid. 9

Naked came I out of my mother's womb, and naked shall I return thither: the Lord gave, and the Lord hath taken away; blessed be the name of the Lord.
Ibid. 21

Skin for skin, yea, all that a man hath, will he give for his life.
Ibid. II, 4

Curse God, and die.
Ibid. 9

Let the day perish wherein I was born, and the night in which it was said, there is a man child conceived.
Job. III, 3

There the wicked cease from troubling, and there the weary be at rest.
Ibid. 17

Who ever perished, being innocent? or where were the righteous cut off?
Ibid. IV, 7

Then a spirit passed before my face; the hair of my flesh stood up.
Ibid. 15

Shall mortal man be more just than God? shall a man be more pure than his maker?
Ibid. 17

Wrath killeth the foolish man, and envy slayeth the silly one.
Ibid. V, 2

Man is born unto trouble, as the sparks fly upward.
Ibid. 7

He taketh the wise in their own craftiness.
Ibid. 13

Thou shalt come to thy grave in a full age, like as a shock of corn cometh in his season.
Ibid. 26

How forcible are right words!
Ibid. VI, 25

My days are swifter than a weaver's shuttle, and are spent without hope.
Ibid. VII, 6

He shall return no more to his house, neither shall his place know him any more.[1]
Ibid. 10

I would not live alway: let me alone; for my days are vanity.
Ibid. 16

But how should man be just with God?
Ibid. IX, 2

[1] When a few years are come, then I shall go the way whence I shall not return. — XVI, 22
The place thereof shall know it no more. — *Psalm CIII, 16*

The land of darkness and the shadow of death.
Job. X, 21

Canst thou by searching find out God?
Ibid. XI, 7

And thine age shall be clearer than the noonday.
Ibid. 17

No doubt but ye are the people and wisdom shall die with you.
Ibid. XII, 2

The just upright man is laughed to scorn.
Ibid. 4

Speak to the earth, and it shall teach thee.
Ibid. 8

With the ancient is wisdom; and in length of days understanding.
Ibid. 12

He discovereth deep things out of darkness, and bringeth out to light the shadow of death.
Ibid. 22

Man that is born of a woman is of few days, and full of trouble.
Ibid. XIV, 1

He cometh forth like a flower, and is cut down: he fleeth also as a shadow, and continueth not.
Ibid. 2

But man dieth, and wasteth away: yea, man giveth up the ghost, and where is he?
Ibid. 10

If a man die, shall he live again?
Ibid. 14

Should a wise man utter vain knowledge, and fill his belly with the east wind?
Ibid. XV, 2

Miserable comforters are ye all.
Ibid. XVI, 2

My days are past.
Ibid. XVII, 11

I have said to corruption, Thou art my father: to the worm, Thou art my mother, and my sister.
Ibid. 14

The king of terrors.
Ibid. XVIII, 14

I am escaped with the skin of my teeth.

Job. XIX, 20

Oh that my words were now written! oh that they were printed in a book!

Ibid. 23

I know that my redeemer liveth, and that he shall stand at the latter day upon the earth.

Ibid. 25

And though after my skin worms destroy this body, yet in my flesh shall I see God.

Ibid. 26

Seeing the root of the matter is found in me.

Ibid. 28

Though wickedness be sweet in his mouth, though he hide it under his tongue.

Ibid. XX, 12

Shall any teach God knowledge?

Ibid. XXI, 22

Is it any pleasure to the Almighty, that thou art righteous?

Ibid. XXII, 3

They are of those that rebel against the light.

Ibid. XXIV, 13

The womb shall forget him; the worm shall feed sweetly on him; he shall be no more remembered.

Ibid. 20

Yea, the stars are not pure in his sight.

How much less man, that is a worm? and the son of man, which is a worm?

Ibid. XXV, 5–6

The land of the living.

Ibid. XXVIII, 13

The price of wisdom is above rubies.

Ibid. 18

And unto man he said, Behold, the fear of the Lord, that is wisdom; and to depart from evil is understanding.

Ibid. 28

When the ear heard me, then it blessed me; and when the eye saw me, it gave witness to me.

Ibid. XXIX, 11

I caused the widow's heart to sing for joy.

Job. XXIX, 13

I was eyes to the blind, and feet was I to the lame.

Ibid. 15

The house appointed for all living.

Ibid. XXX, 23

I am a brother to dragons, and a companion to owls.

Ibid. 29

My desire is, that the Almighty would answer me, and that mine adversary had written a book.

Ibid. XXXI, 35

Great men are not always wise.

Ibid. XXXII, 9

For I am full of matter, the spirit within me constraineth me.

Ibid. 18

One among a thousand.

Ibid. XXXIII, 23

Far be it from God, that he should do wickedness.

Ibid. XXXIV, 10

He multiplieth words without knowledge.

Ibid. XXXV, 16

Fair weather cometh out of the north.

Ibid. XXXVII, 22

Who is this that darkeneth counsel by words without knowledge?

Ibid. XXXVIII, 2

Gird up now thy loins like a man.

Ibid. 3

Where wast thou when I laid the foundations of the earth? declare, if thou hast understanding.

Ibid. 4

The morning stars sang together, and all the sons of God shouted for joy.

Ibid. 7

Hitherto shalt thou come, but no further: and here shall thy proud waves be stayed?

Ibid. 11

Hath the rain a father? or who hath begotten the drops of dew?

Ibid. 28

Canst thou bind the sweet influences of Pleiades, or loose the bands of Orion?

Job. XXXVIII, 31

Canst thou guide Arcturus with his sons?

Ibid. 32

He saith among the trumpets, Ha, ha; and he smelleth the battle afar off, the thunder of the captains, and the shouting.

Ibid. XXXIX, 25

Behold, I am vile; what shall I answer thee?

Ibid. XL, 4

Behold now behemoth, which I made with thee; he eateth grass as an ox.

Ibid. 15

Canst thou draw out leviathan with a hook?

Ibid. XLI, 1

Hard as a piece of the nether millstone.

Ibid. 24

He maketh the deep to boil like a pot.

Ibid. 31

He is a king over all the children of pride.

Ibid. 34

I have heard of thee by the hearing of the ear; but now mine eye seeth thee.

Ibid. XLII, 5

Blessed is the man that walketh not in the counsel of the ungodly, nor standeth in the way of sinners, nor sitteth in the seat of the scornful.

Psalms. I, 1

And he shall be like a tree planted by the rivers of water, that bringeth forth his fruit in his season; his leaf also shall not wither; and whatsoever he doeth shall prosper.

Ibid. 3

The ungodly are not so: but are like the chaff which the wind driveth away.

Ibid. 4

Serve the Lord with fear and rejoice with trembling.

Ibid. II, 11

Blessed are all they that put their trust in him.

Psalms. II, 12

Lord, lift thou up the light of thy countenance upon us.

Ibid. IV, 6

I will both lay me down in peace, and sleep.[1]

Ibid. 8

Out of the mouth of babes and sucklings hast thou ordained strength.

Ibid. VIII, 2

What is man, that thou art mindful of him? and the son of man, that thou visitest him?

Ibid. 4

Thou hast made him a little lower than the angels.

Ibid. 5

How excellent is thy name in all the earth.

Ibid. 9

Flee as a bird to your mountain.

Ibid. XI, 1

How long wilt thou forget me, O Lord?

Ibid. XIII, 1

The fool hath said in his heart, There is no God.

Ibid. XIV, 1; LIII, 1

He that sweareth to his own hurt, and changeth not.

Ibid. XV, 4

The lines are fallen unto me in pleasant places;[2] yea, I have a goodly heritage.

Ibid. XVI, 6

Keep me as the apple of the eye, hide me under the shadow of thy wings.

Ibid. XVII, 8

He rode upon a cherub, and did fly: yea, he did fly upon the wings of the wind.

Ibid. XVIII, 10

The heavens declare the glory of God; and the firmament showeth his handiwork.

Ibid. XIX, 1

[1] I will lay me down in peace, and take my rest. — *Book of Common Prayer, Psalm IV, 9*
[2] The lot is fallen unto me in a fair ground. — *Book of Common Prayer, Psalm XVI, 7*

Day unto day uttereth speech, and night unto night showeth knowledge.
Psalms. XIX, 2

As a bridegroom coming out of his chamber, and rejoiceth as a strong man to run a race.
Ibid. 5

And there is nothing hid from the heat thereof.
Ibid. 6

The judgments of the Lord are true and righteous altogether.
Ibid. 9

More to be desired are they than gold.
Ibid. 10

Sweeter also than honey and the honeycomb.
Ibid.

Cleanse thou me from secret faults.
Ibid. 12

Let the words of my mouth, and the meditation of my heart, be acceptable in thy sight.
Ibid. 14

My God, my God, why hast thou forsaken me? [1]
Ibid. XXII, 1

I may tell all my bones: they look and stare upon me.
Ibid. 17

The Lord is my shepherd; I shall not want.
Ibid. XXIII, 1

He maketh me to lie down in green pastures: he leadeth me beside the still waters.
Ibid. 2

He restoreth my soul: he leadeth me in the paths of righteousness for his name's sake.
Ibid. 3

Yea, though I walk through the valley of the shadow of death, I will fear no evil: for thou art with me; thy rod and thy staff they comfort me.
Ibid. 4

Thou preparest a table before me in the presence of mine enemies: thou

[1] See *Matthew, XXVII, 46,* on page 1055b.

anointest my head with oil; my cup runneth over.
Psalms. XXIII, 5

Surely goodness and mercy shall follow me all the days of my life: and I will dwell in the house of the Lord for ever.
Ibid. 6

The earth is the Lord's, and the fulness thereof; the world, and they that dwell therein.
Ibid. XXIV, 1

For he hath founded it upon the seas, and established it upon the floods.
Ibid. 2

Who shall ascend into the hill of the Lord? or who shall stand in his holy place?
Ibid. 3

He that hath clean hands, and a pure heart; who hath not lifted up his soul unto vanity, nor sworn deceitfully.
Ibid. 4

Who is this King of glory? The Lord of hosts, he is the King of glory.
Ibid. 10

The Lord is my light and my salvation; whom shall I fear? the Lord is the strength of my life; of whom shall I be afraid?
Ibid. XXVII, 1

The Lord is my strength and my shield.
Ibid. XXVIII, 7

Worship the Lord in the beauty of holiness.
Ibid. XXIX, 2

The voice of the Lord is upon the waters: the God of glory thundereth: the Lord is upon many waters.
Ibid. 3

Weeping may endure for a night, but joy cometh in the morning.
Ibid. XXX, 5

I am forgotten as a dead man out of mind: I am like a broken vessel.
Ibid. XXXI, 12

My times are in thy hand.
Ibid. 15

From the strife of tongues.
Ibid. 20

He fashioneth their hearts alike.
Psalms. XXXIII, 15

Keep thy tongue from evil, and thy lips from speaking guile.
Ibid. XXXIV, 13

Rescue my soul from their destructions, my darling from the lions.
Ibid. XXXV, 17

The meek shall inherit the earth.[1]
Ibid. XXXVII, 11

I have been young, and now am old; yet have I not seen the righteous forsaken, nor his seed begging bread.
Ibid. 25

I have seen the wicked in great power, and spreading [2] himself like a green bay tree.
Ibid. 35

Mark the perfect man, and behold the upright.
Ibid. 37

I said, I will take heed to my ways, that I sin not with my tongue.
Ibid. XXXIX, 1

My heart was hot within me, while I was musing the fire burned.
Ibid. 3

Lord, make me to know mine end, and the measure of my days, what it is; that I may know how frail I am.
Ibid. 4

Every man at his best state is altogether vanity.
Ibid. 5

He heapeth up riches, and knoweth not who shall gather them.
Ibid. 6

He brought me up also out of an horrible pit, out of the miry clay, and set my feet upon a rock, and established my goings.
Ibid. XL, 2

Blessed is he that considereth the poor; the Lord will deliver him in time of trouble.
Ibid. XLI, 1

As the hart panteth after the waterbrooks, so panteth my soul after thee.
Ibid. XLII, 1

Why art thou cast down, O my soul? and why art thou disquieted in me?
Psalms. XLII, 5, 11; XLIII, 5

Deep calleth unto deep.
Ibid. 7

My heart is inditing a good matter . . . my tongue is the pen of a ready writer.
Ibid. XLV, 1

God is our refuge and strength, a very present help in trouble.
Ibid. XLVI, 1

Therefore will we not fear, though the earth be removed, and though the mountains be carried into the midst of the sea.
Ibid. 2

Beautiful for situation, the joy of the whole earth, is Mount Zion . . . the city of the great King.
Ibid. XLVIII, 2

Man being in honour abideth not; he is like the beasts that perish.
Ibid. XLIX, 12

Every beast of the forest is mine, and the cattle upon a thousand hills.
Ibid. L, 10

I was shapen in iniquity; and in sin did my mother conceive me.
Ibid. LI, 5

Purge me with hyssop, and I shall be clean: wash me, and I shall be whiter than snow.
Ibid. 7

Create in me a clean heart, O God; and renew a right spirit within me.
Ibid. 10

Open thou my lips; and my mouth shall show forth thy praise.
Ibid. 15

A broken and a contrite heart.
Ibid. 17

Oh that I had wings like a dove!
Ibid. LV, 6

But it was thou, a man mine equal, my guide, and mine acquaintance.[1]
Ibid. 13

---

[1] See *Matthew, V, 5*, on page 1050b.
[2] Flourishing. — *Book of Common Prayer, Psalm XXXVII, 36*

[1] But it was even thou, my companion, my guide, and mine own familiar friend. — *Book of Common Prayer, Psalm LV, 14*
Mine own familiar friend. — *Psalm XLI, 9*

We took sweet counsel together.
Psalms. LV, 14

The words of his mouth were smoother than butter, but war was in his heart:[1] his words were softer than oil, yet were they drawn swords.
Ibid. 21

Put thou my tears into thy bottle: are they not in thy book?
Ibid. LVI, 8

They are like the deaf adder that stoppeth her ear;
Which will not hearken to the voice of charmers, charming never so wisely.[2]
Ibid. LVIII, 4, 5

Vain is the help of man.
Ibid. LX, 11; CVIII, 12

Lead me to the rock that is higher than I.
Ibid. LXI, 2

He only is my rock and my salvation; he is my defence; I shall not be moved.
Ibid. LXII, 6

Surely men of low degree are vanity, and men of high degree are a lie: to be laid in the balance, they are altogether lighter than vanity.
Ibid. 9

Thou renderest to every man according to his work.
Ibid. 12

My soul thirsteth for thee, my flesh longeth for thee in a dry and thirsty land, where no water is.
Ibid. LXIII, 1

Thou crownest the year with thy goodness.
Ibid. LXV, 11

The little hills rejoice on every side.
Ibid. 12

Make a joyful noise unto God, all ye lands.
Ibid. LXVI, 1

[1] The words of his mouth were softer than butter, having war in his heart. — *Book of Common Prayer, Psalm LV, 22*

[2] Like the deaf adder, that stoppeth her ears; which refuseth to hear the voice of the charmer, charm he never so wisely. — *The Book of Common Prayer, Psalm LVIII, 4, 5*

We went through fire and through water.
Psalms. LXVI, 12

God setteth the solitary in families
Ibid. LXVIII, 6

Cast me not off in the time of old age; forsake me not when my strength faileth.
Ibid. LXXI, 9

He shall come down like rain upon the mown grass.
Ibid. LXXII, 6

His enemies shall lick the dust.
Ibid. 9

His name shall endure for ever.
Ibid. 17

As a dream when one awaketh.
Ibid. LXXIII, 20

He putteth down one and setteth up another.
Ibid. LXXV, 7

A stubborn and rebellious generation.
Ibid. LXXVIII, 8

Man did eat angels' food.
Ibid. 25

How amiable are thy tabernacles, O Lord of hosts!
Ibid. LXXXIV, 1

They go from strength to strength.
Ibid. 7

A day in thy courts is better than a thousand. I had rather be a doorkeeper in the house of my God, than to dwell in the tents of wickedness.
Ibid. 10

Mercy and truth are met together: righteousness and peace have kissed each other.
Ibid. LXXXV, 10

A thousand years in thy sight are but as yesterday when it is past, and as a watch in the night.
Ibid. XC, 4

They are like grass which groweth up.
In the morning it flourisheth, and groweth up; in the evening it is cut down, and withereth.[1]
Ibid. 5, 6

[1] See *Isaiah, XL, 6, 8,* on page 1047a.

We spend our years as a tale that is told.[1]

Psalms. XC, 9

The days of our years are threescore years and ten; and if by reason of strength they be fourscore years, yet is their strength labour and sorrow; for it is soon cut off, and we fly away.[2]

Ibid. 10

So teach us to number our days, that we may apply our hearts unto wisdom.

Ibid. 12

Establish thou the work of our hands upon us; yea, the work of our hands establish thou it.

Ibid. 17

He that dwelleth in the secret place of the most High shall abide under the shadow of the Almighty.

Ibid. XCI, 1

I will say of the Lord, He is my refuge and my fortress: my God; in him will I trust.

Ibid. 2

Surely he shall deliver thee from the snare of the fowler, and from the noisome pestilence.

Ibid. 3

His truth shall be thy shield and buckler.

Ibid. 4

Thou shalt not be afraid for the terror by night; nor for the arrow that flieth by day.

Ibid. 5

Nor for the pestilence that walketh in darkness; nor for the destruction that wasteth at noonday.

Ibid. 6

A thousand shall fall at thy side, and ten thousand at thy right hand; but it shall not come nigh thee.

Ibid. 7

[1] We bring our years to an end, as it were a tale that is told. — *Book of Common Prayer, Psalm XL, 9*

[2] The days of our age are threescore and ten; and though men be so strong that they come to fourscore years, yet is their strength then but labour and sorrow; so soon passeth it away, and we are gone. — *Book of Common Prayer, Psalm XL, 10*

He shall give his angels charge over thee, to keep thee in all thy ways.

Psalms. XCI, 11

The righteous shall flourish like the palm tree: he shall grow like a cedar in Lebanon.

Ibid. XCII, 12

Mightier than the noise of many waters.

Ibid. XCIII, 4

In his hand are the deep places of the earth: the strength of the hills is his also.

Ibid. XCV, 4

The sea is his, and he made it: and his hands formed the dry land.

Ibid. 5

We are the people of his pasture, and the sheep of his hand.

Ibid. 7

O sing unto the Lord a new song.

Ibid. XCVI, 1

The Lord reigneth; let the earth rejoice.

Ibid. XCVII, 1

Make a joyful noise unto the Lord, all ye lands.

Ibid. C, 1

As for man, his days are as grass: as a flower of the field, so he flourisheth.

Ibid. CIII, 15

The wind passeth over it, and it is gone; and the place thereof shall know it no more.

Ibid. 16

Wine that maketh glad the heart of man.

Ibid. CIV, 15

The trees of the Lord are full of sap; the cedars of Lebanon, which he hath planted.

Ibid. 16

Man goeth forth unto his work and to his labour until the evening.

Ibid. 23

Such as sit in darkness and in the shadow of death.

Ibid. CVII, 10

They that go down to the sea in ships, that do business in great waters.

Ibid. 23

They reel to and fro, and stagger like a drunken man, and are at their wits' end.

Psalms. CVII, 27

Thy people shall be willing in the day of thy power, in the beauties of holiness from the womb of the morning: thou hast the dew of thy youth.

Ibid. CX, 3

Thou art a priest for ever after the order of Melchizedek.

Ibid. 4

The fear of the Lord is the beginning of wisdom.

Ibid. CXI, 10

From the rising of the sun unto the going down of the same.

Ibid. CXIII, 3

The mountains skipped like rams, and the little hills like lambs.

Ibid. CXIV, 4

Eyes have they, but they see not. They have ears, but they hear not.[1]

Ibid. CXV, 6

I said in my haste, All men are liars.

Ibid. CXVI, 11

Precious in the sight of the Lord is the death of his saints.

Ibid. 15

The stone which the builders refused is become the head stone of the corner.[2]

Ibid. CXVIII, 22

This is the day which the Lord hath made.

Ibid. 24

Blessed be he that cometh in the name of the Lord.[3]

Ibid. 26

I have more understanding than all my teachers: for thy testimonies are my meditation.

Ibid. CXIX, 99

Thy word is a lamp unto my feet, and a light unto my path.

Ibid. 105

I will lift up mine eyes unto the hills, from whence cometh my help.

Ibid. CXXI, 1

My help cometh from the Lord, which made heaven and earth.

Psalms. CXXI, 2

He will not suffer thy foot to be moved: he that keepeth thee will not slumber.

Ibid. 3

Behold, he that keepeth Israel shall neither slumber nor sleep.

Ibid. 4

The sun shall not smite thee by day, nor the moon by night.

Ibid. 6

The Lord shall preserve thy going out and thy coming in from this time forth, and even for evermore.

Ibid. 8

I was glad when they said unto me, Let us go into the house of the Lord.

Ibid. CXXII, 1

Peace be within thy walls, and prosperity within thy palaces.

Ibid. CXXII, 7

They that sow in tears shall reap in joy.

Ibid. CXXVI, 5

He that goeth forth and weepeth, bearing precious seed, shall doubtless come again with rejoicing, bringing his sheaves with him.

Ibid. 6

Except the Lord build the house, they labour in vain that build it.

Ibid. CXXVII, 1

He giveth his beloved sleep.

Ibid. 2

Happy is the man that hath his quiver full of them.

Ibid. 5

Out of the depths have I cried unto thee, O Lord.

Ibid. CXXX, 1

I will not give sleep to mine eyes, or slumber to mine eyelids.[1]

Ibid. CXXXII, 4

Behold, how good and how pleasant it is for brethren to dwell together in unity!

Ibid. CXXXIII, 1

[1] Also in *Psalm CXXXV, 16-17.*
[2] Also in *Matthew, XXI, 42.*
[3] Also in *Matthew, XXI, 9, XXIII, 39; Mark, XI, 9; Luke, XIII, 35.*

[1] Also in *Proverbs, VI, 4.*

By the rivers of Babylon, there we sat down, yea, we wept, when we remembered Zion.[1]

Psalms. CXXXVII, 1

We hanged our harps upon the willows.

Ibid. 2

They that carried us away captive required of us a song; and they that wasted us required of us mirth, saying, sing us one of the songs of Zion.

Ibid. 3

How shall we sing the Lord's song in a strange land?

Ibid. 4

If I forget thee, O Jerusalem, let my right hand forget her cunning.

Ibid. 5

If I ascend up into heaven, thou art there: if I make my bed in hell, behold, thou art there.

Ibid. CXXXIX, 8

If I take the wings of the morning, and dwell in the uttermost parts of the sea.

Ibid. 9

I am fearfully and wonderfully made.

Ibid. 14

Teach me to do thy will.

Ibid. CXLIII, 10

That our sons may be as plants grown up in their youth; that our daughters may be as corner stones.

Ibid. CXLIV, 12

Put not your trust in princes.

Ibid. CXLVI, 3

Let every thing that hath breath praise the Lord.

Ibid. CL, 6

My son, if sinners entice thee, consent thou not.

Proverbs. I, 10

Wisdom crieth without; she uttereth her voice in the streets.

Ibid. 20

[1] By the waters of Babylon we sat down and wept: when we remembered thee, O Sion. — *Book of Common Prayer, Psalm CXXXVII, 1*

Length of days is in her right hand; and in her left hand riches and honour.

Proverbs. III, 16

Her ways are ways of pleasantness, and all her paths are peace.

Ibid. 17

Wisdom is the principal thing; therefore get wisdom; and with all thy getting get understanding.

Ibid. IV, 7

The path of the just is as the shining light, that shineth more and more unto the perfect day.

Ibid. 18

Keep thy heart with all diligence; for out of it are the issues of life.

Ibid. 23

For the lips of a strange woman drop as a honeycomb, and her mouth is smoother than oil:

But her end is bitter as wormwood, sharp as a two-edged sword.

Ibid. V, 3, 4

Go to the ant, thou sluggard; consider her ways, and be wise:

Which having no guide, overseer, or ruler,

Provideth her meat in the summer, and gathereth her food in the harvest.

Ibid. VI, 6–8

Yet a little sleep, a little slumber, a little folding of the hands to sleep.

Ibid. 10; XXIV, 33

Can a man take fire in his bosom, and his clothes not be burned?

Ibid. 27

Can one go upon hot coals, and his feet not be burned?

Ibid. 28

He goeth after her straightway, as an ox goeth to the slaughter.

Ibid. VII, 22

Wisdom is better than rubies.

Ibid. VIII, 11

I love them that love me; and those that seek me early shall find me.

Ibid. 17

Wisdom hath builded her house, she hath hewn out her seven pillars.

Ibid. IX, 1

Reprove not a scorner, lest he hate thee: rebuke a wise man, and he will love thee.

Proverbs. IX, 8

Stolen waters are sweet, and bread eaten in secret is pleasant.

Ibid. 17

A wise son maketh a glad father: but a foolish son is the heaviness of his mother.

Ibid. X, 1

The memory of the just is blessed: but the name of the wicked shall rot.

Ibid. 7

Hatred stirreth up strifes: but love covereth all sins.

Ibid. 12

In the multitude of counsellors there is safety.

Ibid. XI, 14; XXIV, 6

He that is surety for a stranger shall smart for it.

Ibid. 15

As a jewel of gold in a swine's snout, so is a fair woman which is without discretion.

Ibid. 22

He that trusteth in his riches shall fall.

Ibid. 28

A righteous man regardeth the life of his beast: but the tender mercies of the wicked are cruel.

Ibid. XII, 10

The way of a fool is right in his own eyes.

Ibid. 15

Hope deferred maketh the heart sick.

Ibid. XIII, 12

The way of transgressors is hard.

Ibid. 15

He that spareth his rod hateth his son: but he that loveth him chasteneth him betimes.

Ibid. 24

Fools make a mock at sin.

Ibid. XIV, 9

The heart knoweth his own bitterness; and a stranger doth not intermeddle with his joy.

Ibid. 10

Even in laughter the heart is sorrowful.

Proverbs. XIV, 13

The prudent man looketh well to his going.

Ibid. 15

The talk of the lips tendeth only to penury.

Ibid. 23

Righteousness exalteth a nation.

Ibid. 34

A soft answer turneth away wrath.

Ibid. XV, 1

A merry heart maketh a cheerful countenance.

Ibid. 13

He that is of a merry heart hath a continual feast.

Ibid. 15

Better is a dinner of herbs where love is, than a stalled ox and hatred therewith.

Ibid. 17

A word spoken in due season, how good is it!

Ibid. 23

Before honour is humility.

Ibid. 33; XVIII, 12

A man's heart deviseth his way; but the Lord directeth his steps.

Ibid. XVI, 9

Pride goeth before destruction, and an haughty spirit before a fall.

Ibid. 18

The hoary head is a crown of glory, if it be found in the way of righteousness.

Ibid. 31

He that is slow to anger is better than the mighty; and he that ruleth his spirit than he that taketh a city.

Ibid. 32

Whoso mocketh the poor reproacheth his Maker.

Ibid. XVII, 5

A gift is as a precious stone in the eyes of him that hath it.

Ibid. 8

He that repeateth a matter separateth very friends.

Ibid. 9

A merry heart doeth good like a medicine.
Proverbs. XVII, 22

Even a fool, when he holdeth his peace, is counted wise.
Ibid. 28

A fool's mouth is his destruction.
Ibid. XVIII, 7

A wounded spirit who can bear?
Ibid. 14

Whoso findeth a wife findeth a good thing.
Ibid. 22

A man that hath friends must show himself friendly: and there is a friend that sticketh closer than a brother.
Ibid. 24

Wealth maketh many friends.
Ibid. XIX, 4

He that hath pity upon the poor lendeth unto the Lord.
Ibid. 17

Wine is a mocker, strong drink is raging.
Ibid. XX, 1

It is an honour for a man to cease from strife: but every fool will be meddling.
Ibid. 3

The hearing ear and the seeing eye, the Lord hath made even both of them.
Ibid. 12

It is naught, it is naught, saith the buyer: but when he is gone his way, then he boasteth.
Ibid. 14

Bread of deceit is sweet to a man; but afterwards his mouth shall be filled with gravel.
Ibid. 17

Meddle not with him that flattereth with his lips.
Ibid. 19

The glory of young men is their strength: and the beauty of old men is the grey head.
Ibid. 29

It is better to dwell in a corner of the housetop, than with a brawling woman in a wide house.
Ibid. XXI, 9; XXV, 24

A good name is rather to be chosen than great riches.
Proverbs. XXII, 1

Train up a child in the way he should go: and when he is old he will not depart from it.
Ibid. 6

The borrower is servant to the lender.
Ibid. 7

Remove not the ancient landmark.
Ibid. 28

Seest thou a man diligent in his business? He shall stand before kings.
Ibid. 29

Put a knife to thy throat, if thou be a man given to appetite.
Ibid. XXIII, 2

Riches certainly make themselves wings.
Ibid. 5

As he thinketh in his heart, so is he.
Ibid. 7

The drunkard and the glutton shall come to poverty: and drowsiness shall clothe a man with rags.
Ibid. 21

Despise not thy mother when she is old.
Ibid. 22

Look not thou upon the wine when it is red, when it giveth his colour in the cup, when it moveth itself aright. At the last it biteth like a serpent, and stingeth like an adder.
Ibid. 31, 32

A wise man is strong; yea, a man of knowledge increaseth strength.
Ibid. XXIV, 5

If thou faint in the day of adversity, thy strength is small.
Ibid. 10

Rejoice not when thine enemy falleth, and let not thine heart be glad when he stumbleth.
Ibid. 17

Fret not thyself because of evil men.
Ibid. 19

A word fitly spoken is like apples of gold in pictures of silver.
Ibid. XXV, 11

If thine enemy be hungry, give him bread to eat; and if he be thirsty, give him water to drink:

For thou shalt heap coals of fire upon his head.[1]

Proverbs. XXV, 21–22

As cold waters to a thirsty soul, so is good news from a far country.

Ibid. 25

For men to search their own glory is not glory.

Ibid. 27

Answer a fool according to his folly.

Ibid. XXVI, 5

As a dog returneth to his vomit, so a fool returneth to his folly.

Ibid. 11

Seest thou a man wise in his own conceit? There is more hope of a fool than of him.

Ibid. 12

The slothful man saith, There is a lion in the way; a lion is in the streets.

Ibid. 13

The sluggard is wiser in his own conceit than seven men that can render a reason.

Ibid. 16

Whoso diggeth a pit shall fall therein.

Ibid. 27

Boast not thyself of tomorrow; for thou knowest not what a day may bring forth.

Ibid. XXVII, 1

Let another man praise thee, and not thine own mouth.

Ibid. 2

Open rebuke is better than secret love.

Ibid. 5

Faithful are the wounds of a friend; but the kisses of an enemy are deceitful.

Ibid. 6

To the hungry soul every bitter thing is sweet.

Ibid. 7

Better is a neighbour that is near than a brother far off.

Ibid. 10

[1] See *Romans, XII, 20,* on page 1060a.

A continual dropping in a very rainy day and a contentious woman are alike.

Proverbs. XXVII, 15

Iron sharpeneth iron; so a man sharpeneth the countenance of his friend.

Ibid. 17

The wicked flee when no man pursueth; but the righteous are bold as a lion.

Ibid. XXVIII, 1

He that maketh haste to be rich shall not be innocent.

Ibid. 20

To have respect of persons is not good: for for a piece of bread that man will transgress.

Ibid. 21

He that trusteth in his own heart is a fool.

Ibid. 26

He that giveth unto the poor shall not lack.

Ibid. 27

A fool uttereth all his mind.

Ibid. XXIX, 11

Where there is no vision, the people perish.

Ibid. 18

A man's pride shall bring him low: but honour shall uphold the humble in spirit.

Ibid. 23

Accuse not a servant unto his master.

Ibid. XXX, 10

The horseleach hath two daughters, crying, Give, give.

Ibid. 15

The way of an eagle in the air; the way of a serpent upon a rock; the way of a ship in the midst of the sea; and the way of a man with a maid.

Ibid. 19

Give strong drink unto him that is ready to perish, and wine unto those that be of heavy hearts.

Ibid. XXXI, 6

Who can find a virtuous woman? for her price is far above rubies.

Ibid. 10

In her tongue is the law of kindness.

Ibid. 26

She looketh well to the ways of her household, and eateth not the bread of idleness.

Proverbs. XXXI, 27

Her children arise up, and call her blessed.

Ibid. 28

Many daughters have done virtuously, but thou excellest them all.

Ibid. 29

Vanity of vanities; all is vanity.

Ecclesiastes. I, 2; XII, 8

What profit hath a man of all his labour which he taketh under the sun?

Ibid. 3

One generation passeth away, and another generation cometh: but the earth abideth for ever.

Ibid. 4

All the rivers run into the sea; yet the sea is not full.

Ibid. 7

The eye is not satisfied with seeing, nor the ear filled with hearing.

Ibid. 8

There is no new thing under the sun.

Ibid. 9

Is there anything whereof it may be said, See, this is new? It hath been already of old time, which was before us.

Ibid. 10

I have seen all the works that are done under the sun; and, behold, all is vanity and vexation of spirit.

Ibid. 14

In much wisdom is much grief: and he that increaseth knowledge increaseth sorrow.

Ibid. 18

Wisdom excelleth folly, as far as light excelleth darkness.

Ibid. II, 13

The wise man's eyes are in his head; but the fool walketh in darkness.

Ibid. 14

One event happeneth to them all.

Ibid

How dieth the wise man? as the fool.

Ibid. 16

To every thing there is a season, and

a time to every purpose under the heaven.

Ecclesiastes. III, 1

A time to be born, and a time to die.

Ibid. 2

A time to weep, and a time to laugh; a time to mourn, and a time to dance.

Ibid. 4

A time to keep silence, and a time to speak.

Ibid. 7

Wherefore I praised the dead which are already dead, more than the living which are yet alive.

Ibid. IV, 2

Woe to him that is alone when he falleth.

Ibid. 10

A threefold cord is not quickly broken.

Ibid. 12

God is in heaven, and thou upon earth: therefore let thy words be few.

Ibid. V, 2

Better is it that thou shouldest not vow, than that thou shouldest vow and not pay.

Ibid. 5

The sleep of a labouring man is sweet.

Ibid. 12

But the abundance of the rich will not suffer him to sleep.

Ibid.

A good name is better than precious ointment; and the day of death than the day of one's birth.

Ibid. VII, 1

It is better to go to the house of mourning, than to go to the house of feasting.

Ibid. 2

Sorrow is better than laughter: for by the sadness of the countenance the heart is made better.

Ibid. 3

As the crackling of thorns under a pot, so is the laughter of the fool.

Ibid. 6

Better is the end of a thing than the beginning thereof.

Ibid. 8

In the day of prosperity be joyful, but in the day of adversity consider.

Ecclesiastes. VII, 14

Be not righteous over much.

Ibid. 16

There is not a just man upon earth, that doeth good, and sinneth not.

Ibid. 20

One man among a thousand have I found; but a woman among all those have I not found.

Ibid. 28

God hath made man upright; but they have sought out many inventions.

Ibid. 29

There is no discharge in that war.

Ibid. VIII, 8

A man hath no better thing under the sun, than to eat, and to drink, and to be merry.[1]

Ibid. 15

All things come alike to all: there is one event to the righteous, and to the wicked.

Ibid. IX, 2

A living dog is better than a dead lion.

Ibid. 4

The living know that they shall die: but the dead know not any thing, neither have they any more a reward; for the memory of them is forgotten.

Ibid. 5

Whatsover thy hand findeth to do, do it with thy might; for there is no work, nor device, nor knowledge, nor wisdom, in the grave, whither thou goest.

Ibid. 10

The race is not to the swift, nor the battle to the strong.

Ibid. 11

He that diggeth a pit shall fall into it; and whoso breaketh an hedge, a serpent shall bite him.

Ibid. X, 8

A feast is made for laughter, and wine maketh merry: but money answereth all things.

Ibid. 19

[1] Also in *Luke, XII, 19.*

A bird of the air shall carry the voice, and that which hath wings shall tell the matter.

Ecclesiastes. X, 20

Cast thy bread upon the waters: for thou shalt find it after many days.

Ibid. XI, 1

He that observeth the wind shall not sow; and he that regardeth the clouds shall not reap.

Ibid. 4

In the morning sow thy seed, and in the evening withhold not thine hand.

Ibid. 6

Rejoice, O young man, in thy youth

Ibid. 9

Remember now thy Creator in the days of thy youth, while the evil days come not, nor the years draw nigh, when thou shalt say, I have no pleasure in them.

Ibid. XII, 1

While the sun, or the light, or the moon, or the stars, be not darkened, nor the clouds return after the rain.

Ibid. 2

In the day when the keepers of the house shall tremble, and the strong men shall bow themselves, and the grinders cease because they are few, and those that look out of the windows be darkened.

Ibid. 3

The doors shall be shut in the streets, when the sound of the grinding is low, and he shall rise up at the voice of the bird, and all the daughters of music shall be brought low.

Ibid. 4

The almond tree shall flourish, and the grasshopper shall be a burden, and desire shall fail; because man goeth to his long home, and the mourners go about the streets.

Ibid. 5

Or ever the silver cord be loosed, or the golden bowl be broken, or the pitcher be broken at the fountain, or the wheel broken at the cistern.

Ibid. 6

Then shall the dust return to the earth as it was: and the spirit shall return unto God who gave it.

Ecclesiastes. XII, 7

The words of the wise are as goads, and as nails fastened by the masters of assemblies.

Ibid. 11

Of making many books there is no end; and much study is a weariness of the flesh.

Ibid. 12

Let us hear the conclusion of the whole matter: Fear God, and keep his commandments; for this is the whole duty of man.

Ibid. 13

For God shall bring every work into judgment, with every secret thing, whether it be good, or whether it be evil.

Ibid. 14

The song of songs, which is Solomon's.

The Song of Solomon. I, 1

I am black, but comely, O ye daughters of Jerusalem, as the tents of Kedar, as the curtains of Solomon.

Ibid. 5

O thou fairest among women.

Ibid. 8

I am the rose of Sharon, and the lily of the valleys.

Ibid. II, 1

His banner over me was love.

Ibid. 4

Stay me with flagons, comfort me with apples: for I am sick of love.

Ibid. 5

Rise up, my love, my fair one, and come away.

For, lo! the winter is past, the rain is over and gone;

The flowers appear on the earth; the time of the singing of birds is come, and the voice of the turtle is heard in our land.

Ibid. 10–12

The little foxes, that spoil the vines.

Ibid. 15

Until the day break, and the shadows flee away.

The Song of Solomon. II, 17; IV, 6

By night on my bed I sought him whom my soul loveth: I sought him, but I found him not.

Ibid. III, 1

Thy two breasts are like two young roes that are twins, which feed among the lilies.

Ibid. IV, 5

Thou art all fair, my love; there is no spot in thee.

Ibid. 7

Awake, O north wind; and come, thou south; blow upon my garden, that the spices thereof may flow out. Let my beloved come into his garden, and eat his pleasant fruits.

Ibid. 16

My beloved put in his hand by the hole of the door, and my bowels were moved for him.

Ibid. V, 4

His mouth is most sweet: yea, he is altogether lovely. This is my beloved, and this is my friend, O daughters of Jerusalem.

Ibid. 16

Who is she that looketh forth as the morning, fair as the moon, clear as the sun, and terrible as an army with banners?

Ibid. VI, 10

Thy belly is like a heap of wheat set about with lilies.

Ibid. VII, 2

Thy neck is as a tower of ivory.

Ibid. 4

Like the best wine . . . . that goeth down sweetly, causing the lips of those that are asleep to speak.

Ibid. 9

Set me as a seal upon thine heart, as a seal upon thine arm: for love is strong as death; jealousy is cruel as the grave.

Ibid. VIII, 6

Many waters cannot quench love, neither can the floods drown it.

Ibid. 7

We have a little sister, and she hath no breasts.
The Song of Solomon. VIII, 8

Make haste, my beloved, and be thou like to a roe or to a young hart upon the mountains of spices.
Ibid. 14

The ox knoweth his owner, and the ass his master's crib.
Isaiah. I, 3

The whole head is sick, and the whole heart faint.
Ibid. 5

As a lodge in a garden of cucumbers.
Ibid. 8

Bring no more vain oblations.
Ibid. 13

Come now, and let us reason together.
Ibid. 18

Though your sins be as scarlet, they shall be white as snow.
Ibid.

They shall beat their swords into plowshares, and their spears into pruning-hooks; nation shall not lift up sword against nation, neither shall they learn war any more.[1]
Ibid. II, 4

In that day a man shall cast his idols . . . to the moles and to the bats.
Ibid. 20

Cease ye from man, whose breath is in his nostrils.
Ibid. 22

The stay and the staff, the whole stay of bread, and the whole stay of water.
Ibid. III, 1

Grind the faces of the poor.
Ibid. 15

Walk with stretched forth necks and wanton eyes, walking and mincing as they go, and making a tinkling with their feet.
Ibid. 16

In that day seven women shall take hold of one man.
Ibid. IV, 1

[1] Also in *Joel, III, 10* and *Micah, IV, 3.*

Woe unto them that rise up early in the morning, that they may follow strong drink.
Isaiah. V, 11

Woe unto them that draw iniquity with cords of vanity, and sin as it were with a cart rope.
Ibid. 18

Woe unto them that call evil good, and good evil.
Ibid. 20

I saw also the Lord sitting upon a throne, high and lifted up, and his train filled the temple.
Ibid. VI, 1

Holy, holy, holy, is the Lord of hosts: the whole earth is full of his glory.
Ibid. 3

Then, said I, Lord, how long?
Ibid. 11

Behold, a virgin shall conceive, and bear a son, and shall call his name Immanuel.
Ibid. VII, 14

For a stone of stumbling and for a rock of offence.
Ibid. VIII, 14

The people that walked in darkness have seen a great light: they that dwell in the land of the shadow of death, upon them hath the light shined.
Ibid. IX, 2

For unto us a child is born, unto us a son is given: and the government shall be upon his shoulder: and his name shall be called Wonderful, Counsellor, The mighty God, The everlasting Father, The Prince of Peace.
Ibid. 6

The ancient and honourable.
Ibid. 15

And there shall come forth a rod out of the stem of Jesse, and a Branch shall grow out of his roots:
And the Spirit of the Lord shall rest upon him, the spirit of wisdom and understanding, the spirit of counsel and might, the spirit of knowledge and of the fear of the Lord.
Ibid. XI, 1, 2

The wolf also shall dwell with the lamb, and the leopard shall lie down with the kid.
Isaiah. XI, 6

How art thou fallen from heaven, O Lucifer, son of the morning!
Ibid. XIV, 12

Is this the man that made the earth to tremble, that did shake kingdoms?
Ibid. 16

Like the rushing of mighty waters.
Ibid. XVII, 12

Babylon is fallen, is fallen.
Ibid. XXI, 9

Watchman, what of the night?
Ibid. 11

Let us eat and drink; for tomorrow we shall die.
Ibid. XXII, 13

I will fasten him as a nail in a sure place.
Ibid. 23

Whose merchants are princes.
Ibid. XXIII, 8

A feast of fat things, a feast of wines on the lees.
Ibid. XXV, 6

He will swallow up death in victory; and the Lord God will wipe away tears from off all faces.
Ibid. 8

Thou wilt keep him in perfect peace, whose mind is stayed on thee.
Ibid. XXVI, 3

Hide thyself as it were for a little moment, until the indignation be overpast.
Ibid. 20

Leviathan, that crooked serpent . . . the dragon that is in the sea.
Ibid. XXVII, 1

For precept must be upon precept, precept upon precept; line upon line, line upon line; here a little, and there a little.
Ibid. XXVIII, 10

We have made a covenant with death, and with hell are we at agreement.
Ibid. 15

It shall be a vexation only to understand the report.
Isaiah. XXVIII, 19

They are drunken, but not with wine; they stagger, but not with strong drink.
Ibid. XXIX, 9

Their strength is to sit still.
Ibid. XXX, 7

Now go, write it before them in a table, and note it in a book, that it may be for the time to come for ever and ever.
Ibid. 8

The bread of adversity, and the water of affliction.
Ibid. 20

This is the way, walk ye in it.
Ibid. 21

And a man shall be as an hiding place from the wind, and a covert from the tempest; as rivers of water in a dry place, as the shadow of a great rock in a weary land.
Ibid. XXXII, 2

The desert shall rejoice, and blossom as the rose.
Ibid. XXXV, 1

Then the eyes of the blind shall be opened, and the ears of the deaf shall be unstopped.
Ibid. 5

Then shall the lame man leap as an hart, and the tongue of the dumb sing.
Ibid. 6

Sorrow and sighing shall flee away.
Ibid. 10

Thou trustest in the staff of this broken reed.
Ibid. XXXVI, 6

Set thine house in order.
Ibid. XXXVIII, 1

I shall go softly all my years in the bitterness of my soul.
Ibid. 15

Comfort ye my people.
Ibid. XL, 1

The voice of him that crieth in the wilderness, Prepare ye the way of the

Lord, make straight in the desert a highway for our God.[1]

Isaiah. XL, 3

Every valley shall be exalted, and every mountain and hill shall be made low: and the crooked shall be made straight, and the rough places plain.

Ibid. 4

All flesh is grass, and all the goodliness thereof is as the flower of the field.

Ibid. 6

The grass withereth, the flower fadeth:[2] but the word of our God shall stand for ever.

Ibid. 8

He shall feed his flock like a shepherd: he shall gather the lambs with his arm, and carry them in his bosom, and shall gently lead those that are with young.

Ibid. 11

The nations are as a drop of a bucket, and are counted as the small dust of the balance.

Ibid. 15

Have ye not known? have ye not heard? hath it not been told you from the beginning?

Ibid. 21

They that wait upon the Lord shall renew their strength; they shall mount up with wings as eagles; they shall run, and not be weary; and they shall walk, and not faint.

Ibid. 31

They helped every one his neighbour: and every one said to his brother, Be of good courage.

Ibid. XLI, 6

A bruised reed shall he not break, and the smoking flax shall he not quench.

Ibid. XLII, 3

There is no peace, saith the Lord, unto the wicked.

Ibid. XLVIII, 22

[1] See *Matthew, III, 3*, on page 1050a. Also in *Mark, I, 3; Luke, III, 4; John, I, 23.*
[2] See *Psalm XC, 5–6*, on page 1035b.

Can a woman forget her sucking child, that she should not have compassion on the son of her womb?

Isaiah. XLIX, 15

How beautiful upon the mountains are the feet of him that bringeth good tidings, that publisheth peace.

Ibid. LII, 7

They shall see eye to eye.

Ibid. 8

He is despised and rejected of men; a man of sorrows, and acquainted with grief.

Ibid. LIII, 3

All we like sheep have gone astray.

Ibid. 6

He is brought as a lamb to the slaughter.[1]

Ibid. 7

Ho, everyone that thirsteth, come ye to the waters.

Ibid. LV, 1

Let the wicked forsake his way, and the unrighteous man his thoughts.

Ibid. 7

For my thoughts are not your thoughts, neither are your ways my ways, saith the Lord.

Ibid. 8

A little one shall become a thousand, and a small one a strong nation.

Ibid. LX, 22

Give unto them beauty for ashes, the oil of joy for mourning, the garment of praise for the spirit of heaviness.

Ibid. LXI, 3

I have trodden the winepress alone.

Ibid. LXIII, 3

All our righteousnesses are as filthy rags; and we all do fade as a leaf.

Ibid. LXIV, 6

I am holier than thou.

Ibid. LXV, 5

As one whom his mother comforteth, so will I comfort you.

Ibid. LXVI, 13

Saying, Peace, peace; when there is no peace.

Jeremiah. VI, 14; VIII, 11

[1] Also in *Acts, VIII, 32.*

Stand ye in the ways, and see, and ask for the old paths, where is the good way, and walk therein.[1]
Jeremiah. VI, 16

Amend your ways and your doings.
Ibid. VII, 3; XXVI, 13

The harvest is past, the summer is ended, and we are not saved.
Ibid. VIII, 20

Is there no balm in Gilead? Is there no physician there?
Ibid. 22

Oh that I had in the wilderness a lodging place of wayfaring men!
Ibid. IX, 2

I will feed them . . . with wormwood, and give them water of gall to drink.
Ibid. 15; XXIII, 15

Can the Ethiopian change his skin, or the leopard his spots?
Ibid. XIII, 23

Her sun is gone down while it was yet day.
Ibid. XV, 9

A man of strife and a man of contention.
Ibid. 10

Written with a pen of iron, and with the point of a diamond.
Ibid. XVII, 1

He shall be as a tree planted by the waters, and that spreadeth out her roots by the river.
Ibid. 8

The heart is deceitful above all things, and desperately wicked: who can know it?
Ibid. 9

Thou art my hope in the day of evil.
Ibid. 17

He shall be buried with the burial of an ass.
Ibid. XXII, 19

O earth, earth, earth, hear the word of the Lord.
Ibid. 29

The fathers have eaten a sour grape,
[1] Stare super vias antiquas. — *The Vulgate.*

and the children's teeth are set on edge.[1]
Jeremiah. XXXI, 29

With my whole heart and with my whole soul.
Ibid. XXXII, 41

And seekest thou great things for thyself? seek them not.
Ibid. XLV, 5

Is it nothing to you, all ye that pass by? behold, and see if there be any sorrow like unto my sorrow.
Lamentations. I, 12

Their visage is blacker than a coal.[2]
Ibid. IV, 8

As it were a wheel in the middle of a wheel.
Ezekiel. I, 16

As is the mother, so is her daughter.
Ibid. XVI, 44

I will cause you to pass under the rod.
Ibid. XX, 37

The king of Babylon stood at the parting of the way.
Ibid. XXI, 21

Son of man, can these bones live? And I answered, O Lord God, thou knowest.
Ibid. XXXVII, 3

His legs of iron, his feet part of iron and part of clay.
Daniel. II, 33

Shadrach, Meshach, and Abed-nego, fell down bound into the midst of the burning fiery furnace.
Ibid. III, 23

Nebuchadnezzar . . . was driven from men, and did eat grass as oxen.
Ibid. IV, 33

Belshazzar the king made a great feast to a thousand of his lords.
Ibid. V, 1

And this is the writing that was written, MENE, MENE, TEKEL, UPHARSIN.
Ibid. 25

[1] Also in *Ezekiel, XVIII, 2.*
[2] The faces of them all are as the blackness of a kettle.—*Douay Bible* [1609], *Nahum, II,* 10. (The English version of the Roman Catholic Bible was first printed in Douay, France.)

MENE; God hath numbered thy kingdom and finished it.

Daniel. V, 26

TEKEL; Thou art weighed in the balances, and art found wanting.

Ibid. 27

PERES; Thy kingdom is divided, and given to the Medes and Persians.

Ibid. 28

His windows being open in his chamber toward Jerusalem.

Ibid. VI, 10

According to the law of the Medes and Persians, which altereth not.

Ibid. 12

They brought Daniel, and cast him into the den of lions.

Ibid. 16

So Daniel was taken up out of the den, and no manner of hurt was found upon him, because he believed in his God.

Ibid. 23

The Ancient of days.

Ibid. VII, 13

Many shall run to and fro, and knowledge shall be increased.

Ibid. XII, 4

Like people, like priest.

Hosea. IV, 9

They have sown the wind, and they shall reap the whirlwind.

Ibid. VIII, 7

I have multiplied visions, and used similitudes, by the ministry of the prophets.

Ibid. XII, 10

Your old men shall dream dreams, your young men shall see visions.

Joel. II, 28

Multitudes in the valley of decision.

Ibid. III, 14

They sold the righteous for silver, and the poor for a pair of shoes.

Amos. II, 6

Can two walk together, except they be agreed?

Ibid. III, 3

The houses of ivory shall perish.

Ibid. 15

And Jonah was in the belly of the fish three days and three nights.

Jonah. I, 17

They shall sit every man under his vine and under his fig-tree.[1]

Micah. IV, 4

What doth the Lord require of thee, but to do justly, and to love mercy, and to walk humbly with thy God?

Ibid. VI, 8

Write the vision, and make it plain upon tables, that he may run that readeth it.

Habakkuk. II, 2

The Lord is in his holy temple: let all the earth keep silence before him.

Ibid. 20

Ye have sown much, and bring in little.

Haggai. I, 6

He that earneth wages, earneth wages to put it into a bag with holes.

Ibid.

Your fathers, where are they? And the prophets, do they live forever?

Zechariah. I, 5

I have spread you abroad as the four winds of the heaven.

Ibid. II, 6

Not by might, nor by power, but by my spirit, saith the Lord of hosts.

Ibid. IV, 6

For who hath despised the day of small things?

Ibid. 10

They are the eyes of the Lord, which run to and fro through the whole earth.

Ibid.

Behold, thy King cometh unto thee . . . lowly, and riding upon an ass.

Ibid. IX, 9

Prisoners of hope.

Ibid. 12

I was wounded in the house of my friends.

Ibid. XIII, 6

Have we not all one father? hath not one God created us?

Malachi. II, 10

Behold, the day cometh.

Ibid. IV, 1

[1] See *1 Maccabees, XIV, 12,* on page 1067a.

But unto you that fear my name shall the Sun of righteousness arise with healing in his wings.

Malachi. IV, 2

He shall turn the heart of the fathers to the children, and the heart of the children to their fathers.

Ibid. 6

NEW TESTAMENT

And [Joseph] knew her not till she had brought forth her firstborn son: and he called his name Jesus.

Matthew. I, 25

Now when Jesus was born in Bethlehem of Judaea in the days of Herod the king, behold, there came wise men from the east to Jerusalem.

Ibid. II, 1

Where is he that is born King of the Jews? for we have seen his star in the east, and are come to worship him.

Ibid. 2

They saw the young child with Mary his mother, and fell down, and worshipped him; and . . . they presented unto him gifts; gold, and frankincense, and myrrh.

Ibid. 11

Rachel weeping for her children, and would not be comforted, because they are not.

Ibid. 18

Repent ye: for the kingdom of heaven is at hand.

Ibid. III, 2

The voice of one crying in the wilderness, Prepare ye the way of the Lord, make his paths straight.[1]

Ibid. 3

And his meat was locusts and wild honey.

Ibid. 4

O generation of vipers, who hath warned you to flee from the wrath to come?

Ibid. 7

This is my beloved Son, in whom I am well pleased.

Matthew. III, 17

Man shall not live by bread alone, but by every word that proceedeth out of the mouth of God.[1]

Ibid. IV, 4

Follow me, and I will make you fishers of men.

Ibid. 19

Blessed are the poor in spirit: for theirs is the kingdom of heaven.

Blessed are they that mourn: for they shall be comforted.

Blessed are the meek: for they shall inherit the earth.[2]

Blessed are they which do hunger and thirst after righteousness: for they shall be filled.

Blessed are the merciful: for they shall obtain mercy.

Blessed are the pure in heart: for they shall see God.

Blessed are the peacemakers: for they shall be called the children of God.

Ibid. V, 3–9

Ye are the salt of the earth: but if the salt have lost its savour, wherewith shall it be salted?

Ibid. 13

Ye are the light of the world. A city that is set on an hill cannot be hid.

Ibid. 14

Let your light so shine before men, that they may see your good works, and glorify your Father which is in heaven.

Ibid. 16

Think not that I am come to destroy the law, or the prophets: I am not come to destroy, but to fulfill.

Ibid. 17

Till heaven and earth pass, one jot or one tittle shall in no wise pass from the law, till all be fulfilled.

Ibid. 18

Whosoever looketh on a woman to lust after her hath committed adultery with her already in his heart.

Ibid. 28

---

[1] See *Isaiah, XL, 3*, on page 1046b–1047a. Also in *Mark, I, 3; Luke, III, 4; John, I, 23.*

[1] See *Deuteronomy, VIII, 3*, on page 1025b.
[2] See *Psalm XXXVII, 11*, on page 1034a.

If thy right eye offend thee, pluck it out, and cast it from thee: for it is profitable for thee that one of thy members should perish, and not that thy whole body should be cast into hell.

Matthew. V, 29

If thy right hand offend thee, cut it off.

Ibid. 30

Whosoever shall marry her that is divorced committeth adultery.

Ibid. 32

Swear not at all; neither by heaven; for it is God's throne:

Nor by the earth; for it is his footstool.

Ibid. 34, 35

Resist not evil.

Ibid. 39

Whosoever shall smite thee on thy right cheek, turn to him the other also.

Ibid.

Love your enemies, bless them that curse you, do good to them that hate you, and pray for them which despitefully use you, and persecute you.

Ibid. 44

He maketh his sun to rise on the evil and on the good, and sendeth rain on the just and on the unjust.

Ibid. 45

When thou doest alms, let not thy left hand know what thy right hand doeth.

Ibid. VI, 3

After this manner therefore pray ye: Our Father which art in heaven, Hallowed be thy name.

Thy kingdom come. Thy will be done in earth, as it is in heaven.

Give us this day our daily bread.

And forgive us our debts, as we forgive our debtors.

And lead us not into temptation, but deliver us from evil: For thine is the kingdom, and the power, and the glory, for ever. Amen.

Ibid. 9–13

Lay not up for yourselves treasures upon earth, where moth and rust doth corrupt, and where thieves break through and steal.

Matthew. VI, 19

Lay up for yourselves treasures in heaven.

Ibid. 20

For where your treasure is, there will your heart be also.

Ibid. 21

The light of the body is the eye.

Ibid. 22

No man can serve two masters.

Ibid. 24

Ye cannot serve God and mammon.

Ibid.

Behold the fowls of the air: for they sow not neither do they reap, nor gather into barns.

Ibid. 26

Which of you by taking thought can add one cubit unto his stature?

Ibid. 27

Consider the lilies of the field, how they grow; they toil not, neither do they spin.

Ibid. 28

Even Solomon in all his glory was not arrayed like one of these.

Ibid. 29

Take therefore no thought for the morrow: for the morrow shall take thought for the things of itself. Sufficient unto the day is the evil thereof.

Ibid. 34

Judge not, that ye be not judged.

Ibid. VII, 1

And why beholdest thou the mote that is in thy brother's eye, but considerest not the beam that is in thine own eye?

Ibid. 3

Neither cast ye your pearls before swine.

Ibid. 6

Ask, and it shall be given you; seek, and ye shall find; knock, and it shall be opened unto you.

Ibid. 7

Every one that asketh receiveth; and he that seeketh findeth.

Ibid. 8

Or what man is there of you, whom if his son ask bread, will he give him a stone?

Matthew. VII, 9

Therefore all things whatsoever ye would that men should do to you, do ye even so to them: for this is the law and the prophets.

Ibid. 12

Wide is the gate, and broad is the way, that leadeth to destruction.

Ibid. 13

Strait is the gate, and narrow is the way, which leadeth unto life, and few there be that find it.

Ibid. 14

Beware of false prophets, which come to you in sheep's clothing, but inwardly they are ravening wolves.

Ibid. 15

By their fruits ye shall know them.

Ibid. 20

It was founded upon a rock.

Ibid. 25

But the children of the kingdom shall be cast out into outer darkness: there shall be weeping and gnashing of teeth.

Ibid. VIII, 12

The foxes have holes, and the birds of the air have nests; but the Son of man hath not where to lay his head.

Ibid. 20

Let the dead bury their dead.

Ibid. 22

A man, named Matthew, sitting at the receipt of custom.

Ibid. IX, 9

They that be whole need not a physician, but they that are sick.

Ibid. 12

For I am not come to call the righteous, but sinners to repentance.

Ibid. 13

Neither do men put new wine into old bottles.

Ibid. 17

The harvest truly is plenteous, but the laborers are few.

Ibid. 37

Freely ye have received, freely give.

Ibid. X, 8

Be ye therefore wise as serpents, and harmless as doves.

Matthew. X, 16

The disciple is not above his master, nor the servant above his lord.

Ibid. 24

Are not two sparrows sold for a farthing? and one of them shall not fall on the ground without your Father.

Ibid. 29

But the very hairs of your head are all numbered.

Ibid. 30

I came not to send peace, but a sword.

Ibid. 34

He that findeth his life shall lose it: and he that loseth his life for my sake shall find it.

Ibid. 39

He that hath ears to hear, let him hear.

Ibid. XI, 15

A friend of publicans and sinners.

Ibid. XI, 19

Wisdom is justified of her children.[1]

Ibid.

Come unto me, all ye that labour and are heavy laden, and I will give you rest.

Take my yoke upon you, and learn of me; for I am meek and lowly in heart: and ye shall find rest unto your souls.

For my yoke is easy, and my burden is light.

Ibid. 28–30

He that is not with me is against me.

Ibid. XII, 30

The tree is known by his fruit.

Ibid. 33

Out of the abundance of the heart the mouth speaketh.

Ibid. 34

Because they had no root, they withered away.

Ibid. XIII, 6

But other fell into good ground, and brought forth fruit, some a hundredfold, some sixtyfold, some thirtyfold.

Ibid. 8

[1] Also in *Luke, VII, 35.*

The kingdom of heaven is like to a grain of mustard seed.
Matthew. XIII, 31

Pearl of great price.
Ibid. 46

Is not this the carpenter's son?
Ibid. 55

A prophet is not without honour, save in his own country.
Ibid. 57

The daughter of Herodias danced before them, and pleased Herod.
Ibid. XIV, 6

Give me here John Baptist's head in a charger.
Ibid. 8

We have here but five loaves, and two fishes.
Ibid. 17

And they did all eat, and were filled: and they took up of the fragments that remained twelve baskets full.
Ibid. 20

And in the fourth watch of the night Jesus went unto them, walking on the sea.
Ibid. 25

Be of good cheer; it is I; be not afraid.
Ibid. 27

O thou of little faith, wherefore didst thou doubt?
Ibid. 31

Of truth thou art the Son of God.
Ibid. 33

Not that which goeth into the mouth defileth a man; but that which cometh out of the mouth, this defileth a man.
Ibid. XV, 11

They be blind leaders of the blind. And if the blind lead the blind, both shall fall into the ditch.
Ibid. 14

The dogs eat of the crumbs which fall from their masters' table.
Ibid. 27

When it is evening, ye say, It will be fair weather: for the sky is red.
Ibid. XVI, 2

The signs of the times.
Ibid. 3

Thou art Peter, and upon this rock I will build my church.
Matthew. XVI, 18

I will give unto thee the keys of heaven.
Ibid. 19

Get thee behind me, Satan.[1]
Ibid. 23

What is a man profited, if he shall gain the whole world, and lose his own soul?[2]
Ibid. 26

Except ye be converted, and become as little children, ye shall not enter into the kingdom of heaven.
Ibid. XVIII, 3

The ninety and nine.
Ibid. 12, 13

Where two or three are gathered together in my name, there am I in the midst of them.
Ibid. 20

Until seventy times seven.
Ibid. 22

What therefore God hath joined together, let not man put asunder.[3]
Ibid. XIX, 6

If thou wilt be perfect, go and sell that thou hast, and give to the poor, and thou shalt have treasure in heaven.
Ibid. 21

It is easier for a camel to go through the eye of a needle, than for a rich man to enter into the kingdom of God.
Ibid. 24

But many that are first shall be last; and the last shall be first.
Ibid. 30

Borne the burden and heat of the day.
Ibid. XX, 12

Is it not lawful for me to do what I will with mine own?
Ibid. 15

Overthrew the tables of the money changers.
Ibid. XXI, 12

[1] Also in *Luke, IV, 8.*
[2] Also in *Mark, VIII, 36.*
[3] Those whom God hath joined together let no man put asunder.
Book of Common Prayer, Solemnization of Matrimony

My house shall be called the house of prayer; but ye have made it a den of thieves.

Matthew. XXI, 13

They made light of it.

Ibid. XXII, 5

For many are called, but few are chosen.

Ibid. 14

Render therefore unto Caesar the things which are Caesar's.[1]

Ibid. 21

Whosoever shall exalt himself shall be abased; and he that shall humble himself shall be exalted.

Ibid. XXIII, 12

Woe unto you . . for ye pay tithe of mint and anise and cummin.

Ibid. 23

Blind guides, which strain at a gnat, and swallow a camel.

Ibid. 24

Whited sepulchres, which indeed appear beautiful outward, but are within full of dead men's bones.

Ibid. 27

As a hen gathereth her chickens under her wings.

Ibid. 37

Wars and rumours of wars.[2]

Ibid. XXIV, 6

The end is not yet.

Ibid.

Abomination of desolation.[3]

Ibid. 15

False prophets.

Ibid. 24

Wheresoever the carcass is, there will the eagles be gathered together.

Ibid. 28

Heaven and earth shall pass away, but my words shall not pass away.

Ibid. 35

One shall be taken, and the other left.

Ibid. 40

Then shall the kingdom of heaven be likened unto ten virgins, which took

their lamps, and went forth to meet the bridegroom.

And five of them were wise, and five were foolish.

Matthew. XXV, 1, 2

Well done, thou good and faithful servant.

Ibid. 21

Unto every one that hath shall be given, and he shall have abundance; but from him that hath not shall be taken away even that which he hath.

Ibid. 29

And before him shall be gathered all nations: and he shall separate them one from another, as a shepherd divideth his sheep from the goats.

Ibid. 32

For I was an hungred, and ye gave me meat: I was thirsty, and ye gave me drink: I was a stranger, and ye took me in:

Naked, and ye clothed me: I was sick, and ye visited me: I was in prison, and ye came unto me.

Ibid. 35, 36

Inasmuch as ye have done it unto one of the least of these my brethren, ye have done it unto me.

Ibid. 40

An alabaster box of very precious ointment.

Ibid. XXVI, 7

To what purpose is this waste?

Ibid. 8

For ye have the poor always with you; but me ye have not always.

Ibid. 11

What will ye give me, and I will deliver him unto you? And they covenanted with him for thirty pieces of silver.

Ibid. 15

My time is at hand.

Ibid. 18

Verily I say unto you, that one of you shall betray me.

Ibid. 21

It had been good for that man if he had not been born.

Ibid. 24

---

[1] Also in *Mark, XII, 17.*
[2] Also in *Mark, XIII, 7.*
[3] Also in *Mark, XIII, 14.*

Jesus took bread, and blessed it, and brake it, and gave it to the disciples, and said, Take, eat; this is my body. And he took the cup, and gave thanks, and gave it to them, saying, Drink ye all of it;

For this is my blood of the new testament, which is shed for many for the remission of sins.

Matthew. XXVI, 26–28

This night, before the cock crow, thou shalt deny me thrice.

Ibid. 34

O my Father, if it be possible, let this cup pass from me: nevertheless, not as I will, but as thou wilt.

Ibid. 39

Watch and pray, that ye enter not into temptation: the spirit indeed is willing, but the flesh is weak.

Ibid. 41

Hail, Master; and kissed him.

Ibid. 49

All they that take the sword shall perish with the sword.

Ibid. 52

Thy speech bewrayeth thee.

Ibid. 73

Then began he to curse and to swear, saying, I know not the man. And immediately the cock crew.

Ibid. 74

The potter's field, to bury strangers in.

Ibid. XXVII, 7

Have thou nothing to do with that just man.

Ibid. 19

Let him be crucified.

Ibid. 22

He took water, and washed his hands before the multitude, saying, I am innocent of the blood of this just person: see ye to it.

Ibid. 24

His blood be on us, and on our children.

Ibid. 25

A place called Golgotha, that is to say, a place of a skull.

Ibid. 33

This is Jesus the King of the Jews.

Matthew. XXVII, 37

He saved others; himself he cannot save.

Ibid. 42

Eli, Eli, lama sabachthani? that is to say, My God, my God, why hast thou forsaken me? [1]

Ibid. 46

And, behold, the veil of the temple was rent in twain from the top to the bottom; and the earth did quake, and the rocks rent.

Ibid. 51

His [the Angel of the Lord] countenance was like lightning, and his raiment white as snow.

Ibid. XXVIII, 3

Go ye therefore, and teach all nations.

Ibid. 19

Lo, I am with you alway, even unto the end of the world.

Ibid. 20

The latchet of whose shoes I am not worthy to stoop down and unloose.

Mark. I, 7

The sabbath was made for man, and not man for the sabbath.

Ibid. II, 27

If a house be divided against itself, that house cannot stand.

Ibid. III, 25

With what measure ye mete, it shall be measured to you.

Ibid. IV, 24

First the blade, then the ear, after that the full corn in the ear.

Ibid. 28

What manner of man is this?

Ibid. 41

My name is Legion: for we are many.

Ibid. V, 9

Clothed, and in his right mind.

Ibid. 15

My little daughter lieth at the point of death.

Ibid. 23

Knowing in himself that virtue had gone out of him.

Ibid. 30

[1] See *Psalm XXII, 1*, on page 1033a.

I see men as trees, walking.

Mark. VIII, 24

Lord, I believe; help thou mine unbelief.

Ibid. IX, 24

Suffer the little children to come unto me, and forbid them not; for such is the kingdom of God.[1]

Ibid. X, 14

Which devour widows' houses, and for a pretense make long prayers.

Ibid. XII, 40

And there came a certain poor widow, and she threw in two mites.

Ibid. 42

For many bare false witness against him.

Ibid. XIV, 56

Go ye into all the world, and preach the gospel to every creature.

Ibid. XVI, 15

Hail, thou that art highly favoured, the Lord is with thee; blessed art thou among women.

Luke. I, 28

And blessed is the fruit of thy womb.

Ibid. 42

My soul doth magnify the Lord.

Ibid. 46

For he hath regarded the low estate of his handmaiden: for, behold, from henceforth all generations shall call me blessed.

Ibid. 48

He hath put down the mighty from their seats, and exalted them of low degree.

Ibid. 52

He hath filled the hungry with good things; and the rich he hath sent empty away.

Ibid. 53

And she brought forth her firstborn son, and wrapped him in swaddling clothes, and laid him in a manger; because there was no room for them in the inn.

Ibid. II, 7

Shepherds abiding in the field, keeping watch over their flock by night.

Luke. II, 8

And, lo, the angel of the Lord came upon them, and the glory of the Lord shone round about them; and they were sore afraid.

Ibid. 9

Fear not: for, behold, I bring you good tidings of great joy, which shall be to all people.

Ibid. 10

Glory to God in the highest, and on earth peace, good will toward men.[1]

Ibid. 14

Lord, now lettest thou thy servant depart in peace.

Ibid. 29

A light to lighten the Gentiles.

Ibid. 32

Wist ye not that I must be about my Father's business?

Ibid. 49

His mother kept all these sayings in her heart.

Ibid. 51

The axe is laid unto the root of the trees.

Ibid. III, 9

Physician, heal thyself.

Ibid. IV, 23

Woe unto you, when all men shall speak well of you!

Ibid. VI, 26

Nothing is secret, that shall not be made manifest.

Ibid. VIII, 17

No man, having put his hand to the plough, and looking back, is fit for the kingdom of God.

Ibid. IX, 62

Peace be to this house.

Ibid. X, 5

The labourer is worthy of his hire.[2]

Ibid. 7

A certain man went down from Jerusalem to Jericho, and fell among thieves.

Ibid. 30

---

[1] Also in *Matthew, XIX, 14*, and *Luke, XVIII, 16*.

[1] The Douay Bible has "peace to men of good will."

[2] Also in *1 Timothy, V, 18*.

He passed by on the other side.
Luke. X, 31

A certain Samaritan . . . had compassion on him.
Ibid. 33

Go, and do thou likewise.
Ibid. 37

But one thing is needful; and Mary hath chosen that good part which shall not be taken away from her.
Ibid. 42

Soul, thou hast much goods laid up for many years; take thine ease, eat, drink, and be merry.
Ibid. XII, 19

Thou fool, this night thy soul shall be required of thee.
Ibid. 20

Let your loins be girded about, and your lights burning.
Ibid. 35

The poor, and the maimed, and the halt, and the blind.
Ibid. XIV, 21

Which of you, intending to build a tower, sitteth not down first, and counteth the cost, whether he have sufficient to finish it?
Ibid. 28

Rejoice with me; for I have found my sheep which was lost.
Ibid. XV, 6

Wasted his substance with riotous living.
Ibid. 13

Bring hither the fatted calf, and kill it.
Ibid. 23

For this my son was dead, and is alive again; he was lost, and is found.
Ibid. 24

The children of this world are in their generation wiser than the children of light.
Ibid. XVI, 8

He that is faithful in that which is least is faithful also in much; and he that is unjust in the least is unjust also in much.
Ibid. 10

The beggar died, and was carried by the angels into Abraham's bosom.
Luke. XVI, 22

It were better for him that a millstone were hanged about his neck, and he cast into the sea.
Ibid. XVII, 2

Out of thine own mouth will I judge thee.
Ibid. XIX, 22

This do in remembrance of me.[1]
Ibid. XXII, 19

Father, forgive them; for they know not what they do.
Ibid. XXIII, 34

Father, into thy hands I commend my spirit.
Ibid. 46

He gave up the ghost.
Ibid.

He was a good man, and a just.
Ibid. 50

Did not our heart burn within us, while he talked with us?
Ibid. XXIV, 32

In the beginning was the Word, and the Word was with God, and the Word was God.
John. I, 1

And the light shineth in the darkness; and the darkness comprehended it not.
Ibid. 5

There was a man sent from God, whose name was John.
Ibid. 6

The true Light, which lighteth every man that cometh into the world.
Ibid. 9

The Word was made flesh, and dwelt among us.
Ibid. 14

Can there any good thing come out of Nazareth?
Ibid. 46

Woman, what have I to do with thee? mine hour is not yet come.
Ibid. II, 4

Make not my Father's house an house of merchandise.
Ibid. 16

[1] Also in *1 Corinthians, XI, 24.*

The wind bloweth where it listeth, and thou hearest the sound thereof, but canst not tell whence it cometh, and whither it goeth: so is every one that is born of the Spirit.
John. III, 8

For God so loved the world, that he gave his only begotten Son, that whosoever believeth in him should not perish, but have everlasting life.
Ibid. 16

Rise, take up thy bed, and walk.
Ibid. V, 8

He was a burning and a shining light.
Ibid. 35

What are they among so many?
Ibid. VI, 9

Gather up the fragments that remain, that nothing be lost.
Ibid. 12

I am the bread of life.
Ibid. 35

Judge not according to the appearance.
Ibid. VII, 24

He that is without sin among you, let him first cast a stone at her.
Ibid. VIII, 7

Neither do I condemn thee: go, and sin no more.
Ibid. 11

I am the light of the world: he that followeth me shall not walk in darkness, but shall have the light of life.
Ibid. 12

The truth shall make you free.
Ibid. 32

There is no truth in him.
Ibid. 44

The night cometh, when no man can work.
Ibid. IX, 4

Whether he be a sinner or no, I know not: one thing I know, that, whereas I was blind, now I see.
Ibid. 25

I am come that they might have life, and that they might have it more abundantly.
Ibid. X, 10

I am the resurrection and the life: he that believeth in me, though he were dead, yet shall he live:

And whosoever liveth and believeth in me shall never die.[1]
John. XI, 25, 26

Jesus wept.
Ibid. 35

Walk while ye have the light, lest darkness come upon you.
Ibid. XII, 35

That thou doest, do quickly.
Ibid. XIII, 27

A new commandment I give unto you, That ye love one another.
Ibid. 34

Let not your heart be troubled.
Ibid. XIV, 1

In my Father's house are many mansions: if it were not so, I would have told you. I go to prepare a place for you.
Ibid. 2

I will come again, and receive you unto myself; that where I am, there ye may be also.
Ibid. 3

I will not leave you comfortless.
Ibid. 18

Peace I leave with you.
Ibid. 27

Greater love hath no man than this, that a man lay down his life for his friends.
Ibid. XV, 13

Whither goest thou?
Ibid. XVI, 5

Ask, and ye shall receive, that your joy may be full.
Ibid. 24

Be of good cheer; I have overcome the world.
Ibid. 33

Now Barabbas was a robber.
Ibid. XVIII, 40

Behold the man!
Ibid. XIX, 5

It is finished.
Ibid. 30

[1] Also in Book of Common Prayer, Burial of the Dead.

And suddenly there came a sound from heaven as of a rushing mighty wind.

Acts. II, 2

And there appeared unto them cloven tongues like as of fire, and it sat upon each of them.

And they were all filled with the Holy Ghost, and began to speak with other tongues.

Ibid. 3, 4

Thy money perish with thee.

Ibid. VIII, 20

In the gall of bitterness, and in the bond of iniquity.

Ibid. 23

Saul, Saul, why persecutest thou me?

Ibid. IX, 4

It is hard for thee to kick against the pricks.

Ibid. 5

God is no respecter of persons.[1]

Ibid. X, 34

Come over into Macedonia, and help us.

Ibid. XVI, 9

Certain lewd fellows of the baser sort.

Ibid. XVII, 5

Men of Athens, I perceive that in all things ye are too superstitious.

Ibid. 22

For as I passed by, and beheld your devotions, I found an altar with this inscription, To the Unknown God.

Ibid. 23

For in him we live, and move, and have our being.

Ibid. 28

Mighty in the Scriptures.

Ibid. XVIII, 24

All with one voice about the space of two hours cried out, Great is Diana of the Ephesians.

Ibid. XIX, 34

It is more blessed to give than to receive.

Ibid. XX, 35

I am . . . a Jew of Tarsus, a city in Cilicia, a citizen of no mean city.

Ibid. XXI, 39

[1] See *Romans, II, 11*, on page 1059b.

Brought up in this city at the feet of Gamaliel.

Acts. XXII, 3

And the chief captain answered, With a great sum obtained I this freedom. And Paul said, But I was free born.

Ibid. 28

I am a Pharisee, the son of a Pharisee.

Ibid. XXIII, 6

When I have a convenient season, I will call for thee.

Ibid. XXIV, 25

I appeal unto Caesar.

Ibid. XXV, 11

Much learning doth make thee mad.

Ibid. XXVI, 24

Words of truth and soberness.

Ibid. 25

For this thing was not done in a corner.

Ibid. 26

Almost thou persuadest me to be a Christian.

Ibid. 28

Wherein thou judgest another, thou condemnest thyself.

Romans. II, 1

There is no respect of persons with God.

Ibid. 11

These, having not the law, are a law unto themselves.

Ibid. 14

God forbid.

Ibid. III, 31

Where no law is, there is no transgression.

Ibid. IV, 15

Who against hope believed in hope.

Ibid. 18

Where sin abounded, grace did much more abound.

Ibid. V, 20

Death hath no more dominion over him.

Ibid. VI, 9

Speak after the manner of men.

Ibid. 19

The wages of sin is death.

Ibid. 23

For the good that I would I do not; but the evil which I would not, that I do.

Romans. VII, 19

Heirs of God, and joint-heirs with Christ.

Ibid. VIII, 17

For we know that the whole creation groaneth and travaileth in pain together until now.

Ibid. 22

All things work together for good to them that love God.

Ibid. 28

If God be for us, who can be against us?

Ibid. 31

Neither death, nor life, nor angels, nor principalities, nor powers, nor things present, nor things to come,

Nor height, nor depth, nor any other creature, shall be able to separate us from the love of God, which is in Christ Jesus our Lord.

Ibid. 38, 39

Hath not the potter power over the clay, of the same lump to make one vessel unto honour, and another unto dishonour?

Ibid. IX, 21

Given to hospitality.

Ibid. XII, 13

Be not wise in your own conceits.

Ibid. 16

Recompense to no man evil for evil.

Ibid. 17

If it be possible, as much as lieth in you, live peaceably with all men.

Ibid. 18

Vengeance is mine; I will repay, saith the Lord.

Ibid. 19

If thine enemy hunger, feed him; if he thirst, give him drink: for in so doing thou shalt heap coals of fire on his head.[1]

Ibid. 20

Be not overcome of evil, but overcome evil with good.

Ibid. 21

[1] See *Proverbs, XXV, 21–22,* on page 1041a.

The powers that be are ordained of God.

Romans. XIII, 1

Render therefore to all their dues; tribute to whom tribute is due; custom to whom custom; fear to whom fear; honour to whom honour.

Ibid. 7

Owe no man anything, but to love one another.

Ibid. 8

Love is the fulfilling of the law.

Ibid. 10

Make not provision for the flesh, to fulfill the lusts thereof.

Ibid. 14

Doubtful disputations.

Ibid. XIV, 1

Let every man be fully persuaded in his own mind.

Ibid. 5

None of us liveth to himself.

Ibid. 7

Let us therefore follow after the things which make for peace.

Ibid. 19

God hath chosen the foolish things of the world to confound the wise; and God hath chosen the weak things of the world to confound the things which are mighty.

1 Corinthians. I, 27

As it is written,[1] eye hath not seen, nor ear heard.

Ibid. II, 9

I have planted, Apollos watered; but God gave the increase.

Ibid. III, 6

Every man's work shall be made manifest.

Ibid. 13

Not to think of men above that which is written.

Ibid. IV, 6

We are made a spectacle unto the world, and to angels, and to men.

Ibid. 9

Absent in body, but present in spirit.

Ibid. V, 3

[1] In *Isaiah, LXIV, 4.*

A little leaven leaveneth the whole lump.[1]

         1 Corinthians. V, 6

It is better to marry than to burn.

         Ibid. VII, 9

The fashion of this world passeth away.

         Ibid. 31

Knowledge puffeth up, but charity edifieth.

         Ibid. VIII, 1

I am made all things to all men.

         Ibid. IX, 22

Let him that thinketh he standeth take heed lest he fall.

         Ibid. X, 12

If a woman have long hair, it is a glory to her.

         Ibid. XI, 15

Though I speak with the tongues of men and of angels, and have not charity, I am become as sounding brass, or a tinkling cymbal.

         Ibid. XIII, 1

Though I have all faith, so that I could remove mountains, and have not charity, I am nothing.

         Ibid. 2

And though I bestow all my goods to feed the poor, and though I give my body to be burned, and have not charity, it profiteth me nothing.

         Ibid. 3

Charity suffereth long, and is kind; charity envieth not; charity vaunteth not itself, is not puffed up.

         Ibid. 4

Beareth all things, believeth all things, hopeth all things, endureth all things.

         Ibid. 7

Charity never faileth.

         Ibid. 8

We know in part, and we prophesy in part.

         Ibid. 9

When I was a child, I spake as a child, I understood as a child, I thought as a child: but when I became a man, I put away childish things.

         Ibid. 11

[1] Also in *Galatians, V, 9.*

For now we see through a glass, darkly; but then face to face: now I know in part; but then shall I know even as also I am known.

         1 Corinthians. XIII, 12

And now abideth faith, hope, charity, these three; but the greatest of these is charity.

         Ibid. 13

If the trumpet give an uncertain sound, who shall prepare himself for battle?

         Ibid. XIV, 8

Let all things be done decently and in order.

         Ibid. 40

And last of all he was seen of me also, as of one born out of due time.

         Ibid. XV, 8

But by the grace of God I am what I am.

         Ibid. 10

But now is Christ risen from the dead, and become the firstfruits of them that slept.

For since by man came death, by man came also the resurrection of the dead.

For as in Adam all die, even so in Christ shall all be made alive.

         Ibid. 20–22

The last enemy that shall be destroyed is death.

         Ibid. 26

Evil communications corrupt good manners.

         Ibid. 33

That which thou sowest is not quickened, except it die.

         Ibid. 36

One star differeth from another star in glory.

         Ibid. 41

It is sown in corruption, it is raised in incorruption.

         Ibid. 42

The first man is of the earth, earthy.

         Ibid. 47

Behold, I show you a mystery; We shall not all sleep, but shall all be changed,

In a moment, in the twinkling of an

eye, at the last trump: for the trumpet shall sound, and the dead shall be raised incorruptible, and we shall be changed.
1 Corinthians. XV, 51–52

Death is swallowed up in victory.
Ibid. 54

O death, where is thy sting? O grave, where is thy victory?
Ibid. 55

Watch ye, stand fast in the faith, quit you like men, be strong.
Ibid. XVI, 13

Not of the letter, but of the spirit; for the letter killeth, but the spirit giveth life.
2 Corinthians. III, 6

We have such hope, we use great plainness of speech.
Ibid. 12

The things which are seen are temporal; but the things which are not seen are eternal.
Ibid. IV, 18

We walk by faith, not by sight.
Ibid. V, 7

Now is the accepted time.
Ibid. VI, 2

By evil report and good report.
Ibid. 8

As having nothing, and yet possessing all things.
Ibid. 10

God loveth a cheerful giver.
Ibid. IX, 7

Though I be rude in speech.
Ibid. XI, 6

For ye suffer fools gladly, seeing ye yourselves are wise.
Ibid. 19

Forty stripes save one.
Ibid. 24

A thorn in the flesh.
Ibid. XII, 7

My strength is made perfect in weakness.
Ibid. 9

The grace of the Lord Jesus Christ, and the love of God, and the communion of the Holy Ghost, be with you all.
Ibid. XIII, 14

The right hands of fellowship.
Galatians. II, 9

Weak and beggarly elements.
Ibid. IV, 9

It is good to be zealously affected always in a good thing.
Ibid. 18

Ye are fallen from grace.
Ibid. V, 4

But the fruit of the Spirit is love, joy, peace, longsuffering, gentleness, goodness, faith,

Meekness, temperance.
Ibid. 22, 23

Every man shall bear his own burden.
Ibid. VI, 5

Whatsoever a man soweth, that shall he also reap.
Ibid. 7

Let us not be weary in well doing.
Ibid. 9

Carried about with every wind of doctrine.
Ephesians. IV, 14

Be ye angry, and sin not: let not the sun go down upon your wrath.
Ibid. 26

Put on the whole armour of God.
Ibid. VI, 11

For we wrestle not against flesh and blood, but against principalities, against powers, against the rulers of the darkness of this world, against spiritual wickedness in high places.
Ibid. 12

Wherefore take unto you the whole armour of God, that ye may be able to withstand in the evil day, and having done all, to stand.
Ibid. 13

To live is Christ, and to die is gain.
Philippians. I, 21

Work out your own salvation.
Ibid. II, 12

Whose God is their belly, and whose glory is in their shame.
Ibid. III, 19

The peace of God, which passeth all understanding.
Ibid. IV, 7

Whatsoever things are true, whatsoever things are honest, whatsoever things are just, whatsoever things are pure, whatsoever things are lovely, whatsoever things are of good report; if there be any virtue, and if there be any praise, think on these things.
Philippians. IV, 8

I have learned, in whatsoever state I am, therewith to be content.
Ibid. 11

Touch not; taste not; handle not.
Colossians. II, 21

Set your affections on things above, not on things on the earth.
Ibid. III, 2

Let your speech be alway with grace, seasoned with salt.
Ibid. IV, 6

Luke, the beloved physician.
Ibid. 14

Labour of love.
1 Thessalonians. I, 3

Study to be quiet, and to do your own business.
Ibid. IV, 11

Putting on the breastplate of faith and love; and for an helmet, the hope of salvation.
Ibid. V, 8

Prove all things; hold fast that which is good.
Ibid. 21

The law is good, if a man use it lawfully.
1 Timothy. I, 8

Not greedy of filthy lucre.
Ibid. III, 3

Drink no longer water, but use a little wine for thy stomach's sake.
Ibid. V, 23

We brought nothing into this world and it is certain we can carry nothing out.
Ibid. VI, 7

The love of money is the root of all evil.
Ibid. 10

Fight the good fight.
Ibid. 12

Rich in good works.
Ibid. 18

Science falsely so called.
1 Timothy. VI, 20

A workman that needeth not to be ashamed.
2 Timothy. II, 15

I have fought a good fight, I have finished my course, I have kept the faith.
Ibid. IV, 7

Alexander the coppersmith did me much evil: the Lord reward him according to his works.
Ibid. 14

Unto the pure all things are pure.
Titus. I, 15

Making mention of thee always in my prayers.
Philemon. I, 4

Such as have need of milk, and not of strong meat.
Hebrews. V, 12

Strong meat belongeth to them that are of full age.
Ibid. 14

Faith is the substance of things hoped for, the evidence of things not seen.
Ibid. XI, 1

We also are compassed about with so great a cloud of witnesses.
Ibid. XII, 1

The author and finisher of our faith.
Ibid. 2

Whom the Lord loveth he chasteneth.
Ibid. 6

The spirits of just men made perfect.
Ibid. 23

Be not forgetful to entertain strangers, for thereby some have entertained angels unawares.
Ibid. XIII, 2

Yesterday, and today, and forever.
Ibid. 8

For here we have no continuing city, but we seek one to come.
Ibid. 14

Let patience have her perfect work.
James. I, 4

Blessed is the man that endureth temptation; for when he is tried, he shall receive the crown of life.

James. I, 12

Every good gift and every perfect gift is from above.

Ibid. 17

No variableness, neither shadow of turning.

Ibid.

Be swift to hear, slow to speak, slow to wrath.

Ibid. 19

Unspotted from the world.

Ibid. 27

Faith without works is dead.

Ibid. II, 26

How great a matter a little fire kindleth!

Ibid. III, 5

The tongue can no man tame; it is an unruly evil.

Ibid. 8

This wisdom descendeth not from above, but is earthly, sensual, devilish.

Ibid. 15

Resist the Devil, and he will flee from you.

Ibid. IV, 7

Behold, we count them happy which endure. Ye have heard of the patience of Job, and have seen the end of the Lord.

Ibid. V, 11

The effectual fervent prayer of a righteous man availeth much.

Ibid. 16

Hope to the end.

1 Peter. I, 13

Abstain from fleshly lusts, which war against the soul.

Ibid. II, 11

Fear God. Honour the king.

Ibid. 17

Ornament of a meek and quiet spirit.

Ibid. III, 4

Giving honour unto the wife, as unto the weaker vessel.

Ibid. 7

Charity shall cover the multitude of sins.

Ibid. IV, 8

A crown of glory that fadeth not away.

1 Peter. V, 4

Be sober, be vigilant; because your adversary, the Devil, as a roaring lion, walketh about, seeking whom he may devour.

Ibid. 8

And the day star arise in your hearts.

2 Peter. I, 19

The dog is turned to his own vomit again.

Ibid. II, 22

Bowels of compassion.

1 John. III, 17

He that loveth not, knoweth not God; for God is love.

Ibid. IV, 8

There is no fear in love; but perfect love casteth out fear.

Ibid. 18

Be thou faithful unto death.

Revelation. II, 10

He shall rule them with a rod of iron.

Ibid. 27

Behold, I stand at the door and knock.

Ibid. III, 20

A pale horse: and his name that sat on him was Death.

Ibid. VI, 8

All nations, and kindreds, and people, and tongues.

Ibid. VII, 9

As the voice of many waters.[1]

Ibid. XIV, 2

They may rest from their labours; and their works do follow them.

Ibid. 13

And he gathered them together into a place called in the Hebrew tongue Armageddon.

Ibid. XVI, 16

Another book was opened, which is the book of life.

Ibid. XX, 12

I saw a new heaven and a new earth.

Ibid. XXI, 1

The holy city, new Jerusalem.

Ibid. 2

[1] The noise of many waters. — *Psalm XCIII, 4*

I am Alpha and Omega, the beginning and the end, the first and the last.
Revelation. XXI, 6

There shall be no night there.
Ibid. XXII, 5

Without are dogs.
Ibid. 15

THE APOCRYPHA [1]

How exceeding strong is wine! it causeth all men to err who drink it.
1 Esdras. III, 18

Ye must know that women have dominion over you: do ye not labour and toil, and give and bring all to the woman?
Ibid. IV, 22

Great is truth, and mighty above all things.[2]
Ibid. 41

Do right to the widow, judge for the fatherless, give to the poor, defend the orphan, clothe the naked.
2 Esdras. II, 20

What is past I know, but what is for to come I know not.
Ibid. IV, 46

Unto you is paradise opened.
Ibid. VIII, 52

Now therefore keep thy sorrow to thyself, and bear with a good courage that which hath befallen thee.
Ibid. X, 15

I shall light a candle of understanding in thine heart, which shall not be put out.
Ibid. XIV, 25

If thou hast abundance, give alms accordingly: if thou have but a little, be not afraid to give according to that little.
Tobit. IV, 8

[1] These books form part of the sacred literature of the Alexandrian Jews, and with the exception of *2 Esdras* are found interspersed with the Hebrew Scriptures in the ancient copies of the Septuagint, or Greek Version of the Old Testament. — *The Apocrypha According to the Authorized Version, Preface* (Oxford University Press)

[2] Magna est veritas et praevalet. — *The Vulgate, Book III* (uncanonical)

Honour thy father and thy mother in law, which are now thy parents.
Tobit. X, 12

Ye cannot find the depth of the heart of man, neither can ye perceive the things that he thinketh: then how can ye search out God, that hath made all these things, and know his mind, or comprehend his purpose?
Judith. VIII, 14

Put on her garments of gladness.
Ibid. X, 3

Our time is a very shadow that passeth away.
Wisdom of Solomon. II, 5

Let us crown ourselves with rosebuds before they be withered.
Ibid. 8

The souls of the righteous are in the hand of God, and there shall no torment touch them. In the sight of the unwise they seemed to die: and their departure is taken for misery, and their going from us to be utter destruction: but they are in peace.
Ibid. III, 1–3

They that put their trust in him shall understand the truth.
Ibid. 9

Wisdom is the gray hair unto men, and an unspotted life is old age.
Ibid. IV, 9

When I was born, I drew in the common air, and fell upon the earth, which is of like nature, and the first voice which I uttered was crying, as all others do.
Ibid. VII, 3

All men have one entrance into life, and the like going out.
Ibid. 6

Who can number the sand of the sea, and the drops of rain, and the days of eternity?
Ecclesiasticus. I, 2

If his understanding fail, have patience with him.
Ibid. 13

Observe the opportunity.
Ibid. IV, 20

Let not thine hand be stretched out to receive, and shut when thou shouldest repay.
Ecclesiasticus. IV, 31
A faithful friend is a strong defence: and he that hath found such an one hath found a treasure.
Ibid. VI, 14
Be not slow to visit the sick.
Ibid. VII, 35
Whatsoever thou takest in hand, remember the end, and thou shalt never do amiss.
Ibid. 36
Rejoice not over thy greatest enemy being dead, but remember that we die all.
Ibid. VIII, 7
Miss not the discourse of the elders.
Ibid. 9
Forsake not an old friend, for the new is not comparable to him. A new friend is as new wine: when it is old, thou shalt drink it with pleasure.
Ibid. IX, 10
In the day of prosperity there is a forgetfulness of affliction: and in the day of affliction there is no more remembrance of prosperity.
Ibid. XI, 25
He that toucheth pitch shall be defiled therewith.
Ibid. XIII, 1
A rich man beginning to fall is held up of his friends: but a poor man being down is thrust also away by his friends.
Ibid. 21
The heart of a man changeth his countenance, whether it be for good or evil: and a merry heart maketh a cheerful countenance.
Ibid. 25
Wine and women will make men of understanding to fall away.
Ibid. XIX, 2
Whether it be to friend or foe, talk not of other men's lives.
Ibid. 8
Gladness of the heart is the life of man, and the joyfulness of a man prolongeth his days.
Ibid. XXX, 22

Consider that I laboured not for myself only, but for all them that seek learning.
Ecclesiasticus. XXXIII, 17
Leave not a stain in thine honour.
Ibid. 22
Honour a physician with the honour due unto him.
Ibid. XXXVIII, 1
When the dead is at rest, let his remembrance rest; and be comforted for him, when his spirit is departed from him.
Ibid. 23
How can he get wisdom . . . whose talk is of bullocks?
Ibid. 25
Look upon the rainbow, and praise him that made it.
Ibid. XLIII, 11
Let us now praise famous men, and our fathers that begat us.
Ibid. XLIV, 1
These were honoured in their generations, and were the glory of their times.
Ibid. 7
There be of them that have left a name behind them.
Ibid. 8
And some there be, which have no memorial.
Ibid. 9
Their bodies are buried in peace; but their name liveth for evermore.
Ibid. 14
His word burned like a lamp.
Ibid. XLVIII, 1
A scarecrow in a garden of cucumbers keepeth nothing.
Baruch. VI, 70
Was not Abraham found faithful in temptation, and it was imputed unto him for righteousness?
1 Maccabees. II, 52
With the God of heaven it is all one, to deliver with a great multitude, or a small company: For the victory of battle standeth not in the multitude of an host; but strength cometh from heaven.
Ibid. III, 18, 19

When he was at the last gasp.

1 Maccabees. VII, 9

The noble acts which he did, and his greatness, they are not written: for they were very many.

Ibid. IX, 22

Ask and learn.

Ibid. X, 72

Every man sat under his vine and his fig tree.[1]

Ibid. XIV, 12

We have been careful that they that will read may have delight, and that they that are desirous to commit to memory might have ease, and that all

[1] See *Micah, IV, 4,* on page 1049b.

into whose hands it comes might have profit.

2 Maccabees. II, 25

It is a foolish thing to make a long prologue, and to be short in the story itself.

Ibid. 32

Nicanor lay dead in his harness.

Ibid. XV, 28

If I have done well, and as is fitting, . . . it is that which I desired; but if slenderly and meanly, it is that which I could attain unto.

Ibid. 38

Speech finely framed delighteth the ears.

Ibid. 39

BOOK OF COMMON PRAYER [1]

The Scripture moveth us, in sundry places to acknowledge and confess our manifold sins and wickedness.

Morning Prayer. Minister's Opening Words

We have erred, and strayed from thy ways like lost sheep.

Ibid. General Confession

We have left undone those things which we ought to have done; and we have done those things which we ought not to have done.

Ibid.

The noble army of Martyrs.

Ibid. Te Deum

Make them to be numbered [2] with thy Saints, in glory everlasting.

Ibid.

I believe in God the Father Almighty, Maker of Heaven and earth: And in Jesus Christ his only Son our Lord: Who was conceived by the Holy Ghost, Born of the Virgin Mary; Suffered under Pontius Pilate, Was crucified, dead, and buried: He descended into hell; The third day he rose again from the dead: He ascended into heaven, And sitteth on the right hand of God the Father Almighty: From thence he shall come to judge the quick and the dead.

Ibid. The Apostles' Creed

Begotten of his Father before all worlds, God of God, Light of Light, Very God of very God; Begotten, not made; Being of one substance with the Father; By whom all things were made: Who for us men and for our salvation came down from heaven, And was incarnate by the Holy Ghost of the Virgin Mary, And was made man.

Ibid. The Nicene Creed

The author of peace and lover of concord, in knowledge of whom standeth our eternal life, whose service is perfect freedom.

Morning Prayer. A Collect for Peace

Afflicted, or distressed, in mind, body, or estate.

Ibid. A Prayer for All Conditions of Men

Lighten our darkness, we beseech thee, O Lord; and by thy great mercy defend us from all perils and dangers of this night.

Evening Prayer. Collect Against Perils for Aid

From envy, hatred, and malice, and all uncharitableness,
Good Lord, deliver us.

The Litany

The world, the flesh, and the devil.

Ibid.

From battle and murder, and from sudden death.

Ibid.

Give to all nations unity, peace, and concord.

Ibid.

The kindly fruits of the earth.

Ibid.

Almighty God, unto whom all hearts are open, all desires known, and from whom no secrets are hid.

Holy Communion. Collect

Miserable sinners.[1]

Holy Communion. Exhortation

Read, mark, learn, and inwardly digest.

Collect for the Second Sunday in Advent

Renounce the devil and all his works, the vain pomp and glory of the world,

---

[1] American Revision [1928].

[2] In the Latin, this word is *munerari* (rewarded), and was mistaken, perhaps, by an early copyist, for *numerari* (numbered).

[1] The invocation, "Have mercy upon us, miserable sinners," was included in the Litany prior to the Revision of 1928. "Miserable offenders" appears in *Morning Prayer, A General Confession.*

with all covetous desires of the same, and the sinful desires of the flesh.
Holy Baptism. Of Children
The pomps and vanity of this wicked world and all the sinful lusts of the flesh.
Offices of Instruction (Catechism)
To keep my hands from picking and stealing.
Ibid. Answer 8
To do my duty in that state of life unto which it shall please God to call me.
Ibid. Answer 10
An outward and visible sign of an inward and spiritual grace.
Ibid. (On the Sacraments)
Forsaking all others, keep thee only unto her, so long as ye both shall live.
Solemnization of Matrimony
Let him now speak, or else hereafter for ever hold his peace.
Ibid.
To have and to hold from this day forward, for better for worse, for richer for poorer, in sickness and in health, to love and to cherish, till death us do part.
Ibid.
With this Ring I thee wed.
Ibid.
In the midst of life we are in death.[1]
Burial of the Dead. At the Grave

[1] This is derived from a Latin antiphon, said to have been composed by Notker, a monk of St. Gall, in 911, while watching some workmen building a bridge at Martinsbrücke, in peril of their lives. It forms the groundwork of Luther's antiphon *De Morte*.

Earth to earth, ashes to ashes, dust to dust; in sure and certain hope of the Resurrection unto eternal life.
Burial of the Dead. At the Grave
Show thy servant the light of thy countenance.
The Psalter. Psalms, XXXI, 18
God that maketh men to be of one mind in an house.
Ibid. LXVIII, 6
The iron entered into his soul.
Ibid. CV, 18
God, in whom we live and move and have our being.
Family Prayer. Morning
O Lord, support us all the day long, until the shadows lengthen and the evening comes, and the busy world is hushed, and the fever of life is over, and our work is done. Then in thy mercy grant us a safe lodging, and a holy rest, and peace at the last.[1]
Ibid. At Night

BOOK OF COMMON PRAYER, ENGLISH

Grant that the old Adam in these persons may be so buried, that the new man may be raised up in them.
Holy Baptism. Of Those of Riper Years
With all my worldly goods I thee endow.
Solemnization of Matrimony

[1] By Cardinal Newman.

THE KORAN

Translated [1734] by GEORGE SALE
[1697–1736]

Turn, therefore, thy face towards the holy temple of Mecca; and wherever ye be, turn your faces towards that place.

Chap. 2

Wherever ye be, God will bring you all back at the resurrection.

Ibid.

As for him who voluntarily performeth a good work, verily God is grateful and knowing.

Ibid.

Your God is one God; there is no God but He, the most merciful.

Ibid.

O true believers, take your necessary precautions against your enemies, and either go forth to war in separate parties, or go forth all together in a body.

Chap. 4

Fight for the religion of God.

Ibid.

O men, respect women who have borne you.

Ibid.

Wheresoever ye be, death will overtake you, although ye be in lofty towers.

Ibid.

Whosoever flieth from his country for the sake of God's true religion, shall find in the earth many forced to do the same, and plenty of provisions.

Ibid.

God loveth not the speaking ill of any one in public.

Chap. 4

Let not thy hand be tied up to thy neck; neither open it with an unbounded expansion, lest thou become worthy of reprehension, and be reduced to poverty.

Chap. 17

Of his mercy he hath made for you the night and the day, that ye may rest in the one, and may seek to obtain provision for yourself of his abundance, by your industry, in the other.

Chap. 28

If God should punish men according to what they deserve, he would not leave on the back of the earth so much as a beast.

Chap. 35

God obligeth no man to more than he hath given him ability to perform.

Chap. 65

Woe be unto those who pray, and who are negligent at their prayer: who play the hypocrites, and deny necessaries to the needy.

Chap. 107

O unbelievers, I will not worship that which ye worship; nor will ye worship that which I worship. . . . Ye have your religion, and I my religion.

Chap. 109

INDEX

INDEX

INDEX

Entries are arranged alphabetically, with hyphenated words indexed as
one word. Note the order for possessives and plurals of identical spelling.

Bird, another, sings better, 222a
  or devil, 545a
Bird-cage, summer, 100a
Bird's, sweet, throat, 160a
Birds about a ruined place, 978a
  were mad with glee, 673b
Birds' cries, 896a
Bird-song at morning, 752a

The letter *a* after the page number means that the entry is in the left
column of the page cited; *b* indicates the right column.

Archaic, dialect, and other variant spellings in the text are retained in the
index, with one exception: In the case of two standard modern variables of
the same word, entries are combined under the preferred Webster spelling.
For example, *bisy larke* appears under *bisy;* but references to *defence* and
defense are combined under *defense*.

1073

Affection's strong, 230b
Affections dark as Erebus, 147a
  hath not a Jew, 145a
  history of the, 446a
  holiness of the heart's, 478a
  mild, 278b
  of flesh, 240b
  of mild, 315b
  of so many millions, 472a
  old offences of, new, 207a
  on things above, 1063a
  robbed of our, 670a
  stronger hold on the, 515b
  untamed, 17a
  which attend human life,
    301b
Affects to nod, 280a
Affinity with the soul of man, 560a
Affirmative, minds are naturally,
    688b
Afflict, how dost thou, me, 128b
  mischiefs that, mankind, 290b
  our souls, 57b
  passion, our natures, 173a
  the best, 347b
  vertebrata who, the universe,
    909a
Afflicted humanity, destinies of,
    888a
  or distressed in mind, 1068b
Affliction, acquainted with, 687a
  alters, 208b
  comforts us in our, 29a
  consoling in the depths of,
    538b
  enamour'd of thy parts, 137a
  forgetfulness of, 1066a
  in the day of, 1066a
  is digested, 346a
  may smile again, 132b
  or defect, 858a
  water of, 1046b
  we cherish and brood over,
    446b
Affliction's sons, 391b
Afflictions sorted, 233a
Affluence, rising from, to poverty,
    677b
Afford, all that life can, 342a
  good whiskey, 760a
  more than people could, 931b
  to go to Corinth, 41b
  unnecessary luxuries, 840a
Affords more striking conviction,
    336b
Affrayed me out of slepe, 77b
Affright, pain and, 935b
  the bad, 347b
Affrighted skies, rend th', 312b
Affront, fear is, 307a
  no woman can bear, 108b
Afire, bush, with God, 520a
  set the Thames, 817b
A-fishing, gone, 235a
  stream I go, in, 590a
A-flutter, my heart is all, 995b
A-flying, old time still, 230b
Afoot and light-hearted, 608b
  game's, 155a
  swiftest traveller goes, 589b
  the game is, 782a
Afore, let pride go, 15a
Afraid, anything I should be, to
    do, 329b
  be not, 1026a, 1065a
  be not, ye waiting hearts, 633a
  for the terror by night, 1036a
  I am sadly, 71b
  in a world I never made, 787a

Afraid, it is I be not, 1053a
  keep from being, 279b
  many are, of God, 616a
  of snakes, 940a
  of whom am I, 648a
  of whom shall I be, 1033b
  sir because I am not myself,
    656a
  so I was, 569b
  stand, and start at us, 240b
  stranger and, 787a
  they were sore, 1056a
  to be, basest of all things, 977a
  to feel, 901b
  to strike, 319a
  wait death nor be, 572a
  what profit me to be, 945b
Africa and her prodigies, 240a
  we knew, 992a
African descent, Americans of,
    666a
Afric's burning shore, 419b
  sunny fountains, 445b
After this therefore because of this,
    1010b
After-dinner talk, 546b
After-dinner's sleep, 184b
After-life, letter of that, to spell,
    532b
Aftermark of almost too much
    love, 881a
Aftermath of war, 874a
Afternoon, all in the golden, 655b
  how softly runs the, 890b
  my custom always of the, 172b
  of her best days, 128a
  repeat in vacant, 358b
  rude multitude call the, 133b
  summer, 804b
  tea, ceremony known as, 718a
  took long to die, 972a
Afton, flow gently sweet, 392b
Against, he not with me is, me,
    1052a
  who can be, us, 1060a
Agamemnon, brave men after,
    956a
  brave men before, 40a
Agate, eyes like, lanterns, 982a
Agate-stone, no bigger than, 134b
Age a burden, 23b
  accurate about her, 769a
  ache penury and imprisonment,
    185a
  all the misery of his, 326a
  and body of the time, 175b
  and dust, pay us with, 111b
  and hunger, 161a
  and memories of eld, 544a
  and youth are reconciled, 747b
  as lusty winter, 160a
  belongs only to his own, 473a
  best in four things, 119a
  cannot wither her, 200b
  carries all things away, 36a
  certain, 456b
  comfort to my, 160a
  common vice in old, 33a
  cradle of reposing, 319b
  dallies like the old, 164b
  dawn in happy old, 498a
  decrepit, 232a
  disease or sorrows strike, 595b
  draw out his old, 31a
  each, a lens, 649a
  each, each kindred, 601b
  every, and race, 821a
  every, has its pleasures, 286b
  excel in pride of life, 620b

Age finds out was dew, 575a
  folly in all of every, 287a
  folly of the, 287a
  frittering away his, 419a
  give me bless'd, 780b
  golden, in imagination, 494a
  Golden, once more may live,
    39b
  good old, 1023a
  green old, 5b, 276a
  growing infirmities of, 431a
  grows torpid in old, 342a
  harvest of old, 34a
  he was not of an, 219b
  heritage of old, 511a
  I make light of it, 627b
  in a virtuous person, 301b
  in every, adored, 320b
  in ev'ry, and clime, 7a
  in the flower of their, 1027a
  in which art is immobile, 767b
  in which their lot has fallen,
    494a
  is a dream that is dying, 730a
  is dull and mean, 527a
  is grown so picked, 178b
  is in wit is out, 158a
  is opportunity, 525a
  is terrible misfortune, 491a
  joys with, diminish, 574b
  labour of an, 244b
  leave my name to the next,
    121b
  leaves us friends and wine,
    440a
  like distance, 534b
  lingers into old, 16a
  man's common, 566b
  master spirits of this, 167b
  message for the, 822b
  narrative with, 4a
  needs of the, 822b
  next Augustan, 493a
  occupy, with the dream, 572b
  of atomic energy, 965b
  of chivalry is never past, 599a
  of comfort and violence, 941b
  of discord and strife, 124b
  of ease, 355b
  of foolishness, 580a
  of giants, 817b
  of Gold, fetch the, 244b
  of miracles, 475b
  of ours not numbered by years,
    103a
  of poverty, 146b
  of revolution and reformation,
    374b
  of troubles losses anxieties,
    702a
  of wisdom, 580a
  old, and experience, 289a
  old, can do no spoil, 156b
  old, continued faithful until,
    25b
  old, crept over them, 794b
  old, has so great authority, 34a
  old, is a regret, 512a
  old, is consummation of life,
    34b
  old, is out, 280b
  old, is second childhood, 23a
  old, may come after you, 609a
  old, of an eagle, 32b
  old, remote from infancy, 118b
  old, should burn and rave, 997a
  old, they abuse, 16b
  or country, 339b
  physician of the Iron, 620a

Age, point of view of the, 701b
 proper, of my life, 285a
 ripe, gives tone, 638a
 scarce expect one of my, 401a
 shall not weary them, 843b
 silver'd o'er with, 308a
 sixth, shifts, 161b
 skepticism of a skeptical, 701a
 smack of, 152b
 small for its, 69b
 soul of the, 219a
 spirit of his, 326a
 staff of, 144b
 strong meat to them of full, 1063b
 summon, to grant youth's heritage, 572a
 talking, 355b
 tasteless and illbred, 35a
 that has no criticism, 767b
 that, is gone, 932b
 that is waiting before, 463b
 that possesses no art, 767b
 they know your, 775a
 thine, shall be clearer, 1030b
 this is old, 258b
 thou art shamed, 166b
 thou waitedst, 572a
 thoughts that mould the, 599b
 three problems of the, 496b
 time cannot, it, 781a
 to age succeeds, 546b
 to cheated age, 817a
 to come my own, 267a
 too late or cold climate, 258a
 torrent of a downward, 327b
 toys of, 317b
 truth about her, 851a
 'twixt boy and youth, 414a
 ugly, and feeble impotence, 899b
 veracity increases with old, 266a
 viaticum of old, 71b
 what an, this is, 284a
 where youth and manhood, 376a
 wherein he lived was dark, 266b
 whom, doth chill, 262a
 widow of doubtful, 562a
 will perform promises, 337a
 wintry, 365b
 with his stealing steps, 178b
 world's great, begins anew, 467a
 worth an, without a name, 416b
 you live in, 43a
 youth 'gainst time and, 116a
Aged and poor and slow, 760a
 blessed youth becomes as, 184b
 bosom, slow growth in, 335a
 ears play truant, 132b
 face, beauty of an, 912b
 later times more, 118b
 man is but a paltry thing, 827a
 men full loth and slow, 416a
 now we are, and gray, 699b
 nurse, time that, 479a
 phase in the life of the, 966a
 thrush, 705b
 wife, match'd with an, 548a
Ageless and eternal sea, 23b
 and indifferent sea, 986a
 in your heart, 899b
Agencies, widely its, vary, 488b
Agency, bestowed by divine, 27a
 where there is no free, 484a

Agent, none the less the free, 68a
 poor, despised, 182b
 powerful, is the right word, 679b
 trust no, 157b
Agents of the people, 689a
 to Congress, 389a
Age's, old, alms, 116a
 tooth, 147b
Ages, emptiness of, in his face, 755b
 great order of the, 36a
 heir of all the, 549a, 613b
 how many, hence, 167b
 joke for the, 651b
 long ago those lovers fled, 481a
 mighty, of eternity, 626b
 of twenty-five and forty, 744a
 of your sires, 620b
 onward roll, 547b
 our help in, past, 302b
 past a blank would be, 395b
 rock of, 372a
 seven, 161a
 stamp and esteem of, 275a
 thousand, in Thy sight, 303a
 three distant, born, 279b
 to all succeeding, curst, 276b
 unborn, crowd not on my soul, 350a
 wakens the slumbering, 494b
Agesilaus heard the nightingale, 56a
Agglomeration called Holy Roman Empire, 324b
Aggrandizement, countries seek no, 922a
Aggravate choler, 153a
Aggravates ill success, 333a
Aggravation of self, 696b
Aggravations, accept in silence minor, 743b
Aggressions, hostile, 375a
Aggressive fancy working spells, 705b
A-gley, gang aft, 390a
A-glowing, wine with four years, 38a
Agnes, world dear, a strange affair, 270a
Agnes' dreams, sigh'd for, 480b
 St, Eve, 480b
Agnostic, Mohammedan, monist, 774b
 with sympathies, 876a
Agog, round eyes, 959a
Agonies and love, 407a
 doubts and spiritual, 822b
 ere errors, and fears, 673b
 fiercest, 471b
 small talk dies in, 466b
Agonize them in farewell, 812b
Agonized hopes and ashen flowers, 838b
Agonizing, most, spy enemy could send, 646b
Agony, cup of strength in, 596a
 leave off the, 737a
 swimmer in his, 457b
 'tis life for all its, 632b
 with words, 159a
Agree, agreed we can't never, 731b
 birds in their little nests, 302b
 in essential articles, 339b
 in general with my friend, 624b
 in one fact we all, 595b
 let mankind, 280b
 make two clocks, 95a

Agree, the more we didn't, 731b
 thou and I shall never, 1000a
 though all things differ all, 309a
 two of a trade never, 7a, 638b
 verbs and nouns do more, 687a
 with her would not, 824a
 with no man's opinions, 594b
Agreeable addition, 41a
 bright and, children, 64b
 companion on a journey, 43b
 darkness is restful and, 51b
 feetur, haint one, 600b
 few hours in life more, 718a
 indolent but, condition, 65b
 Miss Blachford is, 428a
 nor the best to live with, 757b
 person, idea of an, 513a
Agreeably, speak, with whom we deal, 121a
Agreed, except they be, 1049a
 to differ, 427a
 we can't never agree, 731b
Agreement, entered into a tacit, 495a
 with hell, 517a
 with hell are we at, 1046a
Agrees not with leanness of purse, 125a
 person who, with me, 513a
Agricultural population, 50b
Agriculturist, farmer and not an, 801a
 works the farmer, 713b
Ahab, ran before, 1029a
 went to Ascalon, 894a
Ahkond is dead, 581b
A-hold on the greatness of God, 716b
A-hunting, daddy's gone, 1016b
 go, upon St. David's Day, 1019a
 goes with buskins, 231a
 we daren't go, 638a
 we will go, 332b
Aiblins nae temptation, 391b
Aid, feeble, do join, 311a
 foreign, of ornament, 328a
 from a chink in the floor, 856b
 giving, and comfort, 376a
 help me by their unconscious, 748a
 me for to win her, 857a
 of the party, 1005b
 prepare with mutual, 282b
 small, is wealth, 16b
 the unfortunate, 37a
 to every poor man, 282b
 to the worker, 13a
 win our battles by its, 584a
 wisdom's, 351b
Aiding, benefit myself in, him, 15a
Ail thee knight at arms, 480a
Ailed, what, us O gods, 692a
Ailest, thou, here and here, 620a
Ailing brother, 1005a
Ailments, because our, are the same, 295a
 clod of, and grievances, 765a
Aim and reason, 379b
 at objects in an airy height, 293b
 deliberate, at peace, 797b
 fixed as, or butt, 154b
 forgotten your, 806b
 low, is crime, 602a
 malice never was his, 296a
 mind thine own, 503b

Assyrian, oiled and curled, bull, 553b
Assyrians, in the camp of the, 456a
Asterisk of death, 525a
  to do his dirty work, 952a
  writer owned an, 952a
Astern, look, while they row ahead, 61b
Asthma, gout, and seven maladies, 419a
Astolat, come again to, 962a
  lily maid of, 555a
Astonish, gratify some and, the rest, 679b
  the world, 275a
Astonishment, shalt become an, 1026a
Astray, all we like sheep gone, 1047b
  go, and fall, 566a
  present world go, 76b
  weak women went, 293b
Astride on his reason, 294b
  upon a reed as upon a horse, 60b
Astronomer, undevout, is mad, 306a
Astronomers, confounding her, 854b
  who totter off to bed, 846a
Astronomy compels soul, 24b
Asunder, let not man put, 1053b
  put this man and woman, 296b
Asylum, lunatic, in suburbs of Jerusalem, 784b
  optimism in lunatic, 784a
Asylums, comfortably padded lunatic, 469b, 923a
Atahualpa, knows who strangled, 492b
Atavistic features of college life, 776a
Ate a dozen oysters, 838a
  and drank the precious words, 646a
  elephant, all night, 748a
  his bread in sorrow, 378b
  into itself, 238b
  old man, and prayed not, 264a
  the fellow raw, 647a
  to live, 60b
Athanasian Creed, 513a
Atheism, inclineth man's mind to, 120b
  in art, 630a
  my, is true piety, 807b
  owlet, 422b
  religion and not, 360a
Atheist half believes a God, 306a
  neither, nor rationalist, 400a
  novelist realist, 556b
  superstitious, 571a
  town, 985a
  violent, 975a
Atheist's laugh's a poor exchange, 391b
Atheists in the foxholes, 991b
Athenian, Socrates not an, or a Greek, 61b
Athenians command the rest of Greece, 53b
  may have this story to tell, 59a
  will kill you some day, 57a
Athens a fragile kingdom, 947a
  eye of Greece, 259b
  greatness of, 20a
  maid of, ere we part, 452b
  men of, 1059a

Athens, sending owls to, 71a
Athlete, rayspictable f'r to be an, 834a
Ation, osity and, 400b
Atlanta, from, to the sea, 660b
Atlantic Charter, 922a
  children across the, 566b
  dawn on other side of, 493a
  deep immense, 720b
  Monthly, essay in the, 908b
  Monthly, must read the, 805b
  Ocean for whales, 676a
  on other side of his, 677b
  steep, stream, 247a
  surge, 328a
Atlas, Teneriff or, unremoved, 256a
Atmosphere, create a fresh, 559b
  in thought's, 722a
Atom, in erg and, 977b
  no evil in the, 987a
  of that infinite space, 615b
  to be split, 939b
  why each, knows its own, 721b
Atomic Age, 945b
  and biological warfare, 954b
  bomb, war fought with, 900b
  bombs burst in fumbling hands, 831b
  bombs, catastrophe of the, 831b
  energy, 900b, 965b
  energy, constructive in relation to, 1009b
  energy, release of, 929a
  scientists, 954b
Atomies, count, 162a
  crumbled out again to his, 217a
  team of little, 134b
Atoms, casual concourse of, 292b
  move in the void, 12a
  or systems into ruin hurl'd, 316a
  somewhere up in space, 703a
Atone, pictures for the page, 321b
A-trembling because I got to decide, 677a
Atrocious crime of being young, 334b
  thing, war such an, 642b
Atrophied, sexually, 807a
Atrophy, sporting spirit will, 913a
Atropos of the future, 25b
Attachment, bonds of confidence and, 856b
  constitute so strong an, 375b
  to the country, 758a
  to their government, 360b
Attachments, intense local, 429a
Attack, first to, their neighbours, 270a
  is the reaction, 341a
  prompt in, 360a
  risk, upon them, 26b
  strength lies in, 951a
  we must, 923b
Attacked by naval and air forces, 921a
  than unnoticed, 342a
Attacking and getting well hammered, 765b
  complaining and, one another, 618a
  situation excellent I am, 754b
  vested interests, 672a
Attacks, answer all the, on me, 542b
  on me or my wife, 921b
Attain an English style, 337b
  full purport, 611b

Attain, that which I could, unto, 1067b
Attainable, deem it, by thee, 68a
Attained, best, when all share, 26b
  by sudden flight, 523b
Attainment of a true philosophy, 702b
  of the goal, 784a
Attains the upmost round, 167a
Attempt and not the deed confounds, 196b
  fearing to, 183b
  it was a vain, 628a
  the end, 231a
  to divert only irritates, 341b
  to palliate nor deny, 334b
Attempted, something, something done, 521b
Attend, shooting stars, thee, 231a
  the history of Rasselas, 337a
  to disorders of the eyes, 19a
Attendance, dance, 212a
  repay us for our, 431b
Attendant, little beetle, sail, 318a
Attended by a single hound, 648a
Attending ears, music to, 135b
  good and bad angel, 221b
  softest music to, ears, 135b
Attention like deep harmony, 138b
  of a people, 951a
  socks compelled, 851a
  unremitted, 359b
Attentive eyes closed in death, 338a
  to his own applause, 319a
Attentively, look sharply and, 121a
Attenuate our bodies, 222a
Atthis, I loved thee, 8b
Attic, beauty crieth in an, 670b
  bird trills her notes, 259b
  salt, 271a
  salt, stores of, 661a
  shape fair attitude, 482b
Attire, rich, creeps rustling, 481a
Attired with stars, 249b
Attitude, attic shape fair, 482b
  respectful, toward men and God, 970a
Attitudenize, don't, 343a
Attorney, Hocus an old cunning, 327a
Attorney's firm, office boy to an, 682a
  office door, 585b
Attorneys, district, in dirty business, 710a
Attract to play, 64b
Attraction to one person, 861a
Attraction's power to chain, 792b
Attractive beauty and unspotted fame, 105b
  kinde of grace, 114b
  sweet, grace, 255a
Attribute, first, of a good critic, 602b
  power but, God's, 673a
  to awe and majesty, 146a
  to God himself, 146a
Attributes of God are eternal, 281b
Attuned, string, to mirth, 221a
Attyre bee comely, 112a
Auber, dank tarn of, 545b
Auburn, sweet, 355b
Auction mart, brawlers of the, 767b
Auctions, often when looking on at, 70b

Beggars, deformity which, mimicked, 492a
do away with, 726b
might ride, 999b
mounted, 126a
must be no choosers, 228a
should be no choosers, 92b
when, die no comets seen, 167b
Beggary in the love reckon'd, 200a
Begged, living Homer, his bread, 227a
of the moon, 1003a
Begging bread, 1034a
them to taste brandy, 437b
Begin and cease and then begin, 622a
come back to it and, over, 879b
finish what I, 528a
get up and, again, 569a
in gladness, 406b
to smell a rat, 106b
with usual jokes, 22b
Beginning, from a bad, great friendships, 32a
and the end, 987a, 1065a
art of, 526a
at the, not the end, 986b
ay that's the old, 65b
bad, makes a bad ending, 17b
better the end than, 1042b
each venture is a new, 945a
end depends upon the, 62b
end of the, 871a
farther distance from the, 118b
for a friendship, 768a
grey, of years, 694b
half done who has made a, 41a
hard, maketh good ending, 91b
in my, is my end, 945a
in my end is my, 101b, 945a
in the, God created the heaven, 1021a
in the, was the word, 1057b
is most important part, 24a
long choosing and, late, 258a
love is the, of knowledge, 473a
never ending still, 280a
no great love in the, 180a
of a beginning, 831b
of a fray, 94b
of a new month or year, 882b
of fairies, 792a
of feast, 151b
of good, cometh good end, 92b
of journey, 21a
of life, 788a
of our end, 142b
of the cask, 7b
of the end, 384a
of things longer, 788b
of wisdom, 985b, 1037a
responsibility of, 642b
things best in their, 272a
told you from the, 1047a
Beginnings and endings are untidy, 838a
end to, of all wars, 922a
favorable to bold, 36b
return to our, 16a
small, 229b
Begins, charity, at home, 240b
life is closed life, 610b
life's year, and closes, 440a
nothing, and nothing ends, 789b
to be incredulous, 20a
with an M, 657a
Begone dull care, 1000a
Begot, how, how nourished, 145a

Begot in ventricle of memory, 133a
to whom related by whom, 313b
when they, me, 345b
Begotten by despair, 269a
flowers, 691b
of his Father, 1068a
Son, gave his only, 1058a
Begs pardon first, 162a
Beguil'd, be, by one, 189a
Beguile, light of light, 132a
strumpet's plague to, 189a
the thing I am, 187a
the time look like the time, 195a
you from grief, 541b
Beguiled the leisure of the crew, 681b
Beguiles, the pain of it, 345b
Beguiling, fortune, 343b
Begun for, wonder what I was, 1014a
not yet, to fight, 377b
things ended and things, 610b
Behave, how well I did, 785b
in a quarrel, 764b
in life as at a banquet, 65a
like a pig, 963a
like apes, 939a
mannerly at table, 750a
wish friends to, to us, 71b
Behaving as if you were in heaven, 766a
Behavior, complexion or form or, 505b
immediate check to loose, 301b
standard of, 849b
surfeit of our own, 191a
upon his good, 459a
which appears correct, 965a
Behemoth, behold now, 1032a
Behind, come no more, your scenes, 339a
falls down for those, 924a
get up, him, 345b
led his regiment from, 685b
never gets left, 807a
no longer forward nor, 527b
one must ride, 158a
the times, 830a
Behold a rainbow, 406a
a smile of God, 612a
and hear griefs, 15a
be what they, 312b
heaven and the earth, 83a
her judge for yourselves, 443b
I shall, your face, 660a
it very different from day, 351a
the man, 1058b
thy master, 326a
wandering moon, 246a
you again in dying, 752a
Beholder, heart of the, 984a
Beholders discover everybody's face, 294b
strike an awe into the, 295b
Beholding bright countenance, 250a
myself all rosy red, 842b
Behoving and unbehoving, 519a
Behynde, shame cometh, 15a
Be'ind, less than 'arf o' that, 818a
Being, applause of a single human, 342b
coming into, of composite things, 12a

Being darkly wise and rudely great, 316b
each young and beautiful, 802b
gives, to all things, 229b
is holiness harmony immortality, 616b
live move and have our, 1059a, 1069b
necessary, of Himself, 275a
one principle of, 68a
Penrod was merely a state of, 847a
pleasing anxious, 349a
this, of mine, 66a
Being's end and aim, 317b
Beings now latent in our thoughts, 831b
reasoning, were created, 66b
Belabored hound, cower like a, 583b
Beld, now your brow is, 392a
Beldame nigh to sit for us, 29b
Belfry, bats in the, 804a
clock in the, strikes one, 660b
Belgium's capital, 452b
Belgrave Square, hearts beat in, 683b
Belial, sons of, 252b
with words clothed, 254a
Belican, more than his, 904a
Belie all corners of world, 204a
Belief, believe in, 790b
England restores our, 956a
epoch of, 580a
history is, in falsehood, 622a
history is, in the senses, 622a
hope is, joy will come, 418b
in a beneficent power, 705a
in occurrence of improbable, 909a
in supernatural source of evil, 773a
live and die in this, 84a
my most ethereal, 804b
points of, 438b
prospect of, 194b
ripened into faith, 411a
Beliefs, lightly held, and prejudices, 831b
lost causes and forsaken, 621b
old dead ideas and old dead, 641b
swallow more, than he can digest, 784a
tremulous, agonized hopes, 838b
Believe a woman or an epitaph, 452a
all the fables in legends, 120b
any man than an artificer, 244a
easier to, than to deny, 688b
heard and do in part, 170a
her though I know she lies, 207b
I, in God, 400a
impossible things, 659a
in fairies, 792a
in God the Father, 1068a
in happiness, 889b
in heaven and hell, 774b
in love, 790b
in nothing, 594b
in one God and no more, 371a
in what I can't see, 703a
it or not, 967a
know what he ought to, 75a
make themselves, 98b
man makes us, oath, 13b
man's oath, 35b

Believe, men, that which they desire, 276a
no evil till evil's done, 269b
none, speeches trustworthy,
35b
nothing unless in print, 101a
only possibilities, 240b
that I, and take it, 97b
that which they do not, 98b
what is told him, 51a
what they least understand,
100b
what varies every day, 279a
with all my soul, 601a
with ease, what we wish, 276a
Believed abject and humble, 282a
everything he read, 828b
liar will not be, 10b
not merely, but understood,
616b
nothing so firmly, 98b
who never doubted never half,
552b
Believers, he will get, 752b
O true, 1070a
Believes, atheist half, a God, 306a
each, his own, 261a
yet each, his own, 310a
Believeth all things, 1061a
he that, in me, 1058b
Believing, pleasure of, what we
see, 465b
to pass all men's, 932b
to, souls gives light, 125a
where we cannot prove, 551a
Bell and his book, 451a
as the last, struck, 566a
book and candle, 104b, 148a
clear-toned Baptist, 635a
cowslip's, 210a
crier rings his, 955a
Episcopalian, 635a
for whom the, tolls, 218a
goes to bed by a, 675a
good old Dutch church, 635a
Inchcape, 426b
invites me, 196a
let the, toll, 544a
merry as a marriage, 453a
Methodist, 635b
prompter's, 563b
prompter's hand is on his, 686b
rang out the Unitarian, 635a
rang the temperance, 635b
Roman Catholic, 635b
seems to deplore dying day,
76b
sexton tolled the, 487b
silence that dreadful, 187b
sound as a, 158a
sounds as a sullen, 152a
surly sullen, 205b
swing to and fro, 753b
the Cat, 11a
the widder eats by a, 675a
to toll me back from thee, 482a
tolled the one, only, 786a
twilight and evening, 557a
Universalist, 635b
Bellamy's, Edward, position, 746a
Belle Aurore, 574a
bear away the, 640b
dame sans merci, 480a
Rivière, 898b
vain to be a, 343b
young, of old Natchez, 989b
Belleau Woods, sergeant at, 898b
Bellicose, querulous and, 908b
Bellies, fill their hungry, 229b

Bellies' sake, such as for their,
249a
Belligerent, dissevered discordant,
443b
Bellman, fatal, 196a
so the, would cry, 659b
Bellows like the sea in tempest,
75b
Bells and the Fudges, 493a
Canterbury, 875a
harness, 880b
hear the loud alarum, 546a
in the country, 970a
in your parlours, 187a
knoll'd to church, 161a
music of those village, 365a
noisy, be dumb, 786a
of heaven, 854a
of Old Bailey, 1015b
of St. Clement's, 1015b
on her toes, 1017b
port is near the, I hear, 610a
ring, and fire pistols, 882b
ring happy, 552b
ring it ye, of the kirk, 757a
ring O, 610a
ring out wild, 552b
silver, and cockle shells, 1015b
sound no trumpet ring no,
1006a
sound of all, 429b
sweet, jangled, 175a
they sound on Bredon, 786a
they sound so clear, 786a
tintinnabulation from the, 546a
Belly and brain I lived America,
994b
back and feet, 41a
eye is bigger than the, 235a
fair round, 161b
fill, with the east wind, 1030b
God send thee good ale, 97a
has no ears, 55a
he who does not mind his, 340a
in its dull quiet way, 10a
in the mud, 943b
increasing, 152b
like heap of wheat, 1044b
no, and no bowels, 947a
of the fish, 1049b
spent under the, 90a
wears wit in his, 181b
whose God is their, 1062b
Bellyful of fighting, 204a
Bellywash, felt slippers and warm,
973a
Belonged, the lamb that, to the
sheep, 10b
to church, 996a
Belongs, afterwards it all, to you,
983b
covets what, to another, 48b
to a greater power, 100a
Belov'd, never be, by men, 388a
Beloved child, bed of some, 964b
creature that is, 164b
escape me never, 569a
fill the cup, 531b
giveth his, sleep, 518a
home, free land in our, 613a
loves better than he is, 98b
of a king, 1012a
over all, 816b
Pan and all other gods, 25b
physician, Luke the, 1063a
Beloved's bed, heaped for the,
468b
Below, creatures here, 287b
memory of those who lie, 577a

Below, thoughts remain, 176b
Belshazzar the king, 1048b
Belted knight, prince can make
a, 394a
you an' flayed you, 818a
Belting, lilting at loom and, 992a
Bemocked, beams, the sultry main,
422a
Bemused, parson much, in beer,
318b
Ben Battle was a soldier bold,
487b
Ben Bolt, 597a
Bench, hut with only a, simple,
652a
Benches black with people, 808a
Bend a knotted oak, 298a
acts of government, 399a
low O dusky night, 673b
low, shall I, 144a
on me thy tender eyes, 510a
their will to mischief, 312b
your eye on vacancy, 177a
Bendemeer's stream, 441a
Bending, above the fallen, 662b
my head is, low, 636a
to the force of the wind, 10b
Bends the gallant mast, 447b
though she, him, 523a
to the grave, 355b
Bene qui latuit bene vixit, 795b
Beneath his feet all fears, 36b
look, the surface, 68a
the starry flag, 613a
Benedick the married man, 157a
Benediction, face like a, 104a
Heaven's, 94a
said therefore and for ever,
518b
Benedight, Jhesu Crist and seiynte,
80b
Benefaction, calling to mind a, 21b
Benefactor, first great, 678a
less to blame than his, 265b
was unknown, 430a
Benefactors in newspapers, 427b
love those they benefit, 98b
Beneficence, private, is inadequate, 791a
universal, of grass, 662a
Beneficent force outside ourselves,
782a
power, belief in a, 705a
thing or function, 793b
Beneficial exercise, art derives,
718b
happiness is, 856a
reform, attempting to carry
out, 874a
results, 444b
Benefit another generation, 31a
confers a, 98b
die without, of clergy, 857a
his country, 20a
human, and enjoyment, 360a
in commercial life, 744a
in making failures early, 633b
love those whom they, 98b
myself in aiding him, 15a
of Europe in general, 390a
of individual or party, 442a
of the people, 433b
of the public, 338b
receives a, with gratitude, 48a
to go over in the imagination,
84b
use and, of men, 275a
where benefactor unknown,
430a

Benefit written in water, 86b
Benefits, desire to receive greater, 265b
  disable, 162b
  in refusing, 282b
  liberty of the press ensures, 516a
  of a college education, 505a
  of scientific advances, 929b
  responsibilities and, 965b
  temperate diet will bring, 40b
Benevolence, calls trusting universal, 355a
  full o' beans and, 510a
Bengal, in, to move at all is seldom done, 982a
Benicia Boy, 573a
Benighted, pore, 'eathen, 818a
Benign is solitude, 404b
  nature so mild and, 306b
  sky, under that, 592a
Benignant information is his hobby, 854a
Benison fall on our meat, 231a
  of hot water, 938b
Bennet, Justice, of Derby, 273b
  Mrs., was stirring the fire, 428a
Bent, affection cannot hold the, 164b
  bow cannot always stand, 106b
  classic, 817a
  eyes idly, 140b
  find out the natural, 25a
  his bow, 3a
  just as the twig is, 314a
  mind is, to ill thy, 6b
  on doing evil, 44b
  on pleasure she was, 363b
  orthodox on carnage, 287a
  to make some port, 620b
  top of my, 176b
Benumbs all his faculties, 339a
  care's a canker that, 685b
Be'old this world so wide, 819a
Be-puffed be-painted too alas, 805a
Bequeath my soul to God, 121b
Bequeathed name of Washington, 455b
Bequest of wings was but a book. 646a
Bereavement, anguish of your, 541b
  pain, famine thirst, 654b
  speak comfort for great, 495a
Bereft of beauty, 130b
Berkeley, Bishop, 459b
Berkshire boulders, 960b
Bermoothes, still-vexed, 209a
Bermudas, remote, ride, 269a
Berries, harsh and crude, 248b
  two lovely, moulded, 142a
Berry, bright as a, 858b
  bush, poem hangs on the, 704b
  God could have made a better, 236a
Berry's cheek is plumper, 647b
Berth was of the wombe, 113a
Bertie displayed repugnance, 910a
Berye, broun as is a, 79b
Beseech you of your pardon, 188b
Beset, avoid perils which, them, 282b
Besotted myriads of people, 222b
Bespangling herb and tree, 231a
Bess, bold mare, 576b
  good Queen, 798a
  image of good Queen, 488b
  the landlord's daughter, 909b

Best, acts the, 586a
  administer'd is best, 317b
  advice, worst men give the, 586b
  age, in four things, 119a
  all is, 260b
  all was for, 571b
  all's for the, 561b
  almoner keeps back nothing, 73a
  and brightest come away, 469a
  and brightest leave us, 817b
  and happiest moments, 469a
  and the worst of this is, 694b
  at the greatest and the, 275a
  bear his mild yoke, 251b
  book we've had, 983a
  books haven't been written, 915b
  business you can go into, 562a
  butter, 656b
  cannot go quite true, 338b
  chosen language, 428b
  company when you read, 419a
  could would did, 118a
  days, afternoon of her, 128a
  dearest and the, 789a
  did it for the, 789b
  disguise, go naked is, 297b
  do the very, I know how, 542b
  doctors in the world, 296b
  dress, fair undress, 328b
  dressed in Sunday's, 427a
  fear not to touch the, 111a
  fools be a little wise, 215b
  foot forward, 148b
  forced to do your, 598b
  found her first and, 817a
  friends ever known, 791a
  garment, wears as his, 924b
  gave the people of his, 549b
  give to world the, you have, 723a
  gives his, 336a
  God knows, 841b
  good man with worst-natured muse, 289a
  have seen the, 806b
  he that comes last is, 221b
  his at last who says it, 508b
  hope for the, 418b
  I loved you, 289b
  ideas are common property, 47a
  in four things, 119a
  in kind, 523a
  in this kind but shadows, 142b
  is enemy of good, 325b
  is like the worst, 818b
  is never to be born, 486b
  is yet to be, 572a
  kind of victory, 109b
  lack all conviction, 826b
  laid schemes, 390a
  liar, 671a
  loveliest and the, 532a
  loves, that calls me Tom, 227a
  made the, of this, 394b
  make the, of mankind, 366a
  man among them, 1017a
  marry th', man on earth, 841a
  men men of few words are, 155a
  men moulded out of faults, 185b
  moderation is, 53b
  never to have been born is, 16a
  not to seem but to be the, 13a
  nurse contemplation, 247b
  of all God's works, 258b

Best of all instructors, 44b
  of all possible worlds, 900a
  of all ways, 439a
  of dark and bright, 456a
  of friends must part, 1004b
  of me is diligence, 191a
  of men that e'er wore earth, 215a
  of now and here, 527b
  of our time, 190b
  of possible worlds, 324b
  of the cards at the table, 699a
  of things cloy, 5a
  of times, 580a
  old fashions please me, 130a
  old friends are, 119a
  opinion of the strongest is, 269b
  part of a picture, 507a
  part of valour, 152a
  past and to come seem, 153a
  policy, honesty is always, 108b
  political community, 26b
  portion of a good man's life, 403b
  possession, man's, 17b
  prayeth, who loveth best, 422b
  propagate the, that is known, 621b
  race hasn't been run, 915b
  schoolteachers in the world, 935b
  service for our country, 709b
  she can choose, 60b
  so much bad in the, of us, 711b
  sometimes forget, 187b
  stand and do the, 69a, 786b
  stolen sweets are, 298b
  stomachs not best thinkers, 325b
  subject they treat, 723b
  that has been known and said, 623b
  that is in one, 727a
  the kingdom provides, 839a
  thing between France and England. 509b
  thing, my speech the, 285b
  thing we can do, 994a
  things, in their beginning, 272a
  things upon earth, 653b
  those who love us, 754a
  though the, is bad, 786b
  to forget, 575a
  to live with, 757b
  to the, most beautiful, 619a
  trust that all is, 583a
  use of laws, 562b
  way of doing everything, 505a
  way out is through, 879b
  way to make friends, 990a
  we will do our, 870b
  what began, can't end worst, 573a
  what friend is, 96b
  when he is, 143b
  when people barely know him, 912b
  will come back to you, 723a
  wits greatest scholars, 223a
  women miss the, in life, 771b
  words in best order, 424a
  would heaven seem, 570a
  you get is an even break, 911b
  yuh ever poured, 978b
Best-humour'd man, 289a
Bestial, what remains is, 187b

Books obedient to my hand, 794b
of all time, 605b
of dried plants, 558a
of honour razed quite, 205a
of making, there is no end, 794b,
  912a, 1044a
of the hour, 605b
of universal appeal, 863b
of which the backs and covers,
  576b
old, are best, 780b
old, old wine, old friends, 119a
peace of great, 898b
people die but never, 921b
popular American children's,
  804a
put their names to their, 222b
quit your, 403b
read what, I please, 319a
reading great, 942b
reading my, in originals, 506a
reading valueless, 605b
real war never in the, 611a
rural quiet friendship, 328a
schoolboys from their, 135b
show me the, he loves, 643b
shut his, 800a
shut out from reading good,
  933a
small number of really good,
  782a
some, are drenched sands, 650a
some, are lies, 391b
soul of past time in, 475b
soul that feeds on, alone, 711b
sweet serenity of, 525a
tenets with, 314a
that people give us, 847b
that people talk about, 847b
that we would like to read, 847b
there are no, inside, 761a
think for me, 430b
three, on the soul, 571b
thy toil o'er, 308a
too many, I haven't read, 996b
trees my, 161b
university a collection of, 475b
we think we ought to read, 847b
were woman's looks, 439b
which are no books, 430b
which cannot be adequately reviewed, 700b
which contain no lies, 723a
with obsolete spelling, 776a
you carry to the fire, 338b
Bookseller's, good price from the,
  358a
Book-store, so weak as in the,
  582b
Boon companions, offers made by,
  576a
southern country, 622b
Boone the pioneer, 625b
Boot, appliances and means to,
  153b
heels, bleatin' to your, 821a
hey for, and horse, 598b
saddle to horse, 567b
Booted and spurred to ride, 271a
Booth died blind, 902b
Bootless cries, 205a
Boots and shoes, 596a
body, and britches, 959a
boots boots boots, 819a
died in my, 978b
dying in my, 896b
hauled on his, 587a
long, hard boots, 899a
look at his, 766a

Boots not to resist both wind and
  tide, 126b
what it with incessant care,
  248b
Booze, Georgia, is mighty fine,
  978b
Bo-Peep, little, 1018a
played at, 231a
Borden, Lizzie, took an axe, 1006a
Border, blue bonnets over the,
  650b
nor breed nor birth, 814a
of Prussia, 485b
through all the wide, 414b
Borders, death, upon our birth,
  220b
no, time has, 949a
of my realm, 97a
on the ridiculous, 371a
Bore, all you pitied all you, 750a
cleanliness a, 637a
dead bodies, 149b
every hero becomes a, 504a
first lion thought last a, 420a
life too short to, ourselves, 727a
more contemptible than the,
  670a
not only as sin but as a, 459a
person who talks, 714a
secret of being a, 326a
their children, 766a
to be in society, 769a
to the man with the flute, 736a
waking up the same person,
  822a
we dread being alone with, 603b
without abuse, 553a
Bored, man who lets himself be,
  670a
mankind by thee would be less,
  798a
talk to every man as if he, you,
  769a
very much, if not there, 952b
Boredom did indeed cease, 728b
disease brought on by, 991a
gods struggle against, 394b
inconstancy, anxiety, 272b
pain and, 461b
Bores and bored, 459b
augurs because they were, 600a
through his castle wall, 139b
you and then injects, 801b
Boring to live with, 931a
Born, all men are, free and equal,
  373a
among gypsies or thieves, 959b
an American, 445a
anew, great order is, 36a
as wasteful as tigers, 953b
be, anywhere, 959a
beauty, of murmuring sound,
  405b
because of body's hunger, 930a
before eyes, 939b
begin to die as soon as, 62b
below par, 839b
better had they ne'er been, 417a
better to be lowly, 210b
blackest midnight, 245a
bless'd who ne'er was, 294a
but to die, 316b
Christ the Lord is, 334b
conceived and, in sin, 223a
cross cause why we were, 133b
cry for being, 122a
day wherein I was, 1030a
days, in my, 103b
else wherefore, 554b

Born every minute, sucker, 557b
every one, of the Spirit, 1058a
for success, 506a
for the universe, 357b
friends are, not made, 696a
genius must be, 280a
glad I was not, before tea, 419b
good if he had not been, 1054b
good to be, on, 603a
great, some are, 165a
happiness was, a twin, 457b
hour I was, 1003b
house where I was, 487b
I was being human, alone, 934b
I was free, 1059b
I was, get me, 946b
I was, sneering, 684b
immortal names not, to die,
  462b
in a manger, 271b
in bed, 263a
in Bethlehem, 334b
in Bethlehem of Judaea, 1050a
in other's pain, 789b
in silent darkness, 122a
jealousy, with love, 266a
king of the Jews, 1050a
knew that before you were, 49a
like eagles, to be free, 953b
likenesses in brethren, 16b
makes his own bed ere, 263b
man is, free, 344a
man is, unto trouble, 1030a
Miniver Cheevy, too late, 846b
naked, 49b
never to be, at all, 486b
never to have been, is best, 16a
new, infant's tear, 387b
no great man is, too soon, 840a
no man is, an angler, 235b
no man is, an artist, 235b
nobly, is now a crime, 226b
none of woman, shall harm,
  198b
not, for death, 481b
of a little sin, 963a
of a woman, 1030b
of the sun, 995a
of the Virgin Mary, 1068a
of thee, 798b
of virgin mother, 244a
on a Monday, 1018b
one, out of due time, 1061b
out of my due time, 666b
over and over, 997a
poet's made as well, as, 219b
powerless to be, 621b
so many I love not yet, 990b
some are, posthumously, 729a
souls that were never, 986a
sucker, every minute, 557b
this I was, to do, 122a
three distant ages, 279b
thy light was, 617a
time to be, 1042b
to blush unseen, 348b
to disastrous end, 114b
to fly upward, 76b
to freedom, 921a
to inquire after truth, 100a
to marshal his fellow-men, 663a
to one possession, 679a
to see it right, 173a
to shame, 137a
to sweet delight, 388a
to the manner, 172a
to the purple, 965b
to wander, 953b
to write converse, 318b

Born too soon my dear, 757b
 under a rhyming planet, 159a
 under shadow of a creed, 959a
 under that star, 157b
 unless it's pretty nigh in, 579b
 wept that he was ever, 846a
 when I was, 49b, 1065b
 wit and wisdom, with man, 227b
 with a chronic anxiety, 688b
 with a silver spoon, 109b
 with the gift of laughter, 884b
 would thou hadst ne'er been,
  189b
Borne burden and heat of day,
  1053b
 his faculties so meek, 195b
 like a vapor on the summer air,
  636a
 like thy bubbles onward, 455a
 me on his back, 178b
 one by which it may be, 65a
 respect women who have, you,
  1070a
 short paine well, 113a
 well, without defeat, 154b
Borogoves, all mimsy were the,
  657b
Borough clock, on time with the,
  996a
Borrow, days that need, 263b
 from books surcease of sorrow,
  544b
 good and truth to, 507a
 men who, 429b
 name of the world, 120b
 the money to do it with, 665b
 those who, trouble, 904a
 trouble, 589a
Borrow'd from his enemies, 564a
Borrowed book, in the evening,
  332a
 plumes, 10a
 something, something blue,
  1008a
 the matter, 100b
 wit, 229b
Borrower, bettered by the, 251a
 is servant to lender, 1040b
 nor a lender be, 171b
 of the night, 197a
Borrowers nearly always ill-spenders, 606a
 of books, 429b
 wholesale, 562b
Borrowing, depends on, and debt,
  641a
 dulls edge of husbandry, 171b
 everything of neighbours, 285b
 goes a sorrowing, 330b
 goeth a, 96b
 kind of, 251a
 lingers, 152b
Bosom, Abraham's, 128a, 407a,
  1057b
 angel borne on my, 571b
 carry lambs in his, 1047a
 charge within the, 646a
 frozen, bears, 185b
 glory in his, 597b
 hand on her, 190a
 heart out of the, 785b
 heaves and spreads, 411b
 heroic, beats no more, 458a
 in your fragrant, dies, 236b
 let me to thy, fly, 334a
 love in my, like a bee, 116a
 man take fire in his, 1038b
 ocean's, unespied, 269a
 of God, 112a

Bosom of his Father and his God,
  349b
 of public opinion, 874a
 of the sea, 125b, 220b
 of the urgent west, 721b
 slow growth in an aged, 335a
 slumber in its, 470b
 starves her gen'rous birth, 348a
 stuff'd, 199b
 swell, with thy fraught, 189a
 third in your, 136a
 thorns that in her, lodge, 172b
 unzone thy girlish, 916b
 vale in whose, 438b
 warm cheek and rising, 349b
 wife of thy, 1025b
 wring his, 355a
Bosom'd deep in vines, 322a
 high in tufted trees, 245a
Bosom-friend of the maturing sun,
  482b
Bosom's lord sits lightly, 137b
Bosoms, gold used to hang and
  brush their, 571a
 home to men's, 119b
 lift, higher than shores, 181a
 white, of actresses, 339a
Boss, something to cuss around
  and, 895b
 want tew, the thing, 594b
Boss's daughter, marry the, 947b
Boston asks how much does he
  know, 679b
 audience, appear before a, 674b
 Bassarid of, 695a
 Bostonian who leaves, 690a
 Concord and Lexington, 443b
 Evening Transcript, 943a
 good old, 793a
 if, knew the most, 506b
 is like an English town, 985a
 man, pry that out of a, 536a
 marriage around, 966a
 runs to brains, 760a
 State-house is the hub, 536a
 swimming Charles River to go
  to, 506a
 Thucydides at, 493a
 Transcript, obituary in the,
  805b
Bostonian who leaves Boston, 690a
Bostonitis, a sort of, 697b
Boston's a hole, 573a
Bo'sun tight and a midshipmite,
  682a
Boswell first of biographers, 338b
Botanist, puzzle to the, 668b
Botanize, peep and, 405b
Botany, all their, is Latin names,
  504a
Botch, make a, in trying to swap,
  541b
Boteler, Dr., said of strawberries,
  236a
Both, adventuring, found both,
  143b
 always himself in, 979b
 ends are out of sight, 914a
 of them are thine, 127b
 sides of the street, 921b
 true both wise, 267a
 worlds at once they view, 242b
Bother, baby a blessing and, 675a
 it I may occasionally say, 682a
 the colleges when you die, 535b
Bothered, hot and, 821b
Bottle, a little for the, 377a
 extra, of Johannisberg, 381b
 friend in need nor a, 578b

Bottle, large cold, 747a
 needle in a, of hay, 107b
 of Burgundy, 293a
 of hay, 142a
 of rum, 749b, 750a
 of salvation, 111a
 on the chimley-piece, 577b
 tears into thy, 1035a
 yo-ho-ho and a, of rum, 749b,
  750a
Bottled lightning, 577a
Bottles, beetle balanced, 741a
 narrow-necked, 321a
 new wine into old, 1052a
Bottom, affection hath unknown,
  162b
 bless thee, 142a
 build from, up, 918b
 in one, trusted, 143a
 of my grief, 137a
 of the deep, 149b
 of the deeps, 100a
 of the monstrous world, 249b
 of the woe is deep, 603b
 of the worst, 181b
 remaining at the, 811a
 sits on his, 101a
 stand upon his, 274a
Bottomless gulf of civil pensions,
  442a
 perdition, 252a
 ponds will be thought, 590b
 rise out of the, sea, 610b
Bottoms of my trousers rolled,
  943a
Bough, Apollo's laurel, 123b
 bloom along the, 785a
 blossom that hangs on the, 210a
 blossom-burdened, 814b
 chaffinch sings on the orchard,
  568b
 how white a cherry, 928b
 reddening on the, 8b
 set upon a golden, 827a
 touch not a single, 498b
 wet black, 932b
 when the, breaks, 734a
Boughs are daily rifled, 489a
 bearing, may live, 140a
 hide God, 764a
 lordly cedar green with, 756a
 lowest, and brushwood sheaf,
  568b
 melancholy, 161a
 nests amid the shuddering, 721a
 of love and hate, 824a
 of the may, 725a
 shake against the cold, 206a
 soul into the, does slide, 269a
Bought by judgment of the eye,
  132b
 'er the same, 818a
 fame is not, and sold, 663a
 golden opinions, 195b
 good names to be, 149a
 Hudibras again, 284b
 men who can't be, 899a
Bouillabaisse, a noble dish is,
  565b
Boulder's shade, long in the, 845a
Boulders, Berkshire, 960b
Bound along if you can, 500b
 as is befitting each, 610b
 each to each, 406b
 few paternal acres, 309a
 hand and foot with red tape,
  579b
 hath his, in earth sea sky, 129a
 in duty equally, 345b

Bread, grind his bones to make my, 1020b
half-penny-worth of, 150b
have not to labor for daily, 530a
he is, 110a
I am the, of life, 1058a
I broke with you, 948b
if his son ask, 1052a
in sorrow ate, 521a
in the other hand, 30a
is the staff of life, 292b
it has earned, 374b
Jesus took, 1055a
live by, alone, 1050b
live by, only, 1025b
live for, 506b
living Homer begged his, 227a
loaf of, and thou, 531b
loaves of, ready made, 370a
looked to government for, 361b
Lord shall give thee, 91b
man lives not upon, alone, 749b
of adversity, 1046b
of deceit is sweet, 1040a
of idleness, 1042a
of life, 474a
of others savors of salt, 77a
quarrel with my, and butter, 296b
ravens brought him, 1028b
royal slice of, 917b
should be so dear, 489a
side my, is buttered, 94b
some gave them white, 1015a
spoiled the 629b
strengthens man's heart, 292b
struggle for, 773a
supply you your, and butter, 763a
thou shalt eat, 1022a
to one dying of thirst, 761a
toil and work and earn, 538a
took the, and brake it, 97b
unleavened, 1024a
upon the waters, 1043b
white, and butter, 1016a
whole stay of, 292b, 1045a
Breadlines, heard of unemployment and, 990a
Bread-sauce of the happy ending, 719a
Breadth of heaven betwixt you, 519a
taller by, of my nail, 295a
two fingers', 70a
Breadths, naked, of the ocean, 524b
Break all chains, 746b
an oath he never made, 239a
best you get is an even, 911b
bruised reed shall he not, 1047a
eternal Sabbath, 277b
eyes the, of day, 185b
faith with us who die, 860b
frame of nature round him, 299a
his sleep, 531b
into hundred thousand flaws, 191b
it to our hope, 200a
my staffs, 210a
my troth, 132a
no canon of the social code, 781a
of the wave, 462a
off from entanglement, 23a
off this last kiss, 216b
on thy cold gray stones, 549b
our bonds of affection, 539b

Break out rather than surrender, 872a
shins against it, 160a
study to, it, 132a
that sole bond, 360b
the hearts of kith and kin, 877a
the legs of time, 534b
their eggs at the smaller end, 295b
through Japanese lines, 907b
through, wasps and hornets, 294b
thy word, 66b
up housekeeping, 699a
up under heavy years, 893a
where billows never, 292a
you may shatter, 439b
Breake, better is to bow then, 92a
Breakers, dangerous, of the Euxine, 459a
wantoned with thy, 455a
Breakfast, contentment that comes with, 981b
dare eat, 155b
dinner lunch and tea, 849a
impossible things before, 659a
Michael Angelo for, 674b
project a scheme for her, 305a
where shall we our, take, 1012b
with appetite you have, 211a
Breakfasts and dinners and balls, 632b
at five-o'clock tea, 659b
Breakfast-table, account of itself at your, 507b
ready for the national, 585b
well-provisioned, 514a
Breakfast-tables of people indifferent to press, 838a
Breakfast-time, critical period is, 955a
Breaking of day in the lone east, 881b
out the eternal stars, 609b
shout of our days, 96cb
stop one heart from, 645b
straying and, away, 931a
waves dashed high, 470a
Breaks a leg, 807a
brightest into dawn, 17a
butterfly upon a wheel, 319a
death, every bond, 290a
diseased nature, 150b
his birth's invidious bar, 552b
jest, no bones, 342b
magic chains, 247b
more homes than it, up, 851b
sorrow, seasons, 128a
strain itself until it, 765b
sun, through darkest clouds, 130b
through yonder window, 135a
up in rout, 14a
Breast and countenance, 76a
beat his, 421a
beats in every human, 620b
blush upon thy, 528b
charitable, 935a
court of justice in his, 555b
dwell in my, 379b
encloseth my poor heart, 127b
fair as thine ideal, 454b
fair love's ripening 479b
from my brain and from my, 867a
hairy, 897a
heart at rest within my, 385b
hold me to your deep, 673b
in some quiet, 738a

Breast, knock the, 260b
Madeline's fair, 481a
marble of her snowy, 242a
marched, forward, 575b
mark on his red, 528b
nunnery of thy chaste, 208a
obdur'd, 254a
of doves, 936a
of her gown, 514a
one master-passion in the, 317a
peace within my, 863a
reddened all his, 528b
sail upon her patient, 181a
soft hand and softer, 480a
soothe the savage, 298a
sparkling cross on her white, 312a
springs eternal in the human, 316a
sweet flowing, 936b
tamer of the human, 347b
that gives the rose, 639a
told but to her mutual, 433a
toss him to my, 233b
trembles in the, 413a
truth hath quiet, 138a
two hands upon the, 635b
typical American, 718a
village Hampden with dauntless, 348b
wake in our, living fires, 535a
wanton sweetness through, 328b
wave of life in her, 487b
what his, forges, 202b
where learning lies, 309b
Breast-high amid the corn, 488a
Breastie, panic's in thy, 390a
Breastplate of faith and love, 1063a
stronger, 125a
Breasts are dun, 207b
bore within their, 582b
brown, 961a
oppose gallant, 40b
orbs of heavenly frame, 116a
she hath no, 1044b
the blows of circumstance, 552b
the keen air, 354a
thy two, 1044b
within our, this jewel lies, 330a
Breath, able to take his, away, 572b
and finer spirit, 406a
bated, and whispering humbleness, 144a
blew back, 646b
boldest held his, 433a
breathes with human, 546b
call the fleeting, 348b
can make them, 355b
down and out of, 152a
draught of a, 462a
draw thy, in pain, 179b
enough, for the whole tune, 788a
everything that hath, 1038a
exponent of, 647b
extend a mother's, 319b
fail sun and, 606b
fame is the, of power, 774a
fancy'd life in others', 317b
first, our souls draw, 655a
flatter'd its rank, 453b
gate of, 692b
grown grey from thy, 693a
healthy, of morn, 483a
heaven's, smells wooingly, 195a
his last, 679a
his life a, of God, 585b

Breath, hoarse with tempestuous, 690a
  hot and cold with the same, 11a
  in our mouth, 817a
  is in his nostrils, 1045a
  kept his, to cool his pottage, 60b
  lack of, 260b
  last moment of his, 353b
  life of mortal, 523a
  lightly draws its, 403a
  love's latest, 122b
  moist, of decay, 639a
  most immediate, of life, 379a
  mouth-honour, 199a
  musty, of the multitude, 791a
  my quiet, 481b
  of autumn's being, 466a
  of flowers, 121b
  of kings, 390b
  of life, 1021b
  of morn, 256a
  of self-respect, 986b
  of the night-wind, 622a
  of the wind, 879b
  of vernal shower, 350a
  one mighty, 440b
  orbs would open at thy, 688a
  renown but a, of wind, 76b
  rides on posting winds, 204a
  second life in others', 309b
  servile to skyey influences, 184b
  shine and seek to mend, 217b
  some of us are out of, 658b
  summer's ripening, 135b
  taking or the giving, 949a
  tender-taken, 479b
  terrible as terminations, 157a
  thou no, at all, 194a
  thought takes one's, away, 627b
  till time lose, 754a
  to the latest, 314b
  twilight hour of, 833b
  uninforming, 912b
  unnoticed as the, we draw, 816b
  utter sweet, 142b
  waste of, the years behind, 826a
  what chisel could cut, 208b
  where, most breathes, 206a
  with one, attunes the spheres, 591a
  with panting, has escaped, 75a
  yield up their, 631b
Breath'd, still, in sighs, 313a
Breathe and blow, 550a
  as tho' to, were life, 548a
  content to, his native air, 309a
  his better doth not, 127b
  if such there, 414a
  not his name, 438a
  our evening prayer, 584a
  prayer for all who lie beneath, 820b
  see nor, nor stir, 896b
  the air again, 613a
  the vital air, 6b
  thou thereon didst only, 219a
  thoughts that, 268a
Breathed, first true gentleman that, 215a
  into his nostrils, 1021b
  upon dead bodies, 508b
Breathers of this world, 206a
Breathes a prayer for him, 499a
  a recollection, 806a
  All's-well to these, 705b

Breathes, into the statue that, 667a
  of love, 729b
  of nations saved, 459a
  the foe, 476b
  the man with soul so dead, 413b
  upon a bank of violets, 163b
  who, must suffer, 294a
Breathing bronze, mold the, 37b
  clay, life but, 328a
  closer is He than, 556a
  coeval with the act of, 297b
  eating as well as, 351a
  health and quiet, 478b
  household laws, 407a
  music, from her face, 268a
  of the common wind, 407a
  through the night, 487b
  time of day, 179b
Breathless on thy fate, 522b
  vigil, kept a, 964b
  we flung us, 938a
  with adoration, 407a
Breath's a ware that will not keep, 785b
Breaths, thoughts not, 586a
Bred at Edinburgh, 332a
  at Oxford or Cambridge, 273a
  en bawn in a brier-patch, 738b
  folly without father, 245b
  in the bone, 28b
  pure digestion, 256b
  to the sea, 469b
  where is fancy, 145a
Bredon, bells they sound on, 786a
Breeches, book in, 419b
  cost him but a crown, 187b, 1011b
  pocket, hand in its, 478a
  upon his backside, 346a
  were blue, 427a
  women wear the, 221b
  wouldn't hurt, 782b
Breed a habit in a man, 132a
  border nor, nor birth, 814a
  creatures of a lesser, 973a
  England, again such a king, 122b
  fear'd by their, 139a
  happy, of men, 139a
  Hyla, 880a
  large resolute, of men, 611b
  neglect may, mischief, 234a, 330b
  of horses and dogs, 288a
  the past again, 556a
  where they most, and haunt, 195b
Breede continuall remembrance, 83a
Breeding, due to gentle, 14b
  good, 680a
  lilacs, 943b
  man's want of, 56b
  men of loyal, 632a
  test of a man or woman's, 764b
  write with ease to show, 382b
Breeds, chaos often, life, 696b
  delay, danger, 106a
  familiarity, contempt, 10a, 680a
  feeds and, by composture, 203b
  fine thoughts, 73a
  lesser, without the law, 816a
  valiant creatures, 155b
Breeze, battle and the, 432b
  blew the white foam flew, 421b
  blow through life like a, 989a
  dancing in the, 409a

Breeze, flag to April's, unfurled, 504a
  folds rippling in the, 563a
  free as the, 412b
  freshened fragrant, 961b
  is on the sea, 417a
  playful, drops in the pool, 589a
  tyranny in every tainted, 360a
  without a, 421b
Breezes dusk and shiver, 547b
  genial, 670b
  sunset, shiver, 803b
Breitmann, Hans, gife a barty, 631a
Brekeke-kesh, koash, koash, 22b
Brent, bonie brow was, 392a
Brer Fox he lay low, 738b
Brest, Natur's learned, 103a
Brethren born, likenesses in, 16b
  earthly, 701b
  to dwell together in unity, 1037b
  we be, 1023a
Brevity, body, wit its soul, 423a
  insensible of the, of life, 290a
  soul of wit, 173a
  what is use of, 52a
Brew, soup or broth or, 565b
Brews, as he, so shall he drink, 218a
Bribe, death's boatman takes no, 39a
  too poor for a, 350a
Bribed, public not to be, 502a
Bric-a-brac, among the, 943a
Brick and steel and stone, 978a
  straw to make, 1024a
Brick-dust man with grime o'er-spread, 332b
Bricks are alive to testify, 125b
  by chance and fortune, 61a
  lies supple on the, 978a
  sold him gilded, 894a
  throw, and sermons at, 679b
  throwing, 902b
Brick-yard, dewdrops gathered in a, 801b
Bridal of the earth, 232a
Bridal-cakes, brides and, 230a
Bride, glittering, 410b
  hail the, 685a
  half of the world a, 780b
  hath paced into the hall, 421a
  teeming mistress but a barren, 314b
  to a lad gone down, 962b
  unravish'd, of quietness, 482a
Bride-bed to have deck'd, 179a
Bridegroom coming out of his chamber, 1033a
  fresh as, 149b
  hail the, 685a
  half of the world a, 780b
  in my death, 201b
  went forth to meet the, 1054b
Bride-grooms brides and bridal-cakes, 230a
Brides and bridal-cakes, 230a
  lion woos his, 352b
Bridge, broken arch of London, 492b
  cobweb, flung from his mind, 804a
  demolition of a, 838a
  don't cross the, 524b
  grave is but a covered, 524b
  of asses, 29a
  of blue, 525b
  of Sighs, 453b

Changed, haven't, a bit, 992a
  innocence for innocence, 207b
  into two bright birds, 725a
  not all sleep but all be, 1061b
  people, yet Egdon remained,
    705a
  we have, all that, 270a
  we shall be, 1062a
Changeful potency, 182b
  thing is woman ever, 37a
Changeless, fain keep her, 639b
Changer, morals of a money, 843a
Changers, money, 1053b
Changes are irksome, 367b
  bewildering, 630a
  desire to see no, 922a
  follow, of the moon, 188b
  in her circled orb, 135b
  more constantly than past, 956a
  name changes quarter, 76b
  of circumstances, 444b
  our desire, 856a
  scene, but aspirations persist,
    954a
  sky, when wives, 162b
  territorial, 922a
  with its every whim, 972b
  woman often, 37a
  world's a scene of, 267a
  writes our Fortune's, 41b
Changeth, old order, 547b
Changing demands of economic
    process, 914b
  face, sorrows of your, 824b
  from brown suit to gray, 931b
  guard at Buckingham Palace,
    917b
  lineaments, moulded the, 702a
  one's mind, 875a
  scene, humanity a, 516a
  skies, wind cloud and, 471a
  things according to our desire,
    856a
Channel, butting through the,
    896b
  dream you are crossing the,
    684a
  drum them up, 803b
  thick fog over, 950a
Channels for the stream of love,
    526b
Chanst, give him a, 835b
Chant, do use to, it, 164b
  how can ye, ye little birds, 392b
Chanticleer, crow like, 160b
Chanting faint hymns, 140b
Chants doleful hymn, 148b
Chaos and cosmos, 654a
  black, comes again, 131a
  come, now, 806b
  come of organized disorder,
    995b
  contracted to intricate form,
    893b
  emotional, remembered in tran-
    quillity, 971b
  is come again, 188a
  of thought and passion, 317a
  of Waterloo, 901a
  often breeds life, 696b
  primeval, 557a
  reign of, 253a
  thy dread empire, 322a
  what a, what a contradiction,
    272b
Chaos-like together crush'd and
    bruis'd, 309a
Chap, I am an intellectual, 684a
Chapel, devil builds a, 291b

Chapel, devil would build a, 86b
  God's grand greenwood, 654b
Chapels had been churches, 143b
  legend of the green, 997a
  stolen looks are nice in, 448a
Chap-fallen, quite, 178b
Chaplain, Blue Beard's domestic,
    576a
Chaplet, rose fallen from thy, 416a
Chapmen's tongues, 132b
Chapter, and so on to end of, 90a
  longest, in the book, 324a
  of accidents, 324a
  repeat a complete, 342a
  two, begin with, 861a
Chapters of mankind, 800a
Character, accommodatin', 664b
  appeared in that, 342b
  bestowed by nature, 27a
  bird of bad moral, 331b
  easier kept than recovered, 371a
  everything in solitude except,
    447a
  formation of, 614b
  give an action its, 56a
  habits and manners, 628b
  hand in making southern, 676b
  happiness ennobles the, 875b
  hereditary strokes of, 1001b
  his own, is the arbiter, 35b
  humanizes, 43a
  incongruity of, 54b
  is a caricature, 982b
  is Destiny, 12a
  limitations of his own, 699b
  man that makes a, 305a
  more clearly will his, appear,
    671a
  Negro, 758b
  of the victim, 512b
  of the writer, 472b
  of woman cannot be altered,
    630a
  possesses this talent, 853b
  propagates, by the sword, 1002a
  purify and elevate, 616b
  rag of, they spare, 725b
  say nothing against a, 341b
  set like plaster, 715a
  simplicity of, 700b
  society wholesome for the, 602b
  sow a, 1005b
  tell the, of every man, 47a
  unaffected for the better, 715a
  undecided, 478b
  unhampered by, or conviction,
    641a
Characteristic, charming, of man,
    743b
  faculty of humanity, 722a
  of human nature, 63b
  of the present age, 512b
  of wisdom, 589b
Characteristics, healthy and gen-
    tle, 514b
  of a vigorous mind, 336a
  of the modern spirit, 799a
  two marked, 937b
Characters, fashioning, in the
    wrong way, 715a
  high, 261a
  most women have no, 314b
  of hell to trace, 349b
  of ordinary life, 428b
  people not, 982b
  supernatural, 424b
  venerate four, 372b
Charge, angels, over thee, 1036b
  Chester charge, 415a

Charge, dat's de, 946b
  God's holiest, 352a
  in earnest, 704a
  in peace a, 281a
  is prepar'd, 308b
  once more and then be dumb,
    622b
  transgression to my, 147b
  with all thy chivalry, 433a
  within the bosom, 646a
Chargeable with no exaggeration,
    435b
Charged against us, 52a
  troops of error, 240a
  with punishments the scroll,
    741b
  with spirit and decency, 334b
  with the grandeur of God, 724a
Charger, head in a, 1053a
Charges, die to save, 222a
  matter of, 244a
Chargeships, and foreign missions,
    537b
Charging a blunderbuss, 339a
  of his enemy, 103b
Chariest maid is prodigal enough,
    171a
Charing Cross, betwixt heaven
    and, 790b
Chariot, bring me my, of fire, 388b
  of fire, 1029a
  that bears a human soul, 647a
  time's wingèd, 269a
  wheel, dust beneath thy, 812b
Chariots, wheels of his, 1026b
Charitable breast, 935a
  lie, 992a
  men's, speeches, 121b
  wicked or, intents, 172a
Charities of a kiss or smile, 425b
Charity, anticipate, 74b
  begins at home, 240b
  blubber of, 907a
  Christian pearl of, 528a
  costume, ball, 990a
  cover multitude of sins, 1064a
  depend for subsistence on, 513b
  edifieth, 1061a
  faith hope, 431b, 1061b
  for all, 542a
  frozen as, 427b
  gracious, remains, 669a
  greatest of these is, 1061b
  have faith and have not, 1061a
  holding out hand for, 74b
  lectures or a little, 608a
  liberty like, 965a
  little earth for, 211b
  love friendship, 182a
  mankind's concern is, 317b
  mercy, and love, 577a
  never faileth, 1061a
  pity gave ere, began, 356a
  rarity of Christian, 489b
  rewarded by God of Abraham,
    264a
  scrimped and iced, 729b
  smile of Christian, 808a
  suffereth long, 1061a
  the living need, 664a
  to all mankind, 398b
  when rich concern themselves,
    876b
  with, for all, 845a
  with the world, 296b
Charity's golden ladder, 74b
Charlatan, defamed by every, 553a
Charles Augustus Fortescue, 849b
  gentle-hearted, 429a

Child is father of the man, 406b
  is little, 790b
  Jesus Christ her little, 591b
  keeps a secret so well as a, 497b
  like a tired, 465a
  little, I stand, 231a
  look upon a little, 334a
  Mary she came with her, 1003a
  meet nurse for poetic, 414a
  misses the unsaid good-night, 879b
  Monday's, 1018b
  naked new-born, 377b
  never without an infant, 448b
  of calamity, 676a
  of grandmother Eve, 132b
  of hope, 561a
  of misery, 368a
  of nature, a well-developed, 644a
  of scorn, 846a
  of the pure unclouded brow, 657b
  old man is twice a, 174a
  on a cloud I saw a, 385a
  on the homeless street, 756a
  painted, of dirt, 319a
  ranked as a mere, 594a
  Roland to the dark tower, 192a
  saving a little, 699a
  Shakespeare Fancy's, 245b
  she was a, and I was a child, 546a
  should always say what's true, 750a
  should grow into the man, 323b
  sick, in the basement, 760b
  simplicity a, 278b
  spare rod and spoil, 239a
  spare th' rod an' spile th', 837a
  spend their fury on a, 127a
  spoil the, 84b
  straying of a little, 800a
  strike a, 765a
  sung by any, of song, 732a
  teach the, to doubt, 388a
  tears of a, 853a
  thankless, 191a
  that's born on the Sabbath day, 1018b
  thoughts of a, 660a
  three years', 421a
  trumpet of a, of Rome, 694b
  unborn, 853a
  unto us a, is born, 1045b
  use of a new-born, 912b
  what it is to be a, 790b
  what will a, learn sooner, 320b
  when I was a, 1061a
  whom many fathers share, 308b
  wise father knows own, 144b
  with Mary his mother, 1050a
  wretched, expires, 849a
  you are like a flower, 486a
  you'd say poor, 629b
Childes, no, pley, 81b
Childhood, days of, 428b
  dwarfing of, 497a
  eye of, fears, 196b
  fleet, womanhood and, 522a
  friends of our, 529a
  make glad the heart of, 701b
  manhood and decrepit age, 232a
  noisy impertinence of, 603b
  of the world, 743b
  old age is second, 23a
  scenes of my, 450a
  second, 853a
  shows the man, 259b

Childhood's cheek, tear down, 415b
  hour, ever thus from, 441a
Childish ignorance, 488a
  inconstant, proud, 477a
  joy now lives in me, 913b
  sweet, days, 406b
  things, I put away, 1061a
  toy, religion a, 123b
  treble, 161b
Childishness, second, 161b
Childless and crownless, 454a
  and bland, 686b
Children across the Atlantic, 566b
  and fooles cannot lye, 93a
  and fooles speake true, 93a
  and fools want everything, 286a
  are what the mothers are, 431b
  as living arrows, 924a
  become as little, 1053b
  begin by loving parents, 768a
  behold the chimpanzee, 805a
  blood on us and on our, 1055a
  breed of their, 288a
  breeds contempt and, 680a
  bright and agreeable, 64b
  call her blessed, 1042a
  called the, of God, 1050b
  care of, 825a
  come dear, let us away, 619b
  comfort of thy, 128a
  dear, wives and, 559a
  devise to, yellow shores, 777a
  drinkest tears of, 449a
  fear to go in the dark, 119b
  fits her, with something to do, 600b
  follow'd with endearing wile, 356a
  fonder of their, 27a
  forget they have been, 631a
  had so many, 1017a
  he that hath wife and, 120a
  hear the, weeping, 518b
  heart of, to their fathers, 1050a
  here my, have been born, 538b
  holdeth, from play, 116a
  human soul on the lips of, 498a
  in sorrow thou shalt bring forth, 1022a
  iniquity of fathers upon the, 1024b
  inter parents, 16b
  kind and natural, 154b
  king over all, of pride, 1032a
  know a lot about raising, 836b
  laboring, 886b
  laugh and play, 462b
  learn to walk on frozen toes, 847a
  learne to creepe, 93a
  leave to, the dandelions, 776b
  lips and hearts of little, 565a
  little, of the wind, 762a
  lost slain by arrows of frost, 634b
  mother who talks about her, 513a
  neither, nor gods, 815a
  never forgot his, 1014b
  never let angry passions rise, 302b
  no longer any, 271a
  of a larger growth, 323b
  of an idle brain, 134b
  of his own, till he had, 60b
  of larger growth, 276a
  of men, 620b
  of one family fall out, 302b

Children of the brain, 294b
  of the country, 783a
  of the kingdom, 1052a
  of the light, 621b
  of this world, 1057a
  of yesterday, 711a
  other folks' dogs and, 843b
  parents bore their, 766a
  peacemakers called, of God, 125a
  put our, on wheels, 891b
  saying he would steal his, 677a
  shall wander, 1025b
  sins of the fathers upon, 18a
  so act toward, 65a
  somewhere, shout, 808a
  spoke bad English, 804a
  sports of, 354a
  suffer the little, 1056a
  talking to, in the dark, 976b
  three eldest, of necessity, 672b
  through survival of their, 702b
  to those who are no longer, 777a
  voices of, are heard, 385b
  way to rear up, 519b
  we and they are his, 571a
  weeping for her, 1050a
  who tumble barefooted, 898b
  wife, and friends, 403a
  will burn, 1015b
  will not leave, 985b
  will still have to toil, 739b
  wisdom justified of her, 1052b
  wiser than, of light, 1057a
  with Hyacinth's temperament, 851b
  women and, first, 1003b
  women not used to bear, 54a
  world in which, have existence, 580a
Children's children will have to toil, 739b
  fate, for all our, 821b
  gratitude, 827b
  griefs are little, 790b
  hour, 524a
  popular American, books, 804a
  teeth on edge, 1048b
Child's mistake fancies as lost, 790a
  sob in the silence, 518b
  strength, credulity the, 429b
  tender years, 63a
Child-wife, it's only my, 579b
Chill companionship of waxen vines, 947b
  courtesy grows, 703b
  detraction stirs no sigh, 705b
  icy and, 563b
  in wintry age to feel no, 365b
  November's sky, and drear, 414a
  November's surly blast, 390a
  penury repress'd their rage, 348b
  the warmest heart, 630a
  thy dreaming nights, 480a
  whom age doth, 262a
  wind is, 414b
  you through and through, 747b
Chills, breathed its killing, 751b
  of, and fever she died, 946b
  the lap of May, 354a
Chillun, tun'nin' of de, in de bed, 859b
Chilly, feel, and grown old, 571a
  man's fire, 598b
Chime, guide their, 269a
  hours high heaven doth, 271b

Clothed with derision, 691b
  with integrity, 270a
Clothes and buttons of the man, 68oa
  are to our bodies, 798a
  buying, and groceries, 899a
  cares much for his, 690b
  civilized life without, 798a
  enterprises that require new, 589b
  extravagance was, 741a
  for myself and wife, 284b
  hang your, on a hickory limb, 1008b
  hanging out the, 1017a
  kindles in, a wantonness, 230b
  liquefaction of her, 231a
  loves but their oldest, 215b
  not be burned, 1038b
  nothing to wear but, 775a
  old, are not venerable, 474b
  out of these wet, 941a
  police in citizens', 505b
  put on his Sunday, 464b
  since, came in, 580b
  smell of old, 938b
  spoiling her nice new, 1018a
  state of her, 989b
  stepped out of their, 827b
  swaddling, 1056a
  tatter'd, 193a
  thrown on with a pitchfork, 296b
  walked away with their, 512a
  wear theirs and they our, 223a
  when he put on his, 354b
  without bodies, 798a
Clothespole, more like a bar'l thin a, 836b
Clothing, come in sheep's, 1052a
  corn and, 705b
  lack of decent, 514b
  of delight, 385a
  of the grave, 848a
  wolf in sheep's, 10b
Clotho singing of the present, 25b
Cloths, heavens' embroidered, 825b
Cloud and clod, 922b
  and ever-during dark, 254b
  brightest day a, 125a
  choose a firm, before it fall, 314b
  comes to me or, or sun, 515b
  every, not a storm, 127a
  every wandering, 769b
  fast-flying, 462a
  fiend hid in a, 387b
  fiend in a, 384b
  in shape of a camel, 176a
  inner half of every, 879a
  into night, 706b
  is scattered, 469a
  joy is the luminous, 423a
  lies around us like a, 563a
  lonely as a, 409a
  music and the flying, 650a
  nature is a mutable, 501b
  of ignorance, 978b
  of witnesses, 1063b
  on a, I saw a child, 385a
  out of the, a silence, 733b
  out of the sea, 1029a
  pillar of a, 1024a
  sable, 247a
  scowl of, 575a
  set my bow in the, 1022b
  silver lining to their, 851a
  spirit sits in a foggy, 198a
  stooping through fleecy, 246a

Cloud, sunburnt face is but a, 385a
  that floats on high, 409a
  that's dragonish, 201a
  the happiness of others, 337a
  thickest, earth stretched, 573a
  through the dark, shining, 865a
  which outwept the rain, 467b
  will turn to rain, 525b
Cloud-born squadrons of the gale, 649a
Cloud-calligraphers of windy spirals, 939a
Cloud-capp'd towers, 210a
Clouded hills, shine upon our, 388b
  hours that are, 434b
  majesty, rising in, 255b
  sky, from out yon, 509b
Cloud-kissing Ilion, 131b
Cloudless climes and starry skies, 456a
  sunshine, 39b
Clouds and eclipses, 205a
  and stars and birds, 866a
  are mean, 647b
  billowy, of June, 890b
  blue-massing, 938b
  breaks through a gloom of, 301a
  dark, lower, 498b
  dropping from the, 327b
  fear not, will lour, 394a
  fill sky with black, 39b
  gay castles in the, 328b
  gloomy and portentous, 500a
  hooded, like friars, 521a
  hungry, swag on the deep, 385b
  look black, 380a
  look when the, are blowing, 720b
  looks in the, 167a
  murky, pursue thy way, 617a
  never doubted, would break, 575b
  never king dropped out of, 227b
  new made, 997a
  on the morrow of his battles, 558b
  pack, away, 227a
  pity sitting in the, 137a
  play of colours on, 797a
  prince of the, 618b
  regardeth the, 1043b
  return after rain, 1043b
  robe of, 456b
  sees God in, 316a
  shadows of the, 662a
  silk-sack, 724b
  sit in, and mock us, 153a
  somewhere among the, above, 826a
  sun breaks through darkest, 130b
  take heaven out of the, 996b
  that gather round the setting sun, 408b
  through rolling, to soar, 452a
  trailing, of glory, 408a
  tumult in the, 826a
  turn my, about, 879a
  various, are tost, 332b
  wrapt in, and snow, 453a
Cloud-topped hill, behind the, 316a
Cloudy, skies are not, all day, 730b
  symbols of high romance, 479b
  trophies, among her, 483a
  was the weather, 1020a
Clouted brogues, 204b
Clouts, coppers brooms, and brushes, 886a

Clove, bitter bark and burning, 881a
Cloven clay, 692b
  tongues, 1059a
Clover, how to live in, 27b
  in the, or the snow, 626a
  pressed, leaves, 898b
  to him is aristocracy, 647a
  underneath the, 655a
Cloves, nutmegs and, 232a
Clown, emperor and, 482a
  stupid and the, 713a
Cloy appetites they feed, 200b
  of all meats the soonest, 267a
  the hungry edge, 138b
Cloyless sauce, 200b
Club an assembly of good fellows, 336b
  swamp-elm, 760b
Clubs typical of strife, 365a
Clumsy feet of April, 969a
  vanity, 769a
Clung to their first fault, 567a
Clusium, Lars Porsena of, 493b
Cluster of gifts, 718b
  possession of, of qualities, 718b
  woes, 178a
Clutch, claw'd me in his, 178b
  come let me, thee, 196a
  either hand may rightly, 820b
  of circumstance, 741b
  the golden keys, 552b
Clutching the inviolable shade, 621a
Clyde, bonny banks of, 850a
Coach, clatter with his, 285b
  come my, 178a
  drive a, and six, 1007a
  not too much to keep a, 285b
  rascals in the, 599b
  rattling of a, 218a
  sit in the back of the, 284b
Coaches, turn pumpkins into, 790b
  waggons playhouses, 429a
Coach-house, double, 427a
Coal, cargo of Tyne, 896b
  comes hissing hot from hell, 586a
  glossy cope is black as, 689b
  is a portable climate, 505a
  mine, partners in a, 836a
  to break into fire, 939b
  visage blacker than, 1048b
Coalescing, communicate without, 992a
Coals, blows the, and works, 22a
  can one go upon hot, 1038b
  eyes dead, 208b
  fallen into the, 8a
  heap, of fire, 1041a, 1060a
  to Newcastle, 40b
Coarse complexions, 248a
  familiar but not, 337b
  in substance, 68b
Coast of Coromandel, 493a, 581b
  rough and stormy, 748a
  stern and rock-bound, 470a
  threw upon a desert, 405a
  was clear, 122b
Coaster, dirty British, 896b
Coasts, bristling sea, 538a
  glorious, where ocean tides, 755b
  line the, with lamps, 959b
Coat and bands and hymn-book, 517a
  black, all buttoned down, 498b
  covered with embroideries, 826a
  hold my, and snicker, 943a
  of arms of the Empire, 840b

Commendations, paltry, of mankind, 544b
  satiety of, 203a
Commends the ingredients, 195b
Comment, no, 872a
  upon one another, 101a
Commentator, transatlantic, 493a
Comments, amused, 773b
Commerce and honest friendship, 374b
  disinterested, between equals, 355a
  in matters of, 401b
  long prevails, 353b
  promote, and not betray it, 286b
  saw the heavens fill with, 548b
  war of, and arms, 916b
  wealth and, 592b
  weapons of, 916b
  which attracts envy, 359b
  with our colonies, 359b
  without its folly-swaddles, 714a
Commercial and professional life, 744a
  capital, 594a
  liturgies, 845b
Commercing with the skies, 246a
Commission, encourage, of many, 46a
  partisanship installed in, 661a
Commit adultery, 1025a
  oldest sins, 154a
  to memory, 1067a
  treason nor be outlawed, 110b
Commitments and power in balance, 952b
Committed adultery in his heart, 1050b
  crimes, in thy name, 383a
  flat burglary, 158b
  gross errors, 109a
  never, treason, 86b
  now their sins are all, 660b
  to the task, 987a
  to the will of God, 229b
Committees, intellectual before one of, 900b
  little suspected, 505a
Commodities, cheapening of, 594a
  hateful tax levied upon, 336b
Commodity, ceases to be a mass, 985b
  of good names, 149a
  oil of, 907a
Commodores, proud gods and, 603b
Common affairs of life, 434a
  age, man's, 566b
  air, drew in the, 49b, 1065b
  as light is love, 465b
  bond, universal and, 100b
  buttercup, 936a
  chord, life's, 574b
  clay, inhabits, 804b
  clay, wrought in, 814a
  crude material, 690b
  cure of love, 105b
  day, fade into light of, 408b
  daylight sweet, 738a
  dear, flower, 600a
  diamond has become, 739b
  dotages of human kind, 222a
  earth, her beauty fed my, 896b
  executioner, 162a
  fame, so false as, 289a
  fame, trust to, 504b
  fate of the indolent, 380a
  friendliness, 721b
  German soldier, 951b

Common, good thing make too, 152b
  grave, empires and cities in, 369b
  ground, we stand on, 675b
  grow up through the, 557b
  heap, misfortunes laid in one, 60a
  herd, stand above the, 751a
  hours, success unexpected in, 590b
  ideas and ideals, 983b
  interest, no kind of, 618a
  judges of property, 336b
  law is nothing but reason, 110a
  law not brooding omnipresence, 709b
  law of England, 955a
  life, enlarger of the, 666b
  life, sense of the, 722b
  lot of curs, 533b
  man, best memorial for the, 793b
  man, century of the, 948b
  man, happiness of the, 831a, 900a
  man protection against war, 926b
  man, what is a, 936a
  mass of matter, 6a
  men, crowd of, 237a
  men to greatness, 956a
  mind, education forms the, 314a
  murderer, 851b
  natures, same with, 307a
  new opinions not, 283a
  nothing, did or mean, 268b
  old, arbitrator time, 182b
  organized, peace, 770b
  passage, no act of, 204a
  people, foolish questions of, 735a
  people nod our heads, 803a
  people of the skies, 213a
  power to keep them in awe, 228b
  problem yours and mine, 570b
  proof, 'tis a, 167a
  property, best ideas are, 47a
  right of humanity, 538a
  roll of, men, 150b
  saying among people, 273a
  sense and plain dealing, 502b
  sense, appal your, 794a
  sense, bourn of, 953b
  sense can deal with, 952b
  sense, dictate of, 329b
  sense, God-given trait sound, 644a
  sense is not so common, 325a
  sense kicked out, 294b
  sense, rarest gift to beauty, 639a
  sense, sword of, 640a
  service, too sharp for, 446a
  sight, beauties hid from, 630a
  sight did seem, 408a
  speech, gracious even in, 587a
  steals goose from off the, 712b
  steals the, from the goose, 713a
  stock of intellectual enjoyment, 791b
  sun the air the skies, 349b
  sweets grown, 206b
  talk of the town, 284a
  task, 464a
  things, dull catalogue of, 480b
  thought, too much thinking to have, 314b
  to friends, all things, 33a
  to mankind, 14b

Common touch, nor lose the, 820b
  tree, where is a, 936a
  understanding, 983b
  understanding kicked out, 294b
  use, remote from, 457a
  vice of all in old age, 33a
  weal, contributes not to, 66b
  where the climate's sultry, 457b
  world, men awake are in one, 58b
Commonest but most uncritical faults, 732b
  delight of the race, 664b
  goddamnedest kind, 1004a
Common-looking man, 542b
Commonplace aspect on life, 515a
  I am weary of the, 661a
  life, 734a
  people dislike tragedy, 896a
  poetry of the, 744a
  present estate too, 847a
  things and characters, 428b
  unassuming, of nature, 407b
Commons faithful to their system, 397b
  House of, thrives on criticism, 871b
  kings lords and, 435b
Common-sense, rich in saving, 553a
Commonwealth affairs, 154a
  caterpillars of the, 139a
  lie abroad for the, 213b
  meddle in the, 86a
  pays the freight, 889b
Commonwealths, seed of, 772b
Communicate their mind, 286b
  things worth observation, 300b
  without coalescing, 992a
Communicated by contagion, 617b
  good the more, 256b
Communicatest with dreams, 208a
Communicating, intention of, truth, 424b
Communication of immediate pleasure, 423b
  of the dead, 945a
  of truth, 423b
  unreserved, 359b
Communications, evil, corrupt, 1061b
Communicative, infinitely, 913a
Communing, all our deep, 583a
Communings with nature, 711a
Communion of the Holy Ghost, 1062a
  statesmen flock to, 728b
  that will not grow strange, 730a
  with her visible forms, 470b
Communism, support of advocate of, 919b
Communist, what is a, 441b
Communities, individualities may form, 512b
  industrialized, 910b
  social forces flow over, 700a
Community, best political, 26b
  by the ears, 445b
  in process of dissolution, 860a
  is like a ship, 641b
  marriage a, 714a
  members of the human, 922a
  of place, 26a
  of power, 770b
  of thought, 697a
  privileges which, affords, 874b
  right of the, to regulate, 779b
  rules the, has evolved, 875b
  standing in the, 758a

Community, world, 983b
Commuter, definition of, 984b, 990b
Compact between North and South, 517a
  imagination all, 142b
  majority, 642a
  we make with our fellow, 505b
Compacted, sweets, lie, 232b
Companies, militia, with shotted guns, 760b
Companion, agreeable, on a journey, 43b
  better, than fear, 561b
  dog to be, 417b
  lone man's, 598b
  no better, than the rifle, 628b
  none is like the mind, 95b
  of mean souls, 370a
  peaceful and sweet, 288a
  regarded as a, in ours, 492b
  sad, 203b
  so companionable as solitude, 590a
  to owls, 1031b
Companionable as solitude, 590a
Companioned years, 876a
Companionless strengthless, 16a
Companions, call your, 556b
  few select, 300a
  for middle age, 120a
  gloomy, of disturbed imagination, 1001b
  in misery, 46b
  in my days of childhood, 428b
  innocence and health, 355b
  keep pace with his, 590b
  lovely, 439a
  musing on, gone, 414a
  of our journey, 869b
  of the spring, 378a
  offers of service by boon, 576a
  rather have as, 641b
  slept, 523b
  thou'dst unfold, 189b
  true who studied with me, 401b
Companionship, accident counts much in, 696a
  flag is, 563b
  in peace with honour, 202b
  of waxen vines, 947b
Company, crowds without, 369b
  delighting in your, 999b
  faithful dog shall bear him, 316a
  G, I belong to, 669b
  good, and good discourse, 236a
  good, in a journey, 235b
  great multitude or small, 1065b
  high-lived, 354b
  his, an everlasting pleasure, 29a
  is Spartan, 40b
  jocund, 409a
  keep no bad, 356b
  keeps much company, 284a
  live always in best, 419a
  lost in idle, 284a
  merges into the family, 843a
  no figure in, 338a
  none but women and one parson, 284b
  not so much to enjoy, 337a
  of just and righteous men, 17a
  poverty parts good, 417a
  tell me thy, 108a
  thou keepest, 158a
  tone of the, 323a
  villanous, 151a
  worst of the, 295a
Comparable, new is not, 1066a

Comparative or superlative degree, 579a
Compar'd to Bononcini, 323a
Compare as day with night, 629a
  great things with small, 36a
  thee to a summer's day, 204b
Compared, men, with gods, 35b
Comparison, no, no judgment, 361b
Comparisons are odious, 83b, 216b
  make no, 356b
  thing of contrasts and, 665a
Compass, a narrow, 242a
  mind my, and my way, 326b
  of fifty pounds a year, 284b
  of the notes, 278b
  patience may, anything, 89a
  truth lies within a little, 303b
  wide, round be fetched, 573a
Compass'd by the inviolate sea, 553a
  dangers, round, 257a
Compassed about with a cloud, 1063b
Compasses, stiff twin, 216b
Compassion and sacrifice, 977a
  bowels of, 1064b
  had, on him, 1057a
  on son of her womb, 1047b
  to the poor, 262a
  words of perfidious, 773b
Compassionate pity in this life, 774a
Compassionating those who hold in bondage, 398b
Compatriots, all men my, 100b
Compeer, without a, among swindles, 676b
Compelled to keep on his guard, 729a
Compels, neither, you or me, 345b
Compensation in ever-growing calm, 774b
  world of, 538b
Compensations, paltry, 544b
Competence, health peace and, 317b
Competency lives longer, 143b
Competent judge, 235a
Competition and mutual envy, 229a
  battle of, 594a
Complacencies of the peignoir, 906a
Complacency and satisfaction, 430a
  thoughtlessness optimism, 807a
Complain, I heard him, 302b
  no use to grumble and, 745a
  of deception of the world, 500b
  of ingratitude, 341b
  of injustice of government, 399a
  of oppression, 444b
  of thee I must, 259b
  those who do not, 428a
  wherefore the poor, 427a
Complaining and attacking one another, 618a
  soft, flute, 278b
  wild and weak, 620a
Complains, a narrow wind, all day, 647b
  of his judgment, 265a
  of his memory, 265a
Complaint, most fatal, of all, 985b
  young man's heart's, 608a
Complaints are many and various, 972b
  done with indoor, 608b

Complaints, dust and soot of your, 743b
Complaisance in their hearts, 106a
  servile imitation and, 559b
Complaisant, how humble and how, 303a
Complete and self-sufficient form, 26b
  chapter, repeat a, 342a
  clad in, steel, 247b
  ignorance of everything, 958b
  more than, steel, 123a
  single song and carelessly, 735b
  steel, dead corse in, 172a
  symmetrical, colossal, 676b
Completed, melancholia of everything, 727a
Completely, do evil, and cheerfully, 273a
Completeness of the wild pigeon, 940b
Completer, stolen kisses much, 448a
Completion of their appointed rounds, 19b
Complex, amoebas were not, 854a
  built for two, 928a
  fate being an American, 717b
  problem of the head, 811a
  sound matter in the, 431b
Complexion, adulterate, 214b
  fresh, 208b
  is perfect gallows, 208b
  mislike me not for, 144a
  of the sky, 139b
  of virtue, 72a
  or form or behavior, 505b
  sex or, 517a
  smirch'd, 155a
Complexions, coarse, 248a
Complexities of circumstance and character, 910b
Complicated state of mind, 683a
Complicators, terrible, 665b
Complies against his will, 239b
Compliment, acquaintance that begins with a, 769b
  he began to, 1020a
  heartfelt, 425b
  highest, to the first, 340b
  him about looking young, 446b
  something like a kiss, 498a
Compliments, captain of, 136a
  hollow, and lies, 259b
  only pleasant things to pay are, 768b
Compos'd, decent limbs, 313b
Composed, cruel but, and bland, 622b
  of some ten parts or more, 49b
  of the same particles, 613b
Composer, most imaginative, of fiction, 761a
Composers, by the, they love, 837b
Composing, in, run your pen through, 419b
Composite things, 12a
Composition and fierce quality, 190b
  not a prize, 20a
  regular and orderly, 336b
Compositions, read over your, 341a
  surpassed the rest of his, 431a
Composture stolen from excrement, 203b
Compound for sins, 238b
  of villanous smell, 180b

Conscience does make cowards of us all, 174b
  equity is according to, 227a
  freedom of, 679a
  guardian in the individual, 875b
  guide to man is his, 870a
  has not, in everything, 346a
  hath thousand several tongues, 128b
  is deposit of prohibitions, 930b
  irritate your, 801b
  is a coward, 354b
  laws of, 98a
  live without, 653a
  makes egotists, 768a
  next to a good, 236b
  no more with gallantry, 381b
  of a good, 142b
  of her worth, 257b
  of my race, 916b
  of the king, 174a
  opiates for the, 965a
  policy sits above, 203a
  private, for the guide, 279a
  reason and, of men, 952
  sat alone with my, 733b
  spiral of his, 926b
  still and quiet, 211b
  that dwells in the heart, 31a
  that spark of celestial fire, 366b
  tongue confuted by his, 243b
  upright and stainless, 76a
  wakes despair, 255a
  with injustice is corrupted, 125b
Conscience-calm'd, thou be, 480a
Consciences, cheveril, that will stretch, 224b
  guilty, make cowards, 28b
  historian of fine, 774a
Conscient reason, 722a
Conscientious, matters purely, 262a
  sensible and, men, 339b
Conscious and deliberate, 943b
  energy of selection, 809b
  men are the universe become, 774b
  of no fault, 1010a
  of none, 65b
  of rectitude, 37a
  of virtue, a mind, 37a
  poet, and unconscious, 943b
  something to resent the yoke, 545b
  stone to beauty grew, 503a
  thoughts and actions, 670b
  virtue bold, 312b
  water, 263a
Consciousness in relation with the divine, 617a
  of freedom, 402a
  of having done a day's work, 332a
Conscripted unvictorious ones, 937b
Consecrate their hopes and thine, 803b
  to thee, 431b
  we cannot, this ground, 541a
  with thine own hues, 465a
Consecration and poet's dream, 409b
Consent, exists by geological, 930b
  full reference to one, 154b
  I will ne'er, 457b
  of the governed, 373a
  silence gives, 355a
  taxed without, 353a
  to be slain, 32a

Consent, without, been only tried, 226a
Consenting feet, cadence of, 967a
Consents, poverty not my will, 137b
Consequence, applause is of great, 342b
  betray's in deepest, 194b
  of his crime, 380b
  thing of, 67b
  'tis almost, 648a
  trammel up the, 195b
Consequences, I note and enjoy noting, 720a
  logical, are scarecrows of fools, 633b
  of ignorance, 516a
  serious and alarming, 366b
  there are, 662b
  will be the same, 370b
Consequense, ov no great, 595a
Conservatism, argument of, 502b
Conservative government, 512a
  liberal and, parties, 921a
  little liberal or a little, 684a
  when old, 881a
Conservatives, true, 936a
Consider anything only don't cry, 659a
  day of adversity, 1043a
  end in everything, 269b
  her ways and be wise, 1038b
  how much he has, 301a
  how my light is spent, 251a
  the lilies, 1051b
  the little mouse, 30a
  them most honest and safe, 376a
  this as said to himself, 49a
  too curiously, 179a
  what precedes and follows, 46a
  when I, life, 275b
  your honour, 69b
  your origin, 76a
Considerable, least, man, 1002a
Consideration, Aristotelian, 98b
  equal, for all, 618a
  like angel came, 154a
  of mankind, 366b
Considered present state of things, 55b
Consigned in every place, 337b
Consimility of fancy, 228a
Consistency is a paste jewel, 843a
  is the hobgoblin, 501b
Consistent, noble trustworthy nor, 832a
Consistently inappropriate, 995b
Consists in fear and retreat, 290a
  in mutual and partaken bliss, 248a
  liberality, less in giving, 288b
  of a little flesh, 66a
  of men women and Herveys, 322a
Consolation, edifying words of, 822b
  ever comes too soon, 346a
  in the thanks of the Republic, 541b
  mediocrity has no greater, 379a
  thought of suicide, 727a
  to the wretched, 46b
  we derive from transitoriness, 514b
  well-meant but miserable, 670a
Consoler of the lonely, 666b
  in the depths of affliction, 538b
Consonant, surrendered every, 713a

Consonants, only, and vowels, 947a
Conspicuous by his absence, 63b
  consumption, 775b
  in times of disaster, 56a
  waste, 776b
  wastefulness, 775b
Conspiracies, plots and, of history, 773b
Conspiracy, O, 167a
Conspire against him, less likely to, 25a
  causes which, to blind, 310b
  to grasp this sorry scheme, 533b
Constable with lifted hand, 810a, 854a
Constabulary duty's to be done, 682b
Constancy and valor our shield, 869b
  hope, in wind, 452a
  in a good cause, 240a
  lives in realms above, 421a
  of a friend, 813a
  of the women who love me, 764b
  plain and uncoined, 156b
  to purpose, 512b
Constant as Penelope, 1013b
  as the northern star, 167b
  as various, 972a
  but yet woman, 150a
  cares to increase his store, 352b
  drinking, fresh with, 267a
  force for muddlement, 719b
  friendship is, 157a
  goddess, and glad, 680b
  heart, 999b
  image of creature beloved, 164b
  in human sufferings, 916b
  in nature were inconstancy, 267b
  is a wondrous excellence, 206b
  joy of sudden discovery, 908a
  labor of uniform kind, 593b
  most, of all friends, 655b
  nothing, but inconstancy, 295a
  obeying him, 243b
  repair, keep friendship in, 339b
  to me and so kind, 479a
  to one thing, 157b
  use of actions, 64b
Constantinople, patriarch of, 424b
  Russians shall not have, 635a
Constellation, bright, 374b
  noblest, 626a
  of O'Ryan, 643b
Constellations, want the, any nearer, 609a
Constituents, strictest union with, 359b
Constitute a book, 52a
Constitution, act against the, 353a
  American, most wonderful work, 534a
  between friends, 703b
  British, most subtle organism, 534a
  did not contain word democracy, 865b
  doctor who knows her, 596a
  does not provide, 964a
  duty to support its, 842a
  federal, 516a
  follows th' flag, 834a
  genius of the, 335a
  glittering generalities, 490b
  in actual operation, 331b
  in all its provisions, 528b
  is all sail and no anchor, 494a
  like the British, 705a

Country, serve thy, and mankind, 666a
serves his, best, 4b
serves his, well, 324b
set a, free, 370b
shrink from service of his, 370a
slow sort of, 658a
so virtuous and so wise, 783a
socialism in one, 905a
socialism in capitalist, 850b
soil of an unknown, 842a
that, is the richest, 605b
they touch our, 364a
they've undone his, 299b
to be cherished, 557a
tremble for my, 373b
trouble running any, 895a
undiscovered, 174b
upon earth, 497b
vow to thee my, 788b
when my, grows polite, 816a
with all her faults my, 362b
with its institutions, 539a
Countryman looked for his ass, 109a
Countrymen, all one, 117a
are mankind, 517a
first in hearts of his, 384a
friends Romans, 168a
most unscottified of, 341a
my, Kiltartan's poor, 826a
my, what a fall was there, 168b
Romans, and lovers, 168a
Country's battles, fight our, 1004b
blood, guiltless of his, 348b
by their, wishes bless'd, 351b
call, heard his, 819a
cause, no omen but his, 5a
ends thou aim'st at be thy, 211b
fame, raise his, 96a
fashion, 156b
flag, spare your, 527b
good, I do love my, 202b
good, left for our, 304b
heart, here in the, 800a
historian of my, woes, 6a
mind, touch my, 897b
pleasant, earth, 140a
pride, peasantry their, 355b
ruin, never to see my, 289b
slain in your, wars, 129a
stead, in their suff'ring, 23b
stood for, glory fast, 414a
treasure, squandering of, 561b
Countryside, smiling and beautiful, 782a
Counts, first step which, 327a
his sure gains, 412b
Paris, an author, 287a
County Guy the hour is nigh, 417a
here lies the, slain, 138a
of Warwick, 273b
Couple, it must, or must die, 616a
new-married, 430a
of wallets, 35a
Couple-colour as a brindled cow, 724a
Coupled, stand, for common flight, 87a
Courage a virtue, 290a
and gaiety, 753b
and skill to him that can get it, 274b
be of good, 1047a
bear his, up, 279b
bear with a good, 1065a
bear with, and submission, 633a
blend of, integrity, 981b
brother do not stumble, 582a

Courage exhibited from birth, 27a
fear they call, 855a
fires us, love and joy, 308b
foes proclaim, 277a
fresh, 618a
good of the agent to, 282a
greatness magnanimity, 566b
Heraclean cheerfulness and, 751a
in our own trouble, 661b
in peace, 763a
is better than fear, 685b
is resistance to fear, 678a
is the price life exacts, 981b
is to feel daily daggers, 889d
man, 136b
mercy, kindness mirth, 843b
moral, 705a
mounteth, 147b
my little spark of, dies, 1009a
never to submit, 252a
of conscience, 490a
of heart or holiness, 849a
of making a choice, 858b
of New England, 490a
of the Negro, 562b
screw your, to the sticking-place, 196a
soul nor hold thy strength, 637a
species of, 282a
stout rather than live in snuff, 111b
strong and of good, 1026a
tale to tell of the, 842b
to do it, 20b
to face it, 925b
to forget, 645a
true, consists in fear, 290a
two o'clock in morning, 400a
unmatchable, 155b
weak in, 386a
what is virtue, wit, 303b
which is not true courage, 973b
without ferocity, 451b
Courageous captain of compliments, 136a
captains, 1012a
Couriers, horsed upon sightless, 195b
stays these, 19b
Course, arrest your, 463a
betake myself to that, 286a
chances change by, 118a
each act a, 304a
earth's diurnal, 405b
finished my, 1063b
icy current and compulsive, 189a
impede its quiet, 594b
impediments in fancy's, 183b
in how to live, 805b
my preudunt, is steadied, 601a
of human events, 373a
of nature is art of God, 240a
of one revolving moon, 277a
of true love, 141a
of ultimate extinction, 537b
served to him course by, 868b
war in its, 15b
westward the, of empire, 306b
world's, will not fail, 629b
Coursers like a page of poetry, 647a
Courses from the shore, 610b
like ships steer their, 238b
of the stars, 471b
Court a mistress she denies, 218b
as of Angels, 502a
confession in open, 376b
death keeps his, 139b

Court, envious, 159b
in perpetual session, 927b
King Ballyhoo's, 940b
let her alone she will, you, 218b
love rules the, 413b
more I, it, 261b
news, rogues talk of, 193b
of justice, 3a
of justice in his breast, 555b
pale, in beauty and decay, 467b
rivers and forests, 36b
search in every prince's, 582a
them, men despise those who, 20b
threshold of Jove's, 246b
Courted by all the winds, 260a
in your girls again be, 1013a
Courteous, as, to a man, 505b
retort, 163a
Courtesies, small sweet, 346b
Courtesy, by, a man, 669b
candy deal of, 149b
fine sense which men call, 587a
grace of God is in, 849a
greater man the greater, 555a
grows chill, 703b
heart of, 115b
is the true alchemy, 638b
joints but none for, 181b
mirror of all, 81a, 210b
no defence like elaborate, 842a
pink of, 357b
sinit is ruled be, 837a
stole, 151a
sweet, has done its most, 680b
time enough for, 508a
very pink of, 107b
wins woman, 555a
Courtezan, word love in mouth of a, 504b
Court-house, Appomattox, 643a
Courtier, heel of the, 178b
Courtier's soldier's eye, 175a
Courtiers, our, were good, 298b
upon every road, 565b
Courting new impressions, 702a
Courtliness and the desire of fame, 555b
Courtly nurture, men of, 628a
suit, wear a, 591a
Courts, American, of justice, 515b
camps and, 522a
day in thy, 1035b
forsaken, 985b
justice in their, 566a
of princes, preferments in, 28b
prophecies of what, will do, 709a
shown in, at feasts, 248a
where Jamshyd gloried, 531b
Courtship love matrimony, 588a
requires long and constant, 561a
Cousin of the forest-green, 478b
Cousins, given two, to the war, 664b
his sisters and his, 682a
Covenant between me and the earth, 1022b
with death, 517a, 1046a
words of the, 1025a
Covenants, open, of peace, 771a
Covent Garden, wickedness about, 429a
Cover dunghill with tapestry, 109a
friendless bodies, 225b
great deal of country in books, 725a
her face, 226a
l, all, 898a

Cruel disintegration of slow years, 899b
  doubts more, than truths, 270a
  for a woman, 930b
  love is more, than lust, 692a
  mercies of wicked are, 1039a
  only to be kind, 177a
  place, England is a, 598b
  rule, better no rule than, 9b
  scorn, crowned in, 528b
  sea so, 76a
  snare, 109b
  war is, 613b
Cruellest lies often told in silence, 749b
  month, April called the, 991a
  month, April is the, 943b
Cruell'st she alive, 164a
Crueltie and ambition of man, 111b
Cruelty, direst, 195a
  hanging too good said Mr., 274b
  has a human heart, 387b
  of pirates, 601b
  soldier without, 660a
  to load a falling man, 212a
Cruise, on our last, 749b
Crumb, craved no, 685a
  just a, to me, 646b
  memorial, 648a
Crumble crumble voiceless things, 911b
Crumbled out again to his atomies, 217a
Crumbles, my world, to nothing, 447a
Crumbs, fed with their, 515a
  from their masters' table, 1053a
Crumpetty tree, 581b
Crumpled horn, cow with the, 1020b
Crunch, crackers to, 714b
Crusaders from some infernal clime, 534b
Cruse, neither did the, of oil fail, 1029a
  oil in a, 1028b
Crush amang the stoure, 391a
  the infamous thing, 325a
Crush'd and bruis'd together, 309a
  sweet poison, 247a
Crushed ideals, 878a
  incensed or, 120a
  or trodden, 120a
Crust, nightmare, 992b
  of bread, 953a
  of bread and liberty, 320a
  of earth in earth, 634a
  thin, over a volcano, 783b
  to break through, 939b
  water and a, 480b
Cry against all banks, 444b
  all, and no wool, 83b
  anything only don't, 659b
  creation's, goes up on high, 817a
  every, of every man, 387b
  far, to Lochow, 416b
  fear of having to, 367b
  for being born, 121b
  for hire, 42a
  gladiators', 525a
  good, a great comfort to a woman, 510b
  great, but little wool, 83b
  great, in Egypt, 1024a
  harlot's, 388a
  havoc, 168a
  he'll be sure to, 1016a
  hounds join in glorious, 332b

Cry, in bed we, 263a
  infant's, of fear, 387b
  kitten and, 150b
  liberty, 251a
  little need to, 966b
  man's image and his, 824b
  mum, 109a
  my eyes out, 106a
  my speech as the best thing, 285b
  no language but a, 552a
  nor swoon'd nor utter'd, 550b
  not when his father dies, 338b
  of a child by the roadway, 825a
  of a thousand souls, 890a
  of Absence Absence, 946b
  of bugles going by, 795a
  of energies and hopes, 707b
  of his hounds, 472b
  of home, 994b
  of the critic, 668b
  one haughty, 914b
  out the loudest of its abuse, 283a
  raise a hue and, 105a
  scandal and the, 549b
  Susanna don't you, for me, 636a
  the more it made them, 357b
  there little girl don't, 745b
  too big to, 540a
  war is still the, 452b
  was still more hay, 748a
Cry-babies of the western world, 942a
Crye, moche, and no wull, 83b
Cryin' at the lock, 559a
Crying, first voice was, 49b
  first voice I uttered was, 1065b
  in the wilderness, 1050a
  made her eyes more bright, 801b
  need in humbler ranks, 641b
  over a husband, 814a
  solitary in lonely places, 762a
Cryptic mirth, met rancor with a, 846a
Crystal brooks, golden sands and, 216a
  light, sailed on a river of, 747a
  springs should solace me, 236a
  stair, build the trout a, 892b
  what youth deemed, 575a
Cubia, alone in, 834b
Cubic inch of space, 610b
Cubit, one, unto his stature, 1051b
Cuccu, lhude sing, 999a
Cuckold lives in bliss, 188a
Cuckoo jug-jug, 213a
  mocks married men, 134a
  shall I call thee bird, 409a
Cuckoo-buds of yellow hue, 134a
Cuckoos are cock-sure, 760b
Cucullus non facit monachum, 1010a
Cucumbers, cold as, 228a
  extracting sunbeams out of, 295b
  garden of, 707a, 1045a
  scarecrow in garden of, 1066b
Cud, chew the, and are silent, 361a
Cudgel his own jackass, 708a
  thy brains, 178a
Cudgel's, what wood a, of, 238b
Cue, twisted, 685a
Cuffs, imagination at, with senses, 294b
Culled flowers, nosegay of, 100b
  picked and, 89b
Culprit, affect the, 940a
Cult called Christianity, 705b

Cultivate gift of taciturnity, 743b
  our garden, 325a
  peace and harmony, 367a
  spirit of subordination, 367a
  such a measure of equanimity, 744b
  the mind, 20a
Cultivated and improved, 424b
  classes, malady of the, 617b
  manners, learning without, 932a
  underrated nobleman, 685b
Cultivates the golden mean, 38b
Cultivation, fruit of great, 338a
  of the physical world, 538b
Cultural proper, ivory tower of the, 883a
Culture, dozen years to implant basic, 971a
  essential to high, 637b
  French, 728a
  Germany ruins, 729a
  great law of, 472b
  hall-mark of the national, 908a
  highest stage in moral, 530a
  is in its finest flower, 797b
  not measured by greatness, 753a
  nothing but education and, 21a
  or any knowledge, 611a
  pursue, in bands, 804a
  the acquainting ourselves, 623b
Cultured critics, 672b
  prosperous and, life, 905b
  word, 817a
Cumbrous, archaic, and ineffective, 776b
Cummin, mint and anise and, 1054a
Cumnor Hall, walls of, 368b
Cunning hand, sweet and, 164a
  livery of hell, 185a
  old, attorney, 327a
  passages, 943b
  point of, to borrow, 120b
  point of, to shape answer, 120b
  right hand forget her, 1038a
  seldom gain their ends, 1003a
  sharpening of sense of, 727b
  sin cover itself, 158b
  strong in, 386a
  times, 145b
  tyrant, first, 538a
  valiant and, in fence, 165b
  which we in England call, 120b
Cunning'st pattern, 190a
Cup, between the, and the lip, 223a
  bitterest, of sorrow, 857a
  blue lake brims her, 796b
  clos'd in my love's hand, 138a
  colour in the, 1040b
  come fill the, 531a
  come fill up my, 417b
  death at bottom of the, 690a
  decided over a, of coffee, 381b
  drink a, to Scotland, 489b
  give a, of water, 483b
  glory in a shallow, 533a
  he took the, 1055a
  leave a kiss but in the, 219a
  let this, pass from me, 1055a
  life's bitter, 1014a
  made up of loveliness, 499a
  of hot wine, 202a
  of Samian wine, 458b
  of strength, 596a
  offering his, 532b
  quaffed out of a golden, 772b
  runneth over, 1033b
  secret, of serious thought, 405b
  sun in a golden, 827b

Dear, to me more, 357a
  too, for my possessing, 206a
  we were, we were leal, 762a
  what is so sweet and, 780b
  wisdom is never, 562a
  work good-night, 543a
Dear-bought wisdom, 309a
Dearer, honour is, than my life,
  106a
  than to himself, 219a
Dearest and the best, 789a
  do not think me rude, 893a
  foe in heaven, 171a
  in the grave, 500a
  inheritance, 1001b
  never guess, 876b
  one has perished, 467b
  thing he owed, 194b
  what costs, is most valued,
  106b
  wish to gain, failed my, 615a
  wishes fixed on objects, 424a
Dearie, flew o'er me and my,
  393a
Dear-lov'd lad convenience snug,
  391b
Dearly let or let alone, 231b
Dearness only that gives value,
  370b
Dears, lovely, her noblest work,
  391b
Dearth of woman's tears, 529b
  whom, hath slain, 217b
Death a fast approaching end,
  596b
  a hideous show, 622b
  a necessary end, 167b
  a state of nothingness, 20b
  accustom'd sight of, 162a
  achiev'd by other's, 148b
  after life, 113a
  after life is, 693b
  after the first, 997a
  aims with fouler spite, 231b
  all in the valley of, 553b
  amiable lovely, 148a
  anchor of a love is, 730a
  and chance and thee O time,
  249b
  and failure and fame, 781b
  and his brother sleep, 464b
  and i will coquette, 894b
  and life are one, 848b
  and sorrow will be companions,
  869b
  and taxes, 332a
  and that vast forever, 598a
  and the Roman populace, 525a
  and time bring on the prime,
  742a
  angel of, has been abroad, 561b
  angel of, spread his wings, 456a
  any man's, diminishes me, 218a
  arise from, 217b
  armed with a new terror, 435b
  arms of cool-enfolding, 610a
  artist is in danger of, 982b
  as deep as ever, can be, 652a
  attentive eyes closed in, 338a
  be not proud, 217b
  be of such a nature, 20b
  before you taste of, 359b
  black fancies and thoughts of,
  773b
  blaze forth, of princes, 167b
  blessing men fly from, 626a
  borders upon our birth, 220b
  breaks every bond, 290a

Death, bridegroom in my, 201b
  brief as water falling will be,
  949a
  broke the vital chain, 338a
  brother of quiet, 122a
  brother to, 122a
  brought, into the world, 252a,
  678a
  by beauty made amends, 838b
  by inches, 202b
  by the shadow of, 676a
  calls ye to the crowd, 237a
  came with friendly care, 420b
  can not efface, 973a
  cannot slay, 781a
  cares naught for, 243a
  cast a cold eye on life on, 828a
  caught his, 1014a
  choose slavery or, 299b
  closes a man's reputation, 301a
  come, and welcome, 137a
  comes to all, 96a
  cometh soon or late, 493b
  condemn you to, 656a
  could not daunt, 1012a
  could not stop for, 648a
  covenant with, 517a, 1046a
  creation, and love, 897a
  cruel as, 327b
  cruel, is always near, 1000b
  cure for birth and, 807b
  dark, or dreamful ease, 547b
  day of, better than day of birth,
  1042b
  dear beauteous, 272a
  defend to the, 326a
  delicate, 609b
  desertion and, 484b
  devise for thirty pence, 233a
  devours all lovely things, 961b
  die not poor, 217b
  direst shapes of, 628a
  discourse is of, 285a
  disdainfully of, 68b
  disregard for, 983a
  distance from, 70a
  divide life from, 544b
  doom'd to, 278b
  done to, 159a
  draw the trigger at his, 339a
  draws near, 16b
  dread of something after, 174b
  dull cold ear of, 348b
  dunno about, 896a
  eaten to, with rust, 152b
  éclat of, 648a
  eclipsed gayety of nations, 337b
  enviable, 872a
  equal in the presence of, 43a
  equal piece of justice, 240b
  ere slain another, 230a
  ever truly longed for, 546b
  evergreens associated with,
  672b
  exile in the isles of, 688a
  face to meet, with, 572b
  fair in, 146b
  faith by love's bed of, 122b
  faithful unto, 1064b
  fatal asterisk of, 525a
  fear, and pain, 51b
  fear of, 45a
  fear of, has bygone us, 705b
  fear of violent, 229a
  fear, to feel the fog, 572b
  fed on the fullness of, 693b
  fell sergeant, 179b
  follows life, 625a
  for such as he there is no, 654a

Death, foreknowledge of, 691b
  foretaste of, 461a
  forgotten, 984a
  found, in life, 425b
  friend and enemy is, 938b
  friend, how now, 652b
  frightened to, 510a
  from sudden, 1068b
  from, to life, 122b
  gave all that we possess, 705b
  go with anyone to, 879b
  gone to her, 489a
  grim, 226b
  grim, my son and foe, 254b
  half in love with easeful, 481b
  happened in his berth, 487b
  happy, 84b
  happy people not afraid of,
  823a
  has broach'd him, 377a
  has shaken out the sands, 472a
  hate is like, and avarice, 490b
  hath a thousand doors, 226a
  hath no more dominion, 1059b
  hath so many doors, 226a
  hath ten thousand doors, 226a
  he taketh all away, 627a
  heard name of, 202b
  heaven gives early, 30a
  himself his Maker and angel,
  423b
  homesick unto, 912b
  honours continue after, 34b
  how wonderful is, 464b
  hunt a joy to, 853a
  hymn to own, 148b
  I said, 519a
  i' the other eye, 166a
  improved by, 851b
  in itself is nothing, 275b
  in life, 550b
  in the pot, 1029a
  in the shadow of, 1036b
  in, they were not divided, 596b,
  1027b
  in, your daylight finish, 574b
  interest in disease and, 883a
  intrench'd, 306a
  is a beautiful adventure, 607b
  is a sleep, 693a
  is always a tragedy, 779a
  is an eternal sleep, 396a
  is at the bottom of the cup,
  690a
  is better still, 486b
  is certain to all, 153b
  is dead, 468a
  is eternal sleep, 23a
  is life, 23a
  is master, 731a
  is merciful, 899b
  is no parenthesis, 968b
  is not the worst, 15a
  is only a horizon, 707a
  is only an old door, 910b
  is slumber, 465a
  is that side of life, 884a
  is the ugly fact, 650b
  is the veil, 465b
  is to the dead, 652a
  jaws of, 103a, 553b
  just, kind umpire, 124b
  keeps his pale court, 467b
  keeps, his court, 139b
  kiss of, 864b
  land of the shadow of, 1045b
  last enemy destroyed is, 1061b
  laugh myself to, 209b
  lays icy hand on kings, 237b

Determine, of material nature, 340b
  which is me, 763b
Determined by community of place, 26a
  so long is he, not to do it, 282a
  to know beans, 590b
Determines or indicates his fate, 589b
Determinism, history abhors, 977a
Detest offense, 281a
  the Sabbath-day, 677b
Detestable curiosity, damnable and, 530b
  man is most, 680a
Detestation of the high, 580a
Detested her first husband, 768a
Detests, fashion she, 165a
  my heart, him, 4b
Detraction stirs no sigh, 705b
Detractions, hear, 157b
Deus vult, 1010a
Develop faculties and intelligence, 641b
Development, opportunity of autonomous, 771a
  uneven economic, 850b
Develops, grief, powers of mind, 856a
Deviates, Shadwell never, into sense, 277b
Device, banner with the strange, 522a
  one for all that is our, 131b, 496b
Devil a monk would be, 89a
  abash'd the, stood, 256a
  acquaintances can be the, 842a
  all haste is from the, 1010a
  and all his works, 1068b
  apology for the, 672a
  as a roaring lion, 1064b
  at everything, 106a
  author of confusion, 224a
  beggar outride the, 126a
  bird or, 545a
  black as the, 384a
  brook'd the eternal, 166b
  builds a chapel, 291b
  cite Scripture, 144a
  damn thee black, 199a
  defy the, 165b
  did grin, 422b
  dream of the, 451b
  dress her not, 201b
  eat with the, 82a
  enter the prompter's box, 877b
  every man was God or, 277a
  fears a painted, 196b
  for all, 95a
  give, his due, 104b
  had done for the rest, 750a
  hath not an arrow, 460a
  have all the good tunes, 376b
  having seen the, 676b
  he's a very, 165b
  how then was the, dressed, 427a
  is a gentleman, 192a
  is asleep, 763b
  is gone to look, 427a
  language of the, 473b
  let us call thee, 187b
  looks less terrible than he, 747b
  match for the, 980a
  mischievous, 672a
  must be in that jackdaw, 451a
  outride the, 126a
  play the, 127b
  poor, get thee gone, 345b

Devil, resist the, 1064a
  ringing his knell, 426b
  sends cooks, 91b
  shame the, 89b
  sugar o'er the, 174a
  synonym for the, 239b
  take her, 261a
  take the hindmost, 228a
  talk of the, 425a
  was sick, 89a
  was well, 89a
  wear black, 176a
  what the, was he doing, 271a
  when thou wast made a, 225b
  whispered behind the leaves, 817a
  will come, 123b
  world flesh and the, 1068b
  would build a chapel, 86b
Devil-and-all to pay, 106b
Devildoms of Spain, 556a
Devilish deeds, excus'd his, 255b
  earthly sensual, 1064a
  sly, tough and, 578b
Devill, eat with the, 82a
Devil's back, got over the, 90a
  foot, who cleft the, 215b
  leavings, 321b
  madness war, 877b
Devils being offended, 187a
  in Worms, 86b
  Lord transformed to, 74a
  more, than hell can hold, 142b
  place the, dwell in, 240b
  to ourselves, 182b
Devils'-triumph and sorrow for angels, 567b
Devis'd to keep strong in awe, 128b
  to set a gloss on deeds, 203a
Devise, brain may, laws, 143b
  for thirty pence my death, 233a
  some scheme of life, 939a
  wit write pen, 132b
Devised, plan is, 44a
Deviseth, man's heart, his way, 83a
Devocioun, farewell my, 79a
Devoid of sense and motion, 253b
Devon, Dons sight, 803b
  man, Drake he was a, 803b
  seas, ruled the, 803b
Devote, now to death, 258b
  to daily wants, 25a
Devoted flame, love's, 440a
  to his country upon earth, 497b
  to practicable objects, 613b
  vizier, 673a
Devotee of the gospel of getting on, 764b
Devotees, no genuine, 446b
Devotion, capable of a, to anything, 687a
  despair the twin-born of, 692a
  earnest and entire, 561b
  ignorance the mother of, 224a
  increased, to that cause, 541a
  last full measure of, 541a
  of a lifetime, 769a
  of the patriot soldier, 666a
  perpetual, to business, 749b
  respects piety and, 496a
  still prayer of, 440b
  sweet look of, 701b
  to God almighty, 367b
  to organization, 863b
  to something afar, 468b
  to virtue, 812b
  universal, 446b

Devotion's visage, 174a
Devotions, beheld your, 1059a
Devour, do not, thy heart, 72b
  jaws of darkness, 141a
  seeking whom he may, 1064b
  threat'ning to, me, 255a
  treacherous bait, 158a
  widows' houses, 1056a
Devoured, envious people were, 71b
  small, great ones, 203b
Devouring forces, mercy of all, 917b
  of the weak, 615a
Devours all lovely things, 961b
  his own kind, 374a
  the shore, 963a
Devout, disciples, gaze and adore, 654b
  nun, and pure, 246a
Dew, age finds out was, 575a
  begotten drops of, 1031b
  bespangling herb and tree, 231a
  bright with autumn, 471a
  chaste as morning, 261a
  cool, in his little bill, 528b
  debauchee of, 646a
  fades awa' like morning, 1013a
  fed it with silver, 466b
  from heath-flower dash'd the, 415a
  gently drinking up the, 687b
  glad for the fall of, 764a
  honey-heavy, of slumber, 167a
  hours of, 741a
  into a sea of, 747a
  like the, on the mountain, 415a
  mists of silver, 465b
  not think we dew, 713a
  o'ertrip the, 146b
  of thy birth, 113a
  of thy youth, 1037a
  plenty of, 954a
  plenty to, and did it, 595a
  rain'd a ghastly, 548b
  roses full of, 745b
  shed a honeyed, 7a
  soft falls the, on the dead, 636b
  sun drew the morning, 281a
  thaw and resolve into a, 170b
  timely, of sleep, 255b
  under the sod and the, 637b
  upon a thought, 458b
  vale which the, cumbers, 707a
  walks o'er the, 170a
  was on the lawn, 922b
  will rust them, 186a
  wombe of morning, 113a
  world of fire and, 825a
Dewdrop from lion's mane, 182a
  like, on the rose, 416a
  on its perilous way, 477b
  protects the lingering, 412a
  seek, 141a
  starlight and, are waiting, 636b
  time's corrosive, 634a
  woman like a, 569b
Dewdrops gathered in a brickyard, 801b
  which sun impearls, 256b
Dewey feel discouraged, 713a
  was the admiral, 713a
  was the morning, 713a
  were the regent's eyes, 713a
Dew-pearled, hillside's, 567a
Dews, fall like, 934a
  fresh, of night, 248b
  mother of, 327b
  of solace, 747a

Ear, eye not seen nor, heard, 1066b
  few that only lend their, 122a
  few whom he whispers in the, 572a
  filled with hearing, 1042a
  first the blade then the, 1055b
  flea in mine, 89a
  for verbal delicacies, 908a
  give every man thy, 171b
  good, in music, 142a
  hark in thine, 193a
  hath not heard, 142b
  heard and blessed me, 1031a
  hearing, and seeing eye, 1040a
  I was all, 248a
  I will enchant thine, 131a
  jest's prosperity lies in, 134a
  jewel in Ethiop's, 135a
  left voice in Adam's, 257b
  lend neither, nor glance, 464a
  listening, of night, 560b
  more meant than meets the, 246b
  night's dull, 155b
  of Eve, 256a
  of man hath not seen, 142b
  open vowels tire the, 311a
  pierced through the, 186b
  red, 383a
  silk purse out of sow's, 235a
  so tough-gristled, 574b
  softly her warm, lays, 600a
  to my listening, 411a
  unpleasing to a married, 134a
  velvet cap out of a sow's, 235a
  vexing dull, 148a
  voice so pleasing on their, 6b
  whorlèd, 724b
  won the, of Pluto, 245b
Eare, breed in cat's, 94a
  did heare that tong, 114b
  in at tone, out at tother, 78b
  wrong sow by, 94b
Eares, pitchers have wyde, 94a
  woodes have, 80b
Earl by right by courtesy a man, 669b
  can last but few years, 638a
  of Fitzdotterel's eldest son, 638a
  of Murray, 1013a
Earldom, insignificancy and an, 324a
Earlier creation, by right of an, 492a
  later times more aged than, 118b
Earliest birds, charm of, 256a
  drops, to ground, 145b
  sex's, latest care, 343a
Earls, absent conquering, 604a
  daughter of a hundred, 546b
Early bright transient chaste, 281a
  but enduring monument, 468a
  call me, mother dear, 547a
  called a little, 782b
  days, happy those, 272a
  death, heaven gives favourites, 30a
  education sort of amusement, 25a
  familiarity with the Bible, 783a
  following thee, 982a
  had it been, had been kind, 339a
  in the morning, 332a
  in the morning our song, 445a
  memories, 886a
  nothing to him falls, 224b
  pumpkins blow, 581b
  rising, better than, 108b
  rosy-fingered dawn, 5b
  to bed and early to rise, 330b

Early to rise and early to bed, 971b
  too, or too late, 67a
  too, seen unknown, 135a
  village clock, 128b
Early-Gothic smile, 805a
Earn a little and spend a little less, 752b
  bread and I'll eat it, 538a
  his living by the sweat, 589b
  honest livelihood, 74b
  little to, 598a
  that I eat, 161b
Earned a night's repose, 521b
  hatred of entrenched greed, 919a
  in blood of followers, 954b
  with sweat of my brows, 103b
Earnest about these objects, 931b
  between jest and, 105b
  elements of nature, 939b
  frogs die in, 62a
  grasping, capable of, 480a
  I am in, 517a
  life is, 521a
  occupation, 333b
  of victory of labour, 850b
  'twixt, and joke, 386a
Earneth, he that, wages, 1049b
Earning, learning, and yearning, 978a
  power, 978a
Earnings, France poured its, 628b
  unequal, 441b
Earns his freedom and existence, 379b
  whate'er he can, 521b
Ear-piercing fife, 189a
Ears, aged, play truant, 132b
  belly has no, 55a
  blows in our, 155a
  but they hear not, 1037a
  creep in our, 147a
  delighteth the, 1067b
  earth has stopped the, 786a
  hangs from beauty's, 366a
  have, and hear not, 292b
  have heard the holy word, 386b
  he that hath, to hear, 1052b
  hum about mine, 209b
  I have, in vain, 481b
  last echo dies within our, 764a
  lend me your, 168a
  look with thine, 193a
  music to attending, 135b
  no, for what experience has given no access, 729a
  noise of waters in mine, 128a
  of the deaf unstopped, 1046b
  of the groundlings, 175b
  of the old cur, 238b
  of the world, 694b
  pitchers have, 94a
  porches of mine, 172b
  produce loaves of bread, 370a
  ravish'd, 280a
  setting community by the, 445b
  she gave me, 406a
  shout about my, 867b
  speak while their, can hear, 643a
  tongue edifies his, 311b
  trumpet of time in our, 960b
  trusts, less than eyes, 18b
  two, and but a single tongue, 1006b
  two, but only one mouth, 511b
  two, of corn to grow, 295b
  walls have, 80b
  watching the world with his, 974a

Ears, wolf by the, 33a
  woman's, 12b
  words all, took captive, 183a
Earth a stage, 161a
  abideth for ever, 1042a
  affords or grows, 101b
  air, and skies, 407a
  all Danae to the stars, 551a
  all, forgot, 439b
  all, to love, 816b
  ancients of the, 118b
  and all the stars, 607a
  and dust, 127a
  and every common sight, 408a
  and everything that's in it, 820b
  and sky stand presently, 814a
  and the sky, 889a
  axis of the, 536a
  back of the, 1070b
  be, insensible, 258b
  bears no balsam, 712b
  bears thee dead, 152a
  beauty for, too dear, 135a
  being so good, 570a
  belongs to the living, 375b
  betray a niggard, 347b
  bleeding piece of, 167b
  blessed are peacemakers on, 125a
  blessing of, is toil, 757a
  bound in, sea sky, 129a
  bound us to, to rot, 973b
  bounds of, and sky, 616a
  bowels of the, 220b
  brave of all the, 803b
  bridal of the, 232a
  but the frozen echo, 738b
  circles the, 444b
  cold in the, 592a
  cold the, is, 688a
  comes more near the, 190a
  confines of, 397b
  confound all unity on, 198b
  crawl upon the surface of the, 295b
  crawling between, and heaven, 175a
  creatures walk, unseen, 256a
  crust of, in earth, 634a
  daughter of, and water, 466b
  days on, as a shadow, 1029b
  days when, was young, 584b
  deep-delved, 481a
  demi-Atlas of this, 200a
  detached from the, 973b
  did quake, 1055b
  do her homage, 112a
  doth like a snake renew, 467a
  doth not breathe upon, 127b
  dust return to the, 1044a
  embroil the, 287a
  ends of the, 814a
  English, 820b
  expos'd he lies on bare, 280a
  fall to the base, 139a
  feeble worm of the, 272b
  fell to, 522b
  fell upon the, 49b, 1065b
  felt the, move out, 983a
  felt the wound, 258a
  firm and stable, 229b
  first gentleman on, 853a
  flowers appear on the, 1044a
  forcing, teach heaven's employ, 571b
  fragrant the fertile, 256a
  frame in, 113b
  from this, this grave this dust, 111b
  from, to paradise, 892b

Earth, fruits of the, 12b
full of his glory, 1045b
get away from, awhile, 879b
giants in the, 1022b
glance from heaven to, 142b
glory from the, 408a
God created the heaven and the, 1021a
goodly frame the, 173b
hail element of, 935a
happy like heaven above, 626b
has stopped the ears, 786a
hath bubbles as the water, 194b
hear the word of the Lord, 1048a
heaven and, shall pass away, 1054b
heaven on, 255a
heaven or, or hell, 754b
heavens and, reply, 334a
hell on, 765a
her beauty fed my common, 896b
hold the, from heaven away, 712b
I am the poem of, 610b
I will move the, 29b
if another, he could remove this, 54b
if it be in tune, 600a
in an earthy bed, 554a
in this broad, of ours, 609a
inherit the, 1034a, 1050b
is but a small star, 980a
is but a star, 927a
is here so kind, 509b
is not the steadfast place, 845a
is sepulchre, 20b
is the Lord's, 1033b
job on the top of the, 818b
keep silence before him, 1049b
kindly fruits of the, 1068b
knows a little God the rest, 667b
knows no desolation, 639a
labor in the, 373b
lap of, 349a
lards lean, 150a
latter day upon the, 1031a
lay her i' the, 179a
less of, in them than heaven, 415a
less of, than heaven, 499a
let go hold of the, 978b
let the, rejoice, 1036b
lie lightly gentle, 228b
little, for charity, 211b
lords or kings of the, 606a
lowly, to vaulted skies, 597b
made, to tremble, 1046a
majesty of heaven and, 329b
man marks the, with ruin, 454b
marry th' best man on, 841a
master of, and sea, 823b
may run red, 662a
melt this iron, 992a
model of barren, 139b
moon is more interested in, 756b
my footstool, 316a
my late discovered, 934b
mystery of an unknown, 772b
names of, and heaven, 268a
new enchanted, 888b
new heaven and new, 1064b
no sure happiness on, 114a
none on, above her, 396b
not a thing on, 289a
not anything to show, 406b
not gray but rosy, 574b

Earth, not on things on the, 1063a
o'er, there comes a bloom, 489b
o'erwhelm foul deeds, 171a
of majesty, 138b
of the, earthy, 1061b
on does the old, steer, 845b
on the, the broken arcs, 572a
or air, in sea or fire, 170a
over to the squall of time, 960b
peace on, and mercy mild, 334b
peace on the, 560b
peace to men on, 670a
plants suck in the, 267a
pleasant country's, 140a
poetry of, 477b
pomp but, and dust, 127a
power passing from the, 410b
princes of the, 511b
put girdle round, 141b
put on, a little space, 385a
receive her King, 303a
red, the smack and tang, 756a
reign of mind commence on, 440b
replenish the, 1021a
rid the, of him once, 846a
roast him on, 810a
room upon, for honest men, 370b
sad old, must borrow, 754a
salt of the, 1050b
scum o' the, 904b
secret caves of, 559b
seems no more a mother, 49a
serves me to walk upon, 99a
shall not perish from the, 541a
six feet of, 805b
sleepers in that quiet, 592a
so much of, 406a
some hours after the, 121a
soul of wines of the, 839b
speak to the, 1030b
special good to the, 136a
spirits more vast than, 669b
spot men call, 246b
stained red from veins, 774b
stood hard as iron, 649b
sun is coming down to, 638b
sure and firm-set, 196a
swear not by the, 1051a
symbol of, and of storm, 893b
takes wing with heaven, 695b
ten metres thick, 936b
that hides things old, 896b
that is sufficient, 609a
things learned on, 568b
thirsty, soaks up the rain, 267a
this is the last of, 398b
this, realm England, 139a
thou spirit given on, 543b
though, be removed, 1034b
thought nothing good on, 713b
tideless and inert, 737b
till heaven and, pass, 1050b
to, and thee restore, 787b
to earth, 1069b
to, some special good, 136a
to the listening, 299a
touch of, 555a
touching, with rest, 711a
truth crushed to, 471b
turf of fresh, 243b
'twixt heaven and, 753b
unfolds heaven and, 141a
was nigher heaven, 567b
was without form, 1021a
waters and sky, 287a
way of all the, 1026b
wayside inn of, 808b

Earth, weaned away from, 978b
wears the Parthenon, 503b
weary of watching, 649b
while the, remaineth, 1022b
whose table was, 460b
will live by hers, 619b
with her thousand voices, 423a
word of the, 694b
words are daughters of, 336b
would not hold it, 789a
you are more than the, 626b
Earth-born joy renew, 721b
Earthlier happy is rose, 140b
Earthly ball a peopled garden, 378b
brethren, 701b
brown, hooded in an, 736b
dignities, peace above, 211b
godfathers, 132b
grossness quit, 249b
joy, honey of all, 267a
life, dangers of this, 665b
paragon, 204b
power doth then show, 146a
sensual devilish, 1064a
sum of, bliss, 257b
temple, within my, 763b
things heavenly or things, 274a
vigor, 77a
years, 405b
Earth-made implement, 474a
Earthquake, after the wind an, 1029a
and eclipse, 465a
dam'd by an, 676a
the Lord was not in the, 1029a
Earthquakes with thunder and lightning, 675b
Earth's a thief, 203b
crammed with heaven, 520a
degenerate sons, 4a
diurnal course, 405b
foundations fled, 787a
foundations stand, 787b
full rivers, 649b
golden time changed, 40a
green banner shakes, 640a
green fields, 584a
human shores, 479b
imagin'd corners, 217b
last picture, 814b
paths are cleared, 885a
returns for whole centuries, 568b
shadows fly, 468b
smoothness rough, turns, 572a
sweet flowing breast, 936b
the right place for love, 880a
Earths and skies and seas around, 591a
Earthy bed, earth in an, 554a
of the earth, 1061b
Ear-wax, not so much brain as, 182b
Eas'd the putting off, 256a
Ease a heart like a satin gown, 966a
after warre, 113a
age of, 355b
and pleasure, 484b
and plenty, 16b
and speed in doing, 82a
at, in Zion, 909a
believe what we wish with, 276a
brings long, 113a
come to take their, 212b
confess with, 64b
counselled ignoble, 254a
dark death or dreamful, 547b
despise with the greatest, 461a

Evils, greatest of, is poverty, 765b
  in government, 399a
  less grievous of two, 462a
  of all outward, 473a
  of idleness, 47a
  of two, the less, 27a
  old age accompanied with, 59b
  other, will mend, 491a
  past, and future evils, 264b
  present, triumph over it, 264b
  religion could urge mankind to,
    34b
  three great, 325a
  two, monstrous, 946b
  two weak, 161a
  which never arrived, 507a
  with all its threatening, 611a
  working, for another, 7a
Ev'ning, grateful, mild, 256a
Evolution is not a force, 700a
  of things that wouldn't evolve,
    777b
  some call it, 573b
Evolve, things that wouldn't, 777b
Ev'rywhere, sad and dreary, I
    roam, 636a
Ewe lamb, save one little, 1028a
Ewe-milking, lilting at our, 992b
Ex umbris and imaginibus, 496a
Exact day-labour, 251b
  justice to all men, 374b
  line was rigid and, 613a
  man, writing maketh an, 121b
Exacted through taxation, 689a
Exaction becomes ruthless extor-
    tion, 689a
Exactness and discrimination, 340b
  of beauty, 82a
  with, grinds he all, 522b
Exacts, life, for granting peace,
    981b
Exaggerated, reports of my death
    are, 679a
Exaggeration, become crimes by,
    496b
  chargeable with no, 435b
Exaltation from proximity of dis-
    aster, 868a
  of fortune or feeling, 651a
  of the defective, 776a
Exalted, every valley shall be,
    1047a
  humble shall be, 1054a
  ideas of fancy, 22b
  Satan, sat, 253b
  them of low degree, 1056a
Exalts delights or adorns hu-
    manity, 449b
Examination, manners are always
    under, 505a
  minute, of facts, 897b
  of acts of government, 426a
Examine, I pause I, 101b
  laws of heat, 700a
  medicine has to, disease, 57b
Examined a second time, 18b
Example, annoyance of a good,
    678b
  is the best precept, 10b
  more efficacious than precept,
    10b
  of wit, 284b
  results of his own, 48b
  salutary influence of, 337b
  set us a good, 769a
  take an, from others, 33a
  terrible, 257a
  the school of mankind, 361b
  thy stream my great, 266b

Example you with thievery, 203b
Examples, good, of wise men, 55a
  philosophy teaching by, 304a
  provide bad, 265a
Exceed, flies worms and flowers,
    me, 302b
  never, your rights, 344a
Exceedin' accommodatin' char-
    acter, 664b
Exceeding fair she was not, 116b
  poor man, 144a
  wise fair-spoken, 212a
Exceeds, half, the whole, 7a
  man's might, 182a
Excel, age, in pride of life, 620b
  arts in which the wise, 289b
  how much does one man, an-
    other, 31b
  in any profession, 435a
  in rituals and faith, 635a
  the bees for government, 102b
  those he pursues, 41a
  'tis useless to, 343b
Excellence, based on, of perfor-
    mance, 965a
  claim of, is recognized, 20a
  constant is a wondrous, 206b
  fair divided, 147b
  incredible standards of, 978b
  of what is in their hands, 15a
  to maturity, 46a
Excellencies, dwell upon, than im-
    perfections, 300b
  of lively conversation, 372a
Excellent angler now with God,
    236a
  beauty, 121a
  campaigning weather, 981a
  canopy the air, 173b
  dumb discourse, 209b
  everything that's, 683b
  fancy, 178b
  foppery of the world, 190b
  good, so so is very, 163a
  herb, 820a
  immodesty, 984a
  is thy name, 1032b
  lies before us, 398a
  marriage, 585b
  mastiffe, 284b
  mediocrity of ancient times, 101a
  no, soul is exempt, 48a
  old way, 825a
  original, just to an, 313b
  situation, 754b
  thing in woman, 193b
  things as difficult as rare, 283a
  things that are more, 781a
  to have a giant's strength, 184b
  to make a poet, 240a
  Watson cried, 782a
  wit, proverb old of, 524b
  works, largest number of, 325a
  wretch, 188a
Excellest, thou, them all, 1042a
Excelling nature, pattern of, 190a
Excels all other bliss, 101b
  at a plan or title-page, 353a
  good stomach, them all, 288a
  in something, 43a
  quirks of blazoning pens, 187a
Excelsior, strange device, 522a
Exception, admits not some, 222a
  painful to be an, 558b
Exceptional man deteriorated,
    727a
Excepts, guilty man, 279a
Excess, give me, of it, 163b
  moderation even in, 511a

Excess, not the drinking but the,
    227a
  nothing in, 31b, 69b
  of glory obscur'd, 253a
  of my responsive youth, 720a
  of severity, 700b
  of stupidity, 340a
  of wealth, 124a
  power in, 120a
  reform carried to an, 424a
  scant this, 145b
  surprise by a fine, 478a
  wasteful and ridiculous, 148a
Excessive, dark with, bright, 254b
  literary production, 596b
  politeness, treated me with,
    909a
Exchange, credited to, 912a
  green, 936a
  of good offices, 265a
  of mutual protection, 26a
  one for the other given, 115b
  such wonders to, 949a
Exchanged hearts, 262a
Exchequer of the poor, 139a
  rob, 151a
Excise a hateful tax, 336b
  those to whom, is paid, 336b
Excite my amorous propensities,
    339a
  us to love a woman, 105b
Excited abnormal exhausting con-
    dition, 765b
Excitement, hurried away by, 64b
  insane, at first, 697b
  of the heart, 545a
Excites envy, 290a
  the public odium, 433b
  us to arms, 278b
Exciting, found it less, 685b
Exclaim against second marriages,
    333b
Excludes, infinite day, the night,
    303a
  not till the sun, you, 610a
Exclusion, built colony on princi-
    ple of, 629a
Exclusive predominance, 910b
  worms, 966b
Exclusiveness in our public life,
    20a
Excrement, stolen from general,
    203b
Excrescence superabundance, 981a
Excus'd his devilish deeds, 45a,
    255b
Excuse, any, will serve a tyrant, 9b
  beauty is its own, 503b, 526b
  came prologue, 258b
  coy, 248b
  every man will plead, 227b
  fault worse by, 148b
  I will not, 517a
  in this delay, 136b
  lose without, 861b
  not a single, 816b
  prove an, for the glass, 382a
  thou make in this delay, 136b
Excuses, contests allow no, 12a
  himself, 97a
  ignorance, no man, 227b
  patch'd up your, 200b
Excusing, by, nothing pure love
    shows, 270a
  fault, 148b
Execrable shape, 254b
  scum of all villanies, 329b
Executant, no limit to attempt as
    an, 718b

Fear, courage is mastery of, 678a
  courage is resistance to, 678a
  courage not absence of, 678a
  cuckoo word of, 134a
  darkly-brooding, 851a
  death and pain, 51b
  death we, 184b
  descending darkness of, 917a
  distill'd with act of, 171a
  do from, of the laws, 71b
  everything rustles to him in, 16a
  farewell, 255a
  for one who prospers, 15b
  free from, and apprehension, 722a
  freedom from, 920b
  full of, 1003a
  gave them our love and, 571a
  God and keep his command-ments, 1044a
  God honour the king, 1064a
  Greeks bringing gifts, 37a
  has no need of, 936b
  hate not, not, 972b
  hate whom they, 31a
  I cannot taint with, 198b
  I learnt to, God, 500b
  I to fall, 111a
  imagining some, 142b
  in a handful of dust, 944a
  is affront, 307a
  is most accurs'd, 124b
  is rot, 972b
  is sharp-sighted, 104b
  Job, God for nought, 1029a
  little we, 563b
  littlest doubts are, 176a
  look in hope or, 527b
  love casteth out, 1064b
  love casts out, 554b
  mask for, 51a
  mean actions to, 726a
  men, death, 119b
  men swayed by, 27a
  no, be thine, 595a
  no evil, 1033a
  no, in love, 1064b
  no more heat o' the sun, 204b
  nobility exempt from, 125b
  nor wish for your last day, 52b
  not clouds will lour, 394a
  not lest existence, 532b
  not the sight of it, 627b
  not thou child infirm, 506b
  not to touch the best, 111a
  nothing to be feared as, 589a
  nothing to swear, 35b
  o' hell's a hangman's whip, 224a
  of blame or misunderstanding, 761b
  of change, 253a
  of death, 45a
  of death has bygone us, 705b
  of having to cry, 367b
  of having to repay in kind, 282b
  of ill that may happen, 265b
  of kings, 146a
  of some divine powers, 224a
  of suffering injustice, 265a
  of the dark, 930a
  of the Lord, 1037a
  of the Lord is wisdom, 1031a
  of thine heart, 693b
  of violent death, 229a
  only thing we have to fear is, 918b

Fear or hope from censure, 336b
  possess them not with, 156a
  protect them from, 920a
  provided they, let them hate, 34a
  prudery together with, 673a
  punishment brings increase of, 727b
  put, out of your heart, 842a
  rush in and, to tread, 801b
  serve the Lord with, 1032a
  shame coward, 529b
  shuddering, 145b
  strange and speechless, 747b
  strange that men should, 167b
  that lurks in men's eyes, 939a
  that reigns with the tyrant, 522b
  the force of the wind, 793b
  the foundation of governments, 368a
  the worst oft cures, 181b
  theoretic and visionary, 374b
  they call courage, 855a
  thief, each bush, 127a
  thing of which I have fear is, 97b
  thou not what hap, 379b
  thou shalt, waking, 693b
  throw, to the wind, 23a
  to be we know not what, 275b
  to live or die, 506b
  to love thee sweet, 790a
  to prevent war is not to, it, 425b
  to whom fear, 1060b
  trembled with, at your frown, 597a
  unaccustomed to, 1005a
  we must get rid of, 475b
  where angels, to tread, 312a
  which can engender the thing feared, 1009b
  whom shall I, 1033b
  why, death, 607b
  yet do I, thy nature, 194b
Fear'd by their breed, 139a
  no danger, 278b
Feare may force a man, 91b
  pine with, 114a
Feared God and eschewed evil, 1029b
  just as I, 580b
  lest sky should fall, 32b
  nothing to be, as fear, 589a
  the light, 261a
  to run away, 808b
  twenty times was Peter, 404a
Fearful, come forth thou, man, 137a
  concatenation, 444a
  Death's, forehead, 712a
  fire, saved them from the, 663b
  goodness never, 185a
  innocence, our peace our, 407a
  joy, snatch a, 347b
  lifting up a, eye, 118a
  man, come forth thou, 137a
  night, pilot 'tis a, 485a
  odds, facing, 493b
  our, trip is done, 610a
  pale, pensive not jesting, 66a
  summons, 170a
  symmetry, frame thy, 387a
  thing in winter, 587a
  thing to see, 456b
  unbelief, 474a
  with a, shriek he leaped, 717b

Fearfully and wonderfully made, 1038a
Fearing doubting dreaming dreams, 545a
  to attempt, 183b
  to be spilt, 177b
Fearless, bold and, my eye was, 23b
  eyes, foe that comes with, 803a
  for unknown shores, 610a
  peerless, an army's flower, 781b
  race, names of our, 463b
Fear's as bad as falling, 204a
Fears a painted devil, 196b
  and disquietudes, 41a
  and distastes, 119b
  do make us traitors, 198b
  faith triumphant o'er our, 523a
  fear among, 823b
  friendly soothing of my, 899b
  grown from sudden, 456b
  his fate, 262b
  hopes and, of all the years, 669b
  hopes belied our, 487b
  humanity with all its, 522b
  humble cares and delicate, 406a
  I had no human, 405b
  in ghastly, 386a
  little, grow great, 176a
  loves or, or hates, 412b
  no one loves him he, 27a
  of the world, 861a
  old age with, and ills, 847b
  pains and, 261a
  pangs and, 211b
  past regrets and future, 532a
  present, 194b
  put all, beneath his feet, 36b
  saucy doubts and, 197b
  that I may cease to be, 479b
  to be disgraced, 330a
  to speak of Ninety-eight, 627b
Feast and your halls are crowded, 754a
  as you were going to a, 218b
  beginning of, 151b
  better knew the, to sway, 449b
  continual, 1039b
  enough as good as a, 95a
  for your scholars and sages, 651b
  good man's, 161a
  guests are met the, is set, 421a
  imagination of, 138b
  in thine eternal cell, 179b
  invite man that loves thee to a, 7b
  made for laughter, 1043a
  makes a merry, 129a
  nourisher in life's, 196b
  of Crispian, 156b
  of fat things, 1046a
  of languages, 133b
  of love is song, 668a
  of nectar'd sweets, 247b
  of reason, 319b
  of Stephen, 592b
  of wines on the lees, 1046a
  pomp and, and revelry, 245b
  riseth from a, 144b
  to the Lord, 1024a
  to thousand of his lords, 1048b
  when I make a, 117b
Feaste, tables groan before ye, 852a
Feasters groan, 852a
Feasting, house of, 1042b
  if, rise, 662a

Felt like planets had fallen on me, 929a
  scarcely, or seen, 322b
  shoe troop of horse with, 193a
  slippers and warm bellywash, 973a
  so finely, as injustice, 580b
  the earth move out, 983a
  with spirit so profound, 405b
Female beauty, th' idee iv, 836b
  character, fault of, 461b
  errors fall, some, 312a
  essential, elements, 910b
  friendship, elegance of, 337a
  grandmother Eve a, 132b
  heart can gold despise, 347b
  hundred per cent, 949b
  knee is a joint, 863b
  logic, book of, 566a
  lovely, shapes, 665b
  male and, created he them, 1021a
  murderers, 765b
  of sex, 260a
  of the species, 817b
  pulchritude, 909a
  sex, occupied with the, 923a
  warriors, 325b
Females of all species, 895a
Feminine, eternal, draws us on, 380a
  gender of vessels, 904a
  intuition, 967b
  of genius, 533b
  soul is a queen, 807a
Fen, by lake or moorish, 247b
  of stagnant waters, 407b
  wild-fire dances on the, 395b
Fence against the world, 283b
  dazzling, 248a
  downtrod by trespassers, 12b
  impregnable, 126b
  neighbor breaks your, 573a
  'round the top of the cliff, 701a
  thirty yards of board, 675a
  valiant and cunning in, 165b
Fences, American social, 985a
  good, make good neighbors, 879b
Fenner's, Uncle, family
Fens and the sedges, 935a
Fer from eze fer from herte, 83a
Fere, darling of his, 29b
Ferlie he spied wi' his e'e, 1012b
Ferment, soul is in a, 478b
Ferments of the worst kind, 306b
Fern and flower with silvery dew, 651b
Ferns by these Berkshire boulders, 960b
Ferny, forest's, floor, 862b
  glens, grey flocks in, 592a
Ferocious heroes, land of, 888a
Ferocity, courage without, 451b
  in beasts, 505b
Ferry-boats, street-cars and, 288a
Ferryman, grim, 128a
Fertile, fragrant the, earth, 256a
  in such a fix to be so, 990a
  infinitely, 807a
  soil of man's vanity, 873a
  twice five miles of, ground, 420b
Fertility, suck soil's, 140a
Fertilize the Jordan plain, 893a
Fervent, effectual, prayer, 1064a
  long and, kiss, 486b
Fervently do we pray, 542a
Fester, lilies that, 206a

Festina lente, 1010a
Festival, great anniversary, 367b
  rites, 463b
Festooned with haberdashery of success, 821b
Fetch a pail of water, 1016b
  Age of Gold, 244b
  de mo'ners up higher, 738b
Fetched sea-born treasures, 503a
Fetisly, ful faire and, 79b
Fetter his feet in shackles, 243a
Fettered hope, set wild the, 912b
  poetry, 388b
  to an office stool, 682a
  to her eye, 268a
Fetters human race, 338b
  leaving the, to me, 645a
  servile, 1000b
  throws its last, off, 470b
Feuds, forget all, 494a
  of faith, 850b
  rent with civil, 443b
Fever and the fret, 481b
  beyond the fire and, 780b
  called living, 545b
  famine and war, 743b
  has just left me, 57b
  life's fitful, 197b
  of chills and, she died, 946b
  of life is over, 1069b
  passion is a, in the mind, 788a
  to the questing hound, 897b
Fevered lips, drained by, 483b
  world, 873a
Feverish ardor, 516b
  preoccupation, 910b
  selfish little clod, 765a
Fever-trees, set about with, 819b
Few, angel visits, and far between, 291b, 432b
  are chosen, 1054a
  assume to be deputies, 402a
  capable of education, 774b
  honest men better than numbers, 237b
  honored by the, 602a
  hours, he was within a, 345b
  in science address the, 511a
  laborers are, 1052a
  let thine occupations be, 67a
  let thy words be, 1042b
  love all trust a, 182b
  materials for history, 369a
  men of, words, 155a
  more and the, 887b
  neither too many nor too, 431b
  not in hands of the, 20a
  of us fall very low, 791b
  owed by so many to so, 869b
  privileged, 919a
  profit by advice, 43b
  real friends, women find, 343a
  save the poor, 498b
  shall part where many meet, 433a
  that only lend their ear, 122a
  there be that find it, 1052a
  thoughts of the, 699a
  unpleasant'st words, 145b
  we happy, 156b
  who early in life, 668b
  words are, and often funny, 588a
  words, enormous force of, 508a
Fewest disasters, middle station had, 292a
  those who want the, things, 70b
Fezziwig, in came Mrs., 578a
F.F.V.s, start counting, 980a

Fib, destroy his, or sophistry, 318b
Fibres, multitude of, 497a
Fibs, I'll tell you no, 357b
Fickle and changeful thing, 37a
  and restless as a fawn, 486b
  and unstable subject, 97b
  and wavering, 668a
  as a changeful dream, 415b
  fantastic, fierce and vain, 415b
  fortune's, wheel, 155b
  froward vindictive fellow, 58b
  gypsy, Dame Fortune a, 499b
  whatever is, freckled, 724a
  when Fortune is, 33b
  when Fortune's, 31a
Fickleness of the women I love, 764b
Fico for the phrase, 180a
Fiction, by fairy, drest, 350a
  carries truth in solution, 565b
  chiefly in the form of, 687a
  comforting piece of, 908b
  condemn as improbable, 165b
  dull with homely men, 801a
  fact or, 831b
  lags after truth, 359b
  most imaginative composer of, 761a
  prompts tongue to deal in, 308a
  turns the Muses' mangle, 794b
  up-to-date, 704a
Fiddle all the bugs off, 978b
  cat and the, 1016b
  merry love the, 825b
  play on my, in Dooney, 825b
  second, carrying the air, 889b
  we know is diddle, 695b
Fiddle-de-dee, 659a
Fiddler, chymist, statesman, 277a
  in came a, 578a
Fiddlers three, called for his, 1015a
  weary of it like men, 750a
Fiddlestring, tune-swept, 914b
Fiddling-stick, my master's lost his, 1014b
Fidelity, gossamer, of mere man, 544b
Fidget and no reformer, 795a
Fido, Towser Sport Spot or, 970b
Fie fie upon her, 182b
  foh and fum, 192b
Field, accidents by flood and, 186a
  artilleree, 902a
  corner of a foreign, 938b
  covered by our knowledge, 753a
  cribs from your, 573a
  dedicate a portion of that, 540b
  dignity in tilling a, 767a
  flower of the, 1036b, 1047a
  foul fiend coming over the, 274a
  good animal in the, 341a
  happy, or mossy cavern, 482b
  Hector in the, 525a
  inundate his, 3a
  man for the, 550b
  marriage is a, of battle, 749a
  of a few acres, 370b
  of destiny, 527a
  of human conflict, 869b
  of morals, 908a
  of night, 531a
  of ripe corn, 943a
  potter's, 1055a
  Prussia hurried to the, 383a
  roam'd from, to field, 384b
  shepherds abiding in the, 1056b
  sickle in the fruitful, 386b

Found, hast thou, me O mine enemy, 1029a
he was lost and is, 1057a
her decay, 343b
Him in the shining of stars, 555b
himself out, 792b
his warmest welcome, 341b
I have, it, 29a
in the register of God, 241b
itself a weed, 860a
less often sought than, 461a
looked inwards and, her, 275b
lost time is never, 331a
much that I, 900a
my latest, 256b
myself famous, 455a
no end, 254a
out by seeking, 32b
out my riddle, 1026b
something good may be, 341b
sought but, him not, 1044b
valour, in feasting, 222a
weighed and, wanting, 1049a
where was ever, a mother, 308a
you an argument, 343a
Foundation must be laid in youth, 783a
no, other than the right, 344a
no sure, on blood, 148b
of a religion, 953b
of a state, 951a
of morals and legislation, 324b
of most governments, 368a
or destruction of religion, 951a
superstructure on economic, 850a
Foundations, earth's, stand, 787b
earth's, fled, 787a
laid the, of the earth, 1031b
loosen old, 899a
of all states, 85b
Founded it upon the seas, 1033b
securely, 379a
upon a rock, 1052a
Founder, meant to, 814b
Founders of human civilization, 444b
Fount, level with their, 526a
of joy's delicious springs, 452b
Fountain and a shrine, 544a
choke the dark, 464a
gentle murmur of a low, 649a
I have is a, 729b
let thy voice rise like a, 548a
of industry, 444b
of life in every creature, 559b
of sweet tears, 406a
of wit, 35a
pitcher broken at the, 1043b
silver-fingered, 968b
stirr'd, 182a
stream and sea, 413a
that which the, sends forth, 522b
troubled, 130b
woman is like, troubled, 130b
Fountain's silvery column, 422b
Fountains, Afric's sunny, 445b
large streams from little, 401a
of my hidden life, 507b
of the Nile, 502b
under the, 1013b
Founts, fresher, 777a
Four aces, Christian with, 680b
and twenty blackbirds, 1017a
and twenty letters, 60a
and twenty tailors, 1017a
champions fierce, 254b

Four characters, venerate, 372b
degrees of drunkenness, 497a
doors were five, 971b
drinks, 963a
essential human freedoms, 920b
first acts already past, 306b
friends in the world, 272a
full, seasons, 962a
hours spend in prayer, 110b
larks and a wren, 580b
lean hounds, 968b
limited undergraduates to, 864a
must be one of, 996a
snakes gliding up and down, 501a
speeches, I taught him, 624b
stories, 89b
things come not back, 42a
things I am wiser to know, 966b
twice two be not, 594b
walls limit my vision, 844a
walls, my own, 476b
when angry count, 678a
winds of heaven, 1049b
years a-glowing, 38a
years, short space of, 539b
Foure corners of the worlde, 102a
Four-in-hand, fiery, 424a
Fourscore and seven years ago, 540b
old man, and upward, 193a
years, if they be, 1036a
years, numbered more than, 525a
years, wind him up for, 276a
Four-square to all the winds, 553b
Fourteen hundred years ago, 149a
Fourteenth Amendment, 709b
Fourth dimension, inhabitants of a, 990b
eleventh ninth and sixth, 96a
estate, corporation of the, 565b
estate of the realm, 473a
glass for mine enemies, 300b
is freedom from fear, 920b
of July orations, 795b
safe and sane, 830b
sound, frame not a, 572a
watch of the night, 1053a
Foweles, smale, maken melodye, 79a
Fowl of the air, 1021a
or good red herring, 92a
you elegant, 581a
Fowler, snare of the, 1036a
Fowls, behold, of the air, 1051b
small, flew screaming, 604b
Fox, Brer, he lay low, 738b
build nest on your hearthstone, 857a
from his lair, 472b
know how to play the, 55a
knows many things, 7b
like Aesop's, 221b
like the tailless, 695a
trusted him, 151b
went out in hungry plight, 1003a
when he cannot reach the grapes, 10a
Foxes, fellow, cut off theirs, 221b
have holes, 1052a
honoured among, 997a
little, that spoil vines, 1044a
Foxey our revered father, 577a
Foxholes, atheists in the, 991b
Fox's, patch it out with the, 55a

Fox-terriers born with original sin, 788a
Fra Luca Parioli, 993a
Frabjous day callooh callay, 658a
Fraction, infinitesimal, of a product, 474a
Fractions dhruv him fr'm school, 834a
happiness made of minute, 425a
Fragile but with more vitality, 855a
dew-drop, 477b
form, every, 577a
kingdom, 947a
profound and, lips, 968b
skiff attains the shore, 699b
Fragment, ship a, detached from earth, 772a
Fragmentary blue, 880a
Fragments, death tramples it to, 468b
gather up the, 1058a
live in, no longer, 901b
of a once glorious Union, 443b
practice old lovely, 898b
took up, that remained, 1053a
Fragrance, flowers of transient, 336b
no perfect flower without, 823b
on the glass, 806a
smells to heaven, 330a
spicy, 120a
such as never clings, 961b
you wish to extract, 653a
Fragrant bodice, loosens her, 481a
bosom, 236b
day is done, 831b
flowers, deck with, 526a
freshened, breeze, 961b
most, when incensed, 120a
the fertile earth, 256a
thousand, posies, 123a
Fraid-cat, wasn't a, much, 829b
Frail a thing is man, 1000b
and erring men, 952a
as a bubble, 804b
azures fluttering, 968b
blood, inhabits our, 165b
brief and, and blue, 966b
delight, web of, 866a
gaunt and small, 705b
it may be, 335a
know how, I am, 1034a
mortality, 121b
Frailest, life is, of all things, 272b
Frailties, draw his, from their abode, 349b
framed to reproduce, 640a
Frailty, discovering every, 57b
human, without recreation, 106b
love's but a, of the mind, 298a
of a man, 119b
of our powers, 182b
organ-pipe of, 148b
thy name is woman, 170b
Frame, awful desert's, 602a
by her just standard, 310a
corruption our, consume, 436b
essence of picture is, 866b
goodly, the earth, 173b
his fair replies, 5b
in earth, 113b
it in language, 653b
man of giant, 471a
of adamant, 336a
orbs of heavenly, 116a
quit this mortal, 312a
rapture-smitten, 432a

Fret of existence, 985b
  the fever and the, 481b
  thy soule, 114a
Fretful, love grown faint and, 694a
  porpentine, 172b
Frets, fig for him who, 809a
  his hour upon the stage, 199b
  strives and fights and, 476b
Fretted and kept in a stew, 557b
  pygmy-body to decay, 276b
  vault, 348b
  with golden fire, 173b
Freud, ideas of, 797b
Friar of orders grey, 130b, 1011b
Friars, hooded clouds like, 521a
Fribsbi, Madame, 565a
Friction, keep planet warm by 963a
Friday, I had that fellow, 714b
  my man, 292a
  name should be, 292a
  worse on, 1018b
Friday's child, 1018b
Fried sole, changed oysters to, 838a
Friend a strong defence, 1066a
  after friend departs, 413a
  and a song, 893a
  and enemy is death, 938b
  and I have built a wall, 864a
  angry with my, 387b
  asked what a, was, 72b
  await felicity or doom, 647b
  bachelor's, 598b
  bear friend's infirmities, 169a
  best mirror is an old, 234a
  better your enemy than your, 594b
  candid, 401b
  choose author as you choose a, 283b
  commend so good a, 280b
  constancy of a, 813a
  Death how now, 652b
  death of dear, 143a
  defend your departed, 280a
  easy to find, in prosperity, 33b
  eat peck of salt with, 104a
  enemy and, to hurt you, 679a
  equal to a brother, 7b
  every man will be thy, 220a
  exonerating themselves to a, 223b
  fair fame of, or foe, 745a
  faithful, is found, 31a, 33b
  faithful, is the best, 653b
  fav'rite has no, 347b
  for a, is life too short, 507a
  gained from heav'n a, 349b
  gif ye want ae, that's true, 390b
  good, for Jesu's sake, 212b
  good wine a, or being dry, 288b
  good words said of a, 732a
  guide philosopher and, 318a, 912a
  hast thou a, 96b
  have God thy, 96b
  he that is thy, indeed, 220a
  he that wrongs his, 555b
  house that shelters a, 502a
  I have valued and tried, 438b
  idleness sorrow, and foe, 966b
  in life the firmest, 451b
  in misery, 220a
  in my retreat, 363b
  in need, 30b, 578b
  in power is friend lost, 696b
  in prosperity, 31a

Friend is a person with whom I
    may be sincere, 502a
  Jack loved his, 377a
  keep, under own life's key, 182b
  knew a man who had a, 1008b
  knolling departing, 152b
  little, of all the world, 816b
  loan loses itself and, 171b
  loved his, 1014b
  loved too true to keep a, 520a
  made a, sincere, 558a
  makes no, who never made a foe, 555a
  mine own familiar, 1034b
  much too patient, 817a
  my God my father my, 283b
  my, here didn't see, 873b
  'neath every one a, 602b
  never find a, 826b
  never knowne till man have neede, 93b
  new, is as new wine, 1066a
  no, like music, 988b
  nor a, to know me, 752a
  nor a toy, 602a
  not a, to spare, 73b
  of every country, 401a
  of friendless name the, 337b
  of man, 777b
  of man desires, 620b
  of my better days, 462b
  of pleasure, 351b
  of publicans and sinners, 1052b
  of the race had gone, 735b
  of those that have no friend, 746b
  of woe, 427b
  one, I had, 663a
  one, in a lifetime is much, 697a
  one soul abiding in two bodies, 5a
  one, to another friend, 893a
  or foe that spread these lies, 640b
  plainest, 971a
  praise from a, 4b
  price fixed with a, 7b
  reckoned the masterpiece of nature, 502a
  religious book or, 213a
  services I render to my, 14b
  soul of a, we've made, 799a
  soul unto itself an imperial, 646b
  still let a, be dear, 489b
  stoop to become your, 823b
  striking sometimes a, 233a
  talk as friend to, 486a
  that loved her, 186b
  that sticketh closer, 1040a
  thou art not my, 503a
  time is a kind, 928b
  to close his eyes, 280a
  to genius the stern, 505a
  to her virtues be a, 343b
  to human race, 4b
  to public amusements, 341a
  treat, as if he might become enemy, 44b
  true industrious, 149a
  value a real, 29a
  way to have a, is to be one, 502a
  welcome, 263b
  what, is best, 96b
  who deserts you, 10b
  who hath not lost a, 413a
  who lost no friend, 315b

Friend whose face will never change, 729b
  without treachery, 660a
  world is not thy, 137b
  worth loving, 732a
  wounds of a, 1041a
  yet, to truth, 315a
Friendless bodies of unburied men, 225b
  of, name the friend, 337b
  old solitary widow, 731b
  sick and poor and, 711a
Friendliest to sleep and silence, 256b
Friendliness, common, 721b
  of the British, 681b
Friendly bowl, mingles with my, 319b
  bust, 943b
  counsel cuts off foes, 124b
  cow all red and white, 750b
  door, came to your, 756a
  faces of old sorrows, 891b
  forces in the difficult, 884a
  hand, grasp of a, 729b
  nothing more, 30b
  social, honest man, 390b
  soothing of my fears, 899b
  stroke, feel the, 292a
  universe not hostile nor, 902a
Friend's infirmities, bear his, 169a
  wife, expect from a, 429a
Friends absent speak, 217a
  advanced true, 620b
  advertis'd by our loving, 127a
  again with roses, 692b
  age leaves us, and wine, 440a
  aliens into trusting, 587a
  all things common to, 33a
  alone with his, 294a
  and brother souls, 556b
  and comrades, 484b
  and oh my, 962a
  are born not made, 696a
  are everything, 886a
  are much more dangerous, 748a
  ashamed to look upon one another, 236a
  backing of your, 150a
  be warned by me, 849a
  beautiful are, 897a
  best, ever known, 791a
  best of, must part, 1004b
  best way to make, 990a
  better, I'll not be knowing, 962b
  better than through mortal, 643b
  better to make, at home, 53a
  cakes and, 971a
  cast off his, 358a
  choice makes our, 371a
  comfort, and foes, 354b
  confidence in untried, 576a
  Constitution between, 703b
  could expect of a child, 285b
  country, all quitted, 428b
  death of, 890a
  defend me from my, 401b
  depart, 485a
  distresses of our, 266a
  do with my, as with my books, 502a
  does not make, with you, 340a
  eat and drink as, 130a
  eaten their old, up, 823a
  exultations agonies love, 407a
  faithful, hard to find, 220a
  falling out of, 31b

Girl I left behind me, 1001a
little, by day, 889a
needs good parents, 929b
never looks as well, 966a
never mind the, 829b
not a, goes walking, 915b
protect the working, 775b
spoke I to my, 230b
sweet, graduates, 550a
sweetest, I know, 878a
there little, don't cry, 745b
Tuxedo, 828a
unlesson'd, 145b
who had a little curl, 526a
Girlish bosom, unzone thy, 916b
glee, filled with, 684b
laughter, laugh thy, 780b
Girl's forehead, lie on a, 632b
Girls, all, he can please, 701a
between two, 124b
deck our, for gay delights, 597b
display a shocking freedom, 741a
gayest of gay, 486b
hired, 931b
in your, again be courted, 1013a
lads and, quiet dust was, 648b
rosebud garden of, 554a
servant, in the kitchen, 856b
shires where, are fonder, 787b
that are so smart, 307b
what are little, made of, 1018b
who wear glasses, 966b
wonderful training for, 957a
wretched un-idea'd, 339a
Girt me for the onset, 646b
Git, giggle gabble gobble, 821b
thar fustest, 871b
Gitche Gumee, 523a
Gits, them that has, 735a
Give a little love to a child, 606a
a loving heart, 230a
a man a horse he can ride, 667b
according to that little, 1065a
all thou canst, 411b
alms accordingly, 1065a
ample room and verge enough, 279b
and not count cost, 87b
and take back their word, 785a
annoyeth one to, unto them, 726b
away, what we, 975a
back the lost delight, 673b
better to, than to take, 91b
but a glimpse, 343b
country back to Indians, 980a
devil his due, 104b
dreadful note of preparation, 155b
every man thy ear, 171b
fame for pot of ale, 155a
fortune doth, too much, 117b
freely, 1052a
gets to, 893a
give, daughters crying, 1041b
good counsel, 223a
harder to, properly, 726b
her such beauty, 912b
her the living child, 1028a
him a chanst, 835b
him a good fight, 914a
him back to his nation, 934a
I generally had to, in, 400a
it an understanding, 171a
it lovingly, 853b
kiss better than you, 182b
law to lovers, 73b
let a man, him a blow, 72a
let him, on, 277a

Give matter for virtuous deeds, 117a
me a face, 218b
me a fruitful error, 740a
me a home where buffalo roam, 730b
me a light, 881b
me a look, 218b
me a private station, 299b
me an ounce of civet, 193a
me an understanding wife, 226a
me another horse, 128b
me but two brigades, 626a
me give me, 377b
me high noon, 914b
me just another whiskey, 717a
me my hollow tree, 320a
me, stamped foot and cried, 648b
me that piece of chalk, 717a
me the daggers, 196b
me the heart to fight, 933b
me the ocular proof, 189a
me the old enthusiasms, 606b
me thus my daily bread, 894a
me to drink mandragora, 200a
me where to stand, 29b
me your hand, 129b
me your tired masses, 724b
men get and, 378b
more blessed to, 91b, 1059a
my regards to Broadway, 892a
no more, the people straw, 1024a
not, up the ship, 441b
of your possessions, 924a
of yourself, 924a
our gold in princely sum, 791a
plenty of what is given to you, 630a
range her gifts and, 966b
reason on compulsion, 150a
receive but what we, 423a
rest to the poor, 88a
services for nothing, 21b
sleep to mine eyes, 1037b
some special good doth, 136a
sorrow words, 198b
strong drink, 1041b
't or take 't, 165a
ten shillings and no more, 284a
thanks for life, 692b
thee peace, 1025b
them your love, 924a
they beg I, 101b
this cheek a little red, 314a
thy worst of thoughts, 188a
to a thief, 995a
to all nations unity, 1068b
to get esteem, 354a
to God each moment, 329a
to me the bouquets, 655a
to the poor, 1053b, 1065a
to the world the best, 723a
up essential liberty, 331a
up the friend, 438b
up the ghost, 105a
us a song to cheer, 666b
us men, 632a
us the daily manna, 76b
us the luxuries of life, 536a
us the tools, 870a
us this day, 1051a
what did we, today, 791a
what you have, 522b
when I, I give myself, 608b
world assurance of a man, 177a
your heart to a dog, 819b
Given, hath, them in wit, 129a
horse in mouth, 88a

Given, it shall be, you, 1051b
promise most, 116b
state may be, up for lost, 344a
the bees the honey, 326a
to hospitality, 1060a
to one that hath shall be, 1054b
to whom nothing is, 333a
world, to lying, 152a
you delight, 822a
Giver, cheerful, 1062a
gift without the, 600a
keep modest as a, 726b
Givers prove unkind, 175a
Gives a child a treat, 896a
a lovely light, 962a
blesseth him that, 146a
greater feeling, 138b
hand that, blow, 277b
he that lends, 234b
its blessing, 330a
light in darkness, 125a
me some kind of content, 285b
much receives but nothing, 350b
quickly gives twice, 106b
somewhere back the thoughts, 938b
stern'st good-night, 196a
to airy nothing, 142b
to her mind, 343b
whate'er he, 336a
Giveth his beloved sleep, 1037b
love that, in full store, 635b
unto the poor, 1041b
Giving, art of, presents, 953b
aught that is worthy to give, 783b
draws power from living and, 490b
Friday's child is loving and, 1018b
his enemies the slip, 345b
manner of, worth more, 243a
more of, 862b
odour, stealing and, 163b
presents is a talent, 853b
Giving's, throb of, sweet, 966b
Gizzard, wife hath something in her, 286a
Glad, comely fashion to be, 612b
confident morning, 568a
did I live, 751a
diviner's theme, 277a
father, wise son maketh a, 1039a
hand in a populous town, 803a
heart too soon made, 569b
I was commanded to turn people, 273a
let a man be, 693a
life's arrears, 572b
make, the heart of childhood, 701b
me with its soft black eye, 441a
mighty, I'm living, 892a
of her coming, 285a
of other men's good, 161b
only a, good morning, 740a
sleep and be, 692b
that I live am I, 764a
to be at friendship, 286a
to be selling fish, 898a
to fall away, 328b
what some folks would be, of, 333a
when they said unto me, 1037b
wine that maketh, 1036b
you liked it, 624b
young mad young futurists, 831b
Gladden his who revisits it, 443a

Glorious epicurean paradox, 536a
  every thing honourable and,
    366b
  eye shines on me still, 509b
  fault of angels, 313b
  gates to, and unknown, 901a
  gifts of the gods, 3b
  haven, 76a
  in a pipe, 460b
  in arms, 132b
  in thy just defence, 299a
  institution, 36ob
  land above the sky, 1008b
  life, crowded hour of, 416b
  long and, past, 789b
  mirror, 455a
  more, the triumph, 370b
  morning, full many a, 205a
  pleasant thrilling, hours, 590b
  song of old, 560b
  summer by sun of York, 127b
  sunsets have birth in cities, 853a
  thing to be a pirate king, 682b
  to be an exception, 558b
  triumphs, win, 778b
  war, circumstance of, 189a
  works, these are thy, 256b
Gloriously drunk, 365a
  false, 39a
  succeeded, 987b
Glory, all things give him, 725a
  all-cloudless, 459a
  among men dies also, 8a
  and blue air, 519b
  and freshness of a dream, 408a
  and grief agree not well, 605a
  and shame of the universe, 273a
  and the dream, 408a
  belongs to our ancestors, 57b
  declare, of God, 1032b
  desire of, clings longer, 63b
  desirous of honour and, 283a
  doesn't mean a knock-down
    argument, 659a
  drown'd, in a shallow cup, 533a
  earth full of his, 1045b
  excess of, obscur'd, 253a
  folded, of his wings, 969b
  forgot was Britain's, 634b
  from his gray hairs gone, 527a
  from the earth, 408a
  full meridian of my, 211a
  glow, in thunder, 724b
  goin' ware, waits, 600b
  gown of, 111a
  greater, of God, 1009b
  guards with solemn round, 613a
  his food was, 494b
  height of her, 444a
  honor and undying fame, 956a
  impressed by spectacle of, 20a
  in a great mistake, 996a
  in hevin' nothin' o' the sort,
    601a
  in his bosom, 597b
  in one day fill the stage, 232a
  in outstripping donkeys, 52b
  in the flower, 408b
  is all moonshine, 613b
  is departed from Israel, 1027a
  is that bright tragic thing, 648a
  is that of all adventurers, 953b
  is their shame, 1062b
  jest and riddle of the world,
    317a
  land of hope and, 798b
  left him alone with his, 464a
  like a circle in water, 124a
  like a shooting star, 139a

Glory, long hair a, to her, 1061a
  love of, is most ardent, 301b
  made the sages smile, 458b
  majesty and might and, 809b
  name thee old, 501a
  no path of flowers leads to, 269b
  nothing so expensive as, 418b
  O the, of the winning, 639b
  of a representative, 359b
  of an April day, 131b
  of Him who moves everything,
    77a
  of his country, 443a
  of honours beauties wits, 216a
  of my crown, 97b
  of rulers or races, 900a
  of the coming of the Lord, 597b
  of the Creator, 118b
  of the Egdon waste, 704b
  of the Lord shone, 1056b
  of the universe, 530b
  of their times, 1066b
  of young men is strength, 1040a
  one, an' one shame, 600b
  or the grave, 432b
  passes away the, of this world,
    1010b
  path of duty was way to, 553b
  paths of, 348b
  prayer gives God, 725a
  rainbow's, is shed, 469a
  search their own, 1041a
  shall not descend after him, 8b
  shows the way, 291a
  Solomon in all his, 1051b
  spread the morning's, 740a
  star differeth in, 1061b
  stars of, 476b
  sudden, 228b
  sun of thy, 500a
  sun question his, 647b
  survives, 20b
  that book doth share the, 134b
  that fadeth not away, 1064a
  that was Greece, 543b, 872b
  the colour the, the gold, 895b
  these in the robings of, 637b
  time's, is to calm, 131b
  to God in the highest, 1056b
  to the king of kings, 334b
  to the new-born king, 334b
  trailing clouds of, 408a
  triumph without, 243a
  true and honorable recompense,
    297b
  vain pomp and, 211a, 1068b
  visions of, 350a
  waits thee, 438a
  walking in an air of, 272a
  who is this king of, 1033b
  who works for, 762b
  wild cataract leaps in, 550a
  wings lose all their, 441b
Glory's page, 437b
  small change, 496b
  thrill is o'er, 438a
Gloss of art, 357a
  on faint deeds, 203a
Glossary necessary to understand
    Chaucer, 933a
Glossy cherished anthracite, 956a
  cope is black as coal, 689b
  plumage dark and sleek, 395b
Gloucester, Doctor Foster went to,
    1019b
Glove, iron hand in velvet, 95a
  upon that hand, 135a
Gloves on ere they touched meat,
    979b

Gloves, through the fields in, 936a
  wear seemly, 534b
Glow, eyes, like sparks of fire,
    231a
  neon, 941b
  of a kindly heart, 729b
Glow'd beyond nature warm, 320b
  the firmament with sapphires,
    255b
Glowing axle, 247a
  embers through the room, 246a
  fire, before a, 864b
  hot, hammer iron when, 43b
  hours, chase the, 453a
  kiss had won, 488a
  life of its own times, 757b
Glow'red, as Tammie, 393b
Glows, in deep thicket's gloom,
    378b
  in ev'ry heart, 305a
  while he reads, 310b
Glow-worm, eyes the, lend thee,
    231a
  shows the matin to be near,
    172b
Glow-worms, glories like, 226a
Glue and lime of love, 230a
Glued, pale student, to his desk,
    628b
Glum, glance was, 685a
Glut sorrow on a morning rose,
    483a
Gluts twice ten thousand caverns,
    478a
Glutted market, 309b
Glutton, drunkard and the, 1040b
  idler and fool, 896a
Glynn, marshes of, 716b
Gnarling sorrow hath less power,
    138b
Gnat, strain at a, 1054a
Gnats, small, mourn, 483a
Gnawing of a mouse, 962b
Gnaws my hat, 902b
Go about but cannot find, 978a
  and catch a falling star, 215b
  and do thou likewise, 1057a
  and find it, 815b
  and sin no more, 1058a
  and teach all nations, 1055b
  at once, 198a
  away, presently they, 889b
  beyond the mark, 266a
  bow thy head in gentle spite,
    629a
  bump in the night, 1003a
  child in way he should, 1040b
  die and, we know not where,
    185a
  don't ever try to, there, 967b
  find out and be damned, 815b
  forth and conquer a crown, 730a
  forth and seek, 897b
  forth in separate parties, 1070a
  forth with crowds, 959a
  from me, 519a
  gentle into that good night, 997a
  get thee to a nunnery, 175a
  I shall, to him, 1028a
  I will not let thee, 330a
  in time let, 812b
  into the house of the Lord,
    1037b
  like to, by myself, 434a
  litel bok, 79a
  little book, 751a
  lovely rose, 242a, 823a, 912a
  mark him well, 414a

God, Hannah, and me, 662b
  has a few of us, 572a
  has designed to ruin, 18b
  has given you one face, 175a
  has hung a sign, 445a
  has written all the books, 672a
  hath chosen foolish things, 1060b
  hath joined together, 1053b
  hath numbered thy kingdom, 1049a
  hath raised me high, 97b
  have mercy on the sinner, 947a
  have mercy on this sot, 74b
  have seen, face to face, 1023b
  have, thy friend, 96b
  he for, only, 255b
  he thinks that I am, 655b
  heirs of, 1060a
  help me Amen, 86b
  help our darkened country, 883b
  helps them that help themselves, 330b
  helps those, 13a
  himself can't kill them, 42a
  himself from, could not free, 503a
  himself scarce seemèd, 422a
  his father and his, 349b
  his life a breath of, 585b
  holy Lamb of, 388b
  homely verse to, is dear, 830b
  house of, 1023a
  how should man be just with, 1030a
  how they speak of, 890b
  I believe in, 400a
  I believe that, is overhead, 652a
  I b'lieve in, and the angels, 699a
  I never spoke with, 648a
  if, be for us, 1060a
  if, did not exist, 275a, 325b
  if this were enough, 752a
  in apprehension how like a, 173b
  in faces of men and women, 608b
  in his mercy lend her grace, 547b
  in his works and word, 304a
  in, is our trust, 436a
  in my flesh shall I see, 1031a
  in place of, to her child, 565a
  in Three Persons, 445b
  in whom we live, 1069b
  incomprehensibility of, 490b
  insult to, 567b
  is a verb not a noun, 972a
  is always there, 822a
  is an unutterable sight, 782b
  is and all is well, 528b
  is for big battalions, 325b
  is grateful and knowing, 1070a
  is here, 334a
  is in heaven, 1042b
  is living working still, 583a
  is love, 672a, 1064b
  is mightiest in power, 27b
  is not a man, 12b, 1025b
  is our refuge and strength, 1034b
  is seen God in the star, 571b
  is the only mind, 616b
  is their belly, 1062b
  is they are, 572b
  is thy refuge, 1026a
  is within, 63b
  jealous, 1024b
  Job fear, for nought, 1029b
  joy is grace we say to, 612b

God, joyful noise unto, 1035a
  just are the ways of, 260a
  justify ways of, 252a
  keeps thee from thy, 495b
  kindliest thing, ever made, 873a
  know what, and man is, 556a
  knows best, 841b
  knows it I am with them, 767b
  knows thou art a collop, 92b
  laid down His life, 737a
  laws of nature's, 373a
  laws of, the laws of man, 787a
  leap up to my, 123b
  leapt to life a, 463b
  learnt to fear, 500b
  lends aid to the worker, 13a
  lesser, had made the world, 555b
  let not, speak with us, 1025a
  let us be back'd with, 126b
  let us worship, he says, 390a
  lets them down, 952a
  lifetime of his, 604a
  Lion of, 73b
  live as if, beheld you, 47a
  looks after fools drunkards, 1008a
  looks up to nature's, 318a
  Lord, Almighty, 445b
  Lord, made them all, 591b
  loses faith in, and woman, 650a
  love and be wise, 43a
  loves an idle rainbow, 854b
  loves to help him who strives, 13a
  loveth a cheerful giver, 1062a
  loveth not knoweth not, 1064b
  loveth not speaking ill, 1070b
  lower law than, 655a
  made a heart of gold, 877b
  made a little garden, 647a
  made all the creatures, 571a
  made him, 143b
  made it for this man, 558b
  made love, 804b
  made man, 804b
  made man upright, 1043a
  made men to enjoy felicity, 65a
  made the country, 121a, 364a
  made the vine, 805a
  made them high or lowly, 591b
  make our blunders wise, 903a
  make the will of, prevail, 623a
  makes all things good, 344a
  makes sech nights, 601a
  man in the bush with, may meet, 503a
  man is a fallen, 463a
  man sent from, 1057b
  man with, in majority, 95b
  man's word is, in man, 554a
  many are afraid of, 616a
  may be had for the asking, 600a
  may forgive sins, 507b
  men that, made mad, 867b
  Mencken Nathan and, 915b
  mighty fortress is our, 86b
  mills of, 522b
  ministers who spoke of, 590b
  mistake young man for Greek, 908b
  more just than, 1030a
  mother is the name for, 565a
  moves in a mysterious way, 362b
  must forever bless, 540b
  my, my Father and my Friend, 283b
  name of, upon his lips, 344b
  nature is the art of, 240a

God, near the Church far from, 92a
  nearer my, to thee, 515b
  necessary Being of Himself, 275a
  neglect, and his angels, 218a
  nest on the greatness of, 716b
  never made his work for man to mend, 280b
  never spoke of, 996a
  no, but God, 950a
  no, dare wrong a worm, 506b
  no, found stronger than death, 693a
  no respecter of persons, 1059a
  noblest work of, 224b, 318a, 390b
  not the, of nature, 233b
  not willing to do everything, 85b
  not worshipped by the herd, 897b
  nothing not, is greater, 608b
  nothynge more dyspleaseth, 84b
  now, alone knows, 688a
  obedience to, 1002b
  obligeth no man to more, 1070b
  o'erhead, 521a
  of Abraham, 264a
  of glory thundereth, 1033b
  of God, 1068a
  of heaven, worship the, 264a
  of music, 759b
  of my idolatry, 135b
  of nature placed in our power, 369a
  of our fathers, 816a, 260a
  of slep, 77b
  of storms, 534b
  of the Congo, 903a
  on our side, 427a
  on side of best digestion, 895a
  on whom each one depends, 655b
  once loved a garden, 917a
  one, and no more, 371a
  one, created us, 1049b
  one, in it all, 68a
  one nation under, 762b
  one, one law one element, 553a
  one towards, 619a
  only, can make a tree, 936b
  only who made us rich, 519b
  others call it, 573b
  our fathers, to thee, 529b
  our mind is, 28a
  out in the fields with, 1006a
  out of me, and man, 694b
  owe, a death, 153b
  pack and label men for, 790a
  Pan is dead, 61b
  peace of, 1062b
  peacemakers children of, 125a
  planted a garden, 695b
  plays upon this string first, 274b
  pleased, to visit us, 229b
  praise, sang Theocrite, 569b
  praises sing to, the King, 670a
  praising, with sweetest looks, 488a
  pray, keep me from being proud, 284a
  presume not, to scan, 316b
  prevail as sure as, reigns, 771b
  proportions the wind, 234b
  put another in for luck, 802b
  put your trust in, 434a
  reflect that, is just, 373b
  register of, 241b

Good-bye God bless you, 746b
 night goodbye, 772b
 Piccadilly, 878a
 proud world, 502b
 to care, 862a
 to the bar, 598a
 dwelling on, 976a
Good-day, and so, 665b
Goodest man ever you saw, 745b
Goodfellowship, nauseous sham,
 766a
Good-fortune, I ask not, 608b
 is a giddy maid, 486b
Good-humored stomach, 47b
Goodliest man of men, 255b
Goodliness as flower of the field,
 1047a
Good-looking men more beautiful,
 55a
Goodly act long buried, 655a
 act, some kindly word or, 655a
 apple rotten at the heart, 144a
 are thy tents, 1025b
 frame the earth, 173b
 heritage, 1032b
 outside falsehood hath, 144a
 thing, doing some, 591a
 thou art, O love, 691b
Good-morrow, and so, 666a
 to sorrow I bade, 479a
 to thy sable beak, 395b
Good-nature, full of, 136b
 it's as full of, 136b
 more agreeable than wit, 300b
Good-natured a soul as e'er trod,
 104a
 and cheerful, 332a
 lounging, 405a
 woman, 429a
Goodness and mercy shall follow
 me, 1033b
 and the grace, 442b
 armed with power, 963b
 crownest the year with, 1035a
 does not perish, 18a
 gentleness, faith, 1062b
 greatness and, not means, 423b
 His vaunted, to declare, 612a
 how awful, is, 256a
 I find so much of, still, 711b
 in things evil, 155b
 infinite, has such wide arms, 76a
 is the only investment, 590b
 more, in her little finger, 296b
 never fearful, 185a
 no truth or, dies, 475a
 not enough of love and, 596b
 of the physician, 22a
 recanting, 203a
 soul of, in things evil, 614b
 tainted, odor from, 589b
 that comes by nature, 27a
Good-night air, 705b
 and so, 665b
 Annette sweetheart, 749a
 bid me, and be kissed, 714b
 dear work, 543a
 gives stern'st, 196a
 sweet prince, 179b
 thousand times, 135b
 to all a, 437a
 to all to each a fair, 415a
 unsaid, 879b
Goods and services can be paid
 for, 864a
 bestow, to feed the poor, 1061a
 conspicuous consumption of valuable, 775b
 deliver the, 766b

Goods, half his, on the counter,
 437b
 he has to sell, 1006b
 he's got the, 802a
 imperfections of hand-wrought,
 776a
 laid up for many years, 1057a
 lead him not, 233b
 man who delivers the goods,
 803a
 with all my worldly, 1069b
 you're the, 800b
Good-will complacency thoughtlessness, 807a
 no one returns with, 48b
Goodwin, Captain, 1001a
Goolden days has passed, 836b
Goose, all the gold the, could give,
 11a
 cried in, alas, 946b
 every, a swan, 598b
 hangs high, 1007b
 look, where gott'st that, 199a
 Mother, 1014b
 royal game of, 356b
 steals, from off the common,
 712b
 steals the common from the,
 713a
 why may not a, say thus, 99a
Goosegirl, ermined, 981b
Goose-quill, corporation of the,
 565b
Goosey goosey gander, 1017a
Goot gifts, 180a
Gooth, forth it, 82b
Gopher Prairie, 931b
 wood, ark of, 1022b
Gorboduc, niece of King, 166a
Gor'd mine own thoughts, 206b
Gordian knot, Alexander cut the,
 56b
 knot he will unloose, 154a
Gore, preserved his, 685b
 shedding seas of, 459a
Gored, ox is, 87a
Gorge, my, rises at it, 178b
Gorgeous as sun at midsummer,
 151a
 dyes, mingled with its, 476b
 East, 253b
 east in fee, 407a
 palace, deceit in such a, 137a
 palaces, 210a
 tragedy, 246a
Gorging Jack and guzzling Jimmy,
 564b
Gorgonized me from head to foot,
 553b
Gorilla, distinguishable from a,
 564b
Gory, all with battle-blood, 637b
 bed, welcome to your, 394a
 locks, never shake thy, 197b
Gospel, brown bread and the, 292b
 of getting on, 764b
 of labour, 757a
 preach the, 1056a
 speak, 88b
Gospell, all is not, 88b
Gospel-light dawn'd from Bullen's
 eyes, 348a
Gossamer fidelity of mere man,
 544b
Gossip, accepts rumor and, 860a
 babbling, of the air, 164a
 give no faith to, 398a
 ill-natured, 851a
 most knowing of persons, 47a

Gossip, to, I'll give no faith, 633a
 within everybody's reach, 989a
Gossipees, other kind is, 989a
Gossipers, one kind is, 989a
Gossip-ground, held from general,
 apart, 882a
Gossip's bowl, 141b
Got a wolf by the ears, 33a
 away, one that, 967a
 oft, without merit, 187b
 penny saved is a penny, 328b
 the better of himself, 109b
 things ill, 126a
 up and gone to bed, 875b
Goth and the shameless Hun,
 816b
 Hercules and, and Moor, 703a
Gotham, three wise men of, 1016b
Goths of Germany, 18b
Gott, und, on high, 734b
Gotta love for Angela, 852b
Göttingen, University of, 401b
Gourd, sugar in the, 1003b
Gout asthma and seven maladies,
 419a
 or stone, 275a
Govermint gives too little amusemint, 837a
 offices, floats over th', 835b
Govern, he that would, others,
 226b
 king reigns but does not, 101b
 legitimate right to, 425b
 lesser restless minds, 586a
 most make least noise, 227b
 my passions, 275a
 people who think they ought to
 be free, 359a
 right of kings to, wrong, 322a
 syllables, the world, 227b
 those that toil, 354a
 thou my song Urania, 257a
 tongues with difficulty, 282a
 tyrants safely, home, 126b
Governed, consent of the, 373a
 happiness of the, 494b
 nation is not, 360a
 power from the, 425b
 powers derived from consent of,
 842a
 with little wisdom the world is,
 227b
Governing, just demand made of,
 475b
 men's, principles, 67b
 the nation, 986a
Government, all, every human benefit, 360a
 all persons share in the, 26b
 art of, 325a
 at Washington still lives, 652a
 attachment to their, 360b
 basis of our, 373b
 be upon his shoulder, 1045b
 bend acts of, 399a
 best, desires to make people
 happy, 491b
 better than good, 761a
 blessings a, can confer, 491b
 burden, the was laying, 789b
 by a great aristocracy, 780a
 by a mob, 780a
 by a plutocracy, 780a
 by crony, 874a
 by divine right, 425b
 cannot be stronger, 987a
 cannot endure half slave, 537b
 charming form of, 25a
 conservative, 512a

Grin, dead men, by the wall, 909b
  ending with the, 656b
  firm of, and Barrett, 777a
  how cheerfully he seems to, 656a
  I began to, 1020a
  of all hard things to bear and, 630b
  owned with a, 427a
  smile which is not a, 773b
  so merry draws one out, 371b
  universal, 332b
  wear so wide a, 811b
Grind, axe to, 437b
  exceeding small, 234b, 522b
  faces of the poor, 1045a
  his bones, 1020a
  in the mill of a truism, 501a
  one demd horrid, 577a
  their souls, 729b
  with water that's past, 233b
Grinders cease, 1043b
Grinding, sound of the, 1043b
Grinds, God's mill, slow, 234b
Grindstone, noses to the, 91b
Grinning, mock your own, 178b
Grins, unrepentant sits and, 763b
Grip, lost your, 829a
  middlin' tight, 698b
Griping griefs, 999b
Grips with half her purpose, come to, 897b
Grisildis, in trust to fynde, 81b
Grisly gang, 870b
  thing, face the, 914b
Gristle, people still but in the, 359b
Grizzled, beard was, 171a
  hair just, 276a
Groan, anguish pour'd his, 338a
  condemn'd alike to, 347b
  howl or a, 659b
  nor sigh nor, 224b
  of a martyr's woe, 389a
  sit and hear each other, 481b
  tables, 852a
Groan'd, my mother, 387b
Groaneth, creation, 1060a
Groans, dying, 362a
  more loudly, 920b
  of the wounded, 613b
  sending forth dreadful, 9b
  sighs and, 133a
Groceries, buying clothes and, 899a
Grocer's assets swell, 803a
  golden, boy, 936b
Grog-shop, wild-blazing, 487a
Groined the aisles of Christian Rome, 503a
Gromboolian plain, 582a
Groom there was none to see, 786a
Grooves, ringing, of change, 549a
Grope with little faith, 933b
Gross errors, committed many, 109a
  flattery to name a wretch, 403a
  hungry population violent and, 633b
  people, do not find among, 338a
  things rank and, in nature, 170b
Grossly, close it in, 147a
Grossness, by losing all its, 361a
  earthly, quit, 249b
  measureless, 609a
Grosvenor Gallery, greenery-yallery, 683b
Grot, ferned, 645b
  fringed pool ferned, 645b
Grotesque, result has been, 618a

Grotesque, so, a blunder, 878b
  so striking and so, 493b
Grotesquely wrong, discovered she was, 718a
Ground, call it holy, 470a
  choose thy, 461a
  color of the, 756a
  drops earliest to, 145b
  enough to rot upon the, 307a
  every vice on Christian, 322a
  fallen unto me in a fair, 1032b
  fathom-line never touch, 149b
  fell into good, 1052b
  firm, of result and fact, 868a
  gazes on the, 755b
  holy, 1023b
  kingdoms in a foot of, 979b
  least willing to quit the, 371b
  let us sit upon, 139b
  little patch of, 177b
  lodging is on the cold, 308a
  looks ahead to see kind of, 982a
  lose tomorrow, won today, 621a
  loving hearts in the hard, 962b
  no holier spot of, 644b
  passion that left the, 572a
  plat of rising, 246a
  purple all the, 249b
  return unto the, 1022a
  six foot of, 564a
  sons of dark and bloody, 613a
  spot of, where one grew, 295b
  stand on your own, 585b
  stand your, 358b
  that looked like Eldorado, 545b
  thing we cast to the, 639a
  tiller of the, 1022a
  to own a bit of, 664b
  Tom Tiddler's, 591a
  tread on classic, 298b
  upon one's own sole, 703a
  walks on hallowed, 965a
  water spilt on the, 1028a
  we cannot hallow this, 541a
  when he has reached, 339a
  where is sorrow there is holy, 770a
  withering on the, 4b
Grounded on just and right, 257b
Groundlings, split ears of the, 175b
Grounds are virtue and talents, 375b
Group of seven words, 778b
Grout, here lies Sir Jenkin, 1014b
Grove, Jemmy, 1012b
  meadow, and stream, 408a
  of myrtles, 220a
  olive, of Academe, 259b
Grovel in abject submission, 851b
Groves, o'er shady, they hover, 225b
  of Academe, 41b
  of laurel and myrtle, 378b
  were God's first temples, 471a
Grow, ask me where they, 230a
  asked how pearls did, 230b
  beneath their shoulders, 186b
  both, in one, 138a
  cherries, none may buy, 220b
  enter to, in wisdom, 666a
  find time to, old, 306b
  if left alone, 985a
  ills, milder, 16a
  infernal power to, 847a
  laugh, fat, 159a
  lets, her wings, 247b
  libraries are not made they, 746a

Grow lovely growing old, 891a
  mischievous and kill him, 167a
  my wrath did, 387b
  oaks from little acorns, 401a
  old along with me, 572a
  old and die, 826a
  old, last thing to, 8a
  old learning something new, 8a
  out at heels, 191a
  pleasant fruits do, 220b
  poets by their sufferings, 239b
  resolved to, fat, 275b
  riches, in hell, 253a
  straight, 694b
  to what they seem, 354a
  up as soon as you can, 949a
  upon a spot of ground, 295b
  virtuous in their old age, 321a
  warmer among ruins of Iona, 337b
  whylst grass doth, 93a
  wiser and better, 275a
  world do not, old, 285b
Growed, I 'spect I, 563a
Groweth, flourisheth and, up, 1035b
  sed and bloweth med, 999a
Growing boy, close upon the, 408b
  darling I am, old, 740a
  deeds the circle, 638b
  fonder of my staff, 587b
  I'm, old I've sixty years, 615a
  infirmities of age, 431a
  judgment instruct me, 17a
  old, 587b
  old, loves life like him, 16a
  old, say I'm, 448a
  old, think he is, 446b
  older every minute, 714a
  plants, beauty of, 282b
  potentiality of, rich, 342b
  strength of that people, 516b
  tender and, night, 608a
  when ye're sleeping, 416b
Growl, bears and lions, and fight, 302b
Growled and roared and howled, 421a
Grown by what it fed on, 170b
  calm and very coldly wise, 928b
  from sudden fears, 456b
  men understand it, 107a
  might have, full straight, 123b
  taller from walking, 891a
  world is, so bad, 127b
Grown-up people correct on fact, 784b
  people ought to be more careful, 785a
  people's feet, 750a
Grows and smells not of itself, 219a
  and spreads, 473a
  bald by nature, 129a
  fairer than at first, 207a
  familiar to the lover, 299b
  harder to write, 975a
  lives dies, 140b
  memory as it, fainter, 856a
  no profit, 130a
  nodding violet, 141b
  old and worn with usage, 650a
  on mortal soil, 249a
  one fat, old, 150a
  praise, not old, 20b
  small experience, 130a
  the face, old, 687b
  the mind, old, 26a
  torpid in old age, 342a

Hand, greater things produced by
   His, 229b
handle toward my, 196a
harp within my, 611b
hat in his, 338b
hath made our nation free, 535a
heart in his, 561a
heavier, than kings, 331a
heaving up my either, 231a
heav'n's, or will, 251b
here's my, 209b
hold fire in his, 138b
hold readily in your, 338b
holding out, for charity, 74b
hurts my, 189b
idle thunder in his lifted, 275b
immortal, or eye, 387a
imposition of a mightier, 492a
in hand with God, 889b
in hand with wand'ring steps,
   259a
in its breeches pocket, 478a
industrious, from England, 641a
infection and the, of war, 138b
infinity in palm of your, 388a
iron, in velvet glove, 95a
keep the lifted, in awe, 305a
larger heart the kindlier, 553a
lays icy, on kings, 237b
leans cheek upon her, 135a
leaves thy, in mine, 519a
lend a, 624b
lets the curtain fall, 322b
licks the just raised, 316a
lift up one, to heaven, 744a
like the dyer's, 207a
little thing in, 11a
living, warm and capable, 480a
man's, not able to taste, 142b
mortality's strong, 148b
muckrake in his, 274b
my time is at, 1054b
my times are in thy, 1033b
nature's sweet and cunning, 164a
Nelson's, 695b
not able to taste, 142b
not the, but the understanding,
   107a
of God, 881b
of very healing, 873a
old nonchalance of the, 826b
on her bosom, 190a
one heart one, one nation, 535a
one iron, less, 735a
open, an easy shoe, 795a
our times are in his, 572a
over the lamp of life, 34b
paid for what his mouth ate,
   1014b
papers in each, 318a
prompter's, is on his bell, 686b
raise a, against Rome, 887b
rash, in evil hour, 258a
red right, 253b
richest, showers, 253b
right, offend thee, 1051a
rosy, unbarr'd the gates, 256b
seen God's, through a lifetime,
   571b
shake of the, 943b
so various, 260a
soft, and softer breast, 480a
stretch a, in hour of death, 857a
stretch out your, 65a
stretched out to receive, 1066a
strong as your, can make it,
   888b
sweeten this little, 199a
sweeter in air than in, 121b

Hand, take a pen in his, 339a
tender inward of thy, 207a
that bore a nation, 663a
that hath made you fair, 185a
that held the dagger, 920b
that is honest and hearty, 412b
that kindles, 456a
that made us is divine, 299a
that ope'd the gate, 737a
that rocks the cradle, 606b
that rounded Peter's dome, 503a
things made entirely by, 886a
thoughtless, brush'd away, 387a
three lilies in her, 640b
threw a pearl away, 190b
time hath a taming, 495b
to execute, 369a, 1002a
to mouth, 102b
to one unfriended, 796a
to the plough, 1056b
touch of a vanish'd, 549b
tricks by sleight of, 298a
true love's, 138a
turn your, to, 106a
unbless'd thy, 6b
unearthly, presses the snib, 791b
unfriendly to tyrants, 271b
upon his head, 518b
upon my heart, 524b
upon thy mane, 455a
was on the oar, 23b
wash blood clean from my, 196b
waved her lily, 308a
we in God's, 155b
welcoming, 803a
whatsoever thou takest in, 269b
when he had not a pen in, 342b
whip in every honest, 189b
who hath seen her wave her,
   547b
willow in her, 146b
win the, of woman, 514a
with his, the vessel made, 533a
work of our head and, 816b
Handclasp's a little stronger, 862b
Handel, care a farthing candle for,
   430b
sings wisdom, 507b
Handel's, Mynheer, but a ninny,
   232a
Handfasted, when we are, 417a
Handfasting, this we call, 417a
Hand-flung spears, 584b
Handful, fling us a, of stars, 933b
o' things I know, 698b
of ashes, 895b
of dust, 944a
of grey ashes, 627a
of meal in a barrel, 1028b
of sand, 977b
of silver, 567b
to the tribes that slumber, 470b
Handicap, poverty is a, 929b
Hand-in-glove, you and he were,
   297a
Handiwork, firmament showeth
   his, 1032b
you give to God, 755b
Handkerchief of the Lord, 607b
Handle, lie, which fits them,
   536a
of a broom, 903a
of the big front door, 682a
one old jug without a, 581b
right and wrong, 65a, 370a
taste not, not, 1063a
toward my hand, 196a
Handled with a chain, 646a
Handler, nation's freight, 898a

Handles, everything has two, 65a
everything hath two, 223a
Handmaid and nurse of enterprise,
   925a
Handmaiden, low estate of his,
   1056a
Hands, aching, and bleeding feet,
   620a
acrost th' sea, 833b
administration in, of the many,
   20a
all the rights in their, 517b
are blue, 581a
bearer's, otherwise employed,
   776a
blesseth with two happy, 115a
business goes off a man's, 285b
by fairy, knell is rung, 351b
clap your, 792a
clasp, and weep a little, 486a
clasps the crag with crooked,
   553a
clean, and a pure heart, 1033b
defended by all our, 557a
entergraft our, 216b
extended in straight line, 50a
failing, 86ob
feed out of your tribe's, 821b
feel that I must wash my, 729a
fold my, and wait, 688b
foreign, clos'd thy dying eyes,
   313b
formed the dry land, 1036b
from our, have power, 411b
from picking and stealing, 1069a
full, fortune with both, 153b
hammer away ye hostile, 754b
happiness in the, of others, 434a
hath not a Jew, 145a
hold much of heat, 946b
horny, of toil, 599b
if time be heavy on your, 547a
in your own, 817a
into thy, I commend, 1057b
join your, 127a
kiss her lips and take her, 825a
laid hold of by greedy, 537b
large and sinewy, 521b
lay thy soul full in her, 606b
laying violent, upon ship, 294b
lift up the, in prayer, 725a
little, make vain pretence, 656a
little, were never made, 302b
made before knives, 296b
many, make light worke, 94a
mischief for idle, 302b
mouths without, 281a
musket moulds in his, 747a
my own fair, 295a
nearer than, and feet, 556a
new heraldry is, not hearts, 189a
nobody has such small, 968b
not built with mortal, 279a
not without men's, 596a
now join your, 127a
of America, 888a
of Esau, 1023a
of mem'ry weave, 698b
of sisters death and night, 609b
of the higher classes, 376a
old, to young, 707a
on, and knees follow in it, 500b
on that golden key, 246b
oozing out at palms of my, 381a
pale, I loved, 812b
palms of your, will thicken,
   793b
predatory human, 784b
reach out, amid the stars, 831b

Happiness of society, 368a
    of the common man, 831a, 900a
    of the governed, 494b
    of the human race, 360b
    oh what, to live, 404b
    on earth is no sure, 114a
    on this terrestrial ball, 989b
    or misery of mortal life, 650b
    or our misery, 444a
    our being's end and aim, 317b
    overexpecting, in married estate,
        244a
    particular mood of, 970a
    pastime and, will grow, 410b
    philosophy to attain, 702b
    political prosperity and, 538b
    profligate of, 849b
    pursuit of, 373a, 921a
    recollection of vanished, 711a
    result, 579a
    rob him of his, 642a
    she does not find, 336a
    so much, is produced, 341b
    so perfect as the martyr's, 800b
    solid, we prize, 330a
    soul saw a glimpse of, 243b
    special, of each day, 886a
    sum of human, 780b
    supreme, of life, 497a
    talk, 753b
    that makes heart afraid, 488a
    thirst after, 345a
    thought of tender, 410a
    too swiftly flies, 347b
    true, is of retired nature, 300a
    unforeseen, 447a
    virtue sufficient for, 235b
    was born a twin, 457b
    was never lost, 711a
    what right have we to, 641b
    wherein lies, 479a
    work out, for themselves, 437b
Happy a man as any in the world,
        284b
    accident, 908a
    alchemy of mind, 326b
    always was it for that son, 126a
    as a lover, 409b
    as kings, 750b
    as the daisies that dance, 636b
    as the grass was green, 997a
    as the heart was long, 997a
    autumn-fields, 550b
    born to be, with others, 65a
    bounding flea, 941b
    breed of men, 139a
    call no man, 18b
    called thee so, 427b
    capacity to become, 264b
    Christian child, 442b
    Christmas to all, 437a
    convents bosom'd deep, 322a
    count myself in nothing else so,
        139a
    count them, which endure, 1064a
    dawning of her thigh, 231a
    days that make us, 896b
    days, those were, 301b
    days, world of, 127b
    dead, how fares it with the, 552a
    death, 84b
    desires to make people, 491b
    devote itself to making you,
        765a
    dreams, mother tells me, 747b
    duty of being, 749b
    duty to make him, 585a
    earth, like heaven above, 626b
    ending, bread-sauce of the, 719a

Happy endings, romantic plays
        with, 830b
    existence you wanted, 978b
    families resemble one another,
        642a
    fam'ly, still a, 836b
    feel, deep down, 952b
    fellow-creatures, 371a
    field or mossy cavern, 482b
    fireside clime, 393a
    goes as lucky goes, 887a
    good-night air, 705b
    happy tree, too, 478a
    he alone, 278a
    he is, who hath this only, 58b
    he who could learn causes, 36b
    he who has once been, 703a
    he who knows the country gods,
        36b
    he with such a mother, 551a
    health unto the, 809a
    high majestical, 465b
    highways where I went, 786a
    how, could I be with either, 308b
    human beings, 605b
    human eyes, 751b
    I and wretched he, 584b
    in the United States, 909a
    inexperience, hope of, 576a
    is he born and taught, 213a
    is he who knows them not, 84a
    is rose distill'd, 140b
    is that city, 223a
    is the blameless vestal's lot,
        313a
    is the man possessing a judg-
        ment, 23a
    Isles, touch the, 548b
    land, hail Columbia, 402b
    land, seek the, 584a
    learn'd is, nature to explore,
        317a
    let us all be, 665a
    let us be, as we can, 342b
    letter tell him the page, 647b
    life, spent a, 220a
    lines, lord once own the, 311b
    live completely, 9a
    lived, can say he has, 40a
    living things, 961b
    made him, as a married man,
        340b
    make two lovers, 315b
    man be his dole, 91a
    man cannot be, alone, 720b
    man confines himself, 514b
    man happy dole, 91a
    man in modern world, 914a
    man, pride ever taints, 202b
    man's without a shirt, 90b
    mixtures, 457a
    more, if we had never met, 485a
    morn, this the, 244a
    morn, yields darkness to, 723b
    moron, 1008b
    needed to make, life, 68a
    never so, as we imagine, 265a
    never was so, 1003b
    New Years, 580b
    no birds so, as we, 582a
    no man is, 45b
    no one can be, till all are happy,
        614b
    noise to hear, 786a
    not a place so, as America, 370b
    old age, 498a
    pair live while ye may, 255b
    parents are able to think calmly,
        702b

Happy past, not in forgetting, 670a
    people, in their work, 605a
    people not afraid of death, 823a
    place, hope hath, 592b
    place to be, is here, 662b
    ports and, havens, 138a
    prospects in view, 65b
    recall, time in wretchedness, 75b
    remote from the, 993b
    sad and, days of yore, 750a
    say that man is, 15b
    sleep, 84b
    songs, wrote my, 385a
    state, full description of a, 283b
    the farmers, 36b
    the heart that sighed, 122a
    the house that shelters a friend,
        502a
    the man, 326b
    the man that hath quiver full,
        1037b
    the man who can call today his
        own, 39b, 278a
    the man who has learned his
        place, 51a
    the man whose wish and care,
        309a
    the people whose annals are
        blank, 476b
    they that hear detractions, 157b
    they whose walls already rise,
        36b
    thing to be father, 126b
    those early days, 272a
    though married, 804b
    thrice, they, 38b
    time to be, is now, 662b
    to be, 909a
    to have been, 73b
    'twere now to be most, 32a, 187a
    warrior, 409b, 864b
    warrior sleeps, 924b
    way to be, 662b
    ways of doing things, 505a
    we, few, 156b
    were but little, 157b
    where we ust to be so, 746a
    which is, in this world, 565a
    who crowns in shades, 355b
    who in his verse can steer, 286a
    winds upon her played, 549b
    workaday people, 959b
    young are, never, 780b
Harangue, telling nothing in a
        great, 270a
Harangued, exhibited and, 22b
Harass the distrest, 335b
Harbinger, amber scent her, 260a
    love's, 259a
Harbingers, pious thoughts as,
        243b
Harbor, arrived in a good, 229b
    bar be moaning, 598a
    cleared, 421a
    is a good thing, 742a
    more virtue than doth live, 218b
    never one in, as white, 740a
    put up in New York, 766b
    ship comes into the, 229b
    where lies the final, 604b
    with my Sylvia nightly, 132a
Harbors wealth of valued verse,
        960a
Hard as for a camel, 140b
    as piece of nether millstone,
        1032a
    beginning maketh good ending,
        91b
    beset, I am being woman, 934b

Haunt, public, 159b
  the rich man's door, 38b
  where they most breed and, 195b
  you yet, 890b
Haunted air, 948b
  by a demoniac throng, 731a
  by ghosts they have depos'd,
  139b
  houses, 523b
  me like a passion, 404a
  spring and dale, 244b
  stream, 245b
  waning moon was, 420b
Haunts and obsesses my brain,
  486a
  busy, of men, 470a
  love seldom, the breast, 309b
  me like a face half known, 780b
  me night and day, 928b
  suspicion, guilty mind, 127a
  the tempest, 618b
  thy days, 480a
Have, all we, and are, 821b
  more than thou showest, 191a
  not what we, 780b
  nought venter nought, 93a
  they lack I, 101b
  to, to hold, 812b, 1069a
  what we would have, 184b
Have-beens, no sense of, 706a
Have-much and Have-little, 108a
Haven, down to the, 556b
  glorious, 76a
  in sunny Palestine, 896b
  safe into the, glide, 334a
  under the hill, 549b
Haven's gate, people wait at, 862a
Havens dumb, green swell in the,
  724b
  ports and happy, 138a
Having nothing nothing can he
  lose, 126b
  nothing yet possessing, 1062a
Having-been-in-danger, 884a
Having-gone-to-the-very-end, 884b
Havoc, cry, 163a
Hawk, know a, from a handsaw,
  174a
  or a buzzard, 983a
  their wares, 949a
  wild, to the wind-swept sky,
  815a
Hawk'd at and kill'd, 197a
Hawk-eyes and cheek of apple-
  blossom, 554b
Hawk's the darling of his fere,
  29b
Hawks, between two, 124a
  such hounds such, 1012b
Hawthorn bush with seats, 355b
  hedge, 938a
  in the dale, 245a
  snow of the, 777a
Hawthorne to Montaigne to Baudelaire, 751b
Hay, bottle of, 142a
  cry was still more, 748a
  dance the antic, 123a
  farmers make, 803a
  for the cattle, 59a
  live on, 1009a
  make, when the sunne shineth,
  91a
  needle in a bottle of, 107b
  turkey in the, 1003b
  world is a bundle of, 460a
  worth a load of, 1000a
Haycock, needle in the, 957b
Haydn, some cry up, 430b

Haystack, under the, fast asleep,
  1016a
Hazard, art's long, 846b
  march to the unseen, 809a
  not the, but the play, 829b
  of concealing, 391a
  of new fortunes, 147b
  of the die, 128b
  runs a very great, 107a
  when a nation's life's at, 625a
Hazardous, definitions are, 336b
Haze, shimmering golden, 849b
  that side of the, 647a
Hazel, Glenartey's, shade, 415a
Hazel-switch for discovery of treasure, 823b
Hazlitt to Lamb to Wordsworth,
  751b
He, faithful only, 256b
  for God only, 255b
  forget the, and she, 215b
  has given bees honey, 326a
  has invented history, 327a
  let's eat, 564b
  poorest, in England, 228b
  that is thy friend indeed, 220a
  that is without sin, 1058a
  think of yourself as, 844b
  who does not mind his belly,
  340a
  who goes to bed sober, 225a
Head aches, when the, 107a
  and front of my offending, 186a
  and shoulders, bring in by, 100a
  and the hoof of the law, 815b
  anointest my, with oil, 1033b
  as full of quarrels, 136b
  at his, a grass-green turf, 177b
  audacious, is lifted, 661a
  binds so dear a, 467a
  bow thy, in gentle spite, 629a
  bowed his comely, 268b
  center the hub the king pin,
  661a
  chills upon the, or heart, 751b
  chop off her, 656b
  chop off your, 1016a
  coals of fire upon his, 1041a
  complex problem of the, 811a
  concerned with outer weather,
  881a
  contempt comes from the, 461a
  crack like that in her, 732a
  crotchets in thy, 180a
  crown in heart not, 126b
  crown of his, 158a, 451a
  crown of the, 50a
  crown old Winter's, 263b
  disorders of the, 19a
  dissever from the fair, 312b
  erect beneath the tragic years,
  774a
  fame over his living, 468a
  gently falling on thy, 302b
  give him a blow on the, 72a
  good gray, 553a
  great, of things, 49a
  grown gray in vain, 468a
  guts in his, 181b
  hair of yon gray, 528a
  hair on my, stands up, 16a
  hairs of their owner's, 708a
  hand upon his, 518b
  hang the, as discontent, 220b
  hangs his, for shame, 627b
  hat upon my, 338b
  heaven upon earth to weary,
  488b
  heels higher than my, 101a

Head, heels up to the, 750b
  hide his, under his wing, 1018a
  hit nail on the, 89a
  hoary, 529a
  hoary, is a crown of glory,
  1039b
  horror's, 189a
  humour not more from the, 472b
  if she'd but turn her, 825b
  I'll eat my, 576b
  imperfections on my, 172b
  in my heart not on my, 126b
  in the heart or in the, 145a
  inside a wolf's mouth, 9b
  is bloody but unbowed, 741b
  keep good tongue in your, 209b
  kicked in, by a mule, 828b
  King Charles's, 579a
  lay my, upon my grave, 241a
  lift my, till it strikes, 38a
  lock upon the shapely, 717b
  made up the lilac out of my,
  934a
  man with the, 550b
  Medusa's, 960b
  my, is bending low, 636a
  no roof to shroud his, 227a
  not silver'd o'er, 364b
  not so long by the, 133b
  of the army, 400a
  of the table, 501a
  of this great widespread family,
  812a
  off with her, 657a
  off with his, 128a
  old gray, 527b
  on her knee, 190a
  one small, 356b
  over, and heels, 35a
  plant thou no roses at my, 649b
  planted in the human, 461a
  pleasing land of drowsy, 328b
  ragged, seld-shaven, 429a
  repairs his drooping, 249b
  seems no bigger than his, 193a
  she bow'd, 246a
  shot it through the, 1019b
  silent doctor shook his, 308a
  silver'd o'er with age, 308a
  smote off his, 1026b
  some once lovely, 531b
  stand on your, 656a
  statuaries loved to copy, 492a
  stone of the corner, 1037a
  stroked down with a slipper,
  32a
  stuff, with all such reading, 322a
  sweete tooth in his, 112b
  that wears a crown, 153b
  thing comes in his, 127a
  thoughts in our, 817a
  thoughts into a lover's, 405a
  tired her, 1029b
  to contrive, 369a
  trickled through my, 659a
  turned her little, aside, 1014a
  twenty years, of a household,
  816a
  upon the lap of earth, 349a
  useful lesson to the, 365b
  very staid, 146a
  where to lay his, 1052a
  whole, is sick, 1045a
  wild ass stamps o'er his, 531b
  wires grow on her, 207b
  wise man's eyes in his, 1042a
  work of our, and hand, 816b
  worst fall on, 148b
  young body with old, 146a

Headache, lying awake with a dismal, 684a
or sciatica, 505b
Headdress, lady's, 300b
Headlines, read the, 990a
Headlong, hurled, 252a
Heads, all the, in the world, 510a
are green, 581a
are just as bare, 955b
baskets on their, 949a
diminish'd, 255a
get gray, 707a
grow beneath shoulders, 186b
houseless, 192a
hung their, 485b
land of broken, 867b
monster with uncounted, 152a
of the same material, 937b
on your own, 817a
over the, of people you meet, 632a
put our, together, 881a
seat on people's backs and, 726b
see without turning their, 922b
so little there is no room, 243b
so many, so many wits, 32b
tall men had empty, 89b
tossing their, 409a
touch heaven, 186a
two, better than one, 92a
we common people nod our, 803a
wooden, arc inherited, 857b
Headstones, milestones into, change, 602b
Headstrong as an allegory, 381a
liberty, 129a
Heal, fame can never, 582b
full many a strife, 329b
heart may, or break, 558a
physician, thyself, 1056b
the blows of sound, 534b
the rod must, the sin, 712b
the tortured mind, 471b
Healed of a suffering, 856a
the heart that's broken, 558a
Healer, Death the, 13a
Healers, best of, 13b
Healing, hand of very, 873a
in his wings, 1050a
is matter of time, 21b
tears that bring no, 620a
virtue, 526b
Wordsworth's, power, 620b
Heals, prayer that, the sick, 616b
the heart, 993a
Health, accidents of, 812a
and a day, 501a
and good sense, 46a
and quiet breathing, 478b
and wealth have missed me, 448a
blessed, 346b
blossom of, 462a
by his, sickness, 385b
double, to thee, 456b
drink a, to the wonders, 856b
ease, and life resign, 309b
enjoy good, 40b
good, and mind's content, 285b
grace affordeth, 101b
heart's, is to be sick with love, 961b
heaven vouchsafe me, 763b
holy, 9a
horse's, 192b
in, in sickness, 336a
in sickness and in, 1069a
innocence and, 355b

Health is the second blessing, 236b
it might hurt, 358a
lead a sick man to, 16b
look to your, 236b
medicine to produce, 57b
of nations, 930b
of the people, 513a
on both, 197b
peace and competence, 317b
perfect state of, 65b
physic to preserve, 121a
protect the, of community, 919b
rather out of, 788a
recover their, 21b
sinlessness and immortality, 616b
strength and life itself, 933b
talk, 753b
that mocks, 527a
time nor, nor life, 428b
to fond deceit, 810b
to sick men, 110a
unbought, 280b
unto the happy, 809a
vital principle of bliss, 329a
wealth and beauty, 263a
Healthful and his wits about him, 264b
ease, 488b
members, 107a
Healths, urge no, 356b
Healthy and gentle characteristics, 514b
breath of morn, 483a
care for the, 22a
free the world before me, 608b
hatred of scoundrels, 476a
imagination of a boy is, 478b
instinct for it, 672a
sick danger for the, 727b
wealthy and dead, 971b
wealthy and wise, 330b
Heap, choose badness in a, 7a
coals of fire, 1041a, 1060a
dead beneath the, 790a
dig and, lay stone on stone, 620a
high the farmer's hoard, 526b
misfortunes laid in one common, 60a
o' livin', 913b
of dust alone remains, 313b
of stick and stone, 706a
of wheat, 1044b
on more wood, 414b
struck all of a, 381b
thrown on the scrap, 765a
undistinguished, of ruins, 353a
Heaped for the beloved's bed, 468b
Heapeth up riches, 1034a
Heaps of couch grass, 706b
of things have bitten me, 22a
soul's wealth lies in, 650a
unsunn'd, of treasure, 247b
Hear a little song, 378b
a sudden cry of pain, 922b
afeard to, worst, 148b
an old man, 60a
be silent that you may, 168a
beyond the range of sound, 591a
detractions, 157b
go with them to, the priest, 273a
greater inclination to, you, 301b
have ears and, not, 292b
have ears but, not, 1037a
he that hath ears to, 1052b
I, America singing, 607a
list'ning they seemed to, 6b
loves to, himself talk, 136a

Hear me for my cause, 168a
moves more than, them told, 131b
not my steps, 196a
of me before three, 301b
one may, 502a
one to speak another to, 588b
quickness to, to move, 809a
rather, thy discourse, 223b
repeat but half of what you, 1006b
sea-maid's music, 141b
see a sermon than, one, 913b
seldom, good of themselves, 292b
so many hollow compliments, 259b
the angels sing, 560b
the daisies grow, 767a
the griefs of kin, 15a
the latest Pole, 943a
thee and rejoice, 409a
time will come when you will, me, 511b
time's wingèd chariot, 269a
what you say to the contrary, 508a
world might, and stare, 751a
you I will come, 786a
your prayers, 11a
Heard a bird at break of day, 932b
ain't, nothin' yet, 936a
by the hearing of the ear, 1032a
chimes at midnight, 153b
eye of man hath not, 142b
have ye not, 1047a
I will be, 517a
idly spoken and so coldly, 510b
in tale or song, 246b
less he spoke the more he, 876b
melodies are sweet, 482a
never was it spoken never, 840a
of my going to plays, 286a
one side of the case, 672a
reasons manifold, 141a
so have I, 170a
the laughter of her heart, 958b
the nightingale, 56a
the other side, 18a
the world around, 244b
woman seen not, 14b
Heare, eare, that tong, 114b
fooles talke to, 113a
neither, nor see, 94b
Hearer thinks he can do as well, 20a
Hearers, anxious to convince, 21a
dying, such as you, 1014a
like my books, 117b
that our merits know, 4b
too deep for his, 357b
Hearing ear and seeing eye, 1040a
ear filled with, 1042a
passionate my sense of, 133a
posterity will give a fair, 672a
world that was within my, 285b
Hearken, to, better than the fat of rams, 1027a
to the voice of charmers, 1035a
Hearkeners seldom hear good, 292b
Hears, ear of him that, it, 134a
speak to Him thou for He, 556a
tell all he sees or, 284a
thy faintest word, 263a
Hearse, marriage, 387b
sable, 230a

Heart, absence absence in the, 946b
abundance of the, 1052b
ageless in your, 899b
alike conceived and dared, 570a
all thy, lies open unto me, 551a
and stomach of a king, 97a
and the soul and the senses, 571a
and voice oppressed, 593a
and voice would fail me, 645a
anniversaries of the, 526a
another heart divines, 524b
arrow for the, 460a
as a seal upon thine, 1044b
as great as the world, 508a
as he thinketh in his, 1040b
as that of a little child, 566a
at rest within my breast, 385b
balm of the bruised, 122a
batter my, 217b
beating of my own, 543a
beats the, so kindly, 582b
because my, is pure, 549a
best, best brain, 662b
bitten me to the, 22a
blessed are pure in, 1050b
breast encloseth my poor, 127b
broken and contrite, 1034b
broken, lies here, 494a
bruis'd, was pierced, 186b
build on the human, 567a
burn within us, 413b
burning at the, of living, 977b
can push the sea, 961b
captain with the mighty, 756a
carries my, as stowaway, 876b
caused widow's, to sing, 1031b
change the, from red, 712b
changeth man's countenance, 1066a
chill the warmest, 630a
chills upon the head or, 751b
clean, 1034b
clean hands and a pure, 1033b
cold of his, 802a
command my, and me, 263a
committed adultery in his, 1050b
congenial to my, 357a
constant, 999b
consume my, away, 827a
courage of, or holiness, 849a
cracks a noble, 179b
crown is in my, 126b
cruelty has a human, 387b
cure thy, of love, 500a
cutting the, asunder, 923b
dark as one's own, 514a
darkies how my, grows weary, 636a
darling of my, 307b
deceitful and wicked, 1048a
depth of the, of man, 1065b
detests him, 4b
devils dwell in, of man, 240b
disease, housemaid's knee to, 862a
distress touching his, 371a
distrusting asks, 357a
do not devour thy, 72b
dry of blood, 480a
ease a, like a satin gown, 966a
ease thine, of love, 500a
eat not thy, 57b
eate thy, 114a
enrich not the, of another, 522b
everywhere he feels his, 3a
excitement of the, 545a
expends his whole, 379a

Heart fail because of Goliath, 1027b
faint, ne'er won fair lady, 107b
faint, never won fair lady, 684a
falsehood leads to the, 373b
felt along the, 403b
female, can gold despise, 347b
find thy, at home, 232a
find your, despair, 591a
fire that in the, resides, 620a
flaw'd, 193b
flowers of Thy, 441b
fond, till we meet, 329a
for any fate, 521a
for every fate, 456b
fountain of sweet tears, 406a
from itself kept, 689b
gathered to thy, 736b
give a loving, 230a
give me back my, 452b
give not your, away, 785b
give your, to a dog, 819b
gives his, and soul away, 785b
glad with all my, 122b
gladness of the, 1066a
glow of a kindly, 729b
glows in ev'ry, 305a
God made a, of gold, 877b
good, is better than all the heads, 510a
great thoughts come from, 115b
grieve his, 198b
grown cold, 468a
gushed from my, 422a
hand and, to this vote, 443a
happiest, that ever beat, 738a
happy as the, was long, 997a
happy the, that sighed, 122a
hard, of a child, 934b
hardened Pharaoh's, 1024a
has hidden treasures, 586b
has its love, 486a
has its reasons, 272b
hath but one eye, 755a
hath ne'er within him burned, 413b
hath 'scap'd this sorrow, 206a
hatred comes from the, 461a
have its say, 760b
healed the, that's broken, 558a
heals the, 993a
here in the country's, 800a
heresy of, 527b
hid in the, of love, 824b
high as my, 162a
his grave a nation's, 629a
hit a woman's, 509a
how dear to this, 450a
how goes it, 849a
how many a, must pass me by, 733b
humble and a contrite, 816a
humble human, in pain, 830b
hurt you to the, 679a
I told her all my, 386a
if every, were just frank, 270a
if, fails thee climb not, 111a
if guilt's in that, 439b
if one has no, 486b
imagination of man's, 1022b
in each, a little heaven, 294a
in every true woman's, 446a
in his hand, 561a
in the midst of crowds, 431a
in the, or in the head, 145a
in unison with all mankind, 741a
incense of the, 330a
infant, 431b

Heart, into her, too easy, 258a
is a lonely hunter, 762a
is all a-flutter, 995b
is getting softer, 606a
is Highland, 436a
is in a whirl, 829b
is inditing a good matter, 1034b
is like a singing bird, 649b
is made better, 1042b
is not here, 392b
is on the mountain still, 796b
is open wide tonight, 767a
is slow to learn, 962a
is sorrowful, 1039b
is there with thee, 797a
is turning home again, 757a
is wax moulded, 110a
is where the hills fling up, 796b
jot of, or hope, 251b
joys of our, 487b
keep thy, with diligence, 1038b
keep, when all have lost it, 566b
kep' goin' pity-pat, 601a
kept these sayings in her, 1056b
key to your, 519a
kind and gentle, 354b
knocked on my sullen, 751b
know truth by the, 272b
knoweth his own bitterness, 1039a
laid his hand upon my, 524b
language of the, 319b
languor is not in your, 623a
larger, the kindlier hand, 553a
larger was his, 277b
laughter of her, 958b
leaps up when I behold, 406a
leave the, aglow, 830a
let every, prepare Him room, 303a
let not thine, be glad, 1040b
let not your, be troubled, 1058b
level in her husband's, 164b
like bowl brimming over, 659b
little body with a mighty, 154b
live without, 653a
living, and hearth-stone, 539b
lock'd my, in a case o' gowd, 1013a
look in thy, 115b
look into any man's, 641a
looked into his father's, 987a
Lord looketh on the, 1027b
love lays hold on gentle, 75b
love that is in my, 486a
love-sick, dies, 961a
make glad the, of childhood, 701b
makes the, afraid, 488a
makes the, grow fonder, 485a
makes the, run over, 372a
maketh glad the, of man, 1036b
man after his own, 1027a
manly, 521b
man's, deviseth his way, 83a
man's, is small, 816b
may give a useful lesson, 365b
may go where it will, 43a
may heal or break, 558a
may she find all one, 624b
meditation of my, 1033a
meek and lowly in, 1052b
meet a mutual, 328b
memory plays tune on, 591a
mend the, 312b
merry, doeth good, 1040a
merry, goes all the day, 208a
merry, hath a continual feast, 1039b

Hunger and thirst after righteous-
　　ness, 1050b
　　and war and weather, 781b
　　because of the body's, 930a
　　bodily, in his eyes, 765b
　　fer 'em somehow, 913b
　　for a well-stored mind, 741a
　　for self-approval, 679b
　　if any chance to, 110a
　　if thine enemy, 1060a
　　is staring her in the face, 963a
　　man be done with, 16b
　　no sauce like, 107b
　　teacher of the arts, 24a
　　toil, nakedness, 484b
　　untroubled by, 980a
Hungered, for I was an, 1054b
Hungry and he gave him not meat,
　　352b
　　and squalid population, 633b
　　and thin of face, 953a
　　as the grave, 327b
　　bellies, fill their, 229b
　　clouds swag on the deep, 385b
　　eats when he is not, 1006b
　　edge of appetite, 138b
　　filled, with good things, 1056a
　　generations tread thee down, no,
　　481b
　　guests, like, 304a
　　had to go to bed, 841a
　　if thine enemy be, 1041a
　　judges the sentence sign, 312b
　　lean and, look, 166b
　　lean, men, 445b
　　lean-faced villain, 129b
　　lion gives a grievous roar, 420a
　　makes, where she satisfies, 200b
　　man is not a free man, 986b
　　man's food, 598b
　　meat for the, 109b
　　mouth is prest, 936a
　　packs of wolves, 697b
　　plight, 1003a
　　poet should always be, 981b
　　poor, phantom of the, 674a
　　rich when he is, 72a
　　sheep look up, 249a
　　sinner, 459b
　　soul, to the, 1041a
　　tigers are getting, 868b
　　younguns allus, 930b
Hungry-looking men, 57b
Hunt a joy to death, 853a
　　down love together, 693a
　　for a desert isle, 995b
　　in fields for health, 280b
　　the house through, 569a
Hunted, all day they, 1019a
　　and hollo'd, 333a
　　little, hares, 854a
　　past reason, 207a
Hunter, Bahram that great, 531b
　　home from the hill, 751b
　　horn of the, 491b
　　Indian, pursued the deer, 464a
　　man is the, 550b
　　my heart is a lonely, 762a
　　night the dark-blue, 839b
　　Nimrod the mighty, 1023a
　　of the east, 531a
Hunters of dreams, 777b
　　who hunt for gunless game,
　　777b
Hunter-state of man, 430a
Hunting big game, 950a
　　form of war on the weak, 876b
　　handsome, man, 863a
　　weary wi', 1013a

Huntlie Bank, true Thomas lay on,
　　1012b
Hunts in dreams, 548b
Huntsman, as a, his pack, 358a
　　winds his horn, 332b
Huntsmen are up in America, 241b
　　three jolly, 1019a
　　three jovial, 332b
Hurdy-gurdies make it their own,
　　739b
Hurdy-gurdy, violin is not a, 653a
Hurl, the halt and the, 815b
Hurl'd, atoms or systems into
　　ruin, 316a
　　raised aloft, in the dust, 623a
Hurled, Almighty Power, head-
　　long, 252a
　　gods out of their skies, 266b
　　in ruin and confusion, 299a
　　Pelion from Ossa, 6a
　　world and her train were, 272a
Hurlyburly's done, 194a
Hurrah for the next that dies,
　　627b
　　we bring the jubilee, 660b
Hurricane, one night came on a,
　　377a
　　sired by a, 676a
　　win' can blow lak, 758b
Hurried and worried until buried,
　　892a
　　away by excitement, 64b
Hurries back for more, 412b
Hurry at the touch of fate, 897a
　　being in a, 976a
　　never, 557b
　　never in a, 329b
　　to get up when we fall, 923b
　　to that fatal fall, 15a
　　try to, history, 986b
　　up, American motto, 906b
　　up please its time, 944a
Hurrying, delaying not, not, 609a
　　feet, clang of, 582b
　　two, shapes met, 680b
　　world, parted by the, 404b
Hurt cannot be much, 136b
　　do a mortal little, 798a
　　do nothing for to, her, 564a
　　fact that you're, 829b
　　help with things that, 719b
　　little wren, 388a
　　minds, balm of, 196b
　　more frayd than, 91b
　　never, a hair of Him, 926a
　　no, found upon Daniel, 1049a
　　no living creature, 12b
　　rather frightened than, 671a
　　sweareth to his own, 1032b
　　that honour feels, 548b
　　too badly, to laugh, 540a
　　what he finds, 121a
　　why should I, thee, 345b
Hurteth not toung to give faire
　　words, 92a
Hurtful power o'er virginity, 247b
Hurting himself and others, 222a
Hurtles in the darken'd air, 350a
Hurts my hand, 189b
　　you have cured, 507a
Husband a whole-time job, 832b
　　and wife and lover, 638b
　　at all times your faithful, 301b
　　bad, and ill-provider, 505a
　　chaste to her, 314b
　　commandeth her, 243b
　　crying over a, 814a
　　delight of her, 946b
　　detested her first, 768a

Husband, endure, with beard, 157a
　　frae the wife despises, 393b
　　heavy, 147b
　　lover in the, may be lost, 343a
　　ne'er answers till a, cools, 314b
　　not oftener to church, 931b
　　shape a, 564b
　　woman oweth to her, 131a
Husbanded, so father'd and so,
　　167b
Husbandry, advised my father to
　　good, 284b
　　dulls edge of, 171b
　　in heaven, 196a
Husband's eye, looks lovely in her,
　　403a
　　heart, level in her, 164b
　　sister's, niece, 660a
Husbands look behind and wish,
　　955a
　　too carefully to waste it, 671a
Hush my dear, 302b
　　whisper who dares, 917b
　　with the setting moon, 554a
Hushaby Street, Rock-a-By Lady
　　from, 747a
Hush'd and smooth, 479a
Hushed are the stars, 890b
　　busy world is, 1069b
　　every thought that springs, 411b
Husking, laws of, 383a
Husks, strew'd with, 182b
Husky, stormy, brawling, 898a
　　whisper, breathed the, 753b
Hustings, world's, 604a
Hustle the East, 814b
Hustled, Indian summer of life
　　never, 698a
Hustles, he tells you how he, 867b
Huswife's wool, 248a
Hut, dear, our home, 330a
　　give me a log, 652a
　　I only wish a, of stone, 536a
　　love in a, 480b
　　of the peasant, 759a
Huxley, Thomas Henry, 981a
Huzza'd out of my seven senses,
　　90a
Hwang, Emperor, 725a
Hyacinth hair, 543b
　　the garden wears, 531b
Hyacinth's temperament, 851b
Hyacinths to feed thy soul, 734a
Hybla bees, 169a
Hyena skin, sold a, 871b
　　voice of the, 117a
Hyla breed that shouted, 88oa
Hymettus, honey of, 661a
Hymn, can sing half a, 845a
　　chants doleful, 148b
　　sober as a, 741b
　　the Brahmin sings, 507a
Hymn-book, coat and bands and,
　　517a
　　skin and bones and, 517a
Hymns, chanting faint, 140b
Hymself, ech man for, 80a
Hyperion to a satyr, 170b
Hyperion's curls, 176b
Hyphenated Americanism, 780a
Hypocrisy, base alloy of, 537b
　　Christian without, 660a
　　in the wurruld, 836a
　　is homage vice pays, 265b
　　organized, 512a
　　sincerity and, 370b
　　supercilious, of a bishop, 1002a
　　world safe for, 987b
Hypocrite falls into sin, 73a

Industrious, obscure, men of let-
    ters, 832a
Scots, 116b
to make themselves uneasy,
    105b
true, friend, 149a
Industry, brooding, 807a
cultivated, and frugality, 624a
delving in patient, 707a
fountain of, 444b
his, his judgment, 359b
in art a necessity, 668b
in position of predominance,
    910b
life without, is guilt, 606a
love of bustle is not, 47a
manured with, 186b
provision by your, 1070b
race of modern, 593b
regulate their pursuits of, 374b
without art, 606a
Indyans, presarved fr'm th', 834a
Inebriate, cheer but not, 306b,
    364b
of air am I, 646a
Inebriated virtue, 695a
with the exuberance, 513a
Ineffable, mystic sees the, 875a
Ineffective, archaic cumbrous and,
    776b
Ineffectual, beautiful and, angel,
    623b
yesterdays, 742a
Inelegance, continual state of,
    427b
Ineluctable problem of human
    folly, 914a
Inequalities, shams, and unfair-
    nesses, 679b
Inert, earth tideless and, 737b
facts, 697a
hidden handful of the, 604a
Inertia of matter, 883a
Inestimable blessing, a baby is an,
    675a
Inevitability of gradualness, 791a
Inevitable, arguing with the, 603b
defeat, 908a
hour, await the, 348a, 973a
war is, 900b
war is not, 799b
Inexactitude, terminological, 868a
Inexhaustible, city was, 958b
sensibility, 720a
Inexorability of a law of nature,
    594a
Inexorable as one's self, 514a
more fierce and more, 137b
Inexperience, hope of happy, 576a
Inexplicable dumb-shows and
    noise, 175b
Inexpressible as sweet, 762a
desire, give me my, 739b
Inextinguishable passion of
    woman, 297b
Infallibility, faith in her own,
    900a
Infallible proceeding, 651b
rule, 330b
test of blameless style, 425a
Infamous are fond of fame, 362b
delay, chides his, 305b
peace with cowardice is, 31a
rich quiet and, 493a
thing, crush the, 325a
Infamy be heaped on my memory,
    562a
date which will live in, 921a
lived without, and praise, 75a

Infamy of his nature, 241b
worst of the city's, 845b
Infancy, heaven about us in our,
    408b
nations have their, 304a
not only around our, 600a
old age remote from, 118b
terror to, is solitude, 715b
tetchy and wayward thy, 128a
Infant crying in the night, 552a
heart, 431b
heir to the whole world, 578a
mewling and puking, 161a
of three, 946b
sagacity brooding, 935b
soul unfolds, 565a
those who have lost an, 448b
year, firstling of the, 237a
Infantry, moved out that match-
    less, 740a
Infantryman's eyes, look at an,
    997b
Infant's breath, regular as, 423b
cry of fear, 387b
new born, tear, 387b
Infants, canker galls, of the
    spring, 171a
unbaptized, 705a
who but, question, 640b
Infatuated and besotted, 222b
luck is, with the efficient, 505b
Infect, false words, the soul, 21a
sickness, 151a
to north star, 157b
Infected, all seems, 311b
Infecting the city at large, 55b
Infection and the hand of war,
    138b
moral, 580a
Infelicity seem'd to have years too
    many, 226a
Inferior, bear yourself as gods',
    39a
books, life too short for, 605b
grievances, 1001b
lest it prove, 536b
of any man, 662a
providence of the, 662b
Inferiority, acknowledgment of,
    442a
moral, 679b
senator seldom proclaims, 696a
to the choice hidden handful,
    604a
Inferiors, advantages over their,
    108b
live with your, 566a
revolt to be equal, 26b
Infernal clime, crusaders from
    some, 534b
constancy, 764b
licentious abominable, 382a
power to grow, 847a
serpent, 252a
Inferno, Dante of the dread, 571b
Infest, cares that, the day, 522a
Infidelity, fanatic in his, 496a
Infidels, Jews kiss and, adore,
    312a
sextillions of, 608a
Infinite, as good as, 473b
book of secrecy, 200a
capacity for taking pains, 476a
capacity of the human mind,
    382a
day excludes the night, 303a
echo of the, 709a
faculties of man, 474a
forms, evil has, 272b

Infinite goodness has such wide
    arms, 76a
heart's ease, 156a
height in divine knowledge,
    100a
in faculty, 173b
in his desires, 463a
in wealth and depth of tone,
    697b
jest, fellow of, 178b
love, marvellous mercies and,
    692b
meadows of heaven, 522b
mercy on the day of judgment,
    774a
movement, time is, 642b
number of worlds, 58a
pain, good out of, 716a
passion, only I discern, 569a
possibilities that are, 797b
power, individualize, 617a
primary cause was the, 70b
riches in little room, 124a
space, atom of that, 615b
space, king of, 173b
spaces, silence of these, 272b
though, can never meet, 269a
we aim at the, 710b
what is that to the, 497a
while men believe in the, 590b
wrath and despair, 255a
Infinitesimal fraction of a prod-
    uct, 474a
Infinitesimals, countless, of feel-
    ing, 425b
Infinitude of silence, 614a
Infinity in palm of your hand,
    388a
which moves us, 806b
Infirm, minstrel was, and old,
    413a
of purpose, 196b
weak and despised old man,
    191b
Infirmities, bear his friend's, 169a
of age, 431a
Infirmity, last, of noble mind,
    249a
Infix'd and frozen round, 254b
Inflame and fix its barbarism,
    832b
Inflaming wine pernicious, 4b
Inflation is repudiation, 859a
reckless, 783a
Inflexible, we must be, 869b
Inflexibly committed to the task,
    987a
Inflicting one calamity, 44a
Inflicts, life, its worst, 654b
Influence, against his own per-
    sonal, 490a
cock has great, 44b
commands all, 224b
destiny exercises its, 726a
make sure of power and, 341a
of an author, 696b
of lawyers, 516a
of music, 809b
of poverty or wealth, 24b
of wealth, 444b
of wise and good men, 471b
our, may fall, 717b
over minds of men, 925a
people, 942b
powerful and enduring an,
    925a
rain, 245b
salutary, of example, 337b
stars have, upon me, 99a

Influence, unaw'd by, 436b
　widest helpful, 605b
　wise man have so little, 19b
Influences, good humor of outside,
　838b
　of Pleiades, 1032a
　past that, our lives, 956a
　skyey, 184b
　wide world-embracing, 473a
Inform, occasions do, against me,
　177b
Information, benignant, 854a
　know where we can find, 341a
　only ask for, 579a
　private, 769b
　speak from chance, 19b
Infortune, worste kynde of, 78b
Infuse, raptures that yourselves,
　290b
　themselves in trunks of men,
　146a
Infused opinions, learning and,
　154a
Ingenious assembly of portable
　plumbing, 957a
　machine for turning, 930a
　speculation, 84b
Ingenuity avails, how much, 48b
Ingenuously confess, 119a
Inglorious arts of peace, 268b
　mute, Milton, 348b
　mute, Miltons, 908b
Ingratiate deeply with the mind,
　298a
Ingratitude, hate, more in a man,
　165b
　man's, 161b
　of those risen above him, 341b
　thou marble-hearted fiend, 191a
Ingredient of genius, 334a
Ingredients of our poison'd chal-
　ice, 195b
　three, in the good life, 978a
Ingress, man's, into the world,
　378a
Inhabit, house we, together, 569a
　soul, bird, 146a
　this bleak world, 439a
　void of fellow men to, 15a
Inhabitants, horizon for its, 424b
　of a fourth dimension, 990b
　only, of the field, 361a
　town that boasts, like me, 524a
Inhabited by writers of small his-
　tories, 336b
Inhabits our frail blood, 165b
Inharmonious, sickness sin and
　death, 616b
Inhere as do the suns, 649a
Inherit, all which it, shall dis-
　solve, 210a
　good as it is to, a library, 746a
　pain, 132a
　the earth, 1034a, 1050b
　vasty hall of death, 621a
　wits, after death, 309b
Inheritance, dearest, 1001b
　divided an, with him, 372a
　learn extent of our, 613b
　meek to enter into their, 855a
　questions of taste of, 696b
Inherited from our fathers, 641b
　tradition cannot be, 943b
　wooden legs are not, 857b
Inhibit thy taboo, 928a
Inhuman, ev'y thin' thet's done,
　600b
Inhumanity, essence of, 765a
　man's, to man, 390a

Inhumanity, sport of it not the,
　494a
Inimies, if we didn't keep our,
　833b
Inimy, threated as an, 836b
Iniquities, permit judge to allow,
　710a
Iniquity and idolatry, 1027b
　bond of, 1059a
　draw, with cords of vanity,
　1045b
　grey, 150b
　know more about, 813b
　laurel of approved, 846a
　of oblivion, 241b
　of the fathers, 1024b
　shapen in, 1034b
Initial of creation, 647b
Initials, cockney, 602a
Injects a stinging drop, 801b
Injers all on 'em the same, 600b
Injunction, I can get out an,
　835a
　parting, of mothers and wives,
　872b
Injur'd, distant Trojans never, 3b
　lover's hell, 256b
Injure the government, 539b
　the state, who mutually, 19a
　yourself, you will only, 10a
Injured, forgiveness to the, 47b
　hate whom they, 47b
　no one, save by himself, 73a
　woman who has, you, 714a
Injures, never pardons those he,
　47b
　when A annoys or, B, 909a
Injuries, forget and forgive, 106a
　saints in your, 187a
Injurious, beauty though, 260b
Injury, added insult to, 10a
　and sullenness against nature,
　250b
　and violence, defence against,
　110b
　had Aristides done him, 54b
　engraved in metal, 86b
　never forget an, 851a
　shelter from all, 606a
　sooner forgotten than insult,
　323a
　the one does them no, 603a
　without, to meaning, 425a
Injustice, conscience with, is cor-
　rupted, 125b
　done to an individual, 1002a
　easy to bear, 908b
　extreme law extreme, 32b
　fear of suffering, 265a
　jealousy, 307a
　makes democracy necessary,
　963b
　mankind censure, 24a
　national, 534a
　nothing so finely felt as, 580b
　of our fellows, 270a
　rigorous law often rigorous,
　32b
　sense of justice and, 326a
　threatened with a great, 495a
Injye other people's sufferin',
　836a
Ink, gall enough in thy, 165a
　had not faded, 793a
　he hath not drunk, 133a
　hermit never saw pen and,
　166a
　in formal, 226b
　shelter of his, 771b

Ink, small drop of, 458b
Inkstand, Vesuvius' crater for an,
　604a
Inky cloak, 'tis not alone my,
　170b
Inlaid with patines, 147a
Inland, though, far we be, 408b
Inlets, creeks and, 595b
Inmate of the skies, 6b
Inn, a book's an, 889b
　die drinking in an, 74b
　gain the timely, 197b
　good tavern or, 341b
　no room in the, 1056a
　place to die should be an,
　341b
　remember an, Miranda, 849a
　strange charm in a county,
　505a
　take mine ease in mine, 91b
　warmest welcome at an, 341b
　wayside, of earth, 808b
　world not an, 241a
Innate desire to live beyond in-
　come, 671b
Inn-door, riding up to the old,
　909b
Inner air an inner light, 986b
　blindness, signifies, 942b
　chamber, heart's, 529a
　conflicts, resolve, 930b
　half of every cloud, 879a
　life, refreshment of your, 637b
　man, contentment of the, 981b
　vision quick to find, 630a
　weather, 881a
　worth, a poor substitute for,
　10a
Innisfail, harp of, 432b
Innisfree, go to, 824b
Innocence and health, 355b
　ceremony of, 826b
　changed innocence for, 207b
　closing up his eyes, 122b
　dream of sleeping, 649a
　has nothing to dread, 287b
　her, a child, 278b
　ignorance is not, but sin, 574b
　mirth and, 457a
　of love, 164b
　of our neighbors, 590b
　our own recovered, 590b
　our peace our fearful, 407a
　silence of pure, 208a
　timid, 287b
Innocency, next thing to, 46b
Innocent amusement, death pro-
　vides, 967b
　armed without that's, 320a
　as a new-laid egg, 682a
　condemn an, one, 324b
　death strikes down the, 577a
　faces, pensive looks, 490b
　flower, look like the, 195a
　grieves not at ills, 326b
　I am, of the blood, 140a–140b,
　1055a
　merriment, source of, 685a
　minds, and quiet, 268b
　moon, 789b
　nose, 159b
　of the blood, 140a–140b
　officious, sincere, 337b
　rich shall not be, 1041b
　shames, 158b
　skin of an, lamb, 125b
　sleep that knits, 196b
　something so homely and, 512b
　species of wit, 372a

Judas Iscariot Simon's son, 233a
Judas's heart, 704b
Judea, wild, stretches far, 560b
Judee, down in, 600b
Judge above his shoe, 51a
  amongst fools, 53a
  any public servant, 778b
  by a small sample, 103b
  by complexion of the sky, 139b
  competent, 235a
  fitter to invent than, 121a
  for the fatherless, 1065a
  for yourselves, 443b
  forbear to, 125b
  himself the, and jury, 555b
  I'll be, I'll be jury, 656a
  in his own cause, 45a
  is condemned, 44b
  justice, or vicar, 381b
  learned, 146b
  men only by their success, 265b
  neutrality of impartial, 361b
  never dare to, 18a
  no man can, another, 802b
  not according to appearance,
    1058a
  not that we be not judged, 542a
  not that ye be not judged, 125b,
    1051b
  of a man by his foes, 772b
  of all things, 272b
  of authors' names, 311b
  of my regret, 485a
  of the highest matters, 25b
  proper, of the man, 48a
  should not be young, 24a
  sober as a, 332b
  sole, of truth, 317a
  supreme, of their lives, 447a
  that no king can corrupt, 210b
  the deeds of others, 802b
  the prize, 245b
  the quick and the dead, 1068a
  them as they grow older, 768a
  to allow iniquities, 710a
  upright, 146b
  whole piece by pattern, 718b
  will I, thee, 1057b
  you as you are, 184a
Judged from point of view of the
    age, 701b
  in light of the final issue, 27b
  not by their tint of skin, 812b
  that we be not, 542a
  that ye be not, 125b, 1051b
Judge's robe, 184a
Judges, a fool with, 53a
  alike of facts and laws, 306b
  all ranged, 309a
  are apt to be naif men, 709b
  common, of property, 336b
  do and must legislate, 709b
  hungry, the sentence sign, 312b
  of important causes, 26a
  vain, we are, 324a
Judgest, wherein thou, another,
    1059b
Judging, fatigue of, 382a
  people by appearances, 269b
Judgment, angry with his, 240a
  blind man's erring, 310b
  Book, leaves of the, 634b
  come to, 146b
  day, 557b
  day of, by that name, 927b
  day of, infinite mercy on the,
    774a
  day of, style of the, 750b
  day of, vulgarize the, 509a

Judgment day, waiting the, 637b
  defend against your, 280a
  difficult, 378b
  diversity of, 262a
  every work into, 1044a
  falls upon a man, 227b
  fled to brutish beasts, 168a
  force, on the few, 511a
  frame by her just standard,
    310a
  gets the better of my, 17a
  God's great, seat, 814a
  green in, 200a
  holy blessing of a, 23a
  I will execute, 1024a
  in, old, 144b
  infinite mercy on the Day of,
    774a
  intelligence, reflection and, 34a
  no one complains of his, 265a
  not only industry but, 359b
  of the eye, 132b
  or intuition more subtle, 709b
  persons deprived of, 28b
  practical, of Americans, 516a
  reserve thy, 171b
  right, of any man or thing,
    472b
  shallow spirit of, 124b
  skill and, thrown away, 347a
  style of the day of, 750b
  thunders split the house, 756a
  top of, 184a
  vulgarize the day of, 509a
  we still have, here, 195b
  will be, enough for me, 733b
Judgments as our watches, 261a
  brawling, 554b
  men's, are a parcel, 201a
  of the Lord are true, 542a,
    1033a
  selling, of the English law, 856b
  so in our very, 261a
  with our, as our watches, 310a
Judicial power distinct from legis-
    lative, 368a
Judicious care, 390a
  epicure, 430a
  grieve, 175b
  readers, content with few, 40b
Judicyous, a little, swearin', 836a
Judy O'Grady, 818b
Jug of wine loaf of bread, 531b
  w'en it gits loose fum de, 738b
  without a handle, 581b
Jugglery, nickname for, 327a
Juggling fiends, 199b
Juice, buried in his own, 52a
  nectarean, 483b
Julia, in silks my, goes, 231a
Julia's lips do smile, 230a
Juliet bleeding, 138a
  is the sun, 135a
  philosophy can make a, 137a
  wills it so, 137a
Julius Caesar thou art mighty yet,
    169a
  Caesar to mesilf, fr'm, 836b
  live first with, 900a
July, second day of, 1776, 367b
July-flowers, June and, 230a
July's day short as December,
    208a
Jumblies, lands where the, live,
    581a
Jump both sea and land, 205a
  good wits, 109a
  see him, before me, 750b
  the life to come, 195b

Jumped into a bramble bush,
    1020b
Jumps into the train, 807a
Junctions, changed at, 754a
June and July-flowers, 230a
  billowy clouds of, 890b
  blossom, and rapture pass, 878a
  clouds of, 652a
  end of an Indian, 813a
  flowers of, 652a
  leafy month of, 422a
  'long about knee-deep in, 745b
  longest day is in, 721a
  newly sprung in, 391b
  old sophistries of, 647b
  Romany in, 887a
  seek ice in, 452a
  so rare as a day in, 600a
Junes, golden, and bleak Decem-
    bers, 740b
Jungle, law of the, 877a, 958a
  laws of the, 815b
  pack meets pack in the, 815b
Junior deacon in my mother-
    lodge, 818b
Juniper-tree, sat under a, 944b
Jupiter, if, were to speak, 57a
  laughs at perjuries, 135b
  loaded us with couple of wal-
    lets, 35a
Jupiter's statue by Phidias done,
    1007b
Jurgen opened the door, 899a
Juries fill their stomachs, 856b
  trial by, 374b
Jurisprudence, gladsome light of,
    110a
Jury, appear before a qualified,
    766b
  himself the judge and, 555b
  I'll be judge I'll be, 656a
  'll pitch th' tistimony, 833b
  passing on prisoner's life, 184a
  thins his, 279a
Jurymen may dine, 312b
Just, actions of the, 237a
  admission of topics, 431b
  and firm of purpose, 39a
  and lasting peace, 542a
  and right well-managed, 257b
  and righteous men, 17b
  are the ways of God, 260a
  Aristides, the, 55a
  battled for the true the, 552b
  be, and fear not, 211b
  before you're generous, 382a
  coldly sublime intolerably, 720b
  death kind umpire, 124b
  defence, glorious in thy, 299a
  demand of governing, 475b
  friends and brave enemies, 375a
  gentle and merciful and, 471b
  gods are, 193b
  good man and a, 1057b
  hair, grizzled, 276a
  hath his quarrel, 125a
  he who is merely, 324b
  how should man be, with God,
    1030a
  if all the world were, 56a
  jewel of the, 272a
  man, nothing to do with that,
    1055a
  man upon earth, 1043a
  man will pay more, 24a
  memory of the, is blessed,
    1039a
  men, 307b
  men, light for, 17a

Kindle a brighter than its own, 701a
   cannot, when we will, 620a
   fires to warm it, 630b
   soft desire, 280b
Kindled by the master's spell, 396b
   light here, 229b
   love, by virtue, 76b
Kindles a wantonness, 230b
   hand that, 456a
   true genius, 318b
Kindleth little fire, 1064a
Kindlier hand, larger heart the, 553a
Kindliest thing God ever made, 873a
Kindliness of sheets, 938b
Kindling her undazzled eyes, 250b
Kindly as well as frosty, 603a
   frosty but, 160a
   fruits of the earth, 1068b
   had we never lov'd sae, 392a
   heart, glow of a, 729b
   stars given a form so fair, 499a
   use 'em, they rebel, 307a
   wanderer loved and known, 654b
   word or goodly act, 655a
Kindness and love, 403b
   any, I can show, 300a
   Christ took the, 573b
   from the unkind, 924b
   full of valour as of, 156a
   have you had a, shown, 703a
   in another's trouble, 661b
   in women, 130b
   kill wife with, 130b
   large and plain, 979a
   lavish, 445b
   law of, 1041b
   little deeds of, 626b
   little word in, spoken, 557b
   master-art of, 726b
   mercy courage, mirth, 843b
   milk of human, 195a, 950b
   natural, 826b
   no man show him any, 281b
   not quite free from ridicule, 540b
   road into his, 202b
   save in the way of, 403a
   tak a cup o', 392b
   tempered every blow, 688a
   to his majesty, 463a
   treated with special, 932a
   what wisdom greater than, 344b
   who does a, not therefore kind, 314a
Kindnesses, for these, do me small mischief, 58b
   great persons able to do great, 108b
   proclaims, received, 109a
   series of, 372a
   which most leave undone, 599a
Kindred, brothers sons and, slain, 266b
   comrades lovers friends, 630a
   drops mingled into one, 364a
   each age each, 601b
   flower of her, 439a
   gloom, 327b
   medley of, 105a
   only should behold, 15a
   points of heaven, 412a
   to the great God, 539b

Kindreds people and tongues, 1064b
Kine, lean and ill-favoured, 1023b
   learn from the, ruminating, 726b
   Pharaoh's lean, 150b
   seven fat, 1023b
King a thing men have made, 228a
   acts like a, 345a
   and farewell, 139b
   and shepherd even, 109b
   Arthur ruled this land, 1020a
   asked the queen, 917b
   balm off from anointed, 139b
   belovèd of a, 1012a
   Belshazzar the, 1048b
   best, of good fellows, 79b
   by your own fireside, 103b
   came not, 652b
   cat may looke on a, 94a
   catch conscience of the, 174a
   Charles's head, 579a
   chief defect of Henry, 849a
   Christ, 969a
   city of the great, 1034b
   Cole, 1015a
   Cophetua, 549b, 1011b
   cotton is, 499b
   dainty dish to set before the, 1017a
   David and King Solomon, 794b
   David wrote the psalms, 794b
   discharge my duties as, 972a
   divinity doth hedge a, 178a
   earth receive her, 303a
   easily as a, 166b
   every inch a, 193a
   fellow with the best, 79b
   follow the, 554a
   for our rightfu', 392a
   fought my, 266b
   George, dead soldiers of, 821a
   glorious to be a pirate, 682b
   glory to the new-born, 334b
   glory to, of kings, 334b
   God save the, 307b, 1027a
   gold crowned, 928b
   Gorboduc, niece of, 166a
   government without a, 490a
   great as a, 377a
   great God our, 530a
   greater than the, 335a
   grew vain, 280a
   he is rightful, 754b
   heart and stomach of a, 97a
   heart of the, 759a
   heaven's all gracious, 560b
   Heav'n's eternal, 244a
   honour the, 1064a
   I am the Roman, 271a
   I was a, in Babylon, 742a
   idle, by this still hearth, 548a
   in a carriage may ride, 533b
   James call for old shoes, 119a
   judge that no, can corrupt, 210b
   lad that's born to be, 781b
   Lear, by reading, 373a
   long live our noble, 307b
   long live the, 364a
   man the, delighteth to honour, 1029b
   mockery, of snow, 140b
   more royalist than the, 1010b
   mortal temples of a, 139b
   never, dropped out of clouds, 227b
   of all kings, 999a

King of artists, 669a
   of Babylon, 1048b
   of Boyville, 843a
   of England cannot enter, 335a
   of France went up the hill, 1015a
   of hearts, 900a
   of infinite space, 173b
   of kings, 465a
   of pain, 693a
   of realms of endless joy, 936b
   of shreds and patches, 177a
   of Spain's daughter, 1017b
   of terrors, 1030b
   of the Jews, 1050a, 1055b
   of the sea, 904a
   old, dead, 154a
   one's own sole, 703a
   over children of pride, 1032a
   pageantry of a, 1002a
   Pandion is dead, 220a
   pin the main spring, 661a
   praises sing to God the, 670a
   precedent a, of men, 696a
   rank no, can give, 591a
   reigns but does not govern, 101b
   ruin seize thee ruthless, 349b
   sad-eyed Hindu, 673a
   sent me his dirty linen, 324b
   serve my, and master, 211b
   shake hands with a, 462b
   show 'em who is, 894a
   sits in Dunfermline town, 1011a
   Solomon, King David and, 794b
   Solomon loved many women, 1028b
   Solomon wrote the proverbs, 794b
   sovereign lord the, 288b
   spider and, 591b
   state without, or nobles, 490a
   Stephen was a worthy peer, 187b, 1011b
   still am I, of those, 140a
   such a, Harry, 122b
   sword of an angel, 388b
   they were all looking for a, 631b
   'tis so much to be a, 100a
   title running 'fore the, 156a
   was a fortunate soldier, 324b
   was in his counting-house, 1017a
   Wenceslas, 592b
   when George the Third was, 39b
   when I am, dilly dilly, 1019b
   when you strike at a, 508b
   who is law is, 117a
   who is this, of glory, 1033b
   who seeks to bestride the people, 538a
   will not leave country, 985b
   worm that hath eat of a, 177b
   would change with me, 584b
   year's pleasant, 212b
Kingdom, a little, I possess, 654a
   almost in every, 223a
   best the, provides, 839a
   both crown and, 117b
   by the foam, 947a
   by the sea, 546a
   children of the, 1052a
   come, palaces in, 896a
   enter, of God, 140b
   enter, of heaven, 1053b
   fit for the, of God, 1056b
   for a horse, 128b

Law, kept, by transgressing, 251a
 lesser breeds without the, 816a
 life of the, 110a
 life of the, not logic, 708b
 locks up both man and woman, 712b
 maxims of civil, 336b
 measure for, 227a
 must be stable, 851b
 necessity has no, 70a
 nor duty bade me fight, 826a
 of conspicuous waste, 776b
 of culture, 472b
 of duty, 709a
 of God the law of good, 617a
 of kindness, 1041b
 of Medes and Persians, 1049a
 of nature, 594a
 of the jungle, 877a, 958a
 of the Yukon, 877a
 old father antic the, 149a
 old, sad but not bitter, 888a
 one God one, one element, 553a
 orderly change of, 709b
 ought, to weed it out, 119b
 patience to, will go, 329b
 persecution is first, of society, 960a
 preserves the earth a sphere, 396b
 provision in its organic, 539a
 public opinion's in advance of, 837b
 reason is our, 258a
 redress by mob, 537a
 religion liberty and, 436b
 remoter aspects of the, 709a
 rich men rule the, 354a
 rigorous, often rigorous injustice, 32b
 scarecrow of the, 183b
 secures equal justice, 20a
 selling judgments of English, 856b
 seven hours to, 110b
 sharp quillets of the, 124b
 so general a study, 360a
 spoke too softly, 55a
 strongest tenure of the, 29a
 sword of war or of the, 375b
 there can be no less acknowledged, 112a
 to ourselves, 258a
 unalterable, 943a
 unchanging, of God, 560b
 underneath the, 816b
 unto themselves, 1059b
 wedded love mysterious, 256a
 what I mean by the, 709a
 where no, is, 1059b
 wherein we see reflected, 708b
 which moulds a tear, 396b
 who himself is, 117a
 will admit of no rival, 561a
 will never be strong, 698a
 windy side of, 157b, 165b
 with literature as with, 543b
 world's, not thy friend, 137b
 written and an unwritten, 71a
 written in the Book of the, 281b
Law-abiding, law-givers and the, 987a
Lawd God Jehovah, 954a
Lawes, love knoweth no, 92a
Lawful, all ambitions are, 773b
 eyes, hooks forsake their, 708a
 guns aren't, 966b
 is it not, for me, 1053b
 wives, ships his, 904a

Lawfully, if a man use it, 1063a
Lawlands, ye Highlands and ye, 1012b
Lawless linsey-woolsey brother, 238b
 wing'd and unconfin'd, 386b
Lawlessness, epidemic of world, 919b
Lawn canapie, 102b
 dew was on the, 922b
 house with, enclosing it, 751a
 purpled o'er the, 6a
 satyrs grazing on the, 123a
Lawns, daisied, 927a
Law's delay, 174b
 grave study, 110b
Laws, abhor makers and, approve, 279a
 alien or accidental, 866b
 and customs, 406a
 and learning die, 592b
 are dumb, 33b
 are like cobwebs, 294b
 are with us, 427a
 base, of servitude, 275b
 best use of, 562b
 better for us to have no, 101a
 cage of, 953b
 care not who makes its, 290b
 care not who makes th', 835a
 change from old to new, 26a
 curse on all, 313a
 discrete not reconciled, 503b
 do from fear of the, 71b
 equal, which it framed, 490b
 every cause stands on, 436b
 execute, is a royal office, 361b
 execute, people have made, 689a
 fewer, less confided power, 502b
 for blood, 143b
 for themselves and not for me, 787a
 from phenomena of nature, 916a
 gives his natural senate, 319a
 good, and good arms, 85b
 good, lead to better ones, 344a
 government of, not men, 368a
 grind the poor, 354a
 grow by natural, 702a
 impartial, 307b
 instruction in, of nature, 633a
 judges alike of the facts and, 306b
 keeps his self-made, 615b
 kinder, to bring us back, 578b
 know not whether, be right, 770a
 money in its effects and, 502b
 nature's, lay hid in night, 321a
 no, he ever keeps so well, 383a
 obedient to their, 9a
 obey its, respect its flag, 842a
 of conscience, 98a
 of France, 287a
 of God the laws of man, 787a
 of heat, 700a
 of husking, 383a
 of nature and nature's God, 373a
 of revered righteousness, 12b
 of the jungle, 815b
 or kings can cause, 337b
 ought not remain unaltered, 26a
 ourselves have made, 551a
 precept of her peaceful, 287b
 purer science holier, 598b
 regard to unwritten, 20a
 repeal of obnoxious, 623b

Laws, respect for authority and the, 20a
 rules of game are, of nature, 633b
 sweeter manners purer, 553a
 territory people and, 540a
 that lacqueys make, 781a
 true friendship's, 6b
 unequal, unto a savage race, 548a
 were like cobwebs, 69b
 without origin in the mind, 916a
 world abounds with, 1002b
Lawsuit mania, 688a
Lawyer, deceive not thy, 233b
 every quarrel to the, 234a
 religion of my physician or, 98a
 skull of a, 178b
 tells me I may do, 360a
 that's wurruked twinty hours, 835a
 without history or literature, 416a
Lawyers are met, 308b
 Cantilena of, 437a
 defy historians heroes, 459b
 disguise matters, 86a
 in public business, 516a
 kill all the, 125b
 take what they would give, 535a
 university men, 322a
Laxity, relative, of mothers, 741a
Lay a trap for it, 650b
 a wager, 333b
 cleric before and, behind, 238b
 Doric, 249b
 down his life, 1058b
 down in a certain cave, 70b
 enough to, up, 307a
 her i' the earth, 179a
 heroic, is tuneless, 458a
 him low lay him low, 626a
 it bare to the bone, 983b
 it on thick in right places, 671a
 last to, the old aside, 311a
 me down as in mother's lap, 258b
 me down in peace and sleep, 1032b
 me down in peace to sleep, 451a
 me down to bleed a while, 1012a
 me down to take my sleep, 1000b
 me low my work is done, 661b
 me on an anvil, 899a
 my ashes at the roots, 886b
 my head on my grave, 241a
 not flattering unction, 177a
 not transgression, 147b
 not up treasures, 1051a
 on Macduff, 200a
 out money on a rope, 222a
 pierced the strong tower, 612b
 simple and heartfelt, 522a
 stone on stone, 620a
 the proud usurpers low, 394a
 up a little upon a little, 7b
 up treasures in heaven, 1051b
 waste our powers, 410a
 weary bones among ye, 211b
Layer-up, ill, of beauty, 156b
Layes soule to sleepe, 113a
Layette to mound, 993a
Laying on our backs, 677a
 violent hands upon the ship, 294b
Layings-out in clothes, 284b
Lays hand upon a woman, 403a
 on disarray it, its wing, 866a

Line, slanting silver, 961b
stretch to crack of doom, 198b
upon line, 1046a
upon line they reach the roof, 725a
ye grave for me, 910a
Lineage, damsel of high, 554b
proud old, 927a
Lineaments, moulded the changing, 702a
of Gospell bookes, 114b
of gratified desire, 386b
Lined himself with hope, 153a
with good capon, 161b
Linen, dirty, to wash, 324b
lifetime of, 993b
old, wash whitest, 119a
wash their dirty, 399b
you're wearing out, 489a
Liner she's a lady, 814b
Liners, luxury, laden with souls, 993b
Lines and life are free, 233a
are fallen unto me, 1032b
close in dial's centre, 154b
dry desert of a thousand, 320b
epigram of two, 52a
for all your deathless, 912a
ghosts creeping between the, 641b
hard stiff, of life, 528a
in every angle greet, 269a
level, of woodwork, 794b
lord once own the happy, 311b
these, made I, 37b
town-crier spoke my, 175a
washed my, away, 462a
Linger and labor there, 782b
in our northern clime, 414b
meadows where you, 749a
on the flathouse roof, 995b
out a purpos'd overthrow, 206a
they do not live but, 222a
to caress him, 584a
Lingered round them, 592a
Lingering dewdrop, protects the, 412a
sit, here, 272a
spirit so, 858a
Lingers, borrowing, 152b
into old age, 16a
last rose, 38b
Lingo, outlandish, 389a
unless you know the, 488a
Ling'ring bays, 335b
flying, 312a
Lining, inside out to show the, 879a
there's a silver, 865a
turn forth her silver, 247a
Link, each fresh, progress, 708b
silver, the silken tie, 413b
strength of one, in the cable, 840b
Linkèd sweetness long drawn out, 245b
Linnet, tear the, from the leaf, 826b
Linnet's wings, 824b
Linnets, pipe but as the, sing, 551b
Linsey-woolsey brother, 238b
brothers, 322a
Lint, invisible strand of, 801b
Lintel low enough, 757a
Lion among ladies, 142a
and the cock, 893a
and the lizard, 531b
and the unicorn, 1015a

Lion, beard the, in his den, 414b
bearing, 464a
bold as a, 1041b
carcase of the, 1026b
dead, 1043a
devil as a roaring, 1064b
fawns upon lamb, 127a
from his lair, 417b
hind mated by the, 183a
in the chase, 403a
is in the streets, 1041a
is not so fierce, 234a
lip of, 155b
look no larger than the cat, 556b
not a, but a pard, 934b
of God, 73b
old, is dead, 378a
on your old stone gates, 547a
painting a, from the claw, 8a
prince must be a, 55a
roar like a, 963a
roast, 589a
rouse a, 149b
vapour sometime like a, 201a
wine, 497a
woos his brides, 352b
wrath of, is wisdom of God, 386a
Lioness opening up an antelope, 990b
Lionlike March, 690a
Lion's mane, dew-drop from the, 182a
Nemean, nerve, 172a
ruddy eyes, 385b
saw, shadow, 146b
skin will not reach, 55a
wear, hide, 148a
Lions, bears and, growl and fight, 302b
den of, 1049a
my darling from the, 1034b
stronger than, 1027b
talks of roaring, 147b
Lip, between the cup and the, 223a
contempt and anger of his, 165a
coral, admires, 237a
frown and wrinkled, 465a
hair upon the upper, 950b
is curved with pain, 686a
keep a stiff upper, 630b
language in her, 182b
nectar on a, 381b
not a, or eye we beauty call, 310b
of lion, 155b
reproof on her, 485a
'twixt the cup and the, 223a
vermeil-tinctur'd, 248a
Lippincut, Miss Fawn, 841a
Lips are dumb, 547a
are now forbid to speak, 485a
bearded, 523b
but half regretful, 694a
closed, hurt no one, 58a
crimson in thy, and cheeks, 138a
divine persuasion flows from, 4b
drained by fevered, 483b
drew my soul through my, 123b
drop gentle words from his, 7a
eternity was in our, 200a
far from the, we love, 439a
flattereth with his, 1040a
for your, to drink, 692b
forth to your, to quaff, 532b
from speaking guile, 1034a
Helen's, are drifting dust, 844b
her, were red, 421b

Lips, her, were so near, 736a
how came your, 854b
Julia's, do smile, 230a
kiss her, 825a
let me put my, to it, 577b
listen at its, 529a
love at the, 880b
mouldered the, 947a
murmuring with its foamy, 625b
name of God upon his, 344b
of a strange woman, 1038b
of children, 498a
of dying men, 621b
of inebriated virtue, 695a
of those that are asleep, 1044b
of truth, 440b
once sanctified by hers, 533b
ope my, 143a
open thou my, 1034b
part her, 230b
persuasion hung upon his, 345b
poverty to the very, 189b
profound and fragile, 968b
red mournful, 824b
say God be pitiful, 518b
smile on her, 414b
smily round the, 601a
suck forth my soul, 123b
sweet, soft hand, 480a
take cup to your, 219a
take those, away, 185b
talk of the, 1039b
that are for others, 550b
that I have kissed, 178b
that love thy name, 803b
that those, had language, 366a
that touch, 948b
that touch liquor, 828b
that were dead, 953a
to your attentive ear, 411a
touch, and part with tears, 693b
truth from his, 356a
upon my, a song, 936a
very good words for the, 580a
weary, I close, 350a
were red, 261b
whispering with white, 453a
words from his, 3b
would keep from slips, 737a
Lips' red, 207b
remark was oh you kid, 936b
Lipstick, when you've got too much, 990b
Liquefaction of her clothes, 231a
Liquescent and nebulous lustre, 545b
Liquid, bitter, recommended, 978a
dew of youth, 171b
fire and distilled damnation, 397a
history, 776b
lapse of murmuring streams, 257b
manure and guano, 954a
notes, 250a
surge, 203b
Liquidation of the British Empire, 871a
Liquor, brews livelier, than the muse, 786b
bumper of good, 381b
claret is the, for boys, 342a
gives genius discerning, 357a
is quicker, 989b
lips that touch, 828b
love or fights, 787a
mint is in the, 806a
swims enough good, 690a
taste a, never brewed, 646a

Love, dull sublunary lovers', 216b
each time we, 650a
earth's the right place for, 880a
ebb to humble, 189a
ectasy of, 173a
emphasis of passionate, 431b
end of a, or a season, 879a
ennobles all, 1006a
enough of woman's, 827b
every leaf, 618a
everything, 618a
everything that's old, 119a
exultations agonies and, 407a
fall out with those we, 550a
falleth from, 83b
falling in, at first sight, 813b
false or true, 824b
fans it, 781a
far from the lips we, 439a
fear to, thee sweet, 790a
feast of, is song, 668a
fickleness of the women I, 764b
fight for, 141b
finds comfort in despair, 125a
first learned in lady's eyes, 133b
fitter, for me, 216a
flies out the window, 1000a
flowers and fruits of, 461a
for a woman you respect, 761b
for Angela, 852b
for fellow-citizens, 367a
for ladies', unfit, 281a
for sake of being loved, 463a
for things afar, 13b
for this flag, 852b
for thy, I will not grieve, 693b
for timber, 962b
for your, to her, 130a
free as air, 313a
freedom comrades, 897a
freedom in my, 268b
friendship and marriage, 434a
friendship charity, 182a
friendship is, 451b
friendship needs emotion to become, 673a
from too much, of living, 694a
from whom the world begun,
721b
from whose eyelids dropped, 7a
fulfilling of the law, 1060b
fulsome, for gain, 309b
gather the rose of, 230b
gave them our, and fear, 571a
gilds the scene, 381a
gin, be bonnie, 1013a
give a little, to a child, 606a
give me a sign his, to prove,
611b
God from necessity is, 561a
God gave them, 884b
God gives us, 547b
God if You wish for our, 933b
God is, 672a, 1064b
God made, 804b
God the world and, 672b
goes toward love, 135b
good creditable acquaintance,
295a
good man's, 162b
good-night must thou go, 686a
great, with a little gift, 29b
greater, hath no man, 1058b
greater than his power, 673a
greatest, of life, 371b
greybeards call divine, 127a
grief bound up with our, 670a
grown faint and fretful, 694a
grows bitter with treason, 693a

Love had been sae ill to win,
1013a
hail wedded, 256a
half in, with easeful death, 481b
half makes, to you today, 781a
hang level in balances of, 673a
hardly seem worth thinking of,
825b
harvests that our, had sown,
899b
harvest-time of, 427b
has found its home, 42a
hate traitors and treason, 279a
have not found my thing to,
885a
he bore to learning, 356b
he had to her, 1023b
he was all for, 377a
heart that gives it, 872b
her till I die, 999a
her was a liberal education,
301b
he's my, forevermore, 1020b
hid in the heart of, 824b
him because he is good, 797a
him for enemies he has made,
636b
him so as if to hate him, 14b
hold, in, 933b
honesty and, doth mince, 187b
hope faith and, 394b
hope nor, nor a friend, 752a
hopeless, finds comfort, 382a
how do I, thee, 519b
how vast a memory has, 310a
human, thou spirit given, 543b
hunt down, together, 693a
I am sick of, 1044a
I and my, wont to gae, 1013a
I could not, thee dear so much,
268a
I hate and I, 35b
I told my, 386a
if ever thou shalt, 164a
if love be perfect, 554b
if, means affection, 953a
if music be the food of, 163b
if my, were in my arms, 999a
if she, me I will die, 229a
if there's delight in, 298a
if thou must, me, 519a
if, were what the rose is, 693a
if you speak, 157a
in a golden bowl, 384b
in a hut, 480b
in law or in, 587b
in my bosom, 116a
in search of a word, 716b
in, with the janitor's boy, 995b
innocence of, 164b
is a boy by poets styl'd, 239a
is a flame, 897a
is a greater law, 73b
is a mood to man, 754a
is a sickness, 122b
is anterior to life, 647b
is bitter, 948b
is blind, 144b
is blynd, 81b
is enough, 667a
is flower-like, 425a
is full of showers, 118a
is God's essence, 672b
is grown to ripeness, 547b
is heaven, 413b
is immortal, 707a
is in his heart, 761a
is indestructible, 427b
is left alone, 547b

Love is like a dizziness, 402b
is like a lovely rose, 649b
is like the wild rose-briar, 591b
is love, 892b
is more cruel than lust, 692a
is nature's second sun, 116b
is not all, 963a
is not love which alters, 207a
is of a birth as rare, 269a
is something so divine, 366b
is strong as death, 1044b
is sweet for a day, 693b
is swift sincere pious, 83b
is the coldest of critics, 631a
is the jewel, 885a
is the only priest, 662b
is then our duty, 308b
it I love it, 591a
its essence is, 472b
itself possess'd, 137b
itself shall slumber on, 468b
iz like the meazles, 594b
jealousy born together with,
266a
jot of former, 122b
joy and, triumphing, 254b
kelson of creation is, 607b
kept in, 893b
kindled by virtue, 76b
kindness shall win my, 130b
kisses tears and smiles, 409a
know her was to, her, 396b
knoweth no lawes, 92a
labour of, 1063a
land that I, 941b
laws of life truth and, 616b
lay thy phobias to rest, 928a
lays hold on gentle heart, 75b
learn to bear beams of, 385a
least that let men know, 131b
let him, tomorrow, 304b
let the warm, in, 482b
let those, now, 304b
let thy, be younger, 164b
let's contend no more, 568a
liberty to those who, it, 444a
light and calm thoughts, 423b
lightly turns to thoughts of, 548b
like death levels ranks, 510a
like everybody not in, 855b
like friendship steady, 440a
like, is warm, 440a
like ours can never die, 813a
like sunshine after rain, 131a
lime of, 230a
limited by limited strength, 490b
liquor, or fights, 787a
little, my love come to me, 892b
little words of, 626b
live and, 35a
live with me and be my, 123a,
992b
live with thee and be thy, 110b
live without, 653a
lodged in a woman's breast,
213a
look of, alarms, 386b
look with as much, as friends,
284a
looks not with eyes, 141a
Lord of, came down, 757a
lose the power to, 583b
lose thy, I lose my all, 313a
lost to, and truth, 819a
love alone can pore, 716b
love for the woman you, 761b
love, in others they, 266a
lovers who, truly, 723a
loves in higher, endure, 552a

Loved her that she did pity them, 186b
him as he loved his own soul, 1027b
him for himself, 381b
his country as no other, 624b
his friend, 1014b
I saw and, 123a
I, you best, 289b
idols I have, 533a
if you, me ever so little, 693a
in vain, 451b
Jack, his friend, 377a
laughed often and, much, 905b
life, 891b
like not only to be, 596b
long since and lost, 495b
love and be, by me, 546a
love for sake of being, 463a
loves that we have, before, 885a
man I, in Rome, 962b
many, 887b
many strange women, 1028b
marked of many, of one, 706a
me for dangers I had pass'd, 186b
me still the same, 483b
memory of the, and lost, 541b
money and knew how to keep it, 106a
nature I, 432a
never to have been, 552a
no sooner, but they sighed, 163a
none, but at first sight, 123a
not wisely but too well, 190b
nothing to have, 552a
one he, in secret, 767a
one, time and place and the, 575a
ones, come before their, 774a
only after constructed, 866b
pale hands I, 812b
palpable thou hast never, 673a
passing well, 174a
Pharaoh's lean kine be, 150b
Rome more, 168a
saw and, 369b
see the souls we, 554a
sigh'd to many, but one, 452b
so long as we are, 752a
so many I, were not dead, 990b
some we, 532a
talk to every woman as if you, her, 769a
the beggar-maid, 1011b
the prairie, 898b
thee Atthis once, 8b
these I have, 938b
those who always, 304b
thou hast, and suffered, 632b
three whole days, 261b
to be, be lovable, 42b
to have, to have thought, 620b
to plead lament and sue, 414a
too true to keep a friend, 520a
treachery, 279a
use him as though you, him, 236b
way to know is to have, 720a
we that had, him so, 567b
when all was young, 599a
when I, you, 988a
who never, before, 304b
wish I, the human race, 796b
with a love more than love, 546a
you better than you knew, 654b
you dear as well as he, 833a
you so long, 999b

Loved you Wednesday, 519a
your moments of glad grace, 824a
Love-gift of a fairy-tale, 657b
Love-in-idleness, 141b
Love-knot, dark red, 909b
Love-lamps in the casement hung, 564a
Lovelier flower on earth never sown, 405b
no, hills than thine, 863a
things have mercy shown, 455a
Loveliest and the best, 532a
fantasy, 863a
lassie that trips, 484b
last still, 454a
of lovely things, 471a
of trees the cherry, 785a
tune becomes vulgar, 739b
Love-light lies and lies and lies, 439b
Loveliness, Adonis in, 447b
believe in, 790b
dream of, descending, 631a
fade as it will, 438b
he made more lovely, 468a
I never knew, 483b
increases, 478b
keeps house, 810b
lay down in her, 420b
needs not foreign aid, 328a
not without such, 879a
one made up of, 499a
spend all you have for, 928b
that, is enough, 708b
web of, 866a
within hath found, 215b
Lovely, amiable, death, 148a
and more temperate, 204b
and pleasant in their lives, 1027b
and soothing death, 609b
apparition, 409a
April of her prime, 204b
as a Lapland night, 409b
as you are, 972a
being scarcely formed, 460a
companions, 439a
corpse, 577b
days, made such, 513b
dears her noblest work, 391b
eyes are Cupid's arms, 1000b
fair and smell'st so sweet, 189b
female shapes, 665b
fighting along the whole line, 663a
floating hair, 660a
flowers are, 425a
fragments, practice old, 898b
grow, growing old, 891a
he is altogether, 1044b
I say the world is, 708b
in a lonely place, 863b
in thy youthful grace, 471b
in your strength, 453b
is the rose, 408a
lady garmented in light, 466b
language, 931a
laughter shows, 220b
light, it gives a, 962a
living boy, 103a
loveliness he made more, 468a
Mary Morison, 393b
of yore, 535a
organ of her life, 158b
rose, go, 242a, 823a
rose, love is like a, 649b
single, action, 603a
so be, 972a

Lovely stars the forget-me-nots, 522b
Thais, 280a
the brave deserve the, 631b
thing, memory of a, 928b
thing, order is a, 866a
things like that, 967b
things will have an ending, 948b
two, berries moulded, 142a
whatsoever things are, 1063a
who shall be, as she, 912b
wise and, 962b
woman stoops to folly, 944a
Lovely-asunder starlight, 724b
Love-match generally a failure, 840a
Love-quarrels in pleasing concord end, 260b
Lover, all mankind love a, 502a
and his lass, 163a
and no adventurer, 772a
and sensualist, 741b
angel appear to each, 304b
days dividing, and lover, 691b
everything disturbs absent, 104a
fond, 261a
for an hour, 935a
give repentance to her, 355a
grows familiar to the, 299b
happy as a, 409b
having been your, 823b
husband and wife and, 638b
I am a, 885a
in the husband, 343a
like an island shore, 864a
loose or hold me fast, 693b
lunatic, and poet, 142b
magnetic peripatetic, 683a
no, of poetry can spare Chaucer, 508a
no, of pompous title, 97b
of Concord, 1068b
of his mistress, 270b
of men the sea, 692b
of my soul, 334a
of trees, 568b
or nightingale, 758a
plagues a, bears, 293a
propositions of a, 162a
required in every, 106a
rooted stays, 507b
scratch a, 966b
searching for a new, 991a
sighing like furnace, 161a
sulk no more, 993b
tame, unlocks his heart, 231b
what woman says to ardent, 35b
without indiscretion, 705a
woman loves her, 458a
Love-rhymes, regent of, 133a
Lover's, act a, or a Roman's part, 313b
bed, 201b
every, a soldier, 42b
ghost, some old, 216b
hire, win the, 386b
injur'd, hell, 256b
loss, woe for a, 592b
on her, arm she leant, 549a
pinch, 202a
quarrel with the world, 881b
thoughts into a, head, 405a
Lovers admire naked beauties, 460b
alas for, 83b
all other, being estranged, 827b
all true, such as I am, 164b
anger of, 31b
are commonly industrious, 105b

Man is a prisoner, 20b
is a reasoning animal, 47a
is a rope, 726b
is, an ape or an angel, 512b
is as old as he's feeling, 637a
is better than a book, 793b
is born free, 344a
is born into the world, 599b
is born unto trouble, 1030a
is but a beast, 1013b
is but a thinking reed, 272b
is by no means poor, 41a
is cause of the work, 857a
is dead, 527a
is equal iv ivry other man, 837b
is first-rate, 596b
is happy, 15b
is his own star, 224b
is like a phonograph, 765b
is like company he keeps, 18a
is little to be envied, 337b
is man and master of his fate,
35b, 554b
is most detestable, 680a
is neither angel nor brute, 272b
is, no more than this, 192a
is not the creature of circumstances, 511a
is not upon oath, 341b
is only animal that blushes, 679a
is so in the way in the house,
558a
is stark mad, 99a
is the dream of a shadow, 13b
is the hunter, 550b
is tired of London, 342a
is very apt to complain, 341b
it is so between, and man, 121a
it means a, 876a
Jesus was most scientific, 616b
joy in, in leaf in star, 780b
just upright, 1030b
justify God's ways to, 786b
kills the thing he loves, 769b
kind of, the country turns out,
507b
knew a, who had a friend, 1008b
know end of day's business, 169a
know myself a, 213b
know what God and, is, 556a
knows nothing without being
taught, 49b
knows right from wrong, 679b
laborin', 600b
large-hearted, 518a
last, on earth'll be lost, 737b
last thing civilized by, 638b
law for, and law for thing, 503b
law not the, 484b
laws of God the laws of, 787a
lay down his life, 1058b
laying down his life, 984b
least considerable, 1002a
leave his father and mother,
1021b
let God and, decree, 787a
let no such, be trusted, 147a
let not, put asunder, 1053b
life of, less than a span, 121b
life of, solitary, 229a
little, what now, 965b
little worse than a, 143b
live by bread alone, 1050b
lives not upon bread alone, 749b
living-dead, 129b
look sad, 143a
looketh on outward appearance,
1027b
looking for a, 72a

Man looks small at a wedding,
978b
lopsided, runs fastest, 811b
Lord is a, of war, 1024b
lord of over his fellow, 774b
lose neither past nor future, 66a
loseth other life, 66a
lot of, but once to die, 232a
lot of, to suffer, 5b
love a, who is zealous, 342a
love is a mood to, 754a
love such a, 323b
love the, I marry, 906a
low, seeks a little thing, 570a
machine called, 578b
made him happy as a married,
340b
made the town, 121a, 364a
majority can never replace the,
951a
make a, spring, 262b
make a weak, your enemy, 594b
make, in our image, 1021a
make one worthy, my foe, 319a
makes no noise over good deed,
67b
makes the circumstances, 473b
makes us believe oath, 13b
manage a clever, 814a
manners makyth, 77a
man's inhumanity to, 390a
marks the earth with ruin, 454b
marries again, 768a
marry any sort of white, 562a
marry this, and woman together,
296a
matters not how, dies, 340b
may benefit his country, 20a
may escape from rope and gun,
308b
may redeem the past, 757b
may tak a neebor's part, 391a
may work from sun to sun,
1001a
meddles with them, 344a
memory of, 352a
middle-aged, concludes to build,
589a
mildest manner'd, 458a
military, in world, 155a
mind is the, 33a
mind of, a musical instrument,
613b
mind's the standard of the, 302b
mine equal, 1034b
misfortunes occasioned by, 49b
mistakes of a good, 1002a
moral, and man of honor, 909a
moral, was Werther, 564a
morality of vulgar, 727b
more sinn'd against, 191b
most married, I ever saw, 665a
most precious thing possessed
by, 344b
must be a non-conformist, 501b
must eat peck of salt, 104a
must have his faults, 51b
must learn, 957a
must please himself, 616a
my, Friday, 292a
my mother's life made me a,
896b
nae, can tether time or tide, 91a
named Matthew, 1052a
natural, has two primal passions,
743a
need to see a woman, 953a
never extinguished in heart of,
345a

Man never falls so low, 560a
never is but always to be blest,
316a
never met a, I didn't like, 904b
never was harmed by truth, 68a
no beard less than a, 157a
no, became wicked all at once,
62b
no, but a blockhead, 341b
no, can feel himself alone, 791a
no, can serve two masters, 1051b
no, ever wetted clay and left it,
61a
no, is a hero to his valet, 61b
no, is an island, 218a
no, is happy, 45b
no, is happy without a hobby,
744b
no longer the, you were, 995a
no, loves life like him, 16a
no right to be a public, 577b
no, ruleth safely, 83a
no, so good, 100b
no, speak write to him, 281b
no such thing as an honest, 306b
no time for, to recover hair, 129a
no, truly knows another, 802b
no, was more foolish, 342b
no wedded, so hardy be, 81b
no, will supply thy want, 220a
no wise, quit a certainty, 337a
no, wiser for learning, 227b
no, worth having is true, 294b
no, written out of reputation,
292b
no young, believes he shall die,
434b
noblest work of, 662b
none more wonderful than, 14a
nor proudest of his works, 369b
not a, that lives, 404b
not afraid of the sea, 857a
not always actions show the,
314a
not good that, should be alone,
1021b
not trusted with government,
374b
nothing more fun than a, 967a
nothing out of artist not in, 909a
nothing yet contrived by, 341b
of absolute genius, 908a
of achievement, 478a
of action in state of thought,
838a
of all modern poets, 275b
of business, clergyman also a,
73a
of genius makes no mistakes,
917a
of genius sees the world, 784a
of genius seldom ruined, 339b
of giant frame, 471a
of God's own mould, 663a
of great estate, 42a
of knowledge increaseth strength,
118a
of letters must make up his
mind, 690a
of letters, physician and, 534a
of letters, skin of the, 651a
of mettle, 307a
of might, 584b
of my kidney, 180b
of peace, 891a
of profound feeling, 644a
of rank, 342b
of sorrows, 1047b
of sovereign parts, 132b

Meals, getting, and washing plates, 980b
  make no long, 357a
  short and sparing at, 262a
  unquiet, 129b
Mealy boys and beef-faced boys, 576b
Mean actions to fear, 726a
  age is dull and, 527a
  all books else appear so, 289b
  and self-conscious, 931a
  as cat's meat, 876a
  birth, reviled for his, 59a
  cultivates the golden, 38b
  license they, 251a
  no creature's made so, 574a
  nothing common did or, 268b
  observances of decorum, 418a
  occupations, busies himself in, 54a
  poem should not, but be, 960b
  proper, 38b, 325b
  say what you, 656b
  so trifling or so, 442b
  souls, companion of, 370a
  speak not what we, 184b
  stupid dastardly, 434a
  things, meanly admires, 565a
  to have a war, 358b
  what do you, to do, 706b
  what I say, 656b
  what may this, 172a
  words, many different things, 659a
Meander's margent green, 247a
Meaner, ambition of the, sort, 124b
  beauties of the night, 213a
  creatures kings, 128b
  law than Brotherhood, 655a
  pelf, ask thee for no, 588b
Meanest flower that blows, 409a
  floweret of the vale, 349b
  lives for mortal known, 711b
  motives and petty causes, 491a
  of his creatures, 571b
  of mankind, 318a
  of your sons inspire, 310b
  peereth in, habit, 130b
  slave, dreads like the, 314a
  sorts of labor, 476a
  thing in his hull life, 735a
Meaning, blunders round about a, 318b
  doesn't matter, 683a
  fresh, for every situation, 920b
  honour, and import, 369b
  in saying he is good man, 143b
  intricate, and pith, 651b
  it's what you please, 651b
  new feeling and new, 618a
  of a word, 518a
  of life has been lost, 728a
  to some faint, make pretence, 277b
  when poetry has a, 787b
  without injury to, 425a
Meaningless universe, 872b
Meanings, hell is full of good, 233b
Meanly, slenderly and, 1067b
  they live within doors, 285b
  wrapt in rude manger, 244b
Meanness in the argument, 502b
  poverty is parent of, 24b
Meannesses, worst weaknesses and, 580b
Means, all, permitted to fight an evil, 949b

Means, appliances and, to boot, 153b
  bad, and bad men, 370b
  by all the, you can, 329b
  end must justify the, 293b
  find, of evil, 252b
  great show with little, 565a
  increased, 513a
  live content with small, 557b
  live within our, 665a
  make it fair up to our, 571a
  may lie too low for envy, 267a
  money, and content, 161b
  much more the, he raises, 319a
  no one, all he says, 697b
  not but blunders, 318b
  of destruction, 929b
  of livelihood, 875a
  of our own destruction, 11b
  of subsistence, 792b
  placed in our power, 369a
  save, to live, 209b
  to do ill deeds, 148b
  to enjoyments of life, 925a
  to make us one, 216b
  visible, of support, 714a
  what I choose it to mean, 659a
  whereby I live, 146b
  will not say all it, 846b
Meant, more is, than meets ear, 246b
  well tried a little, 753a
Measels, did you ever have the, 664b
Measles, stars like, fade, 955b
Measure, all life moving to one, 893a
  days by dreams, 810b
  delightful, or dance, 138b
  fate thy, takes, 602b
  for law we have a, 227a
  God gives wind by, 234a
  most moderate, most perfect, 101a
  narrow, 787a
  not the work, 520a
  of a play, 42a
  of latitude and opulence, 508b
  of my days, 1034a
  of our torment, 819a
  of the value of a nation, 743a
  of this thought, 709a
  services I render, 14b
  shrunk to this little, 167b
  sighed to, 406b
  take thine own, 232b
  uncertain, would this be, 227a
  undertaken with temerity, 19b
  we call a foot, 227a
  with what, ye mete, 1055b
  your mind's height, 567a
Measured back to you again, 28b
  by my soul, 302b
  language, use in, 551b
  out my life, 942b
  phrase, 406b
  speeches, by the hour, 375b
Measureless, caverns, to man, 420b
  content, shut up in, 196a
  grossness and slag, 609a
Measures bind the pow'r of pain, 617a
  in short, life may perfect be, 219b
  Lydian, 280a
  not men, 323a, 355b
  not men but, 359a
Meat, abstract truths are strong, 561a

Meat, after, comes mustard, 105a
  and he gave him not, 352b
  appointed to buy the, 228a
  benison fall on our, 231a
  buys opinions as it buys, 672a
  chew our, for us, 98b
  diggy but no, dar, 738b
  dined upon cold, 285a
  drink and cloaths, 1002b
  drink and cloth, 90a
  easy, and drink, 817a
  eat but little, 97a
  eaten without mirth, 417a
  egg is full of, 136b
  for the hungry, 109b
  God sendeth, 91b
  in the hall, 751a
  mean as cat's, 876a
  no stomach for such, 704a
  nor drink nor slumber, 963a
  one man's poison is another's, 34b
  out of the eater came forth, 1026b
  outdid the, 231a
  packer, talent of a, 843a
  provideth her, in summer, 1038b
  sit down and taste my, 232b
  so dressed and sauced, 92a
  some hae, and canna eat, 393b
  strong, 1063b
  this dish of, 236b
  'tis not the, 261b
  upon what, doth Caesar feed, 166b
  was locusts and wild honey, 1050a
  ye gave me, 1054b
Meats, digests experiences like, 727b
  funeral baked, 170b
  of all, the soonest cloy, 267a
Meazles, love iz like the, 594b
Mebbe an' mebbe not, 735a
Mecca, holy temple of, 1070a
Mechanic a mere working mason, 416a
  art, poetry a mere, 363a
  mere, operation, 239b
  pacings to and fro, 548a
  sad, exercise, 551b
  slaves, 201b
Mechanical art, surest test afforded by, 484a
Mechanician, visible sage, 592b
Mechanics and laborers, 399a
  shivering bicycle, 974a
Mechanism, battles transacted by, 474b
Mechanized automaton, 464b
Med, groweth sed and bloweth, 999a
Medal, dangling that bright hard, 719b
Med'cinable gum, 190b
  some griefs are, 204a
Meddle in the commonwealth, 86a
  make or, 434a
  not with him that flattereth, 1040a
Meddles, man, with them, 344a
  with cold iron, 113a
Meddlesome tongues, 557b
Meddling, every fool will be 1040a
  government, paternal or, 492a
  with another man's folly, 813b
Medea gather'd herbs, 147a
Medes, law of, and Persians, 1049a

Mist, grey, on the sea's face, 895b
  here a, there a mist, 645b
  in my face, 572b
  mantled in, 993b
  of light hides what they are, 543a
  of tears, 790a
  resembles the rain, 522a
  Scotch, 603a
  shouted in the, 880a
Mistake, as if there is some, 880b
  blue and gold, 647b
  glory in a great, 996a
  God's second, 728b
  great thoughts, 586a
  he never overlooks a, 633b
  in the translation, 294a
  there is no, 400b
  thy child's, 790a
  without music life a, 727b
Mistaken, holy, zeal in politics, 1002a
  path to happiness, 461b
  pronounce him to be, 266a
Mistakes, genius makes no, 917a
  lament, of a good man, 1002a
  make, I will protect you, 965b
  name everyone gives to their, 768b
  no balsam for, 712b
  of their own lives, 698a
  string of, called memoirs, 597a
Mr. Clay, yes said, 433b
  Finney had a turnip, 1004b
  Hennessy, 836a
  Lear, pleasant to know, 580b
  Micawber, never will desert, 579a
  Reilly, 1005a
  Watson come here, 736a
  Webster, eloquence of, 980a
Mrs. Bennet was restored, 428a
  Fezziwig, in came, 578a
  Porter and her daughter, 944a
Mistress, art is a jealous, 505a
  court a, she denies you, 218b
  in my own, 816a
  law is a jealous, 560b, 561a
  lover of his, 270b
  master, and two slaves, 714a
  moderately fair, 267a
  most deceitful, 697b
  O, mine, 164a
  of herself though china fall, 315a
  of mistresses, 618b
  of the months and stars, 691a
  such, such Nan, 96b
  teeming, 314b
  to the man I love, 313a
  unlocks his heart unto his, 231b
Mistress' eyebrow, 161a
  eyes nothing like the sun, 207b
  order to perform, 322a
Mistresses, hardly any, 851a
  mistress of, 618b
  wives are young men's, 120a
Mistrust a subordinate, 738a
  ignominious to, friends, 265a
Mistrusts, he who, most, 8b
Mists and mellow fruitfulness, 482b
  of silver dew, 465b
  soft, in her hair, 860b
  the Apennine, 646b
Misty flats, in between on, 796b
  incomprehensible wavering and, 772b
  island, sheiling of the, 435b

Misty, moisty morning, 1020a
  morn, old autumn in the, 488a
  tiptoe on, mountaintops, 137a
Misunderstand, no fate willfully, me, 879b
Misunderstanding, fear of blame or, 761b
Misunderstood, criticized vilified and, 763a
  grief may be joy, 520a
  misrepresented and, 722b
  to be great is to be, 501b
Misuse of words, 861b
Misused, poison of, wine, 247a
Mites, threw in two, 1056a
Mithridates, half, half Trissotin, 493b
  he died old, 876b
Mitigate the billows, 46a
Mitigated by reason and evaluation, 954a
Mix and amalgamate, 497b
  little folly with wisdom, 100b
  subtlest parts, 262a
  unwilling to, my fortune, 284a
Mixed everywhere, 269a
  shades and shadows, 604b
  yust get, in wrong, 946a
Mixt, with embraces curses oft I, 309b
Mixture, come to us with a, 431a
  of Christian sorrow, 932b
  of fools and angels, 801b
  of sorrow, 106b
  of water or worse, 702b
  stir the, well, 536b
Mixtures of more happy days, 457a
Mizpah the Lord watch, 1023b
Moan a sigh a sob a storm, 655b
  delicious, 482b
  English mother made her, 601b
  eternal, 584a
  for rest, 655b
  frosty wind made, 649b
  made sweet, 480a
  of doves in immemorial elms, 551a
  of thunder, 468a
  paid with, 789b
  texts of joy or, 601b
  the little ones, 619b
Moaning, bar and its, 598a
  of the bar, 557a
  on ilka green loaning, 992b
Moans, orphans', 362a
  tugs and, 971b
Moat-by-the-Castle, 883b
Moated grange, 185a
Mob, amphibious ill-born, 291b
  government by a, 780a
  is varied and inconstant, 282b
  jokes at which, laughs, 866b
  law, redress by, 537a
  of gentlemen, 320b
  opinion of the, 282b
  the crowd the mass, 898a
  turbulent, 445b
Moby Dick, great diplomat a, 907a
Moche Crye and no Wull, 83b
Mock at sin, 1039a
  meat it feeds on, 188a
  not Eros, 956b
  on Voltaire Rousseau, 387b
  sit in clouds and, 153a
  the air with idle state, 349b
  Turtle, 657a
  your own grinning, 178b

Mock'd himself and scorn'd, 166b
  in ev'ry thing, 213b
Mocker, wine is a, 1040a
Mockeries, human, 440b
Mockery and the contradiction, 807a
  delusion a, and a snare, 437a
  hence unreal, 198a
  king of snow, 140b
  monumental, 182a
  of monumental stone, 468a
Mocketh, whoso, the poor, 1039b
Mockin'-bird, lovesick, 859b
Mocking air, 148b
  pencil, 588b
  to ashes, 829a
Mocking-bird's throat, 609a
Mockings or arguments, 607b
Mocks, cuckoo, married men, 134a
  lightning that, the night, 469a
  man that, at it, 138b
  my loss of liberty, 384b
Mode, beautiful, of saying things, 621b
  futile decalogue of, 781a
  heat as a, of motion, 613b
  it began à la, 704a
  maintain miserable, 75a
Model, draw the, 153a
  of a modern major-general, 682b
  small, of barren earth, 139b
  to inward greatness, 154b
Moderate, be, 182b
  haste, one with, 171a
  measure the most perfect, 101a
  O love be, 145b
  pleasant food and drink, 282b
Moderately, love, 136b
  mistress, fair, 267a
Moderation even in excess, 511a
  is best, 53b
  is best in all things, 8b
  is the silken string, 220b
  noblest gift of Heaven, 17a
  observe, 7b
  stoutness in, 683b
Moderator of passions, 235b
  reasonable, 240b
Modern and ancient poets, 275b
  capitalists, class of, 593b
  classic literature is always, 511a
  inconveniences, all the, 676a
  industry, race of, 593b
  instances, 161b
  large, fortune, 769b
  life, strange disease of, 621a
  manners of expression, 314a
  no idea is so, 873a
  notions, 817a
  old or, bard, 247a
  oratory, vice of, 375b
  phrase, caskets a vile, 515a
  politics a struggle of forces, 697b
  spirit, characteristics of the, 799a
  world, happy man in, 914a
  world, supreme ecstasy of, 987b
Modernity to feel priggish about, 923b
Moderns, speak of, without contempt, 323a
Modes, nobler, of life, 553a
  of worship in Roman world, 369a
Modest cough of a minor poet, 765b
  crimson-tipp'd flow'r, 391a
  doubt, 181b

Modest front of this small floor, 264a
keep, as a giver, 726b
looks the cottage adorn, 357a
men are dumb, 395b
not the presumptuous inquirer, 304a
pride, 255b
quip, 163a
simple, manly true, 602a
stillness and humility, 155a
woman in all her finery, 357a
Modestly conceals her beauties, 343b
Modestus said of Regulus, 65a
Modesty and unselfishness, 932b
bounds of, 137b
clemency are species of nobility, 282a
downcast, conceal'd, 328a
of nature, 175b
true school of, 449b
vanity of more benefit than, 878a
virtue not found among poets, 108a
with meekness and, bore him, 23a
Modification, bad plan of no, 44b
of my oft-expressed wish, 540a
Modified by whatever modifies life, religions, 702a
Modify, have time to, his shape, 679b
Moe the merrier, 94b
Mogul and Mugwump, 661a
Mohammed is his prophet, 950a
Mohammedan agnostic monist, 774b
Mohammed's truth, 543a
Moidhered head an' brains, 859b
Moiling, toiling and, 568b
Moist breath of decay, 639a
cabinet, lark from his, 131a
eye a dry hand, 152b
hot and cold and, and dry, 102a
hot cold, and dry, 254b
unpleasant body, 576b
Moisty, misty, morning, 1020a
Molar to molecular motions, 709b
Molasses catches flies, 747b
Mold a mighty state's decrees, 552b
a world of fire and dew, 825a
arts and sciences not cast in, 99a
cast in same, 99a
damp and, 885b
force into one, 95a
grew out of the, 820a
home of fairest, 877b
how large of, 663a
man of God's own, 663a
men's thought and purpose, 700a
mildew, and stain, 772a
mouthful of, 895b
nature broke the, 456a
of a man's fortune, 36a
of form, 175a
of its vulgarity, 939a
our lives, 670b
smell the rose above the, 489b
splashing the wintry, 825a
the breathing bronze, 37b
the secret mind, 695a
to break away from, 939b
verge of the churchyard, 488b

Molded by some plastic force, 703a
formed or, 460a
meal-drift, 724b
nation be, to last, 696a
on one stem, 142a
out of faults, 185b
wax, as she pleases, 110a
Molder piecemeal on the rock, 455b
Moldered into oblivion, 446a
the lips, 947a
Moldering bones, 853a
in the grave, 401b
Molders hemp and steel, 416b
Molding her mighty fates, 845b
Sheridan, 456a
Molds, love that is hoarded, 975a
musket, in his hands, 747a
Moldy chestnut, salute each, 661a
damnable, 263a
rolls of Noah's ark, 277a
world would grow, 556a
Mole, velvet, 934b
wilt thou go ask the, 384b
Molecular motions, molar to, 709b
Mole-hill and mare's nest, 704a
Moles and bats, 1045a
Molière pleases all the world, 286b
Mollify, strive to share and, 763b
Molly, blades to Meg and, 663a
Pitcher, bright name of, 748b
Stark is a widow, 358b
true to his, 377a
Molten blue, inns of, 646a
bowels, 866a
mass, 939a
Mome raths outgrabe, 657b
Moment as it flies, 329a
before it's ripe, 386b
creature of the, 434a
deem of no, 25b
endurance for one, more, 732b
endures a, or a day, 827a
eternity was in that, 297b
glitters for a, 301a
great pith and, 175a
hold every, sacred, 883b
horror of that, 657b
I would rather be thy, 648b
in some blithe, 735b
last, of his breath, 353b
lose eternity in the passing, 994a
myself and the lucky, 95a
never can spare you a, 876a
no, more annihilating, 853b
not the briefest, 863a
of difficulty and danger, 1001b
of my greatness, 943a
of strength of romance, 772b
only a, 772b
present, the least happiest, 577a
psychological, to say nothing, 768a
to decide, 599b
when all had succeeded, 400a
white then melts forever, 393b
without a, of rest, 642b
work of a, 103b
yet the actor stops, 563b
Momentary, beauty is, 906a
effect on man, 479a
in endurance, 68b
Moment's monument, sonnet is a, 640b
ornament, 409a
Moments, best and happiest, 469a
day is bursting with, 985a

Moments, great, are not turning points, 878a
highest quality to your, 702a
little, humble though they be, 626b
make the year, 305a
of error or alarm, 375a
of glad grace, 824a
of high proud exultation, 940b
of surplus power, 914b
one by one the, fall, 634a
small seeds of, 797a
ugliest trades have, of pleasure, 509b
when he is only stupid, 487a
Momentum, psychological, or factor, 768a
Monads of Leibniz, 932a
Monan's, moon on, rill, 415a
Monarch, does not misbecome a, 350a
eastern, charged his wise men, 538b
hears with ravish'd ears, 280a
is night, 935b
it becomes the throned, 146a
merry, scandalous and poor, 289a
morsel for a, 200a
no, but would give crown, 242a
of all I survey, 363b
of mountains, 456b
of the vine, 201a
page and, 593a
richest, in Christian world, 394b
sceptred, of the dead, 6b
statesman warrior or, 515a
teach a, to be wise, 348a
Monarchs must give place, 591a
must obey, 277b
perplexes, 253a
seldom sigh in vain, 414a
Monastic aisles, 503a
Monday, betwixt a Saturday and, 307b
born on a, 1018b
going to do on, 911a
Monday's child is fair of face, 1018b
Money, accept, from a woman, 732b
alms were, put to interest, 427b
answereth all things, 1043a
as long as, can be made, 983a
bet, on de bobtail nag, 636a
blessing that, cannot buy, 236b
borrow the, to do it with, 665b
built without, or toil, 587b
business and, 783a
can't appreciate, 801a
changer, morals of a, 843a
changers, 1053b
changers have fled, 919a
comes withal, 130a
comparable to paper, 784a
cost me much, 284a
counting out his, 1017a
dear friends I write for, 736b
disease called lack of, 88b
do not mind his, 868a
does not pay for anything, 864a
doth not stay but wastes, 84a
ever wrote except for, 341b
exchange their ware for, 702b
fool and his, 999b
from one class of citizens, 325a
get, 41a
give, to colleges, 535a
good provision of, 88b

Moon, begged of the, to give him light, 1003a
behold wandering, 246a
brilliant, and milky sky, 824b
build a bridge to the, 589a
by yonder blessed, 135b
climbing, upon empty sky, 825a
cold fruitless, 140b
come from the dying, 550a
comes over Brooklyn, 995b
commanded, to stand still, 331b
course of one revolving, 277a
cow jumped over the, 1016b
crimson, and azure eye, 395b
danced by the light of the, 581a
daughter of the, 523a
ebb and flow by the, 193b
error of the, 190a
everyone is a, 679a
fair as the, 1044b
follow changes of the, 188b
horned, 421b
hush with the setting, 554a
in a silver bag, 827b
inconstant, 135b
innocent, 789b
is like a flower, 385b
is my sister, 848b
kneaded by the, 705a
Lady, where are you roving, 543a
lies fair upon the straits, 622a
like to a silver bow, 140b
lucent as a rounded, 602b
made of green cheese, 88a
make guilty the, the stars, 191a
marsh beneath the, 935a
minions of the, 149a
more interested in earth, 756b
mortal, 206b
mortals call the, 466b
moving, went up the sky, 422a
nor the, by night, 1037b
ode to the, 854a
on Monan's rill, 415a
or stars be not darkened, 1043b
or sun or what you please, 130b
pale-faced, 149b
resolves into salt tears, 203b
revisit'st glimpses of the, 172a
rising in clouded majesty, 255b
said the wind to the, 631b
saw the new, late yestreen, 1011b
shine at full or no, 239b
shone bright on Mrs. Porter, 944a
shown the wintry, 481a
sigh for the, 665a
silent as the, 260a
silver apples of the, 825a
slowly silently now the, 862b
small, lightens more, 721a
sun and, should doubt, 388a
sun and stars brother, 500b
sun and, were sunk, 247b
sun stood still the, stayed, 1026a
swear not by the, 135b
sweet regent of the sky, 368b
takes up the wondrous tale, 299a
talk by a poet, 676b
that looks for us again, 533b
the stars the planets, 929a
thou climb'st skies, 115b
to the, complain, 348a
unmask her beauty to the, 171a
very wide awake the, and I, 684b
waning, was haunted, 420b
was a ghostly galleon, 909b
when the, shall rise, 213a

Moon, white, beams, 952a
will wax, 525b
Moon-calf, 209b
Moone, cast beyond the, 91b
Moonlecht necht, 850a
Moonlight and feeling are one, 469a
come to thee by, 909b
is divine, 995b
is softest in Kentucky, 725b
lulled by the, 636b
meet me by, 484b
not of the, 556b
ribbon of, 909b
rotten mackerel by, 425b
shade, beck'ning ghost along, 313b
sleeps upon this bank, 147a
unto sunlight, 549a
visit it by the pale, 413b
Moonlit cedar, from that, 621a
door, knocking on the, 862b
Moonrise, gradual as the, 616a
Moon's an arrant thief, 203b
unclouded grandeur, 464b
Moons, among the suns and, 994a
my old, and my new moons, 724a
reason has, 854b
while stars burn, increase, 547b
Moonshine, find out, 142a
its glory is all, 613b
Moon-struck madness, 258b
Moor, Hercules and Goth and, 703a
I never saw a, 648a
over the purple, 909b
wild, 1003a
your bark with two anchors, 43b
Moor'd, fleet was, in the Downs, 308a
Moore, Tom, a health to thee, 456b
Moorish fen, by lake or, 247b
Moorsfield London, 336b
Moping melancholy, 258b
mum, 685a
owl does complain, 348a
Mops, seven maids with seven, 658a
Moral and intellectual powers, 733a
and material welfare, 779b
artistic, personality, 611a
authority, basis of, 617b
character, bird of bad, 331b
conflict, van of every, 588a
courage with physical timidity, 705a
culture, highest stage in, 530a
effort, golf a form of, 844b
ends by settling the, 696a
Englishman thinks he is, 765a
enterprise, success of, 517b
everything's got a, 657a
evil and of good, 403b
free from, obligations, 420a
habits in men's lives, 55a
indifference is the malady, 617b
infection, 580a
inferiority, 679b
intellectual and, achievements, 637b
is what you feel good after, 982b
issues, 983b
losses of expediency, 964a
man and a man of honor, 909a
man was Werther, 564a
no one can be, till all are moral, 614b
obligation to be intelligent, 901a

Moral or an immoral book, 768a
persons attempting to find a, 676b
philosophy makes men grave, 121b
physical and, standard, 616b
point a, 336a
question for the heart, 811a
satire ever, ever new, 287a
sense of work of art, 719a
sense, women have, 696a
sensible well-bred man, 363a
sentiments, 472a
soil for aesthetic growth, 866a
spark out of stone easier than a, 689a
story with a, 801b
test, perception of beauty a, 589a
things, or things evangelical, 274a
world, intellectual and, 538b
Moralist set up the ignoble maxim, 783b
statesman cannot be a, 930b
Moralities, never mind about, 679a
Morality, blunderbuss against, 339a
enliven, with wit, 300a
foes of popular, 617b
in courage of making choice, 858b
is a private luxury, 697a
knows nothing of boundaries, 614b
middle class, 766a
needs emotion to become religion, 673a
no, where there is no free agency, 484a
of his actions, 344b
of vulgar man, 727b
periodical fits of, 492a
pernicious to general, 514b
sexless orgies of, 695a
temper wit with, 300a
thou deadly bane, 390b
treat politics and, apart, 700a
unawares, expires, 322a
veracity is heart of, 633b
wear his, 924b
which suits him, 778a
Moralize my song, 113a
Moralizing, philosopher's, 812b
Morals, about, 982b
and legislation, 324b
faith and, 407a
falsified by conventional, 861a
field of, 908a
make you dreary, 753a
of a money changer, 843a
of the market place, 849b
self-interest was bad, 919b
simply blind obedience, 784a
Morbid doubt, 753b
Morbidity, disgusting, 925b
Mordre wol out, 82a
More abundant life, 919a
and more about less and less, 799a
and more and more, 658b
and the few, 887b
blessed to give, 1059a
books upon books, 101a
brawn than brain, 36a
by hoping, they have less, 131a
easy to take, than nothing, 657a
elder than looks, 146b
giving thy sum of, 159b

Mouth, one's, what one becomes, 838a
  opened the, of the ass, 1025b
  out of the heart the, speaketh, 1052b
  out of thine own, 1057b
  over the, blown, 944b
  pebbles in his, 57a
  playwrights, 794b
  purple-stained, 481b
  right which your, utters, 14a
  sad kissed, 692b
  shall be filled with gravel, 1040a
  show forth thy praise, 1034b
  silver spoon in his, 109b
  take from the, of labor, 374b
  tiresome, 722a
  two ears but only one, 511b
  what his, ate, 1014b
  wickedness sweet in his, 1031a
  wine comes in at the, 826a
  with his verb in his, 677b
  words of his, smoother, 1035a
Mouth-filling oath, 151a
Mouthful of mould, 895b
Mouth-honour breath, 199a
Mouths a sentence, 362a
  in other, was rough, 599b
  made, in a glass, 191b
  of nations yet unborn, 96a
  of wisest censure, 187b
  put enemy in their, 187b
  without hands, 281a
Movable types, device of, 473b
Mov'd, vast shadow, 272a
  with concord of sweet sounds, 147a
Move, all things work and, 583b
  and have our being, 1059a, 1069a
  desire to, in harmony, 633a
  doubt the sun doth, 173b
  each gay turn thy rapture, 311a
  easiest who learn'd to dance, 311a
  forward with strong faith, 922a
  in cloud of ignorance, 978b
  in the void, 12a
  makes no show to, 216b
  on a rigorous line, 621b
  only in command, 199a
  quickness to hear to, 809a
  shadows, over the slopes, 37a
  stars, still, 123b
  the earth, 29b
  times do, 114a
  with leaden feet, 689b
Moved, any given weight might be, 54b
  beyond endurance, 925a
  heart, with a trumpet, 116a
  I shall not be, 1035a
  in perfect phalanx, 253a
  suffer thy foot to be, 1037b
  to smile at anything, 166b
  woman, like fountain troubled, 130b
Movement, a palpable, 704b
  every great, on this globe, 950b
  from unity, 697b
  new, is not a stampede, 811a
  new, of human activity, 722b
  produces a few great men, 941a
  time is infinite, 642b
  with great aims, 951a
Movers and shakers of the world, 730a
Moves, cursed be he that, my bones, 212b

Moves more to see sad sights, 131b
  she, a goddess, 4a
Moveth itself aright, 1040b
  might of the gods, 17a
Movin' up and down again, 819a
Moving accidents by flood and field, 186a
  ever, spheres of heaven, 123b
  every passion, 57a
  finger writes, 533a
  forward to greater freedom, 919a
  in form and, how express, 173b
  in opposite directions, 419b
  land, seems a, 257a
  moon went up the sky, 422a
  pitch my, tent, 413a
  row of magic shadow-shapes, 533a
  slow and, finger, 189b
  time a thing steadfast, 404b
  to measure of his thought, 709a
  vitalizing work, 744a
  waters at priestlike task, 479b
  why they do it, 391b
  yet and never stopping, 609a
Moving-delicate and full of life, 158b
Mow, plow and sow and reap and, 1000a
Mown grass, 1035b
Mozart, some cry up, 430b
  tried to play, 955b
Much, asking too, 401b
  book not worth, 605b
  faithful also in, 1057a
  fortune doth give too, 117b
  has lain outside our ken, 706a
  have I seen and known, 548a
  I owe, 88a
  I want which most would have, 101b
  in another man's purse, 107b
  know, and think for nothing, 220b
  little more, too much, 151a
  little time to do so, 921b
  made of a Scotchman, 341a
  may be said on both sides, 300b
  men who know, 344b
  must not do too, of it, 605a
  nothing too, 60b
  of a muchness, 294a, 657a
  outcry little outcome, 9b
  so, is he sure of, 109a
  so, owed by so many, 869b
  so, to do, 552b
  some have too, 101b
  talk too, 277a
  that I sought, 900a
  that which had too, 159b
  to do, 758a
  too, and too little education, 272a
  too, of a good thing, 103b
  unjust also in, 1057a
  unkindness may do, 189b
  upon his back, 220a
  world where, to be done, 338a
  you get is small, 630a
Muchness, much of a, 294a, 657a
Muck of sweat, 354b
  stop raking the, 779b
Muckle, twice as, 's a' that, 394a
Muckrake in his hand, 274b
  men with the, 779b
Mud, belly in the, 943b
  garlic and sapphires in the, 944b
  in, eel is, 1019a

Mud, learn or his name is, 957a
  marble and, 514a
  me name is, 886b
  silver fountains, 205a
Muddied oafs at the goals, 816b
Muddle, brain is in a, 829b
  manage to, through, 561b
Muddled state sharpest reality, 719b
Muddlement, constant force for, 719b
Muddy ill-seeming thick, 130b
  vesture, 147a
  water, Mississippi is, 776b
Mudville nine, 807b
  no joy in, 808a
Muffet, little Miss, 1018b
Muffin man, 1019b
Muffins, inspiration in a plate of, 765a
Muffled and dumb, 506b
  drums, 521a
  oar, I wait the, 528a
  roar, 808a
Muffler afore her eyes, 121a
Mugwump educated beyond his intellect, 661a
  mogul and, of final plot, 661a
Mulberry-trees, amid her, 525b
Mule, brown Missouri, 854a
  Democratic Party like a, 361a
  kicked in the head by a, 828b
  reason with a, 758b
Mules, facts are contrary 'z, 297b
Mulleary, Shake, and Go-ethe, 761a
Mulligan Guard, march'd in the, 732a
Mulligrubs, die merely of the, 109b
Multifold, dying, without respite, 648b
Multiplication is vexation, 999a
Multiplicity in uniformity, 806b
  unity into, 697b
Multiplied visions, 1049a
Multiplieth, words without knowledge, 103b
Multiply, be fruitful and, 1021a
  each through endless years, 441a
  sentinels, 497b
Multitude always in the wrong, 283b
  Antony addressing a, 57b
  by the sea in, 1028b
  fool, 145a
  gathering, that shrunk, 471a
  hoofs of a swinish, 361a
  into unity of effect, 424b
  long-lost, of ships, 625b
  many-headed monster, 115b
  men and the, of words, 70a
  musty breath of the, 791a
  of an host, 1066b
  of counsellors, 1039a
  of days, 336a
  of fibres, 497a
  of friends, 218a
  of projects, 44a
  of sensations, 493a
  of sins, 1064a
  of words wanteth not sin, 70a
  or small company, 1066b
  rude, call afternoon, 133b
  still-discordant wavering, 152a
  underlings of the, 57a
  washed hands before the, 1055a
  wear another face to the, 514a
Multitudes, I contain, 608b
  in valley of decision, 1049a
  of hours pilfered away, 405a

Necessity has no law, 70a
 industry in art is a, 668b
 knows no law, 45a
 legs for, 181b
 mother of invention, 24a
 nature obey, 169a
 none sorer than, 14b
 of being ready increases, 539b
 of subduing again, 360a
 prepare for days of, 10b
 progress not an accident but, 614a
 refuses anything to, 45a
 region of absolute, 861a
 sharp fumes of, 791a
 stress of, 45a
 strive against, 70a
 tyrant's plea, 45a, 255b
 villains by, 191a
Necessity's sharp pinch, 191b
Neck as a tower of ivory, 1044b
 drip huge drops on your, 959a
 fall on the, or kiss, 815a
 humbled, 162a
 millstone hanged about his, 1057b
 of a vinegar-cruet, 338a
 some chicken some, 871a
 tied up to thy, 1070b
 yield not thy, 126b
Necks, stretched forth, 1045a
Necktie, left my, God knows where, 786b
Nectar I can make into honey, 689a
 Jove's, 219a
 on a lip, 381b
Nectar'd sweets, perpetual feast of, 247b
Nectarean juice, 483b
Ned's and the Squire, 705a
Neebor's part, man may tak a, 391a
Need, another man's intimate, 772b
 crying, in humbler ranks, 641b
 day and light, thee so, 686a
 deserted at his utmost, 280a
 friend in, 30b
 help thee in thy, 220a
 hour of dire, 715a
 how little we, in this world, 792a
 mass response out of mass, 985b
 most, of blessing, 196b
 no law, 117a
 no, of ancestors, 324b
 no, of valour, 56a
 nothing, 608b
 nothing can, a lie, 232b
 of a world of men, 568a
 of milk, 1063b
 of the sky, 808b
 of woman, 966b
 pray in thy, 924b
 satisfies no normal, 975a
 thou hast in life of me, 812b
 which I do not, 70b
Neede, friend never knowne till man have, 93b
Needed, all are, by each one, 503a
 not the spectacles of books, 275b
 to make happy life, 68a
Needful motions, 102a
 one thing is, 1057a
Needin', raison like, th' money, 836a
Needle, eye of, 140b, 1053b
 for the, she, 550b
 hinders, and thread, 489a
 in a bottle of hay, 107b

Needle in the haycock, 957b
 plying her, and thread, 489a
 true as the, to the pole, 239b
Needle-note, silver, of a fife, 976a
Needle's eye, hold the, 957b
 small, eye, 140b
Needless Alexandrine ends the song, 311a
Needs, daily cares pleasures and, 594b
 each according to his, 594a
 fault which, it most, 232b
 fear no fall, 238b
 for its, and woes, 704a
 in search of what he, 756b
 men must, abide, 126b
 must when Devil drives, 89b
 neither bush nor preface, 46b
 of the age, 822b
 optics sharp it, 380b
 when, he must, 319a
Needy, deny necessaries to the, 1070b
 hollow-eyed wretch, 129b
 money in the stomachs of, 73a
 relief not for the, 921b
 wealth to the, 110a
Neer to church further from God, 92a
Negation, begets its own, 594a
Negative capability, 478a
 criticism, 518a
 yet no slight virtue, 474a
Negatives, make much of, 611a
Neglect and oblivion, 431a
 creeping hours, 161a
 God and his angels, 218a
 hired girls, 931b
 kings, heart's ease, 156a
 may breed mischief, 234a, 330b
 perpetual, of many things, 749b
 such sweet, more taketh me, 218b
 wise and salutary, 359b
Neglecting worldly ends, 208b
Neglects learning in youth, 18a
Negligence and indisposition, 54a
 and silence, 342b
Negligences, noble, teach, 294a
Negligent at their prayer, 1070b
 more admir'd than by the, 201a
Negotiate, every eye, for itself, 157b
Negotiation, Anglo-American, 950b
Negro character, 758b
 courage of the, 562b
 dehumanizing the, 537b
Negroes, all men created equal except, 537a
 learned nothing more democratic, 964a
 oppression of, 537a
Negro's sword, 563a
Neighbor, bad, is a misfortune, 7b
 breaks your fence, 573a
 desirous of being good, 919a
 do our, all the good, 28a
 eye his, as possible enemy, 860a
 false witness against thy, 1025a
 hate your, 492b
 helped every one his, 1047a
 helping every feeble, 661b
 his hungering, and me, 600a
 let your, carve for you, 296a
 love my, well, 438b
 love thy, 1025a
 love your, 233b
 loves his, as himself, 763b
 nor angry with our, 20a

Neighbor, policy of good, 919a
 rob a, 493a
 says does thinks, 67a
 struck into back of its, 920b
 that is near, 1041a
 whom we have disliked, 886a
 without reproach, 660a
 wrangle with a, 99a
Neighborhood, first entering a, 428a
 London, 495a
Neighboring, cynosure of, eyes, 245a
Neighborly, keep up our spirits and be, 577b
Neighbor's, any thing that is thy, 1025a
 creed, 503a
 grandfather a Syrian, 264b
 heart, what is in, 66a
 house, covet thy, 1025a
 wife, covet thy, 1025a
 wife, love your, 492b
Neighbors, bad feelin's between, 843b
 borrowing everything of, 285b
 buried brother John, 690b
 call your, in, 1016b
 central empires into good, 925a
 first to attack their, 270a
 good fences make good, 879b
 innocence of our, 590b
 knowing too much of his, 697b
 lending confidentially to, 341a
 live together as good, 998a
 made, very miserable, 723a
 make sport for our, 428a
 more right than his, 588b
 next-door, yet strangers, 405a
 showed his, peace, 584b
 simply hold their own, 715b
 what will the, think, 956b
 where would my, go, 859b
Neighing far off on haunted air, 948b
 in likeness of a filly foal, 141a
 steed, farewell the, 189a
Neighs, boastful, 155b
Neither is most to blame, 694b
 sun nor death, 264b
Nellie, know, like I do, 850a
Nelson gave orders for boarding, 389b
Nelson's hand, 695b
Nemean lion's nerve, 172a
Neon glow, 941b
Neptune, flatter, for his trident, 202b
 floods which, obey, 1013b
 shall never sink this ship, 47b
 watery, 139a
Neptune's ocean wash this blood, 196b
Nerve brings us out of it, 616b
 iron, to true occasion true, 553b
 me who am as a, 465b
 mortal arm and, 416b
 Nemean lion's, 172a
 stretch every, 329a
 tense American, 994b
Nerves, ganglion in, of society, 709a
 my firm, shall never tremble, 198a
 sensitive, of receiving, 667a
 strengthens our, 361b
 the nerves, 578b
Nervous and intellectual system, 784a

Outline, dowager's was a demd, 576b
Outlines, two countesses had no, 576b
Outliv'd doctor's pill, 308b
Outlive, desire, performance, 153a
 his wealth, 146b
 life half a year, 176a
Outlives, he that, this day, 156b
 in fame the pious fool, 241b
 no structure, a book, 713a
Outlook, could man, that mark, 272a
 wasn't brilliant, 807b
Outmost margins, 939b
Outnumber, shapes the busy thoughts, 465a
Outnumbered, we are so, 923b
Out-of-doors, no house like God's, 750a
Out-paramoured the Turk, 192a
Outrage on the spirit of justice, 757b
 when man destroys, 888a
 worse than death, 423a
Outraged art, 937b
Outrageous fortune, 174b
Outrageously virtuous, 302a
Outride, beggar, the Devil, 126a
Outrider, torch-bearing, 718b
Outset, use medicines at the, 46b
Outshone wealth of Ormus, 253b
Outside, furside is the, 855a
 goodly, falsehood hath, 144a
 influences, good humor of, 838b
 martial, 159b
 show is a poor substitute, 10a
Outsider, tremendous, 953b
Outsoared shadow of our night, 468a
Outspoken, honest, pride, 748a
Outstretch'd, arms, as he would fly, 182a
Outstripping donkeys, 52b
Out-topping knowledge 619a
Outvalues, possession which, all others, 679a
Outvenoms worms of Nile, 204a
Outward, all goes onward and, 607b
 all, loathes, 215b
 and visible sign, 1069a
 appearance, 1027b
 difficulties, 98b
 evils, of all, 473a
 form and feature, 423b
 shewith bright, 77b
 showing an, pity, 140a
 side, angel on the, 185b
 touch, soiled by any, 72b
 virtue on, parts, 145b
Outwardly decent, 801a
 flame appear, 76b
Outweighs whole years, 318a
Outwept the rain, 467b
Outworn creed, 410a
 theory, dominated by the, 857a
Ouzel, crag where the, sings, 598b
Oven, put it in the, for baby and me, 1015a
Over head and heels, 35a
 hill over dale, 901b
 the hills and far away, 1017b
 the hills we'll bound, 638b
 the race is, 710b
 there, 892a
 violent or over civil, 277a
 well if the thing is, 911a

Overawed, not to be entreated and, 502a
Overbearing word is a spur, 13b
Over-board, mast be now blown, 127a
Overcame, came saw and, 153b
 his natural bonhomie, 878b
Over-canopied with luscious woodbine, 141b
Overcoat, put on your, 603b
Over-coloured and over-voluminous narrative, 700a
Overcome, be not, of evil, 1060a
 its internal difficulties, 905a
 the Romans, 59a
 the world, 1058b
 things taken together cannot be, 55b
 to persuade to prevail to, 765a
Overcomes, who, by force, 253a
Overdressed and underbred, 796a
Over-emphasis, free from, 994b
Overexpecting happiness in married estate, 244a
Overfed overdressed and underbred, 796a
Overflowing and dripping with coolness, 450a
 streams, love has, 526b
Over-great a wit, 82b
 pleasure in being popular, 559b
Over-grey wi' moss, 896a
Overhead, I believe that God is, 652a
Overloaded undermanned, 814b
Overlooked and neglected, 65b
Overlooks, he never, a mistake, 633b
Over-mastered with piece of dust, 157a
Overmatch, wisdom is, for strength, 48b
Over-measure, enough with, 202b
Over-offended ladies, 302a
Overpast, indignation be, 1046a
Over-poetical for poetry, 567a
Over-polite to his customers, 437b
Overpowering knell, 459a
Over-praise of others, 603a
Over-praised season, spring an, 670b
Oversoul well in the van, 654a
Overtaxed patience gives way, 44a
Overthrew tables of money changers, 1053b
Over-thrifty, shrewd and, 924a
Overthrow, beget the greater for its, 640a
 of militarism, 839a
 purpos'd, 206a
 right to dismember or, 539a
 the tallest oaks, 112b
Over-use, use and, the word new, 675b
Over-voluminous narrative, 700a
Overwhelm myself in poesy, 477b
Overwhelming, grief of a loss so, 541b
 let it be, 881a
 sense of the uselessness, 821a
 task is, 984a
Overwhelms the son, 219b
Overwise, keep my talk from getting, 881a
Overwork, killed by, 814a
Ovide, Venus clerk, 78a
Ow'd great obligation, 294a
Owe a cock to Asclepius, 21a
 a debt, if a man, 3a

Owe God a death, 153b
 I can, 90b
 much, 88a
 no man anything, 1060b
 no man hate, 161b
 ourselves partly to society, 99b
 sum two married people, 379a
Owed by so many to so few, 869b
Owes, grateful mind by owing, not, 255a
 it the most precious thing, 344b
 me another form of existence, 379b
 no homage unto the sun, 241a
 not any man, 521b
 nothing to the land, 344b
 two buckets, 140a
Owest, lend less than thou, 191a
Owing, grateful mind by, owes not, 255a
Owl and the pussy-cat, 580b
 bloody, 983a
 clamorous, 141b
 for all his feathers, 480b
 I'm an, you're another, 587a
 moping, does complain, 348a
 mousing, hawk'd at, 197a
 nightly sings the staring, 134a
 night's herald, 131a
 that shriek'd 196a
 very gravely got down, 587a
 wise old, 876b
Owlet Atheism, 422b
Owls, companion to, 1031b
 couch when, do cry, 210a
 no, in the island, 342a
 sending, to Athens, 71a
 two, and a hen, 580b
Owl-songs or the midnight blast, 459b
Own a bit of ground, 664b
 few rich men, their property, 662b
 he has been in the wrong, 321a
 my, and only love of you, 595b
 my, shall come to me, 688b
 nothing we can call our, 139b
 soft impeachment, 381a
 the hearth and stool, 913a
 up to a lack of humor, 811a
 whether I come to my, 607b
Owner, gives its, passport, 587a
 in fee, 587b
 makes, stoop, 147b
 of the sphere, 507a
 ox knoweth his, 1045a
 was Giant Despair, 274b
 write to that nigger's, 677a
Owner's head, hairs of their, 708a
Owners, down went the, 681b
 kick their, over, 380b
 of the means of social production, 593b
 relinquished them for good, 470a
Ownership, act of woman to proclaim, 801b
Owns, his estate, him, 71a
Ox, dog barked at the, 10b
 eateth grass as an, 1032a
 fish sold for more than an, 59b
 goeth to the slaughter, 1038b
 heels of the laureled, 695a
 is gored, 87a
 knoweth his owner, 1045a
 nor his, 1025a
 stalled, and hatred, 1039b
 steal an, 235a
Oxen bear the yoke, 37b
 eat grass as, 1048b

Perfect in bud as in bloom, 668b
   inaction, succeed to, 306b
   indifference, matter of, 402a
   it was, it was rounded, 676b
   life may, be, 219b
   limousine, 966b
   love casteth out fear, 1064b
   love casts out prudery, 673a
   maiden most, 690b
   man, honest soul the only, 224b
   man, mark the, 1034a
   mind, not in my, 193b
   moved in, phalanx, 253a
   music, in quality, 746a
   peace, wilt keep him in, 1046a
   place for a writer, 963a
   poem round and, 650a
   practice makes, 44b
   rest, blessed with, 757a
   rose, 966b
   round, in the heaven a, 572a
   social tact, 769a
   song, golden orb of, 519b
   spirits of just men made, 1063b
   state of health, 65b
   strength made, in weakness, 1062a
   understanding almost extinguish pleasure, 787b
   union, form a more, 376a
   union one and inseparable, 842a
   woman nobly planned, 409a
   woman, woman, 225b
   word, searches for the, 908a
   work, patience have her, 1063b
Perfected by degrees, 99a
   functions of his own life, 605b
Perfectest herald of joy, 157b
Perfectibility of man, 516a
Perfection, fulness of, 147b
   greatness and, of soul, 739b
   in him was a, 972b
   is reached, 988a
   nestles the seed, 609a
   never lead you to, 741a
   of reason, 110b
   of ten, 182a
   pink of, 357a
   pursuit of, 623a
   pursuit of unattainable, 823a
   right praise and true, 147a
   sanity and, of living, 617a
   songs spring thought, 575b
   take her own way to, 359b
   through art we realize our, 767b
   what's come to, perishes, 568b
Perfectionism obstruct paths to peace, 922a
Perfections, sweete, caught, 114b
Perfectly feel even at finger's end, 89b
Perfects it makes amends, 568b
Perfidious bark, 249a
   compassion, words of, 773b
   friends, 119b
Perform, ability to, 1070b
   Almighty's order to, 298b
   each word, 12b
   for sake of our friends, 33b
   in the wet, 105b
   mistress' order to, 322a
   never promise more than you can, 45a
   patient to, 6a
   promises of youth, 337a
Performance, based on excellence of, 965a
   desire outlive, 153a
   lovers swear more, 181b

Performance of every act of life, 67a
   of pleasant actions, 922b
   prove easy to, 337a
   takes away the, 196b
   viewing them as a literary, 611b
   without precedent, 344b
Performed to a T, 89a
Performeth a good work, 1070a
Performing a public duty, 624a
   great and illustrious actions, 56a
Performs it perfects it, 568b
Perfume, do best, the air, 121b
   on violet, 148a
   owest the cat no, 192a
   puss-gentleman that's all, 363a
   scent of odorous, 260a
   subtle sad, 686b
   warm, for vapour cold, 489b
Perfumed like a milliner, 149b
   old women should not be, 54a
   Paris, 525a
   sea, gently o'er a, 543b
Perfumes, all the, of Arabia, 199a
   rarely come from the flowers, 739b
   take pleasure with, 282b
   the bower, 417a
Perhaps, going to seek a great, 87b
Peri at the gate of Eden, 441a
Peril, for those in, on the sea, 634b
   free from, 159b
   in, of my life, 144b
   more, in thine eye, 135b
   ships in, 84b
   to his body, 494b
Perilous fight, 436a
   lie, and beautiful, 947a
   seas in faery lands, 482a
   stuff, 199b
   to conduct, 85a
   way from a tree's summit, 477b
Perils and dangers of this night, 1068b
   avoid, which beset them, 282b
   delivered from, and miseries, 229b
   doe enfold, 113a
   have this beauty, 498a
   of camp march and battle, 666a
   past, 903a
   sordid, of actual existence, 767b
   when our, are past, 401a
Period, belonged to our, 910a
   brief, of sleep, 766b
   dim murky, 594b
   of history, 798a
   of life is long enough, 34a
   sleep during a prosperous, 344b
Periodical convulsions, 746a
Peripatetic, magnetic, lover, 683a
Perish, all his thoughts will, 737b
   as one of the vulgar herd, 702b
   day, wherein I was born, 1030a
   fall and, 19a
   fight it out or, 753a
   from the earth, 541a
   goodness does not, 18a
   hero, or a sparrow fall, 316a
   him that is ready to, 1041b
   houses of ivory shall, 1049a
   in it if needful, 500b
   in our own pain, 789b
   in the dust, 427a
   in the fight, 529b
   in this wilderness, 229b

Perish, no seed shall, 707b
   one of thy members, 1051a
   people, 1041b
   should not, 1058a
   survive or, 443a
   that thought, 298b
   the steadfast, 911b
   things that had better, 731a
   though I, truth is so, 595b
   through eternal peace, 951a
   thy money, with thee, 1059a
   to, rather, 253b
   twice, 880b
   wake to, never, 408b
   weak shall, 877a
   what I preserve can, never, 412b
   with him the folly, 527b
   with the sword, 1055a
   world fit to, 783b
Perished, all my friends have, so, 668a
   at sea, 585a
   once, enough to have, 37b
   passion, phantom pains of, 809b
   the ship, 3a
   to make us men, 689b
   weapons of war, 1027b
   who ever, being innocent, 1030a
Perishes, everything, 1010b
   what's come to perfection, 568b
   with the flesh, 20b
Perishing, when a society is, 559a
Periwig, make great show with new, 285b
Periwig-pated fellow, 175b
Perjur'd, till action lust is, 207a
Perjuria ridet amantium Jupiter, 135b
Perjuries, heed not their, 35b
   Jove laughs at lovers', 135b
Perjury, Jove laughs at lovers', 135b
Perked up in glistering grief, 210b
Permanence, ancient, 704b
   of matter, 883a
   terrible, 945b
Permanent alliances with foreign world, 367a
   and certain characteristics, 336a
   equality of property, 515b
   grandeur of these states, 607a
   invaluable, invalid, 769a
   more delightful than, 490b
   nothing, except change, 12a
   nothing is or ought to be, 516a
   yearning for something, 886a
Permit nature her own way, 101a
   to heaven, 259a
   transports of a British muse, 290b
Pernicious influence of wealth, 444b
   live and actively, bird, 840b
   more, than love of flattery, 302a
   race of little vermin, 295b
   to general morality, 514b
   to mankind, 4b
   weed, 363a
Perpetual charm in a letter of yours, 681a
   devotion to business, 749b
   exile, condemned to, 690a
   feast of nectar'd sweets, 247b
   morning, day is a, 590a
   motion, scoured with, 152b
   night, kingdom of, 128a
   night, 'tis with us, 218b
   peace, work us a, 244b
   priesthood, literary men a, 472b

Perpetual quarrel, 360b
  rack, 222a
  session, 927b
  steady and, serenity, 301a
  struggle for room and food,
    53oa
Perpetually damned, 123b
Perpetuate, repair and, it, 753a
Perplex and dash, 253b
Perplex'd in the extreme, 190b
Perplexed, souls, and distressed,
    722b
  with error, 19b
Perplexes monarchs with fear,
    253a
Persecute, pray for them which,
    you, 1051a
Persecutes the mind, 279a
Persecutest, why, thou me, 1059a
Persecution a bad and indirect
    way, 240b
  christened it, 596b
  first law of society, 960a
  will lead to strengthening, 951b
Persecutor, zealot may commence,
    373b
Perseverance and soothing lan-
    guage, 374a
  in a good cause, 345b
  in disguise, 776b
  keeps honour bright, 182a
  more prevailing than violence,
    55b
Persevere, strength to forbear and,
    753b
Persia, past their first sleep in,
    241b
  throne of, 491a
Persian carpet, 53b
  Gulf the Red Sea, 581b
  gulfs pearls of thought in, 602b
  messengers, 19b
Persian-lambed, ermined and
    minked and, 805a
Persian's heaven, 439b
Persians, antique, 460a
  truth-loving, 972b
Persistent, more, more faithful,
    855a
Person, age in a virtuous, 301b
  bore is, who talks, 714a
  easiest, to deceive, 510a
  esteemed, nod from a, 57a
  in the first, 1005b
  isolated naked, 917b
  master owns only your, 497b
  of respectable connections, 670b
  portrait of a, one knows, 379a
  really busy, 758a
  sacrificed to individual, 917b
  set thy, forth to sell, 212b
  there's no such a, 578a
  to know what a, wants, 853b
  umble, 579a
  waking up always the same,
    822a
  well-conducted, 564a
  which each, deserved, 71b
  who agrees with me, 513a
  who can't pay, 580a
  who disliked gravy, 270b
  wise, and a fool, 31b
Personage, less imposing, 435b
  play their, 103a
Personages, risk everything with
    great, 297b
Personal arrogance, 910b
  beauty a better introduction,
    71a

Personal considerations, 623b
  experience should not be guide,
    24b
  ideals, three, 744b
  immortality, endow myself with,
    841b
  intercourse, correspondence and,
    558a
  life as an individual, 882a
  likings, graves of his, 651a
  Northwest Passage, 933b
  opinions, rawness of his, 787b
  possessions, decline, 807b
  presence everywhere, 734b
  relationship, 988a
  ridicule is a shaft, 784b
  significance or insignificance,
    540a
  slim and crooked but, 718a
Personalities, greater, than them-
    selves, 895a
  trivial, decomposing, 923a
Personality, artistic moral, 611a
  creates outside of his own, 756b
  native, endows a man, 611a
  needs a good, 930a
  newspaper-man a double, 696b
  poetry an escape from, 943b
Personally defeated, 517a
  one to become, attach'd to,
    610b
Persons, addressed to private,
    487a
  attempting to find a motive,
    676b
  deprived of judgment, 28b
  divers, 162a
  duty of all, to reflect, 32b
  eleven thousand, 295b
  first must be forgotten, 425b
  God in three, 445b
  great, able to do great kind-
    nesses, 108b
  grown old in business, 431a
  living on annuities, 457b
  money rather than their, 344a
  more lives of obscure, 798b
  most knowing of, 47a
  no respect of, with God, 1059b
  no respect of place, nor time,
    164a
  no respecter of, 1059a
  of good sense, 332a
  respect of, is not good, 1041b
  two distinct, 221b
  without education, 435a
Perspicuity of language, 74a
Perspicuous, enough if a work be,
    425a
Perspiration, ninety-nine percent,
    735b
Perspire, dig till you gently, 820a
Persuade, beauty doth of itself,
    131a
  to woo to, prevail, 765a
  tongue to, 369a
Persuaded his enemy, 1014b
  in his own mind, 1060b
Persuades, every man, himself,
    338a
  when speaking fails, 208a
Persuadest, almost thou, me,
    1059b
Persuading, by, others, 1002a
  fair-spoken, 212a
  revolting instead of, 375b
Persuasion and belief, 411a
  divine, flows from lips, 4b
  hung upon his lips, 345b

Persuasion shine all silver, 9a
  tries force because, fails, 574a
Persuasions, winged, 467b
Persuasive sound, magic numbers
    and, 298a
Pert as a schoolgirl, 684b
Perturbed spirit, 173b
Perturbs their minds, 516b
Peru, from China to, 335b
  Newton at, 493a
  with its riches, 484b
Pervades, spirit, public acts, 20b
Perverse as a legislature, 989b
  as human nature, 989b
  depravity of their nature, 290b
  imp of the, 545a
  opinion, men of, 15a
Perverseness one of primitive im-
    pulses, 544b
Perversion, enormous and inner-
    most, 728b
  of the mind, 961a
Perverted by selfishness of man,
    914b
  woman's cold, will, 469b
Pessimism as agreeable as op-
    timism, 832b
  name men give to wisdom, 976b
Pessimist fears this is true, 900a
  not a, but a pejorist, 785a
  sees the hole, 891a
Pest of love, 479a
Pester'd with popinjay, 149b
Pestiferous superlatives, 808a
Pestilence, like a desolating, 464b
  noisome, 1036a
  that walketh in darkness, 1036a
Pestilence-stricken   multitudes,
    466a
Pestilent congregation of vapours,
    173b
Petal, each finger nail a crimson,
    973a
  root to crowning, 736a
  sleeps the crimson, 551a
  tip-tilted like the, 554b
Petals from blown roses, 547a
  on a wet black bough, 932b
Petar, hoist with his own, 177b
Peter, call him, 147b
  denied his Lord, 1000b
  Peter Pumpkin-eater, 1018b
  Piper, 1018a
  robbing, he paid Paul, 88b
  the thought that, spoke, 722b
  thou art, 1053b
  twenty times was, feared, 404a
  Uncle, Daniels, 1014a
Peterkin, quoth little, 426b
Peter's dome, hand that rounded,
    503a
Petition government for a redress,
    376b
Petrarch's wife, 458a
Petrified opinion, loyalty to, 680a
  truth, 674a
Petrifies the feeling, 391a
Petticoat, feet beneath her, 261a
  government, 446a
  tempestuous, 230b
Pettifogger, one produces the,
    433b
Petty artery in this body, 172a
  causes, meanest motives and,
    491a
  done the undone vast, 570a
  men walk under his legs, 166a
  minds, good fortune will ele-
    vate, 55b

Pocket full of rye, 1017a
  hand in its breeches, 478a
  into some wan's, 833b
  little in one's own, 107b
  Lucy Locket lost her, 1019a
  scruple to pick a, 291a
  touches the purse or, 573a
  very sling in my, 370a
  watch in a private, 323a
  wid a, full of tin, 636a
Pocketbook, full, often groans, 92b
Pocketed by most newspaper critics, 472b
Pocket-handkerchief before his streaming eyes, 658b
Pocket-knife, magic tool the, 450a
Pockets, changing contents of, 931b
  compensated out of their, 425b
Poe with his raven, 600b
Poem, discussing poet not, 933a
  explanation of, 961a
  fain would write a, 571b
  for one single good, 379a
  God wrote His loveliest, 888b
  hangs on the berry bush, 704b
  heroic, a biography, 474b
  I recall by its rhythm, 508b
  illuminated reader is the, 865a
  lonely as a tree, 936a
  make his life a heroic, 472b
  marred by superfluous verse, 526a
  music of, along with words, 857a
  not necessarily obscure, 425a
  of earth, 610b
  ought to be a true, 250a
  read a good, 378b
  round and perfect, 650a
  shot a, into the air, 912a
  should not mean but be, 960b
  to which we return, 424a
  United States the greatest, 607a
  works and does some, 476a
Poems are made by fools, 936b, 942a
  he who would write heroic, 472b
  Ibid's prose or, 855a
  in every volume of, 341b
  living, 524a
  more, produced, 880a
  no man reads, 52a
  seldom consist of poetry, 787b
  temporary, 336b
  Whitman's, 973a
Poesy, a drainless shower of light, 477b
  forgetting the great end of, 477b
  have participation of divineness, 118b
  heavenly gift of, 278b
  overwhelm myself in, 477b
  pleasures of heroic, 243a
Poet against poet, 7a
  and saint, 268a
  bad, is super-abundant, 923a
  bad, unconscious and conscious, 943b
  binds together, 406a
  bit by him that comes behind, 296a
  broad famous English, 214a
  buffoon and, 741b
  business of a comic, 297b
  cannot die, 549b
  can survive everything, 767b
  commend so great a, 280b

Poet could not but be gay, 409a
  creates outside of his own personality, 756b
  despised, 515a
  dies mute nature mourns, 413a
  discussing, not poem, 933a
  gathers fruit, 780b
  Goldsmith, naturalist, 337b
  he was a, 884a
  how does the, speak to men, 473a
  joyful let the, be, 592b
  liberty of a, 243a
  lies beneath this sod, 425b
  like the prince of the clouds, 618b
  limbs of the mangled, 40a
  lunatic lover and, 142b
  make a, excellent, 240a
  modest cough of a minor, 765b
  moon talk by a, 676b
  more confident than a bad, 52a
  more than the, expressed, 515a
  must be a chameleon, 791a
  no, and they died, 320b
  not a musician, 827a
  not the way of the great, 897b
  octogenarian, 823a
  of the difficult, 993b
  perhaps no person can be a, 492a
  pleasantest sort of a, 936b
  proof of a, 607a
  secure of a few copyists, 559b
  short-haired, 713a
  should always be hungry, 981b
  should avoid religion, 630a
  shuts the past against the, 516b
  soaring in high reason, 250a
  tadpole, 695a
  the priest the soldier the, 619a
  twirls them in his mind, 704a
  vision arose, 722a
  was ever, so trusted, 341a
  who's old and wise, 936b
  will follow the rainbow, 729b
  with so many felicities, 403a
  with the coward's tongue, 781a
  without love, 473a
  worthy of the name of, 476a
Poeta nascitur non fit, 424b
Poetess, maudlin, 318b
Poetic faith, which constitutes, 424b
  fields encompass me, 298b
  flights, 436b
  genius, good sense body of, 424b
  imagination, higher, 556b
  justice with lifted scale, 321b
  license, freer utterances of, 33a
  meet nurse for, child, 414a
  names, have given them less, 599a
  nook, 448a
  pains, pleasure in, 277b
  pearl, 604a
  wine-scented and, soul, 751b
Poetical, gods made thee, 162a
Poetics, never indulge in, 30b
Poeticule, tenth-rate, 695a
Poetry a criticism of life, 732b
  a medium for writing prose, 767b
  a mere mechanic art, 363a
  an escape from emotion, 943b
  architecture sculpture, 614b
  art, intrigue, 702a
  as well written as prose, 933a

Poetry, attainable in, 545b
  be a poet or enjoy, 492a
  beautiful mode of saying things, 621b
  breath and finer spirit, 406a
  brisker pipes than, 786b
  change in body of, 941a
  Chinese, 799a
  comes fine spun, 42b
  consist of, and nothing else, 787b
  cradled into, by wrong, 239b, 466a
  dawn of music, and art, 502a
  definition of pure, 756b
  definitions of prose and, 424a
  essential, 424a
  essential gaudiness of, 906a
  fettered, 388b
  fleshly school of, 708a
  forged slowly, 869a
  genius for painting, 505a
  gives pleasure, 702a
  good religious, 787b
  great things in, are song, 824a
  I know that is, 649b
  if, comes not naturally, 478a
  in the hearts of all men, 475b
  is comforting piece of fiction, 908b
  is difficult to read, 573b
  is man's rebellion, 900a
  is what Milton saw, 895b
  life's prose, 654a
  like a page of prancing, 647a
  line of, strays into my memory, 788a
  live without, music and art, 653a
  made subsequent, 250a
  melancholy madness of, 1001b
  music resembles, 310b
  never become popular art, 967a
  no lover of, can spare Chaucer, 508a
  nobody ought to read, 515a
  not a purpose but a passion, 544b
  not, but prose run mad, 318b
  not proper antithesis, 423b
  of earth, 477b
  of Lord Byron, 492b
  of speech, 454a
  of the commonplace, 744a
  of words, 546a
  old-fashioned, 236a
  over-poetical for, 567a
  painting and music, 388b
  prophecy and religion, 605a
  record of the best moments, 469a
  refreshment with a bit of, 637b
  Shakespeare wrote better, 798a
  she that with, is won, 239a
  should surprise, 478a
  silent, 62a
  speak as one who fed on, 510a
  speaking painting, 62a
  spontaneous overflow, 406a
  teaches the force of few words, 508a
  that has palpable design, 478a
  their universal pastime, 520b
  thinking in its higher forms is, 784a
  when, has a meaning, 787b
  where the Greeks had, 449b
  whining, 215b
  wit hope virtue, 501a

Poetry, writing of, 943b
  written, unless out of health, 788a
Poet's darling, 407b
  dignity and ease, 319a
  dream, consecration and the, 409b
  ear, flattery lost on, 413b
  eye in fine frenzy, 142b
  eye, muse on nature with a, 432a
  food is love and fame, 466a
  inward pride, 992a
  made as well as born, 219b
  pen turns them to shapes, 142b
  possess a, brain, 122b
  song and prophet's word, 832b
  visions, 812b
Poets, all that, sing, 510b
  an' useful men, 969a
  and romancers, 808a
  are people who despise money, 792a
  are sultans, 266b
  are the hierophants, 432b, 468b
  autumn, sing. 647a
  avoid citations from, 22a
  by their sufferings grow, 239b
  creatures most absurd, 320b
  desire to teach, 41b
  experience choked feeling, 984b
  fail in reading their verses, 518a
  ferryman, write of, 128a
  few, were so mated before, 791a
  generals or, or statesmen, 675b
  hallucinations of, 908b
  historians biographers, 423b
  Homer first of heroic, 338b
  in our youth, 406b
  in their misery dead, 406b
  Irish, learn your trade, 828a
  light but lamps, 648b
  like stinking fish, 425b
  long-haired, 713a
  lose half the praise, 242b
  love is a boy by, styl'd, 239a
  make men witty, 121b
  makes men, and sages, 638a
  modern and perhaps ancient, 275b
  of the proud old lineage, 927a
  only great, can read them, 590a
  pensive painful vigils keep, 321b
  pleasure only, know, 277b
  seem more business-like, 880a
  souls of, dead and gone, 482b
  steal from Homer, 221a
  stones and, 790b
  that lasting marble seek, 242a
  things that the first, had, 122b
  three, in three ages born, 279b
  to have great, 611b
  touchy tribe of, 41b
  two classes of, 508a
  unacknowledged legislators, 469a
  virtue not often found among, 108a
  women and, see the truth, 996a
  works of the great, 590a
  youthful, dream, 245b
Poets' forms of beauty pass, 605a
  orchestra, 735b
Poignancy to pleasure, 290a
Point a moral, 336a
  as with silent finger, 411a
  highest, of my greatness, 211a
  lieth at, of death, 1055b
  man at the, of death, 290a

Point, men at, of death, 138a
  of a diamond, 1048a
  of cunning to borrow, 120b
  of cunning to shape answer, 120b
  of doctrine, 68b, 339b
  of time, 58a
  of view, someone else's, 901a
  of wisdom to be silent, 58a
  refined, of felicity, 294b
  slow and moving finger, 189b
  too fine a, to your wit, 110a
  too fine a, upon it, 579b
Pointed firs, great army of the, 742b
  pleasure, 751b
  satire, Buckhurst for, 289a
  spires of many temples, 443a
Points, arm'd at, exactly, 171a
  daggers with, downward, 224a
  eleven, in the law, 29a
  of belief, 438b
  of gravest import yielded, 686a
  out some circumstance, 266a
  out the soul's eternal sleep, 383a
  to yonder glade, 313b
  trifling, 436b
Poise, keep an equal, 736a
Poised, remain, a long time, 855a
Pois'ning of a dart, 267a
Poison, bathe before I drink the, 21a
  crush'd sweet, 247a
  dream has power to, sleep, 469a
  England at her roots, 865b
  it is a, 559b
  make use of, to show skill, 28b
  more deadly, 129b
  ounce of, in one pocket, 493b
  persons for whom truth is, 932b
  power is, 697b
  steel nor, can touch him, 197b
  sweet, 147b
  the butter, 802a
  their lives, 872b
  to his mind, 494b
  to others, 34b
  us do we not die, 145a
  which acts upon serpents, 50a
Poison'd by their wives, 139b
  chalice, 195b
Poisoned rat in a hole, 296a
Poisonous Nessus shirts, 474b
  sting, critics with, 606b
  wine, wolf's-bane for its, 483a
Poison-weeds, vilest deeds like, 770a
Poke, buy pig in the, 95a
  dial from, 160b
  poor Billy, 873b
Poky dull and dry, 847b
Polar day, through the long, 626a
Pole, behold each, 213b
  beloved from, to pole, 422a
  embrace a, as a Frenchman, 100b
  pleasure trip up to the, 707a
  sigh from Indus to the, 313a
  so tall to reach the, 302b
  spread truth from, to pole, 299a
  to Cape Columbia, 763b
  transmit the Preludes, 943a
  true as the needle to the, 239b
Poles, wheel between the, 556b
Police in citizens' clothes, 505b
  international, power, 779b
  legacies left to strange, 872b
  spies lie in the bushes, 84b
Policeman Day, 820a

Policeman, heard a, on his beat, 1008b
  tall, of my mind, 968b
Policeman's lot is not a happy one, 682b
Policemen stand and purr, 955a
Policy, cause of, 154a
  economy exercised over men becomes, 55b
  Fabian, 30b
  honesty is always best, 108b
  of repression of ideas, 984a
  of the good neighbor, 919a
  sets no hand to best, 14a
  sits above conscience, 203a
  stratagems and, are allowable, 108a
Polish, felony to buy stove, 835b
  her until she glimmers, 739a
  independent, state, 771a
  of far-reaching ancestry, 628a
Polish'd horde, society is now one, 459b
Polished dart, laughter winged his, 688a
  idleness, frivolous work of, 397b
  razor keen, 322b
  through act and speech, 637b
  up the handle, 682a
  up the silver plate, 956a
Polish't lips, apply its, 411a
Polite, costs nothing to be, 872b
  phrases and poses, 644a
  safe, obedient and sterile, 931b
Politeness, pine-apple of, 381a
  treated me with excessive, 909a
  wind in French, 754b
Politic, the body, 344a
Political animal, man is, 26a
  appeasement, 917b
  assemblies, tyranny of, 515b
  bands, dissolve the, 373a
  calculation, variable of, 633b
  campaigns, 806a
  community, best, 26b
  decisions, 811b
  democracy in America, 611a
  discussions, 811a
  distorted into, subjects, 418b
  education, 696b
  executive magistracy, 361b
  freedom was business of government, 919a
  independence, guarantees of, 771a
  institutions a superstructure, 850a
  life, right to his own, 921a
  man is a, animal, 26a
  or religious privilege, 588a
  party, test of a, 986b
  party that works both sides, 921b
  pills, 831a
  preach upon subjects, 418b
  prosperity, social and, 538b
  rather, than religious, 339b
  spine-character, 611a
  system, basis of our, 367a
  uneven, development, 850b
  unit, United States is a, 977a
  volcanic, instinct, 767a
  world, natural and, 361a
  world, necessary in the, 374a
Politically, power, fer years, 841a
Politician, coffee makes the, wise, 312b
  I am not a, 664b
  proper memory for a, 700b

Prayed, thing we have, for, 519b
Prayer assist me, 76a
  be not forgetful of, 618a
  breathe our evening, 584a
  breathes a, for him, 499a
  burden of a sigh, 413a
  comes around again, 827b
  conclude the, 279b
  erects house of, 291b
  every wish is like a, 520a
  fear anger pleasure joys, 62b
  feeling which prompts, 613b
  for all who lie beneath, 820b
  four hours spend in, 110b
  great deeds be thy, 562a
  homes of silent, 552a
  house of, 1054a
  is an education, 618a
  let the, re-echo, 489b
  lift up the hands in, 725a
  made his, even as you and I, 816b
  make our earnest, 367a
  more things are wrought by, 548a
  my, some daily good to do, 617a
  my, will somewhat vary, 906a
  negligent at their, 1070a
  of a righteous man, 1064a
  of thanks, 898b
  offices of, and praise, 410b
  one, to God, 325b
  or two in English, 755b
  people's, 277a
  reduces itself to this, 594b
  rises from, a better man, 638b
  shall have a widow's, 612a
  shrine where a sin is a, 692a
  steeped their souls in, 543a
  still, of devotion, 440b
  teach to render, 146a
  that reforms the sinner, 616b
  the soul's sincere desire, 413a
  when I say a, 822a
  wing and a, 997a
  would fulfilment know, 615a
Prayer-books, beads and, 317b
Prayers, angry, 854a
  feed on, 116a
  for death, 16b
  for pretense make long, 1056a
  gods answer our, 11a
  hate you enough to hear, 11a
  lives are faithful, 552a
  mention of thee in my, 1063b
  more, to heaven, 541a
  nor daring nor reason, 953b
  of the Church to preserve, 297a
  our tears, 523a
  profit by losing of our, 200b
  saying his, 917b
  sharp and sudden on some, 519b
  this was in my, 40b
  whose, would make me whole, 820a
  without words, 665b
  wouldn't say his, 1017a
Prayer-time, Christ's progress and his, 271b
Prayeth well who loveth well, 422b
Praying, be brief in, 231a
  God on high, 913a
Prays for a miracle, 594b
  thus the suppliant, 336a
Preach, all, none practise, 227a
  never sure to, again, 266b

Preach, practise what we, 822b
  practise what you, 653b
  the gospel, 1056a
  upon subjects political, 418b
Preached as never sure to preach again, 266b
Preacher, dying, I have been, 1014a
  never denied the, 996a
  sacred, cries, 329a
Preachers, itinerant, 332a
  jangle, 794b
  pirates, poteen-makers, 856b
Preaches contentment to that toad, 813a
  in her gown, 489a
  nature teaches more than, 688b
  well that lives well, 108a
  what he and hearers practise, 822b
Preaching, a woman, 340a
  by-word for dull conversation, 418b
  down a daughter's heart, 548b
  practising so different from, 587b
Precarious things, dinners were, 430a
Precautions against your enemies, 1070a
Precede, lead the way and we'll, 381a
Precedent a king of men, 696a
  embalms a principle, 512b
  one, creates another, 1001a
  performance without, 344b
  solitary, 433b
  well-established, 777a
Precedents deliberately established, 433b
  supported by, 55b
Precedes and follows, consider what, 46a
Precept, example is the best, 10b
  more efficacious than, 10b
  of her peaceful laws, 287b
  that's the true business, 577b
  upon precept, 1046a
Precepts, all other, depend upon these, 60b
  glorious, draw, 436b
Precession of the equinoxes, 557a
'Preciate things ye lef' behind, 913b
Precincts, warm, of the cheerful day, 349a
Precious as the stuff they sell, 533a
  as the truths she reveals, 856a
  bane, 253a, 915a
  blood, moistened with, 528b
  damn your, soul, 89b
  fumes more, 890b
  habit, apparell'd in, 158b
  in sight of the Lord, 1037a
  jewel, 159b
  jewel carved curiously, 723b
  jewels into a garret, 89b
  liberty is, 850b
  life is too, 596a
  life-blood of a master-spirit, 250b
  make vile things, 191b
  nose, that's his, 489a
  nothing so, as time, 71b
  odours, virtue like, 119b
  ointment, better than, 1042b
  ointment, box of, 1054b

Precious ointment, good name like, 120a
  past, all the, 878b
  porcelain of human clay, 279b
  seed, bearing, 1037b
  seeing to the eye, 133b
  so, life is, 680b
  stone, a gift is as a, 1039b
  stone set in silver sea, 139a
  thing possessed by man, 344b
  thing that was, 690a
  three unspeakably, things, 678b
  treasure of eyesight, 134b
  truth is, and divine, 239a
  words, ate and drank the, 646a
Precipice, draw chair up to edge of, 975a
Precise, art is too, 230b
  in promise-keeping, 183b
  psychological moment, 768a
  too, about birds, 611b
Precluded from offering sentiments, 366b
Precocity, miracle of, 49b
  some price is demanded for, 560a
Preconceived, waiting in vain for the, 720b
Predatory human hands, 784b
Predecessor, illustrious, 333b
Predestined, beyond what fate has, 400a
  elect, thinned down the, 675a
  intimates are, 696b
  of the will, 884b
Predicts ruin of the state, 388a
Predilection and love, 705a
  for painting, 712a
Predominance among human interests, 910b
Predominant feature in British fleet, 390a
Pre-eminence in Germany, 950b
Pre-eminent lustre, 63a
Prees, greet, at market, 81a
Preest oghte ensample for to yive, 171b
Preface to make it welcome, 46b
Prefer life to honor, 63a
  to err with Plato, 34a
Preferable, delay is, to error, 374a
  ignorance is, to error, 373b
Preferment, riches and, 1002b
Preferments in the courts of princes, 28b
Preferred the man of worth, 53b
  to public service, 20a
Preferreth all countries before his own, 226b
Prefers service of princes, 28b
Pregnant fancies of your world, 992b
  hinges of the knee, 175b
  in matter, 436b
  quarry, 320b
  with thought inbreathed, 632b
Prejudice a vagrant opinion, 714a
  editorial, 861b
  popular, in favour of two, 576b
  that quite cut off the view, 794a
  this pretension a great, 723a
Prejudices, honest, 301a
  lightly held beliefs and, 831b
  man without any, 723a
  traced back to intestines, 729a
  travel ought to soften, 637a
Prelate, religion without a, 490a

Qualities, possession of cluster of, 718b
  various, and advantages, 855b
Quality, composition and fierce, 190b
  counsels not in such a, 145a
  diversity is most universal, 99a
  evidence a blemish not a, 668b
  exact, of strength, 772b
  greatness a certain, 670a
  happiness has one useful, 856b
  highest, to your moments, 702a
  indifference to, 863b
  irregular and intimate, 886a
  music perfect in, 746a
  noble, we call valor, 616b
  none of any, 284a
  of mercy, 146a
  of the stupid, 461b
  of thought they think, 812b
  pleasure regarded as the, 806b
  rather than quantity, 47a
  royal banner and all, 189a
  several, of a thing, 68a
  taste of your, 174a
  to form a man of achievement, 478a
  true-fix'd and resting, 167b
  white, talk, 946b
Qualms, many many, 794b
Quangle wangle, 581b
Quantities, such, of sand, 658a
Quantity, all their, of love, 179a
  quality rather than, 47a
  they do not write, 475a
  unlimited in, 746a
  vast, of nonsense, 580a
  worship of, 863b
Quantum o' the sin, 391a
Quarantine of the patients, 919b
Quare, God's ways is very, 969a
Quarelets of pearl, 230b
Quarles is sav'd by beauties, 321b
Quarrel between past and present, 869a
  during each successive, 789b
  entrance to a, 171b
  every, to the lawyer, 234a
  find, in a straw, 177b
  hath his, just, 125a
  how they behave in a, 764b
  justice of my, 123a
  let them who make the, 520b
  lover's, with the world, 881b
  or reprimand, 503b
  over water in Arkansass, 929a
  perpetual, 360b
  sudden and quick in, 161b
  take up our, with foe, 860b
  very pretty, 381a
  with my bread and butter, 296b
  with the shirt, 782b
Quarreling, chickens quit, over food, 894b
Quarrels, breeds more, 562b
  cut fiercest, short, 108a
  head as full of, 136b
  of lovers, 31b
  pick no, 356b
  put, on others, 165b
  sedition idleness, 290b
  those who in, interpose, 308a
  unsevered by bitter, 38b
  would not last long, 266a
Quarrelsome, countercheck, 163a
  mutinous and, 332a
Quarry it shall find, 935b
  marked-down, 765a
  never found, 897b

Quarry, not the, but the chase, 829b
  pregnant, 320b
Quarry-slave at night, 470b
Quart, drank off his, 447b
  of myghty ale, 81a
Quarter, give no, to tyrants, 517a
  I always drop a, 713a
Quarter-dollar, finds a long-hidden, 800b
Quarter-staff, wield a, 862a
Quarto, beautiful, page, 381b
Quarts of Ludlow beer, 786b
Quasi-sovereign, 710a
Quay, sit on the busy, 852a
Que scais-je? 101a
Quean, flaunting extravagant, 381b
Queen and huntress, 218a
  Anne's dead, 395b
  asked the dairymaid, 917b
  been to London to look at the, 1018a
  beggar maid shall be my, 549b
  Bess, image of good, 488b
  can you guess who that could be, 889a
  cold, of England, 867a
  come not near our fairy, 142a
  every lass a, 598b
  feminine soul is a, 807a
  good, Bess, 798a
  grace a summer's, 415b
  if you were, of pleasure, 693a
  I'm to be, o' the May, 547a
  insipid as a, upon a card, 555b
  Mab hath been with you, 134b
  Mary's saying, 568b
  not a, for all the world, 210b
  of France, 520b
  of Hearts, 1016a
  of secrecy the violet, 478b
  of Sheba, 1028b
  of swell society, 828a
  of the waters, 500b
  our rose our star, 499b
  rose of the rosebud garden, 554a
  shall be as drunk, 332b
  she looks a, 4a
  turned crimson with fury, 657a
  was in the parlor, 1017a
  you shall be, 1019b
Queen's, delight, sing for their, 780b
  Navee, ruler of the, 682a
Queens have died young and fair, 213a
  who die with Antony, 900a
Queer, all the world is, 1006b
  formless, and incomplete, 811b
  how strange it seems and, 569b
  ill-tempered and, 580b
  monster the artist, 700a
  sense of relief and shame, 980b
  suburban streets, 956a
  thee is a little, 1006b
  you look so, 1004a
Queerest folk of all, 794a
  little craft, 722b
  schap, 713b
  they ever did see, 877a
Quell, music raise and, 278b
Quench appetite, 68b
  my great love, 684a
  rivers cannot, 127a
  smoking flax shall he not, 1047a
  the flame, 456a
Quench'd the open truth, 415a
Querulous criticisms, 608b

Querulous, newspapers are, 908b
  serenity, 428a
Quest for righteousness, 745a
  of that one beauty, 896a
  to have extreme, 207a
  vain but hopeful, 933b
  wherefore is a hopeless, 781a
Questing hound, 897b
Question all things, 518a
  beautiful, 968b
  cares nothing about rights of, 21a
  deserves an answer, 45b
  dies without, in his heart, 811a
  greatest, debated in America, 367b
  ignorance never settles a, 512b
  interrupt with a silly, 345b
  is ever settled, 754a
  marriage an open, 504b
  moral, for the heart, 811a
  not but live and labour, 661b
  nothing to say on the, 802a
  of loving them enough, 976a
  others abide our, 619a
  school nor creed, 438b
  settle a, rightly, 492a
  start a, 750b
  that is the, 174a
  two sides to every, 72b
  who but infants, 640b
Questionable shape, 172a
  superfluity, 125b
Question'd me story of my life, 186a
Questioning before he speaks, 17b
  if I lack'd anything, 232b
Questions, ambiguous, 958b
  answered three, 656a
  answered your, briefly, 785a
  ask me no, 357b
  asking, and writing them, 846b
  complex, dismays doubts, 822b
  feel strongly about putting, 750b
  foolish, of common people, 735a
  love that asks no, 789a
  of taste of feeling, 696b
  old, of why and whence, 833a
  prove him with hard, 1028b
  them that asks no, 357b
Quhat say thai, 112a
Qui ante diem periit, 803b
  procul hinc, 803b
Quick and easy death, 794a
  and far, ill news goes, 61a
  and fresh art thou, 163b
  and the dead, 1068a
  as a flash 'tis gone, 775a
  bright things, 141a
  delivery stamp, 811b
  feeling is, and transient, 570b
  in quarrel, 161b
  Jack be, 1019a
  mint of joy, 448b
  of all time is the instant, 931a
  'ow, we'd drop 'er, 819a
  touched to the, 569b
  waters pass away, 111a
Quicken his perception though dull, 787b
Quickened, that which thou sowest not, 1061b
Quickens mental demand, 720a
  spirit that, him, 490a
Quicker, liquor is, 989b
  than their brains, 915b
Quick-ey'd love, 232b
Quickly, gives, gives twice, 106b
  little fire, trodden out, 127a

Reading, contemplation more than his, 273b
  curst hard, 382b
  decent, room and a library, 844b
  distinguish what is worth, 888a
  easy writing makes hard, 983b
  employ themselves by, 290a
  enthusiasms about, 910a
  great books, 942b
  greatest part of the night, 332a
  he that I am, has most force, 99a
  I prefer, 823a
  is to the mind, 299a
  King Lear, 373a
  left off, 430b
  maketh a full man, 121b
  men of thought and, 632a
  much, is an oppression, 288b
  no, easier than a catalogue, 723a
  of a book, 590a
  peace is poor, 706a
  shut out from, good books, 933a
  soul of, 345b
  tyrannical the habit of, 603b
  valueless books, 605b
Reading-matter, sheer casual, 864a
Reads, all books he, 312a
  as a task, 340a
  but one book, 235a
  glows while he, 310b
  he, much, 166b
  nothing but detective stories, 942a
  poems no man, 52a
  though running, 102a
Read'st black where I read white, 388b
Ready, Abra was, 294a
  fire when, Gridley, 689b
  for war, 290a
  hands, true faith and, 597b
  I wait until I am, 940a
  in case of anything turning up, 579a
  is heaven to stoop to him, 790b
  man, conference maketh a, 121b
  minds, becks our, 479a
  money is Aladdin's lamp, 459b
  money makes the man, 303b
  money, sparing use of, 565a
  necessity of being, 539b
  to believe what is told him, 51a
  to die with you, 39a
  to ride, 524a
  to smite once, 249b
  to try fortunes, 153b
  wait till that other is, 589b
  way to virtue, 240b
  when trouble came, 787a
  with every nod to tumble, 128a
  you'll find us, 578b
Ready-made opinions, 617b
Real and permanent grandeur, 607a
  and safe progress, 304a
  fight, if life be not a, 715b
  friends, women find few, 343a
  life is, 521a
  life never was begun, 890b
  nothing, till it is experienced, 478b
  Simon Pure, 297a
  spirit is the, and eternal, 616b
  thing, 982a
  thing, hiss the, 11b
  utility in ships, 333a
  war never in the books, 611a

Realist rhymester play your part, 556b
Realities are less dangerous, 861b
  loves not, and creators, 501b
  seeking only to face, 770b
  sharpest of the, 719b
Reality, bill drawn on nature's, 474b
  brings us joy of discovery, 856a
  encounter, of experience, 916b
  human kind cannot bear, 944b
  idea and the, 944a
  more than a small part of, 622a
  of creatures, 939b
  of distress, 371a
  regulate imagination by, 338b
  sail into the wind of, 991b
Realization of tomorrow, 922a
Realm, in any coin of any, 845b
  moves to that mysterious, 407b
  of France, ill unto, 84a
  of silence, 596b
  riding o'er the azure, 350a
  we have never conquered, 931a
Realms, Anna whom three, obey, 312b
  constancy lives in, above, 421a
  of gold, 477a
  whatever, to see, 353b
Reap an act, 1005b
  as we have sown, 527a
  as you sow ye are like to, 239a
  blessings of freedom, 370b
  by force, 105a
  he that regardeth clouds shall not, 1043b
  in joy, 1037b
  neither do they, 1051b
  our sowing, 666a
  plow and sow and, and mow, 1000a
  so shall he also, 29a
  stranger came to, 930b
  that shall he also, 1062b
  the whirlwind, 1049a
Reap'd, chin new, 149b
  harvest that I, 532a
Reaped the evil fruit, 7a
Reaper whose name is death, 521a
Reapers, gather after the, 1027a
Reaping, grew the more by, 201b
Reaps the bearded grain, 521a
Rear, remains forever in the, 855a
  scatters, of darkness, 245a
  shall march tomorrow, 638a
  the tender thought, 328a
Rear'd the stage, 335b
Rearward of a conquer'd woe, 206a
Reas'ning but to err, 316b
  pride our error lies, in, 316a
Reason a bird can sing, 889b
  according to soundest, 67b
  against it instinct for it, 672a
  aim and, 379b
  and conscience of men, 95a
  and evaluation, 954a
  and the will of God prevail, 623a
  and welcome, 572a
  art has as much, for being, 507b
  astride on his, 294b
  but from what we know, 316a
  conscient, 722a
  discourse of, 170b
  easiest victory over, 950b
  faith in supremacy of, 860a
  feast of, 319b
  fifty times to one does err, 289a
  firm the temperate will, 409a

Reason for its own existence, 698b
  for loving as well as working, 596b
  godlike, 177b
  has moons, 854b
  high, of his fancies, 250a
  human, needs only to will, 882b
  humanity, and justice, 360a
  ignis fatuus of the mind, 289a
  I'll not listen to, 558a
  irritable reaching after, 478a
  is left free to combat it, 374b
  is life of the law, 110a
  is of no use to us, 366b
  is our law, 258a
  is the card, 317a
  kills, itself, 250b
  know the, why, 509a
  know truth not only by, 272b
  knows nothing of, 272b
  let us, together, 1045a
  lies between spur and bridle, 234b
  men have lost their, 168a
  never has failed men, 843a
  no other but woman's, 131b
  no sooner knew the, 163a
  noble and most sovereign, 175a
  noble in, 173b
  nothing reasonable from pure, 866a
  of so many senseless scholars, 288b
  on compulsion, 150a
  or any other, why, 288b
  panders with, 177a
  past, hunted, 207a
  perfection of, 110b
  psychological, 718b
  pursue my, to an O altitudo, 240a
  render a, 1041a
  render a, for faith, 418b
  rhyme nor, 115a
  ruling passion conquers, 315a
  sanctity of, 257a
  scorn to give other, why, 462b
  shapes and regulates, 64a
  shared by thinking creatures, 68a
  surprise the better, 977b
  takes the, prisoner, 194b
  theirs not to, why, 553b
  to apprehend, 340a
  to rule, 279a
  under its own control, 68b
  why I cannot tell, 293a
  with a mule, 758b
  with reasonable men, 517a
  worse appear better, 253b
  yield with a grace to, 879a
Reasonable, everything, may be supported, 63b
  kills a, creature, 250b
  man, the figure of the, 955a
  men, assembly of, 375b
  men, reason with, 517a
  moderator death, 240b
  nothing, from pure reason, 866a
  number of fleas, 735a
  the figure of the, 955a
  women rather be right than, 989b
  words, speak a few, 378b
  wrong way seems the more, 756b
Reason'd high of providence, 254a
Reasoned errors, more harmful than, 634a

Reply, theirs not to make, 553b
  this our sole, shall be, 643a
  to our intelligence, 460b
Report, by evil, and good report,
  1062a
  country of fair, 9a
  falsehood of, 37a
  heart not able to, 142b
  louder, than thunder, 106b
  me and my cause aright, 179b
  of fashions in proud Italy, 138b
  retort rejoinder repartee, 704a
  vexation to understand the,
  1046b
  whatsoever things of good,
  1063a
  who knows how he may, 260b
Reporter's gallery yonder, 473a
Reporters, gallery in which, sit,
  473a
  speaking through, to Buncombe,
  476a
Reports of my death are exaggerated, 679a
Repose, dragon-fly's, 602b
  earned a night's, 521b
  expects the issue in, 411b
  foster-nurse of nature is, 192b
  hush'd in grim, 350a
  is insupportable, 697b
  is not destiny of man, 709a
  is taboo'd by anxiety, 684a
  manners had not that, 547a
  oblivion and divine, 668a
  of passions, 434b
  placid, under liberty, 271b
  pleasures satisfaction, 359b
  wakes from short, 354a
  worship of world but no, 467a
  you here in rest, 129b
Reposes, in quiet she, 621a
Reposing age, cradle of, 319b
  hours, 128a
Reprehension, worthy of, 1070b
Represent, novel attempts to, life,
  718a
  really see and really, 719b
  things as we wish them to be,
  10a
Representation, taxation without,
  353a
Representative, happiness and
  glory of a, 359b
  of our country, 331b
  of the people, 399b
  owes you his industry, 359b
Representatives of the people,
  463b
Represented as so hard to learn,
  333a
Reprimand, quarrel or, 503b
Reprinted everywhere, 912a
Reproach, cheerfully bear the,
  494a
  neighbor without, 660a
  no defence against, 300b
  people for talking, 723b
  receives, of being, 207a
  to remind man of good turns,
  27b
Reproached, when a man, him, 72a
Reproachful words, 54b
Reprobation, fall to, 190a
Reproduce, frailties framed to,
  640a
Reproduction of formal types,
  767b
Reproof on her lip, 485a
  valiant, 163a

Reprove not a scorner, 1039a
Reptile, haunt of every noxious,
  353a
  struck with instant death, 50a
Republic could hope to exist, 516a
  democracy in a, 842a
  for which it stands, 762b
  gave the, her station, 499a
  is a dream, 898b
  O good, 1014b
  of letters, 333a, 446b
  safety of the whole, 557a
  they died to save, 541b
Republican form, change its,
  374b
  form of government, 615a
  leaders attacks on me, 921b
  only form of government, 374a
  Party, baseball or the, 931b
Republicans, we are, 575b
Republics, free, of America, 603a
  kings, and emperors, 99b
  most factious of all, 446b
  vice of, 522b
Repudiate support of any advocate, 919b
  wisdom will, thee, 722a
  with indignation and abhorrence,
  512b
Repudiation, inflation is, 859a
Repugnance to mental exertion,
  910a
Repuls'd our final hope, 126a
Reputability, canons of, 776b
  to the gentleman of leisure,
  775b
Reputation, act and scheme to retain his, 282b
  at every word a, dies, 312b
  author's literary, 358a
  bubble, 161b
  death closes a man's, 301a
  easiest way to get a, 975a
  for being clever, 851b
  for my life and art, 21b
  good, is more valuable, 43b
  I have lost my, 187b
  is an idle imposition, 187b
  lost comes not again, 430b
  maligner of his fair, 662a
  no luck in literary, 502a
  not carefully preserved dies,
  282b
  of possessing social tact, 769a
  purest treasure spotless, 138a
  sold my, for a song, 533a
  survive their own, 99a
  that hardly comes up to a celerity, 597a
  written out of, 292b
Repute, half his present, 600b
  thing of good, 776a
Reputed wise, 143a
Request, fit, should be followed,
  76a
  virtue in, is conformity, 501b
Requiem, to thy high, become a
  sod, 481b
Requir'd with gentle sway, 255b
Require, equal syllables alone,
  311a
  what he thought 'e might, 821a
Required, can nothing be, 333a
  in every lover, 106b
Requirements of women, 642b
Requisite of a good citizen, 779a
Re-read and loved, 606a
Rere-mice, war with, 141b
Re-resolves, resolves and, 305b

Rescue my soul from destructions,
  1034a
Research, experimental method of,
  530b
Resemblance, philosophy of sympathy and, 759a
  showy, 371a
Resemble, imitation of those we
  can not, 336b
  when I, her to thee, 242a
Resembling my father as he slept,
  196b
Resembleth uncertain glory of
  April day, 131b
Resent, do not, criticism, 870a
  no individual could, 296a
Resentful, thermometer at, 993b
Resentment a bitter memory, 770b
  endure contumely without, 763a
  passion of, 728b
Reserv'd to blame or to commend,
  319a
Reserve a little complaisance, 106a
  ability they never perform, 181b
  cultivated, 748a
  hold the deadlier, 640a
  side of the last, 325b
  thy judgment, 171b
Reservedly, read deliberately and,
  590a
Reservoir of good will, 964a
  of maxims, 715a
Residence, forted, 185b
  in someone else's point of view,
  901a
Resident, card-playing, 417b
Resides, brief period here he,
  839a
  fire that in the heart, 620a
Residue, starve upon the, 955b
Resign, nor when we will, 621b
  refuse nor, an office, 332a
  title and profit, 299b
Resignation, bearing with heroic,
  788b
  die with graceful, 434b
  gently slopes the way, 355b
  vacancies by, 375a
Resign'd when ills betide, 330a
Resigned all hopes, 935a
  but I am not, 962b
  to the shutting away, 962b
Resist, boots not to, 126b
  both wind and tide, 126b
  everything except temptation,
  768b
  him in authority, 3a
  it steadily, 419a
  not evil, 1051a
  the devil, 1064a
  useful knowledge, 382a
Resistance, courage is, to fear,
  678a
  refinement on principles of, 360a
  spirit of, 1001b
  to the herd spirit, 863b
Resisted, rejoice that America has,
  334b
Resk forty dollars, 674a
Resolute and great in small things,
  602b
  bloody bold and, 198a
  breed of men, 611b
  gentle plain just and, 610a
  sagacious blue-stocking, 493b
Resolution in war, 872a
  native hue of, 174b
  never tell your, beforehand,
  227b

Seasoned timber, 232b
  with Attic salt, 271a
  with salt, 1063a
Seasoning of all enjoyments, 270a
Seasons all alike to him, 672b
  as, fleet, 125a
  depends on, and on days, 889b
  forget, and their change, 255b
  full four, 962a
  lovers', 215b
  makes love at all, 1007a
  mercy, justice, 146a
  return with the year, 254b
  seven, back, 817a
  sorrow breaks, 128a
  swift, roll, 536b
  vernal, 250a
Seat, ancient, of pedantry, 755a
  he held his, 4b
  in some poetic nook, 448a
  is the bosom of God, 112a
  made the throne her, 302a
  of desolation, 252b
  of Mars, 138b
  of the scornful, 1032a
  of this sensation, 788a
  proud, of Lucifer, 258b
  sit in the scorner's, 777b
  this castle hath a pleasant, 195a
  wild sequester'd, 351b
  yourselves on people's backs,
    726b
Seated, grace, on this brow, 176b
  heart knock at my ribs, 194b
  in the heart of courtesy, 115b
  in thy silver chair, 218a
  one day at the organ, 634a
Seats beneath the shade, 355b
  mighty from their, 1056a
  steal to their sovran, 721a
Seaward among the outer islands,
    742b
  fly, 944b
  light woods go, 447b
Seawards, my road leads me, 896a
  salt tides, flow, 619b
Seceded states, say to the, 450b
Second birth, fresh as from a,
    440b
  childhood, fools have their,
    853a
  childhood, old age is, 23a
  childishness, 161b
  class carriage, 684a
  Daniel, 146b
  day of July 1776, 367b
  draught makes him mad, 163b
  edition, if life had a, 469b
  fiddle carrying the air, 889b
  glass for my friends, 300b
  God's, mistake, 728b
  he is a, Hercules, 53a
  is freedom to worship God,
    920b
  life in others' breath, 309b
  live in very, of present, 983b
  man in Rome, 56b
  marriages, exclaim against, 333b
  million, 344a
  Mrs. Tanqueray, 849b
  nature, custom is almost, 60a
  nature's, course, 196b
  of desire, 525b
  place, no disgrace to stop at,
    33a
  race, appointed for my, 272a
  state, great have no, 853a
  thought, as if it were a, 448b
  thoughts are ever wiser, 17b

Second time is examined, 18b
  time, look up a, 412a
  time will confirm it, 953a
  time, wishes to be so a, 340b
  valor's, prize, 51b
  wife, by taking a, 340b
Seconded with will and power,
    181a
Second-hand quote, 510b
  three busts all, 761a
Seconds, slow drip the, 992b
Secrecy, for, no lady closer, 150a
  human dress, 387b
  nature's infinite book of, 200a
  queen of, the violet, 478b
Secret aims of nature, 721a
  and self-contained, 578a
  anniversaries of the heart, 526a
  as the grave, 109b
  be, and exult, 826a
  black and midnight hags, 198a
  bread eaten in, 1039a
  caves of earth, 559b
  cup of still serious thought,
    405b
  dark, love, 387a
  death, of nature, 67a
  dread, whence this, 299b
  faults, cleanse me from, 1033a
  guilt by silence is betrayed,
    279a
  harmony between its tides, 759a
  history of our enemies, 523b
  in, it rolls, 438a
  in, kept in silence sealed, 586b
  in, to be great, 602a
  is not having bad manners,
    766a
  isolated joy, 709a
  keeps a, so well as a child, 497b
  keeps the, it betrays, 524b
  knows my, knows it well, 762a
  lives, men who lead, 773b
  love, 1041a
  loved in, and apart, 767a
  no, grief is there, 687b
  nothing is, 1056b
  of being a bore, 326a
  of eloquence and virtue, 617b
  of success in life, 738a
  of success is constancy, 512b
  of the riddle for successes, 889b
  of the sun, 721b
  of uniform, 946a
  of your looks, 534b
  open or, war, 374a
  phrases of the soul, 915b
  place of the most High, 1036a
  profound, and mystery, 580a
  receive. whispers, 155b
  reference to intelligent persons,
    515a
  satisfaction of thinking, 300a
  source of humor, 678b
  sympathy the silver link, 413b
  that if suspected, 515a
  thing, joy a, 853a
  things belong unto God, 1026a
  thoughts, impart our, 29a
  thoughts of a man, 228b
  trusted, to a woman, 55a
  unrest tortured thee, 485b
  way, shows her the, 231b
  window whence the world, 867a
  wound, 760a
Secretaries of Nature, 236b
Secretary of nature and learning,
    236b
Secret's safe 'twixt you me, 574b

Secrets, betrayeth not thy, 632b
  from whom no, are hid, 1068b
  intrust women with, 28b
  learned, of the grave, 701b
  of the nether world, 66a
  reveal no, 356b
  tell what, they know, 324a
  tested by a hundred, 751a
  that everybody guesses, 764b
  that they do not know, 891b
  trust not him with your, 372b
  weighty, 734a
  yield, to grasping imagination,
    717b
Sect, melt not in an acid, 528a
  slave to no, 304a, 318a
Sector, desolate, of the Somme,
    960a
Sects, other, I can win, 273b
  two-and-seventy jarring, 532b
  vicissitude of, 121b
Secular, music neither, nor re-
    ligious, 862a
Secure access to the sea, 771a
  amidst a falling world, 299a
  from worldly chances, 129b
  guilty conscience never feels,
    28b
  he is, 468a
  public good, 382b
  sea that once made her, 876a
  their reign, 266b
  whate'er he gives, 336a
  within, 278a
Secured, blessing previously, 34a
Secures equal justice to all, 20a
Security, advantage and, to all,
    380a
  against future violations, 335a
  against pride of knowledge,
    543a
  collateral, to virtue, 323b
  eat our chestnuts in, 862a
  for the future, 335a
  for the, of the future, 652a
  greater, for average man, 919a
  little, have we, 434a
  of a god, 119b
  permanent system of, 922b
  principle of collective, 887b
  true, in social solidarity, 618a
  upon nobleness of another,
    885b
Sed, groweth, and bloweth med,
    999a
Sedate ignorance, 336a
Sedentary life is real sin, 729a
Sedge has withered from the lake,
    480a
Sedges, fens and the, 935a
Sedition idleness aversion to
    labour, 290b
  spread, in Russia, 840b
Seducer, sea always a, 904a
Seductive, literature most, of
    professions, 700a
Sedulous ape, played the, 751b
See a fine picture, 378b
  all I, is mine, 630b
  all that we, or seem, 543b
  and approve better things, 42b
  another's woe, 385b
  become what we now, him,
    340a
  beyond the range of sight, 591a
  by the dawn's early light, 436a
  can I boast I, 924b
  come up and, me sometime,
    968a

Serene I fold my hands and wait, 688b
  peaceful state, 294b
  purest ray, 348b
  ways of death are, 741b
Serenely arriving, 609b
  full the epicure would say, 39b
Serenity of books, 525a
  of death, 662a
  of Shangri-La, 985b
  pure, of mind, 236b
  querulous, 428a
  steady and perpetual, 301a
Serfs, vassals and, at my side, 483b
Serge, old blue, 890a
  piece of scarlet, 983a
Sergeant at Belleau Woods, 898b
Series of congratulatory regrets, 513a
  of kindnesses, 372a
Serious air, Cervantes', 321b
  and alarming consequences, 366b
  and the smirk, 576b
  importance, no human thing is of, 25b
  in ridiculous matters, 59b
  nothing, in mortality, 197a
  occupation, 402a
  strenuous and, 952b
  takes himself, 904b
  writer and a solemn writer, 982b
Sermon, him who a, flies, 232b
  implies absence of everything agreeable, 418b
  improve delivery of a, 332a
  preach a better, 504b
  read a song not a, 232b
  see a, than hear one, 913b
  turn out a, 391a
Sermons and soda-water, 458a
  in stones, 159b
  no, in stones, 688b
  throw bricks and, 679b
  worth all, in the world, 446a
Serpent, Aaron's, 317a
  be the, under 't, 195a
  beguiled me, 1022a
  biteth like a, 1040b
  crooked, 1046a
  infernal, 252a
  more, than dove, 124a
  of old Nile, 200a
  shall bite him, 1043a
  sting twice, 145b
  strike at a, that hisses, 761a
  tempted me and I did eat, 573a
  trail of the, 441a
  upon a rock, 1041b
  was more subtile, 1021b
  wise as a, 829a
Serpent-detector, Bonaparte sent for a, 50a
Serpent's egg, think him as a, 167a
  tongue, woman with the, 781a
  tooth, sharper than a, 191a
Serpents, poison which acts upon, 50a
  remove two, seen in house, 50a
  strangled, 981a
  they become, 317a
  wise as, 124a, 1052b
Servant, accuse not a, to his master, 1041b
  accustom, to tell a lie, 340a
  borrower is, to lender, 1040b

Servant depart in peace, 1056b
  faithful and good, 87a
  girls in the kitchen, 856b
  good and faithful, 1054b
  in love, 82a
  is thy, a dog, 1029a
  judge public, by one act, 778b
  nor, above his lord, 1052b
  of God, well done, 256b
  of God's holiest charge, 352a
  of the scattered family, 666b
  pass not away from thy, 1023a
  show thy, the light, 1069b
  thy, heareth, 1027a
Servant's title, 526b
Servants, all sorts of, 577b
  and agents of the people, 689a
  as good as themselves, 108b
  fire is the best of, 475b
  made them obedient, 946a
  of light, 655a
  of regrets, 949b
  of sovereign or state, 120a
  of their human interests, 807b
  public, serve you right, 986b
  sons and, 83b
  usefulest of all, 475b
  what his, robbed, 1014a
Serv'd no private end, 315a
Serve a hitch in hell, 762b
  and not to dominate world, 929a
  any excuse will, a tyrant, 9b
  for sweet discourses, 137a
  God and mammon, 1051b
  his time to every trade, 452a
  in heaven, 252b
  my king and master, 211b
  on his knees, 116a
  other people, 642b
  so long as we love we, 752b
  state in choosing men to, 237b
  the future hour, 411b
  the Lord with fear, 1032a
  Thee as Thou deservest, 87b
  these woes shall, 137a
  they also, who only stand, 251b
  they, him best, 251b
  thy country and mankind, 666a
  time to, and to sin, 691b
  to ply the sampler, 248a
  two masters, 1051b
  us or cut us, 603a
  willing faithfully to, 237b
  with their money, 344a
Served God with half the zeal, 211b
  his kind by word and deed, 654b
  public must and will be, 288b
  you are, right, 207b
Serves a certain purpose, 697a
  and seeks for gain, 191a
  as paste and cover, 139b
  his country well, 324b
  it in the office of a wall, 139a
  literature, beyond all, 611a
  me most who serves his country best, 4b
  take current when it, 169a
Serveth not another's will, 213a
Service, ability for good, 361a
  as soon as public, ceases, 344a
  best, for our country, 709b
  beyond all recompense, 243b
  done the state some, 190a
  dyvyne, 79b

Service, essential, to his country, 295b
  greater than the god, 181b
  hard, must be done, 495b
  high and anthems clear, 246b
  is no heritage, 183a
  mutual, 794a
  of my love, 789a
  of our great imperial family, 997b
  of princes, 28b
  of the greatest, 21a
  offers of, so freely made, 576a
  pressed into, 879b
  ranks the same with God, 567b
  school of the Lord's, 73b
  shrink from, of his country, 370a
  small service is true, 412a
  strength of the ship is the, 840b
  strong for, still, 364b
  to others, 972a
  to the state, 295b
  want for, unforeseen, 442b
  weary and old with, 211a
  whose, is perfect freedom, 1068b
  yeoman, 179a
Serviceability, beauty or, 776a
Serviceable according to his folly, 773a
  to God and His people, 237b
Services, give, for nothing, 21b
  goods and, can be paid for, 864a
Servile fetters, 1000b
  imitation and complaisance, 559b
  insurrection, inciters of, 666a
  status and vicarious life, 776a
  to skyey influences, 184b
Serving, betrays instead of, 359b
  to die for her is, Thee, 535a
Serving-men, six honest, 819b
Servitors, nimble and airy, 250a
Servitude and license, 516a
  base laws of, 275b
  consequence of his crime, 380b
  freedom and not, 360a
Sesame, open, to every portal, 743b
  your open, 86ob
Sesoun priketh every gentil herte, 80a
Sesquipedalianism is natural to Americans, 795b
Session, perpetual, 927b
Sessions of sweet silent thought, 205a
Sesun, somer, 78a
Set a beggar on horseback, 126a
  a thief to catch a thief, 58a
  among high tides, 148a
  candle in the sun, 223b
  faults, in note-book, 169a
  feet on firm earth, 229b
  foundation, on blood, 148b
  free half-regain'd Eurydice, 245b
  gloss on faint deeds, 203a
  gray life and apathetic end, 548a
  her on even keel, 14a
  his light little foot, 842a
  his seal, 177a
  honour, to leg, 151b
  in a garden wall, 910b

Soul, naked, of Tomlinson, 817b
  narrates adventures of his, 723b
  never yet freed a human, 680a
  no coward, is mine, 592a
  no excellent, is exempt, 48a
  no higher than the, is high, 961b
  no thought has satisfied my, 739b
  nobility of, miscalled, 914a
  not a, to search himself, 35a
  not knowing a, 792b
  nothing like a, as a bee, 498a
  O my prophetic, 172b
  of a friend we've made, 799a
  of a journey is liberty, 434a
  of Adonais, 468b
  of all the kindly wines, 839b
  of Annabel Lee, 546a
  of fire, 336a
  of goodness, 155b
  of goodness in things evil, 614b
  of grandam inhabit bird, 146a
  of man a kind of harmony, 476a
  of man is immortal, 25b
  of man larger than sky, 483b
  of man like the rolling world, 650a
  of music shed, 438a
  of music slumbers, 396b
  of Orpheus sing, 246a
  of reading, 345b
  of Richard, 128b
  of, sincere, 315a
  of the age, 219a
  of the sculptor is bidden, 667a
  of the whole past time, 475b
  of truth in things erroneous, 614b
  offends me to the, 175b
  on fire, 533a
  once my, possess, 673b
  one, abiding in two bodies, 5a
  one, as good as another, 766a
  one drop would save my, 123b
  oppresses my, 659b
  palace of the, 242b, 452b
  panteth my, after thee, 1034a
  perches in the, 646b
  perdition catch my, 188a
  perished in his pride, 406a
  pilgrim, in you, 824b
  poor, sat sighing, 189b
  portions of the, of man, 599b
  possess your, with patience, 279b
  pour'd her pensive, 351b
  pouring forth thy, abroad, 481b
  pray the Lord my, to keep, 1000b
  primitive, 599b
  prison that can bind the, 757b
  prophet of the, 503a
  prophetic, 206b
  proud, ne'er pays, 149b
  Psyche my, 545b
  pure, unto his captain, 140a
  ragged meadow of my, 969a
  rapt, sitting in thine eyes, 246a
  real dark night of the, 974b
  receive my, at last, 334a
  remembering good friends, 139a
  rest her, she's dead, 178b
  restoreth my, 1033a
  reticence of, 914a
  returned to me, 532b
  rolled from thought to, 262b
  sad lucidity of, 620a

Soul, sad, take comfort nor forget, 674a
  saddest thing befall a, 650a
  sail leagues beyond, 640b
  save your, 996b
  saw a glimpse of happiness, 243b
  search the, and die, 829a
  secret phrases of the, 915b
  seed the, hath sown, 707b
  seeking, 895a
  selects her own society, 646a
  sell your, 14a
  sent my, through the invisible, 532b
  sets the, in tune, 274b
  shall taste the sadness, 483a
  she has her, to keep, 736a
  shell disdained, had gained, 602a
  shorten stature of my, 638b
  sigh'd his, 146b
  sinews of the, 244a
  sings, and body, 148b
  small-town, 987a
  smithy of my, 916b
  so warm and true, 437b
  soft intercourse from, to soul, 313a
  sooth'd his, to pleasures, 280a
  speech is a mirror of the, 47a
  stands shivering, 291b
  startled heaven of my, 894a
  still flies above me, 935b
  strong is the, 619a
  studies each commonplace, 734a
  subject's, his own, 155b
  superior, 931a
  sweet and virtuous, 232b
  sweetest, that ever took'd, 552b
  swell the, to rage, 280b
  takes nothing with her, 21a
  that can be honest, 224b
  that can render an honest man, 224b
  that feeds on books alone, 711b
  that has not learned to read, 711b
  that o'er him planned, 503b
  that rises with us, 408a
  the fixt foot, 216b
  the world the race the, 610b
  thirsteth for thee, 1035a
  this, its body off, 827b
  thou hast much goods, 1057a
  three books on the, 571b
  thy, be required of thee, 1057a
  thy, was in me, 694b
  time for, to stretch and spit, 994b
  time the, of this world, 62a
  timid, 934a
  to solitude retires, 531a
  to the, that maketh all, 316b
  tocsin of the, 459a
  truth and his great, 573b
  twilight, between, 949a
  two bodies with one, 5a
  unacquainted with our own, 213b
  unconquerable, 741b
  under the ribs of death, 248a
  unlettered small-knowing, 132b
  unto itself an imperial friend, 646b
  upward longing of my, 859b
  veils of the, 691b
  virtue of the, distributing, 71b
  visit the, in sleep, 465a
  waiteth for one lone, 655b

Soul, wake, by tender strokes, 312b
  war against the, 1064a
  was like a star, 407b
  was not spoken of the, 521a
  way his, shall go, 796b
  we too take ship O, 610a
  what each, conquered, 574b
  what will satisfy the, 610b
  why cast down O my, 1034b
  why shrinks the, 299b
  wild of, 981a
  will to do the, to dare, 415a
  windows of my, 527b
  windows of the, 102b
  wine-scented and poetic, 751b
  wit its, 423a
  with all its maladies, 701b
  with all thy, 1025b
  with my whole, 1048b
  with rapture takes my, 689b
  with sorrow laden, 545a
  with the saints, 425a
  wretched, bruised, 129a
  your, in her firm white hands, 857b
Soul-destroying hatred, 869b
Soule bodie forme, of the, 115a
  fret thy, 114a
  is forme, 115a
  layes the, to sleepe, 113a
Soul-hungry, worse to be, 1007b
Soul's arrest, 867a
  calm retreat, 271b
  dark cottage, 242b
  eternal sleep, 383a
  eternity, memorial from the, 640b
  invincible surmise, 806b
  prayer the, sincere desire, 413a
  wealth lies in heaps, 650a
Souls, adorn and beautify our, 702b
  afar, borne inward into, 518a
  all the, that were, 184a
  apart, custom presses on, 897b
  are now acting enduring, 655b
  are portions of eternity, 599b
  assembled, 242b
  beyond reaches of our, 172a
  companion of mean, 370a
  corporations have no, 110b
  cry of a thousand, 890a
  do not think about their, 959b
  evil only in men's, 987a
  fatted, of the English, 816a
  find rest unto your, 1052b
  first breath our, draw, 655a
  flame of freedom in their, 707b
  forbids to afflict our, 57b
  friends and brother, 556b
  good morrow to our waking, 215a
  great liberty inspire our, 299a
  harmony in immortal, 147a
  house bodies but not, 924a
  in hell their, may dwell, 625b
  in house of tomorrow, 924a
  in the self-same mill, 729b
  jewel of their, 188a
  left your, on earth, 482b
  letters mingle, 217a
  like, ready to remind us, 855b
  luxury liners laden with, 993b
  mounting up to God, 640b
  must be saved, 187b
  mysteries in, do grow, 216b
  numberless infinities of, 217b
  nurse of full-grown, 599b

Spirit, music gentlier on the, lies, 547a
my, felt thee there, 422b
my, is too weak, 477b
needs, lack all life behind, 574b
no, can walk abroad, 170a
noble and resolved, 55b
not the letter but the, 1062a
nought so much the, calms, 457b
O, of love, 163b
of a youth, 201a
of an ancient, 314a
of Beauty, 465a
of delight, 468b
of general suspicion, 860a
of God, 1021a
of heaviness, 1047b
of his age, 326a
of liberty, 360a
of man suffer annihilation, 793a
of mortal be proud, 462a
of party, 367a
of prophecy, 21a
of resistance, 1001b
of reverence pervades, 20a
of revolt, 641b
of romance is dead, 599a
of subordination, 367a
of the Constitution, 900b
of this world, 351a
of truth and of freedom, 641a
of wine sang, 742a
of wisdom and understanding, 1045b
of youth in everything, 206b
old Grecian, 583b
one fair, for my minister, 454b
outrage on the, of justice, 757b
Oxford, 858a
pard-like, 468a
passed before my face, 1030a
perturbed, rest, 173a
poor in, 1050b
present in, 1060b
preserve the, and form, 382b
renew a right, 1034b
return unto God, 1044a
roughness and, of defiance, 611b
ruleth his, 1039b
scorn'd his, 166b
shallow, of judgment, 124b
sits in a foggy cloud, 198a
so lingering and searching, 858a
so profound, 405b
so still and quiet, 186a
soft meek patient, 215a
stab my, broad awake, 751b
streaming from the waters of baptism, 790b
strongest and fiercest, 253b
subtle, has my path attended, 934b
swiftness of the, 883a
task undertaken in adventurous, 773b
that always denies, 379b
that answered your every mood, 819b
that on life's rough sea, 117a
that quickens him, 490a
that remembers, 592a
too much, to be e'er at ease, 314b
vexation of, 1042a
walks abroad, 169a
what voice did on my, fall, 552a
which prized liberty, 538a
who might be within there, 788b
who pities me, 924b

Spirit, wild, moving everywhere, 466a
with calm, seek rest, 34b
with more, chased, 144b
with spirit can meet, 556a
within constraineth me, 1031b
wounded, who can bear, 1040a
Spiriting, do my, gently, 209a
Spiritless, so faint so, so dull, 152a
Spirit-like eludes embrace, 629b
Spirit's, care, soothe my, 591b
vestal grace provokes, 629b
Spirits, actors were all, 210a
all unselfish, heed, 654b
apothecary never be out of, 381b
black, and white, 214b
brave, there are, 723a
bravest, in our annals, 223a
by our own, are we deified, 406a
can either sex assume, 252b
cheered my, 733a
choice and master, 167b
choice, carry germ of it, 723b
clad in veils, 583a
day of, 271b
exuberant, 727b
from vasty deep, 150b
good, and good temper, 577b
keep up our, 577b
learn that we are, 870b
like two, 207b
make us preserve remembrance, 34b
man's animal, 593b
meet, 262a
more vast than earth, 669b
not finely touch'd, 183b
of just men made perfect, 1063b
of the wise, 153a
poor, who neither enjoy much, 778b
quaint, 142a
that tend on mortal thoughts, 195a
throw, into the Irish Channel, 744b
tobacco nor, ever made appeal, 841b
vanish like evil, 375b
wanton, look out, 182b
Spirit-stirring drum, 189a
Spiritual cause, found the, 616b
content, proportion to, 948a
creatures, millions of, 256a
effect physical as well as, 679b
food, pray for, 625a
interposition, 782a
inward and, grace, 1069a
is stronger than material force, 506a
level, adapt its, 951a
physical and, night, 497a
significance to objects, 722a
the divine the, and the eternal, 617a
unbidden and unconscious, 557b
understanding of Him, 616b
unlocated, area, 821b
virtue of a sacrament, 72a
when nothing, remains, 948a
wickedness in high places, 1062b
wild oats, sow our, 671b
Spiritually as well as economically, 473b
indispensable, toiling for, 474a
Spit brown, 897a
for us, to sit and, 29b
in face, 150a

Spit there glorifies your face, 533b
time for soul to stretch and, 994b
Spite, death aims with fouler, 231b
doctor's peaceful mission, 747a
in, of every sage, 286b
O cursed, 173a
of my teeth, 85a
of nature and their stars, 238b
the world, 197b
Spiteful envious ungrateful, 434a
Spites do not harm true genius, 725b
Spitting in Niagara Falls, 964b
with lips once sanctified, 533b
Spleen, meditative, 411a
of race, 850b
wit and mirth and, 300a
Splendid a star, 575a
and unselfish action, 888a
eloquence, 324a
hearts, men with, 938a
in ashes, 241b
shilling, retains a, 358b
shilling's praise, 358b
silence clings around me, 838b
silent sun, 609b
stars, 927b
was its station, 789b
wife, would have made a, 801b
Splendidly null, 553b
Splendor and speed of thy feet, 691b
around the world, 940b
falls on castle walls, 550a
guilty, 364b
in the grass, 408b
not in lone, hung, 479b
of a sudden thought, 572b
world's, and wonder, 725a
Splendors, ancient, fling, 560b
and glooms, 467b
heaven with all its, 600a
old homes old names and old, 842a
Splenetive and rash, 179a
Splinter of steel, 964a
Split, atom to be, 939b
ears of the groundlings, 175b
pea, nothing left but one, 564b
sides with laughter, 106a
the sky in two, 961b
Splits, welkin, apart, 854a
Splitting air with noise, 202b
caraway, 29b
Spoil all, historians, 98b
by trying to explain it, 381a
foxes that, the vines, 1044a
like bales unopen'd, 306a
lives of better people, 753a
of me, 151a
reaches for his, 831a
spare rod and, child, 84b, 239a
upon my face, 156b
will not share the, 9b
Spoil'd my best array, 309b
Spoiled, pagan, 810a
the bread, 629b
the form, 100b
Spoilers of symmetry of shelves, 429b
Spoiling her nice new clothes, 1018a
its bloom, 774a
Spoils a romance, 769a
conquests glories triumphs, 167b
of nature, 240a

Sterile truth, you can keep your, 740a
  with idleness, 186b
Sterilized, it wasn't, 853b
Sterling page, refine her, 287a
  worth, most of, 549a
Stern and distant shore, 808a
  and rock-bound coast, 470a
  and stubborn pride, 933b
  Caledonia, and wild, 414a
  daughter of the voice of God, 409b
  friend, to genius the, 505a
  joy, rule it with, 928a
  joy which warriors feel, 415b
  partisan, Hugo, 903b
  proconsul of intractable provinces, 993b
  resolve, 39a
  ruin's ploughshare, 391a
  severe and, to view, 356a
  true-born Englishman, 138b
Sterner days, speak rather of, 870b
  soldiers, 781b
  stuff, ambition made of, 168a
Sternest, nature's, painter, 452a
Stern-faced men, 488a
Stern'st good-night, 196a
Sterres, writen in the, 81a
Sterte, oon hole for to, 30a
  out of his sleep to, 80a
Sterves, seely steede, 93a
Stevenson was a roadmender, 753a
Stew is smokin' hot, 859b
  kept in a, 557b
  onions in the, 950a
Steward falls into the soup-tureen, 819b
Stewed prunes, longing for, 184a
Sthreet railrood comp'nies, 835a
Sthrong arm men iv th' Sinit, 835a
Stick, beat with fist instead of a, 238a
  carry a big, 779a
  close to your desks, 682a
  cobbler, to his last, 51a
  fell like a, 371a
  heap of, and stone, 706a
  man whose acquisitions, 715b
  more close than a brother, 819b
  on conversation's burs, 534b
  party, the less, 120b
  serge draped over a, 983a
  tattered coat upon a, 827a
  there I'll, 105a
  this old cove throwed, 612a
  to what you're at, 897a
Sticketh closer than a brother, 1040a
Sticking, aye, in a tree, 416b
Sticking-place, screw your courage to the, 196a
Stickle, perversely, at parts, 429a
Sticks in the heart's deep core, 388a
  nix hicks pix, 864b •
  of sealing-wax, 578a
  to my own bones, 607b
  to the pot, 109a
Sticky, gilded and, 935a
Stiel, trewe as, 78b
Stiff in opinions, 277a
  lines of life, 528a
  new wasps, 997b
  'twill civilize thim, 834b
  twin compasses, 216b
  upper lip, keep a, 630b
  wrist grows, and old, 615b
Stiffen sinews, 155a

Stiffened worm, 640a
Stiffening of the vertebrae, 763a
Stiffens and rejoices, 944b
Stiffnecked people, 1025a
Stiffness and the soul's arrest, 867a
Stifle, creed would, me, 891a
  opinion we are endeavoring to, 517b
Stifling snow, sleet or, 567a
Stigmatize, wallop and, 912a
Stile, before you come to, 104b
  crooked, 1019a
Still and awful red, 422a
  and lovely face, 863a
  and quiet conscience, 211b
  and serious thought, 405b
  commanded sun to stand, 331b
  days are, and bright, 509b
  evening and twilight gray, 255b
  falls the rain, 941a
  how, we see thee lie, 669b
  nights all white an', 601a
  nodding night, 608a
  not to sit, 820a
  question'd me the story, 186a
  quiet and, air, 250a
  raven, is sitting, 545a
  sad music of humanity, 404a
  small voice, 1029a
  small voice of gratitude, 350a
  small voice spake unto me, 546b
  sowe eats up draffe, 92b
  spirit so, and quiet, 186a
  stand, you ever moving spheres, 123b
  stars move, 123b
  to be neat to be drest, 218b
  waters, 1033a
  waters, take heed of, 111a
  woman should be, 887a
Still-discordant wavering multitude, 152a
Stille, fol can not be, 78a
Stilled the rising tumult, 808a
Stiller town, townsman of a, 786a
Stillness, air a solemn, holds, 348a
  modest, and humility, 155a
  soft, and night, 147a
  world in solemn, lay, 560b
Still-remembered olden days, 849b
Still-soliciting eye, 190b
Still-vexed Bermoothes, 209a
Stilly, hum, sounds, 155b
  night, 439b
Stimulating, science, to imagination, 959b
Stimulus, we need some imaginative, 702b
Sting, a, a resentment, 770b
  bitter, is a little fault, 76a
  cold doth not, 213a
  O death where is thy, 775a, 1062a
  of a tiny insect, 10a
  of the rowelled steel, 813b
  serpent, twice, 145b
  stare and, forever, 960b
  that bids nor sit nor stand, 572a
  thorns to prick and, her, 172b
  with a little, 935a
Stinger, 'tis a, 214b
Stingeth like an adder, 1040b
Stinging drop, injects a, 801b
Stings, disturb it it, 307a
  endure, crowd and buzz, 267a
  hope that, 780b
  in the very flowers, 35a

Stings, stinks and, 319a
  wanton, and motions, 183b
  what, is justice, 908b
  you for your pains, 307a
Stingy with your blooming hair, 894a
Stink, stand by the fire and, 191a
  that thy name may not, 3a
Stinking fish, poets like, 425b
  mackerel, 150b
Stinks and stings, 319a
  like rotten mackerel, 425b
  stenches and several, 425a
Stipple, rose-moles all in, 724a
Stir a flower, 790a
  best not, the rice, 109a
  do not, fire with sword, 72b
  hell shall, for this, 156b
  make the greatest, 777b
  men's blood, 168b
  of echoes, 960b
  of the great Babel, 364b
  sap begins to, 795a
  see nor breathe nor, 896b
  smoke and, of this dim spot, 246b
  soft potential, 648a
  the fire, 364b
  the mixture well, 536b
  without great argument, 177b
Stirr'd, her face, with her dream, 458b
  like a fountain, 182a
  up with envy and revenge, 252a
Stirred with high hopes of living, 250a
Stirring, die when so much was, 60a
  living embers, 535b
  up some war, 25a
Stirrup, sprang to the, 568a
Stirs, affection, her spirit, 427b
  divinity that, within us, 300a
  of discontented strife, 220b
  this mortal frame, 423a
  to rouse a lion, 149b
Stitch, every, takes up its slack, 977b
  in time saves nine, 46b
  stitch stitch, 489a
Stitches, laugh yourselves into, 165a
Stithy, Vulcan's, 176a
Stock, common, of intellectual enjoyment, 791b
  dove whose echo resounds, 392b
  how his, went on, 427a
  of harmless pleasure, 337b
  words once my, 280b
Stocking all the day, 353b, 356b
  draws a, up, 943b
Stockings, blue in, 520a
  coming out of her, 714a
  silk, and white bosoms, 339a
  went to bed with his, on, 1019a
  were hung by the chimney, 437a
  with long silk, 909b
  yellow, 165a
Stocks and stones, worship, 251b
Stoic backs, 947a
  bird, 934a
  of the woods, 433a
  or a satyr, 761b
Stoicism, no, and no philosophy, 605a
  Romans call it, 299b
Stoic's pride, 316b
Stoics, after manner of the, 119b
Stole a piece of beef, 1016b

Sweat, who casts to write must, 219b
Sweating palm to palm, 969b
Sweats easier than I do, 589b
  Falstaff, to death, 150a
  wild regrets and bloody, 769b
Swedish steel, recourse to, 641a
Sweeney to Mrs. Porter, 944a
Sweep and turn and fly, 813a
  forces flow with a tidal, 700a
  over thee in vain, 454b
  your chimneys I, 385a
Sweeping by in sceptred pall, 246a
  triumph, rushed past in, 511b
  up the heart, 648a
Sweeps a strain low sad and sweet, 617a
Sweet, adversity's, milk, 137a
  Alice, 597a
  all love is, 465b
  and bitter fancy, 163a
  and cunning hand, 164a
  and fair she seems to be, 242a
  and gracious, 587a
  and honourable to die, 39a
  and low, 550a
  and musical as Apollo's lute, 133b
  and pure and fair, 486a
  and twenty, 164a
  and virtuous soul, 232b
  and voluble in discourse, 133a
  approach of even, 254b
  are the slumbers, 300a
  are thoughts of content, 117b
  are uses of adversity, 159b
  are words of love, 673a
  as bright Apollo's lute, 247b
  as English air could make her, 550a
  as honey, 3b
  as love, 384a
  as summer, 212a
  as the primrose, 357a
  as those by hopeless fancy, 550b
  aspect of princes, 211a
  attractive grace, 255a
  beauty's best, 206b
  bee doth suck his, 116a
  bells jangled, 175a
  bird that shunn'st noise, 246a
  bird's throat, 160a
  bread of deceit is, 1040a
  but then how it was, 572b
  by distance made more, 351b
  cement glue and lime of love, 230a
  childish days, 406b
  civilities of life, 281a
  closing of an eye, 563a
  compulsion, 142a
  concord of, sounds, 147a
  content passing all wisdom, 509a
  counsel together, 1035a
  courtesy has done its most, 680b
  cruelly, are the echoes, 591a
  crush'd, poison, 247a
  day so cool, 232a
  days and roses, 232b
  delight, born to, 388a
  discourse, showers of, 263b
  discourses in our time, 137a
  disorder in dress, 230b
  dividing throat, 236b

Sweet dream when the long trick's over, 896a
  dreams and health, 478b
  ease in misery, 122a
  Echo sweetest nymph, 247a
  every bitter thing is, 1041a
  every, its sour, 501b
  food of knowledge, 116a
  found the common daylight, 738a
  friends farewell, 76b
  friendship, steady and loyal, 678a
  Genevieve, 698b
  girl graduates, 550a
  hard way, and delectable, 139a
  has its sour, 501b
  hay hath no fellow, 142a
  Helen make me immortal, 123b
  Highland Mary, 393a
  his mouth is most, 1044b
  his ways are, 13a
  how charmingly, you sing, 581a
  how passing, is solitude, 363b
  how, the summer, 899b
  if truth offend my, 892b
  indifference, full of a, 708b
  inexpressible as, 762a
  is a grief well ended, 12b
  is death, 555a
  is every sound, 551a
  is love itself possess'd, 137b
  is peace so, 369a
  is pleasure after pain, 280a
  is revenge, 258a, 457b
  is the breath, 350a
  is the breath of morn, 256a
  is true love, 555a
  Jerusalem, 127a
  keen smell, 640b
  kinde of grace, 114b
  land of liberty, 529b
  leaves to the air, 134a
  less than to remember thee, 439a
  lies of Paradise, 439b
  life did and does smack, 574b
  life is, 693b
  life, life is the same, 800a
  life more, 159b
  little doll dears, 599a
  look of devotion, 701b
  lords sweet lovers, 133a
  love is, for a day, 693a
  love remember'd, 205a
  lovers love the spring, 163a
  magic of a cheerful face, 535a
  make end most, 138a
  Marie, 762a
  memory, 396a
  mercy nobility's badge, 129b
  mermaid, 129a
  milk of concord, 198b
  mirage that lured me, 606b
  moan, made, 480a
  more welcome is the, 183b
  morsel, 292b
  mountain nymph, Liberty, 245a
  music, 132a
  music, how sour, 140b
  music, never merry when I hear, 147a
  music that softer falls, 547a
  music's melting fall, 350a
  musk-roses, 141b
  my own my, 554a
  naught in this life, 221a, 225b
  naught so, as melancholy, 221a
  neglect more taketh me, 218b

Sweet o' the year, 208a
  oblivious antidote, 199a
  of bitter bark, 881a
  opposition may become, 596b
  ornament truth doth give, 205b
  pangs, 164b
  parting is, sorrow, 136a
  peace is crowned, 271b
  perfections caught, 114b
  person adorning, 464b
  Phosphor bring the day, 231b
  psalmist of Israel, 1028a
  rather have my, 932b
  reluctant amorous delay, 255b
  remembrance of the just, 237a, 290b
  retired solitude, 247b
  return, urges, 258a
  revenge at first though, 258a
  robin I heard them say, 528b
  sacrifice, 210b
  self, talking about his, 814a
  serenity of books, 525a
  silent thought, 205a
  simplicity of three per cents, 377a
  singing in the choir, 1004b
  sleep, music that brings, 547a
  sleep thou ow'dst yesterday, 188b
  slug-a-bed, 231a
  small clumsy feet of April, 969a
  so, a tongue, 956b
  so coldly, so deadly fair, 455a
  so, love seemed, 721b
  softly, in Lydian measures, 280a
  sorrow, parting is such, 136a
  sound that breathes upon violets, 163b
  sounding name of patria, 774b
  sour adazzle dim, 724a
  spring full of sweet days, 232b
  stolen waters are, 1039a
  strains of music, 777a
  strains or pensive smiles, 503a
  Swan of Avon, 219b
  sweet poison, 147b
  sweets to the, 179a
  sweets with, war not, 204b
  Te Deums, 875a
  tell me not, I am unkind, 268a
  the coming on of ev'ning, 256a
  the memory is to me, 525a
  the pleasure, 280a
  their memory still, 362b
  things, night and day both, 500b
  things should be fleet, 694b
  things, to taste, 138a
  though in sadness, 466a
  thoughts led to woeful pass, 75b
  thunder, 142a
  tired nature's, restorer, 305a
  to dance to violins, 769b
  to the sense, 262b
  to think where'er we rove, 439a
  to unbend, 40a
  too simple and too, for words, 629b
  touch as, as I could bear, 880b
  touches of, harmony, 147a
  understanding, 132b
  unmemoried scents, 721b
  unrest, awake for ever in, 479b
  upon the ear in cadence, 365b
  utter, breath, 142b
  valley so, 438b

Things, new, succeed, 231a
  not always what they seem, 48b
  not made for sake of words, 70a
  not on, on the earth, 1063a
  not seen are eternal, 1062a
  not to do desperate, 589b
  now are as they were, 68b
  of little or no use, 54a
  old unhappy far-off, 407b
  ordinary commonplace, 428b
  outward draw inward quality, 201a
  part of the, that please, 341b
  past or things to come, 274a
  past redress, 139a
  poor foolish, that live a day, 824a
  possessing all, 213a, 422b
  present nor things to come, 1060a
  present worst, 153a
  pretty state of, 684b
  profane, things sacred or, 274a
  proposed as things forgot, 311b
  quick bright, 141a
  rank and gross in nature, 170b
  release from little, 981b
  remembrance of, past, 205a
  sacred or things profane, 274a
  secret, belong unto God, 1026a
  seen are temporal, 1062a
  shadows of the, to be, 630b
  shape of, to come, 832a
  small, make base men, 125b
  smell and taste of, 855a
  so full of a number of, 750b
  so many fine, to do, 891a
  some, are of that nature, 274b
  soul of goodness in, evil, 614b
  soul of truth in, erroneous, 614b
  standing thus unknown, 179b
  strange, come out, 394b
  such, to be, 552b
  sum of human, 376b
  surfeit of sweetest, 142a
  sweet to taste, 138a
  talk of, heavenly, 274a
  thank Thee for the, I miss, 627b
  that almost happen, 513b
  that are more excellent, 781a
  that didn't occur, 777b
  that feed the mind, 720a
  that go bump in the night, 1003a
  that haven't been done before, 913b
  that he thinketh, 1065b
  that help with things that hurt, 719b
  that mar or bless, 780b
  that ne'er were, 261a
  that stand, 888b
  that trouble us now, 661b
  that wouldn't divide, 731b
  these, shall be, 707b
  think on these, 1063a
  thinking how, may be, 338b
  those are the, to try, 913b
  those who want the fewest, 70b
  thoughts and, look older, 499b
  three, for salvation of man, 75a
  three, in a building, 379a
  three silent, 892b
  time for all, 108b
  time for some, 108b
  to be remembered by, 959b
  to come, giant mass of, 181b
  to come, things past or, 274a

Things, to talk of many, 658b
  to their destruction draw, 216a
  trophies and dead, 226a
  two, at once, 43a
  two, excite us to love, 105b
  two noblest, sweetness and light, 294b
  two, people desire, 63a
  two, stand like stone, 661b
  unattempted yet, 252a
  uncomely and broken, 825a
  under ground, 104b
  unknown proposed, 311b
  very much as always, 858b
  vicissitudes in all, 31b
  violently destroyed, 406a
  voiceless, 911b
  we have seen and have known, 721b
  we live through all, 654b
  we never do for our own sake, 33b
  we see are shadows, 630b
  wee unimportant, 987a
  well said songs well sung, 930a
  what mean the, unseen, 733b
  what were the most necessary, 70b
  whatsoever, are true, 1063a
  which are Caesar's, 1054a
  which elemented it, 216b
  which I have seen, 408a
  which they put in practice, 70b
  who knows at, 722a
  why and wherefore in all, 156b
  why, are as they are, 722a
  with more spirit chased, 144b
  without all remedy, 197b
  words are, 458b
  worst, 974b
  worth their observation, 301a
  write well in laudable, 250a
  ye lef' behind, 913b
Thing-um-a-jig, 659b
Think above that which is written, 1060b
  always talk who never, 219b
  and ne'er disclose her mind, 187a
  another, talk one thing and, 44a
  as though we stayed home, 901a
  because I, him so, 131b
  before thou speakest, 106a
  beyond our circle of ideas, 740a
  by fits and starts, 787a
  clear feel deep, 620b
  difficult to, nobly, 345a
  do not try to, consciously, 822a
  feel do as one pleases, 434a
  fellows whom it hurts to, 786b
  for yourselves, 326b
  free to, and act, 669b
  free to, speak and write, 376a
  freedom to, 600b
  great thoughts, 709a
  greatly, or bravely die, 313b
  he still has found, 341b
  him as a serpent's egg, 167a
  how much we, of ourselves, 680a
  I, therefore I am, 237a
  if one, it important, 715b
  in the morning, 386a
  in this batter'd caravanserai, 531b
  is to be full of sorrow, 481b
  it worth enjoying, 280a
  know much and, for nothing, 220b
  last opinion right, 311b

Think, later than you, 877b
  men, all men mortal, 305b
  men will say or, 262a
  must not, of thee, 736b
  no more, 786a
  none, the great unhappy, 302a
  not God at all, 260a
  of your forefathers, 398b
  of yourself as he, 844b
  on these things, 1063a
  only this of me, 938b
  pleasant too to, on, 261b
  quietly talk gently, 557b
  say what other people, 638a
  so then, 582a
  sooner or later begins to, 846b
  talk and never, 219b
  talk for one who can, 605a
  that day lost, 305b
  their little set mankind, 376b
  there is a God, 595b
  they're thinking, 895b
  those who, must govern, 354a
  thousands perhaps millions, 458b
  thy swan a crow, 134b
  thy thought, 568a
  too little, 277a
  too little and talk too much, 219b
  town that made feeling, 957a
  upon dangers of the seas, 214a
  we have enow, 220b
  we have thoughts in our head, 817a
  well of him, 763a
  well of oneself, 944a
  what is true, 633b
  what others, of us, 530a
  what thought can, 117b
  what we, fits us for future, 586a
  when I, I must speak, 162a
  while we stop to, 43b
  who dares, one thing, 4b
  with the thoughts of the few, 699a
  young, old men fools, 116b
Thinker, deep, or great ventriloquist, 822b
  new, 811b
  secret isolated joy of the, 709a
Thinkers, best stomachs not best, 325b
  greatest, often amateurs, 784a
Thinketh, as he, in his heart, 1040b
  he standeth, 1061a
  perceive things that he, 1065b
Thinking, a mere pause from, 460b
  curtsey while you're, 658a
  effort of, 698a
  fantastic summer's heat, 138b
  future, must be world-wide, 964a
  God does that, 604b
  high, outcome of fine living, 784a
  how things may be, 338b
  I have not lived in vain, 300a
  in another sense, 697a
  in its lower grades, 784a
  is but an idle waste, 436b
  is coolness and calmness, 604b
  is very rare, 956b
  lays lads underground, 786a
  made, feel, 957a
  madness caused by, 774a
  make people think they're, 895b
  makes it so, 173b

Truth never yet fell dead, 560a
  no escaping into, 994a
  no mask like open, 297b
  no, or goodness dies, 475a
  noonday light and, 587b
  not so popular, 460a
  nothing powerful as, 444a
  nutritive or suggestive, 719a
  obedient to command of, 614a
  object of philosophy, 738a
  of history, 628b
  of imagination, 478a
  of, thou art Son of God, 1053a
  offend my sweet, 892b
  on war's red techstone, 601b
  one being law reason, 68a
  one, is clear, 316b
  opposeth no man's profit, 229a
  or satisfaction of the intellect,
    545a
  patriot, 436b
  peeps over the glass's edge,
    570b
  persons for whom, is poison,
    932b
  petrified, 674a
  philosophy conformable to,
    722a
  possession of, 240a
  possession of the, 283a
  profession of, by each one, 643a
  pure, cannot be assimilated,
    617b
  put to the worse, 251a
  quench'd the open, 415a
  rather than love than money,
    590b
  receives new, as an angel, 437a
  regard for, 849b
  ridicule is the test of, 323b
  search after, 68a
  see the, arrive, 996a
  seeming, 145b
  semblance of, 424b
  serve her in the ranks of, 624b
  severe, 350a
  shadows and symbols into, 496a
  shall be thy shield, 1036a
  shall be thy warrant, 111a
  shall ever come uppermost, 584a
  shall make you free, 1058a
  show of, 158b
  simple, his utmost skill, 213a
  sits upon the lips, 621b
  snap like vixens at the, 935a
  so absolutely good is, 574a
  sole judge of, 317a
  sometimes improbable, 460a
  soul of, in things erroneous,
    614b
  speak a disagreeable, 372a
  speak, and nothing but truth,
    106a
  speak, as much as I dare, 99b
  speak the, 89b, 460a
  speech is, 414a
  spirit of, and of freedom, 641a
  spread the, from pole to pole,
    299a
  stood on one side, 560a
  stood up instead, 569b
  strife of, with falsehood, 599b
  suffers by heat of defenders,
    288a
  swear to the, of a song, 293b
  sweet ornament, doth give, 205b
  takes two to speak the, 588b
  tell the, or trump, 677b
  test of, 710a

Truth, there is no, in him, 1058a
  this, at least we know, 846a
  those blessed strains are telling,
    584a
  though I perish, is so, 595b
  time will teach thee the, 109b
  told with bad intent, 388a
  took for, test of ridicule, 383b
  trick of, 892b
  unbidden, 977b
  understand the, 1065b
  unflattering, 771b
  urge him with, 5b
  using words to convey, 752b
  vantage-ground of, 119b
  verse of, or beauty, 845a
  was felt by instinct, 573b
  well fixed in the minds, 428a
  well of true wit is, 639b
  were he to tell the, 846b
  whatever remains must be the,
    781b
  when in doubt tell the, 678b
  where doubt there, is, 552b
  where is the, we seek, 465b
  which he apprehends, 897b
  white, in simple nakedness,
    554b
  who speaks the, 599b
  whole of, and knowledge, 701a
  will come to light, 82b
  will conquer, 83a
  with gold she weighs, 321b
  with him who sings, 551b
  wither into the, 826a
  within thy mind rehearse, 546b
  write an unpleasant, 761a
  write, on tablet of heart, 617a
  yet friend to, 315a
  you can keep your sterile, 740a
Truthful James, my name is, 687a
  to be, is easy, 885b
Truthfulness, refining of the sense
    of, 885b
Truth-loving Persians, 972b
Truth's a dog must to kennel,
    191a
  ends thou aim'st at, 211b
  sad ashes, 605a
Truths, abstract, are strong meat,
    561a
  all, are half-truths, 797b
  are portions of the soul, 599b
  bear all naked, 483a
  customary fate of new, 634a
  discovery of divine, 304a
  doubts more cruel than, 270a
  eternal, 735a, 920b
  great, begin as blasphemies,
    766a
  hearts believe the, I tell, 351a
  in and out of favor, 879b
  instruments of darkness tells us,
    194b
  irrationally held, 634a
  no whole, 797b
  not for all men, 325a
  old universal, 977a
  precious as the, she reveals,
    856a
  principles the, the history, 582b
  spring of capital, 857a
  that wake, 408b
  to be self-evident, 373a
  verities and, of the heart, 977a
  without world's believing, 373b
Try bravely again, 591b
  end, the man, 153a
  fair adventure, 148b

Try first thyself, 13a
  no certainty until you, 15b
  our fortunes, 153b
  something, 918b
  tempers of men, 57a
  the whole cause, 656a
  times that, men's souls, 370a
  to please and please not, 974b
  tropic for your balm, 971a
  with all my might, 442b
Trying, gone on, 945a
  instrument to perform upon,
    788a
  there's no use, 659a
  to be Greek, 947a
  to sit on two stools, 88a
Tryst so faithful, 864a
Trysted, the wish'd the, hour, 393b
Trysting day, named a, 493b
Tu, et, Brute, 167b
Tub, fling him out an empty, 294b
  must stand upon its bottom,
    274a
  tale of a, 89a
  three men in a, 1019a
Tubal Cain was a man of might,
    584b
  fashioned hand-flung spears,
    584b
Tubes are twisted and dried, 814b
Tubing, lengths of piping or, 736b
Tuckahaw, twist 'em up a high,
    1003b
Tucked, tail, in, 853b
Tucker, little Tommy, 1016a
Tuckt up she a-hunting goes, 231a
Tucson and Deadwood, 979a
Tuesday, christened on, 1018b
  is to be the day, 284b
Tuesday's child, 1018b
Tuffer it goes with us, 594b
Tuffet, sat on a, 1018b
Tufted, high in, trees, 245a
Tug of war, 291a
Tugg'd with fortune, 197b
Tugs and moans, 971b
  in a different way, 460a
Tuileries or the Escurial, 502b
Tulgey wood, whiffling through
    the, 657b
Tumble, another, 489a
  barefooted and bareheaded, 898b
  on heather, 416a
  ready with every nod to, 128a
Tumbler, clean, and a corkscrew,
    577a
  pouter, and fantail, 530b
Tumbling, Jill came, after, 1016b
Tumor that ends by killing, 696b
Tumors of a troubl'd mind, 12b
Tumult and the shouting, 816a
  in the clouds, 826a
  of the soul, 411b
  of thy mighty harmonies, 466a
  stilled the rising, 808a
  there was, in the city, 625a
Tumultuous privacy of storm,
    503b
Tune, all the, that he could play,
    1017b
  dancers dancing in, 554a
  earth if it be in, 600a
  enough breath for the whole,
    788a
  incapable of a, 429b
  instrument here at door, 217b
  keep in, so long, 303a
  loveliest, becomes vulgar, 739b
  new piano's, 813a

Two strong men stand face to
face, 814a
styles of portrait painting, 576b
takes, to speak the truth, 588b
things at once, 43a
things believed of any man,
847a
things excite us to love, 105a
things people desire, 63a
things stand like stone, 661b
things they disliked, do, 875a
things to aim at, 822b
thy, breasts, 1044b
towers of sail, 595a
tragedies in this world, 768b
trick worth, 150a
twice, be not four, 594b
unbodied essences, 262b
vast and trunkless legs, 465a
walking apart forever, 612b
ways of spreading light, 804a
ways out iv an argymint, 836a
weak evils, 161a
went to pray, 263a
when the clock strikes, 686b
where, or three are gathered,
1053b
who love are parted, 486a
witnesses, testimony of, 376a
words im-possible, 916a
words wait and hope, 496b
world knows only, 218b
worlds, wandering between,
621b
worth, in the box, 835a
worth, in the bush, 11a
years ten years, 898a
young roes, 1044b
Two-and-seventy jarring sects,
532b
stenches, 425a
Two-and-twenty, and I am, 785b
Two-eared crock, 38a
Two-edged sword, 1038b
Two-gun man, 935b
Two-handed engine, 249b
Two-legg'd, unfeather'd, thing,
276b
Two-legged animal without feathers, 72a
Twopence a week, 658b
colored, 752a
Twopenny damn, 400b
Tyger's hart in player's hide,
126a
Tying her bonnet under her chin,
66oa
Tyme fleeth, 81b
that may not sojourne, 77b
ylost not recovered, 78b
Tyne coal road-rail pig-lead, 896b
Type, careful of the, she seems,
552b
I am, 812b
noble, of good, 524a
nowhere existing, 615a
of all her race, 558a
Types, device of movable, 473b
reproduction of formal, 767b
Typewriting machine, 897b
Typical American breast, 718a
essayist, 793b
literary product a refined essay,
908b
Tyrannical principle, 538b
the habit of reading, 603b
Tyrannies on human kind, 279a
shams and inequalities, 679b
whom, hath slain, 217b

Tyrannize another day, 231b
Tyrannous and rough in proof,
134b
to use it like a giant, 184b
Tyranny and oppressions of body,
375b
begins, 335a
eternal hostility against, 374a
Frederick without his, 660a
is a habit, 618a
like hell, 370a
may always enter, 611b
Nazi, 870b
of facts, 795b
of Mrs. Grundy, 614b
of political assemblies, 515b
reliance against, 538a
short-lived, 71a
snuff the approach of, 360a
taxation without representation
is, 353a
Tyranny's disease, 12b
ecclesiastic, worst plague, 291b
Tyrant, any excuse will serve a,
9b
by, fate on victim thrust, 615b
custom, 103a
disappear for ever in the, 618a
disposed of foreign enemies,
25a
fear that reigns with the, 522b
first cunning, 538a
force beget the greater, 640a
if you are a, 895a
impassive-faced, 773a
like intemperance, 517a
of his fields, 348b
public opinion is a weak, 589b
springs, root from which, 25a
threatening, 39a
Tyrant's plea, necessity the, 45a,
255b
Tyrants and slaves, 355a
blood of patriots and, 374a
fall in every foe, 394a
from policy, 361a
give no quarter to, 517a
hand unfriendly to, 271b
necessity the argument of, 255b
rebellion to, 1002b
safely govern home, 126b
scepter from, 330b
Sicilian, 41a
thus ever to, 1010b
watered by the blood of, 384a
Tyre, Nineveh and, 816a

Ubi saeva indignatio, 297a
Ubiquitous press, 565b
Ucalegon, Melchizedek, 846a
Uffish thought, 657b
Uglier yet is the hump we get,
820a
Ugliest of trades, 509b
Uglification and derision, 657a
Ugliness, success hides all, 261b
Ugly age and feeble impotence,
899b
as sin, 616a
fact, death is the, 650b
indisputably, 323b
sights, full of, 127b
sights of death, 128a
toad, and venomous, 159b
why wasn't I born old and,
577b
yahoo tricks, 902b
Ultimate and sacred thing, 866b
extinction, course of, 537b

Ultimate good desired, 710a
justice of the people, 539a
powers of the society, 375b
Ultimum moriens of respectability,
536a
Ulysses' absence, yarn spun in,
202a
Umbered face, 155b
Umble, not only humble but, 579a
person, 579a
pie, 579b
Umbrella is of no avail, 603a
Umbris et imaginibus, 496a
Umpire, kind, of miseries, 124b
Unaccommodated man, 192a
Unaccustomed to fear, 1005a
Unacknowledged legislators of the
world, 469a
Unacquainted, not, with sorrow,
37a
with our own soul, 213b
with the A.B.C., 410a
Unadorn'd, adorn'd the most,
256a, 328a
Unadvertised, leave the work,
709b
Unafraid, gentlemen, 814b
Unalienable, certain, rights, 373a
Unalloyed, bliss, for none, 615a
Unalterable days, nor mourn the,
506b
determination, 443a
law, 943a
law, army of, 639a
Unaltered, laws ought not to re-
main, 26a
Unaneled, unhousel'd disap-
pointed, 172b
Unanimity, feel their way to-
wards, 812a
Unanimous chorus of praise, 844a
Unapprehended inspiration, 468b
Unapproachable in the White
House, 925a
Unarm Eros, 201b
Unarmed, being, brings evils, 85b
Unassisted merit advances slowly,
335b
Unassuming commonplace of na-
ture, 407b
Unattached, primitive, state, 882a
relatives, vagaries of, 966a
Unattainable perfection, pursuit
of, 823a
Unattained, how vast the, 552b
Unattempted, things, yet, 252a
Unavailing star, life on this,
823a
Unavoidable and imminent death,
794a
conflict is, 850b
Unavenged, insults, 410b
Unaware, blessed them, 422a
of proverbs, 956b
Unawares, entertained angels,
1063b
morality expires, 322a
spoken some mischievous thing,
59b
Unaw'd by influence, 436b
Unbaptized infants, 705a
Unbarr'd gates of light, 256b
Unbearable for the enemy, 905b
Unbegotten souls, work through,
720b
Unbeguiled I saw the snare, 546b
Unbehoving, behoving and, 519a
Unbelief, fearful, 474a
help thou mine, 1056a

Weary leagues two hearts divide, 729a
  life, grunt and sweat under, 174b
  life, wheels of, 276b
  life's, way, 810b
  lips I close, 350a
  listlessness, 290a
  of breath, 489a
  of days and hours, 694a
  of the chill companionship, 947b
  of the existing government, 539a
  of thinking, 673a
  of watching earth, 649b
  people, sunless pleasures of, 701b
  pilgrimage, 232a, 342b
  pondered weak and, 544b
  ragged and, and swarthy, 793b
  rich and, 233b
  run and not be, 1047a
  search to find bliss, 354a
  stale flat and unprofitable, 170b
  warld, 791b
  warld to rest are gone, 380a
  way, through mony a, 487a
  way, trudgin' my, 731b
  wayworn wanderer, 543b
  weight is lightened, 403b
  wi' hunting, 1013a
  with age and travel, 264a
  with disasters, 197b
  world is, of the past, 467a
  years decline from it, 761b
Weasel, it is like a, 176a
  pop goes the, 1004a
  sucks eggs, 160a
Weasels bats and ferrets, 262a
Weather, always fair, 808b
  Austerlitz, 558b
  bitter, 593a
  blue unclouded, 547b
  brook the, 133a
  campaigning, 981a
  chronic anxiety about the, 688b
  different kinds of, 675b
  dominions of westerly, 773a
  dreadful hot, 427b
  English, in his heart, 807a
  eyes blue to any, 947a
  God sorts out the, 745b
  God's own chosen, 742a
  how the, was, 983b
  hunger and war and, 781b
  inner, 881a
  is a literary speciality, 677b
  is thrust upon us, 802a
  less, than when I was a boy, 975a
  may make heavy, 957a
  nature of foul, 229a
  New England, 675a
  no such thing as bad, 775a
  October's bright blue, 652b
  pipe to smoke in cold, 377b
  prove fair, 261b
  sad or singing, 693a
  sharp be the, 416a
  that would sink them, 991b
  things and, taken together, 503b
  through pleasant and cloudy, 372b
  trying to get behind the, 772b
  under this window in stormy, 296a
  warm, when one's in bed, 295a
  why the, alters so, 863b
  will be dry, 803a

Weather, winter and rough, 160a
  without, 563b
Weathercock of the church steeple, 369b
  on a steeple, 132a
Weather'd every rack, 610a
Weathered the storm, 401a
Weather-glass is set at alas, 993b
Weave a circle round him, 420b
  blissful dreams of long ago, 698b
  me a spell, 788b
  nets to catch the wind, 226a
  no more silks, 597b
  robes ye, another wears, 466a
  the sunlight, 943a
  the warp, 349b
  their shadows overhead, 803b
  their thread with bones, 164b
  with colors all our own, 527a
Weaver's shuttle, 1030a
Weaves one music, 735b
Weaving and unweaving, 596a
  the web of days, 693b
  what are you, 711a
Web of frail delight, 866a
  of loveliness, 866a
  of our life, 183a
  she left the, 547b
  tangled, we weave, 414b
  weaving the, of days, 693b
Web's centre, confin'd in her, 102b
Webs from their own entrails, 102b
  of more than common size, 362a
  trafficked for strange, 701b
Webster, Daniel, a steam-engine, 419a
  eloquence of Mr., 980a
  much possessed by death, 943b
  word liberty in mouth of Mr., 504b
Wed, December when they, 162b
  in leisure, 130a
  the fair Ellen, 414b
  with this ring I thee, 1069a
  wooed not, 569a
Wedded fast to falsehood, 441a
  love, hail, 256a
  maid and virgin mother, 244a
  to calamity, 137a
  to him not through union, 845a
Wedding day, dance barefoot on, 130a
  in the church, 285a
  is destiny, 91a
  man looks small at a, 978b
Wedding-day is absolutely fixed on, 333b
Wedding-gown, chose my wife as she her, 354b
Wedding-guest stood still, 421a
Wedding-ring, small circle of a, 298b
Weder for to slepen inne, 78b
Weders, wintres, overshake, 78a
Wedge, tough, 45b
Wedged in that timber, 283b
Wedlock compared to public feasts, 100a
  forced a hell, 124b
Wedlock-treachery, 260b
Wednesday, he that died o', 151b
  loved you, 519a
  married on, 1018b
Wednesday's child, 1018b
Wee doch-an'-dorris, 850a
  modest crimson-tipp'd, 391a
  sleekit cowrin beastie, 390a

Wee unimportant things, 987a
  Willie Winkie, 559a
Weed, dull and flowerless, 526b
  duller than the fat, 172b
  found itself a, 860a
  heart like that delicate, 653a
  is a flower in disguise, 508b
  is but an unloved flower, 508b
  law ought to, it out, 119b
  pernicious, 363a
  salt, sways in the stream, 619b
  sworn to, and pluck, 139a
  that grows beside thy door, 812b
  that grows in every soil, 360b
  tobacco is a dirty, 975a
  votarist in palmer's, 247a
  what is a, 508b
  whiskers of, 904a
  who art so lovely fair, 189b
Weede, ill, growth fast, 92b
Weeds are shallow-rooted, 125a
  let them not pass like, 441b
  noisome, 140a
  now grown over with, 353a
  of the river, 898b
  sleep beneath these, 845a
  smell worse than, 206a
  winter, outworn, 467a
  wiped away the, and foam, 503a
Week, argument for, 150a
  eighth day of the, 777b
  food enough for a, 904a
  from once a day to once a, 577a
  of all the days in the, 307b
  of passionate humility, 718a
  Thursday come and, is gone, 234b
  tried all, to be good, 398b
  twopence a, 658b
  was seven domes, 972a
Weekend, rhythm of the, 974b
Weekly from Southampton, 819b
Week's, good, labour, 214b
Weeks, six, to frost, 957b
Weep a people inurned, 493a
  all around thee, 377b
  and you weep alone, 754a
  at joy, 157a
  away the life of care, 465a
  awhile if ye are fain, 655a
  but never see, 431b
  clasp hands and, 486a
  death makes men, 459b
  do nothing but, 49b
  for Adonais, 777b
  for their sins, 608a
  I, for you, 658b
  if you wish me to, 362a
  little sorrows sit and, 386a
  made them and myself, 284b
  make angels, 184b
  men that laugh and, 694a
  no more, 478b
  no more my lady, 636a
  no more nor sigh, 224b
  not for me, 495b
  not for the silent dead, 397a
  now or never more, 544a
  on, 437b
  she must, or she will die, 550b
  some, because they part, 680b
  stricken deer go, 176a
  strive nor, 568a
  tears such as angels, 253a
  therefore must we, and wail, 748b
  thy girlish tears, 780b
  time to, 1042b

White, black spirits and, 214b
　boards, coffin out of the, 856b
　bosoms of actresses, 339a
　bread and butter, 1016a
　bread, some gave them, 1015a
　breast, sparkling cross on her,
　　312a
　candle in a holy place, 912b
　canoe, paddles her, 437b
　chameleon cannot appear, 54a
　cheeks were so red and so, 599a
　church above thin trees, 875a
　circles of delight, 984a
　clear white inside, 818a
　cliffs of Dover, 876a
　curd of ass's milk, 319a
　dipping sails, 896a
　fire laden, 466b
　flannel trousers, 943a
　flesh tinder, 947a
　flower of a blameless life, 554a
　foam flew, 421b
　Gilbert, discovered the formula,
　　806a
　great steamers, and gold, 819b
　great, way, 1007b
　hairs, comes sooner by, 143b
　hairs ill become fool, 154a
　horse, fine lady upon a, 1017b
　House, unapproachable in, 925a
　if snow be, 207b
　in, in black in green, 1000a
　is for purity, 563b
　man, appeal to any, 352b
　man, marry any sort of, 562a
　man's burden, 817a, 833b
　moon beams, 952a
　my soul is, 385a
　nights all an' still, 601a
　nor grew it, 456a
　nose, three white feet and a,
　　1006b
　officers cast in their lot, 666a
　one black the other, 260b
　one, foot, 1006b
　or black stone, 107b
　pair that once was, 534b
　people, degrading classes of,
　　537a
　plates and cups, 938b
　plume and a green lance, 976a
　plume shine, 491b
　pure celestial, 476b
　quality talk, 946b
　radiance of eternity, 468b
　raiment, as snow, 1055b
　read'st black where I read, 388b
　rose breathes of love, 729b
　rose is a dove, 729b
　roses and, lilies blow, 220b
　sail's shaking, 895b
　sails, as white can be, 740a
　sails crowding, 721a
　sails still fly seaward, 944b
　seas do show, 226a
　sewing her long, seam, 612b
　shall not neutralize black, 574a
　she keeps them, 736a
　silence below, 934a
　silence, thunders of, 519a
　silken turbans, 259b
　singing hour of peace, 929a
　slaves, half-a-hundred, 780b
　so very white, 401a
　sullen, surf, 604b
　their, stays for ever, 703b
　then melts forever, 393b
　three, leopards, 944b
　too, for hell, 279a

White truth in simple nakedness,
　554b
　warned off, House grounds, 837a
　wench's black eye, 136a
　wild horses play, 619b
Whited sepulchres, 1054a
Whiteness, angel, 158b
　pearls are not equal in, 635a
Whiter grows the foam, 721a
　swans seem, 102a
　than snow, 1034b
　than the driven snow, 347a
Whites of their eyes, 353a
Whitest blanket wraps him in ice,
　485b
　old linen wash, 119a
White-walled tent, 969b
　town, one last look at the, 619b
Whitewash, bucket of, 674b
Whitewash'd wall the sanded floor,
　356b
Whither every coffin asks us, 662b
　goest thou, 1058b
　O splendid ship, 721a
　thou goest, 1027a
　whence and, give no rest, 781a
Whithersoever thou goest, 1026a
Whiting to a snail, 656a
Whitman and Melville, 973a
Whitman's poems, 973a
Whittington Lord Mayor of Lon-
　don, 999b
Whittled out of hickory sticks,
　974a
Who are you I'm nobody, 646a
　how and where and, 819b
　killed Cock Robin, 1016a
　killed John Keats, 1816a
　knows the thoughts of a child,
　　660a
　lives it safely anywhere, 963a
　loses who wins who's in, 193b
　or why or which or what, 581b
　says it what he says, 700b
　thought of the lilac, 934a
Whoe'er thou art, 326a
Whole and every grain of sand,
　618a
　animate the, 419b
　armour of God, 1062b
　better had I stol'n the, 751a
　book, does not say in a, 728a
　cannot grasp at a, 429a
　course of love, 186a
　creation, up and down the, 636a
　dies when the heart is, 961a
　duty of man, 1044a
　dwarfish, 423a
　earth is full of glory, 1045b
　entire and, and perfect, 789a
　half exceeds the, 7a
　head is sick, 1045a
　heart, with my, 1048b
　I am equal and, 694b
　in faith, 84a
　judge, piece by pattern, 718b
　makes His beautiful, 734a
　new life, you sell him a, 956b
　of truth and knowledge, 701a
　one beautiful perfect, 655b
　parts of one stupendous, 316b
　saw life steadily and, 619a
　skin, come off with a, 104b
　soul, with my, 1048b
　they that be, 1052a
　'tis not the, of life to live, 413a
　tribe of fops, 190b
　truths, 797b
　vocation were imitation, 408b

Whole wit in a jest, 228a
　world in state of chassis, 928a
　world kin, 182a
　world, love the, 618b
Wholeness of the human problem,
　883a
Wholesale borrowers, 562b
Wholesome flowers, 140a
　for the body, 243b
　nights are, 170a
　restraint, 445a
　to digest, 714a
　wold, deer to the, 815a
Wholesomest, old wine, 119a
Wholly, heartily and, laughed,
　473b
Whom should I knock, 130a
　to, you speak, 737a
Whooping, out of all, 162a
Whore, pity she's a, 228b
　tarnish, and thief, 804b
Whore's oath, 192b
Whores artists saints and wives,
　996a
　were burnt alive, 293b
Whoring, other folks', 931a
Whorlèd ear, 724b
Who's master who's man, 297a
　Who in America, 960a
Whoso says in his heart, 344a
Whosoever believeth in him, 1058a
Why and wherefore, folly asks,
　499b
　and wherefore in all things,
　　156b
　every, hath a wherefore, 129a
　moving, they do it, 391b
　or wherefore, 51a
　questions of, and whence, 833a
　should I today repine, 798a
　the, is plain, 160b
　the weather alters so, 863b
　things are as they are, 722a
　what and, and when, 819b
　why why, 917a
Wicked are wicked no doubt, 566a
　cease from troubling, 1030a
　contemplating, act, 63a
　extremely, all at once, 62b
　fire of lust, 81a
　flee when no man pursueth,
　　1041b
　forsake his way, 1047b
　have done some, thing, 71b
　heart deceitful and, 1048a
　in great power, 1034a
　I's mighty, 563a
　man Hitler, 869b
　men from out thee go, 267b
　mercies of, are cruel, 1039a
　name of the, shall rot, 1039a
　no peace unto the, 1047a
　not that men are, 840b
　or charitable intents, 172a
　people, dead bodies or, 967b
　persons, Philip betwixt two, 59a
　punishin' th', 836a
　righteous and the, 1043a
　something, this way comes, 198a
　too, for a smile, 423a
　war regarded as, 767b
　wight, 262a
　will betrayed and baffled, 689b
　world, vanity of this, 1069a
　worldliness, 585b
　would the, be so bad, 703b
Wickedness about Covent Garden,
　429a
　be sweet in his mouth, 1031a

Wild, malign and, 76b
  moor, 1003a
  native wood-notes, 245b
  New England shore, 470a
  oats, sow our spiritual, 671b
  oats will get sown, 830b
  of soul, 981a
  pigeon, 940b
  piping down the valleys, 385a
  regrets and bloody sweats, 769b
  religion without creeds, 879a
  revenge is, justice, 119b
  rose-briar, 591b
  sanctuary, within a, 873a
  sea-banks, 147a
  spirit moving everywhere, 466a
  spring air, 911a
  surmise, look'd with, 477b
  thing sorry for itself, 931a
  things, den of, 854a
  thyme blows, 141b
  tongues that have not thee in
    awe, 816a
  uproar, sun sand and, 503a
  vicissitudes of taste, 335b
  waves reach their hands, 674a
  waves saying, what are the,
    582b
  waves whist, 209a
  tail, waving his, 820a
  west wind, 466a
  wet, woods, 820a
  whistling blackbirds, 392b
  white horses play, 619b
  wind blows, 592a
  wind sweep, 470a
  witches, 826b
  with all regret, 550b
  with leaves, 934a
  words ought to be a little, 925b
  young scamp, 853a
Wild-blazing grog-shop, 487a
Wild-cats in your kitchens, 187a
  whip his weight in, 746b
Wilderness, crying in the, 1050a
  first flower of their, 463b
  forth to the, 898a
  highway in the, 753a
  if the world's a, 630b
  in the, a lodging-place, 454b,
    1048a
  lodge in some vast, 364a
  man in the, 1015b
  man is never alone in a, 63b
  oceans mingling with the sky,
    628a
  of human flesh, 796a
  of monkeys, 145a
  of sweets, 256b
  of this world, 274a
  other side of the, 784a
  perish in this, 229b
  savage, into a glorious empire,
    360b
  scapegoat into the, 1025a
  seek a barren, 652b
  send choice grain into this, 281b
  singing in the, 531b
  to this, we bring, 490a
  voice that crieth in the, 1046b
  wander in the, 1025b
  went into the, 808b
  were paradise enow, 531b
Wildernesses, shores and desert,
  247a
Wildest blow, contempt for the,
  714b
  eddies and tangles, 690a
  freedom, not restraint but, 501b

Wildest peal for years, 854a
Wild-fire dances on the fen, 395b
Wild-goose chase, 105a
  run the, chase, 136a
Wildly striking sometimes a
  friend, 232b
Wilds, her waters her woods her,
  460b
Wile, evil habit's earliest, 464a
  follow'd with endearing, 356a
  gather gear by ev'ry, 391a
Wiles, by crooked, 13b
  cranks and wanton, 245a
  of the stranger, 990a
  simple, 409a
Wilhelmine, grandchild, 426b
Will, a woman, or won't, 307a
  across the sky in stars, 946a
  and intellect are same, 281b
  as God wills, 371b
  be firmly bent, 893b
  be there a, 383b
  betrayed and baffled, 689b
  boy's, 523b
  broad-based upon her people's,
    553a
  city obedient to his, 24b
  committed to the, of God, 229b
  complies against his, 239b
  conviction and, to carry on,
    952b
  diligence and strength of, 598b
  fanatical, power, 951b
  flaw in a donkey's, 535b
  foreknowledge, and fate, 254a
  freedom of the, 77a
  God's, be done, 371b
  good, for the deed, 89a
  good or ill lies within, 64a
  has woven with absent heed,
    705b
  heav'n's hand or, 251b
  Honeycomb, 302a
  if the, of man were free, 642b
  immanent, and its designs, 705b
  in, threat or promise dwells,
    1005b
  into appetite, 181a
  knowing that we do Thy,
    87b
  laid me down with a, 751a
  last, and testament, 776b
  leads the, to desperate under-
    takings, 173a
  left free the human, 321a
  live by one man's, 112a
  lived at your single, 819b
  lose the power to, 583b
  my poverty not my, 137b
  necessity and free, 473b
  not as I, 1055a
  not when he may, 91a
  nothing good save in the, 65a
  of majority of the people, 921a
  of the Yukon, 877a
  opinions and a, 597b
  our, that enchains us, 465b
  peace in His, 944b
  power into, 181a
  predestined of the, 884b
  puzzles the, 174b
  reason panders, 177a
  serveth not another's, 213a
  set the, on fire, 897a
  settling the moral, 696a
  sister calls me, 747b
  teach me to do thy, 1038a
  Thy, be done, 241a

Will, Thy, be done in earth,
  1051a
  Thy, not mine be done, 515b
  to do the soul to dare, 415a
  to fashion as we feel, 915b
  tool that did his, 712b
  unconquerable, 252a
  unconquerable, of occupied ter-
    ritories, 870b
  undisappointed, 64b
  unless to thought is added, 507a
  was strong, 1014b
  without the, to win, 907b
  woman's cold perverted, 469b
  women's love and men's, 216a
  you won't you join the dance,
    657a
Willas, in the spring the, cather,
  977b
Willed, little wife well, 377b
Willer, fat ole weepin', 886b
Willful crime, banished for my,
  259a
  men, little group of, 770b
  thorns, rosebud set with, 550a
  waste, 442b
Willful-wavier meal-drift moulded,
  724b
William, father calls me, 747b
  you are old Father, 426a, 656a
Willie, mother calls me, 747b
  Winkie, wee, 559a
Willin', Barkis is, 579a
Willing faithfully to serve it, 237b
  hart, 91b
  in day of thy power, 1037a
  suspension of disbelief, 424b
  to die, 16b
  to wound, 319a
Willingly, not, let it die, 250a
Willingness is great, 85b
Willow in her hand, 146b
  pattern, 525b
  sing, 190a
  sing all a green, 189b
  titwillow, 685a
  under the, the Gray, 637b
  underneath the abject, 993b
  willow waly, 683a
Willow-cabin at your gate, 164a
Willows, hanged our harps upon
  the, 1038a
  southern, 366a
  tearful, 662a
  whiten aspens quiver, 547b
Willow-tree, weeping, 1004b
Willowy brook that turns a mill,
  396b
Wills and bodies sold to state,
  946a
  are gardeners, 186b
  burn out human, 897a
  choose executors and talk of,
    139b
  if an endless sleep He, 633a
  Juliet, it so, 137a
  nature, death, 68b
Willy, leave the lady, 829a
Wilson could write notes, 925a
Wimpled whining purblind boy,
  133a
Wimpling wing, 724a
Win, aid me for to, her, 857a
  all I fail of, 528a
  friends and influence people,
    642b
  glorious triumphs, 778b
  kindness shall, my love, 130b
  know how to, 31a

Wisdom never dwelt below, 286b
  never lies, 5b
  no human, can calculate, 371a
  no joy even in beautiful, 9a
  nor, in the grave, 1043a
  nor much their, teaches, 549a
  of a just content, 654a
  of human contrivances, 360a
  of its framers, 812a
  of mankind creeps slowly, 509a
  of many, 1007a
  of our ancestors, 359a, 578a
  of our sages, 374b
  of tomorrow, 743a
  or its fairest flower, 509a
  part not dependent on, 772a
  pessimism is name given to,
    976b
  pray for, and guidance, 625b
  pray for, yet, 645a
  prime, 257b
  Raphael paints, 507b
  that will never die, 669b
  the mirrored shield, 468a
  therefore get, 1038b
  to be only wise, 806b
  to be silent, 58a
  to believe the heart, 806b
  to love to live, 812b
  too full of, 845a
  unerring, never dwelt below,
    286b
  wealth of mankind is, 729b
  what, can you find, 344b
  where love and, dwell, 583a
  whose lessons, 333a
  will repudiate thee, 722a
  wiser turn a larger, lends, 643b
  with the ancient is, 1030b
  world is governed with little,
    227b
  wrath of lion is, of God, 386a
Wisdom's aid, 351b
  part, 330a
  school, 214b
  self seeks solitude, 247b
Wise, absolute strong and, 816b
  all things, and wonderful, 591b
  amazed temperate furious, 197a
  among fools, 52b
  among women, 692a
  and frugal government, 374b
  and good men, 471b
  and good, must first be, 251a
  and lovely, 962b
  and masterly inactivity, 397b
  and pious patience, 543a
  and salutary neglect, 359b
  and understanding heart, 1028a
  and virtuous man, 57a
  are never without friends, 1003a
  arts in which the, excel, 289b
  as a serpent, 829a
  as serpents, 124a, 1052b
  at fifty, 234a
  be, soar not too high, 226b
  be, today, 298a
  be, with speed, 305a
  beacon of the, 181b
  become, from contemplation,
    805b
  bids fair to grow, 45b
  bitter grave or over, 825a
  book but a blast from the lungs,
    949b
  both true both, 267a
  by nature, 226a
  coffee makes the politician, 312b
  confound the, 1060b

Wise, consider her ways and be,
    1038b
  country so virtuous and, 783a
  crack that knows its father,
    959b
  darkly, and rudely great, 316b
  days that make us happy make
    us, 896b
  defer not till tomorrow to be,
    298a
  enough to keep own counsel,
    106a
  enough to play the fool, 165a
  fair-spoken, 212a
  father knows own child, 144b
  five of them were, 1054b
  folly to be, 347b
  fool doth think he is, 163a
  fool is counted, 1040a
  for cure on exercise depend,
    280b
  gamester, 16b
  God make our blunders, 903a
  good to be merie and, 90b
  government, 343b
  great men not always, 1031b
  guid to be merry and, 394b
  he who thinks himself, 326a
  healthy wealthy and, 330b
  histories make men, 121b
  I'm growing, 587b
  in show, 251a
  in the foreboding of evil, 12b
  in the use of his pronouns, 699a
  in their own craftiness, 1030a
  in their own eyes, 351a
  in your own conceits, 1060a
  learn from foes, 23b
  little, the best fools be, 215b
  love and be, 43a
  love that's, 846b
  man, died like a, 110a
  man does not try to hurry, 986b
  man even, fool and, 109b
  man have little influence, 19b
  man, how dieth the, 1042a
  man, hundred fools do not
    make, 951a
  man is strong, 118a, 1040b
  man knows himself a fool, 163a
  man never loses anything, 98b
  man never refuses, 45a
  man, rebuke a, 1039a
  man say, heard a, 785b
  man to discover, 72b
  man utter vain knowledge,
    1030b
  man who lets contest fall, 18a
  man's eyes, 1042a
  man's son, every, 164a
  man's task, 64a
  man's verdict, 571a
  men as silly and as, 541b
  men, beacons of, 633b
  men from the east, 1050a
  men have little foolery, 159a
  men, not the part of, 62a
  men, precedents established by,
    433b
  men profited by fools, 55a
  men, prophecy of, 463a
  men refrain to meddle, 86a
  men say nothing, 227b
  men, speech given to, 286b
  men's counters, 228b
  more, when he had a pen, 342b
  never was so, a man. 524b
  no, man quit a certainty, 337a
  not, to let friendship die, 342b

Wise, not to the, the light, 757a
  not wisdom to be only, 806b
  old and, 936b
  old and crafty and, 825a
  old bird, 876b
  old owl, 876b
  one, nor ever does a, 289a
  ones, gifts of the, 829b
  passiveness, 403b
  pause from learning to be, 336a
  penny, pound foolish, 221b
  person and a fool, 31b
  philanthropists, 509a
  reputed, 143a
  safeguard known to the, 380a
  saws, 161b
  scepticism, 602b
  seeing ye yourselves are, 850a
  seem foolish among the, 52b
  so young never live long, 128a
  son maketh a glad father,
    1039a
  spirits of, 153a
  stand to your work and be,
    815a
  statesmen foresee, 700a
  strong, foolish, 777b
  teach a monarch to be, 348a
  the reverend head, 303a
  though a man be, 14a
  three, men of Gotham, 1016b
  through time, 4a
  thrush, that's the, 568b
  to be, and love, 182a
  to be swift is less than to be,
    5b
  to be the wealthy, 25b
  to learn, 588a
  to, man ports and happy havens,
    138a
  to resolve, 6a
  too, to be a dogmatist, 496a
  very coldly, 928b
  what leisure to grow, 621b
  who knows that he knows is,
    754b
  who soar, 412a
  woman never yields, 447a
  wondrous, 1020b
  word to the, 109a, 331a
  words of, are goads, 1044a
  words taught in numbers, 114a
  worldly, 231b
  wretch, 314b
  ye yourselves are, 1062a
  you're sure to be, 440b
Wisely, act, on the thing appre-
    hended, 797b
  and slow, 136a
  loved not, but too well, 190b
  thrown away, 336b
  who reasons, not therefore wise,
    314a
  worldly, 231b
Wiser being good than bad, 573a
  cannot be, than the people,
    987a
  French, than they seem, 121a
  grow, and better, 275a
  in his own conceit, 1041a
  in their generation, 1057a
  left me none the, 907a
  man, instruct a, 49a
  man, sadder and a, 422b
  no man, for learning, 227b
  no. than a daw, 124b
  Satan now is. 315a
  second thoughts are, 17b
  sorry you are, 945b

Worm a mere nothing, 329b
  bud bit with envious, 134a
  cannot make a, 99a
  feeble, of the earth, 272b
  feed sweetly on him, 1031a
  he stiffened, 640a
  i' the bud, 164b
  invisible, 387a
  its hero the conqueror, 544b
  man that is a, 1031a
  man to a, 714a
  mounts through all the spires of
    form, 506a
  no god dare wrong a, 506b
  or beetle drought or tempest,
    731a
  that hath eat of a king, 177b
  the canker and the grief, 461a
  thou art my mother, 1030b
  to a toad, 714a
  tough, in your little inside, 685a
  want to be a, 794a
  will turn, 107a
Worms and shrouds, 477b
  banqueter on, 772a
  destroy this body, 1031a
  devils in, 86b
  eaten men not for love, 162b
  enough, 854a
  flies, and flowers exceed me,
    302b
  life of the very, 633a
  most exclusive, 966b
  of Nile, 204a
  talk of graves, epitaphs, 139b
  tasted two, 730a
  try preserved virginity, 269a
  vilest, 205b
Worm's-eye point of view, 986a
Wormwood, bitter as, 1038b
  feed them with, 1048a
Worn, fancies sooner lost and,
    164b
  him to the bones, 137b
  old and, with usage, 650a
  out and old, 825a
  out, being thoroughly, 765a
  out or broken with service, 55a
  out with eating time, 276b
  ring so, as you behold, 384a
Worn-out soil, same, 513b
  word, alone that, 510b
Worried and fretted, 557b
  hurried and, until buried, 892a
  the cat, 1020b
Worries me to beat the band, 914a
Worry, i should, and fret, 894b
  over trivial things, 914a
  the interest paid, 904a
  two days I never, 722a
Worrying society, 445b
  what's the use of, 906b
Worse, all the, for the fishes, 536b
  appear the better reason, 70b,
    253b
  bad ones bring about, 344a
  better hap to, 118a
  boundless better boundless, 546b
  confusion, confounded, 254b
  gone further and fared, 93b
  greater feeling to, 138b
  he can't be, 835b
  know for better or, 893b
  little, than a man, 143b
  make fault, 148b
  makes the man no, 67a
  nobody one penny the, 451b
  none the, nor the better, 67a
  not much, for wear, 364a

Worse off than yourself, 9b
  on Friday, 1018b
  pen, than the sword, 222b
  shod than shoemaker's wife, 93a
  sometimes a great deal, 107b
  than being talked about, 768a
  than grandsires' age, 39a
  than I was last month, 284b
  than the disease, 44a
  the better the day, the, deed,
    214a
  they change for, 116b
  things in life, 146a
  things waiting for men, 692b
  truth put to the, 251a
  what must be, 355a
  woman goes by the, 260a
Worser ills to face, 808b
Worship, come to, him, 1050a
  duty to, the sun, 700a
  every one's true, 23b
  freedom to, God, 470a, 920b
  gods of the place, 224a
  gods with fruits, 12b
  her by years of golden deeds,
    555a
  in beauty of holiness, 1033b
  in the Roman world, 369a
  justice is the only, 662b
  knew how to, a woman, 690a
  of quantity, 863b
  of the world, 467a
  of vanity, 948a
  stated calls to, 337b
  that which ye worship, 1070b
  to the garish sun, 136b
  too fair to, 463b
  wonder is the basis of, 473b
  your, is your furnaces, 866a
Worshipp'd, angels, be, 216a
  sun, 134a
Worshipped fire only, 264a
  God not, by the herd, 897b
  in a tuneful carol, 979a
  rising sun, 56a
Worshipper, nature mourns her,
    413b
  wiser the silent, 669b
Worshippers, dies among his, 471b
  gain her, 933a
  suffer'st more than thy, 156a
Worship'st at temple's inner
    shrine, 407a
Worshipt stocks and stones, 251b
Worst, afeard to hear, 148b
  and best are both inclined, 935a
  best and, of this is, 694b
  best is like the, 818b
  bottom of the, 181b
  cliques consist of one man, 766b
  come to the, 104b
  darn stuff I've seen, 975b
  death is not the, 15a
  do your, 870b
  fear the, oft cures, 181b
  friend and enemy is death, 938b
  full of passionate intensity,
    826b
  furnished, 89b
  his, he kept, 549b
  is better than none, 338b
  is death, 139b
  is yet to come, 555b, 830a
  kind, ferments of the, 306b
  knew the, too young, 819a
  life inflicts its, 654b
  like to be told the, 870a
  men give the best advice, 586b
  more cruel than, of truths, 270a

Worst of all frauds, 586a
  of crimes is poverty, 765b
  of madmen, 320b
  of the city's infamy, 845b
  of the company, 295a
  of thoughts worst of words,
    188a
  of times, 580a
  of tyrannies on human kind,
    279a
  part of an eminent man's con-
    versation, 510b
  pursue the, 42b
  sin towards fellow creatures,
    764b
  so much good in the, of us,
    711b
  sure rivals are the, 293a
  thing about him, 184a
  thing you can do to, author,
    342a
  things, 974b
  things at the, will cease, 198b
  things present, 153a
  this is the, 192b
  tomorrow do thy, 39b, 278a
  treason has done his, 197b
  use a man could be put to,
    213b
  way to improve the world, 586a
  what began best can't end, 573a
  when he is, 143b
Worsted, though right were, 575b
Worst-humour'd muse, 289a
Worst-natured muse, 289a
Worth a month in town, 649b
  all these toils, 35a
  and choice of friends, 218a
  as he esteems himself, 89a
  as much as my life was, 346a
  boasts its supreme, 574a
  cannot be, much, 728a
  conscience of her, 257b
  doing at all, 323a
  estimated by its intrinsic, 57a
  fighting for, 983a
  good words are, much, 233b
  heart's, gold, 153a
  his labour, 216b
  his salt, 51b
  immortal, mortal thing of, 629b
  improving British, 358b
  is life, living, 673a
  life is, living still, 669b
  little, a sigh, 661b
  living, life unexamined not,
    20b
  living, whether life is, 709a
  lore, the knowing, 706a
  makes the man, 317b
  man of, 14a
  man's, something, 571a
  most of sterling, 549a
  never knew the, of him, 846a
  New York asks how much is
    he, 679b
  nobler yet in his own, 277b
  not, going to see, 342b
  not nearly as much as it's, 995a
  not, the search, 143b
  noted for acknowledged, 22b
  nothing, a tear, 661b
  nothing, the lying awake, 841b
  on foot, 599b
  one hour's sleep before midnight,
    three after, 234b
  opinion of our own, 99a
  Paris, a mass, 115b
  pleasant memory of their, 471b